Shortly before her death, one of Canada's greatest writers finally set aside fictional characters and told her own story. This candid portrayal of Gabrielle Roy's first thirty years—from her poverty-filled childhood in St. Boniface, Manitoba, as one of eight children, through her travels in Europe on the brink of war, to her return home just a few years before she began writing *The Tin Flute*—is an honest, deeply moving account of a young woman's search for a purpose...and a voice.

Enchantment and Sorrow is a brilliant portrait of a vanished era, filled with the exquisitely drawn scenes for which Gabrielle Roy is renowned. Through stories of her family, her schooling, her work as a teacher, her early struggles to write, discovering the magic of Europe and the passion and heartbreak of love, we follow the young Gabrielle as she first asserts her independence and then struggles to come to terms with it.

Enchantment and Sorrow is a superbly crafted, intensely personal story, and a major literary autobiography.

"No French-Canadian writer has ever touched the hearts of so many people across Canada. Roy's settings may partly account for her wide readership—such books as *Where Nests the Water Hen* and *The Road past Altamont* lovingly evoke Western Canada. But her popularity also pays tribute to her lasting faith in human nature. Only a few modern writers, notably Isaac Bashevis Singer, could match her gift of portraying warmth without sentimentality, joy without delusion. Even when her work described alienation and loneliness, it also reached out in hope."

Mark Abley, *Maclean's*

"Here is an autobiography [which] is a lesson in frankness and courage...."

La Presse

"This is a larger-than-life epic—a chronicle of great cultural significance for Canada."

Sarah Chesterman, *The Vancouver Sun*

"One wishes...Gabrielle Roy's *Enchantment and Sorrow* could not be recommended, but required reading."

Ronald Sutherland, *The Globe and Mail*

ENCHANTMENT AND SORROW

The Autobiography of Gabrielle Roy

Translated by Patricia Claxton

LESTER
&ORPEN
DENNYS
PUBLISHERS

Originally published in French under the title *La Détresse et l'enchantement* by Les Editions du Boréal Express, copyright © Fonds Gabrielle Roy, 1984

FIRST EDITION

Canadian Cataloguing in Publication Data

Roy, Gabrielle, 1909–1983
Enchantment and sorrow

Translation of: La Détresse et l'enchantement.
ISBN 0-88619-101-7 (bound) ISBN 0-88619-167-X (pbk.)

1. Roy, Gabrielle, 1909–1983 — Biography.
2. Authors, Canadian (French) — 20th century — Biography.* I. Title.

PS8535.095Z5313 1987   C843'.54   C87-094273-5
PQ3919.R74Z46613 1987

The Publisher wishes to thank the Canada Council for its support in the translation of this book.

Design by Gordon Robertson
Typeset in 11 pt Aldus by Q Composition Inc.

Printed and bound in Canada by Metropole Litho Inc. for

Lester & Orpen Dennys Limited
78 Sullivan Street
Toronto, Ontario M5T 1C1

Foreword

THIS BOOK is the last that Gabrielle Roy wrote, the autobiography in two parts which she began in 1976 and at which she worked virtually until she died in 1983. It completes her literary estate – consisting of all her works – which she bequeathed to the Fonds Gabrielle Roy, a non-profit trust established to administer the estate and distribute its revenues to various charities.

Of the three or four parts she initially planned, she was able to complete only the first two before illness forced her to cease her work. These two, "The Governor's Ball" and "A Bird Knows Its Song", retrace what might be called her formative years, from her Franco-Manitoban childhood to her return from Europe on the eve of the Second World War. She began her first novel, *Bonheur d'occasion* (*The Tin Flute*), three or four years later.

This, then, is the story of the first thirty years of Gabrielle Roy's life, her discovery of herself as an individual and, gradually, her vocation as a writer. The story is interwoven with memories: in the first part, memories of her family, especially her mother, and the milieu in which she taught school, took part in amateur theatre productions, and became aware of her identity; in the second, of Europe in the late thirties and the two years she spent there, which for her were decisive. Much of this story has been hitherto unknown.

Gabrielle Roy was most anxious that this book be considered an *autobiography*, not memoirs, for what she wanted to write was not a historical reconstitution of a time gone by, but rather a re-creation or re-enactment of the past from memory and imagination, strongly flavoured with emotion and subjectivity: a past that never fails to quicken and live in the very process of its recall.

Foreword

The original French text of the autobiography was taken directly from the typewritten manuscript, of which she left two copies, corrected by the author's own hand. She entrusted one of these to me shortly before her death; the other was found among her papers. When it was first published in Montreal in the autumn of 1984, the book was enthusiastically acclaimed by critics and public alike.

Patricia Claxton's translation has been patiently researched and thoughtfully rendered. No finer tribute could be paid to Gabrielle Roy and her work.

FRANÇOIS RICARD
Executive Director
Fonds Gabrielle Roy

Translator's Note

A FEELING of urgency underlies this book, an anxiety to set down, before time runs out, as much as possible of the things that Gabrielle Roy wanted the world to know about her life, her urge to seek beyond an increasingly confining milieu, her large and small discoveries, and above all, perhaps, about the strong, often conflicting emotional forces at work in her – the things that led her, or drove her, towards the vocation she was destined for.

A translator has a curious position in such an intensely personal book. Although I met and talked to Gabrielle Roy at some length years ago, in a context of no importance here, I would not for a moment imagine that I knew her personally. Yet for more than a year I lived in her left-hand pocket, so to speak, and now must remind myself that I really did not know her, that she really was not there in the flesh sometimes, telling me her story so I could pass it on.

The first French edition of *La détresse et l'enchantement*, published in 1984, reproduced Gabrielle Roy's personally corrected typescript almost exactly as she left it, which is to say, without editing of any kind except for minor spelling and grammatical tidying. From time to time the author expresses worry that her dervish will fail to finish what he has started. Indeed, there was only time to complete part of what she had planned, and as this translation progressed it became clear that time had run out also for the honing and polishing her work habitually received. For instance, in dialogue spoken in 1938, before the outbreak of the Second World War, characters speak of the "First World War".

Such potentially distracting anomalies have been corrected in the course of translation.

I have also added first names on first mention of real people, which is more customary in English than French, and the names of authors of most books and plays, since French works will be less familiar to English readers. Proper names have been verified for spelling and some have been corrected.

Readers with an academic bent would no doubt like to see footnotes to justify such apparent divergences from the underlying text, or to add interesting information. If this were a scholarly work it would bristle with indexes and footnotes, which would be only proper. But that was not the kind of book Gabrielle Roy was so anxious to leave.

It would be a pity, nevertheless, not to share at least a few gleanings from my research and reflection. For instance, I was puzzled by the way in which Gabrielle Roy speaks of "Pembina Mountain". I learned that this, in the early days of Manitoba, was the name used collectively for a group of small settlements on the slopes of the Pembina Escarpment, although I found no other reference to an elevation by that name. I also learned that on the Canadian prairies the berries called "pembinas", from which pembina jelly is made, are also known as "mooseberries", and are elsewhere more prosaically called "highbush cranberries".

The need for research has occasionally been more apparent for a person of English heritage than of French. The line of investigation and resolution has often been circuitous. For example, since Charing Cross is at one side of Trafalgar Square, a bus leaving Trafalgar Square and heading north towards Epping Forest will not pass Charing Cross ten minutes or so later, though it will almost certainly pass King's Cross. To Gabrielle Roy, "Saxon" appears to mean "old English" in a broad sense, but "Saxon" cottages, thatched and half-timbered, are more accurately Tudor, and Boadicea lived before the coming of the Saxons and was therefore not a Saxon but a British queen. Still, designating Boadicea as "British" might allow an impression that she was a rather recent queen, whereas if she is identified with the ancient Britons her antiquity is no longer in doubt. Similarly, in 1938 Zambia was Northern Rhodesia; however, in the context it is not so much the name as its exotic aura that is important, and so the missionary with whom Esther

corresponds is located in neither Zambia nor Northern Rhodesia
in the translation, but "somewhere up the Zambezi", which fits
both the tone and the geography.

Where details in the French text are at variance with strict accuracy, a decision on how fastidious to be with correction has
sometimes been difficult. In general, errors of indisputable fact are
corrected, whereas those in grey areas involving Gabrielle Roy's
opinion or impression are left intact. For instance, in a reconstructed
conversation, Esther remarks that the Queen belongs to the "High
Church"; but in 1938 King George VI was on the throne and
therefore "Queen" should more properly be "King and Queen".
On the other hand, the significance given to "High Church" and
"Low Church" is supposition on the author's part, and so this
remains unchanged. When a Swedish girl's parents are mentioned
as being in Oslo, the placename appears to be an error; in this case,
since nothing whatever depends on the placename, the least ob-
trusive solution is for it simply to disappear. A morning's walk
from just outside Nice to St-Tropez is clearly intended to telescope
a distance of some hundred kilometres. Still, such a walk rather
severely taxes the imagination for one who may know the region;
the solution is merely to allow a slightly vaguer impression of the
length of the ride by *micheline* before the walk begins. More complex is the use of the name "Provence" as a synonym for the Midi
or South of France in general. This, while not strictly accurate, is
a common practice among the French themselves, and furthermore
it is "Provence" in this sense that is so dear to Gabrielle Roy's
heart; "Provence" is therefore the term that remains, except when
Ruby's thoughts are being expressed.

Certain socio-cultural situations and allusions have needed pondering and even gentle nudging in order not to leave some readers
thoroughly perplexed. One of these is Madame Jouve's abhorrence
of being labelled a "landlady". Another occurs with the appearance
of Sir John Henry Dunn, Bart, where the comma after "Dunn"
and the period after "Bart" were lost in the French printing, and
where the distinction between a peer and a baronet, no doubt incomprehensible to most French-speaking people, will be important
to many English-speaking readers. In another vein, a *château* is
not necessarily a castle. As to Lillie Road, why the name should
"smack of perdition" remains a mystery, but I suspect that Gladys

planted the notion, the street perhaps having been named for Lillie Langtry, the "Jersey Lily", who was both admired and scorned as an actress, great beauty, and long-time favourite of Edward, Prince of Wales in the late nineteenth century.

Finally, Gabrielle Roy often obtains emphasis or sharpened impression by using tautologies; after due reflection, a few of these have been omitted if, instead of adding something to the text in translation, they intruded to the point of weakening it.

All decisions of an editorial nature have been approved by François Ricard, Gabrielle Roy's literary executor, and have benefited from the opinion of Joyce Marshall, who was general editor for this book. I am indebted to both for their wisdom and guidance on these and other matters. Joyce, who knew Gabrielle Roy and translated three of her books, for example pointed out, when I was inclined to use the word "garret", that an "attic" figures quite prominently in other of Gabrielle Roy's books, notably *Street of Riches*, and recalled that Gabrielle Roy was particularly fond of the word "horizon" and would certainly have preferred it where in some instance I had initially used "skyline".

I have also had occasion to call upon the special expertise of a number of others and could not finish without expressing my gratitude for their generous assistance. I wish in particular to thank Mary and Jack Plaice, Joan Rolland, Anthony Abbott of Debrett's in London, and Vaughan and Sally Turner of London.

PATRICIA CLAXTON

This translation is dedicated
to Jim

I

THE
GOVERNOR'S
BALL

I

WHEN DID IT first dawn on me that I was one of those people destined to be treated as inferiors in their own country? I don't think it was during any of the frequent forays that Maman and I made to Winnipeg, leaving our little French city of St-Boniface and crossing the Red River by the Provencher Bridge. It would be easy to suppose so, since our capital city never really received us otherwise than as foreigners, but when I was a child I rather liked the feeling of crossing a border and being in a strange place, light years away but right next door to home. I think it opened my eyes, trained me to observe things and stimulated my imagination.

Generally we set out early, Maman and I, and if it was summer we went on foot. We didn't do it just to save money. We did it because all of us were natural walkers and loved to stride along with our eyes free to roam, our minds wherever they wished and our thoughts unfettered – and so we do still, those of us who are still of this world.

We almost always set off in high spirits and full of expectation. Maman would have read in the paper or heard from a neighbour that Eaton's was having a sale of curtain-lace, or printed cottons suitable for making aprons or house-dresses, or maybe children's shoes. Always, as we began these shopping expeditions, we were drawn by the hope that so warms the hearts of poor people, that of turning up a real find at the bargain counter. It occurs to me now that we hardly ever ventured into the rich metropolis next door except on buying trips. This was where a good portion of our hard-earned money went – and it was pennies from the pockets of poor people like us that made the city such an arrogant and intimidating neighbour. Later I often went to Winnipeg for a lot of other

reasons, but in my childhood, as I recall, it was almost exclusively for bargain hunting.

As we left, Maman was most often bubbling with merriment and inclined to optimism, even wishful thinking, as if she was set free by leaving the house and city behind along with the usual trammel of constraints and obligations. From that point on she had that capacity for enjoyment which is the lot of every footloose adventurer. To tell the truth, Maman had only to step outside her familiar routine and she was at once on an adventure and open to the whole world.

On the way, she'd talk to me about the things she'd buy if the discounts were really big. But she always let herself imagine much more than our means would allow, thinking perhaps of a rug for the living room, or a new set of china. Since she hadn't yet dipped into the little sum she'd set by for the day, it always felt like enough to satisfy all the wants long kept in check, plus some more that emerged on the spur of the moment. So when we crossed the bridge, we were rich, with all our possible acquisitions still intact in our heads.

But as soon as we were on the other side, we'd undergo a kind of transformation that made us draw together, as though solidarity would help us face a kind of shadow that had fallen over us. It was partly because we were now on dismal Water Street beside the railway sorting yards, undoubtedly the most woebegone part of Winnipeg, full of drunkards, the wails of crying children and the hiss of escaping steam; the hideous face which the haughty city couldn't hide, a mere stone's throw from its broad airy avenues. But there was more to it than that; our discomfort came partly from inside us too. We'd suddenly be less sure of ourselves, the money we were going to spend wouldn't seem so inexhaustible, and our plans for it would have come back down to earth.

We'd arrive at Portage Avenue, which was so inordinately broad it could swallow a throng of thousands without showing it. We'd still be speaking French, of course, but perhaps less audibly, particularly after two or three passersby turned around and stared at us. The humiliation of having someone turn to stare when I was speaking French in a Winnipeg street was something I'd felt so often as a child that I no longer realized it was humiliation. Besides,

I'd often turned around myself to stare at some immigrant whose soft Slavic voice or Scandinavian accent I'd heard. I got so used to it eventually that I suppose I thought of it as natural for us all to feel more or less like foreigners on someone else's ground. That is, until I came around to thinking that if everyone was a foreigner, then none of us was.

Only when we arrived at Eaton's was it decided whether or not there would be a confrontation. It all depended on Maman's frame of mind. Sometimes she'd begin by calling for a saleswoman who spoke our language to serve us. In our patriotic moments, we of St-Boniface claimed it was our right and even our duty to make a point of doing so, and that if all of us did this, industry and department stores would be obliged to hire our people.

So if Maman was having one of her good days, if her confidence was up and her tongue felt nimble, she'd take the offensive and demand one of our compatriots to wait on us. The more forceful she was, I'd observed, the more accommodating the floorwalker would be. He'd lose no time sending for Miss or Mrs. So-and-so, who often turned out to be someone we knew, sometimes even a neighbour. Amid the hustle and bustle of strangers on all sides, the most cordial and composed of conversations would ensue.

"Ah, Madame Phaneuf," Maman would say. "How are you? And how's your father? Is he still living in the country?"

"Madame Roy!" the saleslady would exclaim. "How are you? What can I do for you? It's always such a pleasure to help you."

It seems to me we poor people of St-Boniface had a gift for neighbourly warmth when thrown together, handed down from some gracious society of olden times.

On days like that we probably bought more than we should have, being so grateful to be doing it in our own language that the money slipped through our fingers even faster than usual.

But there were also times when Maman felt beaten before she began, weary of a struggle that had to be taken up again and again and was never won for good and all; at such times she found it simpler and less taxing to "bring out" her English, as she used to say.

We'd move from counter to counter. Using her hands and facial expressions to help, she really managed pretty well, though some-

times a real problem arose, like the time she wanted some chamois ("shammy" to the English) to line a coat, and asked for "a yard or two of Chinese skin to put under the coat."

When a saleswoman failed to understand her, she would call another to help, and sometimes that one would call a third. Passing customers would stop to help too, for Winnipeg, while it treated us as foreigners, was nothing if not quick to fly to our assistance the moment we found ourselves in a fix. These confabulations were intended to solve our predicament, but to us they were pure torture. Sometimes we'd slip away in the middle of it all. Then we'd be overcome with mirth at the thought of all those good-hearted folk no doubt still arguing over how to rescue us, with us already far from the scene.

Once, when she was even more upset than usual by the barrage of solicitousness, Maman opened her umbrella as we escaped, and we ran down the aisles of the store as though caught in a downpour. Only when we got outside to find a beaming sun did she think of closing it, which lent an air of provocation to the harmless escapade. I know now that the paroxysms of laughter she infected me with despite myself were a blessing, an antidote for the bleakness in our lives, but at the time I was quite embarrassed.

In fact, after the umbrella episode – a good few minutes after – I became angry and told Maman that we might both have been laughing, but we'd been making ourselves a laughing stock too.

To which Maman retorted, somewhat stung, that it was not for me to lecture her; I'd had every kind of opportunity for education, while she'd only been able to stay in school long enough to finish sixth grade at her little country school in St-Alphonse-de-Rodriguez, where the teacher herself didn't know much more than the pupils, and how could she, poor girl, when all she earned was four hundred dollars a year. I was the one, with my quick mind and my brain not broken down already from constant figuring, who ought to start learning English so I could make up for all the rest of us. Later, when I came to Montreal and found things no different in that city's west end department stores, I was dumbfounded and began to feel there was no cure for the misfortune of being French Canadian.

Never had Maman been so voluble on the subject. I was taken aback. I think this was the first time I ever realized that she'd

suffered cruelly from her condition in life and had found comfort only in imagining her children established in circumstances she would have liked for herself.

WE CAME HOME from our expeditions to Winnipeg dog-tired and, in truth, almost always depressed. Either we'd been sane and sensible and had bought only what was essential (and who ever reaped joy from sticking to essentials?), or else we'd done something idiotic (like buying the hat that suited me so well but cost the earth), and then we felt guilty; we'd have to make it up somewhere else, Maman would say, and besides, she would hint, not let Papa know what we'd paid. Being so strapped for money all the time meant that sooner or later we'd overspend and then we'd be more strapped than ever.

In any event, though we crossed the bridge on the way out with our heads full of plans as if we were rich, we never recrossed it feeling anything but poor, three-quarters of our money having slipped through our fingers, very often without our being able to say where it had gone.

"My, how fast it goes!" Maman would sigh. "That's what money's for, of course, but your father's going to say – again – that I can let it go faster than anyone else."

Soon, on the other side of the bridge, we'd see the towers of the cathedral, then the dome of the Jesuit College, then spires and other church towers. The familiar outline of our little city against the intense Manitoba sky revealed much more attachment to prayer and education than to business, and it always gave us comfort. It reminded us that we'd been created for eternity and would be recompensed for having been so hard put to make ends meet.

A few steps more and we'd be on home ground. We may not have been numerous in our pious and studious little city, but this helped us feel of one heart. Now Maman and I would be speaking our own language with all the confidence in the world, neither in whispers nor too loudly as we would in Winnipeg, where our behaviour was governed by our self-consciousness, or by the shame of it. And we'd be hearing the sound of other French voices in harmony with ours. In our relief at being back in our natural surroundings we'd find ourselves greeting almost everyone we met, though it's true that between us we knew practically everyone in

the city, at least by name. The farther we went, the more people Maman would recognize as friends, exchanging greetings and snatches of personal news with this one and that.

There were times, once we were back in our own city, when she'd look up at the tall sky with a kind of rapture. Often the weariness would vanish from her face as if by magic and she'd declare, as if calling me to witness: "It's good to be home!"

At last we'd arrive at Deschambault Street. We must have felt it was something like a miracle to find our house still intact and standing guard over our French way of life, protecting it from the hurly-burly and disparity of the Canadian West, for in the last minute we'd hurry towards it, as though we might arrive to find it had been snatched away from us.

It was a pleasing but unpretentious house, with dormers in the attic, lots of big windows on the second floor, and a wide veranda with a row of white columns around the front and west sides. We always came back to it as though returning from a harrowing expedition. Yet those expeditions from St-Boniface to Winnipeg, however revealing, were not what really opened my eyes to our lot in life, we French Canadians of Manitoba. That happened at another and much more trying time.

II

I HAD BEEN ill with one severe case of indigestion after another, and my stomach still hurt. The day I began to feel a little better, Maman decided to take me to the doctor, as many people in our condition would have done, no doubt. After the questions and the examination, which in those days consisted mostly of palpations, she and I waited on tenterhooks for the verdict. The doctor took a very long time to deliver it. Finally he looked straight at Maman and said crisply and a bit reproachfully:

"Madame, this child will have to have an operation. As soon as possible. Without delay."

I turned my head a mite to glance at Maman and saw her shudder, as though accused of a crime. She turned white, then I think I remember her turning red, and all this time she seemed to be looking for words that wouldn't come. At last she found the usual ones, the ones that came most naturally to us. I can still hear her. I'll always be able to hear her say in that stifled voice:

"How much? How much will it be, Doctor?"

We might have been at the grocer's or the butcher's, but I had the impression that Maman was steeling herself for a much closer contest than with the merchants, with whom she easily had the upper hand.

The doctor shuffled his papers, pen, blotter, as uncomfortable, it seemed, as Maman.

"Well now, in the normal course of these things, for an operation of this kind it's a hundred and fifty dollars."

He must have seen the consternation on Maman's face because he quickly held up his hands, adding, "But..., but...."

Having calmed her a little he continued.

9

"For you, since I know your circumstances, it'll be a hundred dollars."

I could see that this didn't do much to help Maman relax. With a little groan she repeated as if to herself, not complainingly to him, "A hundred dollars! A hundred dollars!"

Helplessly, the doctor gave a shrug. Then I realized she was going to recite the story of our life, which she brought out in public only when she really had nothing else to fall back on, and which always filled me with such shame and distress that I could neither cry nor speak. I wished I could stop her, shut her up somehow, but the time for that had already run out. Sitting on the edge of her chair, her hands clasped tightly in her lap, without once raising her eyes towards the doctor so as not to be distracted in any way from what she had to say, she began.

"My husband was a civil servant with the federal government. He was persecuted behind his back for not hiding his political loyalties. To make it short, he was given the sack, dismissed just six months before he reached retirement age, which meant he would get no pension. So you see, in our old age we were suddenly penniless, with nothing we could count on coming in. We had to live on what we'd been able to put by, which didn't go far as you can imagine, plus some help from my grown children, and whatever I could earn myself from sewing...."

The story went on and the doctor listened. Perhaps he was bored, for his eyes would stray to the ceiling at times, come to rest on me for a moment or two, unsmiling, then turn away again. He'd spoken to me only once, at the beginning of the consultation. "How old are you, little girl?" he'd asked. "Twelve? You don't look it. More like ten, I'd say." And he'd said to Maman sternly, "You should have brought this child to me six months ago."

Now he was looking at me unamiably, one would say. What an absurd idea of Maman's to have me seen by the most expensive doctor in the city!

Now she came to the most painful details, which I couldn't hear without wanting to hide my face in my hands: the mending and alterations she'd sit down to at night after her normal day was over, and which brought in quite a bit of money, she said with curious emphasis, as if the doctor might have household mending jobs to pass along to her in return for his services.

There were times when I really didn't understand Maman. This proudest of women would spend nights on end making dresses for her daughters that were as beautiful as any worn by the daughters of the city's richest and most important figures, and find money Lord knows where for our piano lessons. This most stoical of women, too, never in my hearing admitted to the least physical pain, nor even, at a later time, to the terrible hurt of loneliness. Yet the moment the health, well-being, or future of her children might have been in jeopardy, she could easily have become a street-corner beggar.

Finally, when he could stand no more of her story, which was perhaps much like many others he'd heard in this very place, the doctor raised his hands to silence her.

"Please, Madame, please.... If you can't pay me my fee all at once, then do it bit by bit, as you're able to."

Then she unwound a little.

The moment a monetary obligation – however large – could be broken up and settled in small instalments, she felt she had it beaten. After all, she'd been doing this for years, she'd been trained to it: so much this month for the sewing machine (though sometimes when she was feeling low she'd admit that the machine would probably wear out before it belonged to us); so much for the silverware (as I recall this was only fifty cents every fortnight, but we almost never had it when the salesman came to collect); so much for the ice-box. Having understood that my operation could be fitted into this category, she was immediately soothed and turned to me with a look that seemed to say, "There, you see? We'll manage this too." In her relief, her face even showed a gentle little smile, which included both the doctor and me and made her look almost happy for all her distress. She was like a fine, full-flowing river whose bed is strewn from beginning to end with obstacles – boulders, rocks, and reefs – amid which she'd keep flowing, around them, over them, or wishful-thinking them away. And in the brief spells between obstacles, before the next turbulence caught her, you could hear her calm-water song.

"Well, Doctor, in that case please be assured that I'll manage to pay you...."

The doctor stood up, cutting short her promises. We stood up too. Then she remembered.

11

"When will the operation be? In a few weeks?"

"What can you be thinking of, Madame! I'm going to telephone the hospital immediately. I want her admitted this evening. Tomorrow at the latest."

"Oh, tomorrow, please!" Maman begged.

With the business end of it put in order – or put off – she could at last think of her concern for me and her own anxiety on other counts. She began to plead for more time. Time to make me some clothing suitable for the hospital. Time to get my father used to the idea of the operation. And, who knows, perhaps even to work things out without it, if she was granted enough time.

"We've already waited far too long," snapped the doctor. "We're dealing with a serious crisis that could lead to a ruptured appendix. I'll operate on your child the day after tomorrow at the latest."

WE LEFT. Which little tree-shaded street we came out on, I really don't know. I do remember the day was one of the loveliest that summer can bring – gentle and filled with a breeze that caresses your face. On a day like this it seemed odd to be so taken up with making ends meet, with our terror of hospitals, and our anxiety about what Papa was going to say. Where we should have been, we agreed, was in the country somewhere, sitting on the grass under a tree, having a picnic or just looking at the sky and daydreaming. But with perfectly healthy bodies.

Maman took my hand and asked if I wasn't too tired. "Because," she said, "if you feel strong enough I'd like to walk a bit." We were in an area of small streets where we'd have had to walk farther to find a streetcar than if we went straight home. She must have been really preoccupied not to have considered this. "I'd like to have time," she said, "to think over how I'm going to tell your father."

I tried to talk her into not telling him at all. I told her I was better, that it didn't hurt any more, anywhere. And it was true. Anxiety had galvanized me, borrowed strength for the moment from goodness knows where. There was nothing new about a reaction like that for me, either. A toothache that had kept me awake all night would promptly disappear when I was taken to the dentist. Maman therefore paid no attention to what I was saying. She continued her line of thought.

12

"He's always had a horror of debts, even when he was earning enough to support us, so you can imagine how they terrify him now. Still, when you can pay a bit each month debts aren't the end of the world, it seems to me."

I must have taken after my father on that point because they terrified me too. I'd made up my mind.

"I don't want the operation," I declared. "We can't afford it. And Papa will be against it."

Maman stopped abruptly and shook me gently by the shoulders.

"Don't you ever say such a thing! Your father won't be against it. All I have to do is make him see that this debt's no worse than any other. But it's a tight spot we're in. Don't take away my courage," she begged, "not just when I need it most to get us out of this."

"But we're always in a tight spot," I reminded her.

To my surprise she began to chuckle, as if reviewing all her feats of ingenuity from a distance.

"We've got out of lots of tight spots before."

"It wasn't the same," I insisted, and I couldn't resist a conspiratorial smile.

We'd turned the corner of one quiet little street and were walking down another, which was lined like the first with trees whose leaves we could hear rustling gently despite our preoccupation. One lovely thing about our life was that Nature hardly ever failed to leave a benign mark on us throughout our trials and tribulations. Or perhaps it was because we kept looking to Nature for consolation that she always granted it.

Then, as though talking to herself, Maman astonished me with a sudden admission of defeat.

"Yes, it's true, things have been going hard with us for ages. We'd probably have to go a long way back to find out how it all started. It's a long story."

Stories were so dear to my heart, even in the depths of misery, that I was all ears.

"Tell me," I begged.

She gave me a wry smile which said: it's time I did, here goes.

Then, despite our troubles of the present, a tale of woes from the past began to come forth in snatches, stirred up no doubt by the scene in the doctor's office – at least, that's the way it seemed

13

to me. For suddenly, there in that peaceful street, we were joined by a host of kith and kin, all beset with troubles, and all long dead, yet still living in us. As I listened to Maman, I had the curious impression that our predicament of the moment had summoned hundreds of others, and that all of them were walking with us along the deserted street, they perhaps consoled to find we still cared about them, though they were long gone, and we to find we weren't alone.

"It all started," recounted Maman, "when the English stole our land – the farms we had back there in our first home, when we had one – because they saw how good it was there in the land of Evangeline. So they could get those rich farms for themselves, they rounded us up, tricked us, put us on leaky ships, then took us far away and left us in places we'd never seen before."

"We were Acadians?"

Perhaps she'd already told me the story and I hadn't remembered. Or perhaps I hadn't been ready to listen to awful things like that and hadn't paid much attention.

"That's how our troubles began, a very long time ago," she said. "I don't know the whole story. Only bits, handed down from one generation to another."

"Where were they taken to, Maman?"

"Oh, here and there in America. They didn't even know the language where they ended up. They had to get along however they could. With great difficulty, one group managed to get back together in Connecticut. They used to work in factories, in the bush, and on the railways, wherever there was hard work to be done cheap. But they looked out for each other, and were a comfort to each other in their homesickness."

This was the point in Maman's story at which I began to worry about the notion of home, about what exactly it meant, collectively speaking. In any event, I caught her off-base by asking her point blank if we had a home.

"Why, yes," she replied. Then as soon as she'd said it she didn't seem so sure herself, and she put a hand on my forehead and said, "You haven't got a fever, have you?"

I protested that I hadn't, then persisted in wanting to know what had happened to our people in Connecticut.

"It's a sad old tale and this isn't the moment to make me tell

14

it," she sighed. "I'm discouraged enough as it is. I've got to pack your things for the hospital...." Then with a little groan, "the hospital," she said again, and quickly assured me I'd be all right there..., and then she was back with our people in Connecticut. "In those days," she said, "there were priests called colonizers, whose whole lives you'd swear depended on finding lost flocks and bringing home as many sheep as possible. One of them came to us in Connecticut."

She'd begun to say "we" when she talked of our distant fore-fathers, and it gave me a funny warm feeling.

"In our little church there he preached to us in French. And he told us we'd be welcomed with open arms in Quebec and that land would be granted in a fertile township not far from Joliette, if we wanted to come back."

"So Quebec was our home?"

"Yes and no," said Maman. "It's pretty hard to explain." Then she continued, "There was a split among us. Some said, 'We'll make a home here. We're already half American. Our children will speak English. It's only common sense. If we move around all our lives we'll never get anywhere.' But others were all for giving the Quebec adventure a try. 'They're our brothers up there,' they said. 'We speak the same language. We have the same faith. Let's go and put ourselves in their hands.' "

"So what did they decide?"

"My, how this story's got you interested all of a sudden!" she exclaimed, then continued, "Well, some stayed, so we ought to have some distant cousins in Connecticut, and some came and settled in the lovely, fertile parish of St-Jacques-l'Achigan."

At that point we saw a bench at a street corner under a rustling tree, and Maman said, "Let's sit down for a bit so you can rest." And the gently stirring leaves whispered to us of respite and a moment of cheer in the lives of the exiles.

"You've still got no pain?" Maman asked.

I shook my head, and it was true that I felt none – only the pain in my ancestors' hearts.

"Were our people happy in St-Jacques-l'Achigan?"

"Yes and no," she said again. "They had lots of children. All our relatives brought up big families. Our priests used to tell us it was the price of winning back our place in the sun. In St-Jacques-

15

l'Achigan they were soon pretty cramped for room. Not far north there was a line of barren hills, where the land was poor and full of rocks and all spiky with dark evergreens. But that's where your grandfather Elie and grandmother Emilie went to settle. Nobody on earth ever worked harder than those two," she said with a faraway look, as though still suffering herself from their long, hard labours. "They cleared the trees, they dug thousands of stones from the ground, built fences with some and put the rest in piles, and they planted several fields of oats and buckwheat. They soon replaced their first cabin with the house I was born in, the one you've seen in the album. Your grandfather was good with his hands and it was a fine house. We ate buckwheat cakes more often than white bread, but I think I was a happy little girl in that house."

I heaved a sigh of contentment, I was so glad Maman had been a happy little girl before her troubles began. I wanted to know what had made her happy, and she replied that she didn't remember but she thought children were generally happy because it didn't take much to make them so. Then she felt sorry for me because I was looking at her and wanting to cry, though she'd got me wrong and didn't know it was for her I wanted to cry. She stroked my brow and told me I was going to get better, and then I'd be back at my games and I'd be happy again.

"If you were happy at St-Alphonse-de-Rodriguez, why did you ever leave?" I wanted to know.

"Maybe wandering was in our blood, we'd moved around so much," she replied. "Though nowadays nobody wants to stay put once and for all more than I do. Your grandfather Elie was an adventurous soul. He felt he was too hemmed in by those barren hills and wouldn't be able to settle his sons around him. Then another of those colonizing priests came our way, this time to tell us wonderful things about Manitoba and how we'd be made to feel at home here. He talked about beautiful rich land and all the Canadian West where we should hurry to go and get established before the Scots and English, who were arriving in droves in those days. He told us the whole country from ocean to ocean belonged to us, we of French blood, because of the French explorers who'd been all over it first. Our rights to our language and our religion would be respected. The government of the new province would grant a

quarter-section to each family head and each of his male children who'd turned eighteen. It was tempting for people like us. Your grandfather was all excited. You're like him, the way your imagination can run away with you," she said, stroking my cheek, then she went on, "Your grandmother was the only one against it. But in the end she gave in, and there we were on the move again. You know the rest of the story, I've told it to you a hundred times. They were granted land in the Pembina Mountain settlements."

"And they could take it easy then?"

"Oh, my heavens, they were a long way from taking it easy. They had to start all over again. Your grandfather built the new house exactly like the one at St-Alphonse, your grandmother made all new furniture, the cupboards, the dough-box...."

"And the settle-bed," I put in, remembering.

"When you were little and we went to visit, you'd cry if we wouldn't let you spend the night in the settle-bed.... I always wondered why you so loved sleeping in that thing. It's like a coffin!"

I think I remember feeling totally safe there, as though the hands that had made the rustic old piece held the power to keep away all danger.

"After a few years everything could have been wonderful at St-Léon," said Maman, "because the land was ours. Counting the boys' land, we had a square mile in all. Grandmother used to grow the same flowers in her garden that she'd had in Quebec, the only language we heard spoken around us was the one we knew, and at last we were almost prosperous, and then the Manitoba government turned against us. It passed that dreadful law forbidding French to be taught in our schools. We were trapped, far away from our second home. We couldn't afford to leave, and besides, where would we have gone?"

"So we were without a home again?"

"We still had our land, our customs, our houses...and our language, which we weren't ready to have taken away from us. But that's what ruined us too – that long struggle, and all the money we had to spend to keep our schools. Have you rested enough?" she asked. "We should go. Your father will be worried not to see us back by now."

Gabrielle Roy

When the leaves parted they showed us a patch of high, clear blue sky. We sat watching it side by side, and it made us smile. And Maman continued.

"Your father, now, it was the terrible poverty of his people near Beaumont that drove him away. He had to start working when he was a young child and soon went to the States, like so many of us that Quebec couldn't support. He worked at everything under the sun, but all the time he read and studied, and prepared to do something important when he came back to his country. He ended up in Manitoba. Like the colonizing priest of the old days, when I met him at St-Léon he believed that the whole of the West would be dotted with little colonies, and at least half French from sea to sea. Then he got to know Laurier, who was to become prime minister soon after, and who asked him to work for his election. From that point on your father gave his life to that man, he had so much faith and confidence in him. When Laurier was prime minister and wouldn't take sides in the Manitoba French issue because it was a provincial matter, he kept on believing in him. 'He has his reasons,' he used to say. Religious soul that he was, what really hurt him was hearing an anathema pronounced on Laurier's supporters from the pulpit, and Laurier declared a traitor because of the language quarrel. In the end his political loyalty cost him his job as settlement officer, because just before he reached retirement age he lost it. It was the ruin of us, and I've reasons to suspect it was the doing of our own people, our Manitoba French. You know, perhaps the saddest part of our story is that we still aren't united after all we've been through."

Then she looked at the ground by her feet and spoke without raising her eyes.

"Now perhaps you can begin to understand why I talked about those things to the doctor. I didn't like doing it, I can tell you."

I felt so bad for her, for my father, for all those people we'd been talking about, I couldn't have replied if I'd known how. When she asked me again if we hadn't better get along home and I stood up to follow her, we might have been taking our places in the interminable exodus. Where would we get to by the end of the end?

Suddenly, without any connective, she said, "When I met him your father wasn't young any more, but he had lots of energy and

18

great ideals, a very attractive man, and full of fun when the mood was on him."

Then I remembered that when we were in his consulting room the doctor had asked her, "How old were you when she was born?" and Maman had seemed embarrassed. As though she wasn't sure, she'd answered, "Forty...forty-two, or -three."

"And your husband?"

"Fifty-nine, Doctor."

As if in answer to my unspoken question, she now assured me, "Your father was proud and happy when you came into the world.... They say," she continued, "that the children of older parents are frail and have delicate health, but it seems they're the most gifted too."

At this point we couldn't have been far from the cathedral, because she had a suggestion: "Shall we go in on the way and pray for everything to go right?"

After the daylight, the high-vaulted nave seemed very dark. It seemed to be lit only by the votive candles on stands at the back of the church.

Maman took me almost to the front pews, near the choir. This was where we used to come and pray when we were in desperate need of help, as if here we'd have more chance of being seen and heard. We knelt down. I prayed, I suppose, but most of all I watched Maman pray. I've since seen a few, a very few others pray as she prayed that day, but this was the first time, and my heart ached to see it. She stayed totally motionless, not a muscle moving, yet everything was taut, her face, her eyes, her lips, even her hands as she held them in front of her in suppliant attitude. It was then, I believe I remember correctly, that I resolved in the depths of my soul to make good for her. Or rather, it was then that my resolution must have taken shape from all my impotence and weakness.

When we came out, the brightness of the daylight hurt our eyes, and our souls too. I was beginning to drag, so Maman slowed her step, which normally was so brisk in those days. She scolded herself for having kept me talking so long, for having made me walk a few steps more to get to the church. I was near the end of my strength but my head was still full of my little plan to make good for her. I'd make good for my father, too, and my Beaumont

relatives and my St-Jacques-l'Achigan relatives and my Connecticut ancestors before them. I was far away in the past discovering the hardship of my forebears, and from this I drew the will to place one foot after the other.

BUT IN the hospital, behind a screen which a nun had set in place, when the old priest sat near me and began to talk about life, death, and eternity, I changed my mind. It would be better, I thought, if I died and spared my parents further expense than if I lived, perhaps, only perhaps, to make good for them some day, which at that point looked pretty difficult.

The old missionary was temporarily in the city, having come perhaps from the North. Sometimes I think fate must have had a hand in sending him to me. He talked to me softly, enveloping me with a calm, kindly gaze, his eyes shining from a bearded face in the nightlight's dim incandescence. He talked to me about death without stripping it of solemnity and seriousness, as he might have done since I was a child, and it's perhaps because I heard this old man speak of it with dignity and candour when I was very young that death has lost much of its power of terror over me. He told me that I would almost certainly get better, but that all would happen as God wished it. Tomorrow, when they put me to sleep, I would be like a little bird that the Lord held in His hand. Either He would release me so I could go back to playing and laughing and having fun with other children, or else He would keep me in His mysterious abode.

I'd discovered what I wanted; I asked the old priest to explain what that mysterious abode was like. Today I still bless Heaven for having put someone near me who made no pretence of understanding the inexplicable, but just imagined it.

"Oh, my child," he said, "if only we knew, eh? But then making the long journey wouldn't be worth much, and not very interesting either, don't you think? All I can foresee or imagine myself is that our lives will open into infinity, and all of us want that, I think."

Ah, just to hear him talk about it made me want it myself. I asked him whether we were still responsible for our debts in infinity.

What kind of debts, he wanted to know. Dishonourable debts, which you take on deliberately knowing perfectly well you'll never

be able to repay them? Or poor people's debts, which they have hanging over them because they really can't do otherwise?

I had trouble finding an answer. It seemed to me that our debts didn't fit cleanly into either category, and were perhaps a bit of both.

He stroked my forehead gently and told me not to worry about it. He told me to rest in the Lord and to put all my problems in His hands. I think I'd always known that when you came down to it there was no one else to help us, but it seemed to me, too, that He wasn't doing it. How could that be? Was it because we were too far away from Him, or He from us? I began to imagine that when I arrived in the abode of the Most High, as He was called, I'd be close enough to tell our whole story right into His ear. Then He'd see that you had to take Maman with a grain of salt. How could she pay five dollars a month towards my operation when she already had three to pay for the sewing machine, four for my piano lessons, which she refused flatly to give up, plus arrears at the grocer's, the coal merchant's, and practically all the other trades-men? Besides, she'd just promised me a new coat as a reward for getting better – made out of an old one, it's true, but she was going to give it an astrakhan collar, bought from one of the city's better furriers. If anything was keeping me a mite attached to life it was that coat, and my curiosity to see how Maman was going to manage it as well as everything else.

On the other hand, I still wanted to quit life so I'd stop being an expense to Maman, and that was the substance of what I expected to be my final prayer, which I think really expressed a desire to escape. For thinking about my death – oddly but on the other hand perhaps quite logically – had given me a glimpse of what life might hold for me, and it had frightened me. In order to make good for Maman, I realized that once I was back at school I'd have to work twice as hard, always come first in French and English and all the other subjects, win medals and other kinds of prizes, and keep bringing her trophies. Then I couldn't see anything clear-cut and identifiable before me beyond the end of my studies, only a road leading upward, seemingly deserted, going off into some desolate distance beneath a cloudy sky. My courage failed me.

I'd always loved prairie roads with a passion. They allowed you

to see far ahead and all around because everything was flat; the road of my future as I saw it that night was nothing but steep hills and twists and turns that all disappeared in darkness and never allowed me to look ahead and see where I was going. At a later time, I was to stand one day on a slight rise in the prairie and look out along a little dirt road bathed in sunlight, which seemed to me to have a mysterious connection with my life, buoying me up with a rush of elation. But in the hospital that time, the road of my life – or of any life, perhaps – looked like a road to nowhere, and the terror of it remained with me for many years.

A nun came and gave me a sedative. Soon I felt almost happy, in a waiting state that no longer rattled my nerves. I would go to sleep and wake up in what the old priest called the wonderful abode. The next morning I was in the same tranquil state when they wheeled me into the operating room. I wondered only if God came out to meet people who were dying, or whether He waited for them without budging from His doorstep. Just one step towards them would be reassuring, I thought. When Maman was expecting someone she really loved, she'd watch at the living-room window or sometimes on the veranda, and when they appeared at the end of the street she'd run down the steps and often to the gate. You'd be hugged tight against her breast. You'd hear another heart joyfully beating against yours. You'd be home at last. Had I known that happiness? Or had I only imagined it?

"Breathe deeply, dear," said a strange voice, and I felt myself dissolve.

I CAN'T DENY it was disappointing at first to open my eyes and find I was still of this world. And how very much the world I knew too well became immediately apparent. Beside me there stood a man in white, whom I saw dimly owing to the continuing effects of the anaesthetic. He was talking to me and his voice seemed to come from a great way off.

"I was the one who put you to sleep, dear," he was saying. "When your mother comes, will you give her this? It's my bill. Anaesthesia's separate."

How can anaesthesia be separate? Nobody told us that. I was sure for a minute I'd said it aloud. In fact, I didn't have the strength

to bring the words to my lips, and they stayed inside, resting heavily on my stomach.

Then I noticed he'd slipped a piece of paper between my fingers.

"Don't forget, dear. Anaesthesia's separate, and generally that's what you pay first."

I nodded and groped for somewhere to hide, but where can you hide when you've been sent back to Earth by the Lord Himself after being an inch from His doorstep? Someone came and gave me an ice-cube to suck, then Maman arrived, and I knew I was glad to be still of this world after all. The minute our eyes met, all our cares and troubles were swept away in an outpouring of happiness at being reunited. But when she bent over me, her face very close to mine, I could see the weariness of her life, as if through a magnifying glass, the scars of adding and subtracting, the lines left by evenings of mending and alterations, and it was more than I could bear. I closed my eyes and tried to go back to where there were no expenses, costs, or fees. Alas, I remembered the slip left by the anaesthetist and handed it to her.

She unfolded it, saying, "I'd have thought he could have waited a bit...," then fell silent, with a familiar crease in her forehead.

"Is it much?" I asked, full of apprehension.

She forced a smile.

"No, it's not too bad." Then she tucked the bill away in her handbag.

In a cheerful voice, sitting close to me, she began at once to tell me the good news.

"Listen to this, now. Yesterday, as I was leaving the hospital, who d'you think I met? Madame Bérubé, whose daughter's getting married next month. She needs a dress for the wedding and so does her sister-in-law. So there I am with two big orders, just because I went out by one door rather than another, which God probably put me up to. He gets a finger in the pie sometimes, you know."

I wasn't so sure of that since He'd turned me back from His paradise. Besides, if Maman had got those orders, it was probably more because she was going to do them cheap. But today I didn't have the strength to stand up to her.

"The anaesthetist's bill's going to put a dent in my order before

it's even started," she said, then seemed to find it funny that our money was always spent before it was earned.

Out of a grocery bag she took three oranges. She must have spent ages choosing them because it seemed to me I'd never seen oranges rounder, more flawless, or more perfectly matched.

"You bought them at Mr. Trossi's!" I declared, knowing at once, and my thoughts smiled with me in my affection for the poor immigrant who always treated me like a princess whenever Maman sent me to his shop to buy *à la graine*, as we used to say – one or two of this or that.

A little sadly, she then admitted she'd only bought two, Mr. Trossi having added the third as a present from him to "the little sick girl who has to get better quick if she wants to do her Italian friend a favour." I must have shown more pleasure over the Italian's present than hers, because she seemed a bit jealous, observing that it was curious I should be so fond of someone we really hardly knew.

But that day she had no time to spare for either joy or resentment. She barely seemed to have arrived when she was telling me she'd have to leave and begin her sewing if she was going to finish her order in time and get paid the money we needed so badly. All the same, she delayed going a few moments, long enough to arrange my pillows and give me some encouragement: the doctor had said I'd soon be on my feet and everything would be fine. She asked me several times if I was suffering and I shook my head, and it was partly true; throughout the illness which left such an indelible mark on my life, search my memory as I may, I can recall no trace of physical pain, perhaps because one easily forgets that kind of pain. But I do remember having lived what seemed years in those few days.

Finally Maman fled, so to speak. Perhaps because I hadn't seen her from behind for so long, or else because my illness had given me eyes to see with, her silhouette seemed old, quite different from the one I thought I knew, almost like Grandmother's not long before she died. I couldn't stand it and found voice to call her back. At my feeble call she stopped, hesitated, long enough to compose herself, I think, then turned and came back to me.

"Is there something you want?"

I don't know what I'd had in mind to say to her, but when I saw

traces of the distress she hadn't quite had time to banish from her face, I thought of committing myself to the one promise I was sure would bring back her courage. So I announced that at school from then on I'd always come first in my class...though it was a promise I was far from believing I would keep.

She leaned over me and stroked my hair, and her face, which a moment before had looked so drawn, was now radiant. In her brown eyes shone the pride I so loved to see there.

"If you come first," she promised in return, "you won't only have a new coat in the fall; I'll make you a lovely little skirt, too... the kind you like, a flared one...so full it'll fly...."

Thereupon I could picture the undulations of the light-as-gossamer skirt, I could see it fly up around me as I spun on my heel, my eyes were filled with the graceful image. And the other children in the ward looked on, blind or envious, not understanding how rich we were, Maman and I, for all our poverty.

III

TOWARDS THE END of the day, a time he found soothing, when the light was fading and the outlines of things were beginning to blur, wavering as they do in dreams perhaps, and life seemed less difficult, my father appeared.

He stopped at the door, looked at each of the little girls in the four corners of the hospital ward in turn, then slowly came over to me. For a long moment he stood still and silent by my bedside, looking forlorn.

Yet he couldn't have known that the night before last I'd been hiding outside near the door to the summer kitchen, a kind of small building backed against the house, where my father loved to sit alone on warm evenings. Maman had joined him there and I'd heard them talking about me. Under the low branches of the gooseberry bush, I held my breath the better to hear them.

"What did he say?" my father asked.

"It's an operation, Léon," my mother answered.

I'd noticed that when things were bad they were quite likely to address each other by name, as though a full measure of identity was appropriate to such solemn moments.

There were some murmured words that I missed, but I grasped the subject and it was what I'd expected; such a familiar subject, yet it never failed to deal me a blow.

"How much is it, Mélina? What's he asking?"

I heard in the tone of her voice that Maman was trying to avoid alarming my father.

"He says he'll give us a good price, Léon."

"A good price! What's he mean by 'good'?"

In the end, of course, Maman had to state the figure. Something like a short groan from my father came to my ears.

I could see him without needing to be there. He'd be sitting in the faint light of the little old stove Maman kept there for cooking on in summer if the day was torrid, which helped keep the main house cool. For some time now she'd hardly ever used this room, saying at first that there was always something missing when she needed it, and finally that the inconveniences of preparing meals there outweighed the possible advantages. My father was practically the only one to set foot in it any more and remained strangely attached to the place. Often in the evening we'd go looking for him all over and then find him there, sitting quietly in the darkness with the door open to the back yard, to the gentle rustlings of night. Though it was joined to the main house by a door, this squat little structure was quite different, rather rustic, really a kind of shack which seemed to us like the country or even a cabin in the wilds, with its rough cupboards and exposed beams in the ceiling. Perhaps it gave my father the same feeling he'd had for the crude shelters in settlement areas in his days of arduous travels. In any event, he could stay there for hours, sitting on a little low chair near the stove, which he'd keep just barely lit.

When Maman had joined him she'd been careful not to put on a light, so they weren't really able to see each other as they talked quietly.

"A hundred dollars, Mélina! How are we going to do it?"

Maman's voice was reassuring.

"We'll find it, Léon. Money can always be found. I won't say all at once, but little by little."

Papa seemed to take some courage from this and made a suggestion.

"Maybe I could sell our garden vegetables to the neighbours and not just give them away. That's what you've always told me I should do, Mélina, though I couldn't ever bring myself to...."

Apparently they finally agreed to ask modest prices for the produce of Papa's long summer labours, those beautiful vegetables he'd been so happy to distribute as presents to almost everyone around us.

And now he was standing by my bedside with an anxious look on his face, perhaps not knowing how to talk to children any more. He seemed so old I thought I'd never find the right words to reach him. Yet when I was little I'd loved to make up games to play with old people.

27

I glanced at him in puzzlement. How old was he then? Seventy-one...seventy-two? When he'd fathered me he was already old. Did he sometimes think of this with a kind of regret and, could it be, a certain embarrassment? Was that what stopped him from opening his heart when he talked to me? I've never known. We never revealed any of our deep feelings to one another, he and I – like most human beings living in close proximity, I imagine.

Yet according to what I've been told, when I came into the world he was still full of energy if not in robust health, and sure of the usefulness of his life and his work. I often heard that he was committed in those days to the idea that French Canadians should come in great numbers to the West, despite all the difficulties, in order to ensure the happy balance between French and English that is so assiduously sought today. He'd just founded one of his most impressive settlements, Dollard in Saskatchewan, composed almost entirely of compatriots from the county of Dorchester in Quebec, where he was born, and the rest repatriated from the United States. I was the only one of his children who hadn't known him as a man of great plans, fine accomplishments, and profound hopes which gave life to his clear blue eyes. Or at least, I was so young I could only have had the most tenuous, most shadowy memories of him while he was still that way.

Drowsy with sedative, I dozed off briefly as he stood beside me, or else I had a dream while only half asleep. I thought I was back in the days before I began to be frightened by the aura of tragedy surrounding him. I was still very small. I used to run to him quite happily, not so he'd pick me up and cuddle me, which little children love so much, but just to be near him, sharing a strange kind of solemnity. I think this pleased him. Being in his sixties, he could have felt it unbefitting his advanced age, I suppose, to give me the cuddling that most fathers lavish on their very young children. And yet I seem to recall he'd readily take his grandsons into his arms, my sister Anna's children, the eldest exactly my age, whereas with me all he'd ever do was put his hand on my head and stroke my hair. But in the kind of dream I was drifting in, one day when I had run to him as he was working in the garden, he'd put down his hoe, picked me up and sat me in the wheelbarrow, then pushed me several times round the house, with me clutching my fat grey cat to my chest. The strange, slow ride had shown me several totally

new things about a landscape I knew better than anything else in the world. I was so enthralled I begged for "More!" after the third turn, and off we went again, my old father puffing a bit harder than before. That day being so bright a flower amid all the dark ones, the reawakening of the memory must have caused me more pain than happiness, for I couldn't hold back a moan.

With a distraught look, my father asked at once if I was suffering that much. I told him no, all I felt was a little burning where they'd opened me up.

Then he urged me to eat well as soon as I could so I'd soon get my strength back, and reminded me I'd have to avoid too-vigorous games for a time. And he even dared report to me part of what the doctor had told him, that I'd be weak for quite some time, and that I'd have to look after my health because it would always be fragile.

I was a little more awake now and turned my head towards him, trying to give him a reassuring smile. I saw then that he was holding three roses. They were the kind we used to call "cemetery roses" because he'd bought some roots to plant on the graves of the two little girls named Agnès in our family plot, and they'd flowered so successfully that he'd taken some cuttings to plant around the house. Maman didn't like them and neither did I. Nobody in our house liked them, in fact, except my father. What did we have against them? Probably the fact that they came from the cemetery, but not only that. They weren't really very pretty. They had a lot of small petals which curled too tightly against each other, they faded as soon as they bloomed, and became blotched for no reason, a drop of rain or a brisker wind than usual. They really didn't have anything to recommend them except their smell, and even that was sickly sweet and reminded us of flowers at funerals.

None the less, to me that day, those roses in my father's hand were beautiful. Perhaps I realized he must have chosen them with as much care as Maman had her oranges. Or else I'd learned how to see at last. I was sorry now I'd never helped him care for them. They didn't need much, I remembered, only the soapy water poured over them after you'd washed your hands, which had an insecticidal effect. I reflected that I'd hardly ever bothered to do so, either because I forgot or because I didn't want to put myself out for flowers which to my mind didn't deserve it. But at the moment I

was moved by their eagerness to live despite our indifference, and I promised Papa I really would try to collect soapy water for them in the future.

"It doesn't take much effort," he replied, "and the soap that's so dear gets used twice that way."

I remembered then that as the days went by I'd seen him being careful not to waste things, though he was never mean about it, and working hard to acquire skills that weren't entirely natural to him, like gardening. The thought crossed my mind that now, perhaps more than when he was admired, he was showing nobility. Having fallen low, his hopes fled, he'd been devoting himself to such modest endeavour as might still be useful. Was fever making me ten times more perceptive that day about people and things? Or was the sedative blunting my natural heartache, allowing me to see more clearly than usual? With his callused hands, his lined face, and his stooped back, my father seemed to have a courage that even yesterday I'd been incapable of seeing. I'd have liked to tell him so but didn't know how.

When he'd put the three roses in my water glass, their heads already drooping a little, he walked slowly away, looking rather like those tired roses, I thought. I buried my face in my pillow, trying to hide from the pain so it wouldn't ever find me again.

IV

WHY IS IT that we who were so often unhappy could also be so happy? That's what astonishes me most, even today. Just as I also find the coming of happiness more surprising than the coming of sorrow, not because it's more unusual but perhaps because it's less easily explained.

Happiness came to us like the wind, from nothing and from everything. Summer was a festival in itself for us. When I was a child I didn't know anyone who cherished summer as we did. Whatever worries or sorrows Maman had, as soon as summer came she'd drop everything to gather up the geraniums and fuchsias that had spent the winter on the windowsills and plant them in the earth around the house. We'd soon see the pale, sickly things return to health. Papa used to plant a big vacant lot not far from our house, having obtained permission from the municipal council to cultivate it until it was sold, which couldn't have happened for a long time because I seem to remember our always having that big, beautiful vegetable garden. And summer repaid our efforts. Our fruit trees gave us sweet-smelling flowers and then tart little apples from which Maman made an exquisite jelly, and also cherries and small blue plums. Our yard behind the house was surrounded by a wooden fence and was always full of robins and sparrows, which sang so loudly and cheerfully we couldn't help hearing them, even when our troubles were many. It wasn't a very big yard but it bordered a lane which in turn bordered an unsubdivided meadow, so that all the open space behind the house looked just like a glimpse of green prairie. My father would sit in the half-darkness by the open door of the little summer kitchen and contemplate it endlessly. And sometimes you could see a red glow in the sky between two street corners beyond, mysteriously deepening the narrow cleft

between the houses and making it seem to reach into a kind of limitless space, right in the middle of the city. If we ever went to talk to Papa at that hour as he sat at his observation post, there was a strange and surprising peacefulness in his voice. It was as if we'd brought him back from some infinite distance, from his youthful excursions in the wilds, perhaps.

But it was the summer holidays above all that used to bring us the most intense happiness. We'd set off, Maman and children and later just Maman and I together, for Pembina Mountain. Papa would stay behind to watch the house, quite happy to have it to himself, I think, to be free to wander from room to room, engrossed in the reveries often encouraged by solitude. Then, probably, those dreams that still dared stir his heart seemed less surely doomed.

I think now I can see what it was that made us the way we were, and in a sense made things so hard for us. Just as we were rich although poor, we were unfortunate people with a flair for happiness.

In the time I remember best, we used to spend the summer holidays with my uncle Excide, the youngest of the Landry sons.

We used to take the train at the domed CN station, which we called *le dépôt*, though I don't know why. In no time we'd reach the flat land around Winnipeg. From above, the train must have looked like some black caterpillar crawling into eternity beneath the immense prairie sky. I loved the open prairie; I've always been fascinated by it. For all its reticence, it's always had more to say to me than any other landscape. But on these train trips to the settlement area called Pembina Mountain, the centre of attraction to which all our thoughts turned was the mountain itself. About an hour out of Winnipeg, shadowy hills would begin to show against the pale blue sky. A little later the train would enter those hills so gradually that we wouldn't notice it. Only when we were in the middle of them would we realize we were in broken and even mountainous country, or so it seemed to us, who were so used to flatness. We'd come to a place of no importance called Babcock. The train would stop for a minute or two, and I still wonder why, for as I recall there was nothing there except a shack and an abandoned quarry. But also the mountain. Just an elevation really, crowded against the railway line, its flanks forming rocky escarpments. To see its summit, Maman and I would crouch till we were almost kneeling, our eyes level with the bottom of the

window. That way we could see all of it. It took our breath away. Such altitude! Such soaring height! On the way there, we'd talk about nothing else, Maman and I. We'd be watching for it from the moment the train left the station. Afterwards it so dominated what we remembered of the ride that it banished all other recollection. On a visit to Manitoba a few years ago, I felt an intense desire to see the mountain that had stirred my soul more, I'm sure, than the Rocky Mountains did later, or even perhaps the Alps. I found myself in a tiny out-of-the-way place closed in by heaps of quarried stone left lying about and hiding the skyline. But I could see absolutely no mountain! Finally, among the piles of stone, I did distinguish a more or less natural butte.

I'm still not sure who had the better vision, the impassioned child with her nose pressed against the train window, or the seasoned traveller who had to have a real mountain before her eyes to believe in it.

After Babcock we'd leave the little hills almost immediately. Now another kind of prairie unfolded before us, rolling towards infinity in wide, flowing undulations. We'd arrive at the village of Somerset. On one of these trips it was here that I heard the jangle of a handbell being rung on the doorstep of the hotel next to the station, signalling that the noonday meal was about to be served. This was a detail I used in *Enchanted Summer*. The Somerset of those days has become very dim in my mind, but if I retained nothing else, this would be enough to make me remember it with affection.

My uncle Excide with his big black moustache would be waiting for us, pacing up and down the wooden platform, as high-strung as he'd always been. He'd drive us to the farm, which wasn't much more than two miles from the village, in his little high Ford with mica windows in its canvas doors. But our hearts lightened because we were really going much, much farther than two miles, back into time past, through the generations, almost to the beginnings of our family. We were finding something from the old days still alive in the brisker air of the plateaux, here in the third of the homes our forebears had built since they began their wanderings.

This third home in fact began near the village of St-Léon, six or seven miles beyond the farm. It was there that Grandfather obtained his concession and built his house, which was exactly like

33

the one at St-Alphonse-de-Rodriguez, with a wing of the same shape but smaller and lower. Those people were amazing, I must say; they'd leave everything behind, then begin all over again to make everything just the way it had been at the other end of the earth. I've always been touched by this. It reminds me of the birds, who always build the same nest wherever they go in the vast expanses open to them.

Grandmother, who was as good at working with wood as with dough or yarns, soon turned out cupboards, hutches, and a dough-box patterned after those she remembered from years past. Their neighbours, almost all compatriots from Quebec, spoke only French; in all the years she spent in Manitoba, I doubt that Grandmother learned more than a dozen words of English, and from those she fashioned others for her own use, words like *ouaguine* (for wagon), *mitaine* (a Protestant church, from "meeting"), *bécosse* (outhouse, from "backhouse").... The neighbours' names were Lafrénière, Labossière, Rondeau, Major, Généreux, Lussier. Oddly enough, they had a parish priest from France, Théobald Bitsche, born in Nieder-Bernhaupt in the diocese of Strasbourg, and later, for the education of their daughters, a religious community from France, the Chanoinesses Régulières. Out in the country, they had a counterpart of the little country school in Quebec, called *l'école Théobald* after the parish priest, which was often the custom in Quebec. My eldest sister, Anna, attended it when she was very young, before my parents moved with their children to St-Boniface.

I came to know and love the third home of the Landrys long after those early days. I was fourteen or fifteen. Grandfather had been dead for about ten years. With the help of his sons, in a little more than a generation he'd brought a whole section under cultivation, which is to say a square mile of marvellously black earth, the wheat-growing soil of the West, which yielded prodigiously. He'd built an impressive farm with its house and barn, fine outbuildings, a well with a rim, and silos, and he must have died happy in the belief that he'd left his descendants a lasting home. After he died Grandmother went to live in the village of Somerset in a little house that her sons built for her just the way she wanted it. I knew that little house. This was the one I had more or less in mind when I wrote "My Almighty Grandmother" in *The Road past Altamont*. It too was in the French-Canadian style, once again

34

perpetuating the memory of the beloved house in St-Alphonse which Grandmother had left with such regret, but which had never really been left behind, since it was reborn twice on faraway soil. As I recall, it had a mansard roof and a smaller, lower wing in the same style. From its chimney to the plants around it, it proclaimed Quebec very loudly in Somerset, which in those days was at least half English.

When the railway was built to pass through here rather than St-Léon, Somerset's growth was assured, to the detriment of the little French-Canadian village, which thereupon began to decline.

My grandmother lived alone until she was very old in her little Quebec house in Somerset. Immediately after her death a buyer came forward who'd had his eye on that house for some time, without wishing Grandmother's demise I should hope, but keeping himself posted nevertheless. He was an elderly retired Englishman for whom, it seems, Grandmother's house was a strong reminder of the dear old England he'd left years before. He surrounded it with honeysuckle and planted rosemary where Grandmother's dill had been and lived happily there without any other change. Thus the house that had comforted Grandmother in her homesickness gave him comfort in his. All of which made me also want to buy the house that had been such a haven. The last time I was in Manitoba I learned that Grandmother's successor had finally died. I hadn't exactly wished for his death, but I'd been waiting my turn with some impatience, since the old Englishman lived to be very old indeed.

I arrived in Somerset. I managed to find the house on my own. By now it was only a tumble-down ruin. And yet, deserted and mournful though it was, surrounded by high yellow autumn grasses and long-overgrown honeysuckle, there seemed to be some mysterious collusion between that house and nostalgic stirrings of my own which I'd never really admitted to myself. I came close to buying it. Then my cousin pointed out that it was only good for taking down and I'd have to rebuild from scratch if I really wanted a house in Somerset.

"And what would you do with a house here when you live in Quebec?" he wanted to know.

I had to give in to reason. Nevertheless, the deserted house long reproached me for having abandoned it. But more than the crum-

bling house I'd so wanted to buy because it touched the very heart of my most precious memories, perhaps it was the sound of the wind that voiced all those generations of longing for a home so often sought and so often lost, a gentle, wistful September wind I heard plucking at the vestiges of Grandmother's garden, one day when I passed that way.

It seems to me sometimes as if the episode of our existence in Manitoba had no more substance than dreams that blow away with the wind, and if anything's left of it, it can only be in dreams.

AT THE TIME I myself remember best, we found the spirit of my pioneer grandparents still almost intact in Uncle Excide. For all that, he'd given up the much-loved paternal house and built one to his own liking on a new farm just a few miles from Somerset. And so we began to oscillate between Somerset for reasons of business, which was done mostly in English, and St-Léon for the good of our souls. Sometimes we'd go to one and sometimes to the other, and finally we went to Somerset almost always; it was closer and really more convenient.

My uncle, who'd become a widower at a very young age, was always happy to see Maman arrive. She'd at once take the running of the house in hand, much to the relief of my cousin Léa, who at the age of fourteen had found that weighty responsibility on her shoulders. The house was spacious, pleasant, and very comfortable for the time, with a hand pump which brought water inside from a well under the summer kitchen, and central heating too. It was in the middle of a little wood, which my uncle had long sought, he'd so missed having trees over his head as at St-Alphonse. Though he'd left there when very young, only five, he'd apparently been longing ever since to have at least a grove of trees around him.

In truth, the little wood around my uncle's house played almost as important a role in my life as did the mountain at Babcock. It was probably rather sparse as woods go, composed mostly of poplars and small oaks, but for years it was the archetypal forest to me, embodying all the shadowy and magical things I used to imagine about a forest. I loved it, but I think most of all I loved the contrast it provided, always renewing the feeling of space you'd get from the open prairie beyond. When you came out of that little wood at the end of the farm road, you'd instantly feel you were entering

infinity. From there the prairie stretched away as far as you could see; in one immense, rolling plain it unfolded in a series of long, fluid waves sweeping unendingly to the horizon. I've seen nothing more harmonious anywhere, except perhaps where the downs of Dorset flow down to the sea.

In that permanence in constant motion, in that tranquil yet beckoning immensity, there was a beauty that tugged at my heart like a magnet, even when I was still very young. I kept returning to that vista as if it might get away from me if I left it alone too long. I'd arrive at the end of the farm road, reach the place where the trees parted, and the vast, magnetic expanse would appear, and each time it was the world laid at my feet again. But really much more than the world, I know that now.

Eventually I discovered another road I could take to find that unaccountable excitement. A little section road bordering my uncle's farm climbed a slope to a high point from which the view across the prairie was even more breathtaking. I told no one of my discovery. I'd pretend I was going there to gather hazelnuts and wild cherries. The happiness awaiting me at the end of my walk was so mysterious I seemed to feel I'd risk losing it if I talked to anyone at all about it; perhaps even if I admitted it to myself.

I'd set off along that rutted little road. Nothing was more ordinary. It consisted only of two cart tracks with weeds growing rife between them and bushes on either side. There was no horizon, nothing but the sound of the wind imprisoned in the dense shrubbery, intoning a kind of tedium. Then all at once the revelation, the magnitude, the endless unfolding of naked earth! That little road to nowhere took me to the edge of eternity. A wave of inexplicable joy would sweep over me. Where it came from, why it was granted me, what it was made of, I don't know and I've never known.

For a long time I believed the excitement I was promised, there at the end of the little dirt road when I was sixteen, was a joy of this world, to be seized while I was alive. Now I'm not so sure. Perhaps that kind of joy awaits us elsewhere.

THOUGH we still felt at home in the high country near the sky, little by little the things that made it home were eroding, wasting away, without our really doing much about it. When we went into

Somerset we'd see how many of our people were defecting, putting up signs in English only and taking the initiative in speaking first in that language to almost everyone. The young men were going to Winnipeg, Chicago, or Vancouver; nearly all my uncle's sons settled permanently in one or another. The poles of attraction were the West and the United States. We would come back to the farm discouraged and depleted. The comforting vastness, as if suffused with dreams, would take us in hand and bring us a kind of confidence – or forgetfulness – with the sound of a gently plaintive wind. In my mind I can still hear that wind from the high plateaux, one that unfailingly seemed to soothe the pain of great but fruitless efforts.

Often I'd go alone to where my dead grandparents had felt at home. I'd learned to ride a little roan mare that I'd trained myself. I'd gallop off, crossing an old dried-up lake bed at the bottom of my uncle's farm, then skirting some other little lakes whose beds were barely wet and were ringed with tattered bulrushes – a curious landscape in the midst of the rich wheat farms – and soon reach the village of St-Léon. It was so sleepy and deserted it might have been under some grim kind of spell. The only time I ever saw it wake up and show signs of life was after high mass on Sundays. Yet when the colonists arrived in my grandparents' day it must have been bustling with life. Then progress passed it by and established its banks, its trade, and the railway in Somerset. There was no longer even a hotel in St-Léon, or a single shop or store of any consequence. Yet there stood a presbytery better suited to a city than this isolated country setting, along with the church and the convent. The three of them were so dominant you really saw nothing else. At the end of the main street, the only street in the village, I'd come to a house of considerable size but unfinished, covered in black insulating paper. It stayed that way through all the time I knew it. That house alone, better than anything else, showed the depth of despondency that must have weighed on that poor village shorn of its expectations. For St-Léon had been something of a Ville-Marie of Manitoba, destined to grow into the Montreal of the West under the guidance of stern priests with visions, I have no doubt, of human communities that would be rigorously pure.

The tarpapered house was a friendly place for me, despite all. This was where the Majors lived, the parents of Uncle Excide's dead wife whom we'd loved so much, the gentle, tender-hearted Luzina whose name I gave in affection to one of the most lovable of all the characters in my books. Luzina had died young but her old mother was still living, and everyone in the village called her "Mémère", meaning "Granny". I almost always found her making blood pudding or soap in an enormous black cauldron over a brush fire. Here, against the Manitoba sky that was so very blue, everything was black: the cauldron, the billows of smoke escaping from under it, the house, the old woman in her long skirts. I'd always supposed she had a bit of gypsy in her, but it must have been the effect of the outdoor life she loved that made it seem so, or perhaps a nomadic instinct that was rare in those days in our old people, whose hardships in early life had made them more inclined to seek all the comfort possible. She alone seemed to take pleasure – for a few months of the year at least – in living the way my grandmother probably had when she first came to St-Léon. She used to keep some of her kitchen pots hung on the outer walls of the house so they'd be at hand when the spirit moved her to take her knitting outdoors in summer. Her laundry tub was also hung up outside, and all kinds of utensils and other objects were strewn around her as if she were camping.

With her eyes reddened by the smoke, Mémère glared at me.

"Who's that riding this way like Saint Michael at the end of the world for the Last Judgement?" she demanded.

That bantering manner alone told me she'd recognized me. I didn't say a word. At last she greeted me in her characteristic way.

"Black damnation! If it isn't Elie Landry's wife Emilie Jeansonne's girl Mélina's girl! And where is it you've come from galloping hell-bent on your great black steed?"

She knew my little mare wasn't black, or damnation either, and I didn't bother to put her right, I was so entranced with her colourful language and the kind of rich earthy spirit it showed. Besides, I'd come for quite a different reason. I dismounted from my little Nell and approached the old woman.

"Tell me my fortune with your cards, Mémère Major," I begged. "Tell me what's in the future for me."

39

"What's in the future for you, my little charmer of the highways and byways, I can tell you that without cards! You're going to live, get old, and die."

That sent chills down my spine.

"No, no, my own future, Mémère!" I insisted.

She burst out laughing, sounding like a cackling hen.

"What's the matter with you young people, wanting to know what's in the future, you that's got a future. It'll come anyway, it'll come, then one day you'll turn round and it'll be gone. Serve you right, too!"

Sometimes she'd consent to peer into my open palm, her old face crackled like gumbo in a drought. I'd catch the still-bright sparkle in her old, worn eyes.

"Yes, I see," she'd say, raising my expectations, then she'd continue, "You'll travel...you'll make friends with young men...fair-haired ones...and dark-haired ones...."

I wonder what it was that made me want so much to have my future predicted by this ancient matriarch who never did anything but poke fun at me about it, unless it was the persistent rumour that she was capable of seeing everything that was going to happen...if she really wanted to...once in a while....

But in the end I was drawn to her perhaps more because of the past than the future. Mémère Major, who was so different from my tidy grandmother and just a little older, had been her friend and remembered hundreds of details from a time long before I'd known her, and I never tired of hearing her tell me about them. Tight-lipped though she was about my future, she didn't have to be asked twice to recount what had gone before me. She'd relate the story of the journey from St-Norbert by ox-cart, the clouds of mosquitoes around the tent they'd just pitched, the darkness of the prairie pierced only by the travellers' campfire, the first winter at St-Léon which six families spent under one roof, the squabbles, the kindnesses exchanged, the help from God, the devil's tricks....

There weren't many left of those Mémère Major talked about, only a few frail old relics. They made me think of survivors of a long-ago shipwreck. I used to love those poor old souls from Quebec who were living out their days here in the middle of nowhere; who, though they still spoke only their own language among themselves, had watched many of their children switch irrevocably

to English, and their children's children grow up unable to communicate with their old grandmother or grandfather. They seemed so isolated, as the anchorites of Patmos seemed to me later. Their extreme fragility made me cherish them; they were like leaves held just barely to a branch, which the first little shake will carry away. I realize now that what drew me to them was their past, which would soon be vanishing with them. Their gentleness and resignation have stayed as indelibly in my heart as the intense blue of the sky above their pensive faces, and the wind lamenting round them, recounting tales of wasted lives, it seemed to me. So many times they'd been brought to the middle of nowhere, there to disappear without a sound and almost without a trace.

I'D COME BACK from those trips to St-Léon wrapped in thought and bearing affectionate messages as if from a much-loved distant country. We were too close to write letters and too far away to see each other very often. My uncle was glad to have the fresh news I'd bring back to him. Soon, though, he began to look at me and frown. The idea of a girl in pants riding through the pious little village scandalized him. He said as much to Maman. She, whom I'd had such trouble winning over, now stood up to her brother in my defence. "For goodness' sake, Excide, don't be such an old fogey! If she's going to ride, better she do it in pants than a skirt flying in the wind."

When I'd first talked to her about a pair of riding jodhpurs, though, she'd been against it, then one day she changed her mind: "Let's go and see how they're made, it won't do any harm." And there we were in a very exclusive shop catering to a small carriage trade. In those days there weren't many riders in Winnipeg. We'd never been so out of place. Yet Maman looked around and very quickly singled out the finest ensemble in the shop, and probably the most expensive too. She asked to have me try it on. The saleslady consented but not with good grace. She'd unmasked us immediately, perhaps because we were speaking French, though quietly between ourselves, but more probably because Maman didn't even ask the price, being so certain she wouldn't be tempted to buy anything there. I could have sunk through the floor, but I wanted a pair of jodhpurs so badly that in the end I put them on, then came and modelled them in the light of a bay window overlooking

41

the street, watched with sudden enthusiasm by Maman and disdain by the pinch-lipped saleslady. To prepare her retreat, Maman then began to find fault with them. "They wrinkle here, they bulge there."

We were barely outside when she told me they suited me beautifully, that she'd had time to really study the cut and thought she remembered it and could make me a pair exactly like them from some old putty-coloured trousers of my brother Rodolphe's, the material being still in very good condition. And she did, so successfully that no one in the world would ever have recognized Rodolphe's old trousers in my jodhpurs. I used to wear them with a pastel blouse open at the neck and a little kerchief knotted cowboy style, with the ends blowing in the wind. When I wore the outfit I felt ready to face the world, ready to cope with life, and it gave me confidence. When Maman saw the effect it had on me, making me stand straighter and hold my head higher, she came to love it too.

So my uncle's criticism didn't bother either of us very much. We knew he was a grouch about propriety, boy-girl friendships, and young folk in general, who he felt had too much freedom, though really he was far from ill-disposed towards them. There was a puritan streak in him, tempered by a merry disposition, a love of life, and a healthy sexual urge.

How he managed to reconcile those conflicting inclinations was rather odd. For example, in order not to disobey the village priest, who forbade parents to allow their children to dance under their roofs, he'd declare an absolute ban to his children, then go out square-dancing himself in the houses of less punctilious neighbours; when called upon to swing his partner, he'd grasp her with gusto and squeeze her so tight against his chest he'd half stifle her.

His widowed state was certainly hard on him. More than once he was on the point of remarrying, but in the end he wouldn't allow himself to, remaining faithful to his gentle Luzina whose idealized image he carried in his heart all his life, and also for fear of giving his children a stepmother they might not like.

If there was no dance in the neighbourhood in the evening, after the interminable family prayers were done he'd take up his violin and for hours on end try to play rollicking tunes like "Turkey in the Straw" by ear, though all his bow ever produced were doleful

lays with practically no melody at all. Even at summer's end after the exhausting work of harvesting, rare were the evenings when he failed to try his hand at playing jolly tunes, which, alas, always turned so diabolically into laments.

He was a handsome man, tall, well built, and dark-complexioned, with glossy black hair parted in the middle and a superb black moustache. His eyes were black too, like shiny dark marbles, and he was constantly casting them about, as if following a thought that darted first in one direction, then another. Watching him pursue his thoughts like that, dogging them this way and that, became obsessive after a while.

He could be full of fun one minute, telling hilarious jokes to us children, then suddenly become moody and glum for a time, during which no one could get a word out of him; then just as suddenly his eyes would begin to turn this way and that again, and he'd be out of his spell of depression as quickly as he'd fallen into it.

I was very fond of him just as he was. When I came to read the Russian authors I found him, with his bouts of giddy merriment and a moody side plunging him abruptly into devastating silences, to be the image of so many of their characters, excessive at one minute in their devotions and equally excessive the next in letting off steam.

Later I used to wonder what he was seeing so far away during those moody contemplations, whether it was the future lying in store for his people and his family. His children, if anything, spoke better English than French, while he knew only a few words of English at most. Towards the end of his life, this last of the Landry sons who'd come to Manitoba from Quebec began recalling the faint memories he had of St-Alphonse-de-Rodriguez. The older he became, the more came back to him. He became obsessed with a desire to go back to the village of his ancestors before he died. He used to talk about it often, but as if it were a joy too great to be attained in this world. When, at the age of eighty-four, he died where he'd spent his whole life except his early childhood, he did so, one might say, with his soul turned towards his almost-forgotten source.

A FEW YEARS ago when I was in Manitoba attending to my sister Clémence, who lives in a home, I took time to run up to Somerset.

The fascination the village and its surroundings had and still have for me always outweighs the disillusionments they've brought me. The few relatives who are still there complain that if I find the time to go there it's always to see places first, and people after. It was true again this time. My first visit was to my uncle Excide's farm, which, while one couldn't say it was abandoned, was now a lonely place.

My uncle's eldest son lives in the village two and a half miles away and comes there every day at a fixed time, like a civil servant going to the office, to plough, harrow, and seed the fields, and, when appropriate, to mow and harvest the crops, all by machine, of course. Except on rare occasions, he can do it all himself. So work that used to require an army of farm labourers is now done in uncanny silence, without a sound other than that of a motor, in an atmosphere that's almost other-worldly. It numbs the mind to see a man just sitting at the controls of a tractor – his sole companion – turning, turning, again and again, alone in all that vastness, without the least sign of anything one might call human. Almost as punctually as he leaves in the morning, my cousin is scheduled to come home, his day's work done.

Around the silent farmhouse all was clean and tidy, the yard in perfect order, the machines put away, and the barn doors closed this late autumn day. I meandered around the house. A high sliding door had been installed in one of its walls. By standing on a log I managed to look in through a window. I was thunderstruck by what I discovered. With the ceiling removed and the partition walls demolished, the house was now just a huge shed, almost entirely filled by the Massey-Harris tractor.

The sight might have hurt less if a particularly delightful memory of this house in happier days hadn't superimposed itself on the present. One evening during the year I was a teacher in the neighbouring village of Cardinal, I arrived when I probably wasn't expected. It was mild and snowing abundantly, one of those tranquil, silent snowfalls that come straight down, undeflected by any wind, and as steadily as if to smother all traces of uncleanliness. There must have been some happy gathering, because all the lamps were lit and the house was resplendent, and through this same window I could see silhouettes bustling about cheerfully. But the most beguiling part of the scene was outside, where a delicate stream of

44

light from the brightly lit windows was falling on five or six horse-drawn sleighs lined up by the door. Since there was no real cold in the air, no one had bothered to take the horses to the stable. They'd been left hitched to their sleighs, with blankets thrown over their backs, and more blankets had been spread over the sleighs to keep the snow off the seats. Ever so gently, the snow was piling up like an additional warm, fluffy blanket over the covered seats and over the animals standing there with their heads drooping, asleep on their feet, you'd swear, if you hadn't spied their eyelids blinking now and then.

Just as I'd stood at the end of the little dirt road from where I could see all that boundless space and been certain I'd find happiness some day, when I witnessed the scene on the night I describe my heart was flooded with longing for something still more wonderful, which was peace of mind. But now, standing on a log with my hands cupped around my eyes the better to see through the window, I was discovering something I couldn't believe: the ultimate, un-suspected fate of one of the most-loved houses of my life.

I stopped at my cousin's in the village. He lives in a pleasant, very modern, ranch-style house. The West is covered with them. In a friendly way I took him to task for having turned the house associated with our childhood memories into a tractor shed. He laughed as he defended himself.

"The wood's all rotted," he said. "It may as well at least be used for that."

There was nothing to be done about it. Just as he could justifiably have accused me of having no practical sense, I could have accused him of having nothing else.

Soon after that, I left him and went looking in a rather haphazard way for places and things I kept remembering out of the blue. I hunted for ages for a corner bakery where my grandmother had sent me for a loaf of bread one day when I was very small. I described it as I remembered it to people in the street, who would have liked to help me but didn't remember any bakery answering my description. Perhaps, with time, I'd imagined it to be quite different than it really was. Or else it had long ago ceased to exist. I can't describe the grief I felt at not being able to find that bakery, a grief quite disproportionate to its cause. Yet out there under the high, pure sky, the wind was still dusting up the dirt along the

edges of the highway, as it used to when I was a child – except that then the whole highway was dirt. Dust raised by the feet of some invisible walker tramping endlessly along the deserted road, one might imagine.

I found my way to the cemetery on an isolated butte not far from the village, exposed to all the winds and watched over by a few spruce trees, which aren't native here and must have been brought from very far away. Companions in death at last for folk like Grandmother Landry, who'd pined all her life for the dour trees of her childhood that grew on the hillsides at St-Alphonse-de-Rodriguez. Now at least they were reunited, those sombre trees and my grandmother, who was so untalkative and undemonstrative, yet so faithful to her attachments.

I had no difficulty finding her grave and Grandfather Landry's, though I hadn't been to visit them since the distant day when Maman had brought me as a little girl to pray and meditate beside them. I found myself reading aloud what amounted to their abbreviated life stories: that Emilie Jeansonne, born at St-Jacques-l'Achigan in 1831, had died at St-Boniface on March 7, 1917; that her beloved husband, Elie Landry, born in St-Jacques-l'Achigan in 1835, had died at Somerset on August 6, 1912. I noted the fact that my grandfather, though four years younger than Emilie, had died five years before her. How much he'd accomplished in so little time! And besides, having left St-Alphonse-de-Rodriguez almost penniless, he'd managed to put aside a little sum to leave to his children which was quite respectable for those days.

I felt better. Slender and fragile though it was, the bond was still holding fairly well between us, we wanderers across the centuries. I managed to picture their two old faces to some extent, but in that I was probably helped by having seen their photographs.

I moved along a few paces, staying inside the Landry family plot. A few feet away there rose two large monuments, recent ones certainly, in modern style and more ostentatious too: no doubt Luzina's and my uncle Excide's. I took another step and received such a shock I thought I must be seeing things. Two high, matching stones confronted me, standing on end side by side. In characters that leapt out at me, one bore the word "Father" and the other one "Mother". In English! I searched in the back of my memory for Luzina's angular face, already lined by illness in my childhood

but glowing with a warmth of heart that the relentless advance of tuberculosis never snuffed out. I saw my uncle with his eyes always in pursuit of some thought, either a jovial or an inconsolably sorrowful one. Those two who had never been called Father and Mother in English by anyone while they were living would be identified that way for ever, here in this little cemetery beneath the unsullied sky in the middle of nowhere. They'd been taken from me more surely that day than on the day they died.

I left the cemetery. High in those imported trees the wind was rising. Its long recitative, murmured in a far-off voice, gripped my heart. A voice retelling a pathetic tale of human lives, lost on the earth's face and in history.

AS MUCH as I'd let myself go during the holidays, with my endless rides on the prairie and the airy castle building they lent themselves to, as soon as school began I'd fling myself into my schoolwork with equal abandon. Having wandered to my heart's content all summer, I now stayed riveted every evening to my little desk in my secluded room, reading and getting as much of the material into my head as possible. I learned by heart with extraordinary ease. Very often I'd read a paragraph attentively but effortlessly and then realize that that was all I'd had to do to remember it word for word. However, I soon forgot a text I'd learned without a lot of effort.

I'd promised Maman I'd apply myself so totally to studying that I'd always come first in future, having resolved to make it up to her that way for all her sacrifices for my benefit. However, I didn't begin to do so in the year following my appendectomy. Before coming to that I had to have more time, and even another illness which kept me at home for several months and made me lose a school year. Now I was a year behind my former classmates and quite crushed by the fact. I also had to see my father, who was very ill now, worrying constantly about my future, to the point of confiding to Maman that he was afraid they'd never be able to get me through my studies. But most of all, I think, I had to realize that my mother was driving herself mercilessly, trying to run the house.

How did she do it? I think it was mostly by taking lodgers and sometimes boarders. It seems to me we always had strangers living

47

with us. Sometimes they were well mannered and pleasant. That kind we treated like family, and some we made friends of and missed long after they left. Others we disliked, finding them coarse or loud, and those we had the greatest difficulty enduring under our roof. In either case, independent as we were by nature, I wonder how we put up with not having our house to ourselves for years. The fact was that the money it brought in was practically all we had, apart from the help Maman got from Rodolphe and Adèle. So, as she'd often remind us, she on whom it was hardest, we just had to swallow our pride and learn that our house wasn't entirely our own. But she promised us it would be one day, once all the strangers had gone. But when all the strangers had gone it was because the house had been sold. Now we ourselves were like the strangers we'd had under our roof all those years, people who had no real home. Now we knew what it was like and felt sorry for them.

From Rodolphe at this time, Maman sometimes received really lavish sums, so big she'd pale and exclaim almost dolefully, "How could he have guessed that today's the day we have to buy coal for the winter?" or "that today's the last day for paying the taxes?"

Alas, the time would come when a crestfallen Rodolphe, the day after one of his shows of largesse, after a poker game with friends and a thousand other foolish things, would ask for it back, and she, with shattered face, would give it to him, saying in his defence, "He isn't obliged to support the family. He isn't at all."

I don't know how we could have carried on for so long with so little if it hadn't been for one of the chimeras the weary soul cherishes so. On our horizon there was always a kindly mirage to bolster our flagging hopes. When I came to read Georges Duhamel's *Le Notaire du Havre* (*Letter from Havre*), how well I recognized us all in the Pasquiers, who were also living on an illusion. Our illusion was "the land" in Saskatchewan. My father had acquired it when he was establishing his settlement at Dollard, along with other acreages he had had to let go one by one as our need for money became urgent. To this piece of land, *the* land, he remained doggedly, unshakeably attached. When things were at their worst, he who was not an optimist by nature was the one to offer encouragement.

"Anyway, Mélina," he'd say, "we've still got our land in Sas-

katchewan. If we can hold on long enough it'll save us in the end, you'll see."

To which Maman, emboldened by such confidence, would reply, "Yes, thank God, we've still got the land in Saskatchewan. When we absolutely have to, we'll sell it, but we don't have to do it now, the time's not come yet."

That faraway piece of land, transfigured by our fancies, daily given new reality in our imaginations, was for years the invincible refuge that saved us from total demoralization.

Sometimes, when the sun was setting at the end of the lane, spilling its rays into our back yard, we were sure we could also see its golden light filtering through the high, waving wheat on our land in Saskatchewan.

The oddest part of this whole story is that when I finally saw that land with my own eyes, long after it had ceased to belong to us, it looked just the way we'd seen it in our most rapturous daydreams. It really was a vision of intense blue sky, flaxen harvest, and wide-open space to comfort the heart.

V

I MUST HAVE been about fourteen when I began to immerse myself in my schoolwork the way one enters a cloister. I'd been beating around the bush, telling myself over and over that I'd get down to business next month. Then there came a day when I began to suspect that Maman was losing ground, and that she wouldn't be able to hold on if she didn't soon get some encouragement to brace her. The year-end examinations were approaching. I began reviewing my schoolwork in earnest. I'd get up well before the rest of the household and come down to study in the peace and quiet of the kitchen while I had it to myself for an hour or two. When Maman came to put the morning porridge on the stove, she'd find me at the big kitchen table with my books spread around me. So as not to disturb me she'd greet me simply with a nod, as she might one of our boarders, and a look of approval and commendation. Then she'd set to work with as little noise as possible.

At the end of that year I came first in my class for the first time in my life. I even won a medal for some subject or other. But what I'll never forget is Maman's face when I brought home the first instalment of her reward. It was immediately as though I'd lifted the weight of years past from her, and her anxiety about the years to come as well. She didn't pay me any lavish compliments, but she was radiant. Though she didn't know it, two or three times I heard her boasting about me to neighbours, artfully finding an appropriate opening in the conversation for the disclosure that "my daughter won the Bishop's medal this year." Once I appeared on the scene just as she was dropping a reference to that ordinary everyday medal, and I was struck by the expression in her eyes. They were shining as I'd rarely seen them do, like two deep pools

of tender radiance from which all the dark, bitter waters of hardship seemed to have been drained.

That was the support I was able to give her. How could I not have wanted to keep on giving it? She'd spared nothing in her support of me. It made me giddy to see myself able to lighten her step at so little cost. Coming first made me giddy, too. I even wonder if this wasn't the beginning of a habit that wasn't altogether good, because I took it very badly when I came second one year, uncovering a weakness in needing to come first that I had to learn to fight.

In any case, coming first wasn't such a remarkable feat as it might seem. What, apart from studying, could I have flung myself into with such abandon at the age of fifteen or sixteen in those days? We didn't engage in any sports to speak of. I did have a pair of skates, a present from my brother Rodolphe, and I learned to skate more or less in time to the lovely *Blue Danube Waltz* they used to play over the loudspeakers at public skating rinks. But that was all. I had to wait till I was earning my own money before I could buy myself a tennis racket, and later a light bicycle which was my pride and joy, and finally second-hand skis which were much too long for me but on which, for lack of hills in those parts, I was a very solitary pioneer of cross-country skiing years before it became the vogue.

But that wasn't until my young adulthood, my early twenties or even a bit older. I was late growing up, as often happened in those days. At fifteen I was a little old woman always buried in my books, with a weak upper back already, and my outlook cluttered by a hodgepodge of useless knowledge.

Even Maman came to think I was overdoing it. To make me leave my books and get to bed at a reasonable hour she'd sometimes cut off my electricity by taking out the fuse for the circuit my room was on. This way she could retire in peace, knowing I wouldn't be putting on my light again that night.

But at last I was keeping the promise I'd made her some years earlier in the hospital; year after year I was bringing home the medal awarded by the Manitoba French Canadian Association for the highest marks in French. Then I won the most coveted of all, the one given by the Quebec Department of Education to the stu-

dent with the highest year-end marks in French in all Manitoba. If I remember correctly, it bore in effigy the rather Roman head of Cyrille Delage, the noted Quebec writer on wines and gastronomy. My collection of medals was impressive by now, almost filling a drawer. Maman kept them carefully there, where they wouldn't get covered with dust. She who'd attended only a humble little village school and never won anything more than a fifty-cent book, which she still cherished, was quite dazzled by my drawerful of big fat medals; I suspect that when she was alone she often opened that drawer so she could admire them at her leisure.

Later I was to cause her much grief over those medals, and therein lies a tale I may recount if I have time. Now that I've begun to spin out my memories, they're tumbling out so thick and fast it frightens me, like a never-ending thread. It isn't going to stop, I tell myself. I'll never get down more than a particle of it all. Can it be possible to have enough inside you to fill tons of paper, if only you get hold of the right end of the thread?

In grades eleven and twelve, the Manitoba French Canadian Association prizes were fifty and one hundred dollars respectively. These were handsome sums in those days, almost comparable to today's Canada Council and Cultural Affairs grants, and you didn't have to apply for them, which was especially nice. I won both of them, which covered my enrolment at normal school and the purchase of the necessary books, so that I cost my parents practically nothing after I finished school, and that was essential, since by then they'd come to the end of their meagre resources.

When we were so far from Quebec, for those of us who finished school the achievement wasn't so much to have done so but to have done it in French as well as in English. And despite the law that allowed only an hour a day for the teaching of French in public schools in French-speaking neighbourhoods, it seems to me that the French we spoke was every bit as good as in Quebec, in the same period and for similar social strata.

Who or what was responsible for this almost miraculous situation? Certainly our collective fervour, the presence of some outstanding French immigrants among us, too, which brought distinction to our milieu, but most of all the zeal and tenacity of our schoolteachers, mostly nuns but also some lay teachers, who used to give extra, unpaid time to the teaching of French despite already onerous

schedules. A few used to take quite brazen liberties with the law; passionate and defiant, some of them drew the ire of the school board; they may have done us more harm than good.

When the provocation was not too visible, the Department of Education closed its eyes. As long as the children were able to show they were learning some English when the inspector came, the rest was more or less accepted. We were always vulnerable, of course, to an upsurge of hostility from small groups of fanatics calling for strict application of the law. For a time there was a rumour that there was an investigator on the warpath. The standing order at the time was that if the investigator or indeed anyone from the school board appeared unexpectedly, all our French textbooks were to be hidden, evidence of lessons in French erased from blackboards, and our English books prominently displayed. No doubt there were tense moments of that kind in some schools and perhaps even in mine before my time, but personally I was never aware of any such dramatic visit. Yet the danger was quite real and it galvanized us. We used to feel it around us; perhaps our teachers had something to do with maintaining the feeling. Then it would fade and our passive resistance would resume, which perhaps wore down the enemy more effectively than an open revolt. Sometimes I wonder if the opposition we were subjected to wasn't a service rather than a disservice to us. There were so few of us that if we'd been left alone the easy route would have been the fastest one to perdition, it seems to me. We were certainly spared the easy route. And we managed to learn and preserve the French language in all its beauty and elegance, but to tell the truth it was for the pride of it, the dignity; it couldn't equip us for everyday life.

In any event, if we were going to pass our exams and get our degrees or certificates, we had to comply with the program laid down by the Department of Education, which meant learning most subjects in English: chemistry, physics, mathematics, and most history. So we were more or less English in algebra, geometry, the sciences, and Canadian history, but French in Quebec history, French literature, and particularly history of religion. This gave us an odd turn of mind, constantly alert to readjusting our focus. It was like being a juggler with all those plates to keep in the air.

Sometimes this was a blessing. I remember the keen interest I took in English literature as soon as I had access to it. And for good

reason. Our French literature textbooks acquainted us with Veuillot and Montalembert, pages and pages of them, and very little else; practically nothing of Zola, Flaubert, Maupassant, even Balzac. And what idea could we have of French poetry when it was reduced almost exclusively to François Coppée, Sully Prudhomme, and La-martine's "Le Lac", which we parroted so many times that today, by some curious reaction – mental block perhaps – I couldn't recite a single line of it. And yet I remember getting 99% for my essay on that poem in a competition sponsored by the Manitoba French Canadian Association.

The doors to English literature, however, were open wide and gave us access to its greatest minds. I'd soon read Thomas Hardy, George Eliot, the Brontë sisters, Jane Austen. I knew Keats, Shelley, Byron, and the Lake poets, and adored them. Fortunately for French literature, our program of study did include the sparkling Alphonse Daudet. At fifteen I fell upon his *Lettres de mon moulin* (*Letters from My Mill*) and learned it by heart from beginning to end. Sometimes I wonder if the soft spot in my heart for Provence, which has taken me to every corner of it, isn't partly owing to my enchantment at my first encounter with graceful French prose when I was fifteen. Without this, French prose would have seemed very dreary beside the English. If, at that age, I'd been able to read Rimbaud, Verlaine, Baudelaire, and Radiguet, I can only imagine what it would have done to me.

My first literary encounter was with Shakespeare. He profoundly repelled my classmates and, it seems to me, hardly enthused the nun who was our literature teacher either. But I was enthralled by his passionate earthiness, joined sometimes to such sensitivity it would melt your heart, the expression of the soul's upwelling, with all its tenderness and turmoil.

I had the good fortune to attend a performance of *The Merchant of Venice*, presented by a London company that was touring Canada. The magic began for me at the Walker Theatre in Winnipeg – which in itself predisposed me to the sorcery of the stage, with its rows and rows of ornate balconies, its immense chandeliers, and its heavy crimson velvet curtain. All question of French or English or forbidden or imposed language disappeared. There was only a language that transcended languages, like that of music. In the highest balcony, leaning over the rail towards the actors – who

from that height looked very small – I could barely catch the words, which for me were pretty obscure anyway, yet I was spellbound. I've never really been able to fathom the fascination of my very first evening of Shakespeare, a fascination which is as much a mystery to me today as it ever was.

From then on the teacher, who had trouble comprehending the Bard, would rely on my insight, which wasn't all that great, but then I made up for the shortfall with enthusiasm. She maintained that if you were enthusiastic – or seemed enthusiastic – you could make the inspector swallow anything. What it took was memorizing. We were then into *Macbeth*. Since she couldn't help us understand the play, there was another recourse.

"Learn bits of it by heart," she implored us. "Then the inspector won't think about asking questions."

One evening I came upon a "bit" which was just about incomprehensible but which captivated me anyway with the indescribable shade of darkness I was sure I could see in it. The next day, burning with excitement, I recited the whole of Macbeth's great monologue, "Is this a dagger which I see before me...."

The teacher couldn't get over finding me so passionately enamoured of that remote poet of Elizabethan times. She seemed a bit put out, in a way, but was quick to see the benefit she might draw from my aptitude. Subsequently, in fact, whenever we were expecting one of our Visiting Mothers with a particular penchant for English, or some important gentleman from the Department of Education, she would put me on notice.

"Save the class, Gabrielle. Stand up and give him 'Is this a dagger....' "

I was already saving the class through the Manitoba French Canadian Association's year-end competition. I thought it was a lot to be saving it in English too. But I was a bit of a show-off, I think, perhaps owing partly to our collective inferiority complex, which led me to seek approval at every opportunity.

The inspector arrived. He addressed us in English, of course.

"How are you getting along with Shakespeare, Sister? *Macbeth*? Oh, fine, fine! Does anyone remember by which names the witches on the heath hail Macbeth?"

I was like a cat on hot bricks and shot up my hand. I was the sole volunteer. The evening before I'd been turning the pages of

my *Macbeth* and by happy coincidence had lighted upon those gloriously resonant salutations.

The inspector smiled as he looked at me. Who else would he have looked at? All the class but me practically had their backs turned to him. I jumped to my feet and pronounced, "Thane of Glamis, Thane of Cawdor."

That I should know those strange-sounding salutations seemed to make him unbelievably happy. It appeared he felt himself to be in enemy territory and was as much afraid of our reactions as we were of his. He asked me if I knew some passage of the play by heart. I lost no time drawing the mask of tragedy over my face and launching full tilt into "Is this a dagger...."

Strangest of all, when I first saw *Macbeth* performed in London many years later I discovered that I hadn't been too bad a Macbeth way back then, in my tone, delivery, in everything but accent, which was straight out of Deschambault Street and must have been excruciatingly funny.

But the inspector didn't laugh. He seemed moved. Perhaps he sensed a significance in that classroom scene which was as strange as that of the witches on the heath. Perhaps he had an inkling of what it was like to be a little French Canadian in those days in Manitoba, and perhaps he felt compassion for us, a secret admiration, even.

"Why do you love Shakespeare so, young lady?" he asked me.

The young lady was hearing herself so addressed for the first time in her life, and was overcome. She replied with something off the top of her head, having no doubt heard it somewhere.

"Because he's the greatest."

"And why is he the greatest?"

That bothered me and I thought a bit before risking a reply.

"Because he knows all about the human soul."

That seemed to make him even happier than my answer about the witches. He studied me with touching benevolence. That was when I first discovered how dearly our English-speaking adversaries can love us, providing we play the game and show what good, obedient children we are.

"Are there any other English poets you like?" he asked me.

I knew Coleridge's "Ancient Mariner" by heart. I'd learned to love it the year before from an elderly nun who adored fine allit-

eration, and who would recite it to us in a dreamy voice with a faraway look in her eyes.

"We were the first that ever burst into that silent sea...."

I recited the old ballad for him as he'd certainly never heard it before, swaying to the rhythm of the lines, picturing the sailing ship lost in the Sargasso Sea.

The inspector had apparently lost sight of the fact that there were thirty-five pupils in that class, thirty-four of whom were as silent as posts.

When he took his leave, accompanied to the door by the teacher, on whom he was lavishing warm felicitations and much "Madame..., dear Madame...," I told myself, "Soon I'll be the one getting the compliments. Sister must be pleased with me."

At the door he redoubled his effusions. The teacher beamed. I thought I heard snatches that just might have been about me: "brilliant young lady...will go far...."

Ah, far was certainly where I'd decided to go. But in what direction?

At last the teacher came back to her place behind the desk high up there on the platform, up the two steps I so constantly tripped on in my years at school. Her face still bore a hint of triumph. Was it because we'd hoodwinked the inspector, or because she fancied she'd suddenly become a superlative English literature teacher? Who could say? I approached her, a bit too eager to learn what had been said at the door about me.

"Was the inspector pleased with me, Sister?"

She glared at me, suddenly all disapproval. The demon pride was what the nuns used to hunt down in us most diligently, all the while reminding us relentlessly that as French Canadians we must lift our heads and hold them high – so how were we supposed to know when to bow them?

Then she softened a little, proud of me but feeling she shouldn't show it. She shot an almost affectionate rebuke at me which made her the first to recognize my natural inclination, though neither she nor I knew where it would lead me.

"Get out of my sight, you little romancer!"

THAT WAS in my last year at the Académie Saint-Joseph, grade twelve, which I very nearly never took. When I'd finished grade eleven, I overheard my father and mother talking about me. Once

again their voices reached me from the little summer kitchen, through the open door on a mild summer evening in late June or early July. I always found it profoundly disconcerting to suddenly hear them talking frankly about me in the belief that they were alone. I was on the point of moving away but curiosity kept me hovering near the door, trembling; a curiosity mixed with much heartache, and fear of learning the worst.

My father was admitting that he had neither strength nor courage left, saying wearily to Maman, "If I'm going to live to see her able to earn her living as a teacher as you've always wanted, Mélina, she'll have to get there soon. I won't be able to wait much longer."

I think by then he'd conveyed the land in Saskatchewan to my sister Adèle in repayment of loans she'd advanced him. So we didn't even have that illusion any more. Papa was therefore arguing that I should go straight into normal school that autumn.

But Maman was being stubborn.

"When she's doing so well at school, getting the highest marks and all, taking her out now would be so unfair! And then, have you considered that without grade twelve she'll only get a school leaving certificate, not matriculation, and that'll make problems for her later when she wants to teach in the city to be near us."

"You talk as if I can choose how long I'm going to live," grumbled my father.

I ached to rush out and tell them I was going to get a job, any job, to relieve them of spending all that money on me. I think I couldn't stand the idea of their being here together again because of me, like refugees from their lovely big house in this kind of shack, even though they felt at home here, perhaps because it was more their style. What held me back was fear, most likely. Fear of life, which so often looked appealing, even exciting, but so often like a dark, tormented landscape ahead of me. And then once again came the thought that if I was going to repay Maman for the endless sacrifices she'd imposed on herself, nothing less than dazzling success on my part would do.

My father heaved a long-suffering sigh.

"Have it the way you want, Maman." He called her that, as we children did, in the last years of his life. "I'd have liked to see her standing on her own feet before I go."

SO I TOOK grade twelve despite all the obstacles – a ridiculous expense, an outrageous luxury for people in almost desperate straits as we were. Fortunately I won the hundred-dollar scholarship given by the Manitoba French Canadian Association. I'd come first in French five years in a row. It occurred to our principal to check my year-end marks in the Department of Education examinations, and she found what she'd expected, that I'd come first in English too in those five years. This was cause for rejoicing at school and among the nuns. But for my part, as I remember, all I felt was a kind of indifference. I must have begun to realize that coming first didn't really mean very much. The honour brought me another trophy, of course, which went to fatten the collection in my medal drawer.

Then there came the long-awaited day of what we called *la graduation*. There were twelve or fifteen of us graduating, I think, a fairly big group in those days when not many girls of our milieu went that far in school, often by choice but mostly for lack of means. The principal, who loved an excuse for holding celebrations and receptions, decided she couldn't let the occasion pass without making a big splash that "would for ever be remembered in the annals of the school."

A large number of both French and English dignitaries were to be invited. The commencement ceremony was to take place in the auditorium, with parents and guests seated in the audience and we, *les graduées*, sitting or standing on the stage where everyone could see us, with all the ferns from the convent arranged behind and around us. It must have given us a sylvan setting indeed, since the big backdrop behind us, I think I recall, was painted with tall interlacing trees as well. We were to be dressed all in white, including our shoes. In the crook of the left arm, near the heart, we were to hold identical bouquets of red roses, bought all together at a small discount and costing us five dollars each. And we were to be photographed up there on the stage in all our glory, holding our bouquets, and it was all to be so beautiful that some of our teachers were already close to tears as they coached us in the bows we were to make, "bending from the waist, but never looking down...."

And so for the day that should have been one of pure delight for her, Maman was obliged to eke even more than usual out of

59

nothing. How she did it I'd rather not know, but I had my two dollars for the photograph. "Smile, you pretty liddel ladies," beseeched the Armenian photographer, for there was always one of us drifting wistfully off as the shutter snapped. He never did get us all smiling together at "the beautiful life waiting for you, just think, liddel ladies, like a morning in June." I had my white shoes. I had my bouquet of roses, the first bought flowers I'd ever held. A florist's delivery still makes my heart skip a beat, and it's probably because of those roses.

And the dress. Where could Maman's thoughts have been when she sat down to make it? I think I recall that Papa's condition worsened about that time, although I myself didn't really notice, I was in such a turmoil over pleasing him by coming first. Increasingly, everything was falling on Maman's shoulders and on hers alone.

From up there on the stage, I searched and searched through the faces in the crowd. Finally I caught sight of her, and she remains for ever in my memory as I saw her then. Her poor face was grey with fatigue – she may have finished my dress only late the night before – but was lifted, straining towards me, smiling at me across the distance. For all its sunken eyelids and drawn cheeks, it shone with pride, and that hurt more than anything I'd seen before because suddenly I knew how much all this had cost. The wave of cruel realization swept over me, gripped me in vice-like anguish, robbed me of all my joy in the day, then faded, leaving me to my insouciant youth up there in my place of honour.

I seem to have forgotten all the rest of that scene. To bring it back I have to look at the photograph. It shows pretty well how things were. My dress isn't very stylish. The hem is rather uneven. The collar's a bit askew as well, as though Maman had cut it wrong and not been able to fix it. But the girl seems not to know she's awkwardly dressed. The large, anxious eyes look far away towards the vast unknown called life, and it's her confidence that overcomes a kind of shadow from the future hanging like a cloud, darkening this, her greatest day.

I can talk about her without embarrassment. The child that I was is as much a stranger to me as I would have been to her if she, at the dawn of life as they say, had been able to see me as I

am today. But from birth to death and from death to birth, through remembrance on my part and hopes and dreams on hers, the two of us keep moving closer to a common meeting ground, as the distance between us grows.

VI

I ENTERED the Winnipeg Normal Institute that autumn. It was a big building in barracks or firehall style, on Logan Street as I recall. For a time we'd had a normal school in St-Boniface, where the courses were given in French and the goal was to prepare a body of teachers to teach in French. My elder sisters, Anna and Adèle, had studied there. Now all that was in the past. So from a school run by French-speaking nuns, where despite all the obstacles placed in our path we managed to live pretty well as we did at home, we now passed into an institution which was strictly English. Well, no; we did have one French-speaking instructor. She came a number of times to pronounce three or four laborious sentences reminiscent of Ionesco's comically mechanical verbalizations in *The Bald Soprano*. Perhaps they even originated in the same textbook. Having by mistake posed questions to one or other of our little French-speaking contingent and got real answers in real French, she ceased thenceforth to call on us at all, and the lessons proceeded as previously, between people talking at cross-purposes without understanding a word of what they were saying.

But we weren't just passing from one language to another. We were passing from one climate to another. We were leaving a little world in which the nuns overprotected us perhaps, sheltered us too much from reality, and venturing into the lion's mouth, one might say.

There, the most apprehensive of our teachers had led us to believe, our faith and our fidelity to our past would be sorely tried. We would need to show unshakeable determination. More important, there in the enemy camp we'd be duty bound to do honour to our community by our fineness of character, our exemplary conduct, our excellence in all things. And if confrontation proved inevitable, we'd have to face it courageously.

That was the foolish state of mind I was in when I took the streetcar one fine morning for the long ride, interrupted by an aggravating transfer, to the gloomy building on Logan Street. Though it terrified me at the time, today I really have no clear recollection of the building itself.

Sometimes, when she was not too "hard-up" as she used to say – she knew so little English that it was significant she'd picked up the expression – Maman would give me twenty-five cents for my lunch at the school canteen; the rest of the time she'd make me a sandwich to eat with a piece of cheese and an apple.

In my class of about seventy-five students, only five or six of us were French-speaking. Two were country girls and were so shy they'd shrink into the ground if one of our instructors so much as looked at them. What could be expected of comrades-in-arms like that? I saw from the beginning that if ever I should have to do battle here, I'd have to do it with a very small army. For a time I saw the school as the scene of a battle to be waged, and nothing else. Hitherto, the tactics we'd been taught to use against our English adversaries had been tact, diplomacy, cunning strategy, and polite disobedience. In my imagination, the time had now come to cross swords. I was soon presented with my opportunity.

After perhaps a week of classes, the school's principal, the kindly old Dr. Mackintyre whom I became so fond of later, came to give us his principal's word of welcome. He was a teacher of psychology, and he delivered an hour-long, rambling peroration consisting merely, to me at that time, of an old duffer's well-intentioned maunderings. In fact, long before the notion of self-fulfilment came to be common currency, this man was talking of nothing else, using terms like "an opening out" and "a blossoming of self". Once started on his favourite topic, which was that a child is not made to suit a school and so the school must suit the child, that "those dear young creatures before everything else should be happy in school", he could go on for hours on end.

He had a strong Scottish brogue, a fine head of white hair, and, I was soon to learn, a warm, kind heart.

As he spoke, I was waiting for an opening. Suddenly, there it was. I put up my hand, asking to speak.

Agreeably surprised at such interest in the midst of the prevailing

somnolence, he adjusted his spectacles and turned to the seating chart showing each student's name and place in the room.

"Miss Roy," (pronounced the English way in that milieu) "you have a question to ask?"

I stood up. My knees were shaking, only barely holding me up. But there was no turning back. It was now or never for my profession of faith. My voice sounded very weak, as if rising into a vast acoustical void and coming back from afar distorted and quite unrecognizable.

"I agree with you, sir," I said, "that a child's education must first take account of his own personality."

"Well," said he, all smiles, "I see you've been closely following what I've been saying. Have you something to add?"

"Yes, that I see a terrible contradiction between theory and practice. For example, take the case of a little French-speaking child coming to school for the first time in his life, and it's an English school. From the minute he arrives he'll have to be put in the mould designed for little English Canadians. What chance will there ever be for his personality to blossom?"

A deathly silence fell around me. I'd touched the forbidden subject. Woe to the one who lets scandal through the door. I had the impression the whole class was turning away from me. Dr. Mackintyre studied me with a look of surprise, but one in which there was neither animosity nor disapproval.

"Quite so! Quite so!" he said. Then he invited me to consider that the subject hardly lent itself to class discussion and suggested that I stop by his office after four o'clock; we'd talk about it then.

I sat down and the aftershock of my audacity hit me. I was sure I was done for. I'd be expelled from the school, dashing Maman's hopes and proving that my father's gloomy misgivings had been right after all. Ah, how well inspired I'd been to go looking for martyrdom! In my agitation, I even began gathering up my books and notes, getting ready for my inevitable dismissal.

At four o'clock I went to the principal's office. The stoop-shouldered old man with the shock of white hair gave me a weary smile as he waved me to the chair on the other side of the huge desk.

"Brave girl!" he muttered. In my surprise I didn't realize at first that he was speaking of me.

Then he confided that when he was a young man in Scotland

he'd experienced the same racial and linguistic injustices suffered by the French community of Manitoba. And that he'd often been laughed at for his burr, too.

"Language is the vehicle of communication," he observed, "but it's created more misunderstanding in the world than anything else, except perhaps faith."

He then pointed out that since our French contingent was not a large one, it would probably be better not to waken the sleeping hounds of fanaticism on either side; that he could see only one course for us to follow, which was to excel in everything, always to be better than others.

"Work at your French," he said. "Always be faithful to it. Teach it when you get the chance and as much as you can...without getting caught. But don't forget, you'll have to excel in English too. The tragic thing about minorities is that they have to be better, or disappear.... Can you yourself, dear child, see another way out for you?"

I shook my head.

Adroitly, he then questioned me about my family, the position my father had held, my studies with the nuns, all the way down to what we lived on, as I recall. He seemed to be better at patching together my pathetic story than I was myself.

"Poor gerrrl," he was saying now. "Poor young gerrrl."

He shook my hand very warmly. And when I was out in the corridor he called after me in a loud voice, "Never give up!"

I left with much to think about. It hadn't escaped me that the extremists on our side, who were pushing for French teaching exclusively, and for a refusal to learn English, would have us driven to tragic isolation or else, sooner or later, to the point of packing up and leaving. While there were still a few Québécois coming to join our ranks in Manitoba, far more often it was the opposite: our young people, raised in French, leaving to settle in the mother province. I myself dreamed of it. Dr. Mackintyre, it seemed to me, had been talking the language of friendship, and it matched the counsel given us by some of the most astute of our teachers at school.

After that I stopped trying to provoke our teachers, although there was one who seemed determined to provoke me. This teacher's history lectures seemed to be aimed at me from the ill-starred

day when, on the strength of what we'd learned from the nuns, I insisted there couldn't have been any bad popes. Thereafter, at every opportunity the teacher would trot out the schemers, the poisoners, the quarrelsome, the fornicators, and the incestuous among the popes. Though I was no papist, I could have become one at the goading of that rabid anti-papist. But I kept choking back my indignation. I was determined to take what was worth taking while I was there and leave the rest. Ruefully, I'd discovered I could be liked, and even considered charming and lovable, as long as I stayed in my place, second place that is, and showed I was content to be there. All I was trying to do after that was get good marks. The hard, solitary path I'd seen ahead of me when I was a child was indeed mine, there was no getting away from it.

My father's health was declining day by day. This had been going on so long that I hadn't yet realized how fast his condition was deteriorating now. But his heavily lined face and his deeply sunken eyes, in which there was only suffering now, used to follow me throughout my morning streetcar ride, when I'd sometimes open my books and try to review my work. They haunted me still at the school during lectures, and I had to summon every ounce of will to rivet my attention on what at the time seemed to be the most important and pressing parts of the course material. I was working hardest on my English accent, having made the class laugh several times at my expense. I finally threw myself totally into my work and lost sight of my father's suffering image.

That's the way it's been too often in my life. In my haste to accomplish and thus bring support, comfort, or reason for pride to those I love, I haven't been attentive enough to see that they couldn't wait.

DURING the second term we were sent out into various schools of the Winnipeg School Commission, where each of us was to take charge of a class under the supervision of the regular teacher, who would evaluate our teaching prowess and ability to keep order. The marks we'd get from the teacher were to count heavily in our final marks for the year. Most of us were terrified by the prospect, because if we happened to get a harpy for a teacher it could be disastrous. Which is what happened to me.

I'd barely opened my mouth to introduce myself when she wanted

to know what nationality I was, because of what she called my peculiar accent. And when I spelled my name for her she snorted, "French, eh!" Without further ado she told me to carry on with the lesson where she'd left off; I don't remember what the subject was, geography perhaps. All I recall of that class is the horror of it. The pupils were from a district known to be a rough one. They were fairly big, aged twelve to fourteen, and half boys, half girls. They quickly saw how shy and frightened I was, and went wild. I've never heard such an uproar in a classroom. They slammed the lids of their desks. They slapped the sides of them with their rulers. They made buzzing sounds in unison or whistled. The teacher didn't lift a finger to help me. She stood a little to the side with her arms crossed and a hard little smile on her lips, appearing to enjoy watching me getting deeper and deeper into trouble. Beyond my despair of the moment, another still more devastating was rearing its head: if I have to cope with this to be a teacher I'll never make it, I was telling myself, I'll never be able to stand it. And I saw the door to the only occupation I'd been prepared for closing before me. In truth, I was losing my grip on everything: this classroom full of children making fun of me, my rapidly vanishing future, my confidence in my capabilities, and even my hope of passing my final examinations.

But most devastating of all was the haunting image of my ailing father. His pulmonary edema had suddenly worsened and he'd been hospitalized for several days. On account of his age, he'd refused the operation that had been proposed to him. After receiving treatments merely to give him some relief, he'd been allowed to return home. This had made him so happy that in my youthful obliviousness I thought he had recovered. The improvement lasted a few days and then, two nights previous, he'd stopped pacing the downstairs hallway and come, towards dawn, to the foot of the stairs, calling to Maman in distress. She'd gone to him at once and immediately had a little bed from upstairs brought down for him so he'd be close by and she could care for him while continuing to go about her work. In resisting his illness he'd stayed on his feet so long I was very alarmed to see him take to bed, but I couldn't believe this phase wouldn't last at least a few months. Before leaving the house that morning I'd gone to look at him as he slept, still under the sedation given him during the night. I'd been struck by

the change in his face and had asked Maman if I hadn't better stay at home that day, but knowing what a hard day was awaiting me and how nerve-racking it would be to put it off, she took it on herself to reassure me, not realizing herself, perhaps, how close the end really was.

"Go and do your best," she'd told me. "When this day's behind you you'll be happier and in better shape to help me."

Those images and anxious words were large in my mind as I faced that roomful of rebellious children and tried once again to get their attention, to no avail. My voice, weakened by fear and the turmoil inside me, didn't reach them. I wonder if the words I was trying to speak even got past my lips. Perhaps they did, because I seem to recall a boy laughing loudly as he mimicked me.

Then, at the point where I could take no more and was perhaps about to break down in tears, throw in the sponge, turn tail and run, the door opened a crack. The school principal beckoned to the teacher, who went to join him in the hall. She returned with a very different face. First in surprise and then in fright, I thought I saw sympathy for me in her expression now. She bent forward and said softly in my ear:

"Go now. Go quickly. They've just telephoned to say your father...is...very ill...."

VII

I TOOK THE streetcar. It must have been just a thrifty reflex, because I think I remember the principal, or perhaps even the dragon-teacher, offering to lend me the money to go home by taxi.

The trip was slow and the stops at practically every street corner drove me frantic. I was tempted two or three times to get off and walk, I was so sure I'd get there faster.

At the transfer point for St-Boniface, just before the Provencher Bridge, I saw my nephew Fernand, my sister Anna's eldest son who'd just become an office clerk, getting on my streetcar – or perhaps I was getting on his. Our eyes met across the crowd. We realized we'd been called to the house for the same reason. We elbowed our way through the crowd to be together. The closeness of our ages, only three months apart, had earned us a lot of teasing, and consequently we'd felt uncomfortable and tended to avoid each other. He didn't like being called my nephew any more than I liked being called his aunt. But now, though neither of us said a word or even looked at the other, we joined our little fingers on the seat between us and kept them joined.

The room where my father was dying adjoined the living and dining room. At one time he'd used it as an office and we continued to call it *l'office*. I don't know who first used the English term. Perhaps my father himself, since he was accustomed to using English for anything related to his office work in Winnipeg, where it was the only language of work permitted; or my mother, out of a kind of ingenuous respect for the sort of thing he did at work, which was so far removed from her lowly domestic occupations. Now that I've at last come to wonder about it, who is there to tell me? The room was furnished at that time with a big roll-top desk and a safe, and its walls were covered with very detailed maps of

Saskatchewan and Alberta and others of the townships, on which the locations of his settlements were marked with circles. It was here that my father had often worked far into the night, writing reports to the government or lists of supplies of all kinds needed by the next group of settlers who'd be starting out for their new homes under his guardianship. Maman had probably established him there for the sake of convenience, so she could look after him without constantly having to run up and down stairs, but perhaps also having thought it fitting that his life should end here, where he'd known his hours of greatest hope.

When we reached the house, Fernand and I, still with our little fingers joined, it was full of people. I'd be at a loss to recall exactly who was there, for I had eyes only for the head on the pillow. I have never seen such an avowal of pain on a human face. Not physical pain; from that, at least, he'd been delivered by a strong sedative, which was no doubt also affecting the thinking realms of his being since he appeared unconscious, though from time to time he'd still give a little moan as if in recollection of suffering more than from its present effects. But what his face expressed, now that all defences were down, was the incredible accumulation of suffering in a single human life. I was fascinated by that defenceless face; as I looked at it, I was hearing a soul's long, soundless lamentation for the first time in my life. So that's what life is, I said to myself, a torment so frightful one's face can no longer mask it when the end comes. And I think it was that extraordinary, other-worldly openness which must at last have made me see death as something majestic and beautiful.

We had a little tabby cat which had come to adore my father – it's a mystery why cats are instinctively drawn to melancholy souls. He kept jumping up onto the pillow despite my mother's efforts to shoo him away. He'd crouch very close to the dying man's face and watch it intensely. When Maman was out of the room for a minute, he put out his tongue and gently began to lick the fine white fringe of hair on the still temple, remembering, perhaps, all the fondling my father had lavished on him. I left him alone. It seemed to me our little Mephisto was showing the tender familiarity we ourselves shrank from in the face of approaching death, and in his innocence was the only one still treating my father like a friend, the rest of us having more or less abandoned him.

Not far from the bed, some neighbours were kneeling and praying aloud. I watched the little animal stretch out a soft paw and touch my father's forehead, perhaps in his way trying to get him to pay attention. I heard sweet voices asking God to receive my father's soul. Then Maman came back. Scandalized to find Mephisto occupying so prominent a place in such a tragic scene, she picked him up and took him away, and shut him behind some door. Long afterwards, we could still hear him mewing disconsolately through the murmur of prayers.

At last I knelt down with the others, not so much to pray, I think, but to be closer to the event, this end of a life which was so engrossing me. This was the first time I was to witness death and, as happens with everyone, I think, the first feeling it awakened in me was such a burning, infinite, and prodigious curiosity that for the moment it was distracting me from grief. I'd been hauled away from the insignificant tussle we call life and brought face to face with the total mystery of existence, and this death on this day was telling no more about existence than had the first death to come upon humankind.

Scattered among these painful thoughts came all kinds of other ordinary ones, some almost trite. Now that I was closer to my father's face, I observed again how much he looked like photographs I'd seen of Tolstoy in his latter years: the same high forehead and receding hairline, the same furrowed cheeks, the same eyes deeply sunk in their sockets – and, not so long ago, the same piercing gaze which seemed to look deeper into the soul than any other I've known. Naïvely, it also pleased me to liken the love that both of them had for the Doukhobors, for whose settlement in Canada Tolstoy had contributed the royalties from one of his great novels. Despite their fractiousness, my father had always defended them and continued to attend to their needs long after conducting them to the virgin lands on which they were to settle. It occurred to me, too, that in French he and Tolstoy bore the same given name, Léon.

Suddenly my father's death throes became more pronounced. His chest sagged. His mouth opened wide and gasped for air with a rattling sound. His eyes, however, remained closed as if from exhaustion. For several seconds his body remained still, then with a longer rattle the terrible struggle resumed. It was as if someone were trying desperately to tear himself away from life, and when

I thought of it that way, as a struggle to be free, it seemed to me that life had been impossibly cruel to him. At last he lifted his hands limply as if to push everything away. He opened his eyes, not seeing anyone around him, I think. Though unseeing, they seemed to follow a light across the room. Another breath, not as deep or from as far away, more like a sigh this time, came just as far as his lips like a last little ripple fading on a beach. His head fell to the side. There was no sound, no struggle now. Silence at last.

Then Maman approached. She looked at the face of her lifelong companion with a curious fervour that I had never before seen in her, one which saw much more in this dead man than any of us had ever seen in his lifetime. Gently she closed his half-open eyes. Then in the midst of the prayerful silence there rose a high-pitched wail which I didn't realize at first was mine. Astonished to hear me cry out that way, Maman dropped everything and rushed to comfort me. Kneeling beside me, she put an arm around my shoulders and drew me to her, rocking us both as if to lull our pain.

I couldn't yet understand why my grief was so acute. I hadn't thought I'd loved my father so deeply. It was now my turn to have my eyes opened, and I couldn't stand the hard reality that death was teaching me in so short a lesson. Does a man need to die for his life to become important in a way unsuspected mere seconds earlier? And must one's own soul be laid bare, stripped of its cover in relation to that life? In this moment I discovered a thousand and one lost opportunities for showing my father the affection now pouring out of me like a pent-up torrent. Only last week he'd asked Maman why I hadn't been to see him in the hospital. She'd made excuses for me, saying I was very worried about the lesson I had to give in one of the city schools, working every night preparing all kinds of approaches because I didn't really know what would be asked of me, that he'd soon be home in any event. There was truth in all this, but it was also true that I hadn't gone to see him because I didn't know how to behave or what to say to him when he was so sick. We'd never learned to talk to each other, each always hoping the other would start and break the ice. Only now I realized he'd craved affection, wanting it so badly he couldn't ask for it for fear of being rejected. Now I knew it was this fear which used to make him seem so severe. I knew because I could see that I'd always

been that way myself. The truth was that we were two of a kind, each living in fear of finding our poor, shy love for each other misunderstood.

I began to cry in great sobs, I was so distraught that life should be such a tissue of misunderstanding. Thinking perhaps that my misery came from feeling my father hadn't loved me, Maman now tried to persuade me otherwise. Still kneeling beside me and rocking me as she held me to her, she whispered that two nights ago when he'd begun to suffer so much he'd told her she could depend on me because I was really a brave, hard-working child; that two or three weeks ago, when I was running a bit of a fever but had gone to the school as usual, he'd been very upset, saying, "She's got my delicate health, poor child. I'm afraid she's going to have a hard life." And so on, not suspecting she was wringing my heart, because my grief lay in seeing no possibility of making amends. My relationship to my father would remain for ever as it was when death separated us. Nothing could ever be added, taken back, corrected, or wiped away.

If only I'd had just one visit with him in the hospital. "One little visit," I told myself pleadingly as if it just might be possible, as if the lost opportunity might miraculously be recaptured. Or perhaps I resented his not waiting, not giving me a little more time to bring him my teacher's certificate. So I wept as I thought about the joy we could have had together.

Now there was no going back. All I had to console me was my memory of that wheelbarrow ride with my old father holding the handles high and me in the box, lifting to him what I really believe was a beaming face.

MY FATHER'S remains were exposed at the house in an open coffin, as was the custom then. In the house on Deschambault Street there had been similar observances for two other members of the family: my much-loved Grandmother Landry, who'd come to die there at the age of eighty-four when I was eight and whom I remembered well, and my sister Marie-Agnès, who'd died as the result of burns when I was a baby. The house was therefore no stranger to the simple yet dignified preparations occasioned by a death in those days.

Maman had removed everything removable from the living room,

and the rest, just the piano as I recall, was draped in black, as was the big window looking onto the street. In the middle of the room stood the coffin, surrounded by tapers whose flickering light played night and day on my father's stone-still face, now and then creating a fleeting impression of life. He looked very distinguished in his best navy-blue suit; he'd worn it so little in latter years that it looked brand new, though it was very loose around his wasted shoulders. Although this was no longer the fashion, he had on a hard wing collar which held his neck and head very straight, reminding me of the picture I still had of him wearing a collar like that for some evening event, which would have been a rare occasion indeed. Or perhaps I wasn't really remembering such an occasion, just imagining it from the story Maman had told us a dozen times about the invitation she and my father had received to the lieutenant-governor's ball, and about the extraordinary adventure this had led to.

Yes, some twenty years or more before, when my father was already well on in years and my mother still young, though old enough to have given birth to almost all her children, they really had been invited to a ball for the first and only time in their lives. I loved the story. Maman used to tell it as though it were funny, something to laugh over, but I'd always thought it rather sad. Why did it keep popping into my mind out of the blue at this time, during meals for instance, or now, when the flood of callers was about to begin and I was here alone in the stillness and quiet beside my father's open coffin? Alone, that is, except for the little tabby cat. For he'd been quick to learn to make his visits to his dead master at times when Maman was too busy to see him slip by, and when no one was there but me; he knew I'd never chase him away. He'd jump up on the coffin and crouch on its edge with all four feet together, and stay there motionless, his eyes big and reflecting the light of the tapers, staring at my father's face. He never touched it now. He just watched it intently. I think he and I were equally engrossed in the drama of death, he on one side of the coffin and I on the other.

But what had made me think about the ball just then? Perhaps the big gilt-framed photograph of my father when he was young, which Maman had hung on the living-room wall. It must have been taken about the time they met, or perhaps earlier, because he

couldn't have been much more than thirty. He was a stranger to me as he appeared in that picture, a handsome young man with curly hair, a trace of a smile in his eyes, and an honest, open face alive with hope and ideals. The face of a man with a sense of fun and also hope, confidence, and, to a certain extent, ambition: all the things that nourish the soul. I'd have been very surprised if anyone had told me then how much I was like the young man in the heavy gold-leafed frame, especially around the eyes.

On the same wall Maman had also hung photographs of my grandfather Charles Roy and his sad-faced wife, Marcelline. The portraits upset me terribly every time I looked at them, and I resented Maman's having given them that place of honour.

We'd never known those two except through those awful portraits and the occasional disclosure let drop by my father. I felt such an antipathy towards them that I refused to recognize anything about myself in them. I imagined I was descended only from the Landrys, a breed in striking contrast, light-hearted, fun-loving, romantic, even a little fey, as well as gentle, loving, and passionate.

But at this moment, having turned my eyes to the grandmother I'd never known, I found I was suddenly deeply moved by that cheerless face with lips closed tight as though holding back too deep a sorrow to convey in words, a sorrow perhaps never confessed except in this silent photograph. From the frame beside Marcelline's, the face of her husband glared down, Charles Roy, my grandfather, grimly stern and uncompromising. Yet however hard his eyes, they seemed to be brimming with the misty sadness of never having known what it is to love or be loved; a self-appointed judge of morality, he was alone in the world. The little I knew of him, gleaned from scraps my father let fall in emotional moments, was that he was hostile to anything that was joyful or mind-broadening, and particularly to books, which he considered to be the most evil things on earth.

One day something very strange happened between my father and me. I'd escaped to some corner of the house and was reading; I seemed happy, I suppose, as one always is when borne off by the magic of a well-told story, or merely the elation of seeing oneself in words more adroit than one's own. My father appeared and stood looking at me. In a voice that was a bit husky and full of despondency, he asked, "D'you know how lucky you are?"

I looked up at him, astonished. Then he blurted out this extraordinary revelation:

"When I was about the age you are now, I was reading one night in a corner the way you're doing, only by candlelight, and I was happy for a while, when all of a sudden my father was standing over me, shouting, 'There you are again filling your head with lies and bad influence instead of getting on with honest work! Give me that cursèd book! All that's written there is lies!' And he snatched it out of my hands. He lifted a lid from the stove. The flame was high because the night was cold and we'd made the fire roar. My father threw my book in it, the only book I had. I can still see it burn, all my life I've seen it burn."

Now, alone in this room with his remains, I finally grasped all the bitterness of that outpouring so many years before. I began to weep softly, not for me and my omissions and regrets but for a thirteen-year-old's grief borne for a lifetime without real consolation, and now beyond consolation.

Not long after that incident, according to Maman, young Léon left the paternal home and went to Quebec City, where he took employment as a junior salesman in a shop. He was paid so little that he couldn't afford a room in the city and slept on a pallet under the counter on which, by day, he displayed merchandise for sale. This surely must be the story I was told, yet I'm so accustomed to stringing out facts and story-telling that a doubt has crept into my mind, and there are times when I tell myself it just couldn't have been so. Now I have no one left to resolve my hesitation and corroborate the story as I believe I heard it.

In due course my father was taken under the wing of a compassionate and generous priest who bore the cost of two years of study for him in a classical college, though whether in Quebec City or elsewhere I don't know. Then he went to the United States, where for the next few years he was so constantly on the move that who knows where he'd been, as Maman used to say.

Despite my distaste, I returned to the latter-day Savonarola, the burner of books who was at the root of those misfortunes. I began to understand where my father's gloomy side had come from, the side that showed increasingly as he aged. Also his fear of being misunderstood, which made him touchy. As for my book-burning

grandfather, to whom could he have owed such bitterness of soul that all he'd ever spread around him was more bitterness? My feeling was that one would have to go back indefinitely, into the far, far distant past, to discover the real source of ill, or of good.

My eye fell again on the portrait of my father as a young man, the one I was comparing with his face in death, and despite myself the story of the lieutenant-governor's ball returned to my thoughts.

The invitation had come to the house. My parents must have been living in the house they rented when they first came to St-Boniface, before the one on Deschambault Street was built. I imagine that house filled with young children, and with tears, laughter, and rumpus. I can see Maman, a bit frazzled, perhaps doing the laundry, wiping her hands hurriedly on her apron before opening the large envelope with the gold crown on the flap. Then a bolt from the blue! "Mr. and Mrs. Léon Roy are requested to attend a ball at...."

Did she begin at once to picture the dress she'd wear, and how she'd make it, and what fabric she'd use? What is certain, because she told us a hundred times, is that her mind was made up immediately: nothing in the world would keep her from going to that ball. My father was away at the time for a week or two, visiting his settlements. He might come back bone-weary, as he often did, and not much interested in getting himself all dandied up for an evening like that, one which would surely intimidate him, unaccustomed as he was to social gatherings. Maman set out to persuade him to accept, and she succeeded. How did she do it? Had she already made her dress of peach-coloured satin? Did she put it on to show him, with her beautiful black hair done up in a chignon? And did his heart melt to see the radiance of the young woman, who'd never in her life known a single hour of social triumph? I had the strongest urge to run to her in the kitchen, where, mastering her grief, she'd be preparing supper for the country relatives who'd come for the funeral and for whom the least she could do was keep them for a meal or two. I could imagine the look she'd give me if, in the midst of her grief and her concern for her guests, I appeared with questions like, "Maman, the night of the ball, how had you done your hair? Surely you had some little bit of jewellery to wear, didn't you?"

At the time it really did seem important to me to get all the details of the story right then, as if this were its last chance, like a dying fire's, to give a final little flare of warmth to our hearts.

In any event, she'd enquired of a number of civil servants' wives who were better versed in the customs of polite society than she was, and had ascertained which of the social graces were important to observe on arrival at Government House and during the course of the evening. She made herself what she called a *sortie de bal* or evening wrap, which was probably a long, voluminous cape to throw on over her dress. For inspiration in her sewing she no doubt went to the evening-wear departments of the fashionable shops in the city, perhaps trying on some dresses, and why not the most expensive while she was at it, just the way she did when she made my jodhpurs. But this time, for once in her life, the place of honour was to be hers.

At last it was the night of the ball. She must have been radiant, with her eyes sparkling, as she still was nowadays when confronted by some happy surprise. Father must have worn his best plain, dark blue suit, like the one he was to be buried in – I couldn't remember ever seeing him wear any other colour. His black tie would have been fastened, as at present, with a tie pin finely set with an opal, a gift from a group of grateful settlers, a possession he cherished beyond any other in his life and which, the day after tomorrow, before the coffin was closed, Maman would take from him to keep in remembrance.

So they left for the ball arm in arm, young again perhaps, both light of step as though released from their constant burdens of duty, cares, and frugality. At the corner they took the streetcar. Maman didn't feel the incongruity of being all dressed up in her ballgown, rubbing shoulders with weary-faced, sleepy labourers in the dimly lit, rattling and lurching little streetcar. It let them off fairly far from Government House. They continued on foot. Only when they reached the gates to the grounds, with the imposing house blazing with lights from every window at the end of the driveway, did they begin to feel intimidated. Carriages were passing to right and left of them, splattering them with mud as they went. They pressed on to the entrance, where an aide-de-camp was opening the carriage door for each arriving couple, who then, the man supporting his lady by the elbow, had only to advance a step or

two to find themselves, gay and resplendent, in the shelter of a marquee, with the sound of music issuing in great gusts whenever the door opened on the glittering interior. Father was the first to want to turn back. "Let's go, Mélina, we don't belong here." But she was not to be persuaded, not yet. The vision still shimmered in her head. She dragged my protesting father almost to the bottom step. The only thing that finally won out over her vision was the disdainful gaze the splendidly uniformed usher cast down his nose at them. Maman then looked at her dress and saw the spattered mud, and at her shoes and saw that they were soiled. She whispered to my father, "Léon, let's ignore him. Let's walk by as though we're just looking. After all, this is where the representative of the people lives; anyone can come just to look. We'll walk around, then go out again."

Around the corner she spied a low window looking into the great reception room. She found that by standing on a stone she could get a fine view of the interior. My father, overcome by embarrassment, kept saying, "Come away...," but she remained standing under the window, one hand on the casement to balance her. Later, when she told me the story of that already distant evening, she laughed merrily at herself as she said, "Can't you see me watching through the window as the men in tail coats and the women in dresses with trains came forward, and then the women curtseying to the lieutenant-governor and the men bending their heads a bit haughtily, and all of it in English; you know, I could even hear the aide-de-camp announcing 'Mr. and Mrs. Hugo McFarlane....' Then another couple would come up, the woman covered in pearls and diamonds and the man in decorations.... Can't you see me in my little homemade dress," she said, "can't you see the two of us, your father mortified and me all muddy as though I'd come straight from the fields...." She laughed and laughed and there didn't seem to be a trace of rancour or bitterness, only the natural sense of fun in someone who could look at herself with perfect clarity and humour.

"Your father kept telling me we should leave," she said, "but I wanted to see the ball begin, and the couples dancing."

The orchestra struck up a waltz. The lieutenant-governor bowed to a lady. Then, she holding her train in a gloved hand – "To think," recalled Maman, "that I never knew you had to have long gloves" – and the lieutenant-governor a bit starchily, together they

led off the dancing. Then other couples formed and Maman watched them waltzing about beneath the great chandeliers while everything sparkled, the crystal drops of the chandeliers, the diamonds around the necks of the dancing ladies, the medals against the dark suits, the eyes of men in love and of women conscious of being desirable....

I returned from my curious journey into the past hoping to have discovered perhaps an hour or two of happiness in my father's life.

They came home by streetcar; they weren't unhappy, insisted Maman, not at all unhappy; she, indeed, still felt all lit up by the festive spectacle. Even with her hair a bit mussed and her dress a bit muddied she must have been very beautiful that night to my father, who had so seldom seen her dressed up for a party, scintillating with excitement. Who knows, perhaps that night was one of the great nights of their lives. My sister Marie-Agnès was born less than a year after the lieutenant-governor's ball.

I was endlessly amazed, there beside my father's remains, to find myself already so eagerly engrossed in searching back for the smallest scraps I could recall of his life. I didn't know then that death's first effect is to bring the deceased to life in the minds of those who have loved that person, and with a clarity and intensity never again equalled.

I leaned forward and by the flickering light of the candles studied the poignantly fine face my father would present ever after in my memory. Great dignity emanated from it. It had calmed my grief and even my regrets. I was fascinated. This face of death, like many others later in my life, never spoke to me of a void, or of nothingness. Neither did it speak to me of another life, or another world. To me, what was there was total mystery, something never even to be glimpsed, total release at last, darkness intact, and for this reason, perhaps, more beautiful than anything I'd ever seen on earth. When I looked at my father's face I had the impression that life, almost everything about life, was one distraction after another, all meant to conceal the essential truth from us.

ALMOST AS SOON as the funeral was over I had to get back to my studies to prepare for the approaching examinations. To my great surprise, I passed them without difficulty. Perhaps the dragon-teacher had repented at the last minute and given me a good mark.

Or perhaps Dr. Mackintyre had intervened. I'll never know, but I finished not far from the top of the class.

If the news had come in time it would have brightened my father's last days, but now I didn't know what to do with it. I longed to be able to bring him back to life so I could tell him. What was so great about it if it was just for me? Later it was Maman I longed to bring back, so I could tell her about all the wonderful things that were happening with *The Tin Flute*. In my imagination she wouldn't believe me as I told her, and I'd be saying, "Come on now, Maman, I'm almost rich, so you can rest in peace now." And she, back there in the shadows, would be shaking her head sadly, not believing I wasn't still poor and defenceless. Later still it was my sister Anna, who'd always been so worried about what love, marriage, and family ties would do to me; I'd have been able to tell her those shackles had in fact been rather good for me. But she wouldn't have heard and would have kept right on worrying about me as always. Nowadays it's Dédette I keep calling to in vain, wanting so much to tell her it's all right about a particular sorrow in my life, the one she knew about and was so upset by. But however many times I tell her that I've got over it, that it doesn't hurt much any more, she never hears me. I've learned from life that we don't so much want our loved ones back when we're unhappy as to soothe the worries they had for us in life. For it seems to me we can't free them of those worries, even when we've been freed of them ourselves.

Which is probably why I feel so much better if I see Maman or my sisters with happy, untroubled faces in my dreams at night. But no dream has ever let me see my father young again and smiling, as I've seen the others.

VIII

JUST BEFORE the school year finished at the end of May, Dr. Mack-intyre called me to his office. When my father died he'd written me a beautiful letter full of affection and comforting thoughts, which I regret not having kept. In those days I was so obsessed with having my hands free that I kept nothing.

I entered and thanked him for his letter. Visibly moved himself, he waved aside my thanks and gestured me to a chair. Quite a few seconds passed before he began telling me almost excitedly that he had news for me, not just good but excellent news.

I must have looked at him unbelievingly because he quickly confirmed it, then explained.

At that time of the year, he told me, a school board without enough substitute teachers sometimes asked the Normal Institute to send them one of its graduating students. He'd just had such a request and had thought of me. The school was in a little village about fifty miles from the city. The trip wouldn't cost much. I'd earn five dollars for each school-day. But the best part of it was that when I applied for a permanent teaching job, which would be soon, I'd be able to show I'd had a little experience, without, he observed artfully, having to specify that it had only been for a month.

As I listened to him I felt that my life had already turned a corner. The ink on my teacher's certificate wasn't yet dry and already I had a school. *My* school! Suddenly I was so overcome with joy I could have flung my arms around his neck. And at the time I didn't even know what a rare piece of luck this was; only three schools had made such a request and there were three hundred students finishing the year at the Normal Institute. In my case, of course, the school and village were French, so I fitted the bill per-

fectly. All the same, getting my own school when I was barely out of teachers' college, what a stroke of luck!

I literally ran home, and I think I was even skipping when there was nobody ahead on the sidewalk, the way I used to as a little girl.

I came bounding into the kitchen.

"Maman! Maman! Guess what!"

I wonder how many times I'd burst in on her that way, all youth, verve, and excitement, when she was coping with her worries and grief. I think she was making jam. The wood stove had been stoked to the limit and was giving off a searing heat. Her face was almost as cooked as her jam and her cheeks were beet red, which emphasized the joylessness in her eyes, the still-fresh memories of bereavement. There had been no triumph, no achievement since my father's death to help her cope with her grief, it's true. I was rather ashamed of my euphoria but I really couldn't contain it.

"Guess what! A school, Maman! My first school!"

"Stop your babbling about a school!" she retorted, losing patience. "We're still a long way from September. And you're just out of school yourself."

"That's what's so wonderful! I've got one already. For the month of June. I start the day after tomorrow. *My* school, Maman!" And I tried to throw my arms around her, tried to spin her round with me.

It was too much. She shoved me away almost roughly.

"A school? Where?"

"At Marchand."

"Marchand!"

All of a sudden she was bristling and hostile. I was bewildered. Hadn't her life been focused on seeing me get a school at last so I could stand on my own feet? Suddenly, as if to emphasize her disapproval, or revulsion as it seemed, she tore off her apron.

"Not Marchand," she flung at me. "Never! It's a dreadful place! I've heard about it. The boondocks! You're not going there!"

"The boondocks?" I said. "It's only for a month, for goodness' sake, and I've got to start somewhere. You can't expect me to start at the top after all."

"But Marchand! Ugh!" She looked as though she might be sick.

In the end she came and sat down at the kitchen table. She folded her hands and stared in front of her, not believing what was hap-

83

pening, hurting with the pain for which she herself had laid the groundwork. And finding distress when I thought I was bringing her pleasure, I reminded her of this, not thinking I was rubbing salt in her wounds.

"You're the one who's wanted me to be a teacher all your life."
She was weakening, about to give in.
"When is it?" she asked in a small, resigned voice.
"Well, I really have to leave tomorrow."
"Tomorrow!"
A shower of exhortations began to fall on me. With all those uncouth people out there I'd have to be careful to keep my distance. Be polite, yes, but never familiar. Make sure I didn't get put upon, either. "Oh dear," she sighed, "you're too young to start off surrounded by tough, bad-mannered hicks."
"Maman, so what if I have to learn fast?"
In the end she mustered up a smile for me and left everything she'd been doing to come and help me pack.

By the next day she'd found an acquaintance who was going to be driving in the direction of Marchand and had agreed to take me.

Such was her distress over seeing me leave the house that I think she forgot to kiss me. All that mattered was that I should look out for myself, keep my place, stand on my rights, and, if the going got too tough out there, come home.

ONCE THERE, it was abundantly clear that the only place I could stay was the hotel, since there was nothing else except some wretched wooden shacks built right on the sandy ground, scattered among clumps of scrawny spruce trees. Forty years later I would draw on this mournful setting and the sorrowful event that marked my first day of school at Marchand to write "The Dead Girl", the episode that came to light so strangely in *Enchanted Summer*.

But that day when I set foot in Marchand, terrified and homesick already, how far I was from having any sense of the aptitude I had – or would have, like a seed lying dormant in the ground long before germinating – for turning moments of my life into stories that would create a bridge between me and other people. And those moments that have made me feel the most alone have often won me the most hearts among strangers. One knows less about one's own destiny than about anything else on earth.

Not until I was halfway up the precipitous stairs on the way to my room, behind the hefty figure of the lady hotel-keeper, who was lugging up my two suitcases, did I suddenly remember one of Maman's most specific enjoinders.

"Before you take a room find out the price," she'd said. "Be very careful they don't take advantage of your inexperience. Considering what you're going to earn, don't let yourself in for more than twenty-five dollars a month, room and board."

Behind the ample back I heard myself pipe up with the question in a voice so faint and shy that scorn was the only reaction it could draw from a person so unmistakably sure of herself.

"Madame, the rent...what will it be? How much will you be asking?"

Perhaps irritated that I should bring it up in the middle of the staircase, and to her back, and in any case being of a nature to want to take me down a peg, she plonked the bags down right there.

"First off you can do yer own fetchin' and carryin'."

Several steps farther up, when it was my turn to be out of breath, she deigned rudely to tell me what I wanted to know.

"Anyway, young miss, you needn't think I'm gonna feed you and give you a bed and light and...and...for less than twenty-five dollars a month."

I heaved a sigh of relief despite her offensive manner. That was the limit Maman had fixed. I could accept it without argument, and Lord knows I had no heart to haggle with that awful woman.

My room was small and almost bare, but clean. A clean little prison cell. My landlady cocked her chin at it and left without a word. I sat down on the foot of the narrow iron cot with its dreary white coverlet just like the ones in convent dormitories. But all I really saw was the window. It looked out on one of the most lifeless vistas I've ever seen. Nothing moved in that landscape. Nothing even stirred. There were trees all over, standing alone or in sparse clumps, and all of them were still, petrified, waiting for something to happen. As though the wind had stopped outside the village, not daring to cross a mysterious, invisible line, while all within lay paralysed, struck with some terrible foreboding.

I went downstairs and, taking a wrong turn, found myself in a big, bright, airy kitchen, certainly the most pleasant room in that whole peculiar hotel, where elsewhere the blinds stayed depress-

ingly drawn, leaving everything in deep gloom. My landlady was getting a snack for the children, five of them, I think, who would be my pupils the following morning. But they paid no more attention to me than to a stranger whose business here was and would remain no concern of theirs.

The mother was cutting thick slices of beautiful white bread which couldn't have looked more appetizing. Since the people who'd brought me were in a hurry to go about their business and get home before dark, we hadn't made any stops where we could get a bite to eat. I was dying of hunger. Next she spread each slice of bread thickly with strawberry jam. My mouth was watering. Each of the children was given one and then ran outside, taking big bites and licking the jam off their lips as they passed me. When they'd all been served I raised my eyes humbly to the provider. The bread was so generously cut and spread and smelled so delicious, I wonder if I've ever wanted a slice of bread and jam so much in my whole life. My landlady looked me straight in the eye. She took the bread and wrapped it in a clean towel to keep it fresh, then put it in its tin box and slammed the lid. She took the pot of jam, screwed the lid back on tight, and put it in the cupboard.

"Mind you don't get yourselves dirty now," she called after the children. Then to me she said crisply, "Supper's at six."

I went outside. I took the path leading to the schoolhouse, which was not far from the houses and, like them, built right on the sandy ground. I went in. I sat down at a desk that was up two steps on a dais if I remember correctly, unless I'm confusing it with the school at the Little Water Hen. The silence around me was oppressive. It weighed heavily on my stomach. It even invaded my thoughts, frightening them and preventing them from taking shape. Through the row of windows in the south wall of the schoolhouse I could see a straggly troop of those puny spruce trees standing as motionless as one could imagine, stuck in their woebegone poses. And sitting there I peered into the obscurity ahead of me, trying to catch a glimpse of the life awaiting me.

IX

THE FOLLOWING September I began teaching at Cardinal, a larger and less indigent village but no livelier, located on the opposite side of the province. I was dreadfully homesick there and uncomfortable besides, for I was boarding in a flimsily built house with the barest suggestion of heating, even when winter set in and its winds blew through the thin walls. If I didn't freeze to death it was because my landlady took pity on me and made me a voluminous feather comforter. Pulled up over me in bed, it felt like a light and marvellously soft mountain. After that I wasn't cold any more, not at night anyway, even when the water in the pitcher beside my bed froze hard.

In the last chapter of *Street of Riches* I think I recreated the atmosphere of that village fairly accurately. It also figures briefly in *Children of My Heart,* the book I'm putting the final touches to at present. Nowhere, however, have I tried to describe it exactly as it was. That's something I don't think I could do any more. Nowadays I need to break up the elements of my own experience, separate them, reassemble them, add to them, leave this or that out and perhaps invent things. That's often the way I manage to convey the most authentic mood, an intangible depending neither on any precise detail nor on the sum of the parts, but somehow on an almost equally intangible and seemingly strange composition. It would bore me to death now to describe a house faithfully just as I see it, or a street or a corner bar, the way I did in *The Tin Flute*. I made myself do it then, partly for the sake of realism, it's true, but also to discipline an overactive imagination, to make myself look carefully at everything and not allow myself to get into sloppy habits of describing things with no roots in reality.

I'm therefore not inclined to dwell further on the village of

Cardinal, though the year I spent there was one of the most important in my life. That year turned a spoiled child into an industrious young teacher, perhaps even a first-rate one, since the inspector's report must have had something to do with my getting a position the following year at the Académie Provencher in St-Boniface, just a stone's throw from our house. Now Maman could stop worrying about my living in the boondocks.

One of the good things about Cardinal – the best thing, as I saw it – was that it wasn't very far from my uncle Excide's farm where I'd spent such happy summer holidays and which I loved so much. That year I spent almost every weekend there. I'd take the train on Saturday morning and get off fifteen minutes later at the next station, which was Somerset. From there I'd find some way to get to the farm a few miles away. Or I might just wait, knowing that my cousins hardly ever missed coming to town to shop on Saturdays. We really would have had to try very hard not to run into each other, either at the general store or at the Chinese restaurant, where one of us was always having an ice cream. After sleepy little Cardinal, where the only sound for hours on end was the wind, setting foot in Somerset seemed like coming to a mini-metropolis, and I'd be in a lather of excitement.

Sometimes, when he had business with the blacksmith-cum-garage mechanic in Cardinal whose work he liked best, my uncle would come and get me on Friday evening. Then we'd speed off in the high old Ford, the hard tires pitching us constantly one against the other on the bumpy roads he'd take because they got us there fastest. There'd be total silence during the short trip. Though he could be talkative when he wished, he never spoke to me when he drove, and I learned to leave him to his silent woolgathering, having soon realized that he didn't like it intruded on when driving. At first I found his moodiness disconcerting, but I'd still be happy and excited because I was headed for a little piece of heaven, so to speak. I'd have two whole days at the farm, perhaps a bit more, because occasionally my cousins would take me home very early Monday morning to give me a blissful, unbroken Sunday. All week I'd be obsessed with the thought that a treat like that should be earned, and I'd work twice as hard to deserve it. I would have worked as hard anyway, perhaps, but not as eagerly.

So I spent the weeks working like a Trojan and the weekends laughing, singing, and dancing, and time went by very quickly.

My uncle's house was well heated; I could wash my hair and walk around as it dried without risk of catching cold. My cousin Léa and I would spend hours playing duets over and over on the old piano in the living room, ready at any minute to collapse in paroxysms of laughter when we'd hear a squeak like a mouse's among the high notes. That squeak had been the piano's distinguishing feature ever since a mouse had chewed the felt from one of the strings and made a nest with it in that corner.

On Saturday morning, Léa and I would go out and stroll up one side of the main street and back again, pretending we didn't know that the eyes of the young bucks of the village were on us. If we didn't do that, it was because the young bucks came calling on us. There was a great deal of ceremony involved in these visits, which amused me no end, though I could never be persuaded to play the role expected of me. If a young suitor came calling for the first time and we liked him, we were supposed to let him know without saying so, by handing him his hat with our own hands when he left at the end of the evening. This meant he could come again. Not handing him his hat at the door when he'd sung us a song with his eyes fixed on ours, having sort of dedicated it to us with a bow before beginning, was nothing less than a serious breach of hospitality, of which I was guilty many times. My uncle, who was so freewheeling himself in some ways, scolded me for it, even predicting I'd never find a man to marry me if I kept brushing off honourable intentions so clearly demonstrated. But to me it was all too comical. Whenever a young man stood before me, gazing at me with sheep's eyes as he sang one of those western laments that all seem to have the same tune, it was all I could do to keep from laughing in his face. And it was even harder to contain myself when he stood at the door waiting with his hand out for his hat.

That's the way it was at my uncle's; I'd be light-hearted, playful, and teasing again, disrespectful of customs and no doubt enjoying making myself conspicuous. During the week I'd come back down to earth in the freezing cold house in Cardinal. I'd do my preparation for the next day at the school, where there was a bit of heat at least, and return to the house as late as possible. There were no

books or music in that house; the only entertainment the family had was telling each others' fortunes with cards or reading palms or teacups: a distraction common to those in whose lives nothing ever happens – I wrote about it in *Street of Riches* – endlessly asking inanimate objects for promises of a future filled with adventure and fantasy.

THE COMINGS and goings between Cardinal and the farm went on all autumn, and to my immense joy were not interrupted when winter came. By then we'd become too attached to each other, I to my cousins and they to me, to give up our evenings together. But winter soon turned very harsh. One Sunday night I was taken home in a "cabin" sleigh through a raging snowstorm. Years later I used that episode as the basis of "The Storm" in *Street of Riches*. Another time when we made the trip in an open box-sleigh, the cold was so perishing that my cousin and I, sitting side by side on the single seat, pulled the fur robes over our heads and virtually buried ourselves in them, leaving the horses unguided. I was rather worried they might not find their way.

It was Cléophas who was taking me home that night.

"Bah," he retorted, "if we're going to freeze to death, what's the difference whether we know where we are or not? You needn't worry, though. The poor beasts have taken you home so many times they know the road by heart, you can be sure of that. And they're in such a hurry to get back to the stable they'll keep up a good trot, too."

Luckily it was a perfectly clear night. The crusted snow shone almost as brightly as the vast expanse of stars I could see twinkling busily any time I opened our fur tent to get a little air. The night was so resplendent with its crisp, steel-sharp bite and its blazing lights that I felt something like shame to be hiding from it like that. But the cold burned when it reached my lungs and I'd duck back under cover. My cousin, who'd be half asleep, would growl at me for letting in the cold and beg me to keep still. We must both have slept a good part of the trip, partly torpid from the cold and partly asphyxiated, no doubt. A sudden stop jolted us awake. Dazed and alarmed, we sat up, rubbing our eyes. The horses had come to a stop at the door of my boarding house.

I jumped out.

"Bye," I said to Cléophas.

"Bye," he replied.

I could hardly hear him. He'd already pulled the fur robes back over his head. Then, of their own accord, the horses turned the sleigh around and trotted briskly away.

Since one or another of my cousins always had to take me home – though it often seemed to be Cléophas's turn – I should have recognized how much trouble I was giving them and considered not coming so frequently. But the good-hearted fellows never complained. And when Friday came around you'd think I was possessed; I'd hear the irresistible call of the piano and violin in my uncle's house, the chases upstairs and down, the laughter, the singing, the harmless giddiness of our time of life.

IN MARCH the weather became abominable. It poured with rain for two or three days, and when the countryside had become as pitted and potholed as a muddy cattle-pen, the cold returned and froze all the humps and hollows rock-hard. Then again mild weather came and turned all that surface into a huge swamp of wet snow and mud. One Monday morning, Cléophas wondered whether to take a sleigh or the buggy to drive me home. Luckily he decided on the buggy, because there were long stretches of road without a trace of snow, which we never could have navigated with a sleigh. But those were still the most difficult. We would inch ahead through a morass, with each turn of the wheels flinging splatters of mud onto our clothes, down our necks, and into our hair. Soon we couldn't help laughing when we looked at one another, because our faces were black with mud and our eyes showed through as if we had masks on.

My uncle warned me that this was the worst time of the year, that nothing, either sleigh or buggy, could get through, and even less a car, so I should wait a bit; he would come and get me as soon as the roads were passable.

When I wrote *Where Nests the Water Hen*, I gave my stout-hearted Luzina that dreadful kind of weather to travel in, and I think I knew what I was talking about when I described the problems she and the unsociable Nick Sluziuk had to face.

I waited two, then three weeks. A bright, unclouded April sky was enough to convince me that the whole countryside should now

be dry enough for travel. In the village it was hardly muddy at all any more. In any event, I could go at least four miles of the distance to my uncle's in a nice, dry train. Then, by taking shortcuts, I'd have only about as far again to walk. I told myself there'd be no trouble getting there, even if the ground was still a bit wet. Besides, I'd been planning to do that last leg to the farm on foot one day. That Friday, at five minutes past four, I was lucky enough to catch the hand-car going to Somerset. So there I was with the railway hands on a little mobile platform driven by a lever vigorously pumped up and down by one of them. We bowled along in the warm spring breeze between brimming ditches, accompanied by the song of water freed from the bonds of winter.

Where the railway crossed the little section road which was the shortest route to my uncle's, I said goodbye to the kind and helpful men. In a twinkling they were gone, far away already, and I was alone at the edge of what looked like an endless expanse of mud and puddles of water. It was a lonely spot. There was a house nearby, but it had a forbidding air. I had never seen any signs of life there when I passed. In front of the silent house the road was flooded; a usually docile little brook had swelled to the size of a raging river and was sweeping across with rumbling sounds. I was testing the footing with a toe when a man rushed out of the house.

"The road's blocked. Where d'you think you're going?"

I shouted my reply.

"You won't make it," he shouted back. "Stay here for the night. Tomorrow the water may have gone down."

Nothing in heaven or earth was going to stop me from attempting to cross that watercourse. I advanced a few steps and the water came up to my ankles. A few steps more and it was nearing the tops of my knee-high boots. I felt it on the point of spilling into them. I kept advancing very slowly, bracing myself against the current with a stick I'd picked up at the edge of the swollen brook. By now I was afraid I'd be swept off my feet at any minute. Then suddenly the strength of the current slackened. I'd passed the deepest part. Now with each step the water was getting much shallower. I reached solid ground.

On his veranda, his dog beside him now, the man raised a hand as if calling on heaven to confirm that there'd been magic in the feat. The dog was standing half-upright with his front paws on the

veranda rail, watching without a sound through the tangle of long hair over his face, as stupefied as his master. Just a couple of hours before, I was told later, those two had watched from the same veranda as another traveller had been forced to retreat, a tall, husky man who'd had water almost up to his waist at the place I'd victoriously crossed. I turned slightly to wave at my silent audience of two, then continued down that totally deserted road as the daylight began to fade. There was no other house on the road between there and my uncle's.

At first I walked along the edge of the road and hardly sank in at all. Under what was left of the snow, my feet were finding spongy but fairly firm ground, and I kept up a pretty regular pace. I was buoyed by the lingering glow of light in the sky, too.

In fact, despite the dismal sight of fields half-clad in shreds of dirty snow, the ominous woods in the distance, and the uniformly muddy colour of everything except that little band of light in the sky, for no reason that I can comprehend the magic of that mysterious time of day was working on me as it has so often in my life, lifting me on a wave of irrepressible confidence. So I walked along that deserted road with no more fear than if help had been at hand on all sides.

Soon I realized that those forbidding woods, that line of sodden black tree-trunks I'd been seeing for some time at the far edge of fields still covered with snow, must be none other than the woods fringing a dried-up lake on the edge of my uncle's farm. Even in summer we didn't often cross through those woods, though I didn't know why. That's the reason I hadn't recognized them at first. If I cut through there, I thought idiotically, I'd reach the house much sooner, saving myself almost two miles by road. My boots were beginning to be very heavy because I was walking in gumbo now, and at each step I was lifting enormous gobs of it which were very hard to shake off. I was getting tired. The witching hour had yielded to a uniform ashen greyness, darkening minute by minute. The shortcut was looking more and more attractive. Suddenly, without further thought, I left the road and struck off across the field towards the dark woods.

At first the snow carried me reasonably well. Only when I'd walked perhaps half-way across the field did it give way beneath me, suddenly, as if to swallow me up. I was up to my hips in a

kind of crack that was very hard to get out of because the sides were as soft as the bottom. I managed to crawl out and get to my feet, but just a few steps farther on I sank in again, this time to my waist. Then I found my feet weren't touching bottom any more. My boots began to fill with ice-cold water. I remembered then having heard my uncle grumble one day about a spot on his land where it was still impossible to grow anything, a kind of rotten swamp that he'd never been able to drain. This was what I must have ventured into. Lying flat on my stomach, I realized I was on a thin, semi-frozen layer of snow, no doubt barely covering a small lake, perhaps a deep one. I looked at the line of trees not far away. My only salvation lay there, I thought. I struck out for it, still on my stomach, inching forward with a kind of swimming motion, now with my arms, now with my legs. Behind me I was leaving a series of large holes like a row of graves for a multiple burial in some weird cemetery. I'd lost my flashlight in one of them. I finally reached the line of trees, but I found no firmer surface there, only shelter, one might say, from the great leaden sky spread across the earth, which was now quite colourless. But there was no shelter from the rain which was beginning to fall, without wind or rumbling thunder but hard and steadily, as if it would go on for ever. The weight of my sodden clothes was dragging me down, closer and closer to the water beneath me – the layer of rain-drenched snow and ice that just barely separated me from it was getting thinner by the minute. Not far away, coyotes hurled their bone-chilling call into the night. It didn't affect me the way it usually did. In a way I think I was already beyond fear. It seems to me the feeling I had was one of waiting for something, or even more, perhaps, an urgent, anxious, and infinite curiosity. So I was mortal! And not just mortal but capable of dying an exceedingly stupid death, just yards from the house I loved so much, so close to people who loved me. I think my most crushing realization was that love gave so little protection. If I had cried out at that time I would have done so in vain. Who in that house with its doors and windows well closed would ever hear me calling for help? At that very moment they were probably gossiping cheerfully in the big, friendly kitchen. Of all that happened that night, what hurt most was probably the thought that they would be blissfully unaware that I was

fighting off death; that their deep affection for me wouldn't warn them that I was in danger.

I stayed still, lying flat and on my back now. The softening layer of ice and snow still supported me, provided I hardly moved. I lay and gathered my strength, and after a while regained a modicum of reason. I realized that I wasn't going to get out of there by pushing ahead, but by going back the way I'd come.

It was horrible. I relive it in my dreams at night sometimes. I retraced my route from hole to hole, making each one deeper. I must have left fifty or more almost full-length imprints of my body. I reached the road. It was perhaps there that I had the most trouble forcing myself to keep going, for I was gripped by an almost irresistible longing to stay lying on the icy ground and go to sleep, at least for a moment. But I managed to get up and, staggering, set off down the road. My clothes were beginning to stiffen on my body. The water in my boots was turning to ice. It kept raining. Sometimes I'd begin to shiver, then I'd feel so hot I'd think of getting rid of my coat. My soaking hair was stuck to my face. I don't know how I made it over the last few hundred yards. I seem to remember dozing off now and then; I'm not sure I wasn't asleep a few seconds at a time as I continued to walk. Finally the house appeared, all lit up and cheerful-looking through the trees of the same wood whose other side had been so disastrous for me. How good and how sweet life seemed at that moment! But my last really clear thought was that I mustn't say anything about my adventure to the people there so as not to frighten them about what might have happened.

I reached the door. It must have been at least ten o'clock. I'd never arrived at the farm on my own so late at night. It seemed to me only proper to knock on the door.

Silence fell in the big kitchen. Then the door opened. In the rectangle of light I could see them all for a moment as they really were, so kind and lovable, but at first they didn't recognize me. They honestly thought I was some unfortunate stranger lost or in flight, someone whom pure chance had led to their door seeking shelter from the vile weather.

I heard a few words as though from very far away, and fell into their arms.

They took care of me, pampered me, and nursed me back to health. Oddly enough, while I was ill under their care, and even later, we never talked about my adventure. Not even the faintest allusion. Not until years later, in any event.

I would never again come to the farm without being invited and brought, but I hasten to add that I didn't have to sit around waiting. Almost every week one or another of the family would turn up, often just as I was dismissing my pupils, giving me barely enough time to go and gather a few things to take with me. They'd realized how I felt. We'll move heaven and earth to return to where we've been happy, even if it costs us our last breath.

X

MY APPRENTICESHIP in the country was not a long one, and in a way
I regret it, for there life taught me its most cogent lessons, administered roughly sometimes, even harshly, lessons I learned well
and never forgot.

Immediately after my year at Cardinal I was engaged to teach
at the Académie Provencher. This was a rather grand name for
what was really a big public school – an elementary and high school
combined – under the jurisdiction of the Manitoba Department of
Education and located in the heart of French-speaking Manitoba,
the old quarter of St-Boniface. I was perhaps jumped over the heads
of more seasoned teachers who had applied before I did, but if there
was any favouritism I owed it undoubtedly to Brother Joseph Hinks,
the school's *principal*, as it pleased us to call him in the English
fashion. The residence of the Brothers was on Cathedral Street
immediately opposite the girls' school I had attended, and Brother
Joseph had been well placed, particularly when working in his
garden, to watch us passing on walks in crocodile formation, arriving one by one, or possibly exchanging confidences, in any event
paying no attention to the gowned figure ostensibly absorbed only
in his roses. It seems that with his natural gift for observation and
judgement of character, he would size us up from a host of small
details and decide long in advance which of us he would favour if
ever we should apply to teach at his school. His opinion carried
much weight in the choice of staff; it was even said that no one
became part of it against his will. He was an Alsatian by birth, a
rather small man who impressed partly with his very elegant cuffed
and buttoned black cassock and white bib, but even more with his
naturally distinguished bearing and profound humanity. In no one
else have I ever seen such goodness of heart combined with such

authority. All it took to calm a roomful of obstreperous school-children was for him to appear and stand composed and quiet with his hands behind his back, a knowing little smile on his face. In Manitoba he soon came to be regarded as one of the most re-markable educators of his time; even today I see schools adopting methods which he had already put to the test and sometimes re-jected as detrimental nearly fifty years ago.

The high marks I'd got from the inspector at Cardinal combined with the principal's recommendation were enough: at twenty, there I was on the teaching staff of our city's major school for boys, which must have had nearly a thousand pupils at the time.

Though Brother Joseph made all the decisions himself, he had a clever way of consulting us and letting us think we'd made our own choices. For instance, he asked me if I didn't think I'd be happy and at my best teaching the youngest children, having decided himself that this was where I'd be most effective. He wasn't mis-taken, but how on earth could he have known when he had seen me only three or four times?

At Provencher we had two first-grade classes. One was for French-speaking children who, first and foremost, were taught the rudi-ments of their own language, which meant taking rather broad liberties with the province's education laws. After that they learned a smidgin of English, at least a few nursery rhymes of the Humpty Dumpty kind, which they'd recite with such verve for the inspector that he'd be quite won over. That was an old trick practised back in my own early school-days, which apparently still worked.

The other baby class was open to all non-French-speaking chil-dren, who were considered English-speaking though there weren't really any of English origin, but rather Russian, Polish, Italian, Spanish, Irish, Czech, Dutch, almost everything imaginable; those who mostly gravitated to the English side eventually, except for some Italian and Walloon families. This motley class was assigned to me. So I, a young French-speaking teacher, trained to serve my own language and culture in every way possible, found myself in charge of a class of children representing nearly all the nations on earth, most of whom knew no more English than they did French. At first we communicated through sign language and a lot of smil-ing. I didn't feel there was anything absurd about this; I thought of my class simply as a mirror of our country, which is about as

rich as any on earth in ethnic variety. I became very attached to it and very close to those children, and they taught me a great deal about the folklore, songs, and dances of their people, as well as something deeper, something both painful and joyous. So much so that when Brother Joseph suggested I move up to a third- or fourth-year class a few years later, I begged him to leave me with my little immigrants. He needed no persuading. I wonder if he'd perceived that I was born to serve the League of Nations in a sense. Or perhaps it was my little charges from all corners of the earth who inspired in me the dream of universal understanding that has been with me ever since.

So I began adulthood already launched on a career, seemingly for life, in conditions that looked almost unbelievably good to Maman after our years of hardship. In fact, because of the Depression, my starting salary at Cardinal, a hundred and ten dollars a month, was reduced to only ninety-six in St-Boniface. Nevertheless, to Maman the life we led was easy and pleasant in comparison to the way it had been before.

"It's almost too good to be true," she'd say from time to time. "Do you think it'll last?"

She had such confidence that things had finally begun to go right for us that she even thought we might manage to "save" the house, as she used to put it. Yet we'd always known that we'd have to resign ourselves to parting with it one day. The taxes and heating bills alone would have eaten up more than half my salary. So Maman had to keep on renting rooms and scrimping and saving to cover a good proportion of our day-to-day expenses. It didn't work. She kept accumulating small debts without my knowledge, just as she'd done behind my father's back.

In our lucid moments we were almost agreed, for a few hours at a time, that we should put the house up for sale. There were only three of us, Maman, Clémence, and I, living there the year round now. Surely we'd be just as comfortable in a small rented apartment which would cost less and cause less work for Maman.

"Yes," she'd say, seeming to have come around to the idea. "I'll get after it tomorrow. I'll go and see So-and-so, who might be thinking of buying.... You never know."

An hour or two later I'd find her up on a table washing a ceiling because it was "smoky", according to her. Or outside giving di-

rections to a neighbour who'd come to dig over our vegetable garden, which just happened to have got bigger that year.

I have to admit that after we'd been talking about selling it, the house had a way of seeming more attractive than ever before, with its row of white pillars, its crab-apple trees in flower, and the elms my father had planted, now as high as the window of my attic room, where I'd spun so many dreams of marvellous accomplishments as a child. That house was part of us as only a house can be whose inhabitants have experienced everything from birth to death within its walls.

"To think," said Maman, "that when your father brought me to see it before it was quite finished, hoping I'd fall in love with it, I couldn't hide my disappointment. 'But it's much too small, Léon,' I said, 'with all the children we've got! Where are we ever going to put them all?' To think that now we're finding fault with it because it's too big!"

My father had spent almost half his life saving enough to build it, penny by penny, then the rest of his days trying not to lose it. There were times when I felt bitterly resentful towards it, the way you do towards a person you love who can wheedle anything out of you. It used to suck us dry. One year it would have to have a new roof. Next it would need repainting, which would have to wait till one of my brothers was free to do it. Then the heating system would begin to wear out. Above all, the taxes ate away at us endlessly. While our earnings were being cut, the taxes increased year after year, especially the school taxes, which did little to benefit us since we of the French-speaking community had to maintain our own French private schools in the largely English suburbs of St-Boniface. So our determination to preserve our French language also helped ruin us in the end.

"Come on now, Maman, you know perfectly well we'll be beaten one of these days. The house is dragging us under."

"But it's home for us in the meantime," she'd say. "As long as we have it, as long as there's a place to come home to, we'll be a family."

And this was true. Adèle, for instance, who was teaching in increasingly far-off corners of northern Alberta, as though doggedly trying to recapture the pioneering days of her youth, still came

back to us often in the summer holidays. Each time she came she'd been converted to a new fad diet; one year it was nothing but spinach, lemons, and apples; another, nothing but prunes and oat-meal. But the year she arrived home with a summer's supply consisting of nothing but oranges, grapefruit, dates, and nuts, it vanished so fast from her cache in the cellar that she had to finish out the season eating at table like the rest of us. I seem to recall this as being one of the rare times she deigned to behave like everybody else. My poor sister! I realize now that she craved affection and longed to be understood and accepted, but everything she did seemed designed to rebuff affection. I've often wondered if people like Adèle are incapable of reaching out to others because there's no love in their lives, or whether their inability to reach out has kept love at bay. I still don't know which it is. It must be the same conundrum I found in my book-burning grandfather's portrait. How far, O Lord, must we go back to find the source of unhappiness in a person? There's a degree of it in all of us, no doubt, but so much more in some than in others.

Rodolphe, who was a telegraphist and then a station-master be-fore having no job at all, like so many others during the Depression, came to visit often, especially when he was posted near St-Boniface. He would arrive in fine fettle, with a song on his lips, just a little tipsy, and his pockets stuffed with bank notes which he'd distribute magnanimously on all sides. "A fifty, Ma, I bet you could use that, got to keep the wolf from the door, you know. No, no, keep it, it's yours, I don't want to hear any more about it!... Clémence dear, how'd you like a nice crisp new ten? Take it, take it.... And Ma, while we're about it, take another fifty, while there's still more where that came from. Need another to fill the gaps, maybe?" And like as not he'd turn out his pockets the next day and take back almost everything he'd given away, and perhaps borrow a little besides so he could get home. But he was always full of devilment, and would play airs from *Rigoletto* by ear, drawing sounds from our old untuned piano that no one else could, or sing a hearty, rollicking toreador song that would have all of us walking or jigging more or less in time to it. When Rodolphe arrived, the whole neighbourhood knew it, and rejoiced.

"Little sister," he'd say to me when I was fifteen or sixteen,

stroking my hair, "you've got the most beautiful hair in the world. Who," he'd demand of some unseen audience, "could have more beautiful hair?"

"Clémence," he'd say to my invalid sister, "one day I'm going to take you to see the Rocky Mountains – the greatest wonder of the world!"

He overflowed with affection, and could inspire it with just a smile from his twinkling brown eyes. But as soon as he'd done so he'd be off to light another spark.

We forgave him everything for so long, so long...until he drove us to despair.

He spent the last years of his life in Vancouver, living on his war veteran's pension and writing us letters that were funny in a way uniquely his, I think, constantly laughing at himself, his youth (one day it was there and the next a thousand miles away), his follies, his vanished hopes, the human merry-go-round, people's good intentions unfulfilled, all of which produced a steady stream of mirth, besides something faintly audible in the background, like a stifled sob.

He was found dead one night in his tiny apartment, which he always left unlocked to allow the cronies around him to come quickly to his aid in case of an asthma attack. His pockets had been emptied, perhaps by those same cronies who'd been supplying him with alcohol and sometimes real help, and who sang with such feeling at his funeral. Or perhaps someone had merely recovered a loan.

Our pious little nun, Dédette, our Sister Purity, the spotless lamb in the muddy barnyard, was then on missionary duty, one might say, at a poor convent at Kenora in Ontario near the Manitoba border; later she spent several years at Keewatin in the same region, where she led a life of real poverty with a single companion in a shack that barely kept out the rain. Yet in all her religious life she was happier there than anywhere else, she confided to me when the time came for revelations, shortly before her death. But occasionally she had to emerge from those faraway woods, where she was almost forgotten even by her community, for gatherings of the community or personal retreats in St-Boniface. Then she'd obtain what she considered a very special permission: almost a

whole day to spend at home with her family. Now that I know what the brief breath of freedom meant to that loving soul, I don't even feel like smiling any more. As fleeting as it was, it was enough to sustain her passion for life.

She'd come to us early in the morning brimming with joy, convinced she was bringing us happiness and would find only that. But before long there would be some little confession let slip by Maman, some family news long concealed from her, a host of little signs, and she'd begin to see the ugly old face of misfortune and suffering she thought she had banished from the earth by the sheer force of prayer before an altar. Poor little nun! We'd always see her leave like a wounded bird trailing a damaged wing, crushed to have been back and seen what the world was like.

But I'd rather talk about when she'd arrive – a delight to behold! I must say Maman had always done everything possible to make sure it would be a day of charm and light-heartedness, almost of luxury, one that would hide as never before all trace of want in our family life. Once, when we were really at a low ebb, she even went as far as to buy a magnificent damask tablecloth for the occasion. For Dédette never came alone but was always accompanied by "one of our sisters", and while Maman was certainly bent on doing honour to Dédette, she was probably more anxious to enhance her image in the eyes of her companion, who might be from a wealthy family, and for whom, in any event, we had to do things nicely.

So one fine morning a pair of dark figures would take shape at the end of Deschambault Street, dressed in the voluminous black habit of those days, with all-concealing skirts and starched white band across the forehead and veil floating in the wind. Soon one of them would detach herself from the other and run forward, dignity and seemliness flung aside – a little flying nun, a real one. Maman too would take off like an arrow. At the gate, usually, they'd come together and embrace like two souls who'd had to cross the desert – or life itself perhaps – in order to be together. Much later, when nuns were beginning to have a great deal more freedom, I wrote to Dédette's Sister General and obtained permission for her to spend a few weeks with me at Petite-Rivière-Saint-François. When I met her at the station in Quebec City, I watched her run

to me with the same eagerness, the same outpouring of joy as when she'd run to Maman on Deschambault Street. I don't think I've ever seen a person run to a loved one the way she used to.

When I was called to her bedside seven years later, as she was dying of cancer, I carefully broached the subject of that deep attachment for her family. Why, I asked her, when she loved life so much, had she become a nun? I'm still haunted by the reply she gave me. When my own time comes, I hope I'll be able to talk about it with as much passionate simplicity as she did.

MAMAN WAS so right when she insisted that as long as we had our house we'd be a family, that happy or unhappy, at least we'd be together.

With the house sold and Maman dead, we did get together a few times more, Adèle, Clémence, Dédette, Anna, and I, at Anna's lovely property in St-Vital, with its house and little outbuildings all white with blue trim, nestled along a lazy loop of the winding Red River. Our old Bell piano had come to rest there. I used to let my fingers wander over its yellowed keys, trying to bring back a tune my father had been particularly fond of. I'd feel a wave of sadness rise up in me, as much for what I sensed I was going to lose as for what I'd already lost. I'd reached an age where one begins to lose much, and being the youngest in the family, I sometimes glimpsed a period in which I'd see all my remaining family depart before my own turn came.

Then Anna died, far away among cactuses and giant saguaros, their arms raised in beseeching gestures to the sky, almost in the desert; she'd fled to Phoenix, where her son Fernand lived, in a last desperate effort to be freed of the cancer that had been eating at her for fifteen years. There it caught up with her, and there under the sunny Arizona skies she was buried. Now our family had no nucleus at all. Clémence, everybody's child, who often saw better and more gravely than we, which was perhaps the source of her trouble, one day in a state of agitation put it another way: "There's no house for us to go to any more."

SO NOW WHEN I go to Winnipeg for my visits to Clémence, who is in a home, I take a room in a hotel. It's a very curious feeling to be in an air-conditioned room a step away from the city where

I was born, grew up, went to school, and earned my living, and suddenly to realize that I'm waiting at least for the phone to ring, though I haven't yet told anyone I've arrived.

I do get invitations and would be received with genuine warmth, but my cousins, my sister-in-law, and various other close or distant relatives, all of whom are getting on in years, live in what amount to tiny cubicles, which serve as living room, dining room, kitchen, and bedroom all in one; when the sofa-bed is folded up and everything is tidily in place, you can move around, but only just. They find it convenient. They say that it's really better that way when you're growing old and can't get help for love or money.

There's no longer really anything to make me feel at home in Manitoba, except the little section roads that stretch away beneath the endless sky, if only I can get to them, and if when I do my friends will just leave me alone for an hour or so to commune with that utterly silent horizon. There are some who understand, who'll take me to the edge of the open prairie and release me as you'd release a bird, then go away pretending they have things to do elsewhere. They know they won't lose me, though many's the time I've longed to go and lose myself for ever out there – that's just a childish fancy; one doesn't put oneself away like that, however strong the urge may be at times.

So I set off, feeling buoyed nevertheless, walking towards the red glow low down in the sky where the prairie ends, because for the magic to work I need not only an illusion of infinite space but also the gentle time of day just before nightfall. Then, for a few moments, my heart may soar once again.

XI

MAMAN WAS HAPPY during the last years we spent together, though less on her own account than because she felt I was content with my lot.

She had seen Adèle, a fine young woman and a striking beauty, enter into the most disastrous marriage; it broke up almost immediately, but the memory – or the shame – drove her all the rest of her life, a hunted creature always on the run to increasingly distant points, the frontiers of civilization, "Adèle's hardship villages" as we called them. She would teach for a year or two, rarely more, and as soon as life began to be a little less harsh, would take off for some other, even more primitive outpost. One would have said she never could punish herself enough for having strayed into love in her tender and vulnerable youth.

Maman had Anna to grieve for as well. Anna had married too young and her husband, though probably a good and affectionate man, was not her equal, in either education or sensitivity; her exceptional gifts were gradually stifled by a dreary, stultifying existence. She always made me think of Chekhov's *Three Sisters*. I often remember seeing her stand motionless at a window, gazing out but seeing nothing, as though knowing she'd been destined for better things and it was now too late. The burden of sorrow in her heart was something I never suspected when I was young. It was a long time before I conceived a great and profound compassion for my sister Anna.

Maman also watched helplessly as our beloved Rodolphe sank into alcoholism, gambling, and all sorts of other folly. Not so long before, he had been the very image of youthful charm: brilliant, funny, irresistible in his exuberance. She died before the worst

happened, thank God, though she had seen enough to hasten her end.

I, the youngest, was to all appearances happy with my work, doing the best I could and finding it satisfying. For recreation I took part in group activities, played tennis, went to parish gatherings. A little later I was to join the Cercle Molière, a purely amateur theatrical group which, under the direction of a marvellous couple, Arthur and Pauline Boutal, came to play a major role in our community. I learned a great deal from that group. Even before then, however, it seemed to Maman that of all her children I was the only one to have a flair for happiness. She had suffered so much on account of her children; distressing failures, Clémence's incurable illness, the vagabond existence of her eldest son, Joseph, from whom we'd hear nothing for years on end. She'd admitted to me one particularly depressing day that she was afraid not one of us would ever find happiness. "I think" she told me, "the biggest cross one can bear is knowing that one's children are unhappy." That was the only lifelong sorrow she ever confided to me; others she quickly dismissed, saying, "It's nothing much, it isn't really so bad.... It'll pass...."

So it was no wonder she took new heart, began to hope again, with me and for me. I could be gay and entertaining, I did wicked parodies of local characters, I often made her laugh till she gasped for breath, and as for love, though I seemed to inspire it then as naturally as I breathed, I wasn't yet letting myself be caught.

Only one thing may have worried her somewhat. That was when I'd shut myself up, night after night for over a month at a time, in the little front room on the third floor, the cherished refuge of my childhood rediscovered when I was twenty-two, the little attic room where I'd been visited by my early reveries. Those workings of my imagination, I know now, had been rich and nebulous enough to nourish a whole lifetime. How curious it is that our childhood reveries come to us at an age when we know nothing about ourselves, and yet, like heralds of things to come, they teach us more about our own nature than anything else ever will.

There in my attic I'd scribble page after page. I had stories of a kind crowding into my head, and I kept trying to put that fermentation into words. It all seemed so alive when I started, so how

did I end up most of the time with empty and pompous words I'd never used before? I'd plunge this way and that, into humour, realism, mystery, and horror in the manner of Edgar Allan Poe. When the excitement passed, having briefly given me the most extravagant notions about what I was doing, I always saw that I'd written only childish prattle, worthless flashy trivialities. Nothing on which I could build a project, or a life, or from which I could even draw a little hope. I'd tear up what I'd written. After a while I bought myself a small portable typewriter, a very light one which almost jumped off its base when I used it, because I imagined that my style, by the very fact of being typed in unerasable characters, so to speak, would stand out more and have better form. I think all it achieved was to make everything shorter, because I'd avoid words whose spelling I'd have to look up in the dictionary. Which was progress of a sort.

Out of all I wrote, sometimes I'd find one phrase rather pleasing. It would come close to having that mysterious life that can sometimes be infused by a fresh new arrangement of everyday words. But it wouldn't seem to be mine. Had it come back to me from something I'd read? Or did it come from a me that didn't yet exist, someone I wouldn't have access to for quite a while, who, from far in the future, occasionally condescended to point briefly in the direction I should be going? I'd lose patience. I'd come down from my perch. Maman, much relieved, would see me leave with my tennis racket under my arm, or go out to the lane, climb on my bicycle, and pedal away, always – a curious clue in itself – towards those little oak woods to the west, where the sun would be setting.

Maman pointed out one day that when I left the house in late afternoon, I always set off towards the west.

"What's so special about that direction?" she wanted to know.

"It's so beautiful, and it stays beautiful long after sunset because the colours don't go for ages."

"Your father loved it too," she said. "In the worst of our bad years he'd always sit facing the west in the evenings, remember? Then he'd start hoping again that some day we'd be free of our troubles and have a little happiness before we died."

Then, as if she hadn't cherished those illusions as much as the rest of us, she flung me a caveat in a tone approaching bitterness.

"You can see whatever you want when you turn that way!"

LIVELY, exuberant, mischievous though I appeared to be, and probably still was at the time, the worm was already in the apple so to
speak; or at least, something was eating away at my merry, carefree
nature. Hardly a day went by without the strange thought entering
my head that I wasn't really at home here, that I had a life to make
for myself elsewhere. I'd been brought up to be French, but what
would I find here to nourish and sustain me? Apart from our
rehearsals at the Cercle Molière, practically nothing. So I'd hurry
to Winnipeg to hear concerts, or to watch entranced as the great
dramatic characters I'd discovered in my teen years came to life
before my eyes: Lear, Richard, and poor Lady Macbeth forever
sniffing her hand, from which all the perfumes of Araby would
not wash away the smell of blood. It was always the same hateful
dichotomy: in French we'd play Labiche, Brieux, Bernard, even
Molière, all rather clumsily, but it was nice, pleasant; in English
I'd hear great words that remained in the heart of the listener
indefinitely.

It didn't escape me that our life was an inward-looking one,
which led almost inescapably to a kind of withering. The watchword
was survival, and the principal standing order, though it was never
formally pronounced, was not to fraternize with the outside world.
I seemed to feel a little more of my lifeblood escaping every day.

I can still recall bits and pieces of the almost constantly carping
and negative preachings of those days: the beach was an accursèd
place, dancing was an abomination (especially the popular slow
waltz of my twenties), going steady was a mortal peril, particularly
between "us" and "them" because it led to mixed marriages, the
direst of calamities.

Sometimes you'd have thought we were living in some walled
enclosure during the wars of religion, Albi withstanding the Sar-
acens, or some other luckless mediaeval city under siege behind a
bulwark of prohibitions, portcullises, and interdicts. Where was the
Joan-of-Arc fervour of the days of my teens, our loyalty to the
best in ourselves and to each other, the spark that fired our enthusiasm and a kind of boldness bordering on open revolt? We
were jaded, I suppose. There had already been many defections...or

departures. Sooner or later every one of us would face the inevitable temptation, either to cross over to the English side and give in peacefully rather than perpetuate a long, drawn-out death, or to leave and go to breathe the air of our origins.

However, one, two, and then three years of teaching in St-Boniface passed very quickly for me. With an eye to a possible departure, I'd begun to put aside a sum of money each year, a minute one, since the circumstances Maman and I were coping with were as difficult as ever. Where would I go? To Quebec? The previous summer, friends had driven me there during the holidays. One night as we neared our destination we were driving late so that we could sleep that night on Quebec soil. The trip had taken almost a week. I was fighting off sleep in the back of the car. It would be an affront to the revered motherland to come to her the first time fast asleep. In the end I lost the battle and my eyes closed in spite of myself. And when I managed to open them again, all the road signs and advertising were still only in English! So I implored my friends, in case I should really go to sleep, to please, please wake me up the minute we crossed the border.

What was I expecting? That everything would suddenly be different? That the language I'd been told was the most beautiful and charming would flow from every mouth? That friendship would beam at me from all eyes? Surely I'd be instantly recognized and accepted. "Ah," they'd say, "she's one of our own who's returning to us." And they'd rejoice over the lost daughter come home.

Instead of which I found I was that curiosity, a little Franco-Manitoban who still spoke French, bully for her! Or sometimes "the little cousin from the West". In vain I'd explain that both my parents were born in Quebec and that I was returning to my roots. Nobody treated me as though I'd come home. I remained pretty much an outsider, in fact. "Very nice, speaks just like us, but not exactly family." I realized then that we French Canadians don't really have a sense of common blood. Of nationality, yes, but not from the heart like the Jews or other scattered people. Our own, once out of sight, are no longer really our own. I have been deeply hurt by the distance that the Québécois kept at that time and continue to keep between themselves and their brothers in the rest of French Canada. But now that I've lived long and happily in Quebec – more happily, at least, than anywhere else in the world

– and have received its government's highest literary honour and many signs of affection besides in return for my deep love for this land, I almost want to smile at my youthful oversensitivity. One of our common characteristics, something all we French Canadians should be able to recognize in ourselves, is that easily wounded sensitivity. Still, in spite of the admiration I receive (perhaps mostly because of *The Tin Flute*), I sometimes sense a kind of disappointment that this rather widely appreciated author wasn't born in Quebec. And perhaps sometimes a kind of vague resentment or disapproval – what else could I call it? – that my loyalty to Quebec, deep as it is, doesn't shut out the rest of Canada, where we as a people have wandered and suffered, yes, but throughout which we have also left our mark.

So the next time I left I wouldn't be returning to Quebec. Why not Europe? Yes, that was it, I'd go to France. Perhaps France would recognize me as her own.

I must have been mad! Yes, raving mad in my frenzy to be loved, wanted, to feel at home somewhere at last. I must have been really dreaming to imagine I'd be more warmly received in France than in Quebec. The astonishing part is that in fact I did get that warm reception, but much later; such an unbelievably warm reception that I very nearly fainted with emotion. Which goes to show that I may have been mad, but not insane.

FOR THE TIME BEING all was confusion in my head, as in a cloud-filled sky. Deep inside me was something I was carefully hiding from myself, I was so frightened of the stern face it would show me. This was my urge to write, when I still hadn't the least idea how to express myself in a personal or engaging manner. I think it was the Quebec writer Paul Toupin who said that discovering the sound of one's own voice is in itself a very difficult experience. Nothing could be more true. Furthermore, I kept longing for a home and not knowing where it was; perhaps even then I was hoping it was the whole world and all mankind. I'd long for a past, and it would slip away from me. I'd long for a future, and see none on the horizon.

Then suddenly I'd emerge from my doleful soul searching, and having stopped searching I'd find everything, and especially the marvellous current of life and youth that buoys us up and sweeps

us along and fills us with joy at every moment, because our hands are free again, ready to take whatever comes our way. When Maman saw me back to my cheerful self, it would make her forget debts, taxes, compound interest, the vicious circle holding us tighter and tighter in its grasp. What can she have been made of? How often I wish I had her capacity to rebound from adversity into the sunlight! One day she'd be overcome by the burden of the bills to be paid, at the end of her tether from "plugging holes", borrowing here to pay there, running hither and thither, a plug here and a patch there, then she'd get up the next morning a different woman, confident we'd get through, she'd seen it in a dream or heard it when she woke, like a great liberating breath. We'd be able to save the house and save us all, the strayed, the lost, the estranged, we'd be together at least once more and be happy together.

And as she used to when I was little, she'd begin to mesmerize me again with her marvellous dreams, in which everyone lived happily ever after. Our rich but hard-nosed uncle, for example, would have a change of heart and leave us part of his fortune in his will. Or Anna, who kept buying Irish Sweepstakes tickets – it was illegal in those days – would win the grand prize and divide it fairly. But I loved her true stories even more. In the ones she made up "for fun" she didn't pay much attention to credibility, but the true stories depended on keen observation and a sense of relevant detail. Where did she find those incomparable little stories she was always telling the moment she had some relief from her worries? She found them everywhere. I never saw her leave the house, if only to pick vegetables in the garden for the soup pot, stopping for a word with the neighbour across the fence, without bringing back some little story, in which each detail had its place and the important thing had the important place, and was always a surprise. So she'd hardly have left before we were watching for her return, knowing she'd bring back some shrewd, very funny, and very true observation, though we could never guess what it would be. Every time she stepped out of the house she was on a kind of adventure that sharpened her perception of life and things around her. She was Scheherazade bringing delight to our captive years in poverty. Now that I think of it, it seems to me that I was rather like her at that time: one day depressed, feeling we'd never

be free of our heavy debts of the moment, the next day walking on air because, as I'd worked in my attic room, a sentence had flowed from my pen that seemed to contain a glimmer of what I wanted to say. A miracle! Could pain be avenged by writing about pain? Could capturing something of life in words bring us to terms with life?

Maman was then getting on for sixty-seven or sixty-eight, my age now, when at last I'm taking time to think about all the grief she must have known. It's all very curious. We don't really empathize with our parents, it seems, until later, when we reach their age at the time in question, not having realized how alone they felt when we were there beside them. (An excruciating truth which is the whole underlying theme of *The Road past Altamont*, in which I didn't really try to say much more.) I thought Maman was happy, I wanted to believe she was happy, because she'd often still give way to gales of laughter, particularly if she was laughing at herself.

This woman who had seen her adorable little daughter burn alive before her eyes (Marie-Agnès, my elder sister by three and a half years), who had watched her handsome son – perhaps her favourite child – ravaged by alcohol, and who had seen her husband slowly die a broken man by her side, this woman who'd hardly spent a day without wondering where the next day's money would come from, is the one I picture with her head thrown back and her mouth wide open in laughter, her eyes glistening with tears of merriment. A woman made young again despite her sorrows. Who had lifted her spirits that day, so that a happy memory prevails in my mind over so many gloomy, grey, and oppressive ones? It may have been me, and come to think of it, it must have been me. I was about the only one left who could make her laugh like that with my nonsense.

My older sisters used to resent it. "Maman will give her anything," they used to say. "Maman's soft on her." Yet it wasn't exactly that. The truth is that she was old and I was young; I'd become the sunshine of her old age, so to speak. And the thought that one can be somebody's sunshine is enough to make one glow more brightly still.

It's true, in fact, that I often made my mother laugh. Now, in

my late years, if all I have to my credit is those moments of genuine laughter that brightened her anxious old age, I can perhaps forgive myself some of the sorrow I caused her.

XII

AT ABOUT this time a group of St-Boniface boys and girls joined forces to form something like a company of strolling players. All of us had talent: some for music, some for dance, and some, like me, for *déclamation*, as it was then called. We used to tour the French-speaking parishes of Manitoba giving variety shows. One could say we were a modest version of today's summer theatres, except that, far from getting any grants from anyone, we were helping a "good cause". Our cause was the Jesuit college of St-Boniface, which was always more or less on the brink of financial disaster, like almost all our confessional institutions.

There were ten or twelve of us, I don't remember exactly. One, a good pianist, had a repertoire to please almost everyone, from the languorous waltzes of those days to boogie-woogie. He was also a clever cartoonist. (It has only now occurred to me how surprising it was that such remarkable talents flowered in our stony soil.) He would set up his easel at an angle on the stage so that the audience could watch as he drew. Then he'd pick a head from the crowd at random and begin sketching with broad strokes. The subject would begin to be recognized by others in the audience, then by the subject himself, and a murmur of approval would run through the room. We had a kind of clown too, a tall, ungainly fellow with dangling arms, long, spindly legs, a dazed expression, and a silly smile. He just had to stand there and the whole room would laugh with that curious, delighted chuckle of a person who sees a comic image of himself. Then our Gilles would begin his gags and wisecracks, partly improvised and all side-splittingly funny. He deserved the laughter he drew.

For my own act, I would make up and deliver monologues, rather in the style of Yvon Deschamps today but much less polished. Still,

they must have had their modest effect if I can judge by the applause. In the days before Culture, Departments of Cultural Affairs, and TV, our public wasn't very demanding, it's true. On the other hand, it wasn't always easy to get a laugh out of those poker-faced little country audiences in their Sunday best.

The rest of our program included skits, songs, accordion music, and dances. In all, an engaging, bubbly product of slightly silly youthful exuberance.

So when our working day was done we'd leave our classrooms, offices, and service counters and take to the highways and byways of Manitoba. In two battered old cars crammed to their roofs with some of our scenery and props, our costumes, our musical instruments, Fernand's easel, and the makeup box, we'd speed off along little secondary roads in the gathering dusk to nearby villages, reserving the more distant locations for the weekends.

In this period I really came to know our little Manitoban French villages, which I realized later were so much like the ones in Quebec, with their invariable focal point of church, presbytery, convent, and cemetery...except that here each village was surrounded by endless space and silence. Fragile and alone beyond an unbroken prairie, they really went to one's heart.

We performed at St-Jean-Baptiste, Letellier, Notre-Dame-de-Lourdes, La Broquerie, Ste-Agathe on the Red River. I think it was at Ste-Agathe that we gave our show in a beautiful hayloft over a brand-new barn on the outskirts of the village. We were christening it, in a sense. There were no cattle yet in the beautiful clean stalls below, in any event. So far only a little hay had been brought in.

When we'd scrambled up the ladder with all our equipment, we found ourselves under a huge arched roof in the biggest, loveliest auditorium imaginable, an uninterrupted vault without windows, openings, or recesses anywhere to break its continuity. We must have been the first to play in a totally modern theatre, like some of the most experimental performances of today. At the same time, the space incorporated one of the older traditions of the theatre, heavy timbers having been laid to form a stage at the front of the hall. On either side we had small areas closed off from view by potato-sack curtains, which served as wings, dressing rooms, loges, whatever. From there, through holes in the potato sacks, we watched

the elegant ladies and gentlemen arriving via the ladder, all a bit breathless, the parish priest hitching up his cassock and the ladies their skirts. But they did look distinguished once settled in their chairs, which had been arranged in rows of fifteen, with three substantial armchairs for the dignitaries in the middle of the front row. How those armchairs had been been hauled up the ladder is something we wondered about long afterwards.

I've never spent as fragrant an evening. It seemed to have captured all the balmy smells of summer, brought in, no doubt, on a handful of grass, in a clod of earth stuck to a boot while crossing a field. Together with the distant lowing of a cow tethered to a stake, this made the summer-theatre atmosphere complete.

In very small or isolated villages, we sometimes performed by gaslight. During one of these shows, the lamp had been dimming imperceptibly for some time before any of us realized what was happening. Finally, poor Fernand was on stage trying to draw a face, not understanding why he could barely see any more. Thinking perhaps that his eyes were failing, he suddenly exclaimed loudly and anxiously, "I can't see, I can't see!"

In a twinkling a burly fellow leapt to the stage and then onto the table beside Fernand, reaching up to pull the lamp down on its chain while a companion approached with a small hand-pump. To resuscitate the lamp, they followed the same procedure I'd watched at my uncle Excide's when I was a child. Air was pumped into the mantle, the flame came back to life, and we were bathed in a harsh light, the lamp buzzing like a swarm of angry insects. We realized then that we'd given part of our show in semi-darkness. There were protests from the audience that people had missed things and hadn't got their money's worth, so we started all over again from the beginning and the crowd laughed just as hard the second time as the first. After that, no wonder I thought I was promised a brilliant career on the stage.

At the end of those evenings we were usually thanked by the parish priest. Some priests, it's true, were hidebound, intolerant, and authoritarian, even despotic. Yet recalling these occasions, probably happy ones for them, I seem to remember kindly, jovial old souls who were paternally good-natured and a bit naïve when surrounded by their parishioners in festive circumstances.

117

One of these elderly priests took it into his head one night to give his parishioners a lecture on the art of succeeding in life, taking us, the performers, as examples, in our presence.

"This fine young dancer, now," he said, referring to one of us who had done a tap-dance number, "this disciple of Terpsichore, do you imagine he rose to the height of his art overnight? No indeed, my friends! He had to spend weeks and months practising all alone in some out-of-the-way corner at home – perhaps in his barn. And there, for hours at a time, it's been step, hop, tap... tap...tap...."

Though addressing a handful of parishioners on a purely friendly occasion about a very nonreligious subject, the old priest assumed his preaching voice, which carried to the farthest corners and brooked no argument. Suddenly he was talking about me, it seemed, and I was trembling in my boots.

"The lovely young person," he thundered, "whom you saw come forward, bow graciously, and then begin, and talk...and talk...and talk...with nothing, not even a scrap of paper to aid her memory.... She had to keep all that in her head, the little rascal! Talk... talk...talk.... We heard every word. We knew exactly what she was saying. Do you think she had all that ready in her head just by getting up one fine morning and saying, 'Today I'm going to see what I can do'? No, no, no! She had to spend hours and hours practising in front of her mirror, saying to herself...now wrinkle your nose...next give your little smile...now that charming little wave.... And that, my brothers, is how you come to succeed in life."

AT LA BROQUERIE, I believe it was, the parish priest was a handsome old man with an opulent, snow-white beard. He spoke in a soft and hesitant voice, pausing in an odd way every few words, as though he'd lost the thread of what he was saying and had to retrieve at least the end of it before he could continue.

"My young and talented friends...," he began and stopped immediately as though puzzled. He bent his head as if perusing his beard. Then, a little smile brightening his gentle face, he looked up, saying, "friends come from so far to be with us...." Again he was lost, looking down into his beard, even pressing it gently here

and there with his fingers. At last the words came forth..."to be with us and bring joy to my old heart...."

The pattern continued until the end of the affable little speech. After "my old heart" we heard... "heart which swells with fatherly regard...," then "regard of an old friend in La Broquerie...." Each phrase tailed off in shy little mumbling sounds. Then he'd find the thread of the thought again, apparently somewhere in the silky folds of his beard, as though it were a hiding place filled with wishes, memories, and gentle words.

THOUGH MAMAN generally went to bed early after her well-filled day, she'd try to stay awake until I came in, no matter how late, so she could hear about the events of the evening right away.

Sometimes fatigue overcame her burning curiosity and I'd find her asleep. How could I have had the heart to wake her as often as I did? I didn't know, it's true, that she was sleeping very little then in any case, three or four hours a night at most. But even if I'd known, I don't think I would have understood any better what it is to sleep poorly.

I'd sit on the edge of her bed and give her an impatient little shake.

"Come on, Maman, wake up!"

I think I did this because I couldn't have stood not sharing my story with her right then, when it was ready and fresh and funny. It would have lost some of its flavour by morning. I was convinced this was so, though I didn't understand why. I've learned since that a story won't wait until you've dealt with something you think is more important: a letter to write, an interview to give, a trip to take. A story's time comes when it comes, and if you're not ready then, it will rarely come again. If it's made to wait, most of the mysterious, elusive life it has when it's fresh will be lost.

So I'd wake her up. She'd have a moment of confusion, during which she'd look every minute as old as she was and I'd be briefly afraid. Then she'd recognize me, and propping herself up slightly on the pillow, she'd say, "Tell me about it."

Often by the faint glow of a nightlight, or even just the light of the moon through the window, I'd recognize in her face the same eager expectation of a story that I'd felt myself as a child. Now it

was my turn to give her relief from the burdens of life. When the evening had been particularly exciting, I'd sometimes take over an hour from the little time I had left for sleep that night so I could bring her my gift still warm and alive. Often, you're only as good at storytelling as you're allowed to be by having a receptive listener; I think I was never listened to so receptively as in the middle of the night by my poor mother after I'd dragged her out of her scant sleep. She'd laugh, she'd lean forward to hear every word, since I kept my voice low to avoid waking Clémence, she'd nod approval, she'd ask for reruns, like slow-motion movie clips of certain episodes. By the time I left her, my excitement would be soothed and I'd be ready for sleep, but she'd be too wound up to go back to sleep. She probably spent the rest of the night remembering the most amusing parts of my story, because sometimes, if I'd left my door open, I'd hear her chuckling to herself. Or else she'd indulge herself with stories of her own, imagining me, as it pleased her to do even in old age, just the way I was then – young, carefree, congenial, and full of fun, as one generally is while still in the flower of youth.

I LEARNED from Maman that you mustn't hold a story back when it's ready, but you mustn't rush it either; that you have to let it ripen naturally, sometimes for quite a while if it's to have all its own special qualities. I was also to learn that when you try to make it too perfect, fiddling with it constantly, overworking it – or just telling it too often – you sap it of its life and in the end, like any living thing, it may simply die.

That's what happened to my story of the venerable priest who kept losing the end of his sentence in his long white beard.

Maman had liked the story so much, and I suppose had made me tell it so often (or perform it, rather), that I'd been putting less of myself into it each time, leaving it to get across on its own.

One evening when she asked for it again, I told her a bit testily that it wasn't funny any longer and wasn't worth telling. She admitted that in fact the last time I'd told it she'd perhaps laughed a bit less spontaneously. Then she pondered a while.

"After all," she said finally, "it's only natural for stories about life to wear a little thin. Just like life."

That exasperated me.

"Stories wearing thin! What am I supposed to do about it?"

She smiled at me soothingly.

"Make up new stories or combine old ones. Or keep telling an old one but made over so it's new."

I think that was the first time I began to see – fortunately still far away and very vaguely – that the road I'd be taking in life wouldn't ever lead tidily to what writers, when they reach the bottoms of certain pages, naïvely or in self-delusion call "The End".

XIII

WAS IT SPRING or late autumn when we went to Otterburne? We left in such haste at the end of the day, we'd barely had time to swallow a quick bite. Either the evenings hadn't lengthened yet or they'd already shortened, but whichever it was we had to hurry so we wouldn't be overtaken by nightfall on the way.

None of us had ever set foot in Otterburne, though it wasn't far from fine villages like St-Pierre-Jolys and St-Malo, which everyone knew because they were on well-travelled highways. Otterburne, however, because it was badly marked or on some out-of-the-way stretch of secondary road, was considered almost impossible to find. It was so isolated, so shrouded in perpetual loneliness, the saying went, that it was sure to be totally forgotten some day. Yet it had once been the site of one of the most important agricultural colleges in the region; my cousin Cléophas had been a boarder there for several years. It also had a school for Indian children run by a religious order. I don't know whether Otterburne's decline had already begun at the time I'm speaking of, or whether there was just a feeling of decline in the air. In any event we'd been told, "For heaven's sake try to go to Otterburne. They're so lonely out there, it'll be a blessing to have you come and make them laugh a little."

Having missed the main highway almost as soon as we'd left the city, we struck off along some secondary roads rather than turn back. None of them had any signs. Soon dusk was upon us. It rolled in from the depths of the prairie like a light mist. The whole countryside took on the appearance of a dream, clothed in a delicate, semitransparent blue. We weren't paying much attention and we went from a secondary road onto little dirt roads, though apparently still heading in the right direction, judging by the brilliant red

streaks left along the horizon by the setting sun. The country around all those little dirt roads was consistently deserted. Gilles, our lovable clown, kept laughing about it and singing one of his crazy, rollicking songs at the top of his lungs. For my part, I recall being stricken with gloom. The same Otterburne which was then so impossible to find was to play a harsh, emotionally charged role in my life one day. Was I foreseeing that, so many years in advance? Probably not. Hindsight is letting me read things into the way I felt on that strange night forty years ago.

At last a light from a lonely farm appeared, seemingly distant but really very near. We knocked at the door. A woman came out.

"Otterburne? It's very close. You're almost there."

She pointed with outstretched arm to a spot in the infinitely deep, blue distance. A faint light seemed suddenly to appear in the spot to which she was pointing.

"There, see it? You can't miss it."

"A thousand thanks, Lady of the Twilight," Gilles carolled in his most ingratiating voice.

We set off again, our eyes glued to that fragile flicker, then we lost it. In those flat surroundings, whatever could have hidden it? A haystack? A wretched little tree? We wandered around for a good half-hour before coming upon another, equally lonely farm.

"Otterburne!" The man stood on his top step and pointed in the direction we'd come from. "You must've gone right through it. It's there, right close. Just gotta folla the light."

The light, the light! We'd no sooner started off again with our eyes fixed on it than we lost it again...and came to yet another farm on the other side of the village. It seems we went through it three or four times before finally stumbling upon it, the way a ball can roll around the rim of a hole before falling in. Three streetlamps unbelievably far apart brought us to a source of information.

"How come you ain't seen us before?"

Two oldtimers were sitting on a wooden bench in front of the station, pipes clenched in their teeth, contemplating the warm evening.

"Where's the hall where the show's being given?"

"The meetin'? You got here too late. Ain't gonna see nothing. She begun two hours ago, maybe more. Reckon she's about over by now."

Gilles put his head out the car window. "It's not finished, it hasn't even started. We're putting it on."

The second oldtimer spat at least three feet.

"You can't be them. Them's actors. They come on time. Must've. They been there in the hall with the people since…since when, Nésime?"

Nésime pulled out his watch and squinted at it in the light of the stars.

"Since half past seven. The time the priest said. There's some got there before so's to get a better place. Must be three hours them's been in there."

"It's my thinkin' them's prob'ly pretty near cooked by now," said the first oldtimer, "what with the heat the way it is, an' all bit by mosquitoes, too. Less'n them's lit their pipes."

"In your thinking, is it worth going?" asked Gilles.

"Depends," replied the younger of the oldtimers. "There's them that says it'll tickle you pretty good, so if you gonna catch a bit you better git over there quick."

"How come you're not there?" demanded Gilles with a frown.

"I ain't got nothing 'gainst playacting," said the older of the oldtimers, "only a night like this'n it's good being outta doors. Better to spend it out with the stars than shut up in some ol' curling rink. Got only me own smoke to bother me here."

We found the old curling rink at last on the other side of the village. People must indeed have been there for a good long time, and been pulling a lot on their pipes, because when we went in all we could see through the dense billows of smoke was a big straw farmer's hat here and there, the same one, it appeared, in every corner of the hall.

The priest stood up at once and addressed his parishioners.

"The performers have arrived at last. They're young people with delicate throats, so everybody stop smoking. Stop right now!"

The smoke diminished infinitesimally.

From the stage we still couldn't see our audience, and they probably couldn't see us either.

"Can you see me?" shouted Gilles, who'd been pulling faces and getting no response.

"Only the nose on your face," shot back a wag.

"We're really sorry we've arrived so late," offered Gilles. "We got lost."

"Ain't the first that's happened to," commented an invisible spectator in the thickest of the smoke at the back of the hall.

Suddenly we heard an anguished cry from Fernand, who'd gone groping around the stage.

"No piano? What am I supposed to do without a piano?"

Usually, as soon as we arrived and while the rest of us were making up, he'd play some rousing marches to put the audience in a good mood, and help us recover from our roadweariness.

Gilles stepped to the edge of the stage. The smoke had begun to lift and the effect was bizarre, no doubt as much so onstage as below, where we could now see nearly whole bodies, but not all with heads yet, or at least not attached to heads.

"Does anyone here have a piano?" asked Gilles.

A lady at the back seemed to feel obliged to speak up.

"I've got one. Last year I lent it when the bishop came. They brought it back all out of tune, so I don't lend my piano any more."

"And quite right, too," said Gilles agreeably.

As the suffocating smoke dispersed, the audience was making a piecemeal discovery of our clown, those long legs and long arms attached to that long body and long sad face, and there was general astonishment. Almost every mouth was open.

"Lend us your piano," Gilles was wheedling, "and if it comes back to you with a single note out of tune, I'll give you a new one."

"Okay then, that's fine," rejoined the lady.

The priest stood up.

Nearly a third of the audience left on the mission. The wait promised to be long, since the lady lived at quite the opposite end of the scattered village. To coax further patience from that most patient of audiences, Fernand began to sketch one of the faces finally emerging in the uncertain light, a strikingly handsome head wearing a tall, wide-brimmed hat. A whisper of amazement swept through the old curling rink.

"It's Ubald!"

Then the piano arrived, borne by eight stalwart men, four on each side, who practically lifted it over the heads of the audience.

It was nearly midnight. Having just finished his sketch, Fernand leapt from his easel to the piano and struck up some introductory chords. A few sleepy people sat bolt upright and rubbed their eyes in surprise to find themselves still there on the hard little wooden chairs. But almost everyone swung into the spirit of the show, as fresh and ready to be entertained as if they'd just arrived. I seem to recall that show as one of the most resoundingly successful we ever gave.

WHY DO I still have such a vivid memory of that evening, with its glimmering lights and shadows, its laughter and sudden silences engraved so deeply in my mind? Perhaps the silent little prairie village of Otterburne was sending me a message that night that I'd be back. That forty years later I'd be driving the same little roads bathed in twilight, hunting once again for a village as impossible to find as ever, chasing after the same light, repeatedly catching sight of it and losing it again, but this time in dread of what was awaiting me. We often do, in fact, return in sadness to places where we've known joy long ago when young.

IT'S SIX YEARS ago now. I'd hurried to Winnipeg on account of Clémence. I was waiting to be picked up at the hotel. The air conditioning filled my ears with a monotonous drone. And big dark shadows were looming in my heart.

Dédette, Sister Léon de la Croix in religion, had died in the spring of that year. She was carried off by a cancer whose first signs were detected too late, when she still seemed young and full of life. As soon as the Mother Superior of her convent telephoned to say that the surgical exploration had revealed an already inoperable cancer, I jumped on the first plane. The medical prognosis gave Dédette only two months to live.

So this was my second trip to Manitoba in less than six months. I had to face up to it. I'd be returning now to the scenes of my childhood only to watch my relatives die, to reap sorrow.

In the spring I'd spent nearly a month at my dying sister's bedside. I saw her every day, often several times a day. All I did, as I recall, was beat a path from Dédette's room to my cousin's, where I was staying, and from my cousin's to the convent. As a

result, Dédette and I, who'd never had much chance to get to know each other, became so close we began to feel inseparable. I'm still amazed that her approaching death finally enabled me to feel her presence, to see her – even to the colour of her remarkable eyes which I'd never really seen before – and conceive an affection for her that deepened from day to day the better I knew her. Why, I used to wonder sometimes, do we get to know someone so well when we're about to lose them? Dédette's death would have caused me less grief if I hadn't come to know her so well – yet I wouldn't for the world have been deprived of that grief.

Her room in the convent's infirmary was not much bigger than it needed to be to die in, but the window – a symbol of opening and liberation – was immense, one of those high windows typical of convents of the old days. Whenever Dédette was drowsy after a sedative, or if I couldn't bear to see signs of pain flickering in her face while we were talking, I'd move a step or two closer to the big window, and each time I'd be astonished at how beautiful I would find the sky in the midst of such sorrow.

So to break the appalling awkwardness between the one who's going to die and the one who's going to survive, I began, hesitantly at first, to talk about the sky. The one we know, or think we know, since it's always there before our eyes.

"I think our Manitoba sky's one of the most beautiful in the world," I said to her one day, "and I think at last I've discovered why, just today. That's odd, isn't it?"

"Why is it one of the most beautiful?" she murmured.

"Because it's so high, Dédette. So free of smoke and dirt, not spoiled yet by the foul breath of industry and big cities. Perhaps because the land it's over is so flat, too. Though the Greek sky is also very high and just as blue. Homer talks about it all the time in the *Iliad* and the *Odyssey*. What made me decide to go to Greece was all the nostalgia in his descriptions of the sky."

"I didn't know that. Tell me more."

"In Russia, too," I went on, "there must be something about the sky that gets inside you, because in *War and Peace* Tolstoy speaks of the 'towering sky' through Prince Andrei as he lies gazing up at it, mortally wounded in battle and dreaming of peace and harmony."

My dying sister listened. Only my stories of travel or accounts of happy moments in life seemed to distract her from the sadness of going.

"Tell me some more," she'd plead. "In my convent I haven't seen or known anything of the world. Tell me more."

UNTIL THEN I'd always thought that when there's serious talk between two people, one about to go and another who'll be staying, the conversation ought to turn to the one who's going, who'll soon know everything. It isn't always like that at all. Anna, just before she died, talked to me at length about the drabness of her life and not having had her due from it, as though hoping at least not to be forgotten. All Dédette wanted was to hear about my life, which she imagined to be successful, happy, and filled endlessly with gay, sparkling events.

To bring a smile back to the emaciated little face with its eyes like deep holes full of suffering, and because she wanted me to, I concocted a fairytale life of uncommon friendships, unqualified success, fame unspoiled by envy. I wasn't really making it up, just picking out the high points, the peaks, and leaving the rest untold, and so it was that I knew my cup had been filled. Yes, on the brink of death Dédette helped me discover that life is, despite everything, an imponderably marvellous thing. But that's another story, which I'd very much like to tell if I'm allowed enough time. I think that every day I become more like the dervish in the desert who had more and more stories to tell the older he got, and less time left to tell them.

But I must return briefly to Clémence and the day Dédette seemed to be rebelling against God Himself, as if He had made a serious blunder and mistaken her for someone else.

"I can't die!" she protested. "God can't let it happen. He knows how much Clémence depends on me. I can't leave Clémence alone!"

I went to the big window. I looked up at the towering sky, hoping to find some inkling of the meaning of Clémence's life on this earth. A gifted, wonderfully sensitive child, full of grace and intuition, whose power of vision was perhaps too great, and whose mind was suddenly struck a dark and terrible blow, leaving her to wander like a lost soul on earth. Not totally, though, and that's perhaps the most dreadful part. Her ravaged mind still showed such

astonishing flashes of intelligence, such clear signals of distress, that we'd be more upset than ever to see her return to her mysterious corridors of escape. How much Maman had suffered on account of Clémence was something Maman herself never really talked about; the pain was probably beyond words. But often she'd look at each of us in turn, beseechingly, pleading for reassurance.

"Who'll look after Clémence when I'm gone?"

Our Clémence has been an enduring sorrow bequeathed by one sister to another, each one, as she dies, passing on the legacy to a younger sister; strange, priceless legacy.

After Maman's death it was Anna who inherited Clémence. She took good care of her, going often to the little room where Clémence lived alone, taking her home to her lovely property in St-Vital for a few days, trying to entertain her, taking her downtown to buy clothes, when she herself was not too ill. But even so, Clémence would sink into silence and deep gloom. In those days so little was known about her disorder. It would send her into phases of over-excitement and agitation, when anything at all would upset her, then plunge her into sombre withdrawal inside herself, where no help could reach her. At that time I'd thrown myself body and soul into writing and was fighting for my life, in a sense, living alone in Montreal. My conscience was fairly clear about Clémence. "Anna's there for the time being," I'd tell myself. "Anna's keeping an eye on her." And as I'd done with my father, and with Maman, I kept thinking I'd have time when I'd done my writing to come and help Anna help Clémence.

But having floundered right and left, grasping desperately for a little happiness, Anna died. As was perhaps befitting for such a life, the end came in an oasis, in a desert. In Arizona. For Phoenix is surrounded by sand, and none of its royal palms or date or grapefruit trees would be there had water not been brought vast distances at great cost. Otherwise probably nothing would survive there except the strange saguaros, some of them empty cactus shells, through which the trapped wind blows with mournful organ sounds. An image of illusion; there's perhaps none more perfect than Phoenix. Anna spent her last few days of human torture gazing at tall trees with red flowers, poincianas, swaying gently against the bluest sky there ever was. "Is it true," she'd murmur, "am I really seeing that marvellous tree, or am I still only dreaming?" I

was at her bedside shortly before her death, staying at a motel not far from the clinic. Her youngest son, Gilles, came to join us and found a room at another motel nearby. Fernand was living with his small family in a trailer park. Paul, the third son, came with his wife and stayed at Fernand's. There we were, a nomadic little group camping on the edge of death, so to speak, not unlike the penniless Mexicans who'd come to a temporary rest around us, not unlike a good many wandering Americans, in fact. I remember feeling that we fitted the situation perfectly.

We had time for only three short bits of conversation, Anna and I, though we'd at last discovered a thousand and one things to tell each other about our lives. Only a brilliant mind, a keen intelligence, a passionate heart could have produced something I heard, bending close one day near the end, when she, groggy with sedatives, an intravenous drip in her heel and a tube somewhere else, fixed her eyes on a patch of blue sky and murmured:

"Everywhere else but here it's winter, it's cold. But here it's spring! Can it be that only here is real?"

"Yes," I said, wanting to comfort her, "it's only here that's real." But she looked at me sharply, the way she used to long ago, when she was letting us know we needn't try to put anything over on her.

"There's something I must tell you," she said to me two or three times, but then she'd fall into a heavy, sedated sleep. I thought, she's going to talk to me about Clémence. She's going to leave her to me. My turn's come.

But no. Not yet. After Anna died I learned that a whole year earlier, knowing she was nearer the end than she'd given us to believe, she had put Clémence in Dédette's hands.

DEDETTE in her convent! How ever could she begin to manage the running around, the shopping, finding clothes for Clémence, bringing them to her, perhaps having to exchange them, all the things Clémence was incapable of doing for herself, or perhaps at some point had simply decided weren't worth the effort.

Those things were on my mind the day we buried Anna. The sky was radiant. Since there were only two of her three sons, one of her daughters-in-law, and myself to attend the ceremony, plus three chance friends of the kind who seem indispensable one day

and are nowhere to be found the next, the priest suggested holding it at the graveside in the cemetery. He arrived wearing a surplice, with a choir boy and his aspergillum. Chairs had been arranged on the grass in the semishade of a slender tree with delicate leaves. We sat down. It was the tenth of January, 1964. Everywhere, not so far from this miraculous oasis, it must have been winter. Here it was perpetual spring. The cemetery was a profusion of giant poinsettias, hibiscus, and clusters of vivid red jacaranda. Insects buzzed merrily, flitting from clump to clump. The buzzing mingled with rather sweet lamenting sounds from a Mexican family weeping at the grave of a loved one in the distance. There was something infinitely tender and trusting in their praying voices. On a branch of a paloverde a mockingbird sang as though his heart would burst, the "gentle bird of youth" so beloved of southerners, and no wonder, once you've heard it sing.

At last our hearts were filled with love for Anna, whose frustrated, demanding nature could no longer alienate us. Why, I asked myself, is she only now getting the love that would have made her life? I hadn't yet completely returned to the faith of my youth from which, I believed, a dictatorial, unfair, and narrow-minded Church had driven me. But now a nagging riddle was drawing me back – what is life, and what is death? It seemed to me that Anna's life and death had made God necessary. No life or death until then seemed to me to have made Him so necessary. In one of her very last moments of consciousness, she had murmured so faintly that I'd had to put my ear to her lips to hear her, "I want to believe, but I'm not sure, that there's someone at the end.... Do...you think...?"

I took it on myself to tell her there was, though I wasn't sure either.

"Yes, Anna, someone's waiting for us, someone who loves us as much as we've hoped and longed to be loved all our lives."

I'd laid the trap and now I was caught in it. Now I needed assurance myself. Perhaps it was in that comforting little cemetery in Arizona, where even an inconsolable grief couldn't block out the mockingbird's beautiful song, that I began again to want God, at any cost....

I SHUDDERED suddenly as I stood by the big window in Dédette's

little infirmary room, startled, here at the bedside of my dying sister, to find I'd been lost in thought about another sister's death six years before. And I'd forgotten what had made me think of it...ah, yes...Clémence!

Well! Dédette had managed to look after her superbly. Convent rules had already begun to be relaxed at that time, but even if they hadn't, dear Dédette, though she observed rules scrupulously, would have found a way to bend a few for Clémence. But she didn't have to. On the contrary, some of "our sisters" had important connections and hence influence, others had friends with cars, others time to spare, and others frequent reason to be in shops, and all of them were trying to outdo the others in looking after, in fact coddling Clémence. What I hadn't foreseen was that when these women who'd renounced the world were given an opportunity to help someone by returning to it, they became like a swarm of bees, each anxious to do her part and each contributing what she could.

This was how Dédette managed to have Clémence admitted to a very good, brand-new government home for old people still able to walk around. Clémence had a lovely ground-floor room with a little flower garden and all the care that her condition required. It was in the pretty village of Ste-Anne-des-Chênes, which I remembered well since Maman had taken me there on pilgrimages, organized perhaps in competition with Ste-Anne-de-Beaupré in Quebec, or perhaps in spiritual affiliation with it.

It was rather far from the city, about fifty miles. Nevertheless, with the help of all her car-driving acquaintances Dédette managed to go there often, bearing a birthday cake for Clémence, or a pair of stockings, or a nice little pink bathrobe unearthed by "one of our sisters" at the clearance counter in Eaton's basement. And what's more, these visits allowed Dédette to work off a bit of the footloose urge shared by everyone in our family.

This is the place where I should tell the story about Dédette's and Clémence's visit to me at Petite-Rivière-St-François in Quebec's Charlevoix County. I rented a little house for them there, next to the cottage I'd had for several years – three weeks of light, of summer, of incomparable, exhilarating happiness before the dark days that followed almost immediately. That will have to wait till later, though, or else my poor dervish will tangle himself in the threads of his interwoven stories. For the moment we'll stay by

the high window in the little infirmary room where I'm looking at the peaceful sky and picturing the ferment, the bustle, the mobilization of kindly zeal that Clémence's humble and apparently pointless existence had guilelessly set in motion.

Before long, all was not well at Ste-Anne-des-Chênes. Despite the activity on her behalf, Clémence was lonely. Then Adèle came on the scene, planting the idea in her head that the two of them would be better off living together in a little apartment in St-Boniface. For the first time in her life, I think, Dédette telephoned me long distance. She was in a frenzy and her voice was high and shrill. "Just imagine! I had all that trouble getting Clémence into Ste-Anne and now Adèle wants to take her out. If she leaves they'll never take her back."

"We can't allow that," said I. "It's madness and we've got to stop it at all costs."

"But how?" pleaded Dédette across the line from Manitoba.

How indeed! We had no power of attorney from Clémence to look after her well-being. For the moment she was free to do anything she chose, however disastrous it might be.

"We'll pray," said Dédette before hanging up. "Who knows, it might work out this time."

It didn't work out, any more than it had before. Those two poor women, for all the love and compassion they really had for one another, were bound to grate on each other's nerves. Feeling that we'd overprotected Clémence, as perhaps we had, Adèle went too far the other way. "You can do that, Clémence," she'd say. "Learn how to do things yourself." Which soon drove Clémence to hysteria, since her nerves invariably went to pieces at the least difficulty. Furthermore, Adèle, taking after Papa, was slow to get moving in the morning but came to life towards evening. Then she'd make strong coffee, go out and come back in, walk around half the night, meditate, bring back the past, write her recollections...while Clémence, having gone to bed "with the chickens", would be trying to sleep. In the early morning Adèle would be tired from her excitement and activity during the night and want to sleep, while Clémence would have had all she could take of staying in bed and want to stir things up a bit. Perhaps the cruellest part was that for too long they were both prepared to suffer each other rather than suffer alone. Dédette tried to spare me and at first didn't tell me what

was going on, which I'd been suspecting, in fact. One evening she called me from Manitoba in great agitation and announced:

"I had to put Clémence in hospital. Don't be too worried."

Then she told me, speaking fast because long distance costs money, that it was perhaps a blessing in disguise...because, through the good offices of "one of our sisters", Clémence had been seen by a psychiatrist, and he had said, "You must put her in a good institution." It was already almost done, a place had been found. A home run by some Sisters of Providence, very dedicated..."and our sisters know their sisters...."

"Where?" I finally managed to put in.

There was a silence. The cost of the unused line time was a measure of Dédette's discomfort.

"Otterburne," she said with a sigh that reached me from beyond the Great Lakes and across part of the Manitoba prairie.

"Oh Lord!"

I could see the little village that was so secluded people had always said it was in danger of being forgotten sooner or later. I could see the shadowy little roads and thought I saw a solitary figure wandering aimlessly along them, perhaps a lonely Clémence, she too trying to patch together the threads of her life.

"Is there at least a bus to get there?"

"No...but one of our sisters has her family there. They come and take her back with them quite often. I'll have opportunities to go. And then, if we don't take the place, there won't be another one."

I sensed she'd reached the end of her tether.

"That's fine, Dédette. Do whatever's best. Whatever you think."

IT WASN'T so bad. The Sisters of Providence were perhaps not the most learnèd or cultivated of women, but they knew how to comfort the suffering, and before long they had begun to win Clémence's trust. She was under the care of a Korean doctor, brought there by heaven knows what saga, who looked after her better than she'd ever been cared for, perhaps, calming her with words of wisdom and medicines that were not too harsh. The fresh air helped. I saw her next when Sister Ross, the Mother Superior of the home, brought her to visit Dédette and me at the convent, when Dédette was dying. I was told she was much improved by then. Still, it was

a great shock to see the frail little figure, the face sunken and toothless because she wouldn't wear her dentures. Her eyes were huge and searching, a little confused, as if the filmy veil drawn by the drug Largactyl between her and the rest of the world didn't keep her mind from groping for her sufferings of old. I wondered how to tell her that Dédette didn't have long to live, and even whether I had to. We entered Dédette's little room together. Clémence knew at first glance. I saw this in a strangely awakened lucidity in her eyes, which were usually expressionless. But she controlled herself well. She even grumbled to us about the food provided by "those sisters". She'd always grumbled about the food wherever she'd been, and we thought it was just a favourite gripe. One day much later I tasted what she had on her plate at the home and, merciful heaven, it was awful! I think now I realize that people don't get really appetizing meals in any home or hospital where many need to be fed at once.

As soon as we'd left the room, Clémence turned to me and with that seeming indifference induced by sedatives, which is perhaps the most distressing form of pain, she said:

"We're not going to keep our Dédette, eh?"

I put my arms around her. It was like holding a little bundle of clothing wrapped around a feebly struggling mass of suffering.

I took her back to the entrance hall where Sister Ross was waiting.

"I'll bring her back to you next week," said Sister Ross.

"That's very kind, Sister."

"Not at all. We have to come into town every week or so. Clémence may as well take advantage of it."

She had a pleasant face and the pleasant, straightforward manner of a sensible country woman. I didn't in the least expect to become as fond of her as I did, only to lose her too, not many years later. Now when I begin to be fond of someone I'm always terribly afraid, because it seems it will never be for long.

When leaving Clémence I told her I'd try to come and visit her in Otterburne.

"If you can," she said.

In the end I didn't go during that trip. What kept me from going? Something that no doubt seemed important at the time: proofs to correct, the English translation of one of my books to review with the translator. My books have taken a lot of time that I might have

given to friendship, love – to obligations of the heart. But friendship, love, personal obligations have also taken a lot of time that I might have given to my books. The result is that neither my books nor my life is well pleased with me these days.

STANDING at the high window, I returned to Dédette's bedside from a memory triggered by another which, though it had lasted perhaps two minutes, had taken me years back over space and time.

"About Clémence," I said to Dédette, "I don't want you to worry. If it…turns out that you can't look after her, I'll do it. It's time I took my turn."

If I'd expected to put her mind at rest with a promise like that, I was sadly mistaken. I still had much to learn about my sister and, through her, about at least one aspect of the eternal enigma, death. In her eyes appeared the intense distress of someone who perceives that she's being abandoned to death, since the living are taking over those of her duties that are still unfulfilled. In that instant I realized that the worst part of dying is feeling abandoned. Though she didn't know it, her eyes were saying: I'm going to die and you're going to live, all of you around me are going to live. So we aren't the same any more, we're separated already, me on one side and you on the other.

It seemed so true I was ashamed to think that I was going to consent to live, while she would be dead; that I'd done so after each of the deaths that had touched me. If we really loved each other, I said to myself, as soon as one of us went, the others would go also. If we really loved each other, we'd all join hands and walk together into the ocean, towards the Creator, saying to Him, "Don't take us one by one, it's gone on so long; take us all at once." God was waiting only for this, I thought, and then would take pity on His creatures and their love for each other.

SUDDENLY the telephone rang at my elbow. I came back with a start to my hotel room in the land of funeral-taper trees and a wind of despair, from the little infirmary room beneath the tall Manitoba sky, and from a time long before that, when my mother's voice was asking, "Who'll look after my sick child?" A glance at the clock told me the journey had taken perhaps fifteen minutes. Yet it had crossed more distance than all my plane trips laid end to

end. What an astonishing amount of ground one's memory can cover!

I lifted the receiver. I heard a gentle, loving voice, like cool water taking the sting from a burn. It was Sister Berthe Valcourt. When Dédette died she was Mother Superior of the convent in St-Boniface. My sister had died in her arms early one Monday morning. She'd opened her eyes very wide, Sister Berthe told me, "like someone who's going to cry for help," then she'd recognized the nun and murmured, "It's strange...strange...," and, as though recovering from some infinite surprise, just had time to pronounce Clémence's name. Then she was asleep for ever.

A few days earlier, however, she had been perfectly lucid and had clearly and unmistakably given Clémence into Sister Berthe's care. "Gabrielle's far away," she had said, "and so busy already with all her obligations, her letters, her books, her public, and her health so delicate, too. How's she ever going to run back and forth doing everything Clémence needs?"

Sister Berthe had accepted responsibility for Clémence as though she hadn't needed to be asked.

Now her soothing voice was saying, "I finished my seminar a bit earlier than I expected. We still have nearly two hours of daylight, and I have the community car. How would you like to run out to Otterburne and give Clémence a hug?"

How would I like it!

Three minutes later I was at the hotel entrance, though Berthe had warned me she'd need a good quarter of an hour to get there.

XIV

ISN'T IT CURIOUS how life repeats itself? It's as if there were re-hearsals for some future event. The first time we have a feeling of *déjà vu*, and the second time, much later, we're confused in the strangest way. Is it because I now know what I thought I knew then, we wonder, or did I really know then what I know now?

In any event, as we left the city Berthe missed the main highway and we found ourselves on the little secondary roads I'd been on long before, roads which she, a good deal younger than I and always in a hurry, didn't know at all. She was upset. "In all the time I've been going to see Clémence in Otterburne, I've never missed the right road before." I smiled vaguely, a little guilty. I and my memories must have led her astray, that was all. Or else I'd talked too much and distracted her. Whatever the case, she didn't know where she was but I remembered it well, even the time of year. No mistake, the first time had also been in early autumn, harvest time, when the fields of high, golden wheat wave gently in the west wind, in the shimmering light at close of day. For all the sorrows I'd accumulated since the last time I'd been here, I still felt a surge of joy to see the waving wheat, a little sadly I might say, because my distant youth was lending me a small piece of all its happiness – or rather a memory of this happiness.

Soon Berthe confessed that we were lost.

"These little roads put me off!" she exclaimed.

"I've always loved them," I said. "The devil must have made you do it just to please me."

"The devil, indeed!"

Twilight was advancing rapidly, flooding the prairie with what might have been a deep blue liquid, from which nothing clear emerged.

I could hear Gilles's voice: "Otterburne – can you tell me where it is?" And the answer: "Over there, don't you see the lights?"

"We're very close, though," insisted Berthe. "I have the impression we passed right by and missed the turn."

"Aren't there just three streetlamps in the village?" I asked.

"I think there are five or six now," she replied, "but there's the home too, three storeys high, and it should be all lit up at this hour. Usually you can see it from a distance."

I began to look for it. With three floors lit up, it should be easy to find across the dark, uniform prairie.

Very shortly I spotted a glimmer.

Sister Berthe was impressed.

"You have good eyes."

"It's because I trained myself very young to look out into the prairie at this hour."

"What were you looking for?" she asked, affably but with genuine curiosity too.

With my thoughts far away I replied:

"Happiness. Maman kept saying some day he'd surely come our way. I was afraid he might miss our little Deschambault Street, so I used to go and wait for him at the corner, looking out on a kind of open space that was there in those days. I thought of it as the prairie because you could see a long way. I never thought happiness could possibly come from any other direction, just across that dreamy open prairie."

"On foot?" asked Berthe softly so as not to disturb my memories.

"Oh, yes, on foot. And I'd recognize him when I saw him.... Later, when I was fourteen or fifteen, I used to go and wait for him at the end of a little dirt road at my uncle Excide's farm. It must have been on the edge of a plateau, because when you came out of the bushes you could suddenly see such a vast expanse of sky and land it made me feel the world was mine."

"Did you ever see him?" asked Berthe more softly still.

"Twice there was a tree in the distance that looked like someone walking, and for some time I thought it could be he. Only he always stayed in the same place, as if he'd stopped to think and hadn't made up his mind to start again."

We were arriving at the door of the home, whose façade was almost entirely lit up. It looked like a strange, brilliant constellation

at the end of the village, which was half in darkness and about as somnolent as when I'd come there the first time. I could hear our gales of laughter then, but dominant in the foreground were unhappy events of years to come, too numerous to count, it seemed.

How many worn-out bodies and minds were contained in that large establishment on the almost empty prairie, how many lives forsaken, stowed away for ever, locked up, forgotten, I learned only later, fortunately. But fortunately too, I also learned how much unfailing kindness was devoted to relieving all that misery.

Sister Berthe went with me to the second floor, as far as Clémence's door. There she left me. I knocked lightly. I heard a cheerless voice telling me to come in.

CLEMENCE WAS SITTING in semidarkness at the foot of her bed, on a grey blanket neatly folded in four, the way one imagines prisoners in the evening in their cells. She seemed to be part of the vast twilight, now deep night-blue, entering unimpeded through the window, a high one here too. I could barely make out her features but saw very well that she was frighteningly thin, her face terribly small, her body all huddled up as if trying to take as little room as possible in this world, perhaps even to disappear completely. Yet she'd held up well at Dédette's funeral. She'd been dressed appropriately, had received condolences with dignity and a perfectly suitable word of thanks for each person. True, at the time she'd felt like part of the family again…whereas here in this lost village she must have felt we'd abandoned her.

It gave my heart such a wrench I really didn't know how to start a conversation with the poor child. She'd barely turned her head towards me when I entered.

"Would you like me to turn on the light?" I asked gently.

She gave a little shrug.

Did she think she was back in our poorest days, when Maman would ask us not to turn on the lights until we really had to? "As long as there's a little light in the sky we can wait," she used to say. Or did the gentle half-light suit her sadness, the way, in fact, it had always suited me?

"It's still light enough, but turn it on if you like," she said with indifference.

"You're right," I said.

I sat down beside her, tried to put my arms around her and found her stiff, unyielding. She barely let me kiss her on the cheek, and as I did so, kept her eyes on the limitless twilight still sweeping in slow waves into the tiny room. With my arm lightly around her waist, I turned and looked at the sky with her, in silence, and thought how much its colour matched our souls.

I was sitting on a corner of that horrid grey blanket, which had probably come from an army surplus store. I made the blunder of finding fault with it, or rather with whoever had given it to her, either to be rid of it or instead of a better present. People often gave her clothes they didn't want any more, and she, imagining perhaps that they'd been given in generosity, would refuse to part with them. Or perhaps she became attached without illusions to her fusty old things, for some obscure reason we could never understand. I know now that unhappy people take pleasure in surrounding themselves with old, dreary, unattractive objects.

"I'll buy you a much prettier one for the foot of your bed, Clémence," I said. "How about a pink one?"

Her hand clung tight to the ugly blanket as if to a dear and faithful friend.

"It's warm and still good," she said. Then after a silence she added, "What more would pink do for me?"

I felt I had to explain that we weren't poor any more and could allow ourselves some indulgences.

"I've got plenty of money now to buy you nice things, Clémence."

"Money!" she said scornfully, and with the look in her eyes, with her whole wasted face, seemed to be rejecting something that had done nothing for humankind in the depths of misery. Then she asked me — and I still don't know whether it was a childish question or one of great wisdom — "Do you think it helps?"

In her presence that day, I was no longer sure of anything. Certainly nothing shakes our confidence more than being with someone who has none; that's why we can't bear it, perhaps.

"You'll see," I told her, as one always does in such circumstances, "you're going to get better, Clémence. I'm going to help you. You're going to get well again."

I was so shaken to find her in this state. I kept blaming myself for it. But there were others I blamed too. In the city there were still family friends and cousins, male and female, who claimed they

cared for me, yet not one of them had taken the trouble to go and see Clémence. "Otterburne's too far," they'd say. "There's no bus to get there." "It's the end of the earth." They treated her as if she were already buried. But had I done any better, always so busy writing my stories, as though this were my most essential duty? How do you know which duty is the most essential? Perhaps each has its turn and you have to keep hurling yourself this way and that, trying to do justice to one at a time, while the rest are screaming all around you for attention.

"You know, I've come from Quebec especially to see you," I said, as if asking to be forgiven.

"You like your Quebec?" she asked without much interest.

"I've made my life there," I said.

"Maman came from there, Papa too," she murmured, as though I didn't know, or perhaps the better to register such an unusual fact in her solitary existence.

"Would you come there to live with me, or near me, if I came and got you?"

She kept gazing at the gradually darkening sky, like someone dreaming of finding a real home at the end of time.

"No," she said. "Papa's here, Maman's here; they're here for ever in the cemetery. I'll stay with them."

Then she reminded me with a degree of defiance:

"There's still a place in our family plot in the old cathedral cemetery. That's where I want you to bury me later."

"I'll do that, Clémence dear."

Then she seemed to feel a little better and I decided to change the subject.

"In the meantime, we have to get you some new clothes. To-morrow morning Sister Berthe and I will come and get you and take you to Eaton's. I'd like to buy you two or three pretty dresses and a coat and some shoes...."

She let me talk on, adrift in a deep sea of indifference. What did she care about shoes, stockings, lovely new handbags, and silk umbrellas? By the last glimmers of daylight, faint rays still filtering through the window, I saw that there was no hope in her eyes. Still beautiful eyes, sombre brown, moist with the tears of life, but empty of the thing that quickens the soul – though who knows what that really is? My heart ached as I looked at her. Without

reflecting that every day hope is disappointed in this life, hope was suddenly what I wanted at all costs to bring back to my poor sister's eyes. I didn't know the price I would pay; the many trips from Quebec to this poor, forgotten little village, the countless letters I'd write, the endless encouragement day by day. But most of all, yes, most of all, once hope was restored to her I would be even more committed, for how can we ever abandon someone we've "saved"?

I left her in the blue half-light she didn't want interrupted, even to see me better before I went.

Sister Berthe was waiting for me in the car. She comforted me with kind and soothing words. Being with me again after so many years, Clémence was bound to be very apprehensive at first. She was frightened by any change in her routine; any emotional ripple in her isolated existence upset her. But she'd get used to it gradually. Even tomorrow I'd probably find her a little less difficult. And it wouldn't really be long before she'd begin being affectionate again.

I listened in astonishment. You'd have said she was talking about her own sister as much as mine, that she knew Clémence perhaps better by now than I did myself.

What strange compensation heartache sometimes brings! My most loving sister, Dédette, who was always best at comforting me, had no sooner been taken from me than a substitute was given me, a stranger, but every bit as tender and as close. Had Dédette known, wanted it so, perhaps? I thought I recalled seeing in her eyes, when the end was near, during the most difficult moments of our separation, a mysterious look of relief.

Gently Sister Berthe squeezed my hand. Then we started home. Moments later, turning off the road from the village onto the highway, what should we see, as visible as could be against the deep blue sky, but a sign saying "Otterburne".

We glanced at one another with a furtive little smile.

"So it really is on the map," I said.

"By the highway too, which I'll never miss again," said Sister Berthe, "and only thirty miles from the convent. We'll come often. And soon you'll see Clémence come back to life."

The twilight resembled a great watery deep that made you think it must have crept over the whole earth by now. I slowly began to

feel better as it worked its old magic upon me. Perhaps this be-witching time of day was reviving fragments of the old dream of my youth. I peered into the blue of the night that now united earth and sky, and imagined that tomorrow would indeed be better.

XV

NOW, TO PICK UP the threads of my story, I must reach far beyond these sorrowful events to what was probably the most sheltered period of my life. Yet I found reasons not to think I was happy, reasons for preparing to leave, for on my little Deschambault Street I was hearing the call of the far-off lands people used to refer to respectfully as the "old countries", those of our earliest ancestors who had come to North America.

It took me seven years – eight counting Cardinal – to scrape together, penny by penny, the sum of money I felt I had to have to contemplate leaving. I had about eight hundred dollars in the bank. I raised this to almost nine hundred by adding the modest proceeds of selling my bicycle, my fur coat, and a few other objects. Maman was alarmed to see me disposing of things she knew I treasured. It didn't help to tell her I was only going for a year, which I earnestly believed; to her I was behaving like someone burning her bridges, or turning a page in her life.

Precisely how my plan to go to Europe developed and why it took over and ruled my life so utterly, I'd still find it difficult to say. So at the time, I suppose, I didn't understand it at all. It was, it must have been, one of the mysterious calls one hears and obeys blindly, half confident, half confused. I was looking for something, but what? The little things I'd written so far were so worthless. On the strength of those alone I'd never have dared announce I was going to devote myself to writing. No, even in my own eyes, this was not something I was cut out for. And yet I was faintly conscious sometimes of seeing myself in the future, not, indeed, as having become a writer, but as struggling and struggling towards this goal. This was perhaps one of the most accurate premonitions I ever had, concerning either myself or anyone else.

On the other hand, I had had some success on the stage with our amateur theatre groups, Le Cercle Molière, where I played in French in *Blanchette* by Brieux, *Le Gendre de Monsieur Poirier* by Augier and Sandeau, *Le Chant du Berceau* and *Les Soeurs Guédonnec*, and then with the Winnipeg Little Theatre in English. Naïvely, I believed that I had some talent for the theatre – and perhaps I did. Since one must always have a plausible explanation to offer for what one does, I would say I was going to London and Paris to study drama. People thought I was very daring, very full of myself to be departing into the blue this way. I wonder what they would have thought if I had admitted that my real purpose was to see what the world was like on the other side of the hill I'd been living behind and that I was counting on this to show me what it was I was looking for.

But I had a feeling my urge to leave hadn't begun with me alone. Often I thought it must have come from previous generations, whose yearning for fulfilment had been sapped by undeservedly obscure lives, an urge reborn in me, inspiring me to strive for their ultimate liberation. Perhaps I was still gripped by my old childhood dream of making it up to my people with my own success. I liked to keep telling myself so during these months of torment, for I was often terrified by the uncharted future towards which I kept driving myself. I suddenly grasped how big, how impenetrable my future was, seen from my peaceful, countrified little Deschambault Street: a misty vastness in the distance, pierced but not dispersed by brilliant lights. I wanted to turn back but it was too late. I had put the inevitable between myself and my fear, as I was learning to do to protect myself from perpetual indecision.

It must have been my last year of teaching, or possibly the next to last. I still had my first-grade class. I was comfortable with my little immigrants and they seemed comfortable with me; we were drawn together by a subtle feeling that we were all strangers – at least, strangers to an absurd element in life that was ruining it for humankind.

Surprisingly, after a tenacious fight to keep me at home, Maman suddenly gave in. I told how her resistance ended in *The Road past Altamont*, partly fictionalized, or transcended rather, but containing the essential truth, and I don't want to return ever again to that old wound.

She resigned herself more readily than I expected to selling the house. From lack of experience, I didn't understand at the time that she was tired out from struggling, but only where material possessions were concerned. Later, although more tired than ever, she found enough energy to come and visit me in Montreal. And if her children were unhappy or in danger, she'd run to them still, even just before she died.

It would have been impossible to keep the house. I was the only one in the family to have a steady income in those Depression years, apart from Adèle, and even she, as I recall, didn't always have a school during that dreadful period. After seven years at the Académie Provencher, I was earning ninety-five dollars a month for only ten months of the year, less pension fund deductions in the last three years. At the time I never expected that the little sum I recovered from the fund, two years later when I returned from Europe, would virtually save my life as I faced an agonizing decision in my wretched little room on Stanley Street: whether to go back to Manitoba or stay in Montreal.

For the moment, our unpaid property and school taxes, plus compound interest, amounted to over a thousand dollars. We also owed a great deal to the wood and coal merchant.

My brother Germain had no school, and to avoid being a further burden to us was obliged to accept a temporary post at the College of St-Boniface, which was in such straits it could offer him only bed and board and a little pocket money in return for twenty hours of classes a week. He reduced his tobacco ration to almost nothing and spent the winter in a coat worn to threads. He often held his hand across the front of that coat, I remember, about halfway down, to hide the shabbiest part; at least, this was a mannerism we'd never seen in him before. When he finally obtained a teaching post in Saskatchewan, I had to lend him the price of his railway ticket, nineteen dollars and fifty cents. I remember the sum exactly, I suppose because it seemed so enormous.

In the course of the year he spent in St-Boniface, his wife Antonia found herself a school of several grades in a remote area, but for a salary that no one would have dared offer a man; there was not much compunction about doing such a thing to a woman in those days. Out of her sixty dollars a month she had to house, feed, and clothe herself, bring up their two-year-old daughter whom she kept

with her, and, of course, pay the cost of travel and their medical care in case of illness. Germain left for Saskatchewan in high spirits. The school he'd been offered was not far from his wife's. He would be able to visit his little family on weekends. For a reasonable sum, a neighbouring farmer rented him an ancient buggy and an equally ancient mare, which rarely went faster than a walk.

Antonia often told me how, when she'd finished school on Friday evening, she'd take Lucille's little hand and they'd walk quite far down the road to the top of the only rise of land in the flat countryside, a perfect lookout point. They'd finally see the rig appear in the distance, moving far too slowly to suit the two who were waiting, to say nothing of the one approaching. As the distance closed, Antonia sometimes thought she saw the whip rise, impatiently perhaps. But Germain had always loved animals and could never bring himself to be harsh with the old farm horse. The lash would fall rather like a caress on Flossie's broad rump. Slow she may have been, but I think all of them, child, father, and mother, fell in love with Flossie that year. They talked about her long afterwards with curious warmth, as of an old friend in hard times.

Waiting on the high ground, the child would soon begin to jump for joy and wave to her father. Though impatient, Antonia and Germain would just watch the distance between them gradually dwindling.

These two had to wait until half their lives were behind them before realizing their modest ambition of working side by side in the same school, he as principal and she as teacher at the elementary level.

It was during those difficult years, when poverty was so prevalent everywhere it came to seem normal, that I began to think only about taking flight.

MAMAN FINALLY found a buyer and the transaction was quickly concluded, almost without hesitation. All my life, or at least since I'd been able to understand such things, I'd been hearing that selling the house was inevitable. Many times the prospect had come close enough to touch us with its clammy wing, then gone away again and left us in peace a while. Then suddenly it was done and there was no turning back. When Maman told me, pretty calmly, "I've sold the house...," the shock I felt was something I've never really

recovered from. For me it's still as though she told me she'd sold a living, breathing part of us that day.

From that point on, Maman seemed to accept the fact with surprising composure. Once liberated from much that she had accumulated in her life, furniture, objects of one kind or another, she perhaps felt for the first time that she could turn to many of the things that she'd been wanting to do. It may have been like casting off a weight. In any event, she seemed to undergo a mysterious and sudden rejuvenation, ready, one might say, for a new, more carefree, airy existence, with no ties but those of the heart.

We didn't get much for the house: once the debts were paid, barely enough to provide Maman with a very small allowance for a year or two – until I came back from Europe, I thought. But we were pleased with an agreement we had made with the new owner. For a modest sum he would rent us three rooms upstairs, made into a convenient little apartment.

Selling the house where I'd been born on March 22, 1909, where I'd first dreamed my most persistent dreams (to which I'm subject even today, tired as I am of pursuing their delusions of beauty), affected me less than I thought it would once the first shock had passed, probably because we were still basically at home. Calmly and without regret it seemed, Maman disposed of our excess furnishings – rugs, lamps, and the big dining-room table. She'd embarked on the course of self-denial that she followed thenceforth until the day she died, when we were stunned to discover that her personal possessions amounted to little more than those of an old nun bound by vows of poverty.

So Maman, Clémence, and I moved into the three upstairs rooms which we ourselves, when we were the owners, had rented so many times to transients for a week or a month, or to people who stayed for years and became friends.

"It's really almost better this way," said Maman. "We still have our trees, our little street, our peace and quiet, without all the worries that go with them." Fortunately, our landlord also loved these things and took good care of them. In short, we were almost happier as tenants in our own house.

THAT YEAR, Maman went as usual to spend the summer with her brother Excide. I went to Camperville, a tiny village of no account

on the shores of the marvellous Lake Winnipegosis, one of the most limpid and also most tempestuous lakes in Manitoba. I was to spend over a month with my cousin Eliane, my uncle Excide's eldest daughter, whose husband, Laurent Jubinville, was principal of the farm school attached to the Oblate mission on the Indian reserve. The house stood alone in the middle of a huge meadow full of rocks: a strange, bleak landscape creating an air of desolation. But by the edge of the lake, listening to its tireless voice, I was soothed and happy.

Eliane had six adorable little children, and she herself was slim, blonde, and beautiful, with eyes full of kindness, still very young and, one would say, imbued with the artless dreams of youth. To amuse myself and help out, I gave lessons to the three eldest. I've never seen children want to learn as badly as they did. Years later when I wrote *Where Nests the Water Hen*, I borrowed many of the details and elements of Camperville to mix with those of the Little Water Hen, the two regions having much in common. The child Joséphine in *Where Nests the Water Hen* was inspired by Eliane's little girl Denise, who, at barely five and a half, used to follow me everywhere, upstairs and down, outside, through the stony meadow, with her reader in her hand, begging me at every step, "Cousin, show me another page." Often I can still hear those children asking, in their sweet, musical little voices, "Cousin, show us how to do this. Show us...." I found my real children for *Where Nests the Water Hen* while staying with my cousin at Camperville, that's certain. And I confess I also took Luzina's blue eyes, which were always "warm" or "full of feeling", from Eliane. I spent a sweet, dreamy summer there, at peace with myself and untroubled by my plans for the future, just content with the moment, which hasn't often been the case.

I wasn't idle, however. I kept my mornings for my writing, since I wasn't giving up, and displeased as I might be with what I wrote I'd take it up again next morning. This must be when I tried my hand at Indian legends, gleaned from the nearby reserve. I attempted every imaginable genre before finding my own. I wrote a great many pages but kept very few, tearing most of them up as I went along because, having only one suitcase, how could I have carried all that away with me?

In the afternoon I'd call my pupils to school in the family room of the house, which Eliane had assigned to us. I'd brought a small blackboard, chalk, and some erasers, which delighted the children. The three youngest would stand at the door as if at the gates of Paradise, in tears, begging "to come to school too." On Fridays we would let four-year-old Réal come in and he'd sit quietly in a corner, following the lessons without a sound.

To reward my little people, I'd take them swimming afterwards in the cold, sparkling-clean waters of the lake. The waves were dangerous, even at the shore, and Elaine wouldn't have allowed the children to go without supervision. It was an exciting treat for them to be able to discover their lake at last, less than ten minutes from the house. We'd come back washed and a bit limp, the eldest boy carrying golden-haired Marielle, who was two.

In the evenings I'd ride my bicycle along the Indian trails. They had probably been there for generations and generations, and were always quiet, winding, springy under the wheels or feet, and as enticing as if they'd just been discovered. The rustling of leaves accompanied me as I rode – soft woodland music played every summer since the days of the "savages".

The wonderful summer holidays came to an end. I went back to my class at the Académie Provencher. This would definitely be my last year of teaching.

By the end of September, Maman had still not come home. That year the threshing had been much delayed by torrential rains. She was no doubt loath to leave her brother before the heavy work was finished. But I imagined that she was also finding consolation for the loss of her house in the permanence there, things that never let her down: the farm, the high, clear sky of Pembina Mountain, the seasonal farmwork which never changed from one year to the next.

When October came I began to feel she was overdoing it. Her brother was so much younger than she, I didn't like to think of her, at sixty-nine, working her fingers to the bone for him. I suspected that before coming home she was putting the house in order, inspecting the curtains, mending the ones that were still holding together, making new ones to replace those beyond saving, filling cupboard shelves with jams, jellies, and vegetable preserves

151

of all kinds. I suppose I was a little jealous, but I resented the fact that she should put herself out so much for a brother who at times, I felt, had taken rather too much advantage of her.

At last she came home. It was a late October evening. There was frost already. The first snow was about to fall. She arrived with a fat suitcase bulging with jams, pembina jelly, sweet butter, fresh cream — to us, priceless presents from the farm, which Maman intended to share with others. Some of these good things had been sent with Maman for Rosalie, her only sister living in Winnipeg, whom Uncle Excide hadn't wanted to forget.

The next morning, with a cold coming on and extremely tired, I thought, she was determined to go that very day to take Rosalie her share of presents. I'd found her looking poorly when she returned from the farm. She'd lost weight and seemed to have worked beyond her strength, as if on purpose, to escape some kind of punishment, perhaps. I tried to keep her from going, telling her that the day was cold, the sidewalks icy, and that my aunt could certainly wait another day for her share of gifts from the farm. To which she replied that she had brought some homemade bread that Rosalie was particularly fond of, and she wouldn't dream of not letting her enjoy it right away, poor soul, after all she'd spent the summer glued to her sewing machine. At that I lost my temper and told her it really was ridiculous, a woman of her age slaving all summer at Uncle's, then when she'd barely set foot inside the door going out in the streets again like a beggar woman.... I stopped short. Dumbfounded, Maman and I looked at each other. She'd always been the one who'd talked to me that way. "D'you think, just because you're young, you can go on burning the candle at both ends the way you're doing?" Or, "Go on then, do what you like, waste your strength and don't listen to reason, only one day, my poor girl, you'll have to pay for it...."

There we were all of a sudden, each in the other's shoes. I was the one who was scolding, and Maman, just as I'd done, was shrugging her shoulders, putting her nose in the air and going right ahead with what she intended to do, as if to say, "When are you ever going to leave me alone!" Then I knew how like her I was. Understanding now why she was arguing, always giving me the same backtalk, I felt the deep compassion for her that one can feel only through one's own helplessness.

I WATCHED her waiting for the streetcar at the corner, her arms full of bulky packages, in a coat that wasn't warm enough, perhaps without gloves, and for the first time in my life she looked to me like a poor woman. Her wealth of dreams had always made her seem rich to me, but out there at the streetcar stop, her eyes cast down and her head bent, she seemed to have reached some unaccountable impasse. In the darkest days of our money troubles, and even our family quarrels, I never saw her so afflicted, less by the winter wind than by a wind of defeat.

XVI

I WAS UNEASY all that day, though I couldn't put my finger on the reason why.

"Maman hasn't phoned?" I asked when I came home.

"No," Clémence said, "she must be on her way. Or else Aunt Rosalie has kept her for supper."

At six o'clock I called my aunt. She told me Maman had left two hours before, presumably by streetcar.

It was seven o'clock when a policeman rang at the door. He was bringing me the news that Maman had had an accident in the street and had been taken to Misericordia Hospital, which was not far from my aunt's. She had been crossing the icy pavement to reach her streetcar and had fallen and broken her hip. The driver of a car had picked her up.

I left immediately for the hospital, which was at the other end of the city, in an English neighbourhood, of course. Riding in the streetcar, I wondered how Maman had managed, since she knew so little English and probably had no money with her. In those days you practically had to have money in your hand to be admitted to hospital, or at least have a guarantor present.

She was in a four-bed ward and there was a French-speaking woman in one of the other beds. They had already been talking, and I think were helping each other to communicate with the nurse.

As soon as she saw me in the doorway, though in pain (and I learned later she was suffering horribly), her face lit up with joy. Yes, it shone with real happiness, all the more visible for having to overcome her concern and remorse for the commotion she was causing, not to mention her physical pain. She had so seldom inconvenienced anyone, asked so little for herself all her life, that the way I ran across the room to her bedside, instead of seeming

natural, was to her perhaps the first real proof that I loved her. It gave her such joy despite her discomfort that my heart ached at the sight. I think she cherished the memory all the rest of her life. And then, she'd arrived in a poor woman's clothes – who cares about underwear when the clothes on top aren't much to look at? – and she must have felt vindicated, comforted to see me appear in my nice little rust-coloured fall suit. She introduced me to the other occupants of the room rather elatedly, partly because of a rising fever but also with a note of pride, the strange, almost painful pride she felt in recognizing her children as unquestionably superior to herself. But in spite of the sedative she'd been given, I sensed she was suffering considerably, which she certainly wouldn't admit. Only later, when the room had been invaded by visitors, first for the Ukrainian, then for the French Canadian from Ile des Chênes, then for the Mennonite, and they were all talking loudly in their several languages, the men even smoking pipes, only then did she give me a message with a look in her eyes that said, "Get me out of here if you can."

"Tomorrow," I said aloud, "I promise I'll see about it. Right now, do try and get some sleep."

At the door I turned to give her a smile. I could see myself, lying as she was now, in another four-bed ward, watching miserably as she left so she could get down to work and save me. And everything today seemed so identical to yesterday, with the roles reversed, that I felt as though it would never be possible to change our lives, and almost all hope abandoned me.

Riding home on the streetcar through the darkness, heaven forgive me, I foresaw that Maman might remain a permanent invalid, or at the very least considerably handicapped, that at best her accident would consume most of the money left from the sale of the house, that I wouldn't be able to leave her under the circumstances, meaning I wouldn't be leaving at all. I saw my dream being snuffed out, like the dreams of many of my forebears no doubt, the curious dreams that had driven me for years to achieve something I couldn't identify, that would allow me to be myself. And I grieved for the part of me that now would never come to life, would remain hidden from me. But I also felt a cowardly kind of relief at being spared that lonely, hazy, difficult road, at being allowed to walk down the comfortable beaten path where I'd have

company and support on every side. In the darkened window of the streetcar, I could see myself far in the future, gazing out a window, docile and resigned, contemplating what I imagined I might have been.

The next morning I sought the advice of the school board nurse who regularly made the rounds of our classes. I asked her who was the best orthopaedist in town. "No question about it," she told me, "it's Dr. Mackinnon."

I went upstairs to the principal's office and asked permission to use the telephone. He waved me benignly to his own big comfortable chair and the telephone on the desk. Then to put me more at ease, he even found a pretext to leave me alone. Soon I heard a thick Scottish brogue at the other end of the line. It reminded me of kindly old Dr. Mackintyre and I was encouraged. I had no difficulty obtaining an appointment for late the same day. Meanwhile, Dr. Mackinnon assured me, he would go and see Maman at the hospital.

Brother Joseph let me leave my classroom an hour early. And there I was again, riding a streetcar through parts of Winnipeg I didn't know – how could anyone know all of that big, sprawling city? If I look back on those years, I very often see myself travelling about the city on a streetcar, by day or in a kind of darkness, but always obsessed by some problem, worry, remorse, or unexplained haste. At a later stage, I see myself on the train, crossing breathtaking reaches of the country, travelling towards a promising future, or returning to watch one of my family die and leaving again with a heavy heart. I sometimes think I've most intensely felt life's great emotions, even the feeling of being alive, vibrantly alive, while travelling somewhere in lurching little streetcars or long, wailing trains. Or walking through unfamiliar streets in cities where I don't know a soul. So the characters in my books move, travel, walk endlessly, which isn't so surprising when I myself have sat still so little, have been on the move virtually all my life. Yet I admit to having been surprised when this was pointed out to me, because I hadn't realized I'd created characters who were like myself in some ways.

I arrived late at Dr. Mackinnon's office, having made the wrong transfer on the way. I was taken aback to see a man who was old and ill-looking, with a crimson face and great bags under his eyes.

In fact, he was to die before Maman. I've rarely seen a man so unmindful of his own ills, thinking only of those of others. I'd hardly sat down facing him in the light of a heavy-shaded lamp when he leaned his big white head towards me.

"Don't worry. Your mother's not in danger."

"Oh! Good! What needs to be done, then?"

"Operate. Reduce the fracture. Then immobilize her in a body cast that will cover her trunk, both arms and one leg."

"Oh, how awful!"

"It is indeed. Especially for an energetic woman like your mother. She's wonderful," he volunteered. "I've met two or three people in my life, not many more, who've given me the impression of loving life as passionately as she does."

So he'd already sized her up. But how?

"She hardly speaks a word of English," I said. "How did you understand each other?"

"The way she can mime with her face and hands, she could make the densest lout understand. I also remembered a few words of French I learned when I was young. And your mother can find the words too, when she really has to."

I was amazed at the picture he was describing. It was so accurate I began to feel great confidence in the old doctor.

"Will she at least walk again?"

"It's not certain," he said, "but I think so."

A decision about Maman had to be mine alone. Anna was already suffering the long, drawn-out illness that eventually led to cancer, and had lengthy periods of apathy and extreme fatigue. Dédette was far away and restricted by the rules of her community, and could really help only through her prayers – and how hard she prayed, poor soul! Adèle was even farther afield, teaching school to settlers' children in an outpost in northern Alberta, so she couldn't help me much more than they could. As for Rodolphe, we hadn't had any word from him for some time. No question about it: Maman's fate rested in my hands alone. It frightened me.

"How much will it be for the operation?" I remembered to ask at last.

Instantly I imagined I'd been whisked back to the doctor's office Maman had taken me to, when I was the one to be cured and Maman was asking the fateful question: "How much, Doctor?"

"Ordinarily," said Dr. Mackinnon, "it's two hundred and fifty dollars, but I see little signs I recognize because my people weren't rich and I can tell you aren't either. How about a hundred dollars?"

I shuddered, not because of the sum but because the past was so vivid in my mind I'd lost sight of where I was for a moment.

"A hundred dollars!"

And suddenly, buoyed by the confidence the doctor had inspired in me, I found myself opening my heart to him as I'd never done to anyone before. I told him I had enough money in the bank to pay for everything if necessary, the hospital, the anaesthesia, the operation too, but it was money I'd scraped together bit by bit over eight years so I could go and spend a year in Europe, I couldn't really say why, even to myself. Perhaps it was to test myself, to see if I had the stuff to become someone or something, though I had only a muddled idea what, and it wasn't certain I even had any talent, but that was the way it was and I couldn't help it, it was like a mania driving me to find a place for myself. And it was now or never because soon I wouldn't have the strength to leave, I had only just enough now; I could feel the bonds of routine, security – and love – closing tighter around me every day, the better to hold me back.

He'd pushed aside the desk lamp a little, in case it was bothering me no doubt, and the soft half-light encouraged me as I talked.

Suddenly he stood up, and with feeling and determination that took me by surprise told me:

"Go! Go before life swallows you the way it's swallowed so many of your people. Mine too," he added sadly. Then his tone brightened as he continued. "Do we have a bargain? I'll cure your mother. I'll put her back on her feet. And you'll leave.... Sometime in the future, if you can and if I'm still in this world, you can repay me whatever you think's right. I'll leave that to your conscience."

I left his office, in one way relieved and in another feeling worse than ever. In the streetcar, rattling through yet another part of the city, since I was going straight from Dr. Mackinnon's to the hospital, tears kept welling up and I could barely hold them back. What was making me want to cry was a measure of human kindness I didn't think I deserved. Had my own operation ever been paid for? I wasn't sure. Would Maman's ever be paid for if I didn't have the

talent I wanted so much to uncover? I was more tortured by self-doubt than ever before during that interminable ride through a part of town I kept trying to identify; when I wiped a patch of the misted window every so often, I'd see mostly my own anxious face, which seemed to say, "All your life you've received love, devotion, and kindness beyond price. Haven't you something to give in return?"

I found Maman less dispirited than the night before, almost cheerful in fact, chatting with the Ukrainian. Her new friend didn't really speak any more English than she did, so how the two of them communicated I've never figured out. Nevertheless, years later Maman still mentioned her often, telling me hundreds of details about her life, which she could only have learned in those few days in the hospital.

As soon as I began to tell her about my visit to the doctor and the decision to immobilize her in a cast, her cheerfulness vanished. For a moment she was dumbfounded, then she rebelled.

"Never! Never!"

At her age, she argued, it would be madness to let herself be shut up that way. She'd never live through it. Better she accept being crippled and in time be able to move around a bit, and, who knows, perhaps it wouldn't turn out to be as serious as all that.

"And make sure you keep me shut up with you," I said cruelly. I'd suddenly realized that this was the only weapon I had against that iron will of hers.

She blanched. The wound in her eyes told me how surely the blow had struck. She looked down.

"Well, if you think I should go through with it...," she said.

But next morning the principal came to my classroom door to tell me Dr. Mackinnon wanted me on the telephone.

"Your mother refuses to have the operation," the kind, gravelly voice told me.

"Oh, dear heaven! Can it wait? Long enough for me to...?"

"One or two days, not much more. I'm afraid of infection. And her heart's showing some signs of fatigue."

"I'll go to the hospital as soon as possible."

That day Brother Joseph had overheard part of what I'd been saying. He suggested I leave at once.

"But...," I said.

159

In those days I would have had to pay the cost of a replacement from my own pocket, unless there were a death in the family or I were seriously ill myself.

"Go on," said Brother Joseph. "I'll have some of your colleagues take turns keeping an eye on your class. Give them plenty of work to do. I'll spend some time with them myself. It'll be good for me."

Once again I was in a jolting, jarring streetcar. At this time of day it stopped at every corner and seemed to take hours to reach the hospital.

From the corridor I could hear Maman and the Ukrainian telling each other the names of their children: "Irena, Olga, Ivan, Anna, Adèle, Bernadette...."

I brought the exchange to a quick end. I was very angry.

"For three days I've been running myself ragged," I told Maman. "I've found you the best orthopaedist in the city. This morning he put himself out. He came very early from the other end of town just for you. And what did he find? An obstinate old woman who said yes yesterday and who's saying no today."

Maman looked away. She mightn't have felt guilty about saying yes and then no, but she did about making the old Scottish doctor come for nothing; she'd begun to think highly of him.

"I've been told bones sometimes mend very well on their own," she said, "that they join by themselves when they're broken and after a month or two you can start walking again, even with a break like mine. A woman in the next room who had it happen came and told me. And it won't cost as much...."

"And supposing what your woman says is true," I retorted derisively, "what are you going to look like when you walk?"

Thereupon, calling up all my powers of mimicry, I turned myself into an old relic; with one hip protruding, my neck twisted, my face contorted, and one leg dragging pathetically, I staggered across the room, clutching, leaning on anything within reach, moaning, and making enough heavy weather to melt the hardest heart.

The Ukrainian guffawed, even the gentle, sad-faced Mennonite laughed a little, and finally Maman laughed too, won over by the others.

"All right," she said, giving in as easily as a child, "but...."

I knew at once what she wanted. I should have thought of it

before. We had a friend who was a nurse, who was very dear to Maman.

"Clérina's free," I said. "I'll go and see her tonight. I'll ask her to be with you tomorrow when they put you to sleep and when you wake up."

She'd never been anaesthetized, not even when her children were born, and I should have realized that what she was most afraid of was perhaps being put to sleep by force.

She woke up as though enclosed in a sarcophagus, totally dependent on others, even for eating; she who'd never depended on anyone had to be spoonfed at first. For several days nothing was more pathetic than to see her following us about with her eyes, as helpless as a prisoner under life sentence. From the moment she found herself in that dependent state until the day she was released from it, in spite of what she said, I don't believe she slept a single whole night, just in snatches now and then. Yet she adamantly refused to take sleeping pills, even the mildest, even after being lectured by Dr. Mackinnon. In the end he gave up, telling me, "I've often seen that kind of woman, in her generation, absolutely dead set against artificial sleep, even sedatives sometimes, and I've wondered if it isn't because of some deep-down pride."

After two weeks he let us take her home. I'll never forget how we had to struggle to get the stretcher up the stairs with Maman strapped to it, and the anxiety in her eyes as she followed the attendants' efforts to get her past the difficult point. But once in her own bed she regained the courage she'd almost lost for good. She learned to manage quite well with her left hand, the free one. But mostly she spent hours with her face turned towards the window, watching the sky which had always been there, endlessly amazed at how much it had to say to her. Like Anna before she died, like Dédette too, whom I saw turn her eyes to the sky so many times, Maman, always too busy before, was now discovering the depth of the Manitoba sky and marvelling at it, marvelling that you can often see better when in prison than when free. One evening I came home from school and found her contemplating that huge empty sky, and she expressed a thought that haunts me still: "Though the sky sees all and knows all it never says anything, but comforts us anyway. Why, do you suppose?"

We had a practical nurse come in the morning to wash her,

freshen her bed, and roll her onto her stomach like a block of cement to give her a few minutes' change of position. One of our neighbours hardly let a day pass without bringing her a cup of hot chicken broth or vegetable soup. Clémence and I managed everything else ourselves, since Maman really asked so little of us, I realize now at last.

Clémence was a treasure. The minute she was really needed, was asked to help, the poor sick child we'd always tried not to burden with responsibility proved to be a hundred times more effective than we'd thought possible. She cooked adequately the minute Maman wasn't hovering over her, ready to do everything so easily. She brought Maman her small tray, helped her eat, kept the apartment reasonably clean. Best of all, throughout the months that might have been exceedingly difficult, she was less nervous and apprehensive, happier, in short, than we'd seen her for years. All because Maman wasn't at her elbow saying, "Here, I'll do it for you." Since I didn't have much time to help, I depended on Clémence too, leaving her little tasks which she managed to do better and better. One day, almost in secret, she tried her hand at making a johnny cake, the cornmeal bread I used to love as a child. It was light and good. Maman, who hadn't much appetite, made herself eat a piece. Clémence was pleased. When she'd gone back to the kitchen with the tray, Maman, who hated letting emotion show, turned to me, her eyes all wet.

"Don't you think it would have been better for Clémence, really, if I'd been an invalid all my life?"

"Maman, what nonsense you get into your head! Too much responsibility for too long would have been just as bad as none at all for someone like her, you know that."

"You're probably right," she sighed. "It's so hard to know how to handle some sick people. A doctor who took care of her a long time ago did suggest I start her doing things, but then if I asked her to do something, or tried to redo something with her, even patiently, she'd get cranky and ready for one of those awful tantrums when she'd throw things around.... And remember the time she ran out of the house and we had to go looking for her, street by street, one district after another, like a poor little lost dog?"

She put her hand over her eyes, as though seeing this again was too much. I calmed her gently, reminding her that such things

were over and done with, the doctor had told us there wouldn't be any more of those crises. She listened, was comforted and, much truer to her nature, was soon pretending she'd quite recovered from the memory and hadn't been nearly as upset as in fact she had.

The only other complaint she made during this time was about her cast. It was much too big and heavy, she said; the doctor had overdone it and he'd have to take some of it off or she'd suffocate.

I telephoned Dr. Mackinnon. To my great surprise he told me he'd come. Even in those days a specialist didn't go out of his way for such small things. He arrived with an impressive array of instruments including long scissors, pliers, and a kind of small hammer. As he laid out his paraphernalia Maman watched, anticipating great relief, it seemed.

Sitting on the edge of her bed, he promised her she'd feel very much better once he'd relieved her of a good piece of her "straitjacket". Privately, he told me that all he could really do was pretend to cut away part of her cast, but that was often enough to make the patient feel better.

It was astonishing how well the two of them had come to understand each other, she speaking in her language and he in his. I'd see them together, he bending his great head towards her, holding her hand, she looking up at him, her eyes shining with confidence and gratitude. I'd say to myself, am I dreaming, or is there something like affection between this elderly patient and her elderly doctor, who's not in much better health than she? Mightn't they have become lovers when they were young? And I thought I could see what an attractive woman my mother must have been.

Dr. Mackinnon took his big scissors and proceeded to cut away a very narrow strip of plaster from around Maman's neck, handing it to me at once with a clear indication that I must dispose of it before Maman saw it.

"I took off *un grand morceau*," he said, "*et vous allez voir* a great improvement."

Maman ran her free hand around her neck.

"Oh, yes," she declared, "it isn't nearly as high. It's really a lot better!"

She liked the feeling so much that a week later she asked, "Would you telephone Dr. Mackinnon? If he could just take off a little bit more...," so humbly I didn't have the heart to refuse.

He came three times from the other end of town, each time to trim off a "chunk" no wider in reality than half an inch. Everything was going to be fine, he told her. She'd soon be let out of that thing. "And then you'll be full of beans, like a young gerrrl again."

At last the day of her deliverance came. Her eyes showed almost uncontainable impatience for the relief to come, and I realized she must have been near the limit of endurance. Without jostling her too much, Dr. Mackinnon, short-winded and crimson-faced, cut into the tough carapace in earnest this time. You'd have said he was freeing a delicate butterfly from its chrysalis with the exquisite pleasure of seeing something born. But he'd warned me that the coming weeks would be among the hardest for Maman, and indeed she could find no rest either in bed or in the comfortable chair we'd carry her to when someone was there to help. Several times I found her sitting on the edge of the bed with her legs dangling, discouraged, not by the severe pain but by still not being able to move around. Once she flung at me as if in accusation, "My legs are dead, you know. They're no good for anything." I didn't see her make any effort to stand up with the crutches we'd got for her. A kind of despair overtook me; it was my fault that she might never walk again, because I'd made her have the operation. Perhaps she was the one who'd known best and I the one who had been blind, wanting to have her cured so I'd be free to leave.

Then one evening I came home to find her walking a few steps with the crutches, followed by Clémence who was biting her lip for fear Maman would fall. The few seconds' effort left Maman exhausted, at the end of her strength. But she had such courage. When she'd recovered a little in her comfortable chair, she looked lovingly and defiantly at the magnificent setting sun whose fiery glow filled the window that evening, as if telling it, "I'll be back, you'll see."

The next day she took three or four steps around the table, holding on for support. Then she began to make rapid progress. One evening she came into the room I was in, walking with mechanical little steps, without support though not too far from the wall. Her face shone with the surprise and delight of a tiny child standing up and taking her first steps all on her own.

From then on, her recovery was unbelievably fast, and when her strength returned it did so almost to excess. Since she'd given so

much of herself all her life, we might have expected her to overdo it out of gratitude when it appeared she'd be allowed a few good years yet. As she sat in her comfortable chair between periods of exercise, she began spending countless hours sewing for her grandchildren. She sent little patchwork quilts to far corners of the country. She knitted layettes for expected grandchildren. She wrote letters to distant cousins with whom we'd lost touch since goodness knows when. When I was at school she'd venture down the winding stairs and back up, which I had forbidden her to do. Before I knew it she'd been over to visit the kind neighbour who'd brought her chicken broth and vegetable soup. Shortly after, I found her kneading piecrust dough. She told me calmly, "Madame Gauthier makes pretty good soup. Now I'm going to show her what a good pie's like." She was beaming.

"We really ought to try and make her do things a bit more reasonably," I said to Clémence.

"I suppose you think that's easy."

Clémence was already being a mite grumpy again.

Early one brisk spring morning, I spied a little figure in a familiar dark coat, rather huddled up but standing fairly straight, apparently waiting for a streetcar at the corner.

"I don't believe it! I never thought she'd try to go downtown by herself at this point."

"You'd better believe it," said Clémence. "Her mind was made up yesterday."

Under Maman's arm was a fat, rather lumpy package which reminded me oddly of the one she'd set out with that ill-starred day the previous autumn.

"What's she got under her arm?"

"A loaf of homemade bread," said Clémence sourly, "and you can be sure she's taking it to Rosalie."

XVII

SUMMER CAME. Maman had always greeted it with a delightful array of flowers attractively planted around the white-columned veranda and in borders and circular beds in the lawn. This year we didn't have even a square foot of ground in which to plant the few bright red geraniums from the apartment, but Maman didn't seem to miss the garden as much as I'd expected. As her possessions dwindled, she had more love and attention to give to those she had left. She took to her freedom far better than I thought she would, in fact; it allowed her to concentrate on inalienable possessions. I only came to understand this when I myself stopped wanting possessions of any other kind.

Maman was to spend the summer at her brother Excide's again. Suspecting she'd be so grateful to be cured she'd fling herself more ardently than ever into serving others, I lectured her about her tendency to overdo whatever she undertook.

"At least," I said to her, "when they're shorthanded don't go and offer to milk the cows."

She gave me that too-ready smile of assent which generally meant she'd do exactly as she liked. She'd become as impossible as Grandmother Landry used to be when anyone tried to keep her from overtaxing herself for others.

I myself was going to a curious region some three hundred miles north of Winnipeg, a low plain consisting mostly of muskeg, a mixture of earth and water; a region covered with rushes, lakes, and rivers, and inhabited by countless birds. That's what I'd been told, at least, and that's what drew me to it. I was the one, I think, who first called it the Little Water Hen country. I'd obtained one of the few schools in Manitoba that the Department of Education kept open only in summertime, owing to the region's remoteness,

166

poor communications, and harsh climate. I was to be boarded by the local people at their expense, and so would pocket my full five dollars a day from the Department. I hoped thus to repair a large part of the dent in my savings made by the unexpected expenses of the winter. For the moment this was all I was counting on, but in fact the Little Water Hen cast an indescribable spell over me which left a lasting imprint. The rest came as a bonus: my discovery of one of the most delightful places in the world; the longing it left with me for a fresh start in human experience on earth; the book which, much later, grew out of my own time there (a novel about a tiny school at the end of the earth, the first on earth in a sense); the book's good fortune in being chosen for study in many schools in Canada and elsewhere. When I left for the Little Water Hen, all these extraordinary developments were as unsuspected on my part as, indeed, are almost all the essential landmarks in our lives to come.

And just as well! If I had had some premonition of what was in store for me, the experience would probably have done me less good. No, I needed to be totally at the mercy of the harsh solitude; it forced me to turn to my seven little pupils, the few adults in the vicinity, the birds, the wind, the island's vast silence, needing companionship so urgently that it was granted me. From this moment, everything changed between me and the remote land I'd thought completely without interest when I arrived. Solitude has so often brought me to a better understanding of people and things.

Maman was worried at first. When I'd had such a good position in the city, I was behaving like Adèle, she said, running off to the most God-forsaken places.

"When are you leaving for the other side?" she wanted to know. That's what we'd acquired the habit of calling the countries of Europe when the two of us talked, and the term suited Maman's feeling about them perfectly.

I was to return to St-Boniface at the beginning of September, leaving shortly after for Montreal, where I would board ship for London and Paris. My passport was applied for and my passage booked.

"Well then," she said, "I'll come back from Excide's in time to...."

I knew the word "goodbye" had stuck in her throat.

She was no longer fighting my decision. She still didn't understand why I'd want to leave my enviable job, my dear little pupils who loved me so, and a life that must have seemed close to heaven in her eyes. But if she didn't understand what was driving me, she'd begun to sense it, I think, to sympathize, without reflecting that she herself had been subject to some hidden imperative all her life. From that point on, if she'd had the means she might have gone so far as to help me leave.

She would have been the only one. No one else gave me any support. Our little French, Catholic city hadn't put such sacrifice, self-denial, and discipline into raising us only to let us leave without raising barriers. There are times when I'm convinced the community would have kept us at home by force if it could have. We were so few that anyone who left was considered to be deserting, abandoning the cause. My sister Adèle, who was inclined to go to extremes and use theatrical language, accused me of betraying my people. Anna was more restrained but thought I was being headstrong and was certainly in for some bitter disappointment. You'd have said they resented my doing what they hadn't dared do when they were young, which they probably regretted now. I can't really blame them. Almost certainly, I'd been held back less than my older sisters.

But it was our poor defenceless Clémence who made things hardest for me. Maman had often kept her home from school in the early stages of her illness, so it was often she who looked after me when I was very young. She used to take me on walks which were much too long for my small legs, but from which I'd come home happy, convinced I'd seen exotic, new, and exciting things. As I recounted in *Street of Riches*, she often took me to the wild side of our little street. Her talk, which upset people because it was full of strange, poetic digressions and weird references to the family dead as though they were living, didn't bother my childhood logic in the least. The two of us were very close when I was small, and I think I recall running to her quite naturally for assurance if I was frightened. Later, when the dreadful illness had left some invisible part of her permanently crippled, it was she who would cling to me, drawing a kind of confidence from my youth and initiative.

She observed my preparations for departure with a peevishness

which in her was a sign of confusion and fear. One evening she stopped at the door of my room and watched as I was putting things in order.

"So it's true you're going?"

She looked at me steadily with those huge, dark-circled eyes which were always so quick to see pain in the offing, far down the road perhaps, in a sense never mistakenly. I didn't fully understand their distress until years later, when in my hour of greatest need I felt the hand I'd most counted on withdraw from mine.

"Come on, Clémence, I'm not going for ever!"

She kept looking at me unbelievingly, having now lost all confidence in me, perhaps, so hurt that she suddenly blurted out her perception of the truth.

"You're leaving us!"

THINGS LIKE THAT come out sometimes, and once they're out you hear them as long as you live. They stick in a corner of your memory and you can't get rid of them. They lie in wait at some turn in your thinking, often at night when you can't get back to sleep, when the old wounds always find you first. Perhaps even when you're only ashes and dust, or an immortal soul, you'll still remember them. And if these words prey on you all your life and perhaps beyond, there surely must be some truth in them.

DEDETTE WAS BACK from Kenora for a brief period about this time. She had come to take over a grade seven or grade eight class at the Académie Saint-Joseph where I had been to school. She still loved especially to teach teenagers, as I loved to teach the youngest children. She used to say, "It's the age when the flesh is wakening, yes, but ideals too." Removed as we might have presumed she was from our preoccupations and anxieties, she was the one who encouraged me. One day when I couldn't cope any longer with my doubts and indecision, I found myself at the big front door of the Académie asking for Sister Léon de la Croix. I always felt peculiar calling her that.

I waited for her in one of the two identical little parlours, each containing a piano, to one or other of which I'd so often been sent to practise my scales and sonatas when I'd been a pupil there. I

heard her bell ringing in the distance: three short and one long ring, or perhaps the reverse. Soon after, I heard her footsteps hurrying down the main hallway.

Dédette's footsteps! In the family we used to say we could have recognized them among thousands. I sometimes imagine that even in the Valley of Jehoshaphat, if things are really as they're said to be, I could pick out Dédette's footsteps from all the others. They weren't the footsteps of a nun at all. Doubtless her community had tried to make her conform in her walk as in many other respects, but luckily it hadn't succeeded in this, at least. Brisk, hurrying, impetuous, sometimes hardly seeming to touch the ground, at intervals heavy on the heel, her footsteps told everything about her nature: her strong will, her diligence at controlling herself, and her perpetual failure to keep the loving, childlike extrovert in her from running passionately towards the world she'd renounced long ago.

Far down the corridor her footsteps would already be hurried, would quicken on the stairs leading down to the parlours and again in the remaining few feet of corridor, then fly irrepressibly as soon as she saw the face of whoever was waiting for her. There'd be a whirlwind with flying skirt and veil, you'd be caught up, spun round joyfully as though you'd had to come a vast distance to be reunited with her, not just across the street. Perhaps she was right. Perhaps there ought to be a whirlwind and spin-around at every meeting of two people who love each other, even if they've been living next door. At the time I didn't realize how surprising it was that Dédette, the most exuberant, most passionate of us all, had been the one to enter religion. Dédette was Dédette, a real phenomenon – pious, boisterous, demonstrative, meditative – I could see no further than this.

She arrived all out of breath and threw her arms around me, crooning, "My little Gabrielle! My little Gabrielle!" rather plaintively as if I'd been restored to her after a long captivity.

Then she became very calm and made me sit down, drawing her chair as close as possible. She had the rare gift of being able to switch instantly from great excitement to seriousness, the most attentive, observant silence. This was probably something she'd learned through constant effort, but deep down it must also have been related to her tendency to foresee the sorrows of this world

more readily than the joys. And to tell the truth, once or twice I saw the ardour, animation, sparkle fall suddenly from her face, to my great surprise leaving instead a sombre, desolate, lightless, and tormented landscape, an ashen waste; then the ardour, animation, and sparkle would return and I'd think my imagination had been playing tricks on me.

At present she was searching my anxious eyes.

"Dédette," I said, as if calling from a distance, "I really don't know what to do any more. Everybody's mad at me for wanting to go.... But...I feel as if my life depends on it."

She took my hand, made me stand up, and led me to the daylight under the high window. In the clear light of the sky, my sister and I really saw each other for the first time in our lives perhaps, for both of us seemed astonished, I to discover the misty grey of her eyes brimming with a wistfulness I'd never noticed before, she to find heaven knows what, for she kept turning my face gently to the light. In order to see what is, do we really need more than the clear, unobstructed light of the sky? Suddenly she clasped me in her arms, drew my head against her shoulder, and as though she had her Lord's assurance of help for me, in whispers as impassioned as if she were putting her eternal salvation at stake, she told me:

"Go! Go! Go!"

SEVEN YEARS AGO, when she was on the point of death and I had come to be with her and was sitting by her bed in the little infirmary room one evening, I asked her if she remembered the scene in the parlour.

She opened her eyes but didn't give me the smile I'd hoped for. Since the moment her physician had told her she had a cancer that was already well advanced, there had been no smile in her eyes. They still showed love, and her deep concern for others, but not the light that only a smile can bring. Of all the relatives I've watched die it was she, the fervent believer, who seemed to put up the most resistance. She gave her last smile soon after her operation, when she thought she was going to live and was contemplating the things in life that are good, tender, sweet, fragrant, delicious, all at once; there was so much beauty in that smile that she made me see them too. Since then I'd been using all my wiles in the hope of bringing a smile to her face once more at least. To no avail. Only gravity

171

ever showed there now, which was strange in one who had been so animated. She just nodded in reply to my question, then added in the same grave voice as always now, "You don't forget things of the heart. Perhaps that's all we have left in the end. And there aren't a lot of them."

I asked her again if, when she'd urged me with such feeling to go my own way, she'd seen some favourable sign for me. She gave a little frown. From Providence, I added.

She told me no. It was just that when she'd seen so much worry in my face – so young and already so worried – she'd remembered a moment in her life when, at the age of eleven, she'd awakened in the country to a crisp summer morning filled with lovely house smells, toast, coffee, jam, mingled with the smells entering through the wide-open window, new-cut hay, phlox in bloom, dew-soaked earth, and she'd felt so heady with life, and so grateful to the Creator for all the joy He'd given His creatures, that of her own free will she decided there and then to give up part of it and enter religion.

"Do I understand," said I quite incredulously, "that you renounced the world because you loved it too much?"

With the grave manner I still found so disturbing, she bent her head in what might have been a nod.

"I was eleven...," she said again with a kind of remote compassion for the child she had been.

Though she wouldn't have admitted it, a sad little quiver in her lip told me she felt she'd been deprived of her share of earthly happiness for having been so trusting as a child.

"You always said that only God could give us total happiness," I protested, trying to comfort her.

"Maybe He wants us to taste happiness on earth too," she said, "or He would have made all those wonderful things for nothing!"

"But who's seen them better than you, Dédette? You've seen more out of the corner of your eye than those of us who've been free but busy with other things...so many distractions."

I saw that I had indeed comforted her a little. After I left, during the weeks she had remaining, I wrote her a letter every day, sometimes twice a day, always trying to persuade her that she'd felt the splendours of life more vibrantly than anyone else. And after she died I kept on trying to talk to her, to find her at least in the wind,

the trees, the world's beautiful things.... From this came *Enchanted Summer*, a strange book, I'll admit, which has an appearance of humour but underneath is deeply serious. Whatever its failings, I think it does capture the essence of Dédette, her open, childlike spirit, her lifetime of yearning so determinedly repressed.

With the long letters she wrote in her few moments of free time, or on her pauper's holidays at the Sisters' little summer camp on Lake Winnipeg, Dédette taught me, in the glow of fireflies, the cry of a bird somewhere in the sky, the song of rippling water or of leaves on the trees, such humble but beautiful things, to see something of God's grand design at work. I have only tried to pass on what her perceptive eyes illuminated for me.

XVIII

I LEFT FOR the Little Water Hen at the end of June, as soon as the school year at Provencher was over. I took the night train to the little town of Dauphin, where I was to change to another bound for Rorketon. It was appallingly hot. I arrived at Dauphin early next morning not having been able to sleep a wink all night, aching with fatigue. For this journey into the wilds, I had rather foolishly put on a white linen suit, which became horribly rumpled from tossing and turning on the seat of the train. I think my face was smeared with coal dust too. But the worst was still to come. I would have a long wait for my train to Rorketon, the station master told me. How long? He couldn't say exactly. It could be two hours or half the day, maybe more. There was no saying with that train. It came when it could and left when it was ready. That was the kind of thing everybody had to put up with here, he said gently, suggesting that I try to do the same.

I didn't know anyone in Dauphin. Besides, since the train could arrive in three hours or at any minute, it would be best not to leave the station. It was stifling inside. Outside, however, there was a wooden bench under the station master's office window. It was short and narrow, but I wrapped myself in my coat and tried to find a position that wasn't too uncomfortable. I was so tired that with my head on the hard armrest, slipping half off the seat at times, I think I did sleep for brief spells. I'd wake, curl myself up some other way, and sleep a minute or two more.

The station master must have been observing me through his window for some time, feeling sorry for me as I tried to get some sleep under the sky like a derelict, in my beautiful little linen suit. I imagine he was really rather shy and hesitated for some time before coming out to give me a startling invitation.

"Listen, Miss. I'm alone at the station because my wife's away on holiday. She put clean sheets on our bed before she left. I haven't had time to go and sleep in it yet. If you'd like to sleep in a good bed, it's yours; lying on that bench, your neck and shoulders and back are going to be sore pretty soon."

As sleepy as I was, I managed to sit up and open my eyes fully so I could look at the man who was saying these things. He was fairly young, nice-looking, with blue eyes showing a kind of warm concern to see someone in discomfort; he seemed like the Good Samaritan in person. All the same, I had wits enough to remember that he'd said his wife had just left so that he had the place to himself. He must have read my thoughts because he told me he had a pile of reports to finish before the train came. And there was the bed doing nothing, he said, while I needed it so.

Besides feeling some shame at the thought of rebuffing a good intention, I wanted that bed so badly I followed him without further hesitation. He led me to the bedroom, took off the counterpane, folded it neatly and put it on a chair, turned down the bed, which had indeed been freshly changed, put the two pillows one on top of the other, plumped them, and said, "There now...." He promised he'd come and wake me before the train arrived and promptly left, closing the door behind him. I took off my suit and slipped between the clean sheets. I think I was asleep the minute my head touched the pillow. Only seconds later, it seemed, I felt the gentle touch of a hand and heard an unfamiliar voice saying:

"Miss, your train will be here in ten minutes."

I dressed hurriedly. I arrived on the little station platform in the middle of a beautiful, warm, fragrant summer day. I'd gone to bed at six in the morning; it was now two in the afternoon. I was well rested, my face was fresh, my eyes bright. I was ready and eager for the remainder of the journey.

The station master beamed.

"You look altogether different than you did this morning," he said. "I was up twice to see how you were doing, and I've never seen anyone sleep so soundly."

I studied him in silence and saw nothing but pleasure in return for the confidence I'd put in him, and something like gratitude for my having let him show me such kindness.

I had this man rather in mind when I had Luzina say, in *Where*

175

Nests the Water Hen, that you need only place yourself under another human being's protection for him to behave towards you as you would wish.

So years before I wrote that book, I'd already unconsciously stored away some scattered, unconnected elements of it. You could say I had them close to my heart, but wouldn't have access to them for years to come. At times I used to feel I was becoming a huge reservoir of almost inexhaustible impressions, emotions, and observations, if only I could have access to them. But though you'd expect having access to what's inside you to be the most natural thing in the world, it's often the most difficult.

From the train I saw the station master standing in the middle of the platform, watching me go, sadly, like a relative – or rather, like one of those strangers who are so unlike strangers, with whom you cross paths and whom you never forget. I gave him a little wave. He lifted his hand to his green visor and smiled slowly, shyly. Sometimes I wonder if, when my first books appeared – particularly *Where Nests the Water Hen* – he made the connection between the author and the young woman to whom he'd given a bed one summer morning, and if he said to himself, "I thought I might hear more of her some day."

Finally the long-awaited little train began to move, and at once I had the impression it was blazing a trail through hitherto virgin Nature.

THAT RORKETON train! My friend Jean-Paul Lemieux has understood and portrayed it superbly in his series of engravings that illustrate the Gilles Corbeil edition of *La Petite Poule d'Eau*, the French text of *Where Nests the Water Hen*. No doubt to emphasize the feeling of isolation – but also of rescue, for the train is the only lifeline men have in those deserted wastes – he's shown it in winter, coming across the low, snow-covered plain, from the ends of the earth it seems. But I made its acquaintance in the season when its lonely path is dotted with countless delicate flowers.

I'll never forget that journey. Like a journey through summer itself, heady with wild smells, fragrant ones, with Nature's warm breath, and some of her most endearing sounds. Sometimes we'd hear the piercing trill of a bird, sometimes a sudden rustling of leaves or a strident signal from some insect.

The big engine, built for pulling a whole convoy, had only one passenger car coupled directly to it, with a caboose right behind that. The caboose was a kind of cookhouse-cum-dormitory for the train crew, who had to shuttle back and forth between Dauphin and Rorketon at constantly changing hours, without a stop between the two; a moving home away from home where the men could eat, sleep, and rest. Sometimes they simply stopped for the night beside a field or a small lake.

Passengers and mail weren't all the train carried. It was a mixed train, as it was called then, and also carried freight. The day I was travelling, a car behind the caboose was loaded with a big pile of railroad ties, replacements for the rotted ones on the line. We went at about the speed of a farm horse because the men were throwing off ties as needed, judging by eye, two or three here, three or four a bit farther on.

When we were on a section of track that was in good repair, the brakeman would go to the caboose and cast an eye at his stew, lifting the lid of a great black pot on the little stove. A mouth-watering smell would waft forward to the passengers. There were four of us in all: myself, the Department of Health nurse, a cattle dealer, who to my great surprise came back to life as Isaac Boussorvsky in *Where Nests the Water Hen*, and an individual with his nose in reports and papers who declined to help us identify him.

The irresistible smell brought me to the door of the caboose. The brakeman looked up from his steaming pot.

"Smells good," I said.

"Hungry?" he asked.

I must have given him a panhandler's smile. Incredibly, I'd embarked on this journey back through time and civilization without bringing anything to eat.

I received a good heaping bowlful, and the brakeman brought similar helpings to the nurse and the cattle merchant. The nurse passed around some homemade cookies, still warm, out of a big bag which she'd put inside a bigger one to keep them fresh. The brakeman came back shortly with cups of scalding-hot tea.

When the cooking smells had disappeared through the wide-open windows and doors of the train, the smells of Nature entered.

It was the season of wild roses. With their bright colour, they

were spread over the countryside like a setting for a never-ending banquet. Their perfume was intoxicating. Above them, insects of every description darted and hovered, buzzing covetously. Then, after the panorama of roses, among the tall grasses there appeared masses of such pretty little blue flowers nodding on their long, delicate stems that I longed to see them more closely. We were going so slowly I decided I'd have time to jump off, run and pick some, then run back and get on again. The engineer was leaning out of his cab enjoying the sights and fresh air of our surroundings. When he saw me scurry into the field, snatching up a flower here and there, he called to me not to be in such a hurry, we had lots of time, and without further ado applied the brakes. The train waited nearly ten minutes while I picked a bouquet.

When I climbed back on with my arms full of flowers, everyone, including the cattle man, smiled at me kindly, as if at some vision of youth, wish-fulfilment, or childhood reverie. The warmth of those smiles made me so happy I've never forgotten it. I sometimes think of my companions that day as a group of new-found friends who are still waiting for me somewhere, on a little train that doesn't exist any more.

The train arrived in Rorketon shortly before suppertime. I hurried to a boarding house kept by a Mrs. O'Rorke, if I remember correctly, where I was to meet Mr. Jos Vermander, formerly the postmaster in St-Boniface, who some years earlier had been promoted to post office inspector for northern Manitoba. Lacking information, I'd telephoned him to ask how to get to the Little Water Hen. He told me to meet him in Rorketon and we would leave together for Portage-des-Près, the last hamlet on the final leg of the journey, and also the site of the last branch post office.

Very early next morning, we left in an ancient Ford driven by a Ukrainian, a Métis guide riding with us. I was getting to know my country in a totally new light. I related some of this journey in my introduction to the George G. Harrap school edition of *La Petite Poule d'Eau* (this introduction has been reproduced as "Memory and Creation" in *Fragile Lights of Earth*). But I'll never really be able to convey how awestruck I was to be travelling deeper and deeper into the wild, the distant, the inaccessible.

At last, among some scrawny little trees along the rutted dirt road, we came to a few mournful wooden houses, a chapel, and a

school made of rough planking; a village of a kind, it seemed. This was Portage-des-Près. My heart sank at the thought of spending the summer here. But I was deluding myself. My place of employment was even farther still, some thirty miles away, on an island separated from the mainland by two rivers. People called it Jeannotte's Ranch. There was only one way to get there and that was by the postman's battered old truck, which had just left and wouldn't be back for another week. I didn't know what to do.

Jos Vermander just laughed. He was used to such difficulties.

"Give me time to look at the postmaster's books," he said (the postmaster was also the general storekeeper), "and I'll drive you to your island on the Little Water Hen myself. You don't think I'd go away and leave you here, do you?"

So it was thanks to him that I reached the Little Water Hen. I imagine that if I'd stayed at some point on the way all summer the Department of Education wouldn't have been any the wiser, and would have paid my salary anyway, just in case.

After adventures far too numerous to recount, we reached the island on the Little Water Hen shortly before nightfall.

Under an already dark sky, I found my destination: a huge, low-lying island, almost indistinguishable from the gurgling rivers full of eerily whispering rushes, and upon it a single house flanked by small outbuildings. I looked at my destination with dismay close to panic.

I'm particularly fond of one of Jean-Paul Lemieux's engravings. Almost negligible at the very bottom of the picture are the three small buildings that show a human presence, the house, the sheepcote, and the tiny, rough cabin that served as a school. Hanging over this frail cluster is an immense, very black sky that takes up two-thirds of the little picture: a primaeval sky. It might be hostile. It might be overpowering. But there are one or two faint stars, even farther from Earth than stars usually appear, and with them hope glimmers, seeks to pierce the great night of the ages.

When I look at this engraving I'm always amazed at how well the artist has conveyed both my feeling of desolation upon arriving at night in a corner of the world that seemed so totally cut off, and the vague hope I was still to discover.

AS AT CAMPERVILLE, I organized myself in a very few days so I'd

have something to do every minute of the day, the only way I could cope with my overwhelming loneliness.

I would wake early – the lambs bleating around the house took care of that – and scribble in my little bedroom with its low window just above floor level, or in the six-by-seven-foot schoolhouse, sitting at my rustic desk carved from wood that still smelled of sprucegum.

Then my pupils would arrive, seven in all. Four came from the house nearby and the three others from beyond the rivers, sometimes brought by their father, sometimes guiding their fragile craft over the rough, fast-running water alone, poor little souls. I taught them reading, writing, arithmetic, and, rather like Mademoiselle Côté in the book, a reawakening to their French ancestry. I could have taught only this for all the Department of Education would have known, being on another planet so to speak. But wanting to be conscientious, I did try to teach a few subjects in English. To tell the truth, it didn't much matter here. The hard, isolated life, the urgent necessities, the ever-present sky, all taught me that school should be a place of coming together and not of division.

Because of the appalling heat that would build up in the schoolhouse, around three o'clock I'd end the lessons and we'd all go swimming together in the Big Water Hen. A more beautiful river I've never seen. It flowed between flat banks covered with succulent grasses, wide and peaceful, but with a restless current one had to be wary of. The water was always crystal clear, sometimes the dark foliage-green of the reeds growing on either side, as Lemieux paints it, sometimes a soft blue blending with the sky, a reflection that made you think there was another river flowing by, bearing an endless flotilla of white clouds. All the time, night and day, you could hear its deep, rich song, which must have remained unchanged since the beginning of time. Its water was good to drink, so transparent you could see yourself in it, so clean you'd come out of it washed as nowhere else. I realized then what a pure river was, and that was before the atrocious things man has done to water, when it was still like the innocent eyes of the earth.

When supper was over and the dishes were done, Madame Côté, my landlady, having nothing now to occupy her thoughts, would sit by a low-silled window and gaze at the beautiful but empty countryside, letting a deep sadness show. She seemed so forlorn,

poor woman, that one evening I made a suggestion, for want of something better:

"Would you like it if we walked a little way by the river together?"

Even today I'm still astonished when I remember the pleasure brought to her face by such a simple invitation. It was as if I'd said, "Let's go downtown. There's a movie...." She went to her room and returned wearing her hat, which I hadn't ever seen before. For a walk on a rough path by a river in the wilds, this was so unexpected that I was speechless for a good long minute. I can see us still, walking one behind the other because of the narrowness of the path, I in my jodhpurs, which I'd taken such care of that they were still perfectly presentable, and Madame Côté ahead in her incongruous velvet hat, telling me all about herself in fragments, pausing often to catch her breath. Furthermore, the walk I'd so innocently proposed seemed to have created a stir in the tranquil atmosphere of our existence: it brought running, to fall into step behind us in single file, four hens, three cats, the dog, a piglet, the rooster, and, inevitably, a good number of the lambs and ewes that roamed free on the island. Our little procession made its way beside the river as though along a village sidewalk. Perhaps this was the fancy that so delighted Madame Côté and roused the envy of the rest of the household, those I hadn't invited, who watched through the windows as if to say, "How lucky you are and why didn't you take us too?"

I WAS BEGINNING to be happy. I was settling down on the island I'd come to in such a frenzy of anxiety. The weather, which can demoralize us more than anything else perhaps, ceased to bother me. It was as though I were shorn of my past and to all intents and purposes had no future. I hardly gave a thought even to my plans for leaving. I'd been set free. Like my island, borne on its waters from one day to the next, I was living in the present. This was one of three or four wonderful pauses in my life when I've had time to rebuild my physical strength and state of mind. Without them my health, always more or less fragile, would perhaps have failed. In any event, this was certainly what I needed before confronting the emotional turmoil awaiting me. I withstood it only because I'd had this period of calm, silence, and concentration on what I was discovering.

But I hadn't yet written a single line from which I could draw the least satisfaction. How long it takes to get where you ought to be going! Then as soon as you arrive it's time to move on.

Still, without realizing it, when I left the Little Water Hen at the very end of August I had almost everything I needed for the novel I wouldn't begin to write until 1948, some of it found here and some at Camperville. Almost everything, that is, except the kind of life I would be leading in the meantime, which would also colour the book. The intriguing thing about the life of a book and that of its author is this: as soon as the book exists even vaguely in the far corners of the unconscious, everything that happens to the author, every emotion, practically every feeling and experience contributes to the book, enters and becomes part of it, like the water from a river's tributaries throughout the river's length. So a book really is a part of its author's life, provided that it's a purely creative work, of course, not built from other elements.

XIX

AT THE BEGINNING of September I was back in St-Boniface, where I had a room with board at the Misses Muller's for a few days while I waited for Maman, who was to join me there. This, of course, was when I fully realized how badly I missed our house and formed some idea of how much Maman must feel its loss.

I didn't go back to see Deschambault Street, thinking it would be too painful. Nowadays when I go to Manitoba, thoughtful friends will drive me there. We slow down, then stop in front of the house that was ours. It's changed somewhat but it's been kept in good condition and I always feel grateful to its buyer, who has obviously taken great care of it. I look up in silence at the little third-floor window, at which I used to listen on spring evenings to the mating songs of frogs from the ponds at the bottom of the street. And I feel compassion, not for the adult I've become, knowing well that the future is only really glorious long before you reach it, but for the child up there who was so dazzled by its glory.

Maman arrived from Somerset. She was to return there after I'd gone and would come back to St-Boniface with Clémence in the autumn, when they would take an apartment in town. Again I found her thinner, her face drawn, as though a little shrunk. I was annoyed to find her looking so tired and chastised her, no doubt rather bitterly, for tending to overdo things at her brother's. She told me it wasn't the little chores at the farm that had tired her; on the contrary, they'd diverted and relaxed her. She'd just recovered from a bad cold she'd caught one evening in a sudden rain while picking wild berries. What she didn't say was that she'd worn herself out defending me against Anna and Adèle, who'd both been nagging at her constantly for having spoiled me, pampered me too much, reaping only my ingratitude, for there I was going off and

leaving her without support when she needed it most. Now, in answer to a rather sharp comment of my own, she defended them against me, begging me not to be cross over the way they felt because they hadn't been as lucky as I had and were a bit envious.... Wasn't it that way in almost all families?

At which I lost my temper, retorting that I'd had enough of families with their everlasting squabbles, that all most of them wanted was to smother the ones who seemed to be trying to break away. Maman looked wounded, and her eyes turned wearily to the big brass bed.

It was the only one in the room. I was going to sleep in the same bed as Maman for the first time in my life, I think, unless I'd done so when I was very young, which is likely, though if I did I don't remember. I'd always been an independent child, insisting on keeping rather to myself, my own bed, my own little place to study, away from everyone else. Maman had understood this need and respected it, perhaps having wanted privacy for herself.

Lying side by side, neither of us could sleep. Fears for the future; sorrows of the past; insecurity, life's constant companion. Being side by side and defenceless in the dark made these things weigh all the more heavily on us, perhaps. Ever since that night I've felt that unless you've lain in the same bed beside someone, even one of those closest to you, you can't know much about that person, and you'll probably know even less about yourself.

I sensed Maman near me, tense, not allowing herself to move for fear she'd keep me awake. I was doing the same for her.

"You're not asleep yet?" I said finally.

Then she admitted to not having slept more than two or three hours a night for a good many years, and some nights not even one hour. She had a little chuckle at her own expense, part grief, part irony. "Life plays some mean tricks, you know," she said, "waiting for us at turning points we've looked forward to for ages, just so it can tell us it's too late now.... When I was a young woman with babies crying at night, I'd have to get up and I'd be just about asleep on my feet, nursing this one, changing that one, and I'd promise myself, 'When the children are grown I'll make up for all this. I'll sleep and sleep at last as much as I want....' "

"Poor Maman! What then?"

"Then by the time the children were grown and I might have

slept through the night, sleep had turned its back on me, caring no more about me than water does about the driftwood it leaves on a lonely beach."

When my turn came to lose my ability to sleep, when I was so ill with a toxic goitre, I kept remembering what Maman had whispered that night in the big brass bed at the Misses Muller's, and I thought it more heartbreaking than anything else she'd ever confided. All those years without ever getting enough sleep, counting on having it later, wanting it, craving it increasingly, then at last when you're free to give in to it, finding it isn't there any more; it's gone and won't be back. It really is like being left behind on an empty beach, with no protection from your racing thoughts. On the other hand, if I hadn't known insomnia, would I have known what it's like for someone who suffers from it? I might never even have been able to imagine Alexandre Chênevert in *The Cashier*, let alone create the tortured soul who never slept and so had no relief from his vision of human suffering. You might say that every sorrow brings enlightenment and each enlightenment reveals more suffering.

We both pretended to be on the verge of sleep a few seconds longer, then abruptly I put an end to the silliness and spoke up about what was bothering me.

"Those two little rooms you've taken for yourself and Clémence – it seems to me you'll be cramped and have no view. I'm afraid it's going to be very depressing for you."

No, she assured me, and tried to convince me that once the house had been sold, the sacrifice made, she'd felt liberated, and perhaps this was true. She didn't much mind now where she lived. There was a lot to be said for getting rid of things. When you can lose nothing more, you can finally relax. She'd taken far too long, she said, to realize that furniture, rugs, and that kind of thing just tied you down as you aged.

I listened, almost more grieved at this detachment than I'd been at her still recent determination to cling to every reminder of the past.

"Don't worry about me," she continued in a semi-whisper. "If it weren't for not knowing what's going to happen to Clémence, I'd be quite content."

She moved closer and whispered more softly as if the walls might have ears.

"She's been cranky all summer at Excide's. Or else she'd go on long walks by herself. I don't know how to handle her any more."

There was a moment of silence, then she continued with almost childlike candour.

"D'you think when people suffer it might be because their parents won't face up to something, and sort of pass it on to their children so they don't have to think about it any longer?"

"What are you trying to say?" I asked.

"Perhaps Clémence was always prone to mental illness," she said, "but something awful must have happened to bring it on so suddenly. The doctor thought at first there'd been some kind of religious trauma. We never knew for sure. Clémence wouldn't ever say a word to give us any idea what might have happened – and that says a lot in itself. But words I heard her say when she had bad dreams, and the look in her eyes sometimes, and the peculiar way she'd refuse to do certain things, made me suspicious that perhaps...one day...at confession.... She was such a pious little girl, so conscientious...she was only fourteen then...maybe...you know...."

"Oh, Lord above, Maman, that's enough!" I exclaimed, wanting more to spare her than to spare myself, as I recall. But I felt deeply for her, having to live with such an idea and keep it to herself, even if, as she hastened to add, it might never have been anything but a figment of her imagination.

"How could you go on praying...and believing...after having an idea like that!" I scolded.

"Turn against the truth of the Church, just because of one priest...one poor, tortured creature, for goodness' sake?" she retorted. "You can't understand much about life to talk that way!"

A few minutes later, wearily and sadly, she asked me to forgive her for letting herself talk about this just before I was to go away. It was just that she was so worried about Clémence.

"Who'll take care of her when I'm gone?" she said. "Sometimes I'm afraid, very afraid, there won't be a soul in the world who'll look after her."

She'd said it, it was over, but the words kept ringing in my ears,

and they'd ring at intervals for the rest of my days, like mournful bell-buoys tossing on the waves at sea.

Then, surprisingly, I saw the procession of lambs and ewes I'd seen a hundred times ambling beside the Big Water Hen, so long a line it must surely have passed the same spot again and again. To me, this scene was all the peacefulness of evening drifting over the sleepy countryside. There was the river in its inexhaustible splendour, its cool green waters flowing ever more extravagantly but always as abundantly, wending through a thousand open pathways in a sea of reeds to the river's mouth, great Lake Winnipegosis. Among the slender stems, the surface splashed with diving waterfowl. Little water hens bobbed for food, heads down, rumps up. Here and there ducks rose in close formation, necks outstretched. And I wondered how life could contain such beauty and also such tragedy as I thought I saw ahead for Clémence. It seemed to me that I could see her lonely figure against the dusky sky, wandering endlessly along unfamiliar little roads bathed in shadow. I had no idea that when I went searching on the darkened prairie for Otterburne again years later, I'd find those little roads just as I saw them that night.

What upset me most, I think, was feeling that the world was too beautiful to allow her tragedy. I lost hope. Lost hope that I'd been born to be happy. There must have been days when Maman also lost hope for me.

"I'm not going," I said. "There are too many obstacles."

Maman sat bolt upright. She reached over my head to turn on the light. It was dim, but her eyes, though still weary and sad with worry over Clémence, burned with renewed energy.

"That's all we need!" she declared. "Your ticket's bought, your passport's ready, everyone's been told, your replacement at school's been found, and now you go and change your mind. You'll have everybody laughing at you, and so they should!"

"Have everybody laughing at me? I'm used to that!"

"You're going," she said emphatically. "Otherwise you'll never forgive yourself, and you'll have me never forgiving myself either."

Now that I was beginning to waver, she found the only argument that could comfort me and raise my hopes again.

"Pay no attention to what people say. The truth is, you're the

only one of my children who's stayed as long with me. Whatever they say, the others all left the first chance they had. Joseph first at barely fifteen, he was a wanderer if ever there was one. Then Rodolphe not much older, though at least he came back once in a while. Anna married when she was nineteen. Adèle left young too. And to answer the call of God, as she put it, Dédette left us at twenty-two. In a way the first Agnès also left us for God; He took her so young, a dear little girl of fourteen. Then Marie-Agnès, lost when she was only four. You can't remember, you were just nine months old when she died, and it's a shame because she was crazy about you. She wanted to carry you around in her arms all the time. I often wouldn't let her. I was afraid she'd drop you. Sometimes she'd come and take you out of your crib thinking I didn't know, and try to hide you somewhere. I let her do it sometimes; she was only three and a half and it was so sweet to see her carrying you with a hand supporting your back as I'd shown her, trembling with the effort because you were already a fat baby.''

I think we both smiled through our tears at the picture that Maman had described so often I used to imagine I remembered it myself. Though I hadn't really known her, I'd always thought of Marie-Agnès as the closest to me of all my sisters, and perhaps the most dear to me.

"You're the only one I kept. Till now." Maman's voice was firmer. "Do you think I could forget you've stayed with me till the age of twenty-eight?"

I didn't tell her it wasn't just because of her that I'd stayed, though she probably knew this as well as I did. It was good I didn't say it. From that night of whisperings we needed to be left with a feeling of lasting closeness, unshakeable tenderness towards each other.

"Go to sleep now," I told her.

"You too," she replied.

Neither of us went right to sleep even then, each still hearing echoes of the things that had passed between us that night, echoes we'd hear ever after. What a little thing it takes sometimes to unite people, or estrange them! If we hadn't lain in that big strange bed together, Maman and I, we might never have known many things about one another.

A moment later Maman spoke again. Once more her voice was a little strained.

"Tomorrow morning, or this morning rather, how about going to mass together, to pray for your plans to work out?"

I was silent. I should have expected this. For some years, though we'd never really talked about it, I'd been avoiding religious observance in what amounted to revolt against a dogmatic attitude that saw evil in everything, laid claim to sole possession of the truth, and, if it could, would have denied us any communication whatever with a generous human disparity. Not wanting to hurt Maman's feelings, though, I'd managed not to lock horns with her over this, and when possible had avoided letting her know I hardly ever went to church now. Nevertheless, she couldn't have failed to see that I'd lost the fervent faith of my early youth that she'd so loved in me. Her own faith, I suppose, was so strong, so thoroughly tested – or else so ingenuous still – that she wasn't distracted by the Church's very human aberrations, but kept her eyes fixed on the bright light at its centre.

Could I refuse her the comfort she was asking? I told myself that it wouldn't be such a crime to go through the motions, and that if I could borrow a bit of her faith to lift me briefly in unison with her, I might not even need to pretend.

I agreed to go, immediately sensed enormous relief on her part, and must have promptly gone to sleep. Minutes later, it seemed, she was shaking me gently, considerately, as she used to when she woke me to go to mass with her when I was a child. But then it might have been winter, still dark outside with a howling wind, and she must have hated to drag me from my nice warm bed out into the cold air with a few stars still twinkling above. What urgent need she must have felt to make herself do it! This same need must be dictating to her now.

We dressed back to back as we used to, and set off in the crisp morning air for the cathedral.

I'd walked this way beside Maman almost since I took my first steps. Suddenly I was imagining what all our walks placed end to end would add up to: the walks to Eaton's on bargain hunts; to church on Sundays of course; to the forty hours' devotion and to gain indulgences; sometimes, at the peak of a torrid summer, to

Assiniboine Park, though it took hours to get there, to enjoy the cool shade of the trees and admire the fountains and perpetually green lawns; to River Park also, where I loved to look at the animals gazing out with captives' eyes from behind their bars; and often, just because we enjoyed it, up and down our own little Deschambault Street when the heat of the day was past.

On one of these pleasant summer evenings, since I was now "a big girl" as she put it, she decided to enlighten me on the facts, or as I think she said, much more appropriately, the "mysteries" of life. She was so ill at ease I could hardly understand a word of what she was trying to tell me, except that being a woman was so humiliating it made you want to die. We shouldn't really blame the women of those days for not knowing how to talk about love and the body; they were very inhibited about such things, and so considerate of their daughters that they thought they were doing us a favour by leaving us as long as possible in ignorance of what was awaiting us. It's taken a long time for the light to reach us women, centuries of obscurity and silence. Our mothers put such toil and determination into achieving a better life, and along the way, I sometimes think, not an ounce of it has been wasted.

I thought about all this as I walked beside Maman, and my heart was full to bursting with memories I hadn't realized I possessed. Going away does so much – almost as much as death – to open our eyes to the people we're about to leave.

Once again we went to a pew at the front of the long nave to be as close to the sanctuary as possible, among the elderly women in black who were counting their beads and saying Hail Marys under their breath in the dim, warm glow of the tapers.

We knelt side by side as we'd done on the day we'd come to pray before my operation. With feelings as confused as they had been then, I watched Maman pray. Today too, she was undoubtedly praying that I be spared suffering. Yet only suffering really teaches us to love.

THAT MASS must have been my last for a long time. Many years later, God's presence throughout this world seemed very clear to me, leading me to consider the Church's practices not so puerile after all, since they had helped keep the light at its nucleus alive for me. I won't deny that when I returned it was partly from a

nostalgic desire to be kneeling again beside my dead mother, and how could I do this except through God? Sometimes I admit to myself that what I like best about the idea of eternity is the chance for me to unburden myself to my loved ones, and them to me, so that all the misunderstandings in life may finally cease.

IT HAD HURT to think that my friends and school colleagues were letting me leave without having a little goodbye party. This was always done when one of us got married. I didn't mind not getting presents. What grieved me was that they should let me go as if I didn't matter any more, the ultimate sign of what I took to be a kind of disapproval.

But when the evening of my departure came and I arrived with Maman at the old Canadian Pacific station, to my surprise there were friends in every corner of the concourse. I was positively jumping with joy, running from one group to another, suddenly overcome with dizzying tenderness for these young men and women of my own age who I hadn't believed were so close to me, but who suddenly were. I was encouraged by their presence to do my utmost to be a credit to them, like others of our little community whose success, we considered, reflected on us all. There were even some friends from the days of our touring shows. Fernand, the pianist-cartoonist, had brought me a little jewel box which, though I had practically nothing to put in it, I would cherish with special fondness, because Fernand lived very meagrely and I was well aware that his gift could represent piano lessons given all over the city.

They all came with me to the platform. I saw with pride that they made quite a little crowd, just for me. The long train gave a shudder from end to end and emitted little bursts of steam, the voice of elation, I thought.

My friends crowded around for a goodbye hug, some bearing little ribboned packages, others slipping into my coat pocket or handbag an envelope in which I'd find a bank note with a few words like "For a pair of stockings..." or "For a square meal some hungry day...." Dear, kind friends. How grateful I was, in the moments of need that inevitably came, to have an essential pair of shoes or solitary meal, thinking, "He doesn't know, but this is Hector's or Valen's present today."

The conductor shouted his "All aboard!" I jumped onto the step

of the train. The little crowd of friends waved and blew kisses, calling out goodbyes and good wishes. I was giddy with joy at the unexpected demonstration of friendship. Then, in the midst of my euphoria, beyond the sea of young, smiling faces, my mother's distraught little countenance caught my eye, suddenly old and creased with the grief she could no longer hide. I'd been so carried away by the affection being shown me I'd forgotten to kiss her goodbye, and with the look in her tired eyes she was allowing herself just barely to remind me of this. I remembered the look we'd exchanged on the day of my graduation, when I searched for her from the stage and our eyes met, hers shining with so much pride that they lit up my whole being. Today the light seemed on the point of going out. I jumped off the train. I ran to her. I put my arms around her. Why hadn't I noticed before how tiny she was? Her body was like a child's. I hugged her as tight as I could. I whispered goodness knows what silly exhortation to take care of herself, which she hadn't ever done, even when life was being relatively kind.

It was she who first loosened our embrace, saying, "Your train...your train!" because it had slowly begun to move. I jumped back onto the step of my car. I clung to the handrail. I looked at but didn't see the young faces, the smiling faces. I could see nothing but the lonely little figure in the midst of happy people. I watched her pull her rather skimpy coat around her, something I realized only now I'd seen her do at least a hundred times. It revealed so well the way she was, proud and diffident at once. Her sorrowful eyes were fixed on me as though they'd never lose me wherever I went. It became unbearable. I saw too well that she knew I wouldn't be coming back, that destiny was taking me away to another life. My courage failed. It was clear now that I wasn't leaving so I could make good for her, as it had pleased me to believe. Dear heaven, it was really so I'd be free of her, wasn't it? Free of her and the family woes clustered about her, in her keeping.

On the platform now I was seeing only people not really there: Anna with the dejected face of a woman of many gifts who'd never used any of them to advantage and would blame herself to the end of her days; Clémence with her brooding eyes dark-ringed by illness; Rodolphe, his face ravaged already; even Dédette in her nun's habit, showing in her saddened face that she was sorry not

192

to have known a bit more of the world before she renounced it. They all seemed to be reproaching me for their failed or unfulfilled lives. "Why is it only happening to you? Why not us? Mightn't we have found happiness too?"

I was even being condemned, I thought, for putting myself beyond the reach of sorrows still years away, waiting here.

Then, at the end of the platform, there appeared a little crowd from the past, dressed in black. There were my forebears, the Landrys and the Roys too, the Connecticut expatriates, their ancestors who'd been deported from Acadia, their descendants repatriated to St-Jacques-l'Achigan, my St-Alphonse-de-Rodriguez relatives and those at Beaumont, even my Savonarola grandfather whom I had time to recognize beside Marcelline, his eyes dark and smouldering as in his photograph...the terrible exodus my mother had introduced me to one day....

Can I deny finding in my heart that perhaps I'd always wanted to break the chain, escape from my poor dispossessed people? Who among us hasn't wanted this at some point? Loyalty is so difficult.

Next I think I shed some tears. Of shame? Compassion? I'll never know. Perhaps it was the bitter taste of desertion that made me cry.

Now, with the rhythmic sound of the train as it travelled through open countryside, the great, comforting dream of my youth, beguiling as ever, took hold of me again. It was showing me a future in which I'd have time for everything. Time first to save myself. If you drown, what use are you to anyone else? Then time to return and save the others. My dream was telling me I'd be allowed plenty of time.

II

A BIRD KNOWS
ITS SONG

I

OF ALL THE foreigners who stream into Paris every day there was surely never one more bewildered than I in the autumn of 1937. I knew absolutely no one. However, a letter had been sent from my faraway Manitoba to prepare the way for me. Meredith Jones, who taught French at the University of Manitoba, had asked one of his former students who was living as an *au pair* in Paris to help me out a bit, find me a boarding house, meet me at the station. We were to recognize each other by a book she was to have in her hand and a Canadian magazine I was to carry under my arm. But I'd lost my magazine. The strangest part is that today I can't remember the name of the young woman with the book whom I sought so frantically, and who helped me so much when I finally found her.

I stepped out into the terrifying horde that gets off a train arriving at the Gare Saint-Lazare from the coast. In the sea of constantly changing faces, I kept trying to recognize one I'd never seen before. I was caught up by the shouts, the hustle and bustle, the powerful surges of movement, at times finding myself somehow going against the current of humanity and being taken to task with "Hey you, can't you watch where you're going!" I recall this as being one of the first things I heard said to me in Paris. I also made the blunder of trying to ask someone in a hurry for information, and was put firmly in my place. "For information, there's Information," snapped the man, then, perhaps feeling a mite remorseful, as he moved on he tipped his chin to indicate a direction. Next I spied a kind of uniform. I had a fleeting moment of hope for rescue, but I'd hardly begun my tale of woe when its wearer sent me packing. So I was looking for someone, was I! Well, the station was full of people looking for each other. Then, obviously hoping for a more open-

handed client, he shouted over my head, "Porter! Porter!" though people on all sides were trying to catch his attention, also calling "Porter! Porter!"

In the end I let myself move with the crowd and before I realized it I was swept past the turnstiles and into the swarming concourse. I lost all hope of finding my compatriot. I went to a wicket, from which I was sent to another, where I was scolded for not knowing enough to read the signs on which, I was told, everything was indicated. And indeed it must have been so, for looking up I was confronted by a forest of symbols, words, and abbreviations that made my head spin.

Eventually I came to my senses and told myself that if my compatriot was still waiting it surely wouldn't be in this enormous concourse but most likely on the platform. I went back. At the turnstile the ticket checker stopped me.

"Where d'you think you're going, little lady?" he demanded.

"The other side."

"What side? The seaside?"

I pointed.

"In that case, little lady, your ticket!"

"My ticket!" I wailed in exasperation. "I gave it to the conductor of the train. The one I just arrived on."

"And you want to get back on already?"

In time I became accustomed to these sparring matches which so many Parisians seem to relish. Eventually I even came to enjoy them myself, but for the moment I was in the depths of despair. It seemed as impossible to get anyone to listen to me as if I'd been whisked to the heart of China. I tried to persuade the man at the turnstile, telling him how I'd lost the magazine that would have allowed my friend to identify me, and finished by begging him at least to let me go and make sure she wasn't still looking for me on the platform.

Perhaps because he considered I'd already taken up too much of his time with my muddled story, during which he'd done nothing but study his fingernails, he thenceforth addressed me in non-sentences.

"Platform ticket...."

"Where?"

"Machine...." He pointed.

I found it. As I approached, it looked well disposed, unlike the impatient people I'd encountered, and thus inspired me with confidence. Above a slot it told me it was a platform ticket distributor. I pulled the lever.

Nothing happened.

An elegant gentleman was passing. Though he seemed in a great hurry he stopped to watch what I was doing.

"It might work better if you put in a franc," he said.

I reddened to the roots of my hair and opened my purse. Alas, I had no French money yet.

The elegant gentleman put his hand in his pocket. He took out a franc and put it in my hand, then was on his way, his face closed over other thoughts, it seemed.

I ran after him crying, "Monsieur, Monsieur, please, your name, your address, so I can repay you!"

Without exactly slowing his pace he turned partway around and gave me the first smile I'd received in Paris.

"Really, Mademoiselle, such a to-do over a franc!"

So the first handout of my life is still a bit on my conscience. My benefactor might have been a Rothschild; sometimes I think I recall a scarf and a pair of gloves of a quality I've rarely seen since.

I went back to the turnstile with my platform ticket. I didn't realize I was approaching a new ticket checker, who'd perhaps only just arrived to relieve the first.

"Where d'you think you're going, little lady?" I heard myself asked again.

Dumbfounded, I looked up at him. Though I myself couldn't tell one face from another any more, I reproached him for not recognizing me.

"I told you before. I'm looking for another Canadian who was supposed to meet me, and you sent me to get a platform ticket."

"But there's nobody left on the platform," said the new ticket checker. "Look, don't you see?" He was nicer than the first, which was why I finally realized I was talking to a different one.

He was quite right. There wasn't a soul in sight all the way down the platform. I came back to the middle of the noisy concourse. I didn't dare approach the wicket I'd been sent from to look at the signs. For a while I wandered around aimlessly in the crowd

just trying to catch someone's eye, for what purpose I'm not sure, but nobody looked my way. In my frustration I took this as evidence that no one wanted anything to do with me. With no local money, not even knowing the address where a room had been reserved for me, faced with the most callous indifference, I was doomed to go around in circles indefinitely, it seemed. In the vast concourse of the Gare Saint-Lazare I was so discouraged that I formed a very black picture of myself leading a most wretched life in Paris.

Then suddenly the crowd began to thin. It happened so quickly that I was surprised and even more distraught. Soon there were only a dozen or so lost-looking souls still wandering about, making the huge space look ten times bigger than before. Finally there were only two little figures left at opposite ends of all that emptiness. Each of us began a hesitant approach towards the other. I didn't have my magazine and she didn't have her book. She'd left it on the Métro, I learned later. We exchanged beseeching looks. She was the first to speak.

"Are you Gabrielle?"

I flung my arms around her neck as if she were suddenly the dearest soul in the world. Yet I'm still trying to find her name. I seem to have had it on the tip of my tongue for years. Perfidious memory! Will it ever give me back that precious name?

As we went to claim my baggage from the checkroom, she was already doing her best to encourage me.

"Don't be upset by the way strangers treat you here. It's always that way in Paris. You think you've come to a city where they're permanently at war with each other. They quarrel and bicker about everything. It's really just a game, though, and you'll find it's almost always in the cause of justice and logic. Logic's a passion with them, they've got it in their blood like a virus. We all get used to it, you'll see. You even start enjoying it, and when you can beat the Parisians at their own game they surrender in a way that's downright disconcerting. Anyway, what you mustn't ever do at any cost is let on you're afraid of them. Got that?"

These astonishing words came piecemeal to my ears, because my companion had outstripped me and I was scurrying to keep up, often separated from her by a pillar or simply by considerable distance.

At the checkroom I retrieved my two heavy suitcases and my

wardrobe trunk, which must have weighed a good two hundred
pounds. However, the porters whose offers of service had rung in
every corner of the station shortly before were now nowhere to be
seen. When we called for their help our voices went unanswered,
piping and pathetic in the cavernous silence.

So my compatriot and I lugged the two suitcases a good distance,
though not so far that we'd lose sight of them. Then we tackled
the trunk, pivoting it on its corners, watched appreciatively by at
least half a dozen sweepers, all leaning on their brooms. They'd
have liked to help us, they said, but that wasn't their job. With
my baggage all together again, we each sat on a suitcase for a
minute to catch our breath. At last we reached the sidewalk and
heaved the baggage into a tall taxi while the driver calmly kept
reading his *Paris-Soir*. One of us climbed in beside him and tugged
while the other pushed strenuously from below. At the last minute
he deigned to rise briefly from his posterior and give us a hand
with the trunk, for which there was only barely room inside the
vehicle.

As we drove into the City of Light at last, along street after
street I saw nothing but tall façades severely shrouded in darkness.
Even the streetlamps yielded no more than a paltry glow.

"I've found you a suitable *pension*, Madame Jouve's," my compatriot told me, "one they'd say here is *tout ce qu'il y a de bien*,
all you could ask for. But tonight for sure Madame Jouve will come
down on you like a ton of bricks for arriving so late. After midnight,
everything's barricaded like a mediaeval fortress there. Have you
seen Carcassone?" she asked, then returned to my landlady. "If
she attacks, you counterattack. If she snarls, snarl louder. That's
the way to get along in Paris."

"How awful!"

"No, because then you're respected."

Something else I've totally forgotten, perhaps significantly, is
my first address in Paris, though I could probably find my way
there with my eyes closed. The building was impressive for the
period, six storeys and U-shaped, with its front gate and the watchman's cubicle on the Rue de la Santé – my memory can be depended
upon for the name of the street.

At this late hour, of course, we found the tall iron gate locked

and the watchman's cubicle as dark as a hut in a forest. My compatriot groped until she found a bell near the gate to wake the watchman. I'd never before had to disturb so many people just to get inside and into bed shortly after midnight. I was astounded that a city supposedly dedicated to nocturnal pleasures could also be so early to bed. All I'd seen from the taxi was a succession of huge buildings fast asleep, blocks of solid shadow without light in a single window.

The watchman appeared, still pulling on his clothes but not grumbling too much.

He opened the gate for us. We were in a murky courtyard now, with all six storeys around us in almost total darkness from top to bottom, showing only a feeble glimmer from a nightlight here and there. Then I saw a young crescent moon rising over the dark building, its golden cusps every bit as pure and brilliant as they were in the deep empty spaces of Canada.

Our taxi-driver's heart was perhaps softened by the absence of witnesses. He hoisted himself from his seat and unloaded my baggage onto the sidewalk. Then, one good deed leading to another, he helped us put it all inside the entrance to the building, having made the door open for us by pressing a button or shouting "Door! Door!" I don't remember which. This done, he left with all possible speed, wishing us, " 'Soir, 'sieur-dame.''

Immediately the electricity went off. Tripping over my scattered belongings, my compatriot groped for the light button. Just as she announced she'd found it the light went on again. "It's timed," she explained, running over to the button to show me what I'd have to do if I was caught alone in a dark entrance. I'd barely grasped what she was teaching me when she urged, "Come on, get ready to move fast...." The elevator, having been summoned, was descending towards us with creaks and groans, rocking like the basket on an early aeronautical contraption. It opened and revealed an interior that was so tiny I couldn't believe my eyes. I just stood there in astonishment, wasting precious time.

My compatriot had blocked the door open with a suitcase and was straining to wrestle my trunk into the elevator cage, because, she said breathlessly, if it didn't go in first it wouldn't go in at all. Finally it was in, filling the space almost totally.

"We'll come back for the rest?" I asked.

"And leave things down here to get pinched? Never! We'll get it all in."

"But there's no one around."

"That's what you think! Climb up on the trunk and I'll hand you one of the suitcases."

Standing on end, the trunk was already pretty high, and when I was perched on top of it I touched the ceiling of the cage. I succeeded in stowing a suitcase beside me.

Thereupon the light went off. My compatriot ran to put it on again. We managed finally to get both suitcases standing precariously on top of the trunk, on end and side by side. Then, flattening ourselves to the limit between the closed cage door and the mountain of baggage which we held steady with outstretched arms, we began to rise gently towards the sixth floor. Then the light went out again.

I began to laugh uncontrollably, certainly one of the least mirthful laughs I've ever experienced. Nevertheless, it echoed upward and downward with singular insolence, amplified by the funnel effect of the elevator shaft. "Not so loud...not so loud!" my compatriot begged me. She was English-speaking, and though she'd made enormous progress with her French in the year she'd been in Paris she would sometimes lapse into her mother tongue when excited. "You'll wake everybody...," she warned, but to no avail, for the fear of doing just that was making my awful paroxysms worse. But they stopped as abruptly as they'd begun.

The elevator came to a halt. "Hold the lift," my compatriot whispered quickly as she stepped out to find the light button. Though dim, the light blinded me when it came on, I'd become so accustomed to moving around in the dark.

"No noise," warned my compatriot, and we began to drag the baggage out into the hall and pile it beside Madame Jouve's door, making as little noise as a pair of thieves. I'll soon have more to say about thieves as it happens, but not until their turn comes. When the baggage was arranged to our satisfaction, not blocking the passageway too much, I put my finger on the bell, above which a fearsomely distinguished card announced, "Madame Jean-Pierre Jouve."

Almost immediately the self-same Madame Jean-Pierre Jouve

opened the door, wearing a dressing gown, her eyes heavy with sleep and a reproach on her lips, although a polite one.

"This is some hour to be arriving! You could at least have let me know you'd be late, sent me a wire...telephoned...."

Now her eyes were suddenly open wider, for what she perceived first was neither my anxious face so earnestly hoping for sympathy, nor my compatriot's pleasant round one still flushed from battle; not, in short, two plucky young women and their heroic achievement in getting themselves to her door, just the mountain of baggage piled beside it. She gave a cry of dismay.

"That's not all yours...? All that...?"

"I've come for a year, Madame," I ventured.

"And you think you need all that...for just one miserable little year?"

I wanted to tell her a year in Paris couldn't be a "miserable little year", but I didn't have time.

"You're all the same, you Americans, with your tons of baggage!"

"I'm Canadian."

"Same thing, you and your enormous wardrobe trunks," she continued. "Don't you know what a Parisian apartment is like? We haven't got all the room in the world the way you do in Canada, you know."

Yet my trunk was the most compact I could find at Eaton's in Winnipeg, designed especially for going to Paris according to the advertisement, since it asked (in English, of course), "Are you going abroad?" and urged, "Take me with you," promising to make itself small, to fit flat under a bed or stand on end in a corner, to serve as the least cumbersome wardrobe ever with its hanger compartment for suits and dresses and drawers for shoes and underwear. My friends had chipped in to help me pay for it. I'd packed everything I valued in it. And attached to it as I may have been when I left home, how could I measure my fondness for it now that we'd been through so much together? Apprehensively, I looked at Madame Jouve who was looking with distaste at the trunk.

"Listen, my child," she whispered, for the whole conversation of reproach and feeble excuse was taking place under our breath so as not to wake the neighbours, "we'll try to put the suitcases somewhere in the apartment for tonight at least, though I don't see how we're going to get them into your room, but the trunk..."

Her voice, though exceedingly well bred, none the less indicated she would not be crossed.

"...has to go to the basement tonight."

So we put it back in the elevator cage, three of us this time, though Madame Jouve hindered more than she helped because her voluminous shaggy dressing gown kept getting caught in the grille-work of the cage. We descended into the bowels of the earth. Here as upstairs, electricity was apparently dispensed in brief periods, and all we had to see by were feeble little lights spaced along a narrow dirt-floored passageway leading away into utter darkness. At the side was a row of small iron-grilled storage lockers that looked like dungeons in this dismal setting. We manoeuvred the trunk along the passageway, pivoting it on its corners, I with the feeling that having barely arrived I was already reliving one of those stories of the murky side of Paris that I recalled having read with such pleasure when I was safe and sound. I said so to Madame Jouve, who chided me amiably for having too much imagination and letting it run away with me. This, she said, was plainly and simply a safe, clean, and very accessible basement. She was beginning to be pleasant in her own way. She predicted that I'd soon find it a thousand times more convenient to have my trunk down here, where I could come and get what I needed at any time and without causing the least trouble, than in my room, which really was very small. How I agreed with her once I'd seen the room!

At last we arrived at a locker with a number above the door that matched the one on Madame Jouve's apartment. She fiddled briefly with the padlock.

"Well!" she said. "It looks as if it's been forced. It'll have to be changed tomorrow without fail."

This should have put me on my guard, but suddenly, as has happened so often in the midst of difficulties over which I have no control, I was only half there; part of me was revisiting books I'd read that this Paris basement reminded me of. When caught in ridiculous or uncontrollable situations I've often found refuge in memories left by books; they seem so much more comfortable than the reality I'm involved in.

As we moved away I glanced back sadly at the trunk. It looked so lonesome standing on its end in the middle of its dungeon. I had a feeling I might never see it again. But the feeling vanished

in the face of a new problem: the electricity in the bowels of Paris had failed. Happily, Madame Jouve had a cigarette lighter in the pocket of her bulky dressing gown. By the light of the tiny flame, for some reason each of us holding the next by an arm like disaster survivors, we returned to the surface.

We let my friend off the elevator at the ground floor and she fled in great haste. She had a long way to go and would only just catch the last bus. As she left she called over her shoulder that she'd be around to pick me up early next morning and we'd go to the police station. On the way we'd have to get me photographed full-face and profile, with my ears showing, and I mustn't forget to bring a residence certificate. If we had time we'd stop and sign the Canadian visitors' book at the embassy.... "Bye-bye till tomorrow...."

At last I was safe and sound in the sixth-floor apartment. Madame Jouve, having made me sit down for a moment, finally took the time to look at me and became almost maternal.

"My poor child, you look all upset. Would you like something to drink to pick you up?"

I think I pictured a lovely steaming hot chocolate, the kind Mother used to bring me, a big brimming cupful, when she too found I looked peaked after a long hard day. I accepted with a smile, I imagine, thinking of the rich, smooth, delicious-smelling drink I could count on when I came in after our evening shows in little Manitoba villages or even in town. And I must have kept smiling a little, because on the heels of this memory came a succession of others which, if I hadn't been woolgathering about finally being in Paris, I would probably never have known were so pleasant or even that they existed.

"I'll make you a lemonade," said Madame Jouve.

A lemonade just before going to bed has always done me more harm than good, since its effect is to make me get up every fifteen minutes. But I didn't have the strength to refuse. Madame Jouve went to the kitchen to squeeze a lemon. She brought me a bitter drink softened just barely with a few grains of sugar. I drank it, managing with difficulty not to grit my teeth.

"Come along now, you must get to bed."

She led me down a corridor to a door at the end, which she opened cautiously, revealing a room faintly and indirectly lit by

the new moon I'd seen rising over the fortifications. I still don't know why I kept thinking of fortifications. Perhaps I felt I'd strayed so far off the course of my life that I'd for ever be prevented from returning to it. I entered the small room without seeing a thing.

"Take the bed on the right," instructed Madame Jouve. "If you can, leave the light off so as not to wake your roommate. She has to get up early in the morning."

"But I said in my letter I had to have a room to myself," I found the courage to remind her.

"And you shall have it, my child. I've been caught short because a Swedish girl came earlier than expected."

She closed the door behind her.

I groped my way to the head of the bed, deposited my clothes around me on what might have been a chair and a night-table, though I wasn't sure, then lay down, my nerves beginning to relax at last. But I'd barely begun to drift off to some peace and quiet when my lemonade made itself felt. I got out of bed, found my way to the door, opened it, closed it noiselessly, and guided by a kind of instinct followed a corridor and found the facilities, where I still didn't put on the light, identifying everything just by touch. All without a sound. Until, having found and firmly grasped the chain, I gave it a good pull. You'd think I'd opened a floodgate and loosed a cataract. Not until broad daylight, when I found the flush tank attached almost at ceiling height, giving the water three metres to fall, did I realize how I had set off such a din.

I retraced my steps, dived back into what my fingers told me was my bed, and heard a grumbling sound from the other bed, caused by ill humour or a disturbed dream, I couldn't tell which. I began to doze off. But the lemonade hadn't done with me yet. It even seemed to be waiting until I was back in bed before giving me its message. Off I went along the unfamiliar route through the unfamiliar apartment. I returned. I went back again. According to what I was soon to be told, the deafening cataract sound reverberated twice more through the apartment. Each time I returned on tiptoe, though the impressive gurgling of the tank, filling almost as noisily as it emptied, was certainly loud enough to cover the sound of my steps. What drove me to cause such expenditure of water for the expulsion of so little? No doubt my fear of not doing,

when in Paris, as civilized Parisians do, while in fact doing the reverse.

Exhausted, I finally fell asleep. But not restfully. I dreamed I was trudging across Paris with my trunk on my back, having become a street porter, one of those poor wretches of days long past whose picture had sprung from the memory of books I'd read. Next I was tripping on the king's cobblestones at Versailles, fleeing from ruffians who'd been set at my heels. Then I was Jean Valjean of Hugo's *Les Misérables* in the sewers of Paris, clinging to my trunk and being swept along on the evil-smelling waters. The flushing water, the basement at Madame Jouve's, and memories of books from my childhood had joined forces to produce one of the most vivid dreams I've ever had. Suddenly I was attending a *bal musette* with accordions playing and my trunk in my arms, trying to make it dance to a rollicking air. I opened my eyes. It was broad daylight. There was a piano a few feet away taking up two-thirds of the room. My roommate was sitting at it playing with gusto, washed and dressed and hair combed, her bed already made.

"*Bonjour, vous, la Canadienne!*" she called through her chords and arpeggios.

She made not the slightest attempt to excuse herself for waking me so rudely. On the contrary, she took me to task, though good-naturedly, for having kept her awake with my comings and goings and "that infernal flushing you were doing all night as if you wanted to drain the Seine.... Are you on the trot like that every night?" She warned me that for her part she liked to go to bed early so she could get up and be at her piano bright and early, practising for her admission to the Conservatory.

So began my life with Charlotte, a young musician from Alsace who used to spend eight hours a day at her piano, whom even so I was to miss when Madame Jouve gave in to my repeated pleas and put me in a little cell by myself at the other end of the apartment.

For the moment I'd have given anything for another hour of sleep, but Charlotte struck up a triumphal march. The wretched girl played well, too. My half-dead nerve-ends quivered, tempted by the music. Besides, my compatriot was arriving.

"What!" I heard her say in a loud voice as soon as she was inside the door, "Gabrielle's not up and ready yet? We've got a lot to do today."

To my surprise, when Charlotte paused briefly I heard Madame Jouve rise to my defence.

"Give the poor child time to pull herself together at least. And first you're going to let her have her breakfast in peace."

I appeared in the dining room barely awake. My place was still set, the only one left, at a long oval table. A dainty bouquet of flowers at its centre immediately caught my eye.

"What are they?" I asked, never having seen flowers like these before.

"Anemones, my child," said Madame Jouve, apparently pleased I'd asked.

She was dressed in black, relieved only by a white edging high on the neck, and her chignon was impeccable. I'd defy anyone to recognize the frowsy lady of our basement prowls.

"Marie," she called towards the kitchen, "Mademoiselle's breakfast. And good and hot, eh!"

I lifted the steaming bowl, half fragrant coffee and half scalded milk, and found its taste exquisite. Then I took a croissant still hot from the oven and, since my compatriot had been served coffee too, followed her example and dipped it in my coffee. It was delicious. A warming sun flooded through the window from which I'd seen the moon as if it were rising over battlements. The anemones I've loved so much ever since kept drawing my eye and I longed to touch them. Though my throat was burning, which meant I was probably in for a cold, this morning I felt myself timidly beginning to find my feet in Paris, like a bruised plant in a protective layer of compost. I would willingly have stayed a while at this table; later I would realize that in a way breakfast in Paris is the pleasantest moment of the day, a time of peace and serenity, a time for reverie almost, a pause at the start of the day before you're caught up in the hustle and bustle of life. Many is the time it would help me take new heart, set me back on my feet when I thought I couldn't cope with Paris any longer.

I had no sooner meticulously gathered together the crumbs from my croissant on the tablecloth, as I'd watched my compatriot do, than she was hurrying me away.

"Come on," she said, "we're going to the police station."

Poor girl, she couldn't help hurrying me. She was always being hurried herself by her mistress, who didn't give her much time

off, wanting her around all the time to speak English to the children in return for meals and a roof over her head.

So there I was, fresh from the tribulations of the night before, running, stumbling after her across Paris. When she had enough breath left, she lost no opportunity to educate me as we went. "See, at bus stops, if you don't want to be at the back of the line all day you pull this lever on the machine and take a number. It's like the days of Frontenac and Bishop Laval. When the bus comes and the conductor shouts, 'Number, number!' everybody shouts their number and you shout yours too. Only war veterans and pregnant women can get on ahead, but look sharp because I've seen cheating.... Get on now, it's our turn.... Look, over here! That's the famous Café du Dôme where the artists and writers meet. Madame Jouve doesn't even suspect but her precious, much too beautiful Swede (the one who took your room), whose parents asked her to keep a close eye on her, spends whole evenings there with strange men.... We get off here.... Watch it!... Silly girl!... You don't cross streets in Paris except at the crossings between the *clous*, those metal disks in the road. Otherwise if you get run over it's your fault. Did you see the Eiffel Tower just then? It's monstrously beautiful, as they say. Here's the Métro.... We go down this way. Look, here's the *maquette*, the map of the Métro. If you don't know how to transfer to go, say, from the Porte des Lilas to Passy, you press this button and this one. See? Those little lights go on to show which trains to take. It's easy. You're in Paris. Everything's uncompromisingly clear." She added that everyone would keep telling me, "You can't go wrong." All of which gave me plenty to dream about for many nights to come.

II

WE'D SPENT two days under and above ground, running, hurrying, riding, and coughing (my cold had ripened), and my compatriot still losing no opportunity to teach me about Paris. "The Sainte Chapelle? No, we've passed it. The most graceful architecture in the world.... There's Notre Dame on the right. Look! The Arc de Triomphe ahead. Over there...that's the dome of Les Invalides. Napoleon's tomb's there, Egyptian red porphyry. What a dreadful man he was! *Un monstre!*... Downright shameful! How about getting off at the Louvre for a few minutes? Just long enough to take a look at the Winged Victory. *Une merveille, n'est-ce pas?* It's got no head and it's more eloquent than any head.... Come on!... That's our bus just leaving.... Jump!" If she couldn't find the right French word she'd often use an English one.

Near the end of the day my wonderful little guide stopped short and turned to me with a suggestion.

"I put a *bourguignon* on the stove early this morning. It should be cooked by now. Would you like to come and share it with me? I have to warn you, though; you'll have to walk up six floors. My place isn't grand like Madame Jouve's."

I was so enchanted at her invitation to have a quiet meal in what she called her own little corner in Paris, just the two of us, that she could have said two hundred floors and I'd have been just as ready to go. I expected to find the kind of respite which to tell the truth only humble places have ever given me. But I was far from expecting it to captivate me as it did. I felt as though I'd been deprived for centuries of the contemplation, the silence, the un-hurried, dreamy communion with myself that I've never been able to do without for long.

I took her arm. She smiled at me. We stopped running. We

210

reverted to what we really were, two little Canadians, both rather slow to come to decisions and act accordingly. We could do as we liked again and we wanted to feel at home. And this, I was to learn, Paris can also provide.

We walked on, no longer hurrying. Dusk was falling when we came to a narrow, shadowy street lined with tall, solemn, centuries-old houses. It must have been very near the Seine, for besides our footsteps I remember hearing soft lapping sounds, and at a corner perhaps even dimly seeing an expanse of water, deep green, a little dirty and sad, like an old face in which a long, long story is reflected. How I've loved Paris whenever it has shown me a face that's the opposite of what is called the gay, carefree Paris!

On the way we stopped once for a loaf of bread that was longer and thinner than any I'd seen before, again for a head of lettuce beaded with great cool drops of water, somewhere else for a bottle of red wine so we could drink to my arrival, and finally for a cheese that was so ripe it oozed into my sleeve as I carried it in my open palm. We also bought a little bunch of daisies of a kind the French call *paquerettes*, they too the first I'd ever seen. I couldn't stop looking at their tiny, perfect faces and saying, "So those are *paquerettes*!..." I was almost as happy to become acquainted with these flowers as I was to have found a friend I could depend on. Nostalgically, I tried for years to grow this kind of daisy in my small garden in Charlevoix County from the many packets of seeds I brought back from my visits to France. They flowered, making an even-surfaced, ravishing carpet of many colours at the foot of a gnarled old apple tree, but our country wasn't meant for them and they all very quickly died. I'd wanted to delight our vast Canadian sky with their delicate faces at any cost, but I finally stopped trying.

Before we started up the stairs to the sixth floor, my compatriot asked if I thought I could help with the wood we'd have to take up with us. We went to a dark little courtyard containing several stacks of firewood, one of them hers. We each took a good armful, and with wood piled up to our chins, the bags we were carrying filled to overflowing with bottles, bread, and lettuce, and the bright daisy faces lighting our way, we climbed the spiral staircase up the middle of the big old house. The worn steps and graffiti and other marks on the walls gave evidence of the thousands of pilgrims who, like

us, had trudged wearily up to their own little corners. I didn't feel my cold, fatigue, or anxiety any longer. My heart became lighter step by step, as happened in those years whenever I was approaching a moment of unexpected happiness.

At the top of the stairs, gripping one of her packages in her teeth, my compatriot drew a massive key from her pocket and slipped it into the keyhole of a shadowy door which was barely visible in the half-light of the landing. To this day I still picture every detail of the little room inside as I first saw it, the sofa-bed pushed against the wall, books all over, a round table with a cover hanging to the floor on which our two places were already set, and in the middle of the room a real little stove which I fell instantly in love with, it so made me think of good company in dreary hours, even with the fire out. I probably hadn't realized how homesick I must have been since leaving my country, for I went to the stove at once and touched it the way one does a living thing.

But the bewitchment of the place came less from anything of this kind in particular than from the way it was lit, small though it was, by a huge skylight in the roof. The room seemed to be in the sky itself, bathed in a soft, peaceful light that was softening further from minute to minute with the end of day. Never had I seen a room as open to the sky. I entered it as if I were entering a dream, one I'd had all my life: the dream of a haven from human malice, from myself and from others. It's surprising how often I've found such a haven...always very briefly. But the real miracle was that I found it this time in the heart of Paris, and it answered both of my irreconcilable needs, for solitude and warm companionship. All the beauty of the little room must have shown in my face, for my compatriot, who was sitting on the floor blowing on an ember in the ashes, stopped and looked at me open-mouthed.

"What's the matter? You look as if you're in a trance!"

What was the matter? The matter was that my heart was full to bursting and at peace both at once, that I had a feeling of belonging here, of unbelievable well-being. All of which I'd experienced only fleetingly before, like anyone else, of course. No, on second thought better than most, for not many people have ever truly had such a feeling, so indescribable yet so real. At the time I thought it came from outside of me, that the feeling belonged to the place it occurred in. I thought you could possess the feeling by

possessing the place, either by staying there or by trying to take it with you – absurd as this may be. My compatriot laughed when I told her I wanted her room so badly I'd exchange it for my all-you-could-ask-for room and board at Madame Jouve's. Otherwise we'd have to find me a room just like it in every way. Then, I thought, I'd be content for the rest of my days.

When she had got the fire going and was preparing the salad, my compatriot gave me her own view of the piece of heaven I thought I had within reach.

"You get all the way up, loaded with as much as you and I brought up together, then you have to go back down to get coal oil for the lamp. You get all the way back up, but you've forgotten to pick up your mail. You go back down. This time you get almost all the way up and have to go half-way back down to find out what the concierge is yapping at you up the stairs. In the end you go all the way down because she's got a registered letter for you. Next you go down to the fourth floor to get water. You make the same trip to throw out the dirty water. Sooner or later you go back down again to the w.c. It's often ten o'clock before you can open your books and start preparing for your next day's classes. You're half asleep over your notes and you'll be half asleep at the Sorbonne while your eminent professor dispenses his wisdom in droning little sentences."

I listened, moved by the pluck she was laughingly revealing, as though poking fun at an absurd quirk in her character. I could now understand how difficult her life was in Paris, but I envied her no less fervently.

We sat down to dine directly under the skylight. To me we seemed to be sitting at table suspended in the sky, as in a surrealist painting. Later, when we were finishing our meal and the last glow of twilight was filtering over us through the opening in the roof, she agreed that when the chores were done a mysterious kind of peacefulness permeated her "little room in the sky", sometimes making her feel it was captured here for ever. Then she told me she had a surprise for me. She made me climb onto a chair beside her and opened the skylight on its hinges. Standing with our heads outside, we could see Paris all around, spread as far as the horizon like a great drowsy monster, sweet and lovable now it had calmed a little, when in any event none of its fretfulness and hurly-burly

could reach us up here. I stood on tiptoe on my chair for a long time, gazing at the city the way a child of the woods might gaze at faraway vistas from the branch of a tree. I still wonder if even from the top of Notre Dame I've ever had a more enchanting view of Paris.

My compatriot gently brought me back to reality, reminding me that the time had passed quickly and if we didn't leave soon we'd find the door tight at Madame Jouve's. I sighed as I tore myself away from the sky.

Early next morning, she told me, she'd be caught up again with her lectures and running from the Sorbonne to her mistress's house in time for meals so she could make the children say, "Pass me the salt if you please.... Thank you so very much...." And perhaps to stay with them in the evening if her mistress decided to go to the theatre, which wasn't part of the agreement, but an agreement was hardly ever respected when you were an *au pair*.

I could see increasingly how difficult a life she led and was embarrassed to realize what a priceless gift I'd received from her with all the time she'd given me, undoubtedly time that would cost her dearly to make up. It was comforting to know she'd take me home once again, for Paris at night frightened me, but I owed her so much already I didn't want to abuse her kindness and assured her I thought I could get home by myself.

She burst out laughing.

"Never!" she said. "Muddlehead that you are, you could just as well end up at La Villette...," and I was relieved that the time hadn't yet come when I'd be turned loose alone in Paris at night.

At the door I turned for a last fond look at the little room, which we were leaving in some disorder. It wasn't my intense longing to curl myself up and stay for ever that made me linger; this, I knew by now, just couldn't be. I was obeying a kind of command, one reaching me from the future, from years I hadn't yet lived, urging me to take what was important from this little room and keep it for later when I'd be able to use it. I'd been getting this curious command for some time and with increasing frequency whenever I said goodbye to places and things, since the Little Water Hen perhaps or even before, making me retain as much as possible of whatever I was leaving, so as to take it away with me in a sense.

It was a long time before I realized what those vague imperatives were leading to.

We hurried down the flights of stairs, ran through silent streets where the echo of our footsteps suddenly became the sound of pursuers, jumped onto a bus as it pulled away. Over the weeks and months that followed I didn't have much occasion to bring back the picture of the little room up there among the high rooftops of Paris. It used to come to my mind as a lovely, fragile memory, the kind one tells oneself is worth nurturing; then, finding me un-available, it would retreat again. After a while I lost sight of it. I think I even ceased to have any conscious recollection of it.

So why did it come back to life twenty years later, exactly as I'd stored it away in my last look from the door, with its footed salamander stove, squat and green, its round table littered with the remains of our meal, everything bathed in a soft twilight glow? For what reason other than to bring Pierre of *The Hidden Mountain* here when his wanderings ceased? To the haven I myself had longed for, I brought this exhausted soul to live his last torments and ecstasies. Or perhaps for the illusion of seeing, through the opening in the roof, the vast Canadian sky that's so often the colour of twilight in the North, as he'd seen it from his trapper's cabin long before.

III

SOON MADAME JOUVE, having my introduction to life in Paris at heart, began to take a hand in it herself. For she not only lodged and fed us. She guided us, counselled us, gave lessons in French to some and in deportment to others, discreetly observed the comings and goings of the youngest, perhaps reporting to their parents, and generally kept watch over us with a certain affection which, if not demonstrative, was well-meaning and sincere.

After a week or two of running hither and thither in Paris, I'd had more than I could stand of everything new. I shut myself in my room and stayed there, which I'm much inclined to do whenever I get beyond my depth. Madame Jouve, worried to see me living a hermit's existence now, came one evening to badger me out of it, bearing a book in her hand.

"My child, since you've come to Paris, the most exciting city in the world, and then chosen to shut yourself up like this, at least read. Here, I've brought you a book. All Paris is talking about it. All Paris adores it."

If I were given Alain-Fournier's *Le Grand Meaulnes* (*The Wanderer*) to read for the first time today I might be ecstatic, but to tell the truth I was then far too much like the hero of the book to have any taste for the sad tale of escape through imagination. I myself was escaping this way, the only escape from life we really have, but my own private door led to the riverbanks of the Little Water Hen; to me at the time, everything there seemed to have been ineffably peaceful and harmonious. So I paid only token attention to the book's fantasizing, which seemed pretty tame stuff compared to my own. If the conversation at table among the dozen boarders from almost as many countries turned to the book, I would

216

feign enthusiasm. But Madame Jouve had a way of putting questions that soon exposed such deception. She was almost beside herself with indignation that a young Canadian just off the boat from her native wilds should dare to be lukewarm about a novel that all Paris adored.

She was even more scandalized to hear my reaction the evening she took some of her brood to a performance of Giraudoux's *Electra*. Was the leap from Deschambault Street to the Athénée in Paris simply too great? Was I so truly lost here that I'd ceased turning a receptive ear to the voices of others? Or was the play too erudite, too boring? I shall never know because I've not been much inclined to expose myself to Giraudoux again. It took me longer to admit that the great Louis Jouvet himself aggravated me with his dry delivery, his little disconnected phrases coming out cold and flat, his mannerisms, and what to me was merely face-pulling. On the way through London I'd been to the Old Vic and also to a little theatre in Shaftesbury Street whose name I've forgotten, where I saw acting that was restrained, understated, one might even say untheatrical, a style that was discreet, all shades and halftones and vastly superior to what I was seeing in Paris, I felt. Yet in due course I found this kind of theatre in Paris too, the kind which is so close to reality that it's almost banal, but which enthralls.

On my own, when I finally found the courage to come out of my room, I hurried to the Théâtre Français. At home we'd always called it the Comédie Française, and we'd held it in such veneration that we looked with awe on anyone who'd crossed its threshold. I think I recall that we knew exactly how many such privileged individuals there were in our community and could name them and even remember which play each had seen.

I was all excited as I queued up behind the people waiting at the ticket office for the cheap seats. Gone was my fear of Paris and of doing the wrong thing, which Paris inspired in me at every turn. I became communicative, even talkative, and informed my neighbours to right and left that this was my first time at the Théâtre Français. Some said politely, "Oh yes?" and others asked where I was from and seemed interested in me, and I in return glowed with a kind of spontaneous friendship towards them. I was discovering the magical thread of brotherhood that unites these little clutches

of strangers at the doors of theatres (elsewhere too, sometimes, but especially around theatres), which was to teach me so much about others and about myself.

What exactly was I anticipating that evening that I should be in such an effervescent state? I don't remember, of course. I recall, however, that I found as much as I'd expected, perhaps more, in the little church of Saint-Julien-le-Pauvre and in Notre Dame, both of which I'd known first of all through great writers; perhaps this is the case with everyone.

My impatience as I sat waiting was almost painful. The curtain rose. Another shameful confession I'm about to make is that I don't recall what play I saw this first time at the Théâtre Français. I remember other plays I saw there, particularly Racine's *Athalie* with Vera Korène, which I saw on another trip to Paris and which enchanted me. But I've retained nothing of what passed on the stage on my first evening at the Théâtre Français except the sight of an old, fat, pot-bellied little actor lending his ridiculous propor- tions to the young hero of the play. He had a voice that could shake the whole building, however. He used it without the least variation, beginning each alexandrine as deep as a voice can descend and rising from one pitch to the next till he reached such a shrill note it made you imagine he was hurling it at you from the top of a tower. Up...down...up...down. Up and down the scale he went, over and over, trembling on his little old legs. His phrasing would start with a kind of subterranean rumble and end with clarion calls from the ramparts. I really couldn't follow the play at all, I was so preoccupied with the elderly young star's antics. In Winnipeg I'd known a French lady, formerly with the Comédie Française, she said, who used to declaim La Fontaine's simple, homespun fables in the same way.

I cast a shy smile around me, looking for smiles of complicity to reinforce my impression that I was watching something ludi- crous, but saw only solemn and respectful faces. Dear heaven, was I the only one in the world to see things as I saw them? If so, my solitude was worse than I'd sometimes suspected. I even suppressed my silly urge to laugh, an urge which rather frightened me since it had almost turned to hysteria in the elevator.

All the same, a few days later I hurried back to see Rostand's *Cyrano*. I knew long passages by heart, which I must have recited

myself with a certain grandiloquence, perhaps at the time thinking them noble and uplifting. But it left me very ill at ease to see Cyrano mortally wounded, yet hours later still standing, still thrusting out his sword and long nose and speechifying. If this was drama, I thought, I'd never believe in it. It was too contrived. Too overdone. Or else I was wrong for it. Little by little this was becoming evident. What was difficult was admitting it. For I was here in Paris to study drama, or so I tried to make myself believe. What other reason could I have to stay?

To make matters worse, Madame Jouve, to whom I'd confided something of my plans to study drama, kept needling me. "You won't get anywhere just dragging your feet around Paris," she scolded me. I had finally emerged from my room and was now tramping endlessly about the city, venting my indecision and doubts about myself. "Come now, child, you're not going to settle your mind that way." In which she was mistaken, for it's often while wandering alone in strange cities that I've best been able to settle my mind, though along lines other than those I had thought I should follow, almost always better ones.

"It's just struck me," she said one day, "why shouldn't you go and make enquiries at the Atelier? They say that Charles Dullin takes students and that he's absolutely extraordinary."

I was caught in my own trap and I'd have to go through with it if I was going to keep a shred of self-respect.

Was it she or I who made the appointment? In any event, the fateful afternoon arrived and I went to Dullin's theatre. There was a rehearsal of *Volpone* by Ben Jonson going on, Jules Romains's adaptation as I recall. On the stage amid the dust and ropes and trappings that lie about at rehearsal time was a curtained four-poster bed. Its drawn curtains were flapping furiously as though in a windstorm, or from a struggle going on inside. I didn't know the play. I had no idea what could be shaking the bed that way. Uncomfortably, I watched the curtains billow, rise almost to the ceiling, then fall back all limp and quivering. Someone called from the stage as I stood in the semi-darkness:

"You're looking for someone?"

I mumbled a frightened reply about an appointment.

"Who with?"

"Monsieur Dullin."

Out of the bed popped a short man, crippled it seemed to me, and rather ugly. He scowled at me from under heavy, dishevelled eyebrows. I've never seen Charles Dullin anywhere else so I can't say whether it was he or Volpone I met face to face.

He spoke to me from the stage, his voice reaching me as though from a world incredibly far off and very different from real life.

"You're the young Canadian who asked to see me? Where are you from? Have you done any theatre?"

I thought about our innocent little tours to tiny villages in Manitoba at twilight time, seeing in particular the lonely country roads around Otterburne, though why these I don't know. At this moment I'd have given anything to be back there out of sight, back in the state I'd been in before having the ridiculous temerity to approach the great Charles Dullin, to what end, dear Lord, I no longer had any idea.

"A little, in St-Boniface in Manitoba," I ventured at the back of the empty hall, which made my voice sound very hollow.

At this point someone onstage laughed, probably an extra. At me or perhaps my accent, I had the impression. Or perhaps at "St-Boniface in Manitoba," which may have sounded as comical as "Timbuctu in Mauretania" to Parisian ears.

"Come on then! Come up here!" Dullin-Volpone called. "You're going to do a little mime for us to show us what you can do, using your imagination. Anything at all. Whatever you like. Come along now!"

I would have chosen death at that moment, or at least torture on the rack, rather than go up there on the stage and do a pantomime. My throat was tight and there wasn't a drop of saliva in my mouth, yet I didn't dare cross the old tyrant who, I learned later, was in fact the most kind-hearted of men.

I might well have mounted to the stage even so. But then luckily – or unluckily, depending on one's point of view – the telephone rang offstage. Someone shouted, "Dullin, it's for you!" Dullin shouted to me, "Just a minute! I'll be back." Onstage, two other actors found some reason to turn their backs. Apparently there was still someone in the bed, a woman as far as I could tell, but for the time being she was quiet, now and then saying only, *"Oh la la! Oh la la!"* I threw a glance behind me. There was no one to block my way. The door was even open still. It made an embrasure framed

in darkness, a little rectangle of tranquil street, almost pastoral, with a plane tree so close it seemed to be half inside the theatre. If I've retained such a sharp picture of this view of the street, it must be because I wanted so badly to be at liberty out there. I began with great caution to back away towards it. Then, hearing Dullin-Volpone raise his voice saying, "Ah yes, that's the way it goes. We'll talk again...," I moved more quickly. I reached the door. I stepped outside. In fact, I must confess, I fled.

I think I even ran for a bit as though in danger of being caught. At last I calmed down, only to realize that if I'd escaped by the skin of my teeth I couldn't escape my own self-judgement, which was savage. Now I was fleeing in earnest, walking and walking for hours without really knowing where I was going, just straight ahead. Madame Jouve was worried to see me come in so late. When she asked me where I could have got to I didn't know what to say.

The state of mind I'd been in would recur fairly frequently in my life. You run, either to lose yourself or to find yourself. It becomes so unbearable, I suppose, that it numbs your mind and leaves you only half aware of what's around you. I came home from Dullin's theatre in this condition. I didn't breathe a word of my adventure, and seeing my face no one dared ask me about it. And for a long time I tried to make myself believe it hadn't happened.

THE NEXT DAY I resumed my long walks through Paris, still with no plan in mind. A fact I had to face up to was that I hadn't fled the Atelier merely because I was terrified of getting up on the stage and giving a pantomime. Something bigger had taken me by the shoulders and pushed me out of there to save me from a destiny I wasn't suited for...a course that wasn't right for me. But then, if the theatre wasn't right for me, what was I doing in Paris? I think I learned then that a certain kind of lonesomeness is better left to itself than surrounded with advice and consolation. In the mass of strangers in the streets I disappeared with my misery about what I ought to be accomplishing in life, whatever that was. I tramped through whole districts of Paris feeling that I'd seen and heard absolutely nothing, enclosed in a kind of vacuum that I kept as tightly sealed as I could from the humanity pressing around me. The anguish I'd be exposed to otherwise would be just too great.

Years later, however, speech intonations, sounds, smells by the

thousand would come back to me from these long walks. I'd see in precise detail a sign at a certain street corner, or the form of a taverner standing in the door of his bistro, beret pulled down over his brow. I had a faculty for storing away details that would be useful to me later, doing it unconsciously, blindly, one might say, thinking all the while that I'd come to Paris just to waste my time. In the long run wasting time has often proved to be its most profitable use for me, but I wasn't conscious of this either yet and kept berating myself bitterly.

BUT THERE were moments. One of those long walks took me to a street whose name I forget, where I looked up at the playbills outside a small theatre and met the beautiful, compassionate eyes of Ludmilla Pitoëff. I stopped to look longer. They were a little sad, the eyes of someone who knows about life, and as they returned my gaze I thought I saw the same warmth towards me that I instinctively felt towards her. Suddenly my indecision, my beating around the bush, my lack of clearheadedness about myself and my inability to get a grip on what I wanted seemed less ridiculous. Ludmilla Pitoëff's big, rather sorrowful eyes were telling me that she herself had known this kind of confusion, that none of us can ever be sure we won't find ourselves in such a state.

The playbill was announcing *The Seagull* by Chekhov. I knew Chekhov through his fine short stories, particularly "The Steppe". But I'd never heard of Georges and Ludmilla Pitoëff.

I'm not sure whether it was evening or still daylight. I seem to remember some bright foliage stirring gently near the beautiful face on the playbill, but I may only be associating a rustling sound with colour. In any event, as though someone had led me by the hand to this friendly little theatre, it was play time when I arrived. I went in. I bought my ticket. I sat down, part of a small, scattered audience. I was as much at ease in this theatre as I'd been apprehensive in Dullin's. The curtain rose. And I was enthralled.

To me this woman, this Ludmilla, wasn't an actress playing a role on a stage, interpreting a character. She *was* the Seagull, come to endure her lot in life before our eyes. Georges Pitoëff, his voice breaking and his face a weary mask, was simply a man, Russian or of any nationality, selected by chance from the overcrowded ranks of day-to-day monotony. Day-to-day existence lived and

222

breathed here as never before, in fact, showing itself to be more powerful than the tumult of high drama, no doubt because it's so much closer to us. The words that gave it life were neither over-blown nor insignificant; they didn't even seem studied, though they must have been carefully chosen to sound so genuinely usual. You'd have said they were words any of us might say on any ordinary day, interspersed with sighs and silences just as in life, where a faraway look through a window suddenly says more than words. As soon as I've heard this ring of truth, how beautiful I've found it, whether in real life or in the theatre. Perhaps most of all in the theatre, which teaches us to look more perceptively at life, to see it laid bare before our eyes in clear daylight. Better than I could have done myself, I felt this performance expressing my own loneliness, my almost constant bewilderment wherever I was, our inability to understand ourselves, all seen through a fine mist of tears, not really bitter ones, almost sweet. Tears welled in my own eyes. I suppose they came from the curious happiness we feel at hearing ourselves expressed so perfectly.

At one point, as we often do when moved, instinctively trying to catch another eye in order to share an impression, I half turned towards a shy-looking young man beside me. Our eyes met and his were wet like mine. "Isn't it beautiful!" we both observed. And the joy that perhaps had brought as large a lump to his throat as to mine in the darkness and silence seemed now to set us free, to lift us in a kind of radiance.

Several times during the play we shared our feelings about it with a whispered word or simply a glance.

"That's what life is like for most people," he breathed in an undertone, simply, quietly, succinctly. "Chekhov's great talent is that he gives life to characters who don't stand out much in a crowd."

At intermission we went outside and walked a little together in front of the theatre. Recalling this, I know beyond possible doubt that it was afternoon, because at the end of the short street I can suddenly and quite distinctly see the tree whose rustling I've been hearing all this time. Still, there are extraordinary blanks in my memory. For example, I really can't picture the young man's face but I can hear him very clearly, always close, speaking in a voice that matched our rather hesitant steps.

He'd come from a village in the Ardèche to study literature at the Sorbonne. He wasn't adapting well to Paris. Until now he'd been feeling absolutely alone here, but he'd recognized himself in Chekhov's world almost as if he were at home.

Then I told him a bit about St-Boniface and how I had dreamed for so long while there of coming to Paris but now had no idea why, which made me hate it.

"That happens to everybody, though," he said.

A bell rang calling us back to our places. The lights went out. Once again we were caught up in the sweet magic of what was really most ordinary. We looked at each other in the darkness several times again, our eyes sometimes moist, sometimes shining with the beautiful things we were hearing. In two and a half hours the stranger beside me became closer to me than almost anyone I'd known before. Did he in his loneliness find me as miraculously close to him?

There was another brief pause in the performance, during which we resumed our conversation.

"How is it," I said, "that a voice that's really as tragic as Chekhov's is so comforting?"

"Because it tells the truth," he replied softly, "and the truth, even if it's tragic, even if it's cruel, is always more comforting than illusions or lies."

When we left we walked a little more together, along with a small crowd of playgoers which quickly dispersed.

With his head on one side he said, "That's the way writing should be, neither louder nor softer. Chekhov found just the note to touch the soul. All his words have their source in a human being's sensitivity. There isn't one that's pretentious. Not one that's false."

"It can't be easy to do," I said. "Why is saying what's true the hardest thing in the world?"

"It is indeed," he replied. "When we start writing we all tend to inflate our voices, try to impress, make ourselves something we aren't. The right note...perhaps one has to have searched all one's life only to find it in the end...."

At this point our hands moved shyly, perhaps as if to join, but a passerby brushed between us, thrusting us apart.

We came to my bus stop. He was going to continue on foot, back to his "hole in the wall" nearby. When I stopped he hesitated

a moment, seeming to be on the point of suggesting something...perhaps just that I might walk a bit farther with him in the
softly approaching darkness. I wanted this more than anything
else, but he lifted his hat and wished me good luck in Paris and in
life...then drew away as if reluctantly. A little farther on, however,
he stopped and turned. I was still waiting in line to get on the bus.
Our eyes met one last time. No doubt too shy to come back, he
raised his hand in a kind of wave and I replied with an equally
mournful gesture. He walked on and soon disappeared among the
other people in the street. One would have said that Chekhov,
having brought us together, had doomed us to the fate of so many
of his characters, vacillating, lost in indecision, incapable of reaching
out unreservedly to one another with a spontaneity that would set
them free.

IV

I NEVER KNEW where I stood with Paris, the cat-city, as Ionesco so aptly called it. One day for no reason at all it would bare its claws and scratch me, and the next it would touch me with a kittenish paw, equally without reason, just because summer was lingering or the sky was kind. I might be rankling from some rebuff when it would disarm me with a toothless smile from an old crone in carpet slippers or the sight of so many flowers on display. I might be warming to it and beginning to think I was happy when I'd get one of those rebukes that so many Parisians use so devastatingly.

Even so, I can't ever forget that I made my first important discovery about myself in Paris; I've never totally lost sight of this.

That day there had been nothing to prepare me for it. I was coming home joylessly in a crowded bus. It was rush hour. Exhausted, the little people of Paris were congregating in weary columns or tight little clusters at almost every bus stop. I followed my compatriot's advice and took a number from the machine. I still don't know if the right it gave was "priority" or "precedence", but "precedence" fits the situation so well I can't help liking it better. I'd no sooner taken my ticket than I realized I was on the wrong side of the street – my bus was just then drawing up on the opposite side. A dense crowd milled about, the conductor standing on the bus platform shouting "Number?" and everybody shouting a number in answer. Each time I saw this incredible scene replayed I was stupefied, but also filled with a kind of admiration to think that every day in Paris little courts of justice held sway in hundreds of places at once, the conductor filling the role of referee, dispenser of justice, and sermonizer, and the injured parties consisting of pregnant women, wounded war veterans, mothers with babes in

arms, unaccompanied old folk, and a few malingerers. All of which, of course, did nothing to improve the bus service.

Without a second thought I bounded across the street and joined the harassed little crowd. The conductor called, "Sixty-eight.... Is there anyone before that?" To which a weak voice replied, straining to be heard from the back, "Sixty-five." "Sixty-five...," bawled the conductor. Then came my call, triumphant in the certainty that for once I was a winner: "Seventeen!" "Seventeen!" exclaimed the conductor. "Make way, *m'sieurs-dames*. Come forward, seventeen." The crowd, suitably impressed, parted as it might have for the maimed and halt. Mine was the last available place, standing shoulder to shoulder with others on the bus platform. The conductor fastened a light rope across the rear entrance, which I imagine was supposed to keep us from tipping off at corners. Suddenly intrigued, he held out his hand and took my number.

"Well I never!" he cried, choking with indignation. "I should have thought as much!" he turned to my fellow passengers, saying, "Some people think they're clever. They go and take a number on the other side of the street, then come and get in the crowd on this side. Is that right now?" The passengers he was addressing gave me a vaguely disapproving look, then left me to my fate. He continued, addressing me directly: "You deserve to be put off, little lady. If you ever do that again you won't get off so lightly, make sure you get that into your head!" I did my best to shrink out of sight in the mass of humanity, but he kept his eyes on me and persisted, "They begin one day by taking a place from some poor mother who's hurrying home to put on the soup, then the next...." As I raised my eyes to him in supplication, to my astonishment he winked at me and carried right on in the same indignant tone, "then the next, it's from one of our country's war heroes...." Backs weary, shoulders jostling other shoulders, faces vacant, the passengers paid no more heed to his harangue than to the buzzing of a fly. Finally he wearied of it himself and seemed to drift away in reverie for a while, gazing at a patch of sky far behind the bus.

From the moment I ran across the street the entire little scene had taken perhaps three or four minutes, but to me it had seemed interminable and it had left my nerves tied in a large knot. Little by little, however, I began to feel better, lulled by the rocking of

the bus and perhaps yielding to the contagion of my neighbours' drowsiness. You'd swear some were asleep on their feet, eyes open but heads empty of thought.

We were arriving at the Place de la Concorde. I craned my neck, trying to catch at least a glimpse between the close-packed heads and shoulders. The stately square had come to represent what I valued most about Paris. It was like a piece of my native prairie, for which my soul yearned deeply here. Its broad expanse in the heart of the cramped city always brought me peace. I would suddenly have a feeling of relief. And the stone statuary enclosing the space perhaps made it seem even bigger and more open. I had never crossed it without beginning to picture what it would be like in a driving, swirling Canadian snowstorm. I used to imagine how beautiful it would be to watch the progress of the white furor.

Peering between the close-packed heads, I'd caught my glimpse of this marvellous space. Then while the bus took a sharp turn which would have flung us on top of each other if we hadn't been packed so tightly, I had a fleeting view of the Tuileries Gardens. As brief as it was, it showed me the pond with children playing around it, the impeccable rows of round-headed chestnut trees, and down at the far, far end, a fiery red sky, extending the space to infinity. It was just like the flaming sunsets at the end of the lane behind the house on Deschambault Street when I was a child, which opened a path I was sure must reach the edge of the world. An incandescent ray from the far horizon even touched my face. It moved me so deeply I turned to see its reflection on the faces around me, forgetting I'd been an object of scorn in their midst only minutes before. Weariness and gloom were all I saw, preoccupation with cares or the bad news in an open newspaper. Apparently no one else had seen the glorious display of sunset at its most intense. In that instant the city had revealed itself to me, the eager stranger, not to its own with their jaded eyes. And I, marvel as I might, didn't know what to do with it. I would need to marvel many more times yet, uselessly one could say, before learning how to share my wonder with others.

What I can't forget is that seeing the beautiful garden of Paris illuminated by a sun straight from my prairies made me realize I had a faculty for observation I hadn't really been aware of before, together with an infinite longing to know what to do with it.

AFTER MY misadventure at Dullin's Atelier, I can hardly believe I could still have imagined I was cut out for the theatre and kept trying to involve myself in it. I must have been very hard of hearing. Or else I was obeying some vague directive to make sure that all doors were closed to me in this direction, thus forcing me to turn finally to the right one. Whichever it was, shortly after my heady afternoon of Chekhov I wrote a long, rather overwrought letter to Ludmilla Pitoëff, like the ones I quite often get nowadays from bewildered young people who don't really know what to expect of themselves or of life. Into it I poured my admiration for her talent, my own disarray, and the doubts and indecision I was living with; a kind of plea for help, in fact. The effort I put into it no doubt cured me for ever of writing this kind of letter, for I don't remember ever again writing to a stranger in the hope of receiving my salvation.

When I'd finished my letter I hurried to the theatre and left it with the cashier, terrified I'd tear it up if I allowed myself a moment of reflection, I suppose. When the cashier asked if I'd like to wait for a reply, since Madame Pitoëff happened to be inside just then, I shook my head in alarm and fled with almost as much haste as I had from Dullin's.

What was I most afraid of, a rebuff or an invitation? Now that I understand myself better I think I was really hoping for a rebuff – or silence – which would have protected me from trying anything else of the kind, letting me believe that I'd done everything possible and that if I'd failed it wasn't my doing but because of adverse circumstances. In short, I was letting my fate be decided by events, a weakness in my nature which has shown itself too often in the course of my life.

When I'd deposited my letter and scurried away, I wandered this way and that once again, still wallowing in my uncertainties. As I had so many times before, I came finally to the Luxembourg Gardens, not far from Madame Jouve's. Near exhaustion, I would often sit down among the old women who used to come there with their knitting, occupying the same chairs day after day. I would also see the same children day after day, engrossed in sailing their frail little paper boats. This tranquil pause in the heart of the high-strung city used to soothe me almost without fail. But this time nothing could soothe me.

THE MINUTE I set foot in the apartment Madame Jouve rushed to meet me in great excitement.

"Where were you? We've been looking for you for hours! Madame Pitoëff's personal secretary has called twice. She finally left a message and I wrote it down. Here, on this piece of paper.... Tomorrow at rehearsal time you're to come to this theatre. Madame Pitoëff will see you."

Was I happy? Or apprehensive? I don't really know any more.

The next day I arrived at the Pitoëffs' theatre in a very odd frame of mind, ecstatic that Madame Ludmilla was willing to see me but also worried sick over what I was going to have to confess to her.

She was in the middle of rehearsing *La Sauvage* by Anouilh, another author she played a great deal, I believe. As soon as she'd been told I was there she broke off the rehearsal and came down from the stage to where I was sitting in the empty theatre. She smiled as she sat down in the next seat. In the half-darkness I saw her small, delicate face searching mine. She told me she'd been very moved by my letter. So had Georges. When they'd read it again last evening they'd both felt very warmly towards the little French-speaking provinces in the heart of faraway Canada, where the people were still struggling so hard not to lose their fragile bond with France. They'd like to help me, give me guidance if I wanted, but they didn't take students. However, they were prepared to let me attend rehearsals as often as I liked, so that I'd gradually learn at least how a play is produced. Would this be of some use? Did I think I'd benefit from it?

Disconcerted, I remained silent. She asked me then what exactly it was I wanted.

What exactly I wanted. That was the trouble! The further I went the less I seemed to know. Even now when Madame Ludmilla was being so kind, offering me a rare opportunity in the theatre, I was racked with anxiety, still not knowing whether I should or should not accept. In the half-darkness she must have seen signs in my face of the torment you feel when you can't see any way clear ahead of you – in contrast to the courage you have when your course is visible, however difficult it looks. Impulsively she put her hand on mine and gave it a sympathetic squeeze.

"Poor child! Of course you don't know! How could you when you've just arrived in this big seething city from your faraway

St-Boniface! I felt lost here myself for such a long time. Lost...
lost...," she repeated plaintively as if she'd never forgotten the
horror. "Even now, if it weren't for Georges and the children...."

She paused, remembering some difficult hurdles she'd crossed,
I think, then came back to her suggestion.

"Come to rehearsals anyway in the meantime. Even if you don't
yet know what you want, they might help you find out. You'll see
your way come clear little by little, believe me."

WITH THE HOPE she'd inspired in me that I really would see my
way clear eventually, I came to rehearsals...eight, ten, a dozen
times. I don't know how many. I was faithful at first in any case.

I always sat more or less in the same place in the middle of the
empty hall. I'd see the actors moving about the stage reading their
cues and probably their movements from little notebooks each held.
Now and then I'd hear Georges admonishing Ludmilla, "No, no,
love, not like that. Listen, you have to get more inside the character...." Try as I might to follow it all and take an interest, I
became depressed. Nearly deserted theatres have always depressed
me with their actors in street clothes groping earnestly for their
characters, and ropes, pulleys, and all the paraphernalia of a play
in plain view. Never would even a very clumsy attempt at writing
bring me such a desolate feeling, perhaps basically because there's
so much less paraphernalia involved in writing than in the theatre,
or else it's a different, subtler kind you hardly notice. But most
distressing of all was discovering such a contrived reverse side, so
to speak, of what I'd found so convincing and wondrous. I might
even like Chekhov less, I thought, if I saw him taken apart and
slowed down this way.

One day I skipped the rehearsal and two days later I skipped it
again and spent the time instead with my old women in the Luxembourg Gardens. With great relief I sat listening to them talking
about everyday things among themselves over their knitting. The
more I saw of the theatre, the more I was drawn by people's simple,
everyday lives and their everyday language; it was so full of rich
discoveries, all so alive and real. Though I didn't realize it, I was
approaching what would prove to be the right, the only school for
me.

I skipped another rehearsal. After that I was afraid to come face

to face with Ludmilla. To escape Madame Jouve's remonstrances I'd go out at the same hours to make it look as though I were going to my rehearsals, but what I was doing was wandering aimlessly about the city. Aimlessly? Not entirely, perhaps, for without conscious effort but with increasing attention I was eavesdropping from door to door, from chair to chair, listening to the voices that tell us about life. But I still couldn't see the way ahead of me any more clearly.

V

AUTUMN IN PARIS was radiant. At least I had mild weather, a kindly sky, and warm rays of sunshine wherever I went. My little beige suit of warm wool with a matching cape to throw around my shoulders in the cooler hours had so far been adequate for my daytime and evening rambles. It became cold late in October, however, and I went to the basement to get my three-quarter-length coat of rabbit fur dyed to look like otter from my trunk. Remembering the problems with the timed lights on my first descent below ground, I borrowed a flashlight from Madame Jouve. It may seem strange that I'd left my trunk alone in its dungeon with such misgiving and then let six weeks go by without going to make sure it was still there. But this was the way it was. Learning to cope with Paris, my persistent uncertainty over what I should be studying, my recurrent, agonizing suspicion that I had no talent and had been deceiving myself with hopes of expanded horizons, all this had so obsessed me that I was spared all other worries.

I walked along the earth-floored corridor with my flashlight beam reaching only a short way ahead of me. This time it was the silence of these cellars which most unnerved me; it was so total I could hear myself breathe. I came to Madame Jouve's locker. Immediately the catastrophe was apparent. The padlock was partly torn off and the iron-barred door was wide open. And my trunk wasn't there! I drew back in dismay. I made sure the number was the right one. No doubt about it, my trunk had been stolen!

I ran back upstairs, raised Madame Jouve, who was perhaps in the middle of a French lesson, and told her the news in a panic-stricken voice which probably everyone in the apartment could hear. Madame Jouve took me aside, begging me to lower my voice so as not to alarm the other boarders and to try to calm down.

Nevertheless, she went at once to get her coat and set off with me for the police station.

As we rode on the bus, Madame Jouve asked me over and over, "You're quite sure you found the door open? You're sure it was your trunk that was missing?"

The constable who interviewed us listened to Madame Jouve explain why we'd come. Then he handed me a long sheet of paper and an old-fashioned pen and sat me down at a bare table.

"Mademoiselle," he instructed me, "write on this paper the entire list of contents of the trunk you declare to have been stolen."

"The list of all there was in my trunk?" I cried in extreme dismay. "That's impossible! It'll take me hours and hours, just trying to remember!"

"To whatever extent possible," he insisted severely.

I sat down, like a suspect about to be interrogated, under a bare, weak lightbulb hanging by its wire from the ceiling. At the long prisoners' table, my bad pen-nib tearing at the paper, I began to write: one coat, rabbit fur dyed dark brown, one navy-blue suit with silver buttons, two pairs of shoes, one brown, one blue to go with the suit.... As the list lengthened, I felt myself sinking into a depression which this time seemed bottomless. I think the reason was less that my clothes had been stolen than discovering suddenly that things I'd paid dearly for, considering my means, weren't really worth much, a pauper's frippery, but they were all I possessed.

As I sat writing, an argument of some kind arose between the constable and Madame Jouve. He was inscribing her replies to his questions and when he'd come to my address Madame Jouve had replied, "With me, at number...."

"So," he concluded, "I'll put you down as landlady."

"Not at all!" protested Madame Jouve. "I'm not a landlady."

At first I didn't pay much attention. I'd just remembered a beautiful little pale ivory satin collar. I'd bought it to brighten up a dark dress one day when I needed to restore my spirits by splurging a bit. Maman, as soon as she examined it, knew it was expensive and demanded almost angrily, "How much did you pay for this? Too much, I'm sure." I was ashamed of being extravagant when she had so little for running the house and I didn't dare tell her. "How much?" she insisted. In the end I told her, shrinking the figure a mite, "Three dollars." She turned pale. "Three dollars!

When I could have made you one just as lovely for less than half the price!"

The incident was one I would have liked to blot out of my life. The reproach, forgotten then brought so vividly to life again, was holding me motionless, pen poised, gazing gloomily into the distance, when I became aware that the constable and Madame Jouve were still arguing.

"You take in boarders and you're not a landlady?"

"I have guests...."

They now had my attention. I turned my head to them. Madame Jouve so detested the taint of commercialism that she used to ask us to have our correspondents address their letters "care of Madame Jouve."

"I am not a landlady, Monsieur!" I heard her say with some heat.

"Yet you've just told me the young lady boards with you. Does she board with you or doesn't she?"

"In a sense, if you like," Madame Jouve allowed, "but I'm not her landlady. I'm responsible for these young ladies. I give them guidance in their studies...."

"And you're going to tell me you do all that for nothing?"

Absorbed though I was with my own distress, I almost pitied Madame Jouve as she fought tooth and nail not to have the abhorrent word appear in the record as her occupation. I felt for her. She had pride. She was making a living in a courageous way, giving a great deal of herself, and she really was far more to us than merely our landlady. But she was trapped, as I had also been so many times, by the merciless logic of the French.

"My young ladies give me something for their meals and their share of the rent, of course, but I don't so much give them board and lodging as...."

"Mademoiselle," the constable said to me, "do you board at Madame Jouve's?"

"I live at Madame Jouve's."

"For nothing? The way you would at your aunt's?"

"Not for nothing...exactly...."

"So you pay for your room and board, you board at Madame Jouve's, therefore Madame Jouve is your landlady, there are no two ways about it. What are you then, Madame, if not a landlady?"

"Oh, for heaven's sake!" exclaimed Madame Jouve with a contained kind of disgust, "You can put me down as former teacher, Lycée..., titular professor of French at the University of...."

She stopped, too aggrieved to keep up the fight.

"All right then, Monsieur, put down 'landlady' if you don't know any better."

"The question is not what you have been or could be, Madame, if you'll forgive me, but what your present occupation is for the record."

I left them to their argument, which didn't seem about to end, and turned back to my list. Now I wasn't sure I'd brought the little ivory satin collar after all. Perhaps I'd forgotten it or decided to leave it at home. At home? Somewhere behind, that meant. Then suddenly I remembered my medals. I'd brought all of them with me in the trunk.

Walls and passage of time at once disappeared. I was far away from Paris. The journey hadn't taken place. I was still safe and sound in St-Boniface. I hadn't yet caused any grief for anyone. It was months before I was due to leave but I already had my trunk and was so delighted I couldn't resist putting some of my things in it already. Maman must have looked now and then when I wasn't there to see what I'd packed. One day she confronted me, very agitated, her finger raised in accusation.

"You're going to take your medals over there! Why? What good are they going to do you in Paris? You'll have them stolen!"

I held my ground.

"But why? Why?"

I couldn't tell her what I had in mind, of course: the medals were gold and if I fell on really hard times in Paris I could always sell them to keep body and sold together for a while, until....

She raised the subject a hundred times over.

"Leave them with me so I can take care of them."

I was just as obstinate, not even trying to understand why she was so determined to keep them.

"What good will they be to you?" I always retorted.

Now, at the other side of the world, I had the answer to this silly question and was filled with remorse for being so stupid. With the medals lost Maman's reward was lost and also, in a way, the special joy I'd been to her.

"Why, oh why didn't I leave my medals at home!" I groaned aloud, forgetting for the moment where I was.

The argument between the constable and Madame Jouve came abruptly to an end. They both looked at me in consternation, their faces keenly sympathetic.

"Your medals! Lost! Oh my poor child!" Madame Jouve cried with feeling.

The constable's manner was now fatherly and he studied me with a kind of friendly but sorrowful expression. Perhaps he had a daughter who'd also won medals, who was his pride and joy....

"Medals meaning prizes for achievement, for good conduct...?" he asked in a solicitous, almost familiar tone.

"Yes, and for history and literature and French...."

"For French! In a country that's all English! Just think of that! Mademoiselle must have been quite a student!"

"Mademoiselle," put in Madame Jouve, "has remained faithful to the language of France in faraway America with a perseverance that deserves our admiration." Afflicted as I already was with remorse, her pride in me left me more disconsolate than ever.

The constable approached and put his hand on my shoulder.

"We'll find your medals for you, Mademoiselle," he said. "Just let me get my hands on whoever took them and he'll pay for it!"

The most extraordinary part of the story is that he did indeed get his hands on the thief, a boy of fifteen who, when he saw he was caught, panicked and tried to dispose of the medals by throwing them through a sewer grate. So their fate was to travel the same course I'd seen in my crazy nightmares of subterranean adventure on my first night in Paris, perhaps stirred up partly because I had left my trunk all alone in its dungeon.

I learned the epilogue only a year later when I was passing through Paris on my return from London.

AFTER I'D REFLECTED on the matter, it occurred to me that the trunk couldn't have been taken out of the building without the watchman's knowledge. By day, when the iron gate was open, he watched constantly from his cubicle beside it. At night he had to come from his room to open it. So I went down and asked him whether he'd seen anyone going out with my trunk.

"Your beautiful trunk from America? Never! I'd have known

it! There isn't another one like it in the whole neighbourhood. It can't have left here, Mademoiselle."

So it was just as I'd thought since I'd decided to do my own investigation. I borrowed Madame Jouve's flashlight and went to the basement. Perhaps a hundred feet beyond our own locker, inside another with its door open, I discovered my trunk, lying on its side, the lock broken, the drawers pulled out, and my belongings strewn about the floor. They were all there too, except my medals and the little jewel box Fernand had given me. In a way losing this hurt almost as much as losing my medals. I went back upstairs, feeling a little better to have recovered my fur coat and some other badly needed clothes and probably pleased besides to have been more expeditious than the police – which wasn't so hard in cases of petty thievery like this.

Madame Jouve, however, was disturbed by my sleuthing. It was her understanding that having signed a complaint at the police station I had no right to retake possession of my things, even though I'd recovered them myself. I groused but eventually had to go back to the police station and cross virtually everything off my patiently detailed list except item: gold medals and item: jewel box.

The poor little jewel box thus achieved a kind of immortality because as far as I know it's still recorded on some slip in the records of the Paris police. I was sharply reprimanded by the constable on duty that day moreover for having regained possession of my goods without police authorization, which made me liable to a fine, but more particularly, I think, for having been ahead of the police with my investigation below ground.

Perhaps I'd become thick-skinned or was too preoccupied with my self-reproach, but in any case the constable's reproofs hardly bothered me at all. I suppose I was insulated from minor hurts by a deepening state of depression.

The real cause of my melancholy wasn't losing my medals; this episode merely made me conscious of being increasingly discontented since my flight from Dullin's theatre. Despite moments of elation such as I'd felt at seeing the transfiguration of the Tuileries Gardens, I was feeling more ill at ease in Paris all the time. It was becoming too much for me. I was sure I wouldn't achieve anything worthwhile here. I began to tell myself I'd probably come to the wrong place. London would perhaps be better.

I had spent a few days in London on my way to Paris in September, the loveliest time of the year, and now it seemed to me that those days had been sheer delight. I'd been shown around by a friend, a young and very talented violinist who'd come from Winnipeg to study at the Royal Academy of Music. This glimpse gave me enough to dream about for a long time. We saw Hyde Park, the lions in Trafalgar Square, Kew Gardens; we poled in a punt on the Thames to Hampton Court; in short, nothing outside the usual tourist circuit, at first anyway. Yet our recollections and persistent dreams are so dependent on first impressions that although the city rarely saw the light of a clear sky at the time, the London I remembered was tenderly sunny, everything bathed in the rosy colour of enchantment. The sun even seemed to be shining on the metopes and ancient Assyrian statues in the British Museum which my friend Bohdan took me to see.

Afterwards, it's true, we did find more of the really entrancing side of London. One evening we went to see *Tobias and the Angel* at the open-air theatre in Regent's Park, with accompaniment provided by the big cats in the zoo next door roaring in their cages, made nervous by an approaching storm. The minute a few drops of rain began to fall a hawker appeared, renting out sturdy woollen blankets at a shilling apiece. Bohdan took one, with which we made a kind of tent, sitting with our heads close and the blanket draped over them. Soon, with almost the whole audience sheltered similarly, the place looked like an encampment. Toby and his dog continued their peregrinations with the rain now falling heavily, seeming to be part of the production.

I felt that everything about my short sojourn in London had been charming and delightful. I told myself that if I was going to return to Manitoba later, as seemed inevitable, I'd do better to study in London than in Paris. Bohdan thought so. He had been writing me saying that I could enroll in a school of drama while taking private lessons in French from an excellent coach he'd been enquiring about for me. Good friend that he was, having read between the lines that I was getting discouraged, he was doing his best to help me with sensible advice. I think this influenced my decision, if one could call it a decision, for I was as restless as the waves of the ocean at the time.

In any event I made up my mind to return to London. Madame

Jouve did all she could to dissuade me. According to her, I was leaving just as I was beginning to settle in. It was pure madness. I was losing everything I'd gained. I was giving up just as my efforts were beginning to bear fruit. If I kept drifting about the world, as I seemed resigned to doing, I'd never amount to anything.

In one sense she was probably right, but not in another. From my gropings, my comings and goings, my aimless wanderings, I learned as I never would have from any straight line I might have followed through pure tenacity.

In November when it was cold, wet, and gloomy, as no doubt my whole life was going to be through my own fault, I embarked on the Calais-to-Dover ferry. The sky was thick with cloud and fog. As the small ship's propeller churned the dark water, gulls cried overhead, close but invisible, expressing so well the pain of departures, and of arrivals. In no time I lost sight of the coast of France. I thought I'd never return and it made me infinitely sadder than I could have imagined.

I would in fact return to France many times. Some of these occasions were the happiest in my life outside Canada; one, probably the best of all, has left me with a glowing memory – of receiving the major literary prize awarded less than ten years later for my first novel. Of these future occasions and the many dear and faithful friends I would make in France, I had no more premonition than I had had of what was awaiting me at the Little Water Hen.

I journeyed for a long time without a compass, but when life itself is the journey, what use is a compass?

VI

STILL WEAK from a devastating case of seasickness, I set foot in London in the worst fog the city had seen for years. Bohdan had found me a room on Wickendon Street in the working-class district of Fulham.

Again I headed towards the unknown with my belongings piled inside a taxi, including my trunk whose lock I'd had repaired after a fashion. We drove through what seemed to be an opaque, unyielding, dirt-coloured cloud. The city was identifiable only through sounds, so deafening in some districts you couldn't tell one from another, so furtive in others they made you think of a blind man feeling his way. The headlights of all the cars and buses were on, but they hardly penetrated the grimy atmosphere at all and looked far away when in fact you were already on top of them. The taxi-driver must have seen many other fogs like this but still took an hour to find Wickendon Street. Oddly, just as we were arriving the dense cloud thinned a little, even formed a kind of clearing around us for a few seconds. As if in a dream, I briefly saw a street of identical two-storey houses, all built of pinkish stone, all surrounded by what looked like reproductions of the same hedge of clipped holly, and in each bay window, identical to the one next door, the same green succulent plant. Then the fog closed again like a curtain across a stage. The street vanished. I wouldn't see it again for more than a week.

With some help from my landlady, Bohdan took my belongings to my room upstairs. He lit my gas heater to show me how it worked. You put a shilling in the slot in the meter, turned the key, and put a lighted match to the jet. This gave enough gas for several hours, after which you had to put another coin in the shilling-hungry slot. He thoughtfully left me a dozen shillings in case I

might run out and suffer from the damp cold which, he said, I should beware of with my susceptible throat. Then he was already leaving, my arrival having come at the worst possible time for him. He'd just been asked to play at the Royal Albert Hall as guest soloist with the London Symphony Orchestra. His future depended on this concert and even if he worked night and day to prepare himself it wouldn't be enough.

"Cheerio! Everything's going to be fine here, you'll see. Poor beginnings always have fine endings."

He was courage itself. He'd left Winnipeg carrying his violin as his only possession. He worked his way over on a cattle boat, tending the animals, shut up with them in the hold in return for his passage. As soon as he reached London he'd found a job with a gypsy orchestra playing for diners in one of the big Lyon's restaurants. He spent his nights cheering the hearts of lonely people and his days practising Bach. When he had twenty-five dollars in his pocket, this being the price of a lesson, he'd seek out what he considered the best violin teacher in London. "Here I am," he would say, "I can pay you for an hour. God knows when I'll be able to afford another." Now, less than a year later, he was on the point of signing a contract with the BBC for a weekly hour-long program.

Yet it seems to me I'd always perceived a foreboding shadow over this frail but remarkably strong young man, this prodigious and tireless worker, who at times could be merrier than anyone else. But perhaps I'm just letting my memories of him be coloured by his tragic death during the war when a bomb burst over the house he was living in, killing all its occupants.

Since he was worried about me though I tried to appear calm and content, before leaving he hurriedly wrote down two or three telephone numbers where I might reach him in case I needed anything. He told me not to hesitate to call if I had the least problem.

I managed to pretend I was sure of myself until he left. But as soon as the door closed I felt as though I were shut away here, through my own fault. I went to the only window in the room which might, I thought, overlook a little garden. I wiped away the condensation but the abominable fog pressed close against the other side of the glass, blocking the view completely. I was perishing with cold only a few steps away from the gas fire. Before I could

feel any heat on my legs I had to get almost close enough to burn myself, and then my back was freezing.

The silence around me was frightful. Apparently I was alone in this strange house except for the landlady, who'd gone back to her kitchen, and she never made the slightest sound to indicate her presence anyway, not even footsteps since she walked around in felt-soled slippers. Have I ever known a more appallingly silent house? No sound outside. No sound inside. Towards evening I heard someone come in very quietly, then perhaps someone else. Footsteps glided towards neighbouring rooms. Water ran. After this I heard nothing more.

I spotted a little teapot in its tea-cosy near the gas fire. On the mantelpiece there was some tea in a tin box, sugar in another, and of course the inevitable dry biscuits in a tin with a rose-covered, thatched Tudor cottage on the lid.

I lit a gas hot-plate beside the fireplace. A short flame sprang up. I put on the kettle. In answer to the sputtering of the gas there was soon a hum from the kettle as the water began to heat. I began to hope the kettle would whistle, in this country a sign of pleasure to come. It didn't whistle. I drank the first of those countless cups of insipid tea that I would make for myself at all hours of the day for weeks on end, perhaps in an effort to warm my body, or my soul.

I sat on the floor as close as I could to the meagre flame in the fireplace, taking what little help it offered. I felt like a lonely cast-away on a desert island in the middle of a white sea which had itself lost all memory of familiar shores. My thoughts went no further than this. I think I soon stopped having thoughts at all. At times, when I've been too completely isolated, hemmed in by too much silence, I've lost even the sense of thinking, as though the frail mechanism of thought – surely always an appeal to others – had jammed somewhere inside me.

HOW LONG WAS I absent this time? A week? Ten days? Two weeks? I lived in a kind of lethargy which I was careful not to break, in terror of letting in some waiting torment. But if I huddled close to my wretched little fire, which I fed with shillings to keep it going, my curious, nameless state of misery was almost bearable. I saw no one and spoke to no one except my landlady.

Early in the morning, an hour when I've never in my life had much appetite, she would enter bringing an unbelievable breakfast consisting of a mountain of pieces of toast – plus the rest of the loaf to slice myself in case I didn't have enough – a pot of marmalade and another of gooseberry jam, butter, cheese, and either eggs and bacon with fried potatoes, or an omelette, boiled eggs, or a fried herring, whose smell alone turned my stomach. The tray was laden further with an enormous pot of tea big enough for at least six cups and a large jug of hot water. She would put it on a small table near the bed, go to the window and open the curtains a little, give a perfunctory glance outside and say, "Foggy again today," then leave. She'd return to get the tray an hour later and finding it almost invariably untouched would comment briefly, neither sympathetically nor disapprovingly, "You don't eat much." At the time of day when I was hungry, she'd return again with a thin slice of ham, a small slice of bread, and nothing else and tell me, always in the same flat, expressionless voice, "You should learn to eat a good breakfast, for in London we don't serve much lunch. But have it your own way."

So in the end I learned to hide some of the excess breakfast to keep for later when I felt like eating. I had caches in the cupboard among my shoes, behind the gas fire, even in my bed, and soon I observed I'd collected enough to eat for the whole day. My landlady, seeing the bread, cheese, and some of the jam and butter gone from the tray, expressed approval with as little feeling as she'd reproached me.

"I see you're eating a sensible breakfast at last."

The next day she added a bowl of porridge and jug of milk to the tray.

I would look at this woman in her drab-coloured clothes, her hair in a hairnet, listen to her saying the same dull things in the same dispassionate voice day after day, and wonder if she was a real person with emotions, senses, hopes, and fears, or if I had an automaton for a landlady.

The rooms around mine really were inhabited, at least in the evening when their occupants came in. I'd listen for sounds that would tell me of human activity. I'd faintly hear a key turning in the front doorlock, almost inaudible footsteps coming up the stairs, another, lighter key-in-lock sound at the door of a room, and this

was all. In their slippers with their tea made, for the rest of the evening the people around me must all have been warming themselves alone at their own miserable little fires, just as I was. I didn't see any of them for nearly a whole week.

It took nothing less than finding myself with my fire out and no shillings left to give me the energy to leave my room at last and go looking for my landlady.

Then, in this house which I'd thought must be half dead, I came to a room that was warm and inviting. A stove was purring. From its oven there rose a delectable smell of roast beef with a pan of Yorkshire pudding, though my landlady had said she made only one meal a day and that was breakfast. There was a man ensconced near the stove, the husband probably, which surprised me because I'd never heard a man's voice in this house. She didn't introduce us. He lowered the paper he was reading just a little and said in the same tone of voice as his wife's, neither warm nor cold, just totally impersonal:

"Evening, Miss," then turned back to his paper.

"How many shillings do you want?" asked the woman.

I'd come downstairs with a one-pound note.

Her only comment was, "That should last you a good long time."

Not as long as all that, I thought, looking enviously at the friendly little stove with its firebox filled with coke. But since neither of them invited me to sit down even for a moment, I went back up to my room. In a city where I'd soon find the most naturally warm, friendly, and talkative people in the world, I had to fall first upon this dour couple and London's most silent house. How often in my life I've first encountered the repellent side of cities, situations, and people! This has been an advantage in a sense because then I could only find things getting better, not worse. Keeping what's good until last has often meant that this is the only memory I'm left with.

One evening I made myself go out. The fog was still as dense as ever. However, I told myself that if I followed the low holly hedges by the sidewalk I could reach the end of the street without getting lost. When I arrived I'd seen a cluster of small shops there, even an Underground station. A glow of illuminated shopfronts, diluting the fog to a slightly thinner consistency, told me I had arrived. I pushed open a fairly well-lit door and found myself in

one of the ABC chain of tea and pastry shops. I didn't have much desire for more tea but I ordered some anyway, with a sticky bun. Here, at least I was eating in the company of a scattering of customers talking among themselves at their tables, and I still remember the comfort I felt in this little bit of human warmth. The sound of voices and the sight of pleasant-looking faces made me feel so much better that I hated to leave.

Finally I was the only customer left and thought I should go. I set off in the direction I'd come from. After a few steps there was no longer any light to guide me and I realized it was going to be impossible to find "my" house. They were already so alike by day, even down to their identical little gardens, how was one to know which was which at night in dense fog except by their numbers? But the numbers were over the doors and I couldn't see them. I'd go up to a door and look carefully, then stand on tiptoe and strike a match. All I could ever see, if anything, was part of a number.

I wandered from door to door, feeling the way I'd felt in the Gare Saint-Lazare, that I'd never find my way out of this impasse. Once again my weary spirit formed a picture of what life was going to be like for me in Paris, London, or anywhere else.

Suddenly I heard a man's footsteps. Danger? Salvation? One of those muggers I'd been warned about so often who prey on women alone in the fog? But perhaps a Good Samaritan! "Help!" I called. A voice replied, "Coming!" and almost immediately a ruddy-faced bobby appeared, identifying himself with his powerful flashlight.

"Lost, Miss? And a mean night 'tis to be lost in!"

He had a pleasant, open face as far as I could see, but what struck me instantly and forcefully was his speech: old world, colourful, and extremely literary. Time and again in England I would be surprised how often I'd hear such speech from the lips of people who were most unlikely to be avid readers or literary buffs. Where could they have found these uncommon words, these metaphoric terms, this almost Shakespearean cadence?

I can still hear this bobby's "mean night" through the foggy darkness, as if resonating under a low ceiling in some make-believe theatre.

"A mean night to be in. And all the houses being practically the same, 'tis hard indeed to find one's own. And what would your number be, would you know that much, Miss?"

Yes, happily I knew that much. Number 72. I've never forgotten it.

We walked along, the bobby aiming his flashlight beam at the numbers from time to time.

Finally he announced, "Here we are, Miss, safe and sound at your very door! May you have a fine sleep. And pleasant dreams as well."

Such was the first friend I made in London. Often still on a foggy night wherever I am, in a far corner of my memory I see a face in a halo of light and hear a solemn voice wishing me a fine sleep and pleasant dreams.

FOR A FEW DAYS more, however, I nurtured my homesickness, my bewilderment, my fear of the great city, and probably my shame at having given in so completely. Fortunately I've always had another self to tell me off, laugh at me if need be. One evening it spoke to me over my shoulder.

"This is the limit!" I can hear it saying. "Here you are in one of the most exciting cities in the world. At this very moment the curtain is about to rise on hundreds of stages; audiences will be enthralled by the words of great playwrights, lifted on the wings of music, and here you are squatting by your silly little fire feeling sorry for yourself. Really worth all the effort to chuck what you thought was such an insignificant existence in Manitoba, isn't it?"

It was as though I'd been slapped. I looked at my watch. It was only seven-thirty. I grabbed my coat. I clattered down the stairs I'd undoubtedly crept down like everyone else until then. I think I even slammed the door. I tied a white handkerchief firmly to a shrub just behind the holly hedge to serve as a marker when I came home. To make sure, I counted the number of doors from Number 72 to the cluster of small shops. There were twenty-eight. The fog seemed thinner, too, as if about to lift.

I took the Underground and was glad to be with some fellow humans, even the most total strangers. I must have come out at Piccadilly Circus because I remember the signs of theatres and movie houses, the garlands of twinkling lights, all the light on every side overcoming the fog so completely that you saw only wisps of it here and there. In those days it was said that Piccadilly Circus was the crossroads of the world. It must have been true

because in the few minutes I stayed at the exit from the Underground, rooted in surprise, I saw a beggar in unspeakable rags straight out of Dickens, a man of rank with a gold-headed cane and black cape lined with white satin, an eccentric lady, probably from Park Lane, clad all in feathers like an exotic bird, a ferocious-looking Sikh, a tattooed sailor, a Highlander in a kilt, some Arabs in turbans, and what I imagine was an Indian princess with a star – or was it a circle? – painted on her forehead. Such an array of faces and forms that I stood transfixed on those steps as though at the edge of Plato's cave watching chimeras come to life before my very eyes. Even today I have trouble separating later impressions of this city I was to grow to love so much from the rich, crazy, sumptuous sight it offered me that night as I emerged from below ground. In London, and in Paris too for that matter, the most marvellous show of all to me was always the one presented by the city itself, on its terraces, strolling its boulevards, or circulating round and round as here, like some unbelievable carousel of improbable humanity in every shape and form.

WHAT PLAY did I see that night? Not *A Midsummer Night's Dream* because that was with Vivien Leigh, still very young, at the Old Vic, which is in quite another part of London. *The Three Sisters* perhaps, or Stravinsky's ballet *The Firebird*. It doesn't matter. I didn't really see anything mediocre in London. I found what was best, instinctively no doubt, and also wisely counselled by Bohdan, who sometimes left a note on his way by and occasionally some tickets he'd been given.

I came back from Piccadilly Circus my head abuzz with images and sounds, though this didn't for a minute hide the fact that I was alone with a wealth of impressions that I would have loved to share with someone. I found my little marker tied to its shrub, dripping with water from the fog. I went up to my room without a single door opening as I passed. I might have not gone out or not come back and no one would have known the difference.

The next day I told myself I'd fiddled enough and while I still had momentum I went at once to enrol at the Guildhall School of Music and Drama; Bohdan had obtained all the information I needed and had been urging me to make a decision. I was obliged to take

the complete course in drama from makeup lessons to fencing and tap dancing as well as the actual study of plays. I had to pay cash in the first term, which made an enormous dent in the small balance I had in the bank. It didn't matter. I'd come to a point where I felt I had to launch myself in some direction at all costs, even a wrong one, in order to find out at last what I needed to know about myself.

I CAN'T RECALL exactly where the school was. Another blank in my memory! It couldn't have been far from the Thames because I remember finding myself beside the river every time I had a moment of freedom after or between classes.

I can picture myself walking endlessly along the embankments on days when I had nothing special to do. I walked from Blackfriars all the way to Big Ben more than once. Several times I even ventured farther east, towards the docks and the bustling seagoing life of the Thames, which fascinated me. I went by river launch to Greenwich and down to the estuary. I became attached to that river as I've been to very few people in this world. I loved it when it shimmered in the sun, as on one of the times I punted upstream with friends as far as Hampton Court, Cardinal Wolsey's palace until he was forced to give it up to Henry VIII – Hampton Court of such terrible memory, today a destination for picnickers with its black swans and thick green lawns. Little floating shops went back and forth constantly on the river. If we waved they'd come alongside and we'd buy tea or sandwiches before continuing on our course. I loved the Thames of these cheery, simple-hearted outings but even more I loved the Thames of misty nights with muffled cries of gulls, faint lappings of water against ancient stonework, and the muted bleat of foghorns barely reaching the embankment. Often I'd stay for hours, leaning on the parapet, trying to guess from the sounds what was going on behind the pall of fog. Or simply lost in some reverie, swept along with the soothing flow of the unseen water.

THEN I BEGAN to look for a more cheerful room. I found one through the classified columns. I was now buying the evening paper from an old cockney who had his stock-in-trade on the sidewalk where I emerged from the Underground. One evening I read a description

that sounded like just what I wanted. "Sunny third-floor room with small coke fireplace," it said. The address was still in Fulham, not very far from dreary Wickendon Street. I hurried over.

After my street of gloom, the heart of old Fulham was such a busy, lively neighbourhood! My room was on the third floor of a high, narrow building which grew narrower from the ground floor up, with space only for my room at the top. The middle floor was occupied by the owners and the ground floor was entirely filled by a repair shop with a single window on the street side, a chaotic scene of inoperative bicycles hanging by the dozen from the ceiling, leaving room below for hundreds of old phonographs and disassembled radios waiting to be repaired some day. I was to see some of these stay over four months in their blanket of rarely disturbed dust. A crudely lettered sign announced "Geoffrey Price's Bicycle and Radio Repair Shop".

The ground floor was on a level with the sidewalk, onto which the repair shop was partially emptied each morning to give Geoffrey Price room to move around inside amid his jumble of old odds and ends. It was also on the bus route and was one of its stops, in fact. You'd hear a rumble like thunder. Around the corner would come a double-decker bus almost as high as the building. Sharp application of the brakes would loose a soul-searing shriek, then the monster would pull up with its back door opening directly in front of the door of Geoffrey Price's Bicycle and Radio Repair Shop. On a rainy day, people of the neighbourhood said, you could get from Geoffrey Price's to Earls Court or Knightsbridge without risk of having a single drop of rain fall on you.

Across the street was another shop which was just as useful to bus passengers going in the other direction. This was the ironmonger's, which I'd learned to call the paint merchant's in Paris, though at the paint merchant's I recall seeing mostly coal and bottles of coarse red wine. On the third corner of the little square was the greengrocer's, the equivalent of the *verdurier* in Paris. The neighbourhood also included a chemist, a physician with office hours posted at his door, and a dentist whose sign was a huge hinged jaw as tall as a man, which kept opening and closing day and night as if in hope of gobbling up some unwary passerby. Just beyond was an open-air market. From there, early each morning, came the rattle of wooden-wheeled carts bringing vegetables to the stalls.

There was a codfish monger's at its edge. The rankest odours mingled in the air with the most delicate.

You couldn't be in the neighbourhood five minutes without hearing a sound such as the tinkling bell of the flower vendor pushing his little cart full of bright-coloured blossoms or the cry of the glazier, tinsmith, or rag-and-bottle man. Along with the street cries you'd often hear the doleful music of a barrel-organ and sometimes, through the din of all the rest, a pious bell from a little church behind high stone walls somewhere in the vicinity. I finally found this little church one day, hidden by stone and ivy, and a cemetery, the most peaceful in the world with its thick walls and shady trees full of birds – death's tranquil place of rest amid all the bustling humanity. I was to go there often seeking silence when there was too little in the noisy house.

My new landlady was like her neighbourhood, an irrepressible Welshwoman full of jokes, pranks, and mischief and always in a hurry. She showed me the room and I loved it immediately. It was high enough to reduce the noise and had a window overlooking the back, which was surprisingly quiet, a hodge-podge of small yards used for storage or junk, a scene as still as the street was busy on the other side. The fireplace was minute but delighted me because it was made to burn something real. Gladys told me she would light me a fire in the morning when she brought my breakfast, then if I stayed during the day it would be up to me to keep it going. I'd have to buy my own coke and a little kindling for starting it sometimes. Well no, she decided, she'd let me have the kindling. For the room, breakfast, and a bit of lunch – just scraps – it would be a guinea a week.

"A guinea?" I said, puzzled, not having heard the term before.

Gladys explained that a guinea meant a pound plus a shilling. I made her scream with laughter when at the end of the week I brought her a cheque for a guinea.

"There's no such thing really," she told me. "We haven't got any note or coin that's worth a guinea. It's just an expression."

"Well, why do you talk about guineas then?" I wanted to know.

She shrugged. I was stuck with the English lack of logic just as I'd been with the unerring logic of the French and I'd just have to adapt to it. I adapted to it more quickly, in fact, than to the endless reasoned arguments of the French.

This first day when we talked business I almost stooped to beggary.

"For a whole guinea, instead of scraps for lunch since I'll often be out at lunchtime," I said, "wouldn't you give me the same scraps for supper instead?"

Gladys laughed loud enough for the whole neighbourhood to hear, she found it all so funny, my accent, my expressions, my little rabbit coat and my beret which was "so Frenchy". In the end she told me that for a guinea a week, because she liked me so much, she'd "throw in supper and even a bite later on in the evening if you're still hungry, dearie." This was how I got myself a place to live for the best price going in all of London.

There was only one drawback to my new arrangement and that was my address: Lillie Road. "I know it smacks of perdition," agreed my landlady, and having roared another of her window-rattling laughs, concluded that I was getting it at a pretty good price at that.

Though I didn't really think the name smacked of perdition, I was shy about giving my address aloud and avoided it, saying, "I live too far to invite people there," or "It's terribly out of the way." I simply had to put up with it since Lillie Road was close to Paradise for me. Laughing, Gladys tried to make me feel better by telling me it would have been even more compromising if I'd taken a room in Petticoat Lane not far away.

Bohdan came and helped me move. He'd been able to unearth a kind of pushcart on his street. We moved everything I had in one load with a great deal of noise, the rubberless wheels clattering loudly over the cobblestones.

"It's a good thing you're staying so close," said Bohdan. "It won't be long now before my concert's over and then we'll catch up on each other."

He helped me put my clothes on hangers in the wardrobe. I tried to boil water for tea, squatting by the fire. One of the things I liked about it here was being able to have visitors, since with the sofa-bed made up the room became a sitting room.

Bohdan was amused and a bit shocked to see me transplanted to this very working-class neighbourhood. He'd have thought, he said, that for my writing I would have been better off in the quiet of the place he'd found for me. He'd been predicting that I'd become a famous writer ever since we'd first known each other.

While I was still trying to make some tea, Gladys arrived with a tray loaded with buttered scones and cakes and little pots of jam.

"As soon as I saw that young man pushing your things in his barrow I liked him," she confided to me later. "There's not another one like him in all England, you can take my word for it, and you'd better get your hands on him while you've got the chance. Cheerio!"

While Bohdan drank his tea, I observed him in silence. There were dark rings under his eyes and he looked tired, thin, and rather older, though he was really so young.

"Bohdan," I said, "if you're going to go as far as you've made up your mind to, you're going to have to learn to look after yourself."

"Am I going very far?" he shot back, trying to make it sound flippant.

It occurred to me then that despite his frequent cheerfulness I'd always sensed a kind of anxiety in him, as though he had a feeling he was going to run out of time.

"I've got a pretty clear picture," he said, still as though poking fun at himself, "of a stretch of road ahead of me, a few years' worth perhaps, then everything stops, disappears, just drops away suddenly."

"But I can't even see a single day ahead of me and every day I change direction," I said lightly, trying to bring him back to his cheerful self.

He turned strangely serious. "Nevertheless," he said, "your future's certain. I only have to close my eyes and I can see your name in big bold letters. I don't seem to see it on the front of a theatre, though I still believe you've done the right thing signing up for drama. But as I foresee, that's not where you're going to shine. So where will it be? I think I can see your name on the cover of a book, quite clearly in big letters."

"A book!" I retorted. "I haven't even written a half-decent simple little story yet."

In the five or six years I'd known him, ever since we'd first met in Winnipeg, he'd been talking this way, rather like a psychic, and I often laughed heartily at his supposed foresight. This time, however, he seemed so sure of himself it gave me the shivers.

"Let's talk about something else," I said, "you frighten me with your prophecies."

What frightened me most was the intense sadness I'd glimpsed

in his blue-grey eyes, a look I never saw again except in the eyes of people destined to die young.

Our tea-time ended cheerfully for all that, with Bohdan pretending to read from the tea-leaves in the bottom of my cup that I was going to write an earthy, populist novel, which wouldn't really be surprising, since I felt so much at home with working people.

Having retrieved this scene in all its detail from the back of my memory, I've come to wonder now why we weren't lovers, Bohdan and I. He was direct, energetic, the soul of loyalty, and sweet, gentle, and charming. I don't know what he saw in me but I think it must have been rather the same things I valued in him, which made me admire him, trust him implicitly, look for his support, want his approval, and cherish him deeply. Perhaps the bond between us was too honest, too limpid, too uncomplicated to lead to love. It may have lacked a weakness or the grain of uncertainty or worry present in almost every love. Bohdan and I never caused each other the least worry except about each other's health. We were just meant to be friends, as they say unfairly. Curious, isn't it, that we place love, which is so fickle, on a higher plane than friendship, which is almost always so faithful.

Faith in each other. It was probably this that basically sustained our affection yet prevented it from turning into love. But in truth I don't understand it any better today than I did then.

Bohdan was more clairvoyant that day than he had ever been, as though he had the answers to my questions of the moment and for some time to come. Just before he left, he leaned against the doorframe and said in his affectionately bantering manner, "By the way, I want very much to introduce you to a young man I met a few days ago. You'll like him as surely as God made little apples. And as soon as he sets eyes on you he'll be forevermore bewitched."

"Another of your predictions!" I bantered back.

"It'll come true in less than three months. Want to bet on it?"

"What's this irresistible young man's name?" I asked, still not taking him seriously.

Halfway down the stairs he called back a name – was I mistaken? – with a tinge of resentment.

I only caught the first name, Stephen.

"Stephen who?" I shouted.

Either Bohdan didn't hear my question or I didn't hear his reply. I wouldn't learn any more about the young man that day, but Bohdan had succeeded in arousing my curiosity.

VII

MY NEW LIFE began, with a scattering of classes here and there over the week. This time I went at it with a stout heart and persistence, though never with enthusiasm. I forced myself.

The times I liked best were still my free days, when I'd escape and go adventuring on the upper deck of a bus. I developed a real passion for these cross-London tours, west to east, north to south. They could take as long as three or four hours and never cost more than a shilling. Invariably, I climbed the little spiral staircase, and if it was free settled myself in the first row at the very front, from where I'd have a commanding view of the sights. The conductor would arrive, find me pretty well alone up there, and ask, "Where to, ma'am?" I nearly always replied, "As far as you go." Often I returned by the same bus without even getting off. Once settled in my seat and in motion I was happy, it seems to me. I came to know a great deal of London this way, as later I would come to know Montreal by riding the streetcars when I arrived there in 1939.

Except for the City and certain hubs like Charing Cross, Trafalgar Square, Chelsea, and perhaps Soho, London was really just a succession of boroughs, each a kind of small town with its own High Street, each joined to the next, an endless procession. I used to love to watch these peaceful-looking towns go by one after the other, their houses attached one to another for whole streets without a break, their flower markets, their everlasting tea shops, and the never-changing vista of chimney pots as far as the eye could see; in the whole city there must have been a staggering number of these small chimneys in the shape of flower pots, because you could often count a dozen on a single roof, or however many little fireplaces like mine there were inside the house. What a curious

city, each person alone by his own feeble little fire instead of to-gether with others around a nice fat stove! So much scot had fallen from all these chimney pots and nearby factory smokestacks that you often couldn't see the colour of the brick the houses were built of.

Sometimes I'd come to a miraculous pink brick square around a small park enclosed in a quickset hedge or low walls. Only the occupants of the sparkling-clean surrounding houses could use the park, since only they had keys for opening the gate. Inside one might see a nanny in a shoulder-length veil pushing a perambulator or an old man walking slowly, leaning on a cane.

Not one of these outings failed to uncover something new for me. Sometimes I'd get off the bus and go exploring on foot in a neighbourhood far from where I lived, feeling so much at home I would have liked to stay. Often I made the round trip without a stop, and was always surprised at how different everything seemed on the way back. At times, looking down as though from a chariot, I'd find myself observing all the things that were intriguing and sad both at once, as one finds in any big city. At other times, lulled by the rocking of the bus, I'd lose all contact with the reality of the moment and drift away in reveries, which were almost always happy ones as soon as the rocking matched the rhythm of my thoughts, like a kind of ocean roll.

I WENT TO my classes at the Guildhall, of course, and made heroic efforts to benefit from these as well. Classes in diction, for example, during which the teacher tried one day for three-quarters of an hour to make me say "little" the way it ought to be said, showing me where to place my tongue, finally in exasperation asking, "Where on earth did you learn your English?" Exhausted by trying, I replied listlessly, "Where I ought to have learned French instead." There were makeup lessons to teach me how to disguise myself as a Sioux or Nipponese, for all the good it would ever do me. Fencing lessons. Readings of texts by the great English playwrights. All this part of my life, the part inside the walls of the school, seems today like merely something I dreamed. The dreaming I did on the Thames embankments, the upper decks of the huge London buses, and even on weekends at Gladys's cabin opposite Hampton Court – the poor people's side of the river giving the finest view of the palace – this

to me was the only real and lasting part of the life I led in these three or four months.

YET THERE are episodes from these days in London that stand out sharply in my memory.

There was the day when I was attending a class conducted by a Miss Rorke, whom we called "the dragon". She used to rail at us without letup, calling us "snails" because we were slow, I suppose, and zombies and phantoms incapable of making ourselves understood. She wasn't alone; a good many other teachers also habitually insulted and ridiculed us. Why was it necessary to treat us like this when we were already trembling in our boots? It seems, I was told later, that by goading us as a picador goads a bull they were supposed to draw reactions full of pain and fire from us.

It was generally accepted that as a teacher of the English classics Miss Rorke was unsurpassable. Nobody taught Shakespeare and especially George Bernard Shaw better than she. She had played Shaw a great deal in her youth and his acerbic humour had certainly left its mark on her character. She never stopped reminding us of our incompetence. "You want to be actors and actresses, hold audiences spellbound, see your names in lights on theatre marquees...yet you can't do anything properly! You can't walk or sit down or even shake hands, let alone speak lines!"

She was right, too. As I watched my fellow students I could see that, indeed, they were unable to walk or sit down or do anything on stage in a way that seemed in the least natural. I was learning that everything has to be recreated on the stage if it's to seem real, that nothing, even blowing your nose, can be done the way you do it in real life.

I hadn't myself been a target for Miss Rorke's attacks. Then one day I suddenly heard myself being summoned.

"You there! Come and read us a passage." We were doing *The Merchant of Venice.* "Hmm.... Ah yes, Portia's plea to the judge."

This time I couldn't escape as I had from Dullin's. I climbed the steps to the stage. I found the passage. I began to read in a voice that seemed to come from another world, faint, far-off, and frail. I didn't recognize myself at all; someone else was reading, gesturing, while I myself was watching from terribly far away, feeling

258

rather sorry for the poor girl in such a predicament. Then my voice firmed, came to my ears perhaps the way others heard it. I can still hear it even now and probably always will, though I don't remember the words. Life has robbed me of them. As Rutebeuf would say, it robs us of everything with advancing age except the memory of having been young, bold, and foolhardy.

Then all became muddled and blurred. I was no longer two people, one reading and the other watching; I'd escaped from everyone present and myself as well. My shyness and anxiety retreated to the periphery. I was back in my childhood, still in class at the Académie Saint-Joseph. The inspector had come to see what we were doing. Sister Agathe had implored me, "Get up and save the class." And at the Guildhall or in St-Boniface, I was doing my utmost to save heaven knows what.

Gradually my voice became more confident. Around me there was total silence. Something was showing at last through the gaiety I was known for at the Guildhall, surely the old, persistent strain of sadness in me. Were the old woes of Deschambault Street revisiting me, emerging so astonishingly in the words of Shakespeare? The class was dumbfounded perhaps. Who in London had ever heard or would ever again hear Shakespeare recited like this, the Bard in a guise never before seen by his countrymen?

When I'd finished my speech the silence persisted for a good few seconds. Then Miss Rorke said rather gruffly:

"It's a pity you've got such a barbaric accent because at times I actually felt something come to life. But child, I could hardly make out a single word with that horrendous accent of yours!"

Aside she told me, "If you want to come to me in the evening I'll give you some tutoring, without a penny of cost to you, of course."

I went two or three times, I think. After making me rhyme off "which, whichever, witches, whence, where, wherever, either, neither, however, beneath, whole, whatever" and an appalling number of others, she plied me with humbugs, bonbons, scones, hot tea, biscuits, and crumpets. At home, the dragon was just a lovable little old lady nestled in a Victorian armchair, her tiny feet propped on a pouf, her dark skirt draped over them, making me repeat between mouthfuls, "witch, which, wither, whither, wisht, whished,

whim, whichever..." or "throne, throw, thorough, through...,"
which I still can't say properly for all the pains she and many others
have taken with me.

I ALSO ENROLLED in a drama course in French with a Madame Gachet
who made me hold a pencil between my teeth while saying, *"Je
veux et je l'exige,"* to loosen up my tongue. She was another dragon
who kept castigating me for "using your face to speak with instead
of your throat, like all you Canadians."

With her I studied Shaw's *Saint Joan* in French translation, which
was ironic in the extreme since Shaw was far more Miss Rorke's
domain. However, Madame Gachet insisted that the shape of my
face and my features and manner were right for it and therefore
Joan was a good role for me. I'd long known Joan's most brilliant
retorts to the Inquisitor by heart but one morning I tried to produce
them and couldn't find anything there any more.

Madame Gachet's interpretation of Saint Joan was like Ludmilla
Pitoëff's, with the delicate features of a little stained-glass-window
saint. It's said that when Shaw went to Paris for the première of
Madame Pitoëff's production he was so enraged that all through a
dinner given in his honour he wouldn't speak a word to her, though
she was sitting beside him. At the Malvern Festival, which I attended
that year, Elizabeth Bergner's Joan was also a little stained-glass
saint and displeased Shaw so thoroughly that he stamped out to
the garden in fury at intermission and went to walk in the maze
in the centre of which this delightful little summer theatre is located.
I had come to Malvern for the day and was in the maze at the
time. Walking along the twists and turns between the high hedges,
every so often I heard angry grumbling sounds and fragments of
sentences through the foliage. At one point I turned a corner and
came face to face with a white-bearded old man who glared at me
for a moment, then continued his tortuous way, muttering angrily.
I stood stock still, overcome with surprise. "That was George Bernard Shaw I just passed!" I said to myself. "And furious too, as
usual."

Each anecdote keeps reminding me of another I'd like to tell, but
my dervish is increasingly aware that he hasn't time to collect
everything coming to him from the past if he's going to finish all

he has begun. What I do want to add is that the only Joan that Shaw ever approved of was Dame Sybil Thorndike's and later Miss Rorke's: a sturdy, rosy-cheeked country girl who was totally rational, reasonable, and realistic: the Catholics' first Protestant saint, as Shaw himself called her.

More sensibly, I also studied Racine with Madame Gachet, until the day she hurled the book at my head in a rage, declaring I didn't understand a thing about this type of drama – which was the very truth.

Madame Gachet had had as pupils such distinguished actors as Vivien Leigh and Charles Laughton. They still quite frequently came to work on their roles with her, of which she made sure her ordinary pupils were aware. In her better moments we were treated to gossip and juicy anecdotes about the great figures of the movie and theatre world, whom she knew and, it must be said, whom she saw with revealing and often merciless clarity.

LOOKING BACK, how hard I tried during this period of my life! Once the weather was milder, I would sometimes go and recite lines from Racine, even after he'd been hurled at my head, in the only place I was sure of neither disturbing anyone nor being laughed at, behind the thick walls of the little Fulham cemetery, so full of dense shady trees and ancient graves. Even here I sometimes had a pang of guilt to be disturbing such long and sacred rest, and stopped to read a few epitaphs here and there instead. They were so plaintive and sweet. Having my Racine interlarded with the echo of these humble, long-forgotten English lives suddenly made me feel that my own story was a thousand times stranger than those I was studying in books. For a little while it would fascinate me more than any mystery.

THIS WAS the pattern of my life during these months in London. I would be lonely and depressed, pushing myself to do things that seemed to be taking me nowhere; then suddenly my youth and the cheerful side of my nature would take over and I'd be finding the humour in things, laughing and making people around me laugh as in the days of our touring shows in Manitoba, as later too, when I was in Provence.

261

The day I read Portia's great plea, I came down from the stage and was still trembling, the students present gaping oddly, when a tall, handsome young man came forward, clapping approval.

"Let them think what they want," he said, "and even laugh if they like. You have everyone's attention right now."

Naïvely, I took the remark as a compliment. Perhaps it was.

"How about a cup of tea?" he suggested after we'd talked for a minute.

Around eleven in the morning and in mid-afternoon, almost everyone at the Guildhall stopped fencing, dancing, or delivering lines and gathered around small four-place tables in the school restaurant to drink endless cups of tea.

Soon nearly all my class was there in little groups. I noticed that most of them were staring at the tall, handsome young man and me as we sat together, separated slightly from the rest. I could hardly believe the new respect, even envy, in their expressions.

He told me his name and that he was Welsh, but his being Welsh is the only way I can remember him today. While we drank our tea, no doubt he told me he'd studied at the Guildhall and since he was making his career in London he returned to his old teachers from time to time for "refresher courses". Today, though he couldn't explain why, he'd dropped in on the dramatic interpretation class in progress and had at once been captivated by this unusual little creature with eyes so full of a different vision of English drama.

What I didn't yet know was that he was one of England's finest baritones, had sung many times at Covent Garden, and was well launched on the royal road to success. There wasn't a girl present who wouldn't gladly have scratched my eyes out, seeing him court me. Several of them had probably been in my shoes; I soon learned that I was far from the first he'd wooed with the same kind of line.

He lost no time taking out his little black book and asking for my address. Grandly, he informed me he'd be in touch one of these days to take me to one of the evening musicals that were given in the most fashionable salons of London in those days; it would round out my artistic training and give me a unique vantage point for observation.

Alas, rather than own up to living on Lillie Road I was vague, evasive, saying, "I'm on the point of moving.... I don't really know where to...or where I'll be tomorrow." Then, not knowing how to

escape from such a fix, I held out my hand, thanked him for the tea, and left almost at a run.

When I recounted the scene to Gladys she told me I was a crazy little nincompoop. The tall, handsome Welshman was well known in London, she said, you could often hear his superb voice on the BBC, and besides, all Welshmen were musically gifted and most attractive. So it would serve me right if I never set eyes on him again.

We hadn't reckoned on our Welshman's determination. He had little trouble obtaining my address and even my telephone number from the registrar of the school. Two or three days later I got off the bus straight into the bicycle shop as always, and almost straight into the arms of Gladys, who'd been waiting for me in a dither of excitement. My Welshman had telephoned. He'd left a message. He really was the one she'd thought, a celebrity! She'd taken down the number. I had to call back as soon as possible from Geoffrey's office.

What she called Geoffrey's office was an ancient roll-top desk ensconced in a corner of the bicycle shop, littered with nuts, bolts, screws, bits of tubing, and an old maul for keeping the pile of unpaid bills in place. Since he knew where I lived and so the harm was done, I called the handsome Welshman.

"Why didn't you want to give me your address?" he asked.

"Because I didn't want people to know I live on Lillie Road."

I heard a hearty laugh that seemed it would never stop, full, deep, and rolling, drowning the traffic sounds from the street.

"Silly little girl!" he said. "Do you know where I come from? The bottom of a coal mine! My father's still an underground miner. I was one myself till I was sixteen. Will you come with me to the Austrian embassy this evening? Watch out though, the ambassador's name is Baron Frankenstein, I'm not pulling your leg."

Without reflecting that he couldn't see me I nodded, but he must have read my silence correctly.

"I'll pick you up at eight o'clock sharp," he said.

We had found a place for my wardrobe trunk on the landing beside the door to my room. I took out my long, bright-red taffeta dress, which Gladys insisted on pressing for me. I found my matching shoes. Gladys did my hair in a bundle of ringlets on top of my head, which made me look like a Reynolds portrait. She had a

reproduction of one on her sitting-room wall. To complete my evening finery I had white gloves and a kind of little cape of black velvet. I was ready long in advance and came down to await my prince in the middle of the bicycle shop, sitting on a chair which Geoffrey had hastened to wipe off with a rag. Dressed as always for work in a grey smock that made him look like a jailbird, Geoffrey sat near the wide-open door and waited with me, too much on edge to do any work at a time of such great excitement.

How the news had spread I really don't know, but the whole neighbourhood knew that "the nice little French lady at Gladys's is going out tonight with that marvellous Welsh singer you hear over the wireless." But the neighbours' imaginations had turned the evening's event into a ball, perhaps even at Buckingham Palace for all they knew, which from minute to minute acquired such grandiose proportions that not a soul among them wasn't on the doorstep watching for the Prince to appear. They must have expected him to draw up in a carriage, or at least a splendid chauffeured limousine. I'd become their fairy-tale, the Cinderella so beloved of ordinary folk because she takes them with her to the ball.

The hour was approaching. From their doorsteps, people kept looking up at the big clock over Smith's Watch Repair.

At eight o'clock precisely, with a rumble like thunder as always, came the bus from Knightsbridge. Windows rattled. The monster pulled up with its open door facing the welcoming portal of Geoffrey Price's Bicycle and Radio Repair Shop. Out stepped my Welshman, straight into the shop among the bicycles hanging from the ceiling, in evening dress with immaculate boiled shirtfront, top hat slightly tilted on his head, gold-headed cane in his hand, and – caught at the neck with a clasp and flipped nonchalantly back from his shoulders – a huge, magnificent black velvet cape that swept all the dust off the floor in one pass.

The bus driver, intrigued with the distinguished figure he must have seen alight out of the corner of his eye, rolled down his window and put out his head to watch him enter the bicycle shop, and waited. My tall Welshman held out his hand, drew me out of my little straw-bottomed chair, and led me up the steps of the waiting vehicle. The driver stepped on the gas and we drove away in the same bus in which the Prince had arrived.

The ironmonger, the flower vendor, the fishmonger, the chemist, and the greengrocer, wide-eyed and open-mouthed, watched us leave as if we were the most ordinary of mortals, and couldn't, perhaps would never, get over their disappointment.

AROUND THIS TIME I made other much dearer friends than the tall, handsome Welshman who entered my life in such spectacular fashion, and who faded from it no doubt just as quickly, for rack my brain as I may I can find no further trace of him after the evening at Frankenstein's.

A little later I became very fond of a sweet girl whose parents were paying her way through the Guildhall course in drama, though they themselves had never set foot in a theatre. One day she invited me home for Sunday dinner with her family in the South End across the Thames, a rather distant part of the city where, curiously, my excursions by bus had never taken me. No doubt like every other household in London on Sunday at the same hour, we ate roast rib of beef and Yorkshire pudding.

Phyllis and I went to see a great many plays together. We used to buy cheap seats in what Phyllis called "the gods", a term acknowledging that the section known in Paris as the *poulailler* or "hen roost" was a very high perch indeed. In some theatres we might hang so precipitously over the stage that all we could see of the actors far below was the tops of their heads, often bald. We had little chance of seeing their faces unless, said Phyllis, they suddenly began to "play to the gods", as did the late illustrious Henry Irving one night when, probably remembering his penniless youth, he threw back his head and looking towards the ceiling spoke directly to the impoverished souls peering down from above.

Personally, I don't think I ever saw an actor look up towards us until the time came for applause, and then it was rather pleadingly.

The cheap seats – a shilling each – couldn't be reserved, of course, and were in great demand, so we had to arrive a good hour ahead of time. Even then, there was often already a long queue outside the theatre. We would take our places in line and in no time the queue would have lengthened so much that it disappeared around the corner into an adjacent sidestreet. I've seen it grow so long that depending on the space or the whims of those involved it might loop twice around the theatre, making a kind of lasso. The two

loops, one of which seemed to be coming and the other going, would often be very close together and people would converse from one group to the other as they passed. On occasion someone turned up to rent out folding chairs. You could have one for sixpence and sit very comfortably two by two by the wall. Or you could write your name on a piece of paper and pin it to your chair, and without danger of having your place stolen go and have a leisurely bite to eat nearby, or just take a walk.

I liked best to stay in my place with the cluster of people in the queue, an instant family of friends on the sidewalk. If it rained, umbrellas would open wide enough to shelter less prudent neighbours. I often slipped under someone else's umbrella, having asked permission with a glance and a smile or having been invited, and almost invariably I'd engage in conversation with the obliging neighbour. There'd be people reading quietly, holding an umbrella in one hand and turning pages with the other. There'd be women knitting scarves already long enough to reach the ground. "Your lovely scarf's dragging in the dirt," we'd warn them. If the evening was mild and without rain, which was the case fairly often in the course of the winter, street performers would appear. They'd do little dances, sing songs in old, cracked voices, or draw pictures on the sidewalk, then pass the hat and we'd give them a penny for their trouble. Phyllis almost always brought something to eat like buttered rolls and sticky buns, and would insist that we share them equally.

From some of those hours of waiting at the doors of theatres, particularly on pleasant evenings, I have memories of such delight that even the plays for which they should have been merely prologue are pale by comparison in my mind. On these occasions the people of London were the kindest, most considerate, most natural companions one could wish for. I still reflect sometimes that the best play in London's repertory was the one being played on the sidewalk about people ready to share everything, their sandwich with whoever seemed hungry, a flap of their coat with the ill-clad when the wind blew cold, a column of their paper with someone who had nothing to read – I can't count the times a neighbour consented with an amused smile to let me read over his shoulder.

Among these fondly remembered evenings, I spent several with

266

Phyllis, some with friends of the moment as my only companions, and some with Bohdan.

Bohdan's concert took place and was hailed as a triumph. The Royal Albert Hall audience applauded him at great length. So calm and reserved in appearance, that evening he threw himself into his playing like a kind of Paganini finally unleashing his passionate soul. I was astounded by the intensity I saw in him that night and I understood why we could never be lovers, he and I; he was already totally possessed by his music, and though I couldn't yet make out what it was, I too was driven by some burning imperative.

After the concert he was in great demand, with invitations to play in London and on tour. Anxious to live up to expectations, he worked harder than ever now. He became increasingly gaunt, and to me his eyes often had a feverish look, as though focusing on something which must have been unbearable, for he would murmur, half-seriously, half-facetiously as always:

"The gods don't wait. They don't wait."

I MYSELF would be in the depths of gloom one day and as gay as a lark the next. It was the sunny side of my nature that won me such affection from Phyllis and would win me affection from many others over the years. Left to herself, Phyllis would never have found anything to laugh at in the myriad comical little scenes to be found any day of the week in London, but when she heard me laugh she'd look again and suddenly begin also to see the comical side. She was very grateful to me for showing her this side of things practically every time we went out together.

Often a play we wanted to see took us to a part of the city that was difficult to reach, and once there we might have to hunt through narrow, poorly lit streets for a tiny, secluded theatre. This was the case when we went to see Eugene O'Neill's *Mourning Becomes Electra*, which was showing somewhere in Westminster, as I recall, at the end of a little-known street off a cul-de-sac with the Thames lapping gently at its foot. Since the play is very long, the performance was given in two parts, the first beginning at seven-thirty, followed by a half-hour intermission to allow people to go and have something to eat; the performance resumed at about ten-thirty and ended only around midnight.

267

At intermission there were already signs of fog, and by the end of the play a real pea-soup had descended on the deserted streets around the theatre. When we came out, a small audience of about fifty, we couldn't see two steps before us and could barely see each other or the streetlight on the square in front of the theatre. Instinctively, all fifty stayed together, walking step by step, elbow to elbow. Apparently no one was really familiar with the area or knew how to find the nearest Underground station. How did I come to be the one leading the group, marching boldly towards a sound I thought I heard ahead of me, which was in fact no more than the fog-projected echo of the steps behind? More to the point, how did the whole troop of Londoners come to be following me as one man, knowing how treacherous a fog can be?

Soon I thought I heard another sound, one not quite masked by the footsteps behind me. Was it ahead? Was it behind? I couldn't tell, but something about it worried me. Suddenly, with all those people behind me, I came to a tall iron grille beyond which a steep slope led straight into the Thames. We'd arrived at one of the low-tide landings for the launches that ply the river. If the watchman had forgotten to close the gate, we could all have marched laughing into the murky water before we realized what was happening. Only when I turned around did I see, by a feeble light reflected off the water, the trusting little band that had followed me all this way, blindly to say the least.

I began to laugh, infecting Phyllis, who began to laugh too. And when Phyllis, in her lovely trained voice, told all those people in the darkness that they'd been letting themselves be led by a Canadian girl who'd never set foot in the district before, everyone else laughed too. Instead of being angry they all crowded around to see what I looked like and wish me well for the future. Then a seasoned Londoner took the lead. We all joined hands and made a chain and, like a band of merry wraiths dancing a farandole, followed him out of the thick of the fog towards the lights of the Underground.

Dear Londoners! Dear isle! How I loved them at this time in my life and at this time in theirs. The English are so warm-hearted, need so urgently to love; on later visits I didn't find the same degree of free-and-easy charm and readiness to laugh at themselves that I remembered, perhaps because I had become too solemn my-

self, perhaps because they, after the trials and hardships of the war, had lost some of their gentle sense of absurdity.

THE TIME passed quickly despite my ups and downs. I persevered along the course I had set for myself, though I kept announcing I was going to give it all up. One day I'd be at peace with the world and the next the old depression would be back and I'd feel I was wasting my life, and time flew by and winter came to an end without my noticing. In the three months I'd been in London, had I ever really seen the sky, the Thames and the embankments, except in short, fleeting glimpses? Perhaps this was really what made them so unforgettable.

One morning on my way to the school I passed beneath an old linden tree as I did almost every day, and through a break in the fog saw that the branches above my head were still bare. Only the dryish creak of its branches told me for certain where I was, but I'd swear my old friend the linden was bare that morning when the breeze was still on the nippy side.

Halfway through the morning, while I was attending my classes, the air suddenly warmed and the sun came out, even shone brightly for a few hours.

When I came out and walked alone to the Underground it was dark. It must have been the fifteenth or perhaps sixteenth of February. The hour did nothing to spoil my surprise and delight as I passed under my linden tree and, suddenly hearing a new, softer sound, slowed my pace and looked up. I thought I was dreaming. The old linden was covered with leaves! Oh, very tiny still, barely open, newly come into the world, but fragile as they were, rustling in the balmy night air, doing their best to warm the heart. I think I was entranced by the coming of spring in a way I'd never known before. What struck me most was its suddenness no doubt. Just a few hours earlier the old tree at the edge of the sidewalk might have been dead, from its appearance, and now I was seeing the shimmer of its young leaves as they turned towards the feeble light of a nearby streetlamp. The joy that swept over me was itself a rebirth, my own, telling me just how dead I myself had been in many ways.

Years later, when I was writing *The Hidden Mountain*, this joy in the coming of spring would return one day and guide me in

conveying Pierre Cadorai's indefinable happiness one evening in the forest at winter's end, when he hears a drop of water fall from a branch to the ground, its tinkling through the silence and darkness seeming to go on for ever.

But for the moment, since there wasn't a soul to share it with, my joy was almost unbearable. I've often enough found suffering difficult to bear by myself, but perhaps solitary joy even more. "I have Gladys, though," I remembered after a moment or two, and I hurried home.

There were two entrances, one through the bicycle shop where Geoffrey, in his eternal iron-grey smock, was working late, and the other by a little side door at the foot of the stairs that led to the kitchen door of Gladys's apartment. From downstairs I could hear Gladys rattling pots.

"Gladys, it's spring, it's spring!" I called.

She appeared at the top of the stairs in her apron, her hands all white with dough.

"So it is, so it is! And I'm throwing in a fine steak and kidney pie for supper besides."

But then she became serious and told me to come up. She whispered that tomorrow was Geoffrey's birthday and she always sent him a birthday card by the post. He liked to get it on the breakfast tray on his birthday with his morning paper and a daffodil. She'd already addressed the card and she asked me, since the weather was so nice, if I wouldn't go back out and put it in a corner letter-box.

I replied that I certainly would if she really wanted me to, but why bother posting it at all? Wouldn't it be simpler just to put it on the tray with the daffodil the next morning without making it do the tour of the district first?

At this she was very put out. Generally such a good-natured soul, she could become cranky for no reason at all. "Because... because...," she almost shouted, then probably against her better judgement blurted, "Because Geoffrey likes it that way, don't ask me why. Half his pleasure's gone if he doesn't get his card with the Fulham Post Office cancellation on it."

"I'll go and post it if you want," I said, "but I confess I find it odd for two people living in the same house to send each other things by the post, unless they're not on speaking terms."

"The envelope's got a stamp," she snapped, to put an end to it. "All I'm asking you to do is pop out and drop it in a letter-box. There's one just two blocks from here."

Even in Fulham, which was all cement, stone, and barred windows with hardly any trees except those in the cemetery, the gentle English spring was in progress. It was showing in almost imperceptible little ways, keeping me in an extraordinary state of exhilaration as though life were new, pulsating, bursting with hope. From the occasional tree along my way came the same tender, caressing murmurs I'd heard from my linden. I was so intoxicated with the spring evening I could have kept walking for ever. I must have passed two or three letter-boxes before realizing I wasn't far now from Fulham Post Office. For the benefit of Gladys's card, to make absolutely sure it would arrive by the first delivery the following morning, I'd best go and post it there, I thought.

Afterwards, still unable to resign myself to going indoors on such a delicious evening, I took a lengthy detour through the cemetery and then along a street where several little gardens were already in bloom. It was a good hour before I arrived home.

Still light of heart, in the best of humour, I opened the little side door and hearing Gladys's voice humming called, " 'Tis done!"

Gladys appeared on the landing above. She seemed happy. Then we both looked down at the doormat at the bottom of the stairs. There under the letter slot in the door lay the birthday card I'd just posted. I bent down and picked it up. It bore the post office cancellation. Had it been delivered by the postman I'd just passed going the other way? I was bewildered.

"I told you to put it in the post," Gladys scolded. "Why did you bring it back yourself?"

"I did put it in the post," I said. "So as to be sure it would arrive in time I even posted it at the main post office."

"You shouldn't have!" groaned Gladys. "They've got a special fast service there. You must have arrived just in time for it to go straight out. Oh, how awful!"

She was inconsolable. Geoffrey's birthday was ruined, his pleasure spoiled, and it was my fault. Or rather, the fault of His Majesty's fearsomely efficient post office.

Sometimes when I wait three or four days for a letter to come from a part of Quebec City right next to mine, or when the single

Gabrielle Roy

daily delivery is suspended by ice, snow, "study session", or rotating strike...I find myself thinking fondly of that lightning-fast Fulham postal service which so totally foiled Gladys and me.

VIII

WAS IT THIS magical springtime that brought love to my life? Perhaps. Although the sudden burgeoning of life exhilarated me beyond words that February evening, it also made me aware of how alone I was in London. I had some friends, yes, but only friends of the moment, a very short moment. I had no one I could really count on in a pinch except perhaps Bohdan. And so the intensity of my exhilaration had a bitter side too, for it showed me how desolate it was to be far from home without anyone to love or give me love. Again I was asking myself some hard questions: why I had come to London, what I was doing here, why I was studying drama, and where it was going to lead me. Again everything I'd undertaken seemed worthless and futile beside what I ought to be undertaking. There was also a listlessness, persistent, corrosive, that prevented me from taking an interest in any effort I made to escape from the mood I was in. When you're listless, nothing is worth the effort. I practically stopped going to the theatre, on bus rides, even reading. I think I sank into the waiting state I've often experienced, during which I do nothing but wait for something unidentified to come and deliver me.

This was my state of mind when I set out one day to meet, if you will, my destiny. For all my inactivity I hadn't stopped going once a week, more or less, to Lady Frances Ryder's on Cadogan Gardens in South Kensington. This generous lady used to open her London apartment every day at tea-time to students, regardless of colour, from every corner of the Empire. Bohdan had taken me there and introduced me to Lady Frances. After this formality I was free to come again whenever I wished.

The copious fare served us at tea was for many students by far the best meal of the week, and many would tuck away quantities

of butter-soaked crumpets, cheese petits fours, and little tarts smothered in Devonshire cream. The spacious drawing rooms also featured a luxury that most of us had learned to do without: warmth, maintained by central heating. So we'd shed the heavy sweaters we wore almost constantly in winter and move around more at ease, both minds and bodies less constrained, ready for friendly conversation.

Lady Frances would preside over these gatherings herself or would delegate other ladies to do so. They always had theatre, ballet, or concert tickets to distribute, having pried them free of charge out of impresarios and theatre owners by playing on their pride of empire. Fairly often they also had an invitation for one of us to dine with a distinguished Harley Street doctor, or spend a weekend as guest of a great landowner in Ireland or a week at some stately home in Shropshire or Monmouthshire. The great dream of unity among brothers within the Empire was so deeply instilled, on the eve of its disappearance, that we only needed to be students from South Africa, New Zealand, Canada, Australia for the doors of noble residences and simple cottages alike to open wide for us.

In the group called, I think, Overseas British Empire Students, I was the only French Canadian. As such, though I don't know why, I received particular consideration. Lady Frances pressed me many times to accept coveted invitations to Wales, the Midlands, and elsewhere, but the idea of tackling life among the English landed gentry filled me with such paralysing shyness that I always shrank from it. In the end, though, I did accept an invitation to spend a week in Monmouthshire near the marvellous ruins of the old Cistercian abbey celebrated by Wordsworth. Perhaps it was my desire to see these ruins that overcame my hesitation. As Lady Curre's guest I was introduced to fox hunting, black-tie dinners, and some famous personalities, all of which in retrospect make my most fantastic dreams at night seem pale by comparison.

For the moment my feeling towards some of the young men I was meeting at Lady Frances's were no more than comradely. Among them was a giant of an Australian with a heart of gold but an appalling cockney accent and a habit of ending every sentence with "You see?" when you didn't see at all because you hadn't understood a word of what he'd been saying.

Another of what one might call my beaux in this circle was a

New Zealander who was in sharp contrast to the Australian, a tall, reserved, polite young man whose voice was impeccably British and who tried so terribly hard to be British with his bowler hat, his trench coat, and his oh-so-tightly-rolled umbrella that we all thought he was laying it on a bit too thick. He had an important position at the Admiralty. When his mother came from New Zealand to visit him, he invited me to join the two of them on a ten-day tour, which enabled me to become acquainted with the south of England: the splendid red-soiled Devon, Cornwall with its ancient shale castles, the moors, the New Forest, Gloucestershire, and everywhere such wonderful little villages that I sometimes think I must have dreamed them, they were so perfectly nestled in silence and verdure with their old arched bridges, rose-covered roofs, and a peacefulness probably unequalled anywhere in the world. David also used to invite me to dine in fashionable restaurants where I felt uncomfortable. Furthermore, he always seemed to be examining, evaluating me, perhaps considering whether I'd do. When his mother came she was even more obviously looking me over. After a while I began to wonder if David, in his strange, cold way, wasn't in fact courting me with honourable intentions as the saying goes, and mightn't solemnly propose marriage some fine day providing his mother pronounced me suitable. But apparently she didn't, for she went back to New Zealand and David began to space out his invitations, sent me roses, then fell silent, and all was well that ended well. Later, however, I would see him again fairly frequently.

A Lady Wells, who was often our hostess in place of Lady Frances, had introduced David to me, but a month later, having twice seen us leave together, she had a warning for me. "Don't get too attached to that boy," she said. "He's very refined, but underneath the polish he's not very good value. Wait. Some day I'll surely have someone better for you to meet."

One day I entered the big drawing room filled with the hum of conversation to find Lady Wells hurrying to meet me, holding out both hands.

"Dear," she said, "I've someone really special for you to meet. Come."

She kept talking but I no longer heard her. My eyes had turned to a little table in the middle of the room. Of the hundred faces

present I was seeing only one – or rather, one pair of dark, burning eyes that were drawing me irresistibly. And perhaps without my realizing, my eyes were drawing him too, this young man I'd never seen before, because once our eyes had met, his never left mine.

I crossed the room with Lady Wells, she holding my hand and I fervidly praying, "If only he's the one she wants me to meet!" As we approached he rose from the table.

Lady Wells said simply, "Stephen, this is Gabrielle whom I told you about...," and probably something else which I didn't register.

He took the hand I held out and the light in his dark eyes shone brighter. He pulled up another chair for me and we sat five at the table. The others began to talk again among themselves. The two of us said nothing. We kept gazing at each other as though too surprised to talk, too astonished at finding each other after coming so far across the globe and through life.

I don't remember anything about the next hour except that soon almost everyone around was looking at us in surprise to see us just sit and gaze at each other endlessly, as if magnetized.

We left together, having agreed with no more than a glance towards the door.

Outside we cast the same wonderstruck gaze on all we saw, as if expecting everything to be different because we ourselves were changed. Stephen laced his fingers with mine and it felt as though our two hands with the fingers joined this way were just one. We walked, swinging our linked hands in time with our steps, not knowing in what direction.

He didn't ask me any of the questions you usually ask people you've just met and who interest you, like where I was from, what I was doing in London, what my full name was, nothing like that. I didn't ask him any of these questions either. It was some time before I learned from piecing together fragments here and there that he was studying political science at the University of London, that he'd been born in Canada of Ukrainian parents and was still a Canadian citizen though he'd lived in New York for years after studying at Columbia. Much of his life remained totally hidden from me for weeks before I began to wonder about it, and then it was very late to turn back and begin over.

For the moment, our fingers interlaced, we were just at the stage of elation at being together. All that mattered was that we'd found

each other. Both of us were trembling, I think. With fear? Anxiety? Joy? Perhaps I'll never know. Through my trembling fingers I could feel his tremble too.

We had covered a great deal of ground walking aimlessly as we'd been doing and at last he said, "Where do you live, dear? I'm going to have to face up to taking you home, though that's the last thing I want to do."

"In Fulham. Lillie Road."

"Well, I never!" he exclaimed. "I live near there and I have a very dear friend who lives in the neighbourhood too, Bohdan Hubicki."

So it was he whom Bohdan had been so keen for me to meet! Yet just a few days before, Bohdan had confided, "He's a funny fellow, fascinating in a way that bothers me a bit because you'd say he's trying to make you forget you know practically nothing about him. I don't really know what to think of him. He could be a very fine person, however.... And yet...."

Clairvoyant Bohdan. Remembering these words, I felt a strange foreboding. I withdrew my fingers from Stephen's. I think I tried to put some distance between us but it was like trying to hold back the wind and the tide. Stephen interlaced his fingers with mine again. Just having mine interlaced with his was enough to send waves through me, destroying me one minute and elating me the next.

Softly, close to my ear, he said, "Will you come with me tomorrow to hear Boris Godunov?" He hummed a few bars of the monk Pimen's great Song of Destiny.

I was going to accept at once. I wanted nothing as much, but I caught myself in time. How would I look, what would he think of me if I leapt at his first invitation?

"Tomorrow.... I don't know."

"The day after tomorrow, then?"

"The day after tomorrow, perhaps...yes."

Already I was bitterly regretting having put it off so long and was ready to retreat if he gave the least sign of pressing me, but he said nothing, as though he too was sad at the thought of more than a day passing before we'd see each other again.

After many zigzags we finally came to an Underground station.

The train started up. I watched the names of the stations parade

by in big letters on the wall of the tunnel, noticing how we passed gradually from darkness to light as we approached each stop. And like someone in a trance, at almost every one I'd stare at the big Guinness poster showing two huge frothy glasses of beer side by side. A face peered out of the froth on each glass, one serious and the other beaming. Under the first it said, "Sometime I sits and thinks...," and under the second it said, "Sometimes I just sits...." I saw serious-looking people getting in and out carrying long furled umbrellas and briefcases. I wondered who were really living, these people with their haste and importance or Stephen and I on our floating island, from where other people's lives looked appallingly grey and humdrum.

When we came to the little side door at the foot of the stairs leading to Gladys's apartment and on up to my room, Stephen's mood seemed to become thoughtful.

"So this is where you live," he said. "It really doesn't surprise me at all. I couldn't imagine you anywhere else."

He looked at the drab walls, the graceless street in a loving kind of way that made me cherish them.

He didn't try to kiss me or even put my fingers to his lips, just kept them interlaced with his. I didn't know, I still don't know whether he held back because the wisdom of experience was telling him that love is most unforgettable when it's just beginning or whether he was already fulfilled, overjoyed. I think it was this because he suddenly, silently laid his forehead on my shoulder, a gesture of submission, like a plea for refuge. And I, who all my life had so often sought refuge, was so overwhelmed that someone should seek it in me that I could have wept as though just discovering that the whole world longs to rest on a loving shoulder. I wanted terribly to stroke this head, the brown hair with its golden sheen so close to my face, but I didn't dare. I hardly dared breathe. At last he stood straight, whispered a hurried "Adieu...till tomorrow!", then had turned the corner and was gone.

The next day I ran home from an errand I couldn't postpone and called from the bottom of the stairs, "Has anyone phoned for me?"

Stephen had scarcely left when I began to hope he'd call next day to see if I wasn't free after all. And in the scenario I imagined I was saying yes, and he was hurrying over and we were leaving the minute he arrived, with our fingers interlaced as they'd been

the night before and our ears still ringing with the least little words we'd exchanged.

But he didn't call either that day or the next. Then I began to be afraid. Afraid he'd been only a figment of my imagination, that he didn't really exist. I'd dreamt him, that was all, and dreaming wouldn't ever bring him back. Or afraid he'd just been trifling with me and had no intention of seeing me again.

But at eight o'clock, all the way from the top of the house, I heard the bell at the little side door. I'd been ready for hours, just in case he did come back into my life, I kept telling myself. I was downstairs in five seconds. I opened the door. There he was, exactly as he'd been when he left two nights before, except that when he saw me his dark eyes seemed to fill with a bright, caressing light.

"So you weren't a dream, thank God! I was horribly afraid, you don't know how afraid I was that you were just someone I'd imagined."

He laced his fingers between mine. We hurried away. We watched the Guinness ads go by at the Underground stations..."Sometimes I sits and thinks.... Sometimes I just sits...." Why is it I still see them so clearly, while so many other details about my dates with Stephen have vanished for ever? Perhaps because Stephen thought them funny and read them aloud so we could laugh together.

All through the opera he kept my fingers interlaced with his and would lift them to his lips and lightly kiss each one. I scarcely knew where I was. I think it must have been the Sadler's Wells Theatre, though I'm not absolutely certain. When Varlaam was singing his song about Kazan and the strings, brasses, woodwinds, and singer were all fortissimo, Stephen softly sang a few bars with them in my ear. I couldn't tell which was the voice from the stage and which was Stephen's, and when I remember sometimes, his is the only one I hear. The opera was being sung in Russian and he was singing the Russian words.

"So you speak Russian too?" I said afterwards.

"A bit of several Eastern European languages," he replied briefly as if he didn't want to pursue the subject.

When he took me home he said at the foot of the stairs, "Don't let's ever stay two days again without seeing each other. It's like an eternity. Promise me we'll see each other every day."

I wanted nothing less myself. At this point I barely glimpsed to

what a submissive, dependent state I was being led by my feeling for this young man I hardly knew. Still, that night I did have an inkling and made an effort to regain control and put off our next meeting at least a little while, but Stephen made a suggestion that was just too appealing. We would go to an ancient dockland pub, the Prospect of Whitby, on the other side of the city in the heart of a large working-class district. The dandies and eccentrics of Park Lane had made it fashionable by going there to drink draft beer and lean on the bar, elbow to elbow with cloth-capped labourers and picturesque wastrels. The spectacle was really worth seeing, said Stephen; nothing more typified a certain stratum of English society than its efforts to mix with the common herd in order to appear sympathetic to the people and their hardships.

The Underground was almost always a magic carpet for me, but never more than on this particular evening. We came out deep in the Port of London, almost down to the Thames Estuary, and made our way through dark streets peopled with shadowy, disconcerting figures to the little old pub built on piles over the grey waters of the river. You could hear the Thames lapping at its base. The pub was filled with acrid pipe smoke, the stench of beer, hysterical laughter, and cockney oaths. If I turned one way I might have been in a Hogarth painting with its ale-drinking working-class faces; if I turned the other I saw Pygmalion in reverse, high society with caps pulled over one ear and cigarette butts dangling from lips, playing at being the proletariat. I remember this evening with Stephen very well indeed; as dotty as certain dreams, no doubt perfectly in tune with my state of almost constant wide-eyed wonder at the time.

On the other hand, I remember very little about going with him to the National Gallery. My most lasting memories of a visit there are of a time when I went alone during my second trip to England. I remember particularly, though I don't know why, the portrait of "Giovanni Arnolfini and His Bride" by Jan van Eyck, which comes to my mind almost every day of my life. When I was there with Stephen I didn't see the works of art very well; we were holding hands all the time, that electric current kept passing between us, Stephen was whispering tender things to me, and all I really heard, all my ears retained, was the tumult of my emotion.

NOW WE WOULD linger at the little side door in the peaceful street. Our lips would meet. It was harder and harder to tear ourselves away from each other. Sometimes it was he who wouldn't let me go, often I was the one who couldn't bear to see him leave.

Were we happy? I don't think so. Our love was too feverish, too tumultuous, too possessive to allow us any rest, and when there are no islands of calm at which to pause, love soon reaches a point of exhaustion. My feeling for Stephen destroyed almost all power of reflection in me. He made me think I was living with great intensity, but in reality he was keeping me away from practically everything beyond his control. I was no longer seeing anything but brief glimpses of the world around us, which seemed more and more distant, strange, and out of reach, though it was we who were cut off, wrapped up in our passion, isolated as if for ever. Later, when I tried to analyse what had happened to us, it seemed to me that Stephen and I had been like butterflies or night-flying moths, those myriad creatures of the air drawn helplessly by some ruse of Nature like wavelengths or a certain smell. I wonder if the electrifying attraction we were subject to isn't one of the cruelest of all life's pitfalls and misconceptions. Because of him, once free of this subjugation I was long in mortal fear of the thing called love; perhaps I always shall be.

At the little side door, soon we couldn't bear to separate our hands, our lips. A storm would break, keeping us clinging to one another like two souls swept away in a raging tempest.

One night I leaned against the door and it gave way, carelessly latched no doubt. It swung open by itself. Stephen looked at me, a question in his eyes. We started up the stairs, still clinging to one another. At the first landing we stayed motionless for a while, our heads pressed together, engulfed in a silent turmoil beyond all rational thought, I suppose. We climbed the last flight of stairs holding each other up as though neither would be able to stand alone.

When he saw my room, Stephen seemed deeply moved. "A little room filled with the dreams of youth," he said pensively.

It was true, not only of this room but of all the others I'd occupied alone for a number of years. All must have been imbued with the universal dream inhabiting the human heart, which asks, what will love be like? Will it be kind? Will it hurt me?

Only then did Stephen realize that he was going to be my first lover. He became quiet and thoughtful, perhaps rather afraid. Holding me gently against his chest, he whispered that I mustn't hold it against him if he disappointed me a little, that love rarely gave as much as it led one to expect.

Then, holding me away slightly, he looked at me with a solemn expression of wonder and tenderness.

"Dear heart," he said, "how is it that you've waited for me? Surely you've been loved many times, and you must have been in love. What made you wait for me?"

We sat at the foot of my sofa-bed with our fingers interlaced, both looking straight ahead, into our own lives, neither seeing what the other was seeing. The thought passed through my mind that two people couldn't be more total strangers than were Stephen and I, brought together against prodigious odds in this almost transiently occupied little room. Now I could see that I'd been kept from love by my fear of it, I thought, the certainty that it was almost never happy; but it hadn't kept me from hoping for someone, some day, to fulfil my yearning for this utter unknown.

I put my head on his shoulder and told him that I was probably old-fashioned, but for me love was always a very serious thing, never frivolous or passing. That I'd always considered it to be irreversible in a way. That you really couldn't recover from love, any more than you can from death. And this was probably why it had made me so afraid while attracting me so irresistibly.

Putting a finger under my chin, Stephen lifted my face and studied it at length. There was concern in his eyes.

"You really believe that love's so serious you can't ever completely recover from it?"

"It seems to me it can't be something you simply forget."

"In that case," he said gently, "we'd better just stay friends a while longer till we can see more clearly inside ourselves. And especially, don't you think, we'd better avoid being in this room alone together, it feels so good to a weary pilgrim like me, or you, or anyone on this earth...."

But as he spoke he held me very close and I heard the throbbing of his heart, and the fervid, dancing flame in our eyes gave each of us a delicate, ethereal image of the other. We left the world

behind, to overturn and sink...rapturously perhaps...but at least there were two of us to sink together.

OUR HAPPIEST DAYS were in the next few weeks perhaps; we were unaware that they were the last we'd be granted of this period of confidence. Stephen rented two bicycles so we could explore large sections of London together. I'd never ventured anywhere more daunting than country paths or peaceful little sidestreets in St-Boniface on a bicycle, and the thought of braving the heavy traffic of London filled me with terror. I'd never be able to do it, I said. But Stephen kept giving me patient reassurance. He'd be the leader; any time there might be a problem he'd go first and make a path for me; I was to keep my eyes glued to his back and not let myself look elsewhere, follow him without thinking of anything else.

We set out one mildly warm day in May. At first all went well. Stephen had plotted a route through a series of sidestreets, avoiding most of the busy thoroughfares. But we had to confront a few. Before we plunged into one, Stephen would give me encouraging words and signs. Trembling, I'd pedal beside the tall buses which used to delight me so when I was riding all over the city on the upper deck. Perched on my flimsy wheels, almost brushing their sides, I discovered they were four times bigger than I'd thought.

Once, one of the monsters slipped between Stephen and me, separating us. I was so frightened I thought of getting off and just staying where I was, but this was impossible. Ahead there was a monster blocking my way and behind was another which seemed determined to run me over. I simply had to move along with the merciless flow of the traffic. Then, a bit to the right of the bus separating us, Stephen appeared, signalling that the way was clear for me there. I screwed up my courage and rode, looking only at Stephen's beckoning hand. The monster was moving pretty fast but I pedalled by, caught up with Stephen, fell in behind him, and followed as he turned into a quiet street where I could stop and catch my breath. I really thought I'd triumphed that day. I still think so and I've been grateful to Stephen ever since. He had the rare gift of putting confidence in people in order to help them find confidence in themselves. I was still shaking from the fright I'd had, but he told me I'd conquered fear that day and I'd never again feel it as before.

In stages, stopping fairly often to give me a chance to rest, we rode to Richmond Park in less than two hours. It was a weekday and there weren't many people there. We had the whole magnificent park almost to ourselves, we and the free-roaming deer, hinds, and fawns. We fed them pieces of bread, which several came and ate out of Stephen's hand. As I watched, I suddenly thought how naturally tender and kind he seemed. It must have surprised me because I found myself saying, as if I'd had reason to doubt it, "You seem so gentle, really. Are you?"

He seemed a bit put out by the question.

"Not very," he said. "In this world you can't allow yourself to be gentle. It makes you too vulnerable."

As we turned away he took my hand and slipped his fingers between mine, rather by habit than with warmth this time, I thought.

"You see...," he began, then broke off, as if he realized he was about to make himself vulnerable. He changed the subject. "Let's go and sit up there on the bank," he suggested.

We pushed our bicycles up a grassy slope. There was a huge tree at the top whose spreading branches were like an umbrella, blocking the heat of the sun. We leaned the bicycles against its sturdy trunk and stretched out on the grass, half in the sun and half in the shade. We lay on our backs with Stephen's head in my lap, forming a kind of cross.

He gazed up at the sky. It was clean and pure above the great island of verdure formed by Richmond Park in the London of those days.

We stayed this way for a quarter of an hour, perhaps more. For the moment we didn't need to look at each other or caress. We were content to lie in a cross and gaze at the tranquil sky, finding such happiness in this that we needed nothing else.

With his eyes still fixed on the clear blue sky, as if the admission were extracted by a kind of infinite goodness in everything around us, or perhaps his own staggering realization, he said:

"I think I love you."

Years, thousands of years it seems sometimes, have passed since that peaceful interlude under the big tree in Richmond Park. Of everything in our relationship, so full of frenzied sensory excitement and its tyrannical power over our lives, two things still stir

my heart more than any others. One is the memory of Stephen softly singing me that aria from Boris Godunov, and the other, which moves me perhaps even more, is this confession made in full view of the sky.

IX

HE LEFT ME at the bottom of the stairs that night. I was so tired I could hardly stand. He seemed very weary also, and still had to return the two bicycles. He left without calling back, "See you tomorrow," as he usually did, and didn't turn to give me a last little wave. For a moment, in the harsh light of the streetlamp near the door, his face seemed preoccupied, I thought, though in view of what followed perhaps hindsight made me imagine this.

The next day I didn't hear from him, though ordinarily not a day went by without Geoffrey calling up the stairs, "Your friend's on the phone...." I used to run down the stairs four at a time, and when I took the receiver all I'd hear at first was the thump of my own pulse, then at the sound of Stephen's voice my heart would calm and beat less frantically. Each time it was as though I were afraid the miracle wouldn't happen again – the proof that Stephen was real – and once it had happened I could relax and breathe normally again.

The day after, still no word. On the third day I had to go out and imagined that Stephen had chosen this very time to telephone, so I ran home in great haste to ask if there hadn't been a call for me.

Geoffrey looked at me with such obvious compassion I was humiliated. I stopped going to the bicycle shop to see if there'd been a call. I stayed in my room and waited, and the hours passed the way they must pass for prisoners in solitary confinement. The simmering anger I feel whenever someone keeps me waiting goes back to this – though I suspect I was no stranger to it even then. Anger at being forced to do nothing but wait, wasting my time, wasting my life.

I hardly even read any more. My ear was constantly listening

for the phone downstairs to ring. Time and again I would think I had heard it, mingled with the sounds of the street, and I'd run to the door of my room holding my breath, waiting for Geoffrey's voice to call, "Your friend...." I would have been downstairs before he'd even finished, and the sky would have cleared for me once more.

At last I decided to call a number Stephen had given me, rather reluctantly I thought, after I told him I'd never be able to reach him in case there had to be a change in our arrangements for going out. It was the number of the people with whom he boarded, a house I'd never set foot in. A woman's voice answered. Stephen was away, she told me. For how long? She had no idea. Where had he gone? She didn't know. Why did he have to leave so suddenly? With a hint of irritation this time, she told me she didn't think she ought to answer that question.

Totally undone, I went back up to my room. A gaping chasm was opening under my feet. Worse than discovering the mystery surrounding Stephen was discovering how I felt about him. In the centre of the thing that had held me captive for over two months, which I'd thought must be love, something ugly and destructive was now growing, like resentment. Inside of me, distrust had declared war on love and I would never totally recover from this. What I was feeling was a thousand times worse than my long-standing fear of loving: the hostility one feels when caught in a trap after being honest and sincere. Yet I realized that I had been much to blame, for even now I knew practically nothing about Stephen except that he attended the University of London, not very regularly, that he was fluent in seven or eight languages, and that he knew a lot about music. When I searched my memory I also discovered a good many allusions to cities he apparently knew, like Paris, Prague, Munich, Vienna, Budapest, Zagreb, though he had never in so many words told me he'd stayed in any of them.

I resigned myself to telephoning again to the lady whose house Stephen lived in, who could have been a friend, an acquaintance, or simply his landlady for all I knew. This time a man answered. No, Stephen hadn't left any message but he'd certainly be back before long and then would no doubt give me an explanation that would set my mind at rest.

This man had a trace of Stephen's slight Slavic accent. I asked

him if he wasn't Ukrainian too. He told me that he and his wife were indeed of Ukrainian origin, though they'd lived in England since the Russian Revolution. Then he urged me not to worry. Stephen would be back any day now and would call me at once.

I was naïve enough to be a mite reassured by all this. I even decided to go out and get some air and was stunned to realize that while I'd been shut up waiting for word from Stephen, summer had arrived and any number of chances for contact with life and Nature had passed me by. Thereupon my feeling towards him turned to something I had never before felt for anyone – active dislike, I think – perhaps even an urge to retaliate, make him suffer even more than he'd hurt me.

But suddenly I imagined him dead as the result of an accident or dying alone in some foreign country, and I gave him back all the love that swelled my heart. Not long after this I imagined the opposite, that he was alive and well and enjoying himself, holidaying beside the sea or in the mountains, and my bitterness towards him returned in full force, more bristling than ever. I wore myself out, by turns loving and hating the same man.

He was away nearly a month. Then one night Geoffrey called up the stairs, "Your friend's on the phone...." I came downstairs, my heart trembling as it had when I felt his eyes pulling me across Lady Frances's drawing room. But this time my trembling emotion was mixed with an indescribably bleak, painful awareness of what a slave I'd become to his phone call.

I heard him speak in his usual voice, the one he used in our daily conversations when nothing special had happened since the night before. He told me the time had seemed long, that it had been hot, that he really wanted to see me. Would it be tomorrow? Or tonight if I didn't think it was too late?

"I've missed you, you know," he added.

I stayed silent so long he asked, "Are you still there?"

Where was I, indeed? Very far away and very much alone in any case, on the kind of barren shore where love leaves you when it ebbs after its floods have sweetly sung, promising happiness. He had only needed to say, "I've missed you...," and I could see the desolation to which this dearest love of my life had led me by the hand and heart. But I didn't want to admit it. I wouldn't want to

admit it for a long time yet. Seeing clearly into one's heart is the last thing love wants.

"All right," I said. "I'll leave right now. You leave right now too. That way we'll meet half-way unless you walk very fast."

He seemed disappointed that I didn't want to have him come to my room, but said he would leave immediately and follow an agreed route so we wouldn't miss each other on the way.

When he came into view he was still quite far away and in the light of a streetlamp I thought his face looked thin and drawn, prematurely showing the wear and tear age would bring, he who was still so young and vigorous. This distressed me so that I ran to clasp him in my arms as if to keep him young for ever. We stood holding each other, cheek to cheek, rocking together almost in dance, murmuring endearments..."Dear heart!..." "Stephen dear!"

The spell was taking hold of me again. The flood was trying to rise once more and I would have quickly yielded if Stephen hadn't slipped his fingers between mine as we turned to walk; it was so mechanical that I suddenly realized it was a habit, acquired for others, not just me, perhaps practised at length before becoming so endearingly natural. I withdrew my hand because it hurt, because to my eyes skill and finesse in love suddenly betrayed experience...perhaps a certain inconstancy. But he took it again and began to question me about what I'd been doing the last few weeks. Had I been to the theatre? To Gladys's cabin? Had I at least been outdoors taking advantage of the beautiful weather? Never a word about what had happened in his life all this time.

Suddenly I heard myself asking in a strained voice why he had left me so long without word.

At this he dropped his pretence of light-heartedness and seemed exceedingly nervous and tired. From the warm brown eyes I loved so much, so dependably twinkling and beguiling, the sparkle vanished.

"I thought sooner or later I'd have to talk to you seriously," he said.

We had come to a kind of little square with a bench, some trees, perhaps a fountain. We sat on the bench. Stephen looked straight ahead. He seemed so miserable, so much at a loss that I felt for him, thinking he was about to give me a plausible and convincing

explanation for his behaviour and I was going to be ashamed of my suspicions. Already eager to make up, I reached out and smoothed a wayward lock of hair from his brow. He took a deep breath and began to tell me a story which even today I wonder if I really heard from his lips.

Well, he said, since I was so insistent, he was going to reveal a secret part of his life, though it would be better for me not to know anything about it. I'd have to keep what he was going to tell me strictly to myself, and it would still be only part of what he considered he had a right to tell me. As for the rest, I'd have to trust him.

I already felt as though I were involved in some far-fetched novel, and now here he was delivering a warning in an impassioned voice I didn't recognize as his.

"It would be best, of course," he said, "if you didn't expect too much of me, and I should have warned you before, because in a way I'm not free and won't be for some years to come. I've committed my life – part of my life – to the cause of my persecuted country, and there'll be no rest or personal life for me till I've avenged the Soviet Union's crimes against my unfortunate brothers."

I listened, thinking, he's making this up, he can't be a secret agent; but I saw in his face that he was serious. I challenged him.

"What's this unfortunate country you're talking about? Weren't you born in Canada? Isn't that your country? Or even the United States since you consider that your second country?"

"I'm talking about the Ukraine," he replied, "which Stalin reduced to one of the worst famines in history because she resisted Bolshevism. Do you know how many of my people died of hunger in a single year just in Kiev?"

"Your people, if you like," I retorted, "but at that rate all suffering people are yours, and mine too, ours. Why the Ukraine any more than any other country? You don't even know it yourself."

From the look on his face I could see I was wasting my breath trying to reason with him. A fierce exaltation was closing his mind to any other voice.

He told me his recent journey had taken him to a Soviet-dominated country to make contact with an agent of the London Ukrainian Association. He'd been tailed by the KGB, which had been after him for some time, and had had to stay hidden in a

peasant's barn for nearly a week, almost without food. It was a miracle he'd escaped alive. This was why he hadn't been able to get in touch with me. Anyway, couriers were forbidden to communicate with anyone outside the network when they were abroad, to avoid endangering lives. He was putting me at peril just talking to me as he was now. He therefore begged me earnestly to keep what I'd learned tonight strictly to myself.

I listened, still thinking it was just a bad dream.

Little by little he revealed fragments of his other life. I learned that he belonged to a group of Ukrainian militants financed by Ukrainian-American patriots, and its cause was nothing less than the overthrow of Soviet power in the Ukraine and the restoration of the independence it had enjoyed for a single day during the First World War.

I had already had a premonition that his dreams, aspirations, and secretiveness made Stephen profoundly alien to me. That night, sitting on the bench in the little square, I was convinced that in all essentials we had nothing in common.

It wasn't simply discovering that I didn't come first in his life that hurt me so. After suffering so much on his account I was wounded even further to learn what kind of passion was standing between us. If I had been able to share it I might have felt less betrayed, but the whole thing seemed totally absurd, unreasonable, particularly when he admitted that his studies at the University of London were partly a cover, since without an ostensible occupation in London he'd be even more suspect in the eyes of the KGB, which had agents in the city.

I said no more that night about my thoughts, however. I couldn't, I'd received such a blow. For sitting on the bench with the leaves rustling softly overhead as in Richmond Park not so long before, as in Rutebeuf's poem, my love had died. There was no mistake; I knew it instantly. What I didn't know was how long after the mortal blow love keeps trying to come back to life, begging to be allowed to live. One of the most terrifying and unfathomable experiences of all to come our way is this stubborn fight, one's poor deluded soul wanting to be rid of what one's body wants to keep.

We began to walk again. What a lovely summer evening it was! The beginning and the end of a love affair…two immortal moments, one might say, which remain for ever in one's memory, while

much of what has occurred between is erased. I still breathe the scent of flowers as we walked beside the old Fulham cemetery. I remember the smell of freshly watered lawns. I hear the sound of our footsteps in the still night. All of this reached me from a world I had lost, as if with love I had lost all that makes the world warm and wonderful.

No doubt relieved to have unburdened himself, Stephen was talking about things we would do together. In his happiness to find everything back as he imagined it would remain, he even whistled a cheerful tune for a few minutes. Then he talked about Cambridge, which we'd have to go and see some day, but especially, no doubt, the famous Magdalen College at Oxford. He had a friend there who would show us around. And we mustn't fail to go to Canterbury, the heart of old England in Chaucer's time. He was even making long-range plans for much later when he'd regain his freedom after three, four, or at most five years devoted to the Cause. He would return to teaching, perhaps in New York. Then, he led me to understand, if I wished we might unite our destinies.

I no longer believed him. I would never believe him now. That night he had shown me a heart far too full of political passion to leave room for a love that was warm and alive.

And yet, at the little side door, when he looked at me with those magnetic eyes and opened his arms, I went to them, taking refuge from the heartache and pain he'd brought me. And in a kind of love which now could only increase the distance between us, we sought the cure for our need for love.

I despised myself for this. I began to struggle with all my strength to detach myself from him. If it was he who telephoned, I wasn't in. I'd be out at times when he might come. I'd return very late, sometimes to find him waiting for me at the little side door, and wearily, yearning to bring back what once had been, I would go to him. And then I'd hate myself more than ever.

Meanwhile I was doing nothing, and seeing with increasing clarity the destructiveness of a love such as mine had been. I had virtually abandoned my studies. I saw no one. Once again I became a solitary creature, but now my disgust with myself nagged me constantly besides.

Worst of all, for a long time I too had to leave someone who loved me almost totally in the dark. During this time I think I

remember receiving anguished letters from my mother, reproaching me either for not writing at all or for sending meagre little letters that weren't much better. Since I couldn't or wouldn't tell her things she would disapprove of, I'd no doubt been writing platitudes which made her suspect I was hiding what was important.

Towards the end of June Stephen had to leave hurriedly on another of his dangerous secret missions. I learned later that this time he'd been to one of the Balkan countries to deliver some tracts to an intermediary. There were no telephone calls or letters, only a note slipped under my door apologizing for not being able to give me any news; the less I knew about his activities, the better for my own safety. Perhaps he was right.

There was total silence for a while, but this time I was gradually becoming used to it, even began to relax a little. I was desperately lonely, however. Phyllis had gone to Dorset. Gladys was almost always at her cabin across from Hampton Court and I didn't feel like going there any more. Even Bohdan was away on a concert tour in the north of England. Affectionate, honest, courageous Bohdan; if only it were he I loved, I kept thinking, how different things would be! But would they really? In Bohdan's life music had always and would always come first. Even in my own life I often sensed that I must keep room for something other than love, something perhaps even more demanding, and so I would be torn just as Stephen was torn. Yet I wanted to be loved exclusively, with an undivided love.

Living longer doesn't teach you much about love. Still, by now I think I understand that if I demanded so much of Stephen and couldn't abide his having another and equally important interest, in a way this was to get even for the bondage imposed on me by my feeling for him. Sooner or later I was bound to rebel against such total domination over my life. Undoubtedly I was already hoping for a tender, dreamy love; a haven and refuge. But can love ever be peace?

X

IN THE END I came to hate the little room I'd thought was so calming at a time when I was more or less calm already. In July under a white-hot roof, it was stifling. It's strange how often I've had little rooms that are made unbearable by the summer sun at times when I've been most alone. Scarcely a year later I would have another room very like this one at the far end of Dorchester Street in Montreal; early in the morning I used to escape from it and go down to the river where it was cool.

There were so few trees and green spaces in Fulham, and its working-class hustle and bustle, its cries, its smells, the incessant growl of lumbering buses arriving or departing at the door and shaking the whole building from top to bottom – in short almost everything I'd rather enjoyed not so long before – came to be more than I could stand now that the heat of summer had settled in.

I fell into the habit of slipping away to Trafalgar Square, where I'd spend whole days. The water from the fountains filled the pools beneath and the pools overflowed, keeping the huge square relatively cool. Like innumerable passing tourists, like a great many poor people of London who had nowhere else to go to taste the pleasure of water, I used to plunge my hands into the overflowing pools, sometimes my arms all the way up to the armpits. I remember how good the water was. I remember it better than the many times I've bathed in the sea in the course of summers filled with the play and pleasure of water.

I would buy something to eat at one of the little mobile canteens that appeared wherever there was a crowd and eat it right there. I'd read, or pretend to. I'd watch clouds of pigeons fluttering around Nelson's Column. I don't think these parasites are as fat anywhere else as they are in Trafalgar Square, where they're fed the best of

everything. In return they never stop cooing. I'd see couples go by with their fingers interlaced. Sometimes I shut my eyes so as not to see them and sometimes I watched with pity. Didn't they know what misery they were courting? I was sure any love was doomed to die of disappointment, heartache, and exhaustion. At least I had escaped, I thought, well armed never to let myself be caught again.

Day after day I'd come back to sit in the square. In the ever-present throngs there were as many Londoners, residents of the neighbourhood and workers from nearby offices, as tourists with guidebooks in their hands and cameras slung over their shoulders. I was soothed by their company, always changing but always the same, like the waves of the sea. Strange how often in my life I've had crowds of strangers as substitutes for friends and family.

In fact I'd begun to yearn for another kind of company, without yet being fully aware of it. Here in this teeming city square, refreshing visions of whole forests of trees, secluded pathways, and water flowing through river grasses were beginning to stir in me. But I'd been deprived of the pleasures of Nature for so long that they might have been coming from a world and time I'd lost for ever.

Eventually, one day when my mind could focus a little better on my surroundings, I noticed small forest-green buses arriving every half-hour from one direction or another. They would drive around the square and come to a stop beside a marker that was also forest green. After letting off passengers and taking on others they would depart again, cheerfully I thought, for a destination which for some reason I took to be a happy one. I had ridden around so much on London buses, how had I failed to discover these before?

This Green Line went close to forty miles into the country, so you could go out and come back in a day, perhaps even half a day. I learned this from an old cockney who came and sat on the bench beside me. The Green Line couldn't be better named, he told me, for its buses travelled only verdant lesser roads around London to enchanting half-forgotten villages, olden-day places, "the lovely old England", leaving speed and thundering traffic to the Great West Road, the Great East Road, and all the evil-smelling major arteries.

Moments later, one of the sprightly little forest-green buses appeared and drew up at the Green Line sign. From where I sat I could easily read the tall letters on the front that announced its destination. "Epping Forest", they read. Why did it make my heart leap, as if this were the place of healing for me and I shouldn't lose a minute getting there? All I remember of this moment which had such a momentous repercussion on my life is an irresistible urge to drive away in that bus. It gave a gentle roar. It would be leaving any minute. Suddenly I raced across the square. The bus was already in motion when I jumped onto its step. The driver took one hand from the wheel, held it out to me, and drew me inside. As he manoeuvred into a free lane, he chided me gently for giving him such a turn, nearly running under his wheels like that.

"This isn't the forest yet, so you can't go running round like a hare without looking right or left."

We left the noisy square behind. Without realizing, I was on my way to one of those blessed havens to which life has steered me over the years, each a place in which to pause and gather strength and momentum before moving on.

"WHERE TO, MA'AM?" asked the driver-cum-conductor with the affable manner so many Londoners used to have with foreigners, as though sensing their vulnerability better than anyone.

"Epping Forest," I said naïvely, clutching the handrail with both hands.

"Epping Forest's a big place," he observed. "Isn't there a special part where you'd like to get off?"

"I don't know the forest," I said. "Could you show me a pretty place where I could walk a while without getting too far from the bus route, so I can catch the bus back after a few hours?"

"So it's just to go walking you want?" He smiled at me approvingly.

We'd been talking loudly enough for several other passengers to have heard. They weren't your usual city bus riders who, though often helpful, are generally people with things on their minds, in a hurry. These were people relieved to be going home to the country after a tiring day in the city, or city folk whose modest means permitted only outings to the country not far from London. To my great surprise, almost all took pains to help the driver and me decide where I should best get off.

"Beechwood's a pretty spot," said an elderly lady sitting three or four rows behind the driver. "Did you know," she added for everyone's edification, "Tennyson used to go there for peace and inspiration."

"Beechwood is a pretty spot, it's true," said another lady who'd stopped her knitting to join the discussion, "but it isn't on this route. The young miss might run into trouble making the transfer and get lost and all worn out when it's peace and quiet she wants."

"That's what we all do," said a man's voice quietly somewhere down the bus.

Someone else was determined to send me to the town of Epping where I could have tea at a reasonably priced inn beside a forest path. There I'd have plenty of time to cool off and recover from the awful city air.

I listened to these kind souls taking such pains for me and wished I could please every one of them by going to all the places they were suggesting.

The lady who was backing Beechwood pressed her point. "Some of the beeches were already big when the village of Beechwood was named for them three hundred years ago," she said.

This wasn't the first time I'd found instant friends in a group of total strangers and it wouldn't be the last. It's like getting a present, and of all the presents I've ever received, probably none has brought me more pleasure. Yet I've never imagined I could make strangers want to help me this way at will. I've always had to have a genuine need for help, which I suppose in some way becomes apparent. My need that day, my unconscious appeal to others, was perhaps apparent the minute I stepped aboard the bus.

An elderly man sitting halfway down the bus, his knobbly hands propped on the crook of his walking stick, suggested I transfer and go to Waltham Abbey, "the oldest church in England, y'know, started by Harold, the last king of the Saxons...a rare gem, y'know...." He kept on in the loud, strangely metallic voice of people who are a little deaf.

"Here now," an ironic voice protested, "when she don't even know the forest yet, what's the sense of sending the poor young foreign miss chasing all over the place after the oldest church in England?... If it really is the oldest."

We passed King's Cross and my fellow passengers still hadn't

decided where they should send me. The driver finally settled the matter in favour of Wake Arms.

"There's only an inn," he told me, "but it's a friendly place. You can stay there if you like till I come back in two hours' time, or you can go for a walk. On the left there's a quiet path mostly in the forest but not too lonely. Sometimes it comes out in the open and there are farms in the distance now and again...oh yes, and a beautiful moor full of red heather. It's a lovely little path that I'm going to come and explore some more soon myself when I've got a day off."

This was how I came to buy a ticket to Wake Arms. I've never been the same since and I still marvel that such a small decision, just agreeing to go to Wake Arms and not Epping or Beechwood, had so many extraordinary consequences that today I get lost when I try to retrace them all.

I sat behind the driver and made a nuisance of myself, I'm sure, asking him over and over not to forget me when we reached Wake Arms. I was suddenly so enamoured of this unknown place that I didn't want to go anywhere else.

The driver kept reassuring me with a friendly glance in the little mirror in front of him, and finally I calmed down. At least, though a twinge of anxiety lingered, I began to feel soothed, an effect that steady motion has always had on me. Now we weren't picking up many people and the bus moved along at a good pace.

The lady sitting beside me asked me what country I was from.

"From Canada," I told her.

"From Canada!" she exclaimed in a tone of real affection, whether for me or my country I didn't know, but I soon found out. "It's one of our countries, Canada is," she concluded.

I returned her smile with what was probably a rather peculiar one of my own, trying to show gratitude for her warmth but also disapproval of her assumption that I and my country were hers. Then I settled down to enjoy the ride.

Curiously enough, after discussing my case so thoroughly the other passengers left me to my thoughts, no doubt returning to the peace and quiet of their own. We rode along in almost total silence, a busful of people freed of each other yet united, all absorbed in nostalgic musings.

The city took a long time to release us, let us escape from it. It

kept catching up. I had never come this way on my long upper-deck bus rides. The endless city suburbs I was discovering sprawled even farther than I had imagined. Each time I thought they were giving way to an unkempt countryside with billboards sprouting in the fields, they would begin again, with the same High Street, the same little huddle of commerce, the same ABC tea-shop. This was the first time London had ever looked to me like life imprisonment for millions of human beings. The faces I saw as we passed were dejected, burdened, blank. But I confess I'd never before been in any of the city's grimiest, most depressing boroughs.

My relief was all the greater when at last we were bowling along roads with little gardens full of tall flowers and half-timbered cottages often half-hidden under masses of climbing clematis. I'd never seen anything like this before except in pictures and I kept turning my head to keep each one in view as long as possible.

Today when I remember so many unexpectedly pretty country scenes, often in the most surprising places, it makes me think that with their thousands of different little pastoral jewels the English must have invented country scenery – though they have undoubtedly also invented the filthiest and most inhuman of cities. For having done such harm to Nature, have they tried to make amends by nurturing and preserving it?

Suddenly we were in the forest. For some time it had looked cool and inviting but rather distant, still inaccessible. Then all at once it came close. Now it was really all around us, branches from either side joining overhead to make a marvellous continuing archway filled with millions of sparkling, winking specks of sunlight. The great trees, the mossy trunks, the deep rich green must all have come down to us from some long-past age. Probably nothing much had changed since the days when Robin Hood and his Merry Men used to leap out to plunder the coaches of the rich to help the poor, as the legend goes.

The driver must have recognized my delight as he watched me watching the forest through his rearview mirror, for when I glanced in it I saw him smile with the genuine pleasure you feel when you find someone enjoying what you enjoy yourself.

"Marvellous, isn't it?" he commented when I turned my eyes gratefully back to the great, serene archway overhead, all my weariness and heartache banished for the moment.

The bus slowed.

"Wake Arms," announced the driver.

The inn was all alone in a small forest clearing by the road. For the time being, with its pub closed and the upstairs windows shuttered, it looked either deserted for the day or abandoned to a deep torpor. It had a very beautiful sign, as did all English inns in those days, which hung well out from the front of the building on a wrought-iron frame. What was on it? I must have known but, alas, I can't remember.

The driver handed me a timetable. He'd marked the return times with a wax crayon and he made sure I noted that after seven o'clock the buses were less frequent.

I don't think I paid very much attention. Perhaps I already had a feeling I wouldn't be going back that night.

He raised his hand in goodbye. He wished me a nice walk and a pleasant day. He closed the door and the bus pulled away. Through its windows I could see hands waving. Perhaps even the elderly man with the walking stick was waving, or was it his raised walking stick that I saw? Sometimes when my thoughts wander, for no reason at all I see that bus disappearing for ever, leaving me at the side of an unfamiliar road. And through the dappled green reflections in its windows I see hands, a little blurred, waving to me still after all these years.

IT NEVER even crossed my mind to disturb the sleepy inn for information or any other reason. I set off at once down the narrow track leading from the bus stop into the forest. It was just a cycle and walking path, in fact, and I didn't meet a soul. At first I enjoyed being completely surrounded by nothing but Nature. I kept seeing swarms of bees, wasps, and butterflies pass by. I walked on and on, loath to turn back, drawn farther and farther down what I would call a trail, at least around the next curve, for it kept bending one way or the other, always in full sunlight, however, since at this hour the sun was directly overhead and the shadows no longer reached me. Soon I felt very tired from the heat and fresh air, and probably from relaxation of nerves long under tension. I was also thinking that I was foolish to venture so far into the deserted forest and that soon I wouldn't have the strength to return to the bus

stop in case this path didn't really lead anywhere, as I was beginning to suspect.

But I couldn't resist walking a little farther, then a little farther still, driven by the excitement, the anticipation of happy surprise that I've always experienced on unknown roads. This couldn't be the path the driver had talked about in any event. I'd seen neither farms in the distance nor heather-covered moors. Either he'd been mistaken or I'd misinterpreted what he'd said. Small bushy trees grew thick and tangled, pressing close on either side, really very wild, and never an opening to any horizon. This appeared to be a part of the forest left to regrow after some blight or other calamity, for it was clear no cutting had been done for some years. I could just as well have been in the bushlands of my own Manitoba as in one of the most populous countries in the world. But my surroundings pleased me greatly because I could imagine I'd never left home, hadn't flung myself so recklessly down the highways of the world and so still had all my opportunities in life and love ahead, undiminished.

I kept on for some time without thinking, so tired that I was dragging my feet, barely conscious of the time and what country I was in. Eventually, however, frightened by the persistent silence and near the end of my strength, I was about to turn back when I saw signs of habitation just ahead, half hidden in the trees. A minute more and I would have turned away from one of the most extraordinary encounters fate ever brought my way – unless the events of that day were all pure chance. But it's even more difficult for me to believe in chance, all things considered, than in the intrusion of the marvellous into my life.

THE LITTLE HOUSE was very low to the ground and surrounded by trees and flowers, the hollyhocks and tall, pale blue delphiniums reaching almost to its thatched roof. It couldn't be made for living in, I thought, just for playing at living in; the humble little Tudor cottage of Old England on the tins of fine biscuits my mother used to buy when I was a child, mostly for the tin I'm sure, because we treasured those tins and kept them for years to hold batch after batch of other, less expensive biscuits.

The minute I saw it I felt as if I'd returned to the safety and

301

peace of my early childhood. There was a sign nailed to a tree, which I can see in every detail, though I've forgotten many more important things. In crude, hand-painted letters it read, "Fresh-cut flowers, tea, scones, crumpets...1 s." Under an arbour at one side there was a rustic wood table with chairs to match. All around, the air was full of the ecstatic humming of bees, wasps, and hornets, drawn undoubtedly by the flower garden from miles around. Perhaps the swarms I'd seen go by were coming here and had arrived not long before me.

I knocked at the squat little door under the low-hanging eaves. It was opened by a young hunchback with the pleading eyes one often sees in the disabled. I asked her if it was too early for tea and she said no, she was just about to put the kettle on, in fact. Barely fifteen minutes later she re-emerged bearing such a heavy tray for her frail arms that I hurried to help her. When I saw all the food on it for such a small price I couldn't help asking if enough people came this far to make so much preparation worthwhile. She told me it was surprising how many came.

"When they get away from London they're keen for fresh air and freedom, I suppose," she said, "but they're not always sure where to get off the bus. A driver I don't know seems to suggest Wake Arms quite often. Perhaps he came himself one day and keeps hoping he'll come by again. People are like that, aren't they, wanting to go places they know about but haven't been to? I'm that way, all my life I've wanted to go to the seaside. In any case, they take the same path as you. Some take it by mistake, I imagine, but the good Lord sends me quite a few customers, whatever it is."

With obvious pleasure she lingered a few minutes more, watching me enjoy my tea, then went back inside the house.

In no time I'd devoured just about everything on the tray, including a little pot of black-currant jam that the wasps descended upon, competing frantically with me until I thought of putting a spoonful aside for them, which they went to and ate delicately, leaving the pot for me. Since then I've known that wasps and humans can eat together peacefully in a garden if one is generous enough to provide a little share just for the wasps.

Made drowsy by the heat and all the food I'd eaten, I had dozed off when the young woman came back with a big pot of hot water for stretching out my tea.

"Sleep, sleep, " she told me with gentle insistence. "I'll just take the tray away so the flies won't bother you."

My eyes were so heavy with sleep I could hardly keep them open, but I still knew vaguely where I was. Would I ever have the strength to stand up, set off, and walk all the way back to Wake Arms? It didn't seem possible. But most of all I simply didn't want to leave. I felt as though no harm could reach me here; the peace of this place would be mine as long as I stayed. I called the young woman back.

"I walked much too far getting here to go all the way back today," I said. "Couldn't you make some room for me for the night?"

"I would with pleasure, but it's a wee place as you can see," she said with a sad little gesture towards the house. "There's hardly room already for my father and my mother, been paralysed for years, she has, and it's me as does for her, then there's my brother, he's a bit simple, poor lad, he comes home late sometimes when they don't keep him the night at a farm where he's worked all day in return for supper and a bit of kindness."

Suddenly I was wide awake and listening with excitement. It was as if an enchanting page from one of the English novels I'd adored were reaching my ears straight from the very person who'd been its source and inspiration. Just twenty miles from London, guided only by my lucky star, could I really have stumbled upon exactly the old-world atmosphere and surroundings described in the works of George Eliot and Thomas Hardy? So thatched cottages weren't the only things surviving from a time I'd thought long past, recorded only in books.

The young woman was worrying about me. "An idea's just come to me, you know," she said. "If you think you can walk a bit more, not far, scarcely a mile by this same path, you'll come to a wee village called Upshire. Don't stop at the inn, it's not much of a place. Look for Century Cottage. Knock and ask for Esther. Esther Perfect. Tell her Felicity sent you. I'll be a deal surprised if she doesn't welcome you with open arms. She's got room. It's big, Century Cottage is."

I was already on my feet, needing no more to make me find fresh new energy. I left a shilling and a few pence on the table and set off. The heat of the day was still heavy, as were my feet, but I was buoyed by the same curious anticipation that had flagged

only briefly all day. Felicity showed me the direction of the village and several times I heard her rather thin little voice calling encouragement after me, saying, "You won't regret it, oh, you surely won't regret it!"

XI

FOR SOMEONE approaching from the south as I did, the village was set on a gentle upward slope tapering away into a beautiful clear sky. Behind, the forest pressed close, a constant companion, but the vista ahead was boundless and the unexpected sight of so much space was probably what made me take an instant liking to Upshire.

It was all on one side of the single street, which must be rather rare in England – old stone cottages, dear little old church and churchyard surrounded by yews, some less ancient cottages, post office, pub, and vicarage standing in endless contemplation of a huge open plain much like the horizon of the Canadian West that I described in "Where Will You Go, Sam Lee Wong?" in *Garden in the Wind*. The sight of this plain rolling away in magnificently broad, fluid waves lifted my spirits with the same kind of magical lift I saw in those waves, perhaps because I came upon it from the forest as I used to come to the open prairie when emerging from the woods on my uncle's farm. Nothing is quite like the downs of Essex, this is certain, their strong earth swell rolling on and on, driven by the same wind since time began.

The forest, patiently beaten back on the near side, dwindled to a slender, dark line in the far distance, blending with the horizon. Between this and the village, as if barely sketched, you could just see some solitary farm buildings with herds in the fields moving so slightly you could mistake them for big rocks at times. In a hollow much closer I saw what looked like a small manor house with a Georgian façade, and on the top of a mound a curious, intriguingly ancient-looking stone slab. I marvelled to think I had found so much of England's long past so unspoiled barely more than an hour from London.

The reason, I was soon to learn, was that everything here – the

fields and pastures and farm buildings, the village, the forest game preserve, the small manor house, even to a point the church and churchyard – belonged to the squire of the manor, who so far had prevented the metropolitan sprawl of London a few short miles away from expanding towards Upshire. With the metropolis chafing to come and spawn more of its narrow building-lots, High Streets like all the others, rows and rows of identical little houses, and of course ABC tea-shops by the dozen, how much longer would he succeed? But for a time at any rate, the powerful swell of the downs would roll on undisturbed, on some days beneath big masses of white cloud scudding to or from the Channel.

I found Century Cottage without difficulty. Though with its second floor it stood much taller than Felicity's little house, it seemed to be no less buried in a tangled profusion of flowers. I walked up a path winding this way and that, perhaps as dictated by the flowers themselves in their determination to grow and spread where it suited them. I must have disappeared, I thought, among the tall delphiniums, giant hollyhocks, and Canterbury bells bearing more big sumptuous bells than I've ever seen anywhere else. I thought it strange that among these tall, haughty flowers were others, tiny and dainty, which seemed perfectly at home growing at their feet. A scent of mint kept wafting my way from some corner of the garden, mingled with rosemary perhaps. As at Felicity's, the air positively vibrated with the buzzing of insects, like the clamour of voices around a banquet table.

I came to a door of dark wood. I reached out for the knocker, but as if I'd had enough strength only to bring me as far as this doorstep, I suddenly drooped against the doorframe. I think I was so tired that tears came to my eyes, so exhausted I felt I was arriving not just from Wake Arms or Fulham, or from a love that had left me more alone than it found me, or from the agonizing uncertainties I'd been living with so long, or from a thousand mistakes on my part, not just from these but from much farther, the very beginning of my life perhaps. This was my last thought before letting my head fall against the door, no longer able to keep my eyes open. This was how Esther must have found me, almost asleep on her doorstep.

CAN I REMEMBER exactly how I saw her for the first time once the

weary haze over my eyes had gone? I don't know. Throughout the twenty-five years I knew her she never seemed to age; her face remained almost unchanged, as if she were made of something that time cannot disfigure.

Her face was rather long and thin as in many Englishwomen, often giving them a pensive air, and was always framed by a bandeau tied at the back of her neck. The effect would have been severe if not for the countless wisps of hair escaping to dance about her brow, cheeks, and slender neck, a kind of halo, a flowering as wayward as her tousled little garden.

But what struck me most from the first were her magnificent hazel eyes. Though warm and gracious, they seemed to look into the depths of one's soul. Wiser and more discerning eyes I've rarely seen, yet they probed with kindness, and I thought that what they must unfailingly discover was the hurt inside one that cries out for help without one's knowing.

I had barely begun to explain how I'd left London on a whim and ventured too far to go back tonight – a tale muddled with odds and ends about Canada and why I'd come to England – when she put out both her hands and drew me inside.

"There I was just a minute ago," she said, "complaining to God that He hadn't sent me any of His creatures to save for so long, and now look, here you are, like a bird that's flown so far and fallen right on my doorstep! Come in, come in! Of course there's room for you here."

A very few minutes later, as if I were a guest she'd been expecting, she said, "Would you like to see your room?"

I followed her up a rather steep staircase. She opened a door. The most inviting country bedroom met my eyes, with a big brass bed, a washstand complete with water jug and soap dish, and a fireplace with a mantel holding a cluster of small old photographs in frames, and other keepsakes. "This is my mother, she's been gone so many years...and this is my brother John who died in the War, gassed, so his lungs burned slowly away...." Then a sprig of Scotch heather, "the brightest colour of any in the world...," a pebble from the shore of the Irish Sea, dried flowers under glass. But best of all were the two big, high windows on the front side overlooking the downs. They were framed, not the least obstructed, by airy white tulle curtains drawn to either side. To me, the great

waves of the downs were even more delightful from this modest height than from ground level. I could see them far into the distance, an endlessly repeating swell of silent stillness flowing to the far horizon. And from here I could also see the intriguing stone slab more clearly.

"What is that, Miss Perfect?"

"A monument to the memory of Boadicea."

"Boadicea?"

"Our dear queen of the ancient Britons. She was fleeing from the Romans in her chariot but they were about to overtake her, and rather than fall into their hands alive she swallowed a mortal draught of poison. They say she gave up her soul about where that stone is standing."

In everything I was discovering this day I didn't know which was more delightful, finding the past so very present or finding a present so steeped in the past. But even the rarest delight couldn't keep me awake, any more than the most nightmarish memory. I was practically asleep on my feet.

Esther pulled down the counterpane, folded it, and draped it over the foot of the bed.

"To look at you I'd say you'd run all the way from your faraway Canada without a single stop for breath," she said. "Come on then, lie down. Rest a while. I'll come and tell you when tea's ready."

My protest was feeble, sleep gaining the upper hand.

"But I've just had an enormous tea at Boadicea's...no, Felicity's."

"I've heard that before," she said, "but I make nice hot scones, and when you've smelt them you'll be like everybody else...you'll eat them by the dozen. Anyway, tea won't be ready for a good hour. Father likes to go to bed early so we usually have what's called high tea. It's later and we eat more than at ordinary tea, more like early supper, really, a bit earlier than supper and a bit later than tea."

"I thought," I said sleepily, "it was only the Anglican Church that was divided into high and low."

For the first time I saw the gentle, reproachful smile I came to love so much, the only expression of censure she ever allowed herself, I think.

"Don't laugh," she said. "The High Church certainly has good sides to it. The King and Queen belong to it, after all. But we're

Low Church. We consider God's too great for us to go trying to show His likeness in images and statues. It's proper to look for Him only in our own hearts."

"But you look for Him through music and your hymns are the most beautiful on earth."

I didn't argue much longer. I barely saw the door close behind her as she tiptoed out. And as at Dauphin at the station master's, it seemed I'd only just gone under when I was being wakened again.

"Gabrielle dear, tea's ready. It's nice out still so we'll have it in the garden."

Today, so far from those enchanted moments, I make myself think I'm telling a fairy story when I talk about them. Yet this is really how it was. I do at times have trouble keeping my imagination from intruding, touching up, improving on my recollections perhaps, but in this case there's nothing to improve. It was all I could possibly desire.

The little back garden was perhaps even more delightful than the one in front. It had a vegetable garden with flowers and delicate herbs growing among the vegetables, a vine-covered garden shed, and an orchard of five or six trees. The tea-table was set in a small open space down at the end, half in sun and half in shade, under a twisted old apple tree whose largest bough was so low I had to bend to reach my place. A tall, elderly man with a smiling face and a beard as white as his hair rose to greet me. Esther must have told him who I was, to the extent she herself knew, because she said simply, "Father, our dear new friend who's just arrived, Gabrielle." And he just as simply said, "May you be happy in our house."

When I spoke to him, I addressed him, of course, as "Mr. Perfect", while Esther with great tenderness called him "Father". I soon felt I was being terribly formal and awkward in the warm familiarity at the table in the shelter of the old apple tree. Yet I couldn't start calling him "Father". Then suddenly I found the name "Father Perfect" on my lips.

The old man gave me a mischievous smile which creased his wrinkled cheeks in a thousand tight little folds and reduced his twinkling blue eyes to tiny slits.

"Generally," he said, "only God the Father gets called anything

like that. He's the only father that's perfect. But it's not irreverent, the way you say it, and I'd like to try to be a kind of Father Perfect to you, my dear, dear child.''

Before long he ceased to be Father Perfect just for me. How the name I'd found for him in affection came into general use I have no idea, but pretty soon no one in the village, at the manor house, or in the countryside around called him anything else. I even believe that this is what is written on his tombstone in the little churchyard surrounded by yews.

A few minutes after the three of us sat down to tea, Father Perfect wiped his fingers carefully and turned to the old family Bible which Esther had just brought to him. He opened it at random as he always did and read aloud. As I recall, the passage was about Joseph's sojourn in Egypt. The air around us hummed with a song of thanksgiving from the insects foraging among the flowers. It also bore the fragrance of the three precious herbs, thyme, rosemary, and marjoram, one of which was for faith, Esther taught me, and the other two associated with which two virtues I now can't for the life of me remember. When he had finished reading, Father Perfect joined his hands before him and said an impromptu prayer, as he did each day.

First he prayed the Lord to take from us the threat of war which appeared to be hanging over Europe. I remembered then the sultry wind of fear that had blown over London not so long before, something of which I'd been barely conscious, absorbed as I'd been in my own selfish misery. So the terrifying shadow creeping over the world really began to reach me only then, at the bottom of the little garden full of flowers, the buzzing of insects, and the most delicate fragrances of summer. But the old man continued his prayer and peace dropped its fragile mantle over us again.

''Lord,'' he said as if talking to a friend sitting beside him, ''from faraway Canada, which, you remember, our John dreamed so much of visiting, you've brought us today a young friend whose heart is sorely troubled, perhaps. Help us, gentle Saviour, to know how to help her. She could have gone to a thousand other places, knocked on many other doors, but she came to ours. We can't help seeing in this a sign that you were giving her into our care. Now that she's part of our household, protect her, dear Lord, as you protect my dear Esther and myself.''

Silence fell. I could no longer see anything in the distance by the remaining light under the branches of the apple tree. While Father Perfect was praying, memories of the months since the day I met Stephen welled up in my throat, threatening to stifle me. But they didn't have the same bitter taste as in recent weeks, and even threatened to dissolve in tears, a few of which fell though I managed to hide them, I think. But I did take a while to clear my eyes enough to see the comforting landscape again.

Since we were at the top of the slope on which Upshire was built, we overlooked the countryside around. Just beyond the old apple tree that marked the end of the little back garden lay a succession of pastures and fields lying fallow, less attractive than the downs in front but broad and open, hardly closed in at all by the faint line of the forest reappearing in the distance.

Beyond this the sky, so pure elsewhere, appeared murky, darkened as though infected with a kind of sickness or sorrow.

"What's that making the sky so dark over there?" I asked.

"London," Esther replied.

"London!"

I already felt as though I'd been away from the city for years. It was still much on my mind as the scene of my feverish entanglement, then such unhappiness I didn't want to live, but I sensed that here I was protected from this confused memory, it was dormant, and as long as I stayed it wouldn't hurt too much.

Esther had hurried to the kitchen and now came back bearing a tray with a steaming teapot in a woollen cosy and a plate of her scones straight from the oven. She was right when she said their smell would revive my appetite. I devoured three or four one after the other, buttered and spread with local honey or plum jam. The wasps were given their little share on a saucer a short distance from the table.

Suddenly something warm and alive brushed against my leg. I lifted the tablecloth. A small black cat with incredibly sad eyes was looking at me.

"Your cat, Esther?"

"Yes and no. She arrived not long before you did, we don't know where from. She doesn't belong in the village or anywhere round, anyway. There are cruel people in this world. Sometimes they come all the way from London just to leave pets they don't want

any more. She came and cried at the front door. I went to see what it was. She seemed hungry. Now it looks as if she wants to stay."

"That's because your welcome is so warm, Esther. Have you given her a name?"

"Not yet. I haven't had time. Why don't you give her one?"

I bent down and stroked the little lost creature.

"I think Guinevere would suit her."

"Guinevere! That's a very grand name for a little cat from the worst slums of London like as not! But then, why shouldn't she have a name that'll put her up a notch or two."

The homeless little animal rose on its back feet, put its front paws on my knee, and rubbed its head there, murmuring a kind of thank-you in the back of its throat.

The heat of summer had arrived. At moments a breath of cool air wafted under the branches of the apple trees, freshened by the broad reaches of the meadows beyond the garden. When we'd eaten our fill we stayed talking peacefully in the advancing twilight. I learned that Father Perfect had been garden boy, then assistant gardener, and eventually head gardener to the squire of the manor, primarily at an estate in Norfolk before being brought to the smaller manor of Upshire. He'd been retired for some years and had the use and enjoyment of the house and a small pension for himself and Esther as long as they lived, as well as certain rights, for instance to gather dead wood and take small game in the part of the forest still belonging to the manor. He still liked to go to the forest every day, partly to help the gamekeeper, who couldn't be everywhere at once, and partly for his own pleasure. He'd bring back mushrooms, bundles of good dry firewood which burned well, and sometimes just flowers. As I listened I came to understand the source of his serenity and goodness of heart, his uncommon gentleness, something like an original innocence preserved for all time. It must have been that he'd spent his whole life just looking after things that make the world more beautiful. "The roses in our rose garden in Norfolk, now...," he said to me, "I wish you could have seen them. They held themselves like queens standing in a row waiting for the daylight. You'd not even be surprised to see them bow to it...imagine!... Though they're proud, roses are...they don't bend much, even in a storm."

Eventually he seemed very weary from revisiting his earliest

memories, perhaps also from the concern aroused by my arrival. He rose, wished us good-night and blessed us both, then went inside to retire for the night.

I offered to help Esther clear the table.

"Oh no!" she said with feeling. "Not yet. Let's stay and talk a little longer. I love listening to Father. You can see what a dear he is. But every evening it's the same, the roses in Norfolk, the hen pheasants that know him in the game preserve and follow him.... What else can you expect? He's lived in a kind of Garden of Eden and the woes of mankind haven't touched him as they have most people. And there really isn't much left to say about Eden once the story's been told, is there? Stay a bit, it's been so long since I had someone to talk to about all sorts of things, at a time of day when words just seem to come by themselves...you know, round twilight, for instance."

To me, twilight was more a time for silence and thinking thoughts that spread out in circles till they disappeared in perfect stillness, as in a pond at night. But this meant that she and I would get along beautifully. She could open her heart and talk, and I could stay quiet and listen.

In fact, she didn't talk very much...a few words at a time between long spells of thinking. But each little phrase rang so true, showed such pertinent reflection, contained so much wisdom, and was so articulate that each time I listened carefully.

"Where did you learn so much, Esther?"

"Well, certainly not in school at any rate. I stopped school at twelve to go into service in the master's house. They had lots of books, the family did. When the young ladies sat in the garden in their chaises longues they sometimes dropped their books and when I picked up after them there were times when I could open one and read a bit. I was surprised they were so careless of such treasures, even then. Later they gave me books, perhaps to be rid of them. Often I'd read by candlelight in my room at the top of the house till I couldn't stay awake."

"What books have you read, Esther?"

"I was so lucky! The master and mistress insisted their young ladies read the best...and the governesses saw to it they did.... I read all of *Paradise Lost*. I still know long parts by heart. I read *The Pilgrim's Progress* too, but I thought some of it rather boring,

I'm ashamed to confess. Then the Brontë sisters, Jane Austen, *Gulliver's Travels*, nearly all of Tennyson, Browning, both Robert and Elizabeth, and of course most of all the Bible, the Book of books, where there's everything we need to know, dearest Gabrielle. But I like to open my Shakespeare every day too, just anywhere, the way I do the Bible. It's a rare time when I don't come across a sentence that delights me, and then you might say it keeps me company all day long. Or one that tells me something I've been thinking but haven't known how to say, so I know I'm not the only one that thinks it. Then my small lonely life begins to open up, and I feel as if I'm rich and suddenly not lonely any more. Is it the same for you, Gabrielle dear?''

I was moved to hear such deeply personal thoughts and didn't know how to reply. Guinevere lay at my feet, asleep but still purring now and then. In the distance, where the sky had been so murky an hour before, lights were beginning to appear, though faintly still. Everything was different now. London had lost its power to terrify me, as had Paris when I stood on a chair and through the open skylight saw it at my feet in a gentle mood. How I've loved big cities when I've seen them not too close, at the approach of darkness when their lights are coming on, telling as nothing else does of brotherhood among men. Minute by minute the lights of London multiplied. Now they were beyond counting.

"I never thought I'd be sitting with London in the distance like this," I said, "as if it's a sweet, quiet friend I'm spending an evening with."

"I go up to London once a year with Father to visit my sister Heather," said Esther. "You can't imagine sisters more different than Heather and me. She left when she was young to make her life there. She's not a bit shy, she's chic and always dresses in style, wears crazy hats and high heels, goes to the theatre and reads magazines that are a bit bold to my way of thinking. I feel very old-fashioned beside her. But I wouldn't change my life for hers any more than she'd change hers for mine, most like. I always come home all worn out. Besides this we go once a year to the seaside, Father and I do. You need a day by the sea every year, don't you, so you won't forget what it looks and sounds like. Father soon gets tired, so we just go to Bradwell-on-Sea because it's near-

est. And we just go to sit and look at it, you know, just look and listen."

At last we went in. Esther wouldn't hear of my helping her.

"Tonight you're like some of my flowers," she said, "wilting suddenly at the end of a day. For them a day's probably like a whole life for us."

She lit a candle for me. As we crossed through the sitting room, I could see by its wavering light some of the books she'd told me she'd read. They seemed to be part of this room there on their shelves, like guests arrived long ago and still welcome.

"Are those the books the master and his family gave you?"

"Not all of them. Father and I manage to save a bit out of our small pension by scrimping on the coal in winter and not going anywhere except London and the seaside, and we've bought a few more modern ones to keep ourselves up a bit with what's going on in the world. We do lead a nice life as you can see...though perhaps there's one thing missing: I've never seen a single Shakespeare play, can you imagine? What's it like? Is it really wonderful?"

"You'd never forget it, Esther!"

"That's what I thought."

One behind the other, we climbed the stairs leading to the narrow landing onto which our three rooms opened, Father Perfect's, Esther's, and mine, which was the biggest and had the finest view.

Esther handed me the candle.

"There's a lamp all ready by your bed, and matches and some books in case you'd like to read a while. But do get to sleep as soon as you can. I'd like to see you looking better in the morning, and specially to see less unhappiness in your eyes."

She kissed me on the forehead, and as she would do many times again when I spent a night under her roof, now and later when I was almost happy and later still when I was less happy again, she said tenderly, "Night-night, Gabrielle."

I blew out my candle. I just had time to marvel that my rudderless little ship had reached such a kindly port, and I was asleep on the breeze off the downs whose crests rolled away to meet the crests of the sea.

XII

WHEN I WOKE I was perhaps more at peace than I had been since the Little Water Hen. No, since long before that – since the days of summer holidays at the farm when I'd wake on my first morning in my uncle's house not knowing where I was; then I'd recognize the inside and outside smells and know for certain I was happy again in the house I loved so much, where I'd known only peace and happiness.

From the big brass bed I could follow the sweep of the downs. In the soft morning light they had a green, silky sheen that made them even lovelier than the day before, I thought. I picked out the stone marking the spot where the queen of the ancient Britons had died. When I craned my neck a little I could see the small manor house, which had been bequeathed to charity and was now an orphanage, Esther had told me; the squire and his family had moved to another house almost hidden in the forest beyond the end of the village I'd arrived by, but down another road.

With the return of this peaceful feeling so long absent from my life, I discovered just as suddenly a burning urge to write. This had happened before. I would wake up happy to be alive, in a tranquil, receptive mood, and there in my head would be a story, ready and waiting, which I was eager to write. I've almost always harvested my best ideas, images, and stories on waking in the morning, as if they were produced by rest, sleep, darkness, or some long quest pursued unknown to me during my dreams. But I've always had to grasp them quickly if I wasn't going to lose them, for though the riches I find on waking are the most precious, nothing slips away more easily.

I hurried to a small table under one of the big windows where there was something to write on. Carefully I detached a few pages

from the middle of a school copy-book so as not to damage it in case Esther was using it for keeping accounts, which seemed to be the case. This table clearly served as her desk. I took a pencil as well and went back to the bed. Propped against a stack of pillows in sight of the marvellous downs, I began to write.

The story I began with such enthusiasm that morning doesn't count for much today. If I dwell on it at all it's because it was at least better than anything I'd written before. It flowed well and, most important, it was irresistibly absorbing, restoring me to a state of contentment I hadn't known for a long time. As I recount this, it occurs to me how curious it is that one can only be happy when one is pleased with oneself. I'm sure it must be the same for everyone.

The story I found waiting when I woke and which flowed so well was coming in my mother tongue, in French. For a time I had thought it might be a good thing to write in English; I had tried with some success and I was torn. Then suddenly there could no longer be any hesitation. The words coming to my lips and from the point of my pen were French, from my lineage, my ancestral bonds. They rose to my soul like the pure waters of a spring filtering through layers of rock and hidden obstacles.

I wasn't surprised that it was in England, however, in an obscure little hamlet in Essex under the roof of people who had been strangers the day before, that I should waken to my destination, perhaps, but certainly to my own identity, of which I would never again have the slightest doubt.

The reason for what happened that morning was crystal clear, a miracle in a way, though the miracle would occur many times in my life. When I arrived the previous afternoon I had found myself with people who loved me instinctively. Where I've felt loved and have loved in return I've felt safe, and where I've felt safe I've found courage. Only affection can bring me such confidence that life no longer frightens me, I've known this for a long time now. Then I'm brave enough to throw myself into the work of writing, which never ends and has no real goal, an ocean without shores. Feeling such support this morning, perhaps I also felt duty bound to return in my own way the love the old man and his daughter were so freely giving me. I had seven or eight pages written when Esther came in with my breakfast tray.

317

She put it on my knees, brushing aside some of the papers littering the covers. It was such a huge meal I was sure I could never eat it and protested, only to get the same lecture I'd had at Wickendon Street, "A good day begins with a good breakfast."

Now that my mind was distracted briefly from my story, I thought about the long road I had travelled since leaving that dreadful street; I had so often reproached myself for going nowhere with my life since then. But tracing the route, I inevitably encountered a memory that brought back the wrenching pain provoked by the merest thought of Stephen; suddenly the downs, the vista I had been admiring, disappeared. Now I could see only myself, alone, bereft, and defenceless. Esther was as quick to read the changes in a face as in the sky which she studied constantly to foresee the weather.

"There you go, back in the dumps again," she said reproachfully. "A minute ago you were as happy as a child in a sandbox. Do come back. And first of all eat up this lovely kipper I've brought you. I went to get it this morning from the fishmonger in Walthamstow, specially for you. Then if you really must you can scribble some more for a while. But don't forget, the beautiful days God is giving you right now won't last for ever. This afternoon we'll go for a walk in the forest if you like...or on the downs...whichever you'd like best."

"Oh I'd love that, Esther! But I really feel I have to earn my joys, and when I woke under your roof this morning I found one of the greatest joys of my life."

WHEN THE LUNCH dishes were done and put away and Father Perfect had gone for his afternoon rest, Esther and I left for the downs. We climbed over a stile and up a little slope and were already alone in an expanse I was sure belonged only to the wind and the clouds. Distant farm sounds reached us now and then, the bark of a dog, the squeal of a pulley, the crow of a cock, just loud enough to keep us pleasantly in touch with the inhabited world. I was amazed how a country considered to be so small and densely populated could have such broad and beautiful spaces – useless spaces one might say, except for contemplation.

The moors of the north were much more rugged, Esther told me. More rugged and more enchanting too. She still missed them. She remembered being strangely carefree and light of heart for

hours on end on long walks over those wild grey expanses, which were desolate yet noble, she said.

She knew everything about the downs, even their most humble plants. At any minute she might bend down and pluck a sprig of some wild herb or grass or a little flower, and tell me its name and what it could be used for, like forage, a medicine or just for making winter bouquets when there weren't many fresh flowers for brightening the house. She made it so easy to learn all these things that I decided to start my first book of pressed flowers that very afternoon. I'd have enough to fill several pages just with what we brought home from this first walk. As soon as I set to work, Father Perfect kept bringing me a veritable harvest day after day: cocklebur, catnip, a specimen of shepherd's purse (which interestingly becomes *bourse-à-pasteur* in French), and many more. Soon he was taking almost as much satisfaction as I myself in seeing the most characteristically English plants as well as the rarest represented in my collection. I worked at it with much pleasure night after night by the light of the lamp in the parlour with Esther helping me, showing me how to dry my specimens and then glue the stems and flowers to the pages. Alas, in the course of my frequent moves I must have lost it. I still grieve over it. With this collection I lost a tangible reminder of a time of most innocent pleasure.

We came home by a path through the forest. By habit Esther was now thriftily gathering pieces of fallen wood for burning rather than flowers. They would do to make the kettle boil for tea and even to build a cosy fire for the first chilly evenings of autumn, she said. It meant buying that much less coal, which was very dear, and even less of the firewood with which the shed would be stocked before winter came. Besides, without much effort on her part she was helping her father, who often felt he had to bring home much heavier bundles of wood from the forest than he ought to. With my inclination for mimicry, I also began gathering wood from the ground. I kept looking for bigger and bigger pieces, even tackling half-trees complete with branches and getting my feet tangled as I dragged them behind me. We entered the village by the upper end, I burdened like a little burro almost invisible under a bristling load of faggots. We passed the vicarage just as the lady of the manor was coming out. She greeted Esther rather briefly, I thought, then gave me a hard, perplexed look. I've often mused that my

319

overenthusiasm may have embarrassed Esther that day, giving the impression that we at Century Cottage were in the direst straits. But Esther said not a word, perhaps so as not to spoil my pleasure in thinking I was being useful. However, in future when we came home loaded with wood, which was often, unless it was the dead of night we arrived by the back fields and the little gate under the apple trees.

I must have piqued the lady's curiosity, for before long she sent a message inviting us to tea. Esther seemed rather vexed.

"I'll have to get out the same old dress again," she said. "It was already out of style when I fixed it up a bit three years ago for the last invitation to tea at the manor. And isn't it a coincidence that I had someone with me then too, who milady couldn't imagine belonged to my social circle."

We were barely inside the cottage when I scurried to my room to pick up the thread of my story while Esther put the kettle on to boil for tea over a fire made from the sticks we'd brought home.

The fire burning in me was inextinguishable. I didn't care if it wasn't yet producing anything of worth despite its ardour, though I suppose I didn't know then that my writings were worthless. I wrote several pages before realizing Esther was calling me.

I came down and took my place at table in the garden. Twilight was rising gently like a peaceful tide at the bottom of the pasture. In the rather misty distance the myriad lights of London would soon be coming on. Closer there were groupings of lights I had learned to recognize as nearby towns: Walthamstow, where Esther often went by bicycle to do her shopping, Waltham Cross, and perhaps part of Waltham Abbey where I'd be going shortly to visit the squat little old abbey, one of England's truly exceptional churches.

It hadn't dawned on me until then that in my too-great contentment here I had forgotten to let Gladys know where I was. I realized she might be desperately worried not to have heard from me for two days.

I hurried at once to the phone booth outside the post office next door.

Perhaps she really had been frantic with worry. When she heard I was alive and apparently well she flew into a frightful rage, loosing such a torrent of reproach I couldn't get a word in edgewise. What kind of girl was I to have left like that without so much as a word?

Would it really have been too much trouble to at least have told the neighbours? She hadn't slept a wink last night. Geoffrey had been all over the place asking if anyone had seen me. And they had been on the point of calling the police when at last I condescended to telephone.

I might say in my own defence that with Geoffrey absorbed in his repairs or off for the day on some errand and Gladys herself in refuge at Hampton Court without giving any sign of life, they quite often went several days without even noticing whether I was there or not. But I felt guilty enough not to try to defend myself. I just said I was terribly sorry to have been a bother and a worry to her and Geoffrey, and I'd be back soon to get my things.

Early next morning I left for Wake Arms by a short cut Esther had shown me. At the bottom of the village hill I was to turn right at a junction which was easy to miss, so I had to be very careful. I was to walk beside the stone wall surrounding the manor house till I came to a big ploughed field. I had to skirt the edge of the field on a kind of beaten path made by people who knew the short cut. Unless I kept to the path I'd sink into the heavy clay soil at every step, which would be exhausting. Then I'd have only a short distance through the forest to the main highway, and I must walk it singing at the top of my lungs because, according to Esther, nothing keeps villains away in a lonely place like a song from a fearless heart, or one trying to appear so. I don't remember whether I sang as I walked along that dark stretch of path or not, but on the way back from London I may have sung with joy to be coming home to the only place in the world that felt like home at this time.

GLADYS WAS STILL in a towering rage. She followed me around while I gathered my belongings, telling me over and over that it was my own fault I'd lost Bohdan and probably Stephen too, such an attractive young man, and my fault I'd lose everyone unfortunate enough to love me like as not, ungrateful girl that I was. What gratitude had I shown her, who'd done so much for me?

But when I'd stuffed practically everything into my two suitcases I'd forgotten my beret, so I put it on my head, and when Gladys saw me looking much as she'd seen me for the first time her attitude changed completely. A tear came to her eye. What would become of me now, poor child, why didn't I stay, all would be forgotten,

and anyway she was much more to blame than I was, leaving me to get along by myself so much of the time while she was off finding some peace and quiet.

I pointed out that I couldn't afford two places at once. She said I could stay at least a little while for nothing. I told her I could never accept that kind of arrangement. She was on the point of turning against me once more but softened and offered to come as far as the bus at least to help me put my luggage on. I was so afraid she'd take it into her head to come all the way to Esther's that I turned her down, assuring her I was quite capable of managing by myself. Then she did another about-turn. Well then I could go to the devil! If I'd come from Canada all by myself and gone running round Epping Forest all by myself, I certainly ought to be able to put my two suitcases on the bus by myself.

Geoffrey, however, came and met me halfway down the stairs and carried the suitcases to the waiting taxi. And he'd keep my wardrobe trunk in a corner of the bicycle shop till I sent for it.

"Bye-bye," he said rather kindly. "Don't take Gladys's temper too hard. She's like the wind, you know, the way she keeps changing, but she can't carry a grudge."

Indeed, she came running to beg me to write, at least to give her my address, to stop and have a cup of tea whenever I came back to Lillie Road.

I left without a single regret, or so I believed at the time. In fact my thoughts would return often to the neighbourhood, for it left me some of my most persistent memories.

THE TAXI RIDE was the most absurd extravagance, but I was in too much of a hurry to get back to Upshire to take the city bus and risk missing the earliest possible Green Line departure for Epping Forest. Miss it I did, however. I descended from the taxi just in time to see my dear little bus reach the end of the square, driving gaily away to the fresh green countryside. I sat down on the same bench I'd sat on the day I sprinted to the bus as it pulled out. I could have cried. I would only be held up for an hour, but another hour away seemed like an eternity. I sometimes wonder if I wasn't so possessed that if the bus I'd just seen disappear had been the last of the day to Epping Forest I would have set out to walk the distance, as I'd once set out for my uncle's farm in the snow and

rain. Such is the pull of the place on this earth where we've felt the peace and happiness of home, however briefly.

THE FIRST THING I saw when I got off the bus at Wake Arms gave my heart a tug. Under the open sky with his fine white hair blowing in the wind, Father Perfect had probably been waiting for me for hours. Beside him was a crude pushcart I imagined he'd made himself years ago, on which to load my belongings. We set off immediately, almost without a word since the old man was saving his breath for pushing the cart when the ground was rough. He said only that he'd thought of bringing the cart just as he was leaving to meet me, in case I'd brought things back from London. I offered to help him push but he shook his head.

We came to the big ploughed field. Twilight was creeping over it. All you could see was a broad space filled with something vaguely blue and fluid, so ethereal it made you think more of a world beyond the visible than of a piece of unused farmland. Here the old man put down the shafts of the cart for a rest and gazed at the field. It was bathed in such gentle, soft light I thought it looked like happiness wrapped in a half-transparent package, yet close and accessible if only we knew how to get inside. He told me that he and Esther had found the day very long, they'd missed me, there were some people you became attached to very quickly and if you lost them you'd probably grieve all your life. Then he took up the shafts again and we continued. When he lowered them a second time to rest and had caught his breath, he told me light-heartedly that Esther was keeping my share of the shepherd's pie in the oven for me, and this time she'd made a particularly good one.

We came to the end of the field and were about to start along the path beside the manor house grounds. We both stopped for a last look back at the mysterious space, by now half dissolved in the gathering darkness. I saw this field in the first light of day when I was leaving for London, I saw it often near nightfall, and in full sun. I think now it must have been a perfectly ordinary field. I've certainly seen bigger and handsomer. How is it that no other has moved me this way, and why do I still treasure its memory as one of life's rare and precious gifts? Perhaps because each time I came to it I felt lightened, purified, though why this should be I simply can't say.

We emerged from the deep shadow of the trees into the feeble light of Upshire's two streetlamps...or were there three? From the pub, still some distance away, we heard men's voices, a kind of low growl. On weekdays there were rarely more than twelve or fifteen men there from the farms around, but they were soon warmed by the beer they drank and then they talked very loudly and apparently all at once.

On nights before Sundays and holidays, in echo to this rough chorus, from the little church surrounded with yews you could hear the choir practising its hymns line by line, expressing a most tender love of God and His creatures.

These tipsy voices and angelic ones were the only sounds I really ever heard in Upshire after eight or nine at night.

Esther was waiting for us at the gate with Guinevere rubbing about her legs.

"She's been looking for you all day," Esther told me. "I had to speak to her quite crossly. She wasn't giving me a minute's peace, wanting me to go out the front door to watch for you."

We sat down at the big table in the dining room in the soft light of the lamp with the écru shade. The best dinner service gleamed on the sideboard, ready for the meal. Though tired out, to celebrate my return Father Perfect had put off going to bed till later so he could have supper with us.

At his place at the end of the table he adjusted his glasses, opened the Bible, and read a passage, then closed his eyes, joined his hands in front of him, and said simply, "We thank thee, O Lord, for bringing back our Gabrielle safe and sound."

Now I no longer had any doubt. These people loved me as tenderly as I loved them. But why? What had I done to deserve the precious gift of their confidence?

THE VERY NEXT morning my day resumed the pattern it had taken before my return to London. I'd get up early, splash my face with cold water from my water jug, then hurry to the window to look fondly at the downs while I untangled my hair. Then I'd get back into bed and, sitting propped against my heap of pillows, I'd immerse myself in my writing. I had brought my light portable typewriter back from London and worked with it balanced on my knees.

More piquant than profound, my phrases weren't very demanding so I wasn't having much trouble with them. They just came more often than I had to hunt for them. Any time I had to wait for them to come I'd lift my eyes instinctively to the downs, and though I was so absorbed I barely saw them, they seemed to give me encouragement. This is the way it has always been, in fact. In order to work I always have to have a window in front of me and the window has to give me a glimpse of sky and space — curiously, instead of *espace* (space) just now I almost wrote *espérance* (hope). Concentrating on what I'm doing, I don't see the landscape, but it doesn't matter. As long as I know it's there I feel refreshed, lightened, perhaps freed of the bondage that is every human being's lot, a condition which probably, whatever people think, weighs most heavily on a writer. Because a writer, an interpreter of human dreams, doesn't always have access to them at will and must often wait hungrily at the door, like a beggar.

When Esther appeared with the breakfast tray I'd often have a dozen pages written, littering the bed. She'd scold me, telling me it wasn't healthy to work on an empty stomach like that.

One day I scolded her in return for tiring herself bringing up my breakfast, and announced that beginning the next morning I'd come downstairs and have breakfast with her at the kitchen table. She forbade me to, saying she liked to have the house to herself in the morning because it was always a bit of a mess and she could take her own good time putting things in order and getting lunch started.

Was this the truth? In the clear light of morning, if I took the time to really study her face, she always looked older than she had in the soft glow of twilight the evening before, sometimes even very tired. With my typewriter put aside and my breakfast on my knees in its place, she didn't linger now to talk at length as she had at first, since, as she said one morning, she could see I was more in my stories than in real life.

"But it's the same thing, Esther!" I retorted indignantly.

"The same thing? In certain very exceptional books, almost, yes. But in spite of all I've got from books, I must say there aren't many that have spoken to me the way life has."

Her perspicacity left me in confusion and disarray, I sensed there was so much truth in this. Was I wasting my time all over again?

Chasing illusions? Three or four cups of tea in quick succession made me feel better, however, my confidence restored; my creations, whatever else they might be, were at least lively.

I finished the long story I'd begun soon after I arrived at Esther's and at once began another. There seemed to be no end to the material coming to my mind and I expected to keep on living in this heady state of excitement. I tackled a series of short articles on Canada, an idea that had occurred to me when I was answering questions from Esther about what it was like, how we did things, what winter was like, and summer, and the people and so forth. I had barely finished three of these without a pause when on an impulse I put them in an envelope addressed to the editor of a Paris weekly I knew only through having bought an occasional issue in London. Then I ran at once to post them for fear I might change my mind if I hesitated even for an hour.

Sometimes I still shudder to think of my nerve at the time. I had no one to advise me or edit me and I hardly even reread anything myself, so my writing must have read like what I consider today to be a first draft and wouldn't dare show to anyone. But on reflection, the path I chose almost unconsciously is an exacting one, and perhaps one ought to set foot on it with a measure of thoughtlessness. Otherwise who would ever take this endless road?

AFTER LUNCH, which was always copious and which I had difficulty swallowing because I was still tense from four or five hours of work, Esther would send me to have a rest while she washed up, again refusing my offer of help, saying she liked to have this time to herself so she could practise parts of the hymns to be sung on Sunday or plan the next day's menu. Then she'd come upstairs and lie down for a rest herself in the bedroom next to mine. About three-quarters of an hour later she'd knock lightly at my door, saying "Ready?" very softly in case I was asleep, and we'd go for the happiest of walks. For Esther, whose life was all prayer, seriousness, and duty, I think they came to be a kind of reward, and I think now that they were this for me as well.

Most often we'd go out onto the downs as we had the first time, but now we went much farther, sometimes so far that we'd come home very late for tea and find Father Perfect waiting famished and worried at the gate.

"Forgive us, Father dear," Esther would say, "but you used to go on much longer walks than you intended yourself, remember?"

We went as far as one of the farms I'd been able to identify in the hazy distance only by the barking of a dog. We brought back some sweet butter and heavy cream, but I still think Esther took me there mostly to let me see a particularly beautiful view. It lay beyond a broad undulation. Below us was an old house with a blue slate roof cradled in some enormous trees, and beside it a fast-flowing stream with a turning water wheel, a mill race, and a moss-covered mill. A chubby-cheeked, half-naked child was sitting in the water playing with the barking dog.

I finally saw the moor of red heather I'd heard about from the bus driver. Esther knew it well and never failed to go there at least once a year when it was prettiest. It was much farther than I expected, though, and that day we didn't get home until nearly nightfall.

On some days Esther was kept at home tending her incomparable suet pudding which took so long to cook, or writing her "ramblings", interminably long letters like the ones to her old aunt in Malvern, for instance, or a friend she'd met thirty years earlier on a trip to Scotland, or a missionary somewhere up the Zambezi – like the many she would write to me later, in my case (since they came by airmail) all consisting of four sheets of onionskin covered on both sides and all the way to the edges with a tiny, crowded hand almost impossible to decipher. Something helpful I discovered was that each paragraph dealt with a particular subject, always in the same order. First came the Upshire weather. It was really astonishing what she could find to say about this, particularly the wind, which she might say was "soft and balmy, a sweet breath laden with the scent of the hayfields," or in autumn like "a nasty, vindictive soul shrieking across the land." Though some might think nothing ever happened in her life she always had countless little pieces of news to give, about each of her flowers for example: "The big pale blue delphinium by the door is as high as the door knocker; a single stalk of Canterbury bells has eighteen bells." Also about the birds, whose songs she knew and transcribed very well in syllables. And in almost every letter there was something about the old plum tree, which was decidedly showing its age. This year it had given practically nothing, but neither she nor Father Perfect

could bear to replace it with a young tree when they remembered all the pots of jam it had given, and there were still some left on the pantry shelves. Thinking of this, she was reminded of a parable in the New Testament which she'd always felt was incompatible with the goodness of the Lord, about the sterile fig tree that was cut down although it had done its best. How unfair! At the very end of her letter, she would express thoughts about God and His mysterious designs for us and the world around. And since by now she'd have come to her last page, she would wind her final sentence around the rest, a minute line in the almost nonexistent margin, shrinking still further, twisting, weaving in and out and ending up written over other words among which, with a magnifying glass, I'd finally discover her signature. What she thought about God, from her letters in any event, I never really managed to make out. Despite her faith, I'm left with the curious impression that when she tried to throw light on her beliefs she became entangled and confused.

ESTHER SHOWED ME another short cut, this one across the fields adjoining the little orchard where we used to have tea. It led to a local road along which a bus ran every hour, serving the neighbouring towns. I went alone this way to Walthamstow and then Waltham Cross, where I found a cross beneath a delicately columned roof, identical to the one at Charing Cross and ten others, all erected by Edward I to the memory of "his dear Queen" wherever her funeral cortège stopped for the night as he brought her remains across England to London: Lincoln, Grantham, Stamford, Diddington, Northampton, Stoney, Shatford, Dunstable, St. Alban's, Waltham, Tottenham, and finally Charing Cross, the word "Charing", according to what I was told in London, being a corruption of *"Chère Reine"*.

I also went alone to Waltham Abbey. The very ancient church was deserted when I entered. I sat down under its low vaulted arches and stayed for several hours in a state of peace I've felt nowhere else, even in the semidarkness of centuries-old romanesque churches in Provence. Here I found something even more ancient, cruder also, more primitive, something reaching out to God which gripped my heart but without hurting, reassuring me on the contrary. I went to Beechwood finally, to see the magnificent

beeches to which Tennyson is said to have raised a contemplative gaze one day.

Thus time went by, so well filled and happy that I didn't notice it pass.

As soon as I was back from London I concluded a kind of agreement with Esther regarding my room and board. I told her my money was almost gone and I could only offer her a pound and a few shillings a week. Could she keep me for this ridiculous sum? If ever it should become possible, I promised, I would double and perhaps triple the amount, though I didn't expect this to happen.

"Why yes," she said, "a guinea's quite enough for food and light, for you don't waste any. And even if you had nothing to give us you could stay and we'd manage. After all, Father can snare hares if necessary. He can get eggs in exchange for mushrooms, too. And then, what you think will feed two will always feed three."

Time kept going by with life so sweet I found myself thinking this couldn't be real everyday life but some likeness of things as I'd subconsciously willed them. And yet I'd still sometimes feel a stab from the memory of the days of happiness and torment I'd known with Stephen. The days of happiness perhaps hurt the most. So happiness prepares the way for sorrow, I told myself rather naïvely. But now I was spared the steady ache I'd thought so unbearable for a time, because I was rediscovering the excitement and pleasure of telling a story. Or because all of a sudden I was filled with emotion to see some splendid aspect of the downs that I hadn't been conscious of just an instant before.

I couldn't have totally broken off my drama studies, at least my lessons with Madame Gachet, because I remember going to London about once a week and reciting lines from Racine and speeches from Molière in the woods on the way back. Now when I stopped reciting and looked around, it wasn't tombstones but great gnarled trees I would see, surprised to find them disapproving of my behaviour, as it seemed.

One day Mrs. Stone the postmistress called to me from her house next door to Century Cottage, "A letter from Canada for you, dearie!" and came and handed it to me over the picket fence between the properties.

It was from my mother. I began to tremble as soon as I recognized the writing. I always trembled when her letters came, not because

I was afraid of reading reproaches or complaints – there never were any – but because seeing her writing was enough to open the door to memories of all the suffering culminating in me. Surely I shouldn't be the only one to escape, I would think, and I'd feel condemned to suffer, as if it were a duty.

I tore open the letter. This time Maman hadn't really been able to hide her anxiety. Why had I come to this insignificant little village, she wanted to know. Was I discouraged? Had I completely run out of money? If only she had a little to send me!...

When I'd read and reread her letter I looked up at nothing in particular and saw – I imagine by one of those miracles of normal life which happen more often than we think – I truly saw my mother, on the other side of the earth, sitting at a wooden table writing to me, a bottle of ink nearby, her glasses slipping down her nose, her face showing anxiety at being unable to help me and determination at least not to upset me. At this, I was so ashamed of having been happy when she was so sad that I was really upset. Dragging my feet, I went where only yesterday the trees had watched me recite and gesticulate, this time to weep in silence.

How long it took me to accept my mercurial nature! Or life itself perhaps. One day all song and freedom from care, the next all torment and distress!

Not long after, the postmistress called across the picket fence, "Another letter for you, dearie! This time from Paris. My, but you're popular!"

What this letter contained was enough to make me jump out of my skin: a cheque and a few electrifying lines. The first of my articles was accepted – for an upcoming issue – and the two others would be published shortly. I thought I would die of excitement. I don't think I've ever felt as truly like a real, honest-to-goodness writer as I did that day in the little yard among the dandelions. I ran and waved the cheque under Esther's nose and I think was piqued that she didn't go as wild with excitement as I was. The sum wasn't large, about five dollars, but none I would ever receive later would seem as fabulous, or arrive more opportunely. For want of human company to appreciate the magnitude of my glory, I went to the forest to dance and sing and perhaps even try a leap or two among the stern trees. I think I really learned then that of all that comes our way, the hardest to bear in solitude is triumph.

Around this time the threat of a second world war began to filter through to Century Cottage, far removed from the world though it was.

Father Perfect came home from the forest with a long face one evening. He'd been talking to both the gamekeeper and the squire, with whom he'd crossed paths separately. Both had been of the same opinion: war seemed imminent. Day by day Hitler's demands were becoming more intolerable and Britain and France weren't going to give in much longer.

Before tea at the bottom of the little garden that evening, the air strongly scented with thyme and rosemary, Father Perfect, his voice breaking, implored the Lord to spare humanity from the scourge of war. "Thou who hast taken our John from us, my only son, dear Lord, who in Thy wisdom caused him to depart this world so soon...so soon...." Then very close, perhaps in the old damson tree, a bird began to sing and its song was so pure and sweet it could only have sharpened the pain in the old man's broken heart. And trying to hide her face with her hand that tender summer evening, Esther wept silently.

But the next day the sun rose on a radiantly beautiful day. Light streamed over everything – the neatly clipped yews beside the church, the grass on the nearest rolling slopes of the downs, the line of shimmering poplars around the old manor house. War no longer seemed possible.

"In such a beautiful world it can't be," declared Esther. "God won't allow it."

In any event, Esther and I were going to take advantage of this incomparable day to embark on a real expedition, taking our sandwiches because it was a long way. We were going to Copped Hall, Henry VIII's estate, whose manor house was destroyed long ago but whose gardens had been maintained over the centuries and that day would likely be at their most magnificent.

According to legend, Esther told me as we strode along, it was at Copped Hall that the dreadful man waited impatiently for the messenger who was to ride in all haste from London with the news that poor Anne Boleyn's head had indeed rolled – God rest her soul! We observed with a certain awe that the roses blooming in this place, inhabited since those days only by that gory memory, were perhaps the most beautiful in the whole kingdom.

Gabrielle Roy

And so, despite the rumours of war that rumbled more ominously every day, despite the painful memories that invaded me from time to time, within a certain radius of me all suffering seemed to have ceased. Nothing happened to break the spell for several weeks. Then from my window one morning, whom should I see approaching, already close, but Stephen.

XIII

HE MUST have taken the long way through the forest past Felicity's, as I had the first time, for he seemed to be tired and suffering from the oppressive late-morning heat. Also, he was carrying so many packages they reached his chin; he'd always hated carrying packages. It seemed they were intended for me. Besides all the boxes and bags apparently from candy and pastry shops, he was awkwardly holding a little bunch of flowers that were half-crushed by the packages.

As I had done when I first arrived in Upshire, he was looking above the doors of the cottages for their names, the only way they were identified.

He came to our gate and paused to rest his laden arms on it. He'd been smiling, or rather his eyes had sparkled at the sight of the exuberant little garden. Now he seemed to be far away in his thoughts.

From where I was standing I had an excellent view of his face, though he didn't know he was being watched. As almost always in such circumstances, I saw things I never could have seen otherwise. I thought briefly that I wasn't looking at Stephen's face at all, it was showing so much that I didn't recognize. Signs of sorrow, perhaps to think he'd lost me, perhaps for some totally different reason. How could I tell? Signs of uncertainty in a man who'd always been so decisive. Perhaps even a bitter, touching kind of regret. I wanted to warn him that I could see him exposed like this and it was unbearable, but the shock of seeing him at my mercy in a way was so great that I couldn't speak. He'd always sparkled so with vitality, but now I thought he looked thinner, almost exhausted. I was even more surprised to discover what had happened to my own feeling about him. Spying on him from the window so

to speak, I felt none of the pathetic magnetism that had passed between us across Lady Frances's drawing room, as though we were hunted creatures exchanging signals leading us to one another. But there was no trace of my harsh resentment towards him either. What I was feeling at the moment seemed to be compassion, regret that he'd suffered because of me; a new and indulgent feeling, the germ of tenderness at last, perhaps.

I was so relieved to discover this kinder feeling in me that I put my head out the window and called cheerily:

"Stephen! Hello there!"

He looked up. Such a wonderful radiance came over his face that suddenly he was as beautiful to me as the downs behind.

I ran downstairs and out the door and threw my arms around him, flimsily tied packages and all. Our first kisses were sweet and grateful. We were both overjoyed, he that I should welcome him so warmly and I that he should be so happy to have found me again.

I relieved him of part of his burden and led him through the house looking for Esther. When we found her she was washing vegetables in the scullery, the small room behind the kitchen for household chores too dirty to do elsewhere. One day I'd said, "What's the point of it? You have to clean that too." She'd answered, "How right! It's most annoying how often you're right!"

She liked Stephen immediately. I saw it in the tenderness of her smile and the light in her grey-green eyes. And he liked the gentle old spinster immediately, I think almost to the point of adoration. He told me she reminded him of a beloved Ukrainian great aunt, of whom he carried a small photograph at all times.

Though always so natural, after a few minutes she said she was embarrassed to be seen in her apron by a visitor and sent us both to the garden to give her time to finish her vegetables and clean herself up a bit, she said. "But come back for lunch in an hour, an hour and a half at the latest," she reminded us.

By then she had put on a clean dress, redone her hairband, put carefully chosen flowers on the table, and as we arrived was carrying in a fragrant minted leg of lamb the like of which I've eaten only at her table.

Lunch was cheerful and lively. Father Perfect shook Stephen's hand with the same ready warmth he'd shown when he first met

me. He enquired of him regarding events in the world, the country, and London with the deference due to someone who certainly had intelligent views on these matters. Naïvely, he and Esther were delighted to find me less alone in the world than I might have seemed, and their eyes kept straying from me to Stephen and from Stephen to me as if to show me they approved of my choice. Stephen could be such a charmer and cajoler, it was undoubtedly easy for him to win them over, but that day I think there was real affection rather than artifice behind his efforts to please under this roof.

When lunch was over Stephen went to the old harmonium at the end of the room, ran a hand over the keys, then sat down on the bench and, pumping at the pedals covered with worn old felt, began to play and sing a hymn, reading from the open book on the music stand. I knew the simple tune well. Esther used to sing it softly as she went about her dusting with a towel around her head to keep the dust out of her hair. Since she kept losing the key she'd go often to the harmonium to find it again, all of which I could hear in my room. Now she sat smiling at her place at table and as if unconsciously soon began to sing along with Stephen. I thought I must be dreaming to hear their voices in unison, one pious and fervent and the other sincere perhaps only for the moment.

The cow's in the meadow,
The sheep's in the pasture,
God's in His Heaven,
All's right with the world....

Abruptly Stephen dropped the song of praise. His hands seemed to be groping for an air he'd remembered. Then suddenly he was playing the beautiful but ominous Song of Destiny. I shuddered and dark forebodings crossed my mind, evil things, huge, inscrutable, faceless things. Then the uneasiness passed. He had begun another tune, a brisk and cheerful one for all the instrument's solemnity. It was amusing to hear the wheezy harmonium producing almost rollicking sounds. Guinevere was terrified by such unaccustomed noises and ran to hide under an old cupboard. Once again Father Perfect had tears in his eyes, tears of laughter this time. Finally Stephen swung his feet nimbly up and over the bench and turned to face us, smiling broadly.

Esther said, "It's such a lovely afternoon, you two had better hurry out for a walk in the forest."

Stephen looked at me in that burning, intense way of his. I looked down at the floor, Esther must so surely have seen and understood. But Stephen's desire to please came to the fore. He'd wash the dishes, he said, while Esther and I went and sat in the garden.

"The very idea!" said Esther. "You haven't come all the way from London to spend the best part of the day scrubbing pots. You ought to be out under the trees where it's cool, both of you. Go on now!"

I had an idea of my own. The moment had come to show Stephen my first finished story, I thought, and especially the cheque from Paris.

When I put the cheque before him the delight he showed almost outdid my own. I must keep it for ever, he said, because it marked the beginning of my literary life. He'd get it framed for me if I liked.

"Are you crazy?" I said. "I need that money for all kinds of things. Shoes to begin with, or I'll be going barefoot pretty soon."

He relented but was still sad at the thought of this memorable cheque coming to a very ordinary end as money, thus vanishing without trace.

Then I told him I had something better to show him, and produced my manuscript. I wanted so badly to get an opinion on my work at last that I think I was trembling with trepidation and hope.

Stephen took the manuscript from me, scanned a few lines, and at once expressed even greater enthusiasm than he had over the cheque.

Esther suggested we go into the parlour, which would be cool to work in since the sun had now moved to the back of the house. The room was rather reverently preserved, making it somewhat intimidating when we first entered, but it turned out to be a pleasant setting, for it was on a level with the front garden and with the window open the air was fresh and fragrant.

At first Stephen tried to kiss me after every sentence but soon became so absorbed in my story he forgot about me, making me happier than he ever had before.

He read aloud with a pencil in his hand, correcting typing errors

as he went, and soon, with my permission, grammatical and careless mistakes. I had known he had an admirable command of French, but not to the point of being able to pick up all kinds of little errors at first reading, even awkward expressions for which he proposed substitutes that suited my text so well I was as pleased as if I'd found them myself.

Eventually he observed that I was inclined to use far too many adjectives. The noun, according to him, being the strong element in the sentence, could do without qualifiers if it was an adequate one. It didn't occur to me at the time that when writing his tracts with their abrupt, incisive style he had developed a manner of writing totally opposed to mine. That day, however, I was so subservient to his views that for a long time I strove to purge almost all adjectives from anything I wrote. That is, until I realized I was making my writing dry and parched, for a well-used adjective makes a phrase live, makes it touch a chord inside a person.

But Stephen wasn't only interrupting his reading to propose corrections. Much more often he'd exclaim, "That's good! That's very good!" with a pride that lifted me as if on the crest of a wave. And afterwards, with the conviction of someone certain of seeing a piece of the future, he told me as Bohdan had once, "You've really got talent. You're going to write something remarkable one day." His confidence in me was encouraging such confidence in myself that I believed it, too.

Later, however, I saw that what he had praised most highly was perhaps not the best in my writing but the facile, the provocative but shallow, the playful, a tendency to caricature, all things I would try to rid myself of later. Still, this hour of work in the little old-fashioned parlour, a cricket singing intermittently outside among tall flowers which seemed almost to be coming in through the window, had a major effect on my life thereafter. In this little room I discovered what a delight it is for two to work side by side at something both truly enjoy. There is no greater delight, in fact. The caresses bestowed by eyes and hands, which are pretty much the same for all lovers, are so banal beside the encounter of two minds, the part of us we keep most ferociously to ourselves most of the time. I think also I was vastly relieved to feel that however solitary the way ahead of me might be, having companionship at least for a while on occasion wasn't out of the question after all.

We had never been as truly united, Stephen and I, as during this hour when both of us were so intently focused on a common goal you'd think we'd forgotten each other. His eyes shining with something quite other than desire, he kept saying things like, "You really have a gift. You'll see, one day you're going to be a well-known author." And I kept laughing, pretending I didn't believe it, thinking he was exaggerating, too. But his approval encouraged me to want to do a hundred times better and so be more deserving.

Around half past three Esther came and almost drove us away from our work, saying it was criminal to stay inside at our scribblings with a summer afternoon like this just begging us to go outside.

At first we stayed walking decorously from one end of the village to the other, but it wasn't long before I'd shown Stephen all there was to see. It was very hot on the road. A footpath led into the forest near the gates to the manor house grounds. After taking a rather long loop it returned behind the village and ended almost in the fields adjoining Esther's little orchard. This was where I'd gone to weep among the unsympathetic trees over my mother's heart-rending letter. This was where I'd gone to dance and shout my triumph which so quickly turned to a kind of emptiness. We stood at the foot of the path and Stephen looked at me questioningly. I resisted, suggesting we go to Waltham Abbey. We could go and be back by tea-time and it really was worth seeing, I told him.

"Some other time," he coaxed.

I walked down the path with him into the forest. It was cool and pleasant. I tried to remember how he had hurt me, I tried to remember as well how the flesh can sometimes bring happiness but can also assuredly bring all manner of woe. But it didn't occur to me to think twice about Stephen's feelings, he had inspired me with such confidence in them this day.

He took my hand. He laced his fingers between mine. All the sadness, all the bleak despair I had known in human love faded from my mind. We reached the sanctum of the oldest trees. In the deep shadow of their raised, still limbs, suddenly we were entwined, clinging to each other as though we were the last of our species left together on earth.

EVERYTHING SEEMED to have changed by tea-time. An almost chilly mist was rising from the pastures that extended towards Walthamstow from the bottom of our orchard. Esther had thrown a sweater around her shoulders when she came out of the house, and now she pulled it closer. "It'll soon be the end of summer," she said, surveying the countryside around, and the sadness in her voice wasn't like the Esther I knew. "It's been such a splendid summer," she went on. "We should give thanks for having received our share, though pretty soon we'll be complaining about it being taken away."

Then she thought to ask us if we'd had a nice walk. Stephen's eyes as he looked at me shone in a way Esther couldn't possibly mistake. She blushed a little and looked away. Her expression wasn't disapproving. I think she was rather worried for me, and in fact she told me later she'd had a very strong feeling at this moment that Stephen and I were going to do each other great harm.

Father Perfect, so animated and talkative at lunch-time, seemed deeply disturbed. He leaned towards Stephen and asked him if it was true that nations were once again getting ready to kill each other. Was it possible they were on the point of starting the slaughters of the Great War again?

Now Stephen's face also changed. Only when he'd confessed his secret political activities had I seen this worried, haggard look that made him seem so much older than he was. Now I couldn't help thinking how often he must be really unhappy, and it made me feel more sorry for him than he had made me feel for myself.

"Yes," I heard him tell the old man, "war is possible. The Germans are arming for it in any case. As for the Allies, they've got their heads in the sand. They're trying not to see the danger, which couldn't suit Hitler better today, or Stalin tomorrow probably."

"Hitler, Stalin," said the old man softly, "are they as bad as all that? Isn't there some good in them if we can only reach it? In all my life I've never known anyone whose heart you couldn't reach if you tried. Hitler, Stalin...and that other one they say is just as bad...Mussolini...is that his name? Couldn't we come to an agreement with them?"

In the old face, the eyes the colour of forget-me-nots had never been more like two innocent little flowers growing in parched ground.

Stephen smiled at their naïvety and now made an effort to re-assure the old man. All the bets weren't in yet, he said. Things could still work out so war could be avoided, at least for a while.

Though Father Perfect was quick to be alarmed he was just as quick to recover, and soon he was talking affectionately about his old damson tree. They'd been going to cut it down in the autumn but it had come to be part of their lives and they'd decided to keep it a little longer, and the birds that loved it so would be back again to make their nests in it.

Several times I'd seen Stephen glance at his watch. Now he jumped up and announced he'd have to leave immediately if he wasn't to miss the last bus back to London.

Esther offered to put him up for the night on the sofa in the parlour, which was narrow and rather hard but he was most wel-come if he thought he could sleep on it. Stephen replied that nothing would please him more than to spend the night amid all the good smells of the garden, lulled by the song of the cricket which he preferred to any music, but he had urgent business in London and had to be there first thing in the morning.

Esther then looked at me and asked if I didn't think it would be a good idea to go with him to the end of the village to show him the short cut; it would take him less than fifteen minutes to reach Wake Arms if he took this path rather than the long way past Felicity's, which was all in the forest and would soon be dark and worrisome. I think she had a feeling we had something important to settle between us and wanted to give us a chance to be alone a few minutes more.

As we left by the front garden, Stephen bent down and picked one of the smallest flowers, a blue one, and put it in his buttonhole.

There was total silence in the village. The pub patrons had no doubt fallen silent all at once, as happened now and then. Without making a sound ourselves, we walked hand in hand in the soft blue semidarkness, which deepened over the downs not far away.

Suddenly I remembered to ask Stephen how he'd found me. "Was it Gladys who gave you my address?" I had told her she mustn't.

It had been much simpler than that, he said. He'd only had to enquire at Canada House, where I'd left a forwarding address for some of my mail.

I imagine we must have laughed heartily at ourselves because I seem to remember our merry voices ringing incongruously in Upshire's sedate silence.

But as soon as the burst of laughter was over, there was tension. As we passed beneath one of the streetlamps, Stephen turned to me in the wan light and took hold of my wrists. His face was grim.

"Go!" he said. "Leave England. Go back to Canada. I didn't want to talk about it seriously in front of Esther and the old man, he's so emotional, but I don't see how we're going to avoid war. It's almost certain, and it will be very soon."

"But how about you?"

"Oh, me.... I'm still a Canadian citizen and there's a good chance I'll find myself in the Canadian army to fight the Germans sooner or later. I'll leave before that if I have to because one of these days you'll find it's Stalin more than Hitler who'll be the enemy we have to destroy. The two of them may go through the motions of a pact but it won't last, and while I'm no friend of the Nazis I'm even less a friend of the Bolsheviks. So if there's war between them I won't be for the Soviets, I'll be for Hitler, because in order to get the Ukraine on his side he'll give guarantees of freedom for my poor country."

"You'd trust Hitler?"

"For a while at any rate – or I'd pretend to. He'll arm us against the Russians. It's already begun, in fact. Then we'll use those arms to free ourselves from the Nazis."

I listened, overcome by the same horror and revulsion I'd felt sitting beside him on the bench in the faintly lit little square when he first revealed his militancy. The shock was worse this time than the first. It hit me just as I'd renewed my trust in him, when I was freshly recaptured. So he had come and played the game of passion with me, I thought with deep resentment, while the only passion he ever had was for some ridiculous utopia. I studied his haggard face, feeling no pity.

"You might even stoop to terrorism, I suppose."

His eyes flashed briefly but fiercely.

"If I had to...perhaps...yes. My people have suffered far too much over the centuries."

But he wanted me as well. He begged me to keep trusting him... until the day when, if the bloody mêlée didn't end in apocalypse,

he'd move heaven and earth to find me, because then he'd have no other thought than to live happily ever after with me.

My only reply was to point out that if he didn't leave soon he'd miss his bus, and perhaps his rendezvous with his Nazi allies tomorrow too.

The look he gave me was pained and reproachful.

I walked with him a little farther without speaking. In these minutes I really thought I hated him and would never stop hating him. I pointed briefly to the path beside the wall bounding the manor house grounds.

He started down it. Several times he turned around and raised a hand. I stood motionless, watching him go out of my life. Soon I lost sight of his form in the deeper darkness under the trees. I stayed for a time waiting for goodness knows what. I no longer heard his footsteps. After a few minutes I imagined him reaching the big ploughed field that had lifted my spirits so mysteriously. The first stars were still rather pale but they'd be brighter down there above the treeless space. Was his heart also touched by this? Was he still moved by the beauty of the world? Could a man's heart have room for a consuming political passion and also tears, laughter, and an unaccountable attachment to a lonely piece of field in a forest? It's strange how often I've wondered whether this field I loved so much didn't in some way establish a link that night between Stephen and me which has endured, though Stephen himself was gone for ever.

Now, I thought, he must be coming out onto the road. He's reaching Wake Arms. He's getting onto the bus this very minute perhaps. I knew I would never see him again.

XIV

THERE WAS NO CLOSING one's eyes any longer. War was coming. Sometimes in those last days of August one would imagine one could hear its horrible breath blowing across the calm, untroubled sky.

David had found my address as well, perhaps also from Canada House. He sent me a note saying he was worried about me and inviting me to have lunch with him two days hence. Lady Frances was also concerned about me, he wrote, and had asked him to let me know she thought I should go back to Canada. We would talk some more about this. He asked me to telephone him at the Admiralty to confirm that we'd meet outside Selfridge's.

I was there at the appointed hour. I wore my navy blue white-flowered linen dress. David had already seen it but I didn't have anything else suitable to wear when going out with him. I carried a small straw handbag which was also navy blue and went well with the dress. To complete the ensemble, I'd just squandered almost my last pennies for the month on a pair of very nice shoes of exactly the same blue, made of latticed strips of raffia; in the first heavy rain they unravelled before my eyes, leaving me practically barefoot in the middle of Oxford Street.

A City gentleman came into view, identical to a thousand others at this hour, a tall, elegant figure in tasteful and impeccably tailored tweed, walking with brisk, light taps ringing from the metal tip of his oh-so-tightly-rolled umbrella. For the hundredth time I asked myself what on earth this flawless product of British civilization could possibly see in me. Who knows, perhaps he was asking himself the same question. In any event, there was a camaraderie between us which seemed to satisfy a part of each of us, for we

always fell easily into our familiar pattern of light joshing and superficial repartee, exactly as we'd left off several months earlier.

Spotting me in the crowd milling about the department store entrance, he greeted me with, "Ah, I say, hello dear girl!"

Without wasting a second he whisked me off to a well-known restaurant. I wonder if it wasn't the Trois-Pruniers, unless lunch at the Trois-Pruniers was another occasion. My memories of this lunch with David and almost everything else about these troubled weeks are rather muddled.

We'd hardly sat down at the table before he let me know, in his fashion, that he was really concerned about me. He'd brought me to London because he wanted to see me, yes, but more important to persuade me to book passage for Canada without delay. I mustn't risk having to go home on a liner converted for troop transport. Or getting torpedoed on the way.

Understatement was so much a part of his nature that I thought I was dreaming, hearing him talk this way.

"Come on David, you're telling me a story! I've just read in the paper that there's no cause for alarm."

He leaned forward so he could speak very quietly.

"Listen! The instructions are to avoid mass hysteria at all cost. If Londoners got wind of how vulnerable they are at this minute they'd lose their heads. You've seen those balloons in the sky over the city that are supposed to form an aerial barrage. Well, they might as well be balloons at a country fair that you could pop with a pin. The truth is we haven't got a single anti-aircraft gun that works, or any other kind of weapon that can do anything worth talking about to protect us from a surprise attack. If it came tonight the city could be wiped out."

The fine meal, the exquisite décor, the sparkling crystal, the attentive maître d'hôtel, the murmur of voices mingling with what David was saying created an atmosphere of confusion in which I felt myself sinking as in a fog.

"You realize," said David, "that as an Admiralty employee I shouldn't be talking to you this way. We're supposed to bend over backwards to reassure the population, but I think it's my duty to warn people who are in a position to leave...and who I care about. I've been in a stew about you, you know," he chided me with a brief smile. "Lady Frances too. Last time I saw her she told me

344

again, 'You must try to get in touch with our little French Canadian and tell her she should leave.' "

Now at last I was feeling remorse over not having kept in touch with people who were genuinely fond of me, who might have thought I'd come to some terrible end when I was really just preoccupied, avoiding all contact with the outside world, even the least suggestion of contact, trying to preserve the fragile spell I was using as a refuge – a serious sin of omission towards others of which I've been guilty many times in the course of my life.

We'd hardly touched our meticulously prepared food. David brought the meal quickly to an end by swallowing his coffee before dessert. He was tense, to the extent that such a thing was ever apparent with him. When we left he apologized for not taking me wherever I was going. He had to get back to the Admiralty as soon as possible. They were working night and day at present. Doing nothing more, he whispered to me in confidence, than preventing people from getting the wind up.

A taxi answered his signal and drew up to the sidewalk. He stepped in, rolled down the window, and said:

"Just in case we don't see each other again, don't forget to leave me your address in Canada."

Thinking I'd be going back to Manitoba and the prairies if at all and trying to keep the tone light between us, I said, "If I do, will you ever come and see me on my steppes?"

He kissed me lightly on the cheek. It was the first kiss he'd ever given me.

"I shall come and sit on your steps."

His taxi pulled away. In the press of people around, I began finally to see the dejection and bewilderment on all the faces. I went my way to wander alone around London.

IN HYDE PARK they were digging trenches. They were already so deep you couldn't see the men, just their shovels as they tossed out the globs of clay they were mining beneath the world's most lovingly nurtured lawns. Sometimes a shovelful would splatter into a bed of flowers. Children brought there by their nannies were hugely entertained by the transformation of the gardens into a battlefield. Playing at throwing grenades, they were hurling lumps of mud in one another's faces. Adults went this way and that,

saying and seeing nothing. Now I was all attention to this strangest of spectacles, the sight of people going about their business though not believing in it any more. The eyes of the whole city were blank. It hurt more to see this blankness than to see pain, which is at least a sign of life.

In Mayfair as elsewhere, as everywhere I went that afternoon in fact, I saw morale-boosting signs at every streetcorner and arrows pointing the way to the nearest air-raid shelter. In the magnificently cloudless, exceptionally clear blue sky I saw the balloons David had mentioned, whose only purpose was to make people think they were protected. There were posters exhorting citizens to go to the nearest distribution centre and get equipped with a gas mask. Some would be adaptable even for babies. I went and picked up one myself, though today I wonder why. I wandered on for hours, through streets so silent you could hear the lightest footstep. Car drivers were no longer honking their horns. Coming back to the shopping districts, I noticed finally that nobody was going in or out of the shops. In curiosity I went briefly into Selfridge's and roamed through a dozen departments without seeing anyone except salespeople standing motionless behind their counters, as if hypnotized. Even in Piccadilly Circus, people and traffic, still as dense as ever, were moving at a snail's pace, like an old merry-go-round getting ready to pack up and depart. In this city I'd found so affable, gay, and ready to joke and banter barely a year before, I hadn't garnered a single smile or even a glance.

I returned late to Upshire and left again two days later with some of my things, intending to come and get the rest little by little. London was drawing me, I think, with the intense fascination worked on the mind by the approach of tragedy. I had just come to realize that the summit of high tragedy is war.

Thus London, where I was becoming acquainted with the world's greatest scourge, was where I would experience human solidarity as never before.

I rented a room in Chiswick. Why did I choose the extreme western edge of London, so far from its centre? Perhaps because the street where I'd be living was a mere step from Kew Gardens, which for some time I'd longed to be able to visit often and at my leisure, I had been so delighted on the few occasions I'd come there

all the way from Fulham. So now I could and did go there almost every day, learning the names, origins, and characteristics of hundreds of trees transplanted from every corner of the world. Yet today I've been robbed of almost all this knowledge acquired so lovingly. What a waste! I must have spent days and days learning thousands of fascinating things about rare trees I'd never have a chance to see again, about others less exotic, about flowers from the remotest corners of the earth, and what have I left to show for it except the rather painful memory of having been enchanted without knowing exactly why?

Perhaps I also chose Chiswick because it was served by the Green Line, and Epping Forest was one of the destinations shown on the bus-stop marker at the end of my street. I could get to Esther's without a transfer on the way, perhaps faster than if I left from a more central point. And then it must also have been because living here was less expensive than in the heart of London.

The house in which I took a room was clean and bright, on a quiet street, and my room was big and comfortable though without much sun. However, my landlord and landlady were of the sort I'd known on Wickendon Street. If they were on their doorstep or in their tiny garden when I went in or out they'd greet me pleasantly enough, adding a word or two about all the beautiful weather we were having, for as this dramatic summer drew to an end we were blessed with invariably sunny skies. I didn't see them at all any other time and never saw the three other boarders in the house. Little by little I fell into the same unsociable habits as on Wickendon Street.

To tell the truth I don't remember much about how I spent my time in this period. I read a lot, I think, getting my books from the municipal library, which was just as well stocked as the one in Fulham. I roamed a great deal around Kew Gardens where I learned almost everything I ever knew about trees. I think I remember a marvellous corner where all the plants of Malaysia were collected together, and how pleasantly removed from reality I felt while there. But most of the time it was as though I was suffering pain and was only half aware of what was around me, even the books and trees perhaps, which may explain why I remember so little about them. The monstrous calamity brewing was carrying per-

347

sonal calamities away in its path, but not only these. It also thrust all enjoyment of life away into the distance, perhaps for ever; it even seemed to remove all meaning from life.

September came. In this house they put my breakfast tray down outside the door and called, "Your breakfast, lady!" If I had the misfortune to go back to sleep, I'd find it stone cold thirty minutes or an hour later. One morning, however, I heard a prolonged rapping at my door and an excited voice announcing, "Great news! Chamberlain and Daladier have gone to meet Hitler. They may still come to terms."

I hurried downstairs to hear more, and my landlord and landlady were suddenly almost friends. They invited me to listen to their small wireless with them. With my own ears I heard that Chamberlain and Daladier were on their way to undertake negotiations with Hitler in hope of preserving peace.

I had the impression that the whole city was holding its breath that day for fear of snuffing out the flicker of hope on the horizon. Then all the newspapers were announcing in front-page headlines that peace had been obtained in exchange for the cession of the Sudetenland to Germany.

There was an explosion of joy in London the like of which I've seen nowhere else. That is, if it can really be called joy to be returning to one's self, one's personal life, one's own interests in the grim knowledge that the event that has made this possible is bringing tears in another country.

Strangers hugged in the streets. Women threw their arms around tipsy sailors' necks. Conga lines formed and wound singing and shouting through parks hitherto reserved for contemplation. The bars were full night and day. A few souls wept in silence. "Those poor, poor unfortunate Czechs!" exclaimed rich ladies at their garden parties. And with rings and bracelets pulled from their fingers and wrists they filled baskets passed from table to table in smart restaurants in aid of the "poor, poor Czechs."

But a few voices cried in the wilderness that England had covered herself with shame by selling out her former friends, thereby encouraging Hitler to make more and more outrageous demands and merely postponing the day of reckoning feared by everyone. It was then, or perhaps a little later, that Churchill said prophetically in

his thundering voice, "If to avoid war we accept dishonour, we shall have war...and dishonour."

They laughed at him then. They said his speeches were purple oratory. They said he revelled in an atmosphere of gloom and doom, that he was never happier than when all was turning to disaster, fulfilling his prophecies. And they kept dancing and getting drunk and celebrating. I think it's since then that every time I see a city rejoice I feel uneasy. Too often, I've observed, the cause for rejoicing is having escaped an evil that has befallen someone else. Later, London in its agony showed a nobler face.

THOUGH THE THREAT of war seemed to have abated, the anxiety it had imparted to me stayed. I had been too frightened by my first glimpse of the monster to forget it so soon. I was also having quite frequent memories of the day with Stephen in Upshire which had begun so beautifully and ended in such bitter parting. Still, I no longer saw his face as clearly, nor heard his voice as plainly in my head. While I knew I'd probably remain scarred for the rest of my life by this unfulfilling love affair, I also knew that I could now envisage life without Stephen – which I had found the most dreadful prospect to accept.

I really had no heart for anything. I couldn't write a single line. I wasn't interested in any of the stories I might have written. I'd lost almost all interest in drama studies, though I still went to the theatre occasionally. When autumn came I may have continued my lessons with Madame Gachet for a time. I have the curious impression of not remembering much about this period. Yet when I stop trying, a fair number of memories do come back, though they're hazy and uncertain. When the weather was mild I must have spent most of my time in Kew Gardens, walking among trees from Ceylon, in tropical forests and through desert oases, where each plant and tree grew in a little soil brought from its native habitat. I loved these trees so much I could recognize them from a distance, like friends, though since then they've fled from my memory.

I missed Century Cottage every minute of the day; Esther had written to say that the lady of the manor had decided to paint the cottage inside and out before it lost too much value. The house

was all upside down as a result. Then she told me Heather was coming to visit, which she hardly ever did, and it was difficult to keep her from coming when the fancy took her. And of course she'd be occupying "my" room.

I just let myself drift, I think. Then I took fright. I began to struggle, looking for a current to take me to shore, any shore. One day I made myself go back to Cadogan Gardens. The drawing room was full to bursting, as on that far, far distant day when I had entered, immediately met Stephen's dark, bright eyes, and been hopelessly caught. I almost turned back, my heart gave such a leap for fear of finding him there with the others and having the torture of ecstasy and doubt begin all over again. But there was Lady Frances coming towards me with her hands outstretched.

"My child! At last! We've missed you so! Why didn't you come and warm your soul with us during those awful days before Munich? Now, listen to me. You must come out of that solitude of yours; you've been far too much alone, if you'll allow me to say so. Your stay in England will be coming to an end before long, I imagine, and like so many other Canadians you'll be leaving without having seen much of our country. I've two marvellous invitations for you – or rather you'll be getting them formally once you've accepted in principle. One is from Lady Curre in Monmouthshire. You'll have to have a long dress for dinner there... but don't worry, it can be anything at all, a sack will do providing it's long. Then before coming back you'll stay with a charming elderly lady in Dorset. You'll get a letter from each of them shortly telling you when you're expected and how long you're invited to stay."

I was astonished – and would be even more astonished later – to be invited as if I were a friend into the homes of people who knew me no more than I knew them.

I accepted because I was too weak-willed to refuse and also out of friendship for Lady Frances, she seemed so anxious for me to go and visit with the gentry; perhaps I was also too surprised to realize what I was agreeing to.

XV

IT WAS STILL warm and lovely that day in November when I took
the train for Chepstow. I had a suitcase with me in the compartment. My wardrobe trunk, which was holding up well despite some
hard knocks, was travelling in the baggage car. It was a very big
piece of baggage to be taking when all it held was my red taffeta
dress which had attended the event at Baron Frankenstein's and
hadn't been out since, my other evening dress in peach mousseline
with a little bolero, matching shoes for both and a few other small
things. I probably seemed rather ignorant of the ways of society
to have arrived with so much baggage for a week's stay, from the
evening of the seventh to the evening of the fourteenth as the letter
had said. Lady Curre must have been startled to see it, which she
did only as I was leaving, in fact. I really made a great deal of
trouble for myself, dragging the bulky thing around just about
everywhere I went. I don't know why I was so determined, unless
it was because I'd paid a lot for the trunk and wanted to be sure I
got my money's worth. And perhaps it gave me courage in a way,
as though the two of us seemed more important together.

In late afternoon I got off the train in the very pretty and ancient
town of Chepstow. The massive towers of a ruined castle of William
the Conqueror's time are still standing there.

An interminably long black automobile was parked in front of
the station. A liveried chauffeur got out and approached me with
his cap in his hand.

"You the young lady for Itton Court?"

I thought I was and told him so.

He introduced himself. He was Ward, and he presented milady's
apologies for not coming to meet me in person. "She was asked at

351

the very last minute to act as judge at a country exhibition, one of those duties one just can't escape."

In no time we left the historic town behind. We drove up the valley of the Wye, one of the most surprising rivers I ever had occasion to see. At low tide it's an ugly ditch with practically no water, just dreary grey mud all pocked as if with the footprints of large, strange beasts come to wallow there. But when the tide rises the Wye becomes a broad and peaceful river, lending a gentle, pastoral air to the valley.

In the distance I could see sky through some high, ancient arches. I asked what those magnificent arches were over there against the horizon.

"Tintern Abbey," replied Ward. "They say it's the oldest church in England."

Lines I had learned at school from Wordsworth's poem on the ancient Cistercian abbey returned to my mind, and more than ever before I was struck by the marvel of the things that were happening to me. I had wondered what this abbey was like that the poet loved so much, and here I was gazing at its ruins as the red of the setting sun beyond began to filter through.

On a peak surrounded by meadows which were still green I could see what looked to me like a castle. It dominated the whole countryside, in fact.

"What's that?" I asked.

"That's ours," said Ward proudly. "Itton Court, where we're heading, Miss."

My heart sank all the way to my boots. I think if there'd been a chance of bribing Ward I would have done it, begging him, "Take me back to the station...," or "Leave me somewhere on the way...," but his steady eye told me he was above that sort of thing. So I abandoned myself to my fate in a state of panic I've rarely exceeded since.

We turned onto a long tree-lined road leading uphill to the mansion. From the front it reminded me rather of Versailles seen from the gardens, but we drove around and pulled up behind where a squat, ancient tower formed an angle. Under a low archway were two postern doors. My suitcase and battered old trunk were whisked away through the smaller of the two by a servant I didn't have

time to see. I myself entered by the larger, and inside was greeted by the butler, who, waving grandly to indicate the direction, enquired with a solicitude which almost seemed sincere if I had had a good trip, and if I wasn't too tired after the train ride on that most wretched of secondary lines.

He left me at the door to a huge room – the sitting room, drawing room, or music room, I don't remember which. It took me so long to distinguish one from another, except for the morning room, which was flooded with sunlight in the morning, that I still wasn't very sure when the time came for me to leave, as I'd arrived, by the postern door.

A little old lady rose and advanced towards me with tiny steps, blinking as if to see me through a fog. I hadn't noticed her at first because she'd been sitting in a high-backed armchair facing the other way. Thinking she must be my hostess and that it would be nice if I immediately showed myself to be both grateful and affectionate, I too advanced and in a trembling voice spoke as warmly as I knew how.

"So glad, dear Lady Curre! How very kind!"

Which merely irritated the little old lady, for she was a governess or penniless cousin or one of those undefined companions harboured in all great houses like Itton Court.

"Lady Curre will be here later, child," she muttered reproachfully. "Please follow me. I'm to show you to your room."

We walked through endless corridors intersected by other corridors, they also intersected by other, slightly narrower corridors, and finally came to my room. By itself it was nearly as big as any dwelling I'd ever lived in. There was an enormous fireplace at one end, in which practically a whole tree trunk was burning. Straight ahead beyond the high window lay the formal gardens with fountains and statues, for my room was on the "Versailles" side.

"Hope you like your room," said the little old lady. "Dinner's at eight. We dress for dinner here. The dinner gong will sound to call us. To find the dining room, just follow the sound. Now try to have a little sleep."

And she disappeared.

Left to myself, I began by sitting on the end of the huge four-poster bed. The chambermaid had been there before me. She'd

unpacked my suitcase and arranged my humble little belongings, my hairbrush with the worn bristles and my slippers and dressing gown which were now far from crisp and new, I noticed.

In an angle of the room I spotted the prettiest little desk I ever had the use of. If I can trust my jumbled memories of that day, I'd say it must have been a Sheraton. Inside I found ink, pens, and some handsome pearl-grey writing paper imprinted with a crown. I sat down and began to write to almost everyone I knew. I began with Maman, telling her not to worry about me, I was fine and at the moment was living like a princess.

IF I HAD TIME it would be no hardship to describe my experiences during my week at Itton Court. For dinner one night I would put on my taffeta dress and the next the red-flowered peach mousseline, another night adding a red sash to the peach dress and the night after a red bolero. This way I imagined I looked different each night and appeared to have quite a varied wardrobe. I was certainly better equipped for dinner than the diffident little old lady – governess, penniless cousin, or companion, I never found out which – whom I saw night after night always in the same long plum-coloured sack.

There were twelve of us at dinner – I forget their names except for two, captains Wolfe and Fox, which were so appropriate to the hunt, Itton Court's principal activity. We sat at a huge table in a huge room at each end of which there were whole trees burning in cavernous fireplaces, each bigger than a country cottage.

We were all in a hurry to arrive because we were coming from distant wings of the house and froze as we navigated the endless glacial corridors. Indeed I lost my way the first time because the sound of the gong seemed to come from everywhere at once, perhaps because it kept echoing. I tuned my ear to it, however, and more important, I established some reference points in the form of lords in wigs and ladies in little lace bonnets along the way to the dining room.

While we were at table the butler and his footmen hovered behind us, so attentive to our every wish that we would hardly wet our lips and put down the glass before a hand would reach forward to fill it again.

Lady Curre was quite the opposite to the wizened little creature I'd mistaken for her. She was a tall, statuesque woman with broad

shoulders and a booming voice, and she walked with a long stride. Very much a horse woman, as I believe was the term in those circles, not because she looked like a horse, heaven forbid, but because she spent as much time with horses as she did with people, and probably liked them better too. She took part in all the hunts in the region, often hosted them, and took me along on one so that, as she said, I could tell people how it was done one day when I went back to Canada. Among my mementos of this time I still have a little photograph of the hounds and riders, with footmen bringing glasses of sherry to the mounted riders before the start of the hunt. The Versailles side of the house is in the background.

One night at dinner two of the guests, writers and supposedly friends of Chesterton whom they called "G.K.", were conversing with a poetess whose hair was tinted pale mauve, and I suddenly thought how extraordinary it was to find myself in this circle. I suppose my mind wandered off totally for a few minutes. I've often been amazed by my experiences – who doesn't think his or her own life is more surprising than anyone else's? But that night I was astounded. I felt as though I were watching myself from a few steps behind, observing myself sitting here among the upper crust, and I couldn't believe my eyes. There must have been bewilderment on my face because Lady Curre suddenly interrupted the poetess and barked quite loudly at me from the far end of the table:

"Child! Lost in your reveries again! A penny for your thoughts!"

I loved this expression. Esther had often said it to me when she saw I was lost in "the ramblings of that wandering mind." Though a little disconcerted I couldn't hold back a smile for Lady Curre, because I had a feeling she wasn't as fearsome as she might seem and possibly no one had ever talked to her spontaneously. To her servants she was "Milady", and if their manner was superficially familiar when they spoke to her, it was always deferential. Her freeloading guests, some of whom she kept under her roof for long periods for want of something better, lavished endearments on her, which made their "dear Geneva" frown a little, I observed. I don't know what made me tell her what I'd really been thinking.

"I was seeing myself as if from a faraway part of my life," I told her, "back in my little prairie city in the Canadian West, and I couldn't believe I was really here with you, Lady Curre. I'm still not sure."

She smiled and told the others that at last she'd heard some talk under her roof that wasn't just chit-chat and what I'd said was so right, nobody really believes the things that happen to them are true.

From this moment she became so attached to me that it made me apprehensive; she talked of keeping me when my week was over so I could attend a ball she was giving the following week, when I could meet the young people of the region. I said I was expected in Dorset next week, which was nothing less than the truth.

Before leaving I sent the chambermaid, a young German girl who'd been assigned to look after my wants, to take my thank-you note and a little goodbye gift to Lady Curre's room. At Cadogan Gardens Lady Frances had thoughtfully let me know it would be considered good manners to leave some little thing as a mark of gratitude to my hostess, anything at all, it was the thought that counted. I'd wandered around Harrod's for hours looking for something for two dollars at most which wouldn't look too cheap. In the end I bought a spray of handmade lily-of-the-valley to wear on a lapel or as a corsage. I thought it was rather lovely, in fact, and I'd had it wrapped in a nice box. However, the moment I finally met my rather horsey hostess I was pretty sure she wouldn't be thrilled with my present.

So I nearly fell over in surprise when I arrived in London and found a note from Lady Curre waiting for me, thanking me effusively in letters at least six inches high for my charming gift. She'd keep it and cherish it all her life, she wrote, for it was "the one and only gift of the kind I've ever been given. So very sweet of you, child!" For a while I thought she might in a way be making fun of me, or else had been writing any old words just to fill up a sheet of her lovely pearl-grey paper. Then gradually I began to wonder if she mightn't in fact have been quite enchanted to receive flowers that weren't real for once in her life. "Only an imaginative girl like you," she'd written, "would have thought of such a gift."

TO GET FROM Chepstow to Dorset it would almost have been simpler to return to London and take the train direct to Weymouth or some other southern town. I had decided to travel cross-country, however, burdened with my trunk as always and changing trains at

little out-of-the-way stations, wasting time in each waiting for the connection. Still, this way I had a glimpse of a profoundly rural part of England which I would never have known otherwise, and despite its inconvenience I have marvellous memories of this bewildering journey.

My hostess was waiting for me at Bridgeport Station, brought by her chauffeur, who was also the gardener and general factotum. She was a short, elderly woman in stout walking shoes and shapeless tweeds, with a face covered in warts and an enormous plush hat pulled down over her ears. She looked so ugly and frumpy that riding in silence beside her in the back of the car I said to myself, it's not going to work, I'll never be able to spend a week with this woman. But when she lifted her face and I saw her eyes under the rim of her enormous hat, I was so struck by their kindness, good humour, wit, and intelligence that I ceased then and there to find her ugly.

She had been born in England and brought up in Australia, where her father had made a fortune raising sheep. When he died she'd come back to settle in England and had chosen Dorset quite simply because this was where she had found and been able to buy an old cottage in pure Elizabethan style, which was just what she'd wanted all her life. With the help of a cook and her chauffeur-gardener she led a peaceful life, entertaining guests like me from time to time to brighten her days, and also to do her share to foster good feeling throughout the Empire.

This was more or less what Miss Shaw told me as we drove towards Matravers Cottage. Every now and then she called me "my lamb", which I thought at first was just a habit, rather natural for someone brought up among sheep. I soon realized that for her it was a term of affection. Soon, in fact, she began referring to me as "my niece", since her favourite "lambs" became family to her, she explained, her own family not amounting to much, consisting in all of a single real niece.

This was how she introduced me to the vicar, the squire of the village, the squire of the uplands we crossed on horseback, and everywhere she took me to have me seen and heard.

We arrived at the most charming cottage I think I ever saw in England. Together perhaps with a farmhouse with a roof of massive red tiles nestled in the foothills of the Alpilles near St-Rémy-de-

Provence and another old house in the Gaspé Peninsula, it was one of the few dwellings in which, the minute I set eyes on it, I imagined I could live all my life without ever wanting to look for something better.

It was a pleasingly proportioned house, built of grey stone rounded by time, rain, and wind, the walls pierced at precise intervals by small-paned windows framed in white. It stood on a kind of natural platform covered with rather stubbly grass, overlooking an expanse of downs which were perhaps even more beautiful than those at Upshire, for in the far distance was a bright line sparkling in the sun, which was the sea. Sometimes I was even sure I could hear it pounding on the very shores from which Robert Louis Stevenson made the *Hispaniola* set sail in search of Treasure Island.

My room was magnificent, big enough but not too big, and through its small-paned, double-casement window I discovered the downs, a vastness of landlocked waves which this time met the waves of the ocean within eyesight. For the first time in my life I slept between linen sheets. The cook-chambermaid had put an ancient stone hot-water bottle in my bed; it had a little woollen cover so it wouldn't burn my feet. Miss Shaw came to see if I had everything I needed, accompanied by her Scotch terrier, whose eyes, behind all his bristly hair, showed almost as much wit as his mistress's.

I've come upon so many oases in the course of my life, it seems to me now that I've only had to set out boldly and follow my nose in order to find one on the horizon and immediately feel at home.

THOUGH IT WASN'T the season at all, Miss Shaw was determined I should see Bath, the renowned watering place of Regency times. Perhaps she really wanted to see it herself, to revisit a scene from her youth. In any event, one fine morning we were on our way to Bath, driven by Jeremiah, who also found us hotel rooms, posted our postcards, and generally looked after us in all manner of ways. From Bath we continued to Bristol where Miss Shaw had a friend she wanted to see, who kept us overnight. Across the Bristol Channel was Wales, which Miss Shaw spotted me straining to see in the distance, probably looking wishful, because she told me that that was where we would go next time.

She asked me which way I'd like to return, by the coast road or

by the moors. I'd already seen much of the coast with David and his hypercritical mother. I said I'd like to go by the moors. We took a long detour to get to Broadmoor and then Exmoor.

These wild reaches with their coarse grass, without a single house or cultivated field, where fierce winds blow incessantly beneath tormented skies, quite exhilarated me. Why do sterile, treeless, disturbing landscapes immediately seem to release pent-up tensions in me, set me free in some way? It happened in Brittany when I saw the moors of Lanvaux, which I felt I never wanted to leave; their desolation so fascinated me I stayed to look and muse for hours. It happened too when from the Col de Vence in Provence I discovered a sweep of whistling grasses raked by the wind from the mountains and inhabited only by great black rocks raised in most enigmatic poses. Why have these rather mournful landscapes almost always lifted my spirits more than vistas considered cheerful, harmonious, or charming? Miss Shaw, who'd been brought up in the Australian outback, seemed to understand this and agree in any event. Many was the time as we drove along, even before I asked, that she would tell Jeremiah to stop the car so I could get out and walk by myself on a path through the brambles towards some dramatic horizon.

No sooner were we back at Matravers Cottage than she took me to see the town of Dorchester, where the cruel Judge Jeffreys presided over the "Bloody Assizes" and sent people by the hundreds to the gallows. We came back through the pretty town of Weymouth. Miss Shaw always had some story to tell me about each place we visited. The stories never seemed very likely, but this didn't matter; I would watch the old lady light up with pleasure to be pleasing me. I thought she was so ugly when I arrived but now I'd come to think of her as quite lovely, her eyes would sparkle so with delight to have a companion through whom she was rediscovering her own youthful enthusiasm. "Those poor, half-dead old souls," she said of neighbours, most of whom were younger than she, "they aren't interested in anything and don't read anything or feel anything any more."

Seeing how much I loved to roam over the downs, she finally let me leave alone in the morning with sandwiches for lunch, but on two conditions: I mustn't be a minute late getting back for tea, and I must take a walking stick to use as a weapon in case I should

have a disagreeable encounter. She even showed me how to use it; to get the better of an assailant, one had to give him a sharp blow to the side of the head. She'd learned this when very young on the lonely sheep station in Australia.

I think I was really always back in time for tea, which she would have been very disappointed to have alone. As for the walking stick, as soon as I was out of sight I'd hide it under the end of a hedge and then retrieve it on the way back; I'd lean on it heavily at each step if I spied Miss Shaw's face at the window. She'd come out to meet me, beaming.

"Good girl! Good girl!" she'd say. "Nothing like a good stick when you're walking rough ground, eh?"

IN RETURN for such generous hospitality, she asked nothing more than for me to listen to her telling me about the glorious hours of her youth, when she'd do twenty miles on horseback without a stop to get to the nearest neighbouring station. She loved it too when I made her laugh by imitating the curious accent of the local people in my own accent, which was already curious enough. "Give me a lilt from your youth," she'd say, "you have some to spare." It was partly from her that I learned how essential we are to each other, old souls who grieve less for their heyday when they have young people near, and young souls who are less afraid of old age when they see the old still capable of enjoyment and delight.

After a copious dinner, Miss Shaw also liked me to play a game of Australian rummy with her, having taught me the game. We would pull the card table almost into the flames of the fireplace, and the little Scotch terrier would come and lie beside us with his nose towards the fire. It was bad for his eyes, said his mistress, but he couldn't be prevented because he was as fascinated by the flames as we were.

We'd begin our game. Almost every night I'd win and she'd be cross. "May you be thoroughly bedevilled!" she'd exclaim. Though she'd learned much about the nature of people and about Nature itself in the Australian outback, she'd also learned habits of speech that set her somewhat apart from her rather starchy social circle in Dorset. From under his mistress's skirt the scottie would growl, scolding me in his own way for beating her.

This was the only shadow on the easy relationship developing between us, Miss Shaw and me, in our lonely abode out there on the downs. The crusty little dog was not inclined to be friendly at all. If I invited him to go for a walk with me, though he loved walks he'd shake his head angrily as if to say, "Keep your distance if you want me to keep mine." I was all the more hurt by his surly manner when Miss Shaw declared him to be the best judge of human nature she'd ever known.

"He's never been wrong," she said. "Whenever he's refused to be polite to someone who's been here, I've been sure to learn nasty things about the person sooner or later. I've found out a good many false friends this way. If he's nice to a guest under my roof on the other hand, I know I can sleep in peace because then I'm sure the person is straightforward and honest."

"That's not a very good sign for me," I protested.

"Ah, but Alec's far from being done with you yet. He takes his time. He takes longer to make up his mind about some people than others. Besides, you mustn't forget Alec's a Scotchman. He's dour. And cautious. All this time he's been studying you deeply, don't you doubt it."

Which made me even more uneasy about my relationship with the scottie, whom I'd renamed "Alec the Intellectual", to the delight of his mistress.

"That's just what he is," she said, "an intellectual! I've been looking for the right word for ages and now you've found it. Come here, Alec-the-Intellectual!"

By nine o'clock or nine-thirty, Miss Shaw would be sleepy and she'd leave for bed. I didn't know how old she was. Later I learned that she must have been about eighty-seven. "Come along, Alec," she'd say. "We're getting old, you and I, it's time for bed."

Halfway up the stairs she'd stop and look back at me curled up in an easy chair with a book I'd just taken from a shelf beside me. She had an extraordinary set of books recounting the most gruesome crimes from all ages and in every country. Once I'd begun to read those books, I was almost impatient for Miss Shaw to retire for the night so I could get back to the horror that kept me in breathless suspense.

Miss Shaw suspected as much and resented it, though she under-

stood my engrossment for she must have read all those books, since she'd taken the trouble to bring them back from Australia, all thirty gold-edged, heavy red-covered volumes.

This was the hour when the wind over the downs and the wind from the sea met in howling combat around our lonely hilltop.

One night Miss Shaw listened to it with her hand on the banister.

"I've lived in ten houses in my life," she said, "and this is the only one where the winds buffet from all sides at once this way. There's a mystery about it no one can explain. Something evil surely happened in this old house at some time in the four hundred years it's been here. You know, I wouldn't be surprised if there was a skeleton hidden somewhere in these thick walls."

I realized she was dramatizing, hoping to get me to leave my book and take to the upper floor with her. But the sound of the curse-driven wind just deepened my contentment to be absorbed in my grisly story beside a gently crackling fire.

Then she flung at me, like a malediction from the top of the stairs:

"May you be thoroughly frightened! Shaken to the bones!"

MANY HOURS after she'd left me one evening, when I was carried away and read on and on into the night, I thought I heard a small sound. A second later I felt a gentle tongue lick my hand. Through all the hair over his eyes, Alec the Intellectual was looking at me kindly, tenderly, lovingly, but also a little mischievously as if to say, "We mustn't let her know. She wants to be the only one I love. She hasn't got many other real friends, and I love her too much to risk making her the slightest bit jealous." And he rested his muzzle trustingly on my knee while I stroked his forehead trying to reassure him.

WHEN MY WEEK was up Miss Shaw invited me to stay another week, and this had hardly begun when she suggested I stay till the end of the month. This time I felt I shouldn't abuse such generous hospitality, and anyway it was time I was getting back to London. But why? I didn't have anyone really waiting for me. I was even afraid of going back, as if the grief, misery, and loneliness I'd known there were just waiting for me to return before falling upon me again, whereas here at Matravers Cottage I was protected, even

happy in a way. What surprised me most about myself at this time was how often I'd been happy despite an almost constant undercurrent of despondency, and how often I'd made other people think I was naturally gay and light-hearted – and no doubt I was, whenever my melancholy waned.

A little scene occurred before I left which I would have given a great deal to have avoided, though it left me with a very touching memory. The Intellectual and I had been observing our agreement; I never patted him and he would even give me a pretend growl as I passed.

But when he saw me come from upstairs with my coat after Jeremiah had brought down my trunk and suitcase, he lost control and threw himself at my feet to lick them, then pawed at my knees trying to scramble up, crying and whimpering inconsolably it seemed. Through his crying I thought I heard him say, "What's to become of us, my mistress and me? We're both very old and lonely in this windblown house." I wanted to comfort him and I didn't dare.

I met Miss Shaw's eye. It showed a kind of satisfaction at seeing the Intellectual confirm her judgement of me...but also shock and disappointment to find me receiving some of his love when she was supposed to have it all.

In the end she came round and laughed, though perhaps not heartily.

"He had our number!" she said. "He fooled us properly, the little scottie devil!"

XVI

BEING BACK in Chiswick was even worse than I had expected. There was no sky, no open country to look at, no voice of the wind in the trees to listen to, not even a sad or raging wind – none of the things that have always most helped me to endure life. My despondency returned and took hold of me even more firmly than before. Everything I'd done to be rid of it, my week at Itton Court and my two weeks at Miss Shaw's, seemed only to have left me feeling more desolate than ever.

It rained almost without pause that late November. We didn't see the sky for two whole weeks. It was too wet to look for solace among all the incredibly beautiful trees and plants in Kew Gardens. How it rained!

I hardly ever saw Bohdan any more. I'd gone to live a very long way from my friends, it's true. Bohdan scolded me for this on the few occasions we met, always at some middle point so as not to take too much of his time when he had a program on the BBC or a rehearsal with the London Symphony. Sometimes he'd take enough time to invite me to an ABC for a quick cup of tea. He did his best to cheer me up, he who had barely three more years to live; you'd have said he sensed this, he seemed so restless, in such a ferment, never relaxed.

We had no word from Stephen. Bohdan thought he must be away on one of his clandestine visits to militants in countries bordering the Ukraine, where some day he'd probably leave his bones. Bohdan was of Ukrainian descent himself and was very attached to the culture of his forefathers; he thought it absurd for a handful of fanatics, as he called them, to dream of liberating the country. After a few brief meetings, I wouldn't see him again for weeks.

I was back in touch with Phyllis and we went to the theatre

together a few times. It says much about the state of mind I must have been in that I don't remember any of the plays we saw. There are whole segments of my life that have disappeared from my memory, I suppose quite simply because I myself had disappeared. I was just drifting across the surface of things, retaining nothing. Still, as in Paris, I must have been unconsciously registering certain moments from this part of my life, for at times some of them do come back, as though rising to the surface from a deeply buried dream.

Phyllis and I were living in opposite ends of London and we both had to take an interminable bus ride in order to meet at Kensington halfway between. Phyllis was very busy with her studies too. She was persevering at the Guildhall, without showing signs of any greater talent I believe. After I stopped hearing from her, I often wondered if even so she'd managed to make a career for herself in the theatre, if you can call it a career when all you ever play are the rather unrewarding little roles that must be played by someone, and whether in the end she felt she'd somehow achieved what she had hoped. But then, why shouldn't she? There are plenty of writers who never write anything but clever banalities all their lives, yet they've probably put as much effort and perseverance into them as others have put into great works. There's no reason why they shouldn't feel a little pride in what to them is an accomplishment.

For my part, I had heard of an experimental theatre not far from Chiswick where they guaranteed registered students small roles under the guidance of a professional director, as well as whatever might be learned by attending rehearsals of a play being prepared for staging. This was almost exactly what I'd had for nothing from the Pitoëffs, but here one paid handsomely for it. Like an idiot I registered and very soon discovered I'd been fleeced. I went to lodge a complaint at Canada House with some other Canadians in the same predicament and we retrieved half of what we'd paid to this so-called drama school.

I wasn't really writing any more. I couldn't even imagine I would ever have anything to say. I had only one persistent desire throughout my last month in London, and that was to return to Upshire. I knew the cottage was cold and damp at this time of year. Esther had told me she couldn't ever heat it adequately and always had a cold all winter long. Her father's longstanding bronchitis was back,

worse every year. I didn't care. I couldn't picture Century Cottage except surrounded with flowers and overlooking perpetually sun-drenched downs. Even if it was cold and miserable I thought I'd be better off with people I loved and who loved me than anywhere else. I wrote to Esther asking if I could come and spend a few weeks.

Two days later she called me on the telephone. In my present boarding house it was rare to hear someone calling up the stairs that I was wanted on the phone. I was seized with apprehension, as though the call could only mean terrible news. I was even more worried when I heard Esther's voice, for she had to telephone from the booth outside the post office and hated it so much she'd only resort to it in the direst circumstances. She sounded far away at the end of the earth, perhaps because of the resonance in the closed booth.

"Dearest, there is nothing I'd love more than to have you here but my dear old aunt in Malvern, Father's sister, is in a very bad way. Father and I are leaving tomorrow to go to her. I wasn't sure we should. Father's not well. He coughs a lot and even has a little fever in the evening but he insists on going to be with his sister. She's the only one left in his family. They need each other at this time."

"But Esther," I protested, "your father's too frail for a trip like that, particularly when it's so damp. He'll be ill when he gets there and then what help will he be?"

"I'll wrap him up in lots of woollies and watch him so carefully he won't be any worse off on the trip than here. Anyway, it's a risk we have to take. Father would never forgive himself if he didn't go to his sister when she's dying."

I don't know what possessed me to keep arguing with her when she must have been shivering with the cold in the icy phone booth.

"But Esther, haven't you told me a hundred times that our immortal souls will meet in ineffable bliss when this life is done? Since they're sure to be reunited then, why expose him to all the fatigue and emotion of the trip? He could die himself as a result."

She was silent for so long I began to be frightened and called, "Esther! Esther!" Finally she spoke in that gentle, reproachful voice.

"Of course we'll meet in bliss when we're gathered to the Lord and our suffering will be forgotten. But I want you to know,

Gabrielle, that I've thought all of this over many times and I feel it's important for people who are going to be separated to meet again one last time in this life...with all their suffering...."

"But since it's going to be forgotten forevermore, as you say...."

"With all their suffering," she repeated gently, compassionately, "and also to say goodbye properly...on this earth."

When I went back upstairs to my room I reflected on these words. They kept ringing in my head. I couldn't get rid of them. I've never been rid of them since. I hear them every time I'm about to lose someone I love.

"Important to meet one last time...in this life...with all our suffering...and say goodbye properly...."

But why, when suffering will be wiped away by happiness in the end? Perhaps so that a trace may remain for us to reflect on.

I thought about my mother, who might this very minute be sitting with pen in hand, trying to compose the difficult words that would leave me free but still bring me back to her. I realized that she'd been in constant fear for us both since Munich. She never said so outright but she was sure that war would break out soon, that I might not be able to return to Canada, that we wouldn't meet one last time, she and I, with all our suffering...and it was clear to me that the prospect grieved her more than all she had suffered in her life.

FINALLY I fell ill. Was it a real physical illness or was I giving up because everything I'd been trying to do seemed so fruitless? Both, no doubt. In the evening I'd have a little fever. My throat was terribly sore. I didn't even go out to eat in the neighbourhood tea-shops and my landlady brought me practically nothing. Phyllis came all the way across London many times to bring me a big jar of soup and biscuits, fruit, and medicines. At times I could have laughed to see myself. Yesterday I'd been living in a grand house, being pampered by a maid who attended to me almost exclusively, running my bathwater, laying out my freshly ironed dress for dinner...and today I was helpless and alone in a single icy room.

Phyllis insisted I consult a doctor. In the end I gave in, too weak to resist. I think it was she who made the appointment. Perhaps she was acquainted with one of the famous Harley Street doctors but I really don't know. All I remember is that one fine day I found

myself in the consulting room of one of London's leading specialists in otorhinolaryngology. He examined my throat, upper throat, and sinuses at length with a head mirror, as was the practice then.

He informed me that my sinuses had probably been infected for years and my mucous membranes were badly damaged. How, he asked me rather severely, could I have allowed this to happen at my age? I thought of the icy rooms I'd slept in, particularly at Cardinal where I'd had to break the ice in my water jug in order to wash myself, but also at Deschambault Street in our most difficult years, when Mother had to turn down the heat as far as possible, even on nights when it was thirty degrees below zero Fahrenheit.

He told me that he didn't want to alarm me unduly, but if I wasn't careful I'd be in for some very serious respiratory problems later.

At this time when my condition was still quite mild, how far I was from taking his warning seriously! How far I was from thinking that these minor aggravations would give rise to the dreadful disease which finally caught up with me six years ago, from which I've suffered ever since. Often when it wakes me on the brink of suffocation at night, I tell myself that this is no doubt what I'll die of, like my brothers Joe and Rodolphe, who died of asthma. Most of all, since it keeps reminding me I'm mortal, this is what has made me want to write this book, because I'm able now to see so much I never saw before, as if when life is threatened – though when, in fact, is it not? – it throws a light on itself which illuminates every nook and cranny.

"But besides," continued my specialist, "you must have been putting a terrible strain on your throat. What kind of work have you been doing to tire it so?"

I told him I'd been a teacher for eight years. He gave me a smile in which there was compassion, and even more, I think, satisfaction in having been right. Since then I've often seen the same curious mixture of reactions on the faces of other doctors.

"Ah yes," he said, "eight years of talking almost constantly from morning till night, and almost always with your voice raised a bit because of the noise, and chalk dust in the air, that's hard on the throat."

One did indeed write on the blackboard a great deal in the days when I was a teacher.

"Now," he went on, "tell me what you're doing in London. The climate, you must realize, is one of the worst in the world for the respiratory passages. What brought you here?"

As he questioned me, I had the eerie, painful impression that everything I'd ever done had been wrong. I'd practised the wrong profession, I was in the wrong city....

I said I was studying drama.

He shuddered, incredulously perhaps, then after studying me at length conceded that I might have a gift for the theatre...in a way, as long as....

"You're not hoping for a career on the stage, I trust," he said abruptly.

I admitted that I might have considered it...vaguely...though I wasn't sure I really wanted it.

"Put the thought out of your mind for good," he said categorically. "Your throat can't stand that profession. Before long you wouldn't have any voice at all."

Then he tried to qualify what he'd said, thinking he'd probably dealt me a blow and upset me.

It was quite the contrary. His words had just lifted a weight from my shoulders that I'd never really known was there. He'd closed the door for ever to something else that was going to be wrong, something I'd felt obliged to keep exploring even after it was clear I wasn't cut out for it. So now there remained the other road, which was really the most frightening one.

I had already made many forays in this direction, yet the way was still anything but clear. I kept pondering this while the doctor was making an attempt to help me.

"Are you planning to go back to Canada soon? The climate here, I repeat, is very bad for you."

"Probably soon," I said, "because I'm going to run out of money."

"Before you do, would you have enough to go and spend a few weeks where it's warm and sunny? In Provence, for example?"

Had he been there himself and liked it, or in the constant oceans of fog that inundate London had he just dreamed of going? In any event, to lure me out of my total indifference he couldn't have done better than to remind me of one of the great delights of my childhood, discovering the stories of Alphonse Daudet. He must have seen my eyes light up. I'd kept them obstinately fixed on the

carpet while he talked about unhealthy climates and occupations I couldn't pursue.

"Why don't you go?" he urged. "You can live there for practically nothing. You'll manage with no trouble at all, I'm sure of it. The sun and *joie de vivre* will do more to cure you than all the medicines I could prescribe."

I found myself outside in a very curious state of mind. Alexandre Chenevert's impressions on leaving the doctor's office as I described them many years later were exactly like my own feelings when I left my distinguished Harley Street doctor. Hearing myself advised to obey my dearest wish had cost me a pound, an enormous sum for me.

I hurried to Cook's travel agency. What I had left in the bank – almost all of it – was enough to pay for a third-class return fare to Nice and two weeks' room and board with a family in Beaulieu-sur-mer. Why there? No doubt because I was dealing with an agency employee who was very persuasive or perhaps just very obliging, a characteristic of Cook's in those days. While on holiday himself he had tried this boarding house; it was inexpensive and he could recommend it to me in all good faith.

Early in January 1939 I left with my wardrobe trunk, which once again was to be more hindrance than help but I couldn't face a decision to part with it. I probably felt it had been too much involved with all the ups and downs of my life. Two railway employees loaded it onto the baggage car. I kept a close eye on them from my compartment in the train, for I was always very careful to make sure it didn't go astray.

I embarked on the Dover-to-Calais ferry in early afternoon. The weather was as grey, wet, and miserable as one could imagine. The cries of gulls reached me from the foggy sky as they had when I'd left the coast of France just over a year before, reinforcing my impression of not having advanced a single step since then, of feebly groping still, in my life as on this mournful day, for an impossible path through the fog and rain, listening to eerie, muffled cries coming from somewhere I couldn't identify and against which they were trying to put me on my guard.

XVII

THE CHANNEL was in the grip of one of the worst storms of the winter. Our small, flat-bottomed ship kept climbing to the crests of monstrous waves which then let us drop abruptly as if to the bottom of the sea. I've never endured such pitching except perhaps in the Aegean, when we were taken from our cruise ship in frail caïques to visit the islands of Delos and Mykonos, against the world's most tumultuous winds. But these were crossings of ten or fifteen minutes, whereas the crossing from Dover to Calais took two hours in those days.

In no time almost everyone was seasick. You'd see passengers turn pale, then green, and finally leave the dining room in haste, holding their hands over their mouths. There was an adjoining room full of little camp cots which one might think had been set up in anticipation of sudden seasickness. I was soon stretched out on one of these, surrounded by other moaning bodies. The ship creaked from stem to stern. Its groans mingled with those of humans and the haunting sound of an errant wind imprisoned in the gangways.

At one point I imagined I was locked inside one of those frightful little vessels of olden days which took months to cross from Europe to North America – a gasping, retching immigrant who probably wouldn't survive the voyage. It was a taste of the incredible sufferings with which our country was built, with each tiny foothold won from the deep silence of coast and forest.

I'd left London with bronchitis and probably a fever. My stubborn cough, splitting headache, and appalling nausea, and even more perhaps the helpless feeling of not being able to pull myself together, all these had combined to defeat me utterly. Harmless though it may be, seasickness can make us believe we're going to

die and even hope we do. I was reduced to a mere bundle of misery and indifference. Still, beneath the indifference I remember observing bleakly that, all things considered, life seemed such a waste of dreams, efforts, enthusiasm, and hope. I've sometimes wondered what would have become of me that day if someone hadn't suddenly been there to save me, as on so many occasions when I've been most in need. I suppose I could have let myself be taken back to England on the same ferry, or simply stayed aboard until I was removed by force.

Out of the moaning all around me came a placid voice. "Come on now, make a little effort! Swallow a sip of this cognac. Nothing makes one feel better than a steady stomach, you'll see."

I opened my eyes. I could just make out the face of a young woman I'd met on deck shortly before leaving port. I'd heard her from a distance speaking to a porter and by her accent had recognized an English-speaking compatriot from Toronto. I'd gone over to greet my fellow Canadian and we'd exchanged a few pleasantries. She was Ruby Cronk, she told me, and she was a nurse. I found the name so odd I remembered it without difficulty this time. She'd just finished a period of training in London and was going to the South of France for a short holiday before returning to Canada. We'd parted, each to go her own way, with a "Bye-bye now, see you later," which might have turned out to be never. Now here she was beside me, intending to force her care on me if necessary. I don't think I made it too difficult for her. In the hopeless condition I was sure I was in, I simply put myself into the hands of the young woman with the kind, calm round face and swallowed the medicines she was insisting I take.

It seemed only minutes later when she was shaking me to get me up.

"We're going to be getting off soon. The crossing's over. We have to be ready."

I tried to sit up but my head spun and I fell back again. I didn't want to leave that wretched little cot for anything in the world. So Ruby opened my handbag, found my passport, and took charge of my affairs as well as her own. She held me up as we went through customs. Instead of my many other potential worries, the only one that came to the surface of my muddled mind was once again about my trunk. I'd so often been afraid of losing it; of all

my fixations this was certainly among those which caused me the most problems. I mumbled a word or two about it to Ruby. She retrieved it, found the key, and opened it for inspection.

With our baggage checked, we left in mid-afternoon on the fast train to Paris. Already it was almost dark. It was pouring. Rivulets of rain streamed down the windows. Nightfall, blotting out all trace of the dark landscape outside, made them seem more doleful still, like floods of tears. Ruby made me take another capsule and I went to sleep with my head on her shoulder as if she were my dearest friend.

It always moves me deeply to remember the tenderness, care, and kindness I've received from so many strangers. It renews my faith in humankind but also makes me sad. For I think people I've barely met have shown me more affection than many of my close relatives, who, it's true, have had to suffer me over a much longer time. Perhaps everyone finds this to be so.

In Paris we had to change stations, retrieving our baggage in one and taking it to the other. How Ruby managed with only the three or four words of French she knew I have no idea; all I could do was follow her. I remember vaguely hearing her shout at the top of her heavily accented voice, *"Porteur! Porteur!"* which made everyone turn around but not come to help, and seeing her pivoting my trunk on its corners towards the taxi at the curb. With everything swimming in my head, I thought I was arriving in Paris for the first time again and it was my other compatriot who had taken charge for me.

On the Paris–Nice express, Ruby took command of an empty compartment. She had me lie on one of the seats with a rolled-up sweater for a pillow and covered me with my coat and hers too. After this I wasn't conscious of anything else all night. While I slept, she told me next day, she mounted guard at the door. When passengers tried to enter she'd gesture at my sleeping form and with a sorrowful but authoritarian face beg their compassion saying, "Poor girl. Very sick. Perhaps contagious!" Our would-be companions would retreat hurriedly and squeeze as best they could into compartments already full. Some remained standing outside in the corridor, leaning on the handrail and gazing out at the darkness flying by. These I still have on my conscience. After Lyon, our only stop on the way, I think, where she had to beat off some

last attempts at invasion, Ruby lay down on the other seat and she too slept like a log. Even the conductor, who came in twice to punch our tickets, as he told us the following morning in his delightful lilting southern voice, couldn't bring himself to wake the "two sleeping beauties so deep in the arms of Morpheus."

When I opened my eyes it was broad daylight. Everything was flooded with light. The sea was very close and sparkling. I thought it was a dream playing tricks on me and began to rub my eyes. I'd left London in a filthy pea-soup fog. I hadn't seen the sky for months. Perhaps I hadn't really seen it since leaving my native Manitoba and my nostalgia for the tall, boundless sky of the prairies had prevented me from really seeing almost any other. I took my hands from my eyes and all the blue was still there, sky and sea together dazzling me. Among the tamarisks, which I recognized from my walks in Kew Gardens, the aloes holding high their single long-stemmed flowers, and the palms, orange trees, and early-flowering mimosas, I kept catching glimpses of pretty villas in glorious colours nestled in their gardens. It was as if they were for ever beyond reach of poverty, suffering...all the unpleasant things in life.

Had my illness run its course? Had Ruby's medicine taken full effect? Or was I cured instantly by the joy of seeing the world as it ought to be? Today I'm almost certain it was my joy that brought me back to life that morning.

Then Ruby woke and she too showed utter astonishment to find herself whisked as if by magic to such a beautiful world. In keeping with her less demonstrative nature, a more contained happiness than mine spread slowly across her wide, good-natured face. We looked at one another, each discovering the other with excitement, we rain-soaked, wind-whipped pilgrims of yesterday arriving to-gether in the mellow South of France. I felt a fondness for her already, and not merely from gratitude. She seemed drawn to me too, as one often is to someone one has cared for and restored to health. Besides, I'd barely recovered and already I was gay and exuberant. I suppose I delighted her as I had Phyllis and would many others on my way through life, people who haven't been granted my capacity for observation, laughter, and exhilaration, and have become the more fond of me for having caught a little

374

of this from me, as it were, while in my company. The Lord be praised for ever if I've been able to share this with others.

I don't know whether we went to the dining car or had coffee and croissants brought to us. I only remember that we enjoyed our breakfast, watching the endless garden of the Côte d'Azur unfold. I was ecstatic over the gracefulness of the shoreline, its coves, steep-sided inlets, and little fishing villages, and most of all the brightness of the sky which I'd never seen so brilliantly and abundantly diffused anywhere else. As the minutes passed I felt myself conceiving a love for this land that would remain with me all my life. But I was apprehensive also that my joy had been too immediate, and I told Ruby I was terribly afraid I'd find myself back in the constricting reality of just a few short hours before. She confessed the same feeling, afraid for her part that she'd find herself back in Toronto, sloshing through the mud and slush in the crowd on Bloor Street with a bitter wind blowing off Lake Ontario. Then we saw that we really had set foot in Paradise, and it was just as real as all the gloomy places where so many people have chosen or are forced to live.

Ruby told me about her hotel in Nice where she'd meet mostly English people and feel more comfortable, not speaking French. I told her about my boarding house in Beaulieu-sur-mer.

Suddenly I exclaimed, "We're crazy, Ruby! We're both going to be bored to death, you with all those old Englishwomen in big hats and sensible shoes and me in my fussy boarding house."

"What else can we do?" she asked, wide-eyed.

I held out my arms to embrace the delightful villages of the Alpilles, the parasol pines, the highway, the beach...the hillsides with ancient olive trees marching in orderly ranks to their summits.

"Hundreds of things, Ruby! It's all ours, if only we put ourselves out a bit. It's up to us. We can have all of Provence."

"How on earth...?"

"By walking it!"

"Walking?"

The idea had just come into my head, but I was already so enchanted I had a glowing picture to paint for Ruby.

"We won't take anything with us. There'll be nothing to tie us down. It's the best possible way to travel. You see everything, hear

everything. And it won't cost much, either. Just look, the country's so rich and warm and inviting. We'll sleep at farmhouses for a pittance. We'll live on olives...."

Ruby stopped me in full flight.

"Oh, but I have to eat well, you know, to sustain myself...,"

I conceded this.

"We shall eat, and even if we eat well, with the money we'd have spent, you at your hotel and I at Beaulieu, we'll have enough to stay a month, maybe two...."

I saw she was wavering but was resisting the idea of walking.

"I've never walked in my life," she said, "and I've got sort of bad feet from years of standing on hard hospital floors."

"Well," I said, "it's high time you got those poor feet in shape, Ruby, and you know better than I do that there's nothing like walking for doing that. Anyway, we'll start out slowly, two or three kilometres a day at first, then working our way up to twenty, thirty...."

"Thirty kilometres!"

"Well, ten...fifteen.... Don't forget, a kilometre's a lot less than a mile."

"How much less?"

"Oh, an awful lot less!"

I felt her softening in my hands. As strong and determined as she was when it came to nursing, for example, she seemed pretty malleable as soon as you got the better of her in imagination and adventurousness. And I was brimming over with these, thanks to the excellent care she'd given me. Perhaps she was the kind who couldn't blow with the winds of chance but deep down had always longed to and was ready to follow as soon as there was someone to lead. She would suit me perfectly if this was the case. I could already see her confidence in me and this made me more daring by the minute.

"Of course," I said, "you can stay in Nice and spend your holidays playing cards with your nice old ladies. Or you and I can be roaming the countryside, getting to know shepherds and violet pickers, exploring the hills and seashore, seeing heathlands and mountains and Avignon, Arles, and Tarascon. There'll be no end of things to do once we're on the road."

I talked so much and so well that by the time we were nearing

Nice she was converted. We would go to her hotel for just one night and leave our baggage there. The next morning we'd set off on the open road in the good Lord's sunshine, free as the air, and go where the wind took us. My knight and saviour of the Channel had become my faithful Sancho Panza.

Had I gone about it with consummate skill, or had Ruby long been subconsciously ready for the role? So far, in any event, she was apparently as happy as could be with her commitment.

XVIII

EARLY NEXT MORNING we went to outfit ourselves inexpensively in the old city. Ruby was enchanted by the clothing and other wares hanging all along the dark, narrow streets. We bought ourselves good strong walking shoes and, to have done with it quickly, matching skirts and identical jackets and finally knapsacks to wear on our backs. In our knapsacks we stowed an extra sweater, a large-scale map, some chocolate bars, a baguette of bread, and some cheese. Scarcely more hampered than a pair of goats, we left Nice by the rail car known as the *micheline*, getting off shortly afterwards and continuing on foot. We were enchanted with everything we saw, no doubt because we were walking in step and our hearts were open to everything.

A kindly sun looked down, warming us just sufficiently through our jackets. Since Ruby was somewhat plump and sturdy and I was rather slight, we must have looked like ill-matched twins in our identical clothes, and all along our way people smiled at us. The air was fragrant with thyme, sage, and rosemary. The postman, a shepherd, and two old women in black greeted us cordially as they passed and we returned their greeting: " 'Jour, 'sieurs-dames."

I didn't know it yet, but that morning my real youth began. I had been so preoccupied with cares and worries I had never felt as totally young before and would never be as giddily young again. For the first time I was far removed from all the harm that had touched me, that was still touching others. I've so loved this dear land of Provence most of all perhaps because only here have I been truly free of anxiety, ambition, maybe even memories, blissfully living for the moment.

Towards the end of the morning we reached St-Tropez or Ste-Maxime, I'm not sure which. I looked up and there was the first

378

Saracen village I'd ever seen, perched on a rocky peak in the mountains of the Maures massif, its houses forming a rampart. At once
this was where I wanted to go. We enquired at a café. Yes, we
could get up there by bus, but it had left an hour ago and there
wouldn't be another until the day after tomorrow. I was pawing
the ground with impatience and couldn't wait that long.

"Come on, Ruby, let's go!"

"We're going to walk?"

"Why not? It can't be more than five or six kilometres. We'll
take it slowly. We've got lots to eat on the way. We'll sleep up
there tonight. The view must be magnificent."

And since I was beginning to know how she loved to eat, I added
an enticement, saying, "Tonight we'll ignore our budget for the
day if we have to and treat ourselves to a real feast. How about a
pepper steak or a sole amandine, with cream puffs for dessert?"

So poor fat Ruby was persuaded to tackle the rugged uphill road,
though she was already dead tired. We didn't see a soul on the
way up and passed not a single habitation, only a long-deserted
hermitage. She whimpered somewhat on the most difficult stretches
of the stony track. I did what I could to make her feel better.

"Just wait till you taste the air we'll be breathing on that peak!"

Alas, the village I'd guessed to be five or six kilometres from the
coast must have been fifteen at least. The farther we dragged ourselves towards it, the farther it seemed to draw away into the
mountains. At times we couldn't even see it, perhaps because we
were tired or it was hidden by a bend in the road.

Ruby began to limp. When she took off her socks we found a
huge blister ready to burst on each heel. Fortunately I'd brought
some adhesive tape. I made her some adhesive bandages, found
some fresh water for her to drink and even a stout walking stick.
When I discovered she'd eaten all her chocolate on the sly I gladly
gave her what was left of mine. What wouldn't I have done to
keep my Sancho by my side? Without her the adventure would
have lost almost all its tang. On the other hand, wasn't she already
so committed to her tormentor that she'd have followed me come
what might? In any event, when I pointed out that we wouldn't
arrive before nightfall at the rate we were going, she got to her
feet and followed me without too much complaint.

Years have passed since I lost Ruby. That we so quickly became

inseparable still amazes me, still draws me to her in even greater friendship.

In late afternoon, the stronger of us leaning heavily on the weaker, with twisted ankles and dishevelled hair, we reached Ramatuelle and almost simultaneously the friendly doorstep of Chez Henri, its only inn.

When he witnessed the arrival of these dust-covered maidens, Henri himself – and eventually everyone in the village – was absolutely convinced we were a pair of eccentric heiresses. Who else would embark on such utter madness just for the fun of it? Certainly not honest-to-goodness poor girls, anyway. Thus was born some local lore regarding us which led to the most ludicrous misapprehension, a source of endless mirth for Ruby and me.

FOR THE PAST three months the inn had been giving shelter to an Irish baronet, Sir John Henry Dunn, Bart., who couldn't pay his bill and therefore couldn't leave. While it was customary not to pay until leaving, there was no exemption from an eventual reckoning and the longer the poor penniless blueblood stayed, the less able he was to pay. With Ruby's and my arrival, it appeared that his day of deliverance might have dawned at last. He invited us to a copious meal the like of which we'd not imagined even in our wildest dreams. Expense was no object, since this was simply added to his account; he'd been brought up to consider it unbecoming to forgo anything you didn't have to pay for on the spot.

Ruby was instantly restored by the feast, which she completed with two *savarins* in quick succession. I kept marvelling at the quantities she could consume, all of which seemed to be transformed into good humour and goodwill. That night I saw how I could make her follow me to the end of the earth if all other means failed.

That very night there was a *bal musette*, a dance to accordion music in the little village square. We attended, one on each arm of our baronet.

In the middle of the square, almost filling it, grew an ancient elm tree seven hundred years old, which was venerated as the ancestor of all in this eyrie. Around it was an enormous wooden bench, well rounded from years of use, on which the oldest villagers were already seated, the women together and the men smoking,

their pipe-smoke rising into the dense arch of branches beneath the great starry arch of the balmy night.

Young and old came to meet us, see us up close, and congratulate us for having climbed all the way up their steep little mountain to come to their party. Though she didn't understand much of what they were saying, Ruby watched the movement of their lips and the expressions on their faces, smiling and showing her delight. Later she told me that she knew she wasn't charming or beautiful or attractive – ah yes, she knew it all too well – but that night for the first time in her life she felt wanted, accepted, liked, and she had to keep pinching herself almost constantly to believe that she was really the one creating this effect.

The accordionist struck up a lively tune. I whirled in the arms of Sir John Henry Dunn, Bart. He danced beautifully. He also had a way with words. He told me I had beautiful eyes, they'd pierced his heart the moment he saw me, he said. And a lot of other such things. I might have let him go on this way except that I wanted Ruby to have a dance too. For the moment she was sitting on the circular bench among the sages, delighted to be on such good terms with them.

"Ruby's much more beautiful," I said.

"The English girl? She's unattractive, poor thing, too short, nose too big, thick lips."

"But her eyes are beautiful, you'll see if you take the trouble to look, and she has a heart of gold."

I didn't yet know he was fortune-hunting, even dower-hunting perhaps, so what possessed me to fabricate at this point?

"And then, she's rich, very rich, which doesn't hurt."

"Oh, really?" he said with ill-concealed interest.

He danced the next dance with Ruby, his face wreathed in his most enchanting smile, and apparently he strung some kind of line to her too. She was quicker than I to see what he was up to.

"He's obviously looking for an heiress," she whispered to me before the next dance. "He thinks you're gorgeous and paid you a bunch of other compliments besides. I told him your father owns the Canadian Pacific Railway. Don't let on he doesn't. Your turn now!"

I said I thought the game was rather cruel but she retorted, "So what! He's probably fishing for some silly little ninny."

During my next dance with him he dropped what was meant to seem a casual question.

"So you say your delightful, entertaining friend Ruby's rich as well as charming?"

"Is she ever! Her father owns the three biggest pulp and paper mills in Canada. I think he supplies all the newsprint for the *Chicago Tribune*."

Between dances we kept comparing notes, agreeing on what our fathers owned and how far we could push our luck with our suitor.

Poor Sir John Henry Dunn, Bart. That surprisingly warm January night, on the little mountaintop beneath the twinkling stars and the equally twinkling gaze of the old folk sitting around the tree, how shamelessly we led him on!

Ruby was having the time of her life. When they saw how avidly she was being courted by the haughty baronet, the young men of the village also decided that she was desirable and flocked to ask her to dance. She had partners aplenty into the wee hours. Her eyes were bright and her face was animated; as I remember her in these moments, she was almost beautiful.

NOT MANY hours later, having arranged a magnificent picnic to take with us, Sir John led us by a goat path to another Saracen retreat tucked away even higher in the Maures massif, the incredible Gassin, so remote and isolated that Ruby and I may have been the first foreign women to set foot in the village.

From this height the view was breathtaking – the blue line of the Mediterranean in the distance and before us jagged mountain ridges, forests, terraces under cultivation. The air was so light, so intoxicating it made me as happy as if sorrow had never crossed my path.

I owed the discovery of all this to the Irish baronet and hated the thought of leaving him with a false impression of Ruby and me. We spent another day at Ramatuelle to give Ruby's feet time to heal before taking the bus to Ste-Maxime. We left behind an abashed Sir John; I had decided to end his awful suspense and confessed to him that we hadn't a sou to spend on staying an hour longer at an inn as luxurious as this. In an attempt to make amends, I said as we left:

"Why don't you write your memoirs while you're here? You've

got lots of time and the memoirs of princes in exile are always in great demand.''

He gave me a look with a very Irish twinkle. Perhaps he was going to take my suggestion.

Two days later, I don't quite remember how, we reached the island of Porquerolles. Ruby took a final potshot at our suitor. She predicted that he'd languish in captivity for ever in his Saracen village, like the Man in the Iron Mask in the dungeon we visited on one of the small Lérins islands. Serve him right, too!

DAY AFTER DAY I was filled with joy, that mysterious visitor whose presence in us after crushing grief is the most puzzling of our experiences. At moments the memory of my tormenting love for Stephen passed through me, like the hoarse cry of a wounded bird, I thought, or I would recall a scene from the days of Deschambault Street and my mother's endless struggle to give us at least a distant glimpse of happiness...which I now possessed in such abundance. Tears of guilt would flow for having allowed myself such joy. Ruby was quite nonplussed, since she clung as if for dear life to my happy self.

She was knowing joy for the first time. Since she firmly believed she would never have found it by herself, she used to say that I had brought it to her by some kind of magic. I didn't realize how deeply grateful she was for this until much later. But already I was having little difficulty leading my Sancho almost anywhere the fancy took me to go. The only grumbling I ever heard from her was mild, for instance when I suggested that we stretch our hikes to twenty-two kilometres a day.

After Agay, Ruby's choice for once, for the odd reason that she had a cousin by the name of Agay in Peterborough, Ontario, where did we go next? Today I find it impossible to recall our whimsical itinerary, if one could call it that. Our rovings took us one day to Hyères, the next to Grasse and Vence, the day after that to the gorges of the River Var. Not even a pair of excited hares would have traced a more erratic route.

I remember a day with a fiercely blowing mistral when against everyone's advice we took it into our heads to rent bicycles. We must have pedalled for hours without advancing an inch, all the time beside the same property with a high bamboo hedge thrashing

as if in torment. Two men passed us on the road, capes flapping, and kept looking back at us in disbelief. It seems we were watched from the tightly shuttered house, through some crack no doubt, because someone finally came out and offered to share the soup pot with us and give us and our bicycles shelter for the night.

Did I fall in love with Provence because I was hungry for consolation and received far more than I ever hoped? Or was it Provence itself that won my heart and made me happier than anywhere else, with its sparkling gaiety and mercurial moods so much like my own, droll one minute and sombre the next? Only here, I think, have I lived purely for the moment – well, perhaps at the Little Water Hen, but there I had to work. Here, my past with its crippling old anxieties might not have existed. The future wasn't important. I didn't care in the least what was to become of me. Have I ever been as free?

One evening in late twilight we came to Mouans-Sartou, a village of no importance except as the site of a boarding house kept by a Madame Viscardi which was so good and reasonably priced that we decided to make it our headquarters. From here we set out according to our whim of the moment, returning at night to a comfortable bed, the warmth of a massive stove, and the congenial company of a half-dozen boarders who immediately became a kind of family to us. I almost persuaded Ruby that we should become shepherds or goatherds and never leave Provence; it would be sheer folly to go elsewhere having found a land of happiness at last, I said, since no success, money, promotion, or diploma would ever bring us what we already had here for nothing. I didn't know enough about life to see that "nothing" was in fact almost everything: a light heart, bubbling enthusiasm, a spring in one's step, and above all – yes, above all – the ultimate injustice, just because you're young, healthy, and happy-faced, of having everyone love you at first sight.

One day when we had left early in the morning for no more than a long walk, having told Madame Viscardi that we'd be back for dinner, we took a succession of little roads of the kind that have always appealed to me, each lonelier than the last, and eventually realized we were lost. The country was wild and so deserted that the only hint of habitation we'd seen was a slim, handwritten sign at the crossing of two dirt roads announcing "Château de Besançon,

8 km." We'd already tramped farther than that, probably turning in circles, trying to find our way out of this wasteland with its impenetrable silence and circle of dark woods all around.

"We aren't in Provence any more," I said. "The devil's tricked us and we're in some godforsaken corner of Asia."

Ruby was cross with me and wouldn't laugh. This was one of the few times she rebelled openly, saying we were going to get what we deserved, that by just following my nose I'd end up leading us into some insoluble predicament. We seemed to have come to that now. In the tall straggly grass beside this dismal road there was a big flat rock. Ruby sat on the rock and, taking off her shoes to rub her sore feet, told me she wouldn't go a step farther with me. I sat down in the grass beside her. That morning we'd put on our identical flaming red pullovers, which could have been seen for miles across these monotonous meadows. I didn't know what to do to mollify her. I pulled a blade of grass and chewed it glumly. Who would ever expect a most unusual opportunity to be heading our way at this very moment? It would prove Ruby's dire predictions wrong and my luck dependable after all.

A car appeared far down the little road. We watched it come like a pair of vultures, heads and shoulders showing above the grass, as red as could be. When it reached us the car stopped and its driver put a smiling face through the window.

"*Mesdames?...mesdemoiselles?*... Pardon me, would you be local folk?"

"Local folk, indeed we are!" said I in my best imitation of the Provençal lilt.

"Well then, *mesdames...mesdemoiselles...*would you know a Château de Besançon hereabouts? It must be hidden away because I've spent two hours already looking and not finding it. I'm from Nîmes," he added with the obliging tendency in this part of France to anticipate and satisfy the curiosity of others. "I'm an agronomist, and I'd stop looking and go home, only they've got a sickness in their vines at the Château de Besançon and wanted me to come without delay."

"Besançon!" I exclaimed. "What a lucky thing, indeed I know how to find it! Keep on the way you're going. Less than a kilometre on you'll see the sign. Be careful though, it's written by hand and very small. You need good eyes to read it."

385

Then, to be authentically local, with firm conviction I added something I'd heard a thousand times in France:

"Can't miss it! It's straight ahead!"

When he'd left I began to shriek with laughter. Ruby, now more curious than resentful, wanted to know what the motorist and I had been gabbling about.

"He was lost and wanted directions."

"So?"

"So...I gave him directions."

Then she began to shriek with laughter too.

Our cheerful relationship was completely restored. Two hours later we'd begun to consider going to beg a meal at Besançon when we saw the agronomist's car reappear. We were still sitting in exactly the same place. The car stopped.

"*Mesdames?... Mesdemoiselles?...* You aren't lost, I know. So why do I find you here again in your lovely red sweaters, giving this country such a pretty bit of life?"

"*Eh oui!*" I said. "Red's cheerful, sure enough," and I enquired after the vines.

"Ah, very sick, poor things! They've waited too long to have them seen to. It's because the owners themselves are poor, poor things!"

"*Eh aussi*, I thought as much!..." I said compassionately.

"You have something like the accent of these parts," he observed, "but not exactly. Where d'you come from then?"

"From.... That is, from near..., Marseille."

"Marseille? Ah, no! I know the accent of Marseille, *allons*! Would you be from Norway? Sweden? No?"

In the end I told him the truth.

"Canada! The land of snows! Of Maria Chapdelaine! And come to think of it, Montcalm too. Your Montcalm, our Montcalm. Before he went and got himself killed in Canada, poor man, he was from Nîmes, you're aware perhaps. At least, from very close to Nîmes. *Allons, mesdames...mesdemoiselles*...you can't leave without coming to pay your respects to the birthplace of Montcalm. *Allons!* Come with me, *mesdames...mesdemoiselles*. I'll take you to Nîmes."

"What's he so excited about?" Ruby wanted to know.

"He wants to take us to Nîmes to pay our respects to Montcalm."

She said she'd rather go and pay her respects to Wolfe but she had nothing against Nîmes, and besides, she'd rather ride with the devil himself than walk all that awful distance back to Madame Viscardi's.

"He isn't the devil," I assured her. "Agronomists are serious people. And just look what a nice face this one's got."

We both sat in front with Monsieur Didier Laroche. He drove us through the prettiest villages, which I never saw again on later trips to Provence. They must have been on some relatively un-travelled road. He made a detour through the radiant countryside near Nîmes to show us the ancient Roman aqueduct, tier after tier of delicate arches striding across a glowing sky. In the city itself he showed us several monuments and the amphitheatre known as Les Arènes, perhaps the best preserved in Europe, and glass in hand on the terrace of a café as the last rays of a golden afternoon fell across the table, invited us to keep a minute of silence in memory of Montcalm. He would find us an inexpensive hotel. The next morning he'd come and pick us up and take us to see parts of Languedoc where there were vines in need of his care. It was very tempting, but if we were going to stay we'd have to let Madame Viscardi know. The waiter brought us a pen, ink, and a kind of express card designed to travel at lightning speed. I composed a few lines assuring Madame Viscardi that in order to see as much as possible of the fair land of France we couldn't be in better hands, those of a physician to the Lord's vines, and advising her not to expect us for any particular day.

When I look back on all I've been able to see without spending a cent in the course of my travels, I realize I owe nearly all of it to the kind Monsieur Didiers I've met along my way.

When our card had been posted, he dropped us at the door of such a pitiful-looking hotel we hesitated to go in.

"D'you feel like going in there?" asked Ruby. "I'm sure it's full of fleas."

We waited till Monsieur Didier's car was out of sight, then turned and went to look elsewhere.

On the way Ruby said, "I don't know what I'd give to sleep tonight in my nice comfortable bed at Madame Viscardi's, after a lovely dinner of her sorrel soup, her sea perch cooked with fennel, and her chocolate mousse."

"D'you think we could still arrive in time?"

"If we run all the way to the station and catch the next *micheline*...."

When we arrived at the station, panting for breath, the *micheline* was on the point of leaving. The conductor saved us from being crushed between the doors, which were about to close. The same conductor had punched our tickets the day before and the day before that. He was a Corsican, a handsome man with a dark complexion and a sad face. He fixed an intense and despairing eye on me.

"Listen," he said. "I can't stand it any longer. I've loved you madly since I first saw you, now you know, I've told you. I've tried my best to forget you. I can't help it. You get on, you get off, you come back. Not a day goes by that you aren't there. Really, I can't stand it any longer. Marry me. I'll make you a good husband, I swear."

I looked at him and abruptly lost my initial impulse to laugh. The poor fellow wasn't joking. Without the least intention, even in fun, I'd cast some kind of spell on him.

He wasn't the only one. We were in an inn one evening finishing our dinner. A young man seated facing me hadn't stopped staring. He tore a page from a notebook, hastily wrote a message, and asked the waiter to bring it to me. It read, "I'm single – electrician – earn a pretty good living. I lay my life at your feet. I know already I'll love only you. You know, don't you? Your enchantment is irresistible."

Even allowing for the emotional Mediterranean temperament, I must admit I made more than my share of conquests along our path, which Ruby called "the trail of broken hearts".

What was going on? What was giving me the power I seemed to have over people, men and women alike? Wherever I went and at all hours of the day I made friends with people I'd barely met. It was partly the impulsive Provençal nature and its harmony with my own, yes, but there was more. What was it? In London too I made many dear friends among strangers who often passed very briefly through my life and then vanished for ever, but I have the impression that it happened there at times of heartache, loneliness, and melancholy, to which the hearts of Londoners are perhaps particularly attuned. Whereas here...!

Today, so far from what I was then, I watch this blithe creature move, live, laugh, and flit about, and can hardly believe it's myself

I see. I think I must have been radiant with happiness at being loved at every turn, and the radiance attracted more love, which made me still more radiant.

From the Mouans-Sartou stop to the boarding house, again we ran all the way, and were out of breath when we arrived just after nightfall. Madame Viscardi and the boarders were gathered around the shaded lamp reading our card, which had just arrived, with even more astonishing dispatch than the Fulham birthday card.

I can still hear Madame Viscardi's comically accented voice reading aloud: "Leaving with kind Monsieur Didier for a tour of Languedoc.... Perhaps the Cévennes.... Don't expect to see us for a day or two.... Or three or four.... Perhaps not until the end of the week...."

She raised her arms towards heaven and exclaimed, "Did you ever see such devilment, especially the little one that speaks French! She's the one who leads the other one on...."

They turned, saw us standing in the doorway, remained stunned for a moment, then opened their arms to give us hugs, rejoicing at our return as if we'd been away for a century.

XIX

THIS WAS the way things continued for more than a month. Life
was so happy that today, after so many trials and bereavements,
my face would turn red with shame except that I've learned that
if you haven't at least briefly known real happiness, you can't feel
for the suffering in this world either.

What made our days so rich, I think, was that everything was
so unexpected. We never knew on one day where we'd be the next.
We entrusted ourselves to each new day, and the day, like life itself,
almost always took us by surprise, happy surprise, a never-ending
delight.

At the end of the second week Ruby talked about leaving, arguing
that she'd soon have to resign herself to getting back to "real life"
and it might as well be now as later, when it would be even harder.
I managed to dissuade her.

"A week more," I begged her, and when that was up, "One
more, Ruby!"

It wasn't so easy, though, to persuade her to leave Madame
Viscardi's nice comfortable bed and excellent table and move on,
not knowing where we'd lay our heads each night until we found
something almost as good in the little village of Castries in Languedoc, at the far side of the region. This was in a house where a
Madame Paulet-Cassan lived with her shy spinster sister whom
she always addressed as "*Ma-de-moi-selle Thérèse.*" We had asked
an obliging gendarme where we might find a good but inexpensive
room and he'd sent us there without hesitation saying, "At Madame
Paulet-Cassan's, that's the place, no doubt about it.... But don't
say I sent you.... I could be in trouble with the hotel, you know...."

At the very end of the village, in a big, pink, rough-plastered
house with brown shutters, we each had a room that was unheated

but huge, with generous windows overlooking a panorama of plains, gardens, and hillsides covered with vineyards. It was here one chilly morning, standing barefoot on the icy tile floor, that I opened the shutters and for the first time in my life saw the dazzling spectacle of an almond tree in flower. I'll always be able to see this young tree, its delicate pink flowers freshly unfolded with the daylight, standing against the clear blue sky of the vibrant South of France.

Our rooms with big brass beds and down comforters and our deliciously fragrant morning coffee cost us each about twenty-five cents a day in our money. Living with the people not only made our money go further but was also very pleasant, since we learned to adopt their customs and live the same peaceful, uncomplicated lives.

Madame Paulet-Cassan had a small vineyard a kilometre from the village, which it was her pleasure to go and tend almost every day. We left together early one fine morning, the little donkey with his bells ringing, Ruby and I, Madame Paulet-Cassan carrying the *serpe* or hooked pruning knife, her sister with bottles of wine wrapped in napkins in a basket, and the dog Fidèle trotting behind. We came to the field of vines in the midst of sweet-smelling *garrigue*, a kind of *maquis*, past the wondrous arches of the Roman aqueduct, where Ruby and I helped with the pruning and tidying up. In the mellowest of twilights, typical of this region, the donkey laden with faggots of pruned vine-shoots, we passed again under the delicate arches. Some old women drawing water in pitchers from the community source called cheerfully, "*Hé ben! Hé là!* So, Madame Paulet, that's what paying guests are for!"

Over a slow fire of the vine prunings we'd brought home, Madame Paulet-Cassan roasted *bouchées* – morsels of lamb, bacon, and cèpe mushrooms sprinkled with thyme – threaded together on a slender spit which she turned with infinite patience by hand, crouching by the hearth. The smell was enough to make one's mouth water for the rest of one's life.

"Madame Paulet-Cassan, keep us for dinner," I pleaded, "it's so much better here than at the hotel."

"I know why," she said. "At the hotel they don't have time to cook over vine shoots, or know how any more."

She had a plan for us.

"Go to the baker's and the grocer's, buy a bit of cheese, a tart.

Wherever you go, make sure they hear you say I let you do your cooking over my fire. They can't complain about that, the jealous things, all ready to send the gendarme round, they are, saying I haven't got a permit. Permit! Permit! Can't blow your nose without one! Go along now, girls. Do as I say and I'll make you *bouchées* you'll still remember when you've got no teeth left."

Before long she decided the daily price she'd fixed for us was too high. Because we were staying the week she reduced it considerably. The longer we stayed the less it was costing to eat better and better, since besides *bouchées* she soon began making us superb crêpes cooked deftly on a griddle heated in the fireplace.

"At this rate, Madame Paulet-Cassan, what's it going to cost us to live this well if we stay a whole month?"

"Why, nothing at all of course, because you'll be family! Which you are already, in fact. You help in the fields, after all."

Help? From me? Giving me any such credit was more than generous. We would barely reach the vineyard when I'd stray off into the *garrigue* nearby. It was warm and fragrant and alive with the chirp of young crickets, not yet their stridulant song of summer. I'd lie on the sun-warmed, rubbly ground. I'd watch the fluffy clouds float by. I'd dream aimlessly, questlessly, thoughtlessly, without remorse, perhaps even without memories. I surrendered willingly, innocently to the drift of time. This humble, stony field, like the big ploughed field on the path to Upshire, is one of the dearest places on earth to me, among those which I still see most often when I let my mind wander or try to picture the best of things in life. Yet the only memory I can attach to it is simply of well-being without apparent cause, indefinable and as vast and calm as the prairie or the ocean.

My radiant happiness was coming to an end, however. There were times now when it was tinged with sadness. I would have many more happy hours after this, more than I've deserved, perhaps, but never as then. It was perhaps because I sensed this end that during these last days I so often stayed hidden in the *garrigue*, as if it could keep me in this state of peace and torpor.

One day, finally, there was no holding Ruby back. She had become perhaps even more attached to the life we were leading than I was. Since she wasn't naturally dreamy like me, it must have seemed magical to her, more of a fairyland than it did to me,

for in a sense I had expected nothing less. But her strong sense of duty made her feel she ought not to stay away from her nursing any longer.

We returned to Nice to collect our belongings. We parted at the station. At the very last minute she pulled down the window of her compartment and called to me with a most uncharacteristic display of emotion:

"Take care! Take care! And oh, Gabrielle, thank you, thank you for the lovely time! And mostly for making me feel young at least once in my life!"

We would never see each other again. We corresponded for quite a while. Perhaps one of our letters went astray. Perhaps Ruby changed her address and didn't let me know. I stopped hearing from her and she stopped hearing from me. Years passed. When *Street of Riches* appeared in English, *Maclean's Magazine* of Toronto published a picture of me on the cover. Ruby saw it and wrote me in care of the magazine. It was a very touching letter. She told me she had a cherished memory of my euphoric face of the days of Provence, but perhaps she liked the one of today even better, since according to the photograph it showed signs of wear, but still at our age seemed unstripped of illusions.

She had married and lived a rather dull life, she thought now, with no great trials or great happiness either, "a life of very ordinary days." If it hadn't been for our spree in the South of France she might believe she'd never really been young at heart. After that, the colour of everything had been very prosaic. She was therefore still grateful to me for having taken her "on the sideroads of enchantment", and always would be. Sadly, since she was such an unadventurous person, whenever she recounted our escapades no one would believe she'd had such experiences, much less with me since I'd become a "famous author". Saddest of all, she had even come herself to doubt that she'd had them. Perhaps she'd only dreamed those adventures in Ramatuelle, Castries, and Nîmes. Perhaps our dear Madame Paulet-Cassan had never really existed. Perhaps everything, the Saracen eyrie in the Maures massif, the brightest of blue skies, kind Monsieur Didier, had only been the product of long years of wishful thinking. Wouldn't I come one day to visit and reminisce with her? Then she could be sure it was true she'd been so happy to be alive at least this once; it wouldn't

seem so much like something she'd made up. She would come herself to see me, she said, only her health was failing. At the very end, as if it weren't important, she mentioned in the briefest terms that she had cancer and didn't know how long she had to live.

I replied at once that I'd come very soon. Did I take too long, or was her illness already more advanced than she'd admitted? She died the day I was preparing to go and assure her that those happy times so long ago were real. And yet I had known since Anna's death and most of all since Dédette's that before dying everyone needs terribly to know that one had been happy occasionally, and how, where, and why. It's not so important to know that one has suffered; what counts is to know how it feels to hold happiness in one's hand, as if it were the key to love and the mystery of our existence. The people who die most alone are those who cannot remember being happy at least for a moment on this earth.

Like a great bird with dark outstretched wings soaring over a parched valley, Ruby's memory often haunts me.

With Sancho gone, Don Quixote wasn't half as enterprising any more. However, I did stay a little longer to roam about Provence, to Nîmes, Montpellier, and elsewhere. In the end I returned to my old ladies in Castries. Madame Paulet-Cassan welcomed me like a daughter returning to the fold. In a way this is what I'd become to her, for her own daughter lived in Marseille and hardly ever came to see her, and when she did come she spent the time scolding her mother for still cooking over the hearth with an iron cauldron and pans from the olden days. And perhaps seeing the face of Mademoiselle Thérèse all crinkled with joy at my return delighted me even more than her sister's effusions, because I'd never before seen a smile on this face that was as grizzled as a rennet apple.

Years later, when I felt the need to revisit earlier scenes of happiness – an incredibly persistent need for me – I went to introduce my husband to the two old sisters. They recognized me immediately, then examined him with great interest, like an object they were turning this way and that for better scrutiny. *"Hé hé*, Mademoiselle Thérèse and I often used to wonder which of your admirers you'd pick. You've chosen well, I'd say!" They went to the cupboard where they kept liqueurs and brought out the finest, one they had made themselves from oranges and kept for the most precious reunions. An hour later they'd already contrived to spread

through the "jealous" village the news that I really had returned, bringing my husband to show them besides, and if that wasn't proof of faithfulness and heart in the right place, what was!

I have made so many unexpected friends in every corner of the world when I've sought affection from simple folk, and afterwards have rarely lost this affection.

ONCE THE MISTRAL had subsided I rented a bicycle and rode in every direction, as far as Béziers and to Sète to visit the *cimetière marin*, a cemetery for sailors by the sea. When I returned from my outings I recounted them to my two old ladies, who had never seen most of their own region and were delighted to learn something about it from me. One of my great and fairly frequent delights has been in helping others to see around them, feel their own happiness, sometimes dream their own dreams.

I went to Carcassonne and spent a whole day walking on the ramparts without once coming down. I missed Ruby quite beyond reason. It made me feel better if I pretended to be telling her about my most amusing discoveries. Sometimes I laughed out loud to myself, startling passers-by. This still happens, moreover, for instance when I'm doing my shopping on Cartier Street in Quebec City and instead of saying hello to someone I know I'll absent-mindedly laugh in her face. Some think it's a slight and hold it against me. I don't know how to make them believe otherwise.

One day I went by bus to Perpignan. Here I was reminded of the woes of the world and of how infinitely more massive and widespread they are than its ephemeral happiness. Yet for two months I'd hardly seen or given them a thought.

I knew indeed that Spain was torn by civil war, and knew that the forces on both sides were committing atrocities. The war in Spain had seemed unreal in the happiness of each new day I'd spent in Provence, but now the Catalan front had broken and refugees were flooding at the rate of ten, fifteen, and twenty thousand a day through a pass in the Pyrenees into the border village of Prats-de-Mollo not far from Perpignan.

This was where I went. Fortunate though I consider myself to have so often had the *joie de vivre* of others reflect on me, I must also hold it a great but painful privilege to have been near the greatest of the world's woes.

I had barely arrived in Prats-de-Mollo when I made friends with some young teachers who were working as volunteers for the Red Cross. They gave me a little badge which identified me as an assistant and allowed me to go everywhere with them.

Oh God! The spectacle I saw! The memory still haunts my nights with fragments of horror as in Picasso's *Guernica*.

The communal school had been turned into a hospital and the wounded lay on the floor, each wrapped in a single blanket. They watched us as we moved about, never complaining. I remember a tiny girl holding her dying mother's hand, calling to her softly as if not to wake her. Behind the barbed wire were the men who were still whole or at least able to stand, thousands and thousands of them. Grotesquely thin, emaciated, they looked back at us as we looked at them in alarm and curiosity, here also without a word of complaint passing their lips. What struck me most forcibly and still comes back with chilling immediacy was the silence that cloaked this gathering of lost souls. Only one uttered a sound, an old woman looking for her son, not knowing whether he was dead or perhaps alive somewhere in this sea of unrecognizable faces. She wandered ceaselessly from camp to camp, peering into the unvarying masses and calling, "Alfonso, where are you? Are you alive, Alfonso my son? Has anyone seen Alfonso dead or alive?" All one day we heard her voice through the cruel silence, like a stone dropped in a bottomless well.

The French government distributed a loaf of bread a day to each refugee. To this, people of the village added what they could, sharing most of their own food with the unfortunates. A drop in the bucket.

Night-time was still cold at the foot of the snow-covered mountains. The refugees beyond the barbed wire made small fires around which they could be seen trying to warm themselves, blankets over their shoulders, hunched motionless in circles as though in the flames they might discern the enigmatic strands of destiny.

Each day the pitiful flood kept swelling, streaming down from the mountain pass, the sorely wounded carried on stretchers of branches, a few slung over the backs of mules, others hobbling, a blood-soaked bandage around head or calf. Women who had given birth on the snow in the mountains the night before carried infants, some still alive, cradled in the folds of their skirts. All had the look

of those who have seen death face to face and found it less unbearable than life. My young friends of the Red Cross assured me
that the human herd straggling all the way from the border to the
village had been pursued and attacked by Franco's planes, perhaps
Hitler's.

Last of all came their wretched animals, cows with bony haunches,
exhausted ewes, lambs newly born perhaps just the night before
like the infants, horses with terror-stricken eyes. I saw a horse that
was all white, blind, with festering sores for eyes, keeping well in
the middle of the herd as if to be sure of not being abandoned.
Only the animals whimpered. Rounded up in great haste, they had
been brought along to be slaughtered one after the other on the
way, cooked over meagre fires and used to nourish suffering a little
longer. In their dim awareness, no doubt they sensed their fate.

There were two separate groups among the men who had escaped
more or less unhurt to Prats-de-Mollo. One group hoped to be
taken by ship to the Spanish coast with help from France, and put
ashore near Barcelona to join the forces supporting Negrin, who
was still resisting. The rest, trusting in the promised armistice, had
chosen to return immediately to Spain. We could see them leaving
in small groups to go back the way they had come, unarmed, each
with his only possession, his blanket, over his shoulders. According
to my friends of the Red Cross, who claimed to have it on good
authority, they were being shot as soon as they reached the border.
All night long we could hear machine-gun fire coming from the
direction of the pass, this much is certain.

I, a stranger, could move about with total freedom through this
inconceivable turmoil. I still wonder how it could have been possible.
I think I remember there being as many as a hundred thousand
refugees on some days, all crammed into the village of Prats-de-
Mollo whose population couldn't have been more than two thousand.
The efforts were phenomenal. The villagers took in orphans and
mothers with small children. Whole convoys kept leaving with the
severely wounded. I did my little bit to help. The suffering and
hardship were too great for the best will in the world to make much
difference. I wandered among these wandering souls a little like
Pierre Bezuhov on the field of battle in Tolstoy's *War and Peace*,
incredulous, confused, in the depths of my soul not believing what
I was seeing. It was a long time before I believed I had seen it. But

I took some photographs with my little Brownie camera. My friends
the teachers gave me theirs. I still have some of these photographs.
They still make me catch my breath when I look at them. I can
barely conceive that I was a witness – should I say a privileged
one? – of those terrible hours in history.

Eventually the French security policy arrived and drove away
everyone who, like me, had no business there. I returned to Perpignan.

The wind was now bitter, like the misery blowing from the
Pyrenees. In my icy room I threw myself into my first writing
dictated by indignation, pity, and the sorrow of belonging to the
human race. I think I put my whole heart in it, though this alone
has never produced anything of note. Not knowing what to do
with what I'd written, in the end I sent it with some photographs
to *La Presse* in Montreal. What a curious decision! In a period
when not even André Malraux himself would have been allowed
to defend socialist Spain in Montreal, I can imagine how promptly
an article by an unknown expressing such sympathies was dropped
into the wastebasket.

Now there was nothing left for me in Provence. To say the least,
I no longer knew what happiness was and wouldn't for a long time
to come. Looking back a mere matter of days, I couldn't believe I
had been so moved to see an almond tree in flower. What was a
tree with delicate pink flowers doing among my memories? The
breath of war affected me here even more deeply than in London
at the time of Munich. Henceforth one couldn't escape feeling that
it was coming relentlessly closer. Even if I were inclined to stay a
little longer, I couldn't in any event. I had hardly a sou left. I
couldn't have stayed even this long without the few dollars Ruby
had slipped into my handbag when I wasn't looking; I found them
after she left.

I took the train to Paris, throughout the trip reviewing all the
happy moments whose memory now seemed so incongruous. I
needed years, almost a lifetime, to see all the beauty of the joys
I'd known in Provence. It takes time to forgive ourselves for being
able to be happy in this world.

I stayed a few days at Madame Jouve's on the way through,
sharing the room with Charlotte who was still working hard at her
piano, beginning at eight in the morning. I really believe she'd

barely heard of the troubles in Spain. Nothing much about Madame Jouve's seemed to have changed. I looked around me with a kind of bewilderment. Madame Jouve observed me sympathetically, perceptively too.

"My child, you go and you come, you appear and you disappear, as though you can't settle down. I'm sure you're listening, looking, learning and absorbing, but what's it all for? Where are you going with it all?"

Did I know – that is with certainty and conviction? Have I ever known? Except during the months and years when I've been harnessed to the writing of a book, have I really felt like a writer? At this time I think I was in one of my muffled waiting states, unaware but available, someone waiting for the train. Occasionally while waiting I've briefly been given my freedom again and been almost happy, then the discontent with doing nothing has taken hold again. Then I've been unhappy not to be writing, or else I've been agonizing over having to begin again with no assurance of doing better this time.

Yet one day Madame Jouve would in a sense have an answer to her own question. After my Prix Femina I searched high and low and finally found her in a wretched little room, running a home for the aged and lonely. She who was so reserved took me by the shoulders and kissed me tenderly.

"You're the only one of my charming young ladies who's sought me out in my old age, my child, and in your hour of triumph too. I'm not really surprised. I always knew you'd go far because you never knew where you were going. But I was afraid you'd lose courage on a path so poorly marked."

Indeed, in the spring of 1939 I left in great perplexity.

I landed in London beneath the same low sky, heavy with fog and soot, as when I'd left nearly three months earlier. Hardly anything here had changed either. After the scare before Munich, it was as though dear old England had simply gone back to dozing over its cup of tea beside its little coke fire.

I had been worrying over whether or not to write to Stephen. I thought about him increasingly the closer I came to where we had loved so deliriously. In the end I wrote him a brief note saying I'd soon be returning to Canada. Did he get my letter? Perhaps it

arrived while he was away on one of his crazy incursions into Soviet-controlled territory. Perhaps he was as much afraid as I of reopening freshly healed wounds.

I went to Century Cottage for a few days. What a distressing sight! The little garden I remembered as overflowing with fragrance and colour was sodden and cold, half of it lying on the ground, stems crushed and dead blossoms in the mud. A smell of swamp hung in the air.

Dampness oozed from the cottage too. Esther couldn't keep things dry inside with her little fireplaces here and there. With all the doors closed to keep in as much heat as possible, we sat by the stove in the dining room, which now seemed small and dark. Father Perfect had a cough. His sister was dead. After the Bible reading each evening, his prayer was still for me, his tears now for his dear departed Norah. He was glad at least to have gone to keep her company as far as one can go in this life, to the mysterious threshold, since otherwise she would have gone with less confidence to meet the Father. During this time he talked to me in words of great wisdom beneath their apparent simplicity, all of which I wish I could recall today. For example, that we must feel loved by our fellow men before we can feel loved by God and not fear death. Sometimes, not often, I could still make him laugh and even bring a smile to Esther's lips with my stories of Provence, which I made as amusing as I could, trying to cheer them up.

The morning I stepped into the taxi that was taking me to Victoria Station with my trunk and two suitcases, I turned my head for a last look. Beyond the rain-soaked garden I saw their pinched faces trying to smile encouragement. They waved through the pouring rain as if from a diluvial realm that was already half engulfed. We thought we would never see each other again.

And yet...life, which can be so cruel, can sometimes be surprisingly kind, leading us by unsuspected paths back to what we have thought was lost.

Nine years later, after *The Tin Flute*, weary of all the fuss, I came to Upshire from Paris to see if the peace, protection, and love I had known were still there.

Once again it was summer. The delphiniums, the sky-blue and the deeper blue so like the far horizon, had retaken possession of the front garden. We had tea in the back garden beside the old

damson tree which had been spared once more, and watched the lights of London come on beyond the pastures. I found Father Perfect not aged too much, still able to set his snares in the forest and bring home mushrooms and flowers. Esther's face below her hairbands had hardly changed at all. And impossible as it seemed, there was Guinevere rubbing against my leg under the tea-table.

Again I had my big airy room with its windows wide open to the downs, which were even more exhilarating than in the picture I'd been cherishing, rolling away as before beyond the stone raised to the memory of Boadicea, beneath the big white clouds scudding to or from the Channel.

And one morning when I woke, calm and at peace in the big brass bed, I found my memories of the Little Water Hen ready for a book, filtered and transfigured by time, in the depths of my unconscious turned into elements of fiction, meaning elements of living truth, perhaps.

Esther came in with the big breakfast tray and put it on my knees, brushing aside some of the scattered pages.

She asked, "Are you pleased with your work this morning, dearest?"

I replied, half light-heartedly, half absently, "I don't know, Esther."

The only thing I've ever been certain of, in fact, is that I've never known and probably never will know what to think of what I find emerging from within me.

XX

I BOARDED ship in Liverpool. At the last minute a cabin boy knocked on my door. He had a long box of flowers for me. Trembling, I untied the string. My poor heart, which I'd thought was so well cured, tugged towards Stephen because he couldn't let me leave without sending a token of the feelings we'd shared. I seized the card. It was from David, whom I'd phoned on my way through London to say a simple goodbye. He was wishing me bon voyage and good luck in life and saying, among other nice things, that he hoped to come and see me one day in Canada. I tore the card into little pieces. I was vexed with poor David for the gesture I would rather had come from Stephen.

Long before we reached the estuary, the waters of the Mersey were tossing us about abominably. The weather was atrocious; rain, fog, howling wind. Almost every minute you could hear the chilling, mournful toll of a bell-buoy, no doubt marking the channel between reefs. On this apocalyptic note I left the shores of England. Sometimes, in the strange dark corner behind my conscious memory, I still hear the great strokes of iron clappers which I associate, I'm not sure why, with the thunderclaps and menacing tone of the Song of Destiny.

In the open sea, such furious waves battered the ship that the cabin boys quickly came to shut the portholes, while deckhands hurried to set in place the heavy panels that closed in the deck completely. I sailed for almost two days on a ship that was blindfold so to speak. I might have felt that nothing could be more depressing, but my heart was too full of its own misery to have room for more. Curiously, I was less seasick than I'd been on the Channel crossing with Ruby. But I was more heartsick.

When the panels were finally removed and we could go and

breathe the fresh air on deck, I remained for a long time, almost alone, gazing in a kind of bewilderment at the vast and disconcerting expanse of endless choppy water. I don't think I've ever liked the ocean when it's all around me, excluding everything except its awesome grandeur. What I love are its shores, gentle or rugged, the tide, seabirds, islands in the distance, harbours, all that the call of the sea implies for someone on land. But on the ocean itself, this vast moving surface, I feel lost. Perhaps it makes me feel something of the same anxiety that "this immeasurable space" aroused in Pascal.

There had probably been other times when I wished I could die. Perhaps everyone has wished this at least once, even in the course of a happy life and especially in one of perpetual adversity or discouragement. But this time it was not a vague wish. I kept looking at the choppy waves buffeting one another, the leaden clouds gathering on the pale horizon; my eyes blurred with tears, I wanted so much to leave this life. Where was it taking me? Nowhere, of this I was certain now. I had left my teaching, hurt my mother unbearably, given up all I had, crossed the ocean, squandered the money I'd so painfully saved, tried all manner of new things, and today was I any further ahead? I felt I had failed in everything, love, drama, writing. Yes, in everything. Why continue the struggle? What would I gain? All I could do now was go back where I had come from and dig myself in, stay quiet, and consider myself lucky in my lot, as most people must in the end. Or I could sink in the waves and let them carry away my grief, remorse, regrets — perhaps also good things to come, which now I would never know. I think my mind was set on this for several days. But would I have had the courage?

I was always alone at the stern of the ship, as though unable to do anything but gaze behind me. Finally a young man approached me, a Scot with a very attractive face and personality, all fun and good humour. His name was Jock. He had the most laughing eyes in the world while I, he chided me affectionately, had the saddest.

"And why is that?" he said. "At your age your troubles have only begun, and your joys besides."

I had no heart for flirtation or new friendship. The following day, however, he drew a smile from me when he said, "Gabrielle," (he must have asked the steward my name) "hold my hand and

talk to me about myself, for isn't that what we all want most, each in our selfish self?"

Perhaps he helped me find my feet by helping me find my sense of humour again, which is the first step out of a persistent depression. I laughed with him a little after a while, though not heartily.

The sea was still very rough. We were going to sail up the St. Lawrence, and despite my mood I was looking forward to rediscovering the route in the steps of Cartier, Champlain, and Maisonneuve. I would be seeing the country from the river again, in reverse order this time, renewing my pleasure in the sight of villages along the shore with their brightly flashing church roofs, which were almost always galvanized in those days. From a distance you'd have thought they were sending friendly signals.

Shortly before the estuary, however, the ship entered a huge field of icebergs and was forced to reduce speed to a crawl. This was the month of April, early April admittedly, yet the Strait of Belle Isle was still icebound. The captain was ordered to go to Saint John, from where a special CPR train would take us to Montreal. So in the end I returned by one of the country's dreariest gateways. Endlessly bleak and lonely beneath a grey sky, what could have looked more forsaken from the moving train than New Brunswick at this unattractive time of year? In the background there were always the same still, monotonous forests, here and there the same little villages of humble, often colourless wooden houses, separated by interminable fields of old snow melting with the rain and leaving muddy puddles, tree stumps, and once in a while a shack, sometimes quite alone in this woeful landscape. How unloved our dear country seemed and still seems in comparison with the countrysides I had seen in Europe, all so tenderly cared for and kept so neat and clean.

MY JOURNEY ended at Windsor Station. During the night there had been a fall of wet snow. It melted under one's feet and made a dirty kind of mash which I quickly learned to call "slush" like everyone else. I soon learned to love this forlorn, lonesome urban landscape with all my soul, yet on this first day I felt as foreign as if I'd never set foot here.

I found a room as close as possible to the station, almost at the door, in fact, on Stanley Street. Strange though it may seem today, I had become such a wanderer that stations, railways, and railway

tracks would feel almost like home to me for some time to come. I never lost heart as long as I could hear the puff of the fat locomotives of those days departing and arriving. I think I entered the dear old station several times just to listen to the powerful engines huffing and puffing by their platforms, and left feeling less alone. If I woke in a daze at night I could go back to sleep, reassured in a way to hear the long whistle of a train, thinking, "Well, the train's not far away, if life gets too difficult I can always jump aboard and in less than two days be back where I came from." I'd forget that I couldn't afford it for the moment.

But I had another reason for not living too far from the station. Since I might be moving any minute, I left my trunk in the checkroom, the poor old cumbersome companion to which I'd become so curiously attached. By now my feeling for it was perhaps what we often feel for certain people and objects we don't know how to part with. In any event, for once it was convenient to have it close at hand, for I could go and take out lighter clothes as the weather became warmer. To keep my tiny room uncluttered, I also had to put into it things I no longer needed, that is, at least as much as I took out. For a few weeks I kept going back and forth between my room and the Windsor Station checkroom. I always dealt with the same station employee who, as soon as he saw me coming, would go and fetch the trunk, pivoting it on its corners to within my reach. I gave him a twenty-five-cent piece for his trouble the first time, but the second, having seen me hesitate, no doubt, he adamantly refused it. It would be a crime when he had nothing to do for hours on end, he said, to accept a tip for a service so small it wasn't worth talking about. Since he had to go and bring it from the back of a huge room so full of baggage he could hardly move, I didn't think it such a small thing. He said he was already being paid anyway by my comings and goings, which entertained him hugely, for in all his years with the CPR he'd never yet seen anyone come and take a pair of beige shoes out of a trunk and the same day come back and put a pair of brown shoes in. The trunk stayed in his care for a little over a month, and by the end he knew its contents almost as well as I did. He was my first friend in Montreal.

It was he who suggested I move into a house on Dorchester Street next to his, where I had a better room for the same price I was paying on Stanley. We had neighbouring windows through

which, since his house adjoined mine, he used to pass me a share of his Irish stew, always saying he had too much. Later still he encouraged me to take a room and board with someone he had found who made even better Irish stew, a Miss McLean. I owe it to Pat Cossack that in her house, compared to what I'd had before, I was in the lap of luxury.

BUT WHEN I first arrived I lived in the most horrid little room imaginable except in a prison. It was so cramped I had to turn sideways to pass between the grey metal bookshelf and the iron bedstead. The window overlooked the yard behind the principal bus station in Montreal, which was then on Dorchester Street. There dozens of buses were drawn up, always some with motors idling noisily, sending clouds of stifling fumes straight through my window. The loudspeaker never stopped announcing departures and arrivals. "Leaving for Rawdon, *traque numéro sept*, track number seven...leaving for Terrebonne, *traque numéro onze*, track number eleven...." Sometimes I used to repeat in my sleep, "*Traque numéro douze*, track number twelve...."

The atmosphere of wayfaring, confusion of tongues, and dizzy whirl of activity wasn't unpleasant. It suited my state of mind and was certainly more congenial, more friendly than some tranquil little street inhabited by equally tranquil people who have lived there for years. I always seem to have had the right place to stay at the right time.

Two letters arrived at the post office general delivery which I didn't dare open until I was back in the safety of my room, fragile haven though it was. One was from the St-Boniface School Board reminding me that I had been allowed a second year's leave of absence without pay and the privilege couldn't be renewed. I must therefore either return to work or resign. The second was from my mother. I can see myself reading her letter, holding it on my knees as I sat at the foot of my little iron cot.

"*Mon enfant*," it read, "so you're back in Montreal, not so far from home now. Home isn't a house any more, of course, but with the bit of money I have left and what you'll be earning we'll be able to live pretty well, you'll see. And with you so independent and me probably too possessive, I'll try to get used to letting you lead your own life. I imagine I can expect you home soon...."

I looked up and inches away, in the mirror on the little chest of drawers, I saw my distorted face. The flaws in the mirror? My own emotion? The old knot was in my throat again, just as in our days of greatest hardship, perpetual fears, and all that futile courage.

I looked at myself and knew that the time had come to make a decision from which, good or bad, there would be no turning back. I couldn't avoid it any longer.

I left the letter on the chest of drawers, the pages filled with the rather untidy writing which alone always told me better than anything else how strained and bruised Maman's nerves had been.

I went out. Aside from kind Mr. Cossack, I didn't know a soul in the city. I wandered the streets though I don't remember which. I must have walked some distance on St. Catherine Street, then up to Sherbrooke, for behind my agitated thoughts I remember the clanging of streetcar bells, then, as had happened once in London, a sudden intrusion which at first I didn't recognize, the rustling of early spring leaves. And as I had in London and Paris, I kept searching the indifferent faces in the crowd, hoping someone would at least glance at me. At last I walked downhill to where the lights were less bright, St. Antoine or Craig Street perhaps. Down here there was less traffic and less bustle on the sidewalks, and instead something like the murmur of a more private, friendlier sort of life. I wonder why I've always felt less lonely among ordinary people than in drawing rooms and society gatherings, however fondly I'm regarded by others present.

What shall I do? What shall I do? I kept asking myself as I walked. The question hammered at my mind, tormented me much as had the Song of Destiny and the mournful sound of the bell-buoy at Liverpool. What shall I do? Stay or go back?

I had no means of support nor assurance of even the most humble employment here, not even a friendly hand to reach out to me now and then. But could I live in Manitoba's suffocating French climate, its suffocating climate altogether, now that I knew there was something better? For it was misfortune enough to have been born French in Quebec, but infinitely worse, I now perceived, to have been born French outside Quebec in our little colonies of the Canadian West. Though I was lonely here, around me as I walked I heard French being spoken with what seemed a very heavy accent

after that of Paris, but with the words and expressions of my people, of my mother and grandmother, and I found this comforting.

Without knowing the way, I somehow reached the banks of the old Lachine Canal. I stopped short, intrigued. Barges were gliding slowly by, their sides scraping against the old timbers lining the canal. Their horns, requesting the opening of the lock gates, raised strange, repeated cries, like lamentations. I think I stayed for hours, dreaming of nothing in particular, as if abandoned by my own thoughts but not distressed by this. The night was rather mild as I recall, far from the miraculous spring of London but with the kindly feel of our Canadian spring. In the little streets of wooden houses and wide-spaced streetlamps where I went to walk, still aimlessly, I heard sounds of water trickling along the gutters, and here and there saw puddles of melting snow.

The bleatings of barge horns were not all I had for company. This district of St-Henri, whose name I had yet to learn, was constantly shaken by passing trains. First you heard a thin warning bell announcing the approach of a train towards each level crossing, then the long black-and-white-striped arms of the safety gates lowered and the crossing lights began to flash. The great trains bound for east and west came thundering down the track, shaking the ground, the windows of the houses, and perhaps something in the soul that remained quivering, in suspense, after the din had ceased.

Everything about the aura of departure and travel that I discovered in Montreal that night and subsequently made me want to stay. This atmosphere was like home to me for some time, consoling me in a way for not having another home, whispering that all of us are wanderers in this life and it's better to possess nothing if we want at least a clear view of the world we're passing through.

Less than a year later I returned deliberately to this district, listening, observing, sensing that it would be the setting and to a degree perhaps the substance of a novel. Already it gripped me in some curious way that I still don't understand. Its cries, smells, and reminders of travel weren't its only fascination. Its poverty moved me. Its poetry touched my heart, strains of guitars and other wistful scraps of music escaping beneath closed doors, the sound of the wind straying through warehouse passageways. I felt less alone here than in the crowds and bright lights of the city.

I walked up the long Atwater hill. I turned along Dorchester Street, passing, as it happens, in front of the house in which I would shortly have a room. After many wrong turns, I found my way back to Stanley Street. Sitting on my bed and leaning against the wall with the writing paper on my knees, I wrote first to the School Board thanking them for keeping my position open for me and herewith resigning. Then I wrote to my mother. What did I tell her? Probably to be patient, to expect me back in a year or two. She would soon be seventy-two. When I returned to St-Boniface after her death and searched among the pitiful remains of her belongings – practically nothing, cards from her children, small photographs – I couldn't find that first letter from Montreal in which I so hoped to have found words at least to soften the blow. Many of my letters were missing, though she kept little except letters in her last years – all, in fact, except the most recent. Some-one must have taken them to use them against me in some way. Or to prevent someone from using them against me. We were a divided family after Maman's death. She had held us more or less together with the strength of her love.

When I had written my letters I counted the money I had left. Fifteen dollars and a few cents. Enough to pay my rent for a week. I wrote to the two friends whom I thought the most dependable. I hated to borrow. I did it very rarely and never without the most agonizing scruples. In reply I received a long letter from one, full of praise for my talent, courage, and sense of initiative...and regret for not being able to help me because she'd had to buy a new fur coat and pay her tennis club fees, she explained, and really had nothing left, nothing! The other wrote hastily, "This is all I have to send you, alas, but I send it gladly...." She enclosed three five-dollar bills. Coming from the poorer of the two, it seemed like a huge sum. With this, I thought, I could hold out for several weeks and have time to see what lay ahead. Better still, because a friend had such confidence in me that she'd sent me her last pennies as it were, my courage was restored.

On the advice of a journalist at *The Gazette* to whom I had a letter of recommendation from a colleague posted in London, I made the rounds of a number of magazines and weekly papers. All I had to show a modicum of talent was the small collection of articles published here and there over the previous couple of years.

At *Le Jour* I was given to understand that they might, when there was room, publish a short column on a subject of my choice, for a fee of three dollars per column. At *La Revue moderne* they would pay up to ten dollars for a longish story if I could write it in the style the readers liked.

I went back to my room. I sat on the bed leaning against the wall with my typewriter on my knees, my thoughts invaded by relentless announcements — "*Traque numéro huit*, track number eight..." — terror-stricken to realize that now there was really no turning back; to earn my living, I would henceforth have to write and keep on writing. I suddenly saw how ill equipped I was.

I began with anecdotal accounts of my adventures in England and France. Alas, in my downcast state of mind, no longer stimulated by elation, I could bring forth only platitudes. It took close to a year before I began to write articles with some substance, given the opportunity by a farmers' publication, the *Bulletin des agriculteurs*, to write on subjects involving fact, reality, close observation.

It was even longer before I began to build on the reveries germinated beside the old canal that April evening, coming by stages to the major task whose prospect filled me with even greater terror than I had felt on Stanley Street when I began to write for a living. But now at least I was totally absorbed in my subject, helped and sustained by all the experience of human nature and other resources I'd acquired, as well as by my feeling of having come home, of oneness with my people, whom my mother had taught me to know and love in my childhood.

But back in my room on Stanley Street, I could only write insipid little pieces in which one would probably have searched in vain for traces of the torment and delight that have been with me since I was born, and no doubt will leave me only when I die.

Yet a bird, almost the minute it's hatched, I'm told, already knows its song.

The Author

GABRIELLE ROY was born in St-Boniface, Manitoba, on March 22, 1909. She was a schoolteacher from 1928 to 1937, the year in which she left on an extended trip of two years in France and England on the eve of the Second World War. Returning to Canada in 1939, she decided to settle in Montreal and became a freelance journalist with *Le Jour, Le Canada, La Revue moderne,* and *Le Bulletin des agriculteurs,* for which she wrote stories and several major series of articles. Her first novel, *Bonheur d'occasion,* was awarded the Prix Femina in France in 1947, and its translation, *The Tin Flute,* was chosen as the Book of the Month by the Literary Guild of America. While in Europe once again from 1947 to 1950 with her husband, Dr. Marcel Carbotte, she wrote her second book, *La Petite Poule d'Eau (Where Nests the Water Hen).* She returned to live in Quebec, where she remained and wrote for the rest of her life. She died in Quebec City on July 13, 1983.

Gabrielle Roy wrote fifteen books besides this autobiography, comprising novels, short stories, children's books, and a collection of essays. She also wrote a number of other essays and articles. Her recognition as one of the leading figures in Canadian and Quebec literature is attested by the many honours she received, including three Governor General's Prizes (1947, 1957, and 1978), the Prix Femina (France, 1947), the Lorne Pierce Medal (Royal Society of Canada, 1947), the Medal of the Académie canadienne-française (1947), the Prix Duvernay (1956), the Prix David (1971), and the Canada Council Prize for Children's Literature (1979).

The Translator

PATRICIA CLAXTON—a translator and teacher of translation—is a member of the Society of Translators of Quebec, and was founding president of the Literary Translators' Association. She has translated books by Nicole Brossard, Fernand Ouellet, and Marcel Trudel, and stories, poems, and articles by Naïm Kattan, Andrée Maillet, André Major, André Roy, France Théoret, and Pierre Trudeau. Patricia Claxton won the 1987 Governor General's Award for Translation for *Enchantment and Sorrow*.

The Works of Gabrielle Roy

Second and subsequent Canadian editions listed are revised editions, excepting special editions as noted.

Bonheur d'occasion, Montreal, 1945, 1947, 1965, 1970, 1977; Paris, 1947, Geneva, 1968. Prix Femina; Book of the Month, Literary Guild of America; Medal of the Académie canadienne-française; Governor General's Prize; Lorne Pierce Medal, Royal Society of Canada. English translation by Hannah Josephson, *The Tin Flute*, Toronto, McClelland & Stewart, 1947. Retranslation by Alan Brown, Toronto, McClelland & Stewart, 1980. Spanish, Danish, Swedish, Norwegian, Slovak, Czech, Romanian, and Russian translations.

La Petite Poule d'Eau, Montreal, 1950, 1957, 1970, 1980; Paris, 1951, 1967; Geneva, 1953; numbered art edition with twenty prints by Jean-Paul Lemieux, Montreal, 1971. English translation by Harry Binsse, *Where Nests the Water Hen*, Toronto, McClelland & Stewart, 1951. German translation.

Alexandre Chenevert, Montreal, 1954, 1973, 1979; Paris, 1954. English translation by Harry Binsse, *The Cashier*, Toronto, McClelland & Stewart, 1955. German translation.

Rue Deschambault, Montreal, 1955, 1956, 1967, 1971, 1980. Governor General's Prize. English translation by Harry Binsse, *Street of Riches*, Toronto, McClelland & Stewart, 1957. Italian translation.

La Montagne secrète, Montreal, 1961, 1971, 1974, 1978; Paris, 1962; numbered deluxe edition illustrated by René Richard, Montreal, 1975. English translation by Harry Binsse, *The Hidden Mountain*, Toronto, McClelland & Stewart, 1962.

La Route d'Altamont, Montreal, 1966, 1979; Paris, 1967. English translation by Joyce Marshall, *The Road past Altamont*, Toronto, McClelland & Stewart, 1966. German translation.

La Rivière sans repos, novel preceded by three short stories, Montreal, 1970, 1971, 1979; Paris, 1972. English translation (novel only) by Joyce Marshall, *Windflower*, Toronto, McClelland & Stewart, 1970.

Cet été qui chantait, Quebec and Montreal, 1972, 1973; Montreal, 1979. English translation by Joyce Marshall, *Enchanted Summer*, Toronto, McClelland & Stewart, 1976.

Un Jardin au bout du monde, Montreal, 1975, 1981. English translation by Alan Brown, *Garden in the Wind*, Toronto, McClelland & Stewart, 1977.

Ma Vache Bossie (children's story), Montreal, 1976, 1982. Illustrated by Louise Pominville.

Ces enfants de ma vie, Montreal, 1977, 1983. Governor General's Prize. English translation by Alan Brown, *Children of My Heart*, Toronto, McClelland & Stewart, 1979.

Fragiles lumières de la terre, Montreal, 1978, 1980, 1982. English translation by Alan Brown, *The Fragile Lights of Earth*, Toronto, McClelland & Stewart, 1982.

Courte-Queue (children's story), Montreal, 1979, 1980. Canada Council Prize for Children's Literature. English translation by Alan Brown, *Cliptail*, Toronto, McClelland & Stewart, 1980. English and French editions illustrated by François Olivier.

De quoi t'ennuies-tu Eveline? suivi de *Ely! Ely! Ely!*, Montreal, 1979, 1982, 1984.

La Pékinoise et l'Espagnole (children's story), Montreal, 1987. Illustrated by Jean-Yves Ahern.

Tell it to the Skies

ERICA JAMES

An Orion paperback

First published in Great Britain in 2007
by Orion
This paperback edition published in 2008
by Orion Books Ltd,
Orion House, 5 Upper St Martin's Lane,
London WC2H 9EA

An Hachette Livre UK company

1 3 5 7 9 10 8 6 4 2

A CIP catalogue record for this book is
available from the British Library.

ISBN 978-0-7528-9399-0

Typeset by Deltatype Ltd, Birkenhead, Merseyside

Printed and bound in Great Britain by
Clays Ltd, St Ives plc

The Orion Publishing Group's policy is to use papers
that are natural, renewable and recyclable products and
made from wood grown in sustainable forests. The logging
and manufacturing processes are expected to conform to
the environmental regulations of the country of origin.

www.orionbooks.co.uk

Praise for Erica James

'Erica James' sensitive story ... is as sparklingly fresh as dew on the village's surrounding meadows ... thoroughly enjoyable and fully deserving of a place in the crowded market of women's fiction' *Sunday Express*

'This book draws you into the lives of these characters, and often makes you want to scream at them to try and make them see reason. Funny, sad and frustrating, but an excellent, compulsive read' *Woman's Realm*

'There is humour and warmth in this engaging story of love's triumphs and disappointments, with two well-realised and intriguing subplots' *Woman & Home*

'Joanna Trollope fans, dismayed by the high gloom factor and complete absence of Agas in her latest books, will turn with relief to James' ... delightful novel about English village life ... a blend of emotion and wry social observation' *Daily Mail*

'Scandal, fury, accusations and revenge are all included in Erica James' compelling novel ... this story of village life in Cheshire is told with wit and humour' *Stirling Observer*

'An entertaining read with some wickedly well-painted cameo characters. It's a perfect read if you're in the mood for romance' *Prima*

'An engaging and friendly novel ... very readable'
Woman's Own

'A bubbling, delightful comedy which is laced with a bitter-sweet tang ... a good story, always well observed, and full of wit' *Publishing News*

Erica James grew up in Hampshire and has since lived in Oxford, Yorkshire and Belgium. She now lives in Cheshire. She is the author of eleven previous bestselling novels, including *Gardens of Delight*, which won the 2006 Romantic Novel of the Year Award.

By Erica James

A Breath of Fresh Air
Time for a Change
Airs & Graces
A Sense of Belonging
Act of Faith
The Holiday
Precious Time
Hidden Talents
Paradise House
Love and Devotion
Gardens of Delight
Tell it to the Skies

To Edward and Samuel
who make it all worthwhile

Acknowledgements

While digging deep to write this book I was fortunate indeed to be supported and encouraged by some wonderful friends.

Endless gratitude to Ray Allen for his many words of wisdom and for making me laugh with such regularity. Who'd have thought he'd be such a wise sage?

My sincere thanks to Sheila and Alan Jones. Alan, whilst we will happily never agree on all manner of subjects, I congratulate you on being married to one of the nicest people in the world.

Thank you to Max and Keith for adding to my enjoyment of Venice last year. Especially for the extravagant bunch of red roses – a gesture I couldn't resist pinching for this book!

Thanks, too, to Kathleen, my 'English Teacher' in Venice.

I wouldn't be the first author to take a few liberties here and there, but hopefully no one will notice. Or if they do, they'll be accepted as the artistic tweakings of a creative mind.

*'Men never do evil so
completely and cheerfully
as when they do it from
religious conviction.'*

BLAISE PASCAL 1623–1662

*'And now these three remain:
faith, hope and love. But the
greatest of these is love.'*

1 CORINTHIANS 13:13

Now

Chapter One

It happened so quickly.

She had been hurrying from the market side of the Rialto Bridge, trying to avoid the crush of tourists in the packed middle section of shops, when a single face appeared in the crowd as if picked out by a bright spotlight entirely for her benefit. She turned on her heel to get a better look. And that was when she missed her footing and ended up sprawled on the wet ground, the contents of her handbag scattered.

Any other time Lydia might have been appalled at this loss of dignity, yet all she cared about, whilst a voluble group of Americans helped her to get back on her feet, was the man who had caused her to slip. She scanned the crowded steps for his retreating figure in the fine, drizzling rain. But he was long gone.

If he'd been there at all, Lydia thought as she relaxed into the chair and felt the downy softness of the cushions enfold her. The doctor had left ten minutes ago, promising the delivery of a pair of crutches in the morning. Her ankle was now expertly strapped and resting on a footstool. *Dottor* Pierili's parting words had been to tell her to keep the weight off her foot for as long as possible. He'd wanted her to go to the hospital for an X-ray, just to be on the safe side, but she'd waved his advice aside, politely yet firmly. Bandages, rest and painkillers would suffice.

'I still don't know how you managed to get home,' Chiara said, coming into the living room with a tray of tea things. She put the tray on a pedestal table between a pair

of tall balconied windows that looked down onto the Rio di San Vio. The weak, melancholy December light had all but faded and the spacious room glowed with a soft-hued luminosity. Strategically placed lamps created a beguilingly serene atmosphere, making it Lydia's favourite room in the apartment. She was a self-confessed lover of beautiful things; it was what brought her to Venice in the first place. Living here she was surrounded by beauty on a scale she had never encountered anywhere else. Venice's glorious but crumbling architecture together with its proud history combined to produce a profoundly sad and haunting sense of identity that appealed enormously to Lydia. It was the apparent isolation of the place that touched her; it was somewhere she felt she could be separate from the rest of the world.

She would always remember her first glimpse of Venice. It was early evening and as the *vaporetto* entered the basin, the city was suddenly there before her, floating like a priceless work of art in the distance, the low sun catching on the gilded domes and *campanili*. It was love at first sight. From then on she was a willing victim to Venice's trembling beauty and the spell it cast on her. Even with the myriad challenges that the city was forced to cope with – the growing threat of *acqua alta*, the ever-increasing crowds that were choking the narrow *calli*, and the graffiti (almost worst of all to Lydia) that was spreading endemically through Venice – it was still a place of dreams for her. Even the relentless chorus of 'Volare' and 'O Sole Mio!' coming from the gondoliers as they cruised the waterways with their cargo of nodding and smiling Japanese tourists could do nothing to diminish her love for her adopted home.

'You're either the bravest woman I know or the stupidest,' Chiara said as she handed Lydia a cup of tea.

Lydia smiled, noting that Chiara had gone to the trouble of digging out her favourite bone china cup and saucer. 'Undoubtedly the latter,' she replied. 'That's certainly what your father would have said.'

4

'You probably did more damage walking on it than when you slipped.'

'He would have agreed with you on that point too. And said that for a forty-six-year-old woman I should have known better.'

Chiara crossed the room for her own cup then came and curled up in the high-backed chair next to Lydia. It was where Marcello always used to sit, his hand outstretched to Lydia as he quietly read the *Gazzettino*.

'I want you to know that this arrangement will only go on for a day or two,' Lydia said, keen to establish that she would soon be back at work, business as usual.

Chiara, all twenty-four years of her, gave Lydia a quelling stare, her eyes dark and shining in the muted light. 'Oh, no you don't. We can manage perfectly well without you.'

'That's what I'm worried about. I don't want you getting too used to my absence.'

'Now there's an idea. A boardroom coup.'

The shrill ring of the telephone in the hall had Chiara getting to her feet. Within seconds it was obvious the call wasn't for Lydia. Selfishly she hoped it wasn't one of Chiara's friends inviting her out for the evening; she could do with the company.

This neediness had nothing to do with her sprained ankle, and all to do with not wanting to be alone. If she was alone, she might dwell on that face in the crowd. And that was definitely something she didn't want to do. An evening with Chiara would be the perfect distraction.

It was a matter of pride to Lydia that she and Chiara didn't have the usual mother and daughter relationship. For a start Lydia wasn't actually Chiara's mother: she was her stepmother. It was a clumsy label Lydia had dispensed with at the earliest opportunity. Chiara had always called her by her Christian name, anyway.

Lydia had never told anyone this, but it had been Chiara who she had fallen for first – her love for Marcello, Chiara's father, had come later. They had met fifteen years

5

ago, when Chiara was nine and Lydia had been employed to teach the little girl English. She received a phone call in response to one of her advertisements offering her services, and three days later a distinguished-looking Signor Marcello Tomasi and his only daughter arrived at her apartment in Santa Croce. She was a painfully shy, introverted child and it didn't take long to realize why: her mother, as her quietly spoken father explained, had died last winter. Nobody could have empathized more with the young girl. Lydia knew exactly how it felt to have your world turned upside down and inside out. Every ounce of her being made her want to take away Chiara's sadness, to make her face light up with a smile.

The lessons always started at four o'clock on a Saturday afternoon and took place in Lydia's tiny kitchen. She thought it would be a less intimidating environment for this fragile child than to sit at the formal desk in the sitting room. There would always be a pot of freshly made hot chocolate on the table, along with a box of delicious almond biscuits from her local *pasticceria*. Lydia's other students were never offered more than tea or coffee, or fruit juice if she happened to have any in the fridge. Gradually her young pupil began to grow in confidence, which meant she looked less likely to burst into tears if she got anything wrong.

Without fail Marcello Tomasi would return for his daughter as the bell from San Giacomo dell'Orio struck five. He would hand over the agreed amount of money, check that they were still on for the following Saturday and then wish Lydia a pleasant evening. However, one day, just as Lydia was opening the door for them to leave, Chiara did something that changed everything. She beckoned her father to bend down to her, cupped her hand around her mouth and whispered into his ear. Straightening up, he cleared his throat, rubbed his hand over his clean-shaven chin and said, 'Chiara would like to invite you to her birthday party next week.'

The thought of a roomful of over-excited, noisy Italian

6

children held no appeal for Lydia. As if reading her mind, Marcello Tomasi said, 'It will be just a small party. I think Chiara would very much like you to be there. And so would I,' he added.

The party was bigger than Lydia had been led to believe, but it was very much a family affair with the only children present being a handful of Chiara's cousins, most of whom were younger than her and blessedly well behaved. After six months of teaching this man's only daughter and forming a strong, protective relationship with her, but exchanging no more than a few words with him, it was strange to be in his home; it felt oddly intimate. She was suddenly seized with the urge to snoop and pry, to find out more about this immaculately dressed, taciturn man. She knew that he worked on the mainland in Marghera, the nearby industrial zone that was generally considered to be the Beast to Venice's Beauty. She also knew, from Chiara, that he was *very*, *very* important and had *lots* of people working for him. Judging from the house – a two-storey, stylishly restored property a stone's throw from Ca'Doro – he had excellent taste and lived in a degree of comfort. But this scant amount of detail wasn't enough for Lydia; she wanted to know what he did for pleasure. Did he read? If so, what books did he read? What music did he listen to? What did he eat for his supper? More to the point, who cooked his supper? Did he cook it himself, or did he have help? Chiara had never mentioned anyone.

Even if she had had the nerve to carry out any actual unseemly rifling through Marcello's personal effects for answers to her questions, there was no opportunity to do so. Chiara took her excitedly by the hand and introduced her in overly rehearsed English to her many relatives, one by one. 'This is Miss Lydia, my very nice English teacher ... This is Miss Lydia, my very nice English teacher.' The responses were all in Italian, which was fine by Lydia; she had been speaking Italian since she was eighteen. She might only have been in Venice for two years but she could manage a passable version of *la parlata*, the local dialect,

7

which seemed to her to be entirely made up on a whim solely to vex outsiders.

Everyone at the party was very welcoming and took it in turns to press plates of tempting food onto her as well as top up her glass of Prosecco. But she took pains not to outstay her welcome; this was a family affair, she reminded herself. Shortly after the children had been called upon to sing for the adults, accompanied on the piano by Fabio, Marcello's brother – apparently a family tradition – she tried to make her exit as discreetly as possible, but Chiara was having none of it and announced to everyone that her *very nice English teacher* was leaving. Endless goodbyes then ensued until at last she was rescued by Marcello who, having instructed Chiara to offer her sweet-toothed great-grandmother another helping of *dolce*, steered Lydia away.

'I hope that wasn't too awful for you,' he said when they were standing outside in the courtyard garden, the cool night air making her realize how warm she'd been inside and how much Prosecco she'd drunk. She could feel the heat radiating from her cheeks.

'I had a lovely time,' she said truthfully, thinking how much she really had enjoyed herself.

'It wasn't too overwhelming?'

'Not at all. It was good to see Chiara so happy. She's a delightful child; you must be extremely proud of her.'

'She is and I am. I don't know if you're aware of it, but she's grown very close to you.'

'The feeling is mutual. She's charming company.'

'Are you busy tomorrow evening?'

'I don't think so. Why?'

'Will you have dinner with me?'

And that, six months after losing her heart to his daughter, was the start of her relationship with Marcello. A man who, ten years older than her, in no way fitted her idea of a typical Italian. He wasn't one of those rumbustious Italian men who constantly argue about politics and corruption in high places and claim they could change everything

8

overnight if only given the chance. Nor did he have the infuriating habit of shouting '*Ascoltami!*' ('Listen to me!') every other sentence. And not once did he grab her arm to make sure he had her full attention during a conversation. Instead there was a quiet and intelligent reserve about him. He was courteous to a fault and very astute. He realized and accepted that there was a part of her he would never know or understand. 'Your life is like a photograph album with occasional blank spaces where some of the pictures have been removed,' he said on the day he asked her to be his wife.

'Does it matter to you?' she replied.

'No,' he answered. 'I think it's those mysterious gaps I love most about you.'

Perhaps if he had pressed her, she might have shared more of herself with him.

The sound of Chiara's happy laughter, as she continued talking to whoever it was on the phone, broke through Lydia's thoughts and, not for the first time, she wondered how the painfully shy child she had met fifteen years ago had grown into this confident, carefree young woman, a young woman who had had to cope with the loss of both her parents before she'd turned twenty-one. Lydia liked to think that she'd played a part in Chiara's recovery from the death of her mother – Marcello always believed she had – but all she'd done was give the child what she had never experienced when she was that age: love and stability.

Having children had never been something Lydia had particularly craved. However, having Chiara in her life had felt exactly the right thing to do.

That night she slept badly, her sleep disturbed by a host of fragmented dreams. In one dream the siren sounded, signalling *acqua alta*. Venice was sinking. The water was lapping at her feet as she tried desperately to make it home to Chiara. But she was lost; every *calle* she ran into was a dead end. The siren continued to ring out. The ancient

9

wooden supports creaked and groaned and finally they gave way and the buildings crumbled and slid slowly but surely into the lagoon.

She woke with a start and lay in the dark remembering a Bible story from her childhood, about the man who built his house upon the sand. Pastor Digby had his long, bony finger raised accusingly to her; he was asking if she understood what the story was teaching her.

Once she'd allowed one memory to enter her thinking, others began flooding in too. Her next mistake was to attach too much meaning to the dream. Was her life disintegrating? Had she built her life on foundations that were about to give way?

She pulled the duvet up over her head, blaming that wretched face in the crowd. Who was he? A ghost?

Chapter Two

The following morning the promised pair of crutches arrived, as did a succession of visitors throughout the day, all of whom had been despatched by Chiara to entertain Lydia.

'Another one who's been sent to keep me company, I presume,' Lydia said tiredly after she'd buzzed up Marcello's brother, Fabio. His wet, bedraggled appearance was a clear indicator of the kind of day it was outside. The lower edges of his overcoat were drenched, his furled umbrella was dripping onto the marble floor, and his trousers were tucked into a pair of black, knee-high rubber boots.

'Would you rather I left you to rest?' he asked. From his coat pockets he retrieved a bag of *biscotti* and a bottle of Vin Santo. Smiling, he dangled them in front of her. 'I could always keep these for myself.'

'Well, seeing as you've gone to so much trouble, perhaps I'll let you stay.' She watched him take off his coat and boots, then set off awkwardly down the length of the hallway on the crutches, negotiating the rugs with care. Fabio followed behind in his stockinged feet. 'What dear, well-meaning Chiara forgot,' Lydia said, conscious that she was sounding less than gracious, 'in her attempt to keep me occupied for the day, was that I would have to be up and down like a yo-yo to let you all in.'

'In that case, I'd better stay until she returns so you won't be further inconvenienced.'

'Now you're just making me feel like an ungrateful bitch.'

He laughed. 'And with so little effort, *cara*.' He put

his gifts down on the coffee table and helped her to get comfortable on the sofa.

'So why aren't you hard at work?' she asked.

'I'm the boss; I can take time off whenever I want.'

'I'll tell Paolo you said that.'

He laughed again. 'It was Paolo who insisted I drop everything and come and see you after Chiara called.'

'Hah, so he's to blame.'

'I think you need a drink to sweeten that sour tongue of yours.' He fetched a pair of glasses from the kitchen and poured out two generous measures of Vin Santo. He opened the packet of *biscotti* and passed it to Lydia. Of all her visitors that day, Fabio was probably the most welcome. As Marcello's younger brother, there had only ever been a vague physical resemblance between the two men, but the bond between them had been a strong one, had marked them out as being cut from the same cloth.

'So how did you hurt yourself?' Fabio asked after he'd chinked his glass against Lydia's and sat down.

'Too silly to say.'

'Oh, come on, I could do with a good laugh.'

'I thought you were here to make *me* laugh?'

'I know a lost cause when I see one. What did you do, kick some poor tourist out of your way and lose your balance?'

She smiled, but didn't say anything. Instead she dunked a biscuit into her drink then sucked on it, aware that Fabio was watching her closely. She knew all too well that he could spot the slightest change in her a mile off.

'What is it, *cara*?' he said. 'You don't seem yourself. You look distracted.'

She wished that her brother-in-law wasn't so sensitive and perceptive. After Marcello's death from a heart attack four years ago it was his shoulder she had cried on, just as it was his hand, along with Chiara's, that she had held during the funeral service. He had always been there for her. She had joked once that it was as well he was gay or people would certainly have got the wrong idea about

them. But right now she would give anything for him not to care so much for her.

'It's being stuck here,' she said, pointing at her ankle. 'I feel so useless.'

Looking far from convinced by her explanation, Fabio sat back and crossed one leg over the other. 'It's nothing to do with Chiara, is it?' he asked.

She took a sip of her drink, enjoying its dry, sweet warmth on her throat. 'Chiara's fine,' she said. 'And anyway, didn't I just say what's wrong with me?'

Fabio stared at her doubtfully. 'So if it's not Chiara,' he persisted, 'is it work? You've built up quite a business there; it's not becoming too much for you, is it?'

She shook her head. 'Work's fine.' Again, she was telling the truth. The business she and Marcello had started together had never looked in better shape. Shortly after he'd proposed to her, Marcello announced his intention to leave the chemical company where he was the research director. He had always felt that the nature of his work was at odds with his love for Venice – given the environmental effect the industrial zone was having on the lagoon – but he had eased his conscience by saying it was better that someone like him had a say in how things were done, than someone who didn't care. 'I want to do something new,' he told her. 'And it has to be something we can do together.' They soon came up with the idea of running a lettings agency, initially acting on behalf of private and individual owners, but eventually investing in property themselves. Before long, they had an impressive portfolio of apartments to offer clients, most of whom were British, American, French and German. After Marcello's death, and as a direct result of working the worst of her grief out of her system, the agency became even more successful. She now had a reliable team of girls working for her in the newly expanded office, including Chiara who joined the agency when she had finished her studies in Bologna two years previously. As architects, Fabio and his partner Paolo had played their part by helping with any restoration

work that was required in the properties. They had also overseen the work carried out on this very apartment, which she and Marcello had moved into only eighteen months before his death.

The irony of her line of work was not lost on Lydia. Like so many Venetians who complained bitterly about the number of visitors to Venice, she actively encouraged tourists to pour in for the sake of her livelihood. There was also the more controversial matter of Venice's dwindling population. Hardly a day went by when there wasn't a piece written in the *Gazzettino* about the plight of young locals being forced to live on the mainland because they couldn't afford the sky-high prices here in Venice. Prices that had been inflated by outside investors. It was a problem that had everyone in agreement: something would have to be done. But meanwhile, life had to carry on and people made their living the best way they knew how, by welcoming tourists with open arms and giving them a thorough fleecing.

'If it's not Chiara or work that's bothering you,' said Fabio, 'is it loneliness?' He paused, and Lydia could see he was choosing his next words with care. 'Do you think it's time to move on?'

For a while now Fabio had been discreetly hinting that she ought to find someone to take Marcello's place. Lydia smiled. 'Oh, Fabio, I know how you worry about me, and I appreciate it, really I do. But it's not that. Not that at all.'

'*Sei sicura?*'

'Yes, I'm sure. To be honest, I'm usually too busy to give it a thought.'

'That's not healthy.'

'It's the way it is.'

'Then perhaps it's time you changed your ways. When was the last time you had a holiday?'

'Don't be ridiculous. What would I do with a holiday?'

He shook his head in what she hoped was defeat, but taking her by surprise, he said, 'Sometimes I think you go

out of your way to punish yourself. For the life of me I can't think why.'

You don't know the half of it, she thought grimly.

Chapter Three

Chiara came home from work early and straight away Lydia sensed there was something different about her. From the moment she had hung up her coat and put her umbrella to dry, the walls of the apartment seemed to reverberate with the sound of laughter and chatter. She greeted Fabio with her customary warmth, but the hug definitely went on for longer than usual and the grin on her face never slipped. She was joyful. Exuberant.

Now that Fabio had gone, Lydia watched Chiara move about the apartment, drawing the curtains, tidying away the debris of a day's worth of visitors, and all the while humming to herself. She was in a world of her own. No doubt about it. But what could have put Chiara into such an exceptionally happy mood?

After pondering on this for several minutes on her own, Lydia went to find Chiara in the kitchen. She was standing in front of the full-length window, staring absently at her reflection in the glass. On the hob, the kettle was boiling furiously, sending up a cloud of steam. Realizing that Chiara wouldn't notice the ceiling falling down on her in her current frame of mind, Lydia went over and switched off the gas.

Chiara slowly turned around to face her. 'Can I ask you something, Lydia? Something personal?'

'Of course,' said Lydia. 'What is it?'

'Have you ever had a real moment of epiphany? When you knew with absolute certainty that a certain thing was meant to happen to you? Or a certain person was meant to be in your life?'

Of all the things she might have expected Chiara to ask her it was not this. Her response was to think of her own life-changing moment and the subsequent terror it had filled her with. It had happened a long time ago, yet she had never forgotten how resolute she had been. Or how utterly convinced she had been that it was the right thing to do.

'I don't know how it happened,' Chiara went on, not seeming to notice that Lydia hadn't answered her, 'but I was looking into his eyes and I knew that nothing would be the same again. Does that sound crazy? Do *I* sound crazy?'

'Well,' said Lydia, the wind taken out of her sails, 'this sounds like something I should be sitting down to hear. Tell me more. And exactly whose eyes are we talking about?'

Splashing hot water over a peppermint teabag in a mug, Chiara said, 'You promise you won't overreact and tell me I'm being silly?'

Settled at the table now, her crutches propped against the back of another chair, Lydia said, 'Have I ever behaved like that before with you?'

Chiara tossed the dripping teabag into the bin. 'No, but there's a first time for everything. Do you want me to make you a drink?'

'No, I'm fine, thank you. But come and sit down and tell me who's had such a devastating effect on you. He must be quite something.'

Chiara laughed and came and joined her at the table. 'Yes, that's exactly how I'd describe it. I knew you'd understand. His name's Ishmael, and I met him today, and he's ... well, he's just, oh, I don't know, he's the first man to knock me off my feet. I can't even tell you exactly what it is about him that's so amazing. But I do know this: he's *Quello Giusto*.'

The One. Lydia didn't know whether to be delighted or alarmed. It was wonderful that Chiara had met someone who could make her feel this way, but a complete stranger? Trying desperately not to pour cold water on

Chiara's excitement, she said, 'How did you meet this extraordinary man?'

'He came into the office this morning; he's one of our clients and is staying in Ca' Tiziano. Maria Luisa was supposed to take him to the apartment but she had an emergency with Luca and had to fetch him home from school because he had a fever, so I stepped in. And—' She paused for breath and Lydia half expected a drum roll to follow. 'And there he was, standing the other side of my desk, and my heart nearly somersaulted clean out of my chest. I swear I'm not exaggerating. It was just as well I was sitting down as otherwise I'm convinced my legs would have gone from under me.'

'Goodness,' Lydia said inadequately. 'Do you think he realized the effect he had on you?' She hated the thought of Chiara wearing her heart so openly on her sleeve and leaving herself exposed to being hurt. But presumably if this so-called *The One* was staying in one of their apartments, his presence in Chiara's life would be no more than transient. He would leave Venice and Chiara's heart would be left relatively unscathed. No sooner had she articulated this thought to herself than Lydia wondered if she was reacting in this negative way because she was frightened of Chiara leaving her. There had been no previous boyfriend who had got anywhere near to threatening their close relationship, so could it be that Lydia was jealous, that she saw Chiara as her best friend and was afraid to lose her? She flinched at this uncomfortable insight and forced herself to join in with Chiara's enthusiasm.

'I'm not sure if he noticed anything,' said Chiara, 'but after I'd shown him round the apartment he asked if it was against company policy to mix business with pleasure, and would it be all right for him to take me for a drink. He said he'd never been to Venice before and would appreciate any local knowledge he could get.'

'Well, we can't fault him for seizing the moment,' Lydia said.

Chiara stared at Lydia over the top of her steaming

mug, her dark eyes flashing defensively. 'You sound disapproving.'

Lydia offered up what she hoped was a reassuring, conciliatory smile. 'I think I'm acting like a very boring middle-aged woman who's just looking out for you. After all, what do you know of him?'

'Quite a bit as it happens,' Chiara said with a show of spirit. 'He's English and arrived in Venice two days ago and has been staying at the Monaco before moving into Ca' Tiziano. He's here to do a crash course in Italian at the Institute because he's starting a new job in Padua in the spring. And don't forget, if he can afford to stay in Ca' Tiziano, he's not exactly a pauper.'

Hardly sufficient evidence in Lydia's opinion to allay her fears. 'When are you having that drink with him?'

For the first time during the conversation Chiara looked awkward. She raised a hand to her long, dark hair and twirled a curly lock of it around her finger, just as she had as a child when she'd been holding something back. 'If it's OK with you, that's if you don't mind being on your own, I was hoping to meet him in half an hour. I thought I'd take him to the Christmas market, you know, to show him a bit of local colour.'

'Of course it's OK with me,' Lydia said. 'You go and have fun. You've earned it putting up with me whilst I've been such a misery.'

'Really?' The dear girl was practically out of her chair.

'I always mean what I say,' Lydia said.

Within minutes, Chiara had made a call on her mobile and was tying a scarf around her neck and buttoning her coat. 'You're sure you'll be all right?'

Lydia smiled. 'Scram! Go on, get out of here! And don't forget your umbrella.'

'*Ciao, ciao.*'

Laughing happily, Chiara slammed the door after her.

In the silence that followed, Lydia could hear one of Renzo's music students playing the violin in the apartment

below. Outside, a motorboat was chugging slowly by, the water slapping against the sides of the canal. Further away, the bells of the Gesuati were pealing the hour.

She closed her eyes and pictured Chiara – breathless and smiling – meeting this unknown man a short walk away in the prettily lit Campo San Stefano. She saw them browsing the specially erected wooden chalets of the Christmas market, a cup of mulled wine in hand as they sampled the many varieties of salami, olives and cheese on offer. Chiara would probably introduce him to her friend, Felice, who was there every day selling his black and white photographs of Venice. Afterwards they would go on to a bar for a spritzer and probably meet more of Chiara's friends. You couldn't go anywhere in this small city without bumping into someone you knew.

Or perhaps they would want to be alone …

She reached for her crutches and stood up decisively. This pathetic behaviour had to stop. Chiara was a grown woman who could fall in love with whomever she chose. Lydia couldn't protect her for ever. Hadn't she made that mistake before, thinking that she alone carried the world on her shoulders and was entirely responsible for those she loved?

Chapter Four

Four days later and Lydia was climbing the walls. Mentally, that was. Her ankle was on the mend but she still couldn't tackle the four flights of stairs that would take her to the outside world. As undignified as the process would be, she was tempted to make her escape on her bottom, but Chiara wouldn't hear of it. The most she had been able to negotiate out of Chiara was the right to work on her laptop at the kitchen table. Really, that girl was turning into quite a tyrant!

Waiting now for Chiara to come home from work, Lydia was bored rigid. She was on edge, too. Chiara was bringing Ishmael back with her for the first time. 'You'll love him,' Chiara had said at breakfast that morning. 'I just know you will.'

Lydia had done her best to walk the fine line of showing a healthy interest in what was making Chiara so happy, and keeping a tight lid on the many questions she was longing to ask. Not that Chiara had given her much of a chance to be interrogated: if she wasn't at work, she was out with Ishmael, often not coming home till late when Lydia was in bed. Frustratingly, she knew no more about this young man than she had four days ago.

Countless times she had had to fight off the urge to go behind Chiara's back and speak to the girls at the office to see if they knew anything about the client staying in Ca' Tiziano. It was the fear of Chiara finding out that she had done something so sneaky that stopped Lydia from picking up the telephone. That and knowing there was a line a parent never crossed: Chiara's privacy had to be respected.

At the sound of a key in the lock, Lydia roused herself from the sofa. Armed with just the one crutch, she stood to attention, a welcoming smile firmly in place.

If Chiara's reaction on meeting Ishmael for the first time had been a somersaulting heart, Lydia's was all-out shock.

While her mind was making wild panicky leaps, her body had lost all of its strength. She leaned heavily on her crutch and felt the blood drain out of her. Her shock must have shown because, mid-introduction, Chiara said, 'Lydia, are you all right?'

'I'm fine.' But she was far from fine. How could this be? How could she be standing in the same room with the man who had caused her to slip on the steps of the Rialto Bridge ... the very man who had meant the world to her?

Except it wasn't the same man. It couldn't be. It wasn't possible. A lifetime had passed since she last saw him; there was no way he couldn't have aged. Yet, to all intents and purposes it *was* him. The dark, intelligent eyes were the same, as was the narrow face, its features delicately etched as if by a great master. His short, fine hair was instantly familiar too, light brown and highlighted with flecks of burnished gold. And just as familiar were his faded corduroy jeans and black polo-neck sweater. She dropped her eyes to his shoes – that all-important indicator of someone's personality. What else, but well-worn black and white baseball boots? Just as she'd known. He was exactly as she remembered him, even down to the angular, insubstantial build of him.

That had been her initial impression when she'd first set eyes on Noah at the age of nine. He'd seemed so insubstantial, quite incapable of taking care of himself. She hadn't known whether to despise him or feel sorry for him. He'd had a strange unearthly quality, which she later came to realize was a formidable inner strength. It was to prove more powerful than any name-calling or fist-waving threats, to which she and their peers frequently resorted.

But that was *Noah*, Lydia reminded herself. This carbon copy's name was Ishmael. He had to be a handful of years older than Noah had been when she'd last seen him. There could be only one explanation for what she was seeing, but could it be?

'I know this will sound like a cliché, Signora Tomasi, but you look as if you've seen a ghost.'

Once again she was assailed by shock. His voice was the same. It was the kind of voice that could convince you nowhere was safer than by his side, that together you could take on the world no matter what it threw at you.

'Please,' she said, conscious that Chiara was staring at her, 'call me Lydia.' She held out her hand. He took it and as their eyes met, she said, 'I don't recall Chiara mentioning your surname to me; what is it?'

'Solomon,' he replied with a beguiling smile – another trait she had seen before. 'I know,' he shrugged. 'I have the most biblical name going: Ishmael Solomon. It's down to my father, who has a weird sense of humour. The name was his choice. He said he'd been similarly afflicted as a child with the name of Noah, and saw no reason to let me off.'

Through a pounding in her ears, Lydia could hear Ishmael talking as if from a great distance. Further and further away his voice was drifting as the years rolled back and the memories struggled to take flight on the wings of incredulity. For twenty-eight years she had consigned Noah Solomon to the darkest, most unreachable depths of her old life. And what courage and heartbreaking effort that had taken. But now, here was a young man who could change all that. Was it coincidence, his being in Venice? Surely it had to be. Yet what were the chances of that happening?

Questions tumbled through her head, but now wasn't the time to deal with them. Perhaps irritated with her odd behaviour, Chiara had taken Ishmael over to one of the windows. Despite the cold, she'd opened it so the two of them could stand on the balcony overlooking the narrow

rio. She began pointing out the landmarks across the water on the Giudecca where lights twinkled invitingly in the darkness. 'That's the Rendentore,' Chiara was explaining, 'a church built by Palladio to celebrate the end of the plague in 1576. Redentore means redeemer. And over there,' she said, warming to her theme and glancing up at Ishmael, 'is the Mulino Stucky.' Lydia caught the soft, lost smile on Chiara's face and the dazzling one Ishmael gave her in return. Almost imperceptibly, the gap closed between them.

Lydia left them to their mutual absorption and hobbled out to the kitchen. She needed time alone. Time to think what the consequences of this evening might be.

'Lydia,' whispered Chiara, 'what on earth's the matter with you? Don't you like him?' Chiara had now joined Lydia in the kitchen, giving Ishmael some privacy to take a call on his mobile.

'Don't be silly, I like him very much. He's an engaging young man.'

'So why all the dramatics earlier? As he said himself, you looked like you'd seen a ghost.'

Lydia had often stretched or skirted round the truth when she thought the occasion warranted it, but never had she told a full-blown lie to Chiara. Now, though, she wanted to lie until she was blue in the face. 'He reminds me of someone I used to know,' she said. 'That's all.'

'Really? Who?'

'Oh, just someone.'

'Is that why you asked what his surname was? To see if there was a connection?'

'My, you are sharp today.'

Chiara threw her arms in the air. 'Sharp? *Stai scherzando!* You're kidding! A deaf, one-eyed drunk would have noticed your reaction. I can't begin to think what Ishmael must have thought of you.'

'I doubt he noticed. He's much more interested in you than—'

'Sorry about that.'

They both spun round to see Ishmael standing in the doorway; he was slipping his mobile into his pocket. 'It was my mother,' he said, 'checking that I was wearing clean underpants.'

Once again the unexpected sight of him caused Lydia a moment's alarm. She laughed politely at his joke but was concerned by the frown on Chiara's face.

'*Ti vedrò più tardi*,' Chiara muttered under her breath, with more than a hint of Wait-till-I-get-you-home to her tone. '*Parleremo*.' To Ishmael, in English, she said, 'Ready?'

'*Sì*,' he replied. 'But I wish you'd speak to me in Italian. It's why I'm here, don't forget.'

From the sitting room window, Lydia watched Chiara and Ishmael walk along the *fondamenta* in the direction of the Zattere. They'd known one another for no more than a few days, but already she could see by the way they shared their umbrella, their heads inclined towards each other, their pace evenly matched and Ishmael's hand at the small of Chiara's back, that they looked like a couple who'd been together for some time. There was a comfortable ease about them that Lydia knew all too well. She sighed and leaned her forehead against the cold glass. Why was he here? What had brought him to Venice? There were any number of language schools in Italy he could have attended; what was so special about the institute in Campo Santa Margherita?

She drew the curtains and chided herself for her paranoia. It was obvious why he'd come here. Venice was one of the most beautiful places in the world. Millions of visitors descended on the small city every year, far outnumbering its 62,000 inhabitants. For all she knew, Noah may well have been one of these tourists; she could have passed him in a *calle* and never known it. She shook her head. Inconceivable. She would have known he was there. She would have felt his presence as keenly as a pinprick.

Standing in the middle of the room, she wondered what to do next. What would best settle and calm her mind? Some work?

Who was she fooling? How could she contemplate working when she had just met Noah's son?

It was risky, given the state of her ankle, but unable to stop herself, she lifted the latch on the door of the store cupboard in the hall and hauled an aluminium stepladder out from the junk. She hobbled slowly to her bedroom, positioned the ladder in front of the built-in wardrobes, and, letting her crutch drop to the floor, made her way painfully up the steps.

Steely determination finally got her to the top, and perspiring and aching, she rewarded herself with a short rest, carefully shifting her balance so as not to put too much strain on her ankle. There were three locker-style cupboards in all, and opening the middle one she prayed that she'd made the right choice, that her memory hadn't failed her. She had to stretch to reach all the way inside the cupboard, and her hands fumbling blindly, she pushed aside a plethora of old handbags, scarves, hats, belts, coat hangers, and unwanted gifts of table linen. Finally her fingers touched what she was hunting for.

With the wooden box tucked under her arm, she descended the stepladder with excruciating care. She was exhausted when she reached the bottom and sat gratefully on the edge of the bed, the olive wood box on her lap. When she'd caught her breath, she ran her hands over its carved surface, released the two small brass clasps and lifted the lid; it swung smoothly on its hinges.

She removed the protective layer of discoloured tissue paper and put it to one side. The first item she picked out was a cheap tarnished powder compact. She pressed the catch on it at the front and the top flipped open. It was more than forty years old but the smell that escaped was instantly evocative of Lydia's mother. She snapped it shut and moved on to the next item, a long thin jewellery case

covered in faded dark blue velvet. Inside, nestling in the folds of white silk, was a necklace, a single pearl hanging like a tear from a delicate silver chain. Next was a slim leatherbound book of poetry – *The Complete Works of Christina Rossetti*. All that now remained in the wooden box was a ripped and battered manila envelope. She put the box on the bed and tipped the contents of the envelope onto her lap.

The first photograph she looked at was a small black and white snap of her parents. Her mother was wearing a pair of white-framed Jackie Onassis-style sunglasses and her hair was backcombed to resemble a cloud of candy-floss. Her father was in his shirtsleeves and had one arm round his wife's belted waist.

The next photo was of Lydia sitting on a doorstep. For such a young child she had surprisingly thick, bushy hair and a pair of dark eyebrows that almost met in the middle. With her lips pressed tightly together, her chin jutting forward as she squinted into the lens, her face was stormy. She was an odd-looking child, the kind of child people didn't always warm to. Cradled in her arms was a much prettier little girl: Lydia's baby sister, Valerie. Valerie was too busy chewing on the foot of a doll that was almost the same size as her to be concerned about the camera.

The remaining photographs were in colour, the smaller of the two showing a pair of grinning teenagers – Lydia and Noah – larking about for the camera. They were in a kitchen, wearing saucepans on their heads.

Lastly there was a picture of Noah on his own and of all the photographs, this was the one in the worst condition. Every crease and rip reminded Lydia that for a while she hadn't let it out of her sight; she had carried it with her everywhere she went, tucked inside a pocket, or sometimes hidden within her bra for fear of losing it. She turned it over. The ink was faded, but she could still make out the shape of a heart and the single word written within it: Noah. She turned it over again and tilted the photograph to catch the light so she could see it more clearly. And yes,

her memory hadn't played a trick on her; Ishmael's face could be perfectly superimposed on Noah's. She stared at the fineness of his features, the introspective intensity of his gaze, the suggestion of a smile concealed beneath the solemnity of his expression. She recalled the day she'd taken the photo. A day, like so many, when they had sworn nothing would ever part them.

But part they did.

One by one she spread the pictures out on the bed, and though it had been a golden rule never to do so, she allowed herself to think of all that she had lost. When tempted to do this in the past, knowing that it would only leave her feeling hollow and bereft, she had resisted the urge by bringing to mind everything she had gained instead – Marcello and Chiara, and the love and support of the Scalatore family. She was lucky, she always reminded herself.

But today was different. Today the golden rule was irrelevant. She felt like the game was up and she could finally give in to the profound sense of loss that had haunted her for most of her adult life. But mixed in with the pain was a new emotion – the cruel sting of jealousy and betrayal. Noah had led a life without her. He had married. He had had a son. All without her. She was being irrational, she knew. What else was he supposed to have done?

Tears filled her eyes and the photographs swam and became blurred. Eventually she could no longer see them. Crying without restraint, she lay on the bed and pressed her face into the bedspread.

The sound of the intercom buzzing had her jumping off the bed. Too late she remembered her ankle and let out a loud yelp as a bolt of pain ripped through her.

The intercom buzzed again. She wiped her face with her hands and reached for her crutch to go and see who it was.

When she heard Fabio's cheerful voice asking if he could come up, she panicked. 'It's not really convenient at the

moment,' she said into the intercom, not wanting to be seen by anyone right now, 'I'm not feeling very well.'

'*Davvero?*' he said. 'I've just bumped into Chiara and she never said anything.'

'It's nothing serious.'

'In that case, and if it's not contagious, let me in and I'll pamper you for a couple of hours. I'm at a loose end; Paolo's deserted me and gone to Milan.'

Lydia knew it was useless to argue with Fabio.

'*Dio mio!*' he exclaimed, after he'd bounded up the four flights of stairs and she'd opened the door to him. 'You do look ill.' And then, '*Cara*, you've been crying, haven't you? What's wrong? What's happened?'

She opened her mouth to make a rush of denials, but all that came out was a strangled cry. Fresh tears were a blink away. She took a step back and instantly regretted it. Her ankle was throbbing with renewed vigour.

Without another word, in one impressive movement, Fabio lifted her off the floor and carried her through to the living room and set her gently on the sofa. He shrugged off his coat, tossed it onto a chair and knelt beside her.

'Of all the people to find me like this,' she said, 'why did it have to be you, Fabio? If it was anyone else, I'd be able to pull the wool over their eyes.'

'I think you rate your ability as an actress just a little too highly,' he said with a smile. 'Now while I decide what my line of attack will be to get to the bottom of what's upset you, why don't you tell me who the good-looking *ragazzo* is I just met with Chiara. Where's he sprung from? They make a handsome couple, don't you think?'

The connection was too great and once more, much to Lydia's mortification, she couldn't hold back the tears any longer. Aware that Fabio was looking helplessly around for a box of tissues, she said, 'My bedroom, next to the bed.'

It was only when he'd left the room that she realized her mistake: she stopped crying in an instant, picturing her bedroom – the open cupboard, the stepladder ... the photographs.

When he reappeared, he had a box of Kleenex in one hand and the photographs in the other. He passed her the tissues and while she blew her nose, he laid out the photographs on the coffee table in front of them as if he were about to play a game of patience. 'You should never have been on that stepladder,' he said, 'you could have hurt yourself.'

'I agree; it was very silly of me.'

'But I must say you look *bellissima* wearing the saucepan.' He smiled. Then pointed to the picture of Lydia holding Valerie. 'And is this you with the *piccolina*?'

She nodded.

'And these people?'

'My parents.'

'And if I didn't know better,' he said, 'I'd say this was the handsome *ragazzo* I've just been talking to with Chiara.' He turned and looked at her. 'You don't have to tell me if you don't want to, but is he your son? A child you've never told us about?'

She almost laughed. 'No! But I strongly suspect,' she indicated the picture of Noah, 'that he's the father of Chiara's new friend.'

'Without a doubt,' Fabio said. 'Did he mean something to you a long time ago?'

Lydia hesitated before replying. Did she really want this conversation to go any further? Or was it too late? In her heart she knew it was. Ishmael Solomon's presence here in Venice was a catalyst for something she couldn't stop. To lie now to Fabio would be plain stupid. 'Yes,' Lydia said. 'He meant everything to me. We thought we'd always be together.'

'What went wrong? Or was it just a case of two young sweethearts growing up and drifting apart?'

'Something like that.' It was the best answer she could give. To tell the truth was far too complicated. Moreover, even after all this time, she still felt that it was better that only she and Noah were the keepers of that particular truth. But what if Ishmael and Chiara became seriously

involved? What then? Could Lydia go on pretending that there was no history between Ishmael's father and herself? It would never work, because once it came out that she had deliberately concealed her relationship with Noah, Chiara would want to know what she had been hiding.

'Lydia,' Fabio said, 'you know I'd never force you to do anything against your will, but Marcello made me promise that if anything ever happened to him I would always be more than just a brother-in-law to you.'

'And you are. You've been the best friend I could have wished for.'

He suddenly looked serious. 'Marcello told me something I've never forgotten. He said he thought you'd spent all your life carrying an impossible burden. My brother was right, wasn't he? And it has something to do with these photographs you've kept hidden away all the time I've known you. Why don't you tell me what that burden is? That way I'd know I'd honoured my brother's wishes to take good care of you.'

That's not fair! Lydia wanted to scream. You can't use Marcello like that. All the same, she felt a chink in her resolve. And then another. Dear sweet Marcello. So caring and intuitive. 'I'm sorry, Fabio,' she rallied, 'I wouldn't know how to. I wouldn't even know where to start. It's such a long story.'

'I disagree. I think you know exactly where to start; you've probably written every word of it in your head a million times over.'

Lydia looked around her, comparing the elegant charm of her home here with its silk damask wall coverings, antique furniture and ornate Murano glass chandeliers to the stark, loveless house in which she'd grown up, the very walls of which had been permeated with hatred and tension. She shivered, feeling the chill as if she were back there now.

She felt Fabio's hand on her arm and knew that if there was one person in the world she could trust, it was him.

31

THEN

Chapter Five

Lydia always blamed herself. If she hadn't pestered her mother for that ventriloquist's dummy none of it would have happened.

It all started when Diane Dixon's parents had given her one for being 'brave' when she'd had her tonsils out. Lydia didn't know what all the fuss was about – you were fast asleep when the doctor removed your tonsils and when you woke up you were allowed to eat nothing but ice-cream. What was so brave about that? When Diane was well enough to return to school, she brought the dummy in with her and they'd all crowded round to take a look at it. Its eyes moved from side to side and its mouth clunked open and shut with a jerky snap, depending on how well you operated the lever hidden in its back. Dressed in a smart red suit with a black bow tie and shiny black shoes, its legs and arms dangled loosely like lanky sausages from its hard body. Lydia didn't think Diane did the voice very well, especially when she tried to make it sing that silly song by The Beatles, something about them all living in a yellow submarine – but maybe that was because Diane didn't have her tonsils any more. Lydia thought she could do a much better job.

With her ninth birthday coming up, Lydia got to work on her mother, dropping hints and reminders whenever she could, saying how she'd give anything in the whole wide world to have a ventriloquist's dummy just like Diane Dixon's. Every time they went shopping she would make a point of lingering in front of the toyshop where Diane had said her parents had bought the dummy, and where

there was one actually displayed in the window, propped up in a box padded with tissue paper. She pointed it out to her mother and from then on whenever they passed the toyshop she would make sure there was always a reason to hang about and look in the window. She would suddenly notice that her shoelace needed tying, or that her sagging socks needed pulling up, and while she was crouched on the pavement she would will her mother to see the dummy looking out at them through the glass, its eyes wide and staring, just begging to be taken home with them.

Home now was a flat in Mr Ridley's house. Lydia didn't like Mr Ridley; he had a weird way of looking at her mother, like he was hungry. He was always licking his lips. He came upstairs to their flat nearly every day saying that he had to make sure everything worked. 'There!' he'd say, as he fiddled with the bath tap. 'I guessed as much: it needs a new washer.' He seemed very concerned that nothing should ever leak – gas or water – and regularly checked for anything that might be faulty. He said he would be failing in his duty as a landlord if he didn't take good care of his tenants. 'And your mother's a very special tenant,' he told Lydia one day when Mum was at the doctor's and Mr Ridley had offered to watch Lydia and her sister while she was gone. 'It's not right that your mum's all alone,' he said, poking around at the back of the electric fire in the lounge, his enormous bottom sticking up in the air.

'She's not alone,' Lydia said indignantly, tempted to give him a kick up the bum, 'she's got me and Valerie.'

'Children are all very well, but what she needs is a man.'

It was when Mr Ridley – Creepy-Ridley, as Lydia secretly called him – said things like that, that she wished her father was still alive. Before he died they'd lived in a pretty house with a garden and a small fishpond which one day her father had covered with green netting. 'We don't want your baby sister falling in, do we?' he said.

'Didn't you worry that I might fall in when I was a

baby?' Lydia had asked him. Babies got all the attention, she was fast learning.

'We didn't live here when you were a baby.'

Babies were dull, in Lydia's opinion. Valerie did nothing more exciting than lie in her cot making funny squawking noises when she wanted her bottle. It was difficult to imagine her getting down the stairs and out to the garden and fishpond when she couldn't even crawl to the end of her cot. Everyone had told Lydia it would be fun having a baby sister. Well, it wasn't.

Their father was killed when a lorry drove into him and knocked him off his motorbike on his way to work. It was raining and the lorry driver said he hadn't seen him, and when he did, it was too late. Lydia had overheard the policewoman telling her mother all this from the top of the stairs. 'Is there anyone who could be with you, Mrs Turner?'

'No,' was her mother's faint reply. 'There's no one.'

It had never seemed odd to Lydia that her parents didn't have any friends or family, although she had once questioned her mother's insistence that they weren't to get too friendly with their neighbours. According to Mum, the last thing they needed was a street of busybodies knocking on the door every two minutes scrounging a bowl of sugar.

'Why would they ask for sugar?' Lydia had wanted to know. 'Why not something nicer, like biscuits or crisps?'

'It doesn't matter what they're asking for, it's so they can poke their noses into our business.'

'Your mum's a very private person,' Lydia's father had often told her, usually when she'd asked if a friend could come to play. He explained that it was because Mum had grown up in an orphanage. Her parents both died when she was very young and being constantly surrounded by other people had made her learn to keep herself to herself. 'Your mum doesn't like a lot of fuss, love.'

Dad had parents but Lydia had never even seen a photograph of them. For some reason Dad hadn't spoken to them since he'd married Mum.

The day after Dad died, the telephone rang and from her permanent position at the top of the stairs – where she could listen out for Valerie in her cot and her mother crying downstairs – Lydia listened to the one-sided conversation. To begin with Mum's voice was trembling with little choking sounds, but then suddenly she became cross, her words coming out loud and snappy. 'I just hope you're happy now. You wished your son dead when he married me, and now he is!' The phone was banged down hard.

Happy. Why would anyone be happy that Dad was dead?

A few days later, for the first time ever, Lydia and Valerie got to go inside a neighbour's house. It was the day of Dad's funeral and Mum had said Lydia and her sister couldn't go with her, and that Mrs Marsh next door had offered to look after them. Mrs Marsh was nice. After she'd settled Valerie in her pram outside by the back door for some fresh air, she tied a frilly apron around her waist and told Lydia they were going to do some baking. She didn't seem at all the kind of person Mum had warned her about, the sort of scrounging, nosy parker who would want to know everything about them.

Lydia was disappointed when Mum arrived to take her and Valerie home: Mrs Marsh had just sat her down at the kitchen table with a cup of milky tea and an iced fairy cake. Mrs Marsh offered Mum a cup of tea but Mum shook her head. 'Well, how about taking some of these cakes with you?' Mrs Marsh asked.

'No thank you.' Mum's voice was clipped and short.

'If there's anything else I can ever do, you've only got to ask.'

'We'll be fine, thank you.'

'Suit yourself.' Now Mrs Marsh's voice sounded like Mum's.

From then on Mum was never the same. She began staying in bed until gone lunchtime, leaving Lydia to feed and change Valerie. When she did come downstairs she would lie on the settee in her nightdress staring up at the ceiling.

Luckily it was the summer holidays and Lydia could take care of her sister. With each day that passed she hoped her mother would get better, but she didn't.

Lydia missed her father so much it hurt deep inside her, but she also missed her mother. She missed her kisses, even the messy ones that left red lipstick on her cheek. She missed her mother's singing and the way she used to spend hours in front of the mirror doing her hair. To try and make Mum feel better, Lydia would kneel on the floor next to the settee and stroke her limp, dry hands, whispering to her that everything would be all right soon.

One morning when Lydia was standing on a chair in the garden hanging out the nappies she'd just washed in the kitchen sink, she heard voices. They were coming from the other side of the fence, from Mrs Marsh's garden. Lydia could hear Mrs Marsh saying that things were definitely sliding at number ten. Another woman's voice said, 'The curtains are pulled across for most of the day. She's probably gone to pieces.'

'But will she ask for help? Not on your Nellie! She's a stuck-up madam, for sure. Thinks she's so much better than the rest of us. It's the children I feel sorry for.'

'She was quick enough to leave them with you for the funeral, wasn't she?'

Lydia hurriedly finished pegging the last of Valerie's nappies on the line, but when she stepped down from the chair she saw that some of them were still dirty. Torn between needing clean, dry ones for Valerie, and giving something else to the neighbours to gossip about, she yanked the worst ones off the line and carried the chair back inside the house. She threw the nappies into the sink to wash again later and after making her mother a cup of tea in the hope it would encourage her to get out of bed, she went upstairs. Valerie was awake in her room and gurgling noisily like a bath emptying, but her mother was still asleep.

'I've brought you some tea, Mum,' Lydia said, putting the cup and saucer on the cluttered, dusty bedside table.

Her mother stirred but didn't open her eyes. Lydia was about to pull back the curtains and let some light in when she changed her mind. Instead she tiptoed over to the dressing table and, holding her breath, she pulled out her mother's purse from her handbag. Very quietly she opened it and took what she hoped would be enough.

Half an hour later, with Valerie sitting up in the pram with a crumbling pink wafer biscuit in her chubby hand, they set off for the shop. The pram was large and bouncy and Lydia could only just see over the top of it. Dad had always been telling her to eat more so that she'd grow big and strong.

She'd come top in her class for arithmetic at the end of term and so she had no trouble adding up the cost of things at the corner shop – some Cow and Gate milk powder for Valerie, a tin of Spam, a packet of Smash, a loaf of Mother's Pride, a pot of jam and a packet of strawberry-flavoured Angel Delight. She hovered by the bottles of drink but decided against a bottle of Tizer. Mum only let her have that on special occasions.

Mr Morris rang up the items on the till and placed them in the red string shopping bag Lydia had brought with her. 'All alone?' he asked after she'd handed over the money and was putting the shopping in the wire tray under the pram.

'No. My mother's at the post office.' The lie slid off her tongue like butter off hot toast.

'Give her my best wishes,' he said, and holding the door open for Lydia, added, 'and tell her I was sorry to hear about your dad.'

Lydia manoeuvred the pram out onto the street and was just thinking how men were always nicer to her mother than women were, when she realized she was almost level with the post office. She slowed her speed and, glancing back over her shoulder, she saw Mr Morris still standing at the door of his shop. She stopped the pram and made a conscious effort to look as if she was waiting for her mother.

There were many more days like that. They were the easy ones. By the start of the new autumn term, they were no longer living at number ten Larch Road. It was something to do with money. Just as Lydia had learned that babies got all the attention, she was now learning that money was the key to everything.

Their new home was Flat A, sixty-four Appleby Avenue. Number sixty-four was a large semi-detached house with a paved garden to the front and back, and the owner, Mr Ridley, had turned the upstairs part of the house into a flat. The day they moved in, he offered to help carry what little furniture they had upstairs. Lydia was so used to hearing her mother say, 'No thank you, we can manage on our own,' she was surprised to see her mother smile and say, 'Thank you, that's very kind of you.'

It didn't take them long to unpack; they had so little. Valerie's cot hadn't made the move with them and Lydia had to share her bed with her sister now, top and tail style. Even the big old pram that had been Mum's pride and joy had been sold and replaced with a second-hand pushchair that stank of sick until Lydia scrubbed it clean with disinfectant. Now it smelled like the toilets at school.

Back at school, everyone treated her differently. She heard them whispering about her in the dinner queue. Her best friend, Jackie, had also moved during the holidays, but to somewhere a long way away. She hadn't written to Lydia as she'd promised. There was no one to play with during break time and no one to talk to about what had happened during the summer. Instead she wrote it all out for their new teacher, Miss Flint, after she told the class that the best way for her to get to know them was to hear all about what they'd got up to during the holiday. So very carefully, as they'd been instructed, Lydia put that day's date – 4 September 1968 – at the top of the page of her brand new exercise book and didn't stop writing until Miss Flint told them to. But when it was Lydia's turn to go up to the front of the class and read out her work, Miss Flint's face turned red. 'Thank you, Lydia,' she interrupted,

even though Lydia had only read a tiny bit of what she'd written. 'That was ... yes, that was ... Goodness. Perhaps you'd like to sit down.'

The subject of money was seldom far from Lydia's thoughts. This was mainly down to her mother constantly reminding her that they didn't have any. 'Our situation has changed,' was a frequent remark, along with, 'We're poor now, Lydia, so please don't even think of asking me for anything trivial.' Bang went the new shoes Lydia desperately needed as well as the school trip to the swimming baths. 'Maybe school will let me go for free if we tell them we can't afford to pay for it,' Lydia had suggested. She received a sharp slap for her comment and was told that no one was to know they had no money. With what she thought was a flash of helpful brilliance, Lydia's next suggestion was: 'I know what the answer is! Why don't you try getting a job?' She was clearly missing something because her mother took another swipe at her.

It couldn't have been such a daft idea because shortly afterwards her mother announced that she'd found herself a job. The following Monday she would start work at the local off-licence. It was owned by a man called Mr Russell and Mum would have to work there from six o'clock until ten. 'Who's going to look after us while you're not here?' Lydia had asked.

'You're a big girl, Lydia; you don't need anyone looking after you.'

'I'm only eight.'

'You'll be nine in a few months' time. And anyway, Mr Ridley will be downstairs if there's a problem.'

Creepy-Ridley had dirty fingernails and was always running them through his greasy, dandruff-speckled hair. She wrinkled her nose at the thought of him. Her mother said, 'You could at least look pleased for me. After all, it was your idea for me to get a job.'

To begin with it was great with Mum going out to work. There were no more comments about being poor. No more cuffs around the ear. And best of all, Mum brought

home the occasional bottle of Tizer and packets of salted peanuts. She was looking much more like her old self, too. Her hair was done nicely and she'd started wearing perfume and make-up again, regularly opening and shutting her powder compact with a businesslike click. They even had a small turkey for Christmas and Lydia was allowed to decorate the plastic tree all on her own.

But then in the New Year, at the end of January 1969, it all went wrong. Lydia had just put Valerie to bed when she heard the front door slamming downstairs. She went to see what was going on. Peering over the banister, she saw Mum leaning back against the front door and then Creepy-Ridley appeared in the hall. Mum was crying.

'What's the matter, Bonnie?' Creepy-Ridley asked. Lydia hated it when he called Mum by her Christian name; it didn't seem right.

'I've been sacked.'

'Why?' Creepy-Ridley was now standing next to Mum.

Her crying got louder and Creepy-Ridley moved closer still. 'Women can be so spiteful,' she spluttered through her tears. 'Mr Russell's wife had no right saying those things to me. As if I'd want her husband! And now I won't be able to pay you this week's rent.'

Creepy-Ridley put his hand on Mum's arm. 'Now don't you go worrying your pretty head over a little thing like that. I'm sure we can come to some other arrangement.'

Chapter Six

Once again they were officially poor. Hardly a day passed without Mum burying her head in her hands and saying how shameful it was to be on the dole. 'Being on the dole' was a new phrase to Lydia and she couldn't understand what the fuss was all about. If someone was prepared to give Mum money for free, surely that was a good thing? Her mother was insistent that no one should ever know that she had to go to the Labour Exchange and stand in line with a lot of other people and wait patiently to be given a cheque which she could then exchange for real money at the post office so she could buy that week's food. When it was a dole day, she always wore her big sunglasses and a chiffon scarf tied under her chin to cover her hair.

Mum was constantly worried about what others thought of her. Every night she made Lydia spend twenty minutes polishing her school shoes. Apparently you could tell a lot from someone's shoes. Especially if they weren't polished. Mum said people would think she didn't care about Lydia if she couldn't see her face in them. Lydia would have preferred a dirty, scuffed pair of shoes that fitted her properly to the gleaming pair that pinched and squashed her toes, but she kept her head down and her hand busy with the polishing brush.

Occasionally Mum took time out from worrying about the state of Lydia's shoes and lay in bed claiming she couldn't get up because the sleeping pills the doctor had given her made her feel too groggy. And if she wasn't groggy from the pills, she had what she called one of her thundery headaches coming on. Then one day she started

to smell different. Whenever Lydia got close to her mother, her breath reminded Lydia of happier times, when there was something special to celebrate, and Mum used to have a glass of sherry and Dad always had what he called a tot of whiskey. But what was Mum celebrating on her own when Lydia was at school?

It did at least mean that her mother was often in a better mood. When it was a Good Mood Day, Lydia would come home from school to be given a handful of loose change and told to run down to the chip shop for their tea. Other treats began creeping into their lives, like Arctic roll for pudding, or trips to the sweet shop where Lydia could spend as long as she liked choosing from the glass jars of pink shrimps, white sugar mice, traffic light gobstoppers and mint humbugs. She was allowed to stay up late too, so long as she was quiet while Mum listened to her Engelbert Humperdinck records – 'Please Release Me', 'There Goes My Everything', and 'The Last Waltz' played over and over. Sometimes, if Mum was in a really happy mood, she would make Lydia dance with her, twirling her round the small room, not caring about the furniture and saying that very soon their uppsy-downsy life would all be sorted out. She would hug and kiss Lydia goodnight, reassuring her that their luck was about to change. With her mother's sweet sherry breath making Lydia's eyes water, she wanted desperately to believe that this was true.

It was during a week of late-night Engelbert Humperdinck sessions that Lydia decided she wasn't getting anywhere with her hints about the ventriloquist's dummy. Her birthday was only a few days away; the time had come for her to catch her mother in one of her 'good moods' and ask her outright for the present. Now seemed as good a moment as any – Mum had just been downstairs to the dustbin with an empty bottle and she was now coming in to kiss Lydia and Valerie goodnight. Humming to herself, she sat down heavily on the bed, not noticing that she was crushing Lydia's feet. Lydia tried to slide her feet out from under her mother's bottom without her noticing. 'Mum,

you know it's my birthday on Friday? Well, I was just wondering if you'd remembered what it was I said I really, *really* wanted.'

She must have totally misjudged her mother's mood because suddenly Mum was slumped forward, her head in her hands and crying. 'How can you ask for a present when we don't have any money?' she cried. 'How can you be so selfish?'

'But I thought we had money. I thought the dole money—'

'It's not enough!' her mother shouted at her. She then jumped off the bed, her arms wrapped around herself. 'And if you really want to know, there's nothing left in my purse and there won't be any more until next week.' She shuddered and sniffed.

Lydia wriggled her toes, confused. Where was all the money going? At the other end of the bed, sensing the change in atmosphere, Valerie had also started to cry.

Mum whipped round on Lydia. 'Now see what you've done!'

Lydia was horrified. Was she selfish? Was it wrong of her to want a present for her birthday?

An hour later when Valerie was sleeping soundly, Lydia heard the bedroom door creak open: light flooded in. 'Are you awake, Lydia?'

Lydia closed her eyes and lay very still.

'Lydia?'

She opened her eyes. Maybe her mother was going to apologize and say that somehow she'd find the money for a present. 'Yes, Mum?' she whispered.

Her mother came in and stood next to the bed. 'Don't be cross with me,' she said. Her voice was thin and wobbly. 'You know how difficult it is for me. Why don't we pretend your birthday's next month? I'll save up some money and buy you whatever you want. How does that sound?'

Lydia said nothing. She simply stared at her mother and thought of all those sherry bottles rattling around in the dustbin downstairs.

The next day when Lydia was walking home from school she stopped to look in the window of the toy shop. Her heart sank. The ventriloquist's dummy had gone. It had been there in the morning, but now in its place was an enormous blonde-haired doll in a shiny pink dress with a yellow sash tied around its waist.

Lydia pushed open the door, setting off the tinkling bell, and went inside. 'Do you have any more ventriloquist's dummies?' she asked the woman behind the counter.

'I'm afraid not. I sold the last one this afternoon. I was glad to see it go, to be honest. We had it in the window gathering dust for weeks. What about a nice dolly?'

A nice dolly? Dolls were for babies! Disgusted that she'd been mistaken for a baby, and furious that there was no hope now of her having what she wanted for her birthday, Lydia stomped home, her satchel banging against her hip. She was about to dig under her school shirt for the door key she wore round her neck on a piece of string, when she saw the dustbins beneath Creepy-Ridley's front window. She glanced up at the top window, then back to the dustbin.

Minutes passed.

Then, throwing her satchel to the ground, she lifted off the lid of their bin, the one with '64a' painted on it. The rubbish stank, but she didn't care. She rummaged through it until she had everything she wanted and when she was finished, she put the lid back on the bin and let herself into the house. From the other side of Creepy-Ridley's door she could hear him speaking on the telephone.

Upstairs, Valerie was asleep on the settee, her thumb tucked inside her mouth, her tongue and cheeks moving rhythmically.

'Is that you, Lydia?' The question coincided with the closing of a cupboard door. With new understanding, Lydia recognized it as a guilty sound and one she'd heard for several months now every afternoon when she'd come home from school.

Her mother appeared in the doorway of the lounge, one hand smoothing her hair, the other covering her mouth. 'How was school today?' she asked.

'I want to show you something,' Lydia said.

'Oh, something you made at school?'

'No. Come with me. It's downstairs.'

'How mysterious you are. Is it a surprise for me?'

Just you wait, Lydia thought nastily. She opened the front door and stepped outside ahead of her mother. She wanted to be able to look back and see the expression on her face. 'There,' she said, 'that's the reason you won't let me have my birthday on the proper day.'

Her mother gasped, then made a strange whimpering sound. But Lydia ignored her. Months and months of keeping her feelings to herself, of missing Dad, and of not saying anything in case she upset her mother, suddenly exploded inside her. 'That's why you wouldn't buy me the only present I ever really wanted,' she screamed. 'I hate you and I wish it was you who'd died and not Dad!' She kicked out at the row of sherry bottles she'd carefully lined up and sent them flying; three of them crashed against the brick wall, and the rest toppled and spun on their sides.

For a split second she was frightened at what she'd said and done. She felt her stomach drop to her knees. As she looked at her mother's shocked face, a tremor ran through her and her breath came out with a shudder. But there was no undoing what had happened and all she could think to do was to run; run from that look on her mother's face. She took to her heels and sprinted down the road. She didn't know where she was going, only that she could never go home again. Never! With tears nearly blinding her, she felt the pain of bottling up all the hurt of wanting Dad to be alive again. Why did he have to die?

She did go home, though, when it got dark and started to rain and her rumbling tummy wouldn't stop reminding her that she hadn't had any tea. She didn't like the way

people were staring at her either, probably wondering why she was out so late.

She quietly closed the front door behind her and bumped straight into Creepy-Ridley coming down the stairs. He was smirking and hitching up his trousers. He looked very pleased with himself. He'd probably been fixing something in the flat again. 'Like a bad penny you've turned up, then?' he said.

Mum was already in her nightdress and shabby old candlewick dressing gown when Lydia let herself in. Funny, Mum didn't usually get ready for bed this early. She was shredding a tissue, letting the pieces drop onto the carpet at her feet. Once again Lydia felt guilty at what she'd done. 'I'm sorry, Mum,' she said.

'So am I,' her mother said tightly. 'More sorry than you'll ever know. I just hope that one day you'll realize what I've done for you and understand how hard it's been for me.'

It's always about her, Lydia thought when she was lying safe and warm in bed with Valerie. Why didn't her mother ever think that it was difficult for her too?

On the morning of her ninth birthday, despite knowing the day wouldn't be any more special than any other, Lydia woke with a sense of anticipation. She couldn't help herself. It was habit. Dad had always made such a big thing of birthdays; he said they were something to enjoy and celebrate. Thinking of her father made her instantly sad. How different their lives were since her last birthday when she'd been eight and Val wasn't yet two. Dad had been alive then and they were living in their lovely house. Everything had been lovely. Now everything was horrible.

Valerie was already out of bed and playing on the floor with Lydia's satchel, the contents of which now lay scattered over the small threadbare rug. She beamed proudly at Lydia, a pencil sticking out of her mouth. Lydia tried to look sternly back at her but found she couldn't. Not

with Val smiling at her like that. She gathered everything together, put on her school uniform and took Valerie through to the kitchen where she sat her in her highchair. For once Mum could change Valerie's first nappy of the day. She would be glad when her sister was properly potty trained. She was sure she hadn't still been in nappies at this age. Within minutes Valerie was protesting, and as if sensing she was being used to get even with their mother, she started to wriggle and cry, her face puckered like an old lady's.

'Oh, all right,' Lydia relented. Ten minutes later, the soaking wet nappy had been replaced. Lydia hadn't been able to find any clean ones so she'd used a hand towel from the kitchen drawer. She wasn't bothered what Mum would say. If she couldn't get out of bed today of all days, then why should Lydia care about anything?

She'd just got Valerie settled back in her highchair and put two slices of bread under the grill when Mum shuffled into the kitchen. She wasn't dressed, but in her hands was a large, badly wrapped box; there was a gap on one side where the paper edges didn't quite meet. 'Happy birthday, Lydia,' she said.

Lydia didn't know what to say. Perhaps she was dreaming. Any minute she would wake and the day would begin again. Yet she knew she wasn't dreaming and what's more, she was sure she knew what was in the box. She would know its shape and size anywhere. She felt her face burn with shame and regret. How could she have doubted her mother? How could she have been so mean to her?

'Don't you want it?' prompted her mother.

'I thought we didn't have any money,' Lydia murmured awkwardly.

After a pause, during which Lydia noticed her mother was looking anywhere but at her, she said, 'You have Mr Ridley to thank. He ... gave me the money.' She held out the present. 'Take it, then.'

Lydia didn't hesitate. She didn't care where the money came from, so long as she finally had what she'd been

wanting all this time. 'Thank you,' she said, remembering her manners. She placed the box on the table and picked at the sticky tape carefully. She never frantically ripped presents open; she liked to take her time, to make the moment last as long as possible.

But when she had the paper off she could have cried. It wasn't the ventriloquist's dummy – it was the ugly blonde-haired doll she'd seen in the toy shop window the other day.

From behind her came the smell of burning toast.

Chapter Seven

It was the summer school holidays and they'd spent the afternoon at Dad's grave. It was exactly a year since Dad had been knocked off his motorbike. Mum cried for most of the bus ride home and then went to bed. It was only six o'clock, but she said she had a headache. Which meant Lydia and Valerie had to be quiet. Valerie was three now and while she wasn't much of a talker – she was more of a watcher – she could kick up a right storm with the pots and pans in the kitchen. Turn your back for two seconds and she'd have the cupboard door open and would be crashing saucepan lids together like cymbals. So while their mother slept off her headache, Lydia didn't dare let Val out of her sight. She kept her occupied with jam sandwiches, a bath, and a very long bedtime story before she finally snuggled her down under the bedclothes with Belinda Bell. Belinda Bell was the ugly doll Mum had bought for Lydia on her birthday; Val had claimed it for herself and rarely went anywhere without it now.

Lydia didn't know how long she herself had been asleep in bed when she was woken by a noise. She sat up, expecting it to be Valerie wanting to be taken to the toilet. She peered into the darkness but at the other end of the bed, Valerie was sleeping soundly. No sooner had she put her head back down on the pillow when she heard the noise again. It was somebody singing. Mum? Lydia sat up again and listened properly. The singing stopped abruptly and the door opened. No light flooded in, but Lydia could just about make out her mother in the darkness. She was still dressed in the clothes she'd worn during the day, but for

some strange reason she was wearing her sunglasses and chiffon scarf.

'I want you both to come with me,' her mother whispered urgently.

'Why? Where are you going?'

'Don't argue with me, Lydia. Not today of all days.'

When Lydia started reaching for her clothes on the floor by the side of the bed, her mother said, 'Don't bother getting dressed; there isn't time. Just put your shoes on and a cardigan over your nightie.'

At her mother's impatient insistence, Lydia then carried a still sleeping Valerie downstairs and tucked her into the pushchair with a blanket.

Her mother quietly unlocked the front door and they stepped outside. The road was quiet; nobody was about. In the light cast from the street lamp, Lydia looked at her watch to see what time it was: it was ten minutes past one in the morning.

'Come on,' her mother whispered. Her breath was sticky sweet. Sherry.

'But where are we going?'

'You'll see.'

'Is it far?'

Without answering her, her mother set off down the road, her high heels clicking in the silence. Lydia chased after her with the pushchair.

They'd been walking for what felt like for ever. A few cars had passed them and one had actually slowed down and the driver had stared hard at Lydia as she ran to keep up with her mother. They were now in an area that Lydia didn't recognize, but at least Mum wasn't walking so fast. Instead she was singing again and making herself angry because she kept getting the words to 'Please Release Me' all muddled up. Each time she got it wrong she would stamp her foot and go back to the beginning and start again. If Lydia hadn't been so jumpy with apprehension, she would have sung along to help her mother.

There were no street lights and the only houses were

set miles back from the road. It was difficult to see where they were going; several times she'd come close to losing Valerie in a ditch. Worry had now turned to fear. What if they got lost and couldn't find their way home?

When they came to what looked like a small bridge, Mum stopped unexpectedly. 'We're here.' She spoke as if suddenly everything made sense, and pushed through a gap in the hedge. Nearly losing control of the pushchair, Lydia found herself sliding down a slope, brambles and twigs scratching at her legs as she tried to stay upright. Oblivious to her daughter's struggle, her mother waited for her at the bottom of the slope. Dizzy with exhaustion, Lydia was close to tears. Why was her mother doing this? Why couldn't she be normal like other mothers?

'Please, Mum, can we sit down for a while and then go home?' she asked.

'Oh, do stop whingeing, Lydia. We're having an adventure. Don't you want an adventure you'll always remember?'

'Y-es,' she said uncertainly, 'but why here?'

'Don't you think it's pretty?'

Lydia looked around her doubtfully. 'It's too dark to see anything.'

Her mother started to poke the grass with her foot as though she was looking for something. 'Your father and I used to come here before you were born. We would lie here and stare up at the stars. Come on, let's do the same.'

Beginning to shiver with the cold, but glad of the chance to rest, Lydia lay in the cushiony, damp grass alongside her mother. Within seconds she felt herself drifting off to sleep, but then a hand was shaking her roughly. 'Look,' Mum said, sitting up beside her now. 'I bought you your favourite, a Marathon bar. It is your favourite, isn't it?'

'Yes, Mum,' Lydia said sleepily, 'it is. Thank you.'

'Aren't you going to eat it?'

Lydia unwrapped the slightly squashed chocolate bar and took a bite. She then offered it to her mother.

Her mother shook her head. 'It's for you. Eat it up.

When Valerie wakes, I've got some chocolate buttons for her.' She took off her sunglasses and worked at the knot of her scarf. She must have done it too tight because she gave up on it. Chewing on a mouthful of chocolate and peanuts and watching her mother staring up at the sky, Lydia wondered how she had managed to find her way here in the dark with those silly glasses on.

'Isn't the sky beautiful?' Mum's voice was suddenly soft. So was her face. Lydia thought how young and pretty she was. She wished that she might be as pretty one day. That people would turn and stare at her the way they did with Mum. Or the way they used to. Recently she'd noticed people often looked away. 'It's like it goes on for ever and ever,' Mum murmured, her face still turned up towards the sky. 'Your father used to tell me that if you have a problem, you shouldn't keep it to yourself; you should tell it to the skies. I want you to promise me something, Lydia.'

Lydia didn't like it when her mother asked her to make promises – they were usually impossible to keep.

'It's important that you remember this moment and what I'm about to say. You must promise you'll always look after your sister for me. Do you promise?'

With her eyelids feeling so heavy nothing in the world would keep them open, and the warm, dreamy sensation of sleep wrapping itself around her, Lydia murmured that of course she would take care of Val. It was an easy promise to keep. Hadn't she been doing exactly that ever since Dad died?

'And something else I want you to remember—'

But Lydia didn't hear what else she was supposed to remember. She was dreaming of Dad. He was carrying her off into the dark night sky, above the trees, over the roof tops and chimney pots, flying higher and higher. He was telling her everything would be all right now. 'Just tell it to the skies, Lydia, and everything will be all right.' It was good to be in his arms again. She felt so safe and happy.

*

Lydia read about it in the newspaper. Nobody knew that she had – they thought they'd hidden the papers – but she'd found one and had read it so many times she could have recited it from memory.

A *twenty-seven-year-old mother of two, not long since widowed, threw herself in front of a train whilst her children slept on the embankment.*

The train driver, a father of two children himself and from Crewe, who wishes to remain anonymous, said there was nothing he could do. 'There was no way I could avoid hitting her,' he said of the tragedy, which took place shortly before five a.m. and approximately two miles from Maywood station. 'I don't think I'll ever get over what happened,' he further added. 'It was horrific.'

It is believed the woman, Mrs Bonnie Turner, of 64a Appleby Avenue, Maywood, had never recovered from the death of her husband, who died in a motorcycle accident a year ago. Neighbours claim that her mental state had been unbalanced for some time before she took her life.

Her mother would have hated for everyone to read about her this way. Lydia hated it too. But then there was so much for her to hate now. Like the people in the children's home who wouldn't listen when she told them she and Valerie didn't need to be there, that they could manage perfectly well on their own back at the flat. She had tried to explain to them that she was perfectly capable of taking care of her sister. But they kept saying she and Valerie couldn't live on their own, that it wasn't allowed; it was against the law. 'And what about school?' they asked. How would she go to school *and* look after Val? And who was going to pay the rent?

Sitting in the back of the car with Valerie and Belinda Bell on her lap – two women from the children's home in the front – Lydia stared out of the car window, watch-

ing the blurry scenery fly by. They were on their way to a place called Swallowsdale in Yorkshire. It was where Dad's parents lived and it was to be their new home. She had read stories about children losing their parents and going to live with complete strangers. They always ended up having exciting adventures.

She rammed her clenched fists against her eyes, remembering her mother's words: 'Don't you want an adventure you'll always remember?'

Chapter Eight

She was sure she had only slept for a few minutes but when Lydia opened her eyes, she awoke to a completely different world. They must have travelled an unimaginable distance. She had never seen anything like it. There was so much of it. Emptiness. Miles of it. It went on and on as far as she could see, nothing but sloping green fields criss-crossed with funny walls that didn't look as if they'd been made properly. They weren't made of bricks like normal walls; they were made of dirty grey stones. Some of the fields had sheep in them. She pointed them out to Valerie, but Valerie wasn't interested; she was clinging to Lydia, her warm, flushed face pushed against Lydia's neck, her mouth making a cool damp patch on her skin.

The road they were driving along kept on twisting this way and that. It went up and down too; it was a bit like that time Dad took her on a ride at the funfair. She'd been sick afterwards. She hoped she wouldn't be ill when they arrived at their grandparents' house.

She closed her eyes and listened to the two women talking in the front: one was telling the other they were almost there. Lydia always made a point of listening hard to other people's conversations now. It was the only way she could find out what was going on. She'd discovered that Dad's parents didn't really want to have Lydia and Valerie living with them. Well, join the club! Lydia didn't want to live with them either. Not if they were the kind of people who could be happy that Dad was dead. She fought the aching tightness in her throat. She would not cry. Not when she knew it would upset Valerie.

She opened her eyes and concentrated on looking at the passing scenery. It had changed. The fields were sort of grubby and patchy and the walls were tumbling down in places. It didn't look a friendly place. In the distance, crouched like a black cat in a hollow, she could see what looked like a town. The buildings all seemed to have been built higgledy-piggledy. Five tall, blackened chimneys puffed out smoke into a dreary grey sky. There was a church slap bang in the middle of the chimneys and its spire looked as though it should have been smoking too. Further into the distance, the ground rose up into a hill that seemed to watch over the town disapprovingly. Dotted across the hillside were clumps of trees and houses, and more of those funny walls. As the car dipped down towards the town, Lydia saw a sign on the side of the road: Swallowsdale.

They came to a stop in front of a house that stood at the end of a long row of terraced houses. Every one of them seemed to have been built with the same sooty stones the rickety walls in the fields had been made with. Hadn't they heard of bricks here? Behind the row of houses was a bump of a hill.

Lydia stared at the house they were parked in front of. It seemed to be bigger than all the others. A twitch of net curtain at one of the downstairs windows made Lydia's stomach churn.

'Well then,' said the woman in the front passenger seat in a stupidly jolly voice, 'here we are.' In the last couple of weeks Lydia had noticed that grown-ups had an irritating habit of stating the obvious when they were nervous and didn't know what else to say.

The front door was opened by a skinny woman with hair the colour of a grey, rainy day. It was scraped back from her pale face into a scruffy bun. Pin-prick eyes skimmed over Lydia and her sister. 'You're later than I was told to expect you,' she said, her hands crossed in front of her.

'Yes, we're sorry about that, Mrs Turner,' said the

woman who had driven them here. 'It took us longer than we thought it would.' She held out her hand. 'I'm Janet and this is my colleague, Deirdre. And of course, these are your grandchildren, Lydia and Valerie.'

Once more Lydia felt the pin-prick eyes skim over her and Val. Lydia suspected they were the kind of eyes that missed nothing.

They were shown through to the lounge. For a few moments no one seemed to know what to say, then Deirdre suggested that 'the girls' might like a drink of orange juice after the long journey.

Their grandmother pursed her lips. 'We don't throw money away on extravagances like orange juice in this house,' she said, 'not when the good Lord provided us with water to drink.'

'I'm sure water will be fine, Mrs Turner.'

Lydia caught the two women exchanging glances when they were left alone. As well as listening to grown-ups, Lydia now made it her business to watch them closely.

'Well then,' Janet said. 'This is nice, isn't it, Lydia? What do you think of your new home?'

Lydia looked round the gloomy room. Cold. Dull. Miserable. Plain. Those were the words that described it best. There was nothing nice to look at, not in this room anyway, just two brown upright armchairs either side of the fireplace, a small brown upright settee that Janet and Deirdre were sitting on and a glass-fronted bookcase that was almost empty. On top of this was a wooden cross and the largest book Lydia had ever seen. The floor was covered with a sludgy green carpet. There was no television in the room, no record player, no ornaments, no pictures. Nothing like the cheerful things Mum used to treasure – her red balloon glass vase, her picture of the gypsy woman playing the guitar, and her collection of Engelbert Humperdinck records. She wondered what these people did in the evening if they didn't watch the television. Without answering Janet's question, she said, 'What do I call them?'

'Who, Lydia?'

'Mr and Mrs Turner. My father's parents. My grand-parents.'

The two women exchanged another look. 'That's prob-ably best sorted out between you and them after we've gone,' Deirdre said.

Lydia went over to the window. She lifted the net cur-tain and stared out at the small front garden. She hadn't noticed much about it between the car and the front door, but now she saw that everything was extremely neat and tidy. A thin border of blue and white flowers ran up either side of the short path. Two circular beds, each with red roses in them, were edged with orange marigolds. Here at least was some colour, she thought. She didn't know why, but the sight of it made her want to rush out there and stamp on every single flower, crushing the petals till there was nothing left of them.

Mr Turner – their grandfather – appeared within minutes of Janet and Deirdre leaving. After a brief conversation with his wife in the kitchen, he returned to the lounge where Lydia and Val had been told to wait.

He instructed Lydia to stand in front of him, and loom-ing over her he stared down, examining her. Like his wife, he was grey-haired, but he wasn't anywhere near as thin as her. He was tall with big shoulders. He looked strong and powerful, like a giant. He had faded, unfriendly blue eyes and his hair, parted at the side, was oily and glued down close to his scalp. He didn't have a particularly big nose, but from where Lydia was standing, he had the biggest nostrils she had ever seen; great caverns of dark hairiness. How could such a horrible-looking man be her father's father? Dad had always had a smile on his face. He had been the kindest, funniest man she knew. This man was none of those things. He was cold. Cold as winter.

As his silent examination of her continued, she became conscious of her thick unbrushed hair, and her clothes that were rucked up from being in the car for so long. She

suddenly remembered her shoes. Not daring to lower her eyes, she couldn't recall when she'd last polished them. Mum would have been furious with her.

Taking her by surprise, the man bent down and pushed his face almost into hers. 'You look just like your mother,' he announced. He spat out the word 'mother' like it would leave a nasty taste in his mouth if he let it stay there for a second longer. It took all of Lydia's willpower not to shrink back from him. 'It remains to be seen if you've inherited her ungodly ways as well,' he added, straightening up. He clicked his fingers and waved her away dismissively, then turned his attention to Valerie, who was cowering behind Belinda Bell on the settee.

He made no comment on Val's appearance other than to clear his throat and tell them tea would be ready soon.

Tea was poached fish, boiled potatoes and cabbage. No one spoke during the entire meal, other than at the start when their grandfather bowed his head and thanked God for the food on the table. Before now, Lydia had only ever heard grace said at school. A clock on the mantelpiece ticked loudly in the unnerving silence. The fish was chewy and bland – not like the lovely cod in batter Lydia used to fetch from the chip shop – and the potatoes were rock hard and covered in something that could have been grass cuttings. What was wrong with chips? Or Smash? Afraid to leave anything on her plate, Lydia forced it down, at the same time trying to help Valerie feed herself. But Val was having none of it. Wobbling on her cushioned seat – there was no highchair for her – she kept her mouth tightly shut, only to open it finally to whisper to Lydia that she needed the toilet.

When the ordeal of tea was over, their grandmother showed them upstairs to their bedroom and told them to unpack their two small cases before putting themselves to bed. Left alone with Val, Lydia got on with the job straight away, but the sight of their few clothes hanging in the big

wardrobe that smelled of something not very nice made her see them with new eyes – they were old and worn, in tatters some of them. She knew what her grandmother would think when she saw them: that Mum hadn't been a good mother.

Was that what her grandfather had meant about 'ungodly ways'?

Chapter Nine

'It's *my* hair and you can't cut it if I won't let you.'

Lydia's grandfather came towards her, the scissors in his hand. 'Close the door, Irene. Let's get this over with.'

They were upstairs in the bedroom; Lydia and Valerie were still in their nightdresses. They'd only been awake a few minutes when the door had opened and their grandparents had come in and found them in bed together. 'But we always sleep together,' Lydia had begun to explain when their grandfather demanded to know what was going on. Ignoring her, he'd pulled back the sheet and blanket as though checking to see if there was anyone else in the bed: all he'd found was Belinda Bell. A woman at the children's home had tried to stop them from sleeping together, but after Val had made herself sick from crying so much, the woman had given in.

'Don't just sit there,' their grandfather had said. 'We haven't got all day.'

What had they done wrong? Had they slept too long? Only then had Lydia seen that her grandmother was holding a pair of scissors and a hairbrush. A cold shiver had run through her. She'd put a hand to her hair, which was wild and tangled after being in bed. She had forgotten to plait it the night before.

Their grandmother had stepped forward. 'I won't have you living under this roof running around like a couple of savages. Shorter hair will be easier to keep clean.'

'But I don't want my hair cut,' Lydia had said. 'I like my hair the way it is.' This wasn't exactly true. She never gave her hair a second thought; she couldn't remember

the last time she'd had it cut. Mum used to trim it when the mood took her, often giving her a fringe as jagged as crocodile teeth.

Her grandfather had sucked in air through his nose, then let it out slowly through his mouth.

'It's *my* hair and you can't cut it if I won't let you,' Lydia had asserted.

That was when her grandfather had taken the scissors from his wife and told her to close the door. 'One thing you're going to have to learn,' he said, addressing Lydia, 'is that what *you* want doesn't count. You're living in *our* house now and by *our* rules. If I say you're having your hair cut, that's exactly what's going to happen. Do I make myself clear?'

With the door now shut, Lydia knew there was no escape. With equal understanding, she realized that the best way to get through this was to act as if she didn't care. Her grandparents could do whatever they wanted and it wouldn't matter to her.

So she stood in the middle of the room, between the two single beds, deliberately facing the mirror on the dressing table so that she could watch her grandfather cut her hair, her chin jutting forward to prove that he didn't scare her. She didn't even flinch when he made the first cut level with the top of her ear and a long, thick hank of hair dropped to the floor. She gritted her teeth, her lips pressed tight, and stared hard at her reflection, telling herself that it didn't matter. It was only hair. She would grow it again one day. For Valerie's sake too, she would stay quiet and calm, as though everything was perfectly normal. Snip, snip, the scissors went. But not a flicker of movement did she make.

When her grandfather had finished and the floor all around her was covered in hair, he said, 'You still look more like a child of Satan than of God, but it's a start.'

I look like a boy, Lydia thought. An ugly, skinny boy. Everything about her face seemed bare and bigger. Her cheekbones were wider apart, her chin was pointier, her

eyes greener, her skin paler. Worst of all her eyebrows looked thicker and darker. She put a hand to the stubby tufts of coarse hair that were sticking up all over her head. She imagined the nicknames she would be taunted with. Hedgehog. Toilet brush. Coconut head.

She was so preoccupied with staring at her reflection – this new person that wasn't her – she didn't notice that behind her Valerie was now having her hair cut. 'No!' she cried, spinning round. 'Not Valerie!' But it was too late; her sister's lovely silky baby-blonde hair lay in wispy ribbons on the floor.

Lydia's heart slammed shut against these people. She had never hated anyone so much in her life.

Two things were decided during breakfast. The first was that Lydia and her sister were to call these hateful strangers Grandfather and Grandmother. Grandma was also allowed. But not Nanny, Nan, Granddad, Grandpa or Gramps. No reason was given. Just as no reason had been given when Lydia had referred to the lounge and was instantly reprimanded and told to call it the front room.

The second decision was that their grandmother was to take them shopping for some new clothes. This, at least, was something to look forward to.

They were instructed to wait at the bottom of the stairs while their grandmother got ready to take them into town. Their grandfather had already left the house to go and do God's work. Lydia didn't have a clue what that meant. Was there an office nearby where her grandfather sat with other men dressed in suits doing God's work? And what exactly was that work? And why couldn't God do it himself?

Sitting next to Lydia on the bottom step, Valerie was stroking Belinda Bell's long, matted hair. Lydia put a hand to her own hair. She wondered how long it would take for her to get used to it being so short. She missed the weight and warmth of it. Mum would hate it.

Wrong! Mum *would have* hated it.

As she continued watching her sister stroking Belinda Bell's hair, she thought of Valerie's lovely blonde hair now lying in the dustbin along with hers. She felt hot and sick. And bad. Very bad. This was all her fault. If only she hadn't pestered Mum for that stupid ventriloquist's dummy none of this would have happened. If she hadn't been so selfish and greedy she would never have upset Mum so much that she had to borrow money from Mr Ridley and then go and ...

She swallowed and tried again; it was important to punish herself with the truth. Her mother had killed herself because of her. There. She'd said it. Her mother had thrown herself in front of that train because of *her*. And Lydia would remind herself of that every day of the rest of her life so that she never forgot what a bad, bad daughter she'd been. To make up for it, she would keep her promise to Mum. She would do her absolute best to look after Valerie.

She felt a hand touching her. It was Valerie. Her pretty little face was screwed up into a frown and she was running her fingers over the top of Lydia's head. Lydia forced herself to smile. 'Do you like it?' she asked.

Valerie shook her head sadly, her blue eyes big and anxious.

Mum had always said that Val was slow to speak because Lydia had never let her get a word in edgeways. But since Mum had died Val had almost stopped talking altogether. It worried Lydia. What if Val forgot how to do it?

There was a bus stop at the end of their grandparents' road. While they waited for the bus in the warm summer sunshine, Lydia noticed that everyone in the queue seemed to know each other and they were chatting happily amongst themselves. The women wore brightly coloured sleeveless dresses, and some had shiny handbags that matched their belts and stiletto-heeled shoes. They reminded Lydia of her mother before Dad died. An older woman with painted-on eyebrows that shot up and down

as she joked and laughed was wearing a pink headscarf; a row of hair-curlers peeped out from underneath it. Lydia had the feeling they were talking about her grandmother, who was dressed in a navy-blue pleated skirt with a grey, long-sleeved cotton blouse buttoned up to her chin. She wore no make-up, except for a dusting of chalky powder, and with her flat black lace-up shoes and a large shopping bag clutched in both hands, she looked so dull she was almost invisible. None of the other women spoke to her, but they all had a good gawp at Lydia and her sister. Never had Lydia been more conscious of what she looked like. Two buttons were missing from her cardigan and both of the cuffs were frayed, the hem on her dress was much too short and the sole on her left sandal was flapping open at the front. Ashamed, she slid behind the pushchair, where no one could see her shoes. A pity there wasn't a way to hide her head.

They were hardly on the bus before they were clambering off. Lydia was disappointed; she had been enjoying the ride. Seeing all that open space with the sun shining down on it had made her want to pull off her socks and sandals and run and run until she was so breathless she would have to lie down in the grass to recover. Then she'd roll down one of the steep slopes and scream and laugh at the top of her voice.

The town was busy. 'Is it always like this?' she asked her grandmother as people jostled around them.

'It's Saturday; market day.'

Lydia had already caught sight of the market stalls with their brightly coloured awnings. Pointing across the road to the stalls of clothes, she said, 'Is that where we're going, to the market?'

'Stop pointing! And no, we're not doing our shopping with the heathens.'

'What's a heathen?'

'An ungodly person.'

'What's an ungodly person?'

Her grandmother came to a stop and stared at her sternly. 'An ungodly person is a person who asks too many questions. Now do as you're told and be quiet.'

Lydia was just turning this thought over when her grandmother took a sharp turn to the right and led them down a narrow street. At the end was a scruffy building with a corrugated iron roof and a large cross above the door with a sign that said: The Church of The Brothers and Sisters in Christ. Her grandmother headed straight for it.

Just inside the door an old woman with glasses and teeth like a rabbit was sitting behind a small trestle table; in front of her was a Quality Street tin and a book of tickets. 'Hello, Sister Irene,' she said, while Lydia's grandmother rummaged around in her purse for some money. She tore off a ticket and after staring at Lydia and Valerie, said, 'Are these the—' she lowered her voice, 'the children you told us about?'

'Yes, Sister Muriel. As you can see, they're badly in need of some decent clothes.'

The goofy woman stared again at Lydia and Valerie through her thick lenses. Especially Lydia. Lydia wanted to cover her head with her hands and shout that it wasn't her fault she looked so awful. 'Sister Vera and Sister Joan are in charge of children's clothing,' the woman said. 'You'll find them next to Pastor John's bookstall.'

Curious, Lydia looked around the hot, stuffy hall. It was packed with people pushing and shoving in front of tables piled high with all sorts of junk. Mum used to say that she would rather die than wear other people's filthy cast-offs from a jumble sale. 'You never know what germs you might catch from wearing someone else's old clothes,' she would say with a shudder. Lydia took a cautious sniff. The air smelled stale. To be on the safe side, she decided to hold her breath whilst they were here.

With her grandmother already moving ahead, Lydia followed behind with the pushchair. Several times she caught the backs of her grandmother's heels and received

a furious look each time. When they made it to the table of children's clothes, Lydia once again found herself flinching under the scrutinizing gaze of two more women. She heard her grandmother greet them as Sister Joan and Sister Vera. They were talking to her grandmother when one of them, a big woman with bosoms as big as pillows, said, 'Is there something wrong with that child? Should she be that colour?'

All three women stared at Lydia. 'Lydia?' her grandmother said. 'Glory be, whatever is the matter with you?'

Lydia couldn't hold on any longer. She let out the breath she'd been holding and coughed and spluttered and breathed in hard. If there were any of those germs here that her mother had warned her about, she'd probably got them now.

Her grandmother tutted and turned away, disgusted. 'That tramp of a mother taught them no manners at all.'

'Praise the Lord that they're now in your hands, Sister Irene.'

'Praise the Lord indeed,' echoed the other woman, who unbelievably had what looked like a moustache growing above her pink, rubbery lips. 'One day they'll thank you.'

'They need to be washed in the blood of Christ; that'll see them right.'

'Amen to that.'

'The youngest one doesn't look too much of a handful,' the big bosomy woman said. 'She has an innocence about her.' Knowing she was being talked about, Valerie hugged Belinda Bell, tucked her chin into her chest and closed her eyes. 'But the other one has a very sour look about her.'

'That's because she takes after her mother.'

Sister Vera and Sister Joan shook their heads. 'We'll pray for you, Sister Irene,' they both said.

Lydia edged away from them. For something to do, she picked up a dress from the pile of clothes. It was a delicate shade of apricot with a cream collar. How could anyone have parted with it? It was just the kind of dress Lydia would love to wear to a party. 'You can put that down for

a start,' her grandmother said, snatching the dress from her hands. 'It's much too fancy. There'll be no vanity in our house. Here, try these on. Go on, go behind the table.'

Lydia was horrified. Not only because the clothes she was being given looked as dowdy as her grandmother's, but because everyone would see her trying them on. 'I'm sure they'll fit,' she said in desperation.

'Your feckless, spendthrift mother may have been stupid enough to fritter away good money on clothes that didn't fit you, but I'm not. Now do as you're told and go behind the table.'

Her face as scarlet as a pillar box, Lydia did as she was told. When she was down to just her knickers, the holey ones with a safety pin holding them up, she wished she could catch some of those lethal jumble-sale germs her mother had warned her about and die right there on the spot.

'She's a bit thin, isn't she?' was one of the comments she heard as her grandmother pushed her head roughly through the neck of a scratchy, red woollen jumper. Next she was forced into a pair of even scratchier blue and green tartan trousers. A heavy grey duffle coat was added to the outfit. It came down well below Lydia's knees and her hands were lost within the miles of sleeves.

While Lydia thought she might faint from the heat, her grandmother stood back to take a better look. 'It'll do for the winter. Maybe even two winters if we're lucky. Now, take it all off and try these on.'

When her grandmother had at last finished with her and had turned her attention to Valerie, Lydia escaped to the bookstall. 'Do you have any children's books?' she asked the man running the stall, wondering if he was the man the woman at the door had referred to as Pastor John.

'Over here,' he said, leading her to the middle section of the long table.

'Are they all stories about God?' she asked after she'd hunted through the box and hadn't found anything of any interest.

He gave her the friendliest smile she'd seen in ages. 'I had

some Enid Blytons earlier,' he said, 'but they've all gone. Don't you like Bible stories? I've got plenty of those.'

She'd never really thought about enjoying Bible stories before. She knew the Christmas and Easter stories and the one about a man being in a lion's den, oh, and the one about Noah's Ark, but liking them had never come into it. It was what they did at school. 'I like some of them,' she said politely. Then noticing a book on the top of a pile at the back of the table, a thought occurred to her. 'Can I look at that one, please?'

He passed the dictionary to her. 'You're a girl of discerning taste, I can see.'

'What does discerning mean?'

He laughed and tapped the book in her hands. 'Why don't you find out for yourself?'

She turned the pages steadily, and when she'd got as far as *disaster* she said, 'How do you spell *discerning*?'

He spelled it out for her. 'D-I-S-C-E-R-N-I-N-G.'

She moved her finger slowly down the page. '*Discern: to see or be aware of something clearly.*' She read on. '*Discerning: having or showing good judgement.*' She thought about this before looking up from the page. 'That sounds like a good thing to be,' she said.

'It is.'

'Are you Pastor John?'

'I am. And with whom do I have the pleasure of talking?'

She blushed. 'I'm Lydia Turner.'

He held out his hand. 'Hello, Lydia, pleased to meet you. I heard you and your sister would be arriving soon.'

Lydia had never shaken hands with anyone before. Embarrassed, she did what she thought she was supposed to do and then said, 'Is Pastor your name? Your Christian name?'

'Strictly speaking it's my title. You know, like a vicar, a Reverend Somebody or other. Officially I'm in charge of the church here.' He laughed. 'Though not everyone would agree with me on that.'

Confused, Lydia said, 'Is it a real church?'

'Oh, yes, as real as any you'll find.'

Lydia wasn't convinced. She was sure churches had to have a proper spire or a tower with bells in it and windows made of coloured glass. 'Why do my grandmother and her friends call one another Sister?'

'It's how we address each other here, because we're all brothers and sisters in Christ. Would you excuse me, please? I think I have another customer.'

He moved away, down to the other end of the table, and remembering the word she wanted to look up, Lydia flicked almost to the end of the dictionary. *Ungodly: wicked; sinful.*

She shut the book. That didn't sound such a good thing to be. Was she wicked? Whilst sitting at the bottom of the stairs with Valerie earlier that morning she had called herself bad. Had she got it wrong? Was she worse than bad?

She said the word several times over inside her head.

Wicked.

Wicked.

Wicked.

The more she said it, the more she knew that it was true. She *was* wicked. Look what she'd made her mother do.

As though to prove just how true it was, she slipped the dictionary under her cardigan and walked away with it.

Chapter Ten

The next morning Lydia saw another bit of herself disappear. Standing in front of the mirror, staring at her exposed, unfamiliar face, she did the buttons up on a stranger's short-sleeved shirt. She wondered who had worn it before her. The buttons were on the wrong side, so it must have been a boy. What kind of a boy? A nice boy? A snivelling, cry-baby boy? Or a mean, nasty bully? The navy-blue shorts her grandmother had picked out for her had a white anchor on each pocket. They were much too big and baggy for her and made her legs look like white sticks. After she'd pulled on a pair of ankle socks, she slipped her feet into a pair of brown sandals with a soft rubbery sole; there was about an inch of free space beyond her toes – growing room, her grandmother had said. They were so comfortable after the torture of her last pair of shoes, Lydia didn't care who had worn them before, or how ugly they were.

Next she helped her sister to get dressed. Lydia was glad that their grandmother had chosen some pretty clothes for Valerie. The pale yellow smocked dress and white cardigan made her look sweet enough to eat and Lydia couldn't resist kissing her smooth cheek in the way Mum used to press her lips against her own cheek.

When they'd got back from the jumble sale yesterday, their grandmother had dragged out the twin-tub washing machine from the corner of the kitchen and hooked it up to the tap at the sink and while their new second-hand clothes – including vests, socks and pants – had been left to stew in a milky brew of Tide and steaming water,

74

Lydia and Valerie had been told to gather their old clothes together so that their grandfather could make a bonfire of them later that evening. They'd gone to bed with the smell of smoke and ashes in their nostrils and a fear of what else might be taken from them to be burned – Valerie wouldn't let Belinda Bell out of her sight now and Lydia had hidden the only photographs she had of Mum and Dad and Valerie, along with Mum's powder compact. She'd climbed onto a chair and hidden them on the dusty curtain pelmet.

Today they were being taken to church. Sitting in the back of their grandfather's car with her legs sticking damply to the sun-warmed vinyl seats, Lydia thought about the dictionary she had stolen from Pastor John. Was there a chance he had seen what she'd done? If so, would he be there today and tell everyone that she was a thief?

She'd smuggled the book home in Valerie's pushchair, under her seat cushion, and had put it in her bedside drawer. When she'd stolen the dictionary she had felt a tingle of excitement, like the time she had once stuck two fingers up behind Creepy-Ridley's back. But the tingle had only lasted a few minutes. When it had gone she'd been left with a bad feeling inside her.

The hall was hot and stuffy just as it had been yesterday, but unlike yesterday, there were no trestle tables to be seen, just rows of wooden chairs laid out in two blocks with an aisle down the middle. Most of the chairs were occupied. There didn't seem to be any other children. Trailing behind her grandparents, Lydia felt everyone's eyes on her. Was it her hair? Or was it because they all knew who she was? Hadn't Pastor John said he'd known that she and Val would be coming here? Or was it far worse than that? Had he told them about the dictionary?

Halfway down the aisle, Lydia recognized Sister Muriel and Sister Joan. Recalling how Sister Joan had seen her in nothing but her tatty old knickers yesterday, she lowered her head and kept her eyes on the wooden floorboards.

When they'd taken their seats, right at the front, Lydia saw another familiar face. And body. Sister Vera was sitting behind an upright piano not five feet away from them and banging out a loud, jangly piece of music that made Lydia want to cover her ears. Next to her, with Belinda Bell on her lap, Valerie did exactly that. With each crash of her massive hands on the keys, the woman's enormous pillowy bosoms shook and wobbled.

Lydia had never been taken to church before. Their father had been dead against it. He'd said that he'd rather walk over hot burning coals than set foot in a church; he'd said he'd had enough of that when he'd been growing up. She supposed this was the church he'd come to as a child. Maybe he'd sat in this very chair. God wasn't something that Lydia had ever heard her parents talk about, but her grandparents seemed to talk about little else. And if it wasn't God, it was Jesus.

Something that had been bothering Lydia for a while now was what the teachers in assembly used to say: that when you died, if you'd been good and believed in God, you went to heaven. But to believe in God properly, did you have to go to church regularly? If that was true, Mum and Dad wouldn't have been allowed into heaven, because they never went to church. And supposing Lydia and her sister were made to go to church every week with their grandparents, would that mean they would go to heaven when they died and not be with Mum and Dad?

The more Lydia thought about that, the more she thought it would be better to be bad. She thought of the stolen dictionary in her bedside drawer and hugged the badness to her.

During the service Lydia looked at anything except Pastor John's face. She stared at the woman who banged a tambourine whilst Sister Vera bashed the keys of the piano. She stared at her unfamiliar sandals, wriggling her toes in the roomy, soft leather. She picked at the anchors on her shorts. She turned the pages of the hymn book looking

for something interesting to read. When everyone else had their heads bowed and their eyes shut to say the Lord's Prayer, she twisted round and watched in fascination as a bald man at the back of the church got to his feet and, with his hands in the air, babbled something she couldn't understand. Was he foreign? When he sat down Lydia heard her grandmother mutter the word 'unhinged'. Lydia made a mental note to look it up in her stolen dictionary. But even with all these distractions, she couldn't stop worrying about Pastor John. She was so convinced that he knew what she'd done, she wished he'd put her out of her agony and get on with whatever punishment he had in mind for her.

At the end of the service, a shutter went up with a clattering rattle and revealed a counter of cups and saucers and a plate of biscuits. Behind the counter, with a large brown teapot in her hands, was a smiling woman wearing a battered little hat decorated with flowers. When Lydia looked closely, she could see there was a tiny pretend robin hidden in amongst the flowers. She was just wondering how many biscuits she could sneak off the plate and into her pockets to share with Val later, without anyone seeing, when she felt a firm hand on her shoulder. 'How did you like the service, Lydia?'

Startled, she looked up to see Pastor John staring down at her. He'd come for her, at last. She stuck out her chin and put on her best stormy face – the one Dad used to say could stop a pack of wild dogs in its tracks. 'It was OK,' she said.

He smiled. 'I expect you found it a bit boring, didn't you?'

The smile wasn't fooling her. Or his friendliness. She knew what he was doing; he was softening her up with some silly conversation before telling her off in front of everyone. Well, if that's what he wanted, she could play along. 'Who was that peculiar man who stood up when we were saying the Lord's Prayer?' she asked. 'Is he

foreign? Or is he—' she decided to try out that new word – 'unhinged?'

The smile got bigger. 'Brother Walter was speaking in tongues. It's a gift from God. Not everyone is given it. And not everyone here appreciates it. I thought you might enjoy these.'

Lydia had been so intent on protecting herself with her stormy face, she hadn't noticed what Pastor John had been holding. He held out a pile of books to her.

'After you'd gone yesterday I found these Enid Blytons in a box under the table. They're not in very good condition, I'm afraid. There's also a children's Bible for you.'

She jammed her hands into her pockets and stared at the books suspiciously. 'But I don't have any money. I can't pay for them.'

'I'm not expecting you to pay for them; they're a present from me to you.'

'But ...'

'But what, Lydia?'

She looked away, down at the floor. 'I don't deserve them,' she said, wishing that he wasn't being so kind. Or was he playing a cruel trick on her? Get her to take these books and then accuse her of stealing them as well? Or ... or was he being genuinely nice and hadn't seen what she'd done yesterday? Was it possible she'd put herself through all that worry for nothing?

'You're not thinking of that dictionary, are you, Lydia?'

Thump! There went that hope.

When she didn't say anything, he said, 'You only had to ask me, and I would have given it to you anyway.'

She looked up and her insides shrivelled. He had such a kind, friendly face. Shame trickled through her like sand in an egg timer. 'Are you going to tell anyone what I did? My grandparents?'

He bent down to her so that his kind, friendly face was level with hers. 'Do you want me to?'

She shook her head, unable to speak.

'Then it will be our secret. Now why don't you take the

78

books and go and get yourself a drink and a biscuit?'

'Thank you,' she managed to say. She took the bundle from him and was about to go when she thought of what had been bothering her earlier. 'Can I ask you something?' she asked.

He was standing up straight now. 'Of course.'

'If someone doesn't believe in God and they don't go to church every week, where do they go when they die?'

He scratched his ear and looked thoughtful. 'I wouldn't worry yourself about that, Lydia. Better to think about how much the Lord Jesus loves you and what a wonderful friend you have in him.'

She didn't know about Jesus, but Lydia decided Pastor John was quite a nice friend to have.

Chapter Eleven

There were lots of bits of their grandparents' long thin garden that were out of bounds – the raspberry canes, the strawberry patch, the shed, the bonfire bin, the chestnut tree and the compost heap. Apparently compost heaps were dangerous; if you fell into one on a hot sunny day you could get badly burned. Lydia and her sister had been ordered never to go near these areas, which made them all the more tempting. When nobody was looking, Lydia deliberately crossed the invisible boundaries and helped herself from the strawberry patch or the raspberry canes. She had even prodded a stick into the compost heap to see if it would burn, but disappointingly it didn't. What she really wanted to do was to unlock the padlock on the shed at the end of the garden and snoop around inside. One day when her grandmother had been standing guard over the twin-tub and her grandfather had been out at work – he had a proper job with the council as well as the Lord's work that kept him busy most evenings – she had stood on tiptoes and peered in through the grimy window. She didn't know why her grandfather bothered to keep the door locked when there didn't seem to be anything valuable in there. From what she could see it was just lots of tools hanging from hooks above two messy shelves. On the top shelf she could see a rusty tin with a picture of a rat on the front and the words 'Rat Poison' underneath it. There was a folding camping stool on the floor next to a stack of dirty old clay pots and a brass lamp suspended from the roof. The lamp was similar to the smelly kerosene one Dad used to have in the shed where he kept his motorbike.

On the floor, under a pile of sacking cloth, Lydia could see what looked like the corner of a magazine poking out. In the two weeks she and her sister had been living with their grandparents, Lydia had only ever seen her grandfather read the Bible, which he did every morning before getting into his car and going off to work, and then again in the evening after supper when Lydia helped her grandmother do the dishes. So what did he read here all on his own?

Today, while Valerie was having her afternoon nap and their grandmother was hammering out wrinkles and creases with a hot spitting iron and complaining about the extra work she now had to do, Lydia was once again breaking her grandfather's boundary rules and climbing the chestnut tree next to the compost heap. It was the first time she'd ever climbed a tree – the children in the books she liked to read were always doing it – and to her delight and amazement she found it was the easiest thing in the world to do. It was as if the branches had been perfectly placed for her to pull herself up onto them; she felt as light and springy as a monkey. Within minutes she was high above the garden, astride a thick solid branch, pretending she was riding a horse, galloping across all that countryside the other side of the garden wall. She still hadn't got used to the big, wide open spaces. Or how different it could look depending on the weather. In the sunshine, the sloping hills and fields appeared green and soft and welcoming, but when it rained they became harsh and wild. Some of the fields weren't fields at all, but moorland; she hadn't worked out which yet.

She opened her mouth wide and gulped back a mouthful of air that was sweet and milky with the smell of freshly mown grass from one of the neighbouring gardens. The air didn't always smell as nice. Some days, when the wind blew in from a different direction, it brought the bitter, sooty smell of the town with it.

Gripping the branch with her legs, she imagined herself galloping far away, leaving behind her the sadness of Mum and Dad and the cruel strictness of her grandparents. She

decided this would be her special place, where a secret sun would always shine down on her through the dancing leaves of the tree.

She wondered how old the tree was. Had her father climbed high into its branches when he'd been a boy? If she looked hard enough, would she find his name carved into the bark somewhere? If she did, she'd carve her name right next to his. The thought that she might be following in her father's footsteps filled her with a mixture of happiness and emptiness. To feel closer to Dad, she often went round the house touching things that he must have touched when he was little – the door knobs, the handrail on the stairs, the bathroom taps, the light switches. It didn't really work. There was nothing to remind her of Dad in the house. No photographs. No old games or jigsaw puzzles he used to play with. No favourite books. It was as if he'd never been here.

Off in the distance she could see an area of woodland that crept up the side of the hill. It looked somewhere interesting to go and play. She wondered what was on the other side of the hill. Were there houses there where other children lived? There was no one the same age as her in her grandparents' road. She'd seen a gang of spotty teenagers hanging around the bus shelter or phone box kicking a tin can between them, cigarettes dangling from their lower lips, but no one she could be friends with. She longed for school to start. All she'd had for company so far had been the books Pastor John had given her.

Her grandparents hadn't approved of the books. They said the only one she needed to read was the one the Good Lord had written. When she'd reminded them that it had been Pastor John himself who had given her the books, her grandfather had banged his fist down hard on the dinner table – so violently even her grandmother had started. Sometimes Lydia thought her grandmother was as scared of her husband as Lydia was. 'You will never answer me back again, young lady,' he'd roared, his huge nostrils flaring. 'Now go to your room and pray that God will save

you from your wickedness.' Lying on her bed, her stomach growling for her supper that lay untouched downstairs, she had tried to make sense of what had just happened. Surely Pastor John, as the leader of their church, was like God and was never wrong? If Pastor John thought Enid Blyton was all right for her to read, why didn't her grandparents?

When she'd woken in the morning, she'd discovered that all her books had disappeared. She'd dashed across the landing to the bathroom and opened the window that looked down onto the garden: smoke was coming out of the blackened chimney of the metal bonfire bin. Downstairs she found that not all of the books had been burned: two had escaped. On the breakfast table there was the children's Bible Pastor John had given her, along with the dictionary. She pushed them casually to one side and got on with her breakfast. She wouldn't give her grandparents the satisfaction of knowing they'd upset her.

Changing her position on the branch, Lydia swung one leg over to join the other and swivelled round to peer into next door's garden at the washing that hung on the line. It was very different from the stuff her grandmother put out to dry. It looked expensive and what Dad, with a wink, would have called racy. Stockings, petticoats and slinky knickers fluttered and rippled like silky flags in the sunshine. There was a black see-through nightie too, along with several lacy brassieres and a girdle. Her mother had worn a girdle after she'd had Valerie; it had made her tummy as flat as a chopping board. It had also made her breathless and Dad had said he preferred her without it.

According to her grandmother, the woman who lived next door was a floozy. Lydia had checked the word in her dictionary and discovered that this meant she was disreputable. Further reading revealed that disreputable meant The Floozy had a bad reputation. But a bad reputation for what?

Lydia had overheard her grandmother talking to Sister Vera about The Floozy at church. Between them they had

a long list of complaints that Lydia didn't understand. What was wrong with having a breakfast bar in your kitchen and a patio made of crazy paving, or buying a fake leopardskin coat from a catalogue?

Lydia now knew that The Floozy was one of the women she had spotted at the bus stop the first time they'd gone into town to buy clothes at the jumble sale. Since then she had dyed her hair an even brighter shade of yellow. Lydia had never seen her without make-up. She wasn't married, but Lydia didn't think she was lonely because now and then, late at night when Lydia couldn't sleep, she could hear music and laughter coming through the wall from next door.

The following Sunday in church, Pastor John reminded everyone that it was the last day to get their money in for the Brothers' and Sisters' Weekend away. 'What weekend away?' Lydia asked her grandmother when the service was over and cups of tea were being passed round. She sensed that people were excited about something; tea and biscuit time wasn't usually this noisy. It was more like a party.

'I've told you before; speak when you're spoken to, child.'

'Oh, go on, Sister Irene, tell the dear girl where we're going.'

This encouragement was from a funny little pink-faced woman who was smiling and nodding so hard she was spilling tea into her saucer. Her hat was sliding about on her head, too. Lydia had learned that Sister Lottie was famous for her hats. She had dozens of them, all decorated with flowers and fruit and tiny birds or animals.

Her grandmother narrowed her eyes to slits and Lydia knew she was far from pleased about something. 'It's nothing to lose one's head over,' she said dismissively to Sister Lottie. 'It's only a weekend in Scarborough.'

'Where's Scarborough?' Lydia asked, forgetting that she was supposed to wait until she was spoken to.

Her grandmother shot her a furious look, but Sister

Lottie beamed and placed one of her white plimsolled feet over the other. Lydia had never seen an adult wear plimsolls before. 'We're going to Yorkshire. To the seaside. Won't that be fun?'

During the drive home Lydia thought of nothing but splashing about in rock pools, throwing herself into waves, building sandcastles and licking chopped nuts off the top of an ice-cream cornet. Sister Lottie was right; it would be fun. She'd been to the seaside before, with Mum and Dad. She'd ridden a donkey and eaten so much candy floss her mother had scolded her and said she'd probably wake up pink in the morning. That was the day Dad had taken her on the ride that had made her sick.

In the days that followed Lydia was careful not to put a foot wrong. Her grandfather was constantly on at her, saying that if she didn't do exactly as he said, she could forget about going to Scarborough. So she helped her grandmother around the house as much as she could, dusting, polishing, ironing, scrubbing out the toilet, as well as taking care of Valerie. Every night she knelt at the side of her bed – making sure the bedroom door was open so that her grandparents could hear – and prayed out loud as they'd taught her. 'God forgive me for my sinful nature. God take away my sin and make me a better person. Thank you, God, for my lovely new home and the kindness of my grandparents, even though I don't deserve it. Amen.' Before hopping into bed, she would silently add: 'Please, please, *please*, God, let me go to the seaside.'

The weekend away blazed like a bright light at the end of a very dark tunnel and she was prepared to do and say whatever it took to be allowed to go.

But then, the day before they were due to leave, and after she'd laid out her and Valerie's clothes to pack later that evening, she did something wrong. Whilst Valerie had been having her usual nap and her grandmother was having a Tea and Sisters Scripture meeting in the front room, Lydia was down at the bottom of the garden. It

was a scorching hot afternoon. There hadn't been any rain for ages and the air was thundery, as thick and sticky as syrup. All the strength seemed to have been sucked out of her body and she couldn't even be bothered to climb the chestnut tree. Instead, she found a stick and played with the compost heap, pretending the sweet-smelling rotting grass cuttings and vegetable peelings were the ingredients for an enormous cake that needed stirring before going in the oven. With the sun beating down on it, the heat from the steaming layered mixture was extraordinary. – hot enough to use as an oven itself. She was so absorbed in what she was doing, she didn't hear her grandfather's footsteps approaching, not until she heard him fitting the key into the padlock on the shed door. She held her breath and kept perfectly still in the hope she would be invisible to him. It didn't work. He'd just opened the door and was pulling something out from inside his jacket when he saw her. At first he looked startled, as though he was the one who had been caught doing something wrong. Then his expression hardened and she knew she was in for it. In a flash, before she'd had time to make a run for it, he'd disappeared inside the shed and was back out and coming for her. He towered over her, hands on hips, blocking her way. Gripping the stick, she did her best to look him in the eye, to disguise how terrified of him she was.

'I warned you about playing with the compost heap,' he said. 'What did I say could happen if you weren't careful?'

There was something scary about the slow, steely tone of his voice and she had to look away from him. 'I can't remember,' she lied.

He took the stick from her. 'Do you want me to remind you?'

She kept her eyes on the stick and shook her head.

'So you do remember what I told you?'

She swallowed. 'I'm very sorry. I won't do it again.'

He prodded her chest with the dirty end of the stick, pushing her back against the boarded side of the compost

heap. 'No, you won't do it again. And do you know why you're not going to come down and play in this part of the garden again?'

'Because I'll get into trouble if I do?'

'You most certainly will. But to make sure you do as you're told, I'm going to have to teach you a lesson that will make you mend your ways. Hold out your hands.'

Her whole body clammy with sweat, her heart beating frantically, Lydia did as he said and braced herself, her eyes closed.

Her screams tore apart the still silent afternoon. On a branch above her head, a startled wood pigeon clattered its wings and flew off into the sultry sky.

Chapter Twelve

She was lucky. That's what people had said yesterday. Lucky that she hadn't hurt herself more. Lucky too that she was well enough to go to Scarborough.

In the back of their grandfather's car, with Valerie on her lap and a suitcase bumping against her shoulder whenever they went round a corner, Lydia kept telling herself that the moment she could smell the tangy sea air, the pain would magically stop. Her hands and arms were bandaged from the elbow down to her fingers and if she concentrated hard on reciting her times tables in her head, she could forget the stinging pain that made her want to rip off the bandages and plunge her arms into two imaginary buckets of icy water.

Grandmother had been furious when her grandfather had taken her into the house and interrupted her Tea and Sisters Scripture meeting. He had explained what had happened – that he'd come home early from work and found Lydia mucking about on the wall behind the compost heap, despite having been expressly forbidden to play in that area of the garden. He told everyone that she'd lost her balance and fallen in when he'd asked her to get down. Her grandmother had been all for sending Lydia – still covered in grass cuttings and rotting peelings – straight to bed without any tea, but then Lydia had felt the room spin and had been sick over the carpet. Sister Lottie had dropped her Bible and knocked over her cup of tea as she rushed to help. 'It's shock!' she cried. 'If she's badly burned we must get the poor girl into a bath of cool water.'

'She certainly requires washing,' said Sister Vera, her face puckered with disgust.

'She's lucky she didn't break her neck,' Sister Joan said. 'She should count herself lucky she didn't kill herself!'

When Lydia was sick again, The Sisters were hurriedly shooed out of the house. Twenty minutes later, shivering with cold, she had begged through chattering teeth to be allowed out of the freezing bathwater. Her grandmother had then rubbed margarine into her rapidly reddening arms and wrapped them roughly in bandages. 'There, that's the best I can do,' she said. 'You should give thanks to the good Lord that it was only your arms you burned.'

As the windscreen wipers scraped backwards and forwards – the weather had finally broken in the night with the loudest thunderstorm Lydia had ever heard – she caught her grandfather looking at her in the rear-view mirror. No longer brave enough to stare back at him, she closed her eyes and tried to pretend he didn't exist. That he was buried deep at the bottom of the compost heap.

In those few short seconds when she had waited for that stick to come cracking down on her hands, she'd found herself suddenly being lifted off her feet and her arms being pushed into the compost heap. Surprise had made her cry out but then, as she'd wriggled to break free from his strong grasp, she'd screamed louder and harder because of the fiery heat that was spreading up her hands and arms. But he'd ignored her cries, saying the punishment was for her own good, that the heat she was experiencing now was nothing like the fires of hell that awaited her if she continued to disobey him. When he eventually put her down, he said, 'Tell anyone about this and I'll punish you again. Do you understand?'

Tears streaming down her cheeks, she'd promised him she wouldn't tell anyone.

For the rest of the journey Lydia kept her gaze glued to the dreary, rain-soaked scenery through the steamed-up side window. Anything but catch her grandfather's glinty eye in the mirror. Anything but wonder why he hated her

so much. Or why she hadn't been brave enough to tell anyone what had really happened to her.

The sky was blue and the sun was shining brightly by the time they arrived in Scarborough. Pastor John greeted them at the boarding house where they were staying. When he saw Lydia, he crouched down in front of her. 'Poor Lydia,' he said, 'Sister Lottie told me about your accident. How do you feel?'

Through a dry raspy throat, and conscious of her grandfather standing behind her – one of the cases he was carrying was digging into the backs of her legs – she said, 'I feel much better now, thank you.'

'She's fine,' her grandfather rumbled, pushing forward with the cases, 'a lot of fuss about nothing. It'll teach her to be more careful in the future. Now then, where are our rooms?'

Lydia and Valerie had a room to themselves. It smelled of cigarette smoke and something fishy. There was no window to let in any fresh air or light, and the only furniture was a pair of bunk-beds. There was a notice pinned to the back of the door that read: 'No sand to be left in the bedrooms or public rooms. No wet towels or bathing costumes put out to dry on the window ledges. No guests back before four o'clock. The front door will be locked at ten thirty p.m. sharp.'

With no chest of drawers to put their clothes in, Lydia explained to her sister it would be best to keep their things in their case under the bottom bunk, which would be Valerie's. With no unpacking to do, they crept quietly back out onto the dimly lit passageway. The door to the right of theirs was shut but Lydia could hear her grandparents' voices. She moved a little nearer to the door, her ears straining to hear what they were saying. They seemed to be discussing Pastor John.

Suddenly the door opposite opened and Sister Lottie appeared. 'Isn't this grand?' she said, clasping her hands

in front of her. She was wearing a pair of lacy gloves and another of her hats covered her curly grey hair. It was made of straw and decorated with real flowers – drooping buttercups and daisies – and was held in place with a yellow ribbon tied under her chin in a large bow. She patted Valerie's head. 'Sweet, darling angel,' she cooed. Then to Lydia: 'And how are your arms today, dear? You gave us all such a terrible fright yesterday. Really you did.'

'They're much better, thank you.'

'I'm so pleased.' She smiled a dimply smile and bent forward. 'Shall we be very naughty and go for a walk before tea?' she whispered. 'I expect you're like me and can't wait to see the sea.'

Much as Lydia wanted to race down to the beach straight away she wasn't sure it was such a good idea to go without letting her grandparents know. Yet she knew that if she asked them for permission to go they would be sure to say no.

Sister Lottie was already off down the passageway with Valerie's hand in hers. 'Come on, Lydia,' she called over her shoulder. 'Let's go and have some fun!'

They passed Sister Joan and Sister Vera on the stairs and grabbing a way to stay out of trouble, Lydia said, 'Could you tell my grandparents Sister Lottie's taking me and my sister to the beach, please?'

'Sister Lottie, you do realize tea is in an hour, don't you?'

'Oh, yes, Sister Joan. We'll be back in plenty of time, won't we, girls?'

Lydia suspected that Sister Joan and Sister Vera didn't really like Sister Lottie. They think they're better than her, Lydia thought as she followed behind Sister Lottie and Valerie. True, there was something perhaps a little batty – that was the word Mum would have used – about the woman, but so what? Sister Lottie and Pastor John were the only really nice people she'd met since coming to live in Swallowsdale.

*

The sun was low in the sky when they made it to the beach and people were packing up their things to go home. Valerie had only been a tiny baby when Mum and Dad had taken them to the seaside and she held on to Lydia's hand tightly as she looked anxiously around her. Staring out to sea, Sister Lottie was standing perfectly still. 'Isn't it beautiful?' she said, her arms stretched out in front of her, her palms held high, a joyful smile on her parted lips. 'This is why I love God. He's so good to us. Alleluia and praise the Lord!' Her voice had risen and around them people had stopped what they were doing and were gawping. They gawped even harder when, without warning, Sister Lottie gathered up her skirt and ran towards the water's edge. Someone sniggered and said, 'Crazy old woman.'

Another said, 'Probably soft in the head and let out from the loony bin for the day.'

'Has to be as nutty as a fruitcake to be wearing that awful hat and those ankle socks and plimsolls.'

Lydia felt her cheeks redden. Part of her wanted to creep away, to pretend she didn't know the woman they were discussing. But something far stronger than embarrassment made her want to stand up for Sister Lottie. So what if she wore a funny hat and children's plimsolls? So what if she was a bit soft in the head? If soft in the head made you kind and nice, then Lydia knew whose side she was on.

'Come on,' she said to Valerie, 'let's go and see what Sister Lottie's doing.'

Valerie looked doubtfully at the sand and pebbles and held up her arms to be carried. 'Sorry, sweetheart,' Lydia said, 'I can't. Not today. Maybe tomorrow.'

By the time they had joined Sister Lottie at the water's edge, she had removed her socks and plimsolls. 'We must have a paddle,' she said.

'But we don't have a towel.'

'Oh, Lydia, we don't need a towel. Don't worry so.'

She's more of a child than me, Lydia thought as she sat down and took off her socks and sandals. Valerie shook her head when Lydia tried to undo the buckles on her

sandals. 'Then you must sit here like a very good girl and don't move. Can you do that for me, Val?'

Valerie nodded. But she didn't sit down. 'Dirty,' she whispered, looking around her.

The water was cold and made Lydia suck in her breath and stand on tiptoe. She let the waves wash over her toes and then ventured in further. She felt the pull of the water and laughed when a rush of sand and stones tickled her feet. She breathed in the salty air, tipped her head back to let the sun stroke her cheeks and felt a tiny chink of happiness burst through the clouds inside her.

'I said it would be fun, didn't I?' Sister Lottie said. The hem of her skirt was wet, but either she hadn't noticed or she didn't care. Lydia was glad she was wearing shorts – at least there was no danger of getting them wet and being told off for it. Looking out at the sea, the waves sparkling in the lowering sun, Lydia realized this was the first time since coming to live at number thirty-three Hillside Terrace that she had been properly alone with someone other than her grandparents. Better still, this was someone who might be able to answer some of the questions she had.

'Sister Lottie?'

'Yes?'

'Have you known my grandparents for a long time?'

'Ooh, I should say so. I knew them when they married.'

'Did you know my father?'

'Of course I did. He was a dear, sweet boy. The apple of your grandparents' eye. Valerie looks a lot like him, you know.'

'Really?'

'Well, not when he was grown up, but when he was little. He had the same lovely blond hair.'

'Do you know why my grandparents were happy when my dad died?'

The old woman gasped and turned round. 'Oh, dear me! Dear, dear me. How could you say such a terrible thing?'

'Because it's true. I heard my mother on the telephone the day after he died.'

'Well ... oh, precious child, you're much too young to understand these things.'

'What things?'

Sister Lottie sighed and, with a trembling hand, touched the silver cross she wore at her neck. 'You have to remember that your grandparents loved their son very much and they wanted the world for him.'

'I don't think that's true. I've never heard them talk about him. They don't even have a photograph of him in the house. I've looked and I can't find anything that belonged to my dad.'

A wave larger than any of the ones before rolled in fast and crashed at their legs. Sister Lottie hitched up her skirt but was too late. Drenched to the waist, she plucked the wet folds of now transparent cotton off her thin legs and began squeezing out the water. 'What a silly goose I am,' she said with a cheerful laugh.

'So why aren't there any pictures of my dad in the house?' Lydia pressed on, at the same time keeping an eye out for any other big waves.

'They used to have lots of photographs of him,' Sister Lottie said, 'all round the house, but then ... but then he changed.'

'How? How did he change?'

'He disappointed them. He met your mother, and I'm afraid to say he turned away from God.'

'Is that all?'

'It meant everything to them.'

'And is that why they hate me and Valerie?'

Sister Lottie looked shocked. 'Wherever did you get that idea? How could they not love you and your sister?'

Lydia wanted to hold out her bandaged arms and say, 'Could someone who loved me do this to me?' But she didn't. She clamped her mouth shut and shrugged.

Chapter Thirteen

They ran all the way, Sister Lottie carrying Valerie and Lydia frantically urging her to go faster. But they were still late for tea. They would have been even later had Lydia not begged Sister Lottie to stop kicking through the waves and put her socks and plimsolls back on.

Her grandmother was waiting for them in the doorway to the dining room. Her thin body looked as taut as a stretched rubber band about to go ping. 'You've delayed tea by twenty minutes,' she said, arms crossed in front of her, eyebrows drawn. 'And for the sake of proprieties, Sister Lottie, you might like to tidy yourself up before eating.'

With her flushed face, her hat tipped to one side and her wet skirt beginning to show a salty tide line, even Lydia had to admit that Sister Lottie did look a bit of a mess. But Sister Lottie didn't seem in the least concerned. 'We had such a glorious time, Sister Irene,' she said breathlessly, her eyes shining. 'Simply glorious. You should have been there with us. We had such fun.'

How wonderful it must be to be Sister Lottie, Lydia thought enviously, so completely unaware that anyone could be cross with her. But all too aware of her grandmother's mood, and anxious to get in her good books, Lydia said, 'I'll take Valerie upstairs so we can wash our hands, shall I?'

'Yes,' her grandmother said snappily. 'Five minutes, mind. And make sure you comb your hair. No messing about up there.'

Tea was a dollop of gloopy shepherd's pie with tinned peas and watery cabbage. For afters there were tinned peaches with evaporated milk. Lydia and Valerie weren't allowed to have any evaporated milk. Their grandmother said it was too rich and would make them sick. 'And the last thing I need, on top of everything else,' this was said with a look in Sister Vera and Sister Joan's direction, 'is another episode like yesterday.' Lydia's ears pricked up at the words *on top of everything else*. What did that mean? She searched her grandparents' faces for clues, then looked about the room.

Sitting at the nearest table was a group of people she didn't know. Apparently they were from their sister church here in Scarborough. There were only two churches like theirs in the whole of the country, but by coming here to spread the word, they hoped to get more people to join and maybe start up a third church. On another table, Pastor John and Sister Lottie were chatting with more unknown people, including a man with silvery-grey hair, deep dark grooves either side of his mouth and a black eye patch. Lydia stared in fascinated horror. What lay behind that patch? A gruesome hole that went straight through to his brain? She shivered and popped a piece of squishy peach into her mouth. Then wished she hadn't.

'What have I told you about staring?'

'Sorry, Grandma,' Lydia said meekly. 'Who's that man with the eye patch?'

'His name's Brother Digby and a man more full of the Holy Spirit you will never meet. He's a truly righteous and scripturally led man. Now stop mythering me with your questions and finish your tea.'

The next morning they were up early and immediately after breakfast they marched in single file down to the beach with a box of tambourines and hymn books, as well as a stack of leaflets inviting people to let Jesus into their lives.

Lydia and Valerie had been given the task of handing

the leaflets out whilst the congregation sang 'Onward Christian Soldiers', 'All Things Bright and Beautiful', and 'For All the Saints'. With it being so early and with a strong wind blowing in off the sea, there weren't many people about. Lydia soon noticed that if she persuaded her sister to offer the leaflets to the few who were on the beach, more people took them. Probably because Valerie looked so sweet. Unlike Lydia, she wasn't cringing with embarrassment and wishing she could dig a big hole in the sand and bury herself.

Brother Digby – his full name was Brother Digby Pugh – led the service and he was very different from Pastor John. He had the loudest voice ever. Several times Lydia jumped out of her skin at his shouted words. She noticed others doing the same, including Sister Lottie. He roared and bellowed at them above the wind about how sly and dangerous the devil could be, that he was the most infectious disease known to mankind. He warned them to be alert and constantly on their guard. Then he thumped his opened Bible with his fist and read from it: 'Finally, brethren, be strong in the Lord, and in the power of his might. Put on the whole armour of God, that ye may be able to stand against the wiles of the devil. For we wrestle not against flesh and blood, but against principalities, against powers, against the rulers of the darkness of this world, against spiritual wickedness in high places.' He jerked his head up, slapped the Bible shut, and with his one piercing eye swept the faces of the congregation as if searching for someone in particular. 'Which of you,' he hissed, his hand raised and a long bony finger pointing, 'has allowed the evil one to feast on the demons within?' Lydia gulped and slid to her left to hide behind Sister Vera. When she thought it was safe to come out, she saw that Brother Digby's eye and bony finger had settled on Pastor John.

Pastor John had turned very pale.

By tea-time it was all anybody could talk about. The Brothers and Sisters in Christ were in crisis. Hovering

in doorways, taking her time over handing out Bibles, lurking behind corners, or pretending she was praying, Lydia gathered information from the rustle of gossip like a thieving magpie.

Shocking!

Disgusting!

Who'd have thought it?

A man we trusted!

He's betrayed us all!

He'll burn in hell for this!

He could have taken us all down with him!

Lucky for us Sister Irene was on to him!

These were just a few of the snippets Lydia overheard until finally she got to the bottom of it. Pastor John was being kicked out of the church, for something to do with indulging in ungodly relations with a married woman in Keighley.

Having been told by her grandparents to go and amuse themselves – they had important business with Brother Digby to discuss – Lydia took Valerie upstairs with her to look for Sister Lottie. They found her sitting on her bed, crying.

'I can't believe the dreadful things they're saying about Pastor John,' she sobbed, flapping her handkerchief. 'He was such a good man. Always so patient and understanding. The kindest man I ever knew. The church won't be the same without him.' She crushed Lydia and Valerie to her. 'Promise me you won't think too badly of him. You mustn't turn against him like everyone else.'

At breakfast the next morning not only did Lydia find out that Pastor John had packed his case in the night and left without saying goodbye, but she learned that Brother Digby was to be their new pastor in Swallowsdale.

Chapter Fourteen

The start of a new term had always made Lydia feel anxious, but the start of a new term in a new school was keeping her awake at night and making her head ache and her tummy tie itself into knots. Dad would have said she was suffering from an attack of the collywobbles. She'd always thought that having the collywobbles sounded like it should be fun, something that made you laugh.

But as she sat at the breakfast table in her second-hand blue and grey uniform, trying to force down a mouthful of toast, and reminding herself that a few weeks ago she had been longing for school to start, she wasn't laughing. It wasn't only herself she was worrying about. This was the first time in ages that she and Valerie would be apart. Lydia was so used to doing everything for her sister, she couldn't imagine how Valerie would cope without her around. Nor could she imagine their grandmother being patient enough to tease out what it was that Val wanted when she would sometimes do nothing more than speak through her eyes.

With her stomach all topsy-turvy, Lydia gave up on the toast and looked at Valerie, who had hardly eaten any of her cornflakes; they were either sticking to the side of the bowl or floating like soggy scabs in the milk. 'Come on, Valerie,' Lydia encouraged her, 'try and eat some more.'

Valerie turned her eyes meaningfully to Lydia's uneaten piece of toast.

'That's different,' Lydia said, 'I don't need to do as much growing as you. Now promise me you'll be good for our grandmother whilst I'm at school.'

Valerie blinked. It was a slow, deliberate movement, just the way Belinda Bell blinked when you tipped her slowly backwards.

From the hallway came the sound of letters being pushed through the letterbox, followed by their grandmother's thwacking footsteps hurrying from the kitchen to the front door. Their grandfather had already left for work; he rarely ate breakfast with them. He complained that they interfered with his routine.

Helping her sister down from her cushioned seat, Lydia kissed her briskly on the forehead. 'I'll be home before you've even missed me.'

There was a queue at the bus stop. Lydia recognized the spotty gang of teenage boys; they looked different in their black blazers and grey trousers, bigger and not so scruffy. They all had the same bristly short haircut with a white rim of pale skin above their ears and round their necks. A group of girls in black blazers and short grey skirts showed off long legs in knee-high white socks and carried duffel bags slung over their shoulders. When they saw Lydia they stopped talking and looked her up and down. For days now Lydia had been practising for just such a moment. Concentrating hard, she narrowed her eyes and stared back, pretending she was casting an evil spell on them. The tallest of the girls, inhaling hard on a cigarette, said, 'Cheeky little tart! I've a good mind to thump her one. She needs to learn to respect her elders. Oi, Tufty, what yer staring at?'

'Give over,' one of the boys said. 'She's nowt but a baby.'

Lydia bristled. She knew she was small, but she wasn't *that* small.

Someone else said, 'Isn't she the granddaughter of them religious loonies? Mad as snakes, my mum says.'

Grateful that the gang of teenagers thundered upstairs to the top deck of the bus, Lydia claimed a seat downstairs next to the window. She had been told by her grandmother

to stay on the bus until the other children with the same uniform as her got off. After a few minutes she risked a glance to her right and then over her shoulder to the seats behind. A blur of blue and grey confirmed she was at least on the right bus. For the rest of the journey she willed her churning, queasy stomach to settle. To distract herself she thought of the good luck card Sister Lottie had made for her. She had given it to Lydia in church yesterday morning. This was after Pastor Digby had put one of his bony hands on her head in front of everyone and prayed that she would be a good child of Christ and that she wouldn't be infected by the ungodly at her new school.

The first thing Pastor Digby had done when he came to Swallowsdale was to walk up and down the aisle of their church sweeping the floor with a broom. It was a symbol of his ministry, he said. He had been sent to them to sweep away the old and to make room for the new. He had then read out a list of changes he wanted to put in place. There was to be no gambling of any sort, not even the buying or selling of raffle tickets. No alcohol was to be drunk. Television was banned, as was smoking, the reading of horoscopes, perms, make-up, perfume and hair colouring, and the wearing of jewellery. Wedding rings were allowed, but nothing in the way of unnecessary accessories. Only hats of a modest and unadorned nature could be worn. Sister Lottie had let out a little gasp at this. Lydia had later looked up the word unadorned and understood her gasp.

According to Pastor Digby these were all instruments of the devil and he was ridding the church of them. 'They encourage the sin of pride and vanity, the sin of slothfulness, and worse, the sin of greed,' he roared at them, making the windows rattle in their frames. He explained that under Pastor John's guidance, the church had been allowed to become flabby and vulnerable to attack. If they were to be a godly church, tough leadership was required. He vowed he would make street evangelists of them all.

Lydia had only found out recently that there had been a question mark over her being allowed to go to school.

She'd overheard her grandmother telling Sister Vera that she was concerned that Lydia would pick up the ways of the heathen at school, that maybe she would be better staying at home. Pastor Digby had then been asked for his opinion on the matter and he'd ruled that as Lydia was the only school-age child in their flock, she would be their secret weapon. It would be her job, on behalf of the Brothers and Sisters, to spread God's Word at school.

As she'd known they would, the lessons flew by and the break times dragged. Out in the playground the boys screamed and ran around like idiots and the girls huddled together, their arms linked, telling Lydia what she already understood all too clearly: friendships had long since been formed and no one needed a new one thank you very much. She'd tried talking to them during morning break, but when one of them had asked her why she had her hair cut like a boy's, she'd scowled and walked off.

For something to do she went for a walk round the field. She took off her cardigan and tied it around her waist – just as her grandmother said she wasn't supposed to do – and pushed up her sleeves. The burns on her arms had healed. She'd been disappointed that she wasn't left with some really good scars that she could show off, but all that remained was a faint blush on the inside of her arms.

Above her, the sun shone down from a pearly blue sky and birds sang in the trees. It was a beautiful day, still very much like summer. Instead of making her feel happy, though, it made her feel uglier and more alone. But perhaps that was how she was meant to feel. Pastor Digby said God saw and heard everything and that he punished those who did wrong. Pastor Digby hadn't said how God punished people, but maybe he just made them unhappy, like her.

In the days and weeks that followed, Lydia gradually got to know some of her classmates, particularly the ones who had been made by their teacher, Miss Dillinger, to take it

in turns to sit next to her. The first had been a blonde girl called Zoe Woolf who spoke in a fancy lah-di-dah voice. She was originally from somewhere in the south of England and said words like bath and glass as though they had an r in them. She already wrote with a fountain pen and was considered one of the cleverer ones in the class. She could ask for directions to the toilet in French, whereas the rest of them were only just learning to count and say *bonjour* and *au revoir*. She had thought she was the only one in the class who had her own dictionary, until Lydia pulled hers out of her satchel.

Next to sit with Lydia was a boy called Peter Day, who had been born with a hole in his heart. Everyone called him Bena, as in Ribena, because he was a funny purply-blue colour. He was excused all games and PE lessons but was never teased.

Then there was a boy called Jimmy Dodson, who was nicknamed Jimmy Fumble because he was so clumsy. Everyone dreaded it – '*Oh, Miss!*' – if he was ever picked to be milk monitor.

After Jimmy came Lisa Fortune, of whom Lydia was secretly terrified. Apparently when she was still inside her mother's tummy, her mother had been given some tablets by her doctor and when Lisa was born she only had one hand. She wore an artificial limb with a hook on the end of it and Lydia had had nightmares about Lisa chasing her round the playground with it.

She'd discovered that there was a girl in the other class in their year who was definitely one to be avoided. She was a big, tall girl with a long ponytail of dull, mousy-brown hair and she never went anywhere without her gang of friends. Her name was Donna Jones and just yesterday she had approached Lydia wanting to know who she was and how much money she had on her. After putting her scowl to good use once again, backed up by an imaginary evil spell, Lydia had walked off as though Donna hadn't spoken. Within seconds she regretted what she'd done and next playtime, despite the awful smell, she'd hidden in the

outside toilet block until the bell rang.

Today, wandering round the school field during morning break, she was keeping an eye out for Donna Jones and her gang. She found trouble sooner than she expected when she came upon a crowd of chanting girls and boys. Curiosity made her draw nearer. When she was close enough she realized that they had a girl pinned down on the grass. Donna Jones was sitting on top of her, undoing the poor girl's blouse. From listening to the chants Lydia soon understood why: it was because the poor girl was wearing a bra for the first time and they wanted to see what she had to put in it. Lydia felt sick at the unfairness of it and badly wanted to do something to stop it. But what? What could she do against all of them? Perhaps they'd do something equally cruel and embarrassing to her. Like ... pull her knickers down.

To her shame, knowing it was the wrong thing to do, she walked away before anyone saw her.

Chapter Fifteen

It was a week later, on a cold, crisp October day, when life at school changed for Lydia.

After morning assembly she and the rest of her class found Miss Dillinger waiting for them in their classroom. She wasn't alone; a pale, thin boy with darting eyes was with her. The most noticeable thing about him was that he was wearing an ugly leg brace, all metalwork and leather straps. Lydia had seen one before, but not close up like this.

'This is Noah Solomon,' Miss Dillinger announced once they were in their seats and sizing up the unknown boy. 'I want you all to make him feel very welcome.'

The only empty chair in the classroom was the one next to Lydia, so it was no surprise when Miss Dillinger instructed the new boy to sit with her, saying, 'Lydia only recently joined the school, so she's the best person to look after you and help you with anything you need to know.'

Lydia watched him make his agonizingly slow way between the desks, the leg brace clanking and squeaking. Sniggers broke out from the other side of the classroom: the word 'spastic' ricocheted off the walls. Jack Horsley and Alfie Stone were immediately told to be quiet. He finally made it and plonked himself down on the chair, his leg sticking out into the narrow aisle. Pretending to give all her attention to turning the pages of her exercise book for that morning's maths lesson, Lydia watched him out of the corner of her eye as he lifted the lid on his desk. A sheen of sweat had appeared on his top lip and he looked paler than ever. He had the darkest eyes she'd ever seen. It

didn't take him long to organize himself. All he seemed to have in his satchel was a notebook and a metal tin. When he opened the tin she could see three pencils, a rubber, a pencil sharpener, a clear plastic six-inch ruler and a pen: a fountain pen like Zoe Woolf used. He caught her looking at his things and flipped the lid shut.

For some reason it was OK for a girl to have something wrong with her, but it wasn't the same for a boy. Jimmy Fumble was always being made fun of for his clumsiness, but Lisa Fortune with her hook was never bothered. Peter Day was the exception. They all knew that because of the hole in his heart, Bena could die any minute just by someone snapping their fingers too loudly. So unless this new boy could prove he had something as impressively wrong with him, he was in for some serious trouble. As the day wore on and the taunts – spaz and spacky – came thick and fast, Lydia soon felt that the task given her by Miss Dillinger was beyond her. How could she possibly look after this new boy? It was hopeless. Everything was against him. From his clanky leg, to his brand new shoes and uniform (ridiculously too big for him), to his posh voice. He rarely spoke, but when he did, he sounded like Zoe Woolf. And why didn't he try and help himself, instead of just standing there with that strange, slightly puzzled expression on his face?

The next day, during morning break, Donna Jones and her gang appeared. 'Go on, then, spacky,' Donna said, 'show us how yer can run with that thing on yer leg.'

'I can't run,' he said simply.

Donna and her friends laughed and crowded round him. 'Then yer'd better learn. If yer not too busy building an ark, that is!'

Lydia couldn't bear to see him standing there so helpless and vulnerable. She went over to make her presence known.

Donna saw her and laughed. 'I see you've got yerself a

midget-sized girlfriend to protect yer. But if that's the best yer can do, yer'd better learn to run extra fast, cos you're gonna need to.' She tossed Lydia a snarling look. 'Yer an all.'

Their point made, Donna and her gang sauntered off to pick on someone else.

'I don't need looking after.' These were the first words this strange new boy had spoken directly to Lydia.

'Could have fooled me,' she retaliated.

'And you're not my girlfriend,' he added sullenly.

By home time, Lydia felt the full sting of his words. He was nothing but an ungrateful snob! As far as she was concerned, he was on his own from now on. Why should she care about him? He could get into whatever trouble he wanted and it was nothing to do with her. Besides, it would be better for her all round if she wasn't seen with him too often. She didn't want anyone else accusing her of being his girlfriend.

But as the days went by she couldn't stop looking out for him. Right now, despite not knowing a single thing about him, he was the nearest she had to a friend. She'd got used to him sitting like a silent shadow next to her in class and having to share books with him. For some reason he never put his hand up to answer any of Miss Dillinger's questions, although Lydia was sure he knew the answers because he was always getting ten out of ten for his work and being awarded gold stars to go on the wall chart. His handwriting was good too, better even than Zoe's. All his letters sat perfectly on the line and slanted evenly to the right; nothing he handed in was ever smudged, creased or torn. When he wasn't looking one day, Lydia had stolen a piece of work from his desk and had tried copying it at home so that she could learn to write neatly and be allowed to use a real pen instead of a pencil. He was better at art than anyone else in the class, too; when he drew something you could easily recognize what it was.

The truth was, even if he didn't have to wear that ugly

leg brace, he would still stick out from the rest of the boys in the class, none of whom was interested in getting to know him because he couldn't play football or bulldog. Bena wasn't interested in him, either. He kept his distance, probably sensing that no good could come of being his friend.

But if Noah was her silent shadow during lessons, Lydia was his secret shadow in the playground. She spied on him round corners and kept her ears pricked not just for the clunky squeak of his brace, but for the name-calling that followed him wherever he went. She suspected that he was on borrowed time, that any day soon the taunts would turn into something worse.

She was proved right.

After lunch one day she came across him at the back of the portable classrooms. He was surrounded by Donna and her gang. They had his blazer and were going through the pockets, tipping whatever they found – mostly bits of paper and loose change – onto the grass. Somebody had already broken his fountain pen and added it to the pile.

'And what have we here?' Donna crowed. 'A drawing of someone? Hey, I know who this is; it's that ugly midget girl with the bog-brush hair and the eyebrows, in't it? Do yer fancy her, then? Is that why yer've drawn her?'

When Noah didn't answer, Donna screwed the picture up and tossed it onto the ground. After another poke around in a pocket she pulled out something else. 'Oh, how *sweet*!' she said sarcastically. 'It's a photo of Mummy and Daddy! Look, everyone!'

'Please give it back,' Noah said quietly.

'Ooh, *please* give it back,' Donna mimicked him. Like sheep, everyone else followed her example.

'If yer want it that badly,' Donna taunted, 'why don't yer come and get it, yer cissy spaz?' She held the photo just out of his reach and when he took a step nearer to take it, she snatched it away.

It still shamed Lydia down to the tips of her toes when she thought of the day when she'd walked away from that

poor girl who'd needed her help in this very same spot, and so when she saw Donna suddenly shove Noah to the ground and rip up the photograph, letting the pieces flutter over him as he struggled to get to his feet, Lydia knew she couldn't make the same mistake twice. She stepped out from her hiding place and with a massive surge of energy, knowing she had the element of surprise on her side, she threw herself at Donna and knocked her flying into a patch of long grass.

Bang! went Donna's head on the soft ground.

Bang! it went again.

Bang!

Bang!

Filled with a violent rage, Lydia could have gone on doing it for ever. Never had anything felt so good or so satisfying. She could hear herself screaming at Donna as she held onto the girl's ears but had no idea what she was saying. She knew, though, that her anger wasn't just about Donna picking on Noah.

Finally the worst of her fury subsided and Lydia released her hold. 'Come after me or my friend again,' she hissed, 'and I'll spread the word about what I've just done to you. And you wouldn't like that, would you? A girl my size embarrassing big tough Donna Jones in front of all her mates?' She pinched Donna's ears hard. 'Got it?'

Donna nodded.

'Good.' Lydia stood up, and knowing it would humiliate Donna further, offered her hand to her so she could pull herself upright. Rubbing the back of her head, Donna refused her help.

'You didn't need to do that,' Noah said when they were alone.

'Somebody had to, or they would have gone on for ever making your life miserable.'

'There's nothing they could do to make my life any worse than it already is,' he said gloomily.

She followed the direction of his gaze. He was staring at

the scattered pieces of the photograph on the ground.

'It would be less embarrassing for me if you would push me over so I could get down there to pick them up,' he said. 'I hate asking for help.'

'So what's wrong with your leg?' she asked after she'd gathered together the pieces of ruined photograph and he'd put them in his pocket.

He looked her square in the eye. 'Are you asking if I'm a spastic? And would it make a difference if I was?'

'I'm only asking you what's wrong with your leg, you idiot.'

He shrugged. 'It was an accident.'

'Are you stuck like that for always? You know, with that thing on your leg?'

He shrugged again. 'I don't know.'

His eyes had now settled on the screwed-up ball of paper. Lydia said, 'Do you want that as well?'

'Not really. It wasn't very good.'

'Can I see it?'

'I'd rather you didn't.'

'Why, because you've made me look even uglier than I am?'

'You're not ugly.'

'Liar.'

'So far you've called me an idiot and a liar. Anything else you want to say?'

She picked up the ball of paper. 'Yes,' she said with a smile. 'Can we be friends?'

Chapter Sixteen

It was the second day of half-term and Lydia was missing Noah.

She had decided to keep quiet about him at home, to keep him as her very own special secret. He was the one really good thing to happen to her in ages and because of that she was frightened he might be taken away from her. Having lost so much already, she hated the thought of losing him as well.

They spent all their break times together at school, usually playing hangman and noughts and crosses, but she still didn't know that much about him. One thing she did know was that he was a Roman Catholic. Every Friday morning he and about nine other children were excused from assembly so that a man in a black dress could come into school to talk to them.

He'd moved to live in Swallowsdale only recently and had had hundreds of operations on his leg, spending ages in hospital because of it. The glimpse of that ripped-up photograph was all Lydia had to go on about his family and she assumed Donna had been right, that it was a picture of his parents. It seemed an odd thing to carry round with you at school – like bringing in your favourite teddy. It was asking for trouble. Sometimes she thought he deliberately made himself a target. He was either very stupid, which she didn't think he was, or he just didn't care what anyone did to him. For all his quiet thoughtfulness and his smashed-up leg, she'd decided he was a lot tougher than she'd initially thought.

But something he'd said that day at the back of the

portable classrooms niggled. *There's nothing they could do to make my life any worse than it already is.* What had he meant by that? His life didn't seem that bad to her. OK, he had to wear that awful contraption and couldn't run about like the rest of them, but was that really so bad? So what that he couldn't play football or go on the climbing frame? He could draw and paint better than anyone else she knew. Compared to her – having to live with her grandparents because both her mother and father were dead – a mangled leg wasn't exactly the end of the world.

She'd deliberately not told him much about her life or her grandparents. She wanted him to think she was as normal as everyone else. If he knew the truth he might not want to be her friend any more. Anyway, it was better to keep everything separate. Their friendship was perfect just as it was. No point in jumbling it all up.

She had kept the crumpled picture he'd drawn of her and at first she hadn't known what to think when she'd looked at it. Her eyebrows certainly stood out, but instead of the cross expression she'd been expecting, he'd made her look ... well, less cross and a bit nicer. Curious, she had asked him when he'd drawn it. With his face turning slightly pink, he'd said he'd done it from memory at home. She felt doubly flattered that he'd not only wanted to draw her, but that he'd been thinking of her outside of school. She now had the picture smoothed out and hidden inside the children's Bible Pastor John had given her.

Lydia was missing Pastor John, too, although she hadn't known him for long. She often wondered where he was. Was he still having 'relations' with that married woman from Keighley? Referring to her dictionary, she'd discovered that this was a way of saying that Pastor John had been having 'sexual intercourse' with the woman. She knew about all that stuff because when Mum had Valerie growing inside her tummy, she'd explained how Valerie had got there – Daddy's 'thingy' had gone inside Mummy and had planted a tiny seed. Lydia also knew that the words 'sexual intercourse' were two words that were

guaranteed to make a grown-up go bright red and change the subject. And because she was bored, bored, *BORED*, she thought it might be interesting to see what kind of reaction she would get if she said those two words now.

She was helping to pass round cups of tea during her grandmother's Tea and Sisters Scripture meeting. As a result of Pastor Rigby's new rules, the Sisters were dressed even more plainly than they used to be. Sister Vera wasn't wearing her beaded necklace or amethyst brooch on her huge wobbly bosom any more and Sister Hilda's hair was no longer that strange mauve colour: it was snowy white. Sister Mildred's hair was also different. Before it had been like a see-through doily of rigid white curls – now her pink, baldy scalp was even more visible through the wisps of hair that lay flat on her head. Lydia felt embarrassed to look at her. And poor old Sister Lottie looked all wrong in her sad flowerless hat. Only Lydia's grandmother looked exactly the same as before.

Whilst concentrating hard on not spilling any tea as she moved amongst the Sisters, Lydia was listening to what was being said, waiting for exactly the right moment. It came just as she was handing Sister Joan her cup and saucer: over by the door, in a hushed tone, Sister Mildred mentioned Pastor John's name. When the tutting and shushing had died away, Lydia said, 'What does sexual intercourse mean, Grandmother?'

Her question was like a bomb going off. In the commotion that followed Lydia immediately regretted what she'd asked. What had got into her? As if seeing it all in slow motion, Lydia watched Sister Joan's cup and saucer slip out of her hands onto the carpet, while next to her Sister Vera started choking on a Rich Tea Finger, causing her bosom to shake so violently Lydia feared it might burst out of her dress, sending buttons popping. Meanwhile, Sister Hilda, who had Valerie sitting on her lap, covered Val's ears with her hands and Sister Mildred quivered like a jelly. Sister Lottie had turned the colour of beetroot and looked as if she was trying not to giggle.

But Lydia's grandmother looked like thunder. Down on her hands and knees at Sister Joan's feet, she was scrubbing furiously at the carpet with a paper napkin. 'Go to your room at once, Lydia. You're not fit to mix in decent company.'

Closing the door after her, Lydia heard her grandmother say, 'I blame that whore of a mother of hers. She painted her nails red, you know.'

Upstairs, Lydia lay on her bed, her hands clasped behind her head. What *had* got into her? What had made her say something so stupid that was bound to cause trouble? Afraid to think how she might be punished, she swung herself off the bed and went to look out of the window. It had started to rain; in the distance she could see it slicing the air at an angle that was almost horizontal. Down in the road, she could see The Floozy tottering along on her high heels, her short mac belted tightly at her waist, an umbrella protecting her beehive hairdo, her bottom swinging from side to side. When she was out of sight, Lydia wondered what Noah was doing. Whatever it was he had to be having more fun than she was.

She went back to lying on the bed. Disappointed, she had half hoped that Valerie would come upstairs after her and keep her company. Since Lydia had started school back in September, Val had changed. There were times when her sister seemed happier to be with their grandmother than with Lydia. She had become everyone's favourite at church and the Sisters couldn't stop cooing over her or chucking her under the chin. Sometimes they squabbled over whose turn it was to have her sit on their lap.

Lydia certainly wasn't jealous – who wanted to sit on Sister Vera's lap and risk being suffocated by that enormous bosom! – but occasionally she did feel left out. At least Valerie was happy and had started to talk more and was sleeping in her own bed with only Belinda Bell for company. But Lydia missed doing things for her, missed being the only one who could understand her nods and

blinks. It upset her that she wasn't as important to Valerie as she used to be.

'Your grandmother's worried about you.'

Normally Lydia didn't have to think too much about where to look when she was being spoken to, but with Pastor Digby it was different. She couldn't stop herself from switching between his good eye and his sinister black eye patch. It was like a game of ping-pong – good eye, black eye patch, good eye, black—

'Lydia, are you listening to me?'

The rapping sharpness of his voice made Lydia concentrate extra hard and stand up straighter. Definitely the good eye. 'Yes, Pastor Digby,' she said.

'Your grandmother has asked me to talk to you because she's concerned that you're succumbing to outside influences.'

'Um ... I'm not sure what you mean, Pastor Digby,' she lied. She knew exactly what this was about. Just hadn't expected Pastor Digby to be the one who told her off.

He rose from his chair, his tall thin body looking like a scarecrow silhouetted in the light from the window as he stood with his back to her. 'I'm talking about wicked people putting filth into your mouth, Lydia. Your grandmother told me that yesterday you uttered words no child of your age should know or dare to say out loud. And I think you know to which words I am referring.'

'I only asked what they meant.'

Pastor Digby slowly turned round. 'But where did you hear such wicked words? That's what your grandparents and I want to know.'

Thinking fast and concerned that he might take her dictionary away if she told him the truth, Lydia said, 'It was the older children at the bus stop.'

His good eye glittered back at her. Did he believe her? Or had she just cooked her goose? Would he now ban her from going to school? Her gaze slid to the black eye patch. From the other side of the closed door she could hear her

grandmother singing to Valerie that Jesus wanted her for a sunbeam.

'Some children are born bad, Lydia. Did you know that?'

She shook her head, wondering where the conversation was going next. He came and sat down again. 'Unfortunately, it's true,' he said. 'Do you have bad thoughts, Lydia?'

She was having one right now. Why couldn't he drop dead and leave her alone?

'Tell me the truth, Lydia.'

'Sometimes,' she said warily.

He leaned forward, resting his elbows on the shiny fabric of his suit trousers. 'I thought as much. What kind of bad thoughts do you have?'

Hoping to shock him into leaving her alone, she said, 'I sometimes wish I was dead so I could be with my mum and dad.'

His good eye bulged like a full moon and he snapped to attention in the chair. 'Only God can decide who lives and dies,' he said sternly. 'That's why what your mother did was such a sin. It was selfish and wrong of her. Surely you don't want to be like her, Lydia, an evil unbeliever who abandoned her children on a railway line?'

Lydia suddenly wanted to run from the room. Why was he saying these things to her? Her mother hadn't been evil. She'd been unhappy. And it was all Lydia's fault that she had been unhappy – that's why she did what she did. That's why she killed herself.

'You know what happens to evil people like your mother, don't you, Lydia? They don't go to heaven to be with our Lord; they go to hell. Is that where you want to go? Lydia? Answer me. Is that where you want to go?'

Tears filled her eyes. She wanted to say yes, if it meant she could be with her mother again and tell her how sorry she was. But she knew that Pastor Digby would only leave her alone if she gave him the answer she thought he wanted to hear. 'No,' she tried.

'Louder, Lydia. I can't hear you.'

'No,' she said, 'I don't want to go to hell.'

'Then you must change. You must be the child God wants you to be, not this wild, disrespectful, feral, devil-child your grandmother tells me your mother allowed you to become. You must put that wretched to-be-pitied person behind you, Lydia. Can you do that?'

She swallowed and nodded.

'When I ask you a question I expect a proper answer, Lydia.'

'Yes, Pastor Digby,' she said. 'I will try to be a better person.'

That Sunday at church it was decided that Lydia would take the leaflets left over from their weekend in Scarborough in to school with her to distribute. She couldn't help but feel this was her grandmother's petty way of punishing her for ruining her Tea and Sisters Scripture meeting. Not that she had any intention of doing anything so embarrassing. She would simply dump them all in a bin.

Chapter Seventeen

Lydia was disappointed when there was no sign of Noah at school the next morning. She had been so looking forward to seeing him after a week of being apart. At first break, having offered to stay behind and help get the classroom ready for their art lesson, she asked Miss Dillinger if she knew what was wrong with Noah.

'His uncle phoned to say he had a hospital appointment,' Miss Dillinger said as Lydia stood at the sink filling jam jars with water from the tap.

'Has he got to have another operation on his leg?' she asked, concerned.

'As far as I'm aware his uncle didn't say anything about that.'

The last of the jam jars filled, Lydia began placing them carefully on the tables that Miss Dillinger had covered with newspaper. Something struck Lydia as being odd. Why wasn't it Noah's mother or father who had left the message? She thought of the photograph he had been carrying round with him, and because Miss Dillinger seemed to be in a chatty mood, she said, 'Is Noah's uncle taking him to the hospital?'

'I assume so.'

'Not his mum or dad, then?'

Miss Dillinger, counting out sheets of grey sugar paper, stopped what she was doing but didn't say anything. Lydia watched the woman's face closely; the hesitant expression was one she had come to know well. She had seen it a million times in other adult faces. If Miss Dillinger didn't want to answer Lydia's question, it could mean only one

thing: she had stumbled across something she wasn't supposed to know about.

'Good heavens,' Miss Dillinger suddenly exclaimed, 'just look at the time, Lydia! We're nowhere near ready. Quick, go and get the paintbrushes; they're on the middle shelf next to the glue.'

The next day another cross was put against Noah's name in the register. As soon as the opportunity arose, Lydia approached Miss Dillinger.

'Sorry, Lydia,' the teacher said. 'I have no idea where he is today; there's been no further message. Don't worry. I'm sure he'll show up tomorrow.'

But Lydia was worried. She was convinced something terrible had happened to Noah and as the day wore on her anxiety grew to the point that by the time she was on the bus going home, she imagined the absolute worst: she would never see her friend again.

The following day there was still no sign of Noah and once again Miss Dillinger claimed not to know where he was. Lydia decided the woman was lying. Nothing else for it; she would have to find out the truth for herself. Knowing that the headmistress insisted on fresh air swirling around every room of the school, no matter what the weather was, she went and hung about outside the open window of the staff room during afternoon break. For ages she breathed in the smell of cigarette smoke and listened to the teachers complaining about some of the children. Alfie Stone and Jack Horsley got the most mentions. As did Donna Jones.

With only a few minutes left before she knew the bell would ring, Lydia was ready to give up, but then she heard her own name being spoken. Jamming herself as near to the window as she dared without being seen, she held her breath and listened hard. They were talking about her and Noah. 'It's easy to see why they took to each other the way they did,' someone said. 'You know, having so much in common.'

'But that's the weird part. I get the distinct feeling Lydia doesn't know anything about Noah's background.' Lydia recognized Miss Dillinger's voice. 'She wouldn't have asked me what she did if she knew.'

'Why, what did she ask you?'

'She wanted to know if his parents had taken him to the hospital. Clearly Noah hasn't told her anything.'

'You're right, that is weird. You'd think he'd want to confide in someone, especially a kindred spirit.'

'Or maybe what happened to his parents is just too awful for him to talk about. Who could blame him?'

The bell rang and somebody inside the staff room sang, 'Hi bloody ho, it's off to teach we go.'

Yet again, the next day Noah's chair remained empty. At first break Lydia went to look for the person most likely to be able to help her. In the short time she had been at the school she had heard many stories about Mr Darby, the school caretaker. You always knew when he was nearby because he stank of disinfectant; it was rumoured that he dabbed it on like aftershave to cover up the smell of the gin that he drank all day. Depending on who you listened to he was either one of the Great Train Robbers who'd managed to escape the police and was hiding here until everyone had forgotten about the robbery, or he was a Russian spy on a secret mission. But the two things he was really famous for were knowing everything that went on in the school, and his stash of lost property pens, especially fountain pens. Some said he went round the classrooms when everyone had gone home and helped himself to them from the desks. If you wanted your pen back, you had to go and see him and pay a forfeit for being stupid enough to lose it in the first place. Lydia had heard that he made the boys hand over a whole sixpence to get a pen back, but made the girls show him their knickers. She had yet to speak to any girl who had actually done this, but perhaps that was because they were too embarrassed to admit it.

As she knocked on Mr Darby's door, Lydia hoped that

she wouldn't have to pay anything in exchange for asking for information.

'Not been with us long, have yer?' Mr Darby said, when she stepped into the dim, fuggy atmosphere of the boiler room. 'Aren't yer the lass who lost her mother?'

She wobbled her head in a yes-and-no kind of way, at the same time fighting the urge to cover her face with a hand. The pong of disinfectant made her want to gag.

'What's the matter? Cat got yer tongue?' He hauled himself from his chair and Lydia was shocked to see two enormous breasts staring back at her from the page of a newspaper laid out on a table he'd been sitting at. Her grandmother said that women who showed their naked bodies like that were filthy, nasty tarts. But Lydia thought the woman looked extremely clean and not at all nasty. In fact she was smiling in a very friendly way. Her breasts must have been quite heavy because she was holding them up with both hands and sort of pointing them towards whoever had taken the photograph.

'So what can I do for yer?' he asked, at the same time turning the page of the newspaper. 'Lost a pen? Is that it?'

Steeling herself, Lydia said, 'I want to know something,' she said.

'Oh, aye?' Staring at her, he scratched his chin; Lydia could hear the scrape of his nail on his bristly skin. 'And what might that be?'

'It's about a friend of mine, Noah Solomon.'

'And what made yer think I'd know owt about him?'

She shrugged helplessly. 'I just thought …' Her voice trailed off. How could she politely accuse him of knowing everything that went on at school because he was such a nosy parker? She began to think coming here hadn't been such a good idea after all. She took a step back towards the door.

He suddenly started to laugh at her. 'It's OK, lass, don't look so scared. I'm not about to eat yer. There's not enough on yer bones to feed a sparrow any road. So what is it yer want to know about this friend of yours?'

'I want to know what happened to his parents.'

'Do yer indeed?'

'Yes I do,' she said with as much conviction as she could. 'It's very important to me.'

He laughed again and sat down. 'Hark at yer with your posh cut-glass voice! "It's very important to me,"' he mimicked.

Lydia had never been called posh before. To her surprise she felt a rush of pride.

'OK, then,' he said. 'I'll tell yer what yer want to know. Sit yerself down.'

Lydia looked around the boiler room, noticing for the first time that the place was a giant slag heap of mess and clutter. Mops, brooms, buckets, tins of polish, grubby towels, boxes of soap, newspapers, punctured footballs, cans of disinfectant and a stack of wastepaper bins gave the impression of swallowing up the room whole. But nowhere could she see another chair.

'Go on,' Mr Darby said, 'pull up a drum. Or are yer too fancy for that?' He pointed to a large drum of cooking oil.

'Shouldn't this be in the kitchens?' she asked when she'd got herself settled.

'Yer accusing me of sommat?' he said sharply.

Aha! So the rumour about him pinching stuff was true. 'Tell me about Noah Solomon,' she said.

'Pushy little thing, aren't yer? Let's hope yer've got a strong stomach, because the way I see it, yer gonna need it. Aye, it's a grim tale and all. Are you sitting comfortably?'

She nodded.

'Then I'll begin.'

Chapter Eighteen

Lydia heard Noah before she saw him. She was hanging up her duffel coat whilst trying to stop Jack Horsley messing about with her hair when she caught the unmistakable sound of clanking footsteps.

Since visiting Mr Darby in his smelly boiler room yesterday afternoon – and escaping without having to give him anything! – she had been wondering what to say to Noah when he did finally return to school. She badly wanted him to know that she *knew*, but had no idea how he would react if she so much as hinted that she did. Now that he was here, though, she felt unexpectedly shy of him and playing for time, she pretended to hunt through her coat pockets for something vitally important whilst listening to the others dishing out their welcome-back comments.

'Look who it is – it's old spacky! ... Not floated off in your ark, then, spaso?'

Not a word did Noah say in response and when everything eventually went quiet and she was sure it was just the two of them left amongst the coats and plimsoll bags, Lydia turned round. He had his back to her and appeared to be doing what she'd just finished doing – hunting through his coat pockets for something vitally important.

'Hello,' she said awkwardly. 'How's your leg?'

He stopped what he was doing and faced her with a puzzled expression. 'My leg? It's the same as ever. Why do you ask?'

'Miss Dillinger said you were at the hospital on Monday. With your uncle.'

'Oh, that. It was nothing.'

The careless flatness of his reply smarted. After all the worry she'd gone through, how could he be so off-hand with her? Didn't he realize how much she cared about him? Her head buzzing with indignation and not minding how he would react, she said, 'Why didn't you tell me about your parents?' Straight off she could see she'd surprised him. And was glad.

'Why didn't you tell me about *your* parents?' he said with a frown.

Two could play at that game! 'You never asked,' she said, quick as a flash.

'Well, neither did you.'

Only then, as she tried to think of something else to fire back at him, did Lydia realize what he'd just admitted: that he knew about Mum and Dad. But how? It certainly wasn't something she had ever discussed with anyone at school. There again, Mr Darby seemed to know all about her.

She watched Noah pick up his bag from the floor and, regretting her outburst, she said, 'Can I ask you *now* about your parents?'

'What? Right now?'

'No, not *now*, silly. Later.'

He gave her a long, hard look. 'OK,' he said, 'after lunch, on the far side of the field. Under the beech tree.'

The morning dragged on. Who cared about long division or what boring old Monsieur Bertillon and his stupid family were getting up to in their *maison* when there was Noah's family to hear about? Break time had passed with Lydia helping him to catch up on the work he'd missed, and although she was brimming over with questions, she kept her mouth firmly shut.

But now, here they were beneath the copper beech tree, the chilly November wind swirling the fallen leaves on the ground at their feet. Noah seemed happy enough just to stand with her in the rustling silence, but Lydia wasn't. She decided to be the one to get things moving, to loosen

that tongue of his. 'My mother killed herself by jumping in front of a train,' she blurted out. She poked at a stone in the dusty hard ground with the toe of her shoe. 'My sister and I were sleeping on the embankment when she did it.'

'I know,' was all he said.

'Who told you?'

'Does it matter?'

'Was it Mr Darby, the caretaker?'

Noah shook his head. 'No. It was Donna Jones.'

The stone popped out of the ground and Lydia gave it a kick. She wished chicken pox, mumps, German measles, tonsillitis, and verrucas the size of golf balls on Donna Jones. All at the same time and with a dose of diarrhoea thrown in. She had no idea how Donna had found out about her mother, or why she hadn't said anything to Lydia, but for now that wasn't important. 'If you knew, why didn't you ask me about it?' she asked Noah.

'Because it would have led to us talking like this.'

'Is that so very bad?'

'Perhaps not for you, but for me, yes. I don't like to talk about what happened.'

'You think it's any easier for me, telling people about my mum's suicide?' As soon as the word was out, Lydia wanted to snatch it back. Never before had she uttered the word 'suicide' aloud. She began poking at another stone in the ground with her shoe, conscious that her cheeks were burning with something that she thought was embarrassed shame, although she couldn't really understand why.

'Was it very bad for you?' Noah asked.

No one had asked Lydia this before. Decisions and assumptions had been made on her behalf because of what her mother had done, but not one single person had actually asked her how she'd felt at the time. Now that someone had, she wasn't sure how to answer. 'There was too much going on to stop and think about it,' she said without looking up. 'Besides, I had my little sister to take care of.'

'You were lucky. I had nothing to distract me.'

She risked a glance at his face. 'Did you have any idea it was going to happen?'

'There'd been lots of arguments and all that kind of thing, but nothing to warn me that one day I'd come home from school and find—' He broke off, his eyes sliding away from hers.

Lydia waited patiently for him to carry on. And waited.

Flexing his clanky leg, he eventually said, 'Mum didn't answer the back door when I knocked so I looked in through the kitchen window and saw my father lying on the floor with his head in the oven. It seems stupid now when I say it, but I thought he was trying to mend it. He was always tinkering with stuff that had stopped working or was broken. I didn't even think it was odd he was home so early from work. I knocked on the window to attract his attention but he didn't seem to hear me.'

'Didn't you notice he wasn't moving?'

Noah shot her a dark look. 'I'd never come across anyone who had killed themselves by sticking their heads in a gas oven before, so perhaps I was a bit slow to act.'

Lydia could have kicked herself for her clumsiness. It had sounded as if she was criticizing, or worse, blaming Noah. How would she like it if he told her she might have been able to save her mother if she hadn't agreed to go for that walk in the middle of the night? 'I'm sorry,' she said. 'Just ignore me and my big mouth.'

He flexed his knee again and took up the story once more. 'I knocked and knocked and when I finally realized something was seriously wrong I smashed a pane of glass in the back door and let myself in. I switched off the gas and dragged my father out to the garden. I tried to give him the kiss of life, the way I'd seen it done in a book, but he was dead ... I was too late.'

Lydia pictured the scene: Noah struggling with his clanky leg and trying to heave his father's heavy body outside. She felt so sorry for him. But something else, too. Envy. There had been no opportunity for her to try and

save her mother. No last touch. No final goodbye. Only the terror of being woken from a deep, fuzzy sleep by the unearthly sound of metal screeching on metal. She'd had a vague feeling that fear had made her let out a scream, but she couldn't be sure. What she had instinctively known at the time was that her mother was in danger. She had leapt to her feet and scrambled pell-mell down the slippery bank towards the railway line. She hadn't given a thought to Valerie who was still strapped into her pushchair on the embankment. It was a while before anyone spotted her and when they did, someone yelled, 'For God's sake, don't let her see!' A man and a woman came and led her away. She'd tried to wriggle out of their grasp, but they wouldn't let go of her. She'd shouted at them: 'But my mother's down there, don't you understand? I have to go to her!'

'God help you, that's not your mother, dearie,' the woman told her. Initially this had given Lydia hope. She'd got it wrong! How silly of her to think her mother would do such a terrible thing, that she would want to kill herself, leaving Lydia and Valerie all alone. But her relief was soon shattered when she understood that the woman had meant something altogether worse: the body she wasn't allowed to see was no longer recognizable as Lydia's mother.

A cold gust of wind brought her back from that dawn morning and a shower of leaves fell like huge pieces of copper confetti at her feet. Her throat had tightened and tears were filling her eyes. Embarrassed, she worked at trying to loosen another stone in the ground. If Noah could tell his story without crying, so could she. 'When did you find your mother?' she asked.

'When I knew there was nothing more I could do for Dad I went looking for her. I found her upstairs on their bed. She'd been ... Dad had strangled her.'

Despite having heard this from Mr Darby, Lydia was still shocked to hear Noah say it. She couldn't imagine her father ever having wanted to do that to Mum. Not even when she accidentally knocked over his motorbike and ruined the paintwork. You'd have to be very cross with

the person you were married to, to want to kill them like that. Curious, she said, 'How did you know she'd been strangled?'

'I didn't at the time. I found that out afterwards. And that it was Dad who had killed her. He wrote me a letter.'

Lydia felt another pang of envy. Her mother hadn't left her a note. 'Do you still have the letter?' she asked.

He hesitated, as if he regretted what he'd just told her. 'I do,' he said slowly, 'but you must swear not to tell anyone.'

'Of course I won't tell anyone. Who would I tell, anyway?'

'You swear?' He suddenly seemed jumpy and anxious.

'I swear on ...' Not her mum or dad's life, so whose? 'On my sister's life,' she said, hoping that she wasn't tempting fate. 'So what did the letter say?' she asked.

'Not much. Mostly that he was sorry for the mess he was leaving behind him and that he hoped I wouldn't hate him for what he'd done.'

'And do you?'

'How can I hate him? He just went a bit crazy, that's all.'

That's all. Lydia wondered about this. Was that what had happened to her mother that night? Had she merely gone a bit crazy? Did it happen to everyone? Would she and Noah go a bit crazy one day? 'What did the police think of the letter when they read it?' she asked.

'I never showed it to them. It was *my* letter. It was private ... between Dad and me. That's why you mustn't tell anyone about it.'

'Could *I* read it?'

One of his eyebrows shot up. 'Why would you want to do that?'

The honest answer was that the more Noah shared with her, the better she felt. It was as if his own dark experience was shining a light on hers. But thinking he wouldn't understand this, she said, 'We're best friends, aren't we? And best friends share everything.'

When he didn't reply right away, Lydia began to worry. Supposing she had got it wrong and Noah didn't consider her his best friend?

'OK,' he said. 'I'll let you read it, but you must remember your promise.'

Suddenly the letter didn't matter to her. All that was important was that he hadn't denied their friendship.

Chapter Nineteen

Noah was very clear about two things.

The first was that Lydia must keep the promise she had made not to tell anyone about the letter and the second was that she had to meet him somewhere outside of school to read it. He said he couldn't risk taking the letter into school and someone getting their hands on it. She suspected he was thinking of Donna Jones's hands in particular. But since that day round the back of the Portakabins, Donna hadn't come near either of them. Lydia had had a heart-stopping scare just the other afternoon, when she'd caught sight of Donna going into a house at the other end of Hillside Terrace – the cheap end, as her grandmother called it. It turned out that Donna had an aunt who lived in the road and that was probably how she'd got to hear about Lydia's mum killing herself.

Following that day in the field beneath the beech tree when Noah had told her about his parents, Lydia had told him more about herself, about Dad, Creepy-Ridley, her mother's sweet sherry breath, and the ventriloquist's dummy. In exchange, he had told her that his parents' deaths had made it into the newspapers, and not just the local ones in Lincoln where he used to live, but into the big papers read by the whole country. Knowing that Noah was sort of famous made Lydia proud to be his friend. His cleverness – which he never showed off about – was something else she was proud of. Secretly she wanted that same cleverness for herself and she had started to work extra hard in class. Nothing pleased her more than when she got a better mark than Noah. Apparently, when he'd spent so

much time in hospital, he'd done nothing but read from a set of encyclopaedias his father had bought for him.

Lydia was glad that her mother's death hadn't made it to the big newspapers – just two paragraphs in the *Maywood Gazette* – as she hated to think of so many people knowing how Mum had died. Particularly people at school. Yet Noah wasn't worried about anyone at school finding out who he was. He said his name and photograph had never appeared in the papers, so why would anyone think he had anything to do with the story? But he wasn't happy that the headmistress and teachers at school had been put in the picture by his uncle. 'I don't like knowing that they're watching me,' he admitted one day. 'They're probably worried I'm going to go loopy and fly off the handle.'

Lydia was fascinated by this remark. 'Do you think you *will* go loopy?' she asked.

'Who knows?'

Something else that fascinated Lydia was Noah's uncle. Noah rarely spoke about him in any real detail, so in the hope he would tell her more, she had thought she could trade with him by telling him about her grandparents and the Sisters and Brothers and their church. Disappointingly, all she'd got in return was that he thought the church she went to sounded a bit weird and that it wasn't like the one his uncle occasionally took him to.

How and where to meet up with Noah to read his letter was proving to be almost impossible. Apart from school and church and the end of the garden, Lydia didn't go anywhere where she could be alone with him.

There's always a way, her father used to say, and a week into December, when every day the sky was the colour of dirty dishwater, an opportunity to meet with Noah outside of school fell into Lydia's lap.

Sister Lottie was ill in bed with bronchitis. The Sisters had been praying for her and taking it in turns to visit with Pyrex dishes of nourishing meals, most of which she was too ill to eat. It was decided that Lydia should

also take her turn to pay a call on Sister Lottie and so on Sunday afternoon she was loaded up with a flask of hot vegetable soup and a copy of Pastor Digby's sermon, which he had written out specially for Sister Lottie. Seeing this as a golden opportunity, Lydia hatched a plan to meet Noah at his uncle's house when she had finished her visit to Sister Lottie.

What she hadn't bargained on was how long it would take her to reach Sister Lottie. From the back of her grandfather's junk-piled wooden garage, a heavy, rusting old bicycle emerged. It was the first thing Lydia had seen which had actually belonged to her father. Despite the half can of oil squirted at the gears and chain, the bicycle still made a deafening racket when the pedals went round. The saddle was as hard and pointy as a rock with a rusting metal spring bursting through the split leather, and there was also the small matter of the crossbar to negotiate.

Ker-lunk, *ker-dunk*, *ker-lunk*, *ker-dunk* went the pedals. Downhill wasn't too bad, but uphill was a nightmare. Several times she had to jump off and push the bike. Eventually, twenty minutes late, she made it to Cuckoo Lane where Sister Lottie lived. Exhausted and steaming like a hot pasty in her enormous duffel coat, she unhooked the basket from the handlebars, left the bike leaning against the gate and panted up the short path to the little terraced house. She'd been told how to let herself in and after slipping her hand through the letterbox, she found the key on the end of a long piece of string. Once inside, she called out to Sister Lottie. 'Up here,' came a faint reply, followed by the sound of coughing.

Feeling a bit like Little Red Riding Hood as she went upstairs with the basket, Lydia held on tightly to the banister; the narrow strip of shabby stair carpet was thin and coming away dangerously in places. Balls of dust and fluff had collected in the corners of the varnished steps. Knowing how fussy her grandmother was about housework and how she was always telling Lydia that cleanliness was next to godliness, she wondered why no

one from church, including her grandmother, had offered to flick a duster round Sister Lottie's house since she'd been stuck in bed.

The poor woman didn't look at all well. She was propped up in bed in a shabby pink bedjacket, her pale face almost lost in the whiteness of the pillows. She smiled when she saw Lydia. 'What a lovely surprise,' she said. 'Is your grandmother with you? Is she downstairs?'

'No. I came on my own. I cycled all the way,' Lydia said proudly, 'on my father's old bicycle.'

'Goodness! What an adventure! But I'm afraid I'm not very good company at the moment.'

'That's all right. I've brought you something to eat. Oh, and Pastor Digby's sermon. I'm supposed to read it to you while you have your soup.'

'That doesn't sound much fun for you. I'm sure you'd rather be somewhere else.'

Lydia thought of Noah. The plan had been to get her visit over and done with as quickly as possible, but here now with Sister Lottie and seeing how unwell she was, Lydia's heart softened. This funny old woman had always been so kind to her. 'I've come here specially to see you,' she said brightly, shrugging off her coat and setting the basket down on the end of the bed. 'Shall I fetch a bowl from the kitchen for your soup?'

Sister Lottie's house was so small it reminded Lydia of a doll's house. The kitchen was particularly tiny; there wasn't even room for the smallest of tables. There was a white china sink with a wooden draining board, a green and yellow gas cooker, two shelves that contained a tea caddy and a small collection of tins and jars – pilchards, butter beans, rice pudding, custard powder, Shippam's paste. A refrigerator hummed noisily in the corner and next to it was a cream cupboard where Lydia found a bowl and a spoon.

On her way back to the stairs she stopped to push open the door to the only other room downstairs and peeped in. It was the front room and was jam-packed with furniture,

big and small. With its flowery wallpaper, fancy frilled and fringed lampshades, doilies and antimacassars, books and ornaments everywhere, it looked a busy sort of room. The framed pictures on the walls were old-fashioned black and white photographs. Some were very old, Lydia decided, judging from the funny clothes the people were wearing. She closed the door after her and carried on carefully up the stairs with the tray. Now that she had taken off her coat and had cooled down she realized just how cold Sister Lottie's house was. Surely that wasn't good for someone so ill?

After she'd poured out the bowl of soup and rearranged Sister Lottie's pillows so she could sit up comfortably, she noticed that behind the chair she was about to sit on there was the teeniest-weeniest fireplace. 'Would you like me to light a fire for you?' she asked. 'It's very cold in here.'

Sister Lottie's pale face brightened. 'Would you? Oh, that would be marvellous. How good you are to me. What an angel you are!'

Lydia had never actually made a fire before, but she didn't let on to Sister Lottie. She gathered up all the equipment she thought she needed – the coal scuttle from the front room, along with a pair of tongs, some kindling in a box by the back door, and a box of matches from the windowsill behind the cooker. Something was missing though. 'I need some paper,' she said to Sister Lottie. 'Do you have any old newspapers?'

Sister Lottie shook her head, and then right at the same time, their eyes fell on Pastor Digby's ten-page sermon, which Lydia had yet to read. 'That will do,' Lydia said decisively.

Sister Lottie gasped, and then coughed painfully, her face turning pink. 'Do you think we ought to?' she croaked when she'd caught her breath.

Already screwing up the sermon into loose balls, Lydia shrugged. 'I won't tell him if you don't. And anyway, I can tell you word for word what his sermon was about.'

Sister Lottie relaxed back into the pillows. 'Of course you can; you're the brightest little girl I know.'

Lydia suspected that apart from Valerie, she was the *only* girl Sister Lottie knew. 'I'm not that little, you know,' she said, adding one last lump of coal to the fire and striking a match.

'You are to an old woman like me. What's more, you're a very special girl whom I'm immensely fond of.'

It was so long since anyone had said anything so nice to her, Lydia didn't know what to say.

Strange, she thought later as she pumped away on the *ker-lunky, ker-dunky* pedals, that an unexpected kindness like that should make her feel sad. You'd think it would have the opposite effect.

It was getting dark when she found herself on the road that, according to the map Noah had drawn for her, would lead directly to Upper Swallowsdale House. He had told her that he lived in the middle of nowhere and that she had to watch out for a stile in the drystone wall on the right and then a large house made of dirty grey stone.

She saw the stile and, finding the hill too steep, she swung her leg over the crossbar and jumped off the bike, pushing it the last few yards. Noah had explained that his uncle would be out, which meant they would have the place to themselves.

Noah was waiting for her at the front door. 'You're late,' he said irritably. 'I thought you weren't coming.'

'Sorry, but I stayed with Sister Lottie longer than I thought I would.'

He instantly cheered up at her apology. 'Oh, well, you're here now, that's all that matters. Let's go up to my bedroom.'

Lydia had never seen Noah tackle stairs before – everything at school was on one level – and she found herself having to look away as he struggled with the steps. Lagging behind, she discreetly looked back down to the gloomy hallway. While it was the largest she had ever seen – in

fact she had never been inside such a big house – she could see the tell-tale signs of something that Noah had kept quiet about: Noah and his uncle were poor. There weren't any carpets anywhere and the floor wasn't even properly made; it was just slabs of worn, shiny stone. They couldn't afford electricity either, by the looks of things. Instead of proper lights there were white candles fixed onto the walls with funny little mirrors behind them. Melting wax was dripping onto the stone floor beneath them as well as making a mess on the top of a scruffy wooden chest. There were strange unframed paintings on the walls. She couldn't really work out what they were pictures of, but it occurred to her that maybe someone had made a mistake and they were actually hanging upside down.

There were more paintings covering the walls on the landing upstairs. One seemed to have been painted with chunks of blue and purple paint and showed a naked woman sprawled across a fancy settee that had only one end to it. But it wasn't the kind of woman Mr Darby had been looking at in his newspaper in the boiler room. This one had two eyeless heads on the end of long thin, bendy necks. Lydia turned away from it quickly. 'You get used to them after a while,' Noah said.

Annoyed that she'd been caught out, she said, 'Who's it of?' She didn't want him to think she was childish enough to be embarrassed.

'My mother.'

'Your mother! She had two heads?'

He smiled. 'No, silly. It's called abstract art.'

'Oh, that,' she said airily. She made a mental note to look up the word 'abstract' when she got home.

'This is another painting of my mother,' he said when they had reached the end of the landing, which was about a mile long and lit with yet more candles. 'It's her on her eighteenth birthday. Do you like it?'

This painting was much more normal. It was a picture of a pretty fair-haired girl wearing a low-necked dress and a necklace. She was sitting on a chair and behind her was

a mirror with the fuzzy reflection of a man in it. The style was very different from the other picture. A lot less paint had been used and the colours were soft and delicate. Lydia decided she liked it.

'See the man in the mirror?' Noah said. 'That's my uncle. He and Mum were twins.'

'So it was both their birthdays?'

'Yes. My uncle says it was the first picture he'd painted that he was actually proud of.'

'Your uncle did it?' Lydia couldn't keep the surprise out of her voice. 'Did he also do the other one?'

Noah nodded. 'All the paintings in the house are his.'

She thought of the upside-down pictures downstairs. 'Is he a proper artist?' she asked doubtfully. 'You know, one who gets paid for his paintings?'

'Oh, yes. He gets paid stacks of money. I'm thinking of being an artist like him one day.'

Thinking of the bare stone floors and all the candles, Lydia kept her mouth shut. For once she felt she knew something that Noah didn't: that her uncle couldn't possibly be rich. Only poor people used candles; that's what had happened to them when Mum ran out of money for the electricity meter.

Noah's bedroom was also lit with candles. There were four lined up along the window ledge, three on the mantelpiece, two on the desk next to his bed and another two on the bookcase that was packed full with books and board games. Shadows played against the walls and the room smelled pleasantly of used matches. But best of all, there was a fire burning in the grate; behind a blackened metal guard logs spat and popped noisily. Drawn to it, she stared into the flickering flames, wanting to say how brilliant it was that he was allowed his very own fire in his bedroom. But she didn't dare. If this was normal for Noah, she didn't want him to think she was so easily impressed. Instead she said, 'You're lucky to have such a big room all to yourself. Mine's much smaller and I have to share it with Valerie.'

'I expect it's better than being on your own all the time.'

'But at least you have your uncle. He sounds as if he's—' She was going to say fun, but remembering the picture of Noah's scary two-headed mother out on the landing, she quickly changed her mind and settled for, 'interesting.'

'He's that all right. Do you want something to eat?'

'What have you got?'

From the bottom drawer of the desk he pulled out a battered old Crawford's biscuit tin. He took the lid off and offered her the tin. Other than in a shop, Lydia had never seen so many sweets all together. There were Spangles, Smarties, Rolos, Opal Fruits, Curly Wurlies and Milky Way bars. 'Help yourself,' he said. 'Or would you rather have something else? I can make you some toast in front of the fire if you'd prefer.'

The idea of making toast by the fire sounded like fun to Lydia, but not if Noah had to go all the way downstairs for the bread and then back up again. 'This will be fine,' she said. She helped herself to a packet of Rolos, took one and returned the packet to the tin.

'No,' he said, 'take them all.'

'Really?'

'Of course. I've got some Tizer if you'd like it.'

She hesitated. 'Will you have to go downstairs for it?'

'I have everything I need up here.' He went over to the massive wardrobe on the far side of the room and opened one of the doors. She stared open-mouthed at what was practically a small larder. Noah had more food in his wardrobe than Sister Lottie had in her entire kitchen. 'Good, isn't it?' he said. 'I'm what you call self-sufficient. But then I have to be; my uncle sometimes forgets I'm here.' He poured out two mugs of Tizer, handed her one and then pointed for her to sit on the bed. 'When you've finished your drink I'll get my dad's letter for you.'

Lydia sipped her Tizer slowly, letting the bubbles fizz up into her nose. She glanced round the comfortably untidy room, taking in the candlelight and the fire, the

well-stocked larder in the wardrobe, the telescope in front of the window, the plastic model aeroplanes hanging on threads of cotton from the ceiling, the chemistry set and spinning globe of the world on his desk, the posters of Concorde and Neil Armstrong on the moon, the shelves of books and games – Mousetrap, Twister, Monopoly – and wondered if she was dreaming. Noah's world was so different from hers. He seemed to have so many interesting things all to himself and so much freedom. There was no one like her grandparents constantly watching over him, stopping him from having fun.

'Where's your uncle?' she asked.

'London. He went down there last night.'

'London? You mean you're here alone?'

'I often am. That's why I couldn't make it to school after half-term.'

'So you didn't have a hospital appointment?'

'Oh, I had that, but the next day Uncle Brad had to be in London to exhibit some of his pictures. Which meant I couldn't get to the bus stop for school.'

'Didn't anyone from school telephone to find out where you were?'

'The phone did ring, but Uncle Brad had left me strict instructions not to answer it, just in case school found out I was here alone. The last thing he wants is them poking their noses in and making things difficult for us.'

'Why didn't you tell me this before?'

'I never think those kinds of things are important.'

'I do. I was worried about you.' Lydia blushed at her own confession and then let out a loud, Tizer-fuelled burp. She slapped a hand over her mouth and giggled.

Noah grinned. 'Bet you can't do that again.'

'I bet I can.' She flexed her throat and belched satisfyingly loudly.

They spent the next ten minutes out-burping each other until their sides ached with laughter. Lydia couldn't

remember the last time she had felt so ridiculously happy.

They were making so much noise, they didn't hear the sound of footsteps or the door opening.

'Fee fie foe fum, I smell the unmistakable whiff of fun,' said a man's voice.

Chapter Twenty

In Lydia's imagination Noah's uncle had been a friendly, jolly, absent-minded, tubby man with spectacles and a beard. She supposed she had wanted to think that her friend had someone nice and kind taking care of him.

Uncle Brad – as Noah had referred to him for the first time that afternoon – was far from being tubby. He was tall. Lanky tall, and as skinny as a drainpipe. His hair was a dull blond colour and Lydia's grandparents would have been disgusted by how long it was; it all but touched the shoulders of his pink and white flowery patterned shirt. He was wearing a purple scarf knotted at his neck and purple trousers made of velvet. They were embarrassingly tight until just below the knee, where they suddenly flared out. Lydia had never seen anything like him before. She'd heard of hippies and something called a beatnik and wondered if he was one of them. She tried not to stare, but he really was so peculiar, like a brightly coloured daddy-long-legs.

'Who's the groovy little friend, Noah?' he asked from the doorway where he stood with one shoulder resting casually against the frame. His voice was not altogether clear. It sounded a lazy can't-be-bothered kind of voice.

'Her name's Lydia.' Unlike Lydia, who was blushing and standing nervously to attention, Noah was still lying on the bed, propped up on one elbow.

Uncle Brad waved at Lydia, just one sweep of his hand, as though wiping a window clean to peer through it. 'Hi, Lydia,' he said. 'Nice to meet you.'

Lydia blushed an even deeper shade of red.

'Why are you home so early?' Noah asked his uncle. 'I thought you weren't coming home till late tonight.'

'I'd had enough. Everyone I met was beyond tedious.' He yawned hugely, not even attempting to cover his mouth with his hand. 'Ma-*a-a-an*, but I'm starving. Don't suppose you have any odds and ends I could scrounge, do you? There's a zero-food situation downstairs.'

'Help yourself.'

Uncle Brad came into the room and ambled over to the wardrobe. He helped himself to a couple of biscuits. 'God knows what I'd do without him, Lydia,' he said as he munched noisily and sprayed crumbs into the air. 'He's a saint for putting up with me. I must be the worst uncle ever. Isn't that right, Noah?'

'You're not so bad,' Noah said with a faint smile.

'See what I mean, Lydia? He's a saint. Anyone else would have told me to sling my hook and buy my own biscuits. Not this boy. Heart of gold.' He pushed a hand through his long blond hair and moved back towards the door. 'Well then, I'll leave you two groovesters to get on with whatever it was you were doing. Sorry to have interrupted you.'

'It's getting late,' Lydia said when they were alone. 'I ought to go.'

'You don't have to go just because my uncle's home.'

'No really, I should. I don't want to be too late and make my grandparents suspicious that I've been somewhere other than Sister Lottie's.'

Rolling off the bed, Noah got awkwardly to his feet. 'Will you come again?'

'If I can find a way, yes.'

'I don't understand why you don't just tell your grandparents about me. Then you could come any time you wanted.'

Lydia picked up her coat from the floor and thought of how they would react to Noah's extraordinary uncle. 'It's better that I don't,' she said. 'Anyway, secrets are fun.'

It was only when she was riding the *ker-lunk*, *ker-dunk*

beast home in the dark that she remembered Noah had forgotten to show her his secret letter.

The next day at tea-time, to Lydia's delight, her grand-parents announced that seeing as everyone at church was busy in the run-up to Christmas, with the strict rota of street evangelizing they had to do, she was to make herself useful and keep Sister Lottie company after school each day. Whilst she wasn't glad that Sister Lottie was ill, it did mean, as she discussed with Noah at school in the morning, she would now be able to see him secretly after every visit she made to the old lady.

Sister Lottie really did seem to be quite poorly. Lydia could see that everything was an effort for her. Perhaps she was bored. The few times Lydia could remember being ill in bed she had always been bored.

While she cleared the ashes out from the grate, made another fire and gave Sister Lottie a bowl of her grand-mother's pearl barley soup, she tried to think what might cheer up the old woman.

'Do you still have all your lovely hats, Sister Lottie?' she asked.

'Don't tell anyone,' the woman whispered, as though she was frightened somebody might hear, 'but I didn't throw them away as I was supposed to. I know Pastor Digby says it's a sin to value anything too much but I just couldn't part with my dear old friends. They're in a box under the bed.'

'Shall we get them out and check they're all right? We could try them on, just to be sure.'

Sister Lottie's face broke into a small smile.

It was dusty under the bed and the box was larger than Lydia had expected. When she'd got the lid off and peeled away the layers of tissue paper, she realized she had seen only a tiny part of Sister Lottie's precious collection. 'Can I try this one on?' she asked, very taken with a pale green hat complete with a veil. She went over to admire herself

in the three-way mirror on the dressing table. 'I've never seen you wearing it,' she said, catching her profile this way and then that way. The veil did a fantastic job of hiding her eyebrows. 'Why's that?'

'Sister Vera once told me it was too grand for church. She was probably right.'

Lydia kept her thoughts about Sister Vera to herself and went back to the box. 'Which one do you want to try on?' she asked.

'You choose for me.'

Lydia searched for the hat that she remembered Sister Lottie wearing most often, the one with the tiny robin peeking out from behind the flowers. 'How about this one? I always liked you in it.'

Sister Lottie put her bowl of soup on the bedside table and took the hat. Lydia fetched the hand mirror from the dressing table. 'See, it makes you look more like your old self. Doesn't that make you feel better?'

Staring at her reflection, Sister Lottie tilted her head from side to side. She put a hand to the bedraggled flowers sewn onto the floppy brim and stroked them gently. Something sad and faraway washed over the old woman's face and Lydia knew then that she had made a mistake. The hats weren't making Sister Lottie feel better at all.

Ten minutes later, guilty that she was rushing away so soon, Lydia said goodbye and set off for Upper Swallowsdale. It was pitch-black and with no street lamps and hardly any cars on the road, she was dependent upon the faint glow of light from her bicycle lamp to guide her to Noah's house.

As before, he was waiting for her at the front door. The candles in the hall flickered and spluttered in the cold draught when he swung the heavy wooden door shut. She could see from the look on his face that he was pleased to see her. Her heart swelled.

'Is your uncle here?' she asked.

'Don't worry about him; he's in his studio working on a new painting. Come on, let's go upstairs.'

Noah's bedroom seemed even more magical than Lydia remembered it. Laid out on a blanket in front of the roaring fire was a plate of sliced white bread, a pot of jam and a packet of butter. 'I'm going to make us some toast,' he said, getting down awkwardly onto the floor. He picked up a long fork and hooked a piece of bread onto it. 'Can you take the guard away for me?'

Lydia did as he said and sat next to him. Within no time at all they were biting into hot toast, their lips shiny with jam and butter. I never want this moment to end, Lydia thought. This is perfect. This is how I want my life to be. Always. 'I wish I could live here with you,' she said shyly when they'd finished eating and were licking their fingers clean.

He smiled. 'You'd soon change your mind after living with my uncle for a week.'

'He seems OK to me. He lets you do whatever you want and he's not at all strict.'

Noah shrugged. 'Sometimes it's as if he's the child and I'm the adult. There are days when I get tired of it.'

'Do you have any grandparents?'

'Nope. All dead. It's just me and Uncle Brad. Do you want to read my dad's letter now?' Without waiting for her to answer, he got to his feet and went over to the desk. She watched him root around in the bottom drawer until he found what he was looking for. She decided to save him the trouble of getting back down onto the floor and went and sat on the bed. Then, very carefully, as if he was handing her the Crown jewels, he gave her the letter. Almost afraid to read it, she unfolded the single sheet of paper. The writing was messy and shaky, almost unreadable in places. Out of the corner of her eye Lydia was aware of Noah moving aimlessly round the room.

Dear Noah,
I'm sorry. Sorry for everything. Please, PLEASE believe me when I say I never meant to do it. I loved your mother but she was going to leave us.

I couldn't let that happen. She was my world. All I ever wanted. Forgive me if you can. Don't hate me for leaving you on your own but I can't live without her. Or with what I've done.

Goodbye, Noah.

Lydia folded the letter and passed it back to Noah, who had now come to a stop and was sitting on the bed beside her. 'When did he write it? I mean, when did it happen?'

'Earlier this year. The third of April.'

A few months before she lost her mother, Lydia thought. 'Did it make you feel angry?' she asked.

'Yes. Was it the same for you?'

'A bit. But I didn't think it was right. If someone dies you're supposed to feel sad, aren't you? Feeling angry with Mum, because of what she'd done, felt like wearing the wrong clothes. Sort of scratchy and too tight.'

He nodded. 'Uncle Brad was angry. So angry he drove his car into a brick wall. He said it made him feel better. But only for a while. He gets drunk quite often. He says it helps.'

Lydia thought of her mother and all those empty sherry bottles. Her mother had only been trying to make herself feel better. 'Do you think we should try it?' she asked, half joking but half curious.

'I already have.'

Lydia was impressed. 'What was it like?'

'Foul. I was sick and woke up with a terrible headache. I don't know how my uncle does it.'

They sat in silence for a few minutes. Lydia was just thinking how much she and Noah had in common, and how that thought made her feel better, kind of happier and less cold and prickly inside, when a painful stab of guilt stopped her short. She had no right to start feeling better or happier, because unlike Noah, who couldn't be blamed for what his father had done, it was entirely her fault that her mother had killed herself. And nothing could ever take away that feeling inside her.

A sudden bone-jumping bang at the door had Noah snatching the letter out of Lydia's hands. He'd just managed to put it safely back in the desk drawer when Uncle Brad burst in, crashing the door against the wall. 'And who might you be, young lady?' he demanded, his hair wild and his face splattered with paint.

'This is Lydia,' Noah said. 'Don't you remember her?'

Uncle Brad staggered into the room on his long, spidery legs. He came right up to the bed where Lydia was still sitting. He stared hard at her, bent down and took her chin in his rough hand. It smelled oily. 'Actually, now you mention it, there is something familiar about her.' Terrified, Lydia allowed him to turn her head slowly to the right and then slowly back to the left. 'Interesting profile,' he said, his breath coming at her in a fiery blast. 'I could do something with that.' He pressed his thumb into her chin. 'What's more, young lady, you're going to be a beautiful woman one day.' He straightened up abruptly.

Lydia's face burned. Was he drunk and making fun of her?

For days afterwards, Lydia replayed Uncle Brad's words in her head. A beautiful woman. She was going to be beautiful one day. A tiny part of her began to believe it and she would often find herself standing in front of the bedroom mirror searching her face for signs of what was to come. Yet the more she studied her reflection, the more she decided Noah's uncle was mad. She was ugly and always would be.

Chapter Twenty-One

In the year Lydia turned eleven four things happened.

It was 1971 and in February everyone in the country had to stop using pounds, shillings and pence and convert to decimal currency. Lydia's grandparents thought it was disgraceful that people were abbreviating the word *pence* to *pee*. Sister Lottie had been so anxious about the new system of money she had begged Lydia to go shopping with her. 'Just until I've got the hang of it,' the old woman had said. 'You know how flustered I get.'

Then during the summer holidays, a few days after Uncle Brad had brought home a television for Noah to watch the astronauts driving round on the moon in a moon buggy, Noah was given the news that he no longer had to wear his leg brace. His leg was nowhere near perfect – he still walked with a bad limp – but without the heavy contraption strapped to it, he could get around much more easily.

A month later in September, Lydia and Noah, along with all of their classmates, started at Swallowsdale Comprehensive. It was very nearly the end of the new autumn term when Lydia came home from school to learn that her grandmother had been taken into hospital for an operation and would be staying there for some time. 'With your grandmother not here, you'll have to look after your sister and take over the running of the house,' her grandfather told Lydia before she'd even got her coat off.

'What's wrong with her?' Lydia asked.

'Never you mind! Just make sure you have her in your prayers. Now out of my way; I have things to do.'

Lydia went upstairs to find her sister. Valerie was five now and with her sweet, angelic face and fine blonde hair – which she had been allowed to grow – she had become the apple of their grandmother's eye. She didn't have a naughty bone in her body and she behaved as perfectly as she looked. Which of course made Lydia, who had grown a whopping five inches in the last year, appear even more of an awkward, gangling tomboy. Unlike Val, she wasn't allowed to grow her hair and she regularly had to sit on a kitchen chair and watch her dark curls drop to the floor as her grandmother wielded the scissors. She didn't care. Nothing that went on at home was of any interest to her. She had long since accepted that what really mattered was what went on beyond the walls of number thirty-three Hillside Terrace. The real Lydia Turner only existed inside her head or when she was away from her grandparents. She was happiest when she was with Noah. Or Sister Lottie, whom Lydia secretly considered to be her proper grandmother.

It was after Lydia had confided in the old lady about Noah being her only real friend that Sister Lottie suggested Lydia bring him to church one Sunday morning. Lydia knew the suggestion was kindly meant, but she couldn't imagine anything worse than letting Noah experience the full embarrassing horror of the Brothers and Sisters. Not wanting to hurt Sister Lottie's feelings, she had said she didn't think he would be interested.

She was wrong. When Lydia asked Noah if he'd like to come to church with her, explaining that if he came her grandparents might approve of him and decide he was a suitable friend for her, he'd said he would but wanted to know why they might think he wasn't a suitable friend.

'Because they only want me to mix with believers,' she'd told him

'What's a believer when he's at home?'

'A believer is someone who believes in God.'

'And do you?'

'Sometimes I do and sometimes I don't.'

'Sounds OK to me. But I thought you wanted to keep our friendship a secret?'

'There's no point in it being a secret if I can only see you at school.'

So it was arranged, and the next Sunday Noah asked his uncle to drop him off in the town centre, having made no mention of where he was going. Lydia had made Noah swear he wouldn't let Uncle Brad come anywhere near the Brothers and Sisters, not when there was no knowing what they would make of him. Sister Lottie was the first to welcome Noah and within minutes of his arrival others were buzzing curiously around him wanting to know who he was. Lydia was amazed how relaxed he was around grown-ups. He seemed to know exactly what to say to get on their right side and gain their acceptance. Throughout the service he sang loudly and said Amen and Praise The Lord with such sincerity she could have believed he'd always been a member of their church. She felt proud that he could put on such a convincing performance for her benefit.

His only blunder, so it seemed, was to cross himself in front of the altar, which was actually nothing more than a table with a wooden cross on it. Lydia had no idea why such a simple gesture should have provoked the reaction it did, but Pastor Digby's swivelling eye nearly popped out of its socket and her grandmother muttered something about Popish nonsense. Even so, everyone was polite to him during tea and biscuits and said they hoped he would come again. He later joked with Lydia that the Brothers and Sisters' acceptance of him was because adults can never resist a crippled child – this had been just before he'd had his leg brace removed.

'Was it very awful for you?' she asked him.

'It wasn't as bad as I thought it would be. They're a weird bunch, though. But then my uncle says most churches are made up of people who don't fit in anywhere else. Misfits, he calls them.'

Lydia thought about this for a few moments. 'But that's

what *we* are, aren't we?' she said. 'We're misfits who don't really fit in with everyone else.'

'I suppose you're right.'

'Does it bother you?'

'Why? Who wants to be the same as everyone else? I'm happy being who I am. By the way, did I pass the test with your grandparents?'

'They haven't said anything bad about you, so hopefully, yes. Will you come to church with me again?'

'I don't think so. That one-eyed coot Pastor Digby gave me the creeps. And anyway, Uncle Brad would rather I went to St Joseph's. He doesn't go regularly himself, but when he does, he insists I go with him.' St Joseph's was the red brick-built Catholic church next to the cinema and Lydia had recently discovered that for some strange reason anyone who went to that church was known as a left-footer. She had never asked Noah why this was, or what it meant, for fear of appearing stupid. Something she was always keen to avoid with him.

'You don't really think God made the world in only seven days, do you?' he once asked her.

He had asked the question with such dismissive author-ity, she'd said, 'Of course not. That's just a story for little children like Valerie.' She'd said nothing about quite liking the idea of a God who had that much power. That with a click of his fingers he could do whatever he wanted and make everything right.

Valerie, on the other hand, believed every word Pastor Digby said about God and Jesus as well as everything their grandmother taught her. 'She's full of the Lord's grace,' their grandmother would say with pride. 'A true child of God.' Every picture Valerie drew or painted portrayed some Bible story or other. The stories she wrote at school – she was now at infant school – always contained charac-ters with biblical names and whenever she sang, it was always a hymn. The Sisters said she had the voice of a

heavenly angel and often encouraged her to sing to them during their Tea and Sisters Scripture meetings. Valerie was nothing like the silent, anxious child she'd once been; she was confident and chatty and completely devoted to their grandmother.

Lydia had learned the hard way to be careful what she now said to Val. Saddened that her sister couldn't remember their mother, she had made the mistake of trying to bring back some of the memories for her. Val had immediately got out her crayons and drawn a picture of their mother from the description Lydia had given her. Their grandfather had been furious when he'd seen it and walloped Lydia on the side of the head so hard her ear had rung for days afterwards. She was accused of brainwashing her sister and sent to bed without any tea. Being punished for the slightest thing was something Lydia was quite used to. There were days, weeks even, when she didn't seem able to do anything right.

When Valerie started becoming aware of the difference in the way they were treated and got upset by it, she was told by their grandmother that Lydia had to be punished for her own good, that it was what God wanted. It was also God's wish that Val's clothes were brand new and Lydia's were all bought from jumble sales because it was pointless wasting good money on new clothes for her while she was growing so fast.

Lydia found Valerie in their bedroom. She was sitting at the dressing table, her head bent in concentration. She looked up when she saw Lydia. 'I'm making a card for Grandmother,' she said. 'She's in hospital.'

'Do you know what's wrong with her?' Lydia asked, at the same time admiring her sister's handiwork. Val had drawn a bed with presumably their grandmother sitting up in it and in the top left-hand corner was a smiling angel, her hands clasped together in prayer.

'Grandfather says she has to have an operation.'

'Did he say what kind of operation?'

'No. There, I've finished. Do you like it?' Valerie held the card up for Lydia to see. 'I want it to be really special so it makes her feel better.'

'It's lovely,' Lydia said. 'And you're a very clever and kind girl to go to so much trouble.' She meant what she was saying, but she hated the way Valerie's kindness always showed up her badness. It made her feel petty and mean-spirited.

But, she reminded herself, if her grandparents treated her the same way they treated Valerie, then maybe it would be different. As it was, Valerie was the favourite and Lydia was the nuisance. And that, she told herself firmly, was not Valerie's fault. She must never, *ever* blame her sister. Valerie was simply too young to understand what was going on.

Over the following days, before and after school, Lydia cooked, washed and ironed. She swept and mopped, she vacuumed and she polished. Valerie did her bit by helping with the washing-up and making the beds while Lydia did her homework. But heaven help Lydia if their grandfather came home from work and found the brass door knocker and letterbox not polished enough or the cushions not straight. And all the while, not a word did he say about when their grandmother might come home.

At church that Sunday everyone said a prayer for Sister Irene's full recovery and afterwards, while her grandfather was busy talking to Pastor Digby, Lydia asked Sister Lottie if she knew what was wrong with her grandmother. Her voice low, Sister Lottie said, 'She'll be home soon. Try not to worry. The Lord has her safely in the palm of his hand.'

'But what's wrong with her?'

Sister Lottie bobbed her head, checking that no one was listening to them. 'It's a woman's operation.' She fluttered a hand over her right breast. 'There was a lump. The doctors thought it was cancer. But thank the Lord, it wasn't. It'll take a long time for your poor grandmother

to convalesce and fully get over the drastic surgery she's undergone. We must all pray extra hard for her. Can you do that, Lydia?'

Pray for a woman who hated her so much? Lydia didn't think so. But what was the alternative? If their grandmother died there would be no let-up for her. She would have to carry on doing all the housework as well as suffer her grandfather's worsening temper.

So pray she did. For herself as much as her grandmother.

Chapter Twenty-Two

Their grandmother didn't come home until the beginning of February of the next year. During the time she had been away she had lost weight and her face had sort of caved in. Her skin was the colour of ash. She held herself differently too; her thin shoulders were hunched and her arms seemed to be wrapped around her body as if holding it together. Lydia had wondered many times about the 'drastic surgery' Sister Lottie had referred to, but she had no idea what it could really mean. Whatever it was, she decided as she watched her grandmother make her way slowly upstairs to get into bed, it had to be bad.

Over the following days, whilst their grandfather was at work, a steady flow of visitors came to the house. A nurse came first thing in the morning to check on their grandmother, and from then on the Sisters took it in turns to come in pairs and sit with her upstairs. Listening at the closed bedroom door, Lydia would hear them praying and singing hymns. But one afternoon, when Sister Lottie and Sister Joan arrived for their shift, they were turned away before Lydia had even got the kettle on to make them some tea. 'Your grandmother's weak and depressed,' Sister Lottie whispered to Lydia as she was leaving. 'We need to be very patient with her.'

The one person their grandmother seemed willing to have around her was Valerie, and so the moment she came home from school, Valerie would rush upstairs to be with her. Only she could tempt their grandmother to eat the lunch their grandfather came home at midday to make specially for his wife.

But the patience they needed to deal with their grand-mother was nothing compared to what Lydia needed to cope with her grandfather. The longer their grandmother remained in bed, the worse his temper became. She had the bruises to show for it. Nothing was ever right for him. The cups of tea she made for him were too weak or too strong. The meals she cooked were inedible, fit only for the bin. The shirts she ironed for him had the crisp creases he insisted on in all the wrong places. He didn't seem able to be in the same room as her without calling her a lazy slut or accusing her of something she hadn't done. Through it all, Lydia held her tongue. Until finally she forgot herself and answered him back.

She was in the middle of cooking tea when he arrived home early and announced that he wanted corned beef hash for his tea and not the mince and onions she was preparing.

'But we don't have any corned beef,' she said.

'Then go and buy some,' he roared. From his trouser pocket he pulled out a handful of change and threw it at her.

She ran all the way in the pouring rain to Gorton's corner shop, launching herself over puddles and hanging onto the hood of her duffel coat, which was much too small for her now.

Mrs Gorton was about a hundred and ten and as deaf as a post. She took ages to serve the customers who were ahead of Lydia in the queue and when at last she stepped back out onto the street the rain had almost stopped. She'd got as far as the phone box when she heard her name being called. Not her real name, but the nickname the gang of older boys and girls had given her on her first day at junior school. Now that she was at the same school as them, she saw even more of them.

'Oi, it's Tufty!' one of the lads yelled. 'Got anything to eat for us?'

Two lads came over. One flipped back her hood and messed up her hair whilst the other checked her pockets.

All he found was the tin of corned beef. Blowing smoke in her face, he said, 'Got any money?'

'No,' she lied.

The other lad grabbed Lydia's clenched fist behind her back and prised her fingers open to reveal a ten pence piece. 'Ta very much,' he gloated.

'Please don't take it,' Lydia said. 'I'll get into trouble if you do.'

'Tough! Yer shouldn't have lied to us. How's your witch of an old gran? I 'eard she had one of her baps cut off. She must look a right sight in t'buff. Bet her old man won't want to do it with her any more.'

Running the rest of the way home, Lydia felt sick. Surely it couldn't be true? How could *that* part of a woman's body be removed? As for her grandparents doing 'it', that was disgusting rubbish. They were much too old.

Out of breath, she let herself in at the back door. Her grandfather was standing at the sink washing his hands. There was no sign of Val. She was probably upstairs with their grandmother. 'What took you so long?' he demanded.

'Sorry,' Lydia panted, pulling the tin of corned beef out of her pocket and shrugging off her coat.

Drying his hands now, he said, 'Where's my change?'

'I'm sorry,' Lydia apologized again. 'But one of the boys outside the phone box took it. I tried to stop him but he wouldn't listen to me.'

He glared at her, his nostrils flaring. He slowly put down the towel. 'You expect me to believe that? You've taken it for yourself, haven't you? You lying bitch. You probably squandered it on sweets and ate them on your way home. That's why you were so long!'

'I didn't. Honestly. One of the boys took—'

'Don't answer me back!'

'I'm not! I'm just telling you what happened!'

The glare intensified and then with a suddenness that took Lydia completely unawares, her grandfather cracked her on the side of her head with the open palm of his

hand. The blow was so powerful, her head whipped round and she staggered, lost her balance and banged her head on the hard, cold floor.

She could feel herself being lifted. Roughly. As though she were a heavy bag of potatoes. There were voices. She tried to open her eyes, but it was too much effort. She didn't know why, but she felt sick and dizzy. Like she'd been spun round too much. A woozy blanket of sleepiness began covering her and she slid deeply beneath its comforting warmth. She saw herself floating away, far, far away. There in the distance she could see her mother beckoning to her. Oh, and there was her father, smiling and holding out his arms for her. They weren't dead after all! The last couple of years had been nothing but a horrible dream. She ran to her father and he swung her round. They were spinning together, high in the sky, so high they were right above the snowy-white clouds. How wonderful it was to know that she would never have to live with those nasty parents of his again. His arms tightened around her and he spoke her name. Over and over. 'Lydia … Lydia … Lydia …'

Except it wasn't her father. The voice was all wrong. Whoever it was, they were spoiling her lovely dream. She reached out to cling to her father, but he'd vanished and she was falling from the sky. And there was no one to catch her.

She snapped open her eyes.

'Ah, there you are,' said a voice she didn't recognize.

Lydia blinked in the bright light and tried to focus on her surroundings. She was in a bed with a brown and orange curtain around her. There was a strange woman in a uniform looking down at her.

But why?

Feeling groggy and confused, she was just about to ask where she was when she heard voices and a gap opened in the curtains at the end of her bed. A man wearing a white coat appeared. Right behind him was her grandfather.

Lydia hardly knew him for the expression of concern on his face.

'Well, young lady,' the man in the white coat said, 'it looks like Nurse Davies has done what I couldn't; she's woken you up. Perhaps now I can get a proper look at you.'

At his request they were left alone. 'You've had a lucky escape,' he said, when he was flashing a light into her eyes. 'You gave your head quite a bump. Not to mention some hefty concussion. You're now the proud owner of nine stitches, every one of them put in by my own fair hand. Your grandfather says you're constantly getting into mischief, that it's a wonder you haven't hurt yourself more seriously before now.' He put his stethoscope to her chest and moved it about.

Lydia swallowed and ran her tongue over her cry lips. 'Did my grandfather say how I hurt myself?'

'I'm afraid not. All he knows is that he came home from work and found you lying on the kitchen floor. Lucky he came home when he did, or who knows what might have happened.' Then, hooking his stethoscope round his neck, he said, 'I don't suppose you can fill me in on the details, can you? For instance, what's the last thing you remember?'

'I ... I'm sorry, I can't remember anything.'

'Not to worry. Temporary memory loss is quite common in these situations. It should return before too long. Meanwhile, I'm going to keep you in overnight and take another look at you in the morning. With any luck you should be sleeping in your own bed tomorrow night. Home's always the safest place to be in my opinion; you never know what you might catch in hospital.' He laughed at his own joke.

But Lydia didn't laugh with him. A tiny, shivery tweak of fear told her that being at home was the last place she would feel safe.

Chapter Twenty-Three

Lydia's grandfather arrived to take her home after he'd finished work. To the doctors and nurses he was all smiles and politeness, thanking them for their help and apologizing for his careless granddaughter who'd put them to so much trouble. But when he was alone with Lydia in the car the smile was gone. With his hands gripping the steering wheel, his expression rigid, he said, 'Have you remembered what happened yet?'

She hesitated, wanting so much to say the right thing. She sensed it was important not to make a nuisance of herself. Or any more of a nuisance than she already had been. Her grandfather probably thought she was pretending to lose her memory just so she could attract attention to herself. But the truth was, she really couldn't remember what had happened. All she had to go on was a hazy picture of being in the kitchen getting tea ready. From then on it was a blank.

When she didn't reply, her grandfather said, 'If you know what's good for you, you won't go causing any trouble. Your grandmother isn't well and the last thing we need is you making life more difficult for her. Do I make myself clear?'

As clear as mud, thought Lydia. What trouble did he think she might cause? 'Yes, Grandfather,' she said dutifully. Turning her face to look out of the side window, she put a hand to her bandaged head, willing it to start working properly. The doctor had assured her that her memory could return at any moment, that all she needed was the right trigger and that it could come in a flash all at once,

or steadily like a dripping tap. There wasn't anything to worry about, he'd said. But she *was* worried. How could you lose a part of yourself like that and not worry? She didn't believe for a single second that she had fallen off a chair reaching for the biscuit tin in one of the high kitchen cupboards as her grandfather had suggested to the doctor. For a start, there weren't any biscuits in the cupboard any more because their grandmother only ever used to buy them for her Tea and Sisters Scripture meetings, and since her operation last year everyone now met at Sister Vera's house.

They were almost home now, and as her grandfather drove past Gorton's corner shop at the end of the road, Lydia saw that the usual gang of teenage lads was hanging about; they were lazily kicking a can to each other across the road. Her grandfather gave the horn a loud blast to make them get out of the way. The two cocky boys who had stolen her money yesterday stayed exactly where they were. When her grandfather banged his fist down on the horn again, they jabbed two fingers in the air and dragged themselves to the kerb. Her grandfather revved the engine noisily and drove on.

Lydia twisted round sharply in her seat, stared back at the gang of boys through the rear window and realized that she had remembered something from yesterday. The two lads ... she'd had some money in her hand ... one of them had taken it. She must have either been on her way to the shop or leaving it. What shopping had she been sent out to do?

Facing the front now, Lydia squeezed her eyes shut and held her breath. This was the trigger the doctor had told her about; she mustn't let it slip away from her. Very gently she tried to tease out these fragile new memories to see what else would come to her. It had been raining ... she'd run home feeling sick about the awful things the boys had said about her grandmother ... her grandfather was in the kitchen ... he was the one who'd sent her to the

shop ... he was angry and accusing her of stealing from him ... he ...

Lydia opened her eyes. Her grandfather had hit her. Not some sharp little prod or slap as she was used to, but a real hard blow that had knocked her off her feet. She shuddered, recalling how much it had hurt, and knowing that it had been no more of an accident than that time her grandfather had claimed Lydia had fallen into the compost heap. Then she'd been burned; this time he'd given her concussion and nine stitches. She supposed she had at least to be grateful that he had taken her to the hospital. Had he been scared into doing that because he couldn't wake her? Had he thought she might die? And that he could be blamed?

The car jolted to a stop. They were home. A tremor of fear ran through Lydia. Watching her grandfather getting out of the car, she wanted to say, *I know what you did to me; I've remembered everything. I know that you lied to the doctor and that you'll lie to everyone else. But I know the truth.* But to her shame she was too frightened of him. Who knew what else he might do to her if she made him angry? Better to keep quiet and let him think he'd got away with it. Because he had, hadn't he?

That night at bedtime, Valerie made Lydia promise she would never do anything to upset their grandparents, especially their grandmother.

'Grandma's very worried,' Valerie whispered when they'd switched off the light. 'She thinks we might be taken away from her.'

Lydia turned over to face Valerie in the dark. 'Why does she think that?'

When Valerie didn't reply, Lydia realized her sister was crying. She went and knelt beside her bed. 'What is it, Valerie? What's wrong?'

'Grandma thinks you're going to go and spoil everything by telling people lies about her and our grandfather.'

'What sort of lies?'

'That they're unkind to you.'

'But they *are* unkind to me.'

'Only because you do wicked things and they're try-ing to save you from provoking the Lord to anger. She says that if you spread bad lies about them someone will knock on the door one day and make us live somewhere else. Somewhere a long way away and not so nice, where we'll never see our friends from church again.' Valerie's cries grew louder. 'I couldn't live anywhere else, Lydia. I couldn't live without Grandma. She says you don't love her. You do love her, don't you, Lydia?'

Lydia hugged her sister and hushed her with a kiss. 'Don't be silly, of course I love her. And we'll live here for ever and ever. Just you see.'

'You promise you won't do anything to upset her?'

'I promise.'

Chapter Twenty-Four

They were playing Monopoly. Lydia was winning. By miles. She had all the best properties and Noah's racing car had just landed on Mayfair with four houses on it. 'Pay up! Pay up! Pay up!' she chanted.

Noah started counting out his money. It was obvious he didn't have enough.

'Tell you what,' she said, 'I'll let you off if you give me Fenchurch Street Station and King's Cross.'

He eyed her long row of property cards. 'That gives you the set.'

'Really?' she said innocently. 'Oh, so it does.'

He laughed and tossed his money onto the board. 'I give in. You win. Again. How about some toast? I'm starving.'

'OK. You get toasting and I'll put this away.'

'Sure you don't want to count your winnings first?' he teased. 'Just to rub in your victory?'

'I don't need to,' she said with a smile. 'I know exactly how much I have: eight thousand, four hundred and seventy-five pounds.' She waved the thick bundle of cash under his nose.

He smiled too and went over to the wardrobe, bringing back a loaf of Mother's Pride, a plate, a knife, and a pot of jam. As she tidied away the board game, Lydia watched Noah light the candles on the mantelpiece and thought how this room, with its every cluttered, shadowy nook and cranny, was so comfortingly familiar to her. It was her absolute favourite place in all the world. Nowhere was she happier.

Right now Noah and his uncle weren't the only ones using candles. According to Lydia's grandfather, the lazy Neo-Marxists who worked in the mines and power stations were holding the country to ransom by making sure there wasn't enough coal and electricity to go round. Some days at school they didn't have a cooked meal and the dinner ladies gave them sandwiches to eat. But according to Noah, who got his information from his uncle, the miners needed their support and what was a little inconvenience compared to fighting for a good cause and bringing down such a useless government? Ted Heath, who in Uncle Brad's opinion was nothing more than a poncy sailor and a social-climbing jackass for signing Britain up for the Common Market, would be the first to be put against the wall if he had his way.

Lydia had understood some time ago that she'd got it wrong about Uncle Brad. He wasn't poor at all. His weird paintings really did sell for lots of money down in London and his preference for candles over lightbulbs was just one of his many peculiarities.

'Would you mind nipping downstairs to get some butter?' Noah asked.

'Is your uncle around?'

'You're not scared of him, are you?'

She stuck out her chin. 'I'm not scared of anything.'

He smiled. 'I know; that's why I think you're so great.'

Lydia absorbed the unexpected compliment like a thirsty sponge and set off, candle in hand, on the trek down to the kitchen. Along the shadowy landing with its strange paintings and rucked-up rugs she went, down the wide staircase, across the hall, and through the freezing cold narrow passageway with Adolf the stag's head looking down on her from his lofty position on the wall. Hooked onto one of his enormous antlers was a policeman's helmet which Noah said Uncle Brad had stolen during a drunken brawl in a pub when he'd been a student.

Noah had been right to tease Lydia about being scared of Uncle Brad: she was. But not in a bad way, like she was

with her grandfather. It was just that he was so unlike anyone she knew. He could be friendly, glamorous and grumpily aloof, all at the same time. She never knew what he was going to say or do next. Sometimes he would greet her with the words, 'Hey, here's the cool cat I'm going to paint one day!' Other times, even after all this time, he treated her as if they'd never met before. That was when he'd been knocking back the drink, Noah said. Or when he'd been smoking one of his special cigarettes.

There was no sign of Uncle Brad in the kitchen, but the sound of music blaring from his studio told Lydia he was nearby. She found an unopened packet of butter in the fridge and hurried back upstairs. One day, she told herself, she was going to live in a big house like this. Just as soon as she was old enough, she would leave Swallowsdale. She would work hard and earn so much money she'd be able to surround herself with lovely things and all her clothes would be new and beautiful. It was why she always concentrated during lessons at school and made a point of doing her homework and revising for any tests they had. Being rich and clever wasn't about being born lucky. She'd learned that from Noah. You only had to see his collection of books – she'd give anything to have all those fantastic encyclopaedias – to know that knowledge was a choice to be grabbed. And it was a choice she had grabbed ages ago, when she'd first tried to copy Noah's handwriting. She didn't do that now, of course. But she was always conscious that the better impression you gave people of yourself, the better they treated you. It was just as Mum used to say: polishing your shoes really did make a difference. It was why she'd taught herself to polish up the way she spoke by secretly mimicking the way Noah spoke. She didn't do it too much at home, not when she'd be accused of getting above herself, but she had it hidden up her sleeve ready for when the time came to leave Swallowsdale. If you wanted to be treated as a lady, you had to sound like one. And that's what she aimed to be one day.

What about Noah and Valerie? a voice inside her head

asked. Where will they be when you're waving goodbye to Swallowsdale?

Oh, that was easy. They'd have to come with her. She couldn't leave them behind. She'd earn enough money to look after all three of them.

Since her 'accident' two weeks ago, Lydia had taken extra care not to put a foot wrong with her grandfather. For Valerie's sake, she did everything that was asked of her, no matter how difficult or unreasonable. But the worst part was knowing that her sister now lived in constant fear of being taken away from their grandmother if Lydia didn't toe the line. How cruel and cunning their grandfather had been to twist the truth round to his advantage. What lies had he told their grandmother to make her put those fears in Val's head? Or had their grandmother, while she lay in bed with the curtains drawn, still too depressed to get up, worked it out for herself? Had she guessed what had really happened and worried what Lydia might tell people? Had she immediately come up with a way to make Lydia keep her mouth shut? Or had the pair of them put the idea together? This thought was doubly chilling because it meant that her grandmother was prepared to let her vicious, foul-tempered husband do whatever he wanted.

At the moment her grandfather's favourite punishment was to force Lydia to stand in the corner of the room during mealtimes and make her watch him and Valerie eat. 'It's for your sister's own good,' he would tell Valerie, while helping himself to another portion of apple pie and custard. 'She's growing too fast because she eats too much. She's a gluttonous pig that needs to have its appetite curbed. You must pray for her.'

And Val did pray for Lydia. Down on her knees at bed-time she would pray aloud for Lydia to be released from Satan's grip. She also prayed that she herself wouldn't be tainted by Lydia's refusal to bow to God's will. It broke Lydia's heart that her sister had been turned against her. What would their poor mother say? And what of the promise she had made Mum to look after Val?

As close as she was to Noah, Lydia never shared with him what went on at number thirty-three Hillside Terrace. Her pride just wouldn't let her. She didn't want him knowing just how shabby her life was compared to his. She'd hate it if he started feeling sorry for her. So she lied to him to stop him finding out. She lied about why her clothes were too small for her – they were her favourite and she couldn't bear to part with them. She said that the bruises she had on her arms and legs were from falling out of bed in the middle of the night, or from slipping on the stairs.

As to how she'd ended up with nine stitches in the side of her head – she'd had them removed last week – she used her grandfather's lie and told him she'd fallen off a chair. She even joked with him that she had turned into a clumsy idiot because she was growing so fast. Which wasn't entirely untrue. Taller than Noah by an inch, she was now the tallest girl in their year at school. For a while she had tried to make herself appear smaller and less obvious, but then one day she'd decided there wasn't any point. With her looks she was always going to stand out.

Just as Noah did. Nobody cared less about his appearance than Noah. His school uniform was smart enough, but his home clothes were scruffy and thrown on any old how, and he never noticed if they were too big or too small or if a button had dropped off. He was proud of the fact that he cut his own hair and made such a poor job of it. 'Oh, clothes,' he'd say with a shrug. 'Who gives a monkey's?'

Whilst Lydia hated lying to Noah, she never had a problem lying to her grandparents, so long as she was sure she wouldn't be found out. The most regular lies she told them were the ones that enabled her to spend time with Noah. Today she was supposed to be playing in an after-school netball match. Later in the week it would be a drama lesson that kept her late at school, or recorder practice.

*

'I've been thinking,' Noah said when she was back in his room and warming herself in front of the fire, 'why don't we make a pact?'

She glanced up from the piece of toast she was buttering. 'What kind of a pact?'

He looked at her steadily, his face glowing in the flickering firelight. His expression was thoughtful with just a hint of eyebrow-raising puzzlement to it. She called it his Question Mark Face. 'A pact that means we'll always be friends. That nothing will ever part us.'

Just as she usually did these days, Lydia took the short cut home from Noah's by climbing over the wall at the end of his garden and making her way across the mile or so of sloping moorland that separated their houses. She could cover the distance far quicker during daylight, but in the dark it took her longer. It didn't frighten her, not now she had perfected her route and knew how to avoid the boggiest, steepest or rockiest areas. The first time she had done it in the dark, she had been petrified and had imagined countless ways she could meet with her death – vampire bats, dangerous prisoners on the run, werewolves, or those strange men she'd heard about who just wanted to unzip their trousers and show her their 'thing'. She'd used Noah's torch on that first occasion, but now she didn't bother; she let instinct and experience guide her, having discovered that the darkness was rarely total.

At the halfway point, at the entrance to the wooded dell, which she and Noah had nicknamed the Dell of the Dead, Lydia shifted her school bag on her shoulder and paused to let her eyes grow accustomed to the gloom; the dreary afternoon light had all but faded. In the freezing February air, her breath formed a ghostly vapour, then vanished. It was always here that her heart skipped a beat and she felt the urge to make a run for it. It was a matter of honour that she didn't, that she kept her nerve and her pace unchanged. It was equally important to keep a lid on her imagination and not dwell on who or what might be

hiding amongst the trees. Normally she hummed 'What Shall We Do With The Drunken Sailor?' inside her head, but this time, as she plunged in, she thought of the pact she and Noah had just made. Using his Swiss Army knife, he'd made a cut in the middle of their palms, then pressed their hands together to share their blood, saying the words, 'No matter what, we'll never be parted.'

Kicking through the thick layers of fallen leaves, within yards of the outer edge of the dell, Lydia touched the plaster Noah had put on her hand. She hoped she'd have a scar to remind her how much Noah meant to her.

A sudden rustle over to her left made her stiffen. Every hair on the back of her neck stood on end. Holding her breath and straining her ears, her heart nearly leapt out of her mouth when a bird with the biggest wingspan she'd ever seen flew out of the trees and swooped by right in front of her. When she heard its screeching call, she relaxed. If an owl was the scariest the Dell of the Dead had to offer, then she had absolutely nothing to fear.

Chapter Twenty-Five

The summer holidays were dragging for Lydia. It was over a week since the end of term, when she'd last seen Noah.

She was sitting in the garden making daisy chains with Valerie, wishing she could find a way to slip over the wall without anyone missing her and go and see him. When she and Noah had worked out that all that separated them was a wooded dell and a stretch of moorland, Lydia had remembered the day she had climbed up into the branches of the out-of-bounds chestnut tree for the first time and wondered who might live on the other side of the sloping hill. Little had she known that her very best friend would soon be living there.

With a sudden uncanny feeling that they were being watched, Lydia turned to look back up at the house. Sure enough, staring down at them through a gap in the bed-room curtains was their grandmother. She was dressed as she always was, in a nightdress and dressing gown. Lydia couldn't remember the last time she had left the house. Other than in March when she'd gone back into hospital for another operation. Just before this had happened she had started to feel better. She had been managing to get dressed and come downstairs for a few hours a day. She'd even had Pastor Digby and the Sisters round for tea a couple of times and was talking about being well enough to go to church again. But apparently the first operation hadn't been done right and there had been complications. When she came home this time, she was even more de-pressed and Lydia often heard her crying at night, a sort of low wailing sound. Their grandfather moved into the

spare room around this time. He'd been sleeping in there ever since.

Another change to the routine was that unlike before when his wife had come home from hospital, he didn't come back during the day to make her lunch. Instead, the Sisters had been encouraged to pop in for an hour or so each day. Lydia had overheard him telling Pastor Digby that his wife might say she didn't want any company, but what she wanted and what she *needed* were entirely two different things. Pastor Digby had agreed and said, 'Sometimes a firm hand is what is needed.' He'd then quoted from the Bible about the importance of wives submitting to their husbands.

Lydia knew all about her grandfather's firm hand. He hadn't lashed out at her anywhere near as badly as he had earlier in the year, but there had been moments when she'd genuinely feared that he might. He seemed to take pleasure in knowing that he could so easily make her cower from him. It was as if it was a game for him, to raise his hand sharply and then watch her reaction. He would laugh at her cruelly, saying she would be scared of her own shadow next.

'Look, Val,' Lydia said, pointing up to the window. 'Grandmother's awake. Do you want to go in and see her?'

Scrambling to her feet, Valerie scooped up the daisy chain necklace she'd been making. 'I'll take this in for her, shall I?'

'Yes, go on, she'll like that.'

Lydia watched her sister skip up the garden path and disappear inside the house. She had only been alone a couple of minutes when Sister Lottie appeared at the back door. Wiping her hands on her apron she called out to Lydia. 'I'm putting a picnic lunch together. Do you want to help bring it out to the garden while I take some sandwiches upstairs to your grandmother?'

Lydia didn't hesitate. Sister Lottie's picnic lunches were the highlight of the day.

Having insisted with their grandfather that Lydia and Valerie couldn't possibly be left alone every day while he was at work during the long summer holiday, Sister Lottie's Morris Minor arrived outside the house every morning bang on ten o'clock. It was wonderful having her around. She was always so kind and cheerful, baking them lovely cakes and biscuits and telling them not to fret, that their grandmother would soon be well again and everything would be back to normal.

Was it so very wrong of Lydia to hope that things never went back to being normal? With their grandmother permanently 'resting' upstairs, life was so much more fun with Sister Lottie around. It was just a shame their grandfather couldn't lock himself away in the spare room as well.

Deliciously full of sardine and tomato paste sandwiches, cheese and onion crisps, fairy cakes and iced gems – something their grandmother would never have approved of – Lydia lay back on the grass and let out a contented sigh. 'Why is a picnic in the garden always so much nicer than sitting at the table inside the house?'

But before Sister Lottie could answer her, a sound Lydia hadn't heard since coming to live in Swallowsdale rang out. It was the sing-song chime of an ice-cream van. She even recognized the tune it was playing: 'Edelweiss'. Her father used to sing it to her. She remembered him telling her edelweiss was the name of a flower that grew in the mountains of Switzerland. The connection with her father, coupled with the excitement of something new and unexpected going on, had her leaping to her feet and racing from the end of the garden, down the path alongside the garage and round to the front garden. Yes! There it was. An ice-cream van parked right outside their house. It was blue and white with chrome so shiny the sun was bouncing off it. High up on the van's roof, lying on its side, was a large light-up plastic ice-cream cornet with a plastic chocolate flake sticking out of it. In red looping writing, the name 'Joey' was written on the cornet. The

music suddenly stopped and the window on the side of the van slid open to reveal a man with a head of curly black hair. He had a thick black moustache and his skin was the colour of brown sugar. He spotted Lydia straight away. 'Hello,' he said. 'And what would you like on thissa beautiful day, leetle girl?'

How strange he looked and sounded. She started to back away.

'Pleeasse, do not run away. Come anda choose some-zing. I have everyzing. Nats, spreenkles, strawberry seerop, weefers, cornots, and lallies. So many lovelee lallies.'

'I don't have any money,' she said, trying not to laugh at his funny pronunciation.

He shook his head of black curls. 'Ah, zat eesa beega problema. Maybe you go inside your lovelee house and aska your mama for money.'

'My mother's dead.' Lydia often said this just to see what reaction she got. It always interested her to see how awkwardly it made people behave.

This man's reaction was different from anyone else's, though. He put a hand to his forehead, then touched his chest and then both shoulders. Just as Lydia had once seen Noah do. 'Oh, *Mama mia*! I ama so sorry, leetle girl. Me anda my beega moutha. For that you can ave what you wanta. Pleeasse, come ana choose somezing.'

Lydia hesitated. 'I don't think I'd be allowed to do that.'

He nodded and was about to say something when foot-steps approached. 'Ah, more customers,' he said, rubbing his hands together. 'Ziss isa good. It was a pleasure to meeta you, leetle girl. Bye, bye.'

Lydia watched her neighbours cluster round the van and then turned on her heel and ran straight to the back gar-den. 'Sister Lottie, can we have an ice-cream, please? Oh, please say yes! It's such a hot day. Wouldn't you like one, too? It would be the perfect end to our lovely lunch.'

Lydia knew Sister Lottie wouldn't let her down and in no time at all, the three of them – Lydia, Valerie and Sister

Lottie – were standing in front of the open window of the ice-cream van. The other customers had all gone. 'So, leetle girl,' said the funny curly-haired man, 'eeza zissa beautiful lady your grandmother?'

Sister Lottie giggled and put a hand to her face.

'No,' Lydia said, 'she's my friend. And this is Valerie, my sister. She's six.'

The man smiled. 'Anda may I know *your* name?'

'Lydia. Lydia Turner.'

'I ama very pleased to meeta you, *Signorina* Lydia Turner. I ama Joey Scalatore. I ama from Italy. Have you heard of Italy?'

'Is that the country that's shaped like a boot?'

'*Sì! Brava!* And my home cana be founda near Napoli. Butta please, you have not introduced me to your beautiful friend.'

'This is Sister Lottie.'

'I ama pleased to meeta you, Sister Lottie. You are a nun?' Lydia noticed the ice-cream man's face had turned serious, sort of respectful. She also noticed that peeping out from his open-necked shirt and dark hairy chest was a gold necklace with a crucifix hanging from it.

'Oh, no,' Sister Lottie laughed, her face now the colour of beetroot. 'I'm much too ordinary for anything like that.'

But she is a saint, Lydia thought when they had said goodbye to the nice man and were licking their double ninety-nines to the sound of 'Edelweiss' tinkling away down the street.

What a perfect day.

Chapter Twenty-Six

For the next fortnight, the sun shone brightly from a clear blue sky and the sound of 'Edelweiss' could be heard every afternoon between two and three o'clock on Hillside Terrace.

Joey Scalatore was just like Sister Lottie, always so cheerful. His real name was Giuseppe but he said Joey was easier for British people to say. She loved it when he called her his *bella* leetle friend in his funny voice. He'd explained to her that *bella* meant beautiful. He was teaching her Italian by giving her a different word to remember whenever he saw her. So far she knew the Italian for hello was *ciao*, or *buon giorno*, and that *arrivederci* meant see you soon. She knew that *va bene* was the same as saying OK, that *gelato* was ice-cream, and that thank you was *grazie*. Oh, and *sì* was yes. She could also count from one to ten and was practising rolling her Rs, just like Joey had taught her, but she didn't think she did it very well. It was quite different from French.

Joey must have decided that Sister Lottie couldn't really afford to buy ice-creams every day, so when he'd finished serving all the other customers from their road, he often gave them the broken lollies he said he couldn't sell. Yesterday he'd promised to bring Lydia some photographs of where he came from in Italy, and now, as she waited her turn at the back of the queue, she hoped he hadn't forgotten. She was curious to know what Italy looked like. The only pictures she'd seen were in a book at school and one of them had showed a tower that was leaning over so much it looked like it was about to topple over.

The Floozy was at the front of the queue and was taking for ever. Perhaps Joey was teaching her some Italian words as well. She was looking particularly smart today, wearing a tight-fitting white halter-neck dress and a pair of red high-heeled sandals. Lydia would have loved a pair of shoes just like that, all pointy and strappy. She could see that The Floozy had been sunbathing; her shoulders were pink and striped with pale white strap marks. From an overheard conversation at the corner shop, Lydia knew that The Floozy had recently changed jobs and was now working shifts at one of the mills, which meant she slept during the morning, had the afternoons free and then went to work at night. Lydia had never once heard anyone mention a husband – not even a dead one – which puzzled her. She would have thought an attractive woman like The Floozy would definitely have had a husband at some time. She certainly didn't seem to be short on men friends. In fact, Lydia had seen any number of different men turning up on a Saturday evening to take her out. Some brought bunches of flowers with them, or boxes of Milk Tray. Lydia couldn't imagine her grandfather ever bringing home a box of chocolates for his wife. He hadn't even done it the two times she'd come out of hospital. So maybe The Floozy had it right, that it was better not to be married. This way, she was independent, earned her own money and could have as many boyfriends giving her presents as she wanted.

The Floozy turned from the hatch with an ice-cream in her hand and exchanged a few words with the other women in the queue. Laughing huskily, she said, 'He could lick my cornet any time he wanted.'

'Mine too,' someone else said.

'For a foreigner, he's a bit of all right, in't he?'

'I'll say. Have yer copped a look at his hairy chest?'

Embarrassed by their talk, Lydia stared hard at the ground. She hoped Joey couldn't hear what they were saying. Or if he could, that he didn't understand it.

'What yer staring at down there, then?'

Lydia started. It was The Floozy. And she was talking to her.

'How're yer getting on? That grandfather of yours taking good care of yer and your sister while your grandmother's getting over her operation?'

'Um ... yes. We have a friend who spends the day with us during the holiday while he's at work.'

'I'm glad to hear it. And yer've only got to knock on my door if yer need sommat. Yer could come in and watch a bit of telly if yer fancied it. I know yer don't have a set. For now, have this. Ta-ra.'

Lydia watched The Floozy tick-tacking away on her high heels, her curvy hips swaying. This was the first proper conversation Lydia had ever had with the woman. She then looked at the money she had just had pressed into her hand: a shiny fifty-pence piece. She decided The Floozy couldn't possibly be any of the bad things her grandparents had said about her.

At last it was Lydia's turn.

'*Ciao*, my leetle *bella* friend,' Joey greeted her.

'*Ciao*,' she replied shyly, even though they were alone.

He wagged a stubby dark finger at her. 'No, no. You musta say it louder anda with more passion. Remember, there is no sucha person as a shy Italiano. Especially not from Napoli, where I ama from.'

Self-consciously she tried the greeting again, then asked if he had remembered the photographs he'd said he'd bring for her to see.

He raised his hands in the air. 'Oh, I ama so sorry. Iya forgot all abouta zat. Forgeeve me, please, but I have hada many zings to zeenk about. I ama to be, how do you say, homeless? Yes, as of next week I will have nowhere to leeve. My landlord says he does nota like my van parked outside zee 'ouse.'

'Does that mean you have to go back to Italy?' Lydia scarcely knew Joey but she couldn't imagine the rest of the summer holidays without him.

'No, but if I cannota find somewhere to leeve, I will have to sleep in zee van.'

Lydia had a thought. Sister Lottie had a spare room – perhaps she'd like a lodger. 'I have an idea,' she said. 'Can you wait here a few minutes?'

'Sì. For you, my leetle *bella* friend, I have all zee time in zee world.'

Within minutes, Lydia had put her idea to Sister Lottie and they were outside talking it through with Joey. 'It's only a small room I can offer you,' Sister Lottie explained, 'so I wouldn't charge you too much rent.'

'Anda mya van, eez is nota problema for you?'

'I have a garage I never use, so you can put it in there.'

The next thing, Joey was out of the van and kissing Sister Lottie on each cheek. 'Sucha kindness! And if zere are any jobs you needa doing in your house, I cana do zem for you. Oh, *Dio mio*, what a lucky day zees is for me! Zank you, zank you!'

Pink-faced and hair all ruffled, Sister Lottie emerged from Joey's dark, hairy arms like a cork popping from a bottle. 'Don't thank me,' she said breathlessly, her voice all wobbly. 'Thank Lydia; it was her idea.'

But it was Sister Lottie who, in Lydia's opinion, came up with the best idea of the day. They were sitting in the garden with the broken strawberry Mivvies Joey had given them – Valerie had gone inside to share hers with their grandmother – when Sister Lottie said, 'I've been thinking, Lydia. You must be getting very bored here with only Valerie and me for company. Wouldn't you like to spend some of the holiday with your friend, Noah?'

'I'm not sure my grandparents would agree to that,' she said carefully, at the same time licking a dribble of melting ice-cream off her thumb.

'Oh, I think your grandparents have much too much on their minds to be bothered with the details of what we get up to during the day. We don't want to make a nuisance of ourselves by burdening them with anything unnecessary, do we?'

About to turn a few cartwheels inside her head, Lydia

suddenly thought of her sister. Val told their grandmother just about everything that went on. Choosing her words with care, not wanting to appear as though she was being disloyal and criticizing her sister, Lydia said, 'But what about Valerie? She might, well, you know, she might just happen to mention it to Grandmother.'

Sister Lottie smiled and patted Lydia's hand. 'You leave little Valerie to me.'

Lydia could hardly believe her luck.

The next morning she climbed over the wall at the end of the garden and set off across the hard, dry ground. It was ages since it had last rained. In the distance the heather was in full bloom and if she squeezed her eyes almost shut, all she could see was a mysterious smoky haze of purple. Sister Lottie had made her a cake to take with her to Noah's and she had this wrapped in foil inside her duffel bag. 'It wouldn't be polite to turn up empty-handed,' Sister Lottie had said. She'd also made several rounds of cheese and pickle sandwiches and slipped in a bag of crisps. Valerie had promised to keep Lydia's visit to Noah a secret because she'd been told that anything out of the ordinary might upset their grandmother, and she didn't want that, did she? Lydia had had no idea that Sister Lottie could be so sneaky.

As they'd agreed on the telephone yesterday afternoon, Noah was waiting for her on his side of the Dell of the Dead. 'I thought we could go up to the beck,' he said. He indicated the small rucksack on his back. 'I've made us a picnic.'

'Snap,' Lydia said. 'Sister Lottie's made us a cake as well.'

They set off through the heather and bracken for the beck and Lydia told Noah all the latest news; about Sister Lottie coming every day and about Joey Scalatore and him teaching her Italian. 'I've decided I'm going to visit Italy when I'm old enough,' she said. 'Joey says I'd love it. He says the weather is always warm and sunny where he's

from and that the food is the best in the world.'

'If it's so great there, why's he here in Swallowsdale, then?'

Taken aback by Noah's question, and the flat tone of his voice, Lydia didn't know what to say. Thinking that maybe she had gone on too much and had bored him with all her chatter, she said, 'So tell me what you've been up to.'

'Not much. Uncle Brad's been away this last week.' His voice still sounded flat and uninterested.

'It must be great having the house all to yourself,' she said, trying to sound enthusiastic to cheer him up.

'It doesn't really feel that different from when he's around.'

'Do you have enough to eat?' she asked, concerned, knowing that he didn't have a shop on the doorstep like she did.

'Oh, yeah. My uncle stocked the fridge and cupboards before he went. And now that I'm more mobile and can get to the bus stop, he's left me a stack of money if things get low.'

'Where's he gone?'

'Bolivia.'

'Bolivia? Where's that?'

'Next door to Brazil and Peru.'

'Blimey, what's he gone there for?'

'Usual thing: inspiration for his paintings.'

'How long's he away for?'

Noah shrugged again. 'Not that long. Just a couple of weeks.'

They walked in silence for a while, and, always conscious that Noah couldn't walk too far or too fast, Lydia slowed her pace and pretended to be interested in watching a buzzard circling overhead. He didn't limp as much as he used to, not compared to this time last year when the brace had been removed, and he never made a fuss about it, but she knew his leg wasn't that strong. Maybe it never would be.

They were almost at the beck when Noah came to an abrupt stop. He put a hand on her arm. 'Lydia,' he said, 'I just want to say that I'm glad you phoned yesterday. I really—' His gaze and words fell away and he suddenly looked awkward and shy. To her surprise his face was turning pink.

'What is it, Noah?' she asked. 'What's the matter?'

'Nothing's the matter,' he said, his eyes coming back to hers. He swallowed. 'It's no big deal, it's just, well, the thing is, I've missed you. Really missed you. And I'm sorry I was so miserable earlier, but I was jealous. You sounded like you'd been having a lot more fun than me. I wish you'd phoned me before.'

'I wanted to, but—'

'It's OK,' he interrupted her, the pressure of his hand increasing on her arm. 'I know you don't want your grandparents to think that I'm anything more than someone who just happens to go to the same school as you. I don't suppose there's any chance they could both conveniently drop down dead, could they? It would solve a lot of your problems.'

She laughed. 'What do you mean? It would solve *all* my problems!'

Except of course, as Lydia knew all too well, it wouldn't. It would just create a whole load of new problems. Such as what their grandmother's death would do to Valerie. But she kept quiet about that and said, 'Anyway, never mind my horrible grandparents, tell me what you've been doing all on your own. You must have done something interesting.'

He took his hand away from her and pushed it down inside his trouser pocket. 'Oh, just the usual messing about stuff. Remember I said I wanted to have a go at making a crystal radio set? Well I have, and it works pretty well too.'

She gave him a light punch on his shoulder. 'Knowing how modest you are, that probably means it works brilliantly.'

'Hey, can I help being a genius?'

'Listen to Einstein!'

Laughing, with all trace of the awkwardness that had passed between them now gone, they walked on.

At the beck, when they were lying on their backs staring up at the puffy white clouds in the sky, Lydia pictured the rest of the summer holiday spent just like this. How blissful it would be.

So long as Sister Lottie kept looking after her and Valerie and their grandmother stayed in bed for ever and ever.

Chapter Twenty-Seven

When their grandmother did finally get out of bed nothing was as it had been. Physically she may have been stronger, but mentally she was very different. Exactly a year after her grandmother's first operation Lydia noticed that she was acting strangely, although with hindsight she realized it had been going on for a while. It was just little things to begin with, like refusing to answer the door or telephone, drawing the curtains during the day or hiding things at the back of the airing cupboard. Things started to disappear with such regularity that if Lydia couldn't find the peg bag, a saucepan lid or the potato peeler, she would go straight to the airing cupboard. Just as strangely, no one but Lydia seemed to think that it was odd. Neither her grandfather nor Val ever said anything about it. Which meant Lydia didn't either. As with so many other things, it was politely swept under the carpet and ignored.

But by the following Christmas, their grandmother's bizarre behaviour had escalated to the point that it was impossible for anyone to ignore it. Now if there was a knock at the door or the telephone was ringing, she would hide, quaking behind the settee, sometimes forcing Valerie to hide with her. Yet it was the fear of catching something that really filled her with the most anxiety. With germs as her number one enemy, she alternated between wearing rubber gloves and using the wooden tongs from the twin tub to pick up the post from the doormat. She was constantly washing her hands – sometimes scrubbing them so hard they bled – and would spend hours disinfecting the pavement outside their house with a mop and bucket.

Some days she would mop the path as well, going right up to the gate. She was getting through so much disinfectant that Lydia and Valerie were always being sent to the shop to buy more. Which was preferable to their grandmother going herself, because the corner shop was now owned by Mr and Mrs Khan, a Pakistani couple. During their first week of taking over from old Mrs Gorton, their grandmother had been embarrassingly rude to them about the colour of their skin.

It wasn't until she started burbling aloud in church on Sunday – just like the people she used to condemn as being unhinged – that their grandfather finally seemed to admit, if only to himself, that something was wrong. On Monday morning, after Lydia overheard him losing his temper with his wife and what sounded like a hard slap, he drove her to Doctor Bunch's surgery. Lydia had no idea what took place there, but in the weeks that followed their grandmother definitely seemed less agitated.

But not for long. By the summer of 1974, their grandmother's moods could switch as easily as turning the pages of a book – one minute she would be sitting calmly with Valerie and the next she would be rampaging round the house, throwing things and shouting at the top of her voice. It was the aggression that frightened Lydia most. Having caught enough of that from their grandfather over the years, Lydia was frightened that she might now have to put up with her grandmother lashing out at her. Or worse, what if she turned on Valerie?

Lydia knew that Valerie must be worried and confused about their grandmother, but try as she might she couldn't get her sister to talk about it. She had tried just now, but Valerie had rebuked Lydia by saying it was disrespectful to talk about their grandmother behind her back. For eight years old she could be remarkably – not to say annoyingly – stubborn and condescending.

Home from school, they were out in the garden, playing a game of jacks. It seemed such a trivial thing to be doing after the news Lydia had heard that morning. During

assembly the headmaster had announced that Bena, who hadn't been at school that week, had died the day before. Everyone had instantly stopped fidgeting or kicking the chair in front of them. Even now, in the warm July sun, Lydia felt a shiver when she thought of it. Fourteen years old. Dead. Bena's heart had finally done what they'd all said it might. It had simply stopped working.

At the sound of raised voices, Lydia caught hold of the small ball and looked up. Their grandmother was arguing with their neighbour; she was pointing over the fence at The Floozy's underwear, which was hanging on the washing line. 'You're nothing but a dirty, filthy whore!' she screeched at the top of her voice.

Lydia had frequently heard her grandmother refer to The Floozy in this way, but she couldn't believe she was actually saying the words out loud to the woman's face.

Removing a cigarette from her red-painted lips, The Floozy shouted back, 'Better than a barmy, dried-up old hag who can't please her old man.'

Riveted by the angry exchange, but sensing it was something Valerie shouldn't witness, Lydia said, 'Why don't we go inside and get a drink, Val?'

They'd got as far as the back door when there was a blood-curdling cry from The Floozy. 'That's it! That's bloody done it! I've had enough. You're gonna cop it now, good and proper. Just yer wait and see.'

Lydia gasped: her grandmother had gone berserk and was throwing soil at The Floozy's clothes line. Great handfuls of it.

Pushing her sister inside the house, just in case Val had any ideas about joining in to defend their grandmother, Lydia wondered what on earth would happen next.

What happened next was that their grandfather arrived home from work to find The Floozy with two policemen banging on the front door and their grandmother hiding in the broom cupboard under the stairs.

'She needs locking up!' The Floozy shouted at their

grandfather as they all burst into the hall where Lydia was standing with her arms around Val. Through the open door, Lydia could see that a small crowd of neighbours had gathered outside to watch. 'She's barmy!' The Floozy continued to yell. 'Off her blooming rocker! I'm telling yer, she's not right in t'head.'

'Thank you, madam, we'll take it from here,' one of the policemen said.

'Yer must be joking! I'm sticking round to make sure justice is done. She's made my life a living hell with her obscene letters she's been shoving through my letterbox these last weeks. Not to mention the rubbish she keeps tipping over the fence into my garden. Give me a bleeding straitjacket and I'll put her in it myself! And while yer're about it, why don't you check out them kiddies? If she hasn't turned them into fruitcakes as nutty as she is, they're certainly not being treated right. Especially the older one. Some days I've heard her being shouted at so loud I can hardly hear my telly.'

Eventually The Floozy was convinced that she had done all she could to help, and it was just the two policemen and their grandfather left to try and coax his wife out of the broom cupboard.

'Lydia,' barked their grandfather, 'take your sister up to your bedroom.'

As soon as they were upstairs, Lydia made Valerie sit on her bed. 'Stay here, Val,' she whispered, 'while I go and find out what's going on.'

Standing at the top of the stairs, safely out of sight, Lydia held her breath and listened. One of the policemen was talking. 'I'm sorry about this, sir, but you're going to have to get your wife out of the cupboard. We need to talk to her.'

'Can't I just go next door and make an apology?'

'No, sir. Allegations have been made and we need to speak to your wife.'

'I'm not sure if you're aware of this, but that woman next door is a woman of ... of dubious morals. I wouldn't

put it past her to make up those things she said about my wife.'

'We don't think that's the case, sir. Now if you'd kindly—'

'Are you saying the word of my wife, a good Christian woman, counts for nothing against that … *tart* next door?'

'Let me ask you a question, sir. Do you think it's natural behaviour for a good Christian woman to hide herself in the cupboard under the stairs?'

There was a long silence, a heavy sigh, and then, 'Look, she hasn't been herself for some time. A lot of fuss and bother over a misunderstanding isn't going to help her.'

'I'm afraid you'll have to let us be the judge of what constitutes a misunderstanding. Now, if you could ask her to come out and answer our questions, we can get on.'

Their grandmother never did answer the questions they had for her. Instead, after biting one of the officers, she was bundled kicking and screaming into their police car and driven away. And all with the neighbours looking on. Staring down onto the street from the bedroom window, Lydia swallowed back the worry that had lodged there ever since the police had arrived. What was going to happen to their grandmother? If she went to prison, would that mean Valerie's worst fears would come true? That they would be taken away to live somewhere else.

And would it mean that Lydia would never see Noah again?

The next morning Pastor Digby, Sister Vera and Sister Joan arrived in a flurry of sympathy and scripture to see what could be done to help. With no school – it was Saturday – Lydia and her sister were once more banished to their room. Which meant Lydia took up her listening position at the top of the stairs. She already knew from eavesdropping on her grandfather's telephone calls last night that their grandmother hadn't been taken to the police station.

Shortly after the police car had driven away yesterday, their grandfather had told Lydia that he had to go out. He didn't return until gone ten. He'd spent the next hour on the telephone, his voice low. One of the calls had been with Doctor Bunch. Now, as Lydia listened to the murmur of voices in the front room, it was clear that their grandmother was in a special hospital. *A mental hospital*.

Mad. Her grandmother was mad. Lydia shuddered. It was worse than she thought. And what if madness could be inherited?

That afternoon, while their grandfather went to visit his wife, Sister Lottie came to spend the afternoon with Lydia and Valerie. But if Sister Lottie was her usual chirpy self as they sat in the garden shelling peas together, Valerie was not. It worried Lydia. She had tried her best to coax Val to come and sit with them in the sunshine, but shaking her head, Val had remained at the bedroom window, as though keeping watch for the moment when her precious grandmother would come home. Lydia was so used to worrying about something and keeping it to herself it came as a shock to hear Sister Lottie suddenly say, 'Lydia, what are we going to do about Valerie? I don't believe she's spoken a single word all afternoon.'

'Actually, she hasn't spoken since last night,' Lydia said.

'Really? Oh, dear. Dear, oh dear. That's not good.'

'I don't know whether it's the same thing, and she was only small then, but I remember her doing this when our mother died.'

Sister Lottie stopped what she was doing. 'Yes,' she said thoughtfully. 'Now I recall it, she was very quiet when you first came to live here. She's such a fragile little thing and being so attached to your grandmother, yesterday must have been a terrible shock for her. I suppose all we can do for now is lift her up to the Lord.'

Lydia knew it was wrong and unworthy of her, but she felt a stab of jealousy. She had always viewed Sister Lottie

as *her* special friend and she didn't want her feeling too sorry for Valerie. Changing the subject, she said, 'I know what kind of hospital our grandmother's been taken to, but is she very ill? You know, in her head?'

Sister Lottie's face turned red. 'Well, oh dear,' she flustered, 'what with those operations, your grandmother's been through a lot. With something like that, it can make a person's mind think in extraordinary ways. It can happen to us all. Why only the other week I couldn't remember if I'd paid the milkman or not. I got myself into a terrible stew.'

'I bet you didn't call him names or send him nasty notes.'

Sister Lottie's face turned even redder. 'You're such a wise child. Much too clever for a simple old woman like me.'

'Then tell me the truth. Please.'

'I'm not sure I can, other than to say that what's probably happened to your grandmother is that her mind has decided it's had enough to cope with and wants a rest.'

'Will she get better?'

'I'm sure she will. The doctors will take wonderful care of her. She'll be home in no time.'

'I hope you're right, because I think Val is worried that if she doesn't come home, we'll be forced to live somewhere else and she'll never see Grandmother again.'

Sister Lottie patted Lydia's hand. 'Nothing like that's going to happen. You're not going anywhere.'

For Valerie's sake, Lydia hoped Sister Lottie was right.

Chapter Twenty-Eight

Their grandmother eventually came home in time for Harvest Festival, but by January, after she was found roaming the street late at night in her nightdress and being described as a danger to herself and possibly to others as well, she was back in hospital again. It was obvious to Lydia that their grandfather was ashamed of his wife's illness. She'd become known as the local nutter. And just as Lydia had known he would, he took out his frustration on her. If the house wasn't cleaned to his specific requirements he would deliberately mess it up and make her do it all over again. Sometimes, to check if she really had cleaned everywhere, he would hide tin tacks round the house for her to find. If she failed to find them all, she would be made to go without any tea. That was when he was in a good mood. He kept a garden cane handy in the kitchen for when he was in a bad mood.

The person who was suffering most in all of this was poor Valerie. She hadn't spoken properly since the first time their grandmother had been taken away. Everything she said was mouthed or whispered. Sometimes not even that and she would resort to writing instead of speaking. Her teachers said it was a phase she was going through and took the view that rather than upset Valerie further by forcing her to speak, they would patiently wait until she was ready to do so herself. Pastor Digby and the Brothers and Sisters were of the opinion that Val's voice would be returned to her when, and only when, the Lord had decided it was right. After all, who knew what God was trying to tell them through Val's silence?

Lydia wasn't convinced. Not by a long way. But since no one at church ever asked for her opinion, she never gave it. Sister Lottie was the only one to say she thought maybe Valerie should see a doctor, but when she was accused by Pastor Digby and Sister Vera of interfering with God's Great Plan for Valerie, she pressed a handkerchief to her trembling lips and said no more on the matter.

Sister Lottie had also been criticized for having an unmarried man living in her house with her. A foreign man, at that. More than once Lydia heard the Sisters whispering amongst themselves at church about the sins of the flesh and that Italian men were no better than savages when it came to women. 'It's well known they have unnatural passions,' Lydia heard Sister Joan saying to Sister Vera during tea and biscuits. 'They're famous for it. Sister Lottie is making a fool of herself.'

To Lydia's delight, Sister Lottie quietly retaliated by telling the Sisters that Joey was a good and godly man and that he always went to mass twice a week at St Joseph's. She could be surprisingly tough at times, Lydia had learned, yet on other occasions she could be reduced to a tearful child. She was a funny old thing, but Lydia was fiercely fond of her and would for ever be grateful for her help and kindness.

It had been Sister Lottie who had taken Lydia 'women's shopping', as she'd called it, to buy her her first bra. Just as it had been Sister Lottie who'd explained what was what when Lydia had started having stomach cramps.

Lydia hated the way her body had changed. It was like a betrayal. Especially her ever-growing chest. Alfie Stone and Jack Horsley were always ogling at it. Jimmy Fumble had even tried touching her. She'd kicked him hard between the legs – so hard he'd been heard throwing up in the toilets afterwards. Jack and Alfie had kept their distance from then on. Lots of other girls in their class were as big as her, but they all seemed quite happy with how they looked and when they could get away with it, they wore their shirts unbuttoned so low you could actually see their bras. Zoe

Woolf even made a big thing of leaning over her desk so that Mr Taylor, their history teacher and the best-looking teacher in the school, could get an eyeful.

Being a woman wasn't much fun, Lydia had decided. You had to shave your legs and armpits or risk being called a gorilla; you felt like you were dying every month; and the boys suddenly thought you were something to be experimented with. 'Go on, give us a feel,' one of the boys on the school bus had said only yesterday when she'd passed him to get off with Valerie. Donna Jones had been waiting at the bus stop, and if ever Lydia needed proof that being a woman was a bad thing, it was all there in the sight of Donna puffing hard on a cigarette, her massive stomach bulging hideously. Donna was pregnant and now living at Hillside Terrace with her aunt because her mother had kicked her out. Lydia couldn't imagine a girl the same age as her – almost fifteen – expecting a baby. There were all sorts of rumours about who the father was, including one about him being the driver of the rusting Jag Donna had been seen getting in and out of at the school gate at lunchtime.

If everything else around Lydia was changing, at least one thing was as constant as ever: Noah. Unlike the rest of the boys in their class, Noah treated her exactly as he always had. She was no longer taller than him; he'd rocketed in the last year and was now a good five inches taller than her. But like her, he was still thin and gangly and hadn't started to get that broad, chunky look so many of the other boys now had. He'd had another operation on his leg, but it hadn't been the success the doctors had hoped it would be. He still walked with a limp and in his own words would always be a complete tosser at sport.

Lydia was on her way to meet him now. It was a jarringly cold March morning. Newborn lambs were huddling against their mothers for warmth in the shelter of a drystone wall as the wind whipped in from the north, carrying with it the acrid smell of the town. It was a depressing smell, but maybe one that might not be around

for too much longer. One of the woollen mills had closed down earlier in the year and there were angry rumours that Marsden's, the biggest producer of worsted cloth in the area, might not make it through the summer. The reports in the local newspaper said Marsden's had borrowed too much money from the bank and couldn't pay back the loans. The owners blamed it on the oil crisis last year, but the workers said it was down to bad management. Either way, it was bad for the town.

Above her, the sky was low and grey and Lydia hoped it wasn't going to snow as she pumped away on the pedals of her father's old bike. It wasn't so difficult for her to ride these days, now that she was so much taller, and since Joey had taken a look at it last autumn before he'd gone home to Italy – as he did every year after the summer was over – it didn't make that awful noise any more. Sister Lottie had received a letter from Joey last week saying that all was well with him and his family in Naples and that he hoped to return to Swallowsdale at the end of April. Lydia looked forward to seeing him and starting up her secret Italian lessons with him again.

So much of her life was wrapped in secrecy. If she didn't protect herself this way, her grandfather would probably ban her from ever leaving the house. Sometimes she thought he was as ill in the head as her grandmother. Particularly when he voiced his disapproval of most of what she was doing at school. 'What's the point in you learning French?' he would say when she was doing her homework. 'It's not like you're ever going to go there, is it?' Chemistry and biology also came in for an equally dismissive blasting. 'Waste of time teaching a girl like you – all you'll amount to is getting yourself pregnant and trapping some fool of a man just as your mother did.'

For someone who was constantly being labelled at home as stupid and lazy, she was doing surprisingly well at school. Along with Noah and Zoe she had been chosen to sit O-levels as well as CSEs. It meant a bigger workload but Mrs Drake, their form teacher, had said she was more

than capable of coping with it. Easy for Mrs Drake to say when she didn't have the home life Lydia did!

One more hill to go and she would be there. Climbing over the garden wall was a much quicker route to Noah's house, but she'd had to drop Valerie off at Sister Lottie's beforehand. It had been hard going with Valerie sitting on the crossbar, but thank goodness her sister was still quite small and as light as a feather.

Today was yet another secret Lydia had to keep from her grandfather. He was away on church business – a last-minute arrangement, he'd said at breakfast – and knowing that this was an unexpected opportunity for her to be able to see Noah on a Saturday, she'd asked Sister Lottie if she would have Valerie for a few hours. Lydia wasn't worried that her sister would blab to their grandfather that she'd disappeared off somewhere else. These days Val was very much aware that it was better not to antagonize their grandfather.

It was Noah's fifteenth birthday today and Lydia really hoped that he'd like the presents she'd got him. By saving some of her dinner money every week and doing some odd jobs for Sister Lottie she'd saved enough to buy him a second-hand copy of Alexander Solzhenitsyn's book, *The Cancer Ward*. She'd also bought him a greatcoat in amazingly good condition at a jumble sale for a pound. She used to hate wearing second-hand stuff, but now she loved snooping through the piles of clothes for something out of the ordinary. She wasn't interested in the latest fashions like the rest of the girls at school. She couldn't understand why they all wanted to look the same in their platform shoes, tank tops, tartan flares, and glittery eyeshadow. Noah too had become a fan of jumble sales and they often scanned the local paper together to see when the next one would take place. She especially looked out for large-sized men's collarless shirts and chunky, dark-coloured cardigans that were much too big for her. Her latest bargain was a charcoal-grey beret which she was wearing for the first time. It helped to pin down her unruly curly hair which,

now that her grandmother wasn't around to insist on cutting it, had grown down to her shoulders.

It sounded like a party was in full swing when Lydia wheeled the bike round to the back of Upper Swallowsdale House. She took the carrier bag from the basket on the handlebars and knocked on the door. When no one answered it, she banged the knocker even harder. Several minutes passed before the door finally opened and Noah appeared with a loud rush of music behind him. Lydia recognized it as one of Noah's favourite King Crimson albums – *In the Court of the Crimson King*. It was one of Uncle Brad's favourites as well.

'Have you been knocking for long?' he asked above the racket.

'For days,' she said with a smile, as he stood back to let her in.

'Sorry about that. Uncle Brad's just remembered it's my birthday and has decided to throw me a party. He's in one of his wild moods, so watch yourself.'

Lydia was quite used to Uncle Brad's moods, even the wild variety. She used to blush at the outrageous things he said, but now she either ignored him or laughed at him. The one thing you could say about Uncle Brad was that he was never dull.

'We're in the kitchen,' Noah said. She shrugged off her coat and followed behind Noah as he pushed open the door into the kitchen and the source of the loud music: it was so loud the china was rattling on the dresser. A record player and two speakers had been rigged up on one of the counters and Uncle Brad – bare-footed and wearing his hair in a ponytail – was standing on the kitchen table pretending to play an imaginary guitar. 'Hi, Lyddie,' he shouted when he saw her, using the name that Noah always called her by these days. 'It's Noah's birthday! We're having a little celebration.'

'I can see that,' she yelled back, noting the opened bottle of whiskey on the draining board and the ashtray with

the smouldering remains of one of Uncle Brad's special hand-rolled cigarettes. She also noticed that the kitchen was its usual disaster zone of mess and muddle. Every inch of space was occupied with books, half-finished paintings, dirty dishes, and electronic gadgets Noah was assembling. It was more of a workshop than a kitchen.

Uncle Brad held out his hands to her. 'Come and play guitar with me.'

'I don't know how,' she shouted.

'There's nothing to it; I'll teach you.'

'Maybe later, after I've given Noah his presents.'

Noah went over to the stereo and turned down the volume. The china stopped rattling but Uncle Brad carried on strumming, his eyes closed, the table creaking ominously.

'What do you want first?' Lydia asked Noah as she tipped the presents out of the large carrier bag.

'I don't mind. You choose.'

She passed him the biggest. 'Happy birthday. I hope you like it.'

He did. She could see it in his face and the eagerness with which he slipped it on and pulled the collar up around his ears. 'What do you think?' he asked, his hands pushed deep into the pockets.

'Um ...' She paused uncertainly. The coat was a bit big for him, as she'd thought it would be, but what made her hesitate was how different it made him appear. He suddenly seemed much older. And sort of, well, more handsome and distinctive-looking. Almost a stranger in a funny kind of way. A tall, dark, very good-looking stranger. 'You look very subversive,' she said, at length. 'Like the good Trotskyite Uncle Brad would want you to be.'

'Excellent,' he said. 'Thanks, Lyddie. It's great. Really great.'

She smiled. 'I know. That's why it's called a greatcoat.' She handed him his next present. 'It's not new,' she apologized, 'like the coat.'

'Brilliant!' he said when he'd removed the wrapping paper. 'Just what I wanted.' Knowing that he meant it,

she blushed with pride and happiness. But then he did something that made her blush even more: he hugged her tightly. It was the first time he'd ever done anything like it before and by the time she'd decided she quite liked the feel of his arms around her, he'd let go. For a moment neither of them seemed to know what to say next, and just stood there staring at one another. She was just thinking that perhaps he'd regretted what he'd done, when behind them the ominous creaking from the table had turned even more ominous. They both yelled at the same time. '*Jump!*'

But it was too late. The splintering of wood followed by an almighty crash happened before Uncle Brad had an inkling of what was going on. 'Whoa!' he cried out as he hit the floor in a tangle of arms and legs that was the funniest thing Lydia had ever seen.

'Bloody hell!' he let rip while they, hysterical with laughter, pulled him from the wreckage. 'Good thing I didn't have a drink in my hand or I might have spilt it. Hey, nice hat by the way, Lydia. Very groovy.'

When she was back on her bike and heading into town for Sister Lottie's, Lydia was still laughing to herself. It was without doubt the best time she'd had in ages. The highlight of the afternoon, other than Uncle Brad smashing up the kitchen table, had been when he announced that he was going to teach Lydia and Noah to waltz. 'You never know when you might need this particular skill,' he told them as he changed the record on the stereo. Still dressed in his coat, Noah had refused point-blank to take part, but then after Lydia had called him a spoilsport and jammed a saucepan on his head, and then one on herself, they pranced around the kitchen according to Uncle Brad's instructions. She didn't know about their footwork, but the music was amazing. 'It's Russian,' Uncle Brad informed her when she asked him what it was. 'Sviridov.'

'Sure you're not talking about a brand of vodka?' Noah said.

'Philistine!' Uncle Brad roared, turning up the music and

then taking a photograph of them. 'Do try and hold Lyddie properly, Noah,' he continued to instruct impatiently. 'You look like you're terrified to touch her!'

Celebrating birthdays was one of the many things Pastor Digby had ruled out of their lives. According to him, celebrating your birthday was a sin rooted firmly in the mire of personal vanity.

Smiling to herself, Lydia couldn't help but wonder what Pastor Digby and the Brothers and Sisters would have made of the party she'd just been to. But the thought of their reaction soon wiped the smile off her face. If they ever got wind of what went on at Upper Swallowsdale House, what limited freedom she had managed to engineer for herself would be taken from her in an instant.

She was almost at Sister Lottie's when she noticed a car parked on the corner of a narrow side street. It was a car she knew all too well and had her pumping the pedals double fast. But what was her grandfather doing in town? He'd told her he was going to Skipton for the day.

Terrified that her grandfather might get home before her and be suspicious that she'd been up to something, she refused Sister Lottie's offer of a drink and a biscuit and set off with Valerie balanced on the crossbar.

They arrived home to find no car on the drive. Relief flooded through Lydia.

'What's wrong?' Valerie mouthed at her.

'Nothing,' Lydia lied as she opened the garage doors and pushed the bike inside.

Going in the back door, Lydia hurriedly started to peel the potatoes for tea. She'd just got the pan on to boil, when the doorbell rang.

She went to the door, opened it cautiously and peered at the man in the two-inch gap. He certainly wasn't anyone she knew. He had bushy sideburns and an ugly leathery face, and on the ground next to him was a battered suitcase. Maybe he was one of those men who came round with brushes and tins of polish.

'G'day sweetheart,' he said in a voice with a drawling accent she didn't recognize. 'I'm your uncle Leonard. Can I come in?'

Chapter Twenty-Nine

Uncle Leonard turned out to be their grandfather's younger brother, which strictly speaking made him not their uncle, but their *great*-uncle. He said he was happy for Lydia and Val to drop the 'great' and just be their common or garden Uncle Leonard.

According to Sister Lottie, he had been something of a rascal when he was a young man. 'He was very charming and could get away with all sorts,' she'd explained to Lydia. 'There was also a lot of rivalry between the two brothers and it caused, well, let's just say it caused ill-feeling between them.'

Lydia didn't think there was anything charming about the man currently staying with them. He was a big slab of a man with a thick neck, thick hands and a thick voice. For years he'd been living in Australia in a place called Wollongong, which didn't sound like a real place at all. He said he'd emigrated there to make his fortune and told them stories about kangaroos jumping out in front of cars, about koala bears and spiders that were as big as dinner plates and hid beneath the toilet seat. 'Oh, it's a great life,' he boasted, shovelling food into his enormous mouth, then helping himself to more from the dishes on the table.

'Then why have you come back to Swallowsdale?' Lydia's grandfather asked grimly.

'To be with my family, of course, Arthur.'

Lydia didn't believe half of what he said. More than that, he gave her the creeps. There was something in his face. Something sly and dangerous. He looked like trouble.

He reeked of the same aftershave nearly all the boys at school doused themselves in: Brut. In fact the whole house seemed to stink of the stuff; there was no escape from it, other than to go into the garden. But often he was out there, too. Banned from smoking inside, he would stand by the back door puffing away. Afterwards he'd spray his mouth with a minty breath freshener.

Within hours of Uncle Leonard's surprise arrival, it became very clear to Lydia that her grandfather hated having his brother around. Even before Uncle Leonard had unpacked his case and tested the firmness of the bed in the spare room, Lydia overheard her grandfather asking him when he would be leaving.

'I must say, Arthur, I don't call that much of a welcome,' Uncle Leonard had said.

'And I don't call you much of a brother,' came the reply. 'You've got a real nerve showing your face back here.'

'Surely you're not still harping on about the past? I told you, I'm a changed man. I've been reborn in the blood of our dear Lord and Saviour, Jesus Christ.'

'That remains to be seen.'

'I'll prove it to you. Just you see.'

Ten days on and Uncle Leonard didn't seem to be in any hurry to leave. He was still stinking the house out with his revolting aftershave and minty breath. This morning he was coming to church with them. Last week he hadn't got out of bed in time. He'd said the long journey had taken it out of him and he needed to catch up on his sleep. He did a lot of that. He was never up before Lydia and Valerie went to school. Lydia was convinced that he stayed in bed for most of the day. The evenings their grandfather visited his wife in hospital, Leonard would get himself all spruced up after tea and go out. He didn't say where he was going, but Lydia suspected it was to the pub.

At church, the Brothers and Sisters greeted Uncle Leonard politely enough, but not with their usual enthusiasm when anybody new appeared. 'I'm afraid his reputation goes before him,' Sister Lottie whispered to Lydia as

they took their seats. 'A lot of people remember why he left Swallowsdale in the first place.'

'What did he do?'

But there was no time for Sister Lottie to say anything more, as Pastor Digby was on his feet, his palms held up before the Lord. It was the signal for them all to do likewise. For some reason Lydia didn't fully understand, she could never find it in herself to come right out and say that she hated going to church. Parts of it she disliked intensely, like the one-eyed, po-faced Pastor Digby for starters and all his silly rules – he'd recently banned them from drinking coffee, saying it was addictive – but when the room was perfectly quiet and everyone was deep in prayer, she felt a strange sense of peace she didn't feel anywhere else. Coming here to this dusty, musty-smelling hall was such a part of her life now, she couldn't really imagine not doing it. Besides, she couldn't bear the thought of disappointing Sister Lottie by not coming.

They were almost at the end of the service when Pastor Digby made his usual announcement that it was Share and Pray time. Lydia hoped that just once, no one would have anything special on their minds that needed praying about. The service was long enough as it was without everybody getting in on the act and wanting, like last week, to pray about the soul of the woman in the dry cleaner's who'd overcharged Brother Derek earlier in the week. A rustle of movement further along the row of seats told Lydia that her wish had not been granted. But when she saw that it was Uncle Leonard who was on his feet with something to say, she sat up straighter, her curiosity sparked. Hello, this should be interesting.

'I'd just like to say what it means for me to be here,' he began. 'As some of you will doubtless remember, I was not a good man in my younger days. Brothers and Sisters, the word sinner doesn't cover what I was then. Let me tell you, I sinned on a scale you can scarcely comprehend. I drank more than was good for me. I drank till I was lying

in the gutter in my own vomit. And then I'd drag myself out of the gutter and drink some more.'

Shocked gasps could be heard.

'Yes, good folk, you have every reason to view me with disgust and loathing. But there's worse to come. I went with women. Hundreds of them. As many as I could lay my hands on.'

More gasps.

'And you know what? The devil had me so firmly in his hot sticky grasp I enjoyed every minute of it. It wasn't until I ended up in the barrel of sin, so near the bottom I was covered in the filth of lust and debauchery, that the Lord finally saved me.'

'Praise the Lord,' someone muttered from the back of the hall.

'But what I really want to share with you is something that's been weighing heavily on my heart for so many years. There's this great need in me to share with you exactly what kind of a man my brother is. You see there are things that need to be said, things that—'

'I think you've said enough, Leonard.'

Along with everyone else, Lydia whipped round to look at her grandfather: his face was puce.

'No, Arthur, I haven't. Please let me do this. Because I fear that if I don't, it can't ever be right between us. Only when it's right between us will I know you've forgiven me from the bottom of your heart.'

From the pin-drop silence around her, Lydia didn't doubt that there wasn't a person in the hall who wasn't on the edge of their seat to hear what else Uncle Leonard had to say. She saw her grandfather look to Pastor Digby for back-up, but Pastor Digby raised a hand and shook his head. 'Go on, Leonard,' he said. 'The Lord is listening. Put your confession before Him.'

He's as nosy as the rest of us, thought Lydia, trying not to smirk.

'Thank you, Pastor Digby. This is difficult for me. Very difficult. But the reason I'm here is not just to seek my

brother's forgiveness but to open your eyes to show you how my brother—'

'This is intolerable! I won't stand for it!'

Doing exactly that, Lydia's grandfather jumped to his feet. He looked like he was about to explode.

'Sit down, please, Brother Arthur.'

'No! I shan't sit here and listen to this rubbish.' He jabbed a finger in the air at Uncle Leonard. 'You're no different from how you always were. After all these years, you still want to make me look bad. To humiliate me in front of my friends. You're no more filled with the spirit than I'm John the Baptist!'

Next to her, Valerie lowered her head and leaned into Lydia. Lydia reached for her hand and squeezed it. Please God, she silently prayed, don't let anyone make us leave the room. Not when it's getting so interesting.

But interesting wasn't the word for what happened next. Uncle Leonard began to cry. 'I knew it,' he wailed, his enormous hands raking through his greasy, dandruffy hair. 'I knew it wouldn't be possible to put the past to rest and be truly forgiven by my own flesh and blood.'

'Don't listen to him! He's a charlatan. A crook and a cheat. He's doing what he always did, weaving a web of lies to take you all in. He's capable of anything. Believe me when I say the devil has many cunning disguises, and this is one of them!'

'Please, Brother Arthur,' Pastor Digby said sternly. 'Sit down. It's our duty at all times to dig out the sin within ourselves and so I suggest we put this into the Lord's hands.' He swivelled his beady eye round to Uncle Leonard. 'Only when the demons have been fully seen off will the Lamb of God reside in our hearts.' The beady eye was back on Lydia's grandfather now. 'There's clearly some devilry at work here and I feel God calling me to exorcise it.'

A small part of Lydia almost felt sorry for her grandfather as he sank back into his chair, defeated. But the greater part of her was all agog to hear what it was Uncle Leonard was so eager to share with them.

'Like I said, this is difficult for me,' Uncle Leonard began. 'But I know I have to confess all. There can be no hiding from God.' He paused and stared straight at his brother.

Get on with it! Lydia wanted to shout. Just tell us what you did. She suspected he was enjoying himself with everyone hanging on his every word.

'Brother Arthur, I just pray you can find it in your heart to say the words, "I forgive you, Brother Leonard." Would that be too much to ask of you?' When he got no reply, not so much as a glance, he addressed the congregation. 'My brother's a proud man, and who can blame him? For what I did to him was despicable. I expect you all think that the reason I emigrated to Australia was because I stole from my brother. Not once. Not twice. But repeatedly. Small amounts of money at first and then I stole his chequebook and wrote out cheques for myself. I all but cleared out his account. Any other brother would have killed me there and then. But not mine. Not my brother Arthur. He turned the other cheek. Yes, that's what he did. And what did I do in return? Oh, let me tell you, I wanted even more from him. I wanted everything he had. Including his wife. His dear sweet wife.'

The congregation gasped as one.

'And still my brother didn't kill me. Instead, he gave me what little money he had left so that I could make a new and decent life for myself in Australia.' He thumped a fist against his chest. 'All this I did to my own precious brother. Oh, what a miserable wretch am I! But what a fortunate group of people you are, having a saint walking amongst you. A man so good of heart that he let me walk away, even though I'd made unseemly advances towards his wife.' He slumped dramatically to the floor and, down on his knees, he clasped his hands together in prayer.

The reaction to this confession was mixed. Some people tutted, some shook their heads, and some, like Uncle Leonard, got down on their knees and prayed. But Lydia's grandfather remained perfectly still in his seat. His gaze

was fixed firmly on Uncle Leonard, and judging from the expression on his face, Lydia didn't think forgiveness was on the cards. But there was something else in his expression that had her wondering. It took her a few minutes to realize what it was: confusion. Why would her grandfather look confused? Unless he was expecting Uncle Leonard to confess to something else.

A few minutes of quiet passed and then Pastor Digby helped Uncle Leonard to his feet. 'I've no time for malingering Christians – those who profess the faith but do nothing to bring others to the Lord. Or those who cannot find it in their heart to forgive. This man has done a brave and virtuous thing here today and it is our duty to take him into our fold and prove to him what our faith really means. Brother Arthur, I invite you to join me here and publicly forgive Brother Leonard.'

'Not bloody likely!'

Chapter Thirty

The Prodigal Son had nothing over the Prodigal Uncle Leonard.

He was now the absolute centre of attention for the Brothers and Sisters in Christ. They couldn't get enough of him and were continually singing his praises. All during Easter week, they'd passed him amongst themselves at hot-pot suppers as a shining example of what the Lord could do for a sinner who had sincerely repented. Even the very worst of sinners. This was what the resurrection was all about: Uncle Leonard had been washed in the blood of Christ. He was truly born again. Hallelujah!

Lydia's grandfather was also coming in for a certain amount of attention. But there wasn't a single voice singing his praises. Pastor Digby was worried about him. As was the rest of the church. They were all busy praying for Brother Arthur.

It was just gone five o'clock in the afternoon and after finishing the ironing, Lydia was now listening to the raised voices behind the closed front room door. Pastor Digby was saying that if her grandfather continued to harden his heart towards Uncle Leonard, he risked letting the devil sneak into his life. 'It's too late for that,' Lydia heard her grandfather say. 'The devil has already wormed his way into my life. He's moved into my spare room and is making fools of the lot of you. I can't believe he's taken you all in.'

'Brother Arthur, I strongly urge you to reconsider your feelings. Search your heart, long and hard, for anything that isn't of our Lord and Saviour. Jealousy is an ugly thing close up. It destroys our walk with God. I say this

not just as your spiritual mentor, but as your friend.'

'You know what they say about people who eavesdrop, don't you?'

The question was whispered hoarsely in Lydia's ear. She spun round, swamped by Uncle Leonard's close-up presence and the sickening smell of Brut and breath freshener.

'I wasn't eavesdropping,' she lied.

'Sure you weren't. You just happened to have your ear firmly pressed against the door, checking for the sound of woodworm. So what are they saying in there?'

He was so close to her she could practically count the gingery hairs in his bushy greying sideburns. There were hairs in his enormous nostrils, too. That much he had in common with his brother. 'I don't know,' she lied, moving away fast.

'Were they talking about me?' he asked, following her to the kitchen.

'I told you I don't know.'

He smiled, the leathery skin crinkling around his eyes. 'Don't look so frightened, Lydia,' he said. 'I'm on your side. I know what kind of a man my brother really is. I just want you to know that I'm your friend. If you want me to be, that is. Do you need a friend, Lydia? Someone you can trust?'

She swallowed nervously, but didn't answer him. What could she possibly say? If her grandfather thought for a single second that she had an ally in his brother, he would make life hell for her. Yet, what if Uncle Leonard really did know what his brother was capable of? Wouldn't it be better to have him on her side? Maybe in the short term, but what about when Uncle Leonard left Swallowsdale, as he surely would? 'I'd better make a start on getting tea ready,' she said non-committally.

If he thought she'd snubbed him, he gave no sign of being offended. 'In that case,' he said, 'don't bother making anything for me; I've been invited out to supper again.'

'Lucky you.'

He winked. 'Lucky me, indeed.'

*

Shortly after Pastor Digby left, Lydia's grandfather came into the kitchen and announced that he would be out for the evening. Excellent, thought Lydia. She and Valerie could have a nice evening together. No grandfather. No Uncle Leonard. The house to themselves. What could be better?

With tea out of the way, Val whispered to Lydia that she was going upstairs to read. Disappointed that her sister didn't want to stay downstairs with her, Lydia decided to leave the washing-up until later. Why not enjoy some time to herself, seeing as it was the last day of the Easter holidays? So whilst it was still light, she went out to the garden and climbed up into the branches of the chestnut tree. She looked out across the moors in the direction of Noah's house. She supposed he'd be home now, back from his holiday down in London with Uncle Brad. London. It was about as foreign to her as Joey's home in Italy. But one day she'd go there. London and Italy. That was a promise. Resting her back against the broad solid trunk of the tree, she played her hands over the large leaves that almost hid her from view. They were still that lovely fresh green colour that you only saw in spring. In the cool evening air, she listened to the birds giving their final burst of busy sing-song before settling down for the night. Then through the chirruping and squawking she became aware of another sound: a car. A car that had stopped nearby. Very nearby. Next she heard the sound of a car door slamming shut.

Remembering the washing-up she hadn't done, she clambered down from the tree and bolted up the garden towards the house, her heart thumping.

But she was too late – her grandfather was already in the kitchen.

'Where have you been?' he demanded.

'I was in the garden,' she said, shutting the back door behind her. She followed the direction of his questioning gaze, to the dishes piled up on the draining board.

'You were in the garden, weren't you?' he said. His tone was slow and menacing and there was a chilling mixture of anger and relish on his face. It made her stomach clench with queasy fear. 'You had better things to do with your time than tidy up, did you?' He took off his jacket and hooked it over a chair.

'I ... I was going to do it when—'

'What?' he interrupted, going over to the door to the hall and closing it. 'Because I wasn't here to keep an eye on you, you were going to do it when you were good and ready? Is that it? Except I came home early and caught you out.' He came and stood directly in front of her.

She pushed up her sleeves to show she was ready to get on with the job now. Right now this very minute, if only he'd get out of the way.

But he made no move to get out of the way, and as if copying her, he began rolling up his own sleeves. She knew what that meant and her stomach clenched even more. 'It makes me wonder what else you get up to while my back is turned,' he said. 'Maybe you haven't been in the garden at all. Maybe you've been somewhere I don't know about.'

'I haven't,' she said, eyeing the cane over by the bin. 'I've been in the garden. And only for a few minutes. Honestly.'

'I don't believe you!' he barked, making her jump. 'I can see it in your face. You're lying.' His eyes blazed and he seemed visibly to swell before her. Then it came: not the cane, but his hand full across her face.

Lydia reeled and nearly lost her balance. She hadn't recovered properly when he came at her again, cracking her on the side of her head. Then the other side too. Dizzy, she could taste blood. She touched her lip; it was split. Shocked, she knew that this was going to be no ordinary beating. The slow, menacing tone he'd used before was gone and he was shouting at her now. Calling her those vile names he always did. She was scum. Worse than scum. She was a whore. She forced her mind to go to that special

place where she went when she needed to detach herself from what was happening. She pictured herself being carried away into the night sky by her father; he was taking her somewhere safe.

But the special place wasn't working for her this time. Her grandfather had her by the shoulders and was shaking her with such violence her head flew backwards and forwards. 'If I don't teach you right from wrong,' he yelled at her, 'who will?' He then shoved her from him so forcibly she fell to the floor, the air knocked clean out of her. Just inches from his feet, instinct made her wrap her arms around her head. But that left the rest of her vulnerable. The first kick was aimed at her stomach. The next at her shoulder. This was new. He'd never kicked her before. He really had lost control and she knew she had to do something. She had to get out of here. Keeping her head protected, she twisted round to look over to the back door. To her surprise, it was open and somebody was standing there watching. It was Uncle Leonard.

'Well, well, well, brother dear,' he said, stepping inside. 'So this is how you get your fun these days, is it?'

Immediately her grandfather stopped what he was doing. Relief flooded through Lydia. It was over. She was safe. But the sense of relief was quickly followed by shame. She didn't want to be seen this way, so degraded and humiliated.

'Keep out of this,' her grandfather snarled at his brother. 'It's got nothing to do with you.'

'Is that so? You wouldn't be taking out your frustration on a defenceless young girl because you're too frightened to pick a proper fight with me, would you?'

Faint with pain and fear, and hardly daring to look at her grandfather or uncle, knowing only that the kitchen was suddenly charged with an explosive tension, Lydia dragged herself off the floor. She began to shiver.

'Not everything in this world is about you, Leonard,' her grandfather said. 'I'm teaching her an important lesson. Not to lie to me. You know how I feel about liars and cheats.'

'I know only too well,' said Uncle Leonard with a tight smile. 'You'll be telling me next that she can only be redeemed through true suffering.' He came over to where Lydia was standing. 'Have you lied to your grandfather, Lydia?'

'No,' she replied; her voice was small and pathetic, little more than a strangled croak from the back of her dry throat. She was a cold mess of fear inside. 'No, I haven't.'

'Of course you haven't. You're much too sweet and innocent to do anything like that.' He turned back to his brother. 'You should be ashamed of yourself, Arthur. Now out of my way while I take Lydia upstairs and make sure she's all right. She might need a doctor.'

Panic seized hold of Lydia. Whilst she was grateful for his intervention, she knew that if she accepted any more help from him, it would only make matters worse for her. 'Thank you,' she murmured, already moving towards the door and the safety of the hall and upstairs, 'but I don't need any help. I'm fine.'

Upstairs she found Valerie crying under her bedclothes. 'It's OK, Val,' she assured her. 'It was just some silly disagreement and Grandfather lost his temper like he always does. You're not to worry. Please, Valerie,' she begged, 'please don't cry. You know I hate to see you upset.'

But when Valerie poked her head out from the covers, she took one look at Lydia's face and started sobbing again.

Knowing what her sister was worried about, Lydia spent the next hour comforting her, telling her everything was going to be OK, that nothing was going to change for them. Stability was what her sister needed and it looked like Lydia was the only one who could provide it. With lies and whatever else it took.

Once Valerie was asleep, Lydia quietly got ready for bed. It was a while before she could get comfortable. Shock must have numbed the worst of the pain earlier – now she was conscious of it throughout the whole of her sore,

tender body. There wasn't a bit of her that didn't ache. She felt sick and her head wouldn't stop spinning. Maybe Uncle Leonard was right and she did need to see a doctor. She put the thought out of her mind and closed her eyes.

Sleep wouldn't come. Staring at the light cast from the street lamp through the gap in the curtains, she started to worry what she could tell Noah to explain away the bruises. She had used the 'falling down the stairs' excuse too often already. And not just to Noah. Miss Drake had asked her about the livid marks on her legs the last time her grandfather had taken the cane to her. On that occasion she had 'tripped' on the carpet on the stairs.

Downstairs she could hear her grandfather arguing with Uncle Leonard and then the sound of a door slamming. One thing she knew for sure was that after what had just taken place, life was going to get a lot more difficult. If only she'd just done the washing-up when she normally did ... if only she hadn't gone out to the garden. She squeezed her eyes shut and jammed her knuckled fists into her sockets. Why was life so unfair to her? What had she done to deserve it?

The answer came back at her in a flash. *You reap what you sow.* If she hadn't driven her mother to suicide, none of this would be happening. But because of what she'd done, this was her punishment: to be a lightning conductor for bad things. She had no one but herself to blame.

Chapter Thirty-One

As she made him his toast and poured out his tea, Lydia was jumpy around her grandfather the next morning. He hadn't said a word to her. He didn't need to. It was there in the grim set of his face. *Just you wait*, it said. Unable to eat any of her own breakfast, she concentrated on making sure Val ate hers.

In the deathly silence, Lydia could hear movement in the room above them, followed by the sound of heavy footsteps on the stairs. Then unbelievably, for the first since he'd arrived, Uncle Leonard appeared for breakfast. 'Now that's what I like to see,' he said in a loud, overly cheery voice, 'a happy family sitting round the table together. Room for me?' he said to his brother.

Without answering him, her grandfather threw down his half-eaten toast and marched out of the room. And the house.

Her cereal bowl empty now, Val also left the room and went upstairs to clean her teeth. Keeping an eye on the time, Lydia started clearing away the dishes.

'How are you this morning, Lydia?' Uncle Leonard asked, sitting in his brother's seat. 'Are you sure you're well enough for school?'

'I'm just a bit stiff, that's all.'

'You wouldn't prefer to stay at home?'

Nothing would have suited her more than to hide herself away in bed for the rest of the week. She didn't know why, but she felt dirty. Dirty all over. Inside and out. No amount of washing would make her feel clean again. 'Best

not,' she said. 'I don't like to miss any lessons if I can help it,' she said.

'Good for you. That's the spirit. Any chance of a cuppa?'

She fetched him a mug and poured out the last of the tea from the pot. 'Thanks, sweetheart,' he said, and after taking a noisy slurp, he rested his elbows on the table. 'You know, I meant what I said yesterday. I'm your friend, Lydia. And I'd bet my last dollar or pound that this isn't the first time my brother has hurt you, is it? And that you've never told anyone. Eh?'

Lydia couldn't speak. It was bad enough that he'd witnessed her humiliation, but to talk about it so openly was too much. When she didn't respond, he said, 'You know he's banking on you being too scared to open your mouth. If he was worried that you'd talk to anyone, do you think he'd let you go to school with that face? No. He's done too good a job on you. But like I said, I'm your friend, Lydia, and if you want me to protect you from my brother, you're going to have to trust me. Do you think you can do that?'

Slightly mesmerized, Lydia surprised herself by nodding. Just a small, barely noticeable nod, as though anything more would expose her dirty shame to the world.

Uncle Leonard smiled at her. A big grin of a smile that showed two rows of badly stained teeth. 'Then why don't you stop what you're doing and keep me company while I pack away some breakfast?'

'I'm sorry but I don't have time, the bus leaves in fifteen minutes.'

All the way to school, Lydia kept thinking how badly she'd misjudged Uncle Leonard when he first came to stay with them. He may have done some terrible things in the past, but at least he wasn't cruel and didn't beat people for no real reason. He may not be able to protect her for ever from her grandfather, but the way she felt now, she would take whatever help she could get.

So what if that help sprang from a situation she didn't fully understand? The relationship between her grandfather and Uncle Leonard was a mystery to Lydia. Given that he had publicly refused to forgive his brother, she couldn't work out why her grandfather allowed him to stay.

From what she had pieced together from snippets of overheard conversation, Uncle Leonard had far from made his fortune in Australia as he'd hoped to and had returned to Britain without a bean to his name. Apparently, having allowed Jesus into his life, he'd been overcome with the need for forgiveness from his brother, as well as a desire to see his family again, particularly the two great-nieces he'd never met before but whom he had learned about through an old school pal in Swallowsdale who had recently got in touch with him. Could his return home really be as simple as that? Or was there more to it?

'What the hell happened to you?' Noah asked the second he saw her.

Wishing that just once he wasn't such a good and caring friend, Lydia busied herself with something at the bottom of her bag. 'Oh, you know what I'm like,' she said lightly. 'I'm such a clumsy idiot. Those stairs are going to be the death of me one day.'

When she couldn't convincingly go on rustling around inside her bag any longer, she looked up. Noah was staring at her. He continued to do so for the longest time, his dark, thoughtful eyes searching hers. Then his eyes travelled slowly over her split lip and her swollen jaw. Thank God the rest of the bruises were hidden beneath her clothes. Trying not to squirm, she saw his expression change. There was ... there was anger in his face. Something she had never seen before. She suddenly realized with total certainty that he didn't believe her. That probably he never had. Shocked, she willed him not to say what he had to be thinking. Please, she silently begged him, please allow me to hang on to what's left of my dignity.

When he did speak, he very gently touched her jaw with

his fingers and said, 'It looks painful, Lyddie. Have you seen a doctor?'

His concern made something deep within her ache far more painfully than her bashed ribs did. 'It looks worse than it really is,' she said, turning away and blinking back the tears. 'I'm OK. Really. How was London? Did Uncle Brad take you to the Planetarium as he said he would?'

Everyone else at school had a field day teasing her, wanting to know who she'd got into a scrap with during the Easter holiday. 'You should see the state of the bloke after I'd finished with him,' she bragged to Alfie Stone, 'so you'd better watch yourself.'

How easy it was to tough it out and be full of bravado when you weren't scared of the person.

On her way home, having stayed late for a French conversation class, Lydia was feeling particularly fed up. She had a letter in her bag about a school trip that she knew she would never be allowed to go on. It had been organized some time ago and her grandfather had thrown the original letter straight in the bin, saying it was too expensive. She hadn't given it another thought. But now some extra places had become available and her French teacher had made a point of urging Lydia to take one up.

When she rounded the corner of the back of the house, she found Uncle Leonard sitting in a deckchair in the garden. Her spirits fizzled even lower. She was tired, and wanted only to go in and lie down on her bed for a while. She had a headache and her ribs were sore and tender, as was her jaw.

'Hello,' he said cheerfully. 'How was your day?'

'OK,' she said politely.

'That doesn't sound too good. Any problems I can help you with?'

'I shouldn't think so.'

'Why don't you try me?'

She sighed and went over to him. 'The French department

at school is arranging a trip to Paris at the end of May.'

'So why the glum face?'

'Do you think for one moment my grandfather will let me go?'

He rubbed his chin, then stroked his ridiculous sideburns. 'Mm ... I see what you mean. Well, perhaps I could find a way to convince my brother that you should go. I could play the education angle. No one knows more than me that travel broadens the mind.'

As tempting as his offer was, Lydia decided not to push her luck. Having Uncle Leonard's protection was more important to her than her grandfather's arm being twisted so she could go on some silly French trip. Besides, something told her that it wasn't a good idea to put all her eggs in one basket. Better not leave herself too much in Uncle Leonard's debt. 'No thanks,' she said, 'it's not that big a deal to me.' She turned to go inside.

'Don't rush off,' he said. 'Stay and chat with me while I finish my illicit fag.'

Seeing as there was only a short stub left to his cigarette, she gave in. 'I wouldn't have thought you'd care less about my grandfather's insistence that you smoke outside the house.'

'Are you suggesting a good Christian man like myself would deliberately antagonize my brother?'

'No ... but—'

'It's about respect, Lydia. Whilst I can't respect my brother for what he's done to you, I'm a guest here in his house and as such I have to respect his rules and abide by them.'

Lydia couldn't help but think his answer was about as plausible as his dramatic confession in church. Reminded of his confession, she said, 'Can I ask you something?'

'Ask away.'

'Did you really try it on with my grandmother when you were younger?'

He took a hard puff on his cigarette, inhaled the smoke, then exhaled it through his nose in two long curling

ribbons. 'I may have been a bad boy back in those days, but I wasn't desperate. No offence, but your grandmother was no looker.'

'So you didn't?'

'In a drunken moment or two I may have wanted to annoy my brother by making the odd pass at her. But nothing serious took place.'

'Then why did you say you did in church?'

He stubbed out his cigarette on the grass at his feet and tapped his nose. 'That's strictly between me and my dearly beloved brother.'

Chapter Thirty-Two

The day before Lydia's fifteenth birthday, Sister Lottie invited her to tea. It was a special occasion: Joey had just returned to Swallowsdale.

When Lydia saw the dainty crustless sandwiches, the chocolate fingers, the butterfly cakes and a Victoria sponge cake in pride of place in the middle of all the plates, she said, 'This looks wonderful, just like a real birthday party.'

Sister Lottie was immediately all a-flutter. 'Oh, goodness gracious no! Pastor Digby wouldn't approve of that. But if anyone asks, we're celebrating the Lord bringing Joey safely back to us.'

Lydia tried not to smile. She loved it when Sister Lottie got round one of Pastor Digby's silly Thou Shalt Nots.

'I have never understood this strange church of yours,' Joey said, 'so many rules, so many ways to stop you enjoying yourselves.'

'Now, now, Joey,' Sister Lottie said, managing to sound quite stern, something that she was rarely capable of pulling off, 'you Catholics have just as many odd rules.'

Joey laughed, shaking his head of black curly hair. 'Yes, but we ignore almost all of them.'

Sister Lottie tutted and passed him the plate of sandwiches. Watching Joey eat, marvelling at how good his English was now compared to when he first came to Swallowsdale, Lydia thought how happily at home he appeared here in this little house. He was like the son Sister Lottie had never had and it always amused Lydia that she mothered him so lovingly. Joey often spoke about his

own mother back in Italy, who had been left to bring up six children single-handedly after her husband died in a gruesome accident with a threshing machine while helping out on a friend's farm. They had been so poor they had regularly gone to bed with only water slopping around in their stomachs. His mother had taught them to imagine the water was a tasty stew of lamb and potatoes. Two of Joey's brothers, like him, had gone in search of work abroad so they could support the family back home – they were now living in America working in the kitchen of a restaurant owned by a cousin.

For all that, Joey was never miserable and not once had Lydia ever heard him complain. He was fiercely proud of his family and utterly devoted to making life easier for them, even if it did mean he had to spend so many months apart from them. He was equally devoted to Sister Lottie, who he claimed was his adopted mother here in England. Continuing to observe him, Lydia listened to the story he was telling about the kind lorry driver who had given him a lift all the way from Dover. He was doing what he always did, punctuating the telling of his tale with wild hand gestures and happy laughter. With his coal-black eyes, straight white teeth, tight jeans and black shirt, he looked impossibly glamorous and Lydia could easily understand why all the women on Hillside Terrace took ages making up their minds when choosing which ice-cream to buy.

The following day it was Lydia's birthday and she was given permission to visit Donna Jones, who had recently come home from hospital with a baby boy. Donna's aunt had put a note through the letterbox asking Lydia to visit her niece that afternoon. Lydia's grandfather had opened and read the note – there was no such thing as privacy in their household – and after a lengthy discussion on the phone with Pastor Digby, who seemed to think the risk of Lydia being tainted and led astray was outweighed by the opportunity of winning a prize sinner for Jesus, Lydia was told she could accept the invitation. She was handed

a selection of Pastor Digby's tracts to give to Donna and informed that it was her duty as a believer, and for the sake of the newborn child, to bring Donna to Christ.

Lydia knew Donna would be no more interested in the religious pamphlets than she was in sharing them with her. Anyway, she had plans. As soon as she could get away, she was going to see Noah.

Lydia knocked nervously on Donna's door. The aunt, decked out in pink fluffy mules, a short silky dressing gown and a headdress of Carmen heated rollers, let her in and showed her through to the front room. 'I'll leave you to it,' she said, closing the door after her.

Donna was stretched out on a scabby PVC settee that looked like it was suffering from a bad case of eczema. Donna's feet were resting on a pouffe, with her eyes glued to a colour television. The only television Lydia was familiar with was Noah's TV, a small portable black and white set that had an aerial like a halo sticking out of it. This one was huge. Balanced on Donna's lap was not a baby, as Lydia had expected, but a can of stout. 'Wotcher,' Donna said, briefly flicking her eyes away from the screen, where a man in a hat like a tea cosy was trying to comfort a tearful blonde woman: their faces were a peculiar shade of orange. 'Come in and park yer bum. It's only *Crossroads*. It'll be over in a mo.'

While she waited for the action to come to an end on the television, Lydia lowered herself into a PVC armchair: it made an embarrassing raspberry sound when she put all her weight on it. She glanced around her. There were lots of signs that a baby had recently moved in – a row of cards on the mantelpiece, a pair of woollen mittens on the floor, a half-empty bottle of milk warming in the sun on the windowsill alongside a bottle of Aqua Manda, but no sign of an actual baby.

Although Lydia had known Donna since they were nine years old, she didn't *know* her one little bit. Donna's bullying days may have been left behind at junior school, but

Lydia had never felt inclined to be friends with the girl. She didn't have a clue why she'd been summoned to visit Donna. As far as she was concerned, the sooner this visit was over, the better.

A twangy theme tune started up from the television, signalling the end of the programme. Donna took a swig from the can of stout. 'Switch it off, will yer? Knob's on t'right.'

Lydia did as she was told, and that was when she saw the baby. He was on the floor at the far end of the settee, loosely wrapped in a crocheted blanket inside a plastic laundry basket: it didn't seem much of a start in life for the poor thing.

'He's an ugly little bleeder, in't he?' Donna said.

Lydia was no expert, but he didn't look that bad. Just a bit scrunched up, that was all. Quoting something she'd heard before, she said, 'I expect he'll grow into his looks.'

'Let's hope you're right.'

Sitting back in her chair again, Lydia said, 'What have you called him?'

'Kirk.'

Lydia repeated the name inside her head. Why did it ring a bell? Ah! Captain Kirk from Noah's favourite TV programme, *Star Trek*. Perhaps Donna was a fan too. 'How was it?' she asked. 'You know, the birth?'

'A bloody nightmare from start t'finish. From now on I'm going on t'pill. Come to that, the way my fanny feels I doubt I'll ever want sex again. I'm as big and rattly as a dustbin down there.'

Lydia wished she hadn't asked. She squeezed her knees together. What on earth was she doing here? Why had Donna's aunt put that note through the letterbox?

But Donna had plenty more to say on the subject of giving birth. 'I've got knockers as hard as spuds and me belly's like a wrinkled balloon at the end of a party. I'm a wreck. Fifteen years old and me body's fit only for t' knacker's yard.'

'Has the father been to see you?' Lydia asked, swearing

to herself she would *never* let anyone get her pregnant.

'Has he 'eck as like! Anyway, I don't want him hanging around me. Take it from me, Lydia, you're better off without them. Men! Selfish, useless bastards one and all.' She raised the can to her mouth and tipped her head back. When it was empty, she lobbed it across the room, where it missed the wastepaper bin by a foot and landed on a Bay City Rollers album cover. She belched loudly. 'Midwife says the best way to build my strength up is to drink stout. Makes yer laugh, doesn't it? Seeing as I'm not officially old enough to drink. Funny old world. What've you done to your face?'

It was a week and a half since that awful night in the kitchen and whilst her lip had healed as good as new, her jaw, legs and back were still coloured by faint blossoms of greenish-yellow bruises. She'd be glad when the marks, especially the one on her face, finally disappeared. She was tired of lying to people. Yesterday it had been Sister Lottie and Joey she'd lied to. Now Donna. 'I wasn't looking where I was going,' she said.

'Yer should be more careful. So what've yer got there, then? Sommat for me?'

Time to get the worst over with and then scarper. 'We wondered if you'd like to read these.' Lydia handed over the pamphlets as though they were red hot and about to burst into flames.

Without looking at them, Donna said, 'Who's *we*?'

'Um ... Pastor Digby, the man in charge of the church I go to.'

'I know about that church of yours. Bit bloody barmy if yer don't mind me saying. Why do yer go? Why not have a lie-in on a Sunday morning like most sensible people do?'

It was a question Lydia had never been able to answer properly, even to herself. 'It's something to do,' she said with a shrug. There was also the small matter of what her grandfather would do to her if she did ever refuse to go. 'You don't have to read them if you don't want to.'

Donna briefly looked at the pamphlets in her hand

before tossing them aside. She let out a short, bitter laugh. 'Chance would be a fine thing.'

'Yes, I suppose you are rather busy at the moment, aren't you? What with the baby and everything.'

Donna picked at the flaking settee. 'It's not that,' she said, her voice oddly unsure all of a sudden, 'it's …' But her words trailed off. She pulled back a thin strip of PVC and flicked it away from her. 'Promise yer won't laugh?'

Lydia nodded, despite not knowing what she was agreeing to.

'The thing is, I can't read. I can make out a few words, but not enough to make sense of it all.'

Amazed, Lydia said, 'But however did you manage at school?'

'If yer play up enough the teachers stop bothering yer and yer can get away with murder. I thought I was the mutt's nuts, all that larking about. But now look at me. Stuck here with a baby that resembles a sodding goblin.'

A world without books wouldn't be worth living in for Lydia and before she knew what she was doing, she was offering to teach Donna to read.

Now it was Donna's turn to be amazed. 'Why would yer want to do that?'

'I don't know,' she said, suddenly embarrassed. 'The idea just popped into my head.' As did a long and distant memory of her father sitting on the edge of her bed reading to her when she was little. 'Don't stop,' she used to beg him, even though she was so sleepy she could hardly keep her eyes open. Swallowing back the tender recollection, she said, 'When Kirk's older, it would be good if you could read to him, don't you think?'

Donna looked doubtful. 'Nobody ever read owt to me when I was little.' She reached for a packet of Silk Cut on the pouffe. 'Maybe it's too late for me.'

'Why don't we give it a go? No harm in that, surely?'

'OK. You're on. But no being bossy with me. Or telling anyone. I'll kill yer if you do. And definitely no homework. I ain't got time for that.'

As if to prove her point, a snuffling sound came from the end of the settee, followed swiftly by a loud, demanding cry.

Lydia took it as her cue to leave.

After saying she'd call round in a few days' time, she let herself out and crossed the road to the phone box. For once it wasn't home to a gang of boys making obscene calls.

When her grandfather answered, she crossed her fingers and explained that she'd been invited to stay for tea and that Donna's aunt was going out for the evening and Donna didn't want to be alone with the baby for too long. 'Why are you calling from a public pay phone?' he wanted to know.

'Theirs isn't working. Can I stay, then? Donna wants to know more about the leaflets.'

Grudgingly he agreed, told her not to be too late and rang off.

She then phoned Noah.

To make sure she wasn't spotted by anyone at home looking out from an upstairs window, she had to take a detour, which meant a longer route across the moors to Noah's. She didn't care: it was a beautiful spring afternoon. The day felt newly washed and the air smelled fresh and earthy. The gorse was nearly in flower, with shy glimpses of tiny clusters of yellow just peeping through on the bushes. A perfect day for a birthday, she thought as she picked up pace and headed towards the Dell of the Dead.

Noah now had a blue and white enamelled 'Private – Keep Out' sign on his bedroom door: Uncle Brad had 'stumbled across' it somewhere and had brought it home for Noah.

As she always did, Lydia made herself at home by kicking off her shoes and sitting cross-legged on Noah's bed. She didn't think she would ever tire of his room. Every time she came here there was something new and interesting to

get to know. He hated to throw anything away and as a result the room was chock-full of the strangest things. More often than not they were objects he collected to draw – a bird's skull, a fir cone, a pile of smooth pebbles, an old gas mask, a stuffed mynah bird, a one-legged action figure from *The Man From U.N.C.L.E.* There were minutely detailed drawings of some of these things on the walls. There were also things he liked to take apart to see if he could meet the challenge of putting them back together again – a cuckoo clock, a radio, a small steam engine, a Stylophone, a record player.

He was nicknamed The Professor at school, but not unkindly. He had long since earned the respect of everyone in their class because there wasn't anything he couldn't fix with a tube of glue or a soldering iron. He had a nice little sideline going, charging fifty pence a repair. He was the most patient person Lydia knew and would spend hours happily inventing some electronic gadget or other, or piecing together a broken ornament. His latest craze was for three-dimensional wooden puzzles. Lydia regularly confounded him by being able to figure them out faster than him. She didn't know why, but she could always see exactly how the pieces fitted together. It was the same with maths equations or algebra. And French. The tenses and verbs just seemed to make perfect sense to her.

'Happy birthday, Lyddie,' he said after he'd foraged in the wardrobe then closed the door. 'I hope you like what I've got for you.'

She took the two wrapped presents and held them, savouring the moment: they were the only presents she'd received. 'Which one shall I open first?' she asked him.

He joined her on the bed. 'Up to you. You choose.'

She opted for the one that was clearly book-shaped. He'd made such a thorough job with the sticky tape it was impossible not to make a mess of the paper and she reluctantly had to tear it off. 'Oh!' she cried with delight when she saw he'd given her a small hardback of the complete poems of Christina Rossetti. 'You remembered,' she said.

He arched one of his eyebrows. 'Of course I did. What do you take me for?'

She smiled and thought of the day when she was supposedly staying late at school for a netball match. She and Noah had gone into town and spent an hour browsing the shelves in the second-hand bookshop. She had discovered this dusty, faded little gem but had returned it to the shelves as being much too extravagant for her pocket.

She longed to throw herself into reading it, but conscious of the other present on the bed next to her she turned her attention to that instead and made quick work of the wrapping paper.

'It's beautiful,' she gasped, her breath truly taken away. She ran a finger lightly over the tiny pearl and delicate silver chain that nestled in the velvet jewellery box. 'But it must have cost you a fortune.'

'It didn't cost me anything,' he said. 'It belonged to my mother.'

Shocked, she snapped the lid shut. 'But you can't possibly give it to me. It's much too precious.'

'I knew you'd say that, but I want you to have it. I can't think of anyone I'd rather see wearing it.'

'Do you really mean that?'

He frowned. 'Lyddie, why do you always doubt me? If I say something, it's because I mean it.'

Confused, she said, 'But I don't doubt you. You're the one person I've never doubted.'

Just inches away from her, he stared at her steadily, his dark, compelling eyes boring right into her. Right down to the depths of her guilty, secretive soul. The bit of her she never wanted him to know. 'I don't think that's true,' he said softly.

There was a troubled sadness to his voice that made her feel she'd let him down. That he was disappointed in her. Disconcerted as to where he might lead the conversation, she opened the box again and took out the necklace. 'Can you help me put it on, please?'

After a moment's hesitation, he took the necklace from

her and told her to turn round. She lifted up her hair. His hands felt warm and sure on the back of her neck. 'There,' he said, 'why don't you go and look in the mirror and see what you think?'

She jumped off the bed and went and stood in front of the wardrobe. She scrutinized her reflection, wishing she was just a fraction as pretty as the necklace. Or, thinking of the painting Uncle Brad had painted of Noah's mother on her eighteenth birthday, as pretty as the girl who had originally worn it. Why did she have to be so gawky? Why couldn't she have silky straight hair and elegant eyebrows that didn't meet in the middle? 'It's lovely,' she said.

Noah came and stood behind her. Their eyes met briefly in the speckled glass before he lowered his gaze to the pearl at her neck.

Maybe it was because she was staring at his reflection and not directly at him, but Lydia found herself seeing Noah with fresh eyes, just as she had last month when she'd given him that coat for his birthday and had thought how different it made him seem. A tall, dark, very good-looking stranger, she remembered thinking at the time. And here was that stranger again. Except he seemed even more handsome now. The more she looked at his face – a face she had believed to be so completely familiar to her – the more new and unique it became. She tried to make sense of this feeling by studying what she'd always known, but perhaps had never actually seen before: the nose that was straight and neither too big nor too small; the eyebrows – so unlike hers – that were expressive and perfectly arched; the smooth cheekbones that narrowed down to form a perfect triangle with his chin; the hair that was light brown and flecked with shades of gold; and best of all, the dark intelligent eyes.

Dark intelligent eyes that were staring back at her in the mirror.

'What are you thinking?' he asked.

Embarrassed to admit the truth, she said the first thing that came into her head. 'I was thinking how we could be

brother and sister,' she said. 'Not in looks. But because we've known one another so long.'

'I suppose we could,' he responded blandly.

Acknowledging that subconsciously she must have been thinking of Uncle Brad's painting of himself and Noah's mother, Lydia said, 'You don't sound very convinced.'

'That's because I'm not.' He put his hands on her shoulders and his expression in the mirror became so intense that she wondered if she'd said something wrong. Something to upset him.

A loud rap at the door had them both jumping.

'Can I come in?' It was Uncle Brad.

'No!' Noah shouted back.

'Come on, Noah, don't be a spoilsport.'

'I've got company.'

'That much I know.'

'Then go away and leave us in peace.'

'But I've got a birthday card for Lydia.'

'You can push it under the door.'

'That's a bit rude, Noah,' Lydia said.

'Is that my sweet Lydia sticking up for me?'

Lydia giggled.

'Ah, message received, loud and clear. You're up to no good in there, aren't you?'

Noah rolled his eyes and ran his hands through his hair so that it was sticking up all over his head. 'Sorry about this. He's probably been drinking.'

Smoothing down his hair for him, Lydia whispered, 'Wouldn't it be easier just to let him in?'

'Not whilst you're wearing that necklace.'

'Then help me take it off.'

'I'll tell him to come back later.'

'But then he really will think we've been up to something.'

'I can hear you whispering in there. Are you making yourselves decent? I hope you're being careful, Noah. If you know what I mean. Nudge, nudge, wink, wink.'

'Go *away*!'

'Hey, no need to blow your cork. I know when to split and leave you crazy cats to enjoy yourselves. Lydia, my sweet, this is for you.' A white envelope appeared under the door.

Listening to his footsteps fading away, Lydia felt doubly bad when she saw that Uncle Brad had gone to the trouble of drawing a card especially for her. It was of a girl who looked remarkably like her and she was shielding her eyes from the glare of the sun, staring into the distance. Inside was written, 'Lucky you, the future is all before you. Make the most of it!'

'He's got a thing about growing old at the moment,' Noah said. 'Worried that time is running out for him. Talking of which, let's make the most of the time you're here and go for a walk before it gets dark.'

While Noah put on his shoes, she fingered the necklace he'd given her and thought of the expression on his face when she'd suggested they could be like brother and sister. Why would that have upset him?

Chapter Thirty-Three

It was dark when Lydia set off on her usual route home across the moors. She hadn't wanted to leave her presents and card behind with Noah, but with no bag in which she could smuggle them safely into the house, she had thought it safer for him to hang on to them for her. She had sensed he had something to say on the matter, but thankfully he didn't. Just as he hadn't commented when she'd told him she definitely wouldn't be going on the school trip to Paris next month, other than to say he hadn't changed his plans either; he was still going away with Uncle Brad for the bank holiday weekend.

More out of curiosity than hope, she'd given her grandfather the letter from school and predictably he'd ripped it in two and said, 'We don't have the money. You're not going.'

'I could get a part-time job and pay for it myself,' she'd suggested. Again, just to see how he'd react.

'I said no. You're not going anywhere and that's an end to it. I'm not having you coming back with your head filled with any foreign nonsense. You've got enough uppity airs and graces as it is. Time you learned your place, that getting above yourself and flying too high never did anyone any good.'

What a contrast to the encouragement Uncle Brad gave Noah. In his opinion you couldn't fly high enough. 'Look at that Margaret Thatcher,' he'd say, 'bloody awful woman, but nothing's stopped her from being the first woman to lead a British political party. OK, she's only been doing the job for a month, but I'll tell you now, she's damned

ambitious. It wouldn't surprise me if we see her running the country one day. God help us if it happens, though. I'll be long gone.'

Uncle Leonard had repeated his offer to help twist his brother's arm in order for her to go to Paris, but Lydia had stood by her original decision not to push her luck. There was enough tension in the house as it was without Uncle Leonard adding to it. Especially as she had the distinct impression that Uncle Leonard was enjoying having his brother where he wanted him: under his thumb. Try as she might, Lydia couldn't allow herself to relax and believe the situation could remain as it was. Always at the back of her mind was the concern that Uncle Leonard's protection would be short-lived. The day would inevitably come when he would want to move on elsewhere. Which meant this period of relative safety was nothing more than the lull before the storm. Everything would go back to how it had been: living in fear and being too ashamed to admit the truth to anyone.

Even though she was confident she wouldn't be seen in the dark, when Lydia climbed over the wall at the end of the garden, she did so as stealthily as she could. After all, she was supposed to have been at Donna's for the evening and the way home from Donna's was straight along the street.

Lydia was just passing her grandfather's shed when she noticed a faint glowing light from inside. Curious, she stopped to peer in through a gap in the manky old curtains at the window. What she saw her had frozen to the spot. Her grandfather was in there and with his trousers undone he was doing that ... that disgusting thing she'd heard the other boys at school boasting about. And he was doing it whilst looking at a magazine like the one Alfie Stone had brought into school once.

Terrified that her presence might be given away by a careless rushed movement, Lydia took a slow, deliberate step back from the shed and promptly knocked over a

flowerpot. The noise had her grandfather whirling his head round.

She should have been running. She should have been running like the wind. But she couldn't move. She could hardly draw breath. All she could do was stare back at her grandfather's shocked expression. Anything but look at that revolting *thing* in his hand.

Then in a split second of clear thinking, she knew she could use this to her advantage. Her grandfather knew that he'd been caught doing something he would be deeply ashamed and embarrassed about. It was something he would never want anyone to know about. For once, his shame might be greater than her own.

This is power, she thought. Real power. All she had to do was hold her nerve.

Chapter Thirty-Four

Lydia did hold her nerve. In the shadowy darkness, she lay in wait for her grandfather to emerge from the shed. To stop herself trembling, she concentrated on thinking how much worse this had to be for him. He was the one who should be nervous. Not her.

She watched him lock the shed and as he came up the path and saw her standing there, his eyes were anywhere but on her.

She decided to tackle him with the least important of the three things she wanted him to agree to. 'I want to go on that school trip to Paris,' she said with icy calm. 'Do you think you might like to change your mind about it?'

He pursed his lips and finally met her gaze, regarding her with a look of pure loathing and contempt. All her old fears ran through her and it was all she could do to stop herself from apologizing and running for safety. But she didn't. This was a crucial moment and she mustn't let it slip from her hands. If she did, she would never forgive herself.

'And if I don't let you go?'

'Then I'll have to ask someone at church what it was I saw you doing in your shed.'

'Bitch!' He stepped towards her, his hand raised.

Somehow she managed not to flinch. 'I'd also have to ask about the magazine you were looking at. I'm sure Pastor Digby would have something to say on that particular subject.'

His hand dropped down to his side. 'Hell's too good for you.'

'I'm sure you're right, but after living here I reckon it'll be an improvement. Tomorrow I want my birth certificate so I can organize a passport as soon as possible. You can give it to me at breakfast.'

She took a quick, deep breath. Now for her most important demands.

'Just so that you know, I'll carry on doing a fair share of the household chores, but you are not to be unreasonable about it. There'll be no more hidden tin tacks. No more shouting at me for forgetting something. Lastly, you will never lay another finger on me again. Is that understood? Not ever.'

With that, she walked away, leaving him standing in the dark.

Things are going to be different round here from now on, she told herself when she was back inside the house. This was certainly a birthday she wouldn't forget in a long, long time.

She was up early the next day. Her grandfather must have been up even earlier, because there on the table alongside his finished breakfast was Lydia's requested birth certificate.

The first lesson at school that morning was French and when it was over, Lydia approached Mrs Roberts and asked if it was possible for her name to be added to the school trip. It was! Overjoyed, she rushed to tell Noah.

He didn't ask how she'd won her grandfather round and she certainly wasn't in any hurry to explain it to him. 'That's brilliant,' he said. 'Do you think there'd be a place for me as well?'

'But I thought you weren't going to be around at the end of May?'

He smiled. 'Sudden change of plan.'

'How come?'

'I'd have thought that was obvious,' he said, still smiling. 'I wasn't going to go without you, was I?'

'You mean, you and Uncle Brad weren't ever going away?'

'Nope. So there it is. I lied to you. Call me a devious bastard if you like, but meanwhile, I'm off to find Mrs Roberts.'

After school, letting Val walk home ahead on her own from the bus stop, Lydia called in at the corner shop. Dressed in a pretty rose-pink sari with an Aran cardigan over the top, Mrs Khan was alone and stacking boxes of Ritz crackers onto a shelf near the counter, behind which a paraffin heater was sending heady fumes into the already fuggy air. 'Hello,' she greeted Lydia brightly in her pretty sing-songy voice. 'I'll be with you in a minute. Whilst it's quiet I must just finish doing this.'

Which was all the opening Lydia required. 'Mrs Khan,' she said, 'I don't suppose you need any extra help here, do you?'

Mrs Khan put the last of the boxes onto the shelf. 'Are you looking for a job?'

'Yes. Only part-time, of course. During term time I could work Saturdays and after school, but in the holidays I could work whenever you wanted me to. I can add up really fast. In my head. You can test me if you want.' Lydia crossed her fingers behind her back, praying that Mrs Khan wouldn't hold her grandmother's crazy rudeness against her.

'As a matter of fact, Mr Khan and I were only saying the other day how we could do with an extra pair of hands. You see, I'm going to have a baby and there'll be days when I'll need to take it a little easier in the coming months. But we need someone reliable.'

'I wouldn't ever let you down.'

Mrs Khan's face broke into a smile. 'In that case, when can you start?'

Without worrying what her grandfather would have to say on the matter, Lydia went ahead and arranged to start work after school the next day.

It wasn't often Lydia got the opportunity to thank God for answering any of her prayers, but walking home, she

felt that at long last he'd actually been paying attention. So now she had a job and what's more, she was going to Paris. And Noah was coming too! She was so very touched that he'd gone to the trouble of lying about not being able to go on the school trip so that she wouldn't feel left out. She was even more touched that he'd immediately signed up for the last place when he knew she was able to go. Now all she had to do was get the money from her grandfather and arrange her passport. And to think, the furthest she'd ever been from Swallowsdale was Maywood, where she was born.

In the days and weeks that followed, what with dividing her time between working at the corner shop, teaching Donna to read, doing her homework, and keeping an eye on Valerie as well as keeping up with her renegotiated rota of chores, Lydia hardly saw anything of her grandfather. She couldn't be sure, but she had the strong feeling he was avoiding her. Well, good! She wouldn't care if she never set eyes on him again. Sometimes when she thought about what she'd caught him doing that night, her stomach would heave. But one day in church she had very nearly burst out laughing when she imagined leaping to her feet and exposing him for the disgusting pervert he was. 'He looks at porn in his garden shed and plays with himself! What do you think to that?!'

She'd noticed that the padlock on the shed had been changed and the tatty old curtains had been replaced with some thick new ones. Obviously he was still at it in there.

Uncle Leonard had quizzed her one day about the surprising U-turn her grandfather had made regarding Paris and she'd shrugged her shoulders and said, 'Search me what goes through his mind. Perhaps it's your presence here that gave him a change of heart.' She was quite happy to let him take the credit for something he hadn't done. No way was she going to say what had really gone on.

Having been extremely grateful to Uncle Leonard, rather uncharitably she was now wishing that he'd leave

Swallowsdale. She no longer needed his protection. She'd acquired that for herself. Several times he'd referred to himself as her knight in shining armour. He'd wink and call her his little damsel in distress. All of which was enough to make her want to stick her fingers down her throat.

Home from work one Saturday afternoon in May, Mr Khan having given her permission to leave early because it was so quiet, Lydia let herself in at the back door. The house was completely silent. She remembered then that Valerie had been invited to Sister Vera's for tea and that her grandfather wouldn't be home until later. Goodness knows where Uncle Leonard was.

After putting the kettle on for a cup of tea, she went upstairs to change out of her work clothes. She was almost at the top of the stairs when she heard a noise. She stood stock still and cocked her ear. There it was again. Someone was in her bedroom.

Lydia thought of all the precious things she had carefully hidden away, including the necklace Noah had given her, and knew that she wasn't going to let some rotten burglar get away with them. She reached for the heavy brass cross on the small window ledge to her left, took the last few steps as silently as a cat, then launched herself across the landing and into the bedroom, hoping to take the burglar by surprise.

The burglar wasn't the only one to be surprised.

Lydia looked at the groaning body on the floor and couldn't believe who it was. Nor could she believe what he'd been doing: snooping through her things. How dare he!

But looking for what?

A frantic search through her underwear drawer revealed that her wages were gone. All of them. She went back to the body on the floor and gave it a vicious kick.

'Get up, Uncle Leonard,' she said.

He put a hand to the back of his head where she'd clunked him with the cross. 'What the hell did you hit me with?'

'God.'

He squinted up at her. 'Are you mad?'

'Yes. Hopping mad. Now give me back my money or I'll hit you again.'

He got to his feet and sat on the edge of Valerie's bed, still rubbing his head. 'Lydia, I'm shocked. How could you accuse me of stealing from you?'

'I saw what you were doing. You were going through my things.'

'I was looking for something.'

'Liar! Now hand over my money or I'll—'

'Or you'll what?'

Lydia reached for the cross that she'd put on the dressing table. 'Or I'll hit you again. Maybe even kill you.'

Raising himself up from the bed, he shook his head and tutted, as though she'd just said something very tiresome. He came and towered over her. 'Now we both know you're not brave enough to do that. If you couldn't stand up to my brother, you're certainly not capable of killing me just for a few lousy quid. Isn't that the truth?'

She swallowed and gripped the cross tighter, furious that he wasn't taking her seriously. He was treating her like a child. 'So you admit it. You *have* stolen my money.'

'I'm admitting nothing, sweetheart. Now give me that cross before I get angry with you. Which would be a terrible shame when we're such good friends.'

'Perhaps it will be a different story when you tell it to the police, Leonard.'

They both turned. Standing in the doorway was Lydia's grandfather.

'He's stolen my money,' Lydia shouted, 'all of it! I came home early and caught him going through my things.' She was shaking with anger.

Her grandfather stepped into the room. There was an expression of triumph on his face. 'A leopard and his spots, Leonard. I always knew.' He held out his hand. 'Give me Lydia's money. Or I'll call the police.'

'No you won't. One word from me and your whole world will come tumbling down on you.'

'I've had enough of your threats. I want you to pack your things and leave my house. At once.'

'But you know what will happen if you try and make me: I'll have to let Pastor Digby know the real Arthur Turner. The Arthur Turner who takes the punishment of his teenage granddaughter just a bit too seriously.'

'And I'll have to tell him and everyone else at church about you stealing from your own kith and kin. Again. And once I've told them that, and Lydia's backed me up, how long do you think it will be before they see through your born-again claims and refuse to believe a word that comes out of your filthy lying mouth?'

Uncle Leonard smirked. 'Sounds like a stalemate to me. Though personally I think you have more to lose. Your hugely misplaced pillar-of-the-community reputation for one thing. But you know what? I was getting bored staying here anyway. I reckon it's time to ship out and go somewhere where my company will be properly valued and appreciated.' He turned to Lydia. 'I just hope you'll be all right, sweetheart. Remember, I'll always be your knight in shining armour.'

Lydia cringed. 'Just give me my money,' she said, her heart hardened towards him. 'That's all I care about.'

'Oh, Lydia,' he said with a sigh. 'I can't tell you how much that hurts. And after all I've done for you. That's quite a betrayal.' He let his gaze linger on her for a moment longer, then switched his attention back to his brother. 'I have to congratulate you, Arthur. You've manipulated her well. You've really got her well trained. I've read that even the most terrified hostage can become dependent on their captor, no matter how cruel they are.'

'That's enough! Lydia, go downstairs and leave me to sort this out.'

Lydia shot her grandfather a look. 'Don't let him leave with my money.'

'Do as I say. Now go!'

Chapter Thirty-Five

Uncle Leonard was gone within the hour and Lydia's money was safely returned to her. At her grandfather's instruction, she and Val stripped the bed in the spare room, washed the sheets and put them out on the line to catch the last of the evening sun. They also opened the window in the spare room to get rid of the cloying smell of Brut and breath freshener.

At church the following morning, the Brothers and Sisters greeted the news of Uncle Leonard's sudden departure with shock and sadness. They soon changed their stance when they were given the facts: that he'd been caught stealing from Lydia. 'I warned you all about him,' her grandfather told the hushed congregation during Share and Pray time. 'I warned you that he was a pernicious liar, and whilst it grieves me to say it, I think we have to accept there are some people in this world who simply aren't capable of being fully redeemed. The devil had a far stronger hold on my brother than any of us could have known. I just wish you'd listened to me.' He'd looked pointedly at Pastor Digby, then sat down. Apologies were duly made and Lydia's grandfather was once more well and truly back in the fold.

This gave Lydia cause for concern. Her hold over her grandfather might come to an end sooner than she'd hoped. After being proved right over his brother, no one at church would ever doubt him again. If he said Lydia was a liar – just like her great-uncle Leonard – his word would be as good as the word of God. So bang would go her threat to share with Pastor Digby what he got up to in

his shed late at night. For the time being, though, the truce remained intact.

With the trip to Paris only a week away, Lydia and Valerie came home from school to find a strange woman in a squashed hat and a raincoat sitting at the table. She seemed hunched with cold, even though it was such a warm day. It was Valerie who was first to recognize who it was. Dropping her satchel to the floor, she flung herself at the woman.

It was four months since they had last seen their grandmother and in the intervening time she looked as if she'd aged by about ten years. Her hair was white all over and she'd lost weight. Beneath her coat, the buttoned collar of her blouse gaped, revealing a scrawny neck like a chicken's. Her hands were knobbly and heavily veined. She looked as brittle as a dried twig. From a chalky-white face, a pair of dull eyes stared at the top of Valerie's head; they didn't seem to be focusing properly. For an awful moment Lydia was worried that her grandmother might not recognize her favourite granddaughter. What would that do to Valerie? Despite repeatedly pleading with their grandfather to take Valerie with him on his hospital visits, he had never allowed her to go, saying it wouldn't be helpful, that maybe it might even be harmful to their grandmother. Now as Lydia watched those unfocusing eyes looking uncertainly at Valerie, she wished he had. Regular contact with her grandmother might have ensured that Valerie wouldn't be forgotten.

But then, as if her brain had just needed time to put two and two together, the arms that had been hanging limply at the old woman's sides came up, wrapped themselves around Valerie and clutched her tightly.

That was when Lydia heard her grandfather coming down the stairs. He came into the kitchen with a lilac cardigan in his hands and seemed surprised to see Lydia and Valerie. 'I didn't know it had got to that time yet,' he muttered, glancing at the clock.

'Why didn't you tell us Grandma was coming home today?' Valerie whispered huskily. Her eyes were shining with tears. 'Is she home for good?'

'Oh, so these days I have to run everything by you, young lady, do I? Now out of the way. Don't go crowding and suffocating your grandmother before she's even got her coat off.'

'Is she home for good?' Valerie repeated insistently.

'How should I know?' he snapped. 'That's for God to decide.' He didn't sound like he was too happy about the situation.

But Valerie, hugging her grandmother again, was delighted. Her happiness made Lydia's throat tighten with love for her.

At school, for those going to Paris, there was only one subject to talk about. The countdown was on. Six days and they'd be crossing the Channel. For most of them it was the first time they would be going abroad. Zoe Woolf had been to Paris before and wasn't slow in showing off her knowledge about the Eiffel Tower or the Champs-Élysées. She took great pleasure in boasting how she'd eaten snails and frogs' legs and how she'd visited a red-light area, where prostitutes sat in shop windows with their legs open. It wasn't long before the boys were all saying that they'd give Mrs Roberts the slip and head straight there.

What came as a revelation was that Noah had also been to Paris before. 'Why didn't you say anything before now?' Lydia asked him when he admitted this would be his second visit.

They'd just bought an ice-cream from Joey's van – which on fine days was always conveniently parked at the gate when school was over – and were on their way into town for a browse round the bookshop and then on to the post office. After Lydia had got her money back from Uncle Leonard, she'd immediately opened a savings account and regularly put her wages into it. 'It hardly counts,' Noah

said in answer to her question. 'I was a baby at the time and can't remember a thing about it.'

It was ages since either of them had spoken about their lives before they came to Swallowsdale and it was difficult for Lydia to imagine that Noah had been brought up by anyone other than Uncle Brad. Sometimes it was difficult to remember that she too had had another life before this one. 'Have you done anything else I should know about?' she asked.

'You make it sound like I deliberately keep things from you.'

She licked at the thick coating of strawberry syrup on the cornet Joey had made for her and said, 'Don't you?'

'No more than you.'

She kept quiet. Why had she even broached the subject?

'Well?' he prompted.

'Well, what?'

'Come off it, Lyddie. I'm not stupid.'

Now she knew for sure they were in dangerous territory. She hurriedly stepped off the pavement to cross the road.

She hadn't noticed the car speeding round the corner and she found herself being yanked back onto the pavement. The driver of the car tooted the horn angrily and sped on.

'Look,' Noah said, keeping hold of her arm as they stood on the pavement, 'I know you've always kept stuff from me. I've no idea why, but I just want you to know that if you ever need my help, you've only got to ask for it.' Frowning, he added, 'You must know that I'd do anything for you.'

Oh, God, she thought, suddenly limp with clammy panic. Not kindness and understanding. Anything but that. Yet at the same time, now that she seemed to have a measure of control over her life, she thought what a relief it would be to confide in Noah. Noah, her closest friend. Her greatest ally. The person whom she respected most in the world. The one person whose respect she wanted and

valued above all else. She stared into the dark pools of his solemn eyes and felt herself tremble inside as she realized something she had always known but never acknowledged – Noah was so much more than a friend. She suddenly felt a powerful surge of love for him. There were so few people she really cared about, but for Noah she'd willingly give her life.

So why not share with him those things she'd kept hidden?

Don't do it, a low, insistent voice growled in her head. *Don't admit to anything. Do that and he'll see the real Lydia Turner. The grubby, ashamed, frightened Lydia Turner. Didn't he once say that the reason he thought you were so great was because you weren't afraid of anything? If he knows the real disappointing you, he'll treat you differently. And what if he begins to wonder if you deserve what goes on at home?* The voice was right. It was too big a risk. She didn't want Noah to know the truth.

'Noah,' she said, 'I really don't have any idea what you're talking about. You've not been at your uncle's marijuana, have you?'

The frown deepened and he shook his head. Very slowly, he let go of her arm. He spread his hands. 'Sometimes I just don't understand you. Or even feel that I know the first thing about you.'

Once more, just as she had on her birthday, she saw that she'd disappointed him. Except this time it was far worse. The pain in his kind, sensitive face was too much for her. It tore at her heart. How could she be so cruel to him? 'I'm sorry,' was all she could say.

'So am I, Lyddie. More than you'll ever know.'

After tea that evening, Lydia went to see Donna under the guise of trying to win her soul for Jesus by teaching her to read.

Captain Kirk, as Lydia secretly called Donna's baby, was no longer the easy-going baby he'd been when Lydia had first visited. Their lessons were frequently interrupted

by his ear-splitting demands to be fed, winded or changed. Donna was not always in the right mood to deal with him and often Lydia would try to soothe the squawking, fractious child. She was reminded of when Valerie had been a baby.

She and Donna had formed an unlikely friendship, given the way they had got to know each other all those years ago in the playground. Lydia supposed the poor girl was desperate for friends. She certainly seemed to be short on them these days. From the moment she'd dropped out of school her so-called friends had dumped her. Maybe they were frightened of catching a baby themselves.

Donna had no qualms about dishing the dirt to Lydia about her family: how her father had walked out years ago and how ever since her mother had had a succession of horrible boyfriends. One of them had broken her mother's nose in a fight over whose turn it was to pay for a drink. Another had been to prison for stealing cars. The most recent boyfriend had been responsible for making Donna's mother kick her out. He worked shifts at Ravencroft's mill and had said he didn't want a baby disturbing his sleep.

'God, this is hard!' Donna exclaimed. 'You don't know how lucky yer are.' She was standing at the open bedroom window trying to read one of Valerie's old Bible story books. She tossed the book onto the floor, lit up a cigarette and inhaled deeply.

'How come I'm so lucky?' Lydia asked.

'Yer might be a bit on the plain side, but you've got brains. And that's gotta be worth more than looks alone.'

Lydia smiled. 'I suppose there's a compliment tucked away in there somewhere.'

Now that Lydia had got Captain Kirk off to sleep, she laid him carefully in his plastic laundry basket and covered him with the blanket. Another couple of weeks and he'd be too big for the basket. She hoped Donna had got something else planned for him. Picking up the discarded book, she joined Donna at the window where she was looking

down onto the rubbish tip of a garden – Donna's aunt was to gardening what Donna was to tact.

'Which bit were you struggling with?' Lydia asked Donna patiently, opening the book at the first page.

Donna waved it aside. 'All of it. Mind if I give yer a word of advice?'

'It's not like you to ask my permission. You usually just go right ahead and inform me that I should do something about my hair, my clothes, oh, and let's not forget my eyebrows.'

Donna cast her damning gaze over Lydia's latest eclectic mix of jumble-sale bargains – a man's collarless shirt belted at the waist over a long tiered skirt – and said, 'Yer'll be calling that clobber yer student look, I s'pose.'

'It's the "I don't give a damn" look. So what's this advice you've got for me?'

Donna took a long hard puff on her cigarette, her lips compressed tightly. After she'd exhaled two rings of smoke into the air, she said, 'I bumped into Alfie Stone the other day and he said that Zoe Woolf is after your Noah. Yer wanna watch that girl. She's trouble with a capital T in my opinion.'

Chapter Thirty-Six

It was generally accepted that Zoe Woolf was gorgeous and that she could have any bloke she fancied. All the boys had a thing for her and like any girl as stunning as she was, it was understood that she could keep her admirers dangling for as long as she wanted and never be called a tease. So far she'd been out with three boys in the year above them but never with anyone her own age.

So why had she suddenly decided Noah was of interest to her? Why not any of the other boys in their year? There were plenty to choose from.

Pastor Digby was constantly warning them that jealousy was one of the widest gateways to hell, and in the blink of an eye, Lydia was consumed by it. She could feel it raging through her body like molten lava. Trying hard to conceal her reaction to Donna's 'word of advice', she said, 'Donna, I don't know why you refer to him as being *my* Noah.'

Donna snorted. 'Yeah, and pull t'other one while you're about it! The two of yer have always been inseparable. You're like cheese on toast, salt and pepper, egg and chips, Tom and—'

'Yes, I get the picture,' Lydia cut her off impatiently, 'but we're just friends. Mates. Pals.' She wasn't going to say anything about the real extent of her feelings for Noah. Donna wouldn't understand anyway.

'And t'rest,' Donna said scornfully. 'So have yer done it with him yet?'

'Done what?'

Donna rolled her eyes. 'Sex. Yer know, had it off with Noah.'

Lydia's cheeks flamed. 'Certainly not!'

'Hey, keep your hair on. No need to go getting your knickers in t'twist. I'm only asking.'

'Well stop asking!'

'Is it that church of yours that's stopping yer?'

'I said stop it.'

'Bloody hell, girl, you're a bit uptight about it all, ain't you?'

'A shame *you* weren't before you went and got yourself pregnant.'

Stubbing out her cigarette on the windowsill outside, Donna pursed her lips tightly shut.

Mortified, Lydia said, 'I'm sorry, I shouldn't have said that.'

'But yer did. Yer bloody well did.'

'I didn't mean it. I know you love Kirk and wouldn't be without him.'

'Yeah, well, maybe that's t'trouble. Maybe I don't love him and maybe I could live without him. Ever thought of that?'

Lydia walked home in a miserable mood. What was wrong with her great big gob today? First she'd upset Noah, now Donna. What kind of friend was she?

But more important than that, what was she going to do about Zoe? Her best hope was that Alfie had got it wrong. On the basis that most days he couldn't be trusted to find the end of his own nose, how could he be trusted to know what was going on around him? It was always possible that he was mixing Noah up with someone else at school.

But that was pointless wishful thinking on Lydia's part. There was no mistaking Noah for anyone else. For a start he was the only boy in the school who walked with a limp. He was also the only one had had an encyclopaedic knowledge of every *Monty Python* sketch and knew *all* the lyrics to *Dark Side of the Moon*. In Lydia's view – now that she'd woken up to it – he was also easily the best-looking boy at school. No one else had eyes like his. Or eyebrows

that could arch the way his did. He had features that were sharp and clean, not like Jack or Alfie's doughy faces with their bristly top lips and spotty chins. And unlike a lot of the other boys in their year, he didn't have a muscly athletic build that the girls would whistle at during games. Instead, he had a strong, almost secret, inner strength to him. As well as an air of mystery. Other than when he was alone with her, Noah never spoke about his home life. He was a very private person.

Lydia slowed her pace and registered that everything she had listed about Noah marked him out from the competition and would attract any number of girls. There was no doubt about it: Noah Solomon was number one fanciable stuff. Of course Zoe would be interested in him. It would be a miracle if she wasn't. But how had Lydia missed what was going on? Was it a new thing, Zoe making a play for Noah, or had it been a long-term thing?

And why should it matter? Why should she feel like a knife had been plunged into her chest and was being slowly twisted round, at the thought of Zoe with Noah? Of Zoe flicking her impossibly straight shiny blonde hair and kissing Noah. Of Zoe—

She called a halt to any other tormenting images.

But was Noah attracted to Zoe?

Lydia had never seen him ogling Zoe in the way the other boys did, but then she'd been so wrapped up in what was happening at home recently, she probably wouldn't have noticed a spaceship crammed full with one-eyed Martians landing in Swallowsdale.

She recalled her conversation with Noah this afternoon and silently groaned. Completely out of the blue, he'd offered to help her and she'd shoved his kindness right back in his face. If she'd wanted to push him into the arms of another girl, she could not have done a better job.

Donna had been right to say that Noah was Lydia's. He *did* belong to her. And not just as a friend. Her mouth went dry and her heart pounded as she thought what that really meant. Very tentatively, she pictured him leaning in

close and kissing her. Suddenly light-headed, she had to catch her breath.

She had no idea if he would find the thought of kissing her utterly repellent or not, but one thing she did know, she now had to find that out. But would it mean having to fight off Zoe? So what if it did? She would do whatever it took.

But how? What did she have to offer Noah that Zoe didn't have? Or perhaps, hadn't already offered?

Exactly, whispered the voice inside Lydia's head. *How can you hope to compete with a perfect girl like that? A perfectly beautiful girl who's led a perfectly beautiful life with no shameful secrets.*

Lydia stamped on the voice hard. Noah was hers. Not Zoe's. And with a flash of inspiration, she knew how she would fight for Noah. Or rather she knew *where* she'd fight for him. Paris. Mrs Roberts had described it as the most romantic city in the world. Lydia would get Noah alone there and Paris would work its magic on him. That would show Zoe!

For the remaining days at school, she watched Zoe like a hawk. Sure enough, the girl was all over Noah: one minute she was asking his opinion on something and the next she was offering to lend him some record or other. It was all Lydia could do not to confront Zoe there and then. But with steely determination she forced herself to wait for her moment of triumph in Paris. Love would win out!

Meanwhile, she became so jittery, she was tempted to knock back some of her grandmother's tablets, the ones that kept the old woman so sleepy she could hardly keep awake. There was something innocent and child-like about her now. Compared to the phases when she'd been scarily aggressive, seeing her this docile was quite unnerving. Outside of school hours, Valerie was constantly by her side, helping her with the simplest of tasks, such as making a cup of tea or bringing in the washing. Her devotion was humbling. The Sisters were frequent visitors again and had roped their grandmother into helping with

a tapestry they were making for church. Lydia often found her sister secretly redoing her grandmother's clumsy stitch work.

The good news, though, was that Valerie's voice had almost returned to normal. It was still a little harsh and husky at times – like a gate gone rusty from not being used – but for the most part, it was just as Lydia remembered it. Or as Sister Lottie described it a lot more poetically, it was as joyful and sweet as the sound of summer birdsong.

On Saturday morning, with only two days to go until the coach would take them down to Dover to catch the overnight ferry for Dieppe, Lydia woke with what felt like a prickly golf ball stuck in her throat. She was hot, too. Very hot. She went to the bathroom and pressed a cold flannel to her face. Bliss. She did this several times and convinced herself that nothing was the matter with her. So long as she didn't swallow, the prickly golf ball wasn't a problem. And so long as she didn't wear too many clothes, the scorching heat rising off her wouldn't be a problem either.

She was wrong.

Mrs Khan took one look at her when she arrived for work and sent her home. 'You're ill, Lydia. You should be in bed.'

'No really, I'm fine,' she said through teeth that were beginning to chatter – the hot sweats had been replaced with goosebump shivers that ran bone-deep.

Mrs Khan was having none of it. 'I don't want you here giving me and my unborn baby your germs.' More kindly, she added, 'Go home and rest, Lydia, or you won't be well enough to go to Paris on Monday.'

Nothing could have galvanized her more. It was unthinkable that she would miss out on the trip. By the time she had staggered home, the hot sweats had returned and the prickly golf ball was bigger and more painful. Sister Lottie's Morris Minor was parked outside the house and Lydia could have wept with relief. Sister Lottie would

know what was wrong with her and know exactly how to cure her.

Her grandmother didn't even bother to look up from the cooking apples she was peeling with Valerie when Lydia walked into the kitchen. But Sister Lottie took one look at her, put down the bag of brown sugar she was tipping into a mixing bowl and said, 'Dear child, whatever is the matter with you? You don't look at all well.'

'I don't know what's wrong with me. My throat hurts and I'm hot one minute and freezing cold the next. Mrs Khan sent me home.'

'Quite right too. Let's get you off to bed and call for Doctor Bunch.'

'Doctor Bunch?' repeated her grandmother, dropping the apple in her hand.

'Not for you, Grandma,' Valerie said. 'For Lydia. She's got a cold.'

'It feels more than a cold,' Lydia said miserably. She was near to tears she felt so ill. She could feel Paris drifting out of her reach.

In the end, to save time Sister Lottie drove Lydia to Doctor Bunch's surgery. Within minutes of seeing him she was diagnosed as having acute tonsillitis. Antibiotics were prescribed. As was plenty of fluids and bed rest. 'Will I be well enough to go to Paris on Monday?' she croaked.

Through the smeary lenses of his spectacles, Doctor Bunch looked at her as if she were mad. Her heart sank. She wouldn't be going to Paris. She cried all the way home but couldn't tell Sister Lottie why.

She slept intermittently for most of the day, thrashing around in a tangled mess of dank bedclothes. Her dreams were nightmarish and fever-fuelled, and held her in an iron grip that dragged her back in time, then forward. She dreamt of Diane Dixon. Diane was telling Lydia that she needed to have her tonsils out just as she had. The girl then offered to do the operation for her so Lydia could

go to Paris. She tipped her head back so that Diane could perform the operation only to then find that it was a ventriloquist's dummy about to do it. The dummy had a menacingly evil look in its eyes as it waved a pair of huge scissors dripping in blood at her. Next she dreamt of Zoe. Zoe was with Noah at the top of the Eiffel Tower. They were holding hands and she was wearing the necklace Noah had given Lydia. Lydia was there in the dream too and she was sneaking up behind Zoe to push her over the edge of the barrier. Except she had got it wrong and it was Noah falling to his death. She tried to reach him, stretching as far as she dared. 'Noah!' she called out as he grew smaller and smaller until he was nothing but a speck in the distance. 'Noah, I'm sorry. Please forgive me.'

She woke with a jolt and found that it was dark. She still felt awful. Her throat was raw and burning and her body was covered in sweat. She turned her face into the pillow to muffle the sound of her choking sobs. 'Oh, Noah,' she wept.

Chapter Thirty-Seven

Lydia could not have prayed harder for a miracle cure, but by the Bank Holiday Monday afternoon, when she should have been arriving at school with her packed case, passport and French francs, all she had the strength for was to sit up in bed for a few minutes or stagger to the toilet. Admittedly her temperature had gone down and the golf ball was less prickly, but her throat still hurt like mad when she swallowed. She could not have felt more sorry for herself. She pictured everyone on the coach larking about and driving Mrs Roberts round the bend, along with the other teachers who'd been roped in for the trip. It wasn't fair. Why had God done this to her? Didn't he understand what was at stake here?

It wasn't until this morning that they had been able to get in touch with school to say that she couldn't go. On her way back from the toilet, hovering at the top of the stairs, Lydia had listened to her grandfather telling the headmistress that she was ill and that he would be expecting a full refund. From the way the conversation went, Lydia could only assume that the headmistress didn't think this would be possible. Her grandfather was in a foul temper from then on.

The most important person whom Lydia wanted to know that she was ill was Noah, but she couldn't bring herself to ask her grandfather to phone him. Not in his current mood, anyway. Arouse his suspicions that she had a friend she really cared about, a boy at that, and he'd probably send for Pastor Digby to fire off twenty rounds of scripture from the hip and then exorcize her. There was

no chance to ask Val to make the call either. With it being half-term, she was downstairs practically glued to their grandmother's side. At one point, when Lydia had been having another of her hallucinogenic dreams, she'd dreamt she had climbed over the garden wall and gone to Noah to tell him that she wouldn't be going to Paris with him after all. She dreamt that he'd hugged her and kissed her on the forehead. 'In that case I won't go either,' he'd said. The dream had felt so real that when she woke, she could have sworn it had really happened.

Even now she could feel the touch of Noah's lips on her forehead and the comfort of his arms around her. She stared up at the ceiling, following the cracks with her eyes as they travelled like veins from one side of the room to the other, and tried not to let herself hope that any minute Noah would appear. That he'd throw a handful of pebbles at her window and call up to her that he wasn't going to Paris without her.

What an idiot she was to give in to such ridiculously romantic nonsense. Noah was going to Paris without her and that was all there was to it.

Yet no matter how true she knew this to be, she couldn't stop herself constantly glancing at the alarm clock on her bedside table. It was four thirty-nine: he'd know by now that she wasn't coming, probably would have checked with Mrs Roberts. Perhaps he'd try to slip away before the coach set off and telephone her, even though he'd promised never to do that. But this was an emergency and he'd call, if only to say how sorry he was that she couldn't come and that he would miss her. Yes, that at least would make her feel a little better, would make the next few days almost bearable.

The cracks in the ceiling began to blur and, exhausted from the effort of so much wishful thinking, Lydia closed her eyes and waited for the sound of the telephone to ring down in the hall. She wanted to die.

It was seven o'clock in the evening and after waking from a deep sleep and yet another dream that had her wondering what was real and what wasn't, she learned

from Valerie that she and their grandparents had been to a meeting at Pastor Digby's house that afternoon. 'But that means no one was here to answer the phone while I was asleep,' Lydia croaked, sounding eerily like Val used to.

Her sister looked at her, confused. 'If it's important they'll try again later.'

No they won't! Lydia wanted to scream. They'll be on a ferry crossing the Channel and heading to God knows what in Paris.

In the days that followed, Lydia didn't know who she hated more: Zoe or herself. She hated herself for making such a mess of things, and she hated Zoe for all the obvious reasons – for being so pretty, for being so perfect, but most of all for setting her sights on Noah.

For a while Lydia even hated Noah. How could he have gone to Paris without her? But her anger with Noah only made her hate herself more. Noah wasn't to blame. It was her. Her track record for messing things up spoke for itself and this one was entirely down to her.

She deliberately punished herself by imagining Zoe and Noah together.

Alone.

Always alone.

To Lydia's knowledge Noah had never kissed a girl before, just as she had never kissed a boy before, but Zoe was much more experienced and would probably enjoy teaching Noah all she knew. There was a rumour at school that she was an expert French-kisser.

The thought of Zoe's perfect little tongue exploring Noah's mouth had Lydia thinking of Pastor Digby and all his warnings about the perils that awaited the ungodly in hell. The stupid man didn't have a clue what he was talking about. Lydia was already there and it was a hundred times worse than anything he'd ever described.

On Friday morning, the day that the French party was due back, Lydia was well enough to go to work. The Khans

were glad because Mr Khan needed to drive his wife to the hospital for her antenatal appointment after lunch, so for most of the afternoon Lydia was on her own listening to Radio One. She was restocking the confectionery display on the counter when the door jangled and in came Donna: Captain Kirk had been parked outside in his pram, next to the Spastic Society's collection box.

'What the sweet Fanny Adams are yer doing here?' Donna asked, her overly plucked eyebrows raised and nearly making contact with her streaked hairline. 'I thought yer were in Paris?'

'I couldn't go. I've been stuck in bed all week with tonsillitis.'

'You poor miserable bugger.'

'Yeah, that about describes it.'

'Hang on a tick. Didn't yer say Zoe Woolf was going on that trip?'

'Please, don't remind me.'

'Bleeding hell! Her and Noah without yer to put a spanner in t'works. No wonder you've a face on yer like a wet weekend in Blackpool. Oh, turn t'radio up, I like this one.'

How fitting, Lydia thought as her friend started singing along to the Bay City Rollers' 'Bye Bye Baby'. 'Thanks, Donna,' she said. 'Can I get you anything or did you just come in to make me feel worse than I already do?'

'Packet of Silk Cut and a box of matches, since you mention it. So what're yer gonna do?'

'Absolutely nothing. Besides, it's probably too late.'

'Come on, girl, I never had yer down as a loser. Thought yer had more fight in yer than that. Stop feeling so sorry for yerself.'

Donna was right. But how to go about it? Nothing Lydia had learned in life had prepared her for this moment. How did you fight for someone whom you now realized you couldn't live without?

The answer, she decided, was to be completely honest with Noah. She would open her heart to him. If he wasn't interested, then at least she could comfort herself by knowing she'd tried.

When the Khans arrived back from the hospital they said she could call it a day. But she didn't go home. Instead, guessing that Noah should be home any minute, she headed for the Dell of the Dead and then on to Upper Swallowsdale House. She was halfway up the garden when she heard the sound of a car pulling onto the gravelled drive. Her heart hammering, she approached the house cautiously and peered round the corner, expecting to see Noah getting out of Uncle Brad's wine-coloured Capri.

What she saw was Noah getting out of an orange Volvo estate car. Lydia recognized not only the car, but also the blonde girl sitting in the passenger seat who was waving madly at Noah as he hoisted his rucksack on his shoulder and patted his jeans pocket for his door key. Just as the car was driving off, Lydia saw that she'd been spotted. At first Zoe merely looked surprised, but then leaning out of the window, she waved back at Noah and pointed in Lydia's direction. '*Bonne chance!*' she shouted.

Lydia wanted to run and hide. Oh, the humiliation! The complete and utter shame of it. Caught like a no-good peeping Tom.

'Lyddie?' Noah had come round to where she was standing like a fool, wishing the ground would open up beneath her feet.

She mustered what little dignity she still had. 'Hi,' she said. 'Thought I'd be here to welcome you home. Doesn't look like you need it, though.'

He threw down his rucksack, and the next thing she knew he had his arms around her and was squeezing her tight.

She wanted to hug him back, but she couldn't. The best she could do was stand stiffly in his embrace and say, 'Did you have a nice time in Paris? You and Zoe?'

He loosened his arms and stepped away from her. 'Why do you ask about Zoe?'

'Because ... because she fancies you and you fancy her. Don't you? Please don't lie to me.'

'Is that what you really think?'

'Well of course you fancy her! What boy doesn't? She's beautiful. She's clever. *And* she knows how to French-kiss.'

He raised an eyebrow. 'That's news to me.'

'I expect you've got that to look forward to then.'

He shrugged. 'I doubt that very much. Can I ask you something?'

'If you want.'

'Do you ...' He cleared his throat and swallowed, suddenly looking anxious. 'Do you fancy me? And is that what this is all about? You being angry and everything?'

Courage, she willed herself. Courage. She looked him squarely in the eye. 'Yes,' she said. 'Yes I do.'

He shook his head, and then he smiled. 'Thank God for that!'

Her cheeks tingling with embarrassment, Lydia said, 'I don't think there's anything to smile about. In fact—'

'Come here, you!' And once again he had her in his arms. 'Lydia Turner, can it be officially put on record that you fancy me and I fancy you?' He tilted her chin up with his hand. 'I'd also like it to be officially recorded that I'm going to kiss you now.'

He did and it was far better than any of her tentative imaginings. His mouth was warm and smooth against hers and she could have gone on kissing him for the rest of time, had she not thought of Zoe. She pulled back from him sharply. 'Did Zoe teach you that?'

'I think you and I need a little talk. Let's go inside.'

'What about Uncle Brad?'

'He's down in London. That's why Zoe's dad gave me a lift home.'

*

They sat at the kitchen table – a new and sturdier version of the one that was destroyed in the dancing-on-the-table incident. It was littered with signs that Uncle Brad had either left in a hurry or, more likely, had forgotten to clear up after his last meal. After Noah had pushed aside the festering remains of a pork pie, along with a mouldy loaf of bread and a piece of dried-out Cheddar cheese, he said, 'You think Zoe and I did stuff together in Paris, don't you?'

'Didn't you?'

'What made you think I would?'

'Alfie told Donna that Zoe had a thing about you, and Donna thought I should know.'

'And it didn't cross your mind to ask me what *I* thought?'

When she didn't say anything, he leaned towards her. 'Look, and this is the truth, OK? God knows why, but Zoe did try flirting with me, and I told her straight that she was wasting her time. I explained that there was only one girl I was interested in and it wasn't her.'

Lydia was incredulous. 'You turned down Zoe? Zoe Woolf? *The* Zoe Woolf? I bet that made her angry.'

'Not really. She guessed who I was talking about and wanted to know why I hadn't got things sorted between us.'

Us, repeated Lydia even more incredulously to herself. 'What did you tell her?'

'I said the trouble was that the girl in question wasn't interested in me. That she always made it very clear we were only friends. Or worse, as she told me on her birthday, brother and sister.'

Lydia gasped. 'You mean ... back then you felt ... but why didn't you say something?'

'I was about to, but my uncle's immaculate timing put the kibosh on my carefully planned speech.'

'Which was?'

He smiled. 'Painfully embarrassing, with hindsight. Uncle Brad did me a favour.'

'I wish I'd known how you felt.'

'Look at it from my point of view. Every time I tried to get closer to you, you pushed me away. Like that day the other week in town when I said I knew you kept things from me.'

She turned from him. 'I'm sorry about that. I was very rude to you.'

'You have to understand, Lyddie, I care about you.' He touched her hand. 'Is that so very difficult for you?'

She returned her gaze to his. 'Maybe not.'

'So can I kiss you again?'

'You might catch my germs.'

'Too late to worry about that.' He lightly brushed her lips with his. She shivered. He kissed her again and she pressed her mouth closer to his. She closed her eyes, lost in the sweet wonder of how magical something as simple as a kiss could make her feel.

'I thought it was supposed to be all bumping noses and clashing teeth,' Noah said when they finally pulled apart.

'I'd heard that it was like having your face wiped with a wet dishcloth.'

'In that case, we're either doing it wrong, or we must be naturals.'

'My stomach felt like it was turning inside out.'

'Mine too. Any butterflies?'

'Masses.'

'I know I'm not supposed to admit to this, being a bloke and all, but kissing you is bloody amazing. You're amazing, too.'

She smiled shyly. 'Why didn't you ring me before you set off for Dover?'

'As soon as Mrs Roberts told me you were ill I nipped off to use the call box by the Co-op. But there was no answer. I tried again the next night from Paris and got your grandfather. I'm sorry, but knowing how much you don't want him to know about me, I lost my nerve when I heard his voice. Did you mind very much that I went without you?'

'Yes,' she said. 'But only because I was convinced you would come back as Zoe's new boyfriend.'

'I knew I shouldn't have gone. The thing was, I had about ten minutes to decide what to do. In the end I reasoned that I wouldn't be able to see you if I stayed, so I might just as well go and bring you back something.' Smiling, he got to his feet.

'You got me a present?'

'Of course.' He pulled out a sweater from his rucksack and unearthed a squashed paper bag. 'It's nothing special. Just a book of postcards to show you what you missed, and a bar of pink and white nougat.'

But to Lydia they were the most special presents in the world.

Chapter Thirty-Eight

A year to the day, they celebrated their first anniversary of being girlfriend and boyfriend by taking a picnic up to the beck near Noah's house to revise for their French oral exam. They'd been there for an hour and all Noah had said so far in French, in what Lydia called his beret-wearing-striped-jersey accent, was *Je t'aime*, Lyddie. *Je t'aime. Je t'aime.*

Lydia could not believe it was possible for two people to be as close as she and Noah were. She loved him and he loved her. It was how it was always meant to be. It was perfect.

Except it wasn't. There was a shadowy darkness creeping ever nearer. A darkness that Lydia knew only too well would eventually eclipse their love for each other. If only she could go on forever keeping Noah at a distance, everything would be all right.

At the age of sixteen, she was embarrassingly ignorant about sex and was convinced that Noah knew far more about it than she did. Certainly he couldn't know less! It stood to reason that Uncle Brad would be a huge potential source of information on the subject, particularly when he was drunk. There was never any actual evidence of Uncle Brad having a sex life, unless the many framed and unframed nudes cluttering the house represented notches on his belt, but Noah said the reason his uncle was in London so frequently was because he had a woman down there.

Most of what Lydia understood about sex – or thought she understood – was based on biology lessons, listening to Pastor Digby's dire warnings at church and Donna's

grubbily explicit tales of her own sexual encounters. Captain Kirk was now a chubby-faced toddler with a baby brother or sister on the way. Donna had confessed to Lydia that she had lost her head in an alleyway on a drunken night out to a club in Bradford. 'Only me bleeding self to blame,' she told Lydia. 'Yer'd think I'd have learnt me lesson, wouldn't yer?'

In Lydia's head sex was to be avoided at all costs, for the following reasons. A) It was dangerous and likely to end in pregnancy, thereby killing all chances of a decent future. B) It was shameful and her grandfather would kill her if he found out. And C) It was wrong. It was a sin. Wasn't it?

But somewhere deeply lodged in the pit of her stomach, where her desire for Noah curled like a wily snake, the message was very different. With guilty greed she wanted him to touch her in those places that in her head were barred with Private No Entry signs and double padlocked for good measure. When they lay together on his bed, their kissing left her breathless, trembling and dizzy, her insides melting, the world forgotten. Lydia and Noah. Noah and Lydia. That was all that mattered. Why worry about the consequences? Remove the No Entry signs, turn the key in the padlock.

But always, just as one of Noah's hands would slowly creep down from her shoulder to slip under her clothes to touch her breast, she would be jolted into a state of rigid panic. She knew that Noah had sensed early on the change in her whenever he tried to touch her and in turn he was always cautious just where he allowed his hands to wander. While his sensitivity reassured and relaxed her, it was still months before she felt comfortable enough to let him touch her bare skin. It wasn't that she didn't trust him. Oh, no, it was Lydia Turner she didn't trust.

Lydia Turner and that wily snake intent on trouble. Give in to it, and who knew what trouble lay ahead for her?

Yet their days together weren't all about sex, or, more precisely, her avoidance of it. Often they would lie on his

bed or on the soft leafy ground in the Dell of the Dead, reading to each other. Some days it was the poems of Blake, John Donne and Shakespeare's sonnets in which they lost themselves. Other days they'd go for something amusing like *The Wind in the Willows* or *Three Men in a Boat*, a copy of which Uncle Brad had given Lydia on her sixteenth birthday. 'No library should be without it,' he'd claimed. 'It's essential reading.' These were some of the most intimate moments she and Noah spent together. Probably because she didn't feel threatened and on her guard.

Now as they lay on their backs beside the beck in the warm sunshine, they each had a leg in the air at a ninety-degree angle. In Noah's case, it was his good leg. It was a regular game they played, seeing who could hold the position the longest. Noah was wearing his faithful old black and white baseball boots with the fraying laces and his drainpipe jeans and Lydia had on a new pair of red clogs. The only contact was between their hands. They'd been going for a long time, had reached that crucial point when it felt as if the very last few drops of blood were draining out of their legs; it was when they had to hold their breath and focus hard. Lydia was always tempted to close her eyes, but do that and the game was lost because her leg would simultaneously drop a couple of inches. There was another reason why it was important to keep her eyes open. Noah, as she'd discovered, wasn't above cheating. She'd caught him out once and had never let him forget it. 'Cheat!' she'd exploded, jumping on him. 'Cheat, cheat, *cheat*!'

'It's only a game, Lyddie,' he'd laughed.

'But a game I won fairly and squarely. Admit it!'

'Never!'

There was a friendly competitiveness between them in most things they did. They were fairly evenly matched: one week she would come top in a subject, another week he would. The two subjects they couldn't compete in were French and art. Lydia knew when she was flogging a dead

horse and had dropped art as soon as the opportunity arose – she was keen not to have a single blemish on her school reports, which repeatedly glowed with As. French was her best subject and she planned to do it at A-level, along with English and maths, but Noah struggled with it, and since it was a compulsory subject, he had no choice but to grit his teeth and do the best he could. There had been no embarrassment on his part when he asked for Lydia's help, which only proved just how close they were. He'd been surprised, though, when she'd admitted to him that when they'd been at junior school together she had aspired to be as clever as him, understanding even then that it was a better way to be. He'd laughed, saying that as far as he'd been concerned it had always been him trying to keep up with her.

Noticing a slight waver in Noah's leg, Lydia knew she was on the home straight. She inhaled one last time, slowly and carefully. It was all in the breathing. All in the focus. Just keep a single goal in mind and anything was possible. This was the philosophy by which she now lived. Her goal was to do as well as she could at school, go on to the local sixth-form college, and then hopefully make it to university to study French and Italian. Noah still hadn't made up his mind whether to study engineering or art.

Predictably Lydia's grandfather had already informed her that he wouldn't be throwing good money after bad on her; if she wanted to go and live in a world of sex and drugs – which was how he viewed university – she would have to pay for it herself. Luckily there were grants available. Noah and Uncle Brad seemed to think she would qualify for one; she just hoped they were right. But there was a lot of hard work to be done before she needed to worry about that. Meanwhile they had their CSEs to get through, followed by just as many O-levels. She, Noah and Zoe, and a handful of others from their year group had been selected to do the two sets of exams. Since January they'd been having extra lessons after school to prepare

for them and that would continue right up until the exams were finally over in June. It was hard grind but worth every minute if it meant Lydia would escape Swallowsdale and her grandparents.

With a thud, the heel of Noah's baseball boot hit the grass. 'You win,' he groaned, clutching his stomach muscles. He rolled onto his side and she slowly lowered her leg and turned to him, her face triumphant. 'You're getting too good at this,' he said.

'Just a case of mind over matter.'

He plucked a long stalk of grass and stroked her cheek with it. 'Tell me what you were thinking all that time.'

'The usual: escaping Swallowsdale. What were you thinking of?'

He ran the stalk of grass over her lips. 'The usual: you.'

'It didn't help, did it?' she teased. 'It didn't keep you focused.'

'True,' he said. But he didn't smile as she expected him to. Something was wrong. She had a feeling she knew what it was.

Anxious, she sat up. 'Do you want something to eat?'

He stayed where he was, on his side. 'No. I want to talk to you.'

'One doesn't rule out the other, you know.'

He touched her wrist. 'Is it me, Lyddie? Am I doing something wrong with you? Tell me if I am. Please.'

She wished that she didn't have a clue what he was talking about, but she knew all too well what was on his mind. It was a measure of how much she loved and respected him that she didn't pretend otherwise. 'No, it's not you, Noah, it's me.'

He sat up and wrapped his arm around her shoulder. 'You know I'd never do anything to hurt you.'

'I know that.'

'Are you worried about getting pregnant? Is that the problem?'

She seized on this and nodded. 'It would ruin everything.

Bang would go my chance of doing A-levels or going to university. It wouldn't make any difference to you, but I'd be stuck here in Swallowsdale like Donna. That's if my grandfather hadn't killed me first. Which, thinking about it, would be the better option by far.'

He squeezed her shoulder. 'Don't *ever* say that. Not even as a joke. But what if I promised you I'd always be careful? That we'd only do it with a—'

She cut him off. 'Donna says they're not always a hundred per cent safe.'

'Not in Donna's hands at any rate,' he said tightly. After a moment's silence, he said, 'Look, we don't have to go all the way if you don't want to. There are other things we can do.'

Lydia's anxiety deepened. Why was it so important? Why couldn't they stay as they were? Just kissing. Just stroking and holding each other. 'What other things?' she asked nervously.

'Well, you know; *other* things.'

She sensed that he was getting impatient with her. 'Tell me, then. Seeing as you're the expert,' she added snippily, not caring now if she seemed naive or stupid.

He swallowed. 'Well ... I ... I could—' He cleared his throat. 'I could give you an orgasm and then you could do the same for me.'

'How?'

He took a breath as if launching himself into an answer, but then seemed to change his mind. 'How do *you* think it might happen?'

She shrugged. 'I've never done it before, so how would I know?'

'Nor have I, but I've a pretty good idea what goes on.'

'Excellent. So tell me how we go about it.' Her tone was even snippier.

He whipped his arm away from her, staring straight ahead. 'God, Lyddie, are you being deliberately difficult? Or just trying to make me look a fool?'

Burning with shame and humiliation, she jumped to

her feet and walked down to the edge of the beck. She'd always known it would come to this. She'd been a fool to hope for anything else. She plonked herself down and scooped up a handful of stones and began hurling them into the gushing water one by one.

Plop! Pastor Digby was right.

Plop! Sex was a curse.

Plop! It really did ruin everything.

Out of stones, she bent her head and buried her face in her hands, wretched with loss. She'd lost Noah now, for sure. Aware of movement beside her, she turned to see him sitting next to her.

Hugging his knees to his chest, he suddenly looked so young and vulnerable. His hair was choppy and all messed up from his hands raking through it. She longed to reach out and smooth it back into place as she often did. To smooth everything back to how it used to be between them. 'I'm sorry,' he said, 'that was a class one pratty thing for me to say. Just call me a pillock.'

She snatched at the grass around her. 'I can't help being the way I am, Noah. You'd be better off with another girl-friend. A more experienced girl who knows what's what and doesn't ask such daft questions.'

'If it's all the same to you I'd rather rip out my eyes and feed them to the crows than be with another girl.'

'So what do we do next?'

'I learn to control my feelings for you.'

She looked at him. 'What do you mean?'

'It means when I kiss you I have to think of something other than how much I love you.'

'Will that work?'

'Search me, because what I feel for you is like nuclear energy. But I don't want to do anything that might result in losing you, Lyddie.'

'What about doing those other things you mentioned? Why don't you explain them to me?'

He smiled and gave her one of his long, thoughtful stares. 'We're sixteen – there's plenty of time for all that

later. How about we get our exams over and done with and then talk about it?'

She blinked back tears, wishing she could be the girl he wanted her to be. 'I don't deserve you.'

'Rubbish. You deserve someone far better than me.' He reached for her hand. 'No worrying. You promise? Not when this is such an important time for us.'

She nodded and to make him think that everything really was OK between them, she wagged a finger at him and said, 'In that case, *mon ami*, give me the imperfect tense of *avoir*.'

'*Merde!*' he shouted, tipping back his head and laughing. 'Anything but that!'

After several attempts, he finally got it right and they rolled back onto the grass and once again found themselves gazing up at the sky.

But for all Noah's caring consideration, Lydia knew that what he'd given her amounted to nothing more than a stay of execution. This painful scene would come round again. Just as humiliating. Just as shameful. And what would she do or say then? To lose Noah was unthinkable. But the other option seemed infinitely worse.

Chapter Thirty-Nine

Lydia had never known a summer to pass as quickly as this one. Nor had she known one to be as hot. Joey was permanently running short of ice-cream and ice lollies and joked that if the heatwave continued he'd be able to return to Italy and never work again.

With what seemed like lightning speed, the homemade calendar stuck on the wall above Lydia's bed gained a big red cross in each box for each exam completed, until finally it was all over and she could throw the calendar in the bin. In truth, the exams had been a much-needed distraction from what really worried her – what lay ahead for her and Noah.

Prayers are always answered, just not how we imagine them to be, was something Sister Lottie would often say, so when, after their last exam, Noah grumbled to Lydia that Uncle Brad was taking him away for the rest of the summer, Lydia breathed a quiet guilty sigh of relief. 'You'll have a great time,' she told him. 'It'll be fantastic.'

'No it won't,' he said miserably. 'I'd much rather be here with you. This will be the longest we've ever been apart.'

Being so geographically apart was not a concept either of them was used to and despite the initial rush of relief, Lydia soon realized she hated Noah being thousands of miles away from her. Letters written on flimsy airmail paper from far-flung places such as Caracas, Nicaragua and Guatemala – sent to Donna's house – had her reaching for her school atlas and measuring the distance growing between them.

As the weeks flew by and she began to anticipate Noah's

return, Lydia pictured a very different boyfriend from the one she had kissed goodbye. This one would be tanned and well travelled, his horizons transformed beyond her comprehension. He would be so drastically changed he would view her through new eyes and would inevitably kick off his feelings for her like a shabby old pair of shoes that no longer fitted.

She comforted herself by thinking that they would at least always be friends and this would let her off the hook from the threat of taking 'things' any further.

Sex may have been a silent worry for Lydia, but it was a subject that was referred to with irritating regularity by Donna, and as Lydia knelt on the dry scrubby grass and leaned over the side of the paddling pool to play with Captain Kirk, Donna let out a loud sigh and cursed whoever it had been who'd got her in the mess she was in. It was a habitual complaint and, as ever, Lydia had to bite her tongue from reminding Donna that she should have been more careful and not allowed herself to be led into that dingy alleyway to have her back pressed against the rough brick wall and her skirt hitched up around her hips. But instead of preaching, as Donna would accuse her of doing, she turned to look at her friend who was fidgeting in a deckchair trying to get comfortable. 'Is the baby moving?' she asked.

'Moving! It's like a bleeding octopus doing the twist in there. I'll be glad when it's out and I can get some peace and quiet.' Donna stroked her enormous bare belly that was baking like a swelling loaf in the hot August sun; her belly button resembled a monstrous currant stuck in the middle of it.

'Bleeding octopus,' echoed Captain Kirk with a toothy grin while handing Lydia the watering can to fill again. Lydia had given up reproving the boy; his limited speech was peppered with as many colourful obscenities as his mother's. She submerged the watering can in the pool to fill it then passed it to him to water the pretend flowers she'd just planted.

'Oh, leave him be,' Donna said bad-temperedly, throwing down the magazine she'd been flicking through – she was an avid reader of women's magazines now that she could read. 'Come and keep me company.'

'I'd better not. It's not safe to leave Kirk on his own in the paddling pool,' Lydia said, trying not to sound as if she knew better than Donna when it came to looking after her son.

Donna puffed out her cheeks. 'Honestly, yer spend more time with that little bugger than yer do with me.'

'That's because I'm always babysitting him.'

'Hey snidey gob, a girl's gotta go out now and then. I can't sit here all day. Where's the fun and excitement in that? It's all right for you: in two years' time yer'll be beggaring off and I'll still be here changing shitty nappies.'

'You could change things if you really wanted to.'

'Oh, don't start banging on about that again. I know what I've done, I've made me bed and now I have to sodding well lie in it.' She sighed. 'If I could just find meself a decent bloke, all my troubles would be over.'

'You could try looking for a bloke who wants more than just sex from you.'

Donna gave her one of her withering looks. 'Until yer've tried it, keep your holier-than-thou opinions to yourself. The way you're carrying on, you're going to end up the oldest virgin in Swallowsdale.'

A nudge at Lydia's elbow told her that Captain Kirk needed a refill of his watering can. She obliged only to be further harangued by Donna. 'I can't believe you and Noah still haven't done it. He's not queer, is he? You know, a screaming great bender? A poof? Playing for the other side?'

Captain Kirk rose up out of the water on his chubby legs and proudly peed into the pool. 'Poof, poof, poof,' he chanted as the stream of wee arced gracefully through the air.

Donna laughed throatily. 'Dirty little beggar.'

Lydia whipped her hand out of the water. 'I don't know

why you should think that of Noah, just because he hasn't forced me to have sex with him.'

'Who said owt about him forcing yer?' Donna snatched up the magazine and began fanning herself with it. 'Strikes me that you're scared of sex. Yer should just get on with it and discover how great it can be. Just bear in mind that the first time is always a disappointment. It'll be over in a matter of seconds. Noah won't have a clue what he's doing and you'll feel like a huge branding iron has been shoved up between your legs.'

And that's supposed to encourage me to have sex, Lydia thought minutes later when she was joining the end of the queue outside Donna's house to buy them ice-creams from Joey's van.

The Floozy was at the front of the queue. She was taking for ever. As usual. When at last it was Lydia's turn, Joey mopped his forehead with a handkerchief from his apron pocket. 'You are not working today?' he asked.

'Not this afternoon. I'm doing the late shift in the shop this evening.'

'And your exam results? When do you receive them?'

'The day after tomorrow. By the way, I did that Italian homework you set me.'

'*Brava!* You are my best student.'

Lydia laughed. 'I'm your *only* student, Joey.'

He laughed too. 'I run a very exclusive school.'

Their lessons were held once a week at Sister Lottie's and although both Joey and Lydia had tried to encourage Sister Lottie to take part, she always declined, saying that God had not given her the gift of learning another language. Joey's English was almost perfect these days and he gave Sister Lottie all the credit. 'She should have been a teacher,' he once said to Lydia. 'She is so patient. A true sainted lady.'

Lydia had often thought that Sister Lottie had thrown away her life on caring for her sick mother when she was younger. But it was only recently that she had learned that Sister Lottie's father had done a runner when she was little

and that she had left school before her fifteenth birthday because her mother insisted she would be of more use to God working in one of the mills than sitting idly in a classroom. What fascinated Lydia was that when Sister Lottie was nineteen she had become engaged to a man who worked in the accounts department where she worked, but within days of the engagement her mother was bedridden with a mystery illness and claimed she couldn't manage without her only daughter. For the next twenty-five years Sister Lottie worked at the mill and cared for her mother. There was no time for marriage. Not surprisingly, her fiancé had married someone else and moved away.

Sister Lottie never spoke ill of her dead mother, but Lydia couldn't imagine there hadn't been moments when she hadn't resented the woman who had denied her the chance she should have had.

No one was ever going to do that to Lydia. There would be no lost opportunities for her.

For all Lydia's mental tough-talking and plans for the future, she was not without her Achilles heel.

Valerie was ten now and as different from other ten-year-old girls as it was possible to be. She wasn't at all shy around anyone from church, but outside of church it was a different matter. Often she wouldn't speak, not even to Joey. Selectively mute, she would use her lovely waist-length blonde hair as a curtain to hide behind. She had made no real friends at school and refused to go some days. Whenever school queried her absences, their grand-mother – who for ages now had been going through a phase of behaving normally, well, normal for her – would say that she was giving Valerie lessons at home of a much higher standard than her teachers were currently provid-ing. These lessons, as far as Lydia could see, were nothing more than hours spent poring over a Bible preparing for the Second Coming.

One such lesson, even though it was the school holi-days, was in progress right now when Lydia let herself in

at the back door. She knew better than to interrupt, so tiptoed upstairs to change her clothes – Captain Kirk had managed to stain her T-shirt with his orange lolly while pretending it was a rocket.

With the bedroom door closed, Lydia did a quick check of the room. Ever since Uncle Leonard had rifled through her things, she was paranoid about anyone else tampering with her belongings. Last week, when she had made the same routine check, she had accidentally knocked a pencil off the dressing table and, retrieving it from under Valerie's bed, she had discovered, next to a long-since-discarded Belinda Bell, a small case she didn't recognize. Intrigued, she'd slid it out from under the bed and opened it: it was packed with a Bible, a set of neatly folded clothes and a toothbrush still in its wrapper. When she later asked Valerie why she had a packed overnight case hidden under the bed, her sister had said it was perfectly obvious what it was for and that if Lydia had any sense she'd have one too for when Judgement Day came.

Lydia was horrified: Valerie was ready and waiting for when she would be saved and taken up to heaven with the rest of God's chosen people! There was no talking her out of it, either. Valerie was convinced she had to be prepared for the awesome Day of Judgement. That meant having a packed case like Grandma had and keeping away from the ungodly in case she got mixed up with them and the Lamb of God overlooked her when the time came.

Lydia had tried explaining that generations of Christians all over the world had been anticipating the end of the world for nearly 2,000 years and to her knowledge no one else had put together an overnight bag like Val had.

'How do you know that?' Valerie had asked.

Floundering for a logical answer, Lydia had replied, 'Show me where in the Bible it tells us to pack clothes and a toothbrush. Give me an exact scripture reference.'

'It tells us hundreds of times to be ready,' Valerie replied patiently.

'*Spiritually* ready, maybe, but not a packed suitcase!'

'Oh, Lydia,' her sister said with a long sigh. 'I wish you wouldn't be so doubting and stubborn. Can't you see what your wilful self is doing to you? Why don't you let me pray for you? Here, give me your hands.'

Too stunned to object, Lydia listened to her sister imploring God to show mercy on her immortal soul. 'Help Lydia to see that your way is the only way, Father,' Val prayed, 'that Jesus has the power to save her if only she'd turn to him and repent of her sins. I don't want to be separated from my sister when the Day of Judgement comes, so please, Lord, help me to put Lydia on the path of righteousness before it's too late. Amen.'

That was what upset Lydia most: Val's genuine belief, coupled with her genuine need to keep her wayward sister from going to hell. It made her feel horribly unworthy. And guilty. Valerie was her responsibility and for a long time now she had neglected her. What with studying for her exams, working for the Khans, babysitting for them as well as Donna, not to mention doing her chores at home and fitting in the odd visit to Noah, she had given poor Valerie nothing of her time. And because of that, she had allowed her to be brainwashed by their grandmother. What kind of sister did that?

A self-absorbed sister who had only one thought in her big, fat, selfish head: escape.

Lydia hardly dared process the thought, but she knew the reality of the situation was that no matter how much she loved Valerie – and more importantly, no matter how much she reminded herself of the promise she had made their mother – she would have to leave Val behind one day. What choice did she have? She couldn't very well take Valerie to university with her, could she? When the sly voice of her conscience told her she shouldn't go to university, that her place was here in Swallowsdale with Valerie, she would drown out the voice with that of her father saying how proud of her achievements he was and that he only wanted the best for her.

But if Lydia had trouble sleeping at night because of the

guilty turmoil she was experiencing, it was a mystery to her how Val managed to get a wink of sleep if she really believed the end of the world was as imminent as she thought it was.

Lydia's own idea of God went through many different shades of belief and disbelief. Some days she was happy to believe there was a God who worked tirelessly in the background of their lives. Other days she thought it was all mumbo-jumbo. Then there were the days when she wanted to give God a ruddy great piece of her mind for making such a mess of things.

Yet strangely, she couldn't ever really dismiss God out of hand. Not the God that she knew Sister Lottie believed in: the God of love who sacrificed his only son for the sake of mankind. If forgiveness was the cornerstone of their faith, then love and sacrifice were the next crucially important building bricks. Sister Lottie claimed that putting others before yourself was what it was all about.

If that was true, then there was no hope for Lydia. All she ever thought about was herself.

Chapter Forty

On the bus after going into town on an errand for her grandmother – she needed some wax circles for the strawberry jam she wanted to make with Valerie – Lydia decided to call in and see Donna before going home. It would have to be a quick visit; she didn't want to get her grandmother all stewed up by keeping her waiting.

Lydia still thought of her grandmother as the crazy, dangerously out of control woman who'd ended up in hospital for so long and she treated her with kid gloves. That bizarre period in their lives was never mentioned or referred to and it amazed Lydia that someone could be so ill like that and then apparently so completely back to normal. Though presumably the tablets her grandmother still took were partly responsible for that. Yet what wasn't quite so 'back to normal' was the relationship between her grandparents. They were still not sharing a bedroom, and now and then, when their grandmother had had a bad day – a tired, fretful, weepy day – Lydia saw the simmering resentment in her grandfather's face. He'd grit his teeth and clench his fists. She'd heard him shouting at his wife, telling her that she was no use to him, that she should pull herself together, or else. Or else what? Have her carted off to hospital again? Where she would no longer be an inconvenience to him?

But whatever was going on between the two of them, Lydia was determined to stay out of it. The more she could blend into the background the better, as far as she was concerned. And just as her grandfather hadn't resumed sleeping in the same room as his wife, nor had he reverted

to bullying Lydia. She didn't think for a minute that it was because of the threat she had once made about his secret hobby in the shed. It seemed more as if he'd become indifferent to her. He was still as irrationally strict as ever, but mercifully they were both out of the house so frequently their paths seldom crossed. She'd like to think he'd had a fit of conscience and regretted what he'd done to her, but like the leopard he'd accused his brother of being, she knew better than to believe he could change his spots entirely.

Off the bus now, Lydia walked the short distance to her friend's house. When she'd seen her yesterday, Donna had been feeling really down. She'd been complaining about everything – the heat, the wasps, the boredom, her swollen ankles, Kirk's refusal to eat anything other than Smash and ketchup, and the fact that her aunt had gone on holiday without her.

Lydia knocked at the door. Knocked again, and then assuming that Donna and Kirk were probably in the garden, she went round to the back of the house. Donna's usual deckchair was empty and floating face down in the paddling pool was a naked Action Man: there was no sign of either Donna or Captain Kirk. Seeing that the back door was ajar, she went inside. 'Donna?' she called out. 'It's me, Lydia.'

Silence.

She went through to the hall and called again to Donna. This time there was a sound from upstairs. Reminded of the day she'd found Uncle Leonard stealing from her, she hoped she hadn't stumbled across a more dangerous and menacing burglar. When Captain Kirk appeared at the top of the stairs, his nappy hanging off him and trailing the floor, her heart stopped pounding so frantically. 'Hello, Kirk,' she said. 'Where's your mum?'

He raised himself onto his toes and pointed vaguely behind him with a pair of kitchen scissors. 'Bed,' he said.

Lydia climbed the stairs. Donna in bed at midday

was not that unusual. Occasionally, when her aunt was at work, she didn't get up till lunchtime and left Kirk to amuse himself. Lydia didn't like to think how her friend was going to cope when the new baby arrived.

'Crying,' Kirk said. 'In there.' He pointed to Donna's bedroom door, which was closed, as were all the others, making the small space feel dark and poky. Lydia noticed that lying amongst the piles of washed clothes and nappies was a telephone lying upside down on the floor with a short stump of cord. Frowning, she asked Kirk to give her the scissors.

She had just slipped them into her pocket when a loud groan, followed by a blood-curdling scream had her hair standing on end.

Lydia didn't wait. She burst into Donna's bedroom, terrified at what she might find.

Donna was lying on her back in nothing but a long T-shirt, her knees bent, sweat pouring off her, her face twisted into a grimace so hideous that it made her almost unrecognizable.

'Thank God you're here,' Donna gasped. 'The baby's coming.'

Lydia froze. 'But it can't be ... you've got more than a month to go.'

The ugly grimace faded from Donna's face and her body went limp. 'Are yer gonna argue with me or do sommat to help?' she snapped.

Never had Lydia felt so helpless or ignorant. Help? How? 'Tell me what to do,' she pleaded.

'Ring for an ambulance. I tried explaining to Kirk how to ring 999 but the silly bugger probably hasn't done it.'

Lydia pictured the telephone out on the landing with its severed cord. Very calmly she said, 'Listen, Donna, I don't think the phone is working. I'll go next door and ask to use theirs.'

Donna's eyes rolled back and she started panting hard. Her face suddenly took on the ugly grimace again and she let out an animal-like scream. Lydia went to her. It scared

her to see her friend in so much pain. Kirk came and stood at the side of the bed as well.

'Contractions,' panted Donna. 'They're coming fast. Don't leave me. *Please*.'

'But I need to call for an ambulance,' Lydia reasoned.

Donna clutched at her hand. 'It's too late. I told yer it's … it's coming.' As if to prove the point, she screamed again, squeezed her eyes shut and crushed Lydia's hand so hard Lydia thought she could feel every bone being crunched to powder. She wanted to let out a cry herself, but in the face of Donna's terrible pain, she didn't dare.

When Donna went quiet and limp again, Lydia stirred herself into action. 'Kirk,' she said, 'I want you to be really helpful. Can you go to the bathroom and bring me all the towels you can find?'

'Yer'll be telling him to bring hot water next,' quipped Donna as she wiped the sweat from her forehead and Kirk scuttled off.

Knowing she had no choice but to take charge, Lydia said, 'Donna, the only one of us who's done this before is you. Now tell me what I have to do.'

'Just catch the little bleeder when it pops out. Which I think …' Her face contorted violently. 'Is about now. Yer'd better get down t'other end, because I'm about to push it out.'

Lydia did as she was told and just as Kirk came back into the room with a bundle of towels dragging on the floor, something dark and bloody began to appear. Lydia's stomach heaved. Oh, God, what was she supposed to do? Catch it as Donna had said? Her friend was really screaming now, one long, terrifying scream after another. Frightened, Kirk began to howl as well and threw himself under the bed. This is madness, Lydia thought. I'm sixteen years old. I can't deliver a baby!

Suddenly the decision was taken out of her hands. The baby was delivering itself. The crown of a small black-haired head had appeared, followed by a bit more. And a bit more. But then it seemed to get stuck. Something was

wrong. 'Stop pushing!' Lydia yelled. She moved in close and saw that there was what looked like a blue and bloody coil wrapped around the baby's neck. It didn't look right. She got to work and carefully unwound the soft, warm, gooey scarf. 'OK,' she said breathlessly, 'push!'

Donna did and in one almighty fluid bloody movement the baby slithered out.

It was only when Donna had stopped screaming that Lydia realized the baby wasn't moving.

Chapter Forty-One

Doctor Bunch said she was a heroine – that if it hadn't been for her quick thinking, the baby girl would most certainly have died. The local paper had picked up the story and plastered right across the front page was a picture of Lydia holding the baby with Donna sitting up in bed beside her. 'Anyone would think you were the mother from looking at that,' Donna had said. 'And just look at the bleeding state of me! They could have waited until I'd got my roots done.'

Donna hadn't been quite so off-hand and cocky at the time, when Lydia had put her mouth to the baby's blue lips, desperately hoping that she could fill its tiny lungs with oxygen. She'd had no idea if she was doing it the right way, but some kind of reflex guided her actions. Donna was crying by then, making a low moaning sound and Kirk was still hiding under the bed, but Lydia didn't waste her breath telling her friend everything was going to be all right, she just kept blowing steady little puffs of air into the baby's mouth. Until suddenly, amazingly, the scrawny little ribcage had quivered and then it had heaved and shuddered.

The next moment the room was filled with the sound of bawling. Lydia couldn't believe that such a deafening racket could come from something that had been totally lifeless a few seconds ago. With fists clenched and punching the air angrily, her stick-thin legs pumping like pistons, Donna's daughter was really kicking up a storm. Wondering what she should do about the cord, Lydia remembered the scissors she'd taken from Kirk. She pulled

them out from her pocket and, praying she was doing the right thing, she cut through the cord. When blood began spurting everywhere she grabbed a rubber band from the dressing table and fumbled wildly to tie it around the slippery cord. Miraculously, the flow of blood slowed, then stopped. Lydia wrapped the baby in one of the towels Kirk had brought her and gave the screaming, wriggling bundle to Donna. 'She's just like her mother,' Lydia said, 'a right shirty piece of work.'

Once both Donna and the baby were calm and Kirk had come out from hiding, Lydia had gone next door to call for an ambulance. The neighbour, an elderly woman with a pair of purring cats weaving in and out of her slippered feet and a hearing aid in one ear, said, 'I thought I heard sommat going on through the wall, but I thought it was the radio or the telly on extra loud.'

It was at the hospital, when mother and daughter had been thoroughly checked over, that Donna announced that she was naming her daughter after Lydia. 'You're not going soft on me?' Lydia asked her friend, trying not to show how touched she was.

'Bloody hell! I name me baby after yer and that's the nicest thing yer can say? There are plenty other names out there I could choose from, yer know.'

Wiping her eyes with the backs of her hands Lydia said, 'Yeah, but none of them as special as mine.'

'Give over, yer daft bitch. Any more crying like that and yer'll have me at it too.'

For days afterwards, Lydia couldn't go anywhere without people stopping to congratulate her for what she'd done. Everyone who came into the shop wanted to hear the story, but Lydia couldn't bring herself to give them the details. It had been bad enough actually being there at the time without having to relive it. She'd been having a recurring nightmare in which it was she who was in labour and screaming like a banshee because the baby wouldn't come out. She didn't think she could ever put herself through the ordeal of what supposedly came naturally to every other

woman on the planet. How could all that pain and blood be natural?

Lydia had often heard Pastor Digby say that the pain of childbirth was God's way of punishing Eve for her disobedience, but until now she hadn't given it much thought. Having witnessed what she had, Lydia couldn't believe God could be so vindictive.

Usually of little interest to anyone at church, Lydia was embarrassed to be called to the front of the congregation the following Sunday. Pastor Digby then proceeded to lay his hands on her head so he could praise God for having channelled a miracle through one of his flock. Lydia wasn't sure if Pastor Digby meant a member of God's flock or his own personal fan club. 'You must thank the Lord for choosing you,' he instructed her when he allowed her to stand up. 'God picked you out specially that day in the hour of your friend's great need. Perhaps he's calling you to pursue a nursing career.'

When she shook her head and said she thought she would make a terrible nurse, he bore down on her with his swivelling eye. 'Helping others is what we're called to do, Lydia. Never forget that. We're not here on this earth to self-serve.'

Publicly Lydia's grandparents said how proud they were of her, but in private her grandfather told her not to let it go to her head. 'Don't be getting above yourself, girl,' he warned her. 'All you did was save a bastard child from going where by rights it should have gone: straight to hell.'

By the time Noah was due home from his travels with Uncle Brad, Lydia's skirmish with local fame was old news and everyone had gone back to complaining about the weather: how sweltering it was and would it ever rain? Even Mrs Khan, who previously had said she didn't think she would ever get used to the cold British weather, had stopped wearing her thick woolly cardies. There were some places in the country where water was being rationed

and you weren't allowed to wash your car or use a hose. But business was booming so well for Joey, he'd bought himself a second-hand car.

The last letter Lydia had received from Noah was from Lima in Peru, to let her know he'd be back late at night, the day before the O-level results would be announced. Right at the end of his letter he'd written: 'I can't wait to see you! Meet me in the Dell of the Dead at 10.00 and we'll go into school together for our results.' The row of slightly smudged kisses made Lydia smile.

The hot August sun blazed down on Lydia's shoulders as she set off to meet Noah. She was so excited about seeing him again, she wanted to run all the way to the Dell of the Dead, but not wanting to greet him red-faced, breathless and sweating, she settled for a steady pace instead.

She was wearing a new outfit in honour of his return – a layered skirt that swished and rustled with each step and a black halter-neck top that her grandparents would most definitely not approve of. Stuffed into her bag was the cardigan she'd been wearing when she left the house. She'd done her hair differently, too. Tied it up on top of her head with a few bits hanging down, just to soften the look. Just to make Noah think she was worth coming back for. As eager to see him as she was, she was still anxious that his feelings for her might have changed. That was why she had made more of an effort with her appearance. Taking Donna's advice for once, she had actually bought some lip gloss as well as going to the excruciating trouble of plucking her eyebrows. Donna had wanted to do it for her, but fearing she would end up with a copy-cat set of spider legs stretched across her forehead like her friend had, Lydia had refused her offer and locked herself in the bathroom two nights ago. She now had neatly arched brows that no longer met in the middle. The difference it made to her face was extraordinary.

Stepping into the welcome dappled shade of the dell and listening to the sound of a woodpecker thrumming

in the distance, Lydia felt her heartbeat quicken. A glance at her watch told her she was two minutes early. Would Noah be here already? Would there be any awkwardness between them? Or had he slept in after all that travelling and forgotten about meeting her?

She pressed on, deeper into the heart of the dell, then veering to the right to the semicircle of fallen trees that was their official meeting place. What they called their special place.

And there he was, sitting on the trunk of the largest of the toppled trees. The second he saw her, his face broke into a smile and he got to his feet. He came towards her, arms outstretched. She melted into his embrace and when they kissed she wondered why she'd been so stupid to doubt him. He held her tightly and she pressed herself closer still to his firm, warm body. Clasping her hands around his neck, she rested her cheek against his and breathed in the familiar smell of him: toothpaste, soap and a tantalizing hint of sweat. 'You're the same,' she whispered. 'Exactly the same.'

He tilted his head back so that he could look into her eyes. 'You're not. You're even more beautiful than I remembered you.' He frowned. 'You've done something to your face. Something different. What is it?'

She blushed. 'One of Donna's hot beauty tips: I plucked my eyebrows.'

He smiled, dipped his head and kissed her again, slowly and deeply. Her love for him made her heart ache and she felt consumed with a dreamy contentedness. Then suddenly, for the first time ever, Lydia felt her body respond to his in a way it had never done before. There was no fear or guilt bound up in her desire for him. No reluctance to let him touch her and hold her. This is what wanting another person is all about, she thought. It was a revelation. A true awakening. But just as she thought this, Noah arched his body away from her.

'What's wrong?' she asked.

His eyes were dark and wide. He swallowed. 'Nothing. Just a bit of a problem going on down ...'

She lowered her gaze and realized what he was referring to. Whereas previously she would have been instantly on her guard, now she smiled, pulled him back into her arms and pressed herself hard against him. He kissed her neck, first one side, then the other. When his hand covered her breast through the thin cotton of her top and held it gently, she felt her insides dissolve. His lips moved lightly over her skin, and he murmured her name. 'Did you miss me?' he asked, drawing away and looking into her eyes.

'Every day. I never want us to be apart again.'

'Me neither. All I could think about during the long flight home was you. But I was afraid. Afraid you might have changed your mind about me.'

'Never. I love you even more.'

'Really? Because before I went away I thought ... I thought maybe you were getting fed up with me. You didn't seem that bothered about me going.'

She should have known he'd be sensitive to any change in the way she treated him. Unable to lie to him, she said, 'It was knowing how much you wanted to ... to have sex. I knew that once our exams were over I'd have to face it. And then when you announced you would be away for the whole of the summer I ...' She paused, blushing guiltily. 'I'm sorry, but I felt relieved.'

He stepped back, putting a small but meaningful distance between them. 'My God, Lyddie, I'd never make you do something you don't want to do. Surely you know that? I'm not some kind of monster.'

'I didn't ever think you were. But I feel differently now. Seeing you again ... well, I'm not scared any more.' She closed the gap between them and kissed him, badly wanting him to know that she meant it.

He held her in his arms and stroked her hair. They didn't speak. Lydia felt safe and cocooned, as though the world beyond the dell didn't exist. Their love was all that mattered.

'Uncle Brad goes down to London at the weekend,' Noah said eventually. 'We'd have the house all to ourselves. How does that sound?'

She pressed herself closer still to him. 'Perfect,' she murmured.

'And remember,' he said. 'I'll always love you and take care of you. No matter what. Don't ever forget that.'

With so few of them having taken any O-levels, there wasn't much of a crowd at school to collect the exam results. It was very different from when the CSE results had been announced. That day the place had been packed. 'Nine grade ones,' Zoe had said gleefully after she'd opened her envelope. 'Mind you, they hardly count really; it's the O-level results that are important.' She'd then pestered Lydia to open her envelope and say how she'd done.

'I'm waiting for when Noah gets back,' Lydia had explained. 'We made a deal to open them together.'

'Yeah, but a little peek wouldn't hurt, would it? I mean, you wouldn't have to tell him, would you?'

But Lydia had stuck to her guns and changed the subject. Apart from the deal she had with Noah, she knew that deep down Zoe wanted to know if she had done better than her. 'So how was your holiday?' Lydia had asked. 'I can't remember where you were going.'

Disappointment had momentarily wrong-footed Zoe, but she soon got over it. All credit to her; she wasn't a girl who harboured a grudge. Not even over Noah.

Zoe arrived soon after Lydia and Noah.

'Hiya!' she greeted them as they waited for the deputy head to hand out the all-important envelopes. 'How was your summer, Noah?'

'Pretty good.'

'And the best bit?'

He laughed, glanced quickly at Lydia and squeezed her hand that had been tucked inside his all the way to school. 'Coming back was easily the best bit.'

Zoe rolled her eyes. 'Honestly, you two!'

Listening with only half an ear to Zoe telling Noah about a great idea she had for a gang of them to go camping together next summer, Lydia stole a moment to observe Noah. Since leaving the Dell of the Dead, they'd been so busy talking – mostly about Noah's holiday – she hadn't actually checked to see if there really was anything different about him. His hair was longer and messier and he was more tanned, but essentially he was the same. She wondered if he had any idea just how good-looking he was. Probably not. And maybe that was part of his attraction. There had never been anything remotely showy about him; he'd never needed to prove himself. Just as she'd once envied him his cleverness, Lydia also envied the comfortable ease he had when he was around other people, and how they naturally warmed to him.

She thought back to when they'd been in the dell and the way her body had reacted when they'd kissed and touched. Just the memory of it caused her mouth to go dry and her stomach to somersault. She replayed the memory again. And again.

'You OK, Lydia?'

Shaken out of her reverie, her cheeks blazing, Lydia snapped to attention. 'Sorry, Zoe, what were you saying?'

'I was just telling Noah about you delivering Donna's baby, that you made the front page of the paper.'

Before she was able to respond, Mr Johnson appeared in the corridor. 'Right, folks, gather round. Time to put you out of your misery. Good luck.' He passed round the envelopes. As already agreed, Lydia and Noah went outside to sit on the tennis court to open theirs. But first they had their CSE results to read. 'I have a confession,' Lydia said when they'd both ripped open the envelopes. 'The results were in the paper and Donna blabbed them out to me. I should never have taught her to read.'

'It doesn't matter,' he said. After a hurried look at his piece of paper, he asked, 'How did you do?'

'Nine grade ones.'

'Snap!' He leaned over and kissed her. 'Now the other ones.'

They were both quiet for a moment.

Lydia was the first to speak. 'Happy with yours?'

'All As except for French. I got a B for that.' He grinned. 'I blame my private tutor. She kept distracting me. How about you? No, let me guess. Straight As. Am I right?'

She nodded. 'You don't mind?'

'Mind what? That I'm in love with the smartest girl in the entire school and that she's smart enough to be in love with me? A local hero into the bargain!'

His words wrapped around her as tightly as his arms. She basked in his praise – and the knowledge that now they really were on their way to escaping Swallowsdale.

One day, she vowed, she would really make something of herself. That would show her grandfather. How was that for getting above herself?

Chapter Forty-Two

With Donna's words echoing in her head as she emerged from the cool shade of the Dell of the Dead – *the first time is always the worst* – Lydia's step faltered. What if it really did hurt and she couldn't go through with it? Or worse, what if she survived it only to get pregnant?

Noah had promised he would never do anything to hurt her, just as he'd sworn he would always be careful. 'The last thing I want is to get you pregnant,' he'd repeatedly assured her. 'It would be a disaster for us both.' She took comfort in the knowledge that he was as paranoid as she was.

Since the birth of her daughter, Donna had vowed she would spend the rest of her life living like a nun, if only because she couldn't be trusted to remember to take the pill every day. Lydia reckoned she wouldn't have the same problem, but what she couldn't bring herself to do was ask Doctor Bunch if she could go on the pill. The thought of him questioning her reasons for wanting to use *any* form of contraception was too mortifying for words. She just knew he would sit there peering at her through his spectacles making her feel dirty and shameful.

But it wasn't shameful what she and Noah were about to do. Nor was it something dirty, as no doubt Pastor Digby would describe it. Anyway, what would Pastor Digby know about sex? He'd probably never done it in his life. Or known what it was like to kiss someone and know that they loved you as much as you loved them. That was the trouble with her grandparents and everyone at church; they went on and on about the right way to live, but had any of them *really* lived?

She pressed on up the hill, the hot sun shining down on her. Overhead, a pair of buzzards circled gracefully, climbing higher and higher in the cloudless sky, their melancholy mewing call the only sound in the still air. She decided that when the moment came, if it did hurt, she would think only of Noah and that this was the sacrifice she was making for him. Wasn't the Bible always talking about sacrificial love?

Why, she wondered crossly, was she thinking of the Bible at a time like this?

Because a small, niggling part of her could not be entirely convinced that what she was about to do was not a sin. She had only to think of the mess Donna had made of her life by not following the supposed rules, to know that she, too, could so easily be punished for throwing caution to the wind.

Enough! she told herself. No more doubts! No more worries! Instead, concentrate on that morning in the dell when everything changed. Yes, that she could do. How could she ever forget the intensity of her feelings when in an instant she had wanted to give herself to Noah? The whole of her. All her reserve gone.

Noah was waiting for her at the end of his garden. He helped her over the wall and kissed her, a light, tantalizing brush of his lips against hers. Then a kiss with more force. His hair was damp and he smelled as if he was fresh out of the bath.

'I can't remember the last time I was this nervous,' he confessed with a fleeting smile when he led her inside the house.

'Me too,' she said.

He turned to face her. 'You're sure you want to do this?'

She swallowed. 'Why, have you changed your mind?'

He took her hands in his. 'No. I just don't want to let you down. What if—'

'I've already played the "what if" game all the way here,' she interrupted him.

'I just don't want anything to change between us. I'm worried we'll do this and everything will be spoilt. You might end up hating me. I'd rather be dead than make that happen.'

'I could never hate you. Not in a million years.' Relieved that it wasn't only her who was plagued with nerves, she added, 'Come on, let's go upstairs. Let's pretend it's just an ordinary day and I've come to see you as usual.'

They lay on the bed as they had countless times before, listening to music, going through Noah's holiday snaps, laughing at how ridiculous Uncle Brad looked riding a donkey, and making plans for when they moved on to sixth-form college in a little over a week's time.

Relaxed and happy, Lydia raised herself onto an elbow and studied Noah, who now had his hands clasped behind his head. His eyes were closed; they were perfectly still, not a flicker. She loved the calm, unhurried pace of him. She let her gaze wander to the curved arches of his eyebrows, then to his cheekbones and his clean-shaven chin, and then to the soft underside of his arms where blue veins snaked beneath the surface of his skin. With his arms raised, his T-shirt had ridden up and she could see the flatness of his stomach. On an impulse she leaned over and planted a light kiss just above the waistband of his jeans. She felt his muscles tense. She did it again and then slowly moved up to kiss him on the mouth. He kissed her back and sweeping her hair away from her face with his hands, he held her face. Their eyes locked and all at once Lydia knew that it was going to be all right.

Chapter Forty-Three

In the following year, a month after her seventeenth birthday, Uncle Brad reminded Lydia of something he'd said to her a long time ago.

She and Noah were making themselves some toast before settling at the kitchen table to do their maths homework together, when Uncle Brad burst in on them. 'Lydia!' he roared so loudly she dropped the knife in her hand. 'Just the girl I've been thinking about all afternoon!'

'Oh, yes?' Noah said, looking and sounding dubious.

'Not like that, you mucky-minded scoundrel!' Uncle Brad remonstrated. Wearing odd shoes – one a battered cowboy boot, the other a black slip-on moccasin – and walking with a comical lopsided gait, he came over to where Lydia was now rinsing the knife under the tap at the sink. Without warning, he grabbed hold of her chin, twisted her head to the right towards the light coming in from the window and then to the left. His hands stank of linseed oil and were dusty with dried-on paint. She laughed when he stroked her nose. 'Perfect,' he declared, prodding a cheekbone with his thumb. 'Absolutely perfect. Come with me. There isn't a moment to be lost. Didn't I promise you I'd paint you one day?' He lunged for her hand and would have swept her out of the kitchen if Noah hadn't intervened.

'All well and good, Uncle B, but here on planet earth, Lyddie and I have homework to do.'

Uncle Brad stared at Noah, bewildered. 'Homework?' he repeated. 'But ... but the light. It's just right.' He appealed to Lydia. 'Lydia, tell him. The light. It's perfect.'

'How long will it take?' she asked, feeling sorry for the

poor man. He looked like a distressed child who had been told by the grown-ups to leave the room.

He shrugged, his hands extended. 'How the hell do I know? It takes as long as it takes. I'm an artist, not a car mechanic!'

Noah shook his head. 'Another time, Uncle B. Our homework has to be handed in tomorrow.'

Uncle Brad took a second or two to think about this. Then: 'Tomorrow!' he cried, leaping on the word as though it was the answer to everything. 'You'll pose for me tomorrow. There, it's decided.'

'You could try actually asking Lydia if she wants to pose for you,' Noah intervened again. 'And you better not have any ideas about asking her to take any clothes off. No nudes. OK?'

'Oh, Lydia, Lydia, he's such a pedant these days. To say nothing of his prudish, high-minded morals. I don't know where he gets them from.'

'Certainly not from you,' muttered Noah, going over to the toaster.

Still addressing Lydia, Uncle Brad said, 'His mother would turn in her grave to know he's grown into such a bourgeois.'

'What kind of picture did you want to paint of me?' Lydia asked. She couldn't pretend she wasn't just a teensy bit flattered that Uncle Brad was so keen to paint her.

'A brilliant one!' he responded without a trace of modesty. 'Maybe my best yet!'

Lydia had heard this kind of talk from Uncle Brad many times over the years. She knew that he spent his every waking moment in pursuit of what he called the ultimate artistic high. His pictures these days tended to be enormous stormy landscapes with paint layered so thick in places it looked like it had been shovelled on with a garden trowel. The last portrait she could remember him doing was one of Noah and that was last year. It was Lydia's favourite picture in the house and was hung in the hall beneath Adolf the Stag.

*

'You don't have to sit for him if you don't want to,' Noah said when they had decamped upstairs to his bedroom to do their homework, whilst Uncle Brad commandeered the kitchen to make a start on cooking one of his ferociously hot curries. Tapping a pencil against his teeth, Noah added, 'If you're not comfortable with the idea, I'll just tell him you're too busy and can't spare the time.'

'I am busy, but so long as it doesn't take for ever, I don't mind doing it. I'm sort of curious, if I'm honest.'

Noah twirled the pencil, flipped it in the air and caught it deftly. 'And if *I'm* honest, I'm jealous. I hate the thought of my uncle doing something that I've wanted to do for ages now.'

'But you're always sketching me.'

He tossed her words aside with a wave of his hand, a dismissive gesture amusingly reminiscent of his uncle. 'They're just sketches. I've had something special in mind to do for some time.'

'Oh?'

'I want to draw you properly, but in a way you might not be happy about. I've tried doing it from memory but it just won't work. I can't do you justice.'

Lydia pushed aside her textbook. Applied maths would have to wait. She gave him her full attention. 'Exactly how do you want to draw me?'

He fiddled with the pencil some more and said just one word: 'Naked.'

When she didn't say anything, he said, 'No one else would ever see the picture. It would be for me. For us.' He paused and let out his breath. 'You hate the idea, don't you? I should never have said anything.'

'I don't hate the idea, it's just ... well, you know, a surprise. How would you feel if it was the other way round and I wanted you to pose for me without any clothes on?'

A ghost of a smile flickered across his face. 'I'd hate it. I'm hardly Mr Universe, am I?'

She smiled too. 'And I'm hardly Miss World.'

'You don't see yourself the way I see you.' He moved away from where he was sitting at his desk and joined her on the bed. He kissed her and when she kissed him back, long and deeply, it was only a matter of seconds before Lydia felt her body go weak then spring to life as a bolt of electric desire ripped through her. She knew, though, that they couldn't take things any further. They had a rule: never do more than kiss when Uncle Brad was around. They always locked the door, but neither of them wanted to risk Uncle Brad hearing what they were up to. Noah said his uncle probably wouldn't give a tinker's cuss what they did, but they stuck to the rule all the same. And anyway, it was so much better when the house was empty. They didn't have to worry about the sound of Noah's ancient bed creaking and squeaking, or the noise either of them made when that wonderfully delicious moment overtook them both.

They had learned a lot about their bodies since that very first time. To Lydia's great relief it hadn't hurt anywhere near as much as she had dreaded. Noah had been as gentle and careful with her as he'd promised he would be, and although he'd been embarrassed that it had been over so fast, the next day when they lay on their sides in bed together, their bodies a perfect fit, Lydia revelled in the extraordinary and totally unexpected beauty of what they were doing. How could it ever be considered a sin when it felt like the most loving thing you could do?

It was several weeks later, when Uncle Brad was away in London, that she experienced her first orgasm. She had cried when it had happened, with surprise and disbelief as much as anything. Noah was concerned that he'd hurt her, but when she'd described the amazing feelings that had flooded through her, he'd admitted with a smile to sneaking a look at one of his uncle's books and trying on her what he'd read.

Whilst babysitting for Donna, she had secretly started to read her friend's magazines, especially the problems pages. Orgasms were every woman's dream, she'd discovered, yet

it wasn't every man who was able to work out how to make it happen. Lucky her, she thought smugly.

The following Saturday after she'd finished work, with Noah's blessing – he was out having a driving lesson – Lydia sat in Uncle Brad's studio modelling for him. She had her hands crossed on her lap, her mouth shut, her breath held, her face pointed towards the window and the soft afternoon light, just as she'd been instructed.

'No, no, *NO!*' Uncle Brad yelled at her. 'Who is this preposterously prim-faced girl I see before me? Where's Lydia? Where's the Lydia I've watched grow from being an awkward, shy child into the beautiful, confident young woman I know?'

Letting out her breath, Lydia flushed. 'I was only doing what you told me to do.'

'Lies. Lies. And damned lies! Did I say anything about looking like a constipated racoon holding its breath? Relax, Lydia. I said *RELAX!*'

'I would if you stopped shouting at me,' she said, flustered.

'Shouting? You call this shouting? Why, this is the gentle murmuring of a—'

'Psychopathic tyrant?' she suggested.

He laughed and she laughed too.

'That's more like it, my girl. Now put your elbow on the arm of the chair, rest your chin on the heel of your palm and stare out of the window. I want you to think of Noah.'

'Why?'

'Because you love him, my sweet, and he loves you. Now get a move on. Elbow up, and think those delectable thoughts of love.'

The session lasted a lifetime, although in real time it was only an hour. 'I feel so stiff,' she complained when he said he'd finished for the day. He immediately covered the easel with a dirty old bit of cloth so she couldn't see what he'd done. 'Same time next week,' he said.

It was an order.

*

They went through the same process again the following Saturday, Uncle Brad shouting his head off at her until she'd adopted the correct relaxed pose. How he expected her to relax when he was so rude, she didn't know, but the moment he ordered her to think of Noah, it worked. While he was painting, Uncle Brad spent a good deal of the time muttering and cursing to himself. She was just thinking that he was oblivious to her as a person and was treating her as an object – like an apple in a still life – when he said, 'Does Noah ever talk to you about his parents?'

Surprised at the question, she turned to answer him, but was immediately yelled at. She adopted the correct position again.

'Well, does he?'

'Hardly ever,' she replied.

'More to the right. Chin up. That's better. Why do you think that is?'

'Because they died so long ago?'

'Are you asking me or telling me?'

'I'm giving you an educated guess.'

He cursed and dabbed viciously at the canvas. A few minutes passed. 'What about you?' he demanded. 'Your parents died more or less the same time; do you talk to Noah about them?'

'Not really.'

'What does *not really* mean?'

'When we first got to know each other at primary school we swapped stories; it was what we had in common. It's what made us friends, I suppose. But now we don't need to do that.'

'You now have each other in common; is that what you're saying?'

'Yes.'

'Mmm ... So way back in the beginning, when you were swapping life histories, did he tell you about his leg?'

'His leg?'

'Don't be obtuse, Lydia. His useless smashed-to-pieces leg. Did he ever tell you about the accident?'

As extraordinary as it was, Noah had never told Lydia how he'd wound up with a limp. More extraordinary perhaps was that she had never asked him for an explanation. She had vaguely assumed it was something he'd been born with, like Lisa Fortune and her artificial hand. 'No,' she answered Uncle Brad. Intrigued, she said, 'Are you going to tell me about it, then?'

'Time's up.'

In the week that followed she could so easily have asked Noah about the 'accident' that Uncle Brad had referred to, but instinct stopped her. If it was something Noah had wanted to share with her, he would have done so by now.

But that didn't stop her wanting to prompt Uncle Brad to pick up where he'd left off when, once again, she was settled into the required position.

The May afternoon light was bright and glittery and a breeze was shaking the last of the blossom from the cherry tree outside Uncle Brad's studio. Lydia watched the petals fall and disappear into the long, unkempt grass. In a nearby patch of earth, a blackbird was tugging at a worm, stretching it like a grubby piece of elastic, until finally it was pulled free from the soil. If this was a cartoon, Lydia thought, the bird would have fallen back onto its feathered behind and the worm would have made a top-speed escape. As it was, the worm stood no chance and because Lydia couldn't turn away or close her eyes, she was forced to watch its grisly demise. For a distraction, she said, 'So tell me how Noah got his bad leg. Was it a car accident?' She winced as she asked the question – right now, Noah was out on his penultimate driving lesson before his test. Her heart skittered at the thought of him coming to any harm.

'No, not a car accident,' Uncle Brad answered her.

'What then?' she asked when several minutes of silence had passed.

'It was an accident that should never have happened. His mother blamed herself. She never got over the guilt.'

Lydia thought of the ugly two-headed portrait upstairs of Noah's mother and felt a stab of hatred. 'She did it deliberately?'

'Of course not! Ingrid would never have wilfully laid a hand on anyone, let alone her own son.'

'What did she do? And how old was Noah at the time?'

'He was five. Nearly six. His father was away on business – he did that a lot. Stephen never grasped how lonely Ingrid became. She was a gregarious girl. She needed company. Lots of it.'

'She had Noah for company,' Lydia interjected.

'He was a child, Lydia.' Uncle Brad's voice was sharp. 'Ingrid needed the stimulating company that only another adult can give.'

Donna's own claim of needing company chimed in Lydia's ears. 'Go on,' she urged.

'Ingrid decided to throw a party. Like the ones we used to have in the old days, before she married Stephen. What you need to know is that Stephen was a good man, but not a charismatic man. He was devoted to Ingrid, but devotion isn't always enough. Anyway, in Stephen's absence, she invited the old crowd from our time at college. They were a pretty wild bunch.'

'Were you there?' Lydia interrupted.

'No. I couldn't make it.' He seemed to think about this for a while, before saying, 'I've often wondered if things might have turned out differently if I had.'

'How do you know what went on in that case, if you weren't there?'

'Ingrid told me later. She poured it all out to me, based on what she knew personally and from what Noah and some of the guests had told her.' He fell silent again. Minutes later, he cursed loudly. 'Damn you, Lydia, I've lost my thread. Where was I?'

'They were a pretty wild bunch.'

'Oh, yes, that's right. Well, the party was in full swing when Noah woke up wanting a drink. It's not difficult to imagine him coming to the top of the stairs, calling for his mother and getting no response. What would any child do in those circumstances? He went downstairs to the kitchen to help himself to a glass of milk from the fridge. The place was crowded with people who all made a big fuss of him. He was on his way back upstairs when he noticed some plates of chocolate cake. When no one was looking, he stuffed his dressing gown pockets full, and went back upstairs to enjoy his illicit feast.'

'Where was his mother when all this was going on?'

'That's irrelevant. Now stop interrupting. What Noah didn't know was that the cakes he ate weren't ordinary cakes. They were jam-packed with LSD.'

'No!'

'God knows how much of the stuff he ate, but the effect it had on him was disastrous. He must have been literally out of his mind, because he ... he opened his bedroom window and for whatever reason – perhaps he thought he could fly, or was being chased by something – he jumped. He wasn't found until the next morning. Ingrid thought he was dead at first. It was a miracle that he was alive and that his only injury was—'

Lydia couldn't sit still any longer. She was consumed with fury for the uncaring, irresponsible mother who should never have allowed such a terrible thing to happen to her child. She jumped up from the chair. 'Your sister was a monster! She should have gone to prison for what she did!'

There were tears in Uncle Brad's eyes. 'Worse, Lydia. She went to hell. She was never the same again.'

'Good! It's where she deserves to be.'

'Perhaps you're right,' he murmured, wiping his eyes with the backs of his hands. 'But it doesn't make me miss her any less. She wasn't only my twin sister; she was my best friend. You have no idea what it feels like to watch someone you love disintegrate before your eyes. She began

having a series of meaningless affairs, shoving them in Stephen's face to force him into punishing her for what she'd done to Noah. She was hell-bent on a course of self-destruction, pure and simple. And then one day, she told Stephen she was leaving him for some new man she'd taken up with. That was when she finally got her wish. Stephen took her by the throat and killed her. He strangled the very last breath out of her. Do you have any idea what that did to me? Knowing that I, who loved her more than anyone, didn't save her from herself? There isn't a day when I don't think I should have tried harder.' He flung down his paintbrush and reached for the cloth to cover the easel.

Seeing the wretched torment etched on Uncle Brad's face, Lydia could feel his guilt as tangibly as her own regarding her mother's death.

'Why have you told me all this?' she said.

'Because Noah heard and saw things a young boy should never see. He was at an extremely impressionable age. I want to know how much of this he's carrying around inside him. I thought if anyone would know, it would be you.'

'You could have just come right out and asked me yourself, Uncle Brad.'

They both turned to see Noah standing in the doorway of the studio.

Chapter Forty-Four

It wasn't until Tuesday the following week, when it was half-term, that Lydia saw Noah again. She had hurriedly made herself scarce on Saturday afternoon when Noah had walked in on that terrible conversation, deciding that whatever was said next was strictly between him and his uncle.

She was working at the shop, and while the Khans were at the wholesalers and there was a lull in customers, she was lugging crates of Coca-Cola out from the stockroom to go on the shelves. She'd just emptied the last of the crates when she noticed a red sports car pull up. The hood was folded back and Noah was waving at her from the driver's seat. He was alone. Which meant only one thing. She rushed outside to congratulate him.

'I thought I'd blown it,' he said, getting out of the car and hugging her. 'I did a lousy three-point turn and my hill start could have been better. Are you working tomorrow?'

'No. I've got the day off.'

'Excellent! Fancy a trip somewhere?'

The car had been a present from Uncle Brad for Noah on his seventeenth birthday and Noah had done all his lessons in it. It was years old, but Lydia knew it was his pride and joy. He spent hours washing and polishing it as well as messing about under the bonnet. It was a Sunbeam Alpine, almost identical to the model Uncle Brad had owned more than a decade ago, before Lydia and Noah had even met. Noah couldn't drive a car with a manual transmission

– because of his leg – and Uncle Brad had secretly phoned round hundreds of garages and private dealers until he'd tracked one down in the right condition with an automatic gearbox. What really mattered to Noah, so he told Lydia, was that for the first time in his life he was truly independent; he could get around without relying on anyone else for lifts.

He never complained about not being able to walk that far or ride a bike any real distance, but Lydia knew it bothered him. She knew also that if he did push himself too much, the pain in his knee and ankle could be excruciating. She'd once seen him turn white with pain and actually be sick after he'd missed his footing. What went through his head when that happened? Did he blame his mother? Did he hate her for what had happened to him?

She waited for Noah to come and pick her up at the end of her road, where she hoped certain prying eyes wouldn't see her. More out of habit than anything else.

Her grandfather had retired from working for the council, yet he rarely seemed to be at home. 'Church matters' kept him busy most days and evenings. When he was at home he bossed them all about as usual – including their grandmother – but Lydia sensed his heart, ironically, wasn't in it. He was merely going through the motions of being a tyrant. Time was he'd have raised merry hell if the tea wasn't ready on time or cooked to his exact liking. Nowadays, he seldom shared a meal with them and showed not the slightest interest in what was going on. If it wasn't for the painful memories Lydia had of all those times when he'd lashed out at her – the cane was still there in the kitchen – she might have taken advantage of his apparent apathy and stayed out later and more often. She might even have asked to be allowed to go to an occasional disco in town. Or a concert like the ones Zoe was always going to. As it was, she counted her blessings that life was so much easier for her. She wasn't greedy. She had as much freedom as she needed these days. No point in pushing her luck.

Lydia couldn't be sure, but she had a feeling that her grandfather stayed out as often as he did because his wife had started behaving oddly again. She was hoarding tins of food in the airing cupboard, refusing to answer the telephone and hiding from anyone who came to the door. The only time she left the house was to go to church. She would scuttle to the car, paranoid that there was someone watching her. Her mood swings were increasing, too. She cried more and seemed restless and agitated. She wasn't sleeping properly, either and would visibly shake and cower if her husband lost his temper and shouted at her. He locked her in the bedroom one day, shouted that he wouldn't let her out until he was satisfied she would behave.

More recently Lydia had heard the old woman downstairs in the kitchen, in the middle of the night, reading aloud from the Bible. For the last two nights, Valerie had been down there with her. It was obvious to Lydia that their grandmother should see Doctor Bunch. So why didn't their grandfather get on and arrange it? Perhaps he simply didn't care. Or worse, was he cruelly waiting for his wife to go completely mad again so that he could be conveniently rid of her like before?

When Noah's red car came into sight, Lydia forgot all about her grandparents and wondered whether it would be Noah or her who would raise the subject of the conversation he'd overheard her having with Uncle Brad.

Noah had always been good at surprising her, and he did so again today.

'I want to see where you lived before you came to Swallowsdale,' he said after she'd stowed a picnic of crusty rolls, a packet of sliced processed cheese, two bags of crisps and several cans of Seven-Up into the boot of the car.

She sat in the front passenger seat, dumbfounded. 'Why?'

He smiled enigmatically. 'It's that kind of a day. A day for getting to know each other even better.'

'But I've never been back to Maywood. I ... it sounds silly, but I don't know the way.'

He reached behind him. 'No problem. I have a map. And it's not that far. I've already checked.'

'You're serious about this, aren't you?'

'Yes.' He hesitated. 'Unless you'd rather not because it would stir up too many bad memories.'

She regarded him levelly. 'Maybe it's time,' she said. 'For both of us.'

He kissed her cheek. 'That's exactly what I thought.'

Lydia couldn't remember much about the journey she and her sister had made from Maywood to Swallowsdale all those years ago, other than the car being hot and stuffy and her falling asleep with Val on her lap.

This time, as map reader, there was no falling asleep. Nor was there any conversation about why they were really making this trip. That would come later, they had both agreed. And with the hood back, the warm May sun shining down on them and the wind tugging at Lydia's hair, they drove out of Swallowsdale and followed the road as it dipped and climbed and twisted across the moors towards Cheshire.

And the past.

It was market day in Maywood and the narrow streets were busy with shoppers. 'Recognize anything?' Noah asked as he negotiated the traffic.

'Sort of. But it doesn't feel real. It's like a dream. Like I've been here before but in my sleep.'

'I'll drive around a bit. Shout if you see something that you want to stop and look at properly.'

Five minutes later she did exactly that.

'What is it?' Noah asked when he'd brought the car to a halt and reversed a few yards at her request.

Lydia couldn't speak. She just stared at the shop window. It hadn't changed. The toys had, of course, but the way they were crammed into the small space, each toy and

board game jostling for position, took her right back to when she'd longed for that awful ventriloquist's dummy. She could see herself standing in front of the window, scheming like mad to get that most prized of possessions for her birthday. She remembered the dummy staring back at her as if it would make everything right in her world. She'd wanted it as a friend, she now understood. Something to fill the gap her father had left behind

'If you take my father's death out of the equation, this is where it all started,' Lydia said, her voice almost inaudible. She felt Noah's hand on hers.

'Do you want to go inside?'

'No. This is enough.' She told him the story. How she'd pushed her mother to the limit because she'd wanted something so badly. He made no comment, just kept hold of her hand.

'I know where I want to go next,' she said resolutely, after they'd sat in silence for a while.

'To the church where your parents are buried?' Noah asked.

'No. Somewhere that means more to me.' She studied the map, then pointed to where she wanted Noah to drive.

It took a few attempts to find the right road, but gradually the houses and buildings thinned and the pavements were replaced with hedgerows and grass verges sprinkled with daisies and dandelions. Lydia wasn't sure she would find what she was looking for; this was navigation by some mysterious instinct, a memory so deeply buried inside her she couldn't believe it would work.

'Slow down!' she said, snapping forward in her seat. 'Here. Pull over, if you can.'

The road was narrow and Noah had to park the car right up against the hedgerow; Lydia had to clamber over his seat to get out. At her suggestion, they took the picnic with them. 'You'll think it's a weird place to eat lunch,' she told him, 'but as you said earlier, it's that kind of a day.'

She led the way and after they'd pushed through the

hawthorn hedge, she said, 'Do you mind if I go on ahead on my own? I need a few minutes alone.'

'I'll wait here. Give me a wave when you're ready.'

When she'd made it down to the level area of long grass, Lydia looked back up at Noah and, remembering how she'd struggled down the steep slope with Valerie in the pushchair that night, she hoped that he wouldn't find it too difficult. Just as her mother had done, she inspected the grass for a likely place to sit down. Having found a suitable spot, she hugged her knees tightly, closed her eyes and tried to picture her mother. Not the anxious, worn-down woman she had become after Dad had died, but the woman who had loved to get dressed up and who smiled when Dad put his arm around her waist and told her how pretty she was and that he was the proudest man in all the world to have such a beautiful wife and two lovely daughters. The image of a delicate exotic bird flew into Lydia's mind. A bird that simply wasn't strong enough to cope with the worst that life could throw at it. Tears filled her eyes. She tried to picture her father, but his face wouldn't come to her. What came to her instead were those words Lydia had drifted away to on that shattering night: *Tell it to the skies, Lydia ... Tell it to the skies ...*

Was that the answer? If she could say the words out loud, here in this place, would it be over? Would it untie the knot of her guilt? Would she stop hating herself for what she'd done?

Only one way to find out. She took a deep breath, opened her eyes, tipped her head back and stared up at a large drifting cloud. 'I haven't forgotten you,' she said softly. 'I still love you both.' And to her mother, with more strength to her voice, she said, 'Please forgive me, Mum. Forgive me for what I did to you. I'm so very sorry. I never meant to hurt you. Please believe me.'

She began to cry. Quietly at first, but then she bowed her head and wept so hard she felt like she was choking on her sobs. As she struggled to breathe, the tears kept coming. It was what she had never allowed herself to do

before now: to grieve for her parents. The wrenching pain was unbearable. It was shredding her heart, tearing her apart. Never had she felt so desolate or alone.

But suddenly she wasn't alone. Noah was there. He had her in his arms. She was shaking but he held her to him. Tightly. Protectively. Unable to speak, she clung to him, pressing her face to his shoulder.

He stroked her hair and soothed her. 'I'm sorry,' he said. 'I'm so sorry. I shouldn't have brought you here. I'll take you home right away. Forgive me, please, Lyddie.' His words were a poignantly haunting echo of her own just minutes earlier and made her cry even harder.

But they didn't go home right away. Once Lydia had recovered, they sat staring down at the railway track. 'This is where she did it,' Lydia said. 'While Valerie and I slept here on the bank, she threw herself under a train. But then you'd probably worked that out for yourself.'

He nodded. 'Are you sure you want to stay?'

'I'm fine.'

'You're not, you know. And you won't be until you stop blaming yourself. It wasn't your fault your mother killed herself. Any more than it was my fault what my parents did to each other.'

Surprised at his words, she said, 'Surely you never blamed yourself for their deaths?'

'I used to. I used to think that if I hadn't eaten that cake, they'd still be alive. Then I decided that I'd probably drive myself mad if I kept thinking that way. I only had to look at my uncle to see what guilt could do to a person.'

She turned and gazed into his eyes. 'Can I ask you about that night and your accident?'

'Not much to tell. It was an accident that could have happened to any family where cakes laced with LSD are served at a party.'

'Did you hate your mother for what happened to you?'

'For a while, yes. I hated everything about her. Her selfishness. Her ineffectualness. The way she treated my

father. But then I understood that she hated herself enough for the two of us. Now I feel sorry for her.'

'What happened immediately afterwards, when you were taken to hospital?'

'Most of it I can't remember. I was quite ill. Children aren't meant to consume that much LSD. The upside, I suppose, was that I didn't feel the pain when I fell.'

'Do you remember jumping from the window?'

'Only vaguely. Or maybe I kid myself I do.'

'Were the police brought into it? You know, there being drugs involved.'

'I don't know how, but that side of things was magically hushed up.'

'And your leg, how bad was it?'

'Smashed to pieces; it took the full brunt of my fall. It was touch and go whether they were going to amputate it.'

Lydia flinched. 'Why did you never tell me this before now?'

'Same reason you've never told me your grandparents use you as a punchbag. You feel useless, worthless. Almost deserving of what they dish out.'

She caught her breath, shocked. Shocked that he'd broken the unspoken rule between them and had come right out with what he'd said, but equally aghast that he'd described exactly how she felt. Shaken, she said, 'You always knew, didn't you?'

'Yeah, me the genius.' He shook his head. 'Trust me, it wasn't difficult, Lyddie. I can't tell you how many times I've wanted to come to your house and beat the hell out of your grandparents. It is both of them hurting you, isn't it?'

Embarrassed, she lowered her head, letting his question hang there between them while she summoned the courage to be honest with him. 'Just my grandfather,' she murmured eventually.

'But your grandmother lets it go on? She's never tried to stop him?'

'I think she's as scared of him as I am.'

'He probably gets off on scaring people. His type do. Does he hit Valerie?'

Lydia looked up sharply. 'He wouldn't dare. My grandmother wouldn't stand for it. Nor would I.'

'That time you came into school with a cut lip and a swollen jaw, that wasn't an accident, was it?'

For all of a split second, out of habit, still wanting to conceal the ugly truth, Lydia considered lying, but she couldn't bring herself to do it. Why bother? Noah had known the real her for a long time. 'No,' she said. 'My grandfather lost control that time.'

'For any special reason?'

Knowing how petty the reason sounded, she felt the last of her pride and dignity being demolished. 'I hadn't done the washing-up when I should have.'

Noah clenched his jaw. 'Bastard! Complete and utter bastard!'

'He hasn't touched me in ages,' she said quickly, wanting to mollify Noah. 'It's almost as if I don't exist to him any more.'

'Good. And it had better stay that way. Because if anything like that happens again, I swear I'll kill your grandfather. That's a promise.'

She saw the intense, fierce conviction in his eyes and felt her heart miss a beat.

Chapter Forty-Five

During that summer term at college, everything in Zoe's world was either a-*maaz*ing, *grrr*eat or phe-*nommm*inal. Lydia and Noah's daily walk with her down to the sandwich shop, where a group of lower-sixth formers congregated at lunchtime, wouldn't be complete unless they had these over-used, over-stretched adjectives thrown at them at least half a dozen times.

Zoe now had jet-black hair, a stud in her nose, and a boyfriend at Exeter University. Rick was an a-*maaz*ing guy, as she never tired of telling them, and was a *grrr*eat guitarist with his own punk band. According to Zoe, the band was so shocking and outrageous they made the Sex Pistols look like founding members of the Val Doonican fan club. They had a string of gigs lined up for the summer in Devon and Cornwall and just as soon as term ended, Zoe was joining the band in Devon. They'd be sleeping on the beach at night. If they slept at all. It was going to be phe-*nommm*inal, the perfect antidote to the Queen's Jubilee and all those stupid street parties.

So much for a gang of them going camping together as Zoe had suggested last year. The casual abandonment of that original plan had come as a relief to Lydia. Asking her grandfather for permission to go would have been more trouble than it was worth. She'd had enough trouble from him when she'd worn her Doc Martens for the first time in the house. He'd snapped and snarled at her like the ferocious Rottweiler that had moved in at number twenty-five and had banned her from wearing them to church. He probably thought she was going to give the Sisters and

Brothers a good kicking and rob them of their pensions, or make off with the collection plate.

In another Rottweiler moment, after a spate of increasingly weird behaviour from their grandmother, he blamed Lydia for her illness, saying that until she had come to live with them – before the strain of having evil under their roof had become too much for her – his wife had been perfectly well.

Finally he got round to sending for Doctor Bunch and some new pills were prescribed. Initially they seemed to do the trick, but then, having grown used to their grandmother being too scared to leave the house, they started suddenly having to watch her all the time in case she slipped out and made a nuisance of herself with the neighbours. Embarrassingly, she had become convinced that God was calling her to root out the ungodly living on Hillside Terrace.

'But what if she really is under God's orders?' Noah had once asked Lydia when she was sharing with him her grandmother's latest escapade, that of shouting scripture through a neighbour's letterbox late at night, urging the neighbour to give up his life of sin and turn to Christ.

'That's not funny, Noah.'

'I'm just playing devil's advocate,' he'd replied. 'What if everyone had dismissed Christ as being clinically insane?'

'There's no mention in the Bible about him going round shouting through letterboxes under cover of darkness, so I'll stick my neck out and say you're barking up the wrong tree. As well as sounding like Val.'

Eleven years old now, an age when she should be much more aware of what was real and not real, Valerie still badly wanted to believe their grandmother's behaviour was rational. It was as if she saw herself as a devoted disciple, and that scared Lydia more than anything their grandmother got up to.

These thoughts came back to haunt Lydia about a fortnight later at two o'clock in the morning, when she discovered

319

her grandmother kneeling on the kitchen floor hacking off her hair with a pair of blunt scissors.

The following night in bed, Lydia was jolted awake by being shaken. She opened her eyes half expecting to discover she was about to die in an earthquake. Instead, perhaps far worse, she saw her grandfather standing over her.

'Get up!' he ordered, at the same time switching on her bedside lamp.

Blinking in the sudden burst of light, she grabbed hold of the bedclothes and held them tightly against her. 'What's wrong?' she asked.

He pointed to Val's bed. It was empty, neatly made as if it hadn't been slept in. 'They've disappeared,' he said. 'I've checked the whole house.'

'They?' she repeated, groggy with sleep.

'Your grandmother and Valerie.'

All grogginess suddenly gone, Lydia leapt out of bed. Down on her hands and knees, she peered under Val's bed.

'Are you mad?' her grandfather exploded. 'You think they're both hiding under there?'

Lydia got to her feet. 'Did you know Grandmother and Val have both had cases packed since last year for when the time came to be taken up to heaven? Val had hers hidden under her bed: it's gone.'

Hardly ever was her grandfather stuck for words, but in this instance he was. He shook his head in disbelief.

'We should go and look for them,' Lydia said, reaching for her jeans and T-shirt, sensing that it would have to be her who took the initiative. With her sister's safety uppermost in her mind, and knowing that their grandmother had been acting even more erratically of late, she added, 'If we can't find Grandmother and Val, we'll have to call the police.'

The police found them several miles away, out on the moors. The scene they later described to Lydia and her grandfather was a chilling one.

Wearing only slippers and her nightdress, Valerie had been found sleeping in the shelter of a drystone wall, while their grandmother, also in only her nightdress, had been down on her knees, praying. It had been her wailed entreaties to God that she and Val be spared Armageddon that had led the two police officers to them. They probably knew her as 'Mrs Turner, that barmy old bat' and though they had tried to handle her respectfully she was having none of it and had whipped out a carving knife from her case.

From then on, they'd had no choice but to treat her as armed and dangerous and had forced her to the ground, her arms cuffed behind her back. They radioed for help, and it was only then that they registered something was wrong with Valerie. She wasn't sleeping peacefully as they'd thought, but was out cold: she'd been drugged. For what purpose, no one liked to say.

Which left Lydia to dwell on the inconceivable. Had Grandma drugged Valerie with her own medication – medication that she had been secretly hoarding in the suitcase – with a view to making some kind of obscene sacrifice? Why else had she packed that knife?

Inevitably the local press got wind of the story. Lydia was glad. It meant that her grandfather could no longer turn a blind eye to what had been going on, or ignore the harm it had done to Valerie.

Valerie was now signed up for weekly sessions with a child psychologist. Lydia had no idea what went on during these visits because, once again, her sister had given up talking altogether. Her loss of voice was officially put down to her suffering from psychological trauma – as if they couldn't work that out for themselves. The Brothers and Sisters rallied, especially Sister Lottie, but to all intents and purposes Val had shut down. She wouldn't go to school – with only a week left of term, no one thought this mattered – but then nor would she venture outside to the garden, let alone leave the house. Which included not

going to church. And since they couldn't leave her on her own, Lydia stayed at home, too.

Meanwhile, their grandmother had been admitted to the psychiatric ward where she had been before. There was talk of her being schizophrenic, of her actions being a response to voices in her head. A month after she'd been taken to hospital, nobody was talking about when she might return home.

'It all stems back to that operation she had,' Sister Lottie said, her voice so hushed Lydia could hardly hear her. 'Your grandmother was never the same after that.'

Lydia grabbed hold of this thought. It was the operation that had caused her grandmother's madness. It wasn't some strange gene that she or Val could inherit. But what if Sister Lottie was wrong? No, she told herself. She must put the fear right out of her head. Anyway, there was a greater fear she had.

'Do you think she would have … you know, actually hurt Valerie?' Lydia's gaze flickered to the ceiling, where above them Valerie was in the bedroom.

Sister Lottie finished pouring herself a cup of tea and carefully put the stainless steel pot down. She straightened the crocheted tea cosy, then added a spoonful of sugar to her cup. 'I can't let myself think that, Lydia dear. Irene loved Valerie so much. And still does. Why, that child is the apple of her eye.'

'Abraham loved his son Isaac, but look at what he was prepared to do.'

'But God stopped him, didn't he?'

'Grandfather says I'm to blame for Grandmother's illness. He says there wasn't anything wrong with her until I showed up.'

Sister Lottie stirred her tea slowly. 'Your grandfather's been under a lot of strain these last few years and is bound to say things he'll later regret. Try not to hold it against him. Anyway, didn't I just say it was that operation your grandmother had that did the damage?'

'You always think so well of people, don't you?'

Sister Lottie blushed. 'Not always.'

'I don't believe you. Who have you ever thought badly of?'

The blush deepened. 'I haven't always seen eye to eye with some of the Brothers and Sisters. I didn't really approve of the way Pastor John was treated. He should have been given a chance to repent. You probably don't remember him, do you? That business happened so long ago. Poor man.'

'No, I do remember him.' And seeing as it was confession time, Lydia said, 'The first time I met Pastor John I stole a book from him. A dictionary.'

Sister Lottie smiled. 'I watched you do it.'

'You did? Why didn't you say anything?'

'You'd just lost your mother. And your father before that. What was a sneaked dictionary compared to what you must have been going through?'

Tears welled up in Lydia's eyes. 'You've always been so kind to me, like a guardian angel. You were my first real friend here.'

The teacup wobbled in the saucer in Sister Lottie's hand, and the old lady pressed her white plimsolled feet together. 'You were kind to me, too,' she said softly. 'You took me just as I was, with all my many faults. Which is something some of the Brothers and Sisters have never managed to do. Oh, yes, I know they call me dotty old Lottie behind my back, and perhaps I am dotty. But that's the way the Lord made me, a simple woman. As Brothers and Sisters in Christ, one of the things we're called to do on this earth is not to judge others. It's not our job.'

'I don't think I'll ever be as good as you. I have terrible thoughts about some people. Really bad thoughts.'

Sister Lottie reached across the table and patted Lydia's hand. 'You're still so very young and with so much to learn.'

'Do you ever regret not getting married and having a family of your own?'

'Sometimes, yes. But then I think how blessed I've been

to have you and Valerie in my life. And of course, there's Joey too. He's been like a son to me.'

'He's very fond of you.'

'And I of him. I shall miss the dear boy when he stops coming to work here in Swallowsdale.'

Lydia sat up straight. 'He's not coming back after this summer?'

'Oh, I don't know about that. But one day he won't return. He'll find a lovely wife in Italy and want to settle down with her there and have a family. It's inevitable.'

'A summer without Joey doesn't seem possible. It just wouldn't be the same.'

Sister Lottie topped up their teacups. 'You'll be leaving soon as well. Off to university. I shall be so proud of you. Didn't I always say you were as smart as paint? Lydia? Whatever is the matter? You suddenly look so serious. Have I said something out of turn?'

Lydia took a deep breath. 'You might just as well know; I won't be applying to university for next year.'

'What?'

'How can I? I have to stay and take care of Valerie. I can't possibly leave her here on her own with our grandfather. It wouldn't be right.'

Chapter Forty-Six

Sister Lottie wasn't the only one to be horrified by Lydia's decision.

Joey spent the rest of the summer being furious with her. In September, when he was packing up his things into the boot of his rusting old car – which didn't look like it would make it to the end of the road, never mind all the way down to Dover through France and Switzerland before finally arriving in his village near Naples – he had stopped what he was doing and told her he would never speak to her again if she didn't change her mind.

'I'll just have to take that risk,' she'd said, tired of everyone telling her what she should do.

Exasperated, he'd thrown his hands in the air. '*Mamma mia!* You have the expression of a stubborn, stupid mule on your face! What is more, you are acting like one!'

It was all very well, Joey going on like this, along with anyone else who wanted to throw in their tuppence worth, but what they refused to see was that this wasn't about her, it was about Valerie. Lydia's duty was to take care of her sister, because their grandfather, for all his outwards displays of piety, didn't give a fig about her or Val. They could both drop down dead tomorrow and he'd feel nothing but relief finally to be rid of them both.

Not so long ago their grandfather would not have delayed Lydia's leaving for university; moreover he would probably have gladly waved her goodbye. But now everything was different. She had heard Doctor Bunch telling him that he doubted their grandmother would ever fully recover from her most recent and dramatic breakdown. Which meant

two things: their grandmother would probably never come home again and their grandfather, as galling as it must be to him to admit, needed Lydia's help with Valerie.

Uncle Brad had been as furious with her as Joey. 'You stupid little idiot!' he'd roared at her. 'Don't you dare come near me with that holy "I have to do the right thing" crap! You're throwing your life away. Don't you understand that?'

'Did you think you were throwing away your life when you stepped in to bring up Noah?'

'That was completely different,' he'd yelled, stomping off to his studio. He'd reappeared five minutes later brandishing the portrait he'd painted of her and announced he'd be selling it at his next exhibition. He'd said he couldn't bear to lay eyes on it knowing that she could be such a bloody useless fool.

Whilst she was hurt by Uncle Brad's condemnation, it was nothing like the sick, empty loneliness Noah's silence invoked. She longed for him to voice his feelings, but all she got from him was an anxious permanently preoccupied look.

The teachers pitched in, but only fleetingly. What could they say, anyway? Other than tactfully murmur about her taking up a university place as a mature student in years to come.

The person who wouldn't let up, though, was Donna. Every time Lydia saw her, Donna would remind her what a mistake she was making. She was doing it now as they sat with the children watching television. 'OK, so tell me what's the one thing yer've dreamt of doing ever since yer came to live in this dump of a place?'

'Change the record, why don't you?' Lydia answered her. 'I've heard it all before and there's nothing you can say to make me change my mind.'

'Like fu—'

'Don't swear in front of the children,' Lydia interrupted, just as Kirk leapt up from the shag pile rug and reached for the money box on top of the telly.

'I'll do as I piggin' well please. This is *my* house, in case it had slipped yer memory.'

It was ironic that as Lydia's life was becoming horribly tangled, Donna's was straightening out nicely. Donna had recently moved out of her aunt's place and was now happily installed in her very own council house. She'd got herself a part-time job in the evenings, stacking shelves at the new supermarket that had opened in town. Noah also worked there, along with Alfie Stone, and sometimes they all stacked shelves together. Occasionally Noah worked on the delicatessen counter on a Saturday, when he had to wear a paper hat with the words 'A Taste of the Continent' printed on it. He had to slice exotic cold meats like peppered salami and hand out samples of Polish sausages. Lydia had bought some once, as well as a round of Camembert in a sort of flimsy wooden case, and had taken it home only to have her grandfather condemn it as foreign muck.

While Donna was doing her shelf-stacking shift, Lydia babysat Captain Kirk, now two and a half, and Lydia Junior, who was thirteen months. If their grandfather was out for the evening, as he so often was, Valerie would come with Lydia. She was wary of Donna – but then who wasn't? – and occupied herself by playing with the children, patiently building towers of wooden blocks for them to knock down. Happy now to leave the house, she was once again attending church. She'd even made the transition to big school and had progressed to speaking in a whispered gruff voice, which fascinated Kirk and Lydia Junior. This evening she was having supper with Sister Vera and Sister Joan.

'Yer know what really bugs me,' Donna said after lighting up a cigarette, 'is that I really believed in yer. I really thought yer knew what yer were about. Idiot that I was, I actually respected and admired yer. Christ on a bike, I thought I wanted to *be* yer at one stage!'

Once again Kirk was on his feet and rattling the money under his mother's nose.

'Give over, Kirky, I didn't swear.'

Sharing a smile with Kirk, Lydia said, 'Blasphemy incurs a fine as well.'

'I'll have to write yer an IOU, Kirky,' Donna said. She then pointed a finger at Lydia. 'Kitchen. Now. We need to have a private conversation.'

Out in the kitchen, Donna began slamming cupboard doors as she made them some coffee.

'You'll have the council round here if you carry on like that,' Lydia commented. 'This being council property.'

Donna thumped the jar of Maxwell House down on the counter. 'Like I give a damn! Now shut up and listen to me for once. Think about what I just said. I believed in yer. It was *you* who taught me to read. *You* who got me to be a better mum. Not some do-gooding, arsed-faced teacher, or some tosspot of a social worker. And that takes something rare and special. You're by far the cleverest person I know, so why the hell do yer want to chuck it all away?'

'I'm not chucking it away; I'm just putting it to a different use.'

'And then what? Yer'll stay at home until Val's eighteen, then what happens?'

'Valerie will go to university and I'll—'

As if she hadn't spoken, Donna stabbed a teaspoon in the air just inches from Lydia's face. 'I'll tell yer what happens. Val's going nowhere when she hits eighteen. After everything that nutty grandmother of yours has put the girl through, she's going nowhere but Swallowsdale for the rest of her life.'

'Well, if that's true, there's even more reason for me to stick around and make sure that doesn't happen.'

The teaspoon nearly made contact with Lydia's nose. 'It's too late!' Donna snapped. Then less angrily, she said, 'Look, Lydia, I know yer love yer sister and want the best for her but the way I see it, she'd be better off being looked after by that church of yours. She's one of them, isn't she? In a way you never were and never will be. Didn't yer once tell me she was never happier than when she was at church?'

Feeling less sure of herself now, Lydia said, 'What you're saying is out of the question. I couldn't abandon her to them.'

'It wouldn't be abandoning her. Your mate Sister Lottie would be there for her. I can always keep an eye on her too. After all, she knows me well enough now. And the kids. And it's not as if yer'd be going to a university on t'other side of the world. Yer'll have holidays and weekends to come home and make sure she's OK.'

Donna's words should have gone in one ear and straight out the other. But they didn't. For days afterwards, they lingered inside Lydia's head, whispering to her that maybe, just maybe, with Sister Lottie's help, it could work. But it was a lot to ask of Sister Lottie. And what about the guilt Lydia would always carry round with her, knowing that she had put her own needs above those of Valerie?

The one person in all of this whose opinion Lydia hadn't asked, was the most important person: Valerie.

Four months had passed since Valerie had gone out that night with their grandmother thinking that they were both about to be snatched up to heaven, their souls to be for ever saved. No one, least of all the child psychologist – whom Valerie no longer visited – had managed to get her to speak about that night. Doctor Bunch said she had probably blocked it out of her memory, like the time Lydia had woken up in hospital and hadn't been able to remember how she'd got there. Except, of course, she had remembered in the end. So maybe Valerie was keeping quiet in just the same way Lydia had.

What she did talk about now was that God spoke to her and that she had visions. Mystical visions. They came to her quite regularly, she said. Her claims made a shiver run up Lydia's spine. God only knew what the child psychologist would have made of it. Sharing her concerns with Sister Lottie, they decided to hope for the best and put it down as a brief phase of attention-seeking by showing off a very special imaginary friend. Although Sister Lottie was

quick to point out to Lydia, there was nothing imaginary about God. And while they also both felt that Val was too old to have an imaginary friend, given the circumstances they didn't think it was that surprising she would want the comfort of one.

Valerie may not have made any real friends at school, but she did have a tentative friendship of sorts at church. A new family had joined them – Brother Gordon and his wife, Sister Prue. They had a son called Brian. Brian was two years older than Valerie and never went anywhere without a droopy-eared rabbit made out of patchwork fabric. He'd latched onto Valerie right at the outset. They always sat together and he trailed round after her when tea and biscuits were being served, his clumsy lumbering body towering above her. Sometimes he got a bit excitable and knocked things over and Valerie would shush him with a single look and a finger pressed to her lips. It was clear to everyone at church that he worshipped the ground Valerie walked on.

'But I want you to know that if you're not happy with what I've suggested, I won't go to university,' Lydia said. 'I'll stay here and take care of you. I'll do whatever you want me to do.'

It was Saturday afternoon and Lydia and Valerie were walking back from the bus stop, having been into town to buy Valerie her first bra. She had grown dramatically this year and Lydia had already given her the 'talk' about what to do when her periods started.

'Of course you must go, Lydia,' Val replied gruffly. 'How could you even think of not going?'

'But I hate the idea of leaving you here alone with our grandfather.'

'But I won't be alone. Grandma will come home soon. And anyway, I don't think your presence here helps.'

Lydia slowed her step. She let the remark about their grandmother go and said, 'Who or what aren't I helping?'

'Please don't be cross, but I'm sure I could take better care of our grandfather if you weren't here. You do seem to have a habit of upsetting him.'

Lydia hung onto her jaw. 'Shouldn't it be *him* taking care of *you*?'

'I'm not a child, Lydia. I really wish you'd stop treating me as one.'

'You're not yet twelve,' Lydia pressed.

'Age is unimportant. It's what the Lord wants of me that counts.'

'And what exactly does the Lord want of you?' Lydia hardly dared think.

'To serve him in all ways. It's time for me to "put childish ways behind me", one Corinthians chapter thirteen, verse eleven. I know you mean well, but you've wrapped me in cotton wool for long enough. I have to learn to stand on my own two feet.'

Every one of Val's responses should have made Lydia feel happier about leaving her, but this irritating I'm-a-big-girl-now routine made her want to scream with frustration. 'It's not as if I'll be leaving home permanently,' she said as calmly as she could. 'I'll be backwards and forwards all the time.' She attempted a light laugh. 'You'll be sick of the sight of me.'

Valerie didn't say anything, she just carried on walking, her eyes straight ahead, her chin up as rain began to fall. She didn't even flinch when the Rottweiler bared its teeth and hurled itself at the gate of number twenty-five.

Feeling hurt and confused, Lydia tried one more time to elicit an emotion from her sister that she felt was genuine and not some evangelical cliché. 'Will you miss me?' she asked.

'Don't be silly, of course I'll miss you. You're my sister. And I'll pray every day for you not to come to any harm. Now let's not talk about it any more. When the time comes, you're going away to university and that's an end to it.'

Chapter Forty-Seven

It was the night before Lydia's first A-level exam when she had a massive shock. In the big scheme of disasters that had so far dotted her life, it was actually pretty small potatoes, but it was still nasty and unwelcome. It came just when she least needed anything to distract her. Ever since both she and Noah had received conditional offers from Oxford University, her every waking thought had been focused on achieving the required grades. Grades that would set her free! Amen and hallelujah with bells on to that!

Their grandfather was out and Valerie had gone to answer the door – Lydia was at the kitchen table trying to cram her head with some last-minute quotes from *Hamlet* – and from the second she heard the hearty greeting Valerie received, she was on her feet. Three years had passed, but she would know that voice anywhere. The last they'd heard, he'd returned to Australia, so what was he doing here? And how did he have the nerve to come back? Heaven only knew what their grandfather would say.

For some inexplicable reason Valerie was welcoming him in. There was cheek-turning and then there was sheer bloody madness!

Lydia went out to the hall. A chilly wind was gusting in through the open door. 'Great-Uncle Leonard,' she said.

She was greeted with a loud wolf-whistle. 'Well, if it ain't my damsel of a grand-niece! Just look at you! Quite the sight for sore eyes. You must be eighteen now; am I right?'

'What brings you to Swallowsdale?' she replied coldly. 'We're hardly on your doorstep, are we?'

'Now if you don't mind me saying, that doesn't sound too friendly. But I can understand your animosity. I was just telling your sweet little sis that the Lord has dragged me here by the scruff of my neck. I told him, "Lord, I can't go back there. I made a terrible mistake during my last stay. I'll go anywhere you want, just not Swallowsdale." You know what he said to me?'

'Surprise me.'

'He said, "Leonard, you may be the blackest of my sheep, but take my word for it: them folk are the only people who can save you. Your salvation depends on them forgiving you."'

'I seem to remember you saying something similar once before.'

'Indeed I did. And I'm ashamed to say I screwed up my chance then.' He laughed. 'But what can I say? God seems intent on saving me.'

And before Lydia could say anything else, Uncle Leonard had deftly closed the door behind him and was shoving his scruffy suitcase towards the bottom step of the stairs, messing up the rug and nearly knocking over the telephone table. He reeked of aftershave. Not Brut, as before. But something just as strong and overpowering.

While Uncle Leonard was upstairs relieving himself in the bathroom – the embarrassingly loud Niagara Falls sound of him suggesting he hadn't done so since he was last here – Lydia was in the kitchen with her sister. 'Val,' she said, 'it's very important that you listen to me. That man is not to be trusted. He lies and steals and he doesn't care who he does it to.'

Her sister stared at her blankly. 'We can't turn him away. That would be wrong. If God has told Uncle Leonard to come here then I'm sure Pastor Digby would say it's our duty to help him.'

Above their heads, Niagara Falls was coming to a trickling stop-start finish. 'Pastor Digby won't want to help him, I guarantee it,' Lydia said.

But Valerie stared serenely back at Lydia. 'He will when I tell him about a vision I had some weeks ago.'

Lydia tried not to overreact. She was tired of her sister's supposed gift of prophecy and had listened patiently to many of these so-called visions. They ranged from simple pronouncements such as God loving everyone, or Valerie foretelling that someone was going to receive good or bad news in the coming days, to more complicated and ambitious predictions to do with angels and plagues and golden cups. The latter Lydia invariably put down to Val's imagination working overtime after Pastor Digby had read from Revelation in church.

'So what was this dream about?' she asked her sister.

Valerie frowned. 'I've told you before; it's a vision, not a dream. God showed me a man knocking on our door, asking to take shelter from the storm that was on its way.'

There'll be a storm all right, thought Lydia, just as heavy footsteps thudded across the landing. But the knocking on the door vision wasn't new. Valerie had described similar scenes before. They were nothing more than dreams influenced by basic New Testament teaching – don't turn anyone away because it could be Christ disguised in filthy tramp's rags on your doorstep.

Uncle Leonard was halfway down the stairs when Lydia heard the sound of their grandfather putting his key in the front door lock.

From the kitchen doorway, she saw it all: the challenging look on Uncle Leonard's face as he continued slowly down the stairs, and the expression of shock and hatred on the other man's face. If looks could kill, Uncle Leonard would be lucky to see the night through.

Their grandfather carefully shut the door. He uttered just three words. 'Lydia. Valerie. Upstairs.'

Some masochistic desire to stick around to watch the fireworks made Lydia say, 'But I was revising.'

'Then do it upstairs!' When neither she nor Valerie had moved so much as an eyelash, he roared at them. '*NOW!*'

*

In the morning, just as soon as she'd finished her breakfast, Lydia was summoned to the front room. Doubtless her grandfather wanted to confide in her so they could devise a way between them to get rid of the sly, deceitful man who, even now, was hogging the bathroom when she needed to brush her teeth before catching the bus for college.

She could not have been more wrong.

'My brother will be staying with us for a while,' her grandfather said, his back to Lydia as he stood looking out onto the front garden, the wind and rain lashing the window as they had done for most of the night. He turned round. 'I expect you to welcome him into our home and treat him with respect. Do you understand?'

Lydia's jaw dropped.

Chapter Forty-Eight

For years now Lydia had had the Brothers and Sisters down as a fickle and naive lot, and so it really should not have come as a surprise when they were once again taken in by Uncle Leonard's claims that without their help and forgiveness he was sunk.

Their forgiveness of him – self-acknowledged and hopeless sinner as he was – was to be decided during an emergency meeting of the most senior members of the church and was being held at number thirty-three Hillside Terrace, exactly twenty-four hours after his arrival. Apparently Uncle Leonard had gone to Pastor Digby earlier in the day and thrown himself on the man's mercy. As a consequence, here they all were, crammed into the front room.

Everyone had had something to say, including Valerie. She had asked to be allowed to give her own personal testimony in support of Uncle Leonard. His return to Swallowsdale had been foretold in a vision God had personally given her, she explained, up on her feet. With her gruff voice strained to its limits, she went into considerable detail about her mystical vision, embroidering her tale with all sorts of extras that interestingly she hadn't given Lydia last night. The whole thing stank of theatrics. Val was enjoying herself just a little too much – her pretty face was utterly animated, her eyes were wide and glittering, her cheeks flushed. But then Val revealed her trump card, and she did it with such a beatific flourish, you'd have thought she'd just turned water into wine. 'God told me that after Uncle Leonard's return,' she paused for dramatic effect, her eyes wider still, her hands extended, 'a terrible storm

would follow in his footsteps.' A gasp went round the room. A storm! And what had happened that very night? While Uncle Leonard had been snoring his head off in the spare room, thunder had cracked and boomed overhead and a deluge of rain had poured from the heavens. Such a torrent, in fact, that part of the church's corrugated roof had given way and water had poured in, taking out the electrics.

How could the assembled gathering not fall for it?

But equally so, how could Lydia's grandfather just sit there and not say anything? Surely he didn't believe any of this ridiculous hokum? Why had he even let the wretched man stay the night in his house?

As the final clincher, just in case there were any doubters lurking amongst the group, Uncle Leonard got to his feet and offered to put his building skills to use free of charge – oh, that was big of him! – by repairing the church roof. 'I sure as heck have no idea what the Lord wants from me, but whilst I'm here, I might just as well try to do something useful,' he said.

'In the light of what we've been told by Sister Valerie,' Pastor Digby said, also rising to his feet, 'I think it would be a good idea if you stepped outside for a while so we can come to a decision.'

Uncle Leonard wasn't the only one to be banished from the room: Lydia and Sister Lottie were asked to go and make some tea. Interestingly, Valerie was allowed to stay. Perhaps they wanted to be held in rapture by her story all over again?

'I do hope we haven't been too hasty in all of this,' Sister Lottie whispered later when she and Lydia were washing up and Uncle Leonard's readmittance into the fold had been confirmed.

Lydia was surprised to hear Sister Lottie, of all people, question what was going on. She was always so generous in wanting to find the best in another person. Her goodwill was endless. 'Why do you say that?' Lydia asked her.

With her head bent over the saucer she was drying so intently, the old lady said, 'False prophets can be very convincing, not to say appealing and ...' Her words trailed off.

Lydia saw why. Val was standing in the doorway. Standing tall and straight-backed, she looked immensely pleased with herself. 'Christ had no time for doubters and gossipers,' she said primly.

Uncle Leonard was behind her. He was smiling directly at Lydia, as if to say, there's not a damn thing you can do to get rid of me. I'm here for as long as I want to be. He even had the cheek to wink at her. She could have punched his ugly face into a bloodied pulp.

As disturbing as this thought was, it was nothing compared to the sight of his proprietorial hand placed on Val's shoulder. He certainly knew which side his bread was buttered. Valerie had stuck up for him in a way he could never have foreseen, so now, all of a sudden, she was his new best friend.

Noah had once said that he didn't understand the first thing about her, when he'd tried to coax out of Lydia what was being done to her at home and she'd refused his offer of help. But since that day last summer when he'd driven her to Maywood and she'd shared with him what she'd hidden for so long, he'd not only made her promise that she would never lie to him again, even by omission, but had apologized for not understanding sooner the reasons for her secrecy. He'd also made her promise that she would never blame herself again for her mother's death. Some days she managed to convince herself that this was true, but then other days the guilt would creep up on her, tap her on the shoulder and say, 'Hi, remember me?' Keeping relentlessly busy was the answer, she'd found. Leave herself with no time to dwell on those old memories and she was able to put them out of her mind.

Revising for her exams was perfect for blocking out anything she didn't want to be reminded of, and today,

with her final exam tomorrow morning, she was in the garden stretched out on her front on an old towel, leaning on her elbows while eating an ice-cream she'd bought from Joey. Discreetly positioned so no prying neighbours could see her over the fence, she was enjoying the warm sun on her back.

She'd just eaten the last mouthful of the ice-cream when a shadow fell across the page of her *Wuthering Heights* study notes. She scrambled to an upright position and grabbed for her top which she'd removed, sure in the knowledge that she had the house and garden to herself for the afternoon – Grandfather was visiting Grandmother, Val was at school, and Uncle Leonard was supposed to be fixing the church roof. He was not supposed to be here, catching her sunbathing while she was half undressed!

But she wasn't quick enough. Smiling, Uncle Leonard dangled her top in front of her. Embarrassed, she stood up to take it from him, but he snatched it away. 'What will you give me in return for it, my little damsel in distress?' he asked.

Embarrassment now turning to anger, she covered herself with the towel, securing it firmly under her arm. She glared at him. 'I'm not your little damsel,' she said.

'Oh, don't be like that. Not after everything I did for you. Here, take it.'

Once again she put her hand out for her top, but just as he'd done before, he flicked it out of her reach. She was close enough to him now to be aware of the cloying smell of his aftershave. And to know that he'd been drinking. He stank of another hard day at the pub.

'Just give it to me,' she said.

'Say please.'

'*Please*,' she said through gritted teeth. But she didn't move her hand. She didn't trust him. She could see he was just going to make her look stupid again.

Grinning, he said, 'Go on. It's yours. Take it.'

Her annoyance growing, she did as he said, only to find herself suddenly caught in his strong grip. Startled, she

let out a cry of alarm. 'That's better,' he said, both of his hands around her now. 'Doesn't that feel nice and cosy?'

'Let go of me,' she gasped.

'Don't be like that. I just want us to be friends. Special friends. Is that too much to ask?'

'Friends don't steal from each other.'

'Everyone else has forgiven me; why can't you?'

'Because I don't trust you. Now let go of me!' She tried again to wriggle out of his revolting hands.

But he just laughed and increased his hold on her. 'A little recognition for when I came to your rescue is what I'm after, Lydia. I reckon you owe me something by way of thanks, don't you?' He trailed a finger along her bare shoulder, stopping at her bra strap. 'How about a kiss? For starters. If you know what I mean.'

In a state of shock and panic, she tried to shove him away. But it was no good. He was so much bigger and stronger than she was. She started to shout at him, hoping one of the neighbours would hear.

He clamped a hand over her mouth. 'Not so loud, my little damsel. We don't want to disturb anyone, do we? And really, you know, you shouldn't go parading your half-naked body round the place without expecting trouble. You have only yourself to blame. But then you know that deep down, don't you?' He then slowly removed his hand from her mouth, and before she was able to draw breath, he slammed his rough, dry lips against hers, and jabbed his fat tongue around inside her mouth. His rank, boozy tobacco breath made her want to gag and she willed herself to be sick over him. She fought to break free, but his enormous hands were holding her fast, digging into her skin. When he started rubbing himself against her and pushed one of his hands under the towel and between her legs, anger turned to paralysing fear. What if he raped her? The house was empty. They were alone. How could she stop him?

Then as suddenly as he'd grabbed her, he let her go. 'That's just a taste of what's to come,' he said. 'Because I'll

tell you this: before I leave Swallowsdale, you're going to pay me back what you owe me. It's my right. My reward. And who knows, you might even enjoy it.'

'I'll kill you before that happens! I swear it.'

He laughed. 'Such tough, brave words from you. But then I've seen you in the woods, Lydia. You're not the innocent girl you make out to be, are you? I've followed you several times now and got a right old eyeful of you and that crippled boyfriend of yours. Oh, don't look so outraged. You put on a nice little show, the pair of you. Really turned up the voltage for me.'

'I'm going to tell my grandfather what you've just done to me,' she hissed, shaking with murderous hatred.

'Tell him whatever you like. It won't make a jot of difference. Haven't you figured it out yet?'

'Figured what out?'

'That it's me who's in charge now. I'm the one calling the shots. Your grandfather will do whatever I ask him to. If I asked him to strip you naked and deliver you to my room, he'd do it. Why do you think he changed his mind about me staying here again?'

'I don't know. Just as I don't understand why you came back in the first place.'

An evil smile oozed across his bloated, leathery face. 'I've always believed a good con is worth trying more than once. You see, a little birdie told me what your grandfather's been up to. He's a very wicked man, you know. Much worse than me. There he is, pretending to be oh-so-good and virtuous, when all the time he's hiding a dark and dirty secret. But that's fine by me because it gives me a nice bit of financial leverage. And that's very handy since I'm down on my luck again.'

The penny dropped for Lydia. 'You've got something on my grandfather? You're blackmailing him?'

'As surely as God made little green apples. It's something he would never want anyone to know about. While his loopy old wife's locked up making raffia baskets, he's at it like a rutting ram, and all the while pretending to

those crackpots at that church of yours that he's whiter than white.'

'He's having an *affair*?' Lydia's voice was nearly as shrill as the blackbird that was innocently singing its heart out in the tree next to them. 'An *affair*?' she repeated. 'I don't believe it.'

'As true as I'm standing here. Been at it for years. If it isn't true, my sweet, voluptuous Lydia, why has he allowed me to move back in? Eh?'

'Why didn't you expose him when you were here three years ago?'

'Because all I had on him then was that he'd been unfaithful to Irene when they were first married. He was terrified I was going to spill the beans on him, but then you went and spoilt everything by siding with him. My word against the two of you ... I knew the odds were stacked against me.'

'And now?'

'Now's different.' He tapped his nose. 'I've got all the information I need to keep my brother just where I want him.'

'So why did you go through with that fiasco of seeking forgiveness from Pastor Digby and the others?'

'In my experience, a little extra insurance never hurt anyone. That, and I can't help myself. They're so naive. So easy to manipulate.'

'You're pure evil, aren't you?'

'If that's the case,' he said with a wink, 'you'd better watch yourself.'

The more Lydia thought about it that night in bed, the more she knew it had to be true. Of course her grandfather had been having an affair. Why else would he be spending so much time away from the house? Why else would he flatly refuse to take Val with him when he claimed to be visiting their grandmother? She recalled a day a long, long time ago when she was cycling home with Val and she'd seen his car parked in town when he was supposed to be away

somewhere. Had he been carrying on then with someone? Was it the same woman now, all these years on? If so, who? Someone from church? Surely not. She ran through the list of Sisters in the congregation and couldn't for the life of her imagine any of them in bed with her grand-father. For that matter, she couldn't imagine her grand-father in bed with anyone other than her grandmother, and then it was only to fall asleep. Wasn't he too old for sex?

Not if his brother was anything to go by.

She shuddered. After what Uncle Leonard had done to her in the garden that afternoon, she'd waited for him to go out again, then locked herself in the bathroom for an hour. She'd scrubbed every inch of her body in the bath and brushed her teeth until her gums bled. But nothing could take away the sense of violation she felt. She felt dirty, inside and out. And ashamed that somehow she'd allowed the situation to happen. Never again would she sunbathe in the garden like that.

But what if he tried it again? What if he really meant to make her pay him back as he'd said? To claim his reward? Oh, God, and to think she'd trusted him once.

She would have to be vigilant. She would make sure she was never alone in the house with him, either. She would arm herself with Val at all times. He would never dare try anything with Val around.

What was almost as sickening as what he'd done to her that afternoon was knowing that he had spied on her and Noah in their special place in the dell. They had always been careful, but she supposed they'd got away with it for so long, they had grown complacent and assumed they had the place to themselves.

Despite her promise not to keep anything from Noah, Lydia had no intention of telling him what Uncle Leonard had said and done to her. She knew he would go ballistic. But the following day at college, when they'd finished their very last exam and he leaned over in his car to kiss her,

she recoiled from him. She hadn't meant to. Her body had simply reacted of its own accord.

As usual, whenever she did something he didn't fully understand, Noah didn't comment on it straight away, just gave her a quick puzzled glance which left her feeling worthless and guilty. He raised the matter later, though, when he'd driven them to his house and they were sitting at the wooden table in the shade of the cherry tree where he was slicing an apple with his Swiss Army knife. Anxious to put his mind at rest, needing him to know that it was nothing he had done to upset her, she reluctantly told him everything. She instantly felt better for sharing it with him.

But not for long. Noah was very still. His face had turned dark with anger. When he spoke, his voice was so low she had to lean forward to hear him. 'I don't want you going back there, Lyddie,' he said. 'Stay the night here with me. Where I'll know you'll be safe.'

'I can't do that, Noah.'

'I don't see why not. You're eighteen. You can do what you want.'

'Thanks, but I'll be fine. So long as I stay on my guard.'

Noah gripped the penknife in his hand and drove the point of it viciously hard into the surface of the table. 'You make sure you do. But I'm telling you now, if he touches you, or threatens you again, I'll go after him. I'll push this knife straight through his ribs and out the other side.' Again his voice was low and tightly controlled.

'Sorry to disappoint you, but if anyone's going to stick a knife in him, it'll be me.'

'I'm serious, Lyddie.'

She walked home, full of regret now that she'd told Noah what she had. She should have lied, made up some story to fob him off. She had never seen him stay angry for so long. They should have been celebrating the end of their exams, but instead, Noah was morose and locked deep in

344

his own thoughts. It was all her fault. Her and her great big mouth. When would she ever learn?

As she climbed over the wall at the end of the garden and wondered what awaited her at home, she considered the possibility of counter-blackmailing her grandfather by insisting that if he didn't get rid of his brother, she would tell everyone at church about the affair he was having. Which, apart from putting her grandfather between a rock and a hard place, did raise an interesting question: whose will would he bend to?

While scraping the potatoes for tea, Lydia listened out for Uncle Leonard's movements upstairs. She knew he was up there, but whatever he was doing, he was very quiet. As was Val. Maybe she was having another of her so-called mystical visions. Immediately Lydia was cross with herself for having such a mean-spirited thought. For all she knew, Val might well turn out to be some kind of modern-day prophet. She smiled at the thought, picturing pilgrims from all over the world visiting number thirty-three Hillside Terrace in search of enlightenment.

She had almost finished the potatoes when the telephone rang. If her grandfather was in the house she wouldn't dream of 'being too big for her boots' and answering the phone, but since he was 'visiting their grandmother' she wiped her hands and went out to the hall.

'Is Mr Turner there, please?' asked a woman with a crisp, well-ironed voice.

'No, I'm sorry, he's out at the moment.' Busy rutting like a ram, she was tempted to add. 'Can I pass on a message for him? I'm his granddaughter.'

'Well, it's a bit awkward, really.' The crisp voice wasn't so crisp now. Lydia wondered fleetingly if this was the object of all the secret rutting. 'But I suppose it will have to do. My name's Mrs Vickers and I'm calling from the hospital. The thing is, his wife has disappeared. We can't find her anywhere.'

The sound of a door opening upstairs momentarily

distracted Lydia and out of the corner of her eye she saw Uncle Leonard crossing the landing to the bathroom. 'We wondered,' continued Mrs Vickers, whose voice had now lost all its professional poise, 'well, to be honest, we're hoping that she might, like a homing pigeon, find her way back to you. If she does, we'd be grateful if you could telephone us right away. Meanwhile, I'm afraid we're going to have to call the police to help us find her. She could be anywhere.'

Within seconds of ending the conversation, Lydia's first thought was how to keep the news from her sister. Val would worry herself sick if she thought their grandmother was wandering the streets, lost and confused. A ring at the doorbell made her jump. For a split second she wondered if their grandmother had found her way home already.

But it wasn't their grandmother: it was Joey. At once Lydia could see something was wrong; he looked so unhappy. 'I didn't want to leave without saying goodbye, Lydia,' he said. 'I wanted to wish you well for when you go to university.'

'Goodbye? But where are you going?'

'I'm going home. I heard today that my mother is very ill. It is not good news. She has had an attack of the head, no, I mean, of the heart. Forgive me; I am so upset, my English is all over the place.'

'Oh, Joey, I'm so sorry. When are you leaving?'

'Tomorrow. Early.' He almost smiled. Just a small flicker. 'But not before breakfast. I do not think the good Sister Lottie will allow me to leave without something to eat before my long journey.'

'Do you think you'll be back next year?'

He shrugged. '*Chi sa?* Who knows? If my poor *mama* dies, then I will have to stay and look after the rest of the family.'

The thought that she might never see Joey again filled Lydia with such sadness, she put her arms around him. 'If you don't come back I'll come and visit you in Italy one day. That's a promise.'

They were just pulling apart when Lydia heard a roar and saw Noah's red sports car hurtling at top speed down the road. Just inches from Joey's rusting old Ford, he swerved to a stop, tyres squealing. Slamming the car door shut, he made his way up the garden path. She could see he had something on his mind. He was so agitated he didn't even acknowledge Joey. 'Lyddie,' he said, 'I want to speak to that bastard uncle of yours. I can't stop thinking about what he said he'd do to you.'

Joey frowned anxiously. 'Would you like me to stay, Lydia?'

'Um ... it's OK, Joey. You go. I can sort this out.'

Noah swung round and faced Joey. 'That's just the point: she can't sort it out. He's threatened to rape her. I mean, he's her great-uncle, for God's sake! What kind of a sick pervert is he? And what kind of a boyfriend would I be to stand by and let that happen?'

Lydia put a hand out to Noah to try and shush him; his raised voice was attracting curious neighbours out on the street. But Noah wasn't having it. 'Please, Lyddie, you've been through enough. I won't let you suffer again at the hands of this twisted family of yours.'

'Is this true?' Joey asked. 'Has this man touched you? Your uncle Leonard?'

'Hello, hello, hello. What's going on here, then? Do my ears deceive me, or do I hear my name being taken in vain?'

Ambling nonchalantly down the stairs was Uncle Leonard. Noah took one look at him and hurled himself over the doorstep. 'You! I want a word with you. And then I'm going to fucking kill you!'

Chapter Forty-Nine

Noah's fist slammed straight into Uncle Leonard's face.

Rocking back on his heels, Uncle Leonard put a hand to his mouth, saw that he was bleeding and then glared at Noah. There was a furious glint in his eye. 'You're gonna bloody well pay for that, sonny.'

'Oh, yeah?' yelled Noah. 'Well, so are you for touching Lydia.' He raised his fist again, but Uncle Leonard was ready for him this time and moved fast. He blocked Noah's arm, then aimed a vicious kick at his leg. His bad leg. Noah crumpled and dropped to the floor. He clutched his ankle and groaned.

'Boys still wet behind the ears shouldn't take on grown men,' Uncle Leonard said dismissively, as if he'd done nothing more than swat an annoying fly out of his way.

A surge of savage rage filled Lydia and she took a swing at him herself. To her amazement, she landed a punch smack on his nose and felt something squish beneath her knuckles. Blood gushed. It was such a satisfying sight, that and the look of astonishment on his face, that she experienced a heady rush to hit him again. She flexed her arm, all set to unleash another punch, but Joey stepped in and took hold of her elbow. '*Basta*,' he said, quietly. 'Enough.' He pointed to the top of the stairs where Valerie was staring down at them. She looked petrified. 'This is not good for her to see.'

Joey was right. And ignoring Uncle Leonard's shout for someone to give him a handkerchief – blood was pouring from his nose and dripping onto his clothes – Lydia bent down to help Noah to his feet.

She'd just got him upright when her grandfather appeared at the door. He took in the scene with a look of icy disapproval. 'What the hell's going on here?' he demanded.

'Try asking your brother,' Lydia flung back at him.

Noah was all for having it out there and then, with both men, but Lydia pleaded with him not to. 'Please.' she begged, dragging him outside with Joey's help. 'It's better that you go.'

'But I can't leave you here like this,' he said, struggling hard to break free and go back inside the house.

'If you stay, you'll only make things worse,' Lydia said firmly. 'I don't want Valerie getting any more upset. Please, just leave everything to me.'

His anger was still palpable, but she could see she'd left him no choice and reluctantly he let her steer him to his car. 'I'll never forgive myself if anything happens to you. Ring me if you need me. Promise?'

'I promise. But only if you promise to calm down and stop worrying.' Remembering that his uncle was away until tomorrow, she added, 'When the dust's settled here, I'll come and see you later tonight. OK?'

He opened the car door and got in. 'No, I've got a better idea; I'll meet you halfway. In the dell. Midnight. That way we'll know we've got the place to ourselves.'

'Will your leg be all right?'

He nodded and reached up to kiss her, his hand on the nape of her neck. 'Take care,' he said. She kissed him back. But only briefly. She was conscious that they still had an audience.

He started the engine, reversed away from Joey's car, then pulled out. 'I'll be waiting for you!' he called to her as he drove off.

She waved at him, then turned to Joey. He looked serious. 'There is real evil in there, Lydia,' he said, glancing back at the house. 'I don't feel happy returning to Italy knowing what I now know. Like Noah, I too do not want to leave you here.'

'But you have to go, Joey. Your mother needs you. Besides, I've a feeling everything's going to be different from now on.'

He looked doubtful. 'I could finish off what Noah started,' he said.

She smiled. 'It was you who stopped it in the first place.'

He didn't return her smile. Instead he hugged her and said, 'Promise me you will look after yourself.'

I've been looking after myself since for ever, she thought, waving him goodbye.

Ignoring the handful of neighbours who were still hanging around in case there was anything else worthwhile seeing, she edged her way around them and found herself face to face with Uncle Leonard, who was standing by the gate. How long had he been standing there with a handkerchief pressed to his nose? 'Perhaps you should get yourself off to the doctor and have that looked at,' she said, barging past him.

'Don't think I won't get my own back,' he snarled.

'My, what a big man you are. Threatening girls and kicking boys wet behind the ears. What's your problem? Got a small willy?'

Inside the house, her grandfather was waiting for her in the front room. 'I'd like an explanation,' he said.

'As I said earlier, why don't you ask your brother for one?' responded Lydia. 'When you've done that, tell him to push off out of Swallowsdale for good.'

Nostrils flaring, he stared at her, then at Uncle Leonard, who'd come in behind her. She tried not to feel as if she was caught between the two of them.

'Just what gives you the right to tell me what to do?' her grandfather said, plumping up his chest to assume his usual air of authority.

She took a step towards him, reminded of that very first time she had stood in this room and cowered beneath his scrutinizing gaze. But that was then. This was now. Never had she felt more sure of herself.

'Your reign of terror is over, Grandfather,' she said. 'You can stick your pompous, self-righteous, holier-than-thou act where the sun doesn't shine. I know about your affair. I also know about your brother blackmailing you. But, and here's the dilemma for you, if you don't agree to get rid of him by this time tomorrow, I will tell everyone, and I mean *everyone*, about your sordid double life. Oh, and you might like to know, the hospital telephoned earlier to say Grandmother's disappeared. They haven't a clue where she is and were calling the police to look for her. But then I suppose it would be wonderful news for you if she were to be found dead in a ditch somewhere. How convenient that would be for you.'

The powerful energy that had fuelled her words in the front room soon fizzled away to nothing, and by the time Lydia reached the top of the stairs she felt emotionally and physically drained.

She tapped on the bedroom door – something she and Valerie always did now as a mark of respect for each other's privacy – and went inside. But Valerie wasn't there.

Nor was she in the bathroom.

Where had she gone? And when? Lydia stood on the landing, concerned. What if her sister had overheard what Lydia had just said about their grandmother? *Wonderful news ... Dead in a ditch ...* Lydia cursed herself. Why couldn't she ever think before she spoke?

Lydia had good cause to be concerned about her sister. She reappeared in time for tea – it was only the two of them eating, thank goodness – but Val refused to say where she'd been. In fact, she refused to speak at all. Not even a whisper. Nor would she write anything down as she'd done before when she'd been upset. All Lydia could assume was that after overhearing her conversation with their grandfather, Valerie had irrationally rushed straight out to look for her precious grandmother. Lydia tried her best to reassure her by saying there wasn't anything to

worry about, that by the morning everything would have been sorted out. But it made no difference to her. Valerie just sat there at the table, glassy-eyed and silent. She was unreachable.

They went to bed early. Lydia didn't want to be downstairs when either her grandfather or Uncle Leonard returned home. Her grandfather had been out all evening, having driven off shortly after she'd given him her ultimatum. Minutes later, Uncle Leonard had left the house, too.

Lydia's plan was that she would snatch an hour or two of sleep, and then when the house was perfectly quiet, she would go and see Noah.

But she ended up sleeping the sleep of the dead. Mid-dream, she woke with a start. It was the kind of start that made her think something – a footstep perhaps – had woken her.

She checked the luminous hands on her alarm clock and saw to her dismay that it was ten minutes past one. Poor Noah, he would have been waiting all this time for her. Worse, he was probably worrying himself sick, imagining that something terrible had happened to her.

After listening for the tell-tale steady breathing sound that told her Valerie was fast asleep, she pushed back the bed covers. From the floor, she picked up her shoes and carefully folded clothes, and quietly padded out of the room downstairs to the kitchen. There, she hurriedly got dressed and turned the key in the back door.

The moon was full and bright and the sky so clear and spangled with stars, she had no trouble making her way to the dell. Once there, following the well-trodden familiar route through the trees, her eyes rapidly adjusting to the change in darkness, she could hear the rustling sound of animal life in the distance. Hearing a noise nearby, off to her right, she turned and saw a pair of unblinking eyes staring back at her. A fox. A second later and it was gone.

She pressed on. A little further and she would be at the

halfway point. From there it was only a short distance to her and Noah's special place. A place now that would be for ever tainted by the knowledge that Uncle Leonard had spied on their every intimate gesture. She would never feel comfortable there again.

It was always possible that Noah had given up waiting for her and gone home, but somehow she doubted it. He was too tenacious for that. She had never known him to go back on his word. She hoped he'd fallen asleep in that case. At least then he wouldn't have been worrying about her.

She allowed herself a small smile when, in the shadowy darkness, she saw a pair of legs sticking out from behind one of the fallen trees. How well she knew Noah! And by the looks of how still he was, he hadn't been able to stay awake whilst he waited for her.

Moving as silently as she could, she inched her way forward, deciding to creep up on him and wake him with a kiss. Sleeping Beauty role reversal, she would tease him. Then she would lie down beside him and they would spend the rest of the night here wrapped in each other's arms to keep warm. It would be their first whole night together and they'd wake in the morning to the sound of birdsong.

It was the smell that alerted her. The sickly smell of aftershave that made her realize it wasn't Noah sleeping against the fallen tree. Shock wrenched a startled cry from her lips and she stepped back clumsily, her only thought to run. And fast. If he caught up with her, alone here in the dell, God only knows what he would do to her. But she'd only taken a few steps when she missed her footing and tumbled headlong over a tree root. Again she let out a cry, louder this time because her fear had turned to wild panic. Scrabbling to get up, her hands clawing at the dry, dusty ground, she was near to tears, terrified that he would come after her.

Once she was back on her feet, a slither of logic

penetrated her brain: with all the noise she'd made, why hadn't he woken and come after her?

And something else. If he'd been sleeping, why hadn't he been snoring? He *always* snored. Just like the revolting pig he was.

Her heart thudding against her ribcage, she summoned all her courage and retraced the steps she'd taken. She was almost back where she'd been before, when she froze. What if he was playing a game with her? Was he drawing her near, biding his time before pouncing on her?

To the left of her, she saw a handy-sized branch. It looked solid, like it could do some damage. 'I know you're there,' she said, gripping the branch with both hands and lifting it, ready to take aim. If she had to, she'd take his head clean off. 'So why don't you just stop messing about?'

When he didn't answer her, she took another step forward. And another. Until finally she was level with not just his legs, but the whole of him.

The first thing she saw was that his head was tilted to one side and his eyes were wide open; they were staring straight at her. Then she saw the blood. It was on the side of his head. The front of his shirt was also soaked in it. Bending down, she could see holes in his blood-soaked shirt. He'd been stabbed. Several times.

There was no doubt in her mind that he was dead.

Chapter Fifty

The enormity of what Noah had done was coming at Lydia in ever-growing waves of horror.

Initially she had been calm, focusing only on what had to be done. But now, the next morning, in the cold light of day – oh, how apt that phrase was – the reality of Noah's actions was hitting her with all the force of an atom bomb.

Noah had killed Uncle Leonard. He had said he would. And he had. He really had.

And yes, she too had threatened to kill the vile man. In the dell last night, when she thought she might have to protect herself against him, she had picked up that branch with the full intention of knocking his head off. But would she really have gone through with it? Wasn't it just something you said in the heat of the moment?

She began to shake uncontrollably, her stomach pitching and heaving. She clamped a trembling hand over her mouth, but it was no good. She went round to the back of the garage, bent over into the bushes and retched until she thought her stomach was going to turn itself inside out.

Exhausted, she leaned against the wall of the garage and closed her eyes, dizzy with the storm that was raging inside her head.

Murder. If caught, Noah would go to prison. He would stay there for the rest of his life, all because of her. He had done this dreadful thing for her sake. Because he loved her.

But how had he thought he would get away with it? He hadn't thought, had he? That was the whole trouble. He had acted on impulse to protect her.

Noah may not have been thinking straight last night, but Lydia had more than made up for that oversight on his part. She had done nothing but look at the situation from every possible angle, trying to work out the best way she could save Noah from going to prison. She had immediately dismissed the two of them running away together. Where would they go? What would they do? The police would find them within days; two young people on the run were much more conspicuous than only one. And if that happened, if they were caught, Noah would confess to killing Uncle Leonard and then that would be it. He'd be locked away for ever. His life finished. Her life over, too.

She just couldn't let Noah suffer for something he'd done out of love for her. The awful truth in all of this was that it was her fault. Everything always came back to her. Whatever she touched, she destroyed. Her mother was dead because of her. Valerie wasn't the happy carefree child she should be because Lydia hadn't taken good enough care of her. And now, because of her, Noah had killed a man. She could not, *would not*, let him be punished for it.

It was this thought that was the driving force behind her actions now; it was all she had to give her the courage to go through with what she had instigated whilst in the dell. There was no other way. The evidence against Noah was enough to condemn him in an instant. How soon would it be before those neighbours came forward and told the police they had witnessed a fight only yesterday afternoon, that they had even heard Noah shouting at Uncle Leonard that he was going to kill him? Her grandfather, too, would be quick to corroborate their claims, saying he'd come home to find a violent young man sprawled on his hall floor. He would do it if only to spite Lydia.

Tears slid down her cheeks. Why did Noah have to love her so much?

Once again, she pieced together what had happened, seeing the events all too clearly in her mind's eye. In the aftermath of the fight, Uncle Leonard had overheard the

two of them arranging to meet in the dell – why else had he been hanging around by the gate, if not to eavesdrop? – and had consequently decided to go there and spy on them. Or just cause trouble. Noah, having got to their special place on time, had then come across Uncle Leonard. There had been words between them. More taunts and insults from Uncle Leonard. Probably still feeling humiliated by that vicious kick to his leg, Noah would have picked up a heavy branch, just as Lydia had, and hit Uncle Leonard with it. The blow would have knocked him unconscious, giving Noah the perfect opportunity to take out his penknife and …

Unable to carry on, Lydia squeezed her eyes shut. Shaking again, she didn't think she would ever forget the sight of all that blood.

Hearing a car approach, she pressed herself against the wall of the garage and watched it rumble out of sight down the cobbled single-track road. Was this what the rest of her life would be like? Always watching over her shoulder? Always wondering if someone was coming for her?

Even if it was, she had no choice but to do everything she could to trick the police into looking the other way. They had to be so convinced that she was the one who had killed Uncle Leonard, they wouldn't consider Noah as a possible suspect.

The first part of her plan had been to plant the right kind of evidence on Uncle Leonard's body. Taking one of those hateful hands of his, she had raked his nails across her arm, pushing them painfully hard into her skin. Next she had pulled out some strands of her hair – nobody could ever confuse her long wavy hair with Noah's – and then she had kicked up the leaves around the body trying to ensure that only her footprints would be discernible. She didn't know how soon it would be before the body would be discovered, but knowing that few people walked through the dell, she hoped to be long gone when it was.

She had then thought about going on to Upper

Swallowsdale House to tell Noah what she'd set in motion. She'd soon changed her mind. Noah would try and stop her by saying it was too big a risk. Instead, exhausted and numb with shock, she had stumbled home, but not to sleep. Sitting at the kitchen table, she had written two letters – one to Sister Lottie and one to Noah – and then going upstairs, taking care not to wake Valerie, she had quietly packed a rucksack, carefully stowing inside it her passport and birth certificate and those few precious things she just couldn't leave behind. Fully dressed, just as dawn was breaking, she had finally gone to bed.

She'd woken up later than she'd intended. Valerie was already out of bed and, judging from the sound of running water, was having a bath. Her grandfather was nowhere to be seen.

The hardest part was leaving without saying goodbye to Valerie, but she just couldn't risk it. One look at her sister and her resolve would have faltered. Shouldering her rucksack, she had shut the back door after her, caught the bus into town and gone straight to the post office. From there she had hidden at the back of Sister Lottie's garage to wait for the one person on whom she was pinning all her hopes.

If Joey did refuse to take her to Italy with him, it wouldn't be the end of the world. Hadn't that happened already? No, she had a plan B to fall back on if need be.

Now, as she patiently waited for Joey to appear, she felt her stomach churn again. Could she really go through with this? Could she really bear to be separated from Noah?

She took a deep breath, played her fingers over the marks she had made on her arm with Uncle Leonard's nails, and shuddered. Yes, she could. If it meant saving Noah from going to prison, then she could. Hadn't they both always promised they would do anything for each other? Was she about to prove that the promise had meant nothing? Just empty words that had tripped off her tongue? It would be a sacrifice, like no sacrifice she had ever thought she would have to make, but do it she would.

Besides, it wouldn't be for ever. Somehow they would find a way to be together again. They just had to be patient. So long as Noah did exactly as she had instructed in the letter she had just posted to him, everything would work out in the end.

Now

Chapter Fifty-One

Lydia's head was zinging. She and Fabio had drunk so many cups of espresso during the telling of her story, she didn't think she would sleep for a week. If it wasn't for her ankle, she would be pacing up and down. As it was, she had to stay frustratingly still and wait for Fabio to ask her the inevitable question. As well as all the others that would follow.

'So what happened next, *cara*? Did Joey bring you here to Italy?'

She nodded. 'It was easy to convince him to take me with him. I told him that I had killed Uncle Leonard, that he had followed me to the dell in the middle of the night and attacked me while I was waiting for Noah. Don't forget, I had those marks on my arm to back up my story.' She paused, remembering the look of explosive anger on Joey's face and how good he'd been to her. 'I've always felt guilty about that lie to Joey,' she continued, 'but I'm afraid I was prepared to do anything to protect Noah.'

'You had no difficulty getting away from England?'

'None at all. My original idea depended upon slipping away before the body was discovered and leaving the country on the ferry for France quite legally, but Joey wouldn't have it. Despite the awful risk he was taking, he was adamant that he would smuggle me across the Channel in the boot of his car. I was totally against it. If we were caught it would have put him in danger of going to prison as well. He argued that it would be better that no one knew that I had left England on the same day as

him. Better that people thought I was hiding somewhere in England.'

'But surely, once the body was found, with the evidence you had placed, the police would have put two and two together and concluded that chances were you had left with Joey?'

'That's exactly what did happen. The British police got in touch with the Italian authorities and two officers from the local *questura* turned up to question Joey in his village. He told them he didn't have a clue where I was, and that he certainly hadn't brought me to Italy.'

'Did they search the house?'

'Yes, in a rather desultory fashion. They really couldn't have cared less, so Joey told me later. I wasn't there, of course. When we arrived in Italy, the first thing he did was to take me to friends of his who lived in Naples. He said Naples was so big and busy no one would find me there; it would be the classic needle in a haystack scenario. Moreover, with my dark hair I'd blend in easily; no one would look twice at me. To earn my keep, I immediately started work, washing dishes in a restaurant. I learned to speak Italian pretty fast, I can tell you.'

'*Dio mio!* You were eighteen years old, Lydia. Anything could have happened to you there. Imagine Chiara at that age and her doing something similar.'

Lydia sighed. 'I know, Fabio. But don't you remember when you were eighteen? You think you're invincible and have all the answers. Bear in mind just how determined I was to keep Noah safe. I was prepared to do anything for him.'

'You did, *cara*. From what you tell me, I'm only too surprised you didn't hand yourself over to the police and confess that you were the murderer.'

'There wouldn't have been any point in doing that. Noah would have immediately told them the truth, that I was trying to protect him. It was my greatest fear all along that he would feel the need to confess.'

'Would you really have gone to prison for him?'

'If I'd had to, yes. But given what kind of a man Uncle Leonard was, I was banking on a jury having some sympathy for me. That they would see me as a distraught young girl trying to defend herself, and as a result I'd be given a lesser sentence. Noah, on the other hand, would have been found guilty of murder.'

'It was an enormous risk.'

'I know, but I was hoping it would never come to that. Everything hung on my escape to Italy. Once I arrived I knew I could disappear for as long as it was necessary and then eventually, when it was safe, Noah would come to me. I thought we'd find a way to be together. Somehow. Somewhere.' She shook her head. 'I know from the expression on your face, Fabio, exactly what you're thinking. As plans go, it sounds wobbly and ill-conceived. But that's with the benefit of hindsight and objective thinking. I was eighteen. Incredibly naive. And very frightened. It made perfect sense to me at the time.'

'Actually you're wrong,' Fabio said. 'I was thinking that Noah is not coming out of this well. He murders a man, you make sure the finger is pointed at you, and he makes no effort to find you and thank you? Where has he been all this time? What has he been doing? Murdering other people?'

'Oh Fabio, you sound so cross.'

'I am! You sacrificed so much for his sake. Why didn't he look for you? A better man would have searched the entire earth until he found the girl he truly loved.'

'You think I never once thought that myself? Believe me, there were many times when I lay in bed at night crying myself to sleep that Noah could have let me down. I couldn't believe it. Not Noah. Then, when at last I had no choice but to accept he'd betrayed me, hurt turned to anger. Then bitterness.'

She fell silent and looked down at her hands; they were balled into ugly, tight fists on her lap. Even now, the pain of Noah's betrayal had the power to hurt her. Relaxing her hands, she cleared her throat. 'You sidetracked me, Fabio.

What I was going on to explain was that the morning I left Swallowsdale, after I'd drawn out all my savings from my post office account, I posted two letters, one to Noah and one to Sister Lottie.'

'Yes, I remember you saying that. Do you want another drink, by the way?'

'No more coffee for me, but a small glass of Vin Santo would be nice.'

While Fabio crossed the room to the console table behind the sofa where she kept a collection of decanters and bottles on a silver tray, Lydia thought of the letter she had written to Sister Lottie. It had been no more than a few lines to put the woman's mind at rest, explaining that after the pressure of all the exams she needed to get away from Swallowsdale for a while. The last thing Lydia had wanted was Sister Lottie worrying about her, imagining that she had been abducted and insisting the police search high and low for her. Lydia had had no such fear that her grandfather would instigate a search. But whether or not her letter would have put the old woman's mind totally at rest, Lydia didn't know. Probably not. Especially after Joey had admitted that when he'd reluctantly left Lydia standing on the pavement of Hillside Terrace, he'd driven straight to Sister Lottie's and shared with her his concerns about the kind of man Uncle Leonard really was. The news had come as a terrible shock to her, so Joey had explained to Lydia, and she'd promised him faithfully that she would do something about it. Whatever it was Sister Lottie had planned to do, Lydia would never know.

The letter she had written to Noah had been harder to write and she had worded it as carefully as she could in case it got into the wrong hands. She had prayed that he would read between the lines and understand the real message she was giving him. She'd told him that he wasn't to worry, she had it all worked out. All he had to do was trust her and everything would be OK. She'd stressed the importance of him keeping quiet and not trying to find

her. She'd also stressed just how much she loved him and that she always would.

When Fabio was back sitting next to her on the sofa, Lydia took up the story once more and explained about the letters. 'I didn't dare write again to Noah, or Sister Lottie, once I was out of the country because I was certain the police would be watching their mail, just waiting for a letter from Italy to arrive and confirm their suspicions. But when Christmas came round, Joey wrote to Sister Lottie as he would normally, except this time he wrote to say he wouldn't be returning to Swallowsdale in the summer because he and two cousins were opening a restaurant in Sorrento. Two months later, his card was returned to him with a solicitor's letter informing him that Sister Lottie was dead and that she'd left him a small amount of money in her will. She'd had a massive stroke and never recovered. I was devastated. I'd known her since I was nine and loved her like—' Lydia's voice broke off abruptly. She put down her glass and tried to compose herself. 'Sister Lottie was always so kind to me.' Her voice wavered again and she covered her mouth with her hand.

Fabio put his arm around her.

'I feel so silly,' Lydia said, trying to make light of it, 'getting so upset after all these years. But she was such a sweet innocent woman who never did a bad thing in her life. By most people's standards she was probably a bit daft, but I loved her. I loved her so much and never got the chance to say goodbye. Or thank her for everything she did for me. I've always regretted that.'

One of the things Lydia loved about Fabio was that he always managed to say and do the right thing. For now he understood that silence was what she needed and so in the welcome quiet, she rested her head companionably against his shoulder. Moments passed. On the canal below, a motorboat was puttering past and someone nearby was closing their shutters for the night. Then Fabio pressed Lydia's forgotten glass of Vin Santo into her hand. 'Here's to Sister Lottie,' he said, touching his glass against hers.

Lydia echoed his words. 'Sister Lottie.'

'And what of Noah?' he asked after she'd taken a restorative sip and was in control of her emotions again.

'I didn't dare risk sending a letter to him in Swallowsdale, so I took a gamble and sent one to Oxford, to the college he'd applied to, not knowing for sure whether he'd got in or not. I gave him an address he could reply to in Naples. I waited weeks for a reply. Then months. Nothing came. By now a year had gone by since I'd left. I tried ringing the house in Swallowsdale, and I knew I had the right number, but it was as if the line was dead. There was no ringing tone at all.'

'Weren't you tempted to go back to England to see him?'

'Only about a hundred times a day, but I was convinced I would be picked up the minute I set foot on British soil.'

'You could have slipped in the same way you left.'

'I've always believed that one shouldn't push one's luck, not when it's such a finite commodity. I'd got away with illegally leaving the country; I certainly wasn't going to try sneaking back in illegally. No, what I did next was to ask a couple of British tourists to post a letter for me when they got back. A letter to Noah in Swallowsdale with a British postmark would be safe enough, I thought. I gave them the money for the postage, but I'll never know if they posted it for me or not. Three months later when I hadn't received a reply, I tried it again with another couple from London, but still nothing. I tried phoning as well, but drew the same blank as before.'

'Why didn't you write to Donna? Didn't you trust her?'

'I thought about it, but she was always so careless about things. What if she now had a boyfriend and he got hold of the letter? I even considered writing to Valerie, if only to let her know I was safe, but decided against it. If my sister believed I was a murderer, heaven only knew how she would react to a letter from me.'

Letting out his breath, Fabio said, 'So in the end, you

did what anyone would have done in the circumstances: you gave up?'

Lydia nodded. 'Yes, I did. I had no way of getting in touch with Noah. And I suppose it was then that the anger crept in and I began to think that if Noah really wanted to get in touch with me he would have. He could have made the same leap the police did and suspected I'd come to Italy with Joey. He could have found out Joey's address from Sister Lottie, before she died, and written to him. He could have tried. It seemed so—'

'Ungrateful of him, after everything you had done?'

'Yes. Exactly. I had to accept that he'd probably weighed up the pros and cons and decided that for us to be together he would have to give up his place at university and everything else he'd planned on doing. Put simply, it was too big a sacrifice for him. He'd had a lucky escape and wanted to put it behind him and move on afresh.'

'Maybe he did write to Joey, and Joey, thinking he was protecting you, didn't pass on that letter?'

'Never. Joey knew my feelings for Noah.'

'But he also believed you were guilty of murder and could go to prison if anyone found out where you were. Perhaps he trusted you, but not Noah?'

Lydia frowned. 'In all these years, I hadn't ever thought of that. How strange.'

They both drained their glasses. 'Another?' asked Fabio.

'Not for me. You go ahead, though.'

'No, I'll pass, thanks.' He leaned back on the sofa, crossed one leg over the other and played absently with a shoelace. But then his expression became serious. He uncrossed his legs. 'Something's just hit me,' he said, looking directly at her. 'You could still be found guilty of a murder you never committed.'

Lydia slowly nodded. 'Now that is a thought that's occurred to me often over the years.'

'How can you be so calm about it?'

'I've had years to come to terms with it. I soon learned

to stop jumping out of my skin whenever there was a knock at the door.'

'But you yourself just said that luck is finite. What if it runs out for you? What then? What if the past does catch up with you?'

'Who knows what I'll do,' she said, suddenly bone-weary, despite the caffeine zapping through her bloodstream. She looked at the photographs still laid out on the table and felt the past drawing and repelling her with equal force.

'I won't let anything bad happen to you, Lydia,' Fabio said. 'I made a promise to Marcello and I intend to keep it.'

'Now you're just being melodramatic.'

At the sound of a key unlocking the front door, and voices – happy laughing voices so at odds with their solemnity – Lydia and Fabio looked at each other.

'You have to tell him you knew his father,' Fabio said as Lydia quickly gathered up the photographs. 'I won't leave until you do.'

'And I suppose you'll then want me casually to drop into the conversation, oh, and by the way, Ishmael, did you know your father's a murderer?'

'Now who's being melodramatic?'

Chapter Fifty-Two

Lydia was spared from having her hand forced by Fabio there and then because Ishmael didn't come in with Chiara; he had merely been doing the gentlemanly thing and seeing Chiara safely home. But when Fabio was putting on his coat to leave and Chiara was conveniently out of earshot, he made Lydia promise that in the next twenty-four hours she would tell Chiara what she'd shared with him.

After a night of predictably restless sleep, Lydia woke the following morning feeling heavy-headed and anxious. Putting on her dressing gown, she slowly made her way to the kitchen. Her mood wasn't helped by having to rely on a crutch again. She found Chiara making breakfast, humming along to the radio, her head and shoulders moving in time to the music, an aura of happiness bouncing off her like sunlight on a spring day.

'I thought I'd cook something special for us tonight,' Chiara said when she saw her. 'If it's OK with you, I'd like to invite Ishmael to join us. Are you all right, Lydia? You don't look so good. Is your ankle very bad again? Uncle Fabio told me about you and the stepladder. Honestly, what on earth did you think you were doing?'

'Heavens! You're chirrupy this morning. Can I have a cup of tea before I submit myself to any further questions? Do you mind if we don't have the radio on?'

Chiara was all smiles. 'Of course. Sorry. Sit down and I'll make you some breakfast. What would you like? Some fruit?'

'Just tea, please.'

Humming to herself again, Chiara finished putting her breakfast together and finally sat down. 'So what do you think about Ishmael joining us for dinner tonight? I thought I'd make your favourite *spaghetti con le vongole*. We could invite Uncle Fabio and Paolo.' Her face dropped. Always an intuitive child, she said, 'What's wrong?'

'Nothing's wrong. Why would you think that?'

'There is something; I can see it in your face. You're worried about something. Is it me? Have I done something to upset you? Have I been too bossy about making you stay away from work?'

Lydia smiled. 'No, Chiara, it's nothing to do with work or you bossing me about. But that will have to stop, you know.'

Dipping a spoon into her pot of yogurt, Chiara smiled, too. 'You're the boss.' Then more seriously, clearly not prepared to let the matter drop, she said, 'So what is worrying you?'

Stalling for time and hoping against all the odds that the answer to her question might let her off the hook, Lydia poked at the slice of lemon floating on the surface of her tea. 'Just how fond of Ishmael are you?' she asked. If there was a chance of Chiara and Ishmael's relationship fizzling out any time soon, then Lydia would never need to take things further. Everything could go back to how it was.

'What does that have to do with anything?' Chiara asked warily.

More than you can imagine, Lydia thought. 'Please, just answer the question. I know it's early days and you really hardly know each other, but do you think it's serious between the two of you?'

Chiara put down her yogurt. 'Yes,' she said. 'Very serious. I've never felt this way about anyone before.' She smiled and relaxed a little. 'We both feel like we've always known each other. It's quite extraordinary.'

'In that case, I have to tell you that I'm one hundred per cent sure I knew his father.'

'Really?' Chiara leaned forward, her elbows resting on

the table. 'How amazing. But how can you be so sure?'

It was time to bring out the photographic evidence. 'In my bedside table drawer, there's an envelope with some photos inside. Could you get them for me, please? When you see them, you'll understand my reaction last night.'

As soon as Chiara had the photographs in her hands, she let out a whistle. 'Now I see why you were acting so strangely. It really could be Ishmael, couldn't it?'

'I didn't tell you before, but Ishmael's the reason I hurt my ankle. I saw him in the crowd and was so stunned I lost my footing.'

'Tell me about the man he looks like.'

'We met at school when we were nine years old. We became inseparable. Like brother and sister. But that changed when we were older ... when we were teenagers ... then our relationship became ... became something else.' Lydia stumbled clumsily over her words. How could she possibly describe what she and Noah had meant to each other in so few inadequate words?

Chiara came to her rescue. Her eyes shining, her expression animated, she said, 'Did you fall in love? Were you lovers?'

Lydia nodded. 'We thought nothing in the world would ever part us.'

'But that's so fantastic!' Chiara cried, her whole demeanour that of a girl newly in love and wanting everyone else to be in love, too. 'How wonderful. If it's true, of course, and Ishmael really is the son of this man you knew.' She looked again at the photograph of Noah on his own. 'But it has to be true. It can't be a coincidence. What a fabulously romantic story!'

Romantic was not the word Lydia could bring herself to use. 'It's not as straightforward as you think, Chiara. There's more to it than that. Ishmael's father and I haven't seen one another since we were eighteen.'

'Why? Did you have a row and a huge falling-out?'

'No. We never argued, we—'

'You're not ... you're not going to tell me Ishmael is—'

Chiara's eyes were wide now. 'He's not your son, is he? A love child you had to give away because you were too young to keep him? Not that that would make any difference to Ishmael and me. It's not as if you and I are blood related.'

Lydia swallowed back the sting of Chiara's remark. She knew Chiara didn't intend any offence, yet nonetheless she couldn't help but feel like she'd only ever been a caretaker mother. But for Chiara to blurt out such a comment meant that the connection she and Ishmael had was real. Lydia knew she hadn't imagined the closeness between them when she'd watched them leaving the apartment together last night. 'No, Chiara,' Lydia said calmly, glad that there was at least one concern she could put to rest, 'Ishmael is definitely not my son. He wasn't a love child I had to give away.'

'So why do you look so miserable? I'd have thought this was something to make you happy. We explain everything to Ishmael and he'll put you in touch with your long-lost love. What could be more exciting and romantic?'

Lydia was about to suggest that Ishmael's mother may have something less enthusiastic to say on the matter, when Chiara's mobile trilled inside her handbag on the other side of the kitchen. She went to it.

'It's a text from Ishmael,' she said, her lovely face blushing with a happy smile. Back at the table, still smiling, she glanced at her watch. 'Hey, I must dash! I want to get to work early so I can leave early this afternoon to shop for tonight's meal. I'll give Fabio and Paolo a call. I can't wait to tell Ishmael everything.' She drained her coffee cup in a single gulp, then kissed Lydia on the cheek. 'I'll ring you during the day.'

Would there have been any point in making Chiara promise not to say anything to Ishmael? Lydia asked herself when once again she was listening to the sound of Chiara's departing footsteps on the stairs.

No. Why not sit back now and see what happened next?

It seemed she was at the centre of a situation over which she had no control.

For the rest of the day, Lydia was on tenterhooks. She was dreading the evening ahead. She couldn't imagine how she would survive the small talk she would have to endure with Noah's son. There would be endless cross-referencing while all the time Fabio would be wanting to chip in impatiently and say, '*Sì sì*, that's all very well, but what about Uncle Leonard?'

A little after lunchtime, while she was testing her ankle to see if she could walk without the aid of her crutch – and finding to her annoyance that she couldn't – the phone rang: it was Chiara. 'I've just been talking with Ishmael and there's been a change of plan for this evening,' she said. 'Ishmael and I are going out for dinner instead. You're not disappointed, are you?'

'Not at all,' Lydia replied, although perversely she was. 'Did you say anything to him about me knowing his father?'

'No, I'm saving it for when we're alone. Anyway, I can't chat for long, I've got someone to show round an apartment in ten minutes. Don't wait up for me tonight.'

'Won't you be back to change for dinner?'

'No, Ishmael's meeting me straight from work. *Ciao, ciao*.'

The rest of the day stretched out long and tediously for Lydia. She tried ringing round a few friends, but no one was at home. They were all out Christmas shopping, she supposed.

After a brief, unintentional nap – not surprising really, considering the bad night she'd had – she woke to find the apartment in darkness. It was nearly six o'clock. Now she had only the evening to get through.

Up on her feet, she negotiated her way round the room carefully, switching on lamps then going over to the windows to draw the curtains. Since Marcello had died,

seldom did she close the shutters as well. She didn't like to shut out too much of the world.

Desperate for some kind of company, she flicked through the TV channels for something to while away the time until she went to bed. Nothing. She then resorted to the phone once more and tapped in Fabio and Paolo's number. Irritatingly, all she got was their voicemail. She tutted. Why was everyone busy except her?

When the front door bell rang, she could have whooped with delight. Saved! Company! And not just any old company – it was probably Fabio here to check up on the promise he'd forced her to make. More fool him. She would hold him captive now for the rest of the evening. Better still, maybe he'd brought Paolo with him.

She went out to the hall, registering that either the main door downstairs had been left open, or one of her neighbours must have let Fabio in. Leaning on her crutch, she turned the lock and pulled open the door.

For an eternity they both stared at each other. It couldn't be. It wasn't possible. Her brain was playing games with her. If she closed the door and opened it again, he would be gone. A figment of her imagination.

'Lyddie,' he said.

She swallowed. 'Noah.'

Chapter Fifty-Three

'Is this when I faint?' she asked.

'I was wondering the same thing myself.'

'In that case you'd better come in.'

He stepped inside and at once she noticed his limp was more pronounced than she remembered and that he carried an elegant silver-topped walking cane. She closed the door and again they stood and stared at each other.

'Snap,' he said, indicating her crutch with his cane.

'I fell,' she said. 'I wasn't looking where I was going.'

'The way I heard it, my son is to blame. I hope you've taken him to task.'

She blinked, then shook her head as if it would make everything clearer. 'I'm sorry,' she said. 'I can't take this in. I need to sit down. Then you have to explain what's going on. How, after all these years, you appear from nowhere on my doorstep.'

He followed her through to the sitting room. She pointed to a chair, but he said, 'If you don't mind, I'd prefer to move around.' He made it sound like he preferred to be a moving target rather than a sitting one.

'At least take off your scarf and coat.'

When he'd removed his coat she could see he still had the same slim build that would compel every Italian *mama* to feed him up. She took his things from him and laid them over the back of a chair, noting that the black woollen coat was beautifully made. Cashmere. Expensive. A far cry from the stiff-as-cardboard jumble sale greatcoat she'd once bought him.

She sat down and tried to pull herself together. If

anything, the shock of seeing him was gaining momentum. 'Twenty-eight years,' she managed to say, 'and you look the same. Different. But the same. If that makes any sense.'

'And you've proved my uncle's prediction absolutely right. You're even more beautiful.'

'Uncle Brad,' she repeated in a small, dazed voice. 'How is he?'

'Living in the south of France with the latest love of his life and still behaving disgracefully. He knocks out an occasional painting when the mood takes him, which isn't very often. He's seventy-two now. Can you believe it?'

'I can believe that more than I can believe I'm looking at you right now.'

Noah prodded at the rug with his cane. 'Nice segue. I suppose it's time to ditch the small talk, isn't it?' He moved stiffly over to one of the windows, then turned to face her. 'Ishmael called me this morning. He told me about a girl he'd met here called Chiara and that her English stepmother was called Lydia. He then asked me if I'd known a Lydia when I was a child, because apparently this Lydia said she'd grown up with a boy called Noah Solomon. I didn't doubt for a second who he was talking about. I'm sorry, but from that moment on, only an apocalypse would have stopped me from coming straight here. Once I knew there was a flight I could get on, I rang Ishmael to meet me at this end. He did, along with your stepdaughter. Don't be cross, but Chiara was the one who suggested I surprise you like this. I wanted to ring you, to give you time to prepare yourself, but Chiara wouldn't hear of it.' He smiled ruefully and went and stood in front of the fireplace. 'She seemed to think it would be more romantic this way.'

'You'll have to excuse her. Her head's full of romantic nonsense just now.'

'If I'm honest, I was frightened that if I did call you first, you might disappear before I got here.'

'Why would I do that?'

'Because ...' He shrugged, and ran a hand through his

hair, oblivious to the fact that it was now all messed up. 'Because I can't believe that after all this time, it could really happen. That we'd be in the same room again.'

He looks so young still, Lydia found herself thinking. And just as handsome. Her hands began to itch to smooth out his ruffled hair and she was reminded of all the times in that other life when she had done exactly that.

'What?' he said.

'Sorry?'

'You're looking at me strangely.'

She relaxed a tiny bit and smiled. 'Take a look in the mirror behind you.'

He spun round and looked at his reflection in the mirror above the mantelpiece. 'Ah, I see what you mean.' He did the necessary and faced her again. 'I think it's fair to say I haven't improved much. I'm about as sartorially aware as a chipmunk.' He raised his walking cane. 'Ishmael bought this for me with the idea it would help to sharpen up my act. He calls it my Jack the Ripper accessory, and then has the nerve to accuse me of having a sick sense of humour.'

'You always had your own look,' she said, taking in the white T-shirt beneath the grey V-neck sweater, and the black jeans rumpled at the knees.

'So did you.'

'Have we reverted to small talk again?'

'It's bound to happen.'

'Perhaps a drink will help.' She levered herself up from the sofa. 'Wine? Or something with more kick?'

'Actually, I don't drink these days.'

'Oh?'

'I had a problem with it for a time.'

'When?'

'When you left Swallowsdale. Or more precisely, when I was finally discharged from hospital.'

They were sitting at the kitchen table now, two omelettes in front of them, as well as a bowl of salad and a bottle of Pellegrino.

Whilst Lydia had prepared their meal, she had asked Noah to stay in the sitting room and listen to some music. She had needed time alone to try and gather her thoughts and steady her nerves. Even without his presence in the kitchen, she had still been a mess. Twice she'd nearly taken the end off a finger when she was slicing the tomatoes. The second time she'd cursed loudly and dropped the knife with a clatter. 'Everything all right?' he'd asked, coming into the kitchen.

'It's nothing,' she'd said, flustered. 'I was being careless.'

'Let me see.'

Embarrassed, she'd held out her hand. 'It's nothing,' she repeated, despite the evidence to the contrary. Blood had already dripped onto her bandaged ankle.

He ripped off a square of kitchen roll, folded it in half and in half again, then wrapped it tightly around her finger. 'Where do you keep the plasters?'

'In the drawer behind you.'

As he bent over her hand to apply the plaster, Lydia had to hold her breath. It was the smell and touch of him. It suddenly made him more real to her. This was no dream. He was really here.

When he'd dealt with her finger, he stooped to pick up the knife she'd dropped. He handed it to her and for a moment, their eyes met. Was he, like her, remembering that night in the dell?

Neither of them said anything. He left her to get their meal ready and only reappeared when she called him.

Sitting opposite him now she was reacquainting herself with his face. She knew a lot of men who, by their mid-forties, had grown paunchy with age and good living; they had developed jowls and lost the distinctive sharpness of their youthful looks. Everything became a little blurred and faded. But not Noah. He had somehow defied the passing of years. There were lines at the corners of his eyes, and a smattering of grey hairs, but if anything, his features were sharper and more defined. His eyebrows were just as

expressive, still perfectly arched, giving him that slightly puzzled expression. Life had not been too harsh for him, she concluded. He looked well. But then she remembered what he'd said earlier, about alcohol having been a problem for him for a time, and that he'd been in hospital.

'How's the finger?' he asked, interrupting her thoughts.

'It's OK,' she lied. It was actually throbbing quite painfully, but there were more important matters to discuss. 'Tell me about the drinking. What made you start? You'd always been so anti. You used to say you hated what it did to your uncle.'

He put down his knife and fork and flung himself back in the chair. 'What a sanctimonious prig I was.'

'You were never that.'

'Oh, yes I was. Uncle Brad drank and used drugs because he needed to escape. Turned out, when push came to shove, that was what I needed to do as well.'

It made sense to Lydia. He'd murdered someone – why wouldn't he want to escape the guilt of what he'd done by drowning his sorrows in the bottom of a glass? But it was much too soon to voice such an opinion. Though how they were ever going to discuss what he'd done that night, she didn't know. Would he expect her to say 'thank you' after all these years? *Thank you, Noah, for wanting to protect me by killing Uncle Leonard. Thank you for screwing up the rest of our lives.*

There it was again. The bitter pain of his betrayal.

'You mentioned you'd been in hospital,' she said, reining in her hostility. 'What was that for?'

He opened his mouth to say something, but then frowned and massaged his temple. 'Sorry to change the subject, but do you have any paracetamol?' he asked.

She went to the same drawer where she kept the plasters, and handed him a packet. He popped two out and downed them with a gulp of water, his head tipped back. At the sight of the smooth, pale skin at his throat, she felt a strong compulsion to put her arms around him.

Stunned that she could feel anything like that for him

still, she sat down quickly, hoping he hadn't noticed, and resumed eating. Noah didn't. He rested his elbows on the table, steepled his hands together, his long slender fingers neatly entwined, and said, 'I'll explain about my stay in hospital later. If you remember I was always a tedious pedant. I haven't changed, so I'll stick to the chronological order of events, if that's OK with you. I spent the journey here trying to remember exactly how things happened.'

If she hadn't known where the conversation would lead them, she would have smiled at his description of himself. 'Nothing wrong in being a stickler for detail,' she said lightly. 'Go on.'

'It all started that awful afternoon when I'd tried to take your uncle on and then your grandfather appeared and you insisted I went home. God, if I'd known what was to follow, I'd never have listened to you. I would have stayed and ...' He paused, breathed in deeply and exhaled with a weary sigh. 'Sorry, no point in stating the obvious, is there? Anyway, I reluctantly drove home, and when I got there I was all over the place. I couldn't stop thinking how I'd never forgive myself if that man did anything else to you. I wanted to get in my car again and drive straight back to you. But instead, and this was when I made the biggest and worst mistake of my entire life, I decided that what I needed was something to calm me down. A glass or two of whatever my uncle currently had stocked in the house. Just something to take the edge off things.'

The corners of his mouth curved into an expression of scathing self-reproach. 'It certainly did that,' he said. Suddenly fidgety, he covered his face, then rubbed his chin. 'My memory's a bit hazy on some of the details of what happened next,' he continued, 'but I do remember that once I'd started, knowing that my uncle wasn't due back from London until the following day, I decided that what I really needed was total oblivion. So I set to with a vengeance. I was on a mission to drink myself into as deep a comatose state as I could. Anything that would take

away the shame of not being able to protect you in the way I'd wanted to. For having failed you so spectacularly. You know, I hadn't appreciated until then just what a proud idiot I was. At some point during all the drinking, I decided I wanted to listen to a record that was in my room. I remember very clearly staggering to the top of the stairs and feeling ridiculously infallible when I got there. I was capable of anything, I thought. Now I could really take on that scumbag and prove myself to the girl I loved.' He paused again and took a long drink from his glass of water.

Lydia felt sick. She wanted to hear the rest of what he had to say, but at the same time she didn't. To hear Noah confess to what he'd done that night was too much.

'So there I was,' Noah went on, 'at the top of the stairs, when I remembered I was supposed to be meeting you in the dell. I had no idea what time it was and as I moved my arm to look at my watch, I somehow lost my balance. The next memory I have is waking up in hospital with Uncle Brad dozing in a chair by the side of my bed. Turned out he'd had a lousy time in London and came home a day early. He rolled up just after eleven o'clock and found me lying unconscious at the bottom of the stairs. Apparently I was lucky not to have broken my neck. As it was, and it was sod's law of course, I'd shattered my already wrecked leg and was on traction for several months afterwards. I've got these metal pins now. Lyddie? You're staring at me again. What is it?'

'But what about—' Lydia stopped herself short. What if he was demonstrating a classic example of selective memory? Was he in denial? Had his brain conveniently put a block on that gruesome part of the night?

'Lyddie,' he repeated. 'What is it? Tell me.'

'But that can't be right. You went to the dell at midnight. Just as we'd arranged.'

An expression of sad regret passed across his face. 'I only wish I had.'

'But you went,' she asserted. 'You went there to meet me at *midnight*.'

He shook his head slowly. 'I didn't. I couldn't have found my way to the back door, never mind to the dell. As I just said, Uncle Brad found me unconscious at the bottom of the stairs a little after eleven.'

'But that's not possible. You were *there*.' Lydia's voice was rising with impatience. How dare he sit here twenty-eight years later and rewrite history!

Once more he shook his head. 'I can't tell you how many times I wished I had gone to meet you. If only I hadn't got drunk, everything would have been so different. That bastard wouldn't have attacked you and you wouldn't have needed to—'

'Needed to do what?' she said when he left the words hanging.

He met her gaze. 'Defend yourself, Lyddie. I just wish you hadn't run off like that without me. I would have gone with you. I'd have done anything you asked. *Anything*.'

Lydia felt like she was drowning in a sea of confusion. None of this was making sense. 'But I didn't do it, Noah. *You* did it. You just don't remember.' She could feel herself shaking. '*You* killed my uncle. Not me.'

He looked baffled. 'But when the police questioned me in hospital, they said they were looking for you. They said there was evidence. It was in the papers.'

Exasperated, Lydia banged her hand down on the table. 'This is how it happened! OK? I overslept. I got to the dell much later than we'd arranged. I found the body. I then put the evidence there to make the police think I had done it.'

'Why? Why would you do that?'

'So they wouldn't think you did it, of course! I covered up for you.'

'But I keep telling you, I didn't do it.' He raked his hands through his hair. 'I couldn't have done it. I swear it.'

'But if you didn't do it, and I know I certainly didn't, who the hell did?'

*

Their omelettes practically untouched, they moved back into the sitting room. Lydia was shivering. 'Here, let me put this around you,' Noah said.

She gratefully accepted the offer of his coat. He sat next to her on the sofa, took her hands in his and rubbed them gently as if to warm them. 'I'm not cold,' she said. 'It's shock.'

'I know,' he said. 'But this gives me something to do while I try and make sense of what you've just told me.'

'I can't believe it,' Lydia murmured. 'I just can't believe it. All this time, you thought I had killed Uncle Leonard.'

'I thought it from the minute I read of the murder in the local paper when I was in hospital. That and your letter, which Uncle Brad eventually brought in for me. He'd forgotten all about the mail piling up at the house and when he got around to bringing me your letter, the local paper was rife with the story of your uncle's body found in the dell and that you were missing and the police wanted to talk to you to help them, as they put it, with their inquiries. He must have recognized your writing and had his suspicions because when he gave me the letter, he said, "Better not let anyone else read it. Keep it hidden. Better still, throw it away afterwards."'

'Do you think he'd steamed it open and read it for himself?'

'Not a hope. Uncle Brad is many things, but he's not a sneak. Do you want to know how I got rid of it?'

She nodded.

'I ate it.'

In spite of everything – in spite of feeling she was hopelessly adrift, that a lifetime of belief had just been swept away – Lydia laughed.

'How else was I to destroy what the police might have thought was important evidence, when I was stuck in bed?'

'So you read the letter and thought what?'

'Relief, initially. It explained why your grandfather had

told Uncle Brad he didn't know where you were when I got him to ring you to tell you I was stuck in hospital. I'd been worried sick something had happened to you. Then it hit me. You were in big trouble. You'd as good as admitted to killing your uncle. You said you had everything all worked out, that I had to keep quiet and trust you. And most importantly, I wasn't to try and look for you.'

'No! That wasn't what I meant. What I was trying to say, without coming right out with it in case someone else read the letter, was that I knew what you'd done and why and that I had it all under control. That so long as you didn't say or do anything, the police would think I did it and you'd be safe. I was protecting you.'

'What would you have done if the police had found you?'

'That was my Plan B. I would have stuck to the story that Uncle Leonard had attacked me and it had been self-defence.'

'Oh, God, Lyddie. You were prepared to do that for me?'

'Without a second thought.' *Would you have done the same for me?* was on the tip of her tongue, but she didn't dare ask him.

He lowered his head and pressed the palms of his hands against his eyes. 'Sorry,' he said, when he looked up. 'I can't seem to shift this headache. Could I have some more water, please?'

She fetched his glass from the kitchen and handed it to him. 'Why didn't you answer any of my letters?' she asked.

'What letters?'

'The ones I sent to Swallowsdale. And the one I sent to the college in Oxford you'd been offered a place at.'

'I never made it to Oxford. I was discharged from hospital at the end of the summer and that's when I hit the booze. I blamed myself for everything. I should have been able to prevent what had happened. Every day I didn't hear from you was another day I blamed and tormented

myself some more and drank some more. By the time I was supposed to take up my place at Oxford I was completely off the rails. The only way I could function was to hit the vodka bottle when I got up in the morning, although it was usually afternoon by the time I surfaced, and then it was a full-time job keeping the levels topped up throughout the rest of the day.'

'Didn't Uncle Brad step in?'

'He tried for a bit, but he was busy down in London. Then one day he announced that he was madly in love with a poet from Cork and he was selling the house and we were moving to Ireland. I think he had some half-cocked notion that the change of scene would do me good. The last thing I wanted was to leave Swallowsdale. I was desperately hanging onto the hope that you might come back. But my uncle insisted. So off we went. Needless to say, he didn't stay madly in love for long, and for about a year we were constantly on the move, going from one place to another. We were like gypsies.'

'Well, that explains why you never got any of my letters.'

'Uncle Brad had organized for our mail to be forwarded, but since we never stopped anywhere very long, there was little chance of it ever catching up with us.'

'I used to hope you'd guess exactly what I'd done and come and find me.'

'I'm sorry, but I was too mired in my own misery to figure out anything useful. I'd even started to think that you were dead. That was when I wished I was dead too. Then occasionally I had drunken moments of bravado when I imagined tracking you down, but then I would sober up and remember your letter. Your instructions were very explicit. I was terrified of doing the wrong thing and leading the police to you.'

'Can you remember when Uncle Leonard's body was discovered?'

'Not exactly. But it must have been nearly a fortnight after you'd disappeared. Shortly afterwards two policemen

came to visit me in hospital. They kept saying how important it was that they found you. They claimed they had compelling evidence that you'd been in some sort of a struggle with your uncle in the dell before he died. I had no idea what evidence they were talking about, but I did my best to convince them they'd got it wrong. I lied and said that, yes, you had been in a struggle with your uncle, but it had taken place that afternoon when I'd turned up at your house, and that was why I'd threatened to kill him, just as your neighbours had told the police. With no one to dispute what I'd said, I just hoped I'd given them something that might help to put you in the clear, or at least distract them. What sort of evidence had you left for the police to find?'

'My skin under Uncle Leonard's nails and some strands of hair. Did it say in the paper who found the body?'

Noah took hold of her hands again, as though she needed to be prepared for yet another shock. 'Yes,' he said. 'It was your sister.'

Chapter Fifty-Four

Valerie. She would be forty now. A grown woman. Married? With children? Still having mystical visions? Lydia had no idea. Yet for peace of mind, and to assuage her guilt for having abandoned Valerie in the way she had, Lydia had to believe that against all the odds, her sister had gone on to live a happy and fulfilling life. The guilt ran deep, though. Not only had she chosen Noah over and above her sister's needs, Lydia had never once in all the years that followed tried to make contact with Valerie. Selfishly, for self-preservation, she had needed to cut the tie. To look back would have given her hope for something that could never be. False hope, as she'd learned, was too costly. It was better to start afresh. To be someone new.

But now Lydia had the added guilt of knowing that her twelve-year-old sister had been the one to discover Uncle Leonard's decomposing body. What further harm could that have done to the poor girl's already fragile state of mind?

'It's not your fault, Lyddie,' Noah said, still holding her hands. She hadn't said a word, hadn't voiced what was in her head, yet he had known what her reaction would be.

'I think I'd like to be alone now,' she said.

He didn't argue with her, merely hauled himself to his feet. 'Of course,' he said.

Grateful for his understanding, she passed him his coat. 'Presumably you're staying with Ishmael?'

'Yes.'

'Will you be able to find your way to the apartment? Venice is a very disorientating place.'

'Not unlike the past,' he said. 'But don't worry. I'll be fine. I have a map.'

At the front door, she watched him doing the buttons up on his coat and suddenly thought of something. 'Have you ever been to Venice before?' she asked.

He shook his head. 'No. It's my first time.'

She allowed herself a secret smile of satisfaction. 'I thought so.'

'Why?'

'I would have known. That's all.'

His gaze held hers and he put a hand out to her arm. 'Can I come back tomorrow? There's still so much more we have to say.'

'Of course. And I'm sorry I'm kicking you out now. It's just that I don't think I'm capable of another coherent thought tonight.'

He increased the pressure on her arm and dipped his head, just the merest hint of movement as if he was going to kiss her, but then he drew back. 'Good night, Lyddie,' he said. 'Sleep well.'

'I doubt I will.'

'Me neither.'

She stood at the window, holding the curtain to one side as she watched him appear on the *fondamenta* below. Again he must have known what she would do and standing in the glow of the street lamp, pausing to tighten his scarf around his neck and to turn up his collar against the cold, he raised his gaze and saw her. He acknowledged her with a small smile and went on his way.

She stayed watching him until he'd vanished out of sight. A profound sense of loss came over her and she felt compelled to open the window and call after him. What if he disappeared in the night and she never saw him again?

She went straight to bed with the intention of pretending she was asleep when Chiara came home. She wasn't capable of dealing with the level of interrogation Chiara would want to pursue. It could keep until morning.

*

As it turned out, she didn't need to fake sleep. She was dead to the world until she became conscious of someone moving around in her room. She heard the swish of curtains being parted, followed by sunlight pouring in. 'I've brought you a cup of tea,' said Chiara.

'What time is it?' Lydia asked with a groggy groan. She felt like she'd been drugged.

'It's half past nine.'

Lydia roused herself into a sitting position. 'But it can't be. I can't have slept so long.' Bleary-eyed, she checked her alarm clock; sure enough it was nine thirty.

'I looked in on you when I got home last night,' Chiara said, settling herself on the bed, 'and you were fast asleep. I must say, I was very disappointed. I was looking forward to a chat.'

'I bet you were.'

Chiara smiled. 'Well? How did it go?'

'For a start you've been a very devious girl, haven't you? You told several whopping great lies yesterday; all that stuff about there being a change of plan. What an understatement! Presumably you and Ishmael cooked the whole thing up between you. It was probably you who let Noah in downstairs, wasn't it?'

'Guilty of every accusation. You're not cross, are you?'

'Not exactly. But it was a huge shock.'

'A good one?'

Lydia sipped her tea thoughtfully. 'I don't know yet.'

'He seemed lovely. A bit serious, maybe, but very handsome. Ishmael really is the spitting image of him, isn't he?'

'No doubt about that.' Then registering Chiara wasn't dressed, Lydia said, 'Shouldn't you be getting ready for work?'

'It's Saturday. Which means I'm going to sit here on your bed until you've told me everything about last night.'

'No! ... You thought he was a murderer all these years! ... You ran away! ... You left everything for him! ... You put yourself at risk of being sent to prison! ... *No!*'

Jumping up and down, twirling round on the spot, and flinging her arms in the air, Chiara was a whirlwind of typically over-the-top Italian reaction to Lydia's story. She finally came to rest and perched on the edge of the bed, and spoke the first calm, reasoned words since Lydia had started speaking. 'Did my father know any of this?' she asked.

'No. But I think he always knew deep down that there was something I was hiding from him. And it's important that you know I never actually lied to your father. He just never asked the kind of questions that would have forced me to lie to him.'

Chiara's face was pensive. 'Which suggests that he did suspect something, but loved you so much he didn't want to ruin things. He accepted you as he saw you.'

Lydia nodded sadly. 'He was a wonderful man who always tried to take others at face value.'

'Uncle Fabio says he was one of the most honourable men he knew.'

'Your uncle's right. Maybe that was what I was attracted to in the first place. Perhaps I was hoping his decency would rub off on me.'

Chiara frowned. 'Why would you, of all people, think that?'

'Because in the early days, long before I came to Venice, the thing I hated most about myself was the lie I was living, not being able to be honest and be the real me.'

'I don't understand.'

'By coming to live in Italy I had to lose my true identity. I'd been living illegally in the country for nearly two years when Joey decided it was time to get my paperwork in order. So, through a friend of a friend in Naples where, as we both know, just about anything can be arranged, a new passport was organized for me, as well as all the other official documents I needed in order to stay in the country legally.'

'Is Lydia your real name?'

'Oh, yes, I kept that, but on my passport it's my middle

name. Before I married Marcello, I was officially Teresa Lydia Jones. If ever I had to explain this to anyone, your father included, I said that I preferred to use my middle name.'

Suddenly concerned by what Chiara might be thinking, Lydia said, 'Are you very shocked by what I've told you? Do you feel I've conned you in some way? That I'm not the woman you thought I was?'

Chiara smiled. 'Not at all. You've been a fantastic mother and friend to me. Nothing could ever change that.'

With tears in her eyes, Lydia leaned forward and hugged Chiara. 'I couldn't bear to lose your love and respect,' she said. 'Or your friendship.'

After telephoning ahead, Noah and Ishmael arrived together just before midday. Seeing the two of them standing side by side, Lydia was rendered speechless. For longer than was polite, she openly stared at them. 'Now I know what it feels like to be a museum exhibit,' Ishmael joked.

Leaving Ishmael and Chiara to chat, Noah came over to where Lydia was standing at the window. 'How are you feeling?' he asked.

'I'm OK, thank you. How about you? Did you sleep?'

'Not a wink. I kept thinking that if I did sleep I'd wake up and find yesterday was a dream and that you were still lost to me.'

'I thought the same when I watched you walk away last night.'

He was standing very close to her. Mixed in with the light scent of his aftershave, she could smell the tangy, crisp winter air on his coat. It made her long to be outside.

'I hope you don't mind,' he said, 'but I've told Ishmael everything.'

'Chiara also knows the whole story now.'

At the sound of their names being mentioned, Chiara and Ishmael glanced over at them. Chiara said, 'What do you want to do about lunch, Lydia? Shall I cook us something?'

Seized with the desire to be anywhere but stuck indoors, Lydia said, 'Why don't you two do your own thing? Seeing as it's the first fine day we've had in ages, it's time for me to tackle the stairs. I'll go stir-crazy if I don't have some fresh air and a change of scene. I promise I'll take it steadily,' she added when she saw the warning expression on Chiara's face. 'Noah will help me, won't you?'

Noah was complicit, and with a hand placed at her elbow, he helped Lydia make her escape. It took them for ever to cover the short distance down to the Zattere, and once there Lydia sank gratefully into a chair at one of the open-air cafés. With their chairs facing the bright December sun, sunglasses firmly in place, Noah said, 'You haven't changed at all, have you? You're as single-minded and determined as ever.'

'I'll probably end up paying for it later when my ankle swells to the size of a football, but for now, this is blissful. You're not too cold, are you?'

'Not at all.' He looked around them. 'It's a popular place, by the looks of things.'

Most of the clientele were smartly dressed Italians; many of the women were wearing full-length fur coats. Her voice low, Lydia said, 'It's a bit of a tourist catch, but on a day like today I don't care. I love to do all the things the snobby purists say you're not supposed to do in Venice.' Seeing a waiter approaching and thinking of what Noah had told her last night, she said, 'Do you mind if I have a glass of Prosecco?'

'Please, go ahead. Have whatever you want. I'll have some hot chocolate.'

Their drinks ordered and delivered to the table, the conversation went the only way it could, with Lydia recounting her life in Naples. 'I then moved to Sorrento, where Joey had opened a restaurant with some cousins,' she explained. 'I worked for him for about three years, then decided it was time to go my own way. I went to Positano, where I got a job working in a hotel and taught

394

English as a sideline. Before long I was teaching English full-time.'

'God only knows you must have had so many regrets, effectively living in exile as you were, and I don't mean to sound insensitive, but did you particularly regret missing out on university? It was such an important goal for you.'

'I never allowed myself to go down that road. I channelled all my energy into sustaining the new life I was creating for myself.'

'And Joey? Are you still in touch with him?'

'Not as much as either of us would like, what with all our commitments, but yes, we talk on the phone now and then. He's married with five children and a grandchild on the way. He owns three restaurants now. I don't suppose you even knew the reason why he had to rush back to Italy so suddenly.'

Noah shook his head.

'His mother had had a heart attack and he dropped everything to get home to her. She not only survived, but is still alive and looking forward to being a great-grandmother.'

An elderly couple with a small dog dressed in a tartan overcoat came and sat at the table nearest to them. When they were settled, Noah said, 'So if it hadn't been for Joey's mother, you wouldn't be here in Italy, would you?'

Lydia stared up at the faultless blue sky; it seemed wonderfully infinite and crystalline, Venetian through and through. This place was so very much home to her. 'Who knows where I would have gone if it hadn't been for Joey's mother,' she said thoughtfully.

'And Positano? How long did you stay there?'

'Oh, for years. Long enough to put down some tentative roots.'

'A man?'

She nodded, aware that Noah was staring hard into his empty cup.

'Did you marry him?'

'He asked me, but that was my cue to start running.

395

Until I met Chiara's father I'd been happy to keep things on a fairly superficial level.'

'Did you leave Positano to come here to Venice?' Through his sunglasses, Noah's gaze was now back on hers.

'No, I went to Sardinia, followed by a brief spell in Rome and then I came here. I've always found work easy to find, whether it's been teaching English, reception work, working as a guide, or doing translation. I've enjoyed the variety. I particularly enjoy what I'm doing now. Chiara's father and I started the agency together.' She turned to look out across the glittering water towards the church of the Redentore where every July she and Marcello used to light a candle along with all their friends and family. 'We were a good team,' she said wistfully. 'He died of a heart attack four years ago. I still miss him.'

'I'm sorry,' Noah said. 'I'm truly sorry that you found happiness, only to have it snatched away.'

Her eyes still on the church across the water, she said, 'Sometimes I think he made me happier than I deserved.'

'That sounds like you're being too hard on yourself.'

'I'm afraid it's true. I never really gave Marcello the whole of me. I always held something back.' She slowly turned and looked straight at Noah. 'I did it once before, handed my heart over, and look where it got me.'

For a few moments, Noah considered the paper serviette in his hands, folded it carefully, then laid it aside on the table. 'How different it could all have been, Lyddie. If only—'

She raised her hand to stop him, suddenly finding it too painful to think what might have been. 'Please, don't say it. Instead, fill me in on what you've done with your life. And your wife. What does she think about you coming here to Venice without her?'

'I don't have a wife.'

'Yes you do, Ishmael's mother.'

'She's my *ex*-wife, Lyddie. We divorced six years ago.'

'Oh. And you haven't remarried?'

He stared at her steadily, her face reflected in his sunglasses. 'No,' he said. 'I've been extremely wary about making another mistake. I married Ishmael's mother for all the wrong reasons. I wasn't a good husband to her. I wasn't a terrible husband, just not a very good one.'

'For ages after I left Swallowsdale I used to have this recurring dream that I would come back to England and discover that you'd just got married.'

'To anyone in particular?'

Lydia chewed on her lip and watched a *vaporetto* pull away from the nearby landing stage. What if by saying the name she made it true? Don't be ridiculous, she told herself. And so what if Noah had found solace in her arms? 'It was someone from school,' she said. 'Maybe you don't remember her. Her name was Zoe Woolf.'

Noah pushed his cup to one side and leaning in close, removed first his sunglasses, then Lydia's. 'I think that would be a coincidence too far, don't you?' He put his hand to her cheek, and kept it there. 'For all these years, I've felt your presence in my subconscious. Sometimes it was in my dreams. Sometimes it was when I heard a song from when we were growing up. And sometimes it was in the fleeting glance of a stranger or a gesture. I tried to forget you. I tried so hard. But you were always there, giving me hope that one day I would be able to do this.' His hand moved to her chin, tilted her mouth towards his, and very tenderly, he kissed her on the lips.

It was as if they'd never spent a day apart.

Chapter Fifty-Five

They ordered something to eat, neither of them caring what it was. It was merely fuel. Something to occupy them through the awkward pauses.

'Why didn't you try to find me?' Lydia asked. 'Not straight away, but later, when maybe you thought it would be safe to do so?'

'Initially I didn't want to do anything that would put you in danger. Then when I reasoned you'd got on with your life without me, that that was probably how you wanted it, I did something careless and in an instant the rest of my life was set on a course that couldn't include you.'

'What did you do?'

'I got a girl pregnant. I met Jane in London while I was kidding myself I could hack it as an art student. She thought she could save me from myself. For a while I almost believed she could. We married within a month of her discovering she was pregnant. The combination of us both being Catholic, no matter how vaguely so on my part, together with my need to be a better person, to get something right just once in my life, meant there was no question of her having an abortion. And, of course, things were different then. Abortion and single-parent families still carried a stigma. Marriage was the answer.'

'You must have had some moments of happiness or you wouldn't have stayed together as long as you did.'

'Jane gave me stability, so yes, therefore a degree of happiness. But it was Ishmael who really made it worthwhile. I wasn't prepared for that. He was born a week before my twenty-first birthday and he just blew me away. I couldn't

get over how this small scrap of life was totally dependent on his mother and father, when we were barely out of our own childhood. I was staggered by the effect he had on me. It made me understand I couldn't go on wallowing in self-pity; I had to pull myself together and shape up. I had to make it work. I couldn't let anyone else down. Which meant no more booze.' He paused for a few moments. 'And no more thoughts of you,' he added, his voice tight.

He turned from her and as he stared out across the water, Lydia could see the haunting sorrow and deep regret in his eyes. All at once, he seemed weighed down by it. Her heart went out to him. He had suffered as much as she had. He hadn't forgotten or abandoned her as she'd believed. The realization sent a whoosh of longing and desire straight through her. It made her want to hold him close to her, to breathe in the smell of him. She wanted to kiss him as he'd kissed her earlier and feel her heart beat a little faster again. Was it really possible that time had done nothing to diminish the powerful effect he had on her? While he continued to be lost in his own thoughts, she allowed herself the indulgence of studying him, absorbing the way his eyes crinkled at the corners, the way the line of his mouth curved, and the firm smoothness of his jaw. She wondered what it would be like to make love with him after all these years. Would he still be as tender and loving as he had once been? Would their bodies fit together as well?

He suddenly turned and looked at her. Alarmed that he might not have lost his talent for reading her mind, she said, 'When I met Ishmael for the first time, he joked that his father had been responsible for his fine Old Testament name. He attributed it to you having a weird sense of humour.'

'He tells everyone that.'

'You're very close, aren't you? You could almost be brothers.'

'I've been lucky in that respect. Did you never want children?'

'For years I had a real aversion to the idea, and then

when I met Marcello I thought a child between us would make everything perfect. But for whatever reason, it didn't happen.'

'But at least you have Chiara.'

'Yes, Chiara has given real meaning to my life. She was only nine when I met her and still missing her mother, who hadn't long since died. She reminded me of myself at that age. I wanted to wrap her in cotton wool and keep her safe from the world. Her father had decided that learning English might work as a distraction for her, something to keep her occupied. That's how I met Marcello: he responded to one of my adverts.'

'And now Ishmael and Chiara have met. What do you make of it?'

'I don't know what it is about the Solomon men,' Lydia said with a smile, 'but Ishmael seems to have swept Chiara off her feet. I've never seen her like this before.'

'The same goes for Ishmael. They've fallen for each other in a big way, haven't they?'

'They're so young, though.'

'Not that young.'

'You sound as if you want to encourage their relationship.'

'I do. For the simple and very selfish reason that if they get seriously involved, you and I will have the perfect excuse to keep seeing each other.'

'Do we need an excuse?'

'I thought maybe you might want one.'

'Oh, Noah, how could you think that?'

He reached for her hand. 'The truth is I'm scared. Scared how unreal sitting here with you feels. It seems too good to be true.'

They paid the bill and left. The moment they were out of the sun, the coldness of the day hit them and by the time they made it back to the apartment – there was no sign of Chiara and Ishmael – they were grateful to be in the warm.

'It's a beautiful apartment,' Noah said, looking appreciatively around him. 'The proportions are grand without being at all ostentatious.'

'Thank you. You're probably thinking that it's a far cry from Hillside Terrace, aren't you?'

'Just a touch.' He went over to take a closer look at the furthest wall, which was covered in silk damask. 'Not old, I presume,' he said, a statement rather than a question. Taking out a pair of glasses, he traced a finger over the Venetian red fabric. 'It's in too good a condition. Polyester in the mix, I'd guess.'

She laughed and sat down so she could rest her ankle. 'You're right on both counts. I bought it locally here in Venice and it's a fraction of the price of the genuine article, but allegedly it'll last longer. You sound like an expert on the subject.'

'I have my moments,' he said with a smile, switching his attention to one of Lydia's favourite watercolours: a picture of San Giorgio at dusk. She watched him appraising the painting as he leaned on his cane. She could see from his expression that he liked and approved of it.

'What kind of house do you live in?' she asked. 'For that matter, where do you live and what do you do for a living?'

He put away his glasses and went over to the window. He seemed to be restless and in a prowling sort of mood. 'Now we really are indulging in small talk, aren't we?' he said.

'I'm sorry. There's so much I know about you, but so much I don't. There's this huge gap I need to fill.'

'OK then, here goes. I live in a Northamptonshire village in a house I had built for me three years ago. Work-wise, I run a textile company making soft furnishing fabrics. We've recently bought a small Italian company near Padua that specializes in a particular finish we want to start using. Which is why Ishmael is here in Venice studying at the language school. He works for me, or as he likes to say, he's my heir apparent, and is going to be based in Padua

for the foreseeable future. You look surprised.'

'I am. I never pictured you in a suit-and-tie kind of job. How did you get into the world of textiles?'

'Blame Uncle Brad; he was the one who encouraged me to have an interest in drawing in the first place. Anyway, when Jane and I got married and I left art school, I dabbled in a bit of graphic design and then my uncle got me a job doing textile design work for an old friend of his. Next thing I knew, I discovered I had a talent for it and started doing stuff on the side that I could easily sell. By the time I was Ishmael's age, I'd set up my own company and had a dozen people working for me. Now we have almost a hundred.'

'Impressive. Do you still do any of the creative work?'

'It's pretty much all I do. Some years ago, I lost my appetite for what I see as the more tedious aspects of running a business, and now have an excellent team to take care of that side of things. I'm in the fortunate position of looking forward to taking more of a back seat before too long.'

'Did your work ever bring you to Italy?'

'There were, and still are, the trade fairs in Milan and Bologna, but since that was always Jane's forte, I opted out of them after a couple of years, happy to leave it to her.'

'Jane worked with you?'

'She still does. She runs the company with me. And that's another reason why we didn't rush into a divorce. What was the point when we were spending every day working together? It would have been different had we been at one another's throats, but we weren't.'

Lydia felt an unexpected twang of jealousy. 'A real family affair, then?'

Noah frowned and walked stiffly across the room. He sat on the sofa next to her. 'It's the way it turned out. Didn't you have the same situation here when Marcello was alive? Except for you it was different: you loved each other. Jane and I have an excellent working relationship, but as to the other, there's been nothing but friendship

between us for years. She remarried eighteen months ago and is happier now than I ever made her.'

Lydia closed her eyes, a surge of reddening shame flushing her face. 'I'm sorry,' she said, her head lowered as she fiddled with the plaster Noah had applied to her finger the previous night. 'I don't know where that came from. I suddenly felt so jealous. Ignore me. I'm just being irrational.'

Putting a hand to her back and working his palm up and down her spine, he said, 'You sound perfectly rational to me.'

Rational or nor, there was one thing Lydia couldn't let go of: the thought that Noah hadn't tried to find her. 'Those times you went to Milan and Bologna,' she said, 'didn't you ever think that I might be in Italy? You must have suspected that this was where I'd run to with Joey.'

Noah's hand came to a stop in the small of her back. He sat very still for a long time, staring ahead of him. Then switching his gaze back to her, his voice low, he said, 'Every place I ever went to, I thought you could be there, Lyddie. When I was living in London, I became convinced you'd deliberately disappeared the same day as Joey to make the police think you'd gone to Italy, whereas really you hadn't left the country at all. The more I thought this, the more I believed you'd gone where every runner-away goes: London. I nearly drove myself crazy imagining that you could be living just around the corner from me. I used to go through the phone book picking out numbers with the name of Turner and ring them. Which was absurd. If you were trying to keep your identity secret, you'd hardly advertise your whereabouts in the telephone directory, would you?' His hand moved to her shoulder. 'I'm sorry, but for the sake of my marriage, and Ishmael, I had to let it go. I had to believe that wherever you were, you were happy.'

The light was beginning to fade when Noah raised the subject that had been eclipsed by everything else they had needed to ask each other.

'Lyddie,' he said. 'You realize, don't you, that you have to come back to England with me? We have to find out who really did kill your uncle. If you don't, people will always think you did it. You have to clear your name. You can't live the rest of your life with this hanging over you.'

It was exactly what Lydia had dreaded Noah saying. She didn't want to go back to Swallowsdale. Not when she was frightened she might never return home to Venice.

Chapter Fifty-Six

Two days later, it was all arranged and Lydia was boarding a BA flight for Heathrow. She was fraught with nerves.
She had never been at ease on planes, something Marcello
hadn't ever understood the few times they had flown together. But then he hadn't known the cause of her anxiety,
had just assumed she nursed the perfectly conventional
fear of their plane crashing. How could he have known
that the sight of a customs official, his or her hand outstretched for her passport, gave Lydia far more anxiety
than the thought of a mid-air explosion.

Staring at the tarmac as she strapped herself into her
seat, Lydia wondered if it wasn't too late to change her
mind. Why couldn't she just take her chances and live out
the rest of her life in Venice never knowing who had killed
Uncle Leonard? After all this time, did it matter?

When she had aired these thoughts over dinner last
night with Fabio and Paolo, she had been met with the
same argument that Noah had given her: that she had to
clear her name. Whilst they'd all been in agreement on this
point, Fabio had added a word of caution and made Noah
promise that he would take good care of Lydia while they
were away. But how would Noah be able to do that if the
police discovered she had entered the country? Whilst he
seemed to think the case would be so long dead and buried
that she could walk into the police station in Swallowsdale
and no one would bat an eyelid, she was not so sure. Nor
was she convinced by his reassurance that her passport
wouldn't set off any alarm bells. 'You've taken out Italian
citizenship, you have an Italian passport, and your married

name is Tomasi. What possible reason would there be for anyone to suspect you of committing a crime in England that happened so many years ago?' was Noah's reasoning. He was one hundred and ten per cent sure that she was safe.

But as the thrust from the aeroplane's engine kicked in and she saw the tarmac rushing away from beneath her, Lydia felt anything but safe. She wished she had never given in to Noah and the rest of them. Now she had proved that she could move around relatively painlessly and without the aid of a crutch, Fabio and Paolo had invited them all to dinner last night. Lydia hadn't been fooled. She had known that Fabio wanted to meet Noah, to check him out. 'And your opinion of Noah?' she had asked him discreetly in Italian when he had been helping her into her coat at the end of the evening. 'I like him, Lydia,' he'd whispered, 'and his son. But please, be careful. You broke your heart over him once before. I don't want to see you hurt again.'

There was no question of Lydia falling in love all over again with Noah. It just wasn't possible, for the simple reason that she had never stopped loving him. She may have succeeded in blocking him out for most of her adult life, but the connection was still there. If anything, the magnetism was even stronger.

The plane was levelling out now with Venice and the lagoon no longer within sight. Its absence tugged at Lydia's heart. Would she ever see it again? Why was she risking everything? As if seeking assurance, she glanced at Noah.

'You OK?' he asked.

'No,' she said. 'I'm terrified.'

He put his hand on her wrist and stroked it lovingly. 'We're in this together. Don't forget that.'

Once they were off the plane, Noah held her hand all the way to passport control. 'Nothing's going to happen,' he whispered in her ear when it was finally her turn to step forward. Sure enough, she and her passport were given no more than a cursory glance and she was waved through.

Their luggage retrieved from the carousel, they took the route signposted 'Nothing to Declare' and emerged into the arrivals hall. An enormous Christmas tree dominated the crowded space. Her nerves all jagged, feeling like a child, Lydia wanted to feel the security of Noah's hand again, but he was pushing the trolley with their luggage on it.

'So far so good,' he said when they had stowed their luggage into the boot of a sleek, silver Mercedes sports car. 'Now all we have to do is negotiate the horrors of the M25.'

When on the mainland, away from Venice, Lydia was quite used to Italian drivers and their love of speed – she was no slouch herself – but the second Noah had negotiated their way out of the confines of the airport, he put his foot down in a way that would have put any one of them to shame. But not once did he frighten her. He drove confidently, never carelessly, his eyes on the road at all times.

'Nice car,' she remarked.

'Thanks. Cars are a weakness of mine I'm afraid, and this is definitely the kind of car a boy can get himself into trouble with.'

Relaxing a little, Lydia smiled. 'Go on, I know you're itching to: give me the specification. What model and what size engine?'

His eyes lit up. 'It's the SL600 with a V12 biturbo 5.5 litre engine that can zap to sixty in 4.5 seconds. I had to wait nearly ten months for it.'

She laughed. 'I loved the car Uncle Brad bought you for your seventeenth birthday. What happened to it?'

'I crashed it. I was very drunk at the time.'

It was dark when Noah eventually brought the car to a stop on a gravelled drive in front of a pillared porch. From what Lydia could see of the house, it looked gracious and individual. Not unlike its owner.

Inside, Noah dumped their luggage in the hallway,

flicked on lights and dealt with an alarm system. 'Sorry it's not very warm,' he apologized. 'I left the heating ticking over on its lowest setting. I'll go and give the boiler a talking to.'

She followed him into a large L-shaped kitchen and while he disappeared through another door, she scanned her surroundings, curious to observe Noah as an adult in his natural habitat. He was meticulously tidy, was her first observation as she took in the uncluttered granite surfaces. How different it was from Uncle Brad's messy workshop of a kitchen at Upper Swallowsdale House. The decor was unfussy, cool and neutral. Nothing jarred. There was an island unit in the middle of the room with a discreet flat-screen television built into the cream-coloured units directly opposite: Lydia imagined Noah eating his supper here whilst watching the evening news. Next to a stainless steel range-style cooker was a shelf of cookery books and a set of professional kitchen knives. He was a cook of some merit, perhaps? On a shelf above the cookery books was a framed photograph of a young Ishmael, ten or eleven years old. It could so easily have been a picture of Noah at that age.

'That's the heating booted up,' Noah said, coming back into the kitchen. 'Coffee?'

'Please.'

She watched him put the kettle on and then go over to an eye-level fridge. 'Excellent,' he said. 'Not only do we have milk, but something to eat for tonight. Shepherd's pie. What would I do without Mrs Massey?'

'And who might she be?'

'My housekeeper. She comes in three times a week and is a godsend. I called her yesterday to ask if she could get some food in for us. Stupidly, I forgot to ask her to turn up the heating, though.'

Mrs Massey had also been asked to prepare the largest of the guest rooms and when Noah took Lydia upstairs they found a vase of prettily arranged flowers on the dressing

table and clean towels hanging on the rail in the en suite bathroom.

'It's a big house just for one,' Lydia commented when they were back out on the spacious landing and she was admiring the dramatic vaulted ceiling.

His hands resting on the oak balustrade, looking down onto the hall with its pale oak floor, Noah said, 'What can I say? I like some space around me.'

'You must have found Venice very cramped. Some people find it claustrophobic and never take to the place.'

'I didn't feel that at all. Quite the reverse in fact. Come with me: there's something I want to show you. But you have to promise you won't freak out when you see it.'

'Why did you think I'd freak out?' Lydia asked, after he'd pushed open the door into his bedroom and they'd gone inside. On the wall opposite his bed, above a chest of drawers, was the portrait Uncle Brad had painted of Lydia shortly after her seventeenth birthday.

'I was worried you might think me a bit weird for still having it,' he said, 'especially as it's hanging in my bedroom. And before you ask, no, I didn't have it on show when I was married. It was carefully stored away then.'

'When did it see the light of day again?'

'When I came to live here. Mrs Massey is the only person who's seen it. No one else ever comes into my room.'

Lydia stepped in closer to get a better look at her seventeen-year-old self. How young she looked. And how serious and melancholy. Was that how Uncle Brad had seen her? She wondered how he would paint her now. Would he exaggerate the lines around her eyes, add in the grey hairs her hairdresser so artfully disguised for her, so as to show the real her? To reveal the life she'd led? 'At the time I was never really sure if Uncle Brad was any good as a painter,' she said, stepping back from the oil painting and her lost youth, 'but now I can see he was more than good. He had a deft touch. No wonder he was always down in London with some exhibition or other.' She suddenly laughed. 'I remember the very first time I came to your

house and seeing all the candles, I thought you were so poor you couldn't afford electricity.'

Noah came and stood behind her. 'I could never tire of looking at that face,' he said. She felt his hand on her shoulder, then her hair being lifted to one side so that he could kiss the nape of her neck. She melted at his touch and wanted to turn round and kiss him, but she knew if she did that, with the bed so conveniently positioned there would be only one outcome. Were they really ready for that? She thought of the guest room Noah had had made up for her. Was that good manners on his part, or an indicator of his reluctance to take that step?

After they'd eaten and tidied everything away, with an early start planned for the morning, they both agreed that an early night would be sensible.

'You're sure you've got everything you need?' Noah asked her on the landing outside her room.

'You've asked me that twice already.'

He smiled, embarrassed. 'I know. I guess I'm just putting off the moment.'

'What moment?'

'The moment when I ask you what I really want to ask you.'

'Which is?'

'Can we dispense with the guest room sham? I thought it was the right thing to do but I can't go through with it. I can't lie in the room next door to you knowing that you're sleeping just yards away from me. I want you in my bed tonight. I want to make love to you. I want to wake up in the morning with you in my arms.'

She leaned towards him. 'I'd like that, too.'

Noah held her in his arms, kissing her, touching her lightly. 'I've missed you so much,' he breathed heavily.

She stroked his face and stared deep into his dark, familiar eyes. 'I've missed you for a lifetime.'

He led her to the bed and started kissing her again, his

hands fumbling with the buttons on her top. 'God, I'm suddenly so nervous,' he said. 'I'm like a teenager again.'

'Me too,' she admitted, and suddenly shy, she took hold of his hands. 'Noah, you realize, don't you, that it won't be the same between us? I'm ... I'm older.'

He raised a questioning eyebrow. 'And your point?'

'I don't look how I used to.'

He smiled, peeled off his T-shirt and threw it on the floor. 'Thank God for that. Because neither do I.' He kissed her again. 'Don't worry,' he whispered, 'it'll be fine.' He went back to the buttons on her top, slipped it off, then reached round to unhook her bra.

'Don't say I didn't warn you,' she said, half joking, half serious.

He silenced her with another long, tender kiss, then lay her down on the bed. His lips moved to her neck and then her throat, tracking a slow path to her breasts. Her head spun.

When they were both fully undressed Lydia pressed her hands flat against his chest, then rested her ear against him. 'I used to love doing this,' she murmured, 'listening to your heart.'

'Your body hasn't changed at all,' he said, taking the whole of her in. 'You still look eighteen.' There was an expression of wonder on his face.

'It's the light in here,' she said. 'It would flatter a rhinoceros.'

'Hey, here's the deal. While you get on with disagreeing with everything I say, I'll apply myself to the business of making love to you. How does that sound?'

Lydia laughed and then gasped when he gently placed his hand between her legs. She wrapped her arms around him. His touch was slick and dexterous, and when he slid down the length of her and she felt the warmth of his mouth on her, her body responded in a way it hadn't done in years. She closed her eyes and gave in to the quivering, intense pleasure.

He took his time, keeping her on the brink until finally

the growing tingling tremors exploded into an orgasm suffused with so much love she could hardly breathe. The release was immense, almost spiritual. When she was still, he lay beside her, crushed her to him.

When at last she could find the words to speak, she said, 'I see you're still a natural genius for conjuring up an orgasm.'

'It helps to be with the right woman,' he said quietly, raising himself up onto an elbow. He stared at her intensely, his eyes dark and penetrating. He stroked her cheek. 'It always felt right with you. It still does.'

Lydia turned her face into the palm of his hand and kissed it. 'I used to dream of us being together again like this. In bed. I always woke up crying. I had to teach myself never to think of you. It was the hardest thing I ever did.'

'I'm sorry,' he said. 'Sorry for all the wasted years.' His voice was thick.

'So am I.' She ran a hand along the length of his long, lean body. In the soft light cast from the lamp behind him, she could see the myriad scars on his badly damaged leg. He saw what she was looking at and reached for the duvet to cover it. She stopped him. 'Please don't,' she said. 'It's a part of you.' She tipped him onto his back and kissed him lightly on the mouth, no more than a teasing whisper of a kiss. His lips parted and she traced them with her tongue. He shivered and opened his mouth wider, wanting more of her, one of his hands on the back of her head pulling her down to him. She resisted with a smile. 'I think you'll find I'm calling the shots on this one,' she said.

He gave her his best Question Mark Face.

Laughing, she hooked a leg over his hips and sat up astride him, her back straight. 'That car of yours, how long did you say it took to get to sixty miles an hour?'

He groaned. 'Be gentle with me, Lyddie. It's been a while.'

Chapter Fifty-Seven

The following morning, a light dusting of snow had turned Noah's garden into a magical winter wonderland. In the dark, Lydia hadn't noticed the formal box hedging or the stone urns that lined the gravel drive. In the distance, beyond the spire of a church, and behind a swell of gently sweeping hills, a ball of shimmering gold light was climbing the pale sky. It was a stunningly beautiful day. With their breath forming in the cold air, they packed their luggage into the boot of the car and hurriedly got in.

At the end of the driveway Lydia turned to take one last look at the house, as though committing it to memory.

'Don't worry,' Noah said. 'I promise you'll see it again.'

Their destination was Swallowsdale. Noah had everything planned, right down to where they would be staying and what their first move would be. Before leaving Venice he'd booked them into the Oak Manor Court Hotel, which was to be their first port of call. Lydia had imagined they would then go to the library in Swallowsdale and spend hours poring over microfilm, reading up on newspaper reports of the murder. But apparently not. Noah said they would nose around first, then check out the library.

They were on the motorway when Noah pressed a button and music filled the car. She didn't recognize it, but then she was more familiar with Italian bands and singers. 'What are we listening to?' she asked.

'It's Thom Yorke's album, *The Eraser*.'

At her blank expression, he said, 'Radiohead?'

'That rings a bell,' she said vaguely.

'Don't tell me we've hit our first cultural divide.'

She smiled and stared out of the window, taking in the landscape. England, twenty-eight years on. She had some catching up to do.

The Oak Manor Court Hotel, with views across a scrubby golf course to the west, and Swallowsdale and the moors to the east, proudly boasted its three-star status with a sign that was hanging off a rusting hinged bracket. It creaked and grated as it swung in the raw, blustery wind that welcomed them with a stinging slap in the face when they stepped out of the car. There was no snow to soften the bleak landscape and it was hard to imagine anywhere more isolated or depressingly remote.

'It's life, Jim, but not as we know it,' Noah murmured as they stood in the small reception area waiting for someone to appear behind the desk. Above their heads, Christmas music tinkled away from a speaker that, like the sign outside, had a perilous tilt to it. Over by the window, an artificial Christmas tree was festooned with decorations and flashing lights. 'I know what you're thinking,' Noah said, 'but believe me, this was the best on offer at such short notice. What's the betting Basil Fawlty's lurking here somewhere?'

'You always did watch too much television,' Lydia said. 'Why don't we ring the bell?' On the desk next to a miniature Christmas tree was a small brass bell. She gave it a light tap and straight away a voice called out, 'Be with you in a jiffy.'

Within seconds the half-glazed door behind the desk opened and a sturdily built woman pulling off a pair of rubber gloves greeted them. 'Sorry about that,' she said, 'plumbing trouble. Right then. Checking in? Or just here for morning coffee?'

'Checking in,' Noah said. 'Mr and Mrs Solomon. We have a reservation.'

The woman consulted something out of sight to Lydia

and Noah and said, 'Ah, yes, here we are.' Still struggling to get one of the gloves off, she pushed a piece of paper towards them. 'If you could just fill out your name and address and car registration then I'll show you to your room. Would you like a wake-up call and a newspaper in the morning?'

'Darling?'

Lydia hesitated, then shook her head.

Putting on his glasses, Noah completed the form and passed it back to the woman. 'Righty ho,' she said, 'that's the formalities dealt with. Now I'll show you upstairs.' She lifted up part of the desk top and came round to join them. When she saw Noah's cane, she said, 'The stairs won't be a problem for you, will they?'

Noah assured her they wouldn't, but even so, she insisted on carrying their luggage. 'I've put you in the Hardcastle Suite,' she said. 'It has the best views and a lovely big jacuzzi bath. I've got you down for three nights. Are you here on holiday?'

'Sort of,' Noah said. 'A trip down memory lane you could say. I used to live in the area.'

'That's nice.'

'How about you?' Noah asked. 'Are you local?'

'Me? No. My husband and I bought this place ten years ago after running a pub in Coventry. We fancied a change. And we certainly got that.'

At the top of the stairs, while the woman unlocked the panelled door to the Hardcastle Suite, Noah exchanged a look with Lydia. She knew what he was thinking: at least there was no danger of the owners of the hotel recognizing her.

They were shown the room with such zeal and attention to detail – everything was superior or deluxe – it was as if they were potential buyers. Alone at last, they both sat on the edge of the four-poster bed. Its flimsy, repro structure creaked ominously. They looked at each other and laughed. 'Sex is definitely off the agenda,' Lydia said. 'Not unless we want to entertain the other guests.'

'There's always the jacuzzi bath to frolic in,' Noah suggested, 'though God knows what deluxe horrors that may have in store for us. More seriously, you don't mind that I booked us in as being married, do you? Only I thought it would be simpler that way. I'd hate for you to think I was being presumptuous when I booked the room back in Venice. Separate rooms, or twin beds, especially twin beds, would have provoked more questions.'

'Of course I don't mind. Although you took me by surprise with that "darling" business.'

'I took myself by surprise.' He smiled. 'Shall we put the superior tea and coffee-making facilities to the test and discuss what we're going to do next, *darling*?'

It wasn't in Lydia's nature to let someone else make so many decisions on her behalf, but she had sensed since leaving Venice that finding out the truth about Uncle Leonard's death was something Noah needed to do. Knowing that she had sacrificed so much for him – even mistakenly so – he probably saw this as his way to try and make amends. Yet for all that, it was difficult for her to take a back seat. As an adult she had always been in control of her life, and rightly or wrongly she had a tendency to make snap decisions – more often than not, snap unilateral decisions. It was a lifetime's habit based on a need to defend and protect not just herself but those she loved.

A shame she had got it so colossally wrong that night in the dell.

They drove the short distance to Swallowsdale, stopping first in Upper Swallowsdale. The engine idling, they stared up at Uncle Brad's old house. White PVC-framed windows had been installed, along with a satellite dish. A handmade poster was tied to the gate; it was advertising a fundraising mince pie and mulled wine do for the local Conservative party.

'Uncle Brad would die on the spot,' Lydia said.

'Wouldn't he just?' Noah agreed, his foot already tweaking the engine. 'Seen enough?'

'Yes.'

'Swallowsdale town centre, here we come. Unless you want to go to Hillside Terrace first?'

She shook her head. 'Let's save that till last.'

In the gloomy half-light, the town was nothing like they remembered. The shabby parade of flat-roofed shops along the main street had gone. As had the scruffy old barber's on the corner opposite the bank. Where was the post office? And the dry cleaner's and the old bookshop? And how about the supermarket where Noah had worked?

The whole place had been transformed beyond recollection. There was now a pedestrianized area where the main street had once been, and as they moved amongst the crowds of Christmas shoppers, they could hear piped carols in the cold afternoon air. There were ye olde street lamps and matching rubbish bins and tea shops galore. There were antique shops aplenty, and a store selling expensive leisurewear and walking boots. Where their favourite second-hand bookshop had been was an Italian restaurant called *Il Trattoria*, complete with red and white chequered table cloths and lots of fake hams and salami hanging from hooks above the bar. Next door to it was a shop claiming to be selling vintage clothing. 'Looks just like the stuff we used to buy from jumble sales,' Lydia said, standing at the window.

'I hate to be the bearer of bad tidings, Lyddie, but those clothes count as genuine vintage these days.'

She gave him a playfun punch. 'And you can keep the ageist comments to yourself. It all looks so much more prosperous than I remember it.'

They went in search of the Church of The Brothers and Sisters in Christ. But it was gone – all trace of it. In its place was a public convenience, complete with a ramp and a pay-on-entry turnstile. The irony was just too fitting to be funny. 'Pastor Digby and his ilk flushed away for all eternity,' Lydia remarked, feeling sadder than she might have expected.

They'd missed out on lunch, but didn't dare risk one of the gentrified tea shops for something to eat. Lydia was paranoid about staying still for too long and being recognized – even with her hat and sunglasses on, and a scarf wrapped high around her neck. They risked a sandwich shop, joined the queue inside and scanned the extensive menu options. Behind them the entire wall was a mirror, probably there to make the shop feel bigger and airier.

'Who's next, then?'

Noah nudged Lydia. 'We are,' he said to a man behind the counter, who had a striped apron tied around his waist. His hair was very short and gelled to form little peaks at the front. 'I'll have a bacon and avocado baguette, please,' Noah said. He turned to Lydia. Lydia dithered. 'Um ... oh, the same for me, please.'

'That'll be five pounds ninety, please.'

They were the only ones in the shop now, and whilst the man made their baguettes for them, Noah glanced at Lydia and frowned. 'What's wrong?' he whispered.

Lydia tipped her head towards the man. 'He reminds me of someone,' she whispered back.

'Who?'

'I don't know. But I want to get out of here. Now.'

'You go on ahead to the car.' He pulled his keys out of his coat pocket and gave them to her. 'I'll catch you up.'

She had been sitting in the car for almost ten minutes, wondering if she had let her paranoia get the better of her, when Noah appeared. He got into the driver's seat beside her. He looked pleased with himself. 'You were right to think there was something familiar about that guy. Remember Donna Jones?'

Lydia nodded. 'Of course. It was her surname I used for my new identity.'

'Well, that was none other than her son, Kirk.'

While Noah explained how he'd got chatting to the sandwich man – after all, they were here to dig up whatever information they could – Lydia did the maths. 'That

makes him thirty-one. I can't believe it! Captain Kirk, thirty-one. It's not possible.'

'Never mind how old Captain Kirk is,' Noah said, 'he told me his mother still lives in Swallowsdale. Now pass me that phone book I pinched from the hotel.'

'I knew my hunch to come here and nose around would pay off,' Noah said when they were negotiating the road system of a smart housing estate. The houses all had the sharp-edged look of having only been in existence for a short time.

They'd found Donna's entry in the phone book under her married name – which Kirk had supplied when Noah had said he'd been at school with Donna and was visiting the area to look up a few old friends – and the plan was for Noah to park the car some distance from Donna's house, leaving Lydia in it while he went and chatted with Donna about the 'old days'. It was inevitable that the conversation would innocently lead to Lydia and the murder of her great-uncle.

It seemed a foolproof plan. All along Noah had been convinced that they'd be better off showing up in Swallowsdale and running into people from the past to get what he called an 'on the ground' perspective about the murder. 'Donna is perfect,' he said now to Lydia as they turned into a road signposted as Lark's Close. 'She's bound to have an opinion, and who knows, she might just know something important.'

Lydia said nothing. She couldn't believe it could be as simple as that.

With Donna's house located – it was a large detached property with a double garage and a BMW on the drive – Noah drove back out of Lark's Close and into an adjoining road. 'Right,' he said with a determined expression. 'I could be a while.'

She watched him walk stiffly away in the fading light.

No clock-watching, she told herself, when after only a few minutes had passed she found she couldn't stop

looking at her watch. Noah had left the keys in the ignition to switch the engine on if she got too cold. Another five minutes and she might have to do exactly that.

To distract herself, she counted the number of houses with lights shaped as icicles attached to them. From there she progressed to counting the illuminated bulbs on the Christmas tree in the garden next to her. Bored of that, she decided to call Chiara and bring her up to date. But all she got was the engaged tone ringing in her ear.

She put her mobile away in her bag, leaned her head back against the headrest and relaxed into the soft, comfortable leather seat. She let her thoughts drift. Swallowsdale. She was really here. Against all the odds and every fiercely made vow, she had actually returned. And to find a killer, of all things. Or at least, discover who the killer had been. It was possible that the person who had brought an end to Uncle Leonard's life was also dead now. Who knows, the two men might even be buried side by side. How they would have hated the idea of that!

Ruling out some random nutter roaming the dell that night, the most obvious suspect was her grandfather. With the most to gain by Uncle Leonard's death, he was certainly not lacking a motive. She and Noah had checked the phone book for an A. Turner and had drawn a blank. If her grandfather was still alive – he'd have to be in his nineties now – he was no longer living at number thirty-three Hillside Terrace. Or if he was, his name had been removed from the listing. The prospect of going to the house to find out filled Lydia with dread. She'd told Noah she wanted to leave driving there until last, and she meant it.

Cold now, she reached across to the driver's seat and turned the key in the ignition to activate the car heater. She put her gloves on and closed her eyes, pondering what Donna's reaction would be to Noah turning up unexpectedly on her doorstep. Immediately, she thought of her own reaction when Noah had appeared on her doorstep in Venice. Shock. Disbelief. Anger even. But most of all,

the sure knowledge that nothing was ever going to be the same again.

Late last night, Noah had confessed to her that after he'd left her apartment that first night in Venice, he'd lain awake in bed thinking how badly he'd wanted to take her in his arms. How he'd wanted to kiss her. He'd wanted to turn her face up to his and kiss her mouth. All that, the first night.

A tap on the car window made her jump. She looked up to see Noah. He opened the door and leaned in. 'I think you'd better come in and hear what Donna's just told me.'

Chapter Fifty-Eight

'Friggin' hell!' Donna roared at the top of her voice. 'Just look what the bloody cat finally dragged in! Who'd have thought it?'

Lydia hugged her old friend, genuinely delighted to see her again. 'And who'd have thought you'd turn into such a shy, retiring little thing?'

Donna laughed. 'Like that was ever gonna happen! Now come in out of the cold and sit down and let me get a proper look at you. Hey, Noah, how about some tea while us girls do some catching up here? You'll find everything you need in all the obvious places. Oh, and there are some mince pies in the tin on the draining board. Chop, chop!' she added with a mischievous wink.

When they were alone, Lydia said, 'You look well, Donna. Really well.'

'I am. A little fatter than I'd like, but I blame that on good living and giving up the fags. But look at you! Quite the classy tart in your finery. You finally got around to doing sommat about your appalling dress sense, then? Just wait till I tell Alfie you were here. You remember Alfie, don't you?'

'Of course. Kirk's grown, hasn't he?'

'Yeah, just a bit. Noah said you'd run into him in town. He's married with a kid of his own now. I'm a grand-mother. How about that?'

'Congratulations. And Lydia Junior?'

Donna pointed to a large framed photograph on the mantelpiece. 'See for yourself.'

Lydia went to have a look at it, along with all the

other pictures that were partially hidden behind a row of Christmas cards. 'She's the smart one,' Donna said. 'Took after you, I reckon. You must have whispered sommat in her ear when you delivered her. She's a teacher. Lives in Birmingham with her boyfriend who's a solicitor.'

'You must be so proud of them both. Did you have any more children?'

'Are you crazy? No, I kept my knickers firmly on and my powder dry after Lydia. I then had the sense to channel my energies into a different direction. I went back to school. Just as you used to nag me! I got myself all educated up and started my own little business. You've caught me on a rare afternoon when I'm home early. I now run a flooring company. Floors Direct, it's called. Doesn't sound very exciting, I know, but I built it up from nowt, and what with everyone currently mad for laminate and wood flooring, business has been booming a treat these last few years. My only disappointment is that Kirk refused to come and work with me like Alfie did a few years back. He's a stubborn whatsit and wants to do his own thing.'

'Good for him,' Lydia said. 'And especially good for you.' Then looking around the spacious sitting room with its cream carpet and oyster-coloured leather three-piece suite and large plasma screen television she said, 'I don't see any wood flooring here.'

'Not on your life! I'm a carpet girl through and through. When I'm not in the kitchen and bathroom, I like a nice bit of wool under my feet. You can't beat it in my opinion.'

Lydia laughed. 'So when did you and Alfie get together?' She picked up a photograph of Donna and Alfie on their wedding day. Donna was sporting a blonde perm of monumental proportions; Alfie's hair looked suspiciously like it had had the same treatment. Donna's hair now was chestnut brown and styled into a softly layered bob that suited her perfectly. As did the silvery-grey roll-necked sweater.

'We started dating about two years after you slung your hook,' Donna said, 'and without so much as a by your leave on your part, I might add.'

Lydia put the photograph back in its place. 'I'm sorry I left without saying goodbye. I had to.'

'So you should be. I was furious with you, but once all that stuff about your uncle hit the papers, it made sense. Later, though, when the truth came out, I thought, right, now she can come—'

'Truth?' Lydia interrupted, leaping on the word. 'You know what happened?'

'Of course. But we'll get to that in a moment. First off, where the hell have you been all this time?'

'Italy.'

Just then, Noah came in unsteadily with a tray of mugs and a plate of mince pies. Donna jumped up from her armchair and took it from him. She placed it on the glass coffee table in front of the sofa. 'Have you got to the point and told her yet, Donna?' he asked.

'Give us a moment to catch up, won't you?' Donna handed Lydia one of the mugs of tea. 'I don't remember him being this bossy and impatient. You want to watch that.'

Amused, Lydia sat down. 'I'll do my best,' she said. How good it was to see Donna again. Time and prosperity may have changed her – certainly her language and broad accent had mellowed – but essentially she was still the same.

'Right then,' Donna said when they were all settled, 'now it's your turn to bring me up to date. Let me guess, you two are married? And I wouldn't blame you if you were, Lydia. Apart from that chronic impatience of his, he's turned out to be quite a looker, hasn't he? Kept himself in good shape as well. If I didn't have Alfie, I might be tempted myself.'

'Donna!' Noah remonstrated, his face a picture of embarrassment. 'Please, just tell Lydia what you told me.'

'Well,' Donna began, 'you can imagine what a big deal it was when the papers got hold of the story of some bloke who'd been murdered in Swallowsdale, right here on our doorstep. Within no time everyone had a theory about

who could have done it. Most folks thought Joey, the ice-cream man, had done it, being foreign and all, and what with him leaving when he did, so sudden-like. Then once it became known you were missing, people said it had been a double murder, that Joey had killed your great-uncle, then killed you and hidden your body. Or carted it off to Italy with him.' Donna laughed. 'I can't tell you how many people went round saying they'd always known Joey had a look about him, that he was a mass murderer just waiting for the right moment to strike.'

'What did you think?' Lydia asked while Donna drew breath and sipped on her tea.

'Me? Oh, I was having no truck with all that nonsense. I reckoned you'd done the old pervert in good and proper. Don't look so shocked. I might have done it myself given half a chance.'

A cold unease crept over Lydia. 'Why do you call him an old pervert?' she asked.

'Because that's what he was. I knew he must have tried sommat on with you.'

'Why would you think that?'

Donna rolled her eyes. 'We girls know these things. Now will you stop interrupting me and let me get on with being the centre of attention? Now then, where was I?'

'The pervert,' prompted Noah.

'That's right, the old perv. Yeah, well, the disgusting tosser tried it on with me. He came to my house one day asking if I wanted any odd jobs doing and when I said he could have a go at sorting out the washer on the kitchen tap, he said he hadn't been thinking of that kind of job. I told him I'd hack his dick off and throw it to the dogs if he came near me again. Next time I saw him he tried to get a cop of my jing-jang when I was on my way home from work one night and I gave him a right mouthful.'

'Why didn't you ever tell me this?'

'Come off it! No girl wants to admit that some horny old perv has tried it on with her. Different story if it's some drop-dead gorgeous guy. Then we're practically shouting

from the rooftops about it. Anyway, the point is, when he was found dead and you were missing, I put two and two together, just as the police did. Next thing we knew from reading the papers was that you were wanted for questioning in connection with the murder. We were all questioned, those who knew you. 'Course, I never said anything. It was never actually printed in the papers, but it got out somehow, as these things do, that there was evidence to put you at the scene of the crime. Well, it was a done deal as far as we were all concerned. But then, and I can't be sure exactly when, but let's say it was some months later, it was in the paper that the murderer had been found. As far as I know, no arrest was actually made, but the police had a confession and the case was closed. End of story.'

'Who was it, Donna? Who confessed?'

'Your grandmother. Crazy as crazy, she stuck a knife in the old devil and then for some reason started bragging about it when everything had gone quiet. She told the police God had made her do it.'

Lydia was stunned into silence. She couldn't believe it. Her grandmother? The night she'd run off from the hospital? It certainly fitted. 'But what about the evidence the police found that made them think it was me?' she asked Donna. 'How did the police think that had got there?'

'They went along with the theory that that fitted in with the fight you'd had earlier with your uncle.'

'Did it come out why my grandmother did it?' Lydia asked.

'Look, and no disrespect, but your grandmother was a complete psycho, capable of doing anything and for any reason. It's a wonder she didn't kill us all! The way the story went, she got lost on the moors, found herself in the dell with your uncle and God spoke to her. He told her that she was his avenging angel and had to kill your uncle. You can't help but think that it was the one good thing she ever did in her life.'

'What happened to her?'

'The case never went to trial because she was considered unfit to plead. Instead she was moved to a secure psychiatric hospital to live out the rest of her life. Her death was reported in the papers three years later, a week after Alfie and I got back from our honeymoon.'

Whilst Lydia was still trying to absorb everything Donna had told her, Noah said, 'Is Lydia's grandfather still alive, Donna?'

'No. He snuffed it a long time back. Before that, he remarried when his batty old wife died, though. To the woman he'd—'

'My sister,' Lydia said abruptly, cutting Donna off mid-sentence. 'Valerie. Do you know what happened to her, where she is and what she's doing?'

'I can't swear to what she's doing now, but back then, when that cranky old church of yours closed down, she moved away and became a nun. And let's face it, there's not a soul alive who could be surprised by that.'

Over dinner in a half-empty dining room at the Oak Manor Court Hotel, accompanied by a CD of schmaltzy Christmas songs, Lydia and Noah were discussing what their next move would be.

'If only Sister Lottie was alive, she'd be able to help us,' Lydia said. 'She would have known where Valerie had gone.' Finding Valerie had now become Lydia's number one priority.

'Donna was pretty sure it was a convent in Staffordshire. Is it too much to hope convents are listed online or in the phone book?'

'After our run of luck today, I could believe anything. How are you feeling, by the way? Any better?' When Noah had been driving them back from Donna's, he had complained of a headache.

'Not really,' he said. 'I'll take some more paracetamol when we go to bed.'

'Are you prone to headaches now? You never used to be.'

'No more than anyone else. I probably just need to get my eyes tested again.'

A waiter brought them their main course, and after he'd left, just as Johnny Mathis started singing 'When a Child is Born', Noah lifted his glass of water and said, 'I think we should celebrate the fact that we cracked the case within a few hours of arriving in Swallowsdale and, more importantly, you're now officially off the UK's most wanted list.'

'No disagreement there.'

They clinked glasses.

'If you don't mind me saying, you don't look too thrilled by our day's work.'

Lydia lowered her glass. 'That's because I feel as if I've been incredibly stupid all this time. All those measures I took to keep myself safe, and you safe, they were for nothing. My whole life has been a mockery. A ridiculous illusion. A cheap joke.'

'Don't be so hard on yourself. What you're feeling is perfectly understandable. It's difficult to change the way you've always thought about things. For so long you've believed something to be true and now you're finding it's turned on its head. It'll take a while to come to terms with it.'

'I suppose it's true for you as well. All these years, you thought I was a murderer.'

He stared at her intensely, his eyes dark and luminous in the flickering light from the candle between them. 'I never thought of it quite like that. I pictured a frightened eighteen-year-old girl trying to protect herself. Did you view me as a cold, calculating murderer?'

'No. Never.' She picked up her knife and fork, but then sighed wearily. 'I'm being morose and ruining the evening, acting like a real killjoy. I'm sorry. God, this beef is tough! Have you tried it yet?'

Noah cut a small piece off his steak and chewed on it. And chewed. 'You're right. It's awful.'

They ate as much as they could and lied politely to the

waiter when he came to clear their plates away. 'We had too much to eat at lunch,' Noah said with an apologetic shake of his head.

They ordered coffee and, serenaded by Bing Crosby singing 'White Christmas', Noah leaned forward, his elbows on the table. 'Tomorrow we try to find your sister. OK?'

Lydia leaned forward as well, pushed the candle out of the way and kissed him. 'Yes, Sherlock.'

Up in their room whilst they were getting ready for bed, Lydia's mobile rang. It was Donna.

'I've just remembered something that might help you find your sister,' she said. 'Do you remember Lisa Fortune? She was the girl at school with the artificial hand.'

'Yes, I used to have nightmares about her.'

'Really?'

'I'll tell you why another time.'

'Well, I often see her at Weight Watchers, and blame it on all the excitement of seeing you again, but I clean forgot that she joined that church of yours. She got really involved with it, too, and despite the age gap became quite pally with your sister. I've just been on the phone with her. Have you got a pen and a bit of paper handy? You might want to write this down.'

The weather was even colder the next morning. It was raining, too. It was a real misery of a day, not helped by the restless night they'd passed.

Everything had been fine until they'd got into bed and realized just how creaky the wretched thing was. Spreading the duvet on the carpet, they'd made love as discreetly as they could, given that the floorboards were almost as indiscreet as the four-poster bed. For sleeping purposes, they'd risked the bed, but if it wasn't that that had disturbed them every time one of them moved, it was the sound of the wind rumbling down the chimney or rattling the not-so-deluxe windows in their rotting frames. The headache that Noah had complained of earlier also kept

him awake. It was made worse by lying down, so he'd snatched what little sleep he could by sleeping upright.

They were the only people in the dining room for breakfast, which suited them fine. They were served by the same waiter as the previous night. He was probably the only waiter the hotel had.

By the time they drove into Swallowsdale, the rain had turned to sleet. They were early enough to beat the traffic and managed to park directly outside the chemist. Noah was in and out within minutes. He passed a paper bag to Lydia. 'The pharmacist thought I might have a migraine,' he said, starting the engine.

Their next stop was to fill up with petrol and to buy a bottle of water. Whilst still on the forecourt, Noah swallowed two of the tablets and chased them down with a gulp of water. 'Soon be as right as rain,' he said with a half-smile, driving out of the petrol station and into the wintry sleet that was coming down harder and faster. 'Which way for Sister Lottie's house? I hope you can remember, because I can't.'

'Left,' Lydia said, the instruction surfacing from her unconscious mind without hesitation. 'And then right into Cuckoo Lane.'

But Sister Lottie's house was no more. Where once her little house had formed part of a row of terraced houses, there was now a video rental shop with a large car park to one side. Noah turned off the road and pulled onto the car park.

'It's all so depressing,' Lydia said, staring at where her dear old friend used to live. 'So much change.'

'Would you like to try and find where she's buried?'

Her throat painfully bunched up, Lydia shook her head. After a few minutes had passed, she said, 'I was so close to her, yet I could never be completely honest with her. I never once told her what my grandparents were really like. It would have upset her too much. I wanted to protect the belief she had that we lived in a beautiful world, where nobody meant any real harm. She accepted that people

made mistakes, but she didn't believe they could ever be cruel and wicked to the core. "No one is beyond redemption," she used to say. I've always wondered about that.'

'You wouldn't be the first. Do you want to go on to Hillside Terrace now?'

She shook her head again. 'No. I've had enough of Swallowsdale. Why don't we cut short our stay here? Let's drive back to the hotel for our stuff and then head for Staffordshire to find Valerie.'

According to Donna, Valerie had entered the convent when she was eighteen and the last time Lisa Fortune had been in touch with her was ten years ago. The sensible thing to do would be to ring the convent, to establish whether Valerie was indeed still there, but – call it instinct – Lydia knew that she was.

The child in her wanted to arrive unannounced and surprise her sister.

Chapter Fifty-Nine

Lydia had been expecting the convent to be a gloomy, forbidding place in a remote location, heavily gated to keep out the rest of the world, and to keep the nuns inside from escaping.

But no, here they were looking up at an impressive Victorian house at the end of a quiet residential road. It was an affluent neighbourhood with substantial houses well set back from the road. Discreetly tucked behind tidy hedges and high walls, they had enormous plots of land all to themselves.

There was a gate to the Order of St Agnes, but unlike the one of Lydia's imagination it was wide open and welcoming. The front garden was immaculate, mostly laid out with well-established rhododendrons and conifers. They parked alongside a filthy white Transit van on the tarmac drive. Someone had written in the grime on the back of it, *I'm a dirty slag!*.

Out of the car, Lydia slipped her hand through Noah's and they approached the house. Either side of an imposing front door there were two stained-glass windows. One portrayed a spindly-legged lamb and the other, the Tree of Life. On closer inspection, Lydia could see some gardening implements propped against the tree: a hoe, a rake and a spade.

There was a polished brass ship's bell hanging from a wall bracket. Lydia gave it a polite ring and tried to quell the hostility that had been rising within her during the journey from Swallowsdale. No matter what had brought her sister here when she was eighteen years old, Lydia

didn't feel it was right that Val had wasted the best years of her life in a place like this, shut off from the rest of the world, a virtual prisoner.

'I think you might have to give it a bit more welly than that,' Noah said, indicating the bell.

Lydia expended some of her anger and gave the short piece of rope a vicious tug.

Shortly afterwards, the door was opened to them by a woman dressed in a black, full-length habit. Only her ageing bespectacled face and hands were visible. It wasn't Valerie, was Lydia's first thought. As briefly as she could, she explained why they were here. With a nod of her head, the other woman invited them inside. Her habit swishing and her shoes squeaking on the polished wooden floor, she showed them into a room across a spacious hall with a wide staircase leading off from it. 'Please help yourselves to coffee,' she said, indicating a surprisingly high-tech piece of equipment on an oak sideboard. 'Just press the appropriate button, and Bob's your uncle.'

When the door closed silently behind her, Noah approached the coffee machine and Lydia read the plaque on the wall next to a painting of the convent's namesake. 'Listen to this,' Lydia said. 'It says here Saint Agnes is the patron saint of betrothed couples, gardeners and virgins.'

'That's a relief,' Noah said. 'Imagine if she'd been the patron saint of lost causes. It wouldn't have felt like a good omen, would it?'

'Not funny,' Lydia said. 'Anyway, you're the Catholic: you should know all this stuff.' She continued reading from the plaque. 'Since the sixth century, because Agnes's name is so like the Latin name for lamb, the lamb has been her emblem.'

'Hence the stained-glass window at the front door. Coffee's up.'

Lydia took the small china cup from him and sat down. 'But gardeners. That's a funny thing to be a saint of, isn't it?' She took a cautious sip of the hot coffee. 'What if visitors aren't allowed?' she said anxiously.

'Drink your coffee and stop worrying. We know visitors are allowed because we were invited in as visitors and we're sitting in what feels suspiciously like a visitors' lounge. I could be wrong, of course.'

What they thought would be a ten-minute wait turned into twenty, then thirty, then forty minutes. Almost an hour later the nun they had seen earlier reappeared and said that Mother Superior would see them now.

Mother Francis Ann was a real cold fish. She had the word 'BOSS' chiselled deep into her icy, detached demeanour. With her wimple framing her perfectly oval face, she sat behind her desk and listened impassively to what Lydia had to say, her sharp grey eyes fixed on her at all times. Lydia put her at about sixty. There was an underlying air of the imperious headmistress about her. Perhaps running a convent wasn't that different from being in charge of a school? Her office, if that was what it was called, was sparsely furnished with a desk, four chairs and two book-cases. The wood was all shining with the kind of lustre that came with constant polishing. Pride of place above the fireplace was an oil painting of the Christ child in his mother's arms.

'I wonder you didn't think to telephone ahead,' the woman said when Lydia had finished speaking. 'You might have saved yourself the trouble of a long journey, as well as a great deal of disappointment.'

Lydia's heart sank. Valerie wasn't here after all. So much for her instinct.

'But as it is,' Old Frosty Knickers continued, her tone as impassive as her manner, 'your journey has not been in vain. I've spoken to Sister Valerie Michael and she says she'll see you.'

And the point of this interview? Lydia wanted to ask. But what did the process matter, when the end result was seeing Valerie again? Suddenly filled with heart-skipping excitement, Lydia couldn't believe it was really going to happen.

The woman rose from her chair, smoothed down her habit and straightened the crucifix hanging around her neck. There was something so controlled and sure about her; she didn't look like she'd ever experienced a moment's doubt or fluster. It riled Lydia. Made her want to shake the woman out of her trouble-free complacency and explain to her just how tough the real world was.

'I don't know if you know anything about us,' Mother Francis Ann said, as Lydia and Noah joined her at the door, 'but we're an Anglican order and we don't isolate ourselves from the rest of the world; we do a lot of work in the wider community. Having said that, we do have a few contemplatives who have taken the decision never to step beyond our walls here. Sister Valerie Michael is one such contemplative.'

Lydia had already discussed with Noah that she wanted to meet her sister on her own, so he was invited to return to the visitors' lounge to play with the coffee machine again. Lydia was led outside to where a man was at the top of a long ladder fixing a broken window. Presumably he was the owner of the Transit van on the drive. 'Follow the path round to the chapel,' she was instructed, 'then go through the arch in the wall, which will take you into the kitchen garden. You'll find Sister Valerie Michael in the greenhouse.'

They may have left the worst of the weather behind them in Swallowsdale, but the wind was just as bitterly cold here; it whipped at Lydia's face, making her eyes water. She passed several nuns wearing navy-blue fleecy jackets; they were busy raking leaves from the lawn, at the same time doing their best to stop the skirts of their habits from flying up in the wind. An irreverent image of Marilyn Monroe dressed as a nun popped into Lydia's mind. In the kitchen garden, another gang of workers was hard at it, staking and tying what looked like Brussels sprout plants. One of the women acknowledged Lydia with a wave and pointed to the large greenhouse in the distance. Word must have got round.

The door of the greenhouse slid back as Lydia drew near and a nun stood to one side to let her in. Lydia was about to thank her when she realized she was face to face with Valerie.

Seized with a split second of uncertainty, Lydia didn't know what the etiquette was in these situations. Did nuns hug people? She made an instant judgement call. What the hell! Valerie had been her sister long before she ever became a bride of Christ! Bursting with euphoria, she threw her arms wide and embraced Valerie.

But Valerie didn't return the hug. If anything, she stiffened in Lydia's arms and Lydia found herself awkwardly letting go of her. 'Sorry,' she said, embarrassed, 'is that not allowed?'

'Let me close the door,' Valerie said, without answering her question. 'It's cold out there. Please, come and sit down.' She led the way to where two wooden chairs were placed next to a small, ineffectual heater in the aisle of the greenhouse. Lydia made no move to take off her coat. Valerie, she noticed, wasn't wearing anything over her habit. 'How do you do it?' she asked, holding her hands out to the heater. 'Don't you feel the cold?'

'You get used to it. Thermal underwear helps.'

'Oh, this is much too surreal,' Lydia burst out. 'I haven't seen you in twenty-eight years and we're talking about the weather and thermal underwear!'

A flicker of a smile passed across Valerie's face as she straightened her habit around her. Beneath the severity of her clothing, Lydia could discern the pretty child she had once been. If anything, her delicate face was enhanced by the wimple. She looked fragile and vulnerable, much younger than her forty years. And quite beautiful. Presumably her lovely, long, blonde hair was no more, cut short to ward off the threat of vanity. But at least her voice was normal. Thank God she'd lost that ugly rasp of a voice.

'You look well, Valerie,' Lydia said.

Her back ramrod straight and her hands crossed on her

lap, making her seem almost child-like, Valerie said, 'So do you. I knew God would take care of you. I never doubted that one day he would bring you safely back to me and we'd—' Her voice wavered and tears suddenly filled her eyes. 'I just wasn't ever sure how it would make me feel when I saw you again,' she managed to add.

Lydia instantly leaned forward to comfort her but Valerie jerked away. 'Please don't,' she said. 'It's the shock. That's all.' She closed her eyes, clenching her hands tightly together. Feeling shut out, Lydia watched helplessly as her sister struggled to regain her composure. It was painful to see. Eventually Valerie opened her eyes. 'Where have you been all this time?' she asked quite calmly.

Tears filling her own eyes now, Lydia fumbled inside her bag for a tissue. 'Italy,' she said.

'*All* this time?' Valerie's tone had changed. Gone was the poignancy of just moments ago. Now she sounded polite, almost formal, as if they were strangers. She had clearly won the battle over her emotions.

But Lydia was losing her battle fast. This wasn't how she had imagined her reunion with her sister. Where was the spontaneous outpouring of love and joy over finding each other again? 'Yes,' she said, wiping her eyes. 'This is the first time I've been back to England since ... since I left Swallowsdale.'

'Really?'

The cold, indifferent way she said the word made Lydia think her sister didn't believe her. It made her worry all the more over Valerie's reaction to what she was about to say next. 'I'm sorry I left without saying goodbye to you,' she said. 'I've never forgiven myself for that.'

'The past is so long ago,' Valerie replied mechanically, without appearing to consider Lydia's words. 'It isn't something we should allow ourselves to dwell on.'

Lydia didn't know whether she admired her sister's extraordinary self-control or was angered by it. Was this what shutting yourself away from the real world taught you? To stamp hard on your emotions and bury them

437

deep? 'I disagree,' she said. 'The past is right here in this greenhouse. It's us, Val. You and me. It's why we haven't seen one another in twenty-eight years. Don't you want to know why I left without saying goodbye? Aren't you curious? Just a little?'

'It's enough that you're here,' Valerie said smoothly. 'That's all that matters to me.'

'Are you saying you've forgiven me?'

'Is that what you came here for?'

Surprised by Valerie's blunt frankness – and the truth of it – Lydia caught her breath. 'I ... I came because you're my sister and I love you.'

'But you also want me to forgive you, don't you?'

'Is that so very bad?'

Valerie stared back at Lydia in silence.

Lydia knew then that she had hurt her sister profoundly. Maybe irrevocably so. It was what she had always feared. Hanging on to that initial display of emotion Valerie had given way to, she said, 'I can't undo what I did, Val, but please, let me try and explain why I did what I did. Will you let me do that?'

'If you think it will help you, yes.'

'I hope it will help us both,' Lydia said, trying not to feel so unnerved or disappointed by her sister's coolness towards her. 'It's important to me that you know that my actions weren't premeditated. I didn't wake up that morning with the intention of hurting you.' Then, in as few words as she could, Lydia outlined the events in the dell and everything that immediately followed.

When she finished, a tiny crease of a frown appeared on Valerie's face, just between her eyebrows. 'But everyone knew straight away Noah couldn't have done it,' she murmured. 'The police had ruled him out because he'd fallen down the stairs and knocked himself unconscious. I don't understand why you went on protecting him.'

'I only discovered very recently about Noah falling down the stairs and ending up in hospital. From Noah himself.'

The frown deepened. 'But why didn't he tell you before?'

'We hadn't seen or spoken to each other until last week. All this time he thought I'd killed Uncle Leonard and I thought he'd done it. And that's why I'm here back in England. I came home to find out who really did kill that dreadful man. Noah and I saw Donna yesterday. Do you remember Donna Jones?'

'Yes.'

'She told me about Grandmother. That it was she who'd killed Uncle Leonard the night she'd escaped from the hospital. Donna said Grandmother confessed to the police that she had been acting according to God's wishes.'

Some of the tension went out of Valerie's body. 'You have to understand, Grandma was very ill,' she said quietly, a small tremor to her voice. 'She didn't know what she was doing. For so long the balance of her mind had been kept stable by the use of drugs. How could she possibly have any control over her actions?'

'I'm not judging her,' Lydia said quickly, sensitive to Valerie's devotion to their grandmother, even now. 'Please don't think that. I decided many years ago that it was probably our grandfather who helped to make her so ill. He was a very cruel man. I can't begin to think what kind of a god he believed in.'

Valerie took a moment to respond. 'You never really did have a faith, did you?'

'Actually, I did. And still do. Just not as clear-cut as yours. I was told that you're a contemplative nun; does that mean you've never left the order since you came here?'

Valerie nodded. 'That's right. And I never will leave it.'

'Don't you ever wonder what's going on out there?' Lydia very nearly said, 'in the real world', but she stopped herself. This place, for Valerie, *was* the real world.

'I have all I need here. This is where I belong.'

Intrigued, Lydia said, 'What do you spend your days doing?'

'Apart from serving God through prayer, we're committed to sharing our love of the Lord with our neighbours. And as well as baking communion wafers and making candles, we grow all our own fruit and vegetables and sell it to a number of local shops. We do the same with the honey we produce. We're not idle here, Lydia, if that's what you're thinking.'

Lydia caught the defensiveness in her sister's voice and changed the subject. 'Donna said that both our grandparents are dead now. Which makes us the end of the line.' She smiled ruefully. 'When we're gone, there'll be no more Turners.'

'I assumed you'd have children.'

'I have a stepdaughter called Chiara. She's beautiful, very clever, and I love her dearly.'

'How old is she?'

'Twenty-four. She was nine when she came into my life.'

'What about her father?'

'He died four years ago.'

'And now Noah has come back into your life?'

'More amazing than that, he has a son more or less the same age as Chiara.' She then told Valerie the full story of how she'd first seen Ishmael on the steps of the Rialto Bridge and everything that had fallen into place since.

Valerie looked thoughtful, and suddenly a lot less tense. 'When God wants something to happen, there's no obstacle that can get in his way,' she said.

'You're right; it does feel like fate.'

Valerie tutted. But she was smiling too, making her face quite radiant. 'Don't you remember what Pastor Digby used to say about fate? He said it was the heathen's way of rejecting God's existence.'

'Maybe I'll concede that one to you and Pastor Digby. But as to the vast majority of that man's teaching, I wouldn't give you tuppence. He was a dangerously malign influence on a lot of vulnerable people and he certainly enjoyed the power of his position.'

The sound of the greenhouse door sliding open had them both turning.

A breathless, red-faced nun burst in. Valerie gave her a disapproving look. 'Sister Peter Margaret,' she said, 'I specifically asked not to be disturbed.'

'Please, it's Mr Solomon. He's not well. We found him on the floor.'

Chapter Sixty

Lydia took back every bad thought she'd had about Mother Francis Ann. The woman's cool efficiency could not be faulted and by the time Lydia was by Noah's side, she had the situation under control. An ambulance had been called for and the two young nuns who had found Noah had been interrogated and sent on their way. After a brief exchange with Lydia, she also made a discreet exit in order to give them some time alone.

Lydia had been warned that Noah was groggy and disorientated, and keeping her voice level, she said, 'They seem to think you had some kind of a seizure, Noah. Have you ever had one before?'

She could see his dazed eyes trying to focus on her, as if he were drunk. 'Where's Lydia?' he murmured.

'I'm here, Noah. Right here with you.' She put her arm around his shoulder. His body was taut.

'Where's Lydia?' he repeated. 'I want Lydia here with me.'

All the way to the hospital in the ambulance, he remained in a weakened state of confusion. He still didn't know who Lydia was, but once he'd been checked over by the paramedic, he was happy for her to hold his hand. He kept murmuring to himself and closing his eyes, but if his eyes were shut for any length of time, because she was terrified what that might mean, Lydia would squeeze his hand to wake him.

He was seen immediately at the hospital. 'Mr Solomon,'

the young doctor said, whilst shining a light into his eyes, 'do you know where you are?'

The doctor's words seemed to bring Noah to his senses and he suddenly looked more alert. He opened his mouth to say something but then hesitated. He glanced uncertainly at Lydia. 'My office?' he said, like a small, anxious boy desperately wanting to give the right answer. Lydia smiled back at him encouragingly.

The doctor put away her torch and came and stood at the end of the bed with Lydia. 'What's wrong with him?' Lydia asked, her voice hushed even though she was sure Noah had no idea he was being talked about. 'It's as if he has amnesia.'

'I'm fairly confident that the loss of memory will pass, as will his general state of disorientation. The real concern is that the discs at the back of his eyes are swollen. It's called papilledema and is caused by a rise in pressure of the cerebrospinal fluid in the skull. I'm going to arrange for a CT scan first thing tomorrow morning.'

Suddenly amnesia was sounding a much better option. Lydia swallowed. 'What do you suppose the scan will show?'

'It's highly likely it will indicate the presence of a brain tumour.'

The world began to slide away from Lydia. 'But not always. Right?' Please God, not always.

'When we factor in what you've told us, the persistent headache, the seizure he experienced earlier, coupled with the subsequent confused and disorientated state, I'm afraid the evidence is stacking up. I think it would be best if he stays here with us tonight so we can keep an eye on him.'

Within the hour Noah had been transferred to a main ward. It was eight o'clock, visiting time, and Lydia was allowed to stay with him. They had the curtains pulled around the bed and Lydia was just pouring a glass of water from the jug on the locker when, in a sleepy faraway voice, Noah said, 'Lyddie, what's going on?'

443

She stopped what she was doing and sat on the bed. 'You know who I am now?'

He frowned. 'Of course I do. But how have we ended up here?' His words were slow and blurred around the edges as if he'd woken from a deep sleep. 'Have we had an accident?' He raked a hand through his hair. 'I feel so tired.'

'What's the last thing you remember?'

He blinked. 'Your sister. We were ... we were somewhere and I was waiting for you. And then ... Oh, God, I remember being scared. I was shaking. I thought I was going to die.' Each tiny fragment of memory seemed to weigh on him as heavy as a great boulder. Lydia could see him exhausting himself with the sheer effort of so much concentration. Her heart ached for him and she desperately wanted to prompt him, but she kept quiet, hoping he'd be able to find his way through the fog. Eventually he looked at her in despair. 'Help me, Lyddie, please. Tell me what's going on.'

Lydia wasn't allowed to stay the night with Noah, and when she took the lift down to the ground floor of the hospital she was tempted to rush back and defy anyone who tried to kick her out. But she knew it was useless. She had to trust what the doctor had said: that Noah was in safe hands.

The lift opened onto the main reception area and she was met by the sound of singing. Carol singers were gathered around a Christmas tree, giving voice to 'Away in a Manger'. It was so reminiscent of school carol services – standing next to Noah and smirking their way through the verses – it made Lydia want to burst into tears. She had nowhere to stay for the night. No transport. And worst of all, so very, very worst of all, maybe no Noah.

Going outside into the dark and the cold, she dug around in her handbag for her mobile to make the all-important call to Chiara, who would then have to explain things to Ishmael.

She woke the next morning feeling stiff and hung-over. Not from alcohol, but from fear. Letting her eyes grow accustomed to the light filtering in through the badly fitting curtains at the window, she lay very still, gathering her senses and willing the tension out of her body. She could hear a television through the wall at her head and voices in the corridor the other side of the door. Signs that for some people this was just another ordinary day. She pushed back the bedclothes and hauled herself off to the bathroom in need of a hot, reinvigorating shower. What she got was little more than a lukewarm trickle. Afterwards, to add insult to injury, she had to put on the same clothes she'd worn yesterday.

A porter at the hospital last night had recommended this soulless hotel because it was within easy walking distance. Its location was pretty much all it had going for it. Downstairs, in the faux Mediterranean dining room where badly painted sunny scenes of al fresco dining adorned the walls, Lydia endured a breakfast of tinned grapefruit and floppy toast whilst watching overweight men gorging themselves on piled-high plates of fried food. Lydia imagined sharing the horribleness of the place with Noah later that morning, joking with him that they would never again bad-mouth the Oak Manor Court Hotel.

She checked out and retraced her steps along the busy road of nose-to-tail traffic to the hospital. She was almost there when her mobile rang. It was Fabio. Without preamble he said that Chiara had told him everything. Above the roar of traffic noise, the sound of his dear voice, so full of love and concern, was too much for her and she thought she might choke with the strain of not giving in to her fears. Throughout the conversation, passers-by threw odd glances in her direction, and it was only when she was saying goodbye to Fabio that she understood why: she had been speaking in Italian. She had forgotten how British people stared at anyone different from themselves.

Passing the locked gate of a church on her left, Lydia

thought of her sister. She couldn't even remember saying goodbye to Valerie yesterday; she had somehow melted away into the background with all the other nuns. Lydia hoped that the next time they met, Valerie's chilly reserve might have thawed. She couldn't hope to be forgiven so soon, but surely now that Valerie knew the truth she would gradually come to accept the sacrifice Lydia had made, and would let go of the hurt she had hung on to all these years. After all, hadn't Lydia done the same with Noah? Hadn't she harboured feelings of hostility and angry resentment towards him when she'd been blinded by misunderstanding?

Noah was definitely in better shape than when she'd left. He was still experiencing a degree of tiredness, causing his movements to appear slow and leaden, but he was mentally alert and fully aware of what was going on. Lydia was given permission to go with him for the CT scan and held his hand when it was confirmed that he did indeed have a tumour. In layman's speak it was situated at the front of his skull, above his left eye and was about the size of a satsuma. The good news was that it was highly probable it wasn't malignant. Even better, it was in an accessible spot where it could be removed. Given the seizure Noah had experienced and the prolonged spell of grogginess he'd undergone, the recommendation was that the tumour should be dealt with sooner rather than later. With his healthcare cover, he was to be referred to a private neurosurgeon near to home in Northamptonshire. He could expect to be admitted for surgery in a couple of days. It was made to sound so commonplace. They could have been sitting in a travel agent's office booking a holiday.

But what about the What Ifs?

This was brain surgery they were discussing, not some trip to the dentist for a filling. Start opening up a person's skull and anything could happen. What if the operation went wrong and Noah ended up in a vegetative state for the rest of his life? Or what if the tumour turned out to

be malignant? What would Noah's chances of survival be? And the biggest What If of all: what if Noah was taken away from her? For ever.

Officially discharged from the hospital, they took a taxi back to the convent where they'd left Noah's car. The dirty white van was still there on the drive alongside his Mercedes. The words on the back of it had been wiped off.

Lydia paid the driver and they went and rang the bell. Noah had said he'd wanted to thank Mother Francis Ann for her help yesterday and to apologize for creating such a commotion. And, of course, Lydia wanted to speak to her sister again.

Back into Old Frosty Knickers mode, the woman disregarded Noah's thanks with an airy wave of the hand. Then without another word on the subject, she turned her attention to Lydia. 'While you're talking with Sister Valerie Michael, I'll take Mr Solomon to the chapel to pray with him.'

Lydia might have been less surprised if the woman had offered her a marker pen to scribble a moustache and a pair of glasses on the Madonna and Child painting above the fireplace. However, while she was glad of the opportunity to see Val again, she was less than enthusiastic about letting Noah out of her sight. Those What Ifs were never far from her mind. He was definitely much more his old self, which was what the doctor had said would happen as the day wore on, but what if he had another seizure? As though reading her mind, Noah said, 'I'll be fine, Lyddie. Don't worry.'

To confirm matters, Old Frosty Knickers said, 'I'll send for Sister Valerie Michael. You can talk to her here.'

Left on her own to wait for her sister, Lydia brooded anxiously. Why was Old Frosty Knickers so keen to get Noah alone with her in the chapel? He hadn't mentioned his tumour to the nun – they hadn't even had the chance

to discuss it properly themselves yet – but did the woman suspect his life hung in the balance and want to encourage him to put some serious petitioning in before it was too late?

The minutes ticked slowly by whilst Lydia waited patiently for Valerie to appear. She mentally began compiling a list of all the things she needed to ask her sister. For instance, who had their grandfather married after their grandmother had died?

A faint knock at the door, followed by the appearance of a frail, elderly nun interrupted her list-making. 'I'm very sorry, but Sister Valerie Michael says she's unable to see you today. Can I get you a drink instead?'

'And she gave no reason why she couldn't see you?' Noah asked when they were on the road once more. This time, though, it was Lydia at the wheel of the expensive car. Having never driven on the left-hand side of the road before, she was taking it steadily, finding her way cautiously with the powerful engine.

Her gaze glued to the road ahead, she said, 'No reason given at all.'

A mile sped by and Noah said, 'You haven't told me how it went yesterday with your sister. Being the unthinking bugger I am, I rather stole the show on your reunion, didn't I?'

Seething with a potent mix of disappointment and anger that Valerie could have snubbed her so pettily, Lydia said, 'If you don't mind, I don't want to talk about Valerie just now. I'd rather talk about you.' She hated to think this was her sister's way of getting her own back. See, this is how it feels to be tossed aside!

'You sound cross, Lyddie.'

'I am.'

'Then don't be. Especially when you're driving my car.'

She slid him a sideways glance and saw that he was smiling. She smiled back at him.

'That's better,' he said.

Several miles later, after Noah had directed her onto the motorway, she was feeling more confident behind the wheel. 'You haven't told me what you and Mother Superior got up to in the chapel.'

'Funnily enough, she did exactly what she'd offered to do. She prayed for me. And for the coming days.'

'Did you tell her what the doctors had diagnosed?'

'That was the odd thing. It was as if she already knew that it was pretty serious.'

Another silence lapsed between them. Minutes later, when Lydia glanced across at Noah, she saw that his eyelids were closed. She hoped he wouldn't sleep for long; she needed his directions to get home.

From its hands-free cradle on the dashboard, Noah's mobile let out a sudden loud trill. He leaned forward immediately – as if he hadn't been asleep at all – and pressed the answer button. A voice Lydia knew straight away filled the car. It was richer and fuller than when she'd last heard it, but unmistakable all the same.

'Noah, it's me, Brad. Ishmael's been on the blower. What's the latest news? Bearing in mind these doctors don't know their arse from their elbow these days.'

'They certainly know a brain tumour when they see one. I've seen the picture of it myself.'

'I don't believe it!'

'I'm having trouble believing it myself.'

'What's the next step?'

'Surgery. There's talk of an operation the day after tomorrow.'

'Bloody hell! They're not messing about, are they? How do you feel?'

'Like I've been hit with both barrels.'

'Has the C word been mentioned at all?'

'It's not been ruled out. Although they seem to think it's unlikely. They'll know for sure when they open me up.'

'Is Lydia there with you?'

'Yes she is. You can speak to her if you want.'

But Lydia couldn't speak to anyone. She was having

trouble seeing, too; her eyes were brimming with tears. Spotting an exit slip road for a service station, she swerved into the inside lane and shot off the motorway. When it was safe to do so, she brought the car to a stop. She was crying so hard now she was shaking.

'I'll call you back later, Uncle Brad.' Noah ended the call. 'Lyddie?'

'I'm sorry,' she said, her forehead against the top of the steering wheel. 'I just can't bear to hear you talking about it so calmly. You sound so in control, whereas I feel utterly useless. You need me to be strong and supportive, and I'm a pathetic emotional wreck.'

Very gently, he pulled her head away from the steering wheel and turned her to face him. 'I was going to wait until we got home,' he said, 'but I might just as well say it now. I want you to listen very carefully to what I'm about to say and understand that this is what I want. What I *need*. OK, Lyddie?'

She wiped her eyes with her hands. 'I'm listening.'

'We've done exactly what we came here to do. We found out who really did kill your great-uncle Leonard and you now have nothing hanging over you. From here on you're free to get on with the rest of your life and enjoy it to the full. No more guilt. No more regret.' He paused and took a breath. 'I want you to go home to Venice tomorrow.'

'Are you mad? I'm not going anywhere tomorrow unless it's with you.'

He shook his head impatiently, as if he'd explained this several times already. 'Look, the truth is, I don't need you here. I want you to go home. I want you to promise me you'll stay there in Venice and get on with your life and live happily ever after.'

Chapter Sixty-One

Nothing could have more effectively knocked the feeble-
ness out of Lydia. She wiped her eyes again and blew her
nose. 'I thought it was me who had the habit of making
misguided unilateral decisions,' she said.

He turned away from her and stared straight ahead.
'You don't need to be involved.'

'I am already. So just accept I'm not leaving you. I'm
here for the long haul.'

'I mean it, Lyddie. I don't want you around if things get ...'
He didn't finish. Lydia waited. 'Sticky,' he said finally.

'I'm not arguing with you, Noah. So you can forget
about me going back to Venice. And anyway, who says
things are going to get sticky? The doctor says this is a
perfectly routine operation with a good rate of success.'

He turned and settled his fractured gaze on hers. Seconds
passed before he spoke. 'Then why are you so scared?'

She covered his hand with hers. 'Because I wouldn't be
human if I wasn't. I love you, Noah. I don't want anything
bad to happen to you. Ever.'

'And I don't want you to see me if it goes wrong and I
become some dribbling—'

'Don't say it,' she said, cutting him short. 'We're both
stunned and exhausted and latching on to worst-case
scenarios. Besides, how would it be if the boot was on the
other foot? If it was me facing this?'

Rain began to patter lightly against the windscreen.
He breathed in deeply, then exhaled slowly. 'Damn you,
Lyddie.' He raised her hand to his lips. 'I'd be there with
you every step of the way. As well you know.'

Twisting round in the small space, she took him in her arms and kissed him. 'We've been through too much not to survive this little glitch, Noah.' She kissed him again. 'What's more, we have your birthday to celebrate next year. I want you to be in Venice with me and we'll do something special. Something outrageous.'

'I'm not bungee jumping off the bell tower in St Mark's. Not even for you.'

She smiled. 'Spoilsport.'

Lydia was not the only one who was taking matters into her own hands. They were twenty minutes from home when Ishmael phoned to say that he would be flying over tomorrow. 'Any chance I can persuade you not to?' Noah asked him.

'Absolutely none whatsoever,' came back Ishmael's reply. 'Oh, and I've told Mum. She's going to ring you in the morning.'

When the call was over, Noah said, 'You're all ganging up against me.'

'Are you surprised? My advice is to give in gracefully.'

He put a hand on Lydia's leg and kept it there for the rest of the journey.

It had been a long day and they went to bed early. But neither of them could sleep. Noah's head ached more when he lay down and Lydia's was too full of What Ifs to sleep. 'Only one thing for it,' Noah said, gently easing Lydia onto her back and dispensing with her nightdress. 'Better make hay whilst we can, because after tomorrow who knows when I'll be able to get you in bed again?'

'And don't forget all the years we need to catch up on.'

'Good point,' he said, pushing away the duvet so he could look at her. He placed the palm of his hand on her stomach. 'Do you remember those nude sketches I did of you?'

'You haven't still got them, have you?'

452

'Of course I have. I could never have parted with them. And before you ask, no one else has ever seen them.'

'Where are they?'

'Hidden at the back of Uncle Brad's portrait of you. I put them there when I resigned myself to the unthinkable: that I was never going to see you again.'

'I kept the few photographs I had of you,' she admitted. 'I hadn't looked at them in years. Not until last week, after meeting Ishmael. Do you still draw?'

'When I have the time. I'd love to draw you again.' He lowered his head and kissed her.

For a brief blissful time they lost themselves in each other, banishing the strain and anxiety of the last twenty-four hours from their minds. Yet there was a poignant, bittersweet intensity to their lovemaking. With every touch, every kiss, was the fear their newfound happiness might be cut short.

They were still in bed when the telephone rang just before nine o'clock the next morning. It was the hospital, to say Noah's operation was booked for the following day.

Not ten minutes later, when they were still in bed, the phone rang again. This time it was Noah's ex-wife, Jane. Lydia left him to take the call in private while she went downstairs to make some breakfast. In response to a call from Noah yesterday, Mrs Massey had once more worked her magic and stocked the fridge for the coming days. A cafetiere of coffee and scrambled eggs on toast seemed a fitting way to start the day.

Lydia put the kettle on first, and while opening the fridge for the eggs, her attention was caught by the framed photograph of Ishmael. As he smiled back at her, she thought how different his childhood must have been from his father's. Did he even know about Noah's parents and the way they died? Or was that something Noah never discussed? Just as she had never shared with Marcello and Chiara the truth of her upbringing, glossing over it with a highly edited version of the truth. Lydia had read about

people who became obsessed with their ancestry as a way to affirm who they were themselves, but she had never felt the urge to dig deeper than her own parents. Her mother had been an orphan and Lydia didn't have a clue who her maternal grandparents had been. Nor did she care. She had always been more concerned with the present.

When she had everything on a tray, Lydia carried it upstairs. Noah was still on the phone when she nudged open the door. He beckoned her in when she held back, not wanting to intrude. 'Thanks, Jane,' he said. 'No, I promise I won't worry about work; I know you've got it covered. And yes, I'll get Ishmael to give you a call just as soon as he knows anything. You take care as well. I'll see you soon. Bye.'

'Do you think we ought to take the phone off the hook?' he asked when Lydia put the tray on the end of the bed and passed him his breakfast. 'I'm not sure how convincing I am at reassuring people that everything is going to be fine. Poor Jane was trying her hardest not to sound like she was saying goodbye to me for the last time.'

'You're still very fond of one another, aren't you?' Lydia said, sliding back into bed with him and surprising herself that she didn't feel any jealousy now towards the woman who'd been lucky enough to be married to Noah.

'We may not have been ideally suited as husband and wife, but in other ways we get on extremely well. I told her about you. About *us*.'

'What did she say?'

'She said that it explained everything. She never suspected me of being unfaithful, but she'd always known that there had been someone else. She wished us luck. She meant it, too.'

'I'd like to meet her one day.'

Noah smiled. 'That's what she said about you.'

They showered together, got dressed and decided to go for a walk. They left their mobiles behind, not wanting to be disturbed.

It was a bitterly cold day. The sun was scarcely more than a faint white glow in the grey sky. The fields and hedgerows were still covered in a thick white frost. Puddles were iced over and bare tree branches looked blackened and petrified.

At the end of Noah's drive they took the main road, following it until the cottages and houses – all dressed for Christmas with holly wreaths on their doors and cards at the windows – ran out either side of them. Leaving the road, they slowly meandered their way towards a large oak tree on the crest of a hill.

At the top, they stopped to take in the far-reaching views; the only sound to be heard, other than their breathing, came from the crows cawing loudly from the highest branches of the tree. The landscape was very different from Swallowsdale. There was a beguiling softness to it. No bleakness. No dark stretches of treacherous moorland. Just a satisfying sense of peace.

Noah leaned his cane against the tree and came and stood behind Lydia. He wrapped his arms around her, resting his chin on the top of her head. 'The day seems frozen in time, doesn't it?' he said.

Wishing that it really could always be this moment – the day before Noah's operation when he was still safe – Lydia said, 'You must be very happy living here. It's so beautiful.'

'I'd be happier with you here.'

She pulled his arms more tightly around her.

'I know what you're thinking,' he said. 'You're trying to figure out how we can make it work, aren't you? Well don't. I've got it licked. We divide our time between our respective homes and businesses. I come to you. You come to me. See, it couldn't be easier.'

She turned and faced him. 'Smart-arse Solomon, you always did have all the answers, didn't you?'

Ishmael arrived just as Lydia's mobile rang. She left Noah and his son to talk and went upstairs to take the call.

She was slow to pick up on the voice. 'Valerie?' she said uncertainly.

'Lydia, I want to talk to you again.'

The hurt and anger Lydia had felt before surfaced at once and multiplied. 'Why wouldn't you see me yesterday?'

'I couldn't.'

'Couldn't or wouldn't?'

'Please don't make this any more difficult for me than it already is. Come here tomorrow and I'll explain properly.'

'I'm sorry, I can't. I'm with Noah. He goes into hospital tomorrow morning for an operation and I'm afraid there's nothing on this earth that will tear me away from his side.'

There was a long silence. It went on for so long that Lydia thought the connection had been broken. 'Val?' she said. 'Are you still there?'

'Yes, I'm still here. I was just recalling how you always did choose Noah over me.'

The accusation scythed through Lydia. 'Please don't say that to me. I did everything I could for you, Val. *Everything!*'

'Did you? Did you really?'

Again the scything blow. Whoever came up with the phrase 'the truth always hurts' knew what they were talking about. 'I know you'll never forgive me for leaving you the way I did, but remember, I was eighteen. I did my best. For the rest of my life I'll have to live with the knowledge that it wasn't enough for you.'

Hearing herself pleading with her sister made Lydia even more upset. What she was feeling was too deep for rational argument and so she flung at Valerie her one last desperate attempt to make things right between them. 'If only for everything your faith must mean to you, Valerie, can't you find it in yourself to forgive me?'

When even that failed to elicit a response from her sister, Lydia said, 'If you really want to speak to me, why don't you come and see me here?'

'You know that's not possible.'

'Nothing's impossible, Val. Not if you want it badly enough.'

In the morning, Ishmael drove the three of them to the hospital in his car. They met the surgeon who was going to operate. His manner was confident and reassuring, and he spared no effort in describing what the procedure would be during and after the operation, saying that if everything went according to plan, Noah was looking at approximately five hours on the operating table followed by ten days' recovery in hospital. It was the word 'recovery' that Lydia focused on as she listened to the soothing voice of the surgeon, at the same time sizing up the man's hands – the hands that Noah's life now rested in. Just how capable and experienced were they?

At last it was the moment Lydia had been dreading; she had to say goodbye to Noah. Ishmael had already spent some time alone with his father. Now it was Lydia's turn.

'Just in case you don't recognize me when I see you next, I'll be the one who looks like a boiled egg with the top cracked open,' Noah joked with her.

'Now I know what to buy you for Christmas,' she said. 'A hat.' She bent down and squeezed his hand. 'I'll be waiting for you.'

He beckoned her closer.

She bent down. 'Yes?'

'Closer,' he said. 'There's something important I want to say.'

She did as he said and bent so close that his mouth was brushing against her ear. 'Just in case there's any doubt in your mind,' he whispered, 'I love you, Lyddie. Always have. Always will.'

She forced a smile to her trembling lips. 'I love you too, Noah.'

*

Three hours into the operation, Lydia left Ishmael in the waiting room and took the stairs down to the ground floor. At the bottom of the stairs, she followed the signs. Several corridors later, a set of automatic doors let her into the reception area. The doors hadn't even swished behind her when she spotted two nuns sitting with their backs to her.

She went over and whilst she didn't know the one who was knitting and talking to a young mother with a child in a pushchair, the other nun wasn't a stranger. Sitting rigidly with her hands on her lap, no one could have looked more thoroughly out of place than Valerie. Lydia felt a pang of pity towards her. And empathy. Because ironically they were both experiencing a similar culture clash – after twenty-eight years of living in Italy, Britain was just as alien to Lydia as it must be to Valerie.

She went over and touched her sister lightly on the shoulder.

Valerie visibly started. Seeing the strain in her face, Lydia could see that this visit was costing her dearly. The other nun broke off from her conversation with the young mother, shoved her knitting to one side and introduced herself as Sister Catherine John. She was possibly ten years Valerie's junior and was altogether more relaxed and assured. 'I've travelled down with Sister Valerie Michael,' she explained in a jolly voice. 'We had an excellent journey, didn't we? And met some fascinating people.'

Lydia detected annoyance in Valerie's face. Lydia didn't blame her. Doubtless Sister Catherine John thought she was being a helpful, friendly minder but two seconds in her company and it was obvious to Lydia that she was a stone's throw from patronizing and insulting her nervous charge. Lydia stepped in. 'You're probably desperate for something to eat or drink,' she said to Sister Catherine John. 'There's an excellent coffee bar here on the ground floor.' Lydia had no idea how good or bad the refreshments on offer were – she and Ishmael had been using the vending machine on their floor – but the sooner she got Valerie alone, the better.

'Thank you,' Valerie said, when Lydia was leading the way to where she hoped her sister would feel more at ease. 'Sister Catherine John means well, but she has yet to learn the rich reward of silence.'

'How very tactfully put,' Lydia said with a smile. 'Was your journey very awful?'

'I pretended to sleep for part of it.'

The hospital chapel was empty and with only the simple altar and wooden cross subtly lit from an overhead light, even Lydia felt a soothing calm embrace her when they entered. She felt glad now that Noah had had the presence of mind to give Mother Francis Ann their mobile phone numbers so that Valerie would be able to get in touch at a later date if she so wanted. If he hadn't, she and Valerie wouldn't be here now. The fact that Valerie had made the sacrifice of leaving the convent meant everything to Lydia. It meant her sister must have had a change of heart.

They sat down in the front row of seats and in their different ways offered up an act of prayer. Lydia didn't know what Valerie might be sharing with God, but she was in the mood for some straightforward blackmail: take Noah from me, she warned God, and our relationship will be over. *Finito!*

Valerie lifted her head long after Lydia had finished dishing out her threats, and with both hands holding on to the cross round her neck, she said, 'You were right the other day when you said the past is always with us, that we can't pretend otherwise. It never leaves us, no matter how hard we try to isolate ourselves from it.'

'What made you change your view?'

'You. You stirred up too many memories. Memories I didn't want to relive.'

'I'm sorry.'

'Don't be. I've spent a lifetime being penitent and I'm ashamed to say it hasn't worked entirely.'

Surprised by this admission, but deciding to address it later, Lydia voiced the first of so many questions she had

to ask. 'Why did you accuse me on the phone yesterday of not taking care of you?'

'I was suddenly reminded how, as a child, you had what I always wanted, a friend. A real friend.'

'But you gave the impression of not needing one. You had the Brothers and Sisters. And our grandmother. You were close to her in a way I never was. She adored you.'

'You're describing relationships I had with adults. Is that normal for a young girl?'

'I've come to know there's nothing normal in this world, Val. When we were children I thought everyone else was normal except for me.'

'But you had Noah. You could share things with him.'

'I didn't always. For a time there were things I was so deeply ashamed of I hid them even from Noah, because I was convinced I'd lose him if he knew the truth. I've since discovered we all do it. We're all scared and vulnerable. In fact, we're all so abnormal we're completely normal.'

Looking down at her hands, her voice low, Valerie said, 'I tried so hard to be what Grandma wanted me to be. I trusted her and believed everything she ever said. And all the time, she was ill. Deluded.' She raised her eyes and faced Lydia. 'Do you ever worry that we may have inherited that from her? That maybe we could be the same?'

'Schizophrenic, you mean?'

Valerie nodded.

'As an adult I've never considered it. But as a teenager, when we were coping with Grandmother's illness, yes, I did sometimes worry about it. I also had the memory of our mother's behaviour after Dad died. I could see that on both sides of our family there were problems.'

'Don't you worry about it now?'

'No. Do you?'

'Constantly. I've suffered with depression for years. Sometimes I sink so low with it I feel I can't face another day.'

'Oh, Val, I'm so sorry. Is there help available to you? At the convent?'

'I have a spiritual mentor. She's very patient and kind but we both know that our sessions together are never going to heal the sickness that lies at the heart of my problems.'

'Are you honest with her?'

Valerie shook her head.

Very tentatively, Lydia said, 'Could you be honest with me?'

As though she hadn't heard, Valerie said, 'For two nights now, since you came to St Agnes, I've had nightmares. Terrible nightmares. I've been screaming out aloud and walking in my sleep. It hasn't happened in a long time. Mother Francis Ann heard about it yesterday morning and suggested it might be useful for me to speak to you again.' She swallowed. 'Actually, it was more of an order than a suggestion.'

Once again Lydia had to think well of Old Frosty Knickers. Whatever the source of the woman's intuition, Lydia was happy to go along with it. Choosing her words with care, she said, 'In what way did she think a meeting between us would be useful to you, Val?'

An eternity passed before Valerie answered her. 'I can't speak on behalf of Mother Francis Ann,' she began, 'but I've ...' She faltered and squeezed her eyes shut. Then opened them. 'I've reached the conclusion that you're my only hope. You're the only person I can tell this to. And I'm afraid that if I don't, I'll end up just like Grandma.'

Chapter Sixty-Two

The door of the chapel opened, spilling light in as well as a breathless old man. He sat in a chair on the back row of seats, his head bowed, his wheezy, laboured breathing dominating the small space. He didn't stay long. When the door closed after him, Lydia said, 'We could go somewhere else if you'd rather?'

'No, this is fine.'

Before picking up where they'd left off, Lydia had something she needed to say, something that on top of everything else had been bothering her enormously. 'I'm sorry I was so short with you on the telephone yesterday,' she said. 'I was angry with you. Which I know is no excuse. But I was just so upset not to see you again.'

'We do many things through anger,' Valerie said faintly. 'It's a powerful emotion. Possibly the most dangerous weapon anyone can ever be in possession of. Even our Lord wasn't above it.'

Lydia had always thought that episode of Christ's pique – when he turned over the tables in the temple – was every bad-tempered Christian's over-played Get Out of Jail card. She kept this to herself, though.

'I also need to apologize,' Valerie said, 'for being distant with you when you came to see me. I hope that by the end of this conversation you'll understand why I found our meeting so difficult. Not that this one is going to be any easier. Suddenly I don't know where to start.'

'How about those nightmares you mentioned?'

Valerie's hands returned to her cross, her eyes fixed firmly on the altar. She swallowed. 'They're to do with

Uncle Leonard. He wasn't killed by our grandmother as everyone thinks.'

'But she confessed to it,' Lydia said. 'Donna told me it was in the newspapers, and that she was moved to a secure hospital after the police had to accept she was too ill to stand trial.'

'I know all that,' Valerie said, her gaze now coming slowly round to Lydia's. 'Don't forget I was there living and breathing it. I saw how the hospital was only too happy to let our grandmother be moved somewhere else and the whole case hushed up. The last thing they wanted was anyone pointing the finger at them for allowing her to escape in the first place. But I'm telling you, I know who really murdered Uncle Leonard. I've always known. And I can promise you it wasn't our poor sick grandmother.'

The intensity of Valerie's words carved out a momentary silence between them. Lydia's mind raced. If not their grandmother, who? Her grandfather? Of course it had to be him. Just as she'd thought.

'Aren't you going to ask me who it was?' Valerie said.

'It was our grandfather, wasn't it?' Lydia replied.

Valerie sighed and shook her head wearily as if Lydia had just got the simplest of questions wrong. 'No, Lydia, it wasn't our grandfather. It was me. I murdered Uncle Leonard.'

An icy sliver of shock pierced Lydia's heart. She battled it. It couldn't be true. But why would Valerie say it was? Was it possible she was displaying some kind of extreme misplaced devotion for their grandmother? 'But you couldn't have done it,' Lydia reasoned. 'You were a child. You were only twelve years old.'

'I was an angry, confused and very scared child. I was perfectly capable of committing murder.'

Another sliver of shock found its target. Bewildered, Lydia said, 'But why?'

Valerie's gaze, which had been rock solid until now, wavered. 'That afternoon ... Uncle Leonard came into

463

our bedroom, he ... he made me—' She clasped her cross tighter still, her knuckles as white as her face.

Lydia felt the colour drain from her own face. No! He wouldn't have dared. Not Valerie. 'Val,' she said, 'tell me he didn't touch you. Please God, tell me it wasn't that.'

Valerie shuddered. But she didn't speak. Her eyes were wide and Lydia could see the horror and anguish in them. 'Tell me what he did, Val.'

She opened her mouth to speak but no sound came out. Instead her face twisted in a grimace of anguish. Tears spilled down her cheeks. 'I ... I tried to make him stop, but—' Her shoulders heaved. 'But he wouldn't. He kept saying it was in the name of Jesus. He said it was what God wanted for me and I would enjoy it. He said I was special. His special friend.' She began to shake violently, wrapping her arms around her body.

Cold, implacable anger gripped at Lydia's insides. 'Are you saying he raped you?'

Valerie let out a low-pitched groan of immense pain. Tears rushed to Lydia's eyes and she put her arms around Valerie. But Valerie's body was like stone and Lydia could feel her cowering away from her. 'I'm sorry,' she sobbed, gulping for air. 'Even now I can't bear to be touched.'

Lydia let go of her. She frantically hunted through her bag for some tissues, then, risking a hand on her sister's shoulder, she gently dabbed at Valerie's face, wiping away her tears. 'Why didn't you say anything to me?' Lydia asked when at last Valerie seemed able to speak. 'I would have done something. I would have gone to the police. I would have killed him myself!'

'I was in shock. Then immediately after it had happened, Noah appeared at the house and of course all that mattered to you then, was him.'

Lydia froze, remembering with awful clarity the way Uncle Leonard had sauntered down the stairs. She remembered, too, Valerie standing on the landing. At the time she and Joey had thought her sister was alarmed by the commotion going on in the hall, when really ...

when really she'd just been raped by that monster and was traumatized. Another sickening realization hit home. The evil act had taken place when Lydia, she, who had promised their mother she would always look after Valerie, was downstairs in the kitchen getting tea ready, oblivious to what was going on above her head.

'It was while we were washing up after tea that I decided to kill him,' Valerie said quietly. 'It came to me so clearly I was convinced it was the right thing to do. I'd heard Noah shouting on the doorstep that Uncle Leonard had done something to you, too and I knew he had to be stopped. All I had to do was wait for the right moment. It came sooner than I expected. That very night. I couldn't sleep and when I heard footsteps on the stairs, then the sound of the back door being opened, I crept to the bathroom window where I could look out onto the back garden. I saw Uncle Leonard climbing over the garden wall. I didn't bother to get dressed. I went downstairs, grabbed my shoes and anorak and the carving knife from the drawer and followed him.'

'But how did you ever think you would be able to overpower him?' Lydia asked. 'He was such a big man.'

'If you had been in my place, would you have worried about a trivial detail like that? All I could think about was plunging that knife deep into his chest. The very thought of it was hypnotic and it guided me through the darkness as much as the moonlight did. It was as if I was being led. I really had no choice in the matter.'

Lydia watched her sister closely. Watched her lips. Watched her hands. She was very still now. Very calm. Very composed. Unnaturally so. It was as if she had gone into a trance, hypnotized again by the memory of reliving that dreadful night.

'Again luck was with me,' Valerie continued, 'because when he got to the area of fallen trees, he sat down behind one of them, as if he was waiting for someone. It was so much easier than I'd thought it would be. I watched him get comfortable, then silently crept up behind with a thick

branch in my hand. I thought if I could stun him first, then I'd stab him. And I did. With both hands, I pushed the knife into his heart as hard as I could. I did it several times. Just to be sure. Just to be sure he'd never come near me ever again. Or you.' She turned to Lydia. 'Are you very shocked by what I've told you?'

Lydia swallowed. 'He deserved it, Val. He really did. What did you do next?'

'I ran home. I washed the knife in the sink, put it back in the drawer and then stuffed my anorak and nightdress under my bed to clean in the morning. I hadn't bargained on there being so much blood. I'd been in bed for no more than a few minutes when I saw you get up in the darkness. I pretended to be asleep. When I heard you go downstairs and open the back door, I went to the bathroom window again and looked down onto the garden. There you were, climbing over the wall. I assumed you were meeting Noah and I thought of going after you and telling you what I'd done. I suddenly wanted your assurance. I needed someone to tell me it wasn't wrong what I'd done. But then I lost my nerve. What if you told me it was wrong? What if you were angry with me?'

'Oh, Val, I would have helped you any way I could. Just as I had thought I was helping Noah.'

'Really?'

Her heart and throat tight with sorrow, Lydia said, 'Of course.' She stretched out a tentative hand to her sister, palm upwards. A moment passed and then Valerie placed her own hand lightly on top of it. With extreme gentleness, Lydia curled her fingers around Valerie's. In a muffled, faltering voice, she said, 'Do you want to carry on talking or have you had enough for now?'

Valerie blinked her eyes rapidly, chasing away more tears. 'I want to tell you everything,' she said. 'That's why I've come here. I'm not leaving until I have. I want to tell you what else I did that was so wicked.'

'Don't ever say that. It wasn't wicked.'

'Hear me out and then you might change your mind.

After I'd watched you climb over the wall, I got back into bed and prayed and prayed that you wouldn't discover the body. The next thing I knew, it was morning and the only thing on my mind was to lock myself in the bathroom and wash myself clean. Over and over. When I finally came out from the bathroom, you were gone. I thought you'd left for work early. I never dreamt it would be so long before I'd see you again.'

'When did our grandfather notice his brother was missing?'

'He didn't start to wonder where either of you were until that evening when I was bringing in the washing. When you still didn't show up at bedtime he became angry, saying you'd catch it from him in the morning. Two days later he spoke to Sister Lottie to see if she knew anything, but she said she hadn't seen you. But at church, she said something odd to me, something that made me think she knew more than she was letting on. She said I wasn't to worry, that she knew with total certainty that God had you tightly in his hand.'

Lydia nodded. 'I sent her a letter saying I needed to get away from Swallowsdale for a while. I asked her not to tell anyone that I'd written to her. She was a surprisingly good keeper of secrets.'

'As far as I know she kept that letter a complete secret. You know she died the same year, don't you?'

Lydia nodded again. 'It was very brave of you, but why did you go back into the dell and then pretend to discover Uncle Leonard's body?'

'Do you remember Brian from church?'

'The lad with the toy rabbit?'

'Yes. While his parents were having a meeting with Pastor Digby and our grandfather at our house, I suggested Brian and I went for a walk. I was sure the police would never suspect me, a twelve-year-old girl, of being the murderer, but just to be on the safe side I'd got it into my head that it might look better if I innocently stumbled across the body when somebody was with me. But it all went wrong. People

started saying that you must have killed Uncle Leonard. And that was why you'd disappeared. Then it dawned on me. You'd run away because you thought Noah had killed Uncle Leonard just as he'd threatened to do, and you were protecting him. I couldn't believe the mess I'd made of everything. I didn't know what to do. The last thing I'd wanted was for you to be blamed for something I had done. I wanted to go to the police and tell them the truth, but the thought of explaining why I'd done it made me feel ill. I couldn't do it. I even thought of talking to Noah, but he was in hospital. And to be honest I couldn't bring myself to tell anyone what had happened.' She bowed her head. 'I'm sorry, Lydia. I ruined everything. I ruined your life by turning you into an exile. I never meant to do that. Believe me, please.'

'It was my love for Noah that turned me into an exile,' Lydia said. 'It was my decision entirely.'

'But if I hadn't killed Uncle Leonard you would never have had to make that decision. I committed the very worst crime of all, murder, and didn't confess to it. I deliberately allowed you to be my scapegoat.' Valerie's eyes were brimming with tears and she looked so vulnerable, Lydia glimpsed the frightened little girl who hadn't been able to go anywhere unless she had Belinda Bell in her arms.

'It doesn't matter,' Lydia said. 'None of that matters now. What's important is that you try and put it behind you. It's understandable what you did. You were a child who was raped and struck back in the only way you knew how.'

But Lydia could see Valerie wasn't listening to her. She had let go of Lydia's hand and was rummaging around inside her habit. She drew out a handkerchief and wiped her eyes. After she'd tucked the handkerchief away, she grasped Lydia's hand again. 'I still haven't told you everything,' she said. 'As time went by, I came up with a way to make amends to you. All I needed was to make someone else confess to the crime. That way it would be safe for you to come home and everything would be normal again.'

'And that someone was Grandmother?'

'A month after she'd been found lost and confused wandering the moors for two whole days and nights, I started visiting her. Our grandfather had stopped going to see her, so I went on my own, and very slowly, but very surely, I poisoned what was left of her mind. I used to sit and pray aloud with her. I would pray that God would forgive her for killing Uncle Leonard. Sometimes I prayed that she would free herself fully and confess to the crime, and other times I prayed that God would have mercy on her for having believed she was acting as his avenging angel. Oh, Lydia, what could be more evil and twisted than taking advantage of such a sick mind? But I desperately wanted you to come home. I missed you so much. But you didn't come home. And so it was all for nothing. Grandma died with everyone thinking she was a killer and my guilt and shame grew and grew. I began to hate you. I blamed you for what I did to Grandma. If only you had come back, it would have been worth it.'

What words of comfort could Lydia possibly offer her sister? Other than to say the words she'd been saying nearly all her life. 'I'm sorry, Val. I should have been a better sister to you. I let you down in so many ways.'

'No you didn't. It was me who was at fault. I wasn't an easy sister. I got all the attention from our grandmother and there wasn't any left for you. Only hatred from our grandfather. The worst of it was, I was so desperate to be Grandma's favourite, I couldn't show you how much I loved you. I knew that if I tried to, it would have made her jealous, and that would have made life more difficult for you. Then whenever she was really ill and taken away, a part of me was taken away as well. I wanted to turn to you, but I couldn't; it would have been a betrayal of Grandma's love for me. I convinced myself you didn't really care about me so that I could justify not caring about you. Your love for Noah was all I needed to harden my resolve. And when things just got too difficult for me, it was easier to block everything out and disappear inside

469

myself. Losing my voice was a defence mechanism. Even now I find that difficult to understand.'

'How did you know Noah and I were more than just friends?'

'Don't be cross, but I followed you into the dell once and saw you kissing. I wanted to know where you were going.'

'And those visions you claimed to experience?'

'They felt real at the time, is all I can say. And, of course, I enjoyed the attention everyone gave me because of them.'

Once more they were disturbed by the opening of the door. This time a couple came in; the woman was quietly crying with a tissue pressed to her face. The man looked like he'd been crying too. Their whispered exchange rose and fell. Ten minutes later they left.

The interruption enabled Lydia to steer the conversation in another direction, to fit yet another piece into the puzzle. 'Why did the police never seriously consider our grandfather as a suspect?' she asked.

'He had a good alibi. He didn't come home that night. In fact, he didn't come back until almost lunchtime the next day.'

'Where had he been?'

'With a woman. Not that I was supposed to know that. But I overhead him telling the two police officers who came to the house after Brian and I had supposedly discovered the body in the dell. He'd been having an affair with this woman for some time.'

'Was it anyone we knew?'

Valerie shook her head. 'He used to work with her at the council offices. She was one of the women from the typing pool. The real details of their relationship only came out when Pastor Digby was exposed for stealing money from the new roof fund. To get his own back he went round telling tales about the Brothers' and Sisters' weaknesses and transgressions, including our grandfather's. Apparently Sister Vera suffered from kleptomania, Brother Walter had

gambled nearly all his savings away in the betting shop, and Sisters Mildred and Hilda were more than just close friends. I have no idea how he knew all this.'

'Was that why the church folded? Pastor Digby helping himself to money and the aftermath?'

'Yes and no. When he went, there was no one suitable to take his place. People just drifted away. For all his faults, he did have excellent leadership skills. He kept the church together.'

'That's what people said about Hitler and the Third Reich,' Lydia said bitterly.

They fell into a long, reflective silence. Beyond the white-painted walls of the chapel, Lydia was conscious of a distant other world. Here, with Val, she felt locked in the past. It was beginning to stifle her. She would need to escape soon. Perhaps Valerie was experiencing the same sensation. 'How are you feeling?' she asked her sister.

'Numb. And frightened. I'm afraid of the consequences of this conversation. I could go to prison for what I did.'

'By rights Uncle Leonard should have gone to prison for what *he* did.'

Valerie shook her head. 'Please don't say anything about an eye for an eye and a tooth for a tooth. I couldn't bear that.'

'I won't, but you have to start believing that you've been punished enough for what happened that day. You mustn't go on blaming yourself. Not for any of it. As for the consequences of this conversation, I think they'll be positive ones. You don't have to tell anyone else what you've shared with me, but never again will you have to feel that this is something you have to deal with on your own. From now on, I'll always be there for you, Valerie. I mean it.'

'But do you understand now why I behaved the way I did when you came to see me? I knew that if I showed you how genuinely pleased I was to see you I would fall apart. I just didn't think I could risk it. It seemed too painful.'

Again they were interrupted by the door opening and

light flooding in. This time it wasn't a stranger seeking solace in the chapel. It was Ishmael.

He came over, his handsome young face tight with anxiety. 'I'm sorry to disturb you, Lydia,' he said quietly, 'but you said I was to come here if there was any news. I've just heard that Dad's out of surgery.'

And Then ...

Chapter Sixty-Three

Lydia sat at the table alone. It was eleven o'clock at night and Caffe Florian was doing good business. Dressed in their smart white jackets and chattering discreetly amongst themselves, the waiters were keeping a casual watch over the tables of customers.

It had been a pleasantly warm March day but now it had turned into a chilly, damp night. An impenetrable mist had started to roll in from the Adriatic and the piazza of San Marco had acquired a melancholy feel that was greatly at odds with what the musicians were playing – 'New York, New York'. It was a perennial favourite with the tourists who flocked here as persistently as the pigeons did.

Lydia had always preferred the piazza at night: fewer tourists, and zero pigeons. After Marcello had died, unable to sleep, she had often come here to the deserted square in the dead of night, wandering through the colonnaded arcades, her footsteps echoing in the haunting emptiness.

She watched the mist continue to roll in; the top of the Campanile had magically vanished, as had two of the domes on the basilica. It was an extraordinary and eerie sight, which she had seen many times before. She touched the pearl hanging from the delicate chain at her neck and wished Noah was here to see it.

More than three months had passed since that day when she had tripped on the steps of the Rialto Bridge. In some ways the time had sped by as fast as a blink of an eye, but in other ways, she felt she had lived an entire lifetime during those few months. It had been a period of great change and adjustment.

Not least of all for Chiara. She and Ishmael were even more in love and with Ishmael now working in Padua they were planning to move in together. Selfishly Lydia was delighted that there was no question of Chiara leaving Venice to be with Ishmael in Padua. Padua was only thirty minutes away on the train, yet Chiara was adamant she wasn't moving to the mainland. Venice was her home, she'd told Ishmael; it was also where the agency was and now that she was easing Lydia's workload, she wanted to remain on its doorstep. She was a girl who knew her own mind and fortunately Ishmael was quite prepared to commute from Venice. They'd found a recently restored apartment to share and Lydia couldn't be happier for Chiara.

Another source of happiness for Lydia was that she and Valerie were in regular touch by letter. All these years on, they were finally getting to know each other properly. Her greatest hope was that Valerie could now find the peace of mind she deserved. Absolution, too. As a result of their correspondence, Lydia had reviewed her opinion of the Order of St Agnes. Gone now was her hostility regarding the closed world Valerie had chosen to live in. Where once Lydia had viewed the convent as little better than a prison depriving her sister of the rich and varied life she was meant to experience, she now understood it had been a place of sanctuary for Valerie, somewhere she had been surrounded by compassion and kindness. Somewhere she felt safe.

The exchange of letters was also enabling them to fill in the gaps in their lives. Lydia now knew that their grandfather had remarried four years after that dreadful night in the dell, a year after their grandmother's death, and the year Valerie turned sixteen. Life at number thirty-three Hillside Terrace changed dramatically when Doris moved in. The house was redecorated from top to bottom, the kitchen was knocked through to the dining room and a breakfast bar installed, the shed in the garden was replaced with a summer house, and part of the lawn was dug up to make room for a pond and a patio of crazy paving. While

Doris was not an unsympathetic woman, she had had no idea how to deal with a sixteen-year-old girl, especially one as complex as Valerie. When Valerie announced on her eighteenth birthday that she was leaving Swallowsdale to join the Order of St Agnes, it had come as a huge relief to all concerned.

Lydia had promised her sister faithfully that the truth about Uncle Leonard's death would always remain their secret. It may have been unfair that their grandmother had died with everyone believing her to be a murderer but then it wasn't fair that poor Valerie had had her innocence so cruelly stolen, or that her life had been blighted as a consequence.

The one person who seemed not to have been affected in any way by what had gone on was their grandfather. Lydia hated that. She hated knowing that he hadn't suffered for what he'd done. She would never know what had made him into the cold-blooded, vicious sadist he'd been, or what had made his brother into an abusive monster who preyed on young girls, but she knew she would never find it within her to forgive them. If there really was such a place as hell – especially the nightmarish place of torment Pastor Digby used to rant about – she hoped they were both there.

The night before his operation, Noah had joked of his preference not to go to hell if anything went wrong. As to be expected, neither of them had been able to sleep. All day Lydia had managed to stop her thoughts from becoming maudlin, but alone in bed with Noah, she couldn't keep up the act any more. 'I know what you're worrying about,' he'd said in the darkness. 'You're wondering, in a worst-case scenario, whether I'm hell or heaven-bound, aren't you?'

'Please don't joke about tomorrow,' she'd said, rolling onto her side to look at him. 'Everyone I've ever really cared about has been taken from me long before they should have.'

Ignoring her, and clasping his hands behind his head,

he'd said, 'I have to say, heaven's my preferred choice. That way I'll get the chance to meet your parents at long last, as well as catch up with mine. And then there's Marcello. I'd give him a high-five and let him know that he had impeccable taste in women. I'd be discreet, of course; I wouldn't—'

She'd silenced him with a kiss. A very long kiss. Anything but listen to him making light of what was so precious to her.

It pained her unbearably to think of that conversation now and she let her thoughts drift to the people whose lives had touched her so deeply, and the link that connected them all – Lydia's mother had been orphaned at a very young age, Lydia and Valerie had lost their parents, as had Noah and Chiara. Was it coincidence they had all been brought together? Or fate? She suddenly smiled to herself, imagining Valerie admonishing her for using the F word.

From high up in the dark, misty sky, the bells in the tower struck the half hour: it was half past eleven. Lydia looked across the piazza, its damp surface gleaming in the bright lights spilling out from the colonnaded arcades. That was when she saw that her wait was over. Spontaneously, her heart beat a little faster and she felt a wave of tender love wash over her. She knew that for as long as she was able to draw breath, the effect that face had on her would never diminish. She put a hand in the air to show where she was and received an acknowledging wave in return.

Even though they'd been apart only briefly, Noah kissed her before pulling out a chair for himself. 'Did you get Uncle Brad safely back to his hotel?' she asked.

'I left him ordering a drink at the bar. He'll be nicely settled in for the night I shouldn't wonder.'

Now that she was no longer alone, a waiter materialized at their table and they ordered two espressos.

Staring up at the partially hidden campanile and basilica, Noah said, 'I've never seen a mist roll in as fast as this.'

'That's Venice for you. Utterly unique.' Suddenly anxious,

Lydia said, 'You *do* like it here, don't you? Truthfully.'

He leaned in close and grazed his lips against her cheek. 'I've told you before: it feels like home.'

It was exactly what she'd said about his house in England. When the medical staff at the hospital had said he was well enough to go home after Christmas, Lydia had stayed with him the whole time, almost afraid to let him out of her sight. She didn't think she would ever forget those agonizing hours while she and Ishmael had waited for him to come round from the operation. Despite the emphatic assurance from the surgeon that there had been no complications throughout the five-hour operation – the tumour had been benign – and that there was no reason to doubt Noah wouldn't make an excellent recovery, she had convinced herself that he would never wake up, or, if he did, he wouldn't be the man he'd once been. Never had she been happier to be proved wrong. And on both points.

It was during Noah's convalescence that she had grown to love his house and the village where he lived. She had felt very much a part of it. As soon as he was strong enough, friends and neighbours began dropping in, and again, Lydia became part of those friendships. Noah's ex-wife, Jane, stopped by regularly, and whilst they initially tiptoed warily around one another, they quickly became firm allies in their determination to get Noah well again, mainly by enforcing as much bed rest on him as they could get away with.

Three weeks after Noah's operation Uncle Brad flew over to England from France. It was an emotional reunion for Lydia. His first words were to tell her and Noah what a pair of bloody fools they'd been for not finding each other before now. He'd then presented Noah with a smart fedora to wear until his hair grew back. Age had not mellowed him in the slightest. If anything, he'd turned into an even more irascible old devil and Lydia loved him for it. Now here he was in Venice, no expense spared, pitching his tent at the Gritti Palace for the weekend. Good for him!

Noah had been staying with Lydia in Venice for the last fortnight. It was the start of things to come. Just as he'd said on that cold winter's day when they'd gone for a walk before his operation, they planned to divide their time between here and England. Noah had already taken steps to hand over more of the day-to-day running of his business and with Chiara proving to be a force to be reckoned with at the agency, they had high hopes of being able to make their slightly unconventional new life work.

Their coffee arrived, and while the waiter placed the tray of drinks on the table, he bent down and whispered in Lydia's ear. '*Grazie*,' she said, glancing over the top of Noah's head towards the musicians. The violinist gave her a questioning look. She nodded.

'Have you and the waiter got something going I should know about?' Noah asked when they were alone. 'If I'm in the way, just say the word.'

She flashed him a smile. 'I have something going with every waiter in Venice; it's how I avoid paying the full price for anything.'

Whilst they drank their coffee, a Sri Lankan teenage boy approached them with a bunch of red roses. They were a sitting target. 'A rose for the pretty lady?' the boy said hopefully to Noah.

Noah reached for his wallet from inside his coat, but then hesitated. 'How much for the whole bunch?' he asked.

The boy looked astonished.

'I'm serious,' Noah said, his wallet in his hand now.

'Twenty euros,' the boy said hurriedly, seeing the unexpected opportunity of an early night.

Noah handed over the money and gave Lydia the flowers. People sitting around them smiled approvingly. 'Cheesy as hell, I know,' he said quietly, 'but if a man can't make romantic gestures in Venice to the woman he loves, where can he?'

She laughed happily and kissed him. 'If you thought

that was corny, just wait and see what I've got in store for you.'

With perfect timing, the musicians came to the end of the number they'd been playing and in the sudden silence, the bells in the campanile pealed the hour. It was midnight. 'Happy birthday,' Lydia said. She pushed back her chair and got to her feet, just as the musicians started playing their next piece. She held out her hand. 'Noah Solomon, may I have the pleasure of this dance?'

Recognition dawned on Noah's face. He looked horrified. He shook his head. 'Lyddie, *no*!'

She grabbed his hands. 'Oh yes!'

'But I can't. Not in front of everyone.'

'Yes, you can. Imagine we're here on our own.'

'But my leg. All I'll manage is a clumsy shuffle.'

'That'll do for me.'

In the space next to their table – the table Lydia had chosen specially when she'd arrived earlier and had made her request to the lead violinist – they held each other closely, their gaze unbroken. They settled into the rhythm, and to the delight of everyone around them, they danced to the waltz from Sviridov's Snow Storm, just as a drunken Uncle Brad had taught them to do on Noah's fifteenth birthday in the kitchen at Upper Swallowsdale House.

'Lyddie?' Noah said.

'You're not going to say you'd rather be bungee jumping off the campanile, are you?'

'No. But I am glad it wasn't a tango Uncle B taught us.'

She smiled. 'I thought you were going to thank me for not forcing you to wear a saucepan on your head.'

He smiled too and she felt him relax against her. 'You know, I think I'd like to do this again sometime,' he said.

'When were you thinking?'

'How about when we get married?'

'I didn't know we were.'

'I thought it was a given.'

'A girl likes to be asked.'

481

He held her closer, his expression intensely solemn. 'Will you marry me, Lyddie? Marry me so that we can finally be together, man and wife, just as we always should have been.'

'Yes,' she said, almost before he'd finished speaking.

'You might like to think about your answer.'

'I have. Since for ever.' She stopped moving and kissed him.

They were still standing there, wrapped in each other's arms, long after the music had stopped.

Tell it to the Skies

Reading Group Notes

In Brief

Lydia saw him and fell. As simple as that. A face amongst the crowd of tourists around the Rialto Bridge had so caught her attention that she'd turned, captivated, and down she'd gone. The result: a sprained ankle, the promise of crutches, and a growing disbelief in what she'd seen.

Stuck in the apartment, Lydia can't help dwelling on the uneasy feelings the sight of that face caused. Is her world about to come tumbling down? She dreams of a sinking Venice, the water lapping around her as her world disappears. It is, after all, such a fragile world she has created.

Then her step-daughter, Chiara, brings home her new love, and suddenly Lydia is taken back twenty-eight years to a man she would have done anything for – a man for whom she gave up her future.

In Detail

C hiara's new boyfriend is not Noah. Clearly he can't be. But he looks just like him. After they leave, Lydia is drawn inexorably to her past. Despite her ankle, she clambers up to reach down an olive wood box and looks through the only remains of her life before Italy – her life in England.

Amongst the things in the box is an envelope of photographs, of her parents, and her sister Valerie. One of them is of her and Noah messing around as teenagers, another, creased, torn and worn, is just of Noah. Now Lydia can see the startling similarity between Noah and the man Chiara has fallen in love with. He can only be Noah's son. Lydia always knew that the past would catch up with her one day . . .

It was the ventriloquist's dummy that did it. That was the start of so many years of unhappiness and guilt. With her ninth birthday coming up, Lydia had set her heart on the one in the toy shop window. If only she hadn't gone on so about it to her mother, but everything had changed since that rainy day when her father had been taken from them, and she had to do so much to help her mother. Surely, now, the ventriloquist's dummy wasn't too much to ask for? But it turned out that it was. Her mother got worse and worse until a frightening middle-of-the-night

walk ended in the piercing screech of metal wheels trying too late to stop on metal rails. And Lydia and Valerie were sent to live with their grandparents – the same couple who were so bitter about who their son had married, they were glad he was now dead.

Swallowsdale was so much worse than she could ever have thought. Her grandparents were impossibly strict. They were members of The Church of The Brothers and Sisters in Christ and were convinced that Lydia was cursed in the same way that her mother had been. They couldn't punish her mother for taking their son from them, but they could hurt Lydia. And they did. Small windows of light shone into Lydia's world: Pastor John seemed kind, and batty Sister Lottie was good to her, but it wasn't until the arrival of a new boy at school that Lydia found a focus in her life. Noah was an outsider like her, and an alliance grew.

Over the years they drew closer and closer together, and made plans for the future – until one awful night when the simmering violence in Swallowsdale exploded and Lydia ran away. She'd started running and never really stopped . . .

About the Author

E rica James grew up on Hayling Island in
Hampshire, and has since lived in Oxford,
Yorkshire and Belgium. She is the author of eleven
bestselling books, and says her main qualification for
writing is that she's 'a nosy devil and loves watching
and eavesdropping on other people's conversations'.
  She now lives in Cheshire.

For Discussion

- If you're a child of the seventies, were you transported back? How does the author achieve this? How does she recreate the past?

- 'Since Marcello died, seldom did she close the shutters as well. She didn't like to shut out too much of the world.' Doesn't she? Why would Lydia want to see what was outside her apartment?

- How does the author use water in the novel?

- 'In fact, we're all so abnormal we're completely normal.' If Lydia had realised this earlier, how do you think her life would have been different?

- How is the concept of sanctuary used in *Tell it to the Skies*?

- Lydia believes she is 'a lightning conductor of bad things'. Is she? Is any of it her fault? Could she have made her life better by making different decisions or behaving differently?

- What do you think the author thinks about religion?

- 'Keeping relentlessly busy was the answer, she'd found. Leave herself with no time to dwell on those old memories and she was able to put it out of her mind.' Does this save Lydia, or curse her never to move forward?

- Why do you think the author named Noah's son Ishmael?

- *Tell it to the Skies* is a novel of consequences. As a tale of those 'roads not taken', whose lives could have been different?

Suggested Further Reading

Pillow Talk by Freya North

A Gathering Light by Jennifer Donnelly

Starter For Ten by David Nicholls

The Pact by Jodie Picoult

A Party in San Niccolò by Christobel Kent

The Villa in Italy by Elizabeth Edmondson

VENICE AND THE ROLE IT PLAYED IN THE WRITING OF *TELL IT TO THE SKIES*.

Although the vast majority of *Tell it to the Skies* takes place in Yorkshire, Venice played a crucial part in pulling together the story. In fact, it was the trigger for writing the book in the first place.

I had written eleven books in as many years and reached the point when I needed time out to recharge my creative batteries. I knew I needed to step back from my writing because when I came to the end of the book I was then working on – *Gardens of Delight* – I didn't know what I was going to write next. Usually I know exactly

what I want to write next but, scarily, my mind was blank this time round. So I decided I would go and stay in my favourite city for a month. I was also in the mood for a bit of an adventure. And where better to do that than Venice?

I had already been having Italian lessons but, conscious that I had a long way to go yet in learning the language, I signed up for a week's course at the Istituto Venezia – the language school in Campo Santa Margherita – which in due course became the language school where Noah's son Ishmael takes lessons.

Just about every other person in Venice seems to be a

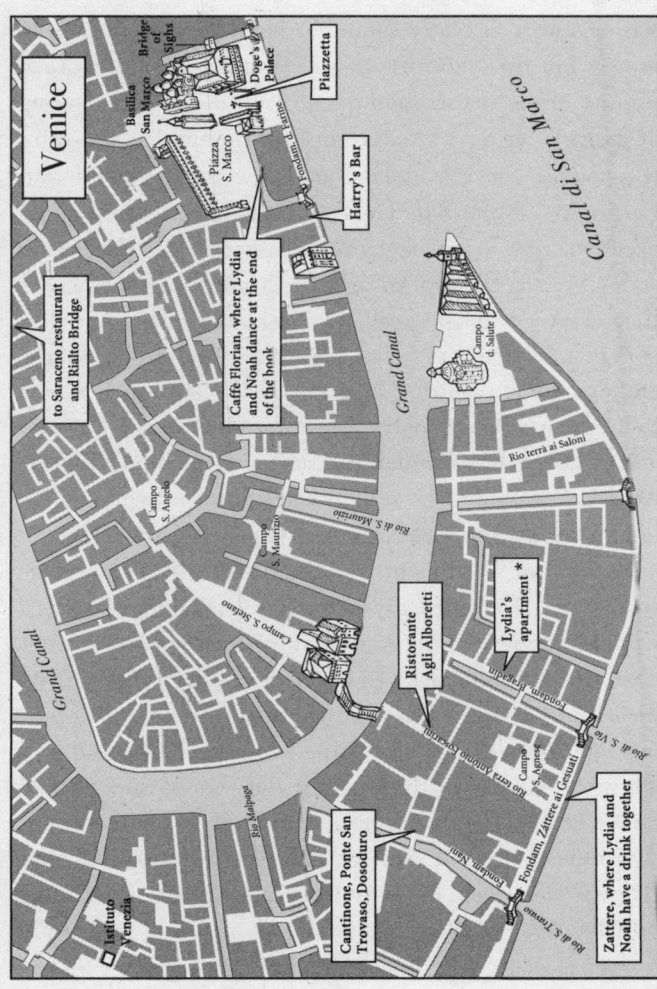

Venice

Isfituto Venezia

Grand Canal

to Saraceno restaurant and Rialto Bridge

Campo S. Angelo

Rio Malpaga

Campo S. Maurizio

Campo S. Stefano

Rio di S. Maurizio

Cantinone, Ponte San Trovaso, Dosoduro

Ristorante Agli Alboretti

Fondam. Bragadin

Campo S. Agnese

Rio terra Antonio Foscarini

Fondam. Nani

Rio di S. Trovaso

Zattere, where Lydia and Noah have a drink together

Fondam. Zattere ai Gesuati

Rio di S. Vio

Lydia's apartment *

Grand Canal

Rio terra ai Saloni

Campo d. Salute

Caffè Florian, where Lydia and Noah dance at the end of the book

Piazza S. Marco

Basilica San Marco

Bridge of Sighs

Doge's Palace

Piazzetta

Fondam. d. Farine

Harry's Bar

Canal di San Marco

* There isn't a specific building which I used, just the row/area

writer and so it really shouldn't have been a surprise to me on my first morning at the language school to turn around in the registration queue and find myself looking at a crime writer I knew from back home. He was later responsible for introducing me to a great cicheti bar, Cantinone, Ponte San Trovaso, Dosoduro, as well as an excellent restaurant near the Accademia, the Ristorante Agli Alboretti (Dosoduro 882, Rio Terà Foscarini), where they serve the most excellent baccala and offer the best cheese selection I've ever eaten in Italy. Much to my embarrassment, during a recent visit I got stuck in the toilet in that particular restaurant, but that's another story! It was also through this crime writer that I met an American woman who taught English for a living, which later gave me the idea for how Lydia meets Marcello.

It was once I had survived the rigours of the language school that I applied myself to the challenge of what I would write next. I was sitting in the Saraceno restaurant next to the Rialto Bridge, when the first glimmer of an idea came to me. It was mid October, the light was fading and the weather had turned unexpectedly cold and wintry. I started to think of all the things that I loved about Venice, how it can be enchantingly seductive yet at the same time quite sinister, giving the impression that there is so much more hidden behind the crumbling facades than at first appears. I thought of the proud resilience of the city and its people, how against all the

*Erica on the Rialto Bridge, with the Saraceno restaurant
in the background*

odds Venice was still standing. I thought how claustrophobic the city can be with the narrow *calli* jam-packed
with tourists, but then how late at night one could have

Detail of the Rialto Bridge

the place practically to oneself, catching little more than a shadowy glimpse of a solitary, ghost-like figure walking home.

My thoughts had just moved on to thinking how melancholy and secretive the city can feel when I suddenly pictured a woman about the same age as me living there and having a secret that she had never shared with anyone. I held on tight to this thought and reflected how easy it would be to lose oneself in Venice. The more I thought about this, the more I could imagine that this was the perfect place for someone with a secret, a person

who had a very real reason to hide from their past.

A glass of wine later, I had a strong mental image of my central character stumbling on the steps of the Rialto Bridge after she catches sight of a face in the crowd. From then on, there was no stopping the ideas, they kept on coming.

Over the following weeks, I became a regular at the Saraceno. I felt it was a 'lucky' place for me and returned again and again, notepad and pen in hand. The waiters, once they realised I was a writer, were great and never hustled me on to make room for other diners, despite the restaurant always being busy. It's a restaurant I still like to visit as it now holds very special memories for me. Plus, the waiters are always so charming!

ﮩﮩﮩ

Before I can really start writing a new book, I have to experience an emotional pull to the characters and the setting. Venice instilled within me a strong sensation of sadness and loss – which essentially sets the tone of the novel, that and a sense of mystery – and to underpin this feeling, when I was back at home and writing in my study, I listened endlessly to the following pieces of music:

Waltz from Georgi Sviridov's *Snowstorm*
Onegin's Theme from the soundtrack to the film
   Onegin

She Devil by Natalie Merchant

Cowboy Romance by Natalie Merchant

Motherland by Natalie Merchant

Photograph by Natalie Merchant and R.E.M.

Stop by Lizz Wright

A Living Prayer by Alison Krauss

Exit Music (For a Film) performed by Brad
  Mehldau, written by Radiohead

When it Rains by Brad Mehldau

I Will Wait For You performed by Laura Fygi,
  written by Michel Legrand

It's an eclectic mix but what these tracks all have in common, whether it's through the melody of the singer's voice or the lyrics, is an air of mournful longing, bitter regret and melancholy. They conjure an atmosphere that is haunting and dreamlike. Just as Venice does.

On the whole, my books are known for having a feel-good quality to them – admittedly that takes a long time to happen in *Tell it to the Skies* – and consequently people tend to think that to write books with a happy ending I must be of a permanently sunny disposition. It always comes as a surprise when I reveal the darker side to my nature, in that I feel things acutely and have a natural inclination to tap into those gloomier and more sombre emotions and explore them through my characters. I think that's why I feel so at home in Venice; I'm able to

Erica outside the Basilica San Marco

connect with the place, recognising that beneath the surface of faded grandeur and fairy-tale beauty, there lurks a very different soul. There's an intriguing sense of drama and tragedy about Venice; why else would so many crime writers choose the city as the setting for their novels?

But Venice isn't all gloom and mystery. There's plenty of fun to be had. Venetians have a raucous sense of humour and many would claim they need it, given the challenges they face on a daily basis, whether it's coping with the hoards of tourists that descend on the city, or the increasing threat of *acqua alta*.

For a fun night out, one of my favourite places to eat is Harry's Bar (San Marco 1323, Calle Vallaresso). It really isn't the tourist trap people think it is. Yes, a lot of Americans have it on their 'must do' list, but on the occasions I've been there Italians have always outnumbered foreigners. I've eaten the best risotto of my life in this restaurant. But a word of warning, it is colossally expensive. I burst out with near hysterical laughter when I first ate there and asked for the bill afterwards. 'I only wanted to pay for my meal, not everybody else's,' I felt like saying. It's by no means large inside and the décor is nothing to write home about, but there's always a fantastic buzz to the place. I'd advise booking ahead and dressing smartly. Definitely no shorts or flip flops! Personally I'm not a huge fan of the Bellini cocktail the bar is

The Piazzetta

famous for, and prefer a glass of Prosecco or a vodka martini.

Another favourite place of mine is Florian's (Caffè Florian, San Marco 56–59, Piazza San Marco). How could it not be? After all, it is *the* place in the Piazza San Marco. The toasted sandwiches are sublime as is afternoon tea. The cosy interior is excessively kitsch and is the perfect place to people-watch when it's too cold to sit outside. Again, it's off-the-chart expensive but somehow I can always justify it. Especially when the musicians are playing their repertoire of catchy crowd pleasers. I'm a total sucker for anything cheesy or romantic.

I had written about a quarter of *Tell it to the Skies*
when I pictured the final scene with Lydia and Noah
dancing in the Piazza. One of the artistic liberties I had
to take with that particular scene was having the musicians playing when strictly speaking they wouldn't be
there until a few months later when the weather is
warmer. What few people realise is that the musicians
who play in the Piazza aren't Italian, let alone Venetian.
They're from Eastern Europe, all classically trained but
unable to find work at home. Request a Russian piece of
music and see their faces light up.

There's a lot of snobbery regarding Venice. The so-
called experts will tell you to avoid any of the tourist
spots to eat, drink or shop. But frankly, I'll eat, drink and

shop exactly where I feel most comfortable. Nor do I try to put as many ticks as possible in the cultural boxes each time I visit. In my view, Venice is like a large box of very rich chocolates – eat too much in one go and the pleasure is spoilt. I like to pace myself, knowing that I have a store of new gems to enjoy on a return trip. I hate it when people look at me in horror and say, 'What do you mean you haven't seen the Carpaccios at the Scuola di San Giorgio degli Schiavoni?' Which, for the record, I have now seen.

వ.ఴ

There have been so many books written about Venice, and the ones I've enjoyed the most are:

The City of Falling Angels by John Berendt
A Thousand Days in Venice by Marlena De Blasi
Miss Garnet's Angel by Salley Vickers
Venice by Francesco da Mosto
Venice Revealed: An Intimate Portrait by Paolo Barbaro

It would be presumptuous of me to align myself with any of these authors, but it would be nice to think that my own book might tempt someone who hasn't yet been to Venice to go there and discover for themselves just how unique a place it is.

With very best wishes
Erica James

Foreword

Wang Yang-ming (1472–1529) is generally credited with a revolution in Confucian thinking, inaugurating a philosophical project that dominated China for two hundred years and Japan down into this century. Strange as it may seem to Westerners, the vehicle of his revolution was an attack on an editorial change that Chu Hsi (1130–1200) had made in the order of items in a list in the text of the ancient *Great Learning*. Wang restored the text to its supposed original order. By implication, Chu Hsi's original editorial change was a core component of his own revolution which has been even more influential than Wang's and is usually thought now to be truer to the heart of Confucianism than Wang's. One way of looking at these two events is to see a tradition with enormous creativity and diversity punctuating its radical turning points by scholarly moves that appear to be aiming at continuity.

Professor Tu Wei-ming sees himself as transmitting the Confucian tradition and introducing it to the West. This volume like his others is interpretive of Confucian ideas and figures. Unlike many scholars, however, he understands that the true meaning of transmission is not merely translation and the conveying of "knowledge about." It is also the conveying of the felt merit of the ideas and practices, a transmission of the reasons why they are true and worthy of adoption. This is not a simple matter.

The reasons why a great figure such as Wang Yang-ming said what he did are given only in part in his explicit expressions. The rest come from his feeling for his age, from the way his own parents treated him, from the things that made him dream the dreams he had. True transmission of Wang's thought would require a thorough, empathetic social and psycho-history of his own situation. Of course that is impossible. The records are simply inadequate and most of what one would need to get inside Wang's mind probably was never recorded. Nevertheless, with careful scholarship an expert can come close to understanding the context and thereby grasping the affect in Wang's ideas. Professor Tu set the standard in the par-

1

ticular case of Wang with his own *Neo-Confucian Thought in Action: Wang Yang-ming's Youth (1472-1509)* (Berkeley: University of California Press, 1976). One might go so far as to say that a great scholar can understand a previous time even better than most of us can understand our own. The usual effect of coming to understand a prior age and its tastes is that our own minds are put back in that age, perhaps with considerable empathy. In rare cases our own experience is simply expanded so as to include that age as well as ours. The historical interest does not directly answer the question, however, whether Confucian ideas in any form have merit as a contemporary philosophical option. To answer that question one might begin with a thorough engagement with contemporary life, an engagement often avoided (unconsciously?) by the historical orientation.

The opposite transmission strategy is to bracket the historical dimension, assuming that human nature and social context are pretty much the same everywhere and always. Books such as the recently popular *Tao of Physics* by Fritjof Capra allow for great comparative generalizations. Truly sophisticated philosophical studies in this genre can apply analytical methods to unravel and state the meanings of ideas. Again, Professor Tu has offered us a fine example of this genre, his *Centrality and Commonality: An Essay on Chung-yung* (Honolulu: the University Press of Hawaii, 1976). The limitation of this approach is that without strict historical controls it allows the questions that nudge our own minds to guide the hermeneutics of the old texts. These might not be the questions in the minds of the original authors at all. And then since the understanding of the text in turn guides our own self-understanding, this a-historical approach to ideas may lead us recursively to delusions about our own situation.

Students of hermeneutics have argued in this century that we need to unite both approaches in an ever-circling process of interpretation. To this I would like to add one emphasis, that we have a particular responsibility to engage our own time from more angles than those of hermeneutical circles catching up ancient texts. The very habit of interpreting the past puts a bias on our participation in the present. Please do not think I believe we can effectively engage the present without bringing it into relation with the past and our understanding of it. But there are other approaches, theoretical, appreciative, and practical, by which we come to terms with ourselves and our time; each approach has its own strength which corrects

and completes the others. These many approaches need to be registered in any metaphysics for our own time to be embodied in an adequate philosophy of life.

Now it is Professor Tu's particular interest to present Confucianism as an adequate philosophy of life. This requires him both to be faithful to the tradition's texts and to present Confucianism as a responsible resource for our own philosophic needs. There are two stages, as I see it, to this interest. The first is to present Confucianism as a world class philosophy, not just the historic expression of Chinese culture. To do this requires developing Confucian ideas to address the major issues and life situation of the major groups of people in the contemporary era. Professor Tu, I believe, is well along in doing this, as Whitehead did it for Platonism and McKeon for Aristotelianism.

The second stage goes beyond showing the relevance of a set of basic ideas to the explicit elaboration of them from an idiosyncratic author's point of view. This means the creation of a new authorial perspective that allows us to grasp our situation in new and improved ways. Whitehead and McKeon also did this, the former by developing process metaphysics and the latter by establishing a school of historical criticism. Professor Tu is now in this stage, a stage of creativity in which he stands in danger of being rejected by the mere repeaters of Confucianism. I know of no one more successful at developing a twentieth-century Confucian philosophy than he.

Like Wang and Chu Hsi, Professor Tu's creative revolution centers around a point of authority within the tradition. As mentioned before, Chu Hsi's philosophy has generally been taken to be the orthodox line of Confucian interpretation, despite two hundred years of competition from Wang Yang-ming. Chu Hsi's interpretation, for instance, formed the examination system in China up to our own century. Professor Tu, however, in his *Humanity and Self-Cultivation: Essays in Confucian Thought* (Berkeley: Asian Humanities Press, 1979), argues that Wang's is the more faithful interpretation of the line beginning with Confucius and Mencius. What this means for Professor Tu's philosophy is the importance he thus can put on the will and its cultivation. Wang said that the decision to become a sage is itself the root of sagehood, not just the beginning but the stuff, as it were, of which sagehood is made. This leads Professor Tu in the current volume to focus on the transformation of the self. As much as any scholar, he has told us that Confucianism is a social philosophy, a philosophy of practice and engagement with the moral

affairs of the world. With striking parallels to Dewey's pragmatism, Confucianism as it comes to us through Mencius, Wang, and Tu emphasizes the transformation of the moral quality of action through careful learning. But whereas Dewey moved from there to considerations of public policy, Tu turns instead to the cultivation of the self. This volume, even more than his earlier ones, displays this orientation.

Questions of authentic Confucianism aside, what does Professor Tu's emphasis mean for Confucianism as a contemporary philosophy? For one, it means a corrective emphasis to pragmatism, one that can capture and discipline the often silly and narcissistic personal "seeker" phenomenon which arose in reaction against crude pragmatism. Confucian self-cultivation is a rigorously disciplined path. Another meaning of Professor Tu's emphasis is that the religious dimensions of self-cultivation can be given new expression in an avowedly atheistic cosmology. To be sure, there are categories in Neo-Confucianism's ontology (the topic of one of the chapters here) that function like the "ultimate" categories of Western thought. But there is not the belief in a God with a definite, historically particular will such as characterized most non-mystical Western religion and philosophy. Insofar as we live after the "death of God," Professor Tu's reconstruction of a viable religio-philosophy is appropriate.

I mentioned earlier the need for an authentic metaphysics to be embodied in any philosophy which is viable for our time. By that I mean that we need to discern the most general thought forms expressed in the assumptions that make life vital today — assumptions in science, economics, efforts at distributive justice, and the like — because these thought-forms must also be embodied in the philosophies by which we can reflect on and guide that vital life. The most devastating criticism of a philosophy is that its root patterns are not those which engage the vital activities of life. This is not to assume that there is a single consistent set of assumptions, or only one metaphysics, or only one philosophy of life. Yet a philosophy which is metaphysically connected to nothing vital is of no serious interest. The Confucian tradition would be the first to acknowledge this. (It may be of great playful interest. The Taoists insist on this point.)

The formation of a metaphysics is no easy matter, coming as it does both from a dialectic with past metaphysical ideas and from an articulation and extrapolation of vigorous areas of inquiry and ac-

tivity. In this volume Professor Tu makes significant strides toward a metaphysics that would make Confucianism a way of wisdom for our common life. Ethical considerations constitute a good starting point for a metaphysical construction where the sources come from such diverse traditions as those of China and the West. Professor Tu makes ingenious uses of psychology as well in this volume. The Neo-Confucian tradition presents many notions concerning principle and nature that will move him on to basic issues of aesthetics and cosmology.

The essays in this volume present themselves as attempts at transmission and interpretation, Confucius' own self-understanding. But embodied in that task is one of the most exciting and creative philosophical projects of our time: the evocation of a world philosophy for the twentieth century from Confucian roots.

Robert C. Neville
Professor of Philosophy and Religious Studies
SUNY Stony Brook

Introduction

In the opening discussion of the final meeting of the five-year Berkeley-Harvard program in the comparative study of social values,[1] Robert Bellah, my teacher and friend for over two decades, in commenting on my paper, "The 'Moral Universal' From the Perspectives of East Asian Thought" (Chapter 1), raised the challenging question, "What is the Confucian self?" The nine essays included in this book attempt to answer this question. They do not, however, offer a simple answer. Rather, they explore dimensions of Confucian thought which illuminate the meaning of Confucian selfhood as creative transformation.

If we Confucians have a coherent conception of the self, why was it difficult for me to give Bellah a straightforward answer? Part of the problem is contextual. Unless we fully understand a question, we cannot hope to offer the right answer. Often the way a question is posed is deceptively simple, but the background that gives meaning to it is immensely complex. Because the question emanates from the *Problematik* of the questioner, we need to know not only the propositional content of the question but also the thinking person behind it. For me, then, Bellah's question occasioned a living encounter rather than a mere exchange of information. The essays in this book are, in this sense, all living encounters. To be sure, they offer basic information on the Confucian tradition; but, primarily, they are self-consciously "Confucian" responses to perennial human concerns.

Had I been asked the same question by someone else, by a language student for example, I could have answered the question by simply listing the cluster of terms which, for all practical purposes, can be accepted as functional equivalents of the classical or modern Chinese terms for the English word "self." (This may have been what the student was really after, although he might have continued to wonder whether a one-to-one translation would work in some cases.) But, the weight of Bellah's question lies elsewhere, for in reflecting on my attempt to discern the shared orientations of East Asian thought, he was troubled by the centrality of "self-cultiva-

tion" in my characterization of the Mencian line of Confucian thought, Chuang Tzu's version of Taoism, and Ch'an (Zen) Buddhism. What about the other salient features of East Asian culture: the sense of community, the importance of the sacred texts, the power of tradition, convention and sharable values, the significance of the exemplary teacher, and the primacy of the political order? Moreover, self-cultivation smacks of preoccupation with one's individuality, one's inner spirituality, indeed one's own private self. Bellah, a most eloquent critic of individualism in our society, is particularly concerned about the radical individualistic tendencies that have been undermining the social fabric of American civil religion.[2]

In light of this *Problematik*, one of the most intriguing areas for me to explore is the authentic possibility of a new vision of the self which is rooted in the reality of a shared life together with other human beings and inseparable from the truth of transcendence. Chapter 1, which was prepared as a background paper for an interdisciplinary examination of the truth claims of sociobiologists, sketches the rationale for a twofold approach to self-realization in East Asian thought. (1) Each human being has sufficient internal resources for ultimate self-transformation; we can become a sage, a buddha, or a true person through our self-effort because sageliness, buddhahood, or the *Tao* is inherent in our human nature. (2) The path to the highest good, to *nirvāna*, or to oneness with the *Tao* is long and strenuous. Self-cultivation is ceaseless. We can never say at any juncture of our life that we have already made it. This interplay between faith in the strength of humanity in ordinary daily existence and the wisdom of infinite human potential for personal growth enables the three East Asian traditions to perceive the self as a dynamic, holistic, open system, just the opposite notion of the privatized ego. However, whether such a self can be grounded in society without losing sight of the transcendent reality remains problematical. In order to address this issue, we need to examine the metaphysical assumption underlying this conception of the self.

Chapter 2 propounds the thesis that the "continuity of being," a characteristic of Chinese cosmological thinking, frames the whole question of self-cultivation in a specific context. Particularly noteworthy is the implicit conceptual apparatus which allows a vision of the self significantly different from what Bellah, following Alasdair MacIntyre, calls "bureaucratic individualism."[3] The familiar dichotomies such as self/society, body/mind, sacred/profane, culture/nature, and creator/creature, in light of the

"continuity of being," are relegated to the background. A different mode of thinking, which emphasizes part/whole, inner/outer, surface/depth, root/branches, substance/function, and Heaven/man, becomes prominent. The central question does not involve static, mechanistic, analytical distinctions but subtle relationships, internal resonance, dialogical interplay, and mutual influence. As a result, the cosmos envisioned by Chinese thinkers is a "spontaneously self-generating life process." Inherent in such a life process "is not only inner connectedness and interdependence but also infinite potential for development."[4] Thus, the Chinese conceive of the cosmos, like the self, as an open system. "As there is no temporal beginning to specify, no closure is ever contemplated. The cosmos is forever expanding; the great transformation is unceasing."[5] The message for us humans is as follows:

> The precondition for us to participate in the internal resonance of the vital forces in nature is our own inner transformation. Unless we can first harmonize our own feelings and thoughts, we are not prepared for nature, let alone for an "interflow with the spirit of Heaven and Earth." It is true that we are consanguineous with nature. But as humans, we must make ourselves worthy of such a relationship.[6]

The Confucian emphasis on humanism may seem to be in conflict with Taoist naturalism. However, in light of their shared concern for self-cultivation, we cannot say that the Confucian insistence on social participation and cultural transmission is incompatible with the Taoist quest for personal freedom. Both the Taoist critique of Confucian ritualism and the Confucian critique of Taoist escapism are dialogical interplays reflecting a much deeper point of convergence. This is not to deny the nuanced differences between the two spiritual traditions; but, despite their divergence, they belong to the same symbolic universe in which they not only co-exist but help each other to grow through mutual influence.

"A Confucian Perspective on Learning to be Human" (Chapter 3) was written for a collection of essays intended to offer some current perspectives in religious studies in honor of the work of Wilfred Cantwell Smith.[7] Bellah's question, against the background of Smith's concerted effort to address the dual problem of cumulative tradition and faith in human religiosity,[8] takes on new significance. The Confucian project of learning to be human, defined by Con-

fucius as "learning for the sake of the self," takes the concrete person living here and now as its point of departure. This seemingly particularistic, temporal, secular, and individualistic focus is predicated on a holistic vision of humanity which transcends not only self-centeredness, nepotism, ethnocentrism, nationalism, and culturalism but also anthropocentrism. Indeed, the Confucian vision of "forming one body with Heaven and Earth and the myriad things"[9] is anthropocosmic in the sense that the complete realization of the self, which is tantamount to the full actualization of humanity, entails the unity of humankind with Heaven. Therefore, the Confucian insistence that the journey of self-realization begins with the concrete experience of the self should not be construed as an assertion of the finite, historical, and culturally specific to the exclusion of the infinite, trans-historical, and universal. The significance of the Confucian project of learning to be human, in a comparative religious perspective, lies in its insight into the creative tension between our earthly embeddedness and our great potential for self-transcendence.

As Bellah notes, "bureaucratic individualism" is "the logical consequence of that process of instrumental rationalization that Max Weber analyzed so profoundly."[10] The economic and psychological mobilization of resources for the purpose of mastering the world, as portrayed in Weber's *The Protestant Ethic and The Spirit of Capitalism*, may have so much distorted the spirit of Calvinism that, to use Weber's vivid expression, the cloak lightly placed on the shoulder of the modern West has now become an "iron cage" for the industrial world.[11] This is certainly not the place to assess the historical accuracy of Weber's interpretation. Nor can we take much comfort in noting that the Confucian ethic did not contribute to that process of instrumental rationalization that fundamentally transformed the West and, by extension, the world at large. However, Weber's depiction of the Confucian spiritual orientation as "adjustment to the world"[12] in his *The Religion of China* is relevant here. The Confucian recommendation for harmonizing society appears to be a reasonable corrective to the rampant individualism seen in the West. What Weber detected as a deficiency in the rationalizing potential of Confucian ethics is now recognized as a strength for forging social solidarity.

Notwithstanding the possible relevance of the Confucian message to us, "The Value of the Human in Classical Confucian Thought" (Chapter 4) addresses much broader concerns. Such a discussion, in

the context of the symbolic resources of the Confucian tradition itself, may provide a fresh perspective on the idea of the self without evoking sentiments about individualism. As I observe in the conclusion of this Chapter,

> Historically, the emergence of individualism as a motivating force in Western society may have been intertwined with highly particularized political, economic, ethical, and religious traditions. It seems reasonable that one can endorse an insight into the self as a basis for equality and liberty without accepting Locke's idea of private property, Adam Smith's and Hobbes' idea of private interest, John Stuart Mill's idea of privacy, Kierkegaard's idea of loneliness, or the early Sartre's idea of freedom.[13]

Recent scholarship, notably Thomas Metzger's *Escape from Predicament*, suggests that Weber was probably wrong in making such a sharp distinction between the inner asceticism of the Calvinist Puritan and the this-worldliness of the Confucian literatus.[14] The Confucian, like the Puritan, was greatly energized by an internal measure of self-worth. His rationalizing potential was as high as the Puritan's, even though it did not engender a comparable spirit of capitalism. In fact, the Confucians may have fashioned the East Asian world into a particular kind of socio-political order through their transformative ethics, even though they did not shape their society in the direction of bourgeois capitalism.

If the Confucian project, either in its spiritual self-definition or in its historical function, is not "adjustment to the world," what is the ontological status of the human community in its ultimate concern? Herbert Fingarette's seminal study on *Confucius — The Secular as Sacred* persuasively argues that the Confucian perception of society as the "holy rite" makes the presumption of an inner psyche superfluous.[15] By implication, there is no need to posit the idea of the psychological self in our understanding of the "personal locus" in Confucius' *Analects*. While I have enormously benefited from Fingarette's insightful observations, I do not totally share his interpretation of the core value in Confucian thought, *jen* (humanity). My attempt to study "*Jen* as a Living Metaphor in the Confucian *Analects*" (Chapter 5) is thus both an appreciation and a critique of Fingarette's treatment of the initial formulation of the Confucian project.

A major contribution of Fingarette's study is his emphasis on the universality of the Confucian idea of "ritual" (*li*). This underscores the significance of Hsün Tzu as a contributor to the Confucian Way.[16] However, traditional as well as modern Chinese interpretive literature repeatedly notes that without self-cultivation as the root of a participatory moral community, the imposition of the rules of decorum by the elite on the unsuspecting masses easily degenerates into authoritarianism. Mencius, the transmitter of the Confucian Way, was also intensely interested in the continuation of the moral community, the preservation of the classics, the vitality of the sagely tradition, of well-established rituals and of the good common sense of the people, the respect for the teacher, and the stability of the political order. Nevertheless, he took the ultimate self-transformation of the person as the key to the realization of social and political values. His theory of human nature, far from being a romantic advocacy of human perfectibility, calls our attention to our internal resources for spiritual growth. Learning to be human, in the Mencian perspective, is to refine ourselves so that we can become good, true, beautiful, great, sagely, and spiritual. Chapter 6, intended to suggest an approach to Chinese aesthetics for a research conference in theories of the arts in China, depicts the Mencian self as body, heart, and spirit.

The first six chapters in this book should demonstrate why, in answering Bellah's challenging question, I felt reluctant to shift my emphasis from self-cultivation in order to avoid a possible misunderstanding. The difference between the Confucian perception of the self as a center of relationships and Western individualism is so obvious that by stressing the sociality of Confucian selfhood we may have further deepened the mistaken impression that personal dignity, independence, and autonomy are not deep-rooted Confucian values. A more serious reason for my insistence on the centrality of self-cultivation is the rightness that I sense in articulating the Confucian project as I best understand it. I must hasten to add that this sense of rightness is not momentary. It is neither a heuristic device nor an expedient corrective, but a personal realization. In other words, my deliberate choice to proceed in such a manner is not only dictated by a desire to adopt the best interpretive strategy but also prompted by my own understanding of what the Confucian spiritual orientation is all about.

I do not believe that we can discuss Confucian ideas in English in the twentieth-century United States as if the terms used by Con-

fucius, Mencius, and Wang Yang-ming in classical Chinese were transparently clear through translation. Whenever my compatriots teaching in American universities assure me that a distinctive advantage of discussing Confucian ethics with an English-speaking audience is that we are unencumbered with layer after layer of commentary and sub-commentary sedimentation, I feel extremely uneasy. For one thing, I do not believe that it is possible to present an undifferentiated Confucian position on vital issues, such as the idea of the self, as if there were a trans-temporal wisdom which, once revealed, would remain essentially the same. There is no monolithic Confucian self to speak of.

My attempt to explore those dimensions of Confucian thought that are particularly relevant to Confucian selfhood has been painstakingly difficult. I am critically aware that to understand Confucius in the light of the Mencian rather than the Hsün Tzuan interpretation or to understand Mencius in the Wang Yang-ming rather than the Chu Hsi line impels me to reason from a particular vantage point. Thus, my intellectual claim to universality or, if you will, ecumenicalism, even within the Confucian tradition, is limited. Nevertheless, the parochialism in which I am inevitably circumscribed provides a concrete basis for encountering perennial human concerns in a comparative perspective. Of course, I did not hold these views as self-evidently true when I was first attracted to them. Nor do I intend to defend them, if I am persuaded that they are untenable. I have come to realize that they are sharable, indeed universalizable, mainly because I have been inspired to speak on their behalf by those who challenge me to relate my particularistic study to broad interpretive issues.

How could Confucius, informed by Mencius' *Problematik* which had been, in turn, informed by Wang Yang-ming's *Problematik* have responded to the question of the self that is framed by Bellah's *Problematik*? Chapters 7 and 8 intend to show that the possibility to imagine such a response is itself profoundly meaningful. Chapter 7 addresses the common assumption that the Confucian self, in the context of a hierarchical structure of social roles, is inevitably submerged in the group. The father-son relationship seems to provide an excellent case in which the Confucian son submits himself to the parental authority for the maintenance of social order. Bellah suggests that "the Confucian phrasing of the father-son relationship blocks any outcome of Oedipal ambivalence except submission — submission not in the last analysis to a person but to a pattern

of personal relationships that is held to have ultimate validity."[17] This emphasis on the primacy of political and familial authority leads Bellah to the view that in Confucian culture "creative social innovation as in the Protestant case was precluded by the absence of a point of transcendent loyalty that could provide legitimation for it."[18]

However, if we take seriously the centrality of self-cultivation in the Confucian tradition, the governing principle of the father-son relationship is reciprocity rather than subjugation. It is the realization of the father's ego-ideal, not merely the respect for the father in the flesh, that defines the son's filial piety. Furthermore, a social dyad, in the Confucian sense, "is not a fixed entity but a dynamic interaction involving a rich and ever-changing texture of human-relatedness woven by the constant participation of other significant dyadic relationships."[19] Viewed in this broader context, the father-son relationship in Confucian thought specifies a given and yet transformable human condition for self-realization. Nevertheless, to say that Confucian selfhood entails the participation of the other is not to imply that it is pre-eminently sociological and thus devoid of any profound religious import.

> The answer lies in the Confucian conception of the self not only as a center of relationships but also as a dynamic process of spiritual development. Ontologically, selfhood, our original nature, is endowed by Heaven. It is therefore divine in its all-embracing fullness. Selfhood, in this sense, is both immanent and transcendent. It is intrinsic to us; at the same time, it belongs to Heaven.[20]

Chapter 8, "Neo-Confucian Religiosity and Human-Relatedness" presents further reflections on the same theme. Learning, to reiterate an earlier point, is for the sake of the self. Since the self as a center of relationships is an open system, self-realization involves the establishment of an ever-expanding circle of human-relatedness. Such a circle must develop through the structures of the self, the family, the country, and the world; it must also transcend selfishness, nepotism, ethnocentrism, and anthropocentrism to maintain its dynamism and authenticity.[21] This broadening and deepening of the self can be characterized, in Mencian terminology, as the manifestation of the "great self" and the concomitant dissolution of the "small self."[22]

Mencius maintained that the unlimited sensitivity of the human heart-and-mind provides the basis for ceaseless self-growth.

Through the full realization of our human sensitivity, we can truly understand our nature and, by understanding our nature, we can know Heaven. By taking the self-cultivation of a single person as the root of not only human self-understanding but also divine knowledge, Mencius suggested that ultimate self-transformation, instead of being a lonely quest for one's inner spirituality, is a communal act. Human-relatedness is thus an integral part of one's quest for spiritual fulfillment. To take one's situatedness in a particular network of dyadic relationships as the given is not total submission to the prescribed social roles but a recognition of the most immediate and fruitful way of initiating and completing one's task of learning to be human. After all, in the Confucian view, the ultimate meaning of life is never found in a radical otherness, for it is inseparable from our ordinary daily existence.

The final essay, "Neo-Confucian Ontology: A Preliminary Questioning," explores the metaphysical foundation of humanity as perceived by the principal Neo-Confucian thinkers. Intent on transmitting the Mencian faith in the perfectibility of human nature through self-effort, the central question for them is, How do I learn to become a sage? Since sagehood means the most genuine and authentic manifestation of humanity, the question is virtually identical with, How do I learn to be fully human? Furthermore, since, as we have already discussed, learning to be human, in the Confucian sense, entails learning for the sake of the self, the question is tantamount to, How do I really know myself? or, in more elaborate Neo-Confucian terminology, How do I cultivate my "body and mind" so that I can truly understand my human nature and, by implication, know Heaven?

In a comparative perspective, it seems that Neo-Confucian ontology, grounded in the ultimate certitude of human sensitivity, our ability to feel, sense, and experience an ever-enlarging reality as an integral part of our selfhood, is diametrically opposed to Kantian metaphysics in which the objectivity of the moral will, devoid of any emotional content, features prominently. Yet, since I wrote my "preliminary questioning" almost ten years ago, I have been continuously encouraged by the points of convergence lurking behind the two apparently conflicting metaphysical visions. If we probe Kant's awe-inspiring attempt to lay the metaphysical foundation for autonomous morality in "the realm of ends,"[23] Kant's deep concern for the form and principle from which "the categorical imperative" results may find a sympathetic echo in the Neo-Confucian insistence that the "Heavenly Principle" inherent in human nature is the real

source of moral creativity. The alleged Kantian formalism, which provoked a strong negative response from Bellah in the aforementioned Berkeley-Harvard meeting, may turn out to be a surface manifestation of Kant's, and I believe also Neo-Confucian thinkers', fully justified anxiety about selfish desires, private interests, and self-deception.

I have learned, through numerous conversations with my mentor, Benjamin I. Schwartz, that, in broad comparative study. the clear boundaries that define East and West, or for that matter North and South, usually do not provide the necessary intellectual impetus for deep thinking. Rather, the subtle, nuanced differences in between offer greater opportunity for critical scholarship. The "fruitful ambiguity"[24] of Confucian selfhood may prevent us from giving a straightforward answer to Bellah's challenging question, but it can prompt us to consider the question itself in fresh perspectives. The nine essays, written over a fairly long period of time for a variety of purposes are, in the kind words of Robert C. Neville. "attempts at transmission and interpretation, Confucius' own self-understanding."[25] However, these attempts, far from transmitting and interpreting the Confucian conception of selfhood, suggest ways of exploring the rich resources within the Confucian tradition so that they can be brought to bear upon the difficult task of understanding Confucian selfhood as creative transformation.

Notes

1. The Berkeley-Harvard program in the comparative study of social values (also referred to as the comparative ethics project) has been co-directed by Mark Juergensmeyer, Associate Professor of Religious Studies at the Graduate Theological Union and the University of California, Berkeley, and John Carman, Professor of Comparative Religion and Director of the Center for the Study of World Religions at Harvard University.

2. For Bellah's recent reflection on "civil religion," see R. N. Bellah and P. E. Hammond, *Varieties of Civil Religion* (San Francisco: Harper & Row, 1980). For his criticism of individualism, see his "Religion and the University: The Crisis of Unbelief" (The W. B. Noble Lectures; Harvard University, 1982).

3. Bellah, "Discerning Old and New Imperatives in Theological Education" (Address to the Association of Theological Schools, Pittsburgh, June 21, 1982), p. 8. See A. MacIntyre, *After Virtue* (Notre Dame, Ind.: University of Notre Dame Press, 1981), p. 33.

4. Chapter 2, "The Continuity of Being: Chinese Visions of Nature," p. 39.

5. Ibid.

6. Ibid., p. 47.

7. *The World's Religious Traditions; Current Perspectives in Religious Studies; Essays in Honor of Wilfred Cantwell Smith,* ed. Frank Whaling (Edinburgh: T.&T. Clark, 1984).

8. W.C. Smith's scholarly proposal is succinctly set forth in *The Meaning and End of Religion: A New Approach to the Religious Traditions of Mankind* (New York: Macmillan, 1963). Since its publication, the book has been reissued: New York, New American Library (Mentor Books), 1964; San Francisco, Harper & Row, 1978.

9. Wang Yang-ming, "Inquiry on the Great Learning," in *Instructions for Practical Living and Other Neo-Confucian Writings,* trans. Wing-tsit Chan (New York: Columbia University Press, 1963), p. 272.

10. Bellah, "Discerning Old and New Imperatives in Theological Education," p. 8.

11. Weber's original statement reads:

The Puritan wanted to work in a calling; we are forced to do so. For when asceticism was carried out of monastic cells into everyday life, and began to dominate worldly morality, it did its part in building the tremendous cosmos of the modern economic order. This order is now bound to the technical and economic conditions of machine production which today determine the lives of all the individuals who are born into this mechanism, not only those directly concerned with economic acquisition, with irresistible force. Perhaps it will so determine them until the last ton of fossilized coal is burnt. In Baxter's view the care for external goods should only lie on the shoulders of the saint "like a light cloak, which can be thrown aside at any moment." But fate decreed that the cloak should become an iron cage.

See Max Weber, *The Protestant Ethic and the Spirit of Capitalism,* trans. T. Parsons (New York: Scribners, 1958), p. 181.

12. Max Weber, *The Religion of China: Confucianism and Taoism,* trans. Hans H. Gerth (Glencoe, Ill.: Free Press, 1951), p. 235.

13. Chapter 4, p. 78.

14. Thomas A. Metzger, *Escape from Predicament; Neo-Confucianism and China's Evolving Political Culture* (New York: Columbia University Press, 1977), pp. 3-4, 18-19, 198-204.

15. Herbert Fingarette, *Confucius — The Secular as Sacred* (New York: Harper & Row, 1972), pp. 1-17.

16. Fingarette's interpretation of Confucius is based on his hermeneutic reading of the *Analects*. He does not himself associate his interpretive position with the Hsün Tzu tradition. However, his emphasis on ritual as communal performance helps us to appreciate an important dimension of Hsün Tzu's moral education.

17. Robert Bellah, "Father and Son in Christianity and Confucianism," in his *Beyond Belief: Essays on Religion in a Post-Traditional World* (New York: Harper & Row, 1976), p. 95.

18. Ibid.

19. Chapter 7, p. 118.

20. Ibid, p. 125.

21. Chapter 8, p. 137.

22. *Mencius*, 6A:15.

23. *Immanuel Kant, Foundations of the Metaphysics of Morals*, trans. Lewis White Beck (New York: Bobbs-Merrill, 1959), pp. 58–61.

24. I am indebted to B. I. Schwartz for this thought-provoking idea. His refusal to tie up loose ends prematurely both as a style of scholarship and as an intellectual commitment to a sympathetic and sophisticated method of comparative intellectual history has been a major inspiration for my own work. His *The World of Thought in Ancient China* (Cambridge, Massachusetts: Harvard University, 1985) gives us further insight into his brilliant critique of reductionism.

25. R. C. Neville, Foreword, p. 5.

I. The "Moral Universal" from the Perspectives of East Asian Thought

A defining characteristic of East Asian thought is the widely accepted proposition that human beings are perfectible through self-effort in ordinary daily existence. This proposition is based on two interrelated ideas: (1) The uniqueness of being human is an ethicoreligious question which cannot be properly answered if it is reduced to biological, psychological, or sociological considerations; and (2) the actual process of self-development, far from being a quest for pure morality or spirituality, necessarily involves the biological, psychological, and sociological realities of human life. For the sake of convenience, the first idea will be referred to as an ontological postulate and the second as an experiential assertion. I begin this chapter with a few general observations on the proposition. After I have noted some of the salient features of the East Asian mode of thinking relevant to the present deliberation, I will proceed to a more focused investigation of the two basic ideas. For brevity, the discussion of East Asian thought will be confined to the Mencian line of Confucianism, the Chuang Tzu tradition of Taoism, and the Ch'an (Zen) interpretation of Buddhism.

It should be mentioned from the outset that the primary focus of the "Three Teachings" under study is self-knowledge. Since the conception of a Creator as the ultimate source of morality or spirituality is not even a rejected possibility, there is no appeal to the "wholly other" as the real basis of human perfectibility. Rather, the emphasis is on learning to be human, a learning that is characterized by a ceaseless process of inner illumination and self-transformation. The Confucian ideal of sagehood, the Taoist quest for becoming a "true person," and the Buddhist concern for returning to one's "original mind" are all indications that to follow the path of knowledge backward, as it were, to the starting point of the true self is the aim of East Asian thought.

Knowledge so conceived is not a cognitive grasp of a given structure of objective truths; nor is it an acquisition of internalized skills. It is basically an understanding of one's mental state and an appreciation of one's inner feelings. Since presumably a genuine knowledge of the self entails a transforming act upon the self, to know in this sense is not only to reflect and comprehend, but also to

19

shape and create. To know oneself is simultaneously to perfect oneself. This, I think, is the main reason that East Asian thought lays as much stress on how to cultivate oneself as on who and what the true self is. To the Confucians, Taoists, and Buddhists, self-knowledge is predominantly an ethicoreligious question, although it is inevitably laden with epistemological implications.

In a deeper sense, self-knowledge is neither "knowing that" nor "knowing how"; it is, in essence, an objectless awareness, a realization of the human possibility of "intellectual intuition." Self-knowledge is nothing other than the manifestation of one's real nature (inner sageliness in Confucianism and buddhahood in Ch'an), and that real nature is not only a being to be known but also a self-creating and self-directing activity. However, although self-knowledge does not depend upon empirical knowledge, it is not incompatible with sense experience, or the "knowledge of hearing and seeing." Thus the relation between self-knowledge and empirical knowledge can be either mutually contradictory or mutually complementary. In an extreme formulation, the Taoist maintains that in the pursuit of the Way one must first lose all that one has already acquired in order to embody the Tao. But it is one thing to lose the fragmented and confusing opinions of the world and quite another to lose a sense of reality by enclosing oneself in a totally narcissistic state. Generally speaking, East Asian thought takes empirical knowledge seriously, while focusing its attention on the supreme value of self-knowledge.

The idea of "intellectual intuition" needs some elaboration. For one thing, it is significantly different from either irrationalism or esoterics. It does claim a direct knowledge of reality without logical reasoning or inference. But, unlike what is commonly associated with mysticism, it has very little to do with revelation. Actually, the whole tradition of contemplation as a way of coming to an immediate cognizance of the true essence of God without rational thought is alien to the East Asian mode of thinking. Rather, the possibility for each human being to have "intellectual intuition" is predicated on the presumption that since humanity forms an inseparable unity with heaven, earth, and the myriad things its sensibility is in principle all-embracing. The theological distinction between Creator and creature, signifying an unbridgeable gap between divine wisdom and human rationality, is here transformed into what Joseph Needham characterizes as an organismic vision.[1] Human beings are therefore thought to have as their birthright the potential power and insight to penetrate the things-in-themselves,

or, in Ch'an terminology, the suchness and thusness of *samsāra*. This resembles the Christian notion of divinity inherent in human nature: in the prelapsarian state man is created in the image of God; and in medieval Christian thought man is sometimes defined as divinity circumscribed.

It would be unfortunate if this organismic vision were understood as no more than a form of primitive animism, a doctrine which apparently conflicts with the scientific explanations of natural phenomena. Far from being an unexamined belief in the continued existence and mutual interaction of individual disembodied spirits, organismic vision here seems to have been the result of a philosophical anthropology which neither denies nor slights the uniqueness of being human. As a matter of fact, it subscribes to the non-evolutionary observation that human phylogeny has its own specific structure which cannot be fully explained in terms of the general laws governing the animal kingdom as a whole. Needless to say, it also rejects the attribution of a discrete indwelling spirit to any material form of reality. It is perhaps not far-fetched to consider the organismic vision as an ecological insight, locating humanity in a highly complex web of interdependency.

It would be equally unfortunate if, instead of animism, the organismic vision were taken as a form of anthropocentrism. The human possibility of "intellectual intuition" must not be viewed as a license for manipulative imposition of the human will upon nature. Promethean defiance and Faustian restlessness are not at all compatible with the cherished value of harmony, as both societal goal and cosmic ideal, in East Asian thought. On the contrary, the authentic manifestation of the human will is thought to be ultimate self-transformation, a liberation rather than a conquest. To Confucians, Taoists, and Buddhists, knowledge is enlightenment, a power of self-illumination. And only in its corrupt form does knowledge become a power of conquest. According to this line of thinking, to be fully human requires the courage and wisdom of constantly harmonizing oneself with an ever-enlarging network of relationships, which necessitates a perspective going beyond the restrictions of anthropocentrism.

Yet the transcending perspective never allows a departure from the lived world here and now. This is part of the reason why all major spiritual traditions in East Asia emphasize inner experience as a basis for ethicoreligious deliberation, not only the abstract "inner experience" as a category of thought for systematic analysis but also the concrete inner experience of the thinker engaged in philosophizing.

The line between religion and philosophy is inevitably blurred. What is normally associated with the discipline of psychoanalysis becomes religiously and philosophically relevant and significant. The conscious refusal or, if you will, the inability of East Asian thought to submit itself to the academic compartmentalization characteristic of modern universities is not simply a sign of its lack of differentiation but also an indication of its wholeness with all of its fruitful ambiguities. Indeed, common experiences, such as eating and walking, are respected as having great symbolic significance for moral and spiritual self-development.

For example, to the Confucian every human act is perceived as the reenactment of a time-honored ritual. Each gesture, such as eating, requires numerous practices before it takes the proper form. Only through socially recognized forms can one establish the communication necessary for self-cultivation. Human growth can thus be described as a process of ritualization. However, it is misleading to characterize Confucianism as a kind of ritualism. A coercive imposition of well-established social norms upon the individual who cannot choose but adjust to the all-powerful society is at best the result of a highly politicized Confucian ideology of control. Confucian ethics, on the contrary, is built upon commonly shared human feelings, such as empathy. Ritual in this connection is not a fixed norm but a flexible and dynamic procedure by which self-realization as a concrete means for communal participation rather than as an isolated quest for inner truth becomes possible. The Ch'an teaching of *satori* may on the surface seem diametrically opposed to the ritualized world, but, as the Ch'an masters have never failed to note, the enlightening experience is a confirmation rather than a rejection of common sense because simple acts such as carrying water and chopping wood are the Way of Buddha. Taoism, too, for that matter, affirms the intrinsic value of ordinary human existence. They are all, in a sense, involved in the art of practical living.

It is vitally important to mention at this juncture that the East Asian concept of the human as a self-perfectible being in common ordinary existence without the intervention of a transcendent God is atheistic only in a profoundly religious sense. The ultimate concern of self-realization actually necessitates a ceaseless process of inner moral and spiritual transformation. The purposefulness of life, however, is not a form of teleology in the sense of a preconceived cosmic design. In fact, human beings often remain tragically aimless and helpless, like "rudderless ships on restless waves." It is

misleading to define sageliness or buddhahood in the language of entelechy. Human beings can become sages and buddhas because they are endowed with the "germinations" of morality or "seeds" of enlightenment, but it is highly problematical to perceive these germinations and seeds as the functional equivalents of what some vitalists claim to be the suppositiously immanent but immaterial agency responsible for the achievement of maturity in the human organism. For one thing, in both Confucianism and Buddhism, the duality of spirituality and materiality is meaningless. The Confucian *hsin*, which must be awkwardly rendered as "heart-mind," is a case in point. Intent on integrating the emotive aspects of human life with other dimensions of self-development, Mencius considers the fulfillment of the "bodily design" the highest manifestation of self-cultivation. In Ch'an, the assertion that *nirvāna* is *samsāra,* with all its ramifications, clearly rejects the artificial dichotomy between the body and the enlightened mind. Suggestively, the root metaphor shared by all Three Teachings in East Asian thought is the Way.

In light of the above discussion, the rhetorical situation in which the East Asian Way is articulated has, at least, the following features: (1) the inquirer is as much an inside participant as an outside observer. It is inconceivable that the general question of self-knowledge can be completely independent of the questioner's own self-knowledge. Indeed, as the questioning process unfolds, the inquirer deepens and broadens his understanding of the general issue only to the extent that his personal transformation confirms it. However, (2) it would be mistaken to infer that the East Asian Way is subjectivistic because it lays much emphasis on inner experience. Actually, the idea of "intellectual intuition" does not give any particular individual privileged access to truth. Indeed, the concept of individuality is not at all compatible with it. Rather, it is predicated on a strong sense of sharability and commonality. In other words, the experience that is considered truly personal is not at all private to the individual; self-knowledge is a form of inner experience precisely because it resonates with the inner experiences of others. Accordingly, internality is not a solipsistic state but a concrete basis of communication, or, in the Taoist expression, of "spiritual communion."

It is in this sense that (3) the aforementioned organismic vision is the result of neither animism nor anthropocentrism but of a transcending perspective which seeks the ultimate meaning of life in ordinary human existence. Of course, it is often taken for granted that the ultimate meaning of life is never found in ordinary human

existence. The commonly observed distinctions between soul and body or between sacredness and profanity are clear indications that this is so. Paradoxically, all Three Teachings of the East Asian Way endorse the view that everydayness is not only the point of departure but also the eventual return of any significant moral and spiritual journey. They believe that the true test of lasting values in any ethicoreligious tradition is common sense and good reasons. But they by no means glorify the trite and plain languages of everyday speech. It is actually in what Herbert Fingarette calls the "secular as sacred"[2] that the spirit of their concern for ordinariness really lies.

Against this background, the ontological postulate can be introduced with one more observation. The uniqueness of being human must first transcend many familiar forms of reductionism. It is fallacious to define human nature merely in terms of biological, psychological, or sociological structures and functions because, viewed holistically, a more comprehensive grasp of its many-sidedness is required. However, an empirical enumeration of as many "human" traits as is practically feasible is not satisfactory either. Such a procedure cannot address our question without in principle changing it in a fundamental way. To put it differently, the question about the uniqueness of being human will always be scientifically unanswerable, as advances in biology, psychology, and sociology never intend to provide it with an answer.

The postulate about the perfectibility of human nature is thus empirically unprovable. Yet it is certainly not an unexamined faith in something beyond rational comprehension. Its status is ontological because it specifies a mode of understanding the being of the human. To be sure, perfectibility presupposes malleability and changeability. Ordinarily it is quite conceivable that malleation or change may not lead to the desired perfection. As a result, it seems that human nature can be seen as corruptible no less than as perfectible. However, common to all Three Teachings is the further claim that inherent in human nature is the moral and spiritual propensity for self-development. Only when this original propensity is frustrated by a complexity of internal and external causes is human nature destroyed or led astray. It is in this connection that Mencius insists upon the goodness of human nature as the real basis for self-realization. The Mencian thesis deserves a brief exposition.

Each human being, Mencius asserts, is endowed with a "moral sense," also known as the sensibility of the *hsin*. Inherent in the *hsin* are the four germinations of the four basic human feelings: commiseration, shame and dislike, deference and compliance, and right

and wrong. Although environment, both social and psychological, features prominently in human growth, the germination power of these feelings is the structural reason for moral and spiritual self-development. In a strict sense, morality or spirituality is not internalized by but expressed through learning. Learning to be human in the Mencian tradition is therefore conceived of as the "mutual nourishment" of inner morality and social norms rather than the imposition of external values upon an uncultured mind. Indeed, *hsin* is both a cognitive and an affective faculty, symbolizing the functions of conscience as well as consciousness. For it not only reflects upon realities but, in comprehending them, shapes and creates their meaningfulness for oneself.

Similarly, in the view of Taoism, the inner illumination of the mind is the real basis for self-liberation. Confucian values, such as humanity and righteousness, are rejected by Chuang Tzu as unnecessary and are considered harmful social and cultural constraints detrimental to the spontaneity of nature. However, the pursuit of the Way requires a process of ultimate self-transformation which appeals neither to the immortality of the soul nor to the existence of God but to the "intellectual intuition" inherent in the true self. The *prajñā* in Ch'an, commonly rendered as "intuitive wisdom" or "nondual knowledge," also refers to an inalienable quality of the mind which manifests itself as the true buddha nature in each person.

Accordingly, despite divergent approaches to the actual process of moral and spiritual self-development, Confucianism, Taoism, and Buddhism all share this fundamental belief: Although existentially human beings are not what they ought to be, they can be perfected through self-cultivation; and the reason that they can become fully realized is inherent in what they are. Therefore, the human condition here and now, rather than either the original position in the past or a utopian projection into the future, is the central concern. It is in this sense that the ontological postulate of human perfectibility must be supplemented by an experiential assertion about the concrete path by which one's own "germinations" and "seeds" can eventually be brought to fruition. This may account for some of the deceptively simple paradoxes in East Asian thought, such as:

(a)   There is sageliness in every human being/Virtually no one, not even Confucius, can claim to be a sage.

(b)   Every sentient being is endowed with buddhahood/*Nirvāna* can never be attained except through Great Death.

(c)   *Tao* is everywhere/Only the most sensitive and subtle mind can hear the Way.

It should be mentioned that germinations and seeds constitute only one of the many forms of the metaphorical language used in this connection. A frequently used analogy is the digging and drilling of a well, suggesting many degrees and layers of personal knowledge. Only after one has penetrated the deepest ground of one's existence can one truly experience the "taste" of one's enlightening self, which significantly also provides the authentic possibility for communicating with others and understanding things as they really are. The self so conceived, far from being an isolated and enclosed individual, signifies a sharable commonality accessible to every member of the human community. However, it is vitally important to note that commonality here by no means implies sameness, for it inevitably assumes different shades of meaning as it is perceived and manifested in different persons. The idealists' claim that all rational beings will finally agree is too restrictive a notion to account for the complex structure of common selfhood in East Asian thought. It is also in this sense that all Three Teachings assume that moral and spiritual self-development involves not only a convergence of stages to be perfected but also a multiplicity of ways to be pursued. Exclusivism in ethicoreligious thought is rejected mainly because by insisting upon a single path it would be incapable of accommodating the divergent interests and concerns of human beings as a whole. The recognition that the best way for me is not necessarily the best for my neighbor is a psychology essential for the peaceful coexistence of different and even conflicting beliefs in East Asian society and culture. The Confucian Golden Rule, for instance, is deliberately stated in a negative form: "Do not do to others what you would not want others to do to you."

The reluctance to impose one's own way on others is a consideration for the integrity of the other, and also a recognition that one can never fully comprehend another to the same extent and in the same degree as one can comprehend oneself. The veil of ignorance, however, must not prevent one from constantly trying to empathize with other human beings as an integral part of one's own quest for self-knowledge. Indeed, a sense of community, which is a manifestation of the organismic vision, is absolutely essential for moral and spiritual self-development. Only Confucianism among the Three Teachings unequivocally asserts that society is both necessary and intrinsically valuable for self-realization. Taoism and Ch'an do not seem to have attached much importance to human relations. But neither Taoism nor Ch'an belittles the lived world as a meaningful context in which ethicoreligious developments are assessed, as prob-

lems of afterlife, heaven and hell are deliberately relegated to the background. It is this sense of togetherness in the secular world, I suppose, that accounts for much of the concerted efforts of the Three Teachings to eradicate the alleged fallacy of "individualism." The Confucian instructions on the falsehood of self-centeredness, the Ch'an warning against egoist attachments, and the Taoist advocacy of self-forgetfulness all seem to point to the necessity of going beyond the private in order to participate in a shared vision.

The underlying thesis, then, is equality without uniformity. Moral and spiritual self-development can be understood as a process toward an ever-deepening subjectivity, but this must not be taken as a quest for pure morality or spirituality. The idea that inner truth is mysteriously connected with a transcendent reality not accessible to the human community at large does not feature prominently in East Asian thought at all. The perfected self is never conceived of as a depersonalized entity assuming a superhuman quality. This partly explains the absence of priesthood, presumably a spiritual elite mediating between the secular and the sacred, in any of the Three Teachings. Confucian, Taoist, and Ch'an masters are supposed to be exemplary teachers. They may try to instruct, discipline, and enlighten the student. But the purpose is always to inspire the self-effort of the student because the ultimate reason for self-realization is one's own inner strength.

The "Moral Universal," viewed from these perspectives, assumes a twofold significance: (1) Human beings are moral because, as self-perfectible beings, they cannot be circumscribed merely by the instinctual demands for survival or, for that matter, by the necessities and needs for the solidarity of the group or the perpetuation of the species. The meaning of being human is so uniquely personal that functional explanations, no matter how broad the scope they attempt to encompass, rarely escape the danger of reductionism. Indeed, simple human acts such as eating and walking have profound symbolic significance, making them qualitatively different from similar "acts" in other animals. Human hunger, for example, may from a naturalistic point of view be no more than a common physiological condition in the animal kingdom, but symbolically it is a phenomenon *sui generis*. Human development, therefore, involves much more than the combination of biological growth, psychological maturation, and the continuous internalization of social norms. (2) However, human beings are also inescapably biological, psychological, and social; and in order to realize themselves they must transform these circumscriptions into

necessary "instrumentalities" for self-development. To learn to become what one ought to be, far from being a total rejection of what one is, must begin with a critical self-examination, "a reflection on things at hand." Commonly experienced feelings are therefore the points of departure for cultivating personal knowledge. It is not asceticism but perhaps a balanced diet, and certainly not occultism but a disciplined mind, that can really broaden one's vision and sharpen one's awareness. Methods of "quiet-sitting," "regulated breathing," or *zazen*, notwithstanding their varying degrees of seriousness in different traditions, all seem to suggest that the given "body and mind" is after all the concrete place where great ethicoreligious insight occurs. Pure morality and spirituality, admitting no biological, psychological, or sociological factors, is a kind of formalism as unacceptable to the East Asian mode of thinking as an extreme kind of behavioral reductionism would be. Mencius may have a point when he claims that if we can fully extend the common experience of feeling unable to bear the sufferings of others, our humanity will become inexhaustibly abundant.

FURTHER THOUGHTS

Having prepared this general statement on East Asian thought as a background paper for a workshop on the "biological foundations of morality," I propose to offer in retrospect, especially in the light of Clifford Geertz's thought-provoking comments on my presentation, some observations that may have a direct bearing on the psychological and philosophical issues raised in our joint endeavor.[3] For expediency, I would call our attention to the thought of Wang Yang-ming, who is said to have combined the wisdom of Ch'an Buddhism and the aesthetic sensitivity of Taoism with the humanist concerns of Confucianism. This may help us to focus more sharply on the salient features of the so-called Three Teachings. To begin, it should be remarked that Yang-ming, hailed as a most original and influential thinker in premodern China, was a distinguished scholar-official who consciously and conscientiously put into practice his metaphysical vision and demonstrated through his own personal spiritual development the beliefs he held. Indeed, his life history was an ex-

emplification of the "unity of knowledge and action" idea which he advocated as a defining characteristic of his mode of thinking.

I. *The Great Man Regards Heaven, Earth, and the Myriad Things as One Body.* Thus begins the first line of Wang Yang-ming's "Inquiry on the *Great Learning*," a synoptic view of the central theme he had been formulating throughout his life.[4] What he intends to convey here is neither an intellectual ideal nor an ethical injunction but, as Geertz noted, primarily "a common experience of feeling that undergirds morality."[5] This shared feeling is explicitly described as the "emotional inability to bear the sufferings of others." Underlying these deceptively simple experiential assertions is an ontological claim about the "humanity of the heart." The reason that the great man can manifest his empathic and sympathetic feelings toward another (human being, animal, plant, or stone) in a genuine and spontaneous manner is thought to be in the structure of the heart (*hsin*) itself. Indeed, following Mencius, Yang-ming maintained that the "emotional inability to bear the sufferings of others" is an inborn capacity, not acquired (although it must be enhanced and refined) through imitative learning. Of course this does not mean, to paraphrase P. H. Wolff, that human sensitivity "matures in isolation from specific socioenvironmental influences."[6] On the contrary, from a developmental point of view, it is like a delicate bud which can be easily frustrated without proper nourishment.

The opposite of this kind of unpremeditated human sensitivity is often depicted as selfishness (or self-centeredness), a deliberate refusal to share with, care for, and show affection toward others. Selfish acts are obviously in conflict with what H. L. Rheingold and D. F. Hay call the "prosocial behavior of the very young." Viewed from this perspective, the humane qualities of the infant as empirically identified by Rheingold and Hay are ontologically as well as ontogenetically inherent in the original capacity of the heart. Understandably, the growth of a human being depends as much upon the active participation of the learner (the infant, for example) as a "partner," indeed a "socializer" (a sharing, caring, and feeling "great man" in process) as on what we commonly call "socialization" from outside. This middle path must also reject both "normative biologism" and "normative sociologism."[7]

Yang-ming's interpretive position is actually predicated on a metaphysical vision. If properly understood, such a vision is in accord with the Aristotelian, and for that matter Kantian, assertion

that what makes "reason" most valuable and essential to human beings is precisely the fact that it is beyond genetic constraints and thus
"biologically irrelevant." For one thing, the innateness of universalizable feelings shared by the human community is conceived as a
manifestation of the same "principle" (*li*) which underlies Heaven,
Earth, and the myriad things. Indeed, there is only one "principle" in
all beings and that "principle" is inherently in and intrinsically
knowable to the "humanity of the heart." Unlike the Platonic idea,
the "principle" that is embodied in each concrete thing is the "principle" in its all-embracing fullness. There is no distinction here between man and animal, plant or stone. The uniqueness of man,
however, lies in his ability to know and manifest through self-effort
the "principle" in him.

Man has this ability because ontologically he is endowed with the
"humanity of the heart" for self-realization which, in the tradition of
Chung-yung (Doctrine of the Mean), necessitates a concomitant realization of the other. But, in practice, unless a consistent and strenuous
effort at self-development is applied, man can in actuality become as
insensitive as stone. This metaphor, widely used in Chinese
literature, seems to imply that although man is the most sentient being that embodies the "principle" in the cosmos, what he is existentially may turn out to be a parody of what he can and ought to
become. It is therefore not only man's right but also his duty to be
moral. This reminds us of Kant. However, unlike Kant, Yang-ming
believed that the "principle," which has also been rendered as
"reason," is what human nature in the ultimate sense really means.
As a result, the formalist approach in Kantianism is here replaced by
an appeal to the universality of moral feelings which are biologically
based but not genetically determined. For the "principle" and the
"humanity of the heart" are one and the same reality.

II. *The Preservation of the Heavenly Principle and the Elimination of
Human Desires*. Implicit in the claim that the "humanity of the heart"
is universal and that the greatness of being human lies in the maximum development of this commonly shared feeling are two conflicting images of man. He can "embody" (*t'i*) the cosmos in his heart as
a concretely lived experience rather than a mere intellectual projection. Man so conceived symbolizes, in the words of Chou Tun-i
(1017–73), "the highest excellence" of the creative process of the
universe. Unfortunately, it is also probable that man is so cir-

cumscribed and corrupted by his "human desires" (*jen-yü*), biologically rooted and socioenvironmentally conditioned as well, that he can in fact inflict inhumanity upon himself and his closest kin. Even without the myth of the Fall, the range of human possibility for morality and immorality is frightfully extensive. Man can go beyond anthropocentrism (let alone egoism and ethnocentrism) and serve as a guardian of nature; or he can exhibit an aggression toward himself as well as all other beings as the most destructive force in the universe.

The contrast between the "Heavenly Principle" and "human desires" is of great significance in light of the above. Yang-ming took it for granted that what is truly human necessarily manifests the "principle" in its most generalized sense. Paradoxically "human desires," as limited and distorted expressions of the self, are detrimental to the original rhythm of the heart. This is why "human desires" are also described as "selfish desires" (*ssu-yü*). Just as selfishness endangers the authentic development of the self, "human desires" frustrate the true manifestation of humanity. Thus Yang-ming stated that learning to become a great man "consists entirely in getting rid of the obscuration of selfish desires in order by his own efforts to make manifest his clear character, so as to restore the condition of forming one body with Heaven, Earth, and the myriad things, a condition that is originally so, that is all."

Actually, the preservation of the Heavenly Principle and the elimination of human desires must be taken as a unitary effort of self-cultivation, signifying a holistic process of ultimate personal transformation. A key concept in this connection is *i* (intention), especially an act of the will to manifest one's "clear character" informed by the Heavenly Principle. For without a continuous quest for self-knowledge by an ever deepening psychology of purification, selfish desires cannot be eliminated and the quality of one's life, so far as the "principle" is concerned, remains obscure. This, I suppose, is the main reason why Yang-ming attached so much importance to "establishing the will" (*li-chih*) as the first essential step in the ceaseless process of learning to be truly human. This view seems remarkably similar to F. A. Jenner's observation in which he suggests that "we cannot live in everyday life without acting as though the moral depends on intention,"[8] indeed intentionality. For Yang-ming, we can surmise, morality entails intending, both as a state of conscious knowing (directionality of the mind) and as a process of conscientious acting (transforming effect of the heart). Perhaps in

this sense we can follow E. Turiel's distinction between morality and convention without necessarily committing ourselves to the claim that they are "different aspects of social regulation."⁹

III. *The Full Realization of Primordial Awareness.* I mentioned earlier that the Confucian *hsin* must be glossed as "heart-mind" because it involves both cognitive and affective dimentions of human awareness. This "fruitful ambiguity" is perhaps the result of a deliberate refusal rather than an unintended failure to make a sharp distinction between conscience and consciousness. To Yang-ming, consciousness as cognition and conscience as affection are not two separable functions of the mind. Rather, they are integral aspects of a dynamic process whereby man becomes aware of himself as a moral being. Indeed, the source of morality depends on their inseparability in a pre-reflective faculty. Borrowing a classical term from Mencius, Yang-ming defines this pre-reflective faculty as *liang-chih* (commonly translated as "innate knowledge" but here rendered as "primordial awareness"), signifying an innermost state of human perception wherein knowledge and action form a unity. This primordial awareness, which can also be understood as a more subtle way of characterizing the "humanity of the heart," creates values of human understanding as it encounters the world. Learning to be human, in this sense, involves a continuous development of one's "primordial awareness." The expression *chih liang-chih*, often translated as "the extension of innate knowledge," may be more appropriately interpreted here as the full realization of one's primordial awareness. I do not see any obvious conflict between this line of thinking and T. Nagel's analysis that "a capacity to subject their prereflective or innate responses to criticism and revision, and to create new forms of understanding"¹⁰ is that unique quality that human beings have discovered in themselves. Yet I must admit that Yang-ming's "primordial awareness" is not merely a rational capacity; nor is it simply a perceptual and motivational starting point. Needless to say, it also has little to do with biological nativism. Rather, it is a mode of perceiving which I earlier noted as the function of "intellectual intuition." A feature of it is that, as a critical self-awareness, it can understand our true nature and apprehend the thing-in-itself, a capacity which Kant thought is humanly impossible.

The justification for this seemingly outrageous claim is relatively simple: "Knowing thyself" means to realize the "principle" inherent in one's nature. Since the same "principle" also underlies humans

and things in general, the procedure by which other forms of understanding are created is, in the ultimate sense, identical to that of self-knowledge. But the assumption that the level of self-knowledge attained entails a comparable depth of knowledge about humans and things in general is not an expression of subjective idealism. The true self so conceived is never an isolated entity. The solipsistic predicament (an extreme case of self-centeredness perhaps), so far as it may have a bearing on this, is rejected by a direct appeal to the common experience of feeling. The sense of cosmic togetherness, or in Chang Tsai's (1020–77) poetic expression that "Heaven is my father and Earth is my mother . . . . All people are my brothers and sisters, and all things are my companions," is a primary background understanding in this tradition. As a result, the whole philosophical activity centered around the skeptic's questions about the outside world and about other minds is never developed. Whether or not this mode of thinking will eventually lead to a form of panpsychism is beyond the scope of our present discussion. It is clear, however, that the position introduced here is basically at odds with the view that biological or any physical structures can in themselves explain human morality.

The apparent divergence between this line of inquiry, focusing on the commonality and sharability of human experience, indeed on the unity and continuity of being, and Charles Fried's plea for a greater tolerance of diversity is perhaps a matter of emphasis.[11] I wonder, however, whether the centrality of recognizing the identity of persons as a background assumption for the morality of free, rational choosing beings does not itself presuppose a primordial awareness that despite the distinctness of persons, equality of respect is possible. After all, Kant "who sees in freedom the heart of moral value" feels it is fitting to define moral *choice* as a duty, a categorical imperative. A fiduciary commitment (in Michael Polanyi's sense) to the value of the human, I believe, is a basis for the "principle of the autonomy of morals."

NOTES

1. Needham, J. and Wang, L., *Science and Civilization in China*, 6 vols. (Cambridge: Cambridge University Press, 1954–), 2–287.

2. Fingarette, H., *Confucius: The Secular as Sacred* (New York: Harper & Row, 1972).

3. Professor Geertz's comments have been published in *Philosophy East & West* 31.3 (July 1981), 269–272.

4. For Wang Yang-ming's "Inquiry on the *Great Learning*," see Wing-tsit Chan, trans., *A Source Book in Chinese Philosophy* (Princeton: Princeton University Press, 1973), pp. 659–667.

5. Geertz, p. 271.

6. See P.H. Wolff, "The Biology of Morals from a Psychological Perspective," in *Morality as a Biological Phenomenon*, edited by Gunther S. Stent (Berlin: Dahlem Konferenzen, 1978; reprinted Berkeley, CA: Univesity of California Press, 1980), pp. 83–92, especially pp. 88–89.

7. See H.L. Rheingold and D.F. Hay, "Prosocial Behavior of the Very Young," in *Morality as a Biological Phenomenon*, pp. 93–108.

8. F.A. Jenner, "Psychiatry, Biology and Morals," in *Morality as a Biological Phenomenon*, p. 143.

9. E. Turiel, "The Development of Moral Concepts," in *Morality as a Biological Phenomenon*, p. 120.

10. T. Nagel, "Ethics as an Autonomous Theoretical Subject," in *Morality as a Biological Phenomenon*, p. 204.

11. See C. Fried, "Biology and Ethics: Normative Implications," in *Morality as a Biological Phenomenon*, pp. 186–195, especially p. 194.

II. The Continuity of Being: Chinese Visions of Nature

The Chinese belief in the continuity of being, a basic motif in Chinese ontology, has far-reaching implications in Chinese philosophy, religion, epistemology, aesthetics, and ethics. F. W. Mote comments:

> The basic point which outsiders have found so hard to detect is that the Chinese, among all peoples ancient and recent, primitive and modern, are apparently unique in having no creation myth; that is, they have regarded the world and man as uncreated, as constituting the central features of a spontaneously self-generating cosmos having no creator, god, ultimate cause, or will external to itself.[1]

This strong assertion has understandably generated controversy among Sinologists. Mote has identified a distinctive feature of the Chinese mode of thought. In his words, "[t]he genuine Chinese cosmogony is that of organismic process, meaning that all of the parts of the entire cosmos belong to one organic whole and that they all interact as participants in one spontaneously self-generating life process."[2]

However, despite Mote's insightfulness in singling out this particular dimension of Chinese cosmogony for focused investigation, his characterization of its uniqueness is problematic. For one thing, the apparent lack of a creation myth in Chinese cultural history is predicated on a more fundamental assumption about reality; namely, that all modalties of being are organically connected. Ancient Chinese thinkers were intensely interested in the creation of the world. Some of them, notably the Taoists, even speculated on the creator (*tsao-wu chu*) and the process by which the universe came into being.[3] Presumably indigenous creation myths existed although the written records transmitted by even the most culturally sophisticated historians do not contain enough information to reconstruct them.[4] The real issue is not the presence or absence of creation myths, but the underlying assumption of the cosmos: whether it is continuous or discontinuous with its creator. Suppose the cosmos as we know it

35

was created by a Big Bang; the ancient Chinese thinkers would have no problem with this theory. What they would not have accepted was a further claim that there was an external intelligence, beyond human comprehension, who willed that it be so. Of course the Chinese are not unique in this regard. Many peoples, ancient and recent, primitive and modern, would feel uncomfortable with the idea of a willful God who created the world out of nothing. It is not a creation myth as such but the Judeo-Christian version of it that is absent in Chinese mythology. But the Chinese, like numerous peoples throughout human history, subscribe to the continuity of being as self-evidently true.[5]

An obvious consequence of this basic belief is the all-embracing nature of the so-called spontaneously self-generating life process. Strictly speaking, it is not because the Chinese have no idea of God external to the created cosmos that they have no choice but to accept the cosmogony as an organismic process. Rather, it is precisely because they perceive the cosmos as the unfolding of continuous creativity that they cannot entertain "conceptions of creation *ex nihilo* by the hand of God, or through the will of God, and all other such mechanistic, teleological, and theistic cosmologies."[6] The Chinese commitment to the continuity of being, rather than the absence of a creation myth, prompts them to see nature as "the all-enfolding harmony of impersonal cosmic functions."[7]

The Chinese model of the world, "a decidedly psychophysical structure" in the Jungian sense,[8] is characterized by Joseph Needham as "an ordered harmony of wills without an ordainer."[9] What Needham describes as the organismic Chinese cosmos consists of dynamic energy fields rather than static matter-like entities. Indeed, the dichotomy of spirit and matter is not at all applicable to this psychophysical structure. The most basic stuff that makes the cosmos is neither solely spiritual nor material but both. It is a vital force. This vital force must not be conceived of either as disembodied spirit or as pure matter.[10] Wing-tsit Chan, in his influential *Source Book of Chinese Philosophy*, notes that the distinction between energy and matter is not made in Chinese philosophy. He further notes that H. H. Dubs's rendering of the indigenous term for this basic stuff, *ch'i*, as "matter-energy" is "essentially sound but awkward and lacks an adjective form."[11] Although Chan translates *ch'i* as "material force," he cautions that since *ch'i*, before the advent of Neo-Confucianism in the eleventh century, originally "denotes the

psychophysiological power associated with blood and breath," it should be rendered as "vital force" or "vital power."[12]

The unusual difficulty in making *ch'i* intelligible in modern Western philosophy suggests that the underlying Chinese metaphysical assumption is significantly different from the Cartesian dichotomy between spirit and matter. However, it would be misleading to categorize the Chinese mode of thinking as a sort of pre-Cartesian naïveté lacking differentiation between mind and body and, by implication, between subject and object. Analytically Chinese thinkers have clearly distinguished spirit from matter. They fully recognize that spirit is not reducible to matter, that spirit has an independent ontological status, and that axiomatically spirit is of more enduring value than matter. There are of course notable exceptions. But these so-called materialist thinkers are not only rare but also too few and far between to constitute a noticeable tradition in Chinese philosophy. Recent attempts to reconstruct the genealogy of materialist thinkers in China have been painful and, in some cases, far-fetched.[13] Indeed, to characterize two great Confucian thinkers, Chang Tsai (1020–1077) and Wang Fu-chih (1619–1692), as paradigmatic examples of Chinese materialism is predicated on the false assumption that *ch'i* is materialistic. Both of them did subscribe to what may be called philosophy of *ch'i* as a critique of speculative thought but, to them, *ch'i* was not simply matter but vital force endowed with all-pervasive spirituality.[14]

The continuous presence in Chinese philosophy of the idea of *ch'i* as a way of conceptualizing the basic structure and function of the cosmos, despite the availability of symbolic resources to make an analytical distinction between spirit and matter, signifies a conscious refusal to abandon a mode of thought that synthesizes spirit and matter as an undifferentiated whole. The loss of analytical clarity is compensated by the reward of imaginative richness. The fruitful ambiguity of *ch'i* allows philosophers to explore realms of being which are inconceivable to people constricted by a Cartesian dichotomy. To be sure, the theory of the different modalities of *ch'i* cannot engender ideas such as the naked object, raw data, or the value-free fact, and thus cannot create a world out there, naked, raw, and value-free, for the disinterested scientist to study, analyze, manipulate, and control. *Ch'i*, in short, seems inadequate to provide a philosophical background for the development of empirical science as understood in the positivistic sense. What it does provide,

however, is a metaphorical mode of knowing, an epistemological attempt to address the multidimensional nature of reality by comparison, allusion, and suggestion.

Whether it is the metaphorical mode of knowing that directs the Chinese to perceive the cosmos as an organismic process or it is the ontological vision of the continuity of being that informs Chinese epistemology is a highly intriguing question. Our main concern here, however, is to understand how the idea of the undifferentiated *ch'i* serves as a basis for a unified cosmological theory. We want to know in what sense the least intelligent being, such as a rock, and the highest manifestation of spirituality, such as heaven, both consist of *ch'i*. The way the Chinese perceive reality and the sense of reality which defines the Chinese way of seeing the world are equally important in our inquiry, even though we do not intend to specify any causal relationship between them.

The organismic process as a spontaneously self-generating life process exhibits three basic motifs: continuity, wholeness, and dynamism.[15] All modalities of being, from a rock to heaven, are integral parts of a continuum which is often referred to as the "great transformation" (*ta-hua*).[16] Since nothing is outside of this continuum, the chain of being is never broken. A linkage will always be found between any given pair of things in the universe. We may have to probe deeply to find some of the linkages, but they are there to be discovered. These are not figments of our imagination but solid foundations upon which the cosmos and our lived world therein are constructed. *Ch'i*, the psychophysiological stuff, is everywhere. It suffuses even the "great void" (*t'ai-hsü*) which is the source of all beings in Chang Tsai's philosophy.[17] The continuous presence of *ch'i* in all modalities of being makes everything flow together as the unfolding of a single process. Nothing, not even an almighty creator, is external to this process.

The motif of wholeness is directly derived from the idea of continuity as all-encompassing. If the world were created by an intelligence higher than and external to the great transformation, it would, by definition, fall short of a manifestation of holism. Similarly, if the world were merely a partial or distorted manifestation of the Platonic Idea, it would never achieve the perfection of the original reality. On the contrary, if genuine creativity is not the creation of something out of nothing, but a continuous transformation of that which is already there, the world as it now exists is the authentic manifestation of the cosmic process in its all-embracing fullness. Indeed, if the Idea for its own completion entails that it realize itself

through the organismic process, the world is in every sense the concrete embodiment of the Idea. Traditional Chinese thinkers, of
course, did not philosophize in those terms. They used different conceptual apparatuses to convey their thought. To them, the appropriate metaphor for understanding the universe was biology
rather than physics. At issue was not the eternal, static structure but
the dynamic process of growth and transformation. To say that the
cosmos is a continuum and that all of its components are internally
connected is also to say that it is an organismic unity, holistically integrated at each level of complexity.

It is important to note that continuity and wholeness in Chinese
cosmological thinking must be accompanied by the third motif,
dynamism, lest the idea of organismic unity imply a closed system.
While Chinese thinkers are critically aware of the inertia in human
culture which may eventually lead to stagnation, they perceive the
"course of heaven" (*t'ien-hsing*) as "vigorous" (*chien*) and instruct people to model themselves on the ceaseless vitality of the cosmic process.[18] What they envision in the spontaneously self-generating life
process is not only inner connectedness and inter-dependence but
also infinite potential for development. Many historians have
remarked that the traditional Chinese notion of cyclic change, like
the recurrence of the seasonal pattern, is incompatible with the
modern Western idea of progress. To be sure, the traditional Chinese
conception of history lacks the idea of unilinear development, such
as Marxian modes of production depicting a form of historical inevitability. It is misleading, however, to describe Chinese history as
chronicling a number of related events happening in a regularly
repeated order.[19] Chinese historiography is not a reflection of a
cyclic world view. The Chinese world view is neither cyclic nor
spiral. It is transformational. The specific curve around which it
transforms at a given period of time is indeterminate, however, for
numerous human and nonhuman factors are involved in shaping its
form and direction.

The organismic life process, which Mote contends is the genuine
Chinese cosmogony, is an open system. As there is no temporal
beginning to specify, no closure is ever contemplated. The cosmos is
forever expanding; the great transformation is unceasing. The idea
of unilinear development, in this perspective, is one-sided because it
fails to account for the whole range of possibility in which progress
constitutes but one of several dominant configurations. By analogy,
neither cyclic nor spiral movements can fully depict the varieties of
cosmic transformation. Since it is open rather than closed and

dynamic rather than static, no geometric design can do justice to its complex morphology.

Earlier, I followed Mote in characterizing the Chinese vision of nature as the "all-enfolding harmony of impersonal cosmic function" and remarked that this particular vision was prompted by the Chinese commitment to the continuity of being. Having discussed the three basic motifs of Chinese cosmology — wholeness, dynamism, and continuity — I can elaborate on Mote's characterization by discussing some of its implications. The idea of all-enfolding harmony involves two interrelated meanings. It means that nature is all-inclusive, the spontaneously self-generating life process which excludes nothing. The Taoist idea of *tzu-jan* ("self-so"),[20] which is used in modern Chinese to translate the English word *nature*, aptly captures this spirit. To say that *self-so* is all-inclusive is to posit a nondiscriminatory and nonjudgmental position, to allow all modalities of being to display themselves as they are. This is possible, however, only if competitiveness, domination, and aggression are thoroughly transformed. Thus, all-enfolding harmony also means that internal resonance underlies the order of things in the universe. Despite conflict and tension, which are like waves of the ocean, the deep structure of nature is always tranquil. The great transformation of which nature is the concrete manifestation is the result of concord rather than discord and convergence rather than divergence.

This vision of nature may suggest an unbridled romantic assertion about peace and love, the opposite of what Charles Darwin realistically portrayed as the rules of nature. Chinese thinkers, however, did not take the all-enfolding harmony to be the original naïveté of the innocent. Nor did they take it to be an idealist utopia attainable in a distant future. They were acutely aware that the world we live in, far from being the "great unity' (*ta-t'ung*) recommended in the *Evolution of the Rites*,[21] is laden with disruptive forces including humanly caused calamities and natural catastrophes. They also knew well that history is littered with internecine warfare, oppression, injustice, and numerous other forms of cruelty. It was not naïve romanticism that prompted them to assert that harmony is a defining characteristic of the organismic process. They believed that it is an accurate description of what the cosmos really is and how it actually works.

One advantage of rendering *ch'i* as "vital force," bearing in mind its original association with blood and breath, is its emphasis on the life process. To Chinese thinkers, nature is vital force in display. It is

continuous, holistic, and dynamic. Yet, in an attempt to understand the blood and breath of nature's vitality, Chinese thinkers discovered that its enduring pattern is union rather than disunion, integration rather than disintegration, and synthesis rather than separation. The eternal flow of nature is characterized by the concord and convergence of numerous streams of vital force. It is in this sense that the organismic process is considered harmonious.

Chang Tsai, in his celebrated metaphysical treatise, "Correcting Youthful Ignorance," defines the cosmos as the "Great Harmony":

> The Great Harmony is called the Tao. It embraces the nature which underlies all counter processes of floating and sinking, rising and falling, and motion and rest. It is the origin of the process of fusion and intermingling, of overcoming and being overcome, and of expansion and contraction. At the commencement, these processes are incipient, subtle, obscure, easy and simple, but at the end they are extensive, great, strong and firm. It is *ch'ien* ("heaven") that begins with the knowledge of Change, and *k'un* ("earth") that models after simplicity. That which is dispersed, differentiated, and discernible in form becomes *ch'i*, and that which is pure, penetrating, and not discernible in form becomes spirit. Unless the whole universe is in the process of fusion and intermingling like fleeting forces moving in all directions, it may not be called "Great Harmony."[22]

In his vision, nature is the result of the fusion and intermingling of the vital forces that assume tangible forms. Mountains, rivers, rocks, trees, animals, and human beings are all modalities of energy-matter, symbolizing that the creative transformation of the Tao is forever present. Needham's idea of the Chinese cosmos as an ordered harmony of wills without an ordainer is, however, not entirely appropriate. Wills, no matter how broadly defined, do not feature prominently here. The idea that heaven and earth complete the transformation with no mind of their own clearly indicates that the harmonious state of the organismic process is not achieved by ordering divergent wills.[23] Harmony will be attained through spontaneity. In what sense is this what Mote calls "impersonal cosmic function"? Let us return to Chang Tsai's metaphysical treatise:

> *Ch'i* moves and flows in all directions and in all manners. Its two elements (yin and yang) unite and give rise to the concrete. Thus

the multiplicity of things and human beings is produced. In their
ceaseless successions the two elements of yin and yang constitute
the great principles of the universe.[24]

This inner logic of *ch'i*, which is singularly responsible for the production of the myriad things, leads to a naturalistic description of the
impersonal cosmic function. Wang Fu-chih, who developed Chang
Tsai's metaphysics of *ch'i* with great persuasive power, continues
with this line of thinking:

> The fact that the things of the world, whether rivers or mountains,
> plants or animals, those with or without intelligence, and those
> yielding blossoms or bearing fruits, provide beneficial support for
> all things is the result of the natural influence of the moving power
> of *ch'i*. It fills the universe. And as it completely provides for the
> flourish and transformation of all things, it is all the more spatially
> unrestricted. As it is not spatially restricted, it operates in time and
> proceeds with time. From morning to evening, from spring to
> summer, and from the present tracing back to the past, there is no
> time at which it does not operate, and there is no time at which it
> does not produce. Consequently, as one sprout bursts forth it
> becomes a tree with a thousand big branches, and as an egg
> evolves, it progressively becomes a fish capable of swallowing a
> ship. . . .[25]

The underlying message, however, is not the impersonality of the
cosmic function, even though the idea of the moving power of *ch'i* indicates that no anthropomorphic god, animal, or object is really
behind the great transformation. The naturalness of the cosmic function, despite human wishes and desires, is impersonal but not inhuman. It is impartial to all modalities of being and not merely anthropocentric. We humans, therefore, do not find the impersonal
cosmic function cold, alien, or distant, although we know that it is,
by and large, indifferent to and disinterested in our private thoughts
and whims. Actually, we are an integral part of this function; we are
ourselves the result of this moving power of *ch'i*. Like mountains and
rivers, we are legitimate beings in this great transformation. The
opening lines in Chang Tsai's *Western Inscription* are not only his article of faith but also his ontological view of the human:

> Heaven is my father and earth is my mother, and even such a
> small being as I finds an intimate place in their midst. Therefore,

that which fills the universe I regard as my body and that which
directs the universe I regard as my nature. All people are my
brothers and sisters, and all things are my companions.[26]

The sense of intimacy with which Chang Tsai, as a single person,
relates himself to the universe as a whole reflects his profound
awareness of moral ecology. Humanity is the respectful son or
daughter of the cosmic process. This humanistic vision is distinctively
Confucian in character. It contrasts sharply with the Taoist idea of
non-interference on the one hand and the Buddhist concept of
detachment on the other. Yet the notion of humanity as forming one
body with the universe has been so widely accepted by the Chinese,
in popular as well as elite culture, that it can very well be
characterized as a general Chinese world view.

Forming one body with the universe can literally mean that since
all modalities of being are made of *ch'i*, human life is part of a continuous flow of the blood and breath that constitutes the cosmic process. Human beings are thus organically connected with rocks,
trees, and animals. Understandably, the interplay and interchange
between discrete species feature prominently in Chinese literature,
notably popular novels. The monkey in the *Journey to the West* came
into being by metamorphosis from agate,[27] the hero in the *Dream of
the Red Chamber* or the *Story of the Stone*, Pao-yü, is said to have been
transformed from a piece of precious jade,[28] and the heroine of the
Romance of the White Snake has not completely succeeded in transfigur-
ing herself into a beautiful woman.[29] These are well-known stories.
They have evoked strong sympathetic responses from Chinese audiences young and old for centuries, not merely as fantasies but as
great human drama. It is not at all difficult for the Chinese to imagine that an agate or a piece of jade can have enough potential
spirituality to transform itself into a human being. Part of the pathos
of the White Snake lies in her inability to fight against the spell cast
by a ruthless monk so that she can retain her human form and be
united with her lover. The fascinating element in this romance is
that she manages to acquire the power to transfigure herself into a
woman through several hundred years of self-cultivation.

Presumably, from the cosmic vantage point, nothing is totally fixed.
It need not be forever the identity it now assumes. In the perceptive
eye of the Chinese painter Tao Chi (1641–1717), mountains flow
like rivers. The proper way of looking at mountains, for him, is to
see them as ocean waves frozen in time.[30] By the same token, rocks
are not static objects but dynamic processes with their particular

configuration of the energy-matter. It may not be far-fetched to suggest that, with this vision of nature, we can actually talk about the different degrees of spirituality of rocks. Agate is certainly more spiritual than an ordinary hard stone and perhaps jade is more spiritual than agate. Jade is honored as the "finest essence of mountain and river" (*shan-ch'uan ching-ying*).[31] By analogy, we can also talk about degrees of spirituality in the entire chain of being. Rocks, trees, animals, humans, and gods represent different levels of spirituality based on the varying compositions of *ch'i*. However, despite the principle of differentiation, all modalities of being are organically connected. They are integral parts of a continuous process of cosmic transformation. It is in this metaphysical sense that "all things are my companions."

The uniqueness of being human cannot be explained in terms of a preconceived design by a creator. Human beings, like all other beings, are the results of the integration of the two basic vital forces of yin and yang. Chou Tun-i (1017–1073) says, "the interaction of these two *ch'i* engenders and transforms the myriad things. The myriad things produce and reproduce, resulting in an unending transformation."[32] In a strict sense, then, human beings are not the rulers of creation; if they intend to become guardians of the universe, they must earn this distinction through self-cultivation. There is no preordained reason for them to think otherwise. Nevertheless, the human being, in the Chinese sense of *jen* which is gender neutral, is unique. Chou Tun-i offers the following explanation:

> It is man alone who receives [the Five Agents] in their highest excellence, and therefore he is most intelligent. His physical form appears, and his spirit develops consciousness. The five moral principles of his nature (humanity, rightness, propriety, wisdom, and faithfulness) are aroused by, and react to, the external world and engage in activity; good and evil are distinguished; and human affairs take place.[33]

The theory of the Five Agents or the Five Phases (*wu-hsing*) need not concern us here. Since Chou makes it clear that "by the transformation of yang and its union with yin, the Five Agents of Water, Fire, Wood, Metal, and Earth arise" and that since "the Five Agents constitute a system of yin and yang."[34] they can be conceived as specific forms of *ch'i*.

That humankind receives *ch'i* in its highest excellence is not only manifested in intelligence but also in sensitivity. The idea that humans are the most sentient beings in the universe features prominently in Chinese thought. A vivid description of human sensitivity is found in the "recorded sayings" (*yü-lu*) of Ch'eng Hao (1032–1085):

> A book on medicine describes paralysis of the four limbs as absence of humanity (*pu jen*). This is an excellent description. The man of humanity regards heaven and earth and all things as one body. To him there is nothing that is not himself. Since he has recognized all things as himself, can there be any limit to his humanity? If things are not part of the self, naturally they have nothing to do with it. As in the case of paralysis of the four limbs, the vital force (*ch'i*) no longer penetrates them, and therefore they are no longer parts of the self.[35]

This idea of forming one body with the universe is predicated on the assumption that since all modalities of being are made of *ch'i*, all things cosmologically share the same consanguinity with us and are thus our companions. This vision enabled an original thinker of the Ming Dynasty, Wang Ken (1483–1540), to remark that if we came into being through transformation (*hua-sheng*), then heaven and earth are our father and mother to us; if we came into being through reproduction (*hsing-sheng*), then our father and mother are heaven and earth to us.[36] The image of the human that emerges here, far from being the lord of creation, is the filial son and daughter of the universe. Filial piety connotes a profound feeling, an all-pervasive care for the world around us.

This literal meaning of forming one body with the universe must be augmented by a metaphorical reading of the same text. It is true that the body clearly conveys the sense of *ch'i* as the blood and breath of the vital force that underlies all beings. The uniqueness of being human, however, is not simply that we are made of the same psychophysiological stuff that rocks, trees, and animals are also made of. It is our consciousness of being human that enables and impels us to probe the transcendental anchorage of our nature. Surely, the motif of the continuity of being prevents us from positing a creator totally external to the organismic cosmic process, but what is the relationship between human nature and heaven which serves as the source of all things? Indeed, how are we to understand the on-

tological assertion in the first chapter of the *Doctrine of the Mean* that
our nature is decreed by heaven?[37] Is the Mandate of Heaven a onetime operation or a continuous presence? Wang Fu-chih's general
response to these questions is suggestive:

> By nature is meant the principle of growth. As one daily grows,
> one daily achieves completion. Thus by the Mandate of Heaven is
> not meant that heaven gives the decree (*ming*, mandate) only at the
> moment of one's birth. . . . In the production of things by heaven,
> the process of transformation never ceases.[38]

In the metaphorical sense, then, forming one body with the
universe requires continuous effort to grow and to refine oneself. We
can embody the whole universe in our sensitivity because we have
enlarged and deepened our feeling and care to the fullest extent.
However, there is no guarantee at the symbolic or the experiential
level that the universe is automatically embodied in us. Unless we
see to it that the Mandate of Heaven is fully realized in our nature,
we may not live up to the expectation that "all things are complete in
us."[39] Wang Fu-chih's refusal to follow a purely naturalistic line of
thinking on this is evident in the following observation: "The profound person acts naturally as if nothing happens, but . . . he acts
so as to make the best choices and remain firm in holding to the
Mean."[40] To act naturally without letting things take their own
course means, in Neo-Confucian terminology, to follow the "heavenly
principle" (*t'ien-li*) without being overcome by "selfish desires"
(*ssu-yü*).[41] Selfish desires are forms of self-centeredness that belittle
the authentic human capacity to take part in the transformative process of heaven and earth. In commenting on the *Book of Change*,
Ch'eng Hao observes:

> The most impressive aspect of things is their spirit of life. This is
> what is meant by origination being the chief quality of goodness.
> Man and heaven and earth are one thing. Why should man pur-
> posely belittle himself?[42]

Forming a trinity with heaven and earth, which is tantamount to
forming one body with the myriad things, enjoins us from applying
the subject-object dichotomy to nature. To see nature as an external
object out there is to create an artificial barrier which obstructs our
true vision and undermines our human capacity to experience

nature from within. The internal resonance of the vital forces is such that the mind, as the most refined and subtle *ch'i* of the human body, is constantly in sympathetic accord with the myriad things in nature. The function of "affect and response" (*kan-ying*) characterizes nature as a great harmony and so informs the mind.[43] The mind forms a union with nature by extending itself metonymically. Its aesthetic appreciation of nature is neither an appropriation of the object by the subject nor an imposition of the subject on the object, but the merging of the self into an expanded reality through transformation and participation. This creative process, in Jakobson's terminology, is "contiguous," because rupture between us and nature never occurs.[44]

Chuang Tzu recommends that we listen with our minds rather than with our ears; with *ch'i* rather than with our minds.[45] If listening with our minds involves consciousness unaffected by sensory perceptions, what does listening with *ch'i* entail? Could it mean that we are so much a part of the internal resonance of the vital forces themselves that we can listen to the sound of nature or, in Chuang Tzu's expression, the "music of heaven" (*t'ien-lai*)[46] as our inner voice? Or could it mean that the all-embracing *ch'i* enables the total transposition of humankind and nature? As a result, the aesthetic delight that one experiences is no longer the private sensation of the individual but the "harmonious blending of inner feelings and outer scenes"[47] as the traditional Chinese artist would have it. It seems that in either case we do not detach ourselves from nature and study it in a disinterested manner. What we do is to suspend not only our sensory perceptions but also our conceptual apparatus so that we can embody nature in our sensitivity and allow nature to embrace us in its affinity.

I must caution, however, that the aesthetic experience of mutuality and immediacy with nature is often the result of strenuous and continual effort at self-cultivation. Despite our superior intelligence, we do not have privileged access to the great harmony. As social and cultural beings, we can never get outside ourselves to study nature from neutral ground. The process of returning to nature involves unlearning and forgetting as well as remembering. The precondition for us to participate in the internal resonance of the vital forces in nature is our own inner transformation. Unless we can first harmonize our own feelings and thoughts, we are not prepared for nature, let alone for an "interflow with the spirit of Heaven and Earth."[48] It is true that we are consanguineous with nature. But as humans, we must make ourselves worthy of such a relationship.

NOTES

1. Frederick F. Mote, *Intellectual Foundations of China* (New York: Alfred A. Knopf, 1971), pp. 17–18.

2. Ibid., p. 19.

3. For a thought-provoking discussion on this issue, see N J. Girardot, *Myth and Meaning in Early Taoism* (Berkeley: University of California Press, 1983), pp. 275–310.

4. For a suggestive methodological essay, see William G. Boltz, "Kung Kung and the Flood: Reverse Euhemerism in the *Yao Tien,*" *T'oung Pao* 67 (1981): 141–53. Professor Boltz's effort to reconstruct the Kung Kung myth indicates the possibility of an indigenous creation myth.

5. Tu Wei-ming, "Shih-t'an Chung-kuo che-hsüeh chung te san-ko chi-tiao" [A preliminary discussion on the three basic motifs in Chinese philosophy], *Chung-kuo che-hsüeh shih yen-chiu* [Studies on the history of Chinese philosophy] (Peking: Society for the Study of the History of Chinese Philosophy) 2 (March 1981): 19–21.

6. Mote, *Intellectual Foundations of China*, p. 20.

7. Ibid.

8. See Jung's Foreword to the *I Ching (Book of Changes)*, translated into English by Cary F. Baynes from the German translation of Richard Wilhelm, Bollingen Series, vol. 19 (Princeton, N.J.: Princeton University Press, 1967), p. xxiv.

9. Needham's full statement reads as follows: "It was an ordered harmony of wills without an ordainer; it was like the spontaneous yet ordered, in the sense of patterned, movements of dancers in a country dance of figures, none of whom are bound by law to do what they do, nor yet pushed by others coming behind, but cooperate in a voluntary harmony of wills." See Joseph Needham and Wang Ling, *Science and Civilization in China*, 6 vols. (Cambridge: Cambridge University Press, 1954–), 2:287.

10. Actually, the dichotomy of spirit and matter does not feature prominently in Chinese thought, See Tu, "Shih-t'an Chung-kuo che-hsüeh," pp. 21–22.

11. Wing-tsit Chan, trans. and comp., *A Source Book in Chinese Philosophy* (Princeton, N.J.: Princeton University Press, 1969), p. 784.

12. Ibid.

13. For a notable exception to this general interpretive situation in the People's Republic of China, see Chang Tai-nien, *Chung-kuo che-hsüeh fa-wei* [Exploring some of the delicate issues in Chinese philosophy] (T'ai-yuan, Shansi: People's Publishing Co., 1981), pp. 11–38; 275–306.

14. For a general discussion on this vital issue from a medical viewpoint, see Manfred Porkert, *The Theoretical Foundations of Chinese Medicine: Systems of Correspondence* (Cambridge, Mass.: MIT Press, 1974).

15. Tu, "Shih-t'an Chung-kuo che-hsüeh," pp. 19–24.

16. A paradigmatic discussion on this is to be found in the *Commentaries on the Book of Changes*. See Wing-tsit Chan, *Source Book in Chinese Philosophy*, p. 264.

17. See Chang Tsai's "Correcting Youthful Ignorance" in Wing-tsit Chan, *Source Book in Chinese Philosophy*, p. 501.

18. For this reference in the *Chou I,* see *A Concordance to Yi-Ching,* Harvard-Yenching Institute Sinological Index Series Supplement No. 10 (reprint; Taipei: Chinese Materials and Research Aids Service Center, Inc., 1966), 1/1.

19. The idea of the "dynastic cycle" may give one the impression that Chinese history is nondevelopmental. See Edwin O. Reischauer and John K. Fairbank, *East Asia: The Great Tradition* (Boston: Houghton Mifflin Co., 1960), pp. 114–18.

20. Chuang Tzu, chap. 7. See the Harvard Yenching Index on the *Chuang Tzu,* 20/7/11.

21. See William T. de Bary, Wing-tsit Chan, and Burton Watson, comps., *Sources of Chinese Tradition* (New York: Columbia University, 1960), pp. 191–92.

22. Wing-tsit Chan, *Source Book on Chinese Philosophy,* pp. 500–1.

23. Ibid., pp. 262–66. This idea underlies the philosophy of change.

24. Ibid., see. 14, p. 505. In this translation, *ch'i* is rendered "material force." The words *yin* and *yang* in parentheses are added by me.

25. Ibid., pp. 698–99.

26. Ibid., p. 496.

27. Wu Ch'eng-en, *Hsi-yu chi,* trans. Anthony C. Yü (Yü Kuo-fan) as *Journey to the West,* 4 vols. (Chicago: University of Chicago Press, 1977–), 1:67–78.

28. Ts'ao Hsüeh-ch'in (Cao Xueqin), *Hung-lou meng* [Dream of the Red Chamber], trans. David Hawkes as *The Story of the Stone,* 5 vols. (Middlesex, England: Penguin Books, 1973–), 1:47–49.

29. For two useful discussions on the story, see Fu Hsi-hua, *Pai-she-chuan chi* [An anthology of the White Snake story] (Shanghai: Shanghai Publishing Co., 1955) and P'an Chiang-tung, *Pai-she ku-shih yen-chiu* [A study of the White Snake story] (Taipei: Students' Publishers, 1981).

30. P. Ryckmans, "Les propos sur la peinture de Shi Tao traduction et commentaire," *Arts Asiatique* 14 (1966): 123–24.

31. Teng Shu-p'in, "Shan-ch'uan ching-ying—yü te i-shu" [The finest essence of mountain and river—the art of jade], in *Chung-kuo wen-hua hsin-lun* [New views on Chinese culture] (Taipei: Lien-ching, 1983), Section on Arts, pp. 253–304.

33. Ibid.

34. Ibid.

35. Ibid., p. 530.

36. Wang Ken, "Yü Nan-tu chu-yu" [Letter to friends of Nan-tu], in *Wang Hsin-chai hsien-sheng ch'üan-chi* [The complete works of Wang Ken] (1507 edition, Harvard-Yenching Library), 4.16b.

37. Wing-tsit Chan, *Source Book in Chinese Philosophy,* p. 98.

38. Ibid., p. 699.

39. *Mencius,* 7A4.

40. Wing-tsit Chan, *Source Book in Chinese Philosophy,* pp. 699–700.

41. For example, in Chu Hsi's discussion of moral cultivation, the Heavenly Principle is clearly contrasted with selfish desires. See Wing-tsit Chan, *Source Book in Chinese Philosophy,* pp. 605–6.

42. Ibid., p. 539.

43. For a suggestive essay on this, see R. G. H. Siu, *Ch'i: A Neo-Taoist Approach to Life* (Cambridge, Mass.: MIT Press, 1974).

44. Roman Jakobson, "Two Aspects of Language and Two Types of Aphasic Disturbances," in Roman Jakobson and Morris Halle, *Fundamentals of Language* ('sGravenhage: Mouton, 1956), pp. 55–82. I am grateful to Professor Yu-kung Kao for this reference.

45. *Chuang Tzu*, chap. 4. The precise quotation can be found in *Chuang Tzu ying-te* (Peking: Harvard-Yenching Institute, 1947), 9/4/27.

46. *Chuang Tzu*, chap. 2 and *Chuang Tzu yin-te*, 3/2/8.

47. For a systematic discussion of this, see Yu-kung Kao and Kang-i Sun Chang (Sun Kang-i), "Chinese 'Lyric Criticism' in the Six Dynasties," American Council of Learned Societies Conference on Theories of the Arts in China (June 1979), included in *Theories of the Arts in China*, eds. Susan Bush and Christian Murck (Princeton, N.J.: Princeton University Press, 1984).

48. *Chuang Tzu*, chap. 33 and *Chuang Tzu ying-te*, 93/33/66.

III. A Confucian Perspective on Learning to be Human[1]

In the modern pluralistic cultural context, the Confucian "faith" in the intrinsic meaningfulness of humanity may appear to be finite, historical, secular, and culturally specific. However, to the living Confucian, this faith is an articulation of truth, an expression of reality and, indeed a view of life so commonly accepted in East Asia for centuries and so obviously rational that it is singularly self-evident. In this essay, I intend to demonstrate, based upon my own understanding of the Confucian project, that this humanistic claim about faith is of profound significance to the study of religion as an evolving and developing discipline which may, in the long run, establish a unity of understanding and appreciation of ultimate concerns despite the seductiveness of sophisticated relativism currently espoused by some of our most brilliant and open-minded colleagues in social sciences and the humanities.

I. *Learning for the Sake of the Self.* The Confucian approach to perennial human questions has generally been considered finite, if not miserably parochial. In part, this is because Confucius, in response to the queries of his students, refused to speculate on the subjects of death and spirits on the grounds that our understanding of life and human beings should be of primary importance.[2] The Confucian point of departure which focuses on the person living here and now is, however, predicated on a broadly conceived notion of life and human beings in which death and spirits feature prominently as constitutive elements. In other words, a genuine appreciation of the Confucian perception of the living person necessarily involves sensitivity to death and spirits. The significance of this will be discussed later but it is important to note here that it is not only inadequate but misleading to assert that because Confucius did not overtly answer questions about death and spirits he was unmindful of those profound human concerns. In fact, it is difficult to imagine what shape the Confucian tradition would have assumed had the mourning rituals and the ancestor cult been left out.

Yet, despite the outsider's view that traditional Confucians were under their ancestors' shadow,[3] the Confucian commitment to the

human community is firm and comprehensive. This commitment
may mean instrumentally that the whole Confucian enterprise begins with the person living here and now. It may also mean substantively that the person in ordinary daily existence is the basis for the
full realization of humanity. The Confucian insistence that learning
is for the sake of the self,[4] an end in itself rather than a means to an
end, speaks directly to this. Learning, for the Confucian, is to learn
to be human. We are, to be sure, inescapably human, and in a
naturalistic sense it is our birthright to be so. But in an aesthetic,
moral or religious sense, being human necessitates a process of learning. Learning to be human then means becoming aesthetically
refined, morally excellent and religiously profound. I am critically
aware that the terms and categories I have just used are not Confucian
although they can be shown to be compatible with the original
Confucian insight. Perhaps it is simply a matter of emphasis, but the
primary concern of Confucian learning is character formation defined in ethical terms.

If the primary Confucian concern is to learn to become a good
person, what does this entail? It is vitally important to know, from
the outset, that learning to become a good person in the Confucian
context is not only the primary concern but also the ultimate and
comprehensive concern. Therefore, it does not make much sense to
compare and contrast the idea of the good person with that of the
wise, strong, sensitive, intelligent, or creative person. To the Confucian, the good person is necessarily wise, strong, sensitive, intelligent, creative, and more. If we prefer to use the word "good" to
designate a quality that can be distinguished from other desirable
qualities such as wise and creative, we may have to redefine the
primary Confucian concern in more neutral terms such as "learning
to become more authentically or more fully human." With due
respect to the interpretive consensus among Sinologists that Confucianism is a form of social ethics, the word "authenticity" even with
its modern existential implications seems to me more appropriate
than narrowly conceived moralistic terms such as "honesty" and
"loyalty" to convey the original Confucian sense of learning for the
sake of the self.

To learn to become an authentic person in the Confucian sense is
certainly to be honest with oneself and loyal to others, but it also entails a ceaseless process through which humanity in its all-embracing
fullness is concretely realized. This dimension of Confucian learning
is not reducible to any particular virtue; nor is it an aggregate of
those that are distinctively Confucian. Yet, taking the living person

here and now as a point of departure inevitably imposes constraints on the Confucian intention to universalize its project: How can a Confucian assume that learning to be human, a process which varies according to country, history, culture, social class, and a host of other factors, is a universally valid conception? Traditional Confucians were of course not aware of the significance of this question. They believed that the idea was sound; they put it into practice; they demonstrated its validity through exemplary teaching; they embodied it; indeed, they lived it.

II. *Understanding through Inquiry.* The living Confucian in the twentieth century, who responds to the challenge of pluralistic relativism, with heightened critical self-awareness, cannot take for granted that the Confucian message is self-evidently true. The idea of learning for the sake of the self may have been a reflection of the perceived privilege of the cultural elite in the later half of the Spring and Autumn period (722–481 B.C.).[5] It may have been an integral part of the ideology of the newly emerging feudal bureaucracy (or the declining slave-owning aristocracy) designed to monopolize the channel of upward social mobility. It may also have been a manifestation of the peculiar Sinic predilection for moral education at the expense of scientific knowledge and institution building. It is difficult, after all, to determine whether the Confucian idea of humanity was really inclusive in a sense comparable to the idea of "all men are created equal" or whether it signified a rather exclusivistic "we Chinese" or even "we the educated classial scholars in the state of Lu."

Furthermore, the living Confucian is also aware that the idea of learning for the sake of the self could not have meant a quest for one's individuality. Even in the West, individualism as a positive doctrine is a relatively recent phenomenon.[6] Self, in the classical Confucian sense, referred to a center of relationships, a communal quality which was never conceived of as an isolated or isolable entity. Since the social basis, the cultural background, and the ethicoreligious context in which the Confucian idea of learning for the sake of the self emerged were all so radically different from what we experience in the modern West as "learning" and as "self," how can we retrieve its meaning without distorting its original intent in order to make it relevant to us here and now?

The task of trying to understand what Confucius meant when he said that true learning was for the sake of the self requires painstaking archaeological digging. Many disciplines—etymology, textual

analysis, exegesis and commentary, just to mention a few of the traditional Sinological tools — will have to be brought to bear on the process. If we extend our task to include an appreciation of the traditional Confucian understanding of the Master's statement over the centuries, other disciplines such as cultural history, comparative religion, hermeneutics, and philosophy will also be required. Even then, we can never be sure that we have gotten it right. For the gap between the two radically different epistemic eras, to use a fashionable expression, may forever remain wide and open. However, the responsibility of the scholarly community is precisely to struggle against overwhelming odds in order to reach an understanding, no matter how partial and how imperfect that understanding turns out to be. For the living Confucian, such an intellectual endeavor is not only desirable but necessary for spiritual self-definition.

The matter, however, is complicated by the fact that what is at stake goes beyond the need of the scholarly community to extend its intellectual horizons and the desire of the Confucian to search for his or her meaning in life. The challenge all members of the scholarly community who are actively involved in comparative studies must face is whether or not, in principle, we can really understand such a deceptively simple Confucian statement as "learning is for the sake of the self" out of context. The answer, unfortunately, must be in the negative. We cannot know what it means if we do not situate it in its proper context: Why was the statement made? What did it want to affirm? Was it a response to a different kind of learning prevalent at the time? How central is it to the Confucian mode of thinking? Is it a code for something much more elaborate and significant? There is no guarantee that we can fully appreciate what Confucius meant to convey even after we have found satisfactory answers to these questions, for there will be numerous other questions that demand our attention, if we are serious about our inquiry.

These issues are also relevant to the Confucian living today. The sort of difficulty that scholars encounter in moving from one linguistic universe to the other pertains to modern Confucians as well. The age of certainty in which the educated person in China would be expected to know what it means to be a Confucian is forever gone. In today's pluralistic world, the Confucian, like his or her counterpart in the Buddhist, Jewish, Christian, Islamic, or Hindu community, must learn to live an ethicoreligious life as a deliberate choice. However, unlike those in other faith communities, all Confucians must also try to apprehend the meanings of the

statements in the classical texts with the same kind of conscientiousness that critical scholars of Confucian learning display. This is partly due to the absence of a functional equivalent to the priesthood in the Confucian tradition; perhaps an even more significant factor is the lack of tangible religious institutions responsible for standardizing and transmitting Confucian precepts. It is therefore interesting to note that the Chinese term for Confucian, *ju*, generically means "scholar".[7]

It may not be far-fetched to suggest that the modern approximation of the traditional Chinese idea of *ju* is the scholar in the humanities. However, in the highly professionalized atmosphere of the academic setting, a scholar in the humanities captures only one aspect of what *ju* purports to stand for. The contemporary use of the term "intellectual," especially in the sense of one who is engaged in and concerned with the well-being of humanity, comes close to the idea of *ju*. In fact, this communal dimension of Confucianism is preeminently a social philosophy.[8] Understandably, Confucian learning is often characterized as altruistic, for its primary purpose is thought to be for the sake of others.

III. *Centrality of Self-Cultivation.* The prevalent view that Confucianism is a form of social ethics which particularly emphasizes human-relatedness is basically correct, but it fails to account for the centrality of self-cultivation as an independent, autonomous and inner-directed process in the Confucian tradition. Confucians do maintain that one becomes fully human through continuous interaction with other human beings and that one's dignity as a person depends as much on communal participation as on one's own sense of self-respect. But the Weberian characterization of the Confucian spiritual orientation as "adjustment to the world"[9] because of its alleged teaching of submission to established patterns of human relationships seriously undermines the Confucian capacity for psychological integration and religious transcendence. In fact, the ability of the Confucian tradition to undergo profound transformations without losing its spiritual identity lies in its commitment to the inner resources of humanity.

The self as the center of relationships has always been the focus of Confucian learning. One's ability to harmonize human relations does indeed indicate one's self-cultivation, but the priority is clearly set. Self-cultivation is a precondition for harmonizing human relations; if human relations are superficially harmonized without the

necessary ingredients of self-cultivation, it is practically unworkable and teleologically misdirected. The common Chinese expression that the friendship of small-minded people is as sweet as honey and the friendship of profound persons is as plain as water suggests that the relationships dictated by need are far inferior to disinterested fellowship dedicated to moral growth. One enters into communication with other human beings for a variety of reasons, many of which are, to some modern sociologists, morally neutral and thus irrelevant to the inner lives of the persons involved. Confucians recognize that human beings are social beings, but they maintain that all forms of social interaction are laden with moral implications and that self-cultivation is required to harmonize each one of them.

The heuristic value of learning for the sake of the self can perhaps be understood as an injunction for self-cultivation. Since self-cultivation is an end rather than a means, learning motivated by reasons other than self-knowledge, such as fame, position and wealth, cannot be considered true learning. An archer who fails to hit the mark and turns around introspectively to rectify the mistake from within enacts the Confucian concern that to know oneself internally is the precondition for doing things right in the external world.

If human relations are harmonized, it is because the people involved have cultivated themselves. To anticipate a harmonious state of affairs in one's social interaction as a favorable condition for self-cultivation is, in the Confucian sense, not only unrealistic but illogical. Self-cultivation is like the root and trunk, and harmonious human relations are like the branches. Both temporally and in terms of importance, the priority is irreversible.[10] Strictly speaking, learning for the sake of others as a demonstration of altruism cannot be truly altruistic, unless it is built on the foundation of self-knowledge. The Confucian Golden Rule, "Do not do unto others what you would not want others to do unto you,"[11] does not simply mean that one should be considerate to others; it also means that one must be honest with oneself. It was perhaps for this reason that Confucius felt that some of his best disciples still had a great deal to learn in order to put the Golden Rule into practice.

What is the status of the Confucian Golden Rule in self-cultivation, if it cannot be uniformly applied? It is certainly not a categorical imperative in the Kantian sense; nor is it the guiding principle for action to which one is enjoined to conform. Rather, it is a standard of inspiration and an experienced ideal made meaningful to the students through the exemplary teaching of their master. Self-cultivation may mean different things to different people at different

stages of moral development, and its realization may also assume many different forms. Yet, self-cultivation remains the locus of Confucian learning. Learning to be human, as a result, centers on the self, not the self as an abstract idea but the self as the person living here and now.

IV. *From a Personal Point of View*. One of the most intriguing insights of Confucian learning is that learning to be human entails learning for the sake of the self and that the self so conceived is not the generic self but I myself as an experiencing and reflecting person here and now. To turn the mode of questioning from the impersonal self to the personal I requires intellectual sophistication as well as existential commitment. The safe distance between what I as a person speculate about in propositional language and what I speak as a concrete human being is no longer there. I am exposed, for what I think I know is now inevitably intertwined with what I do know. If I am wrong, it is not simply because what I have proposed is untenable but also because of a defect in the way I live. However, the psychoanalytical procedure of allowing my deep-rooted private self to be scrutinized by another intelligence is not part of the Confucian tradition. Confucian self-cultivation presupposes that the self worth cultivating is never the private possession of a single individual but a sharable experience that underlies common humanity.

It is not at all surprising then that, despite the centrality of self-cultivation in Confucian learning, autobiographic literature exhibiting secret thoughts, private feelings, and innermost desires and drives is extremely rare in the Confucian tradition. Obviously, the cultivated self is not private property that we carefully guard against intrusion from outside. The ego that has to be protected against submersion in the waves of social demand is what the Confucians refer to as *ssu* (the privatized self, the small self, the self that is a closed system). The true self, on the contrary, is public-spirited, and the great self is the self that is an open system. As an open system, the self in the genuine sense of the word is expansive and always receptive to the world at large. Self-cultivation can very well be understood as the broadening of the self to embody an ever-expanding circle of human relatedness. However, it would be misleading to conclude that the Confucian self broadens horizontally only to establish meaningful social relations. The concentric circles that define the self in terms of family, community, country, and the world are undoubtedly social groups, but, in the Confucian perspec-

tive, they are also realms of selfhood that symbolize the authentic human possibility for ethicoreligious growth.

Ethicoreligious growth, for the Confucian, is not only a broadening process but also a deepening process. As I myself resonate with other selves, the internal resources inherent in me are multiplied. I acquire an appreciation of myself through genuine communication with the other; as I know more of myself, I apprehend more of the other. The Confucian dictum, "in order to establish myself, I establish others; in order to enlarge myself, I enlarge others,"[12] is therefore not only an altruistic idea but also a description of the self in transformation. The quest for inner spirituality as a lonely struggle belongs to a radically different rhetorical situation. Confucian self-cultivation is a deliberate communal act. Nevertheless, the self is not reducible to its social roles. The dramatic image of the modern person who assumes a variety of social roles is definitely unConfucian. The idea of my assuming the role of son in reference to my father and simultaneously assuming the distinct and separate role of father in reference to my son is unnatural, if not distasteful. From my own experience, as far as I can remember, I have always been learning to be a son. Since my son's birth, I have also been learning to be a father and my learning to be a son has to take a new significance as a result of becoming a father myself. Futhermore, my being a son and a father is also informed and enriched by being a student, a teacher, a husband, a colleague, a friend, and an acquaintance. These are ways for me to learn to be human.

Normally we do not talk about these matters in public. They are too personal. We should not reveal too much of our private feelings; they are not intellectually interesting. Yet, at the same time, we are obsessed with what we think, feel, and want. We often doggedly assert our opinions, nakedly express our emotions, and unabashedly demand our wants. We take rights seriously but we have to be persuaded by authority or law to accept our duties. We are estranged from our own cultural traditions and, as alienated humans in post-industrial societies, from our own communities. As we become increasingly subjectivistic, individualistic, and narcissistic, we can neither remember the old nor instruct the young. We are politically isolated and spiritually alone. Yet in our scholarly endeavors we assume that we have to take an impersonal stance in order to reason objectively in the abstract.

V. *Confucius as an Exemplar.* Confucius was willing to speak as a self-reflective human being. He opted for an intensely personal style of communication. And, by conscious choice, he shared his thoughts and feelings with those around him: "My friends, do you think I am secretive? There is nothing which I hide from you, my friends. There is Ch'iu (Confucius' first name) for you."[13] Confucius interacted openly with his students not by pedagogical design but as a reflection of his attitude toward life. We may suspect that he could afford to reveal himself thoroughly because he spoke from the lofty position of an accomplished sage. The truth of the matter, however, is quite different. Confucius never believed that he had attained sagehood. He was, like us, struggling to learn to be human. His self-image was that of a fellow traveller, committed to the task of realizing humanity, on the way of becoming fully human. As he continued to refine himself in living the life of a *ju*, he frankly confessed that he failed to learn to do the ordinary things that like-minded human beings ought to do:

> There are four things in the Way of the profound person, none of which I have been able to do. To serve my father as I would expect my son to serve me: that I have not been able to do. To serve my ruler as I would expect my ministers to serve me: that I have not been able to do. To serve my elder brother as I would expect my younger brothers to serve me: that I have not been able to do. To be the first to treat friends as I would expect them to treat me: that I have not been able to do.[14]

Confucius' humility is also shown in his clear perception of what he could do:

> There are presumably men who innovate without possessing knowledge, but that is not a fault I have. I use my ears widely and follow what is good in what I have heard; I use my eyes widely and retain what I have seen in my mind. This constitutes a lower level knowledge.[15]

By assigning himself to the "lower level knowledge," Confucius removed himself from "the best who are born with knowledge" and allied himself with "those who get through learning."[16] As a learner, Confucius took himself seriously as a concrete living person in

transformation. He approached with sincerity and critical self-awareness his task as a witness to common humanity:

> In practicing the ordinary virtues and in the exercise of care in ordinary conversation, when there is deficiency, the profound person never fails to make further effort, and when there is excess, never dares to go to the limit. His words correspond to his actions and his actions correspond to his words.[17]

As a seer and a listener, Confucius used his sensory perception wisely to reach a standard of moral excellence in which the virtue of modesty is taken for granted and the vital importance of constantly reflecting on things near at hand is fully recognized. Confucius' genuineness as a person is a source of inspiration to those who share his humanist wisdom not because of its abstract idealism but because of its concrete practicality.

VI. *Ultimate Meaning in Ordinary Existence.* The Confucian project, as exemplified by the lived reality of the Master, is a personal approach to human learning. Its message, simply put, is that we can realize the ultimate meaning of life in ordinary human existence. What we normally do on a daily basis is precisely the activity in which humanity manifests the highest excellence of itself. To initiate the whole process of learning to be human with the person living here and now is to underscore the centrality of self-cultivation at each juncture of moral growth. Implicit in this project is the injunction that we should take full responsibility for our humanity, not for any external reasons but for the very fact that we are humans.

The living person, in the Confucian order of things, is far more complex and meaningful than a mere momentary existence. The idea of an isolated individual who eventually dies a lonely death in the secularized biophysiological sense is not even a rejected possiblity in the Confucian perception of human reality. A human being is an active participant of an agelong biological line, a living witness of a historical continuum, and a recipient of the finest essences in the cosmos. Inherent in the structure of the human is an infinite potential for growth and an inexhaustible supply of resources for development. Ontologically a person's selfhood embodies the highest transcendence within its own reality; no external help is needed for the self to be fully realized. The realization of the self, in the ultimate sense, is tantamount to the realization of the complete unity between

humanity and Heaven. The way to attain this, however, is never perceived as the establishment of a relationship between an isolated individual and God. The self as a center of relationships in the human community must recognize that it is an integral part of a holistic presence and, accordingly, work its way through what is near at hand.

Mencius, in a suggestive passage, observes:

> All the ten thousand things are there in me. There is no greater joy for me than to find, on self-examination, that I am true to myself. Try your best to treat others as you wish to be treated yourself, and you will find that this is the shortest way to humanity.[18]

The ontological assertion that one's selfhood is totally sufficient does not lead to the existential complacency that self-realization involves no more than the quest for inner spirituality. On the contrary, while through self-cultivation, I, as a person, can take great delight in realizing that I have been in touch with my genuine humanness, I must endeavor to relate conscientiously to others as the most efficacious way of apprehending our commonly shared humanity. The implied soteriology, if we dare employ such a loaded concept, is found in another Mencian statement:

> For a man to give full realization to his heart is for him to understand his own nature, and a man who knows his own nature will know Heaven. By retaining his heart and nurturing his nature he is serving Heaven. Whether he is going to die young or to live to a ripe old age makes no difference to his steadfastness of purpose. It is through awaiting whatever is to befall him with a perfected character that he stands firm on his proper destiny.[19]

Two terms in the quotation above, "steadfastness of purpose" and "proper destiny," deserve our special attention. First, however, a caveat must be noted: the Chinese text cannot be so neatly dissected as the English translation seems to permit us to do in this analysis. Since our goal is a general discussion of the sort of soteriological intent implicit in the Mencian conception of the human condition, the nuanced linguistic features should not concern us here. Mencius fully recognizes the distinctness of the person in his ontological assertion that through knowing one's own nature, one can know Heaven. People are unique. Just as there are no two identical faces, there are also

as many paths of self-realization as there are human beings. There are numerous factors, internal as well as external, that determine the shape of a unique person. Yet, "steadfastness of purpose," as Mencius would have it, is the direct and immediate result of a person's will power and is, therefore, available to all members of the human community without reference to any differentiating factor. The example that Confucius used to illustrate a similar point is pertinent here: "The Three Armies can be deprived of their commanding officer, but even a common man cannot be deprived of his purpose."[20]

This "steadfastness of purpose" is all that is needed for self-cultivation. All human beings are equal so far as this dimension of human reality is concerned. A severely handicapped person may exert a great deal of effort to coordinate his physical movements, but his will power is absolutely independent, autonomous, and self-sufficient. We admire a Helen Keller not only for what she in fact managed to overcome but for the steadfastness of purpose that makes her awe-inspiring performance possible in the first place. Actually there are numerous cases where self-improvement in the physical sense is an unsurmountable task. Many people die before they can reach their potential. We are all, in this sense, fated to be unfulfilled. Confucius' best disciple, for example, died young and the Master lamented: "There was one Yen Hui who was eager to learn. . . . Unfortunately his alloted span was a short one and he died. Now there is no one. No one eager to learn has come to my notice."[21] Yet, one's steadfastness of purpose can not only transcend the structural limitations of one's existence but also transform them into instruments of self-realization. The case of Yen Hui is particularly suggestive here. His poverty, premature death, and lack of any tangible accomplishments by the perceived Confucian standards of public service did not at all deter the Master from praising, time and again, his eagerness to learn and his resolve to become a *ju*:

> How admirable Hui is! Living in a mean dwelling on a bowlful of rice and a ladleful of water is a hardship most men would find intolerable, but Hui does not allow this to affect his joy. How admirable Hui is![22]

In the light of this, one's "proper destiny" is inseparable from one's willingness and ability to take oneself to task inwardly. One's calling, as it were, is none other than the inner voice that enjoins one to

become what one ought to be. This critical self-awareness, informed by one's openness to an ever-expanding circle of human-relatedness, is the authentic access to one's proper destiny. The reality of the human is such that an eagerness to learn in order to give full realization to one's heart, to know one's own nature and to appreciate the meaning of humanity is the surest way to apprehend Heaven. Since our nature is conferred by Heaven, it is our human responsibility to participate in the cosmic transformation so that we can form a trinity with Heaven and Earth.[23] Our proper destiny, personally and communally, is not circumscription. We are not circumscribed to be merely human. Rather, our proper destiny is an invitation, a charge to take care of ourselves and all the beings in the world that is our abode. We must learn to transcend what we existentially are so that we can become what we ontologically are destined to be. We need not depart from our selfhood and our humanity to become fully realized. Indeed, it is through a deepening and broadening awareness of ourselves as humans that we serve Heaven.

The underlying structure of this mode of thinking is analogically presented in a key passage in the Confucian classic, *Centrality and Commonality*, better known as the *Doctrine of the Mean*:

> The way of Heaven and Earth is extensive, deep, high, brilliant, infinite, and lasting. The heaven now before us is only this bright, shining mass; but when viewed in its unlimited extent, the sun, moon, stars, and constellations are suspended in it and all things are covered by it. The earth before us is but a handful of soil; but in its breadth and depth, it sustains mountains like Hua and Yüeh without letting them leak away, and sustains all things. The mountain before us is only a fistful of straw; but in all the vastness of its size, grass and trees grow upon it, birds and beasts dwell on it, and stores of precious things (minerals) are discovered in it. The water before us is but a spoonful of liquid, but in all its unfathomable depth, the monsters, dragons, fishes, and turtles are produced in them, and wealth becomes abundant because of it.[24]

By analogy, what we see in front of us is but the physical presence of a changing body. However, those who are absolutely sincere in the sense that they, through ceaseless learning to be human, have become witnesses of humanity as such, "can order and adjust the great relations of mankind, establish the great foundations of humanity, and know the transforming and nourishing operations of

Heaven and Earth." The reality that the perfect sage symbolizes is not a superhuman reality but genuine human reality: "all embracing and extensive, and deep and unceasingly springing, these virtues (wisdom, generosity, tenderness, firmness, refinement and so forth) come forth at all times. All embracing and extensive as heaven and deep and unceasingly springing as an abyss!"[25]

The Confucian "faith" in the intrinsic meaningfulness of humanity is a faith in the living person's authentic possibility for self-transcendence. The body, the mind, the soul, and the spirit of the living person are all laden with profound ethicoreligious significance. To be religious, in the Confucian sense, is to be engaged in ultimate self-transformation as a communal act. Salvation means the full realization of the anthropocosmic reality inherent in our human nature.

NOTES

1. This essay is intended to be a response from a Confucian point of view to Wilfred Cantwell Smith's recent treatise on *Faith and Belief* (Princeton: Princeton University Press, 1979). I am deeply impressed by Smith's assertion: "Thus it is faith, in a form appropriate to our day, that enables one to cope intellectually and personally with pluralistic relativism — with, for instance, truth as that to which all accounts of it approximate — so that acceptance of diversity enriches rather than undermines one's own apprehension of truth" (p. 170). Although I cannot claim to have understood the theological implications of his historical reflection, I find myself in sympathetic resonance with his thought-provoking observation: "Truth is ultimately one, although the human forms of truth and the forms of faith decorate or bespatter our world diversely. Our unity is real transcendently; whether history will so move that we approximate it more closely actually in the construction on earth of a world community, not merely a world society already virtually with us, is a question of our ability to act in terms of transcending truth, and love."

2. "Chi-lu asked how the spirits of the dead and the gods should be served. The Master said, 'You are not able even to serve man. How can you serve the spirits?' 'May I ask about death?' 'You do not understand even life. How can you understand death?'" *Analects*, XI:12. All translations from the *Analects* are based on D. C. Lau, trans., *Confucius: The Analects* (Middlesex, England: Penguin Classics, 1979).

3. The expression is borrowed from Francis L. K. Hsü, *Under the Ancestors' Shadow; Kinship, Personality, and Social Mobility in China* (Stanford: Stanford University Press, 1971).

4. *Analects*, XIV:24.

5. Hou Wai-lu, et al., eds., *Chung-kuo ssu-hsiang t'ung-shih* (History of Chinese thought), 5 vols. (Peking: Jen-min Publishing Co., 1937–59), vol. I, pp. 131–190.

6. See Steven Lukes, *Individualism* (Oxford: Blackwell, 1973).

7. For a discussion of the meaning of *ju*, see Hu Shih, "Shuo ju" (On the concept of *ju*) in *Hu Shih wen-ts'un* (Preserved works of Hu Shih; reprint, Taipei: Yüan-tung Publishing Co., 1953), IV, pp. 1–103. For a comprehensive treatment of the origins of *ju* in English, see D. B. Obenchain, *Ministers of the Moral Order: Innovations of the Early Chou Kings, the Duke of Chou, Chung-ni and Ju* (unpublished Ph.D. dissertation, Committee on the Study of Religion, Harvard University, 1984).

8. See Étienne Balazs, "La crise de fin des Han," in his *La bureaucratie céleste; Recherches sur l'économie et la société de la Chine traditionnelle* (Paris: Gallimard, 1968), p. 180.

9. Max Weber, *The Religion of China*, trans. Hans H. Gerth (New York: The Free Press, 1964), p. 235. For a general assessment of Weber's interpretation of Confucianism, see Wolfgang Schuluchter, ed., *Max Webers Studie über Konfuzianismus und Taoismus* (Frankfurt: Suhrkamp, 1983).

10. The *Great Learning* states in its main text: "From the Son of Heaven down to the common people, all must regard cultivation of the personal life as the root or foundation." See Wing-tsit Chan, trans. and comp., *A Source Book of Chinese Philosophy* (Princeton: Princeton University Press, 1969), p. 87.

11. *Analects*, XII:2; XV:24.

12. *Ibid.*, VI:30.

13. *Ibid.*, VII:23.

14. *The Doctrine of the Mean*, chap. 13. See Wing-tsit Chan, p. 101. A statement comparable in spirit is found in the *Analects*, XIV:28.

15. *Analects*, VII:28.

16. *Ibid.*, XVI:9.

17. *The Doctrine of the Mean*, chap. 13; Wing-tsit Chan, p. 101.

18. *Mencius*, VIIA:4.

19. *Mencius*, VIIA:1; D. C. Lau, p. 182.

20. *Analects*, IX:26.

21. *Ibid.*, VI:3.

22. *Ibid.*, VI:11.

23. *The Doctrine of the Mean*, chap. 22; Wing-tsit Chan, pp. 107–108.

24. *The Doctrine of the Mean*, chap. 26; Wing-tsit Chan, p. 109.

25. *The Doctrine of the Mean*, chap. 31; Wing-tsit Chan, p. 112.

IV. The Value of the Human in Classical Confucian Thought

The root metaphor in the Confucian classic, the *Analects*, is the Way (*tao*).[1] The Confucian Way suggests an unceasing process of self-transformation as a communal act. It is specified as a human way, a way of life. The Way of Heaven also features prominently in Confucian literature and an understanding of the meaning of death is essential for a comprehensive appreciation of the Confucian perception of humanity. But it seems that the ontic weight in the Confucian spiritual orientation falls on the lived experience of ordinary human existence.

The *Analects* places a great deal of emphasis on commonly shared human concerns. It characterizes the method of humanity as an analogical reflection on that which is near at hand as its point of departure. One's own existence, body and mind, provides the primary context wherein the Way is pursued concretely. Without this basic grounding, the Way can never be found and one's humanity can never be realized. The Way does not in itself give full expression to humanity; it is through human effort that the Way is manifest.

Analogy, in this sense, far from being an imperfect form of deductive reasoning, signifies a mode of inquiry significantly different from linear logic but no less rigorous and compelling. To think analogically is to develop self-understanding by a continuous process of appropriating insights into the human situation as a whole and one's particular "location" in it. This involves systematic reflection and constant learning.

As an integral part of a comprehensive quest for self-knowledge, Tseng Tzu, a disciple of Confucius, is recorded to have engaged in daily self-examination on three points: "Whether, in transacting business for others, I may have been not faithful; whether, in intercourse with friends, I may have been not truthful; whether I may have not mastered and practiced the instructions of my teacher."[2] This attempt to inform one's moral self-development by constantly probing one's inner self is neither a narcissistic search for private truth nor an individualistic claim for isolated experience. Rather, it is a form of self-cultivation which is simultaneously also a communal act of harmonizing human relationships.

By implication, the centrality of learning (*hsüeh*) in the *Analects* must also be interpreted as a process of training the self to be responsive to the world and culture at large. Thus, one studies *Poetry* (*Shih*) in order to acquire "language" (*yen*) as a necessary means of communication in the civilized world, and *Ritual* (*Li*) in order to internalize the "form of life" characteristic of one's own community. Accordingly, learning is a way to be human and not simply a program of making oneself empirically knowledgeable. The whole process seeks to enrich the self, to enhance its strength and to refine its wisdom so that one can be considerate to others and honest with oneself.

Needless to say, learning in the Confucian perspective is basically moral self-cultivation. It is a gradual process of building up one's character by making oneself receptive to the symbolic resources of one's own culture and responsive to the sharable values of one's own society. Thus, Confucius observes, "In order to establish oneself, one should try to establish others; in order to enlarge oneself, one should try to enlarge others."[3] This sense of mutuality is predicated on the belief that learning to be human is by no means a lonely struggle to assert one's private ego. On the contrary, human beings come into meaningful existence through symbolic interchange and reciprocal relationship which affirms a commonly experienced truth.

Inherent in this belief is a deep-rooted concern for the human as a communicable and sharable value. It is inconceivable that one's humanity could be realized in isolation or expressed by a private language. Of course, periods of self-imposed moratorium, such as the observance of the mourning ritual, are a highly respected aspect of life in virtually all schools of Confucian thought. But even there, the primary focus is on social solidarity through an elaborate reenactment of commonly experienced roles and scenes. Indeed, the memory of the dead intensifies the care for the living.

The central concern of knowledge in this connection is to cultivate the human way and the way of life. Understandably, teaching and learning by example is considered the authentic and perhaps also the most effective method of education. One learns to be benevolent, truthful, courageous and firm not by following a set of abstract moral rules but by a continuous encounter with the multiplicity of existential situations exemplified in the life of the teachers. The teacher, who must also be a dedicated student, responds to specified questions about self, society, politics, history, and culture not merely

as an informed elder but also as an experiencing and loving fellow wisdom-seeker on the way.

This is probably the main reason that the value of ritual assumes such a central significance in the *Analects*. Like language, ritual is a form of communication and self-expression. Without a growing awareness of the ritual language, one cannot become a fully participating member of one's own society. Maturation entails a creative appropriation of the prescribed values shared by the community at large. Ritual as a non-verbal mode of human interaction is particularly emphasized in Confucian literature because it involves a commitment not only synchronically to a form of life but also diachronically to a living tradition.

However, despite the apparent indication that the ontic weight of the *Analects* tends toward human sociality, it is misleading to characterize the Confucian perception of learning as sociological. For one thing, Confucius himself maintains that real learning is for the sake of the self (*wei-chi*) rather than for the sake of others (*wei-jen*).[4] Indeed, the learning of the profound person is a learning to gain personal knowledge, which implies a way of life that can never be completely objectified as a blueprint for behavior. Exemplary teaching so conceived necessitates a sense of discovery. After all, the dialogical encounter as an incessantly confirming and renewing process of self-understanding always involves creativity. The way of the profound person is therefore as much a process of internal self-transformation as a demonstrable communal act. The internality and immediacy of the way to be human is such a recognized value in the *Analects* that Confucius unequivocally asserts, "Is humanity (*jen*) indeed far away? If I wish to be human, and lo! humanity is at hand."[5]

It is also in this sense that ritual is thought to come afterwards because it has to be built upon humanity.[6] And without humanity, ritual practice easily degenerates into formalism. Confucius' response to Yen Hui's inquiry into the meaning of humanity is most instructive. Instead of characterizing humanity as loving and caring as he does in other contexts, Confucius explains to his best disciple that humanity consists in self-mastery and returning to ritual.[7] In the light of this seminal idea, it is vitally important to note that if ritualization is the Confucian way to be human, it is inseparable from a more fundamental Confucian concern for self-mastery.

A significant development of the Confucian concern for self-mastery is found in Mencius' philosophical anthropology. By con-

ceptualizing learning as nothing other than the quest for the lost heart, Mencius underscores the centrality of heart in his thought.[8] To him, the way of learning to be human is primarily a purification and nourishment of the heart. But since the Chinese word *hsin* in *Mencius* connotes conative as well as cognitive and affective meanings, the cultivation of the heart involves not only harmonizing one's feelings but also refining one's consciousness and establishing one's will. Actually the Mencian heart, far from being merely a physiological or a psychological idea, is an ontological basis for moral self-cultivation. Mencius claims that it is because of the heart, which is also set forth as the "great body" (*ta-t'i*), that morality is not drilled into us from outside, but inherent in our nature.[9]

It is in this connection, I think, that Mencius insists upon a fundamental distinction between inability (*pu-neng*) and unwillingness (*pu-wei*).[10] While Mencius fully acknowledges differences in temperament, talent, intelligence, and environmental influences among human beings, he refuses to grant that the ability of learning to be human as a quest for moral self-development is not readily available to each member of the human community. The willing faculty itself, namely the inner decision of the heart, is not only the ultimate reason but also the actual strength for self-realization. Indeed, Mencius' moral philosophy further articulates the Confucian belief in the power of the human will: "Although the commander of the three armies can be snatched away, the will of even a commoner cannot be snatched away."[11] As I have noted elsewhere, Mencius' unflagging faith in human perfectibility through self-effort is a direct result of his commitment to the view that no matter how disturbed and destroyed the human heart has become, its inner strength for rejuvenation can never be subdued.[12] Actually this deceptively simple appeal to what may be called the indestructibility of the true self is closely related to a theory of human nature which emphasizes the commonality and universality of the value of the human.

By focusing his attention on "what is common in all our hearts," Mencius wishes to show that moral goodness is not merely a potential inherent in human nature but a universally experienced reality. Surely Mencius is critically aware of "all too human" atrocities against nature, mankind, and the self. After all his age is historically designated as the period of the "Warring States," known for its numerous cases of internecine struggles among those of the same surname and of the same family. The allegory of the Niu Mountain, denuded of trees by wood-cutters and even of buds and sprouts by

browsing cattle and goats, clearly indicates that Mencius knows well the deprivation of the human condition. However, notwithstanding his realistic appraisal of the actual state of humanity, he propounds the thesis that "the sage and I are the same in kind."[13] Implicit in this assertion is the message that our existential situation, no matter how degenerate it has become, does not deny us the same reality that enables ordinary human beings to become sages.

This fiduciary commitment to the inner resources of the self is based upon an observation that common human feelings such as commiseration, shame, deference, and a sense of right and wrong, relative and feeble as they are at times, are the concrete foundations of moral self-cultivation.[14] The very fact that we, as ordinary human beings, can experience alarm and concern when we suddenly see a child about to fall into a well sufficiently demonstrates that we are endowed with an ability to sympathize with others. To be sure, our sympathy is sometimes latent, and occasionally it is no more than a "spark" buried in the dust of selfish worries. Yet, the nature and function of the heart is such that it can regain its vitality as soon as it is preserved and nourished. Although one can lose one's heart, it is inconceivable that one cannot find it upon willing. Needless to say, the act of willing itself is also an activity of the heart. The apparent circularity of thinking is subtle but not vicious. Mencius is absolutely serious in claiming that if anyone with moral feelings "knows how to give them the fullest extension and development, the result will be like fire beginning to burn or a spring beginning to shoot forth."[15] This is actually the way by which an ordinary human being can eventually become a sage, symbolizing humanity in its all-embracing fullness. The primary concern of learning in Mencius is thus the quest for self-knowledge. To seek the lost heart is a spiritual discipline whereby primordial feelings, such as commiseration, shame, deference, and a sense of right and wrong are transformed into moral qualities, such as humanity, righteousness, propriety, and wisdom.

However, it is misleading to conclude that in Mencius' thought knowledge has lost its objective validity and self-knowledge is no more than the self-awareness of an isolated self in transformation. For one thing, the prominence of "internality" (nei) as Mencius would have it is neither a concern for privacy nor an attachment to individuality. Rather, it intends to show that personal knowledge is an authentic way to genuine communication as well as to deep self-understanding. This is in accord with the Confucian instruction that

learning for the sake of the self is the best way to manifest common humanity: the ability to take one's own feelings as a guide is the course of human-relatedness.[16]

Undeniably, strong human feelings are often associated with instinctual demands, such as appetite for food or sex. Although Mencius strongly recommends that the cultivation of the heart depends on making our desires few,[17] he never advocates asceticism. On the contrary, he not only recognizes but proposes that basic physiological and psychological needs be properly fulfilled. Actually he insists that it is the duty of the political leader to feed and enrich the people as a prior condition for educating them. Without an adequate livelihood, Mencius maintains, it is senseless to impose moral standards upon the people.[18] Yet it is vitally important to point out that the gratification of animal desires is no more than the minimum requirement of being human. If one is preoccupied with food and sex at the expense of one's "great body," one can hardly appreciate the value of the human in its full expression. This is like the shortsighted man who is fixated on nourishing his finger to the exclusion of rest of the body.[19] In response to the question, "Since we are all human beings, why is it that some follow their great body and others follow their small body?" Mencius states, "When our senses of sight and hearing are used without thought and are thereby obscured by material things, the material things act on the material senses and lead them away."[20]

By implication, it is "thinking" (ssu) that can free us from the limitation of the small body. Lest we should mistake this view for a kind of intellectualism, thinking in the Mencian context involves not only the heart and the mind but also the body. It signifies a holistic and integrated way of learning. Thus, Mencius observes that "if we first establish the great body in us, then the small body cannot overcome it. It is simply this that makes a person great."[21] It is also in this sense that Mencius maintains that only the sages can fully realize their "bodily designs" or their "human forms."[22] In other words, the development of the true self, as differentiated from the expansion of the privatized ego, is a process that opens oneself up to an ever broadening and deepening horizon of values shared by the enlarging community of like-minded moral persons. This is a concrete path leading towards a universalizable experience of personal identity and communication. Against this background, it seems fitting that Mencius concludes that if we can fully develop our hearts, we can completely realize our human nature; and if we completely realize our human nature, we will know Heaven.[23]

This seems on the surface no more than a naïve faith in the ability of the heart to fully develop itself and in so doing not only to realize humanity in general but also to know the ultimate reality, Heaven. However, a fundamental assumption in classical Confucian thought underlies this seemingly unbridled romantic assertion on the unity of the human way and the Way of Heaven. The prescriptive reason is given in a short but highly suggestive text, *Chung-yung*, commonly known as the *Doctrine of the Mean*. In my study on *Chung-Yung*, which I translate as "centrality and commonality," I have made the following observation:

> Professing the unity of man and Heaven, *Chung-yung* neither denies nor slights a transcendent reality. Actually, since human nature is imparted from and confirmed by Heaven, it is inconceivable in *Chung-yung's* view that man can be alienated from Heaven in any essential way. As an integral part of Heaven's creative process, man is not only endowed with the "centrality" (the most refined quality) of the universe but is charged with the mission of bringing the cosmic transformation to its fruition. Therefore the Way is nothing other than the actualization of true human nature. In a strict sense, the relationship between Heaven and man is not that of creator and creature but one of mutual fidelity; and the only way for man to know Heaven is to penetrate deeply into his own ground of being. Consequently, an inquiry into philosophy or religion must begin with a reflection on the problem of man here and now.[24]

This rudimentary formulation of *Chung-yung's* philosophical anthropology may give the impression that the Mencian line in the Confucian tradition, of which *Chung-yung* is a part, seems to advocate the thesis that "man is the measure of all things." But as I have further observed:

> One can [certainly] argue that learning and teaching in *Chung-yung* are basically concerned with the problem of how to become a person, and that doctrines such as the unity of man and Heaven and the harmony of man and nature are manifestations of this humanistic concern. Spiritualism and naturalism as such do not play a key role in *Chung-yung*. But we would be ill-advised to interpret *Chung-yung's* humanism as a form of anthropocentrism, ignoring its spiritualist and naturalist dimensions.[25]

Actually it is not difficult to see that in the perspective of *Chung-yung*, the realization of the deepest meaning of humanity entails a process transcending the anthropological realm. The logic is readily comprehensible: since human nature is imparted from Heaven, it shares a reality that underlies the myriad things. To actualize this underlying reality, therefore, is not to transcend humanity but to work through it. This is predicated on the belief that ontologically human nature is endowed with the "original ability" and the "original wisdom" to realize the ultimate meaning of Heaven in ordinary human existence. But the task of actualizing the ontological truth of humanity in concrete, everyday experience requires a continuous process of self-cultivation which is reminiscent of Tseng Tzu's description of the way and burden of the profound person: "For humanity (*jen*) is the burden he has taken upon himself; and must we not grant that it is a heavy one to bear? Only with death does his journey end; then must we not grant that he has far to go?"[26]

It is in this sense that the person who realizes his own nature to the full necessarily becomes a paradigm of authentic humanity. "What is being realized, then, signifies not only his personal humanness but humanity as such and as a whole. And since humanity is an integral part of the 'myriad things,' a complete realization of humanity must lead to the realization of things as well."[27] Against this background, the sincere, true, and real persons are thought, through their quests for self-knowledge, to have transformed the universe as well. The following statement from the *Chung-yung* can thus be taken as an articulation of the Confucian faith in human perfectibility.

> Only those who are absolutely *sincere* can fully develop their nature. If they can fully develop their nature, they can fully develop the nature of others. If they can fully develop the nature of others, they can then fully develop the nature of things. If they can fully develop the nature of things, they can then assist in the transforming and nourishing process of Heaven and Earth. If they can assist in the transforming and nourishing process of Heaven and Earth, they can thus form a trinity with Heaven and Earth.[28]

Indeed, "The profound person, through a long and unceasing process of delving into his own ground of existence, discovers his true subjectivity not as an isolated selfhood but as a true source of creative transformation."[29]

The apparent conflict between the search for inner spirituality and the commitment to social responsibility is no longer relevant.

Even the tension between self and society, one of the most salient characteristics of "religious" experience, also assumes a rather different shade of meaning. "Internality" in the Mencian tradition of Confucian thought denotes an experienced human value, a personal knowledge of the good. It is inconceivable that the ripening of one's inner moral sense of humanity and righteousness does not lead to a growing concern for social well-being. Indeed, the real threat to the maturation of the self is selfishness. A privatization of the self is, in Mencius' terminology, the frustration of the great body by the small one. The cultivation of the heart, then, is to make it receptive to the universal power of the self to communicate with other structures of being.

The humanist vision which first appeared in the *Analects,* then developed in the *Book of Mencius*, and eventually attained a remarkable fruition in *Chung-yung*, is a holistic approach to the perennial human concern for self-understanding and self-realization. Confucian humanism is therefore fundamentally different from anthropocentrism because it professes the unity of man and Heaven rather than the imposition of the human will on nature. In fact the anthropocentric assumption that man is put on earth to pursue knowledge and, as knowledge expands, so does man's dominion over earth is quite different from the Confucian perception of the pursuit of knowledge as an integral part of one's self-cultivation. To be sure, the belief that knowledge implies power is not totally absent in the Confucian tradition. Hsün Tzu, for example, strongly advocates the position that since culture is man-made, the human transformation of nature is not only necessary but also highly desirable. Yet, what Hsün Tzu proposes is hardly a form of aggressive scientism. Indeed, he is so painfully aware of the principle of scarcity that his general attitude towards natural resources is not manipulative but conservationist.[30]

The human transformation of nature, therefore, means as much an integrative effort to learn to live harmoniously in one's natural environment as a modest attempt to use the environment to sustain basic livelihood. The idea of exploiting nature is rejected because it is incompatible with the Confucian concern for moral self-development. Once our attention is focused upon the external, as the argument goes, our internal resources will be dissipated. In Mencius' words, the interaction between material things and material senses can form a vicious circle. As the things act upon the senses, the senses will demand more things for gratification. This will lead to an uncontrollable expansion of the "small body," a kind of inflated ego. As

a result, the true self (the human heart), will be lost. This seems to support the modern sociological observation that the glorification of the technocratic power may produce a protean creature whose flexibility is disproportional to his miserably limited inner freedom. In other words, his adaptability is merely symptomatic of the brute fact that, having been shaped into many unnatural forms by man-made environments, he is no longer capable of experiencing his own selfhood.

However, it is helpful to note that the Confucian quest for a vision of the whole from a humanist point of view is by no means incongruous with the scientific spirit of acquiring empirical knowledge, although it is certainly in conflict with the dogmatic positivistic assertion that only verifiable knowledge is philosophically sound. Actually empirical knowledge is such a cherished value in the Confucian tradition that its way of learning to be human entails a comprehensive program of education which includes, among other subjects, the natural world of grass, trees, birds and animals. Also, it should be mentioned that the Confucian "six arts," prerequisites for the educated person, involve arithmetic, as well as ritual, music, archery, charioteering and calligraphy.[31] Furthermore, it is not difficult to see that the Five Classics are rich sources for the study of astronomy, geography, government, history, poetry and art. Understandably the *Great Learning*, a highly compact essay on Confucian education, begins its instruction with the precept of "investigating things."[32] To be sure, the extension of knowledge in the Confucian sense is always conceived as an integral part of a holistic way of humanization. But the value of knowledge is absolutely irreducible in Confucian humanism; it is inconceivable that one can become fully human without going through a conscious process of learning to do so.

Implicit in this spiritual orientation is a concerted effort to maintain a delicate balance between freedom as an inner moral direction and knowledge as a self-disclosure to the cosmos as a whole. It rejects both an introspective affirmation of the self as an isolable and complacent ego and an unrestrained attachment to the external world for the sake of a limitless expansion of one's manipulative power. The myth of the Faustian drive or of the unbound Prometheus, symbolizing the human passion to know, to change, and to conquer, is alien to the Confucian concept of man not because it dramatizes self-transcendence but because it glorifies a complete destruction of the primordial order. When Mencius observes that the great man does not lose his childlike heart, he is perhaps also

making a general statement about knowledge and its relationship to human nature.[33] To him, the value of knowledge lies in its contribution to the wisdom of self-fulfillment, of communality, and of union with Heaven. In other words, knowledge helps us to realize our original nature. If knowledge is pursued for its own sake to the extent that it becomes completely beyond human self-understanding, it will turn out to be a serious threat to our inner freedom.

On the other hand, the appropriation of knowledge in the Confucian tradition never intends to be a possession, as a way of controlling nature. Rather, it implies a movement of opening up the self to nature. To live a full life, then, requires the willingness and the courage to transform the limited and limiting structure of the ego into an ever deepening and broadening self. It is in this sense that true subjectivity is not only compatible with but also essential for the development of an experienced universality. The real challenge to self-realization is not the external world but self-ignorance and egoism. The Confucian Way, suggesting an unceasing process of self-transformation as a communal act,[34] is therefore an attempt to show that knowledge, properly understood as a humanist value, can ultimately free us from the constrictions of the privatized ego.

This approach to the problem of the self naturally leads us to a comparative observation: the Confucian tradition either omits or rejects a large category of Western ideas which is thought to have been the necessary outgrowth of a more refined philosophical understanding of humanity. The category includes ideas of self-interest, private property, spiritual loneliness, and psychological egoism as positive contributions to the formulation of respectively political, economic, religious, and ethical individualism. Indeed, it can be further pointed out that a conflicting, if not contradictory, category of ideas assumes great prominence in Confucian thought: for example, duty-consciousness, public service, mutuality between man and Heaven, and a sense of community. Of course, we need to examine the different stages of Chinese history to determine the genetic reasons found in economic conditions, political organizations, social structures, and other relevant constraints for the seeming asymmetry, mainly from the Western viewpoint, between ideas of individualism and their social practices.

Does this imply that the Confucian perception of the dignity of man is separable from the individual's autonomy, privacy, and self-development? Surely, equality in Confucianism is defined in terms of man's inner worth, his inherent ability to attain moral excellence.

Since the ontological basis as well as the actual strength of self-realization is considered to be anchored within the structure of human nature and mind, respect for the dignity of man, as a corollary, is believed to be egalitarian in a universal sense. However, it does not necessarily follow that since respect is equally due to all persons in virtue of their being persons, there is no way of criticizing autonomy as self-centeredness, privacy as self-isolation, and self-development as an expression of egoism.

It is difficult to argue that a man's dignity can be preserved if he does not decide and choose in a self-determined way. Yet, to say that his dignity depends on the fact that his actions are solely determined by his conscious "self" is not without serious ambiguity. Specifically when and how a person acts autonomously is often problematic. More intriguing is the ethicoreligious question: What kind of person can really experience a sense of inner freedom and thus claim to be autonomous? Similarly, to define privacy as freedom from interferences and obstacles is predicated on the belief that, in Isaiah Berlin's words, "a frontier must be drawn between the area of private life and that of public authority." Unfortunately the notion of "frontier" is morally debatable and can be easily abused in the political sphere. Even in the case of self-development, although the practice of egoism does not seem to us as dangerous as the inculcation of ideologically-controlled collectivistic ideas in the unsuspecting mind, it is nevertheless a perversion of human growth.

Historically, the emergence of individualism as a motivating force in Western society may have been intertwined with highly particularized political, economic, ethical, and religious traditions. It seems reasonable that one can endorse an insight into the self as a basis for equality and liberty without accepting Locke's idea of private property, Adam Smith's and Hobbes' idea of private interest, John Stuart Mill's idea of privacy, Kierkegaard's idea of loneliness, or the early Sartre's idea of freedom. While I am sympathetic to Steven Luke's conclusion that "the only way to realize the values of individualism is through a humane form of socialism,"[35] I suspect that the task may have to begin with an inquiry into the value of the human with all its far-reaching philosophical implications.

NOTES

1. For a general discussion on this root metaphor, see Herbert Fingarette, *Confucius — The Secular as Sacred* (New York: Harper & Row, 1972), pp. 18–36. I have

also written on the subject in reference to Confucius' spiritual self-identification; see my essay on "The Confucian Perception of Adulthood," *Daedalus: Journal of the American Academy of Arts and Sciences*, 105:2 (Spring 1976), 109–123. This essay is included in *Adulthood*, ed. Erik H. Erikson (New York: W. W. Norton & Company, 1978), pp. 113–127. I wish to note that Paul Ricoeur's "multi-disciplinary studies of the creation of meaning in language" have been most inspiring to me in my research on this particular aspect of Confucian thought; see his *The Rule of Metaphor*, trans. by Robert Czerny (Toronto: University of Toronto Press, 1977).

2. *Analects*, 1:4.

3. Ibid., 6:28.

4. The statement in the *Analects* reads: "The scholars of antiquity studied for the sake of the self; nowadays scholars study for the sake of others" (14:25). Arthur Waley correctly interprets this to mean that "[i]n old days men studied for the sake of self-improvement; nowadays men study in order to impress other people." See *The Analects of Confucius*, trans. by Arthur Waley (London: George Allen & Unwin, 1938), p. 187.

5. *Analects*, 7:29.

6. The statement in the *Analects* reads: "Tzu-hsia asked, saying, what is the meaning of 'Oh the sweet smile dimpling,/The lovely eyes so black and white!/Plain silk that you would take for colored stuff.' The Master said, The painting comes after the plain groundwork. Tzu-hsia said, Then ritual comes afterwards? The Master said, Shang [Tzu-hsia] it is who bears me up. At last I have someone with whom I can discuss the Songs!" (3:8). For this translation see Waley, pp. 95–96. It should be noted that "the Songs" here refers to the *Book of Poetry*, which symbolizes the natural expression of basic human feelings.

7. *Analects*, 12:1. For a consideration of the philosophical significance of this passage in Confucian thought, see my paper "The Creative Tension between *Jen* and *Li*," *Philosophy East and West*, 12:1-2 (January–April 1968), 29–39.

8. *Mencius*, 6B:11.

9. For a discussion of Mencius' moral philosophy, see my paper "On the Mencian Perception of Moral Self-Development," *The Monist*, 61:1 (January 1978), 72–81. Also see *Mencius*, 6A:15.

10. *Mencius*, 1A:7.

11. *Analects*, 9:25.

12. "On the Mencian Perception of Moral Self-Development," p. 76.

13. *Mencius*, 6A:7.

14. The term "fiduciary commitment" is here used in Michael Polanyi's sense; see his *Personal Knowledge: Towards a Post-Critical Philosophy* (New York: Harper & Row, 1962), pp. 30–31. See *Mencius*, 6A:6.

15. *Mencius*, 2A:6.

16. *Analects*, 6:28.

17. *Mencius*, 7B:35.

18. Ibid., 1A:7.20; 3A:3.

19. Ibid., 6A:14.

20. Ibid., 6A:15.

21. Ibid., 6A:15.

22. Ibid., 7A:38.

23. Ibid., 7A:1.

24. Tu Wei-ming, *Centrality and Commonality: An Essay on Chung-Yung* (Honolulu: The University Press of Hawaii, 1976), p. 9.

25. Ibid., p. 10.

26. *Analects*, 8:7.

27. Tu Wei-ming, *Centrality and Commonality*, p. 118.

28. *The Doctrine of the Mean*, chapter 22. For this translation, see Wing-tsit Chan, trans., *A Source Book in Chinese Philosophy* (Princeton: Princeton University Press, 1973), pp. 107–108.

29. Tu Wei-ming, *Centrality and Commonality*, p. 140.

30. For a brief account of Hsün Tzu's political and social thought, see Fung Yu-lan. *A History of Chinese Philosophy*, trans., Derk Bodde (Princeton: Princeton University, 1952), vol. I, pp. 294–302.

31. This refers to the famous "six arts" in Confucian education, see the "Ta-ssu-t'u" section of the "Ti-kuan" chapter in the *Chou-li*.

32. The precept of *ko-wu* ("investigation of things") was one of the most important foci of intellectual debate in Neo-Confucian thought. It is the first of the "eight steps" of education in the *Great Learning*. See Wing-tsit Chan, *A Source Book*, pp. 84–94.

33. *Mencius*, 4B:12.

34. For a more comprehensive treatment of this point, see my paper on "Ultimate Self-Transformation as a Communal Act: Comments on Modes of Self-Cultivation in Traditional China," *Journal of Chinese Philosophy* (1979), 237–245.

35. Steven Lukes, *Individualism* (New York: Harper & Row, 1973), p. 157.

V. *Jen* as a Living Metaphor in the Confucian *Analects*

In an article surveying Chinese and Western interpretations of *jen* (humanity), Wing-tsit Chan maintains that Confucius in the *Analects* was the first to conceive of *jen* as the general virtue "which is basic, universal and the source of all specific virtues." "Although Confucius' concept of *jen* as the general virtue is unmistakable," Chan further observes, "he never defined it."[1] Chan's position that in the hierarchy of values in Confucian symbolism *jen* occupies the central position around which other cardinal virtues are ordered, although *jen* in itself is never specified, seems self-evidently true in light of traditional Chinese and Japanese exegeses.

To my knowledge, the only serious challenge to this interpretive consensus is Herbert Fingarette's focused investigation on *li* as the "holy rite" in the human community. In *Confucius — The Secular as Sacred*, Fingarette argues that the metaphor of an inner psychic life is not even a "rejected possibility" in the *Analects* and that the way of Confucius' *jen* should be understood as "where reciprocal good faith and respect are expressed through the specific forms defined in *li*."[2] The purpose of the present article is to conduct a new inquiry into *jen* as a living metaphor, while bearing in mind Fingarette's highly provocative reflections.

I. *The Rhetorical Situation.* To the modern inquirer who has been steeped in the art of argumentation, Confucius may appear to be "a prosaic and parochial moralizer," his collected sayings "an archaic irrelevance."[3] This initial response is likely to become an unreflective fixity, if the inquirer is mainly concerned with philological issues as matters of fact.[4] Needless to say, a study geared only to explicating the stylistic nuances of the original text leaves many questions unasked. And since "unasked questions are unlikely to be answered,"[5] the impression that Confucius was an outmoded ethical teacher, the study of whom is only *historically significant*,[6] will remain persistent. In what sense can Confucius be understood and appreciated as, for example, in Fingarette's words, "a thinker with profound insight and with an imaginative vision of man equal in its grandeur to any I know"?[7]

To begin, I would suggest that the mode of articulation in the *Analects* is a form of what Wayne C. Booth has forcefully argued for as "the rhetoric of assent."[8] In such a rhetorical situation, the internal lines of communication are predicated on a view of human nature significantly different from that of the pseudo-scientific assertion that ideally man is a rational atomic mechanism in a universe that is value-free. Rather, the basic assumptions are as follows: human beings come into existence through symbolic interchange. We are "created in the process of sharing intentions, values, meanings; in fact more like each other than different, more valuable in our commonality than in our idiosyncrasies: not, in fact, anything at all when considered separately from our relations."[9] Viewed from this perspective, the whole world defined in terms of the polarities "individual" and "society" shifts: "even usage of words like *I, my, mine, self*, must be reconsidered, because the borderlines between the self and the other have either disappeared or shifted sharply."[10]

It is in this connection that Fingarette's perceptive observation becomes singularly pertinent:

> The images of the inner man and of his inner conflict are not essential to a concept of man as a being whose dignity is the consummation of a life of subtlety and sophistication, a life in which human conduct can be intelligible in natural terms and yet be attuned to the sacred, a life in which the practical, the intellectual and the spiritual are equally revered and are harmonized in the one act—the act of *li*.[11]

Indeed, intent on underscoring the commonality, communicability, and community of the human situation, the rhetoric of assent affirms not only the malleability of human nature but also the perfectibility of undivided selves through group sharing and mutual exhortation. Yet this is neither a license for unbridled romantic assertion nor a belief in dogmatic scientistic manipulation, but an attempt to establish "a commonsensical defense of the way we naturally, inescapably, work upon each other,"[12] without resorting to the "clean linearity" of an argumentative procedure. Elsewhere, I have used the notion of "fiduciary community" as opposed to an "adversary system" in describing this kind of psychic as well as social ethos.[13]

The philosophical anthropology predicated on this rhetorical insight maintains that "man is essentially a self-making-and-remaking, symbol-manipulating [worker], an exchanger of information, a com-

municator, a persuader and manipulator, an inquirer."[14] The symbolic exchange wherein self-identification and group awareness in both cognitive and affective senses take place thus becomes the primary human milieu. Against this background, the dialogical encounters couched in analogical reasoning are by no means "an unsound form of the inductive argument."[15] For their persuasive power lies not in the straightness of a logical sequence devoid of emotion but in its appeal to common sense, good reasons, and a willingness to participate in the creation of sharable values.

Of course, as Wayne Booth observes, "we have no reason to assume that the world is rational in the sense of harmonizing all our 'local' values; in fact we know that at every moment it presents . . . sharp clashes among good reasons."[16] Actually, there is no assumption in the *Analects* like the one found in the objectivists' claim that "all truly reasonable men will always finally agree."[17] On the contrary, it is taken for granted that reasonable men of diverse personalities will have differing visions of the Way. As I have pointed out in my reflection on the Confucian perception of adulthood, "[s]ince the Way is not shown as a norm that establishes a fixed pattern of behavior, a person cannot measure the success or failure of his conduct in terms of the degree of approximation to an external ideal."[18] Consequently, "[e]ven among Confucius' closest disciples, the paths of self-realization are varied. Between Yen Hui's premature death and Tseng Tzu's longevity, there are numerous manifestations of adulthood."[19]

However, the multiplicity of paths in realizing the Way is not at all in conflict with the view that the pursuit of the Way necessitates a continuous process of symbolic exchange through the sharing of communally cherished values with other selves. The self as a center of relationships rather than as an isolable individual is such a fundamental premise in the *Analects* that man as "an ultimately autonomous being" is unthinkable, and the manifestation of the authentic self is impossible "except in matrices of human converse."[20]

The conversations in the *Analects* so conceived are not merely instructive sayings of the Master but intersubjectively validated ideas, communal values exemplified by life experiences of the speakers in the act of *li*. Since the act of *li* entails the participation of others, the rhetorical situation in the *Analects* is, in an existential sense, characterized not by the formula of the teacher speaking to the student but by the ethos in which the teacher answers in response to the student's concrete questioning. And the exchange as a whole echoes

a deep-rooted concern, a tacit communal quest, for self-realization as a collaborative effort. Understandably, in the Confucian tradition, teaching (*chiao*) and learning (*hsüeh*) for both the teacher and the student are inseparable, indeed interchangeable

II. *The Semiotic Structure: Jen as a Sign.* It is commonly accepted that etymologically *jen* consists of two parts, one a simple ideogram of a human figure, meaning the self, and the other with two horizontal strokes, suggesting human relations.[21] Peter Boodberg, obviously following this interpretive tradition in "Semasiology of Some Primary Confucian Concepts," proposes that *jen* be rendered as "co-humanity." And, based upon a phonological analysis of related words in ancient Chinese pronunciation, he further proposes that a root meaning of *jen* should be softness, weakness, and, I presume by implication, pliability.[22]

Boodberg's claims, far from being a novel reading of the classics, can be substantiated by the vast lore of Chinese and Japanese scholarship on the subject. In a recent study on the evolution of *jen* in pre-Confucian times, the author summarizes her findings by identifying the original meanings of *jen* in terms of two semictic foci (1) as the tender aspect of human feelings, namely, love and (2) as an altruistic concern for others, and, thus a mature manifestation of humanity.[23] But in either case, *jen* functions as a particular virtue, often contrasted with other equally important virtues, such as *li* (propriety), *hsin* (faithfulness), *i* (righteousness), *chih* (intelligence), and *yung* (bravery). Therefore, it is quite conceivable that a man of *jen* could be neither brave nor intelligent, for his tenderness may become a sign of weakness and his altruistic concern for others, an obstacle in achieving a realistic appraisal of the objective conditions.

The author then concludes that the concept of *jen* in the *Analects* seems to have been a crystallization of these two trends in the early Spring and Autumn period. In her words, the creative synthesis of Confucius skillfully integrates *jen* as "*ai-jen*" (love and care for others) and *jen* as "*ch'eng-jen*" (fully human or adult in the ethical sense).[24] Thus, in the *Analects, jen* is elevated to a general virtue, more embracing than any of the other core Confucian virtues. Surely, "love" remains a defining characteristic of *jen*, but as the scope of *jen* becomes qualitatively broadened, it is no longer possible to conceive of *jen* merely as a localized value. Indeed, a man of *jen* is necessarily brave and intelligent, although it is not at all impossible that a brave man or an intelligent man falls short of being a *jen* man. In a deeper

sense, through the general virtue of *jen*, such values as bravery and intelligence are being transvalued. Bravery and intelligence as contributing elements in the symbolic structure of *jen* must now be understood as courage and wisdom.

Genetic reasons aside, this quantum leap of intellectual sophistication is perhaps the main reason *jen*, in the *Analects*, appears to be discouragingly complex. Methodologically, it seems that one problem is particularly germane to the complexity of the semiotic structure of *jen*: let us call it the problem of linkage. Before undertaking a brief analysis of this problem, however, it should be noted from the outset that the lack of a definitional statement about what *jen* is in itself in the *Analects* must not be construed as the Master's deliberate heuristic device to hide an esoteric truth from his students: "My friends, I know you think that there is something I am keeping from you. There is nothing at all that I keep from you. There is nothing which I do that is not shown to you, my friends" (7:23). On the contrary, Confucius seems absolutely serious in his endeavor to transmit the true sense of *jen*, as he understood and experienced it, to his students. After all, as numerous scholars have already stated, it is *jen* rather than *chih, yung*, or *li* that really features prominently and uniquely in the *Analects*.

Although Confucius "rarely spoke of profit, fate, or *jen*," (9:1) his recorded remarks on *jen* by far surpass his comments on any other virtues in the *Analects*. Of course, each recorded articulation on the subject is but a clue to the all-inclusive virtue, or in Waley's words, the "mystic entity."[25] Among the hundred and five references to *jen* in 58 out of 498 chapters of the *Analects*,[26] there are, to be sure, statements that appear to be conflicting or paradoxical assertions. A mechanistic cataloguing of these statements is not likely to develop a coherent interpretation of *jen*. A more elaborate strategy is certainly required.

First, we must not pass lightly over what seem to be only cliché virtues ascribed to those who are thought to manifest *jen*: "courteous," "diligent," "faithful," "respectful," "broad," and "kind" (13:19, 14:5, 17:6). For these traditional virtues provide the map of common sense and good reasons on which *jen* is located.[27] However, the tenderness of *jen* is also closely linked with such virtues as "brave," "steadfast," and "resolute." Accordingly only those of *jen* know how to love men and how to hate them (4:3), for the feelings of love and hate can be impartially expressed as fitting responses to concrete situations only by those who have reached the highest level of morality.[28] This is predicated on the moral principle that those

who sincerely strive to become *jen* abstain from evil will (or, if you wish, hatred); as a result, they can respond to a value-laden and emotion-charged situation in a disinterested but compassionate manner. The paradox, rather than obscurity, is quite understandable in terms of Confucius' characterization of the accommodating and compromising hyperhonest villager as the spoiler of virtue (17:13). A man of *jen* refuses to tolerate evil because he has no evil will toward others; his ability to hate is thus a true indication that he has no penned up hatred in his heart.[29]

The problem of linkage is particularly pronounced when *jen* is connected with two other important concepts, *chih* and *li*. Our initial puzzlement over the precise relationship of *jen* to *chih* or *li* can be overcome, if *jen* is conceived of as a complex of attitude and disposition in which the other two important concepts are integral parts or contributing factors. In other words, *jen* is like a source in which symbolic exchange comes into existence. By implication, it is in *jen's* "field of influence"[30] that the meanings of *chih* and *li* are shaped. They in turn enrich *jen's* resourcefulness. Without stretching the point, I would suggest that the relationship of *jen* to *chih* or to *li* is analogous to the statement that "a man of *jen* certainly also possesses courage, but a brave man is not necessarily *jen*" (14:5). To be sure, in the courts of communal exchange, as exemplified in the rhetorical situation of the *Analects*, the presence of *jen* without *li* and *chih* is illegitimate. Furthermore, the examples of *li* as ritualism and *chih* as cleverness clearly indicate that *li* or *chih* without *jen*, easily degenerates into formalism or insensitivity. Thus, a man who is not *jen* can have nothing to do with *li* (3:3), because the true spirit of *li* is always grounded in *jen*.

Whether or not *jen* and *chih* are like "two wings, one supporting the other,"[31] in the Confucian ethical system, the two frequently appear as a pair (4:2, 6:21, 9:28, 12:22, 15:32, 14:30). The contrast between mountain, tranquility, and longevity symbolizing the man of *jen* on the one hand, and water, movement, and happiness symbolizing the man of *chih*, on the other (6:21), gives one the impression that *jen* and *chih* seem to represent two equally significant styles of life. Confucius' preference, however, becomes clear when he asserts that without *jen*, a man cannot for long endure either adversity or prosperity and that those who are *jen* rest content in *jen*; those who are *chih* pursue *jen* with facility (4:2). The necessity for *jen* to sustain *chih* and the desirability for *chih* to reach *jen* is shown in a crucial passage which states that "even if a man's *chih* is sufficient for him to attain it, without *jen* to hold it, he will lose it again" (15:32).

Chih in the *Analects* may occasionally be put in a negative light to mean fragmented or nonessential knowledge (15:33); sometimes the absence of *chih* can convey a sense of receptivity and flexibility (9:7), and even its opposite, *yü* (stupidity or folly), may in extraordinary situations be applauded as a demonstration of inner strength (5:20). *Jen*, by contrast, is always understood as "Goodness" (Arthur Waley), "Human-heartedness" (E. R. Hughes), "Love" (Derk Bodde), "Benevolent Love" (H. H. Dubs), "Virtue" (H. G. Creel), and "Humanity" (W. T. Chan). The practice of qualifying *jen* with such adjectives as "false" (*chia*) and "womanish," (*fu-jen chih jen*) which appear in later writings in ancient China, is completely absent in the *Analects*. In the light of the preceding discussion, it seems that, while *jen* and *chih* appear as mutually complementary virtues in Confucian symbolism, *jen* is unquestionably a more essential characterization of the Confucian Way.

Therefore, it may not be far-fetched to suggest that *jen* is in a subtle way linked up with virtually all other basic Confucian concepts. Yet its relation to any of them is neither obscure nor mystical. I believe that a systematic inquiry into each occurrence of the linkage problem should eventually yield the fruit of a coherent semiotic structure of *jen*. The matter involved is no less complex than what the scholarly tradition of *ko-i* has demonstrated. But through "matching concepts" or, more dramatically, through a series of wrestlings with the meanings of each pair of ideas in terms of comparative analysis, *jen's* true face should not be concealed for long.

At the present juncture, we may tentatively conclude: Confucius refused to grant *jen* to Tzu-lu despite his talents in political leadership and to Jan Ch'iu despite his virtuosity in state rituals (5:7); he also resisted the temptation to characterize the loyalty (*chung*) of Tzu-wen and the purity (*ch'ing*) of Ch'en Wen Tzu as *jen* (5:18), not because *jen* implies "an inner mysterious realm" but because *jen* symbolizes a holistic manifestation of humanity in its commonest and highest state of perfection.

III. *The Semantic Locus: Jen as a Symbol.* When we shift our attention from the linkage problem to focus on *jen* as a problem in itself, we are easily struck by the assurance that *jen* is immediately present if desired: "Is *jen* far away? As soon as I want it, there it is right by me" (7:29). Also, we are told that although it is difficult to find one who really loves *jen*, each person has sufficient strength to pursue its course without relying upon external help (4:6). This sense of im-

mediacy and infallibility assumes a new shade of meaning when, in
Tseng Tzu's imagery, *jen* becomes a heavy burden to be shouldered
throughout one's life (8:7). Indeed, *jen* can be realized only after one
has done what is difficult (6:20).

The paradoxical situation in which *jen* presents itself both as a
given reality and as an inaccessible ideal is further complicated by
a group of passages in the *Analects*, orienting our thoughts to the absolute seriousness with which *jen* is articulated. Thus, the *chün-tzu*
(profound person) is instructed never to abandon *jen* "even for the
lapse of a single meal;" instead, "he is never so harried but that he
cleaves to this; never so tottering but that he cleaves to this" (4:5). *Jen*
must come before any other consideration (4:6); it is a supreme
value more precious than one's own life and therefore an idea worth
dying for (15:8).

Yet the pursuit of *jen* is never a lonely struggle. It is not a quest for
inner truth or spiritual purity isolable from an "outer" or public
realm. From the *jen* perspective, "a man of humanity, wishing to
establish his own character, also establishes the character of others,
and wishing to fully manifest himself, also helps others to fully
manifest themselves. The ability to take what is near at hand as an
example may be called the method of realizing *jen*" (6:28). The task
of *jen*, far from being an internal, subjectivistic search for one's own
individuality, depends as much on meaningful communal inquiry as
on self-scrutiny.

Tseng Tzu's daily self-examination is a case in point. The effort of
personal cultivation certainly suggests a spiritual-moral dimension
not reducible to social considerations, but the three areas of concern — loyalty to others, faithfulness to friends and commitment to
learning (1:4), are so much an integral part of the "symbolic interchange" mentioned earlier that Master Tseng's message is clearly in
the realm of human relations. The self so conceived is a kind of
value-creating field in which the fiduciary community exists and is
realized by a tradition of selves in continuous interaction with selves.
It is in this connection, I believe, that Confucius insisted that true
learning be specified as learning for the sake of the self (14:25).

However, an essential characterization of *jen* impels us to go
beyond the behavioristic approach, no matter how comprehensive it
purports to be. In fact, the reason *jen* seems to be "surrounded with
paradox and mystery in the *Analects*"[32] is also relevant here. The
four-word phrase, *"ke-chi fu-li,"* wrongly rendered by Arthur Waley
as "he who can himself submit to ritual,"[33] clearly shows that the at-

tainment of *jen* involves both self-mastery and returning to ritual. The interpretation that "the man who can submit himself to *li* is *jen*" misses the point in a fundamental way.[34] And, by implication, the portrayal of *jen* as a disposition "after one has mastered the skills of action required by *li*" is probably an inadequate view of the linkage problem.[35] *Jen* is not simply "a matter of the person's deciding to submit to *li* (once he has the objective skill to do so);"[36] rather, it is a matter of inner strength and self-knowledge, symbolizing an inexhaustible source for creative communal expression.

The primacy of *jen* over *li* and the inseparability of *li* from *jen*, a thesis I tried to develop in my study "*Li* as Process of Humanization,"[37] can be substantiated by Confucius' response to Lin Fang who asked about "the foundation of li." After having noted the importance of the question, the Master recommended that "in ceremonies, be thrifty rather than extravagant, and in funerals, be deeply sorrowful rather than shallow in sentiment" (3:4). Obviously the emphasis is not on role performance but on "the raw stuff of humanity." Therefore, it is not at all surprising that the Master was very pleased with Tzu-hsia when he understood that "just as the painting comes from the plain groundwork, ritual comes afterwards" (3:8).

The centrality of self-mastery to the practice of *jen* can be shown in Confucius' remark that "a man who is strong, resolute, simple, and slow to speak is near to *jen*" (13:27). In fact, notwithstanding the danger of psychologizing the *Analects*, it is important to note that the text contains many ideas specifying that the mature personal stance is determined not merely by social approval but more importantly by personal integrity, as in freeing oneself from arbitrariness of opinion, dogmatism, obstinacy, and egoism (9:4). Accordingly, dispositional qualities resulting from spiritual-moral cultivation, such as cordiality, frankness, courteousness, temperance, and deference, are thought to be bases upon which proper human intercourse should be conducted (1:10). This particular concern for self-improvement clearly underlies Confucius' suggestion that looking out for faults is a way of recognizing *jen* (4:7). The vigilant way of overcoming one's moral and spiritual "sickness" is nothing other than constantly "looking within" (12:4).

It is in this sense, I think, that the controversial notion of *yu* (sorrow, worry, trouble, anxiousness) in the *Analects* does signify a "subjective state" not provable or demonstratable by ordinary hard tests.[38] In fact it is a reflection of personal knowledge or inner

awareness, comparable to what Michael Polanyi calls a kind of in-dwelling.[39] Surely, *yu* is related to "the notion of objective uncertain-ty and unsettledness with possible ominous import,"[40] but it is much more than a matter of objective comportment. The characterization that the man of *jen* is not *yu* (9:28, 14:30) suggests, at least on the surface, that *yu* is the opposite of *jen*.[41] However, Confucius makes it clear that virtue without proper cultivation, ignorance of the task of learning, inability to change according to the words of the righteous, and failure in rectifying faults are examples of *yu* (7:3).

The context in which "the man of *jen* is not *yu*" occurs should put the issue in proper perspective. Two passages conveying essentially the same idea have a parallel syntactical structure: The wise are not perplexed; the brave are not fearful; the *jen* are not *yu*. To be sure, the brave are not fearful, but Confucius instructed the fearless Tzu-lu that his "associate must be able to approach difficulties with a sense of fear and eventually manage to succeed by strategy" (7:10). Similarly, since the person who is aware of his ignorance really knows (2:17), the wise is he who can put aside the points of which he is in doubt (2:18). Along the same line of thinking, Confucius can speak of himself as so joyful and eager in learning and teaching that he forgets *yu* and ignores the onset of old age (7:18), precisely because he is *yu* with regard to the *Tao* and not to his private lot (15:31).[42]

The absence of the language and imagery of a purely psycholog-ical nature, or for that matter of a purely sociological nature, should not trouble us in the least. After all, recent developments in psychology and sociology as well as in philosophy in the West have already rendered the sharp contrast between "individual" and "socie-ty" not only undesirable but empirically unsound.

IV. *The Interpretive Task.* It should become obvious by now that "the deepest meaning of the thought of Confucius and, paradoxi-cally, its application to our time" is yet to be discerned by a sys-tematic and open-minded inquiry into the *Analects*. Fingarette is certainly right in concluding that "[t]he noble man who most perfectly [has] given up self, ego, obstinacy and personal pride (9:4) follows not profit but the Way."[43] Nevertheless, I cannot help wondering whether such a man, having come to fruition as a person, is really a "Holy Vessel."[44] I would rather contend that it is precisely in the recognition that "the profound person is not a vessel" (2:12) that the interpretive task of true humanity in the *Analects* begins.

NOTES

1. Wing-tsit Chan, "Chinese and Western Interpretations of *Jen* (Humanity),"
Journal of Chinese Philosophy 2 (1975), 109.

2. Herbert Fingarette, *Confucius — The Secular as Sacred* (New York: Harper &
Row, 1972), p. 42.

3. Ibid., vii. Of course, Fingarette makes it clear that this initial response of his to
the *Analects* was short-lived.

4. The word "philological" is used here simply to designate the methods of
linguistic analysis in the Ch'ien-Chia tradition of Ch'ing scholarship. I am aware
that "philology" in terms of the principles of Böckh's *Philologie*, signifying "the recognition of that which was once cognized," can be philosophically meaningful. I am
indebted to Masao Maruyama for this insight. See his *Studies in the Intellectual History
of Tokugawa Japan*, trans. Mikiso Hane (Princeton: Princeton University Press,
1974), xx.

5. Fingarette, *Confucius*, ix.

6. It is important to note that "historically significant" in the Levensonian sense is
comparable to the idea of "traditionalistic," which means that the "heritage" in question has little modern relevance, because it is no longer a living tradition.

7. Fingarette, *Confucius*, vii.

8. Wayne C. Booth, *Modern Dogma and the Rhetoric of Assent* (Chicago: The University of Chicago Press, 1974). I am indebted to my colleague, Leonard Nathan, for
calling my attention to this seminal work.

9. Ibid., p. 134.

10. Ibid. Also, cf. Fingarette, pp. 72–73.

11. Fingarette, *Confucius*, p. 36.

12. Booth, *Modern Dogma*, p. 141.

13. Tu Wei-ming, *Centrality and Commonality: An Essay on Chung-yung* (Honolulu:
The University Press of Hawaii, 1976), pp. 52–99.

14. Booth, *Modern Dogma*, p. 136.

15. Based on Monroe C. Beardsley's *Thinking Straight: Principles of Reasoning for
Readers and Writers* (Englewood Cliffs, N.J.: Prentice-Hall, 1966), pp. 130–36; 284,
quoted in Booth, *Modern Dogma*, p. 141.

16. Booth, *Modern Dogma*, p. 110.

17. Ibid., p. 111.

18. Tu Wei-ming, "The Confucian Perception of Adulthood," *Daedalus* 105, no. 2
(Spring, 1976), 110.

19. Ibid., 121.

20. Booth, *Modern Dogma*, p. 132. Also, see Fingarette, *Confucius*, p. 34.

21. I am aware that this etymological reading of the sign, traceable to the Han
lexicographer Hsü Shen, may itself have been influenced by the Confucian tradition. See Wing-tsit Chan, "Chinese and Western Interpretations," 108–109.

22. Peter Boodberg, "The Semasiology of Some Primary Confucian Concepts,"
Philosophy East and West 2, no. 4 (October, 1953), 317–332. For Chan's critical

remarks on Boodberg's phonological analysis of *jen*, see Wing-tsit Chan, "Chinese and Western Interpretations," 125.

23. Fang Ying-hsien, "Yüan-jen lun—tzu Shih Shu chih K'ung Tzu shih-tai kuan-nien chih yen-pien," (On the origins of *jen*—the transformation of the idea from the time of the *Poetry* and the *History* to the time of Confucius) *Ta-lu tsa-chih* 52, no. 3 (March, 1976), 22–34.

24. Ibid., 33.

25. Arthur Waley, *The Analects of Confucius* (London: Allen & Unwin, 1938), p. 28.

26. Based upon Wing-tsit Chan, "Chinese and Western Interpretations," 107.

27. Cf. Fingarette, *Confucius*, p. 41.

28. Ibid., p. 40.

29. Thus, I cannot go along with Fingarette's observation that "it becomes all too evident that the concept *jen* is obscure." See ibid.

30. Booth, *Modern Dogma*, p. 126n.

31. Wing-tsit Chan, *A Source Book in Chinese Philosophy* (Princeton: Princeton University Press, 1973), p. 30.

32. Fingarette, *Confucius*, p. 37.

33. Waley, p. 162. See my critique of Waley's interpretive account, "The Creative Tension between Jen and Li," *Philosophy East and West* 18, no. 2 (April, 1968), 30–31.

34. Fingarette, *Confucius*, p. 42.

35. Ibid., p. 51.

36. Ibid.

37. "Li as Process of Humanization," *Philosophy East and West* 22, no. 2 (April, 1972): 188.

38. Booth, *Modern Dogma*, p. 116.

39. Michael Polanyi, *Personal Knowledge: Towards a Post-Critical Philosophy* (New York: Harper & Row, 1964), pp. 173, 344, 378.

40. Fingarette, *Confucius*, p. 46.

41. Ibid., p. 43.

42. It is in this sense that I must take issue with Figarette's interpretive position, see ibid., pp. 45–47.

43. Ibid., p. 79.

44. Ibid.

VI. The Idea of the Human in Mencian Thought: An Approach to Chinese Aesthetics

In his *Chung-kuo i-shu ching-shen* (Spirit of Chinese aesthetics), Hsü Fu-kuan states that Confucians and Taoists share the belief that self-cultivation is basic to artistic creativity.[1] This is contrary to the trite and commonplace observation that the essential purpose of art is to assist in the perfection of the moral and spiritual personality. It suggests a way of perceiving what art is rather than what its function ought to be. Art, in this sense, becomes not only a technique to be mastered but also an articulation of a deepened subjectivity. It moves and touches us because it comes from a source of inspiration which humanity shares with heaven, earth, and the myriad things. Proponents of this view assert that the manifestation of true subjectivity depends on a complete transformation of the self, which they attempt to achieve by various methods: the establishing of the will, the emptying of the mind, the fasting of the heart, and the nourishing of the great body. Deepened subjectivity centers upon the "great foundation" (*ta-pen*) of the cosmos. As a result, it harmonizes different forms of life and brings humanity into tune with nature, so that the distinction between subject and object is dissolved.

Hsü Fu-kuan adds that a root idea in Chinese aesthetics is precisely this insistence that the dichotomies of subject/object, self/society, and man/nature are unreal and thus transformable.[2] True subjectivity opens up the privatized ego so that the self can enter into fruitful communion with others. The ultimate joy of this communicability allows us, in Chuang Tzu's phrase, to roam around with the Creator.[3] Since even the gap between Creator and creature is bridgeable,[4] when human beings create art they participate "in the transforming and nourishing process of heaven and earth."[5]

Hsü maintains that philosophically and historically the *Chuang Tzu* text epitomizes the emergence of aesthetic subjectivity in China. He is aware, of course, that the moral subjectivity established in Confucian teachings is also laden with far-reaching aesthetic implications, and he alludes to Confucius' fascination with music and the relevance of the six arts to the development of Chinese aesthetics.[6] However, he says little about Mencius. In the present

chapter, I would like to examine the ways that the Mencian perception of self-cultivation is pertinent to theories of art in China.

My purpose is twofold: to explore the idea of the human in classical Confucian thought with particular emphasis on Mencius, and to suggest that such an exploration could be fruitful for an understanding of Chinese aesthetics. I intend neither to offer a thorough analysis of the Mencian image of man nor to argue that Mencius, rather than Chuang Tzu for example, is particularly relevant to Chinese aesthetics. I do hope to show, however, that in China philosophical anthropology has provided much of the symbolic resources for the development of theories of art. As I focus on some of the insights found in a text which is central to ethics and hitherto ignored with regard to aesthetics, my immediate concern is simply to present an orientation or a method of analysis. It is possible that such an approach will eventually lead us to belief that Chinese arts have deep humanist roots.

I. *Tao (The Way).* The principle of the human way in its all-embracing fullness underlies Mencian thought.[7] As a metaphor in Mencian language, the Way is never a static category, signifying something external and objective. It is a process, a movement, and, indeed, a dynamic unfolding of the self as a vital force for personal, social, and cosmic transformation. Rather than a norm to be conformed to, Mencius sees the Way as a standard of inspiration that must be reenacted by ceaseless effort. We do not achieve humanity purely and simply by being alive. We must learn to cultivate ourselves so that we can fully realize those humane possibilities inherent in our nature. Only then can we say that we are on our way to becoming authentically human. This unending process led Tseng Tzu to describe the mission of a resolute scholar as a long road and a heavy burden: "For humanity (*jen*) is the burden he has taken upon himself; and must we not grant that it is a heavy one to bear? Only with death does his journey end; then must we not grant that he has far to go?"[8]

What will we become, if we commit ourselves to this long and strenuous task of learning to be human? There must be people who have no interest whatsoever in this sort of effort. Is there really any serious deficiency in their lives, if they never entertain the possibility of self-improvement? Mencius does not speculate on what kind of miserable creatures human beings can degenerate into. The rampant inhumanity among men during the period of the Warring

States was probably indication enough of the lower end of the scale. Mencius is acutely aware of the internecine struggle for wealth and power throughout the country, but he maintains that ordinary human beings can become sages by directly applying the inner resources of their hearts (*hsin*) for their own moral and spiritual cultivation. He asserts that the sages and we are the same in kind.[9] Even if we learn to become sages, we do not ascend to a different kind of being. We are still human to the core. Even though Mencius denounces those who choose not to improve themselves as committing inexcusable self-abasement,[10] he fully recognizes their right to be human. Between sagehood and self-deprivation, the range of humanity is truly vast.

A defining characteristic of Mencian thought is the belief that human beings are perfectible through self-effort.[11] He appeals neither to the existence of God nor to the immortality of the soul, but sees the spontaneous feelings of the heart as sufficient for the task. It seems that there is a moral "deep structure" inherent in human nature that can be fully developed, without forcing, as a natural process of growth.[12] This deceptively simple and easy way of self-development is, however, not a quest for isolated inner spirituality. Rather, it is a holistic process of learning through which the privatized ego is transformed into a feeling and caring self. We have here, in addition to the idea of a deep structure, also the image of natural growth. Learning so conceived not only encompasses the sudden emergence of one's innate qualities but also unhurried nourishment of "buds" and "sprouts" of humanity. For example, we are all capable of feelings of commiseration when suddenly confronted with the tragedies and misfortunes of other human beings, as seen in our immediate response to a child who falls into a well.[13] But unless we cultivate our sense of commiseration, it will be limited in its capacity and it will not flow beyond a small circle of close associates. Often, it takes an unusually powerful impact from outside to awaken us from our ordinary insensitivity. Developing the deep structure, like learning a moral language or acquiring a ritual form, requires a balanced ("neither forgetting nor assisting")[14] approach. Just as the usefulness of the five kinds of grain depends upon their ripeness, "the value of humanity depends upon its being brought to maturity."[15]

Even the mature person does not cease to learn, for the development of our innate qualities necessitates continuous refinement. To learn a moral language proficiently or to acquire a ritual form thoroughly is a perpetual challenge. Just as we require daily practice in order to develop the ability to generate new linguistic patterns or

to create new modes of human interaction, we must constantly
cultivate the capacity of the self in order to enter into fruitful communion with others. Maturity, as a value in human learning, thus
includes an authentic possibility for further growth. There is a
multiplicity of paths to be pursued in the process of moral development, but they converge at various states to give us standards of inspiration that we can look up to, not as fixed models but as ways of
witnessing the excellence in humanity.[16] This leads us to the following characterization in *Mencius*:

> He who commands our liking is called good (*shan*).
> He who is sincere with himself is called true (*hsin*).
> He who is sufficient and real is called beautiful (*mei*).
> He whose sufficiency and reality shine forth is called great (*ta*).
> He whose greatness transforms itself is called sagely (*sheng*).
> He whose sageliness is beyond our comprehension is called
> spiritual (*shen*).[17]

From the good to the spiritual there are numerous degrees of
subtleties. A sophisticated appreciation must also take into consideration the dynamic process that underlies all of them, as a more
detailed explanation of the idea of the human in classical Confucian
thought will make clear.

II. *Shen (Body)*. It is often assumed that the Confucian method of
self-cultivation (*hsiu-shen*) is sociological, since it teaches a child to be
obedient to his parents, to respect authority, and to accept societal
norms. This common-sense observation fails to account for a large
amount of literature in the Confucian tradition that repeatedly
stresses the importance of taking care of one's body as a necessary
condition for learning to be human. Tseng Tzu's symbolic gesture of
showing his hands and feet to his disciples shortly before he died
clearly indicates the reverence he had for what was given to him by
his parents.[18] It is not merely out of a sense of filial piety that one
must respect one's physical body as a sacred vessel, to borrow an image from the *Analects*.[19] The self as a concrete living reality is inseparable from the body. Since self-cultivation in its literal meaning
refers to the cultivation of the body, there is a rich reservoir of body-
related language in the Confucian classics. Indeed, without an
awareness of the importance of the body, we can hardly appreciate
the significance of the six arts (*liu-i*)[20] in classical Confucian thought.

Etymologically the character "*i*," which is commonly rendered as "art," signifies the activity of planting, of cultivating fields.[21] It seems that the agricultural origin of the character later gave rise to its meaning of acquired skills. Thus a man of *i* is a talented person capable of performing unusual tasks.[22] The Confucian emphasis on literary accomplishments may have provided the impetus to define *i* in terms of fine arts.[23] In the classical educational context, however, the six arts are disciplines that have particular reference to physical exercises. They are activities to be performed as well as subjects to be mastered mentally. The learning of the six arts seems to be a deliberate attempt to allow civilizing influences to work through our bodies as well as our minds. Of course, we are not necessarily aware of the underlying philosophical import of these disciplines. But the idea that the arts implant prosocial attitudes in us as a one-way subjugation is misleading. We are not simply being socialized; we are actively engaged in our own socializing by planting and cultivating the "buds" and "sprouts" within us. This is part of the reason for Mencius' insistence that "rightness" is not drilled into us but is inherent in the deep structure of our human nature.[24]

Accordingly, ritual, the first of the six arts, is a discipline of the body. It is intended to transform the body into a fitting expression of the self in our ordinary daily existence. The practice of ritual, which involves such simple activities as sweeping the floor and answering short questions,[25] trains us to perform routine functions in society as fully participating members. We learn to stand, sit, walk, and eat properly so that we can live in harmony with those around us. We do so not to seek their approval but to respond to the standards that have inspired us to become an integral part of the community. Some of those around us may use ritual language in a clumsy way. That should not discourage us from trying to perfect our own arts, however, because we ourselves are primarily responsible for what we can and ought to become. On the other hand, if we fail to live up to the expectations of our community, it should be a grave concern for us, because we cherish the reciprocal relationship as a necessary condition for our own moral and spiritual self-cultivation. Thus, we emulate those who are worthy of our admiration and turn our gaze within to scrutinize ourselves in the presence of a bad man.[26] The Confucian golden rule—"Do not do to others what you would not want others to do to you!"[27]—supports the attitude of altruism as a corollary of being honest with oneself.

Confucian thought values the heuristic function of ritual so highly that it seems to have characterized ritualization as the concrete pro-

cess whereby we learn to become mature human beings.[28] In fact, even though verbal instructions are common in Confucian teachings, the preferred method is to conduct them in an atmosphere suffused with nonverbal forms of communication. Exemplary teaching (*shen-chiao*), which is superior to teaching by words (*yen-chiao*), literally means to teach by one's body. Finely executed ritual acts as performative demonstrations of what one should do in given situations have greater educational force than verbal descriptions of them can ever have. The *Analects* is full of vivid examples of Confucius in action. The "Hsiang-tang" chapter, for instance, portrays in delightful detail how the Master dressed, sat, stood, bowed, walked, and ate. The care with which it depicts even the slightest gestures of the Master on solemn occasions is particularly illustrative:

> When carrying the tablet of jade, he seems to double up, as though borne down by its weight. He holds it at the highest as though he were making a bow, at the lowest, as though he were proffering a gift. His expression, too, changes to one of dread and his feet seem to recoil, as though he were avoiding something. When presenting ritual-presents, his expression is placid. At the private audience his attitude is gay and animated.[29]

If ritualization disciplines the body, music (the second of the six arts) is intended to harmonize the body so that it can appropriately express our emotions in tune with the rhythm of life. The importance of music in Confucian education cannot be exaggerated. Together with ritual it symbolizes the civilizing mode, the proper way of learning to be human. Since all authentic music is said to arise from the human heart,[30] it can shape the movements of the body into a graceful manifestation of the inner self. In Confucian literature, not only the performances of the court dancers but also the demeanors of cultured men are thought to be melodious.[31] Musical instruments, ranging from weighty stone chimes to the delicate lute, produce an infinite variety of sound patterns to channel all our "seven feelings" into their proper courses.[32]

One learns to play the lute or to sing lyric songs in order to communicate with others and, more importantly perhaps, to experience the internal resonance one shares with nature. Far from being a mere fleeting impression on our senses, the sound of the great music that we hear is an enduring virtue (*te*).[33] As harmony of heaven and earth, it brings us into accord with the primordial order. Music—

the right kind of music, and not the excessively sensuous songs of the state of Cheng[34] — can transform the human body into an articulation of beauty. As the *Analects* reports, after being exposed to the charming music of Shao, Confucius was in such a state of beatific enchantment that he did not notice the taste of meat for three full months.[35]

Although the arts of archery and charioteering may not have comparable cosmic significance, the physical exercises involved are, nevertheless, laden with far-reaching implications. An exemplary archer, for example, is not merely a skillful marksman but a "profound person" (*chün-tzu*) who, having mastered all the techniques of the art, constantly turns inward to examine himself, especially when he fails to hit the target.[36] If the case of Wang Liang in *Mencius* is any indication, the art of charioteering also involves complex rituals of self-mastery.[37] The discipline required builds one's sense of the proper forms of conduct as well as developing physical strength. By analogy, calligraphy and arithmetic can also be conceived as ways of refining one's body by acquiring the necessary dexterity with the brush or abacus to use it resourcefully.[38]

The "six arts" are therefore ways of cultivating the body. They transform the body from its original state where, like the rustic Shun before he was exposed to good words and good deeds,[39] it has merely the "buds" and "sprouts" of human possibility, into a center of fruitful relationships. As a center, a person never loses his proper location whenever and wherever he happens to be: the profound person always feels at home.[40] At the same time, he is sensitive and responsive to the human network around him. Through dialogical encounters, he deepens his self-awareness and enriches the lives of those who have entered into communion with him: "A man of humanity, wishing to establish himself, establishes others; wishing to enlarge himself, enlarges others."[41] To him, the "six arts" are not merely acquired skills; they are instrumental in establishing and enlarging himself. In the Mencian perspective, the person whose body is transformed by ritual, music, archery, charioteering, calligraphy, and arithmetic has created truth and beauty in and for himself. And as he is both a producer and an appreciator of the idea of the human, he is eminently qualified to be called a "good," "true," and "beautiful" person.

Yet, self-cultivation involves much more than the transformation of the body. It is true that Mencius explicitly states, "Form and color (our body) are nature endowed by Heaven. It is only the sage who can fully realize his physical form."[42] But "physical form" (*hsing*) here

symbolizes the self as a whole. The body is often a limited figure of speech in which the subtler and finer aspects of the self are deliberately relegated to the background. Paradoxically the sage can fully realize his physical form precisely because he has transformed and transcended it. The possibility of self-transformation and self-transcendence leads us to the language of the heart.

III. *Hsin (Heart)*. If the body is a spatial concept, occupying a specific location, a distinctive character of the heart is its remarkable ability to wander: "It comes in and goes out at no definite time and without anyone's knowing its direction."[43] Since the body is observable, it is possible for us to establish behavioral criteria to describe it. Exemplary teaching is, in a sense, model learning. The student learns proper ritual, right music, or good calligraphy by imitating the movements of the hands, feet, and body of the master. An outsider observing a Confucian student's learning the six arts may easily conclude that he is engaged in a sort of mimetic dance. But, presumably, the Confucian master is interested not only in the correctness of the form but also in the mental attitude behind it. He is keenly aware of the difference between a rote performer and an active participant, even though both follow instructions correctly. There is something missing in the rote performer. We might say that his heart is not in it. How does the master know that form-likeness is not the real thing? If the student knows exactly how ritual acts are to be performed and does so proficiently, how can we not conclude that his heart is in it all the time? Yet the master, with his discerning attentiveness, is able to pick up signs here and there that enable him to conclude that the student still lacks the intensity necessary for a virtuoso execution of the ritual. This seems to imply that form itself can be a sufficient basis for judging the truth and beauty of a performer. The Confucian master does not focus solely on the result, however, but also on the whole process by which the result is attained. His primary concern is the well-being of the student as a total person in transformation.[44]

In moral education, knowing manifests itself in acting, and through action one authenticates one's knowledge. It is inconceivable for one to will oneself to be polite, courteous, respectful, and humble, yet not have the inner strength to learn to be so. The Mencian distinction between "inability" (*pu-neng*) and "unwillingness" (*pu-wei*) is particularly relevant here. One may excuse oneself for one's inability to move a mountain single-handedly, but one cannot say that

one is incapable of showing deference to an elder.[45] Since behavioral criteria are deficient in matters of intention, the master is never content simply to show his students the correct form. He tries to enable the student to create his own style and his own interpretation. A truly inspired student should be like Yen Hui, who perceived Confucius' teaching in mystic terms:

> The more I strain my gaze up towards it, the higher it soars. The deeper I bore down into it, the harder it becomes. I see it in front; but suddenly it is behind. Step by step the Master skillfully lures me on. He has broadened me with culture, restrained me with ritual. Even if I wanted to stop, I could not. Just when I feel that I have exhausted every resource, something seems to rise up, standing out sharp and clear. Yet though I long to pursue it, I can find no way of getting to it at all.[46]

As words (*yen*) can never fully explain the hidden meanings of intentions (*i*), the body can hardly express the inner feelings of the heart.

Although the body, no matter how ritualized, melodious, strong, and dexterous, is not able to encompass the activities of the heart, it is the proper place for the heart to reside. Mencius emphatically states that the way of learning consists of nothing other than the quest for the lost heart.[47] In this sense, the six arts are efforts to "preserve the heart" (*ts'un-hsin*). They are training for the heart as well as discipline for the body. While the body requires a long and gradual process to assume a proper form, the transformation of the heart appears to be swift, since the heart is amorphous: "Hold it fast and you preserve it. Let it go and you lose it."[48] It is misleading, however, to believe that an act of willing is by itself sufficient to preserve the heart. Mencius does appeal time and again to the king's "unbearing heart" (*pu-jen chih hsin*) to establish "humane government" (*jen-cheng*), as if we could solve the problem of tyranny by a natural extention (*t'ui*) of the king's inability to bear the suffering of others.[49] But we must not confuse this strategic attempt to pinpoint a basic feeling shared by all members of the human community, even by an insensitive king, with Mencius' philosophy of the heart. As the parable of the farmer in the state of Sung points out, the cultivation of the heart is a delicate matter. If we exert too much artificial effort to help a plant grow, it will soon wither. In the same way there is a natural course for the development of the heart. One should neither forget (*wang*) nor assist (*chu*) in one's daily effort to preserve it.[50]

"Hold it fast and you preserve it" should therefore be understood as the art of steering, involving a process of adjusting and balancing on unpredictable currents.

Despite its changing configuration, Mencius asserts that the structure of the heart is knowable through direct experience. He tells the story of I Ch'iu, a superior chess player who failed to instruct an absent-minded student, to show that the mere presence of "buds" and "sprouts" of humanity in us cannot guarantee our actually knowing and preserving our hearts.[51] Since "even a plant that grows most readily will not survive if it is placed in the sun for one day and exposed to the cold for ten," without sustained effort of cultivation, nothing much can be done with the few new shoots that come out.[52] To use a different analogy, the spring that is about to dry up can hardly overflow a small pond. On the other hand, in times of flooding, water can be extremely powerful. It is a matter of quantity as well as quality. Here lies a unique Mencian insight about the structure of the heart: if cultivated, it is capable of virtually unlimited expansion. This is the reason that, to Mencius, the heart is the "great body" (ta-t'i), whereas our physical form is only the "small body" (hsiao-t'i).[53] To know and preserve the heart is therefore to hold fast to a dynamic and ever-enlarging structure. The growth of the heart, unlike the maturation of the body, is infinite. Between self-deprivation and sagehood, the range of humanity is indeed vast. It is not the body but the heart that makes the real difference. Just as we eat to nourish the whole body rather than just a small portion of the belly, Mencius claims, self-cultivation allows the development of the "great body" rather than just the small.[54]

Mencius suggests that we can best nourish the heart by making our desires few.[55] What he advocates is not a kind of asceticism but a sense of priority. He fully recognizes the importance of such instinctual demands as the appetite for food and sex, but he insists that human fulfillment requires a holistic vision in which other equally compelling propensities—notably humanity, rightness, the rites and wisdom—ought to be satisfied as well. While the same instinctual demands we share with other animals define us in terms of what we are born with, the moral propensities inherent in our nature make us uniquely human.[56] This observation leads to two interrelated ideas: (1) the uniqueness of being human is a moral and spiritual question which cannot be properly answered if it is reduced to biological or social considerations; and (2) the actual process of self-development, or the nourishment of the heart, far from being a

quest for pure morality or spirituality, necessarily involves the biological and social realities of human life. Consequently, if we satisfy only our instinctual demands, we can never realize the potential of the human heart. If we cultivate the "great body," however, our physical form will also be fulfilled:

> That which a profound person follows as his nature, that is to say, humanity, rightness, the rites and wisdom, is rooted in his heart, and manifests itself in his face, giving it a sleek appearance. It also shows in his back and extends to his limbs, rendering their message intelligible without words.[57]

The sage dwells in the peaceful abode of humanity and walks on the path of rightness.[58] Mencius claims that we learn to appreciate the greatness of such a person by an analogical reflection of the germinations of the four basic human feelings inherent in our own hearts: commiseration, shame and dislike, deference and compliance, and right and wrong. The germinating power of these feelings provides us with an intellectual intuition to perceive truth and beauty in ourselves as well as in sages and worthies.[59] The body-language must now ascend to the language of the heart to explain the educational functions of moral excellence in the human community: "A profound person transforms where he passes, and works wonders where he abides. He is in the same stream as Heaven above and Earth below."[60]

This cosmic reference opens up a new vista, adding a transcending perspective to the heart. Indeed, the Mencian heart is both a cognitive and an affective faculty, symbolizing the functions of conscience as well as consciousness. It not only reflects upon realities but, in comprehending them, shapes and creates their meaningfulness for the human community as a whole. In this way, the person who realizes his "great body" and "whose sufficiency and reality shine forth is called great." However, Mencius also maintains that "the great man does not lose his child-like heart"[61] and that the "great body" is, in the last analysis, our original nature. This twofold assertion that the great man has become a spiritlike being flowing with the cosmic transformation of heaven and earth and that, at the same time, what he manifests is no more than authentic humanity gives rise to what some Sinologists call mysticism in Mencian thought.

IV. *Shen (Spirit)*. We may recall that Mencius characterizes those whose greatness transforms itself as "sagely" and those whose sageliness is beyond our comprehension as "spiritual." Sageliness and spirituality are therefore, like goodness, truth, and beauty, symbols of human perfection. These are standards of inspiration to be continuously enacted as we learn to realize ourselves. In the Mencian perspective, they are not objective criteria for judging human worth but aesthetic appraisals of what human beings can attain and, by implication, what we ought to learn to become. Since sages and we are the same in kind, we should applaud Yen Hui's courage: "What sort of man was Shun (a sage-king)? And what sort of man am I? Anyone who can make anything of himself will be like that."[62] Indeed, it is not only the great man whose sufficiency and reality shine forth, for we possess the same internal resources:

> All the ten thousand things are there in me. There is no greater joy for me than to find, on self-examination, that I am true to myself. Try your best to treat others as you would wish to be treated yourself, and you will find that this is the shortest way to humanity.[63]

Profound insight into the human condition, rather than naïve moral optimism, prompts Mencius to articulate his philosophical anthropology. Human beings "survive in adversity and perish in ease and comfort."[64] We learn to mend our ways only after we have made mistakes. "It is only when a man is frustrated in mind and in his deliberations that he is able to innovate. It is only when his intentions become visible on his countenance and audible in his tone of voice that others can understand him."[65] We learn to know ourselves, to communicate with others, and to assume responsibility for humanity through endeavor. Mencius observes that many of the ancient sages and worthies experienced personal ordeals before they emerged as spiritual models:

> That is why Heaven, when it is about to place a great burden on a man, always first tests his resolution, exhausts his frame and makes him suffer starvation and hardship, frustrates his efforts so as to shake him from his mental lassitude, toughen his nature and make good his deficiencies.[66]

In addition to the mandate of heaven, Mencius fully acknowledges that both the social and the psychological en-

vironments play important roles in human growth, but his faith in the possibility of moral and spiritual self-development leads him to perceive the matter in a hopeful light:

> For a man to give full realization to his heart is for him to understand his own nature, and a man who knows his own nature will know Heaven. By retaining his heart and nurturing his nature he is serving Heaven. Whether he is going to die young or to live to a ripe old age makes no difference to his steadfastness of purpose. It is through awaiting whatever is to befall him with a perfected character that he stands firm on his proper destiny.[67]

The profound person, accordingly, steeps himself in the Way in order to be able to find it within his own heart. "When he is at ease with it, he can draw deeply upon it; when he can draw deeply upon it, he finds its source wherever he turns."[68] The spring that did not have enough water to overflow a small pond before is now in a state of abundance: "Water from an ample source comes tumbling down, day and night without ceasing, going forward only after all the hollows are filled, and then draining into the sea."[69]

To continue the water analogy, self-cultivation in Mencian terms is an attempt to cultivate one's "floodlike *ch'i*." At this level it does not consist merely of developing the proper form or the right mental attitude. It aims, rather, at nourishing the inner resources, enhancing the power of the will and building up the reserve of one's psychic energy. The character *ch'i*, variously rendered as "material force" (W. T. Chan), "matter-energy" (H. H. Dubs), and "vital spirit" (F. W. Mote), denotes a kind of psycho-physiological power associated with breathing and the circulation of the blood. In the Mencian usage, it refers to a "strong, moving power" generated by moral and spiritual self-cultivation.[70]

Mencius' discourse on the "floodlike *ch'i*" was occasioned by Kung-sun Ch'ou's question about the method of attaining the state of the "unperturbed heart" (*pu-tung-hsin*). At the outset, Mencius asserts that "the will is commander over the *ch'i* while the *ch'i* is that which fills the body." Ordinarily the *ch'i* follows where the will directs. It is therefore important to "take hold of your will and do not abuse your *ch'i*." However, it is conceivable that when the *ch'i* is blocked, it also affects the will. Even though "the *ch'i* rests where the will arrives," nourishing the *ch'i* is essential to the well-being of the heart. What, then, is this floodlike *ch'i*?

It is difficult to explain. This is a *ch'i* which is, in the highest
degree, vast and unyielding. Nourish it with integrity and place no
obstacle in its path and it will fill the space between Heaven and
Earth. It is a *ch'i* which unites rightness and the Way. Deprive it of
these and it will collapse. It is born of accumulated rightness and
cannot be appropriated by anyone through a sporadic show of
rightness. Whenever one acts in a way that falls below the standard
set in one's heart, it will collapse. . . . You must work at it and
never let it out of your mind. At the same time, while you must
never let it out of your mind, you must not forcibly help it grow
either.[71]

As we can see, even in this brief passage, Mencius claims that within
the structure of the human body and the human heart, there is the
real potential and great possibility of enlarging the self to become
one with heaven and earth. Humanity so conceived is not an
unrealizable ideal but an inexhaustibly abundant power of moral
and spiritual transformation. To use an image found in *Chung-yung*,
since humanity can assist in the transforming and nourishing process of heaven and earth, it can form a trinity with them.[72]

Does such an approach to self-perfection suggest that there was a
deep humanist base for the arts in China? Since neither Mencius nor
Chuang Tzu was interested primarily in aesthetics, we must resort
to interpretive reconstruction to discover what theory of art, if any,
lies in these rich sources. Hsü Fu-kuan's successful effort to show by
recontextualizing the text that there are indeed aesthetic insights in
Chuang Tzu has encouraged me to raise questions about truth and
beauty in terms of the human self-images in works such as *Mencius*.
This kind of endeavor may ultimately broaden the scope of aesthetic
studies. But my real purpose has not been to explore the possibility
of a Confucian aesthetics, in contrast with or complementary to a
Taoist aesthetics. Rather, I have sought to tap those symbolic
resources that are common to both traditions. To pursue Hsü's
analysis further, self-cultivation as a mode of thinking may have
predated any systematic attempt to formulate a tradition later identified as either Taoist or Confucian. In one of the most significant
events in classical Chinese intellectual history, Mencius creatively
appropriated some of these early insights to develop his integrated
idea of the human.

We can easily see how the use of Mencius' definition of the human way affects aesthetic terminology. The body and "the sentience that infuses the human frame"[73] become primary points of reference in conceptualizing the idea of beauty, and any impulse to objectify a norm of beauty as a static category is relegated to the background. Beauty, like all good and true qualities of human growth, exists as a standard of inspiration. It forms our sense of sufficiency and reality not as a fixed principle but as a dynamic interplay between the experiencing self and the perceived entity. We see beauty in things. In describing it, we move from its physical existence to its underlying vitality and, eventually, to its all-embracing spirit. The thing can be a tree, a stream, a mountain, or a stone. Its aesthetic effect on us, however, is not that of a silent object, but a living encounter and, indeed, a "spiritual communion" (shen-hui). This is not simply a form of anthropomorphism, and to interpret such encounters as the imposition of human characters on the external world limits and distorts the dialogical relationship that underlies the aesthetic experience. The idea of the human in *Mencius* is not anthropocentric. It does not subscribe to Protagoras' principle that man is the measure of all things. Instead, it intends to show that self-realization, in an ultimate sense, depends on a mutuality between man and nature. As Hsü Fu-kuan points out, a basic assumption in Confucian thought is that the completion of the self (ch'eng-chi) necessitates the completion (ch'eng), rather than the domination (ts'ai), of things (wu).[74]

Perhaps this is the reason that auditory perception features so prominently in classical Confucian thought. As I have noted in a different context, the Confucian Way is not perceptible if we cast our gaze outward;[75] the objectifying act of visualization alone cannot grasp the subtle manifestations of cosmic transformation. To be sure, the brilliant insight of a sage-king, such as that of the great Shun, is capable of penetrating the incipient activation of the universe by probing into minute signs of nature.[76] But, it is through the art of hearing that we learn to participate in the rhythm of heaven and earth. The "virtue of the ear" (erh-te), indeed the "virtue of hearing" (t'ing-te)[77] enables us to perceive the natural process in a nonaggressive, appreciative, and mutually supportive mode. Through the mental as well as physical discipline of listening, we open ourselves up to the world around us. By broadening and deepening our nonjudgmental receptivity, rather than by projecting our limited visions onto the order of things, we become co-creators of the cosmos.

Mencius' choice of music as a metaphor to characterize the
sageliness of Confucius, in the light of the above discussion, seems to
have been a deliberate attempt to present the Master's form of life in
auditory images:

> Po Yi [Po I] was the sage who was unsullied; Yi Yin [I Yin] was
> the sage who accepted responsibility; Liu Hsia Hui [Liu-hsia Hui]
> was the sage who was easygoing; Confucius was the sage whose ac-
> tions were timely. Confucius was the one who gathered all that was
> good. To do this is to open with bells and conclude with jade tubes.
> To open with bells is to begin in an orderly fashion; to conclude
> with jade tubes is to end in an orderly fashion. . . .[78]

Bells and jade tubes, or chimes, are musical instruments symbolizing the proper way of opening and concluding a ritual performance.
A performance that accords with the highest standard of excellence
requires both the "strength" to carry it out and the "skill" to make it
right. It is not only the power and ability to complete the whole process but also the "timing" at each moment as the music unfolds that
gives the quality of "an orderly fashion" to the performance. Thus
Mencius further comments:

> To begin in an orderly fashion is the concern of the wise while to
> end in an orderly fashion is the concern of a sage. Wisdom is like
> skill, shall I say, while sageness is like strength. It is like shooting
> from beyond a hundred paces. It is due to your strength that the
> arrow reaches the target, but it is not due to your strength that it
> hits the mark.[79]

To return to the earlier metaphor, the perfect "timing" of Confucius'
sageness goes beyond the unsullied, the responsible, and the easy-
going, precisely because it symbolizes a great concert, "gathering
together all that is good." If the single note properly produced can
enlighten the mind — "Hence, hearing of the way of Po I, a covetous
man will be purged of his covetousness and a weak man will become
resolute" or "hearing of the way of Liu-hsia Hui, a narrow-minded
man will become tolerant and a mean man generous"[80] — how much
more so can a great concert inspire us?

The followers of this kind of approach would consider analogical
thinking and the lyric mode, with their emphases on internal
resonances, to be the supreme forms of aesthetic communication.

They would deliberately deprecate the art of argumentation, seeking beauty in understanding. A smile between two resonating hearts or an encounter between two mutually responding spirits cannot be demonstrated to the insensitive eye or the unattuned ear. Aesthetic language is not merely descriptive: it suggests, directs, and enlightens. It is not the language itself that is beautiful. Indeed, words need not be eloquent or ingenious, for they merely carry and convey (*ta*) the meaning (*i*).[81] It is the extralinguistic referent—the inner experience, the joy of the heart, or the transforming spirit— that is the real basis of beauty, either in artistic creativity or in aesthetical appreciation.

NOTES

1. Hsü-Fu-kuan, *Chung-kuo i-shu ching-shen* (Taichung: Tunghai University Press, 1966), p. 132.

2. Ibid.

3. *Chuang Tzu* 6. See Wing-tsit Chan, trans., *A Source Book in Chinese Philosophy* (Princeton: Princeton University Press, 1973), pp. 196–198.

4. F. W. Mote observes: "The basic point which outsiders have found so hard to detect is that the Chinese, among all peoples ancient and recent, primitive and modern, are apparently unique in having no creation myth; that is, they have regarded the world and man as uncreated, as constituting the central features of a spontaneously self-generating cosmos having no creator, god, ultimate cause or will external to itself." Even if we believe that this claim is too strong, it is undeniable that the perceived gap between man and heaven is bridgeable. See Mote, *Intellectual Foundations of China* (New York: Alfred A. Knopf, 1971), pp. 17–18.

5. *Chung-yung*, 22.

6. Hsü Fu-kuan, *Chung-kuo*, pp. 1–40, 48–49.

7. See Tu Wei-ming, "On the Mencian Perception of Moral Self-Development," *The Monist* (January, 1978), 61 (1): 72–81.

8. *Analects*, 8:7.

9. "The sage and I are of the same kind" and "The sage is simply the man first to discover this common element in my heart" (*Mencius* 6A:7). For this translation, see D. C. Lau, trans., *Mencius* (Middlesex, England: Penguin Classics, 1970), p. 164.

10. *Mencius*, 4A:10.

11. For a critical reflection on this Mencian claim, see Donald J. Munro, *The Concept of Man in Early China* (Stanford: Stanford University Press, 1969), pp. 72–77.

12. For a classical formulation of this belief in the goodness of human nature, see *Mencius* 6A:6.

13. *Mencius*, 2A:6.

14. Ibid., 2A:2.

15. Ibid., 6A:19.

16. Tu, "On the Mencian Perception of Moral Self-Development," pp. 80–81.

17. *Mencius*, 7B:25.

18. *Analects*, 8:3.

19. For a perceptive analysis of this, see Herbert Fingarette, "A Confucian Metaphor—the Holy Vessel," in his *Confucius—The Secular as Sacred* (New York: Harper & Row, 1972). pp. 71–79. See *Analects*, 2:12, 5:3.

20. *Chou-li chu-chu* (Shih-san-ching chu-shu ed., 1815), 10:24b and 14:6b.

21. This is the original meaning found in Hsü Shen's *Shuo-wen*. See Morohashi Tetsuji, *Dai Kan-wa ji-ten*, 13 vols. (Tokyo: Daishū Kan Book Co., 1955–1960), 9:987.

22. *Analects*, 6:6.

23. For example, the early Yüan scholar Liu Yin (1249–1293) observes that the meaning of the "arts" has undergone a fundamental change since the time of Confucius: While the Master used it to refer to the practices of ritual, music, archery, charioteering, calligraphy, and arithmetic, nowadays the arts mainly include poetry, prose, calligraphy, and painting. See "Hsü-hsüeh", in *Ching-hsiu hsien-sheng wen-chi* (1897 ed.) 1:3b–10b.

24. *Mencius*, 6A:6.

25. For a vivid description of some of the daily ritual practices, see Wang Meng-ou, *Li-chi chin-chu chin-i*, 2 vols. (Taipei: Commercial Press, 1970), 1:1–39.

26. *Analects*, 4:17.

27. Ibid., 15:23.

28. For an interpretation of ritual from this point of view, see Tu Wei-ming, "Li as Process of Humanization," *Philosophy East and West* (April, 1972), 22(2): 137–201. For a thought-provoking analysis of ritual, see Erik H. Erikson, *Toys and Reasons: Stages in the Ritualization of Experience* (New York: W. W. Norton & Company, 1977), pp. 67–113.

29. *Analects*, 10:5. For this translation, see Arthur Waley, *The Analects of Confucius* (London: George Allen & Unwin, 1953), p. 147.

30. See the beginning line of the "Yüeh-chi", in Wang Meng-ou, *Li-chi chin-chu chin-i*, 2:489.

31. For an interesting description of the demeanors of the *chün-tzu* by using jade as a metaphor, see Wang Meng-ou, *Li-chi chin-chu chin-i*, 2:827.

32. See Hsü Fu-kuan, *Chung-kuo*, pp. 1–8.

33. Ibid., pp. 12–33.

34. *Analects*, 15:10.

35. Ibid., 7:13, 3:25.

36. *Chung-yung*, 14.

37. *Mencius*, 3B:I.

38. Of course, there is no historical evidence to support the view that the abacus, or a kind of calculating machine, was actually used then. This apparently anachronistic observation is intended to note that it is highly likely that arithmetic was not conceived of only as a mental activity but also as a technique to be

mastered. The term *suan-shu* "technique of calculating" — to be sure, a later coinage — seems to convey this sense well. A form of finger exercise may have been involved in the study of arithmetic.

39. *Mencius*, 4B:1, 7A:16.

40. *Analects*, 9:13; *Chung-yung*, 14.

41. *Analects*, 6:28.

42. *Mencius*, 7A:38.

43. Ibid, 6A:8.

44. For a relevant study on this subject, see Herbert Fingarette, *The Self in Transformation* (New York: Harper & Row, 1965), pp. 244–293.

45. *Mencius*, 1A:7.

46. *Analects* 9:10 (see Waley, p. 140).

47. *Mencius*, 6A:11.

48. Ibid., 6A:6.

49. Ibid., 1A:7.

50. Ibid., 2A:2.

51. Ibid., 6A:9.

52. Ibid.

53. Ibid., 6A:14, 15.

54. Ibid., 6A:14.

55. Ibid., 7B:35.

56. Ibid., 6A:3.

57. Ibid., 7A:21.

58. Ibid., 6A:11.

59. Ibid., 2A:6.

60. Ibid., 7A:13 (see D. C. Lau, p. 184).

61. Ibid., 4B:12.

62. Ibid., 3A:1.

63. Ibid., 7A:4.

64. Ibid., 6B:15.

65. Ibid.

66. Ibid.

67. Ibid., 7A:1.

68. Ibid., 4B:14.

69. Ibid., 4B:18.

70. See Wing-tsit Chan, *Source Book*, p. 784, and F. W. Mote, *Intellectual Foundations*, p. 60.

71. *Mencius*, 2A:2 (see D. C. Lau, pp. 77–78).

72. *Chung-yung*, 22.

73. Huston Smith, *Forgotten Truth: The Primordial Tradition* (New York: Harper & Row, 1976), p. 63.

74. Hsü Fu-kuan, *Chung-kuo*, pp. 132–133.

75. Tu Wei-ming, "The Confucian Perception of Adulthood," *Daedalus* (April, 1976), 105(2):110.

76. *Mencius*, 4B:19.

77. It should be noted that these two terms do not appear in *Mencius*; they are found in the so-called "Lost Confucian Text" in the newly discovered Ma-wang-tui silk manuscripts. However, a preliminary investigation indicates that the "Lost Confucian Text" may very well have been in the Mencian tradition. For a brief reference, see Tu Wei-ming. "The 'Thought of Huang-Lao': A Reflection on the Lao Tzu and Huang Ti Texts in the Silk Manuscripts of Ma-wang-tui," *The Journal of Asian Studies* (November, 1979), 34(1), 96, n. 5.

78. *Mencius*, 5B:1 (D. C. Lau, p. 150).

79. Ibid. (D. C. Lau, pp. 150–151).

80. Ibid. (D. C. Lau, pp. 149–150).

81. *Analects*, 15:50.

VII. Selfhood and Otherness: The Father-Son Relationship in Confucian Thought

This chapter is an inquiry into the idea of the self in the Confucian tradition, the Confucian tradition as a mode of thinking and a way of life that still provides a standard of inspiration for people in East Asian societies. In presenting such an inquiry, I am aware that it must take place within a complex historical landscape and an equally complex modern intellectual discourse. I am also aware that the elasticity of Confucianism, as it has undergone the vicissitudes of more than two millennia, inhibits generalizations about its views on perennial issues such as the idea of the self. Notwithstanding the special problems one encounters in articulating a particularly "Confucian" idea of the self, I shall nevertheless try to show that a characteristic Confucian selfhood entails the participation of the other and that the reason for this desirable and necessary symbiosis of selfhood and otherness is the Confucian conception of the self as a dynamic process of spiritual development.

I have elsewhere defined the Confucian quest for sagehood, in the ethicoreligious sense, as ultimate self-transformation as a communal act.[1] This definition involves two interrelated assumptions: (1) the self as a center of relationships and (2) the self as a dynamic process of spiritual development. Since the former has been more fully studied by cultural anthropologists, social psychologists, and political scientists in subjects such as family, socialization, and authority patterns in premodern and contemporary China,[2] our attention here will be focused on the Confucian idea of the self as development.

To differentiate the Confucian project from a variety of psychological technologies — transcendental meditation, holistic healing, rebirthing, dynamic living, and the like, currently in vogue throughout North America — which also claim self-development as an underlying assumption, it is helpful to note that, in the Confucian sense, self as development is a lifelong commitment which necessitates a ceaseless process of learning. Furthermore, Confucian learning is not only book-learning, but also ritual practice. It is through the disciplining of the body and mind that the Confucian ac-

113

quires a taste for life, not as an isolated individual, but as an active participant in the living community — the family, the province, the state, and the world. The idea of "ritualization," which implies a dynamic process of self-cultivation in the spirit of filiality, brotherhood, friendship, discipleship, and loyalty, seems to capture well this basic Confucian intention.[3]

A distinctive feature of Confucian ritualization is an ever-deepening and broadening awareness of the presence of the other in one's self-cultivation. This is perhaps the single most important reason that the Confucian idea of the self as a center of relationships is an open system. It is only through the continuous opening up of the self to others that the self can maintain a wholesome personal identity. The person who is not sensitive or responsive to the others around him is self-centered; self-centeredness easily leads to a closed world, or, in Sung-Ming terminology, to a state of paralysis.[4] Therefore, to encounter the other with an open-minded spirit is not only desirable; it is as vital to the health of the self as is air or water to one's life. The well-known statement in the *Analects*, "Wishing to establish oneself, one establishes others; wishing to enlarge oneself, one enlarges others,"[5] enjoins us to help others to establish and enlarge themselves as a corollary of our self-establishment and self-enlargement. Strictly speaking, to involve the other in our self-cultivation is not only altruistic; it is required for our own self-development.

It is commonly assumed that by stressing the importance of social relations, Confucian thought has undermined the autonomy of the individual self. In this view, a Confucian self devoid of human-relatedness has little meaningful content of its own. Since the self in Confucian literature is often understood in terms of dyadic relationships, a Confucian man's self-awareness of being a son, a brother, a husband, or a father dominates his awareness of himself as a self-reliant and independent person. If we pursue this line further, the Confucian man is seen predominantly as a social being whose basic task is to learn the science and art of adjusting to the world.[6] If this is accepted as the reason that the presence of the other is significant in Confucian self-cultivation, Confucian ethics would hardly be differentiable from the common-sense notion that we are inescapably bound in a human community.

That the Confucian tradition has attached great importance to sociality, both in its formative years and in its subsequent developments, is beyond dispute. Surely a defining characteristic of

Confucian thought is its concern for social ethics.[7] But underscoring the significance of this particular dimension of Confucian thought should not lead to the conclusion that social ethics is all-embracing in the Confucian mode of thinking. In actuality, the evidence seems to show that, in a comprehensive understanding of the Confucian project, the social dimension, on the other hand, is rooted in what may be called a Confucian depth psychology and, on the other, must be extended to a realm of Confucian religiosity in order for its full significance to unfold. In other words, if we choose to employ terms derived from disciplines established in modern secular universities to characterize the Confucian idea of learning to be human, it is vitally important to realize that notions such as social adjustment hardly tell us the whole story. Concepts such as personal integration, self-realization, and ultimate concerns must also be used. It is outside the scope of this chapter to further pursue the art and strategy of interpreting Confucianism. Let it suffice to suggest that the Confucian emphasis on sociality is laden with fruitful ambiguities and that, if we do not prematurely tie up loose ends, Confucian sociality is laden with profound psychological and religious implications.[8]

We now return to our earlier question, what is the significance of the other in the Confucian project of self-cultivation? Since it is no longer satisfactory simply to note that the Confucian approach to ethics is sociological, we need to explore another track. To begin, let us examine in some detail the father-son relationship in the context of self-cultivation. The conventional belief is that since "filial piety" is a cardinal value in Confucianism, a salient feature of the father-son relationship is the unquestioned obedience of the son to the authority of the father. For the son to cultivate himself, in this view, he must learn to suppress his own desires, anticipate the wishes of his father, and take his father's commands as sacred edicts. His receptivity to his father is thus the result of his concerted effort to internalize his "superego," to the extent that his conscience automatically dictates that he do what his father wishes. Latent aggressiveness toward, not to mention hatred of, his father is totally repressed in belief and attitude as well as suppressed in behavior. Understandably, the Confucian son, overpowered by the authority of the father, evokes images of weakness, indecision, dependency, and conformity.

However, even if we accept this one-sided interpretation of the father-son relationship, the subjugation of the son involves a mobilization of internal resources which implies a complex process of internal adjustment, as well as accommodation and harmoniza-

tion. For one thing, it is the willing participation of the son, socialized by a long and strenuous education supported by the community and sanctioned by the political leadership, that underlies the whole enterprise. Imagine, in Freudian terms, the complicated mechanism required to transform, indeed purify, the Oedipus complex in the Confucian son. The common impression that traditional Chinese society, steeped in Confucianism, managed to impose the unquestioned authority of the father on generation after generation of submissive sons is predicated on the false assumption that since the Confucian son had little choice, there was no opportunity for him to exhibit any voluntarism on matters of filial piety. One wonders if the control, even in its most efficacious phase, could really accomplish this without turning the so-called filial sons into hypocrites and psychopaths. Can a society survive, let alone provide a healthy environment for personal growth, if a large portion of its population is instructed to follow the dictates of gerontocratic dogmatism with no appeal to any transcendent authority?

Furthermore, the son's obedience to his father is not only restricted to the world of the living. For example, in the *Analects*, filial piety is attributed to a son because he chooses to follow his father's will for three years after the father's death.[9] But even this is only the beginning of a continuous reenactment of a memorial ritual in which the presence of the father, through the art of imagining, is made real throughout the rest of one's life. The *Book of Rites* describes in some detail the psychological state of the filial son in mourning:

> The severest vigil and purification is maintained and practised in the inner self, while a looser vigil is maintained externally. During the days of such vigil, the mourner thinks of the departed, how and where he sat, how he smiled and spoke, what were his aims and views, what he delighted in, and what he desired and enjoyed. By the third day he will perceive the meaning of such exercise. On the day of sacrifice, when he enters the apartment [of the temple], he will seem to see [the deceased] in the place [where his spirit-tablet is]. After he has moved about [to perform his operations], and is leaving by the door, he will be arrested by seeming to hear the sound of his movements, and will sigh as he seems to hear the sound of his sighing. . . .[10]

As Fung Yu-lan notes, "to gain communion with the dead through abstraction in this way, hoping that '*peradventure* they could enjoy his

offerings,' is nothing more than to give satisfaction to the emotions of 'affectionate longings.'"[11]

The commitment of the son to the father is therefore a lifelong commitment and a comprehensive one at that. If the father, or at least the image of the father, is forever present, what symbolic act does the son employ to "kill" his father so that he can eventually declare his independence? Normally one would think that when the son begins to care for his aged father, he can then take the comfort of realizing himself as a provider, a giver. However, the ability to support one's father is classified as the lowest among the three degrees of filial piety in the *Book of Rites*, the other two being honoring him and not disgracing him.[12] After all, it is not only the father in the flesh that the son must learn to obey and respect. The father's ego-ideal must also be realized. It is precisely in this sense that Fung Yu-lan explains:

> On the spiritual side, filial piety consists, during the lifetime of our parents, in conforming ourselves to their wishes, and giving them not only physical care and nourishment, but also nourishing their wills; while should they fall into error, it consists in reproving them and leading them back to what is right. After the death of our parents, furthermore, one aspect of it consists in offering sacrifices to them and thinking about them, so as to keep their memory fresh in our minds.[13]

This normative view of filial piety seems incompatible with the well-known Confucian proverb: "There are no erroneous parents under Heaven." If what the proverb conveys is simply that, in the obedient eyes of the son, the father is incapable of committing mistakes, then its meaning is certainly in conflict with the idea of "reproving him" and even "leading him back to what is right." However, since Confucians do recognize that it is human to err, a corollary of the Confucian belief in human perfectibility,[14] they can certainly accept the plain truth that their fathers do sometimes fall into error. The "erroneous parents" then must be taken to mean wrong parents in the sense that they do not fit our ideals of parenthood. Surely the Confucians recognize that there are unfit parents. Common observation as well as legal judgment helps us to detect that this is not at all unusual. Traditional China certainly had a fair share of this kind of human tragedy also, and Confucians have not been blind to the blatant reality of unfit parents. However, what is one to do if one's father

falls short of being fatherly? It is not at all difficult to condemn unfit fathers, but when and how can I say that my own father is unfit for me? Indeed, what is the significance of committing myself to the value that my father, no matter what he is or does, is always my father?

The Confucian perception of this matter deserves our attention because the "reality principle" applied to the father-son relationship addresses not only the question of the superego but also that of the ego-ideal in a thought-provoking way. Especially noteworthy, in this connection, is the underlying assumption that a social dyad is not a fixed entity, but a dynamic interaction involving a rich and ever-changing texture of human-relatedness woven by the constant participation of other significant dyadic relationships. Methods of analysis based upon either the theory of conflict resolution or a sort of hydraulic mechanism of damming and releasing only scratch the surface manifestation of the father-son dyad. Usually these methods do not address the embedded meaning structure, let alone the spiritual values that sustain it.

The Confucian approach takes as its point of departure that the father-son relationship is absolutely binding. Unlike the minister in the ruler-minister relationship, whose overriding concern for righteousness may compel him to openly criticize, indeed remove himself from the relationship as public protest, the son ought not to sever his ties to his father under any circumstances. The trite and commonplace observation that one cannot choose one's father is here maintained as a core value. The Confucian proverb that there are no erroneous parents clearly indicates that since we owe our origins to our parents and since our existence itself is inextricably linked to our parental relationships, we must recognize the continuous presence of our parents in every dimension of our lived reality. Our bodies, for instance, are not our own possessions pure and simple; they are sacred gifts from our parents and thus laden with deep ethicoreligious significance:

> The body is that which has been transmitted to us by our parents. Dare anyone allow himself to be irreverent in the employment of their legacy? If a man in his own house and privacy be not grave, he is not filial; if in serving his ruler he be not loyal, he is not filial; if in discharging the duties of office he be not serious, he is not filial; if with friends he be not sincere, he is not filial; if on the field of battle he be not brave, he is not filial. If he fail in these five

things, the evil [of the disgrace] will reflect on his parents. Dare he but be serious?[15]

Filial piety so broadly conceived as the source of all virtues may be the result of politicized Confucian ethics,[16] but the idea of continuing a biological reality because of its spiritual meaning as well as its social and political significance is unmistakably an original Confucian insight.

An important feature of this insight is the recognition that the father's ego-ideal, his wishes for himself as well as what he has created as standards of emulation for his family, is an integral part of the legacy that the son receives. The idea of continuity must not be taken literally to mean the continuity of a biological line. An unbroken genealogy for several generations surely calls for celebration, not to mention the happy outcome of establishing and enlarging the family fortune to include numerous talented and prosperous descendants. Yet it is the scholarly achievements, the cultural attainments, and the quality of life of the family that really define a successful Confucian father. Enhancing the father's reputation entails a set of conditions beyond the cherished value of allowing the family line to continue. Mencius is perhaps misinterpreted as having subscribed to the simple view that producing male progeny is the most important duty of the filial son.[17] In a patriarchal society, the birth of a son may have been conceived as a minimum requirement for continuing a family line, but the transmission of the father's legacy clearly involves a much more complex process of symbolic interaction.

The plight of the legendary Sage-King Shun is a case in point.[18] Born as the son of a brutish man in the Eastern Barbarian region, Shun, in response to the exemplary teachings of the Sage-King Yao, became a paradigm of filial piety through self-development. He was able to do so against overwhelming odds. For one thing, his father colluded with his stepmother and his half-brother in a series of plots to murder him. Due to divine intervention, or in Confucian terminology, his extreme sincerity that reached to Heaven, he escaped each threat of calamity unscathed. Never was his filial love for his undeserving father compromised. For this exceptionally inspiring expression of virtue, not to mention inner strength and personal dignity, he was offered the throne by Yao to rule the Middle Kingdom as an exemplar. For our purpose, it is illuminating to note that in this legend Shun does not appear merely as an obedient son, for had he been unquestioningly submissive to the brutality of his

father, he would have endangered his life, which in turn would have implicated his father in further unworthiness. It is precisely in this sense that in the *Sayings of the Confucian School*, Confucius instructs the filial son to endure only light physical punishment from an enraged father.[19] To run away from a severe beating, the argument goes, is not only to protect the body which has been entrusted to him by his parents but also to respect the fatherliness in his father that may have been temporarily obscured by rage.

The dilemma by which Shun was confronted was, of course, much more difficult to escape. There was hardly any indication that the old brute was a caring person. Shun's strategy was to do what his moral sense judged the best possible course of action at the moment. On the solemn matter of marriage, for example, he chose not to inform his father beforehand. Mencius, in defense of this apparently unfilial act, suggested to his students that allowing the father to interfere could have brought about more serious consequences.[20] Shun, in Mencius' view, appealed to a personality ideal for guidance which transcends all ordinary rules of civilized conduct and provides ultimate justification for the meaningfulness of any particular rule of conduct in the human community. He was deemed a paradigm of filial piety because, even though he was not submissive and by established convention might even be thought disobedient his action showed concern and respect for what must have been the wishes of this father's ego-ideal. In this sense, Shun never challenged his father's authority, nor did he ignore it; he conscientiously rectified it and thus restored it. The continuous presence of the father, both actual and ideal, in Shun's moral consciousness enabled him to develop his inner strength through a constant symbolic interaction with this significant other. Shun could not have realized his filial love alone. For this, he was grateful not only to his father but also to his step-mother and half-brother.

The legend of Shun can be conceived of as the worst possible case for maintaining that filial piety is a natural expression of the son's spontaneous love and care for his father. The Confucian interpretation stresses the possibility of self-realization even if involved in the most unwholesome dyadic relationship. The moral is clear: we should all be inspired by Shun's example in adjusting himself to an extremely difficult relationship, harmonizing himself with it in his own quest for moral excellence, and using it to transform creatively himself and those around him. Thus the legend of Shun conveys the twofold message that the father-son relationship is inescapable and

that it engenders an inexhaustible supply of symbolic resources for self-cultivation. Implicit in this message is a typical Confucian paradox. The father-son tie is a constraint, a limitation, and a bondage; yet through its constraining, limiting, and binding power, it provides a necessary means for self-cultivation for the father as well as the son. This seemingly arbitrary imposition of the superego upon the individual is rooted in a perception of the human condition as one in which the father-son relationship itself implies a transcendence beyond the psychosocial dynamics that envelops it. Shun's actions clearly show a realized possibility for the Confucian son to appeal to his father's ego-ideal, an appeal which in turn informs his own conscience of the best course of action.

In a thought-provoking essay, "Father and Son in Christianity and Confucianism," Robert Bellah remarks on the "truly heroic loyalty" of an unwavering minister in demonstrating the supreme value of filial piety in political protest as an indication of "the roots of the strength and endurance of a great civilization."[21] However, he also observes that in

> the Confucian attitude toward political and familial authority, there does not seem to be any point of leverage in the Confucian symbol system from which disobedience to parents could be justified. This does not mean parents could not be criticized. When they did not live up to the pattern of their ancestors there was indeed a positive duty to remonstrate, but they could not be disobeyed.[22]

This observation leads him to conclude:

> [T]he Confucian phrasing of the father-son relationship blocks any outcome of Oedipal ambivalence except submission — submission not in the last analysis to a person but to a pattern of personal relationships that is held to have ultimate validity. An outcome that could lead to creative social innovation as in the Protestant case was precluded by the absence of a point of transcendent loyalty that could provide legitimation for it. In the West, from the time of the Mosaic revelation, every particular pattern of social relations was in principle deprived of ultimacy. In China filial piety and loyalty became absolutes. In the West it was God alone who in the last analysis exercized power. In China the father continued to dominate.[23]

If we follow Bellah's insightful observation, the Confucian orientation clearly fails to account for the multilayered meaning of the
Oedipus complex: the sentiments and pathos of love and fear,
respect and guilt, and obedience and rebellion generated in man's
relationship to his father. The reason for its alleged failure, however,
is quite subtle. As Bellah notes in the beginning of his essay, "in
Chinese religious symbolism familial figures are far from central.
Though there is no civilization that has placed greater emphasis on
the father-son tie, it is not reflected in the ultimate religious symbolism."[24] This apparent asymmetry between social structure and
religious symbolism can serve as a reference point for a more focused
investigation of the father-son relationship in Confucian thought.
Again, it is helpful to take Bellah's essay as a point of departure.
"Having sampled briefly some of the implications of the father-son
symbolism in Christian belief and ritual," Bellah warns us against a
literal reading of the Freudian thesis:

> Nevertheless it becomes obvious upon reflection that the Christian
> symbolism is not explained by the Oedipus complex. If it were
> simply a direct projection of the Oedipus complex, then since the
> Oedipus complex is universal so would be Christian symbolism.
> But this is clearly far from the case. Christian symbolism is in fact
> highly unique, emerging from a particular historical context and
> bearing a particular historical role, a fact that Freud seems to have
> recognized. The particular qualities of the Christian symbolism
> emerged in the first instance from the Christian notion of God,
> around which the whole symbolic structure hangs.[25]

It seems that the explanatory power of the Oedipus complex as
Freud envisioned it was greatly enhanced by Christian symbolism
both as a background understanding and as a particular manifestation, if not direct projection, of a unique perception of the father-son
relationship. To be sure, Christian symbolism can hardly be *explained*
by the simple notion of a direct projection of the Oedipus complex.
The very fact that the Oedipus complex makes a great deal of sense
for the analysis of basic Christian motifs in psychodynamic terms
seems to suggest that its own conceptualization may have been deeply
influenced by Judaeo-Christian symbolism in the first place. The
Oedipus complex may not be as universal as Freud supposed it to
be. It is neither "the nucleus of all neurosis," nor the "origin" of the
major aspects of human society and culture as he asserted in *Totem*

and Taboo.[26] Nevertheless, the Oedipal situation, the highly charged emotional ambivalence inherent in the father-son relationship, does appear to have universal significance. The projection theory, however, is too simple-minded a causality to account for the tremendous power and influence that cultural symbolism exerts upon social structure.

Despite the centrality of the family in Confucian society, it is not conceived as an end in itself. The Confucians regard the family as the natural habitat of humans; it is the necessary and the most desirable environment for mutual support and personal growth. The father-son relationship, viewed in this context, is a defining characteristic of the human condition: it is human to have a father. The ultimate purpose of life is neither regulating the family nor harmonizing the father-son relationship, but self-realization. Indeed, only through self-cultivation can one's family be regulated and, by implication, one's relationship to one's father harmonized. Understandably the *Great Learning* takes self-cultivation as the root and regulating the family, governing the state, and bringing peace to the world as the branches.[27] The implicit logic that self-cultivation can eventually bring about universal peace under Heaven, as branches are the natural outcome of a healthy root, need not concern us here. It will suffice to note that, while there is no evidence that cultural symbols such as *T'ien* (Heaven) and *Tao* (Way) in Confucianism are projections of familial values, the father-son relationship and the other "five relationships" must be understood in terms of a transcendence that gives meaning to this particular social structure.

Unlike Christian symbolism, which tends to undermine the significance of familial relationships in its soteriology, with Jesus as saviour, Confucian salvation, as it were, takes the basic dyadic relationships in the family as its point of departure. The emphasis is on the concrete path by which one learns to be human rather than on the final goal of self-realization. The idea of the *Analects* that filiality and brotherliness are the bases of humanity, properly interpreted, means that being filial and brotherly is the initial step towards realizing one's humanity.[28] Mencius, in criticizing Moist universalism, argues against the ethics of treating people on the street as dearly as one would treat one's father.[29] It is not the ethical idealism that bothers Mencius but the impracticality of the whole procedure. If we reduce the richness, including the fruitful ambiguities, of the father-son relationship to the one-dimensional encounters we normally have with people on the street, our good intention of caring for strangers as dearly as we care for our parents may result in treating

our dear ones as indifferently as we treat strangers. The insistence that we begin our tasks of self-realization in the context of the immediate dyadic relationships in which we are inevitably circumscribed is a basic principle underlying the father-son relationship in Confucian symbolism.

An equally basic principle governing the father-son relationship is reciprocity.[30] The impression of the father as the socializer, the educator, and thus the authoritarian disciplinarian is superficial, if not mistaken. It is true that the Confucian son is not permitted to express his rebellious feelings toward his father, but to describe the explosion of age-long repressed aggression of sons against fathers as a central problem in modern as well as traditional Confucian society is misleading. According to the norm, the father should act fatherly so that the son can follow in a manner most appropriate to his self-identification. The son's filiality is conceived as a response to the father's kindness. The father must set an example for the son as a loving and respectable person before he can reasonably expect his son to love and respect him. Indeed, he should, in his son's mind, be seen as an exemplary teacher. On the other hand, he is not encouraged to instruct his son personally for fear that the intimacy between father and son be damaged as a result.[31] For this reason, exchanging sons for the purpose of formal instruction has been a common practice in Chinese society.

The sternness of the father image in Confucian culture must not be confused with aloofness or indifference. The father is not supposed to be physically close to the son. Physical closeness seems to be a prerogative of mother and son. Nevertheless, the father remains intimate with the son as his constant companion in the most critical stages of his development. The caring father guides the son's education, oversees his maturation, assists in his marriage arrangements, and prepares him for his career. The son in turn endeavors to fulfill his father's aspirations by internalizing them as goals in his own life. Reciprocity so conceived seems common in many other societies. A peculiar justification in the Confucian symbolism is that this reciprocal intimacy is not only absolutely necessary but also highly desirable for personal spiritual growth. This is diametrically opposed to the idea that the quest for inner spirituality requires that one transcend or forsake all primordial ties. The centrality of the father-son relationship in Confucian thought can thus be seen as a paradigmatic expression of the Confucian perception that selfhood entails the participation of the other.

Does this mean that since in Confucian symbolism there is no obvious shift of the ultimacy (e.g., Heaven or Way) from the natural social order to a transcendent reference point (such as God), there is no resultant capacity to ask ultimate questions? If this is the case, Confucian selfhood is, in the last analysis, a category in social ethics and one which does not seem to have any profound religious import. On the other hand, if Confucian selfhood is itself a transcendent reference point, a line of thought I intend to pursue further here, how are we to understand its linkages with ultimate ideas such as Heaven and Way?

The answer lies in the Confucian conception of the self not only as a center of relationships but also as a dynamic process of spiritual development. Ontologically, selfhood, our original nature, is endowed by Heaven.[32] It is therefore divine in its all-embracing fullness. Selfhood, in this sense, is both immanent and transcendent. It is intrinsic to us; at the same time, it belongs to Heaven. So far, this conception may appear to be identical to the Christian idea of humanity as divinity circumscribed. By analogy, Confucian selfhood, or original human nature, can be seen as God's image in man. However, the transcendence of Heaven is significantly different from the transcendence of God. The Mencian thesis that a full realization of our minds can lead us to a comprehension of our nature and eventually to an understanding of Heaven is predicated on the belief that our selfhood is a necessary and sufficient condition for us to appreciate in total the subtle meanings of the Mandate of Heaven. To translate this into Christian terms, it means that humanity itself, without God's grace, can fully realize its circumscribed divinity to such an extent that the historical Jesus as God incarnated symbolizes no more than a witness of what people ought to be able to attain on their own. After all, Christ is also called the Great Exemplar. However, this claim exhibits a family resemblance to the notorious Confucian pelagianism: the denial of original sin, the assertion that we are endowed with the freedom of will not to sin, and the avowal that we as human beings have the unassisted initiating power to appropriate the necessary grace for salvation. Indeed, the Confucian position does not even consider grace relevant to self-realization.

Though we do not take transcendence to mean an external source of authority, not to mention a "wholly other," there is still a distinctly transcendent dimension in Confucian selfhood, namely that Heaven resides in it, works through it and, in its optimal manifestation, is

also revealed by it. Selfhood so conceived maintains a tacit communication with Heaven. It is the root from which great cultural ideals and spiritual values grow. Understandably, subjectivity in the Confucian sense is not particularistic and is, paradoxically, the concrete basis for universality.

Since I have elsewhere elaborated on this point,[33] let us here inquire only into the significance of transcendence in selfhood for the idea of dynamic spiritual development. If goodness is intrinsic to human nature, why is there any need for self-realization? A direct response is simply to note that the intrinsic goodness in our nature is often in a latent state: only through long and strenuous effort can it be realized as an experienced reality. In a deeper sense, however, a distinction between ontological assertion and existential realization must be made. Self-realization is an existential idea, specifying a way of bringing into existence the ontological assertion that human nature is good. Precisely because human nature is good, the ultimate basis for self-realization and the actual process of initiating self-cultivation are both located in the structure of the self. Pelagian fallacy notwithstanding, Confucian selfhood contains the necessary inner resources for its own dynamic spiritual development.

There is an implicit circularity in this conception of the self: human nature is good so that there is an authentic possibility for dynamic spiritual development and vice versa. If we accept that the above-mentioned distinction of ontological assertion and existential realization also involves a dialectic relationship, the circularity is no longer a vicious one. Rather, we can well see that inherent in the structure of the self is a powerful longing for the transcendent, not for an external supreme being but for the Heaven that has bestowed on us our original nature. This longing for the transcendent, in a deeper sense, is also an urge for self-transcendence, to go beyond what the self existentially is so that it can become what it ought to be. Although we are, in ontological terms, never deficient in our internally-generated capacity for spiritual development, we must constantly open ourselves up to the symbolic resources available to us for pursuing the concrete paths of self-realization. The participation of the other is not only desirable but absolutely necessary. For as centers of relationships, we do not travel alone to our final destiny; we are always in the company of family and friends, be they remembered, imagined, or physically present.

The ultimate question for the Confucians then is, how can I, in the midst of social relations, realize my selfhood as the Heaven-

endowed humanity? The reason that the father-son relationship is so central to Confucian symbolism is itself a reflection of this mode of questioning. Since I can never realize myself as an isolated or even isolable individual, I must recognize as a point of departure my personal locus with reference to my father among other dyadic relationships.[34] My relationship to my father is vitally important for my own salvation, because if it is ignored, I can no longer face up to the reality of who I am in a holistic sense. After all, my Heaven-endowed nature can only be manifested through my existence as a center of relationships. For my own self-cultivation, I cannot but work through, among other things, my relationship to my father with all its fruitful ambiguities. The Sage-King Shun certainly had a more difficult task than most, but he, like us, could not bypass his social relationships in order to establish an intimate connection with Heaven directly. He was able to reach Heaven in the sense of fully realizing his selfhood precisely because he courageously faced up to the challenge of his social relationships near at hand. Social relationships are not in themselves ultimate concerns. They become prominent in Confucian symbolism because they are, on the one hand, rooted in one's depth psychology and, on the other, extended to one's religiosity.

The father-son relationship, in this sense provides a context and an instrumentality for self-cultivation. It is not because our fathers dominate or because we dare not disobey them that we cultivate our sense of respect for them. We respect them for our own projects of self-realization and, with gentle persuasion, they may be convinced that it is also for theirs. Indeed, our ego ideals come into existence as a result of our discipleship, friendship, ministership, brotherhood, and a host of other social roles. The father-son relationship, central as it is, constitutes but one among them. Like Shun, we take our relationships to our fathers as absolutely binding, but we do not submit ourselves to their arbitrary rule. For their own sake as well as ours, we must appeal to our Heaven-endowed nature, our conscience, for guidance. After all, it is for the ultimate purpose of self-realization that we honor our fathers as the source of the meaningful life that we have been pursuing. Indeed, there is a sense of a "creative fidelity"[35] in our relationships to our fathers. We are all involved in a joint venture to bring about the good life for our society. We know that we have to rise above the self-centeredness of our limited world views really to appreciate the universal Mandate of Heaven inherent in our human nature. We take our dyadic relation-

ships seriously because they, in concrete ways, help us to enrich our supply of internal resources with symbolic content. Filiality, brotherliness, friendship, and the like are thus integral parts of our spiritual development. It is in this sense that Confucian selfhood entails the participation of the other.

Lest we should misconstrue the symbiosis of selfhood and otherness as a still-undifferentiated organismic notion, it is important to note that the Confucian perception of the self, without ideas of original sin and God's grace, is far from being an assertion of prelapsarian naïveté. The lack of a myth of the Fall notwithstanding, human frailty, fallibility, and diabolism are fully recognized in Confucian symbolism. The Confucians are acutely aware of the human propensity for self-destruction, not to mention slothfulness, wickedness, arrogance, and the like. Indeed, it is this deep sense of the tremendous difficulty that one encounters in one's self-cultivation that prompts the Confucians to define personal spiritual development as a communal act. The idea of a loner trying to search for salvation in total isolation, without the experiential support of a community, is not inconceivable in Confucian society. The more cherished approach, however, is self-cultivation through communication with and sharing in an ever-expanding circle of human-relatedness. Even at the risk of losing one's individual autonomy, the Confucian chooses fellowship of companionable people and "like-minded friends" to develop themselves jointly through mutual exhortation. In this connection, the father-son relationship, not unlike the teacher-student relationship, or for that matter the husband-wife relationship, is in the last analysis a "covenant" based upon a fiduciary commitment to a joint venture. Through the significant other, one deepens and broadens one's selfhood. This is the meaning of the Confucian self not only as center of relationships, but also as a dynamic process of spiritual development.

NOTES

1. Tu Wei-ming, "Ultimate Self-Transformation as a Communal Act," *Journey of Chinese Philosophy* 6 (1979), 237–246.

2. For representative works in these areas, see Emily M. Ahern, *Chinese Ritual and Politics* (Cambridge: Cambridge University Press, 1981); Francis L. K. Hsü, *Americans and Chinese: Purpose and Fulfillment in Great Civilizations* (Garden City N.Y.: Doubleday Natural History Press, 1970) and *Under the Ancestors' Shadow: Kinship, Per-*

sonality, and Social Mobility in China (Stanford: Stanford University Press, 1971); Lucian W. Pye, *The Spirit of Chinese Politics; A Psychocultural Study of the Authority Crisis in Political Development* (Cambridge, Mass.: M.I.T. Press, 1968); Arthur P. Wolf, *Religion and Ritual in Chinese Society* (Stanford: Stanford University Press, 1974) and A. P. Wolf, ed., *Studies in Chinese Society* (Stanford: Stanford University Press, 1978).

3. Tu Wei-ming, "Li as Process of Humanization," *Philosophy East and West*, XXII:2 (April 1972), 187–201. For "ritualization" in a psychoanalytical sense, see Erik H. Erikson, *Toys and Reasons; Stages in the Ritualization of Experience* (New York: W.W. Norton & Company, 1977).

4. Wing-tsit Chan, trans., *A Source Book of Chinese Philosophy* (Princeton: Princeton University Press, 1969), p. 530.

5. *Analects*, 6:30.

6. Max Weber, *The Religion of China: Confucianism and Taoism*, trans. Hans H. Gerth (Glencoe, Ill.: Free Press, 1951), p. 235.

7. Étienne Balazs, *Chinese Civilization and Bureaucracy; Variations on a Theme*, trans. H.M. Wright and ed. Arthur F. Wright (New Haven: Yale University Press, 1964), p. 195.

8. Huston Smith, "Transcendence in Traditional China," *Religious Studies*, 2 (1967), 185–196.

9. *Analects*, 1:11.

10. Fung Yu-lan, *A History of Chinese Philosophy*, trans. Derk Bodde (Princeton: Princeton University Press, 1952), I, pp. 351–352.

11. Ibid., p. 352.

12. Ibid., p. 359.

13. Ibid.

14. Donald J. Munro, *The Concept of Man in Early China* (Stanford: Stanford University Press, 1969), pp. 49–83; also see his *The Concept of Man in Contemporary China* (Ann Arbor: University of Michigan Press, 1977), pp. 15–25.

15. Fung Yu-lan, p. 360.

16. Hsü Fu-kuan, "Chung-kuo hsiao-tao ssu-hsiang te hsing-ch'eng yen-pien chi-ch'i tsai li-shih chung te chu-wen-t'i" ("The formation, development and historical issues of filial thought in China"), in his *Chung-kuo ssu-hsiang shih lun-chi* (collected essays on Chinese thought; Taichung, Taiwan: Tunghai University Press, 1968), pp. 155–200. Although Professor Hsü later significantly modified his historical interpretation, his claim that a broadly conceived notion of filial piety as the source of all virtues may have been the result of politicized Confucian ethics is still valid.

17. *Mencius*, 4A:26, 4B:30.

18. Ibid., 5A:2.

19. *K'ung Tzu chia-yü* (Sayings of the Confucian school), comp. Wang Su (reprint of the Shu edition of the Sung dynasty; Taipei: Chung-hua Book Co., 1968), 4:5a-6a.

20. *Mencius*, 5A:2.

21. Robert N. Bellah, *Beyond Belief: Essays on Religion in a Post-Traditional World* (New York: Harper & Row, 1976), p. 95.

22. Ibid., p. 94.

23. Ibid., p. 95.

24. Ibid., p. 78.

25. Ibid., p. 82.

26. S. Freud, *Totem and Taboo*, trans. James Strachey (New York: W.W. Norton & Company, 1952), p. 157.

27. Wing-tsit Chan, pp. 86–87.

28. *Analects*, 1:2.

29. *Mencius*, 3B:9.

30. Lien-sheng Yang, "The Concept of *Pao* as a Basis for Social Relations in China," in *Chinese Thought and Institutions*, ed. John K. Fairbank (Chicago: University of Chicago Press, 1957), pp. 291–309, 395–397.

31. *Mencius*, 4A:19.

32. Wing-tsit Chan, p. 98.

33. Tu Wei-ming, *Centrality and Commonality: An Essay on Chung-yung* (Honolulu: The University Press of Hawaii, 1976), pp. 100–141.

34. This focused investigation of the father-son relationship is meant to underscore the centrality of the parent-child relationship (mother-son, father-daughter or mother-daughter) as a whole. Indeed, all dyadic relationships in the family, including an extended family, are taken seriously in Confucian humanism.

35. Gabriel Marcel, *Creative Fidelity*, trans. Robert Rosthal (New York: Farrar, Strauss & Co., 1964).

VIII. Neo-Confucian Religiosity and Human-Relatedness

The primary purpose of Neo-Confucian learning is "for the sake of one's self" (*wei-chi*).[1] One learns to be human not to please others or to conform to an external standard of conduct. Indeed, "learning to be human" (*hsüeh tso-jen*) is a spontaneous, autonomous, fully conscious, and totally committed intentional act, an act of self-realization. It gives its own direction and generates its own form and creates its own content. Virtually all root precepts in Neo-Confucian thought, in both the Ch'eng-Chu and the Lu-Wang traditions, take self-realization as a background assumption. Ch'eng I's "Self-cultivation requires reverence; the pursuit of learning depends on the extension of knowledge";[2] Chu Hsi's "dwelling in reverence and fathoming principle";[3] Lu Hsiang-shan's "establishing first that which is great in us";[4] Wang Yang-ming's "full realization of one's primordial awareness";[5] and Liu Tsung-chou's "effort of vigilant solitariness"[6] are paradigmatic examples. Yet, even though Neo-Confucianism asserts that the center of creativity in the ethicoreligious realm is human subjectivity, it is neither subjectivistic nor individualistic.

For one thing, the self in Neo-Confucian thought, instead of being the private possession of an isolated individual, is an open system. It is a dynamic center of organismic relationships and a concrete personal path to the human community as a whole. In this essay I intend to explore the ethicoreligious significance of this insight by addressing some of the perennial issues of religion and family from the perspective of Neo-Confucian philosophical anthropology.

A defining characteristic of Neo-Confucian thought is its reenactment of the classical Mencian learning of the mind as a ceaseless process of deepening and broadening self-knowledge. This involves an ontological justification for the enterprise of personal cultivation and an existential description of how to pursue it. In Neo-Confucian terminology, learning for the sake of one's self involves two inseparable dimensions: "original substance" (*pen-t'i*) and "moral effort" (*kung-fu*). On the level of original substance, the justification for learning of the mind is predicated on the Neo-Confucian perception of humanity as "sensitivity."[7] Human beings, like any other modalities of being in the cosmos, are endowed with the reality known as the

"principle" (*li*). Human beings are thus an integral part of the "chain of being," encompassing Heaven, Earth, and the myriad things. However, the uniqueness of being human is the intrinsic capacity of the mind to "embody" (*t'i*) the cosmos in its conscience and consciousness. Through this embodying, the mind realizes its own sensitivity, manifests true humanity and assists in the cosmic transformation of Heaven and Earth.[8]

Far from being a romantic assertion about the unity of all things, this Neo-Confucian commitment to the unlimited sensitivity of the mind is a deliberate attempt to accord human nature a kind of godlike creativity.[9] In theological terms, although Neo-Confucians do not believe in a transcendent personal God who is sometimes characterized as the "wholly other," they have faith in the ultimate goodness and all-embracing divinity of human nature, which is decreed by Heaven to be fully realized through the conscious and conscientious activity of the mind. An obvious background assumption here is what may be called the idea of the "continuity of being."

The reality of Heaven so conceived is by no means radically alien and therefore incomprehensible to the willing, feeling, and knowing functions of the mind. The mind may never understand the subtlety of the workings of Heaven through its intellectual faculty alone, but the nourished and cultivated mind, like the attuned ear, can perceive even the most incipient manifestations of the voice of God. Of course, Neo-Confucianism, being significantly different from any style of theologizing, depicts the course of Heaven as devoid of sound and fragrance.[10] Furthermore, following the Mencian tradition, it insists that Heaven sees as the people see and Heaven hears as the people hear.[11] This mutality of Heaven and man defines Neo-Confucian religiosity.

Wilfred Cantwell Smith, in his seminal study on the meaning and end of religion, makes a helpful distinction between "a religion" as an institution characterized by a set of objectifiable dogmas and "being religious" as spiritual self-identification of the living members of a faith community.[12] Accordingly, the problem of whether Neo-Confucianism is a religion should not be confused with the more significant question: what does it mean to be religious in the Neo-Confucian community? The solution to the former often depends on the particular interpretive position we choose to take on what constitutes the paradigmatic example of a religion, which may have little to do with our knowledge about Neo-Confucianism as a spiritual tradition; the question of being religious is crucial for our apprecia-

tion of the "inner dimension" of the Neo-Confucian project. For the sake of expediency, being religious in the Neo-Confucian sense can be understood as being engaged in *ultimate self-transformation as a communal act.*[13] Since the self, as already mentioned, is an open system, this process entails a continuous enlargement of the self.

We can perhaps envision the enlargement of the self diagrammatically as a series of constantly expanding concentric circles which symbolize the unplumbed sensitivity of the mind to embrace Heaven, Earth, and the myriad things. To enlarge oneself is therefore to purify, enlighten, and bring to fruition the ultimate capacity of the mind to "embody" the cosmos. The self so conceived is not a static structure but a dynamic process. It is a *center* of relationships, not an enclosed world of private thoughts and feelings. It needs to reach out, to be in touch with other selves, and to communicate through an ever-expanding network of human-relatedness. Yet, even though the Neo-Confucian self can be understood very well in terms of social roles, it is primarily an ethicoreligious idea with far-reaching cosmological and ontological implications.

The concrete path to actualize human nature through the learning of the mind involves a dynamic interplay between contextualization and decontextualization. This unique feature of Neo-Confucian ethics and religiosity can be further characterized as a dialectic of structural limitation and procedural freedom which emerges at each stage of self-cultivation. The necessity of recognizing the interrelated conditions, the context, in which the self as a center of relationships initiates its own realization is based on the aforementioned "continuity of being." Self-transformation is by definition not simply a departure from but also a return to one's "locale." It is not a quest for pure spirituality nor is it a liberation from the flesh, the mundane, or the profane. The dichotomy of secular and sacred, or for that matter of body and mind, is rejected as heuristically misleading. The real task, perceived by the Neo-Confucians, is to manifest the ultimate meaning of life in ordinary human existence.[14]

The Neo-Confucian universe is certainly not without locale and date. Time and space experienced by the "self in transformation"[15] provide an inalienable context — thus the centrality of primordial ties in Neo-Confucian self-definition. Surely, the sense of being situated in a definite place at a particular moment involves more than the awareness of one's physical presence. The human mind may resemble a *tabula rasa,* but a person is always born to a complex

social network. The self, not as an abstract concept but as a lived reality, must be aware of the others around it as integral parts of its own existence. The situation of the self requires not only a passive acceptance but also an active recognition. Once the fact of human-relatedness is recognized, one can begin to assume personal responsibility for one's social role. The structural limitation that we are inevitably contextualized need not be perceived merely as an external imposition on our freedom of choice; it also provides us the nourishment for survival, the environment for growth, and the symbolic resources for creativity.

In a deeper sense, however, the meaning of the self in Neo-Confucian thought cannot be determined by the social roles that contextualize it. At any particular juncture of one's development, no matter how coercive one's structural limitation is or is perceived to be, there is always the possibility to transcend it and overcome its negative influence. The self is situated, but neither enclosed nor enslaved, in its sociality. The texture of the dyadic relationships that define its social roles is never fixed. It has to be constantly interwoven with the changing configuration of disappearing and emerging threads which the self encounters in its life situations. To be sure, there are underlying permanent webs, such as the father-son relationship, that must endure all contingencies. Even this, however, is by no means fixed because as it shapes other relationships, it is also being shaped by them. The interaction of a variety of dyadic relationships generates the dynamism for personal integration earlier referred to as procedural freedom.

To pursue this further, the enlargement of the self, with its eventual union with Heaven as the most generalized universality, travels the concrete path of forming communions with a series of expanded social groups. The *locus classicus* for this ethicoreligious insight is the *Great Learning*:

> When the personal life (*shen*) is cultivated, the family (*chia*) will be regulated; when the family is regulated, the state (*kuo*) will be in order; and when the state is in order, there will be peace throughout the world (*t'ien-hsia*).[16]

The Neo-Confucian reading of the text, true to the spirit of learning for the sake of self-realization, puts great emphasis on the issues directly relevant to the cultivation of one's personal life. Thus, much hermeneutic effort is focused on the "inner dimension" of the

enlargement of the self. This consists of the "investigation of things" (*ko-wu*), "extension of knowledge" (*chih-chih*), "sincerity of the will" (*ch'eng-i*), and "rectification of the mind" (*cheng-hsin*).[17] A kind of archaeological digging, with the expressed purpose of acquiring a deep understanding of the self, features prominently in the writings of virtually all major Neo-Confucian thinkers.

The Neo-Confucian faith in the perfectibility of the self is extended to the family, the state, and the world. Cultivation of the self as the "root" (*pen*) conveys not only personal but also social, political, and religious import. The corollary to this belief in the great transformative potential of the self is an awareness of the necessary form for its manifestation. Implicit in the statement that "when the personal life is cultivated, the family will be regulated" is an assertion that, as long as the family is not yet regulated, the cultivation of the personal life must be continued. By analogy, if the body politic is not yet in order or if peace has not yet pervaded all under Heaven, the effort of self-cultivation should not be interrupted. Learning (*hsüeh*), in the Neo-Confucian sense, requires an ultimate and a continuous commitment.

Robert N. Bellah has argued that Neo-Confucian religiosity is limited by the lack of transcendent leverage in Confucian symbolism. As a result, "there is no basis for a structurally independent religious community."[18] Since there is little in the Confucian position which justifies going beyond socially sanctioned norms, the authentic possibility for creative social innovation is often "precluded by the absence of a point of transcendent loyalty that [can] provide legitimation for it."[19] Recent scholarship, including Bellah's own reflection on the matter, has significantly revised this broadly conceived Weberian interpretation of Confucian ethics. Thomas Metzger, for example, argues with energy that there is indeed a functional equivalent to the Puritan ethic in Neo-Confucianism.[20] Max Weber's claim that the spiritual orientation of Confucianism is adjustment to the world, rather than mastery over the world, is no longer tenable. Nor is his overall assessment of the Confucian life-orientation:

> A well-adjusted man, rationalizing his conduct only to the degree requisite for adjustment, does not constitute a systematic unity but rather a complex of useful and particular traits. . . . Such a way of life could not allow man an inward aspiration toward a "unified personality," a striving which we associate with the idea of personality. Life remained a series of occurrences.[21]

However, even though Weber was misinformed when he insisted that in the Confucian ethic "there was no leverage for influencing conduct through inner forces freed of tradition and convention,"[22] his basic thesis still merits our attention. Weber argues that by harmonizing the conflict between the self and society, Confucian ethics lacks

> any tension between nature and deity, between ethical demand and human shortcoming, consciousness of sin and need for salvation, conduct on earth and compensation in the beyond, religious duty and socio-political reality.[23]

Whether or not the Neo-Confucian masters themselves managed to overcome the conflict between their commitment to moralizing politics through spiritual self-transformation and the autocratic demand for loyal participation in the political order, it was not conceivable to them, as it was taken for granted in Christianity, that "every particular pattern of social relations was in principle deprived of ultimacy."[24] And, historically, it is undeniable that under the influence of highly politicized Confucian symbolism, "filial piety and loyalty became absolutes."[25] The inability of even the most brilliant minds in Confucian China to develop a soteriology beyond politics clearly indicates that the idea of transcendence, as radical otherness, was not even conceived as a rejected possibility in Neo-Confucian thought.

To criticize Neo-Confucian symbolism for lack of transcendent leverage is to impose a Christian and, therefore, alien perspective. It would be indeed difficult for modern Confucians to appreciate fully the idea of the "wholly other," the sentiment of absolute dependency, or the justification for total faith in an unknowable God. However, within the symbolic resources of the Neo-Confucian tradition, the authentic possibility exists for developing a transcendent leverage which can serve as the ultimate basis for an intellectual community, or the community of the like-minded followers of the Way, structurally independent of the political order and functionally inseparable from the lived realities of society and politics. Despite the difficulty of conceptualizing transcendence as radical otherness, the Confucian commitment to ultimate self-transformation necessarily involves a transcendent dimension. The idea of going beyond the usual limits of one's existential self so that one can become true to one's Heavenly endowed nature entails the transformative act of

continuously excelling and surpassing one's experience here and now. This transformative act is predicated on a transcendent vision that ontologically we are infinitely better and therefore more worthy than we actually are. In the ultimate sense we, as persons, form a trinity with Heaven and Earth. From this transcending perspective, it is not at all inconceivable that every particular pattern of social relations is only instrumentally important and is therefore deprived of ultimacy.

We can perhaps restate Neo-Confucian religiosity in terms of a twofold process: a continuous deepening of one's subjectivity and an uninterrupted broadening of one's sensitivity. Ultimate self-transformation as a communal act, in this connection, entails a series of paradoxes. The cultivation of the self assumes the form of mastering the self; for the self to realize its original nature, it must transform its self-centered structure. Accordingly, to deepen one's subjectivity requires an unceasing struggle to eliminate selfish and egoistic desires. By inference, just as cultivation of the personal life impels us to go beyond egoism, regulation of the family, governing the state and bringing peace throughout the world impel us to transcend nepotism, racism, and chauvinism. The Neo-Confucians may not have been as sensitive to the bigotry of these limited and limiting collective consciousnesses as we are in our pluralistic global village. Yet, it is vitally important to note that, in their perception, broadened sensitivity should also enable one to rise above anthropocentrism. To them, the real meaning of being human lies in the mutuality of Heaven and man and the unity of all things.

From this anthropocosmic perspective, the Neo-Confucian idea of the family is laden with ethicoreligious as well as social and political implications. Chang Tsai's (1020–1077) *Western Inscription*, which Wing-tsit Chan describes as "the basis of Neo-Confucian ethics," speaks directly to this:

> Heaven is my father and Earth is my mother, and even such a small creature as I finds an intimate place in their midst. Therefore that which fills the universe I regard as my body and that which directs the universe I consider as my nature. All people are my brothers and sisters, and all things are my companions.[26]

The family and, by extension, the state and the world are integral parts of the "fiduciary community" where organismic connections unite all modalities of being in a common bond. A natural applica-

tion of this anthropocosmic vision to human society recognizes that:

> Even those who are tired, infirm, crippled, or sick; those who have
> no brothers or children, wives or husbands, are all my brothers
> who are in distress and have no one to turn to.[27]

However, as Chu Hsi (1130–1200) points out, the underlying assumption in Chang Tsai's all-embracing humanity is not undifferentiated "universal love," but the Neo-Confucian thesis: "principle is one but its particularizations are diverse" (*li-i fen-shu*).[28] Without going into the technical issues, this thesis means that, from the perspective of the "original substance," the organismic unity pervades everything. There is absolute equality among things and the mind's sensitivity can and should embody all of them without discrimination. From the functional viewpoint, on the other hand, the exertion of "moral effort" necessitates a concrete analysis of a given situation. As a result, the diversity in which the principle is particularized becomes the central concern. Since it is thought to be humanly impossible for one to care for a stranger in the same degree and to the same extent that one cares for one's closest kin, a proper way to express one's sensitivity requires a differentiated manifestation.

The "five human relations" (*wu-lun*), understood in this light, point to five structurally and functionally distinct dyadic relationships.[29] A sense of priority or an order of hierarchy can be assigned to the five relations. The prominence of the father-son dyad seems indicative of a prioritized or hierarchical pattern which underlies all the relationships. It is misleading, however, to suggest that the father-son dyad provides a model for the other four. Rather, each has a uniqueness which cannot be reduced to or subsumed under any other. A common mistake in interpreting traditional Chinese political culture, presumably under the influence of Neo-Confucianism, is to assume that the ruler-minister relationship is modelled on that of the father-son. The father-son or, generally speaking, the parent-child relationship is a primordial tie, absolutely binding and inescapably given. While one cannot choose one's parents, the freedom not to enter a ruler-minister relationship and the choice to sever a political obligation is always available. Thus, the guiding principle between father and son is "affinity" (*ch'in*), whereas the governing virtue between ruler and minister is "righteousness" (*i*). It may be more appropriate to understand the

ruler-minister in terms of the father-son and the friend-friend relationships combined.

Another common mistake in analyzing the five relations is to exaggerate the importance of asymmetry in all the dyads. This gives rise to the general impression that the "three bonds" (*san-kang*),[30] emphasizing the one-dimensional dependency of the minister on the ruler, the son on the father and the wife on the husband, are defining characteristics of Neo-Confucian ethics. Historically, Neo-Confucianism as a political ideology may have contributed to despotic, gerontocratic, and male-oriented practices in premodern Chinese society; however, the value that underlies the five relations is not dependency but "reciprocity" (*pao*).[31] The filiality of the son is reciprocated by the compassion of the father, the obedience of the minister reciprocated by the fair-mindedness of the ruler and so forth. Friendship, in this connection, is a reciprocal relation *par excellence*. It is mutuality rather than dependency that defines "trust" (*hsin*) between friends.

The fiduciary community which friends enter into is not a "trust" created to achieve a narrowly defined economic or social goal. The modern idea of a religious fellowship, rather than a professional association or an academic society, comes close to the Neo-Confucian "way of the friend" (*yu-tao*), which is intimately connected with the "way of the teacher" (*shih-tao*). Friendship as well as the teacher-student relationship exists for the sake of communal self-transformation. Its purpose is moral education:

> Master Lien-hsi (Chou Tun-i, 1017–1073) said: Righteousness, uprightness, decisiveness, strictness, and firmness of action are examples of strength that is good, and fierceness, narrow-mindedness, and violence are examples of strength that is evil. Kindness, mildness, and humility are examples of weakness that is good, and softness, indecision, and perverseness are examples of weakness that is evil. Only the Mean brings harmony. The Mean is the principle of regularity, the universally recognized law or morality, and is that to which the sage is devoted. Therefore the sage institutes education so as to enable people to transform their evil by themselves, to arrive at the Mean and to rest there.[32]

This idea of moral education "for the sake of one's self" also features prominently in the relationship between brothers. The application of the principle of reciprocity in the pursuit of self-

knowledge involves altruism as well as fairness. The pervading spirit is empathetic understanding of the other which implies considerateness and forgivingness (*shu*).[33] The idea of vengeance is diametrically opposed to the Neo-Confucian value of reciprocity. To the question: "Suppose the older brother is respectful toward his younger brother but the younger brother is not reverent toward the older brother. Should the older brother imitate his brother's lack of reverence and stop being respectful?" Chu Hsi emphatically stated, "The older brother should be respectful to the highest degree." This, he insisted, is the true meaning of the verse in the *Book of Odes*: "Brothers should be good to each other but should not imitate each other."[34]

It would be misleading to suppose that self-sacrifice or a simple psychology of detachment is the message here. A fiduciary community means that the moral well-being of each member is the personal concern of all. In a specific dyadic relationship where an obvious asymmetry occurs, as in the case of the younger brother's lack of reverence, conscious effort is required of the righteous (the older brother) for his own self-cultivation to help the other (the younger brother) to resume his course of moral learning. The *locus classicus* for this is the Confucian *Analects*: "In order to establish oneself, one helps others to establish themselves; in order to enlarge oneself, one helps others to enlarge themselves."[35] Therefore, in the light of self-education, the reciprocal relationship is always a two-way communication. The ruler, the parent, the teacher, the senior friend, and the older brother are as much involved in making themselves obedient, faithful and dedicated to the shared values of the community as are the minister, the child, the student, the junior friend, and the younger brother.

It is conceivable that occasionally one may have to find a way to help one's parent and, by implication, one's teacher (not to mention one's ruler who often falls short of a minimum standard of rulership) to behave properly. The necessity and desirability of doing so is taken for granted, but the actual style to bring the necessary and desirable result requires careful deliberation and, of course, finesse. Commenting on the line from the *Book of Change*: "In dealing with troubles caused by one's mother, one should not be too firm," Ch'eng I (1033–1107) had this to say:

> In dealing with his mother, the son should help her with mildness and gentleness so she will be in accord with righteousness. If he

disobeys her and the matter fails, it will be his fault. Is there not a way to obey with ease? If one goes forward with his strength and abruptly resists or defies her, the kindness and love between mother and son will be hurt. That will be great harm indeed. How can he get into her heart and change her? The way lies in going backward, bending his will to obey, and following his mother so that her personal life will be correct and matters well managed. The way for strong ministers to serve weak rulers is similar to this.[36]

This concern for the irreparable damage to the amiable relationship between mother and son caused by the son's blunt confrontation in order to right the wrongs of the mother is a concern for the moral well-being of the mother as well as the harmony of the family. Voluntary change of attitude is preferred; an arbitrary imposition of an external standard, despite its possible heuristic value for self-discipline, can never bring about genuine self-transformation. Thus,

In teaching people, Confucius "would not enlighten those who are not eager to learn, nor arouse those who are not anxious to give an explanation themselves."[37] For if one arouses them without waiting for them to become eager to learn and anxious to give an explanation themselves, their knowledge will not be firm. But if one waits for them to be eager and anxious before arousing them, they will learn irresistibly like the rush of water. A student must think deeply. If he has thought deeply but cannot understand, it will then be all right to tell him.[38]

On the surface, the conjugal relationship seems to be a significant departure from the principle of reciprocity. The common impression that the wife and daughter-in-law in a male-oriented society has no "rights" of her own is, however, a misconception of how the normative system actually works in Neo-Confucianism. It is true that, in response to the loaded question: "In some cases the widows are all alone, poor, and with no one to depend on. May they remarry?" Ch'eng I, apparently troubled by the questioner's intention to establish the strong claim that remarriage is sometimes necessary if not desirable, stated in an unusually stern manner: "This theory has come about only because people of later generations are afraid of starving to death. But to starve to death is a very small matter. To lose one's integrity, however, is a very serious matter."[39] This un-

compromising articulation of faith in the sacredness of marriage as a total commitment was probably in Ch'eng I's mind applied equally to husband and wife. Furthermore, it was meant to be a critique of a common practice which seemed to have taken too lightly the true meaning of matrimony by using a simple economic justification. The very fact that Ch'eng I cited approvingly his father's decision to remarry a widowed relative as a manifestation of kindness[40] indicates that, while he was in principle against remarriage, he did not make a dogma out of it.

Ideally, in the Neo-Confucian order of things, the conjugal relationship is the most fundamental of all human relations. The Neo-Confucians argue that it is from husband and wife that all other familial ties are engendered.[41] Failure to establish genuine reciprocity between husband and wife destroys domestic harmony and indeed social stability. Therefore, in underscoring its importance, their emphasis is on mutual responsibility rather than romantic love. Injunction against devoting too much attention to the affective aspect of the conjugal relationship is readily available in Neo-Confucian literature:

> Tranquillity and correctness are the ways to enable husband and wife to live together for a long time, whereas indecent liberties and improper intimacies result in disrespect and cause husband and wife to drift apart.[42]

Reciprocity in the conjugal relationship is often characterized by "respect" (*ching*). A common expression in describing a proper husband-wife relationship is that they treat each other respectfully as guests. For example, Ch'eng I summarized his mother's relationship to his father as follows: "she and father treated each other with full respect as guests are treated. Grateful for her help at home, father treated her with even greater reverence. But mother conducted herself with humility and obedience."[43]

Like all other forms of dyadic relationships, the idea of mutual respect between husband and wife conveys a profound ethicoreligious import. Although it is basically correct to interpret the Neo-Confucian perception of the conjugal relationship in terms of social values such as the creation, maintenance and perpetuation of the family, the mutuality of husband and wife should also be taken as an integral part of the self-education of both of them. One

wonders if Ch'eng I did not somehow simplify the complexity of the actual situation in his praise of the virtue of his mother as wife:

> She was humane, altruistic, liberal, and earnest. She cared for and loved the children of my father's concubines just as she did her own. My father's cousin's son became an orphan when very young, and she regarded him her own.[44]

Nevertheless, despite the male-centeredness of the culture, the active participation of the wife in shaping the form of human-relatedness in the family is fully recognized and strongly encouraged. The division of labor between the inner (domestic) and the outer (public) realm of responsibility makes it functionally necessary for the wife to assume a major role at home. Thus, Ch'eng I's mother's preference in consulting her husband even in small matters was noted as an indication of extraordinary considerateness.[45] Needless to say, the ultimate self-transformation of the wife-mother, like that of the husband-father, provides a standard of inspiration for the family and for society at large.

The Neo-Confucian conception of the proper conduct of a wife differs from the accepted standards of behavior in pre-modern China. Although no convincing evidence has been found to establish a causal relationship between the rise of Neo-Confucian culture in the tenth century and the prevalence of such appalling social customs as footbinding, the charge that Neo-Confucian ideology significantly contributed to the decline in the status of women in China has not yet been cleared. Certainly, the Neo-Confucian advocacy of a hierarchical ordering of the human community according to prescribed social roles may have oriented society to adopt what seems to us an unwarranted policy of sex differentiation. However, it is the structural limitation of the human condition, to which we earlier referred, that actually provides the justification for perceiving society as a highly differentiated "organic solidarity" of which sex differentiation is only a part. People are also differentiated by age, profession, wealth, power, reputation, family connections, and so forth. One does not choose but is simply fated to be a particular person. Yet, the recognition that one is inescapably situated in one's primordial ties, far from being an acceptance of fatalism, is a realistic understanding of the context in which one begins the task of learning to be human. This task involves a dynamic process of

growth rather than mere submission to assigned social roles. In this sense, the dialectic interplay between contextualization and decontextualization for the wife-mother, like that for the husband-father, can also function creatively at each stage of her self-realization. Like her male counterpart, she realizes herself through the "procedural freedom" that she cultivates despite (we may even say paradoxically because of) her structural limitation.

This Neo-Confucian position on the role of woman is predicated on a vision of society in which women, like men, actively shape its moral character. One cannot exaggerate the importance of the mother in nourishing and educating the young and the wife in harmonizing and managing the family in traditional China. The transformation of a daughter into a responsible wife-mother, like the transformation of a son into a responsible husband-father, is a major concern in Confucian culture. Indeed, within the symbolic resources of the Neo-Confucian tradition, there is a wellspring of insights on how to cultivate true mutuality between man and woman. The functional cosmology that the Neo-Confucians subscribe to is not anthropomorphic; therefore it is not wedded to a male-dominated symbolism. A natural consequence of the lack of a fully institutionalized mediating structure (such as the priesthood) between the mundane and the transcendent in the Confucian tradition is the absence of any theological justification for the creation of an exclusively male spiritual leadership. While women were long excluded from state examinations and from higher education, these practices are not prescribed by Confucian moral metaphysics. Rather, a society of like-minded followers of the Way is and ought to be open to all members of the human community. The universalistic claim that every human being (in the sense of the sexually neutral form *jen*) has the potential to form a unity with Heaven, Earth, and the myriad things is thus not only an intellectual assertion but also a spiritual commitment of the Neo-Confucian masters.

Nevertheless, we cannot ignore the historical fact that Confucian China was unquestionably a male-dominated society. The education of the son received much more attention than the education of the daughter, the husband was far more influential than the wife, and the father's authority significantly surpassed that of the mother. The idea that a woman passed through three stages of dependency: dependency on the father in youth, on the husband when married,

and on the son in old age clearly indicates her inferior status in the so-called hierarchical ordering of the human community. Surely, to criticize Neo-Confucian ideology as male-oriented is to introduce a modern feminist perspective beyond the realm of imagination in most traditional discourses Eastern or Western. Yet, if we take Neo-Confucian religiosity seriously as a viable persuasion rather than merely as a historical phenomenon, we must criticize the outmoded Neo-Confucian ideology in order to retrieve the deep meaning of its universal humanistic teachings. Only then will we encounter no theological or scriptural difficulty in stressing the necessity and desirability of the participation of women in influencing, shaping, and leading the Confucian Way in the future. Chu Hsi or Wang Yang-ming may not have adopted a conscious policy of training women to become Confucian masters, but their legacy speaks loudly in favor of such a tendency. While they may not have been egalitarian in the modern sense, the suggestion that they subscribed to a kind of class consciousness that prevented women and the uneducated masses from becoming fully human is a misreading of their message. Indeed, their insistence that respect is the governing virtue between husband and wife is based not only on the idea of the division of labor but also on the value of mutual appreciation. This, by implication, requires the formation of a functionally differentiated and substantively unified relationship between woman and man.

I have suggested that, in the perspective of Neo-Confucian thought, human-relatedness is an essential dimension of religiosity. As an ultimate self-transformation, being religious entails being actively engaged in a communal act. Religious consciousness so understood is a quest for the identity and continuity of one's communality as well as one's selfhood. Paradoxically, for the self to be ultimately transformed, it must travel the concrete path defined in terms of its primordial ties such as parentage, ethnicity, locale, historical moment, and so forth. Strictly speaking, if the self fails to transform the primordial ties into "instruments" for moral cultivation, it can only be contextualized and structured to assume a predetermined social role. Yet, its creativity as a moral agent cannot be manifested merely by transcending the context and the structure that determines its center of relationships. The authentic approach is neither a passive submission to structural limitation nor a Faustian activation of procedural freedom but a conscientious effort to make the dynamic interaction between them a fruitful dialectic for self-

realization. Learning for the sake of one's self is ethicoreligious because it takes as its root idea the inseparability of the ethic of human-relatedness and the religiosity of the quest for personal knowledge.

NOTES

1. The idea occurs in the *Analects* (14:25) and is accepted as an underlying assumption by virtually all schools of Neo-Confucian thought.

2. This phrase, *"han-yang hsü-yung ching chin-hsüeh tsai chih-chih,"* is characteristic of the Ch'eng-Chu approach to moral self-cultivation. See Wing-tsit Chan, *A Source Book in Chinese Philosophy* (Princeton: Princeton University Press, 1963), p. 562.

3. The idea of *"chü-ching ch'iung-li"* can be taken as Chu Hsi's interpretation of Ch'eng I's method of education. Wing-tsit Chan notes: "Like Ch'eng I, Chu Hsi struck the balance between seriousness and the investigation of things in moral education. He said that seriousness is the one important word transmitted in the Confucian school, that it is the foundation in Ch'eng I's teachings, and that it is Ch'eng's greatest contribution to later students." See *A Source Book*, p. 607. It should be mentioned that the word *"ching"* is rendered as "reverence" or "respectfulness" in this essay, whereas Chan has chosen "seriousnessness" to convey its many-sided meanings.

4. It is commonly known that Lu Hsiang-shan builds his moral philosophy on the Mencian idea, *"hsien li-hu ch'i ta-che," Mencius*, 6A:15.

5. *"Chih liang-chih"* has been variously rendered as "extension of innate knowledge," "extension of conscientious consciousness," "extension of knowledge of the good," and "extension of intuitive knowledge." In this essay, *liang-chih* is rendered as "primordial awareness" and *chih* as "full realization." See *Mencius*, 7A:15.

6. Liu Tsung-chou's teaching of *shen-tu* is based on the *Great Learning* and the *Doctrine of the Mean*.

7. See Ch'eng Hao's essay, "On Understanding Humanity" ("Shih-jen"), in *Erh-Ch'eng i-shu*, 2A:3a-b.

8. This is based on the anthropocosmic vision in the *Doctrine of the Mean*, chap. 22. See Tu Wei-ming, *Centrality and Commonality: An Essay on Chung-Yung* (Honolulu: The University Press of Hawaii, 1976), chap. IV.

9. Thomé H. Fang, *Chinese Philosophy: Its Spirit and Its Development* (Taipei: Linking Publishing Co., 1981), pp. 446–469.

10. This is also based on the *Doctrine of the Mean*, chap. 33. However, the idea originally came from the *Book of Poetry*, no. 235.

11. *Mencius*, 5A:5. It should be noted that this "democratic" or "populist" idea is found in the *Book of History*; see James Legge, trans., *The Shoo King* in the *Chinese Classics*, vol. 3 (Oxford: Clarendon Press, 1865), p. 292.

12. Wilfred Cantwell Smith, *The Meaning and End of Religion* (New York: The Macmillan Company, 1964), pp. 19–74.

13. Tu Wei-ming, "Ultimate Self-Transformation as a Communal Act: Comments on Modes of Self-Cultivation in Traditional China," *Journal of Chinese Philosophy* 6 (1969), 237–246.

14. Tu Wei-ming, "The Neo-Confucian Concept of Man," in *Humanity and Self-Cultivation: Essays in Confucian Thought* (Berkeley: Asian Humanities Press, 1980), pp. 71–82.

15. An expression borrowed from the title of Herbert Fingarette's thought-provoking book, *The Self in Transformation: Psychoanalysis, Philosophy and the Life of the Spirit* (New York: Basic Books, 1963).

16. *The Great Learning*, chap. 1.

17. Ibid.

18. Robert N. Bellah, "Father and Son in Christianity and Confucianism," in his *Beyond Belief: Essays on Religion in a Post-Traditional World* (New York: Harper & Row, 1976), p. 81.

19. Ibid., p. 95.

20. Thomas Metzger, *Escape from Predicament: Neo-Confucianism and China's Evolving Political Culture* (New York: Columbia University Press, 1977), pp. 29–47.

21. Max Weber, *The Religion of China*, trans., from the German and ed., Hans H. Gerth (New York: Free Press, 1964), p. 235.

22. Weber, p. 236.

23. Weber, pp. 235–236.

24. Bellah, p. 95.

25. Ibid.

26. Wing-tsit Chan, *A Source Book in Chinese Philosophy* (Princeton: Princeton University, 1963), p. 497.

27. Ibid.

28. Ibid., p. 550. This phrase is often rendered as "principle is one and its manifestations are many." In this essay, I follow Wm. T. de Bary's translation. See his *The Liberal Tradition in China* (Hong Kong: The Chinese University Press and New York: Columbia University Press, 1983), p. 51.

29. The *locus classicus* for this is again *Mencius*: "According to the way of man, if they are well fed, warmly clothed, and comfortably lodged but without education, they will become almost like animals. The sage (emperor Shun) worried about it and he appointed Hsieh to be Minister of Education and teach people human relations, that between father and son, there should be affection; between ruler and minister, there should be righteousness; between husband and wife, there should be attention to their separate functions; between old and young, there should be a proper order; and between friends, there should be faithfulness." (3A:4) See Wing-tsit Chan, *A Source Book*, pp. 69–70.

30. The "three bonds" are those binding the minister with the ruler, the son with the father, and the wife with the husband. The Han philosopher, Tung Chung-shu (c. 179 - c. 104 B.C.) discusses these relations in terms of moral education. The idea

of one-dimensional dependency is a highly politicized interpretation of the whole matter. See Wing-tsit Chan, *A Source Book*, pp. 277–278.

31. Lien-sheng Yang, "The Concept of 'Pao' as a Basis for Social Relations in China," in *Chinese Thought and Institutions*, ed., John K. Fairbank (Chicago: The University of Chicago Press, 1957), pp. 291–309, 395–397.

32. Wing-tsit Chan, trans., *Reflections on Things at Hand: The Neo-Confucian Anthology Compiled by Chu Hsi and Lü Tsu-ch'ien* (New York: Columbia University Press, 1967), p. 260.

33. *Analects*, 4:15 reads: "The Way of our Master is none other than conscientiousness (*chung*) and altruism (*shu*)." See Wing-tsit Chan, *A Source Book*, p. 27.

34. Wing-tsit Chan, trans., *Reflections*, pp. 181–182.

35. *Analects*, 6:28.

36. Wing-tsit Chan, trans., *Reflections*, pp. 171–172.

37. *Analects*, 7:8.

38. Wing-tsit Chan, trans., *Reflections*, p. 226.

39. Ibid., p. 177.

40. Ibid., p. 179.

41. The underlying philosophy of this assertion is found in the *Book of Change* where it states: "The great characteristic of Heaven and Earth is to produce." See Wing-tsit Chan, *A Source Book*, p. 268.

42. Wing-tsit Chan, trans., *Reflections*, p. 173.

43. Ibid., p. 179.

44. Ibid.

45. Ibid.

IX. Neo-Confucian Ontology: A Preliminary Questioning

The mode of questioning in Neo-Confucian thought may give us the impression that metaphysical or ontological problems are either relegated to the background or subsumed under the category of ethics. One can easily point to the dialogues between masters and disciples in the "recorded sayings" (*yü-lu*) of the Neo-Confucian thinkers to confirm such an impression. Indeed, it seems that the central concern of the Neo-Confucians, motivated by a strong will to fully realize themselves (*chien-hsing*),[1] is simply an all-encompassing psychological process: *how* to become a sage. Questions of what and why, it seems, do not feature as prominently as the practical considerations of how.[2] Understandably it is commonly observed that Neo-Confucianism is predominantly a moral philosophy. Even though it may occasionally depart from the concrete issues of everyday existence, it seems always to return to the ethical realm.[3] And it is in moral philosophy, we are told, that the strength of Neo-Confucian thought really lies.

Viewed from this perspective, discussions of ultimate reality in Neo-Confucianism such as Chou Tun-i's (1017–1073) treatise on the "great ultimate" (*t'ai-chi*) and Chang Tsai's (1020–1077) reflection on the "great harmony" (*t'ai-ho*) are sometimes explained, or explained away, in terms of conscious responses to the metaphysical challenges of Buddhism and Taoism. The argument, in a simplified form, is that these Neo-Confucian masters were not primarily interested in these problems but that they were compelled to take up the task of investigating them because the Buddhists and the Taoists, having developed highly sophisticated metaphysical systems, had already set the shape of intellectual discourse in those terms. Unless Buddhist and Taoist methods of metaphysical speculation were confronted directly, the argument continues, the Confucian position could not be securely established. Therefore, the Neo-Confucian thinkers, for the sake of delivering their message, learned the art of metaphysicizing as a strategic necessity. According to this interpretation, Neo-Confucian metaphysics, if the term is permissible, is at best a preparation for social ethics, which is to them, as it were, the real thing.

Although such a genetic explanation is unsatisfactory in many respects, it has contributed much to the wide currency of the view that the Neo-Confucian tradition is an outstanding example of ethical thought in China. The textbook account of the Chinese mind as exemplifying an effortless eclecticism of Taoist or Buddhist sacredness on the one hand and Confucian secularity on the other further enforces the belief that Neo-Confucianism, far from being concerned with the problem of reality, focuses its attention on man's everyday existence. Neo-Confucian thought so conceived seems not unlike a Chinese counterpart of the later Stoa with its insistence on the practical and moral principles of human life.[4]

The intention of this essay is to present an analysis of the Neo-Confucian approach to ontology. It is based on the belief that Neo-Confucian ethics, in its effort to formulate a holistic way of being human, is indeed predicated on an ontological vision without which its moral philosophy would be incomplete and its social thought groundless. The purpose, however, is not so much to work out a systematic critique of the "common-sense" interpretation of Neo-Confucianism as to show that if we undertake a serious inquiry into the underlying structure of Neo-Confucian ethics it is not difficult to see that precisely because its moral and social ideas are anchored on a highly integrated metaphysical plane they take on meanings significantly different from those of other ethical systems.

I. *The Metaphysical Grounding of Sagehood.* A defining characteristic of the Neo-Confucian mode of questioning is, as already mentioned, its emphasis on the problem of attaining sagehood. It may not be far-fetched to suggest that sagehood, as the highest and the profoundest manifestation of humanity, is the philosophical locus wherein all the major realms of concern in Neo-Confucian thought converge. And it is probably in this sense that the Neo-Confucians characterize their "learning" (*hsüeh*) and "teaching" (*chiao*) as the Sagely Way.[5] Therefore, in a strict sense, the Neo-Confucians do not simply *follow* the way of the ancient sages; they try to embody it so that they can manifest it in their own ways of life.[6] Sagehood so conceived is not an inaccessible ideal but a realizable state of existence. The alleged founder of the Neo-Confucian tradition, Chou Tun-i, has made it explicit that sagehood is attainable through learning:

Can one become a sage through learning?

Yes.

Is there any essential way?

Yes.

Please explain it to me.

The essential way is to [concentrate on] one thing. By [concentrating on] one thing is meant having no desire. Having no desire, one is vacuous (*hsü*, being absolutely pure and peaceful) while tranquil, and straightforward while in action. Being vacuous while tranquil, one becomes intelligent and hence penetrating. Being straightforward while active, one becomes impartial and hence all-embracing. Being intelligent, penetrating, impartial, and all-embracing, one is almost a sage.[7]

Whether or not "desirelessness" (*wu-yü*) is an authentically Confucian way of self-realization should not concern us here. Suffice it to note that Chu Hsi (1130–1200) has raised serious doubts about the suitability of defining oneness, a concentrated state of mind, in terms of having no desire.[8] But the insistence on the centrality of sagehood and the presumption that it can be attained by self-effort indicates such a general belief in Neo-Confucianism that all schools of thought within the tradition, despite serious arguments concerning issues such as whether or not having no desire is the right method of spiritual cultivation, subscribe to this belief as self-evidently true.

However, sagehood in the Neo-Confucian sense is much more than a simple personality-ideal, and its implications cannot begin to unfold if the proposed inquiry remains only at the levels of psychology and ethics. It is true that Chou Tun-i states that "sagehood is nothing but sincerity (*ch'eng*)."[9] Taken at its face value, this may be interpreted to mean that honesty is all that is required to become a sage. But sincerity, far from being just a psychological or ethical idea, is actually an ontological concept. Thus Chou continues:

It [Sincerity] is the foundation of the Five Constant Virtues (humanity, righteousness, propriety, wisdom, and faithfulness) and the source of all activities. When tranquil, it is in the state of non-being, and when active, it is in the state of being. It is perfectly correct and clearly penetrating. Without sincerity, the Five Constant Virtues and all activities will be wrong. They will be depraved and obstructed.[10]

The term which is here translated as "sincerity" has also been rendered as "truth" or "reality."[11] After all the English word itself connotes the meaning of honest genuineness, signifying in a poetic sense a heartfelt feeling grounded not on semblances but on realities.

Indeed, Chou further states that "the sage is the one who is in the state of sincerity, spirit (*shen*), and subtle incipient activation (*chi*)."[12] This may be taken as a refinement of the earlier assertion that sagehood is nothing but sincerity. Quoting from the "Appended Remarks" of the *Book of Change*, Chou defines sincerity as "the state of absolute quiet and inactivity" and spirit as that which "when acted on, immediately penetrates all things."

> And the state of subtle incipient activation is the undifferentiated state between existence and non-existence when activity has started but has not manifested itself in physical form. Sincerity is infinitely pure and hence evident. The spirit is responsive and hence works wonders. And incipient activation is subtle and hence abstruse.[13]

This mode of presentation, as evident in Chou's other remarks in his highly acclaimed *Penetrating the Book of Change (T'ung-shu)*, is not only characteristic of Neo-Confucian thought but also reminiscent of the Mencian tradition of classical Confucianism. The following statement in Mencius is a case in point:

> The desirable is called "good." To have it in oneself is called "true." To possess it fully in oneself is called "beautiful," but to shine forth with this full possession is called "great." To be great and be transformed by this greatness is called "sage;" to be sage and to transcend the understanding is called "divine" ["spiritual"].[14]

One might easily infer from these explanatory sentences that just as the sage symbolizes a continuous perfection of the good, the true, the beautiful, and the great, the spiritual is a further refinement on the sage. But, as Chu Hsi maintains, the idea of the spiritual in this connection by no means signifies a "spiritual being" (*shen-jen*) which rises above the sage. Rather, it indicates that the transforming power of the sage is beyond ordinary human comprehension.[15] This line of thinking is in perfect accord with the "moral metaphysics" of the *Doctrine of the Mean (Chung-yung)*:

Only those who are absolutely *sincere* can fully develop their nature. If they can fully develop their nature, they can then fully develop the nature of others. If they can fully develop the nature of others, they can then fully develop the nature of things. If they can fully develop the nature of things, they can then assist in the transforming and nourishing process of Heaven and Earth. If they can assist in the transforming and nourishing process of Heaven and Earth, they can thus form a trinity with Heaven and Earth.[16]

It can therefore be argued that Chou Tun-i's deceptively simple statement, "Sagehood is nothing but sincerity," is actually buttressed by a fully developed metaphysical vision. To be sure, sagehood as a mode of experience rather than as an abstract principle is not devoid of psychological and ethical implications. Yet since it is as much an idea about ultimate reality as one about the deepest meaning of human existence, it should be understood and appreciated from a much broader perspective. Indeed, no matter how much weight one puts on the psychological and ethical dimensions of it, sagehood in Neo-Confucian thought is always grounded in a metaphysical structure. Only then do concepts such as "sincerity," "spirit," and "subtle incipient activation" seem compatible with it.

II. *Kantian Mode of Questioning Compared.* In the light of the above, although it is true that one can interpret the Neo-Confucian spiritual orientation as a form of philosophical anthropology, the metaphysical grounding of sagehood must be construed as the ultimate fruition of an ethicoreligious insight wherein the conventional distinction between ethics and religion becomes merely a heuristic device. The central questions underlying the attainment of sagehood are, then, Who am I? and What can I become? Or, in other words, What is it to be human? Even though the Neo-Confucian masters do not appear to have posed their questions in precisely such terms, a brief survey of their main concerns should be sufficient to illustrate this point.

The question which is alleged to have been first raised by Confucius' best disciple, Yen Yüan, is most instructive in this connection: "What sort of man was Shun (the Sage-King)? And what sort of man am I? Anyone who can make something of himself will be like that."[17] Intent on expounding the philosophical implication of Yen Yüan's questioning, Ch'eng I (1033–1107) wrote the famous treatise

entitled "What Master Yen Loved to Learn." Despite his seemingly simple answer that "it was to learn the way of becoming a sage," Ch'eng I elaborates on the reason why every person is in essence a sage and therefore in practice can well become one. The argument, as we shall see, is very much in the spirit of Chou Tun-i:

> From the essence of life accumulated in Heaven and Earth, man receives the Five Agents (Water, Fire, Wood, Metal, and Earth) in their highest excellence. His original nature is pure and tranquil. Before it is aroused, the five moral principles of his nature, called humanity, righteousness, propriety, wisdom, and faithfulness, are complete.[18]

Therefore, Ch'eng I continues, "the way to learn is none other than rectifying one's mind and nourishing one's nature. When one abides by the Mean and correctness and becomes sincere, he is a sage."[19]

We may, at this particular juncture, insert a comparative note. On the basis of what has been said so far, the Neo-Confucian problematic does not seem directly responsive to any of the three Kantian questions:

1. What can I know?
2. What ought I do?
3. What may I hope?

To be sure, the Neo-Confucian concerns, so far as they have been mentioned above, may be subsumed under question 2, since they seem to fall into the category of human activity involving the personality and freedom of moral choice. Accordingly, one can go so far as to conclude that Neo-Confucianism, instead of focusing its attention on cosmology or on theology, is exclusively preoccupied with psychology. Yet this kind of unexamined assertion does a serious injustice not only to Neo-Confucian metaphysics but also to the Kantian perception of morality.

Kant, in his *Foundations of the Metaphysics of Morals*, insists that the ground of obligation (pure morality) "must not be sought in the nature of man or in the circumstances in which he is placed, but sought *a priori* solely in the concepts of pure reason."[20] Problems of translation and equivalence of terms aside, this would seem to conflict with the Neo-Confucian teaching that morality is deeply rooted in human nature. While Kant stresses "the utmost necessity to construct a pure moral philosophy which is completely freed from everything which may be only empirical and thus belong to an-

thropology,"[21] the Neo-Confucians strongly believe that moral cultivation is inseparable from man's knowledge of himself as an integral and "natural" being. However, these apparent incompatibilities only scratch the surface of a much more fundamental difference.

Viewed from a Neo-Confucian perspective, it seems that Kant is particularly concerned about the secret incentives undiscoverable even by the most searching self-examination. For the "dear self," which is capable of eluding the strictest scrutiny, remains powerful behind our thoughts and aspirations, although they are often falsely believed to have been dicated solely by the idea of the good.[22] Therefore, the stern command of duty (which would often require self-denial) becomes the only basis for moral action.[23] And this is predicated on the conviction that "reason of itself and independently of all appearances commands what ought to be done."[24] Perhaps this is why Kant, for fear that the will might not of itself be in complete accord with reason, stipulates the categorical imperative, an objective principle which acts as a command of reason.[25] Since the categorical imperative, or the imperative of morality, "concerns not the material of the action and its intended result but the form and the principle from which it results," it can be taken as a practical *law* rather than merely a principle of the will.[26]

Time and again, Kant urges us not to think that the reality of this law can be derived from "the constitution of human nature."[27] Indeed, "we cannot too much or too often warn against the lax or even base manner of thought which seeks principles among empirical motives and laws, for human reason in its weariness is glad to rest on this pillow."[28] Therefore it is extremely important to stress that the categorical imperatives, either as conformity to law by actions or as the prerogative of rational beings as such, must "exclude from their legislative authority all admixture of any interest as an incentive."[29] This leads Kant to the observation that

> Man is subject only to his own, yet universal, legislation, and that he is only bound to act in accordance with his own will, which is, however, designed by nature to be a will giving universal laws.[30]

With this background in mind Kant introduces the principle of *autonomy of the will* and the concept of a *realm of ends*.

Whether or not Heidegger is justified in depicting Kant as "recoiling in fear, in the second edition [of his *Critique of Pure Reason*], from

the abyss of human subjectivity opened up by the schematizing imagination,"[31] his perception of Kant's problematic is worth noting:

> Through the laying of the foundation of metaphysics in general,
> Kant first acquired a clear insight into the character of the "univer-
> sality" of ontologico-metaphysical knowledge. . . . In the struggle
> against the superficial and palliative empiricism of the reigning
> moral philosophy, Kant attached increasing importance to the
> distinction which he established between the a priori and the em-
> pirical. And since the essence of the subjectivity of the subject is to
> be found in personality, which last is identical with moral reason,
> the rationality of pure knowledge and of [moral] action must be af-
> firmed. All pure synthesis, indeed, all synthesis in general, must as
> relevant to spontaneity depend on that faculty which in the strictest
> sense is free, the active reason.[32]

Heidegger is suggestive in maintaining that a fourth question,
What is man? must be added to the three previously cited Kantian
questions.[33] But in the light of the above discussion, one can at least
doubt whether, without stretching the truth, it is possible to contend
that metaphysics, in the Kantian sense, belongs to "human
nature."[34] Of course, this is not to deny that by underscoring the impossibility "for the subtlest philosophy as for the commonest reasoning to argue freedom away,"[35] Kant in a sense has grounded his a
priori synthetical practical proposition on the "inner man." However, it is
highly problematic whether Kant ever believed that human intelligence can really know the "inner man," or the "true self," if such
a being actually exists:

> The subjective impossibility of explaining the freedom of the will is
> the same as the impossibility of discovering and explaining an in-
> terest which man can take in moral laws. Nevertheless, he does ac-
> tually take an interest in them, and the foundation in us of this in-
> terest we call the moral feeling. This moral feeling has been er-
> roneously construed by some as the standard for our moral judg-
> ment, whereas it must rather be regarded as the subjective effect
> which the law has upon the will to which reason alone gives objec-
> tive grounds.[36]

III. *The Ontological Status of Human Nature.* Undeniably,
Heidegger's attempt to describe the real result of the Kantian laying

of the foundation in terms of the discovery of an "[essential] connection between the question of the essence of man and the establishment of metaphysics"[37] requires an unusually rigorous intellectual effort. And Heidegger himself admits that "the indefiniteness of this question [What is man?] indicates that even now we are not yet in possession of the decisive result of the Kantian laying of the foundation."[38] As we have seen, however, in Neo-Confucian thinking, the inseparability of human nature and ontological reality is a point of departure. This does not necessarily imply that the Neo-Confucian mode of questioning can be better understood and appreciated in the Heideggerian language. Actually, Professor Mou Tsung-san of New Asia Research Institute, in a powerfully argued monograph, asserts positively that the Heideggerian course of establishing a fundamental ontology on the basis of developing a metaphysics of *Dasein* is incompatible with the Neo-Confucian insistence on the "nontemporality" of human essence.[39] But the issue involved is not merely a mapping out of similarity and difference in a kind of typological analysis of philosophical systems. Rather, the task is to see how a real 'confrontation' of two fundamentally different modes of questioning can deepen our awareness of the limits as well as the strengths of our own chosen approach to ontology.

Chang Tsai, in one of the most celebrated essays in Chinese literature, sets forth the Neo-Confucian position in a highly condensed form:

> Heaven is my father and Earth is my mother, and even such a small being as I finds an intimate place in their midst. Therefore that which fills the universe I regard as my body and that which directs the universe I consider as my nature. All people are my brothers and sisters, and all things are my companions.[40]

This eloquent and condensed expression may appear simply to introduce an "organismic" vision, advocating that human beings are integral parts of a cosmological whole.[41] To be sure, that human beings are intrinsically related to Heaven, Earth, and the myriad things is essential to Chang's insight. And what he propounds can in a general way befit an organic structure. However, the *Western Inscription (Hsi-ming)*, as the essay is commonly known, is first of all a statement on man's ontological status.

A human being so conceived is not merely a creature who, by

definition, has no knowledge of his ontological ground of existence. Rather, as the son or daughter of Heaven and Earth (the receiver of the cosmic forces in their highest excellence),[42] humanity is the embodiment of that which is most refined in the creative process of the universe. This is in perfect accord with the assertion in the *Doctrine of the Mean* that human nature is what Heaven imparts to man.[43] And it is in this sense that Chang Tsai reminds us that no matter how small a being we find ourselves to be in the vastness of the cosmos, there is not only a locus but also an intimate place for each of us. For we are all potentially guardians and indeed co-creators of the universe. In this holistic vision of man, an ontological gap between Creator and creature would seem to be almost inconceivable. It appears that there is no post-lapsarian state to encounter and that alienation as a deep-rooted feeling of estrangement from one's primordial origin is nonexistent. Furthermore, the idea of man as a manipulator and conqueror of nature would also seem to be ruled out.[44]

This apparently childlike belief in the euphonious continuum of Heaven, Earth, man, and things is predicated on the cosmology of "great harmony." However, if we examine Chang's cosmos clearly, it is not so much the sweet sounds of an innocent garden as the powerful currents of the mighty ocean:

> [The Great Harmony as the Way] embraces the nature which underlies all counter processes of floating and sinking, rising and falling, and motion and rest. It is the origin of the process of fusion and intermingling, of overcoming and being overcome, and of expansion and contraction. At the commencement, these processes are incipient, subtle, obscure, easy, and simple, but at the end they are extensive, great, strong, and firm. It is *ch'ien* (Heaven) that begins with the knowledge of Change, and *k'un* (Earth) that models after simplicity.[45]

The influence of the *Book of Change* behind the whole conceptualization is readily noticeable. The metaphor, far from being static, seems to suggest a dynamic process of transformation. This is clearly shown even in his notion of the "Great Vacuity" (*t'ai-hsü*), the original substance of material force (*ch'i*). For "its integration and disintegration are but objectifications caused by Change."[46]

Yet it would be a mistake to suppose that since the cosmos is in a constant flux the idea of permanence is not applicable to Chang's

cosmology. In fact, he unequivocally notes that "as an entity, material force simply reverts to its original substance when it disintegrates and becomes formless. When it integrates and assumes form, it does not lose the eternal principle (of Change)."[47] This is because "although material force in the universe integrates and disintegrates, and attracts and repulses in a hundred ways, nevertheless the principle (*li*) according to which it operates has an order and is unerring."[48] Underlying the discussion, then, is the famous thesis attributed to Chang that *principle is one but its manifestations are many (li-i fen-shu).*[49]

The phenomenal world, from this perspective, exhibits an infinite variety of dynamic interactions through which things come into existence. The act of creation as a conscious design by a supernatural being completely beyond the comprehension of human intelligence, which is undoubtedly a rather simplistic reading of Christian theological doctrine, is absolutely incompatible with this cosmological insight. Contrary to the idea of creation as a divine function which brings things into existence *ex nihilo*, the process of transformation in Chang Tsai's thought is an unceasing operation of creativity. Thus a thing comes into existence not because it has been molded by a mysterious agent. Rather, it is the result of a continuous procedure of differentiation. In this sense, a thing becomes a thing only after it has achieved, as it were, a state of differentiatedness:

> According to principle nothing exists alone. Unless there are similarity and difference, contraction and expansion, and beginning and end among things to make it stand out, it is not really a thing although it seems to be. To become complete (to attain individuality), a thing must have a beginning and an end. But completion cannot be achieved unless there is mutual influence between similarity and difference (change) and between being and non-being (becoming). If completion is not achieved, it is not really a thing although it seems to be. Therefore it is said [in the *Book of Change*], "Contraction and expansion act on each other and thus advantages are produced."[50]

However, to achieve its thingness, so to speak, a thing must endeavor to become itself; it is not enough simply to leave the whole matter to its natural course. This is predicated on the following premise:

> Sincerity implies reality. Therefore it has a beginning and an end.
> Insincerity implies absence of reality. How can it have a beginning
> or end? Therefore it is said [in the *Doctrine of the Mean*], "Without
> sincerity, there will be nothing."[51]

One may suspect that this is a case of transposing the realm of
nature into the context of morality. But it is misleading to interpret
this line of reasoning in terms of a moralization of natural
phenomena. What is exemplified here, to borrow from Heidegger,
signifies "the endeavor to make being manifest itself."[52] Whether or
not such an idea represents merely "the last cloudy streak of
evaporating reality,"[53] to Chang Tsai, reflecting on the "highest concepts" such as the Great Vacuity is the authentic way of understanding the true meaning of concrete things.

Therefore, it is vitally important to note that by positing the
oneness of ultimate reality and the multiplicity of its manifestations
Chang Tsai by no means advances a doctrine of dualism. On the
contrary, he envisions that "the integration and disintegration of
material force is to the Great Vacuity as the freezing and melting of
ice is to water."[54] And he further states that "if we realize that the
Great Vacuity is identical with material force, we know that there is
no such thing as non-being."[55] This mode of thought has clear implications for the concept of man: human nature as well as the
nature of things lies in the unity of the Great Vacuity and material
force.[56] With this basic assumption in mind, Chang contends that
"one's nature is the one source of all things and is not one's own
private possession."[57] Thus, in an exceedingly interesting passage,
Chang depicts the ontological status of man as follows:

> The Heavenly endowed nature in man is comparable to the nature
> of water in ice. It is the same whether the ice freezes or melts.
> Water's reflection of light may be much or little, dark or bright,
> but in receiving the light, it is the same in all cases.[58]

To be sure, as Professor Wing-tsit Chan has pointed out, Chang
Tsai's philosophy of "vacuity" has never been propagated by any
later Neo-Confucianist.[59] But, notwithstanding this idiosyncrasy,
Chang's postulate that since all human beings are endowed with the
same essence which underlies the creative transformation of Heaven
and Earth, each person has the inner ability to know and experience

ultimate reality in its all-embracing fullness, remains a defining characteristic of Neo-Confucian thought.[60]

IV. *Humanity as the Fundamental Question*. In an essay 'On Understanding Humanity' (*Shih-jen*), Ch'eng Hao (1032–1085) asserts emphatically that true humanity actually "forms one body with all things without any differentiation." For the sake of underscoring man's inner ability to know and experience ultimate reality, Ch'eng further suggests that "the purpose of (Chang Tsai's) 'Western Inscription' is to explain this substance (of complete unity) fully."[61] Humanity, or *jen*, so conceived is not only the innermost sensitivity but also an all-pervading care. Citing the description of paralysis as "absence of humanity (*pu-jen*)" in traditional Chinese medicine, he uses the following analogy to illustrate this point:

> The man of *jen* regards Heaven and Earth and all things as one body. To him there is nothing that is not himself. Since he has recognized all things as himself, can there be any limit to his humanity? If things are not parts of the self, naturally they have nothing to do with it. As in the case of paralysis of the four limbs, the vital force no longer penetrates them, and therefore they are no longer parts of the self.[62]

At first sight the statement seems to refer to "a subject which cancels out everything objective, transforming it into mere subjectivity."[63] However, far from advocating subjectivism or even anthropocentrism, what Ch'eng intends to convey here is simply that "since man and Heaven and Earth are one thing, why should man purposely belittle himself?"[64] In fact, he freely admits that "man is not the only perfectly intelligent creature in the universe. The human mind (in essence) is the same as that of plants and trees, birds and animals."[65] For once a thing is produced, it by necessity possesses the complete principle.[66] Therefore, the Mencian idea that "all things are already complete in oneself" is not only applicable to man but to things as well.[67] The difference merely lies in the fact that man can extend the principle in him to others whereas things in general cannot do so. Even then, Ch'eng notes that "although man can extend [the principle], when has he augmented it to any extent? And although things cannot extend it, when have they diminished it to any extent?"[68]

Indeed, Ch'eng Hao further observes that existentially "everyone's nature is obscured in some way and as a consequence he cannot follow the Way. In general the trouble lies in resorting to selfishness and the exercise of cunning. Being selfish, one cannot take purposive action to respond to things, and being cunning, one cannot be at home with enlightenment."[59] Although Ch'eng repeatedly urges the student (one who learns to be human) not to seek afar but to search within himself so that he can enlarge his humanity through self-cultivation,[70] he never denies the necessity of what Heidegger suggestively terms the "right time, i.e. the right moment and the right perseverence."[71] In his own words, "Not the slightest effort is exerted!"[72] For Mencius has made it clear, "Always be doing something without expectation. Let the mind not forget its objective, but let there be no artificial effort to help it grow."[73]

Ch'eng Hao's way to preserve humanity so that the self and the other can be identified[74] does bear some resemblance to the Heideggerian notion of "waiting." To be sure, Heidegger's effort to confront the ontological challenge resulting from modern man's "forgetfulness of being" symbolizes a shape of thought significantly different from the Neo-Confucian insistence on the inseparability of being (principle) and being-human (humanity). But Ch'eng's caution that "to force things and to drag things along is naturally not to be in accord with the Way and principle" and that "as soon as [the Way and principle] is obscured by selfish ideas, it will be diminished and feeble"[75] reminds us of Heidegger's perceptive observation on how men have become alienated from being:

> They thrash about amid the essence, always supposing that what is most tangible is what they must grasp and thus each man grasps what is closest to him. The one holds to this, the other to that, each man's opinion [Sinn] hinges on his own [eigen]; it is opinionatedness [Eigen-sinn]. This opinionatedness, this obstinacy, prevents them from reaching out to what is gathered together in itself, makes it impossible for them to be followers [Horige] and to hear [horen] accordingly.[76]

Similarly Ch'eng observes that "simply because of selfishness, man thinks in terms of his own person, and therefore, from the point of view of principle, belittles [things]. If he lets go this person of his and views all things in the same way, how much joy would there be!"[77]

For "what is gathered together in itself" is the principle which enables "all things [to] form one body."[78]

Nevertheless, what Ch'eng Hao advocates and, for that matter, what his teacher Chou Tun-i and his uncle Chang Tsai also advocate is that, despite man's finitude in his everyday existence, ontologically his ability to apprehend in the sense of "embodying" ultimate reality is unlimited: "the reason why the man of humanity can serve Heaven and be sincere with himself is simply that he is unceasing in his humanity."[79] This vision of humanity differs in a fundamental way from Parmenides' image of man as "historical being (as the historical custodian of being)," which Heidegger hails as a crucial definition of being human for the West.[80] The governing perspective in Neo-Confucian thought is neither historicity nor temporality but the (non-temporal) unfolding of humanity as the self-disclosure of ultimate reality. This, perhaps, is what Mou Tsung-san means when he identifies as a basic assumption of the Chinese mode of thinking: all human beings are endowed with the ability of "intellectual intuition" (*chih te chih-chüeh*).

Indeed, Neo-Confucian thought, with its single-minded concern for the realization of sagehood, is an outstanding example of "intellectual intuition" at work. The following statement from Chang Tsai is a case in point:

> By enlarging one's mind, one can enter into all the things in the world [to examine and understand their principle]. As long as anything is not yet entered into, there is still something outside the mind. The mind of ordinary people is limited to the narrowness of what is seen and what is heard. The sage, however, fully develops his nature and does not allow what is seen or heard to fetter his mind. He regards everything in the world to be his own self. This is why Mencius said that if one exerts his mind to the utmost, he can know nature and Heaven. Heaven is so vast that there is nothing outside of it. Therefore the mind that leaves something outside is not capable of uniting itself with the mind of Heaven. Knowledge coming from seeing and hearing is knowledge obtained through contact with things. It is not knowledge obtained through one's moral nature. Knowledge obtained through one's moral nature does not originate from seeing or hearing.[81]

This possibility, that one can enter into all the things in the world

and that one can obtain knowledge through one's moral nature without the sensory perceptions of seeing and hearing, is never allowed in Kant's philosophy. In fact, the kind of intellectual intuition that is necessary for apprehending things as they are is, from the Kantian point of view, humanly impossible.

Kant's considered opinion that it is impossible that human beings are capable of apprehending things-in-themselves through intellectual intuition seems to signify not only his own idiosyncratic approach to philosophy but a basic assumption in Western thought. To be sure, following Heidegger's interpretation, the reason why Kant is barred, in principle, from actually bringing the "fundamental ontology" to fruition is in a way connected with this:

> In the broadest terms, the reason lies in Kant's inability or perhaps his ultimate reluctance to shake loose from the metaphysics of objectivity, from the assumption that the meaning of being is adequately determined in function of the relation of being-an-object-for-subjectivity.[82]

However, as Ernst Cassirer observes, Kant's alleged "turning from the metaphysical realism of the external world to a concern about man, the basis of his finitude, and the relationship between his finitude and the question of being which he is ontologically structured and impelled to raise"[83] is basically a Heideggerian imposition on the philosophical intention of Kant.[84]

It should be mentioned in this connection that Husserl, not unlike Fichte on this particular point, also sharply criticized Kant's failure or refusal to acknowledge an intuitive knowledge of the acting ego.[85] In the words of James Collins, Husserl's argument is as follows:

> The Kantian method of regressive reconstruction of the conditions of possibility for judgments in the mode of scientific objectivity is lacking precisely in that *intellectual intuition* which could save it from becoming lost in objectivity, and could complete the turn toward the life of subjectivity. Hence there is no Kantian experience of the transcendental life of the ego, the I-actuality which is not just the ego-pole correlated with the objective world.[86]

Whether or not Husserl's "transcendental phenomenology" can furnish both the method of understanding and the reflective experience itself of the pure ego, the central problem of Kant and by extension a most important issue in Western philosophy is now identified.

The claim that the "simple and easy" method of the Neo-Confucians consists fundamentally in taking intellectual intuition for granted as an inner ability of man is not likely to satisfy the critical mind of a Husserl or a Heidegger, but as Mou Tsung-san suggests, if taken seriously this mode of thinking, by whatever name one calls it, has the potential of bringing forth a philosophical vision more congenial to Kant's original insight than either the Husserlian phenomenology or the Heideggerian ontology.[87]

As already mentioned, the fourth Kantian question, What is man? must be added to the three major problem areas in philosophy. It can be further argued, as Heidegger has already done in his reflection on Kant, that the question of human nature, in terms of the magnitude of philosophical importance, actually precedes problems of knowing (epistemology), doing (psychology), and hoping (theology). Of course, this by no means suggests that the science of man (anthropology) alone is the fundamental discipline of philosophy. In Neo-Confucianism as well as in Heidegger's thought, there is the necessity of developing an intrinsic relationship between the problem of man and a laying of the foundation of metaphysics.[88] However, while Heidegger focuses his attention on the finitude in man and thus on the importance of *Dasein* as temporality, the governing perspective in Neo-Confucian thought is the realization of humanity in the absolute unity of man and Heaven. The central question for the Neo-Confucians is, then, How can I really know my true self? or, put in the context of the above discussion, How can I cultivate my capacity for intellectual intuition as a way of manifesting my true self and participating in the fundamental unity of the cosmos? To borrow from Mou Tsung-san, the question can be simply restated as the ontological possibility of intellectual intuition for human beings.[89]

NOTES

1. Although the expression first occurs in the *Book of Mencius*, "Our body and complexion are given to us by Heaven. Only a sage can give his body complete fulfillment (*chien-hsing*)," the concept is widely used in Neo-Confucian literature. Literally meaning to bring one's bodily design to fulfillment, *chien-hsing* makes it clear that self-cultivation in the Confucian sense, far from being a form of asceticism, is aimed at a complete realization of the person, body as well as mind. See D. C. Lau, trans., *Mencius* (Middlesex, England: Penguin Classics, 1970), VIIA:38, p. 191.

2. For a brief discussion of this issue, see Tu Wei-ming, "Toward an Integrated Study on Confucianism," *Aken des XIV. Internationalen Kongresses für Philosophie* (Wien, 1968), VI, 532–537.

3. For instance, the late Snologist Étienne Balazs characterized all Chinese philosophy as preeminently social philosophy; "even when it attempts to detach itself from the temporal world and arrive at some form of pure, transcendental metaphysics there can be no hope of understanding it without recognizing its point of departure to which sooner or later it returns." See his "Political Philosophy and Social Crisis in the End of Han," in Étienne Balazs, *Chinese Civilization and Bureaucracy: Variations on a Theme*, trans. by H. W. Wright, ed. by Arthur F. Wright (New Haven: Yale University Press, 1964), p. 195.

4. For a discussion on the Later Stoa, see Frederick Copleston, S. J., *A History of Philosophy: Greece & Rome*, Vol. I, Pt. II (New York: Doubleday, 1962), pp 172–181. It is interesting to note that Marcus Aurelius' *Meditations*, so far as its aphoristic statements are concerned, is compatible with some of the collected sayings of the Neo-Confucian masters.

5. The Sagely Way (*sheng-jer chih tao*) is also known as the "learning of the body and mind" (*shen-hsin chih hsüeh*) or the "teaching of mind and human nature" (*hsin-hsing chih chiao*). The emphasis in all three cases is on the problem of how to become a sage through moral self-cultivation.

6. It is interesting to compare this observation with the following statement in the *Book of Mencius*: "[The Sage-King Shun] followed the path of morality. He did not just put morality into practice," D. C. Lau, trans., *Mencius*, IVB:19, p. 131. Of course, the idea of "following" in this connection signifies that, instead of putting morality into practice as an object, Shun, who had embodied morality in his life, was able to walk in its path without exerting any artificial effort.

7. See *Chou Tzu t'ung-shu*, SPPY edition (Taipei: Cheng-chung Book Co., 1966; reprint), XX, 4b. For this translation, see W. T. Chan, *A Source Book in Chinese Philosophy* (Princeton: Princeton University Press, 1969), p. 473.

8. For Chu Hsi's comment, see the *Cheng-i-t'ang ch'üan-shu* (1896) edition of *T'ung-shu* or the *Wan-yu wen-k'u* edition of *Chou Tzu ch'üan-shu*, p. 165. Also see Wing-tsit Chan, *A Source Book*, pp. 473–474.

9. *Chou Tzu t'ung-shu*, II, 1a

10. *Ibid.* See Wing-tsit Chan *A Source Book*, p. 466.

11. I have made a general analysis of the concept of *ch'eng* in a monographic study of the *Doctrine of the Mean* in *Centrality and Commonality: An Essay on Chung-yung* (Honolulu: The University of Hawaii Press, 1976), pp. 106–141.

12. *Chou Tzu t'ung-shu*, IV, 1b. See Wing-tsit Chan, *A Source Book*, p. 457.

13. *Chou Tzu t'ung-su*, IV, 1b Wing-tsit Chan, p. 467.

14. D. C. Lau, trans., *Mencius*, VIIB:25, p. 199. It should be noted that the Chinese character *shen* is more commonly rendered as "spiritual."

15. See Chu Hsi's comment on this statement in his *Ssu-shu chi-chu*, quoted in Shih Tz'u-yün, annotated *Meng Tzu chin-chu chin-i* (Taipei: Commercial Press, 1973), p. 403, note 7. It should be noted that in making this remark, Chu Hsi cites a statement from Ch'eng Tzu (either Ch'eng Hao or Ch'eng I) to support his point.

16. *Chung-yung*, XXII: Wing-tsit Chan. *A Source Book*, p. 107–108. The concept of "moral metaphysics" (*tao-te hsing-shang-hsüeh*) is developed by Mou Tsung-san in the light of Kant's *Foundations of the Metaphysics of Morals*; see his *Hsin-t'i yü hsing-t'i* [Mind and Nature] in 3 vols. (Taipei: Cheng-chung Book Co., 1968), I, 115–189.

17. D. C. Lau, trans., *Mencius*, IIIA:1, p. 96.

18. For a reference to Yen Yüan (Yen Hui or Yen Tzu), see *Analects*, 6:2. The complete essay is found in *I-ch'üan wen-chi*, 4:1a–2a. According to Chu Hsi, the essay was composed by Ch'eng I when he was only eighteen years old; see *Chu Tzu yü-lei* (1880 edition), 93:9a Yao Ming-ta contends that it can be dated even earlier; see his *Ch'eng I-ch'uan nien-p'u*, p. 16. The above information is taken from W. T. Chan, *A Source Book*, p. 547, note 19. For the translated statement, see W. T. Chan, p. 547.

19. See W. T. Chan, p. 548.

20. Immanuel Kant, *Foundations of the Metaphysics of Morals*, trans. Lewis White Beck (New York: The Bobbs-Merrill Co., 1959), p. 5.

21. Ibid.

22. Ibid., p. 23.

23. Ibid., pp. 23–24.

24. Ibid., p. 24.

25. Ibid., pp. 29–30.

26. Ibid., p. 33. For a brief discussion on the idea of a practical *law*, see *ibid.*, p. 37.

27. Ibid., p. 43.

28. Ibid., p. 44.

29. Ibid., p. 50.

30. Ibid., p. 51.

31. In the words of James Collins, see his *Interpreting Modern Philosophy* (Princeton: Princeton University Press, 1972), p. 310. Also see Heidegger, *Kant and the Problem of Metaphysics*, trans. by James S. Churchill (Bloomington: Indiana University Press, 1962), p. 222.

32. Heidegger, *Kant*, pp. 173–174.

33. Ibid., pp. 214–215.

34. It is interesting to note that while Kant makes it explicit that the categorical imperative cannot be derived from the constitution of human nature (*Metaphysics of Morals*, p. 43), Heidegger asserts that "metaphysics, with the laying of the foundation of which we are concerned, belongs to 'human nature.'" (*Kant*, p. 176).

35. Kant, *Metaphysics of Morals*, p. 75.

36. Ibid., pp. 79–80.

37. Heidegger, *Kant*, p. 220.

38. Ibid., p. 221.

39. For Mou Tsung-san's interpretive position, see his *Chih te chih-chüeh yü Chung-kuo che-hsüeh* [Intellectual intuition and Chinese philosophy] (Taipei: Commercial, 1971), pp. 346–367. It should be noted that although in his *Hsin-t'i yü hsing-t'i* (1968) Professor Mou hardly mentions Heidegger, his recent study on "intellectual intuition and Chinese philosophy" takes Heidegger's reflection on Kant as its point of departure; see *Chih-te chih-chüeh yü Chung-kuo che-hsüeh*, pp. 24–59.

40. These are the opening lines of the *Hsi-ming* ("Western Inscription"). Originally entitled *Ting-wan* ("Rectifying Obstinacy"), the essay was inscribed on the western wall of Chang Tsai's study. Thus Ch'eng I later gave it the new title "Western Inscription." See Wing-tsit Chan, *A Source Book*, p. 497; also cf. note 2 on the same page. It should be noted that the same lines are rendered somewhat differently by Siu-chi Huang: "Heaven (*ch'ien*) is my father, and earth (*k'un*) is my mother; I, as a small, finite being, occupy a central position between them. Therefore, what fills heaven and earth is my body (*t'i*), and what commands heaven and earth is my Nature (*hsing*). All men are my brothers, and all things are my companions." See her "The Moral Point of View of Chang Tsai," *Philosophy East and West* XXI (1971), 141.

41. Joseph Needham has made some very insightful observations on this point. For his characterization of the Neo-Confucian view of the universe as "organic," see his "History of Scientific Thought" in *Science and Civilization in China* (Cambridge: Cambridge University Press, 1969), II, 412, 502. Although Needham here only refers to the "organic naturalism" of the Ch'eng-Chu (or Hsing-li) school, it can well be argued that the Lu-Wang (or Hsin) school also subscribes to this cosmological view.

42. Actually Chou Tun-i states, "It is man alone who receives (the Five Agents) in their highest excellence, and therefore he is most intelligent." See his *T'ai-chi-t'u shuo*, which is translated in full by Wing-tsit Chan, *A Source Book*, p. 463.

43. *Chung-yung*, I.

44. See Tu Wei-ming, *Centrality and Commonality*, pp. 1–2, 19–22.

45. *Cheng-meng*, I:1. See Wing-tsit Chan, *A Source Book*, p. 500.

46. *Cheng-meng*, I:2, See Wing-tsit Chan, p. 501.

47. Ibid., I:3; see Wing-tsit Chan, p. 501.

48. Ibid.

49. The idea of the oneness of reality and the multiplicity of its manifestations has exercised tremendous influence on Neo-Confucian thought. However, the implication of this seminal idea has to be understood in the context of Chang Tsai's philosophy. For some helpful suggestions in this regard, see T'ang Chün-i, "Chang Tsai's Theory of Mind and Its Metaphysical Basis," *Philosophy East and West* VI (1956), 113–136; T'ang Chün-i, "Spirit and Development of Neo-Confucianism," in Arne Naess and Alastair Hannay, eds., *Invitation to Chinese Philosophy* (Oslo: Universaitets-forlaget, 1972), pp. 56–83; Siu-chi Huang, "Chang Tsai's Concept of Ch'i," *Philosophy East and West* SVIII (1968), 245–259; Siu-chi Huang, "The Moral Point of View of Chang Tsai," *Philosophy East and West* XXI (1971), 141–156; Wing-tsit Chan, "Neo-Confucian Solution to the Problem of Evil," *Studies Presented to Hu Shih on His Sixty-fifth Birthday* (Tapei: Academia Sinica, 1957), pp. 780–783; Wing-tsit Chan, *A Source Book*, p. 495; and Joseph Needham, *Science and Civilization in China*, II, 472–485.

50. *Cheng-meng*, V, SPPY edition, 2:16b. See Wing-tsit Chan, *A Source Book*, p. 515. In Chan's translation, *I Ching* is rendered as *Book of Changes*.

51. Wing-tsit Chan, p. 508. For the quotation from the *Doctrine of Mean*, see *Chung-yung* XXV.

52. Martin Heidegger, *An Introduction to Metaphysics*, trans. by Ralph Manheim (New York: Doubleday, 1961), p. 34.

53. Quoted by Heidegger from *The Twilight of Idols*, in Nietzsche's *Complete Works* (Edinburgh and London: Heinemann, 1911)). XVI, 19. See Heidegger, *Metaphysics*, p. 29.

54. Wing-tsit Chan, *A Source Book*, p. 503.

55. Ibid.

56. Ibid., p. 504.

57. Ibid., p. 508.

58. Ibid., p. 59.

59. Ibid., pp. 504–505.

60. To be sure, it is still problematical whether by identifying the principle solely with human nature and by characterizing the mind as a refined stuff of material force, Chu Hsi has emphasized man's ability to attain sagehood through self-effort as strongly as the Neo-Confucian thinkers in the Lu-Wang tradition. But it is undeniable that, although Chu Hsi time and again stresses the importance of learning, he strongly believes that "each person has the inner ability to know and experience ultimate reality in its all-embracing fullness." For a thought-provoking interpretation of Chu Hsi's position on this issue, see Mou Tsung-san, *Hsin-t'i yü hsing-t'i*, III, 464–485.

61. "Shih-jen" in *Erh-Ch'eng i-shu*, 2A:3a–b. See Wing-tsit Chan, *A Source Book*, p. 524.

62. Ibid., p. 530.

63. Heidegger, *Metaphysics*, p. 117.

64. Wing-tsit Chan, *A Source Book*, p. 539.

65. Ibid., p. 527.

66. Ibid., p. 533.

67. The whole statement reads as follows: "All the ten thousand things are there in me. There is no greater joy for me than to find, on self-examination, that I am true to myself. Try your best to treat others as you would wish to be treated yourself, and you will find that this is the shortest way to benevolence [humanity]." See D. C. Lau, trans., *Mencius*, VIIA:4, p. 182, Also see Wing-tsit Chan, *A Source Book*, p. 534.

68. Wing-tsit Chan, *A Source Book* p. 534.

69. Ibid., p. 526.

70. Ibid., p. 532.

71. Heidegger, *Metaphysics*, p. 172.

72. Wing-tsit Chan, *A Source Book*, p. 524.

73. D. C. Lau, trans. *Mencius*, IIA:2, p. 78.

74. Wing-tsit Chan, *A Source Book*, p. 524.

75. Ibid., p. 532.

76. Heidegger, *Metaphysics*, p. 110.

77. Wing-tsit Chan, *A Source Book*, p. 533.

78. Ibid.

79. Ibid., p. 508. It should be noted that some deletions have been made. The original statement reads: "The reason why the man of humanity and the filial son can serve Heaven and be sincere with himself is simply that they are unceasing in their humanity and filial piety."

80. Heidegger, *Metaphysics*, p. 119.

81. Wing-tsit Chan, *A Source Book*, p. 515.

82. James Collins, *Interpreting Modern Philosophy*, p. 301.

83. Ibid. For a brief discussion of the Cassirer-Heidegger Seminar of 1929 in Davos, Switzerland, see ibid., pp. 201–203.

84. For a summary of Cassirer's critique of Heidegger's interpretation of Kant as well as other Heideggerian themes, see Carl H. Hamburg, "A Cassirer-Heidegger Seminar," *Philosophy and Phenomenological Research* XXV (1964–65), 208–222.

85. James Collins, *Interpreting Modern Philosophy*, p. 295.

86. Ibid., Italics added.

87. See Mou Tsung-san, *Chih-te chih-chüeh yü Chung-kuo che-hsüeh*, pp. 184–202. Although Professor Mou does not seem to have discussed Husserl's phenomenology in his published studies, it is clear that in his forthcoming monograph on "phenomenon and thing-in-itself," his single-minded attention to Kant's problematics is by implication a critique not only of Heidegger but also of Husserl.

88. Heidegger, *Kant*, p. 225.

89. Mou Tsung-san, p. 157.

Epilogue, "Embodying the Universe: A Note on Confucian Self-realization"

Personality, in the Confucian perception, is an achieved state of moral excellence rather than a given human condition. An implied distinction is made between what a person is by temperament and what a person has become by self-conscious effort. A person's natural disposition — whether introverted or extroverted, passive or aggressive, cold or warm, contemplative or active, shy or assertive — is what the Confucians refer to as that aspect of human nature which is composed of *ch'i-chih* (vital energy and raw stuff). For the sake of convenience, we may characterize the human nature of vital energy and raw stuff as our psychophysiological nature, our physical nature, or simply the body.[1]

The Confucian tradition — in fact, the Chinese cultural heritage as a whole — takes our physical nature absolutely seriously. Self-cultivation, as a form of mental and physical rejuvenation involving such exercises as rhythmic bodily movements and breathing techniques, is an ancient Chinese art. The classical Chinese concept of medicine is healing in the sense not only of curing disease or preventing sickness but also of restoring the vital energy essential for the wholeness of the body. Since the level of vital energy required for health varies according to sex, age, weight, height, occupation, time, and circumstance, the wholeness of the body is situationally defined as a dynamic process rather than a static structure. The maintenance of health, accordingly, is a fine art encompassing a wide range of environmental, dietary, physiological, and psychological factors. The delicate balance attained and sustained is the result of communal as well as personal effort. To become well and sound is therefore an achievement.

171

However, the centrality of the physical nature (the body) in the Confucian conception of the person is predicated not only on the irreducibility of the vital energy and raw stuff for personal growth but also on the potentiality of the body to become an aesthetic expression of the self. The wholeness of the body, often understood as allowing the vital energy to flow smoothly, is not only a measuring standard but also a unique accomplishment. Indeed, the idea is laden with ethico-religious as well as psychophysiological implications.[2] When Mencius defines the sage (who has attained the highest moral excellence in the human community) as the person who has brought the bodily form to fruition,[3] he assumes that the body is where the deepest human spirituality dwells. Yet, it is important to note that the Mencian conception of sagehood involves much more than our physical nature.

It seems that the conscious refusal to accept, rather than the lack of conceptual apparatus to perceive, the exclusive dichotomy between body and mind prompts the Confucians to endow rich resources to the idea of the body as the proper home for human flourishing. The ascetic rigor deemed necessary for reaching a higher spiritual state in virtually all major religions is practiced in the Confucian tradition, but the attention is not focused on self-denial, let alone immolation of the body. The Confucians do not take the body as, by nature, an impediment to full self-realization. To them, the body provides the context and the resources for ultimate self-transformation.

Understandably, Confucian education takes the "ritualization of the body" as the point of departure in the development of the person.[4] Lest the purpose be misconstrued as the imposition of well-established societal norms of behavior upon the innocent youth, "ritualization" as a dynamic process of interpersonal encounter and personal growth is not passive socialization but active participation in recognizing, experiencing, interpreting, and representing the communicative rationality that defines society as a meaningful community. In other words, through ritualization we learn not only the form of the accepted behavior but the grammar of action underlying the form as well. Surely, on the surface at least, it seems that we are socialized unsuspectingly, if not totally against our will, to become members of a linguistic and cultural community. We really do not have much choice in adopting the linguistic specificities of our mother tongue and the cultural particularities of our fatherland.

Nevertheless, the Confucians believe that if we make a conscientious effort to actively incorporate the societal norms and values in our own conduct, we will be able to transcend the linguistic and cultural constraints of our society by transforming them into instruments of self-realization. Like poets who have mastered the subtleties of the language, articulating their innermost thoughts through them, Confucians who have become thoroughly proficient in the nuances of the ritual are said to be able to establish and enlarge others as well as themselves by bringing this personal knowledge to bear on daily practical living. The seeming naïveté of the Confucians in accepting their own linguistic and cultural universe as intrinsically meaningful and valuable is based on the collective judgment that the survival and continuation of their civilization is not a given reality but a communal attainment. This judgment is itself premised on a fundamental faith in the transformability and perfectibility of the human condition through communal self-effort.

Actually, for the Confucians, the intellectual recognition and experiential acceptance of the body as the point of departure for personal growth are the result of a strong commitment to a holistic view of self-realization. The body, as our physical nature, must be transformed and perfected so that it can serve as a vehicle for realizing that aspect of our nature known as the nature of *i-li* (rightness and principle), the moral nature, or simply the heart-mind (*hsin*).[5] Even though the body is a constitutive part of our nature, it is the heart-mind that is truly human.

A person's temperament may significantly determine his natural disposition in a social environment. Whether he is introverted, passive, cold, contemplative, and shy, or extroverted, aggressive, warm, active, and assertive may very well be a reflection of his native endowments. Quite a few Chinese thinkers, for pragmatic and bureaucratic considerations as well as for social and aesthetic ones, have been fascinated by the classification and evaluation of distinctive character traits. A third-century treatise on the categorization of human beings according to talent and disposition remains to this day a comprehensive treatment and sophisticated analysis of personality types.[6] However, despite the importance and irreducibility of the vital energy and raw stuff (the physical nature or the body) that we are endowed with, the main concern of Confucian education is the process through which we realize ourselves by transforming and perfecting what we are born with.

THE HEART-MIND AND HUMAN SENSITIVITY

As Mencius notes, in regard to physical nature, the difference between humans and animals (birds or beasts) is quite small. What truly distinguishes human beings from animals is not the body but the heart-mind. Since the body is the proper home in which the heart-mind dwells, it is perhaps more appropriate to say that the heart-mind (in addition to the body or the body fully informed by the heart-mind) specifically defines the uniqueness of being human. Learning to be human means that the self-consciousness of the heart-mind initiates a process by which the body is transformed and perfected. The ritualization of the body can thus be understood as the active participation of the heart-mind to help the body to become a fitting expression of the self in a social context. To be sure, an act of the will or an existential decision is required when the heart-mind becomes fully aware of its role and function in bringing this process to fruition. For Confucius, the critical juncture occurred when he "set his heart upon learning" at fifteen.[7] However, even the very young, when involved in simple rituals such as sprinkling water for the adults to sweep the floor or giving answers of yes or no to easy questions, exercise their hearts and minds in ritualizing their bodies. It is precisely because the heart-mind is housed in the body (although in practice it can be absent from it) that the human body takes on the profound spiritual significance that distinguishes it from the physical nature of birds and beasts. As a corollary, the body devoid of the heart-mind, is, strictly speaking, no longer human and can easily degenerate into a state of unreflexivity indistinguishable from the physical nature of birds and beasts.

The most prominent feature of the heart-mind is sympathy, the ability to share the suffering of others. This is why the Chinese character *hsin* — like the French word *conscience*, which involves both cognitive and affective dimensions of consciousness — must be rendered as "heart-mind": For *hsin* signifies both intellectual awareness and moral awakening. By privileging sympathy as the defining characteristic of true humanity, Confucians underscore feeling as the basis for knowing, willing, and judging. Human beings are therefore defined primarily by their sensitivity and only secondarily by their rationality, volition, or intelligence.

EXPANDING SENSITIVITY: THE PERFECTION OF THE SELF

Learning to be human, in this sense, is to learn to be sensitive to an ever-expanding network of relationships. It may appear to be a consciousness-raising proposition, but it entails the dynamic process of transforming the body as a private ego to the body as an all-encompassing self. To use the Confucian terminology of Master Ch'eng Hao (1032–1085), the whole enterprise involves the realization of the authentic possibility of "forming one body with Heaven, Earth, and the myriad things."[8] Concretely, for Confucians, in learning to be human beings by cultivating the capacity to empathize with the negative feelings of one's closest kin—namely, by directly referring to our own hearts and minds—we should understand the reasonableness of the following dictum: "Do not do unto others what I would not want others to do unto me!"[9]

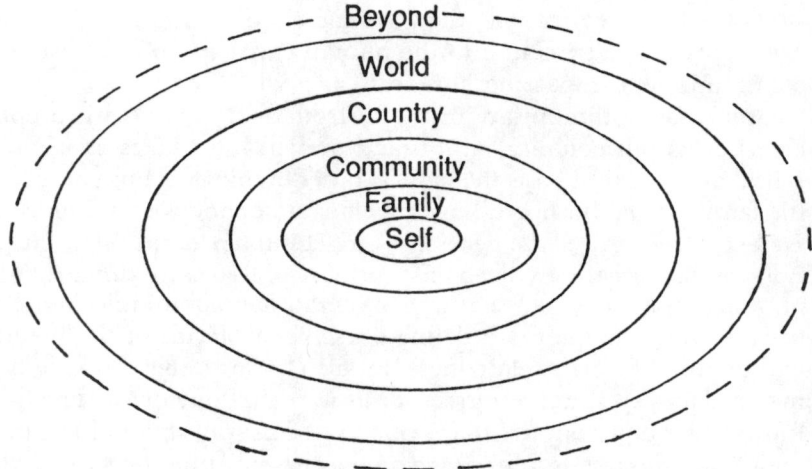

Figure 1. The Broadening Process of the Self

The ability to feel the suffering of others or the inability to endure their suffering empowers us to establish an experiential connection with another human being. This provides a great resource for realizing our moral nature (the nature of rightness and principle). The Confucians believe that our sympathetic bonding to our parents is

not only biologically natural but morally imperative, for it is the first step in learning to apprecate ourselves not in isolation but in communication. Indeed, since the Confucians perceive the self as a center of relationships rather than as an isolable individuality, the ability to show intimacy to those who are intimate is vitally important for allowing the closed private ego to acquire a taste for the open communicating self so that the transformation of the body can start on a concrete experiential basis.

But if we extend sympathy only to our parents, we take no more than the initial step toward self-realization. By embodying our closest kin in our sensitivity, we may have gone beyond egoism, but without the learned ability to enter into fruitful communication outside the immediate family, we are still confined to nepotism. Like egoism, nepotism fails to extend our sensitivty to embody a larger network of human relationships and thus limits our capacity for self-realization. Similarly, parochialism, ethnocentrism, and chauvinistic nationalism are all varying degrees of human insensitivity. In the dymanic process of self-realization, they are inertia or limitation. In either case, they are detrimental to the human capacity for establishing a community encompassing humanity as a whole.

Confucian communitarianism, far from being a romantic utopian assertion about equality, unity, and universality, takes as its theoretical and practical basis the natural order of things in human society: the family, neighborhood, kinship, clan, state, and world (Figure 1). In fact, it recognizes the necessity and legitimacy of these structures, both as historically evolved institutions and socially differentiated organizations. They are natural to the human community not only because they enable us to define ourselves in terms of the breadth and depth of human-relatedness but also because they provide both material and spiritual resources for us to realize ourselves. The Confucians do not accept the status quo as necessarily rational. Actually their main mission is to improve on the current situation by bridging the gap between what the status quo is and what it can and ought to be. Confucians are in the world but not of the world. They take an active role in changing the world by managing it from within; instead of adjusting themselves to the status quo, they try to transform it according to their moral idealism.

A salient feature of Confucians' moral idealism is their commitment to the efficacy of education as character building. The Confucian faith in the transformability and perfectibility of the human

condition through communal self-effort implies that personal growth has not only ethical value but political significance. The ritualization of the body is relevant to political leadership as well as to social harmony in the family, neighborhood, and clan. Since Confucians believe that exemplary teaching is an integral part of political leadership, the personal morality of those involved is a precondition for good politics. Politics and morality are inseparable. What political leaders do at home is closely linked not only to their styles of leadership but also to the very nature of their politics. Self-realization, in this sense, is not a lonely quest for one's inner spirituality but a communicative act empowering one to become a responsible householder, an effective community worker, and a conscientious public servant. Confucians may not be successful in their political careers or may choose not to seek office, but they can never abandon their vocation as concerned intellectuals.

A concerned intellectual, the modern counterpart of the Confucian *chün-tzu* (nobleman or profound person), does not seek a spiritual sanctuary outside the world. He is engaged in this world, for total withdrawal from society and politics is not an option. Yet, although to be part of the "secular" world is the Confucian vocation, the Confucian calling is not to serve the status quo but to transform the "secular" world of wealth and power into a "sacred" community in which, despite egoistic drives, the quest for human flourishing in moral, scientific, and aesthetic excellence continuously nourishes our bodies and uplifts our hearts and minds.

THE CEASELESS PROCESS OF HUMAN FLOURISHING

Understandably, to become a mature person (an adult), in the Confucian sense, is not to attain a limited professional or personal goal but to open oneself up to the ceaseless process of human flourishing. The becoming process, rather than an attained state of being, defines the Confucian personality. One's critical self-awareness in the later stages of one's maturation (e.g., at the age of fifty, when Confucius confessed to have known the Mandate of Heaven)[10] ought to be directed to the authentic possibilities of further growth in moral development. Unlike scientific and aesthetic talents, sensitivity

in ethics never declines and, properly cultivated, it becomes more subtle and refined.

Nevertheless, a person becomes a personality not by conscientiously obeying conventional rules of conduct but by exemplifying a form of life worth living; indeed by establishing a standard of self-transformation as a source of inspiration for the human community as a whole. The interchange between an exemplary teacher and the students aspiring to become householders, community workers, or public servants is never one-way. As fellow travelers on the Way, they form a community of the like-minded so that the project of human flourishing becomes a joint venture, mutually admonishing and mutually encouraging. The exemplary teacher as an achieved personality in the eyes of the students must continue to cultivate his inner resources for self-transformation. Confucians do not believe in fixed personalities. While they regard personalities as accomplishments, they insist that the strength of one's personality lies not in its past glories but in its future promises. Real personalities are always evolving. This is why fundamental improvement in the quality of existence is possible for even a human being a breath away from death: "Thou shall not judge the person conclusively before the coffin is sealed!"[11]

This faith in and commitment to the transformability and perfectibility of the human condition through communal self-effort enables Confucians to perceive each person as a center of relationships who is in the process of *ultimate* transformation as a communal act. The "ultimacy" in this seemingly humanistic enterprise is premised on the ability of the human heart-mind, without departing from its proper home (the body), to have the sensitivity to establish an internal resonance with Heaven by fully comprehending its Mandate. Sensitivity so conceived is a "silent illumination." It is neither a gift from an external source nor a knowledge acquired through empirical learning. Rather, it is an inner quality of the heart-mind, the shining wisdom that a ritualized body emits for its own aesthetic expression. Such an expression is neither private nor individualistic, but communal.

As mentioned, for the Confucian to bring self-transformation to fruition (to its ultimacy), he must transcend not merely egoism but nepotism, parochialism, ethnocentrism, and chauvinistic nationalism. These undesirable habits of thought, perceived as varying degrees of human insensitivity, limit the full potential of the silent il-

lumination of the human heart-mind to manifest itself. The Confucian insistence that we must work through our families, communities, and nations to realize ourselves is not at all incompatible with the Confucian injunction that we must go beyond nepotism, parochialism, and chauvinistic nationalism to fully embody our humanity. Actually, the seemingly contradictory assertions signify a dynamic process that defines the richness of the Confucian way of learning to be human.

On the one hand, Confucians, in contrast to individualists, take the communal path by insisting that, as a center of relationships, a personality comes into being by fruitfully interacting with its natural human environment — the family, kin, community, and the state. This process of continuously communicating with an ever-expanding network of human relationships enables the self to embody an increasingly widening circle of inclusiveness in its own sensitivity. On the other hand, Confucians, as opposed to collectivists, firmly establish the "subjectivity" of the person as *suit generis*. No social pro-

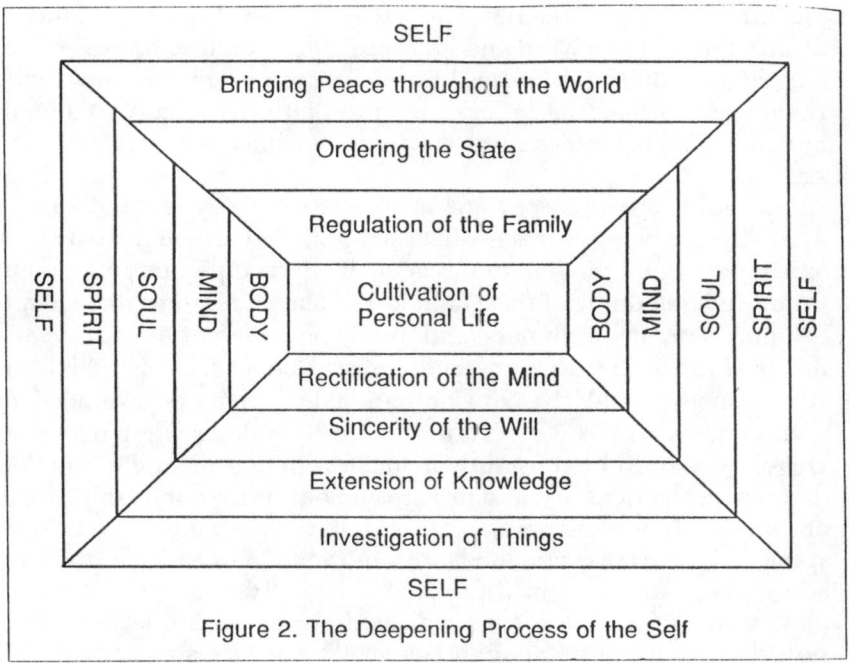

Figure 2. The Deepening Process of the Self

gram, no matter how lofty, can undermine the centrality of selfhood in Confucian learning. After all, Confucians see learning for the sake of the self as the authentic purpose of education. To be sure, the self as an open and communicating center of relationships is intimately connected with other selves; far from being egoistic, it is communal. However, by stressing the centrality of the self in learning to be human, the Confucians advocate ultimate self-transformation, not only as social ethics but also as the flourishing of human nature with profound religious significance.

FORMING ONE BODY WITH EARTH AND MYRIAD THINGS

For Confucians to fully realize themselves, it is not enough to become a responsible householder, effective social worker, or conscientious political servant. No matter how successful one is in the sociopolitical arena, the full measure of one's humanity cannot be accommodated without a reference to Heaven. The highest Confucian ideal is the "unity of Man and Heaven," which defines humanity not only in anthropological terms but also in cosmological terms. In the *Doctrine of the Mean (Chung-yung)*, the most authentic manifestation of humanity is characterized as "forming a trinity with Heaven and Earth."[12]

Yet, since Heaven does not speak and the Way in itself cannot make human beings great—which suggests that although Heaven is omnipresent and may be omniscient, it is certainly not omnipotent—our understanding of the Mandate of Heaven requires that we fully appreciate the rightness and principle inherent in our heart-minds. Our ability to transcend egoism, nepotism, parochialism, ethnocentrism, and chauvinistic nationalism must be extended to anthropocentrism as well. To make ourselves deserving partners of Heaven, we must be constantly in touch with that silent illumination that makes the rightness and principle in our heart-minds shine forth brilliantly. If we cannot go beyond the constraints of our own species, the most we can hope for is an exclusive, secular humanism advocating man as the measure of all things. By contrast, Confucian humanism is inclusive; it is predicated on an "anthropocosmic" vision. Humanity in its all-embracing fullness "forms one body with

Heaven, Earth, and the myriad things." Self-realization, in the last analysis, is ultimate transformation, the process which enables us to embody the family, community, nation, world, and cosmos in our sensitivity (Figure 2).[13]

NOTES

1. According to Chu Hsi (1130–1200), the idea of "physical nature" originated with Chang Tsai (1020–1077). For a general discussion on this, see Wing-tsit Chan, "The Neo-Confucian Solution to the Problem of Evil," *Bulletin of the Institute of History and Philology* 28 (1957), 780–83.

2. For a thought-provoking attempt to formulate an Eastern mind-body theory, see Yuasa Yasuo, *The Body*, ed. T.P. Kasulis (Albany, New York: State University of New York, 1987). It should be noted that Professor Yuasa's attempt is based on his understanding of Japanese Buddhism in general and the thoughts of Dōgen and Kūkai in particular.

3. *Mencius*, 7A:38.

4. For a general discussion on ritualization as humanization, see Tu Wei-ming, "Li as Process of Humanization, *Philosophy East and West*, 22, no. 2 (April 1972), 187–201.

5. *Mencius, 6A:7.*

6. Unfortunately, Liu Shao's *Treatise on Personalities (Jen-wu chih)* is still not yet available in English translation.

7. *Analects*, 2:4.

8. See his essay on "Understanding the Nature of *Jen* (Humanity)," in *A Source Book in Chinese Philosophy*, trans. and comp. Wing-tsit Chan (Princeton: Princeton University Press, 1963), p. 523.

9. *Analects*, 15:23.

10. *Analects*, 2:4.

11. This common expression is still widely used in China. Although it is a popular idiom rather than an assertion in the Confucian classics, it vividly captures the Confucian spirit that self-realization never completes and that, as long as a person lives, he is still redeemable.

12. *Chung-yung (Doctrine of the Mean)*, XXII. For a discussion of this idea in the perspective of Confucian "moral metaphysics," see Tu Wei-ming, *Centrality and Commonality: An Essay on Chung-yung* (Honolulu: The University Press of Hawaii, 1976), pp. 100–141.

13. The two figures in this Epilogue first appeared in Tu Wei-ming, *Confucian Ethics Today: The Singapore Challenge* (Singapore-Federal Publications, 1984), pp. 219 and 221.

Glossary

ai-jen 愛人

Bito Masahide 尾藤正英

Cao Xueqin (see Ts'ao Hsüeh-ch'in)

Chan Wing-tsit 陳榮捷

Ch'an 禪

Chang Li-wen 張立文

Chang Tai-nien 張岱年

Chang Tsai 張載

Ch'en Wen Tzu 陳文子

Cheng 鄭

Cheng-chung 正中

cheng-hsin 正心

Cheng-i-t'ang ch'üan-shu 正誼堂全書

ch'eng (sincerity) 誠

ch'eng (complete) 成

chèng-chi 成己

Ch'eng-Chu 程朱

Ch'eng Hao 程顥

Ch'eng I 程頤

chèng-i 誠意

Ch'eng I-ch'uan nien-p'u 程伊川年譜

chèng-jen 成人

Ch'eng Tzu 程子

chi 幾

Chi-lu 季路

ch'i 氣

chia (family) 家

chia (false) 假

chiao 教

chien 健

chien-hsing 踐形

ch'ien 乾

Ch'ien-Chia 乾嘉

chih (intelligence) 知

chih (extension) 致

chih-chih 致知

chih liang-chih 致良知

chih te chih-chüeh 智的直覺

Chih te chih-chüeh yü Chung-kuo che-hsüeh 智的直覺與中國哲學

ch'in 親

ching 敬

Ching-hsiu hsien-sheng wen-chi 靜修先生文集

Ch'ing 清

Ch'iu 丘

Chou I (see *Chou-i*)

Chou-i 周易

Chou Li (see Chou-li)

Chou-li 周禮

Chou-li chu-shu 周禮注疏

Chou Tun-i 周敦頤

Chou Tzu ch'üan-shu 周子全書

Chou Tzu t'ung-shu 周子通書

chu 助

Chu Hsi 朱熹

Chu Tzu yü-lei 朱子語類

chü-ching ch'iung-li 居敬窮理

chün-tzu 君子

Chuang Tzu 莊子

Chuang Tzu yin-te 莊子引得

chung 忠

Chung-hua 中華

Chung-kuo che-hsüeh fa-wei 中國哲學發微

Chung-kuo che-hsüeh shih yen-chiu 中國哲學史研究

"Chung-kuo hsiao-tao ssu-hsiang te 中國孝道思想

    hsing-ch'eng yen-pien chi-ch'i 的形成演變及其

    tsai li-shih chung te chu-wen-t'i" 在歷史中的諸問題

Chung-kuo i-shu ching-shen 中國藝術精神

Chung-kuo ssu-hsiang t'ung shih 中國思想通史

Chung-kuo ssu-hsiang shih lun-chi 中國思想史論集

Chung-kuo wen-hua hsin-lun 中國文化新論

Chung-yung 中庸

Dai Kan-Wa ji-ten 大漢和字典

Daishū Kan 大修館

erh-te 耳德

Fang K'e-li 方克立

Fang Ying-hsien 方穎嫻

Feng Ch'i 馮契

Fu Hsi-hua 傅惜華

fu-jen chih jen 婦人之仁

Fung Yu-lan 馮友蘭

Han 漢

han-yang hsü yung ching 涵養須用敬

   chin-hsüeh tsai chih-chih 進學在致知

Hou Wai-lu 侯外廬

Hsi-ming 西銘

Hsi-yu chi 西遊記

"Hsiang-tang" 鄉黨

hsiao-t'i 小體

Hsieh 契

hsien li-hu ch'i ta-che 先立乎其大者

hsin (heart-and-mind) 心

hsin (true, faithfulness) 信

hsin-hsing chih chiao 心性之教

Hsin-t'i yü hsing-t'i 心體與性體

hsing (nature) 性

hsing (form) 形

Hsing-li 性理

hsing-sheng 形生

hsü 虛

"Hsü-hsüeh" 叙學

Hsü Fu-kuan 徐復觀

Hsü Shen 許慎

hsüeh 學

hsüeh tso-jen 學作人

Hsün Tzu 荀子

Hu Shih 胡適

Hu Shih wen-ts'un 胡適文存

Hua 華

hua-sheng 化生

Huang-Lao 黃老

Huang Siu-chi 黃秀璣

Huang Ti 黃帝

Hung-lou meng 紅樓夢

Hui 回

i (art) 藝

i (righteousness) 義

i (meaning, intention) 意

I Ching (see *I-ching*)

I-ching 易經

I-ch'uan wen-chi 伊川文集

I Yin 伊尹

Jan Ch'iu 冉求

jen 仁

jen-cheng 仁政

Jen-min 人民

jen-yü 人欲

ju 儒

kan-ying 感應

Kao Yu-kung 高友工

k'e-chi fu-li 克己復禮

ko-i 格義

ko-wu 格物

k'un 坤

kung-fu 工夫

Kung Kung 共工

Kung-sun Ch'ou 公孫丑

K'ung Tzu chia-yü 孔子家語

kuo 國

Lao Tzu 老子

Lee Kwang Kyu 李光奎

Lee Sang-eun 李相殷

Li (the *Book of Rites*) 禮

li (ritual) 禮

li (principle) 理

Li-chi chin-chu chin-i 禮記今註今譯

li-chih 立志

li-i fen-shu 理一分殊

liang-chih 良知

Lien-ching 聯經

Lien-hsi 濂溪

Lin Fang 林放

Liu-hsia Hui 柳下惠

liu-i 六藝

Liu Tsung-chou 劉宗周

Liu Yin 劉因

Lu Hsiang-shan 陸象山

Lu-Wang 陸王

Lü Tsu-ch'ien 呂祖謙

Ma-wang-tui 馬王堆

Maruyama Masao 丸山眞男

mei 美

Meng Tzu chin-chu chin-i 孟子今註今譯

Ming 明

ming 命

Morioka Kiyomi 山根常男

Morohashi Tetsuji 諸橋轍次

Mou Tsung-san 牟宗三

nei 內

Pai-she-chuan chi 白蛇傳集

Pai-she ku-shih yen-chiu 白蛇故事研究

P'an Chiang-tung 潘江東

P'ang P'u 龐樸

pao 報

Pao-yü 寶玉

Park Song-bae 朴性培

pen 本

pen-t'i 本體

Po I 伯夷

pu-jen 不仁

pu-jen chih hsin 不忍之心

pu-neng 不能

pu-wei 不爲

san-kang 三綱

shan 善

shan-ch'uan ching-ying 山川精英

"Shan-ch'uan ching-ying — 山川精英 —

    yü te i-shu" 玉的藝術

Shang 商

Shao 韶

shen (spirit) 神

shen (body) 身

shen-chiao 身敎

shen-hsin chih hsüeh 身心之學

shen-hui 神會

shen-jen 神人

shen-tu 愼獨

sheng 聖

sheng-jen chih tao 聖人之道

Shih 詩

"Shih-jen" 識仁

Shih-san-ching chu-shu 十三經注疏

"Shih-t'an Chung-kuo che-hsûeh 試談中國哲學

　　chung te san-ko chi-tiao" 中的三個基調

shih-tao 師道

Shih Tz'u-yün 史次耘

Shu 蜀

shu 恕

Shun 舜

"Shuo ju" 說儒

Shuo-wen 說文

Sofue Takao 祖父江孝男

Song-bae Park (see Park Song-bae)

ssu (think) 思

ssu ("self") 私

Ssu-shu chi-chu 四書集註

ssu-yü 私欲

suan-shu 算術

Suenari Michio 末成道穗

Sun K'ang-i 孫康宜

Sung-Ming 宋明

ta (great) 大

ta (convey, reach) 達

ta-hua 大化

Ta-lu tsa-chih 大陸雜誌

ta-pen 大本

"Ta-ssu-t'u" 大司徒

ta-t'i 大體

ta-t'ung 大同

t'ai-chi 太極

T'ai-chi-t'u shuo 太極圖說

t'ai-ho 太和

t'ai-hsü 太虛

Tai-yüan 太原

Takao Sofue (see Sofue Takao)

T'ang Chün-i 唐君毅

T'ang I-chieh 湯一介

Tao 道

Tao Chi 道濟

tao-te hsing-shang-hsüeh 道德形上學

te 德

Teng Shu-p'ing 鄧淑蘋

"Ti-kuan" 地官

t'i 體

T'ien 天

t'ien-hsia 天下

t'ien-hsing 天行

t'ien-lai 天籟

t'ien-li 天理

Ting-wan 訂頑

t'ing-te 聽德

ts'ai 宰

tsao-wu chu 造物主

Ts'ao Hsüeh-ch'in 曹雪芹

Tseng Tzu 曾子

ts'un-hsin 存心

Tu Wei-ming 杜維明

t'ui 推

Tung Chung-shu 董仲舒

T'ung-shu 通書

Tunghai 東海

Tzu-hsia 子夏

tzu-jan 自然

Tzu-lu 子路

Tzu-wen 子文

Wan-yu wen-k'u 萬有文庫

wang 忘

Wang Fu-chih 王夫之

Wang Hsin-chai hsien-sheng ch'üan-chi 王心齋先生全集

Wang Ken 王艮

Wang Liang 王艮

Wang Ling 王鈴

Wang Meng-ou 王夢甌

Wang Su 王肅

Wang Yang-ming 王陽明

wei-chi 爲己

wei-jen 爲人

wu 物

Wu Ch'eng-en 吳承恩

wu-hsing 五行

wu-lun 五倫

wu-yü 無欲

yang 陽

Yang Lien-sheng 楊聯陞

Yao 堯

Yao Ming-ta 姚名達

Yao Tien (see *Yao-tien*)

Yao-tien 堯典

yen 言

yen-chiao 言教

Yen Hui 顏回

Yen Yüan 顏淵

Yen Tzu 顏子

Yi Ching (see *I-ching*)

yin 陰

yu 憂

yu-tao 友道

yü 愚

Yü Kuo-fan 余國藩

yü-lu 語錄

"Yü Nan-tu chu-yu" 與南都諸友

Yüan 元

"Yüan-jen lun—tzu Shih Shu chih 原仁論—自詩書至

   K'ung Tzu shih-tai kuan-nien 孔子時代觀念

   chih yen-pien" 之演變

Yüan-tung 遠東

Yüeh 岳

"Yüeh-chi" 樂記

yung 勇

Zen (see Ch'an)

Bibliography of Tu Wei-ming

1968

"The Creative Tension between *Jen* and *Li*", *Philosophy East and West*, XVIII: 1-2 (January–April 1968), 29-39.

The Quest for Self-Realization — A Study of Wang Yang-ming's Formative Years (1472-1509), thesis presented to the Committee on the Degree of Doctor of Philosophy in History and Far Eastern Languages (Harvard University, 1968), 271 pp.

"Towards an Integrated Study on Confucianism", paper presented to the 14th International Congress of Philosophy (Wien: Akten des XIV Kongresses für Philosophie, 2-9 September, 1968), V:532-537.

1970

Traditional China, coedited with James T. C. Liu (Prentice-Hall, 1970), 179 pp.

San-nien ti hsü-ai 三年的畜艾 (Three years of cultivating the moxa; Taipei: Chih-wen 志文 Book Co., 1970), 191 pp.

"The Unity of Knowing and Acting — From a Neo-Confucian Perspective", in *Philosophy: Theory and Practice*, ed., T. M. P. Mahadevan (Madras: Proceedings of the International Seminar on World Philosophy, December 7-17, 1970), pp. 190-205.

1971

"The Neo-Confucian Concept of Man", *Philosophy East and West* XXI:1 (January 1971), 79-87.

"Mind and Human Nature", review article, *The Journal of Asian Studies*, XXX:3 (May 1971), 642–647.

1972

"*Li* as Process of Humanization", *Philosophy East and West*, XXII:2 (April 1972), 187–201.

1973

"Jih-pen T'ien-li ta-hsüeh ts'ang 'Wang Yang-ming chiang-hsüeh ta-wen ping ch'ih-tu' chüan ch'u-t'an 日本天理大學藏王陽明講學答問並尺牘卷初探 (A preliminary examination of Wang Yang-ming's unpublished letters from the T'ien-li University collection in Japan), *Ta-lu tsa-chih* 大陸雜誌, XLVI:3 (March 1973).

"Subjectivity and Ontological Reality — An Interpretation of Wang Yang-ming's Mode of Thinking", *Philosophy East and West*, XXIII: 1–2 (January–April 1973), 187–205.

"Wang Yang-ming ta Chou Tao-t'ung shu wu-feng" 王陽明答周道通書五封 (Wang Yang-ming's five unpublished letters to Chou Tao-t'ung), *Ta-lu tsa-chih*, XLVII:2 (August 1973).

"On the Spiritual Development of Confucius' Personality", paper read at the XXVII International Congress of Orientalists in Ann Arbor, Michigan (August 7, 1967), *Ssu-yü yen* 思與言 (Thought and Word), XI:3 (September 1973), 29–37.

1974

"An Introductory Note on Time and Temporality", *Philosophy East and West*, XXIV:2 (April 1974), 119–122.

"Reconstituting the Confucian Tradition", review article, *The Journal of Asian Studies*, XXXIII:3 (May 1974), 441–454.

"An Inquiry into Wang Yang-ming's Four-Sentence Teaching", *The Eastern Buddhist*, new series VII:2 (October 1974), 32–48.

1975

"Yen Yüan: From Inner Experience to Lived Concreteness", in *The Unfolding of Neo-Confucianism*, ed., Wm. T. de Bary (New York: Columbia University Press, 1975), pp. 511–541.

1976

"Ou-yang Te", in *Dictionary of Ming Biography*, eds., L. Carrington Goodrich and Chaoying Fang (New York: Columbia University Press, 1976), pp. 1102–1104.

"The Confucian Perception of Adulthood", *Daedalus*, 105:2 (April 1976), 109–123.

Centrality and Commonality: An Essay on Chung-yung, monograph no. 3 of the Society for Asian and Comparative Philosophy (Honolulu: The University Press of Hawaii, 1976), 181 pp.

"Hsiung Shih-li's Quest for Authentic Existence", in *The Limits of Change*, ed., Charlotte Furth (Cambridge: Harvard University Press, 1976), pp. 242–275; 396–400.

"Transformational Thinking as Philosophy", review article, *Philosophy East and West*, XXVI (January–April 1976), 75–80.

"Confucianism: Symbol and Substance in Recent Times", *Asian Thought and Society: an International Review*, I:1 (April 1976), 42–66.

Jen-wen hsin-ling te chen-tang 人文心靈的震盪 (The resonance of the humanist mind; Taipei: China Times Publication Co., 1976), 197 pp.

Neo-Confucian Thought in Action: Wang Yang-ming's Youth (1472–1509) (Berkeley: University of California Press, 1976), 218 pp.

"Wang Yang-ming's Youth: A Personal Reflection on the Method of My Research", *Ming Studies*, no. 3 (1976), 11–17.

1977

"Inner Experience: The Basis of Creativity in Neo-Confucian Thinking", in *Artists and Tradition, Uses of the Past in Chinese Culture*, ed.,

Christian Murck (Princeton: The Art Museum, Princeton University, 1977), pp. 9–15.

"Chinese Perceptions of America", in *Dragon and Eagle: United States-China Relations, Past and Future*, eds., Michel Oksenberg and Robert B. Oxnam (New York: Basic Books, 1977), pp. 87–106.

1978

"On the Mencian Perception of Moral Self-Development", *The Monist*, 61.1 (January 1978), 72–81.

"The *Problematik* of Kant and the Issue of Transcendence: A Reflection on 'Sinological Torgue'", *Philosophy East and West*, XXVIII:2 (April 1978), 215–221.

"The 'Moral Universal' from the Perspectives of East Asian Thought", in *Morality as a Biological Phenomenon*, ed., Gunther S. Stent (Berlin: Dahlem Konferenzen, 1978), pp. 187–207.

"Yi Hwang's Perception of the Mind", *T'oegye Hakpo*, No. 19 (October 1978), 76–88. [Also available in Korean translation].

"T'oegye hsin-hsing lun shu-hou" 退溪心性論書後 (Further thoughts on Yi Hwang's perception of the mind), *T'oegye Hakpo*, No. 20 (December 1978), 18–21 [Available in Korean translation only].

1979

Humanity and Self-Cultivation: Essays in Confucian Thought (Berkeley: Asian Humanities Press, 1979), 364 pp.

"Shifting Perspectives on Text and History: A Reflection on Shelly Errington's Paper", *Journal of Asian Studies*, XXXVIII:2 (February 1979), 245–251.

"The Value of the Human in Classical Confucian Thought", *Humanitas*, XV:2 (May 1979), 161–176.

"Ultimate Self-Transformation as a Communal Act: Comments on Modes of Self-Cultivation in Traditional China", *Journal of Chinese Philosophy*, 6 (1979), 237–246.

"*Hsi-yu Chi* as an Allegorical Pilgrimage in Self-Cultivation", review, *History of Religions*, 19.2 (November, 1979), 177–184.

"The 'Thought of Huang-Lao': A Reflection on the Lao Tzu and Huang Ti Texts in the Silk Manuscripts of Ma-wang-tui", *The Journal of Asian Studies*, XXXIX:1 (November 1979), 95–110.

"A Note on Wittfogel's Science of Society", *Bulletin of Concerned Asian Scholars*, 11.4 (October–December 1979), 38–39.

1980

"Neo-Confucian Ontology: A Preliminary Questioning", *Journal of Chinese Philosophy* 7 (1980), 93–114.

"A Religiophilosophical Perspective on Pain", in *Pain and Society*, eds. H.W. Kosterlitz and L.Y. Terenius (Berlin: Dahlem Konferenzen, 1980), pp. 63–78.

1981

"*Jen* as a Living Metaphor in the Confucian *Analects*", *Philosophy East and West*, 31.1 (January 1981), 45–54.

"Ts'ung i tao yen" 從意到言 (From intention to word), *Chung-hua wen-shih lun-ts'ung* 中華文史論叢 (Shang-hai: January, 1981), 225–261.

"Shih-t'an Chung-kuo che-hsüeh chung ti san-ko chi-tiao" 試談中國哲學中的三個基調 (A preliminary discussion on the three basic motifs in Chinese philosophy), *Chung-kuo che-hsüeh shih yen-chiu* 中國哲學史研究 (Beijing, March 1981), 19–25.

"Kung Tzu jen-hsüeh chung ti tao hsüeh cheng" 孔子仁學中的道學政 (The Way, Learning and Politics in Confucius' Learning of Humanity), *Chung-kuo che-hsüeh* 中國哲學 (Beijing, 1981), 17–32.

1982

"T'oegye's Creative Interpretation of Chu Hsi's Philosophy of Principle", *Korean Journal*, XXII:2 (February 1982), 4–15.

"Towards an Understanding of Liu Yin's Confucian Eremitism", in Hok-lam Chan and Wm. T. de Bary, eds., *Yüan Thought: Chinese Thought and Religion under the Mongols* (New York: Columbia University Press, 1982), pp. 233–277.

1983

"Perceptions of Learning (*hsüeh*) in Early Ch'ing Thought", in *Symposium in Commemoration of Professor T'ang Chün-i* (Taipei: Student Book Co., 1983), pp. 27–61.

"Die neokonfuzianische Ontologie", in Wolfgang Schluchter ed., *Max Webers Studie über Konfuzianismus und Taoismus* (Frankfurt: Suhrkam, 1983), pp 271–297. A German translation of "Neo-Confucian Ontology: A Preliminary Questioning" published in 1980.

1984

"The Idea of the Human in Mencian Thought: An Approach to Chinese Aesthetics", in Susan Bush and Christian Murck, eds., *Theories of the Arts in China* (Princeton: Princeton University Press, 1984), pp. 57–73.

"A Confucian Perspective on Learning to be Human", in *The World's Religious Traditions*, ed., Frank Whaling (Edinburgh: T. & T. Clark, 1984), pp. 55–71.

"On Neo-Confucianism and Human-Relatedness", in *Religion and Family in East Asia*, eds., George De Vos and T. Sofue (Osaka: The National Museum of Ethnology, 1984), pp. 111–125.

"The Continuity of Being: Chinese Visions of Nature", in *On Nature*, Vol. 6 of *Boston University Studies in Philosophy and Religion*, ed., Leroy S. Rouner (Notre Dame, Ind.: University of Notre Dame Press, 1984), pp. 113–129.

"Wei-Chin Hsüan-hsüeh chung ti t'i-yen ssu-hsiang — shih-lun Wang Pi 'sheng-jen t'i-wu' kuan-nien ti che-hsüeh i-i" 魏晉玄學中的體驗思想－試論王弼'聖人體無'觀念的哲學意義 (Personal experiential thought in the Wei-Chin period — a preliminary discussion on the

philosophical meaning of Wang Pi's concept, "the sage embodies nothingness"), *Yen-yüan lun-hsüeh chi* 燕園論學集 (Essays in memory of T'ang Yung-t'ung's ninetieth birthday; Beijing: Peking University Press, 1984), pp. 197–213.

"Ts'ung shen-hsin-ling-shen ssu ch'en-tz'u k'an Ju-chia ti jen-hsüeh" 從身心靈神四層次看儒家的人學(Confucian humanist learning in the four related perspectives of body, mind, soul and spirit; Hong Kong: *Ming-pao yüeh-kan* 明報月刊, December 1984), 41–44.

Confucian Ethics Today: The Singapore Challenge (Singapore: Federal Publications, 1984) 247 pp.

1985

"Sung-Ju chiao-yü kuan-nien ti pei-ching" 宋儒教育觀念的背景 ("A Background for Understanding the Idea of Education in the Sung"), trans., Lin Cheng-chen 林正珍 , *Historical Review* (Taiwan University), no. 9 (January 1985), pp. 43–57.

Confucian Thought: Selfhood as Creative Transformation (Albany, New York: State University of New York Press, 1985), 203 p.

"Subjectivity in Liu Tsung-chou's Philosophical Anthropology", in *Individualism and Holism: The Confucian and Taoist Perspectives*, ed. Donald J. Munro (Ann Arbor: University of Michigan Press, 1985), pp. 215–235.

"Yi T'oegye's Perception of Human Nature: A Preliminary Inquiry into the Four-Seven Debate in Korean Confucianism", in *The Rise of Neo-Confucianism in Korea*, eds., Wm. T. de Bary and Jahyun Haboush (New York: Columbia University Press, 1985), pp. 261–281.

1986

"Ju-hsüeh ti-san-ch'i fa-chan ti ch'ien-ching wen-ti" 儒學第三期發展的前景問題 ("On the so-called 'Third Epoch of Confucian Humanism'"), *Ming-pao Monthly* 明報月刊(Hong Kong), no. 21.1 (January 1986), pp. 27–32; no. 21.2 (February 1986), pp. 36–38; no. 21.3 (March 1986), pp. 65–68.

"An Inquiry on the Five Relationships in Confucian Humanism", in *The Psycho-Cultural Dynamics of the Confucian Family*, edited by Walter

H. Slote (Seoul: International Cultural Society of Korea, 1986), pp. 175–190.

"Ts'ung shih-chieh ssu-ch'ao k'an Ju-hsüeh yen-chiu de hsin fa-chan" 從世界思潮看儒學研究的新發展 ("New Directions in Confucian Studies in the Perspective of World Thoughts"), *Chiu-chou hsüeh-k'an* 九州學刊 (Chinese Cultural Quarterly; Hong Kong: The Hong Kong Institute for Promotion of Chinese Culture, 1986), vol. 1, no. 1.

"Toward a Third Epoch of Confucian Humanism: A Background Understanding", in *Confucianism: The Dynamics of Tradition*, ed. Irene Eber (New York: Macmillan, 1986), pp. 3–21.

"The Structure and Function of the Confucian Intellectual in Ancient China", in *The Origins and Diversity of Axial Age Civilizations*, ed., S.N. Eisenstadt (Albany, New York: State University of New York Press), pp. 360–373.

"Lun Ju-chia de t'i-chih — te-hsing chih chih de han-i" 論儒家的體知－德性之知的涵義 ("On the 'Experiential Knowing' in Confucian Thought — The Implications of Moral Knowledge"), in *Ju-chia lun-li yen-t'ao-hui lun-wen chi* 儒家倫理研討會論文集 (*Collection of Essays on Confucian Ethics*), ed. Liu Shu-hsien 劉述先 (Singapore: The Institute of East Asian Philosophies, 1987), pp. 98–111.

"Profound Learning, Personal Knowledge, and Poetic Vision", *The Vitality of the Lyric Voice*, eds., Shuen-fu Lin and Stephen Owen (Princeton: Princeton University Press, 1986), pp. 3–31.

1987

"The Chinese Intellectual's Way of Being Religious", *Faith*, May 1987, vol. 1, issue 1, 25–28.

"Iconoclasm, Holistic Vision, and Patient Watchfulness: A Personal Reflection on the Modern Chinese Intellectual Quest", *Daedalus*, vol. 116, no. 2 (spring 1987), 75–94.

"The Religious Situation in the People's Republic of China Today", in *Religion in Today's World*, ed. Frank Whaling (Edinburgh: T & T Clark 1987), pp. 279–291.

"A Chinese Perspective on Pain", *Acta Neurochirurgica*, Suppl. 38, 147–151 (1987).

"Confucian Studies in the People's Republic", *Humanities*, VIII: 5 (September/October 1987), 14–16, 34–35.

1988

"Confucius and Confucianism", *Encyclopaedia Britannica*, Macropaedia (15th edition, 1988), vol. 16, pp. 653–662.

"Nature in Confucian Humanism", *Essays on Perceiving Nature*, ed. Diana Macintyre Deluca (Honolulu: The Perceiving Nature Conference Committee, 1988), pp. 99–110.

"A Confucian Perspective on the Rise of Industrial East Asia", 1687th State Meeting Report, *Bulletin of the American Academy of Arts and Sciences*, vol. XLII, no. 1 (October 1988), 32–50.

"Lun Lu Hsiang-shan ti shih-hsüeh" 論陸象山的實學 (On the real learning of Lu Hsiang-shan), *Chung-kuo che-hsüeh-shih yen-chiu*, no. 32 (July 1988), 56–69.

1989

Ju-hsüeh ti-san-ch'i fan-chan de ch'ien-ching wen-ti 儒學第三期發展的前景問題 (The *Problematik* of the development of the "third epoch" of Confucian learning; Taipei; Lien-ching 聯經, 1989).

"Embodying the Universe: A Note on Confucian Self-Realization," *World & I* (August 1989), 475–485.

"Chi-ch'eng wu-ssu fa-chan Ju-hsüeh" 繼承五四發展儒學 (Carry forward the May Fourth and develop Confucian learning; *Dushu Magazine*, Beijing, June 1989), 114-120.

Centrality and Commonality: An Essay on Confucian Religiousness, a revised and enlarged edition of *Centrality and Commonality: An Essay on Chung-yung* (Albany, New York: State University of New York Press, 1989), 165 pp.

The Way, Learning and Politics: Perspectives on the Confucian Intellectual (Singapore: Institute of East Asian Philosophies, 1989).

Index

adulthood, 83

aesthetics, 93–99, 106–109, auditory perception, 107–108; Confucian and Taoist, 93, 106; harmony of inner and outer, 47; self-cultivation and, 104

alienation, 58, 158; Heidegger on, 162

altruism, 55–58, 84, 97, 114, 140; based on self-knowledge, 57; and Confucian Golden Rule, 56, 97; *jen* as, 84

Analects, 67–70, 81–92; on the body, 96; centrality of learning in, 68; on establishing oneself and others, 58, 68, 114, 140; Fingarette on, 11, 81–82, 90; *jen* in, 69, 74, 81–92; on music, 99; on purpose, 62, 70; ritual in, 69, 79 n.6; passages from, 56, 58, 59, 62, 64 n.2, 67, 68, 69, 70, 74, 79 n.4,6, 85, 86, 87, 88, 89, 90, 94, 98, 101, 104, 114, 140, 148 n.33

analogy, *see* reasoning, analogical

animism, 21

anthropocentrism, 14, 21, 31, 42, 75, 137, 161; critique of, 10, 73

anthropocosmic vision, 10, 64, 137–8; in *Chung-yung*, 73; *see also* one body

anthropology, philosophical, 69, 73, 82, 94, 104, 153

anthropomorphism, 107, 144

anxiety, (*yu*), 89–90

Aristotle, 29

art, *see* aesthetics; six arts

asceticism, 28, 72, 102, 165 n.1; Calvinist, 11

atheism, 22

auditory perception, 107–108

Aurelius, Marcus, 166 n.4

authenticity, 52

authoritarianism, 12

authority: of the father,13, 115–6, 120; transcendent, 116

autonomy, 12, 78, 83, 114, 128; of the will, 62; *see also* freedom

Balazs, Etienne, 166 n.3

beauty (*mei*): human, 103, 106; as Mencian standard of inspiration, 12, 96–109, 152

Bellah, Robert N., 7–16, 135; on father-son relationship, 13, 121–2

Berlin, Isaiah, 78

bigotry, 137

biological lineage, 60, 119

biological traits, 102

Bodde, Derk, 87

body (*shen*), 96–100; given by parents, 118; Mencius on, 107; protection of, 120; relation with heart, 101; six arts and, 98–99

body-language, 103

Boodberg, Peter, 84

Book of Change (I Ching), 46, 140, 148 n.41, 152, 158

Book of History (Shu Ching), 146 n.11

Book of Odes (Shih Ching), 140

Book of Rites (Li-chi), 117; mourning ritual, 116

Booth, Wayne C., 82, 83

bravery (*yung*), 84–86

buddahood, 22, 25; in Ch'an, 20; inherent in human nature, 8

buddha nature, 25

Buddhism: contrast with Confucianism, 43; metaphysical challenge of, 149; Neo-Confucianism and, 150; *see also* Ch'an

"bureaucratic individualism," 8, 10

capitalism, 11

Cassirer, Ernst, 164

categorical imperative, *see* Kant, Immanuel

chain of being, 38, 132; degrees of spirituality, 44

Chan, Wing-tsit, 36, 87, 105, 137, 146 n.3; on Chang Tsai, 160; on *jen*, 81

Ch'an, 8, 19–25; buddahood in, 20; compared with Christianity, 21

Chang Tai-nien, 48 n.13

Chang Tsai, 33, 138; on *ch'i*, 37, 158–60;

211

Correcting Youthful Ignorance (*Cheng-meng*), 41; on the Great Harmony (*t'ai-ho*), 41, 149, 158; on the Great Vacuity (*t'ai-hsü*) 38, 158–60; on knowledge through the moral nature, 163; on *li*, 159; on moral ecology, 43; ontology, 157; on sincerity, 160; "Western Inscription" (*Hsi-ming*), 42, 137, 157, 161, 168 n.40
Ch'en Wen Tzu, 87
ch'eng (sincerity), 151–3
Ch'eng Hao, 161–3; on human sensitivity, 45; metaphor of paralysis, 114, 161; on origination, 46; on selfishness, 162; On Understanding Humanity (*Shih-jen*), 161
Ch'eng I, 131, 153, 146 n.3; on learning to become a sage, 154; on mother-son relationship, 140; on persuasion, 141; praise of his mother, 142–3; on re-marriage, 141–2; "What Master Yen Loved to Learn," 154
ch'i: as blood and breath, 36–38, 43–45; Chang Tsai on, 37, 158–60; and empirical science, 37; floodlike (*hao-jan chih ch'i*), 105–106; as material force, 36, 105 158–60; as medium of perception, 47; translations of, 36–37; 105; underlying all beings, 38, 45; as vital force, 37–47; Wang Fu-chih on, 42; will and, 105
chih (intelligence), 84–87, 102; criticism of, 87; relation to *jen*, 86
chih liang-chih, 32, 146 n.5
ching (respect), 146 n.3; between brothers, 140; between husband and wife, 142
Ch'ing scholarship, 91 n.4
Chou Tun-i, 30, 44, 150–4, 163; on the Five Agents, 44, 168, n.42; on the great ultimate, 149; on the Mean, 139; *Penetrating the Book of Change* (*T'ung-shu*), 152; on sagehood, 150–1; on sincerity (*ch'eng*), 151–3
Christ, as the Great Exemplar, 125
Christianity, compared with Confucianism, 123–5, 136
Chu Hsi, 13, 131, 138, 146 n.3; on having no desire, 151; on Heavenly Principle, 49 n.41; on inner ability to know ultimate reality, 169 n.60; on respect between brothers, 140; on sagehood, 152; on women, 145
Chuang Tzu, 8, 19, 25, 106; on listening with *ch'i*, 47; on the Creator, 93
chün-tzu, see profound person
chung, see loyalty
Chung-yung (*Doctrine of the Mean*), 30, 46, 63, 73–75, 106, 158; moral metaphysics, 152–153

civil religion, 8
Collins, James, 164
commiseration, 71, 95, 103
concentric circles, *see* human relations
conflict resolution theory, 118
Confucianism, *passim*; as adjustment to the world, 10, 55, 114, 135; critique of, 53, 145; in the modern world, 54, 77; politicized, 119, 136, 139; translation of terms in, 13; women in, 142–5
Confucius: actions of, 98; on death and spirits, 51, 64 n.2; on establishing oneself and others, 58, 68, 114, 140; as exemplar, 59–60; humility of, 25, 59, 85; on *jen*, 69, 81, 85; on learning for the sake of the self, 79 n.4; and music, 99; mystic appreciation of teaching, 101; praise of Yen Hui, 62; on *yu*, 90; see also *Analects*
conscience, 127; and consciousness, 25, 103, 132
contextualization, 133
continuity of being, 8, 33, 35–36, 132–3
Correcting Youthful Ignorance, 40–41
cosmogony, 35–39; Big Bang, 36; continuous, 39, 159; organismic process, 36
cosmos: in *Chung-yung*, 63; as father and mother, 45; humans as co-creators of, 107, 158; harmony, 36, 40–41; impersonal but not inhuman, 42; as open system, 9; as organismic process, 38, 43; transformation, 44, 107; wholeness, dynamism and continuity, 38–40
creation: continuous, 159; *ex nihilo*, 36, 159; *see also* cosmogony
creation myth, in Chinese thought, 35, 48 n.4
Creator, 19, 35, 38, 73, 93; and creature, 20, 158
Creel, Herrlee G., 87
cycles, historical, 39

Darwin, Charles, 40
death, 60, 62, 67, 74; and spirits, 51; mourning ritual, 68, 116
Descartes, Rene, 37
desires: elimination of (*wu-yü*), 31, 102, 151; human (*jen-yü*), 30–31, 72; selfish (*ssu-yü*), 16, 31, 46, 137
destiny, 61, 62, 63
dignity, human, 77–78
Doctrine of the Mean, see *Chung-yung*
Dream of the Red Chamber (*Story of the Stone*), 43

dualism, 160; of spirit and matter, 36
Dubs, H. H., 36, 87, 105
duty, 58, 155; consciousness of, 77

ecology, 21, 75, 76
education, *see* learning
"eight steps," of the *Great Learning*, 135
empirical knowledge, 76
environment, 25
epistemology, 19, 20, 38
equality, 78
ethics: political, 72; social, 55-56, 115
evil, 86, 128
Evolution of the Rites, 40
exemplary teacher: Christ as, 125; father
    as 124; in Three Teachings, 27
exemplary teaching (*shen chiao*), 53, 56,
    68-69, 98; model learning, 100
existential commitment, 57

faith, 9, 24, 132; Confucian, 51, 64; in
    humanity, 8
Fall, myth of, 31, 128
family, 15, 113, 131, 137; centrality of,
    123; division of labor in, 143;
    perpetuation of, 142
father-son relationship, 13, 58, 113-30,
    134, 138; absolutely binding, 11;
    Christian symbolism, 122; as covenant,
    128; reciprocity in, 14, 124; and self-
    cultivation, 120, 127; and transcendence,
    121; *see also* Oedipus complex
feminism, 145
feudalism, 53
Fichte, Johann Gottlieb, 164
fiduciary community, 82, 88, 137, 140
filial piety, 14, 115-21, 136, 139; in
    spiritual development, 128; of Shun,
    120; toward the universe, 45
Fingarette, Herbert, 11, 12, 17 n.16, 24,
    81-82, 90
five agents (*wu-hsing*), 44
Five Classics, 76
five relations (*wu-lun*), 123, 127-8,
    138-40; Mencius on, 147 n.29;
    persuasion in, 140
footbinding, 143
four germinations (*ssu-tuan*), 24, 71, 95, 103
freedom, 76-78, 125, 133-4, 138, 145;
    autonomy and, 78, 114; Kant on, 156;
    modern limitation, 76; of moral choice,
    154; political, 138; procedural, 133;
    Taoist quest for, 9; of women, 144
Freud, Sigmund, 116, 117; *Totem and
    Taboo*, 122-3
Fried, Charles, 33

friendship, 114, 139
Fung Yu-lan: on filial piety, 117; on
    mourning ritual, 116

Geertz, Clifford, 28, 29
God, 20-22, 61, 95; as unknowable, 136;
    Creator, 36; existence of, 25; human in
    image of, 125; voice of, 132
Golden Rule, Confucian, 26, 56, 61, 97
good (*shan*), as a Mencian standard of
    inspiration, 12, 96-107, 152
great (*ta*), as a Mencian standard of
    inspiration, 12, 96, 99, 152
great body (*ta-t'i*) and small body
    (*hsiao-t'i*), 70-75, 102-103; Mencius on,
    72, 103; nourishing of, 93
Great Harmony (*t'ai-ho*), 41, 47, 149, 158
Great Learning, 65 n.10, 76, 123, 134, 135
great transformation (*ta-hua*), 38-40, 42
great ultimate (*t'ai-chi*), 149
great unity (*ta-t'ung*), 40
Great Vacuity (*t'ai-hsü*), 38, 158-60
ground of being, 73, 74

harmony, 21; of cosmos, 40-41; of human
    relations, 56
Hay, D. F., 29
heart, see *hsin*
Heaven, 119, 123, 125-137; and Hell, 27;
    course of (*t'ien hsing*), 39; in *Chung-
    yung*, 73; knowing, 15, 61, 63, 72-73;
    sees as the people see, 132; serving, 63,
    163; transcendence of, 125; union with,
    134, 144, 157; Way of, 67
Heaven and Earth: forming one body with,
    see one body; human oneness with, 160;
    principle in, 30
heavenly principle (*t'ien-li*), 15, 30, 31, 46
Heidegger, Martin, 155-163; on *Dasein*,
    165; on Kant, 155-157, 164
hermeneutics, 54
historiography, 39
Hobbes, Thomas, 78
holy rite: society as, 11
honesty, 52, 151-152; hyperhonest villager,
    86; with oneself, 56, 68, 97
Hou Wai-lu, 64 n.5
hsin (heart and mind), 23, 32, 70-73, 95;
    capacity to embody the cosmos, 133;
    empathy of, 29; fasting of, 93; known
    through direct experience, 102;
    preserving (*ts'un-hsin*), 101; quest for the
    lost, 70-71, 101; rectification of (*cheng-
    hsin*), 135; sensitivity of, 24, 132; and the
    six arts, 100; unbearing (*pu-jen chih hsin*),
    101; unperturbed (*pu-tung-hsin*), 105

hsin (faithfulness), 84; *see also* true
Huang, Siu-chi, 168 n.40
Hsü Fu-kuan, 106–107; *Chung-kuo i-shu
   ching-shen*, 93
Hsün Tzu, 12, 13, 17 n.16; on culture, 75
Hughes, E. R., 87
humans: co-creators of the universe, 158;
   guardians of creation, 44; intimacy with
   cosmos, 43, 158; sensitivity of, 45;
   uniqueness, 61
human desires (*jen-yü*), ·see desires
human nature: divinity of, 132; endowed
   by Heaven, 127; intrinsic goodness of,
   126; obscured by selfishness, 162
human relations, concentric circles of, 14,
   55–58, 63, 134
humanity, see *jen*
"humanity of the heart," 29–32
husband-wife relationship, 128, 142, 145
Husserl, Edmund, 164–5

i (art), 97; *see also* aesthetics; six arts
i (intention), 31, 101, 131
i (righteousness), 25, 84, 102, 138
I Ching, see *Book of Change*
I Yin, 108
idealism, 33
individualism, 8–12, 27, 31, 53, 58, 67,
   77–78, 114
innate knowledge, see *liang-chih*
intellectual intuition (*chih te chih-chüeh*),
   20–21, 25, 32, 103; impossibility for
   Kant, 164; Mou Tsung-san on, 163–65;
   shareability of, 23
intelligence, see *chih*
intention, see *i*
internality (*nei*), 75; Mencius on, 71

Jakobson, Roman, 47
Jan Ch'iu, 87
jen (humanity), 11, 25, 74, 81–92, 94, 106,
   161; in the *Analects*, 69, 81–92; buds and
   sprouts, 102; centrality of, 81; contrast
   with *yu*, 90; evolution of the concept, 84;
   Fingarette on, 81; as general virtue,
   84–85; and *li* (ritual), 86, 89; relation to
   chih (knowledge), 86–87; translations of,
   87; Tzeng Tzu on, 88, 94; Wing-tsit
   Chan on, 81
Jenner, F. A., 31
Jesus, 123, 125
Journey to the West, 43
ju (scholar), 55, 59, 62, 65 n.7
Jung, Carl G., 36

Kant, Immanuel, 15–16, 29–33, 153–165;

categorical imperative, 55, 155; *Critique
   of Pure Reason*, 155; *Foundations of the
   Metaphysics of Morals*, 154; freedom of the
   will, 156; on reason, 154–5
Keller, Helen, 62
Kierkegaard, Soren, 78
knowledge: as power, 75–77; authenticated
   by action, 100; empirical, 20; extension
   of (*chih-chih*), 135; *see also* self-knowledge
ko-i (matching concepts), 87
ko-wu (investigation of things), 76, 80 n.32, 135
kung-fu (moral effort), 131, 138
Kung-sun Ch'ou, 105

learning (*hsüeh*): aesthetics of, 52; by
   example, 68; to be human (*hsüeh tso-jen*),
   9, 15, 19, 25, 51–65, 76, 88, 94, 131,
   162; Mencian stages of, 12, 96–109,
   152–3; music in, 98; natural growth and,
   95; for the sake of the self (*wei-chi*),
   10–14, 51–57, 69, 72, 131–4, 139, 146;
   ultimate commitment to, 135
Levenson, Joseph, 91 n.6
li (ritual), 12, 68, 83–84, 95, 102, 113;
   as communication, 22, 69; as discipline
   of the body, 97; as exemplary teaching,
   98; Fingarette on, 81–82; formalism, 86;
   as gesture, 22; mourning, 68, 116; music
   and, 108; relation to *jen*, 69, 86, 89
Li-chi, 116–7
li-chih (establishing the will), 31
li-i fen-shu (principle is one but its
   manifestations are many), 138, 159
liang-chi (primordial awareness), 32, 131
Lin Fang, 89
lineage, 60
Liu Tsung-chou, 131
Liu-hsia Hui, 108
Locke, John, 78
love, *jen* as, 84
loyalty (*chung*), 52, 114, 121, 136; and
   jen, 87
Lu Hsiang-shan, 131
Luke, Steven, 78

Ma-wang-tui silk manuscripts, 112 n.77
MacIntyre, Alasdair, 8
Mandate of Heaven, 46, 104, 125, 127
marriage, reciprocity in, 142
Marxism, view of history, 39
materialism, in Chinese thought, 37
matter: and energy, 36; dichotomy with
   spirit, 36–37
maturity, in Mencian learning, 96
Mencius, 93–112, *passim*; aesthetics of, 94,
   107; on the body, 23, 165 n.1; on

childlike heart, 76, 103; on floodlike *ch'i*
106; on four germinations (*ssu-tuan*), 103;
on the great and small body, 72; on
inability to bear the suffering of others,
28–29; on *liang-chih*, 32; line of
Confucian tradition, 13, 19, 132; and
Mo-tzu, 123; on ordeals of sages, 104;
quest for the lost heart, 101; on self-
examination, 61, 104; on Shun, 120, 166
n.6; on stages of learning to be human,
96–109, 152; on types of sagehood, 108;
theory of human nature, 12, 24, 70, 97;
on the will, 62, 70, 100; *Book of Mencius*,
passages from, 61, 71, 72, 95–108, 109
n.9, 147 n.29, 165 n.1, 166 n.6,
169 n.67
metaphysics, 15, 35, 149–70
methodology, 53–54
Metzger, Thomas, 11, 135
Mill, John Stuart, 78
mind, see *hsin*
Mo-tzu, 123
morality, inherent, 70
Mote, Frederick W., 35–51, 105, 109 n.4
mother-son relationship, 124, 140–1
Mou Tsung-san: on Heidegger and Neo-
Confucianism, 157, 167 n.39; on
intellectual intuition, 163, 165; on Kant
and Husserl, 170 n.87; on moral metaphysics, 167 n.16
music, 93, 98–99; as metaphor for
Confucian sageliness, 108
mysticism, in Mencius, 103

Nagel, T., 32
nature (*tzu-jan*), 40–41; dichotomy of man
and, 93; human consanguinity with, 47;
spontaniety of, 25
Needham, Joseph, 20, 36, 41, 48 n.9,
168 n.41
Neo-Confucianism, *passim*
Neville, Robert C., 16
nirvāna, 8, 23, 25
Niu Mountain allegory, 70

obedience, 115, 119, 122, 139
Obenchain, Diane B., 65 n.7
Oedipus complex, 13, 116–7, 122–31
"one body," 10, 29, 43–46, 60–61, 165;
Ch'eng Hao on, 161, 163; predicated on
ch'i, 45; as process of growth, 46
ontology, see metaphysics
organismic vision, 20–23, 26, 157
original mind, 19
original sin, 128

Parmenides, 163
patriarchy, 144–145
Pelagianism, 126
pen-t'i (original substance), 131, 138
Penetrating the Book of Change, 152
perception, as resonance of *ch'i*, 47
perfectibility, human, 19, 22–27, 82, 95,
104, 117, 135; *Chung-yung* on, 74;
Mencius on, 70
Plato, 30, 38–39
pluralism, 54, 137
Po I, 108
Poetry (*Shih*), 68; see also *Book of Odes*
Polyani, Michael, 33, 79 n.14, 90
positivism, 76
practical living, 60–61, 97, 133; Three
Teachings on, 22
prajña, 25
priesthood, absence of, 27, 55, 144
primordial awareness, *see liang-chih*
principle (*li*), 30–32, 132, 138; Chang Tsai
on, 159; Ch'eng Hao on, 161–2; and *jen*
(humanity), 162
privacy, 77–78
private property, 77
profound person (*chün-tzu*), 56–60, 74, 88,
90, 99; learning of, 69; Confucius on the
Way of, 59
progress in history, 39
Prometheus myth, 76
propriety, *see li* (ritual)
Protagoras, 107
psychology, 115, 127, 149
punishment, 120
purpose, see will

quiet sitting, 28

reason, 30; Kant on, 154–5
reasoning: analogical, 67, 83; based on
shared values, 82–83; deductive, 67
reciprocity, 14, 124, 139–40; in
marriage, 142
reductionism, 24, 27–28
relativism, as challenge to Confucian
tradition, 53
religion, 64, 131–2
remarriage, 141
repression, 115
respect (*ching*), 146 n.3; between brothers,
140; between husband and wife, 142
Rheingold, H. L., 29
"rhetoric of assent," 82
Ricoeur, Paul, 79 n.1
righteousness, see *i*
rights, 58, 141

ritual, see *li*
ritualization, 22, 114
Romance of the White Snake, 43
romantic love, critique of, 142
ruler-minister relationship, 138

sage, 8, 19, 25, 64, 104, 113; learning to
    become, 15, 95, 150-1; metaphysical
    grounding of, 153; ordeals of, 104;
    realizing physical form (*hsing*), 100;
    sincerity of, 152; single-minded
    concern, 163
sagely (*sheng*), as a Mencian standard of
    inspiration, 12, 96, 104, 152-3
salvation, 127-8; *see also* soteriology
samsāra, 21, 23
Sartre, John Paul, 78
satori, 22
Sayings of the Confucian School (*K'ung Tzu
    chia-yü*), 120
Schwartz, Benjamin I., 16, 18, n.24
scientism, 75-76
secular and sacred, 27, 133
self, 7-16, *passim*; as center of relation-
    ships, 12, 53, 55, 61, 83, 113, 133; the
    great and the small, 14, 57; as an open
    system, 8, 14, 26, 57, 114, 131; as
    process of spiritual development, 113,
    125, 128; and society, 75, 93; and
    transcendence, 8, 60, 126
self-cultivation (*hsiu-shen*), 7-9, 14, 23-27,
    55-61, 67-68, 74, 99, 102, 106; artistic
    creativity and, 93; and the body, 96;
    Ch'eng Hao on, 162; *ch'i* and, 105;
    deepening and broadening, 23, 57-58,
    63, 114; elimination of selfish desires,
    31; germinations and seeds, 23, 25; and
    jen, 89; leading to immediacy with
    nature, 47; through ordinary experience,
    22; participation of the other, 115, 126,
    128; primordial ties and, 115, 126-8,
    133; ritual and, 12, 97; as the root
    (*pen*), 123, 135; and self-knowledge, 75;
    steadfastness of purpose and, 62; Tseng
    Tzu on, 67, 88
self-development, *see* self-cultivation
self-knowledge, 33, 56; analogy of digging
    a well, 26; as transforming the universe,
    74; *see also* self-cultivation
self-realization, 10, 30, 60-61, 107, 115,
    120-7, 134; and family relationships, 14,
    120-4, 145; as existential, 126;
    autonomy and, 131; communal effort,
    26, 84; many paths, 62, 83; of women,
    143-4; the will and, 70; *see also* self-
    cultivation

self-transcendence, 64, 76, 100, 126;
    concrete experience, 10
self-transformation: as a communal act, 19,
    58, 64-69, 77, 100, 113, 133, 137,
    141-5; and friendship, 139; and
    transcendence, 136; as voluntary, 141
selfhood, modern dilemmas of, 76
selfish desires (*ssu-yü*), 16, 46, 137;
    elimination of, 31
selfishness, 14, 29, 75; Ch'eng Hao on, 162
Semiology, 84
senses, Mencius on, 72, 75
sensory perception, in self-cultivation,
    60-61
seven feelings, 98
sex, differentiation by, 143-145
shen (body), *see* body
Shih Ching, 140
Shu Ching, 146 n.11
Shun, 104, 107, 153; filial piety of,
    119-121, 127; morality of, 166 n.6; as
    rustic, 99
sincerity (*ch'eng*), 151-3
six arts (*liu-i*), 76, 93; discipline in, 99,
    110 n.23; as physical exercises, 96-97;
    training for the heart, 100-101
Smith, Adam, 78
Smith, Wilfred Cantwell, 9, 64, n.1, 132
social ethics, 55, 56, 113-5
sociobiology, 8
soteriology, 61, 64, 136; Confucian and
    Christian, 123
spirits, 21; Confucius on, 51
spiritual (*shen*), as a Mencian standard of
    inspiration, 12, 96, 104, 152-3 ,
spiritual communion (*shen-hui*), 107
Spring and Autumn period, 53, 84
ssu (privatized self), 57
ssu-tuan, *see* four germinations
Stoicism, 150
subject and object, 46, 93
subjectivity, 74, 126, 131, 137; deepening,
    27, 93
suffering of others, inability to bear, 28,
    29, 95, 101
superego, 115, 118, 121

ta-hua (great transformation), 38-40, 42
ta-t'ung (great unity), 40
t'ai-chi (great ultimate), 149
t'ai-ho, *see* Great Harmony
t'ai-hsü (Great Vacuity), 38, 158-60
T'ang Chün-i, 168 n.49
t'i (embodying), 30, 132-3, 150; ultimate
    reality, 163

t'ien, *see* Heaven
Tao, 8, 20, 25, 67, 73, 90, 123, 125;
    creative transformation, 41; standard of
    inspiration, 94; within one's own heart,
    105
Tao Chi, 43
Taoism, 20, 22, 35, 106; Confucianism
    and, 9, 43; inner illumination, 25;
    metaphysical challenge of, 149; Neo-
    Confucianism and, 150
te (virtue), in music, 98
technology, 76
three bonds (*san-kang*), 139, 147 n.30
Three Teachings, 19–28; exemplary
    teacher in, 27; practical living, 22;
    rejection of exclusivism, 26; Wang
    Yang-ming and, 28
time and space, in self-cultivation, 133
transcendence, 45, 123, 137; as radical
    otherness, 136
trinity, with Heaven and Earth, 46, 63,
    74, 137, 153
true (*hsin*), as Mencian standard of
    inspiration, 12, 96, 99, 106–107, 152
true person (*chen jen*), 19
Tseng Tzu, 67, 74, 83, 96; on *jen*, 88, 94
Tung Chung-shu, 147, n.30
Turiel, E., 32
tyranny, 101
Tzu-hsia, 89
tzu-jan, *see* nature
Tzu-lu, 87, 90
Tzu-wen, 87

ultimate concern, in Confucian tradition,
    52
ultimate self-transformation, *see* self-
    transformation
"On Understanding Humanity," (*Shih-jen*)
    161
unity, *see* one body
unity of knowledge and action (*chih-hsing
    ho-i*), 28–29
universalism, 53

vengeance, 140
virtues, relation to *jen*, 84–85

vital force, *see ch'i*
vitalism, 23

Waley, Arthur, 79, n.4, 85, 87, 88
Wang Fu-chih, 37, 46; on metaphysics
    of *ch'i*, 42
Wang Ken, 45
Wang Liang, 99
Wang Yang-ming, 13, 30; on establishing
    the will, 31; "Inquiry on the *Great
    Learning*," 29; on primordial awareness,
    32, 131; Three Teachings in, 28; on
    women, 145
Warring States, 70, 94, 95
Way: of Buddha, 22; of profound person,
    59; diversity of, 83; *see also* Tao
Weber, Max: "adjustment to the world,"
    10–11, 17 n.11, 55, 135–6; *Protestant
    Ethic and the Spirit of Capitalism*, 10;
    Religion of China, 10
"Western Inscription," (*Hsi-ming*), 42, 137,
    157, 161, 168 n.40
"What Master Yen Loved to Learn," 154
will, 21, 41, 116; autonomy of, 155; *ch'i*
    and, 105; establishment of, 93; freedom
    of, 125, 156; Mencius on, 70–71;
    sincerity of (*ch'eng-i*), 135; steadfastness
    of, 61–62; Wang Yang-ming on, 31
wisdom, *see chih*
Wolff, P. H., 29
women: rights of, 141; self-realization of,
    144; status of, 143–145
wu-hsing, *see* five agents

Yao, 119
Yen Hui, 69, 83; courage of, 104;
    eagerness to learn, 62; mystic
    appreciation of Confucius' teaching,
    101; on Shun, 153
Yen Yüan, *see* Yen Hui
yin and yang, 44
yu (anxiousness), 89–90
yung (bravery), 84–86

zazen, 28

Index prepared by Thomas W. Selover

Religion and the Family in East Asia, eds., George A. De Vos and Takao Sofue (Osaka: National Museum of Ethnology, 1984). Copyright © 1984 by the National Museum of Ethnology. Reprinted by permission.

"Neo-Confucian Ontology: A Preliminary Questioning" was first presented at the Berkeley Regional Seminar in Confucian Studies, under the sponsorship of the American Council of Learned Societies, on March 5, 1976. I am indebted to my colleagues and friends there for their searching criticisms and constructive suggestions. The paper was subsequently published in *Journal of Chinese Philosophy* (1980). A German translation is included in *Max Webers Studie über Konfuzianismus und Taoismus*, edited by Wolfgang Schluchter (Frankfurt and Main: Suhrkamp, 1983). Reprinted by permission of *Journal of Chinese Philosophy*.

The Epilogue, "Embodying the Universe: A Note on Confucian Self-realization," is reprinted, with permission, from *World & I* (August 1989), 475–485.

I am indebted to Song-bae Park for taking the initiative of recommending this book to the SUNY Series in Philosophy, to David Hall for his insightful comments, to Betsy Scheiner and Rosanne V. Hall for editing both the published and unpublished portions of the manuscript, to Thomas Selover for his painstaking effort at proofreading and indexing and to Robert Neville for his encouraging Foreword.

"A Confucian Perspective on Learning to be Human" was written as a current perspective in religious studies for a collection of essays in honor of Professor Wilfred Cantwell Smith. It is included in *The World's Religious Traditions*, ed., Frank Whaling (Edinburgh: T. & T. Clark, 1984). Copywright © by T. & T. Clark, 1984. Reprinted by permission.

"The Value of the Human in Classical Confucian Thought" first appeared in *Humanitas*, vol. XV, no. 2 (May 1979). I am grateful to Professor John R. MacCormack, Director of the Institute of Human Values at Saint Mary's University in Halifax, Nova Scotia for his kind invitation which enabled me to share my thoughts with scholars of a variety of disciplines in the humanities.

"*Jen* as a Living Metaphor" was first presented at the Harvard Workshop on Classical Chinese Thought in August 1976. I benefited from inspiring comments by Professors H. G. Creel, Herbert Fingarette, Henry Rosemont, and Benjamin I. Schwartz. The article was published in *Philosophy East and West*, vol. XXXI, no. 1 (January 1981). Copyright © 1981 by the University Press of Hawaii. Reprinted by permission.

"The Idea of the Human in Mencian Thought: An Approach to Chinese Aesthetics," was first presented at a conference on "Theories of the Arts in China," sponsored by the American Council of Learned Societies in June 1979. Useful suggestions from Professors James Cahill, Mary Mothersill, Stephen Owen, and Maureen Robertson enabled me to revise the paper for publication in *Theories of the Arts in China*, eds., Susan Bush and Christian Murck (Princeton: Princeton University Press, 1984). Copyright © 1983 by Princeton University Press. Reprinted by permission.

"Selfhood and Otherness: Father-Son Relationship in Confucian Thought" was written as a response to Robert Bellah's seminal essay on "Father and Son in Christianity and Confucianism." It is included in *Culture and Self*, eds., Anthony Marsella, George De Vos and Francis Hsü (London: Tavistock Press, 1985). Copyright © 1984 by Tavistock Press. Reprinted by permission.

"On Neo-Confucian Religiosity and Human-Relatedness" was first presented at the 5th Annual Taniguchi Symposium for the Promotion of Ethnology, held at the National Museum of Ethnology, Osaka, in September 1981. I learned much from the fellow participants of the Symposium. I am particularly grateful to Professors Bito Masahide, Lee Kwang Kyu, Morioka Kiyomi, and Suenari Michio for their enlightening thoughts on the Confucian family in East Asia. The article, under a slightly different title, is included in

Acknowledgements

"The 'Moral Universal' from the Perspectives of East Asian Thought" was originally published in *Morality as a Biological Phenomenon*, edited by Gunther S. Stent, as *Life Sciences Research Report* 9 of the Dahlem Konferenzen (Berlin, 1978). The article was reprinted, with commentary by Clifford Geertz, in *Philosophy East and West*, vol. XXXI, no. 3 (July 1981). I am grateful to Professor Geertz for his thought-provoking comments and to the Dahlem Konferenzen for its permission to have the article included in this volume.

"The Continuity of Being: Chinese Visions of Nature" was first presented as one of the basic motifs in the Chinese mode of thinking at a meeting of the Association of the History of Chinese Philosophy in Beijing in the summer of 1980 during my six-month research tour of China under the sponsorship of the Committee on Scholarly Communication with the People's Republic of China of the National Academy of Sciences. My conversations on the subject with Professors Chang Li-wen, Fang Ke-li, Feng Ch'i, P'ang P'u, and T'ang I-ch'ieh encouraged me to write an essay in Chinese on the three basic motifs in Chinese philosophy. The essay was published in the *Study of the History of Chinese Philosophy*, a newly established journal of the Institute of Philosophy in the Chinese Academy of Social Sciences. The invitation from Leroy S. Rouner, Director of the Boston University Institute for Philosophy and Religion, to deliver a public lecture on the Chinese visions of nature in the Institute's Wednesday Evening Series of 1983 enabled me to share my thoughts with an English-speaking audience. I benefited greatly from discussions with Professors Peter Berger, John Carman, Ewert Cousins, L. S. Rouner, and Huston Smith. The article is included in *On Nature*, ed., Leroy S. Rouner (Notre Dame: Ind., University of Notre Dame Press, 1984). Copyright © 1984 by University of Notre Dame Press. Reprinted by permission.

Contents

Acknowledgements   *ix*

Foreword by Robert C. Neville   *1*

Introduction   *7*

I   The "Moral Universal" from the Perspectives of East Asian Thought   *19*

II   The Continuity of Being: Chinese Visions of Nature   *35*

III   A Confucian Perspective on Learning to be Human   *51*

IV   The Value of the Human in Classical Confucian Thought   *67*

V   *Jen* as a Living Metaphor in the Confucian *Analects*   *81*

VI   The Idea of the Human in Mencian Thought: An Approach to Chinese Aesthetics   *93*

VII   Selfhood and Otherness: The Father-Son Relationship in Confucian Thought   *113*

VIII   Neo-Confucian Religiosity and Human-Relatedness   *131*

IX   Neo-Confucian Ontology: A Preliminary Questioning   *149*

Epilogue   *171*

Glossary   *183*

Bibliography of Tu Wei-ming   *201*

Index   *211*

IN MEMORY OF

T'ang Chün-i, an exemplary teacher at New Asia College in Hong Kong

and

Lee Sang-eun, an inspiring scholar at Korea University in Seoul

Published by
State University of New York Press, Albany

© 1985 State University of New York

Fourth printing — 1990
Fifth printing — 1991

For information, address State University of New York
Press, State University Plaza, Albany, N.Y., 12246

Library of Congress Cataloging in Publication Data

Tu, Wei-ming.
  Confucian thought.

  (SUNY series in philosophy)
  Bibliography: p.
  Includes index.
  1. Philosophy, Confucian. I. Title. II. Series.
B5233.C6T8 1985   181'.09512   84-16263
ISBN 0-88706-005-6
ISBN 0-88706-006-4 (pbk.)

CONFUCIAN THOUGHT:
Selfhood As Creative Transformation

Tu Wei-Ming

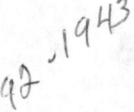

State University of New York Press

SUNY Series in Philosophy
Robert C. Neville, Editor

CONFUCIAN THOUGHT:

Selfhood as Creative Transformation

the lobby. Subdued gold lettering on richly gleaming walnut doors stated:

CONTEMPORARY LIFE INSURANCE, INC.
Hours Mon.—Sat. 9 a.m. — 6 p.m.

"Ralph," Kate said, coming back to the elevators, "can you give me any reason why a piece of evidence establishing the time the victim entered these premises hasn't been collected yet?" She nodded curtly toward the guard desk and the ledger.

Hansen shock his head unhappily. She stepped onto an elevator; Hansen inserted a key to release the sixteenth floor, and she rode up.

Pete Johnson was sketching the lobby on graph paper. She nodded to him, her gaze raking the lobby; uninterested in decor, she gauged the distance from the entryways to the elevators, noted the absence of a stairway. One of the double doors was propped open—not the usual procedure judging from the stapler used as a doorstop. She stepped through the doorway. A wooden sawhorse barricaded the hall to the right; she followed the murmur of male voices to her left, moved carefully around the chalk-encircled pieces of a glass coffee pot scattered across the stained carpet, and entered the corner office.

The area was being processed. The fingerprint man, his back turned, delicately brushed an edge of the ebony desk; the photographer was repacking his case. The deputy coroner talked to a bored ambulance crew, two burly black men who leaned up against the wall near their stretcher, waiting. Kate's eyes drifted over the corpse which sat with arms outstretched, the hands enclosed in paper bags tied at the wrists, an ivory-handled implement protruding from the chest. She nodded to the men in the room.

Ed Taylor, pencil poised over his notebook, completed a yawn and strolled over, skirting the smashed glass and

alcohol-stained carpet. Taylor never did anything quickly. Kate watched him, disapproving of his ballooning bulk. An eighteen-year man, tall and blond, calm and humorous, he was resigned more than dedicated to his responsibilities, wanting to get the twenty years in and pull the pin. She would wager anyone that Taylor would not retire after he'd put in the twenty. Taylor would always be a cop.

"Finished," said the photographer.

She said, "You get plenty of angles of all this glass?"

The photographer did not turn around. "Everything. Dammit, check my log. I got everything."

The ambulance crew moved to the body. Kate looked at the deputy coroner.

"He's been stabbed," Everson said.

The men chuckled, and Kate smiled. The ambulance crew, ready to hoist the corpse onto the stretcher, paused to guffaw.

"Time of death between seven-thirty and eight," Everson said, grinning.

Kate said, "Blood on the killer?"

"Possible. Could very well be. Bleeding was localized but there's a stain on the desk—on impact, from the directionality. A spurt got the killer's hand or sleeve at the very least."

"Victim sitting like that when he got it?"

Everson hesitated, fingering a pencil-thin moustache. "It's odd, Kate. A hundred and eighty degree wound." He flicked a well-manicured hand at the corpse, and she walked over to have a closer look. "Usually there's a downward angle to a knife thrust but this one's almost level. He might've been standing, leaned back from the blow, fell back into the chair. Or sitting, in the process of getting up. The weapon's a beaut, isn't it?" She was bent down, examining the curved, intricate ivory handle. "Too faceted to pick up a print."

"The office manager ID'd the body," Taylor said. "Says it's the victim's letter opener. Wide blade, edges like a razor, he says."

Kate stepped back, and the black men hoisted the body. Everson continued, "A weapon like that, a two-year old could've done it. Went through that whale blubber like butter."

"Fat fucking son of a bitch," one of the black men grunted as they wrapped and secured the hulk on the stretcher.

Again, Kate surveyed the desk, the shattered glass. "That kind of wound, Walt, any possibility of suicide?"

"Kate," Taylor said, "a witness heard somebody—"

"Walt?" Kate interrupted, ignoring Taylor.

Again Everson hesitated. "Could explain the level entry of the weapon, and no defensive cuts on him, either. But there're no experimental wounds, no visible sign of other pricking of the skin. The shirt's nice and neat, no cuts anywhere from hesitation marks. And you know how they hesitate, Kate. How often they take clothing off, or at least push it aside. No evidence of cadaveric spasm—no death grip of the weapon, no immediate rigor like there sometimes is with suicide." Everson glanced at his chain-bracelet watch. "Three hours now and no sign of it yet."

"But still, is it possible?"

"Possible. We'll both need a much closer look."

"Sure." She turned to Taylor. "Ed, how many people in this office?"

Taylor consulted his notes. "Forty-one."

"That's a lot of interviews, Walt."

"And if it's homicide," Taylor said, "we got a lot of people we can't segregate and not much time before they ignore instructions and start gabbing to each other."

"Meaning you want an immediate autopsy." Everson pursed his lips, stroked his moustache again, glanced at the stretcher. "This one looks clean and tidy enough. And it's Tuesday, it's always slow on Tuesdays. Call you as soon as we set it up."

The group soon left, talking and chuckling among themselves as they followed the ambulance crew and stretcher.

Taylor turned back pages of his notes, and Kate settled a hip on the edge of the teak credenza and took out her notebook. She asked, not looking up, "You heard?"

"Yeah. I figured they'd plea bargain down to second, but involuntary manslaughter—Jesus Christ, God damn it, Kate—"

She tuned him out, taking in details of the room again as he continued his diatribe on the insanities of the court system. She had been in court this morning, expecting to testify. The case had been continued to May. The victim had been only seventeen, her killer twenty-two and with a rap sheet as long as her arm; he'd been in trouble since Kate's days in Juvenile. He was typical of today's criminal—and that was what disturbed her, more than the plea bargain. Younger—they were younger, with drugs in their past and present, and they were casual about their crimes, committing without thought acts of utter savagery. And while female crime was also increasing, she had read projections that soon one out of three American men would have in his past a perpetration of violence. . . . The thin blue line of men and women who did their best to protect and to serve—how much longer could they hold back such ferocity? Well, she did her job, it was all she could do. "Ed," she finally said, her tone harsh, "it's history."

He sighed, looked at his notes. "This one's not suicide, Kate. Doesn't feel right. And that corpse looked as surprised as hell."

"True," she conceded. "What've you got so far?"

"Code three all units at seven-forty-two." Taylor read dispassionately from the crime report and his notes. "A one-eighty-seven, suspect on premises. Premises secured approximately eight a.m. We have a complete list of everyone on the upper floors of the building after it was sealed—"

Kate interjected acidly, "For all the good that'll do."

Taylor glanced up only briefly and then continued, "Ellen Rose O'Neil arrived approximately seven-twenty a.m.,

heard noise, found the victim approximately seven-forty. Did not observe the killer . . ."

Taylor's notes were always factual if not comprehensive, and she listened with concentration. Overall examination of the scene was virtually complete: photographs, sketches, measurements, descriptions, fingerprinting. The necessity for elimination fingerprints had been explained to the employees; all had expressed cooperation. Kate jotted one- and two-word notes.

"Hair tidy, body slightly turned but trunk position normal," Taylor droned. "Eyes open. Diamond ring, Cartier wrist watch, three hundred cash in the desk drawer. No signs of disorder except for blood smears on the desk, victim's fingers sliding off. Blood marks on the liquor cart, victim's left hand, it looks like."

Kate walked around behind the desk, gauging the distance and angles between the desk, chair, spilled cart.

Taylor consulted a sketch spread across the seat of a chair in front of the desk. "The cart was pushed from its usual position of nine feet eight inches to a proximity of twenty-six inches from the body, according to the tracks."

Kate knelt next to the overturned cart which was covered with fingerprint powder, lifted a corner with her pen, glanced at the glossy dried reddish-brown stains.

"Blood marks are along the railing," Taylor said unnecessarily. "Indicating the victim grabbed it, pulled it over."

She nodded and moved on her knees, scrutinizing the wheel marks in the carpet. She sank her pen into a set of deep grooves. "Cart usually sits right here. When was it moved? Why? Why would it be so close to his desk at seven o'clock in the morning? Let's check with the cleaning people to see where it was last night."

Taylor made a note.

She got to her feet, brushed at the knees of her gray pants. "Lots of prints on the cart."

Taylor shrugged. "Dozens."

"Desk contents?"

"All itemized, nothing unusual except for the cash. Ditto the credenza. Nothing's missing from the office, according to the office manager. But then he's black—"

"Anything else?" she said curtly. Taylor's racial prejudice, which surfaced at any opportunity, continually irked her.

Taylor flipped note pages. "Cigar butt and ash. Appears to be the victim's but we collected it."

She nodded, her glance again traversing the room: the cream-colored leather sofa and armchair, the glass table topped by an abstract silver sculpture, the bookcase containing a clutter of plaques and trophies. Her gaze lingered on the fouled blond carpet; the darkening bloodstain outlined in chalk on the ebony desk dirty with fingerprint powder and barren except for two Cross pens imbedded in a marble base; the immense leather chair forever divested of its daily occupant. She strolled over and examined three black-framed, autographed photographs on the wall—Fergus Parker shaking hands with Lyndon Johnson, Barry Goldwater, Richard Nixon. She moved to the family photograph on the bookcase. "Notification?"

"Wife. His third marriage. A boy eleven, girl thirteen, in schools back East. The office manager drove out there. Santa Monica. Insisted on going. Hansen took him. The wife is nicely alibied. From six-thirty to eight she was at the next door neighbor's. And I'd say she didn't use a pro."

Kate nodded. "I'd say not. He'd use his own weapon. And make the hit on familiar, predictable territory." She continued to study the photograph of Fergus Parker's family.

Taylor said, "Spend a lot of time with bibs tucked under their chins, don't they? All three porkers, like him."

You should talk, Kate thought. "What about the O'Neil woman?"

"Nice lady. Thirty-one. Cool. Attractive, smart. Handles herself very calm and determined."

Delicately, Taylor cleared his throat. Alerted, Kate

glanced at him; but his gaze was fixed on the Santa Monica mountains, clear and vivid in the distance. "A roommate came. Girl friend."

Gay, she thought. Or at least he thinks so.

"Spent half an hour with her, wanted her to go home, *insisted*. Left mad as hell." He glanced at her. "She's a prof at UCLA. Economics."

So they may be gay, Kate thought in amusement, but apparently not card-carrying dykes. She said bluntly, "The O'Neil woman, she a possible?"

Taylor's grin was swift, ingratiating. "She'd have to get a mad on awful quick. She's new, second day here. Unless it's her period." He grinned again, then shrugged as Kate did not smile. "We're gonna have a good time with this one, Kate. This Fergus Parker's popular as Hitler. These people here, when they heard, I thought they were gonna join hands and sing ding dong the witch is dead. The only one who looked sorry was his secretary—" Taylor looked through his notes. "—Billie Sullivan. Weird. Walks like she's got her body on backwards."

Kate chuckled. "It *is* a little different, Ed. A pillar of the community instead of the usual, like MacKenzie on Friday."

Taylor pushed out his fleshy lips. "Mrs. MacKenzie calls nine times a day. Husband gets bashed with a tire iron in the May Company parking lot, no witnesses, she can't understand why we haven't made a collar yet. One of these people you talk to, you're on Wilshire, she's on Sunset. I explain the May Company parking lot was not exactly loaded with clues, she keeps saying she's a taxpayer."

Kate said impatiently, "Don't waste any more time with her, have her talk to Lieutenant Bell. What's the situation with the employees here?"

"They're plenty nervous. Working, more or less." Taylor ran a hand through lank blond hair, pausing a moment to scratch. "The black office manager, he seems sharp enough. He got 'em all calmed down. Hansen took the O'Neil

woman's statement, I talked to her, we took her in but she didn't give us much—"

"Wait a minute," Kate said. "Go back in your notes about her. About finding the victim."

Taylor turned over two pages in his notebook. "She was in the kitchen getting coffee. Stepped out into the north hallway, walked up to the west hallway carrying the coffee pot to offer some to Guy Adams who she thought was in. Heard running steps, a door slam, the sound coming from the southwest end of the corridor, then crashing glass. Ran down the hallway, saw the vicitm and dropped the coffee pot—"

"Okay," Kate said. "You said she was in the kitchen getting coffee. Who made the coffee?"

"Why she, uh, I assu—" Taylor caught himself. "I don't have a note on that, Kate."

"I want the coffee pot. And the glass in here. I want the coffee pot dusted. I assume," she said, placing sarcastic emphasis on the word as Taylor busily wrote, "no one went through the other office waste baskets for paper cups, checked desks for warm coffee?"

Taylor shifted his feet. "The wastebasket in here was clean. The executive washroom, no signs of blood but we chemical tested, we collected some used paper towels—"

"Maybe the victim's," Kate said shortly.

"Yeah, right." Taylor's broad face was slightly flushed. "Myself, I saw a coffee mug on the kitchen counter, fancy hunting scene on it. Empty. We can still bag all the other trash, Kate."

Kate thought: I suppose I *am* a bitch to work with, but people can be so *damn* stupid. "Think about it, Ed," she said coldly, "what earthly good would that do now?" She asked after a deepening silence, "Press been and gone?"

Taylor's voice was stiff. "Kovich handled it."

"Ed, remember the one three months ago, the guy who shot his way out of the Bank of America?"

"Yeah, oh God yeah, crazy Garcia." Taylor's hostility

softened as he remembered. "God, the mess. God, the wit-nesses." His blue eyes rolled up in mournful memory. "God, the paperwork."

"There's a lot of people here too, Ed. We need to find a handle fast, a pattern, a direction to go."

Taylor nodded. "The office manager's set us up in the conference room. You pull down the shades, it's a fancy interrogation room."

"Suggestions?" She was being only partly conciliatory; she was team supervisor, and she had worked with Taylor—who had reached Detective-one nine years ago and had re-mained there—on too many investigation teams.

"You'll want to talk to Ellen O'Neil and the office manager. This one shouldn't take long, Kate. Whoever did it knew this guy—it figures. And that means we're in Amateur City. And that means we'll get him. So we split up, move fast. You take the managers, they're more your style. I'll take the service people. Anybody that looks like a half-way possible we take down for interrogation."

"Good." She was pleased. "I'll talk to the black office manager first. He have a name?"

"Girl's name," Taylor temporized, flipping pages. "Gail. Freeman. Right now he's in the conference room with the other managers. Figuring a way to handle things till their home office names a new head honcho."

Kate accompanied Taylor down the hall to the door marked CONFERENCE ROOM. Through the door could be heard, faintly, laughter. She said wryly, "They're not exactly holding a wake for Mr. Fergus Parker."

She rapped, opened the door. A woman, and five men, one of them black, stared at her with rapidly sobering faces. Taylor said easily, "This is my partner, Detective Delafield. She'll be coordinating our investigation."

Well aware of the psychological value of her badge, especially in a group, Kate extracted the leather case from her shoulder bag and flipped it open to display her shield and ID card.

"Gail Freeman." The black man had immediately stood, and he leaned over the wide glossy table to shake hands.

Swiftly, she evaluated him: Light-skinned, no more than five-eight, maybe one-thirty-five. Late thirties, early forties—possibly older. Erect posture, dapper. Simple dark suit, crisp beige shirt, subdued tie. Cropped, well-barbered hair. Buffed nails, firm handshake.

He had begun introductions, and she turned her attention to the group around the conference table.

Fred Grayson, wearing a green striped shirt and green tie, adjusted horn-rimmed glasses over owlish hazel eyes as he rose to shake hands. He nodded, his head a mass of regular waves of thick gray-brown hair.

Harley Burton, pristine white shirtsleeves rolled up over thick arms knotted with muscles, seized her hand and pumped it vigorously; as he sat down he yanked on a black and white patterned tie, and stared at her with piercing dark eyes.

Duane Fletcher ran a tidying hand over the dark fringe circling his perfectly spherical bald head, and shook hands with a moist hand. His smile was shy. He wore a bright yellow shirt with a tie of yellow and purple stripes.

Gretchen Phillips, dark-haired, tiny, very pretty in a filmy lilac blouse, nodded and smiled, her delicate lips accented by pale lipstick; she looked at Kate with cool blue-gray eyes alert with appraisal and curiosity.

Guy Adams' handshake was warm and firm, and several seconds longer than necessary. His jacket and tie were the color of rich cream, his shirt the color of coffee. She took in the reddish-blond hair carefully styled to compensate for its thinness, the green eyes not quite focused on her. Turned out like a Brooks Brothers ad, she thought, unsuccessfully resisting the impulse of dislike.

She said, "I trust all of you understand the importance of giving any information you have to us, not discussing it with each other until our interviews are complete. Any of you may possess information of a value—"

There was a sharp rap, and the door swung open. In increasing amazement Kate stared at the young woman who sidled into the room. A tight fuzzy aqua sweater covered thin slouched shoulders and almost imperceptible breasts; bare bony knees poked out from below a wrinkled khaki skirt that outlined stick-like thighs receding toward a pelvis and stomach which were thrust forward. A pointed chin jutted aggressively. The woman held a stack of folders carelessly under one arm; smoke drifted upward from a cigarette cupped in the palm of the other hand.

"Detective Delafield, this is Billie Sullivan," Gail Freeman said in a flat tone. "Fergus Parker's secretary."

"A lady dick," Billie Sullivan rasped, extending a hand. "The boss would be pissed as hell."

Kate managed to smother a laugh, but not her smile. She grasped skeletal fingers that felt like a collection of dry twigs. From around the conference table there were coughs and cleared throats; Gretchen Phillips chuckled softly.

Billie Sullivan said, "So how do you like the Modern Office way of terminating employees?" Her laugh was like the snapping and breaking of glass.

Gretchen Phillips chuckled again. Gail Freeman said sternly, "Billie, did you finish that special report for Philadelphia?"

"About. I gave the shit part to Ellie." She added, "The office idiot, likes to type numbers." This last remark seemed directed at Kate, but Billie Sullivan's wide-set greenish eyes looked off each in a different direction, and Kate was not quite certain. Billie Sullivan pushed wispy carroty hair off a pale freckled forehead, and dragged at her cigarette, cheeks sinking inward with the suction; she hissed out smoke in a thin jet stream.

"Billie, watch that ash on this light carpet," Fred Grayson warned.

Casting a glance of undisguised contempt at Fred Grayson, she deposited the folders in an untidy heap on the conference room table and flicked inch-long ash into a palm

without flinching; then she moved in two long loping strides, cadaverous body slouched into the shape of a question mark, and released the ash from her palm into a wastebasket. She lifted a thick sandal and stubbed out her cigarette against the serrated sole, sending sparks cascading. She dropped in the blackened butt.

"For chrissake," muttered Fred Grayson.

"Thank you, Billie." Gail Freeman's voice was distant and formal. "Please bring me that report the moment it's finished."

"Certainly. Sir," she added, and grinned, revealing wolfish yellow teeth. A blue eyelid drooped over an unfocused eye. For whom the wink was intended, Kate could not guess. Billie Sullivan loped to the door, and turned. "Pleasure meeting you, lady copper." The door swung shut on a sound that was again like shattering glass—Billie Sullivan's laughter.

"Gail," Fred Grayson, said, "that—that woman—"

"One of the first items on the new agenda," Gail Freeman said curtly. He rose. "Why don't we continue this meeting in your office, Fred? I've promised use of this room to the detectives."

Guy Adams immediately got to his feet; Gretchen Phillips gathered up the folders on the table. "Mr. Freeman," Kate said, "would you please remain."

The managers trooped out, Duane Fletcher casting a nervous glance over his shoulder at Gail Freeman, as if at a victim facing an uncertain but surely grim fate.

Kate said quietly, "An ugly business, Mr. Freeman."

"Gail." Freeman crossed his arms and looked directly at her. "Worst thing I ever saw was a guy that rolled into my foxhole without a head and his guts falling out."

Kate said softly, "I was in Da Nang. Marine Supply Corps. But I didn't see things like that till I joined LAPD."

"Pusan," Freeman said, and grinned at her puzzlement. "Different war. Korea. I'm older than I look."

"Fifty-three, Kate," Taylor said.

Taylor was already wasting time, she thought with irritation. "Mr. Freeman, would it be possible to make another room available to us in addition to this one?"

"Luther Garrett left for San Francisco yesterday. His office is in the service bay."

"I'll take that one, Kate," Taylor said. "Be in there interviewing the service people if you need me."

"We have a paging system," Freeman said.

"Good." She nodded dismissal at Taylor. "Mr. Freeman, I understand the victim was VP of operations. Who's in charge now?"

"No one, officially. That decision'll have to come out of Philadelphia, the home office. May take several days."

"Understandable. But didn't Fergus Parker delegate when he was gone or on vacation?"

Freeman shook his head. "You could always get him by phone. But if he decided it wasn't urgent, he'd have your ass hanging from a flagpole."

Kate grinned. "I worked for somebody like that years ago. We called him Insecure Sam."

"I'd never call Fergus Parker insecure," Freeman said drily. "Paranoid, maybe."

"Sounds like you didn't care much for him," she said casually, watching him.

Freeman looked at her steadily. "Let me put it this way. I made the identification of the body. I thought the knife looked well in him."

Kate cleared her throat vigorously to avoid laughing. "You must not be too concerned about being a suspect."

Freeman's laugh was short. "I'll just be one on a list."

"Really?" She tucked her notebook into her bag to encourage response. "Who else would like to see Fergus Parker dead?"

Freeman shook his head, and leaned against the table, hands in his pockets. "I speak only for Gail Freeman. Especially under the circumstances. I listen to gossip, I don't spread it."

She studied his austere face, the carmel flesh drawn across ascetic bones. Even with his jacket unbuttoned and tie slightly askew, he managed a tidy elegance. She said coolly, "Don't you want to see a killer caught?"

Freeman shrugged. "All I am is curious. Who it was that popped his cork."

"Not necessarily he. A woman just as easily."

"Yes. Forgive my prejudiced and sexist remark."

Kate was amused, but she said sternly, "Mr. Freeman, I expect you to be cooperative, within reason."

"I will be, within reason." There was not the slightest hint of sarcasm in his tone.

"Do you know of any reason why the dead man would want to harm himself?"

"Harm himself? You mean . . . *suicide*?" Gail Freeman chuckled; his chuckle became a laugh, gaining rapidly in volume and resonance and infectiousness.

Kate found herself grinning. "I take it the answer is no."

"Most emphatically no. The man was lord of his universe. Loved using and abusing his power. Somebody did it to him and you can take that to the bank."

Kate said, "Would you mind taking me around the office so I can get a better feel for the layout? To the lobby first, I think."

"Sure." He opened the door for Kate, walked with her down the corridor. "One question. Do you have any objection if I fire Billie Sullivan?"

"Why now? Wouldn't you want her for continuity's sake, when the new man comes in?"

"She wouldn't contribute anything useful, just spread poison." Freeman's voice rose in forcefulness. "She does no work to speak of. And creates personnel problems. The little work Parker gave her she always farmed out to the other women. If I ever challenged her, Parker always said she was too busy. The other employees despise her."

"I can well understand," Kate said. "My—I had a friend in an office politics situation like that. Ended up quitting.

But I ask you to hold up just a little longer. Over the span of the initial investigation. Because of her position in relation to the victim. She may have useful information you're not aware of."

"Your objections are well within reason." Freeman nodded toward the hallway. "Can I have that office cleaned up? Smells like a sewer with all that spilled booze."

"Afraid not. The crime scene will have to be sealed pending review of our reports, till we notify you. We'll close and seal the door, release the hallway as soon as our team finishes. All those bottles in there, I assume Fergus Parker was a drinking man?"

"Not to my knowledge. At least not during working hours. We kept ice for him in the kitchen refrigerator but he used it only for visitors."

Kate took out her notebook and roughly sketched the main features of the lobby: the elevators, the doors, the receptionist's desk. Gail Freeman said conversationally, "Being a female detective must present its challenges."

She felt the familiar heavy weariness at being reminded of her singularity. The tired knowledge that always she was silhouetted against her background. Always.

Always. Growing up, she had been taller and stronger, more aggressive than the other girls; in look and manner, hopelessly unfeminine by their standards. Among similarly uniformed women in the Marine Corps, she had been resented for her unusual physical strengths and command presence. She had been the woman reluctantly singled out in her division of the Los Angeles Police Department for one advancement after another as LAPD, in stubborn fighting retreat, gradually succumbed to increasing pressures for change.

And always there had been that one most essential difference: she was a woman who desired only other women.

That she had always stood out in her differentness had no longer mattered after Anne. As long as there had been Anne to love her for all of her differentness . . .

She looked at Gail Freeman. Had she welcomed a discussion of this topic, there was no time, and with Gail Freeman currently a suspect, it was hardly appropriate. She said, gauging the distance in both her voice and her face, "Being a black manager must present its challenges."

Freeman did not reply. He leaned against the reception desk, arms crossed, watching her.

This man is a very class act, she decided. She said, "The receptionist, would you ask her to come out here?"

"Sure. Judy's filing in the service bay." He picked up the receiver on the console behind the black desk, punched a number; his amplified voice came out of the loudspeaker in the ceiling interrupting the Muzak: "Judy Markham, please come to the lobby."

Scant moments later, a blue-eyed, large-breasted young woman Kate judged to be in her early twenties came into the lobby, tucking the tail of a white silken blouse into a red plaid skirt, flinging long straight blonde hair off her face with a practiced toss of her head. Kate looked at her with pleasure.

"Judy Markham, this is Detective Delafield."

Judy Markham looked at her in consternation. "Jeez, this mean I can't come back on the desk yet? Filing's the *pits.*"

Some people, Kate thought sadly, should never be allowed to open their mouths. But she smiled and said gently, "I think everyone feels that way about filing. I'd like you to explain some things about your job. Would you answer a few questions?"

"Sure. I heard we had a lady cop here, it's great. Uh, what do I call you?" She looked Kate over doubtfully.

"Detective," supplied Gail Freeman.

"Oh." She brightened, then shrieked, "Like *Cagney and Lacey!*"

"Somewhat," Kate said, gritting her teeth.

"Judy," Gail Freeman said, grinning, "stop wasting the detective's time. Just answer her questions."

Kate learned that Judy Markham first recorded, then announced all visitors; that she controlled entry through the doors on either end of the lobby by dialing a two-digit code on her console to release the electronic locks, which relocked after a thirty-second delay. And that employees had their own key for after hours, but she customarily dialed them in during the day.

"So no one can get in before or after hours unless they have a key," Kate said.

"Nope."

"What about ex-employees?"

"I collect their keys as a matter of routine," Freeman said. "For security."

Kate smiled. "Ever change the locks?"

Freeman shook his head, his chuckle rueful. "I hear you."

Kate examined the visitor's log. "Miss Markham, anybody unusual visit Mr. Parker recently?"

Judy Markham flicked a glance at Gail Freeman. "Whaddya mean, recently?"

"The past few weeks or so. Mr. Freeman," Kate said casually, "why don't I call you in a few minutes when I'm through out here?"

"Sure." Hands in his pockets, Gail Freeman strolled off and let himself out of the far end of the lobby with his key.

Judy Markham jabbed at a name in the book. "*This* creep. This bald sweaty little *shit*! Did he come on to me? I like told him *four times* I gotta *boyfriend.* He said El Grosso in there—" She gestured violently at Fergus Parker's office, "—said I gave him *head jobs*! All the *time*! He offered me *fifty bucks*! I hope El Grosso took six *hours* to die!"

Kate said soberly, impressed by her fury, "Did Mr. Parker ever come on to you?"

"With his big fat fucking mouth," she spat. "Remarks, you know? Couldn't say hello, he'd say something about my tits. 'Good morning, Mr. Parker,' she mimicked. " 'Good

morning, Judy, nice sweater, color makes you look tasty as ice cream, yum yum.' *Ychhh*! And *look* at me? Like he's *fucking* me with those piggy popeyes!''

Will I ever get used to how easily the young women use the language, Kate thought. "You didn't want to tell me this in front of Mr. Freeman. Why not?"

"He'd of got upset. He's a good guy."

"Miss Markahm, it's his *job* to get upset. Why didn't you complain to him?"

"What was I s'poseta complain about?"

"Harassment. There are increasingly stringent penalties in this state against sexual harassment."

She laughed, mocking peals. "Come on, Cagney. You know how it is. I'm a blonde, a receptionist. I'd be up shit's creek, I ever complain. Laws don't make anything any different. You think I take shit? I gotta good friend, Susie's a stewardess. Cabin attendants they call 'em now. You oughtta hear Susie. Guys figure they got a license. Not all of 'em like El Grosso but I get remarks all the time. And anyway, you think any place's any different from this? You really think that?"

"I really don't know, Miss Markham," Kate said softly. "I only know laws are meant to protect people."

"Hey, Cagney, you're nice." Judy Markham tossed the hair back from her face again, ingenuous blue eyes focused ambiguously on Kate's. "You can call me Judy."

She kept her face expressionless, her voice carefully toneless. "I appreciate that, Miss Markham. Would you page Mr. Freeman?"

"Ah shit. You gonna make me go back and file?"

"Just a little longer. Until we can release the floor for public entry. I'll appreciate your patience."

"Sure, Cagney." Again the ambiguous gaze. Judy Markham sauntered from the lobby, hips swaying.

Sketching in her notebook with intense concentration, ignoring curious faces peering at her, Kate silently walked the hallways, recording names, pacing distances to the stair-

case, the lobby. Gail Freeman strolled beside her, hands in his pockets, lacorically giving names and titles. Again they walked past the crime scene; past Billie Sullivan who sat at her desk running raw-boned fingers through strings of carroty hair as she spoke on the phone; past a door marked MEN PRIVATE.

"The executive washroom," Gail Freeman said. "Opens with a key, of course. Quite a flap when Gretchen Phillips was promoted to sales manager but excluded from the washroom. She didn't care a fig but the rest of the women were mad as hornets." He chuckled reminiscently.

"What did you do?"

"Nothing. I only do something about what I can do something about." He paused before the next door. "Like here. This is word processing. Quite an operation." He pushed open the heavy door.

An incessant rat-a-tat echoed from the machines operated by a row of women attached to earphones. White print blipped frantically down a half dozen luminous green computer screens. One of the operators, a tiny black woman, left her computer to rush to a giant orange trash can, dump an armload of paper, rush back to her console. Two telexes chugged out yellow paper. An Oriental woman gesticulated in eloquent frustration as she spoke on the phone. A telefax whirred rhythmically.

Kate gazed at the maelstrom of activity, noting the relatively low noise level. The ceiling and walls were of sound-absorbent porous cork; the brown carpet, unsightly with excisions—apparently for the movement of electrical outlets—was unusually thick. Four or five women had looked up as the door opened; they waved to Gail Freeman, who acknowledged them with a smile and an upraised hand. He let the door swing shut; the sound cut off abruptly.

"A factory," Kate said.

"Yes. And that group in there, they're such good people, they work so hard . . . Ever been in a factory?"

"No." She walked slowly on down the hall with him.

"I come from a blue-collar town. Toledo. Worked in a wheel factory. The noise—enough to explode your brains. That's how that room used to be, till I managed to get the composition walls, the carpet. But without Guy's help I could never have made those changes."

"Why not, Mr. Freeman?"

"Budget." He said the word the way she had heard other people utter the word fuck. "Fergus Parker told me there was no room in the budget. But even in this uncertain economy, sales down, earnings down, Fergus Parker thought nothing of taking the entire sales staff to San Francisco for a quote business meeting unquote, thousands of dollars, all expenses paid, nothing's too good. And I've been to those quote meetings unquote and know how little quote business unquote is done. But he couldn't find any room in his budget for a few thousand bucks to make that room liveable. Guy Adams was the one who told me to do it, just give him the bills and he'd have the company take care of it."

"How does Mr. Adams have that authority?"

"Had that authority," Gail Freeman corrected sadly. "He's a nephew of the owner—but old Guy Adams died last year and the company's been reorganizing ever since." He paused in the hallway. "This is Guy's office. It's quite an office."

Kate did not look at the office, but at the man sitting on the corner of his desk talking on the phone, facing the windows, his back to them. Again fighting the impulse of dislike, she studied the carefully combed reddish-blond hair, the elegant breadth of the shoulders, the tapered slenderness of the body, the trim waist and hips emphasized by the perfectly cut cream-colored jacket. "I'll take care of it, consider it done," Guy Adams was saying, his voice soft and husky, reminiscent of an actor's voice she had heard in an old war movie during the late hours of the last sleepless night. Aldo Ray, she remembered with satisfaction. Then Guy Adams hung up and turned around and looked at her with startled, widening eyes. She inventoried his features:

thin straight nose, a wide mouth with finely shaped lips, a thin face of fine bones. The features of an aristocrat. She nodded to Guy Adams and walked on.

She went into the kitchen, studied its layout, then continued down the hall. She paused outside the closed door of Gail Freeman's corner office. "Do all the managers close their doors when they're away from the office?"

"Only when they leave for the night, usually. I always close mine if I leave during the day because I have personnel information in my office. The other managers will too if they've been working on something confidential."

"Like what?"

"Oh, salary projections, for instance. I don't believe many of them actually lock their doors at night. I'm always reminding Guy to close and lock his, I chewed him out again just yesterday. It's the only one with anything of real value. But the elevators and staircase are secured at night, the cleaning people are very reliable, we've had no instances at all of theft."

"I see. What—" She broke off. In the office next to Gail Freeman's she saw a woman with shoulder-length wavy brown hair, her chair swiveled so that her gaze was apparently fixed on the gray towers of downtown Los Angeles. Kate took Gail Freeman's arm, led him down the hall a few steps. "Who is that?"

"Ellen O'Neil, my new assistant. She found the—well, you know that, of course. She's very upset, as you can imagine."

"Yes. Detective Taylor mentioned that you informed Mrs. Parker. How did she take the news?"

Freeman cleared his throat. "Well, she was shocked, of course." He gave Kate a gauging look, then said, "She told me first thing she'd do would be to call her kids back East, have them come home. Then she told me she had lots of black, it was the color she mostly wore once she married Fergus Parker. Then she poured herself a highball glass full of scotch, no water, no ice. Then the grieving widow asked

how much insurance I thought Fergus Parker might have."

Kate was unable to smother a smile. "How much does he have?"

"The home office'll call her with the exact figure. But at his salary I'd say at least a quarter million automatically, more if he picked up any of the electives. The widow Parker should be pretty comfortable. Might even buy herself a red dress."

"Indeed. Mr. Freeman, I'd like you to supply a complete list of current employees and their addresses, and all transferred and ex-employees over the period of time the victim has worked in this office."

"We can punch that out of the computer with no problem."

"Are the employment records on file in this office, or Philadelphia?"

"Here."

"We'll have to have those files pulled for our inspection."

Freeman frowned slightly. "I believe I'd better run that one past the legal people in Philly."

"Whatever. I imagine a simple search warrant will be sufficient to satisfy them. Are you filling the breach for Mr. Parker? Since he doesn't have a designated successor?"

"We've decided that two of us should. Myself and Fred Grayson."

Kate consulted her sketch. "Sales manager, southeast corner office."

"That's the one. Senior manager in service time. Anything you need in terms of office functions or personnel, that's my bailiwick normally."

"Good. I'd like to see Miss O'Neil now. Would you have her come to the conference room?"

33

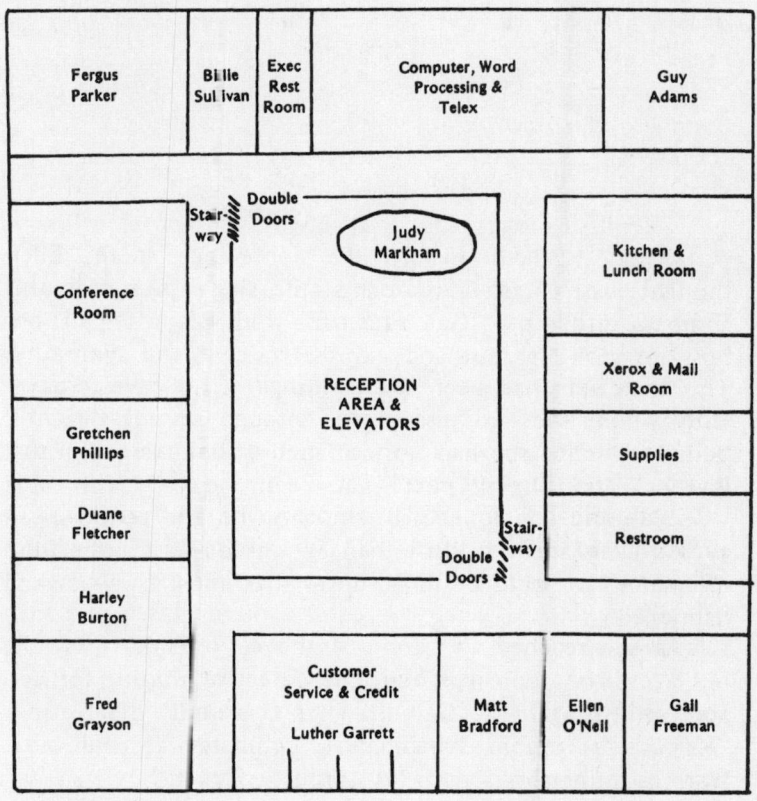

3

As she walked toward the conference room, Ellen thought warmly of Guy Adams, the single person in this company other than Gail Freeman—who was, after all, her boss—to seek her out and express concern and sympathy. This man who had been so charmingly at ease yesterday— with whom she had discovered, through several elegantly bound volumes she had noticed in his bookcase, a mutual love for the English poets—had been today scarcely able to speak and had looked ill, she thought, the gentle green eyes tricken and dull. But then he was obviously the kind of man who would be more upset than most by what had happened.

As she reached the door of the conference room she felt a pull of curiosity about the detective waiting for her, and smiled again at Gail Freeman's sardonic description: "Kojak's a lovable marshmallow compared to this lady. Warmest thing about her is her corduroy jacket."

Ellen opened the door. "Detective Delafield," she said.

The woman sitting across from her at the conference table, her dark hair salted with gray, her corduroy jacket a light soft green, was examining a sketch, holding a leather-bound notebook sideways in strong square hands. She looked at Ellen with light blue eyes that were cool, level, and candid.

Ellen stared at her. *Stephie can talk all she wants about not being able to tell for sure, but if this woman's not a lesbian then neither am I.*

At the sight of Ellen O'Neil, Kate felt a twisting sensation, an excruciating pleasure-pain that became mostly pain. The same height—give or take half an inch. Hips only a little thinner, well-shaped breasts like Anne's, the contours outlined by the soft beige blouse. Lips a little fuller, nose straighter. Prettier. But then Anne had looked like no one else with those features that all tilted upward—delicate bow lips and eyes darker than Ellen O'Neil's—slanty like a Chinaman's, Anne had always said . . . Anne's hair lighter and not so neat as Ellen O'Neil's, with those unruly curls clustered at the nape of her neck . . .

Ellen was startled, puzzled; the detective had looked up from her notebook, her eyes swiftly traveling up Ellen's body to focus on her face, the light blue eyes narrowing in what appeared to be pain.

"Detective Delafield," she said again.

Not much different from Anne's voice, that low throatiness of Anne's . . .

"Detective Delafield?" Ellen looked at her intently, in concern.

Kate cleared her throat. "Excuse me, you reminded . . . I was thinking about something else."

"With great concentration." Ellen smiled, to coax softness into that strong face, those grim features.

Oh God, it's so unfair . . . her smile is like Anne's. She smoothed a fresh page in her notebook and cleared her throat again. "Sit down please, Miss O'Neil. I know this has been hard for you, I know you've told your story several times already, had it recorded. But I'd like you to go over it again. Very slowly. Include every detail you can think of. Starting with where and when you parked your car."

Ellen relaxed. She had always been comfortable around people—especially women—like Stephie, like Kate Delafield, with authority in their voices, strength in their faces,

deliberation in their gestures and manner. "Well, I parked in the garage at twenty after seven—"

"How did you know the time?"

She spoke glibly, having already answered this question twice, "I was listening to the news on KFWB. They announce the time constantly in the morning. And I was annoyed I hadn't figured the time better, I could've slept a little longer. This is my first job in more than a year. I'm not used to getting up this early." She thought, if she pursues this she'll find out I live with a woman . . .

But Kate Delafield said, "I see. Was there anyone in the garage or lobby that you recognized?"

"No, but I'm new. I know hardly anyone."

"What about the people that you do know? Did you see any of them?"

"No."

"Who would you recognize? Name them."

In expanding warmth and pride, she was absorbing the knowledge that this impressive and highly professional woman was the detective in charge of this murder investigation—and a lesbian. "Well, Gail of course. And Guy. Guy Adams. I'm not used to calling managers by first name but that's the custom here—" She broke off her attempt at conversation as she met the cool blue glance, and continued hurriedly, "I was introduced to Luther Garrett yesterday. Some people from the service bay and word processing. I don't know their names but I'd know their faces. Billie Sullivan. That's all."

"Are you sure?"

After a moment's pause, she nodded.

"Positive?"

"Positive." She was annoyed.

"What about Judy Markham?"

"Oh. Yes. I forgot about her."

Knowing Kate Delafield's silence was deliberate, Ellen felt heat rise to her face.

Kate watched her; her face had a slight ruddiness like

Anne's, natural hea thy color without need of the sun. Kate allowed herself to briefly wonder about Ellen O'Neil's "roommate," as Taylor had termed her. She said, "That's why I want you to take your time with your answers, Miss O'Neil. Give them thought, reflection. Something may have registered in your mind that you've simply forgotten, something obvious, like Judy Markham. And at the present time you're our single witness, the only source we have."

"All right," she murmured, chastened.

"Go on, Miss O'Neil."

"I took the elevator up. The first elevator as you come into the lobby," she added, attempting a grin.

Oh God she is so like Anne, Kate thought wrenchingly, and closed her eyes for a moment against her pain. "Back up a moment. Was there anyone in the building lobby? Anyone at all?" She watched Ellen O'Neil bend her head over her lap in thought, the soft dark hair separating into currents of subtle browns.

"No. No one."

"What about the guard?"

"There was no guard. The first time I saw Rick and Mike was when they came up on the elevator to get me."

Ellen O'Neil had lifted her head; her gaze was direct, the voice quavery but decisive. "Go on," Kate said. "You got off the elevator."

"I stayed out there for a minute or two, just looking around."

"What did you look at? Describe it to me as well as you can."

Kate held up a hand twice to slow her as she made meticulous shorthand notes of descriptions of furniture and color and fabric; she would check the accuracy of Ellen O'Neil's memory from these notes. Some women pay attention to the damnedest things, she thought; they can describe the most intricate weave in a fabric . . . She asked, "Did you smell anything?"

"Not that I remember," she said after a moment.

"Perfume? Men's cologne?"

"No. Men's cologne I'd remember. I don't like it."

"I don't either," Kate said with a smile. "Go on."

Ellen was surprised by the smile—magnetically attractive on Kate Delafield's strong face—and surprised by the remark, which made her seem not nearly so bloodless. "I went back to my office—"

"How much time had elapsed by now?" Kate interrupted. "Since you parked your car?" She watched Ellen O'Neil raise both hands, slender, prettier than Anne's, and touch to her temples long fingers tipped with clear polish.

"Three or four minutes."

"Okay. So now it's seven twenty-five. Go on."

As Ellen O'Neil reviewed each move she had made, Kate drew dotted lines on the drawings in her notebook. She tapped her Flair pen on her sketch of the conference room. "Why did you stop here? Why take the long way back around to the kitchen?"

Memory formed vividly in Ellen's mind of her introduction to Fergus Parker. He had leaned back in his immense leather chair, lifted a fat black shiny shoe to one corner of his black slab of a desk, then inserted a black cigar between his wide thick lips, clicking flame from a gold lump of a lighter, holding the cigar between porcine fingers, jowls quivering as he puffed clouds of odoriferous smoke at her. His voice had rumbled out of a chest ringed in fat and encased in a pale yellow suede vest. But she had not heard his words, only seen his eyes: gray and protruding and fixed on her, fixed precisely between her legs.

"Well," Ellen said to Kate Delafield, "I, uh, don't know my way around the office yet."

Kate noted her hesitation and said mildly, "Understandable. But still, why retrace your steps? Why not just continue?"

The hell with it, Ellen decided. "Well, to tell you the truth—"

"Please do."

She doesn't give an inch. In irritation Ellen met the dispassionate blue eyes shaped somewhat like Stephanie's Irritation intensified at the thought of Stephanie. *Damn her, treating me like some powder puff excuse for a woman . . .* "I didn't want to run into Fergus Parker," she stated. "I didn't want to risk being alone with him."

The ever-charming Fergus Parker, Kate thought. "I understand you met him only yesterday."

Ellen said dourly, "With some men it doesn't take long." When Kate smiled the unexpectedness of it again warmed her.

Indicating with her pen on the sketch, Kate said, "So you came back along this way to your office, down the north corridor . . . Did you smell anything?"

"Coffee. Just as I got to the kitchen."

"The coffee pot, Miss O'Neil. Concentrate. Picture it as you walked into the kitchen, as you walked over to pour yourself a cup. How full was the pot? How much coffee was left?"

She touched the slim fingers again to her temples. "Better than half."

"Which means how many cups would you say were gone?"

She sighed, thinking, her unseeing eyes on the green-gold painting covering the wall behind Kate. "Well, styrofoam cups, maybe four. Two or so, if you're filling a mug."

"But a person could make half a pot, isn't that true? Wouldn't someone be more likely to do that early in the morning when no one else was due in till eight o'clock?"

"Not with that kind of coffee maker." She was decisive. "The coffee's premeasured. And the pot of water you put in to make the coffee doesn't make that same pot, but the one after it."

Pleased, Kate paused to complete several notes. "Now, you walked out into the hallway carrying the coffee pot, thinking Guy Adams was in. Why did you think so?"

"Since there were only two offices I hadn't walked past,

and the rest of the office doors were closed, that left him
and Fergus Parker. And I didn't think Fergus Parker would
make coffee." It occurred to her that she had lost personal
awareness of Kate Delafield. What was going on had nothing
to do with either of them as lesbians.

Kate tapped her pen on her sketch. "What about these
people in word processing? You didn't walk past this room.
Any of them could be in, couldn't they?"

"Well, yes. Possibly. If they got here early for some
reason. But Gail told me yesterday their overtime is pre-
approved by him. And one of my duties is to send overtime
reports daily by teletype to Philadelphia. He approved overtime yesterday for only two people in credit who had to
work last night."

"But someone could have been in there."

"Someone could have been in any of the offices. Working
behind a closed door."

"Was Guy Adams' door closed?"

"Uh, yes." She bit her lips; her response had been pure
impulse.

Kate looked at her in surprise. Training and experience,
every instinct told her Ellen O'Neil was lying. The eye shift.
The change in facial set, vocal intonation. And she had been
unprepared for the question, had not taken enough time to
consider it if she were genuinely uncertain. Kate watched her,
allowing silence to accumulate.

What did Guy have to do with this, Ellen thought. Why
should I put him through all this? Why should I give that dear
man a problem?

Kate thought: She's looking at me the way people do
when they're lying. Why in God's name would she want to
protect Guy Adams? Maybe Taylor's wrong about her and
her roommate. Maybe they're just that, roommates. "How
long have you known Mr. Adams?"

"Just since yesterday, of course."

Belligerence had been in the tone. Hesitating, Kate
looked down at her notes. Her training told her to bring all

the weight of her authority upon Ellen O'Neil's stiffening resistance, back her into a corner, suggest—no, threaten—a charge of obstruction of justice, of perjury. That worked with the majority of witnesses in the world of crime and criminals, and certainly would work here in Amateur City, as Taylor had termed it. It would also charge—chill—her tenuous relationship with this woman, a witness with a strong appearance of honesty and credibility if and when a case was put together to present for prosecution. She would come back to Guy Adams; perhaps later Ellen O'Neil would correct her story voluntarily. Strictly a judgment call, she told herself.

A scrupulous inner voice asked, is it a judgment call, or are you avoiding confrontation because she reminds you of Anne?

She said, "What made you first think something was wrong?"

"Thudding sounds, vibration under my feet from somebody running. A door slamming. Loudly."

Ellen O'Neil had shifted in her chair with the new direction of the question, and Kate noted the easing of her posture. "At what point did you hear the thudding? Where were you exactly in the hallway?"

"Right outside Guy's office." Ellen sat up again, remembering that she had been looking at that moment through Guy's window at the green of the mountains, the mist over the ocean.

"And the slamming door?"

"The same. It was only a few seconds later."

"I see. What did you do then?"

"Nothing. It came from Fergus Parker's direction, so I figured it was his office door and none of my business."

"But did you move at all? Where were you in the hallway? Had you gone back toward the kitchen?"

She concentrated. "I might have taken a step in that direction. But then I heard glass breaking and I ran down the hall."

"Ran?"

"I was carrying the coffee pot, but I moved as fast as I could. I slowed up as I got to his office."

Deliberately, Kate stared at her. Then she said, injecting a note of cold skepticism into her tone, "You decided not to investigate thudding feet and a slamming door but yet you *ran* down the hall because glass was breaking?"

Those ice-blue eyes—like being on a skewer. Does she think I'm making this up, for God's sake? "Look, the noise was so *loud*. There was a kind of . . . I don't know, *violence* to the way it was smashing, like something awful was happening."

"Something awful *was* happening," Kate said quietly, seizing the moment. "A man was dying. Miss O'Neil, have you left anything out that you heard or saw in that hallway? Anything?"

Ellen hesitated; the blue eyes held hers, the voice was compelling. But anything she said now would only compound matters, and Guy had been so kind to her . . . "That's all I can remember now," she said. "But I'll give it—give everything more thought."

"Good." The moment was gone, but the answer had been temporizing. "What happened next?"

Tears sprang to Ellen O'Neil's eyes. Kate allowed her to speak uninterrupted, not taking notes; she listened without moving to the details of discovering the body; the realization that a killer might be anywhere on the floor; her actions in the lobby; the arrival of the guards. As Ellen O'Neil described the two guards backing toward her with guns drawn and then the descent to safety on the elevator, her voice broke.

"Many people—most people—would have screamed, run in panic, perhaps—probably—gotten themselves killed." Kate spoke slowly, turning and smoothing pages of her notes to allow Ellen O'Neil time. She had always considered her lack of reaction to tears an advantage she held over male detectives, most of whom dissolved in the presence of a

sobbing woman, and conversely treated a sobbing man with cold contempt. Tears were a healthy manifestation, that was all; she envied anyone, male or female, who could do something she could not do at all. "In most crimes of murder," she said, "the killer will protect himself at all cost. You handled yourself with the kind of presence of mind we teach to police officers."

Flushing with the pleasure of a compliment from this forbidding woman, Ellen murmured, "Thank you." Then she stared as Kate Delafield buried her face in her hands and took a deep shuddering breath, ran her hands through the graying hair. Could she be suffering from some illness?

Like a swimmer coming up from a depth and gasping for air, Kate surfaced from the agony of memory—Anne's face flushed after lovemaking. "Miss O'Neil?" Her voice seemed to echo in her chest. "I know this has been very difficult. But would you show me in the office what you've described to me?"

"Of course," Ellen said gently.

They went into the lobby, through the far doors and into Ellen's office, then down the corridor. Ellen paused before Matt Bradford's office. "I came in here first."

A balding portly man, jacketless, a well-loosened tie hanging from the unbuttoned collar of a white shirt, was bent over his desk examining blueprints. He did not look up. Kate took Ellen's arm and led her along the corridor.

"Miss O'Neil, Matt Bradford's office. Was it open?"

"Yes, but he wasn't in yesterday and it was open all day."

"Do you know why?"

She shook her head. Kate jotted a notation to ask Gail Freeman.

"Then I looked in here." She pushed open the door to Customer Service and Credit.

"Hi Cagney!" shrieked Judy Markham.

Activity halted; a sea of faces turned up to them. People nudged one another, pointed. Ellen stepped back, let the

44

door swing shut.

"Jesus," she whispered.

Kate said calmly, "Who was it that predicted everyone'd be famous for twenty minutes?"

"Andy Warhol," Ellen answered automatically, still stunned by the staring faces.

"In a day or two everything will be back to normal. Try not to let that part bother you. Let's go on."

Kate verified a few notes as they walked slowly past open offices, and she looked in. Fred Grayson glanced up, then bent over his work. Harley Burton's office was empty. Duane Fletcher, broad yellow-shirted back turned to them, hands behind his bald head, sat with his feet up on his credenza and stared out the window. Gretchen Phillips talked on the phone in low calm tones as she searched through mounds of paper burying her desk.

Billie Sullivan passed them with her dipping, loping gait, stringy carrot-colored hair swaying. She had added a new element to her costume of khaki skirt and fuzzy aqua sweater: her legs were covered by ripply gray leg warmers.

"That's Billie Sullivan," Ellen said, chuckling at the amazement on Kate Delafield's face.

"Yes, I know." Kate watched Billie Sullivan until she vanished around a corner. "Unreal."

Remembering the events of this day, Ellen said soberly, "Gail wants to fire her."

"Yes, he told me," Kate said thoughtfully. Billie Sullivan could be an interesting interview. Perhaps two interviews— one before, one after her termination.

At the conference room Ellen said, "I came only this far."

Kate glanced back down the hallway, then walked toward Fergus Parker's office at the end of the corridor, to a lighted EXIT sign; she pulled open the heavy metal-weighted door that led to a staircase, let it swing shut, cushioning the momentum with pressure from her foot. She moved briskly across to Fergus Parker's office, pacing off the distance.

The door of the executive washroom was flung open and Harley Burton strode into the hall, rolling down the sleeves of his chalk white shirt. He nodded curtly as he came toward her; she felt pierced by his dark stare. He continued down the corridor toward his office. She heard Ellen murmur a greeting and Harley Burton's gruff-voiced rejoinder.

They retraced their steps, Ellen moving impatiently ahead, past Gail Freeman who was on the phone and tossed Kate a mock-military salute in passing. In the kitchen, Ellen reconstructed her actions of the morning, pouring coffee and then carrying the styrofoam cup and a half-filled coffee pot into the hallway toward Guy Adams' office.

Ellen smiled; Guy sat at his desk gesturing emphatically to a thin young woman with mountainous frizzy hair. He glimpsed Ellen and rose, murmuring apology to his visitor, and walked into the hallway.

"Ellen, is everything all right? Are you okay?"

Tension in the voice, thought Kate. And the way he stares at her . . .

"Is there anything I can do?" He had directed his question at Kate, then focused his gaze again on Ellen O'Neil.

Perhaps tense by nature, Kate thought. And he seems totally smitten by her . . . "I'll have questions for you later, Mr. Adams." When he did not move she added in a tone of dismissal, "Now if you'll excuse us."

Obediently, Guy Adams walked into his office, but remained just over the threshold, looking on. Kate said, "Miss O'Neil, I want you to tell me if what you hear is what you heard this morning."

Ellen turned to face Guy's office as she had that morning, then glanced back to see Kate Delafield walking down the corridor, straight and trim in her gray pants and corduroy jacket, her walk compact and purposeful. "I was facing this way," she said in a low tone to Guy. "As I recall, your office door was closed."

She searched his face; his green eyes stared dully into hers. She turned away to look down the hallway. Perhaps he

doesn't know it was open, she thought; maybe he doesn't even remember.

Kate had reached the lobby door. She pulled it fully open, released it. Cushioned by an air brake, it closed with stately progress, securing itself with a solid *thunk.*

"Much louder than that," Ellen called.

Kate walked across to Fergus Parker's office, grasped the doorknob, slammed the door violently.

Ellen walked part way down the hall. "It was loud like that, but not quite so close, you made the floor vibrate under my feet. I didn't feel that before, only from the footsteps. And besides, that door was wide open when I got to it."

Reflecting, Kate absently shifted the holster chafing her hip under her jacket. "The killer might've started to come out, spotted you, slammed the door in panic. Then decided you might come anyway, so he opened it again and hid behind it, waiting."

Ellen O'Neil shuddered, and Kate said quickly, "It's very unlikely, that scenario. There'd be no reason for him to open the door again. He'd be more likely to wait with it closed."

Ellen sipped coffee, calming herself and thinking. "Well, no. He might think he'd be more helpless that way, he'd have to judge when to come out and I might see him and escape, there might be someone else on the floor by now to help me. And the way Fergus Parker was killed, I don't know if he'd even have another weapon, unless it was a bludgeon of some kind."

Disagreeing with her, Kate nodded in respect for her logic. "Possible. But doubtful a killer would act so deliberately and coolly after committing such a crime. Natural instinct would almost certainly compel him to run. Miss O'Neil, I'd like to try something else. Would you go back to where you were before?"

She waited until Ellen had again stationed herself outside Guy Adams' office. Adams stood in his doorway still

looking on, his frizzy-haired visitor gone. Kate walked around the corner toward the conference room and the EXIT stairway. She pulled the EXIT fire door fully open, released it. Accumulating rapid momentum, the door hit the jamb with an echoing thunder of sound.

"That's it! That's it!" Ellen O'Neil shouted.

Kate glimpsed movement; Gretchen Phillips popped out of her doorway, then as swiftly vanished into her office. As Kate rounded the corner of the hallway, Ellen was trotting awkwardly toward her cradling the coffee pot.

"I'm positive that's what it was. The stairway door?"

"Right. Here, let me take the coffee pot." Kate smiled. "I won't need you to show me how you dropped it." She was pleased when Ellen O'Neil laughed.

"The killer ran down the stairs, then?"

"Probably. Exited in the garage, I would think."

"But sixteen floors? How would he have enough time? Rick and Mike said—"

"Excuse me." Gail Freeman had come up to them. "All the info you want, all the files are locked in the conference room." He tossed a key to Kate, who deftly caught it in her free hand. "They're confidential."

Kate pocketed the key. "I'll see they're properly safeguarded." She glanced at her watch. "Miss O'Neil, I'll have further questions. Let's say one-thirty. In the conference room." She turned to Gail Freeman. "If Detective Taylor is looking for me, 'll be with Mr. Grayson."

Ellen watched admiringly until Kate Delafield disappeared around the corner of the corridor.

4

Kate looked around slowly, amazed by the lackluster furnishings in the large corner office of Fred Grayson, senior sales manager of Modern Office, Inc. The prosaic square sofa and armchairs were of matching beige corduroy; a plain walnut coffee table matched two lamp tables; the pale blue lamps also matched. Books in groups of three or four were clustered between wood-block bookends, photographs huddled in small groups on the vast expanses of wall. A tiny table with a philodendron trailing from it had been placed indecisively along one wall; a number of sharp leg marks were visible and recent in the carpeting. On the credenza behind Fred Grayson, who sat at a massive oak desk, was a carefully posed photograph of a brown-haired woman perched at the far end of a beige sofa, three children stiffly erect beside her in descending order of height.

Fred Grayson puffed on a small cigar, a fine sprinkle of ash falling onto his dark green tie and over his desk blotter. "I'm surprised as hell you're letting people go in and out, even out to lunch."

Kate took out her notebook. "Not much choice. We can't keep people cooped up when we're still developing and evaluating background."

Fred Grayson raised bushy brown-gray eyebrows. "Well," he said.

The word had been said in two drawn-out syllables, the insinuation almost comical. "Any information you might have could be valuable," Kate encouraged. "Might even catch us a killer."

Grayson adjusted his horn rims, puffed on his little cigar, surveyed her. "My nephew's wife, she's in police work, maybe you know her? Denise Grayson. Pasadena. She's in, uh, traffic enforcement."

Meter maid, Kate thought. "Afraid not. I've never worked that division. With almost seven thousand of us in law enforcement—"

"Sure." Grayson nodded additional emphasis. "Denise's a little thing—bright girl, I'll concede that. She's talking more and more about a police career now that the politics of these times have forced the standards so much lower."

Kate looked at Grayson, and remained silent.

"Don't mean you of course," Grayson said hurriedly, his glance sliding away. "At least you're a decent height, what, five-eight? And look like you handle yourself fine. Not that I'd ever need that kind of help, but I'd sure hate to have one of these new five-foot lady cops try and bail me out of a tough situation."

"She wouldn't try," Kate said mildly, assessing the wide shoulders under the green striped shirt, the bulging biceps. "Every major police department today has trained teams for things like that. But if she did help, you might be surprised. In a contest with even a good-sized man, training can make all the difference."

"Too dangerous a line of work for women," Fred Grayson declared.

Kate shrugged. Why waste time trying to raise the consciousness of a person like Fred Grayson? But she said, "It's cop shows that promote the idea of danger. All the police in L.A. put together don't fire as many shots in a year as they do in some of those shows. The mortality rate's higher in many other professions. Mining. Construction. Even agriculture."

"I read all the time about you cops getting shot."

"From ambush, almost always. And it doesn't matter then whether you're five feet tall or seven feet tall. But there's accumulating evidence to suggest that the presence of women actually helps some situations—" Fred Grayson's scowl was deepening. He had hinted at information he possessed; she would lead him back to this subject.

"My nephew," Grayson said heavily, "he's not about to let Denise ever get into a situation like that. Little thing that she is, she ought to have more damn sense."

Kate chose her words, deciding to skirt the edge of hypocrisy. "Decisions like that are up to the people best informed and most directly involved, don't you think?"

"Damn right." Fred Grayson adjusted his glasses again. "Now don't misunderstand, I don't discriminate—"

"Mr. Grayson," Kate said impatiently, then paused to soften her tone. "You have information relevant to this investigation?"

"Say anything today somebody hollers discrimination," Grayson continued doggedly. "People misunderstand, you know." He was looking at her intently, hazel eyes owlish behind the thick lenses. "Tell somebody a damn *fact* about some minority group and they holler stereotype. They holler *bigot.*"

Understanding, Kate sat comfortably back in her chair, resisting an urge to lift an ankle to her knee. This was familiar ground. She smiled. "I may be a woman, but nobody's ever given me anything. I've worked for everything I have. And it's a statistical fact who's responsible for most crime in our fair city."

Fred Grayson beamed. "By God it's good to meet somebody who understands. Somebody you can talk to, not one of those bleeding hearts . . . I put stock in statistics, myself, you know."

"Somebody was knocking statistics to me just last week. Said just because the tables say a man's life expectancy's sixty-five doesn't mean he won't live a day beyond." Kate

chuckled; she was enjoying herself.

Fred Grayson's thick eyebrows almost met in a fierce beetling. He gestured with his cigar, dropping ash. "People know *shit* about statistics, they *always* argue with crap like that. Excuse my language but—"

Wanting to deemphasize the male–female aspects of this interview, Kate interrupted, "Forget the language. You can't say anything I haven't heard and plenty more." Abruptly she switched direction, saying bluntly, "You've got what, five, six blacks? A few Latinos?"

"The three beaners are okay. Quiet, mind their own business, aren't trying to take over the company. But the coons . . . " Puffing out an enormous cloud of smoke, he watched Kate. "Pardon me, I believe in calling a spade a spade."

Deliberately, Kate smiled. Grayson laughed, slapping his desk with heavy thwacks of a thick-fingered hand. "Good to meet somebody that understands," he repeated. "Cops, it takes cops to know the real world. We got five coons here in the office, two more outside. One's insolent as hell, the inky bastard. Works for Duane, southeast territory, no self-respecting white man'd ever take that territory. Gretchen's got one too, a cu—a woman named Cassie Franklin." He looked meaningfully at Kate's notebook. "I see you take a lot of notes. Important, what I'm telling you?"

"Good notes are very important in a case of homicide. You're telling me you think the black employees are involved?"

"Come on, Fergus was stabbed. You cops know how the jungle bunnies like knives. Niggers love cutting up whitey."

Kate turned to a fresh page in the back of her notebook and wrote four words, and looked up to see Grayson gazing at her in satisfaction. She said, "You know statistics and suspicion never got anyone arrested."

"Sure, I'm not that stupid. I got a top suspect for you. The head nigger.'

"Mr. Grayson, I'm not totally familiar with your

organization, your personnel—"

Grayson said impatiently, "The guy you were with in the hallway, the spade with the girl's name. The nigger they pushed into the wrong goddamn job." Grayson jabbed his cigar at a metal ashtray; ash teetered on the edge, fell onto the desk.

"Does Gail Freeman do a poor job?"

"Listen. A man in my position, I *need* a secretary. Before he got here, I *had* a secretary. Then he . . . reorganized." The word dripped acid. "He said Helen wasn't . . . productive." He seized the ashtray; sparks leaped onto the desk as he stabbed the life from his cigar. "So now he's got her in that damn big room back there. Working with Christ knows what all, Filipinos, niggers. Some Jap supervisor tells her what to do. Helen hates it."

"That's too bad," Kate said evenly. "But what motive would Freeman have for wanting Fergus Parker dead?"

"Hate, pure and simple. Hated his guts. The nigger reports to Philadelphia, you know. So Fergus couldn't get him fired. But he made that coon's life miserable. Argued every capital equipment item he asked for, every change he made in the office. But those damn fools back East, they want these damn computers, they love these damn word processors. Everything's in the computer today. A man can't even have his girl open a file drawer and take out a damn piece of paper. Don't get me wrong, computers are okay. Amazing, I'll even say. But the fun's gone. Time was you could bullshit, wing it. If you guessed right, you'd make yourself look like a hero when the year-end numbers came out. Nowadays you do that and some pissant kid that doesn't even shave, he's gonna punch his pocket calculator and make you look like fresh shit from Mrs. Astor's horse—"

"I'm investigating a murder," Kate interrupted, bored and exasperated. "I need an adequate motive for murder. People don't kill people they hate. Or," she added with a covert, baleful glance at Fred Grayson, "most of us would be dead."

"I was getting to it," Grayson said in an injured tone. "We were in the coon's office, Fergus and me. About the coon's latest brainstorm, he wanted to knock down a lobby wall, make more room for those flunkies in the service bay. Modular work areas, can you believe it? We need a lobby, for chrissake. Imagine our customers coming in to buy office interiors and we've got this dinky little lobby all because bright boy—"

"Mr. Grayson," Kate said coldly.

"I was just trying to show you how he thinks, our *efficient* office manager." Grayson glared at her, thick fingers drumming on the desk. He fumbled in the drawer, took out a package of Tipa-illos. "You smoke at all?"

"Not for years. My—I gave it up."

"Wife's been after me. I switch off to these things once in a while. They taste like horseshit. But somebody like Fergus dies, only forty-eight, you realize . . ." He extracted a cigar, inspected it, inserted it between his fleshy lips, fumbled in another drawer for matches.

Kate shifted, and no longer caring about Grayson's opinion, lifted an ankle onto a knee, reflecting blackly that men in power always inflicted petty tyranies, always arrogantly assumed no one's time could be as valuable as their own.

"Story's kind of funny, really." Grayson puffed on his thin cigar. "Like I said, we were in the head nigger's office, arguing, and Fergus's warning him not to use Guy as a go-between like he did wasting money on that word processing room, which is another story. Then Fergus gets up and walks around and picks up the picture of the coon's family. 'Pretty woman,' Fergus says, 'pretty daughters. Makes me think of the first time I ever went to bed with a black woman.' See? Fergus is being nice and proper, using all the proper words, not saying the words he usually would, like—well, you know. So this coon can't take offense, know what I mean?"

Kate, writing in her notebook, nodded response.

" 'Looked a lot like Marian,' Fergus says. Marian's Mrs.

54

Coon. 'Same size tits,' Fergus said. 'Built just like Marian, too. Loved it, she did. Said she just loved a white man doing it to her.' See how Fergus was going on?''

"Yes," Kate said.

"Then Fergus says, 'This's your older daughter, right? Pauline, isn't that her name?' Fergus was always good about names. And the coon nods, his Adams apple's bobbing up and down from swallowing, he's staring at Fergus, eyes about popping out of his head. 'I had one just about exactly her age too,' Fergus says. 'Did it to her doggy-style. She said she liked it that way best from a white man.' '' Grayson brayed laughter. "And Fergus went on and on, I won't go into all the detail, you can figure it out. Ever see a spook turn white, Detective? This spook was white under that shit-colored skin. This coon was a puddle on the floor. And Fergus strolled out, and I followed him, but I hung back a little and peeked around the corner and this coon was standing there rigid as a post and saying 'I'll kill him I'll kill him I'll kill him . . .' ''

Kate asked, "When was this?"

"Friday. You think the spook had enough motive?"

Kate finished her notes and added another word to the page in the back of her book. "Yes," she said.

"Thought so," Grayson said.

"What was your relationship to the victim?"

Fred Grayson's eyebrows beetled again. "Meaning . . . like what?"

"It's a simple question, Mr. Grayson. Were you friendly? Cordial? Or did you have a business relationship? Or was it cooler than that?"

"Of those choices," Grayson said, looking at her warily, "a business relationship."

"From what I understand, Fergus Parker was detested around here."

"A man in my position doesn't make friends in the office. Fergus Parker was one management level above me." Grayson puffed on his cigar. "Draw your own conclusions."

"No friends, that's one thing. Outright hatred is some-

thing else."

Grayson studied his cigar, adjusted his horn rims. "His style was . . . well, he didn't care about being liked. He must've . . . I think he worked at not being liked. Him and his damn tests—"

"What tests?"

"If you argued, protested something he'd done, he'd look at you like you just shot his mother. Then he'd tell you he'd been testing you and you'd just failed . . . It was a stinking little game of his, to make you afraid of him. I think he thought fear made him effective, gained him respect—"

"Did you respect him?"

"No," Grayson said immediately.

"Did he ever co anything to you?"

Grayson stared at Kate, opened his mouth, closed it firmly, stubbed out his cigar and looked away. "Lots of his . . . tests. Nothing I can think of specifically."

Lying, she knew. "Did any other employee other than Mr. Freeman have reason to harm Mr. Parker?"

"Harm him?" Grayson's bray of laughter ended abruptly. "Break both his legs if they thought they could do it some way and get away with it. Fergus stomped everybody. A game, like I said, a game . . . Me thinking that, it's the only thing that made some of it . . . tolerable."

Kate asked with light irony, "Can you name individuals who might not have reached your state of tolerance?"

"Like I said, Fergus stomped everybody. But he didn't dislike everybody, if you get the difference. Except for the coon. And Guy Adams. Called him a fag all the time."

She asked with interest, remembering Guy Adams' too friendly handshake, his staring at Ellen O'Neil, "Is he?"

Grayson shrugged. "Sometimes he seems a little faggy. But I think he's okay. And I never heard that from anybody else, just Fergus." He added with a challenging glare, "But he'd never make a pass at me, now would he?"

"I doubt it," she said drily. "Anyone else Fergus Parker

did things to?"

Grayson picked up a memo from his desk in an unsubtle hint that he wished to return to his work. "Let me think about it, get back to you."

Politics, she guessed. Except for Gail Freeman and Guy Adams there could be political consequences if he named anyone else. "I'm investigating a homicide," she said, stressing the words and tapping her pen on her notebook in an unsubtle reminder that the business at hand took precedence. "I don't think I have to tell you that withholding of any information by any individual regardless of his motivation is obstruction of justice."

Grayson's bushy eyebrows met. He slammed down the memo. "I'm not obstructing justice, goddammit. I'm just telling you I have to think about it."

She pulled a card from the pocket of her notebook, tossed it onto the desk. "One more question," she said as Grayson slid the card into his shirt pocket. "What time did you arrive this morning?"

Grayson glared at her. "Why? You think I've got something to do with this?"

"At this point I don't think anything. I'm gathering facts."

"Well, I gave you a pretty good lead, didn't I?"

"Remains to be seen. All the information you supply will be given the attention it deserves. Please answer my question."

"About ten to eight. Cops all over the place. Couldn't get in the lobby or upstairs for one hell of a long time."

"Were other company employees there?"

"The head nigger. Acting like Mr. Bigshot rounding everybody up, taking charge. He got the guards to open up that insurance company down there, he herded everybody in. Except for me. He wasn't about to tell Fred Grayson—"

"Mr. Grayson," she said, barely controlling her impatience, "just answer my question. At ten minutes to eight, who exactly did you see?"

"Just watch your tone there, lady detective. I'm a tax-paying citizen, a damn good taxpaying citizen. I don't have to take any crap from any—"

"I'm doing my job, Mr. Grayson, as efficiently as possible. I have many more interviews after yours. If you'd prefer to give your information to another investigator, I'll have an officer take you to the station."

"Oh shit. Come on, let's back off, okay? I've got a short fuse."

She did not reply; she waited with Flair pen poised.

"What was the question?"

She did not answer.

"Who did I see, that it? The head nigger, Guy Adams. Matt, Matt Bradford. I was glad to see him, I needed to—" Grayson met Kate's upward glance and said hurriedly, "Judy with the big tits, I don't know her last name, the receptionist. Gretchen was there, cracking jokes. We didn't know what was going on yet and she said she bet they were arresting Fergus Parker for indecent exposure which in his case would be a felony."

Grayson chuckled; Kate understood that he was trying to be ingratiating. She smiled. "Anyone else?"

"Harley, I mentioned Harley, didn't I? And Duane. Some of those people in the back bay, the Jap supervisor in word processing, I can give you first names is all."

"Whatever.'

"Uh, Ralph. Bill. They're service people in the back bay. John, he's in credit. Betty, she's word processing. I don't know the Jap supervisor's name. That's all I can remember right now."

"How long have you had your present position, Mr. Grayson?"

"Seven years," Grayson said proudly. 'Came out of St. Louis. Been in this corner office four months. Harley used to have it. That's Harley Burton next door. You plan on talking to him?"

"Yes. Of course. Why do you ask?"

Grayson sighed. "Might not have many good things to say about me. I took his job, his office."

"I'm investigating a murder, not office politics," she said curtly. But she made a note. The demotion of Harley Burton probably would have been Fergus Parker's decision. She rose. "Mr. Grayson, let me know if you remember any other facts relevant to this case."

"Sure." Grayson got to his feet, leaned over the desk to shake hands, sat down and again picked up the memo.

In the hallway, Kate glanced at the page in the back of her notebook and the five words she had written: Coon. Spade. Jungle bunny. Nigger. Spook.

"Left out jigaboo," she murmured, and flipped the notebook closed. Lunch, she thought, I could really use a break.

5

Ellen's mother said, "So I had to hear the news from the *perfessor.* Are you sure you're all right? Why didn't you call me?"

"I haven't had time, they've been questioning me. I'm fine, Mother." Ellen shifted the receiver to the other ear, picturing her mother in the customary pink robe, sitting amid the orange and yellow floral pillows of her sofa, platinum hair in curlers as it always was until early afternoon; soon she would comb out the hair, don culottes and a jersey top, and venture out of her Valley apartment with the *Times* under her arm to pass the afternoon with her poolside neighbors.

"You're incredible," her mother said, "you and the perfessor." She had always called Stephanie that, always pronouncing the word sarcastically. "So what was it like, darling?" Her voice lowered dramatically. "Tell me all about it."

"I found a man with a knife in his chest."

"Dear, oh dear. Why ever are you still there?"

"Mother, murder isn't a normal part of their daily routine here."

"Don't be disrespectful. There's a murderer on the loose, maybe right there with you. That wonderful intelligent perfessor told me she's leaving town tonight anyway. I know I

don't understand the life you lead, but how she can leave you alone at a time like this—"

"Dammit, Mother—"

"Well, they haven't arrested anybody yet, have they?"

"I'm sure they will soon. The detective in charge, she seems very good at her work, very tough and capable—"

"A woman detective? In charge? A tough and capable *woman?* What's happening to this world? Where have all the men gone? Why couldn't you find yourself a tough and capable man instead of this other craziness in your head? Or even a tough and capable woman, if it has to be that. Anybody who wouldn't drape herself all over you, drain you dry—"

Ellen sighed, cradled the receiver between her shoulder and ear, began to sort the mail. Her mother had managed to accept her lesbianism only by taking refuge in the belief that some day Ellen would recover from it.

"Two years of college, you're educated—a bright girl, darling. But one part of your head—it's that marijuana, you can't tell me you don't smoke it, all people your age do. Why can't you drink gin? Or even scotch? Like a normal person? First it's Lydia the bum and seven years to come to your senses, then this perfessor—"

Out of patience, Ellen said firmly, "Mother, take it to the cleaners."

"I don't like it, a murder where you work and you all alone in that apartment, I'm worried about you, darling. And I was going out tonight but instead I think I'll—"

"You go right ahead and go out, Mother. I mean it. This isn't an episode of *The A Team.* I'm hardly an eye-witness anyone needs to knock off. I didn't see a thing. So there's no reason to—"

"Even so, it's a crazy world we live in, full of John Hinckleys and Pope killers—"

Ellen changed the subject. "Who are you going out with? The one with the wrist watch that plays *The Yellow Rose of Texas?*"

"Yes. Sam, who wants to marry me. And be nice to your poor mother who only loves you and wants you to be married."

"A diabetic recommending sugar," Ellen twitted. Her mother had been married five times; Ellen's Irish father had been husband number two.

"I'm still right. You and that perfessor, you're so far off base—"

"Mother, would you really be happier if I were miserably married to some man?"

"I was brought up in a generation that believed we take on responsibilities in life, and—"

Ellen sighed again. "Mother, I'm a child of a freer generation. You're a child of yours."

"Bullcrap," said her mother.

Ellen glimpsed baggy leg warmers, a fuzzy aqua sweater; Billie Sullivan loped by, sandwich in hand. "Mother, I have to go to lunch now."

Coming out of the kitchen with a cellophaned ham salad sandwich, she saw Kate Delafield down the hallway just outside Guy Adams' office. She also had a sandwich, and stood talking to the detective who had questioned Ellen earlier—Ed Taylor, she remembered.

Kate Delafield was very trim, about five-eight, she judged, younger than Taylor—perhaps late thirties—and more conservative in bearing and dress. Her solid body was straight, and she wore a simple open-throat white blouse with her green corduroy jacket and gray slacks. Taylor, beefy shoulders slouched, wore a suit of brown checks, a blue shirt, a wide tie of blues and yellows. Kate Delafield gestured impatiently with a compact, kinetic motion of her arm; Taylor listened, head bent, shifting his bulk from one foot to the other. Kate Delafield walked off, around the corner, Taylor following.

Ellen returned to her office, ate her sandwich at her desk. She thought about the faces she knew at Modern

Office, scarcely familiar faces—strangers. Her mother's melo-
dramatics notwithstanding, a killer knew who she was, that
she had been here this morning . . . She told herself there
was no reason for fear. But it would be good if someone was
arrested, and soon.

Taylor said, "The people I'm talking to, clerks, service
reps, they're just the peons. I'm trying to get the gossip,
get a line on somebody who really had it in for this bird."

"Good idea, Ed." Kate had finished the recap of her
morning, and she and Taylor were walking toward the conference room.

"But Christ, Kate. Nothing but garbage so far. Betty-
somebody lives with a wop, every full moon he beats the
living shit out of her. Bill-somebody's got a wife that bets
both their paychecks in the Gardena poker parlors—"

"Why in God's name do good people stay with rotten
people?" Kate said, striding into the conference room.

"Beats me. Marie ever did anything like that, they'd
have to scrape up the pieces."

Kate said drily, "You wouldn't consider just leaving
her?"

"Yeah, that too." Taylor threw his notebook onto the
conference room table. "Mabel-somebody, she guzzles gin
out of her thermos all day long, Fred-somebody, he—"

"Wait a minute. Narcotics. Anybody give you anything
at all? Coke? Pills? Grass? Anything at all?"

"You mean somebody stoned could've . . ." Taylor
rubbed his jaw. "Just that weird Sullivan dame, June-
somebody told me Billie Sullivan smokes reefers in the
john, that's all I've got."

"Watch that angle, Ed. Anything's as possible as anything
else till we get a handle."

"Amateur City," Taylor said disgustedly.

Kate unwrapped her sandwich, spread a napkin on the
table.

"Kate, come out to lunch, you don't want that machine

shit, loaded with all those preservatives. What's an hour for lunch? Whoever d d this isn't gonna run. Amateur City, they never run. Let's go eat Chinese, get a beer—"

Taylor's face showed concern. Some of the men Kate worked with, with whom she had never and would never discuss her private life, had shown similar corcern over the past months. Through her coating of numbness she had felt their reaching out to her in a common humanity—awkward expressions of caring from men who had seen every kind of grisly horror and had layered themselves with deep protective coats of cynicism. Kate said quietly, "Thanks Ed, I appreciate it. But I want to look through these files, get some background on a few people, save some time."

"Okay. See you later."

She made a swift inspection of the folders Gail Freeman had supplied, pocketed the printout of employees to run a check. Then she propped her feet on a chair, contemplated the soothing greens and yellows of the huge painting covering the opposite wall, picked up half of her sandwich. She reviewed what she had learned so far about the death of Fergus Parker.

The killer was by all odds a Modern Office employee—or a relative of an employee—present or past; entry could not have been gained to the sixteenth floor without possession of a key.

The notation would have been made on the guards' log if anyone had preceded or accompanied Fergus Parker, and the killer could not have remained on the premises the night before without discovery by the guards or cleaning personnel; therefore he or she had arrived between seven and seven-forty, before or after Ellen O'Neil. In all probability, pending verification of Fergus Parker's personal habits, he or she was a current employee who had arrived in time to make and drink coffee.

Robbery was not an apparent motive. There was no evident sign of struggle, no blood smears or splatter. The hands were bloody, but it was the usual involuntary reflex

of a victim to clutch at a mortal wound. The damage in the office had been caused by Fergus Parker himself, in the final moments of his life. And he had been murdered by someone he knew, someone he did not fear—he had been totally surprised by the act.

She finished the half of her sandwich, threw the other half into the wastebasket, and pulled the stack of folders toward her. She paused, thinking about Ellen O'Neil. In all good conscience she could no longer be anything but rigorously professional. And that meant taking off the gloves.

6

Ellen returned to the conference room. Feeling Kate Delafield's blue eyes on her, she walked self-consciously, awkwardly. She sat down and rubbed her palms over the rough tweed of her skirt.

Without preamble, Kate asked, "Have you reconsidered your statements of this morning, Miss O'Neil?" She had planned her approach, and continued before Ellen O'Neil could respond, "I'll make it easier for you by reconstructing a few facts."

She laced her fingers together and leaned forward on her elbows. "This morning a man—or woman—was in Fergus Parker's office at seven-forty, and for an undetermined length of time before that. For reasons unknown at this point, this person fatally stabbed Fergus Parker. Then this person came out of the office into the hallway."

Kate sat back and pushed Pete Johnson's sketch of the sixteenth floor to the center of the table. "It's my opinion that this person saw you in the hallway, and in that same instant saw that he or she would have to move—" Kate scowled at Johnson's tiny print. "—eighteen feet toward you to exit into the lobby. Therefore, this person gambled on a dash across the hallway, a distance of only—" she scowled again. "—seven feet to the intersecting hallway. In the anxiety for escape, this person then flung the stairway

door fully open, causing the slam which we duplicated a while ago, and fled down the stairs.''

Kate folded the sketch and fixed her eyes on Ellen O'Neil. "In the meantime, Miss O'Neil, a man was dying. And these are the things we know so far about how he died." Kate brought her hands to her chest. "He instantly clutched at the knife plunged into him. Then he took his hands from his mortal wound and grabbed at the desk to pull himself up." Kate reached to the table in front of her, still staring at Ellen O'Neil. "His slick bloody hands slipped off the desk."

Ellen buried her face in her hands, unable to bear the images.

Kate continued relentlessly, "Then he reached for something he could grasp, the portable bar which was quite near his desk. Perhaps he was able to rise somewhat, perhaps not at all. But he pulled the bar over, causing the enormous crashing of glass which you heard next. Then he turned his chair, tried to reach behind him to the phone on the credenza. Look at me, Miss O'Neil.''

Unwillingly, she raised her head, opened her eyes.

Kate sat with her chair turned slightly, arms outstretched as Fergus Parker's arms had been in death. "He managed to turn his chair only a few degrees, to reach out. And you found him just as he died.''

Again Ellen buried her face in her hands.

"Please look at me, Miss O'Neil.''

Again she raised her head. Kate Delafield sat with arms crossed, elbows resting on the table. Her light blue eyes were not cold, they were not hostile, but they bored into Ellen's as if she were seeing all the way to the back of her head.

"There was a reason why a murderer got across that hallway to safety, why you never saw who it was. Your back was turned. And your back was turned because you were looking into Guy Adams' office. Through his open door into his office." Her voice rose slightly. "Isn't that true?''

"Yes," she whispered, "it's true."

Kate said with a hint of a smile, "I'm not that clever." She flipped open the sketch. "Officer Johnson drew the main features of the sixteenth floor soon after the premises were secured. His sketch shows Mr. Adams' door open."

With difficulty, Ellen managed a smile. Then she said venomously, "Where did you learn your questioning technique, the KGB?"

Kate chuckled. "Maybe law school. I went for a year." Anxious to reestablish cordiality, she pushed the sketch and her notes aside, away from Ellen O'Neil's direct view, and smiled again.

"Really?" Anger faded; Kate Delafield seemed suddenly more accessible, and Ellen was interested and curious. "Why did you quit?"

"Criminal law was the one aspect that appealed to me. But I learned I wouldn't be comfortable on either side, defending or convicting."

"Why? I don't understand."

"I started law school in 'seventy-nine when women were finally being allowed into the more challenging areas of police work. By then I'd advanced far enough in my work to realize there was little appeal in spending my energy and ingenuity defending a possible criminal. The other choice was prosecution—learning to tolerate all the sloppy evidence-gathering procedures I was coming to know only too well, all the serious defects in our court system. So I chose to stay where I could be more effective."

Ellen asked anxiously, "Do you suspect Guy?"

Kate observed her concern with regret. "I suspect everyone. Even you."

"*Me?*"

"This scenario. You came in this morning, made coffee. Fergus Parker came into the kitchen, took you back to his office on some pretext, did something offensive, something obscene, something bad enough to cause you to pick up his letter opener . . . and then you took it from there."

Ellen said furiously, "You can't be serious!"

"Just a scenario to prove a point," Kate said as gently as she could, remembering her usually futile attempts to soothe Anne's temper. "Miss O'Neil, don't be upset."

"You surely can't think—"

"The motivation is a little weak, don't you think?" She was smiling, trying to pacify her, but Kate was amused by her ire; the light brown eyes were narrowed and sparking in anger. "I'd like to be your lawyer if you were arrested on that basis. If what I described actually happened, I see total disgust on your part, I see someone's face being slapped, I see you even resigning from your job. I don't see murder. Why did you try to protect Mr. Adams?"

"I don't see Guy's motivation, either. He disliked Fergus Parker, but everybody did, from what I hear." She hesitated, feeling foolish. "It was pure impulse. He's been very kind to me, I thought I might create an awful problem for him he didn't deserve, make him a suspect."

"When you looked into Mr. Adams' office, was he in there?"

"No! As God is my witness!"

"Was there any evidence of his presence?"

"No. Nothing I can remember."

"Anything on his desk? Papers? A coffee mug?"

She narrowed her eyes in concentration, trying to picture his desk that morning. "No."

"No, there was nothing on the desk, or no you don't remember?"

"No I don't remember," she said, shaking her head. "I was looking out the window at the mountains."

"Are you in love with Mr. Adams?"

"What?" She gaped at Kate Delafield. She stammered, "I—no, I'm—For God's sake, we only just met!"

"His attraction to you is quite evident."

"Really," she said sarcastically, with a vague feeling of offense. She could not reveal to Kate Delafield that she was a lesbian; Kate Delafield's own sexual orientation was not an

established fact, and any information furnished might not be subject to confidentiality.

Kate had been carefully watching the range of emotion on Ellen O'Neil's face, assessing the vocal intonations. For now, she decided, Taylor had been correct in his assessment of Ellen O'Neil and her "roommate." She asked sternly, "Since you're so intent on defending him, did it never occur to you that Mr. Adams might be the killer of Fergus Parker?"

"That's *absurd*. He'd have trouble killing a mosquito. He's not the kind to do anything like that."

"How can you make such a judgment when you've only just met?" The spirit and conviction of Ellen O'Neil's responses was consistent and impressive. Yes, she would make an excellent witness.

"I just *know*. From his temperament, the way he *is*."

Soberly, Kate looked at Ellen O'Neil. She had learned that many people—perhaps most—lived decent lives under pressures that kept them on the perilous edges of control; that for many, simply to get through each day with their human decency still intact was the significant triumph of their lives. But for some, the day came when the control crumbled, when they were propelled into acts . . . "Miss O'Neil," she said with quiet emphasis, "believe me, *anyone* is capable. Some of the most despicable murderers of this century were men who were kind to their children, loved their parents, cherished their wives."

"I suppose you're right," Ellen conceded, unconvinced. "I swear I've told you everything else truthfully."

Kate sighed inaudibly. She knew she could not give anyone else her experience and intuitions. Suddenly weary, she rubbed her face with both hands. "Will you be here the remainder of the day? Home this evening?"

Ellen nodded. "I have to take . . . somebody to the airport." She added, "But I'll be home after eight."

"There'll be another statement to sign later. And possibly more questions. Thank you for your time, Miss O'Neil."

Ellen rose, moved to the door, turned back. "You're

a tough one, Detective Delafield.''

Kate smiled. ''I take it you don't mean that as a compliment.''

''Yes, I do mean it as a compliment.''

''Then thank you.''

As the conference room door clicked shut, Kate sat in utter stillness, disoriented, drifting in a void. The moment passed; and she sagged in her chair, enervated, profoundly depressed. She struggled against the feeling, shaking her head violently and squaring her shoulders. She had work to do, a lot of work. Reports. Interviews with the other managers and the security guards. Review of the information Taylor had compiled, of the files stacked high on the conference room table. An interview with Mrs. Fergus Parker, who had told her on the phone a few minutes ago in a soft apologetic voice that she had to pick up her children on two different flights at the airport, but would be glad to see Kate at seven o'clock.

7

Harley Burton's office was a melange of overcrowded and mismatched furnishings. The desk, huge and oblong, was too large for the room; the chairs too small as if in compensation. Beside the desk were boxes overflowing with books and bookends, plaques, other office paraphernalia. Dozens of photographs crowded the walls and were stacked on the floor, the credenza, the bookcase. A photo in a silver filigree frame dominated the credenza: a woman with whitish hair and cornflower blue eyes stood with arms draped around the shoulders of two teenage boys.

Her hand feeling bruised from Harley Burton's handshake, Kate sat down opposite him and leaned back in the spindly chair, propping her elbows on the metallic armrests. Harley Burton's intense dark stare riveted her to the chair.

"About time you came in. Probably your best suspect, right?" The broad grin uncovered strong but uneven teeth. Like a prizefighter's face, his eyebrows and the bridge of his nose were ridged with bone; a few acne scars pitted his cheeks and chin. Wiry brown hair was clipped short and receded in an even semi-circle from a wide round forehead. His pristine shirt was monogramed in tiny black letters on the pocket, the sleeves rolled up to the elbows of muscular arms covered thickly with brown hair. A large wrist watch

72

of polished stainless steel bristled with gauges and dials. He picked up a huge mug bright with the scene of mounted huntsmen, steam rising from its contents, and took a long draught with evident satisfaction. The rich strong scent of coffee reached Kate.

She asked easily, "Did you want to make a confession, Mr. Burton?"

Harley Burton's laugh came from deep in his broad chest. He was not a tall man, perhaps five-ten, but he projected impressive physical power and energy. "Nope, can't confess. But the man got what he deserved. Helen Parker won't find six pallbearers unless she advertises."

He shook a pack of Carltons vigorously, probed with a finger in the inner recesses and extracted the last cigarette. "Everybody in this damn company smokes mine," he complained with good-natured disgust, crumpling the pack and hurling it into a wastebasket beside the credenza. "Fred's been mooching since Friday, always does when he smokes those stupid little cigars. Gretchen quits every other week, I gave her a pack Monday to keep those begging blue eyes out of my office. Guy's quitting too, he's always in here." He chuckled briefly, drank from his huge mug of coffee.

"For a smoker, you look like a man who takes care of himself."

"Work out on the Nautilus. Play baseball in the summer, semi-pro league. A little basketball, one on one with Gail if I want some real exercise."

"Is Mr. Freeman that good?" Kate took out her notebook.

"Hell yes. The man's a super athlete. He was four, five inches taller, he could've played in the NBA, in my opinion. Base welterweight champ in the Marines." Harley Burton's eyes surveyed her impersonally. "Terrific shape you're in. Cops, even the women, I hear you have to work out. Calisthenics every day?"

Kate chuckled; she understood that Harley Burton's staccato speech pattern was a symptom of shyness. "Only

in police academy. But we have to pass physical tests twice a year. I swim mostly. And like you, play baseball in summer league." She realized that she liked the man across from her and she asked abruptly, to formalize the conversation, "How long have you worked for Modern Office, Mr. Burton?"

"Harley. Fifteen years, September. Started in the Kansas City plant. Life—all luck and timing, you know. Transfer me anywhere but here, who knows? Might've had Wesley Miller's job by now—he's division head in Philly. Vested in September though, family all taken care of pension-wise. Then I can move on."

"Why do you want to?"

"Long story. You don't understand our business."

"Try me."

"Well, it started months ago, Tampa opened. Sales manager slot. Recommended Pete Webber. Leader, damn fine performer, my top man. Always exceeded his PAF—that's performance against forecast, meaning—"

"I follow. Go on."

He picked up his huge coffee mug again. His cigarette had burned halfway down; he had not taken a puff since lighting it.

"You're quite a coffee hound, Mr. Burton," she observed. "That's the biggest coffee mug I ever saw. Must hold half a pot."

"Just about. Damn inefficient use of time, back and forth to the kitchen a dozen times a day. Anyway, Fergus claimed Pete needed more seasoning, wouldn't pass my recommendation on to Philadelphia. Said he wanted to keep the West Coast team intact till we saw which way the economic climate looked."

Harley Burton sucked breath into his broad chest. "Well, that was acceptable to me. Not agreeable, you understand, just acceptable. But damn hard to sell to Pete Webber, let me tell you. Know the toughest thing I ever do as a manager? Support the stupid decisions of upper management. But I talked Pete into accepting it. Then Fergus changed Pete's

account assignments. I don't care what anybody says about sales being nothing but price and delivery, it's a good part personal credibility, customer trust. Some of Pete's accounts he'd been nursemaiding along went to our competitors. And Pete's bonus money went down, his PAF didn't look too good all of a sudden—"

"Did you protest? Argue?"

"Argue? *Argue?* Pounded Fergus's desk to splinters! He said people in Philly orchestrated it, wanted to see how Pete would perform, how he'd react to adversity. You ever hear anything so goddamn *stupid* in all your life? Well Pete reacted all right. Quit. Went to Acme, tried to take our best people with him. They didn't go—loyalty, some of 'em, not all of 'em have Pete's ambition, some of 'em with too much service to quit."

Kate heard a faint cracking sound; her eyes were drawn to Harley Burton's hand which had tightened so powerfully around the handle of his mug that the knuckles and fingers were white.

"Then he demoted me. Said he wanted to shake things up, and I didn't handle my subordinates properly, didn't keep Pete Webber motivated, it was my fault, letting a man like that get away."

Harley Burton, dark eyes narrowed and glittering, stubbed out his cigarette. He fumbled in a drawer for a new pack, ripped off the cellophane and foil, and lit another cigarette, flinging the match; it pinged into the side of a metal ashtray the size of a dinner plate and loaded with ash and cigarette butts of varying lengths. "Sales manager seven years. Seven goddamn years moving from district four—that's Gretchen's job now, the bottom rung—to district one, the corner office. Worked my *ass* off. Even set up an office in my house. Once in a while my wife would come in and introduce herself." Harley Burton's grin was accomplished with obvious effort. "Then Fergus Parker demoted me. And he destroyed it all. All that work, all that commitment, all those years. Men in positions more responsible

than mine don't have nearly my ability, I know that. I know
what I can do. But Fergus Parker destroyed any hope I ever
had for a career with this company."

Profoundly sympathetic, Kate asked quietly, "Is it unusual, what happened to you? Don't things like that happen
all the time in business? Isn't that why they call it a jungle?"

"Detective, that's a damn fine question." Harley Burton
emphasized the sincerity of his statement with vigorous
nods. "A *damn* fine question. Let me tell you, if it only were
a jungle. A jungle's a good place, a fine place to be. That's a
pretty good set of rules, survival of the fittest. Good clean
competition, may the best man be the leader. The smartest,
strongest, the best. But nobody's got a chance against the
man who cheats his way to power, who's unpredictable,
deceitful, bullies to keep his power."

"Seems self-defeating," Kate said, admiring this man. "It
seems a man would soon lose his good strong people, soon
damage his own performance."

"Be surprised how long they get away with it. Sometimes
they break spirited men, use what's left of their talent. Some
people have no guts to begin with. But most people just believe what's told 'em for one hell of a long time. Want to
know something about Fergus? He had ability. Didn't need
us hating him. He understood how to handle people right.
A natural for sales, a hell of a competitor, compete with
anybody in this world man to man. Why wasn't that good
enough?"

"To be big and strong is never good enough," Kate said,
"for a bully."

Harley Burton took a quick puff from his cigarette,
tipped up his mug for a final draught. "Hurt all of us,"
he said quietly, staring at Kate with his piercing dark eyes.
"Destroyed Fred's confidence. Tormented Duane within an
inch of his life. Duane looks like an idiot, won't rise above
where he is but damn good at his job, fine teacher of young
people. His people love him. One of his sales meetings, his
sales group got up and marched around the table singing their

own company version of the USC fight song."

Kate chuckled, and Harley Burton grinned. "That's how well Duane motivates his people. Gretchen . . ." He frowned, rubbed his craggy face. "Whenever I feel really bitter I remind myself I could've been a woman working for Fergus Parker. Or I could've been Gail Freeman. This region's up in sales, Gail's a big part of it. Good administrative mind, treats his people with dignity, they're damn productive, finest support group I ever worked with. Gail computerized our sales forms and reports, freed up our sales reps from all kinds of paperwork, they just feed in figures now. Figured out a way to get orders into the plant earlier. Our requests for quarterly schedule beat the pants off the other regions. Gail's the best thing ever happened to this office, but Fergus bad-mouthed him all over the company, fought every change, hated every new idea."

"What about Guy Adams? Did he do anything to him?"

"Not that I know of. Guy has his own power sources, Fergus had less control over him than Gail. I think Fergus envied him, maybe hated him for his name, all that class Guy has. I keep telling him he should chuck that PR crap and get into sales. Give me those looks, that charm—hell, I'd drive the competition into the Mojave. I heard Fergus bad-mouth him. I heard him tell *customers* Guy's a fag. From what I see, Guy goes strictly for women—but what the hell, who cares? I mean—what matters? Now Duane, he took Matt Bradford's three kids in for a month when Matt's wife cracked up. I mean, what matters about somebody?"

Kate said, "Police work, you see people from one side only, and always from the negative perspective."

"Some damn good people live in this world. And some of them work right here."

Harley Burton looked at his elaborate wrist watch, began to roll down his shirt sleeves. "Pick this up later? Have to drive to Inglewood, customer visit. Be back at four."

Finishing her notes, Kate nodded.

"Tomorrow all the sales managers are having lunch,

pre-funeral celebration. Taking that new girl, what's her name—"

"Ellen O'Neil, I presume you mean."

"Right. Taking her to lunch, Guy's idea. Convince her it's not our habit around here, knocking people off. Like to come?"

Kate said with regret, "It wouldn't really be appropriate. I appreciate it. One last question. What's your assessment of Billie Sullivan?"

"Viper." Harley Burton buttoned his shirt cuffs. "Always wondered if most of the crap Fergus dished out wasn't her idea."

Kate said carefully, "She seems . . . an unusual personality."

Harley Burton snorted. "Damn kind of you. She offends even Philadelphia people. I figure she had to know something, had some kind of hold on Fergus. What I hear, the women here all hate her guts. Surprised Gai hasn't tossed her out on the street yet."

Kate said mildly, "I've tied his hands somewhat."

Harley Burton pulled a black suit coat from the hanger on the back of his door and shrugged into it and fastened the buttons across his muscular torso. "Well, hurry up and arrest somebody." He yanked open his door. "People here know damn well one of us did it. Everybody in the place is damn nervous, I'll tell you that. Hell, I even threw my own letter opener away."

Kate said, grinning, "I'll do my best."

The objects on Duane Fletcher's curved desk were arranged with mathematical precision: the marble-based pens centered exactly at the outer edge, the jar of jelly beans next to them set slightly in; the stack of typed letters at the exact edge of the royal blue blotter; below the pen set telephone messages in overlapping tiers, apparently in the order they would be returned. To one side of the desk a double-unit bookcase was lined with catalogues identified on their spines

by neatly inked tape. Pictures hung along one wall in a straight row and displayed interior designs, one large photograph apparently a project of much pride to the company— Kate remembered seeing it on the wall in Matt Bradford's office. On the credenza was a single photograph, at least ten by thirteen, of a dark-haired, moon-faced woman and two small curly-haired children.

Duane Fletcher hung up his telephone and patted it. "Greatest invention in the history of the world." He stood, smiling, to shake Kate's hand. "Reach out, reach out and touch someone." His tenor voice contained the treble of pre-puberty.

The inch-wide dark hair ringing Duane Fletcher's bald head extended into thick gray sideburns. His bright dark eyes were set close together, giving him a slightly startled aspect, a comical monkishness; a small mouth was tucked up under a nose that had been surely broken at least once. He wore a purple suit jacket with light blue pinstripes over his bright yellow shirt, the yellow and purple striped tie folded into a wide knot under his short fat neck.

Kate made herself comfortable in one of the two soft leather chairs in front of the desk, and took out her notebook. "What time did you arrive today, Mr. Fletcher?"

Taking a jar of Laura Scudder peanuts from a drawer, Duane Fletcher shook out a handful, offered the jar to Kate. "Call me Duane. Everybody calls me Duane. Always get here at ten to eight. Early bird gets the worm. Just like Avis, I try harder." He tossed several peanuts up and caught them in his mouth.

Amused, Kate waved away the offer of the peanut jar. "You like your job, Mr. Fletcher?"

"So don't call me Duane. The job? Like the saying goes, I've come a long way, baby." His high voice was earnest. "But some days, you know, there've been times . . . well, you always figure you could be better off. Put a tiger in your tank, reach for all the gusto you can."

Careful not to smile, Kate asked, "How would you

describe your relat onship with Fergus Parker?"

Duane Fletcher raised both hands in a gesture of supplication. "How do you spell relief? D–E–A–D. I nate to speak
ill of the dead, but plop plop, fizz fizz, oh what a relief it is."

I'm straight man in a comedy act. Kate dropped her
voice into stern solemnity. "I understand Fergus Parker made
your life very difficult."

Duane Fletcher sighed, a wheezing like an air brake on
a door, and ate more peanuts. "He always liked to flick my
Bic. But I took a licking and kept on ticking. I tried every
way I knew to fly the friendly skies, but the man never spoke
a complimentary word. He never threatened to fire me—I
must've done a decent job. I guess I had ring around the
collar that was stronger than dirt."

Duane Fletcher munched more peanuts. "But I didn't
kill him," he said, "if that's what you mean. Not that I didn't
want to. I know too well why Helen Parker's stayed drunk
all these years, how she suffered with that man. I can imagine
how she feels now. We're all well rid of him. We deserve a
break today."

"Mr. Fletcher, do you always speak in advertising
jingles?"

"*Jingles?*" Duane Fletcher's choirboy voice was incredulous, indignant. "Madam, progress is our most important product. Business had put this country in the driver's
seat, made this country snap crackle and *pop*. The best
ideas in this country are business ideas. Ford has a better
idea—"

Will he ever run out? Kate wondered.

Duane Fletcher gazed at his desk and ran a tidying hand
around his fringe of hair. "You really had to take a joke
when you were around Fergus. He was really a kidder, you
know. Sometimes a little . . . tough to take." He looked up;
his dark brown eyes had the nervous vulnerability of a deer.

Kate asked gently, "Did you ever consider sitting down
with him to tell him how much his behavior bothered you?"

"You'd never do that with Fergus. He was always testing

you, he'd say it was just a test. Got to thicken that skin my boy, he'd say. Got to be smart and tough or your subordinates'll put their boots in your back."

Kate asked with a smile, "Ever have a subordinate try to put a boot in your back?"

Duane Fletcher's answering smile was shy, boyish. "My subordinates don't even wear boots. And we all love each other."

"Love? Isn't that a little strong? For the business world?"

"Not for my people. They're wonderful, my sales group."

He leaned toward Kate, and even though the office door was closed, lowered his tenor voice to a whisper. "Know the worst thing Fergus ever did to me? I've never been able to tell a soul. Promise you'll keep it a secret?"

Kate said cautiously, "I can't really make a promise like that."

But she closed her notebook and waited. People confessed their most hidden secrets to priests—and to cops. And this was even a more common occurrence for her than for the male cops she knew. People revealed themselves as they never would to their husbands and wives and lovers, their parents, their friends.

"He told me . . . " Duane Fletcher lowered his voice further, so that Kate had to lean toward him. "He told me . . . " He swallowed. "He told me he went to bed with Marge. My wife."

He asked in his normal high pitch, "Can you imagine that? Saying that to a man? And that's all he said. Not when or why, he just stared at me with those gray popeyes and said . . . " He dropped his voice again. " 'Duane my boy, I've been to bed with Marge. And she sure hasn't got much to peddle.' " He wheezed a sigh and looked at Kate with dark button-round eyes that had become moist. "Can you imagine?"

"No, Mr. Fletcher," Kate said softly, "I can't."

"You know, it's kind of different, being called Mister.

Maybe people don't do that enough anymore. Here, have some peanuts."

"Maybe all people should have more respect for one another." She accepted the jar and shook several peanuts into her palm.

"I assumed it was just another test, what he said. But I asked Marge. I had to. Just out of the blue I asked her, thinking if it was true I might surprise it out of her. But all she did was get mad as hell and want to come down here and—well, I talked her out of *that*. I mean it would have been my *job*. Detective Delafield?" He fixed his soft misted eyes on Kate. "I'm pretty sure it was another kind of test and he was kidding. Think he was kidding?"

"Yes, Mr. Fletcher," Kate said in her most official voice, summoning all the authority she could muster "I'm sure he was kidding."

Duane Fletcher reached into his breast pocket, removed a bright purple handkerchief, dabbed at his eyes. "I think so, too."

Kate ate the peanuts. Then she asked, "Did any other employees that you know of—were they given similar . . . tests?"

Duane Fletcher coughed, cleared his throat. "Well, we all hated him. But poor Gretchen . . . I heard rumors. But I just can't repeat them. I think . . . I think she got . . . special treatment. I think he . . . did some pretty shitty things to her. And Harley, maybe you've heard about Harley Burton?"

Kate noted that Duane Fletcher had moved from the subject of Gretchen Phillips with evident relief. "I understand Harley Burton was demoted," she said.

"Fergus took Harley out of his job and gave it to Fred Grayson for no good reason, just sheer meanness. Harley's a damn hard worker, I was waiting for the day Fergus would move on and Harley'd succeed him, I was *counting* on it. And Fred, once he got that corner office, it was like Fergus had a license to kill him. Pick on me? You should've seen the way he picked on Fred. Called him six ways an idiot in

every meeting, even in front of Philadelphia people. And that's career damage, you know. Those Philadelphia people—well, they decide your *career* outside of this office. So I don't know who'll take Fergus's place, what I'll have to put up with now . . ."

Duane Fletcher gazed mournfully at his empty peanut jar. "I can't believe I ate the whole thing."

Kate smiled, rose. "Anything else comes to mind, Mr. Fletcher, I'll be around." She pulled a card from her notebook. "If there's anything you think of, want to add to what you've said—"

"Right. Nice jacket you got there." Duane Fletcher smiled and touched the fat knot of his tie. "Look sharp, feel sharp, be sharp." He slid Kate's card into his breast pocket.

Kate walked to the door struggling against irresistible temptation. "My card," she said, "don't leave home without it."

Duane Fletcher's high-pitched laughter followed her down the hall.

Gretchen Phillips was on the phone, but she waved Kate in and pantomimed instructions to close the door. She said into the phone, chuckling, "Sure I'll wait, are you kidding? The customer's threatening to throw me out my sixteenth floor window."

Kate sat down, and with increasing pleasure studied Gretchen Phillips, who was drumming almond-shaped coral nails impatiently on the pearl gray cover of an appointment book. Her delicate features were dominated by blue-gray eyes, large and serious, covered by oversize glasses with square bluish frames resting part way down her nose. Glossy black hair framed her face in stark simplicity and elegance. Her lips were finely shaped thinness and lightly lipsticked; in unconscious sensuality she caught her lower lip momentarily in even white teeth. To Kate she was reminiscent of exotic Oriental women with their slight bodies and

luminous white skin. The white suit jacket was well-cut gabardine over her filmy lilac blouse, a strand of tiny pearls at the throat.

Her desk was a functional square, and dwarfed by folders, letters, purchase orders, catalogues, notes, messages. The matching credenza was also piled from end to end. The shelves of her bookcase were stuffed with haphazardly arranged catalogues, some splayed open. Strangely, a stapler and staple remover—perhaps vestiges of previous secretarial days, Kate speculated—sat beside two gold Cross pens in a marble base. One painting hung on a wall, a geometric city of striking purples and grays; three other frames leaned against a wall waiting to be hung, their canvas faces turned in. Kate glanced around the chaotic office for a framed photo—all the managers seemed to have one—but there was none. Again she looked at Gretchen Phillips, at her hands: ringless, except for a delicate thin gold band on the ring finger of her left hand, fashioned into a tiny heart.

"Yes, Jerry." Gretchen Phillips sat erect, slender shoulders straight, and picked up a thin black pen with slim fingers. "Wait, wait just a minute." She stood, an immaculately neat anomaly amid the disarray of her office, and took the phone cord to its limit as she pulled a folder out of a pile on the far end of the credenza.

"You're a doll, Jerry," she cooed into the receiver. "What? Hey listen, you got it. Thanks a lot, the customer really appreciates this . . . Hey, sure. It's a promise. Talk to you soon."

Gretchen Phillips hung up her phone and groaned, sat down and crossed her arms and lowered her head into them and groaned again.

Amused by her dramatics, Kate inquired, "Rough day?"

She lifted her head, removed her glasses, sighed. "Actually, no. Just routine." She extended a hand. "How are you?"

Smiling, Kate took the delicate soft hand, thinking that she was equally lovely with or without her glasses. "Miss

Phillips, I won't feel bad at all taking you away from your work for a few minutes."

Gretchen Phillips inclined her head toward the phone. "Jerry Burns. Floor superintendant in Kansas City. If he ever comes to L.A., I'll arrange to be out of town. I've promised him my body and any number of acrobatic sex acts to expedite orders out of that miserable excuse for a factory."

Kate chuckled, and Gretchen Phillips said, "How long did I talk on that call, ten minutes? Twenty, twenty-five calls I handle when I'm in the office, and only one minute of each call with any substance. That's what, three to four hours? Of nothing but bullshit. Know the first thing I do when I get home? Take a shower. Then and only then Chris fixes me a drink."

Kate chuckled again and said sympathetically, "I'm lucky about my work, or at least aspects of it. It seems a lot of people find themselves in jobs they dislike."

"Oh, don't misunderstand, I love it. I really do. I'm very good at my job. I just care too much. I care about the reps who work for me, I really work for my customers. I'm good at finesse work, actually. I think women usually are, don't you?" Kate nodded and smiled. "I'm aggressive and damn thorough. I bet you are too." Again Kate smiled. "And my people, my customers, one thing they know about me, they know I care. They know I work hard and worry about them and *care.*"

"You're an increasing rarity today." She was impressed by Gretchen Phillips. "How long have you been a sales manager?" She knew the answer, but wanted to steer the conversation.

Gretchen Phillips smiled. "Two long, interesting years."

"Is that how long you worked under Fergus Parker?"

The smile faded; her eyes were remote, cold. "Was your choice of words deliberate?"

Surprised, Kate said in a controlled, even tone, "I thought nothing of them one way or the other."

Gretchen Phillips leaned back in her chair, crossed her legs, shook a cigarette from a pack of Carltons and said tiredly, "That wasn't even a test, and I failed. I'm still getting used to not having any more . . . tests." The word was expelled in a sibilant hiss. "I worked directly for him two years, indirectly for three before that when I reported to Harley Burton."

Kate decided to temporarily deflect her questions into an area that would not invite resistance or animosity. "What time did you arrive this morning, Miss Phillips?'

"Traffic on the Pasadena Freeway was, you should excuse the expression, murder. About a quarter to eight."

"What time do you usually arrive?"

"Seven, seven-thirty. Guess what?" She smiled. "It wasn't me."

Kate returned her smile. "Why not?"

"No motive."

The direction of the conversation was now Gretchen Phillips' choice. "Really? That's not what I hear."

Gretchen Phillips leaned on her elbows and cupped her chin in both hands and looked at Kate with a coyness that seemed self-mocking. "And what is it that you hear?"

"People tell me about Fergus Parker's tests. And that he singled you out for . . . special treatment."

Gretchen Phillips picked up her cigarette and a thin silver lighter, then tucked the cigarette back into the pack. "No, dammit. Chris wants me to quit and this time I'm really trying to. Guy and I, we're suffering together, helping each other. He's down to three or four a day now. We've decided to keep a pack so we know we've got some, but he keeps the pack half the day, I keep it the other half We count the cigarettes missing at the end of the day."

"Good idea, reinforcing each other like that."

Gretchen Phillips placed her arms on the desk, leaned forward. Perfume reached Kate, a sweet flowery scent. The eyes looking into hers were a clear and lovely gray-blue.

"Special treatment," Gretchen Phillips said quietly. "I'm

glad it's a woman detective asking me about that. Let me try to describe Fergus Parker's special treatment." Her voice was low, calm. "His body was like a big sweaty soft slug. He'd take off his jacket and there would be these huge patches of sweat under his arms. He had a sour smell, like rancid yeast. My God, men can smell like sewers." Her tone was uninflected, her eyes cool, expressionless. "His mouth was big and wet, like one of those fish, what do you call them, groupers? And the cigar smoke on his breath, like burnt feathers. And tasted like varnish."

Kate sat in rapt stillness, compelled by the icy calm, the eloquent ugliness of the words.

"He thought he was wonderfully masculine because he had arms that suffocated me, hands that pawed and hurt. And he'd have his hot perspiration all over me by the time he was finished."

As silence lengthened, Kate cleared her throat. "Miss Phillips, why did you put up with that? I don't see why you had to do that."

Gretchen Phillips smiled.

"You could have complained," Kate said. "Wouldn't quitting have been better?"

Gretchen Phillips swung her chair around so that she sat in profile, looking off toward the horizon of the sun-splashed city below them. She crossed her legs and said in a voice that was dreamlike in its lack of expression, "To want the kind of jobs men have . . . you surely know how it feels. That hunger for a sense of accomplishment . . . you surely know about that, too. To have that job you know you would love, know you'd be good at . . . And then a man tells you he wants you, a man with everything to say about whether you get that job, whether you keep that job. How do you react? How do you handle a man with that kind of power over you, over your life? So many women have even fewer options than I had, they're alone, with children . . ."

Gretchen Phillips sighed, turned and looked at Kate, hands clasping the sides of her chair. "Complain? Deana

French complained. She was in sales when I was still a service rep. When she first complained she was laughed at because she was overweight and not particularly attractive. Then the men found out she'd actually written a letter to Philadelphia, and Deana just wasn't a good *sport*. After all, she just had to say no, didn't she? What was the big deal? Then the subtleties began. She was ostracized. Given problem accounts, customers who produced more headaches than profit. Her expense accounts were questioned, checked and rechecked. Her performance appraisals—well, Deana quit. But she couldn't leave L.A. because her mother was ill. And draw your own conclusions, she couldn't find another sales job or any other job in our industry. So then she filed a lawsuit. And some men in this office said things under oath in depositions that simply weren't true. And then her mother died and she had a nervous breakdown. She's pulled herself together, the last I heard she was in partnership with another woman in an employment agency."

Kate said, "I had assumed things were better for women in business now."

"For women with stomach, women willing to pay a price. Or with the strength and wherewithal to draw a line. That's what it really comes down to—what are you willing to go through, to accept? Frequently it's easier to quit, give up that job you love, abandon the dreams. But don't feel badly for me. He didn't want me often, and the man didn't really want sex, he wanted the power. He wanted the rumors that he was laying his lady sales manager. His ejaculation was never sex, it was power."

"Miss Phillips," Kate said gently, "there's something I still don't understand. How can you tell me you had no motive for wanting him dead?"

"I may be wrong, and it doesn't matter one way or the other," Gretchen Phillips said, "but I think . . . I'm pretty sure, you're a lesbian."

Caught totally off-guard, Kate managed to say, "My private life has nothing to do with my work, I don't—"

"I understand. You have no idea how well I understand, it's how I live, too. And you're a police officer, I can't even begin to imagine the pressures on you." She leaned her slender body forward, sending sweet perfume toward Kate once more. "I had no motive because I'm one of the few women who could afford Fergus Parker's price for my job. I met the woman I live with in college. We've been together nine years. Chris and her brother own a small greenhouse, we all live in a little house in Pasadena. She's the reason I won't leave L.A. Chris does wonderful things with plants and flowers. She touches a plant and it's like a miracle."

The gray-blue eyes were again looking directly into Kate's eyes. "The times with Fergus Parker, I'd go home afterward and bathe and douche and then ask Chris to give me a massage. She loves to massage me. She has big hands, soft and healing. I can't begin to describe how they feel on my body. And when she massages me, there's not a part of me she doesn't stroke and love. And it's like he was never there. As long as there was Chris, Fergus Parker never . . . mattered."

"This investigation," Kate said. "Your office has been an education."

"I don't think our office is so unusual."

Kate shook her head. "Fergus Parker's replacement will have to be an improvement from your point of view."

Gretchen Phillips shrugged. "At least a different kind of devil. Somebody from another office, I expect. Harley should have the job, but his demotion had to hurt him badly back East. I worked for him when I was a sales rep, he's a terrific guy, a pro, a hard worker who makes all his people want to produce. Duane has no chance. It's the way he handles himself. He's so crazy about his wife you'd think he'd listen to her and have the sense not to wear those gaudy clown suits. Me, I won't be considered. I think this company will be ready for a Martian in higher management before they'll accept a woman. And I don't have enough service anyway. It may very well be Fred." She sighed, donned her big square glasses. "Fred's such an ass. Insecure, afraid to make a decision.

It'll be everyone for themselves if he gets the job."

"It would seem Harley Burton has an excellent motive for murder," Kate probed.

"I think the world of Harley Burton. If he did it to Fergus Parker, more power to him. I hope you never prove it."

The phone rang. Gretchen Phillips said irritably, "I told Judy to hold my calls." She picked up the receiver. "Gretchen Phillips." She listened for a few moments, then covered the receiver with a hand. "This is really urgent, it won't take long. I've been working on this customer's problem since—"

"It's all right." Kate rose, took a card from her notebook. "Call me if there's anything you'd like to add."

Gretchen Phillips put her phone on hold. She gave Kate her small delicate hand, then clasped Kate's hand in both hers. As Gretchen Phillips' hands slowly tightened, Kate held the level blue-gray gaze with all the impersonality she could muster. The soft hands finally released her, and Kate walked from the office.

Casting a surveying glance over the ornate furnishings of Guy Adams' office, Kate closed the door behind her. She sat down across from him, and in deliberate silence turned the pages of her notebook, one at a time, to a blank page. *Deep tan* were the first words she wrote. After a moment she added *in February.* No doubt a perfect tan, she thought, probably not even a tan line. A tanned peacock sitting in a bright nest of an office with everything designed to enhance his plummage.

Reminding herself of her obligation to objectivity, she straightened her jacket and looked up at Guy Adams. He was taking a swallow of coffee from a mug of translucent bone china shaped like a loving cup. She examined him more closely. Under the tan, the face was drawn, with an off-color pastiness; under the immaculate tailoring, the shoulders sagged. Pallor could indicate guilt—or shock. Cold

judgment told her that when it came to certain of life's realities, Guy Adams was the perfect type to be squeamish, to be lacking in the stomach department. Unlike herself, totally unqualified for garbage collecting. It was comforting irony to think of herself as following in her father's footsteps—in a better paying job, but still cleaning up other people's messes. Her father—dead seven years—had been a sanitation worker in Michigan.

"Mr. Adams, what can you tell me about Fergus Parker's death?"

"I don't—" Guy Adams shook his head and said in a husky whisper, "I'm stunned."

She sighed inaudibly. So much for her best open-ended question. "What time did you arrive this morning?"

"I'm not really sure." Adams' voice was hushed, and he raised it to add, "I had car trouble on the way."

"What kind of trouble?"

"Radiator. My radiator light came on."

"Did you stop at a gas station? Or call an auto club?"

"Neither. It wasn't necessary. I pulled off the freeway and took care of it myself."

Kate made a note, and observed Adams' fretful glance at her notebook. It was not an infrequent reaction. She had always used bound notebooks, believing that her interview subjects were more impressed with the gravity of their statements; and the non-detachable pages impressed juries whenever the notes were entered in evidence.

Deliberately, she made another note, then studied Adams' well-cared-for hands which lay flat on a small, deep green desk blotter edged in gold. "You repaired your own radiator?" She did not soften the sarcasm.

Adams replied with irritation, "I'm perfectly capable of unscrewing a radiator cap. The water level was normal, so obviously the indicator light was malfunctioning." He smiled suddenly, touched fingers to his empty breast pocket. "I can prove it. The radiator cap didn't seem greasy, but I used my handkerchief to wipe my fingers anyway. I tossed

it onto the back seat of the car."

Kate made a note in caps. "We'll just pick up the hand-kerchief. Is your car locked?"

"Do you always presuppose people lie to you?"

Kate reappraised the man across from her. Guy Adams was tense and upset, but he had managed a smile; his poise and confidence were inbred and automatic. 'It's a good idea in police work, Mr. Adams." She repeated, "Is your car locked?"

"No, no reason to lock it. Nothing in it. It's parked on the first floor of the garage." The smile contained indulgence. "It's a company car," he added.

Meaning you can be careless and not lock it. "Make and license number?"

"Eighty-four Olds Cutlass. Black. One-MEL-something."

"Mr. Adams, try to give me a rough estimate of when you arrived this morning."

"I don't know . . . There was so much confusion, police cars, police officers . . . They wouldn't let us up here for a long time . . ."

Seven-fifty or later, Kate wrote. "I'm sure. How well did you know the victim?"

Guy Adams pondered the question. "Not very well. I didn't want to, you see. I didn't work directly for him and I haven't been in the L.A. office long, only three months. We didn't care much for each other. But—"

"Why not?"

"He's not—he wasn't my kind of person." His finely-shaped mouth pinched downward in distaste. "Crude—very. All the class of a street thug. He treated his subordinates shamefully. Excused his inexcusable behavior by always claiming he was testing people. As far as I know, hardly anyone liked him. I've seen other people like him in offices I've worked in, but no one quite so . . . so ugly as this man. I did what I could, discussed him with people I know in Philadelphia—but he had a very successful record here. Of course, the people who worked for him made that success,

but he got the credit. That's how these things work—"

Guy Adams was now speaking freely, but rambling, and to no useful end. "Yes, I know how it works," she interrupted. "What other company offices have you worked in?"

There was a slight smile. "Quite a number. I started in Philadelphia straight out of college, worked there almost three years. Then they sent me to . . . let's see, Dallas, Seattle, Chicago—no, Atlanta, then Chicago. Then New York, then out here."

Adams was a relative, Kate remembered—a nephew. "A lot of transferring. How long have you been with the company?"

"Eight years."

"What exactly is your function?"

Guy Adams sat up straighter and said heartily, "Public relations. Promoting good will with customers. And I work with civic organizations, schools, charities, all that kind of thing. I do lobbying when it's necessary—"

Defensive about his usefulness, she concluded. She prodded, "Why were you sent to so many cities?"

"I carry out assignments given me by the company just like any other employee," Adams said stiffly. "They want me to use my name for the company's benefit, and I use it. They've chosen to spread me around quite a bit."

"That they have," Kate said agreeably. She prodded again, "But still, Adams is such a common name. I don't see why it would be useful except in a company with a name like Adams Furniture."

"My family name is a very great name, to those who *know*." A glint of anger was evident in Adams' green eyes. "My family's English, Guy is an ancient Celtic name, we're descendants of a family branch of Samuel Adams." He paused, his eyebrows raised as if in challenge.

Amused, Kate made an off-hand guess. "The Declaration of Independence."

Adams looked surprised, slightly crestfallen. "Almost everybody thinks of John Adams. Few people know Samuel's

name is just above his, the sixth row of signatures. Our family moved from Boston to Philadelphia around the turn of the nineteenth century and started the family business, fine crafted furniture back then." Guy Adams was speaking easily, as if he had related this background many times. "Around nineteen-ten there was a big family squabble and old Guy Adams bought out his two brothers. Unfortunately, my grandfather was one of the brothers who broke away, so I'm not connected to the great Adams fortune. My father was a lawyer. I've had to earn my living just like anyone else."

Only a tiny silver spoon in your mouth, Kate thought acidly. Merely a pedigree that dates back beyond the Revolutionary War, a job handed to you right after college, travel and a big salary and a car and expense account, enough feeding at the rich end of the Adams trough to indulge a taste for expensive tailoring and these glossy office trappings . . .

She took her time over her notes. She had always disliked men like Guy Adams, not because their money and position and opportunities were unearned, but because of their assumption that this was the way things should be for them, that advantage and important connections were laws of nature, like leaves growing on trees. There was no knowledge in them—not the slightest conception—of what it was like to have money worries, family worries, to work full time and carry a full load of college classes, to live and work week after month after year on the raw edge of exhaustion. Not for Guy Adams to have parents who suffered guilt at what they could not give, to have a mother who on her deathbed whispered, "Kate, our one dream was to find the money somewhere to send you to college . . ."

Pen poised over her notes, Kate asked, bitterly anticipating the answer, "Any wartime service, Mr. Adams?"

Guy Adams shook his head. "College deferment. Sometimes I wish I'd gone, even to a war like Vietnam. War, what it does to a man, that's something I'll never experience."

Undoubtedly this perfect man will go into politics some day, she thought with furious disgust, and take his romanticized view of war with him. "Ever been married, Mr. Adams?"

"Briefly. Divorced. One broken engagement. The lady figured I was one of the moneyed Adamses." His smile was self-deprecating. "A lot of people do misread my proximity to the Adams money, my ability to influence decisions made by the company. I work here just like anybody else."

Just exactly like anybody else, she thought, with a brief and poisonous glance around the ornate office. She decided to proceed quickly with her questions before her contempt for this man became obvious. "This morning when you were allowed upstairs, was your office door open?"

Guy Adams' eyes widened, became blank.

"Mr. Adams, it's an easy question." Kate raised her voice, pursued him. "When you came in was your office door open? Or closed?" She watched acutely as Adams rested an elbow on his desk, rubbed his forehead. He had had the opportunity to compare notes with Ellen O'Neil. Would he lie, as she had lied?

"Gail's always reminding me to close it." His husky voice had dropped to a rasp, seemed distant and tired. "He told me again just yesterday. I can't remember if I did or not. Opening, closing doors, it's so automatic . . . and when you have things on your mind . . ."

It was hard to argue with that, Kate conceded as she recorded Adams' answer. But still unlikely he would not remember. "What did you have on your mind that affected your memory?"

"Last night, you mean? When I left? A report I had to finish today . . . I was supposed to play racquetball with this guy in my building . . . I live at the beach now, so I don't have to use the tanning parlors. I swim, play tennis, all that, I play a little golf—"

Kate interrupted the ramble in a pleasant tone. "You're managing to meet people in L.A.?"

"It's a friendly city. Especially the women." He smiled, a tentative, conspiratorial boys-will-be-boys smile.

"Was Fergus Parker a womanizer, Mr. Adams?"

Adams' smile froze. She was gratified that the implied association with Fergus Parker had given such grievous offense. Adams said tightly, "There were rumors. None I care to repeat."

Kate thought of Ellen O'Neil, that she was the kind of warm, enduring woman a Guy Adams would pursue, the kind of woman who possessed resilience and the qualities of character he did not. She felt a gladness about Ellen O'Neil's "roommate," and that she was not attracted to this French poodle of a man. "All right. Whom did you see when you first came into the building this morning?"

Again the green eyes turned blank. Again Adams rubbed his forehead. "Uh, Gail. Fred, I think. Fred Grayson. And the police, of course... I just can't remember. Gretchen and Harley... but I don't know if they were there already or came later. There was so much confusion, Gail took charge of things and by that time more and more people were arriving—"

"All right. Do you know of any person with a reason for wanting to harm Fergus Parker?"

"Well, he was disliked, as I said. How deep it went with any individual, I'm not in the best position to say—"

"Or don't want to say?"

"Well, maybe both. Ellen—Ellen O'Neil, she was here when it—when he—hasn't she been helpful?"

"Mr. Adams," Kate said sternly, "I believe Lieutenant Kovich explained the necessity for strict confidentiality in an investigation of this kind. It can only help the killer to know what information or evidence is known about—"

"I haven't discussed it," Adams protested. "I've been with Ellen, we didn't talk about it at all."

She rose. "I'll appreciate your continued cooperation." She took a card from her notebook, dropped it on the ornate desk. "Let me know if anything else comes to mind.

If I'm not around you can find me or leave a message at the number on the card."

"How long do you think . . ." Guy Adams trailed off, rubbed a hand again across his forehead.

"We hope to make an arrest soon. I imagine we'll be here several days. Possibly longer."

As she walked to the door she heard the sound of a receiver being picked up, digits being punched. As she opened the door and walked into the hall, she heard Guy Adams: "Ellen? This is Guy. Are you busy?"

8

Wearily, Ellen closed her eyes. The day had been eventful enough without this added complication from Guy Adams. "I really can't, Guy. I appreciate—"

Her other line flashed and rang. The button remained lit as Gail Freeman in the next office picked it up.

Guy Adams said, "You might not feel like eating something, that's understandable. God knows, who does? But how about just a drink? We should talk. There's this place—"

"What I really need is to get my mind off what's happened," she said firmly. "I think that's best, and—"

"Ellen . . . she suspects me, Ellen. That detective."

"Of course she does, Guy," she soothed. "They have to suspect everybody. Don't be upset."

"Ellen? Change your mind." His husky voice was soft.

"I really can't." She chose her words carefully, depressed and annoyed by the necessity: "It would give me a problem . . . in my personal life."

He sighed. "I understand. Okay, I'll call you later, check on you. Promise to call if you change your mind? Maybe you'd like to just get out of the building. I could—"

Gail Freeman had appeared in her doorway. In relief she interrupted, "It's dear of you. Sorry, I do have to go." She hung up and said to Gail Freeman, "Poor Guy, he's so upset."

"I know. He's like that. He'll never know how much Fergus Parker hated him—Guy simply can't conceive of people like Fergus Parker." He smiled. "That was our good detective on the other line."

"Did she ask if Matt Bradford's office was open this morning?"

He nodded. "It's always open whether Matt's here or not. The managers need access to those miniature mockups of our office designs, his material samples."

She said wryly, "Detective Delafield has this fetish about closed doors." She stacked several pages together. "I need you to sign last month's overtime report. Philadelphia called this morning—it's a week overdue."

There was no answer; she looked up to see Gail Freeman staring at her, dark eyes lidded in thought. Then he smiled and walked to her, taking a gold Cross pen from the breast pocket of his jacket.

She remembered sitting across from Gail Freeman in his office moments after her introduction to Fergus Parker. "I know I've accepted this job," she had said, "and as much as I'd like to work here, there's no way I could work for that man. I don't see how any woman could. I don't even want to be in the same city."

He had answered in a low firm voice and ticked off points on slender brown fingers tipped with lighter, well-cared for nails. "You'll be working for me, not him. Short of murder, whatever you do is judged by me, not him. His management style offends everyone in the office, it's not restricted to gender or color, and not all of that is necessarily bad. You'll find the dynamics of this place fascinating."

His intelligence and candor had impressed her in the first meeting, and she looked at his ascetic face with reawakened admiration. "Gail . . ." She hesitated, unaccustomed to addressing a boss by first name, and groping for tactful words to express her distress at Fergus Parker's disdain for Gail Freeman, a contempt he had not bothered to conceal even in front of Gail Freeman's new assistant. "Gail, he treats

you . . ." Again she hesitated, then selected a word. ". . . shamefully."

He steepled his graceful fingers. "A few years ago this company was grateful to have a promotable black man to push into a visible position. But now the climate's changed. And I've changed—older, more cautious, more at stake." He smiled, gestured to the family photo on the credenza. "Two years ago I could've walked out, pretty easily duplicated what I have here. But today—maybe not at all. Ellen, years ago I worked in a wheel factory. The memory's just like yesterday. And that takes a lot of the independence out of your attitude, confidence from your step."

He looked at her from thickly fringed, calm dark eyes. "It's Fergus Parker's mean little talent to pick out vulnerability, smell fear like a vampire smells blood. And he hates anything he considers alien." He chuckled, a low, pleasant resonance. "Anything off-white, for example. Please stay, Ellen. I need your help. You won't have a problem with Fergus Parker. Your independence is too obvious. Fergus Parker never plays a hand that's not a sure winner."

"I want to work for you," she had told him. "You're so straightforward, my first honest boss."

"Let's hear it for management," he had said ironically.

Reflecting on this conversation, she watched Gail Freeman read and sign the overtime report. He said, "Our good detective also told me she'd interview Billie Sullivan tomorrow. Know what? I think she just wants to give Billie Sullivan another day on payroll."

Ellen chuckled. "That doesn't quite fit your ogre image of her."

Gail Freeman looked penitent. "I made some flippant remark about her to her partner. I thought he'd pick me up by my tie and slam me against the wall. He told me Kate Delafield was one of the best cops and finest people he'd ever worked with, and the citizens of this city should pray for a thousand more just like her. He did explain that she's been recovering from the death of someone close to her. A

flaming wreck on the Hollywood Freeway, a really God-awful accident."

Her lover. Ellen knew it instantly. The image of Kate Delafield's strong, suffering face filled her mind. Ellen gazed at her desk. "She's very professional, very good at her job," she murmured. She tried to push away her vision of Kate Delafield's anguish, her unspoken, lonely grief.

Again there was no answer; again she looked up to see Gail Freeman staring at her. Hands in his pockets, he strolled back into his office.

Stephanie Hale said, "You embarrassed me today."

Ellen, folding underwear into a suitcase, stopped and confronted her, hands on her hips. "*I* embarrassed *you*?"

Stephanie looked at Ellen, ocean-gray eyes cool. "As soon as you called, I came. Didn't I? You were upset enough to call me in the middle of a class, weren't you? I came all that way as fast as I could. Through that rotten Westwood traffic."

"I didn't *ask* you to come. I just needed to *talk* to you. We *love* each other, don't we? But no, super butch has to try and drag her little hot house flower home, her little shrinking violet!"

"Ellen, you found a *dead* man. You could've been killed yourself!"

They were shouting; Ellen lowered her voice and hissed, "Well, I *wasn't*. And the detective in charge told me I handled myself with great presence of mind."

"So what does she know? When I got there you'd been crying."

Stephanie had taken her jogging shoes from the closet to bring with her, and Ellen picked them up off the bed and hurled them into the suitcase. "For God's sake, you of all people should know tears are *emotion*, not weakness!"

Calmly Stephanie picked up the shoes and slid them into

a plastic sack and stacked it neatly on top of her socks. "I had every right to want you out of there, not have you any more upset than you already were."

"Answer me this," Ellen said icily. "If you'd been me, if this had happened in the hallowed halls of UCLA, would you let me take you home because you were upset?"

"There are simply some things I handle better than you."

"What goddamn bullshit."

"So you can swear like a man," Stephanie said contemptuously. "I'm impressed."

"Good," Ellen said. "Fuck you."

She stalked into the living room and sat on the sofa with her arms crossed, furious, as Stepahnie finished packing and walked past her into the kitchen.

Carrying plates of food, Stephanie came into the living room. She deposited the plates on TV trays and sat in her usual armchair, eyes drifting to the television screen as she pushed at the contents of her plate. She lifted a forkful of Stouffer's pasta shells and looked at it. "This stuff," she said.

"You used to love it, raved about the sauce," Ellen said nastily. "Good for jogging, you used to say. Before I decided to go back to work."

"You really want to get into all that again? The food's fine, my taster's off. Okay?"

For some minutes they ate in silence. Grudging the conciliation of changing the subject, Ellen muttered, "I can't stand Dan Rather."

Stephanie contemplated the TV screen, drawing curly strands of graying hair over her forehead with the absentmindedness of habit. Twin furrows formed between her deep set gray eyes. "Honey, what do we do next week when Julie comes and you're not here?"

Ellen sighed inaudibly. "What we did before when I was working. Stephie, why do we have to do anything? She's nineteen. Your kids are both old enough to amuse themselves."

"Ellen honey, we see little enough of them."

Ellen smothered a yawn and tucked her legs up under her, thinking that she was exhausted from this day, and that she saw more than enough of Stephanie's teenage daughters.

Stephanie rose, pulling a gray UCLA sweatshirt down over pale blue jogging pants, and carried their dishes to the kitchen, padding off in her stocking feet, wide shoulders slightly bowed. To the sound of plates being scraped, water running, Ellen punched the remote control impatiently, flipping the TV from channel to channel. She thought: Is it really worth it? Is my heart really into working? Since she hates it so much?

Stephanie came back and sat next to her, thin legs folded under her yoga-style. They sat in silence, watching Richard Dawson joke with contestants on *Family Feud.* Stephanie gestured at the TV. "Turn that idiot off, will you?"

Ellen punched the channel selector. "Right there," Stephanie directed as USC cheerleaders danced across the screen in their maroon-lettered white sweaters and gold skirts, and basketball players shot dozens of basketballs in pregame warmup. "Business is Death Valley," she said. "I don't know what I'd do if I couldn't teach. Be a gardener, maybe." Her eyes were fixed on the screen where players were stripping off their warmup suits.

"I don't feel that way. I wish you'd respect that. What I want to do, I wish you'd take it seriously."

"Baby, I do."

"Last night," Ellen accused, "my first day on the job, you expect a home-cooked meal and a night out on the town."

"Oh for Christ's sake, Ellen. You're not running the damn company. If I can work all day and go out so can you."

Ellen said with dignity, "I had material to read. Technical manuals."

"All in one night?"

"I don't like feeling stupid on a job any more than you

would." Anger was swiftly gathering.

Stephanie rose and walked toward the bedroom, pulling her sweatshirt over her head, to change clothes for her flight.

On the way to the airport Ellen rolled down the window, the traffic on the San Diego Freeway drowning out possibility for conversation. They did not speak until they had threaded their way through the airport traffic and pulled up in front of the PSA terminal.

Stephanie set the handbrake on the Fiat. "Ellen darling, it's been too long since we talked. Really talked."

"Months," Ellen conceded sulkily. "For that kind of talking."

"I get back Thursday, Julie comes out next week. Let's talk this weekend. Okay?"

They got out of the car. Stephanie pulled her luggage out of the tiny trunk and then kissed Ellen's forehead, her lips warm and firm. "We have orientation meetings till late tonight. I'll call you tomorrow."

Ellen touched Stephanie's face, suddenly afraid of her leaving, and kissed her cheek, smoothing the fine gray-brown hair back into place behind her ear. She gripped her shoulders.

Stephanie's eyes searched her face gravely. "Ellen? Are you okay?"

She nodded. "Sure." But she was not okay, and did not know what was wrong, nor how to tell her.

She watched Stephanie walk away, garment bag slung over a shoulder; Stephanie looked dignified and distinguished in her herringbone jacket and gray slacks. Stephanie Lewis Hale, Professor of Economics at the University of California at Los Angeles—Ellen was proud of her.

At five minutes to seven, Kate parked off Colorado Boulevard in Santa Monica, and walked around the corner and down the half block to Fergus Parker's house. She was comfortable in her jacket even this late in a February day, even in usually cool Santa Monica; warm Santa Ana winds had blown in from the desert that afternoon. A large woman in a dark blue muumuu paced the driveway beside the house. Gray roots showed along the part in the neatly combed, curly reddish-brown hair that framed a puffy face.

"Mrs. Fergus Parker?"

Red-rimmed sapphire eyes looked her over, glanced at the shield she had extended along with her ID card, and met Kate's eyes. "Detective Delafield," she said in a soft girlish voice, "I've already answered questions—an officer this morning, and the Coroner's office a little while ago. My children have just arrived. Do they have to be involved in this?"

"Will we need to question them? I can't think why we would."

"They're very upset, especially my son. Could we possibly talk in the backyard, leave them to unpack?"

"Certainly."

Kate followed her through a latched wooden gate next to the garage, down a path to a tiny yard containing a narrow

swimming pool perhaps fifteen feet in length.

"It's a lovely night," Helen Parker said, lowering herself into a deck chair and gathering her voluminous dress around her; rolls of fat settled around her midriff. "The Santa Anas are a lovely and unexpected respite from the winter."

"Indeed," Kate said, sitting across from her and taking out her notebook, thinking that under the circumstances her lyrical praise of the weather fit Gail Freeman's ironic description of the ungrieving Widow Parker, but the red-rimmed eyes did not.

"I don't have much progress to report," Kate said, "or even many questions to ask. We're still putting facts together, gathering evidence which may point to the person responsible. Perhaps we can begin with any persons you know of who were enemies of your husband."

She was taken aback by soft peals of laughter.

Helen Parker said, "His wife. His entire management staff. Most people he came into contact with. Don't be misled by the fact that I've been crying. Those were tears for my children. I *have* them now, and they're never going away from me again."

Kate cleared her throat. "I see."

"No, you really don't. You don't even begin to see." She fished in the pocket of her dress and took out a box of Marlboros with a pack of matches tucked into the cellophane, and lit a cigarette. She glanced at Kate's left hand. "Have you ever been married?"

Warily, Kate shook her head.

"Even so . . . you'll understand better than a man would." Helen Parker drew on her cigarette. Her lips were well-shaped, with a trace of lipstick; she held the cigarette gracefully in long plump fingers.

"I haven't had a drink today, Detective Delafield. When Gail told me this morning, I poured myself a stiff one. But then after he left I dumped it into a humidor filled with stinking cigars. I realized I didn't have to drink anymore. Or have to smell stinking cigars in my home anymore. Four

hundred thousand in insurance," she said in a musical, contented voice. "The mortgage on the house will be paid, covered by insurance. Stocks and other assets I've yet to find out about. No will, of course. Fergus never thought he would ever die. It's all mine and the children's, as soon as this is over and his body's been disposed of. It's been a difficult choice between letting the worms go at him, or reducing him to ashes. But it's still so hard to believe he's dead I think I'll feel better with the ashes."

Kate cleared her throat again and closed her notebook to concentrate on this remarkable woman. "Feeling as you do, why did you stay married to him?"

The jewel-like eyes glittered. "As you've already surmised, Mrs. Parker drinks a little. Nine years ago the first time, then four years after that he put me in one of those places they advertise on television. Of course I came home and took one look at him and started all over again. But the point is, it's documented. I did leave him once, you see, and took the children. He went crazy. Somebody actually did something to *him*. My lawyer convinced me that I'd never win a custody battle, not with my drinking history, and Fergus swore he'd get witnesses to say I'd done everything from molesting children to masturbating in public."

She drew deeply from her cigarette. "I wish I could get you something to drink."

"I'm fine, thank you. I appreciate it."

"Anyway, when I came back after trying to leave, Fergus made new conditions for our marriage. In exchange for being allowed to keep my own children, all I had to do was cook and clean and perform other . . . services on demand, certain . . . practices which I had always before refused to do. And Fergus's appetites were far more gross than anyone could ever imagine."

A light ocean breeze disturbed Kate's hair and rustled the folds of Helen Parker's dress. Helen Parker raised her face to the wind, closed her eyes, inhaled deeply, and smiled.

"When this is over," she said quietly, "I'm going to treat myself to a very expensive month at a place called *The Golden Door*. It's a spa in Escondido where they perform miracles with diet and exercise to get you back in shape. I'm only forty-four. I used to be an attractive woman. I intend to be again."

Dreamily, she smoked her cigarette, gazing into a distance beyond the swimming pool. Kate remained silent. Cigarette smoke carried to her on the wind. It had been twelve years since she smoked, and she still sometimes missed it.

"Your children," she said finally. "What was their relationship to their father?"

"Fergus loved them. His children and his parents and his two brothers, they were flesh of his flesh, and they saw a side of Fergus none of the rest of us ever did."

Kate was unable to resist asking, "Why did you marry him?"

Helen Parker dropped the cigarette into the grass. "If there's a reason, I've blanked it out of my mind. I refuse to acknowledge any good I might have once seen."

Kate remained silent again, and Helen Parker smiled. "Aren't you going to ask my whereabouts before eight o'clock this morning? I'd be disappointed if you didn't."

Kate smiled and opened her notebook. "Why don't you tell me."

She gestured vaguely. "I was with Rita Jensen next door fixing pancakes for her kids. I do that sometimes if I'm up early."

"Mr. Parker arrived at the Becker Building at six-fifty-three. Did he often leave the house so early?"

"Unfortunately, no."

"Do you know why he went in early this morning?"

"Not specifically. He mentioned a phone call from the East he had to take before the office opened. He seemed unusually cheerful."

Kate touched her pen to her chin, thinking. Gail Freeman could contact the appropriate people in Philadelphia to check

calls from there to Fergus Parker. She made a note, then asked, "What did he have for breakfast?"

"A light snack of ham, sausage, three eggs, three slices of toast, orange juice, and two Cokes."

Kate smiled as she busily wrote. "Coffee?"

"Never drank coffee. He was a Coca-Cola addict. Drank gallons of it. Beginning first thing in the morning. Belched gas from both ends day and night."

The mention of Coca-Cola reminded Kate of the overturned bar in Fergus Parker's office. "What were his drinking habits?"

"He'd have a little rum in his Coke at night, but not much. Drink a little red wine if he was really celebrating something, like cheating a customer."

"What about the people at Modern Office? Did you see them much? Did you entertain frequently?"

"Not frequently. Fergus preferred to have one or two over occasionally. He loved to make the ones who weren't invited nervous and suspicious. Once a year there was a command performance, all his staff. Fancy, catered, everybody eating tiny canapes, edgy and worried about saying something he'd jump on and ridicule all night."

"Did you notice animosity from any employee that seemed especially intense?"

She sighed. "That's so hard to say. Like measuring inches of evil. I know he did something despicable to Harley Burton. Harley's a fine man, a good person. I think poor Duane suffered the most. Duane's one of those roly-poly foolish little bald men you sort of automatically tease anyway, but Fergus used a cleaver, not a needle."

"Mrs. Parker—"

"Helen."

She decided that this one time she would violate her rule about first names. "Helen, I'd like to at least walk through your home, it would take perhaps five minutes. To gain a better picture of the various facets of your husband's life. Perhaps I could be . . . a tax assessor?"

"You're very kind, Detective Delafield."

She let Kate in the back door, into a roomy and well-equipped yellow kitchen aromatic with cooking food. Kate realized she was hungry. Fergus Parker's house was split-level, three bedrooms and a family room, and in a disarray that aroused in Kate memories of several pain-blurred days in her own house. In the living room, cardboard boxes were half-filled with books and plaques. Desk accessories, golf trophies, photographs were strewn across an overstuffed velvet sofa and loveseat. A big square desk stood bare, pushed against a wall which had been stripped of its pictures; Kate could see the lighter squares in the paint. In one of the bedrooms, a plump young girl with reddish-brown hair unpacked a suitcase; her dark-haired younger brother, his eyes the color of Helen Parkers, lolled on the bed.

"Tax assessor," Helen Parker said as the young people looked at Kate.

The boy scowled. "You picked a fine time."

The girl said, "Aren't you working a little late?"

Kate said, "You know how inefficient the government is."

There were chuckles, and Kate walked on, to the master bedroom.

The bed was stripped down to the mattress, the room was a chaos of boxes filled with men's clothing and toiletries.

Helen Parker said in a thick voice, "I don't know if I can live here anymore."

"Helen, it's a nice house. A good area to bring up kids." Kate spoke in a low firm tone. "Get a new bed, new bedroom set if you want, paint the place. It's a real nice house for a family."

Helen Parker nodded. "You could be right."

"Give it some time."

At the front door Kate said, "I'll call if I have any more questions. We'll bother you as little as possible."

Without a word, Helen Parker extended her hand. Kate held the big soft hand moments longer than necessary and looked into the beautiful sapphire eyes. "Helen," she said, "I hope your children will always be good to you."

11

Kate drove off for dinner.

She had never realized until the past few months the difficulties, the dispiriting awkwardness of dining alone in a good restaurant. Because of her profession she had had to be cautious, circumspect in her personal life, but there were a few close friends who had been fully supportive; there had been no lack of offers of companionship. But she had discovered that she was less and less able to be with women who brought back memories of Anne and herself together, and the recent months had been a time of gradually increasing isolation.

Patiently, she drove around Santa Monica searching for a place lacking formality but not a coffee shop or cafe, and finally stopped on the edge of Venice near the beach. *Seaspray* lacked a liquor license but had bright curtains and hanging plants and white tablecloths. She settled herself gratefully in a small leather booth.

She liked Santa Monica, always had; but Anne had disliked the misty moodiness of oceanside towns. The rent control controversy had quieted somewhat, and maybe she should try to move here now, rent an apartment. Sell, get out of Glendale regardless of the uncertain Southern California housing market. Unlike Helen Parker, what did she want now with two bedrooms and a convertible den and two

baths and three orange trees in the backyard? An excellent investment, the real estate agent had congratulated them eight years ago. A real home and a good neighborhood, Anne had exulted, brown eyes glowing . . .

She had not clung to other mementoes. Anne's clothing, her jewelry, had gone immediately to her sister in Santa Barbara. Snapshots and other recorded memories of their lives had been packed in boxes, placed in storage. She had packed away certain dishes and books, odds and ends that had transfixed her with the agony of memory, until the day came when she could bear to look at everything again. Only Barney was still there, the collie they both had loved, who had protected Anne all the evenings and nights Kate was called away to protect and to serve others . . . Why should she continue to hold onto the house she was so unwilling to return to each night?

She opened her menu. Preferring a double scotch, she settled with little regret for half a carafe of wine. She read her notes of the Fergus Parker case and evaluated the newest pieces of the mosaic as she selected the crispest pieces of lettuce from her salad.

She had taken the file photos of Modern Office employees downstairs to the garage. The attendant, she had quickly discovered, could just as well have stayed home and collected his paycheck for all the care and attention he gave to his job. Every face in the photographs was familiar to him; he could not remember seeing anyone in particular that morning, had not seen anyone running in the garage. Nothing unusual at all—except for someone coughing.

"Man or woman?" she had asked.

"Man."

"Where in the garage was it coming from?"

"I dunno, behind me somewhere."

"Why did you notice?"

"Coughing his lungs out."

"Why didn't you investigate?"

"What the hell do I care about somebody coughing?

Besides, cops were pulling in, they could do their own damn investigating."

Taylor's analysis of the guards' ledger had not revealed any unusual pattern to off-hours activity at Modern Office. Fergus Parker had made no previous early morning visits this year, only four last year. Each of the managers had come in early from time to time, none recently.

At her request, the two guards had recreated their actions after Ellen O'Neil's phone call. Rick Carlson had been on duty; Mike Sutherland had finished his final inspection and was in the guard station. When Ellen O'Neil's call came, Carlson called the police, shouting for Sutherland who came out of the guard office, heard Carlson on the phone with the police, and immediately secured all four elevators, placing them out of service. Sutherland ran to the staircase and released the hydraulic mechanism that lowered the mesh gate on the garage level. Sutherland then refused to wait for the police, insisted that they go up together to check on the safety of Ellen O'Neil. The guards' estimate of how long it had taken to fully close off the upper floors of the building after receiving the call from Ellen O'Neil: forty-five seconds to a minute, no more.

Using a stopwatch, Kate and Taylor had experimented, Taylor's face comically unhappy at having to hurtle his two hundred and twenty pounds down sixteen flights of stairs. They took turns, Kate first; but she had stopped abruptly on the fifteenth floor and called for Taylor. Rolled up against a wall was a Carlton cigarette butt which had burned almost to the filter, a three-quarter length of ash. On the pale green wall was a small black smear: the cigarette had been flung, not merely discarded. Taylor collected the cigarette and ash in separate envelopes, and Kate began her run again. She made the garage in a minute and fifty-two seconds; Taylor's time was two minutes, eight seconds. At Kate's insistence they made the run one more time. Her time was a minute-fifty; Taylor, two minutes-fifteen.

The cleaning personnel, who arrived at five o'clock,

had provided two pieces of information. The stairway was swabbed twice a week, Tuesdays and Fridays. And the portable bar in Fergus Parker's office had been in its usual position away from the desk when the office was cleaned Monday night.

Kate's veal chop arrrived; she put her notes away.

Ellen worked her way through the airport traffic and back out onto Century Boulevard, thinking about the weekend Stephanie had proposed. They had had eight such weekends in their two years together—spiritual housecleanings, Stephanie had called them. Naked in bed, eating delicatessen food, smoking joints, drinking wine, exploring each other's bodies and psyches, a weekend of loving, sleeping, talking. Hour after hour, warmed in the concentrated glow of Stephanie's attention . . . Why was she not as eager as she had always been before?

Troubled, depressed, she parked and walked through the underground garage, cautiously watching the shadows as she always did since the rapist had come from behind a parked car a month ago and seized a woman who lived on the top floor.

The raspy voice of Bob Seger seeped into the upstairs hallway; the erratic guitar rhythms of *Night Moves* seemed aggressive, ominous. Her apartment was inky black, seemed possessed of a sinister silence. She walked quickly through the rooms turning on all the lights. She switched on the TV, searched through the stack of economics periodicals in the rack beside the sofa for the latest *Time.* But she stared at the curtain billowing over the slightly open balcony door, alert and uneasy.

Kate ate her meal with enjoyment, and continued to contemplate the pieces of evidence in the Fergus Parker case. So many aspects were puzzling. Why had Fergus Parker arrived early? Why had he—or someone else—pushed the portable bar close to his desk at seven o'clock in the morning? Most inexplicable of all, why was there no sign of

struggle? Fergus Parker must have known well the specific emnity each individual in the company felt for him. How could a killer catch him so off-guard that he did not—or could not—defend himself?

And another problem—the killer was a coffee drinker, had finished nearly half a pot, according to Ellen O'Neil. Wouldn't he or she bring coffee to Fergus Parker's office? How could the killer run down sixteen flights with a container of coffee in hand? There were no signs of spilled liquid anywhere on the upper stairs—she had checked on hands and knees. Possibly the killer had carried an empty container. But that bespoke too much coolness. Amateur City, Taylor had called this homicide, and experience told her that premeditated or not, after the crime this amateur killer had reacted without thought to what circumstances had dictated.

Ellen O'Neil had responded instantly to sounds of flight and Fergus Parker's death throes—but how long had she delayed in calling the guards? That was the other essential element to be added to the mosaic. If she had acted swiftly, the killer would have had precious few seconds to get down and out of the building before every escape route was cut off.

Kate finished her coffee, reflecting. Except for Luther Garrett, the outside sales group, and a computer operator who had been out since Friday with the flu, she had met or seen all current employees. Depending on the timing of Ellen O'Neil's actions, she could at least place the killer's physical condition within certain parameters.

She glanced at her watch, decided to call Ellen O'Neil.

Her scrupulous inner voice whispered, you don't need to. You can wait until tomorrow. You just want to call her because she is like Anne and you want to hear her voice . . .

Someone came down the hall; footsteps paused outside Ellen's apartment; something brushed against the door. For

some moments she sat frozen; then she tiptoed to the door and peered through the peephole. There was no ore visible. Chilled and frightened, she checked the lock, the security chain.

She leaped as the phone shrilled.

"Miss O'Neil? This is Detective Delafield."

"Oh. Yes, how are you?" She was absurdly happy to hear the calm, authoritative voice.

"I have a few questions about the timing of some events this morning. Am I disturbing you? The questions could wait till tomorrow."

"No, really, I'm—no, you're not disturbing me at all." Her own voice seemed high-pitched, foreign.

"Miss O'Neil, are you all right? You sound—"

"To tell you the truth—" She broke off, remembering the sarcastic response the last time she had used that phrase. "I'm alone tonight, I feel very nervous. I don't know why. I've been alone many times before and it's never bothered me, but I thought I heard someone just now . . ."

"It would be very strange if you weren't strongly affected by what happened today. But isn't there someone—" Kate cleared her throat. "Don't you . . . usually have someone there with you?"

Ellen called herself a fool. Of course this detective in charge of a major investigation would know about Stephanie. Detective Taylor—any of the police officers on the scene— would have passed along the information that Stephanie had come this morning to be with her. Ellen said, "She left tonight for an economics seminar in Berkeley."

"I see. Let me suggest this. Perhaps I can make you feel more assured about your safety. I'm in the area, I'll be glad to come over and check things out where you live. Or perhaps you should call a friend, stay with someone tonight."

"Would you come over?" she asked very softly. "I'd be very grateful." She was not about to call Marcie and Janice. Stephanie would find out and she'd never hear the end of

it, especially after what they had quarreled about tonight. "I can answer your questions, give you something to drink. Would that be all right?"

Kate Delafield was no more than five minutes away; Ellen gave her directions.

12

The apartment building was fronted by a date tree on a postage-stamp lawn divided by a sidewalk. Four evergreens clung to the building, sparse ivy climbed over the roof. From the mail slots Kate saw that Ellen O'Neil lived on the first floor, which was elevated above ground by a subterranean parking level. She surveyed both sides of the structure, frowning at the presence of balconies, then buzzed the apartment.

Ellen answered her knock immediately, smiling. "Hi. Thanks for coming."

To Kate she looked younger and even more feminine in jeans and a man-tailored shirt—much like Anne used to look; but Anne had liked khaki pants, the kind with back pockets that buttoned. "No trouble at all," she said. "Miss O'Neil, you should always ask who it is before you buzz someone into this building. And use your peephole every time, even when you expect someone."

Ellen was momentarily irked. "You're right, I suppose. You know what you're talking about. I just hate living that way."

"Understandably." Kate examined the door lock. "It's not the way I grew up, either. I come from a small town in Michigan. This lock," she said. "Sturdy but not deep enough into the frame. Tell your apartment manager LAPD says you

need a dead bolt half an inch in." She took a card from her notebook. "Give them this. Tell them also the garage needs higher wattage."

"Thank you." She watched, smiling, as Kate went over to the balcony. She felt at ease and secure with this woman.

Kate frowned at the balcony door and the transparent curtain over it, a slow billowing in the night air. She pushed the curtain aside. Several plants were visible on the balcony, a small wooden table and two light aluminum chairs. A broom handle leaned against a wall on the inside track of the door.

"The brace is a good idea," Kate told her. "Be sure you always use it, don't get careless. One case I saw . . ." She decided not to describe the apartment just off Pico and the body of a young woman in a room awash with blood. "Even though you're a good fifteen feet above ground level, you should consider keeping the balcony door closed and locked when you're in here alone at night. This curtain—with lights on, you can see right into the room."

"Feel free to close it now," Ellen said. The room had become chill with the night air.

Kate did so, and moved to the window. "Get some locking devices at a hardware store, Miss O'Neil. They're easy to use, fit right over the runners. A few more safeguards will make you feel that much more secure." As secure as anyone could feel in this city . . . And assuming someone didn't really want to get in here, didn't use glass cutters or a suction cup.

"Thank you. I'll do everything you say. What can I get you? We have beer, fruit juice, coffee . . ." She shrugged apologetically. "Stephanie won't allow liquor or soft drinks in the house." The righteous Stephanie also kept a stash of marijuana in the den, but she couldn't very well offer that to a detective from LAPD.

"Any of those is fine. I'll have what you're having."

Ellen said with a grin, "I'm not having any of those. I like a cup of hot chocolate at night."

Kate's throat closed. She swallowed and managed to say, "Fine. I'd like that. I haven't had hot chocolate for . . . months."

I've struck a memory again, Ellen thought helplessly, moved by the pain she had heard in Kate Delafield's voice. But I don't know how not to. How very much she must have loved her . . .

Reluctant to leave, Ellen said, "Why don't we take care of business first? What did you want to ask?"

Kate sat on the sofa next to Ellen and leafed through her notes, gathering her thoughts. She was suddenly bone-tired; her throat still ached with the anguish of memory, there was a stinging under her eyelids. Emotion had been ambushing her all day, seemed perilously close to the surface again. And she was exhausted. The wine, she thought, I should never drink when I'm working.

She cleared her throat. "It's possible the killer didn't have much time to exit the building. How long would you say it took you to go from the hallway to the lobby after you saw the body?"

Ellen touched her fingers to her temples, concentrating, reliving the moments. "Fifteen to twenty seconds," she said finally.

Kate nodded. Better than she had hoped. "How long did it take to find the number and call the guards?"

"I found the number right away, but I didn't call right away. I was too scared. Of being seen, heard. Another fifteen seconds . . . Maybe twenty."

"How long did it take Carlson to answer?"

"He picked up the phone before it finished a ring."

"And the conversation?"

"Brief. He had trouble hearing me, I was whispering. But it was brief Fifteen seconds at the outside."

Kate sat tapping her pen against her chin. Now that the detective was preoccupied, Ellen murmured, "Excuse me," and rose to fix their hot chocolate.

"Sure," Kate said absently, adding numbers on a blank

page of her notebook. Using Ellen O'Neil's figures, it had taken a total of forty-five seconds to complete the call to Rick Carlson, another minute at the outside for Carlson and Sutherland to close off the building—allow another ten to fifteen seconds error factor. A minute fifty-two it had taken her, Kate Delafield, to get down those steps in reckless flight. The killer had exited from the staircase with scant seconds to spare before the gate had come down. The killer therefore had to be above average in physical condition. Kate leaned back and reviewed her physical impressions of the employees of Modern Office, Incorporated.

In the kitchen, Ellen scalded the milk, spooned and stirred mix until the chocolate was thick and perfect; she poured it into two mugs, arranged a plate of shortbread biscuits, and carried a tray into the living room. And stopped, staring at Kate Delafield.

Kate had looked up at the sound of footsteps. The face was indistinct in shadows, but framed in the light of the kitchen doorway was the small lithe body, the soft wavy hair. And she held the tray of hot chocolate just as she had for so many nights of Kate's life.

"Anne," she breathed.

Carefully, Ellen set the tray on the coffee table. Kate Delafield had dropped her head into her hands. In the anguish of her understanding Ellen reached blindly, gripped shoulders, squeezed them hard with her fingers. Kate Delafield raised her face, a waxen mask of suffering, her light blue eyes glittering with tears.

"I look like her," Ellen said. "Like Anne. Your lover."

Kate closed her eyes in her struggle, but the supports gave way, beginning deep in her stomach, and as Ellen sat down and took her into her arms, her entire body trembled, then shook violently. "Oh God," she choked.

Ellen whispered, "Have you never cried for her?"

The head pressed into the side of her neck shook no.

"You need to. You need to cry for her." She lay back and drew Kate to her.

Ellen held her, rocked her, clasped the shuddering body close against hers. "It's okay," she murmured again and again, "it's okay. Cry, it's okay."

The pain was in layers. She cried through the pure agony, then reached the images, and the words were forced from her: "Burned, burned, parts of her melted, charred . . . she didn't have a chance . . . the tanker fell on the hood, she couldn't get out . . . the metal was all fused, she burned, she burned . . ."

Ellen unbuttoned her shirt, gave her her bare breasts; they were quickly wet with hot tears.

For a long time after the tears stopped Kate took deep wracking breaths, her face buried in the deep soft warmth of Ellen's breasts; Ellen's hands were in her hair, holding Kate's face to her. Then Kate's hands took Ellen's hands away and she sat up, her eyes red, her face splotchy. Her eyes met Ellen's, glanced away.

"Here." Ellen reached to her, held Kate's head with one hand on the back of her neck, dried her face with her shirt. Kate took the shirt, gently wiped the wet breasts.

Ellen said, "Do you have a handkerchief?"

Kate nodded, reached into a jacket pocket.

"You need to blow your nose," Ellen said. "You're terrible at crying. You don't know how to do it at all."

Kate managed a smile. To allow her some moments of privacy, Ellen picked up the mugs and took them to the kitchen. She poured the chocolate back into the saucepan to reheat, went back through the living room and into the bedroom. Kate was sitting with her head bowed; she turned slightly when she heard Ellen, but did not look up.

Ellen pulled on a sweatshirt, returned to the kitchen. She served their hot chocolate again. Kate's eyes were still reddened but her skin coloring had returned to normal.

Ellen sat beside her. "When did she die?"

"Five months ago. You do resemble her."

"I feel honored to look like someone who was loved so very much."

Tears sprang again to Kate's eyes but she sipped her chocolate, her hands steady. "How did you know?"

"About Anne?"

With effort, Kate smiled. "Among other things."

"Gail—my boss said that Detective Taylor mentioned you'd lost someone close to you not very long ago. I—I just knew. Somehow I just did."

"Do I have an L on my forehead? What made you think I'm a . . . lesbian?" She could not prevent the slight hesitation; reticence and caution had become ingrown—self-protective behavior on which her professional survival depended.

"I guessed when we first met. I can sometimes tell. I think I tend to see it in women—" Seeing she was trapped, she admitted, "—that I find attractive."

Kate smiled again. "Thank you. After twelve years with one person you wonder if you're still attractive to anyone else."

Ellen sipped her chocolate, awkward and uncomfortable with what she had confessed, even though she knew that by physical definition at least, she herself was attractive to Kate Delafield.

Kate said, "I haven't cried since I was small . . . You must be clairvoyant, knowing that as well."

"I lost my father a little over two years ago. He was an enormous presence in my life, we were very very close. Now I know I was in deep shock. I went through his funeral but I don't remember much—"

"Anne's was like a dream."

"One night a full four months later I realized my father was dead. And I just fell apart. I cried and cried. For hours. I think when a person means that much the only way you can live through it at first is to have your mind blank it out. Like an anaesthetic during an operation. But then the anaesthetic wears off—"

"Yes," Kate said. "I'm sorry."

"Don't do that." Ellen's voice was firm, quiet. "I think

it would be good if you stayed here tonight."

There had been nothing even faintly sexual in the invitation. Kate looked at her unbelievingly.

Ellen said, "I understand what you're feeling right now about Anne. And you understand my anxieties. Both of us should be with someone tonight—tonight we have mutual needs. You said I should stay with a friend. I feel very safe with you. I don't think you're dangerous, Detective Delafield. Am I wrong?"

Kate said tiredly, "You're not wrong. I don't have a halo. No cop does. But no, you're not wrong."

Ellen's voice softened. "Tomorrow I'll go back to being me, you go back to being a tough cop. Deal?"

"Deal," she said, resisting the impulse to apologize again. "But I did come here tonight to see that you're safe. I give you my word on that—you'll be safe in every way."

"Thank you." She realized that dealing with a sexual advance from Kate Delafield was a possibility that had not occurred to her. "One thing we do need to get settled first—I refuse to spend the night with a woman I have to call Detective Delafield."

It was the first time she had heard Kate laugh, and she grinned, liking the warmth of the sound.

"You're right, Ellen."

"Make yourself comfortable, Kate. I'll get a few things ready in the bathroom."

Thinking of the waxen suffering on Kate Delafield's face, she laid out a towel and a disposable toothbrush, took a pair of Stephanie's pajamas from a drawer. Would it be worse to lose a lover than a parent? She caught herself—told herself guiltily that of course she would go to pieces if anything happened to Stephanie; it was simply too difficult to conceive of such a thing.

She came back to find Kate watching television. She had taken off her jacket; the sleeves of her simple white blouse were rolled to the elbow. The jacket was neatly folded over the back of an armchair, but a thin leather strap was visible,

part of the holster apparatus of her gun, Ellen realized; Kate had tucked the weapon under the jacket to be out of sight. Kate looked drawn and exhausted; but she sat erect, body tilted slightly forward as she gazed at the television screen.

She had always liked the alert features of intelligent women, but she wondered if many other women would find Kate Delafield as attractive as she did. The tight polished planes of her face would be too hard for some; even her mouth, which was full, was set in a firm straight line; and her eyes were that cool color of blue . . . But there was one endearing element of physical vulnerability: the graying hair was so fine that it had the unruly shapelessness of a child's hair.

She sat beside Kate, smothering a yawn as she tried to discern what she was watching—PBS, something about evolution. They were both being polite, she realized. "Look," she said, "I know it's only a little after nine, but it's been a long bad day for both of us."

Kate picked up the remote control, extinguished the picture.

"Bathroom's all yours, Kate."

Hearing the shower run, Ellen remembered her father again, the night she had spent alone crying for him. Kate came out of the bathroom; Ellen motioned with her head toward the bedroom and brushed past her into the bathroom.

Kate contemplated the king-sized bed, decided the side with the digital clock radio on the nightstand was probably Ellen's. She turned down the heavy satin spread. Her guess was confirmed by two economics texts on the other nightstand, the box of man-sized kleenex behind the lamp. She lay in bed cool and relaxed, strands of her hair pleasantly damp from the shower, Listerine still strong in her mouth, and wondered about the woman Ellen O'Neil lived with. A professor of economics at UCLA, Taylor had told her—who had been mad as hell when Ellen refused to leave with her. The pajamas were long enough but too snug; their owner was

as tall, but more slender than she. The owner's first name was Stephanie—and that was all she knew about her.

Exhausted from her spent emotion, warm and drowsy, she watched Ellen come in wearing a thigh-length rose nightshirt; she turned out the light and got in beside Kate, smelling of soap and a sweet and pleasant scent that was not perfume—body lotion or face cream, Kate sleepily decided.

Ellen's hand grasped hers. "Good night, Kate."

Kate turned on her side toward her. "Good night, Ellen."

Her hand still clasped in Ellen's, she plunged into sleep as if bludgeoned.

Ellen was awakened by the blanket being pulled off. The clock digits glowed 12:05. Kate lay rigid beside her, breathing in gasps, tangled in the sheet and blanket, arms and legs twitching.

"Kate," she murmured, rising on an elbow, leaning toward her, knowing not to touch her. "Kate, wake up."

Released from a dream of freezing, of clawing at a transparent glass cage, Kate jerked awake and sat up, her body tense and chilled.

In the street light from the window Ellen saw the pallor of Kate's skin, the faint sheen. She sat up, brushed fingertips over the light film of perspiration on Kate's forehead. She touched an arm and felt gooseflesh through the thin cotton pajamas. Kate shivered, and Ellen took her into her arms and drew her down, pulled the blanket over them, slid her hands under the pajama top and smoothed the cold pimpled flesh with her palms.

Increasingly aware of the soft contours of Ellen's body under hers, the clean scent of the silky hair against her cheek, Kate relaxed under the warm hands soothing coldness and tension from her.

The planes of Kate's back were firmly muscled, her body full and solid—much different from Stephanie's. Curious, Ellen curved her hands around her ribs, and as Kate raised herself slightly in a welcoming of her touch, she explored the

softness of her stomach, flatter, tighter than Stephanie's despite all Stephanie's jogging. She slid her hands up to Kate's shoulders and gripped them, enjoying the breadth and fleshiness of them, their unmistakable strength.

Kate watched her. Ellen's eyes had been closed as her hands moved, but now as she grasped .Kate's shoulders, her eyes were wide and dark in the dimness of the room. Her body warming with desire, Kate cupped the delicate face, strands of curling hair thick around her fingers. Her fingertips caressed a silken throat. Ellen's eyes closed.

Kate took her hands away. Regardless of who had initiated this, it had already gone too far. She had given her word.

Ellen gazed into the shadowed face poised gravely above hers. She moved a hand over Kate's forehead and into fine hair feathery in her fingers. Images of Kate came to her—the steeliness of her during this day. All thought narrowed into a single focus: to feel that strength. Her arms encircled the broad shoulders. "I'm not glass," she murmured, "I won't break."

In the tightening embrace of Ellen's arms Kate kissed the silken throat, and her hands found the silkiness under the nightshirt. Soon Kate slid the nightshirt off, impatiently stripped off her own pajamas. To a soft sound in Ellen's throat, she took Ellen fully into her arms.

She was supple and delicate like Anne, but nothing like Anne. Yielding and responsive in these first moments when Anne would have been tigerish and aggressive. Ellen's gentle yielding was utterly different, her lips melting sweetness, her soft arms warm, and trusting. Hunger rose, distinct in its shape: to give more and more pleasure, to feel every response from the tender woman in her arms. Her lips left Ellen's; desire sharpened as Ellen arched to the first touch of Kate's mouth on her breasts.

Ellen had become accustomed to making slow love with Stephanie, to eroticism sustained by periods of conversation, interruptions of mood. She was overwhelmed by the insistence of Kate's body and arms, the contrasting tenderness

of Kate's hands so subtly caressing her breasts, her mouth that touched lightly in the hollow of her throat, her tongue sweetly stroking. Slowly, Kate's mouth moved down again, to her breasts. All thought vanished.

Kate turned over, to have Ellen on top of her, to clasp and caress the firm swelling of her hips. Ellen's thigh was between hers, and her own thighs closed convulsively; arousal had become an ache. With Anne, she would bring Anne's hand to her now, or turn over and press rhythmically until orgasm released her to continue making love . . . Kate's hands slid down to curve around the thigh between hers. But Anne had never breathed like this, in such gasps . . .

Ellen lay on Kate's body breathing against her desire, against the possessive hands undulating her hips. A thought passed through her, clear and desire-quenching: *I'm Anne.*

"Ellen."

Ellen looked at her.

"Ellen." Kate's eyes were closed. "Ellen . . ."

Ellen turned and pulled Kate on top of her, seeking the full substance of her.

Kate moved her body away. The soft cupping of her hand became her only connection to Ellen. She took her hand away only to know again the crisp softness warmly filling her palm; and yet a second time.

There was a sound—from Kate—as her fingertips touched, were enveloped in warm wetness. The fierce throbbing of her own flesh had eased; her mouth was dry with another want, single and specific.

"Ellen?"

Kate's eyes were burning, hypnotic. The moving, caressing fingertips created ever-widening erotic waves. Ellen answered helplessly, "Yes."

There was another sound—from Ellen—at the first touch of Kate's mouth.

In the ecstasy of tasting her, inhaling her, Kate knew a moment of fear that Ellen would not speak or somehow signal what she needed. Then she heard the sharp intakes of

breath, felt the unmistakable stiffening of Ellen's body. Joyfully, slowly, Kate savored her, pressing the quivering thighs against her face.

She had not been with many women—and never with one who did not want her to readily come; repeatedly sensation intensified and then varied before Ellen realized that for now climax was secondary. She succumbed to sensation, became pure response. Tension became exquisitely unbearable. "Kate," she said in an agonized whisper. Then her body was gathered up into an intensity that ebbed only with the ebbing of orgasm.

She lay in Kate's arms, strength only slowly seeping back into her. Never had a woman's mouth so entirely possessed her.

Ellen's soft hands were warm pleasantness on her breasts, but not arousal; feeling oddly satiated, Kate murmured, "I don't need . . . You were beautiful. I don't need anything else."

Remembering the wetness cool on her thigh as Kate had lifted her body from her, Ellen said simply, "I want to touch you."

Except for her hand which stroked in Ellen's hair, Kate received her caresses without moving. Ellen's fingers traced her breasts, Ellen's mouth took a nipple. Then, as if a veil had been suddenly stripped away, desire powerfully stirred. Kate pressed Ellen's mouth to her.

Ellen lightly stroked the smooth columns of thighs, gripping them again and again, pleasurably feeling their muscular strength. Questing fingers reached higher, explored hair finer than her own and thick—soft damp fur. Kate's legs jerked, and as Ellen's fingers caressed, her heels moved up and down the sheet, her legs opening with each rise and fall of her thighs. Ellen sat up, away from Kate's embrace, and bent to her.

She hung on a precipice of exquisite sensation, her hand clutching Ellen's hair. Tantalized beyond all endurance, she

pulled Ellen's mouth away. "I can't," she gasped. "Not . . . like that."

"Then show me," Ellen said, coming to her, taking her in her arms. "Kate . . . want me . . ."

Again she felt Kate's wetness on her thigh, felt a tremor in Kate's body. She tightened her arms and strained up into her, as if to absorb her excitement.

Sensations dormant for long months had rekindled into brilliance. Ellen's arms fully embraced her, Ellen's body was satin under hers. Ellen's breath was hot against her throat. She felt soft lips press into her shoulder, the light imprint of teeth. Kate groaned from the satin friction, her body surging. Moments later she groaned again.

Her body arched into Kate's, Ellen felt the paroxysm, the sudden relaxation.

Soon afterward Kate managed to say, "You're wonderful."

"So are you." She loosened her grip, but held Kate closely during the long quiet moments that followed.

"Kleenex," Kate finally said. She added in a low mutter, "I've never been so wet."

Pleased, Ellen reached to the nightstand for the man-sized box of tissues.

Later Kate whispered, "Ellen?"

But Ellen, an arm across Kate, her head nestled into Kate's shoulder, was asleep. Anne had never liked sleeping close, even after lovemaking. Kate tightened her arm, drawing the warmth of Ellen even closer.

Kate was disturbed by the stirring of the warmth against her, then awakened by the chill of her body. In predawn light the digital clock read 5:22. Ellen had moved away but lay toward her on her side; in slumbering unawareness she shifted a breast from beneath her. Then she turned, her body curved away from Kate, arms outflung, hair in tangles, face buried in her pillow. The sweeping line of back was only partly

exposed; other contours were suggested by the blanket. Irresistibly, hungrily, Kate ran a hand down the length of her. She stroked and kissed her back.

Ellen murmured part-pleasure, part-protest, but soon turned and gave Kate her arms. She received in return gentle caresses that warmed her and only gradually dissipated the somnolence of her body. Warmth became vague arousal, and memory returned of the pleasure she had known from Kate, body memory that rekindled desire.

Emboldened by her knowledge of Ellen, Kate took new and deeper pleasure in her, allowing herself to be led, rewarded by response even more quickly triggered. The tender prelude between them turned seamlessly into passion.

"Now," Ellen soon whispered, "now."

Kate gave all the pleasure she knew how to give, Ellen's gasps coming swiftly, her hips alternately rising then grinding into the bed.

Afterward in Kate's arms Ellen breathed "Kate . . . Kate," in thick-voiced exhaustion.

Profoundly content, Kate fell asleep.

Voices—the sound of the television—and the unaccustomed smell of coffee awakened Kate. Memory returned; and as she searched for something to cover herself, a feeling of bleakness enveloped her.

Ellen was in the living room curled up on the sofa in a blue robe, watching *Today*. Her glance swept the terry robe Kate wore; she raised her coffee cup in greeting. The gesture seemed ironic to Kate, and soberly, she nodded.

"Good morning." Ellen's voice was low and expressionless.

"Is it?"

Not very, Ellen thought. She said, "Coffee's ready."

Kate shook her head. "For once I wish I were in uniform. I can't go to work in the same clothes. Have to drive to Glendale."

"Glendale might as well be Bakersfield in rush hour

traffic. Look." She ticked off on her fingers, "White blouse, gray slacks, green corduroy jacket. All you really need is another jacket. Borrow one of Stephanie's."

And why not, Ellen thought, glancing again at the familiar terry robe that covered a woman who was not Stephanie. She's already made use of everything else.

Kate plucked at the robe. "Even this is too snug."

"She's not that much smaller. She's got several jackets you could try. You'll get by."

She was pleased that Ellen did not consider Stephanie's superior slenderness of much consequence, and she knew she would not refuse if Stephanie's jackets fit her like a straight-jacket. "Why don't I cook breakfast? What do you like?"

Thinking churlishly that she could not stand cheeriness in the morning, Ellen held out her coffee cup. "Just coffee."

Kate took the cup and looked down at Ellen. "You know, I wasn't young when things changed in the sixties. All my upbringing, my influences, were from the fifties. I'm glad times have changed. There weren't many women in my life before Anne—none of them of any meaning. You're a different level of experience."

"That can be very dangerous to weak egos," Ellen said nastily, stung by Kate's words.

She had expected anything but this response. Not understanding how she had erred, Kate said in a hasty effort to atone, "But I admire you. I liked it . . . how you were . . . in every way. That's what I meant, all I meant. I thought you knew—could tell how much I liked it."

"At least you're honest." She muttered the words grudgingly, only partly mollified. She was angry that she seemed unable to prevent the opening of herself to this woman.

Kate exhaled, remembering her full schedule of activity for the day. "Time for me to be a cop again."

"I think I'll just go on being a loose-living sixties woman," Ellen said gratingly, anger rising again. "As well as your star witness."

Finally, she understood; and wondering how she could have been so stupid, Kate sat down beside her, careful not to touch her. "One time, Ellen, when I was off duty, I found a woman lying on the ground with a crowd of people standing around just staring at her. She'd been hit by a girder from a highrise, both arms smashed, internal injuries, bleeding—she couldn't be touched or moved. It was raining hard, the rain just pouring down on her. She was unconscious, but I spread my raincoat over her, I didn't care about her blood on it or anything else except she was helpless . . . Then somebody else thought to hold an umbrella over her till an ambulance—"

"Am I the raincoat?" Ellen interrupted, smiling. "Or the umbrella?"

Kate said, "This morning when I woke up, the first thing I felt was lousy. What happened between us was because you'd felt sorry for me—"

"That's not true," Ellen interrupted vehemently. "That's the *last* reason—"

"Then the next thing I thought," Kate continued, "was that I'd done something to betray Anne."

"I felt like shit this morning," Ellen said quietly, her voice low and tense. "But you had no reason to feel bad, Kate—not for a second."

"Neither of us did, that's the point. But it was my first instinct, too. Last night was unconnected to anything else in our lives, Ellen. It was—"

Ellen reached to Kate, touched her cheek. "At least I have good taste in the people I find out in the rain."

Kate smiled at Ellen. "You know, I can't imagine why I ever thought you were anything like Anne. You're not—at all."

"Yesterday was a bad emotional time for you. Anybody who resembled Anne might've triggered . . . what I did."

"But that's what I mean. You really *don't* look like her. Not at all."

Immensely pleased, Ellen touched Kate's cheek again.

13

Taylor said, "Know how you can tell it's Sunday?"

Kate sighed and did not answer. She sat at her desk sorting through a day's accumulation of paper, and reading crime scene reports and interviews with Modern Office employees.

"The niggers are in church, the Jews are in Palm Springs, the beaners are fixing their cars, and the Polacks think it's Tuesday."

Kate sighed again. "The autopsy report. Give."

"Hey, I'm part Polack," Taylor protested, "I gotta right." He looked injured. "You ever gonna laugh at one of my jokes?"

"Never. Why do you keep trying?"

"One of these days I'm gonna make you laugh." Taylor dropped the report on Kate's desk and trudged back to his own paper-strewn desk to pick up a ringing phone.

Taylor had attended the autopsy of Fergus Parker; Kate scanned the preliminary report, picked out its conclusion: death by cardiac puncturation. Entrance wound in the left ventricle, flooding of the pericardial cavity exacerbated by the victim's movements.

She skimmed Fergus Parker's vital statistics, noting only that he was five feet nine inches and weighed two hundred and thirty-two pounds. Aortic arteriosclerosis present.

Distended urinary bladder. External hemorrhoids. Obesity. Semen level normal. Fingernail scrapings negative. Blood and all blood samples O Positive, all preliminary tests normal.

But there was one new element, and Kate recorded it in her notebook: among undigested food in Fergus Parker's stomach was several ounces of red wine. She sat tapping her pen against her chin, thinking of Helen Parker's remark that Fergus Parker would drink a little red wine if he were celebrating something . . .

She read over other test reports. A partial palm print had been lifted from the glass coffee pot, value pending. Cigarette ash was found along with cigar ash in Fergus Parker's ashtray. Of the employees past and present, only ex-employee James W. Scott had a prior, 1978. ADW, the assault on his wife, the deadly weapon a poker, charges dropped. Probability zero there, she decided, tugging her cuffs down below the sleeves of her too-tight jacket.

How could anyone leave Ellen O'Neil under these circumstances, she thought as she organized the reports. No matter how important that seminar was, Stephanie should have known to stay with her. Or she should have taken Ellen with her.

She picked up the photographs. After several minutes of scrutiny she spread the closeups of the corpse over her desk and looked carefully at the wound, at the curved and faceted handle of the protruding knife. The autopsy report had listed measurements of the wound, its size slightly larger than the blade—normal for a double-edged weapon. The wound was clean, no tear. The slight curve of the handle was up and down, not sideways, the heavy handle almost perfectly squared with the body.

She stood and pushed her chair back, and using a pocket knife she kept in her desk, feinted in the air with both right and left-handed thrusts, trying to duplicate the entry of the knife into Fergus Parker. Standing at varied distances from an imaginary victim, she could only make the knife go in at a downward angle. And it seemed that plunging the knife

with an upward thrust would create a slashing, jagged entry—when the actual wound was a clean puncture. She stood beside the chair and plunged her knife into her imaginary victim from the side. That worked—if she cocked her wrist at an awkward angle and held the handle sideways to duplicate the position of the curved handle.

Taylor got up from his desk and strolled over. "Kate, maybe I can help you stab whoever you got sitting in your chair."

Kate chuckled. "Fergus Parker."

"I figured."

Kate showed him the photographs and demonstrated the problem again. Taylor tried a few experimental thrusts of his own.

"Kate, what about this?" He stood behind the desk chair and plunged the knife downward.

"Good idea, Ed. It would explain why he didn't struggle. Sit down and let me try. You're more Fergus Parker's size."

"Thanks a lot, partner." Taylor sat. "And be careful with that blade, will you?"

Kate dangled the pocket knife playfully. "This? Don't worry, it doesn't slice baloney."

She took her place behind Taylor, held the blade over his head, plunged it in an arc that ended at Taylor's blue plaid lapel. "Closest yet, Ed. But look at the angle." She held the blade poised against Taylor. "Still upward. And I think it would tear the body. And splatter blood all over the killer's arms."

"Maybe. What about the victim standing? Fell back into the chair?"

"That was Everson's theory, remember? Let's try."

A few minutes later Taylor said, "It's possible. If he stood there leaning back with his chest puffed out and said here, stab me."

"There's still suicide."

"You don't believe that any more than me. Doesn't figure, the coroner doesn't think so, either."

"Right, it's not likely. Unless we discover something totally off the wall." Kate stacked the photographs. "I'm waiting for a phone call from Philadelphia, Gail Freeman's checking out a call Fergus Parker received from there yesterday morning. I'll meet you at Modern Office. We get anything on the cigarette butt yet?"

"Nope. Nice jacket."

Kate tugged again at her cuffs. "You really like it?"

"Fits nice. Like a glove."

Kate grinned. "Too much like one. Think I'll take it back."

"Kidding, aren't you? You're in a hell of a good mood this morning, Kate. Bet you got laid last night."

"Nope," Kate said cheerfully. Last night had been many things—but she would never term it that.

Her phone rang. "Detective Delafield? This is Wesley Miller in Philadelphia."

"Yes sir. Are you the individual who talked to Fergus Parker yesterday morning?"

"Yes I did, called Fergus at seven sharp. Just like I told him I would. I understand from Gail you're actually heading up the investigation. Quite a responsibility. Very progressive city you have there."

The effervescence of Kate's mood vanished. "Lieutenant David Bell is available to give you my qualifications, Mr. Miller, if that's a concern to you." She concentrated on the pleasantness of her tone. "None of us at LAPD like to work with unqualified people, whoever they may be."

"Yes indeed, and I do admire that. I do admire your attitude about that. Wish more people in power thought that way. Gail speaks very highly of you. Now, how can I help you?" Wesley Miller spoke easily, his tone bland.

"Your conversation with Fergus Parker, what was the substance of it?"

"Miss, uh, Detective Delafield, can I have your assurance it'll be kept confidential?"

She made no attempt to soften the hard edges of her

tone. "No. Not if it's relevant to the solution and eventual resolution of this case."

"Oh, I agree with that. I just don't think it will be. I don't see how it could be. Let me explain. I called Fergus to offer him a new position. He was to head up all the company operations west of the Mississippi. But you see, now that he's, ah, not on board, we've had to, ah, reshuffle our plans. And t wouldn't do for, ah, certain people in the organization to know what we had in mind, they wouldn't understand why they weren't chosen in the first place, won't be chosen now."

"I see. Whose decision was it to offer this position?"

"It was my recommendation. But in business this kind of decision is never made autonomously." Wesley Miller's tone was condescending. "I had enthusiastic approvals from the entire executive board including Jonathon. Jonathon Wagner, our president."

"Enthusiastic approvals on what basis?"

"The firmest basis." Wesley Miller's voice strengthened. "The profit of western operations rose fourteen percent the past two years. The numbers from our other regional centers showed a decline."

Numbers, Kate thought. Always numbers. "Did you speak with anyone out here about this promotion? Ask their opinion of Fergus Parker?"

"Certainly not, Detective Delafield. The business world is not a democracy. Our country's democracy is not a democracy."

"Thank you Mr. Miller, but at least one of your employees found a way to vote. Did Fergus Parker accept the job?"

"Yes, yes he did. With a few provisos."

"Which were?"

"Oh, that he'd have some autonomy in certain areas of hiring and firing, that he'd still be based in L.A."

"And did you agree to his conditions?"

"Substantially. With a quibble here and there."

"Exactly what were his conditions and what were your quibbles?"

"Detective, I can't see how this is relevant to anything, the information is confidential—"

"Mr. Miller." Kate stared unseeingly at the drab clutter of the detectives' room, concentrating on reading the cadences and tones of Wesley Miller's voice. "Mr. Miller, let me put it to you this way. I'm conducting a murder investigation out here, and a good part of that inquiry involves the motive for killing Fergus Parker. An employee who learned he would be dismissed from the company—"

"Even so—"

"Let me put it this way, Mr. Miller." Men in power, she thought in disgust. "We have a fine working arrangement with the Philadelphia police. You can cooperate and answer my questions fully, or I can arrange to have my counterparts there—"

"Madam, it was never my intention to interfere with your investigation. We're absolutely appalled back here by this incredible event, the loss of so valuable a man. I'm sure you can understand that I have to consider the best interests of the company . . . The first thing Fergus wanted was final say on manpower levels and all job assignments in Los Angeles." Wesley Miller's voice had changed from sharpness to caution.

"Isn't that partly Gail Freeman's territory?"

"I see you've informed yourself about the office there. It's primarily Gail's territory, but it wasn't really a problem. In areas of disagreement we'd have simply arbitrated the matter here without either man knowing. We do that more often than subordinates realize. But Fergus also demanded that Freeman be fired. Of course I couldn't agree to that, I explained how extremely careful we have to be with black terminations. Even with the Reagan presidency. Particularly when a man's record has been as exemplary as Freeman's. We still need to act with caution in the area of equal—"

"What commitment did you make about Mr. Freeman?"

Wesley Miller cleared his throat with a protracted harrumph. "I agreed we'd try to work out an, ah, attractive transfer opportunity."

Simply move a cog to another part of the machine, she thought, recording the answer in her notes. "What else, Mr. Miller?"

"I presume you've met Guy Adams, nephew of our founder. Done an outstanding job wherever we've sent him, but apparently there'd been some conflict with Fergus. I told Fergus, and I was very adamant about this, even though old Guy Adams passed on some months back there's no way we can simply kick his nephew out the door, I mean, how would it look?"

"What commitment did you make about Mr. Adams?"

Wesley Miller harrumphed again. "Fergus finally backed off some and said he wanted him at least out of his territory, maybe we could bury him some place like the Savannah office. I agreed to discuss it with Jonathon and see what we could work out."

"Do you feel Fergus Parker was justified in either of those demands?"

"Justified?" Wesley Miller was indignant. "Justice doesn't apply here, madam. It's a maxim of management that a man has to have loyalty and support from the men around him. By the same token, it's a definite reflection on the two men who didn't have the good judgment to work out a satisfactory relationship with a man in the position of Fergus Parker."

"Anything else you discussed?"

"He wanted some say in naming his successor. And said he'd be making some key changes in his own sales managers in the coming months."

"Did he say what those changes would be?"

"Not specifically. He mentioned Fred Grayson and Harley Burton as the ones he had in mind. We always discussed his decisions about his people, of course, but it was pretty much his prerogative to operate as he wished in his

own area, so long as he kept turning in good profit numbers."

"Anything else?" She began a fresh page of notes.

"Not really. We discussed remuneration, but I don't think—" Wesley Miller hurriedly amended, "Do you need to know about that?"

"Not at the moment."

"And the effective date of his promotion. We agreed on March thirty-first. And that he should travel around his new territory immediately after—"

"Thank you, Mr. Miller. One more question. Will you be taking any action now about Mr. Freeman or Mr. Adams?"

"Well, possibly Guy. Now that his uncle—now that we're under no obligation to—well, public relations is an expensive proposition even in the best economic times. But Gail—well, if we have to have a black manager, L.A.'s a good city, very liberal and all, more accepting—well, you know. And continuity's very important till we adjust to this very tragic—I think you can see now why I was concerned about confidentiality."

"You have my word on that if your information proves irrelevant. Mr. Miller, I may call you again with further questions?"

"Ah, one thing. We're discussing a replacement for Fergus, we're all wondering back here who you might've eliminated as suspects so that—"

"I can't discuss the investigation," Kate said curtly. "I'm sure you understand."

"Oh certainly," Wesley Miller said resignedly. "I hope you'll soon—"

"I'm sure we will. Good day, sir."

14

Kate reviewed her caseload, thoughts of Ellen O'Neil frequently intruding on her concentration. As she drove to Modern Office, she pondered the few personal facts she had learned about Ellen that morning. Six years with an alcoholic lover. Within a month of that breakup, the death of her father. Stephanie Hale had come on the scene soon afterward; six months later Ellen had quit a responsible job and spent the next year and a half helping Stephanie Hale write an economics text, acting as her research assistant.

Kate had asked, "Aren't books on economic theory soon obsolete?"

"Yes, usually. But this one's a study of information used to develop and formulate theory."

That would put an owl to sleep, Kate had thought. "Well, I hope she dedicated it to you."

"Oh no, she couldn't do that . . . that would be—It's not the kind of book you dedicate, anyway. But I'll get a nice note on the acknowledgement page."

Kate turned onto Merlin Street, parked, and looked with pleasure at the oak trees. She got out and locked the Plymouth. *A year and a half of her life. For a nice note on the acknowledgement page.*

"Hi, Cagney! Where ya been?"

"Good morning, Miss Markham." Kate waved at Judy Markham, who flung back her blonde hair, breasts bouncing, and buzzed her through the lobby doors.

She stopped at the crime scene. The stench of alcohol had heightened several fold over the past hours. Breathing with difficulty, she examined Fergus Parker's desk and chair and credenza. The red wine listed on the autopsy report meant that somewhere amid the smashed glass of Fergus Parker's bar were pieces of a wine bottle. Also a cork, if the bottle had been opened yesterday morning. And the wrapping from around the cork. And wine glasses. Possibly that was why the killer, a coffee drinker, had not brought coffee into Fergus Parker's office—he and his victim were drinking wine. As the host, Fergus Parker would probably have opened the bottle—but if he had not . . . There should be fingerprints, regardless; either Fergus Parker's or someone else's. The bottle and glasses could be reconstructed. Baker was the best fingerprint technician in the division. If there were prints of value in all that glass, Baker would find them.

She closed the door quietly after her and glanced down the hall. Guy Adams' office door was open. Guy Adams, who was infatuated with Ellen, she remembered. She turned and walked the other way, past the conference room, glancing into offices as she walked. Gretchen Phillips, chin held pensively in a hand tipped with coral fingernails, stared into space, smoke curling up from an ashtray hidden by mounds of paper. Duane Fletcher, gesticulating with a cigarette, talked on the phone in high-pitched enthusiasm. Harley Burton's office was empty; he was next door arguing with a stony-faced Fred Grayson.

She paused. Both men looked up with irritated expressions. Reaching toward an ashtray, Fred Grayson growled, "You arrest anybody yet?"

She shook her head and walked on. Grayson, she noted, had abandoned Tiparillos.

Kate slowed, hands in her jacket pockets, to peer into Ellen O'Neil's office. She was on the phone, and waggled

three fingers at Kate, then used them to cover the receiver. "Nice jacket," she whispered, and grinned.

"A friend gave me the use of it," she said solemnly, and winked, and strolled into Gail Freeman's office.

"Good morning." Gail Freeman rose to shake hands. "Did Wesley Miller call?"

"Yes, and thank you for your good work."

"Thank Ellen. She got on the problem like a bulldog."

Kate said, smiling, "Miss O'Neil seems very capable for a new person."

"Terrific. Sharp and quick."

"Yes." She added in an objective tone, "A very attractive person."

To her surprise, Freeman shrugged. "Guess I'm old-fashioned. I like to work with women like her, but that's all. I admire women like you, like her. Women who can fix their own cars, that sort of thing. Forgive me, but I wouldn't marry you."

Kate chuckled. "That's all right. But I think Ellen—" She caught herself. "Ellen O'Neil doesn't look like the mechanic type to me."

"Not literally. I just meant she's very much her own person."

"Do you think so? I've found people can be in control only of certain facets of their lives."

"I suppose you're right." Gail Freeman grinned. "I'll confess I'm not only a chauvinist, but a racist. I adore dark-skinned women." He turned, took the picture of his family from the credenza and displayed it for Kate. "My wife, see how beautiful she is? I think God made her the loveliest of any human creature."

"Beautiful indeed, Mr. Freeman," Kate said truthfully, gazing at the chocolate-skinned woman in the photo. "Your daughters are also very pretty."

"Thank you. My family is the world—" He broke off. "How's the case coming? Any suspects yet? Other than me?"

"Sure," Kate said, smiling.

"Seriously, is there anything I can tell the employees? You can imagine how they feel, all the rumors flying around. The idea of a killer in our office—"

"Yes, I can well imagine. There aren't any definite views of what constitutes a killer's mentality, but based on my experience—this is by no means an official position of any kind—this appears to be an impulse crime, we aren't dealing with a homicidal maniac likely to commit multiple crimes. All I can give you to tell your people is that we're working on every possible lead, we welcome any information anyone might have. And we hope to make an arrest soon."

"Sounds impressive," Freeman said lightly.

Kate smiled. "Best I can do." She glanced at her watch. "I see it's almost lunch time here. I'll finish looking over the files in the conference room. Then interview Billie Sullivan."

"Does that mean I can fire her afterward?"

"You seem very anxious."

"I don't trust her. I want her out of here. I think she's got something up her sleeve."

Taylor was pacing the conference room with buoyant steps. "All kinds of news, Kate. We broke the MacKenzie case. Picked up two Latinos doing their act in Ohrbach's parking lot. One of 'em was rearranging the victim's skull when Forster and Deems rolled up. One's already blaming the other for MacKenzie. The Lieutenant's hopping and skipping with joy. Been a year since he got his mug on TV. Maybe he'll get off our backs for a while, all the followup paper—"

"Don't hold your breath. He's moving to Foothill in June, remember? He'll keep his nose squeaky clean till then." She was leafing through the personnel file on Billie Sullivan, imagining Lieutenant David Bell's tenor voice lowered to factual grimness for the benefit of radio station reporters' tape recorders, the boyish features drawn into solemnity for the television cameras from all seven local stations. Not for her; never would she be interested in the

PR of police work. She said to Taylor, "What else've you got?"

"ID on the cigarette butt. Carlton."

"Terrific," she said ironically. "That narrows it down only to Guy Adams, Gretchen Phillips, Fred Grayson and Harley Burton." But Taylor was still grinning. "We luck out?"

"Yep. Good ABO reading. Blood type B."

Kate smiled and nodded, pleased at the unusual blood type lifted from the saliva on the cigarette butt. "This one may be solved by the lab, the way it looks right now."

"Circumstantial? Shit. Ohrbach's this morning, that's my idea of a good case."

Kate said absently, flipping through her notebook for a note she had made yesterday, "They convict more and more on circumstantial, Ed."

"Yeah, and the appeals take into the next century."

She had found her note, and was uninterested in pursuing this tired subject. "You mentioned a coffee mug you saw in the kitchen yesterday, English hunting scene on it. Empty, you said. What did you mean by empty?"

There was a pause. "An absence of liquid, Kate."

Obligingly, she chuckled. "Was it bone dry? As in washed and dried? Or with dregs in it that sat all night and dried out?"

Taylor ran his hands through his thin blond hair. "Shit. I see what you mean. No, it wasn't bone dry, I don't remember if the liquid was fresh or not quite dried out from the day before."

"Filmed over? Any residue on the bottom of the mug?"

"God damn it, I can't remember. Shit." His voice was heavy with self-reproach. "Whose mug?"

"Harley Burton. Saw it in his office yesterday."

"Shit. That was the other piece of news, Kate. The partial on the coffee pot—his. God damn it."

"Relax, Ed. We're not mind readers."

"Second thing I've blown. Yesterday the crime scene—"

"Forget it. All of us do it, it's tough to guess what's significant in a case like this one. Even the print—could be days old. We have to establish who washes the coffee pot and when they do it."

"Let me handle that, check it out."

Kate knew that yesterday she would have pilloried Taylor for carelessness; in recent months she had been a driven perfectionist, a misery to work with. Taylor would never know how much he owed to Ellen O'Neil for this newly rational perspective.

"Harley Burton is a possible," she said. "The one who seems most doubtful is Guy Adams. Unless Fergus Parker filled him in on a scheme he had to ship him off to the boondocks. And I don't see what difference that would make to Adams—he's worked all over the country. He's got the weakest motive of anybody so far. Friction, yes. But Fergus Parker didn't do the things to Adams he did to people who worked directly for him. I know he referred to Adams as a fag, but I can't see that being enough to kill anybody."

"It would be for me," Taylor growled. "I got nothing against it," he said with a quick glance at Kate, "to each his own. But anybody ever suggested I had a limp wrist, I'd paint cement red with the bastard's face."

Kate thought of Gretchen Phillips, her struggle for her success. How can women ever be equal, she thought, when the accusation of femininity is always the ultimate insult to men?

Taylor said, "Funny, I thought we'd make a quick collar here and never put the MacKenzie case to bed. Besides Harley Burton, we got any other good possibles?"

Kate's sigh was partly a groan. "With the exception of Ellen O'Neil and Helen Parker, everybody I've talked to so far."

"Take 'em all in for heavy duty interrogation?"

"Not yet. I want to hear what Billie Sullivan has to say.

Right now from a physical standpoint—if we go by the time element we worked out yesterday—Duane Fletcher isn't likely. He's more your typical out-of-shape, middle-age-spread executive type. And Gretchen Phillips doesn't look likely. But Fred Grayson and Harley Burton and Guy Adams and Gail Freeman—all good physical specimens. Especially Freeman—small, wiry, athletic. Except for Adams, all with very strong motives."

"This case reminds me of that movie, all those people on a train, all suspects. Turns out all of 'em did it."

"*Murder on the Orient Express.* Agatha Christie." Kate was smiling; Anne had loved the movie.

"Maybe all of 'em did do it, Kate." Taylor was serious; his voice had risen in eagerness. "Or at least a couple. They all have a motive?"

"Motive, malice, intent. All of them from similar backgrounds, too—education, intelligence, moral values—except maybe Fred Grayson. Grayson has to take off his Ku Klux Klan hood to come to work."

"I don't mind a little prejudice," Taylor said.

"I wish I'd known about him before, you could've interviewed him instead of me. Enough to gag a maggot."

Taylor accepted the insult with a good-natured shrug. "My theory, Kate—what do you really think? Somebody held Fergus Parker's arms, somebody else plowed him. Wouldn't that explain the stab wound? And no struggle?"

"It's possible, Ed. But then we have all kinds of problems with Ellen O'Neil's story. And the psychology's all wrong. These people aren't roving thugs like the two we got this morning."

"Amateur City." Taylor exhaled noisily. "I'm leaving, gotta put the MacKenzie case to bed. I'll be glad to get outta here permanently, back on the street. My calm dignity act is a fat bore. These white-collar business types are one big yawn."

"It doesn't seem very likely these white-collar types

would get together and commit premeditated murder."

"Kate, we've seen some pretty strange—"

"I know, Ed. I'm not dismissing any possibilities. See you later."

15

Painted British flags festooned *The White Cliffs of Dover*, a blue and white A-frame with a bright red door. The bar and tables and chairs were of coarse-grained wood; the lighting was subdued. The place was crowded but quiet, filled with murmuring conversations.

"Ellen, this isn't where I'd have taken you," Guy said apologetically. "It's pretty masculine here, sort of male-clubby."

"I like it," Ellen declared, thinking that Stephanie would judge it low class, would sneer at the homely interior, the roughly dressed customers.

Stephanie had called the office that morning; they had spoken briefly, Ellen pleading the press of work (which was true) and a deadline on a report (which was not true). Conscience-stricken at her betrayal of fidelity to Stephanie, she was certain that she would give herself away, certain that Stephanie would somehow hear the guilt in her voice and know that she had spent the night giving comfort and intimacy to another woman.

"It's a regular British pub," Guy said. "Most of the patrons have their own mugs, see?" Above the bar, on a long double rack, hung dozens of beer mugs, all sizes and styles, some plain, some pewter, some glistening painted porcelain. "Nice custom, isn't it? We'd never take our customers here,

but everybody in the office loves the place. And they've sort of adopted us. This table's always reserved at lunch. And one of the dart boards."

Guy was on one side of her, Gail on the other. The round table, large enough for eight, was close to the bar and next to the game area. Behind them the billiard table was deserted. To taunts from the bartender, a paunchy man in khaki pants and a pea jacket intermittently hurled bullet-like darts at one of two black and white sectioned dart boards.

"It was nice of you to ask me here." Ellen had raised her voice to include everyone at the table. She suspected this invitation had been a ploy of Guy's—she could hardly refuse an offer to join all the managers for lunch. "You've been very kind to me," she said. "Very good about . . . everything."

"We try harder," Duane Fletcher said. "The quality goes in before the name goes on."

Forewarned about Duane Fletcher, Ellen chuckled.

"You may not believe this," Gretchen Phillips said, smiling affectionately at Duane Fletcher, "but Duane's name is actually Granny Goose."

"No, he's the Aqua Velva man," Harley Burton said heartily. "There's something about an Aqua Velva man."

"A little dab'll do ya." Gail Freeman directed a playful punch at Duane Fletcher.

"Please don't squeeze the Charmin," Duane Fletcher squealed amid the laughter, avoiding Gail Freeman's feint.

A leather-aproned waiter brought a tray of heavy glass beer mugs foamed well above the rim. "It's Miller time," Fred Grayson said, to more laughter.

Guy Adams raised his mug and said with exaggerated irony, "To a better Modern Office."

"To the late unlamented," Gail Freeman offered.

"Everything you never wanted in a boss, and less." Duane Fletcher clinked mugs with Gail.

Harley Burton said cheerfully, "Bet he's already general manager of hell."

"All that lard should burn forever," Gretchen Phillips said.

Laughing helplessly, Ellen took refuge in her beer mug, the smell pleasantly acrid, the coolness wet and sharp.

"Another toast," Gail Freeman said. "To whoever did it."

Movement at the table stopped. Ellen realized numbly that she could be sitting with a murderer. The person who had been in the office with her yesterday, who had plunged a blade into Fergus Parker's heart. She looked from Guy Adams to Gretchen Phillips to Fred Grayson, to Harley Burton, to Duane Fletcher, watching their stares freeze on Gail Freeman. His gaze traversed his companions coolly, and he continued in a soft voice, "I hope the cops give up soon and get back to more urgent concerns, like giving tickets."

Duane Fletcher said, "I'm Chiquita Banana and I'm here to say that bananas have to ripen in a certain way."

Ellen burst into laughter. Accompanying loud laughter from around the table broke the tension.

"Guy sweetie?" Gretchen Phillips' smile was coaxing. "Why don't you give me one of Harley's cigarettes? Preferably without a lecture. Then let's win more of his money."

"Not today." Harley Burton's tone was abrupt. "Don't much feel like playing today."

"Nor me," Guy Adams said, his face sobering.

"Terrific," Gretchen Phillips said imperturbably. "Best time to take you both on."

"You don't need any advantage," Harley Burton growled.

"Guy sweetie? A cigarette please?"

"Sure, Gretchen." Guy extracted a cigarette from his inside blazer pocket, lit it, and with a charming smile tucked it between Gretchen Phillips' lips. She patted his cheek. Ellen watched them with pleasure, admiring their grace and beauty.

Gail got up and went over to the bar to pick up the darts. Fred Grayson said to Ellen, "We put up a dollar a game.

Total points takes the money."

Ellen watched Gail draw each dart back behind his ear, launch it in a swift graceful arc. Harley Burton was next, hurling his in a single powerful motion, rattling the dart board against the wall. Coming back to the table, he tossed a dollar down with a snort of disgust.

"Try accuracy instead of velocity," Fred Grayson taunted.

"It's both," Harley Burton grunted. He said to Ellen, "Played baseball in college, hell of a fastball. Only pitch I had, could fire that damn ball through a needle in those days."

"I believe you," Ellen murmured, gazing at his bulging arms and chest.

Their food arrived, shaved roast beef on two halves of a thick sourdough roll. Guy spread his sandwich with horseradish so pungent the odor made Ellen's eyes water. Gail cut his sandwich into eighths, then bit fastidiously into one of his mini-snacks. Ellen ate her sandwich with enjoyment, listening to shop talk, some of it already familiar terminology.

"Tell me," she asked, her eyes fixed on the center of the table, her question directed to no one in particular, "the people in Philadelphia—doesn't it matter to them what goes on out here? What kind of man Fergus Parker was?"

"The eastern people," Harley Burton answered, "they come out once, twice a year for a few days. We send 'em back wined, dined, entertained."

"And unenlightened," Gretchen Phillips added, taking a bite from her sandwich.

Fred Grayson had scowled at the candor of his fellow managers. But he said, "Numbers. All they ever want is the numbers. How we did against Apex. What our market share is, how we plan to improve it."

Guy Adams' face was somber. "All the direction and energy went out of the company when my uncle died. All the moral force. Bookkeepers, accountants." His voice was

bitter. "A caretaker management for a once great company. A company that's become a still-life."

Fred Grayson got up. Before each toss of a dart he swung his arm back and forth in a vigorous pendulum, then sighted along it as if over the sights of a rifle. Each dart traveled in a swift straight trajectory, crowding around the bullseye area.

"Not bad, Fred." Gretchen Phillips retrieved the darts and walked quickly to the line. She released her darts quickly, in an economy of motion, each soft toss winging straight into the bullseye.

"Tough," muttered Harley Burton. "Women's equality is one thing. Damn superiority's something else."

Guy asked Ellen, "Would you like to try?"

"I'll leave it to you athletes," Ellen said, smiling at Gretchen Phillips.

"Me too." Duane Fletcher drained his beer mug. "Let it be Lowenbrau for Duane. Good to the last drop. The champagne of bottled beers. Put a little weekend in your—"

"Stuff it, Duane," Fred Grayson said through a bite of his sandwich.

Guy took his place behind the line. In a blur of movement Ellen did not completely follow, a dart flew straight and true and thudded just inside the bullseye. Gretchen Phillips applauded. Ellen watched him, her eyes following the seam of shirt that outlined his shoulders; the planes of his back down to his hips; his long legs. He was extraordinarily attractive, for a man.

Guy finished his darts, the others thrown not nearly so accurately as the first, and tossed his dollar down onto the table. With a grin and a wink at Ellen, Gretchen Phillips picked up all the money. Gail pulled the darts out of the board for another game. They continued to play as they finished lunch, Gail barely outpointing Gretchen Phillips in the next contest.

"Sorry boys," Gretchen Phillips said, "I have to get back. Got to call East before they all leave."

156

Scraping his chair back to get up, Gail said, "Back to the not-so-tender mercies of Detective Delafield."

Ellen started guiltily; she had been remembering Kate Delafield, her thoughts intimate and lingering. She said, half-humorously, "She's very good at her job."

Six pairs of eyes looked at her. Disconcerted, she leaned over and picked up her purse.

16

Billie Sullivan called from the storage closet in her office, "Gimme two more seconds."

Kate caught glimpses of stringy red hair and a pink man-tailored blouse, its tail hanging out over a green skirt so wrinkled the pattern was indiscernible. Sitting down in the single chair in front of Billie Sullivan's desk, she watched, fascinated, as from the closet into a huge cardboard box were flung nylon stockings, tennis shoes, a sweater, two candles, four cans of Budweiser, a pillow, a clock radio, a set of wind chimes, and a sack of pistachio nuts.

Billie Sullivan emerged from the closet smacking her hands together in satisfaction, and moved to her desk in liquid loping strides. She folded herself into her chair. "So grill me, lady copper."

She was the thinnest woman Kate had ever seen, the bones of the arms she propped on the desk protruding whitely through the skin. She looked at Kate with raised reddish eyebrows, neither green eye precisely focused. Kate asked, "How come you're packing?"

"I figure that dink manager's gonna toss my ass any second."

"Why would he want to do that?" Kate's voice was expressionless.

"I do even less around here than Fred Grayson. The world

champion brown-noser and dumb shit."

A woman with nothing whatever to lose, Kate saw. "Hasn't he been sales manager here a number of years?" She stuffed her hands into the pockets of her undersize jacket and arranged herself comfortably in the chair. For now she would take no notes.

"So what if he has? He's an asshole. And *dumb?* I bet his wife has to write directions on her body."

Kate hastily removed a hand from a pocket to rub it across her grin. "Miss Sullivan—"

"I won't talk to anyone that calls me that." Her tone was adamant. "I'm Billie."

"Billie," she conceded. "Who would want to kill your boss?" She gritted her teeth against the screeching laugh.

"You want I should list them in order?"

"It would be helpful," Kate said drily.

Several of the fingernails Billie Sullivan tapped on the desk were broken, the sharp edges unfiled. "Hard to say," she said finally. "Harley Burton's number one easy if he knew how much shit the boss actually did him. But I'd have to say . . . Well, the boss all but pulled out his cock and pissed all over Gail Freeman."

Billie Sullivan picked up a desk dictionary and hurled it into the cardboard box. Kate waited.

"The boss did everything we could think of. Believe me, together we could be pretty cute. Only a matter of time before we figured a way to airmail his ass."

"Why do *you* dislike Mr. Freeman?"

"Not because he's colored, if that's your drift," she said immediately. "The boss and dumbshit Grayson, they hate blacks—but I don't. Colored, female—I figure that's a trade-off." She gyrated on her chair, pulling bony fingers through her hair. "Gail Freeman bullshits everybody that works for him. Claims we all do something *valuable,* for chrissakes." Her tone was withering. "A boss gave me that snowjob just *once.* Before I found out what a stinking cesspool business really is. Men," she sneered, "it's their fucking world, all

their fun and games. Men have it *all* and they aren't about to give it up, I don't care what kind of stupid movements come along to try and stop them. All the bastards ever want to do is kill each other and fuck every woman they see."

Kate cleared her throat and said mildly, "Don't you think Mr. Freeman is at least sincere?"

"Sincere? *Sincere?*" Her out-of-focus eyes glared at Kate. "What does *sincere* have to do with anything? Lady copper, you wear a gun?"

Warily, Kate nodded. "Regulations."

"I wish to Christ I could. Wear it right out on my hip like a cowboy. Right where everybody can see it. Eat or get eaten, that's all there is, nothing more. Five minutes after you're dead nobody knows your name."

Cynical as any cop, Kate thought, watching her.

"Gail Freeman took away the boss's fun, lots of his games. Made the boss have to *think*. Every change he made, the boss had to call in brown-noser Grayson and learn all about it so nobody could get a leg up on him. He *hated* Gail Freeman."

"Sounds like your boss had more motive to murder Gail Freeman than the other way around," Kate commented as she took out her notebook and consulted her brief profile of Billie Sullivan. "Billie, you've worked here three years, two months. Two years longer than any other job. Why did you get along so well with Fergus Parker?"

"Tell you a story. Few months back, Pete Webber wised up and quit. Gave the boss a gift, a shovel with a red ribbon on it. Said the boss should dig up his own mother and screw her too, she was the only person he hadn't done it to, what difference did it make she was dead?"

"You're making that up," Kate said.

Screeching with laughter, Billie Sullivan shook a cigarette from a pack of Benson & Hedges. "Yeah, but it's a neat story, right? I knew exactly what I had to deal with in the boss. Other bosses I had, they were assholes too but they'd do nice things once in a while, help somebody, give money

to charity, that kind of shit. Not the boss." She exhaled smoke in a thin jet, placed a blade sharp elbow on the desk, and cupped her chin. "I could depend on the boss to be a total stinko."

Kate smiled. "It's nice to have consistency in this world. Who's number two on your list?"

"The brown-noser," she said promptly. "You know where you stand with him, too. Absolutely nowhere. If he was going down for the last time, had to decide between a rope and life preserver, he'd drown."

Kate smiled again. "How could a successful manager like Fred Grayson be indecisive?"

"Easy. Real easy." Billie Sullivan flicked ash in the direction of a battered metal ashtray. "He didn't used to be indecisive. The boss and me, we punched him into the perfect company man. Anybody can do it—even to you, lady copper. You make a decision and your boss stands up in front of other people and says you're wrong and stupid besides."

Kate said evenly, "That would happen exactly once."

Billie Sullivan surveyed her with a glance. "Yeah, maybe not you. Maybe not some other people. But the brown-noser caved right in. A man's got to stand up at least once and put his balls on the table, right? That asshole never had the guts to stand up *once*." Her voice was vibrant with contempt. "In return for giving up his balls and licking the boss's ass, the boss kept him around and made all his decisions for him."

"You seem to have a special distaste for Mr. Grayson."

"Wouldn't you? How can anybody give his balls away? God damn it, if I was a man I'd run this fucking world."

Indeed you might, Kate thought. "Why would Fred Grayson want to kill the man who was taking care of him?"

"Oh come on." Billie Sullivan bared her teeth in a humorless grin. "You're a woman. Don't shit me. Don't let on you don't understand all about getting fucked and being taken care of. How it feels, what you think about it."

Kate cleared her throat. "Who's next?"

"Gretchen I suppose. Only because she didn't know how well off she was."

"You didn't even try to at least protect *her*?" With calculation she added, "From . . . that?"

"Then you heard, I guess." Kate did not respond. Billie Sullivan again gyrated on her chair. "Why? Why should I?"

Kate said bluntly, "Because she's a woman."

"And we have enough trouble without doing it to each other, right? He never wanted to fuck any woman here except her. Never made a move on anybody except her. He heard she liked girls and that turned him on. Explain that one to me."

Kate shrugged. "I can't even begin to understand the way people are about sex."

"He fucked her maybe once every couple weeks, she got a sales manager job out of it. And he didn't do anything else to her, I saw to that, made sure he never saw anything in her but some harmless fluff to fuck once in a while."

"Have you ever been raped?"

"I've been married. Does that count?"

Kate ignored the retort. "I've seen raped women. I would think that another woman—"

"Hey lady copper, there's rape and there's sex you don't want. You don't believe there's a difference? Ever been married? No? Ask married women. Like me, I was, twice. I liked sex but I didn't want the fucking, getting that done to me. All the women I know don't want it either, at least some of the time. The bastards all say they don't know what women want today. We don't want anything more than we ever did. All we are is honest now about the shit they do in bed."

"Not all women feel that way."

"Show me one that doesn't, she's had a lobotomy. Look, lady copper. The boss fucked everybody. If he didn't do it to Gretchen that way he'd have figured out some other way. He fucked everybody some way. Understand?" Her voice was

exasperated, as if she were explaining a simple concept to a dull child. "He *had* to do it. It was him, see that? He had to have his brand on everybody's ass." She flicked ash again, pulled at her hair. "I did what I could for her. It was the best I could do. It was *all* I could do."

"Did you never want to change things?"

"Change things," Billie Sullivan repeated.

Kate remained silent; she watched the intake of smoke as Billie Sullivan drew from her cigarette, and the eyes that stared at her in unblinking, unfocused scorn.

"All the Fergus Parkers out there and you want me to change things. What kind of cop are you? This your first case? They had you walking old ladies across the street, right?"

Kate smiled at her. "Who's next?" Surely it would be Harley Burton.

"Maybe . . . Guy Adams. Not that he could've done it," she added. "I'm talking pure motive here, pure and simple. Guy Adams is a *type*."

The word had been spoken venomously. "What kind of type?" Kate asked, suspecting that Billie Sullivan's view of Guy Adams was not dissimilar to her own.

"Pretty clothes, pretty face, his mama sent him to one of those Eastern charm schools—"

Kate resisted the impulse to nod, to add that his type also never got mugged or violated, never even conceived of such outrages happening to them. They never even got traffic tickets . . .

"Now he looks for women to keep on taking care of him," Billie Sullivan sneered. "Just like my own Daddy does to my Mama. The Ashley Wilkes type, you follow me?"

Kate said, grinning, "The character from *Gone With the Wind* that Scarlett thought was so noble."

"The *wimp* from *Gone With the Wind*," she corrected her. "A dear old Daddy type. You'd never think I had a Daddy with class, would you? Graduate of Yale? With a daughter who stomped out of Vassar her first year."

Screeching with laughter, heedless of the skirt that hiked well above her large-jointed knees, she raised broomstick thin legs encased in red plaid knee socks, and propped transparent plastic sandals on the desk.

"Daddy hasn't talked to me since the day I explained to him what he was doing to Mama and what a world-class asshole he really was. I got more balls than my Daddy and Guy Adams combined. You know how Guy Adams thinks? He thinks he can make phone calls to Philadelphia knocking the boss and get away with it, not have it get back. Guy Adams thinks people like the boss aren't dangerous at all, he thinks they just have bad manners. He doesn't have a *clue*."

"Do you think any of the people here except you really had a clue about that?"

She contemplated Kate. "Good question, lady copper. I'd say . . . maybe. But I'd guess they never compared notes, put it all together. Too embarrassed to admit what they all put up with, all the shit they ate."

"Harley Burton," Kate prodded. "You mentioned before he had the most motive of anybody—if he knew. Knew what?"

"What about me?" she parried. "Aren't you curious why the boss kept me around? Why he liked me?"

"I expect because you understood each other," Kate said drily. "Was there another reason?"

"My source. That's why he really needed me. Milly in Philly. Jonathon Wagner's secretary. He's the president, you know. Me and Milly in Philly are like *that*." She held up two intertwined fingers. "She was the one that told me about each and every phone call Guy Adams made. Months ago Milly in Philly told me they were reorganizing, the boss was top choice for a big promotion, his region looked so good. That was because the boss's managers were all busting their asses—but anyway, the boss knew six months ago something was breaking and he could plan."

"I see." Kate turned to a fresh page in her notebook.

"No you don't, but you will. Everybody was afraid of the boss except the one guy around here who handles himself. Harley Burton. And he was worse than trouble, he was competition. One more promotion and he'd of been gone, somewhere else in the country, same as the boss in position and title. Who knows from there? Someday the boss might even have to work for a guy who was once under him. Can you imagine that? Then Tampa opened, Harley Burton wanted Pete Webber to get the job, the boss saw his chance. He turned Webber down. Transferred him to new accounts, figuring he might get pissed enough to quit. Which he did and the boss blamed Harley Burton, demoted him out of that corner office, moved brown-noser Grayson in. And so he had all the talent in his region right under his thumb. Neat?"

"Neat," Kate agreed, making rapid notes.

"There's more. He figured he could walk on Harley Burton—his best man—because Harley Burton wouldn't quit with only a few months left before he had fifteen years in, got vested in the pension plan. Then the boss could move him back into the corner office after the promotion, could afford to then, he'd be two organization levels higher, could always control him. And Harley Burton would see that he had a career again and wouldn't quit. See how cute the boss was?"

"Indeed," Kate said. "What did he plan to do about Fred Grayson?"

She shrugged. "Kick him back down where he came from. Or palm him off on some unsuspecting fool in another region." She grimaced. "The brown-noser came out of this even better than he knows . . ."

"Did Fergus Parker have plans for anyone else?"

She made a slitting motion across her throat. "That, for Gail Freeman and Guy Adams. If it was the last thing he ever did."

Kate remained silent, diagramming the machinations of Fergus Parker and recording several direct quotes from Billie

Sullivan. "Billie," she said, "you didn't place Duane Fletcher anywhere on your list."

"Poor Duane," she said mockingly, "that's what everybody always calls him. Poor Duane. Yeah, the boss kicked his ass all over the office. You know, we sell office furniture here. You'd think Duane was peddling the cure for cancer. Let me tell you about poor Duane. At my house I got cats. Strays come around, two decided to stay. I'd rather have cats than a man anytime, but I'm no Doris Day, I don't even like animals much. Wouldn't have a dog if you paid me. But cats are different. Cats stay because they want to be there. Dogs—you kick a dog and it licks your foot. That's Duane Fletcher."

"You're telling me he didn't have a motive for killing Fergus Parker?"

"Oh shit yes he had a motive," she said impatiently, glaring at Kate, then discarding her butt into the ashtray without bothering to extinguish it. "Don't you catch my drift at all? Not much wonder you cops never catch anybody. What the boss did to Duane, anybody'd want to kill him fifteen times over. But the dog you kick, does it ever kill you? Shit no. Whoever knocked off the boss—you better look for a cat, not a dog like Duane Fletcher."

"I see. So you're telling me Gretchen Phillips and Harley Burton and Gail Freeman are capable."

"Gretchen and Gail Freeman are," she said after a moment. "Some people can take a lot, but only so much . . ."

"But not Harley Burton?" She suspected that Billie Sullivan felt an admiration for Harley Burton she would not admit.

"He's capable. More capable than anybody. But I see him walking out the door, saying fuck the pension. I can see him punching the boss's lights out. I don't see—well, Harley Burton wouldn't use a knife, that's all."

"You've been very helpful," Kate said.

"Snitching is what I do best," Billie Sullivan said.

"What'll you do after you leave Modern Office?"

"Go back to work for a while and behave." With a sigh, she removed her feet from the desk. "The typing and dictation shit again. It's been a three-year vacation with the boss. But don't waste any sympathy on me. Milly in Philly laid the word on me a little while ago about the boss's replacement. Would you believe Fred Grayson?"

Kate murmured, "That seems somehow . . . appropriate."

Again Billie Sullivan bared her teeth in a grin. "I don't figure it'll be long before I find another Fergus Parker and I'll be on vacation again. In the meantime, I have a special farewell in mind when the dink manager comes down here to toss my ass. But don't say anything, okay? Don't spoil my fun."

"There's no reason to say anything. My business is police business."

Kate got up and gave her one of her cards. With a disdainful flip of her wrist, Billie Sullivan tossed it into her cardboard box.

17

Ellen had placed her purse in the bottom desk drawer and was sorting through the phone messages for Gail Freeman when her phone rang.

"Ellen, this is Guy. I really need to see you." His voice was low and husky with strain.

"Guy—we just had lunch." *Why me, God? Why this?*

"We didn't get a chance to talk. Can I see you later?"

"Later? You mean—" She broke off; Gail Freeman had strolled by, glanced in, and paused, watching her.

"I'll call you tonight," Guy said. "How about that?"

That would give her time to think of how she could best discourage this man's gentle, if annoying, persistence. "All right," she said, giving Gail Freeman a sign that she would be off the phone quickly. But he waved and sauntered away.

As she walked down the hall from Billie Sullivan's office, Kate glimpsed Guy Adams on his phone, and she realized with pleasure that Ellen would be back from her lunch with the managers. For some minutes longer Kate strolled up and down the hallway, her head down, pondering, assimilating her conversation with Billie Sullivan. Then she went into the lobby.

"Hey Cagney," Judy Markham said softly, smiling, blinking her large blue eyes, "you gonna make a collar soon?"

Kate smiled. "Maybe."

"I always thought it was a joke, people in business stabbing each other. You got an idea who did it?"

"We're working on it," she answered, and walked on, to Gail Freeman's office.

"You can do what you wish now about Billie Sullivan," she told Gail Freeman. "I'm finished interviewing her."

"Good." He pushed a button on his intercom. "Ellen, I'll be in Billie Sullivan's office a few minutes. Don't switch any calls up there."

"Right, Gail."

Ellen, again looking through the phone messages taken by Judy Markham, smiled gladly at the sight of Kate Delafield in her doorway.

"I was wondering," Kate said, "perhaps you'd like to have dinner tonight, give me a chance to—" Repay you, she was going to say, and broke off in irritation at her clumsiness. "Talk to you," she finished. "Give me a chance to show you something besides a browbeating detective." She added in her mind: And a sobbing mess.

"I'd like that, Kate." She thought rapidly, then said, "I absolutely have to stay a little late tonight, I'm so backed up with all that's been going on. Could we get an early sandwich or something?"

"A sandwich would be fine," Kate said, disappointed.

Ellen remembered *The White Cliffs of Dover.* "There's a British pub near here, where I went for lunch." She added with enthusiasm, "I think you might really like it. How about that? Is six-thirty okay?"

"Fine."

"It's over on Washington, it's called—"

"This is Billie Sullivan speaking."

The voice came out of the speaker in the hallway ceiling.

"I just had my ass fired from this fucking company and before I go there's a few things I'm gonna tell you suckers."

"Oh dear God," Ellen said, and stood up.

"You're a bunch of dumb assholes, you have to be. You're working here. But I'm gonna give you dumb shits the lowdown on a few things once and for all. None of you peons in word processing could get a two dollar raise last quarter, right? All because of the economy, right? Wrong, assholes. It's because fuckers like Fred Grayson cheat on their expense accounts—"

"Oh holy God," whispered Ellen.

"Indeed," Kate agreed. So this was Billie Sullivan's special farewell.

Ellen rushed from the office, through the lobby toward Billie Sullivan's office, Kate following.

"—Fred Grayson brown bags it every day of his useless life but he puts in expense account vouchers for lunch every day with customers, rips this company off two hundred bucks a week that's minimum. And so you see, you suckers—"

"Jeez," Jucy Markham said, gazing in awe at the ceiling speaker.

"Buzz this door open!" Ellen shouted, tugging at the far lobby door.

"Break this fucking door down!" Fred Grayson screamed, yanking savagely on the knob of Billie Sullivan's closed office door.

"—the fucking over this company's given all you sorry bastards slaving your asses away for peanuts, here's the straight scoop on the last sales meeting of your caring and concerned management in San Francisco. The liquor bill alone—"

"We'd need a battering ram," Gail Freeman said, rapping his knuckles on the solid door. "Fergus Parker insisted on nothing but the best for his office and hers too."

"—thousand dollars, my dimwitted friends. The food bill alone another five grand, bringing the grand total to a cool eighteen thousand bucks for twenty people to come from the west coast offices and screw around for three days. And I do mean screw around. Furthermore, assholes—"

"God damn it!" screeched Fred Grayson, pounding on the door.

"—nothing's too good for our customers, pretty boy Guy Adams, all he does is come in and sit in his fancy schmancy office and go to lunch, he put in a bill last week, four people at Le Dome, two hundred and forty smackers, you dumb shits—"

"Master key?" Kate suggested.

Several people had emerged from word processing to stare open-mouthed at the group clustered around Billie Sullivan's door. Gretchen Phillips and Harley Burton came around the corner. Guy Adams trotted down the hall.

"Go back to your offices," Gail Freeman called, hands raised in a stop gesture. The word processing people obeyed; Gretchen Phillips, Harley Burton, and Guy Adams did not.

"—fucking lunches could you dumb peons buy for two hundred and forty bucks?"

Gail Freeman said to Kate, "Can you imagine Fergus Parker entrusting me with a key to his office or his secretary's?"

"—and Fred Grayson just put in an expense account for a dinner for five, a modest affair, only a cool six hundred and eighteen—"

Fred Grayson screamed at Kate, "I'm a taxpayer! I *order* you to shoot this goddamned lock off!"

"—long could you dumb shits feed your kids on six hundred and—"

"Mr. Grayson," Kate said, "I don't believe LAPD would consider this police business."

"—beloved senior manager Fred Grayson hates anybody that wears a skirt unless she lets him screw her, hates anybody any color but white. But he's been sniffing after Cassie Franklin's black ass for months—"

"Slander! She's *slandering* me!"

"Then sue her," Kate said.

"—petty cash fund for, you dumb shits? All kinds of interesting activities. Five hundred bucks, that's what Fergus

Parker and Fred Grayson offered Cassie Franklin if she and a soul sister would put out for a certain visiting Philadelphia VP named Bob James who likes his ladies black and preferably two at a time—"

Fred Grayson hurled himself at the door, bounced off, grabbed his shoulder.

"Christ," Gretchen Phillips whispered.

Guy Adams stood unmoving, rigid and staring at the door. Harley Burton began to laugh.

"I'll take care of this," Ellen said, and opened the door into the lobby.

"—petty cash fund for panelling Fred Grayson's family room and den and a new golf cart for—" The voice cut off.

Ellen returned, dusting her hands in satisfaction. "The Muzak speaker, I turned it off."

Gail Freeman laughed. "Ingenious, assistant." He leaned up against the wall, grinning. "A solution your high-priced management couldn't come up with. I'll get you a raise one of these days—if we can ever get the company's expenses down."

Gretchen Phillips and Harley Burton laughed. Guy Adams looked bewildered. Fred Grayson stared at Gail Freeman, his eyes stony and filled with malice.

"Black boy, you just watch it there."

"Fred, cut out that crap," growled Harley Burton.

"Hey Fred," Guy Adams said softly, putting a hand on Fred Grayson's arm.

Fred Grayson flung off the arm. "You just watch it you black son—"

"Mr. Grayson that's enough," Kate snapped. "You're in violation of Mr. Freeman's civil rights. You're an officer of this company, in the presence of witnesses you've made a racially derog—"

"What *is* this shit!" Fred Grayson screamed. He turned on Kate. "You *agree* with me!"

"Hardly," Kate said with cold contempt.

"Tell you what, Fred." Gail Freeman's voice was casual;

he continued to lean against the wall, hands in his pockets. "Let's settle this outside the office. I'll be quite satisfied beating the living shit out of you."

Ellen glanced in alarm from Gail Freeman's slight frame to the huge bulk of Fred Grayson, and turned to Kate. "You can't let Gail—"

"I can handle myself just fine," Gail Freeman said, his calm dark eyes fixed on Fred Grayson. He flexed his fingers, formed his hands into fists. "And Fred knows it."

Fred Grayson took a rapid step backward. Kate remembered that Gail Freeman had been a boxing champion in the Marines. She did not bother to conceal her grin. "Mr. Grayson, I suggest you apologize."

Gretchen Phillips said, "Fred, what you said is disgusting."

"Show at least a little class, man," Guy Adams said. "If I were Gail—"

"Shut up! Shut up all of you." Not looking at Gail Freeman, Fred Grayson muttered, "It was the heat of the moment. I—"

Billie Sullivan's door edged open; she slipped into the hallway, yellow teeth exposed in a grin, hands held high over her head. "I surrender. Tear me limb from limb."

"Bitch," spat Fred Grayson. "All lies. You bitch, you—"

Kate stepped between them. "Miss Sullivan, perhaps you'd like to be escorted from the building."

"You bet your ass, lady copper." She glided toward Kate.

"We'll send your things," Gail Freeman said. "Kindly exit the premises. Now."

Billie Sullivan linked her arm through Kate's. "I've been thrown out of better places. Come on, lady copper. Take me away from all this shit."

19

The phone in the conference room rang; in a throaty
voice Judy Markham announced Wesley Miller calling from
Philadelphia.

Kate glanced at her watch: three-thirty. "Yes sir," she
said cordially. "Working a little late, aren't you?"

"In these hectic economic times we're all working a
little harder," Wesley Miller rumbled. "I know you can't
discuss the case, but I've just come from an extended meeting with Jonathon Wagner and the executive board about
Fergus Parker's successor. Jonathon's asked me to give you
a call and see whether you'd at least answer this question. Is
Fred Grayson a suspect?"

"Yes sir, he's a suspect."

"Ah, is he just a suspect generally, along with a number
of people? Or is he—as I understand it, your normal procedure is that everyone is under suspicion. Isn't that so?"

Kate decided to parry the question while she considered
how she would answer. "Would Mr. Grayson by chance be
your choice to succeed Fergus Parker?"

"A manager in Kansas City with a fine record was our
first choice. But it's near impossible to find people willing
to transfer into your expensive city." Wesley Miller's voice
was aggrieved. "Can't say as I blame Bill for turning down
the job in these uncertain economic times. He and his wife

have a seventy-thousand dollar house in Kansas City they couldn't begin to duplicate in L.A. So we've decided to promote from within. Maybe it's better under these tragic circumstances, give the employees more of a sense of continuity—"

"Isn't Kansas City where Harley Burton came from?" She was searching back through her notes, to her conversation with Fred Grayson.

"Believe it is."

"I understand he's had an outstanding record—"

"Until recently. Can't promote a man who's just been demoted." Wesley Miller's voice had quickened with impatience and annoyance. "And Fred Grayson's our choice. He's senior manager in service, has a record that shows consistency, if not spectacular—"

This isn't police business, Kate thought, shifting the receiver to the other ear as Wesley Miller droned on. Why the hell should she care whom they chose?

But faces drifted through her mind—Harley Burton, Duane Fletcher, Gretchen Phillips—admirable people who had had a Fergus Parker, and now would have a Fred Grayson. And Ellen O'Neil would still be here, would go on working here after this case was closed—if it ever was . . .

"It's none of my business at all whom you choose, Mr. Miller. And I know you're not interested in other opinions—"

"That's absolutely correct."

Kate kept her voice carefully courteous. "I must say that the choice rather surprises me in view of what I've seen of Mr. Grayson's judgment—"

"Meaning what." Wesley Miller's tone was edgy, hostile.

She chose her first point cautiously. "There's been a public accusation that Mr. Grayson pads his expense account."

Wesley Miller's sigh came clearly over the long distance hum. "Listen, I know I'm talking to a police officer. But I think you know, I think it's public knowledge—well, it's

naive to think some expense account padding doesn't go on in every business."

"Yes sir, but two hundred dollars a week seems excessive by any standard."

"*How* much?"

"Two hundred a week. According to Fergus Parker's secretary."

"Oh. Her. Well—"

Kate continued, "And Mr. Grayson's racial prejudice is rather evident."

Wesley Miller spoke slowly, in a tone that seemed bored. "Lots of us fee like we don't want to ah, work with people who get shovec down our throats whether they can do the job or not. With all these damn laws and—"

"Mr. Miller, we don't disagree on that. We talked about it this morning, remember? I feel that way and so do the police officers I work with. I can well understand anyone's feelings on that score." Kate picked up a piece of company stationery from the file folder she had been examining. "What I'm saying is, as an officer of a company with a strongly worded statement on its official stationery promising full commitment to equal opportunity, Mr. Grayson's prejudice is blatant and has become public—"

Wesley Miller interrupted with quiet command, "Blatant in what way?"

He had chosen the first and less important adjective to question; Kate was certain he was now taking notes. She flipped her notebook open to the back page. "Understand, sir, these are rot my personal judgments of Mr. Grayson. After eleven years in police work I'm quite accustomed to hearing considerable racial hatred. In my presence Mr. Grayson referred to Mr. Freeman as a nigger, a spook, a coon, a jungle bunny, a spade."

There was lengthy silence. Then Wesley Miller rumbled, "I don't care what a man's personal opinions are so long as he keeps them out of his business life. So long as he's got the

damn sense to keep private the things that should be private."

Such wonderful tolerance, Kate thought as she again shifted the receiver.

"Other than to yourself," Wesley Miller said slowly, as if deliberating over his words, "how have these . . . opinions . . . of Fred's become public?"

"He called Mr. Freeman 'black boy' before myself, three managers, and one other non-management employee—and would have made another racial slur except that I intervened. It was an ugly and dangerous situation. And I suggest to you that if there is another incident between Mr. Freeman and Mr. Grayson, or if the company ever wishes to take any kind of disciplinary action against Mr. Freeman, this occurrence has made things doubly difficult."

Wesley Miller's breathing was audible, slow and heavy. "Excuse my language, but people find ways to fuck up today I never even heard of when I went into this business." He sighed, an exasperated expulsion of breath. "I'll suggest to Jonathon that we make Grayson acting manager until we can fully discuss this . . . development."

"May I make a suggestion, Mr. Miller?" The image of Ellen O'Neil again floated through her mind. She smiled and added, "Purely as an objective outsider."

"Go ahead, can't hurt." Wesley Miller sounded mournful, tired.

"Perhaps you could arrange to come out here for a few days, do your own on-site observing. Mr. Freeman's fired Billie Sullivan, but—"

"Who's Billie Sullivan?"

"Fergus Parker's secretary."

"Oh. Yes. Her."

"She has nothing to gain or lose now, and I suggest you talk with her. Especially about the reasons surrounding Harley Burton's demotion."

"Fergus's reasons for that weren't very convincing . . . I liked what I saw of Harley Burton. But it was Fergus's

bailiwick and he was adamant..." Wesley Miller trailed off.

Taking more notes, Kate guessed. "Mr. Miller, I'll be as candid as I can under the circumstances. Whom we arrest, or when we make an arrest—that's still problematic, we're processing facts. In some cases we know empirically who committed a crime but we can never develop sufficient evidence to prosecute. But the strongest suspects in this case at this moment are all six members of the management staff—the six people who worked directly for or with Fergus Parker."

There was a soft whistle. "That a fact?"

"Yes sir, that's a fact. My point is, Fergus Parker gave a strong enough reason for homicide—for murder, sir—to all six people who worked with him. I think that should tell you something about Fergus Parker, and about this office."

There was a silence. Kate waited, but the silence continued.

"Mr. Miller, it would be good right now psychologically for you to come out here. In these hectic economic times," she said, placing slight emphasis on the phrase, "it seems like a good move for a company's top management to look into things..."

After a moment Wesley Miller answered in his resonant voice, "That seems not a half-bad idea. I expect we would probably meet, Detective Delafield."

Kate smiled. "I expect we probably would."

"We're always on the lookout, you know, for smart capable wo—people who show confidence and good judgment, handle themselves well, these are rare commodities, you know. We can always find places in our organization for... people like you."

Caught off-guard, Kate was pleased. "I thank you for the high compliment, Mr. Miller. But my field is law enforcement."

"And I think you should stay in law enforcement. We're a big organization, Detective Delafield. With various needs

for that kind of expertise. I don't know how well they're treating you where you are, but you could listen and see if we might not be able to treat you a little better. Never hurts to talk, I always say. Never hurts to listen."

"No sir, indeed it doesn't." Kate sat back in her chair, smiling, looking out over the hazy sun-splashed city. "It's nice out here right now. Santa Ana winds off the desert are expected for the next few days. You bring your swim trunks when you come."

20

The White Cliffs of Dover seemed dimmer at night, the buzz of conversation livelier, friendlier. The patrons, mostly men, were more casually dressed than at lunch—windbreakers and work pants, jeans and sweaters. Two plump middle-aged women, lumpy in woolen skirts and sweaters, were at one of the dart boards; they emitted smothered explosions of giggles as they launched high-arched darts.

Ellen smiled at Kate. "Guy says Modern Office people come here all the time for lunch. To relax, play darts. I can see why—it's so comfortable and homey."

"Harley Burton invited me for your lunch today." Kate drank her ale with enjoyment, amused by the women at the dart board. "I was sorry I couldn't come. I do like it here." She watched the two women return to their table. A mustachioed man in a navy blue cotton jacket made a mocking gesture toward the dart board; one of the women fondled his graying hair and then patted it back into place. Married, Kate thought; you can always tell.

She returned her attention to Ellen, pleased again by the simplicity of her clothes: the severely tailored dark green jacket, short and without collar or lapels; the matching skirt and pale green blouse tied at the throat by a thin dark green ribbon. Her gaze lingered on Ellen's throat, drifted down to her breasts. Memory of the feeling and taste of her was

interrupted by the shifting of Ellen's body as she raised her beer mug. Kate looked at her hands: ringless. She remembered the apartment where Ellen lived with Stephanie Hale. Not Westwood or Beverly Hills, but a very good section on the westside. And well-furnished, spacious.

"Have you never wanted to own a house, Ellen? Rent on your apartment must be fairly close to a house payment."

"I would love to own a house," Ellen said fervently. "I'd give *anything* to have a place to call my own. I *hate* paying rent. You might as well throw all that money out onto the street. But Stephie—she thinks it's too obvious, two women owning a house together."

"Why should she care? She's tenured, isn't she?"

"She still doesn't want anyone to know."

I hate this Stephanie Hale. "She's deluding herself," Kate said shortly. "People know. If we really think people don't know, we're just kidding ourselves. Straight people with half a brain pick up all the signs. Not how we act, but how we don't act—how we don't fit in with all the heterosexual game playing. We put on an act and they all laugh behind our backs. You know it happens, Ellen, you've heard the straight people laugh at us. The men especially. When you're not interested in them they're only too happy to sneer and call you queer."

Ellen asked, "They know then . . . about you?"

Kate chuckled bitterly. "I've never pretended to be heterosexual. But I've never made any announcements either, and never will. Why give anyone a weapon? And it *is* a weapon. I'll give you one possible scenario: Avowed lesbian denies accusation of making sexual advance to female prisoner."

"Kate . . . could that really happen? I mean—"

"Yes, Ellen, it could happen. And yes, I'm paranoid. But with good reason. And yes they know about me—without my telling them, and they're much happier that way. The brass loves me because I don't call in with problems about my kids, I don't take maternity leave. And the men love me

because they're convinced any woman who wants to be a cop must be suffering from penis envy and my being a lesbian confirms that. And the men can tell their wives, 'Yeah, honey, I'm working with a woman but not to worry because she's a lez.' And so the men's wives love me too. So I'm the perfect woman cop. Everyone can respect my work but still be contemptuous. So women can do the job, they tell themselves, but only because they're pseudo-men. But gay male cops can't do the job at all—and they'll prove *that* if they have to kill them to do it."

"You can't mean that," Ellen said in an appalled whisper.

"Yes, I do mean it. I'm not nearly as bad off as the men, Ellen. All gay male cops are in the deepest darkest end of the closet. You think there's resistance to women? Think about the fact that being a cop is one of the big macho trips of the western world, the cop is today's cowboy. They *pay* you to wear that uniform, all that leather, that gun on your hip. They *pay* you to control and intimidate. Ever ask yourself why anyone would *want* to be a cop? The psychological tests screen out many pathological types, but there's still a whole masculine self-image built up around being a cop."

Kate stared into her beer mug, rotating it in her hands. Then she spoke with the firm swiftness of utter conviction. "All the straight cops I know hate the idea of gay male cops with a rage that's simply indescribable. How dare any faggot invade their macho world and think he can be brave and strong and tough? The gay men out on the lines are all in the closet, Ellen, they have to be. You're a gay man in a dangerous situation and all that has to happen is your partner doesn't do what he's supposed to do quite soon enough, the backup you've called for doesn't get there quite soon enough. And you're one dead gay cop who just wasn't *man* enough to be a cop."

Kate looked up to see Ellen staring at her with stricken eyes. "Straight cops . . . would do that? They're all . . . like that?"

"Not all. But enough."

"Then why do you stay? Why did *you* want to be a cop?"

Kate spoke more slowly, remembering, and gathering her thoughts. "After Vietnam, after all I'd seen over there, I felt serious about people, Ellen. I wanted to . . . help. I joined LAPD in 'seventy-two and worked in juvenile, that's where most women in law enforcement worked then, it was all we could expect. Then the courts mandated numbers, which was the only way I'd have ever gotten into the more challenging areas of police work. I became fascinated by what I saw, the raw edge of lives I could never imagine. People different from me, and other people just like me, but caught in cross currents that turned their lives in directions they never conceived of. All our lives are under thread-thin control that can snap so easily—by something as simple as an oil tanker jack-knifing on a freeway." It was the first time she had freely spoken of Anne's death, and she was astonished at the calmness of her voice.

Ellen said earnestly, "But you're so *good* at what you do. What you do is so *important*."

Kate shook her head. "I don't feel that way anymore. For too long I've made the common mistake of all gay people. Believed if I was good enough, being gay wouldn't matter. Well, being good doesn't matter, makes no difference at all. Nothing I do makes any real difference to anybody."

"That's not true, Kate," Ellen said softly, "that's just not true. I think you're just tired . . . and maybe it's time for you to think about getting out of it. Maybe it's time to do other things you're good at."

Kate was silent, thinking of Gretchen Phillips. *I'm one of the few women*, Gretchen Phillips had said, *who could afford to pay Fergus Parker's price for my job.*

Kate looked down at the hands curved around her beer mug. *I paid that price too—because of Anne. I no longer have to pay any price for any job.*

"You're right," she said, smiling at Ellen and raising her beer mug in a toast. "I don't even have to care about the

mortgage anymore." She took a deep draught of her beer, feeling suddenly light and free. She thought of Wesley Miller, of his promise of other opportunities.

Ellen said in alarm, "You will give it a lot of thought, won't you, Kate? You need to get a good perspective on things before you do anything. After all the years you've given to your work, it's too important a decision."

"I will. And you should give a lot of thought to your own life. None of us should surrender our dreams to other people. Anne's dream was to finish college, get her degree. Anne thought a college degree would confer some magical mark on her." Kate smiled, remembering; then she looked directly into Ellen's eyes. "I was the selfish one in our relationship. I kept telling her next year—she had plenty of time. You're thirty-one. Anne was thirty-two when she died."

Their food arrived; gratefully, Ellen attended to salting her french fries, tasting her fish. But the somberness of Kate's face continued to disturb her. "Billie Sullivan," she said lightly, "that was quite an exit." She was gratified when Kate chuckled.

"I've never met anyone remotely like her."

Ellen asked carefully, "The case, can you tell me anything about it, how it's coming?"

"Well, a pattern's begun to emerge—as it always does in any case of homicide that isn't random violence." She took a bite of her fish. "Haven't you been upset enough by all this, Ellen?"

"I might be useful," she answered quickly. "Even as a sounding board. I'm getting to know some of these people now. If you feel you can trust me."

"It isn't a question of trust—" She broke off. Of course it was. Hadn't she always told Anne about the cases she was working on? With judicious editing of the grosser detail, of course. How could she not trust Ellen O'Neil?

"There are some problems." She buttered a piece of hot crusty bread. "We're still sifting through fingerprint

evidence—it's still the most conclusive proof we can have in a criminal case." She decided she would not mention Harley Burton's partial print on the coffee pot. "We have a cigarette butt we picked up on the fifteenth floor, the lab's lifted an unusual blood type from the saliva. The butt's of very limited value but I'm certain the killer discarded it in his haste."

"Why limited value? I'd think it would be an important piece of evidence."

"It's presumptive evidence. A defense attorney would argue the butt could be anybody's—anyone from any floor in that building could've dropped it. When we make an arrest we'll use it of course if we can match up the blood type—it's unusual enough to be useful. And everything adds weight to a circumstantial case." She ate a piece of bread. "You never find really good bread like this anymore."

"Kate, do you know who did it?"

Kate watched two young men begin to throw darts, flinging them with easy expertise; then she looked into light brown eyes wide with concern, and decided to speak the truth.

"The evidence points to four management people, Ellen. From your signed statement, the statements of the two guards, we know within a few seconds the elapsed time from the moment of the killing, we know the essential fact that it took the killer less than two minutes to get all the way down those stairs and mingle with arriving employees. On that basis, I've eliminated as suspects Gretchen Phillips and Duane Fletcher."

She said in dismay, "And included my boss—the one person I admire most."

Of the four, Kate reflected, Harley Burton was the man she herself admired most. "Unless something unexpected develops, it would appear to be one of them—from the standpoint of opportunity. But when it comes to criminality, there still has to be motive, malice, intent. I'll concede," she said grudgingly, "that Guy Adams seems the least likely from a motive standpoint."

"I knew it, I just *knew* that," Ellen said triumphantly.

"He's still a strong suspect, Ellen," Kate warned. "There are other problems, inconsistencies. The medical examiner says that blood spurted onto the killer's hand or sleeve. Gail Freeman and Fred Grayson wore dark suits that day, but light shirt cuffs. And Guy Adams wore a cream-colored jacket. But what do you do about bloodstains when you've got only a scant few minutes before police are all over the scene? I'm sorry," she said as Ellen put down her fork. "This isn't appropriate dinner conversation."

"It's not that, it's all right . . . I was just thinking . . ." She said slowly, unwillingly, "Harley Burton doesn't wear a jacket in the office. And he rolls up his sleeves."

Kate nodded, pleased with her. "Yes, I noticed that. And that makes Harley Burton a very strong suspect indeed. But there's still a problem—"

A shout went up from the dartboard; Kate looked over to see three darts crowded into the bullseye. "Nice shooting," she said. "There's the one element that just doesn't make sense, Ellen. No sign of struggle. How could Fergus Parker let Harley Burton or anyone else come at him with a knife? It doesn't make sense. How could he just *allow* himself to be stabbed?"

She ate a french fry, thinking that she would not describe to Ellen the unusual nature of the stab wound. There was another shout from the dart board; she glanced over and then sat utterly motionless, staring at the dart that had thudded into the bullseye and still quivered from the impact. In dawning comprehension she turned and met Ellen's eyes, wide with shock and staring into hers.

"He threw it," Ellen whispered.

"Yes. Of course. Exactly." Kate put down her fork and looked again at the dart board and said wonderingly, "That's just not done. It's not. Not in this day and age. Except in Kung Fu movies . . . and the odds against a fatal wound . . . I've never even heard of a case . . ."

She stared down at her dinner knife, sorting through

and fitting images together. A well-crafted, well-balanced knife could be thrown with deadly effect—especially by someone who was accustomed to throwing objects—like darts—with accuracy. And if thrown with velocity . . . A knife striking Fergus Parker squarely and with force . . . causing him to fall heavily backward . . .

Ellen's mind was filled with images of Gail Freeman, Guy Adams, Fred Grayson, and Harley Burton at lunch, at the dart board. It couldn't be Gail—not the way he threw his darts, the delicate flip from behind his ear. And not with that ironic toast at lunch; he could never have killed and then made a boastful toast . . . But Guy, the way he threw his darts—swiftly, with skill and confidence . . . But dammit, Kate Delafield could talk for a hundred years about meek little men who were monsters, Guy Adams was not *capable*. Then she remembered Fred Grayson sighting along his darts as if they were weapons . . . the powerful thuds of Harley Burton's darts into his target. She shuddered, and glanced at Kate; she was picking at her food, eyes distant with thought. It might very well be Harley Burton. Too bad. It was simply too bad anyone had to be punished for killing a creature like Fergus Parker—Fergus Parker was the monster, not his killer.

Kate ate automatically, her mind absorbed. "I'm sorry," she said, suddenly realizing that considerable time had elapsed.

"I understand perfectly," Ellen told her, smiling.

Kate absently buttered another piece of bread. "I just need to go over my notes, all the details again. And look at the facts—" She looked at the knife, touched her forefinger and thumb lightly to the butter on the blade, held the knife in a clean area as if to throw it; then she inserted the knife into her bread and drew it out, staring at the smeared glossy surface.

"I won't keep you much longer," Ellen teased, watching the fine lines of concentration again deepen between the light blue eyes.

Kate glanced at her watch. "And vice versa. I'll let you get home."

"Kate, if you find out something important from all this . . . Will you call me later?"

"Of course. I'd be glad to." She added, "To know if you feel . . . okay. Safe." She should be careful, not have Ellen think she was moving in on the UCLA professor's territory— even if she was.

After Ellen left, Kate displayed her shield to a bartender in shirt and pants of matching red plaid, who gave her permission to use the phone on the bar. She called Joe D'Amico at the lab, covering one ear; noise had increased with the progression of the evening.

"I hear from the background the big butch cop is out there risking life and limb," D'Amico growled.

Kate grinned; obviously D'Amico was alone in the lab. She jammed the receiver to her ear as a chorus of moans and boos went up from the crowd around the pool table. "Joe you sweet thing, do me a favor? I'll buy you a lovely new apron for Christmas." D'Amico, a burly and snarling presence in his lab, was a gourmet cook who created dishes of lightness and delicacy, a reflection of his true nature.

"How can I resist, dear heart? I'm so tired of the twelve aprons I have. What do you want?"

She cupped a hand around the mouthpiece of the receiver as the noise level rose again. "The guy yesterday, obese, about five-nine—"

"Parker, yeah. Lardass. Took up two slabs."

D'Amico's voice had dropped into its usual gruff toughness; someone had come into his lab.

"The very one. I need a test on the weapon. I need it now."

There was a burst of cheering and applause; a ragged chorus of *For He's a Jolly Good Fellow* rose from the pool table. Kate ground the receiver into her ear. "What, Joe? Can't hear you!"

188

"—fucking kind of test do you want?"

"Screening for any foreign material present," Kate shouted.

"—set up a chromatography—"

Kate shouted, "I'll be at the station in half an hour! That okay?"

"—fucking thing as soon as I can and no sooner." D'Amico hung up.

Kate glanced at her watch. Eight-ten. She was only minutes away from the station. She settled herself at the bar, happy in the realization that no one in this place had taken the slightest note of her presence. She ran a hand pleasurably over the rough-grained wood of the bar, signaled for another ale, and relaxed and watched the dart games, listening to the buzz and shout of conversation, allowing warmth and conviviality to flow over her.

21

Ellen stopped at a supermarket and picked up a six-pack of Michelob. Then, after she had gone through the check-out line, she returned and defiantly chose a bottle of chilled Johannesburg Reisling. It wouldn't kill her to have a relaxing glass or two before bedtime this once. A gift, she would tell Stephanie. From a Modern Office customer.

The phone was ringing as she unlocked the apartment.

"Darling? Is everything okay?"

"Everything's fine, Stephie. I just—"

"I've been ca ling since *six.*"

"I worked overtime." Oh screw it, she thought. "Then I had dinner with a friend."

"Which friend?"

"Are you checking on me?"

"Are you stepping out?" The tone was facetious.

"Do you think I am?"

"I wouldn't be surprised."

As usual, Stephanie was being cynical and self-pitying. Ellen said nastily, "Are you sure you aren't really just tired of you and me?"

"Let's drop this, Ellen. We should never try to talk about anything serious over the phone. Is everything all right? Are they any closer to arresting someone? There was even an item in the papers here."

"I think they're very close." She was suddenly exhausted; she didn't feel like talking to Stephanie, or doing anything at all. "How's the conference coming?"

"Terrific. And here's the big news, baby. Phillips wants me to come up with another book proposal, expanding on what we did before. Isn't that wonderful?" Stephanie's voice quickened with animation. "How'd you like to quit that job in a few more months and help out again?"

"We'll discuss it," Ellen said after a moment.

"Such enthusiasm." She added, "Another *book*, Ellen darling. It means I'll get my full professorship—"

"I'm tired, Stephie. These last two days have been such a strain . . . And didn't you just say we shouldn't talk about anything serious on the phone? Isn't a major commitment of my time serious?"

"You're right. Darling, of course you're absolutely right."

She was being unusually docile, Ellen thought.

"And don't bother about picking me up," Stephanie said. "Jim's wife will drop us both off." She added, "She doesn't work."

Irritated by the subtle pressure, Ellen said, "Tell me how the sessions went."

She walked over to the television, dragging the phone cord, switched on the set. She sat heavily in an armchair and curled her legs up under her and listened, eyelids drooping with tiredness, to the cadence of Stephanie's voice.

After a final "I love you too," she hung up, and disinterestedly opened the *Herald Examiner*. She preferred the *Times*, but Stephanie liked the *Herald's* sports page.

MID WILSHIRE GRAY FLANNEL MURDER

The bold two-column headline leaped at her from page three. A smaller subheading read, OFFICE DESIGN EXEC SLAIN.

Fergus Parker, 48, top ranking west coast executive of Modern Office, Inc. was a victim of stabbing early yesterday.

The body was discovered by Ellen R. O'Neil, 31, an employee, shortly before the highrise suite of offices opened for the day.

Robbery was not an apparent motive, according to Lt. James R. Kovich, who also

The shrill of the phone startled her. Could it be Kate? So soon? She folded the paper before picking up the receiver.

"I've been calling and calling," her mother said. "First you don't answer and I picture you lying there in a pool of blood, the Gray Flannel Murderer has got in there and got you. And then the phone is busy and I'm so relieved, and then it's busy and busy and I'm picturing you calling for help and the Gray Flannel Murderer is strangling you and the phone is dangling off the—"

Laughing, Ellen said, "Mother, you're crazy."

"Did you see the *Herald?* Mrs. Fox next door showed me. The *Times* is too refined to have such a writeup. Gray Flannel Murder," her mother snorted. "And they even put your age in the paper—"

"I don't care at all."

"You will. give you five more years and you'll start forgetting a birthday or two."

"Maybe," Ellen said wearily. She glanced at the wall clock: eight forty-five.

"Ellen sweetheart, are you all right?"

"Sure, Mother. Just tired."

"You sure that's all? Your tough and capable detective, is she ever going to catch anybody?"

"Any time now. I'm really tired, Mother. I think I'll just go to bed and curl up with some nice poetry."

"You sure you're—"

"Don't worry, Mother," she said firmly, "the Gray Flannel Murderer hasn't the slightest interest in me. Good night, I'll call you tomorrow."

She got up and threw the *Herald Examiner* in the trash,

and walked into the bedroom. "God damn it," she muttered, glaring at the jumbled bedclothes, the rumpled blue pajamas. There was no way to explain those pajamas, she'd better wash them. And the sheets, too. She changed into her usual jeans and shirt and tennis shoes, and put fresh sheets on the bed.

As she was returning to her apartment from the laundry room she glimpsed, to her surprise and displeasure, Guy Adams in the hallway, talking with her next-apartment neighbors, Carl and John.

Guy walked quickly to her and in a gesture as naturally affectionate as if she were his sister, placed his hands on her shoulders and touched a smooth-shaven cheek to her face. She was disarmed by his gentleness. His faint scent was of woods and autumn, too delicate for cologne; expensive shaving lotion, she guessed.

"I tried to call you earlier. I was out to dinner—I just came on over. Your friends here were nice enough to let me in."

I'm sure they were, she thought. Their glances lingered covetously on Guy Adams, slender and elegant in a white velour turtleneck and dark brown slacks.

"Let me talk to you, Ellen. Just a few minutes."

He looked tired and dispirited, forlorn as a child. Touched, she impulsively took his hand and led him to her apartment.

He sat on the sofa, his body stiffly erect, his hand still clutching hers.

"Guy, you're so tense."

"This is a nightmare."

She knew she could not so much as hint at Kate's confidences, and she answered softly, "Of course. Would you like something to drink? We don't have liquor, I'm sorry. But there's beer, and I have a very nice bottle of wine, Stonegate—"

He said abruptly, "Beer's fine."

"I can give you some grass if you'd prefer. Very good

stuff. Guaranteed by the UCLA student body and faculty," she added drily.

"Smoking grass'll make me want cigarettes. Dumb as it seems, I'm really trying to quit. Beer's fine."

In the kitchen, as she opened two Michelobs and poured them into glasses, her impulse of generosity toward Guy Adams evaporated. He would not be much of a problem to get rid of, she'd just ease him out as quickly as possible ... She came back to find him morosely gazing at the television screen, his hands repeatedly smoothing the sharp creases in his slacks.

"You can't stay long," she said, and added, hating herself, "My boyfriend will be home soon. He—he's very jealous."

He nodded without looking at her and took a glass from her hand and drank half its contents before setting it down on the table. "Thank you, Ellen. That's good." He took a deep breath. "I'm going absolutely crazy."

She sat down next to him on the sofa.

Taylor sat at his desk in a bright wash of light, finishing reports and cleaning up paperwork. He got up and pursued Kate to her desk.

Her phone was ringing, and he placed a hand over the receiver to prevent her picking it up. "I got big news, Kate."

"Me too, Ed. Our killer threw the knife."

Taylor's eyes widened, then clouded as he made mental connections. "Yeah ... yeah ... Jesus, weird. Simple. Logical. I never thought ... Jesus, this business can make you feel like a damn moron. Paydirt on the wine bottle. Just came in."

Her phone had stopped ringing. Taylor fished in a pocket of his jacket, produced a scrap of paper. He read laboriously, "Robert Mondavi Cabernet Sauvignon ... A seal Baker found in all that glass fit the neck of that bottle perfectly."

Kate's phone rang again. "Prints?" She picked up the receiver.

"Prints?" Taylor repeated rhetorically. His eyes gleamed with satisfaction. "To begin with, latents from Fergus Parker—"

"Kate?" It was Joe D'Amico. "There were microscopic traces in the grooves of the knife handle, traces of undissolved material in the blood sample we wiped from the knife. Chemical analysis shows an organic compound composed of the following—" D'Amico's voice was flat; he was reading. "Phosphorous, sulphur, hydrogen sulphide—"

"Joe," Kate said, "give it to me in English." She sat tensely; the warmth and conviviality of *The White Cliffs of Dover* had evaporated in the harsh reality of the station and D'Amico's impartial voice.

"Oil, Kate. Some kind of petroleum product."

Kate said automatically, "Joe, I owe you." She hung up and turned to Taylor.

"Also on the seal and wine bottle," Taylor gloated, "were clear and perfect prints of fingers contaminated with foreign matter—"

"The lab just gave me the same answer. Found oil traces on the knife, in the blood on the knife. He opened the hood of his car, Ed. Unscrewed his radiator cap—that's where he picked it up on his fingers."

"Yup. You bet we're gonna find matching samples on the handkerchief Hansen collected from his car."

Kate said in consternation, "I asked Joe to run that test thinking it would help clear him."

"Amateur City, you can never tell. But I never figured Guy Adams."

Kate did not answer.

"We'll pick him up," Taylor said.

Guy Adams said, "It's amazing how fast you understood what kind of man Fergus Parker was. It took me up until yesterday to really know. Thank God you understood. Women have been the best people ever to happen to me in my life. Ellen," he said miserably, "I need you to understand

why it happened, how it happened. We share a bond now, Ellen. I owe it to you. I *need* you to know."

Ellen had just begun to lift her beer glass. She dropped it down onto the coffee table where it teetered, rattled, wobbled, righted itself.

His voice was a faint whisper. "I still can't believe it happened."

His eyes were fixed on the television screen, and Ellen glanced over thinking she must have misunderstood, that something on television would surely explain what he had just said. They sat in silence, watching two cops pursue a man down an alley.

He said, "Why have you been avoiding me?"

Out of her numbed mind came a clear warning: *Careful. Just be careful.*

"I wasn't avoiding you, Guy."

"Didn't you know—couldn't you imagine how I felt?"

"I—maybe ... who can—" she stuttered, "maybe ... no one can know that, know—"

"You're upset. Don't be upset." His voice rose. "Why are you upset?"

Be careful. Be very very careful. "I'm fine Guy. I just ... feel bad. For you."

"I hardly ever got there early, Ellen. Just once before so early. But it was a report, a survey they needed in Philadelphia, I just had to get it finished ... I knew he was in. From my office I could hear him shouting and laughing, that awful bray of his. But I figured he wouldn't know I was in. I made coffee—"

She started as the phone rang.

"God," he said. "Not now. Just ignore it."

After five rings he got up. "I'll just unplug it."

"Wait," she said through a dry throat. She got up. "Mother—it's my mother, Guy. She said she'd call now—she's only a few blocks away, if I don't answer she'll come over to ... see why."

He stared at her.

"I'll just tell her I'll call her back, that's all." She walked over to the phone as he did not reply. *Let it be Kate* . . . She picked up the receiver.

"Ellen? Ellen it's—"

"Mother, I've got company." The quaver in her voice caught in her throat, and she coughed to clear it. "I'll call you later." She hung up. She walked back to the man staring at her from the sofa.

Kate looked at the phone in her hand. Guy Adams was with Ellen. If he knew Ellen had tried to protect him . . . If Ellen had told him . . .

He thinks she saw him!

She slammed the phone down.

Taylor called from his desk, "Kate, what—"

Kate came from behind her desk, running.

"I'd just gotten more coffee and was walking into my office as he came out of the executive washroom. 'Leave that coffee and come to my office, boy,' he calls to me. 'I got a job for you.' Like I was a two-year old. I had no idea . . . I went back with him. Harley's talked to me about sales, something I'd really like to get into and—" Guy raised a hand in a gesture of futility, dismissal. "He sat down in his big chair—God, it's indelible, all this. He told me not to sit down, to open a bottle of wine, he couldn't manage his corkscrew. He's sitting there, a foot on his desk, his hands behind his head, grinning like . . . like . . ."

He rubbed his palms back and forth on his dark brown slacks. "I thought there was still a possibility we could talk . . . I went to the cart, he told me to roll it over. He couldn't be bothered getting up. I was his serf. I told him I didn't know what was going on—I'd had enough. He could open his own bottle. And he said, 'You want to work for this company one minute after March thirty-first, boy, you better damn well move that cart over here.'"

He took a deep breath and looked at her. She looked

back steadily, scarcely breathing. His face had a greenish pallor against the white pullover, his eyes were fevered.

"Amateur City!" Kate shouted at Taylor as they roared down Pico leading a caravan of two other flashing police cars. A motorcycle thundered out from a side street to join them. "With an amateur cop who couldn't see past her own nose! If he does anything to her—goddammit!" She swerved around a panel truck.

"Slow down, Kate!" shouted Taylor, clutching the dashboard.

She grated, "Adams was so sick he was *green*. Like a damn fool I listened to my instincts instead of my training. I *assumed* he was in shock! If I'd flatout *asked* if he'd done it, he'd have caved like cardboard!"

Kate hit the brake as she came up behind two cars traveling abreast. Savagely, she pounded the horn. The car in the right lane speeded up and she gunned around the car on the left as it began to pull over—its driver a tiny old man who peered over at her with terrified eyes—and she barely avoided a sideswipe.

"Shit, Kate!" Taylor screamed, again clutching the dashboard.

"So I pulled the cart over. It was heavy, rickety, all those liquor bottles clinking together. Then he wanted to know which of the wines was best. There was a bottle of Robert Mon—I'm rambling."

He took another deep breath. "I had trouble breaking the seal. He slid that big ugly letter opener of his across the desk. He told me I should at least be capable of opening wine. Never, he'd never talked to me like that. I just looked at him. He said to finish, he'd explain. By then I knew what it was—a huge step up the ladder for this hideous man. He poured himself a glass—drank a toast. To himself—the new director of company operations west of the Mississippi. He drank that wonderful wine down like it was his disgusting

198

soda pop. Then he told me for being such a good boy he'd explain how piss-poor my future with the company would be."

He paused, his shoulders heaving. "The company . . . I'm so proud . . . my family . . . My job, Ellen, it's my whole life. It was like . . . like I was . . . it was inconceivable, a nightmare." He picked up his beer and drained it, looked at her. "Could I have more?"

The police caravan was strung out, seconds behind them; and there would be other units at Ellen O'Neil's apartment building probably by now.

"Ed," Kate shouted, "he said he couldn't remember if his damn door was open yesterday, but he *must* have remembered to close it Monday night, Gail Freeman had just *reminded* him, it stands to *reason*—"

"He give you anything in the interview?" Taylor sat back as they sped down a brief stretch clear of traffic.

"Didn't say much at all, my fault. I did a lousy interview, he never really answered my questions, I never gave him a chance to cave, he never tried to justify himself like everybody does, it was all there if I'd just seen it. But I didn't read him right because I *hated* the son of a bitch!"

As Kate weaved through another string of cars she snatched a hand from the steering wheel to clap it to her head. "Sick! Adams was *sick!* He threw a knife into Fergus Parker and ran downstairs—that cretin in the garage, it wasn't somebody coughing—it was Guy Adams throwing up!"

"Maybe the woman's okay, Kate. He's such a piece of dogfood maybe he's not capable—"

"I already made that mistake, Ed. Even a weasel protects itself when it's in a corner—goddammit!" She swerved around a Toyota truck pulling out from a curb, fought the wheel.

"Kate! You goddamn idiot slow down!"

Kate righted the car, stamped the accelerator. The car

leapt forward.

Ellen went into the kitchen and poured another Michelob, straining for the sound of sirens. But they wouldn't come with sirens, she realized. That would panic him and . . .

I'm probably wrong, she thought, God knows I've been wrong about everything else so far, but he won't hurt me— if I just don't do anything, say anything . . . He's on the edge, right on the edge . . .

She returned to the living room with his beer, sat beside him.

He drank, and clutched his beer glass in a white-knuckled hand. "He told me what he'd done to people. Gretchen—oh God, poor Gretchen. Gail was as good as finished, he'd see to that. I was dead in the company—he knew all about my phone calls to Philadelphia. I'd end up in a nowhere office so small I'd be lucky to have a desk let alone a telephone."

He picked up the remote control, clicked off the television. "I walked to the door. He stood up and said, "Where you going, boy? You stealing my letter opener, boy? You gutless little *fag*?' Called me a *fag*." His voice broke. He coughed, swallowed audibly. "I'd put his letter opener in my pocket . . . He started to laugh, and laugh and laugh . . . And he said, I got you right by your so-called balls, you little fag.' "

His breathing was rapid, ragged. "He was standing there— a howling puffed up creature from hell—nothing God could ever mean to have on this earth . . . Ellen, you'd throw a stone at a snake or a rat . . . wouldn't you? I threw what I had in my hand. I threw it . . ."

He got up, and carrying his beer glass, began to pace. "Blood, there was blood. He fell back into his chair. I was . . . I was . . . His eyes bulged out . . . He pointed to me . . . Tried to say something . . . Grabbed at his chest . . . Blood on his hands . . . Red, all red . . ."

Ellen buried her face in her hands. It was worse than

Kate Delafield had described, unimaginably worse . . .

Kate's car screeched to a stop; she shouted to Taylor, "Pull in the driveway! Quick!" She leaped from the car as a squad car and then another pulled up behind them. Kate signalled for two men to cover the rear of the building, the others to enter.

"Ellen, I had to tell you—tell somebody."

She looked at him out of tear-blurred eyes. "I know you did, Guy. It's all right."

"My mind—jelly. I ran into the hall, you were there with the coffee pot . . . looking for me. And then there was this sound . . . this awful sound from his office, from him. And I started to throw up. I ran, just ran, trying to hold it down, to get away from him, all the way down those stairs, my stomach heaving and heaving, all the way down . . . through the garage . . . to my car . . . Threw up everything in me . . . Then the police were arriving. I just waited to be arrested."

He ceased pacing, turned and looked at her. "I didn't understand what was happening till you said you didn't tell anybody my door was open. Then I knew you'd seen me—you were protecting me. Still I thought I'd be arrested, the police would find proof, I thought you'd change your mind. Every cop that came up to me, I thought I'd be arrested, especially that woman detective . . . But nothing's happened."

He stood very still, looking at her. "You're the only one who knows."

Kate raced ahead of the car, held up a hand, jumped onto the hood and then the roof. She braced, then leaped for Ellen's balcony wall, grasped the top, and dangled until she could get leverage for her feet, cursing the smooth soles of her shoes. She pulled herself up and over, onto the balcony.

"All last night I had nightmares. What if they arrest

somebody else? Gretchen. Or Gail. And if I got away with it there'd be a cloud over everybody in that office forever—"

"Give yourself up, Guy." She spoke softly, firmly. "Explain what happened."

"I don't know what they'd—what they'd do to me."

"There are extenuating circumstances." She was calm; she knew her voice had the conviction of utter rightness. "Guy, tell them exactly what you've told me. Exactly. What happened to Fergus Parker you didn't mean to happen, everybody who's ever known you can testify to that. And everybody knew what he was like. What could be worse than what you've been going through?"

He walked toward her. "You see why I needed to talk. Why—"

Through the gauzy curtain Kate saw Guy Adams go toward Ellen with an object in his hand. She seized the small wooden table on the balcony, swung with all her strength.

Ellen screamed as the balcony door exploded in a shower of glass, as Kate Delafield burst into the room and crouched, the gun in her two hands trained on Guy Adams.

"Right there, right there or you're dead."

"Holy God." Guy Adams said, stopping in mid-stride.

The object in Guy Adams' hand, Kate saw, was a beer glass. Ellen ran to her; Kate shifted the gun to one hand and pushed Ellen behind her.

"I'm all right, Kate."

"Stay behind me," Kate ordered.

"I'm fine. He wasn't going to hurt me."

Taylor, gun in hand, breathing loudly, stepped through the shattered balcony door and straightened his jacket and tie. "Jesus Christ you're trying to kill me, Kate." He picked his way through the glass. "Running down sixteen flights of stairs, jumping onto balconies—"

Kate grinned; under stress, Taylor as usual was trying to be funny.

"Lay off me," Taylor said. "I promise never to tell you another joke." He turned to Ellen. "Miss O'Neil, I'm glad you're okay." He holstered his gun and approached Guy Adams. "You want to do Miranda, Kate? Or should I do the honors?"

"Guy Adams," Kate said, "you're under arrest and will be charged with homicide. You have the right to remain silent, anything you say can and will be used against you in a court of law. You have the right—"

Guy Adams began to cry; tears streamed swiftly down his face. Wrenched with pity, Ellen moved toward him, but Kate held her back.

"Kate, it's all right—"

Kate did not relax her grip. "In a minute." She finished reciting Guy Adams' rights to him and asked repeatedly did he understand until he finally responded yes in a voice of misery. She nodded to Taylor.

"Police!" came a shout from the hallway.

Taylor opened the door. Half a dozen blue-uniformed cops milled about the room as Taylor patted his hands routinely down Guy Adams' body. Kate released Ellen only when Guy Adams, still sobbing, was handcuffed.

Ellen went to him, smoothed the tears from his face. "Guy, it'll be okay," she whispered. "Believe me, it'll be okay."

"Will you come with me now . . . down there? Stay with me?"

"Of course I will."

"Put him in the car, Ed," Kate said. "We'll be right along."

"Ellen?"

"I'll be right there, Guy. In just one minute. I promise."

The uniformed cops had gone back into the hallway to disperse the crowd of building tenants, including Carl and John, Ellen's next-apartment neighbors, who watched open-mouthed as Taylor, his hand on a white velour shoulder, led Guy Adams out.

Kate shut the apartment door. Ellen made her way through the glass to the balcony. The curtain was a full billow in the gusty Santa Ana winds, and she pushed it aside, inspected her shattered door, the glass-strewn apartment. With a flick of her tennis shoe she broke off a wicked shard of glass protruding from the bottom of the door. She turned to Kate. "My hero," she said.

Kate, weak with laughter, finally had to sit down.

Ellen said, chuckling, "You have a wonderful laugh."

Kate gasped, wiping her eyes, "It feels terrific."

"As long as you've trashed my apartment," Ellen said, "Mother gave me this lamp. She visits here all the time. Would you mind?"

Kate inspected an orange lamp with a mushroom-shaped wicker shade. "It'll be a pleasure," she said, and hurled it to the floor.

"Thank you. Oh God, thank you. You were right about this apartment. It *is* easy to break into."

"I'll get this boarded up till it can be repaired." She wiped her eyes again. "Tell me what went on."

"He told me how it happened and why."

Kate said without a trace of regret, "We'll have a long night ahead, Ellen. We need a very detailed statement from you on tape and in writing. Everything you can remember, everything he—"

"Kate, I know it doesn't make sense to say that somebody could put a knife into somebody else's heart by accident, but that's really what he did."

"No malice? No intent?"

"No more than somebody stepping on a cockroach. What'll happen to him?"

"My guess is involuntary manslaughter. If adequate provocation can be proved. The test will be actual malice—or whether it was the sudden heat of passion. He may have to do a little time."

"Oh God, Kate. What will jail do to him?"

To soothe her, she said lightly, "He'll come through it

all with class. Probably have a Persian rug in his cell."

Ellen smiled; Kate saw that she was drained. And it would be hours before they were through with the events of this night. She paraphrased Ellen's own invitation to her the night before: "I think it would be a good idea if you didn't stay here tonight." She added, "You have a friend who would like to put you up."

Ellen sighed. "I live with someone, as you very well know." She looked at Kate and smiled. "And I've already misbehaved."

"Might as well be hung for a sheep as a lamb."

"In for a penny, in for a dime?"

"Six of one, half a dozen of another."

"That's enough, that's plenty, thank you."

Ellen went into the bedroom, soon reappeared with an overnight bag.

"Ellen," Kate said. "Before we go, before I have to get really busy on this case tonight—well, my situation . . . the way . . . I—" She groped for words, not minding her awkwardness, only wanting the words to be the right ones. "I need time. But I could use . . . a friend."

Ellen said slowly, "You're not the only one who needs time. I've learned a few things and I need to do some thinking, too . . . about a lot of things. I could use a friend, too."

Kate reached for her bag. "Let me take that."

"Not on your life, Detective Delafield. From now on I intend to handle what I can handle. You have a few things to learn about me."

"You'll take some getting used to."

Ellen said thoughtfully, "You know, my mother may just like you. She likes tough and capable people."

Kate said, grinning, "That's nice."

They left the apartment, Ellen's arm through Kate's. "I put a bottle of wine in my bag," Ellen said. "I'm sure we have something to celebrate."

About the Author

Susan Easterly is an award-winning columnist and contributing editor to *Cat Fancy*, a popular national magazine dedicated to cat care for the responsible owner. She has contributed to several books on pet care, including *New Choices in Natural Healing for Dogs* and Cats (Rodale, 1999) and *Petspeak, Share Your Pet's Secret Language!* (Rodale, 2000). She is the author of *The Guide to Handraising Kittens* (TFH, 2000), a 2001 Certificate of Excellence winner from the Cat Writers' Association. She has written hundreds of pet articles in magazines and online, ranging from *Modern Maturity* and *KittensUSA* to Pets.com and the Popular Dogs series.

Easterly holds BA degrees in journalism and English (creative writing). She frequently covers animal welfare issues and could not imaging living without a cat or dog. She lives in Newberg, Oregon, with her family and six pets. Her companion animals sometimes find themselves described in Easterly's articles but they aren't alone. The late Cleveland Amory refers to Easterly and her tongue-in-cheek article about giving a cat a pill in his international best seller, *The Cat Who Came for Christmas*.

Photo Credits

Keith Brofsky: 6, 52, 80

Courtesy of Cape Ann Animal Aid Association, Inc.: 79, 94, 100

Janis Christie / PhotoDisc / PictureQuest: 111

Corbis / PictureQuest: 6, 7, 8, 10, 14, 23, 25, 29, 63, 96, 103, 123

DigitalVision / PictureQuest: 6, 35, 122, 129

Courtesy of Jill Feron: 108

Bill Gallery / Stock, Boston Inc. / PictureQuest: 124

Courtesy of The Glidden Company: 53

Courtesy of Regina Grenier: 50, 59, 65, 77

G.K. & Vikki Hart / PhotoDisc / PictureQuest: 1, 3, 112, 104

Weems S. Hutto: 57, 70, 74

Kent Knudson / PhotoLink / PhotoDisc / PictureQuest: 83

Ryan McVay / PhotoDisc / PictureQuest: 6, 7, 12, 17, 18, 32, 34, 43

Clement Mok / PictureQuest: 26, 55

PhotoDisc: 27, 28, 71, 89, 116, 117, 131

PhotoLink / PhotoDisc / PictureQuest: 114

Tony Ruta / Index Stock Imagery / PictureQuest: 66, 97, 127

Courtesy of Holly Schmidt: 16

Courtesy of Barbara States: 60, 62, 67, 119, 125, 132

Stock South / PictureQuest: 105

Betsy Stowe: 37, 38, 107, 120

Michael W. Thomas / Focus Group / PictureQuest: 45

Sandra L. Toney: 22, 44, 46, 49

pills, how to give, 101
plants, poisonous, 87
play, *see* exercise
Poison Control Center, 87
poisoning, 87–88, 90
prescription diets, 39
preventive care
    comfort, 52–59
    exercise, 44–51
    home checkups, 19–20, 24, 56
    nutrition, 34–42
    priorities for, 30
    veterinary checkups, 20, 22

Q

quiet, importance of, 59, 79

R

recipe, for healthy snack, 40
Reiki, 72, 75
Rescue Remedy, 72
respiratory system, 30. *See also* breathing
Reynolds, Rita, 127

S

safety tips, 58
scratching post, 46
senility, 30
shock, 85
skin
    aging of, 29
    examining of, 19
sleep, 59
snacks, healthy, 39, 40
Snuggle Kitties, 54
spaying, 58
stress
    pain and, 118
    reduction of, 58–59
stretching movements, 44, 46
supplements, 39–40, 42
    in home-prepared diet, 64, 66

T

teeth
    aging of, 28
    care of, 57

common problems of, 98–99
    examining of, 19
    foods to clean, 40
Tellington-Jones, Linda, 75
temperature, of cat
    how to take, 99
    normal, 94
Thermo Kitty Bed, 54
toys
    for comfort, 54
    for play, 48, 49
T Touch, 75–76

U

United States Pharmacopoeia (USP), 42
urinary system, 30–31, 99
urine, normal appearance of, 20
Usui, Dr. Mikao, 72

V

vaccination, 110, 112
veterinarian
    emergencies and, 84
    half-yearly checkup by, 20, 22
    health insurance and, 113
    holistic, 64, 69
    keeping feline history for, 19
Veterinary Pet Insurance (VPI), 113
vision loss, 28, 56
vital signs, normal, 20, 94

W

water, 20, 37–38
weight, *see also* weight loss; weight gain
    comparison chart, 47
    monitoring of, 19–20
weight gain, 38–39
    neutering and, 58
weight loss, 39
    supplements for, 40
    ten steps to, 51

holistic healing, 62,64
    botanical medicine, 68
    chiropractic, 68
    homeopathy, 68
    home-prepared foods, 64, 66
    massage therapy, 68
    medical care, 66, 68–69
    nutraceuticals, 68
    physical therapy, 68
    practitioners of, 69
homeopathy, 68
hospice care, 121
hotlines, for grief counseling, 130
hypertension, 30
hyperthyroidism, 109

I

illness, 104, 106, 109–110. *See also* pain
    cancer, 108, 109
    cardiovascular disease, 106, 108
    chronic, 116, 118, 121
    diabetes mellitus, 108–109
    hyperthyroidism, 109
    inflammatory bowel disease (IBD), 109
    kidney disease, 106
    liver disease, 109–110
    nutrition and, 39
    warning signs of, 20, 31
immune system, 30
incontinence, 99
inflammatory bowel disease (IBD), 109
injections, how to give, 110
injury, *see* first aid
insurance, health, 113
iris atrophy, 28

J

joints, 29, 86

K

kidney disease, 106

L

labels, on pet food, 41–42
leukemia, 112
lifespan, *see* aging process
litter box, 58–59, 99
liver disease, 109–110

M

Manx Meatball recipe, 40
Marano, Nancy, 12
massage, 68, 72, 73
meat
    in home-prepared diet, 64
    need for, 36–37
medication
    administering injections, 110
    administering pills/liquids, 101
    human, poisonous to cats, 88
mourning, by cats, 127
mouth, *see* gums; teeth
muscles, aging of, 29

N

nails, *see* claws
natural medicine
    alternative treatments, 70–79
    holistic healing, 62–69
neutering, 58
new pet, 59, 128
nose, 29
nuclear sclerosis, 28
nutraceuticals, 68
nutrition, 34. *See also* commercial foods
    fresh snacks, 39, 40
    home-prepared foods, 64, 66
    illness and, 39
    importance of good, 36–37
    supplements and, 39–40, 42
    water and, 37–38
    weight and, 38–39

O

obesity, *see* weight gain
Omega fatty acids, 40
"On a Cat Aging" (Gray), 15
osteoarthritis, 98

P

pain
    management of, 118–119, 121
    signs of, 118, 119
permethrin, 88
personality change, 102
Pet Food Institute (PFI), 11
physical therapy, 68

CPR, 88–93

D

death, of cat, 122, 125
    euthanasia, 125
    grief about, 127
    support hotlines, 130
dental hygiene, *see* teeth
detoxifiers, 40
diabetes mellitus, 108–109
diet, *see* nutrition
digestive system, 30
dislocations/fractures, 86

E

Ear TTouch, 76
ears
    aging of, 28
    examining of, 19
elimination, *see* bowel movements; urinary system
emergencies, *see* first aid
endocrine system, 31
euthanasia, 125
exercise, 44, 46, 49
    toys for, 48
    weight loss and, 51
eyes
    aging of, 28
    examining of, 20
    nutrition and, 37

F

Feline Leukemia Virus (FeLV), 112
fever, *see* temperature, of cat
first aid, 82
    basics of, 84
    for bleeding, 85
    for burns, 86
    for choking, 85–86
    CPR, 88–93
    for fractures/dislocations, 86
    for frostbite, 86–87
    kit for, 88, 95
    kit for homeopathic, 68
    for poisoning, 87–88
    safety tips, 90
    for shock, 85
flea products, poisonous, 88
flower essences, 72, 75
flowers, poisonous, 87
foods, *see* commercial foods; nutrition
fractures/dislocations, 86
frostbite, 86–87
fur
    aging of, 29
    clipping of, around wound, 86
    examining of, 19

G

gases, poisonous, 88
gastrointestinal system, 30
glucosamine sulfate, 40
Gray, Alexander, 15
"green" foods, 40
grief, 127, 130
grooming
    by cats, 29
    of cats, 56–58
gums
    care of, 57
    common problems of, 98–99
    examining of, 19

H

hair balls, 56
health insurance, 113
health problems, common, 96–97. *See also* first aid; illness;
    natural medicine; preventive care
    arthritis, 98
    cognitive dysfunction syndrome (CDS), 102
    constipation, 102
    incontinence, 99
    with litter box, 99
    personality change, 102
    with teeth and gums, 98–99
health, signs of good, 128
Healthy Pets 21 Consortium, 11
hearing loss, 28, 56
heart, *see* cardiovascular system
Heimlich maneuver, 86

Index

A

Academy of Feline Medicine (AFM), 20
acetaminophen, 88
acupuncture/acutherapy, 66, 68, 121
aging process
    compared to human, 21
    lifespan and, 11, 16
    physiology of, 29–31
    signs of, 26, 28–29
alternative treatments, 70
    aromatherapy, 76
    flower essences, 72, 75
    massage, 72, 73
    for pain, 121
    Reiki, 72, 75
    TTouch, 75–76
American Association of Feline Practitioners (AAFP), 19, 20, 30
    vaccination guidelines of, 110, 112
American College of Veterinary Nutrition (ACVN), 42
American Holistic Veterinary Medical Association (AHVMA), 62
American Society for the Prevention of Cruelty to Animals (ASPCA), 87, 127
American Veterinary Medical Association (AMVA), 11, 66
Amory, Cleveland, 101
Animal Protection Institute (API), 41, 64
antifreeze, 88
antioxidants, 40, 42
aromatherapy, 76
arthritis, 55, 98
asana, 44
Association of American Feed Control Officials (AAFCO), 36, 40, 41

B

Bach, Dr. Edward, 72
behavior, as indicator of illness, 20, 31
biotin, 40
bleeding, 85
body language, 78
bones, 29
botanical medicine, 68
bowel movements, 57, 102

B (cont.)

breathing, *see also* CPR
    aging and, 30
    normal, 20, 94
breeds, aging of, 19
brushing, *see* grooming
burns, 86

C

Callahan, Sharon, 72, 79
cancer, 108, 109
cardiomyopathies, 108
cardiopulmonary resuscitation (CPR), 88–93
cardiovascular system
    aging of, 30
    diseases of, 106, 108
    nutrition and, 37
carnitine, 40
Cat Sitter video, 54
Cat Who Came for Christmas, The (Amory), 101
cats
    adopting new, 59, 128
    benefits of owning, 11–12
    signs of healthy, 128
central nervous system, 30
chiropractic, 68
choking, 85–86
chondroitin sulfate, 40
chromium, 40
claws
    aging of, 29
    care of, 58
cleaning supplies, poisonous, 88
cleansers, in diet, 40
cognitive dysfunction syndrome (CDS), 102
comfort, 52, 54, 56
    grooming for, 56–58
    neutering and, 58
    stress and, 58–59
commercial foods, 36–38
    label "rules" for, 42
    liquid in, 38
    shopping guide for, 41
constipation, 102
Cornell Feline Health Center, 30
    healthy cat guidelines of, 19–20, 24

Shojai, Amy. *The Purina Encyclopedia* of Cat Care. Ballantine Books, 1998.

Thornton, Kim Campbell and Calloway, Jane. *Cat Treats*. Main Street Books, Doubleday, 1997.

MAGAZINES AND NEWSLETTERS

Cat Fancy
P.O. Box 6050
Mission Viejo, CA 92690
(949) 855-8822

Cat World
Avalon Court, Star Road,
Partridge Green,
West Sussex
RH13 8RY England
(507) 288-2430 (U.S.)
+44 (0) 1403 711511 (U.K.)

Catnip Newsletter
Tufts University School of Veterinary Medicine
P.O. Box 420234
Palm Coast, FL 32142-0234
(800) 829-8893

Cat Watch Newsletter
Cornell University College of Veterinary Medicine
P.O. Box 420235

Palm Coast, FL 32142-0235
(800) 829-8893

laJoie
(quarterly publication dedicated to promoting appreciation for all beings)
laJoie and Company
P.O. Box 145
Batesville, VA 22924
(540) 456-6204

The Whole Cat Journal
P.O. Box 420235
Palm Coast, FL 32142-0235
(800) 829-8893

VIDEOS

Your Cat Wants a Massage by Maryjean Ballner and Champion (Tape Worm Studios, 1999). For more information, call 1-877-Meow-Meow.

Pet Emergency First Aid: Cats by Apogee Communications. Approved by the American Society for the Prevention of Cruelty to Animals (ASPCA). For more information, call 1-888-380-9966, or visit www.apogeevideo.com/cats/

Suggested Reading

BOOKS

Ballner, Maryjean. *Cat Massage: A Whiskers-To-Tail Guide to Your Cat's Ultimate Petting Experience*. St. Martin's Press, 1997.

Callahan, Sharon. *Healing Animals Naturally with Flower Essences and Intuitive Listening*. Sacred Spirit Publishing, 2001.

Commings, Karen. *The Cat Lover's Survival Guide: Helpful Hints for Solving Your Most Pesky Pet Problems*. Barron's, 2001.

Commings, Karen. *Shelter Cats*. Howell Book House, 1998.

Hoffman, Matthew (editor). *PetSpeak: Share Your Pet's Secret Language!* Rodale Inc., 2000.

Mammato, Bobbie, D.V.M, M.P.H. *Pet First Aid*. The American Red Cross and The Humane Society of the United States (HSUS), 1997.

McKay, James E. *Comprehensive Health Care for Cats*. Creative Publishing International, 2001.

Messonnier, Shawn, D.V.M. *Natural Health Bible for Dogs & Cats*. Prima Publishing, 2001.

Moore, Arden. *50 Simple Ways to Pamper Your Cat*. Storey Books, 2000.

Pitcairn, Richard H., D.V.M, and Susan Hubble Pitcairn. *Dr. Pitcairn's Complete Guide to Natural Health for Dogs & Cats*. Rodale Inc., 1995.

Reynolds, Rita. *Blessing the Bridge: What Animals Teach Us About Death, Dying, and Beyond*. NewSage Press, 2001.

Schwartz, Cheryl, D.V.M. *Four Paws Five Directions: A Guide to Chinese Medicine for Cats and Dogs*. Celestial Arts Publishing, 1996.

Siegal, Mordecai (editor). *The Cornell Book of Cats, A Comprehensive and Authoritative Medical Reference for Every Cat and Kitten (2nd edition)*. Villard Books, 1997.

Shojai, Amy. *New Choices in Natural Healing for Dogs and Cats*. Rodale Inc., 1999.

Canadian Cat Association (CCA)
www.cca-afc.com/

Cat Fanciers' Association
www.cfainc.org

Cat Fancy On-Line Feline Library
www.animalnetwork.com/cats
Cat Massage
www.catmassage.com

Cornell Feline Health Center
http://web.vet.cornell.edu/Public/FH
C/FelineHealth.html

directline.com
(pet policy information in the UK)
www.directline.com

Federation Internationale Feline
(FIFE)
(international cat fanciers society
with members in 40 countries)
www.fifeweb.org/

Feline Advisory Bureau
(promotes the health and welfare of
cats; offers more than 50 information sheets on feline diseases, behavior, and breeding)
www.fabcats.org

Feline CRF Information Center
(Chronic Renal Failure)
www.felinecrf.com

insure.com
(pet policy information)
www.insure.com/personal/pets.html

The International Cat Association,
Inc. (TICA)
www.tica.org/

MyPetTribute.com
(mature pet articles, products, and
services)
www.mypettribute.com

Pet Food Institute (PFI)
www.petfoodinstitute.org

Tellington TTouch
www.TellingtonTouch.com
(Check 'Directory of Practitioners'
to find your nearest TTouch practitioner)

Cat Fanciers' Association (CFA)
(largest registry of pedigreed cats)
P.O. Box 1005
Manasquan, NJ 08736
(732) 528-9797

Cornell Feline Health Center
(veterinary medical specialty center
devoted to improving the health and
well-being of cats)
College of Veterinary Medicine
Cornell University, Box 13
Ithaca, NY 14853
(607) 253-3414
Consultation: (800) 548-8937,
M,W,F 9 am to 12 pm, and 2-4 pm
(EST)

Reiki Alliance
(to find a Reiki practitioner in your
area)
P.O. Box 41
Cataldo, ID 83810
(208) 783-4848

Royal Society for the Protection of
Cruelty to Animals (RSPCA)
Animal Centre
Weoley Castle
Birmingham B29 5UP
www.rspca.com

ONLINE RESOURCES

American Animal Hospital
Association (AAHA)
www.healthypet.com

American Association of Feline
Practitioners (AAFP)
www.aafponline.org
American Cat Fanciers Association
(ACFA)
www.acfacat.com/

American College of Veterinary
Nutrition (ACVN)
www.ACVN.org

American Pet Products
Manufacturers Assoc., Inc.
(APPMA)
www.appma.org

American Veterinary Medical
Association (AVMA)
www.avma.org

Anaflora
(flower essence therapy for animals
& animal communication)
www.anaflora.com

Animal Protection Institute (API)
www.api4animals.org

Association for Pet Loss and
Bereavement (APLB)
www.aplb.org

Australian Cat Federation, Inc.
(ACF)
www.acf.asn.au/

Resources

ASSOCIATIONS AND ORGANIZATIONS

American Cat Fanciers Association (ACFA)
P.O. Box 203
Point Lookout, MO 65726
(417) 334-5430

American Association of Feline Practitioners (AAFP)
(professional organization of veterinarians who share an interest in providing excellence in care and treatment of cats; supports American Board of Veterinary Practitioners (ABVP) certification in feline practice)
200 4th Avenue N., Suite 900
Nashville, TN 37219
(615) 259-7788
(800) 204-3514

American Pet Products Manufacturers Assoc., Inc.
255 Glenville Road
Greenwich, CT 06831
(203) 532-0551

American Veterinary Medical Association
1931 North Meacham Road, Suite 100
Schaumburg, IL 60173
(800) 248-AVMA

Animal Protection Institute (API)
P.O. Box 22505
Sacramento, CA 95814
(916) 447-3085

ASPCA Animal Poison Control Center
1717 South Philo Road, Suite 36
Urbana, IL 61802
(888) 4 ANI-HELP
(888)-426-4435

Association for Pet Loss and Bereavement, Inc. (APLB)
(worldwide clearinghouse on pet bereavement)
P.O. Box 106
Brooklyn, NY 11230
(718) 382-0690

Australian Cat Federation, Inc. (ACF)
P.O. Box 3305
Port Adelaide, SA 5015
Australia
08-8449-5880

Canadian Cat Association (CCA)
289 Rutherford Road South, Unit 18
Brampton, Ontario
Canada L6W 3R9
(905) 459-1481

Pet-Loss Support Hotlines

The following pet-loss hotlines can offer support and a listening ear. Best of all, the people on the other end of the line truly understand what you're going through.

University of California, Davis
(800) 565-1526 or (530) 752-4200

University of Florida, School of Veterinary Medicine
(800) 798-6196

Michigan State University
(517) 432-2696

Chicago Veterinary Medical Association
(630) 603-3994

Virginia-Maryland Regional College of Veterinary Medicine
(540) 231-8038

Ohio State University School of Veterinary Medicine
(614) 292-1823

Tufts University School of Veterinary Medicine
(508) 839-7966

Cornell University Pet-Loss Support Hotline
(607) 253-3932

Iowa State University
(888) 478-7574

Colorado State University Veterinary Teaching Hospital
(970) 491-1242

Learn all you can about a new cat
before introducing her into your home.

STARTING OVER

Bringing a new cat into the family can never replace a beloved older cat. Don't rush into adopting a new pet. Take time to heal, and let some time pass. Wait until you feel ready, or until fate once again scratches at your door. Many cat lovers never look for a new cat; the right cat just seems to find them.

But where can you find a new cat or kitten? Shelters, rescue groups (including purebred rescue), reputable breeders, your veterinarian, a friend, responsible pet stores, and perhaps your own doorstep are all viable options. Keep in mind that animal shelters and rescue organizations throughout the country are full of adult cats who long for good homes. And, as you already know, senior cats have plenty to offer.

While it is easy to fall in love with a cat or kitten that needs a home, be patient and remember you owe it to your potential pet to choose wisely. Learn all you can about a new cat before introducing her into your home. If possible, spend time with her in a private room to see how she interacts with you and your family. Whether finding your cat is the result of research or fate, with proper care and a lot of love, the end of your search will be the beginning of a beautiful, long relationship once again.

Of course, cats, like people, aren't perfect. Don't discount a kitten or cat you like for minor medical problems. Fleas, ear mites, and worms may make your cat seem a little less desirable, but such problems are easily solved with professional veterinary help. Visit a veterinarian to treat the cat and get her started on a long, healthy life with you.

Spotting a Healthy Cat

Examine your potential cat or kitten before you sign adoption papers. A healthy kitten has the following qualities:

Eyes are bright and clear

Ears are clean and free of discharge

Nose is clear and free of discharge

Mouth has clean teeth and pink gums (unless naturally pigmented)

Coat is smooth, soft, and clean

Anal area is without discoloration or dried waste

Body is lean but not skinny, no potbelly

UNDERSTANDING GRIEF

The bond we share with our older cats is deep and wonderful. We have been blessed with many years together, sometimes so long that we do not even remember life without our cat. Ironically, this can also set us up for a deeper level of grief when our beloved pet dies or we choose euthanasia to peacefully end our cat's life. An overwhelming sense of sadness, as well as guilt and loneliness, may pervade our days. The feeling that other people, often those who don't have pets, do not understand what we are going through may make us feel isolated.

DO CATS MOURN?

Those who live with more than one cat, as many cat lovers do, are not alone in their grief. Animal behaviorists agree that cats often mourn when a companion animal dies. They report that cats may become depressed, or stop eating and grooming. The cat may wait in a mutually familiar place day after day, waiting for a companion to return. The grieving can be short, or may last for weeks, depending on the cat and relationship.

In 1996, the American Society for the Prevention of Cruelty to Animals (ASPCA) conducted a Companion Animal Mourning Project, surveying the caregivers of 165 pets. The study found that 65 percent of the cats surveyed showed four or more behavioral changes after losing a pet companion. Seventy percent of cats changed the amount of vocalizations—meowing more or less. Nearly 50 percent ate less and in a few extreme cases, the cats starved.

Author Rita Reynolds recalls the following story: "Years ago, we had two cats, Thomas and Benjamin. They were inseparable. One day we came home to find them 'spread out' on the neighbor's lawn. Both cats looked dead, but as we approached we noticed that only Benjamin was gone, apparently struck by a car. Our neighbor had kindly taken his body out of the road. Thomas was lying right next to Benjamin, his front leg draped over his body in a loving embrace. When we removed Benjamin's body to bury it, Thomas followed, watching over him the whole time. He clearly mourned the loss of Benjamin."

DEALING WITH LOSS

When the time comes, take time to say good-bye. Acknowledge your grief, which may equal that associated with the loss of a person. Allow yourself to grieve and keep the following in mind:

- Realize it is okay to grieve in your own way.

- Understand that guilt is a normal by-product of grief. Responsible caretakers often feel the guiltiest.

- Talk to your veterinarian if you have questions, doubts, or worries concerning your cat's death. Many times a vet can give you a concrete explanation and lessen guilt feelings.

- Be honest with your children. Answer their questions and concerns in an age-appropriate way.

- Honor your cat's life in a way that brings you comfort and peace. You may choose to put together a memory book or photo album, or hold a funeral.

- Join a pet-loss support group, or call a pet-loss hotline.

Facing the inevitable loss of a feline family member is a little like savoring the warmth and waning beauty of an Indian summer—time grows short, yet the season remains lovely and precious. Suddenly we pay attention to smells, sounds, and colors. We appreciate what is all around us because it cannot last. It ends too soon.

Most of us outlive our feline companions. Being blessed with the gift of many years with a beloved cat does not make it easier to let go or say good-bye when the time comes. It is a bittersweet time, not always understood by those who haven't been blessed with the enduring company of a cat.

CHOOSING THE TIME

Euthanasia is the act of causing death without pain. It is a humane option for terminally ill cats or for those with a poor quality of life that cannot be improved through medical intervention. Your veterinarian can provide you with the information you need to make an informed decision and may help you plan for the eventual loss of your pet. Veterinary hospitals often set aside a private room where family members can share a pet's last moments, then stay as long as they wish. Many mobile veterinarians conduct euthanasia in the pet's home, which can be comforting, and comfortable, for all concerned.

Many people choose to hold or touch their pet during the euthanasia process. You may want to sing or speak quietly to your cat, reassuring him of your presence and love, and perhaps letting him know that it is okay to go.

CHAPTER TWELVE

Endings and New Beginnings

Elder cats give us the gift of time when no one else has any to spare. Like elder humans, they touch us with their fragility, wisdom, sweetness, and comforting warmth. They curl up close by to be near us. They lay on us when we feel sick or depressed. Old cats ask for little in return, perhaps craving only a little more affection as the years pass. By example, they share basic lessons about life and death—that it is okay to slow down and smell the catnip, that we have no choice but to grow old, too. Older cats teach us about inner listening and watching. They spend more hours sleeping. Some believe they begin their journey with small trips to the other side when they sleep. In the end, senior cats teach us patience and courage, how to let go gracefully and, finally, how to age and die with grace.

where, for instance, degenerative joint problems or arthritis create chronic distress, medications may be prescribed to control or minimize pain.

You may also want to explore alternative therapies for their potential role in treating chronic pain. Acupuncture, for example, has been shown to increase brain endorphin levels and reduce discomfort. In addition, you can take steps to help your older cat deal with chronic pain—or recover from surgery—at home by doing the following:

- Provide tender loving care

- Minimize physical stress—make litter box, food, and water bowls easily accessible

- Provide easy access to favorite perching areas

- Yield to a hurting cat's natural tendency to hide—provide her with a warm, dimly lit place to sleep comfortably.

HOSPICE CARE FOR CATS

A new, welcome idea for cats and their guardians, hospice care for animals—similar to its counterpart for people—encompasses a mix of practical and emotional help supported by love and compassion. No cat should die alone, in pain, or with strangers. Proponents of hospice care say that the passage through death is sacred and in the end, as wonderful as life. While death and dying can be difficult and emotionally trying, especially for pet guardians who must make a life-or-death decision concerning their animal companion, ultimately it should be viewed as a natural part of life.

Providing hospice care for cats often means simply being there for someone who faces the loss of a beloved pet companion. Don't hesitate to ask others for help as well. People are often relieved to have a specific answer to the statement, "Please let me know if there is anything I can do to help." Here are a few suggestions.

Lend a hand. Daily activities can be overwhelming when someone is faced with caring for a chronically ill or dying pet. Assist with simple tasks, like visiting a friend's home to bring a hot cup of tea, coffee, or lunch. Offer to run errands so the pet guardian can stay home with her cat.

Listen. Sit quietly and let the other person share memories. Offer advice only when asked.

Offer moral support. Volunteer to accompany someone to the veterinarian's office. Even better, offer to drive.

Provide a referral. Offer the phone number of a pet-loss hotline or local support group.

Finally, consider these words from a multi-pet guardian who cares for her chronically ill cat, Cleo. "Cleo has lymphosarcoma and was supposed to be dead a year and a half ago. Thinking this event would happen at any time, I have gone above and beyond in telling her how special she is, how loved, and what a magnificent being she is. I make sure everything is as perfect for her as possible—fresh bedding every day, a good and tasty selection of food, spending extra time with her, and playing music for her—often a Gregorian chant. I know her disease could internalize at any time, so I make sure every minute is quality time for her. I don't dwell on her disease in my mind or with her. I just support her living as best I can."

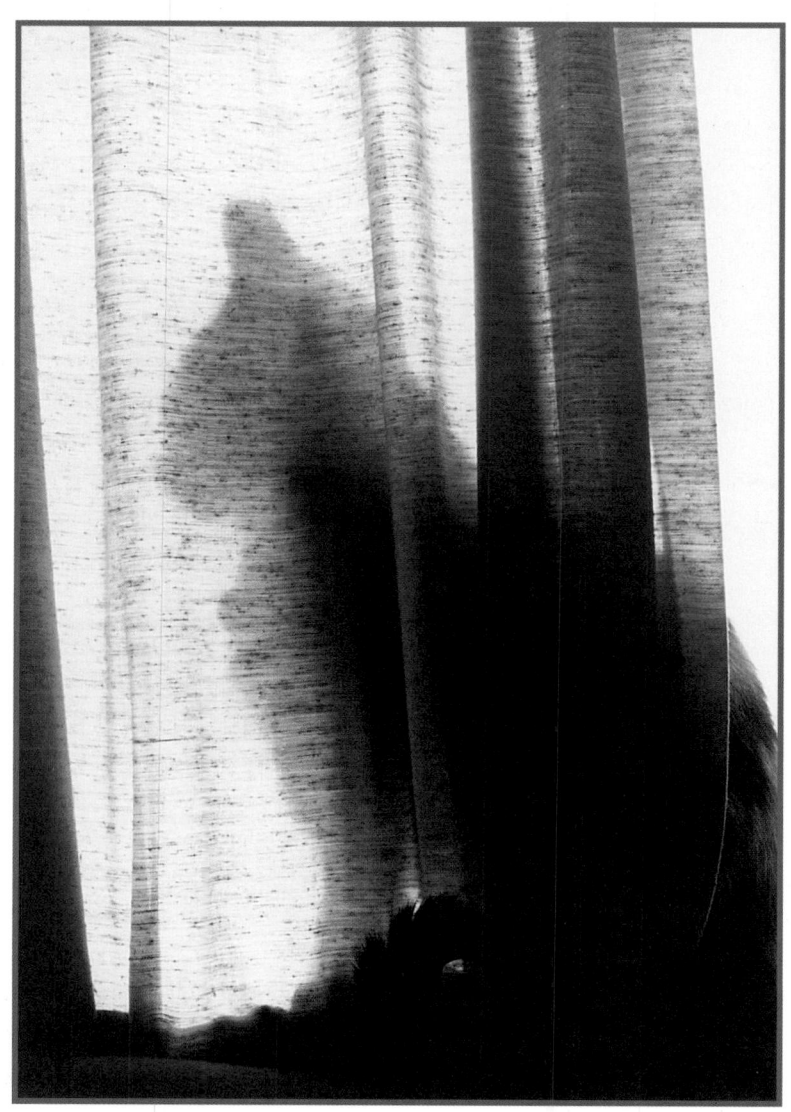

some conditions are more likely to cause cats pain than others. Bone cancers, for example, can be very painful, while blood-formed cancers such as leukemia or lymphoma have little pain associated with them. Acute pain is associated with disease processes such as pancreatitis, gastrointestinal disease, or feline lower urinary tract disease, as well as surgery and trauma. Chronic pain, on the other hand, can stem from musculoskeletal disease, various forms of cancer, and dental problems.

professionals depend on their clients to notice a problem exists and then to do something about it.

Veterinary experts say recognizing pain in cats can be difficult, and each case varies. Unfortunately, the changes caused by pain are often subtle and appear slowly. We may mistakenly attribute these changes to a natural part of aging. Moreover,

To deal with your older cat's pain, you and your veterinarian must team up to identify the source of the discomfort and solve the problem. Your cat's overall health must be evaluated before an intelligent decision on managing pain is reached. In some cases a surgical procedure or treatment can permanently resolve the problem. In others,

Cats feel pain in much the same way that we do.
The difference lies in how each species responds to pain.

How Can I Tell if My Cat Is in Pain?

The following signs can signal discomfort:

- Hiding
- Reduced activity, plays less
- Failure to use a litter box
- Obsessive grooming
- Lameness or reluctance to use a limb
- Lethargy
- Loss of appetite, failure to eat
- Drooling, panting
- Restless, agitated
- Flinches or trembles
- Becomes vocal or cries, may hiss or strike out
- Suddenly irritable or aggressive

Caring for a chronically ill cat can be a struggle and a gift, both physically and emotionally. You may not feel up to the challenge of caring for a seriously ill cat, yet it's important to realize that you are the most qualified person to do so. The loving connection established long ago often grows as life winds down. We realize, more than ever, how precious each moment has become.

PAIN MANAGEMENT

Cats are wired similarly to humans from both a physiological and neuroanatomical standpoint. This means cats feel pain in much the same way that we do. The difference lies in how each species responds to pain. We communicate our discomfort to others, seeking help and relief quickly. Cats, on the other hand, take a different approach. They prefer to hide when they hurt, a carryover from behaviors developed to protect themselves from predators.

THE FOURTH VITAL SIGN

In its simplest terms, pain is stress. Chronic or severe pain significantly stresses the physical body and affects emotions. Pain can impair wound healing and slow recovery. For people and cats, stress can lead to metabolic changes that effect the immune system, which, in turn, can lead to potentially life-threatening complications. Pain can, in a sense, kill a cat.

A cat may display a poker face when it comes to hiding pain, but the understanding of human pain management has grown over the past decade, and veterinary medicine has followed close behind. Veterinarians on the cutting edge of pain management now rate pain as the fourth vital sign in animals, along with temperature, respiration, and blood pressure.

For veterinarians, whose patients do not walk into a hospital or clinic on their own, the tough part is not in understanding the nature of pain, but rather identifying pets that experience it. Veterinary

Coping with Chronic Disease and Pain

Most of us do not think about caring for an ill or dying pet when we bring a young cat into our heart and home. We may not stop to consider that the adoption contract, written or unwritten, is a lifelong commitment to see our cats through illness, injury, or simply old age. Thanks to the bond we share with our cats, though, most of us make this commitment willingly, no matter how hard it may prove to be. Older cats, like other valued family members, deserve nothing less than the best care we can provide during the last stages of their lives.

*Older cats teach us patience and courage,
how to let go gracefully and, finally,
how to heal and begin again.*

THE LAST DANCE

Health Insurance for Cats?

Veterinary care is fresh on the heels of human medicine in terms of technology and development. While veterinary costs haven't escalated as rapidly as have human health-care costs, a chronic feline health problem or disease can quickly drain a wallet. No one wants to be forced to choose between a beloved cat's life and money.

To alleviate the shortfall, a growing number of cat owners carry pet health insurance, similar to the health insurance they use to help shoulder their own medical bills. Several companies now offer some form of pet health insurance. Veterinary Pet Insurance (VPI) in Anaheim, California, was the first, pioneering the concept in 1980 with the support of 750 independent veterinarians. Today VPI policies are licensed in every state and the District of Columbia. The company offers several plans covering everything from cancer treatments to homeopathic medicine, vaccinations, and other routine care. Endorsed by the American Humane Association, VPI has issued more than one million policies and enjoys an 82 percent renewal rate.

VPI recently broadened its coverage to provide additional benefits for cats. Pet owners in 41 states can choose the VPI Superior and VPI Standard Plans featuring lower rates for cats and increased surgical benefits, along with enhanced benefits for specialized diagnostics, such as MRIs and CAT scans. Annual benefit maximums range from $9,000 to $14,000, with monthly rates beginning under $10 for cats.

For more information, call (800) USA-PETS (800-872-7387) or visit www.petinsurance.com

seniors can be vaccinated in the same manner as younger cats.

After receiving the initial vaccination series, and a booster one year after the primary vaccination, healthy senior cats should be revaccinated no more frequently than every three years for the following:

FPV: Feline parvovirus, cause of feline pan-leukopenia

FHV: Feline herpesvirus-1, cause of feline viral rhinotracheitis

FCV: Feline calicivirus

RV: Rabies virus

Several other vaccines exist and are generally considered optional, depending on factors such as age, risk, and the likelihood of infection or disease if exposed. For example, the Feline Leukemia Virus (FeLV) infects domestic cats throughout the world, but outdoor cats that come in contact with other infected cats are particularly vulnerable. The FeLV vaccination, however, is not recommended for older indoor cats with a minimal risk of exposure to FeLV-infected cats.

Giving Injections

Most cat caretakers are a little nervous about giving a cat an injection at first. Don't worry! With practice, you'll soon be able to fill a syringe and inject your cat like a pro. You may be called upon to give injections subcutaneously (meaning under the skin) regularly if your cat is diagnosed with diabetes (insulin injections) or kidney disease (fluid injections under the skin). Your veterinarian will explain the process and help you get started. She will explain that subcutaneous injections are usually placed under the loose skin at the back of the neck or between your cat's shoulder blades. Practice until you feel confident you can handle the procedure. You will soon develop a routine that is comfortable for both of you. Extending your cat's life and maintaining her quality of life are worth overcoming any qualms about giving injections. Here are a few tips.

- Choose a consistent, comfortable room or area in which to give injections.

- Don't rush. Take time to sit quietly and bond with your cat.

- Furnish a healthy treat or a meal after treatment. This will help your cat associate the injection with something pleasant.

Treatment: Immediate veterinary care is needed; force-feeding, then special diet to reduce the need for liver function.

SHOULD I VACCINATE MY OLDER CAT?

Deadly feline viruses can strike cats at any age, and vaccines play a crucial role in controlling these infectious diseases. Immune function declines as cats age, which, in turn, increases a senior cat's vulnerability to infection. Older cats, for example, run a higher risk of developing respiratory disease, which vaccinations can help protect against. Regular booster vaccinations are still recommended for healthy older cats, but vaccination protocols have changed.

Interest in vaccine-related issues has increased, thanks in large part to safety concerns (such as a chance of developing a life-threatening sarcoma—a type of tumor—at the vaccination site) and questions regarding the span of immunity vaccinations provide. For example, one anti-immunization argument reasons that people do not need yearly vaccinations, so why do pets require annual booster shots? These issues will continue to be addressed by national veterinary organizations, scientists, and vaccine manufacturers. According to the latest American Association of Feline Practitioners/Academy of Feline Medicine (AAFP/AFM) Feline Vaccination Guidelines, vaccinations for older cats should be administered based on individual risk assessment and in compliance with local laws. In general, debilitated or ill cats should not be vaccinated, while healthy

produces insulin; diabetes mellitus occurs when the pancreas fails to produce enough of it. Diabetes mellitus is most commonly seen in senior cats. Unspayed female cats are at increased risk, as are overweight cats of both sexes.

Signs: Increasingly thirsty and hungry but losing weight, increased urination.

Treatment: Stabilize with fluids and medications. Oral medications for a lucky few, daily insulin shots for most, along with dietary management.

Hyperthyroidism
A common disease of the feline endocrine system in older cats, hyperthyroidism is associated with overactivity of the thyroid gland. Hyperthyroidism may mask underlying renal, or kidney, disease.

Signs: Increased drinking and ravenous appetite, combined with weight loss, vomiting, diarrhea, hyperactivity, hypertension, and rapid nail growth.

Treatment: Lifelong medication, radioactive iodine therapy (works by destroying the thyroid gland), or surgery (removes affected thyroid lobes).

Inflammatory Bowel Disease (IBD)
A controllable disorder (especially if caught early) of the small intestine, IBD commonly occurs in older cats. Your veterinarian must diagnose this condition after ruling out other causes of gastrointestinal disease.

Signs: Anorexia or weight loss, frequent vomiting, and diarrhea.

The Veterinary Cancer Society's Common Signs of Cancer in Animals

Early cancer detection is critical, because screening tests for specific types of cancer are not yet available in veterinary medicine. Do not attribute the following warning signs to old age.

1. Abnormal swellings that persist or continue to grow
2. Sores that do not heal
3. Weight loss
4. Loss of appetite
5. Bleeding or discharge from any body opening
6. Offensive odor
7. Difficulty eating or swallowing
8. Hesitation to exercise or loss of stamina
9. Persistent lameness or stiffness
10. Difficulty breathing, urinating, or defecating

Treatment: Dietary management, intestinal antibiotic, or anti-inflammatory drug.

Liver Disease
Liver disease refers to any condition that interferes with the liver's normal function. This includes hepatic lipidosis, a common and potentially fatal liver ailment primarily affecting overweight cats.

Signs: Refusal to eat, increased drinking and urination, jaundice, abdominal fluid build-up, vomiting, diarrhea, depression, and lethargy.

makes the system work harder, which can cause heart muscles to weaken. Congestive heart failure is the result, occurring when one of the heart's lower ventricles, or chambers, can no longer do its job.

Cardiomyopathy, a disease of the heart muscle, is the most common heart problem in cats. Hypertrophic cardiomyopathy (HCM), the most frequently diagnosed version, causes portions of the heart to thicken and pump blood less efficiently. While HCM prevents the heart from filling with blood adequately, dilated cardiomyopathy (DCM) affects the heart muscle's ability to contract and thus pump blood. In DCM, the muscle walls thin and the heart enlarges. The rarer restrictive cardiomyopathy (RCM), also known as intergrade or intermediate cardiomyopathy, interferes with both the filling and pumping of the heart.

Signs: Heart and circulatory disorders include labored breathing or panting, lethargy, loss of appetite, rear leg pain or paralysis.

Treatment: Diuretics to remove excess fluid, lifelong drug therapy, dietary management, and possible taurine supplements.

Cancer

Cancer, or neoplasia, is a term covering a group of diseases. Cancer develops when abnormal, or uncontrolled, cell growth replaces normal tissues and disrupts body functions. The growths, or tumors, may be benign or malignant. The care of feline cancer patients is becoming a major component of more veterinary practices as the feline pet population increases and grays. Advances in feline oncology have increased survival times, improved treatment response, and prolonged disease-free intervals. Many cats with cancer can be cured or rendered free of disease for significant periods of time.

Signs: See sidebar on next page.

Treatment: Surgery (to remove tumor), chemotherapy, and radiation therapy. Magnetic resonance imaging (MRI) improves diagnosis. Immunoaugmentive therapy is used in some cases.

Diabetes Mellitus

Diabetes mellitus is a disease in which a cat's body cannot control her blood sugar levels. A common disorder of the endocrine system, diabetes mellitus is caused by a lack of insulin, a hormone that stimulates the movement of glucose (sugar) from the blood into cells. The pancreas

*Early recognition, combined with better diagnostic aids
and treatments, are helping more cats live longer and better.*

Fortunately, cats diagnosed with a serious disease have more treatment options than ever before. Today, new technology is available at the touch of a keyboard to help veterinarians gather expert advice and diagnose illnesses. Despite technical advances, the diagnosis of a serious disease can seem frightening and final. It's important to keep in mind that early recognition, combined with better diagnostic aids and treatments, are helping more cats live longer and better. Thus a diagnosis of cancer is no longer a death sentence but a health challenge that may be contained, treated and, in many cases, cured.

Note: Symptoms of feline disease often have common denominators such as appetite loss, increased thirst, or frequent urination. Do not try to diagnose a health problem yourself. Consult a veterinarian if you suspect your older cat may be ill.

THE BIG FOUR

The four leading causes of death in older cats are renal failure (kidney disease), cardiovascular disease, cancer, and diabetes mellitus. The best defense remains a good offense, however, so let's take a closer look at illnesses your cat may develop.

Kidney Disease

Your cat's kidneys filter waste products from his body; regulate electrolytes; produce a hormone,

erythropoietin, which helps stimulate bone marrow to produce red blood cells; and produce renin, an enzyme that helps regulate blood pressure. Also known as chronic renal failure (CRF) and chronic renal insufficiency (CRI), kidney disease is a progressive and irreversible deterioration of kidney function. Early signs are subtle and easily missed until roughly 70 percent of the kidney no longer functions.

Signs: Increasingly thirsty, excessive urination, loss of appetite, nausea and vomiting, weight loss, decrease in activity, anemia, hypertension, poor hair coat, emaciation, and dehydration.

Cause: Typically age-related, with genetics, environment, and disease as contributing factors.

Treatment: No cure, but manageable with extra fluids, medications, and special diets. With a strong commitment from caregivers, cats with CRF can live for months to years with a decent quality of life. Kidney transplants are an accepted and relatively safe treatment. The success rate for candidates in good condition ranges between 80 and 90 percent.

Cardiovascular Disease

The cardiovascular system is, pun intended, the heart of your cat's body. The ability of the heart to pump blood efficiently decreases with age. This process

CHAPTER TEN

Illnesses Your Older Cat May Develop

Aging increases the odds of contracting a debilitating illness or disease in both people and cats. Our respective bodies simply begin to wear down with time. Because cats age more quickly than we do, it's logical to deduce that feline health problems can develop faster as well. Of course, genetics, environment, nutrition, and preventive care—or the lack of these—all play a part in the way your cat ages. While many cats stay healthy throughout their lives, others will require the help of multiple disciplines—including internal medicine, clinical pathology, surgery, radiology, and nutrition—to maintain health and a good quality of life.

CONSTIPATION

Constipation, though not likely to be life-threatening at first onset, should not be left untreated. This condition can signal a serious underlying, or developing, medical problem. Causes may involve weak muscles, lack of exercise, stress, and poor diet.

Signs: Passes dry stools, crouches and strains while attempting to defecate. May also express soft stools with blood or mucus, and lose appetite and weight.

Treatment: Laxatives and a change to a higher-fiber diet often solve the problem. Surgery may be needed to remove internal blockage. Fluids may be given for dehydration.

What you can do: Seek veterinary help early. Follow veterinary recommendations; in many cases, this means a diet high in fiber and feeding an overall balanced diet.

PERSONALITY CHANGES

Older cats sleep more. They may become less socially inclined and crankier. Sudden or unusual behavior changes, however, are a sign that something is wrong and should be brought to the attention of your veterinarian. For example, a cat that suddenly becomes aggressive may be suffering from a painful dental problem. Other changes may include depression, agitation, lethargy, and Alzheimer's disease-like behavior.

CDS

CDS, or cognitive dysfunction syndrome, is common in elderly cats. A progressive, age-related disease, CDS is caused by physical and chemical changes that affect brain function. Signs of CDS include altered sleep cycles, increased vocalization, confusion, aimless wandering, excessive grooming, aggression, and inappropriate elimination. In addition, a phobia, such as a sudden fear of the dark, may appear. The clinical signs relate to senility or impaired mental function. CDS symptoms can be managed by drug treatments, exercise, and oxygen therapy after other health conditions or diseases are ruled out. A desensitization program can help you deal with your cat's fears. Your veterinarian can help you devise the right course of action. In addition, treat your cat with compassion, understanding, and loving care.

How to Give Your Cat a Pill or Liquid Medications

There's a reason so many stories describe the art and misadventures of giving a cat a pill. Cleveland Amory devoted a whole chapter to the subject of attempting to pill his cat Polar Bear in his international best-seller, *The Cat Who Came for Christmas*. Indeed, cats often seem to be masters at resisting pills. Some go so far as to spit a pill out as soon as the pill-giver smugly leaves the room.

The older your cat becomes, the greater your chance of medicating him grows. While this often comes under the grin-and-bear-it category, pilling your cat doesn't have to be an exercise in frustration or futility. You just need to figure out what works best for both of you. Here are some options.

- Wrap your cat firmly in a towel with only her head exposed. Kneel on the floor, position your cat between your knees, and hold your cat's head away from you, or have someone else hold your cat while you dispense the pill. With the pill in one hand, use the fingers of your other hand to gently pry open your cat's jaws (try the thumb and first finger). Put the pill as far back on the tongue as you can manage, then close her mouth. Keep it closed while you stroke her throat to make sure the medicine goes down. Praise her or give her a treat.

- Package the pill in something that entices your cat to eat it without a second thought. Try a soft cat treat, piece of meat, or cream cheese. Check with your veterinarian for an appropriate food choice for your cat.

- A pill gun, available from veterinarians, can make the pill-popping process easier.

- Turn your pill into liquid medicine by crushing it and mixing with water. To give your cat this solution, or any other liquid medications, fill a medicine dropper or dosing syringe with the correct amount. Restrain your cat as outlined above. Open his mouth, and put the end of the dropper into the corner of the mouth, or cheek pouch. Close the mouth around the dropper and quickly empty the contents. Your cat's natural swallowing reflex will take over.

chew on one side, drop food, or display chattering teeth. Advanced dental problems include mouth ulcers and missing crowns on teeth.

Treatment: Veterinary care includes thorough cleaning under general anesthesia. Decayed or broken teeth are usually extracted, and antibiotics may be given to fight infection.

What you can do: Ask your veterinarian or a veterinary nutritionist whether dietary changes are in order. Seek regular dental check-ups and teeth cleaning, preferably twice a year (See Dental Care, page 57).

LITTER BOX BLUES

An older cat usually has a good reason for urinating or defecating outside the litter box, though humans don't tend to agree. Nothing erodes the relationship between cat and human faster than this problem. A visit to the veterinarian is imperative to rule out possible medical problems, such as cystitis, lower urinary tract disease, diabetes, or kidney disease, and to determine the cause of the problem. If diagnostic testing rules out a medical cause, a behavioral investigation is the next step.

INCONTINENCE

Older cats gradually lose muscle tone, a common cause of incontinence. Painful arthritis may deter an elderly cat from getting up and using the litter box.

Signs: Has frequent accidents, dribbles urine, and defecates while resting or sleeping.

Treatment: Veterinary-approved drugs. Be sure to ask about possible side effects.

What you can do: Seek veterinary help early. Ensure litter box is nearby, clean, and easily accessible.

How to Take Your Cat's Temperature

A fever is part of the body's natural healing process, but it may also indicate a serious health problem. Fever is especially worrisome in fragile older cats that dehydrate easily. A cat's normal temperature ranges from 100°F to 102.5°F.

To take your cat's temperature, lubricate the end of a rectal thermometer with K-Y Jelly and, if possible, ask a family member or friend to help hold your cat steady. Lift your cat's tail and gently rotate the thermometer into the rectum no more than 1 inch deep for one to two minutes. (An electronic thermometer can perform the job quicker, emitting beeps when your mission is accomplished and providing a clear digital reading.) A fever of 103.5°F or higher warrants a call to your veterinarian right away.

*Early intervention can often
enhance and extend the lives of our cats.*

While aging is not a disease, age-related problems are inevitable and generally irreversible. The good news is that early intervention can often enhance and extend the lives of our cats. This new direction in senior care emphasizes healthful living as pets age, not simply the treatment of old, debilitated patients. This means more frequent veterinary exams, diagnostic testing, nutrition counseling, and, most likely, an increased need for age-related medicines. The veterinarian can do none of the above, however, without your participation.

Just as the guardian of a new kitten gradually learns how to properly care for a cat, it's important to pay attention to your cat's needs as she ages. You will need to regularly work with your vet to deal with common health issues that crop up over the years. Catch them early and, above all, do not chalk up the following health and behavior problems to old age. Ignoring them can cause your cat pain and severely reduce your cat's quality of life. The ultimate "solutions" are in your veterinarian's hands, with your help. Working together is the key to your senior cat's health.

ARTHRITIS

Arthritis, defined as the inflammation of the joint, is not nearly as common in cats as in dogs, but it is seen most often in older cats. Osteoarthritis, or degenerative arthritis, can affect one or more joints, making it painful for a cat to move or walk. Traumatic arthritis occurs as result of injury to

joints—a cat who has been struck by a car is a prime candidate for this type of arthritis.

Signs: Legs appear stiff and joints may be warm to the touch. Cats may display reduced physical activity, lameness, difficulty rising and walking, and changes in posture.

Treatment: Veterinary-approved medications are given to reduce inflammation and relieve pain. Surgery may be advised in some cases.

What you can do: Pay attention to early signs of arthritis and seek veterinary help promptly. If your cat is willing, gentle massage may relieve pain and loosen tight muscles (see Massage on page 72). Wrap a towel around a hot-water bottle and apply heat to painful areas. Watch your cat's weight to relieve stress and strain on affected joints. Caution: Do not treat an arthritic cat with human pain relievers of any kind; they can be harmful or fatal to cats.

DENTAL DIFFICULTIES

Dental disorders, or periodontal disease, affect teeth and gums. If ignored, dental problems can eventually spread infection, speed disease, and damage major organs throughout a cat's body.

Signs: Drooling, bad breath, inflamed gums, loss of appetite and drop in weight, and tartar on teeth. Cats with painful mouth conditions may

CHAPTER NINE

Solutions for Common Health and Behavior Problems

More veterinarians now incorporate senior care into their practices. A mix of preventive and therapeutic strategies, senior care is based on the recognition that the needs of older pets are different than those of younger animals and should be addressed—and treated—accordingly. Senior care for cats broadens the medical, nutritional, and overall wellness programs established during the early years of their lives.

First-Aid Kit

Essential Items

Nonstick sterile gauze pads (various sizes)

Gauze elastic tape or adhesive tape to secure bandage

3% hydrogen peroxide (to clean wounds)

Antibacterial ointment

Cotton swabs, cotton balls

Rubbing alcohol

Rectal thermometer

K-Y Jelly (to lubricate thermometer)

Blunt-tipped scissors

Tweezers

Eyedropper

Plastic syringe for liquid medications

Useful to Have on Hand

Nylon cat muzzle, towel (for restraint)

Hairball remedy (paraffin oil)

Kaopectate (for diarrhea—ask your veterinarian for correct dosage)

Styptic pencil or powder (for bleeding claws); —note: It stings!

Activated charcoal capsules (for poisonings; check with vet before using,
    as its use may be contraindicated)

Antihistamine cream/lotion (for insect stings—avoid products containing
    local anesthetics, which can cause methemoglobinemia, a blood disorder, in cats)

Pack the items in a small toolbox or other easy-to-carry storage container, and tape the telephone numbers of your veterinarian, emergency pet clinic, and poison control center to the top of the box. If you aren't sure how to use every item in your first-aid kit, ask your veterinarian for instructions before an emergency strikes.

Extra Rx Tips for Cats

Consult a veterinarian before giving any topical or oral medications to your cat

Induce vomiting only with veterinary approval

Avoid using syrup of ipecac unless your veterinarian specifies its use—
    an excessive amount or repeated doses may have a cardio-toxic effect on cats

Normal Feline Vital Signs
(General Guidelines)

Temperature: 100° F to 102.5°F
Breathing rate (respiration):
20 to 30 per minute
Pulse: 160 to 240 beats per minute

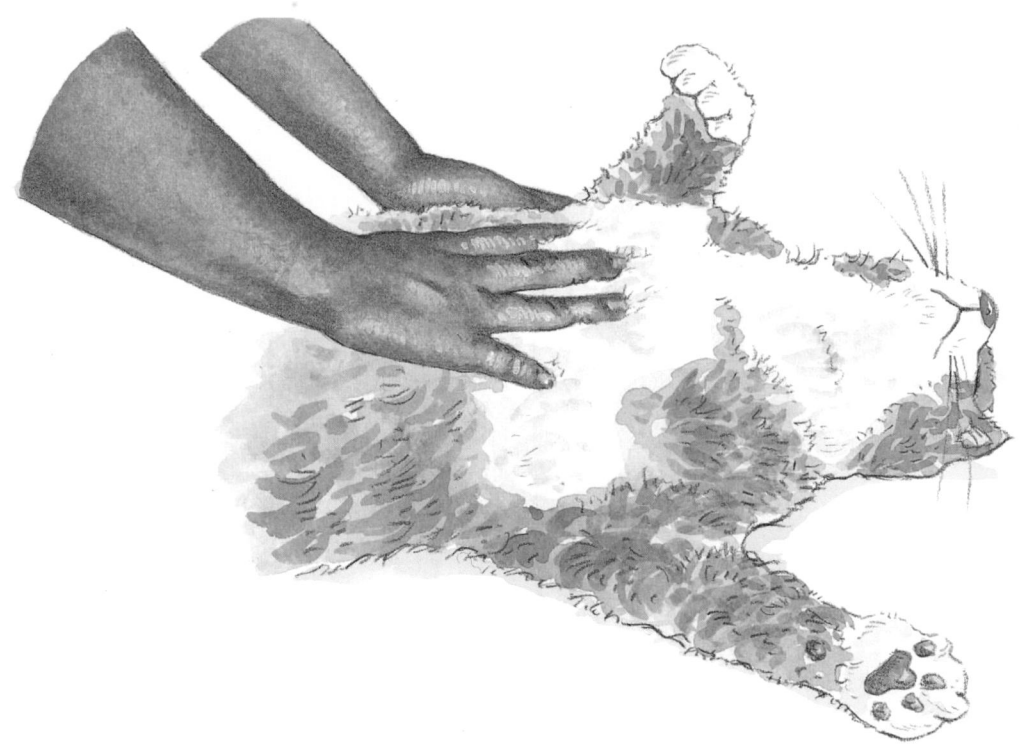

3. Continue this rhythmic sequence until your cat's heart begins to beat or until a veterinarian can be reached. Be sure to check for a pulse frequently while performing CPR.

Last Word on CPR

Keep the following in mind: You don't have to be an expert, and you don't have to perform CPR flawlessly to save your cat's life. Your cat will not die because you fumble through CPR. A cat without a pulse or respiration will surely die, however, if no attempt is made to save his life. One veterinarian in emergency practice for a decade and a half found that numerous caretakers were able to revive their pets by gently blowing into the nose and massaging the chest. Many weren't well versed in how to use CPR. The point is to give your cat a small chance to survive in a situation that would otherwise prove fatal. Enroll in a pet first-aid class to learn more and gain some hands-on experience (and confidence) in pet CPR. To find a class in your area, contact your local humane society or Red Cross chapter.

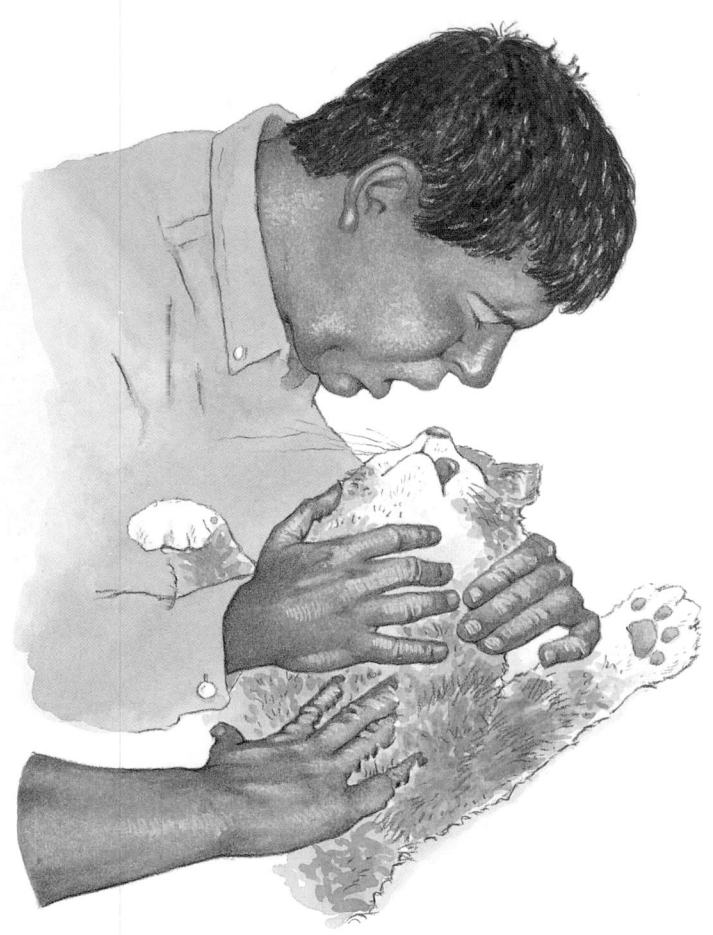

2. Squeeze your hand smoothly (gently but
   firmly) approximately once every second.
   Repeat chest compressions five times, then
   follow with one breath of artificial respiration. (If someone is available to help, divide
   the job.)

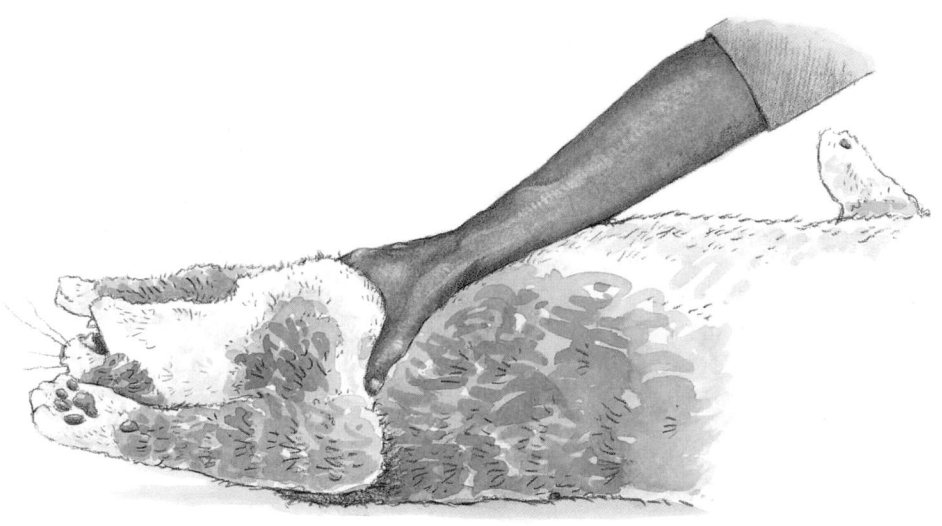

mouth closed and her tongue pulled forward. Place your mouth over her nose and gently but consistently blow into your cat's nose for about three seconds. Her chest will expand; pause to release the air. Repeat once every four to five seconds, or up to fifteen times per minute, until your cat breathes on her own. Veterinary care is a must.

C for circulation: The beating of your cat's heart can be felt by placing your hand (or ear) on the left side of her chest above and behind her elbow, or by pressing arteries in the neck or inside upper hind leg. No pulse and an absence of breathing equal cardiac arrest, and you'll need to begin CPR immediately.

CPR Steps
1. Place the palm of your hand on the cat's chest; rest your thumb on his left side at the point of his elbow while your fingers lay flat on your cat's right side for compression. (See illustration above.)

Pet Safety Kit

Be prepared! Keep a pet safety kit on hand for poisoning emergencies. Place the kit in an easy-to-remember, accessible area and include the following items:

- A fresh bottle of 3% hydrogen peroxide (USP)
- Can of soft cat food
- Turkey baster, bulb syringe, or large medicine syringe
- Saline eye solution to flush out eye contaminants
- Artificial tear gel to lubricate eyes after flushing
- Mild, grease-cutting dishwashing liquid to bathe cat after skin contamination
- Rubber gloves to prevent exposure to skin contaminants
- Forceps to remove stingers
- Restraint (large towel or folded blanket) to keep a cat from hurting you while it is excited or in pain
- Pet carrier to help carry your cat to your veterinarian

—Reprinted with permission,
ASPCA Animal Poison Control Center

three to four minutes exists before permanent brain damage occurs.

Caution: Do not attempt artificial respiration or cardiopulmonary resuscitation (CPR)—a lifesaving procedure combining artificial breathing and chest compressions—on a cat who s conscious and breathing! CPR is a stopgap method to keep your cat alive until her heart and lungs can resume their work; perform CPR only when a cat's heart and breathing have stopped.

What to do: To breathe life back into your cat, think ABC—

- A for Airway

- B for Breathing

- C for Circulation

Is your cat breathing? To decide if your cat requires artificial respiration, check for airflow near the mouth and nose, and observe whether your cat's chest rises and falls. A blue tongue indicates a lack of oxygen. If your cat is not breathing, place her on her side on a flat surface and remove her collar.

A for airway: Remove any obstruction from the mouth or throat (see Choking, page 85). Open her mouth and gently pull her tongue forward to avoid blocking the airway. Gently close her mouth, and pull her head and neck forward. To express old air from her body, gently place hands on ribs and push down quickly. Release. Your cat's elastic recoil mechanism will refill her lungs with air. Repeat approximately once every five seconds.
If the recoil mechanism fails to work (due, for example, to a chest wound or collapsed lungs), you will need to blow air into your cat's lungs.

B for breathing: To perform artificial respiration, support your cat's head in your hands, keeping her

Flea products

Never use insecticides on elderly or debilitated cats without first consulting your veterinarian. Use a vet-recommended flea product, or consider using a nontoxic, hands-on method, such as removing fleas with a flea comb and then submerging the fleas in a small container of soapy water (a time-consuming but much safer alternative). Always read the label before using any product on your cat. A label that reads "do not use on cats" should never be ignored; even a small amount of some canine flea products can be fatal to cats. For example, cats are highly sensitive to permethrin, a common ingredient in flea-control products, and can experience tremors and seizures if only a few drops are applied. (Note: Some products specifically labeled for use on cats do contain tiny amounts of permethrin, usually less than 0.1%. When used according to label instructions, however, these products can be used safely on cats.)

Medicine mix-ups

Caretakers with older cats on prescribed medications sometimes give human medications to their cat unintentionally—a common occurrence in the morning when sleepy people reach for the wrong container. Even something as ordinary as a pain reliever containing acetaminophen (found in Tylenol and similar products) can kill a cat. Keep your medications separate from your cat's pills, and put kitty stickers or bright, colored stickers on the medications to avoid confusion.

Dangerous foods

Don't let your cat ingest moldy or spoiled foods, onions, onion powder, alcoholic beverages, or chocolate.

Auto/garage items

As little as one teaspoon of sweet-tasting conventional antifreeze (which contains ethylene glycol) can be deadly to cats. For a safer alternative, choose the less-toxic version of antifreeze containing propylene glycol.

Household cleaning supplies

Watch out for bleach, ammonia, cleaning fluids, disinfectants, and drain cleaners. While your older cat isn't likely to drink such things, she may haphazardly walk through a product in use, and ingest it as she licks the substance off her paws or fur. Keep the toilet lid on as well, especially if the water is chemically treated.

Gases

Inhaling gases or fumes from ammonia, carbon monoxide, and cooking gas can be toxic to cats, who may show signs of inhalation poisoning with dizziness, difficulty breathing, and bright red lips and tongue. Fresh air is the antidote; then seek veterinary help.

In addition to your pet safety kit (see sidebar, page 90), a well-stocked first-aid kit goes a long way toward protecting your cat during an unexpected crisis. Pre-packaged kits can be purchased at your local pet supply store, or you can create your own. It doesn't take much to build a first-rate first-aid kit for your cat (see page 95).

BREATHING STOPS, NO HEARTBEAT

A cat's basic life functions can cease when she becomes unconscious due to a traumatic injury, accident, or illness. When a cat ceases breathing and her heart stops, a small window of roughly

areas. Look for pale, reddened skin that becomes hot and painful when touched. Swelling also may occur, along with hair loss and peeling skin.

What to do: Place the cat in a warmed area and thaw the frostbitten areas slowly. To do this, use warm, moist towels and replace them frequently. Stop the procedure when the affected tissues become flushed. Wrap your cat in a blanket to conserve her body heat. Warning: Do not apply anything hot to frostbitten skin, and do not rub or massage frozen tissues—it may cause more damage. Consult your veterinarian before applying any topical ointment, and keep your cat out of the cold in the future, as frostbitten tissues are more vulnerable to repeated freezing.

POISONING

The clinical signs of poisoning may be as dramatic and terrifying as a seizure, or as simple as drooling. Symptoms vary from no initial signs at all to staggering, weakness, lack of coordination, depression, vomiting, diarrhea, and convulsion, among others.

What to do: Don't panic if you suspect your cat is exposed to a poisonous substance. Take a minute to collect the material involved, including a product container or anything your cat has chewed or vomited. Put it in a zip-lock bag. If your cat loses consciousness, seizures, or has difficulty breathing, seek immediate veterinary help.

If you are unable to reach your veterinarian or a local animal poison-control center, contact the ASPCA Animal Poison Control Center, an operat-

ing division of the American Society for the Prevention of Cruelty to Animals. The Center hotline provides 24-hour coverage.

888-4ANI-HELP

(888) 426-4435 or (900) 680-0000

Before you call, be ready to provide your name, address, and telephone number; information concerning the exposure (what poison, the amount, and time elapsed since exposure); the age, sex, breed, and weight of your cat; and the symptoms your cat exhibits. Note: The nonprofit Center charges a moderate professional fee per case.

Recipes for Poison

Toxic chemicals, dangerous plants, products, and substances found in our daily environment can prove poisonous or fatal to cats of any age. Watch for the following common but potentially dangerous elements.

Flowers

Lilies are lovely, but several types are highly poisonous to cats, including the Easter and tiger lilies. Ingesting even a small amount can cause kidney failure in cats.

Household plants

Azalea, dieffenbachia, holly, hyacinth, oleander, philodendron, poinsettia, and sweet pea are among common indoor and outdoor plants toxic to cats. For a more complete list, visit the ASPCA Animal Poison Control Center Web site at www.napcc.aspca.org.

or may have a needle attached to it. Instead, rush him to a veterinarian.

Can't reach the blockage? Try a modified Heimlich maneuver to loosen the object. To do this:

1) Place your cat on her side.
2) Position the heel of your hand behind the last rib, angling slightly up. Apply three or four quick thrusts with gentle but firm pressure (you don't want to crack ribs).
3) If the cat does not "cough" out the object, repeat the process. If still unsuccessful, you will need speedy veterinary help.

FRACTURES AND DISLOCATIONS

In an open or compound fracture, the bone breaks and punctures the skin. A simple fracture, which doesn't pierce the skin, usually reveals itself through swelling, painful movement, or a dragging limb (also a symptom of dislocation). A lower jaw that hangs open may signal a broken jaw.

What to do: If your cat appears to have a fractured limb or dislocated hip, carefully place him on a large, flat surface. A cardboard box or clean litter pan works well. Cushion the "gurney" with a towel or blanket and keep your cat as still as possible to avoid further injury. Cover your cat to keep him warm and prevent shock. Transport him to your veterinarian immediately. Leave splinting a fractured limb to a professional, since this process can cause severe pain. If you suspect a fractured jaw, tie gauze tape or a long piece of cloth under the chin and behind the ears.

BURNS

What to do: Prompt veterinary treatment is needed to treat major or minor burns on a cat's body. For minor burns, cover the burned area with cool compresses (don't use ice!) on your way to the veterinary hospital.

For major burns, protect the area with a thick layer of gauze or cloth, cover your cat with a blanket, and seek immediate veterinary help. Protect your hands with rubber gloves if you suspect chemicals caused the burn.

Do not apply antiseptic ointments, butter, or other products to any burned area unless your veterinarian advises you to do so. Never cover any type of burn with cotton balls or pads, because cotton fibers will stick to the affected area.

FROSTBITE

Older cats are more prone to frostbite than younger cats. The extremities are the most likely body parts to be affected; the pads of the feet, tips of the ears, and the tail are the most vulnerable

SHOCK

Shock is a medical emergency that can occur when a cat is severely hurt or ill—especially if she becomes unconscious—and is potentially fatal. Signs include pale or blue lips and gums; a faint but rapid pulse; shallow breathing; staring, unresponsive eyes; a cold body; and lethargy. A cat in shock must be kept warm, as specified above. Quick veterinary care is critical.

BLEEDING

What to do: Apply a pressure bandage to any wound that causes severe external bleeding and rush your cat to the veterinarian. (A minor cut or scratch is likely to stop bleeding on its own and will not bleed profusely unless a larger blood vessel underneath opens.) Apply a sterile gauze pad or clean cloth directly over the wound. Use adhesive or masking tape to secure the bandaged area, or firmly tie the bandage in place with gauze or cloth strips. Unless directed by your veterinarian as a last resort, do not use a tourniquet, which can cut off the blood supply and cause additional damage to the wounded area. Don't

remove an object (such as a bullet) from a wound. Don't lift the bandage to see if the bleeding has stopped. Do take your cat to the veterinarian for additional care.

CHOKING

What to do: The usual suspect is an object lodged in the mouth or throat. If your cat is conscious, proceed cautiously to avoid being bitten. A panicked cat won't appreciate your help. Wrap him in a towel or other restraint and, if available, ask someone else to hold him firmly. Open your cat's mouth by firmly pressing fingers on either side of his jaw. Look inside to determine what's wrong before sticking your fingers in his mouth—you don't want to push a foreign object deeper into the throat. If you can reach the offending item, pull gently with your fingers, tweezers, or long-nosed pliers. Follow the same procedure for an unconscious cat. Caution: If you encounter resistance, do not try to force the object out. If you discover your cat has swallowed string or yarn, do not attempt to remove it. Deeply lodged string or thread can cut through the walls of the intestines,

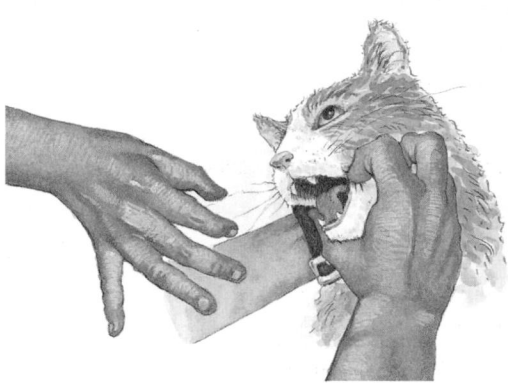

*How you deal with an emergency
can make all the difference in your older cat's survival.*

WHAT DO I DO FIRST?

Contact your veterinarian in an emergency. While this advice seems obvious, it is easy to overlook when you feel panicky or frightened. Take a moment to telephone your vet when your cat is injured or suddenly appears seriously ill. A veterinary professional can offer advice on how to proceed when you may not be thinking clearly. Your call also paves the way for veterinary hospital staff that will anticipate and prepare for your cat's arrival.

Of course, most veterinarians are not available around the clock. You can save precious minutes by knowing your doctor's plan for handling emergency situations ahead of time, especially those occurring after normal business hours and on weekends (when emergencies always seem to happen—see Murphy's Law above). Keep the telephone numbers of your veterinarian, a local emergency veterinary service, local animal poison center, and the national ASPCA Animal Poison Control Center handy at all times.

While getting your cat to your veterinarian quickly is the goal, an unexpected feline accident or injury nevertheless calls for quick, and often challenging, action on your part. For example, you may not have time to get professional help for a choking cat; you must act immediately to save her life. Healthy senior cats can spin into life-threatening shock in an emergency; a debilitated older cat, however, already is in a fragile state. Unless you are a doctor you cannot be expected to act like one. Nevertheless, how you deal with an emergency can make all the difference in your older cat's survival. Studying the basics of first aid can help. First-aid measures for common emergencies you and your cat may encounter follow.

FIRST STEPS

1. Remain calm. Your adrenalin may be running full-tilt, but you need to approach your injured cat quietly and in a nonthreatening way. Take a few moments to assess the situation.

2. Do not lift an injured cat with your bare hands. Pain can cause even the tamest cat to lash out and act defensively.

3. Use a large towel, folded blanket, or small rug to carry your cat to a veterinary hospital.

4. Cover your cat with an emergency "space blanket" or bubble wrap (a jacket or blanket will do) to conserve her body heat and help prevent shock, which occurs when the body cannot maintain sufficient blood pressure.

CHAPTER EIGHT

First-Aid Primer

No matter how carefully you protect your cat, accidents can and do happen. Cats love routine but don't always act predictably, thereby setting in motion the informal version of Murphy's Law, which states that if anything can go wrong, it will. A little forethought and some good planning can help derail this universal principle. Be prepared to treat common injuries your older cat may suffer until the cavalry arrives (or you reach the fort). Possessing the knowledge and tools to handle a feline emergency can ease a traumatic situation for both of you and, in addition, may save your cat's life.

While many cats stay healthy throughout their lives, others will require the help of multiple disciplines—including internal medicine, clinical pathology, surgery, and nutrition— to heal injuries and solve health problems.

AGE-RELATED HEALTH PROBLEMS

CONNECT QUIETLY

Contemplation is your cat's natural state of being.
To better connect and communicate with your
senior cat, try sitting quietly with her, suggests
Sharon Callahan, an internationally recognized
animal communicator in Mount Shasta,
California. Meditation, quiet inner listening, and
centering prayer can help. Your cat will feel your
love and concern, and you will feel and hear
within yourself everything you need to know,
Callahan says.

ABCS OF CAT BODY LANGUAGE

People and cats who live together a long time understand each other well. A simple movement, the blink of an eye, or a single meow evoke secret conversations without words. Yet even those new to a cat's company quickly learn to appreciate the difference between an angry hiss and a cat kiss. Chances are your older cat reads you well. Can you say the same? The following sidebar can help you discern some of her more subtle body signals.

How to Read Your Cat

Calm, relaxed cat:

Eyes—shut (contentment, bliss); stare, slow blink—called cat kiss (happy)

Ears—perky, lean slightly forward

Whiskers—straight out to sides

Tail—soft twitching (comfortable); held high (happy)

Fearful cat:

Eyes—wide open

Ears—flat against head

Whiskers—flattened against face

Tail—tucked low between legs

Curious cat:

Eyes—alert stare

Ears—swivel

Whiskers—fanning

Tail—slightly curved over back (play invitation)

Angry cat:

Eyes—narrow, pupils dilate

Ears—straight back

Whiskers—angled forward, spread apart

Tail—lashing, fluffed (back off)

Ear TTouch

The Ear TTouch, considered one of the most significant touches, is particularly effective for older cats. To start, gently but firmly stroke from the base of the ear to the tip. Supporting your cat's head with one hand, hold your thumb on the outside and folded forefinger on the underside of the ear with the other hand. Repeat this motion several times from the base of the ear to tip, covering different portions of the ear with each slide.

Next, create tiny circles between the thumb and forefinger, covering the entire ear in long lines. Finally, using the tips of the fingers make tiny circles, one at a time, all around the base of the ear.

illness or injury, including problems associated with aging, or to enhance the quality of an animal's life. It also helps establish a deeper rapport between people and companion animals. TTouch can be performed on the entire body, and each circular hand position or movement is considered complete within itself. Certified practitioners around the world teach TTouch techniques to those who want to share them with their companion animals.

AROMATHERAPY

Essential oils, or concentrated pure plant extracts, have been used to benefit the body, mind, and emotions since ancient times. Well-known for their therapeutic value and fragrance, the use of such oils is called aromatherapy.

Although scent therapy has been around for centuries, holistic veterinarians have only recently begun to incorporate its uses in their practices. They have discovered that certain aromas can have a powerful effect on animals through absorption into mucous membranes. For example, lavender can promote relaxation, while other scents can relieve anxiety or reduce blood pressure. Aromatherapy can be applied through diluted drops on the inside of the ear tip or released into the air through a diffuser. Check with a holistic practitioner before treating a pet on your own, though. Some oils, like pennyroyal, can be dangerous to cats.

Flower Essences for Older Cats

Individual Essence	Present State	Desired State
Big Springs Rock Water	Vitality, seniors, indoor animals	Vitality, attunement to nature
Bleeding Heart	Consequences of a broken heart	Heart center opening, trust
Douglas Iris	World-weariness, lethargy, seniors	Enthusiasm for life
Douglas Violet	Withdrawnness in senior animals	Attunement to the present moment
Farewell to Spring	Depression due to aging	Peace of mind, fearlessness
Forget-Me-Not	Loneliness, isolation, accidents	Integration, acceptance, joy
Heartsease	Consequence of abuse, grief	Trust, heart opening
Mallow	Insecurity, anxiety, fear with age	Sense of divine love, protection
Marsh Marigold	Lack of deep attunement	Heart-centered communication
Pine Violet	Shyness, withdrawnness in seniors	Presence in the moment
Shasta White Lupine	World-weariness, senior years	Perseverance, stamina

—Reprinted with permission, Anaflora Individual Flower Essences

During a hands-on treatment, a Reiki practitioner rests his or her slightly cupped hands gently for three to five minutes or more in each of a number of positions corresponding to major organs, chakras (energy points), and endocrine glands of the body. During treatment positions, the fingers are held together and hands rest gently on the animal receiving Reiki. The process is said to work by balancing the energy of the body, then focusing on the injured area, tumor, or incision that may be present. Reiki can also bring comfort and peace to dying animals.

Each cat responds to Reiki in her own way. Some love Reiki and can't seem to get enough; others may back off or appear restless at first. Reiki masters say that animals will communicate what they want and need, often responding to Reiki more quickly than people do. One Reiki master explains that the elder cat is drawn to the energy that supports him. He recognizes and feels the energy, and intuitively knows it helps and heals.

TTOUCH

The Tellington-Touch, or TTouch, is a method based on circular movements of the fingers and hands over the body. Described like turning on the electric lights of the body, TTouch is designed to activate cell functions and awaken cellular intelligence, according to its inventor, internationally recognized animal expert Linda Tellington-Jones. TTouch can be used to assist with recovery from

How to Give Your Older Cat a Massage

Begin by paying attention to specific speeds, hand parts, and pressures. Your cat will patiently guide and encourage your progress.

Speed. Older cats especially enjoy long, slow loving caresses. Begin by stroking your cat down her back. Count how long that stroke takes. Caress again and double the time it takes to complete the stroke. What may seem excruciatingly slow to you feels good to your cat. Slowly explore every bump and contour. You can also try "no-motion" by allowing your cat's head to rest on a single finger or in your cupped palm.

Hand parts. Repeat the same technique with fingertips, finger pads, full palms, four fingers or two fingers together, and thumbs. Use knuckle nooks—a flat surface formed between your knuckles when you bend your fingers—for stroking under the chin, around the cheek, and behind the ears. Take time to discover which hand parts you and your cat prefer and favor.

Cat parts. Explore beyond the familiar regions of your cat's neck, back, and top of the head. Try caressing his furry chest, reach in for an underarm tickle, and slowly weave your fingers around his paws and claws.

Pressures. Frail older bones and bodies need gentler hand pressure. Your older cat prefers a mild pressure. Try using a light pressure (you'll just barely feel the muscles below the fur), or feather-light pressure (a fairy-light touch of the fur).

White gloves and brushes. For an additional massage treat, touch your cat while wearing a soft cotton glove. The different texture adds a refreshing change. Routine brushing, especially important for older cats, will feel better to your cat when combined with cat massage techniques.

Repetition. Don't subject your elderly cat to any sudden changes during a massage session. When you discover a technique that particularly impresses him, repeat it over and over again. For example, instead of stroking along the back two or three times, repeat this motion up to 10 times. Then you can alternate hand parts, speeds, and pressures. Consider devoting an entire massage session around a specific technique.

Friendly feline feedback. It's common for cats to become more affectionate and responsive with frequent massage. Some cats will even bypass the food bowl to demand affection. Others will knead. Pushy head-butts and cat kisses signify your cat's approval. With practice and patience, you may be serenaded with meows or treated to "power purrs."

—Courtesy of Maryjean Ballner, author of *Cat Massage* and *Dog Massage*

CAT MASSAGE

Treated to gentle handling that considers stiff joints and fragile bones, most aging cats learn to appreciate a good massage. Indeed, this hands-on communication may be one of the nicest things you do for your older pet. Touch is powerful—it conveys love and deepens trust while bestowing physical benefits. Massage can help increase your cat's blood circulation while nourishing tissues and soothing aching muscles.

FLOWER ESSENCES

Used for centuries by primitive cultures, flower remedies were rediscovered in 1928 by Edward Bach, M.D., a British physician, bacteriologist, and immunologist. He is perhaps most well known for his popular Bach Rescue Remedy, which combines the essences impatiens, star-of-Bethlehem, cherry plum, rock rose, and clematis. Rescue Remedy is universally used to reduce stress in people and animals (you'll find it at most health food stores). Holistic veterinarians and cat behaviorists often recommend flower essences for healing feline emotions. Made from essential and highly diluted oils, flower remedies—a few drops at a time—are usually added to water or given orally. They are easy to administer and can be used by themselves or with other healing therapies.

While Bach flowers were originally created for people, Anaflora flower essences are made especially for animals by Sharon Callahan, an author, internationally recognized animal communicator,

and pioneer in treating animals with flower essences. She describes flower essences as non-aromatic vibrational tinctures made from the blossoms of flowering plants. Each plant—the flower is the most potent part—has individual healing properties. To make a flower essence, the healing properties of the plant are transferred to water by a process of sunlight infusion. The resulting essence can be rubbed on the skin, ingested, or sprayed around the animal being treated. Anaflora offers 118 individual flower essences and 32 flower essence formulas that address the physical, mental, emotional, and spiritual needs of animals. (See Resources.)

REIKI

The name for this ancient hands-on healing modality (pronounced ray-key) sounds mysterious, yet it has a straightforward premise: a simple, gentle transfer of energy that accelerates the body's ability to heal physical and mental disorders. Dr. Mikao Usui, a minister, scholar, and philosopher in Japan, brought Reiki's origins to light. In the mid-1800s—after a long search—Dr. Usui found a Sanskrit sutra written by a disciple of Buddha more than 2,500 years ago. He called his discovery Reiki and began what became the Usui System of Natural Healing. Reiki is not a spiritual belief system; rather it is used for self-healing and for offering healing to others. Many Reiki practitioners believe it is also a powerful way to help animals, supporting both conventional and holistic treatments.

CHAPTER SEVEN

Hands-On Alternative Treatments

Feeding, petting, and holding are all comforts your hands provide. Use this knowledge to help heal your cat: Petting can become a comforting massage, or you and your cat can discover the natural healing power of Reiki, TTouch, aromatherapy, and flower essences. Often used in conjunction with holistic healing methods and conventional treatments, these hands-on modalities help promote peace and healing. In addition, observing your cat's body language can bring understanding and a deeper level of communication between you.

What to Look For

Searching for a natural practitioner in your area? Look for a licensed practitioner who has received formal training. For example, the International Veterinary Acupuncture Society (IVAS) maintains a list of all certified veterinary acupuncturists. Formed and chartered in 1974, the nonprofit IVAS strives to establish uniformly high standards of veterinary acupuncture through educational programs and accreditation. The following list will help point you in the right direction.

Academy of Veterinary Homeopathy (AVH)
6400 East Independence Blvd.
Charlotte, NC 28212
(866) 652-1590 • www.theavh.org

American Holistic Veterinary Medical Association (AHVMA)
2218 Old Emmorton Road
Bel Air, MD 21015
(410) 569-0795 • www.ahvma.org

American Veterinary Chiropractic Association (AVCA)
P.O. Box 563
Port Byron, IL 61275
(309) 658-2958 • www.animalchiropractic.org

Animal Natural Health Center
1283 Lincoln Street
Eugene, OR 97401
(541) 342-7665 • www.drpitcairn.com

The British Association of Homeopathic Veterinary Surgeons
Chinham House
Stanford in the Vale
Oxon SN7 8NQ
01367 718115 • www.bahvs.com

International Veterinary Acupuncture Society (IVAS)
P.O. Box 271395
Fort Collins, CO 80527
(970) 266-0666 • www.ivas.org

the body of animals by use of acupuncture needles, moxibustion (heat used to stimulate acupuncture points by burning different materials indirectly on the needle or directly on the skin), injections, low-level lasers, magnets, and a variety of other techniques for the diagnosis and treatment of numerous conditions in animals.

Chiropractic

Veterinary chiropractic is the examination, diagnosis, and treatment of animals through manipulation and adjustment of specific joints and cranial sutures. The term veterinary chiropractic should not be interpreted to include dispensing medication, performing surgery, injecting medications, recommending supplements, or replacing traditional veterinary care.

Physical Therapy

Veterinary physical therapy is the use of noninvasive techniques, excluding veterinary chiropractic, for the rehabilitation of injuries in animals. Veterinary physical therapy performed by nonveterinarians should be limited to the use of stretching; massage therapy; stimulation by use of low-level lasers, electrical sources, magnetic fields, and ultrasound; rehabilitative exercises; hydrotherapy; and applications of heat and cold.

Massage Therapy

Massage therapy is a technique in which the person uses only the hands and body to massage soft tissues. (More on this in the next chapter.)

Homeopathy

Veterinary homeopathy treats nonhuman animals by administering substances that are capable of producing clinical signs in healthy animals similar to those of the animal to be treated. These substances are used therapeutically in minute doses.

Botanical Medicine

Veterinary botanical medicine is the use of plants and plant derivatives as therapeutic agents.

Nutraceuticals

Nutraceutical medicine is the use of micronutrients, macronutrients, and other nutritional supplements as therapeutic agents.

Homeopathic First-Aid Kit

Homeopathy, a complex system of holistic medicine using small doses of natural substances to stimulate the body's natural defenses, operates on the premise that like cures like. In a highly diluted form, homeopathic remedies are said to cure what they might cause in a larger amount, thus stimulating the body to heal itself. Though you should always consult a homeopathic veterinarian for correct dosages before treating your older cat, the following items can be kept on hand for emergencies.

- Arnica for wounds
- Hypericum for traumatic injury/possible nerve damage
- Nux vomica for diarrhea
- Silicea for abscesses due to fights

Holistic veterinary medicine incorporates, but is not limited to, the principles of acupuncture and acutherapy, botanical medicine, chiropractic, homeopathy, massage therapy, nutraceuticals, and physical therapy, as well as conventional medicine, surgery, and dentistry.

- 1 cat-size dose of multiple vitamin-mineral supplement (human quality) or cat vitamin

- 1 probiotic/digestive enzyme supplement

- 80 mg taurine (about one 250 mg taurine capsule or tablet, powdered). Omit if using cat vitamin.

IMPORTANT: Go slowly and proceed gradually with any diet change. Your animal companion's tastes and digestive system need time to adjust to new foods. Too rapid a change may result in diarrhea, vomiting, refusal to eat, or other problems. This is especially important for older or sick cats.

HOLISTIC CARE

Holistic veterinary medicine is a comprehensive approach to health care employing alternative and conventional diagnostic and therapeutic modalities, according to American Veterinary Medical Association (AVMA) Guidelines for Alternative and Complementary Medicine. In practice, the guidelines specify that holistic veterinary medicine incorporates, but is not limited to, the principles of acupuncture and acutherapy, botanical medicine, chiropractic, homeopathy, massage therapy, nutraceuticals, and physical therapy, as well as conventional medicine, surgery, and dentistry. The AVMA recommends that holistic veterinary medicine be practiced only by licensed veterinarians educated in the modalities employed.

In 1996, the AVMA revised its guidelines for alternative and complementary veterinary medicine. Below are the organization's brief descriptions of alternative therapies.

Acupuncture and Acutherapy
Veterinary acupuncture and acutherapy involve the examination and stimulation of specific points on

Holistic veterinarians, who often begin their careers as mainstream practitioners, search beyond conventional Western medicine's focus on fixing or eliminating symptoms of illness to encompass a "bigger picture" of an animal's overall health and well-being.

Preventing disease is a primary goal of natural health. For older cats, a holistic approach can be particularly advantageous, because of the strong focus on nutrition and supportive therapies.

In fact, nutrition is the foundation upon which holistic healing therapies are built. Many holistic veterinarians and practitioners advocate a well-prepared homemade diet if a pet guardian has the time and commitment to do it properly. A complete understanding of feline nutrition is essential, however, which means you'll need to do some research first.

Another option is to choose a commercially prepared high-quality, all-natural cat food, such as Innova or Wysong, which are available in some pet supply stores or natural food outlets and through mail order.

HOME-PREPARED DIET FOR ADULT CATS

CAUTION: Before you begin feeding your cat a home-prepared diet, discuss the decision with your veterinarian or a holistic veterinarian in your area. The following ingredients, recommended by the Animal Protection Institute (API), make approximately three servings. Feed an adult cat as much as she will eat in 20 to 30 minutes, and refrigerate leftovers promptly. Feed adult cats twice a day.

Choose One Protein Source
(Meat amounts given in raw weight)
1/2 lb. boneless chicken breast or thigh, minced
6 oz. ground turkey or minced turkey (dark meat)
1/2 lb. beef, chicken or turkey heart, ground or minced (About 3 times a week, include 1 chopped hard-boiled or scrambled egg.)

Optional: once a week, substitute 4 oz. organic liver for 1/2 of any meat source

Optional: once every two weeks, substitute 4 oz. tuna (packed in water, no salt), 6 oz. sardines (canned), or 5 oz. salmon (canned, with bones) for any meat source. Do not use canned fish as a protein source for cats prone to urinary tract problems.

Optional: for cats needing a lower protein diet, add 1 cup cooked white rice.

Supplements
- 2 tsp. olive oil, or 1 tsp. olive and 1 tsp. flaxseed oil

- 300 mg calcium (as carbonate or citrate), or about 1 slightly rounded tsp bonemeal (human grade). If using canned fish with bones, decrease calcium to 1/4 regular amount.

- 1 to 2 tbsp. pureed vegetables—many cats prefer their veggies lightly steamed—or vegetable baby food (without onion powder!)

- 1/4 tsp. salt substitute (potassium chloride)— give 3 or 4 times a week

CHAPTER SIX

Holistic Healing Therapies

Natural care may be a new concept to many cat owners, but alternative treatments have been around for thousands of years. According to legend, the first nonhuman acupuncture patient was an elephant treated for a stomach disorder about 3,500 years ago. In the twenty-first century, holistic healing therapies for people and animals are gaining ground in the United States for several reasons. The American Holistic Veterinary Medical Association (AHVMA) points out that holistic medicine, by its very nature, is humane to the core. Techniques used in holistic medicine are gentle, minimally invasive, and incorporate patient well-being and stress reduction. Holistic thinking centers on empathy, respect, and loving care. One natural practitioner notes that as more people embrace these therapies for themselves, they naturally want them for their pets.

*Preventing disease is a primary
goal of natural health. A gentler, holistic
approach to care can be particularly
advantageous for older cats, because
of the strong focus on nutrition
and supportive therapies.*

SECTION 3

NATURAL RELIEF

than a clean box. Cat food should not be kept in the vicinity of a litter box. If you must move his litter box to another area, show him the new location— stir the litter to make sure he gets the message.

Keep it quiet

Loud noises or commotion easily scare older cats with diminished hearing or sight. They may be unable to move quickly or get out of the way. Avoid the startle factor and advise others, especially kids, to keep things as calm as possible.

Help her sleep

Aging cats nap more but they may also be subject to sporadic sleep, which can cause you stress. Give your cat a warm, soft bed in a draft-free zone, play classical music before sleep and a provide night light.

Introduce new pets gradually

The jury is out on whether adding a younger cat to the household constitutes positive or negative stress. Some experts believe introducing a new pet is a traumatic experience best avoided; others believe a younger cat can encourage an older one to be more alert and playful. If you elect to introduce a new kitty, be patient, take things slowly, and don't leave the two cats alone together until you are sure they can give peace a chance.

Soothe sudden changes

ometimes a big upheaval, like moving to a new home, is unavoidable. Keep your cat in a quiet area of the new location at first. Try to keep everything else, such as food and bedding, the same as before. Lighten your older cat's stress level during a major transition by giving him extra affection, attention, and playtime with you.

Finally, check your senior cat's nails regularly. A weekly trim is in order if your aging kitty clicks her nails across the floor. To trim claws, choose nail clippers designed for cats. Grip a paw and press gently on the footpads to extend a claw. Carefully snip the sharp edge just below the quick, or pink area, of the nail. (Cutting into the quick will result in pain and bleeding—apply styptic powder to stop bleeding if this occurs.) If you're not sure where the quick begins on your cat's nails, you can safely clip the tips of her long nails.

SHOULD I SPAY OR NEUTER MY OLDER CAT?

Yes! Although spay-and-neuter advocates generally focus on how young a cat can handle the operation, spaying (removal of ovaries, uterus, and tubes that carry eggs—stitches required) or neutering (removal of both testes and part of the tubes that carry the sperm—no stitches needed) will make your pet more comfortable at any age—and improve your cat's longevity, health, and behavior. Pre-admission blood work, a checkup and other tests deemed necessary by your veterinarian are a must, however, to help ensure your cat is healthy enough to undergo the surgery. Placing a cat under anesthesia can be risky no matter what his age, but the risk is thought to increase as your cat ages; your veterinarian will take every precaution to minimize negative effects. The benefits outweigh any danger when you consider the alternative: An older female cat can have potentially fatal uterus problems, such as pyometra (pus and bacteria in the uterus); continuing pregnancies (seen in cats up to 15 years old), which take a terrible toll on bones, teeth, and body; and increased susceptibility to breast cancer. Unaltered male cats experience fewer health problems, but they continue to fight, howl, and spray urine to mark territory as long as testosterone rules them, making them less-than-pleasant housemates.

On the other hand, spaying eliminates heat cycles and the often-irritable behavior that accompanies them. Neutered male cats are more affectionate and roam less. Weight gain can be a side effect of spaying or neutering. The operation doesn't cause it, but your cat's newly relaxed attitude may result in a less-active lifestyle. You can avoid this problem by feeding proper amounts of food and making time for daily play sessions with your cat.

REDUCE STRESS

For older cats, a good day is one that is calm and predictable. From your cat's perspective, however, life with humans is often filled with stressful events. The worst offenders include moving to a new home or adding another pet to the household. Here are a few ways to de-stress your cat's environment.

Clean his litter box
Cats believe cleanliness is next to, well, you know. Neat and picky, cats won't settle for anything less

clotted fur. One veterinarian who works with geriatric cats advises working mats out gently and
slowly with a wide metal-tooth comb instead of
scissors. Take your time, let your cat be your guide,
and honor her request to stop. You can always try
again tomorrow. Offer her a healthy treat or a nip
of catnip and praise her for her patience.

Last but not least, don't forget the bottom line.
Unsightly knots can bunch like grapes around your
longhaired cat's anal area—a place that many
aging cats find tough to clean after a bowel movement. If she's not too insulted by your behavior,
try a quick, gentle swab under her tail (baby wipes
work well) after she uses the litter box. Remove
existing clumps as gingerly as you can, or consult
a professional groomer for advice.

TOOTH AND NAIL

Don't forget the other important brushing your
senior cat needs. A cat's teeth play a critical role
in her life. Dental problems are not only painful,
they also are a prime factor in cat behavior problems, illness, and disease. Left untreated, bacteria
in a cat's mouth may infect other organs, such as
the heart or kidneys, and shorten her life. On the
other hand, healthy teeth and gums can significantly extend the quality and length of life.

Veterinarians agree that good dental care is one
of the most important things you can provide for
your aging cat. Evidence indicates that brushing a
cat's teeth and gums daily or weekly reduces tartar formation. Many diligent cat lovers use a piece
of gauze to gently rub their cat's teeth and gums

with toothpaste made for cats (don't use human
toothpaste on your cat's teeth). If you've never
done this and don't want to, or your cat makes it
clear her mouth is off-limits, you have other
options. Most cats like the feline dental chews
available at pet-supply stores, or ask your veterinarian about a prescription food approved by veterinary dentists to help keep teeth clean. Whether
or not you brush your cat's teeth, schedule a dental exam. Regular dental checkups—at least once
a year—and professional cleanings are vital to
maintain your cat's good health.

- For cats with cataracts or poor vision, leave a light on during the night to help your nocturnal cat see. Don't routinely pick up a blind cat; he is likely to be disoriented when you set him down.

- For cats with hearing problems, flick a flashlight on and off to help train or "call" your cat. Your hard-of-hearing cat may also respond to a high-pitched dog whistle.

- Piles of pillows can ease a handicapped cat's path to a higher location.

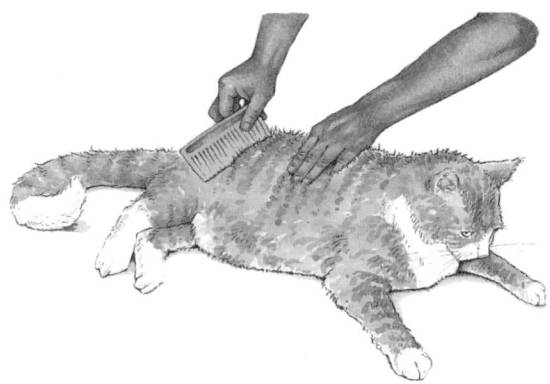

When it comes to making your senior cat more comfortable, you are truly the expert. No one knows your cat, or her needs, like you do. Use the suggestions listed above to launch your own creative ideas.

GOOD GROOMING

Cats enjoy training their human companions in the delicate art of grooming them properly. One lovely 12-year-old calico announces grooming time to her human with a demanding meow and a flop onto her side twice a day. When one side is properly attended to, she rolls over to the other side. She imposes no time limit on this procedure, reluctantly moving along only when the hand brushing her tires. Not all cats enjoy this much pampering, but older cats often need some hands-on help to pick up where their self-grooming duties stop. You'll know your cat needs your help when she begins to look like a person who just got out of bed in the morning—a little sleepy and unkempt. Pay attention to any abrupt change in your cat's grooming habits, though. A sudden lack of groom-

ing may signal the onset of a health problem. Check with your veterinarian if this occurs.

Bathing your older cat isn't necessary unless he becomes dirty. Brushing or a gentle combing every day will make him feel more comfortable in his skin and closer to you. He'll enjoy the attention, and you will do the good work of stimulating his blood circulation and sebaceous gland secretions, removing scales next to the skin and returning a luster to his coat. Brushing also removes dead or loose hairs that otherwise might play a starring role in your cat's next hairball. And hairballs can cause potentially serious problems—like recurring impaction—to aging gastrointestinal tracts.

Finally, daily grooming can help you catch flea or tick problems early. Once-a-month flea and tick "spot" products, available by prescription through your veterinarian, can help prevent any infestation.

DON'T PULL!

Brushing a shorthaired cat usually doesn't present much of a challenge, but the aging longhaired variety can be infamous for mats or clumps of

Consider the following sample of comfort toys for feline couch potatoes:

Snuggle Kitties. Originally designed for use with foster kittens, this stuffed kitty has a hook-and-loop closed cavity under its belly with a disposable heat pouch that stays warm up to 20 hours, or a cloth pouch that holds rice and can be microwaved to keep your cat warm. Comes with a plastic, battery-operated heart that fits into the under-belly opening and simulates a real heartbeat.

Thermo Kitty Bed. This round bed with tall sides includes a removable dual thermostat heater with a super-soft, orthopedic foam base and removable faux lambskin cover for easy washing. The heater is also removable, plugs into any outlet, and uses only four watts of power.

Cat Sitter Video. Mice, squirrels, birds, and fish entertain your cat in this colorful video available in both one-hour or six-hour versions.

Of course, you don't have to spend a lot of money to make your older cat more comfortable; you just need to look at life from her point of view.

Following are some comforting suggestions for older cats, including those with disabilities:

- For stiff or arthritic cats, create steps or use footstools to help them reach their favorite hangouts or resting places. Securely attach carpet to wooden steps to prevent slipping, and ease her transition over steps or stairways with carpet-covered ramps. A paint tray used as a litter box can provide a painless step into the low side, and an elevated food bowl can relieve pain associated with bending down.

CHAPTER FIVE

Comfort Zone: Making Life Easier

To a great extent, a senior cat's quality of life centers on her ability to continue to get around, reach her favorite places, and live as comfortably as possible. You can contribute to your older cat's physical and mental well-being in numerous ways. As the old saying goes, it's the little things that count.

Visit any well-stocked pet supply store or pet-related Web site, and you may be amazed to find several product lines designed specifically for the needs of older animals. You will spot everything from microwaveable heating pads and orthopedic beds to stylish cotton overalls with disposable pads (for incontinent cats) and specially designed ramps and steps.

10 Steps to Help Your Older Cat Lose Weight

Just like people, older cats often add pounds with the years. You can do a lot to help your plump cat drop those extra pounds and regain her svelte shape. Follow these 10 steps suggested by the Iams Company to help your cat reach a healthier weight. Remember to check with your veterinarian first, though, to establish goals and ensure your cat is otherwise healthy. Follow-up visits can help you and your veterinarian monitor your cat's progress.

1. Let the games begin. Playing can help your cat burn calories. Toss her toys to chase, wiggle a wand for high jumps, or provide a taller cat scratching post to climb.

2. Go for a walk. Take your cat for a walk, even if it's just inside the house. Many cats learn to enjoy walking on a leash, and it's a great opportunity for you to get some exercise too.

3. Ease into shape. Watch how your overweight cat handles increased activity. Don't let him become exhausted, overheated, or out of breath. Older cats may not be able to exercise vigorously.

4. Replace treats with praise. When your cat begs for treats, she may be begging for attention. Substitute play, grooming, stroking, or conversation for food treats as expressions of love. You can also try catnip as a nonfood treat.

5. Resist those pleas. Is your cat an expert at begging for table scraps? Keep your cat in a separate room during your meals if you find it difficult to ignore those pleas or wails.

6. Feed cats individually. If you have more than one cat, consider keeping them in separate rooms during mealtimes. This will prevent the greediest cat from overeating and ensure that the slower-eating cat gets fed.

7. Play fetch. Toss kibble to your cat, one piece at a time, to combine exercise with mealtime.

8. Avoid fiber overload. Many reduced-calorie pet foods include increased levels of fiber that can interfere with a cat's ability to absorb and digest nutrients. Food with the proper balance of animal-based protein, fat, carbohydrates and moderately fermentable fiber sources, such as beet pulp, is a healthier choice.

9. Smaller meals, more often. Feeding your cat several small meals each day, rather than one large serving, can help burn more calories through meal-induced thermogenesis. This process of heat produced by the body during digestion, absorption, metabolism, and storage of nutrients causes more calories to be used.

10. Tip the scales. Keep track of your cat's weight by using a baby scale. Or, take your cat in your arms, step on your scale, and subtract your weight from the total weight shown to find your cat's weight. Check your cat's weight-loss progress every two weeks.

health. Increased blood circulation and improved muscle tone are precious gifts to older cats, who become less mobile as arthritis sets in and muscles atrophy. People jog, bike, or swim, but a cat's best activity is playing with you. The act of playing comes naturally to kittens instinctively developing survival skills, but older cats who mastered these techniques long ago (and haven't found much use for them in the meantime) may need more encouragement to get moving. This isn't usually a problem if you've played together since your longtime companion was a kitten. Give him toys that invite him to stalk, climb, leap, and pounce.

These playthings can run the gamut from the simple and cost-free brown-paper shopping bag, cardboard box, or wad of paper on a string to commercially made cat toys. Fortunately, cats are just as content with paper bags and cardboard boxes as they are with expensive or elaborate store-bought toys. If you have a limited budget, tour pet-supply stores for inspiration and make your own.

IT'S NEVER TOO LATE

If you've adopted an older cat or never thought to play with your cat during his early years, it's not too late to start. Begin slowly, perhaps with a strip of paper to encourage the smallest swipe of a paw. Gradually increase the length of time you play with your cat. Schedule regular play sessions at approximately the same time every day to give your routine-loving cat something to look forward to besides meals. Try playing before a meal to kindle her appetite, which simulates feline predatory behavior in the wild, or play in the evening to discourage nighttime activity.

Remember to challenge your cat's brain as well as his body. (This may call for some brain stretching on your part, too.) Positive reinforcement is the key. For instance, choose a simple trick or action you want your cat to perform when asked and consistently reward him every time he does it. The reward doesn't have to be a food treat; reward him with a pat or a verbal "yes!" instead.

Check with your veterinarian before you enlist your cat in a feline exercise program, especially if he is overweight and sedentary or becomes easily winded and tires quickly. Once you get the green light, choose games that are appropriate for your senior's age and condition. Start with simple exercises and slowly build up to more challenging games when your cat appears fit and ready.

Toys to Fit Your Cat's Personality

Wonder what sort of toys match your older cat's personality? Here are some thoughts on the subject, courtesy of CatToys.com. To spark your senior cat's interest in a new toy, sprinkle or rub a small amount of catnip on the toy or in the wrapping paper.

Extremely active cats: If your senior cat springs to life occasionally, try pounceable catnip pillows, an unpredictable rolling activity ball, a bird door hanger, or a realistically squeaky toy mouse.

Moderately active cats: Try soft fabric catnip mice with leather tails; free-standing bird on a spring that rocks back and forth; and motion-sensitive blinking ball with light, bell, and yarn tail.

Couch potato cats: Snacking toys can get your cat off the bed. Consider a hollow ball—the opening at each end allows treats to fall out as he plays. Even couch potatoes love a good feather toy—try furry catnip mice with feather tails.

Plays well with others: Cats who play well with others enjoy interactive play with people too. Choose toys that you and your cat can play with together, or toys that work well for multiple-cat households. Try a feather and felt "chaser" toy packed with catnip, kitty-size catnip pillows to swat or pounce on, or soft fabric catnip mice with leather tails.

Prefers to play alone: Even the most independent aging cat can have a healthy appetite for play. Interest your cat in a reshapeable "messy" toy mouse made of natural sheep's wool with a leather tail, nose, and ears; or try a full-body wrestle (front paws, hind legs) "mollusk" made from fleecy material, topped with feathers and stuffed with catnip.

Insists on playing at night: Nighttime toys for the cat who has a sudden burst of playful energy in the wee early hours include a blinking laser ball; a catnip-refillable, glow-in-the-dark ball; and a flashing toy ball that lights up on impact.

CAUTION: Your cat may be older and wiser, but she still needs supervision during playtime, especially when she plays with toys containing wire, string, or mechanical parts. Remember to put these types of toys safely away when play ends.

How Does Your Cat Measure Up?

Very Thin

- Ribs, backbone, and pelvic bones easily visible, with no fat cover
- Thin neck and narrow waist
- Obvious abdominal tuck
- No fat in flank folds, folds often absent

Underweight

- Backbone and ribs can be easily felt
- Minimal fat covering
- Minimal waist when viewed from above
- Slightly tucked abdomen

Ideal

- Ribs can be felt, but not visible
- Slight waist line observed behind ribs when viewed from above
- Abdomen tucked, flank folds present

Overweight

- Moderate fat cover over ribs, but can still feel ribs
- Abdomen slight rounded, flanks concave
- Flank folds hang down with moderate amount of fat, jiggles when walks

Obese

- Ribs and backbone not easily felt due to a thick fat covering
- Abdomen distended; waist barely visible or absent
- Prominent flank folds which sway from side to side when walking

Of course, cats don't need exercise videos to show them how to stay in shape. Keeping fit comes naturally to them, thanks to a never-forgotten need to survive in the wild. And they manage it without doing anything resembling strenuous exercise such as aerobics or long daily runs. What's their secret? You've probably already guessed that stretching is the key. Cats have the wonderful ability to gracefully stretch every part of their body so powerfully that their muscles vibrate. For people and cats, stretching movements can help strengthen muscles, reduce excess weight, and release nervous stress.

A feline preference for warmth (due to its origins in warm climates) is one theory that may help explain why cats stretch frequently. Aging cats, however, may need a little help to stay sleek and supple, especially if they live in cold climates unkind to stiff joints. You can encourage your older cat to stretch in a warm area, or invite her to join in as you stretch or perform yoga. An enticing scratching post (try a sisal-covered one with a secure base and a small amount of catnip rubbed or scattered on the post) can spark a spine-tingling stretch, or you can simply encourage your cat to reach up to you. An older female cat may enjoy balancing on her front paws while you gently stretch her back paws.

THE ART OF PLAY

Just like us, cats need exercise to lift their spirits and keep them fit. Regular, moderate exercise is the not-so-secret key to weight control and overall

CHAPTER FOUR

Exercise and Play
to Keep Your Cat Active

Your cat rouses from a long nap, yawns, and stands on all fours with her feet apart. She exhales while arching her back. Holding this pose for a few timeless seconds, she then inhales as she slowly curves into a concave position. She raises her head and looks up in a luxuriously slow, flowing movement. If you swear your balletic cat just performed a perfectly lovely yoga posture, you're absolutely right. Human yoga postures, called asanas, have been drawn from natural sources for thousands of years. It has been said there are millions of creatures—and as many yoga postures. "The Cat" asana your cat performs strengthens the back and pelvic area, promotes spinal flexibility, and energizes the feline body. It's no wonder that humans adapted this beautiful stretch from cats.

Pet-Food Label Rules

The 95 percent rule: If the product label says "Salmon Cat Food," 95 percent of the product must be the named ingredient.

The 25 percent or "dinner" rule: Ingredients named on the label must comprise at least 25 percent of the product (but less than 95 percent) when a qualifying "descriptor" term such as dinner, entrée, formula, platter, or nuggets is used. In "Turkey Dinner for Cats," turkey may or may not be the primary ingredient. If two ingredients are named, they must total 25 percent; there must be more of the first ingredient listed than the second; and the lesser ingredient must be at least 3 percent of the total.

The 3 percent or "with" rule: A product may be labeled "Cat Food with Salmon" if it contains at least 3 percent of the named ingredient.

The "flavor" rule: A food may be labeled "Turkey Flavor Cat Food" even if the food does not contain turkey, as long as there is a "sufficiently detectable" amount of flavor. This may be derived from meals, by-products, or "digests" of various parts from the animal species indicated on the label.

—Reprinted with permission from the Animal Protection Institute

Keep in mind that pet-food manufacturers are often one step ahead of us. For example, antioxidants, known for combating destructive free radicals—cells implicated in a weakened immune system, degenerative arthritis, and a host of diseases from cancer to cardiovascular disease—have hit the mainstream pet-food industry with a wallop. Accordingly, pet-food manufacturers increasingly proclaim the addition of antioxidants to their list of ingredients.

To help ensure you're buying quality nutritional supplements:

1. Look for three important letters on the label: USP (which stands for United States Pharmacopoeia). This not-for-profit organization sets standards for prescription and nonpre-scription medicines, including dietary supplements for veterinary use.

2. Ask your veterinarian or consult a veterinary nutritionist. (Your veterinarian can recommend one or refer you to a holistic veterinarian who specializes in nutritional therapy.)

3. Do some research. Contact a nutritionist at a veterinary college or consult a veterinary nutritionist at the American College of Veterinary Nutrition (ACVN). The ACVN Web site is ACVN.org. If you have a specific question about cat nutrition, you can contact the ACVN office and be referred to a Diplomate who specializes in that area.

Pet-Food Shopping Guide

For your cat's sake, don't let pet food labels intimidate you. The Animal Protection Institute (API), based in Sacramento, California, is a nonprofit animal advocacy organization with 85,000 members nationwide. API recommends that you keep the following guidelines in mind when shopping for commercial cat food.

- Make sure the label displays an AAFCO (American Association of Feed Control Officials) guarantee, preferably one that references "feeding tests" or "feeding protocols" rather than "nutrient profiles."

- Avoid cat food containing "byproduct meal" or "meat and bone meal." These rendered products are the most inexpensive sources of animal protein and are not reliable sources of nutrition.

- Look for a specifically named meat or meal, such as lamb or chicken meal, as the first ingredient.

- Avoid generic or store brands. These may be repackaged rejects from big manufacturers and generally contain cheaper, poorer quality, ingredients.

- Bypass "light," "senior," "special formula," or "hairball formula" foods unless specifically recommended by your veterinarian. These foods may contain acidifying agents, excessive fiber, or inadequate fats that can result in skin, coat, and other health problems.

- In general, select brands promoted to be "natural." Look for cat foods preserved with vitamins C and E instead of chemical preservatives like BHA, BHT, ethoxyquin, and propyl gallate.

- Check the expiration date to ensure freshness.

- When you open a bag of dry food, sniff it. If the food smells rancid (bad or "funny"), return it immediately for an exchange or refund.

- Store dry cat food in a sealed nonporous container in a cool, dry place. Remove canned food from the can and refrigerate in a glass or ceramic container.

—Reprinted with permission of the Animal Protection Institute

Manx Meatballs

1 lb. extra-lean ground beef or turkey
1/4 cup chopped fresh parsley
1 egg
2 tablespoons ketchup
1/2 cup dry breadcrumbs
1/4 teaspoon garlic powder

Preheat oven to 450°F. Combine all ingredients in a large bowl and mix well. Shape into small balls, and place on broiler pan rack. Bake until brown, 10 to 15 minutes. Serve at room temperature. Store in the refrigerator.

growing usage of dietary supplements by humans has influenced a similar boom in the pet products industry. The recent flood of diet supplements for pets is the reason the AAFCO created the Novel Ingredients Regulatory Framework Task Force, whose chief job is to research new products and determine appropriate labeling. A selection of popular supplements that pay health dividends for older cats may include the following:

- Antioxidants—Vitamins A, C, E, and the mineral selenium help fortify the immune system, deflect environmental toxins, and reduce the risk of developing some cancers

- Biotin—Aids in digestion, skin repair, muscle formation, cellular growth

- Cleansers and detoxifiers—Greens such as chlorophyll, wheat grass, algae, spinach, and broccoli help strengthen the immune system and cleanse the blood

- Glucosamine sulfate and chondroitin sulfate—Helpful in battling arthritis, these supplements lessen joint swelling, stimulate circulation, and build fluid that lubricates joints

- Omega fatty acids—Omega-3s help itchy skin caused by allergies; Omega-6s can help a dull coat shine.

Also new on the scene are dietary supplements to help your overweight cat lose pounds: Carnitine, now added to cat foods designed for weight loss, can increase fat loss and decrease muscle loss; chomium, a glucose-burner potentially beneficial in feline weight-loss programs if used in small amounts; and the better-known fiber, used in place of carbohydrates and fats.

While supplements can benefit cats, do not add any dietary supplement to your cat's food without consulting a veterinarian, holistic practitioner, or veterinary nutritionist. He or she will help you determine an appropriate dosage based on your cat's age, size, and physical condition. If you are tempted to bypass this advice, be aware that giving your cat vitamins or minerals in incorrect amounts can disrupt the nutritional balance of her diet and may have toxic repercussions. Make sure you help, not hurt, your cat.

Weight loss is the opposite scenario for many cats in the later senior years. Again, a health check will rule out potential diseases that can cause weight loss or a dental problem affecting your cat's ability to eat. At this point, your veterinarian may advise an "energy-dense" food containing higher amounts of fat with adequate amounts of essential fatty acids. These fatty acids, tantalizing to cats, can also help jump-start flagging appetites.

SPECIAL DIETS FOR AILING CATS

Aging cats with conditions such as diabetes, heart disease, or cystitis—to name just a few—may require short- or long-term special diets available through your veterinarian. Prescription diets are formulated to be highly palatable, though some cats manage to resist them quite well. A special diet will not help a cat who refuses to eat it. Work with your veterinarian to establish the best possible diet for an ill or ailing older cat.

HEALTHY SNACKS

It's okay to offer your older cat, and even your dieting older cat, an occasional treat. Try a healthy, low-calorie snack consisting of fresh fruit (an apple slice, grapes, or small balls of cantaloupe or watermelon) or bite-size pieces of raw vegetables (carrot, broccoli, or green beans). A holistic veterinary secret: Raw foods such as carrots can help keep teeth clean.

You'll probably need to experiment to find a healthy treat your cat is willing to eat, but it's worth the effort. When your cat receives treats, remember to reduce his regular food intake slightly to balance the extra food he eats. Snacks should make up no more than 5 to 10 percent of your cat's regular diet. Limit servings to no more than 1/4 cup. On the next page you'll find a popular recipe for a healthy snack, a favorite among feline taste-testers, from *Cat Treats*.

SUPPLEMENTS—TO GIVE OR NOT TO GIVE?

We humans love to pop pills, especially if we believe those pills or capsules may help solve a medical problem, reduce the risk of disease, or keep us healthier longer. Not surprisingly, the

Many people don't realize that cats also obtain water from the food they eat. This is particularly true of canned cat food, which contains large amounts of liquid. Cats who eat canned food drink less water than cats who regularly eat dry kibble. There is some debate concerning the merits of feeding your cat wet (canned) over dry (kibble) food. No formal research proves that one is better than the other for healthy cats, though many cat caretakers recommend feeding older cats canned food for at least a portion of their diet. Your cat or veterinarian may do the choosing for you, or your pet may fare better on one or the other. The most important factor is that your older cat eats the right amount of a nutritionally complete diet.

WEIGHT GAIN AND LOSS

A premium diet created for older cats can help balance your cat's nutrition without adding unneeded calories. (Contrary to some recommendations, protein levels in an older cat's diet should be reduced only if your cat is diagnosed with kidney disease—more on this subject in Chapter 10). Obesity may be the most common nutritional problem veterinarians face with older cats. Feline obesity peaks between 6 and 8 years of age, decreases slightly by 10 years, then declines sharply after that age. If your cat gains weight, a physical exam is needed to rule out health problems. Your veterinarian will then recommend an appropriate senior cat food.

eat more protein than dogs and, unlike dogs, cannot survive without meat-based nutrients. While the feline body can synthesize 12 amino acids found in proteins, 10 essential amino acids must come from a cat's diet. For example, the lack of one amino acid, taurine, can lead to blindness and a heart condition called dilated cardiomyopathy. In addition, your cat's critical requirements for arachidonic acid (an unsaturated fatty acid found in most animal fats) and vitamin A also must come from meat.

But cats do not live by meat alone (and certainly not dog food or table scraps). Your cat's optimal diet consists of a balance of protein, carbohydrates, and fats, as well as vitamins and minerals, all of which address the needs outlined above. Because it isn't easy to create and cook regular, nutritious meals for cats, veterinary nutritionists generally recommend that cats be fed a complete, balanced, high-quality commercial food. The trick is to figure out what constitutes a high-quality commercial food (see sidebar on page 41).

THE MOST IMPORTANT NUTRIENT

Along with nutritious food, always provide your older cat with an abundant supply of clean, fresh water to help his body function properly. An aging cat can dehydrate quickly if he experiences vomiting or diarrhea. Encourage him to drink water by using a shallow bowl, offering cold water, or flavoring the water with an ice cube made of something tasty like tuna broth. Because water is so important to your cat's health, go the extra mile and provide him with filtered or bottled water.

Physical signs of aging can accelerate
when a cat eats a feline version of human junk food.

If your cat is active, healthy, and in good shape, you don't automatically need to adjust her diet based on numerical age. While it's essential to discuss your cat's individual needs with your veterinarian, veterinary nutritionists agree that thriving older cats can continue to eat their regular adult maintenance diet well into their senior years. The general rule of thumb is to select a nutritionally balanced and complete diet for your cat's particular life stage and needs. The diet you choose should be formulated according to guidelines established by the Association of American Feed Control Officials (AAFCO), which provides uniform pet-food regulations throughout the country. Feeding test protocols provided by the AAFCO allow pet food manufacturers to furnish proof of nutritional adequacy before marketing their products.

To date, only a few studies address the nutritional needs of aging cats during the last stages of life. Luckily, as the number of senior cats continues to rise, veterinarians are focusing more attention on older pets. Reversing the aging process may be the goal of researchers investigating gene splicing and other technologies, but the most important factor in a good, long life is less dramatic. New research now proves that nutrition supports immune function and serves as an effective treatment for disease—a core belief long held by holistic veterinarians. The veterinary goal is, or should be, to improve the quality of your cat's life, not just keep her living longer.

Nutritional requirements do change during a cat's lifetime, of course, thanks to increases in body fat and decreases in lean body tissues. For example, a senior cat's metabolic rate decreases with the years, resulting in a reduction of caloric needs by 30 to 40 percent in the last one-third of her life. Adjusting your older cat's diet to fit her changing needs can help prevent or delay degenerative diseases associated with aging. Even more, optimal nutrition is now the latest—and one of the most effective—tools to help critically ill companion animals recover their health.

Put simply, good nutrition means more vital years for your cat. Don't underestimate the importance of nutrition in your cat's diet—any old grocery-store brand will not do. Physical signs of aging can accelerate when a cat eats a feline version of human junk food. Not surprisingly, many people notice visible improvement in their cat's health when they begin feeding their cat a diet filled with nourishing ingredients.

To keep your cat looking and feeling his best, feed him the highest-quality cat food you can afford. Typically, the more expensive the food, the better the quality, though this isn't always true. You still need to check labels and be an informed consumer (see sidebar on page 42). Keep in mind that your cat is an obligate carnivore, which means she requires nutrients provided by meat. Cats need to

CHAPTER THREE

Diet for an Older Cat

Food is at the top of your cat's list of good things in the world. Pop open a can of cat food, pour kibble into a bowl, assemble a homemade feline meal, or reach for a healthy kitty treat, and suddenly your sleepy senior resembles a lively, young Cheshire cat, toothy grin and all. Whether you share life with a take-charge cat, whose "Show me the food!" meow greets you more reliably than your alarm clock, or a quieter being who magically appears at feeding time, it's safe to say your older cat cherishes routine days and regular meals. A creature of habit and timing, she prefers to keep things consistent.

*Lead your cat to the
feline fountain of youth—
preventive care can help her enjoy
her senior years and increase
quality of life as she ages.*

PREVENTIVE CARE

Behavioral Red Flags

It's often hard to tell the difference between warning signs of illness or normal signs of aging. Call your veterinarian if your cat displays any of the following signs of illness.

- Coughs frequently

- Loses or gains weight

- Loses appetite

- Drinks abnormal amounts of water

- Frequently urinates

- Fails to use his litter box

- Has trouble walking

- Becomes lethargic

- Increased vomiting or diarrhea

- Experiences constipation

- Has trouble sleeping

- Becomes aggressive or disoriented, or suddenly displays other sudden personality change.

flow decline in cats as part of the normal aging process. Disorders of potassium balance occur frequently in elderly cats. Cats, fortunately, do not experience many of the lower urinary tract changes found in human and canine senior patients.

Endocrine System
Physiological changes in the aging feline thyroid gland are not yet well studied. Impaired glucose tolerance increases as cats age.

FELINE FORTITUDE
It's important to keep in mind that cats are generally strong, healthy creatures. Learning about your cat's age-related changes can help you understand how your cat's body works and what your cat is likely to encounter over the years. Knowledge, combined with preventive care (covered in the following chapters), can help you deal quickly with any health problems that develop. A close relationship with your veterinarian can ensure your older cat remains healthy and happy for many years to come.

brief system-by-system overview of age-related changes observed in other species, and believed to occur in cats as well, is listed below, courtesy of the Cornell Feline Health Center and the American Association of Feline Practitioners (AAFP).

Immune System

The aging process is associated with a decline in normal immune function and host defense mechanisms, which means older cats become ill more quickly and experience longer recovery times than younger cats. The weaker immune system of a senior cat is less able to fend off infection and disease.

Central Nervous System

In humans, age-related changes in the brain can contribute to loss of memory and alterations in personality commonly referred to as senility. Similar symptoms are seen in elderly cats; they may wander, meow excessively, appear disoriented, and avoid social interaction.

Cardiovascular System

There is no change in normal heart rate associated with aging. Hypertension, or abnormally high blood pressure, is usually the result of kidney failure or hyperthyroidism, a disease associated with overactivity of the thyroid gland.

Respiratory System

Aging lungs display reduced elasticity, tidal volume (the volume of air passing in and out of body during normal breathing), and expiratory reserve. Expiratory reserve is the volume of air that can be forcefully expelled after a normal, unforced expiration. That is, exhale during normal breathing, then force out as much air as you can; the amount forced out is the expiratory reserve. A diminished cough reflex is associated with aging. Primary pulmonary disease is rarely a cause of mortality in older cats.

Gastrointestinal System

It is not clear whether a significant age-related decline in ability to digest and absorb nutrients occurs in all healthy geriatric cats. Protein synthesis and metabolic functions decline in the aging liver, but most common feline liver problems are not routinely associated with age-related changes in hepatic (liver) function.

Urinary System

The feline kidneys undergo several age-related changes that may ultimately lead to impaired function of the organ. Kidney size and renal blood

*To your aging cat, climbing stairs may
now seem like climbing Mount Everest.*

Nose

In healthy senior cats, it's possible a reduced
sense of smell may partially cause loss of
appetite, though a refusal to eat is more likely
associated with dental problems or other diseases.

Skin and Fur

A decline in the metabolic rate can cause your cat's
skin to become dry and less elastic. An aging cat's
skin thins and blood flow decreases, leaving the skin
more prone to infection. The skin may appear flaky,
and the fur may become thinner and a little dull or
rough. As often occurs in aging dogs, your cat's
muzzle may turn gray. Older cats groom less efficiently than younger cats, which sometimes results
in hair matting, skin odor, and dermatitis.

Muscles, Bones, and Joints

Older cats lose muscle tone and can appear
unsteady or wobbly on their feet. The loss of muscle mass may result in a thinner appearance—or
the opposite may happen, as your cat's metabolism slows and your pet puts on weight. Older cats
often display stiffness in their joints as tissues lose
moisture and cartilage gradually deteriorates.
Degenerative joint disease, or arthritis, is common.
Bones become brittle. Senior cats may have trouble getting up, lying down, or stepping into their
litter box. To your aging cat, climbing stairs may
now seem like climbing Mount Everest and his

favorite perch on your couch even harder to reach.
Aging cats may not enjoy being picked up or cud-
dled if they experience pain. Finally, grooming may
become more challenging as stiffness impedes a
cat's ability to bend or stretch.

Nails

The nails, or claws, of an aging cat can become
thicker, brittle, and overgrown. A senior cat is less
able to retract her claws. Be sure to clip her nails
(or have them trimmed) to prevent the nails from
sticking to textured materials such as carpet or
from growing into her paws.

PHYSIOLOGY OF AGING

Research on the physiology of aging in cats is
lacking—most of what is known has been learned
by observation of diseases associated with aging. A

BODY TOUR: HOW YOUR OLDER CAT AGES

Unfortunately, your older cat can't describe the age-related changes she experiences. A good way to understand your cat's season of changes is to take a quick tour of her outer and inner workings. Here is what happens as your cat's body ages.

Eyes

The eyes may display the most visible age-related changes. Stare into your older cat's eyes and you may notice a lacy, or moth-eaten, appearance in the iris where the formerly solid, dark swatch of green, blue or gold once appeared. Cats with nuclear sclerosis may develop a bluish cast in the eyes. Iris atrophy and nuclear sclerosis are common age-related traits that may not decrease your cat's vision to any appreciable extent, though several diseases—especially those related to high blood pressure—can seriously impair a cat's ability to see.

Ears

Hearing loss commonly occurs in elderly cats for a variety of reasons, including chronic inflammation due to infection. As a result of hearing loss, your cat may vocalize more loudly and may not respond when you call him. Sudden moves, noises, or touches may startle him.

Teeth

Paying attention to your older cat's dental health in his younger years will pay huge dividends down the road. Dental disease, which can hamper or prevent eating and cause pain, is extremely common in senior cats. In older cats, some teeth may be missing, or look worn and yellow.

CHAPTER TWO

Season of Changes

The cooler, shorter days, colorful leaves, and dusting of snow during fall and winter signal the aging of the year. These seasons are no less important, or less beautiful, than spring and summer; they are simply part of the year's life cycle. As your cat ages, she also will show physical signs of change; some obvious, some subtle. She will devote more time to sleeping in your lap and less time to chasing balls across the floor. Her coat may thin and the iris, or colored portion of her eye, may seem less vibrant. Eating habits may shift and water intake decrease. If, in her younger years, she couldn't watch a spider scuttle by without batting a paw, she may now be content to watch it spin a web.

Healthy-Cat Checklist

If you can't answer yes to all of the following statements, call your veterinarian as soon as possible.

My cat:
- acts normally; seems active and in good spirits
- does not tire easily with moderate exercise
- does not have seizures or fainting episodes
- has a normal appetite
- has had no significant change in weight
- has a normal level of thirst and drinks the usual amount of water
- does not vomit often
- does not regurgitate undigested food
- has no difficulty eating or swallowing
- has normal-looking bowel movements
- defecates without difficulty
- urinates in normal amounts and with normal frequency; urine color is normal
- urinates without difficulty
- always uses a clean litter box
- has not developed new offensive behavioral tendencies, such as aggression or urine-spraying
- has pink gums with no redness, swelling, or bleeding
- does not sneeze and has no nasal discharge
- has bright eyes that are clear and free of discharge
- has a coat that is full, glossy, and free of bald spots and mats; no excessive shedding is evident
- doesn't scratch, lick, or chew excessively
- has skin that is not greasy and has no offensive body odor
- is free of fleas, ticks, lice, and mites
- has no persistent abnormal swelling
- has no sores that do not heal
- has no bleeding or discharge from any body opening
- has ears that are clean and odor-free
- doesn't shake his head or scratch his ears
- hears normally and reacts as usual to his environment
- walks without stiffness, pain, or difficulty
- has feet that appear healthy, with claws of normal length
- breathes normally without straining or coughing

—Reprinted with permission from the Cornell Feline Health Center, Cornell University's College of Veterinary Medicine

physical condition and weight. A complete medical and behavioral history will be gathered, along with a thorough physical evaluating every organ system. The results will then be compared to previous evaluations. At least once a year certain tests — including blood tests, urinalysis, and fecal exam — will be suggested.

Prevention — and early detection — is the key. Catching and treating disorders early, as well as monitoring ongoing medical conditions, is the aim of veterinarians who want to keep your older cat healthy.

Do not dismiss significant changes
in appetite, weight, elimination,
or water intake, even if your cat seems fine.

The Aging Process:
Human Years and Cat Years

You can generally correlate your cat's age in human years using the chart below. A 1-year-old cat is physiologically similar to a 16-year-old person; age-wise, a 2-year-old cat resembles a 21-year-old human. After the age of 2, each cat year equals about 4 human years.

COMPARATIVE AGES
OF CATS AND HUMANS

Cats	Humans
1	16
2	21
5	33
10	53
11	57
12	61
13	65
14	69
15	73
16	77
17	81
18	85
19	89
20	93

Cat 1 • Human 16

Cat 10 • Human 53

Cat 13 • Human 65

Cat 16 • Human 77

Cat 19 • Human 89

weigh yourself on your scale and then hold your cat, weigh again, and subtract the difference.) If there's a significant variation — a pound or more — contact your veterinarian.

- Face him. Are his eyes clear and bright? Any discharge from the eyes or nose indicates a health problem.

AGE OR ILLNESS?

Just like older people, cats tend to sleep longer, eat and drink less, and tire more easily as the years pass. They may experience changes in sight, smell, and taste, and be more sensitive to stress. Vision and hearing may deteriorate. Never assume, though, that changes you notice in your senior cat are simply due to old age and can be ignored. While aging is a normal process, illness is not. Only your veterinarian can tell the difference, and sometimes even she may have a tough time distinguishing between the two. If you notice any physical or behavioral changes, alert your veterinarian.

Unfortunately, cats hide disease well. This normal protective mechanism is an inheritance from their wild ancestors. Cats will hide signs of illness that make them appear weak, even from human companions they know and trust. Cats with chronic disease can look healthy until the illness becomes very serious. Luckily, many common feline diseases are treatable if caught early enough. Do not dismiss significant changes in appetite, weight, elimination, or water intake, even if your cat seems fine. Other red flags are changes in behavior, hearing, walking, or breathing. Early detection especially benefits older cats, whose age-related susceptibility to bodily changes can make them vulnerable to disease within a short time.

PREVENTION IS THE BEST MEDICINE

The AAFP and the Academy of Feline Medicine (AFM) have developed senior care guidelines to promote optimal health in older cats by setting minimal standards of care for cats with and without clinical signs of disease. The guidelines recommend initiating a preventive health-care program for cats between 7 and 11 years of age, one that should continue for the duration of the cat's life. Older cats also should receive a thorough physical exam every six months, a recent departure from traditional care standards.

During the half-yearly checkup, you can expect your veterinarian to assess your cat's general

Lifestyle, environment, and whether a cat is spayed or neutered, along with the general wear and tear of daily life, all play a part in the aging process. We may know people who seem younger than their age, and others who look older than their years. Similarly, a stray cat who has endured a hard life may appear older than a pampered housecat who ages gracefully. The same factors that contribute to human longevity—including a well-balanced diet, moderate exercise, and weight control—also can extend a cat's life. A cat who eats nutritious meals, maintains a normal weight, plays, and lives in a healthy environment can enjoy an active life long after she is considered "old." This is especially true when human companions recognize and respond to their cat's changing health needs.

WHAT YOU CAN DO

The aging process occurs gradually, so it's easy to overlook signs of change. Now, before problems begin, is a good time to pay attention to your cat's normal patterns. Gauge his sleeping, eating, and playing habits. Make mental notes of your cat's physical appearance and behavior. Better yet, write your observations down and store them in your cat's health file. Someday your veterinarian will thank you for the feline history notes. In addition, you can do a few simple things on a daily or weekly basis to keep tabs on your senior cat's general health. The Cornell Feline Health Center and the American Association of Feline Practitioners (AAFP) recommend performing a mini health exam as an extension of the way you normally interact with your cat.

> ### Did You Know?
>
> Small dogs live longer lives than large dogs, but this isn't the case with cats, whose body shape remains roughly the same from breed to breed. While a cat's breed does not affect the rate at which he ages, genetic predispositions to different diseases in some cat breeds can result.

- While stroking your cat, check his skin for odd lumps, bumps, sores, and dryness.

- Brush your older cat's fur to remove loose hair, assist grooming, and to stimulate blood circulation and sebaceous gland secretions. Is his fur shiny and soft, or dry and lackluster?

- If she cooperates (try scratching her chin), check your cat's teeth and gums by gently raising her upper lips with your thumb or forefinger. Gums should be pink. Red gums, tartar (a thick coating on your cat's teeth), bad breath, or a broken tooth warrant a vet's attention.

- Look in his ears and examine his ear canals. Healthy ears are clean and odorless.

- Monitor your cat's weight. Run your hands gently over her ribs. Do they feel bony? Try weighing her monthly on a scale sensitive enough to detect small changes. (You can use a kitchen baking scale with a large capacity bowl for very small or slender cats of 7 pounds or less; or

CHAPTER ONE

The Aging Process

Cats age better than we do. They don't worry about wrinkles or fret over thinning hair. Perhaps in their quiet wisdom they realize aging is a natural process and not a disease. Cats are individuals and, just like people, age in their own ways. Setting a date for old age can be arbitrary and even a bit controversial. In general, veterinarians consider a cat to be a senior beginning around age 7. This does not mean your 7-year-old cat is old; rather, he's at a midlife benchmark. Seven is the age when metabolic changes begin to surface in mature cats, with noticeable physical changes occurring somewhere between 7 and 10 years. Most cats are considered elderly at age 12, but, again, the label can be misleading. The average feline life lasts about 15 to 18 years, but cats who live well into their 20s are no longer considered rare or unusual.

On a Cat Aging

He blinks upon the hearth-rug
And yawns in deep content,
Accepting all the comforts
That Providence has sent.

Louder he purrs and louder,
In one glad hymn of praise
For all the night's adventures,
For quiet, restful days.

Life will go on forever,
With all that cat can wish;
Warmth, and the glad procession
Of fish and milk and fish.

Only—the thought disturbs him—
He's noticed once or twice,
That times are somehow breeding
A nimbler race of mice.

—Sir Alexander Gray, Scottish professor and poet,
from Gossip, 1928

SECTION 1

HOW YOUR CAT AGES

Just as the aging baby-boomer population causes changes in health-care systems and social-security programs, an increasingly older pet cat population deserves notice as well. This means that as your cat moves into middle age and beyond, you may need to change the way you treat him. If you've picked up this book, you may want to learn more about the joys and challenges of living with an older cat. Perhaps you are interested in discovering simple ways to make your senior cat more comfortable and increase her quality of life. You may be concerned about dealing with a chronically ill cat, considering holistic healing therapies, or seeking solutions for common health problems. You may simply want to understand the feline aging process, from nose to tail. You'll find it in *Your Older Cat*. Our cats are living longer. With this book, you can help them live better.

"Older cats hold wonderful surprises and gifts for the people they live with and love."

10 Cat Wishes for Responsible Pet Owners

1. My life is likely to last 10 to 15 years. Any separation from you will be very painful.
2. Give me time to understand what you want of me.
3. Allow me to place my trust in you—it is crucial for my well-being.
4. Don't be angry with me for long, and don't lock me up as punishment. You have work, your friends, and your entertainment. I have only you.
5. Talk to me. Even if I don't understand your words, I understand your voice when it's speaking to me.
6. Be aware that however you treat me, I'll never forget it.
7. Don't hit me. Remember that I have teeth but I choose not to bite you.
8. Before you scold me for being lazy or uncooperative, ask yourself if something might be bothering me. Perhaps I'm not getting the right food, I've been in the sun too long, or my heart is getting old and weak.
9. Take care of me when I get old. You, too, will grow old.
10. Stay with me on difficult journeys. Never say, "I can't bear to watch it," or "Let it happen in my absence." Everything is easier for me if you are there.

—Author unknown

In return, evidence supports the idea that cat companionship provides meaningful comfort to us, offering protection against depression and loneliness. At least one study indicates that living with a pet may lengthen human life. Of course, those of us who live with older cats don't need surveys and studies to tell us how much we love our cats or how much they add to our lives. We already know how lucky we are to share this precious time with our feline companions.

"Older cats hold wonderful surprises and gifts for the people they live with and love," says Nancy Marano, a writer who lives with two mature cats in Albuquerque, New Mexico. Marano recently conducted an informal inquiry of people with older cats. Here's what she discovered:

"The bond between the person and cat deepens dramatically. You have accommodated each other for so many years that living together becomes very comfortable. You know each other's moods and needs without guesswork or false steps. You just look at your cat and know if something is wrong or amiss, even if he tries to hide it.

their pet's overall health was good, and on average, cat owners take their cats to the veterinarian 1.6 times a year.

A LITTLE TLC GOES A LONG WAY

Not surprisingly, people who closely interact with their older cats tend to be aware of their pet's needs—physically, mentally, and emotionally. These pet guardians are more likely to seek veterinary care, purchase nutritious cat food, and groom their cats. They take time to play with their cats and keep them safe.

"By the time a cat reaches a certain age, he has you wrapped around his paw. He's trained you to do all the right things. You know where he wants to be rubbed and scratched, how pillows should be arranged on the bed, where his favorite sunning spots are, and when he doesn't want to be disturbed. Your cat doesn't have bursts of kitten energy—but he doesn't knock over lamps, either. It's like a good, long marriage where words aren't necessary to know the depths of the other person."

"How old is your cat?" *Cat Fancy* magazine asked in its search for the oldest cat in America. In the months preceding the June 2001 issue announcing the winner, 316 entries for senior cats turned up in the magazine's editorial in box. Some surprising numbers soon emerged: More than half of these cats were 18 or more years old, and a third were 20 or older. The oldest was Starbuck, a handsome 27-year-old striped male cat with bright blue eyes and a hearty appetite. The California resident's veterinarian pronounced him to be "in very good shape," and his lifelong guardian attributed a large part of Starbuck's longevity to "good care and genetics."

Today it is not unusual for a healthy cat to live well into her teens and beyond. Veterinarians across the country report seeing an increasing number of senior cats in their practices, a trend that is sparking new interest in feline geriatric care. Thanks to progress in preventive medicine, nutrition, and knowledge of animal behavior, older cats are blowing out more candles on their birthday cakes. Despite these wonderful advances, the most important part of your senior cat's life, as Starbuck's best friend proves, is you. A well-cared-for older cat can give you just as much pleasure as he did when he was a kitten—as long as he maintains his vitality. Whether you've lived with your aging cat since he was 8 weeks—or 8 years—old, it's up to you to make the most the most of your cat's later years.

CHERISHED RELATIONSHIPS

People began forging relationships with cats more than 4,000 years ago. Over the centuries, cats have survived both our persecution and our adoration. In modern times, the close bond between us is being explored, acknowledged, and respected. Nowhere is this more apparent than in the cherished relationships between senior cats and their human companions.

Today more people live with older cats than ever before. The Pet Food Institute (PFI), which represents companies producing 95 percent of the commercial cat and dog food made in the United States, began keeping track of the number of pets in 1981. Since that time, the feline pet population has jumped by more than 30 million cats! PFI confirms that the number of pet cats reached an all-time high in the year 2000—more than 75 million cats, with over 34 percent of all households living with at least one pet cat. In addition, an American Veterinary Medical Association (AVMA) study shows the percentage of pet cats 6 years of age and older increased from 24 percent in 1983 to just over 47 percent in 1996. There's no denying our graying pet population now lives longer.

Another recent pet study (conducted by the Healthy Pets 21 Consortium, an alliance including the American Animal Hospital Association, the Delta Society, Ralston Purina, and the Center to Study Human-Animal Relationships and Environments, among others) called "The State of the American Pet," reports that most cat owners hug or pet their cat daily (91 percent of 1,000 cat owners). The study also noted that Americans list companionship as their number-one reason for having pets. Most respondents (97 percent) said

LIVING LONGER,
LIVING BETTER

When I graduated from veterinary school, a "short" quarter-century ago, cats were just a minor species, rarely given more than the last 10 minutes of an hour-long lecture. As pets, they were often relegated to the role of outdoor pest controllers, and they rarely achieved the status they enjoy today. Health care was minimal, nutritional information was lacking, and life expectancies were often limited by disease, accidents, or encounters with other animals, including other cats.

During the last decade, however, cats have attained new popularity as the number-one animal companion in the United States. Longer working days, single-parent households, and the urbanization of the workforce have contributed to the popularity of a creature that can live within a home, often never venturing beyond its walls. The simplicity of dealing with a cat's daily needs, along with its egalitarian spirit and entertaining personality, makes more and more Americans choose felines as their new companions.

Along with changes in the owner's lifestyle, cats have enjoyed changes of their own. No longer second-class citizens, they now benefit from advances in nutrition and disease prevention. Today, veterinarians treat their patients with the concept of wellness in mind. Wellness simply means providing care that optimizes cats' lifestyles so they can maintain consistent good health and a long life. With this kind of care, owners can feel confident that their cat will enjoy a high quality of life well into their golden years.

We all have fallen in love with a cuddly kitten who soon becomes a rambunctious adolescent. That same spry young cat will enter middle age calmer and more reserved. And as your cat begins to age, he may begin to face the first real health challenges of his adult life. Just like aging humans, aging cats can experience more health problems than their younger relatives. The problems are familiar—arthritis, vision and hearing loss, even cancer. But the growing senior cat population (which nearly doubled between 1983 and 1996) has changed the face of feline veterinary care. Though it may be difficult for owners to adjust to this new stage in their cat's life, "getting old" doesn't mean that a cat is dying. Advances in nutrition, medical and behavioral care all contribute to the longevity many cats (and owners) now enjoy. With conscientious care and an eye for prevention, owners can help their cats enjoy long, healthy lives.

FOREWORD

BY
GERARD K. BEEKMAN, D.V.M.

CONTENTS

Foreword: by Gerard K. Beekman, D.V.M.   8
Introduction: Living Longer, Living Better   10

Section 1 How Your Cat Ages   14
Chapter One: The Aging Process   16
Chapter Two: Season of Changes   26

Section 2 Preventive Care   32
Chapter Three: Diet for an Older Cat   34
Chapter Four: Exercise and Play to Keep Your Cat Active   44
Chapter Five: Comfort Zone—Making Life Easier   52

Section 3 Natural Relief 60
Chapter Six: Holistic Healing Therapies   62
Chapter Seven: Hands-On Alternative Treatments   70

Section 4 Age-Related Health Problems   80
Chapter Eight: First-Aid Primer   82
Chapter Nine: Solutions for Common Health and Behavior Problems   96
Chapter Ten: Illnesses Your Older Cat May Develop   104

Section 5 The Last Dance   114
Chapter Eleven: Coping with Chronic Disease and Pain   116
Chapter Twelve: Endings and New Beginnings   122

Resources   133
Suggested Reading   136
Index   138
Photo Credits 142
About the Author 143

ACKNOWLEDGMENTS

My deep appreciation and thanks go to all the veterinarians and animal behaviorists who generously shared their time and expertise, particularly James R. Richards, D.V.M.; Shawn Messonnier, D.V.M.; Jill A. Richardson, D.V.M.; and J. Michael McFarland, D.V.M. Without your assistance, this book would not have been written. Any technical errors are my own.

In addition, I would like to thank writers Mary Lidden and Pat Miller for their contribution to the exercise and play section of this book. Special thanks to author Rita Reynolds, whose love of older animals knows no bounds, and to Wendy Simard, for her valuable editorial direction. To fellow members of the Cat Writers' Association (you know who you are), especially Karen Commings and Nancy Marano, I thank you for your encouragement and help. Finally, loving thanks to my family—human and animal—for their great patience and faithful support. My apologies to anyone I have overlooked.

FIRESIDE
Rockefeller Center
1230 Avenue of the Americas
New York, NY 10020

For information regarding special discounts for
bulk purchases, please contact Simon & Schuster
Special Sales at 1-800-456-6798 or
business@simonandschuster.com

Printed in China

10 9 8 7 6 5 4 3 2 1

Library of Congress Cataloging-in-Publication
data available.

ISBN 0-7432-2455-8

Designed by Jill Feron
Illustrations by Todd Bonita
TMBONITA@aol.com

Your Older Cat

A Complete Guide to Nutrition,
Natural Health Remedies,
and Veterinary Care

Susan Easterly

A Fireside Book
Published by Simon & Schuster

NEW YORK   LONDON   TORONTO   SYDNEY   SINGAPORE

6 The Mass Media   132

Sociological Perspectives on the Media   134
Functionalist View   134
Conflict View   139
Feminist View   142
Interactionist View   143

The Audience   144
Who Is in the Audience?   145
The Segmented Audience   145
Audience Behavior   146

The Media Industry   147
Media Concentration   147
The Media's Global Reach   149

SOCIAL POLICY AND THE MASS MEDIA: Media Violence   151

Photo Essay: How Does Television Portray the Family?   136

Social Inequality: The Color of Network TV   141

Sociology in the Global Community: Al Jazeera Is on the Air   150

7 Deviance and Social Control   156

Social Control   158
Conformity and Obedience   159
Informal and Formal Social Control   160
Law and Society   161

Deviance   163
What Is Deviance?   163
Explaining Deviance   168

Crime   173
Types of Crime   174
Crime Statistics   177

SOCIAL POLICY AND SOCIAL CONTROL: The Death Penalty in the United States and Worldwide   179

Sociology on Campus: Binge Drinking   162

Photo Essay: Who Is Deviant?   166

Research in Action: Labeling A Behavior as a Crime: Road Rage   172

Taking Sociology to Work: Tiffany Zapata-Mancilla, Victim Witness Specialist, Cook County State's Attorney's Office   176

8 Stratification and Social Mobility in the United States   184

Understanding Stratification   186
Systems of Stratification   186
Perspectives on Stratification   189
Is Stratification Universal?   192

Stratification by Social Class   194
Measuring Social Class   194
Wealth and Income   195
Poverty   196
Life Chances   200

Social Mobility   201
Open versus Closed Stratification Systems   201
Types of Social Mobility   201
Social Mobility in the United States   201

SOCIAL POLICY AND STRATIFICATION: Rethinking Welfare in North America and Europe   203

Research in Action: The Shrinking Middle Class   190

Sociology in the Global Community: It's All Relative: Appalachian Poverty and Congolese Affluence   198

Sociology on Campus: Social Class and Financial Aid   202

9 Global Inequality   209

The Global Divide   211

**Stratification in the World
System   212**
The Legacy of Colonialism   214
Multinational Corporations   215
Worldwide Poverty   216
Modernization   217

**Stratification within Nations: A
Comparative Perspective   220**
Distribution of Wealth and Income   221
Social Mobility   221

**Case Study: Stratification in
Mexico   223**
Mexico's Economy   223
Race Relations in Mexico: The Color
Hierarchy   224
The Status of Women in Mexico   224
The Borderlands   225

SOCIAL POLICY AND GLOBAL
INEQUALITY: Universal Human
Rights   227

*Sociology in the Global Community:
Cutting Poverty Worldwide   219*

*Sociology in the Global Community:
The Global Disconnect   220*

*Social Inequality: Stratification in
Japan   222*

10 Racial and Ethnic
Inequality   232

**Minority, Racial, and Ethnic
Groups   234**
Minority Groups   234
Race   235
Ethnicity   236

**Prejudice and
Discrimination   237**
Prejudice   237
Discriminatory Behavior   238
The Privileges of the Dominant   239
Institutional Discrimination   240

Studying Race and Ethnicity   241
Functionalist Perspective   241
Conflict Perspective   242
Interactionist Perspective   242

**Patterns of Intergroup
Relations   243**
Amalgamation   243
Assimilation   243
Segregation   244
Pluralism   245

**Impact of Global
Immigration   245**

**Race and Ethnicity in the
United States   246**
Racial Groups   247
Ethnic Groups   253

SOCIAL POLICY AND RACIAL
AND ETHNIC INEQUALITY:
Racial Profiling   255

*Taking Sociology to Work: Prudence
Hannis, Liaison Officer, National
Institute of Science Research,
University of Québec   241*

*Research in Action: Interracial and
Interethnic Friendships   244*

*Social Inequality: Native Americans
Gamble on Gaming   250*

11 Stratification by Gender
and Age   260

**Social Construction of
Gender   262**
Gender Roles in the United States   263
Cross-Cultural Perspective   265

**Explaining Stratification by
Gender   266**
The Functionalist View   266
The Conflict Response   266
The Feminist Perspective   267
The Interactionist Approach   267

**Women: The Oppressed
Majority   268**
Sexism and Sex Discrimination   268
Sexual Harassment   269
The Status of Women Worldwide   269
Women in the Workforce of the United
States   271

Aging and Society   273

Explaining the Aging Process   274
Functionalist Approach: Disengagement
Theory   274
Interactionist Approach: Activity Theory   276
The Conflict Approach   276

**Role Transitions throughout the
Life Course   277**
The Sandwich Generation   277
Adjusting to Retirement   278
Death and Dying   280

**Age Stratification in the
United States   281**
The "Graying of America"   281
Wealth and Income   281
Ageism   282
Competition in the Labor Force   282

SOCIAL POLICY AND GENDER
STRATIFICATION: The Battle over
Abortion from a Global
Perspective   283

*Research in Action: Differences in Male
and Female Physicians' Communication
with Patients   269*

*Sociology in the Global Community: The
Head Scarf and the Veil: Complex
Symbols   270*

*Sociology in the Global Community:
Aging Worldwide: Issues and
Consequences   275*

*Research in Action: Naturally Occurring
Retirement Communities (NORCs)   279*

12 The Family and Intimate Relationships 289

Global View of the Family 291
Composition: What Is the Family? 291
Kinship Patterns: To Whom Are We Related? 294
Authority Patterns: Who Rules? 295

Studying the Family 295
Functionalist View 295
Conflict View 296
Interactionist View 296
Feminist View 296

Marriage and Family 298
Courtship and Mate Selection 298
Variations in Family Life and Intimate Relationships 301
Child-Rearing Patterns in Family Life 302

Divorce 305
Statistical Trends in Divorce 305
Factors Associated with Divorce 305
Impact of Divorce on Children 305

Diverse Lifestyles 306
Cohabitation 306
Remaining Single 307
Marriage without Children 308
Lesbian and Gay Relationships 308

SOCIAL POLICY AND THE FAMILY:
Gay Marriage 309

Photo Essay: What Is a Family? 292

Sociology in the Global Community: Domestic Violence 297

Research in Action: Arranged Marriage, American-Style 300

Research in Action: The Lingering Impact of Divorce 307

13 Religion and Education 314

Durkheim and the Sociological Approach to Religion 316

World Religions 320

Sociological Explanations of Religion 321
The Integrative Function of Religion 321
Religion and Social Support 323
Religion and Social Change 323
Religion and Social Control: A Conflict View 324

Components of Religion 324
Belief 324
Ritual 325
Experience 326

Religious Organization 327
Ecclesiae 327
Denominations 327
Sects 328
New Religious Movements or Cults 329
Comparing Forms of Religious Organization 330

Case Study: Religion in India 332
The Religious Tapestry in India 332
Religion and the State in India 333

Sociological Perspectives on Education 333
Functionalist View 333
Conflict View 335
Interactionist View 337

Schools as Formal Organizations 339
Bureaucratization of Schools 339
Teachers: Employees and Instructors 340
Student Subcultures 340
Homeschooling 341

SOCIAL POLICY AND RELIGION:
Religion in the Schools 342

Photo Essay: Why Do Sociologists Study Religion? 318

Research in Action: Income and Education, Religiously Speaking 322

Research in Action: Islam in the United States 328

Sociology on Campus: The Debate over Title IX 338

14 Government and the Economy 347

Economic Systems 349
Capitalism 349
Socialism 351
The Informal Economy 352

Case Study: Capitalism in China 353
The Road to Capitalism 353
The Chinese Economy Today 354
Chinese Workers in the New Economy 354

Power and Authority 355
Power 355
Types of Authority 355

Types of Government 356
Monarchy 356
Oligarchy 356
Dictatorship and Totalitarianism 356
Democracy 357

Political Behavior in the United States 357
Participation and Apathy 357
Race and Gender in Politics 358

Models of Power Structure in the United States 359
Power Elite Models 361
Pluralist Model 362

War and Peace 362
War 362
Peace 363
Terrorism 364

The Changing Economy 365
The Changing Face of the Workforce 365
Deindustrialization 367

SOCIAL POLICY AND THE ECONOMY:
Global Offshoring 368

Taking Sociology to Work: Richard J. Hawk, Vice President and Financial Consultant, Smith Barney 351

Research in Action: Why Don't More Young People Vote? 359

Sociology in the Global Community: Gender Quotas at the Ballot Box 360

Social Inequality: Affirmative Action 366

15 Population, Communities, and Health 373

Demography: The Study of Population 375
Malthus's Thesis and Marx's Response 376
Studying Population Today 376
Elements of Demography 377

World Population Patterns 377
Demographic Transition 377
The Population Explosion 379

Fertility Patterns in the United States 380
The Baby Boom 380
Stable Population Growth 380

How Have Communities Changed? 381
Preindustrial Cities 382
Industrial and Postindustrial Cities 382

Urbanization 383
Functionalist View: Urban Ecology 384
Conflict View: New Urban Sociology 386

Types of Communities 387
Central Cities 387
Suburbs 388
Rural Communities 389

Sociological Perspectives on Health and Illness 390
Functionalist Approach 391
Conflict Approach 392
Interactionist Approach 393
Labeling Approach 394

Social Epidemiology and Health 395
Social Class 396
Race and Ethnicity 397
Gender 398
Age 398

SOCIAL POLICY AND HEALTH: The AIDS Crisis 399

Sociology in the Global Community: Population Policy in China 380

Research in Action: Store Wars 391

Social Inequality: To Inform or Not to Inform? How Race and Ethnicity Affect Views of Patient Autonomy 394

Taking Sociology to Work: Jess Purmort, Research Assistant, New York Academy of Medicine 396

16 Globalization, the Environment, and Social Change 405

Social Movements 407
Relative Deprivation Approach 408
Resource Mobilization Approach 408
Gender and Social Movements 409
New Social Movements 410

Theories of Social Change 411
Evolutionary Theory 411
Functionalist Theory 411
Conflict Theory 412

Resistance to Social Change 413
Economic and Cultural Factors 413
Resistance to Technology 414

Global Social Change 414
Privacy and Censorship in a Global Village 415
Biotechnology and the Gene Pool 416

Social Change and the Environment 418
Environmental Problems: An Overview 418
Conflict View of Environmental Issues 420
Environmental Justice 420

SOCIAL POLICY AND GLOBALIZATION: Transnationals 421

Sociology in the Global Community: A New Social Movement in Rural India 410

Research in Action: The Human Genome Project 417

Glossary 427
References 435
Acknowledgments 458
Photo Credits 461
Name Index 463
Subject Index 468

chapter opening EXCERPTS

Every chapter in this textbook begins with an excerpt from one of the works listed here. These excerpts convey the excitement and relevance of sociological inquiry and draw readers into the subject matter from each chapter.

Chapter 1
Nickel and Dimed: On (Not) Getting By in America by Barbara Ehrenreich   2

Chapter 2
Paradise Laborers: Hotel Work in the Global Economy by Patricia A. Adler and Peter Adler   29

Chapter 3
Born to Buy: The Commercialized Child and the New Consumer Culture by Juliet B. Schor   54

Chapter 4
Black Picket Fences: Privilege and Peril among the Black Middle Class by Mary Pattillo-McCoy   78

Chapter 5
"Pathology of Imprisonment" by Philip Zimbardo   100

Chapter 6
Growing Up Digital: The Rise of the Net Generation by Don Tapscott   133

Chapter 7
Wallbangin': Graffiti and Gangs in L.A. by Susan A. Phillips   157

Chapter 8
The Working Poor: Invisible in America by David K. Shipler   185

Chapter 9
"Arnold Schwarzenegger, Ally McBeal and Arranged Marriages: Globalization on the Ground in India" by Steve Derné   210

Chapter 10
Asian American Dreams: The Emergence of an American People by Helen Zia   233

Chapter 11
Lipstick Jihad: A Memoir of Growing Up Iranian in America and American in Iran by Azadeh Moaveni   261

Chapter 12
Unequal Childhoods: Class, Race, and Family Life by Annette Lareau   290

Chapter 13
For This Land: Writings on Religion in America by Vine Deloria Jr.   315

Chapter 14
Diversity in the Power Elite: How It Happened, Why It Matters by Richard L. Zweigenhaft and G. William Domhoff   348

Chapter 15
Sidewalk by Mitchell Duneier   374

Chapter 16
Ruling the Waves: Cycles of Discovery, Chaos, and Wealth from the Compass to the Internet by Debora L. Spar   406

boxed features

sociology IN *the Global Community*

1-2 The Global Response to the 2004 Tsunami 21
3-1 Life in the Global Village 59
3-2 Cultural Survival in Brazil 61
4-2 Raising Amish Children 90
5-3 McDonald's and the Worldwide Bureaucratization of Society 122
6-2 Al Jazeera Is on the Air 150
8-2 It's All Relative: Appalachian Poverty and Congolese Affluence 198
9-1 Cutting Poverty Worldwide 219
9-2 The Global Disconnect 220
11-2 The Head Scarf and the Veil: Complex Symbols 270
11-3 Aging Worldwide: Issues and Consequences 275
12-1 Domestic Violence 297
14-2 Gender Quotas at the Ballot Box 360
15-1 Population Policy in China 380
16-1 A New Social Movement in Rural India 410

research IN *action*

1-1 Looking at Sports from Three Theoretical Perspectives 19
2-1 Polling in Baghdad 36
2-3 What's in a Name? 41
5-2 Adolescent Sexual Networks 111
7-2 Labeling a Behavior as a Crime: Road Rage 172
8-1 The Shrinking Middle Class 190
10-1 Interracial and Interethnic Friendships 244
11-1 Differences in Male and Female Physicians' Communication with Patients 269
11-4 Naturally Occurring Retirement Communities (NORCs) 279
12-2 Arranged Marriage, American-Style 300
12-3 The Lingering Impact of Divorce 307
13-1 Income and Education, Religiously Speaking 322
13-2 Islam in the United States 328
14-1 Why Don't More Young People Vote? 359
15-2 Store Wars 391
16-2 The Human Genome Project 417

2-2   Researching Privilege and Discrimination in Employment   39

5-1   Disability as a Master Status   104

6-1   The Color of Network TV   141

9-3   Stratification in Japan   222

10-2   Native Americans Gamble on Gaming   250

14-3   Affirmative Action   366

15-3   To Inform or Not to Inform? How Race and Ethnicity Affect Views of Patient Autonomy   394

3-3   A Culture of Cheating?   68

4-1   Impression Management by Students   85

7-1   Binge Drinking   162

8-3   Social Class and Financial Aid   202

13-3   The Debate over Title IX   338

Dave Eberbach, Research Coordinator, United Way of Central Iowa   44

Rakefet Avramovitz, Program Administrator, Child Care Law Center   91

Tiffany Zapata-Mancilla, Victim Witness Specialist, Cook County State's Attorney's Office   176

Prudence Hannis, Liaison Officer, National Institute of Science Research, University of Québec   241

Richard J. Hawk, Vice President and Financial Consultant, Smith Barney   351

Jess Purmort, Research Assistant, New York Academy of Medicine   396

social policy SECTIONS

Chapter 2

Social Policy and Sociological Research: Studying Human Sexuality   45

Chapter 3

Social Policy and Culture: Bilingualism   71

Chapter 4

Social Policy and Socialization: Child Care around the World   94

Chapter 5

Social Policy and Organizations: The State of the Unions   125

Chapter 6

Social Policy and the Mass Media: Media Violence   151

Chapter 7

Social Policy and Social Control: The Death Penalty in the United States and Worldwide   179

Chapter 8

Social Policy and Stratification: Rethinking Welfare in North America and Europe   203

Chapter 9

Social Policy and Global Inequality: Universal Human Rights   227

Chapter 10

Social Policy and Racial and Ethnic Inequality: Racial Profiling   255

Chapter 11

Social Policy and Gender Stratification: The Battle over Abortion from a Global Perspective   283

Chapter 12

Social Policy and the Family: Gay Marriage   309

Chapter 13

Social Policy and Religion: Religion in the Schools   342

Chapter 14

Social Policy and the Economy: Global Offshoring   368

Chapter 15

Social Policy and Health: The AIDS Crisis   399

Chapter 16

Social Policy and Globalization: Transnationals   421

MAPS summingUP tables photo essays

Mapping Life Nationwide

Educational Level and Household Income in the United States   32

Non-English Speakers at Home   73

Union Membership in the United States   127

The Status of Medical Marijuana   163

Executions by State Since 1976   180

The 50 States: Haves and Have-Nots   187

Active Hate Groups in the United States   238

Census 2000: The Image of Diversity   247

Distribution of the Arab American Population by State   253

Twenty-eight Floridas by 2030   282

Restrictions on Public Funding for Abortion   284

Unmarried-Couple Households by State   306

Discriminatory Marriage and Anti–Gay Discrimination Laws   310

Largest Religious Groups in the United States by County, 2000   330

Availability of Physicians by State   398

Mapping Life Worldwide

Languages of the World: How Many Do You Speak?   62

The Internet Explosion   144

Gross National Income per Capita   213

Poverty Worldwide   218

The Borderlands   226

The Global Divide on Abortion   285

Religions of the World   317

The Global Reach of Terrorism   365

Global Urbanization 2015 (projected)   384

Adults and Children Living with HIV/AIDS   400

Labor Migration   422

SUMMINGUP Tables

Major Sociological Perspectives   18

Existing Sources Used in Sociological Research   40

Major Research Designs   42

Major Sociological Perspectives on Culture   71

Theoretical Approaches to Development of the Self   86

Comparison of Primary and Secondary Groups   108

Comparison of the Gemeinschaft and Gesellschaft   116

Stages of Sociocultural Evolution   117

Characteristics of a Bureaucracy   121

Sociological Perspectives on the Mass Media   146

Modes of Individual Adaptation   168

Sociological Perspectives on Deviance   174

Sociological Perspectives on Social Stratification   194

Three Approaches to Global Inequality   221

Sociological Perspectives on Race   243

Sociological Perspectives on Gender   268

Sociological Perspectives on Aging   277

Sociological Perspectives on the Family   298

Major World Religions   320

Sociological Perspectives on Religion   325

Characteristics of Ecclesiae, Denominations, Sects, and New Religious Movements   331

Sociological Perspectives on Education   339

Characteristics of the Three Major Economic Systems   352

Comparing Types of Cities   383

Sociological Perspectives on Urbanization   387

Sociological Perspectives on Health and Illness   395

Contributions to Social Movement Theory   411

Sociological Perspectives on Social Change   413

Photo Essays

Are You What You Own?   4

Are You What You Eat?   56

Why Do We Gather Together?   106

How Does Television Portray the Family?   136

Who Is Deviant?   166

What Is a Family?   292

Why Do Sociologists Study Religion?   318

preface

Without a doubt, you have thought about sociological issues before opening this book. Have you or a childhood friend ever spent time in day care? Are your parents or a friend's parents divorced? Are you concerned about plagiarism or binge drinking on your campus? Did you need a student loan to attend college? Chances are you have been touched by most or all of these issues. If you are like most students, you've also spent a great deal of time thinking about your future career. If you major in sociology, what occupations can you choose from?

These are just some of the topics of immediate personal interest that are dealt with in this book. Sociologists also address broader issues, from bilingual education to the existence of slavery in the 21st century. Sociology includes the study of immigration, poverty, overpopulation, and the process and problems of growing old in different cultures. In the aftermath of disasters such as Hurricane Katrina and the terrorist attacks of September 11, 2001, sociologists have been called on to explain their social consequences—how they affected people of different ages, social classes, and racial and ethnic groups, and how our government responded. These topics, along with many others, are of great interest to me, but it is the sociological explanations for them that I find especially compelling. The introductory sociology class provides the ideal laboratory in which to study our own society and those of our global neighbors.

Making Sociology Relevant

Sociology examines and questions even the most familiar patterns of social behavior. It can help students to better understand their own lives and those of people from other cultures.

After more than 30 years of teaching sociology to students in colleges, adult education programs, nursing programs, an overseas program based in London, and even a maximum-security prison, I am firmly convinced that the discipline can play a valuable role in teaching critical thinking skills. The distinctive emphasis on social policy found in this text shows students how to use the sociological imagination in examining such public policy issues as the death penalty, welfare reform, racial profiling, gay marriage, and the AIDS crisis.

My hope is that through their reading of this book, students will begin to think like sociologists and will be able to use sociological theories and concepts in evaluating human interactions and institutions. From the introduction of the concept of sociological imagination in Chapter 1, this text stresses the distinctive way in which sociologists examine human social behavior, and how their research can be used to understand the broader principles that guide our lives.

Sociology: A Brief Introduction was developed to meet the need for a concise introduction to the discipline, one that permits instructors to assign additional material or projects. The seventh edition brings the research into the 21st century and introduces a number of features designed to appeal to today's students. One thing that remains unchanged, however, is the steady focus on three especially important goals:

- **Comprehensive and balanced coverage of theoretical perspectives throughout the text.** Chapter 1 introduces, defines, and contrasts the functionalist, conflict, and interactionist perspectives. We explore their distinctive views of such topics as social institutions (Chapter 5), deviance (Chapter 7), the family (Chapter 12), education (Chapter 13), and health (Chapter 15). In addition, the feminist perspective is introduced in Chapter 1. Other theoretical approaches particular to certain topics are presented in later chapters. Summing Up tables at the end of these sections help students to grasp and compare the major theories.

- **Strong coverage of issues pertaining to gender, age, race, ethnicity, and class in all chapters.** Examples of such coverage include Social Policy sections on bilingualism (Chapter 3), welfare (Chapter 8), racial profiling (Chapter 10), and gay marriage (Chapter 12); chapter-opening excerpts on globalization in India (Chapter 9), the so-called Lipstick Jihad in Iran (Chapter 11), and the unequal childhoods of young people in the United States (Chapter 12); boxes on the shrinking middle class (Chapter 8), interracial and interethnic friendships (Chapter 10), naturally occurring retirement communities (Chapter 11), and domestic violence (Chapter 12); and sections on the social construction of race (Chapter 10), the social construction of gender (Chapter 11), and the informal economy (Chapter 14).

- **Emphasis on cross-cultural and global content throughout the book.** The seventh edition greatly extends coverage of globalization. Chapters 1, 9, and 16 provide expanded coverage of global terms and concepts, as well as of social, economic, and technological issues that increasingly influence cultural encounters around the world. A new world map, found on the inside front cover of the book, provides a quick guide to passages that consider sociological issues as they are manifested in other countries and in transnational encounters between businesses, states, and cultures. Among the topics examined are:

- The global McDonaldization of society (Chapters 3 and 5).

- The controversy over the Muslim headscarf in France (Chapter 4).

- The global reach of the media (Chapter 6).
- Transnational crime (Chapter 7).
- Poverty in the United States and Congo (Chapter 8).
- The borderlands between the United States and Mexico (Chapter 9).
- Global immigration (Chapter 10).
- Aging worldwide (Chapter 11).
- Arranged marriage in Asia, Africa, and the United States (Chapter 12).
- Religion in India (Chapter 13).
- The economic effects of globalization (Chapter 14).
- The brain drain (Chapter 15).
- Global social movements (Chapter 16).
- The impact of globalization on the environment (Chapter 16).

I take great care to introduce the basic concepts and research methods of sociology and to reinforce this material in all chapters. The most recent data are included, making this book more current than all previous editions.

Special Features
Integrated Learning System

The text, the *Reel Society* Interactive Movie CD-ROM, and the Online Learning Center Web site work together as an integrated learning system to bring the theories, research findings, and basic concepts of sociology to life for students. Offering a combination of print, multimedia, and Web-based materials, this comprehensive system meets the needs of instructors and students with a variety of teaching and learning styles. The material that follows describes the many features of the text, CD-ROM, and Online Learning Center, as well as the supplementary materials that support those resources.

Poster Art

Each chapter opens with a reproduction of a poster or piece of graphic art that illustrates a key theme or concept of the chapter. Accompanying captions help readers to grasp the relevance of the artwork to the chapter.

Chapter-Opening Excerpts

The chapter-opening excerpts convey the excitement and relevance of sociological inquiry by means of lively passages from writings of sociologists and others who explore sociological topics. These excerpts are designed to expose students to vivid writing on a broad range of topics and to stimulate their sociological imaginations. For example, Chapter 1 opens with Barbara Ehrenreich's account of her experiment in survival as a low-wage worker, drawn from her best-selling book *Nickel and Dimed*. Chapter 3 begins with an excerpt from Juliet B. Schor's *Born to Buy: The Commercialized Child and the New Consumer*

Culture. And Chapter 5 opens with a description of Philip Zimbardo's now-classic mock prison study.

Chapter Overview

The opening excerpt is followed by a chapter overview that provides a bridge between the opening excerpt and the content of the chapter. In addition, the overview poses questions and describes the content of the chapter in narrative form.

Research in Action

These sections present sociological findings on topics such as divorce, political apathy among young people, and naturally occurring retirement communities (NORCs).

Sociology in the Global Community

These sections provide a global perspective on topics such as aging, domestic violence, Al Jazeera, and the 2004 tsunami.

Social Inequality

These sections illustrate various types of social stratification. Featured topics include discrimination in employment, Native American casinos, and affirmative action.

Taking Sociology to Work

These sections profile individuals who majored in sociology and use its principles in their work. While these people are employed in a variety of occupations and professions, they share a conviction that their background in sociology has been valuable in their careers.

Sociology on Campus

These sections apply the sociological perspective to issues of immediate interest to today's students. Title IX, plagiarism, and financial aid are among the featured topics.

Social Policy Sections

The Social Policy sections that close all but one of the chapters play a critical role in helping students to think like sociologists. They apply sociological principles and theories to important social and political issues being debated by policymakers and the general public. Five sections are new to this edition. All the Social Policy sections now present a global perspective. All close with a feature called Getting Involved, which refers students who want to become active in the debate to relevant material on the book's Web site.

Use Your Sociological Imagination

In the spirit of C. Wright Mills, these short, thought-provoking sections encourage students to apply the sociological concepts they have learned to the world around them. Through open-ended "what-if" questions, students step into the shoes of researchers, famous sociologists, and people of other cultures and generations.

Summing Up Tables

Twenty-eight summary tables help students to grasp the main point, compare major sociological perspectives, and comprehend the differences between economic systems, types of cities, and forms of religious organization. From distinguishing between the *Gemeinschaft* and *Gesellschaft* to applying sociological theory to culture, race, or religion, readers will find these study aids invaluable.

Illustrations

The photographs, cartoons, figures, and tables are closely linked to the themes of the chapters. The maps, titled Mapping Life Nationwide and Mapping Life Worldwide, show the prevalence of social trends. A world map highlighting those countries used as examples in the text appears on the inside front cover.

Think About It

Selected tables and figures include stimulating questions that prompt students to interpret the data and think about their deeper meaning. Students search for trends in the data, wonder about the underlying reasons for the trends, and apply the implications to their own lives.

Photo Essays

Seven photo essays enliven the text. Each begins with a question that is intended to prompt students to see some part of everyday life with new eyes—those of a sociologist. For instance, the essay in Chapter 1 asks "Are You What You Own?" and the essay in Chapter 7 asks "Who Is Deviant?" The photos and captions that follow suggest the answer to the question.

Cross-Reference Icons

When the text discussion refers to a concept introduced earlier in the book, an icon in the margin points the reader to the exact page.

Chapter Summaries

Each chapter includes a brief numbered summary to aid students in reviewing the important themes.

Critical Thinking Questions

After the summary, each chapter includes critical thinking questions that will help students analyze the social world in which they participate. Critical thinking is an essential element in the sociological imagination.

Key Terms

I have given careful attention to presenting understandable and accurate definitions of each key term. These terms are highlighted in bold italics when they are introduced. A list of key terms and definitions in each chapter—with page references—follows the end of the chapter. In addition, the glossary at the end of the book includes the definitions of the textbook's key terms and the page references for each term.

Self-Quizzes

Each chapter includes a 20-item quiz that allows students to test their comprehension and retention of core information presented in the chapter. Answers to the questions are presented at the end of the quiz.

Technology Resources

Suggested activities at the end of each chapter take students online to analyze pertinent social issues. Updates, exercises, and hyperlinks related to these Web-based activities are displayed on the book's Web site (**www.mhhe.com/schaefer7**).

Inside Covers

The inside front cover features a new world map highlighting selected countries mentioned in the book. Page numbers indicate the relevant passages, many of which stress the effects of globalization in the United States and other countries. The inside back cover features two summary tables: one that highlights the book's coverage of race, class, and gender and another that summarizes its applications of sociology's major theoretical approaches.

What's New in the 7th Edition?

The most important changes in this edition include the following (refer as well to the chapter-by-chapter list of changes on pages xxii–xxv and to the *Visual Preview* on pages xxvii–xxxii).

Content

- Coverage of globalization has been greatly expanded. The book now includes an entire chapter on global inequality (Chapter 9), featuring major sections on global poverty and the global divide between the West and developing nations. Chapter 16 offers expanded coverage of global issues, including global social movements, global social change, and the impact of globalization on the environment, as well as a Social Policy section on transnationals. A new *Sociology's Global View* map on the inside front cover of this book highlights some of the many other passages related to globalization.

- Eight new chapter-opening excerpts, drawn from sociological writings, convey the excitement and relevance of sociological inquiry: *Paradise Laborers: Hotel Work in the Global Economy* by Patricia A. Adler and Peter Adler (Chapter 2); *Born to Buy: The Commercialized Child and the New Consumer Culture* by Juliet B. Schor (Chapter 3); *Growing Up Digital: The Rise of the Net Generation* by Don Tapscott (Chapter 6); *The Working Poor: Invisible in America* by David K. Shipler (Chapter 8); "Arnold Schwarzenegger, Ally McBeal and Arranged Marriages: Globalization on the Ground in India" by Steve Derné (Chapter 9); *Lipstick Jihad: A Memoir of Growing Up Iranian in America and American in Iran* by Azadeh Moaveni (Chapter 11); *Unequal Childhoods: Class, Race, and Family Life* by Annette Lareau (Chapter 12); and *Diversity in the Power Elite: How It Happened, Why It Matters* by Richard L. Zweigenhaft and G. William Domhoff (Chapter 14).

- Five new Social Policy sections help students to apply sociological principles and theories to important social and political issues currently under debate by policymakers and the general public: The Death Penalty in the United States and Worldwide (Chapter 7); Universal Human Rights (Chapter 9); Racial Profiling (Chapter 10); Global Offshoring (Chapter 14); and Transnationals (Chapter 16).

- A new photo essay—How Does Television Portray the Family?—helps to spark students' interest in sociology.

Pedagogy

- Eight new Summing Up tables help to pull together coverage of the major theoretical perspectives.

- Eight new U.S. and world maps illustrate important sociological trends and developments.

- Twenty-six new boxes cover a wide selection of topics, including road rage, arranged marriage, Native American casinos, adolescent sexual networks, social class and financial aid, and the contrast between Appalachian poverty and Congolese affluence.

- At the end of every chapter, a 20-item self-quiz allows students to test their comprehension and retention of core information presented in the chapter. Answers to the questions are presented at the end of the quiz.

- On the inside front cover, a world map highlights selected countries mentioned in the book. Page numbers indicate the relevant passages, many of which stress the effects of globalization.

Supplements

- **Audio Abridgement CD Set for Study and Review.** The Audio Abridgement CD Set is an abridged, spoken version of *Sociology: A Brief Introduction,* seventh edition. Developed with today's multitasking students and instructors in mind, this "book on tape" was designed to serve as a tool for review while commuting, working out, or just sitting down to study. Each chapter runs approximately 15 minutes and focuses on key chapter concepts. The chapter summaries from the text served as the framework for this abridgement.

- **NBC News Archive Lecture Launcher VHS Video and DVD.** A fourth NBC videotape is available with the seventh edition. This 60-minute video, along with three earlier volumes, offers brief clips (5–10 minutes each) from NBC News and *The Today Show* that dramatize sociological concepts, serve as lecture launchers, and generate class discussion. The new NBC video clips, along with some of the clips that have appeared in earlier volumes, are now available in DVD format.

This edition has been thoroughly updated. It includes the most recent data and research findings, many of which were published in the last three years. Recent data from the Census Bureau, Bureau of Labor Statistics, Current Population Reports, the Population Reference Bureau, the World Bank, the United Nations

Development Programme, and the Centers for Disease Control have been incorporated.

A more complete, chapter-by-chapter listing of the most significant new material in this edition follows.

What's New in Each Chapter?

Chapter 1: Understanding Sociology

- Discussion of how sociologists and other social scientists study events such as Hurricane Katrina, with map: "Poverty Rate in Hurricane Katrina Disaster Area."

- Discussion of the functionalist perspective on cow worship in Indian society.

- Updated discussion of the feminist perspective.

- Discussion of the interactionist perspective on the new NBA dress code, with figure: "Enforcing Symbols: The NBA Dress Code."

- Use of Elijah Anderson's work to illustrate how a sociologist's theoretical viewpoint guides research.

- Section on applied and clinical sociology, including discussion of new research on illegal drug use and the spread of HIV/AIDS.

- "Thinking Globally" section, with key-term treatment of globalization.

- Sociology in the Global Community box: "The Global Response to the 2004 Tsunami."

- Discussion of the radically different survival rates of men and women in the 2004 tsunami.

- Appendix on careers in sociology, with two figures: "Sociology Degrees Conferred in the United States by Gender" and "Occupational Fields of Sociology BA/MA Graduates."

Chapter 2: Sociological Research

- Chapter-opening excerpt from *Paradise Laborers: Hotel Work in the Global Economy,* by Patricia A. Adler and Peter Adler.

- Expanded discussion of independent versus dependent variables, with new example.

- Social Inequality box: "Researching Privilege and Discrimination in Employment," with figure.

- Research in Action box: "What's in a Name?" with figure.

- Two "Use Your Sociological Imagination" exercises.

- Discussion of content analysis of gender differences in the use of sexually explicit language, with photo.

- Appendix: "Using Statistics, Tables, and Graphs," with figure and table.

- Appendix: "Writing a Research Report."

Chapter 3: Culture

- Chapter-opening excerpt from Juliet B. Schor, *Born to Buy: The Commercialized Child and the New Consumer Culture.*

- Discussion of the trends toward coffee drinking and consumerism in non-Western societies as an example of globalization, with photo.
- Sociology in the Global Community box: "Cultural Survival in Brazil."
- Discussion of gendered speech, illustrated by the Lakota dialect.
- Discussion of cross-cultural studies of values.
- Discussion of New York City sanitation workers' argot.
- Discussion of the new subculture that has developed in India among employees at international call centers, with photo.
- Updated Social Policy section on bilingualism, with discussion of legislative proposals regarding treatment of undocumented workers.

Chapter 4: Socialization

- New chapter-opening poster: Shoppers in Bangalore stroll past a Jockey billboard.
- Discussion of Genie, a neglected 13-year-old discovered in 1970, with sketch she did at age 18.
- Discussion of the prolonged transition from adolescence to adulthood in the United States.
- Taking Sociology to Work box: Rakefet Avramovitz, Program Administrator, Child Care Law Center.
- Discussion of the strains on adolescent peer groups in wartime Iraq.
- Figure: "How Young People Use the Media."
- Expansion of the subsection on the state to include religion.

Chapter 5: Social Interaction, Groups, and Social Structure

- Shortens and combines Chapters 5 and 6 from brief sixth edition.
- Relation of Zimbardo's prison study to the Abu Ghraib prison scandal in Iraq.
- Discussion of the role strain Navajo Nation police officers experience in their contacts with conventional law-enforcement officials.
- Research in Action box: "Adolescent Sexual Networks," with network chart.
- Discussion of blogging by U.S. soldiers and Iraqis as a form of electronic networking.
- Sociology in the Global Community box: "McDonald's and the Worldwide Bureaucratization of Society."
- Discussion of how electronic communication is contributing to the fragmentation of work.

Chapter 6: The Mass Media

- Chapter-opening excerpt from *Growing Up Digital: The Rise of the Net Generation* by Don Tapscott.

- Photo Essay: "How Does Television Portray the Family?"
- Discussion of a new children's television program in Gaza, sponsored by Hamas.
- Section on media monitoring.
- Discussion of a UNESCO proposal to combat the homogenizing effect of the media.
- Discussion of audience networks, with figure: "Two Audience Networks."
- Discussion of the social implications of *egocasting*—individual management of media exposure through the Internet.
- Summing Up table: "Sociological Perspectives on the Mass Media."
- Updated Sociology in the Global Community box: "Al Jazeera Is on the Air."

Chapter 7: Deviance and Social Control

- Discussion of the Abu Ghraib prison scandal in connection with conformity and obedience.
- Discussion of new research on routine activities theory.
- Research in Action box: "Labeling Behavior as a Crime: Road Rage," with cartoon.
- Discussion of new research on the connection between crime and social inequality.
- New section on transnational crime, including key-term treatment and table.
- Table: "U.S. Crime Rates."
- Social Policy section on the death penalty, with figure: "Executions by State."

Chapter 8: Stratification and Social Mobility in the United States

- Separate chapter on stratification in the United States—splits old Chapter 9 in two.
- Chapter-opening excerpt from David K. Shipler, *The Working Poor: Invisible in America.*
- Research in Action box: "The Shrinking Middle Class."
- Updated discussion of the real value of the minimum wage, with figure: "U.S. Minimum Wage Adjusted for Inflation, 1950–2005."
- Sociology in the Global Community box: "It's All Relative: Appalachian Poverty and Congolese Affluence."
- Updated discussion of the accuracy of the federal government's definition of poverty.
- Discussion of the effect of social class on people's vulnerability to natural disasters, such as Hurricane Katrina.
- Sociology on Campus box: "Social Class and Financial Aid."
- Discussion of Latino household wealth versus White household wealth.

Chapter 9: Global Inequality

- Separate chapter on global inequality—expands coverage in old Chapter 9.
- Chapter-opening excerpt from "Arnold Schwarzenegger, Ally McBeal and Arranged Marriages: Globalization on the Ground in India," By Steve Derné.
- Section, "The Global Divide," with figure, "Fundamental Global Inequality."
- Subsection, "Worldwide Poverty," with Mapping Life Worldwide map, "Poverty Worldwide."
- Sociology in the Global Community Box: "Cutting Poverty Worldwide."
- Subsection, "Modernization."
- Sociology in the Global Community box: "The Global Disconnect," with table, "Network Readiness Index."
- Summing Up table: "Three Approaches to Global Inequality."
- Expanded section, "Stratification within Nations: A Comparative Perspective," with two new subsections, "Distribution of Wealth and Income" and "Social Mobility," and new figure, "Distribution of Income in Nine Nations."
- Social Inequality box: "Stratification in Japan."
- Social Policy section on universal human rights.

Chapter 10: Racial and Ethnic Inequality

- Discussion of discriminatory classified ads posted on Craigslist.org and Roommate.com.
- Research in Action box: "Interracial and Interethnic Friendships."
- Summing Up table: "Sociological Perspectives on Race."
- Section, "Impact of Global Immigration."
- Social Inequality box: "Native Americans Gamble on Gaming."
- Section on Arab Americans.
- Social Policy section on racial profiling.

Chapter 11: Stratification by Gender and Age

- Opening excerpt from *Lipstick Jihad: A Memoir of Growing Up Iranian in America and American in Iran* by Azadeh Moaveni.
- Summing Up table: "Sociological Perspectives on Gender."
- Sociology in the Global Community box: "The Head Scarf and the Veil: Complex Symbols."
- Discussion of gender inequality in various industrial nations, with figure.
- Expanded discussion of comparative compensation of women and men in the United States.
- Discussion of research on voluntary leave time for women versus men, with figure.

- Major section, "Aging throughout the Life Course," with three subsections: "The Sandwich Generation," "Adjusting to Retirement," and "Death and Dying."
- Research in Action box: "Naturally Occurring Retirement Communities (NORCs)."

Chapter 12: The Family and Intimate Relationships

- Chapter-opening excerpt from Annette Lareau, *Unequal Childhoods: Class, Race, and Family Life.*
- Photo essay: "What is a Family?" featuring photos from Uwe Ommer, *1000 Families.*
- Updated figure: "U.S. Households by Family Type, 1940–2010."
- Research in Action box: "Arranged Marriage, American-Style."
- Discussion of *ala kachuu,* the kidnapping of brides in Kyrgyzstan.
- Updated treatment of single-parent families.
- Updated figure: "Trends in Marriage and Divorce in the United States, 1920–2004."
- Updated Social Policy section on gay marriage, with updated Mapping Life Nationwide map, "Discriminatory Marriage and Anti–Gay Discrimination Laws."

Chapter 13: Religion and Education

- Discussion of the nonreligious segment of the population.
- Research in Action box: "Income and Education, Religiously Speaking," with two-part figure.
- Figure: "Religious Participation in Selected Countries, 1981 and 2001."
- Research in Action box: "Islam in the United States," with photo.
- Updated discussion of use of the Internet for religious purposes.
- Updated case study, "Religion in India," including discussion of Hindu tolerance of cloning and stem cell research as a factor in India's leadership in biotechnology.
- Expanded figure: "Percentage of Adults Ages 25 to 64 Who Have Completed Higher Education."
- Discussion of the recent decline in the number of foreign students in the United States.
- Updated Social Policy section on religion in the schools, including key-term treatment of *intelligent design* and a new cartoon.

Chapter 14: Government and the Economy

- Devoted entirely to government and the economy (coverage of the environment moved to Chapter 16).

- Chapter-opening excerpt from Zweigenhaft and Domhoff (2006), *Diversity in the Power Elite: How It Happened, Why It Matters.*
- Summing Up table: "Characteristics of the Three Major Economic Systems."
- Updated case study of capitalism in China, with new figure, "World's Largest Economies, 2020," and discussion of government censorship of the Internet.
- Section on types of government (monarchy, oligarchy, dictatorship, totalitarianism, and democracy).
- Subsection, "Race and Gender in Politics," with figure, "Women in National Legislatures, Selected Countries, 2006."
- Sociology in the Global Community box: "Gender Quotas at the Ballot Box."
- Social Inequality box: "Affirmative Action," with cartoon.
- Social Policy section on global offshoring.

Chapter 15: Population, Communities, and Health

- Updated Sociology in the Global Community box: "Population Policy in China."
- Mapping Life Worldwide map: "Global Urbanization, 2015 (projected)."
- Discussion of depopulation and economic stagnation in the northern Rockies and Western Great Plains.
- Social Inequality box: "To Inform or Not to Inform? How Race and Ethnicity Affect Views of Patient Autonomy."
- Summing Up table: "Sociological Perspectives on Health and Illness."
- Taking Sociology to Work box: "Jess Purmort, Research Assistant, New York Academy of Medicine."
- Social Policy section on the AIDS crisis (moved from Chapter 5), with updated Mapping Life Worldwide map: "Adults and Children Living with HIV/AIDS."

Chapter 16: Globalization, the Environment, and Social Change

- Includes coverage of the environment (moved from Chapter 14).
- Chapter-opening excerpt from *Ruling the Waves: Cycles of Discovery, Chaos, and Wealth from the Compass to the Internet* by Debora L. Spar.
- Discussion of global social movements.
- Sociology in the Global Community box: "A New Social Movement in Rural India."
- Table: "The United States: A Changing Nation."
- Summing Up table: "Sociological Perspectives on Social Change."
- Expanded section on global social change.

- Subsection on the environmental impact of globalization.
- Updated subsection on environmental justice.
- New Social Policy section on transnationals, with Mapping Life Worldwide map: "Labor Migration."

Support for Instructors and Students

Print Resources

Annotated Instructor's Edition   An annotated instructor's edition (AIE) of the text, prepared by Rebecca Matthews, Ph.D. Sociology, Cornell University, offers page-by-page annotations to assist instructors in using textbook material.

Study Guide   The study guide, prepared by Rebecca Matthews, Ph.D. Sociology, Cornell University, includes standard features such as detailed key points, definitions of key terms, multiple-choice questions, fill-in questions, and true–false questions. All study guide questions are keyed to specific pages in the textbook, and page references are provided for key points and definitions of key terms.

In addition to the questions in the study guide, students can test their mastery of the subject matter by taking the end-of-chapter self-quizzes and the quizzes on the *Reel Society* CD-ROM and the Online Learning Center Web site. Students therefore have four different sets of questions to draw on for review.

Primis Customized Readers   An array of first-rate readings are available to adopters in a customized electronic database. Some are classic articles from the sociological literature; others are provocative pieces written especially for McGraw-Hill by leading sociologists.

McGraw-Hill Dushkin   Any of the Dushkin publications can be packaged with this text at a discount: Annual Editions, Taking Sides, Sources, Global Studies. For more information, please visit the Web site at www.dushkin.com.

Digital and Video Resources

Audio Abridgement CD Set For Study and Review
The Audio Abridgement CD Set is an abridged, spoken version of *Sociology: A Brief Introduction,* seventh edition. Developed with today's multitasking students and instructors in mind, this "book on tape" was designed to be a tool for review while commuting, working out, or just sitting down to study. Each chapter runs approximately 15 minutes and focuses on key chapter concepts. The chapter summaries from the text served as the framework for the abridgement.

NBC News Archive Lecture Launcher VHS Videotapes and DVD   Three 60-minute VHS videotapes feature brief clips (5–10 minutes each) from *NBC News* and the *Today Show*

that dramatize sociological concepts, serve as lecture launchers, and generate class discussion. Each is accompanied by a guide that is available on the Online Learning Center Web site (**www.mhhe.com/schaefer7**). The new NBC video clips, along with some of the clips that have appeared in earlier volumes, are now available in DVD as well as VHS format.

PageOut: The Course Web Site Development Center

All online content for *Sociology,* seventh edition, is supported by WebCT, eCollege.com, Blackboard, and other course management systems. Additionally, McGraw-Hill's PageOut service is available to get you and your course up and running online in a matter of hours, at no cost. PageOut was designed for instructors just beginning to explore Web options. Even the novice computer user can create a course Web site with a template provided by McGraw-Hill (no programming knowledge necessary). To learn more about PageOut, ask your McGraw-Hill representative for details, or visit **www.mhhe.com/pageout.**

eInstruction: The Classroom Performance System

The Classroom Performance System (CPS) is a wireless response system that allows instructors to receive immediate feedback from students. CPS units include easy-to-use software for instructors' use in creating questions and assessments and delivering them to students. The units also include individual wireless response pads for students' use in responding. Suggested questions, prepared by Rebecca Matthews, Ph.D. Sociology, Cornell University, appear on the Instructor's Edition of the Schaefer Web site, **www.mhhe.com/schaefer7,** and on the Instructor's Resource DVD-ROM. CPS also runs alongside the PowerPoint slides that supplement Schaefer's *Sociology: A Brief Edition.* For further details, go to **www.mhhe.com/einstruction.**

Reel Society: Interactive Movie CD-ROMs, Version

2.0 This two-disk set features an interactive movie that demonstrates the sociological imagination through the use of actors and scenarios involving campus life. The program allows students to interact with the concepts described in the textbook in a relevant and meaningful context. Students are asked to take on the role of one of the characters and influence key plot turns by making choices for the character. A wide variety of issues and perspectives (such as culture, socialization, deviance, inequality, race and ethnicity, social institutions, and social change) are addressed in order to relate major sociological concepts and theories to the students' lives. There are also interactive quiz questions on the CDs. These CD-ROMs, a breakthrough in the use of media to teach introductory sociology students, can serve as an integral companion to the book. An instructor's guide to using the CD-ROMs, written by Rebecca Matthews, is available as well as on the Instructor's Resource DVD-ROM.

John Tenuto of College of Lake County (in Illinois) served as the academic consultant throughout the development of this program. The script for *Reel Society* was reviewed by the following instructors: Jan Abu Shakrah, Portland Community College;

Grant Farr, Portland State University; Rebecca Matthews, Ph.D. Sociology, Cornell University; Kenneth L. Stewart, Angelo State University (in Texas); and Cheryl Tieman, Radford University (in Virginia). In addition, students from George Mason University in Virginia offered their reactions to the script during a focus group.

There are several ways for instructors and students to use Reel Society. Students can follow the storyline from start to finish or choose only those scenes for a given chapter or topic. In either case, the movie segments are augmented by a robust array of review and assessment features, including self-quizzes. Instructors are provided with their own version of *Reel Society,* which allows them to choose which of the program's review features to show in class, if any. Additional quizzes and critical thinking activities are located on the *Reel Society* Web site, and instructors will find test questions related to the movie on the Instructor's Resource DVD-ROM. *Reel Society* video clips with accompanying questions are also included on the book's Web site.

Online Learning Center Web Site

The Online Learning Center Web site that accompanies this text (**www.mhhe.com/schaefer7**) offers a rich array of resources for instructors and students, which were developed by Lynn Newhart of Rockford College in Illinois and Rebecca Matthews. Here you will find the author's audio introductions to each chapter, as well as interactive quizzes and maps, social policy exercises, PowerPoint slides, census updates, chapter glossaries, vocabulary flash cards, video clips, additional information about the chapter-opening excerpts and their authors, diagnostic midterm and final exams, links to the book's Internet exercises, and other resources. You can use any of the material from the Online Learning Center in a course Web site that you create using PageOut.

PowerPoint Slides

Adopters of *Sociology* can also receive a set of more than 600 PowerPoint slides developed especially for this edition by Richard T. Schaefer and Gerry Williams. The slides are included on the Instructor's Resource DVD-ROM (described below) and in the Instructor's Edition of the Online Learning Center Web site. The set includes bulleted lecture points, graphs, and maps, and video clips. Instructors are welcome to generate overhead transparencies from the slides if they wish to do so.

Instructor's Resource DVD-ROM with Computerized Test Bank

This DVD-ROM includes the contents of the Instructor's Resource Manual, a test bank in computerized and Word formats, the instructor's guide to the *Reel Society* CD, and PowerPoint slides for instructors' convenience in customizing multimedia lectures. The Instructor's Resource Manual, prepared by Richard T. Schaefer, Clayton Steenberg of Arkansas State University, and Rebecca Matthews, Ph.D. Sociology, Cornell University, provides sociology instructors with detailed chapter outlines, learning objectives, additional lecture ideas

(among them, alternative social policy issues), class discussion topics, essay questions, topics for student research (along with suggested research materials for each topic), and suggested additional readings. Media materials are suggested for each chapter, including videotapes and films. The test bank was written by Clayton Steenberg of Arkansas State University and Rebecca Matthews, Ph.D. Sociology, Cornell University. Multiple-choice and true–false questions are included for each chapter; they will be useful in testing students on basic sociological concepts, application of theoretical perspectives, and recall of important factual information. Correct answers and page references are provided for all questions.

McGraw-Hill's EZ Test is a flexible and easy-to-use electronic testing program. The program allows instructors to create tests from book-specific items. It accommodates a wide range of question types, and instructors may add their own questions. Multiple versions of the test can be created, and any test can be exported for use with course management systems such as WebCT, BlackBoard, or PageOut. EZ Test Online is a new service that gives you a place to easily administer your EZ Test–created exams and quizzes online. The program is available for Windows and Macintosh environments.

Primis Online   Professors can customize this book by selecting from it only those chapters they want to use in their courses. Primis Online allows users to choose and change the order of chapters, as well as to add readings from McGraw-Hill's vast database of content. Both custom-printed textbooks and electronic eBooks are available. To learn more, contact your McGraw-Hill sales representative, or visit our Web site at **www.mhhe.com/ primis/online.**

Acknowledgments

Since 1999, Elizabeth Morgan has played a most significant role in the development of my introductory sociology books. Once again, in the seventh edition, Betty has been involved from the preliminary plans for the vast array of changes right through checking the page proofs with me. Her impact is found on literally every page of this book.

I deeply appreciate the contributions to this book made by my editors. Rhona Robbin, director of development and media technology, has continually challenged me to make each edition better than its predecessor.

I have received strong support and encouragement from Phillip Butcher, publisher; Sherith Pankratz, sponsoring editor; and Dan Loch, senior marketing manager. Additional guidance and support were provided by Trish Starner, Kathy Blake, and Tara Maldonado; Diane Folliard, senior project manager; Marianna Kinigakis, designer; Nancy Garcia Hernandez, media producer; Stacy Dorgan Bentz, media project manager; David Tietz and Sonia Brown, photo editors; Emma Ghiselli, art editor; Carol Bielski, senior production supervisor; and Judy Brody, permissions editor. I would also like to express my appreciation

to DePaul University Program Assistant Valerie Paulson and student Rachel Hanes.

I would also like to acknowledge the contributions of the following individuals: Rebecca Matthews, Ph.D. Sociology, Cornell University, for her work on the annotated instructor's edition, the study guide, and the Online Learning Center; Lynn Newhart of Rockford College in Illinois for her work on the Online Learning Center; Clayton Steenberg of Arkansas State University and Rebecca Matthews for their work on the Instructor's Resource Manual and the Test Bank; Rebecca Matthews for her work on the Study Guide; Thom Holmes of McGraw-Hill and John Tenuto of Lake County College in Illinois for their work on the *Reel Society* CD-ROM; Rebecca Matthews for her work on the instructor's guide to accompany the *Reel Society* CD-ROM, and on a series of exam questions based on *Reel Society* scenarios; and Gerry Williams for his work on the PowerPoint slides.

This edition continues to reflect many insightful suggestions made by reviewers of the first nine hardcover editions and the six paperback brief editions. The current edition has benefited from constructive and thorough evaluations provided by sociologists from both two-year and four-year institutions. These include Dale Anderson, University of Memphis; Andrew Cho, Tacoma Community College; Richard Davin, Riverside Community College; Nancy Greenwood, Indiana University–Kokomo; Garrett Jones, Oklahoma State University; James Knapp, SE Oklahoma State University; Diane Pike, Augsburg College; Ralph Pyle, Michigan State University; John Rice, University of North Carolina, Wilmington; and John Zipp, University of Akron.

As is evident from these acknowledgments, the preparation of a textbook is truly a team effort. The most valuable member of this effort continues to be my wife, Sandy. She provides the support so necessary in my creative and scholarly activities.

I have had the good fortune to be able to introduce students to sociology for many years. These students have been enormously helpful in spurring on my own sociological imagination. In ways I can fully appreciate but cannot fully acknowledge, their questions in class and queries in the hallway have found their way into this textbook.

Richard T. Schaefer
www.schaefersociology.net
schaefert@aol.com

As a full-service publisher of quality educational products, McGraw-Hill does much more than just sell textbooks to your students. We create and publish an extensive array of print, video, and digital supplements to support instruction on your campus. Orders of new (versus used) textbooks help us to defray the cost of developing such supplements, which is substantial. Please consult your local McGraw-Hill representative to learn about the availability of the supplements that accompany Sociology. If you are not sure who your representative is, you can find him or her by using the Rep Locator at www.mhhe.com.

Visual Preview

Teaching Students to Think Sociologically

The 7th edition of *Sociology* continues its tradition of teaching students how to think critically about society and their own lives from a wide range of classical and contemporary sociological perspectives.

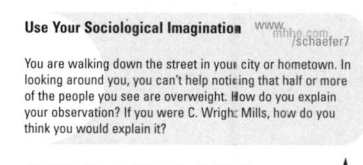

"USE YOUR SOCIOLOGICAL IMAGINATION" SECTIONS

Each chapter contains thought-provoking questions designed to stimulate a student's sociological imagination. Students can respond to these questions using the associated Online Learning Center for the book and e-mail their answers to their instructors.

PROVOCATIVE BOOK EXCERPTS

Each chapter opens with a lively excerpt from the writings of sociologists and others, clearly conveying the excitement and relevance of sociological inquiry. These excerpts are effectively linked to the content of the chapter.

NEW SOCIOLOGY'S GLOBAL VIEW MAP

This edition of *Sociology* offers expanded coverage of globalization. This map, which appears on the inside front cover, serves as a quick guide to selected passages that focus on global issues and topics.

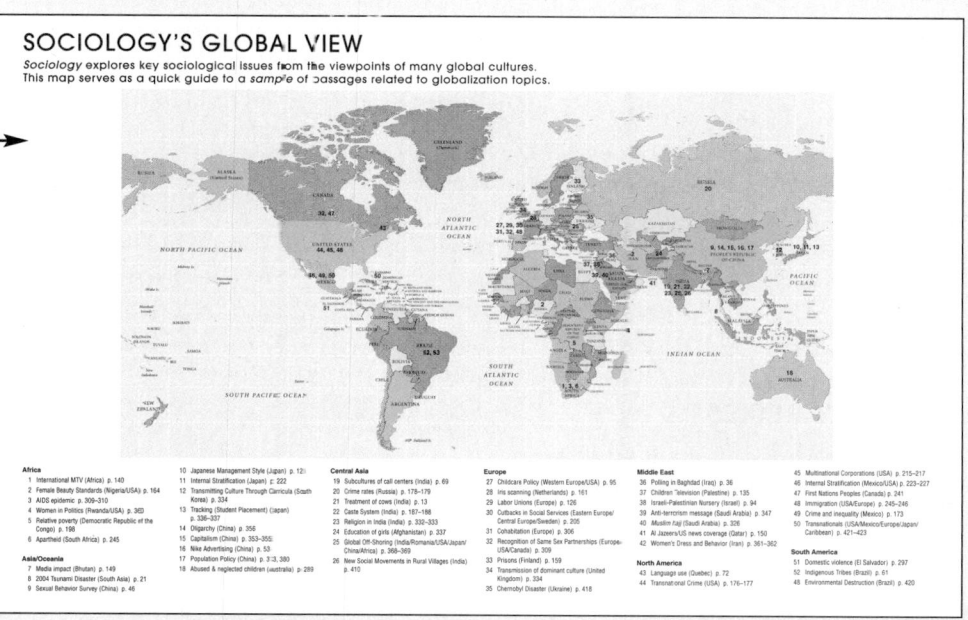

Analyzing a Broad Range of Contemporary Issues

(socialPolicy)
and the Family

Gay Marriage

The Issue
In the United States, attitudes toward marriage are complex. As always, society and popular culture suggest that a young man or woman should find the perfect mate, settle down and marry, and live "happily ever after." But young people are also bombarded by messages implying the frequency of adultery and the acceptability of divorce. In this atmosphere, the idea of same-sex marriage strikes some people as only the latest of many attacks on traditional marriage. To others, it seems an overdue acknowledgment of the formal relationships that faithful, monogamous gay couples have long maintained.

The Setting
In 2004, in his State of the Union message, President George W. Bush warned "activist judges" against attempts to broaden the definition of marriage to include same-sex couples. The only recourse to such measures, he said, would be a constitutional amendment banning same-sex unions.

What made gay marriage the focus of national attention? Events in two states brought the issue to the forefront. In 1999, Vermont gave gay couples the legal benefits of marriage through civil union, but stopped short of calling the arrangement a marriage. Then, in 2003, the Massachusetts Supreme Court ruled 4–3 that under the state's constitution, gay couples have the right to marry—a ruling the U.S. Supreme Court has refused to review.

Sociological Insights
Functionalists have traditionally seen marriage as a social institution that is closely tied to human reproduction. Same-sex marriage would at first appear not to fit that arrangement. But many same-sex couples are entrusted with the socialization of young children, whether or not their relationship is recognized by the state. Functionalists also wonder whether religious views toward marriage can be ignored. The courts have focused on civil marriage, but religious views are hardly irrelevant, even in a country like the United States, which observes a separation between religion and the state. Indeed, religious teachings have led even some staunch supporters of gay rights to oppose same-sex marriage on spiritual grounds.

Conflict theorists have charged that denial of the right to marry reinforces the second-class status of gays and lesbians. Some have compared the ban against gay marriage to past policies that until 1967 banned interracial marriage in 32 states (Liptak 2004a).

Interactionists generally avoid the policy question and focus instead on the nature of same-sex households. They ask many of the same questions about gay partner relations and child rearing that they raise about conventional couples. Of course, much less research has been done on same-sex households than on other families, but the studies published to date raise the same issues as those that apply to conventional married couples, plus a few more. For gay couples, the support or opposition of family, co-workers, and friends looms large (Dundas and Kaufman 2000; Dunne 2000).

Recently, national surveys of attitudes toward gay marriage have been showing volatile shifts in public opinion. Typically, people are more opposed to gay marriage than to civil union: about one-fourth of respondents favor legal recognition of gay marriage, while as many as half favor civil union. Still, as of 2005, the majority of the population endorsed a constitutional amendment to ban gay marriage (Saad 2005).

Policy Initiatives
The United States is not the first nation to consider this issue. Recognition of same-sex partnerships is not uncommon in Europe, including Belgium, Denmark, France, Germany, Great Britain, Italy, the Netherlands, Portugal, and Spain. Today, as many as 8 percent of all marriages in the Netherlands are same-sex. The trend is toward recognition in North America as well, since gay couples can marry legally in Canada.

Many nations strongly oppose such measures, however. For example, when Kofi Annan, secretary general of the United Nations (UN), proposed extending the benefits that married UN employees receive to employees' same-sex partners in 2004, so many countries rose in protest that he reneged. Annan decided that such benefits would extend only to those UN employees whose member nations extend the same benefits to their citizens (Cowell 2005; Farley 2004; Wines 2005).

In the United States, many local jurisdictions have passed legislation allowing for the registration of domestic partnerships, and have extended employee benefits to those relationships. Under such policies, a **domestic part**... unrelated adults who share a mutu... together, and agree to be jointly... dents, basic living expenses, and c... mestic partnership benefits can... parenting, pensions, taxation, ho... fringe benefits, and health care... ate support for domestic partners... lesbian and gay male activists, th... such benefits would be cohabiting...

In the United States, marriage h... jurisdiction of state lawmakers. ...

The Family and Intimate Relationships

HALLMARK SOCIAL POLICY SECTIONS

These discussions provide a sociological perspective on contemporary social issues such as gun control, racial profiling, gay marriage, and offshore service jobs. Providing a global view of the issues, each section includes an overview of the subject plus questions to stimulate critical thinking and discussion.

---

social**INEQUALITY** ●●●

10-2 Native Americans Gamble on Gaming

On Native American reservations, economic opportunity is virtually nonexistent. For many tribes, the only viable source of employment and income is commercial gambling. When gaming began on reservations, it was an industry of last resort, a way for Native Americans to earn a living in an isolated area blessed with few natural resources. But in recent years, gaming has proved to be more than a way of getting by; for some tribes, it has become a bonanza.

Native Americans got into the gaming industry in 1988, when Congress passed the Indian Gambling Regulatory Act. The law stipulates that states must negotiate agreements with tribes interested in commercial gaming; they cannot prevent tribes from engaging in gambling operations, even if state law prohibits such ventures. By 2004, 224 tribal governments had opened a variety of gaming operations in 28 states, including off-track betting, sports betting, and telephone betting; casino games such as blackjack and roulette; high-stakes bingo; slot machines; lotteries; and video games of chance. The gamblers who patronize these operations, almost all of whom are not Native American, sometimes travel long distances for the opportunity to wager money.

Though reservation casinos are tribally owned enterprises, most are not operated by Native Americans. Nationally, 75 percent of tribal gaming operations are run by outsiders, and almost all the reservation casinos are operated by White-owned businesses. In 2004, receipts from these casinos amounted to $18.5 billion nationwide—about one-fourth the revenues from other legal gambling operations.

The income from these lucrative operations is not evenly distributed, however. About two-thirds of recognized Indian tribes are not involved in gambling ventures. Those tribes that earn substantial revenues from gambling constitute only a small fraction of Native Americans. On these reservations, about 25 very successful casinos have produced staggering windfalls. The profits from the Foxwoods Resort Casino, whose annual gaming receipts total well over $1.5 billion, are shared by 820 members of the Connecticut Mashantucket Pequot Indians. The tribe provides generous benefits to anyone who can establish that he or she is at least one-sixteenth Pequot. Revenues from successful casinos have also been used to buy back tribal lands and to support the Smithsonian Museum of the American Indian, which opened in 2004.

For most Native Americans, however, income from gaming has not brought dramatic changes in lifestyle. Typically, they see a drop in unemployment and increases in household income from their moderately successful operations—benefits that are not seen on nongaming reservations. But the impact of the additional revenue is limited, given these tribes' overwhelming social and economic needs.

> *From some people's point of view, Native Americans have learned to play the White man's game of politics only too well.*

Even on those reservations that benefit from gambling enterprises, unemployment levels are substantially higher than for the nation as a whole, and family income is significantly lower.

Criticism of Native American gambling operations exists even among Native Americans. Some feel that the tribal-themed casinos trivialize and cheapen their heritage. Native Americans gambled during tribal ceremonies and celebrations long before Europeans arrived in the Western Hemisphere, but their games were an integral part of their culture, not a commercial amusement. Other Native Americans oppose gambling on moral grounds. They are concerned about the development of compulsive gambling among members of their tribe, although the majority of gamblers are not Native American. Finally, in some tribes, the issue of who should share in the gambling prof-its has led to heated debates over who is or is not a member of the tribe.

Not surprisingly, gaming on reservations has been a magnet for criticism from outsiders. Even though nationwide, Native Americans generate only 23 percent of the total revenue from legal gambling, including profits from lotteries and racing, White gaming interests have lobbied Congress to restrict tribal operations. They question the special status afforded to Native Americans, complaining of an uneven playing field. Tribal members counter that over the last 200 years, government policy created a playing field on which Native Americans were at a distinct disadvantage.

Though Native Americans' voting clout is weak compared to that of African Americans and Latinos, their lobbying power is significant. Casino money fueled the 2006 scandal involving lobbyist Jack Abramoff, who cheated several tribes by pretending to lobby on their behalf. But while many of the political donations Native Americans make are aimed at protecting reservation casinos, federal grants for education, roads, housing and other projects also occupy tribes' political agendas. From some people's point of view, Native Americans have learned to play the White man's game of politics only too well.

Let's Discuss
1. What do you think of the commercial gaming operations that Native Americans run from their reservations? Would your opinion differ depending on whether you yourself were a Native American?
2. Analyze the Native American gaming industry from the functionalist, conflict, and interactionist viewpoints. Which perspective do you find most helpful?

Sources: Bartlett and Steele 2002; Grinkard 2006; Glionna 2004; National Indian Gaming Association 2004; Sahagun 2004; J. Taylor and Kalt 2005.

SOCIAL INEQUALITY BOXES

These boxes on social issues such as disability as a master status, privilege and discrimination in employment, and Native Americans and gambling highlight an important area of analysis for sociologists today.

Providing Expanded Coverage of Globalization

NEW CHAPTER AND NEW SECTIONS ON GLOBAL ISSUES

In addition to a new chapter on global inequality (Chapter 9), every chapter in the book has been revised with an aim toward embracing examples and sociological issues affecting world cultures. Especially important are new sections providing contemporary terms and definitions for thinking globally (Chapter 1); understanding fundamental global inequality (Chapter 9); the impact of global immigration (Chapter 10); and global change and environmental issues (Chapter 16).

Distribution of Wealth and Income

In at least 26 nations around the world, the most affluent 10 percent of the population receives at least 40 percent of all income. The list includes the African nation of Namibia (the leader, at 65 percent of all income), as well as Colombia, Mexico, Nigeria, and South Africa. Figure 9-5 compares the distribution of income in selected industrialized and developing nations.

Women in developing countries find life especially difficult. Karuna Chanana Ahmed, an anthropologist from India who has studied women in developing nations, calls women the most exploited of oppressed people. Beginning at birth women face sex discrimination. They are commonly fed less than male children, are denied educational opportunities, and are often hospitalized only when they are critically ill. Inside or outside the home, women's work is devalued. When economies fail, as they did in Asian countries in the late 1990s, women are the first to be laid off from work (J. Anderson and Moore 1993; Kristof 1998).

Surveys show a significant degree of *female infanticide* (the killing of baby girls) in China and rural areas of India. Only one-third of Pakistan's sexually segregated schools are for women, and

In a pluralistic society, a subordinate group does not have to forsake its lifestyle and traditions. *Pluralism* is based on mutual respect for one another's cultures among the various groups in a society. This pattern allows a minority group to express its own culture and still participate without prejudice in the larger society's level of intergenerational mobility (Ganzeboom et al. 1991; Haller et al. 1990; Hauser and Grusky 1988).

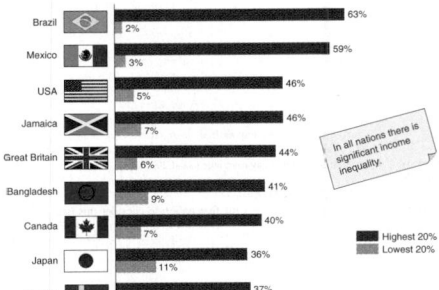

FIGURE 9-5
Distribution of Income in Nine Nations

Nation	Highest 20%	Lowest 20%
Brazil	63%	2%
Mexico	59%	3%
USA	46%	5%
Jamaica	46%	7%
Great Britain	44%	6%
Bangladesh	41%	9%
Canada	40%	7%
Japan	36%	11%
Sweden	37%	9%

In all nations there is significant income inequality.

Note: Data are considered comparable although based on statistics covering 1993 to 2001.
Source: World Bank 2005a:72–74.

Impact of Global Immigration

Worldwide, immigration is at an all-time high. Each year, about 2.3 percent of the world's population, or 146 million people, moves from one country to another. A million of them enter the United States legally, to join the 12 percent of the U.S. population who are foreign born (Schmidley and Robinson 2003; Walker 2000).

In the 1960s, following decades of restrictive immigration policy, Congress overhauled the immigration law. U.S. policy now encourages the immigration of relatives of U.S. residents, as well as of people who have desirable skills. This change has significantly altered the pattern of sending nations. Previously, Europeans had dominated, but for the last 40 years immigrants have come primarily from Latin America, India, and Asia. Thus, in the future, an ever-growing proportion of the U.S. population will be Asian or Hispanic (see Figure 10-5, page 246). Fear and resentment of this growing racial and ethnic diversity is a key

What Is a Family?

What makes a family? Not race, because families can be transracial. Not two generations, because families can be extended. Not the number or age of the members, because families can be big or small, young or old. Around the world, families may eat, dress, and worship differently, but all are united by a special intergenerational bond and an acknowledged responsibility to care for their kin.

German photographer Uwe Ommer (2000) took the photographs on this page and the next. For four years he traveled the world, visiting 130 countries on five continents in search of families who are typical of their societies. These three photographs, taken from Ommer's book *1000 Families*, only hint at the tremendous diversity of families around the world. The interracial family from Botswana (below) represents a departure from the norm in their society; in a country where politics is based on race, they feel they are outsiders. Still, their love for one another holds the family together. The thoroughly modern Syrian family (top right) has three children in college; of the three girls, one aspires to become a journalist, another an engineer, and the third a professional basketball player. The extended family from Armenia (bottom right) combines shoemaking, teaching, and farming to support three generations. Working with their hands and their heads, they are optimistic about the future and plan to have more children.

[Botswana]

292

[Syria]

[Armenia]

REVEALING PHOTO ESSAYS

Six photo essays (three new to this edition) provide glimpses of ways of life in different countries. Each begins with a question intended to prompt students to see some part of everyday life with new eyes—those of a sociologist. The accompanying photos and captions suggest the answer to the question.

SOCIOLOGY IN THE GLOBAL COMMUNITY BOXES

These boxes provide a global perspective on topics such as the worldwide response to the 2004 tsunami disaster, cultural survival in Brazil, cutting poverty worldwide, and the impact of global media such as the Al Jazeera network.

sociologyIN *the Global Community*

9-1 Cutting Poverty Worldwide

The goal of the United Nations' Millennium Project is to cut the world's poverty level in half by 2015. The project has eight objectives:

1. *Eradicate extreme poverty and hunger.* Poverty rates are falling in many parts of the globe, particularly in Asia. But in sub-Saharan Africa, where the poor are hard pressed, millions more have sunk deeper into poverty. As of 2001, more than 1 billion people worldwide were living on less than $1 a day. These people suffer from chronic hunger. As of 2006, an estimated 100 million of the world's children were malnourished—a statistic that has negative implications for their countries' economic progress.

2. *Achieve universal primary education.* While many parts of the developing world are approaching universal school enrollment, in sub-Saharan Africa, less than two-thirds of all children are enrolled in primary school.

3. *Promote gender equality and empower women.* The gender gap in primary school enrollment that has characterized the developing world for so long is slowly closing. However, women still lack equal representation at the highest levels of government. Worldwide, they hold only about 16 percent of all parliamentary seats. Nu-

toward reducing child mortality has slowed in recent decades.

5. *Improve maternal health.* Each year more than half a million women die during pregnancy or childbirth. Progress has been made in reducing maternal death rates in some developing regions, but not in countries where the risk of giving birth is highest.

6. *Combat HIV/AIDS, malaria, and other diseases.* AIDS has become the leading cause of premature death in sub-Saharan Africa, where two-thirds of the world's AIDS patients reside. Worldwide, the disease is the fourth most frequent killer. Though new drug treatments can prolong life, there is still no cure for this scourge.

As of 2001, more than 1 billion people worldwide were living on less than $1 a day.

Moreover, each year malaria and tuberculosis kill almost as many people as AIDS, severely draining the labor pool in many countries.

7. *Ensure environmental sustainability.* While most countries have publicly com-

water has increased, half the developing world lacks toilets and other forms of basic sanitation.

8. *Develop a global partnership for development.* The United Nations Millennium Declaration seeks a global social compact in which developing countries pledge to do more to ensure their own development, while developed countries support them through aid, debt relief, and improved trade opportunities. However, despite the much publicized G8 summit (a meeting of the heads of state of the 8 major economies) in Gleneagles, Scotland, in 2005 and the accompanying LIVE 8 global concerts, the developed nations have fallen far short of the targets they set themselves.

Let's Discuss

1. Do you think the Millennium Project's objectives are realistic, given the enormity of the obstacles that must be overcome? Why do you think the project's founders gave themselves only 15 years to accomplish their goal?

2. How are the project's eight objectives related to one another? Could some of the objectives be reached successfully without addressing the others? If you were a

Relating Sociology to Students' Lives

sociologyON*campus*

8-3 Social Class and Financial Aid

Today's young people have been dubbed Generation Y, but a more appropriate name for them could be Generation Debt. Every year, millions of prospective college students and their parents struggle through the intricate and time-consuming process of applying for financial aid. Originally, financial aid programs were intended to level the playing field—to allow qualified students from all walks of life to attend college, regardless of the cost. But have these programs fulfilled their promise?

In 2004, 40 percent of first-year students at major state universities came from families with incomes of more than $100,000 a year. In other words, close to half of all students came from high-income families. This statistic should not be surprising, given the high cost of tuition, room, and board at state universities. For students from families with the lowest incomes, the cost can be prohibitive. At any school, students from households with incomes of $75,000 and over are three times as likely to graduate as students from households with incomes under $25,000. Those moderate-income students who do graduate, and even those who fail to complete their degrees, are often saddled with heavy postgraduate debt. As of 2006, the average college graduate owed a total of $19,000 in student financial aid.

Besides the spiraling cost of an education, the widespread difficulty in paying for college

stems from three trends. First, over the past few decades, colleges and universities have been moving away from making outright grants, such as scholarships, to deserving students, and toward low-interest student loans. Second, much of the assistance schools offer in the form of loans is not based strictly on need. Since 1982, non-need-based state aid has grown by 336 percent, while need-based assistance has grown by only 88 percent. Third, interest rates on federally guaranteed

Statistics that show the educational level in the United States rising overall obscure the widening gap between the advantaged and the less advantaged.

loans have risen steadily, increasing the burden of repayment.

These trends in financial aid for higher education are closely tied to trends in social inequality. As noted earlier in this chapter, over the past half century, rather than declining, inequality in income and wealth has actually increased. According to one analysis of U.S. economic trends over the last 30 years, this increase in wealth and income inequality has

contributed to a modest increase in educational inequality, as measured by the number of years of formal schooling students achieve. In a variation on the truism that the rich tend to get richer while the poor get poorer, the rich are getting better educations and the poor are getting poorer educations. Statistics that show the educational level in the United States rising overall obscure the widening gap between the advantaged and the less advantaged.

Let's Discuss

1. Take a poll in your class: How many students are receiving some form of financial aid? How many have a scholarship and how many have a loan?
2. Aside from a reduction in individual social mobility, what might be the long-term effects of the shortage of need-based financial aid? Relate your answer to the trend toward globalization.

Sources: Boushey 2005; Campbell et al. 2006; Leonhardt 2004; Michals 2003; Tru...

SOCIOLOGY ON CAMPUS BOXES

These boxes on topics such as cheating, social class and financial aid, binge drinking, and the debate over Title IX apply a sociological perspective to several issues of immediate interest to students.

research*IN*action

5-2 Adolescent Sexual Networks

If you drew a chart of the sexual network at a typical American high school, what would it look like? In the mid-1990s, sociologists Peter Bearman, James Moody, and Katherine Stovel asked themselves that question. While studying romantic relationships at a high school with about 1,000 students, they had found that about 61 percent of the boys and 55 percent of the girls had been sexually active over the past 18 months. Those percentages did not differ much from the results of similar studies done during the period. What surprised the research team was what they saw when they began to chart the students' relationships.

To obtain their data, Bearman and his colleagues conducted in-home interviews with the respondents. Instead of asking students for a face-to-face interview—a technique that might have embarrassed them or distorted their answers—the researchers gave them an

A particularly significant implication of this study is the risk of sexually transmitted diseases (STDs) to those who participate in such a network.

audio recording of the questions, a pair of earphones, and a laptop computer on which to record their answers. The research team also asked respondents to look at a list of all the students at the high school and identify those with whom they had had romantic or sexual relationships.

The results showed that 573 of the 832 students surveyed had had at least one sexual relationship over the past 18 months. Among those respondents, the sociologists found only 63 steady couples, or pairs with no other partners. A much larger group of 288 students—almost a third of the sample—was involved in the free-flowing network of relationships [...] the accompanying chart. (Note the [...] e absence of tightly closed loops of [...] ividuals.) Not shown on the chart [...] er 90 students who were involved in [...] ps outside the school.

A particularly significant implication of this study is the risk of sexually transmitted diseases (STDs) to those who participate in such a network. Through the complicated chain of relationships, even students who have only one or two sexual partners are exposing themselves to a relatively high degree of risk. But while parents and even students may be alarmed by the data, public health officials are encouraged. Experts at the Centers for Disease Control who have reviewed the network charts from this and other studies see them as blueprints for change. If experts can alter participants' behavior anywhere along these chains—by counseling abstinence, condom use, or treatment of STDs—they can significantly reduce transmission of the diseases.

Let's Discuss

1. Do the results of the study surprise you? How does the sexual network described in this study compare to the network where you went to high school?
2. Do you see any problems with the research methods used in this study? Can you think of anything that might have compromised the validity of the data?

Sources: Bearman, Moody, and Stovel 2004; C. F. Turner et al. 1998; Wallis 2005.

Each dot represents a boy or girl at "Jefferson High." The lines that link them represent romantic and sexual relationships that occurred over an 18-month period. While most of the teenagers had had just one or two partners, 288 of the 832 students interviewed were linked in a giant sexual network.

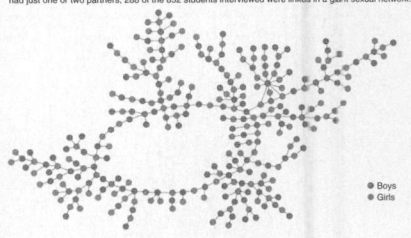

● Boys
● Girls

Other relationships (If a pattern was observed more than once, numeral indicates frequency)

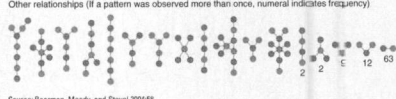

2   2   12   63

Source: Bearman, Moody, and Stovel 2004:58.

RESEARCH IN ACTION BOXES

These boxes present sociological findings on relevant topics such as adolescent sexual networks, the challenge of doing research polling in Baghdad, road rage, and the shrinking middle class.

taking SOCIOLOGY TO WORK

Rakefet Avramovitz
Program Administrator
Child Care Law Center

Rakefet Avramovitz has been working at the Child Care Law Center in San Francisco since 2003. The center uses legal tools to foster the development of quality, affordable child care, with the goal of expanding child care options, particularly for low-income families. As a support person for the center's attorneys, Avramovitz manages grants, oversees the center's publications, and sets up conferences and training sessions. One of her most important tasks has been to organize a working group that brings together people from all parts of the child care community. "The documents that come out of this forum inform the organization's work for the year," she explains.

Avramovitz graduated from Dickinson College in 2000. She first became interested in sociology when she took a social analysis course. Though she enjoyed her qualitative courses most, she found her quantitative courses fun, "in that we got to do surveys of people on campus. I've always enjoyed field-work," she notes. Avramovitz's most memorable course was one that gave her the opportunity to interact with migrant farm workers for an entire semester. "I learned ethnography and how to work with people of different cultures. It changed my life," she says.

Avramovitz finds that the skills she learned in her sociology courses are a great help to her on the job. "Sociology taught me how to work

with people . . . and how to think critically. It taught me how to listen and find the stories that people are telling," she explains. Before joining the Child Care Law Center, Avramovitz worked as a counselor for women who were facing difficult issues. "My background in ethnography helped me to talk to these women and listen effectively," she notes. "I was able to help many women by understanding and being able to express their needs to the attorneys we worked with."

Avramovitz is enthusiastic about her work and her ability to make a difference in other people's lives. Maybe that is why she looks forward to summer at the center, when the staff welcomes several law students as interns. "It is really neat to see people learn and get jazzed about child-care issues," she says.

Let's Discuss

1. What might be some of the broad, long-term effects of the center's work to expand child care options? Explain.
2. Besides the law, what other professions might benefit from the skills a sociology major has to offer?

TAKING SOCIOLOGY TO WORK BOXES

These boxes underscore the value of an undergraduate degree in sociology by profiling individuals who majored in sociology and use its principles in their work.

Offering Distinctive Pedagogy and Illustrations that Reinforce Content

SUMMING UP TABLES

More than 20 Summing Up tables recap coverage of the major theoretical perspectives on key topics.

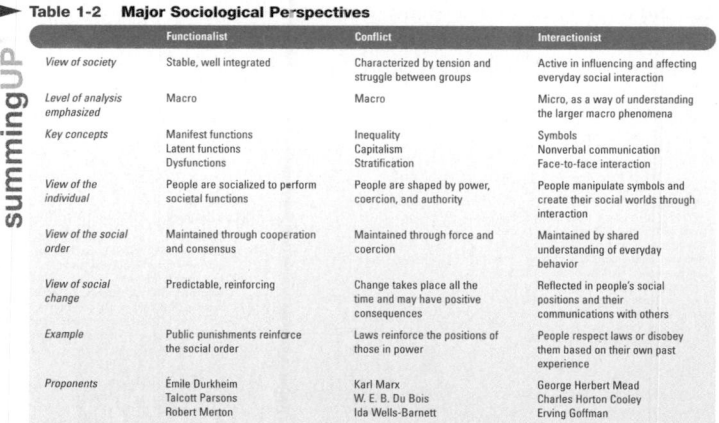

summingUP

Table 1-2   Major Sociological Perspectives

	Functionalist	Conflict	Interactionist
View of society	Stable, well integrated	Characterized by tension and struggle between groups	Active in influencing and affecting everyday social interaction
Level of analysis emphasized	Macro	Macro	Micro, as a way of understanding the larger macro phenomena
Key concepts	Manifest functions Latent functions Dysfunctions	Inequality Capitalism Stratification	Symbols Nonverbal communication Face-to-face interaction
View of the individual	People are socialized to perform societal functions	People are shaped by power, coercion, and authority	People manipulate symbols and create their social worlds through interaction
View of the social order	Maintained through cooperation and consensus	Maintained through force and coercion	Maintained by shared understanding of everyday behavior
View of social change	Predictable, reinforcing	Change takes place all the time and may have positive consequences	Reflected in people's social positions and their communications with others
Example	Public punishments reinforce the social order	Laws reinforce the positions of those in power	People respect laws or disobey them based on their own past experience
Proponents	Émile Durkheim Talcott Parsons Robert Merton	Karl Marx W. E. B. Du Bois Ida Wells-Barnett	George Herbert Mead Charles Horton Cooley Erving Goffman

DEMOGRAPHIC MAP PROGRAM

Two kinds of maps—Mapping Life Nationwide and Mapping Life Worldwide—are featured throughout the text. Interactive versions of many of these maps, along with accompanying questions, appear on the book's Online Learning Center.

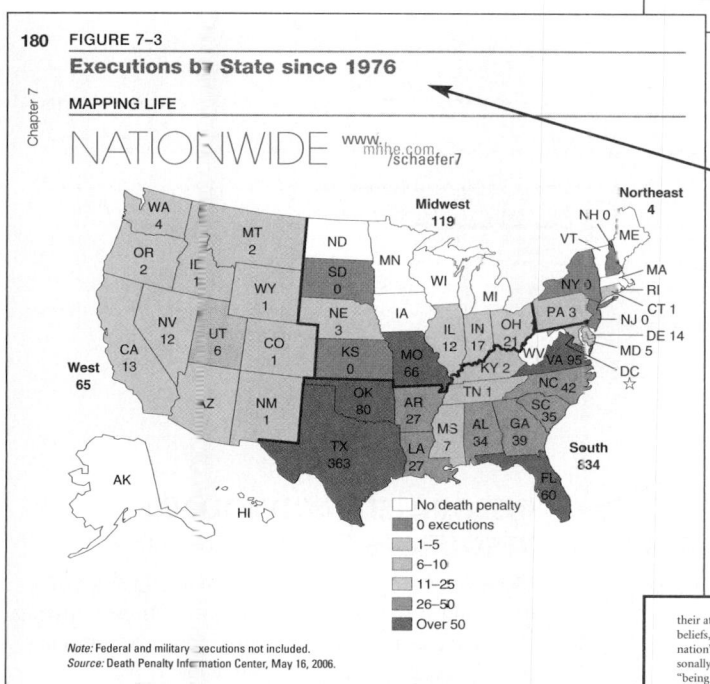

180   FIGURE 7–3

Executions by State since 1976

MAPPING LIFE

NATIONWIDE   www.mhhe.com/schaefer7

Chapter 7

No death penalty
0 executions
1–5
6–10
11–25
26–50
Over 50

Note: Federal and military executions not included.
Source: Death Penalty Information Center, May 16, 2006.

"THINK ABOUT IT" FIGURE CAPTIONS

These captions, which accompany many of the book's maps, graphs, and tables, encourage students to think critically about information presented in figures.

their attitudes. Because this survey focuses on an array of issues, beliefs, and life goals, it is commonly cited as a barometer of the nation's values. The respondents are asked what values are personally important to them. Over the last 39 years, the value of "being very well-off financially" has shown the strongest gain in popularity; the proportion of first-year college students who endorse this value as "essential" or "very important" rose from 44 percent in 1967 to 74.5 percent in 2005 (see Figure 3-2). In contrast, the value that has shown the most striking decline in endorsement by students is "developing a meaningful philosophy of life." While this value was the most popular in the 1967 survey, endorsed by more than 80 percent of the respondents, it had fallen to seventh place on the list by 2005, when it was endorsed by 45 percent of students entering college.

During the 1980s and 1990s, support for values having to do with money, power, and status grew. At the same time, support for certain values having to do with social awareness and altruism, such as "helping others," declined. According to the 2005 nationwide survey, only 39 percent of first-year college students stated that "influencing social values" was an "essential" or "very important" goal. The proportion of students for whom "helping to promote racial understanding" was an essential or very important goal reached a record high of 42 percent in 1992, then fell to 33 percent in 2005. Like other aspects of culture, such as language and norms, a nation's values are not necessarily fixed.

Recently, cheating has become a hot issue on college campuses. Professors now take advantage of computerized services that can identify plagiarism, such as the search engine Google, have been shocked to learn that many of the papers their students

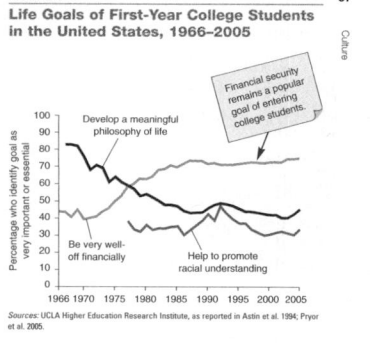

FIGURE 3–2   67

Life Goals of First-Year College Students in the United States, 1966–2005

Culture

Financial security remains a popular goal of entering college students.

Develop a meaningful philosophy of life

Be very well-off financially

Help to promote racial understanding

Percentage who identify goal as very important or essential

Sources: UCLA Higher Education Research Institute, as reported in Astin et al. 1994; Pryor et al. 2005.

Think About It

Why do you think values have shifted among college students in the last few decades? Which of these values is important to you?

Featuring Meaningful Resources that Promote Active Learning and Review

NEW SELF-QUIZZES

At the end of every chapter, a twenty-question self-quiz allows students to test their comprehension and retention of core information presented in the chapter.

Read each question carefully and then select the best answer.

1. From the functionalist perspective, the media can be dysfunctional in what way?
   - a. They enforce social norms.
   - b. They confer status.
   - c. They desensitize us to events.
   - d. They are agents of socialization.

2. Sociologist Robert Park studied how newspapers helped immigrants to the United States adjust to their environment by changing their customary habits and by teaching them the opinions held by people in their new home country. His study was conducted from which sociological perspective?
   - a. the functionalist perspective
   - b. the conflict perspective
   - c. the interactionist perspective
   - d. the dramaturgical perspective

3. There are problems inherent in the socialization function of the mass media. For example, many people worry about
   - a. the effect of using the television as a babysitter.
   - b. the impact of violent programming on viewer behavior.
   - c. the unequal ability of all individuals to purchase televisions.
   - d. both a and b

4. Media advertising has several clear functions, but it also has dysfunctions. Sociologists are concerned that
   - a. it creates unrealistic expectations of what is required to be happy.
   - b. it creates new consumer needs.
   - c. advertisers are able to influence media content.
   - d. all of the above

5. Gatekeeping, the process by which a relatively small number of people control what material reaches an audience, is largely dominant in all but which of the following media?
   - a. television
   - b. the Internet
   - c. publishing
   - d. music

6. Which sociological perspective is especially concerned with the media's ability to decide what gets transmitted through gatekeeping?
   - a. the functionalist perspective
   - b. the conflict perspective
   - c. the interactionist perspective
   - d. the dramaturgical perspective

7. Which of the following is *not* a problem feminist theorists see with media coverage?
   - a. Women are underrepresented, suggesting that men are the cultural standard and that women are insignificant.
   - b. Men and women are portrayed in ways that reflect and perpetuate stereotypical views of gender.
   - c. Depictions of male–female relationships emphasize traditional sex roles and normalize violence against women.
   - d. The increasing frequency of single moms in the media is providing a negative role model for women.

8. Which of the following sociological perspectives helps us to understand more about one important aspect of the entire mass media system—the audience?
   - a. the functionalist perspective
   - b. the conflict perspective
   - c. the interactionist perspective
   - d. the feminist perspective

9. Sociologist Paul Lazarsfeld and his colleagues pioneered the study of
   - a. the audience.
   - b. opinion leaders.
   - c. the media's global reach.
   - d. media violence.

10. In his study of how the social composition of audience members affected how they interpreted the news coverage of riots in Los Angeles in 1992, sociologist Darnell Hunt found what kind of differences in perception?
    - a. racial
    - b. gender
    - c. class
    - d. religious

11. The mass media increase social cohesion by presenting a more or less standardized, common view of culture through mass communication. This statement reflects the _____ perspective.

12. Paul Lazarsfeld and Robert Merton created the term _____ to refer to the phenomenon whereby the media provide such massive amounts of information that the audience becomes numb and generally fails to act on the information, regardless of how compelling the issue.

13. _____ is the term used to describe the set of cultural beliefs and practices that helps to maintain powerful social, economic, and political interests.

14. Sociologists blame the mass media for the creation and perpetuation of _____, or generalizations about all members of a group that do not recognize individual differences within the group.

15. The _____ perspective contends that television distorts the political process.

16. We risk being _____ if we overstress U.S. dominance and assume other nations do not play a role in media cultural exports.

17. Both _____ and _____ theorists are troubled that the victims depicted in violent imagery are often those who are given less respect in real life: women, children, the poor, racial minorities, citizens of foreign countries, and even the physically disabled.

18. The _____ perspective examines the media on the micro level to see how they shape day-to-day social behavior.

{ TECHNOLOGY RESOURCES }

 ### Online Learning Center

1. Everyone has been a member of in-groups and out-groups. Visit the student center in the Online Learning Center (**www.mhhe.com/schaefer7**) and link to the Interactive Activity entitled "In-Groups, Out-Groups, and Un-words." In this activity, you will be asked to discuss your experiences as a member of an in-group and an out-group. You can also do the word scramble, which contains key words and phrases from this chapter.

2. Proponents of educational programs in prisons argue that the social structure of a classroom environment can be used to rehabilitate people who have been incarcerated. Visit the Web site of the Center

for the Study of Correctional Education (**www.csusb.edu/coe/cg/csce/index.html**)—especially the link to Research. Contrast these programs with the social environment of Zimbardo's prison experiment.

3. The Web site of the Illinois Labor History Society (**www.kentlaw.edu/ilhs/index.html**) contains extensive information on labor unions, strikes, and disasters in that state, past and present. Visit the site for an overview of labor history in Illinois.

*Note: While all the URLs listed were current as of the printing of this book, these sites often change. Please check our Web site (**www.mhhe.com/schaefer7**) for updates, hyperlinks, and exercises related to these sites.*

 ### *Reel Society* Video Clips

Reel Society video clips, which appear on this book's Web site, can be used to spark discussion about the following topics from this chapter:
- Social Roles
- Groups

INTEGRATED TECHNOLOGY RESOURCES

These resources include Internet exercises and brief descriptions of specific content on the Online Learning Center Web site, including a listing of relevant topics that are explored in *Reel Society* video clips.

Understanding Sociology

inside

What Is Sociology?

What Is Sociological Theory?

The Development of Sociology

Major Theoretical Perspectives

Applied and Clinical Sociology

Developing a Sociological
Imagination

Appendix: Careers in Sociology

Boxes

Sociology in the Global Community:
The Global Response to the 2004
Tsunami

Research in Action: Looking at
Sports from Three Theoretical
Perspectives

LA AND THE SOUTH PACIFIC // UNITED

THREE DAILY NONSTOPS TO THE SOUTH PACIFIC.

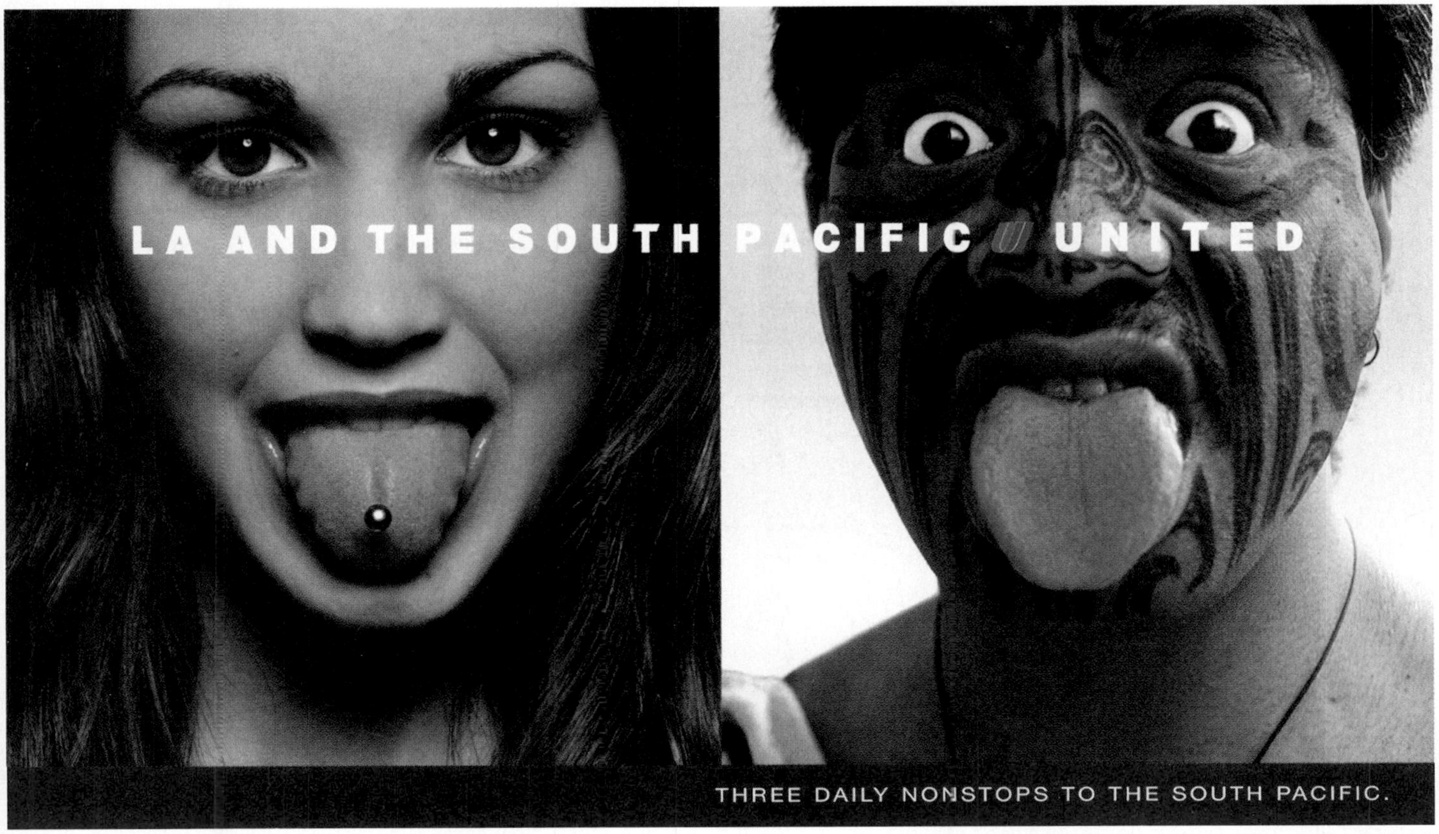

Social behavior varies, both around the world and within societies. Sociologists are interested in both the similarities and the differences in human behavior among different societies. In this billboard for an international airline, a young woman from Los Angeles shows off her tongue stud and a South Pacific islander displays a ceremonial tattooed face.

I am, of course, very different from the people who normally fill America's least attractive jobs, and in ways that both helped and limited me. Most obviously, I was only visiting a world that others inhabit full-time, often for most of their lives. With all the real-life assets I've built up in middle age—bank account, IRA, health insurance, multiroom home—waiting indulgently in the background, there was no way I was going to "experience poverty" or find out how it "really feels" to be a long-term low-wage worker. My aim here was much more straightforward and objective—just to see whether I could match income to expenses, as the truly poor attempt to do every day. . . .

In Portland, Maine, I came closest to achieving a decent fit between income and expenses, but only because I worked seven days a week. Between my two jobs, I was earning approximately $300 a week after taxes and paying $480 a month in rent, or a manageable 40 percent of my earnings. It helped, too, that gas and electricity were included in my rent and that I got two or three free meals each weekend at the nursing home. But I was there at the beginning of the off-season. If I had stayed until June 2000 I would have faced the Blue Haven's summer rent of $390 a week, which would of course have been out of the question. So to survive year-round, I would have had to save enough, in the months between August 1999 and May 2000, to accumulate the first month's rent and deposit on an actual apartment. I think I could have done this—saved $800 to $1,000—at least if no car trouble or illness interfered with my budget. I am not sure, however, that I could have maintained the seven-day-a-week regimen month after month or eluded the kinds of injuries that afflicted my fellow workers in the housecleaning business.

In Minneapolis—well, here we are left with a lot of speculation. If I had been able to find an apartment for $400 a month or less, my pay at Wal-Mart—$1,120 a month before taxes—might have been sufficient, although the cost of living in a motel while I searched for such an apartment might have made it impossible for me to save enough for the first month's rent and deposit. A weekend job, such as the one I almost landed at a supermarket for about $7.75 an hour, would have helped, but I had no guarantee that I could arrange my schedule at Wal-Mart to reliably exclude weekends. If I had taken the job at Menards and the pay was in fact $10 an hour for eleven hours a day, I would have made about $440 a week after taxes—enough to pay for a motel room and still have something left over to save up for the initial costs of an apartment. But were they really offering $10 an hour? And could I have stayed on my feet eleven hours a day, five days a week? So yes, with some different choices, I probably could have survived in Minneapolis. But I'm not going back for a rematch.

(Ehrenreich 2001:6, 197–198) Additional information about this excerpt can be found on the Online Learning Center at www.mhhe.com/schaefer7. ●

> *With all the real-life assets I've built up in middle age—bank account, IRA, health insurance, multiroom home—waiting indulgently in the background, there was no way I was going to "experience poverty" or find out how it "really feels" to be a long-term low-wage worker.*

In her undercover attempts to survive as a low-wage worker in different cities in the United States, journalist Barbara Ehrenreich revealed patterns of human interaction and used methods of study that foster sociological investigation. This excerpt from her book *Nickel and Dimed: On (Not) Getting By in America* describes how she left a comfortable home and assumed the identity of a divorced, middle-aged housewife with no college degree and little working experience. She set out to get the best-paying job and the cheapest living quarters she could find, to see whether she could make ends meet. Months later, physically exhausted and demoralized by demeaning work rules, Ehrenreich confirmed what she had suspected before she began: getting by in this country as a low-wage worker is a losing proposition.

Ehrenreich's study focused on an unequal society, which is a central topic in sociology. Her investigative work, like the work of many other journalists, is informed by sociological research that documents the existence and extent of inequality in our society. Social inequality has a pervasive influence on human interactions and institutions. Certain groups of people control scarce resources, wield power, and receive special treatment. The poster that opens this chapter illustrates another common focus of sociologists, the variations in social behavior from one part of the world to another.

While it might be interesting to know how one individual is affected by the need to make ends meet, or even by the choice to wear a tongue stud or tattoo, sociologists consider how en-

tire groups of people are affected by these kinds of factors, and how society itself might be altered by them. Sociologists, then, are not concerned with what one individual does or does not do, but with what people do as members of a group or in interaction with one another, and what that means for individuals and for society as a whole.

As a field of study, sociology is extremely broad in scope. You will see throughout this book the range of topics sociologists investigate—from suicide to TV viewing habits, from Amish society to global economic patterns, from peer pressure to genetic engineering. Sociology looks at how others influence our behavior; how major social institutions like the government, religion, and the economy affect us; and how we ourselves affect other individuals, groups, and even organizations.

How did sociology develop? In what ways does it differ from other social sciences? This chapter will explore the nature of sociology as both a field of inquiry and an exercise of the "sociological imagination." We'll look at the discipline as a science and consider its relationship to other social sciences. We'll meet three pioneering thinkers—Émile Durkheim, Max Weber, and Karl Marx—and examine the theoretical perspectives that grew out of their work. We'll note some of the practical applications for sociological theory and research. Finally, we'll see how sociology helps us to develop a sociological imagination. For those students interested in exploring career opportunities in sociology, the chapter closes with a special appendix. ●

What Is Sociology?

"What has sociology got to do with me or with my life?" As a student, you might well have asked this question when you signed up for your introductory sociology course. To answer it, consider these points: Are you influenced by what you see on television? Do you use the Internet? Did you vote in the last election? Are you familiar with binge drinking on campus? Do you use alternative medicine? These are just a few of the everyday life situations described in this book that sociology can shed light on. But as the opening excerpt indicates, sociology also looks at large social issues. We use sociology to investigate why thousands of jobs have moved from the United States to developing nations, what social forces promote prejudice, what leads someone to join a social movement and work for social change, how access to computer technology can reduce social inequality, and why relationships between men and women in Seattle differ from those in Singapore.

Sociology is, very simply, the scientific study of social behavior and human groups. It focuses on social relationships; how

those relationships influence people's behavior; and how societies, the sum total of those relationships, develop and change.

The Sociological Imagination

In attempting to understand social behavior, sociologists rely on an unusual type of creative thinking. A leading sociologist, C. Wright Mills, described such thinking as the *sociological imagination*—an awareness of the relationship between an individual and the wider society, both today and in the past. This awareness allows all of us (not just sociologists) to comprehend the links between our immediate, personal social settings and the remote, impersonal social world that surrounds and helps to shape us. Barbara Ehrenreich certainly used a sociological imagination when she studied low-wage workers (Mills [1959] 2000a).

A key element in the sociological imagination is the ability to view one's own society as an outsider would, rather than only from the perspective of personal experiences and cultural biases. Consider something as simple as sporting events. On college

Classroom Tip See "Stimulating Classroom Discussions about *Nickel and Dimed*" (Class Discussion Topics).

Web Resource Encourage students to visit the Online Learning Center at **www.mhhe.com/schaefer7** and explore the student center. Note that it offers several kinds of valuable learning aids, including quizzes, puzzles, audio clips, and activities.

Classroom Tip Tell students when your department was founded, how many sociology majors you have, and how many degrees were presented last year.

Classroom Tip Share with students how you came to be interested in sociology.

Key Person C. Wright Mills (Mills's power elite model of the United States is analyzed in Chapter 14).

Are You What You Own?

Use your sociological imagination to analyze the "material world" of three different societies. These photos come from the book *Material World: A Global Family Portrait*. The photographers selected a "statistically average" family in each country they visited and took pictures of that family with all the possessions in the household. Shown here are families in Japan, Mexico, and South Africa.

What do the material goods in these photographs tell you about the food, shelter, and lifestyle in each culture? Which possessions are geared toward recreation and which toward subsistence? What means of transport and communication are available to each family? What items do all three families own,

and how are those items similar? What does the clothing family members are wearing tell you about their social class? What effect might each family's size have on its economic position? Do all three families have enough material goods to meet all their members' needs? How do you think each family would react if they lived with the belongings of the other two households?

These photos make us aware that when we look at people's material possessions, we learn something about the social, economic, and geographic factors that influence their way of life. The photos may also prompt us to think sociologically about our own material possessions, and what they say about us and about our society (Menzel 1994).

{ The Ukita family, Tokyo, Japan }

{The Qampie family, Soweto, South Africa}

{The Castillo Balderas family, Guadalajara, Mexico}

campuses in the United States, thousands of students cheer well-trained football players. In Bali, Indonesia, dozens of spectators gather around a ring to cheer on well-trained roosters engaged in cockfights. In both instances, the spectators debate the merits of their favorites and bet on the outcome of the events. Yet what is considered a normal sporting event in one part of the world is considered unusual in another part.

The sociological imagination allows us to go beyond personal experiences and observations to understand broader public issues. Divorce, for example, is unquestionably a personal hardship for a husband and wife who split apart. However, C. Wright Mills advocated using the sociological imagination to view divorce not simply as an individual's personal problem but rather as a societal concern. Using this perspective, we can see that an increase in the divorce rate actually redefines a major social institution—the family. Today's households frequently include stepparents and half-siblings whose parents have divorced and remarried. Through the complexities of the blended family, this private concern becomes a public issue that affects schools, government agencies, businesses, and religious institutions.

The sociological imagination is an empowering tool. It allows us to look beyond a limited understanding of human behavior to see the world and its people in a new way and through a broader lens than we might otherwise use. It may be as simple as understanding why a roommate prefers country music to hip-hop, or it may open up a whole different way of understanding other populations in the world. For example, in the aftermath of the terrorist attacks on the United States on September 11, 2001, many citizens wanted to understand how Muslims throughout the world perceived their country, and why. From time to time this textbook will offer you the chance to exercise your own sociological imagination in a variety of situations. We'll begin with one that may be close to home for you.

Use Your Sociological Imagination
www.mhhe.com /schaefer7

You are walking down the street in your city or hometown. In looking around you, you can't help noticing that half or more of the people you see are overweight. How do you explain your observation? If you were C. Wright Mills, how do you think you would explain it?

Sociology and the Social Sciences

Is sociology a science? The term *science* refers to the body of knowledge obtained by methods based on systematic observation. Just like other scientific disciplines, sociology involves the organized, systematic study of phenomena (in this case, human behavior) in order to enhance understanding. All scientists, whether studying mushrooms or murderers, attempt to collect precise information through methods of study that are as objective as possible. They rely on careful recording of observations and accumulation of data.

Reel Society See Sociological Imagination in the Topic Index.
Classroom Tip/Contemporary Culture See Class Discussion Topics for exercises on the sociological imagination.
Let's Discuss Ask students why they are taking a sociology class. Did they take any sociology or social problems courses in high school?

Of course, there is a great difference between sociology and physics, between psychology and astronomy. For this reason, the sciences are commonly divided into natural and social sciences. *Natural science* is the study of the physical features of nature and the ways in which they interact and change. Astronomy, biology, chemistry, geology, and physics are all natural sciences. *Social science* is the study of the social features of humans and the ways in which they interact and change. The social sciences include sociology, anthropology, economics, history, psychology, and political science.

These social science disciplines have a common focus on the social behavior of people, yet each has a particular orientation. Anthropologists usually study past cultures and preindustrial societies that continue today, as well as the origins of humans. Economists explore the ways in which people produce and exchange goods and services, along with money and other resources. Historians are concerned with the peoples and events of the past and their significance for us today. Political scientists study international relations, the workings of government, and the exercise of power and authority. Psychologists investigate personality and individual behavior. So what do *sociologists* focus on? They study the influence that society has on people's attitudes and behavior and the ways in which people interact and shape society. Because humans are social animals, sociologists examine our social relationships with others scientifically.

Let's consider how different social sciences would study the impact of Hurricane Katrina, which ravaged the Gulf Coast of the United States in 2005. Historians would compare the damage done by natural disasters in the 20th century to that caused by Katrina. Economists would conduct research on the economic impact of the damage, not just in the Southeast but throughout the nation and the world. Psychologists would study individual cases to assess the emotional stress of the traumatic event. And political scientists would study the stances taken by different elected officials, along with their implications for the government's response to the disaster.

What approach would sociologists take? They might look at Katrina's impact on different communities, as well as on different social classes. Some sociologists have undertaken neighborhood and community studies, to determine how to maintain the integrity of storm-struck neighborhoods during the rebuilding phase. Researchers have focused in particular on Katrina's impact on marginalized groups, from the inner-city poor in New Orleans to residents of rural American Indian reservations (Laska 2005). The devastating social impact of the storm did not surprise sociologists; as Figure 1-1 (page 8) shows, the disaster area was among the poorest in the United States. In terms of family income, for example, New Orleans ranked 63rd (7th lowest) among the nation's 70 largest cities. When the storm left tens of thousands of Gulf Coast families homeless and unemployed, most had no savings to fall back on—no way to pay for a hotel room or tide themselves over until the next paycheck. For a sociological treatment of another natural disaster, see Box 1-2 (page 21) on the 2004 tsunami.

Let's Discuss Ask students for a show of hands: How many students are majoring in a natural science? In a social science?
Classroom Tip Take a topic (e.g., suicide, religion, crime) and demonstrate how each social science examines that topic.

On August 29, 2005, shortly after Hurricane Katrina swept through the Gulf of Mexico, the U.S. Coast Guard took this aerial photograph of New Orleans. The widespread flooding shown in the photo grew worse as the week wore on, hampering the efforts of rescue teams. Sociologists want to know how the storm affected people from different communities and social classes, as well as how its impact varied with residents' income, race, and gender.

Sociologists have a long history of advising government agencies on how to respond to disasters. Certainly the poverty of the Gulf Coast region complicated the huge challenge of evacuation. With Katrina bearing down on the Gulf Coast, thousands of poor inner-city residents had no automobiles or other available means of escaping the storm. Added to that difficulty was the high incidence of disability in the area. New Orleans ranked 2nd among the nation's 70 largest cities in the proportion of people over age 65 who are disabled—56 percent. Moving wheelchair-bound residents to safety requires specially equipped vehicles, to say nothing of handicap-accessible accommodations in public shelters. Clearly, officials must consider these factors in developing evacuation plans (Bureau of the Census 2005f).

Sociologists put their sociological imaginations to work in a variety of areas—including aging, the family, human ecology, and religion. Throughout this textbook, you will see how sociologists develop theories and conduct research to study and better understand societies. And you will be encouraged to use your own sociological imagination to examine the United States (and other societies) from the viewpoint of a respectful but questioning outsider.

Sociology and Common Sense

Sociology focuses on the study of human behavior. Yet we all have experience with human behavior and at least some knowledge of it. All of us might well have theories about why people become homeless, for example. Our theories and opinions typically come from "common sense"—that is, from our experiences and conversations, from what we read, from what we see on television, and so forth.

In our daily lives we rely on common sense to get us through many unfamiliar situations. However, this commonsense knowledge, while sometimes accurate, is not always reliable, because it rests on commonly held beliefs rather than on systematic analysis of facts. It was once considered common sense to accept that the earth was flat—a view rightly questioned by Pythagoras and Aristotle. Incorrect commonsense notions are not just a part of the distant past; they remain with us today.

Contrary to the saying "The love of money is the root of all evil," for example, sociologists have found that in reality, affluence brings not only nicer cars and longer vacations but also better health and a significantly reduced exposure to pollution of all types. Another commonsense belief, "Love knows no reason," does not stand up to sociological research on courtship and marriage. The choice of a lifetime partner is generally limited by societal expectations and confined within boundaries defined by age, money, education, ethnicity, religion, and even height. Cupid's arrow flies only in certain directions (Ruane and Cerulo 2004).

In the United States today, "common sense" tells us that young people flock to concerts featuring Christian rock because religion is becoming more important to them. However, this particular "commonsense" notion—like the notion that the earth is flat—is untrue, and is not supported by sociological research. Through 2005, annual surveys of first-year college students show a decline in the percentage who attend religious services even occasionally. Increasing numbers of college students claim to have no religious preference. The trend encompasses not just organized religion but other forms of spirituality as well. Fewer students pray or meditate today than in the past, and fewer consider their level of spirituality to be very high (Sax et al. 2005).

Similarly, disasters do not generally produce panic. In the aftermath of disasters such as 9/11 and Hurricane Katrina, most people respond responsibly, even heroically, by following the authorities' directions and reaching out to those in need. Some emergency responses go more smoothly than others. On September 11, 2001, New York City's command and control structures were re-created quickly, but in 2005, amid Katrina's much vaster destruction, social organizations from the local to the federal level struggled to communicate and coordinate. Regardless of the type of catastrophe or its location, however, decision making becomes more centralized in times of disaster.

Like other social scientists, sociologists do not accept something as a fact because "everyone knows it." Instead, each piece of information must be tested and recorded, then analyzed in relationship to other data. Sociologists rely on scientific studies in order to describe and understand a social environment. At

Young people of marriageable age mingle at a social get-together. Though it is common wisdom that "love knows no reason," sociological research shows that the choice of a marriage partner is heavily influenced by societal expectations.

Fewer college students attend religious services today than in the past, despite the presence of on-campus ministries such as this Jesuit center at Fairfield University, Connecticut. Sociological research confirms the downward trend in religious observance.

times, the findings of sociologists may seem like common sense, because they deal with familiar facets of everyday life. The difference is that such findings have been *tested* by researchers.

Common sense now tells us that the earth is round. But this particular commonsense notion is based on centuries of scientific work that began with the breakthroughs made by Pythagoras and Aristotle.

FIGURE 1–1

Poverty Rates in Hurricane Katrina Disaster Area

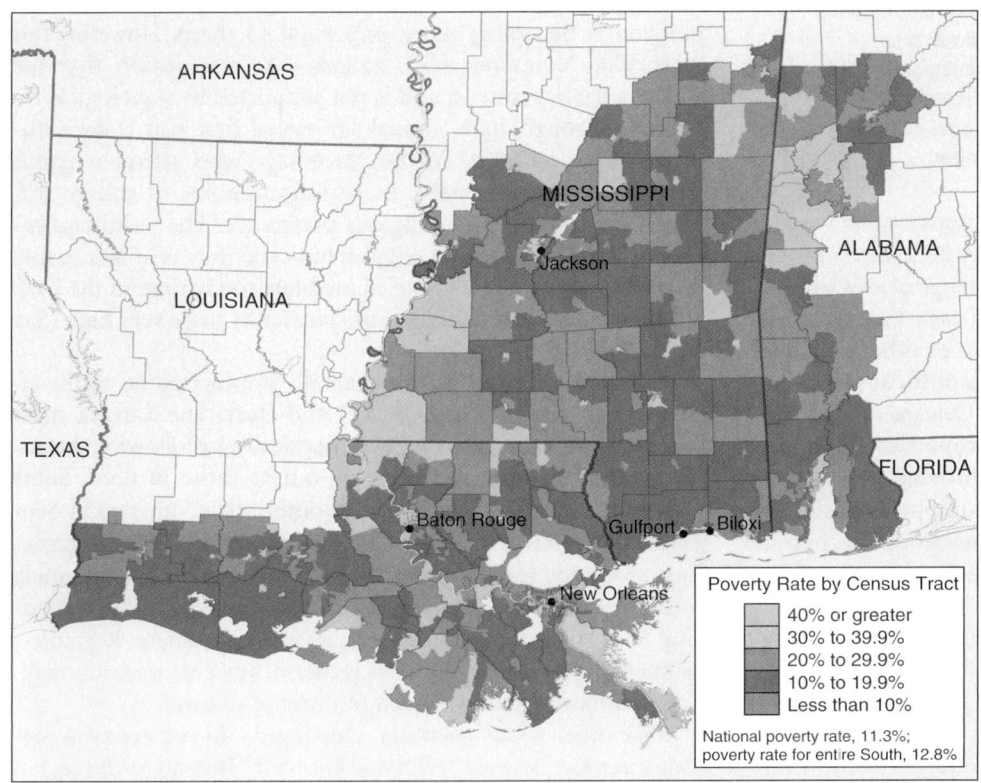

Poverty Rate by Census Tract
- 40% or greater
- 30% to 39.9%
- 20% to 29.9%
- 10% to 19.9%
- Less than 10%

National poverty rate, 11.3%; poverty rate for entire South, 12.8%

Note: Poverty data for 2000, reported in 2001. Disaster area defined by the Federal Emergency Management Agency as of September 14, 2005.
Source: Bureau of the Census 2005g.

What Is Sociological Theory?

Why do people commit suicide? One traditional commonsense answer is that people inherit the desire to kill themselves. Another view is that sunspots drive people to take their own lives. These explanations may not seem especially convincing to contemporary researchers, but they represent beliefs widely held as recently as 1900.

Sociologists are not particularly interested in why any one individual commits suicide; they are more concerned with identifying the social forces that systematically cause some people to take their own lives. In order to undertake this research, sociologists develop a *theory* that offers a general explanation of suicidal behavior.

We can think of theories as attempts to explain events, forces, materials, ideas, or behavior in a comprehensive manner. In sociology, a **theory** is a set of statements that seeks to explain problems, actions, or behavior. An effective theory may have both explanatory and predictive power. That is, it can help us to see

the relationships among seemingly isolated phenomena, as well as to understand how one type of change in an environment leads to other changes.

The World Health Organization (2002) estimated that a total of 815,000 people committed suicide in 2000. More than a hundred years earlier, a sociologist tried to look at suicide data scientifically. Émile Durkheim ([1897] 1951) developed a highly original theory about the relationship between suicide and social factors. Durkheim was primarily concerned not with the personalities of individual suicide victims, but rather with suicide rates and how they varied from country to country. As a result, when he looked at the number of reported suicides in France, England, and Denmark in 1869, he also noted the total population of each country in order to determine the rate of suicide in each nation. He found that whereas England had only 67 reported suicides per million inhabitants, France had 135 per million and Denmark had 277 per million. The question then became: "Why did Denmark have a comparatively high rate of reported suicide?"

Durkheim went much deeper into his investigation of suicide rates. The result was his landmark work *Suicide,* published in 1897. Durkheim refused to accept unproved explanations regarding suicide, including the beliefs that cosmic forces or inherited tendencies caused such deaths. Instead, he focused on social factors, such as the cohesiveness or lack of cohesiveness of religious, social, and occupational groups.

Durkheim's research suggested that suicide, while a solitary act, is related to group life. Protestants had much higher suicide rates than Catholics; the unmarried had much higher rates than married people; and soldiers were more likely to take their lives than civilians. In addition, there seemed to be higher rates of suicide in times of peace than in times of war and revolution, and in times of economic instability and recession rather than in times of prosperity. Durkheim concluded that the suicide rates of a society reflected the extent to which people were or were not integrated into the group life of the society.

Émile Durkheim, like many other social scientists, developed a *theory* to explain how individual behavior can be understood within a social context. He pointed out the influence of groups and societal forces on what had always been viewed as a highly personal act. Clearly, Durkheim offered a more *scientific* explanation for the causes of suicide than that of sunspots or inherited tendencies. His theory has predictive power, since it suggests that suicide rates will rise or fall in conjunction with certain social and economic changes.

Of course, a theory—even the best of theories—is not a final statement about human behavior. Durkheim's theory of suicide is no exception. Sociologists continue to examine factors that contribute to differences in suicide rates around the world and to a particular society's rate of suicide. For example, although the overall rate of suicide in New Zealand is only marginally higher than the rate in the United States, the suicide rate among young people is 41 percent higher in New Zealand. Sociologists and psychiatrists from that country suggest that their remote, sparsely populated society maintains exaggerated standards of masculinity that are especially difficult for young males. Gay adolescents who fail to conform to their peers' preference for sports are particularly vulnerable to suicide (Shenon 1995).

Use Your Sociological Imagination   www.mhhe.com/schaefer7

If you were Durkheim's successor in his research on suicide, how would you investigate the factors that may explain the increase in suicide rates among young people in the United States today?

The Development of Sociology

People have always been curious about sociological matters—how we get along with others, what we do for a living, whom we select as our leaders. Philosophers and religious authorities of ancient and medieval societies made countless observations about human behavior. They did not test or verify those observations scientifically; nevertheless, their observations often became the foundation for moral codes. Several of the early social philosophers predicted that a systematic study of human behavior would emerge one day. Beginning in the 19th century, European theorists made pioneering contributions to the development of a science of human behavior.

Early Thinkers

Auguste Comte   The 19th century was an unsettling time in France. The French monarchy had been deposed in the revolution of 1789, and Napoleon had suffered defeat in his effort to conquer Europe. Amid this chaos, philosophers considered how society might be improved. Auguste Comte (1798–1857), credited with being the most influential of the philosophers of the early 1800s, believed that a theoretical science of society and a systematic investigation of behavior were needed to improve society. He coined the term *sociology* to apply to the science of human behavior.

Writing in the 1800s, Comte feared that the excesses of the French Revolution had permanently impaired France's stability. Yet he hoped that the systematic study of social behavior would eventually lead to more rational human interactions. In Comte's hierarchy of the sciences, sociology was at the top. He called it the "queen," and its practitioners "scientist-priests." This French theorist did not simply give sociology its name; he presented a rather ambitious challenge to the fledgling discipline.

Harriet Martineau   Scholars learned of Comte's works largely through translations by the English sociologist Harriet Martineau (1802–1876). But Martineau was a pathbreaker in her own right. She offered insightful observations of the customs and social practices of both her native Britain and the United States. Martineau's book *Society in America* ([1837] 1962) examined religion, politics, child rearing, and immigration in the young nation. It gave special attention to social

Key Person Émile Durkheim
Let's Discuss Introduce the topic of suicide by asking what types of people are more likely to commit suicide (common sense) and note Durkheim's findings.
Classroom Tip See "Émile Durkheim's Analysis of Suicide" (Additional Lecture Ideas).

Global View Durkheim's landmark study of suicide rates examines variations in suicide rates in several European countries.
Classroom Tip Indicate how Durkheim used the sociological imagination in his study.
Classroom Tip See "Using Maps to Understand Sociological Theory" (Class Discussion Topics) and "Founders of Sociology" (Class Discussion Topics).
Key Persons Auguste Comte, Harriet Martineau

class distinctions and to such factors as gender and race. Martineau ([1838] 1989) also wrote the first book on sociological methods.

Martineau's writings emphasized the impact that the economy, law, trade, health, and population could have on social problems. She spoke out in favor of the rights of women, the emancipation of slaves, and religious tolerance. Later in life, deafness did not keep her from being an activist. In Martineau's ([1837] 1962) view, intellectuals and scholars should not simply offer observations of social conditions; they should *act* on their convictions in a manner that will benefit society. That is why Martineau conducted research on the nature of female employment and pointed to the need for further investigation of the issue (Deegan 2003; M. Hill and Hoecker-Drysdale 2001).

Herbert Spencer   Another important early contributor to the discipline of sociology was Herbert Spencer (1820–1903). A relatively prosperous Victorian Englishman, Spencer (unlike Martineau) did not feel compelled to correct or improve society; instead, he merely hoped to understand it better. Drawing on Charles Darwin's study *On the Origin of Species,* Spencer applied the concept of evolution of the species to societies in order to explain how they change, or evolve, over time. Similarly, he adapted Darwin's evolutionary view of the "survival of the fittest" by arguing that it is "natural" that some people are rich while others are poor.

Spencer's approach to societal change was extremely popular in his own lifetime. Unlike Comte, Spencer suggested that since societies are bound to change eventually, one need not be highly critical of present social arrangements or work actively for social change. This viewpoint appealed to many influential people in England and the United States who had a vested interest in the status quo and were suspicious of social thinkers who endorsed change.

Émile Durkheim

Émile Durkheim made many pioneering contributions to sociology, including his important theoretical work on suicide. The son of a rabbi, Durkheim (1858–1917) was educated in both France and Germany. He established an impressive academic reputation and was appointed one of the first professors of sociology in France. Above all, Durkheim will be remembered for his insistence that behavior must be understood within a larger social context, not just in individualistic terms.

As one example of this emphasis, Durkheim ([1912] 2001) developed a fundamental thesis to help explain all forms of society. Through intensive study of the Arunta, an Australian tribe, he focused on the functions that religion performed and underscored the role of group life in defining what we consider to be religious. Durkheim concluded that like other forms of group behavior, religion reinforces a group's solidarity.

Another of Durkheim's main interests was the consequences of work in modern societies. In his view, the growing division of labor in industrial societies, as workers became much more specialized in their tasks, led to what he called anomie. *Anomie*

{ Harriet Martineau, an early pioneer of sociology, studied social behavior both in her native England and in the United States. }

refers to the loss of direction felt in a society when social control of individual behavior has become ineffective. The state of anomie occurs when people have lost their sense of purpose or direction, often during a time of profound social change. In a period of anomie, people are so confused and unable to cope with the new social environment that they may resort to taking their own lives.

Durkheim was concerned about the dangers that alienation, loneliness, and isolation might pose for modern industrial societies. He shared Comte's belief that sociology should provide direction for social change. As a result, he advocated the creation of new social groups—mediators between the individual's family and the state—which would provide a sense of belonging for members of huge, impersonal societies. Unions would be an example of such groups.

Like many other sociologists, Durkheim did not limit his interests to one aspect of social behavior. Later in this book we will consider his thinking on crime and punishment, religion, and the workplace. Few sociologists have had such a dramatic impact on so many different areas within the discipline.

Max Weber

Another important early theorist was Max Weber (pronounced "VAY-ber"). Born in Germany, Weber (1864–1920) studied legal

Classroom Tip See "Women Sociologists in the 20th and 21st Centuries" (Additional Lecture Ideas).
Gender Harriet Martineau was an early female pioneer of sociology.
Global View Martineau studied social practices of both her native Britain and the United States.
Key Persons Herbert Spencer, Charles Darwin, Émile Durkheim

Theory Émile Durkheim's functional analysis of religion is examined in more detail in Chapter 13.
Let's Discuss Does Weber's view of *verstehen* mean that sociologists can never "take sides"? The issue of neutrality and politics in research is discussed in Chapter 2.
Student Alert Ideal types are valuable in studying human behavior. But point out that *ideal,* as used here, means "typical of a genre" (not "best").

and economic history, but gradually developed an interest in sociology. Eventually, he became a professor at various German universities. Weber taught his students that they should employ *verstehen* (pronounced "fair-SHTAY-en"), the German word for "understanding" or "insight," in their intellectual work. He pointed out that we cannot analyze our social behavior by the same type of objective criteria we use to measure weight or temperature. To fully comprehend behavior, we must learn the subjective meanings people attach to their actions—how they themselves view and explain their behavior.

For example, suppose that a sociologist was studying the social ranking of individuals in a fraternity. Weber would expect the researcher to employ *verstehen* to determine the significance of the fraternity's social hierarchy for its members. The researcher might examine the effects of athleticism or grades or social skills or seniority on standing within the fraternity. He or she would seek to learn how the fraternity members relate to other members of higher or lower status. While investigating these questions, the researcher would take into account people's emotions, thoughts, beliefs, and attitudes (L. Coser 1977).

We also owe credit to Weber for a key conceptual tool: the ideal type. An **ideal type** is a construct or model for evaluating specific cases. In his own works, Weber identified various characteristics of bureaucracy as an ideal type (discussed in detail in Chapter 5). In presenting this model of bureaucracy, Weber was not describing any particular business, nor was he using the term *ideal* in a way that suggested a positive evaluation. Instead, his purpose was to provide a useful standard for measuring how bureaucratic an actual organization is (Gerth and Mills 1958). Later in this textbook, we will use the concept of *ideal type* to study the family, religion, authority, and economic systems, as well as to analyze bureaucracy.

Although their professional careers coincided, Émile Durkheim and Max Weber never met and probably were unaware of each other's existence, let alone ideas. Such was not true of the work of Karl Marx. Durkheim's thinking about the impact of the division of labor in industrial societies was related to Marx's writings, while Weber's concern for a value-free, objective sociology was a direct response to Marx's deeply held convictions. Thus, it is not surprising that Karl Marx is viewed as a major figure in the development of sociology, as well as several other social sciences (see Figure 1-2, page 12).

Karl Marx

Karl Marx (1818–1883) shared with Durkheim and Weber a dual interest in abstract philosophical issues and the concrete reality of everyday life. Unlike the others, Marx was so critical of existing institutions that a conventional academic career was impossible. He spent most of his life in exile from his native Germany.

Marx's personal life was a difficult struggle. When a paper he had written was suppressed, he fled to France. In Paris, he met Friedrich Engels (1820–1895), with whom he formed a lifelong friendship. They lived at a time when European and North American economic life was increasingly dominated by the factory rather than the farm.

While in London in 1847, Marx and Engels attended secret meetings of an illegal coalition of labor unions known as the Communist League. The following year they prepared a platform called *The Communist Manifesto,* in which they argued that the masses of people with no resources other than their labor (whom they referred to as the *proletariat*) should unite to fight for the overthrow of capitalist societies. In the words of Marx and Engels:

> The history of all hitherto existing society is the history of class struggles. . . . The proletarians have nothing to lose but their chains. They have a world to win. WORKING MEN OF ALL COUNTRIES UNITE! (L. Feuer 1989:7, 41)

After completing *The Communist Manifesto,* Marx returned to Germany, only to be expelled. He then moved to England, where he continued to write books and essays. Marx lived there in extreme poverty. He pawned most of his possessions, and several of his children died of malnutrition and disease. Marx clearly was an outsider in British society, a fact that may well have colored his view of Western cultures.

In Marx's analysis, society was fundamentally divided between two classes that clashed in pursuit of their own interests. When he examined the industrial societies of his time, such as Germany, England, and the United States, he saw the factory as the center of conflict between the exploiters (the owners of the means of production) and the exploited (the workers). Marx viewed these relationships in systematic terms; that is, he believed that a system of economic, social, and political relationships maintained the power and dominance of the owners over the workers. Consequently, Marx and Engels argued that the working class should *overthrow* the existing class system. Marx's influence on contemporary thinking has been dramatic. His writings inspired those who would later lead communist revolutions in Russia, China, Cuba, Vietnam, and elsewhere.

Even apart from the political revolutions that his work fostered, Marx's significance is profound. Marx emphasized the *group* identifications and associations that influence an individual's place in society. This area of study is the major focus of contemporary sociology. Throughout this textbook, we will consider how membership in a particular gender classification, age group, racial group, or economic class affects a person's attitudes and behavior. In an important sense, we can trace this way of understanding society back to the pioneering work of Karl Marx.

Modern Developments

Sociology today builds on the firm foundation developed by Émile Durkheim, Max Weber, and Karl Marx. However, the field certainly has not remained stagnant over the last hundred years. While Europeans have continued to make contributions to the discipline, sociologists from throughout the world and especially the United States have advanced sociological theory and research. Their new insights have helped us to better understand the workings of society.

Charles Horton Cooley Charles Horton Cooley (1864–1929) was typical of the sociologists who came to prominence in

Early Social Thinkers

	Émile Durkheim 1858–1917	**Max Weber 1864–1920**	**Karl Marx 1818–1883**
Academic training	Philosophy	Law, economics, history, philosophy	Philosophy, law
Key works	1893—*The Division of Labor in Society*	1904–1905—*The Protestant Ethic and the Spirit of Capitalism*	1848—*The Communist Manifesto*
	1897—*Suicide: A Study in Sociology*	1922—*Wirtschaft und Gesellschaft*	1867—*Das Kapital*
	1912—*Elementary Forms of Religious Life*		

the early 1900s. Born in Ann Arbor, Michigan, Cooley received his graduate training in economics but later became a sociology professor at the University of Michigan. Like other early sociologists, he had become interested in this "new" discipline while pursuing a related area of study.

Cooley shared the desire of Durkheim, Weber, and Marx to learn more about society. But to do so effectively, he preferred to use the sociological perspective to look first at smaller units—intimate, face-to-face groups such as families, gangs, and friendship networks. He saw these groups as the seedbeds of society, in the sense that they shape people's ideals, beliefs, values, and social nature. Cooley's work increased our understanding of groups of relatively small size.

Jane Addams In the early 1900s, many leading sociologists in the United States saw themselves as social reformers dedicated to systematically studying and then improving a corrupt society. They were genuinely concerned about the lives of immigrants in the nation's growing cities, whether those immigrants came from Europe or from the rural American South. Early female sociologists, in particular, often took active roles in poor urban areas as leaders of community centers known as *settlement houses*. For example, Jane Addams (1860–1935), a member of the American Sociological Society, cofounded the famous Chicago settlement, Hull House.

Addams and other pioneering female sociologists commonly combined intellectual inquiry, social service work, and political activism—all with the goal of assisting the underprivileged and creating a more egalitarian society. For example, working with the Black journalist and educator Ida Wells-Barnett, Addams

successfully prevented racial segregation in the Chicago public schools. Addams's efforts to establish a juvenile court system and a women's trade union reveal the practical focus of her work (Addams 1910, 1930; Deegan 1991; Lengermann and Niebrugge-Brantley 1998).

In a photograph taken around 1930, social reformer Jane Addams reads to children at the Mary Crane Nursery. Addams was an early pioneer both in sociology and in the settlement house movement.

Race/Ethnicity Jane Addams and Ida Wells-Barnett joined forces to block the implementation of a racial segregation policy in Chicago's public schools.
Key Person Jane Addams

By the middle of the 20th century, however, the focus of the discipline had shifted. Sociologists for the most part restricted themselves to theorizing and gathering information; the aim of transforming society was left to social workers and activists. This shift away from social reform was accompanied by a growing commitment to scientific methods of research and to value-free interpretation of data. Not all sociologists were happy with this emphasis. A new organization, the Society for the Study of Social Problems, was created in 1950 to deal more directly with social inequality and other social problems.

Robert Merton Sociologist Robert Merton (1910–2003) made an important contribution to the discipline by successfully combining theory and research. Born to Slavic immigrant parents in Philadelphia, Merton won a scholarship to Temple University. He continued his studies at Harvard, where he acquired his lifelong interest in sociology. Merton's teaching career was based at Columbia University.

Merton (1968) produced a theory that is one of the most frequently cited explanations of deviant behavior. He noted different ways in which people attempt to achieve success in life. In his view, some may deviate from the socially approved goal of accumulating material goods or the socially accepted means of achieving that goal. For example, in Merton's classification scheme, "innovators" are people who accept the goal of pursuing material wealth but use illegal means to do so, including robbery, burglary, and extortion. Merton based his explanation of crime on individual behavior that has been influenced by society's approved goals and means, yet it has wider applications. It helps to account for the high crime rates among the nation's poor, who may see no hope of advancing themselves through traditional roads to success. Chapter 7 discusses Merton's theory in greater detail.

Merton also emphasized that sociology should strive to bring together the "macro-level" and "micro-level" approaches to the study of society. **Macrosociology** concentrates on large-scale phenomena or entire civilizations. Émile Durkheim's cross-cultural study of suicide is an example of macro-level research. More recently, macrosociologists have examined international crime rates (see Chapter 7), the stereotype of Asian Americans as a "model minority" (see Chapter 10), and the population patterns of developing countries (see Chapter 15). In contrast, **microsociology** stresses the study of small groups, often through experimental means. Sociological research on the micro level has included studies of how divorced men and women disengage from significant social roles (see Chapter 5); of how conformity can influence the expression of prejudiced attitudes (see Chapter 7); and of how a teacher's expectations can affect a student's academic performance (see Chapter 13).

Today sociology reflects the diverse contributions of earlier theorists. As sociologists approach such topics as divorce, drug addiction, and religious cults, they can draw on the theoretical insights of the discipline's pioneers. A careful reader can hear Comte, Durkheim, Weber, Marx, Cooley, Addams, and many others speaking through the pages of current research. Sociology

has also broadened beyond the intellectual confines of North America and Europe. Contributions to the discipline now come from sociologists studying and researching human behavior in other parts of the world. This geographical expansion can be seen in the current list of sections of the American Sociological Association (see Table 1-1, page 14), which reflects the wide range of interests common to sociologists today. In describing the work of these sociologists, it is helpful to examine a number of influential theoretical approaches (also known as *perspectives*).

Major Theoretical Perspectives

Sociologists view society in different ways. Some see the world basically as a stable and ongoing entity. They are impressed with the endurance of the family, organized religion, and other social institutions. Other sociologists see society as composed of many groups in conflict, competing for scarce resources. To still other sociologists, the most fascinating aspects of the social world are the everyday, routine interactions among individuals that we sometimes take for granted. These three views, the ones most widely used by sociologists, are the functionalist, conflict, and interactionist perspectives. Together, these approaches will provide an introductory look at the discipline.

Functionalist Perspective

Think of society as a living organism in which each part of the organism contributes to its survival. This view is the **functionalist perspective,** which emphasizes the way in which the parts of a society are structured to maintain its stability.

Talcott Parsons (1902–1979), a Harvard University sociologist, was a key figure in the development of functionalist theory. Parsons was greatly influenced by the work of Émile Durkheim, Max Weber, and other European sociologists. For over four decades, he dominated sociology in the United States with his advocacy of functionalism. Parsons saw any society as a vast network of connected parts, each of which helps to maintain the system as a whole. His functionalist approach holds that if an aspect of social life does not contribute to a society's stability or survival—if it does not serve some identifiably useful function or promote value consensus among members of a society—it will not be passed on from one generation to the next.

Let's examine an example of the functionalist perspective. Many Americans have difficulty understanding the Hindu prohibition against slaughtering cows (specifically, zebu). Cattle browse unhindered through Indian street markets, helping themselves to oranges and mangoes while people bargain for the little food they can afford. What explains this devotion to the cow in the face of human deprivation—a devotion that appears to be dysfunctional?

The simple explanation is that cow worship is highly functional in Indian society, according to economists, agronomists, and social scientists who have studied the matter. Cows perform two essential tasks: plowing the fields and producing milk. If eating their meat were permitted, hungry families might be tempted to slaughter their cows for immediate consumption, leaving

Key Person Robert Merton
Let's Discuss Who might be an "innovator" in the academic world? In Merton's typology, would a student who cheats on exams be an innovator? What about a person who claims a degree that he or she does not have? Would someone who plagiarizes be an innovator?

Classroom Tip See "Talking with the Experts" (Class Discussion Topics).
Theory Functionalist perspective introduced
Reel Society See Sociological Perspectives in the Topic Index.
Key Person Talcott Parsons
Theory Discuss how a functionalist would explain some of the oddities of U.S. culture.

ables, or *dalit,* who sometimes resort to eating beef in secrecy. If eating beef were socially acceptable, higher-status Indians would no doubt bid up its price, placing it beyond the reach of the hungriest.

Manifest and Latent Functions   A college catalog typically states various functions of the institution. It may inform you, for example, that the university intends to "offer each student a broad education in classical and contemporary thought, in the humanities, in the sciences, and in the arts." However, it would be quite a surprise to find a catalog that declared, "This university was founded in 1895 to assist people in finding a marriage partner." No college catalog will declare this as the purpose of the university. Yet societal institutions serve many functions, some of them quite subtle. The university, in fact, *does* facilitate mate selection.

Robert Merton (1968) made an important distinction between manifest and latent functions. ***Manifest functions*** of institutions are open, stated, conscious functions. They involve the intended, recognized consequences of an aspect of society, such as the university's role in certifying academic competence and excellence. In contrast, ***latent functions*** are unconscious or unintended functions that may reflect hidden purposes of an institution. One latent function of universities is to hold down unemployment. Another is to serve as a meeting ground for people seeking marital partners.

Dysfunctions   Functionalists acknowledge that not all parts of a society contribute to its stability all the time. A ***dysfunction*** refers to an element or process of a society that may actually disrupt the social system or reduce its stability.

We view many dysfunctional behavior patterns, such as homicide, as undesirable. Yet we should not automatically interpret them in this way. The evaluation of a dysfunction depends on one's own values, or as the saying goes, on "where you sit." For example, the official view in prisons in the United States is that inmate gangs should be eradicated because they are dysfunctional to smooth operations. Yet some guards have actually come to view prison gangs as a functional part of their jobs. The danger posed by gangs creates a "threat

Cows (zebu), considered sacred in India, wander freely through this village, respected by all who encounter them. The sanctity of the cow is functional in India, where plowing, milking, and fertilizing are far more important to subsistence farmers than a diet that includes beef.

themselves without a means of cultivation. Cows also produce dung, which doubles as a fertilizer and a fuel for cooking. Finally, cow meat sustains the neediest group in society, the untouch-

Table 1-1   Sections of the American Sociological Association

Aging and the Life Course	Marxist Sociology
Alcohol, Drugs, and Tobacco	Mathematical Sociology
Animals and Society	Medical Sociology
Asia and Asian America	Mental Health
Children and Youth	Methodology
Collective Behavior and Social Movements	Organizations, Occupations, and Work
Communication and Information Technologies	Peace, War, and Social Conflict
Community and Urban Sociology	Political Economy of the World-System
Comparative and Historical Sociology	Political Sociology
Crime, Law, and Deviance	Population
Culture	Race, Gender, and Class
Economic Sociology	Racial and Ethnic Minorities
Education	Rationality and Society
Emotions	Religion
Environment and Technology	Science, Knowledge, and Technology
Ethnomethodology and Conversational Analysis	Sex and Gender
Family	Sexualities
History of Sociology	Social Psychology
International Migration	Sociological Practice
Labor and Labor Movements	Teaching and Learning
Latino/a Sociology	Theory
Law	

The range of sociological issues is very broad. For example, sociologists who belong to the Animals and Society section of the ASA may study the animal rights movement; those who belong to the Sexualities section may study global sex workers or the gay, bisexual, and transgendered movements. Economic sociologists may investigate globalization or consumerism, among many other topics.
Source: American Sociological Association 2007.

to security," requiring increased surveillance and more overtime work for guards, as well as requests for special staffing to address gang problems (G. Scott 2001).

Conflict Perspective

Where functionalists see stability and consensus, conflict sociologists see a social world in continual struggle. The **conflict perspective** assumes that social behavior is best understood in terms of conflict or tension between competing groups. Such conflict need not be violent; it can take the form of labor negotiations, party politics, competition between religious groups for new members, or disputes over the federal budget.

Throughout most of the 1900s, the functionalist perspective had the upper hand in sociology in the United States. However, the conflict approach has become increasingly persuasive since the late 1960s. The widespread social unrest resulting from battles over civil rights, bitter divisions over the war in Vietnam, the rise of the feminist and gay liberation movements, the Watergate political scandal, urban riots, and confrontations at abortion clinics have offered support for the conflict approach—the view that our social world is characterized by continual struggle between competing groups. Currently, the discipline of sociology accepts conflict theory as one valid way to gain insight into a society.

The Marxist View   As we saw earlier, Karl Marx viewed struggle between social classes as inevitable, given the exploitation of workers under capitalism. Expanding on Marx's work, sociologists and other social scientists have come to see conflict not merely as a class phenomenon but as a part of everyday life in all societies. In studying any culture, organization, or social group, sociologists want to know who benefits, who suffers, and who dominates at the expense of others. They are concerned with the conflicts between women and men, parents and children, cities and suburbs, Whites and Blacks, to name only a few. Conflict theorists are interested in how society's institutions—including the family, government, religion, education, and the media—may help to maintain the privileges of some groups and keep others in a subservient position. Their emphasis on social change and the redistribution of resources makes conflict theorists more "radical" and "activist" than functionalists (Dahrendorf 1959).

An African American View: W. E. B. Du Bois   One important contribution of conflict theory is that it has encouraged sociologists to view society through the eyes of those segments of the population that rarely influence decision making. Some early Black sociologists, including W. E. B. Du Bois (1868–1963), conducted research that they hoped would assist the struggle for a racially egalitarian society. Du Bois believed that knowledge was essential in combating prejudice and achieving tolerance and justice. Sociology, he contended, had to draw on scientific principles to study social problems such as those experienced by

This postage stamp honors W. E. B. Du Bois, who challenged the status quo in both academic and political circles. The first Black person to receive a doctorate from Harvard University, Du Bois later helped organize the National Association for the Advancement of Colored People (NAACP).

Blacks in the United States. Du Bois made a major contribution to sociology through his in-depth studies of urban life, both White and Black.

Du Bois had little patience with theorists such as Herbert Spencer, who seemed content with the status quo. He advocated basic research on the lives of Blacks, to separate opinion from fact. In this way he documented their relatively low status in Philadelphia and Atlanta. Du Bois believed that the granting of full political rights to Blacks was essential to their social and economic progress in the United States. Because many of his ideas challenged the status quo, he did not find a receptive audience within either the government or the academic world. As a result, Du Bois became increasingly involved with organizations whose members questioned the established social order. He helped to found the National Association for the Advancement of Colored People, better known as the NAACP (Wortham 2005).

The addition of diverse views within sociology in recent years has led to some valuable research, especially on African Americans. For many years, African Americans were understandably wary of participating in medical research studies, because those studies had been used for such purposes as justifying slavery or determining the impact of untreated syphilis. Now, however, African American sociologists and other social scientists are working to involve Blacks in useful ethnic medical research on diabetes and sickle cell anemia, two disorders that strike Black populations especially hard (A. Young and Deskins 2001).

The Feminist View Sociologists began embracing the feminist perspective only in the 1970s, although it has a long tradition in many other disciplines. The *feminist view* sees inequity in gender as central to all behavior and organization. Because it clearly focuses on one aspect of inequality, it is often allied with the conflict perspective. Proponents of the feminist perspective tend to focus on the macro level, just as conflict theorists do. Drawing on the work of Marx and Engels, contemporary feminist theorists often view women's subordination as inherent to capitalist societies. Some radical feminist theorists, however, view the oppression of women as inevitable in *all* male-dominated societies, whether *capitalist, socialist,* or *communist.*

An early example of this perspective (long before the label came into use by sociologists) can be seen in the life and writings of Ida Wells-Barnett (1862–1931). Following her groundbreaking publications in the 1890s on the practice of lynching Black Americans, she became an advocate in the women's rights campaign, especially the struggle to win the vote for women. Like feminist theorists who succeeded her, Wells-Barnett used her analysis of society as a means of resisting oppression. In her case, she researched what it meant to be African American, a woman in the United States, and a Black woman in the United States (Wells-Barnett 1970).

Feminist scholarship has broadened our understanding of social behavior by extending the analysis beyond the male point of view. In the past, studies of physical violence typically failed to include domestic violence, in which women are the chief victims. Not only was there a void in the research; in the field, law enforcement agencies were ill-prepared to deal with such violence. Similarly, feminists have complained that studies of "children having children" focus almost entirely on the characteristics and behavior of unwed teenage mothers, ignoring the unwed father's role. They have called for more scrutiny of boys and their behavior, as well as their parents and their role models (Ferree 2005; Fields 2005).

Use Your Sociological Imagination

www.mhhe.com /schaefer7

You are a sociologist who uses the conflict perspective to study various aspects of our society. How do you think you would interpret the practice of prostitution? Contrast this view with the functionalist perspective. Do you think your comments would differ if you took the feminist view, and if so, how?

Interactionist Perspective

Workers interacting on the job, encounters in public places like bus stops and parks, behavior in small groups—all these aspects of microsociology catch the attention of interactionists. Whereas functionalist and conflict theorists both analyze large-scale, societywide patterns of behavior, theorists who take the *interactionist perspective* generalize about everyday forms of social interaction in order to explain society as a whole. In the

Ida Wells-Barnett explored what it meant to be female and Black in the United States. Her work established her as one of the earliest feminist theorists.

1990s, for example, the workings of juries became a subject of public scrutiny. High-profile trials ended in verdicts that left some people shaking their heads. Long before jury members were being interviewed on their front lawns following a trial, interactionists tried to better understand behavior in the small-group setting of a jury deliberation room.

Interactionism (also referred to as *symbolic interactionism*) is a sociological framework in which human beings are viewed as living in a world of meaningful objects. Those "objects" may include material things, actions, other people, relationships, and even symbols. Interactionists see symbols as an especially important part of human communication (thus the term *symbolic* interactionism). Symbols have a shared social meaning that is understood by all members of a society. In the United States, for example, a salute symbolizes respect, while a clenched fist signifies defiance. Another culture might use different gestures to convey a feeling of respect or defiance. These types of symbolic interaction are classified as forms of *nonverbal communication,* which can include many other gestures, facial expressions, and postures.

Symbols in the form of tattoos took on special importance in the aftermath of September 11, 2001. Tattoo parlors in lower Manhattan were overwhelmed with requests from various groups for designs that carried symbolic significance for them. New York City firefighters asked for tattoos with the names of their fallen colleagues; police officers requested designs incorporating their distinctive NYPD shield; recovery workers at Ground Zero sought tattoos that incorporated the image of the giant steel cross, the remnant of a massive cross-beam in a World Trade Center building. Through symbols such as these tattoos,

Key Person Ida Wells-Barnett
Gender Stress the relevance of conflict theory to feminist scholarship.
Gender Feminist scholarship offers insights into the behavior of both women and men.
Classroom Tip Distinguish between the Marxist, the African American, and the feminist versions of conflict theory.

Theory Interactionist theory introduced

people communicate their values and beliefs to those around them (Scharnberg 2002).

Another manipulation of symbols can be seen in dress codes. Schools frown on students who wear clothes displaying messages that appear to endorse violence or drug and alcohol consumption. Businesses stipulate the attire employees are allowed to wear on the job in order to impress their customers or clients. In 2005, the National Basketball Association (NBA) adopted a new dress code for the athletes who play professional basketball—one that involved not the uniforms they wear on court, but the clothes they wear off court on league business. The code requires "business casual attire" when players are representing the league. Indoor sunglasses, chains, and sleeveless shirts are specifically banned. Figure 1-3 illustrates the new dress code for the millionaire athletes, which the NBA hopes will improve the image of its players, presenting them as responsible, serious-minded adults rather than as overgrown teens one step removed from the neighborhood court.

FIGURE 1-3

Enforcing Symbols: The NBA Dress Code

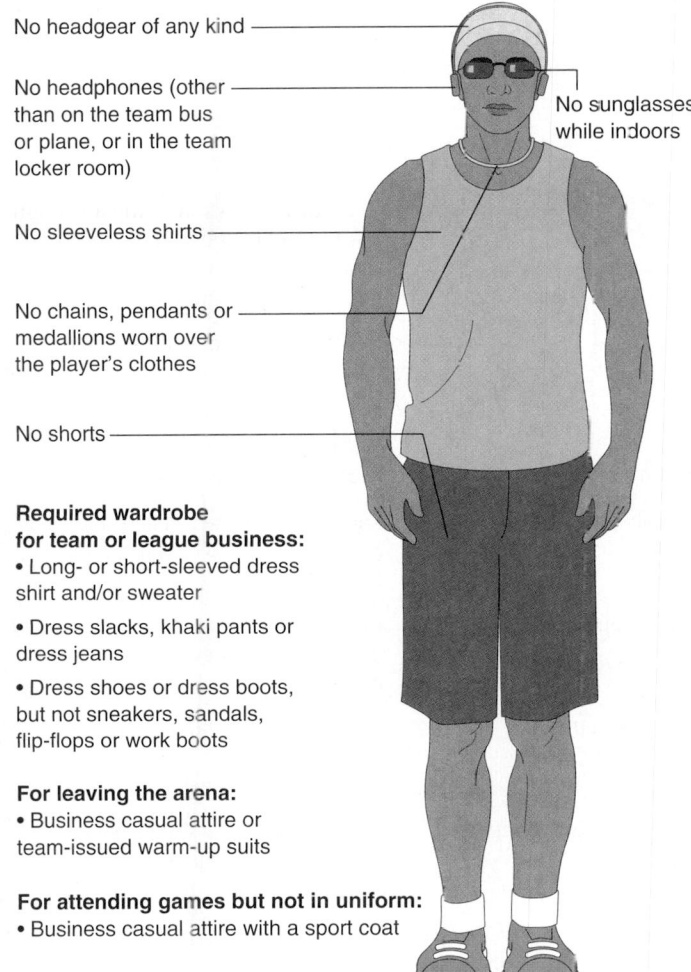

No headgear of any kind

No headphones (other than on the team bus or plane, or in the team locker room)

No sunglasses while indoors

No sleeveless shirts

No chains, pendants or medallions worn over the player's clothes

No shorts

Required wardrobe for team or league business:
• Long- or short-sleeved dress shirt and/or sweater
• Dress slacks, khaki pants or dress jeans
• Dress shoes or dress boots, but not sneakers, sandals, flip-flops or work boots

For leaving the arena:
• Business casual attire or team-issued warm-up suits

For attending games but not in uniform:
• Business casual attire with a sport coat

Source: Crowe and Herman 2005:A23.

Key Person George Herbert Mead
Classroom Tip For more on the interactionist approach, see "Breaching Experiments" (Additional Lecture Ideas).
Key Person Erving Goffman
Classroom Tip For more on Goffman's work and the dramaturgical approach, see "An Interactionist View of Sidewalk Etiquette" (Additional Lecture Ideas).

While the functionalist and conflict approaches were initiated in Europe, interactionism developed first in the United States. George Herbert Mead (1863–1931) is widely regarded as the founder of the interactionist perspective. Mead taught at the University of Chicago from 1893 until his death. As his teachings have become better known, sociologists have expressed greater interest in the interactionist perspective. Many have moved away from what may have been an excessive preoccupation with the large-scale (macro) level of social behavior and have redirected their attention toward behavior that occurs in small groups (micro level).

Erving Goffman (1922–1982) popularized a particular type of interactionist method known as the *dramaturgical approach,* in which people are seen as theatrical performers. The dramaturgist compares everyday life to the setting of the theater and stage. Just as actors project certain images, all of us seek to present particular features of our personalities while we hide other qualities. Thus, in a class, we may feel the need to project a serious image; at a party, we want to look relaxed and friendly.

The Sociological Approach

Which perspective should a sociologist use in studying human behavior? Functionalist? Conflict? Interactionist? In fact, sociologists make use of all the perspectives summarized in Table 1-2 (page 18), since each offers unique insights into the same issue. We gain the broadest understanding of our society, then, by drawing on all the major perspectives, noting where they overlap and where they diverge.

Although no one approach is correct by itself, and sociologists draw on all of them for various purposes, many sociologists tend to favor one particular perspective over others. A sociologist's theoretical orientation influences his or her approach to a research problem in important ways—including the choice of what to study, how to study it, and what questions to pose (or not to pose). (See Box 1-1 on page 19 for an example of how a researcher would study sports from different perspectives.) Whatever the purpose of sociologists' work, their research will always be guided by their theoretical viewpoints. For example, sociologist Elijah Anderson (1990) embraces both the interactionist perspective and the groundbreaking work of W. E. B. Du Bois. For 14 years Anderson conducted fieldwork in Philadelphia, where he studied the interactions of Black and White residents who lived in adjoining neighborhoods. In particular, he was interested in their "public behavior," including their eye contact—or lack of it—as they passed one another on the street. Anderson's research tells us much about the everyday social interactions of Blacks and Whites in the United States, but it does not explain the larger issues behind those interactions. Like theories, research results illuminate one part of the stage, leaving other parts in relative darkness.

Applied and Clinical Sociology

Many early sociologists—notably, Jane Addams, W. E. B. Du Bois, and George Herbert Mead—were strong advocates

Student Alert The list of "proponents" in Table 1-2 is only illustrative; hundreds of names could be used.
Classroom Tip See "Sociologists and Their Theoretical Preferences" (Additional Lecture Ideas).
Classroom Tip See "Theory Triumvirate" (Class Discussion Topics).

for social reform. They wanted their theories and findings to be relevant to policymakers and to people's lives in general. For instance, Mead was the treasurer of Hull House for many years, where he applied his theory to improving the lives of those who were powerless (especially immigrants). He also served on committees dealing with Chicago's labor problems and public education. Today, *applied sociology* is the use of the discipline of sociology with the specific intent of yielding practical applications for human behavior and organizations.

Often, the goal of such work is to assist in resolving a social problem. For example, in the last 40 years, eight presidents of the United States have established commissions to delve into major societal concerns facing our nation. Sociologists are often asked to apply their expertise to studying such issues as violence, pornography, crime, immigration, and population. In Europe, both academic and governmental research departments are offering increasing financial support for applied studies.

One example of applied sociology is the growing interest in the ways in which nationally recognized social problems manifest themselves locally. Since 2003, sociologist Greg Scott and his colleagues have been seeking to better understand the connection between illegal drug use and the spread of HIV/AIDS. The study, which will run through 2009, has so far employed 14 researchers from colleges and public health agencies, assisted by an additional 15 graduate and 16 undergraduate students. By combining a variety of methods, including interviews and observation, with photo and video documentation, these researchers have found that across all drug users, HIV/AIDS transmission is highest among users of crystal methamphetamine. Meth users are also most likely to engage in risky sexual behavior, and to have partners who do so. Fortunately, of all drug users, meth users are the ones most closely connected to health care treatment programs, which allows them to receive substance abuse education and treatment from their regular health care providers. However, their cases, brought to the forefront by Scott and his team, highlight the need for public health officials to identify other individuals who engage in high-risk sexual behavior and get them into appropriate treatment programs (G. Scott 2005).

Growing interest in applied sociology has led to such specializations as medical sociology and environmental sociology. The former includes research on how health care professionals and patients deal with disease. As one example, medical sociologists have studied the social impact of the AIDS crisis on families, friends, and communities (see Chapter 15). Environmental sociologists examine the relationship between human societies and the physical environment. One focus of their work is the issue of "environmental justice" (see Chapter 16), raised when researchers and community activists found that hazardous waste dumps are especially likely to be situated in poor and minority neighborhoods (M. Martin 1996).

Table 1-2   Major Sociological Perspectives

summingUP

	Functionalist	Conflict	Interactionist
View of society	Stable, well integrated	Characterized by tension and struggle between groups	Active in influencing and affecting everyday social interaction
Level of analysis emphasized	Macro	Macro	Micro, as a way of understanding the larger macro phenomena
Key concepts	Manifest functions Latent functions Dysfunctions	Inequality Capitalism Stratification	Symbols Nonverbal communication Face-to-face interaction
View of the individual	People are socialized to perform societal functions	People are shaped by power, coercion, and authority	People manipulate symbols and create their social worlds through interaction
View of the social order	Maintained through cooperation and consensus	Maintained through force and coercion	Maintained by shared understanding of everyday behavior
View of social change	Predictable, reinforcing	Change takes place all the time and may have positive consequences	Reflected in people's social positions and their communications with others
Example	Public punishments reinforce the social order	Laws reinforce the positions of those in power	People respect laws or disobey them based on their own past experience
Proponents	Émile Durkheim Talcott Parsons Robert Merton	Karl Marx W. E. B. Du Bois Ida Wells-Barnett	George Herbert Mead Charles Horton Cooley Erving Goffman

Student Alert Applied sociology is not the same as social work.

1-1 Looking at Sports from Three Theoretical Perspectives

We watch sports. Talk sports. Spend money on sports. Some of us live and breathe sports. Because sports occupy much of our time and directly or indirectly consume and generate a great deal of money, it should not be surprising that sports have sociological components that can be analyzed from the various theoretical perspectives.

Functionalist View

In examining any aspect of society, functionalists emphasize the contribution it makes to overall social stability. Functionalists regard sports as an almost religious institution that uses ritual and ceremony to reinforce the common values of a society:

- Sports socialize young people into such values as competition and patriotism.
- Sports help to maintain people's physical well-being.

Professional racer Danica Patrick. Women often have difficulty entering what are considered men's sports.

Despite their differences, functionalists, conflict theorists, and interactionists would all agree that there is much more to sports than exercise or recreation.

- Sports serve as a safety valve for both participants and spectators, who are allowed to shed tension and aggressive energy in a socially acceptable way.
- Sports bring together members of a community (supporting local athletes and teams) or even a nation (as seen during World Cup matches and the Olympics) and promote an overall feeling of unity and social solidarity.

Conflict View

Conflict theorists argue that the social order is based on coercion and exploitation. They emphasize that sports reflect and even exacerbate many of the divisions of society:

- Sports are a form of big business in which profits are more important than the health and safety of the workers (athletes).
- Sports perpetuate the false idea that success can be achieved simply through hard work, while failure should be blamed on the individual alone (rather than on injustices in the larger social system). Sports also serve as an "opiate" that encourages people to seek a "fix" or temporary "high" rather than focus on personal problems and social issues.
- Sports maintain the subordinate role of Blacks and Latinos, who toil as athletes but are less visible in supervisory positions as coaches, managers, and owners.
- Gender expectations encourage female athletes to be passive and gentle, qualities that do not support the emphasis on competitiveness in sports. As a result, women find it difficult to enter sports traditionally dominated by men, such as Indy or NASCAR.

Interactionist View

In studying the social order, interactionists are especially interested in shared understandings of everyday behavior. Interactionists examine sports on the micro level by focusing on how day-to-day social behavior is shaped by the distinctive norms, values, and demands of the world of sports:

- Sports often heighten parent–child involvement; they may lead to parental expectations for participation and (sometimes unrealistically) for success.
- Participation in sports provides friendship networks that can permeate everyday life.
- Despite class, racial, and religious differences, teammates may work together harmoniously and may even abandon previous stereotypes and prejudices.
- Relationships in the sports world are defined by people's social positions as players, coaches, and referees—as well as by the high or low status that individuals hold as a result of their performances and reputations.

Despite their differences, functionalists, conflict theorists, and interactionists would all agree that there is much more to sports than exercise or recreation. They would also agree that sports and other popular forms of culture are worthy subjects of serious study by sociologists.

Let's Discuss

1. Have you experienced or witnessed discrimination in sports based on gender or race? How did you react? Has the representation of Blacks or women on teams been controversial on your campus? In what ways?
2. Which perspective do you think is most useful in looking at the sociology of sports? Why?

Sources: Acosta and Carpenter 2001; H. Edwards 1973; Eitzen 2003; Fine 1987.

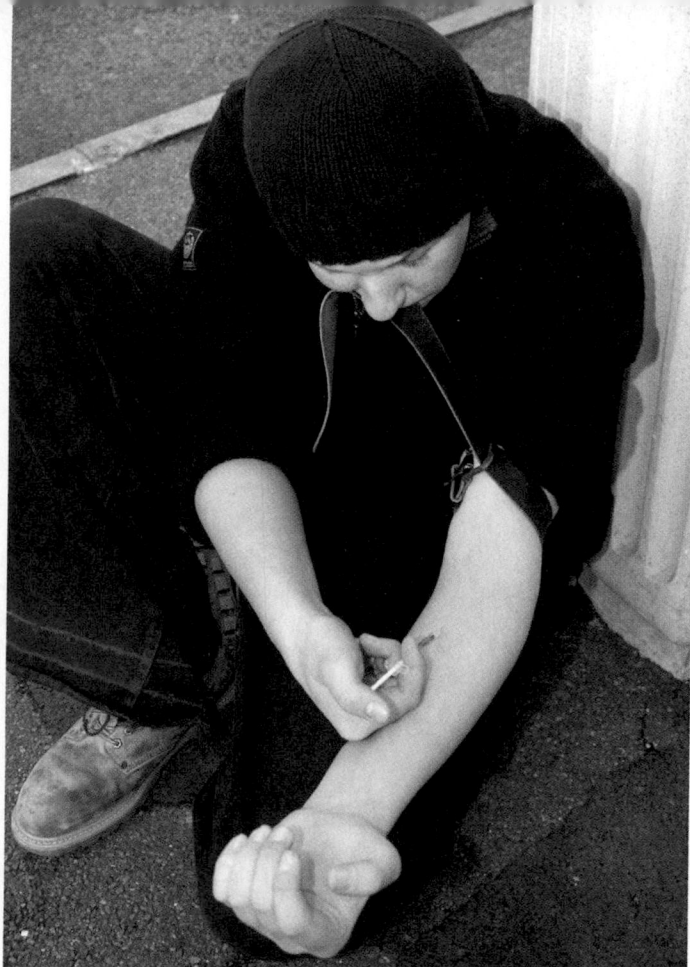

An intravenous (IV) drug user shoots up. Sociologists have studied the link between IV drug use and infection with HIV/AIDS in an attempt to develop guidelines for treatment and prevention.

The growing popularity of applied sociology has led to the rise of the specialty of clinical sociology. Louis Wirth (1931) wrote about clinical sociology more than 75 years ago, but the term itself has become popular only in recent years. While applied sociology may simply evaluate social issues, *clinical sociology* is dedicated to facilitating change by altering social relationships (as in family therapy) or restructuring social institutions (as in the reorganization of a medical center).

The Sociological Practice Association was founded in 1978 to promote the application of sociological knowledge to intervention for individual and social change. This professional group has developed a procedure for certifying clinical sociologists—much as physical therapists or psychologists are certified. In 1999 a new journal was published called *Sociological Practice: A Journal of Clinical and Applied Sociology.*

Applied sociologists generally leave it to others to act on their evaluations. By contrast, clinical sociologists take direct responsibility for implementation and view those with whom they work as their clients. This specialty has become increasingly attractive to graduate students in sociology because it offers an op-

portunity to apply intellectual learning in a practical way. A shrinking job market in the academic world has made such alternative career routes appealing.

Applied and clinical sociology can be contrasted with *basic* (or *pure*) *sociology,* which seeks a more profound knowledge of the fundamental aspects of social phenomena. This type of research is not necessarily meant to generate specific applications, although such ideas may result once findings are analyzed. When Durkheim studied suicide rates, he was not primarily interested in discovering a way to eliminate suicide. In this sense, his research was an example of basic rather than applied sociology.

www.mhhe.com /schaefer7

Use Your Sociological Imagination

What issues facing your local community would you like to address with applied sociological research? Do you see any global connections to these local issues?

Developing a Sociological Imagination

In this book, we will be illustrating the sociological imagination in several different ways—by showing theory in practice and research in action; by thinking globally; by exploring the significance of social inequality; by speaking across race, gender, and religious boundaries; and by highlighting social policy throughout the world.

Theory in Practice

We will illustrate how the major sociological perspectives can be helpful in understanding today's issues, from capital punishment to the AIDS crisis. Sociologists do not necessarily declare "Here I am using functionalism," but their research and approaches do tend to draw on one or more theoretical frameworks, as will become clear in the pages to follow.

Research in Action

Sociologists actively investigate a variety of issues and social behavior. We have already seen that research can shed light on the social factors that affect suicide rates and decision making in the jury box. Sociological research often plays a direct role in improving people's lives, as in the case of increasing the participation of African Americans in diabetes testing. Throughout the rest of the book, the research performed by sociologists and other social scientists will shed light on group behavior of all types.

Thinking Globally

Whatever their theoretical perspective or research techniques, sociologists recognize that social behavior must be viewed in a global context. *Globalization* is the worldwide integration of government policies, cultures, social movements, and financial markets through trade and the exchange of ideas. While pub-

Student Alert Clinical sociologists typically do not work out of clinics.
Let's Discuss Why is it necessary to distinguish among applied, clinical, and basic sociology?
Classroom Tip Explain whether your own research is applied, clinical, or basic.

Student Alert Explain the relationship between the sociological imagination and "theory in practice," "research in action," "thinking globally," "social inequality," "speaking across race, gender, and religious boundaries," and "social policy."

1-2 The Global Response to the 2004 Tsunami

On December 26, 2004, an earthquake beneath the Indian Ocean set in motion a series of events that affected hundreds of millions of people around the world. The shifting ocean floor sent a series of gigantic tsunami waves toward the coasts of South Asia and Africa, completely engulfing many populated islands along the way. As the weeks passed, the outside world looked on in horror as the death toll climbed to more than 225,000.

The international relief effort that mobilized to rescue the injured, provide shelter to the homeless, and address long-term economic needs was one obvious sign of globalization. Through volunteer labor and donated money, sympathetic people and governments around the world could gain some sense of control in the face of the massive natural disaster. Beyond the humanitarian effort, however, lay more complicated aspects of globalization, including social interrelationships that span the globe and vast economic disparities between one part of the world and another.

Most of the devastation caused by the tsunami hit relatively poor areas of the world. As a result, the global economy barely flickered, and the insurance and financial markets escaped virtually unscathed. Had the tsunami hit the coast of North America or Europe, the results would have been far different. In fact, to guard against such catastrophe, a sophisticated tsunami detection and warning system had been in place in the Pacific Ocean for about 40 years, to offer some measure of protection to industrial giants Japan and the United States. No such network existed in the Indian Ocean, where neighboring countries lacked the resources to create one. Expensive warning systems and risk management plans, also common in affluent countries, were nonexistent in the area hit by the 2004 tsunami.

Though the areas affected by the tsunami were populated by some of poorest, most vulnerable people in the world, pockets of incredible affluence could be found there as well. From the vantage point of the region's expensive resorts, vacationing Westerners used their camcorders to videotape the 30-foot waves as they pounded the coast and swept

> *The same borders that tourists cross so effortlessly confine those left homeless by the disaster to their impoverished, flood-ravaged nations.*

through the streets. Because such resorts offer almost the only form of economic development in the coastal areas, within weeks of the calamity, nations like Indonesia, Thailand, and Sri Lanka were urging tourists to return to the stricken zone. Their desperate attempt to restart the shattered tourism industry underscored the privileges that citizens of wealthy nations enjoy. Globalization permits them to pass effortlessly across national borders to visit such luxury resorts, where they pay for a single night's lodging with a sum the local people must work a year to earn. The same borders that tourists cross so effortlessly confine those left homeless by the disaster to their impoverished, flood-ravaged nations.

Another aspect of globalization was the political reaction to the disaster. Within days of the arrival of the first foreign assistance, the government of Indonesia, a predominantly Muslim country, announced that U.S. soldiers would be permitted in the disaster area only without their sidearms. All Western relief organizations were to be out of the country by March 30, whatever the needs in the stricken areas. This unusual step of turning away assistance must be viewed in a global context. At that time, the United States occupied two Muslim countries, Afghanistan and Iraq. Indonesian officials wanted to make clear that their country would not be subject to a similar occupation, however unlikely that scenario. Today, events in one part of the world impact people everywhere, in ways that cannot always be predicted.

Let's Discuss

1. Have you ever lived in or traveled to a place where the very wealthy lived side by side with the desperately poor? If so, where was it—in a foreign country or the United States? Explain the economic relationship between the two groups.
2. Which of the three major theoretical perspectives would be most useful in analyzing the social effects of the 2004 tsunami? Explain your answer.

Sources: Geist et al. 2006; Seabrook 2005; Swiss Re 2005; *The Economist* 2005a.

---

lic discussion of globalization is relatively recent, intellectuals have been pondering its social consequences for a long time. Karl Marx and Friedrich Engels warned in *The Communist Manifesto* (written in 1848) of a world market that would lead to production in distant lands, sweeping away existing working relationships.

Today, developments outside a country are as likely to influence people's lives as changes at home. For example, though much of the world was already in recession by September 2001, the terrorist attacks on New York and Washington, D.C., caused an immediate economic decline not just in the United States, but throughout the world. One example of the massive global impact was the downturn in international tourism, which lasted for at least two years. The effects have been felt by people far removed from the United States, including African game wardens and Asian taxi drivers. Some observers see globalization and its effects as the natural result of advances in communications technology, particularly the Internet and satellite transmission of the mass media. Others view it more critically, as a process that allows multinational corporations to expand unchecked. We examine the impact of globalization on societies throughout the world, including our own, in Box 1-2 (on the tsunami disaster of December 2004) and throughout this text (Fiss and Hirsch 2005).

Classroom Tip Relate Marx and Engels's predictions about globalization to their ideas on social class.

Let's Discuss Why would terrorism in the U.S. affect African game wardens or Asian taxi drivers?

Let's Discuss Compare the number of people killed in natural disasters in the U.S. and Europe to the number killed in the 2004 tsunami. Why the disparity?

Theory How might a conflict theorist interpret the social and economic consequences of the 2004 tsunami?

Theory What might be the manifest and latent functions of sending U.S. soldiers to tsunami-stricken areas?

Let's Discuss Should governments be able to restrict the assistance they receive after a natural disaster?

The Significance of Social Inequality

Who holds power? Who doesn't? Who has prestige? Who lacks it? Perhaps the major theme of analysis in sociology today is *social inequality,* a condition in which members of society have differing amounts of wealth, prestige, or power. The tsunami that hit countries on the Indian Ocean in 2004 highlighted the huge social gap between the impoverished people who live there and the wealthy Westerners who visit the area's luxury resorts (see Box 1-2 on page 21). Likewise, in 2005 Hurricane Katrina drew attention to the social inequality among U.S. residents of the Gulf Coast. Predictably, the people who were hit the hardest by the massive storm were the poor, who had the greatest difficulty evacuating before the storm and have had the most difficulty recovering from it. Barbara Ehrenreich's research among low-wage workers uncovered some other aspects of social inequality in the United States.

Some sociologists, in seeking to understand the effects of inequality, have made the case for social justice. W. E. B. Du Bois ([1940] 1968:418) noted that the greatest power in the land is not "thought or ethics, but wealth." As we have seen, the contributions of Karl Marx, Jane Addams, and Ida Wells-Barnett also stressed this sentiment for the overarching importance of social inequality and social justice. Joe Feagin (2001) echoed it in a presidential address to the American Sociological Association.

Throughout, this book will highlight the work of sociologists on social inequality. Many chapters also feature a box on this theme.

Speaking across Race, Gender, and Religious Boundaries

Sociologists include both men and women, people from a variety of ethnic, national, and religious origins. In their work, sociologists seek to draw conclusions that speak to all people—not just the affluent or powerful. Doing so is not always easy. Insights into how a corporation can increase its profits tend to attract more attention and financial support than do, say, the merits of a needle exchange program for low-income inner-city residents. Yet today more than ever, sociology seeks to better understand the experiences of all people.

Sociologists have noted, for example, that the 2004 tsunami affected men and women differently. When the waves hit, moth-

ers and grandmothers were at home with the children; men were outside working, where they were more likely to become aware of the impending disaster. Moreover, most of the men knew how to swim, a survival skill that women in these traditional societies usually do not learn. As a result, many more men than women survived the catastrophe—about 10 men for every 1 woman. In one Indonesian village typical of the disaster area, 97 of 1,300 people survived; only 4 were women. The impact of this gender imbalance will be felt for some time, given women's primary role as caregivers for children and the elderly (BBC 2005a).

Social Policy throughout the World

One important way we can use a sociological imagination is to enhance our understanding of current social issues throughout the world. Beginning with Chapter 2, each chapter will conclude with a discussion of a contemporary social policy issue. In some cases, we will examine a specific issue facing national governments. For example, government funding of child care centers will be discussed in Chapter 4, Socialization; racial profiling in Chapter 10, Racial and Ethnic Inequality; and religion in the schools in Chapter 13, Religion and Education. These Social Policy sections will demonstrate how fundamental sociological concepts can enhance our critical thinking skills and help us to better understand current public policy debates taking place around the world.

In addition, sociology has been used to evaluate the success of programs or the impact of changes brought about by policymakers and political activists. For example, Chapter 8, Stratification and Social Mobility in the United States, includes a discussion of research on the effectiveness of welfare reform experiments. Such discussions underscore the many practical applications of sociological theory and research.

Sociologists expect the next quarter of a century to be perhaps the most exciting and critical period in the history of the discipline. That is because of a growing recognition—both in the United States and around the world—that current social problems *must* be addressed before their magnitude overwhelms human societies. We can expect sociologists to play an increasing role in government by researching and developing public policy alternatives. It seems only natural for this textbook to focus on the connection between the work of sociologists and the difficult questions confronting policymakers and people in the United States and around the world.

APPENDIX   Careers in Sociology

For the last two decades the number of U.S. college students who have graduated with a degree in sociology has risen steadily (see Figure). In this appendix we'll consider some of the options these students have after completing their undergraduate education.

An undergraduate degree in sociology doesn't just serve as excellent preparation for future graduate work in sociology. It also provides a strong liberal arts background for entry-level positions in business, social services, foundations, community organizations,

Policy Pointer Underscore the textbook's social policy focus. Other social policy sections include such topics as human sexuality, bilingualism, and the AIDS crisis.
Global View Have students note the global aspects of the social policy sections.
Policy Pointer The issue of social inequality is explored in Chapter 8.

Web Resource Alert students to the "Social Policy" component in the student center of the Online Learning Center **(www.mhhe.com/schaefer7)**. "Social Policy" presents overviews of current, and sometimes controversial, social policies, as well as graphs and charts.

not-for-profit groups, law enforcement, and many government jobs. A number of fields—among them marketing, public relations, and broadcasting—now require investigative skills and an understanding of the diverse groups found in today's multiethnic and multinational environment. Moreover, a sociology degree requires accomplishment in oral and written communication, interpersonal skills, problem solving, and critical thinking—all job-related skills that may give sociology graduates an advantage over those who pursue more technical degrees.

Consequently, while few occupations specifically require an undergraduate degree in sociology, such academic training can be an important asset in entering a wide range of occupations (American Sociological Association 2005b). To emphasize this point, a number of chapters in this book highlight a real-life professional who describes how the study of sociology has helped in his or her career. Look for the "Taking Sociology to Work" boxes.

The Figure below summarizes the sources of employment for those with BA or BS degrees in sociology. It shows that the areas of social services, education, business, and government offer major career opportunities for sociology graduates. Undergraduates who know where their career interests lie are well advised to enroll in sociology courses and specialties best suited to those interests. For example, students hoping to become health planners would take a class in medical sociology; students seeking employment as social science research assistants would focus on courses in statistics and methods. Internships, such as placements at city planning agencies and survey research organizations, afford another way for sociology students to prepare for careers. Studies show that students who choose an internship placement

FIGURE

Occupational Fields of Sociology BA/MA Graduates

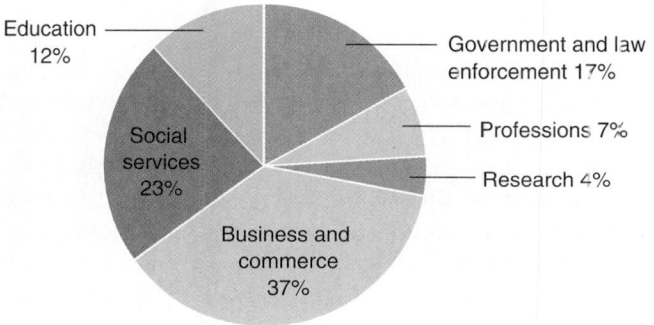

Source: Schaefer 1998b.

FIGURE

Sociology Degrees Conferred in the United States by Gender

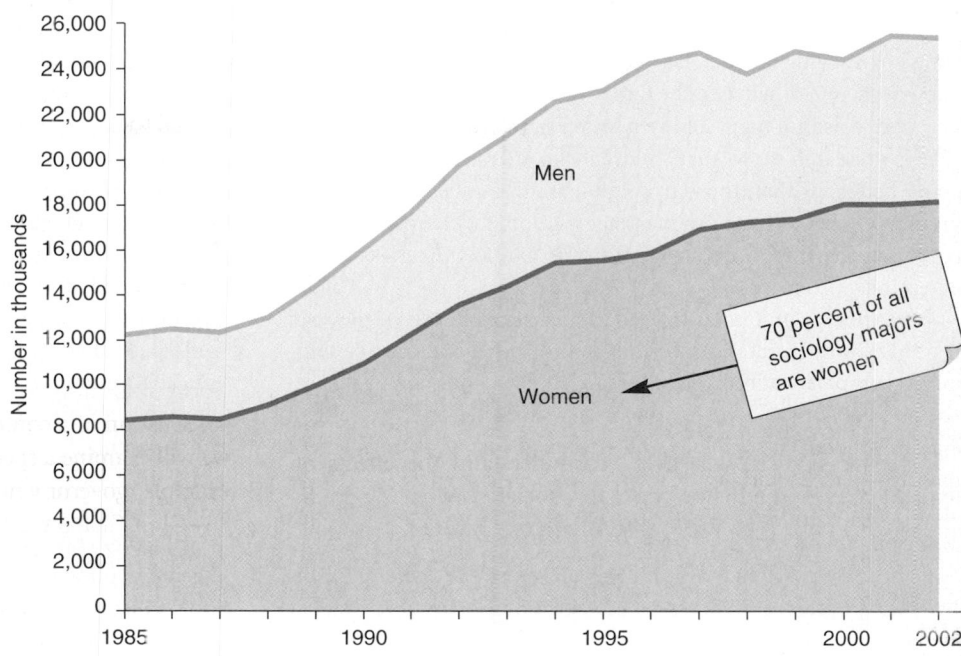

Source: American Sociological Association 2005c.

have less trouble finding jobs, obtain better jobs, and enjoy greater job satisfaction than students without internship placements (Salem and Grabarek 1986).

Many college students view social work as the field most closely associated with sociology. Traditionally, social workers received their undergraduate training in sociology and allied fields such as psychology and counseling. After some practical experience, social workers would generally seek a master's degree in social work (MSW) to be considered for supervisory or administrative positions. Today, however, some students choose (where it is available) to pursue a bachelor's degree in social work (BSW). This degree prepares graduates for direct service positions, such as caseworker or group worker.

Many students continue their sociological training beyond the bachelor's degree. More than 250 universities in the United States have graduate programs in sociology that offer PhD and/or master's degrees. These programs differ greatly in their areas of specialization, course requirements, costs, and the research and teaching opportunities available to graduate students. About 61 percent of the graduates are women (American Sociological Association 2005c, 2007).

Higher education is an important source of employment for sociologists with graduate degrees. About 83 percent of recent PhD recipients in sociology seek employment in colleges and universities. These sociologists teach not only majors committed to the discipline but also students hoping to become doctors, nurses, lawyers, police officers, and so forth (American Sociological Association 2005c).

Sociologists who teach in colleges and universities may use their knowledge and training to influence public policy. For example,

sociologist Andrew Cherlin (2003) recently commented on the debate over proposed federal funding to promote marriage among welfare recipients. Citing the results of two of his studies, Cherlin questioned the potential effectiveness of such a policy in strengthening low-income families. Because many single mothers choose to marry someone other than the father of their children—sometimes for good reason—their children often grow up in stepfamilies. Cherlin's research shows that children who are raised in stepfamilies are no better off than those in single-parent families. He sees government efforts to promote marriage as a politically motivated attempt to foster traditional social values in a society that has become increasingly diverse.

For sociology graduates interested in academic careers, the road to a PhD (or doctorate) can be long and difficult. This degree symbolizes competence in original research; each candidate must prepare a book-length study known as a dissertation. Typically, a doctoral student in sociology will engage in four to seven years of intensive work, including the time required to complete the dissertation. Yet even this effort is no guarantee of a job as a sociology professor.

The good news is that over the next 10 years, the demand for instructors is expected to increase because of high rates of retirement among faculty from the baby-boom generation, as well as the anticipated slow but steady growth in the college student population in the United States. Nonetheless, anyone who launches an academic career must be prepared for considerable uncertainty and competition in the college job market (American Sociological Association 2005b; Huber 1985).

Of course, not all people working as sociologists teach or hold doctoral degrees. Take government, for example. The Census Bureau relies on people with sociological training to interpret data for other government agencies and the general public. Virtually every agency depends on survey research—a field in which sociology students can specialize—in order to assess everything from community needs to the morale of the agency's own workers. In addition, people with sociological training can put their academic knowledge to effective use in probation and parole, health sciences, community development, and recreational services. Some people working in government or private industry have a master's degree (MA or MS) in sociology; others have a bachelor's degree (BA or BS).

Currently, about 22 percent of the members of the American Sociological Association use their sociological skills outside the academic world, whether in social service agencies or in marketing positions for business firms. Increasing numbers of sociologists with graduate degrees are employed by businesses, industry, hospitals, and nonprofit organizations. Studies show that many sociology graduates are making career changes from social service areas to business and commerce. As an undergraduate major, sociology is excellent preparation for employment in many parts of the business world (American Sociological Association 2001).

Whether you take a few courses in sociology or actually complete a degree, you will benefit from the critical thinking skills developed in this discipline. Sociologists emphasize the value of being able to analyze, interpret, and function within a variety of working situations—an asset in virtually any career. Moreover, given rapid technological change and the expanding global economy, all of us will need to adapt to substantial social change, even in our own careers. Sociology provides a rich conceptual framework that can serve as a foundation for flexible career development and assist you in taking advantage of new employment opportunities (American Sociological Association 2005b).

For more information on career opportunities for individuals with a background in sociology, visit the Online Learning Center at **www.mhhe.com/schaefer7.** Go to "Student Edition," and in the section titled "Course-wide Content," click on "Web Resources." Then click on "Career Opportunities," which will provide you with numerous links to sites offering career advice and information.

{ MASTERING THIS CHAPTER }

Summary

Sociology is the scientific study of social behavior and human groups. In this chapter, we examine the nature of sociological theory, the founders of the discipline, theoretical perspectives in contemporary sociology, practical applications for sociological theory and research, and ways to exercise the "sociological imagination."

1. The *sociological imagination* is an awareness of the relationship between an individual and the wider society. It is based on the ability to view our own society as an outsider might, rather than from the perspective of our limited experiences and cultural biases.

2. In contrast to other *social sciences,* sociology emphasizes the influence that groups can have on people's behavior and attitudes and the ways in which people shape society.

3. Knowledge that relies on "common sense" is not always reliable. Sociologists must test and analyze each piece of information they use.

4. Sociologists employ *theories* to examine relationships between observations or data that may seem completely unrelated.

5. Nineteenth-century thinkers who contributed sociological insights included Auguste Comte, a French philosopher; Harriet Martineau, an English sociologist; and Herbert Spencer, an English scholar.

6. Other important figures in the development of sociology were Émile Durkheim, who pioneered work on suicide; Max Weber, who taught the need for "insight" in intellectual work; and Karl Marx, who emphasized the importance of the economy and social conflict.

7. In the 20th century, the discipline of sociology was indebted to the U.S. sociologists Charles Horton Cooley and Robert Merton.

8. *Macrosociology* concentrates on large-scale phenomena or entire civilizations, whereas *microsociology* stresses the study of small groups.

9. The *functionalist perspective* emphasizes the way in which the parts of a society are structured to maintain its stability.

10. The *conflict perspective* assumes that social behavior is best understood in terms of conflict or tension between competing groups.

11. The *interactionist perspective* is concerned primarily with fundamental or everyday forms of interaction, including symbols and other types of nonverbal communication.

12. Sociologists make use of all three perspectives, since each offers unique insights into the same issue.

13. *Applied* and *clinical sociology* apply the discipline of sociology to the solution of practical problems in human behavior and organizations. In contrast, *basic sociology* is sociological inquiry that seeks only a deeper knowledge of the fundamental aspects of social phenomena.

14. This textbook makes use of the sociological imagination by showing theory in practice and research in action; by thinking globally; by focusing on the significance of social inequality; by speaking across race, gender, and religious boundaries; and by highlighting social policy around the world.

Critical Thinking Questions

1. What aspects of the social and work environment in a fast-food restaurant would be of particular interest to a sociologist because of his or her sociological imagination?

2. What are the manifest and latent functions of a health club?

3. How might an interactionist study a place where you have been employed or an organization of which you are a member?

Key Terms

Anomie The loss of direction felt in a society when social control of individual behavior has become ineffective. (page 10)

Applied sociology The use of the discipline of sociology with the specific intent of yielding practical applications for human behavior and organizations. (18)

Basic sociology Sociological inquiry conducted with the objective of gaining a more profound knowledge of the fundamental aspects of social phenomena. Also known as *pure sociology*. (20)

Clinical sociology The use of the discipline of sociology with the specific intent of altering social relationships or restructuring social institutions. (20)

Conflict perspective A sociological approach that assumes that social behavior is best understood in terms of conflict or tension between competing groups. (15)

Dramaturgical approach A view of social interaction in which people are seen as theatrical performers. (17)

Dysfunction An element or process of a society that may disrupt the social system or reduce its stability. (14)

Feminist view A sociological approach that views inequity in gender as central to all behavior and organization. (16)

Functionalist perspective A sociological approach that emphasizes the way in which the parts of a society are structured to maintain its stability. (13)

Globalization The worldwide integration of government policies, cultures, social movements, and financial markets through trade and the exchange of ideas. (20)

Ideal type A construct or model for evaluating specific cases. (11)

Interactionist perspective A sociological approach that generalizes about everyday forms of social interaction in order to explain society as a whole. (16)

Latent function An unconscious or unintended function that may reflect hidden purposes. (14)

Macrosociology Sociological investigation that concentrates on large-scale phenomena or entire civilizations. (13)

Manifest function An open, stated, and conscious function. (14)

Microsociology Sociological investigation that stresses the study of small groups, often through experimental means. (13)

Natural science The study of the physical features of nature and the ways in which they interact and change. (6)

Nonverbal communication The sending of messages through the use of gestures, facial expressions, and postures. (16)

Science The body of knowledge obtained by methods based on systematic observation. (6)

Social inequality A condition in which members of society have differing amounts of wealth, prestige, or power. (22)

Social science The study of the social features of humans and the ways in which they interact and change. (6)

Sociological imagination An awareness of the relationship between an individual and the wider society, both today and in the past. (3)

Sociology The scientific study of social behavior and human groups. (3)

Theory In sociology, a set of statements that seeks to explain problems, actions, or behavior. (8)

Verstehen The German word for "understanding" or "insight"; used to stress the need for sociologists to take into account the subjective meanings people attach to their actions. (11)

Read each question carefully and then select the best answer.

1. Sociology is

    a. very narrow in scope.
    b. concerned with what one individual does or does not do.
    c. the systematic study of social behavior and human groups.
    d. an awareness of the relationship between an individual and the wider society.

2. Which of the following thinkers introduced the concept of the sociological imagination?

    a. Émile Durkheim
    b. Max Weber
    c. Karl Marx
    d. C. Wright Mills

3. Émile Durkheim's research on suicide suggested that

    a. Catholics had much higher suicide rates than Protestants.
    b. there seemed to be higher rates of suicide in times of peace than in times of war and revolution.
    c. civilians were more likely to take their lives than soldiers.
    d. suicide is a solitary act, unrelated to group life.

4. Max Weber taught his students that they should employ which of the following in their intellectual work?

    a. anomie
    b. *verstehen*
    c. the sociological imagination
    d. microsociology

5. Robert Merton's contributions to sociology include

    a. successfully combining theory and research.
    b. producing a theory that is one of the most frequently cited explanations of deviant behavior.
    c. an attempt to bring macro-level and micro-level analyses together.
    d. all of the above

6. Which sociologist made a major contribution to society through his in-depth studies of urban life, including both Blacks and Whites?

    a. W. E. B. Du Bois
    b. Robert Merton
    c. Auguste Comte
    d. Charles Horton Cooley

7. In the late 19th century, before the term *feminist perspective* could even be coined, the ideas behind this major theoretical approach appeared in the writings of

    a. Karl Marx.
    b. Ida Wells-Barnett.
    c. Charles Horton Cooley.
    d. Carol Brooks Gardner.

8. Thinking of society as a living organism in which each part of the organism contributes to its survival is a reflection of which theoretical perspective?

    a. the functionalist perspective
    b. the conflict perspective
    c. the feminist perspective
    d. the interactionist perspective

9. Karl Marx's view of the struggle between social classes inspired the contemporary

    a. functionalist perspective.
    b. conflict perspective.
    c. interactionist perspective.
    d. dramaturgical approach.

10. Erving Goffman's dramaturgical approach, which postulates that people present certain aspects of their personalities while obscuring other qualities, is derivative of what major theoretical perspective?

    a. the functionalist perspective
    b. the conflict perspective
    c. the feminist perspective
    d. the interactionist perspective

11. While the findings of sociologists may at times seem like common sense, they have been _____ by researchers.

12. Within sociology, a _____ is a set of statements that seeks to explain problems, actions, or behavior.

13. In _____ _____'s hierarchy of the sciences, sociology was the "queen," and its practitioners were "scientist-priests."

14. In *Society in America,* originally published in 1837, English scholar _____ _____ examined religion, politics, child rearing, and immigration in the young nation.

15. _____ _____ adapted Charles Darwin's evolutionary view of the "survival of the fittest" by arguing that it is "natural" that some people are rich while others are poor.

16. Sociologist Max Weber coined the term _____ _____ in referring to a construct or model that serves as a measuring rod against which actual cases can be evaluated.

17. In *The Communist Manifesto,* _____ _____ and _____ _____ argued that the masses of people who have no resources other than their labor (the proletariat) should unite to fight for the overthrow of capitalist societies.

18. _____ _____, an early female sociologist, cofounded the famous Chicago settlement house called Hull House and also tried to establish a juvenile court system.

19. The university's role in certifying academic competence and excellence is an example of a _____ function.

20. The _____ _____ draws on the work of Karl Marx and Friedrich Engels in that it often views women's subordination as inherent in capitalist societies.

{ TECHNOLOGY RESOURCES }

Online Learning Center

1. Visit the Online Learning Center, this textbook's specific Web site, at **www.mhhe.com/schaefer7.** The student center in the Online Learning Center offers a variety of helpful and interesting resources and activities for each chapter. The resources include chapter outlines and summaries, quizzes with feedback, direct links to Internet sites, including those found in the Technology Resources sections at the end of each chapter in your text, relevant news updates, and audio clips by the author. The activities include flashcards, crossword puzzles, interactive maps, and interactive exercises. Don't pass up this opportunity to learn more about sociology and to take advantage of resources that will help you master the material in your text and get a better grade in the course!

2. The Web site of the Hull House Museum (**www.uic.edu/jaddams/hull/hull_house.html**) provides a wealth of information about Jane Addams and her life work. To view historical photographs of Hull House and the people Addams served, click on "Urban Experience in Chicago."

3. Descriptions of the major sociological theorists in this chapter only begin to scratch the surface of these fascinating and creative people. Learn more at Sociology Professor (**www.sociologyprofessor.com**), a Web site where you can find biographical information on a variety of historical figures in the discipline.

*Note: While all the URLs listed were current as of the printing of this book, Web sites often change. Please check our Web site (**www.mhhe.com/schaefer7**) for updates, hyperlinks, and exercises related to these sites.*

Reel Society CD and Video Clips

Exercise your imagination and step into the world of *Reel Society,* a professionally produced movie on CD-ROM that demonstrates the sociological imagination through typical scenarios drawn from campus life. In this movie you will become part of the exploits of several college students, and will influence the plot by making key choices for them. You'll learn to relate sociological thought to real life through a variety of issues and perspectives. In addition to the interactive movie, *Reel Society* includes explanatory text screens and a glossary, as well as quizzes and discussion questions to test your knowledge of sociology. The CD also includes a link to the Online Learning Center for *Reel Society.*

Reel Society video clips, which appear on this book's Web site, can be used to spark discussion about the following topics from this chapter:

- The Sociological Imagination
- Major Theoretical Perspectives
- Speaking across Race, Gender, and Religious Boundaries

2

Sociological Research

inside

What Is the Scientific Method?

Major Research Designs

Ethics of Research

Technology and Sociological Research

Social Policy and Sociological Research: Studying Human Sexuality

Appendix I: Using Statistics, Tables, and Graphs

Appendix II: Writing a Research Report

Boxes

Research in Action: Polling in Baghdad

Research in Action: What's in a Name?

Social Inequality: Researching Privilege and Discrimination in Employment

Taking Sociology to Work: Dave Eberbach, Research Coordinator, United Way of Central Iowa

The data social scientists collect often confirm what people think, but sometimes—as this 1992 billboard suggests—they surprise us. Today, the percentage of homes in the United States with two children, a working father, and a homemaker mother remains relatively unchanged.

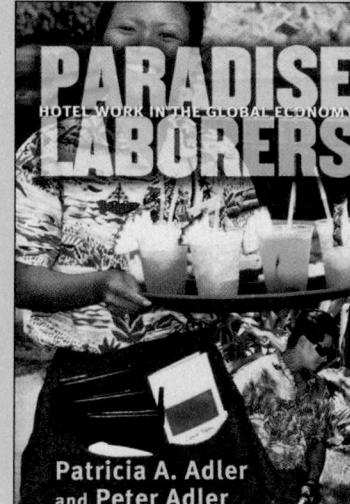

You land in paradise. Departing the airport in your canary-yellow rented convertible, you . . . head toward your vacation destination: an exclusive Hawaiian hotel. . . . Turning off the main road onto the winding driveway, you see the rich, vibrant colors of the beautiful trees and flowers lining the peaceful path. As you drive up to the lobby, a potpourri of pleasurable sensations assaults you. You smell the fragrant plumeria and gardenia blossoms, indications that you are in a tropical Eden. You hear the rumble of the waterfall and then behold its magnificence, a torrent of rushing streams tumbling over rocks and crashing into a pool below. The cascading water and its splash fill the air with moisture and your nostrils with the hydrated aroma. You have entered paradise.

As you pull up . . ., a smartly dressed bell captain approaches and opens your door, welcoming you with a resounding "aloha." A bellman wheels up his cart and unloads your bags. You give your name and hand your keys to the valet and wander toward the lobby. . . . Immediately, a beautiful Polynesian woman appears and, in soft tones, welcomes you, slipping a colorful and sweet-smelling lei over your head. . . .

You are steered toward the front desk where another Polynesian employee greets you and begins your check-in process. Discreetly, your lei greeter returns, carrying a silver tray from which she offers you glasses filled with tropical fruit punch and a sugarcane swizzle stick to chew on. . . . You gaze around at the impressive space, the many workers bustling around in diverse uniforms. They range among the different Hawaiian hotels from the flowing raiment of traditional Polynesian garb to the starched, dignified British uniforms summoning images of old-world butlers and high service.

After you complete your transaction, the front desk clerk summons a bellman who appears with your luggage. . . . Your bellman takes you to your room, . . . brings in your bags, lays them atop the unfolded luggage holders, and fills your ice bucket. You have arrived in the lap of luxury.

This surreal guest experience is made possible by a set of carefully planned structures surrounding and underlying what customers see. Most guests do not notice the precise ethnic and racial stratification of those attending them. They do not recognize that the lei greeters and front desk clerks are locals, selected for their Polynesian appearance; that many valets and the bell captain are "haoles" (Caucasians), selected to give an atmosphere of continental service; and that the bellmen are a combination of these two groups. At the same time guests may completely overlook the new immigrants: outdoor housekeepers sweeping the lobby or gardeners raking the leaves. . . .

Guests are also usually unaware of the complex systems that organize and track the services they receive. Valets and bellmen work on a rotation that calls them forth to fetch luggage or cars in a careful order. . . . Unbeknownst to guests, the passage of every bag through the hotel is meticulously charted . . . . All this constitutes the complex underground functioning of a large resort that makes the guest experience invisibly smooth.

(P. Adler and Adler 2004:1–2, 4) Additional information about this excerpt can be found on the Online Learning Center at www.mhhe.com/schaefer7. ●

> " *Immediately, a beautiful Polynesian woman appears and, in soft tones, welcomes you, slipping a colorful and sweet-smelling lei over your head.* "

This description of a tourist's arrival at a Hawaiian resort, taken from Patricia A. Adler and Peter Adler's (2004) *Paradise Laborers: Hotel Work in the Global Economy,* is based on extensive research into the global tourism industry. Over an eight-year period, the two sociologists conducted extensive fieldwork at five Hawaiian hotels, studying the staff and operations in minute detail. They interviewed employees and members of the corporate management team, took extensive notes, and spent considerable time observing the social organization of the resort business. Their research allowed them to go well beyond the postcard observations that a typical tourist might send home from vacation.

The Adlers' work in Hawaii reflects all three major sociological approaches. In noting the resorts' relatively smooth operation, despite continual employee turnover even at the highest levels, the Adlers adopt a functionalist perspective. When they focus on how members of the hotel workforce relate to one another on the job, they are employing the interactionist perspective. And when they note that those employees are divided by social class, gender, ethnicity, and immigration status, they are relying on the conflict and feminist approaches.

The Adlers' work also illustrates the enormous breadth of the field of sociology. Over the course of their careers, Patricia A. Adler and Peter Adler (1991, 1993, 1998, 2005) have published studies of college athletes, illicit drug traffickers, preadolescent peer groups, and people who engage in self-mutilation (self-described cutters, burners, and so on). Their choice of the global tourism industry as their latest subject indicates the tremendous freedom sociologists have to explore and open up new topics of inquiry.

Effective sociological research can be quite thought-provoking. It may suggest many new questions that require further study, such as why we make assumptions about people's suitability for certain jobs based merely on their gender or race. In some cases, rather than raising additional questions, a study will simply confirm previous beliefs and findings. Sociological research can also have practical applications. For instance, research results that disconfirm accepted beliefs about marriage and the family may lead to changes in public policy.

This chapter will examine the research process used in conducting sociological studies. How do sociologists go about setting up a research project? And how do they ensure that the results of the research are reliable and accurate? Can they carry out their research without violating the rights of those they study?

We will first look at the steps that make up the scientific method used in research. Then we will take a look at various techniques commonly used in sociological research, such as experiments, observations, and surveys. We will pay particular attention to the ethical challenges sociologists face in studying human behavior, and to the debate raised by Max Weber's call for "value neutrality" in social science research. We will also examine the role technology plays in research today. The Social Policy section considers the difficulties in researching the controversial subject of human sexuality.

Whatever the area of sociological inquiry and whatever the perspective of the sociologist—whether functionalist, conflict, interactionist, or any other—there is one crucial requirement: imaginative, responsible research that meets the highest scientific and ethical standards. ●

What Is the Scientific Method?

Like all of us, sociologists are interested in the central questions of our time. Is the family falling apart? Why is there so much crime in the United States? Is the world falling behind in its ability to feed a growing population? Such issues concern most people, whether or not they have academic training. However, unlike the typical citizen, the sociologist has a commitment to use the *scientific method* in studying society. The scientific method is a systematic, organized series of steps that ensures maximum objectivity and consistency in researching a problem.

Many of us will never actually conduct scientific research. Why, then, is it important that we understand the scientific method? The answer is that it plays a major role in the workings of our society. Residents of the United States are constantly bombarded with "facts" or "data." A television news report informs us that "one in every two marriages in this country now

ends in divorce," yet Chapter 12 will show that this assertion is based on misleading statistics. Almost daily, advertisers cite supposedly scientific studies to prove that their products are superior. Such claims may be accurate or exaggerated. We can better evaluate such information—and will not be fooled so easily—if we are familiar with the standards of scientific research. These standards are quite stringent, and they demand as strict adherence as possible.

The scientific method requires precise preparation in developing useful research. Otherwise, the research data collected may not prove accurate. Sociologists and other researchers follow five basic steps in the scientific method: (1) defining the problem, (2) reviewing the literature, (3) formulating the hypothesis, (4) selecting the research design and then collecting and analyzing data, and (5) developing the conclusion (see Figure 2-1). We'll use an actual example to illustrate the workings of the scientific method.

It seems reasonable to assume that these Columbia University graduates will earn more income than high school graduates. But how would you go about testing that hypothesis?

Defining the Problem

Does it "pay" to go to college? Some people make great sacrifices and work hard to get a college education. Parents borrow money for their children's tuition. Students work part-time jobs or even take full-time positions while attending evening or weekend classes. Does it pay off? Are there monetary returns for getting that degree?

The first step in any research project is to state as clearly as possible what you hope to investigate—that is, *define the problem*. In this instance, we are interested in knowing how schooling relates to income. We want to find out the earnings of people with different levels of formal schooling.

Early on, any social science researcher must develop an operational definition of each concept being studied. An **operational definition** is an explanation of an abstract concept that is specific enough to allow a researcher to assess the concept. For example, a sociologist interested in status might use membership in exclusive social clubs as an operational definition of status. Someone studying prejudice might consider a person's unwillingness to hire or work with members of minority groups as an operational definition of prejudice. In our example, we need to develop two operational definitions—education and earnings—in order to study whether it pays to get an advanced educational degree. We'll define *education* as the number of years of schooling a person has achieved, and *earnings* as the income a person reports having received in the last year.

Initially, we will take a functionalist perspective (although we may end up incorporating other approaches). We will argue that opportunities for more earning power are related to level of schooling and that schools prepare students for employment.

Reviewing the Literature

By conducting a *review of the literature*—relevant scholarly studies and information—researchers refine the problem under

study, clarify possible techniques to be used in collecting data, and eliminate or reduce avoidable mistakes. In our example, we would examine information about the salaries for different occupations. We would see if jobs that require more academic training are better rewarded. It would also be appropriate to review other studies on the relationship between education and income.

The review of the literature would soon tell us that many other factors besides years of schooling influence earning potential. For example, we would learn that the children of rich parents are more likely to go to college than those from modest backgrounds, so we might consider the possibility that the same parents may later help their children secure better-paying jobs.

We might also look at macro-level data, such as state-by-state comparisons of income and educational levels. In one macro-level study based on census data, researchers found that in states whose residents have a relatively high level of education, household income levels are high as well (see Figure 2-2, page 32). This finding suggests that schooling may well be related to income, though it does not speak to the micro-level relationship we are interested in. That is, we want to know whether *individuals* who are well educated are also well paid.

Formulating the Hypothesis

After reviewing earlier research and drawing on the contributions of sociological theorists, the researchers may then *formulate*

FIGURE 2–1

The Scientific Method

```
            ┌ ─ ─ ─ ─ ─ ─ ─ ─ ─ ─ ─ ─ ─ ─ ┐
            ↓                               |
      Define the problem                    |
            ↓                               |
      Review the literature                 |
            ↓                               |
   Formulate a testable hypothesis          |
            ↓                               |
     Select a research design               |
     Collect and analyze data               |
   ┌────────┬──────────┬──────────┐         |
 Survey  Observation  Experiment  Existing sources |
            ↓                               |
     Develop the conclusion                 |
            └ ─ ─ ─ ─ ─ ─ ─ ┐              |
                      Ideas for  ─ ─ ─ ─ ─ ─ ┘
                   further research
```

The scientific method allows sociologists to objectively and logically evaluate the data they collect. Their findings can suggest ideas for further sociological research.

Educational Level and Household Income in the United States

MAPPING LIFE

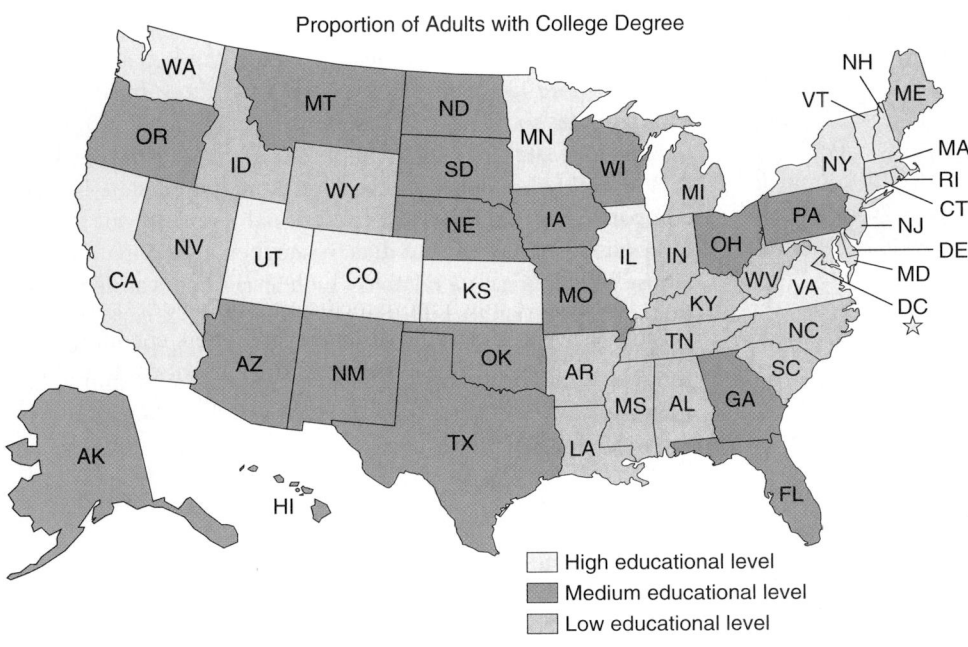

Proportion of Adults with College Degree

☐ High educational level
■ Medium educational level
▨ Low educational level

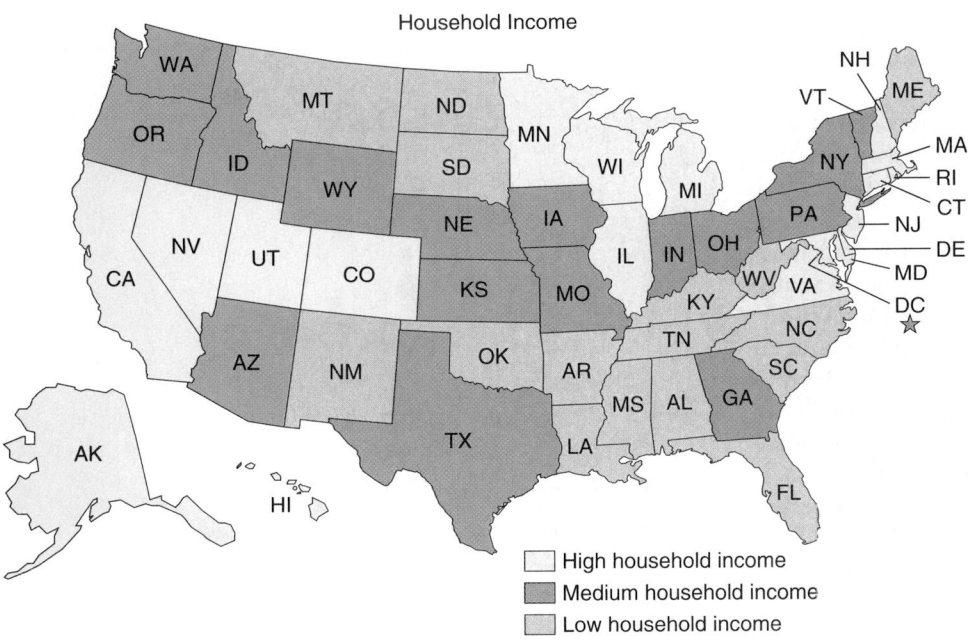

Household Income

☐ High household income
■ Medium household income
▨ Low household income

Notes: Education data are for 2003. Cutoffs for high/medium and medium/low educational levels were 27 percent and 24 percent of the population with a college degree, respectively; median for the entire nation was 27.2 percent. Income data are 2002–2004 three-year average medians. Cutoffs for high/medium and medium/low household income levels were $45,700 and $41,000, respectively; national median household income was $44,473.

Sources: Bureau of the Census 2004a:143; DeNavas-Walt et al. 2005:23, 76.

In general, states with high educational levels (top) also have high household incomes (bottom).

Student Alert A hypothesis is not the same as a guess or hunch, because a hypothesis is based on a review of scientific studies.
Classroom Tip Make sure that students understand the differences between independent and dependent variables. This is often a problem!

the hypothesis. A **hypothesis** is a speculative statement about the relationship between two or more factors known as variables. Income, religion, occupation, and gender can all serve as variables in a study. We can define a **variable** as a measurable trait or characteristic that is subject to change under different conditions.

Researchers who formulate a hypothesis generally must suggest how one aspect of human behavior influences or affects another. The variable hypothesized to cause or influence another is called the **independent variable.** The second variable is termed the **dependent variable** because its action *depends* on the influence of the independent variable. In other words, the researcher believes that the independent variable predicts or causes change in the dependent variable. For example, a researcher in sociology might anticipate that the availability of affordable housing (the independent variable, *x*) affects the level of homelessness in a community (the dependent variable, *y*).

Our hypothesis is that the higher one's educational degree, the more money one will earn. The independent variable that is to be measured is the level of education. The variable that is thought to depend on it—income—must also be measured.

Identifying independent and dependent variables is a critical step in clarifying cause-and-effect relationships. As shown in Figure 2-3 (opposite), **causal logic** involves the relationship between a condition or variable and a particular consequence, with one event leading to the other. For instance, being less integrated into society may be directly related to, or produce a greater likelihood of, suicide. Similarly, the time students spend reviewing material for a quiz may be directly related to, or produce a greater likelihood of, getting a high score on the quiz.

A **correlation** exists when a change in one variable coincides with a change in the other. Correlations are an indication that causality *may* be present; they do not necessarily indicate causation. For example, data indicate that people who

Let's Discuss What other independent variables could be used in a study of income?

prefer to watch televised news programs are less knowledgeable than those who read newspapers and newsmagazines. This correlation between people's relative knowledge and their choice of news media seems to make sense, because it agrees with the common belief that television "dumbs down" information. But the correlation between the two variables is actually caused by a third variable, people's relative ability to comprehend large amounts of information. People with poor reading skills are much more likely than others to get their news from television, while those who are more educated or skilled turn more often to the print media. Though television viewing is correlated with lower news comprehension, then, it does not *cause* it. Sociologists seek to identify the *causal* link between variables; the suspected causal link is generally described in the hypothesis (Neuman 2000:139).

Collecting and Analyzing Data

How do you test a hypothesis to determine if it is supported or refuted? You need to collect information, using one of the research designs described later in the chapter. The research design guides the researcher in collecting and analyzing data.

FIGURE 2–3

Causal Logic

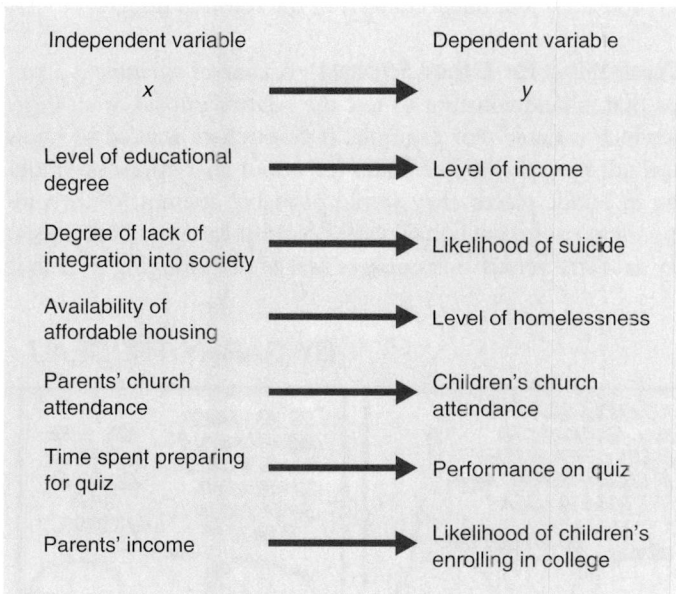

In *causal logic* an independent variable (often designated by the symbol *x*) influences a dependent variable (generally designated as *y*); thus, *x* leads to *y*. For example, parents who attend church regularly (*x*) are more likely to have children who are churchgoers (*y*). Notice that the first two pairs of variables are taken from studies already described in this textbook.

Think About It

Identify two or three dependent variables that might be influenced by this independent variable: number of alcoholic drinks ingested.

Selecting the Sample In most studies, social scientists must carefully select what is known as a sample. A ***sample*** is a selection from a larger population that is statistically representative of that population. There are many kinds of samples, but the one social scientists use most frequently is the random sample. In a ***random sample,*** every member of an entire population being studied has the same chance of being selected. Thus, if researchers want to examine the opinions of people listed in a city directory (a book that, unlike the telephone directory, lists all households), they might use a computer to randomly select names from the directory. The results would constitute a random sample. The advantage of using specialized sampling techniques is that sociologists do not need to question everyone in a population.

It is all too easy to confuse the careful scientific techniques used in representative sampling with the many *nonscientific* polls that receive much more media attention. For example, television viewers and radio listeners are often encouraged to e-mail their views on headline news or political contests. Such polls reflect nothing more than the views of those who happened to see the television program (or hear the radio broadcast) and took the time, perhaps at some cost, to register their opinions. These data do not necessarily reflect (and indeed may distort) the views of the broader population. Not everyone has access to a television or radio, time to watch or listen to a program, or the means and/or inclination to send e-mail. Similar problems are raised by the "mail-back" questionnaires found in many magazines and by "mall intercepts," in which shoppers are asked about some issue. Even when these techniques include answers from tens of thousands of people, they will be far less accurate than a carefully selected representative sample of 1,500 respondents.

For the purposes of our research example, we will use information collected in the General Social Survey (GSS). Since 1972, the National Opinion Research Center (NORC) has conducted this national survey 24 times, most recently in 2004. In this survey, a representative sample of the adult population is interviewed on a variety of topics for about one and a half hours. The author of this book examined the responses of the 1,875 people interviewed in 2002 concerning their level of education and income.

Ensuring Validity and Reliability The scientific method requires that research results be both valid and reliable. ***Validity*** refers to the degree to which a measure or scale truly reflects the phenomenon under study. A valid measure of income depends on the gathering of accurate data. Various studies show that people are reasonably accurate in reporting how much money they earned in the most recent year. ***Reliability*** refers to the extent to which a measure produces consistent results. Some people may not disclose accurate information, but most do. In the General Social Survey, only 5 percent of the respondents refused to give their income or indicated they did not know what their income was. That means 95 percent of the respondents gave their income, which we can assume is reasonably accurate (given their other responses about occupation and years in the labor force).

Scientific studies, including those conducted by sociologists, do not aim to answer all the questions that can be raised about a particular subject. Therefore, the conclusion of a research study represents both an end and a beginning. It terminates a specific phase of the investigation but should also generate ideas for future study.

Supporting Hypotheses In our example, we find that the data support our hypothesis: People with more formal schooling *do* earn more money than others. Those with a high school diploma earn more than those who failed to complete high school, but those with an associate's degree earn more than high school graduates. The relationship continues through more advanced levels of schooling, so that those with graduate degrees earn the most.

The relationship is not perfect, however. Some people who drop out of high school end up with high incomes, whereas some with advanced degrees earn modest incomes, as shown in Figure 2-4. A successful entrepreneur, for example, might not have much formal schooling, while a holder of a doctorate may choose to work for a low-paying nonprofit institution. Sociologists are interested in both the general pattern that emerges from their data and exceptions to the pattern.

Sociological studies do not always generate data that support the original hypothesis. In many instances, a hypothesis is refuted, and researchers must reformulate their conclusions. Un-

FIGURE 2-4

Impact of a College Education on Income

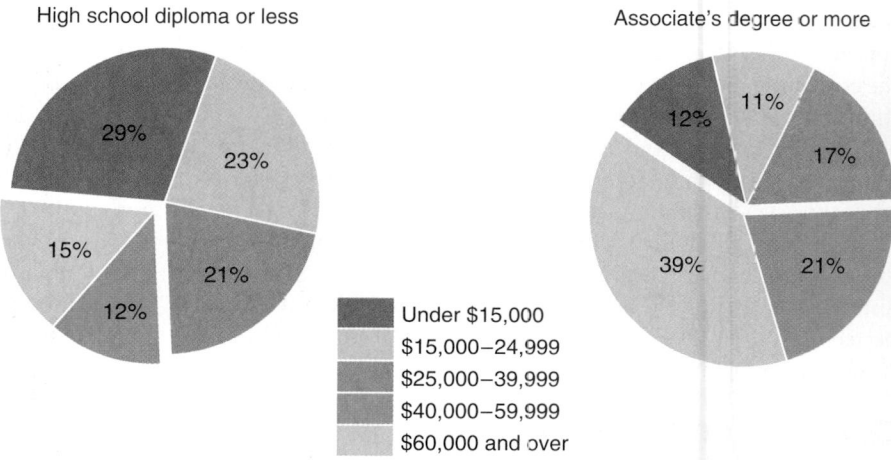

High school diploma or less

Associate's degree or more

Legend:
- Under $15,000
- $15,000–24,999
- $25,000–39,999
- $40,000–59,999
- $60,000 and over

Source: Author's analysis of General Social Survey 2004 in J. A. Davis et al. 2005.

Fifty-two percent of people with a high school diploma or less (left) earn under $25,000 a year, while only 27 percent earn $40,000 or more. In contrast, 60 percent of those with an associate's degree or higher (right) earn $40,000 or more, while only 23 percent earn less than $25,000.

expected results may also lead sociologists to reexamine their methodology and make changes in the research design.

Controlling for Other Factors A ***control variable*** is a factor that is held constant to test the relative impact of an independent variable. For example, if researchers wanted to know how adults in the United States feel about restrictions on smoking in public places, they would probably attempt to use a respondent's smoking behavior as a control variable. That is, how do smokers versus nonsmokers feel about smoking in public

Doonesbury

BY GARRY TRUDEAU

Think About It
What would constitute a less biased question for a survey on smoking?

Student Alert Note the value of discovering that a hypothesis is proved incorrect by research.

places? The researchers would compile separate statistics on how smokers and nonsmokers feel about antismoking regulations.

Our study of the influence of education on income suggests that not everyone enjoys equal educational opportunities, a {p.22 disparity that is one of the causes of social inequality. Since education affects a person's income, we may wish to call on the conflict perspective to explore this topic further. What impact does a person's race or gender have? Is a woman with a college degree likely to earn as much as a man with similar schooling? Later in this textbook we will consider these other factors and variables. That is, we will examine the impact that education has on income while controlling for variables such as gender and race.

In Summary: The Scientific Method

Let us briefly summarize the process of the scientific method through a review of the example. We *defined a problem* (the question of whether it pays to get a higher educational degree). We *reviewed the literature* (other studies of the relationship between education and income) and *formulated a hypothesis* (the higher one's educational degree, the more money one will earn). We *collected and analyzed the data,* making sure the sample was representative and the data were valid and reliable. Finally, we *developed the conclusion:* The data do support our hypothesis about the influence of education on income.

Use Your Sociological Imagination
www.mhhe.com /schaefer7

What might be the effects of a college education on society as a whole? Think of some potential effects on the family, government, and the economy.

Major Research Designs

An important aspect of sociological research is deciding *how* to collect the data. A *research design* is a detailed plan or method for obtaining data scientifically. Selection of a research design is often based on the theories and hypotheses the researcher starts with (Merton 1948). The choice requires creativity and ingenuity, because it directly influences both the cost of the project and the amount of time needed to collect the data. Research designs that sociologists regularly use to generate data include surveys, observation, experiments, and existing sources.

Surveys

Almost all of us have responded to surveys of one kind or another. We may have been asked what kind of detergent we use, which presidential candidate we intend to vote for, or what our favorite television program is. A *survey* is a study, generally in the form of an interview or questionnaire, that provides researchers with information about how people think and act. Among the United States' best-known surveys of opinion are the Gallup poll and the Harris poll. As anyone who watches the news during presidential campaigns knows, these polls have become a staple of political life.

Theory Discuss race and gender as possible control variables in the relationship between education and income.
Reel Society See Scientific Method in the Topic Index.
Classroom Tip See "Defending Surveys" (Class Discussion Topics).
Classroom Tip See "Coding" (Class Discussion Topics).
Methods The Gallup poll is an example of a survey.

When you think of surveys, you may recall seeing many person-on-the-street interviews on local television news shows. Although such interviews can be highly entertaining, they are not necessarily an accurate indication of public opinion. First, they reflect the opinions of only those people who happen to be at a certain location. Such a sample can be biased in favor of commuters, middle-class shoppers, or factory workers, depending on which street or area the newspeople select. Second, television interviews tend to attract outgoing people who are willing to appear on the air, while they frighten away others who may feel intimidated by a camera. As we've seen, a survey must be based on precise, representative sampling if it is to genuinely reflect a broad range of the population.

In preparing to conduct a survey, sociologists must not only develop representative samples; they must exercise great care in the wording of questions. An effective survey question must be simple and clear enough for people to understand. It must also be specific enough so that there are no problems in interpreting the results. Open-ended questions ("What do you think of the programming on educational television?") must be carefully phrased to solicit the type of information desired. Surveys can be indispensable sources of information, but only if the sampling is done properly and the questions are worded accurately and without bias. Box 2-1 on page 36 describes the special challenges of conducting a public opinion poll in Iraq after the defeat of Saddam Hussein's regime in 2003.

There are two main forms of the survey: the *interview,* in which a researcher obtains information through face-to-face or telephone questioning, and the *questionnaire,* in which the researcher uses a printed or written form to obtain information from a respondent. Each of these has its own advantages. An interviewer can obtain a higher response rate because people find it more difficult to turn down a personal request for an interview than to throw away a written questionnaire. In addition, a skillful interviewer can go beyond written questions and probe for a subject's underlying feelings and reasons. On the other hand, questionnaires have the advantage of being cheaper, especially in large samples.

Studies have shown that the characteristics of the interviewer have an impact on survey data. For example, women interviewers tend to receive more feminist responses from female subjects than do male researchers, and African American interviewers tend to receive more detailed responses about race-related issues from Black subjects than do White interviewers. The possible impact of gender and race indicates again how much care social research requires (D. W. Davis 1997; Huddy et al. 1997).

The survey is an example of *quantitative research,* which collects and reports data primarily in numerical form. Most of the survey research discussed so far in this book has been quantitative. While this type of research can make use of large samples, it can't offer great depth and detail on a topic. That is why researchers also make use of *qualitative research,* which relies on what is seen in field and naturalistic settings, and often focuses on small groups and communities rather than on large groups or whole nations. The most common form of qualitative

research IN action

2-1 Polling in Baghdad

In 2003, as the U.S. Army launched the war in Iraq, pollsters watched President George W. Bush's approval rating carefully. Such periodic measures of the public pulse have become routine in the United States—an accepted part of presidential politics. But in Iraq, a totalitarian state ruled for 24 years by dictator Saddam Hussein, polling of public opinion on political and social issues was unknown until August 2003, when representatives of the Gallup Organization began regular surveys of the residents of Baghdad. Later in the occupation, Gallup extended its survey to other areas in Iraq.

Needless to say, conducting a scientific survey in the war-torn city presented unusual challenges. Planners began by assuming that no census statistics would be available, so they used satellite imagery to estimate the population in each of Baghdad's neighborhoods. They later located detailed statistics for much of Baghdad, which they updated for use in their sampling procedure. Gallup's planners also expected that they would need to hire trained interviewers from outside Iraq, but were fortunate to find some government employees who had become familiar with Baghdad's neighborhoods while conducting consumer surveys. To train and supervise these interviewers, Gallup hired two seasoned executives from the Pan Arab Research Center in Dubai.

To administer the survey, Gallup chose the time-tested method of private, face-to-face interviews in people's homes. This method not only put respondents at ease; it allowed women to participate in the survey at a time when venturing out in public may have been dangerous for them. In all, Gallup employees conducted over 3,400 person-to-person interviews in the privacy of Iraqis' homes. Respondents, they found, were eager to offer opinions, and would talk with them at length. Only 3 percent of those who were sampled declined to be interviewed.

The survey's results are significant, since the more than 6 million people who live in Baghdad constitute a quarter of Iraq's population. Asked which of several forms of government would be acceptable to them, equal numbers of respondents chose (1) a multiparty parliamen-

> Needless to say, conducting a scientific survey in the war-torn city presented unusual challenges.

tary democracy and (2) a system of governance that includes consultations with Islamic leaders. Fewer respondents endorsed a constitutional democracy or an Islamic kingdom. At a time when representatives of the Iraqi people had convened to establish a new form of gov-

ernment for the nation, this kind of information would prove invaluable.

In 2005, building on its experience in Iraq, Gallup began to expand its overseas polling operations. Gallup employees are currently working on a public opinion survey in China.

Let's Discuss

1. The 97 percent response rate interviewers obtained in this survey was extremely high. Why do you think the response rate was so high, and what do you think it tells political analysts about the residents of Baghdad?
2. What might be some limitations of this survey?

Sources: Gallup 2004; O'Brien 2005; Saad 2003.

A Gallup employee interviews an Iraqi army veteran at his home in Baghdad. Pollsters had to carefully estimate the population of Baghdad's many districts, subdistricts, and neighborhoods to obtain a statistically representative sample of respondents.

---

research is observation, which we consider next. Throughout this book you will find examples of both quantitative and qualitative research, since both are used widely. Some sociologists prefer one type of research to the other, but we learn most when we draw on many different research designs and do not limit ourselves to a particular type of research.

Contemporary Culture Discuss the questions that students would add to a survey of Iraqi public opinion.
Gender How might men and women respond differently to questions in the Baghdad poll?

Observation

As we saw in the introduction to this chapter, Patricia A. Adler and Peter Adler gathered their information on the Hawaiian resort industry by *observing* the everyday interactions among employees. Investigators who collect information through direct participation and/or by closely watching a group or community

Methods Discuss other research methods through which social scientists could or could not assess Iraqi public opinion.
Let's Discuss Why is it important to gauge Iraqi public opinion?

Peter and Patricia Adler's book *Paradise Laborers,* featured in the opening excerpt for this chapter, was based on careful detailed observation of Hawaiian resort workers. The Adlers spent five years studying receptionists, housekeepers, and other resort employees as they went about their daily work.

are engaged in **observation.** This method allows sociologists to examine certain behaviors and communities that could not be investigated through other research techniques. Though observation may seem a relatively informal method compared to surveys or experiments, researchers are careful to take detailed notes while observing their subjects.

An increasingly popular form of qualitative research in sociology today is ethnography. **Ethnography** refers to the study of an entire social setting through extended systematic observation. Typically, the emphasis is on how the subjects themselves view their social life in some setting. The Adlers' study of the Hawaiian resort industry, described in the opening to this chapter, was an ethnographic study that covered hotel workers' leisure time and family lives as well as their on-the-job behavior (P. Adler and Adler 2003, 2004).

In some cases, the sociologist actually joins a group for a period to get an accurate sense of how it operates. This approach is called *participant observation.* In Barbara Ehrenreich's study of {pp.2–3} low-wage workers, described in Chapter 1, as well as in the Adlers' study of the Hawaiian resort industry, the researchers were participant observers.

During the late 1930s, in a classic example of participant-observation research, William F. Whyte moved into a low-income Italian neighborhood in Boston. For nearly four years he

was a member of the social circle of "corner boys" that he describes in *Street Corner Society.* Whyte revealed his identity to these men and joined in their conversations, bowling, and other leisure-time activities. His goal was to gain greater insight into the community that these men had established. As Whyte (1981:303) listened to Doc, the leader of the group, he "learned the answers to questions I would not even have had the sense to ask if I had been getting my information solely on an interviewing basis." Whyte's work was especially valuable, since at the time the academic world had little direct knowledge of the poor, and tended to rely for information on the records of social service agencies, hospitals, and courts (P. Adler et al. 1992).

The initial challenge that Whyte faced—and that every participant observer encounters—was to gain acceptance into an unfamiliar group. It is no simple matter for a college-trained sociologist to win the trust of a religious cult, a youth gang, a poor Appalachian community, or a circle of skid row residents. It requires a great deal of patience and an accepting, nonthreatening type of personality on the part of the observer.

Observation research poses other complex challenges for the investigator. Sociologists must be able to fully understand what they are observing. In a sense, then, researchers must learn to see the world as the group sees it in order to fully comprehend the events taking place around them.

This raises a delicate issue. If the research is to be successful, the observer cannot allow the close associations or even friendships that inevitably develop to influence the subjects' behavior or the conclusions of the study. Anson Shupe and David Bromley (1980), two sociologists who have used participant observation, have likened this challenge to that of walking a tightrope. Even while working hard to gain acceptance from the group being studied, the participant observer *must* maintain some degree of detachment.

The feminist perspective in sociology has drawn attention to a shortcoming in ethnographic research. For most of the history of sociology, studies were conducted on male subjects or about male-led groups and organizations, and the findings were generalized to all people. For example, for many decades studies of urban life focused on street corners, neighborhood taverns, and bowling alleys—places where men typically congregated. Although the insights gained were valuable, they did not give a true impression of city life because they overlooked the areas where women were likely to gather, such as playgrounds, grocery stores, and front stoops. The feminist perspective focuses on these arenas. Feminist researchers also tend to involve and consult their subjects more than other researchers, and they are more oriented to seeking change, raising consciousness, and trying to affect policy. In addition, feminist researchers are particularly open to a multidisciplinary approach, such as making use of historical evidence or legal studies as well as feminist theory (Baker 1999; L. Lofland 1975; Reinharz 1992).

Experiments

When sociologists want to study a possible cause-and-effect relationship, they may conduct experiments. An **experiment** is an

artificially created situation that allows a researcher to manipulate variables.

In the classic method of conducting an experiment, two groups of people are selected and matched for similar characteristics, such as age or education. The researchers then assign the subjects to one of two groups: the experimental or the control group. The *experimental group* is exposed to an independent variable; the *control group* is not. Thus, if scientists were testing a new type of antibiotic, they would administer the drug to an experimental group but not to a control group.

Sociologists don't often rely on this classic form of experiment, because it generally involves manipulating human behavior in an inappropriate manner, especially in a laboratory setting. However, they do try to re-create experimental conditions in the field. For example, to see the effect of a criminal background on a person's employment opportunities, sociologist Devah Pager (2003) devised an experiment in which she sent four young men out to look for jobs, each with a carefully crafted background story (see Box 2-2).

In some experiments, just as in observation research, the presence of a social scientist or other observer may affect the behavior of the people being studied. The recognition of this phenomenon grew out of an experiment conducted during the 1920s and 1930s at the Hawthorne plant of the Western Electric Company. A group of researchers set out to determine how to improve the productivity of workers at the plant. The investigators manipulated such variables as the lighting and working hours to see what impact the changes would have on productivity. To their surprise, they found that *every* step they took

seemed to increase productivity. Even measures that seemed likely to have the opposite effect, such as reducing the amount of lighting in the plant, led to higher productivity.

Why did the plant's employees work harder even under less favorable conditions? Their behavior apparently was influenced by the greater attention being paid to them in the course of the research, and by the novelty of being subjects in an experiment. Since that time, sociologists have used the term *Hawthorne effect* in referring to the unintended influence that observers of experiments can have on their subjects (S. Jones 1992; Lang 1992; Pelton 1994).

Use Your Sociological Imagination
www.mhhe.com/schaefer7

You are a researcher interested in the effect of TV watching on schoolchildren's grades. How would you go about setting up an experiment to measure this effect?

Use of Existing Sources

Sociologists do not necessarily need to collect new data in order to conduct research and test hypotheses. The term *secondary analysis* refers to a variety of research techniques that make use of previously collected and publicly accessible information and data. Generally, in conducting secondary analysis, researchers use data in ways that were unintended by the initial collectors of information. For example, census data are compiled for specific uses by the federal government but are also valuable to marketing specialists in locating everything from bicycle stores to nursing homes. And Social Security registrations, originally meant for government use in administering the nation's retirement system, have been used to track cultural trends in the naming of newborn children (see Box 2-3, page 41).

Sociologists consider secondary analysis to be *nonreactive*—that is, it does not influence people's behavior. For example, Émile Durkheim's statistical analysis of suicide neither increased nor decreased human self-destruction. Researchers, then, can avoid the Hawthorne effect by using secondary analysis.

There is one inherent problem, however: the researcher who relies on data collected by someone else may not find exactly what is needed. Social scientists who are studying family violence can use statistics from police and social service agencies on *reported* cases of spouse abuse and child abuse. But how many cases are not reported? Government bodies have no precise data on *all* cases of abuse.

How do people respond to being observed? Evidently these employees at the Hawthorne plant enjoyed the attention paid them when researchers observed them at work. No matter what variables were changed, the workers increased their productivity—even when the level of lighting was *reduced.*

Classroom Tip See "The Personal Implications of Ethnographic Research" (Additional Lecture Ideas).

Classroom Tip See "Role Conflict and Observation Research" (Class Discussion Topics).

Gender Sexism sometimes restricts female sociologists from conducting effective observation research in predominantly male environments. Is the opposite true, too?

Methods The research in the Hawthorne plant is an example of an experiment.

Methods Was the Hawthorne study valid? Was it reliable?

Contemporary Culture Ask students how they would study racial profiling.

2-2 Researching Privilege and Discrimination in Employment

At the University of Wisconsin, Devah Pager, a doctoral candidate in sociology, was looking for a topic for her dissertation. Pager was a volunteer at a homeless shelter, where she distributed mail and listened to residents' hard-luck stories. Frequently, she heard men who had prison records talk about their difficulty finding work. Moved by their stories, she wondered if there was something she could do. What if she could demonstrate a clear link between a criminal background and reduced employment prospects?

Pager set out to devise a field experiment to do just that—an experiment that would become the basis for her dissertation. She sent four polite, well-dressed young men out to look for an entry-level job in Milwaukee, Wisconsin. All four were 23-year-old college students, but they presented themselves as high school graduates with similar job histories. Two of the men were Black and two were White. One Black applicant and one White applicant claimed to have served 18 months in jail for a felony conviction—possession of cocaine with intent to distribute.

As one might expect, the four men's experiences with 350 potential employers were vastly different. Predictably, the White applicant with a purported prison record received only half as many callbacks as the other White applicant— 17 percent compared to 34 percent (see the accompanying figure). But as dramatic as the effect of his criminal record was, the effect of his race was more significant. Despite his

prison record, he received slightly more callbacks than the Black applicant *with no criminal record* (17 percent compared to 14 percent). Race, it seems, was more of a concern to potential employers than a criminal background.

These results stunned Pager, along with other academicians and public policy experts. (Indeed, a parallel study, in which researchers merely asked employers their hiring intentions, showed no racial difference.) "I expected there to be an effect of race, but I did not expect it to swamp the results as it did," Pager told an interviewer. Her finding was especially

> *Race, it seems, was more of a concern to potential employers than a criminal background.*

significant because the majority of convicts who are released from prison each year (52 percent) are, in fact, Black men. Pager's research, which was widely publicized, eventually contributed to a change in public policy. In his 2004 State of the Union address, President George W. Bush announced a $300 million mentoring program for ex-convicts who are attempting to reintegrate into society.

In August 2004, Pager received the American Sociological Association's award for best dissertation of the year. She is currently teaching at Princeton University, where she plans to replicate her groundbreaking study.

Let's Discuss

1. Do you see any weaknesses in Pager's research method? Does her study prove conclusively that prison time reduces a man's employment prospects?

2. Can you think of another method for investigating the link between a prison record and difficulty finding work? Explain how you would do it.

Sources: Bordt 2005; Bureau of Justice Statistics 2004; Kroeger 2004; Pager 2003; Pager and Quillian 2005.

White Privilege in Job Seeking

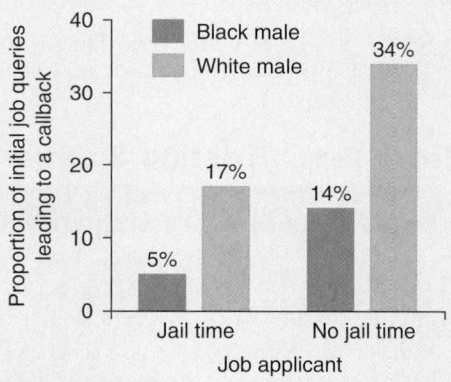

Source: Pager 2003:958.

Many social scientists find it useful to study cultural, economic, and political documents, including newspapers, periodicals, radio and television tapes, the Internet, scripts, diaries, songs, folklore, and legal papers (see Table 2-1, page 40). In examining these sources, researchers employ a technique known as **content analysis,** which is the systematic coding and objective recording of data, guided by some rationale.

Using content analysis, Erving Goffman (1979) conducted a pioneering exploration of how advertisements portray women. The ads he studied typically showed women as subordinate to or dependent on others, or as taking instruction from men. They engaged in caressing and touching gestures more than

men. Even when presented in leadership roles, women were likely to be shown striking seductive poses or gazing out into space.

Today, researchers who analyze film content are finding an increase in smoking in motion pictures, despite heightened public health concerns. Other researchers have found a growing difference in the way men and women use sexually explicit language. For example, an analysis of the lyrics of *Billboard* magazine's top 100 hits indicates that since 1958, male artists have increased their use of such language, while female artists have decreased theirs (American Lung Association 2003; Dukes et al. 2003).

Table 2-2 on page 42 summarizes the major research designs.

Key Person Devah Pager
Gender Suppose some of the job seekers in Pager's study were women. What patterns would you expect?
Contemporary Culture Can students think of other examples from U.S. society that are consistent with Pager's findings?
Policy Pointer Pager's research had a direct impact on public policy.

Methods Sociologists' use of existing sources is introduced.
Classroom Tip See "Content Analysis of the Rodney King Beating" (Additional Lecture Ideas).
Key Person Erving Goffman

Use Your Sociological Imagination
www.mhhe.com /schaefer7

Imagine you are a legislator or government policymaker working on a complex social problem. What might happen if you were to base your decision on faulty research?

Ethics of Research

A biochemist cannot inject a drug into a human being unless it has been thoroughly tested and the subject agrees to the shot. To do otherwise would be both unethical and illegal. Sociologists, too, must abide by certain specific standards in conducting research, called a *code of ethics.* The professional society of the discipline, the American Sociological Association (ASA), first published the society's *Code of Ethics* in 1971 and revised it most recently in 1997. It puts forth the following basic principles:

1. Maintain objectivity and integrity in research.
2. Respect the subject's right to privacy and dignity.
3. Protect subjects from personal harm.
4. Preserve confidentiality.
5. Seek informed consent when data are collected from research participants or when behavior occurs in a private context.

summingUP

Table 2-1 Existing Sources Used in Sociological Research

Most Frequently Used Sources

Census data

Crime statistics

Birth, death, marriage, divorce, and health statistics

Other Sources

Newspapers and periodicals

Personal journals, diaries, e-mail, and letters

Records and archival material of religious organizations, corporations, and other organizations

Transcripts of radio programs

Videotapes of motion pictures and television programs

Web pages, Weblogs, and chatrooms

Song lyrics

Scientific records (such as patent applications)

Speeches of public figures (such as politicians)

Votes cast in elections or by elected officials on specific legislative proposals

Attendance records for public events

Videotapes of social protests and rallies

Literature, including folklore

6. Acknowledge research collaboration and assistance.
7. Disclose all sources of financial support (American Sociological Association 1997).

These basic principles probably seem clear-cut. How could they lead to any disagreement or controversy? Yet many delicate ethical questions cannot be resolved simply by reading these seven principles. For example, should a sociologist who is engaged in participant-observation research always protect the confidentiality of subjects? What if the subjects are members of a religious cult allegedly involved in unethical and possibly illegal activities? What if the sociologist is interviewing political activists and is questioned by government authorities about the research?

Because most sociological research uses *people* as sources of information—as respondents to survey questions, subjects of observation, or participants in experiments—these sorts of questions are important. In all cases, sociologists need to be certain they are not invading their subjects' privacy. Generally, they do so by assuring subjects of anonymity and by guaranteeing the confidentiality of personal information. In addition, research proposals that involve human subjects must now be overseen by a review board, whose members seek to ensure that subjects are not placed at an unreasonable level of risk. If necessary, the board may ask researchers to revise their research designs to conform to the code of ethics.

We can appreciate the seriousness of the ethical problems researchers confront by considering the experience of sociologist Rik Scarce, described in the next section. Scarce's vow to protect his subjects' confidentiality got him into considerable trouble with the law.

Confidentiality

Like journalists, sociologists occasionally find themselves subject to questions from law enforcement authorities because of knowledge they have gained in the course of their work. This uncomfortable situation raises profound ethical questions.

In May 1993, Rik Scarce, a doctoral candidate in sociology at Washington State University, was jailed for contempt of court. Scarce had declined to tell a federal grand jury what he knew—or even whether he knew anything—about a 1991

Theory Goffman's study is an example of microsociology and the interactionist perspective.
Classroom Tip See Class Discussion Topics for several activities about content analysis.
Contemporary Culture Have students illustrate content analysis by examining music videos.
Classroom Tip See "Teaching the Ethics of Sociological Research" (Class Discussion Topics).
Classroom Tip Analyze the ethical problems of having a researcher conduct observation research in your classroom.

researchINaction

2-3 What's in a Name?

Sociologists can learn a great deal using available information. For example, every year the Social Security Administration receives thousands of registrations for newborn babies. Using these data, we can identify some cultural trends in the popularity of children's names.

As the accompanying figure shows, for example, John has been an extremely popular boy's name for over a century. In 2004, over 5,000 babies were named John, making the moniker the 18th most popular name that year. Though only about half as many babies were named Juan in 2004, that name has been gaining in popularity in recent generations, reflecting the growing impact of the Latino population in the United States.

We can see some other patterns in the annual data on name giving. In many ethnic and

> In 2004, over 5,000 babies were named John, making the moniker the 18th most popular name that year.

racial groups, parents choose names that display pride in their identity or the uniqueness they see in their children. Among African Americans, for example, names such as Ebony and Imani are the most popular ones for girls.

The public data contained in name registries also reveal a trend toward "American-sounding" names among immigrants to the United States. In Italy, for example, Giuseppe is a very popular boy's name. Among Italian immigrants to the United states, the English form of Giuseppe, Joseph, is the third most popular boy's name, though it ranks only 15th among other Americans. The pattern of selecting names that will allow children to "fit in" is not uniform, however. In some immigrant groups, parents tend to favor names that symbolize

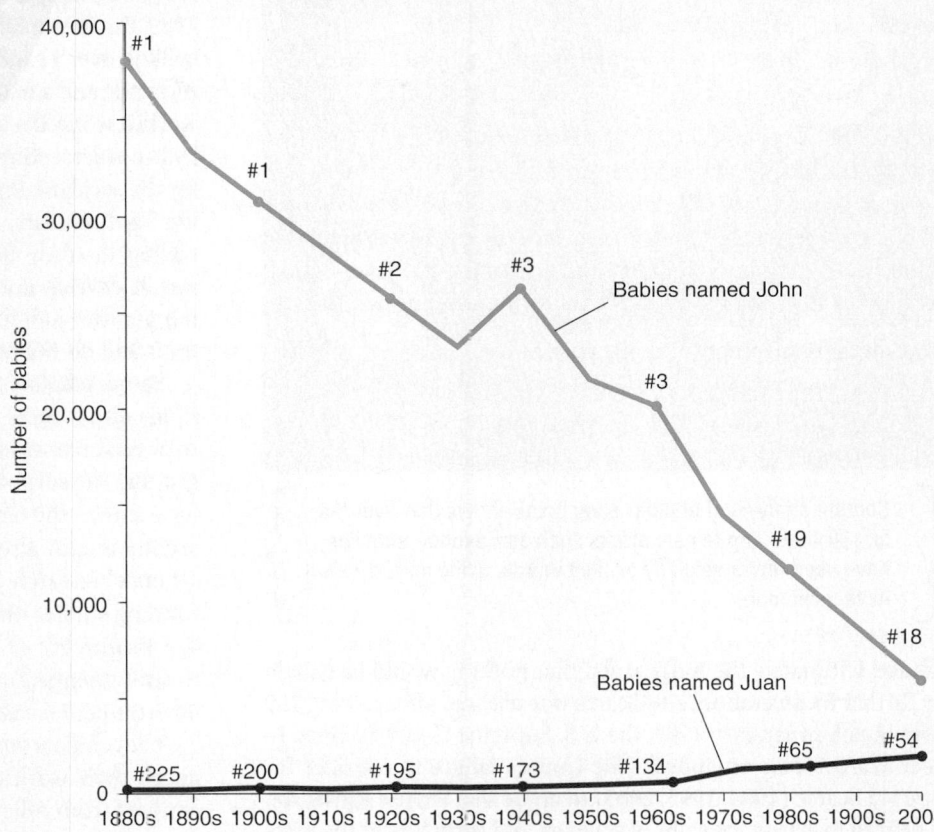

Popularity of John versus Juan

Note: Numbers indicate rank in popularity among all boys' names in that year.
Source: Baby Name Wizard 2006.

their ethnicity. For example, Kelly is popular among Irish Americans, even though it isn't a traditional girl's name in the home country. Thus, the available data on newborns' names allows sociologists to detect cultural trends that reflect changing group identities.

Let's Discuss

1. Visit www.babynamewizard.com on the Internet, and click on "NameVoyager." According to this Web site, how popular is your first name? Is it becoming more or less fashionable over time?

2. What might be the pros and cons of choosing a first name that is associated with a particular ethnic or racial group? Would your answer differ depending on whether the chosen name was Sean or Juan?

Sources: Baby Name Wizard 2006; Levitt and Dubner 2005; Lieberson 2000.

---

raid on a university research laboratory by animal rights activists. At the time, Scarce was conducting research for a book about environmental protestors and knew at least one suspect in the break-in. Curiously, although he was chastised by a federal judge, Scarce

won respect from fellow prison inmates, who regarded him as a man who "wouldn't snitch" (Monaghan 1993:A8).

The American Sociological Association supported Scarce's position when he appealed his sentence. Scarce maintained his

Race/Ethnicity What can or cannot be said about race or ethnicity from a person's name?
Let's Discuss Do sociological factors drive changes in the popularity of names?

Classroom Tip One study shows that job applicants with names like Lakisha and Jamal have more difficulty than others in getting jobs. See the 2003 study by Marianne Bertrand and Sendhil Mullainathan at www.nber.org.
Classroom Tip The discussion of names uses the most common spellings, but other variations (e.g., Johnny, Eboni) are included in the data.

Content analysis of popular song lyrics shows that over the last 50 years, top female artists such as Beyoncé Knowles have used fewer sexually explicit words, while male artists have used more.

silence. Ultimately the judge ruled that nothing would be gained by further incarceration, and Scarce was released after serving 159 days in jail. In January 1994, the U.S. Supreme Court declined to hear Scarce's case on appeal. The Court's failure to consider his case led Scarce (1994, 1995, 2005) to argue that federal legislation is needed to clarify the right of scholars and members of the press to preserve the confidentiality of those they interview.

Research Funding

Sometimes disclosing all the sources of funding for a study, as required in principle 7 of the ASA's *Code of Ethics,* is not a sufficient guarantee of ethical conduct. Especially in the case of both corporate and government funding, money given ostensibly for the support of basic research may come with strings attached. Accepting funds from a private organization or even a government agency that stands to benefit from a study's results can call into question a researcher's objectivity and integrity (principle 1).

The Exxon Corporation's support for research on jury verdicts is a good example of this kind of conflict of interest. On March 24, 1989, the Exxon oil tanker *Valdez* hit a reef off the coast of Alaska, spilling over 11 million gallons of oil into Prince William Sound. A decade and a half later, the *Valdez* disaster is still regarded as the world's worst oil spill in terms of its environmental impact. In 1994 a federal court ordered Exxon to pay $5.3 billion in damages for the accident. Exxon appealed the verdict, and began approaching legal scholars, sociologists, and psychologists who might be willing to study jury deliberations. The corporation's objective was to develop academic support for its lawyers' contention that the punitive judgments in such cases result from faulty deliberations and do not have a deterrent effect.

Some scholars have questioned the propriety of accepting funds under these circumstances, even if the source is disclosed. In at least one case, an Exxon employee explicitly told a sociologist that the corporation offers financial support to scholars who have shown the tendency to express views similar to its own. An argument can also be made that Exxon was attempting to set scholars' research agendas with its huge war chest. Rather than funding studies on the improvement of cleanup technologies or the assignment of long-term environmental costs, Exxon chose to shift scientists' attention to the validity of the legal awards in environmental cases.

The scholars who accepted Exxon's support deny that it influenced their work or changed their conclusions. Some received support from other sources as well, such as the National Science Foundation and Harvard University's Olin Center for Law, Economics, and Business. Many of their findings were published in respected academic journals after review by a jury of peers. Still, at least one researcher who participated in the studies refused monetary support from Exxon to avoid even the suggestion of a conflict of interest.

Table 2-2　Major Research Designs

summingUP

Method	Examples	Advantages	Limitations
Survey	Questionnaires Interviews	Yields information about specific issues	Can be expensive and time-consuming
Observation	Ethnography	Yields detailed information about specific groups or organizations	Involves months if not years of labor-intensive data
Experiment	Deliberate manipulation of people's social behavior	Yields direct measures of people's behavior	Ethical limitations on the degree to which subjects' behavior can be manipulated
Existing sources/ Secondary analysis	Analysis of census or health data Analysis of films or TV commercials	Cost-efficiency	Limited to data collected for some other purpose

Key Person Rik Scarce
Let's Discuss Should there be limits on scholars' control over their research notes? If so, under what circumstances should researchers be forced to violate confidentiality? Was Scarce correct in declining to testify before the grand jury? Was the court correct in sending him to jail?

Contemporary Culture How do students feel about corporate sponsorship of social science research?
Let's Discuss Discuss Exxon's sponsorship of social science research from a conflict perspective.
Let's Discuss Would students discount the results of an Exxon-funded study if the results supported Exxon's point of view?

A floating containment barrier encircles the Exxon oil tanker *Valdez* after its grounding on a reef off the coast of Alaska. Exxon executives spent a million dollars to fund academic research that they hoped would support lawyers' efforts to reduce the $5.3 billion judgment against the corporation for negligence in the environmental disaster.

To date, Exxon has spent roughly $1 million on the research, and at least one compilation of studies congenial to Exxon's point of view has been published. As ethical considerations require, the academics who conducted the studies disclosed Exxon's role in funding the research. In 2001, drawing on their studies, Exxon's lawyers succeeded in persuading an appeals court to reduce the corporation's legal damages from $5.3 to $4 billion. The case is now under appeal by Exxon in an attempt to further reduce the damages (Freudenburg 2005; Sunstein et al. 2003; Zarembo 2003).

Value Neutrality

The ethical considerations of sociologists lie not only in the methods they use and the funding they accept, but in the way they interpret their results. Max Weber ([1904] 1949) recognized that personal values would influence the questions that sociologists select for research. In his view, that was perfectly acceptable, but under no conditions could a researcher allow his or her personal feelings to influence the *interpretation* of data. In Weber's phrase, sociologists must practice *value neutrality* in their research.

As part of this neutrality, investigators have an ethical obligation to accept research findings even when the data run counter to their own personal views, to theoretically based explanations, {pp.8–9} or to widely accepted beliefs. For example, Émile Durkheim challenged popular conceptions when he reported that social (rather than supernatural) forces were an important factor in suicide.

Some sociologists believe that neutrality is impossible. They worry that Weber's insistence on value-free sociology may lead the public to accept sociological conclusions without exploring researchers' biases. Others, drawing on the conflict perspective, as Alvin Gouldner (1970) does, have suggested that sociologists may use objectivity as a justification for remaining uncritical of existing institutions and centers of power. These arguments are attacks not so much on Weber himself as on the way his goals have been misinterpreted. As we have seen, Weber was quite clear that sociologists may bring values to their subject matter. In his view, however, they must not confuse their own values with the social reality under study (Bendix 1968).

Let's consider what might happen when researchers bring their own biases to the investigation. A person investigating the impact of intercollegiate sports on alumni contributions, for example, may focus only on the highly visible revenue-generating sports of football and basketball and neglect the so-called minor sports, such as tennis or soccer, which are more likely to involve women athletes. Despite the early work of W. E. B. Du Bois and Jane Addams, sociologists still need to be reminded that the discipline often fails to adequately consider all people's social behavior.

In her book *The Death of White Sociology* (1973), Joyce Ladner called attention to the tendency of mainstream sociology to treat the lives of African Americans as a social problem. More recently, feminist sociologist Shulamit Reinharz (1992) has argued that sociological research should be not only inclusive but open to bringing about social change and to drawing on relevant research by nonsociologists. Both Reinharz and Ladner maintain that researchers should always analyze whether women's unequal social status has affected their studies in any way. For example, one might broaden the study of the impact of education on income to consider the implications of the unequal pay status of men and women. The issue of value neutrality does not mean that sociologists can't have opinions, but it does mean that they must work to overcome any biases, however unintentional, that they may bring to their analysis of research.

Peter Rossi (1987) admits to having liberal inclinations that direct him to certain fields of study. Yet in line with Weber's view of value neutrality, Rossi's commitment to rigorous research methods and objective interpretation of data has sometimes led him to controversial findings that are not necessarily supportive of his own liberal values. For example, his measure of the extent of homelessness in Chicago in the mid-1980s fell far below the estimates of the Chicago Coalition for the Homeless. Coalition members bitterly attacked Rossi for hampering their social reform efforts by minimizing the extent of homelessness. Rossi (1987:79) concluded that "in the short term, good social research will often be greeted as a betrayal of one or another side to a particular controversy."

Technology and Sociological Research

Advances in technology have affected all aspects of our lives, and sociological research is no exception. The increased speed and

Key Person Max Weber
Student Alert Relate Weber's concept of value neutrality to the discussion of *verstehen* in Chapter 1.
Classroom Tip Relate Weber's concept of value neutrality to the concept of cultural relativism that is introduced in Chapter 3.
Key Persons Alvin Gouldner, Joyce Ladner, Shulamit Reinharz

Key Person Peter Rossi
Let's Discuss What other types of sociological research might be greeted as a betrayal by one or another side to a particular controversy?

Dave Eberbach
**Research Coordinator,
United Way of Central Iowa**

As a research specialist, Dave Eberbach uses his training in sociology to work for social change. Eberbach looks for small pockets of poverty that are generally hidden in state and county statistics. By zeroing in on conditions in specific neighborhoods, he empowers state and local agencies that work on behalf of the disadvantaged.

Eberbach, who is based in Des Moines, Iowa, was hired to establish a "data warehouse" of social statistics for the local United Way. Part of his job has been to demonstrate to agencies how the information in the database can be of use to them. "We have moved most of our data presentations away from charts and graphs, and on to maps of the county, the city and the neighborhood," he explains. "This allows people to truly 'see' the big picture."

When Eberbach entered Grinnell College in 1985, he had already taken a sociology course and knew that the subject interested him. Still, he could not have foreseen all the practical uses he might have had for what he learned. "Never assume that you'll never need to know something (including statistics)," he advises. "Life has a funny way of bringing things around again."

At Grinnell, Eberbach benefited from the presence of several visiting professors who exposed him to a variety of cultural and racial per-

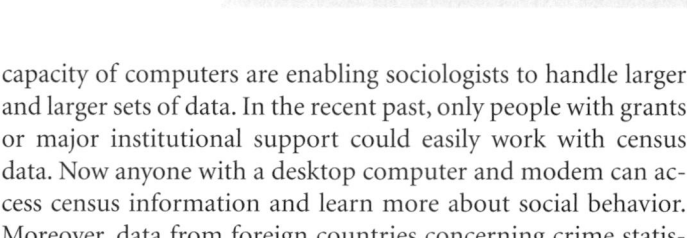

spectives. His personal acquaintance with them complemented the concepts he was learning in his sociology classes. Today, Eberbach draws on his college experiences at the United Way, where his work brings him into contact with a diverse group of people.

Sociology has also helped Eberbach in his chosen specialty, research. "I believe that I am a better 'data person' because of my sociology background," he claims. "The human context for data is as important and can get lost or misdirected by pure statistics," he explains. "My sociology background has helped me ask the appropriate questions to make effective change in our community."

Let's Discuss

1. Do you know what you want to be doing 10 years from now? If so, how might a knowledge of statistics help you in your future occupation?
2. What kinds of statistics, specifically, might you find in the United Way's data warehouse? Where would they come from?

---

capacity of computers are enabling sociologists to handle larger and larger sets of data. In the recent past, only people with grants or major institutional support could easily work with census data. Now anyone with a desktop computer and modem can access census information and learn more about social behavior. Moreover, data from foreign countries concerning crime statistics and health care are sometimes as available as information from the United States.

Researchers usually rely on computers to deal with quantitative data—that is, numerical measures—but electronic technology is also assisting them with qualitative data, such as information obtained in observational research. Numerous software programs, such as Ethnograph and NVivo 7, allow the researcher not only to record observations but to identify common behavioral patterns or concerns expressed in interviews. For example, after observing students in a college cafeteria over several weeks and putting her observations into the computer, a researcher could group all the observations according to certain variables, such as "sorority" or "study group."

The Internet affords an excellent opportunity to communicate with fellow researchers, as well as to locate useful information on social issues that has been posted on Web sites. It would

{
Computers have vastly extended the range and capability of sociological research, both by allowing large amounts of data to be stored and analyzed and by facilitating communication with other researchers via Web sites, newsgroups, and e-mail.
}

Student Alert How does a researcher or student verify the validity of information found on the Internet?

Methods Are there ethical concerns with using computers for sociological research?

Classroom Tip See "NORC and the Internet" (Class Discussion Topics).

be impossible to calculate all the sociological postings on Web sites or Internet mailing lists. Of course, researchers need to apply the same critical scrutiny to Internet material that they would to any printed resource.

How useful is the Internet for conducting survey research? That is still unclear. It is relatively easy to send out a questionnaire or post one on an electronic bulletin board. This technique is an inexpensive way to reach large numbers of potential respondents and get a quick response. However, there are some obvious dilemmas. How do you protect a respondent's anonymity? How do you define the potential audience? Even if you know to whom you sent the questionnaire, the respondents may forward it to others.

Web-based surveys are still in their early stages. Even so, the initial results are promising. For example, InterSurvey has created a pool of Internet respondents, initially selected by telephone, to serve as a diverse and representative sample. Using similar methods to locate 50,000 adult respondents in 33 nations, the National Geographic Society conducted an online survey that focused on migration and regional culture. Social scientists are closely monitoring these new approaches to gauge how they might revolutionize one type of research design (Bainbridge 1999; Morin 2000).

This new technology is exciting, but there is one basic limitation to the methodology: Internet surveying works only with those who have access to the Internet and are online. For some market researchers, such a limitation is acceptable. For example, if you were interested in the willingness of Internet users to order books or make travel reservations online, limiting the sample population to those who are already online makes sense. However, if you were surveying the general public about their plans to buy a computer in the coming year or their views on a particular candidate, your online research would need to be supplemented by more traditional sampling procedures, such as mailed questionnaires.

We have seen that researchers rely on a number of tools, from time-tested observational research and use of existing sources to the latest in computer technologies. The Social Policy section that follows will describe researchers' efforts to survey the general population about a controversial aspect of social behavior: human sexuality. This investigation was complicated by its potential social policy implications. Because in the real world, sociological research can have far-reaching consequences for public policy and public welfare, each of the following chapters in this book will close with a Social Policy section.

Studying Human Sexuality

The Issue

Reality TV shows often feature an attempt to create a relationship or even a marriage between two strangers. In a picturesque setting, an eligible bachelor or bachelorette interviews potential partners—all of them good-looking—and gradually eliminates those who seem less promising. The questions that are posed on camera can be explicit. "How many sexual partners have you had?" "How often would you be willing to have sex?"

The Kaiser Family Foundation conducts a study of sexual content on television every two years. The latest report, released in 2005, shows that more than two-thirds of all shows on TV include some sexual content, up from about half of all shows seven years earlier (see Figure 2-5, page 46). Media representations of sexual behavior are important because surveys of teens and young adults tell us that television is a top source of information and ideas about sex for them; it has more influence than schools, parents, or peers.

In this age of devastating sexually transmitted diseases, there is no time more important to increase our scientific understanding of human sexuality. As we will see, however, this is a difficult topic to research because of all the preconceptions, myths, and beliefs people bring to the subject of sexuality. How does one carry out scientific research on such a controversial and personal topic?

The Setting

Sociologists have little reliable national data on patterns of sexual behavior in the United States. Until recently, the only comprehensive study of sexual behavior was the famous two-volume Kinsey Report prepared in the 1940s (Kinsey et al. 1948, 1953). Although the Kinsey Report is still widely quoted, the volunteers interviewed for the report were not representative of the nation's adult population.

In part, we lack reliable data on patterns of sexual behavior because it is difficult for researchers to obtain accurate information about this sensitive subject. Moreover, until AIDS emerged in the 1980s, there was little scientific demand for data on sexual behavior, except for specific concerns such as contraception. Finally, even though the AIDS crisis has reached dramatic proportions (as will be discussed in the Social Policy section of Chapter 15), government funding for studies of sexual behavior is controversial. Because the General Social Survey concerns sexual attitudes rather than behavior, its funding has not been jeopardized.

Classroom Tip Discuss the purpose and value of Social Policy sections.
Contemporary Culture Have students cite and critically analyze the treatment of human sexuality on television and in popular music.
Classroom Tip Explain to students how innovative the Kinsey reports were at the time they were conducted and published.
Methods The General Social Survey is an example of survey research.

Policy Pointer Note the relevance of the American Sociological Association's *Code of Ethics*.
Web Resource Encourage students to try the crossword puzzle in the student center of the Online Learning Center (**www.mhhe.com/schaefer7**). Remind them that the crossword puzzle provides an enjoyable way to review important terms and concepts found in the chapter.

Percent of Television Shows That Contain Sexual Content

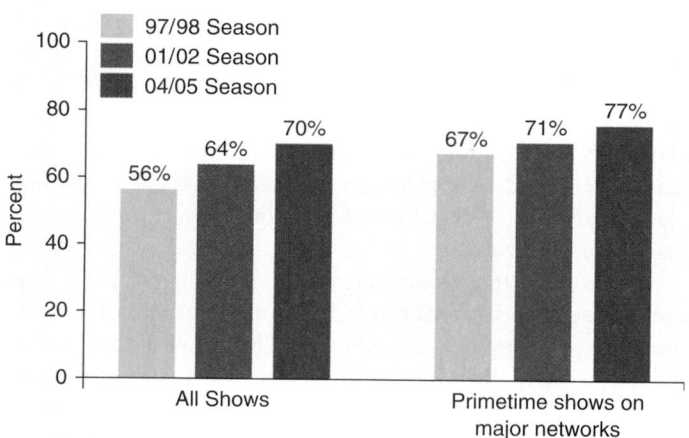

Source: Kaiser Family Foundation 2005:4.

Sociological Insights

The controversy surrounding research on human sexual behavior raises the issue of value neutrality (see page 43), which becomes especially delicate when one considers the relationship of sociology to the government. The federal government has become the major source of funding for sociological research. Yet Max Weber urged that sociology remain an autonomous discipline and not become unduly influenced by any one segment of society. According to Weber's ideal of value neutrality, sociologists must remain free to reveal information that is embarrassing to the government, or for that matter, supportive of government institutions.

Although the American Sociological Association's *Code of Ethics* requires sociologists to disclose all funding sources, it does not address the issue of whether sociologists who accept funding from a particular agency or corporation may also accept the agency's perspective on what needs to be studied. As we saw in our discussion of research funded by the Exxon Corporation (pages 42–43), this question is a knotty one. As the next section will show, applied sociological research on human sexuality has run into political barriers.

Policy Initiatives

In 1987 the National Institute of Child Health and Human Development sought proposals for a national survey of sexual behavior. Sociologists responded with various plans that a review panel of scientists approved for funding. However, in 1991, the U.S. Senate voted to forbid funding any survey on adult sexual practices. Two years earlier, a similar debate in Great Britain had led to the denial of government funding for a national sex survey (A. Johnson et al. 1994; Laumann et al. 1994a:36).

Despite the vote by the U.S. Senate, sociologists Edward Laumann, John Gagnon, Stuart Michaels, and Robert Michael developed the National Health and Social Life Survey (NHSLS) to

Policy Pointer Note the sometimes critical role of funding in determining which subjects are studied.
Let's Discuss What are the advantages and disadvantages of private funding for research?
Let's Discuss Why is government-supported sociological research an ethical issue?

better understand the sexual practices of adults in the United States. The researchers raised $1.6 million of *private* funding to make their study possible (Laumann et al. 1994a, 1994b).

The NHSLS researchers made great efforts to ensure privacy during the interviews, as well as confidentiality and security in maintaining data files. Perhaps because of this careful effort, the interviewers did not typically experience problems getting responses, even though they were asking people about their sexual behavior. All interviews were conducted in person, although a confidential form included questions about sensitive subjects such as family income and masturbation. The researchers used several techniques to test the accuracy of subjects' responses, such as asking redundant questions at different times and in different ways during the 90-minute interview. These careful procedures helped to establish the validity of the NHSLS findings.

The authors of the NHSLS believe that their research is important. They argue that using data from their survey allows us to more easily address public policy issues such as AIDS, sexual harassment, welfare reform, sex discrimination, abortion, teenage pregnancy, and family planning. Moreover, the research findings help to counter some "commonsense" notions. For instance, contrary to the popular beliefs that women regularly use abortion for birth control, and that poor teens are the most likely socioeconomic group to have abortions, researchers found that three-fourths of all abortions are the first for the woman, and that well-educated and affluent women are more likely to have abortions than poor teens (Sweet 2001).

Scholars in China, aware of the NHSLS, have begun to collaborate with sociologists in the United States on a similar study in China. The data are just now being analyzed, but responses thus far indicate dramatic differences in the sexual behavior of people in their 20s, compared to behavior at the same age by people who are now in their 50s. Younger-generation Chinese are more active sexually and have more partners than their parents did. Partly in response to these preliminary results, the Chinese Min-

{ Increasingly, researchers who study human sexual behavior are examining same-sex relationships. }

Gender In research on human sexuality, gender is often a key variable.
Classroom Tip See "Using Humor" (Class Discussion Topics).

istry of Health has sought U.S. assistance on HIV/AIDS prevention and research (Beech 2005; Braverman 2002).

Let's Discuss

1. Do you see any merit in the position of those who oppose government funding for research on sexual behavior? Explain your reasoning.

2. Exactly how could the results of research on human sexual behavior be used to control sexually transmitted diseases?

3. Compare the issue of value neutrality in government-funded research to the same issue in corporate-funded research. Are concerns about conflict of interest more or less serious in regard to government funding?

GettingINVOLVED

To get involved in the debate over research on human sexuality, visit this text's Online Learning Center, which offers links to relevant Web sites. Check out the Social Policy section on the Online Learning Center as well; it provides survey data on U.S. public opinion regarding this issue

www.mhhe.com/schaefer7

APPENDIX I   Using Statistics, Tables, and Graphs

In their effort to better understand social behavior, sociologists rely heavily on numbers and statistics. How large is the typical household today, compared to the typical household of 1980? If a community were to introduce drug education into its elementary schools, what would be the cost per pupil? Such questions, and many others, are most easily answered in numerical terms.

Using Statistics

The most common summary measures used by sociologists are percentages, means, modes, and medians. A *percentage* shows a portion of 100. Use of percentages allows us to compare groups of different sizes. For example, if we were comparing financial contributors to a town's Baptist and Roman Catholic churches, the absolute numbers of contributors in each group could be misleading if there were many more Baptists than Catholics in the town. By using percentages, we could obtain a more meaningful comparison, showing the proportion of persons in each group who contribute to churches.

The *mean,* or *average,* is a number calculated by adding a series of values and then dividing by the number of values. For example, to find the mean of the numbers 5, 19, and 27, we add them together (for a total of 51), divide by the number of values (3), and discover that the mean is 17.

The *mode* is the single most common value in a series of scores. Suppose we were looking at the following scores on a 10-point quiz:

10	7
10	7
9	7
9	6
8	5
8	

The mode—the most frequent score on the quiz—is 7. While the mode is easier to identify than other summary measures, it tells sociologists little about all the other values. Hence, you will find much less use of the mode in this book than of the mean and the median.

The *median* is the midpoint or number that divides a series of values into two groups of equal numbers of values. For the quiz just discussed, the median, or central value, is 8. The mean, or average, would be 86 (the sum of all scores) divided by 11 (the total number of scores), or 7.8.

In the United States, the median household income for the year 2004 was $43,389; it indicates that half of all households had

Table   Percentage of Respondents for or against Legalization of Marijuana

Age of Respondent	For	Against
18–24 years	31%	59%
25–39 years	44	56
40–54 years	42	58
55–64 years	38	72
65 and over	21	79

Source: General Social Survey in J. A. Davis et al. 2005.

Chapter 2

Percentage of Respondents Favoring the Legalization of Marijuana

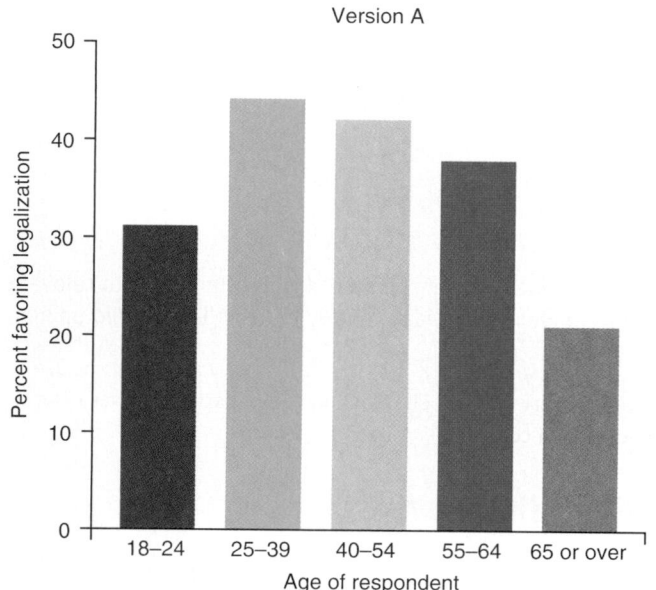

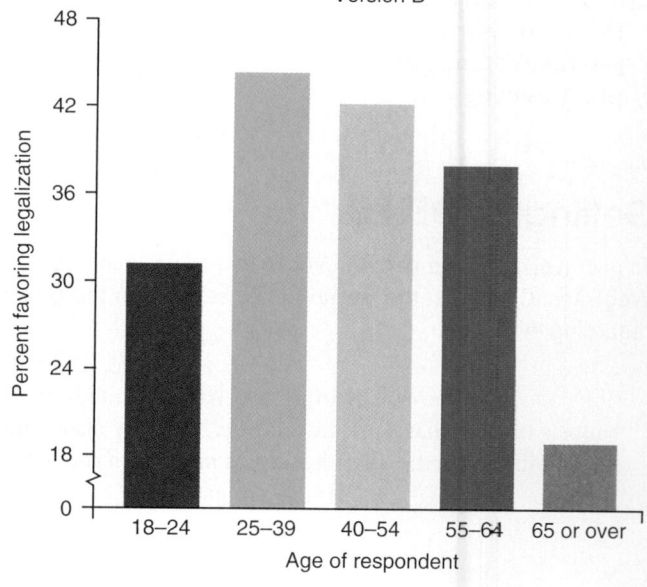

Source: General Social Survey in J.A. Davis et al. 2005.

incomes above $43,389, while half had lower incomes (DeNavas-Walt et al. 2005:31). In many respects, the median is the most characteristic value. While it may not reflect the full range of scores, it does approximate the typical value in a set of scores, and is not affected by extreme scores.

Some of these statistics may seem confusing at first. But think how difficult it is to comb an endless list of numbers to identify a pattern or central tendency. Percentages, means, modes, and medians are essential time-savers in sociological research and analysis.

Reading Tables and Graphs

Tables allow social scientists to display data and make it easier for them to develop conclusions. A *cross-tabulation* is a table that shows the relationship between two or more variables. During 2004, the National Opinion Research Center interviewed 873 people in the United States, ages 18 and over. Each respondent was asked: "Do you think the use of marijuana should be made legal or not?" With-

out some type of summary, there is no way that analysts could examine the hundreds of individual responses and reach firm conclusions. However, through the cross-tabulation presented in the Table on page 47, we can quickly see that older people are less likely to favor the legalization of marijuana than younger people.

Graphs, like tables, can be quite useful to sociologists. And illustrations are often easier for the general public to understand, whether they are in newspapers or in PowerPoint presentations. Still, as with all data, we need to be careful how they are presented. For example, the two bar graphs in Figure above present the same data concerning the legalization of marijuana as the table. Yet the differences in attitudes between the age groups seem much more striking in version B than in version A. Both figures are accurate, but because the vertical axis in B is based on a different scale, it appears that many fewer older respondents favored legalization, compared to the youngest respondents. In reality, about 2 in 10 older respondents favored legalization, compared to about 3 in 10 of the youngest respondents.

APPENDIX II   Writing a Research Report

Let's say you have decided to write a report on cohabitation (unmarried couples living together). How do you go about doing the necessary library research? Students must follow procedures similar to those used by sociologists in conducting original re-

search. First, you must define the problem that you wish to study—perhaps in this case, how much cohabitation occurs and what its impact is on later marital happiness. The next step is to review the literature, which generally requires library research.

Classroom Tip Point out to students that this appendix, "Writing a Research Report," should be helpful in many of their courses, though the main focus is on research reports for a sociology course.

Finding Information

The following steps will be helpful in finding information:

1. Check this textbook and other textbooks that you own. Don't forget to begin with the materials closest at hand, including the Web site associated with this textbook, **www.mhhe.com/ schaefer7.**

2. Use the library catalog. Computerized library systems now access not only the college library's collection but also books and magazines from other libraries, available through interlibrary loans. These systems allow you to search for books by author or title. You can use title searches to locate books by subject as well. For example, if you search the title base for the keyword *cohabitation,* you will learn where books with that word somewhere in the title are located in the library's book stacks. Near these books will be other works on cohabitation that may not happen to have that word in the title. You may also want to search other related keywords, such as *unmarried couples.*

3. Investigate using computerized periodical indexes if available in your library. *Sociological Abstracts* online covers most sociological writing since 1974. A recent search of just this one database found more than 1,258 documents having either *unmarried couples* or *cohabitation* as keywords. Some dealt with laws about cohabitation, while others focused on trends in other countries. If you limited your topic to same-sex couples, you would find 111 citations. Other electronic databases cover general-interest periodicals (*Time, Ms., National Review, Atlantic Monthly,* and so forth), reference materials, or newspapers. These electronic systems may be connected to a printer, allowing you to produce your own printout complete with bibliographic information and sometimes even complete copies of articles.

4. Examine government documents. The United States government, states and cities, and the United Nations publish information on virtually every subject of interest to social science researchers. Publications of the Census Bureau, for example, include tables showing the number of unmarried couples living together and some social characteristics of those households. Many university libraries have access to a wide range of government reports. Consult the librarian for assistance in locating such materials.

5. Use newspapers. Major newspapers publish indexes annually or even weekly that are useful in locating information about specific events or issues. Academic Universe News is an electronic index to U.S. and international newspapers.

6. Ask people, organizations, and agencies concerned with the topic for information and assistance. Be as specific as possible in making requests. You might receive very different information on the issue of cohabitation from talking with marriage counselors and with clergy from different religions.

7. If you run into difficulties, consult the instructor, teaching assistant, or reference librarian at your college library.

A word of caution: Be extremely careful in using the Internet to do research. Much of the information on the Internet is simply incorrect—even if it looks authoritative, is accompanied by impressive graphics, or has been widely circulated. Unlike the information in a library, which must be screened by a highly qualified librarian, "information" on the Internet can be created and posted by anyone with a computer. Check the sources for the information and note the Web page sponsor. Is the author qualified to write on the subject? Is the author even identified? Is the Web page sponsor likely to be biased? Whenever possible, try to confirm what you have read on the Internet through a well-known, reputable source or organization. If the accuracy of the information could be affected by how old it is, check the date on which the page or article was created or updated. Used intelligently, the Internet is a wonderful tool that offers students access to many of the reliable print sources noted earlier, including government documents and newspaper archives extending back over a century.

Writing the Report

Once you have completed all your research, you can begin writing the report. Here are a few tips:

- Be sure the topic you have chosen is not too broad. You must be able to cover it adequately in a reasonable amount of time and a reasonable number of pages.

- Develop an outline for your report. You should have an introduction and a conclusion that relate to each other—and the discussion should proceed logically throughout the paper. Use headings within the paper if they will improve clarity and organization.

- Do not leave all the writing until the last minute. It is best to write a rough draft, let it sit for a few days, and then take a fresh look before beginning revisions.

- If possible, read your paper aloud. Doing so may be helpful in locating sections or phrases that don't make sense.

Remember that you *must* cite all information you have obtained from other sources, including the Internet. If you use an author's exact words, it is essential that you place them in quotation marks. Even if you reworked someone else's ideas, you must indicate the source of those ideas.

Some professors may require that students use footnotes in research reports. Others will allow students to employ the form of referencing used in this textbook, which follows the format of the American Sociological Association (ASA). If you see "(Merton 1968:27)" listed after a statement or paragraph, it means that the material has been quoted from page 27 of a work published by Merton in 1968 and listed in the reference section at the back of this textbook. (For further guidance, consult the "Preparation checklist for ASA manuscripts," under "Publications," at the ASA Web site www.asanet.org.)

Summary

Sociologists are committed to the use of the *scientific method* in their research efforts. In this chapter we examined the basic principles of the scientific method and studied various techniques used by sociologists in conducting research.

1. There are five basic steps in the *scientific method:* defining the problem, reviewing the literature, formulating the hypothesis, collecting and analyzing the data, and developing the conclusion.

2. Whenever researchers wish to study abstract concepts, such as intelligence or prejudice, they must develop workable *operational definitions.*

3. A *hypothesis* states a possible relationship between two or more variables.

4. By using a *sample,* sociologists avoid having to test everyone in a population.

5. According to the scientific method, research results must possess both *validity* and *reliability.*

6. An important part of scientific research is devising a plan for collecting data, called a *research design.* Sociologists use four major research designs: surveys, observation, experiments, and existing sources.

7. The two principal forms of *survey* research are the *interview* and the *questionnaire.*

8. *Observation* allows sociologists to study certain behaviors and communities that cannot be investigated through other research methods.

9. When sociologists wish to study a cause-and-effect relationship, they may conduct an *experiment.*

10. Sociologists also make use of existing sources in *secondary analysis* and *content analysis.*

11. The *Code of Ethics* of the American Sociological Association calls for objectivity and integrity in research, confidentiality, and disclosure of all sources of financial support.

12. Max Weber urged sociologists to practice *value neutrality* in their research by ensuring that their personal feelings do not influence their interpretation of data.

13. Technology plays an important role in sociological research, whether it be a computer database or information from the Internet.

14. Despite failure to obtain government funding, researchers developed the National Health and Social Life Survey (NHSLS) to better understand the sexual practices of adults in the United States.

Critical Thinking Questions

1. Suppose your sociology instructor has asked you to do a study of homelessness. Which research technique (survey, observation, experiment, or existing sources) would you find most useful? How would you use that technique to complete your assignment?

2. How can a sociologist genuinely maintain value neutrality while studying a group that he or she finds repugnant (for example, a

White supremacist organization, a satanic cult, or a group of convicted rapists)?

3. New technologies have benefited sociological research by facilitating statistical analysis and encouraging communication among scholars. Can you think of any potential drawbacks these new technologies might have for sociological investigation?

Key Terms

Causal logic The relationship between a condition or variable and a particular consequence, with one event leading to the other. (page 32)

Code of ethics The standards of acceptable behavior developed by and for members of a profession. (40)

Content analysis The systematic coding and objective recording of data, guided by some rationale. (39)

Control group The subjects in an experiment who are not introduced to the independent variable by the researcher. (38)

Control variable A factor that is held constant to test the relative impact of an independent variable. (34)

Correlation A relationship between two variables in which a change in one coincides with a change in the other. (32)

Cross-tabulation A table that shows the relationship between two or more variables. (48)

Dependent variable The variable in a causal relationship that is subject to the influence of another variable. (32)

Ethnography The study of an entire social setting through extended systematic observation. (37)

Experiment An artificially created situation that allows a researcher to manipulate variables. (37)

Experimental group The subjects in an experiment who are exposed to an independent variable introduced by a researcher. (38)

Hawthorne effect The unintended influence that observers of experiments can have on their subjects. (38)

Hypothesis A speculative statement about the relationship between two or more variables. (32)

Independent variable The variable in a causal relationship that causes or influences a change in a second variable. (32)

Interview A face-to-face or telephone questioning of a respondent to obtain desired information. (35)

Mean A number calculated by adding a series of values and then dividing by the number of values. (47)

Median The midpoint or number that divides a series of values into two groups of equal numbers of values. (47)

Mode The single most common value in a series of scores. (47)

Observation A research technique in which an investigator collects information through direct participation and/or by closely watching a group or community. (37)

Operational definition An explanation of an abstract concept that is specific enough to allow a researcher to assess the concept. (31)

Percentage A portion of 100. (47)

Qualitative research Research that relies on what is seen in field or naturalistic settings more than on statistical data. (35)

Quantitative research Research that collects and reports data primarily in numerical form. (35)

Questionnaire A printed or written form used to obtain information from a respondent. (35)

Random sample A sample for which every member of an entire population has the same chance of being selected. (33)

Reliability The extent to which a measure produces consistent results. (33)

Research design A detailed plan or method for obtaining data scientifically. (35)

Sample A selection from a larger population that is statistically representative of that population. (33)

Scientific method A systematic, organized series of steps that ensures maximum objectivity and consistency in researching a problem. (30)

Secondary analysis A variety of research techniques that make use of previously collected and publicly accessible information and data. (38)

Survey A study, generally in the form of an interview or questionnaire, that provides researchers with information about how people think and act. (35)

Validity The degree to which a measure or scale truly reflects the phenomenon under study. (33)

Value neutrality Max Weber's term for objectivity of sociologists in the interpretation of data. (43)

Variable A measurable trait or characteristic that is subject to change under different conditions. (32)

Self-Quiz

Read each question carefully and then select the best answer.

1. The first step in any sociological research project is to
   a. collect data.
   b. define the problem.
   c. review previous research.
   d. formulate a hypothesis.

2. An explanation of an abstract concept that is specific enough to allow a researcher to measure the concept is a(n)
   a. hypothesis.
   b. correlation.
   c. operational definition.
   d. variable.

3. The variable hypothesized to cause or influence another is called
   a. the dependent variable.
   b. the hypothetical variable.
   c. the correlation variable.
   d. the independent variable.

4. A correlation exists when
   a. one variable causes something to occur in another variable.
   b. two or more variables are causally related.
   c. a change in one variable coincides with a change in another variable.
   d. a negative relationship exists between two variables.

5. Through which type of research technique does a sociologist ensure that data are statistically representative of the population being studied?
   a. sampling
   b. experiments
   c. validity
   d. control variables

6. In order to obtain a random sample, a researcher might
   a. administer a questionnaire to every fifth woman who enters a business office.
   b. examine the attitudes of residents of a city by interviewing every 20th name in the city's telephone book.
   c. study the attitudes of registered Democratic voters by choosing every 10th name found on a city's list of registered Democrats.
   d. do all of the above.

7. A researcher can obtain a higher response rate by using which type of survey?
   a. an interview
   b. a questionnaire
   c. representative samples
   d. observation techniques

8. In the 1930s, William F. Whyte moved into a low-income Italian neighborhood in Boston. For nearly four years, he was a member of the social circle of "corner boys" that he describes in *Street Corner Society*. His goal was to gain greater insight into the community established by these men. What type of research technique did Whyte use?
   a. experiment
   b. survey
   c. secondary analysis
   d. participant observation

9. When sociologists want to study a possible cause-and-effect relationship, they may engage in what kind of research technique?
   a. ethnography
   b. survey research
   c. secondary analysis
   d. experimental research

10. Émile Durkheim's statistical analysis of suicide was an example of what kind of research technique?

   a. ethnography
   b. obervation research
   c. secondary analysis
   d. experimental research

11. Unlike the typical citizen, the sociologist has a commitment to the use of the _____ method in studying society.

12. A(n) _____ is a speculative statement about the relationship between two or more factors known as variables.

13. _____ refers to the degree to which a measure or scale truly reflects the phenomenon under study.

14. In order to obtain data scientifically, researchers need to select a research _____.

15. If scientists were testing a new type of toothpaste in an experimental setting, they would administer the toothpaste to a(n) _____ group, but not to a(n) _____ group.

16. The term _____ _____ refers to the unintended influence that observers of experiments can have on their subjects.

17. Using census data in a way unintended by its initial collectors would be an example of _____ _____.

18. Using content analysis, _____ _____ conducted a pioneering exploration of how advertisements in 1979 portrayed women as being inferior to men.

19. The American Sociological Association's *Code of* _____ requires sociologists to maintain objectivity and integrity and to preserve the confidentiality of their subjects.

20. As part of their commitment to _____ neutrality, investigators have an ethical obligation to accept research findings even when the data run counter to their own personal views or widely accepted beliefs.

Answers

1 (b); 2 (c); 3 (d); 4 (c); 5 (a); 6 (c); 7 (a); 8 (d); 9 (d); 10 (c) 11 scientific; 12 hypothesis; 13 Validity; 14 design; 15 experimental, control; 16 Hawthorne effect; 17 secondary analysis; 18 Erving Goffman; 19 Ethics; 20 value

TECHNOLOGY RESOURCES

Online Learning Center

1. When you visit the student center of the Online Learning Center (**www.mhhe.com/schaefer7**), one of the Interactive Activities for this chapter gives you an opportunity to participate in a brief survey. After you submit your responses, you'll be able to see how other students using this book and participating in the survey answered the same questions.

2. Oral history is a type of qualitative research that is often used in ethnographic studies. Go to the Web site of the Oral History Society (**www.oralhistory.org.uk**) and read the section that guides you through the process of recording an oral history.

3. The Substance Abuse and Mental Health Services Administration (SAMHSA) conducts a national household survey on drug abuse. To read about ecstasy use among adolescents and young adults, link to **http://oas.samhsa.gov/2k3/ecstasy/ecstasy.htm.**

Note: While all the URLs listed were current as of the printing of this book, these sites often change. Please check our Web site (www.mhhe.com/schaefer7) for updates, hyperlinks, and exercises related to these sites.

Reel Society Video Clips

Reel Society video clips, which appear on this book's Web site, can be used to spark discussion about the following topics from this chapter:
   • The Scientific Method
   • Ethics of Research

Culture

inside

Culture and Society

Development of Culture around
the World

Elements of Culture

Culture and the Dominant Ideology

Cultural Variation

Social Policy and Culture:
Bilingualism

Boxes

Sociology in the Global Community:
Life in the Global Village

Sociology in the Global Community:
Cultural Survival in Brazil

Sociology on Campus: A Culture of
Cheating?

While this Hong Kong pedestrian appears not to notice the Nike billboard behind him, featuring NBA star LeBron James wearing the Air Zoom sneaker, the Chinese people certainly did notice. The Oregon-based Nike corporation was forced to pull its "Chamber of Fear" promotion, based on a Bruce Lee movie, after an outraged public objected to the image of a U.S. athlete defeating a kung fu master. In the global marketplace, cultural differences can undermine even the most elaborate promotional campaign.

The United States is the most consumer-oriented society in the world. People work longer hours than in any other industrialized country. Savings rates are lower. Consumer credit has exploded, and roughly a million and a half households declare bankruptcy every year. There are more than 46,000 shopping centers in the country, a nearly two-thirds increase since 1986. Despite fewer people per household, the size of houses continues to expand rapidly, with new construction featuring walk-in closets and three- and four-car garages to store record quantities of stuff. According to my estimates, the average adult acquires forty-eight new pieces of apparel a year. (She has also been discarding clothes at record rates, in comparison to historical precedents.) Americans own more television sets than inhabitants of any other country—nearly one set per person. Observers blame TV for plummeting levels of civic engagement, the dearth of community, and the decline of everyday socializing. Heavy viewing has also resulted in historically unprecedented exposure to commercials. And ads have proliferated far beyond the television screen to virtually every social institution and type of public space, from museums and zoos, to college campuses and elementary school classrooms, restaurant bathrooms and menus, at the airport, even in the sky.

The architects of this culture—the companies that make, market, and advertise consumer products—have now set their sights on children. Although children have long participated in the consumer marketplace, until recently they were bit players, purchasers of cheap goods. They attracted little of the industry's talent and resources and were approached primarily through their mothers. That has changed. Kids and teens are now the epicenter of American consumer culture. They command the attention, creativity, and dollars of advertisers. Their tastes drive market trends. Their opinions shape brand strategies. Yet few adults recognize the magnitude of this shift and its consequences for the futures of our children and of our culture. . . .

Plenty of evidence now confirms how far-reaching this process of commercialization has become. Contemporary American tweens and teens have emerged as the most brand-oriented, consumer-involved, and materialistic generations in history. And they top the list globally. A survey of youth from seventy cities in more than fifteen countries finds that 75 percent of U.S. tweens want to be rich, a higher percentage than anywhere else in the world except India, where the results were identical. Sixty-one percent want to be famous. More children here than anywhere else believe that their clothes and brands describe who they are and define their social status. American kids display more brand affinity than their counterparts anywhere else in the world; indeed, experts describe them as increasingly "bonded to brands.". . .

(Schor 2004:9, 13, 25) Additional information about this excerpt can be found on the Online Learning Center at www.mhhe.com/schaefer7. ●

> *Contemporary American tweens and teens have emerged as the most brand-oriented, consumer-involved, and materialistic generations in history.*

In this excerpt from the book *Born to Buy: The Commercialized Child and the New Consumer Culture,* sociologist Juliet B. Schor describes how young people in the United States grow up learning to consume. Through the media, young children learn about animals, food, and community, absorbing their culture's values in the process. But they are also exposed to commercial advertising. At a formative age, they experience pressure to acquire things they may not need—things their parents may not really be able to afford. Hence the image of a toddler peeking out of a shopping bag.

Schor used several research methods to develop her book. She did participant observation in the advertising industry, attending focus groups, shadowing market researchers, and interviewing those who create children's advertising. She also surveyed fifth and sixth graders to measure their involvement with the consumer culture, and she interviewed some of their parents. To supplement her original research, Schor analyzed data from existing sources published by government and business agencies.

More and more, the consumer goods and brand loyalty that drive our culture are spreading to other societies. In our rapidly globalizing world, people of other cultures now recognize and covet international brands such as Sony and Nike. Someday, the children of Russia, Singapore, and South Africa may be just as materialistic as American children. What are the implications of this trend toward globalization? In what other ways do other cultures resemble our own, and in what ways do they differ? How do our own lifestyles change as we encounter other cultures?

In this chapter we will study the development of culture around the world, including the cultural effects of the worldwide trend toward globalization. We will see just how basic the study of culture is to sociology. We will examine the meaning of culture and society, as well as the development of culture from its roots in the prehistoric human experience to the technological advances of today. We will define and explore the major aspects of culture, including language, norms, sanctions, and values. We will see how cultures develop a dominant ideology, and how functionalist and conflict theorists view culture. Our discussion will focus both on general cultural practices found in all societies and on the wide variations that can distinguish one society from another. In the Social Policy section we will look at the conflicts in cultural values that underlie current debates over bilingualism. ●

Culture and Society

Culture is the totality of learned, socially transmitted customs, knowledge, material objects, and behavior. It includes the ideas, values, and artifacts (for example, DVDs, comic books, and birth control devices) of groups of people. Patriotic attachment to the flag of the United States is an aspect of culture, as is a national passion for the tango in Argentina.

Sometimes people refer to a particular person as "very cultured" or to a city as having "lots of culture." That use of the term *culture* is different from our use in this textbook. In sociological terms, *culture* does not refer solely to the fine arts and refined intellectual taste. It consists of *all* objects and ideas within a society, including slang words, ice cream cones, and rock music. Sociologists consider both a portrait by Rembrandt and the work of graffiti spray painters to be aspects of culture. A tribe that cultivates soil by hand has just as much culture as a people that relies on computer-operated machinery. Each people has a distinctive culture with its own characteristic ways of gathering and preparing food, constructing homes, structuring the family, and promoting standards of right and wrong.

The fact that you share a similar culture with others helps to define the group or society to which you belong. A fairly large number of people are said to constitute a *society* when they live in the same territory, are relatively independent of people outside their area, and participate in a common culture. Metropolitan Los Angeles is more populous than at least 150 nations, yet sociologists do not consider it a society in its own right. Rather, they see it as part of—and dependent on—the larger society of the United States.

A society is the largest form of human group. It consists of people who share a common heritage and culture. Members of the society learn this culture and transmit it from one generation to the next. They even preserve their distinctive culture through literature, art, video recordings, and other means of expression. If it were not for the social transmission of culture, each generation would have to reinvent television, not to mention the wheel.

Having a common culture also simplifies many day-to-day interactions. For example, when you buy an airline ticket, you know you don't have to bring along hundreds of dollars in cash. You can pay with a credit card. When you are part of a society, you take for granted many small (as well as more important) cultural patterns. You assume that theaters will provide seats for the audience, that physicians will not disclose confidential information, and that parents will be careful when crossing the street with young children. All these assumptions reflect basic values, beliefs, and customs of the culture of the United States.

Language is a critical element of culture that sets humans apart from other species. Members of a society generally share a common language, which facilitates day-to-day exchanges with others. When you ask a hardware store clerk for a flashlight, you

Classroom Tip See "Stimulating Classroom Discussions about *Born to Buy*" (Class Discussion Topics).

Student Alert Note that the use of the term *culture* is much broader in sociology than in everyday speech.

Classroom Tip Do we live in a society *and* a culture? Have students discuss the difference between these two concepts.

Let's Discuss Who teaches a society's culture? Parents, teachers, the media, religious and government leaders, peers, and others?

Are You What You Eat?

The foods people eat, along with the customs they observe in preparing and consuming their meals, say a great deal about their culture. In some cultures, such as that of Papua New Guinea, roast pork is a delicacy reserved for feasts; in others it is forbidden food. In U.S. culture, genetically modified food is accepted without much question, but in Europe it is banned. Because Swedish people put great value on natural, organic foods, 99 percent of mothers in Sweden breast-feed their infants—a rate much higher than that in the United States.

In India, people generally dine while sitting on the floor, as shown here, or on very low stools. Instead of utensils such as forks or chopsticks, they eat with the fingers of the right hand. While Indians have accepted some aspects of U.S.-style fast-food culture, they go to McDonalds for McCurry and McVeggie sandwiches—not for hamburgers, a food that is prohibited by the Hindu religion.

In some cultures, such as France, fine cuisine is a cultural institution. The French prefer fresh local produce lovingly prepared, consumed slowly along with good conversation and a bottle of wine. To the French and to gourmets around the world, great chefs are celebrities.

Given their reverence for food, the French would be most unlikely to participate in a contest designed to see who can gobble down the most hot dogs. In the United States and Japan, these public events are quite popular. But though the Japanese admire American culture, they stop short at copying the American habit of eating fast food on the street while rushing from one place to another. The Japanese will purchase food from a street vendor, but they will not walk around while eating it, because doing so would show disrespect for the preparer.

{India}

56

{Coney Island, New York}

{Paris}

don't need to draw a picture of the instrument. You share the same cultural term for a small, portable battery-operated light. However, if you were in England and needed this item, you would have to ask for an "electric torch." Of course, even within the same society, a term can have a number of different meanings. In the United States, *pot* signifies both a container that is used for cooking and an intoxicating drug.

Development of Culture around the World

We've come a long way from our prehistoric heritage. The human species has produced such achievements as the ragtime compositions of Scott Joplin, the novels of V. S. Naipaul, the paintings of Jan Vermeer, and the films of Akira Kurosawa. As we begin a new millennium, we can transmit an entire book around the world via the Internet, clone cells, and prolong lives through organ transplants. We can peer into the outermost reaches of the universe or analyze our innermost feelings. In all these ways, we are remarkably different from other species of the animal kingdom.

Cultural Universals

All societies have developed certain common practices and beliefs, known as *cultural universals.* Many cultural universals are, in fact, adaptations to meet essential human needs, such as the need for food, shelter, and clothing. Anthropologist George Murdock (1945:124) compiled a list of cultural universals, including athletic sports, cooking, funeral ceremonies, medicine, marriage, and sexual restrictions.

The cultural practices Murdock listed may be universal, but the manner in which they are expressed varies from culture to culture. For example, one society may let its members choose their own marriage partners; another may encourage marriages arranged by the parents.

Not only does the expression of cultural universals vary from one society to another; within a society, it may also change dramatically over time. Each generation, and each year for that matter, most human cultures change and expand through the processes of innovation and diffusion.

Innovation

The process of introducing a new idea or object to a culture is known as *innovation.* Innovation interests sociologists because of the social consequences of introducing something new. There are two forms of innovation: discovery and invention. *Discovery* involves making known or sharing the existence of an aspect of reality. The finding of the DNA molecule and the identification of a new moon of Saturn are both acts of discovery. A significant factor in the process of discovery is the sharing of newfound knowledge with others. By contrast, an *invention* results when existing cultural items are combined into a form that did not exist before. The bow and arrow, the automobile, and the television are all examples of inventions, as are Protestantism and democracy.

Globalization, Diffusion, and Technology

The familiar green Starbucks logo beckons you into a comfortable coffee shop, where you can order decaf latte and a cinnamon ring. What's unusual about that? This Starbucks happens to be located in the heart of Beijing's Forbidden City, just outside the Palace of Heavenly Purity, former residence of Chinese emperors. In 2000 it was one of 25 Starbucks stores in China; four years later there were more than 90. The success of Starbucks in a country in which coffee drinking is still a novelty (most Chinese are tea drinkers) has been striking (*China Daily* 2004).

The emergence of Starbucks in China illustrates the rapidly escalating trend of globalization, introduced in Chapter 1. It affects not only coffee consumption patterns but the international trade in coffee beans, which are harvested mainly in developing countries. Our consumption-oriented culture, described in the opening to this chapter, supports a retail price of two to three dollars for a single cup of premium coffee. At the same time, the

Customers enjoy a cup of premium coffee at a Starbucks franchise in China. Through the process of diffusion, the Chinese, traditionally tea drinkers, have begun to appreciate a beverage associated with Western cultures.

sociologyIN *the Global Community*

3-1 Life in the Global Village

Imagine a "borderless world" in which culture, trade, commerce, money, and even people move freely from one place to another. Popular culture is widely shared, whether it be Japanese sushi or U.S. running shoes, and the English speaker who answers questions over the telephone about your credit card account is as likely to be in India or Ireland as in the United States. In this world, even the sovereignty of nations is at risk, challenged by political movements and ideologies that span nations.

There is no need to imagine this world, for we are already living in the age of globalization. African tribal youngsters wear Simpsons T-shirts; Thai teens dance to techno music; American children collect Hello Kitty items. Ethnic accessories have become a fashion statement in the United States, and Asian martial arts have swept the world.

What caused this great wave of cultural diffusion? First, sociologists take note of advances in communications technology. Satellite TV, cell phones, the Internet, and the like allow information to flow freely across the world, linking global markets. In 2006, this process reached the point where consumers could surf the Internet on their wireless cell phones, shopping online at Amazon.com, eBay, and other commercial Web sites from cars, airports, and cafeterias. Second, corporations in the industrial nations have become multinational, with both factories and markets in developing countries. Business leaders welcome the opportunity to sell consumer goods in populous countries such as China. Third, these

multinational firms have cooperated with global financial institutions, organizations, and governments to promote free trade—unrestricted or lightly restricted commerce across national borders.

Globalization is not universally welcomed. Many critics see the dominance of "businesses without borders" as benefiting the rich, particularly the very wealthy in industrial countries, at the expense of the poor in less developed nations. They consider globalization to be a successor to the imperialism and colonialism that oppressed Third World nations for centuries.

Another criticism of globalization comes from people who feel overwhelmed by global

> *Even James Bond movies and Britney Spears may be seen as threats to native cultures.*

culture. Embedded in the concept of globalization is the notion of the cultural domination of developing nations by more affluent nations. Simply put, people lose their traditional values and begin to identify with the culture of dominant nations. They may discard or neglect their native language and dress as they attempt to copy the icons of mass-market entertainment and fashion. Even James Bond movies and Britney Spears may be seen as threats to native cultures, if they dominate the media at the expense of local art forms. As Sembene Ous-

mane, one of Africa's most prominent writers and filmmakers, noted, "[Today] we are more familiar with European fairy tales than with our own traditional stories" (World Development Forum 1990:4).

Globalization has its positive side, too. Many developing nations are taking their place in the world of commerce and bringing in much needed income. The communications revolution helps people to stay connected and gives them access to knowledge that can improve living standards and even save lives. For example, people suffering from illnesses are now accessing treatment programs that were developed outside their own nation's medical establishment. The key seems to be finding a balance between the old ways and the new—becoming modernized without leaving meaningful cultural traditions behind.

Let's Discuss

1. How are you affected by globalization? Which aspects of globalization do you find advantageous and which objectionable?
2. How would you feel if the customs and traditions you grew up with were replaced by the culture or values of another country? How might you try to protect your culture?

Sources: Dodds 2000; Giddens 1991; Hirst and Thompson 1996; Ritzer 2004b; Sernau 2001; Tedeschi 2006.

---

price of coffee beans on the world market has fallen so low that millions of Third World farmers can barely eke out a living. Worldwide, the growing demand for coffee, tea, chocolate, fruit, and natural resources is straining the environment, as poor farmers in developing countries clear more and more forestland to enlarge their fields.

While people in Asia are beginning to drink coffee, people in North America are discovering sushi. Some have become familiar with the *bento box,* a small lunchbox that is often used to serve sushi. More and more cultural expressions and practices are crossing national borders and having an effect on the traditions and customs of the societies exposed to them. Sociologists use the term **diffusion** to refer to the process by which a cultural

item spreads from group to group or society to society. Diffusion can occur through a variety of means, among them exploration, military conquest, missionary work, and the influence of the mass media, tourism, and the Internet (see Box 3-1).

Sociologist George Ritzer coined the term *McDonaldization of society* to describe how the principles of fast-food restaurants developed in the United States have come to dominate more and more sectors of societies throughout the world (see Chapter 5). For example, hair salons and medical clinics now take walk-in appointments. In Hong Kong, sex selection clinics offer a menu of items, from fertility enhancement to methods of increasing the likelihood of having a child of the desired sex. Religious groups—from evangelical preachers on local stations or Web

Chapter 3

sites to priests at the Vatican Television Center—use marketing techniques similar to those that are used to sell Happy Meals.

McDonaldization is associated with the melding of cultures, through which we see more and more similarities in cultural expression. In Japan, for example, African entrepreneurs have found a thriving market for hip-hop fashions popularized by teens in the United States. In Austria, the McDonald's organization itself has drawn on the Austrians' love of coffee, cake, and conversation to create the McCafe, a new part of its fast-food chain. Many critical observers believe that McDonaldization and globalization serve to dilute the distinctive aspects of a society's culture (Alfino et al. 1998; Ritzer 2002, 2004a).

Technology in its many forms has increased the speed of cultural diffusion and broadened the distribution of cultural elements. Sociologist Gerhard Lenski has defined **technology** as "cultural information about how to use the material resources of the environment to satisfy human needs and desires" (Nolan and Lenski 2006:37). Today's technological developments no longer await publication in journals with limited circulation. Press conferences, often carried simultaneously on the Internet, trumpet the new developments.

Technology not only accelerates the diffusion of scientific innovations but also transmits culture. The English language and North American culture dominate the Internet and World Wide Web. Such control, or at least dominance, of technology influences the direction of diffusion of culture. Web sites cover even the most superficial aspects of U.S. culture but offer little information about the pressing issues faced by citizens of other nations. People all over the world find it easier to visit electronic chat rooms about the latest reality TV shows than to learn about their own governments' policies on day care or infant nutrition.

Sociologist William F. Ogburn (1922) made a useful distinction between the elements of material and nonmaterial culture. **Material culture** refers to the physical or technological aspects {pp.4–5} of our daily lives, including food, houses, factories, and raw materials. **Nonmaterial culture** refers to ways of using material objects and to customs, beliefs, philosophies, governments, and patterns of communication. Generally, the nonmaterial culture is more resistant to change than the material culture. Consequently, Ogburn introduced the term **culture lag** to refer to the period of maladjustment when the nonmaterial culture is still struggling to adapt to new material conditions. For example, the ethics of using the Internet, particularly issues concerning privacy and censorship, have not yet caught up with the explosion in Internet use and technology.

Resistance to technological change can lead not only to culture lag, but to some very real questions of cultural survival (see Box 3-2).

Use Your Sociological Imagination
www.mhhe.com/schaefer7

If you grew up in your parents' generation—without computers, e-mail, the Internet, pagers, and cell phones—how would your daily life differ from the one you lead today?

Key Persons Gerhard Lenski, William Ogburn
Let's Discuss Is the United States resistant to the "invasion" of cultural characteristics from other societies?
Global View/Theory The Internet and television enter homes throughout the world, and both are dominated by the English language. Examine from a conflict perspective.

Biological Bases of Culture

While sociology emphasizes diversity and change in the expression of culture, another school of thought, sociobiology, stresses the universal aspects of culture. **Sociobiology** is the systematic study of how biology affects human social behavior. Sociobiologists assert that many of the cultural traits humans display, such as the almost universal expectation that women will be nurturers and men will be providers, are not learned but are rooted in our genetic makeup.

Sociobiology is founded on the naturalist Charles Darwin's (1859) theory of evolution. In traveling the world, Darwin had noted small variations in species—in the shape of a bird's beak, for example—from one location to another. He theorized that over hundreds of generations, random variations in genetic makeup had helped certain members of a species to survive in a particular environment. A bird with a differently shaped beak might have been better at gathering seeds than other birds, for instance. In reproducing, these lucky individuals had passed on their advantageous genes to succeeding generations. Eventually, given their advantage in survival, individuals with the variation began to outnumber other members of the species. The species was slowly adapting to its environment. Darwin called this process of adaptation to the environment through random genetic variation *natural selection.*

Sociobiologists apply Darwin's principle of natural selection to the study of social behavior. They assume that particular forms of behavior become genetically linked to a species if they contribute to its fitness to survive (van den Berghe 1978). In its extreme form, sociobiology suggests that *all* behavior is the result of genetic or biological factors and that social interactions play no role in shaping people's conduct.

Sociobiologists do not seek to describe individual behavior on the level of "Why is Fred more aggressive than Jim?" Rather, they focus on how human nature is affected by the genetic composition of a *group* of people who share certain characteristics (such as men or women, or members of isolated tribal bands). In general, sociobiologists have stressed the basic genetic heritage that *all* humans share, and have shown little interest in speculating about alleged differences between racial groups or nationalities (E. Wilson 1975, 1978).

Some researchers insist that intellectual interest in sociobiology will only deflect serious study of the more significant influence on human behavior, the social environment. Yet Lois Wladis Hoffman (1985), in her presidential address to the Society for the Psychological Study of Social Issues, argued that sociobiology poses a valuable challenge to social scientists to better document their own research. Interactionists, for example, could show how social behavior is not programmed by human biology, but instead adjusts continually to the attitudes and responses of others.

Certainly most social scientists would agree that there is a biological basis for social behavior. But there is less support for the extreme positions taken by certain advocates of sociobiology. Like interactionists, conflict theorists and functionalists believe that people's behavior rather than their genetic structure defines social

Classroom Tip See "Biological Influences on Human Behavior" (Additional Lecture Ideas).
Theory Note the conflict theorists' concerns about sociobiology.

3-2 Cultural Survival in Brazil

When the first Portuguese ships landed on the coast of what we now know as Brazil, more than 2 million people inhabited the vast, mineral-rich land. They lived in small, isolated settlements, spoke a variety of languages, and embraced many different cultural traditions.

Today, over five centuries later, Brazil's population has grown to more than 180 million, only about 500,000 of whom are indigenous peoples descended from the original inhabitants. Over 200 different indigenous groups have survived, living a life closely tied to the land and the rivers, just as their ancestors did. But over the last two generations, their numbers have dwindled as booms in mining, logging, oil drilling, and agriculture have encroached on their land and their settlements.

Many indigenous groups were once nomads, moving around from one hunting or fishing ground to another. Now they are hemmed in on the reservations the government confined them to, surrounded by huge farms or ranches whose owners deny their right to live off the land. State officials may insist that laws restrict the development of indigenous lands, but indigenous peoples tell a different story. In

Mato Grosso, a heavily forested state near the Amazon River, loggers have been clear-cutting the land at a rate that alarms the Bororo, an indigenous group that has lived in the area for centuries. According to one elder, the Bororo are now confined to six small reservations of about 500 square miles—much less than the area officially granted them in the 19th century.

> In Mato Grosso, a heavily forested state near the Amazon River, loggers have been clear-cutting the land at a rate that alarms the Bororo.

Indigenous tribes are no match for powerful agribusiness interests, one of whose leaders is also governor of Mato Grosso. Blairo Maggi, head of the largest soybean producer in the world, has publicly trivialized the consequences of the massive deforestation occurring in Mato Grosso. Though Maggi recently said he would propose a three-year morato-

rium on development, opponents are skeptical that he will follow through on the promise.

Meanwhile, indigenous groups like the Bororo struggle to maintain their culture in the face of dwindling resources. Though the tribe still observes the traditional initiation rites for adolescent boys, members are finding it difficult to continue their hunting and fishing rituals, given the scarcity of fish and game in the area. Pesticides in the runoff from nearby farms have poisoned the water they fish and bathe in, threatening both their health and their culture's survival.

Let's Discuss

1. Compare what is happening in Brazil today to the development of the North American West in the 19th century. What similarities do you see?
2. What does society lose when indigenous cultures die?

Sources: Chu 2005; Instituto del Tercer Mundo 2005.

---

reality. Conflict theorists fear that the sociobiological approach could be used as an argument against efforts to assist disadvantaged people, such as schoolchildren who are not competing successfully (Guterman 2000; Segerstråle 2000; E. Wilson 2000).

Elements of Culture

Each culture considers its own ways of handling basic societal tasks to be "natural." But in fact, methods of education, marital ceremonies, religious doctrines, and other aspects of culture are learned and transmitted through human interaction within specific societies. Parents in India are accustomed to arranging marriages for their children; parents in the United States leave marital decisions up to their offspring. Lifelong residents of Naples consider it natural to speak Italian; lifelong residents of Buenos Aires feel the same way about Spanish. Let's take a look at the major aspects of culture that shape the way the members of a society live: language, norms, sanctions, and values.

Language

Seven thousand languages are spoken in the world today—many more than the number of countries. Within a nation's political

boundaries, the number of languages spoken may range from only one (as in North Korea) to several hundred (as in Papua New Guinea, with 820—see Figure 3-1 on page 62). For the speakers of each one, whether they number 2,000 or 200 million, language is critical to their shared culture (R. Gordon 2005).

The English language, for example, makes extensive use of words dealing with war. We speak of "conquering" space, "fighting" the "battle" of the budget, "waging war" on drugs, making a "killing" on the stock market, and "bombing" an examination; something monumental or great is "the bomb." An observer from an entirely different and warless culture could gauge the importance that war and the military have had in our lives simply by recognizing the prominence that militaristic terms have in our language. On the other hand, in the Old West, words such as *gelding, stallion, mare, piebald,* and *sorrel* were all used to describe one animal—the horse. Even if we knew little of that period in history, we could conclude from the list of terms that horses were important to the culture. Similarly, the Slave Indians of northern Canada, who live in a frigid climate, have 14 terms to describe ice, including 8 for different kinds of "solid ice" and others for "seamed ice," "cracked ice," and "floating ice." Clearly, language reflects the priorities of a culture (Basso 1972; Haviland 2002).

Theory Discuss the importance of language to functionalists, interactionists, and conflict theorists.
Let's Discuss What does the extensive use of words dealing with war say about U.S. culture?

Classroom Tip Introduce the field of environmental sociology.
Contemporary Culture Are there conflicts in the United States that are similar to the one in Mato Grosso? Who is involved?

FIGURE 3–1

Languages of the World: How Many Do You Speak?

MAPPING LIFE

WORLDWIDE www.mhhe.com/schaefer7

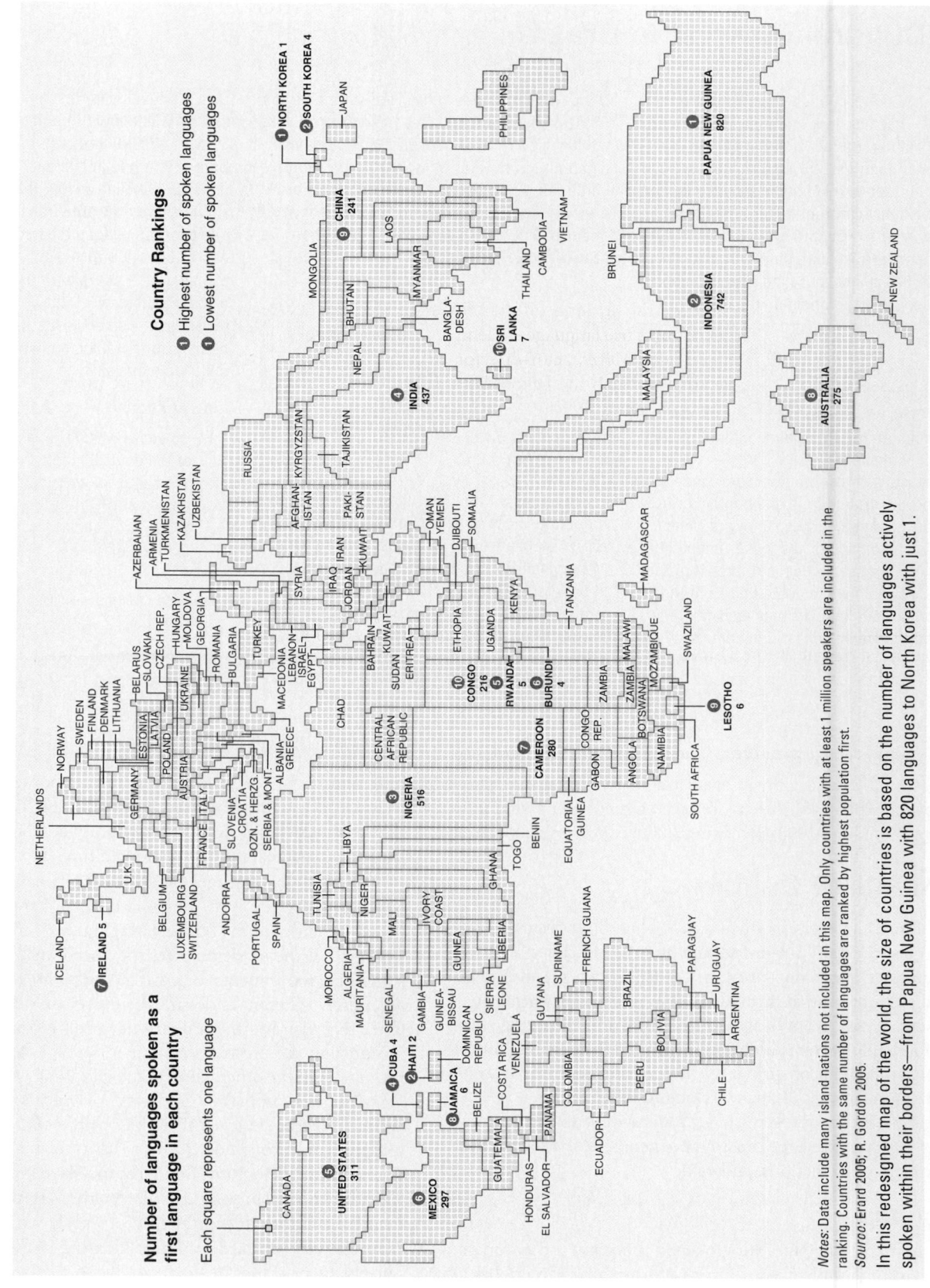

Number of languages spoken as a first language in each country

Each square represents one language

Country Rankings

① Highest number of spoken languages

① Lowest number of spoken languages

Notes: Data include many island nations not included in this map. Only countries with at least 1 million speakers are included in the ranking. Countries with the same number of languages are ranked by highest population first.

Source: Erard 2005; R. Gordon 2005.

In this redesigned map of the world, the size of countries is based on the number of languages actively spoken within their borders—from Papua New Guinea with 820 languages to North Korea with just 1.

Think About It

Considering how many languages are spoken in the United States, why do you think people in the United States are much less likely to master more than one language than people in other parts of the world?

Language is, in fact, the foundation of every culture. ***Language*** is an abstract system of word meanings and symbols for all aspects of culture. It includes speech, written characters, numerals, symbols, and nonverbal gestures and expressions. Because language is the foundation of every culture, the ability to speak other languages is crucial to intercultural relations. Throughout the Cold War era, beginning in the 1950s and continuing well into the 1970s, the U.S. government encouraged the study of Russian by developing special language schools for diplomats and military advisers who dealt with the Soviet Union. And following September 11, 2001, the nation recognized how few skilled translators it had for Arabic and other languages spoken in Muslim countries. Language quickly became a key not only to tracking potential terrorists, but to building diplomatic bridges with Muslim countries willing to help in the war against terrorism.

While language is a cultural universal, striking differences may be found in the way different cultures use language. To lend authenticity to his 1990 film *Dances with Wolves,* actor-director Kevin Costner hired a Lakota woman to teach the Lakota language to the cast. Lakota is a gendered language in which women and men speak slightly different dialects. The cast members found the language so difficult to learn that the teacher decided to dispense with the complexities of gendered speech. When members of the Lakota Sioux tribe saw the film, they could not help laughing at the resulting gender confusion (Haviland et al. 2005:109).

Sapir-Whorf Hypothesis Language does more than simply describe reality; it also serves to *shape* the reality of a culture. For example, most people in the United States cannot easily make the verbal distinctions concerning ice that are possible in the Slave Indian culture. As a result, they are less likely to notice such differences.

The ***Sapir-Whorf hypothesis,*** named for two linguists, describes the role of language in shaping our interpretation of reality. According to Sapir and Whorf, since people can conceptualize the world only through language, language *precedes* thought. Thus, the word symbols and grammar of a language organize the world for us. The Sapir-Whorf hypothesis also holds that language is not a given. Rather, it is culturally determined and encourages a distinctive interpretation of reality by focusing our attention on certain phenomena.

In a literal sense, language may color how we see the world. Berlin and Kay (1991) have noted that humans possess the physical ability to make millions of color distinctions, yet languages differ in the number of colors they recognize. The English language distinguishes between yellow and orange, but some other languages do not. In the Dugum Dani language of New Guinea's West Highlands, there are only two basic color terms—*modla* for "white" and *mili* for "black." By contrast, there are 11 basic terms in English. Russian and Hungarian, though, have 12 color terms. Russians have terms for light blue and dark blue, while Hungarians have terms for two different shades of red (Roberson et al. 2000).

Feminists have noted that gender-related language can reflect—although in itself it does not determine—the tradi-

tional acceptance of men and women in certain occupations. Each time we use a term such as *mailman, policeman,* or *fireman,* we are implying (especially to young children) that these occupations can be filled only by males. Yet many women work as *letter carriers, police officers,* and *firefighters*—a fact that is being increasingly recognized and legitimized through the use of such nonsexist language.

Language can also transmit stereotypes related to race. Look up the meanings of the adjective *black* in dictionaries published in the United States. You will find *dismal, gloomy or forbidding, destitute of moral light or goodness, atrocious, evil, threatening, clouded with anger.* By contrast, dictionaries list *pure* and *innocent* among the meanings of the adjective *white.* Through such patterns of language, our culture reinforces positive associations with the term (and skin color) *white* and negative associations with *black.* Is it surprising, then, that a list meant to prevent people from working in a profession is called a *blacklist,* while a lie that we think of as somewhat acceptable is called a *white lie?*

Language can shape how we see, taste, smell, feel, and hear. It also influences the way we think about the people, ideas, and objects around us. Language communicates a culture's most

A native speaker trains instructors from the Oneida Nation of New York in the Berlitz method of language teaching. Many Native American tribes are taking steps to recover their seldom-used languages, realizing that language is the essential foundation of any culture.

important norms, values, and sanctions to people. That's why the death of an old language or the introduction of a new one is such a sensitive issue in many parts of the world (see the Social Policy section at the end of this chapter).

Nonverbal Communication

If you don't like the way a meeting is going, you might suddenly sit back, fold your arms, and turn down the corners of your mouth. When you see a friend in tears, you may give a quick hug. After winning a big game you probably high-five your teammates. These are all examples of *nonverbal communication,* the use of gestures, facial expressions, and other visual images to communicate.

We are not born with these expressions. We learn them, just as we learn other forms of language, from people who share our same culture. This statement is as true for the basic expressions of happiness and sadness as it is for more complex emotions, such as shame or distress (Fridlund et al. 1987).

Like other forms of language, nonverbal communication is not the same in all cultures. For example, sociological research done at the micro level documents that people from various cultures differ in the degree to which they touch others during the course of normal social interactions. Even experienced travelers are sometimes caught off guard by these differences. In Saudi Arabia, a middle-aged man may want to hold hands with a partner after closing a business deal. The gesture, which would shock an American businessman, is considered a compliment in that culture. The meaning of hand signals is another form of nonverbal communication that can differ from one culture to the next. In Australia, the thumbs-up sign is considered rude (Passero 2002).

Norms

"Wash your hands before dinner." "Thou shalt not kill." "Respect your elders." All societies have ways of encouraging and enforc-

ing what they view as appropriate behavior while discouraging and punishing what they consider to be improper behavior. **Norms** are the established standards of behavior maintained by a society.

For a norm to become significant, it must be widely shared and understood. For example, in movie theaters in the United States, we typically expect that people will be quiet while the film is shown. Of course, the application of this norm can vary, depending on the particular film and type of audience. People who are viewing a serious artistic film will be more likely to insist on the norm of silence than those who are watching a slapstick comedy or horror movie.

Types of Norms Sociologists distinguish between norms in two ways. First, norms are classified as either formal or informal. **Formal norms** generally have been written down and specify strict punishments for violators. In the United States, we often formalize norms into laws, which are very precise in defining proper and improper behavior. Sociologist Donald Black (1995) has termed **law** "governmental social control," meaning that laws are formal norms enforced by the state. Laws are just one

Let's Discuss Why is the norm of "distance" at an ATM important?

example of formal norms. The requirements for a college major and the rules of a card game are also considered formal norms.

By contrast, *informal norms* are generally understood but not precisely recorded. Standards of proper dress are a common example of informal norms. Our society has no specific punishment or sanction for a person who comes to school, say, wearing a monkey suit. Making fun of the nonconforming student is usually the most likely response.

Norms are also classified by their relative importance to society. When classified in this way, they are known as *mores* and *folkways*. **Mores** (pronounced "MOR-ays") are norms deemed highly necessary to the welfare of a society, often because they embody the most cherished principles of a people. Each society demands obedience to its mores; violation can lead to severe penalties. Thus, the United States has strong mores against murder, treason, and child abuse, which have been institutionalized into formal norms.

Folkways are norms governing everyday behavior. Folkways play an important role in shaping the daily behavior of members of a culture. Society is less likely to formalize folkways than mores, and their violation raises comparatively little concern. For example, walking up a "down" escalator in a department store challenges our standards of appropriate behavior, but it will not result in a fine or a jail sentence.

In many societies around the world, folkways exist to reinforce patterns of male dominance. Various folkways reveal men's hierarchical position above women within the traditional Buddhist areas of southeast Asia. In the sleeping cars of trains, women do not sleep in upper berths above men. Hospitals that house men on the first floor do not place women patients on the second floor. Even on clotheslines, folkways dictate male dominance: women's attire is hung lower than that of men (Bulle 1987).

Use Your Sociological Imagination www.mhhe.com/schaefer7

You are a high school principal. What norms would you want to govern the students' behavior? How might these norms differ from those appropriate for college students?

Acceptance of Norms People do not follow norms, whether mores or folkways, in all situations. In some cases, they can evade a norm because they know it is weakly enforced. It is illegal for U.S. teenagers to drink alcoholic beverages, yet drinking by minors is common throughout the nation. (In fact, teenage alcoholism is a serious social problem.)

In some instances, behavior that appears to violate society's norms may actually represent adherence to the norms of a particular group. Teenage drinkers are conforming to the standards of their peer group when they violate norms that condemn underage drinking. Similarly, business executives who use shady accounting techniques may be responding to a corporate culture that demands the maximization of profits at any cost, including the deception of investors and government regulatory agencies.

Norms are violated in some instances because one norm conflicts with another. For example, suppose that you live in an apartment building and one night hear the screams of the woman next door, who is being beaten by her husband. If you decide to intervene by ringing their doorbell or calling the police, you are violating the norm of minding your own business, while at the same time following the norm of assisting a victim of violence.

Even if norms do not conflict, there are always exceptions to any norm. The same action, under different circumstances, can cause one to be viewed as either a hero or a villain. Secretly tapping telephone conversations is normally considered illegal and abhorrent. However, it can be done with a court order to obtain valid evidence for a criminal trial. We would heap praise on a government agent who used such methods to convict an organized crime figure. In our culture, we tolerate killing another human being in self-defense, and we actually reward killing in warfare.

Acceptance of norms is subject to change as the political, economic, and social conditions of a culture are transformed. Until the 1960s, for example, formal norms throughout much of the United States prohibited the marriage of people from different racial groups. Over the last half century, however, such legal prohibitions were cast aside. The process of change can be seen today in the increasing acceptance of single parents and growing support for the legalization of marriage between same-sex couples (see Chapter 12).

When circumstances require the sudden violation of long-standing cultural norms, the change can upset an entire population. In Iraq, where Muslim custom strictly forbids touching by strangers for men and especially for women, the war that began in 2003 has brought numerous daily violations of the norm. Outside important mosques, government offices, and other facilities likely to be targeted by terrorists, visitors must now be patted down and have their bags searched by Iraqi security guards. To reduce the discomfort caused by the procedure, women are searched by female guards and men by male guards. Despite that concession, and the fact that many Iraqis admit or even insist on the need for such measures, people still wince at the invasion of their personal privacy. In reaction to the searches, Iraqi women have begun to limit the contents of the bags they carry or simply to leave them at home (Rubin 2003).

Sanctions

Suppose a football coach sends a 12th player onto the field. Imagine a college graduate showing up in shorts for a job interview at a large bank. Or consider a driver who neglects to put any money into a parking meter. These people have violated widely shared and understood norms. So what happens? In each of these situations, the person will receive sanctions if his or her behavior is detected.

Sanctions are penalties and rewards for conduct concerning a social norm. Note that the concept of *reward* is included in this definition. Conformity to a norm can lead to positive sanctions such as a pay raise, a medal, a word of gratitude, or a pat on the

Gender Differential treatment of males and females in Buddhist cultures
Classroom Tip For a dramatic example of norm violation, see "Socially Approved Cannibalism" (Additional Lecture Ideas).
Classroom Tip See "Smoking" (Class Discussion Topics).
Classroom Tip See "Conflicting Cultures" (Additional Lecture Ideas).

Gender Impact of the gay and lesbian movement in changing social norms
Student Alert Emphasize that sanctions can be positive (e.g., a pay raise, a bigger office, a medal, a pat on the back) as well as negative.
Reel Society See Sanctions in the Topic Index.

Sanctions can be positive as well as negative. In 2000, the British actor Sean Connery was knighted by Queen Elizabeth II in recognition of his work in motion pictures.

back. Negative sanctions include fines, threats, imprisonment, and stares of contempt.

Table 3-1 summarizes the relationship between norms and sanctions. As you can see, the sanctions that are associated with formal norms (those that are written down and codified) tend to be formal as well. If a coach sends too many players onto the field, the team will be penalized 15 yards. The driver who fails to put money in the parking meter will receive a ticket and have to pay a fine. But sanctions for violations of informal norms can vary. The college graduate who goes to the bank interview in shorts will probably lose any chance of getting the job; on the other hand, he or she might be so brilliant that bank officials will overlook the unconventional attire.

The entire fabric of norms and sanctions in a culture reflects that culture's values and priorities. The most cherished values will be most heavily sanctioned; matters regarded as less critical will carry light and informal sanctions.

Values

Though we each have our own personal set of standards—which may include caring or fitness or success in business—we also share a general set of objectives as members of a society. Cultural

values are these collective conceptions of what is considered good, desirable, and proper—or bad, undesirable, and improper—in a culture. They indicate what people in a given culture prefer as well as what they find important and morally right (or wrong). Values may be specific, such as honoring one's parents and owning a home, or they may be more general, such as health, love, and democracy. Of course, the members of a society do not uniformly share its values. Angry political debates and billboards promoting conflicting causes tell us that much.

Values influence people's behavior and serve as criteria for evaluating the actions of others. The values, norms, and sanctions of a culture are often directly related. For example, if a culture places a high value on the institution of marriage, it may have norms (and strict sanctions) that prohibit the act of adultery or make divorce difficult. If a culture views private property as a basic value, it will probably have stiff laws against theft and vandalism.

The values of a culture may change, but most remain relatively stable during any one person's lifetime. Socially shared, intensely felt values are a fundamental part of our lives in the United States. Sociologist Robin Williams (1970) has offered a list of basic values. It includes achievement, efficiency, material comfort, nationalism, equality, and the supremacy of science and reason over faith. Obviously, not all 290 million people in this country agree on all these values, but such a list serves as a starting point in defining the national character.

In the last 20 years, extensive efforts have been made to compare values in different nations, recognizing the challenges in interpreting value concepts in a similar manner across cultures. Psychologist Shalom Schwartz has measured values in more than 60 countries. Around the world, certain values are widely shared, including benevolence, which is defined as "forgiveness and loyalty." In contrast, power, defined as "control or dominance over people and resources," is a value that is endorsed much less often (Hitlin and Piliavin 2004; S. Schwartz and Bardi 2001).

Each year more than 289,000 entering college students at 440 of the nation's four-year colleges fill out a questionnaire about

Table 3-1 Norms and Sanctions

Norms	Sanctions	
	Positive	Negative
Formal	Salary bonus	Demotion
	Testimonial dinner	Firing from a job
	Medal	Jail sentence
	Diploma	Expulsion
Informal	Smile	Frown
	Compliment	Humiliation
	Cheers	Belittling

Classroom Tip See "Youthful Values" (Class Discussion Topics).
Theory Functionalist analysis of the values of a culture
Key Person Robin Williams

their attitudes. Because this survey focuses on an array of issues, beliefs, and life goals, it is commonly cited as a barometer of the nation's values. The respondents are asked what values are personally important to them. Over the last 39 years, the value of "being very well-off financially" has shown the strongest gain in popularity; the proportion of first-year college students who endorse this value as "essential" or "very important" rose from 44 percent in 1967 to 74.5 percent in 2005 (see Figure 3-2). In contrast, the value that has shown the most striking decline in endorsement by students is "developing a meaningful philosophy of life." While this value was the most popular in the 1967 survey, endorsed by more than 80 percent of the respondents, it had fallen to seventh place on the list by 2005, when it was endorsed by 45 percent of students entering college.

During the 1980s and 1990s, support for values having to do with money, power, and status grew. At the same time, support for certain values having to do with social awareness and altruism, such as "helping others," declined. According to the 2005 nationwide survey, only 39 percent of first-year college students stated that "influencing social values" was an "essential" or "very important" goal. The proportion of students for whom "helping to promote racial understanding" was an essential or very important goal reached a record high of 42 percent in 1992, then fell to 33 percent in 2005. Like other aspects of culture, such as language and norms, a nation's values are not necessarily fixed.

Recently, cheating has become a hot issue on college campuses. Professors who take advantage of computerized services that can identify plagiarism, such as the search engine Google, have been shocked to learn that many of the papers their students hand in are plagiarized in whole or in part. Box 3-3 (page 68) examines the shift in values that underlies this decline in academic integrity.

Another value that has begun to change recently, not just among students but among the public in general, is the right to privacy. Americans have always valued their privacy and resented government intrusions into their personal lives. In the aftermath of the terrorist attacks of September 11, 2001, however, many citizens called for greater protection against the threat of terrorism. In response, the U.S. government broadened its surveillance powers and increased its ability to monitor people's behavior without court approval. In 2001, shortly after the attacks, Congress passed the Patriot Act, which empowers the FBI to access individuals' medical, library, student, and phone records without informing them or obtaining a search warrant.

Culture and the Dominant Ideology

Functionalist and conflict theorists agree that culture and society are mutually supportive, but for different reasons. Functionalists maintain that social stability requires a consensus and the support of society's members; strong central values and common norms provide that support. This view of culture became popular in sociology beginning in the 1950s. It was borrowed from British anthropologists who saw cultural traits as a stabilizing element in a culture. From a functionalist perspec-

FIGURE 3–2   **67**

Culture

Life Goals of First-Year College Students in the United States, 1966–2005

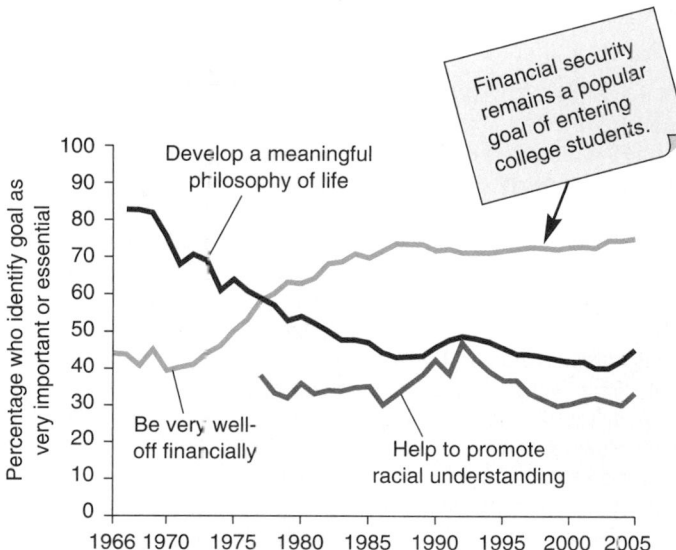

Sources: UCLA Higher Education Research Institute, as reported in Astin et al. 1994; Pryor et al. 2005.

Think About It
Why do you think values have shifted among college students in the last few decades? Which of these values is important to you?

tive, a cultural trait or practice will persist if it performs functions that society seems to need or contributes to overall social stability and consensus.

Conflict theorists agree that a common culture may exist, but they argue that it serves to maintain the privileges of certain groups. Moreover, while protecting their own self-interest, powerful groups may keep others in a subservient position. The term *dominant ideology* describes the set of cultural beliefs and practices that helps to maintain powerful social, economic, and political interests. This concept was first used by Hungarian Marxist Georg Lukacs (1923) and Italian Marxist Antonio Gramsci (1929), but it did not gain an audience in the United States until the early 1970s. In Karl Marx's view, a capitalist society has a dominant ideology that serves the interests of the ruling class.

From a conflict perspective, the dominant ideology has major social significance. Not only do a society's most powerful groups and institutions control wealth and property; even more important, they control the means of producing beliefs about reality through religion, education, and the media. Feminists would also argue that if all a society's most important institutions tell women that they should be subservient to men, this dominant ideology will help to control women and keep them in a subordinate position.

A growing number of social scientists believe it is not easy to identify a "core culture" in the United States. For support, they point

Theory Functionalist view of culture and why certain cultural traits persist over time
Theory Conflict view of how a common culture maintains the privileges of some groups and keeps others subordinate
Theory Contrast the feminist view to the functionalist view of cultural traits.

sociologyONcampus

3-3 A Culture of Cheating?

On November 21, 2002, after issuing several warnings, officials at the U.S. Naval Academy seized the computers of almost 100 midshipmen suspected of downloading movies and music illegally from the Internet. Officers at the school may have taken the unusually strong action to avoid liability on the part of the U.S. government, which owns the computers students were using. But across the nation, college administrators have been trying to restrain students from downloading pirated entertainment for free. The practice is so widespread, it has been slowing down the high-powered computer networks colleges and universities depend on for research and admissions.

Illegal downloading is just one aspect of the growing problem of copyright violation, both on campus and off. Now that college students can use personal computers to surf the Internet, most do their research online. Apparently, the temptation to cut and paste passages from Web site postings and pass them off as one's own is irresistible to many. Surveys done by the Center for Academic Integrity show that from 1999 to 2005, the percentage of students who approved of this type of plagiarism rose from 10 percent to 41 percent. At the same time, the percentage who considered cutting and pasting from the Internet to be a serious form of cheating fell from 68 percent to 23 percent.

Other forms of cheating are becoming rampant, as well. The Center for Academic Integrity estimates that at most schools, more than three quarters of the students engage in some form of cheating. Students not only cut passages from the Internet and paste them into their papers without citing the source; they share questions and answers on exams, collaborate on assignments they are supposed to do independently, and even falsify the results of their laboratory experiments. Worse, many professors have become inured to the problem and have ceased to report it.

To address what they consider an alarming trend, many schools are rewriting or adopting new academic honor codes. According to the Center for Academic Integrity, cheating on tests and papers is considerably less common

> Cheating is considerably less common at schools with honor codes than at schools without honor codes.

at schools with honor codes than at schools without honor codes. Cornell, Duke, and Kansas State University are just three of a growing number of schools that are instituting or strengthening their honor codes in an attempt to curb student cheating.

This renewed emphasis on honor and integrity underscores the influence of cultural values on social behavior. Observers contend that the increase in student cheating reflects widely publicized instances of cheating in public life, which have served to create an alternative set of values in which the end justifies the means. When young people see sports heroes, authors, entertainers, and corporate executives exposed for cheating in one form or another, the message seems to be "Cheating is OK, as long as you don't get caught." More than proctoring of exams or reliance on search engines to identify plagiarism, then, educating students about the need for academic honesty seems to reduce the incidence of cheating. "The feeling of being treated as an adult and responding in kind," says Professor Donald McCabe of Rutgers University, "it's clearly there for many students. They don't want to violate that trust."

Let's Discuss

1. Do you know anyone who has engaged in Internet plagiarism? What about cheating on tests or falsifying laboratory results? If so, how did the person justify these forms of dishonesty?

2. Even if cheaters aren't caught, what negative effects does their academic dishonesty have on them? What effects does it have on students who are honest? Could an entire college or university suffer from students' dishonesty?

Sources: Argetsinger and Krim 2002 Center for Academic Integrity 2006; R. Thomas 2003; Zernke 2002.

---

to the lack of consensus on national values, the diffusion of cultural traits, the diversity within our culture, and the changing views of young people (look again at Figure 3-2). Yet there is no way of denying that certain expressions of values have greater influence than others, even in so complex a society as the United States.

Cultural Variation

Each culture has a unique character. Inuit tribes in northern Canada, wrapped in furs and dieting on whale blubber, have little in common with farmers in Southeast Asia, who dress for the heat and subsist mainly on the rice they grow in their paddies. Cultures adapt to meet specific sets of circumstances, such as climate, level of technology, population, and geography. This adaptation to different conditions shows up in differences in all elements of culture, including norms, sanctions, values, and language. Thus, despite the presence of cultural universals such as courtship and religion, great diversity exists among the world's many cultures. Moreover, even *within* a single nation, certain segments of the populace develop cultural patterns that differ from the patterns of the dominant society.

Aspects of Cultural Variation

Subcultures Rodeo riders, residents of a retirement community, workers on an offshore oil rig—all are examples of what sociologists refer to as *subcultures*. A **subculture** is a segment of society that shares a distinctive pattern of mores, folkways, and values that differs from the pattern of the larger society. In a

sense, a subculture can be thought of as a culture existing within a larger, dominant culture. The existence of many subcultures is characteristic of complex societies such as the United States.

Members of a subculture participate in the dominant culture while at the same time engaging in unique and distinctive forms of behavior. Frequently, a subculture will develop an **argot,** or specialized language that distinguishes it from the wider society. For example, New York City's sanitation workers have developed a humorous argot for use on a job that is so dirty and smelly, most people wouldn't consider doing it. Terms such as *g-man,* *honey boat* (a garbage scow or barge), and *airmail* (trash thrown from an upper-story window) date back to the 1940s and 1950s. More recent coinages include *disco rice* (maggots) and *urban whitefish* (used condoms). Administrators at the sanitation department practice a more reserved humor than those who work on the trucks. When they send a *honey boat* to New Jersey, they're not dumping the city's garbage; they're *exporting* it. And policymakers at the department have invented some novel acronyms to describe New Yorkers' attitude toward the construction of new sanitation facilities: *banana* ("Build absolutely nothing anywhere near anyone") and *nope* ("not on planet earth") (Urbina 2004).

Such argot allows insiders—the members of the subculture—to understand words with special meanings. It also establishes patterns of communication that outsiders can't understand. Sociologists associated with the interactionist perspective emphasize that language and symbols offer a powerful way for a subculture to feel cohesive and maintain its identity.

In India, a new subculture has developed among employees at the international call centers established by multinational corpo-rations. To serve customers in the United States and Europe, the young men and women who work there must be fluent speakers of English. But the corporations that employ them demand more than proficiency in a foreign language; they expect their Indian employees to adopt Western values and work habits, including the grueling pace U.S. workers take for granted. In return they offer perks such as Western-style dinners, dances, and coveted consumer goods. Significantly, they allow employees to take the day off only on U.S. holidays, like Labor Day and Thanksgiving—not on Indian holidays like Diwali, the Hindu festival of lights. While most Indian families are home celebrating, call center employees see only each other; when they have the day off, no one else is free to socialize with them. As a result, these employees have formed a tight-knit subculture based on hard work and a taste for Western luxury goods and leisure-time pursuits. Increasingly, they are the object of criticism from Indians who live a more conventional lifestyle centered on family and holiday traditions (Kalita 2006).

Functionalist and conflict theorists agree that variation exists within a culture. Functionalists view subcultures as variations of particular social environments and as evidence that differences can exist within a common culture. However, conflict theorists suggest that variations often reflect the inequality of social arrangements within a society. A conflict perspective would view the challenge to dominant social norms by African American activists, the feminist movement, and the disability rights movement as a reflection of inequity based on race, gender, and disability status. Conflict theorists also argue that subcultures sometimes emerge when the dominant society unsuccessfully tries to suppress a practice, such as the use of illegal drugs.

Employees of an international call center in Simla, India, socialize after finishing a seven-hour shift on the telephone. Call center employees, who are isolated from other Indians by their unusual holidays and working hours, have formed a tight-knit subculture based partly on their appreciation for Western-style consumer goods

Countercultures By the end of the 1960s, an extensive subculture had emerged in the United States, composed of young people turned off by a society they believed was too materialistic and technological. This group included primarily political radicals and "hippies" who had "dropped out" of mainstream social institutions. These young men and women rejected the pressure to accumulate more and more cars, larger and larger homes, and an endless array of material goods. Instead, they expressed a desire to live in a culture based on more humanistic values, such as sharing, love, and coexistence with the environment. As a political force, this subculture opposed the United States' involvement in the war in Vietnam and encouraged draft resistance (Flacks 1971; Roszak 1969).

When a subculture conspicuously and deliberately opposes certain aspects of the larger culture, it is known as a

Classroom Tip See "The Skinhead Counterculture" (Additional Lecture Ideas).
Classroom Tip Another example of a counterculture is the "survivalists" who see nuclear war as inevitable and have, in some cases, created armed camps to defend themselves from city dwellers after a nuclear attack.

counterculture. Countercultures typically thrive among the young, who have the least investment in the existing culture. In most cases, a 20-year-old can adjust to new cultural standards more easily than someone who has spent 60 years following the patterns of the dominant culture (Zellner 1995).

In the wake of the terrorist attacks of September 11, 2001, people around the United States learned of the existence of terrorist groups operating as a counterculture within their country. This was a situation that generations have lived with in Northern Ireland, Israel and the Palestinian territory, and many other parts of the world. But terrorist cells are not necessarily fueled only by outsiders. Frequently people become disenchanted with the policies of their own country, and a few take very violent steps.

Culture Shock Anyone who feels disoriented, uncertain, out of place, or even fearful when immersed in an unfamiliar culture may be experiencing *culture shock.* For example, a resident of the United States who visits certain areas in China and wants local meat for dinner may be stunned to learn that the specialty is dog meat. Similarly, someone from a strict Islamic culture may be shocked upon first seeing the comparatively provocative dress styles and open displays of affection that are common in the United States and various European cultures.

All of us, to some extent, take for granted the cultural practices of our society. As a result, it can be surprising and even disturbing to realize that other cultures do not follow our way of life. The fact is that customs that seem strange to us are considered normal and proper in other cultures, which may see our own mores and folkways as odd.

Use Your Sociological Imagination

"IT'S ENDLESS. WE JOIN A COUNTER-CULTURE; IT BECOMES THE CULTURE. WE JOIN ANOTHER COUNTER-CULTURE; IT BECOMES THE CULTURE..."

Cultures change. Fashions we once regarded as unacceptable—such as men wearing earrings and people wearing jeans in the workplace—or associated with fringe groups (such as men and women with tattoos) are now widely accepted. These countercultural practices have been absorbed by mainstream culture.

www.mhhe.com /schaefer7

You arrive in a developing African country as a Peace Corps volunteer. What aspects of a very different culture do you think would be the hardest to adjust to? What might the citizens of that country find shocking about your culture?

Attitudes toward Cultural Variation

Ethnocentrism Many everyday statements reflect our attitude that our own culture is best. We use terms such as *underdeveloped, backward,* and *primitive* to refer to other societies. What "we" believe is a religion; what "they" believe is superstition and mythology.

It is tempting to evaluate the practices of other cultures on the basis of our own perspectives. Sociologist William Graham Sumner (1906) coined the term *ethnocentrism* to refer to the tendency to assume that one's own culture and way of life represent the norm or are superior to all others. The ethnocentric person sees his or her own group as the center or defining point of culture and views all other cultures as deviations from what is "normal." Westerners who think cattle are to be used for food might look down on India's Hindu religion and culture, which views the cow as sacred. Or people in one culture may dismiss as

unthinkable the mate selection or child-rearing practices of another culture.

Ethnocentric value judgments have complicated U.S. efforts at democratic reform of the Iraqi government. Before the 2003 war in Iraq, U.S. planners had assumed that Iraqis would adapt to a new form of government in the same way the Germans and Japanese did following World War II. But in the Iraqi culture, unlike the German and Japanese cultures, loyalty to the family and the extended clan comes before patriotism and the common good. In a country in which almost half of all people, even those in the cities, marry a first or second cousin, citizens are predisposed to favor their own kin in government and business dealings. Why trust a stranger from outside the family? What Westerners would criticize as nepotism, then, is actually an acceptable, even admirable, practice to Iraqis (J. Tierney 2003).

Conflict theorists point out that ethnocentric value judgments serve to devalue groups and to deny equal opportunities. Functionalists, on the other hand, point out that ethnocentrism serves to maintain a sense of solidarity by promoting group pride. Denigrating other nations and cultures can enhance our own patriotic feelings and belief that our way of life is superior. Yet this type of social stability is established at the expense of other peoples. Of course, ethnocentrism is hardly limited to citizens of the United States. Visitors from many African cultures are surprised at the disrespect that children in the United States show their parents. People from India may be repelled by our practice of living in the same household with dogs and cats. Many Islamic fundamentalists in the Arab world and Asia view the United States as corrupt, decadent, and doomed to destruction. All these people may feel comforted by membership in cultures that in their view are superior to ours.

Chapter 3

Table 3-2 Major Sociological Perspectives on Culture

summingUP

	Functionalist Perspective	Conflict Perspective	Interactionist Perspective
Norms	Reinforce societal standards	Reinforce patterns of dominance	Are maintained through face-to-face interaction
Values	Are collective conceptions of what is good	May perpetuate social inequality	Are defined and redefined through social interaction
Culture and society	Culture reflects a society's strong central values	Culture reflects a society's dominant ideology	A society's core culture is perpetuated through daily social interactions
Cultural variation	Subcultures serve the interests of subgroups; ethnocentrism reinforces group solidarity	Countercultures question the dominant social order; ethnocentrism devalues groups	Customs and traditions are transmitted through intergroup contact and through the media

Cultural Relativism   While ethnocentrism means evaluating foreign cultures using the familiar culture of the observer as a standard of correct behavior, **cultural relativism** means viewing people's behavior from the perspective of their own culture. It places a priority on understanding other cultures, rather than dismissing them as "strange" or "exotic." Unlike ethnocentrists, cultural relativists employ the kind of value neutrality in scien- {p.43} tific study that Max Weber saw as so important.

Cultural relativism stresses that different social contexts give rise to different norms and values. Thus, we must examine practices such as polygamy, bullfighting, and monarchy within the particular contexts of the cultures in which they are found.

While cultural relativism does not suggest that we must unquestionably *accept* every cultural variation, it does require a serious and unbiased effort to evaluate norms, values, and customs in light of their distinctive culture.

Table 3-2 summarizes the major sociological perspectives on culture. How one views a culture—whether from an ethnocentric point of view or through the lens of cultural relativism—has important consequences in the area of social policy. A hot issue today is the extent to which a nation should accommodate nonnative language speakers by sponsoring bilingual programs. We'll take a close look at this issue in the Social Policy section, next.

and Culture

Bilingualism

The Issue

All over the world, nations face the challenge of how to deal with residential minorities who speak a language different from that of the mainstream culture. **Bilingualism** refers to the use of two or more languages in a particular setting, such as the workplace or schoolroom, treating each language as equally legitimate. Thus, a teacher of bilingual education may instruct children in their native language while gradually introducing them to the language of the host society. If the curriculum is also bicultural, it will teach children about the mores and folkways of both the dominant culture and the subculture. To what degree should schools in the United States present the curriculum in a language other than English? This issue has prompted a great deal of debate among educators and policymakers.

The Setting

Because languages know no political boundaries, minority languages are common in most nations. For example, Hindi is the most widely spoken language in India, and English is used widely for official purposes, but 18 other languages are officially recognized in the nation of about 1 billion people. According to the 2000 Census, 47 million residents of the United States over the age of five—that's about 18 percent of the population—speak a language other than English as their primary language. Indeed, 32 different languages are each spoken by at least 200,000 residents of this country (Bureau of the Census 2003d; Shin and Bruno 2003).

Schools throughout the world must deal with incoming students who speak many different languages. Do bilingual

programs in the United States help these children to learn English? It is difficult to reach firm conclusions because bilingual programs in general vary so widely in their quality and approach. They differ in the length of the transition to English and in how long they allow students to remain in bilingual classrooms. Moreover, results have been mixed. In the years since California effectively dismantled its bilingual education program, reading and math scores of students with limited English proficiency rose dramatically, especially in the lower grades. Yet a major overview of 17 different studies, done at Johns Hopkins University, found that students who are offered lessons in both English and their home languages make better progress than similar children who are taught only in English (Slavin and Cheung 2003).

Sociological Insights

For a long time, people in the United States demanded conformity to a single language. This demand coincided with the functionalist view that language serves to unify members of a society. Immigrant children from Europe and Asia—including young Italians, Jews, Poles, Chinese, and Japanese—were expected to learn English once they entered school. In some cases, immigrant children were actually forbidden to speak their native languages on school grounds. Little respect was granted to immigrants' cultural traditions; a young person would often be teased about his or her "funny" name, accent, or style of dress.

Recent decades have seen challenges to this pattern of forced obedience to the dominant ideology. Beginning in the 1960s, active movements for Black pride and ethnic pride insisted that people regard the traditions of all racial and ethnic subcultures as legitimate and important. Conflict theorists explain this development as a case of subordinated language minorities seeking opportunities for self-expression. Partly as a result of these challenges, people began to view bilingualism as an asset. It seemed to provide a sensitive way of assisting millions of non-English-speaking people in the United States to *learn* English in order to function more effectively within the society.

The perspective of conflict theory also helps us to understand some of the attacks on bilingual programs. Many of them stem from an ethnocentric point of view, which holds that any deviation from the majority is bad. This attitude tends to be expressed by those who wish to stamp out foreign influence wherever it occurs, especially in our schools. It does not take into account that success in bilingual education may actually have beneficial results, such as decreasing the number of high school dropouts and increasing the number of Hispanics in colleges and universities.

Policy Initiatives

Bilingualism has policy implications largely in two areas: efforts to maintain language purity and programs to enhance bilingual education. Nations vary dramatically in their tolerance for a variety of languages. China continues to tighten its cultural control over Tibet by extending instruction of Mandarin, a Chinese dialect, from high school into the elementary schools, which will now be bilingual along with Tibetan. By contrast, nearby Singapore establishes English as the medium of instruction but allows

Throughout Canada, official signs are bilingual, even in regions where almost everyone speaks only English or French.

students to take their mother tongue as a second language, be it Chinese, Malay, or Tamil.

In many nations, language dominance is a regional issue—for example, in Miami or along the Tex-Mex border, where Spanish speaking is prevalent. A particularly virulent bilingual hot spot is Quebec, the French-speaking province of Canada. The Québécois, as they are known, represent 83 percent of the province's population, but only 25 percent of Canada's total population. A law implemented in 1978 mandated education in French for all Quebec's children except those whose parents or siblings had learned English elsewhere in Canada. While special laws like this one have advanced French in the province, dissatisfied Québécois have tried to form their own separate country. In 1995, the people of Quebec voted to remain united with Canada by only the narrowest of margins (50.5 percent). Language and language-related cultural areas both unify and divide this nation of 32 million people (*The Economist* 2005b; Schaefer 2006).

Policymakers in the United States have been somewhat ambivalent in dealing with the issue of bilingualism. In 1965, the Elementary and Secondary Education Act (ESEA) provided for bilingual, bicultural education. In the 1970s, the federal government took an active role in establishing the proper form for bilingual programs. However, more recently, federal policy has been less supportive of bilingualism, and local school districts have been forced to provide an increased share of funding for their bilingual programs. Yet bilingual programs are an expense that many communities and states are unwilling to pay for and are quick to cut back. In 1998, voters in California approved a proposition that all but eliminated bilingual education: it requires instruction in English for 1.4 million children who are not fluent in the language.

In the United States, repeated efforts have been made to introduce a constitutional amendment declaring English as the nation's official language. In 2006, the issue arose once again during debates over two extremely controversial congressional

Theory Bilingualism is examined from a functionalist and conflict view.
Web Resource Encourage students to try the interactive activities in the student center of the Online Learning Center (www.mhhe.com/schaefer7). They will be asked to imagine that they are in need of bilingual education.

Classroom Tip See "Bilingualism" (Class Discussion Topics).
Global View Conflict over separatism in Quebec

FIGURE 3-3　　　　　　　　　　　　　　　　　　　　　　　　　　　　　　　73

Non-English Speakers at Home

MAPPING LIFE

NATIONWIDE ^{www.} mhhe.com /schaefer7

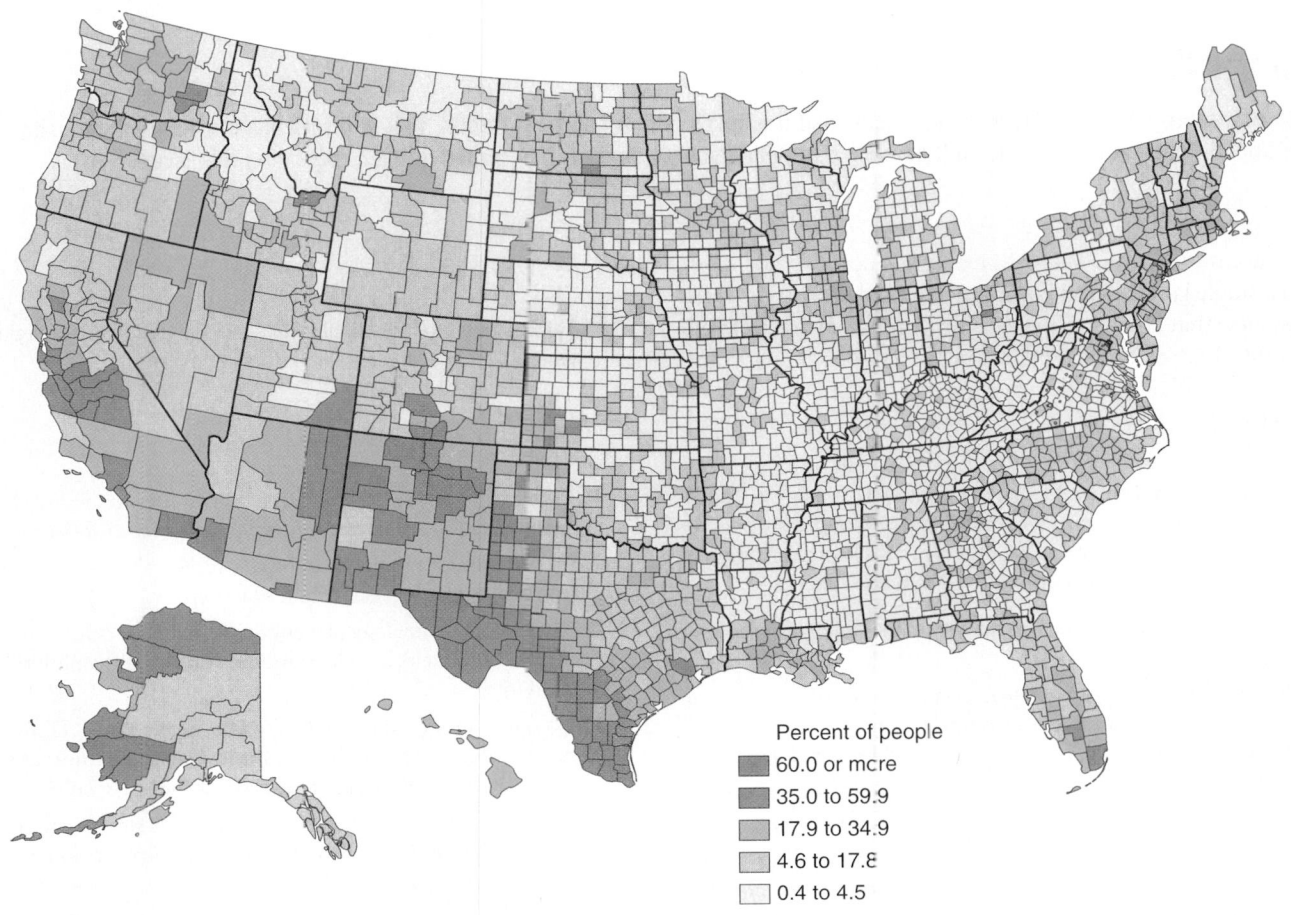

Percent of people
- 60.0 or more
- 35.0 to 59.9
- 17.9 to 34.9
- 4.6 to 17.8
- 0.4 to 4.5

Note: Data are from 2000 Census for people 5 years and over. National average was 17.9 percent.
Source: Shin and Bruno 2003:8.

proposals—a House bill that would have criminalized the presence of illegal immigrants in the United States and expanded the penalties for aiding them, and a Senate bill that offered some illegal immigrants a path to citizenship. In an attempt to reach a compromise between the two sides, legislative leaders introduced a proposal to make English the national language. As they described it, the legislation would not completely outlaw bilingual or multilingual government services. It would, however, require that such services be called for specifically in the Voting Rights Act of 1965, which requires that voting information be printed in multiple languages.

As Figure 3-3 shows, non-English speakers tend to be clustered along the U.S.-Mexican border, in urban areas, and in rural areas populated by Native American tribal groups. Yet bilingualism stirs passions nationwide. The release in 2006 of "*Nuestro Himno*," the Spanish-language version of the "Star-

Spangled Banner," produced a strong public reaction: 69 percent of those who were surveyed on the topic said the anthem should be sung only in English. In reaction against the Spanish version, at least one congressman defiantly sang the national anthem in English—with incorrect lyrics. And the proprietor of a restaurant in Philadelphia posted signs advising patrons that he would accept orders for his famous steak sandwiches only in English. Throughout the year, passions ran high as policymakers debated how much support to afford people who speak other languages (Carroll 2006).

Let's Discuss

1. Have you attended a school with a number of students for whom English is a second language? If so, did the school set up a special bilingual program? Was it effective? What is your opinion of such programs?

Let's Discuss Should all states have official English laws?
Classroom Tip See "Using Humor" (Class Discussion Topics).

2. The ultimate goal of both English-only and bilingual programs is for foreign-born students to become proficient in English. Why should the type of program students attend matter so much to so many people? List all the reasons you can think of for supporting or opposing such programs. What do you see as the primary reason?

3. Besides bilingualism, can you think of another issue that has become controversial recently because of a clash of cultures? Analyze the issue from a sociological point of view.

GettingINVOLVED

To get involved in the debate over bilingualism, visit this text's online Learning Center, which offers links to relevant websites. Check out the Social Policy section in the OLC as well; it provides survey data on U.S. public opinion regarding this issue.

www.mhhe.com/schaefer7

{ MASTERING THIS CHAPTER }

Summary

Culture is the totality of learned, socially transmitted customs, knowledge, material objects, and behavior. This chapter examines the basic elements that make up a culture, social practices common to all cultures, and variations that distinguish one culture from another.

1. A shared *culture* helps to define the group or society to which we belong.
2. Anthropologist George Murdock compiled a list of *cultural universals,* or common practices found in every culture, including marriage, sports, cooking, medicine, and sexual restrictions.
3. Human culture is constantly expanding through the process of *innovation,* which includes both *discovery* and *invention.*
4. *Diffusion*—the spread of cultural items from one place to another—has fostered globalization. But people resist ideas that seem too foreign, as well as those they perceive as threatening to their own values and beliefs.
5. *Language,* an important element of culture, includes speech, written characters, numerals, and symbols, as well as gestures and other forms of nonverbal communication. Language both describes culture and shapes it.

6. Sociologists distinguish between *norms* in two ways, classifying them either as *formal* or *informal* or as *mores* or *folkways.*
7. The formal norms of a culture will receive the heaviest *sanctions;* informal norms will carry light sanctions.
8. The *dominant ideology* of a culture is the set of cultural beliefs and practices that help to maintain powerful social, economic, and political interests.
9. In a sense, a *subculture* can be thought of as a small culture that exists within a larger, dominant culture. *Countercultures* are subcultures that deliberately oppose aspects of the larger culture.
10. People who assume that their own culture is superior to others engage in *ethnocentrism.* By contrast, *cultural relativism* is the practice of viewing other people's behavior from the perspective of their own culture.
11. The social policy of *bilingualism* calls for the use of two or more languages, treating each as equally legitimate. It is supported by those who want to ease the transition of non-native language speakers into a host society, but opposed by those who adhere to a single cultural tradition and language.

Critical Thinking Questions

1. Select three cultural universals from George Murdock's list (see page 58) and analyze them from a functionalist perspective. Why are these practices found in every culture? What functions do they serve?
2. Drawing on the theories and concepts presented in this chapter, apply sociological analysis to one subculture with which you are familiar. Describe the norms, values, argot, and sanctions evident in that subculture.

3. In what ways is the dominant ideology of the United States evident in the nation's literature, music, movies, theater, television programs, and sporting events?

Key Terms

Argot Specialized language used by members of a group or subculture. (page 69)

Bilingualism The use of two or more languages in a particular setting, such as the workplace or schoolroom, treating each language as equally legitimate. (71)

Counterculture A subculture that deliberately opposes certain aspects of the larger culture. (70)

Cultural relativism The viewing of people's behavior from the perspective of their own culture. (71)

Cultural universal A common practice or belief found in every culture. (58)

Culture The totality of learned, socially transmitted customs, knowledge, material objects, and behavior. (55)

Culture lag A period of maladjustment when the nonmaterial culture is still struggling to adapt to new material conditions. (60)

Culture shock The feeling of surprise and disorientation that people experience when they encounter cultural practices that are different from their own. (70)

Diffusion The process by which a cultural item spreads from group to group or society to society. (59)

Discovery The process of making known or sharing the existence of an aspect of reality. (58)

Dominant ideology A set of cultural beliefs and practices that helps to maintain powerful social, economic, and political interests. (67)

Ethnocentrism The tendency to assume that one's own culture and way of life represent the norm or are superior to all others. (70)

Folkway A norm governing everyday behavior whose violation raises comparatively little concern. (65)

Formal norm A norm that has been written down and that specifies strict punishments for violators. (64)

Informal norm A norm that is generally understood but not precisely recorded. (65)

Innovation The process of introducing a new idea or object to a culture through discovery or invention. (58)

Invention The combination of existing cultural items into a form that did not exist before. (58)

Language An abstract system of word meanings and symbols for all aspects of culture; includes gestures and other nonverbal communication. (63)

Law Governmental social control. (64)

Material culture The physical or technological aspects of our daily lives. (60)

Mores Norms deemed highly necessary to the welfare of a society. (65)

Nonmaterial culture Ways of using material objects, as well as customs, beliefs, philosophies, governments, and patterns of communication. (60)

Norm An established standard of behavior maintained by a society. (64)

Sanction A penalty or reward for conduct concerning a social norm. (65)

Sapir-Whorf hypothesis A hypothesis concerning the role of language in shaping our interpretation of reality. It holds that language is culturally determined. (63)

Society A fairly large number of people who live in the same territory, are relatively independent of people outside it, and participate in a common culture. (55)

Sociobiology The systematic study of how biology affects human social behavior. (60)

Subculture A segment of society that shares a distinctive pattern of mores, folkways, and values that differs from the pattern of the larger society. (68)

Technology Cultural information about how to use the material resources of the environment to satisfy human needs and desires. (60)

Value A collective conception of what is considered good, desirable, and proper—or bad, undesirable, and improper—in a culture. (66)

Self-Quiz

Read each question carefully and then select the best answer.

1. Which of the following is an aspect of culture?
   a. a comic book
   b. the patriotic attachment to the flag of the United States
   c. slang words
   d. all of the above

2. People's need for food, shelter, and clothing are examples of what George Murdock referred to as
   a. norms.
   b. folkways.
   c. cultural universals.
   d. cultural practices.

3. What term do sociologists use to refer to the process by which a cultural item spreads from group to group or society to society?
   a. diffusion
   b. globalization
   c. innovation
   d. cultural relativism

4. The appearance of Starbucks coffee houses in China is a sign of what aspect of culture?
   a. innovation
   b. globalization
   c. diffusion
   d. cultural relativism

5. Which of the following statements is true according to the Sapir-Whorf hypothesis?
   a. Language simply describes reality.
   b. Language does not transmit stereotypes related to race.
   c. Language precedes thought.
   d. Language is not an example of a cultural universal.

6. Which of the following statements about norms is correct?
   a. People do not follow norms in all situations. In some cases, they evade a norm because they know it is weakly enforced.
   b. In some instances, behavior that appears to violate society's norms may actually represent adherence to the norms of a particular group.
   c. Norms are violated in some instances because one norm conflicts with another.
   d. all of the above

7. Which of the following statements about values is correct?
   a. Values never change.
   b. The values of a culture may change, but most remain relatively stable during any one person's lifetime.
   c. Values are constantly changing; sociologists view them as being very unstable.
   d. all of the above

8. Which of the following terms describes the set of cultural beliefs and practices that help to maintain powerful social, economic, and political interests?

   a. mores
   b. dominant ideology
   c. consensus
   d. values

9. Terrorist groups are examples of

   a. cultural universals.
   b. subcultures.
   c. countercultures.
   d. dominant ideologies.

10. What is the term used when one places a priority on understanding other cultures, rather than dismissing them as "strange" or "exotic"?

   a. ethnocentrism
   b. culture shock
   c. cultural relativism
   d. cultural value

11. A _____ is the largest form of human group.

12. _____ is the process of introducing a new idea or object to a culture.

13. The bow and arrow, the automobile, and the television are all examples of _____.

14. Sociologists associated with the _____ perspective emphasize that language and symbols offer a powerful way for a subculture to maintain its identity.

15. "Put on some clean clothes for dinner" and "Thou shalt not kill" are both examples of _____ found in U.S. culture.

16. The United States has strong _____ against murder, treason, and other forms of abuse that have been institutionalized into formal norms.

17. From a(n) _____ perspective, the dominant ideology has major social significance. Not only do a society's most powerful groups and institutions control wealth and property; more important, they control the means of production.

18. Countercultures (e.g., hippies) are typically popular among the _____, who have the least investment in the existing culture.

19. A person experiences _____ _____ when he or she feels disoriented, uncertain, out of place, even fearful, when immersed in an unfamiliar culture.

20. From the _____ perspective, enthocentrism serves to maintain a sense of solidarity by promoting group pride.

⟨ TECHNOLOGY RESOURCES ⟩

Online Learning Center

1. In this chapter you have learned that language is the foundation of every culture. For a long time, people in the United States demanded conformity to a single language. One of the interactive exercises in the student center of the Online Learning Center (**www.mhhe.com/ schaefer7**) asks you to assess how well you would adjust, as an immigrant to a non-English-speaking country. Try the assessment and see whether it changes your ideas about the need for bilingual education in the United States.

2. Although certain cultural universals exist in every society, they may be expressed quite differently from place to place. Visit BuddhaNet (**www.buddhanet.net/e-learning/history/funeral1.htm**) to find out how Buddhist funeral ceremonies differ from the Western traditions with which you are probably familiar.

3. One of the more interesting examples of a subculture in the United States is the Gullah culture of South Carolina. Read about Gullah history, culture, and language at the Web site of the Beaufort County (South Carolina) Public Library (**www.co.beaufort.sc.us/bftlib/ gullah.htm**).

*Note: While all the URLs listed were current as of the printing of this book, these sites often change. Please check our Web site (**www.mhhe.com/schaefer7**) for updates, hyperlinks, and exercises related to these sites.*

Reel Society Video Clips

Reel Society video clips, which appear on this book's Web site, can be used to spark discussion about the following topics from this chapter:

   • Cultural Universals
   • Norms

4

Socialization

inside

The Role of Socialization

The Self and Socialization

Socialization and the Life Course

Agents of Socialization

**Social Policy and Socialization:
Child Care around the World**

Boxes

Sociology in the Global Community:
Raising Amish Children

Sociology on Campus: Impression
Management by Students

Taking Sociology to Work: Rakefet
Avramovitz, Program Administrator,
Child Care Law Center

On a busy commercial street in Bangalore, India, pedestrians dressed in traditional garb stroll past a shop and billboard advertising Western fashions. Socialization comes from corporate influences as well as from those who are closest to us, such as family and friends. In today's globalized world, Western media expose children to cultural values that their parents and other authorities may not embrace.

BLACK PICKET FENCES

PRIVILEGE AND PERIL AMONG THE BLACK MIDDLE CLASS

MARY PATTILLO-McCOY

Charisse . . . is sixteen and lives with her mother and younger sister, Deanne, across the street from St. Mary's Catholic Church and School. Charisse's mother is a personnel assistant at a Chicago university, and is taking classes there to get her bachelor's degree. Mr. Baker is a Chicago firefighter. While her father and mother are separated, Charisse sees her father many times a week at the afterschool basketball hour that he supervises at St. Mary's gym. He and Charisse's mother are on very good terms, and Charisse has a loving relationship with both parents. Mr. Baker is as active as any parent could be, attending the father/daughter dances at Charisse's high school, never missing a big performance, and visiting his daughters often.

Charisse and her sister are being raised by the neighborhood family in addition to their biological parents. "We [are] real close. Like all our neighbors know us because my dad grew up over here. Since the '60s." Charisse is a third-generation Grovelandite just like Neisha Morris. Her grandparents moved into Groveland with Charisse's then-teenage father when the neighborhood first opened to African Americans. . . . Now Charisse is benefiting from the friends her family has made over their years of residence in Groveland, especially the members of St. Mary's church, who play the role of surrogate parents. When Charisse was in elementary school at St. Mary's, her late paternal grandmother was the school secretary, and so the Baker girls were always under the watchful eye of their grandmother as well as the staff, who were their grandmother's friends. And in the evenings Charisse's mother would bring her and her sister to choir practice, where they accumulated an ensemble of mothers and fathers.

After St. Mary's elementary school, Charisse went on to St. Agnes Catholic High School for girls, her father's choice. St. Agnes is located in a suburb of Chicago and is a solid, integrated Catholic school where 100 percent of the girls graduate and over 95 percent go on to college. . . .

Most of Charisse's close friends went to St. Mary's and now go to St. Agnes with her, but her choice of boyfriends shows modest signs of rebellion. . . . Many of Charisse's male interests are older than she, and irregularly employed—although some are in and out of school. She meets many of them hanging out at the mall. One evening, members of the church's youth choir sat around talking about their relationships. Charisse cooed while talking about her present boyfriend, who had just graduated from high school but did not have a job and was uncertain about his future. But in the middle of that thought, Charisse spontaneously changed her attentions to a new young man that she had just met. "Charisse changes boyfriends like she changes her clothes," her sister joked, indicating the impetuous nature of adolescent relationships.

(Pattillo-McCoy 1999:100–102) Additional information about this excerpt can be found on the Online Learning Center at www.mhhe.com/schaefer7. ●

> " Charisse is a third-generation Grovelandite just like Neisha Morris. Her grandparents moved into Groveland with Charisse's then-teenage father when the neighborhood first opened to African Americans. "

This excerpt from *Black Picket Fences: Privilege and Peril among the Black Middle Class* describes the upbringing of a young resident of Groveland, a close-knit African American community in Chicago. The author, sociologist Mary Pattillo, became acquainted with Charisse while living in the Groveland neighborhood, where she was doing ethnographic research. Charisse's childhood is similar to that of other youths in many respects. Regardless of race or social class, a young person's development involves a host of influences, from parents, grandparents, and siblings to friends and classmates, teachers and school administrators, neighbors and churchgoers—even youths who frequent the local mall. Yet in some ways, Charisse's development is specifically influenced by her race and social class. Contact with family and community members, for instance, has undoubtedly prepared her to deal with prejudice and the scarcity of positive images of African Americans in the media.

Sociologists, in general, are interested in the patterns of behavior and attitudes that emerge *throughout* the life course, from infancy to old age. These patterns are part of the lifelong process of *socialization,* in which people learn the attitudes, values, and behaviors appropriate for members of a particular culture. Socialization occurs through human interactions. We learn a great deal from those people most important in our lives—immediate family members, best friends, and teachers. But we also learn from people we see on the street, on television, on the Internet, and in films and magazines. From a microsociological perspective, socialization helps us to discover how to behave "properly" and what to expect from others if we follow (or challenge) society's norms and values. From a macrosociological perspective, socialization provides for the transmission of a culture from one generation to the next, and thereby for the long-term continuance of a society.

Socialization also shapes our self-images. For example, in the United States, a person who is viewed as "too heavy" or "too short" does not conform to the ideal cultural standard of physical attractiveness. This kind of unfavorable evaluation can significantly influence the person's self-esteem. In this sense, socialization experiences can help to shape our personalities. In everyday speech, the term *personality* is used to refer to a person's typical patterns of attitudes, needs, characteristics, and behavior.

How much of a person's personality is shaped by culture, as opposed to inborn traits? In what ways does socialization continue into adulthood? Who are the most powerful agents of socialization? In this chapter we will examine the role of socialization in human development. We will begin by analyzing the interaction of heredity with environmental factors. We pay particular attention to how people develop perceptions, feelings, and beliefs about themselves. The chapter will also explore the lifelong nature of the socialization process, as well as important agents of socialization, among them the family, schools, peers, and the media. Finally, the Social Policy section will focus on the socialization experience of group child care for young children. ●

The Role of Socialization

What makes us who we are? Is it the genes we are born with, or the environment in which we grow up? Researchers have traditionally clashed over the relative importance of biological inheritance and environmental factors in human development—a conflict called the *nature versus nurture* (or *heredity versus environment*) debate. Today, most social scientists have moved beyond this debate, acknowledging instead the *interaction* of these variables in shaping human development. However, we can better appreciate how heredity and environmental factors interact and influence the socialization process if we first examine situations in which one factor operates almost entirely without the other (Homans 1979).

Social Environment: The Impact of Isolation

In the 1994 movie *Nell,* Jodie Foster played a young woman hidden from birth by her mother in a backwoods cabin. Raised without normal human contact, Nell crouches like an animal, screams wildly, and speaks or sings in a language all her own.

This movie was drawn from the actual account of an emaciated 16-year-old boy who appeared mysteriously in 1828 in the town square of Nuremberg, Germany (Lipson 1994).

Isabelle and Genie: Two Cases Some viewers may have found the story of Nell difficult to believe, but the painful childhood of Isabelle was all too real. For the first six years of her life, Isabelle lived in almost total seclusion in a darkened room. She had little contact with other people, with the exception of her mother, who could neither speak nor hear. Isabelle's mother's parents had been so deeply ashamed of Isabelle's illegitimate birth that they kept her hidden away from the world. Ohio authorities finally discovered the child in 1938, when Isabelle's mother escaped from her parents' home, taking her daughter with her.

When she was discovered at age six, Isabelle could not speak. She could merely make various croaking sounds. Her only communications with her mother were simple gestures. Isabelle had been largely deprived of the typical interactions and socialization experiences of childhood. Since she had seen few people, she initially showed a strong fear of strangers and reacted almost

like a wild animal when confronted with an unfamiliar person. As she became accustomed to seeing certain individuals, her reaction changed to one of extreme apathy. At first, observers believed that Isabelle was deaf, but she soon began to react to nearby sounds. On tests of maturity, she scored at the level of an infant rather than a six-year-old.

Specialists developed a systematic training program to help Isabelle adapt to human relationships and socialization. After a few days of training, she made her first attempt to verbalize. Although she started slowly, Isabelle quickly passed through six years of development. In a little over two months she was speaking in complete sentences. Nine months later she could identify both words and sentences. Before Isabelle reached the age of nine, she was ready to attend school with other children. By her 14th year she was in sixth grade, doing well in school, and emotionally well-adjusted.

Yet without an opportunity to experience socialization in her first six years, Isabelle had been hardly human in the social sense when she was first discovered. Her inability to communicate at the time of her discovery—despite her physical and cognitive potential to learn—and her remarkable progress over the next few years underscore the impact of socialization on human development (K. Davis 1940, 1947).

Unfortunately, other children who have been locked away or severely neglected have not fared so well as Isabelle. In many instances, the consequences of social isolation have proved much more damaging. For example, in 1970 a 14-year-old Californian named Genie was discovered in a room where she had been confined since the age of 20 months. During her years of isolation, no family member had spoken to her, nor could she hear anything other than swearing. Since there was no television or radio in her home, she had never heard the sounds of normal human speech. One year after beginning extensive therapy, Genie's grammar resembled that of a typical 18-month-old. Though she made further advances with continued therapy, she never achieved full language ability. Figure 4-1 shows a sketch Genie made of her teacher five years after she was discovered (Curtiss 1977, 1985; Rymer 1993).

Isabelle's and Genie's experiences are important to researchers because there are only a few cases of children reared in total isolation. Unfortunately, however, there are many cases of children raised in extremely neglectful social circumstances. Recently, attention has focused on infants and young children from orphanages in the formerly communist countries of Eastern Europe. In Romanian orphanages, babies once lay in their cribs for 18 to 20 hours a day, curled against their feeding bottles and receiving little adult care. Such minimal attention continued for the first five years of their lives. Many of them were fearful of human contact and prone to unpredictable antisocial behavior. This situation came to light as families in North America and Europe began adopting thousands of the children. The adjustment problems for about 20 percent of them were often so dramatic that the adopting families suffered guilty fears of being ill-fit adoptive parents. Many of them have asked for assistance in dealing with the children. Slowly, efforts are being made to introduce the de-

prived youngsters to feelings of attachment that they have never experienced before (Groza et al. 1999; Talbot 1998).

Increasingly, researchers are emphasizing the importance of the earliest socialization experiences for children who grow up in more normal environments. We now know that it is not enough to care for an infant's physical needs; parents must also concern themselves with children's social development. If, for example, children are discouraged from having friends even as toddlers, they will miss out on social interactions with peers that are critical for emotional growth.

Primate Studies   Studies of animals raised in isolation also support the importance of socialization in development. Harry Harlow (1971), a researcher at the primate laboratory of the University of Wisconsin, conducted tests with rhesus monkeys that had been raised away from their mothers and away from contact with other monkeys. As was the case with Isabelle, the rhesus monkeys raised in isolation were fearful and easily frightened. They did not mate, and the females who were artificially inseminated became abusive mothers. Apparently, isolation had had a damaging effect on the monkeys.

A creative aspect of Harlow's experimentation was his use of "artificial mothers." In one such experiment, Harlow presented monkeys raised in isolation with two substitute mothers—one

FIGURE 4-1

Genie's Sketch

Source: Curtiss 1977:274.

This sketch was made in 1975 by Genie—a girl who had been isolated for most of her 14 years, until she was discovered by authorities in 1970. In her drawing, her linguist friend (on the left) plays the piano while Genie listens. Genie was 18 when she drew this picture.

Gender Researchers who study isolated upbringings note that children who have been isolated are disproportionately female, reflecting the less-valued position of girls and women in many societies.
Classroom Tip See "Early Socialization in Orphanages" (Additional Lecture Ideas).
Let's Discuss Are the studies of children in Romanian orphanages comparable to the case of Isabelle? What type of care do children need to develop normally?

Key Person Harry Harlow
Methods Harlow's research with rhesus monkeys is an example of an experiment.
Classroom Tip For more information on Harlow's work, see the interview in *Psychology Today*, April 1973, pp. 65–68, 70, 72–74, and 76–77.

cloth-covered replica and one covered with wire that had the ability to offer milk. Monkey after monkey went to the wire mother for the life-giving milk, yet spent much more time clinging to the more motherlike cloth model. It appears that the infant monkeys developed greater social attachments from their need for warmth, comfort, and intimacy than from their need for milk.

While the isolation studies just discussed may seem to suggest that heredity can be dismissed as a factor in the social development of humans and animals, studies of twins provide insight into a fascinating interplay between hereditary and environmental factors.

Use Your Sociological Imagination   www.mhhe.com/schaefer7

What events in your life have had a strong influence on who you are?

The Influence of Heredity

Identical twins Oskar Stohr and Jack Yufe were separated soon after their birth and raised on different continents, in very different cultural settings. Oskar was reared as a strict Catholic by his maternal grandmother in the Sudetenland of Czechoslo-

{ Two twins celebrate their special identity at the annual Twins Day Festival in Twinsburg, Ohio. Every year, social scientists descend on Twinsburg to study the 3,000 pairs of twins who gather at the festival. Research points to some behavioral similarities between twins, but little beyond the likenesses found among nontwin siblings. }

**Classroom Tip** For another example of the interplay between heredity and environment involving a chimpanzee, see "Nature versus Nurture" (Additional Lecture Ideas).

vakia. As a member of the Hitler Youth movement in Nazi Germany, he learned to hate Jews. By contrast, his brother Jack was reared in Trinidad by the twins' Jewish father. Jack joined an Israeli kibbutz (a collective settlement) at age 17 and later served in the Israeli army. But when the twins were reunited in middle age, some startling similarities emerged: they both wore wire-rimmed glasses and mustaches. They both liked spicy foods and sweet liqueurs, were absent-minded, flushed the toilet before using it, stored rubber bands on their wrists, and dipped buttered toast in their coffee (Holden 1980).

The twins also differed in many important respects: Jack was a workaholic; Oskar enjoyed leisure-time activities. Whereas Oskar was a traditionalist who was domineering toward women, Jack was a political liberal much more accepting of feminism. Finally, Jack was extremely proud of being Jewish, while Oskar never mentioned his Jewish heritage (Holden 1987).

Oskar and Jack are prime examples of the interplay of heredity and environment. For a number of years, the Minnesota Twin Family Study has been following pairs of identical twins reared apart to determine what similarities, if any, they show in personality traits, behavior, and intelligence. Preliminary results from the available twin studies indicate that *both* genetic factors *and* socialization experiences are influential in human development. Certain characteristics, such as temperaments, voice patterns, and nervous habits, appear to be strikingly similar even in twins reared apart, suggesting that these qualities may be linked to hereditary causes. However, identical twins reared apart differ far more in their attitudes, values, chosen mates, and even drinking habits; these qualities, it would seem, are influenced by environmental factors. In examining clusters of personality traits among such twins, researchers have found marked similarities in their tendency toward leadership or dominance, but significant differences in their need for intimacy, comfort, and assistance.

Researchers have also been impressed with the similar scores on intelligence tests of twins reared apart in *roughly similar* social settings. Most of the identical twins register scores even closer than those that would be expected if the same person took a test twice. At the same time, however, identical twins brought up in *dramatically different* social environments score quite differently on intelligence tests—a finding that supports the impact of socialization on human development (McGue and Bouchard 1998; Minnesota Center for Twin and Family Research 2006).

We need to be cautious in reviewing studies of twin pairs and other relevant research. Widely broadcast findings have often been based on extremely small samples and preliminary analysis. For example, one study (not involving twin pairs) was frequently cited as confirming genetic links with behavior. Yet the researchers had to retract their conclusions after they increased the sample and reclassified two of the original cases. After those changes, the initial findings were no longer valid.

Critics add that studies of twin pairs have not provided satisfactory information concerning the extent to which separated identical twins may have had contact with each other, even though they were raised apart. Such interactions—especially if

**Let's Discuss** What do twin studies tell us about the influence of nature and nurture in the development of personality? What do they not tell us about the influence of nature and nurture in the development of personality?
Methods Observation research on twins reared apart was conducted by the Minnesota Center for Twin and Family Research.

Children imitate the people around them, especially family members they continually interact with, during the *preparatory stage* described by George Herbert Mead.

they were extensive—could call into question the validity of the twin studies. As this debate continues, we can certainly anticipate numerous efforts to replicate the research and clarify the interplay between heredity and environmental factors in human development (Horgan 1993; Plomin 1989).

The Self and Socialization

We all have various perceptions, feelings, and beliefs about who we are and what we are like. How do we come to develop them? Do they change as we age?

We were not born with these understandings. Building on the work of George Herbert Mead (1964b), sociologists recognize that our concept of who we are, the *self,* emerges as we interact with others. The *self* is a distinct identity that sets us apart from others. It is not a static phenomenon, but continues to develop and change throughout our lives.

Sociologists and psychologists alike have expressed interest in how the individual develops and modifies the sense of self as a result of social interaction. The work of sociologists Charles { pp.11–12, 17 Horton Cooley and George Herbert Mead, pioneers of the interactionist approach, has been especially useful in furthering our understanding of these important issues.

Sociological Approaches to the Self

Cooley: Looking-Glass Self   In the early 1900s, Charles Horton Cooley advanced the belief that we learn who we are by interacting with others. Our view of ourselves, then, comes not only from direct contemplation of our personal qualities but also from our impressions of how others perceive us. Cooley used the phrase **looking-glass self** to emphasize that the self is the product of our social interactions.

The process of developing a self-identity or self-concept has three phases. First, we imagine how we present ourselves to

Theory Interactionist view of the self introduced
Key Person Charles Horton Cooley
Theory Cooley's interactionist view of the looking-glass self

others—to relatives, friends, even strangers on the street. Then we imagine how others evaluate us (attractive, intelligent, shy, or strange). Finally, we develop some sort of feeling about ourselves, such as respect or shame, as a result of these impressions (Cooley 1902; M. Howard 1989).

A subtle but critical aspect of Cooley's looking-glass self is that the self results from an individual's "imagination" of how others view him or her. As a result, we can develop self-identities based on *incorrect* perceptions of how others see us. A student may react strongly to a teacher's criticism and decide (wrongly) that the instructor views the student as stupid. This misperception may be converted into a negative self-identity through the following process: (1) the teacher criticized me, (2) the teacher must think that I'm stupid, (3) I *am* stupid. Yet self-identities are also subject to change. If the student receives an A at the end of the course, he or she will probably no longer feel stupid.

Mead: Stages of the Self   George Herbert Mead continued Cooley's exploration of interactionist theory. Mead (1934, 1964a) developed a useful model of the process by which the self emerges, defined by three distinct stages: the preparatory stage, the play stage, and the game stage.

The Preparatory Stage   During the *preparatory stage,* children merely imitate the people around them, especially family members with whom they continually interact. Thus, a small child will bang on a piece of wood while a parent is engaged in carpentry work, or will try to throw a ball if an older sibling is doing so nearby.

As they grow older, children become more adept at using symbols to communicate with others. **Symbols** are the gestures, objects, and words that form the basis of human communication. By interacting with relatives and friends, as well as by watching cartoons on television and looking at picture books, children in the preparatory stage begin to understand symbols. They will continue to use this form of communication throughout their lives.

Like spoken languages, symbols vary from culture to culture, and even from one subculture to another. In North America, raising one's eyebrows may communicate astonishment or doubt. In Peru, the same gesture means "money" or "pay me," and may constitute an unspoken request for a bribe. In the Pacific island nation of Tonga, raised eyebrows mean "yes" or "I agree" (Axtell 1990).

In multicultural societies, such differences in the meaning of symbols create the potential for conflict. For example, the symbolic headscarf that is worn by Muslim women recently became a major social issue in France. For years French public schools have banned overt signs of religion, such as large crosses, skullcaps, and headscarves. Muslim students who violated the informal dress code were expelled. In 2003, amid growing controversy, a government advisory panel recommended that the French Parliament strengthen the ban by writing it into law. The issue is a particularly thorny one because of the conflicting cultural meanings these symbols carry. To many of the French, the

Key Person George Herbert Mead
Theory Mead's interactionist view of the self
Theory Interactionists' view of symbols

headscarf symbolizes the submission of women—an unwelcome connotation in a society that places a high value on egalitarianism. To others it represents a challenge to the French way of life. Thus, 69 percent of the French surveyed on the issue supported the ban. But to Muslims, the headscarf symbolizes modesty and respectability. Muslim schoolchildren take this symbol very seriously (*The Economist* 2004a).

The Play Stage Mead was among the first to analyze the relationship of symbols to socialization. As children develop skill in communicating through symbols, they gradually become more aware of social relationships. As a result, during the *play stage*, they begin to pretend to be other people. Just as an actor "becomes" a character, a child becomes a doctor, parent, superhero, or ship captain.

Mead, in fact, noted that an important aspect of the play stage is role playing. ***Role taking*** is the process of mentally assuming the perspective of another and responding from that imagined viewpoint. For example, through this process, a young child will gradually learn when it is best to ask a parent for favors. If the parent usually comes home from work in a bad mood, the child will wait until after dinner, when the parent is more relaxed and approachable.

The Game Stage In Mead's third stage, the *game stage*, the child of about eight or nine years old no longer just plays roles but begins to consider several tasks and relationships simultaneously. At this point in development, children grasp not only their own social positions but also those of others around them—just as in a football game the players must understand their own and everyone else's positions. Consider a girl or boy who is part of a scout troop out on a weekend hike in the mountains. The child must understand what he or she is expected to do but must also recognize the responsibilities of other scouts as well as the leaders. This is the final stage of development under Mead's model; the child can now respond to numerous members of the social environment.

Mead uses the term ***generalized other*** to refer to the attitudes, viewpoints, and expectations of society as a whole that a child takes into account in his or her behavior. Simply put, this concept suggests that when an individual acts, he or she takes into account an entire group of people. For example, a child will not act courteously merely to please a particular parent. Rather, the child comes to understand that courtesy is a widespread social value endorsed by parents, teachers, and religious leaders.

At the game stage, children can take a more sophisticated view of people and the social environment. They now understand what specific occupations and social positions are and no longer equate Mr. Williams only with the role of "librarian" or Ms. Sanchez only with "principal." It has become clear to the child that Mr. Williams can be a librarian, a parent, and a marathon runner at the same time and that Ms. Sanchez is one of many principals in our society. Thus, the child has reached a new level of sophistication in observations of individuals and institutions.

According to George Herbert Mead, children begin to communicate through symbols at an early age, and continue to use them throughout their lives. This French girl is protesting a law that forbids public school students to wear Islamic headscarves and other religious insignia. The ban against the deeply symbolic head covering has sparked considerable controversy in France.

Mead: Theory of the Self Mead is best known for his theory of the self. According to Mead (1964b), the self begins at a privileged, central position in a person's world. Young children picture themselves as the focus of everything around them and find it difficult to consider the perspectives of others. For example, when shown a mountain scene and asked to describe what an observer on the opposite side of the mountain might see (such as a lake or hikers), young children describe only objects visible from their own vantage point. This childhood tendency to place ourselves at the center of events never entirely disappears. Many people with a fear of flying automatically assume that if any plane goes down, it will be the one they are on. And who reads the horoscope section in the paper without looking at their own horoscope first? Why else do we buy lottery tickets, if we do not imagine ourselves winning?

Nonetheless, as people mature, the self changes and begins to reflect greater concern about the reactions of others. Parents, friends, co-workers, coaches, and teachers are often among those who play a major role in shaping a person's self. The term ***significant others*** is used to refer to those individuals who are most important in the development of the self. Many young

people, for example, find themselves drawn to the same kind of work their parents engage in (Sullivan [1953] 1968).

In some instances, studies of significant others have generated controversy among researchers. For example, some researchers have contended that African American adolescents are more "peer-oriented" than their White counterparts because of presumed weaknesses in Black families. However, investigations indicate that these hasty conclusions were based on limited studies focusing on less affluent Blacks. In fact, there appears to be little difference in who African Americans and Whites from similar economic backgrounds regard as their significant others (Giordano et al. 1993; Juhasz 1989).

Use Your Sociological Imagination

www.mhhe.com /schaefer7

How do you view yourself as you interact with others around you? How do you think you formed this view of yourself?

Goffman: Presentation of the Self How do we manage our "self"? How do we display to others who we are? Erving Goffman, a sociologist associated with the interactionist perspective, suggested that many of our daily activities involve attempts to convey impressions of who we are. His observations help us to understand the sometimes subtle yet critical ways in which we learn to present ourselves socially. They also offer concrete examples of this aspect of socialization.

Early in life, the individual learns to slant his or her presentation of the self in order to create distinctive appearances and satisfy particular audiences. Goffman (1959) referred to this altering of the presentation of the self as ***impression management.*** Box 4-1 (opposite) describes an everyday example of this concept—the way students behave after receiving their exam grades. In analyzing such everyday social interactions, Goffman makes so many explicit parallels to the theater that his view has been termed the ***dramaturgical approach.*** According to this perspective, people resemble performers in action. For example, a clerk may try to appear busier than he or she actually is if a supervisor happens to be watching. A customer in a singles' bar may try to look as if he or she is waiting for a particular person to arrive.

Goffman (1959) also drew attention to another aspect of the self—***face-work.*** How often do you initiate some kind of face-saving behavior when you feel embarrassed or rejected? In response to a rejection at the singles' bar, a person may engage in face-work by saying, "There really isn't an interesting person in this entire crowd." We feel the need to maintain a proper image of the self if we are to continue social interaction.

In some cultures, people engage in elaborate deceptions to avoid losing face. In Japan, for example, where lifetime employment has until recently been the norm, "company men" thrown out of work by a deep economic recession may feign employment, rising as usual in the morning, donning suit and tie, and heading for the business district. But instead of going to the office, they congregate at places such as Tokyo's Hibiya Library, where they pass the time by reading before returning home at the usual hour. Many of these men are trying to protect family members, who would be shamed if neighbors discovered the family breadwinner was unemployed. Others are deceiving their wives and families as well (French 2000).

Goffman's work on the self represents a logical progression of sociological studies begun by Cooley and Mead on how personality is acquired through socialization and how we manage the presentation of the self to others. Cooley stressed the process by which we create a self; Mead focused on how the self develops as we learn to interact with others; Goffman emphasized the ways in which we consciously create images of ourselves for others.

Psychological Approaches to the Self

Psychologists have shared the interest of Cooley, Mead, and other sociologists in the development of the self. Early work in psychology, such as that of Sigmund

A prospective employer reviews an applicant's qualifications for the job. To present themselves in a positive manner, both interviewer and applicant may resort to *impression management* and *face-work,* two tactics described by the interactionist Erving Goffman.

Race/Ethnicity Studies of African American adolescents and whom they regard as their significant others
Key Person Erving Goffman
Theory Goffman's interactionist view of impression management

Let's Discuss Can you think of situations in which people in the United States engage in elaborate deceptions to avoid losing face?
Let's Discuss In what way does Goffman's work build on the earlier work of Cooley and Mead?

4-1 Impression Management by Students

When you and fellow classmates get an exam back, you probably react differently depending on the grades that you and they earned. This distinction is part of *impression management,* as sociologists Daniel Albas and Cheryl Albas have demonstrated. The two explored the strategies college students use to create desired appearances after receiving their grades on exams. Albas and Albas divided these encounters into three categories: those between students who have all received high grades (Ace–Ace encounters); those between students who have received high grades and those who have received low or even failing grades (Ace–Bomber encounters); and those between students who have all received low grades (Bomber–Bomber encounters).

Ace–Ace encounters occur in a rather open atmosphere, because there is comfort in sharing a high mark with another high achiever. It is even acceptable to violate the norm of modesty and brag when among other Aces, since as one student admitted, "It's much easier to admit a high mark to someone who has done better than you, or at least as well."

Ace–Bomber encounters are often sensitive. Bombers generally attempt to avoid such exchanges, because "you . . . emerge looking like the dumb one" or "feel like you are lazy or unreliable." When forced into interactions with Aces, Bombers work to appear gracious and congratulatory. For their part, Aces offer sympathy and support to the dissatisfied Bombers and even rationalize their own "lucky" high scores. To help Bombers save face, Aces may emphasize the difficulty and unfairness of the examination.

> *When forced into interactions with Aces, Bombers work to appear gracious and congratulatory.*

Bomber–Bomber encounters tend to be closed, reflecting the group effort to wall off the feared disdain of others. Yet, within the safety of these encounters, Bombers openly share their disappointment and engage in expressions of mutual self-pity that they themselves call "pity parties." They devise face-saving excuses for their poor performance, such as "I wasn't feeling well all week" or "I had four exams and two papers due that week." If the grade distribution in a class in-cludes particularly low scores, Bombers may blame the professor, attacking him or her as a sadist, a slave driver, or simply an incompetent.

As is evident from these descriptions, students' impression management strategies conform to society's informal norms regarding modesty and consideration for less successful peers. In classroom settings, as in the workplace and in other types of human interaction, efforts at impression management are most intense when status differentials are pronounced, as in encounters between the high-scoring Aces and the low-scoring Bombers.

Let's Discuss

1. How do you react with those who have received higher or lower grades than you? Do you engage in impression management? How would you like others to react to your grade?
2. What social norms govern students' impression management strategies?

Source: Albas and Albas 1988.

Freud (1856–1939), stressed the role of inborn drives—among them the drive for sexual gratification—in channeling human behavior. More recently, psychologists such as Jean Piaget have emphasized the stages through which human beings progress as the self develops.

Like Charles Horton Cooley and George Herbert Mead, Freud believed that the self is a social product, and that aspects of one's personality are influenced by other people (especially one's parents). However, unlike Cooley and Mead, he suggested that the self has components that work in opposition to each other. According to Freud, our natural impulsive instincts are in constant conflict with societal constraints. Part of us seeks limitless pleasure, while another part favors rational behavior. By interacting with others, we learn the expectations of society and then select behavior most appropriate to our own culture. (Of course, as Freud was well aware, we sometimes distort reality and behave irrationally.)

Research on newborn babies by the Swiss child psychologist Jean Piaget (1896–1980) has underscored the importance of so-cial interactions in developing a sense of self. Piaget found that newborns have no self in the sense of a looking-glass image. Ironically, though, they are quite self-centered; they demand that all attention be directed toward them. Newborns have not yet separated themselves from the universe of which they are a part. For these babies, the phrase "you and me" has no meaning; they understand only "me." However, as they mature, children are gradually socialized into social relationships, even within their rather self-centered world.

In his well-known ***cognitive theory of development,*** Piaget (1954) identified four stages in the development of children's thought processes. In the first, or *sensorimotor,* stage, young children use their senses to make discoveries. For example, through touching they discover that their hands are actually a part of themselves. During the second, or *preoperational,* stage, children begin to use words and symbols to distinguish objects and ideas. The milestone in the third, or *concrete operational,* stage is that children engage in more logical thinking. They learn that even when a formless lump of clay is shaped into a snake, it is still the

---

Theory Interactionist view of students' impression management after exams
Methods The study of impression management by Albas and Albas is an example of observation research.

Key Persons Sigmund Freud, Jean Piaget
Student Alert Make sure that students understand the difference between the psychological and sociological approaches to socialization.
Let's Discuss In what ways are the views of psychologists similar to and different from the views of Cooley, Mead, and Goffman?

same clay. Finally, in the fourth, or *formal operational*, stage, adolescents become capable of sophisticated abstract thought, and can deal with ideas and values in a logical manner.

Piaget suggested that moral development becomes an important part of socialization as children develop the ability to think more abstractly. When children learn the rules of a game such as checkers or jacks, they are learning to obey societal norms. Those under eight years old display a rather basic level of morality: rules are rules, and there is no concept of "extenuating circumstances." As they mature, children become capable of greater autonomy, and begin to experience moral dilemmas and doubts as to what constitutes proper behavior.

According to Jean Piaget, social interaction is the key to development. As children grow older, they pay increasing attention to how other people think and why they act in particular ways. In order to develop a distinct personality, each of us needs opportunities to interact with others. As we saw earlier, Isabelle was deprived of the chance for normal social interactions, and the consequences were severe (Kitchener 1991).

We have seen that a number of thinkers considered social interaction the key to the development of an individual's sense of self. As is generally true, we can best understand this topic by drawing on a variety of theory and research. Table 4-1 summarizes the rich literature, both sociological and psychological, on the development of the self.

Socialization and the Life Course

The Life Course

Among the Kota people of the Congo in Africa, adolescents paint themselves blue. Mexican American girls go on a daylong

Body painting is a ritual marking the passage to puberty among young people in Liberia, in western Africa.

Table 4-1   Theoretical Approaches to Development of the Self

Scholar	Key Concepts and Contributions	Major Points of Theory
Charles Horton Cooley 1864–1929 sociologist (USA)	Looking-glass self	Stages of development not distinct; feelings toward ourselves developed through interaction with others
George Herbert Mead 1863–1931 sociologist (USA)	The self Generalized other	Three distinct stages of development; self develops as children grasp the roles of others in their lives
Erving Goffman 1922–1982 sociologist (USA)	Impression management Dramaturgical approach Face-work	Self developed through the impressions we convey to others and to groups
Sigmund Freud 1856–1939 psychotherapist (Austria)	Psychoanalysis	Self influenced by parents and by inborn drives, such as the drive for sexual gratification
Jean Piaget 1896–1980 child psychologist (Switzerland)	Cognitive theory of development	Four stages of cognitive development; moral development linked to socialization

Global View Adolescent males paint themselves blue in a rite of passage among the Kota people of the Congo.

Freshman cadets at the Virginia Military Institute crawl up a muddy hill in the school's gritty indoctrination into strict military discipline, a rite of passage at the school.

religious retreat before dancing the night away. Egyptian mothers step over their newborn infants seven times, and students at the Naval Academy throw their hats in the air. These are all ways of celebrating **rites of passage,** a means of dramatizing and validating changes in a person's status. The Kota rite marks the passage to adulthood. The color blue, viewed as the color of death, symbolizes the death of childhood. Hispanic girls celebrate reaching womanhood with a *quinceañera* ceremony at age 15. In the Cuban American community of Miami, the popularity of the *quinceañera* supports a network of party planners, caterers, dress designers, and the Miss Quinceañera Latina pageant. For thousands of years, Egyptian mothers have welcomed their

newborns to the world in the Soboa ceremony by stepping over the seven-day-old infant seven times. And Naval Academy seniors celebrate their graduation from college by hurling their hats skyward.

These specific ceremonies mark stages of development in the life course. They indicate that the process of socialization continues through all stages of the life cycle. In fact, some researchers have chosen to concentrate on socialization as a lifelong process. Sociologists and other social scientists who take such a **life course approach** look closely at the social factors that influence people throughout their lives, from birth to death, including gender and income. They recognize that biological changes mold but do not dictate human behavior.

Several life events mark the passage to adulthood. Of course, these turning points vary from one society and even one generation to the next. According to a national survey done in 2002, in the United States the key event seems to be the completion of formal schooling (see Table 4-2). On average, Americans expect this milestone to occur by a person's 23rd birthday. Other major events in the life course, such as getting married or becoming a parent, are expected to follow three or four years later. Interestingly, comparatively few survey respondents identified marriage and parenthood as important milestones (S. Furstenberg et al. 2004).

One result of these staggered steps to independence is that in the United States, unlike some other societies, there is no clear dividing line between adolescence and adulthood. Nowadays, few young people finish school, get married, and leave home at about the same age, clearly establishing their transition to adulthood. The term *youthhood* has been coined to describe the prolonged ambiguous status that young people in their twenties experience (Côté 2000).

Table 4-2 Milestones in the Transition to Adulthood

Life Event	Expected Age	Percentage of People Who View Event as Extremely/ Quite Important
Financial independence from parents/guardians	20.9 years	80.9%
Separate residence from parents	21.1	57.2
Full-time employment	21.2	83.8
Completion of formal schooling	22.3	90.2
Capability of supporting a family	24.5	82.3
Marriage	25.7	33.2
Parenthood	26.2	29.0

Note: Based on the 2002 General Social Survey of 1,398 people.
Source: T. W. Smith 2003.

Think About It
Why did so few respondents consider marriage and parenthood to be important milestones? Which milestones do you think are most important?

Race/Ethnicity The *quinceañera* as a rite of passage for Mexican American and Cuban American girls
Classroom Tip See "Reverse Socialization and Gender Roles" (Additional Lecture Ideas).

Classroom Tip See "Lifeline" (Class Discussion Topics).
Classroom Tip For some recent views of changes in the conceptualization of the life course, see "Rethinking the Life Course" (Additional Lecture Ideas).

We encounter some of the most difficult socialization challenges (and rites of passage) in the later years of life. Assessing one's accomplishments, coping with declining physical abilities, experiencing retirement, and facing the inevitability of death may lead to painful adjustments. Old age is further complicated by the negative way that many societies, including the United States, view and treat the elderly. The common stereotypes of the elderly as helpless and dependent may well weaken an older person's self-image. However, as we will explore more fully in Chapter 11, many older people continue to lead active, productive, fulfilled lives, whether in the paid labor force or as retirees.

Anticipatory Socialization and Resocialization

The development of a social self is literally a lifelong transformation that begins in the crib and continues as one prepares for death. Two types of socialization occur at many points throughout the life course: anticipatory socialization and resocialization.

Anticipatory socialization refers to processes of socialization in which a person "rehearses" for future positions, occupations, and social relationships. A culture can function more efficiently and smoothly if members become acquainted with the norms, values, and behavior associated with a social position before actually assuming that status. Preparation for many aspects of adult life begins with anticipatory socialization during childhood and adolescence, and continues throughout our lives as we prepare for new responsibilities.

You can see the process of anticipatory socialization take place when high school students start to consider what colleges they may attend. Traditionally, this task meant looking at publications received in the mail or making campus visits. However, with new technology, more and more students are using the Web to begin their college experience. Colleges are investing more time and money in developing attractive Web sites through which students can take "virtual" campus tours and hear audio clips of everything from the college anthem to a sample zoology lecture.

Occasionally, assuming a new social or occupational position requires us to *unlearn* an established orientation. *Resocialization* refers to the process of discarding former behavior patterns and accepting new ones as part of a transition in one's life. Often resocialization occurs during an explicit effort to transform an individual, as happens in reform schools, therapy groups, prisons, religious conversion settings, and political indoctrination camps. The process of re-

socialization typically involves considerable stress for the individual—much more so than socialization in general, or even anticipatory socialization (Gecas 1992).

Resocialization is particularly effective when it occurs within a total institution. Erving Goffman (1961) coined the term *total institution* to refer to an institution that regulates all aspects of a person's life under a single authority, such as a prison, the military, a mental hospital, or a convent. Because the total institution is generally cut off from the rest of society, it provides for all the needs of its members. Quite literally, the crew of a merchant vessel at sea becomes part of a total institution. So elaborate are its requirements, so all-encompassing its activities, a total institution often represents a miniature society.

Goffman (1961) identified four common traits of total institutions:

- All aspects of life are conducted in the same place under the control of a single authority.
- Any activities within the institution are conducted in the company of others in the same circumstances—for example, army recruits or novices in a convent.
- The authorities devise rules and schedule activities without consulting the participants.
- All aspects of life within a total institution are designed to fulfill the purpose of the organization. Thus, all activities in a monastery might be centered on prayer and communion with God. (Davies 1989; P. Rose et al. 1979)

People often lose their individuality within total institutions. For example, a person entering prison may experience the

Prisons are centers of resocialization, where people are placed under pressure to discard old behavior patterns and accept new ones. These prisoners are learning to use weights to release tension and exert their strength—a socially acceptable method of handling antisocial impulses.

Let's Discuss Discuss anticipatory socialization for people headed to college for the first time. Does this process vary for older students who have been out of school for many years?
Classroom Tip See "The Nunnery as a Total Institution" (Class Discussion Topics).

Let's Discuss Examine college hazing and entrance into the military with respect to degradation ceremonies.

humiliation of a *degradation ceremony* as he or she is stripped of clothing, jewelry, and other personal possessions. From this point on, scheduled daily routines allow for little or no personal initiative. The individual becomes secondary and rather invisible in the overbearing social environment (Garfinkel 1955).

Agents of Socialization

As we have seen, the culture of the United States is defined by rather gradual movements from one stage of socialization to the next. The continuing and lifelong socialization process involves many different social forces that influence our lives and alter our self-images.

The family is the most important agent of socialization in the United States, especially for children. In this chapter, we'll also discuss six other agents of socialization: the school, the peer group, the mass media, the workplace, religion, and the state. We'll explore the role of religion in socializing young people into society's norms and values more fully in Chapter 13.

Family

Children in Amish communities are raised in a highly structured and disciplined manner. But they are not immune to the temptations posed by their peers in the non-Amish world—"rebellious" acts such as dancing, drinking, and riding in cars. Still, Amish families don't become too concerned; they know the strong influence they ultimately exert over their offspring (see Box 4-2, page 90). The same is true for the family. It is tempting to say that the "peer group" or even the "media" really raise children these days, especially when the spotlight falls on young people involved in shooting sprees and hate crimes. Almost all available research, however, shows that the role of the family in socializing a child cannot be overestimated (W. Williams 1998; for a different view see J. Harris 1998).

The lifelong process of learning begins shortly after birth. Since newborns can hear, see, smell, taste, and feel heat, cold, and pain, they are constantly orienting themselves to the surrounding world. Human beings, especially family members, constitute an important part of their social environment. People minister to the baby's needs by feeding, cleansing, carrying, and comforting the baby.

Cultural Influences As both Charles Horton Cooley and George Herbert Mead noted, the development of the self is a critical aspect of the early years of one's life. But how children develop this sense of self can vary from one society to another. For example, most parents in the United States do not send six-year-olds to school unsupervised. But that is the norm in Japan, where parents push their children to commute to school on their own from an early age. In cities like Tokyo, first-graders must learn to negotiate buses, subways, and long walks. To ensure their safety, parents carefully lay out rules: never talk to strangers; check with a station attendant if you get off at the wrong stop; if you miss your stop stay on to the end of the line,

then call; take stairs, not escalators; don't fall asleep. Some parents equip the children with cell phones or pagers. One parent acknowledges that she worries, "but after they are 6, children are supposed to start being independent from the mother. If you're still taking your child to school after the first month, everyone looks at you funny" (Tolbert 2000:17).

While we consider the family's role in socialization, we need to remember that children do not play a passive role. They are active agents, influencing and altering the families, schools, and communities of which they are a part.

The Impact of Race and Gender In the United States, social development includes exposure to cultural assumptions regarding gender and race. African American parents, for example, have learned that children as young as two years old can absorb negative messages about Blacks in children's books, toys,

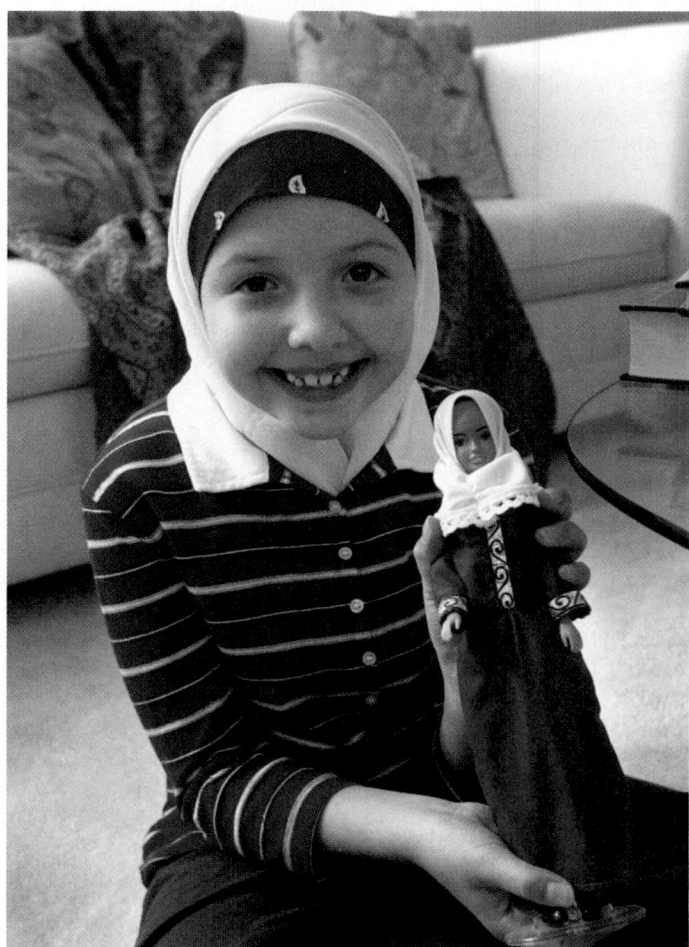

In her Michigan home, a young girl displays Razanne, a modestly dressed doll made especially for Muslim children. Because girls learn about themselves and their social roles by playing with dolls, having a doll that represents their own heritage is important to them.

4-2 Raising Amish Children

Jacob is a typical teenager in his Amish community in Lancaster County, Pennsylvania. At 14 he is in his final year of schooling. Over the next few years he will become a full-time worker on the family farm, taking breaks only for three-hour religious services each morning. When he is a bit older, Jacob may bring a date to a community "singing" in his family's horse-drawn buggy. But he will be forbidden to date outside his own community and can marry only with the deacon's consent.

Jacob is well aware of the rather different way of life of the "English" (the Amish term for non-Amish people). One summer, late at night, he and his friends hitchhiked to a nearby town to see a movie, breaking several Amish taboos. His parents learned of his adventure, but like most Amish they are confident that their son will choose the Amish way of life. What is this way of life, and how can his parents be so sure of its appeal?

Jacob and his family live in a manner very similar to their ancestors, members of the conservative Mennonite church who migrated to North America from Europe in the 18th and 19th centuries. Schisms in the church after 1850 led to a division between those who wanted to preserve the "old order" and those who favored a "new order" with more progressive methods and organization. Today the old order Amish live in about 50 communities in the United States and Canada. Estimates put their number at about 80,000, with approximately 75 percent living in three states—Ohio, Pennsylvania, and Indiana.

The old order Amish live a simple life and reject most aspects of modernization and contemporary technology. That's why they spurn conveniences such as electricity, automobiles, radio, and television. The Amish maintain their own schools and traditions and do not want their children socialized into many norms and values of the dominant culture of the United States. Those who stray too far from Amish mores may be excommunicated and shunned by all other members of the community—a practice of social control called *Meiding*. Sociologists sometimes use the term *secessionist minorities* to refer to groups like the Amish, who reject assimilation and coexist with the rest of society primarily on their own terms.

The socialization of Amish youths pushes them to forgo movies, radio, television, cosmetics, jewelry, musical instruments of any kind, and motorized vehicles. Yet, like Jacob did, Amish youths often test their subculture's boundaries during a period of discovery called

> The old order Amish live a simple life and reject most aspects of modernization and contemporary technology.

rumspringe, a term that means "running around." Amish young people attend barn dances where taboos like drinking, smoking, and driving cars are commonly broken. Parents often react by looking the other way, sometimes literally. For example, when they hear radio sounds from a barn or a motorcycle entering their property in the middle of the night, they don't immediately investigate and punish their offspring. Instead, they pretend not to notice, secure in the comfort that their children almost always return to the traditions of the Amish lifestyle. Research shows that only about 20 percent of Amish youths leave the fold, generally to join a more liberal Mennonite group. Rarely does a baptized adult ever

leave. The socialization of Amish youths moves them gently but firmly into becoming Amish adults.

Let's Discuss

1. What makes Amish parents so sure that their children will choose to remain in the Amish community?
2. If you lived in an Amish community, how would your life differ from the way it is now? In your opinion, what advantages and disadvantages would that lifestyle have?

Sources: Meyers 1992; Remnick 1998; Zellner and Schaefer 2006.

---

and television shows—all of which are designed primarily for White consumers. At the same time, African American children are exposed more often than others to the innercity youth gang culture. Because most Blacks, even those who are middle class, live near very poor neighborhoods, children such as Charisse (see the chapter-opening excerpt) are susceptible to these influences, despite their parents' strong family values (Linn and Poussaint 1999; Pattillo-McCoy 1999).

Race/Ethnicity Depiction of African Americans in children's books, toys, and television shows

The term **gender roles** refers to expectations regarding the proper behavior, attitudes, and activities of males and females. For example, we traditionally think of "toughness" as masculine—and desirable only in men—while we view "tenderness" as feminine. As we will see in Chapter 11, other cultures do not necessarily assign these qualities to each gender in the way that our culture does.

As the primary agents of childhood socialization, parents play a critical role in guiding children into those gender roles

Gender Concept of gender roles is introduced.

Rakefet Avramovitz has been working at the Child Care Law Center in San Francisco since 2003. The center uses legal tools to foster the development of quality, affordable child care, with the goal of expanding child care options, particularly for low-income families. As a support person for the center's attorneys, Avramovitz manages grants, oversees the center's publications, and sets up conferences and training sessions. One of her most important tasks has been to organize a working group that brings together people from all parts of the child care community. "The documents that come out of this forum inform the organization's work for the year," she explains.

Avramovitz graduated from Dickinson College in 2000. She first became interested in sociology when she took a social analysis course. Though she enjoyed her qualitative courses most, she found her quantitative courses fun, "in that we got to do surveys of people on campus. I've always enjoyed field-work," she notes. Avramovitz's most memorable course was one that gave her the opportunity to interact with migrant farm workers for an entire semester. "I learned ethnography and how to work with people of different cultures. It changed my life," she says.

Avramovitz finds that the skills she learned in her sociology courses are a great help to her on the job. "Sociology taught me how to work with people . . . and how to think critically. It taught me how to listen and find the stories that people are telling," she explains. Before joining the Child Care Law Center, Avramovitz worked as a counselor for women who were facing difficult issues. "My background in ethnography helped me to talk to these women and listen effectively," she notes. "I was able to help many women by understanding and being able to express their needs to the attorneys we worked with."

Avramovitz is enthusiastic about her work and her ability to make a difference in other people's lives. Maybe that is why she looks forward to summer at the center, when the staff welcomes several law students as interns. "It is really neat to see people learn and get jazzed about child-care issues," she says.

Let's Discuss

1. What might be some of the broad, long-term effects of the center's work to expand child care options? Explain.
2. Besides the law, what other professions might benefit from the skills a sociology major has to offer?

---

deemed appropriate in a society. Other adults, older siblings, the mass media, and religious and educational institutions also have a noticeable impact on a child's socialization into feminine and masculine norms. A culture or subculture may require that one sex or the other take primary responsibility for the socialization of children, economic support of the family, or religious or intellectual leadership. In some societies, girls are socialized mainly by their mothers and boys by their fathers—an arrangement that may prevent girls from learning critical survival skills. In South Asia, fathers teach their sons to swim to prepare them for a life as fishermen; girls typically do not learn to swim. When a deadly tsunami hit the coast of South Asia in 2004, many more men survived than women.

Interactionists remind us that socialization concerning not only masculinity and femininity but also marriage and parenthood begins in childhood as a part of family life. Children observe their parents as they express affection, deal with finances, quarrel, complain about in-laws, and so forth. Their learning represents an informal process of anticipatory socialization in which they develop a tentative model of what being married and being a parent are like. (We will explore socialization for marriage and parenthood more fully in Chapter 12.)

Theory Explain the socialization process for marital roles as developed by interactionists.

School

Where did you learn the national anthem? Who taught you about the heroes of the American Revolution? Where were you first tested on your knowledge of your culture? Like the family, schools have an explicit mandate to socialize people in the United States—and especially children—into the norms and values of our culture.

As conflict theorists Samuel Bowles and Herbert Gintis (1976) have observed, schools in this country foster competition through built-in systems of reward and punishment, such as grades and evaluations by teachers. Consequently, a child who is experiencing difficulty trying to learn a new skill can sometimes come to feel stupid and unsuccessful. However, as the self matures, children become capable of increasingly realistic assessments of their intellectual, physical, and social abilities.

Functionalists point out that schools, as agents of socialization, fulfill the function of teaching children the values and customs of the larger society. Conflict theorists agree, but add that schools can reinforce the divisive aspects of society, especially those of social class. For example, higher education in the United States is costly despite the existence of financial aid programs. Students from affluent backgrounds therefore have an

Theory Bowles and Gintis's view of schooling, an example of conflict theory, is discussed more fully in Chapter 13.
Theory Functionalist and conflict views of education as an agent of socialization

Chapter 4

advantage in gaining access to universities and professional training. At the same time, less affluent young people may never receive the preparation that would qualify them for the best-paying and most prestigious jobs. The contrast between the functionalist and conflict views of education will be discussed in more detail in Chapter 13.

In other cultures as well, schools serve socialization functions. Until the overthrow of Saddam Hussein in 2003, the sixth-grade textbooks used in Iraqi schools concentrated almost entirely on the military and its values of loyalty, honor, and sacrifice. Children were taught that their enemies were Iran, the United States, Israel and its supporters, and NATO, the European military alliance. Within months of the regime's fall, the curriculum had been rewritten to remove indoctrination on behalf of Hussein, his army, and his Baath Socialist Party (Marr 2003).

Peer Group

Ask 13-year-olds who matters most in their lives and they are likely to answer "friends." As a child grows older, the family becomes somewhat less important in social development. Instead, peer groups increasingly assume the role of Mead's significant others. Within the peer group, young people associate with others who are approximately their own age, and who often enjoy a similar social status (Giordano 2003).

We can see how important peer groups are to young people when their social lives are strained by war or disaster. In Baghdad, the overthrow of Saddam Hussein has profoundly changed teenagers' world, casting doubt on their future. Some young people have lost relatives or friends; others have become involved with fundamentalist groups or fled with their families to safer countries. Those youths who are left behind can suffer intense loneliness and boredom. Confined to their homes by crime and terrorism, those fortunate enough to have computers turn to Internet chat rooms or immerse themselves in their studies. Through e-mail, they struggle to maintain old friendships interrupted by wartime dislocation (Sanders 2004).

Gender differences are noteworthy among adolescents. Boys and girls are socialized by their parents, peers, and the media to identify many of the same paths to popularity, but to different degrees. Table 4-3 compares male and female college students' reports of how girls and boys they knew became popular in high school. The two groups named many of the same paths to popularity but gave them a different order of importance. While neither men nor women named sexual activity, drug use, or alcohol use as one of the top five paths, college men were much more likely than women to mention those behaviors as a means to becoming popular, for both boys and girls.

Mass Media and Technology

In the last 80 years, media innovations—radio, motion pictures, recorded music, television, and the Internet—have become important agents of socialization. Television, and increasingly the Internet, are critical forces in the socialization of children in the United States. One national survey indicates that 68 percent of U.S. children have a television in their bedroom, and nearly half of all youths ages 8 to 18 use the Internet every day (see Figure 4-2).

These media, however, are not always a negative socializing influence. Television programs and even commercials can introduce young people to unfamiliar lifestyles and cultures. Not only do children in the United States learn about life in "faraway lands," but inner-city children learn about the lives of farm children, and vice versa. The same goes for children living in other countries.

Sociologists and other social scientists have also begun to consider the impact of technology on socialization, especially as it applies to family life. The Silicon Valley Cultures Project studied families in California's Silicon Valley (a technological corridor) for 10 years, beginning in 1991. Although these families may not be typical, they represent a lifestyle that more and more households probably will approximate as time goes by. This study has found that technology in the form of e-mail, Web pages, cellular phones, voice mail, digital organizers, and pagers

Table 4-3 High School Popularity

What makes high school girls popular?		What makes high school boys popular?	
According to college men:	According to college women:	According to college men:	According to college women:
1. Physical attractiveness	1. Grades/intelligence	1. Participation in sports	1. Participation in sports
2. Grades/intelligence	2. Participation in sports	2. Grades/intelligence	2. Grades/intelligence
3. Participation in sports	3. General sociability	3. Popularity with girls	3. General sociability
4. General sociability	4. Physical attractiveness	4. General sociability	4. Physical attractiveness
5. Popularity with boys	5. Clothes	5. Car	5. School clubs/government

Note: Students at the following universities were asked in which ways adolescents in their high schools had gained prestige with their peers: Cornell University, Louisiana State University, Southeastern Louisiana University, State University of New York at Albany, State University of New York at Stony Brook, University of Georgia, and the University of New Hampshire.
Source: Suitor et al. 2001:445.

Theory Interactionist view of peer groups and their role in socialization
Gender Gender differences in the peer groups of adolescent females and males
Theory Examine the negative and positive functions of television on children and society in general.

Contemporary Culture Discuss the appropriate age at which children should be allowed to surf the Internet.
Classroom Tip See "Mass Media and Socialization" (Class Discussion Topics).
Let's Discuss As the media become more common in both the home and the classroom, will families and schools weaken as agents of socialization?

FIGURE 4-2

How Young People Use the Media

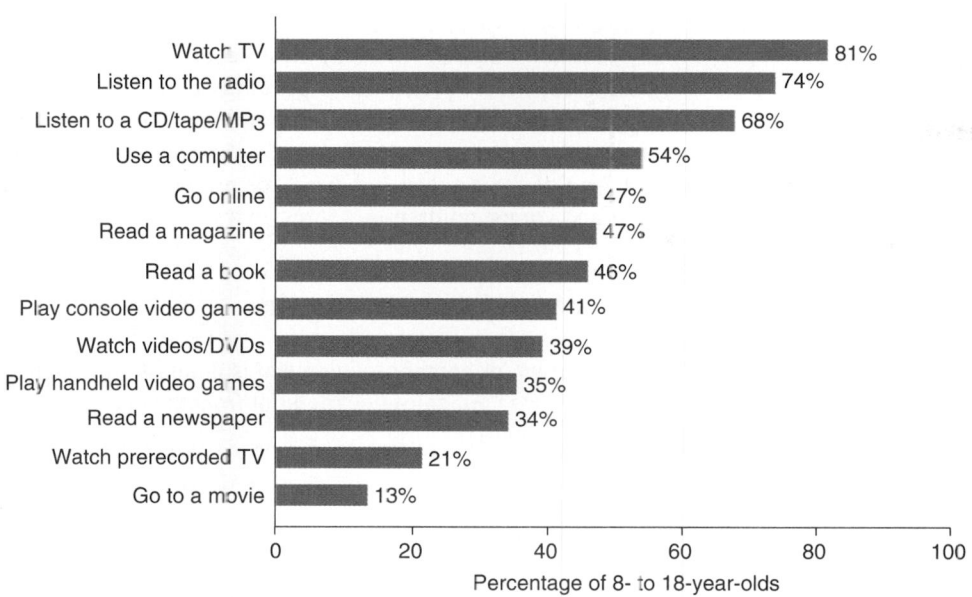

Activity	Percentage
Watch TV	81%
Listen to the radio	74%
Listen to a CD/tape/MP3	68%
Use a computer	54%
Go online	47%
Read a magazine	47%
Read a book	46%
Play console video games	41%
Watch videos/DVDs	39%
Play handheld video games	35%
Read a newspaper	34%
Watch prerecorded TV	21%
Go to a movie	13%

Percentage of 8- to 18-year-olds

Note: Based on a national representative sample of 2,032 people surveyed between October 2003 and March 2004.
Source: Rideout et al. 2005:7.

is allowing householders to let outsiders do everything from grocery shopping to carpooling. The researchers are also finding that families are socialized into multitasking (doing more than one task at a time) as the social norm; devoting one's full attention to one task—even eating or driving—is less and less common on a typical day (Silicon Valley Cultures Project 2004).

Workplace

Learning to behave appropriately in an occupation is a fundamental aspect of human socialization. In the United States, working full-time confirms adult status; it indicates that one has passed out of adolescence. In a sense, socialization into an occupation can represent both a harsh reality ("I have to work in order to buy food and pay the rent") and the realization of an ambition ("I've always wanted to be an airline pilot") (W. Moore 1968:862).

It used to be that going to work began with the end of our formal schooling, but that is no longer the case, at least not in the United States. More and more young people work today, and not just for a parent or relative. Adolescents generally seek jobs in order to make spending money; 80 percent of high school seniors say that little or none of what they earn goes to family expenses. These teens rarely look on their employment as a means of exploring vocational interests or getting on-the-job training.

Some observers feel that the increasing number of teenagers who are working earlier in life and for longer hours are finding the workplace almost as important an agent of socialization as school. In fact, a number of educators complain that student

time at work is adversely affecting schoolwork. The level of teenage employment in the United States is the highest among industrial countries, which may provide one explanation for why U.S. high school students lag behind those in other countries on international achievement tests.

Socialization in the workplace changes when it involves a more permanent shift from an after-school job to full-time employment. Occupational socialization can be most intense during the transition from school to job, but it continues throughout one's work history. Technological advances may alter the requirements of the position and necessitate some degree of resocialization. Today, men and women change occupations, employers, or places of work many times during their adult years. Occupational socialization continues, then, throughout a person's years in the labor market.

College students today recognize that occupational socialization is not socialization into one lifetime occupation. They anticipate going through a number of jobs. The Bureau of Labor Statistics (2002) has found that from ages 18 to 36, the typical person holds 10 different jobs. This high rate of turnover in employment applies to both men and women,

This girl's day doesn't end when school lets out. So many teenagers now work after school, the workplace has become another important agent of socialization for that age group.

and to those with a college degree as well as those with a high school diploma.

Religion and the State

Increasingly, social scientists are recognizing the importance of both government ("the state") and religion as agents of socialization, because of their impact on the life course. Traditionally, family members have served as the primary caregivers in our culture, but in the 20th century, the family's protective function was steadily transferred to outside agencies such as hospitals, mental health clinics, and child care centers. Many of these agencies are run by the state or by groups affiliated with certain religions.

Both government and organized religion have impacted the life course by reinstituting some of the rites of passage once observed in agricultural communities and early industrial societies. For example, religious organizations stipulate certain traditional rites that may bring together all the members of an extended family, even if they never meet for any other rea-

son. And government regulations stipulate the ages at which a person may drive a car, drink alcohol, vote in elections, marry without parental permission, work overtime, and retire. These regulations do not constitute strict rites of passage: most 18-year-olds choose not to vote, and most people choose their age of retirement without reference to government dictates.

In the Social Policy section that follows, we will see that government is under pressure to become a provider of child care, which would give it a new and direct role in the socialization of infants and young children.

Use Your Sociological Imagination   www.mhhe.com/schaefer7

You are Muslim (or another religion that is different from your own). How does your self-concept differ from the one you developed as a child?

social**Policy**
and Socialization

Child Care around the World

In Israel, Aisheh and Eliza run a nursery for 29 Israeli and Palestinian children, ages 4 to 6. Aisheh, who is Palestinian, speaks to the children in Arabic. Eliza, who is Jewish, speaks to them in Hebrew. The result: a bilingual, binational classroom that supports both Arab and Jewish culture—a first for Israel.

This unusual educational setting underscores the importance of early childhood socialization outside the home. Child care programs are not just babysitting services; they have an enormous influence on the development of young children—an influence that has been growing with the movement of more and more women into the paid labor force.

The Issue

The rise in single-parent families, increased job opportunities for women, and the need for additional family income have all propelled an increasing number of mothers of young children into the paid labor force of the United States. Who takes care of the children of these women during work hours?

FIGURE 4–3

Child Care Arrangements for Preschoolers

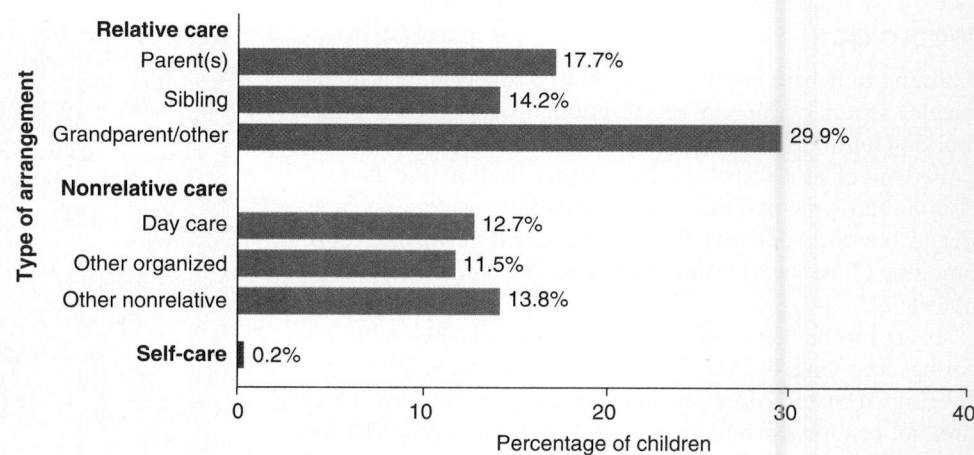

Note: Data for 2002, reported in 2005.
Source: J. Johnson 2005:2.

Preschoolers typically are not cared for by their parents. Seventy-three percent of employed mothers depend on others to care for their children, and 30 percent of mothers who aren't employed have regular care arrangements. As Figure 4-3 shows, children under age 5 are more likely to be cared for on a daily

plore macro-level implications for the functioning of social institutions like the family. But some of the issues surrounding day care have also been of interest to those who take the conflict perspective.

In the United States, high-quality day care is not equally available to all families. Parents in wealthy neighborhoods have an easier time finding day care than those in poor or working-class communities. Finding *affordable* child care is also a problem. Viewed from a conflict perspective, child care costs are an especially serious burden for lower-class families. The poorest families spend 25 percent of their income for preschool child care, while families who are *not* poor pay only 6 percent or less of their income.

Feminists echo the concern of conflict theorists that high-quality child care receives little government support because it is regarded as "merely a way to let women work." Nearly all child care workers (95 percent) are women; many find themselves in low-status, minimum-wage jobs. Typically, food servers, messengers, and gas station attendants make more money than child care workers, most of whom earn less than $8.00 per hour. Not surprisingly, turnover among employees in child care centers runs at about 30 percent per year (Bureau of the Census 2005a:403; Clawson and Gerstel 2002).

Policy Initiatives

Policies regarding child care outside the home vary throughout the world. Most developing nations do not have the economic base to provide subsidized child care. Thus, working mothers rely largely on relatives or take their children to work. In the comparatively wealthy industrialized countries of Western Europe, government provides child care as a basic service, at little or no expense to parents. But even those countries with tax-subsidized programs occasionally fall short of the need for high-quality child care.

When policymakers decide that child care is desirable, they must determine the degree to which taxpayers should subsidize it. In Sweden and Denmark, one-third to one-half of children under age three were in government-subsidized child care full-time in 2001. In the United States, where government subsidies are very limited, the total cost of child care can easily run between $5,000 and $10,000 per family per year (Mencimer 2002).

We have a long way to go in making high-quality child care more affordable and accessible, not just in the United States but throughout the world. In an attempt to reduce government spending, France is considering cutting back the budgets of subsidized nurseries, even though waiting lists exist and the French public heartily disapproves of cutbacks. In Germany, reunification has reduced the options previously open to East German mothers, who had become accustomed to government-supported child care. Experts in child development view such reports as a vivid reminder of the need for greater government and private-sector support for child care (Hank 2001; L. King 1998).

{ People in Sweden pay higher taxes than U.S. citizens, but they have access to excellent preschool day care at little or no cost. }

basis by their grandparents than by their parents Over a third of these children are cared for by nonrelatives in nursery schools, Head Start programs, day care centers, family day care, and other arrangements.

The Setting

Few people in the United States or elsewhere can afford the luxury of having a parent stay at home, or of paying for high-quality live-in child care. For millions of mothers and fathers, finding the right kind of child care is a challenge both to parenting and to the pocketbook.

Researchers have found that high-quality child care centers do not adversely affect the socialization of children; in fact, good day care benefits children. The value of preschool programs was documented in a series of studies conducted in the United States. Researchers found no significant differences in infants who had received extensive nonmaternal care compared with those who had been cared for solely by their mothers. They also reported that more and more infants in the United States are being placed in child care outside the home, and that overall, the quality of those arrangements is better than has been found in previous studies. It is difficult, however, to generalize about child care, since there is so much variability among day care providers, and even among policies from one state to another (Kirp 2004; Loeb et al. 2004; NICHD 1998).

Sociological Insights

Studies that assess the quality of child care outside the home reflect the micro level of analysis and the interest of interactionists in the impact of face-to-face interaction. These studies also ex-

Theory Interactionist and conflict analyses of child care
Theory Feminists and conflict theorists note that male-dominated governments place little priority on child care issues.
Gender The impact of child care decisions falls most heavily on women who work or wish to work.

Global View Child care issues in developing countries and around the world

Let's Discuss

1. Were you ever in a day care program? Do you recall the experience as good or bad? In general, do you think it is desirable to expose young children to the socializing influence of day care?

2. In the view of conflict theorists, child care receives little government support because it is "merely a way to let women work." Can you think of other explanations?

3. Should the costs of day care programs be paid by government, by the private sector, or entirely by parents?

GettingINVOLVED

To get involved in the debate over day care, visit this text's Online Learning Center, which offers links to relevant Web sites. Check out the Social Policy section on the Online Learning Center as well; it provides survey data on U.S. public opinion regarding this issue.

www.mhhe.com/schaefer7

{ MASTERING THIS CHAPTER }

Summary

Socialization is the process through which people learn the attitudes, values, and actions appropriate for members of a particular culture. This chapter examined the role of socialization in human development; the way in which people develop perceptions, feelings, and beliefs about themselves; the lifelong nature of the socialization process; and the important agents of socialization.

1. *Socialization* affects the overall cultural practices of a society; it also shapes the images that we hold of ourselves.

2. Heredity and environmental factors interact in influencing the socialization process.

3. In the early 1900s, Charles Horton Cooley advanced the belief that we learn who we are by interacting with others, a phenomenon he called the *looking-glass self.*

4. George Herbert Mead, best known for his theory of the *self*, proposed that as people mature, their selves begin to reflect their concern about reactions from others—both *generalized others* and *significant others.*

5. Erving Goffman has shown that in many of our daily activities, we try to convey distinct impressions of who we are, a process called *impression management.*

6. Socialization proceeds throughout the life course. Some societies mark stages of development with formal *rites of passage.* In the cul-

ture of the United States, significant events such as marriage and parenthood serve to change a person's status.

7. As the primary agents of socialization, parents play a critical role in guiding children into those *gender roles* deemed appropriate in a society.

8. Like the family, schools in the United States have an explicit mandate to socialize people—especially children—into the norms and values of our culture.

9. Peer groups and the mass media, especially television, are important agents of socialization for adolescents.

10. Socialization in the workplace begins with part-time employment while we are in school and continues as we work full-time and change jobs throughout our lives.

11. Religion and the state shape the socialization process by regulating the life course and influencing our views of appropriate behavior at particular ages.

12. As more and more mothers of young children have entered the labor market, the demand for child care has increased dramatically, posing policy questions for many nations around the world.

Critical Thinking Questions

1. Should social research be conducted on issues such as the influence of heredity and environment, even though many investigators believe that this type of analysis is potentially detrimental to large numbers of people?

2. Drawing on Erving Goffman's dramaturgical approach, discuss how the following groups engage in impression management: athletes, college instructors, parents, physicians, and politicians.

3. How would functionalists and conflict theorists differ in their analysis of socialization by the mass media?

Key Terms

Anticipatory socialization Processes of socialization in which a person "rehearses" for future positions, occupations, and social relationships. (page 88)

Cognitive theory of development The theory that children's thought progresses through four stages of development. (85)

Degradation ceremony An aspect of the socialization process within some total institutions, in which people are subjected to humiliating rituals. (89)

Dramaturgical approach A view of social interaction in which people are seen as theatrical performers. (84)

Face-work The efforts people make to maintain the proper image and avoid public embarrassment. (84)

Gender role Expectations regarding the proper behavior, attitudes, and activities of males and females. (90)

Generalized other The attitudes, viewpoints, and expectations of society as a whole that a child takes into account in his or her behavior. (83)

Impression management The altering of the presentation of the self in order to create distinctive appearances and satisfy particular audiences. (84)

Life course approach A research orientation in which sociologists and other social scientists look closely at the social factors that influence people throughout their lives, from birth to death. (87)

Looking-glass self A concept that emphasizes the self as the product of our social interactions. (82)

Personality A person's typical patterns of attitudes, needs, characteristics, and behavior. (79)

Resocialization The process of discarding former behavior patterns and accepting new ones as part of a transition in one's life. (88)

Rite of passage A ritual marking the symbolic transition from one social position to another. (87)

Role taking The process of mentally assuming the perspective of another and responding from that imagined viewpoint. (83)

Self A distinct identity that sets us apart from others. (82)

Significant other An individual who is most important in the development of the self, such as a parent, friend, or teacher. (83)

Socialization The lifelong process in which people learn the attitudes, values, and behaviors appropriate for members of a particular culture. (79)

Symbol A gesture, object, or word that forms the basis of human communication. (82)

Total institution An institution that regulates all aspects of a person's life under a single authority, such as a prison, the military, a mental hospital, or a convent. (88)

Self-Quiz

Read each question carefully and then select the best answer.

1. Which of the following social scientists used the phrase *looking-glass self* to emphasize that the self is the product of our social interactions with other people?

    a. George Herbert Mead
    b. Charles Horton Cooley
    c. Erving Goffman
    d. Jean Piaget

2. In what he called the *play stage* of socialization, George Herbert Mead asserted that people mentally assume the perspectives of others, thereby enabling them to respond from that imagined viewpoint. This process is referred to as

    a. role taking.
    b. the generalized other.
    c. the significant other.
    d. impression management.

3. George Herbert Mead is best known for his theory of what?

    a. presentation of the self
    b. cognitive development
    c. the self
    d. impression management

4. Suppose a clerk tries to appear busier than he or she actually is when a supervisor happens to be watching. Erving Goffman would study this behavior from what approach?

    a. functionalist
    b. conflict
    c. psychological
    d. interactionist

5. According to child psychologist Jean Piaget's cognitive theory of development, children begin to use words and symbols to distinguish objects and ideas during which stage in the development of the thought process?

    a. the sensorimotor stage
    b. the preoperational stage
    c. the concrete operational stage
    d. the formal operational stage

6. On the first day of basic training in the army, a recruit has his civilian clothes replaced with army "greens," has his hair shaved off, loses his privacy, and finds that he must use a communal bathroom. All of these humiliating activities are part of

    a. becoming a significant other.
    b. impression management.
    c. a degradation ceremony.
    d. face-work.

7. Which social institution is considered to be the most important agent of socialization in the United States, especially for children?

    a. the family
    b. the school
    c. the peer group
    d. the mass media

8. The term *gender role* refers to

    a. the biological fact that we are male or female.
    b. a role that is given to us by a teacher.
    c. a role that is given to us in a play.
    d. expectations regarding the proper behavior, attitudes, and activities of males and females.

9. Which sociological perspective emphasizes that schools in the United States foster competition through built-in systems of reward and punishment?

    a. the functionalist perspective
    b. the conflict perspective
    c. the interactionist perspective
    d. the psychological perspective

10. Which of the following statements about peer groups is *not* true?

    a. Peer groups can ease the transition to adult responsibilities.
    b. Peers can be the source of harassment as well as support.
    c. Peer groups increasingly assume the role of Mead's generalized other.
    d. Boys and girls are socialized differently.

11. _____ is the term used by sociologists in referring to the lifelong process whereby people learn the attitudes, values, and behaviors appropriate for members of a particular culture.

12. In everyday speech, the term _____ is used to refer to a person's typical patterns of attitudes, needs, characteristics, and behavior.

13. Studies of twins raised apart suggest that both _____ and _____ influence human development.

14. _____ are gestures, objects, and/or words that form the basis of human communication.

15. Those individuals who are most important in shaping a person's identity (e.g., parents, friends, co-workers, coaches, and teachers) are referred to as _____ _____.

16. Early work in _____, such as that by Sigmund Freud, stressed the role of inborn drives—among them the drive for sexual gratification—in channeling human behavior.

17. Preparation for many aspects of adult life begins with _____ socialization during childhood and adolescence, and continues throughout our lives as we prepare for new responsibilities.

18. Resocialization is particularly effective when it occurs within a(n) _____ institution.

19. The _____ perspective emphasizes the role of schools in teaching the values and customs of the larger society.

20. As children grow older, the family becomes less important in social development, while _____ groups become more important.

Answers:
1 (b); 2 (a); 3 (c); 4 (d); 5 (b); 6 (c); 7 (a); 8 (d); 9 (b); 10 (a)
11 Socialization; 12 personality; 13 heredity, environment; 14 Symbols; 15 significant others; 16 psychology; 17 anticipatory; 18 total; 19 functionalist; 20 peer

---

TECHNOLOGY RESOURCES

Online Learning Center

1. The rise in single-parent families, increased job opportunities for women, and the need for additional family income have combined to propel more and more mothers of young children into the paid labor force. In the Social Policy exercise for this chapter in the Online Learning Center (**www.mhhe.com/schaefer7**), you can read about the controversies surrounding child care and working mothers.

2. Though cases in which children grow up with limited human contact are tragic, they provide valuable and fascinating information about the importance of childhood socialization. FeralChildren.com (**www.feralchildren.com/en/index.php**) provides extensive information on a number of such children.

3. Parents are a key agent of socialization. The National Fatherhood Initiative (**www.fatherhood.org**) is an organization whose purpose is to educate fathers about their crucial role in socializing their children. Explore this site to learn more about the organization's efforts.

*Note: While all the URLs listed were current as of the printing of this book, these sites often change. Please check our Web site (**www.mhhe.com/schaefer7**) for updates, hyperlinks, and exercises related to these sites.*

Reel Society Video Clips

Reel Society video clips, which appear on this book's Web site, can be used to spark discussion about the following topic from this chapter:
    • Agents of Socialization

5

Social Interaction, Groups, and Social Structure

inside

Social Interaction and Reality

Elements of Social Structure

Social Structure in Global Perspective

Understanding Organizations

The Changing Workplace

Social Policy and Organizations: The State of the Unions

Boxes

Sociology in the Global Community: McDonald's and the Worldwide Bureaucratization of Society

Research in Action: Adolescent Sexual Networks

Social Inequality: Disability as a Master Status

Social interaction is critical to society; without it, there is no shared sense of meaning or purpose. This poster, sponsored by the nonprofit group America's Promise, encourages people to reach out to the youths in their community.

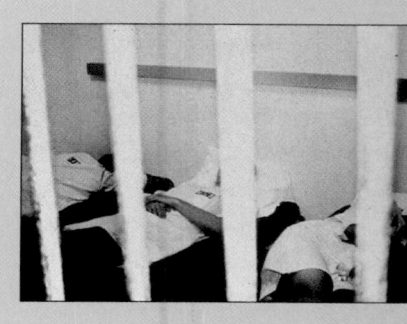

The quiet of a summer Sunday morning in Palo Alto, California, was shattered by a screeching squad car siren as police swept through the city picking up college students in a surprise mass arrest. Each suspect was charged with a felony, warned of his constitutional rights, spread-eagled against the car, searched, handcuffed and carted off in the back seat of the squad car to the police station for booking.

After being fingerprinted and having identification forms prepared for his "jacket" (central information file), each prisoner was left isolated in a detention cell to wonder what he had done to get himself into this mess. After a while, he was blindfolded and transported to the "Stanford County Prison." Here he began the induction process of becoming a prisoner—stripped naked, skin searched, deloused, and issued a uniform, bedding, soap and towel. By late afternoon when nine such arrests had been completed, these youthful "first offenders" sat in dazed silence on the cots in their barren cells. These men were part of a very unusual kind of prison, an experimental or mock prison, created by social psychologists for the purpose of intensively studying the effects of imprisonment upon volunteer research subjects. When we planned our two-week-long simulation of prison life, we were primarily concerned about understanding the process by which people adapt to the novel and alien environment in which those called "prisoners" lose their liberty, civil rights, independence and privacy, while those called "guards" gain social power by accepting the responsibility for controlling and managing the lives of their dependent charges. . . .

Our final sample of participants (10 prisoners and 11 guards) were selected from over 75 volunteers recruited through ads in the city and campus newspapers. . . . Half were randomly assigned to role-play being guards, the others to be prisoners. Thus, there were no measurable differences between the guards and the prisoners at the start of this experiment. . . .

At the end of only six days we had to close down our mock prison because what we saw was frightening. It was no longer apparent to most of the subjects (or to us) where reality ended and their roles began. The majority had indeed become prisoners or guards, no longer able to clearly differentiate between role playing and self. There were dramatic changes in virtually every aspect of their behavior, thinking and feeling. In less than a week the experience of imprisonment undid (temporarily) a lifetime of learning; human values were suspended, self-concepts were challenged and the ugliest, most base, pathological side of human nature surfaced. We were horrified because we saw some boys (guards) treat others as if they were despicable animals, taking pleasure in cruelty, while other boys (prisoners) became servile, dehumanized robots who thought only of escape, of their own individual survival, and of their mounting hatred for the guards.

(Zimbardo 1972:4; Zimbardo et al. 1974:61, 62, 63)

Additional information about this excerpt can be found on the Online Learning Center at www.mhhe.com/schaefer7. ●

> *" The quiet of a summer Sunday morning in Palo Alto, California, was shattered by a screeching squad car siren as police swept through the city picking up college students in a surprise mass arrest. "*

In this study directed and described by social psychologist Philip Zimbardo, college students adopted the patterns of social interaction expected of guards and prisoners when they were placed in a mock prison. Sociologists use the term *social interaction* to refer to the ways in which people respond to one another, whether face to face or over the telephone or on the computer. In the mock prison, social interactions between guards and prisoners were highly impersonal. The guards addressed the prisoners by number rather than name, and they wore reflective sunglasses that made eye contact impossible.

As in many real-life prisons, the simulated prison at Stanford University had a social structure in which guards held virtually total control over prisoners. The term *social structure* refers to the way in which a society is organized into predictable relationships. The social structure of Zimbardo's mock prison influenced how the guards and prisoners interacted. Zimbardo and his colleagues (2003:546) note that it was a real prison "in the minds of the jailers and their captives." His simulated prison experiment, first conducted more than 30 years ago, has subsequently been repeated (with similar findings) both in the United States and in other countries.

Zimbardo's experiment took on new relevance in 2004, in the wake of shocking revelations of prisoner abuse at the U.S.-run Abu Ghraib military facility in Iraq. Graphic photos showed U.S. soldiers humiliating naked Iraqi prisoners and threatening to attack them with police dogs. The structure of the wartime prison, coupled with intense pressure on military intelligence officers to secure information regarding terrorist plots, contributed to the breakdown in the guards' behavior. But Zimbardo himself noted that the guards' depraved conduct could have been predicted simply on the basis of his research (Zarembo 2004; Zimbardo 2004, 2005).

The two concepts of social interaction and social structure are central to sociological study. They are closely related to socialization (see Chapter 4), the process through which people learn the attitudes, values, and behaviors appropriate to their culture. When the students in Zimbardo's experiment entered the mock prison, they began a process of resocialization. In that process, they adjusted to a new social structure and learned new rules for social interaction.

In this chapter we will study social structure and its effect on our social interactions. What determines a person's status in society? How do our social roles affect our social interactions? What is the place of social institutions such as the family, religion, and government in our social structure? How can we better understand and manage large organizations such as multinational corporations? We'll begin by considering how social interactions shape the way we view the world around us. Next, we'll focus on the five basic elements of social structure: statuses, social roles, groups, social networks, and social institutions such as the family, religion, and government. We'll see that functionalists, conflict theorists, and interactionists approach these institutions quite differently. We'll compare our modern social structure with simpler forms, using typologies developed by Émile Durkheim, Ferdinand Tönnies, and Gerhard Lenski. Next, we'll examine how and why formal organizations, such as a corporation or the college you attend, came into existence, touching on Max Weber's model of the modern bureaucracy in the process. Finally, we'll discuss recent changes in the workplace. The Social Policy section at the end of the chapter focuses on the status of organized labor today. ●

Social Interaction and Reality

When someone in a crowd shoves you, do you automatically push back? Or do you consider the circumstances of the incident and the attitude of the instigator before you react? Chances are you do the latter. According to sociologist Herbert Blumer (1969:79), the distinctive characteristic of social interaction among people is that "human beings interpret or 'define' each other's actions instead of merely reacting to each other's actions." In other words, our response to someone's behavior is based on the *meaning* we attach to his or her actions. Reality is shaped by our perceptions, evaluations, and definitions.

These meanings typically reflect the norms and values of the dominant culture and our socialization experiences within that culture. As interactionists emphasize, the meanings that we attach to people's behavior are shaped by our interactions with them and with the larger society. Social reality is literally constructed from our social interactions (Berger and Luckmann 1966).

How do we define our social reality? Consider something as simple as how we regard tattoos. At one time, most of us in the United States considered tattoos weird or kooky. We associated them with fringe countercultural groups, such as punk rockers, biker gangs, and skinheads. Among many people, a tattoo elicited an automatic negative response. Now, however, so many people have tattoos—including society's trendsetters and major sports figures—and the ritual of getting a tattoo has become so legitimized, that mainstream culture regards tattoos differently. At this point, as a result of increased social interaction with tattooed people, tattoos look perfectly at home to us in a number of settings.

The ability to define social reality reflects a group's power within a society. In fact, one of the most crucial aspects of the relationship between dominant and subordinate groups is the ability of the dominant or majority group to define a society's values. Sociologist William I. Thomas (1923), an early critic of theories of racial and gender differences, recognized that the "definition of the situation" could mold the thinking and personality of the individual. Writing from an interactionist perspective, Thomas observed that people respond not only to the objective features of a person or situation but also to the *meaning* that person or situation has for them. For example, in Philip Zimbardo's mock prison experiment, student "guards" and "prisoners" accepted the definition of the situation (including the traditional roles and behavior associated with being a guard or prisoner) and acted accordingly.

As we have seen throughout the last 50 years—first in the civil rights movement of the 1960s and since then among such groups as women, the elderly, gays and lesbians, and people with disabilities—an important aspect of the process of social change involves redefining or reconstructing social reality. Members of subordinate groups challenge traditional definitions and begin to perceive and experience reality in a new way. For example, the world champion boxer Muhammad Ali began his career as the creation of a White male syndicate, which sponsored his early matches when he was known as Cassius Clay. Soon, however, the young boxer rebelled against those who would keep him or his race down. He broke the old stereotypes of the self-effacing Black athlete, insisting on his own political views (including refusing to serve in the Vietnam War), his own religion (Black Muslim), and his own name (Muhammad Ali). Not only did Ali change the world of sports; he also helped to alter the world of race relations. Viewed from a sociological perspective, then, Ali was redefining social reality by rebelling against the racist thinking and terminology that restricted him and other African Americans.

Elements of Social Structure

All social interaction takes place within a social structure, including those interactions that redefine social reality. For purposes of study, we can break down any social structure into five elements: statuses, social roles, groups, social networks, and social institutions. These elements make up social structure just as a foundation, walls, and ceilings make up a building's structure. The elements of social structure are developed through the lifelong process of socialization described in Chapter 4.

Statuses

We normally think of a person's "status" as having to do with influence, wealth, and fame. However, sociologists use the term *status* to refer to any of the full range of socially defined positions within a large group or society, from the lowest to the highest. Within our society, a person can occupy the status of president of the United States, fruit picker, son or daughter, violinist, teenager,

Symbols of status and power, such as this judge's robes, tend to reinforce the position of the dominant groups in society. When such symbols are associated with a member of a racial minority, they challenge prevailing racial stereotypes, changing what the interactionist William I. Thomas called "the definition of the situation."

resident of Minneapolis, dental technician, or neighbor. A person can hold a number of statuses at the same time.

Ascribed and Achieved Status Sociologists view some statuses as *ascribed* and others as *achieved* (see Figure 5-1). An ***ascribed status*** is assigned to a person by society without regard for the person's unique talents or characteristics. Generally, the assignment takes place at birth; thus, a person's racial background, gender, and age are all considered ascribed statuses. Though these characteristics are biological in origin, they are significant mainly because of the *social* meanings they have in our culture. Conflict theorists are especially interested in ascribed statuses, since they often confer privileges or reflect a person's membership in a subordinate group. The social meanings of race and ethnicity, gender, and age will be analyzed more fully in Chapters 10–11.

In most cases, we can do little to change an ascribed status. But we can attempt to change the traditional constraints associated with such statuses. For example, the Gray Panthers—an activist political group founded in 1971 to work for the rights of older people—have tried to modify society's negative and

Key Person William I. Thomas
Let's Discuss How does the "definition of the situation" surface in discussions of religion, poverty, and terrorism?
Race/Ethnicity/Gender Reconstructing social reality is related to various civil rights movements since the 1960s.
Race/Ethnicity The way in which Muhammad Ali redefined social reality

Let's Discuss With respect to the events of September 11, 2001, would you say that we have accepted the "definition of the situation"? Have we had to reconstruct social reality in relation to air travel and safety?
Classroom Tip See "Alternative Social Structure" (Class Discussion Topics).
Classroom Tip See "Social Statuses and Social Roles" (Class Discussion Topics).
Theory Conflict view of the impact of ascribed statuses

confining stereotypes of the elderly (see Chapter 11). As a result of their work and that of other groups supporting older citizens, the ascribed status of "senior citizen" is no longer as difficult for millions of older people.

An ascribed status does not necessarily have the same social meaning in every society. In a cross-cultural study, sociologist Gary Huang (1988) confirmed the long-held view that respect for the elderly is an important cultural norm in China. In many cases, the prefix "old" is used respectfully: calling someone "old teacher" or "old person" is like calling a judge in the United States "your honor." Huang points out that positive age-seniority language distinctions are uncommon in the United States; consequently, we view the term *old man* as more of an insult than a celebration of seniority and wisdom.

Unlike ascribed statuses, an *achieved status* comes to us largely through our own efforts. Both "bank president" and "prison guard" are achieved statuses, as are "lawyer," "pianist," "sorority member," "convict," and "social worker." We must do something to acquire an achieved status—go to school, learn a skill, establish a friendship, invent a new product. But as we will

{ Whom do you see in this photo: a food service worker, an elderly food service worker, or an elderly woman? Our achieved and ascribed statuses determine how others see us. }

see in the next section, our ascribed status heavily influences our achieved status. Being male, for example, would decrease the likelihood that we would consider child care as a career.

Master Status Each person holds many different and sometimes conflicting statuses; some may connote higher social position and some, lower position. How, then, do others view one's overall social position? According to sociologist Everett Hughes (1945), societies deal with inconsistencies by agreeing that certain statuses are more important than others. A *master status* is a status that dominates others and thereby determines a person's general position in society. For example, Arthur Ashe, who died of AIDS in 1993, had a remarkable career as a tennis star, but at the end of his life, his status as a well-known personality with AIDS may have outweighed his statuses as a retired athlete, author, and political activist. Throughout the world, many people with disabilities find that their status as "disabled" receives undue weight, overshadowing their actual ability to perform successfully in meaningful employment (see Box 5-1, page 104).

Our society gives such importance to race and gender that they often dominate our lives. These ascribed statuses frequently influence our achieved status. The African American activist Malcolm X (1925–1965), an eloquent and controversial advocate of Black power and Black pride during the early 1960s, recalled that his feelings and perspectives changed dramatically while in eighth grade. When his English teacher, a White man,

FIGURE 5–1
Social Statuses

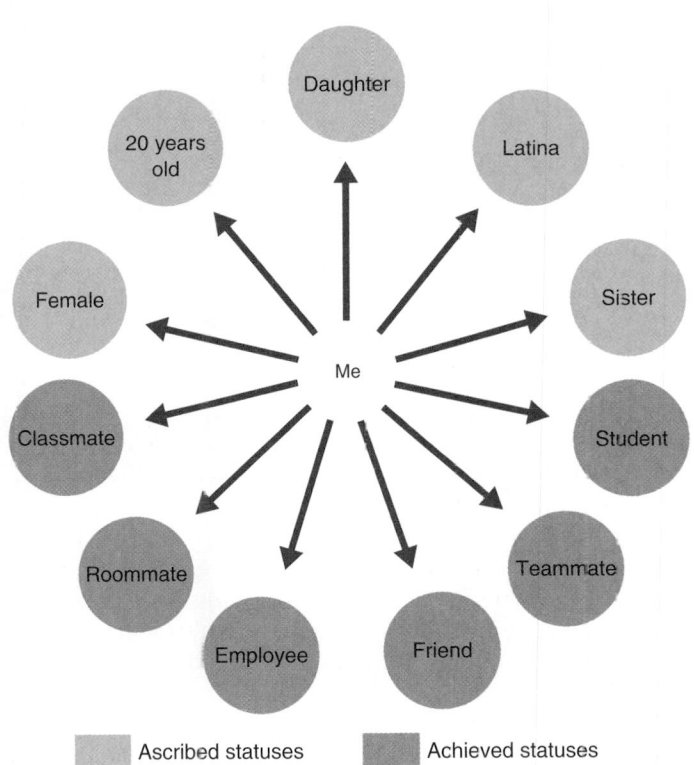

Ascribed statuses   Achieved statuses

Think About It
The young woman in this figure—"me"—occupies many positions in society, each of which involves distinct statuses. How would you define your statuses? Which have the most influence in your life?

social INEQUALITY

5-1 Disability as a Master Status

When officials in New Hampshire required a handicap access ramp for a mountain shelter, they were ridiculed for wasting taxpayers' money. Who could climb a mountain in a wheelchair? critics asked. In the summer of 2000 that challenge impelled several intrepid climbers, some in wheelchairs, to make a 12-hour trek over rocks and rough trail so that they could enter the shelter in triumph. As a result of such feats, stereotypes of the disabled are gradually falling away. But the status of "disabled" still carries a stigma.

Throughout history and around the world, people with disabilities have been subjected to cruel and inhuman treatment. For example, in the 20th century, the disabled were frequently viewed as subhuman creatures who were a menace to society. In Japan more than 16,000 women with disabilities were involuntarily sterilized with government approval from 1945 to 1995. Sweden apologized for the same action taken against 62,000 of its citizens in the 1970s.

Such blatantly hostile treatment of people with disabilities has given way to a *medical model,* in which the disabled are viewed as chronic patients. Increasingly, however, people concerned with the rights of the disabled have criticized this model as well. In their view, it is the unnecessary and discriminatory barri-ers present in the environment—both physical and attitudinal—that stand in the way of people with disabilities, more than any biological limitations. Applying a *civil rights model,* activists emphasize that those with disabilities face widespread prejudice, discrimination, and segregation. For example, most voting places are inaccessible to wheelchair users and fail to provide ballots that can be used by those unable to read print.

> *In Japan more than 16,000 women with disabilities were involuntarily sterilized with government approval from 1945 to 1995.*

Drawing on the earlier work of Erving Goffman, contemporary sociologists have suggested that society attaches a stigma to many forms of disability, a stigma that leads to prejudicial treatment. People with disabilities frequently observe that the nondisabled see them only as blind, wheelchair users, and so forth, rather than as complex human beings with individual strengths and weaknesses, whose blindness or use of a wheelchair is merely one aspect of their lives.

Though discrimination against the disabled occurs around the world, attitudes are changing. The African nation of Botswana has plans to assist its disabled, most of whom live in rural areas and need special services for mobility and economic development. In many countries, disability rights activists are targeting issues essential to overcoming this master status and becoming a full citizen, including employment, housing, education, and access to public buildings.

Let's Discuss

1. Does your campus present barriers to disabled students? If so, what kind of barriers—physical, attitudinal, or both? Describe some of them.
2. Why do you think nondisabled people see disability as the most important characteristic of a disabled person? What can be done to help people see beyond the wheelchair and the seeing-eye dog?

Sources: Albrecht et al. 2001; Goffman 1963a; D. Murphy 1997; *Newsday* 1997; E. Fosenthal 2001; Shapiro 1993; Waldrop and Stern 2003.

---

advised him that his goal of becoming a lawyer was "no realistic goal for a nigger" and encouraged him instead to become a carpenter, Malcolm X (1964:37) found that his position as a Black man (ascribed status) was an obstacle to his dream of becoming a lawyer (achieved status). In the United States, the ascribed statuses of race and gender can function as master statuses that have an important impact on one's potential to achieve a desired professional and social status.

Social Roles

What Are Social Roles?
Throughout our lives, we acquire what sociologists call social roles. A ***social role*** is a set of expectations for people who occupy a given social position or status. Thus, in the United States, we expect that cab drivers will know how to get around a city, that receptionists will be reliable in handling phone messages, and that police officers will take action if they see a citizen being threatened. With each distinctive social status—whether ascribed or achieved—come particular role expectations. However, actual performance varies from individual to individual. One secretary may assume extensive administrative responsibilities, while another may focus on clerical duties. Similarly, in Philip Zimbardo's mock prison experiment, some students were brutal and sadistic guards; others were not.

Roles are a significant component of social structure. Viewed from a functionalist perspective, roles contribute to a society's stability by enabling members to anticipate the behavior of others and to pattern their own actions accordingly. Yet social roles can also be dysfunctional if they restrict people's interactions and relationships. If we view a person *only* as a "police officer" or "supervisor," it will be difficult to relate to him or her as a friend or neighbor.

Role Conflict
Imagine the delicate situation of a woman who has worked for a decade on an assembly line in an electrical plant, and has recently been named supervisor of her unit. How

Student Alert Clarify the difference between the medical and the civil rights models of disability.
Let's Discuss What is the difference between referring to someone as "disabled" or as a "person with a disability"?
Key Person Erving Goffman
Classroom Tip See "China and People with Disabilities" (Additional Lecture Ideas).

Classroom Tip See "Social Roles amidst Disasters" (Additional Lecture Ideas).
Theory Functionalist view of social roles and society's stability
Global View Treatment of people with disabilities in Botswana
Gender Role conflict and gender roles for males and females
Reel Society Several of the *Reel Society* characters experience role conflict and role strain.

is this woman expected to relate to her longtime friends and co-workers? Should she still go out to lunch with them, as she has done almost daily for years? Is it her responsibility to recommend the firing of an old friend who cannot keep up with the demands of the assembly line?

Role conflict occurs when incompatible expectations arise from two or more social positions held by the same person. Fulfillment of the roles associated with one status may directly violate the roles linked to a second status. In the example just given, the newly promoted supervisor will most likely experience a sharp conflict between her social and occupational roles.

Such role conflicts call for important ethical choices. The new supervisor will have to make a difficult decision about how much allegiance she owes her friend and how much she owes her employers, who have given her supervisory responsibilities.

Another type of role conflict occurs when individuals move into occupations that are not common among people with their ascribed status. Male preschool teachers and female police officers experience this type of role conflict. In the latter case, female officers must strive to reconcile their workplace role in law enforcement with the societal view of a woman's role, which does not embrace many skills needed in police work. And while female police officers encounter sexual harassment, as women do throughout the labor force, they must also deal with the "code of silence," an informal norm that precludes their implicating fellow officers in wrongdoing (Fletcher 1995; S. Martin 1994).

Use Your Sociological Imagination

www.mhhe.com/schaefer7

If you were a male nurse, what aspects of role conflict might you experience? Now imagine you are a professional boxer and a woman. What conflicting role expectations might that involve? In both cases, how well do you think you would handle role conflict?

Role Strain   Role conflict describes the situation of a person dealing with the challenge of occupying two social positions simultaneously. However, even a single position can cause problems. Sociologists use the term *role strain* to describe the difficulty that arises when the same social position imposes conflicting demands and expectations.

People who belong to minority cultures may experience role strain while working in the mainstream culture. Criminologist Larry Gould (2002) interviewed officers of the Navajo Nation Police

Department about their relations with conventional law enforcement officials, such as sheriffs and FBI agents. Besides enforcing the law, Navajo Nation officers practice an alternative form of justice known as Peacemaking, in which they seek reconciliation between the parties to a crime. The officers expressed great confidence in Peacemaking, but worried that if they did not make arrests, other law enforcement officials would think they were too soft, or "just taking care of their own." Regardless of the strength of their ties to traditional Navajo ways, all felt the strain of being considered "too Navajo" or "not Navajo enough."

Role Exit   Often, when we think of assuming a social role, we focus on the preparation and anticipatory socialization a person undergoes for that role. Such is true if a person is about to become an attorney, a chef, a spouse, or a parent. Yet until recently, social scientists have given little attention to the adjustments involved in *leaving* social roles.

Sociologist Helen Rose Fuchs Ebaugh (1988) developed the term *role exit* to describe the process of disengagement from a role that is central to one's self-identity in order to establish a new role and identity. Drawing on interviews with 185 people—among them ex-convicts, divorced men and women, recovering alcoholics, ex-nuns, former doctors, retirees, and transsexuals—Ebaugh (herself a former nun) studied the process of voluntarily exiting from significant social roles.

Ebaugh has offered a four-stage model of role exit. The first stage begins with *doubt*. The person experiences frustration, burnout, or simply unhappiness with an accustomed status and the roles associated with the social position. The second stage involves a *search for alternatives*. A person who is unhappy with his or her career may take a leave of absence; an unhappily married couple may begin what they see as a temporary separation.

The third stage of role exit is the *action stage* or *departure*. Ebaugh found that the vast majority of her respondents could identify a clear turning point that made them feel it was

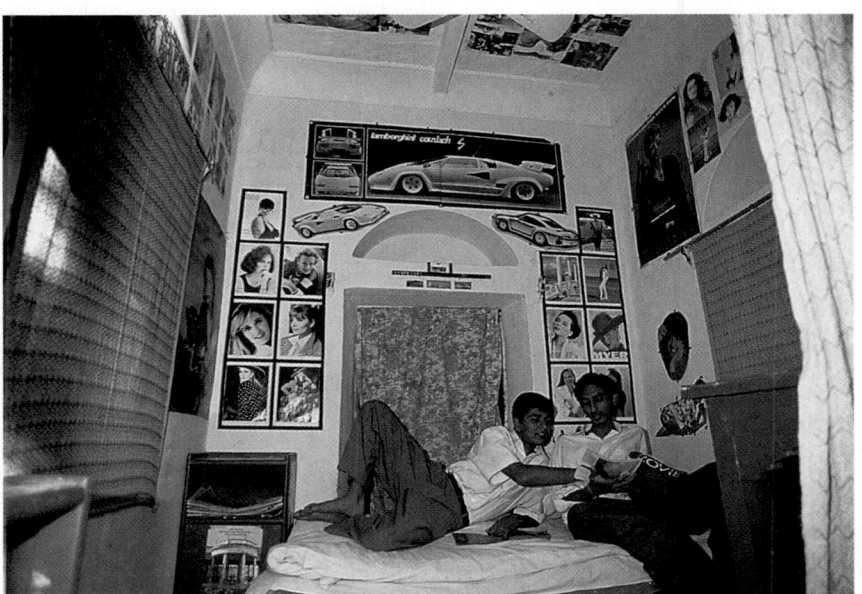

This college student in India has decorated his dorm room with photos of beautiful women and fast cars. They may signify his attempt to create a new identity, the final stage in his exit from the role of high school student living at home.

Why Do We Gather Together?

Around the world, people cluster at bus stops, in schools, and at houses of worship. Others gather at malls, movie theaters, and government offices. They do so for many reasons—to earn a living, get an education, or just to have fun. But there is a larger purpose to these gatherings. Humans are social creatures, with a social fabric that is knit together by the give-and-take of even the most common encounters. The people we meet with, the places where we gather, our purposes in seeking others' company—these are fundamental building blocks of our society.

Our social interactions are also defined by the social structures in which they take place. Social interactions may be rela-tively casual and unstructured, as they are when friends spend time hanging out together at the park. Or they may be carefully organized, as they are when tribal musicians compete for the ti-tle of best drum circle at the powwow, or when mountain climbers attempt to reach the summit of the world's highest peak. In each case, the social interaction is defined by the larger social structure, whether it be the neighbors who live around the park, the organizers of the intertribal competition, or the govern-ment officials who grant climbers permission to ascend a peak.

{Base camp for a Mt. Everest expedition}

{Teen gathering at an urban park}

{Upper Mattaponi tribal powwow, Virginia}

essential to take final action and leave their job, end their marriage, or engage in another type of role exit. Twenty percent of respondents saw their role exit as a gradual, evolutionary process that had no single turning point.

The last stage of role exit involves the *creation of a new identity.* Many of you participated in a role exit when you made the transition from high school to college. You left behind the role of offspring living at home and took on the role of a somewhat independent college student living with peers in a dorm. Sociologist Ira Silver (1996) has studied the central role that material objects play in this transition. The objects students choose to leave at home (like stuffed animals and dolls) are associated with their prior identities. They may remain deeply attached to those objects, but do not want them to be seen as part of their new identities at college. The objects they bring with them symbolize how they now see themselves and how they wish to be perceived. IPods and wall posters, for example, are calculated to say, "This is me."

Groups

In sociological terms, a *group* is any number of people with similar norms, values, and expectations who interact with one another on a regular basis. The members of a women's basketball team, a hospital's business office, a synagogue, or a symphony orchestra constitute a group. However, the residents of a suburb would not be considered a group, since they rarely interact with one another at one time.

Groups play a vital part in a society's social structure. Much of our social interaction takes place within groups and is influenced by their norms and sanctions. Being a teenager or a retired person takes on special meanings when we interact within groups designed for people with that particular status. The expectations associated with many social roles, including those accompanying the statuses of brother, sister, and student, become more clearly defined in the context of a group.

Primary and Secondary Groups   Charles Horton Cooley (1902) coined the term ***primary group*** to refer to a small group characterized by intimate, face-to-face association and coopera-

A pizza delivery crew is an example of a *secondary group*—a formal, impersonal group in which there is little social intimacy or mutual understanding. While waiting for the next delivery, members of this crew will become well enough acquainted to distinguish those who see the job as temporary from those who view it as permanent. They will learn who looks forward to deliveries in perceived high-risk areas and who does not. They may even spend time together after work, joking or boasting about their exploits on the job, but their friendship typically will not develop beyond that point.

tion. The members of a street gang constitute a primary group; so do members of a family living in the same household, or a group of "sisters" in a college sorority.

Primary groups play a pivotal role both in the socialization process (see Chapter 4) and in the development of roles and statuses. Indeed, primary groups can be instrumental in a person's day-to-day existence. When we find ourselves identifying closely with a group, it is probably a primary group.

We also participate in many groups that are not characterized by close bonds of friendship, such as large college classes and business associations. The term ***secondary group*** refers to a formal, impersonal group in which there is little social intimacy or mutual understanding (see Table 5-1). Secondary groups often emerge in the workplace among those who share special

Table 5-1   Comparison of Primary and Secondary Groups

Primary Group	Secondary Group
Generally small	Usually large
Relatively long period of interaction	Relatively short duration, often temporary
Intimate, face-to-face association	Little social intimacy or mutual understanding
Some emotional depth to relationships	Relationships generally superficial
Cooperative, friendly	More formal and impersonal

Key Person Charles Horton Cooley
Student Alert See Cooley's concept of the looking-glass self in Chapter 4. Explain why *primary group* is a related concept.
Classroom Tip For analysis of primary group life in ethnic and urban communities, see "Primary Groups and Subcultures" in Topics and Sources for Student Research.

Let's Discuss Ask students to list the primary and secondary groups of which they are members. Discuss some of these groups.
Classroom Tip See the discussion of agents of socialization, particularly schools and peer groups, in Chapter 4.
Classroom Tip For a sociological study of pizza deliverers, see Kinkade and Katovich 1997.

Members of New York City's Unatics, a unicycle club, often gather in Central Park to ride their cycles. These accomplished riders may serve as a reference group for onlookers who become interested in the sport.

actions that hurt civilians, which the first group will then condemn.

Conflict between in-groups and out-groups can turn violent on a personal as well as a political level. In 1999 two disaffected students at Columbine High School in Littleton, Colorado, launched an attack on the school that left 15 students and teachers dead, including themselves. The gunmen, members of an out-group that other students referred to as the Trenchcoat Mafia, apparently resented taunting by an in-group referred to as the Jocks. Similar episodes have occurred in schools across the nation, where rejected adolescents, overwhelmed by personal and family problems, peer group pressure, academic responsibilities, or media images of violence, have struck out against more popular classmates.

In-group members who actively provoke out-group members may have their own problems, including limited time and attention from working parents. Sociologists David Stevenson and Barbara Schneider (1999), who studied 7,000 teenagers, found that despite many opportunities for group membership, young people spend an average of three and a half hours alone every day. While youths may claim they want privacy, they also crave attention, and striking out at members of an in-group or out-group, be they the wrong gender, race, or friendship group, seems to be one way to get it.

understandings about their occupation. The distinction between primary and secondary groups is not always clear-cut, however. Some social clubs may become so large and impersonal that they no longer function as primary groups.

In-Groups and Out-Groups

A group can hold special meaning for members because of its relationship to other groups. For example, people in one group sometimes feel antagonistic toward or threatened by another group, especially if that group is perceived as being different either culturally or racially. To identify these "we" and "they" feelings, sociologists use two terms first employed by William Graham Sumner (1906): *in-group* and *out-group*.

An **in-group** can be defined as any group or category to which people feel they belong. Simply put, it comprises everyone who is regarded as "we" or "us." The in-group may be as narrow as a teenage clique or as broad as an entire society. The very existence of an in-group implies that there is an *out-group* that is viewed as "they" or "them." An **out-group** is a group or category to which people feel they do *not* belong.

In-group members typically feel distinct and superior, seeing themselves as better than people in the out-group. Proper behavior for the in-group is simultaneously viewed as unacceptable behavior for the out-group. This double standard enhances the sense of superiority. Sociologist Robert Merton (1968) described this process as the conversion of "in-group virtues" into "out-group vices." We can see this differential standard operating in worldwide discussions of terrorism. When a group or a nation takes aggressive actions, it usually justifies them as necessary, even if civilians are hurt or killed. Opponents are quick to label such actions with the emotion-laden term of *terrorist* and appeal to the world community for condemnation. Yet these same people may themselves retaliate with

Use Your Sociological Imagination

www.mhhe.com/schaefer7

Try putting yourself in the shoes of an out-group member. What does your in-group look like from that perspective?

Reference Groups

Both in-groups and primary groups can dramatically influence the way an individual thinks and behaves. Sociologists call any group that individuals use as a standard for evaluating themselves and their own behavior a **reference group.** For example, a high school student who aspires to join a social circle of hip-hop music devotees will pattern his or her behavior after that of the group. The student will begin dressing like these peers, listening to the same music, and hanging out at the same stores and clubs.

Reference groups have two basic purposes. They serve a normative function by setting and enforcing standards of conduct and belief. The high school student who wants the approval of the hip-hop crowd will have to follow the group's dictates, at least to some extent. Reference groups also perform a comparison function by serving as a standard against which people can measure themselves and others. An actor will evaluate himself or herself against a reference group composed of others in the acting profession (Merton and Kitt 1950).

Reference groups may help the process of anticipatory socialization. For example, a college student majoring in finance may read *The Wall Street Journal,* study the annual reports of

corporations, and listen to midday stock market news on the radio. Such a student is using financial experts as a reference group to which he or she aspires.

Often, two or more reference groups influence us at the same time. Our family members, neighbors, and co-workers all shape different aspects of our self-evaluation. In addition, reference group attachments change during the life cycle. A corporate executive who quits the rat race at age 45 to become a social worker will find new reference groups to use as standards for evaluation. We shift reference groups as we take on different statuses during our lives.

Coalitions As groups grow larger, coalitions begin to develop. A *coalition* is a temporary or permanent alliance geared toward a common goal. Coalitions can be broad-based or narrow and can take on many different objectives. Sociologist William Julius Wilson (1999b) has described community-based organizations in Texas that include Whites and Latinos, working class and affluent, who have banded together to work for improved sidewalks, better drainage systems, and comprehensive street paving. Out of this type of coalition building, Wilson hopes, will emerge better interracial understanding.

Some coalitions are intentionally short lived. Short-term coalition building is a key to success in popular TV programs like *Survivor*. In *Survivor I*, broadcast in 2000, the four members of the "Tagi alliance" banded together to vote fellow castaways off the island. The political world is also the scene of many temporary coalitions. For example, in 1997 big tobacco companies joined with antismoking groups to draw up a settlement for re-imbursing states for tobacco-related medical costs. Soon after the settlement was announced the coalition members returned to their decades-long fight against each other (Pear 1997).

Social Networks

Groups do not merely serve to define other elements of the social structure, such as roles and statuses; they also link the individual with the larger society. We all belong to a number of different groups, and through our acquaintances make connections with people in different social circles. These connections are known as a *social network*—that is, a series of social relationships that links a person directly to others, and through them indirectly to still more people. Social networks can center on virtually any activity, from sharing job information to exchanging news and gossip or to sharing sex (see Box 5-2). Some networks may constrain people by limiting the range of their interactions, yet networks can also empower people by making vast resources available to them (Watts 2004).

Involvement in social networks—commonly known as *networking*—is especially valuable in finding employment. Albert Einstein was successful in finding a job only when a classmate's father put him in touch with his future employer. These kinds of contacts—even those that are weak and distant—can be crucial in establishing social networks and facilitating the transmission of information.

In the workplace, networking pays off more for men than for women because of the traditional presence of men in leadership positions. One survey of executives found that 63 percent of the men used networking to find new jobs, compared to 41 percent of the women. Thirty-one percent of the women used classified advertisements to find jobs, compared to only 13 percent of the men. Still, women at all levels of the paid labor force are beginning to make effective use of social networks. A study of women who were leaving the welfare rolls to enter the paid workforce found that networking was an effective tool in their search for employment. Informal networking also helped them to locate child care and better housing—keys to successful employment (Carey and McLean 1997; Henly 1999).

With advances in technology, we can now maintain social networks electronically; we don't need face-to-face contacts. Online network-building companies emerged in 2004, offering their services free of charge at first. People log in to these sites and create a profile. Rather than remaining anonymous, as they would with an online dating service, users are identified by name and encouraged to list friends—even trusted friends of friends—who can serve as job

{ *Panama: Exile Island,* the 2006 version of the popular reality TV show *Survivor,* pitted 16 competitors against one another in a mock struggle for survival. Short-term coalition building has been one of the keys to success in the long-running unscripted television series. }

Contemporary Culture Do college students today have the same reference groups as college students of a generation ago?

Classroom Tip See "Group Behavior" (Class Discussion Topics).

Key Person William Julius Wilson (see Chapter 8 for Wilson's discussion of the underclass)

Let's Discuss Have any students in the class been members of a coalition? If so, what was the common goal of the coalition members?

Theory Functionalist view of the role of groups in social structure

Web Resource Remind students that the student center in the Online Learning Center (www.mhhe.com/schaefer7) has crossword puzzles and quizzes that serve as useful learning tools.

5-2 Adolescent Sexual Networks

If you drew a chart of the sexual network at a typical American high school, what would it look like? In the mid-1990s, sociologists Peter Bearman, James Moody, and Katherine Stovel asked themselves that question. While studying romantic relationships at a high school with about 1,000 students, they had found that about 61 percent of the boys and 55 percent of the girls had been sexually active over the past 18 months. Those percentages did not differ much from the results of similar studies done during the period. What surprised the research team was what they saw when they began to chart the students' relationships.

To obtain their data, Bearman and his colleagues conducted in-home interviews with the respondents. Instead of asking students for a face-to-face interview—a technique that might have embarrassed them or distorted their answers—the researchers gave them an

> *A particularly significant implication of this study is the risk of sexually transmitted diseases (STDs) to those who participate in such a network.*

audio recording of the questions, a pair of earphones, and a laptop computer on which to record their answers. The research team also asked respondents to look at a list of all the students at the high school and identify those with whom they had had romantic or sexual relationships.

The results showed that 573 of the 832 students surveyed had had at least one sexual relationship over the past 18 months. Among those respondents, the sociologists found only 63 steady couples, or pairs with no other partners. A much larger group of 288 students—almost a third of the sample—was involved in the free-flowing network of relationships shown on the accompanying chart. (Note the comparative absence of tightly closed loops of 3 to 5 individuals.) Not shown on the chart were another 90 students who were involved in relationships outside the school.

A particularly significant implication of this study is the risk of sexually transmitted diseases (STDs) to those who participate in such a network. Through the complicated chain of relationships, even students who have only one or two sexual partners are exposing themselves to a relatively high degree of risk. But while parents and even students may be alarmed by the data, public health officials are encouraged. Experts at the Centers for Disease Control who have reviewed the network charts from this and other studies see them as blueprints for change. If experts can alter participants' behavior anywhere along these chains—by counseling abstinence, condom use, or treatment of STDs—they can significantly reduce transmission of the diseases.

Let's Discuss

1. Do the results of the study surprise you? How does the sexual network described in this study compare to the network where you went to high school?
2. Do you see any problems with the research method used in this study? Can you think of anything that might have compromised the validity of the data?

Sources: Bearman, Moody, and Stovel 2004; C. F. Turner et al. 1998; Wallis 2005.

Each dot represents a boy or girl at "Jefferson High." The lines that link them represent romantic and sexual relationships that occurred over an 18-month period. While most of the teenagers had had just one or two partners, 288 of the 832 students interviewed were linked in a giant sexual network.

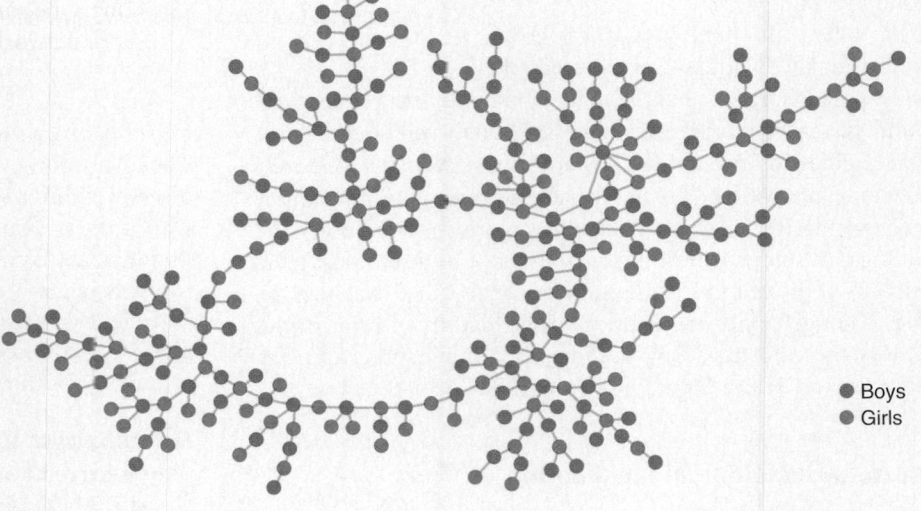

● Boys
● Girls

Other relationships (If a pattern was observed more than once, numeral indicates frequency)

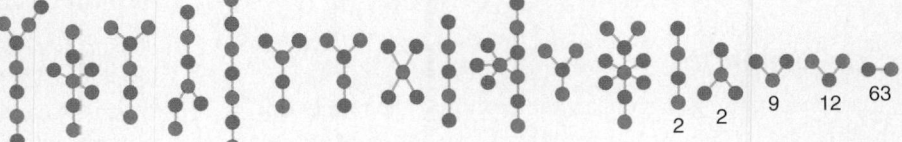

2   2   9   12   63

Source: Bearman, Moody, and Stovel 2004:58.

Contemporary Culture To what extent do the patterns found in this study reflect changing values?

Gender What differences would you expect in male and female adolescent sexual networks?
Policy Pointer The study of adolescent sexual networks can be useful to policy analysts.

111

contacts, offer advice, or simply share interests. One site creates "tribes" of people who share the same characteristic—a religion, hobby, music preference, or college affiliation (Tedeschi 2004).

Sociologist Manuel Castells (1997, 1998, 2000) views these emerging electronic social networks as fundamental to new organizations and the growth of existing businesses and associations. One such network, in particular, is changing the way people interact. *Texting* refers to the exchange of wireless e-mails over cell phones. It began first in Asia in 2000 and has now taken off in North America and Europe. Initially, texting was popular among young users, who sent shorthand messages such as "WRU" ("Where are you?") and "CU2NYT" ("See you tonight"). Now the business world has seen the advantages of transmitting e-mails via cell phones or PalmPilots. However, sociologists caution that such devices create a workday that never ends, and that increasingly people are busy checking their digital devices rather than actually conversing with those around them.

In 2003, the deployment of U.S. troops in the Middle East increased many people's reliance on e-mail. Today, digital photos and sound files accompany e-mail messages between soldiers and their families and friends. Well-established networks have developed to help those who are novices at electronic communication to connect to the Internet. Meanwhile, more seasoned users, including U.S. soldiers and Iraqi citizens, have begun to post their opinions of the war in Iraq in online journals called Web logs, or blogs. Though critics are skeptical of the identity of some of the authors, these postings have become yet another source of news about the war (Faith 2005; O'Connor 2004).

The Internet has added a massive new dimension to social interaction—even though you may not be totally sure whom you are "talking to."

Use Your Sociological Imagination

www.mhhe.com/schaefer7

If you were deaf, what impact might instant messaging, or texting, have on you?

Social Institutions

The mass media, the government, the economy, the family, and the health care system are all examples of social institutions found in our society. *Social institutions* are organized patterns of beliefs and behavior centered on basic social needs, such as replacing personnel (the family) and preserving order (the government).

Theory Functionalist view of social institutions introduced

A close look at social institutions gives sociologists insight into the structure of a society. Consider religion, for example. The institution of religion adapts to the segment of society that it serves. Church work has very different meanings for ministers who serve a skid row area and those who serve a suburban middle-class community. Religious leaders assigned to a skid row mission will focus on tending to the ill and providing food and shelter. In contrast, clergy in affluent suburbs will be occupied with counseling those considering marriage and divorce, arranging youth activities, and overseeing cultural events.

Functionalist View One way to understand social institutions is to see how they fulfill essential functions. Anthropologist David F. Aberle and his colleagues (1950) and sociologists Raymond Mack and Calvin Bradford (1979) have identified five major tasks, or functional prerequisites, that a society or relatively permanent group must accomplish if it is to survive:

1. *Replacing personnel.* Any group or society must replace personnel when they die, leave, or become incapacitated. This task is accomplished through such means as immigration, annexation of neighboring groups, acquisition of slaves, or sexual reproduction. The Shakers, a religious sect that came to the United States in 1774, are a conspicuous example of a group that has *failed* to replace personnel. Their religious beliefs commit the Shakers to celibacy; to survive, the group

Theory The list of functional prerequisites reflects a functional analysis of social institutions.

must recruit new members. At first, the Shakers proved quite successful in attracting members, reaching a peak of about 6,000 members in the United States during the 1840s. As of 2004, however, the only Shaker community left in this country was a farm in Maine with five members—three men and two women (Sabbathday Lake 2004).

2. *Teaching new recruits.* No group or society can survive if many of its members reject the group's established behavior and responsibilities. Thus, finding or producing new members is not sufficient; the group or society must also encourage recruits to learn and accept its values and customs. Such learning can take place formally, within schools (where learning is a manifest function) or informally, through interaction in peer groups (where instruction is a latent function).

3. *Producing and distributing goods and services.* Any relatively permanent group or society must provide and distribute desired goods and services to its members. Each society establishes a set of rules for the allocation of financial and other resources. The group must satisfy the needs of most members to some extent, or it will risk the possibility of discontent and ultimately disorder.

4. *Preserving order.* Throughout the world, indigenous and aboriginal peoples have struggled to protect themselves from outside invaders, with varying degrees of success. Failure to preserve order and defend against conquest leads to the death not only of a people, but of a culture.

5. *Providing and maintaining a sense of purpose.* People must feel motivated to continue as members of a group or society in order to fulfill the first four requirements. After the September 11, 2001, attacks on New York City and Washington, D.C., memorial services and community gatherings across the nation allowed people to affirm their allegiance to their country and bind up the psychic wounds inflicted by the terrorists. Patriotism, then, assists some people in developing and maintaining a sense of purpose. For others, tribal identities, religious values, or personal moral codes are especially meaningful. Whatever the motivator, in any society there remains one common and critical reality: if an individual does not have a sense of purpose, he or she has little reason to contribute to a society's survival.

This list of functional prerequisites does not specify *how* a society and its corresponding social institutions will perform each task. For example, one society may protect itself from external attack by amassing a frightening arsenal of weaponry, while another may make determined efforts to remain neutral in world politics and to promote cooperative relationships with its neighbors. No matter what its particular strategy, any society or relatively permanent group must attempt to satisfy all these functional prerequisites for survival. If it fails on even one condition, the society runs the risk of extinction.

Conflict View Conflict theorists do not agree with the functionalist approach to social institutions. Although proponents of

both perspectives agree that social institutions are organized to meet basic social needs, conflict theorists object to the idea that the outcome is necessarily efficient and desirable.

From a conflict perspective, the present organization of social institutions is no accident. Major institutions, such as education, help to maintain the privileges of the most powerful individuals and groups within a society, while contributing to the powerlessness of others. To give one example, public schools in the United States are financed largely through property taxes. This arrangement allows more affluent areas to provide their children with better-equipped schools and better-paid teachers than low-income areas can afford. As a result, children from prosperous communities are better prepared to compete academically than children from impoverished communities. The structure of the nation's educational system permits and even promotes such unequal treatment of schoolchildren.

Conflict theorists argue that social institutions such as education have an inherently conservative nature. Without question, it has been difficult to implement educational reforms that promote equal opportunity—whether bilingual education, school desegregation, or mainstreaming of students with disabilities. From a functionalist perspective, social change can be dysfunctional, since it often leads to instability. However, from a conflict view, why should we preserve the existing social structure if it is unfair and discriminatory?

Social institutions also operate in gendered and racist environments, as conflict theorists, as well as feminists and interactionists, have pointed out. In schools, offices, and government institutions, assumptions about what people can do reflect the sexism and racism of the larger society. For instance, many people assume that women cannot make tough decisions—even

This memorial service for the victims of the September 11, 2001, terrorist attack incorporated many patriotic elements, all of which helped New Yorkers to maintain a sense of purpose in extremely difficult times.

those in the top echelons of corporate management. Others assume that all Black students at elite colleges represent affirmative action admissions. Inequality based on gender, economic status, race, and ethnicity thrives in such an environment—to which we might add discrimination based on age, physical disability, and sexual orientation. The truth of this assertion can be seen in routine decisions by employers on how to advertise jobs, as well as whether to provide fringe benefits such as child care and parental leave.

Use Your Sociological Imagination
www.mhhe.com/schaefer7

Would social networks be more important to a migrant worker in California than to someone with political and social clout? Why or why not?

Interactionist View Social institutions affect our everyday behavior, whether we are driving down the street or waiting in a long shopping line. Sociologist Mitchell Duneier (1994a, 1994b) studied the social behavior of the word processors, all women, who work in the service center of a large Chicago law firm. Duneier was interested in the informal social norms that emerged in this work environment and the rich social network these female employees created.

The Network Center, as it is called, is a single, windowless room in a large office building where the law firm occupies seven floors. The center is staffed by two shifts of word processors, who work either from 4:00 p.m. to midnight or from midnight to 8:00 a.m. Each word processor works in a cubicle with just enough room for her keyboard, terminal, printer, and telephone. Work assignments for the word processors are placed in a central basket and then completed according to precise procedures.

At first glance, we might think that these women labor with little social contact, apart from limited breaks and occasional conversations with their supervisor. However, drawing on the interactionist perspective, Duneier learned that despite working in a large office, these women find private moments to talk (often in the halls or outside the washroom) and share a critical view of the law firm's attorneys and day-shift secretaries. Indeed, the word processors routinely suggest that their assignments represent work that the "lazy" secretaries should have completed during the normal workday. Duneier (1994b) tells of one word processor who resented the lawyers' superior attitude and pointedly refused to recognize or speak with any attorney who would not address her by name.

Interactionist theorists emphasize that our social behavior is conditioned by the roles and statuses we accept, the groups to which we belong, and the institutions within which we function. For example, the social roles associated with being a judge occur within the larger context of the criminal justice system. The status of "judge" stands in relation to other statuses, such as attorney, plaintiff, defendant, and witness, as well as to the social institution of government. Although courts and jails have great

symbolic importance, the judicial system derives its continued significance from the roles people carry out in social interactions (Berger and Luckmann 1966).

Social Structure in Global Perspective

Modern societies are complex, especially compared to earlier social arrangements. Sociologists Émile Durkheim, Ferdinand Tönnies, and Gerhard Lenski developed ways to contrast modern societies with simpler forms of social structure.

Durkheim's Mechanical and Organic Solidarity

In his *Division of Labor* ([1893] 1933), Durkheim argued that social structure depends on the division of labor in a society—in other words, on the manner in which tasks are performed. Thus, a task such as providing food can be carried out almost

Social institutions affect the way we behave. How might the worshippers at this mosque in Egypt interact differently in school or at work?

Theory Interactionist view of social institutions introduced
Key Person Mitchell Duneier
Gender Social behavior of women working as word processors at a large law firm
Theory Duneier drew on the interactionist perspective in studying women working as word processors.

Key Person Émile Durkheim
Theory Durkheim's view of social structure is an example of functionalist analysis.

totally by one individual, or it can be divided among many people. The latter pattern is typical of modern societies, in which the cultivation, processing, distribution, and retailing of a single food item are performed by literally hundreds of people.

In societies in which there is minimal division of labor, a collective consciousness develops that emphasizes group solidarity. Durkheim termed this collective frame of mind *mechanical solidarity,* implying that all individuals perform the same tasks. In this type of society, no one needs to ask, "What do your parents do?" since all are engaged in similar work. Each person prepares food, hunts, makes clothing, builds homes, and so forth. Because people have few options regarding what to do with their lives, there is little concern for individual needs. Instead, the group is the dominating force in society. Both social interaction and negotiation are based on close, intimate, face-to-face social contacts. Since there is little specialization, there are few social roles.

As societies become more advanced technologically, they rely on greater division of labor. The person who cuts down timber is not the same person who puts up your roof. With increasing specialization, many different tasks must be performed by many different individuals—even in manufacturing a single item, such as a radio or stove. In general, social interactions become less personal than in societies characterized by mechanical solidarity. People begin relating to others on the basis of their social positions ("butcher," "nurse") rather than their distinctive human qualities. Because the overall social structure of the society continues to change, statuses and social roles are in perpetual flux.

Once society has become more complex and division of labor is greater, no individual can go it alone. Dependence on others becomes essential for group survival. In Durkheim's terms, mechanical solidarity is replaced by *organic solidarity,* a collective consciousness resting on the need a society's members have for one another. Durkheim chose the term *organic solidarity* because in his view, individuals become interdependent in much the same way as organs of the human body.

Tönnies's *Gemeinschaft* and *Gesellschaft*

Ferdinand Tönnies (1855–1936) was appalled by the rise of an industrial city in his native Germany during the late 1800s. In his view, the city marked a dramatic change from the ideal of a close-knit community, which Tönnies termed a *Gemeinschaft,* to that of an impersonal mass society, known as a *Gesellschaft* (Tönnies [1887] 1988).

The *Gemeinschaft* (pronounced guh-MINE-shoft) is typical of rural life. It is a small community in which people have similar backgrounds and life experiences. Virtually everyone knows one another, and social interactions are intimate and familiar, almost as among kinfolk. In this community there is a commitment to the larger social group and a sense of togetherness among members. People relate to others in a personal way, not just as "clerk" or "manager." With this personal interaction comes little privacy, however: we know too much about everyone.

Social control in the *Gemeinschaft* is maintained through informal means such as moral persuasion, gossip, and even gestures. These techniques work effectively because people genuinely care how others feel about them. Social change is relatively limited in the *Gemeinschaft;* the lives of members of one generation may be quite similar to those of their grandparents.

In contrast, the *Gesellschaft* (pronounced guh-ZELL-shoft) is an ideal community that is characteristic of modern urban life. In this community most people are strangers who feel little in common with other residents. Relationships are governed by social roles that grow out of immediate tasks, such as purchasing a product or arranging a business meeting. Self-interest dominates, and there is little consensus concerning values or commitment to the group. As a result, social control must rest on more formal techniques, such as laws and legally defined punishments. Social change is an important aspect of life in the *Gesellschaft;* it can be strikingly evident even within a single generation.

Table 5-2 (page 116) summarizes the differences between the *Gemeinschaft* and the *Gesellschaft.* Sociologists have used these terms to compare social structures that stress close relationships with those that emphasize less personal ties. It is easy to view the

In small communities like this one in Merida, Venezuela, people maintain social control through informal means such as gossip. Tönnies referred to this type of community as a *Gemeinschaft.*

Key Person Ferdinand Tönnies

Global View Tönnies's typology of *Gemeinschaft* and *Gesellshaft* was based on his observations in Germany in the late 1800s.

Contemporary Culture Relate *Gemeinschaft* and *Gesellschaft* to reconstruction issues in Iraq.

Web Resource Students can take a survey to help them determine if their home communities are *Gemeinschaft* or *Gesellschaft* communities. Direct them to the first Interactive Activity in the student center of the Online Learning Center (**www.mhhe.com/schaefer7**).

Chapter 5

Gemeinschaft with nostalgia, as a far better way of life than the rat race of contemporary existence. However, the more intimate relationships of the *Gemeinschaft* come at a price. The prejudice and discrimination found there can be quite confining; ascribed statuses such as family background often outweigh a person's unique talents and achievements. In addition, the *Gemeinschaft* tends to distrust individuals who seek to be creative or just to be different.

Lenski's Sociocultural Evolution Approach

Sociologist Gerhard Lenski takes a very different view of society and social structure. Rather than distinguishing between two opposite types of society, as Tönnies did, Lenski sees human societies as undergoing a process of change characterized by a dominant pattern known as *sociocultural evolution.* This term refers to long-term trends in societies resulting from the interplay of continuity, innovation, and selection (Nolan and Lenski 2006:361).

In Lenski's view, a society's level of technology is critical to the way it is organized. Lenski defines *technology* as "cultural information about the ways in which the material resources of the environment may be used to satisfy human needs and desires" (Nolan and Lenski 2006:361). The available technology does not completely define the form that a particular society and its social structure take. Nevertheless, a low level of technology may limit the degree to which a society can depend on such things as irrigation or complex machinery. As technology advances, Lenski writes, a community evolves from a preindustrial to an industrial and finally a postindustrial society.

Preindustrial Societies How does a preindustrial society organize its economy? If we know that, we can categorize the society. The first type of preindustrial society to emerge in human history was the *hunting-and-gathering society,* in which people simply rely on whatever foods and fibers are readily available. Technology in such societies is minimal. Organized into groups, people move constantly in search of food. There is little division of labor into specialized tasks.

Hunting-and-gathering societies are composed of small, widely dispersed groups. Each group consists almost entirely of people who are related to one another. As a result, kinship ties are the source of authority and influence, and the social institution of the family takes on a particularly important role. Tönnies would certainly view such societies as examples of the *Gemeinschaft.*

Social differentiation within the hunting-and-gathering society is based on ascribed statuses such as gender, age, and family background. Since resources are scarce, there is relatively little inequality in terms of material goods. By the close of the 20th century, hunting-and-gathering societies had virtually disappeared (Nolan and Lenski 2006).

Horticultural societies, in which people plant seeds and crops rather than merely subsist on available foods, emerged about 10,000 to 12,000 years ago. Members of horticultural societies are much less nomadic than hunters and gatherers. They place greater emphasis on the production of tools and household objects. Yet technology remains rather limited in these societies, whose members cultivate crops with the aid of digging sticks or hoes (Wilford 1997).

Table 5-2   Comparison of the *Gemeinschaft* and *Gesellschaft*

summing**UP**

Gemeinschaft	*Gesellschaft*
Rural life typifies this form.	Urban life typifies this form.
People share a feeling of community that results from their similar backgrounds and life experiences.	People have little sense of commonality. Their differences appear more striking than their similarities.
Social interactions are intimate and familiar.	Social interactions are likely to be impersonal and task-specific.
People maintain a spirit of cooperation and unity of will.	Self-interest dominates.
Tasks and personal relationships cannot be separated.	The task being performed is paramount; relationships are subordinate.
People place little emphasis on individual privacy.	Privacy is valued.
Informal social control predominates.	Formal social control is evident.
People are not very tolerant of deviance.	People are more tolerant of deviance.
Emphasis is on ascribed statuses.	Emphasis is on achieved statuses.
Social change is relatively limited.	Social change is very evident, even within a generation.

Think About It

How would you classify the communities with which you are familiar? Are they more *Gemeinschaft* or *Gesellschaft?*

Key Person Gerhard Lenski
Classroom Tip See "Gerhard Lenski" in Topics and Sources for Student Research.

Classroom Tip See "Daily Life in a Hunting-and-Gathering Society" (Additional Lecture Ideas).
Let's Discuss How might gender inequality vary across different types of preindustrial society?

At first glance, this scene may seem a throwback to agrarian society, but look more closely. Today's farm is actually a highly mechanized, computer-dependent operation that is networked into the global economy.

The last stage of preindustrial development is the *agrarian society,* which emerged about 5,000 years ago. As in horticultural societies, members of agrarian societies are engaged primarily in the production of food. However, new technological innovations such as the plow allow farmers to dramatically increase their crop yields. They can cultivate the same fields over generations, allowing the emergence of larger settlements.

The agrarian society continues to rely on the physical power of humans and animals (as opposed to mechanical power). Nevertheless, its social structure has more carefully defined roles than that of horticultural societies. Individuals focus on specialized tasks, such as the repair of fishing nets or blacksmithing. As human settlements become more established and stable, social institutions become more elaborate and property rights more important. The comparative permanence and greater surpluses of an agrarian society allow members to create artifacts such as statues, public monuments, and art objects and to pass them on from one generation to the next.

Table 5-3 summarizes Lenski's three stages of sociocultural evolution, as well as the stages that follow, which are described next.

Industrial Societies Although the industrial revolution did not topple monarchs, it produced changes every bit as significant as those resulting from political revolutions. The industrial revolution, which took place largely in England during the period 1760 to 1830, was a scientific revolution focused on the application of nonanimal (mechanical) sources of power to labor tasks. An ***industrial society*** is a society that depends on mechanization to produce its goods and services. Industrial societies rely on new inventions that facilitate agricultural and industrial production, and on new sources of energy, such as steam.

As the industrial revolution proceeded, a new form of social structure emerged. Many societies underwent an irrevocable shift from an agrarian-oriented economy to an industrial base. No longer did an individual or a family typically make an entire product. Instead, specialization of tasks and manufacturing of goods became increasingly common. Workers, generally men but also women and even children, left their family homesteads to work in central locations such as factories.

Table 5-3 Stages of Sociocultural Evolution

Societal Type	First Appearance	Characteristics
Hunting-and-gathering	Beginning of human life	Nomadic; reliance on readily available food and fibers
Horticultural	About 10,000 to 12,000 years ago	More settled; development of agriculture and limited technology
Agrarian	About 5,000 years ago	Larger, more stable settlements; improved technology and increased crop yields
Industrial	1760–1850	Reliance on mechanical power and new sources of energy; centralized workplaces; economic interdependence; formal education
Postindustrial	1960s	Reliance on services, especially the processing and control of information; expanded middle class
Postmodern	Latter 1970s	High technology; mass consumption of consumer goods and media images; cross-cultural integration

Student Alert Be sure to clarify the distinction between horticulture and agriculture.
Theory From a conflict view, surpluses contribute to differential rewards and power.

The process of industrialization had distinctive social consequences. Families and communities could not continue to function as self-sufficient units. Individuals, villages, and regions began to exchange goods and services and to become interdependent. As people came to rely on the labor of members of other communities, the family lost its unique position as the source of power and authority. The need for specialized knowledge led to more formalized schooling, and education emerged as a social institution distinct from the family.

Postindustrial and Postmodern Societies

When Lenski first proposed the sociocultural evolutionary approach in the 1960s, he paid relatively little attention to how maturing industrialized societies may change with the emergence of even more advanced forms of technology. More recently, he and other sociologists have studied the significant changes in the occupational structure of industrial societies as they shift from manufacturing to service economies. In the 1970s sociologist Daniel Bell wrote about the technologically advanced *postindustrial society,* whose economic system is engaged primarily in the processing and control of information. The main output of a postindustrial society is services rather than manufactured goods. Large numbers of people become involved in occupations devoted to the teaching, generation, or dissemination of ideas. Jobs in fields such as advertising, public relations, human resources, and computer information systems would be typical of a postindustrial society (D. Bell 1999).

Bell views the transition from industrial to postindustrial society as a positive development. He sees a general decline in organized working-class groups and a rise in interest groups concerned with national issues such as health, education, and the environment. Bell's outlook is functionalist, because he portrays the postindustrial society as basically consensual. As organizations and interest groups engage in an open and competitive process of decision making, Bell believes, the level of conflict between diverse groups will diminish, strengthening social stability.

Conflict theorists take issue with Bell's functionalist analysis of the postindustrial society. For example, Michael Harrington (1980), who alerted the nation to the problems of the poor in his book *The Other America,* questioned the significance that Bell attached to the growing class of white-collar workers. Harrington conceded that scientists, engineers, and economists are involved in important political and economic decisions, but he disagreed with Bell's claim that they have a free hand in decision making, independent of the interests of the rich. Harrington followed in the tradition of Marx by arguing that conflict between social classes will continue in the postindustrial society.

Sociologists have recently gone beyond discussion of the postindustrial society to the ideal of the postmodern society. A *postmodern society* is a technologically sophisticated society that is preoccupied with consumer goods and media images (Brannigan 1992). Such societies consume goods and information on a mass scale. Postmodern theorists take a global perspective, noting the ways that culture crosses national boundaries.

For example, residents of the United States may listen to reggae music from Jamaica, eat sushi and other Japanese foods, and wear clogs from Sweden.

The emphasis of postmodern theorists is on observing and describing newly emerging cultural forms and patterns of social interaction. Within sociology, the postmodern view offers support for integrating the insights of various theoretical perspectives—functionalism, conflict theory, feminist theory, interactionism, and labeling theory—while incorporating other contemporary approaches. Feminist sociologists argue optimistically that with its indifference to hierarchies and distinctions, the postmodern society will discard traditional values of male dominance in favor of gender equality. Yet others contend that despite new technologies, postindustrial and postmodern societies can be expected to display the same problems of inequality that plague industrial societies (Denzin 2004; Smart 1990; B. Turner 1990; van Vucht Tijssen 1990).

Durkheim, Tönnies, and Lenski present three visions of society's social structure. While they differ, each is useful, and this textbook will draw on all three. The sociocultural evolutionary approach emphasizes a historical perspective. It does not picture

{ In a postmodern society, people consume goods, information, and media images en masse. In Paris, Disneyworld is popularizing U.S. media images abroad, illustrating another characteristic of postmodern societies—globalization. }

Key Person Daniel Bell
Theory Bell's functionalist view of postindustrial societies as basically consensual
Theory Conflict critique of Bell's analysis of postindustrial society
Student Alert Clarify the distinction between postindustrial and postmodern societies.
Let's Discuss How can the concept of diffusion be related to postmodernism?

Theory Postmodernism integrates the insights of functionalism, conflict theory, interactionism, labeling theory, and feminist theory.
Theory Feminist sociologists' view of postmodernism and its possible impact on gender inequalities
Theory The work of Durkheim, Tönnies, and Lenski examines the macro and micro levels of social structure.

different types of social structures coexisting within the same society. Consequently, one would not expect a single society to include hunters and gatherers along with a postmodern culture. In contrast, Durkheim's and Tönnies's theories allow for the existence of different types of community—such as a *Gemeinschaft* and a *Gesellschaft*—in the same society. Thus, a rural New Hampshire community located 100 miles from Boston can be linked to the city by modern information technology. The main difference between these two theories is a matter of emphasis. While Tönnies emphasized the overriding concern in each type of community—one's own self-interest or the well-being of the larger society—Durkheim emphasized the division (or lack of division) of labor.

The work of these three thinkers reminds us that a major focus of sociology has been to identify changes in social structure and the consequences for human behavior. At the macro level, we see society shifting to more advanced forms of technology. The social structure becomes increasingly complex, and new social institutions emerge to assume some functions that once were performed by the family. On the micro level, these changes affect the nature of social interactions. Each individual takes on multiple social roles, and people come to rely more on social networks and less on kinship ties. As the social structure becomes more complex, people's relationships become more impersonal, transient, and fragmented.

Understanding Organizations
Formal Organizations and Bureaucracies

As contemporary societies have shifted to more advanced forms of technology and their social structures have become more complex, our lives have become increasingly dominated by large secondary groups referred to as *formal organizations*. A *formal organization* is a group designed for a special purpose and structured for maximum efficiency. The U.S. Postal Service, McDonald's, and the Boston Pops orchestra are examples of formal organizations. Though organizations vary in their size, specificity of goals, and degree of efficiency, they are all structured to facilitate the management of large-scale operations. They also have a bureaucratic form of organization, described in the next section.

In our society, formal organizations fulfill an enormous variety of personal and societal needs, shaping the lives of every one of us. In fact, formal organizations have become such a dominant force that we must create organizations to supervise other organizations, such as the Securities and Exchange Commission (SEC) to regulate brokerage companies. While it sounds much more exciting to say that we live in the "computer age" than to say that ours is the "age of formal organization," the latter is probably a more accurate description of our times (Azumi and Hage 1972; Etzioni 1964).

Ascribed statuses such as gender, race, and ethnicity can influence how we see ourselves within formal organizations. For example, a study of women lawyers in the nation's largest law firms found significant differences in the women's self-images,

depending on the relative presence or absence of women in positions of power. In firms in which fewer than 15 percent of partners were women, the female lawyers were likely to believe that "feminine" traits were strongly devalued, and that masculinity was equated with success. As one female attorney put it, "Let's face it: this is a man's environment, and it's sort of Jock City, especially at my firm." Women in firms where female lawyers were better represented in positions of power had a stronger desire for and higher expectations of promotion (Ely 1995:619).

Characteristics of a Bureaucracy

A *bureaucracy* is a component of formal organization that uses rules and hierarchical ranking to achieve efficiency. Rows of desks staffed by seemingly faceless people, endless lines and forms, impossibly complex language, and frustrating encounters with red tape—all these unpleasant images have combined to make *bureaucracy* a dirty word and an easy target in political campaigns. As a result, few people want to identify their occupation as "bureaucrat," despite the fact that all of us perform various bureaucratic tasks. In an industrial society, elements of bureaucracy enter into almost every occupation.

Max Weber ([1913–1922] 1947) first directed researchers to the significance of bureaucratic structure. In an important sociological advance, Weber emphasized the basic similarity of structure and process found in the otherwise dissimilar enterprises of religion, government, education, and business. Weber saw bureaucracy as a form of organization quite different from {p.11} the family-run business. For analytical purposes, he developed an ideal type of bureaucracy that would reflect the most characteristic aspects of all human organizations. By *ideal type* Weber meant a construct or model for evaluating specific cases. In actuality, perfect bureaucracies do not exist; no real-world organization corresponds exactly to Weber's ideal type.

Weber proposed that whether the purpose is to run a church, a corporation, or an army, the ideal bureaucracy displays five basic characteristics. A discussion of those characteristics, as well {p.14} as the dysfunctions of a bureaucracy, follows.

1. Division of labor. Specialized experts perform specific tasks. In your college bureaucracy, the admissions officer does not do the job of registrar; the guidance counselor doesn't see to the maintenance of buildings. By working at a specific task, people are more likely to become highly skilled and carry out a job with maximum efficiency. This emphasis on specialization is so basic a part of our lives that we may not realize it is a fairly recent development in Western culture.

The downside of division of labor is that the fragmentation of work into smaller and smaller tasks can divide workers and remove any connection they might feel to the overall objective of the bureaucracy. In *The Communist Manifesto* (written in 1848), Karl Marx and Friedrich Engels charged that the capitalist system reduces workers to a mere "appendage of the machine" (L. Feuer 1989). Such a work arrangement, they wrote, produces extreme *alienation*—a condition of estrangement or dissociation from the surrounding society. According to both Marx and conflict theorists, restricting workers to very small tasks also

weakens their job security, since new employees can be easily trained to replace them.

Although division of labor has certainly enhanced the performance of many complex bureaucracies, in some cases it can lead to *trained incapacity;* that is, workers become so specialized that they develop blind spots and fail to notice obvious problems. Even worse, they may not care about what is happening in the next department. Some observers believe that such developments have caused workers in the United States to become less productive on the job.

In some cases, the bureaucratic division of labor can have tragic results. In the wake of the coordinated attacks on the World Trade Center and the Pentagon on September 11, 2001, Americans wondered aloud how the FBI and CIA could have failed to detect the terrorists' elaborately planned operation. The problem, in part, turned out to be the division of labor between the FBI, which focuses on domestic matters, and the CIA, which operates overseas. Officials at these intelligence-gathering organizations, both of which are huge bureaucracies, are well known for jealously guarding information from one another. Subsequent investigations revealed that they knew about Osama bin Laden and his al-Qaeda terrorist network in the early 1990s. Unfortunately, five federal agencies—the CIA, FBI, National Security Agency, Defense Intelligence Agency, and National Reconnaissance Office—failed to share their leads on the network. Although the hijacking of the four commercial airliners used in the massive attacks may not have been preventable, the

Whistle-blower Colleen Rowley, an FBI agent, tried unsuccessfully to bring her superiors' attention to a French Moroccan who had signed up for pilot training at a local flight school, keen to operate a 747. The man later used his training to crash a hijacked jet into the World Trade Center. Rowley was photographed as she testified before the Senate Judiciary Committee in June 2002.

"Frankly, at this point in the flow chart, we don't know what happens to these people..."

A hierarchy of authority may deprive individuals of a voice in decision making, but it does clarify who supervises whom.

Contemporary Culture Pay attention to campaign promises to reform government bureaucracies.

Let's Discuss Have working students discuss the hierarchical structure of their companies in terms of power and lines of communication. What informal chains of command exist?

bureaucratic division of labor definitely hindered efforts to defend against terrorism, undermining U.S. national security.

2. Hierarchy of authority. Bureaucracies follow the principle of hierarchy; that is, each position is under the supervision of a higher authority. A president heads a college bureaucracy; he or she selects members of the administration, who in turn hire their own staff. In the Roman Catholic Church, the pope is the supreme authority; under him are cardinals, bishops, and so forth.

3. Written rules and regulations. What if your sociology professor gave your classmate an A for having such a friendly smile? You might think that wasn't fair, that it was against the rules.

Rules and regulations, as we all know, are an important characteristic of bureaucracies. Ideally, through such procedures, a bureaucracy ensures uniform performance of every task. Thus your classmate cannot receive an A for a nice smile, because the rules guarantee that all students will receive essentially the same treatment.

Through written rules and regulations, bureaucracies generally offer employees clear standards for an adequate (or exceptional) performance. In addition, procedures provide a valuable sense of continuity in a bureaucracy. Individual workers will come and go, but the structure and past records of the organization give it a life of its own that outlives the services of any one bureaucrat.

Let's Discuss Analyze your college's hierarchical structure in terms of power, lines of communication, and informal chains of command.

Of course, rules and regulations can overshadow the larger goals of an organization to the point that they become dysfunctional. What if a hospital emergency room physician failed to treat a seriously injured person because he or she had no valid proof of U.S. citizenship? If blindly applied, rules no longer serve as a means to achieving an objective, but instead become important (and perhaps too important) in their own right. Robert Merton (1968) used the term *goal displacement* to refer to overzealous conformity to official regulations.

4. Impersonality. Max Weber wrote that in a bureaucracy, work is carried out *sine ira et studio*, "without hatred or passion." Bureaucratic norms dictate that officials perform their duties without giving personal consideration to people as individuals. Although this norm is intended to guarantee equal treatment for each person, it also contributes to the often cold and uncaring feeling associated with modern organizations. We typically think of big government and big business when we think of impersonal bureaucracies. In some cases, the impersonality that is associated with a bureaucracy can have tragic results. More frequently, bureaucratic impersonality produces frustration and disaffection. Today, even small firms screen callers with electronic menus.

5. Employment based on technical qualifications. Within the ideal bureaucracy, hiring is based on technical qualifications rather than on favoritism, and performance is measured against specific standards. Written personnel policies dictate who gets promoted, and people often have a right to appeal if they believe that particular rules have been violated. Such procedures protect bureaucrats against arbitrary dismissal, provide a measure of security, and encourage loyalty to the organization.

In this sense, the "impersonal" bureaucracy can be considered an improvement over nonbureaucratic organizations. College faculty members, for example, are ideally hired and promoted according to their professional qualifications, including degrees earned and research published, rather than because of whom they know. Once they are granted tenure, their jobs are protected against the whims of a president or dean.

Although any bureaucracy ideally will value technical and professional competence, personnel decisions do not always follow that ideal pattern. Dysfunctions within bureaucracy have become well publicized, particularly because of the work of Laurence J. Peter. According to the *Peter principle,* every employee within a hierarchy tends to rise to his or her level of incompetence (Peter and Hull 1969). This hypothesis, which has not been directly or systematically tested, reflects a possible dysfunctional outcome of advancement on the basis of merit. Talented people receive promotion after promotion, until sadly, some of them finally achieve positions that they cannot handle with their usual competence (Blau and Meyer 1987).

Table 5-4 summarizes the five characteristics of bureaucracy. These characteristics, developed by Max Weber more than 80 years ago, describe an ideal type rather than an actual bureaucracy. Not every formal organization will possess all five of Weber's characteristics. In fact, wide variation exists among actual bureaucratic organizations.

Bureaucracy pervades modern life. Through McDonaldization —the worldwide diffusion not only of the fast-food restaurant, but of the principles of operating such an establishment— bureaucratization has reached new heights (see Chapter 3). As Box 5-3 (page 122) shows, the McDonald's organization provides an excellent illustration of Weber's concept of bureaucracy.

Bureaucratization as a Process Have you ever had to speak to 10 or 12 individuals in a corporation or government agency just to find out which official has jurisdiction over a particular problem? Ever been transferred from one department to another until you finally hung up in disgust? Sociologists have used the term *bureaucratization* to refer to the process by which a group, organization, or social movement becomes increasingly bureaucratic.

Normally, we think of bureaucratization in terms of large organizations. But bureaucratization also takes place within small-group settings. Sociologist Jennifer Bickman Mendez (1998)

Table 5-4 Characteristics of a Bureaucracy

summingUP

Characteristic	Positive Consequence	Negative Consequence	
		For the Individual	For the Organization
Division of labor	Produces efficiency in a large-scale corporation	Produces trained incapacity	Produces a narrow perspective
Hierarchy of authority	Clarifies who is in command	Deprives employees of a voice in decision making	Permits concealment of mistakes
Written rules and regulations	Let workers know what is expected of them	Stifle initiative and imagination	Lead to goal displacement
Impersonality	Reduces bias	Contributes to feelings of alienation	Discourages loyalty to company
Employment based on technical qualifications	Discourages favoritism and reduces petty rivalries	Discourages ambition to improve oneself elsewhere	Fosters Peter principle

Key Person Robert Merton
Let's Discuss Have students provide examples of *trained incapacity* and *goal displacement* at their college or places of work.
Classroom Tip "Employment based on technical qualifications" is also referred to as *tenure* or *security of position.*

Classroom Tip See "Nepotism" (Class Discussion Topics).
Let's Discuss Have students discuss their own jobs with respect to bureaucratization and McDonaldization.
Key Person Jennifer Bickman Mendez

sociologyIN *the Global Community*

5-3 McDonald's and the Worldwide Bureaucratization of Society

In his book *The McDonaldization of Society*, sociologist George Ritzer notes the enormous influence of a well-known fast-food organization on modern-day culture and social life. Ritzer defines **McDonaldization** as " the process by which the principles of the fast-food restaurant are coming to dominate more and more sectors of American society as well as of the rest of the world" (Ritzer 2004a:1). Through this process, the business principles on which the fast-food industry is founded—efficiency,

> *Worldwide, McDonald's brand of predictability, efficiency, and dependence on nonhuman technology have become customary in a number of services, ranging from medical care to wedding planning to education.*

calculability, predictability, and control—have changed not only the way Americans do business and run their organizations, but the way they live their lives. For example, busy families have come to rely on the takeout meals served up by fast-food establishments, and social groups from adolescents to senior citizens now meet at McDonald's.

Max Weber's five characteristics of bureaucracy are apparent in McDonald's restaurants, as well as in the global corporation behind them. Food preparation and order-taking reflect a painstaking *division of labor,* implemented by a *hierarchy of authority* that stretches from the food workers up to the shift manager and store operator, and ultimately to the corporate board of directors. Store operators learn McDonald's *written rules and regulations,* which govern even the amount of ketchup or mustard placed on a hamburger, at McDonald's Hamburger University. Little bonding occurs between servers and customers, creating a pervasive sense of *impersonality.* Together with McDonald's cookie-cutter architectural designs, this lack of personal character tends to disguise a restaurant's locale—not just the town or city it serves, but often the country or continent as well. Finally, employ-

ees are expected to have specific *technical qualifications,* although most of the skills they need to perform routine tasks can be learned in a brief training period.

The real significance of McDonaldization is that it is not confined to the food-service industry. Worldwide, McDonald's brand of predictability, efficiency, and dependence on nonhuman technology have become customary in a number of services, ranging from medical care to wedding planning to education. Even sporting events reflect the influence of bureaucratization. Around the world, stadiums are becoming increasingly similar, both physically and in the way they present the sport to spectators. Swipe cards, "sports city" garages and parking lots, and automated ticket sales maximize efficiency. All seats offer spectators an unrestricted view, and a big screen guarantees them access to instant replays. Scores, player statistics, and attendance figures are updated automatically by computer and displayed on an automated scoreboard. Spectator enthusiasm is manufactured through digital displays urging applause or rhythmic chanting. At food counters, refreshments include well-

known brands whose customer loyalty has been nourished by advertisers for decades. And of course, the merchandising of teams' and even players' names and images is highly controlled.

McDonald's reliance on the five characteristics of bureaucracy is not revolutionary. What is new is the bureaucratization of services and life events that once were highly individualized, at times even spontaneous. More and more, society itself is becoming McDonaldized.

Let's Discuss

1. Do you patronize McDonald's and other fast-food establishments? If so, what features of these restaurants do you appreciate? Do you have any complaints about them?
2. Analyze life at your college using Weber's model of bureaucracy. What elements of McDonaldization do you see? Do you wish life were less McDonaldized?

Sources: Ormond 2005; Ritzer 2004a.

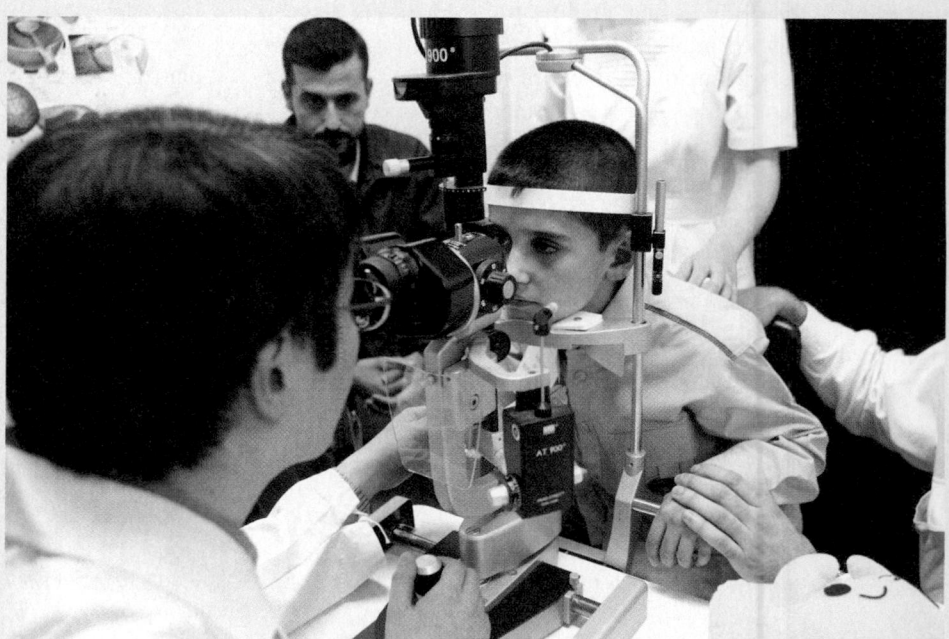

The worldwide success of highly efficient fast-food operations has led to the bureaucratization of many other services, including eye care and other forms of medical treatment.

Let's Discuss Ask students who have worked at a McDonald's to discuss examples of bureaucracy there.
Classroom Tip Share your experiences from college. In what ways is a college education more McDonaldized today?
Contemporary Culture Discuss some local businesses. Are they McDonaldized?

Global View Based on student travels, how McDonaldized are other countries?

studied domestic houseworkers employed in central California by a nationwide franchise. She found that housekeeping tasks were minutely defined, to the point that employees had to follow 22 written steps for cleaning a bathroom. Complaints and special requests went not to the workers, but to an office-based manager.

Oligarchy: Rule by a Few Conflict theorists have examined the bureaucratization of social movements. The German sociologist Robert Michels (1915) studied socialist parties and labor unions in Europe before World War I and found that such organizations were becoming increasingly bureaucratic. The emerging leaders of the organizations—even some of the most radical—had a vested interest in clinging to power. If they lost their leadership posts, they would have to return to full-time work as manual laborers.

Through his research, Michels originated the idea of the *iron law of oligarchy,* which describes how even a democratic organization will eventually develop into a bureaucracy ruled by a few (called an oligarchy). Why do oligarchies emerge? People who achieve leadership roles usually have the skills, knowledge, or charismatic appeal (as Weber noted) to direct, if not control, others. Michels argued that the rank and file of a movement or organization look to leaders for direction and thereby reinforce the process of rule by a few. In addition, members of an oligarchy are strongly motivated to maintain their leadership roles, privileges, and power.

Michels's insights continue to be relevant today. Contemporary labor unions in the United States and Western Europe bear little resemblance to those organized spontaneously by exploited workers. Conflict theorists have pointed to the longevity of union leaders, who are not always responsive to the needs and demands of the membership, and seem more concerned with maintaining their own positions and power. (The Social Policy section at the end of this chapter focuses on the status of labor unions today.)

Bureaucracy and Organizational Culture

How does bureaucratization affect the average individual who works in an organization? The early theorists of formal organizations tended to neglect this question. Max Weber, for example, focused on the management personnel in bureaucracies but had little to say about workers in industry or clerks in government agencies.

According to the *classical theory* of formal organizations, also known as the *scientific management approach,* workers are motivated almost entirely by economic rewards. This theory stresses that only the physical constraints on workers limit their productivity. Therefore, workers may be treated as a resource, much like the machines that began to replace them in the 20th century. Under the scientific management approach, management attempts to achieve maximum work efficiency through scientific planning, established performance standards, and careful supervision of workers and production. Planning involves efficiency studies but not studies of workers' attitudes or job satisfaction.

Not until workers organized unions—and forced management to recognize that they were not objects—did theorists of formal organizations begin to revise the classical approach. Along with management and administrators, social scientists became aware that informal groups of workers have an important impact on organizations (Perrow 1986). An alternative way of considering bureaucratic dynamics, the *human relations approach,* emphasizes the role of people, communication, and participation in a bureaucracy. This type of analysis reflects the interest of interactionist theorists in small-group behavior. Unlike planning under the scientific management approach, planning based on the human relations perspective focuses on workers' feelings, frustrations, and emotional need for job satisfaction.

The gradual move away from a sole focus on the physical aspects of getting the job done—and toward the concerns and needs of workers—led advocates of the human relations approach to stress the less formal aspects of bureaucratic structure. Informal groups and social networks within organizations develop partly as a result of people's ability to create more direct forms of communication than under the formal structure. Charles Page (1946) used the term *bureaucracy's other face* to refer to the unofficial activities and interactions that are such a basic part of daily organizational life.

A series of classic studies illustrates the value of the human {p.38 relations approach. The Hawthorne studies alerted sociologists to the fact that research subjects may alter their behavior to match the experimenter's expectations. The major focus of the Hawthorne studies, however, was the role of social factors in workers' productivity. One aspect of the research concerned the switchboard-bank wiring room, where 14 men were making parts of switches for telephone equipment. The researchers discovered that these men were producing far below their physical capabilities. The discovery was especially surprising because the men would have earned more money if they had produced more parts.

What accounted for such an unexpected restriction of output? The men feared that if they produced switch parts at a faster rate, their pay rate might be reduced, or some of them might lose their jobs. As a result, this group of workers had established their own (unofficial) norm for a proper day's work and created informal rules and sanctions to enforce it. Yet management was unaware of these practices and actually believed that the men were working as hard as they could (Roethlisberger and Dickson 1939).

Today, research on formal organizations is following new avenues. First, the proportion of women and minority group members in high-level management positions is still much lower than might be expected, given their numbers in the labor force. Researchers are now beginning to look at the impact this gender and racial/ethnic imbalance may have on managerial judgment, both formal and informal. Second, a company's power structure is only partly reflected in its formal organizational charts. In

Key Person Robert Michels
Global View Michels developed his "iron law" after studying socialist parties and labor unions in Europe before World War I.
Theory Michels's iron law of oligarchy draws on the conflict perspective.
Student Alert Sociologists do not regard the *iron law* as inviolate.

Theory Interactionists emphasize the importance of informal relations within formal organizations (bureaucracy's "other face").
Methods The Hawthorne studies are an example of an experiment (introduced in Chapter 2).

practice, core groups tend to emerge to dominate the decision-making process. Very large corporations—say, a General Electric or a Procter & Gamble—may have hundreds of interlocking core groups, each of which plays a key role in its division or region. Third, these organizations have traditionally been viewed as having fairly fixed boundaries. But today's production and service systems stretch across networks of independent or semi-independent companies—a fact that must be considered in studying corporate culture (Kleiner 2003; W. Scott 2004).

The Changing Workplace

Weber's work on bureaucracy and Michels's thinking on oligarchy are still applicable to the organizational structure and culture of the workplace. But today's factories and offices are undergoing rapid, profound changes unanticipated a century or more ago. Besides the far-reaching impact of technological advances such as computerization, workers must cope with organizational restructuring. This section will detail the dramatic changes evident in today's workplace.

Organizational Restructuring

To some extent, individual businesses, community organizations, and government agencies are always changing, if only because of personnel turnover. But since the late 20th century, formal organizations have been experimenting with new ways of getting the job done, some of which have significantly altered the workplace.

Collective decision making, or the active involvement of employee problem-solving groups in corporate management, first became popular in the United States in the 1980s. Management gurus had noted the dazzling success of Japanese automobile and consumer products manufacturers. In studying these companies, they found that problem-solving groups were one key to success. At first, such groups concentrated on small problems at

specific points in the production line. But today, these groups often cross departmental and divisional boundaries to attack problems rooted in the bureaucratic division of labor. Thus, they require significant adjustment by employees long used to working in a bureaucracy (Ouchi 1981).

Another innovation in the workplace, called *minimal hierarchy,* replaces the traditional bureaucratic hierarchy of authority with a flatter organizational structure. Minimal hierarchy offers workers greater access to those in authority, giving them an opportunity to voice concerns that might not be heard in a traditional bureaucracy. This new organizational structure is thought to minimize the potential for costly and dangerous bureaucratic oversights.

Finally, organizational *work teams* have become increasingly common, even in smaller organizations. There are two types of work team. *Project teams* address ongoing issues, such as safety or compliance with the Americans with Disabilities Act. *Task forces* pursue nonrecurring issues, such as a major building renovation. In both cases, team members are released to some degree from their regular duties in order to contribute to the organizationwide effort (W. Scott 2003).

The common purpose of work teams, minimal hierarchy, and collective decision making is to empower workers. For that reason, these new organizational structures can be exciting for the employees who participate in them. But these innovations rarely touch the vast numbers of workers who perform routine jobs in factories and office buildings. The 22 million part-time workers and 1 million full-time workers who earn the minimum wage or less know little about organizational restructuring (Bureau of Labor Statistics 2004).

Telecommuting

Increasingly, in many industrial countries, workers are turning into telecommuters. **Telecommuters** are employees who work full-time or part-time at home rather than in an outside office, and who are linked to their supervisors and colleagues through computer terminals, phone lines, and fax machines. One national survey showed that next to on-site day care, most office workers want virtual offices that allow them to work off-site. Not surprisingly, the number of telecommuters increased from 8.5 million in 1995 to 28 million in 2001 (D. B. Davis and Polonko 2001).

What are the social implications of this shift toward the virtual office? From an interactionist perspective, the workplace is a major source of friendships; restricting face-to-face social opportunities could destroy the trust that is created by "handshake agreements." Thus, telecommuting may move society further along the continuum from *Gemeinschaft* to *Gesellschaft.* On a more positive note, telecommuting may be the first social change that pulls fathers and mothers back into the home rather

> Work teams are becoming an increasingly common form of organizational restructuring. Members of this team are brainstorming ways to address the needs of the disabled.

than pushing them out. The trend, if it continues, should also increase autonomy and job satisfaction for many employees (Castells 2001; DiMaggio et al. 2001).

Use Your Sociological Imagination

www.mhhe.com/schaefer7

If your first full-time job after college involved telecommuting, what do you think would be the advantages and disadvantages of working out of a home office? Do you think you would be satisfied as a telecommuter? Why or why not?

Electronic Communication

Electronic communication in the workplace has generated some heat lately. On the one hand, e-mailing is a convenient way to push messages around, especially with the CC (carbon copy) button. It's democratic, too: lower-status employees are more likely to participate in e-mail discussions than in face-to-face communications, giving organizations the benefit of their experience and views. But e-mail doesn't convey body language, which in face-to-face communication can soften insensitive phrasing and make unpleasant messages (such as a reprimand) easier to take. It also leaves a permanent record, which can be a problem if messages are written thoughtlessly (DiMaggio et al. 2001).

Electronic communication has contributed significantly to the fragmentation of work. Today, work is frequently interrupted by e-mail, pagers, and pop-up windows, as well as face-to-face interruptions. In one observation study of office workers, researchers found that employees spent an average of only 11 minutes on any given project before being interrupted. Typically, 25 minutes passed before they returned to their original tasks. While multitasking may increase a person's efficiency in some situations, it has become an integral and not necessarily helpful feature of work for many employees (Mark et al. 2005; C. Thompson 2005).

The State of the Unions

The Issue

How many people do you know who belong to a labor union? Chances are you can name a lot fewer people than someone could 50 years ago. In 1954, unions represented 39 percent of workers in the private sector of the U.S. economy; in 2004 they represented only 12.5 percent (see Figure 5-2). What has happened to diminish the importance of organized labor? Have unions outlived their usefulness in a rapidly changing global economy that is dominated by the service sector (AFL-CIO 2001; Bureau of Labor Statistics 2005)?

FIGURE 5–2

Union Membership in the United States

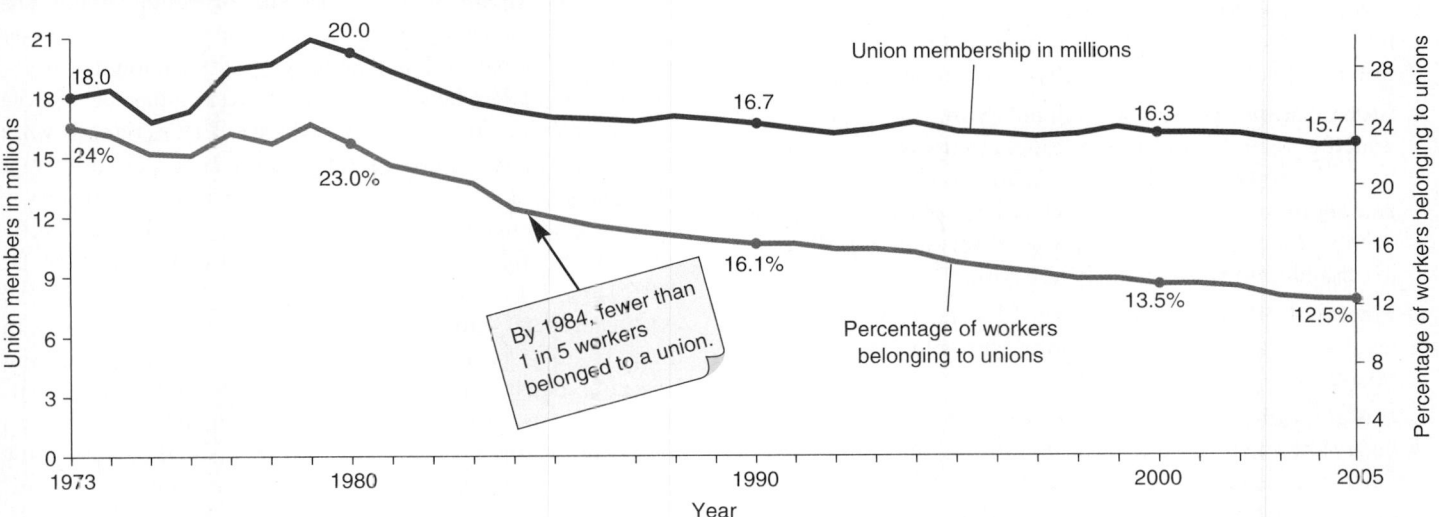

Source: Hirsch and Macpherson 2006.

Contemporary Culture Discuss telecommuting and its impact on friendship networks.

Let's Discuss Has someone ever seriously misinterpreted an e-mail of yours? Would the message have been clearer if delivered in person?

The Setting

Labor unions consist of organized workers who share either the same skill (as in electronics) or the same employer (as in the case of postal employees). Unions began to emerge during the Industrial Revolution in England, in the 1700s. Groups of workers banded together to extract concessions from employers (e.g., safer working conditions, a shorter workweek), as well as to protect their positions. They frequently tried to protect their jobs by limiting entry to their occupation based on gender, race, ethnicity, citizenship, age, and sometimes rather arbitrary measures of skill levels. Today we see less of this protection of special interests, but individual labor unions are still the target of charges of discrimination, as are employers.

The power of labor unions varies widely from country to country. In some countries, such as Britain and Mexico, unions play a key role in the foundation of governments. In others, such as Japan and Korea, their role in politics is very limited, and even their ability to influence the private sector is relatively weak. In the United States, unions can sometimes have a significant influence on employers and elected officials, but their effect varies dramatically by type of industry and even region of the country: see Figure 5-3 (M. Wallerstein and Western 2000).

Few people today would dispute the fact that union membership is declining. Among the reasons for the decline are the following:

1. **Changes in the type of industry.** Manufacturing jobs, the traditional heart of the labor union, have declined, giving way to postindustrial service jobs.

2. **Growth in part-time jobs.** Between 1982 and 1998 the number of temporary jobs in the United States rose 577 percent, while total employment increased only 41 percent. Only in 2000 did laws governing collective bargaining allow temporary workers to join a union.

3. **The legal system.** The United States has not made it particularly easy for unions to organize and bargain, and some government measures have made it more difficult. A dramatic example was President Ronald Reagan's firing of 11,000 air traffic controllers in 1981, when their union threatened they would walk off the job while seeking a new contract.

4. **Globalization.** The threat of jobs leaving the country has undercut the ability of union leaders to organize workers at home. Some say that labor union demands for wage increases and additional benefits have themselves spurred the exodus of jobs to developing nations, where wages are significantly lower and unions are virtually nonexistent.

5. **Employer offensives.** Increasingly hostile employers have taken court action to block unions' efforts to represent their members.

6. **Union rigidity and bureaucratization.** In the past, labor has been slow to embrace women, minorities, and immigrants. Furthermore, in some unions the election of leaders seems to dominate the organization's activity (Prah 2005).

Sociological Insights

Both Marxists and functionalists would view unions as a logical response to the emergence of impersonal, large-scale, formal, and often alienating organizations. This view certainly characterized the growth of unions in major manufacturing industries with a sharp division of labor. However, as manufacturing has declined, unions have had to look elsewhere for growth.

Worldwide, today's labor unions bear little resemblance to those early unions organized spontaneously by exploited workers. In line with Robert Michels's iron law of oligarchy (see page 123), unions have become increasingly bureaucratized under a self-serving leadership. Conflict theorists would point out that the longer union leaders are in office, the less responsive they are to the needs and demands of the rank and file, and the more concerned with maintaining their own positions and power. Yet research shows that under certain circumstances, union leadership can change significantly. Smaller unions are vulnerable to changes in leadership, as are unions whose membership shifts in composition from predominantly White to African American or Latino.

Many union employees encounter role conflict (see pages 104–105). For example, they may agree to provide a needed service and then organize a strike to withhold it. Role conflict is especially apparent in the so-called helping occupations: teaching, social work, nursing, law enforcement, and firefighting. These workers may feel torn between carrying out their professional responsibilities and enduring working conditions they find unacceptable.

Policy Initiatives

U.S. law grants workers the right to self-organize via unions. But the United States is unique among industrial democracies in allowing employers to actively oppose their employees' decision to organize (Comstock and Fox 1994).

A major barrier to union growth exists in the 22 states that have so-called right-to-work laws (see Figure 5-3). In these states, workers cannot be *required* to join or pay dues or fees to a union. The very term *right to work* reflects the anti-union view that a worker should not be forced to join a union, even if the union may negotiate on his or her behalf and achieve results that benefit the worker. This situation is unlikely to change. That is, right-to-work states will remain so; those without such laws typically have a strong union tradition or restrict union activities in other ways.

On the national level, union power is waning. In the security buildup that followed the terrorist attacks of September 11, 2001, federal officials created many new jobs and reorganized existing agencies into the Department of Homeland Security. In doing so, they specified that some 170,000 workers would not have collective bargaining rights, and that 56,000 newly federalized airport security screeners could not be unionized. Though these stipulations may not stand up to legal challenges, many observers see them as another sign of growing anti-union sentiment at all levels of government (Borosage 2003).

FIGURE 5–3

127

Social Interaction, Groups, and Social Structure

Union Membership in the United States

MAPPING LIFE

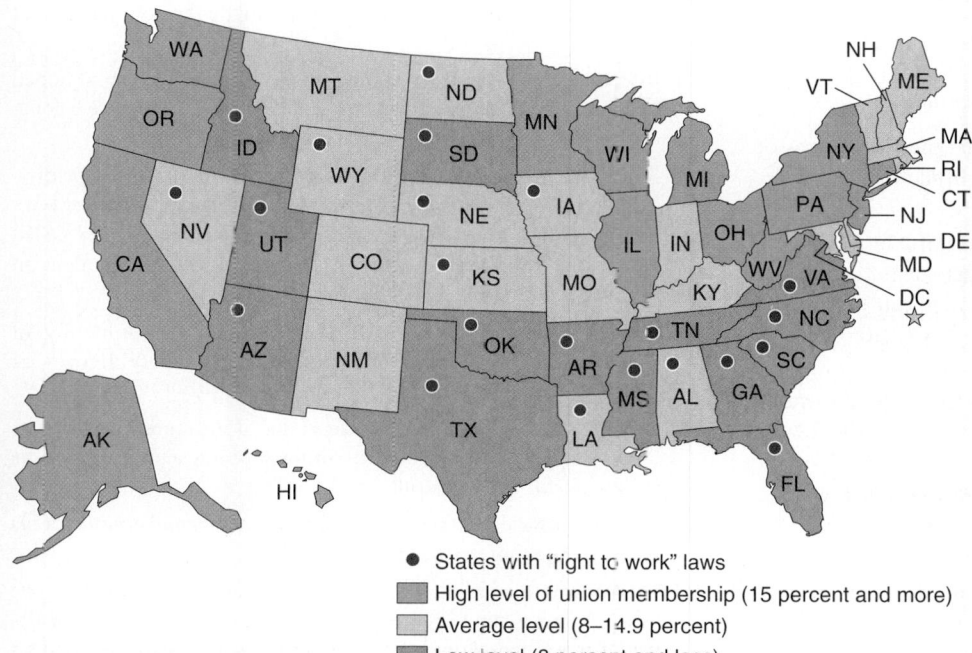

● States with "right to work" laws

▨ High level of union membership (15 percent and more)

▨ Average level (8–14.9 percent)

▨ Low level (8 percent and less)

Note: "Right to work" means that legally, workers cannot be required to join a union or pay union dues.
Source: Developed by the author based on data from Bureau of Labor Statistics 2005; National Right to Work Legal Defense Foundation 2006.

Think About It
What is the relationship between the level of union membership in a given state and the presence of right-to-work laws?

In Europe, labor unions tend to play a major role in political elections. (The ruling party in Great Britain, in fact, is called the Labour Party.) Although unions play a lesser political role in the United States, they have recently faced attacks for their large financial contributions to political campaigns. Debate over campaign finance reform in Congress in 2001 raised the question of whether labor unions should be able to use dues to support a particular candidate or promote a position via "issue ads" that favor one party, usually the Democrats.

Let's Discuss

1. What unions are represented on your college campus? Have you been aware of union activity? Has there been any opposition to the unions on the part of the administration?

2. Do you think nurses should be allowed to strike? Why or why not? What about teachers or police officers?

3. If a union is working on behalf of all the workers of a company, should all the employees be required to join the union and pay dues? Why or why not?

GettingINVOLVED

To get involved in the debate over the labor movement, visit this text's Online Learning Center, which offers links to relevant Web sites. Check out the Social Policy section in the Online Learning Center as well; it provides survey data on U.S. public opinion regarding this issue.

www.mhhe.com/schaefer7

Summary

Social interaction refers to the ways in which people respond to one another. *Social structure* refers to the way in which a society is organized into predictable relationships. This chapter examines the basic elements of social structure: *statuses, social roles, groups, social networks, social institutions,* and *formal organizations.*

1. People shape their social reality based on what they learn through their *social interactions.* Social change comes from redefining or reconstructing social reality.

2. An *ascribed status* is generally assigned to a person at birth, whereas an *achieved status* is attained largely through one's own effort. Some ascribed statuses, such as race and gender, can function as *master statuses* that affect one's potential to achieve a certain professional or social status.

3. With each distinctive status—whether ascribed or achieved—come particular *social roles,* the set of expectations for people who occupy that status.

4. Much of our social behavior takes place in *groups.* When we find ourselves identifying closely with a group, it is probably a *primary group.* A *secondary group* is more formal and impersonal.

5. People tend to see the world in terms of *in-groups* and *out-groups,* a perception often fostered by the very groups to which they belong.

6. *Reference groups* set and enforce standards of conduct and serve as a source of comparison for people's evaluations of themselves and others.

7. Interactionist researchers have noted that groups allow *coalitions* to form and serve as links to *social networks* and their vast resources.

8. *Social institutions* fulfill essential functions, such as replacing personnel, training new recruits, and preserving order. The mass media, the government, the economy, the family, and the health care system are all examples of social institutions.

9. Conflict theorists charge that social institutions help to maintain the privileges of the powerful while contributing to the powerlessness of others.

10. Interactionist theorists stress that our social behavior is conditioned by the roles and statuses we accept, the groups to which we belong, and the institutions within which we function.

11. Émile Durkheim thought that social structure depends on the division of labor in a society. According to Durkheim, societies with minimal division of labor have a collective consciousness called *mechanical solidarity;* those with greater division of labor show an interdependence called *organic solidarity.*

12. Ferdinand Tönnies distinguished the close-knit community of *Gemeinschaft* from the impersonal mass society known as *Gesellschaft.*

13. Gerhard Lenski thinks that a society's social structure changes as its culture and technology become more sophisticated, a process he calls *sociocultural evolution.*

14. As societies have become more complex, large *formal organizations* have become more powerful and pervasive.

15. Max Weber argued that in its ideal form, every *bureaucracy* has five basic characteristics: division of labor, hierarchical authority, written rules and regulations, impersonality, and employment based on technical qualifications. Carefully constructed bureaucratic policies can be undermined or redefined by an organization's informal structure, however.

16. Organizational restructuring and new technologies have transformed the workplace through innovations such as *collective decision making* and *telecommuting.* At the same time, major shifts in the economy have reduced the power of *labor unions.*

Critical Thinking Questions

1. People in certain professions seem particularly susceptible to role conflict. For example, journalists commonly experience role conflict during disasters, crimes, and other distressing situations. Should they offer assistance to the needy or cover breaking news? Select two other professions and discuss the role conflicts people in them might experience.

2. The functionalist, conflict, and interactionist perspectives can all be used in analyzing social institutions. What are the strengths and weaknesses in each perspective's analysis of those institutions?

3. Are primary groups, secondary groups, in-groups, out-groups, and reference groups likely to be found within a formal organization? What functions do these groups serve for a formal organization? What dysfunction might occur as a result of their presence?

Key Terms

Achieved status A social position that a person attains largely through his or her own efforts. (page 103)

Agrarian society The most technologically advanced form of preindustrial society. Members are engaged primarily in the production of food, but increase their crop yields through technological innovations such as the plow. (117)

Alienation A condition of estrangement or dissociation from the surrounding society. (119)

Ascribed status A social position assigned to a person by society without regard for the person's unique talents or characteristics. (102)

Bureaucracy A component of formal organization that uses rules and hierarchical ranking to achieve efficiency. (119)

Bureaucratization The process by which a group, organization, or social movement becomes increasingly bureaucratic. (121)

Classical theory An approach to the study of formal organizations that views workers as being motivated almost entirely by economic rewards. (123)

Coalition A temporary or permanent alliance geared toward a common goal. (110)

Formal organization A group designed for a special purpose and structured for maximum efficiency. (119)

Gemeinschaft A close-knit community, often found in rural areas, in which strong personal bonds unite members. (115)

Gesellschaft A community, often urban, that is large and impersonal, with little commitment to the group or consensus on values. (115)

Goal displacement Overzealous conformity to official regulations of a bureaucracy. (121)

Group Any number of people with similar norms, values, and expectations who interact with one another on a regular basis. (108)

Horticultural society A preindustrial society in which people plant seeds and crops rather than merely subsist on available foods. (116)

Human relations approach An approach to the study of formal organizations that emphasizes the role of people, communication, and participation in a bureaucracy and tends to focus on the informal structure of the organization. (123)

Hunting-and-gathering society A preindustrial society in which people rely on whatever foods and fibers are readily available in order to survive. (116)

Ideal type A construct or model for evaluating specific cases. (119)

Industrial society A society that depends on mechanization to produce its goods and services. (117)

In-group Any group or category to which people feel they belong. (109)

Iron law of oligarchy A principle of organizational life under which even a democratic organization will eventually develop into a bureaucracy ruled by a few individuals. (123)

Labor union Organized workers who share either the same skill or the same employer. (126)

Master status A status that dominates others and thereby determines a person's general position in society. (103)

McDonaldization The process by which the principles of the fast-food restaurant are coming to dominate more and more sectors of American society as well as of the rest of the world. (122)

Mechanical solidarity A collective consciousness that emphasizes group solidarity, characteristic of societies with minimal division of labor. (115)

Organic solidarity A collective consciousness that rests on mutual interdependence, characteristic of societies with a complex division of labor. (115)

Out-group A group or category to which people feel they do not belong. (109)

Peter principle A principle of organizational life according to which every employee within a hierarchy tends to rise to his or her level of incompetence. (121)

Postindustrial society A society whose economic system is engaged primarily in the processing and control of information. (118)

Postmodern society A technologically sophisticated society that is preoccupied with consumer goods and media images. (118)

Primary group A small group characterized by intimate, face-to-face association and cooperation. (108)

Reference group Any group that individuals use as a standard for evaluating themselves and their own behavior. (109)

Role conflict The situation that occurs when incompatible expectations arise from two or more social positions held by the same person. (105)

Role exit The process of disengagement from a role that is central to one's self-identity in order to establish a new role and identity. (105)

Role strain The difficulty that arises when the same social position imposes conflicting demands and expectations. (105)

Scientific management approach Another name for the classical theory of formal organizations. (123)

Secondary group A formal, impersonal group in which there is little social intimacy or mutual understanding. (108)

Social institution An organized pattern of beliefs and behavior centered on basic social needs. (112)

Social interaction The ways in which people respond to one another. (101)

Social network A series of social relationships that links a person directly to others, and through them indirectly to still more people. (110)

Social role A set of expectations for people who occupy a given social position or status. (104)

Social structure The way in which a society is organized into predictable relationships. (101)

Sociocultural evolution Long-term trends in societies resulting from the interplay of continuity, innovation, and selection. (116)

Status A term used by sociologists to refer to any of the full range of socially defined positions within a large group or society. (102)

Technology Cultural information about the ways in which the material resources of the environment may be used to satisfy human needs and desires. (116)

Telecommuter An employee who works full-time or part-time at home rather than in an outside office, and who is linked to supervisor and colleagues through computer terminals, phone lines, and fax machines. (124)

Trained incapacity The tendency of workers in a bureaucracy to become so specialized that they develop blind spots and fail to notice obvious problems. (120)

Self-Quiz

Read each question carefully and then select the best answer.

1. In the United States, we expect that cab drivers will know how to get around a city. This expectation is an example of which of the following?

    a. role conflict
    b. role strain
    c. social role
    d. master status

2. What occurs when incompatible expectations arise from two or more social positions held by the same person?

    a. role conflict
    b. role strain
    c. role exit
    d. both a and b

3. In sociological terms, what do we call any number of people with similar norms, values, and expectations who interact with one another on a regular basis?

    a. a category
    b. a group
    c. an aggregate
    d. a society

4. Which sociological perspective argues that the present organization of social institutions is no accident?

    a. the functionalist perspective
    b. the conflict perspective
    c. the interactionist perspective
    d. the global perspective

5. Social control in what Ferdinand Tönnies termed a *Gemeinschaft* community is maintained through all but which of the following means?

    a. moral persuasion
    b. gossip
    c. legally defined punishment
    d. gestures

6. Sociologist Daniel Bell uses which of the following terms to refer to a society whose economic system is engaged primarily in the processing and control of information?

    a. postmodern
    b. horticultural
    c. industrial
    d. postindustrial

7. The U.S. Postal Service, the Boston Pops orchestra, and the college or university in which you are currently enrolled as a student are all examples of

    a. primary groups.
    b. reference groups.
    c. formal organizations.
    d. triads.

8. One positive consequence of bureaucracy is that it reduces bias. Reduction of bias results from which characteristic of a bureaucracy?

    a. impersonality
    b. hierarchy of authority
    c. written rules and regulations
    d. employment based on technical qualifications

9. According to the Peter principle,

    a. all bureaucracies are notoriously inefficient.
    b. if something *can* go wrong, it *will.*
    c. every employee within a hierarchy tends to rise to his or her level of incompetence.
    d. all line workers get burned in the end.

10. What are the social implications of a shift toward the virtual office as a result of the increasing number of telecommuters?

    a. Supervisors will find that performance goals must be defined more clearly, which may lead to further bureaucratization.
    b. It should increase autonomy and job satisfaction for many employees.
    c. It will lead to greater worker privacy and job security.
    d. both a and b

11. The term _____ _____ refers to the way in which a society is organized into predictable relationships.

12. The African American activist Malcolm X wrote in his autobiography that his position as a Black man, an _____ status, was an obstacle to his dream of becoming a lawyer, an _____ status.

13. Sociologist Helen Rose Fuchs Ebaugh developed the term _____ _____ to describe the process of disengagement from a role that is central to one's self-identity in order to establish a new role and identity.

14. _____ groups often emerge in the workplace among those who share special understandings about their occupation.

15. In many cases, people model their behavior after groups to which they may not belong. These groups are called _____ groups.

16. In studying the social behavior of word processors in a Chicago law firm, sociologist Mitchell Duneier drew on the _____ perspective.

17. According to Émile Durkheim, societies with a minimal division of labor are characterized by _____ solidarity, while societies with a complex division of labor are characterized by _____ solidarity.

18. In Gerhard Lenski's theory of sociocultural evolution, a society's level of _____ is critical to the way it is organized.

19. A(n) _____ society is a technologically sophisticated society that is preoccupied with consumer goods and media images.

20. Max Weber developed a(n) _____ _____ of bureaucracy, which reflects the most characteristic aspects of all human organizations.

{ TECHNOLOGY RESOURCES }

Online Learning Center

1. Everyone has been a member of in-groups and out-groups. Visit the student center in the Online Learning Center (**www.mhhe.com/schaefer7**) and link to the Interactive Activity entitled "In-Groups, Out-Groups, and Un-words." In this activity, you will be asked to discuss your experiences as a member of an in-group and an out-group. You can also do the word scramble, which contains key words and phrases from this chapter.

2. Proponents of educational programs in prisons argue that the social structure of a classroom environment can be used to rehabilitate people who have been incarcerated. Visit the Web site of the Center for the Study of Correctional Education (**www.csusb.edu/coe/cg/csce/index.html**)—especially the link to Research. Contrast these programs with the social environment of Zimbardo's prison experiment.

3. The Web site of the Illinois Labor History Society (**www.kentlaw.edu/ilbs/index.html**) contains extensive information on labor unions, strikes, and disasters in that state, past and present. Visit the site for an overview of labor history in Illinois.

*Note: While all the URLs listed were current as of the printing of this book, these sites often change. Please check our Web site (**www.mhhe.com/schaefer7**) for updates, hyperlinks, and exercises related to these sites.*

Reel Society Video Clips

Reel Society video clips, which appear on this book's Web site, can be used to spark discussion about the following topics from this chapter:
- Social Roles
- Groups

6

The Mass Media

inside

Sociological Perspectives on the Media

The Audience

The Media Industry

Social Policy and the Mass Media: Media Violence

Boxes

Sociology in the Global Community: Al Jazeera Is on the Air

Social Inequality: The Color of Network TV

Though the mass media reflect society, they do not necessarily represent all of society. To highlight films by the native peoples of the United States, the American Indian Film Institute, founded in 1979, holds an annual motion picture festival. This poster, created by Michael Horse of the Yaqui, Zuni, and Mescalero Apache tribes, promotes the AIFI's 2003 Festival.

growing up digital

The Rise of the Net Generation

DON TAPSCOTT
Author of the International Bestseller
The Digital Economy

The Net Generation has arrived! The baby boom has an echo and it's even louder than the original.

What makes this generation different from all others before it? It is the first to grow up surrounded by digital media. Computers can be found in the home, school, factory, and office and digital technologies such as cameras, video games, and CD-ROMs are commonplace. Increasingly, these new media are connected by the Internet, an expanding web of networks which is attracting a million new users monthly. Today's kids are so bathed in bits that they think it's all part of the natural landscape. To them, the digital technology is no more intimidating than a VCR or toaster.

For the first time in history, children are more comfortable, knowledgeable, and literate than their parents about an innovation central to society. And it's through the use of the digital media that the N-Generation will develop and superimpose its culture on the rest of society. Boomers stand back. Already these kids are learning, playing, communicating, working, and creating communities very differently than their parents. They are a force for social transformation.

. . . If left purely to market forces, the digital economy could foster a two-tiered society, creating a major gulf between information haves and have-nots—those who can communicate with the world and those who can't. As information technology becomes more important for economic success and societal well-being, the possibility of "information apartheid" becomes increasingly real. Such a "digital divide" may mean that for many children *N-Gen* means *Not-Generation.*

For example, in the United States there is a direct relationship between family income and access to computers and the Net. This correlation also exists between the higher- and lower-income schools. Some observers argue that this is just a temporary problem, but our research shows that the digital divide is actually widening, not disappearing. As the new technology trickles into poorer neighborhoods and schools, the better-off children are leapfrogging others—getting not only better access, but a wider range of services, faster access, the best technology, and, most importantly, increasing motivation, skills, and knowledge. This not only exacerbates the fluency gap but also the gap in different economic classes' capacity to learn and to have successful lives. Have-nots become know-nots and do-nots. . . .

Globally, most children of the new generation are not growing up digital. In fact many of them will not grow up at all. One billion people were born over the last decade—the biggest increase in human history. However, 97 percent of them were born in developing countries that often lack the ability to feed, house, and educate them. More than half of the 1.2 billion children in the world aged six to eleven have never placed a phone call.

(Tapscott 1998:1–2, 11, 12) Additional information about this excerpt can be found on the Online Learning Center at www.mhhe.com/schaefer7. ●

> " *For the first time in history, children are more comfortable, knowledgeable, and literate than their parents about an innovation central to society.* "

In his book *Growing Up Digital: The Rise of the Net Generation,* Don Tapscott confronts the sweeping social change caused by the introduction of new means of communication. The head of New Paradigm, a Canadian think tank devoted to information technology, Tapscott sees a huge generational divide between Baby Boomers and "N-Gen"—those who were children, adolescents, or young adults at the turn of the 21st century. Like their parents the boomers, who grew up with a new means of communication called television, the young people of N-Gen are defined by the Internet. These "children of a digital age," he writes, will change the way we live and work in ways that marketers, employers, and government planners have not even begun to imagine.

Both TV and the Net are ***mass media,*** a term that refers to the print and electronic means of communication that carry messages to widespread audiences. Print media include newspapers, magazines, and books; electronic media include radio, satellite radio, television, motion pictures, and the Internet. Advertising, which falls into both categories, is also a form of mass media.

The social impact of the mass media is obvious. Consider a few examples. TV dinners were invented to accommodate the millions of "couch potatoes" who can't bear to miss their favorite television programs. Today *screen time* encompasses not just television viewing but also playing video games and surfing the Internet. Candidates for political office rely on their media consultants to project a winning image both in print and in the electronic media. World leaders use all forms of media for political advantage, whether to gain territory or to bid on hosting the Olympics. In parts of Africa and Asia, AIDS education projects owe much of their success to media campaigns. And during the 2003 war in Iraq, both the British and U.S. governments allowed journalists to be embedded with frontline troops as a means of "telling their story."

Few aspects of society are as central as the mass media. Through the media we expand our understanding of people and events beyond what we experience in person. The media inform us about different cultures and lifestyles and about the latest forms of technology. For sociologists, the key questions are how the mass media affect our social institutions and how they influence our social behavior.

Why are the media so influential? Who benefits from media influence and why? How do we maintain cultural and ethical standards in the face of negative media images? In this chapter we will consider the ways sociology helps us to answer these questions. First we will look at how proponents of the various sociological perspectives view the media. Then we will examine just who makes up the media's audience, as well as how the media operate, especially in their global reach. In the Social Policy section we will consider whether the violence shown in the media breeds violent behavior in the audience. ●

Sociological Perspectives on the Media

Over the past decade, new technologies have made new forms of mass media available to U.S. households. These new technologies have changed people's viewing and listening habits. People spend a lot of time with the media, more and more of it on the Internet. Viewers have moved away from broadcast TV and toward cable outlets. Americans now spend less time listening to recorded music than they did just a few years ago; they spend more time surfing the Internet. These patterns tend to vary by age group, however. Among 18- to 34-year-olds, for example, time spent watching prime-time TV—both broadcast and cable—declined by 19 percent between 1991 and 2003, as video games and the Internet took up more of their media time. What do these changes in people's viewing and listening habits signify? In the following sections we'll examine the impact of the mass media and changes in their usage patterns from the three major sociological perspectives (E. Nelson 2004).

Functionalist View

One obvious function of the mass media is to entertain. Except for clearly identified news or educational programming, we often think the explicit purpose of the mass media is to occupy our leisure time—from newspaper comics and crossword puzzles to the latest music releases on the Internet. While that is true, the media have other important functions. They also socialize us, enforce social norms, confer status, and promote consumption. An important dysfunction of the mass media is that they may act as a narcotic, desensitizing us to distressing events (Lazarsfeld and Merton 1948; C. Wright 1986).

Agent of Socialization The media increase social cohesion by presenting a common, more or less standardized view of culture through mass communication. Sociologist Robert Park (1922) studied how newspapers helped immigrants to the United States adjust to their environment by changing their customary habits and teaching them the opinions of people in their new home country. Unquestionably, the mass media play a significant role in providing a collective experience for members of society. Think { p.92–93 about how the mass media bring together members of a community or even a nation by broadcasting important events and ceremonies (such as inaugurations, press conferences, parades, state funerals, and the Olympics) and by covering disasters.

Which media outlets did people turn to in the aftermath of the September 11, 2001, tragedy? Television and the telephone

were the primary means by which people in the United States bonded. But the Internet also played a prominent role. About half of all Internet users—more than 53 million people—received some kind of news about the attacks online. Nearly three-fourths of Internet users communicated via e-mail to show their patriotism, discuss events with their families, or reconnect with old friends. More than a third of Internet users read or posted material in online forums. In the first 30 days alone, the Library of Congress collected from one Internet site more than half a million pages having to do with the terrorist attacks. As a Library director noted, "The Internet has become for many the public commons, a place where they can come together and talk" (D. L. Miller and Darlington 2002; Mirapaul 2001:E2; Rainie 2001).

Of course, the socializing effects of the media can be used to promote the goals of dissident, even militant minorities. In the Palestinian-held Gaza Strip, Hamas—a group better known for its suicide bombing campaigns—has launched a television program meant to familiarize children with the Palestinian position on the disputed territories. In between lectures on revered sites such as Nablus and Al Aksa Mosque, the show's host, known as Uncle Hazim, takes on-air phone calls from viewers and talks with animal characters reminiscent of those on *Sesame Street*. A soft sell, the show omits all mention of violence and armed conflict in pursuit of Hamas's goals (Craig Smith 2006).

Other problems are inherent in the socialization function of the mass media. For instance, many people worry about the effect of using television as a babysitter and the impact of violent programming on viewer behavior (see the Social Policy section). Some people adopt a blame-the-media mentality, holding the media accountable for anything that goes wrong, especially with young people.

Enforcer of Social Norms

The media often reaffirm proper behavior by showing what happens to people who act in a way that violates societal expectations. These messages are conveyed when the bad guy gets clobbered in cartoons or is thrown in jail on *Law and Order*. Yet the media also sometimes glorify disapproved behavior, whether it is physical violence, disrespect to a teacher, or drug use.

The media play a critical role in shaping people's perceptions about the risks of substance use. Increases in substance use among youths during the 1990s were linked to a decline in warnings and antidrug messages from the media; the proliferation of pro-use messages from the entertainment industry; and high levels of tobacco and alcohol product advertising and promotion. Media content analysis shows that in the 200 most popular movie rentals of 1996 and 1997, alcohol use appeared in 93 percent, tobacco use in 89 percent, and illicit drug use in 22 percent, with marijuana and cocaine use shown most often. An analysis of the 1,000 most popular songs during the same period showed that 27 percent referred to either alcohol or illicit drugs. In 1999, 44 percent of entertainment programs aired by the four major television networks portrayed tobacco use in at least one episode (Ericson 2001; D. F. Roberts et al. 1999).

On Al Aksa TV in Gaza, two animal characters interact with Uncle Hazim, the popular host of a local children's show. Sponsored by the militant group Hamas, the show is meant to inculcate in the young the Palestinian people's claim to disputed territories in the Mideast.

In 1997, a federal law required television networks to provide one free minute for every minute the government bought for a public service announcement with an antidrug message. The networks subsequently persuaded the government to drop the free minutes in exchange for aggressive antidrug messages embedded in their programs, such as *ER* and *The Practice*. Some people objected, saying that the networks were evading their legal responsibility in using the public airwaves, but criticism really mounted when word got out that a government agency was screening scripts in advance and even working on the story lines. Many critics felt the practice could open the way for the government to plant messages in the media on other topics as well, such as abortion or gun control (Albiniak 2000).

Conferral of Status

The mass media confer status on people, organizations, and public issues. Whether it is an issue such as the homeless or a celebrity such as Cameron Diaz, they single out one from thousands of other similarly placed issues or people to become significant. Table 6-1 (page 138) shows how often certain public figures are prominently featured on weekly magazine covers. Obviously, *People* magazine alone was not responsible for making Princess Diana into a worldwide figure, but collectively, all the media outlets created a notoriety that Princess Victoria of Sweden, for one, did not enjoy.

Another way the media confer celebrity status on individuals is by publishing information about the frequency of Internet searches. Some newspapers and Web sites carry regularly updated lists of the most heavily researched individuals and topics of the week. The means may have changed since the first issue of

How Does Television Portray the Family?

The media don't just present reality; they filter and interpret it. A good example of the media's interpretive portrayal of content is the way the family has been presented on television, from the 1950s to the present.

One of the earliest and biggest hit shows on TV, *I Love Lucy* (1951–1957), starred a real-life married couple, Lucille Ball and Desi Arnaz. In a nod to audience sensibilities in the prim and proper 1950s, the two characters slept in separate beds and avoided the word *pregnant,* even when in real life Lucille was carrying the couple's first child. Viewers did glimpse signs of the cultural tension inherent in an Anglo-Latino relationship.

As the decades passed and Americans' concept of family life changed, television families changed with it. While the emphasis was on humor in *The Brady Bunch* (1969–1974), the show did foreshadow what would become a common phenomenon by the century's end—the blended family—as character Michael Paul Brady merged his family of three sons with Carol Ann Tyler Martin's family of three daughters. And though *The Cosby Show* (1984–1992) did not always embrace social commentary, it did

present a realistic picture of a dual-career couple (physician and attorney) whose family was firmly rooted in the Black upper middle class.

More recent shows have continued to expand the boundaries of the televised portrayal of family life. *Family Guy* (1999–2002, 2005–present), an animated series about a dysfunctional Rhode Island family with a clueless dad, a talking dog, and a frighteningly precocious infant, offers an irreverent and relatively rare look at a working-class family. And through the story of a family that belongs to a crime syndicate, *The Sopranos* (1999–present) provides a dramatic illustration of the impact of work on the home. Finally, in *Two and a Half Men* (2003–present), two brothers, one of whom retains custody of his son after a divorce, show that today's household comes in all varieties.

Television has also shown Latino, Korean-American, childless, extended, single-father, single-mother, public-housing-project, and gay households. What TV family looks most like yours? What kinds of family are rarely, if ever, shown on television?

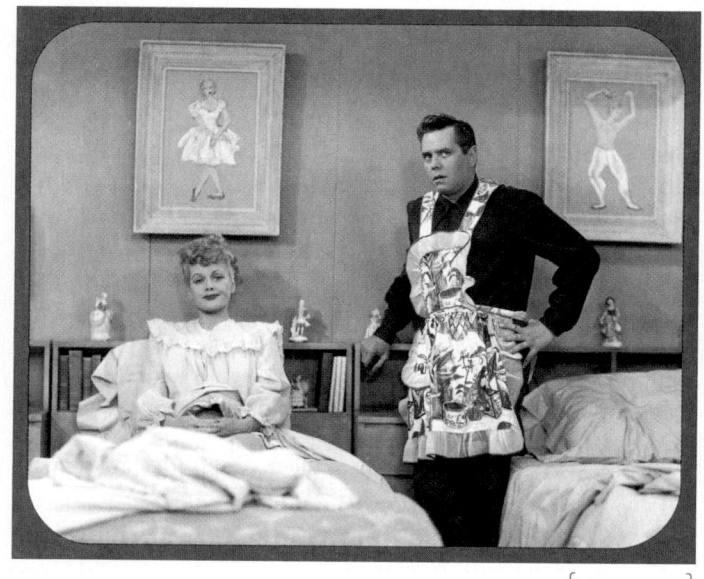

{I Love Lucy}

{The Brady Bunch}

{The Cosby Show}

{Family Guy}

{The Sopranos}

{Two and a Half Men}

137

Table 6-1 Status Conferred by Magazines

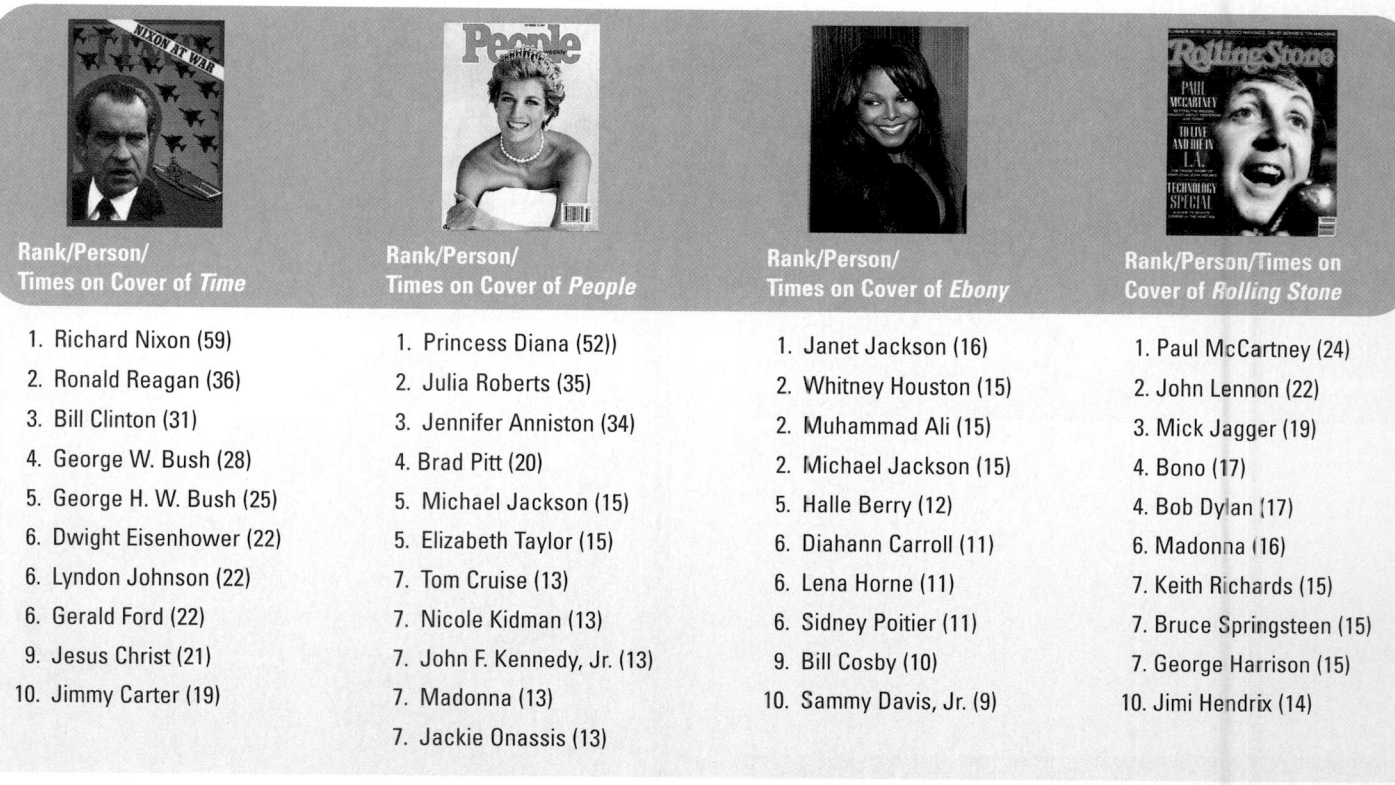

Rank/Person/ Times on Cover of *Time*	Rank/Person/ Times on Cover of *People*	Rank/Person/ Times on Cover of *Ebony*	Rank/Person/Times on Cover of *Rolling Stone*
1. Richard Nixon (59)	1. Princess Diana (52))	1. Janet Jackson (16)	1. Paul McCartney (24)
2. Ronald Reagan (36)	2. Julia Roberts (35)	2. Whitney Houston (15)	2. John Lennon (22)
3. Bill Clinton (31)	3. Jennifer Anniston (34)	2. Muhammad Ali (15)	3. Mick Jagger (19)
4. George W. Bush (28)	4. Brad Pitt (20)	2. Michael Jackson (15)	4. Bono (17)
5. George H. W. Bush (25)	5. Michael Jackson (15)	5. Halle Berry (12)	4. Bob Dylan (17)
6. Dwight Eisenhower (22)	5. Elizabeth Taylor (15)	6. Diahann Carroll (11)	6. Madonna (16)
6. Lyndon Johnson (22)	7. Tom Cruise (13)	6. Lena Horne (11)	7. Keith Richards (15)
6. Gerald Ford (22)	7. Nicole Kidman (13)	6. Sidney Poitier (11)	7. Bruce Springsteen (15)
9. Jesus Christ (21)	7. John F. Kennedy, Jr. (13)	9. Bill Cosby (10)	7. George Harrison (15)
10. Jimmy Carter (19)	7. Madonna (13)	10. Sammy Davis, Jr. (9)	10. Jimi Hendrix (14)
	7. Jackie Onassis (13)		

Source: Author's content analysis of primary cover subject for full run of the periodicals beginning with *Time,* March 3, 1923; *People,* March 4, 1974; *Ebony,* November 1945; and *Rolling Stone,* September 1967 through June 30, 2006. In case of ties, the more recent cover person is listed first.

Think About It
How do these magazines differ in the types of people they feature on their covers? Which type do you think enjoys the most status? Why?

Time magazine hit the stands in 1923, but the media still confer status—often electronically.

Promotion of Consumption
Twenty-thousand commercials a year—that is the number the average child in the United States watches on television, according to the American Academy of Pediatrics. Young people cannot escape commercial messages. They show up on high school scoreboards, at rock concerts, and as banners on Web pages. They are even embedded in motion pictures (remember Reese's Pieces in 1982's *E.T.: The Extra-Terrestrial?*). Such *product placement* is nothing new. In 1951 *The African Queen* prominently displayed Gordon's Gin aboard the boat carrying Katherine Hepburn and Humphrey Bogart. But commercial promotion has become far more common today. Moreover, advertisers are attempting to develop brand or logo loyalty at younger and younger ages (Lasn 2003; Quart 2003).

Media advertising has several clear functions: it supports the economy, provides information about products, and underwrites the cost of media. In some cases, advertising becomes part of the entertainment industry. A national survey showed that 14 percent of those who viewed the 2003 Super Bowl did so *only* for the commercials. Yet related to these functions are dysfunctions. Media advertising contributes to a consumer culture that creates "needs" and raises unrealistic expectations of what is required to be happy or satisfied. Moreover, because the media depend heavily on advertising revenue, advertisers can influence media content (FAIR 2001; Horovitz 2003).

Use Your Sociological Imagination
www.mhhe.com/schaefer7

You are a news junkie. Where do you gather your facts or information—from newspapers, tabloids, magazines, TV newscasts, or the Internet? Why did you choose that medium?

Dysfunction: The Narcotizing Effect
In addition to the {p.14} functions just noted, the media perform a *dysfunction.* Sociologists Paul Lazarsfeld and Robert Merton (1948) created the term **narcotizing dysfunction** to refer to the phenomenon in which the media provide such massive amounts of coverage that the audience becomes numb and fails to act on the information, regardless of how compelling the issue. Interested citizens may

Contemporary Culture What contemporary celebrities have gained fame or notoriety through media coverage?
Contemporary Culture For a comparison of historical and modern movie theaters, see "*Gemeinschaft* and *Gesellschaft*" (Additional Lecture Ideas).
Classroom Tip See "Something Doesn't Quite Ad Up" (Additional Lecture Ideas).

Theory Dysfunction of the media
Key Persons Paul Lazarsfeld, Robert Merton

take in the information but make no decision or take no action.

Consider how often the media initiate a great outpouring of philanthropic support in response to natural disasters or family crises. But then what happens? Research shows that as time passes, viewer fatigue sets in. The mass media audience becomes numb, desensitized to the suffering, and may even conclude that a solution to the crisis has been found (Moeller 1999).

The media's narcotizing dysfunction was identified over 50 years ago, when just a few homes had television—well before the advent of electronic media. At that time, the dysfunction went largely unnoticed, but today commentators often point out the ill effects of addiction to television or the Internet, especially among young people. Street crime, explicit sex, war, and HIV/AIDS apparently are such overwhelming topics that some in the audience may feel they have acted—or at the very least learned all they need to know—simply by watching the news.

Conflict View

Conflict theorists emphasize that the media reflect and even exacerbate many of the divisions in our society and world, including those based on gender, race, ethnicity, and social class. They point in particular to the media's ability to decide what is transmitted through a process called gatekeeping.

Gatekeeping   What story appears on page 1 of the morning newspaper? Which motion picture plays on three screens rather than one at the local cineplex? What picture isn't released at all? Behind these decisions are powerful figures—publishers, editors, and other media moguls.

The mass media constitute a form of big business in which profits are generally more important than the quality of the pro-

gramming. Within the mass media, a relatively small number of people control what eventually reaches the audience through a process known as *gatekeeping.* This term describes how material must travel through a series of checkpoints (or gates) before reaching the public. Thus, a select few decide what images to bring to a broad audience. In many countries the government plays a gatekeeping role. A study done for the World Bank found that in 97 countries, 60 percent of the top five TV stations and 72 percent of the largest radio stations are government-owned (World Bank 2001:183).

Gatekeeping prevails in all kinds of media. As sociologist C. Wright Mills ([1956] 2000b) observed, the real power of the media is that they can control what is being presented. In the recording industry, gatekeepers may reject a popular local band because it competes with a group already on their label. Even if the band is recorded, radio programmers may reject the music because it does not fit the station's "sound." Television programmers may keep a pilot for a new TV series off the air because they believe it does not appeal to the target audience (which is sometimes determined by advertising sponsors). Similar decisions are made by gatekeepers in the publishing industry (Hanson 2005).

Gatekeeping is not as dominant in at least one form of mass media, the Internet. You can send virtually any message to an electronic bulletin board, and create a Web page or Web log (blog) to advance any argument, including one that insists the earth is flat. The Internet is a means of quickly disseminating information (or misinformation) without going through any significant gatekeeping process.

Nevertheless, the Internet is not totally without restrictions. In many nations laws regulate content on issues such as gambling, pornography, and even politics. Popular Internet service providers will terminate accounts for offensive behavior. After the terrorist attack in 2001, eBay did not allow people to sell parts of the World Trade Center via its online auction. A World Bank study found that 17 countries place significant controls on Internet content. For example, China routinely blocks search engines like Google and AltaVista from accessing the names of groups or individuals critical of the government (French 2004; World Bank 2001:187).

Critics of the content of mass media argue that the gatekeeping process reflects a desire to maximize profits. Why else, they argue, would movie star Julia Roberts, rather than Afghanistan's leader Hamid Karzai, make the cover of *Time* magazine? Later in this chapter we will consider the role that corporate structure plays in the content and delivery of mass media. Another criticism of the gatekeeping process is that the content that makes it through the gates does not reflect the diversity of the audience.

Product placement ("brand casting") is an increasingly important source of revenue for motion picture studios. This scene from *Austin Powers: The Spy Who Shagged Me* (1999) doubles as a commercial for Starbucks.

Media Monitoring   In the past, the term *media monitoring* has been used to refer to interest groups' monitoring of media content. Recently, however, use of the term has expanded to include monitoring of individuals' media usage and choices without their knowledge. New technologies related to video

on demand, downloading of audio/video clips, and satellite programming have created records of individual viewing and listening preferences. In 2006, Google opposed U.S. government efforts to obtain company records of users' Web-browsing activities. At the same time, members of the general public expressed concern both that companies such as Google were maintaining such records and that government agencies were interested in them. In Chapter 9 we will see that media and computer giants don't always oppose government efforts to monitor media usage. For example, Yahoo, Google, Microsoft, and Dell have cooperated with the Chinese government's efforts to restrict and monitor Internet use, raising human rights concerns in the process.

The federal government has also come under criticism recently for authorizing wiretaps of U.S. citizens' telephone conversations without judicial approval. Government officials argue that the wiretaps were undertaken in the interest of national security, to monitor contacts between U.S. citizens and known terrorist groups following the terrorist attacks of September 11, 2001. But critics who take the conflict perspective, among others, are concerned by the apparent invasion of people's privacy (Gertner 2005).

What are the practical and ethical limits of media monitoring? In daily life, parents often oversee their children's online activities and scan the blogs they read—which are, of course, available for anyone to see. Most parents see such monitoring of children's media use and communications as an appropriate part of adult supervision. Yet their snooping sets an example for their children, who may use the technique for their own ends. Some media analysts have noted a growing trend among adolescents: the use of new media to learn not-so-public information about their parents (Delaney 2005).

Dominant Ideology: Constructing Reality

Conflict theorists argue that the mass media maintain the privileges of certain groups. Moreover, while protecting their own interests, powerful groups may limit the media's representation of others. The term { pp.67–68 *dominant ideology* describes a set of cultural beliefs and practices that helps to maintain powerful social, economic, and political interests. The media transmit messages that virtually define what we regard as the real world, even though those images frequently vary from what the larger society experiences.

Mass media decision makers are overwhelmingly White, male, and wealthy. It may come as no surprise, then, that the media tend to ignore the lives and ambitions of subordinate groups, among them working-class people, African Americans, Hispanics, gays and lesbians, people with disabilities, overweight people, and older people. Worse, media content may create false images or stereotypes of these groups that then become accepted as accurate portrayals of reality. *Stereotypes* are unreliable generalizations about all members of a group that do not recognize individual differences within the group.

Television content is a prime example of this tendency to ignore reality. How many overweight TV characters can you name? Even though in real life one out of every four women is

obese (30 or more pounds over a healthy body weight), only 3 out of 100 TV characters are portrayed as obese. Heavyset television characters have fewer romances, talk less about sex, eat more often, and are more often the object of ridicule than their thin counterparts (Hellmich 2001).

Minority groups are often stereotyped in TV shows. Almost all the leading roles are cast as White, even in urban-based programs such as *Friends*, which is situated in ethnically diverse New York City. Asian Americans and Native Americans rarely appear in general roles; Blacks tend to be featured mainly in crime-based dramas; Latinos are virtually ignored. Box 6-1 discusses the distorted picture of society presented on prime-time television programs.

Another concern about the media, from the conflict perspective, is that television distorts the political process. Until the U.S. campaign finance system is truly reformed and the law enforced, the candidates with the most money (often backed by powerful lobbying groups) will be able to buy exposure to voters and saturate the air with commercials attacking their opponents.

Dominant Ideology: Whose Culture?

In the United States, on the popular television contest *The Apprentice*, the dreaded dismissal line is "You're fired." In Finland, on *Dilli (The Deal)*, it's "*Olet vapautettu*" ("You're free to leave"); in Germany, on *Big Boss*, it's "*Sie haben frei*" ("You're off"). Although people { pp.58–60 throughout the world decry U.S. exports, from films to

In Johannesburg, South Africa, musical artist Lebo Mathosa celebrates MTV's launch of the first local music channel on the African continent. African artists hope the channel will offer greater exposure to indigenous musicians. Like the mass media in most parts of the world, African television is dominated by Western constructions of reality, including Western musical styles.

6-1 The Color of Network TV

Today, 40 percent of all youths in the United States are children of color, yet few of the faces they see on television reflect their race or cultural heritage. According to a content analysis of prime-time television, 74 percent of all the characters shown in the 2003–2004 season were White non-Hispanics. What is more, the programs shown earlier in the evening, when young people are most likely to watch television, are the *least* diverse of all.

When minority groups do appear on television and in other forms of media, their roles tend to reinforce the stereotypes associated with their ethnic or racial groups. In 2004, nearly half of all Middle Eastern characters shown on television were criminals, compared to only 5 percent of White characters. Latino roles were just as stereotyped. Recently, Latinas have been featured as maids on *Will and Grace* (Rosario), *Dharma and Greg* (Celia), and even the animated *King of the Hill* (Lupino), to name just three shows.

In a rare exception to this pattern, in 2006 *The West Wing* featured the election of a Latino president, played by Puerto Rican American Jimmy Smits. Ironically, the character of Jed Bartlett, who was president through most of the long-running series, is played by Martin Sheen. Sheen, born Ramon Estevez, rarely mentions his Hispanic roots.

Producers, writers, executives, and advertisers blame one another for the rampant underrepresentation of racial and ethnic minorities. Television programming is dictated by advertisers, a former executive claims; if advertisers said they wanted blatantly biased programming, the networks would provide it. Jery Isenberg, chairman of the Caucus for Producers, Writers & Directors, blames the networks, saying that writers would produce a series about three-headed Martians if the networks told them to.

Beyond these excuses, real reasons can be found for the departure from the diversity exhibited in past shows and seasons. In recent years, the rise of more networks, cable TV, and the Internet has fragmented the broadcast entertainment market, siphoning viewers away from the general-audience sitcoms and dramas of the past. Both the UPN and WB networks produce situation comedies and even full evenings geared toward African American

audiences. With the proliferation of cable channels such as Black Entertainment Television (BET) and the Spanish-language Telemundo and Univision, as well as Web sites that cater to every imaginable taste, there no longer seems to be a need for broadly popular series such as *The Cosby Show,* the tone and content of which appealed to Whites as well as Blacks in a way the newer series do not. The result of these sweeping technological changes has been a sharp divergence in viewer preferences.

Meanwhile, mainstream network executives, producers, and writers remain overwhelmingly White. Most of them live far from ethnically and racially diverse inner-city neighborhoods and tend to write and produce stories about people like themselves. Marc Hirshfeld, an NBC executive, claims some White producers have told him they don't know

> *Marc Hirshfeld, an NBC executive, claims some White producers have told him they don't know how to write for Black characters.*

how to write for Black characters. Stephen Bochco, producer of *NYPD Blue,* is a rare exception. His series *City of Angels* featured a mostly non-White cast, like the people Bochco grew up with in an inner-city neighborhood. The series ran for 23 episodes before being canceled in 2000.

In the long run, media observers believe, the major networks will need to integrate the ranks of gatekeepers before they achieve true diversity in programming. Adonis Hoffman, director of the Corporate Policy Institute, has urged network executives to throw open their studios and boardrooms to minorities. Hoffman thinks such a move would empower Black writers and producers to present a true-to-life portrait of African Americans. There are some signs of agreement from the networks. According to Doug Herzog, president of Fox Entertainment, real progress means incorporating diversity from within.

A rare sight on television: In UPN's *The Parkers*, almost all leading roles are played by African Americans.

Why should it matter that minority groups aren't visible on major network television, if they are well represented on other channels such as UPN, WB, BET, and Univision? The problem is that Whites as well as minorities see a distorted picture of their society every time they turn on network TV. In Hoffman's words, "African Americans, Latinos and Asians, while portrayed as such, are not merely walk-ons in our society—they are woven into the fabric of what has made this country great" (A. Hoffman 1997:M6).

Let's Discuss

1. Do you watch network TV? If so, how well do you think it represents the diversity of U.S. society?

2. Have you seen a movie or TV show recently that portrayed members of a minority group in a sensitive and realistic way—as real people rather than as stereotypes or token walk-ons? If so, describe the show.

Sources: D. Bielby and Bielby 2002; Children Now 2004; Directors Guild of America 2002; A. Hoffman 1997; M. Navarro 2002; Poniewozik 2001.

Race/Ethnicity Lack of Hispanics and African Americans in prime-time series   **Theory** Cultural domination determines which ideas and facts are transmitted.
Classroom Tip See "Hispanic Americans on TV" (Class Discussion Topics).
Student Alert Review the concept of ethnocentrism (see Chapter 3).

language to Bart Simpson, the U.S. media are still widely imitated. Sociologist Todd Gitlin describes American popular culture as something that "people love, and love to hate" (2002:177; Wentz and Atkinson 2005).

This love-hate relationship is so enduring that the U.S. media have come to rely on the overseas market. In fact, many motion pictures have brought in more revenue abroad than at home. Through early 2006, for example, *Titanic* had earned a record-breaking $600 million in the United States and another $1.2 billion at overseas box offices. Some Hollywood movies, however, are so insensitive to the global audience that they fail miserably overseas. The 2005 film *Memoirs of a Geisha,* set in 20th-century Japan, greatly offended Japanese moviegoers because the title role went to the Chinese actress Ziyi Zhang. Ironically, her casting also upset the Chinese, who were outraged to see a leading Chinese actress portray a Japanese geisha. In 2006 Chinese government officials banned the film's release (Barboza 2006).

We risk being ethnocentric if we overstress U.S. dominance. For example, *Survivor, Who Wants to Be a Millionaire,* and *Iron Chef*—immensely popular TV programs in the United States—came from Sweden, Britain, and Japan, respectively. Even *American Idol* originated in Britain as *Pop Idol,* featuring Simon Cowell. And the steamy telenovelas of Mexico and other Spanish-speaking countries owe very little of their origin to the soap operas on U.S. television. Unlike motion pictures, television is gradually moving away from U.S. domination and is more likely to be locally produced. By 2003, all the top 50 British TV shows were locally produced. *The West Wing* may appear on television in London, but it is shown late at night. Even U.S.-owned TV ventures such as Disney, MTV, and CNN have dramatically increased their locally produced programming overseas. The introduction of MTV Romania and MTV Indonesia in 2003 brought the number of local versions of the popular music channel to 38 (*The Economist* 2003b).

Nations that feel a loss of identity may try to defend against the cultural invasion from foreign countries, especially the economically dominant United States. Many developing nations have long argued for a greatly improved two-way flow of news and information between industrialized nations and developing nations. They complain that news from the Third World is scant, and what news there is reflects unfavorably on the developing nations. For example, what do you know about South America? Most people in the United States will mention the two topics that dominate the news from countries south of the border: revolution and drugs. Most know little else about the continent.

To remedy this imbalance, a resolution to monitor the news and content that cross the borders of developing nations was passed by the United Nations Educational, Scientific, and Cultural Organization (UNESCO) in the 1980s. The United States disagreed with the proposal, which became one factor in the U.S. decision to withdraw from UNESCO in the mid-1980s. In 2005, the United States opposed another UNESCO plan, meant to reduce the diminishment of cultural differences. Hailed as an im-

Famed Chinese actress Ziyi Zhang played a Japanese geisha in the U.S.-made film *Memoirs of a Geisha* (2005). The decision to cast her in a Japanese role backfired in both Japan and China. Though U.S. films are usually well received abroad, cultural insensitivity can damage their box-office receipts.

portant step toward protecting threatened cultures, particularly the media markets in developing nations, the measure passed the UN's General Assembly by a vote of 148–2. The United States, one of the two dissenters, objected that the measure's wording was vague (Dominick 2005:455; Riding 2005).

Feminist View

Feminists share the view of conflict theorists that the mass media stereotype and misrepresent social reality. According to this view, the media powerfully influence how we look at men and women, communicating unrealistic, stereotypical, and limiting images of the sexes. Here are three problems feminists believe arise from media coverage (Wood 1994):

Global View Some immensely popular TV shows in the United States actually originated in Sweden, Britain, and Japan.
Classroom Tip For the latest box-office data, visit www.boxofficemojo.com.
Let's Discuss Do students believe that the news and cultural content that cross the borders of developing nations should be monitored?

Theory Feminist analysis of mass media
Gender Media project stereotypes, unrealistic images of the sexes

1. Women are underrepresented, which suggests that men are the cultural standard and women are insignificant.

2. Men and women are portrayed in ways that reflect and perpetuate stereotypical views of gender. Women, for example, are often shown in peril, needing to be rescued by a male—rarely the reverse.

3. Depictions of male–female relationships emphasize traditional sex roles and normalize violence against women.

Educators and social scientists have long noted the stereotypical portrayal of women and men in the mass media. Women are often shown as being shallow and obsessed with beauty. They are more likely than men to be presented unclothed, in danger, or even physically victimized. Responding to the way advertising and the entertainment media objectify and even dehumanize women, Jean Kilbourne argues in her writings and film documentaries that "we [women] are the product." Feminist Vivian Gornick asserts that the portrayal of women in the media reflects "innumerable small murders of the mind and spirit [that] take place daily" (1979:ix; Cortese 1999; Goffman 1979; Kilbourne 2000a, 2000b).

A continuing, troubling issue for feminists and society as a whole is pornography. Feminists tend to be very supportive of freedom of expression and self-determination, rights that are denied to women more often than to men. Yet pornography presents women as sex objects and seems to make viewing women that way acceptable. Nor are concerns about pornography limited to this type of objectification and imagery, as well as their implicit endorsement of violence against women. The industry that creates risqué adult images for videos, DVDs, and the Internet is largely unregulated, putting its own performers at risk. A 2002 health survey of triple-X, as the porn industry refers to itself, found that 40 percent of actors and actresses had at least one sexually transmitted disease, compared to 0.1 percent of the general population. The career span of these women and men is short, usually about 18 months, but the profits for the industry are continuous and enormous (Huffstutter 2003).

As in other areas of sociology, feminist researchers caution against assuming that what holds true for men's media use is true for everyone. Researchers, for example, have studied the different ways that women and men approach the Internet. Though men are only slightly more likely than women ever to have used the Internet, they are much more likely to use it daily. According to a 2005 study, about a third of men use the Internet every day, compared to a quarter of women. Not surprisingly, men account for 91 percent of the players in online sports fantasy leagues. But perhaps more socially significant, women are more likely than men to maintain friendship networks through e-mail (Boase et al. 2006; Fallows 2006; Rainie 2005).

Interactionist View

Interactionists are especially interested in shared understandings of everyday behavior. These scholars examine the media on the

micro level to see how they shape day-to-day social behavior. Increasingly, researchers point to the mass media as the source of major daily activity; some argue that television serves virtually as a primary group for many individuals who share TV viewing. Other mass-media participation is not necessarily face to face. For example, we usually listen to the radio or read the newspaper as a solitary activity, although it is possible to share it with others (Cerulo et al. 1992; Waite 2000).

Interactionists note, too, that friendship networks can emerge from shared viewing habits or from recollection of a cherished television series from the past. Family members and friends often gather for parties centered on the broadcasting of popular events such as the Super Bowl or the Academy Awards. And as we've seen, television often serves as a babysitter or playmate for children and even infants.

The power of the mass media encourages political leaders and entertainment figures to carefully manipulate their images through public appearances called photo opportunities, or photo ops. By embracing symbols (posing with celebrities or in front of prestigious landmarks), participants in these staged events attempt to convey self-serving definitions of social reality (M. Weinstein and Weinstein 2002).

The rise of the Internet has facilitated new forms of communication and social interaction. Grandparents can now keep up with their grandchildren via e-mail. Gay and lesbian teens have online resources for support and information. People can even find their lifetime partners through computer dating services. As Figure 6-1 (page 144) shows, throughout the world, the Internet is casting an increasingly wider net over social interactions.

Some troubling issues have been raised about day-to-day life on the Internet. What, if anything, should be done about terrorists and other extremist groups who use the Internet to exchange messages of hatred and even bomb-making recipes? What, if anything, should be done about the issue of sexual expression on the Internet? How can children be protected from it? Should "hot chat" and X-rated film clips be censored? Or should expression be completely free?

Though the Internet has created a new platform for extremists and pornographers, it has also given people greater control over what they see and hear. That is, the Internet allows people to manage their media exposure so as to avoid sounds, images, and ideas they do not enjoy or approve of. The legal scholar Cass Sunstein (2002) has referred to this personalized approach to news information gathering as *egocasting*. One social consequence of this trend may be a less tolerant society. If we read, see, and hear only what we know and agree with, we may be much less prepared to meet people from different backgrounds or converse with those who express new viewpoints.

Finally, while many people in the United States embrace the Internet, we should note that information is not evenly distributed throughout the population. The same people, by and large, who experience poor health and have few job opportunities have been left off the information highway. Figure 6-2 (page 145) breaks down Internet usage by gender, age, race, income, and

Gender Traditional sex roles emphasized; violence against women normalized
Key Persons Jean Kilbourne, Vivian Gornick
Classroom Tip See "Stimulating Classroom Discussion about Killing Us Softly" (Classroom Discussion Topics).
Gender Gender differences in use of Web sites

Methods Research data suggest that women's use of the Internet is increasing faster than men's.
Theory Interactionists examine media from a micro-level approach.
Student Alert Review with students how they may use the Internet in their future classes. Share with them how you as an instructor have benefited from use of the Internet.

The Internet Explosion

MAPPING LIFE

WORLDWIDE www.mhhe.com/schaefer7

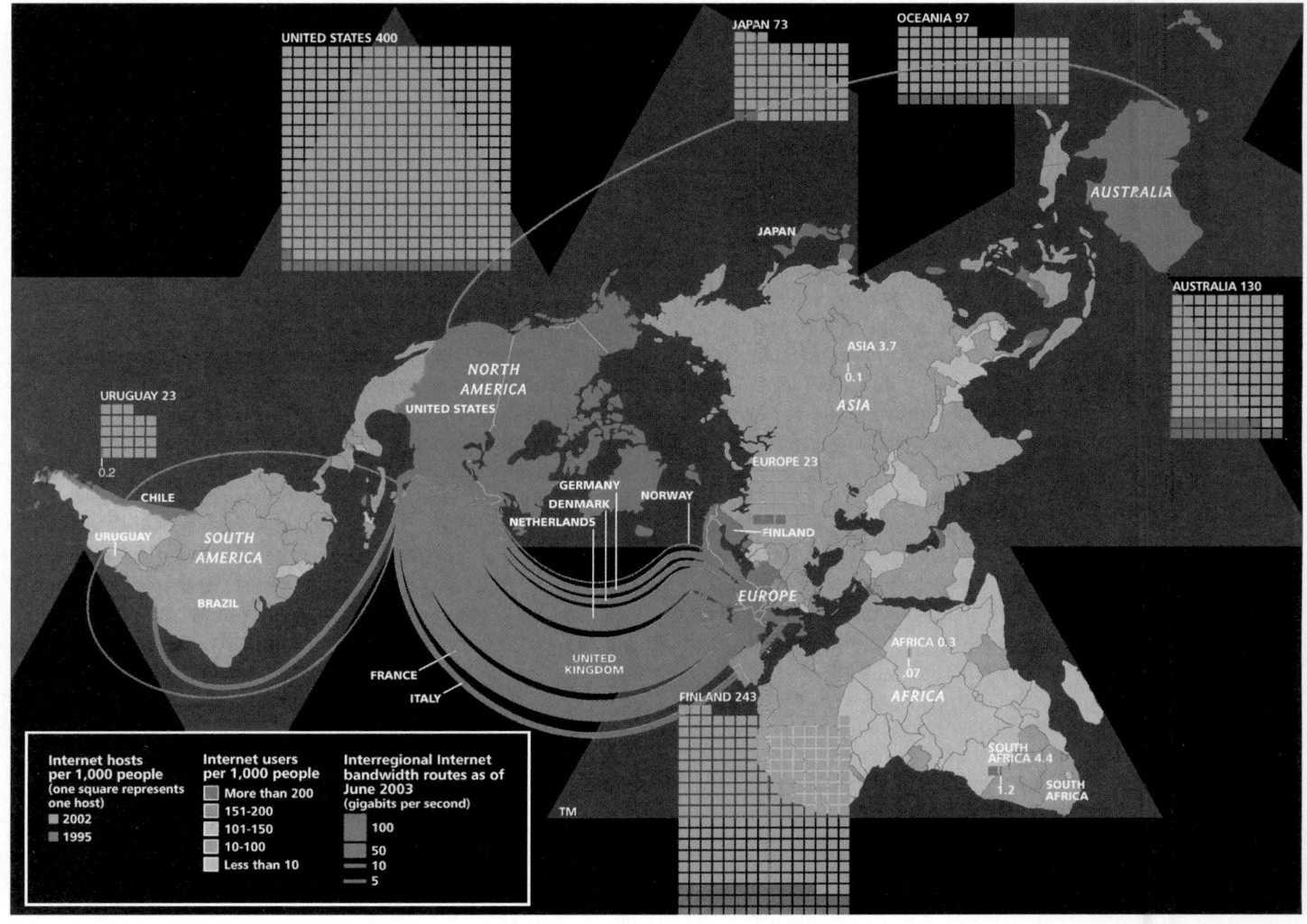

Source: *National Geographic* 2005:21 and the Buckminster Fuller Institute™.
In little more than a decade, the World Wide Web has exploded, touching 600 million users in every single country on earth. Still, a digital divide, measured in the form of relative bandwidth, separates rich countries from poor ones.

education. Note the large disparities in usage between those with high and low incomes, and between those with more or less education. The data also show a significant racial disparity. Though educators and politicians have touted the potential benefits to the disadvantaged, Internet usage may be reinforcing existing social-class barriers.

The interactionist perspective helps us to understand one important aspect of the entire mass media system—the audience. How do we actively participate in media events? How do we construct with others the meaning of media messages? We will explore these questions in the section that follows. (Table 6-2, on page 146, summarizes the various sociological perspectives on the media.)

The Audience

One night a few years ago, I was watching the Chicago Bulls make yet another bid for the NBA championship. Michael Jordan made a spectacular steal and went on to score a game-winning basket. I shouted, but what I remember most were the cheers I heard through the open window from others in Chicago. Earlier that year, my son had been watching *Beverly*

Hills 90210 in his college dorm room. One of the characters revealed that she was going to attend my son's university. As he and his friends screamed, they heard cheers all across the campus. In an unusual way, we had both been reminded that we are part of a larger audience.

Who Is in the Audience?

The mass media are distinguished from other social institutions by the necessary presence of an audience. It can be an identifiable, finite group, such as an audience at a jazz club or a Broadway musical, or a much larger and undefined group, such as VH-1 viewers or readers of the same issue of *USA Today*. The audience may be a secondary group gathered in a large auditorium or a primary group, such as a family watching the latest Disney video at home.

We can look at the audience from the level of both *microsociology* and *macrosociology*. At the micro level, we might consider how audience members, interacting among themselves, respond to the media, or in the case of live performances, actually influence the performers. At the macro level, we might examine broader societal consequences of the media, such as the early childhood education delivered through programming like *Sesame Street*.

Even if an audience is spread out over a wide geographic area and members don't know one another, it is still distinctive in terms of age, gender, income, political party, formal schooling, race, and ethnicity. The audience for a ballet, for example, would differ substantially from the audience for alternative music.

FIGURE 6–2
Who's on the Internet

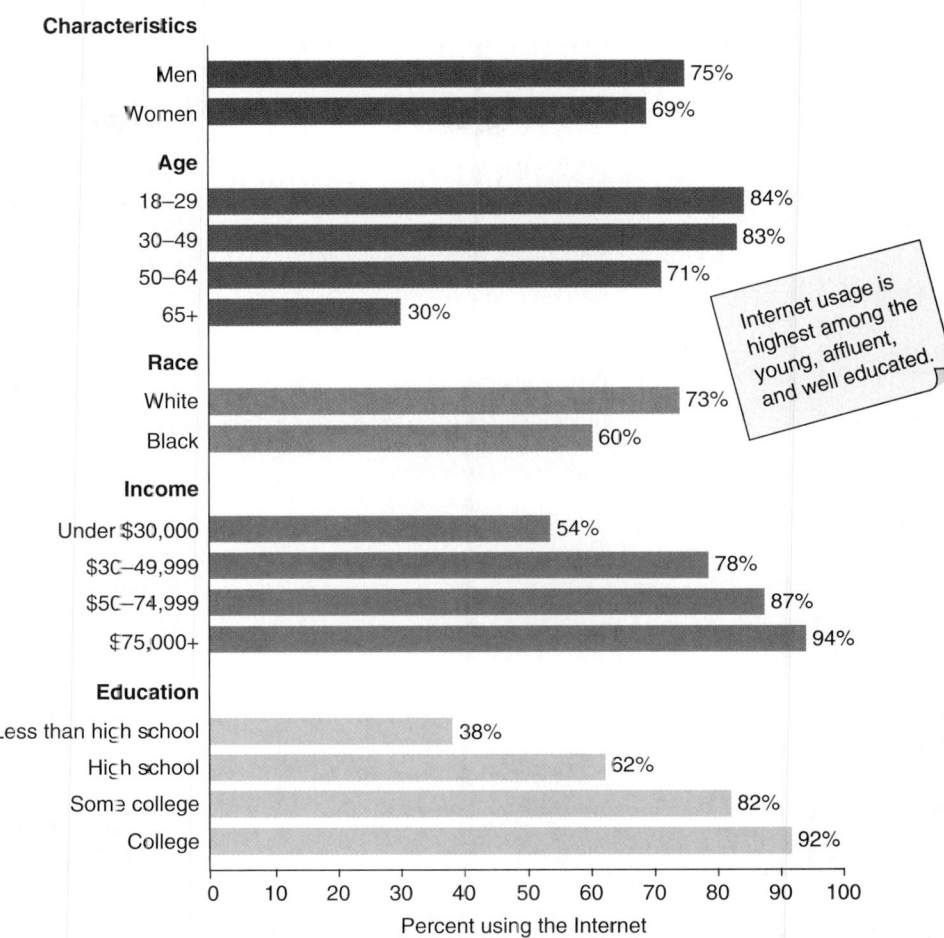

Characteristics

Note: Based on a September 2005 national survey released on December 5, 2005. Data for Blacks and Whites is for non-Hispanics.
Source: Pew Internet Project 2005.

> Internet usage is highest among the young, affluent, and well educated.

Think about the last time you were part of an audience. How similar or different from yourself were the other audience members? What might account for whatever similarities or differences you noticed?

The Segmented Audience

Increasingly, the media are marketing themselves to a *particular* audience. Once a media outlet, such as a radio station or a magazine, has identified its audience, it targets that group. To some degree, this specialization is driven by advertising. Media specialists have sharpened their ability, through survey research, to identify particular target audiences. As a result, Nike would be much more likely to promote a new line of golf clubs on the Golf Channel, for example, than on an episode of *SpongeBob*. The many more choices that the growing Internet and satellite broadcast channels offer audiences also foster specialization. Members of these audiences are more likely to *expect* content geared to their own interests.

Marketing research has developed to the point that those who are interested can estimate the size of the audience for a particular performer. In fact, computer programs have been written to simulate not just specific audiences, but the connections among them. Figure 6-3 (page 146) shows the computer-drawn audience networks for two well-known performing artists, Usher and Shania Twain.

The specialized targeting of audiences has led some scholars to question the "mass" in mass media. For example, the British social psychologist Sonia Livingstone (2004) has written that the media have become so segmented, they have taken on the appearance almost of individualization. Are viewing audiences so

Table 6-2 Sociological Perspectives on the Mass Media

Theoretical Perspective	Emphasis
Functionalist	Socialization
	Enforcement of social norms
	Conferral of status
	Promotion of consumption
	Narcotizing effect (dysfunction)
Conflict	Gatekeeping
	Media monitoring
	Construction of reality
Feminist	Underrepresentation of women
	Misrepresentation of women
Interactionist	Impact on social behavior
	Source of friendship networks

segmented that large collective audiences are a thing of the past? That is not yet clear. Even though we seem to be living in an age of *personal* computers and *personal* digital assistants (PDAs), large formal organizations still do transmit public messages that reach a sizable, heterogeneous, and scattered audience.

Audience Behavior

Sociologists have long researched how audiences interact with one another and how they share information after a media event. The role of audience members as opinion leaders particularly intrigues social researchers. An **opinion leader** is someone who influences the opinions and decisions of others through day-to-day personal contact and communication. For example, a movie or theater critic functions as an opinion leader. Sociologist Paul Lazarsfeld and his colleagues (1948) pioneered the study of opinion leaders in their research on voting behavior in the 1940s. They found that opinion leaders encourage their relatives, friends, and co-workers to think positively about a particular candidate, perhaps pushing them to listen to the politician's speeches or read the campaign literature.

Today, film critics often attribute the success of low-budget independent films to word of mouth. This is another way of saying that the mass media influence opinion leaders, who in turn influence others. The audience, then, is not a group of passive people but of active consumers who are often impelled to interact with others after a media event (Croteau and Hoynes 2003; C. R. Wright 1986).

Despite the role of opinion leaders, members of an audience do not all interpret media in the same way. Often their response is influenced by their social characteristics, such as occupation, race, education, and income. Take the example of the televised news coverage of the riots in Los Angeles in 1992. The riots were an angry response to the acquittal of two White police officers accused of severely beating a Black motorist. Sociologist

FIGURE 6–3

Two Audience Networks

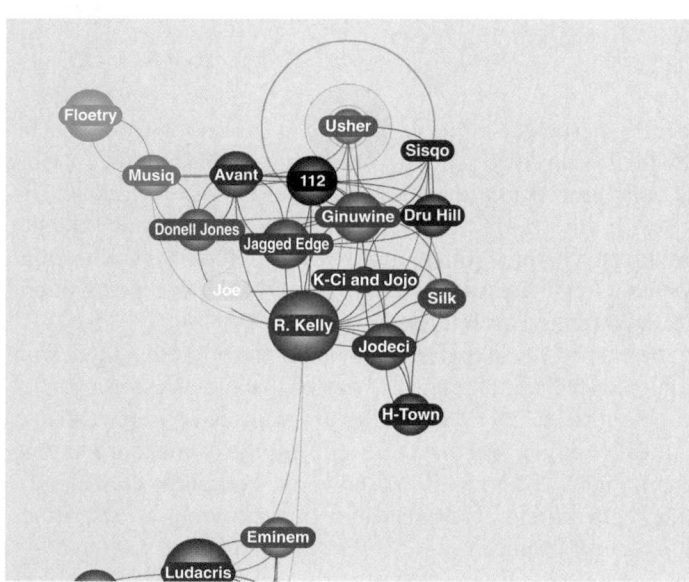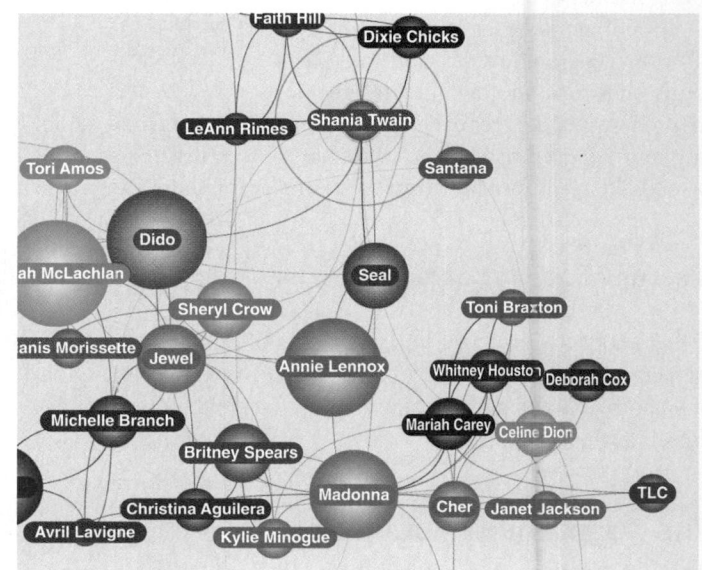

Source: Liveplasma.com 2006.

These maps, which were generated by computer, show the audience networks for two very different performing artists, Usher and Shania Twain. Each circle represents the audience for a particular artist; the larger the circle, the more popular the artist. As the maps show, Usher fans are connected to Shania Twain fans by a series of links, from R. Kelly fans to Eminem fans to Nelly, Justin Timberlake, Madonna, and finally Jewel fans.

Key Person Paul Lazarsfeld

In 2005, 50 Cent's "Candy Shop" became the number-one cell phone ring tone, with 1.9 million downloads. Because today's media provide multiple services, music fans can use the Internet to access recorded music and listen to it on their cell phones (Gunderson 2006).

Darnell Hunt (1997) wondered how the social composition of audience members would affect the way they interpreted the news coverage. Hunt gathered 15 groups from the Los Angeles area, whose members were equally divided among Whites, African Americans, and Latinos. He showed each group a 17-minute clip from the televised coverage of the riots and asked members to discuss how they would describe what they had just seen to a 12-year-old. In analyzing the discussions, Hunt found that although gender and class did not cause responderts to vary their answers much, race did.

Hunt went beyond noting simple racial differences in perceptions; he analyzed how the differences were manifested. For example, Black viewers were much more likely than Latinos or Whites to refer to the events in terms of "us" versus "them." Another difference was that Black and Latino viewers were more animated and critical than White viewers as they watched the film clip. White viewers tended to sit quietly, still and unquestioning, suggesting that they were more comfortable with the news coverage than the Blacks or Hispanics.

The Media Industry

Who owns the media production and distribution process? Increasingly, the answer is a small number of very large corporations. As we will see in the following section, two social consequences of this trend are a reduction in the number of information outlets and an increase in opportunities for cross-promotion.

Media Concentration

Though the United States still has thousands of independent media outlets—small-town newspapers, radio stations, and television broadcasters—the clear trend in the media industry is toward consolidation. A few multinational corporations now dominate the publishing, broadcasting, and film industries, though they may be hard to identify, since global conglomerates manage many different product names. Walt Disney alone owns 16 television channels that reach 140 countries. Media outlets

The 2003 FCC ruling that allowed further consolidation of media outlets by already huge conglomerates may have increased the companies' profitability, but it has had little positive impact on media content.

are likely to become even more concentrated if a 2003 ruling by the Federal Communications Commission (FCC) is allowed to stand. The ruling relaxes restrictions on owning more than one media outlet in the same market area (Carter and Rutenberg 2003; Rutenberg 2002).

A prime example of media concentration was the merger in 2001 of AOL and Time Warner, which created a new corporation that permeates almost every media sector. The AOL network, along with its Netscape Internet browser, operates the most popular Internet sites and boasts more than 32 million online subscribers worldwide. Time Warner is the largest U.S. magazine publisher based on advertising revenue earned. Time Warner's subsidiaries, Warner Brothers and New Line Cinema, rank among the top 10 motion picture producers. Warner Music Group artists accounted for 17 percent of all U.S. album sales in 2002. And Time Warner Cable provides many of the most popular cable channels, including HBO, TBS, CNN, TNT, Nickelodeon, and the WB network (AOL Time Warner 2003; TimeWarner 2004).

AOL Time Warner is only *one* media giant. Add to the list Walt Disney (which includes ABC, ESPN, and Lifetime networks); Rupert Murdoch's News Corporation of Australia (Fox Network Television, book publishers, numerous newspapers and magazines, and 20th Century Fox); Sony of Japan (Columbia Pictures, IMAX, CBS Records, and Columbia Records); and Viacom (Paramount, MTV, CBS, UPN, Black Entertainment Television, Simon and Schuster, and Blockbuster). This concentration of media giants fosters considerable cross-promotion. For example, the release of the Warner Brothers film *The Matrix Reloaded* in 2003 was heavily promoted by both CNN and *Time* magazine. In fact, *Time* managed to devote its cover to the film's release in the midst of the war in Iraq.

Similar concerns have been raised about the situation in countries such as China, Cuba, Iraq, and North Korea, where the ruling party owns and controls the media. The difference, which is considerable, is that in the United States the gatekeeping process is in the hands of private individuals, who desire to maximize profits. In the other countries, the gatekeeping process belongs to political leaders, who desire to maintain control of the government.

We should note one significant exception to the centralization and concentration of the media—the Internet. Research shows that more and more people, especially those under age 35, are receiving their media content through the Internet. Currently, the World Wide Web is accessible through independent outlets to millions of producers of media content. Obviously, the producer must be technologically proficient and must have access to a computer, but compared to other media outlets, the In-

FIGURE 6–4

Media Penetration in Selected Countries

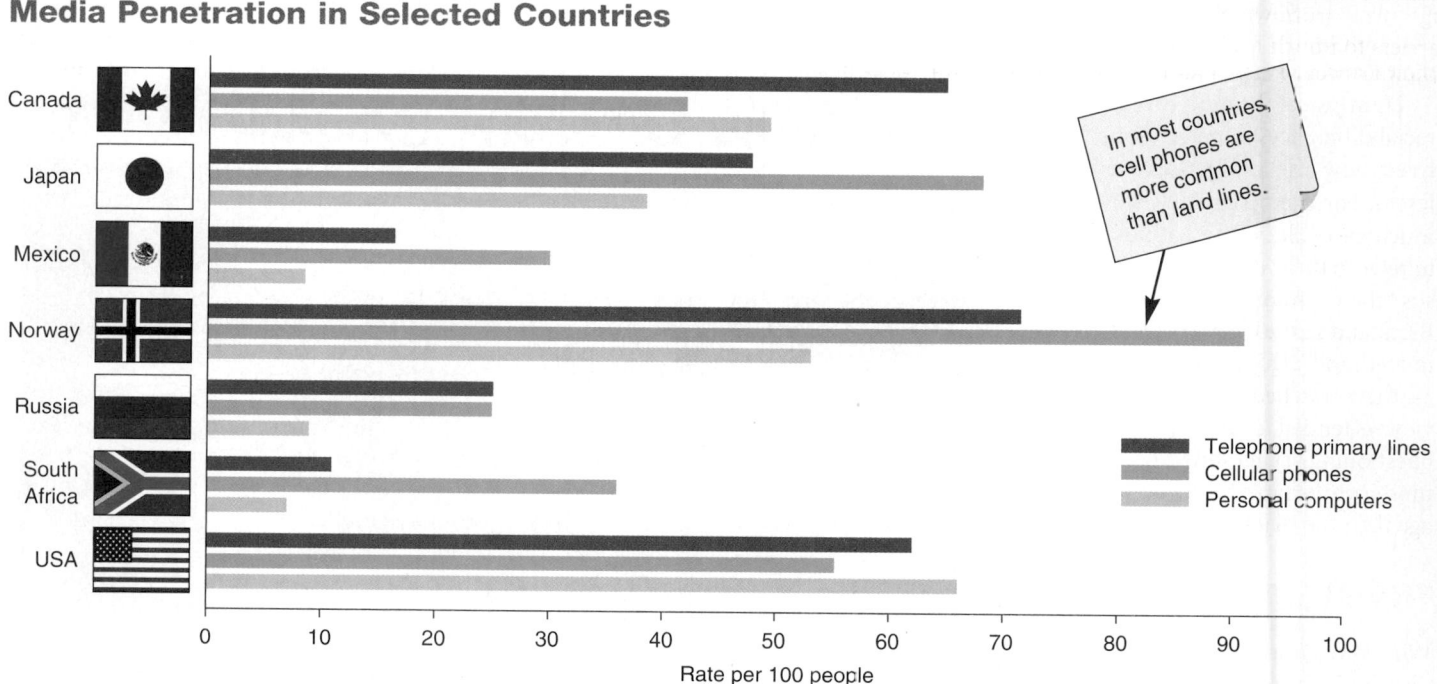

In most countries, cell phones are more common than land lines.

Legend:
- Telephone primary lines
- Cellular phones
- Personal computers

Rate per 100 people

Note: Data for 2003 released in 2005.
Source: Bureau of the Census 2005a:891.

Think About It
What is the economic and political significance of media penetration?

Global View Media in selected countries
Reel Society See Media in the Topic Index.

Global View In China, Cuba, Iraq, and North Korea, the ruling party owns and controls the media.

ternet is readily available. Media conglomerates, well aware of the Internet's potential, are already delivering their material via the Web. Still, for now, the Internet allows the individual to become a media entrepreneur with a potential audience of millions (Gamson and Latteier 2004; J. Schwartz 2004).

The Media's Global Reach

Has the rise of the electronic media created a "global village"? Canadian linguist Marshall McLuhan predicted it would some 40 years ago. Today, physical distance is no longer a barrier, and instant messaging is possible across the world. The mass media have indeed created a global village. Not all countries are equally connected, as Figure 6-4 shows, but the progress has been staggering, considering that voice transmission was just beginning 100 years ago (McLuhan 1964; McLuhan and Fiore 1967).

Sociologist Todd Gitlin considers "global torrent" a more apt metaphor for the media's reach than "global village." The media permeate all aspects of everyday life. Take advertising, for example. Consumer goods are marketed vigorously worldwide, from advertisements on airport baggage carriers to imprints on sandy beaches. Little wonder that people around the world develop loyalty to a brand and are as likely to sport a Nike, Coca-Cola, or Harley-Davidson logo as they are their favorite soccer or baseball insignia (Gitlin 2002; N. Klein 1999).

A highly visible part of the media, whether it be print or electronic, is news. In the past, most people in the United States had little familiarity with news outlets outside their own country, with the possible exception of the British-based Reuters and BBC News. Like so many other things, however, that changed after September 11, 2001, when an Arab news network took center stage (see Box 6-2, page 150).

The key to creating a truly global network that reaches directly into workplaces, schools, and homes is the Internet. Although much of the online global transmission today is limited to print and pictures, the potential to send audio and video via the Internet will increasingly reach into every part of the world. Social interaction will then truly take place on a global scale.

These Bhutanese householders are watching the *Oprah Winfrey Show* on their brand-new television set. The Bhutanese were introduced to television in 1999. Since then, Marshall McLuhan's global village has become a reality in their remote Asian kingdom, where rulers have become concerned about the cultural impact of Western media.

The Internet has also facilitated other forms of communication. Reference materials and data banks can now be made accessible across national boundaries. Information related to international finance, marketing, trade, and manufacturing is literally just a keystroke away. We have seen the emergence of truly world news outlets and the promotion of a world music that is not clearly identifiable with any single culture. Even the most future-oriented thinker would find the growth in the reach of the mass media in postindustrial and postmodern societies remarkable (Castells 2000, 2001; Croteau and Hoynes 2001, 2003).

The lack of one national home for the various forms of mass media raises a potential dilemma for users. People worry that unhealthy influences and even crime pervade today's electronic global village, and that few if any controls prevent them. For example, the leaders of Bhutan worry about the impact of newly introduced television programming on their culture and their people. Similarly, in industrial countries, including the United States, officials are concerned about everything from video poker to online pornography and the menace posed by hackers. In the Social Policy section that follows, we'll consider how the violence that is portrayed in the media can have an undesirable influence on society.

Web Resource Students will find the crossword puzzle in the student center of the Online Learning Center (**www.mhhe.com/schaefer7**) challenging.
Global View Impact of television on the culture and people of Bhutan

sociology IN *the Global Community*

6-2 Al Jazeera Is on the Air

A 24-hour-a-day televised news network with short bulletins every hour, followed by a fast-paced montage of news clips—all broadcast globally by satellite-linked cable stations. This could be CNN, but it's Al Jazeera, the Arabic-language television news network based in the small Persian Gulf state of Qatar. The name Al Jazeera means "island" or "peninsula," in reference to the network's home country. Founded in 1996, the channel now has 230 correspondents based at 30 foreign bureaus and an audience of about 40 million Arabs worldwide, including 150,000 Arab Americans.

Most people in the United States had never heard of Al Jazeera until October 7, 2001. That was when the channel aired the first of several videotaped messages from Osama bin Laden, the mastermind of the Al Qaeda terrorist network. U.S. news outlets also televised the messages, but stopped after the government objected to the airing of bin Laden's calls for violence against U.S. citizens.

Al Jazeera refused to acquiesce to the government request, invoking its motto, "The Opinion, and the Other Opinion Too." Al Jazeera officials insist that they promote a forum for independent dialogue and debate, an unusual practice in the Arab world, where most media outlets are state controlled. In fact, several Arab states, including Saudi Arabia, Jordan, and Bahrain, have banned or restricted Al Jazeera because of the network's critical coverage of affairs in their countries. Other Arab nations criticize Al Jazeera for giving too much airplay to U.S. news.

Though many media observers see Al Jazeera as biased, many viewers around the world might see CNN, ABC, and Fox News as biased. For example, in virtually all media outlets in the United States, the immorality of Palestinian suicide bombings is an unstated assumption. However, many people in the Arab world would regard that assumption as fundamentally wrong. Similarly, most Muslims worldwide would question why CBS's respected news show *60 Minutes* would give exposure to preacher Jerry Falwell, who called the Prophet Muhammad a terrorist. According to Kenton Keith, a former U.S. ambassador to Qatar, Al Jazeera has a slant, but no more than other news organizations. It just happens to be a slant that most Americans aren't comfortable with.

Al Jazeera does offer diverse views. On its popular talk show *The Opposing View*, two women hotly debated polygamy among Muslim men. On another popular program, *Sharia [Islamic Law] and Life,* the speaker dared to reassure Muslim women that the Koran does not force them to marry suitors designated by their parents. Ambassador Keith believes that "for the long-range importance of press freedom in the Middle East and the advantages that will

> *"You have to be a supporter of Al Jazeera, even if you have to hold your nose sometimes."*

ultimately have for the West, you have to be a supporter of Al Jazeera, even if you have to hold your nose sometimes" (Barr 2002:7).

To counter Al Jazeera's influence, in 2004 the U.S. State Department established its own satellite network, Al Hurra, in the Middle East. Based in Springfield, Virginia, and staffed by veteran Arab journalists, the new network promises balanced and objective reporting on regional issues and events. Its ultimate purpose, however, is to win over the hearts and minds of a population that is deeply suspicious of U.S. motives. Al Hurra, whose name means "The Free One," is the latest in a series of U.S. attempts at improving public relations with the Islamic world. Knowledgeable observers view the effort with some skepticism, however. Al Hurra now ranks seventh out of seven among international news channels in the Middle East, with an audience less than 4 percent the size of Al Jazeera's.

Let's Discuss

1. Do you find news outlets in the United States biased? How would you judge?
2. What do you think of the new Al Hurra network in the Middle East? Can it win over the hearts and minds of viewers there? Should the U.S. government be using taxpayers' dollars to fund the effort?

Sources: Al Jazeera 2006; Barr 2002; Daniszewski 2003; Macleod and Walt 2005; McCarthy 2004; MediaGuardian 2001; H. Rosenberg 2003; Urbina 2002.

An Al Jazeera staff member monitors the news at the network's headquarters in Qatar. The Al Jazeera network was featured in the 2004 documentary film *Control Room*.

Global View Arabic-language television
Contemporary Culture Cross-cultural perspectives on controversial political issues
Classroom Tip Visit http://english.aljazeera.net/HomePage to see Al Jazeera's English-language Internet feed.

Global View Have students ever seen news clips or articles that were produced by Al Jazeera?
Let's Discuss Are students concerned about the presence of Al Jazeera in the United States?

socialPolicy
and the Mass Media

Media Violence

The Issue

A blindfolded driver attempts to get a car up a ramp and onto a flatbed semi, depending on the passenger sitting next to him for directions. Two handcuffed people navigate an electrically charged maze of trip wires. Is this some form of torture? No, these episodes are taken from the popular television series *Fear Factor*.

Scenes of violence are not limited to television; they are also common on the Internet, in motion pictures, and in video games. The video game Grand Theft Auto III: Vice City was a virtual urban war game. Companion Internet sites encouraged players to run over pedestrians, shoot the paramedics who show up, and loot the bodies for spare change. Vice City sold 1.4 million copies in the first three days of its release in 2002. Its 2004 sequel, San Andreas, featured crooked cops, rival gangs, and attackers kicking victims as they lay in pools of blood (*The Economist* 2005d; Houghton County 2005; Rainey 2004).

What effects do such violent scenes have on an audience? Will viewers engage in violent acts themselves? Apparently so, since the idea for the electrical maze used in Fear Factor came from the Web site of a college student who had tested the painful experiment 80 times. The question of whether violence in the media leads people, especially youths, to become more violent has been raised since the early days of comic books, when POW! and SPLAT! were accompanied by vivid pictures of fights. Today the

mass media show far more violent and gruesome scenes, and every year the amount of violence seems to increase. A recent study of network television showed an increase in violence at every hour of prime-time TV. Little wonder that in a 2005 national survey, 66 percent of viewers said there is too much violence on television—a higher level of concern than was expressed over cursing, explicit sexual content, or drug and alcohol abuse. Such views have led TV-watch groups to identify the best and worst shows: see Table 6-3 (Lichter et al. 2002; Parents Television Council 2003; Poniewozik 2005).

The Setting

We spend a great deal of time with the media. According to a communications industry study, people spend 10 hours every day with television, videotaped movies, computer games, radio, and other media outlets. At the end of a week, the time averages more than 72 hours—far more than a full workweek (Bureau of the Census 2004a:716).

But does watching hours of mass media with violent images cause one to behave differently? This research question is exceedingly complex, since many social factors influence behavior. Some researchers use an experimental method in which participants are randomly assigned to view either violent or nonviolent media and are later assessed for aggression. Other researchers survey subjects' media habits and aggressive behavior or attitudes. The most comprehensive analysis of more than 200

Table 6-3 **The Best and Worst of TV: Do You Agree?** *Shows from the 2005–2006 prime-time schedule, ranked according to violence, foul language, and sexual content*

Best	Worst
1. *Extreme Makeover: Home Edition*	1. *The War at Home*
2. *Three Wishes*	2. *Family Guy*
3. *American Idol*	3. *American Dad*
4. *The Ghost Whisperer*	4. *The O.C.*
5. *Everybody Hates Chris*	5. *C.S.I. (Crime Scene Investigation)*
6. *Reba*	6. *Desperate Housewives*
7. *Bernie Mac*	7. *Two and a Half Men*
8. *Dancing with the Stars*	8. *That '70s Show*

Source: Parents Television Council 2005.

studies of media violence and aggressive behavior found that exposure to violence causes short-term increases in the aggressive behavior of youths. Another more recent study found that less exposure to television and other media is related to less observed physical aggression (C. Anderson and Bushman 2001; J. Johnson et al. 2002; H. Paik and Comstock 1994; Robinson et al. 2001; U.S. Surgeon General 2001).

Sociological Insights

The controversy surrounding violence and the media raises some basic questions about the functions of the media. If the media's functions are to entertain, socialize, and enforce social norms, how can violence be a part of its programming, especially when the offender rarely sees any consequences?

Even if a viewer does not necessarily become more violent from watching violent images, a kind of desensitization could be taking place. Using the premise of the narcotizing dysfunction, one might suggest that extended exposure to violent imagery leads to an increased tolerance and acceptance of violence in others.

Both conflict and feminist theorists point out that the victims in violent scenes are often those who receive less respect than others in real life: women, children, the poor, racial minorities, citizens of foreign countries, even the physically disabled. The media routinely portray rape in a way that further devalues women. Women are often cast as prostitutes, even in well-regarded motion pictures, from Federico Fellini's *Nights of Cabiria* (1956) to Jodie Foster in *Taxi Driver* (1976), Julia Roberts in *Pretty Woman* (1990), and Elisabeth Shue in *Leaving Las Vegas* (1995).

Interactionists are especially interested in whether violence in the media may become a script for real-life behavior. Because aggression is a product of socialization, people may model themselves after the violent behavior they see, especially if the situations approximate their own lives. Battling Doctor Octopus in *Spider-Man II* is one thing, but what about violence that represents only a slight deviation from normal behavior? In the 1995 film *The Program*, high school football players proved their manhood by lying in the middle of a highway at night. After several young men died trying to prove their own manhood by imitating the scene, Touchstone Films ordered its removal.

Policy Initiatives

Policymakers have responded to the links between media violence and real-life aggression on two levels. In public statements, politicians are quick to call for more family-oriented, less violent content, but on the legislative level, they are reluctant to engage in what could be regarded as censorship. They encourage the media to regulate themselves.

The U.S. Surgeon General's 2001 report on youth violence recommended that parents use V-chip technology to screen the television programs their children watch. Yet despite parental concerns, a 2001 national study showed that only 17 percent of parents use the V-chip to block programs with sexual or violent content. In general, most observers agree that parents should play a stronger role in monitoring their children's media consumption (Kaiser Family Foundation 2001; U.S. Surgeon General 2001).

Often government studies are initiated by violent events we desperately wish to explain. The 2001 Surgeon General's report on youth violence came out of the 1999 Columbine High School shootings in Colorado. Canada launched a serious look at media violence following a 1989 incident at a Montreal university in which 14 young women were shot to death. A senseless beating of a five-year-old girl by three friends in Norway in 1994 led that country to look at violence in the media. In all these cases, initial calls for stiff government regulation eventually gave way to industry self-regulation and greater adult involvement in young people's viewing patterns (Bok 1998; Health Canada 1993).

Much of our knowledge of media violence comes from the study of children who watch traditional television programming. Some more recent studies have tried to assess the impact of video games. We should not lose sight of the fact that media outlets are becoming increasingly diverse, especially given the role the Internet now plays in the delivery of media content. Much of this new content holds great promise for broadening educational horizons, but unfortunately, these new outlets also offer a diet of violence.

Let's Discuss

1. Do you know of anyone whose behavior has become more aggressive from exposure to violence in the media? How was this aggression expressed? Have you noticed any changes in your own behavior?

2. To what extent should government act as a media censor, especially in regard to violent content directed toward young people?

3. What role do you think parents should have in monitoring their children's viewing habits? Would you limit your children's access to media outlets? What alternative activities might children be offered?

GettingINVOLVED

To get involved in the debate over violence in the media, visit this text's Online Learning Center, which offers links to relevant Web sites. Check out the Social Policy section on the Online Learning Center as well; it provides survey data on U.S. public opinion regarding this issue.

www.mhhe.com/schaefer7

Theory Conflict and feminist views of violent imagery in the media
Theory Interactionist perspective on media violence as a script for real-life behavior

Methods Survey conducted by Kaiser shows that only 17 percent of parents use a V-chip.
Methods The 2001 U.S. Surgeon General's report on youth violence was a survey.
Global View Canada and Norway have studied media violence.

Summary

The *mass media* are print and electronic instruments of communication that carry messages to often widespread audiences. They pervade all social institutions, from entertainment to education to politics. This chapter examines how the mass media affect those institutions and influence our social behavior.

1. From the functionalist perspective, the media entertain, socialize, enforce social norms, confer status, and promote consumption. They can be dysfunctional to the extent that they desensitize us to serious events and issues (the *narcotizing dysfunction*).

2. Conflict theorists think the media reflect and even deepen the divisions in society through *gatekeeping,* or control over which material reaches the public; *media monitoring,* the covert observation of people's media usage and choices; and support of the *dominant ideology,* which defines reality, overwhelming local cultures.

3. Feminist theorists point out that media images of the sexes communicate unrealistic, stereotypical, limiting, and sometimes violent perceptions of women.

4. Interactionists examine the media on the micro level to see how they shape day-to-day social behavior. Interactionists have studied shared TV viewing and staged public appearances intended to convey self-serving definitions of reality.

5. The mass media require the presence of an audience—whether it is small and well defined or large and amorphous. With increasing numbers of media outlets has come more and more targeting of segmented (or specialized) audiences.

6. Social researchers have studied the role of *opinion leaders* in influencing audiences.

7. The media industry is becoming more and more concentrated, creating media conglomerates. This concentration raises concerns about how innovative and independent the media can be. In some countries, governments own and control the media.

8. The Internet is the one significant exception to the trend toward centralization, allowing millions of people to produce their own media content.

9. The media have a global reach thanks to new communications technologies, especially the Internet. Some people are concerned that the media's global reach will spread unhealthy influences to other cultures.

10. Sociologists are studying the ways that scenes of violence in the media may promote aggressive behavior or desensitization to violence in viewers.

Critical Thinking Questions

1. What kind of audience is targeted by the producers of televised professional wrestling? By the creators of an animated film? By a rap group? What factors determine who makes up a particular audience?

2. Trace the production process for a new televised situation comedy (sitcom). Who do you imagine are the gatekeepers in the process?

3. Use the functionalist, conflict, and interactionist perspectives to assess the effects of global TV programming on developing countries.

Key Terms

Dominant ideology A set of cultural beliefs and practices that helps to maintain powerful social, economic, and political interests. (page 140)

Gatekeeping The process by which a relatively small number of people in the media industry control what material eventually reaches the audience. (139)

Mass media Print and electronic means of communication that carry messages to widespread audiences. (134)

Narcotizing dysfunction The phenomenon in which the media provide such massive amounts of coverage that the audience becomes numb and fails to act on the information, regardless of how compelling the issue. (138)

Opinion leader Someone who influences the opinions and decisions of others through day-to-day personal contact and communication. (146)

Stereotype An unreliable generalization about all members of a group that does not recognize individual differences within the group. (140)

Read each question carefully and then select the best answer.

1. From the functionalist perspective, the media can be dysfunctional in what way?

    a. They enforce social norms.
    b. They confer status.
    c. They desensitize us to events.
    d. They are agents of socialization.

2. Sociologist Robert Park studied how newspapers helped immigrants to the United States adjust to their environment by changing their customary habits and by teaching them the opinions held by people in their new home country. His study was conducted from which sociological perspective?

    a. the functionalist perspective
    b. the conflict perspective
    c. the interactionist perspective
    d. the dramaturgical perspective

3. There are problems inherent in the socialization function of the mass media. For example, many people worry about

    a. the effect of using the television as a babysitter.
    b. the impact of violent programming on viewer behavior.
    c. the unequal ability of all individuals to purchase televisions.
    d. both a and b

4. Media advertising has several clear functions, but it also has dysfunctions. Sociologists are concerned that

    a. it creates unrealistic expectations of what is required to be happy.
    b. it creates new consumer needs.
    c. advertisers are able to influence media content.
    d. all of the above

5. Gatekeeping, the process by which a relatively small number of people control what material reaches an audience, is largely dominant in all but which of the following media?

    a. television
    b. the Internet
    c. publishing
    d. music

6. Which sociological perspective is especially concerned with the media's ability to decide what gets transmitted through gatekeeping?

    a. the functionalist perspective
    b. the conflict perspective
    c. the interactionist perspective
    d. the dramaturgical perspective

7. Which of the following is *not* a problem feminist theorists see with media coverage?

    a. Women are underrepresented, suggesting that men are the cultural standard and that women are insignificant.
    b. Men and women are portrayed in ways that reflect and perpetuate stereotypical views of gender.
    c. Depictions of male–female relationships emphasize traditional sex roles and normalize violence against women.
    d. The increasing frequency of single moms in the media is providing a negative role model for women.

8. Which of the following sociological perspectives helps us to understand more about one important aspect of the entire mass media system—the audience?

    a. the functionalist perspective
    b. the conflict perspective
    c. the interactionist perspective
    d. the feminist perspective

9. Sociologist Paul Lazarsfeld and his colleagues pioneered the study of

    a. the audience.
    b. opinion leaders.
    c. the media's global reach.
    d. media violence.

10. In his study of how the social composition of audience members affected how they interpreted the news coverage of riots in Los Angeles in 1992, sociologist Darnell Hunt found what kind of differences in perception?

    a. racial
    b. gender
    c. class
    d. religious

11. The mass media increase social cohesion by presenting a more or less standardized, common view of culture through mass communication. This statement reflects the _____ perspective.

12. Paul Lazarsfeld and Robert Merton created the term _____ _____ to refer to the phenomenon whereby the media provide such massive amounts of information that the audience becomes numb and generally fails to act on the information, regardless of how compelling the issue.

13. _____ _____ is the term used to describe the set of cultural beliefs and practices that helps to maintain powerful social, economic, and political interests.

14. Sociologists blame the mass media for the creation and perpetuation of _____, or generalizations about all members of a group that do not recognize individual differences within the group.

15. The _____ perspective contends that television distorts the political process.

16. We risk being _____ if we overstress U.S. dominance and assume other nations do not play a role in media cultural exports.

17. Both _____ and _____ theorists are troubled that the victims depicted in violent imagery are often those who are given less respect in real life: women, children, the poor, racial minorities, citizens of foreign countries, and even the physically disabled.

18. The _____ perspective examines the media on the micro level to see how they shape day-to-day social behavior.

19. We can point to a handful of _____ _____ that now dominate the publishing, broadcasting, and film industries, although they may be hard to identify, since global conglomerates manage many different product names.

20. Some 40 years ago, Canadian linguist _____ _____ predicted that the rise of the electronic media would create a "global village."

{ TECHNOLOGY RESOURCES }

Online Learning Center

1. Visit the student center in the Online Learning Center at **www.mhhe.com/schaefer7** and link to Use Your Sociological Imagination. You will be asked to become a news junkie, and to think about where you will gather your "facts" or information. Next, you will be asked to imagine yourself as part of an audience, and to think about the similarities you might share with other audience members. Use your sociological imagination to answer the questions.

2. Numerous organizations have been formed for the purpose of providing alternatives to mainstream mass media. One of them is Paper Tiger Television (**www.papertiger.org**). Explore this site and become more aware of ways in which media gatekeeping may be challenged.

3. In China, the mass media are largely government controlled. Browse through the English version of China's leading national newspaper, the *People's Daily* (**http://english.peopledaily.com.cn**), to see how government control affects the paper's news coverage.

*Note: While all the URLs listed were current as of the printing of this book, these sites often change. Please check our Web site (**www.mhhe.com/schaefer7**) for updates, hyperlinks, and exercises related to these sites.*

Reel Society Video Clips

Reel Society video clips, which appear on this book's Web site, can be used to spark discussion about the following topics from this chapter:
- Sociological Perspectives on the Media
- The Media Industry

7

Deviance and Social Control

inside

Social Control

Deviance

Crime

Social Policy and Social Control: The Death Penalty in the United States and Worldwide

Boxes

Research in Action: Labeling a Behavior as a Crime: Road Rage

Sociology on Campus: Binge Drinking

Taking Sociology to Work: Tiffany Zapata-Mancilla, Victim Witness Specialist, Cook County State's Attorney's Office

Lick it up.

After rock and rolling all night, we need nourishment. And every drop of chocolate milk has the same vitamins and minerals regular milk has. All the more reason to have a really, really long tongue.

got milk?

KISS © 1999 NATIONAL FLUID MILK PROCESSOR PROMOTION BOARD

Deviance and conformity are relative concepts that can change over time. KISS was a leading example of shock rock in the 1970s, when the band's theatrical costumes and makeup appeared deviant to some. Today, the group's well-known image is less shocking, and the milk industry has enlisted the group to promote its product to young consumers.

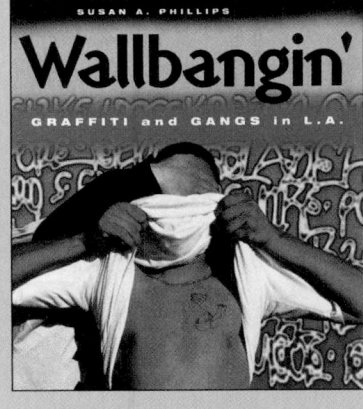

Wallbangin' is a gang term that means, roughly, "gangbangin' on a wall." This can be through straightforward writing or through crossing out the writing of others; either activity enforces relationships of power between gangs. Gang members in Los Angeles generally recognize this as a generic term for the activity of wall writing. . . .

Any type of cultural or artistic production forces change on an environment. Most of the time, people abide by well-established rules for culture-producing activities. They do it through consuming certain products in certain ways or by creating symbols of their identity within the scope of what is legal for the entire society. In general, people who write graffiti produce culture in a different manner. No matter what it says, the manner in which graffiti is produced defines the writer's position as an outsider and alienates that person from the rest of society. . . .

Criminal aspects of graffiti free the writers from constraints that laws would place on their creations. Writers force change on an environment, but without recourse or permission. Their marks are like advertising for groups and individuals who may themselves be outside the law already. Graffiti writers usurp public and private property for their own purposes. The graffitists have not been paid, nor do they pay for the space they use for the privilege. Viewed from the larger society's perspective, graffiti is always just wallbangin': it is cultural production through destruction. . . .

The antisocial nature of graffiti makes its analysis an inherently social endeavor. Graffiti is all about people. It's about relationships, and individuals, and motives. As a researcher, you need to get hold of a social situation on the ground in order to understand the story presented on the walls. . . .

A young man from 29th Street in South Central Los Angeles explained it like this:

It all comes down to basically politics, like everything else. . . . Graffiti . . . to us . . . what we write on the walls . . . is to mark our territory. Which you already know. A way of us marking our territory so people know. See right now we might not be here to represent our neighborhood, but they pass through this, "oh look this is where so and so kicks back." See, it does serve a purpose! That's what we use it for. But yet when we try different styles and different things. Because, believe it or not, we try to make our neighborhood look good. . . . We don't want to write on the wall and just leave it all ugly, we want to write on the wall and make it look nice. . . .

Whether in alleys, around hangouts, parks, on main drags, or on major streets, gang members write graffiti for themselves and others who understand their messages as acts of representing. Gang members use graffiti to organize the spaces in which they reside; in the process, they cover the streets with manifestations of their own identity. Like silent sentinels, the graffiti keep watch and inform onlookers of the affiliations and activities that define a certain area.

(S. A. Phillips 1999:21, 23, 134–135) Additional information about this excerpt can be found on the Online Learning Center at www.mhhe.com/schaefer7. ●

" *Whether in alleys, around hangouts, parks, on main drags, or on major streets, gang members write graffiti for themselves and others who understand their messages as acts of representing.* "

Anthropologist Susan Phillips studied graffiti writing in Los Angeles neighborhoods over a period of six years. In her book *Wallbangin': Graffiti and Gangs in L.A.* she notes that while graffiti writing is regarded as vandalism in the eyes of the law, it serves important social purposes for gang members, from making political statements to identifying home turf and making the "neighborhood look good" (S. A. Phillips 1999:135).

As Phillips makes clear, what should be considered deviant is not always obvious. Wall writing, in fact, has an illustrious history. She begins her book with pages of descriptions of wall writing from such literary sources as the Bible, Mark Twain, Edgar Allan Poe, and George Orwell. Even today, Phillips points out, government authorities sometimes protect graffiti. At Los Angeles harbor, officials do not erase the writing of sailors. Along the Harlem River Parkway in New York City, a playground wall with graffiti by the late artist Keith Haring (who began as a tagger) has been preserved as a work of art.

As another example of the difficulty of determining what is and is not deviant, consider the issue of binge drinking on campus. On the one hand, we can view binge drinking as *deviant*, as violating a school's standards of conduct and endangering one's health. On the other hand, we can see it as *conforming*, or complying with peer culture. In the United States, people are socialized to have mixed feelings about both conforming and nonconforming behavior. The term *conformity* can conjure up images of mindless imitation of one's peer group—whether a circle of teenagers wearing "phat pants" or a group of business executives all dressed in gray suits. Yet the same term can also suggest that an individual is cooperative, or

a "team player." What about those who do not conform? They may be respected as individualists, leaders, or creative thinkers who break new ground. Or they may be labeled as "troublemakers" and "weirdos" (Aronson 1999).

This chapter examines the relationship between conformity, deviance, and social control. When does conformity verge on deviance? How does a society manage to control its members and convince them to conform to its rules and laws? What are the consequences of deviance? We will begin by distinguishing between conformity and obedience and then look at an experiment on obedience to authority. Next, we will analyze the informal and formal mechanisms societies use to encourage conformity and discourage deviance. We will pay particular attention to the legal order and how it reflects underlying social values.

The second part of the chapter focuses on theoretical explanations for deviance, including the functionalist approach employed by Émile Durkheim and Robert Merton; interactionist-based theories; labeling theory, which draws on both the interactionist and the conflict perspectives; and conflict theory.

The third part of the chapter focuses on crime, a specific type of deviant behavior. As a form of deviance that is subject to official, written norms, crime has been a special concern of policymakers and the public in general. We will look at various types of crime found in the United States, the ways crime is measured, and international crime rates. Finally, the Social Policy section considers the controversial topic of the death penalty. ●

Social Control

As we saw in Chapter 3, each culture, subculture, and group has distinctive norms governing appropriate behavior. Laws, dress codes, organizational bylaws, course requirements, and the rules of sports and games all express social norms.

How does a society bring about acceptance of basic norms? The term **social control** refers to the techniques and strategies for preventing deviant human behavior in any society. Social control occurs on all levels of society. In the family, we are socialized to obey our parents simply because they are our parents. Peer groups introduce us to informal norms, such as dress codes, that govern the behavior of their members. Colleges establish standards they expect of students. In bureaucratic organizations, workers encounter a formal system of rules and regulations. Finally, the government of every society legislates and enforces social norms.

Most of us respect and accept basic social norms and assume that others will do the same. Even without thinking, we obey the

instructions of police officers, follow the day-to-day rules at our jobs, and move to the rear of elevators when people enter. Such behavior reflects an effective process of socialization to the dominant standards of a culture. At the same time, we are well aware that individuals, groups, and institutions *expect* us to act "properly." This expectation carries with it **sanctions,** penalties and rewards for conduct concerning a social norm. If we fail to live up to the norm, we may face punishment through informal sanctions such as fear and ridicule, or formal sanctions such as jail sentences or fines.

{ p.65–66 }

The challenge to effective social control is that people often receive competing messages about how to behave. While the state or government may clearly define acceptable behavior, friends or fellow employees may encourage quite different behavior patterns. Historically, legal measures aimed at blocking discrimination based on race, religion, gender, age, and sexual orientation have been difficult to implement, because many people tacitly encourage the violation of such measures.

Functionalists maintain that people must respect social norms if any group or society is to survive. In their view, societies literally could not function if massive numbers of people defied standards of appropriate conduct. In contrast, conflict theorists contend that the "successful functioning" of a society will consistently benefit the powerful and work to the disadvantage of other groups. They point out that in the United States, widespread resistance to social norms was necessary to win our independence from England, to overturn the institution of slavery, to allow women to vote, to secure civil rights, and to force an end to the war in Vietnam.

Conformity and Obedience

Techniques for social control operate on both the group level and the societal level. People we think of as peers or equals influence us to act in particular ways; the same is true of people who hold authority over us or occupy awe-inspiring positions. Social psychologist Stanley Milgram (1975) made a useful distinction between these two levels of social control.

Milgram used the term **conformity** to mean going along with peers—individuals of our own status who have no special right to direct our behavior. In contrast, **obedience** is compliance with higher authorities in a hierarchical structure. Thus, a recruit entering military service will typically *conform* to the habits and language of other recruits and *obey* the orders of superior officers. Students will *conform* to the drinking behavior of their peers and *obey* the requests of campus security officers.

We often think of conformity and obedience as rather harmless behaviors. When members of an expensive health club all don the same costly sportswear, we may see their conformity as unimaginative, but we do not think of it as harmful. Nevertheless, researchers have found that under certain circumstances, both conformity and obedience can have negative consequences. Obedience, in particular, can cause immense damage—a potential that Milgram demonstrated in the laboratory.

If ordered to do so, would you comply with an experimenter's instruction to administer increasingly painful electric shocks to a subject? Most people would say no; yet Milgram's research (1963, 1975) suggests that most of us *would* obey such orders. In his words (1975:xi), "Behavior that is unthinkable in an individual . . . acting on his own may be executed without hesitation when carried out under orders."

Milgram placed advertisements in New Haven, Connecticut, newspapers to recruit subjects for a learning experiment at Yale University. Participants included postal clerks, engineers, high school teachers, and laborers. They were told that the purpose of the research was to investigate the effects of punishment on

Director Michael Moore purchases ammunition at a Kmart store in a scene from his award-winning documentary *Bowling for Columbine,* which questioned the availability of guns in the United States. Many Americans view the private ownership of firearms as a means of social control.

learning. The experimenter, dressed in a gray technician's coat, explained that in each test, one subject would be randomly selected as the "learner," while another would function as the "teacher." However, the experiment was rigged so that the "real" subject would always be the teacher, while an associate of Milgram's served as the learner.

At this point, the learner's hand was strapped to an electric apparatus. The teacher was taken to an electronic "shock generator" with 30 levered switches labeled from 15 to 450 volts. Before beginning the experiment, all subjects received sample shocks of 45 volts, to convince them of the authenticity of the experiment. The experimenter then instructed the teacher to apply shocks of increasing voltage each time the learner gave an

Social control, Finnish style. This young man is relaxing in his prison cell, not in his college dorm room. Thirty years ago Finland rejected the rigid Soviet model of imprisonment and adopted a gentler correctional system meant to shape prisoners' values and encourage moral behavior. Today, Finland's rate of imprisonment is less than half that of England and one-fourth that of the United States.

Chapter 7

incorrect answer on a memory test. Teachers were told that "although the shocks can be extremely painful, they cause no permanent tissue damage." In reality, the learner did not receive any shocks.

In a prearranged script, the learner deliberately gave incorrect answers and expressed pain when "shocked." For example, at 150 volts, the learner would cry out, "Get me out of here!" At 270 volts, the learner would scream in agony. When the shock reached 350 volts, the learner would fall silent. If the teacher wanted to stop the experiment, the experimenter would insist that the teacher continue, using such statements as "The experiment requires that you continue" and "You have no other choice; you *must* go on" (Milgram 1975:19–23).

The results of this unusual experiment stunned and dismayed Milgram and other social scientists. A sample of psychiatrists had predicted that virtually all subjects would refuse to shock innocent victims. In their view, only a "pathological fringe" of less than 2 percent would continue administering shocks up to the maximum level. Yet almost *two-thirds* of participants fell into the category of "obedient subjects."

Why did these subjects obey? Why were they willing to inflict seemingly painful shocks on innocent victims who had never done them any harm? There is no evidence that these subjects were unusually sadistic; few seemed to enjoy administering the shocks. Instead, in Milgram's view, the key to obedience was the experimenter's social role as a "scientist" and "seeker of knowledge."

Milgram pointed out that in the modern industrial world, we are accustomed to submitting to impersonal authority figures whose status is indicated by a title (professor, lieutenant, doctor) or by a uniform (the technician's coat). Because we view the authority as larger and more important than the individual, we shift responsibility for our behavior to the authority figure. Milgram's subjects frequently stated, "If it were up to me, I would not have administered shocks." They saw themselves as merely doing their duty (Milgram 1975).

From an interactionist perspective, one important aspect of Milgram's findings is the fact that subjects in follow-up studies were less likely to inflict the supposed shocks as they were moved physically closer to their victims. Moreover, interactionists emphasize the effect of *incrementally* administering additional dosages of 15 volts. In effect, the experimenter negotiated with the teacher and convinced the teacher to continue inflicting higher levels of punishment. It is doubtful that anywhere near the two-thirds rate of obedience would have been reached had the experimenter told the teachers to administer 450 volts immediately (B. Allen 1978; Katovich 1987).

Milgram launched his experimental study of obedience to better understand the involvement of Germans in the annihilation of 6 million Jews and millions of other people during World War II. In an interview conducted long after the publication of his study, he suggested that "if a system of death camps were set up in the United States of the sort we had seen in Nazi Germany, one would be able to find sufficient personnel for those camps in any medium-sized American town." Though many people

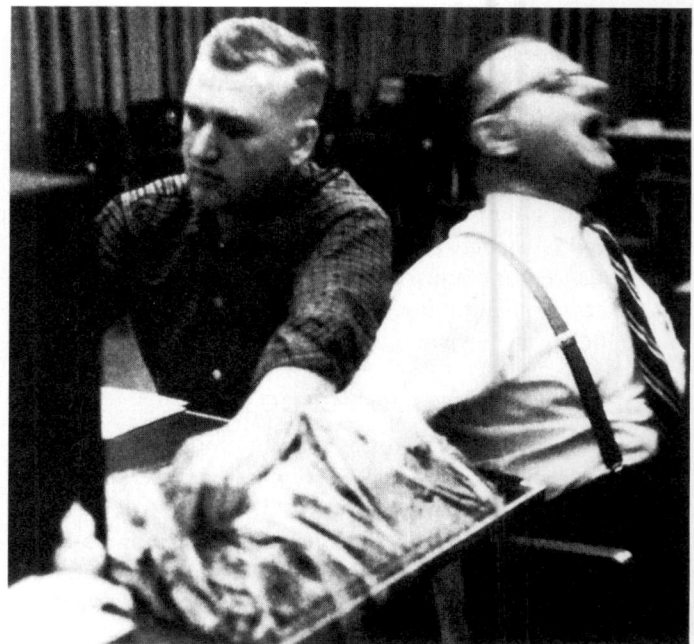

In one of Stanley Milgram's experiments, the "learner" supposedly received an electric shock from a shock plate when he answered a question incorrectly. At the 150-volt level, the "learner" would demand to be released and would refuse to place his hand on the shock plate. The experimenter would then order the actual subject (the "teacher") to force the hand onto the plate, as shown in the photo. Though 40 percent of the true subjects stopped complying with Milgram at this point, 30 percent did force the "learner's" hand onto the shock plate, despite his pretended agony.

questioned his remark, the revealing photos taken at Iraq's Abu Ghraib prison in 2004, showing U.S. military guards humiliating if not torturing Iraqi prisoners, recalled the experiment Milgram had done two generations earlier. Under conducive circumstances, otherwise normal people can and often do treat one another inhumanely (CBS News 1979:7–8; Hayden 2004).

Use Your Sociological Imagination

www.mhhe.com/schaefer7

If you were a participant in Milgram's research on conformity, how far do you think you would go in carrying out orders? Do you see any ethical problem with the experimenter's manipulation of the control subjects?

Informal and Formal Social Control

The sanctions that are used to encourage conformity and obedience—and to discourage violation of social norms—are carried out through both informal and formal social control. As the term implies, people use *informal social control* casually to enforce norms. Examples include smiles, laughter, a raised eyebrow, and ridicule.

Theory Reflecting the interactionist perspective, Milgram's study found that proximity affects subjects' degree of obedience.
Classroom Tip Refer to "Obedience: Another Look" in Topics and Sources for Student Research for material on replications of Milgram's study.

In the United States and many other cultures, adults often view spanking, slapping, or kicking children as a proper and necessary means of informal social control. Child development specialists counter that such corporal punishment is inappropriate because it teaches children to solve problems through violence. They warn that slapping and spanking can escalate into more serious forms of abuse. Yet, despite a 1998 policy statement by the American Academy of Pediatrics that corporal punishment is not effective and can indeed be harmful, 59 percent of pediatricians support the use of corporal punishment, at least in certain situations. Our culture widely accepts this form of informal social control (Wolraich et al. 1998).

Formal social control is carried out by authorized agents, such as police officers, judges, school administrators, employers, military officers, and managers of movie theaters. It can serve as a last resort when socialization and informal sanctions do not bring about desired behavior. An increasingly significant means of formal social control in the United States is to imprison people. During the course of a year, 7 million adults undergo some form of correctional supervision—jail, prison, probation, or parole. Put another way, almost 1 out of every 30 adult Americans is subject to this very formal type of social control every year (Glaze and Palla 2005).

In the aftermath of September 11, 2001, new measures of social control became the norm in the United States. Some of them, such as stepped-up security at airports and high-rise buildings, were highly visible to the public. The federal government has also publicly urged citizens to engage in informal social control by watching for and reporting people whose actions seem suspicious. But many other measures taken by the government have increased the covert surveillance of private records and communications.

Just 45 days after September 11, with virtually no debate, Congress passed the Patriot Act of 2001. Sections of this sweeping legislation revoked legal checks on the power of law enforcement agencies. Without a warrant or probable cause, the Federal Bureau of Investigation (FBI) can now secretly access most private records, including medical histories, library accounts, and student registrations. In 2002, for example, the FBI searched the records of hundreds of dive shops and scuba organizations. Agents had been directed to identify every person who had taken diving lessons in the past three years because of speculation that terrorists might try to approach their targets underwater (Moss and Fessenden 2002).

Many people think this kind of social control goes too far. Civil rights advocates also worry that the government's request for information on suspicious activities may encourage negative stereotyping of Muslims and Arab Americans. Clearly, there is a trade-off between the benefits of surveillance and the right to privacy.

The interplay between formal and informal social control can be complicated, especially if people are encouraged to violate social norms. Box 7-1 (page 162) considers binge drinking among college students, who receive conflicting messages about the acceptability of the behavior from sources of social control.

Law and Society

Some norms are so important to a society that they are formalized into laws regarding people's behavior. *Law* may be defined as governmental social control (Black 1995). Some laws, such as the prohibition against murder, are directed at all members of society. Others, such as fishing and hunting regulations, primarily affect particular categories of people. Still others govern the behavior of social institutions (for instance, corporate law and laws regarding the taxing of nonprofit enterprises).

Sociologists see the creation of laws as a social process. Because laws are passed in response to a perceived need for formal social control, sociologists have sought to explain how and why such a perception arises. In their view, law is not merely a static body of rules handed down from generation to generation. Rather, it reflects continually changing standards of what is right and wrong, of how violations are to be determined, and of what sanctions are to be applied (Schur 1968).

What's next in formal social control—iris checks? At Amsterdam's Schiphol airport, a security official scans a passenger's irises. Like fingerprints, iris patterns are unique, but their greater complexity makes them a more accurate form of identification. This passenger may choose to store her iris patterns on an identification card to expedite her boarding process.

Methods Survey research on physicians' views of corporal punishment
Let's Discuss Canvass students as to whether corporal punishment was used in their elementary schools.
Contemporary Culture Discuss whether students support the Patriot Act.
Classroom Tip See "Field Trips" (Class Discussion Topics).

sociologyONcampus

7-1 Binge Drinking

Danny Reardon's father wasn't worried about his son when he sent him off to the University of Maryland in fall 2001. Danny had been on his own for nine months, traveling through Europe after his high school graduation. But at 5:30 a.m. on February 8, 2002, his father's confidence collapsed. Danny was in the hospital, close to death after drinking too much at a fraternity party the night before.

What had happened? The story was a typical one. When Danny passed out at 11:30 p.m., fraternity members didn't call an ambulance. Instead, they took turns watching him, hoping he would revive on his own. But by 3:30 the next morning, they realized that wasn't going to happen. Danny had stopped breathing. When the ambulance reached the hospital, his brain was no longer functioning. By the end of the week he was dead, another college-age victim of binge drinking.

Danny was not unusual in his behavior. According to a study published by the Harvard School of Public Health in 2002, 44 percent of college students indulge in binge drinking (defined as at least five drinks in a row for men and four in a row for women). For those who live in a Greek fraternity or sorority, the rates are even higher—four out of five are binge drinkers (see the figure). These numbers represent an increase from 1990s data, despite efforts on many campuses across the nation to educate students about the risks of binge drinking. The problem is not confined to the United States—Britain, Russia, and South Africa all report regular "drink till you drop" alcoholic consumption among young people.

Binge drinking on campus presents a difficult social problem. On the one hand, it can be regarded as *deviant,* violating the standards of conduct expected of those in an academic setting. In fact, Harvard researchers consider binge drinking the most serious public health hazard facing colleges. Not only does it cause about 50 fatalities a year and hundreds of cases of alcohol poisoning; it increases the likelihood of falling behind in schoolwork, getting injured, and damaging property.

The other side of this potentially self-destructive behavior is that binge drinking represents *conformity* to the peer culture, especially in fraternities and sororities, which serve as social centers on many campuses. Most students seem to take an "everybody does it—no big deal" attitude toward the

> *44 percent of college students indulge in binge drinking.*

behavior. Many find that taking five drinks in a row is fairly typical. As one student at Boston University noted, "Anyone that goes to a party does that or worse. If you talk to anyone college age, it's normal."

Some colleges and universities are taking steps to make binge drinking a bit less "normal" by means of *social control*—banning kegs, closing fraternities and sororities, encouraging liquor retailers not to sell in high volume to students, and expelling students after three alcohol-related infractions. Yet many colleges still tolerate spring break organizers who promote "All you can drink" parties as part of a tour package.

Let's Discuss

1. Why do you think most college students regard binge drinking as a normal rather than a deviant behavior?
2. Which do you think would be more effective in stopping binge drinking on your campus, informal or formal social control?

Sources: R. Davis and DeBarros 2006; Glauber 1998; Hoover 2002; Wechsler et al. 2002, 2004.

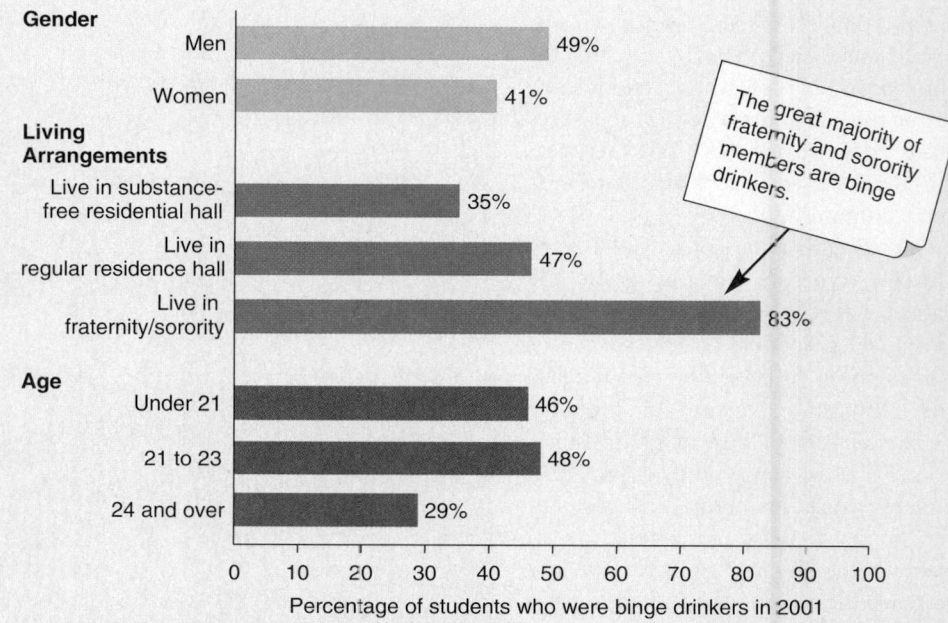

The great majority of fraternity and sorority members are binge drinkers.

Note: Based on a 2001 national survey of more than 10,000 college students. Binge drinking was defined as one drinking session of at least five drinks for men or four drinks for women during the two weeks prior to the self-administered questionnaire.
Source: Wechsler et al. 2002:208.

Global View Binge drinking is a concern in Britain, Russia, South Africa.
Let's Discuss Is binge drinking deviant behavior on a college campus? In a workplace? At home?
Gender Binge drinking is a concern among both male and female college students.

Sociologists representing varying theoretical perspectives agree that the legal order reflects the values of those in a position to exercise authority. Therefore, the creation of civil and criminal law can be a most controversial matter. Should it be against the law to employ illegal immigrants, to have an abortion (see Chapter 11), to allow prayer in public schools (see Chapter 13), or to smoke on an airplane? Such issues have been bitterly debated, because they require a choice among competing values. Not surprisingly, laws that are unpopular—such as the onetime prohibition of alcohol under the Eighteenth Amendment and the widespread establishment of a 55-mile-per-hour speed limit on highways—become difficult to enforce when there is no consensus supporting the norms.

One current and controversial debate over laws governing behavior is whether people should be allowed to use marijuana legally, for medical purposes. Although the majority of adults polled in national surveys support such a use, the federal government continues to regard all uses of marijuana as illegal. In 2005 the Supreme Court upheld the federal government's position. Nevertheless, 11 states have granted citizens the right to use marijuana for medical purposes—even if that privilege rests on dubious legal grounds (see Figure 7-1).

{ p.79 } Socialization is the primary source of conforming and obedient behavior, including obedience to law. Generally, it is not external pressure from a peer group or authority figure that makes us go along with social norms. Rather, we have internalized such norms as valid and desirable and are committed to observing them. In a profound sense, we want to see ourselves (and to be seen) as loyal, cooperative, responsible, and respectful of others. In the United States and other societies around the world, people are socialized both to want to belong and to fear being viewed as different or deviant.

Control theory suggests that our connection to members of society leads us to systematically conform to society's norms. According to sociologist Travis Hirschi and other control theorists, our bonds to family members, friends, and peers induce us to follow the mores and folkways of our society. We give little conscious thought to whether we will be sanctioned if we fail to conform. Socialization develops our self-control so well that we don't need further pressure to obey social norms. While control theory does not effectively explain the rationale for every conforming act, it nevertheless reminds us that while the media may focus on crime and disorder, most members of most societies conform to and obey basic norms (Gottfredson and Hirschi 1990; Hirschi 1969).

Deviance
What Is Deviance?

For sociologists, the term *deviance* does not mean perversion or depravity. *Deviance* is behavior that violates the standards of conduct or expectations of a group or society (Wickman 1991:85). In the United States, alcoholics, compulsive gamblers, and the mentally ill would all be classified as deviants. Being late for class is categorized as a deviant act; the same is true of wearing jeans to a formal wedding. On the basis of the sociological definition, we are all deviant from time to time. Each of us violates common social norms in certain situations.

Is being overweight an example of deviance? In the United States and many other cultures, unrealistic standards of appearance and body image place a huge strain on people—especially adult women and girls—based on how they look. Journalist Naomi Wolf (1992) has used the term *beauty myth* to refer to an exaggerated ideal of beauty, beyond the reach of all but a few females, which has unfortunate consequences. In order to shed their "deviant" image and conform to unrealistic societal norms, many women and girls become consumed with

FIGURE 7–1

The Status of Medical Marijuana

MAPPING LIFE

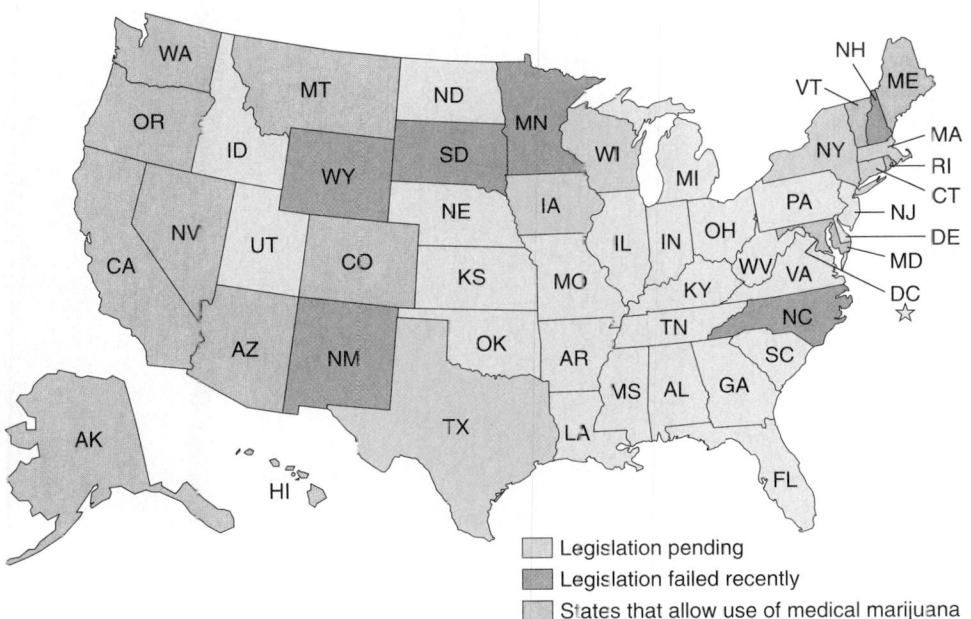

Legislation pending
Legislation failed recently
States that allow use of medical marijuana

Note: Federal law confers a one-year prison sentence on those convicted of possessing a small amount of marijuana. No exception is made for medical use, even if state law allows it, as it does in California. Maryland has not legalized medical use, but has greatly reduced the penalties.
Source: Developed by author based on data from L. Greenhouse 2005 and Marijuana Policy Project 2004, 2006.

Classroom Tip See "Marijuana for Medical Use" (Additional Lecture Ideas).

Theory Control theory introduced
Key Person Naomi Wolf
Gender Impact of the "beauty myth" on women and girls
Let's Discuss In what way is the beauty myth evident on your campus or at your place of work?

adjusting their appearances. Yet what is deviant in one culture may be celebrated in another. In Nigeria, for example, being fat is considered a mark of beauty. Part of the coming-of-age ritual calls for young girls to spend a month in a "fattening room." Among Nigerians, being thin at this point in the life course is deviant (A. Simmons 1998).

Deviance involves the violation of group norms, which may or may not be formalized into law. It is a comprehensive concept that includes not only criminal behavior but also many actions that are not subject to prosecution. The public official who takes a bribe has defied social norms, but so has the high school student who refuses to sit in an assigned seat or cuts class. Of course, deviation from norms is not always negative, let alone criminal. A member of an exclusive social club who speaks out against a traditional policy of excluding women, Blacks, and Jews from admittance is deviating from the club's norms. So is a police officer who blows the whistle on corruption or brutality within the department.

From a sociological perspective, deviance is hardly objective or set in stone. Rather, it is subject to social definition within a particular society and at a particular time. For that reason, what is considered deviant can shift from one social era to another. In most instances, those individuals and groups with the greatest status and power define what is acceptable and what is deviant. For example, despite serious medical warnings against the dangers of tobacco, made since 1964, cigarette smoking continued to be accepted for decades—in good part because of the power of tobacco farmers and cigarette manufacturers. Only after a long campaign led by public health and anticancer activists did cigarette smoking become more of a deviant activity. Today, many state and local laws limit where people can smoke.

While deviance can include relatively minor day-to-day decisions about our personal behavior, in some cases it can become part of a person's identity. This process is called *stigmatization*.

Deviance and Social Stigma

A person can acquire a deviant identity in many ways. Because of physical or behavioral characteristics, some people are unwillingly cast in negative social roles. Once they have been assigned a deviant role, they { p.84 } have trouble presenting a positive image to others and may even experience lowered self-esteem. Whole groups of people— for instance, "short people" or "redheads"—may be labeled in this way. The interactionist Erving Goffman coined the term **stigma** to describe the labels society uses to devalue members of certain social groups (Goffman 1963a; Heckert and Best 1997).

Prevailing expectations about beauty and body shape may prevent people who are regarded as ugly or obese from advancing as rapidly as their abilities permit. Both overweight and anorexic people are assumed to be weak in character, slaves to their appetites or to media images. Because they do not conform to the beauty myth, they may be viewed as "disfigured" or "strange" in appearance, bearers of what Goffman calls a "spoiled identity." However, what constitutes disfigurement is a matter of interpretation. Of the 1 million cosmetic procedures done every year in the United States alone, many are performed on women who would be defined objectively as having a normal appearance. And while feminist sociologists have accurately noted that the beauty myth makes many women feel uncomfortable with themselves, men too lack confidence in their appearance. The number of males who choose to undergo cosmetic procedures has risen sharply in recent years; men now account for 20 percent of such surgeries, including liposuction (American Academy of Cosmetic Surgery 2004).

Often people are stigmatized for deviant behaviors they may no longer engage in. The labels "compulsive gambler," "ex-convict," "recovering alcoholic," and "ex–mental patient" can stick to a person for life. Goffman draws a useful distinction between a prestige symbol that draws attention to a positive aspect of one's identity, such as a wedding band or a badge, and a stigma symbol that discredits or debases one's identity, such as a conviction for child molestation. While stigma symbols may not always be obvious, they can become a matter of public knowledge. Starting in 1994, many states required convicted sex offenders to register with local police departments. Some communities publish the names and addresses, and in some instances even the pictures, of convicted sex offenders on the Web.

Are tattoos a fashion statement, a personal statement, or a barrier to employment? While tattoos may not seem deviant or even unusual to many of us, in some circles they may create quite the opposite impression. Members of the police and the military are often discouraged from displaying tattoos on the job.

Global View Nigerian views of beauty
Classroom Tip See "Positive Deviance" (Class Discussion Topics).
Let's Discuss Are redheads stigmatized? In what way? Are they viewed as deviant? Have students give examples of other stigmatized groups.
Key Person Erving Goffman
Theory Interactionist perspective used to examine stigma and deviance

Gender Females and males both succumb to the beauty myth.

A person need not be guilty of a crime to be stigmatized. Homeless people often have trouble getting a job, because employers are wary of applicants who cannot give a home address. Moreover, hiding one's homelessness is difficult, since agencies generally use the telephone to contact applicants about job openings. If a homeless person has access to a telephone at a shelter, the staff generally answers the phone by announcing the name of the institution—a sure way to discourage prospective employers. Even if a homeless person surmounts these obstacles and manages to get a job, she or he is often fired when the employer learns of the situation. Regardless of a person's positive attributes, employers regard the spoiled identity of homelessness as sufficient reason to dismiss an employee.

While some types of deviance will stigmatize a person, other types do not carry a significant penalty. Some good examples of socially tolerated forms of deviance can be found in the world of high technology.

Deviance and Technology Technological innovations such as pagers and voice mail can redefine social interactions and the standards of behavior related to them. When the Internet was first made available to the general public, no norms or regulations governed its use. Because online communication offers a high degree of anonymity, uncivil behavior—speaking harshly of others or monopolizing chat room "space"—quickly became common. Online bulletin boards designed to carry items of community interest became littered with commercial advertisements. Such deviant acts are beginning to provoke calls for the establishment of formal rules for online behavior. For example, policymakers have debated whether to regulate the content of Web sites featuring hate speech and pornography.

Some deviant uses of technology are criminal, though not all participants see it that way. The pirating of software, motion pictures, and music has become a big business. At conventions and swap meets, pirated copies of movies, CDs, and DVDs are sold openly. Some of the products are obviously counterfeit, but many come in sophisticated packaging, complete with warranty cards. The vendors say they merely want to be compensated for their time and the cost of materials, or that the software they have copied is in the public domain.

"I swear I wasn't looking at smut—I was just stealing music."

Classroom Tip See "Which Acts Are Deviant?" (Class Discussion Topics) and "Deviance or Sport?" (Additional Lecture Ideas).
Reel Society See Deviance in the Topic Index.

Enraged Indiana Pacers basketball player Ron Artest lunges into the stands during the final minute of a 2004 game against the Detroit Pistons. The brawl, which began after a fan hurled a full beverage cup at Artest, raised the questions of how to define improper conduct by fans and what right professional athletes have to defend themselves. Even in highly competitive sports, the amount of violence society will tolerate has limits; those who transgress the limits risk being stigmatized.

Similarly, the downloading of music from the Internet, which is typically protected by copyright, is widely accepted. But file sharing, like the pirating of CDs and DVDs, has grown to the point that it is threatening the profits of copyright owners. Napster, the renegade Web site that allowed thousands of people to download from a wide selection of music files for free, has been shut down, the victim of a court challenge by the music industry. Nevertheless, its fleeting success has encouraged imitators, many of them college students who run file-sharing programs from their dorm rooms. The music industry is fighting back by urging law enforcement agents to track the pirates down and prosecute them.

Though most of these black market activities are clearly illegal, many consumers and small-time pirates are proud of their behavior. They may even think themselves smart for figuring out a way to avoid the "unfair" prices charged by "big corporations." Few people see the pirating of a new software program or a first-run movie as a threat to the public good, as they would embezzling from a bank. Similarly, most businesspeople who "borrow" software from another department, even though they lack a site license, do not think they are doing anything wrong. No social stigma attaches to their illegal behavior.

Deviance, then, is a complex concept. Sometimes it is trivial, sometimes profoundly harmful. Sometimes it is accepted by society and sometimes soundly rejected. What accounts for deviant behavior and people's reaction to it? In the next section we will examine four theoretical explanations for deviance.

Contemporary Culture Deviant behavior on the Internet
Let's Discuss Is viewing pornography on the Internet deviant behavior? Should it be censored? Is viewing it in the library deviant behavior? Should it be censored?
Race/Let's Discuss The expression "black market" uses the word *black* in a negative context that stigmatizes an entire group. Cite other examples of how everyday language stigmatizes groups.

Who Is Deviant?

What if your girlfriend started to elongate her neck by layering it with heavy brass coils? Wouldn't you think she was behaving in a bizarre way? Certainly by the standards of U.S. society, she would be. But not if you were living among the Kayan tribe in northern Thailand, where females traditionally wear up to 12 pounds of coils around the neck as a mark of beauty and tribal identity. Because deviance is socially constructed, it is subject to different social interpretations over time and across cultures.

As these photos show, what is deviant in one culture could very well be celebrated in another. In Latin America, Spain, Portugal, and many other countries, bullfighting is a popular sport. But imagine how Hindus, who consider the cow sacred, would react to the dance of death in the bullring. Even within the same culture, not everyone may share the same idea of what constitutes proper or deviant behavior. For example, cage fighting—a fight staged in a chain-link cage—is banned in some parts of the United States, but in other places it is highly popular and can be seen in person as well as on pay-per-view and commercially produced DVDs. Imagine how bullfighting enthusiasts in Portugal would react to this spectacle of men bloodying one another in a cage. Looking at ourselves and other peoples from their point of view as well as our own helps us to understand deviance as a social construction.

{ "Long-necked" girls of the Kayan tribe in Thailand }

{Matador in the bullring, Portugal}

{Cage fight, Sioux Falls, South Dakota}

Explaining Deviance

Why do people violate social norms? We have seen that deviant acts are subject to both informal and formal social control. The nonconforming or disobedient person may face disapproval, loss of friends, fines, or even imprisonment. Why, then, does deviance occur?

Early explanations for behavior that deviated from societal expectations blamed supernatural causes or genetic factors (such as "bad blood" or evolutionary throwbacks to primitive ancestors). By the 1800s, substantial research efforts were being made to identify biological factors that lead to deviance, and especially to criminal activity. Though such research was discredited in the 20th century, contemporary studies, primarily by biochemists, have sought to isolate genetic factors that suggest a likelihood of certain personality traits. Although criminality (much less deviance) is hardly a personality characteristic, researchers have focused on traits that might lead to crime, such as aggression. Of course, aggression can also lead to success in the corporate world, in professional sports, or in other walks of life.

The contemporary study of the possible biological roots of { p.60 criminality is but one aspect of the larger debate over sociobiology. In general, sociologists reject any emphasis on the genetic roots of crime and deviance. The limitations of current knowledge, the possibility of reinforcing racist and sexist assumptions, and the disturbing implications for the rehabilitation of criminals have led sociologists to draw largely on other approaches to explain deviance (Sagarin and Sanchez 1988).

Functionalist Perspective According to functionalists, deviance is a common part of human existence, with positive as well as negative consequences for social stability. Deviance helps to define the limits of proper behavior. Children who see one parent scold the other for belching at the dinner table learn about approved conduct. The same is true of the driver who receives a speeding ticket, the department store cashier who is fired for yelling at a customer, and the college student who is penalized for handing in papers weeks overdue.

Durkheim's Legacy Émile Durkheim ([1895] 1964) focused his sociological investigations mainly on criminal acts, yet his conclusions have implications for all types of deviant behavior. In Durkheim's view, the punishments established within a culture (including both formal and informal mechanisms of social control) help to define acceptable behavior and thus contribute to stability. If improper acts were not sanctioned, people might stretch their standards of what constitutes appropriate conduct.

Kai Erikson (1966) illustrated the boundary-maintenance function of deviance in his study of the Puritans of 17th-century New England. By today's standards, the Puritans placed tremendous emphasis on conventional morals. Their persecution and execution of women as witches represented a continuing attempt to define and redefine the boundaries of their community. In effect, their changing social norms created "crime waves," as people whose behavior was previously acceptable suddenly faced punishment for being deviant (Abrahamson 1978; N. Davis 1975).

Durkheim ([1897] 1951) introduced the term *anomie* into sociological literature to describe the loss of direction felt in a society when social control of individual behavior has become ineffective. Anomie is a state of normlessness that typically occurs during a period of profound social change and disorder, such as a time of economic collapse. People become more aggressive or depressed, which results in higher rates of violent crime and suicide. Since there is much less agreement on what constitutes proper behavior during times of revolution, sudden prosperity, or economic depression, conformity and obedience become less significant as social forces. It also becomes much more difficult to state exactly what constitutes deviance.

Merton's Theory of Deviance What do a mugger and a teacher have in common? Each is "working" to obtain money that can then be exchanged for desired goods. As this example illustrates, behavior that violates accepted norms (such as mugging) may be performed with the same basic objectives in mind as those of people who pursue more conventional lifestyles.

On the basis of this kind of analysis, sociologist Robert Merton (1968) adapted Durkheim's notion of anomie to explain why people accept or reject the goals of a society, the socially approved means of fulfilling their aspirations, or both. Merton maintained that one important cultural goal in the United States is success, measured largely in terms of money. In addition to providing this goal for people, our society offers specific instructions on how to pursue success—go to school, work hard, do not quit, take advantage of opportunities, and so forth.

What happens to individuals in a society with a heavy emphasis on wealth as a basic symbol of success? Merton reasoned that people adapt in certain ways, either by conforming to or by deviating from such cultural expectations. His *anomie theory of deviance* posits five basic forms of adaptation (see Table 7-1).

Table 7-1   Modes of Individual Adaptation

Mode	Institutionalized Means (Hard Work)	Societal Goal (Acquisition of Wealth)
Nondeviant		
Conformity	Accept	Accept
Deviant		
Innovation	Reject	Accept
Ritualism	Accept	Reject
Retreatism	Reject	Reject
Rebellion	Replace with new means	Replace with new goals

Source: Adapted from Merton 1968:194.

Student Alert Explain how biological theories of deviance can foster stereotyping and prejudice.
Theory Functionalist analysis of deviance
Student Alert In Table 7-1, "deviant" should be viewed in reference to the larger values of the dominant society. A retreatist or ritualist may be viewed as nondeviant by the person's immediate peer group.

Let's Discuss Use Arthur Miller's play *The Crucible* as a basis for a discussion of the meaning of deviance.
Key Persons Émile Durkheim, Kai Erikson, Robert Merton

Under cover of darkness, drag racers await the start signal on a deserted Los Angeles street. Sutherland's concepts of differential association and cultural transmission would both apply to the practice of drag racing on city streets.

Conformity to social norms, the most common adaptation in Merton's typology, is the opposite of deviance. It involves acceptance of both the overall societal goal ("become affluent") and the approved means ("work hard"). In Merton's view, there must be some consensus regarding accepted cultural goals and the legitimate means for attaining them. Without such a consensus, societies could exist only as collectives of people rather than as unified cultures, and might experience continual chaos.

The other four types of behavior represented in Table 7-1 all involve some departure from conformity. The "innovator" accepts the goals of society but pursues them with means that are regarded as improper. For instance, a safecracker may steal money to buy consumer goods and expensive vacations.

In Merton's typology, the "ritualist" has abandoned the goal of material success and become compulsively committed to the institutional means. Work becomes simply a way of life rather than a means to the goal of success. An example would be the bureaucratic official who blindly applies rules and regulations without remembering the larger goals of the organization. Certainly that would be true of a welfare caseworker who refuses to assist a homeless family because their last apartment was in another district.

The "retreatist," as described by Merton, has basically withdrawn (or retreated) from both the goals and the means of society. In the United States, drug addicts and vagrants are typically portrayed as retreatists. Concern has been growing that adolescents who are addicted to alcohol will become retreatists at an early age.

The final adaptation identified by Merton reflects people's attempts to create a *new* social structure. The "rebel" feels alienated from the dominant means and goals, and may seek a dramatically different social order. Members of a revolutionary political organization, such as a militia group, can be categorized as rebels according to Merton's model.

Merton's theory, though popular, has had relatively few applications. Little effort has been made to determine to what extent all acts of deviance can be accounted for by his five modes. Moreover, while Merton's theory is useful in examining certain types of behavior, such as illegal gambling by disadvantaged "innovators," his formulation fails to explain key differences in crime rates. Why, for example, do some disadvantaged groups have lower rates of reported crime than others? Why do many people in adverse circumstances reject criminal activity as a viable alternative? Merton's theory of deviance does not easily answer such questions (Clinard and Miller 1998).

Still, Merton has made a key contribution to the sociological understanding of deviance by pointing out that deviants such as innovators and ritualists share a great deal with conforming people. The convicted felon may hold many of the same aspirations as people with no criminal background. The theory helps us to understand deviance as a socially created behavior rather than as the result of momentary pathological impulses.

Interactionist Perspective The functionalist approach to deviance explains why rule violations continue to happen despite pressure to conform and obey. However, functionalists do not indicate how a given person comes to commit a deviant act, or why on some occasions crimes do or do not occur. The emphasis on everyday behavior that is the focus of the interactionist perspective offers two explanations of crime—cultural transmission and routine activities theory.

Cultural Transmission The graffiti writers described by Susan Phillips in the chapter-opening excerpt learn from one another. In fact, Phillips (1999) was surprised by how stable their focus was over time. She also noted how other ethnic groups built on the models of the African American and Chicano gangs, superimposing Cambodian, Chinese, or Vietnamese symbols.

Humans *learn* how to behave in social situations, whether properly or improperly. There is no natural, innate manner in which people interact with one another. These simple ideas are not disputed today, but such was not the case when sociologist Edwin Sutherland (1883–1950) first advanced the idea that an individual undergoes the same basic socialization process in learning conforming and deviant acts.

Sutherland's ideas have been the dominating force in criminology. He drew on the **cultural transmission** school, which emphasizes that one learns criminal behavior by interacting with others. Such learning includes not only the techniques of lawbreaking (for example, how to break into a car quickly and quietly) but also the motives, drives, and rationalizations of the criminal. The cultural transmission approach can also be used to explain the behavior of those who habitually abuse alcohol or drugs.

Sutherland maintained that through interactions with a primary group and significant others, people acquire definitions of

proper and improper behavior. He used the term *differential association* to describe the process through which exposure to attitudes *favorable* to criminal acts leads to the violation of rules. Research suggests that this view of differential association also applies to noncriminal deviant acts, such as smoking, truancy, and early sexual behavior (E. Jackson et al. 1986).

To what extent will a given person engage in activity that is regarded as proper or improper? For each individual, it will depend on the frequency, duration, and importance of two types of social interaction—those experiences that endorse deviant behavior and those that promote acceptance of social norms. People are more likely to engage in norm-defying behavior if they are part of a group or subculture that stresses deviant values, such as a street gang.

Sutherland offers the example of a boy who is sociable, outgoing, and athletic and who lives in an area with a high rate of delinquency. The youth is very likely to come into contact with peers who commit acts of vandalism, fail to attend school, and so forth, and may come to adopt such behavior. However, an introverted boy who lives in the same neighborhood may stay away from his peers and avoid delinquency. In another community, an outgoing and athletic boy may join a Little League baseball team or a scout troop because of his interactions with peers. Thus, Sutherland views improper behavior as the result of the types of groups to which one belongs and the kinds of friendships one has (Sutherland et al. 1992).

According to critics, however, the cultural transmission approach may explain the deviant behavior of juvenile delinquents or graffiti artists, but it fails to explain the conduct of the first-time impulsive shoplifter or the impoverished person who steals out of necessity. While it is not a precise statement of the process through which one becomes a criminal, differential association theory does direct our attention to the paramount role of social interaction in increasing a person's motivation to engage in deviant behavior (Cressey 1960; E. Jackson et al. 1986; Sutherland et al. 1992).

Routine Activities Theory   Another, more recent interactionist explanation considers the requisite conditions for a crime or deviant act to occur: there must be, at the same time and in the same place, a perpetrator, a victim, and/or an object of property. *Routine activities theory* contends that criminal victimization increases when motivated offenders and suitable targets converge. It goes without saying that you cannot have car theft without automobiles, but the greater availability of more valuable automobiles to potential thieves *heightens* the likelihood that such a crime will occur. Campus and airport parking lots, where vehicles may be left in isolated locations for long periods, represent a new target for crime that was unknown just a generation ago. Routine activity of this nature can occur even in the home. If a parent keeps a number of liquor bottles in an easily accessible place, juveniles can siphon off the contents without attracting attention to their "crime." This theory derives its name from the fact that the elements of a criminal or deviant act come together in normal, legal, and routine activities. It is considered in-

teractionist because of its emphasis on everyday behavior and micro-level social interactions.

Advocates of this theory see it as a powerful explanation for the rise in crime over the last 50 years. That is, routine activities have changed, making crime more likely. Homes left vacant during the day or during long vacations are more accessible as targets of crime. The greater presence of highly portable consumer goods, such as video equipment and computers, is another change that makes crime more likely (L. Cohen and Felson 1979; M. Felson 2002).

Some significant research supports routine activities theory. For example, studies of urban crime have documented the existence of "hot spots" such as tourist destinations and automated teller machines (ATMs), where people are more likely to be victimized because of their routine comings and goings. Furthermore, evidence shows that in cold climates, warmer

Outdoor ATMs invite trouble: They provide an ideal setting for the convergence of a perpetrator, a victim, and an article of property (cash). According to routine activities theory, crimes are more likely to occur wherever motivated offenders meet vulnerable targets.

Theory *Routine activities theory* is a relatively new interactionist explanation of deviance.
Let's Discuss Ask students if they think any of the areas around the World Trade Center site became "hot spots" for crime right after the September 11, 2001, attack.
Classroom Tip See "Social Control on the Streets" (Additional Lecture Ideas).

temperatures are associated with a rise in property crimes and probably violent crimes as well—regardless of a community's population density. In good weather, people are out and about, rendering both themselves and their vacated homes more vulnerable (Cromwell et al. 1995; Hipp et al. 2004).

Labeling Theory The Saints and Roughnecks were two groups of high school males who were continually engaged in excessive drinking, reckless driving, truancy, petty theft, and vandalism. There the similarity ended. None of the Saints was ever arrested, but every Roughneck was frequently in trouble with police and townspeople. Why the disparity in their treatment? On the basis of observation research in their high school, sociologist William Chambliss (1973) concluded that social class played an important role in the varying fortunes of the two groups.

The Saints hid behind a facade of respectability. They came from "good families," were active in school organizations, planned on attending college, and received good grades. People generally viewed their delinquent acts as a few isolated cases of sowing wild oats. The Roughnecks had no such aura of respectability. They drove around town in beat-up cars, were generally unsuccessful in school, and aroused suspicion no matter what they did.

We can understand such discrepancies by using an approach to deviance known as *labeling theory.* Unlike Sutherland's work, labeling theory does not focus on why some individuals come to commit deviant acts. Instead, it attempts to explain why certain people (such as the Roughnecks) are *viewed* as deviants, delinquents, bad kids, losers, and criminals, while others whose behavior is similar (such as the Saints) are not seen in such harsh terms. Reflecting the contribution of interactionist theorists, labeling theory emphasizes how a person comes to be labeled as deviant, or to accept that label. Sociologist Howard Becker (1963:9; 1964), who popularized this approach, summed it up with this statement: "Deviant behavior is behavior that people so label."

How do certain behaviors come to be viewed as a problem? Cigarette smoking, which was once regarded as a polite, gentlemanly activity, is now considered a serious health hazard, not only to the smoker but to others who don't smoke. Box 7-2 (page 172) considers a behavior that has only recently been identified and labeled a crime: road rage.

Labeling theory is also called the *societal-reaction approach,* reminding us that it is the *response* to an act, not the behavior itself, that determines deviance. For example, studies have shown that some school personnel and therapists expand educational programs designed for learning-disabled students to include those with behavioral problems. Consequently, a "troublemaker" can be improperly labeled as learning-disabled, and vice versa.

Traditionally, research on deviance has focused on people who violate social norms. In contrast, labeling theory focuses on police, probation officers, psychiatrists, judges, teachers, employers, school officials, and other regulators of social control. These agents, it is argued, play a significant role in creating the deviant identity by designating certain people (and not others)

as deviant. An important aspect of labeling theory is the recognition that some individuals or groups have the power to *define* labels and apply them to others. This view ties into the conflict perspective's emphasis on the social significance of power.

In recent years the practice of *racial profiling,* in which people are identified as criminal suspects purely on the basis of their race, has come under public scrutiny. Studies confirm the public's suspicions that in some jurisdictions, police officers are much more likely to stop African American males than White males for routine traffic violations, in the expectation of finding drugs or guns in their cars. Civil rights activists refer to these cases sarcastically as DWB (Driving While Black) violations. Beginning in 2001, profiling took a new turn as people who appeared to be Arab or Muslim came under special scrutiny. (Racial profiling will be examined in more detail in the Social Policy section of Chapter 10.)

The labeling approach does not fully explain why certain people accept a label and others manage to reject it. In fact, this perspective may exaggerate the ease with which societal judgments can alter our self-images. Labeling theorists do suggest, however, that the power one has relative to others is important in determining a person's ability to resist an undesirable label. Competing approaches (including that of Sutherland) fail to explain why some deviants continue to be viewed as conformists rather than as violators of rules. According to Howard Becker (1973), labeling theory was not conceived as the *sole* explanation for deviance; its proponents merely hoped to focus more attention on the undeniably important actions of those people who are officially in charge of defining deviance (N. Davis 1975; compare with Cullen and Cullen 1978).

The popularity of labeling theory is reflected in the emergence of a related perspective, called social constructionism. According to the *social constructionist perspective,* deviance is the product of the culture we live in. Social constructionists focus specifically on the decision-making process that creates the deviant identity. They point out that "child abductors," "deadbeat dads," "spree killers," and "date rapists" have always been with us, but at times have become *the* major social concern of policy makers because of intensive media coverage (Liska and Messner 1999; E. R. Wright et al. 2000).

Use Your Sociological Imagination
www.mhhe.com/schaefer7

You are a teacher. What labels, freely used in educational circles, might you attach to your students?

Conflict Theory Conflict theorists point out that people with power protect their own interests and define deviance to suit their own needs. Sociologist Richard Quinney (1974, 1979, 1980) is a leading exponent of the view that the criminal justice system serves the interests of the powerful. Crime, according to Quinney (1970), is a definition of conduct created by authorized agents of social control—such as legislators and law enforcement

Key Person William Chambliss

Methods The study of labeling of people with learning difficulties is an example of survey research.

Let's Discuss Why is the labeling approach sometimes described as the "underdog school"?

Classroom Tip For more on labeling theory, see "Primary and Secondary Deviance" (Additional Lecture Ideas).

Theory Labeling theorists' view of deviance ties into the conflict perspective.

Classroom Tip Carefully distinguish between the societal reaction approach and the social constructionist perspective.

Key Person Richard Quinney

researchIN*action*

7-2 Labeling a Behavior as a Crime: Road Rage

You're cut off by a honking, cursing driver as you try to merge with traffic—road rage in action! Though this kind of antisocial behavior isn't new, the concept of road rage is. Sociologists who have tried to trace its emergence want to know why it became socially significant only recently, even though bad driving dates back to the dawn of the automotive age.

It has been well documented that media portrayals of crime can influence the way we understand crime, even if the social reality is quite different. Serial killers are extremely rare, but you wouldn't know it from watching televi-

> *The concept of road rage resonates with our notion of cars as superpowerful machines.*

sion or the movies. And though news coverage of civil disorders emphasizes the lawlessness of the crowd, most people in the immediate vicinity of such disturbances behave in a law-abiding fashion, even during the largest riots.

Thus we should not be surprised to learn that the provocative term *road rage* emerged in the media, in response to an extreme event: a series of deadly shootings committed by a driver on the Los Angeles Expressway more than 20 years ago. Once the term had become established in everyday usage, the idea that aggressive behavior behind the wheel was on the increase became an accepted truism. In

response to this perception, government officials launched campaigns to control aggressive driving, and legislators passed laws to distinguish road rage from other motor vehicle violations, such as tailgating or forcing another car off the road.

Like the attention the media give to serial killers, the attention given to road rage may be overdone. One research study estimates that the odds of dying because of road rage are only 1 in 9.5 million, compared to the much more significant risk of being killed in an auto accident—a chance of about 1 in 16,000. Yet the concept of road rage resonates with our notion of cars as superpowerful machines. As in Stephen King's novel *Christine* (in which an "evil" car comes to "possess" its owner), cars have acquired almost a personality of their own in the popular imagination.

Once a form of deviance has been designated as unique, it may draw attention away from more pressing concerns. Significantly, more common forms of aggression than road rage—such as "bar rage" or "party rage"—have not been singled out by special expressions. While road rage is far from a trivial or harmless behavior, research suggests that its importance has been exaggerated by the power of labeling.

Let's Discuss

1. What is the role of the audience in the creation of a new label such as *road rage*?

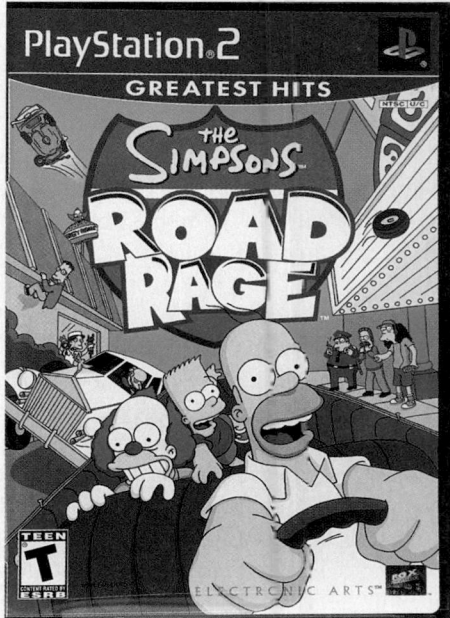

PlayStation2's interactive game Road Rage illustrates the wide usage of a label invented by the media just two decades ago.

2. Can you think of another label for deviant behavior that has come into currency only recently? Do you know how it originated?

Sources: Elliott 1999; Farrar 2005; Lupton 1999, 2001.

---

officers—in a politically organized society. He and other conflict theorists argue that lawmaking is often an attempt by the powerful to coerce others into their own morality (see also Spitzer 1975).

This theory helps to explain why our society has laws against gambling, drug usage, and prostitution, many of which are violated on a massive scale. (We will examine these "victimless crimes" later in the chapter.) According to conflict theorists, criminal law does not represent a consistent application of societal values, but instead reflects competing values and interests. Thus, the U.S. criminal code outlaws marijuana because of its alleged harm to users, yet cigarettes and alcohol—both of which can be harmful to users—are sold legally almost everywhere.

In fact, conflict theorists contend that the entire criminal justice system in the United States treats suspects differently based on their racial, ethnic, or social-class background. In many cases, officials in the system use their own discretion to make biased decisions about whether to press charges or drop them, whether to set bail and how much, whether to offer parole or deny it. Researchers have found that this kind of **differential justice**—differences in the way social control is exercised over different groups—put African Americans and Latinos at a disadvantage in the justice system, both as juveniles and as adults. On average, White offenders receive shorter sentences than comparable Latino and African American offenders, even when prior arrest records and the relative severity of the crime are taken into consideration. The Social Policy section at the end of this chapter notes marked racial disparities in the application of the death penalty (Quinney 1974).

Contemporary Culture How does the perceived threat of road rage change driver behavior?

Theory Use the three perspectives to explain why some people are more likely to express anger to strangers than to people they know.

Let's Discuss Which have you observed the most near campus: road rage, "party rage," or "bar rage"?

Theory Conflict view of criminal law

Theory Conflict perspective on law and inequality

Student Alert Note the difference between *differential justice* and *differential association*.

Race/Ethnicity Differential treatment of African Americans and Hispanics by the justice system

In the 1930s, the Federal Bureau of Narcotics launched a campaign to portray marijuana as a dangerous drug rather than a pleasure-inducing substance. From a conflict perspective, those in power often use such tactics to coerce others into adopting a different point of view.

Feminist Perspective   Feminist criminologists such as Freda Adler and Meda Chesney-Lind have suggested that many of the existing approaches to deviance and crime were developed with only men in mind. For example, in the United States, for many years any husband who forced his wife to have sexual intercourse—without her consent and against her will—was not legally considered to have committed rape. The law defined rape as pertaining only to sexual relations between people who were not married to each other, reflecting the overwhelmingly male composition of state legislatures at the time.

It took repeated protests by feminist organizations to get changes in the criminal law defining rape. Beginning in 1996, husbands in all 50 states could be prosecuted under most circumstances for the rape of their wives. There remain alarming exceptions: for example, in Tennessee a husband may legally use force or coercion to rape his wife as long as no weapon is present and he has not inflicted "serious bodily harm." Despite such exceptions, the rise of the women's movement has unquestionably led to important changes in societal notions of criminality. For example, judges, legislators, and police officers now view wife battering and other forms of domestic violence as serious crimes (National Center on Women and Family Law 1996).

When it comes to crime and to deviance in general, society tends to treat women in a stereotypical fashion. For example, consider how women who have many and frequent sexual partners are more likely to be viewed with scorn than men who are promiscuous. Cultural views and attitudes toward women influence how they are perceived and labeled. The feminist perspective also emphasizes that deviance, including crime, tends to flow from economic relationships. Traditionally, men have had greater earning power than their wives. As a result, wives may be reluctant to report acts of abuse to the authorities, and lose what may be their primary or even sole source of income. In the workplace, men have exercised greater power than women in pricing, accounting, and product control, giving them greater opportunity to engage in such crimes as embezzlement and fraud. But as women have taken more active and powerful roles both in the household and in business, these gender differences in deviance and crime have narrowed (F. Adler 1975; F. Adler et al. 2004; Chesney-Lind 1989).

In the future, feminist scholarship can be expected to grow dramatically. Particularly on topics such as white-collar crime, drinking behavior, drug abuse, and differential sentencing rates between the genders, as well as on the fundamental question of how to define deviance, feminist scholars will have much to say.

We have seen that over the past century, sociologists have taken many different approaches in studying deviance, arousing some controversy in the process. Table 7-2 (page 174) summarizes the various theoretical approaches to this topic.

Crime

Crime is a violation of criminal law for which some governmental authority applies formal penalties. It represents a deviation from formal social norms administered by the state. Laws divide

Such dramatic differences in social treatment may lead to heightened violence and crime. People who view themselves as the victims of unfair treatment may strike out, not against the powerful so much as against fellow victims. In studying crime in rural Mexico, Andrés Villarreal (2004) found that crime rates were high in the areas where land distribution was most inequitable. In areas where land was distributed more equally, communities appeared to suffer less violence and to enjoy greater social cohesion.

The perspective advanced by conflict and labeling theorists forms quite a contrast to the functionalist approach to deviance. Functionalists see standards of deviant behavior as merely reflecting cultural norms; conflict and labeling theorists point out that the most powerful groups in a society can shape laws and standards and determine who is (or is not) prosecuted as a criminal. These groups would be unlikely to apply the label "deviant" to the corporate executive whose decisions lead to large-scale environmental pollution. In the opinion of conflict theorists, agents of social control and other powerful groups can impose their own self-serving definitions of deviance on the general public.

crimes into various categories, depending on the severity of the offense, the age of the offender, the potential punishment, and the court that holds jurisdiction over the case.

The term *index crimes* refers to the eight types of crime that are tabulated each year by the Federal Bureau of Investigation (FBI). This category of criminal behavior generally consists of those serious offenses that people think of when they express concern about the nation's crime problem. Index crimes include murder, rape, robbery, and assault—all of which are violent crimes committed against people—as well as the property crimes of burglary, theft, motor vehicle theft, and arson.

Types of Crime

Rather than relying solely on legal categories, sociologists classify crimes in terms of how they are committed and how society views the offenses. In this section, we will examine five types of crime differentiated by sociologists: victimless crimes, professional crime, organized crime, white-collar crime, and transnational crime.

Victimless Crimes   When we think of crime, we tend to think of acts that endanger people's economic or personal well-being against their will (or without their direct knowledge). By contrast, sociologists use the term *victimless crime* to describe the willing exchange among adults of widely desired, but illegal, goods and services, such as prostitution (Schur 1965, 1985).

Some activists are working to decriminalize many of these illegal practices. Supporters of decriminalization are troubled by the attempt to legislate a moral code for adults. In their view, prostitution, drug abuse, gambling, and other victimless crimes are impossible to prevent. The already overburdened criminal justice system should instead devote its resources to "street crimes" and other offenses with obvious victims.

Despite widespread use of the term *victimless crime*, however, many people object to the notion that there is no victim other than the offender in such crimes. Excessive drinking, compulsive

gambling, and illegal drug use contribute to an enormous amount of personal and property damage. A person with a drinking problem can become abusive to a spouse or children; a compulsive gambler or drug user may steal to pursue his obsession. And feminist sociologists contend that prostitution, as well as the more disturbing aspects of pornography, reinforce the misconception that women are "toys" who can be treated as objects rather than people. According to critics of decriminalization, society must not give tacit approval to conduct that has such harmful consequences (Flavin 1998; Jolin 1994; National Advisory Commission on Criminal Justice 1976; Schur 1968, 1985).

The controversy over decriminalization reminds us of the important insights of labeling and conflict theorists presented earlier. Underlying this debate are two questions: Who has the power to define gambling, prostitution, and public drunkenness as "crimes"? and Who has the power to label such behaviors as "victimless"? The answer is generally the state legislatures, and in some cases, the police and the courts.

Again, we can see that criminal law is not simply a universal standard of behavior agreed on by all members of society. Rather, it reflects a struggle among competing individuals and groups to gain government support for their moral and social values. For example, organizations such as Mothers Against Drunk Driving (MADD) and Students Against Drunk Driving (SADD) have been successful in recent years in modifying public attitudes toward drunkenness. Rather than being viewed as a victimless crime, drunkenness is increasingly associated with the potential dangers of driving while under the influence of alcohol. As a result, the mass media are giving greater (and more critical) attention to people who are found guilty of drunk driving, and many states have instituted severe fines and jail terms for a wide variety of alcohol-related offenses.

Professional Crime   Although the adage "Crime doesn't pay" is familiar, many people do make a career of illegal activities. A *professional criminal* (or career criminal) is a person who pursues crime as a day-to-day occupation, developing

Table 7-2   Sociological Perspectives on Deviance

Approach	Perspective	Proponents	Emphasis
Anomie	Functionalist	Émile Durkheim Robert Merton	Adaptation to societal norms
Cultural transmission/ Differential association	Interactionist	Edwin Sutherland	Patterns learned through others
Routine activities	Interactionist	Marcus Felson	Impact of the social environment
Labeling/Social constructionist	Interactionist	Howard Becker	Societal response to acts
Conflict	Conflict	Richard Quinney	Dominance by authorized agents Discretionary justice
Feminist	Conflict/Feminist	Freda Adler Meda Chesney-Lind	Role of gender Women as victims and perpetrators

Gender Feminist view of victimless crimes, such as pornography
Theory Conflict and labeling views of victimless crimes

skilled techniques and enjoying a certain degree of status among other criminals. Some professional criminals specialize in burglary, safecracking, hijacking of cargo, pickpocketing, and shoplifting. Such people have acquired skills that reduce the likelihood of arrest, conviction, and imprisonment. As a result, they may have long careers in their chosen "professions."

Edwin Sutherland (1937) offered pioneering insights into the behavior of professional criminals by publishing an annotated account written by a professional thief. Unlike the person who engages in crime only once or twice, professional thieves make a business of stealing. They devote their entire working time to planning and executing crimes, and sometimes travel across the nation to pursue their "professional duties." Like people in regular occupations, professional thieves consult with their colleagues concerning the demands of work, becoming part of a subculture of similarly occupied individuals. They exchange information on places to burglarize, on outlets for unloading stolen goods, and on ways of securing bail bonds if arrested.

Organized Crime

A 1978 government report devotes three pages to defining the term *organized crime*. For our purposes, we will consider **organized crime** to be the work of a group that regulates relations among criminal enterprises involved in illegal activities, including prostitution, gambling, and the smuggling and sale of illegal drugs. Organized crime dominates the world of illegal business just as large corporations dominate the conventional business world. It allocates territory, sets prices for goods and services, and acts as an arbitrator in internal disputes. A secret, conspiratorial activity, it generally evades law enforcement. It takes over legitimate businesses, gains influence over labor unions, corrupts public officials, intimidates witnesses in criminal trials, and even "taxes" merchants in exchange for "protection" (National Advisory Commission on Criminal Justice 1976).

Organized crime serves as a means of upward mobility for groups of people struggling to escape poverty. Sociologist Daniel Bell (1953) used the term *ethnic succession* to describe the sequential passage of leadership from Irish Americans in the early part of the 20th century to Jewish Americans in the 1920s and then to Italian Americans in the early 1930s. Recently, ethnic succession has become more complex, reflecting the diversity of the nation's latest immigrants. Colombian, Mexican, Russian, Chinese, Pakistani, and Nigerian immigrants are among those who have begun to play a significant role in organized crime activities (Chin 1996; Kleinknecht 1996).

There has always been a global element in organized crime. But law enforcement officials and policymakers now acknowledge the emergence of a new form of organized crime that takes advantage of advances in electronic communications. *Transnational* organized crime includes drug and arms smuggling, money laundering, and trafficking in illegal immigrants and stolen goods; see the discussion on pages 176–177 (Lumpe 2003; Office of Justice Programs 1999).

White-Collar and Technology-Based Crime

Income tax evasion, stock manipulation, consumer fraud, bribery and extraction of kickbacks, embezzlement, and misrepresentation in advertising—these are all examples of **white-collar crime,** illegal acts committed in the course of business activities, often by affluent, "respectable" people. Edwin Sutherland (1949, 1983) likened these crimes to organized crime because they are often perpetrated through occupational roles.

A new type of white-collar crime has emerged in recent decades: computer crime. The use of high technology allows criminals to carry out embezzlement or electronic fraud, often leaving few traces, or to gain access to a company's inventory without leaving home. In a 2004 study by the FBI and the Computer Security Institute, 74 percent of companies relying on computer systems reported some type of related crime. While computer viruses were the most common, nearly one out of five companies reported embezzlement, fraud, or theft (Rantala 2004).

Sutherland (1940) coined the term *white-collar crime* in 1939 to refer to acts by individuals, but the term has been broadened more recently to include offenses by businesses and corporations as well. *Corporate crime,* or any act by a corporation that is punishable by the government, takes many forms and includes individuals, organizations, and institutions among its victims. Corporations may engage in anticompetitive behavior, environmental pollution, medical fraud, tax fraud, stock fraud and manipulation, accounting fraud, the production of unsafe goods, bribery and corruption, and health and safety violations (J. Coleman 2006).

For many years, corporate wrongdoers got off lightly in court by documenting their long history of charitable contributions and agreeing to help law enforcement officials find other white-collar criminals. In 2003, ten investment firms and two stock analysts

"BUT IF WE GO BACK TO SCHOOL AND GET A GOOD EDUCATION, THINK OF ALL THE DOORS IT'LL OPEN TO WHITE-COLLAR CRIME."

Let's Discuss How are ordinary people impacted by white-collar crime?
Let's Discuss Do you know anyone who has been the victim of a computer crime?

Key Person Edwin Sutherland
Student Alert Distinguish between professional crime and organized crime.
Classroom Tip To learn how a hit man approaches killing as "just a job," see "Being a Hit Man" (Additional Lecture Ideas).
Key Person Daniel Bell
Race/Ethnicity Ethnic succession within organized crime

Tiffany Zapata-Mancilla's typical day brings her into contact with all manner of crime victims—those who have survived murder attempts, domestic assault, child abuse, robbery, and other violent crimes—as well as family members who testify on behalf of victims. She works closely with victims who have witnessed a crime, since they are invariably called to testify in a trial. "My job is to make the courtroom experience for them as comfortable as possible," she says. That may mean offering them referral for crisis counseling, a court escort, court orientation, help with impact statements, assistance with restitution, protection services, transportation, child care, emergency financial assistance, or just a hot lunch. Her caseload of 500 cases comes from the four to eight courtrooms to which she is assigned in Chicago's Cook County.

"My sociological background helps me in all situations on a daily basis," Zapata-Mancilla says. In particular, it helps her to recognize the underlying societal issues, even in what seem to be horrendous individual acts, and to help victims to recognize those issues as well. "I do not judge those who come into the courtroom; I can only judge society," she says. According to Zapata-Mancilla, that doesn't mean that individuals have no personal responsibility for their life choices. But it helps to understand that people are conditioned by the environment and society they live in. One of her cases involved a young man who was called to testify to who killed his younger brother in a gang shootout. At the time of the trial, two years later, he denied knowing

anything about the killing, and afterward went out to eat with the defendant. It appears he might have been offered a drug job in return for not testifying. Instead of taking a judgmental attitude, Zapata-Mancilla recognized the young man's need to survive. Social problems such as poverty dictate to some degree the choices people believe they need to make.

Zapata-Mancilla majored in sociology at DePaul University after becoming hooked by her introductory course. She went on to earn her master's degree in sociology there in 2001. "I was very interested in societal issues such as poverty, crime, organized crime, and gang involvement, and how they influenced the lifestyles and psychology of individuals. Sociology, for me, offers reasons, not excuses, for why individuals act and react in certain ways," she says. She also thinks she has gained a greater understanding of herself as a Latina through her studies.

Her advice for students: "Keep an open mind and don't be judgmental of others."

Let's Discuss

1. Why do you think victim witnesses need special attention?
2. What aspect of sociological study do you think best prepared Zapata-Mancilla for her job?

---

collectively paid a $1.4 billion settlement for issuing fraudulent information to investors. While the magnitude of the fine grabbed headlines nationwide, it must be balanced against the millions of investors who were lured into buying billions of dollars' worth of shares in companies that the accused knew were either troubled or on the verge of collapse. The bottom line is that no individual served a jail sentence as part of the settlement, and no firm lost its license to do business. Prosecutors in other investigations into corporate scandals have pledged to pursue jail sentences for white-collar criminals, but to date most defendants have only been fined (Labaton 2003; J. O'Donnell and Willing 2003).

Conviction for corporate crime does not generally harm a person's reputation and career aspirations nearly so much as conviction for street crime would. Apparently, the label "white-collar criminal" does not carry the stigma of the label "felon convicted of a violent crime." Conflict theorists don't find such differential treatment surprising. They argue that the criminal justice system largely disregards the crimes of the affluent, focusing on crimes committed by the poor. Generally, if an offender holds a position of status and influence, his or her crime is treated as less serious than others' crimes, and the sanction is much more lenient.

Transnational Crime More and more, scholars and police officials are turning their attention to **transnational crime**, or crime that occurs across multiple national borders. In the past, international crime was often limited to the clandestine shipment of goods across the border between two countries. But increasingly, crime is no more restricted by such borders than is legal commerce. Rather than concentrating on specific countries, international crime now spans the globe.

Historically, probably the most dreaded example of transnational crime has been slavery. At first, governments did not regard slavery as a crime, but merely regulated it as they would the trade in goods. In the 20th century, transnational crime grew to embrace trafficking in endangered species, drugs, and stolen art and antiquities.

Transnational crime is not exclusive of some of the other types of crime we have discussed. For example, organized criminal networks are increasingly global. Technology definitely facilitates their illegal activities, such as trafficking in child pornography. Beginning in the 1990s, the United Nations began to categorize transnational crimes; Table 7-3 lists some of the more common types.

Bilateral cooperation in the pursuit of border criminals such as smugglers has been common for many years. The first global effort to control international crime was the International Criminal Police Organization (Interpol), a cooperative network of European police forces founded to stem the movement of political revolutionaries across borders. While such efforts to fight transnational crime may seem lofty—an activity with which any government should cooperate—they are complicated by sensitive legal and security issues. Most nations that have signed protocols issued by the United Nations, including the United States, have expressed concern over potential encroachments on their national judicial systems, as well as concern over their national security. Thus, they have been reluctant to share certain types of intelligence data. The terrorist attacks of September 11, 2001, increased both the interest in combating transnational crime and sensitivity to the risks of sharing intelligence data (Deflem 2005; D. Felson and Kalaitzidis 2005).

Use Your Sociological Imagination

As a newspaper editor, how might you treat stories on corporate or white-collar crime differently from those on violent crime?

Crime Statistics

Crime statistics are not as accurate as social scientists would like, especially since they deal with an issue of grave concern to the people of the United States. Unfortunately, they are frequently cited as if they were completely reliable. Such data do serve as an indicator of police activity, as well as an approximate indication of the level of certain crimes. Yet it would be a mistake to interpret these data as an exact representation of the incidence of crime.

Understanding Crime Statistics   Because reported crime is very high in the United States, the public regards crime as a major social problem. However, there has been a significant decline in violent crime nationwide following many years of increases. A number of explanations have been offered, including:

- A booming economy and falling unemployment rates through most of the 1990s.
- Community-oriented policing and crime prevention programs.
- New gun control laws.
- A massive increase in the prison population, which at least prevents inmates from committing crimes outside prison.

It remains to be seen whether this pattern will continue, but even with current declines, reported crimes remain well above those of other nations, and exceed the reported rates in the United States of just 20 years earlier. Feminist scholars draw our attention to one significant variation: the proportion of major crimes committed by women has increased. In a recent 10-year period (1995–2004), female arrests for major reported crimes

Table 7-3   Types of Transnational Crime   **177**

Bankruptcy and insurance fraud

Computer crime (treating computers as both a tool and a target of crime)

Corruption and bribery of public officials

Environmental crime

Hijacking of airplanes ("skyjacking")

Illegal drug trade

Illegal money transfers ("money laundering")

Illegal sales of firearms and ammunition

Infiltration of legal businesses

Networking of criminal organizations

Sea piracy

Terrorism

Theft of art and cultural objects

Trafficking in body parts (includes illegal organ transplants)

Trafficking in human beings (includes sex trade)

Source: Compiled by the author based on Mueller 2001 and United Nations Office on Drugs and Crime 2005.

increased 9 percent, while comparable male arrests declined 9 percent (Department of Justice 2005:Table 33).

Typically, the crime data used in the United States are based on the index crimes described earlier. The crime index, published annually by the FBI as part of the *Uniform Crime Reports,* includes statistics on murder, rape, robbery, assault, burglary, larceny-theft, motor vehicle theft, and arson (see Table 7-4, page 178). Obviously, many serious offenses, such as white-collar crimes, are not included in this index (although they are recorded elsewhere). In addition, the crime index is disproportionately devoted to property crimes, whereas most citizens are more worried about violent crimes. Thus, a significant decrease in the number of rapes and robberies could be overshadowed by a slightly larger increase in the number of automobiles stolen, leading to the mistaken impression that *personal* safety is more at risk than before.

The most serious limitation of official crime statistics is that they include only those crimes actually *reported* to law enforcement agencies. Because members of racial and ethnic minority groups often distrust law enforcement agencies, they may not contact the police. Feminist sociologists and others have noted that many women do not report rape or spousal abuse out of fear they will be blamed for the crime.

Partly because of these deficiencies in official statistics, the National Crime Victimization Survey was initiated in 1972. The Bureau of Justice Statistics, in compiling this annual report, seeks information from law enforcement agencies, but also interviews members of over 84,000 households and asks if they have been victims of a specific set of crimes during the preceding

year. In general, those who administer *victimization surveys* question ordinary people, not police officers, to determine whether they have been victims of crime.

Unfortunately, like other crime data, victimization surveys have particular limitations. They require that victims understand what has happened to them and are willing to disclose such information to interviewers. Fraud, income tax evasion, and blackmail are examples of crimes that are unlikely to be reported in victimization studies. Nevertheless, 91 percent of all households have been willing to cooperate with investigators for the National Crime Victimization Survey. As shown in Figure 7-2, data from these surveys reveal a fluctuating crime rate with significant declines in both the 1980s and 1990s (Catalano 2005).

International Crime Rates If developing reliable crime data is difficult in the United States, making useful cross-national comparisons is even more difficult. Nevertheless, with some care, we can offer preliminary conclusions about how crime rates differ around the world.

During the 1980s and 1990s, violent crimes were much more common in the United States than in Western Europe. Murders, rapes, and robberies were reported to the police at much higher rates in the United States. Yet the incidence of certain other types of crime appears to be higher elsewhere. For example, England, Italy, Australia, and New Zealand all have higher rates of car theft than the United States. Developing nations have significant rates of reported homicide due to civil unrest and political conflict among civilians (International Crime Victim Survey 2004; World Bank 2003a).

FIGURE 7–2

Victimization Rates, 1973–2004

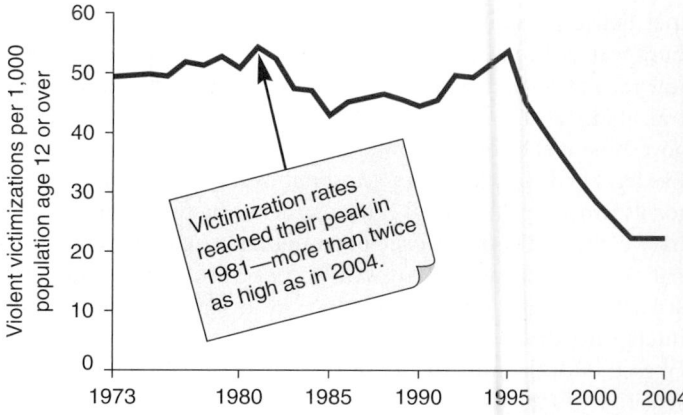

Source: Catalano 2005:1.

Why are rates of violent crime so much higher in the United States than in Western Europe? Sociologist Eliot Currie (1985, 1998) has suggested that our society places greater emphasis on individual economic achievement than other societies. At the same time, many observers have noted that the culture of the United States has long tolerated, if not condoned, many forms of violence. Coupled with sharp disparities between poor and affluent citizens, significant unemployment, and substantial alcohol and drug abuse, these factors combine to produce a climate conducive to crime.

However, disturbing increases in violent crime are evident in other Western societies. For example, crime has skyrocketed in

Table 7-4 National Crime Rates and Percentage Change

Crime Index Offenses in 2004	Number Reported	Rate per 100,000 Inhabitants	Percentage Change in Rate	
			Since 2000	Since 1995
Violent crime				
Murder	16,137	6	−1	−33
Forcible rape	94,635	32	1	−13
Robbery	401,326	137	−6	−38
Aggravated assault	854,911	291	−10	−30
Total	1,367,009	466	−8	−32
Property crime				
Burglary	2,143,456	730	0	−26
Larceny-theft	6,947,685	2,366	−5	−22
Motor vehicle theft	1,237,114	421	2	−25
Total	10,328,255	3,517	−3	−23

Notes: Arson was designated an index offense beginning in 1979; data on arson were still incomplete as of 2004. Because of rounding, the offenses may not add to totals
Source: Department of Justice 2005:Table 1.

Russia since the overthrow of Communist Party rule (with its strict controls on guns and criminals) in 1991. In 1998 there were fewer than 260 homicides in Moscow; now there are more than 1,000 homicides a year. Organized crime has filled the power vacuum in Moscow: one result is that gangland shootouts and premeditated "contract hits" have become more common. Some prominent reformist politicians have been targeted as well. Russia is the only nation in the world that incarcerates a higher proportion of its citizens than the United States. The country imprisons 580 per 100,000 of its adults on a typical day, compared to 550 in the United States, fewer than 100 in Mexico or Britain, and only 16 in Greece (Currie 1998; Shinkai and Zvekic 1999).

socialPolicy and Social Control

The Death Penalty in the United States and Worldwide

The Issue
On June 11, 2001, Timothy McVeigh—the man who took the lives of hundreds of innocent people by bombing the federal building in Oklahoma City—was executed by the federal government. McVeigh was the first federal death row prisoner to be put to death in nearly four decades. His execution and that of others who received the death penalty for their crimes raise many questions, both from supporters and from critics of capital punishment. How can the government prevent the execution of innocent men and women? Is it right to resort to a punishment that imitates the crime it seeks to condemn? Is life in prison enough of a punishment for truly heinous crimes?

Historically, execution has been a significant form of punishment for deviance from social norms and for criminal behavior. The death penalty has been used for centuries in North America to punish murder, alleged witchcraft, and a few other crimes. Yet for most of that time, little thought was given to its justification; capital punishment was simply assumed to be morally and religiously right.

The Setting
Worldwide, fewer than half of all nations allow the death penalty. Yet at least 3,797 prisoners in 25 countries are known to have been executed in 2004 alone, and another 7,395 defendants in 64 nations were sentenced to death that year. Ninety-seven percent of all known executions in 2004 took place in China, Iran, Vietnam, and the United States. Within the United States, 38 states, the military, and the federal government continue to sentence convicted felons to death for selected crimes. On the state level, more than 1,010 prisoners have been executed since 1977.

For many years, the U.S. Supreme Court waffled on the issue of capital punishment. But in 1972, in a landmark 5–4 decision in *Furman v. Georgia*, the Court held that state death penalty laws as they were administered at the time were unconstitutional, because the states allowed judges and juries too much discretion in choosing the death sentence. Before imposing the death penalty, the Justices ruled, lower courts must consider the circumstances of the crime and the character and previous record of the defendant. Four years later, in *Gregg v. Georgia*, the Court ruled specifically that capital punishment is constitutional if administered under these guidelines. According to this ruling, execution can be an appropriate sentence so long as it does not involve needless pain or suffering and is not grossly out of proportion to the severity of the crime. As a result of this ruling, all states that allowed the death penalty changed their statutes to meet the Court's standards. Yet today, state laws regarding the death penalty still vary widely, as Figure 7-3 on page 180 shows (Amnesty International 2006).

Sociological Insights
The debate over the death penalty has traditionally focused on its appropriateness as a form of punishment and its value in deterring crime. Viewed from the functionalist perspective of Émile Durkheim, sanctions against deviant acts help to reinforce society's standards of proper behavior. In this light, supporters of capital punishment insist that fear of execution will prevent at least some criminals from committing serious offenses. Moreover, supporters see the death penalty as justified even if it does not serve as a deterrent, because they believe that the worst criminals deserve to die for their crimes.

While proponents note the functions of the death penalty, there are some dysfunctions. Though many citizens are concerned that the alternative to execution, life in prison, is unnecessarily expensive, sentencing a person to death is not cheap. With hundreds of people housed on death row, the state of Texas spends an estimated $2.3 million *per case*—about three times the cost of imprisoning someone in a single cell at the highest level of security for a period of 40 years (Death Penalty Information Center 2006).

The conflict perspective emphasizes the persistence of social inequality in today's society. Simply put, poor people cannot afford to hire the best lawyers, but must rely on court-appointed attorneys, who typically are overworked and underpaid. With capital punishment in place, these unequal resources may mean the difference between life and death for poor defendants. Indeed, the American Bar Association (1997) has repeatedly expressed concern about the limited defense most defendants facing the death penalty receive. Through 2005, DNA analysis and other new technologies had exonerated 119 death row inmates (Jost 2005:787).

Another issue of critical concern to conflict theorists and researchers is the possibility of racial discrimination. Numerous

Classroom Tip See "Public Opinion on the Death Penalty" (Class Discussion Topics).

179

FIGURE 7–3

Executions by State since 1976

MAPPING LIFE

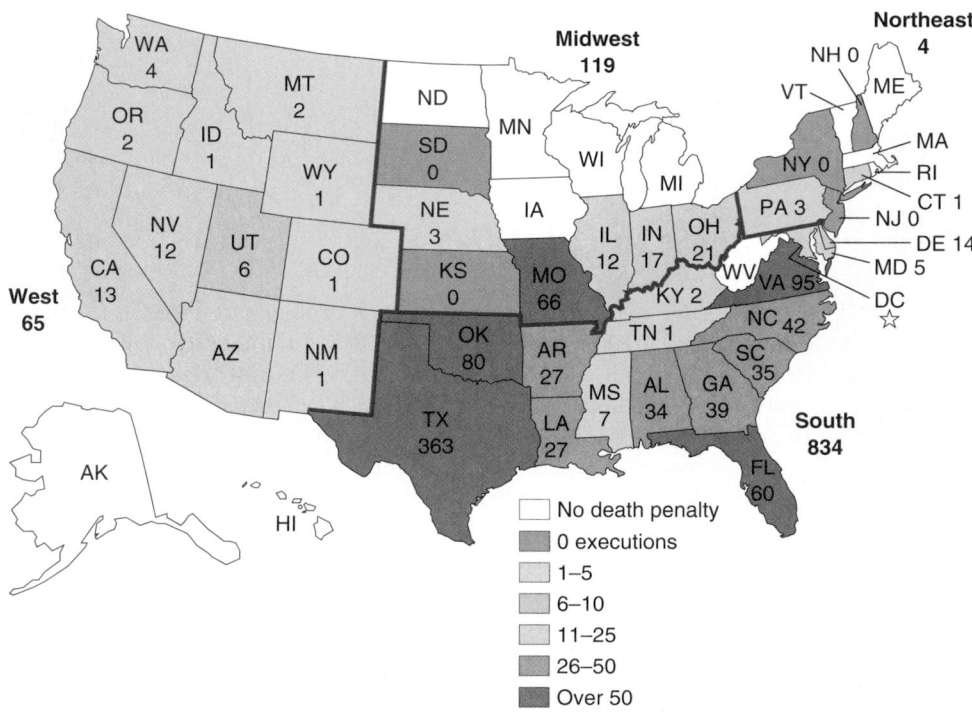

NATIONWIDE www.mhhe.com/schaefer7

Midwest
119

Northeast
4

West
65

South
834

No death penalty
0 executions
1–5
6–10
11–25
26–50
Over 50

Note: Federal and military executions not included.
Source: Death Penalty Information Center, May 16, 2006.

studies show that defendants are more likely to be sentenced to death if their victims were White rather than Black. About 65 percent of the victims in death penalty cases are White, even though only 50 percent of *all* murder victims are White. There is some evidence that Black defendants, who constituted 42 percent of all death row inmates in 2006, are more likely to face execution than Whites in the same legal circumstances. Evidence exists, too, that capital defendants receive poor legal services because of the racist attitudes of their own defense counsel. While racism is never acceptable in the criminal justice system, it is particularly devastating when the legal process results in an execution (Death Penalty Information Center 2006).

Policy Initiatives

Many people hesitate to endorse the death penalty, yet when confronted with a horrendous crime, they feel the death penalty should be available, at least in some cases. In most people's minds, for example, Timothy McVeigh's sentence would be an appropriate use of the death penalty. Surveys conducted in the United States since 1936 have found that the majority of people tend to favor the death penalty for a person convicted of murder, though approval has fluctuated. In 2004 support for the death penalty was at 74 percent (Jeffrey Jones 2005).

Surprisingly, only about 125 death sentences are handed out for the more than 15,000 murders that occur every year. Courts continue to face the question of how this ultimate penalty can be administered in a judicially fair manner. Policymakers, however, do not seem concerned with such questions. In recent years, federal and state legislatures have declared additional crimes to be punishable by death, curtailed appeals by death row inmates, and reimbursed far fewer lawyers for their defense of condemned criminals (Bonczar and Snell 2005).

Internationally, attention has focused on those nations where executions are relatively common, such as China and Iran. Foes of the death penalty see these nations as violators of human rights. In the United States, which usually regards itself as a champion of human rights, pressure to abolish capital punishment has grown, both at home and abroad.

Let's Discuss

1. Does the death penalty serve as a deterrent to crime? If so, why are crime rates in the United States comparatively high?

2. What is your position on the death penalty—should it be legal, or should it be abolished? Why?

3. Should youths who have been convicted of violent crimes be subject to the death penalty? Why or why not?

GettingINVOLVED

To get involved in the debate over the death penalty, visit this text's Online Learning Center, which offers links to relevant Web sites. Check out the Social Policy section on the Online Learning Center as well; it provides survey data on U.S. public opinion regarding this issue.

Summary

Conformity and *deviance* are two ways in which people respond to real or imagined pressure from others. In this chapter, we examined the relationship between conformity, deviance, and mechanisms of *social control.*

1. A society uses *social control* to encourage the acceptance of basic norms.

2. Stanley Milgram defined *conformity* as going along with one's peers; *obedience* is defined as compliance with higher authorities in a hierarchical structure.

3. Some norms are so important to a society, they are formalized into *laws.* Socialization is a primary source of conforming and obedient behavior, including obedience to law.

4. Deviant behavior violates social norms. Some forms of *deviance* carry a negative social *stigma,* while other forms are more or less accepted.

5. From a functionalist point of view, deviance and its consequences help to define the limits of proper behavior.

6. Some interactionists maintain that people learn criminal behavior by interacting with others *(cultural transmission).* To them, deviance results from exposure to attitudes that are favorable to criminal acts *(differential association).*

7. Other interactionists stress that for a crime to occur, there must be a convergence of motivated offenders and suitable targets of crime *(routine activities theory).*

8. An important aspect of *labeling theory* is the recognition that some people are viewed as deviant, while others who engage in the same behavior are not.

9. From the conflict perspective, laws and punishments are a reflection of the interests of the powerful.

10. The feminist perspective emphasizes that cultural attitudes and differential economic relationships help to explain gender differences in deviance and crime.

11. *Crime* represents a deviation from formal social norms administered by the state.

12. Sociologists differentiate among *victimless crimes* (such as drug use and prostitution), *professional crime,* *organized crime, white-collar crime,* and *transnational crime.*

13. Crime statistics are among the least reliable social data, partly because so many crimes are not reported to law enforcement agencies. Rates of violent crime are higher in the United States than in other Western societies, although they have been dropping.

14. The majority of people in the United States approve of the death penalty for particularly horrible crimes. However, sociologists have questioned the effectiveness of capital punishment as a deterrent to crime, and have pointed out that it falls disproportionately on those who are poor and non-White.

Critical Thinking Questions

1. What mechanisms of formal and informal social control are evident in your college classes and in day-to-day life and social interactions at your school?

2. What approach to deviance do you find most persuasive: that of functionalists, conflict theorists, interactionists, or labeling theorists? Why do you consider that approach more convincing than the other three? What are the main weaknesses of each approach?

3. Rates of violent crime are higher in the United States than they are in Western Europe, Canada, Australia, or New Zealand. Draw on as many of the theories discussed in this chapter as possible to explain why the United States is such a comparatively violent society.

Key Terms

Anomie Durkheim's term for the loss of direction felt in a society when social control of individual behavior has become ineffective. (page 168)

Anomie theory of deviance Robert Merton's theory of deviance as an adaptation of socially prescribed goals or of the means governing their attainment, or both. (168)

Conformity Going along with peers—individuals of our own status who have no special right to direct our behavior. (159)

Control theory A view of conformity and deviance that suggests that our connection to members of society leads us to systematically conform to society's norms. (163)

Crime A violation of criminal law for which some governmental authority applies formal penalties. (173)

Cultural transmission A school of criminology that argues that criminal behavior is learned through social interactions. (169)

Deviance Behavior that violates the standards of conduct or expectations of a group or society. (163)

Differential association A theory of deviance that holds that violation of rules results from exposure to attitudes favorable to criminal acts. (170)

Differential justice Differences in the way social control is exercised over different groups. (172)

Formal social control Social control that is carried out by authorized agents, such as police officers, judges, school administrators, and employers. (161)

Index crimes The eight types of crime reported annually by the FBI in the *Uniform Crime Reports:* murder, rape, robbery, assault, burglary, theft, motor vehicle theft, and arson. (174)

Informal social control Social control that is carried out casually by ordinary people through such means as laughter, smiles, and ridicule. (160)

Labeling theory An approach to deviance that attempts to explain why certain people are viewed as deviants while others engaged in the same behavior are not. (171)

Law Governmental social control. (161)

Obedience Compliance with higher authorities in a hierarchical structure. (159)

Organized crime The work of a group that regulates relations among criminal enterprises involved in illegal activities, including prostitution, gambling, and the smuggling and sale of illegal drugs. (175)

Professional criminal A person who pursues crime as a day-to-day occupation, developing skilled techniques and enjoying a certain degree of status among other criminals. (174)

Routine activities theory The notion that criminal victimization increases when motivated offenders and suitable targets converge. (170)

Sanction A penalty or reward for conduct concerning a social norm. (158)

Social constructionist perspective An approach to deviance that emphasizes the role of culture in the creation of the deviant identity. (171)

Social control The techniques and strategies for preventing deviant human behavior in any society. (158)

Societal-reaction approach Another name for *labeling theory*. (171)

Stigma A label used to devalue members of certain social groups. (164)

Transnational crime Crime that occurs across multiple national borders. (176)

Victimization survey A questionnaire or interview given to a sample of the population to determine whether people have been victims of crime. (178)

Victimless crime A term used by sociologists to describe the willing exchange among adults of widely desired, but illegal, goods and services. (174)

White-collar crime Illegal acts committed by affluent, "respectable" individuals in the course of business activities. (175)

Self-Quiz

Read each question carefully and then select the best answer.

1. Society brings about acceptance of basic norms through techniques and strategies for preventing deviant human behavior. This process is termed

   a. stigmatization.
   b. labeling.
   c. law.
   d. social control.

2. Which sociological perspective argues that people must respect social norms if any group or society is to survive?

   a. the conflict perspective
   b. the interactionist perspective
   c. the functionalist perspective
   d. the feminist perspective

3. Stanley Milgram used the word *conformity* to mean

   a. going along with peers.
   b. compliance with higher authorities in a hierarchical structure.
   c. techniques and strategies for preventing deviant behavior in any society.
   d. penalties and rewards for conduct concerning a social norm.

4. Which sociological theory suggests that our connection to members of society leads us to conform systematically to society's norms?

   a. feminist theory
   b. control theory
   c. interactionist theory
   d. functionalist theory

5. Which of the following statements is true of deviance?

   a. Deviance is always criminal behavior.
   b. Deviance is behavior that violates the standards of conduct or expectations of a group or society.
   c. Deviance is perverse behavior.
   d. Deviance is inappropriate behavior that cuts across all cultures and social orders.

6. Which sociologist illustrated the boundary-maintenance function of deviance in his study of Puritans in 17th-century New England?

   a. Kai Erikson
   b. Émile Durkheim
   c. Robert Merton
   d. Edwin Sutherland

7. Which of the following is *not* one of the basic forms of adaptation specified in Robert Merton's anomie theory of deviance?

   a. conformity
   b. innovation
   c. ritualism
   d. hostility

8. Which sociologist first advanced the idea that an individual undergoes the same basic socialization process whether learning conforming or deviant acts?

   a. Robert Merton
   b. Edwin Sutherland
   c. Travis Hirschi
   d. William Chambliss

9. Which of the following theories contends that criminal victimization increases when motivated offenders and suitable targets converge?

   a. labeling theory
   b. conflict theory
   c. routine activities theory
   d. differential association theory

10. Which of the following conducted observation research on two groups of high school males (the Saints and the Roughnecks) and concluded that social class played an important role in the varying fortunes of the two groups?

   a. Richard Quinney
   b. Edwin Sutherland
   c. Émile Durkheim
   d. William Chambliss

11. If we fail to respect and obey social norms, we may face punishment through informal or formal _____.

12. Police officers, judges, administrators, employers, military officers, and managers of movie theaters are all instruments of _____ social control.

13. Some norms are considered so important by a society that they are formalized into _____ controlling people's behavior.

14. It is important to underscore the fact that _____ is the primary source of conformity and obedience, including obedience to law.

15. _____ is a state of normlessness that typically occurs during a period of profound social change and disorder, such as a time of economic collapse.

16. Labeling theory is also called the _____-_____ approach.

17. _____ theorists view standards of deviant behavior as merely reflecting cultural norms; whereas _____ and _____ theorists point out that the most powerful groups in a society can shape laws and standards and determine who is (or is not) prosecuted as a criminal.

18. Organizations such as Mothers Against Drunk Driving (MADD) and Students Against Drunk Driving (SADD) have had success in recent years in shifting public attitudes toward drunkenness, so that it is no longer being viewed as a _____ crime.

19. Daniel Bell used the term _____ _____ to describe the process during which leadership of organized crime was transferred from Irish Americans to Jewish Americans and later to Italian Americans and others.

20. Consumer fraud, bribery, and income tax evasion are considered _____-_____ crimes.

{ TECHNOLOGY RESOURCES }

Online Learning Center

1. If you are interested in what people in the United States think about the death penalty, visit the student center of the Online Learning Center at **www.mhhe.com/schaefer7** and link to the Social Policy exercise for this chapter.

2. Whether or not marijuana should be legal for medicinal purposes is currently a controversial question in the United States. Explore the Web site of a group that advocates legalizing marijuana for such purposes, Americans for Safe Access (**www.safeaccessnow.org**). Do you agree with this group's views?

3. Can ordinary Americans take action to prevent crime? The Neighborhood Watch Program of the National Sheriff's Association believes that they can. Find out how by visiting their Web site at **www.usaonwatch.org.**

*Note: While all the URLs listed were current as of the printing of this book, these sites often change. Please check our Web site (**www.mhhe.com/schaefer7**) for updates, hyperlinks, and exercises related to these sites.*

Reel Society Video Clips

Reel Society video clips, which appear on this book's Web site, can be used to spark discussion about the following topics from this chapter:
- Conformity and Obedience
- Informal and Formal Social Control
- Deviance

8

Stratification and Social Mobility in the United States

inside

Understanding Stratification

Stratification by Social Class

Social Mobility

Social Policy and Stratification: Rethinking Welfare in North America and Europe

Boxes

Sociology in the Global Community: It's All Relative: Appalachian Poverty and Congolese Affluence

Research in Action: The Shrinking Middle Class

Sociology on Campus: Social Class and Financial Aid

Mark Lawson stuffs a 26th hot dog into his mouth, just enough to win an annual contest held in Beachwood, NJ.

ELSEWHERE IN AMERICA, 12 MILLION CHILDREN ARE FIGHTING HUNGER.

THE SOONER YOU BELIEVE IT, THE SOONER WE CAN END IT. Call 1-800-FEED KIDS, or visit feedingchildrenbetter.org to learn about child hunger in America.

In the United States, some people overindulge while others go hungry, as this public service advertisement reminds us. Social class stratification determines the distribution of resources in our society, from necessities such as food and shelter to relative luxuries such as higher education.

The man who washes cars does not own one. The clerk who files cancelled checks at the bank has $2.02 in her own account. The woman who copyedits medical textbooks has not been to a dentist in a decade.

This is the forgotten America. At the bottom of its working world, millions live in the shadow of prosperity, in the twilight between poverty and well-being. Whether you're rich, poor, or middle-class, you encounter them every day. They serve you Big Macs and help you find merchandise at Wal-Mart. They harvest your food, clean your offices, and sew your clothes. In a California factory, they package lights for your kids' bikes. In a New Hampshire plant, they assemble books of wallpaper samples to help you redecorate.

They are shaped by their invisible hardships. Some are climbing out of welfare, drug addiction, or homelessness. Others have been trapped for life in a perilous zone of low-wage work. Some of their children are malnourished. Some have been sexually abused. Some live in crumbling housing that contributes to their children's asthma, which means days absent from school. Some of their youngsters do not even have the eyeglasses they need to see the chalkboard clearly.

. . . While the United States has enjoyed unprecedented affluence, low-wage employees have been testing the American doctrine that hard work cures poverty. . . . Moving in and out of jobs that demand much and pay little, many people tread just above the official poverty line, dangerously close to the edge of destitution. An inconvenience to an affluent family—minor car trouble, a brief illness, disrupted child care—is a crisis to them, for it can threaten their ability to stay employed. They spend everything and save nothing. They are always behind on their bills. They have minuscule bank accounts or none at all, and so pay more fees and higher interest rates than more secure Americans. . . .

Breaking away and moving a comfortable distance from poverty seems to require a perfect lineup of favorable conditions. A set of skills, a good starting wage, and a job with the likelihood of promotion are prerequisites. But so are clarity of purpose, courageous self-esteem, a lack of substantial debt, the freedom from illness or addiction, a functional family, a network of upstanding friends, and the right help from private or governmental agencies. Any gap in that array is an entry point for trouble. . . . The American Myth still supposes that any individual from the humblest origins can climb to well-being. . . .

But the American Myth also provides a means of laying blame. . . . A harsh logic dictates a hard judgment: If a person's diligent work leads to prosperity, if work is a moral virtue, and if anyone in the society can attain prosperity through work, then the failure to do so is a fall from righteousness. . . .

There is an opposite extreme, the American Anti-Myth, which holds the society largely responsible for the individual's poverty. The hierarchy of racial discrimination and economic power creates a syndrome of impoverished communities with bad schools and closed options. The children of the poor are funneled into delinquency, drugs, or jobs with meager pay and little future. The individual is a victim of great forces beyond his control, including profit-hungry corporations that exploit his labor.

(Shipler 2005:3–6) Additional information about this excerpt can be found on the Online Learning Center at www.mhhe.com/schaefer7. ●

> *The man who washes cars does not own one. The clerk who files cancelled checks at the bank has $2.02 in her own account. The woman who copyedits medical textbooks has not been to a dentist in a decade.*

In this excerpt from his book *The Working Poor: Invisible in America*, Pulitzer Prize–winning journalist David K. Shipler highlights a segment of the population often overlooked by social scientists and policymakers. The working poor—Black, White, Asian American, Latino—are in fact a significant segment of the U.S. labor force. Yet as the book's title suggests, they are largely invisible to the better-off people who eat at the restaurants and visit the hotels where they work. Their very presence in an otherwise prosperous economy contradicts the long-held popular belief that in the United States, anyone who works hard can get ahead. Shipler, who clearly wishes this myth were a reality, claims the term *working poor* "should be an oxymoron. Nobody who works hard should be poor in America" (Shipler 2005:ix).

The Working Poor is based on Shipler's interviews with low-income farm, factory, and service workers throughout the United States, from New Hampshire to Chicago and Los Angeles. Shipler began meeting with them in 1997 in the housing projects, sweatshops, and clinics where they lived, worked, and sought medical care. Some of them he spoke with only once or twice; others he interviewed 15 to 20 times over the course of five or six years. Though Shipler's sample population was not necessarily representative, he did study people of all races and ethnic groups. The majority of his subjects were women, as are the majority of the United States' working poor.

Ever since people first began to speculate about the nature of human society, their attention has been drawn to the differences between individuals and groups within society. The term *social inequality* describes a condition in which members of society have different amounts of wealth, prestige, or power. Some degree of social inequality characterizes every society.

When a system of social inequality is based on a hierarchy of groups, sociologists refer to it as *stratification:* a structured ranking of entire groups of people that perpetuates unequal economic rewards and power in a society. These unequal rewards are evident not only in the distribution of wealth and income, but even in the distressing mortality rates of impoverished communities. Stratification involves the ways in which one generation passes on social inequalities to the next, producing groups of people arranged in rank order, from low to high.

Stratification is a crucial subject of sociological investigation because of its pervasive influence on human interactions and institutions. It results inevitably in social inequality, because certain groups of people stand higher in social rankings, control scarce resources, wield power, and receive special treatment. As we will see in this chapter, the consequences of stratification are evident in the unequal distribution of both wealth and income in industrial societies. The term **income** refers to salaries and wages. In contrast, **wealth** is an inclusive term encompassing all a person's material assets, including land, stocks, and other types of property.

Is social inequality an inescapable part of society? How does government policy affect the life chances of the working poor? Is this country still a place where a hardworking person can move up the social ladder? This chapter focuses on the unequal distribution of socially valued rewards and its consequences. We will examine four general systems of stratification, paying particular attention to the theories of Karl Marx and Max Weber, as well as to functionalist and conflict theory. We will see how sociologists define social class and examine the consequences of stratification for people's wealth and income, safety, and educational opportunities. And we will confront the question of social mobility, both upward and downward. Finally, in the Social Policy section, we will address welfare reform, an issue that is complicated by the attitudes that people, particularly those in the United States, hold toward those who do not work. ●

Understanding Stratification

Sociologists consider stratification on many levels, ranging from its impact on the individual to worldwide patterns of inequality. No matter where we look, however, disparities in wealth and income are substantial. Take income and poverty patterns in the United States, for example. As the top part of Figure 8-1 shows, in many states the median household income is 25 percent higher than that in other states. And as the bottom part of the figure shows, the poverty rate in many states is double that of other states. Later in this chapter we will address the meaning of such statistics. We'll begin our discussion here with an overview of the four basic systems of stratification. Then we'll see what sociologists have had to say on the subject of social inequality.

Systems of Stratification

Look at the four general systems of stratification examined here—slavery, castes, estates, and social classes—as ideal types useful for purposes of analysis. Any stratification system may include elements of more than one type. For example, prior to the Civil War, you could find in the southern states of the United States both social classes dividing Whites from Whites and the institutionalized enslavement of Blacks.

To understand these systems better, it may be helpful to review the distinction between *achieved status* and *ascribed status,* explained in Chapter 5. **Ascribed status** is a social position assigned to a person by society without regard for the person's unique talents or characteristics. In contrast, **achieved status** is a social po-

Classroom Tip See "Stimulating Classroom Discussion about *The Working Poor*" (Class Discussion Topics).
Methods Shipler used an interview approach in his study.
Theory The concepts of social inequality and stratification lie at the heart of conflict theory.

Student Alert Clarify the difference between income and wealth by noting that a family's wealth would include a home, car(s), possessions, investments, and insurance.
Theory Four general systems of stratification will be introduced in the chapter.

sition that a person attains largely {pp.102–103 through his or her own efforts. The two are closely linked. The nation's most affluent families generally inherit wealth and status, while many members of racial and ethnic minorities inherit disadvantaged status. Age and gender, as well, are ascribed statuses that influence a person's wealth and social position.

Slavery The most extreme form of legalized social inequality for individuals and groups is ***slavery.*** What distinguishes this oppressive system of stratification is that enslaved individuals are *owned* by other people, who treat these human beings as property, just as if they were household pets or appliances.

Slavery has varied in the way it has been practiced. In ancient Greece, the main source of slaves was piracy and captives of war. Although succeeding generations could inherit slave status, it was not necessarily permanent. A person's status might change, depending on which city-state happened to triumph in a military conflict. In effect, all citizens had the potential of becoming slaves or of receiving freedom, depending on the circumstances of history. In contrast, in the United States and Latin America, where slavery was an ascribed status, racial and legal barriers prevented the freeing of slaves.

Today, the Universal Declaration of Human Rights, which is binding on all members of the United Nations, prohibits slavery in all its forms. Yet around the world, millions of people still live as slaves. In many developing countries, bonded laborers are imprisoned in virtual lifetime employment; in some countries, human beings are owned outright. But a form of slavery also exists in Europe and the United States, where guest workers and illegal immigrants have been forced to labor for years under terrible conditions, either to pay off debts or to avoid being turned over to immigration authorities (Cockburn 2003).

Castes *Castes* are hereditary ranks that are usually religiously dictated, and that tend to be fixed and immobile. The caste system is generally associated with

FIGURE 8– **187**

The 50 States: Haves and Have-Nots

MAPPING LIFE

NATIONWIDE www.mhhe.com /schaefer7

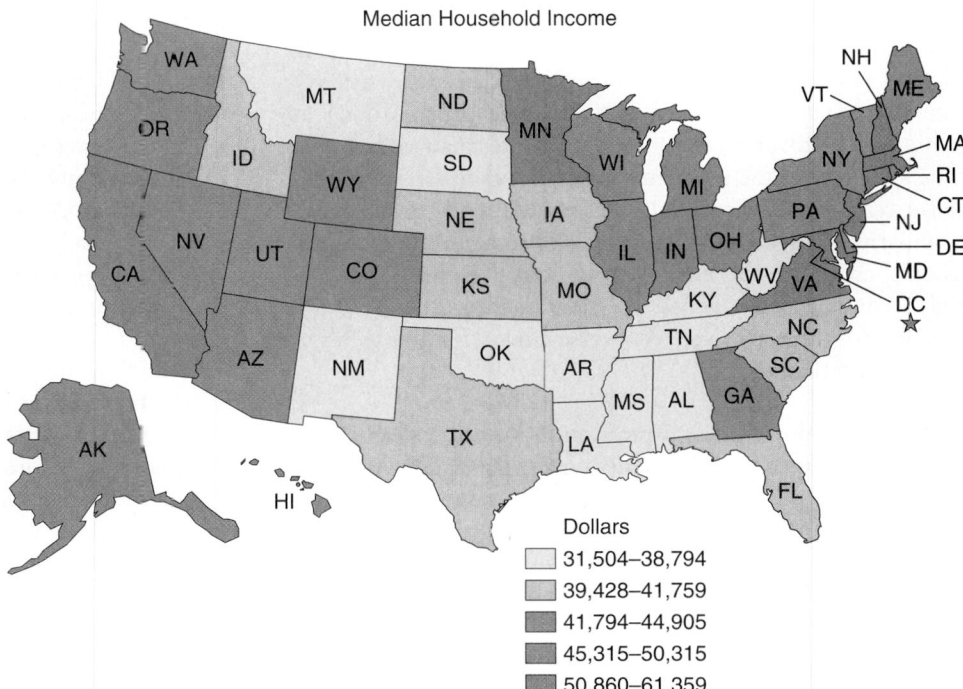

Median Household Income

Dollars
- 31,504–38,794
- 39,428–41,759
- 41,794–44,905
- 45,315–50,315
- 50,860–61,359

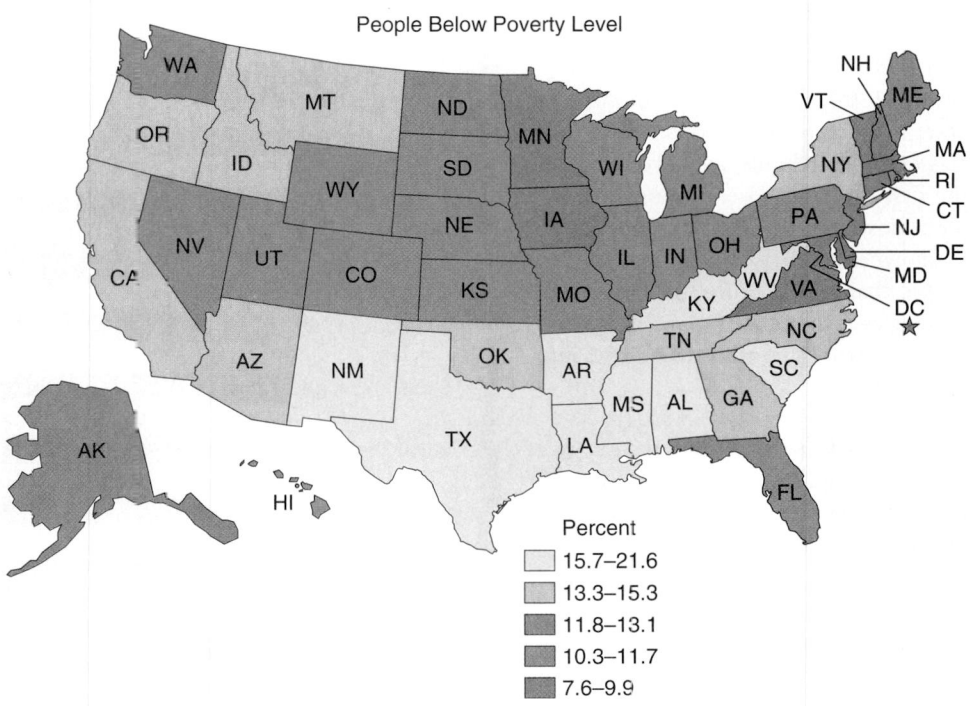

People Below Poverty Level

Percent
- 15.7–21.6
- 13.3–15.3
- 11.8–13.1
- 10.3–11.7
- 7.6–9.9

Source: 2004 census data presented in Fronczek 2005.

Hinduism in India and other countries. In India there are four major castes, called *varnas.* A fifth category of outcastes, referred to as the *dalit,* or *untouchables,* is considered to be so lowly and unclean as to have no place within this system of stratification. There are also many minor castes. Caste membership is an ascribed status (at birth, children automatically assume the same position as their parents). Each caste is quite sharply defined, and members are expected to marry within that caste.

In 1950, after gaining independence from Great Britain, India adopted a new constitution that formally outlawed the caste system. Over the last decade or two, however, urbanization and technological advances have brought more change to India's caste system than the government or politics has in more than half a century. The anonymity of city life tends to blur caste boundaries, allowing the *dalit* to pass unrecognized in temples, schools, and places of employment. And the globalization of high technology has opened up India's social order, bringing new opportunities to those who possess the skills and ability to capitalize on them.

Estates A third type of stratification system, called *estates,* was associated with feudal societies during the Middle Ages. The **estate system,** or *feudalism,* required peasants to work land leased to them by nobles in exchange for military protection and other services. The basis for the system was the nobles' ownership of land, which was critical to their superior and privileged status. As in systems based on slavery and caste, inheritance of one's position largely defined the estate system. The nobles inherited their titles and property; the peasants were born into a subservient position within an agrarian society.

As the estate system developed, it became more differentiated. Nobles began to achieve varying degrees of authority. By the 12th century, a priesthood had emerged in most of Europe, along with classes of merchants and artisans. For the first time there were groups of people whose wealth did not depend on land ownership or agriculture. This economic change had profound social consequences as the estate system ended and a class system of stratification came into existence.

Social Classes A **class system** is a social ranking based primarily on economic position in which achieved characteristics can influence social mobility. In contrast to slavery and caste systems, the boundaries between classes are imprecisely defined, and one can move from one stratum, or level, of society to another. Even so, class systems maintain stable stratification hierarchies and patterns of class divisions, and they, too, are marked by unequal distribution of wealth and power. Class standing, though it is achieved, is heavily dependent on family and ascribed factors, such as race and ethnicity.

Income inequality is a basic characteristic of a class system. In 2004, the median household income in the United States was $44,389. In other words, half of all households had higher incomes in that year and half had lower incomes. But this fact does not fully convey the income disparities in our society. As Figure 8-2 shows, there is a broad range around the median household income. Furthermore, considerable numbers of people fall at the extremes. In 2000, about 240,000 tax returns reported incomes in excess of $1 million. At the same time, about 20 million households reported incomes under $9,000 (Bureau of the Census 2003a:332; DeNavas-Walt et al. 2005).

Sociologist Daniel Rossides (1997) uses a five-class model to describe the class system of the United States: the upper class, the upper-middle class, the lower-middle class, the working class, and the lower class. Although the lines separating social classes in his model are not so sharp as the divisions between castes, members of the five classes differ significantly in ways other than just income level.

Rossides categorizes about 1 to 2 percent of the people of the United States as *upper class,* a group limited to the very wealthy. These people associate in exclusive clubs and social circles. In contrast, the *lower class,* consisting of approximately 20 to 25 percent of the population, disproportionately consists of Blacks, Hispanics, single mothers with dependent children, and people who cannot find regular work or must make do with low-paying work. This class lacks both wealth and income and is too weak politically to exercise significant power.

FIGURE 8–2

Household Income in the United States, 2004

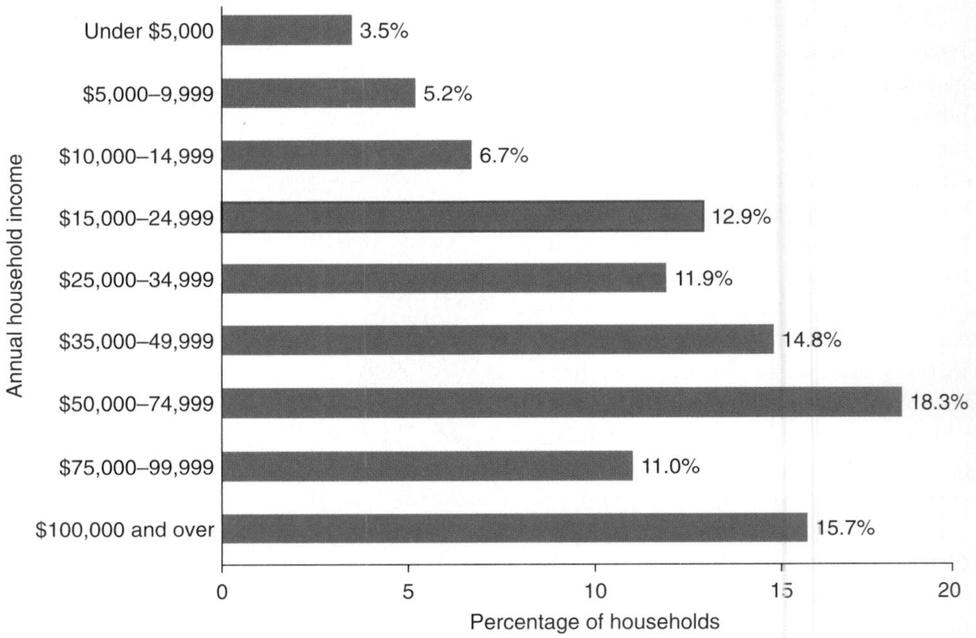

Source: DeNavas-Walt et al. 2005:31.

Global View Caste system in India and other countries.
Let's Discuss How does sexual and racial inequality in today's United States resemble a caste system?
Reel Society Several scenes in *Reel Society* address stratification. See Stratification—Gender, Stratification—Race/Ethnicity, and Stratification—Religion in the Topic Index.

Let's Discuss Can you describe the various social hierarchies that exist on your college campus? Among sororities and fraternities (if any)? In the college's administrative structure?
Let's Discuss If data are available from your admissions office, identify the income distribution of students' families.
Key Person Daniel Rossides

Supersized homes like this one typically belong to upper-middle-class families, who may also enjoy vacation retreats and luxury condos in the city. These conspicuous homes mark their owners as members of a privileged 10 to 15 percent of the population—just shy of the truly wealthy 1 or 2 percent who constitute the upper class.

Both these classes, at opposite ends of the nation's social hierarchy, reflect the importance of ascribed status and achieved status. Ascribed statuses such as race clearly influence a person's wealth and social position. Sociologist Richard Jenkins (1991) has shown how the ascribed status of being disabled marginalizes a person in the U.S. labor market. People with disabilities are particularly vulnerable to unemployment, are often poorly paid, and tend to occupy the lower rung of the occupational ladder. Regardless of their actual performance on the job, the disabled are stigmatized as not earning their keep. Such are the effects of ascribed status.

Sandwiched between the upper and lower classes in this model are the upper-middle class, the lower-middle class, and the working class. The *upper-middle class*, numbering about 10 to 15 percent of the population, is composed of professionals such as doctors, lawyers, and architects. They participate extensively in politics and take leadership roles in voluntary associations. The *lower-middle class*, which accounts for approximately 30 to 35 percent of the population, includes less affluent professionals (such as elementary school teachers and nurses), owners of small businesses, and a sizable number of clerical workers. While not all members of this varied class hold degrees from a

college, they share the goal of sending their children there. This class is currently under a great deal of economic pressure: Box 8-1 (page 190) discusses the shrinking size of the middle class.

Rossides describes the *working class*—about 40 to 45 percent of the population—as people who hold regular manual or blue-collar jobs. Certain members of this class, such as electricians, may have higher incomes than people in the lower-middle class. Yet even if they have achieved some degree of economic security, they tend to identify with manual workers and their long history of involvement in the labor movement of the United States. Of the five classes, the working class is declining noticeably in size. In the economy of the United States, service and technical jobs are replacing those involved in the actual manufacturing or transportation of goods.

Social class is one of the independent or explanatory variables most frequently used by social scientists to shed light on social issues. In later chapters, we will analyze the relationships between social class and child rearing (Chapter 12), religious affiliation (Chapter 13), and formal schooling (Chapter 13), as well as other relationships in which social class is a variable.

Perspectives on Stratification

Sociologists have hotly debated stratification and social inequality and have reached varying conclusions. No theorist stressed the significance of class for society—and for social change—more strongly than Karl Marx. Marx viewed class differentiation as the crucial determinant of social, economic, and political inequality. In contrast, Max Weber questioned Marx's emphasis on the overriding importance of the economic sector, and argued that stratification should be viewed as having many dimensions.

Karl Marx's View of Class Differentiation Karl Marx has been aptly described as both a revolutionary and a social scientist. Marx was concerned with stratification in all types of human societies, beginning with primitive agricultural tribes and continuing into feudalism. But his main focus was on the effects of economic inequality on all aspects of 19th-century Europe. The plight of the working class made him feel that it was imperative to strive for changes in the class structure of society (Beeghley 1978:1).

In Marx's view, social relations during any period of history depend on who controls the primary mode of economic production, such as land or factories. Differential access to scarce resources shapes the relationship between groups. Thus, under the feudal estate system, most production was agricultural, and the land was owned by the nobility. Peasants had little choice but to work according to terms dictated by those who owned the land.

Using this type of analysis, Marx examined social relations within ***capitalism***—an economic system in which the means of production are held largely in private hands and the main incentive for economic activity is the accumulation of profits (D. Rosenberg 1991). Marx focused on the two classes that began to emerge as the feudal estate system declined, the bourgeoisie and the proletariat. The ***bourgeoisie,*** or capitalist class, owns the

Classroom Tip See "Inequality in Taking Quizzes" (Class Discussion Topics).
Classroom Tip See "Status Inconsistency—Janitors and Tenants" (Additional Lecture Ideas).

Classroom Tip Divide the class into four to six groups. Make each group responsible for preparing a slide presentation or picture cutout display illustrating a different economic lifestyle in the area. Prepare the assignment so that the cost to students is minimal.
Key Person Karl Marx
Theory Karl Marx's pioneering work is the basis of contemporary conflict theory.

researchINaction

8-1 The Shrinking Middle Class

The cherished belief that the poor can rise to middle-class status has long been central to the United States' reputation as a land of opportunity. However, according to Lester C. Thurow, noted professor of economics and management at the Massachusetts Institute of Technology, the American middle-class is disappearing. Using a widely accepted definition of a middle-class household as one whose income falls between 75 and 125 percent of the nation's median household income (that is, between $33,300 and $55,500), only about 20 percent of American households would have been classified as middle class in 2004, compared to 28 percent in 1967.

Closer analysis by Thurow indicates that of those who relinquished their middle-class standing during this period, about half rose to a higher ranking in the social class system, while half dropped to a lower position. In Thurow's view, these data mean that the United States is moving toward a "bipolar income distribution." That is, a broadly based middle class is slowly being replaced by two growing groups of rich and poor.

Sociologists and other scholars have identified several factors that have contributed to the shrinking size of the middle class:

- *Disappearing opportunities for those with little education.* In *The Working Poor,* highlighted at the beginning of this chapter, David Shipler tells how his grandfather rose from an eight-cent-an-hour job on the Jersey City docks to the presidency of Bethlehem Steel's steamship lines. Such opportunities are disappearing fast, yet to-

day, less than a third of adults between ages 35 and 44 have prepared themselves with a college degree.

- *Global competition and rapid advances in technology.* These two trends, which began several decades ago, have rendered workers more replaceable than they once were. Increasingly, they are affecting the more complex jobs that were once the bread and butter of middle-class workers. Experts disagree on whether they represent a permanent setback to the workforce or the

> *According to Lester C. Thurow, noted professor of economics and management at the Massachusetts Institute of Technology, the American middle class is disappearing.*

foundation for new industries that will someday generate millions of new jobs. In the meantime, however, U.S. households are struggling.

- *Growing dependence on the temporary workforce.* Some workers depend on temporary jobs for a second income, in order to maintain their middle-class lifestyle. For those workers who have no other job, these positions are tenuous at best, because they rarely offer health care coverage or retirement benefits.

- *The rise of new growth industries and nonunion workplaces.* In the past, workers in heavy industry were able to achieve middle-class incomes through the efforts of strong labor unions. But today, the growth areas in the economy are fast-food restaurants and large retail outlets. Though these industries have added employment opportunities, they are at the lower end of the wage scale.

In response to these concerns, observers note that living standards in the United States are improving. Middle-class families want large homes, college degrees for their children, and high-quality health care—the cost of which has been growing faster than inflation. The answer, for many people, is either to go without or to work longer hours at multiple jobs.

Let's Discuss

1. Does your family belong to the middle class? If so, in what generation did your family achieve that status, and how? Are your parents struggling to maintain a middle-class lifestyle?
2. For the nation as a whole, what are the dangers of a shrinking middle class?

Sources: Bureau of the Census 2005a:148; DeNavas-Walt et al. 2005:HINC-01; Greenblatt 2005; Shipler 2005; Witte 2005.

---

means of production, such as factories and machinery; the **proletariat** is the working class. In capitalist societies, the members of the bourgeoisie maximize profit in competition with other firms. In the process, they exploit workers, who must exchange their labor for subsistence wages. In Marx's view, members of each class share a distinctive culture. Marx was most interested in the culture of the proletariat, but he also examined the ideology of the bourgeoisie, through which that class justifies its dominance over workers.

According to Marx, exploitation of the proletariat will inevitably lead to the destruction of the capitalist system, because the workers will revolt. But first, the working class must develop **class consciousness**—a subjective awareness of common vested interests and the need for collective political action to bring about social change. Often, workers must overcome what Marx termed **false consciousness,** or an attitude held by members of a class that does not accurately reflect their objective position. A worker with false consciousness may adopt an individualistic viewpoint toward capitalist exploitation ("*I* am being exploited by *my* boss"). In contrast, the class-conscious worker realizes that all workers are being exploited by the bourgeoisie, and have a common stake in revolution.

Key Person Lester C. Thurow
Let's Discuss What proportion of this sociology class is middle class? What does the answer imply about income and education?
Race/Ethnicity Explore racial and ethnic patterns in the shrinking middle class.
Let's Discuss How many jobs do you have? Your parents?

Student Alert Labor unions are addressed in the Social Policy section of Chapter 5.

Karl Marx would identify these coal miners as members of the *proletariat,* or working class. For generations, miners were forced to spend their meager wages at "company stores," whose high prices kept them perpetually in debt. The exploitation of the working class is a core principle of Marxist theory.

For Marx, class consciousness was part of a collective process in which the proletariat comes to identify the bourgeoisie as the source of its oppression. Revolutionary leaders will guide the working class in its struggle. Ultimately, the proletariat will overthrow the rule of both the bourgeoisie and the government (which Marx saw as representing the interests of capitalists) and will eliminate private ownership of the means of production. In Marx's rather utopian view, classes and oppression will cease to exist in the postrevolutionary workers' state.

How accurate were Marx's predictions? He failed to anticipate the emergence of labor unions, whose power in collective bargaining weakens the stranglehold that capitalists maintain over workers. Moreover, as contemporary conflict theorists note, he did not foresee the extent to which political liberties and relative prosperity could contribute to false consciousness. Many workers have come to view themselves as individuals striving for improvement within free societies that offer substantial mobility, rather than as downtrodden members of a social class who face a collective fate. Finally, Marx did not predict that Communist Party rule would be established and later overthrown in the former Soviet Union and throughout Eastern Europe. Still, the Marxist approach to the study of class is useful in stressing the importance of stratification as a determinant of social behavior and the fundamental separation in many societies between two distinct groups, the rich and the poor.

Max Weber's View of Stratification Unlike Karl Marx, Max Weber insisted that no single characteristic (such as class) totally defines a person's position within the stratification system. Instead, writing in 1916, he identified three distinct components of stratification: class, status, and power (Gerth and Mills 1958).

Weber used the term ***class*** to refer to a group of people who have a similar level of wealth and income. For example, certain workers in the United States try to support their families through minimum-wage jobs. According to Weber's definition, these wage earners constitute a class because they share the same economic position and fate. Although Weber agreed with Marx on the importance of this economic dimension of stratification, he argued that the actions of individuals and groups cannot be understood *solely* in economic terms.

Weber used the term ***status group*** to refer to people who have the same prestige or lifestyle. An individual gains status through membership in a desirable group, such as the medical profession. But status is not the same as economic class standing. In our culture, a successful pickpocket may belong to the same income class as a college professor. Yet the thief is widely regarded as a member of a low-status group, whereas the professor holds high status.

For Weber, the third major component of stratification has a political dimension. ***Power*** is the ability to exercise one's will over others. In the United States, power stems from membership in particularly influential groups, such as corporate boards of directors, government bodies, and interest groups. Conflict theorists generally agree that two major sources of power—big business and government—are closely interrelated (see Chapter 14). For instance, many of the heads of major corporations also hold powerful positions in the government or military.

The corporate executives who head private companies in the United States earn the highest incomes in the nation. In fact, the gap between their salaries and those of the average worker has widened significantly over time. In 1940, half of all U.S. executives earned more than 58 times the average worker's pay; by 2006, the multiple was 104. These highly compensated individuals represent the pinnacle not just of U.S. society, but of corporate executives around the world. Heads of U.S. corporations are paid significantly better than chief executive officers (CEOs) in other industrial countries. Even when their performance is less than stellar, many of them receive handsome raises. Data reported in 2006 show that of the 49 largest U.S. corporations performing *at a loss* recently, 29 actually increased their CEOs' salaries (Dash 2006; McCall 2006).

To summarize, in Weber's view, each of us has not one rank in society but three. Our position in a stratification system reflects some combination of class, status, and power. Each factor influences the other two, and in fact the rankings on these three dimensions often tend to coincide. John F. Kennedy came from an extremely wealthy family, attended exclusive preparatory schools, graduated from Harvard University, and went on to become president of the United States. Like Kennedy, many people from affluent backgrounds achieve impressive status and power.

This family's expensive lifestyle illustrates Thorstein Veblen's concept of conspicuous consumption, a spending pattern common to those at the very top of the social ladder.

Interactionist View Both Karl Marx and Max Weber looked at inequality primarily from a macrosociological perspective, considering the entire society or even the global economy. Marx did suggest the importance of a more microsociological analysis, however, when he stressed the ways in which individuals develop a true class consciousness.

Interactionists, as well as economists, have long been interested in the importance of social class in shaping a person's lifestyle. The theorist Thorstein Veblen (1857–1929) noted that those at the top of the social hierarchy typically convert part of their wealth into *conspicuous consumption,* purchasing more automobiles than they can reasonably use and building houses with more rooms than they can possibly occupy. Or they may engage in *conspicuous leisure,* jetting to a remote destination and staying just long enough to have dinner or view a sunset over some historic locale (Veblen [1899] 1964).

At the other end of the spectrum, behavior that is judged to be typical of the lower class is subject not only to ridicule but even to legal action. Communities have, from time to time, banned trailers from people's front yards and sofas from their front porches. In some communities, it is illegal to leave a pickup truck in front of the house overnight.

Use Your Sociological Imagination
www.mhhe.com /schaefer7

Refer to the photo essay on pages 4–5. How do you think Thorstein Veblen would answer the question posed in the title? What do you think he would say about the three families pictured in the essay?

Contemporary Culture In what specific ways do Americans engage in conspicuous consumption and conspicuous leisure?

Is Stratification Universal?

Must some members of society receive greater rewards than others? Do people need to feel socially and economically superior to others? Can social life be organized without structured inequality? These questions have been debated for centuries, especially among political activists. Utopian socialists, religious minorities, and members of recent countercultures have all attempted to establish communities that to some extent or other would abolish inequality in social relationships.

Social scientists have found that inequality exists in all societies—even the simplest. For example, when anthropologist Gunnar Landtman ([1938] 1968) studied the Kiwai Papuans of New Guinea, at first he noticed little differentiation among them. Every man in the village did the same work and lived in similar housing. However, on closer inspection, Landtman observed that certain Papuans—men who were warriors, harpooners, and sorcerers—were described as "a little more high" than others. In contrast, villagers who were female, unemployed, or unmarried were considered "down a little bit" and were barred from owning land.

Stratification is universal in that all societies maintain some form of social inequality among members. Depending on its values, a society may assign people to distinctive ranks based on their religious knowledge, skill in hunting, beauty, trading expertise, or ability to provide health care. But why has such inequality developed in human societies? And how much differentiation among people, if any, is actually essential?

Functionalist and conflict sociologists offer contrasting explanations for the existence and necessity of social stratification. Functionalists maintain that a differential system of rewards and punishments is necessary for the efficient operation of society. Conflict theorists argue that competition for scarce resources results in significant political, economic, and social inequality.

Functionalist View Would people go to school for many years to become physicians if they could make as much money and gain as much respect working as street cleaners? Functionalists say no, which is partly why they believe that a stratified society is universal.

In the view of Kingsley Davis and Wilbert Moore (1945), society must distribute its members among a variety of social positions. It must not only make sure that these positions are filled but also see that they are staffed by people with the appropriate talents and abilities. Rewards, including money and prestige, are based on the importance of a position and the relative scarcity of qualified personnel. Yet this assessment often devalues work performed by certain segments of society, such as women's work in the home or in occupations traditionally filled by women, or low-status work in fast-food outlets.

Davis and Moore argue that stratification is universal and that social inequality is necessary so that people will be motivated to fill functionally important positions. But critics say that unequal

Methods Landtman conducted observation research among the Kiwai Papuans. Global View Differentiation among the Kiwai Papuans of New Guinea

rewards are not the only means of encouraging people to fill critical positions and occupations. Personal pleasure, intrinsic satisfaction, and value orientations also motivate people to enter particular careers. Functionalists agree, but they note that society must use some type of reward to motivate people to enter unpleasant or dangerous jobs and professions that require a long training period. This response does not justify stratification systems in which status is largely inherited, such as slave or caste societies. Similarly, it is difficult to explain the high salaries our society offers to professional athletes or entertainers on the basis of how critical those jobs are to the survival of society. And even if stratification is inevitable, the functionalist explanation for differential rewards does not explain the wide disparity between the rich and the poor (Collins 1975; Kerbo 2003; Tumin 1953, 1985).

As popular songs and movies suggest, long-haul truck drivers take pride in their low-prestige job. According to the conflict perspective, the cultural beliefs that form a society's dominant ideology, such as the popular image of the truck driver as hero, help the wealthy to maintain their power and control at the expense of the lower classes.

Conflict View The writings of Karl Marx lie at the heart of {p.11} conflict theory. Marx viewed history as a continuous struggle between the oppressors and the oppressed, which ultimately would culminate in an egalitarian, classless society. In terms of stratification, he argued that under capitalism, the dominant class—the bourgeoisie—manipulates the economic and political systems in order to maintain control over the exploited proletariat. Marx did not believe that stratification was inevitable, but he did see inequality and oppression as inherent in capitalism (E. O. Wright et al. 1982).

Like Marx, contemporary conflict theorists believe that human beings are prone to conflict over scarce resources such as wealth, status, and power. However, Marx focused primarily on class conflict; more recent theorists have extended the analysis to include conflicts based on gender, race, age, and other dimensions. British sociologist Ralf Dahrendorf is one of the most influential contributors to the conflict approach.

Dahrendorf (1959) has modified Marx's analysis of capitalist society to apply to *modern* capitalist societies. For Dahrendorf, social classes are groups of people who share common interests resulting from their authority relationships. In identifying the most powerful groups in society, he includes not only the bourgeoisie—the owners of the means of production—but also the managers of industry, legislators, the judiciary, heads of the government bureaucracy, and others. In that respect, Dahrendorf has merged Marx's emphasis on class conflict with Weber's recognition that power is an important element of stratification (Cuff et al. 1990).

Conflict theorists, including Dahrendorf, contend that the powerful of today, like the bourgeoisie of Marx's time, want society to run smoothly so that they can enjoy their privileged positions. Because the status quo suits those with wealth, status, and power, they have a clear interest in preventing, minimizing, or controlling societal conflict.

One way for the powerful to maintain the status quo is to define and disseminate the society's dominant ideology. The term

{p.67} *dominant ideology* describes a set of cultural beliefs and practices that helps to maintain powerful social, economic, and political interests. For Karl Marx, the dominant ideology in a capitalist society served the interests of the ruling class. From a conflict perspective, the social significance of the dominant ideology is that not only do a society's most powerful groups and institutions control wealth and property; even more important, they control the means of producing beliefs about reality through religion, education, and the media (Abercrombie et al. 1980, 1990; Robertson 1988).

The powerful, such as leaders of government, also use limited social reforms to buy off the oppressed and reduce the danger of challenges to their dominance. For example, minimum wage laws and unemployment compensation unquestionably give some valuable assistance to needy men and women. Yet these reforms also serve to pacify those who might otherwise rebel. Of course, in the view of conflict theorists, such maneuvers can never entirely eliminate conflict, since workers will continue to demand equality, and the powerful will not give up their control of society.

Conflict theorists see stratification as a major source of societal tension and conflict. They do not agree with Davis and Moore that stratification is functional for a society or that it serves as a source of stability. Rather, conflict sociologists argue that stratification will inevitably lead to instability and social change (Collins 1975; Coser 1977).

Table 8-1 (page 194) summarizes and compares the three major perspectives on social stratification.

Theory Functionalist and conflict views of the existence of stratification are contrasted.
Theory Conflict view of stratification introduced
Key Person Ralf Dahrendorf

Theory Conflict view of the social significance of the dominant ideology
Classroom Tip See "Comparison of Perspectives on Stratification" (Additional Lecture Ideas).

Table 8-1 Sociological Perspectives on Social Stratification

	Functionalist	Conflict	Interactionist
Purpose of social stratification	Facilitates filling of social positions	Facilitates exploitation	Influences people's lifestyles
Attitude toward social inequality	Necessary to some extent	Excessive and growing	—
Analysis of the wealthy	Talented and skilled, creating opportunities for others	Use the dominant ideology to further their own interests	Exhibit conspicuous consumption and conspicuous leisure

Lenski's Viewpoint Let's return to the question posed earlier—Is stratification universal?—and consider the sociological response. Some form of differentiation is found in every culture, from the most primitive to the most advanced industrial societies of our time. Sociologist Gerhard Lenski, in his sociocultural evolution approach, described how economic systems change as their level of technology becomes more complex, beginning with hunting and gathering and culminating eventually with industrial society.

In subsistence-based hunting-and-gathering societies, people focus on survival. While some inequality and differentiation are {pp.116–117 evident, a stratification system based on social class does not emerge because there is no real wealth to be claimed. As a society advances technologically, it becomes capable of producing a considerable surplus of goods. The emergence of surplus resources greatly expands the possibilities for inequality in status, influence, and power, allowing a well-defined, rigid social class system to develop. To minimize strikes, slowdowns, and industrial sabotage, the elites may share a portion of the economic surplus with the lower classes, but not enough to reduce their own power and privilege.

As Lenski argued, the allocation of surplus goods and services controlled by those with wealth, status, and power reinforces the social inequality that accompanies stratification systems. While this reward system may once have served the overall purposes of society, as functionalists contend, the same cannot be said for the large disparities separating the haves from the have-nots in current societies. In contemporary industrial society, the degree of social and economic inequality far exceeds what is needed to provide for goods and services (Lenski 1966; Nolan and Lenski 2006).

Stratification by Social Class

Measuring Social Class

We continually assess how wealthy people are by looking at the cars they drive, the houses they live in, the clothes they wear, and so on. Yet it is not so easy to locate an individual within our social hierarchies as it would be in slavery or caste systems of stratification. To determine someone's class position, sociologists generally rely on the objective method.

Objective Method In the *objective method* of measuring social class, class is viewed largely as a statistical category. Re-

searchers assign individuals to social classes on the basis of criteria such as occupation, education, income, and place of residence. The key to the objective method is that the *researcher*, rather than the person being classified, identifies an individual's class position.

The first step in using this method is to decide what indicators or causal factors will be measured objectively, whether wealth, income, education, or occupation. The prestige ranking of occupations has proved to be a useful indicator of a person's class position. For one thing, it is much easier to determine accurately than income or wealth. The term **prestige** refers to the respect and admiration that an occupation holds in a society. "My daughter, the physicist" connotes something very different from "my daughter, the waitress." Prestige is independent of the particular individual who occupies a job, a characteristic that distinguishes it from esteem. **Esteem** refers to the reputation that a specific person has earned within an occupation. Therefore, one can say that the position of president of the United States has high prestige, even though it has been occupied by people with varying degrees of esteem. A hairdresser may have the esteem of his clients, but he lacks the prestige of a corporate executive.

Table 8-2 ranks the prestige of a number of well-known occupations. In a series of national surveys, sociologists assigned prestige rankings to about 500 occupations, ranging from physician to newspaper vendor. The highest possible prestige score was 100; the lowest was 0. Physician, lawyer, dentist, and college professor were the most highly regarded occupations. Sociologists have used such data to assign prestige rankings to virtually all jobs and have found a stability in rankings from 1925 to the present. Similar studies in other countries have also developed useful prestige rankings of occupations (Hodge and Rossi 1964; Lin and Xie 1988; Treiman 1977).

Gender and Occupational Prestige For many years, studies of social class tended to neglect the occupations and incomes of *women* as determinants of social rank. With more than half of all married women now working outside the home (see Chapter 11), this approach seems outmoded. How should we judge class or status in dual-career families—by the occupation regarded as having greater prestige, the average, or some other combination of the two? Sociologists—in particular, feminist sociologists in Great Britain—are drawing on new approaches to assess women's social class standing. One approach is

Key Person Gerhard Lenski
Theory Lenski's view of stratification synthesizes the functionalist and conflict approaches.

Gender Studies of social class tend to neglect the occupations and incomes of women as determinants of social rank.
Theory Feminist sociologists would emphasize the inequality of basing class and status solely on the husband's position.
Classroom Tip For other ways to measure class, see "Measuring Social Class—Subjective and Reputational Methods" (Additional Lecture Ideas).

Table 8-2   Prestige Rankings of Occupations

Occupation	Score	Occupation	Score
Physician	86	Secretary	46
Lawyer	75	Insurance agent	45
Dentist	74	Bank teller	43
College professor	74	Nurse's aide	42
Architect	73	Farmer	40
Clergy	69	Correctional officer	40
Pharmacist	68	Receptionist	39
Registered nurse	66	Carpenter	39
High school teacher	66	Barber	36
Accountant	65	Child care worker	35
Elementary school teacher	64	Hotel clerk	32
Airline pilot	60	Bus driver	32
Police officer or detective	60	Auto body repairer	31
Prekindergarten teacher	55	Truck driver	30
Librarian	54	Salesworker (shoes)	28
Firefighter	53	Garbage collector	28
Social worker	52	Waiter and waitress	28
Dental hygienist	52	Bartender	25
Electrician	51	Farm worker	23
Funeral director	49	Janitor	22
Mail carrier	47	Newspaper vendor	19

Note: 100 is the highest and 0 the lowest possible prestige score.
Source: J. Davis et al. 2005:2050–2051.

to focus on the individual (rather than the family or household) as the basis for categorizing a woman's class position. Thus, a woman would be classified according to her own occupational status rather than that of her spouse (M. O'Donnell 1992).

Another feminist effort to measure the contribution of women to the economy reflects a more clearly political agenda. International Women Count Network, a global grassroots feminist organization, has sought to give a monetary value to women's unpaid work. Besides providing symbolic recognition of women's role in labor, this value would also be used to calculate pension and other benefits that are based on wages received. The United Nations has placed an $11 trillion price tag on unpaid labor by women, largely in child care, housework, and agriculture. Whatever the figure, the continued undercounting of many workers' contributions to a family and to an entire economy means that virtually all measures of stratification are in need of reform (United Nations Development Programme 1995; Wages for Housework Campaign 1999).

Multiple Measures Another complication in measuring social class is that advances in statistical methods and computer technology have multiplied the factors used to define class under the objective method. No longer are sociologists limited to annual income and education in evaluating a person's class position. Today, studies use as criteria the value of homes, sources of income, assets, years in present occupations, neighborhoods, and considerations regarding dual careers. Adding these variables will not necessarily paint a different picture of class differentiation in the United States, but it does allow sociologists to measure class in a more complex and multidimensional way.

Whatever the technique used to measure class, the sociologist is interested in real and often dramatic differences in power, privilege, and opportunity in a society. The study of stratification is a study of inequality. Nowhere is the truth of that statement more evident than in the distribution of wealth and income.

Wealth and Income

By all measures, income in the United States is distributed unevenly. Nobel Prize–winning economist Paul Samuelson has described the situation in the following words: "If we made an income pyramid out of building blocks, with each layer portraying $500 of income, the peak would be far higher than Mount Everest, but most people would be within a few feet of the ground" (P. Samuelson and Nordhaus 2005:383).

Recent data support Samuelson's analogy. Figure 8-3 (page 196) shows the distribution of U.S. income for 2004 in the form of a needle-nosed pyramid. In that year those fortunate Americans who received $1 million or more in income formed a very select group representing only 0.5 percent of the population. The top 20 percent of the nation's population received incomes of $88,029 or more. In contrast, members of the bottom fifth of the nation's population received just $18,500 or less. Note the bottom-heavy nature of the income distribution: except at the base of the graph, the lower the income level, the greater the percentage of the population receiving that income (DeNavas-Walt et al. 2005:40).

There has been a modest redistribution of income in the United States over the past 75 years. From 1929 through 1970, the government's economic and tax policies shifted some income to the poor. However, in the last three decades—especially the 1980s—federal tax policies have favored the affluent. Moreover, while the salaries of highly skilled workers and professionals have continued to rise, the wages of less skilled workers have *decreased* when controlled for inflation. As a result, the Census Bureau reports that regardless of the measure used, income inequality rose substantially from 1967 through the end of

Methods NORC survey data on occupational prestige
Classroom Tip See "NORC Prestige Rankings" (Class Discussion Topics).
Methods Additional scores: engineer 71, veterinarian 62, legislator 61, musician 47, motion picture projectionist 38, miner 29, elevator operator 28
Global View International effort to assign a monetary value to the contribution that women make to the economy

Theory Conflict theorists emphasize that federal budgetary policies have favored the affluent.

U.S. Income Pyramid, 2004

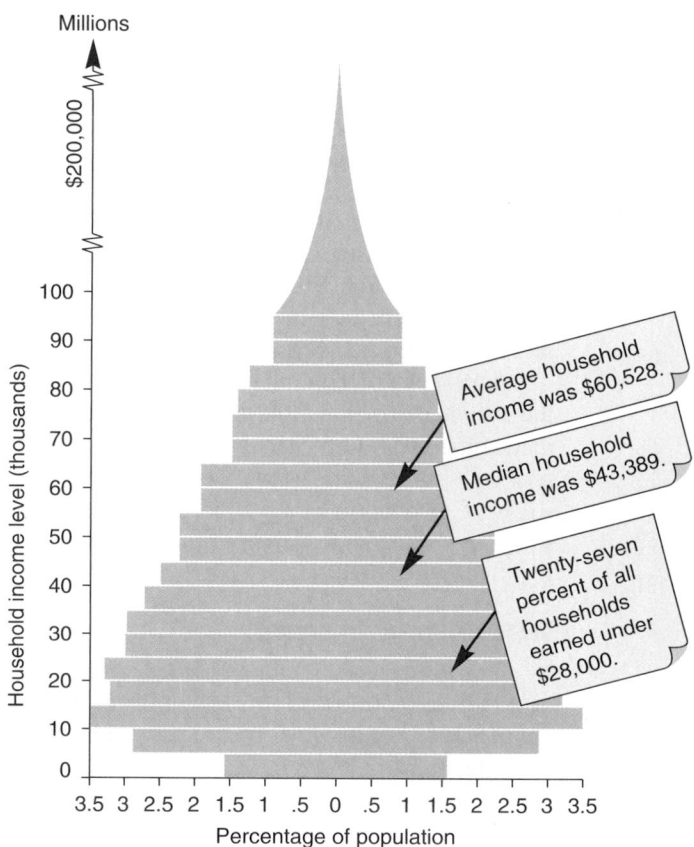

Source: Developed by the author based on data from DeNavas-Walt et al. 2005:HINC-01 and the Internal Revenue Service (2004).

FIGURE 8-4

Distribution of Wealth in the United States, 2001

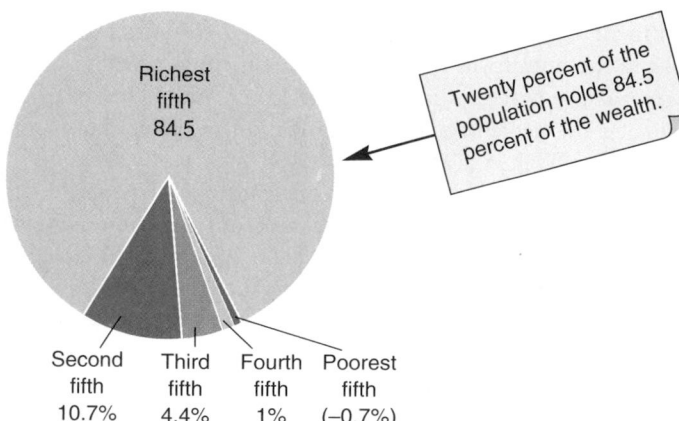

Note: Data do not add to 100 percent due to rounding.
Source: Wolff 2002.

Classroom Tip See "Teaching U.S. Inequality through Games" (Class Discussion Topics).

the century. Former Federal Reserve Board Chairman Alan Greenspan was referring to this increase in income inequality when he told Congress that the gap between the rich and the poor in the United States has become so wide that a democratic society must address it (Greenblatt 2005; Grier 2005).

Survey data show that only 38 percent of people in the United States believe that government should take steps to reduce the income disparity between the rich and the poor. In contrast, 80 percent of people in Italy, 66 percent in Germany, and 65 percent in Great Britain support governmental efforts to reduce income inequality. It is not surprising, then, that many European countries provide more extensive safety nets to assist and protect the disadvantaged. In contrast, the strong cultural value placed on individualism in the United States leads to greater possibilities for both economic success and failure (Lipset 1996).

Wealth in the United States is much more unevenly distributed than income. As Figure 8-4 shows, in 2001, the richest fifth of the population held 84.5 percent of the nation's wealth. Government data indicate that more than 1 out of every 100 households had assets over $2.4 million, while one-fifth of all households were so heavily in debt they had a negative net worth. Researchers have also found a dramatic disparity in wealth between African Americans and Whites. This disparity is evident even when educational backgrounds are held constant: the households of college-educated Whites have about three times as much wealth as the households of college-educated Blacks (Oliver and Shapiro 1995; Wolff 2002).

Poverty

Approximately one out of every nine people in the United States lives below the poverty line established by the federal government. In 2004, 37 million people were living in poverty. The economic boom of the 1990s passed these people by. A recent Bureau of the Census report showed that one in five households has trouble meeting basic needs—everything from paying the utility bills to buying dinner (Bauman 1999; DeNavas-Walt et al. 2005).

One contributor to the United States' high poverty rate has been the large number of workers employed at minimum wage. As Figure 8-5 shows, the federal government has raised the minimum wage over the last half century, from 75 cents in 1950 to $5.15 in 1997. But in terms of its real value, adjusted for inflation, the minimum wage has frequently failed to keep pace with the cost of living. In fact, its real value today is *lower* than it was at any time from 1956 through 1984 (see the figure). Little wonder, then, that the low-income workers David Shipler interviewed could barely scrape by (see the chapter-opening excerpt), or that Barbara Ehrenreich could do no better when she experimented with life as a low-wage worker (see the excerpt that opened Chapter 1). In this section, we'll consider just how social scientists define *poverty*. We'll also take a closer look at the people who fall into that category—including the working poor.

Studying Poverty The efforts of sociologists and other social scientists to better understand poverty are complicated by the difficulty of defining it. This problem is evident even in gov-

Methods Use of a survey to assess dissatisfaction with income disparities in the United States
Global View Dissatisfaction with income disparities examined in the United States, Italy, Germany, and Great Britain

ernment programs that conceive of poverty in either absolute or relative terms. ***Absolute poverty*** refers to a minimum level of subsistence that no family should be expected to live below.

One commonly used measure of absolute poverty is the federal government's *poverty line,* a money income figure that is adjusted annually to reflect the consumption requirements of families based on their size and composition. The poverty line serves as an official definition of which people are poor. In 2004, for example, any family of four (two adults and two children) with a combined income of $19,157 or less fell below the poverty line. This definition determines which individuals and families will be eligible for certain government benefits (Bureau of the Census 2005b).

Although by absolute standards, poverty has declined in the United States, it remains higher than in many other industrial nations. As Figure 8-6 shows, a comparatively high proportion

U.S. Minimum Wage Adjusted for Inflation, 1950–2005

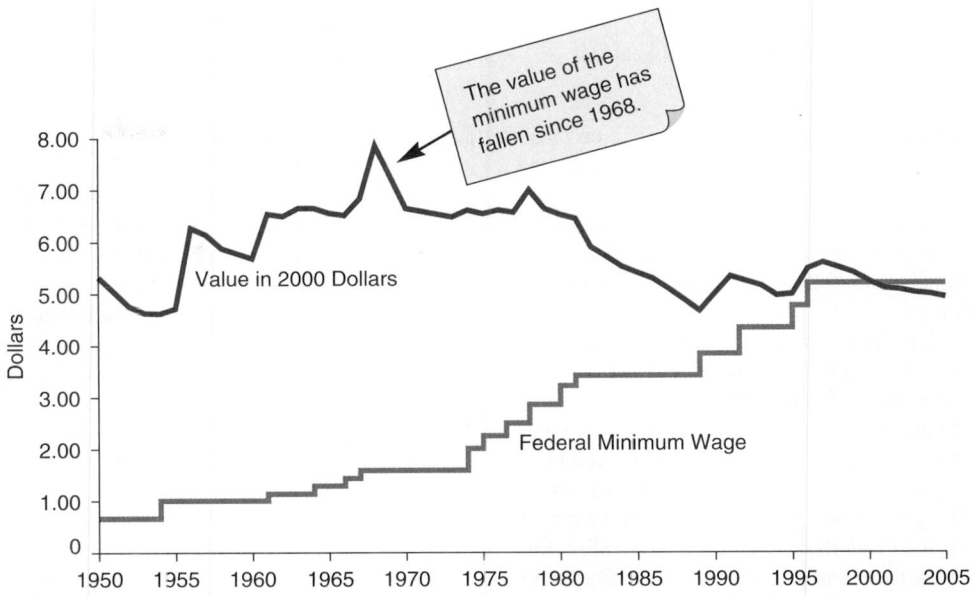

Note: Some states legislate different standards. Minima as of 2005 were actually lower in two states (KS and OH) and higher in 16 states (AK, CA, CT, DE, FL, HI, IL, MA, ME, MN, NJ, NY, OR, RI, VT, WA) and the District of Columbia.
Source: Author's estimate and Bureau of the Census 2005a:413.

FIGURE 8–6

Absolute Poverty in Selected Industrial Countries

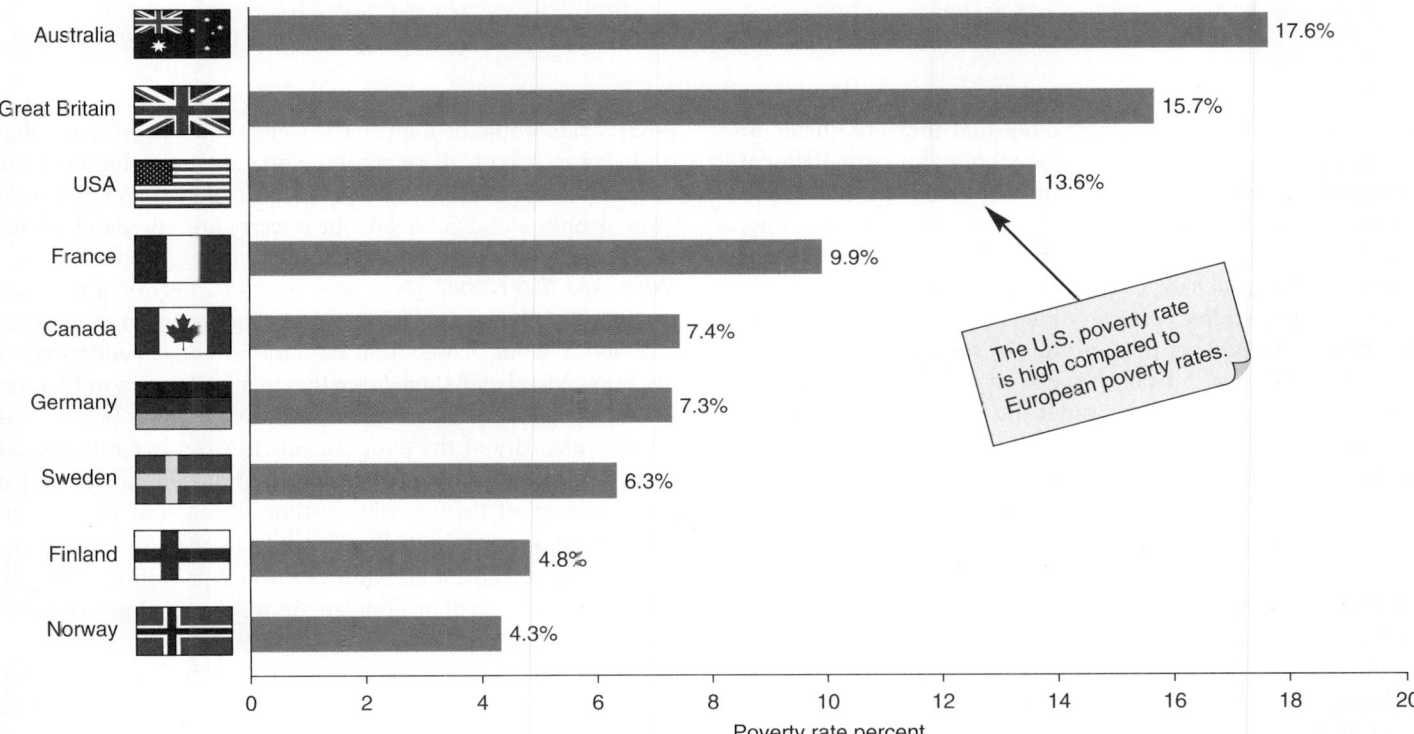

Source: Smeeding et al. 2001:51.

Classroom Tip See "Estimating the Poverty Level for a Family" (Class Discussion Topics); "Poverty and Wealth" (Class Discussion Topics); "Income Levels" (Class Discussion Topics); "Introducing Social Class" (Class Discussion Topics); "Social Stratification—An Active Learning Technique" (Class Discussion Topics); "Homeless Women" (Class Discussion Topics); "Understanding Income and Wealth Inequality"

(Additional Lecture Ideas); "Income Differences by Gender and Race" (Additional Lecture Ideas).
Contemporary Culture What does it say about American society that a working person can still be poor?
Global View Absolute poverty in selected industrial countries

8-2 It's All Relative: Appalachian Poverty and Congolese Affluence

What does it mean to be well off? To be poor? To explore this question, the editors of the London-based publication *The Economist* compared the situations of two men living very different lives: an unemployed truck driver in the Appalachian Mountains and a physician in Congo.

Enos Banks makes his home in a forgotten pocket of rural poverty, described over 40 years ago in Michael Harrington's *The Other America*. Banks once worked for a coal-mining company, but a heart attack forced him to quit his job. In his 60s, he lives in a trailer and gets by on a little more than $500 a month in supplemental security income (SSI). Because he owns a truck, he is not eligible for food stamps.

On the other side of the world, in the Democratic Republic of Congo, Mbwebwe Kabamba earns about $100 or $200 more per month than Enos Banks. Kabamba is a surgeon and head of the emergency room at a hospital in Kinshasa, the country's capital. His hospital salary is only $250 a month, but he supplements it by performing surgery on the side. In Congo, the same income that impoverishes Enos Banks

places Kabamba near the middle of his society's income distribution.

Though Kabamba may seem better off than Banks, especially given the Congo's lower cost of living, such is not the case. Kabamba supports a family of 12, while Banks supports only himself. By U.S. standards, Kabamba's four-bedroom home, spacious compared to Banks's

> By U.S. standards, Kabamba's four-bedroom home, spacious compared to Banks's trailer, is overcrowded with 12 inhabitants.

trailer, is overcrowded with 12 inhabitants. And though Kabamba's home has a kitchen, it lacks running water, dependable electric service, and air-conditioning—services most Americans take for granted. Considered wealthy in his own country, Kabamba is worse off than a poor person in the United States.

Nevertheless, Banks's poverty is real; he occupies a position close to the bottom of the

pyramid in Figure 8-3. In absolute terms defined by his own society, Kabamba is not poor, even though he is less well off than Enos Banks. Relative to most of the world's population, however, both men are doing well.

Let's Discuss

1. Have you ever lived in or traveled to a foreign country where income and living standards were very different from those in the United States? If so, did the contrast give you a new perspective on poverty? What differences between the living standards in the two societies stand out in your mind?

2. If absolute measures of poverty, such as household income, are inconsistent from one country to the next, what other measures might give a clearer picture of people's relative well-being? Should the poverty level be the same everywhere in the world? Why or why not?

Sources: The Economist 2005f; Harrington 1962; Haub 2005.

---

of U.S. households are poor, meaning that they are unable to purchase basic consumer goods. If anything, this cross-national comparison understates the extent of poverty in the United States, since U.S. residents are likely to pay more for housing, health care, child care, and education than residents of other countries, where such expenses are often subsidized.

In contrast, **relative poverty** is a floating standard of deprivation by which people at the bottom of a society, whatever their lifestyles, are judged to be disadvantaged *in comparison with the nation as a whole*. Therefore, even if the poor of 2005 are better off in absolute terms than the poor of the 1930s or 1960s, they are still seen as deserving of special assistance. Box 8-2 explores the difference between relative poverty in Appalachia and relative affluence in the Congo.

Since the 1990s, debate has grown over the accuracy of the federal government's measure of poverty. If noncash benefits such as Medicare, Medicaid, food stamps, public housing, and health care and other employer-provided fringe benefits were included, the reported poverty rate would be lower. On the other hand, if out-of-pocket medical expenses and mandatory work expenses for transportation and childcare were included, the

poverty rate would be higher. The Census Bureau estimates that on balance, if both these recommendations were followed the official poverty rate would be 2 percent higher, and 5 million more people would fall below the poverty line (Bernasek 2006).

Who Are the Poor? Not only does the category of the poor defy any simple definition; it counters the common stereotypes {p.2} about "poor people" that Barbara Ehrenreich addressed in her book *Nickel and Dimed* (see the opening excerpt in Chapter 1). For example, many people in the United States believe that the vast majority of the poor are able to work but will not. Yet many poor adults do work outside the home, although only a small portion of them work full-time throughout the year. In 2004, about 31 percent of all poor adults worked full-time, compared to 66 percent of all adults. Of those poor adults who do not work, most are ill or disabled, or are occupied in maintaining a home (DeNavas-Walt et al. 2005).

Though many of the poor live in urban slums, a majority live outside those poverty-stricken areas. Poverty is no stranger in rural areas, from Appalachia to hard-hit farming regions to Native American reservations. Table 8-3 provides additional

Global View Poverty in the United States and Congo.
Theory Apply Weber's multidimensional view of class to Banks and Kabamba.
Classroom Tip The ascribed status of being disabled often functions as a master status, as was disclosed in Chapter 5.

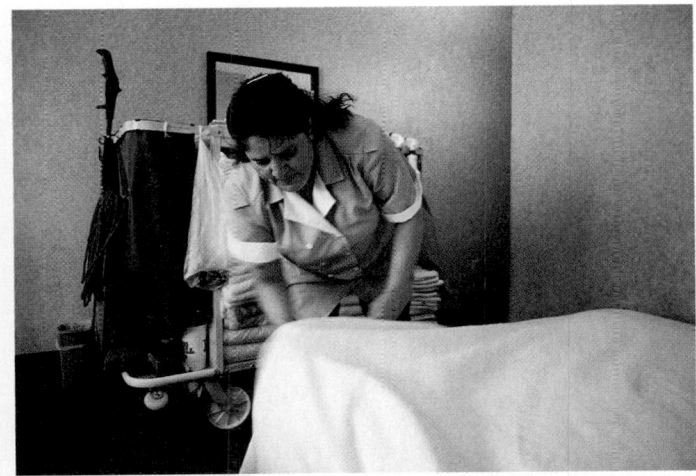

A hotel housekeeper hurries to make the bed and move on to the next room to be cleaned. At low wage rates, even full-time workers have difficulty staying out of poverty, especially if they have families.

statistical information regarding low-income people in the United States.

Since World War II, an increasing proportion of the poor people of the United States have been women, many of whom are divorced or never-married mothers. In 1959, female householders accounted for 26 percent of the nation's poor; by 2004, that figure had risen to 59 percent (see Table 8-3). This alarming trend, known as the *feminization of poverty*, is evident not just in the United States but around the world.

About half of all women living in poverty in the United States are in transition, coping with an economic crisis caused by the departure, disability, or death of a husband. The other half tend to be economically dependent either on the welfare system or on friends and relatives living nearby. A major factor in the feminization of poverty has been the increase in families with women as single heads of the household (see Chapter 12). In 2004, 28 percent of households headed by single mothers lived in poverty, compared to 5.5 percent of married couples in the United States. Conflict theorists and other observers trace the {pp.94–96 higher rates of poverty among women to three distinct factors: the difficulty in finding affordable child care, sexual harassment, and sex discrimination in the labor market.

In 2004, 51 percent of poor people in the United States were living in central cities. These highly visible urban residents are the focus of most governmental efforts to alleviate poverty. Yet according to many observers, the plight of the urban poor is growing worse, owing to the devastating interplay of inadequate education and limited employment prospects. Traditional employment opportunities in the industrial sector are largely closed to the un-

skilled poor. Past and present discrimination heightens these problems for those low-income urban residents who are Black and Hispanic (DeNavas-Walt et al. 2005).

Sociologist William Julius Wilson (1980, 1987, 1989, 1996) and other social scientists have used the term **underclass** to describe the long-term poor who lack training and skills. According to an analysis of Census 2000 data, 7.9 million people live in high-poverty neighborhoods. About 30 percent of the population in these neighborhoods is Black, 29 percent Hispanic, and 24 percent White. In central cities, about 49 percent of the underclass is African American, 29 percent Hispanic, 17 percent White, and 5 percent "other" (Jargowsky 2003:4–5; O'Hare and Curry-White 1992).

Conflict theorists, among others, have expressed alarm at the portion of the nation's population living on this lower rung of the stratification ladder, and at society's reluctance to address the lack of economic opportunities for these people. Often, portraits of the underclass seem to blame the victims for their own plight, while ignoring other factors that push people into poverty.

Analyses of the poor in general reveal that they are not a static social class. The overall composition of the poor changes continually, because some individuals and families near the top edge of poverty move above the poverty level after a year or two, while others slip below it. Still, hundreds of thousands of people remain in poverty for many years at a time. African Americans and Latinos are more likely than Whites to be persistently poor. Over a 21-year period, 15 percent of African Americans and 10 percent of Latinos were persistently poor, compared to only 3 percent of Whites. Both Latinos and Blacks are less likely than Whites to leave the welfare rolls as a result of welfare reform, discussed in the Social Policy section of this chapter (Mangum et al. 2003).

Table 8-3　Who Are the Poor in the United States?

Group	Percentage of the Population of the United States	Percentage of the Poor of the United States
Under 18 years old	30%	36%
18 to 64 years old	61	54
65 years and older	13	10
Whites (non-Hispanic)	83	44
Blacks	12	24
Hispanics	11	25
Asians and Pacific Islanders	4	4
Married couples and families with male householders	82	41
Families with female householders	18	59

Note: Data are for 2004, as reported by the Bureau of the Census in 2005.
Source: DeNavas-Walt et al. 2005:10.

Explaining Poverty Why is it that poverty pervades a nation of such vast wealth? Sociologist Herbert Gans (1995), who has applied functionalist analysis to the existence of poverty, argues that various segments of society actually *benefit* from the existence of the poor. Gans has identified a number of social, economic, and political functions that the poor perform for society:

- The presence of poor people means that society's dirty work—physically dirty or dangerous, dead-end and underpaid, undignified and menial jobs—will be performed at low cost.

- Poverty creates jobs for occupations and professions that serve the poor. It creates both legal employment (public health experts, welfare caseworkers) and illegal jobs (drug dealers, numbers runners).

- The identification and punishment of the poor as deviants {p.163 upholds the legitimacy of conventional social norms and mainstream values regarding hard work, thrift, and honesty.

- Within a relatively hierarchical society, the existence of poor people guarantees the higher status of the more affluent. As psychologist William Ryan (1976) has noted, affluent people may justify inequality (and gain a measure of satisfaction) by blaming the victims of poverty for their disadvantaged condition.

- Because of their lack of political power, the poor often absorb the costs of social change. Under the policy of deinstitutionalization, mental patients released from long-term hospitals have been transferred primarily to low-income communities and neighborhoods. Similarly, halfway houses for rehabilitated drug abusers, rejected by more affluent communities, often end up in poorer neighborhoods.

In Gans's view, then, poverty and the poor actually satisfy positive functions for many nonpoor groups in the United States.

Life Chances

Max Weber saw class as being closely related to people's **life chances**—that is, their opportunities to provide themselves with material goods, positive living conditions, and favorable life experiences (Gerth and Mills 1958). Life chances are reflected in measures such as housing, education, and health. Occupying a higher position in a society improves your life chances and brings greater access to social rewards. In contrast, people in the lower social classes are forced to devote a larger proportion of their limited resources to the necessities of life.

In times of danger, the affluent and powerful have a better chance of surviving than people of ordinary means. When the supposedly unsinkable British oceanliner *Titanic* hit an iceberg in 1912, it was not carrying enough lifeboats to accommodate all passengers. Plans had been made to evacuate only first- and second-class passengers. About 62 percent of the first-class passengers survived the disaster. Despite a rule that women and children would go first, about a third of those passengers were male. In contrast, only 25 percent of the passengers

レオナルド・ディカプリオ　ケイト・ウィンスレット

運命の恋。
誰もそれを裂くことはできない。

タイタニック

「T2」「エイリアン2」のジェームズ・キャメロン監督作品
TITANIC

In the movie *Titanic,* the romantic fantasy of a love affair that crossed class lines obscured the real and deadly effects of the social class divide. This poster appeared in Japan.

in third class survived. The first attempt to alert them to the need to abandon ship came well after other passengers had been notified (D. Butler 1998; Crouse 1999; Riding 1998).

Class position also affects people's vulnerability to natural disasters. When Hurricane Katrina hit the Gulf Coast of the United States in 2005, affluent and poor people alike became its victims. However, poor people who did not own automobiles (100,000 of them in New Orleans alone) were less able than others to evacuate in advance of the storm. Those who survived its fury had no nest egg to draw on, and thus were more likely than others to accept relocation wherever social service agencies could place them—sometimes hundreds or thousands of miles from home (Department of Homeland Security 2006).

Some people have hoped that the Internet revolution would help to level the playing field by making information and markets uniformly available. Unfortunately, however, not everyone can get onto the information superhighway, so yet another aspect of social inequality has emerged—the *digital divide.* The poor, minorities, and those who live in rural communities and inner cities are not getting connected at home or at work. A recent gov-

ernment study found that despite falling computer prices, the Internet gap between the haves and have-nots has not narrowed. For example, while 62 percent of all people could access the Internet at home in 2004, that group included 94 percent of people with incomes over $100,000 but fewer than 40 percent of people with incomes less than $50,000. As wealthier people switch to high-speed Internet connections, they will be able to take advantage of even more sophisticated interactive services, and the digital divide will grow even wider (MRI+ 2005).

Wealth, status, and power may not ensure happiness, but they certainly provide additional ways of coping with problems and disappointments. For this reason, the opportunity for advancement—for social mobility—is of special significance to those on the bottom of society. These people want the rewards and privileges that are granted to high-ranking members of a culture. What can society do to increase their social mobility? One strategy is to offer financial aid to college students from low-income families, on the theory that education lifts people out of poverty. Yet such programs are not having as great an effect as their authors once hoped (see Box 8-3, page 202).

Use Your Sociological Imagination
www.mhhe.com/schaefer7

Imagine a society in which there are no social classes—no differences in people's wealth, income, and life chances. What would such a society be like? Would it be stable, or would its social structure change over time?

Social Mobility

In the movie *Maid in Manhattan,* Jennifer Lopez plays the lead in a modern-day Cinderella story, rising from the lowly status of chambermaid in a big-city hotel to become a company supervisor and the girlfriend of a well-to-do politician. The ascent of a person from a poor background to a position of prestige, power, or financial reward is an example of social mobility. Formally defined, the term *social mobility* refers to the movement of individuals or groups from one position in a society's stratification system to another. But how significant—how frequent, how dramatic—is mobility in a class society such as the United States?

Open versus Closed Stratification Systems

Sociologists use the terms *open stratification system* and *closed stratification system* to indicate the degree of social mobility in a society. An **open system** implies that the position of each individual is influenced by his or her *achieved* status. Such a system encourages competition among members of society. The United States is moving toward this ideal type as the government attempts to reduce the barriers faced by women, racial and ethnic minorities, and people born in lower social classes.

At the other extreme of social mobility is the **closed system,** which allows little or no possibility of individual social mobility. The slavery and caste systems of stratification are examples of

closed systems. In such societies, social placement is based on *ascribed* statuses, such as race or family background, which cannot be changed.

Types of Social Mobility

An airline pilot who becomes a police officer moves from one social position to another of the same rank. Each occupation has the same prestige ranking: 60 on a scale ranging from a low of 0 to a high of 100 (see Table 8-2 on page 195). Sociologists call this kind of movement **horizontal mobility.** However, if the pilot were to become a lawyer (prestige ranking of 75), he or she would experience **vertical mobility,** the movement of an individual from one social position to another of a different rank. Vertical mobility can also involve moving *downward* in a society's stratification system, as would be the case if the airline pilot became a bank teller (ranking of 43). Pitirim Sorokin ([1927] 1959) was the first sociologist to distinguish between horizontal and vertical mobility. Most sociological analysis, however, focuses on vertical rather than horizontal mobility.

One way of examining vertical social mobility is to contrast intergenerational and intragenerational mobility. **Intergenerational mobility** involves changes in the social position of children relative to their parents. Thus, a plumber whose father was a physician provides an example of downward intergenerational mobility. A film star whose parents were both factory workers illustrates upward intergenerational mobility.

Intragenerational mobility involves changes in social position within a person's adult life. A woman who enters the paid labor force as a teacher's aide and eventually becomes superintendent of the school district experiences upward intragenerational mobility. A man who becomes a taxicab driver after his accounting firm goes bankrupt undergoes downward intragenerational mobility.

Social Mobility in the United States

The belief in upward mobility is an important value in our society. Does that mean that the United States is indeed the land of opportunity? Not unless such ascriptive characteristics as race, gender, and family background have ceased to be significant in determining one's future prospects. We can see the impact of these factors in the occupational structure.

Occupational Mobility Two sociological studies conducted a decade apart offer insight into the degree of mobility in the nation's occupational structure (Blau and Duncan 1967; Featherman and Hauser 1978). Taken together, these investigations lead to several noteworthy conclusions. First, occupational mobility (both intergenerational and intragenerational) has been common among males. Approximately 60 to 70 percent of sons are employed in higher-ranked occupations than their fathers.

Second, although there is a great deal of mobility in the United States, much of it is minor. That is, people who reach an occupational level above or below that of their parents usually advance or

Contemporary Culture Besides the movies, what are some ways that belief in upward mobility is perpetuated?
Let's Discuss Who is likely to become president of the United States first: a woman, a Black man, a Hispanic man, an Asian American man, or a Jewish man?
Web Resource Encourage students to take the true–false quiz in the student center of the Online Learning Center (www.mhhe.com/schaefer7).

Student Alert Sociologists are more interested in vertical mobility than in horizontal mobility.
Let's Discuss Intergenerational mobility in students' families
Methods Blau and Duncan and Featherman and Hauser used secondary data.
Reel Society *Reel Society* explores the experiences of a college student whose family is socially mobile.

sociologyONcampus

8-3 Social Class and Financial Aid

Today's young people have been dubbed Generation Y, but a more appropriate name for them could be Generation Debt. Every year, millions of prospective college students and their parents struggle through the intricate and time-consuming process of applying for financial aid. Originally, financial aid programs were intended to level the playing field—to allow qualified students from all walks of life to attend college, regardless of the cost. But have these programs fulfilled their promise?

In 2004, 40 percent of first-year students at major state universities came from families with incomes of more than $100,000 a year. In other words, close to half of all students came from high-income families. This statistic should not be surprising, given the high cost of tuition, room, and board at state universities. For students from families with the lowest incomes, the cost can be prohibitive. At any school, students from households with incomes of $75,000 and over are three times as likely to graduate as students from households with incomes under $25,000. Those moderate-income students who do graduate, and even those who fail to complete their degrees, are often saddled with heavy postgraduate debt. As of 2006, the average college graduate owed a total of $19,000 in student financial aid.

Besides the spiraling cost of an education, the widespread difficulty in paying for college stems from three trends. First, over the past few decades, colleges and universities have been moving away from making outright grants, such as scholarships, to deserving students, and toward low-interest student loans. Second, much of the assistance schools offer in the form of loans is not based strictly on need. Since 1982, non-need-based state aid has grown by 336 percent, while need-based assistance has grown by only 88 percent. Third, interest rates on federally guaranteed

> *Statistics that show the educational level in the United States rising overall obscure the widening gap between the advantaged and the less advantaged.*

loans have risen steadily, increasing the burden of repayment.

These trends in financial aid for higher education are closely tied to trends in social inequality. As noted earlier in this chapter, over the past half century, rather than declining, inequality in income and wealth has actually increased. According to one analysis of U.S. economic trends over the last 30 years, this increase in wealth and income inequality has contributed to a modest increase in educational inequality, as measured by the number of years of formal schooling students achieve. In a variation on the truism that the rich tend to get richer while the poor get poorer, the rich are getting better educations and the poor are getting poorer educations. Statistics that show the educational level in the United States rising overall obscure the widening gap between the advantaged and the less advantaged.

Let's Discuss

1. Take a poll in your class: How many students are receiving some form of financial aid? How many have a scholarship and how many have a loan?
2. Aside from a reduction in individual social mobility, what might be the long-term effects of the shortage of need-based financial aid? Relate your answer to the trend toward globalization.

Sources: Boushey 2005; Campbell et al. 2005; Kamenetz 2006; Leonhardt 2004; Michals 2003; Trumbull 2006.

---

fall back only one or two out of a possible eight occupational levels. Thus, the child of a laborer may become an artisan or a technician, but he or she is less likely to become a manager or professional. The odds against reaching the top are extremely high unless one begins from a relatively privileged position.

The Impact of Education Another conclusion of both studies is that education plays a critical role in social mobility. The impact of formal schooling on adult status is even greater than that of family background (although as we have seen, family background influences the likelihood that one will receive higher education). Furthermore, education represents an important means of intergenerational mobility. Three-fourths of college-educated men in these studies achieved some upward mobility, while only 12 percent of those who received no schooling did (see also J. Davis 1982).

The impact of education on mobility has diminished somewhat in the last decade, however. An undergraduate degree—a B.A. or a B.S.—serves less as a guarantee of upward mobility now than it did in the past, simply because more and more entrants into the job market hold such a degree. Moreover, intergenerational mobility is declining, since there is no longer such a stark difference between generations. In earlier decades, many high school–educated parents successfully sent their children to college, but today's college students are increasingly likely to have college–educated parents (Hout 1988).

The Impact of Race and Ethnicity Sociologists have long documented the fact that the class system is more rigid for African Americans than it is for members of other racial groups. Black men who have good jobs, for example, are less likely than White men to see their adult children attain the same status. The

Let's Discuss In students' own experience, does their school allocate financial aid in a fair way?

Contemporary Culture Explore the implications for future income and wealth of the rich getting a better education.

Student Alert Education is often a means of intergenerational mobility. But an adult returning to school to start a new career is an example of intragenerational mobility.

Race The impact of race on mobility

Race/Ethnicity Limits on occupational mobility among African Americans

Andrea Jung, chairman and chief executive officer of Avon Corporation since 1999, is one of the few women in the United States who have risen to the top of the corporate hierarchy. Despite the passage of equal opportunity laws, occupational barriers still limit women's social mobility.

The Latino population is not doing much better. The typical Hispanic has less than 10 percent of the wealth that a White person enjoys. A 2004 study suggests that in recent years, Latinos have even lost ground. Their continuing immigration accounts for part of the disparity: most of the new arrivals are destitute. But even the wealthiest 5 percent of Latino households have only a third as much net worth as the top 5 percent of White households (Kochhar 2004).

The Impact of Gender Studies of mobility, even more than those of class, have traditionally ignored the significance of gender, but some research findings are now available that explore the relationship between gender and mobility.

Women's employment opportunities are much more limited than men's (as Chapter 11 will show). Moreover, according to recent research, women whose skills far exceed the jobs offered them are more likely than men to withdraw entirely from the paid labor force. Their withdrawal violates an assumption common to traditional mobility studies: that most people will aspire to upward mobility and seek to make the most of their opportunities.

In contrast to men, women have a rather large range of clerical occupations open to them. But the modest salary ranges and few prospects for advancement in many of these positions limit the possibility of upward mobility. Self-employment as shopkeepers, entrepreneurs, independent professionals, and the like—an important road to upward mobility for men—is more difficult for women, who find it harder to secure the necessary financing. Although sons commonly follow in the footsteps of their fathers, women are unlikely to move into their fathers' positions. Consequently, gender remains an important factor in shaping social mobility. Women in the United States (and in other parts of the world) are especially likely to be trapped in poverty, unable to rise out of their low-income status (Heilman 2001).

cumulative disadvantage of discrimination plays a significant role in the disparity between the two groups' experiences. Compared to White households, the relatively modest wealth of African American households means that adult Black children are less likely than adult White children to receive financial support from their parents. Indeed, young Black couples are much more likely than young White couples to be assisting their parents—a sacrifice that hampers their social mobility.

The African American middle class has grown over the last few decades, due to economic expansion and the benefits of the civil rights movement of the 1960s. Yet many of these middle-class households have little savings, a fact that puts them in danger during times of crisis. Studies have consistently shown that downward mobility is significantly higher for Blacks than it is for Whites (Oliver and Shapiro 1995; Sernau 2001; W. J. Wilson 1996).

and Stratification

Rethinking Welfare in North America and Europe

The Issue

- In Milwaukee, a single mother of six has just lost her job as a security guard. Once considered a success story of the welfare reform program, she has fallen victim to the economic recession that followed the boom years of the 1990s. Because she has been on welfare before, she is ineligible to receive additional assistance from the state of Wisconsin. Yet like many other workers who made the transition from welfare to work

in the late 1990s, she does not qualify for unemployment benefits; food stamps are all she can count on (Pierre 2002).

- In Paris, France, Hélène Desegrais, another single mother, waited four months to place her daughter in government-subsidized day care. Now she can seek a full-time job, but she is concerned about government threats to curtail such services in order to keep taxes down (Simons 1997).

Gender Restrictions on mobility among women
Theory Conflict theorists would argue that women's mobility remains more limited than men's because of continuing prejudice and discrimination.

These are the faces of people living on the edge—often women with children seeking to make a go of it amid changing social policies. Governments in all parts of the world are searching for the right solution to welfare: How much subsidy should they provide? How much responsibility should fall on the shoulders of the poor?

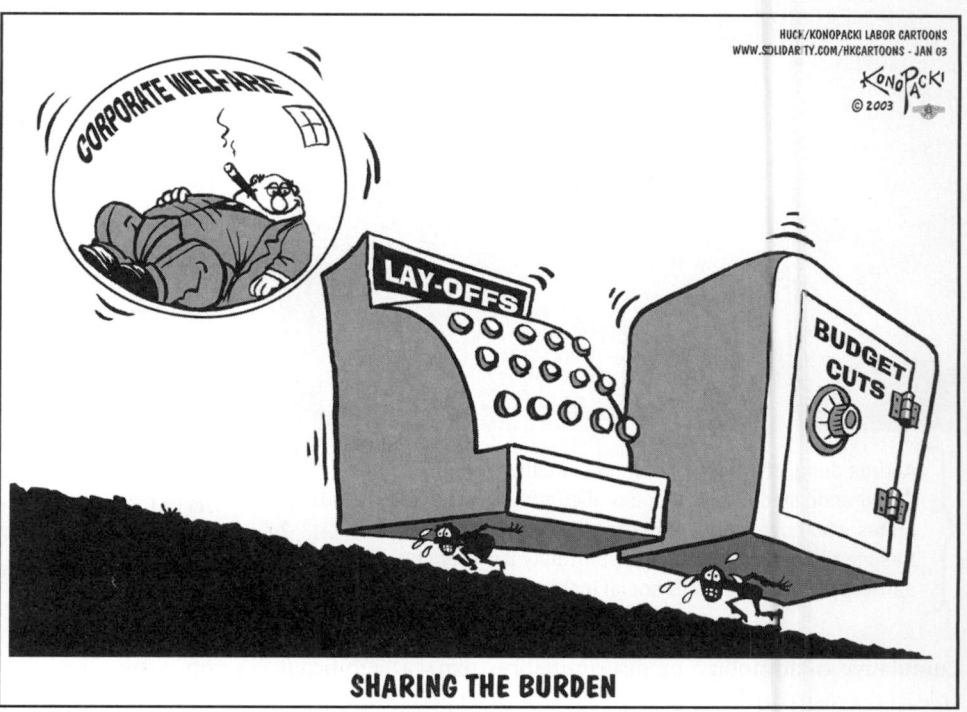

HUCK/KONOPACKI LABOR CARTOONS
WWW.SOLIDARITY.COM/HKCARTOONS - JAN 03

KONOPACKI
© 2003

SHARING THE BURDEN

The Setting

In the 1990s, an intense debate took place in the United States over the issue of welfare. Welfare programs were costly, and concern was widespread (however unfounded) that welfare payments discouraged recipients from seeking jobs. Both Democrats and Republicans vowed to "end welfare as we know it."

In late 1996, in a historic shift in federal policy, Congress passed the Personal Responsibility and Work Opportunity Reconciliation Act, ending the long-standing federal guarantee of assistance to every poor family that meets eligibility requirements. The law set a lifetime limit of five years of welfare benefits, and required all able-bodied adults to work after receiving two years of benefits (although hardship exceptions were allowed). The federal government would give block grants to the states to use as they wished in assisting poor and needy residents, and it would permit states to experiment with ways to move people off welfare.

Other countries vary widely in their commitment to social service programs. But most industrialized nations devote higher proportions of their expenditures to housing, social security, welfare, health care, and unemployment compensation than the United States does. Data available in 2004 indicated that in Great Britain, 82 percent of health expenditures were paid for by the government; in Spain and Canada, 71 percent; but in the United States, only 44 percent (World Bank 2004:88–90).

Sociological Insights

Many sociologists tend to view the debate over welfare reform in industrialized nations from a conflict perspective: the "haves" in positions of policymaking listen to the interests of other "haves," while the cries of the "have-nots" are drowned out. Critics of welfare reform believe that the nation's economic problems are unfairly blamed on welfare spending and the poor. From a conflict perspective, this backlash against welfare recipients reflects deep fears and hostility toward the nation's urban, predominantly African American and Hispanic underclass.

Those who are critical of the backlash note that "welfare scapegoating" conveniently ignores the lucrative federal handouts that go to *affluent* individuals and families. For example, while federal housing aid to the poor was cut drastically in the

1980s, tax deductions for mortgage interest and property taxes more than doubled.

Those who take a conflict perspective also urge policymakers and the general public to look closely at *corporate welfare*—the tax breaks, direct payments, and grants that the government makes to corporations—rather than to focus on the comparatively small allowances being given to welfare mothers and their children. Yet any suggestion to curtail such corporate welfare brings a strong response from special-interest groups that are much more powerful than any coalition on behalf of the poor. One example of corporate welfare is the airline bailout bill that was passed in the wake of terrorist attacks on the United States in September 2001. Within 11 days the federal government had approved the bailout, whose positive impact was felt largely by airline executives and shareholders. Relatively low-paid airline employees were still laid off, and hundreds of thousands of low-wage workers in airports, hotels, and related industries received little or no assistance. Efforts to broaden unemployment assistance to help these marginally employed workers failed (Hartman and Miller 2001).

Policy Initiatives

The government likes to highlight welfare reform success stories. Though many people who once depended on tax dollars are now working and paying taxes themselves, it is much too soon to see if "workfare" will be successful. The new jobs that were generated by the booming economy of the late 1990s were an unrealistic test of the system. Prospects for the hard-core jobless—those people who are difficult to train or are encumbered by drug or alcohol abuse, physical disabilities, or child care needs—have faded as the boom passed and the economy moved into recession (Jencks et al. 2006).

True, fewer people remained on welfare after enactment of the welfare reform law in August 1996. By June 2003, 7.4 million people had left the system, reducing the rolls to under 5 million people. Yet research showed that most adults who had gone off welfare had taken low-wage jobs that did not offer benefits. As they moved off welfare, their Medicaid coverage ended, leaving them without health insurance. Support has also been lacking for working parents who need high-quality child care. And assistance to immigrants, even those who are legal residents, continues to be limited (Department of Health and Human Services 2005; Seefeldt 2004).

European governments have encountered many of the same citizen demands as in North America: Keep our taxes low, even if it means reducing services to the poor. However, nations in eastern and central Europe have faced a special challenge since the end of communism. Though governments in those nations had traditionally provided an impressive array of social services, they differed from capitalist systems in several important respects. First, the communist system was premised on full employment, so there was no need to provide unemployment insurance; social services focused on the old and the disabled. Second, subsidies for housing and even utilities played an important role. With new competition from the West and tight budgets, some of these countries are beginning to realize that universal coverage is no longer affordable and must be replaced with targeted programs. Even Sweden, despite its long history of

social welfare programs, is feeling the pinch. Still, only modest cutbacks have been made in European social service programs, leaving them much more generous than those in the United States (J. Gornick 2001).

Both in North America and in Europe, people are beginning to turn to private means to support themselves. For instance, they are investing money for their later years rather than depending on government social security programs. But that solution works only if you have a job and can save money. Increasingly, people are seeing the gap between themselves and the affluent grow, with fewer government programs available to assist them. Solutions are frequently left to the private sector, while government policy initiatives at the national level all but disappear.

Let's Discuss

1. Do you personally know anyone who has had to depend on public assistance, such as food stamps, now or in the past? If so, what were the circumstances? Would you yourself need government assistance under such circumstances?

2. Do you think welfare recipients should be required to work? If so, what kind of support should they receive? Should any exceptions be granted to the work requirement?

3. Why do you think western and northern European countries have more generous welfare programs than the United States?

GettingINVOLVED

To get involved in the debate over welfare reform, visit this text's Online Learning Center, which offers links to relevant Web sites. Check out the Social Policy section on the Online Learning Center as well; it provides survey data on U.S. public opinion regarding this issue.

www.mhhe.com/schaefer7

{ MASTERING THIS CHAPTER }

Summary

Stratification is the structured ranking of entire groups of people that perpetuates unequal economic rewards and **power** in a society. In this chapter we examined four general systems of stratification, the explanations offered by functionalist and conflict theorists for the existence of **social inequality,** and the relationship between stratification and **social mobility.**

1. Some degree of **social inequality** characterizes all cultures.

2. Systems of social **stratification** include **slavery, castes,** the **estate system,** and social classes.

3. Karl Marx saw that differences in access to the means of production created social, economic, and political inequality, as well as two distinct classes, owners and laborers.

4. Max Weber identified three analytically distinct components of stratification: **class, status group,** and **power.**

5. Functionalists argue that stratification is necessary to motivate people to fill society's important positions. Conflict theorists see stratification as a major source of societal tension and conflict. Interactionists stress the importance of social class in determining a person's lifestyle.

6. One consequence of social class in the United States is that both **wealth** and **income** are distributed unevenly.

7. Many of those who live in poverty are full-time workers who struggle to support their families at minimum-wage jobs. The long-term poor—those who lack the training and skills to lift themselves out of poverty—form an **underclass.**

8. Functionalists find that the poor satisfy positive functions for many of the nonpoor in the United States.

9. One's *life chances*—opportunities for obtaining material goods, positive living conditions, and favorable life experiences—are related to one's social class. Occupying a high social position improves a person's life chances.

10. *Social mobility* is more likely to be found in an *open system* that emphasizes *achieved status* than in a *closed system* that focuses on *ascribed status.* Race, gender, and family background are important factors in social mobility.

11. Today, many governments are struggling with the question of how much tax revenue to spend on welfare programs. The trend in the United States is to put welfare recipients to work.

Critical Thinking Questions

1. Sociologist Daniel Rossides has conceptualized the class system of the United States using a five-class model. According to Rossides, the upper-middle class and the lower-middle class together account for about 40 percent of the nation's population. Yet studies suggest that a higher proportion of respondents identify themselves as middle class. Drawing on the model presented by Rossides, suggest why members of both the upper class and the working class might prefer to identify themselves as middle class.

2. Sociological study of stratification is generally conducted at the macro level and draws most heavily on the functionalist and conflict perspectives. How might sociologists use the *interactionist* perspective to examine social class inequalities in a college community?

3. Imagine you have the opportunity to do research on changing patterns of social mobility in the United States. What specific question would you want to investigate, and how would you go about it?

Key Terms

Absolute poverty A minimum level of subsistence that no family should be expected to live below. (page 197)

Achieved status A social position that a person attains largely through his or her own efforts. (186)

Ascribed status A social position assigned to a person by society without regard for the person's unique talents or characteristics. (186)

Bourgeoisie Karl Marx's term for the capitalist class, comprising the owners of the means of production. (189)

Capitalism An economic system in which the means of production are held largely in private hands and the main incentive for economic activity is the accumulation of profits. (189)

Caste A hereditary rank, usually religiously dictated, that tends to be fixed and immobile. (187)

Class A group of people who have a similar level of wealth and income. (191)

Class consciousness In Karl Marx's view, a subjective awareness held by members of a class regarding their common vested interests and need for collective political action to bring about social change. (190)

Class system A social ranking based primarily on economic position in which achieved characteristics can influence social mobility. (188)

Closed system A social system in which there is little or no possibility of individual social mobility. (201)

Corporate welfare Tax breaks, direct payments, and grants that the government makes to corporations. (204)

Dominant ideology A set of cultural beliefs and practices that helps to maintain powerful social, economic, and political interests. (193)

Estate system A system of stratification under which peasants were required to work land leased to them by nobles in exchange for military protection and other services. Also known as *feudalism.* (188)

Esteem The reputation that a specific person has earned within an occupation. (194)

False consciousness A term used by Karl Marx to describe an attitude held by members of a class that does not accurately reflect their objective position. (190)

Horizontal mobility The movement of an individual from one social position to another of the same rank. (201)

Income Salaries and wages. (186)

Intergenerational mobility Changes in the social position of children relative to their parents. (201)

Intragenerational mobility Changes in social position within a person's adult life. (201)

Life chances The opportunities people have to provide themselves with material goods, positive living conditions, and favorable life experiences. (200)

Objective method A technique for measuring social class that assigns individuals to classes on the basis of criteria such as occupation, education, income, and place of residence. (194)

Open system A social system in which the position of each individual is influenced by his or her achieved status. (201)

Power The ability to exercise one's will over others. (191)

Prestige The respect and admiration that an occupation holds in a society. (194)

Proletariat Karl Marx's term for the working class in a capitalist society. (190)

Relative poverty A floating standard of deprivation by which people at the bottom of a society, whatever their lifestyles, are judged to be disadvantaged *in comparison with the nation as a whole.* (198)

Slavery A system of enforced servitude in which some people are owned by other people. (187)

Social inequality A condition in which members of society have different amounts of wealth, prestige, or power. (186)

Social mobility Movement of individuals or groups from one position in a society's stratification system to another. (201)

Status group People who have the same prestige or lifestyle, independent of their class positions. (191)

Stratification A structured ranking of entire groups of people that perpetuates unequal economic rewards and power in a society. (186)

Underclass The long-term poor who lack training and skills. (199)
Vertical mobility The movement of an individual from one social position to another of a different rank. (201)

Wealth An inclusive term encompassing all a person's material assets, including land, stocks, and other types of property. (186)

Self-Quiz

Read each question carefully and then select the best answer.

1. Which of the following is the term used to describe a condition in which members of a society have different amounts of wealth, prestige, or power?
   a. stratification
   b. status inconsistency
   c. slavery
   d. social inequality

2. In Karl Marx's view, the destruction of the capitalist system will occur only if the working class first develops
   a. bourgeois consciousness.
   b. false consciousness.
   c. class consciousness.
   d. caste consciousness.

3. Which of the following were viewed by Max Weber as analytically distinct components of stratification?
   a. conformity, deviance, and social control
   b. class, status, and power
   c. class, caste, and age
   d. class, prestige, and esteem

4. Which sociological perspective argues that stratification is universal and that social inequality is necessary so that people will be motivated to fill socially important positions?
   a. the functionalist perspective
   b. the conflict perspective
   c. the interactionist perspective
   d. the labeling perspective

5. British sociologist Ralf Dahrendorf views social classes as groups of people who share common interests resulting from their authority relationships. Dahrendorf's ideology aligns best with which theoretical perspective?
   a. the functionalist perspective
   b. the conflict perspective
   c. the interactionist perspective
   d. sociocultural evolution

6. The respect or admiration that an occupation holds in a society is referred to as
   a. status.
   b. esteem.
   c. prestige.
   d. ranking.

7. Approximately how many out of every nine people in the United States live(s) below the poverty line established by the federal government?
   a. one
   b. two
   c. three
   d. four

8. Which sociologist has applied functionalist analysis to the existence of poverty and argues that various segments of society actually benefit from the existence of the poor?
   a. Émile Durkheim
   b. Max Weber
   c. Karl Marx
   d. Herbert Gans

9. The poor, minorities, and those who live in rural communities and inner cities are not as likely to have access to the Internet as other members of the United States. This situation is called
   a. the cybervoid.
   b. electronic redlining.
   c. the digital divide.
   d. none of the above

10. A plumber whose father was a physician is an example of
    a. downward intergenerational mobility.
    b. upward intergenerational mobility.
    c. downward intragenerational mobility.
    d. upward intragenerational mobility.

11. _____ is the most extreme form of legalized social inequality for individuals or groups.

12. In the _____ system of stratification, or feudalism, peasants were required to work land leased to them by nobles in exchange for military protection and other services.

13. Karl Marx viewed _____ differentiation as the crucial determinant of social, economic, and political inequality.

14. _____ _____ is the term Thorstein Veblen used to describe the extravagant spending patterns of those at the top of the class hierarchy.

15. _____ poverty is the minimum level of subsistence that no family should be expected to live below.

16. _____ poverty is a floating standard of deprivation by which people at the bottom of a society, whatever their lifestyles, are judged to be disadvantaged in comparison with the nation as a whole.

17. Sociologist William Julius Wilson and other social scientists have used the term _____ to describe the long-term poor who lack training and skills.

18. Max Weber used the term _____ _____ to refer to people's opportunities to provide themselves with material goods, positive living conditions, and favorable life experiences.

19. An open class system implies that the position of each individual is influenced by the person's _____ status.

20. _____ mobility involves changes in social position within a person's adult life.

{ TECHNOLOGY RESOURCES }

Online Learning Center

1. When you visit the student center in the Online Learning Center at **www.mhhe.com/schaefer7,** link to Author's Audio Overview. Listen to Richard Schaefer, the author of your textbook, talk about some sociology students he taught and their prestige rankings of various occupations. These sociology students were all "lifers" in a maximum-security prison.

2. The question of where to draw the poverty line is a controversial one in the United States. The Economic Policy Institute's Web site (**www.epinet.org**) offers some tools that you can use to explore the issue. Using the online calculators, find out what a budget-conscious family in your community needs to get by. Then read more about the poverty line in the issue guides.

3. This chapter describes the digital divide among various groups in American society. The Digital Divide Network (**www.digital dividenetwork.org**) is an organization that seeks to minimize this emerging dimension of inequality. Explore this Web site to learn more about its efforts.

Note: While all the URLs listed were current as of the printing of this book, these sites often change. Please check our Web site **(www.mhhe.com/schaefer7)** *for updates, hyperlinks, and exercises related to these sites.*

Reel Society Video Clips

Reel Society video clips, which appear on this book's Web site, can be used to spark discussion about the following topics from this chapter:
- Understanding Stratification
- Stratification by Social Class
- Social Mobility

9

Global Inequality

inside

The Global Divide

Stratification in the World System

Stratification within Nations:
   A Comparative Perspective

Case Study: Stratification in
   Mexico

Social Policy and Global Inequality:
   Universal Human Rights

Boxes

Sociology in the Global Community:
Cutting Poverty Worldwide

Sociology in the Global Community:
The Global Disconnect

Social Inequality: Stratification in
Japan

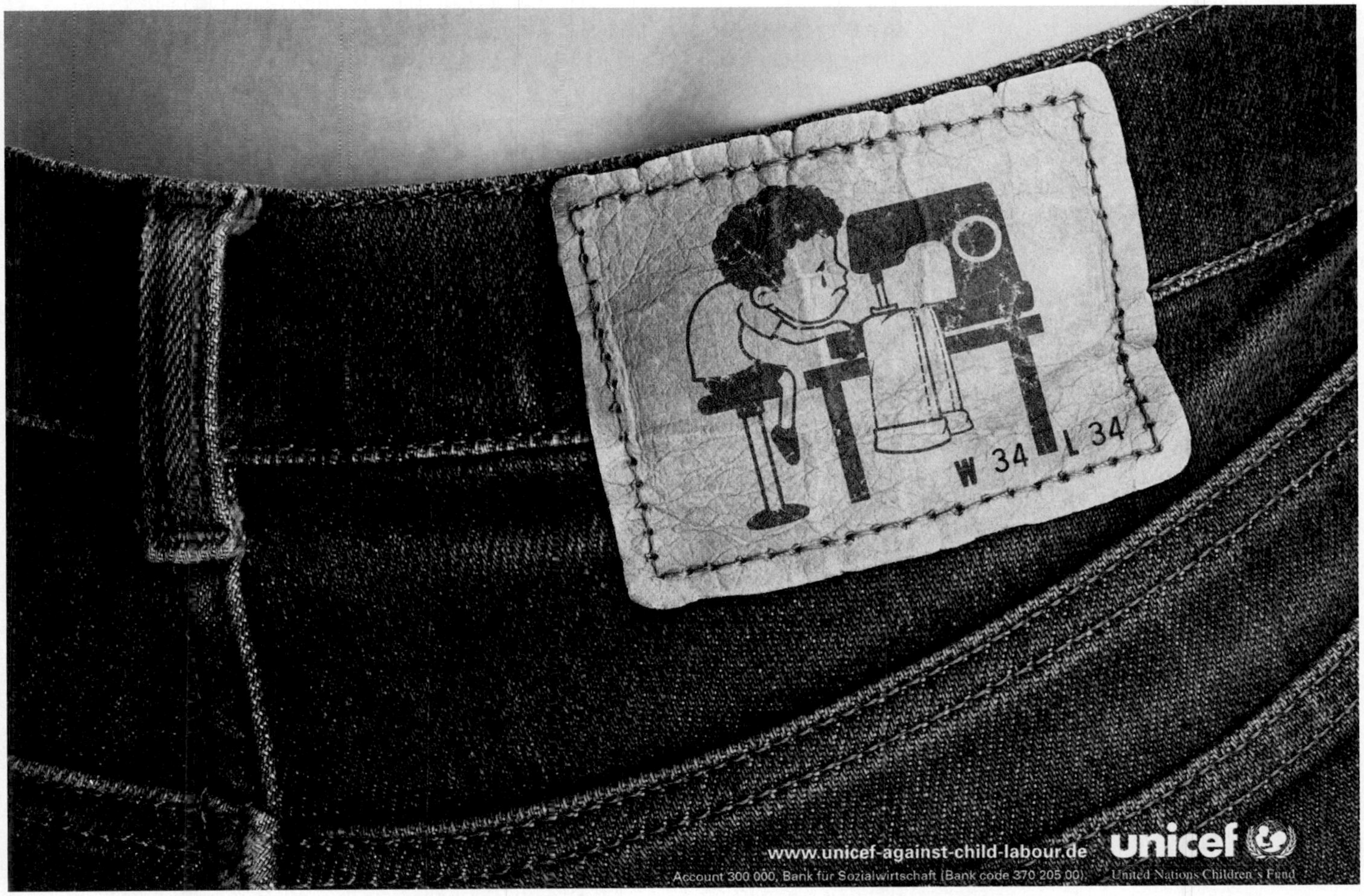

www.unicef-against-child-labour.de **unicef** 🙋

Account 300 000, Bank für Sozialwirtschaft (Bank code 370 205 00)   United Nations Children's Fund

This UNICEF poster reminds affluent Western consumers that the brand-name jeans they wear may be produced by exploited workers in developing countries. In sweatshops throughout the developing world, nonunion garment workers—some of them still children—labor long hours for extremely low wages.

Amit is a member of India's rising middle class. The 22-year-old left his village to study at an urban university and considers himself a connoisseur of Western fashions. He enjoys watching Arnold Schwarzenegger films and National Basketball Association games beamed to India from the United States. The foreign media reaffirm his self-image as a citizen of the world. Yet at the same time Amit complains that the media threaten Indian family arrangements. "I want an arranged marriage," Amit says, "but I fear that Fashion Television, MTV, and [music] channel V are distorting the desires of the younger generation."

India, with a population now in excess of 1 billion, is a massive experiment in "globalization"—the emergence of worldwide markets and communications that increasingly ignore national boundaries. People, jobs, goods, and media move to and from India at unprecedented speed and volume. Global consumer products entice Indians. And Indians, in turn, produce for the global market. Cable and satellite television broadcasts from around the world reach Indian homes and Hollywood has grabbed a significant share of the movie audience (India's huge "Bollywood" film industry notwithstanding). There is a fear that Western images and ideas will undermine traditional Indian culture. . . .

Over the last two decades, more of what people around the world buy and watch is produced elsewhere; more of what they produce is made for a global market; and more local policies are shaped by outside decision makers. In India, a foreign-exchange crisis in 1991 gave the International Monetary Fund leverage to demand the removal of restrictions on foreign investment and trade. With that economic liberalization, once scarce goods rapidly flowed into the Indian market. Taking advantage of cheap, well-trained labor, computer programming jobs appeared. International financiers arrived. Within five years, imports more than doubled, exports more than tripled and foreign capital investment more than quintupled.

Cultural globalization—international media—quickly followed as global advertisers tried to reach the new Indian market and government restrictions eased. In 1991, cable television in India reached 300,000 homes; in 1999, it reached 24 million. In 1991, only a few foreign films showed in the biggest cities, but by 2001 foreign films were dubbed into Hindi and screened throughout the country

Given new opportunities for employment, consumption, and entertainment, affluent urban Indian men aspired to new goods and experimented with changes in family life. In contrast, studies show that the lives of middle-class Indian men have not been significantly transformed and while the research is less conclusive, the contrast seems to apply to women as well. (Unfortunately, the effects of globalization on poor urban and rural Indians have not been sufficiently studied—although we do know that rural and urban poverty have increased slightly since 1991.)

(Derné 2003:12–13) Additional information about this excerpt can be found on the Online Learning Center at www.mhhe.com/schaefer7. ●

> **"** *Amit is a member of India's rising middle class. The 22-year-old left his village to study at an urban university and considers himself a connoisseur of Western fashions.* **"**

In this excerpt from the journal *Contexts,* sociologist Steve Derné describes the effects of globalization on Indian society. Derné conducted observation research in India in 1991 and again in 2001. He found that through Western media, Indians like Amit were being exposed to more and more consumer products, most of which they could not afford to purchase. Indians are considered affluent if their incomes top $2,150 a year; only about 3 percent of the population fits that description. These high-income consumers can afford some foreign goods, as well as an occasional visit to Pizza Hut, where they spend about $6 per person. (In comparison, a full dinner at an Indian restaurant costs about $1.) Even in the United States, most people cannot afford the lifestyle portrayed in movies and on television. But the disconnect between desire and reality is much greater in India and most other countries around the globe (Derné 2003).

At the same time that Western media have been flooding India with images of material wealth, U.S. college students have been questioning the labor conditions in the foreign factories that produce their college-logo-embroidered sweatshirts. Their concerns have given rise to a nationwide coalition called United Students Against Sweatshops, based on college campuses across the country. Because this issue combines women's rights, immigrant rights, environmental concerns, and human rights, it has linked diverse groups on campus. The student movement—ranging from sit-ins and "knit-ins" to demonstrations and building occupation—has been aimed at ridding campus stores of all products made in sweatshops, both at home and abroad. Pressed by their students, many colleges and universities have agreed to adopt antisweatshop codes governing the products they stock on campus. Nike and Reebok, partly in response to student protests, have raised the wages of some 100,000 workers in their Indonesian factories to about 20 cents an hour—still far below what is needed to raise a family (Appelbaum and Dreier 1999; Rivoli 2005).

Together, the apparel industry and the global consumer goods culture focus our attention on worldwide social stratification—on the enormous gap between wealthy nations and poorer nations. In many respects, the wealth of rich nations de-

Students protesting sweatshop labor in developing countries mock Nike with its own slogan: "Just do it."

pends on the poverty of poor nations. People in industrialized societies benefit when they buy consumer goods made by low-wage workers in developing countries. Yet the low wages workers earn in multinational factories are comparatively high for those countries.

What economic and political conditions explain the divide between rich nations and poor? Within developing nations, how are wealth and income distributed, and how much opportunity does the average worker have to move up the social ladder? How do race and gender affect social mobility in these countries? In this chapter we will focus on global inequality, beginning with the global divide. We will consider the impact of colonialism and neocolonialism, of globalization, of the rise of multinational corporations, of grinding poverty, and of the trend toward modernization. Then we will focus on stratification *within* nations, in terms of the distribution of wealth and income and social mobility. In a special case study, we will look closely at social stratification in Mexico, including the social impact of race and gender and the economic effects of industrialization. The chapter closes with a Social Policy section on universal human rights. ●

The Global Divide

In some parts of the world, the people who have dedicated their lives to fighting starvation refer to what they call "coping mechanisms"—ways in which the desperately poor attempt to control their hunger. Eritrean women will strap flat stones to their stomachs to lessen their hunger pangs. In Mozambique, people eat the grasshoppers that have destroyed their crops, calling them "flying shrimp." Though dirt eating is considered a pathological condition (called *pica*) among the well-fed, the world's poor eat dirt to add minerals to their diet. And in many countries, mothers have been known to boil stones in water, to convince their

People's needs and desires differ dramatically depending on where they live. On the left, eager customers line up outside a store in New York City to purchase the newly released edition of Halo 2 for X-Box. On the right, residents of Ethiopia line up to receive water.

hungry children that supper is almost ready. As they hover over the pot, these women hope that their malnourished children will fall asleep (McNeil 2004).

Around the world, inequality is a significant determinant of human behavior, opening doors of opportunity to some and closing them to others. Indeed, disparities in life chances are so extreme that in some places, the poorest of the poor may not be aware of them. Western media images may have circled the globe, but in extremely depressed rural areas, those at the bottom of society are not likely to see them.

A few centuries ago, such vast divides in global wealth did not exist. Except for a very few rulers and landowners, everyone in the world was poor. In much of Europe, life was as difficult as it was in Asia or South America. This was true until the Industrial Revolution and rising agricultural productivity produced explosive economic growth. The resulting rise in living standards was not evenly distributed across the world.

Figure 9-1 compares the industrial nations of the world to the developing nations. Using total population as a yardstick, we see that the developing countries have more than their fair share of rural population, as well as of total births, disease, and childhood deaths. At the same time, the industrial nations of the world, with a much smaller share of total population, have much more income and exports than the developing nations. Industrial nations also spend more on health and the military than other nations, and they emit more carbon dioxide (CO_2) (Sachs 2005a; Sutcliffe 2002).

Stratification in the World System

The divide between industrial and developing nations is sharp, but sociologists recognize a continuum of nations, from the richest of the rich to the poorest of the poor. For example, in 2004, the average value of goods and services produced per citizen (or per capita gross national income) in the industrialized countries of the United States, Japan, Switzerland, Belgium, and Norway was more than $30,000. In at least 12 poorer countries, the value was just $900 or less. But most countries fell somewhere between those extremes, as Figure 9-2 shows.

Still, the contrasts are stark. Three forces discussed here are particularly responsible for the domination of the world marketplace by a few nations: the legacy of colonialism, the advent of multinational corporations, and modernization.

FIGURE 9–1

Fundamental Global Inequality

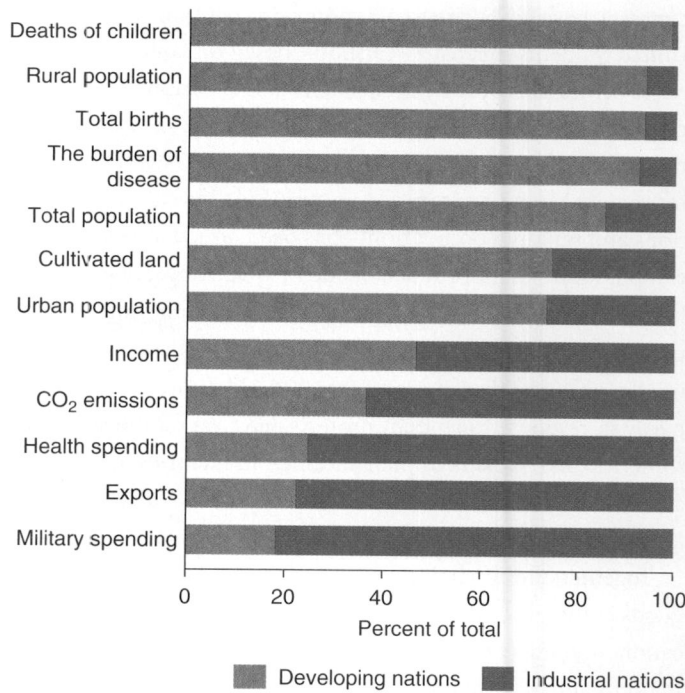

Note: In this comparison, industrial nations include the United States and Canada, Japan, Western Europe, and Australasia. Developing nations include Africa, Asia (except for Japan), Latin America, Eastern Europe, the Caribbean, and the Pacific.
Source: Adapted fom Sutcliffe 2002:18.

Think About It
What is the relationship between health spending, disease, and deaths of children? Between CO_2 emissions, income, and exports?

FIGURE 9–2

Gross National Income per Capita

MAPPING LIFE

WORLDWIDE www.mhhe.com/schaefer7

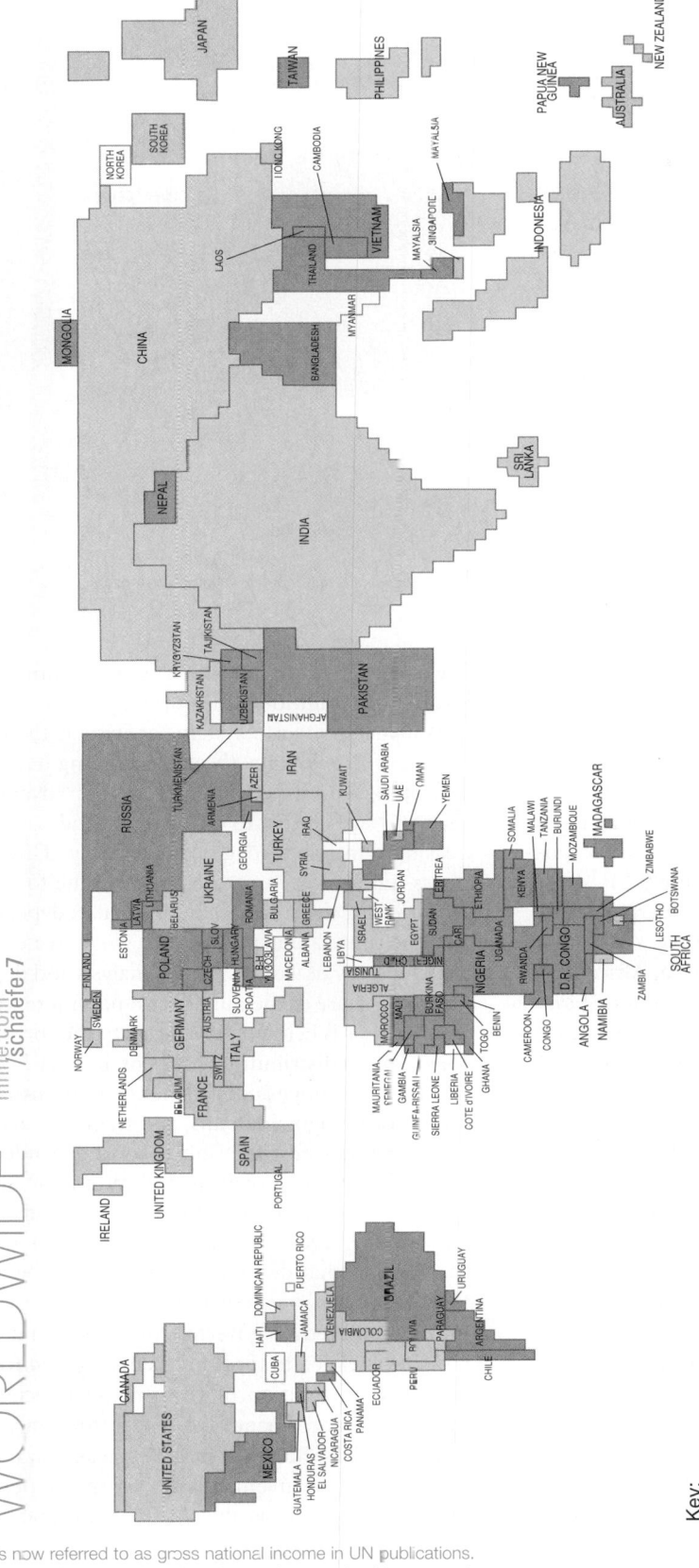

Key:
GNI per capita in 2004

■ $3,000 and below	■ $8,000–$19,100
■ $3,100–$7,995	▨ Over $19,200
□ No available data	

Note: Size based on 2000 population estimates.
Sources: Haub 2005; Weeks 2002:22–23, 2005:32–33.

This stylized map reflects the relative population sizes of the world's nations. The color for each country shows the 2002 estimated gross national income (the total value of goods and services produced by the nation in a given year) per capita. As the map shows, some of the world's most populous countries—such as Nigeria, Bangladesh, and Pakistan—are among the nations with the lowest standard of living, as measured by per capita gross national income.

Student Alert GDP is now referred to as gross national income in UN publications.
Web Resource Remind students that there is an interactive map for this chapter in the student center of the Online Learning Center (**www.mhhe.com/schaefer7**).

Colonialism occurs when a foreign power maintains political, social, economic, and cultural domination over a people for an extended period. In simple terms, it is rule by outsiders. The long reign of the British Empire over much of North America, parts of Africa, and India is an example of colonial domination. The same can be said of French rule over Algeria, Tunisia, and other parts of North Africa. Relations between the colonial nation and colonized people are similar to those between the dominant capitalist class and the proletariat, as described by Karl Marx.

By the 1980s, colonialism had largely disappeared. Most of the nations that were colonies before World War I had achieved political independence and established their own governments. However, for many of these countries, the transition to genuine self-rule was not yet complete. Colonial domination had established patterns of economic exploitation that continued even after nationhood was achieved—in part because former colonies were unable to develop their own industry and technology. Their dependence on more industrialized nations, including their former colonial masters, for managerial and technical expertise, investment capital, and manufactured goods kept former colonies in a subservient position. Such continuing dependence and foreign domination are referred to as *neocolonialism.*

The economic and political consequences of colonialism and neocolonialism are readily apparent. Drawing on the conflict perspective, sociologist Immanuel Wallerstein (1974, 1979a, 2000) views the global economic system as being divided between nations that control wealth and nations from which resources are taken. Through his *world systems analysis,* Wallerstein has described the unequal economic and political relationships in which certain industrialized nations (among them the United States, Japan, and Germany) and their global corporations dominate the *core* of this system (see Figure 9-3). At the *semiperiphery* of the system are countries with marginal economic status, such as Israel, Ireland, and South Korea. Wallerstein suggests that the poor developing countries of Asia, Africa, and Latin America are on the *periphery* of the world economic system. The key to Wallerstein's analysis is the exploitative relationship of *core* nations toward noncore nations. Core nations and their corporations control and exploit noncore nations' economies. Unlike other nations, they are relatively independent of outside control (Chase-Dunn and Grimes 1995).

The division between core and periphery nations is significant and remarkably stable. A study by the International Monetary Fund (2000) found little change over the course of the *last 100 years* for the 42 economies that were studied. The only changes were Japan's movement up into the group of core nations and China's movement down toward the margins of the semiperiphery nations. Yet Immanuel Wallerstein (2000) speculates that the world system as we currently understand it may soon undergo unpredictable changes. The world is becoming increasingly urbanized, a trend that is gradually eliminating the large pools of low-cost workers in rural areas. In the future, core nations will have to find other ways to reduce their labor costs.

FIGURE 9–3

World Systems Analysis at the Beginning of the 21st Century

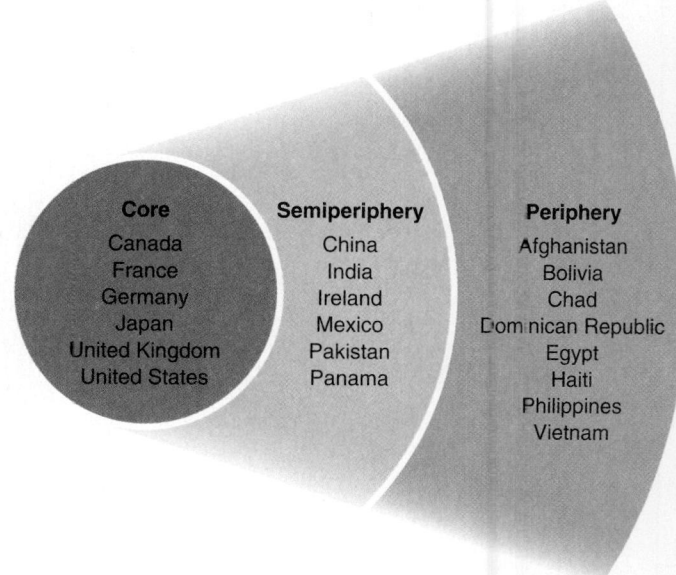

Core	Semiperiphery	Periphery
Canada	China	Afghanistan
France	India	Bolivia
Germany	Ireland	Chad
Japan	Mexico	Dominican Republic
United Kingdom	Pakistan	Egypt
United States	Panama	Haiti
		Philippines
		Vietnam

Note: Figure shows only a partial listing of countries.

The exhaustion of land and water resources through clear-cutting and pollution is also driving up the costs of production.

Wallerstein's world systems analysis is the most widely used version of *dependency theory.* According to this theory, even as developing countries make economic advances, they remain weak and subservient to core nations and corporations in an increasingly intertwined global economy. This interdependency allows industrialized nations to continue to exploit developing countries for their own gain. In a sense, dependency theory applies the conflict perspective on a global scale.

In the view of world systems analysis and dependency theory, a growing share of the human and natural resources of developing countries is being redistributed to the core industrialized nations. This redistribution happens in part because developing countries owe huge sums of money to industrialized nations as a result of foreign aid, loans, and trade deficits. The global debt crisis has intensified the Third World dependency begun under colonialism, neocolonialism, and multinational investment. International financial institutions are pressuring indebted countries to take severe measures to meet their interest payments. The result is that developing nations may be forced to devalue their currencies, freeze workers' wages, increase privatization of industry, and reduce government services and employment.

Closely related to these problems is *globalization,* the worldwide integration of government policies, cultures, social movements, and financial markets through trade and the exchange of ideas. Because world financial markets transcend governance by conventional nation states, international organizations such as the World Bank and the International

{p.20

Theory Conflict view of colonialism and neocolonialism in terms of foreign domination; conflict view of colonized people as equivalent to Marx's proletariat
Key Person Immanuel Wallerstein
Theory The emphasis of world systems analysis on unequal political and economic relationships among nations draws on the conflict perspective.

Student Alert Clarify why dependency theory is similar to world systems analysis.
Theory/Student Alert Note how the global debt crisis illustrates world systems analysis, dependency theory, and conflict theory.
Classroom Tip See "Globalization and Sociology" (Class Discussion Topics).

Ever since violent street demonstrations rocked Seattle in 1999, the annual meetings of the World Trade Organization (WTO) have been accompanied by protests. Dissenters charge that multinational corporations dominate world trade policy at the expense of developing nations, and that industrial nations should be held accountable for the economic and financial problems they create.

and other goods. However, today's multinational giants are not merely buying and selling overseas; they are also *producing* goods all over the world (I. Wallerstein 1974).

Moreover, today's "global factories" (factories throughout the developing world that are run by multinational corporations) may now have the "global office" alongside them. Multinationals based in core countries are beginning to establish reservation services and centers for processing data and insurance claims in the periphery nations. As service industries become a more important part of the international marketplace, many companies are concluding that the low costs of overseas operations more than offset the expense of transmitting information around the world.

Do not underestimate the size of these global corporations. As Table 9-1 (page 217) shows, the total revenues of multinational businesses are on a par with the total value of goods and services exchanged in *entire nations.* Foreign sales represent an important source of profit for multinational corporations, which encourages them to expand into other countries (in many cases, the developing nations). The economy of the United States is heavily dependent on foreign commerce, much of which is conducted by multinationals. Over one-fourth of all goods and services in the United States has to do with either the export of goods to foreign countries or the import of goods from abroad (U.S. Trade Representative 2003).

Monetary Fund have emerged as major players in the global economy. The function of these institutions, which are heavily funded and influenced by core nations, is to encourage economic trade and development and to ensure the smooth operation of international financial markets. As such, they are seen as promoters of globalization and defenders primarily of the interests of core nations. Critics call attention to a variety of issues, including violations of workers' rights, the destruction of the environment, the loss of cultural identity, and discrimination against minority groups in periphery nations.

Some observers see globalization and its effects as the natural result of advances in communications technology, particularly the Internet and satellite transmission of the mass media. Others view it more critically, as a process that allows multinational corporations to expand unchecked, as we will see in the next section (Chase-Dunn et al. 2000; Feketekuty 2001; L. Feuer 1989; Pearlstein 2001).

Use Your Sociological Imagination

www.mhhe.com/schaefer7

You are traveling through a developing country. What evidence do you see of neocolonialism and globalization?

Multinational Corporations

Worldwide, corporate giants play a key role in neocolonialism. The term ***multinational corporations*** refers to commercial organizations that are headquartered in one country but do business throughout the world. Such private trade and lending relationships are not new; merchants have conducted business abroad for hundreds of years, trading gems, spices, garments,

Functionalist View Functionalists believe that multinational corporations can actually help the developing nations of the world. They bring jobs and industry to areas where subsistence agriculture once served as the only means of survival. Multinationals also promote rapid development through the diffusion of inventions and innovations from industrial nations. Viewed from a functionalist perspective, the combination of skilled technology and management provided by multinationals and the relatively cheap labor available in developing nations is ideal for a global enterprise. Multinationals can take maximum advantage of technology while reducing costs and boosting profits.

Through their international ties, multinational corporations also make the nations of the world more interdependent. These ties may prevent certain disputes from reaching the point of serious conflict. A country cannot afford to sever diplomatic relations or engage in warfare with a nation that is the headquarters for its main business suppliers or a key outlet for its exports.

Conflict View Conflict theorists challenge this favorable evaluation of the impact of multinational corporations. They emphasize that multinationals exploit local workers to maximize

Theory Functional and conflict analysis of multinational corporations

The influence of multinational corporations abroad can be seen in this street scene from Manila, capital of the Philippines.

profits. Starbucks—the international coffee retailer based in Seattle—gets some of its coffee from farms in Guatemala. But to earn enough money to buy a pound of Starbucks coffee, a Guatemalan farmworker would have to pick 500 pounds of beans, representing five days of work (Entine and Nichols 1996).

The pool of cheap labor in the developing world prompts multinationals to move factories out of core countries. An added bonus for the multinationals is that the developing world discourages strong trade unions. In industrialized countries, organized labor insists on decent wages and humane working conditions, but governments seeking to attract or keep multinationals may develop a "climate for investment" that includes repressive antilabor laws that restrict union activity and collective bargaining. If labor's demands become too threatening, the multinational firm will simply move its plant elsewhere, leaving a trail of unemployment behind. Nike, for example, moved its factories from the United States to Korea to Indonesia to Vietnam in search of the lowest labor costs. Conflict theorists conclude that on the whole, multinational corporations have a negative social impact on workers in *both* industrialized and developing nations.

Workers in the United States and other core countries are beginning to recognize that their own interests are served by helping to organize workers in developing nations. As long as multinationals can exploit cheap labor abroad, they will be in a strong position to reduce wages and benefits in industrialized countries. With this in mind, in the 1990s, labor unions, religious organizations, campus groups, and other activists mounted public campaigns to pressure companies such as Nike, Starbucks, Reebok, Gap, and Wal-Mart to improve wages and working conditions in their overseas operations (Global Alliance for Workers and Communities 2003; Gonzalez 2003).

Several sociologists who have surveyed the effects of foreign investment by multinationals conclude that although it may initially contribute to a host nation's wealth, it eventually increases economic inequality within developing nations. This conclusion holds true for both income and ownership of land. The upper and middle classes benefit most from economic expansion, whereas the lower classes are less likely to benefit. As conflict theorists point out, multinationals invest in limited economic sectors and restricted regions of a nation. Although certain sectors of the host nation's economy expand, such as hotels and expensive restaurants, their very expansion appears to retard growth in agriculture and other economic sectors. Moreover, multinational corporations often buy out or force out local entrepreneurs and companies, thereby increasing economic and cultural dependence (Chase-Dunn and Grimes 1995; Kerbo 2003; I. Wallerstein 1979b).

Worldwide Poverty

In developing countries, any deterioration of the economic well-being of those who are least well off threatens their very survival. As we saw in Chapter 8 (see Box 8-2, page 198), even the wealthy in the developing world are poor by U.S. standards. Those who are poor in developing countries are truly destitute.

What would a map of the world look like if we drew it to a scale that reflects the number of *poor* people in each country instead of the number of people, as in Figure 9-2 (page 213)? As Figure 9-4 (page 218) shows, when we focus on the poverty level rather than the population, the world looks quite different. Note the huge areas of poverty in Africa and Asia, and the comparatively small areas of affluence in industrialized North America and Europe. Poverty is a worldwide problem that blights the lives of billions of people.

In 2000 the United Nations launched the Millennium Project, whose objective is to eliminate extreme poverty worldwide by the year 2015 (see Box 9-1, page 219). While 15 years may seem a long time, the challenge is great. Today, almost 3 billion people subsist on $2 a day or less. To accomplish the project's goal, planners estimate that industrial nations must set aside 0.7 percent of their **gross national product**—the value of a nation's goods and services—for aid to developing nations. At the time the Millennium Project was launched, only five countries were giving at that target rate: Denmark, Luxembourg, the Netherlands, Norway, and Sweden. To match their contribution proportionally,

Table 9-1   Multinational Corporations Compared to Nations

Rank	Corporation	Revenues ($ millions)	Comparison Nation(s)	Gross Domestic Product ($ millions)
1.	Wal-Mart (USA)	$287,989	Sweden	$301,606
2.	BP-British Petroleum (Britain)	285,059	Saudi Arabia plus UAE	285,708
3.	Exxon Mobil (USA)	270,772	Norway plus Bangladesh	272,768
4.	Royal Dutch/Shell (Britain/Netherlands)	268,690	Poland plus Romania	266,514
5.	General Motors (USA)	193,517	Argentina plus Peru	190,173
6.	DaimlerChrysler (Germany)	176,688	South Africa plus Zimbabwe	177,636
7.	Toyota Motor (Japan)	172,616	Singapore plus Pakistan	174,166
8.	Ford Motor (USA)	172,233	Greece	172,203
9.	General Electric (USA)	152,866	Ireland	153,719
10.	Total (France)	152,609	Portugal	147,899

Notes: Total is an oil, petroleum, and chemical company. UAE refers to United Arab Emirates. Where two nations are listed, the country with the larger GDP is listed first. Revenues as tabulated by *Fortune* are for 2004. GDP as collected by the World Bank are for 2003.
Sources: For corporate data, *Fortune* 2005:119; for GDP data, World Bank 2005a:202–204.

Think About It
What happens to society when corporations grow richer than countries and spill across international borders?

---

the United States would need to multiply its present aid level by 45 (Sachs 2005a).

Privileged people in industrialized nations tend to assume that the world's poor lack significant assets. Yet again and again, observers from these countries have been startled to discover how far even a small amount of capital can go. Numerous microfinance programs, which involve relatively small grants or loans, have encouraged marginalized people to invest not in livestock, which may die, or jewelry, which may be stolen, but in technological improvements such as small cooking stoves. In Indonesia, for example, some 60,000 microloans have enabled families who once cooked their food in a pit to purchase stoves. Improvements such as this not only enable people to cook more food at a more consistent temperature; they can become the basis of small-scale home businesses (*The Economist* 2005g).

Modernization

Around the world, millions of people are witnessing a revolutionary transformation of their day-to-day life. Contemporary social scientists use the term *modernization* to describe the far-reaching process by which periphery nations move from traditional or less developed institutions to those characteristic of more developed societies.

Wendell Bell (1981), whose definition of modernization we are using, notes that modern societies tend to be urban, literate,

Methods The comparison of corporate and national financial data relies on secondary analysis.

Half a century ago, many or most of the garments in U.S. clothing stores carried labels reading "Made in the U.S.A." Today, virtually no clothing is produced entirely in the United States. Despite this store's upscale decor, most of the garments it carries were made in developing nations—in Immanuel Wallerstein's terms, nations at the semiperiphery or periphery of the core nations.

Poverty Worldwide

MAPPING LIFE

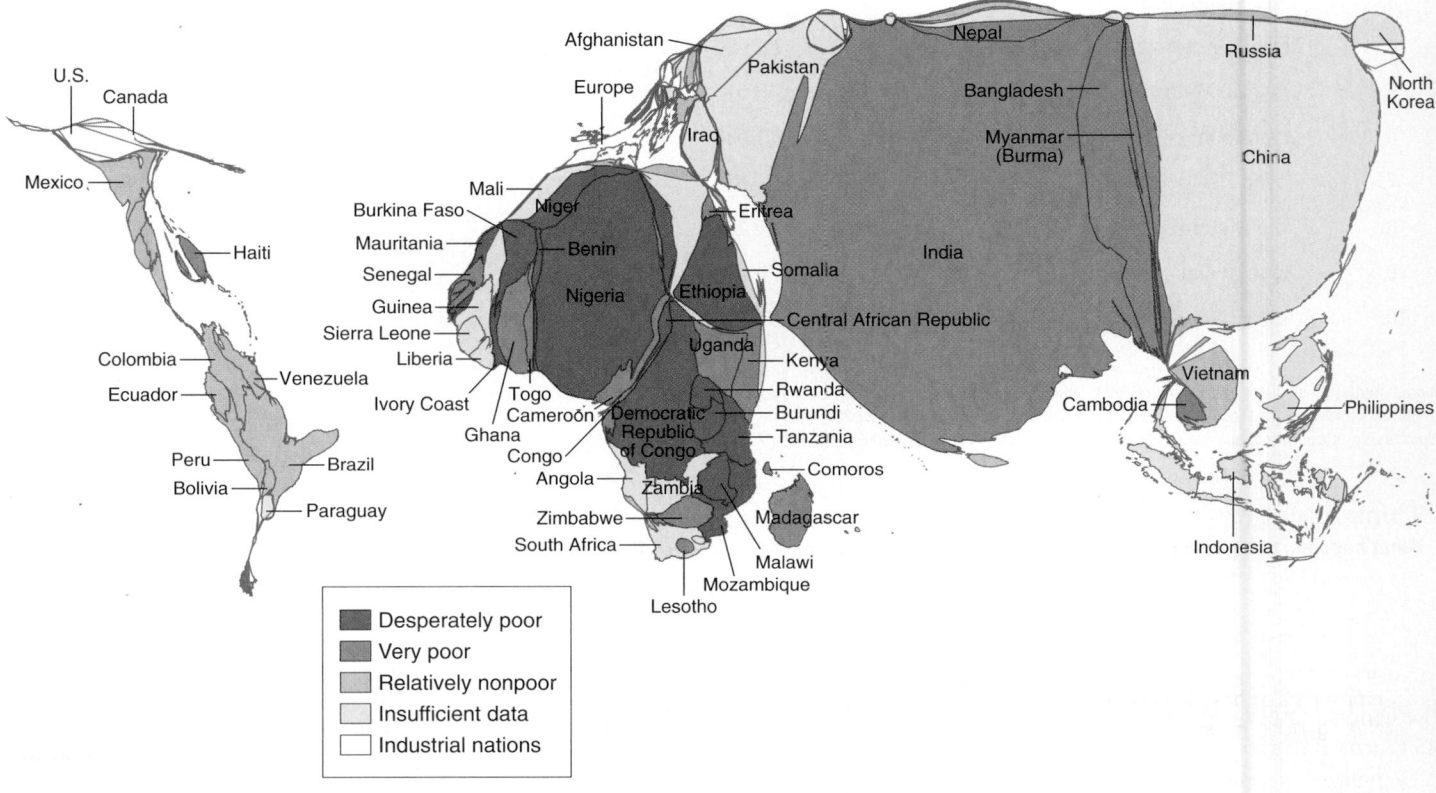

WORLDWIDE www.mhhe.com/schaefer7

Legend:
- Desperately poor
- Very poor
- Relatively nonpoor
- Insufficient data
- Industrial nations

Sources: Chronic Poverty Research Center 2005 in Sachs 2005b.

The scale of this map is based on the number of people in each region who are chronically poor. The colors represent the income levels of those who are poorest.

Think About It

To what degree does this map minimize those countries you have studied or might want to visit? To what degree does it emphasize parts of the world about which you know very little?

and industrial. These societies have sophisticated transportation and media systems. Their families tend to be organized within the nuclear family unit rather than the extended-family model (see Chapter 12). Thus, members of societies that undergo modernization must shift their allegiance from traditional sources of authority, such as parents and priests, to newer authorities, such as government officials.

Many sociologists are quick to note that terms such as *modernization* and even *development* contain an ethnocentric bias. The unstated assumption behind these terms is that "they" (people living in developing countries) are struggling to become more like "us" (in the core industrialized nations). Viewed from

a conflict perspective, these terms perpetuate the dominant ideology of capitalist societies.

The term *modernization* also suggests positive change. Yet change, if it comes, often comes slowly, and when it does it tends to serve the affluent segments of industrial nations. This truism seems to apply to the spread of the latest electronic technologies to the developing world (see Box 9-2, page 220).

A similar criticism has been made of **modernization theory,** a functionalist approach that proposes that modernization and development will gradually improve the lives of people in developing nations. According to this theory, even though countries develop at uneven rates, the development of peripheral coun-

Global View Poverty patterns throughout the world

Theory Modernization theory is an illustration of the functionalist perspective.
Classroom Tip See "Modernization: Kenya, a Case Study" (Additional Lecture Ideas).

9-1 Cutting Poverty Worldwide

The goal of the United Nations' Millennium Project is to cut the world's poverty level in half by 2015. The project has eight objectives:

1. *Eradicate extreme poverty and hunger.* Poverty rates are falling in many parts of the globe, particularly in Asia. But in sub-Saharan Africa, where the poor are hard pressed, millions more have sunk deeper into poverty. As of 2001, more than 1 billion people worldwide were living on less than $1 a day. These people suffer from chronic hunger. As of 2006, an estimated 100 million of the world's children were malnourished—a statistic that has negative implications for their countries' economic progress.
2. *Achieve universal primary education.* While many parts of the developing world are approaching universal school enrollment, in sub-Saharan Africa, less than two-thirds of all children are enrolled in primary school.
3. *Promote gender equality and empower women.* The gender gap in primary school enrollment that has characterized the developing world for so long is slowly closing. However, women still lack equal representation at the highest levels of government. Worldwide, they hold only about 16 percent of all parliamentary seats. Numerous research studies have shown that advances in women's education and governance are critical to improved health and economic development.
4. *Reduce child mortality.* Death rates among children under age five are dropping, but not nearly fast enough. About 59 of every 1,000 children die in the first year of life in developing nations, compared to just 3 of every 1,000 in developed nations. Sadly, evidence indicates that progress

toward reducing child mortality has slowed in recent decades.
5. *Improve maternal health.* Each year more than half a million women die during pregnancy or childbirth. Progress has been made in reducing maternal death rates in some developing regions, but not in countries where the risk of giving birth is highest.
6. *Combat HIV/AIDS, malaria, and other diseases.* AIDS has become the leading cause of premature death in sub-Saharan Africa, where two-thirds of the world's AIDS patients reside. Worldwide, the disease is the fourth most frequent killer. Though new drug treatments can prolong life, there is still no cure for this scourge.

> *As of 2001, more than 1 billion people worldwide were living on less than $1 a day.*

Moreover, each year malaria and tuberculosis kill almost as many people as AIDS, severely draining the labor pool in many countries.
7. *Ensure environmental sustainability.* While most countries have publicly committed themselves to the principles of sustainable development (development that can be maintained across generations), sufficient progress has not been made toward reversing the loss of the world's environmental resources through rampant clear-cutting of forests and other forms of environmental destruction. Even so, many developing countries lack the infrastructure needed to support public health. Though access to safe drinking

water has increased, half the developing world lacks toilets and other forms of basic sanitation.
8. *Develop a global partnership for development.* The United Nations Millennium Declaration seeks a global social compact in which developing countries pledge to do more to ensure their own development, while developed countries support them through aid, debt relief, and improved trade opportunities. However, despite the much publicized G8 summit (a meeting of the heads of state of the 8 major economies) in Gleneagles, Scotland, in 2005 and the accompanying LIVE 8 global concerts, the developed nations have fallen far short of the targets they set themselves.

Let's Discuss

1. Do you think the Millenium Project's objectives are realistic, given the enormity of the obstacles that must be overcome? Why do you think the project's founders gave themselves only 15 years to accomplish their goal?
2. How are the project's eight objectives related to one another? Could some of the objectives be reached successfully without addressing the others? If you were a government planner with the resources to address just one objective, which would you pick, and why?

Sources: Haub 2005; Katel 2005; Sachs 2005a; United Nations 2005a; Weisbrot et al. 2005; World Bank 2006a.

---

tries will be assisted by innovations transferred from the industrialized world. Critics of modernization theory, including dependency theorists, counter that any such technology transfer only increases the dominance of core nations over developing countries and facilitates further exploitation. (Table 9-2, on page 221, summarizes the three major approaches to global inequality.)

When we see all the Coca-Cola and IBM signs going up in developing countries, it is easy to assume that globalization and economic change are effecting cultural change. But that is not always the case, researchers note. Distinctive cultural traditions, such as a particular religious orientation or a nationalistic identity, often persist, and can soften the impact of modernization on a developing nation. Some contemporary sociologists

Policy Pointer Education linked to well-being
Gender Gender inequality linked to health and poverty
Contemporary Culture Crippling impact of HIV/AIDS on sub-Saharan Africa
Theory Relate development goals to world systems analysis.

Classroom Tip Assign students to design programs for eliminating poverty in 15, 50, or 100 years.
Theory Conflict critique of modernization theory

sociologyIN *the Global Community*

9-2 The Global Disconnect

Bogdan Ghirda, a Romanian, is paid 50 cents an hour to participate in multiplayer Internet games like City of Heroes and Star Wars. He is sitting in for someone in an industrialized country who does not want to spend days ascending to the highest levels of competition in order to compete with players who are already "well armed." This arrangement is not unusual. U.S.-based services can earn hundreds of dollars for recruiting someone in a less developed country, like Ghirda, to represent a single player in an affluent industrial country.

Meanwhile, villagers in Arumugam, India, are beginning to benefit from their new Knowledge Centre. The facility, funded by a nonprofit organization, contains five computers that offer Internet access—an amenity unknown until now to thousands of villagers.

Network Readiness Index

Top 10 Countries	Bottom 10 Countries
1. Singapore	95. Ecuador
2. Ireland	96. Mozambique
3. Finland	97. Honduras
4. Denmark	98. Paraguay
5. United States	99. Bolivia
6. Sweden	100. Bangladesh
7. Hong Kong	101. Angola
8. Japan	102. Ethiopia
9. Switzerland	103. Nicaragua
10. Canada	104. Chad

These two situations illustrate the technological disconnect between the developing and industrial nations. Around the world, developing nations lag far behind industrial nations in their use of and access to new technologies. The World Economic Forum's Networked Readiness Index (NRI), a ranking of 104 nations, shows the relative preparedness of individuals, businesses, and governments to benefit from information technologies. As the accompanying table shows, the haves of the world—countries like Singapore, the United

> *For developing nations, the consequences of the global disconnect are far more serious than an inability to surf the Net.*

States, and Japan—are network ready; the have-nots—countries like Ethiopia, Bolivia, and Mozambique—are not.

For developing nations, the consequences of the global disconnect are far more serious than an inability to surf the Net. Thanks to the Internet, multinational organizations can now function as a single global unit, responding instantly in real time, 24 hours a day. This new capability has fostered the emergence of what sociologist Manuel Castells calls a "global economy." But if large numbers of people—indeed, entire nations—are disconnected from

the new global economy, their economic growth will remain slow and the well-being of their people will remain retarded. Those citizens who are educated and skilled will immigrate to other labor markets, deepening the impoverishment of these nations on the periphery.

Remedying the global disconnect is not a simple matter. To gain access to new technologies, people in developing nations typically must serve the world's industrial giants, as Bogdan Ghirda does. Some may benefit from investment by nongovernmental organizations, as the villagers in India have. But progress to date has been slow. In 2005, in an effort to accelerate the diffusion of new technologies, the United Nations launched the Digital Solidarity Fund. The hope is that global information technology companies can be persuaded to set aside some of their profits to help developing nations connect to the Internet.

Let's Discuss

1. For nations on the periphery, what are some of the social and economic consequences of the global disconnect?
2. What factors might complicate efforts to remedy the global disconnect in developing nations?

Sources: Castells 2000; *The Economist* 2005c; T. Thompson 2005; United Nations 2005b; World Economic Forum 2005.

---

emphasize that both industrialized and developing countries are "modern." Researchers increasingly view modernization as movement along a series of social indicators—among them degree of urbanization, energy use, literacy, political democracy, and use of birth control. Clearly, some of these are subjective indicators; even in industrialized nations, not everyone would agree that wider use of birth control represents an example of progress (Armer and Katsillis 1992; Hedley 1992; Inglehart and Baker 2000).

Current modernization studies generally take a convergence perspective. Using the indicators just noted, researchers focus on how societies are moving closer together, despite traditional differences. From a conflict perspective, the modernization of developing countries often perpetuates their dependence on and

continued exploitation by more industrialized nations. Conflict theorists view such continuing dependence on foreign powers as an example of contemporary neocolonialism.

Stratification within Nations: A Comparative Perspective

At the same time that the gap between rich and poor nations is widening, so too is the gap between rich and poor citizens *within* nations. As discussed earlier, stratification in developing nations is closely related to their relatively weak and dependent position in the global economy. Local elites work hand in hand with multinational corporations and prosper from such alliances. At the same time, the economic system creates and perpetuates the

Let's Discuss Relate "The Global Disconnect" to theories of stratification in the world system.
Classroom Tip See "Diffusion into Asia" (Additional Lecture Ideas).

Policy Pointer Efforts by the United Nations to bridge the global digital divide
Contemporary Culture Wide-ranging implications of new technologies

summingUP

Table 9-2 Three Approaches to Global Inequality

Approach	Sociological Perspective	Explanation
World systems analysis	Functionalist and conflict	Unequal economic and political relationships maintain sharp divisions between nations.
Dependency theory	Conflict	Industrial nations exploit developing countries through colonialism and multinational corporations.
Modernization theory	Functionalist	Developing countries are moving away from traditional cultures and toward the cultures of industrialized nations.

exploitation of industrial and agricultural workers. That's why foreign investment in developing countries tends to increase economic inequality. As Box 9-3 (page 222) makes clear, inequality within a society is also evident in industrialized nations such as Japan (Bornschier et al. 1978; Kerbo 2003).

Distribution of Wealth and Income

In at least 26 nations around the world, the most affluent 10 percent of the population receives at least 40 percent of all income. The list includes the African nation of Namibia (the leader, at 65 percent of all income), as well as Colombia, Mexico, Nigeria, and South Africa. Figure 9-5 compares the distribution of income in selected industrialized and developing nations.

Women in developing countries find life especially difficult. Karuna Chanana Ahmed, an anthropologist from India who has studied women in developing nations, calls women the most exploited of oppressed people. Beginning at birth women face sex discrimination. They are commonly fed less than male children, are denied educational opportunities, and are often hospitalized only when they are critically ill. Inside or outside the home, women's work is devalued. When economies fail, as they did in Asian countries in the late 1990s, women are the first to be laid off from work (J. Anderson and Moore 1993; Kristof 1998).

Surveys show a significant degree of *female infanticide* (the killing of baby girls) in China and rural areas of India. Only one-third of Pakistan's sexually segregated schools are for women, and

one-third of those schools have no buildings. In Kenya and Tanzania, it is illegal for a woman to own a house. In Saudi Arabia, women are prohibited from driving, walking alone in public, and socializing with men outside their families (C. Murphy 1993). We will explore women's second-class status throughout the world more fully in Chapter 11.

Social Mobility

Mobility in Industrial Nations Studies of intergenerational mobility in industrialized nations have found the following patterns:

1. Substantial similarities exist in the ways that parents' positions in stratification systems are transmitted to their children.

2. As in the United States, mobility opportunities in other nations have been influenced by structural factors, such as labor market changes that lead to the rise or decline of an occupational group within the social hierarchy.

3. Immigration continues to be a significant factor in shaping a society's level of intergenerational mobility (Ganzeboom et al. 1991; Haller et al. 1990; Hauser and Grusky 1988).

FIGURE 9-5

Distribution of Income in Nine Nations

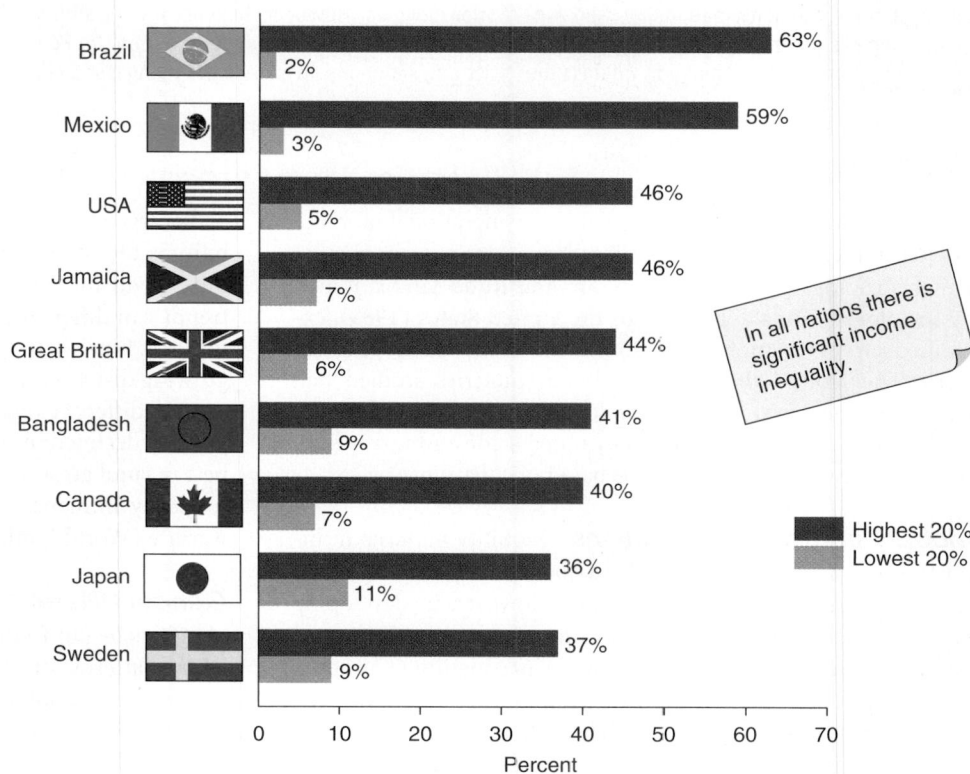

In all nations there is significant income inequality.

Highest 20%
Lowest 20%

Note: Data are considered comparable although based on statistics covering 1993 to 2001.
Source: World Bank 2005a:72–74.

Classroom Tip See "Cross-National Studies of Inequality" (Class Discussion Topics).
Theory From a conflict perspective, worldwide stratification is evident not only between rich and poor nations but between rich and poor citizens within nations.
Classroom Tips See "Gaijin" (Additional Lecture Ideas) and "Lorenz Curve" in Topics and Sources for Student Research.

socialINEQUALITY ● ● ●

9-3 Stratification in Japan

A tourist visiting Japan may at first experience a bit of culture shock after noticing the degree to which everything in Japanese life is ranked: corporations, universities, even educational programs. These rankings are widely reported and accepted. Moreover, the ratings shape day-to-day social interactions: Japanese find it difficult to sit, talk, or eat together unless the relative rankings of those present have been established, often through the practice of *meishi* (the exchange of business cards).

The apparent preoccupation with ranking and formality suggests an exceptional degree of stratification. Yet researchers have determined that Japan's level of income inequality is among the lowest of major industrial societies (see Figure 9-5 on page 221). The pay gap between Japan's top corporate executives and the nation's lowest-paid workers is about 8 to 1; the comparable figure for the United States would be 37 to 1.

One factor that works against inequality is that Japan is rather homogeneous—certainly when compared with the United States—in terms of race, ethnicity, nationality, and language. Japan's population is 98 percent Japanese. Still, there is discrimination against the nation's Chinese and Korean minorities, and the *Burakumin*, a low-status subculture, encounter extensive prejudice.

Perhaps the most pervasive form of inequality in Japan today is gender discrimination. Overall, women earn only about 65 percent of men's wages. Only about 9 percent of Japanese managers are female—a ratio that is one of the lowest in the world. Even in

> *Even in developing countries, women are twice as likely to be managers as women in Japan.*

developing countries, women are twice as likely to be managers as women in Japan.

In 1985, Japan's parliament—at the time, 97 percent male—passed an Equal Employment bill that encourages employers to end sex discrimination in hiring, assignment, and promotion policies. However, feminist organizations were dissatisfied because the law lacked strong sanctions. In a landmark ruling issued in late 1996, a Japanese court for the first time held an employer liable for denying promotions due to sex discrimination.

Progress has also been made in terms of public opinion. In 1987, 43 percent of Japanese adults agreed that married women should stay home, but by 2000 the proportion had dropped to 25 percent. On the political front, Japanese women have made progress but remain underrepresented. In a study of women in government around the world, Japan ranked near the bottom of the countries studied, with only 9 percent of its national legislators female.

Let's Discuss

1. What factors might contribute to the relatively low level of income inequality in Japan?
2. Describe the types of gender discrimination found in Japan. Why do you think Japanese women occupy such a subordinate social position?

Sources: French 2003a, 2003b; Fujimoto 2004; Goodman and Kashiwagi 2002; Inter-Parliamentary Union 2006; Neary 2003.

Cross-cultural studies suggest that intergenerational mobility has been increasing in recent decades, at least among men. Dutch sociologists Harry Ganzeboom and Ruud Luijkx, joined by sociologist Donald Treiman of the United States (1989), examined surveys of mobility in 35 industrial and developing nations. They found that almost all the countries studied had witnessed increased intergenerational mobility between the 1950s and 1980s. In particular, they noted a common pattern of movement away from agriculture-based occupations.

Mobility in Developing Nations Mobility patterns in industrialized countries are usually associated with intergenerational and intragenerational mobility. However, in developing nations, macro-level social and economic changes often overshadow micro-level movement from one occupation to another. For example, there is typically a substantial wage differential between rural and urban areas, which leads to high levels of migration to the cities. Yet the urban industrial sectors of developing countries generally cannot provide sufficient employment for all those seeking work.

In large developing nations, the most socially significant mobility is the movement out of poverty. This type of mobility is difficult to measure and confirm, however, because economic trends can differ from one area of a country to another. For instance, China's rapid income growth has been accompanied by a growing disparity in income between urban and rural areas, and among different regions. Similarly, in India during the 1990s, poverty declined in urban areas but may have remained static at best in rural areas. Around the world, social mobility is also dramatically influenced by catastrophes such as crop failure and warfare (World Bank 2000).

Gender Differences and Mobility Only recently have researchers begun to investigate the impact of gender on the mobility patterns of developing nations. Many aspects of the development process—especially modernization in rural areas and the rural-to-urban migration just described—may result in the modification or abandonment of traditional cultural practices and even marital systems. The effects on women's social standing and mobility are not necessarily positive. As a country

Global View Stratification in Japan
Gender Women earn about 65 percent of men's wages in Japan.
Let's Discuss Ask students to compare gender discrimination in Japan to gender discrimination in the United States.

Theory Conflict view of how there is less mobility in developing nations than in core industrialized nations
Gender Impact of gender on mobility patterns of developing nations
Classroom Tip See "The Informal Economy" (Additional Lecture Ideas).

In developing countries, people who hope to rise out of poverty often move from the country to the city, where employment prospects are better. The jobs available in industrialized urban areas offer perhaps the best means of upward mobility. This woman works in an electronics factory in Kuala Lumpur, Malaysia.

tral land from exploitation by outsiders. Having established their right to its rich minerals and forests, members of indigenous groups had begun to feud among themselves over the way in which the land's resources should be developed. Aided by the United Nations Partners in Development Programme, women volunteers established the Pan-Cordillera Women's Network for Peace and Development, a coalition of women's groups dedicated to resolving local disputes. The women mapped boundaries, prepared development plans, and negotiated more than 2,000 peace pacts among community members. They have also run in elections, campaigned against social problems, and organized residents to work together for the common good (United Nations Development Programme 2000:87).

Studies of the distribution of wealth and income within various countries, together with cross-cultural research on mobility, consistently reveal stratification based on class, gender, and other factors within a wide range of societies. Clearly, a worldwide view of stratification must include not only the sharp contrast between wealthy and impoverished nations but also the layers of hierarchy *within* industrialized societies and developing countries.

Use Your Sociological Imagination

www.mhhe.com /schaefer7

Imagine that the United States borders a country with a much higher standard of living. In this neighboring country, the salaries of workers with a college degree start at $120,000 a year. What is life in the United States like?

develops and modernizes, women's vital role in food production deteriorates, jeopardizing both their autonomy and their material well-being. Moreover, the movement of families to the cities weakens women's ties to relatives who can provide food, financial assistance, and social support.

In the Philippines, however, women have moved to the forefront of the indigenous peoples' struggle to protect their ances-

CASE *study*

(STRATIFICATION IN MEXICO)

In May 2003, on a stretch of highway in southern Arizona, the open doors of an abandoned tractor trailer revealed the dead bodies of 19 Mexicans. The truck had been carrying a group of illegal immigrants across the Sonoran Desert when the people hidden inside began to suffer from the intense desert heat. Their story was not unusual. Each year several hundred illegal immigrants die attempting to traverse the U.S.–Mexican border in the hot, arid corridor that connects the state of Sonora in Mexico to the state of Arizona in the United States.

Why do Mexicans risk their lives crossing the dangerous desert that lies between the two countries? The answer to this question can be found in the income disparity between the two nations—one an industrial giant and the other a partially developed country still recovering from a history of colonialism and neocolonialism. In this section we will look in some detail at the dynamics of stratification in Mexico, a country of 102 million

people. Since the early 20th century there has been a close cultural, economic, and political relationship between Mexico and the United States, one in which the United States is the dominant party. According to Immanuel Wallerstein's analysis, the United States is at the core while neighboring Mexico is still on the semiperiphery of the world economic system.

Mexico's Economy

If we compare Mexico's economy to that of the United States, differences in the standard of living and in life chances are quite dramatic, even though Mexico is considered a semiperiphery nation. Gross national income is a commonly used measure of an average resident's economic well-being. In 2004, the gross national income per person in the United States came to $39,710; in Mexico, it was a mere $9,590. About 87 percent of adults in the United States have a high school education, compared to

Gender Role of Filipina women in protecting ancestral land

Student Alert/Let's Discuss Make sure that students understand why the United States is a core country and Mexico is a semiperiphery country. What implications do these statuses have for interaction between these nations?

A worker cleans the reflecting pool at the opulent Casa del Mar Hotel in San Jose del Cabo, Mexico. Though international tourism is a major industry in Mexico, most Mexicans have not benefited much from it. Mexican workers who are employed in the industry earn low wages, and their jobs are jeopardized by the travel industry's frequent boom and bust cycles.

only 13 percent of those in Mexico. And fewer than 7 of every 1,000 infants in the United States die in the first year of life, compared to about 22 per 1,000 in Mexico (Bureau of the Census 2005a:868, 872; Haub 2005).

Although Mexico is unquestionably a poor country, the gap between its richest and poorest citizens is one of the widest in the world (refer back to Figure 9-5, page 221). According to the World Bank, in 2004, 26 percent of Mexico's population survived on just $2 per day. At the same time, the wealthiest 10 percent of Mexico's people accounted for 43 percent of the entire nation's income. According to a *Forbes* magazine portrait of the world's wealthiest individuals, that year Mexico ranked 10th in terms of the number of the world's wealthiest who lived there (Kroll and Goodman 2005; World Bank 2003b:55, 61).

Political scientist Jorge Castañeda (1995:71) calls Mexico a "polarized society with enormous gaps between rich and poor, town and country, north and south, white and brown (or *criollos* and *mestizos*)." He adds that the country is also divided along lines of class, race, religion, gender, and age. We will examine stratification within Mexico by focusing on race relations and the plight of Mexican Indians, the status of Mexican women, and emigration to the United States and its impact on the U.S.–Mexican borderlands.

Race Relations in Mexico: The Color Hierarchy

Mexico's indigenous Indians account for an estimated 14 percent of the nation's population. More than 90 percent of them live in houses without sewers, compared with 21 percent of the population as a whole. And whereas just 10 percent of Mexican adults are illiterate, the proportion for Mexican Indians is 44

percent (Boudreaux 2002; *The Economist* 2004b; G. Thompson 2001b).

The subordinate status of Mexico's Indians is but one reflection of the nation's color hierarchy, which links social class to the appearance of racial purity. At the top of this hierarchy are the *criollos,* the 10 percent of the population who are typically White, well-educated members of the business and intellectual elites, with familial roots in Spain. In the middle is the large, impoverished *mestizo* majority, most of whom have brown skin and a mixed racial lineage as a result of intermarriage. At the bottom of the color hierarchy are the destitute, full-blooded Mexican Indian minority and a small number of Blacks, some descended from 200,000 African slaves brought to Mexico. This color hierarchy is an important part of day-to-day life—enough so that some Mexicans in the cities use hair dyes, skin lighteners, and blue or green contact lenses to appear more White and European. Ironically, however, nearly all Mexicans are considered part Indian because of centuries of intermarriage (Castañeda 1995; DePalma 1995).

Many observers take note of widespread denial of prejudice and discrimination against people of color in Mexico. Schoolchildren are taught that the election of Benito Juárez, a Zapotec Indian, as president of Mexico in the 19th century proves that all Mexicans are equal. Yet there has been a marked growth in the last decade of formal organizations and voluntary associations representing indigenous Indians (DePalma 1995, 1996; Stavenhagen 1994; Utne 2003).

The Status of Women in Mexico

In 1975, Mexico City hosted the first international conference on the status of women, convened by the United Nations. Much of the discussion concerned the situation of women in developing countries; in that regard, the situation is mixed. Women now constitute 42 percent of the labor force—an increase from 34 percent in 1980, but still less than in industrial countries. Unfortunately, Mexican women are even more mired in the lowest-paying jobs than their counterparts in industrial nations. In the political arena, though they rarely occupy top decision-making positions, women have significantly increased their representation in the national legislature, to 24 percent. Mexico now ranks 30th among 184 nations—well ahead of Great Britain and France (Bureau of the Census 2005a:881; Inter-Parliamentary Union 2006).

Feminist sociologists emphasize that even when Mexican women work outside the home, they often are not recognized as active and productive household members, whereas men are typically viewed as heads of the household. As one consequence, women find it difficult to obtain credit and technical assistance in many parts of the country, and to inherit land in rural areas. Within manufacturing and service industries, women generally receive little training and tend to work in the least-automated and least-skilled jobs—in good part because there is little expectation that women will pursue career advancement, organize for better working conditions, or become active in labor unions (Kopinak 1995; Martelo 1996; see also G. Young 1993).

The economic position of the border-lands is rather complicated, as we can see in the emergence of *maquiladoras* on the Mexican side (see Figure 9-6, page 226). These are foreign-owned factories established just across the border in Mexico, where the companies that own them do not have to pay taxes or provide insurance and benefits to workers. The *maquiladoras* have attracted manufacturing jobs from other parts of North America to Mexico. As of the end of 2004, 1.1 million people were employed in the *maquiladoras,* where the daily take-home pay for entry-level workers was $4 to $5. Since many of these firms come from the United States and sell their products to Mexico's vast domestic market, their operations deepen the impact of U.S. consumer culure on Mexico's urban and rural areas (*Migration News* 2005c).

The *maquiladoras* have contributed to Mexico's economic development, but not without some cost. Conflict theorists note that unregulated growth allows owners to exploit workers with jobs that lack security, possibilities for advancement, and decent wages. Moreover, many of the U.S.-owned factories require female job applicants to take a urine test to screen out those who are pregnant—a violation of Mexican law as well as of NAFTA, and the source of numerous cases of sex discrimination. Social activists also complain that tens of thousands of Mexicans work on *maquiladora* assembly lines for very low wages, raising the issue of sweatshop labor noted earlier in this chapter (Dillon 1998; Dougherty and Holthouse 1999).

Ironically, the *maquiladoras* are now experiencing the same challenge from global trade as U.S. manufacturing plants did. Beginning in 2001, some companies began shifting their operations to China. While Mexican labor costs (wages plus benefits) are just $2 to $2.50 an hour, Chinese labor costs are even lower—50 cents to $1 an hour. Of the 700,000 new *maquiladora* jobs created in NAFTA's first seven years, 43 percent were eliminated between 2000 and 2003 (*Migration News* 2002c, 2004).

When people in the United States think about the border-lands, they generally think about immigration, a controversial political issue in the United States—especially near the Mexican border. For its part, Mexico is concerned about the priorities and policies of its powerful northern neighbor. From the Mexican point of view, the United States too often regards Mexico simply as a reserve pool of cheap labor, encouraging Mexicans to cross the border when workers are needed but discouraging and cracking down on them when they are not. Some people, then, see immigration more as a labor market issue than a law enforcement issue. Viewed from the perspective of Immanuel Wallerstein's

In 2000, a group of masked women demonstrated outside the Mexican Army's barracks in the state of Chiapas, demanding that the soldiers leave. The women were supporters of the Zapatista National Liberation Army, an insurgent group that protests economic injustices and discrimination against the Indian population in Chiapas

In recent decades, Mexican women have begun to organize to address an array of economic, political, and health issues. Since women continue to serve as the household managers for their families, even when they work outside the home, they are well aware of the consequences of the inadequate public services in lower-income urban neighborhoods. As far back as 1973, women in Monterrey—the nation's third-largest city—began protesting the continuing disruptions of the city's water supply. After individual complaints to city officials and the water authority proved fruitless, social networks of female activists began to emerge. These activists sent delegations to confront politicians, organized protest rallies, and blocked traffic as a means of getting media attention. Though their efforts brought improvements in Monterrey's water service, the issue of reliable and safe water remains a concern in Mexico and many developing countries (Bennett 1995).

The Borderlands

Growing recognition of the borderlands reflects the increasingly close and complex relationship between these two countries. The term **borderlands** refers to the area of common culture along the border between Mexico and the United States. Legal and illegal emigration from Mexico to the United States, day laborers crossing the border regularly to go to jobs in the United States, the implementation of the North American Free Trade Agreement, and the exchange of media across the border all make the notion of separate Mexican and U.S. cultures obsolete in the borderlands.

Gender Role of Mexican women in addressing economic, political, and health issues

Theory Conflict analysis of *maquiladoras* in Mexico
Gender Gender discrimination in the *maquiladoras* in Mexico
Let's Discuss Have students explain the *maquiladoras* within the context of Wallerstein's world systems analysis.

The Borderlands

MAPPING LIFE

WORLDWIDE www.mhhe.com /schaefer7

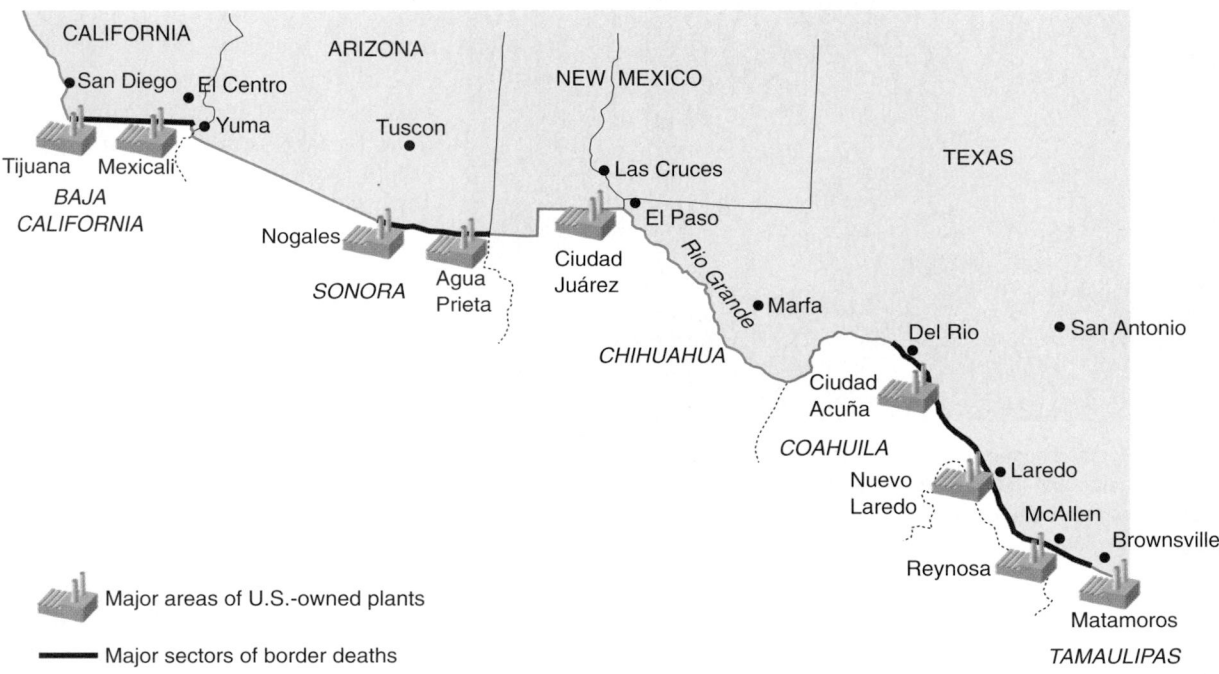

Major areas of U.S.-owned plants

Major sectors of border deaths

Source: Prepared by the author based on Ellingwood 2001; G. Thompson 2001a.

Think About It
How do U.S. consumers benefit from the buildup of factories along the U.S.–Mexican border?

world systems analysis and dependency theory, it is yet another example of a core industrialized nation exploiting a developing country.

As we saw at the beginning of this case, the risks of immigration are considerable. Following September 11, 2001, when the U.S. government increased surveillance at common entry points along the border, migrants without proper documentation moved to more remote and dangerous locations. In all, several hundred illegal immigrants lose their lives every year while attempting to cross the long border, many of them from dehydration in the intense desert heat (Dellios 2002).

The social impact of emigration to the United States is felt throughout Mexico. According to sociological research, the earliest emigrants were typically married men of working age who came from the middle of the stratification system. They had enough financial resources to afford the costs and risks of emigration, yet were experiencing enough financial strain that entering the United States was attractive to them. Over time, kinship ties to migrants multiplied and emigration became less class-selective, with entire families making the trek to the United States. More recently, the occupational backgrounds of Mexican emigrants have widened further, reflecting not only changes in U.S. immigration policy but the continuing crisis in the Mexican economy (Massey 1998).

Many Mexicans who have come to the United States send some part of their earnings back across the border to family members still in Mexico. This substantial flow of money, sometimes referred to as **remittances** or *migradollars*, is estimated at a minimum of $17 billion a year, and is surpassed only by oil as a source of income. If these funds went solely into the purchase of consumer goods, they would underscore the view of dependency theory, that Mexico's economy is little more than an extension of the economy of the United States. In fact, however, some of these migradollars are used by Mexicans to establish and maintain small business enterprises, such as handicraft workshops and farms. Consequently, the transfer of migradollars does stimulate the local and national economies of Mexico (*Migration News* 2005a).

We have seen that inequality is a problem not just in Mexico, but throughout the world. We turn now to an examination of an especially ugly form of social inequality, human rights abuse.

Use Your Sociological Imagination   www.mhhe.com/schaefer7

Imagine a day when the border between the United States and Mexico is completely open. What would the two countries' economies be like? What would their societies be like?

social Policy
and Global Inequality

Universal Human Rights

The Issue

Poised on the third millennium, the world seemed capable of mighty feats, ranging from explorations of distant solar systems to the refinement of tiny genes within human cells. Yet at the same time came constant reminders of how quickly people and their fundamental human rights could be trampled.

Human rights refers to universal moral rights possessed by all people because they are human. The most important elaboration of human rights appears in the Universal Declaration of Human Rights, adopted by the United Nations in 1948. This declaration prohibits slavery, torture, and degrading punishment; grants everyone the right to a nationality and its culture; affirms freedom of religion and the right to vote; proclaims the right to seek asylum in other countries to escape persecution; and prohibits arbitrary interference with one's privacy and the arbitrary taking of a person's property. It also emphasizes that mothers and children are entitled to special care and assistance.

What steps, if any, can the world community take to ensure the protection of these rights? Is it even possible to agree on what those rights are?

The Setting

At first, the United States opposed a binding obligation to the Universal Declaration of Human Rights. The government feared that the declaration would cause international scrutiny of the nation's civil rights controversies (at a time when racial segregation laws were still common). By the early 1960s, however, the United States had begun to use the declaration to promote democracy abroad (Forsythe 1990).

The 1990s brought the term *ethnic cleansing* into the world's vocabulary. In the former Yugoslavia, Serbs initiated a policy intended to "cleanse" Muslims from parts of Bosnia-Herzegovina, and ethnic Albanians from the province of Kosovo. Hundreds of thousands of people were killed in fighting there, while many others were uprooted from their homes. Moreover, reports surfaced of substantial numbers of rapes of Muslim, Croatian, and Kosovar women by Serbian soldiers. In 1996 a United Nations tribunal indicted eight Bosnian Serb military and police officers for rape, marking the first time that sexual assault was treated as a war crime under international law (Power 2002).

In the wake of the terrorist attacks of September 11, 2001, increased security and surveillance at U.S. airports and border crossings caused some observers to wonder whether human rights were not being jeopardized at home. At the same time, thousands of noncitizens of Arab and south Asian descent were questioned for no other reason than their ethnic and religious backgrounds. A few were placed in custody, sometimes without access to legal assistance. As the war on terror moved overseas, human rights concerns escalated. In 2005, the United Nations' secretary-general Kofi Annan criticized the United States and Britain for equating people who were resisting the presence of foreign troops in Afghanistan and Iraq with terrorists. For the foreseeable future, it seems, the United States and other countries will walk a delicate tightrope between human rights and the need for security (Parker 2004; Steele 2005).

Sociological Insights

By its very title, the Universal Declaration of Human Rights emphasizes that such rights should be *universal*. Even so, cultural {p.71 relativism encourages understanding and respect for the distinctive norms, values, and customs of each culture. In some situations, conflicts arise between human rights standards and local social practices that rest on alternative views of human dignity. For example, is India's caste system an inherent violation of human rights? What about the many cultures of the world that view the subordinate status of women as an essential element in their traditions? Should human rights be interpreted differently in different parts of the world?

In 1993, the United States rejected such a view by insisting that the Universal Declaration of Human Rights set a single standard for acceptable behavior around the world. However, in the late 1990s, certain Asian and African nations were reviving arguments about cultural relativism in an attempt to block sanctions by the United Nations Human Rights Commission. For example, female genital mutilation, a practice that is common in more than 30 countries around the world, has been condemned

Policy Pointer A nation's policies regarding treatment of immigrants and refugees often lead to controversies over human rights violations.
Let's Discuss Is the United Nations' definition of human rights culture bound?

Classroom Tip Refer back to the discussion of cultural relativism in Chapter 3.

A Chechen boy who witnessed his father's killing stands outside a refugee camp in Russia, where he and his brother are receiving mental health care from Doctors Without Borders. Civilian assassinations are one of the many violations of human rights that typically occur during wartime.

interfere in human rights issues, especially if they conflict with what are regarded as more pressing national concerns. Stepping up to fill the gap are international organizations such as the United Nations and nongovernmental organizations (NGOs) like Médecins sans Frontières and Amnesty International. Most initiatives come from these international bodies.

Médecins sans Frontières (Doctors without Borders), the world's largest independent emergency medical aid organization, won the 1999 Nobel Peace Prize for its work in countries worldwide. Founded in 1971 and based in Paris, the organization has 5,000 doctors and nurses working in 80 countries. "Our intention is to highlight current upheavals, to bear witness to foreign tragedies and reflect on the principles of humanitarian aid," explains Dr. Rony Brauman, the organization's president (Spielmann 1992:12; also see Daley 1999).

in Western nations as a human rights abuse. This controversial practice often involves removal of the clitoris, in the belief that its excision will inhibit a young woman's sex drive, making her chaste and thus more desirable to her future husband. Though some countries have passed laws against the practice, they have gone largely unenforced. Immigrants from countries where genital mutilation is common often insist that their daughters undergo the procedure, to protect them from Western cultural norms that allow premarital sex. In this context, how does one define human rights (Religious Tolerance 2005)?

It is not often that a nation makes such a bold statement. Policymakers, including those in the United States, more frequently look at human rights issues from an economic perspective. Functionalists would point out how much more quickly we become embroiled in "human rights" concerns when oil is at stake, as in the Middle East, or when military alliances come into play, as in Europe. Governments ratify human rights but resist independent efforts to enforce them within their own borders (Hafner-Burton and Tsutsui 2005).

Because international human rights can be highly contextual, they may also be difficult to enforce within the formal requirements of a country's legal process. Despite the apparent torture exposed in digital camera shots from Iraq and Afghanistan, for example, numerous investigations by the British and U.S. military have been inconclusive. Either because of the tenets of military necessity in wartime or because of an inability to locate the victims, many apparent violations have gone unpunished (Klug 2005).

Policy Initiatives

Human rights issues come wrapped up in international diplomacy. For that reason, many national policymakers hesitate to

In recent years, awareness has been growing of lesbian and gay rights as an aspect of universal human rights. In 1994, Amnesty International (1994:2) published a pioneering report in which it acknowledged that "homosexuals in many parts of the world live in constant fear of government persecution." The report examined abuses in Brazil, Greece, Mexico, Iran, the United States, and other countries, including cases of torture, imprisonment, and extrajudicial execution. Later in 1994, the United States issued an order that would allow lesbians and gay men to seek political asylum in the United States if they could prove they had suffered government persecution in their home countries solely because of their sexual orientation (Johnston 1994).

Ethnic cleansing in the former Yugoslavia, human rights violations in Iraq and Afghanistan, increased surveillance in the name of counterterrorism, violence against women inside and outside the family, governmental torture of lesbians and gay men—all these are vivid reminders that social inequality today can have life-and-death consequences. Universal human rights remain an ideal, not a reality.

Let's Discuss

1. Why do definitions of human rights vary?

2. Are violations of human rights excusable in time of war? In the aftermath of serious terrorist attacks such as those of September 11, 2001? Why or why not?

3. How well or poorly do you think the United States compares to other countries in terms of respect for human rights, both at home and abroad? Has the nation's record improved or declined in recent years?

Theory Functionalist analysis of human rights

Classroom Tip Consider inviting a guest speaker from Amnesty International to discuss the issue of universal human rights.
Theory Conflict view of worldwide human rights violations against women and against lesbians and gay men

GettingINVOLVED

To get involved in the debate over universal human rights, visit this text's Online Learning Center, which offers links to relevant Web sites. Check out the Social Policy section in the Online Learning Center as well; it provides survey data on U.S. public opinion regarding this issue.

www.mhhe.com/schaefer7

{ **MASTERING THIS CHAPTER** }

Summary

Worldwide, stratification can be seen both in the gap between rich and poor nations and in the inequality within countries. This chapter examined the global divide and stratification within the world economic system; the impact of *globalization, modernization,* and *multinational corporations* on developing countries; and the distribution of wealth and income in various nations.

1. Developing nations account for most of the world's population and most of its births, but they also bear the burden of most of its poverty, disease, and childhood deaths.

2. Former colonized nations are kept in a subservient position, subject to foreign domination, through the process of *neocolonialism.*

3. Drawing on the conflict perspective, sociologist Immanuel Wallerstein's *world systems analysis* views the global economic system as one divided between nations that control wealth (core nations) and those from which capital is taken (periphery nations).

4. According to *dependency theory,* even as developing countries make economic advances, they remain weak and subservient to core nations and corporations in an increasingly integrated global economy.

5. *Globalization,* or the worldwide integration of government policies, cultures, social movements, and financial markets through trade and the exchange of ideas, is a controversial trend that critics blame for contributing to the cultural domination of periphery nations by core nations.

6. *Multinational corporations* bring jobs and industry to developing nations, but they also tend to exploit workers in order to maximize profits.

7. Poverty is a worldwide problem that blights the lives of billions of people. In 2000 the United Nations launched the Millennium Project, whose goal is to eliminate extreme poverty worldwide by the year 2015.

8. Many sociologists are quick to note that terms such as *modernization* and even *development* contain an ethnocentric bias.

9. According to *modernization theory,* development in periphery countries will be assisted by innovations transferred from the industrialized world.

10. Social mobility is more limited in developing nations than in core nations.

11. While Mexico is unquestionably a poor country, the gap between its richest and poorest citizens is one of the widest in the world.

12. The subordinate status of Mexico's Indians is but one reflection of the nation's color hierarchy, which links social class to the appearance of racial purity.

13. Growing recognition of the *borderlands* reflects the increasingly close and complex relationship between Mexico and the United States.

14. *Human rights* need to be identified and abuses of those rights corrected in countries throughout the world.

Critical Thinking Questions

1. How have multinational corporations and the trend toward globalization affected you, your family, and your community? List both the pros and the cons. Have the benefits outweighed the drawbacks?

2. Imagine that you have the opportunity to spend a year in Mexico studying inequality in that nation. How would you draw on specific research designs (surveys, observation, experiments, existing sources) to better understand and document stratification in Mexico?

3. How active should the U.S. government be in addressing violations of human rights in other countries? At what point, if any, does concern for human rights turn into ethnocentrism through failure to respect the distinctive norms, values, and customs of another culture?

Borderlands The area of common culture along the border between Mexico and the United States. (page 225)

Colonialism The maintenance of political, social, economic, and cultural dominance over a people by a foreign power for an extended period. (214)

Dependency theory An approach that contends that industrialized nations continue to exploit developing countries for their own gain. (214)

Globalization The worldwide integration of government policies, cultures, social movements, and financial markets through trade and the exchange of ideas. (214)

Gross national product (GNP) The value of a nation's goods and services. (216)

Human rights Universal moral rights possessed by all people because they are human. (227)

Modernization The far-reaching process by which periphery nations move from traditional or less developed institutions to those characteristic of more developed societies. (217)

Modernization theory A functionalist approach that proposes that modernization and development will gradually improve the lives of people in developing nations. (218)

Multinational corporation A commercial organization that is headquartered in one country but does business throughout the world. (215)

Neocolonialism Continuing dependence of former colonies on foreign countries. (214)

Remittances The monies that immigrants return to their families of origin. Also called *migradollars*. (226)

World systems analysis A view of the global economic system as one divided between certain industrialized nations that control wealth and developing countries that are controlled and exploited. (214)

Self-Quiz

Read each question carefully and then select the best answer.

1. The maintenance of political, social, economic, and cultural domination over a people by a foreign power for an extended period of time is referred to as

    a. neocolonialism.
    b. government-imposed stratification.
    c. colonialism.
    d. dependency.

2. In viewing the global economic system as divided between nations who control wealth and those from whom capital is taken, sociologist Immanuel Wallerstein draws on the

    a. functionalist perspective.
    b. conflict perspective.
    c. interactionist perspective.
    d. dramaturgical approach.

3. Which of the following nations would Immanuel Wallerstein classify as a *core* country within the world economic system?

    a. Germany
    b. South Korea
    c. Ireland
    d. Mexico

4. Which sociological perspective argues that multinational corporations can actually help the developing nations of the world?

    a. the interactionist perspective
    b. the feminist perspective
    c. the functionalist perspective
    d. the conflict perspective

5. Which of the following terms is used by contemporary social scientists to describe the far-reaching process by which peripheral nations move from traditional or less-developed institutions to those characteristic of more developed societies?

    a. dependency
    b. globalization
    c. industrialization
    d. modernization

6. In at least 26 nations around the world, the most affluent 10 percent receives at least what percentage of all income?

    a. 20 percent
    b. 30 percent
    c. 40 percent
    d. 50 percent

7. Karuna Chanana Ahmed, an anthropologist from India who has studied developing nations, calls which group the most exploited of oppressed people?

    a. children
    b. women
    c. the elderly
    d. the poor

8. Which of the following terms is used to refer to Mexico's large, impoverished majority, most of whom have brown skin and a mixed racial lineage due to intermarriage?

    a. *criollo*
    b. *indio*
    c. *mestizo*
    d. *zapatista*

9. In Mexico, women now constitute what percentage of the labor force?

    a. 15 percent
    b. 23 percent
    c. 35 percent
    d. 42 percent

10. Which of the following terms refers to the foreign-owned factories established just across the border in Mexico, where the companies that own them don't have to pay taxes or provide insurance or benefits for their workers?

    a. *maquiladoras*
    b. *hombres*
    c. *mujeres*
    d. *toreadors*

11. Colonial domination established patterns of economic exploitation leading to former colonies remaining dependent on more industrialized nations. Such continuing dependence and foreign domination are referred to as _____.

12. According to Immanuel Wallerstein's analysis, the United States is at the _____ while neighboring Mexico is on the _____ of the world economic system.

13. Wallerstein's world systems analysis is the most widely used version of _____ theory.

14. _____ factories are factories found throughout the developing world that are run by multinational corporations.

15. As _____ industries become a more important part of the international marketplace, many companies have concluded that the low costs of overseas operations more than offset the expense of transmitting information around the world.

16. Viewed from a(n) _____ perspective, the combination of skilled technology and management provided by multinationals and the relatively cheap labor available in developing nations is ideal for a global enterprise.

17. In 2000 the United Nations launched the _____ _____; its objective is to eliminate extreme poverty worldwide by the year 2015.

18. Modernization theory reflects the _____ perspective.

19. At the top of the color hierarchy in Mexico are the _____, the 10 percent of the population who are typically White, well-educated members of the business and intellectual elites, and who have familial roots in Spain.

20. The term _____ refers to the area of a common culture along the border between Mexico and the United States.

Answers:
1 (c); 2 (b); 3 (a); 4 (c); 5 (d); 6 (c); 7 (b); 8 (c); 9 (d); 10 (a)
11 neocolonialism; 12 core; semiperiphery; 13 dependency; 14 Global; 15 service; 16 functionalist; 17 Millenium Project; 18 functionalist; 19 criollos; 20 borderlands

{ TECHNOLOGY RESOURCES }

Online Learning Center

1. Test your knowledge of the information in this chapter by visiting the student center in the Online Learning Center at **www.mhhe. com/schaefer7** and taking the multiple-choice quiz. This quiz will not only test your knowledge; it will also give you immediate feedback on the questions that you answered incorrectly.

2. The governments of many industrialized countries—such as the United States—have had a history of subjecting native populations to oppression and mistreatment. The Web site of the Museum Victoria allows you a glimpse into the historical oppression of Aboriginals in Australia. Explore the site at **www.museum.vic.gov.au/** **encounters.** Click on the link to "Coranderrk" and then "Children" to learn about past government policies toward Aboriginal children.

3. In this chapter you have begun to learn about the complex relationship between the United States and Mexico, including some information about the 1993 NAFTA agreement. The NAFTA page on the Public Citizen Web site (**www.citizen.org/trade/nafta**) provides a host of additional resources about this trade policy. Browse through the site to further understand its wide-ranging financial and human impact.

*Note: While all the URLs listed were current as of the printing of this book, these sites often change. Please check our Web site (**www.mhhe.com/schaefer7**) for updates, hyperlinks, and exercises related to these sites.*

10

Racial and Ethnic Inequality

inside

Minority, Racial, and Ethnic Groups

Prejudice and Discrimination

Studying Race and Ethnicity

Patterns of Intergroup Relations

Impact of Global Immigration

Race and Ethnicity in the United States

Social Policy and Racial and Ethnic Inequality: Racial Profiling

Boxes

Social Inequality: Native Americans Gamble on Gaming

Research in Action: Interracial and Interethnic Friendships

Taking Sociology to Work: Prudence Hannis, Liaison Officer, National Institute of Science Research, University of Québec

This advertisement for the American Indian College Fund explodes common stereotypes about Native Americans with its photograph of Blackfeet Indian Carly Kipp, a doctoral candidate in veterinary medicine. Historically, prejudice and discrimination against members of minority groups have prevented them from reaching their full potential.

Ah so. No tickee, no washee. So sorry, so sollee. Chinkee, Chink. Jap, Nip, zero, kamikaze. Dothead, flat face, flat nose, slant eye, slope. Slit, mamasan, dragon lady. Gock, VC, Flip, Hindoo.

By the time I was ten, I'd heard such words so many times I could feel them coming before they parted lips. I knew they were meant in the unkindest way. Still, we didn't talk about these incidents at home, we just accepted them as part of being in America, something to learn to rise above.

The most common taunting didn't even utilize words but a string of unintelligible gobbledygook that kids—and adults—would spew as they pretended to speak Chinese or some other Asian language. It was a mockery of how they imagined my parents talked to me.

Truth was that Mom and Dad rarely spoke to us in Chinese, except to scold or call us to dinner. Worried that we might develop an accent, my father insisted that we speak English at home. This, he explained, would lessen the hardships we might encounter and make us more acceptable as Americans.

I'll never know if my father's language decision was right. On the one hand, I, like most Asian Americans, have been complimented countless times on my spoken English by people who assumed I was a foreigner. "My, you speak such good English," they'd cluck. "No kidding, I ought to," I would think to myself, then wonder: should I thank them for assuming that English isn't my native language? Or should I correct them on the proper usage of "well" and "good"?

More often than feeling grateful for my American accent, I've wished that I could jump into a heated exchange of rapid-fire Chinese, volume high and spit flying. But with a vocabulary limited to *"Ni hao?"* (How are you?) and *"Ting bu dong"* (I hear but don't understand), meaningful exchanges are woefully impossible. I find myself smiling and nodding like a dashboard ornament. I'm envious of the many people I know who grew up speaking an Asian language yet converse in English beautifully.

Armed with standard English and my flat New Jersey "a," I still couldn't escape the name-calling. I became all too familiar with other names and faces that supposedly matched mine—Fu Manchu, Suzie Wong, Hop Sing, Madame Butterfly, Charlie Chan, Ming the Merciless—the "Asians" produced for mass consumption. Their faces filled me with shame whenever I saw them on TV or in the movies. They defined my face to the rest of the world: a sinister Fu, Suzie the whore, subservient Hop Sing, pathetic Butterfly, cunning Chan, and warlike Ming. Inscrutable Orientals all, real Americans none.

(Zia 2000) Additional information about this excerpt can be found on the Online Learning Center at www.mhhe.com/schaefer7. ●

> " *Truth was that Mom and Dad rarely spoke to us in Chinese, except to scold or call us to dinner. Worried that we might develop an accent, my father insisted that we speak English at home.* "

Helen Zia, the journalist and community activist who wrote this reminiscence from her childhood, is the successful daughter of Chinese immigrants to the United States. As her story shows, Zia experienced blatant prejudice against Chinese Americans, even though she spoke flawless English. In fact, all new immigrants and their families have faced stereotyping and hostility, whether they were White or non-White, Asian, African, or East European. In this multicultural society, those who are different from the dominant social group have never been welcome.

Today, millions of African Americans, Asian Americans, Hispanic Americans, and many other racial and ethnic minorities continue to experience the often bitter contrast between the "American dream" and the grim realities of poverty, prejudice, and discrimination. Like class, the social definitions of race and ethnicity still affect people's place and status in a stratification system, not only in this country but throughout the world. High incomes, a good command of English, and hard-earned professional credentials do not always override racial and ethnic stereotypes or protect those who fit them from the sting of racism.

What is prejudice, and how is it institutionalized in the form of discrimination? In what ways have race and ethnicity affected the experience of immigrants from other countries? What are the fastest-growing minority groups in the United States today? In this chapter we will focus on the meaning of race and ethnicity. We will begin by identifying the basic characteristics of a minority group and distinguishing between racial and ethnic groups. Then we will examine the dynamics of prejudice and discrimination. After considering the functionalist, conflict, and interactionist perspectives on race and ethnicity, we'll take a look at common patterns of intergroup relations, and then at the impact of global immigration. The following section will describe the major racial and ethnic groups in the United States. Finally, in the Social Policy section we will explore the issue of racial profiling. ●

Minority, Racial, and Ethnic Groups

Sociologists frequently distinguish between racial and ethnic groups. The term **racial group** describes a group that is set apart from others because of physical differences that have taken on social significance. Whites, African Americans, and Asian Americans are all considered racial groups in the United States. While race does turn on physical differences, it is the culture of a particular society that constructs and attaches social significance to those differences, as we will see later. Unlike racial groups, an **ethnic group** is set apart from others primarily because of its national origin or distinctive cultural patterns. In the United States, Puerto Ricans, Jews, and Polish Americans are all categorized as ethnic groups (see Table 10-1).

Minority Groups

A numerical minority is any group that makes up less than half of some larger population. The population of the United States includes thousands of numerical minorities, including television actors, green-eyed people, tax lawyers, and descendants of the Pilgrims who arrived on the *Mayflower*. However, these numerical minorities are not considered to be minorities in the sociological sense; in fact, the number of people in a group does not necessarily determine its status as a social minority (or a dominant group). When sociologists define a minority group, they are concerned primarily with the economic and political power, or powerlessness, of that group. A **minority group** is a subordinate group whose members have significantly less control or power over their own lives than the members of a dominant or majority group have over theirs.

Sociologists have identified five basic properties of a minority group: unequal treatment, physical or cultural traits, ascribed status, solidarity, and in-group marriage (Wagley and Harris 1958):

1. Members of a minority group experience unequal treatment compared to members of a dominant group. For example, the management of an apartment complex may refuse to rent to African Americans, Hispanics, or Jews. Social inequality may be created or maintained by prejudice, discrimination, segregation, or even extermination.

2. Members of a minority group share physical or cultural characteristics that distinguish them from the dominant group. Each society arbitrarily decides which characteristics are most important in defining groups.

3. Membership in a minority (or dominant) group is not voluntary; { p.102 } people are born into the group. Thus, race and ethnicity are considered *ascribed* statuses.

4. Minority group members have a strong sense of group solidarity. William Graham Sumner, writing in 1906, noted that people make distinctions between members of their own { p.109 } group (the *in-group*) and everyone else (the *out-group*). When a group is the object of long-term prejudice and discrimination, the feeling of "us versus them" can and often does become extremely intense.

5. Members of a minority group generally marry others from the same group. A member of a dominant group is often unwilling to marry into a supposedly inferior minority group. In addition, the minority group's sense of solidarity encourages marriage within the group and discourages marriage to outsiders.

Classroom Tip/Contemporary Culture See "Stimulating Classroom Discussion about *Asian American Dreams*" (Class Discussion Topics).
Student Alert Stress to students that a minority group is not necessarily a numerical minority; the critical factor is unequal treatment in terms of power and influence, access to resources, and life chances (see Chapter 8).

Classroom Tip Integrate with material later in the chapter about discrimination and institutional discrimination.
Theory Functionalist analysis of group solidarity among minorities.
Classroom Tip The term *endogamy* is introduced in Chapter 12 as part of the discussion of in-group marriage.

Table 10-1 Racial and Ethnic Groups in the United States, 2000

Classification	Number in Thousands	Percentage of Total Population
Racial groups		
Whites (includes 16.9 million White Hispanics)	211,461	75.1%
Blacks/African Americans	34,658	12.3
Native Americans, Alaskan Native	2,476	0.9
Asian Americans	10,243	3.6
Chinese	2,433	0.9
Filipinos	1,850	0.7
Asian Indians	1,679	0.6
Vietnamese	1,123	0.4
Koreans	1,077	0.4
Japanese	797	0.2
Other	1,285	0.5
Ethnic groups		
White ancestry (single or mixed)		
Germans	42,842	15.2
Irish	30,525	10.8
English	24,509	8.7
Italians	15,638	5.6
Poles	8,977	3.2
French	8,310	3.0
Jews	5,200	1.8
Hispanics (or Latinos)	35,306	12.5
Mexican Americans	23,337	8.3
Central and South Americans	5,119	1.8
Puerto Ricans	3,178	1.1
Cubans	1,412	0.5
Other	2,260	0.8
Total (all groups)	281,422	

Note: Percentages do not total 100 percent and figures under subheadings do not add up to figures under major headings because of overlap among groups (e.g., Polish American Jews or people of mixed ancestry, such as Irish and Italian). Hispanics may be of any race.

Sources: Brittingham and de la Cruz 2004; Bureau of the Census 2003a; Grieco and Cassidy 2001; Therrien and Ramirez 2001; United Jewish Communities 2003.

Race

The term *racial group* refers to those minorities (and the corresponding dominant groups) set apart from others by obvious physical differences. But what is an "obvious" physical difference? Each society socially constructs which differences are important, while ignoring other characteristics that could serve as a basis for social differentiation. In the United States, we see differences in both skin color and hair color. Yet people learn informally that differences in skin color have a dramatic social and political meaning, while differences in hair color do not.

When observing skin color, many people in the United States tend to lump others rather casually into the traditional categories of "Black," "White," and "Asian." More subtle differences in skin color often go unnoticed. In many nations of Central America and South America, by contrast, people recognize color gradients on a continuum from light to dark skin color. Brazil has approximately 40 color groupings, while in other countries people may be described as "Mestizo Hondurans," "Mulatto Colombians," or "African Panamanians." What we see as "obvious" differences, then, are subject to each society's social definitions.

The largest racial minorities in the United States are African Americans (or Blacks), Native Americans (or American Indians), and Asian Americans (Japanese Americans, Chinese Americans, and other Asian peoples). Figure 10-1 (page 236) provides information about the population of racial and ethnic groups in the United States over the past five centuries.

Social Construction of Race In the United States, it was known as the "one-drop rule." If a person had even a single drop of "Black blood," that person was defined and viewed as Black, even if he or she *appeared* to be White. Clearly, race had social significance, enough so that White legislators established official standards about who was "Black" and who was "White."

The one-drop rule was a vivid example of the *social construction of race*—the process by which people come to define a group as a race based in part on physical characteristics, but also on historical, cultural, and economic factors. For example, in the 1800s, immigrant groups such as Italian and Irish Americans were not at first seen as being "White," but as foreigners who were not necessarily trustworthy. The social construction of race is an ongoing process that is subject to debate, especially in a diverse society such as the United States, where each year increasing numbers of children are born to parents of different racial backgrounds.

Recognition of Multiple Identities In the 2000 census, over 7 million people in the United States (or about 2.6 percent of the population) reported that they were of two or more races. Half the people classified as multiracial were under age 18, suggesting that this segment of the population will grow in the years to come. People who claimed both White and American Indian ancestry were the largest group of multiracial residents (N. Jones 2005).

This statistical finding of millions of multiracial people obscures how individuals are often asked to handle their identity. For example, the enrollment forms for government programs typically include only a few broad racial-ethnic categories. This approach to racial categorization is part of a long history that dictates single-race identities. Still, many individuals, especially young adults, struggle against social pressure to choose a single identity, and instead openly embrace multiple heritages. Tiger

Race/Ethnicity Given the subject matter of Chapter 10, this type of annotation will not be used throughout the chapter.

Global View Color groupings in Central and South America
Theory Labeling theory is inherent in the discussion of the impact of color groupings.
Classroom Tip See "Social Construction of Race" (Class Discussion Topics).
Let's Discuss Ask students to anonymously list their races. Compare the percentage of multiracial people in the class to that of the 2000 census (about 2.6 percent).

Racial and Ethnic Groups in the United States, 1500–2100 (Projected)

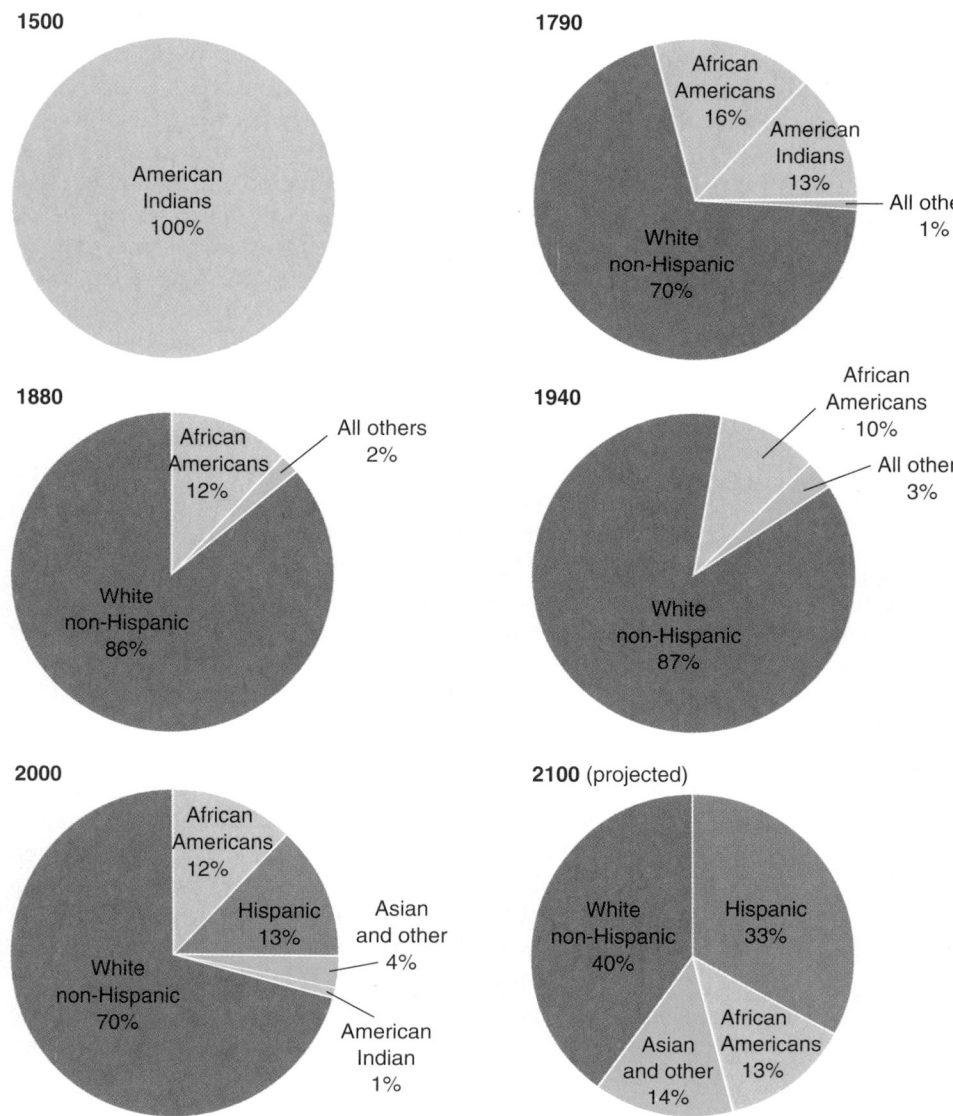

1500
American Indians 100%

1790
African Americans 16%
American Indians 13%
All others 1%
White non-Hispanic 70%

1880
African Americans 12%
All others 2%
White non-Hispanic 86%

1940
African Americans 10%
All others 3%
White non-Hispanic 87%

2000
African Americans 12%
Hispanic 13%
Asian and other 4%
White non-Hispanic 70%
American Indian 1%

2100 (projected)
White non-Hispanic 40%
Hispanic 33%
African Americans 13%
Asian and other 14%

Sources: Author's estimate; Bureau of the Census 1975, 2004a; Grieco and Cassidy 2001; Thornton 1987. Data for 2000 and 2100, African Americans and Asian and other are for non-Hispanics.

The racial and ethnic composition of what is today the United States has been undergoing change not just for the last 50 years, but for the last 500. Five centuries ago the land was populated only by indigenous Native Americans.

Woods, the world's best-known professional golfer, considers himself both Asian and African American.

As we saw in Chapter 5, a dominant or majority group has the power not only to define itself legally but to define a society's values. The interactionist William I. Thomas, observing how we assign social meanings, saw that the "definition of the situation" could mold the individual personality. To put it another way, people respond not only to the objective features of a situation or person but also to the *meaning* that situation or person has for them. Thus, we can create false images or stereotypes that

become real in their consequences. *Stereotypes* are unreliable generalizations about all members of a group that do not recognize individual differences within the group.

In the last 30 years, critics have pointed out the power of the mass media to perpetuate false racial and ethnic stereotypes. Television is a prime example: Almost all the leading dramatic roles are cast as Whites, even in urban-based programs like *Friends* (see Chapter 6). Blacks tend to be featured mainly in crime-based dramas.

Use Your Sociological Imagination

www.mhhe.com /schaefer7

Using a TV remote control, how quickly do you think you could find a television show in which all the characters share your own racial or ethnic background? What about a show in which all the characters share a different background from your own—how quickly could you find one?

Ethnicity

An ethnic group, unlike a racial group, is set apart from others because of its national origin or distinctive cultural patterns. Among the ethnic groups in the United States are peoples with a Spanish-speaking background, referred to collectively as *Latinos* or *Hispanics*, such as Puerto Ricans, Mexican Americans, Cuban Americans, and other Latin Americans. Other ethnic groups in this country include Jewish, Irish, Italian, and Norwegian Americans. While these groupings are convenient, they serve to obscure differences *within* ethnic categories (as in the case of Hispanics), as well as to overlook the mixed ancestry of so many ethnic people in the United States.

The distinction between racial and ethnic minorities is not always clear-cut. Some members of racial minorities, such as Asian Americans, may have significant cultural differences from other racial groups. At the same time, certain ethnic minorities, such as Latinos, may have obvious physical differences that set them apart from other ethnic groups in the United States.

Despite categorization problems, sociologists continue to feel that the distinction between racial groups and ethnic groups is

Not long ago, these children of a White mother and an African American father would automatically have assumed their father's racial identity. Today, however, some children of mixed-race families identify themselves as biracial.

socially significant. In most societies, including the United States, socially constructed physical differences tend to be more visible than ethnic differences. Partly as a result of this fact, stratification along racial lines is more resistant to change than stratification along ethnic lines. Over time, members of an ethnic minority can sometimes become indistinguishable from the majority—although the process may take generations, and may never include all members of the group. In contrast, members of a racial minority find it much more difficult to blend in with the larger society and gain acceptance from the majority.

Prejudice and Discrimination

In recent years, college campuses across the United States have been the scene of bias-related incidents. Student-run newspapers and radio stations have ridiculed racial and ethnic minorities; threatening literature has been stuffed under the doors of minority students; graffiti endorsing the views of White supremacist organizations such as the Ku Klux Klan have been scrawled on university walls. In some cases, there have even been violent clashes between groups of White and Black students (Bunzel 1992; Schaefer 2007). What causes such ugly incidents?

Prejudice

Prejudice is a negative attitude toward an entire category of people, often an ethnic or racial minority. If you resent your roommate because he or she is sloppy, you are not necessarily guilty of prejudice. However, if you immediately stereotype your roommate on the basis of such characteristics as race, ethnicity, or religion, that is a form of prejudice. Prejudice tends to perpetuate false definitions of individuals and groups.

Sometimes prejudice results from *ethnocentrism*—the tendency to assume that one's own culture and way of life represent

{ p.70 the norm or are superior to all others. Ethnocentric people judge other cultures by the standards of their own group, which leads quite easily to prejudice against cultures they view as inferior.

One important and widespread form of prejudice is *racism,* the belief that one race is supreme and all others are innately inferior. When racism prevails in a society, members of subordinate groups generally experience prejudice, discrimination, and exploitation. In 1990, as concern mounted about racist attacks in the United States, Congress passed the Hate Crimes Statistics Act. A *hate crime* is a criminal offense committed because of the offender's bias against a race, religion, ethnic group, national origin, or sexual orientation. In 2004 alone, more than 7,400 hate crimes were reported to authorities. As Figure 10-2 shows, more than half those crimes against persons involved racial bias. Most were carried out by individuals acting alone or with a few friends.

A particularly horrifying hate crime made the front pages in 1998: In Jasper, Texas, three White men with possible ties to race-hate groups tied up a Black man, beat him with chains, and then dragged him behind their truck until his body was dismembered. Numerous groups in the United States have been victims of hate crimes as well as generalized prejudice. In the wake of the terrorist attacks of September 11, 2001, hate crimes against Asian Americans and Muslim Americans escalated rapidly.

As Figure 10-3 (page 238) shows, there is a disturbingly large number of hate groups in the United States. Their activity appears to be increasing, both in reality and in virtual reality. Although only a few hundred such groups may exist, thousands of Web sites advocate racial hatred on the Internet. Particularly troubling are sites disguised as video games for young people or as "educational sites" about crusaders against prejudice. The technology of the Internet has allowed race-hate groups to expand far beyond their traditional southern base to reach millions (Marriott 2004).

FIGURE 10-2

Categorization of Reported Hate Crimes

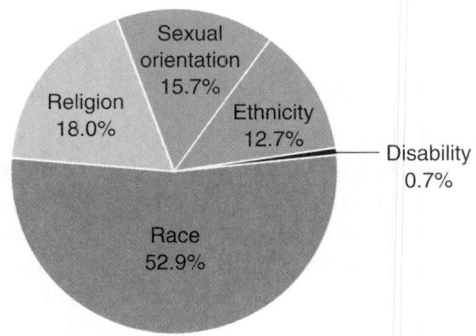

Source: Reported for 2004 in 2005. Department of Justice 2005.

Active Hate Groups in the United States

MAPPING LIFE

NATIONWIDE www.mhhe.com/schaefer7

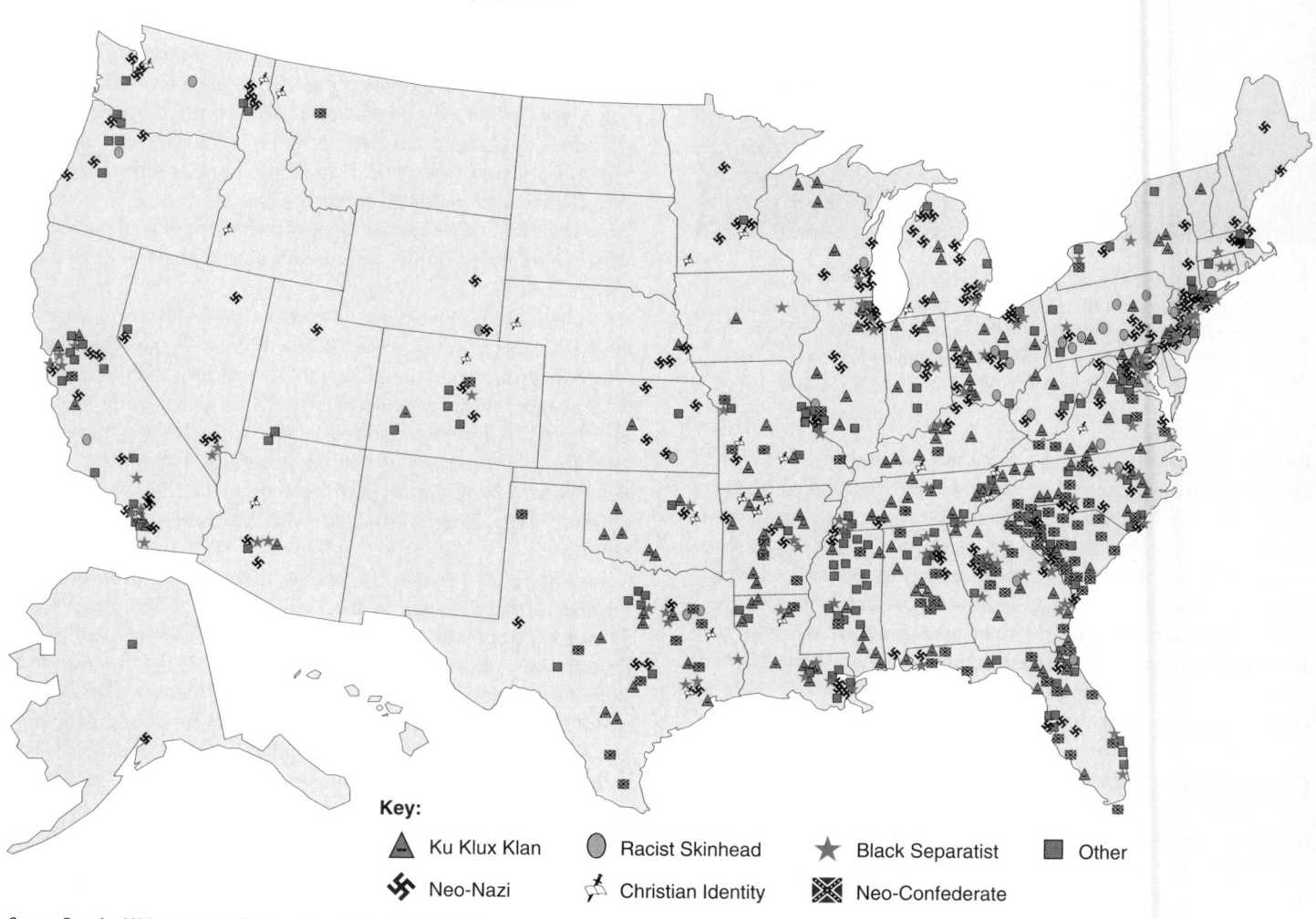

Key:

▲ Ku Klux Klan ⬤ Racist Skinhead ★ Black Separatist ■ Other

卐 Neo-Nazi ⚑ Christian Identity ✖ Neo-Confederate

Source: Data for 2004 reported in Southern Poverty Law Center 2005.

Think About It
Why do you think state legislators enacted special hate crime laws covering acts that already were illegal?

Discriminatory Behavior

Prejudice often leads to ***discrimination,*** the denial of opportunities and equal rights to individuals and groups because of prejudice or other arbitrary reasons. Say that a White corporate president with a prejudice against Asian Americans has to fill an executive position. The most qualified candidate for the job is a Vietnamese American. If the president refuses to hire this candidate and instead selects an inferior White candidate, he or she is engaging in an act of racial discrimination.

Prejudiced *attitudes* should not be equated with discriminatory *behavior.* Although the two are generally related, they are not identical; either condition can be present without the other. A prejudiced person does not always act on his or her biases. The White president, for example, might choose—despite his or her stereotypes—to hire the Vietnamese American. That would be prejudice without discrimination. On the other hand, a White corporate president with a completely respectful view of Vietnamese Americans might refuse to hire them for executive posts

Theory Labeling theory is useful in examining stereotyping of Asian and Muslim Americans.
Classroom Tip See "Discrimination on Television" (Class Discussion Topics).
Reel Society See Stratification—Race/Ethnicity in the Topic Index.

Classroom Tip See "Social Distance Scale" (Class Discussion Topics).
Student Alert Prejudice is attitudinal or cognitive; discrimination is behavioral.

out of fear that biased clients would take their business else-where. In that case, the president's action would constitute discrimination without prejudice.

Sociologist Devah Pager's (2003) experiment, described in Chapter 2, documents racial discrimination in hiring. Recall that in this experiment, a White job applicant with a prison record received slightly more callbacks than a Black applicant with no criminal record. Over time, the cumulative impact of this kind of differential behavior contributes to significant differences in income. Figure 10-4 vividly illustrates the income inequality be-tween White men and everyone else.

Sometimes racial and ethnic discrimination is overt. Internet forums like Craigslist.org or Roommate.com feature classified ads that state "African Americans and Arabians tend to clash with me" or "Clean, Godly Christian men only." While antidis-crimination laws prevent such notices from being published in the newspapers, existing law has not caught up with online big-otry in hiring and renting (Liptak 2006).

Discrimination persists even for the most educated and qual-ified minority group members from the best family back-grounds. Despite their talents and experiences, they sometimes encounter attitudinal or organizational bias that prevents them from reaching their full potential. The term **glass ceiling** refers to an invisible barrier that blocks the promotion of a qualified individual in a work environment because of the individual's gender, race, or ethnicity (Schaefer 2006; Yamagata et al. 1997).

In early 1995, the federal Glass Ceiling Commission issued the first comprehensive study of barriers to promotion in the United States. The commission found that glass ceilings continue to block women and minority group men from top management positions in the nation's industries. While White men constitute 45 percent of the paid labor force, they hold down a much higher proportion of top positions. Even in *Fortune* magazine's 2002 listing of the most diversified corporations, White men held more than 80 percent of both the board of directors seats and the top 50 paid positions in the firms. The existence of this glass ceiling results principally from the fears and prejudices of many middle- and upper-level White male managers, who believe that the inclusion of women and minority group men in management circles will threaten their own prospects for advancement (Bureau of the Census 2004a:371; Department of Labor 1995a, 1995b; Hickman 2002).

The Privileges of the Dominant

One aspect of discrimination that is of-ten overlooked is the privileges that dominant groups enjoy at the expense of others. For instance, we tend to focus more on the difficulty women have get-ting ahead at work and getting a hand at

home than on the ease with which men avoid household chores and manage to make their way in the world. Similarly, we con-centrate more on discrimination against racial and ethnic mi-norities than on the advantages members of the White majority enjoy. Indeed, most White people rarely think about their "Whiteness," taking their status for granted. But sociologists and other social scientists are becoming increasingly interested in what it means to be "White," for White privilege is the other side of the proverbial coin of racial discrimination.

The feminist scholar Peggy McIntosh (1988) became inter-ested in White privilege after noticing that most men would not acknowledge that there were privileges attached to being male—even if they would agree that being female had its disadvantages. Did White people suffer from a similar blind spot regarding their own racial privilege? she wondered. Intrigued, McIntosh began to list all the ways in which she benefited from her White-ness. She soon realized that the list of unspoken advantages was long and significant.

McIntosh found that as a White person, she rarely needed to step out of her comfort zone, no matter where she went. If she wished to, she could spend most of her time with people of her own race. She could find a good place to live in a pleasant neigh-borhood, buy the foods she liked to eat from almost any grocery store, and get her hair styled in almost any salon. She could at-tend a public meeting without feeling that she did not belong, that she was different from everyone else.

McIntosh discovered, too, that her skin color opened doors for her. She could cash checks and use credit cards without sus-picion, browse through stores without being shadowed by secu-rity guards. She could be seated without difficulty in a restaurant. If she asked to see the manager, she could assume he or she would be of her own race. If she needed help from a doctor or a lawyer, she could get it.

FIGURE 10–4

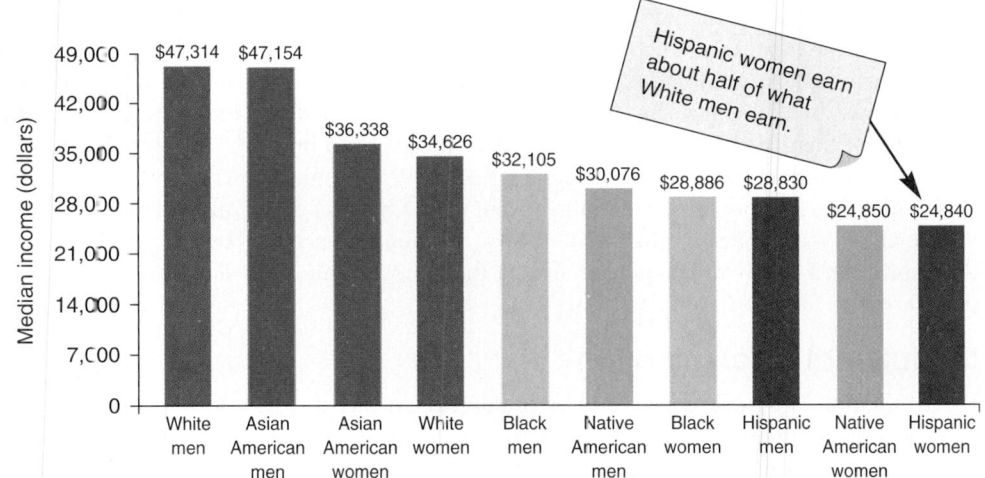

U.S. Median Income by Race, Ethnicity, and Gender, 2004

Note: Includes only people working full-time, year-round, 25 years old and older. White refers to non-Hispanic Whites.
Sources: DeNavas-Walt et al. 2005; for Native Americans, author's estimate based on Bureau of the Census 2003b.

In U.S. retail stores, White customers have different experiences from Black customers. They are less likely than Blacks to have their checks or credit cards refused, and less likely to be viewed with suspicion by security personnel. Whiteness does confer privilege.

cance of race and ethnicity. *Institutional discrimination* refers to the denial of opportunities and equal rights to individuals and groups that results from the normal operations of a society. This kind of discrimination consistently affects certain racial and ethnic groups more than others.

The Commission on Civil Rights (1981:9–10) has identified various forms of institutional discrimination:

- Rules requiring that only English be spoken at a place of work, even when it is not a business necessity to restrict the use of other languages.

- Preferences shown by law and medical schools in the admission of children of wealthy and influential alumni, nearly all of whom are White.

- Restrictive employment-leave policies, coupled with prohibitions on part-time work, that make it difficult for the heads of single-parent families (most of whom are women) to obtain and keep jobs.

McIntosh also realized that her Whiteness made the job of parenting easier. She did not need to worry about protecting her children from people who didn't like them. She could be sure that their textbooks would show pictures of people who looked like them, and that their history texts would describe White people's achievements. She knew that the television programs they watched would include White characters.

Finally, McIntosh had to admit that others did not constantly evaluate her in racial terms. When she appeared in public, she didn't need to worry that her clothing or behavior might reflect poorly on White people. If she was recognized for an achievement, it was seen as her achievement, not that of an entire race. And no one ever assumed that the personal opinions she voiced should be those of all White people. Because McIntosh blended in with the people around her, she wasn't always onstage.

These are not all the privileges White people take for granted as a result of their membership in the dominant racial group in the United States. As Devah Pager's study (see page 39) showed, White job seekers enjoy a tremendous advantage over equally well-qualified—even better-qualified—Blacks. Whiteness *does* carry privileges—to a much greater extent than most White people realize.

Institutional Discrimination

Discrimination is practiced not only by individuals in one-to-one encounters but also by institutions in their daily operations. Social scientists are particularly concerned with the ways in which structural factors such as employment, housing, health care, and government operations maintain the social signifi-

A recent example of institutional discrimination occurred in the wake of the September 11, 2001, terrorist attacks on the United States. In the heat of demands to prevent terrorist takeovers of commercial airplanes, Congress passed the Aviation and Transportation Security Act, which was intended to strengthen airport screening procedures. The law stipulated that all airport screeners must be U.S. citizens. Nationally, 28 percent of all airport screeners were legal residents but not citizens of the United States; as a group, they were disproportionately Latino, Black, and Asian. Many observers noted that other airport and airline workers, including pilots, cabin attendants, and even armed National Guardsmen stationed at airports, need not be citizens. Efforts are now being made to test the constitutionality of the act. At the least, the debate over its fairness shows that even well-meant legal measures can have disastrous consequences for racial and ethnic minorities (H. Weinstein 2002).

In some cases, even ostensibly neutral institutional standards can have discriminatory effects. African American students at a midwestern state university protested a policy under which fraternities and sororities that wished to use campus facilities for a dance were required to post a $150 security deposit to cover possible damages. The Black students complained that the policy had a discriminatory impact on minority student organizations. Campus police countered that the university's policy applied to all student groups interested in using the facilities. However, since the overwhelmingly White fraternities and sororities at the school had their own houses, which they used for dances, the policy indeed affected only African American and other minority organizations.

Theory Conflict view of institutional discrimination by race and ethnicity in the United States
Classroom Tip See "Institutional Discrimination" (Class Discussion Topics).

Contemporary Culture Race relations in colleges and universities

Prudence Hannis
**Liaison Officer, National Institute
of Science Research, University
of Québec**

Prudence Hannis is a First Nations (Native American) woman who serves as an official liaison between her people and Canadian researchers. In her position, she interacts with sociologists, anthropologists, political scientists, legal scholars, and researchers in health and medicine at several Canadian universities, all of whom wish to work with First Nations communities. Hannis is enthusiastic about her job, which gives her an opportunity to educate and sensitize would-be researchers who "never set foot in First Nations communities." In 10 years of work on behalf of the native peoples of Canada, Hannis has seen a dramatic change in their representation in Canadian research and policy. "We are everywhere in research efforts and policy consultation, but whether we are listened to is another matter," she notes.

Before taking her current position, Hannis served as a researcher and community activist with Québec Native Women. There she oversaw the women's health portfolio, organized seminars on sexual abuse for local communities, and produced a resource booklet on the subject. "The purpose of my job was to defend First Nations'

women's concerns, to be their spokesperson when needed, to analyze critical situations for our sisters, and mostly, to determine ways in which women can empower themselves, their families, and their communities," she says.

Hannis has also worked for the Centre of Excellence on Women's Health, Consortium Université de Montréal, where she focused on First Nations women's health issues. A member of the Abenaki tribe, Hannis received her B.A. in sociology from the University of Québec at Montréal. She has found her background in the discipline to be invaluable. "Sociology is now, more than it has ever been, a part of my job," she says.

Let's Discuss

1. Explain the connection between Native Americans' ethnicity and their health.
2. In speaking of empowering First Nations women, what sociological perspective do you think Hannis is drawing on?

Attempts have been made to eradicate or compensate for discrimination in the United States. The 1960s saw the passage of many pioneering civil rights laws, including the landmark 1964 Civil Rights Act (which prohibits discrimination in public accommodations and publicly owned facilities on the basis of race, color, creed, national origin, and gender). In two important rulings in 1987, the Supreme Court held that federal prohibitions against racial discrimination protect members of all ethnic minorities—including Hispanics, Jews, and Arab Americans—even though they may be considered White.

For more than 40 years, affirmative action programs have been instituted to overcome past discrimination. *Affirmative action* refers to positive efforts to recruit minority group members or women for jobs, promotions, and educational opportunities. Many people resent these programs, arguing that advancing one group's cause merely shifts the discrimination to another group. By giving priority to African Americans in admissions, for example, schools may overlook more qualified White candidates. In many parts of the country and many sectors of the economy, affirmative action is being rolled back, even though it was never fully implemented. We will discuss affirmative action in more detail in Chapter 14.

Discriminatory practices continue to pervade nearly all areas of life in the United States today. In part, that is because various individuals and groups actually *benefit* from racial and ethnic discrimination in terms of money, status, and influence. Discrimination permits members of the majority to enhance

their wealth, power, and prestige at the expense of others. Less qualified people get jobs and promotions simply because they are members of the dominant group. Such individuals and groups will not surrender these advantages easily. We'll turn now to a closer look at this functionalist analysis, as well as the conflict and interactionist perspectives on race and ethnicity.

Studying Race and Ethnicity

Relations among racial and ethnic groups lend themselves to analysis from the three major sociological perspectives. Viewing race from the macro level, functionalists observe that racial prejudice and discrimination serve positive functions for dominant groups. Conflict theorists see the economic structure as a central factor in the exploitation of minorities. On the micro level, interactionist researchers stress the manner in which everyday contact between people from different racial and ethnic backgrounds contributes to tolerance or hostility.

Functionalist Perspective

What possible use could racial bigotry have? Functionalist theorists, while agreeing that racial hostility is hardly to be admired, point out that it serves positive functions for those who practice discrimination.

Anthropologist Manning Nash (1962) has identified three functions that racially prejudiced beliefs have for the dominant group:

Policy Pointer Efforts to legislate civil rights laws
Gender The 1964 Civil Rights Act protects women as well as racial and ethnic minorities.

Theory Functionalist perspective on discrimination
Theory Functions that racially prejudiced beliefs have for majority group members

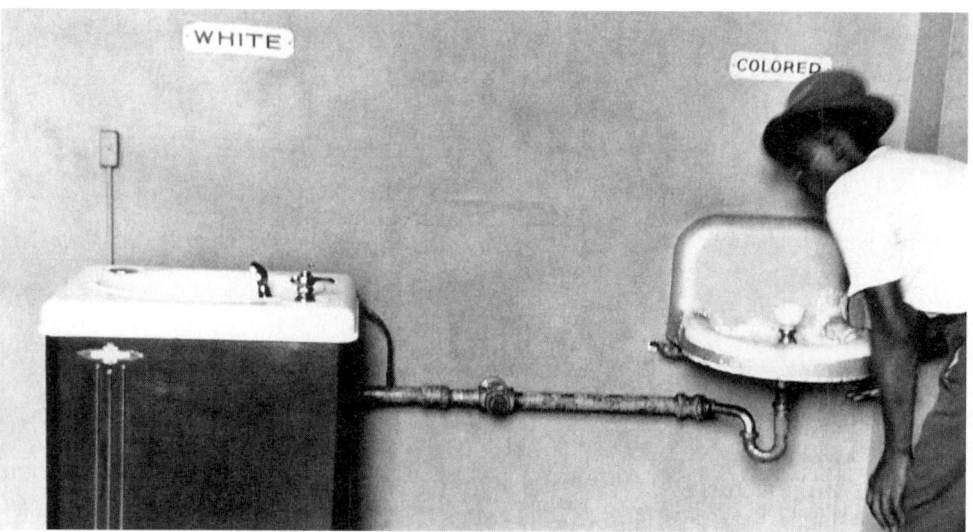

{ Before passage of the Civil Rights Act (1964), segregation of public accommodations was the norm throughout the South. Whites used the most up-to-date bathrooms, waiting rooms, and even drinking fountains, while Blacks ("Colored") were directed to older facilities in inferior condition. Such separate but unequal arrangements are a blatant example of institutional discrimination. }

1. Racist views provide a moral justification for maintaining an unequal society that routinely deprives a minority group of its rights and privileges. Southern Whites justified slavery by believing that Africans were physically and spiritually subhuman and devoid of souls.

2. Racist beliefs discourage the subordinate minority from attempting to question its lowly status, which would be to question the very foundations of society.

3. Racial myths suggest that any major societal change (such as an end to discrimination) would only bring greater poverty to the minority and lower the majority's standard of living. As a result, Nash suggests, racial prejudice grows when a society's value system (one underlying a colonial empire or slavery, for example) is threatened.

Although racial prejudice and discrimination may serve the interests of the powerful, such unequal treatment can also be dysfunctional for a society, and even for the dominant group. Sociologist Arnold Rose (1951) has outlined four dysfunctions associated with racism:

1. A society that practices discrimination fails to use the resources of all individuals. Discrimination limits the search for talent and leadership to the dominant group.

2. Discrimination aggravates social problems such as poverty, delinquency, and crime, and places the financial burden of alleviating those problems on the dominant group.

3. Society must invest a good deal of time and money to defend its barriers to the full participation of all members.

4. Racial prejudice and discrimination often undercut goodwill and friendly diplomatic relations between nations.

Theory Dysfunctions of racism for society
Classroom Tip See "Multicultural Pedagogy" (Class Discussion Topics).

Conflict Perspective

Conflict theorists would certainly agree with Arnold Rose that racial prejudice and discrimination have many harmful consequences for society. Sociologists such as Oliver Cox (1948), Robert Blauner (1972), and Herbert M. Hunter (2000) have used the *exploitation theory* (or *Marxist class theory*) to explain the basis of racial subordination in the United States. As we saw in Chapter 8, Karl Marx viewed the exploitation of the lower class as a basic part of the capitalist economic system. From a Marxist point of view, racism keeps minorities in low-paying jobs, thereby supplying the capitalist ruling class with a pool of cheap labor. Moreover, by forcing racial minorities to accept low wages, capitalists can restrict the wages of *all* members of the proletariat. Workers from the dominant group who demand higher wages can always be replaced by minorities who have no choice but to accept low-paying jobs.

The conflict view of race relations seems persuasive in a number of instances. Japanese Americans were the object of little prejudice until they began to enter jobs that brought them into competition with Whites. The movement to keep Chinese immigrants out of the United States became most fervent during the latter half of the 19th century, when Chinese and Whites fought over dwindling work opportunities. Both the enslavement of Blacks and the extermination and removal westward of Native Americans were, to a significant extent, economically motivated.

However, the exploitation theory is too limited to explain prejudice in its many forms. Not all minority groups have been exploited to the same extent. In addition, many groups (such as the Quakers and the Mormons) have been victimized by prejudice for other than economic reasons. Still, as Gordon Allport (1979:210) concludes, the exploitation theory correctly "points a sure finger at one of the factors involved in prejudice, . . . rationalized self-interest of the upper classes."

Interactionist Perspective

A Hispanic woman is transferred from a job on an assembly line to a similar position working next to a White man. At first, the White man is patronizing, assuming that she must be incompetent. She is cold and resentful; even when she needs assistance, she refuses to admit it. After a week, the growing tension between the two leads to a bitter quarrel. Yet over time, each slowly comes to appreciate the other's strengths and talents. A year after they begin working together, these two workers become respectful friends. This story is an example of what interactionists call the *contact hypothesis* in action.

Theory Conflict view of racial prejudice and discrimination
Theory Interactionist view of racial prejudice and discrimination
Classroom Tip See "Interactionist Approach to Reducing Social Conflict—Robbers Cave Experiment" (Additional Lecture Ideas).

The *contact hypothesis* states that in cooperative circumstances, interracial contact between people of equal status will cause them to become less prejudiced and to abandon old stereotypes. People begin to see one another as individuals and discard the broad generalizations characteristic of stereotyping. Note the phrases *equal status* and *cooperative circumstances.* In the story just told, if the two workers had been competing for one vacancy as a supervisor, the racial hostility between them might have worsened (Allport 1979; Fine 2004).

As Latinos and other minorities slowly gain access to better-paying and more responsible jobs, the contact hypothesis may take on even greater significance. The trend in our society is toward increasing contact between individuals from dominant and subordinate groups. That may be one way of eliminating—or at least reducing—racial and ethnic stereotyping and prejudice. Another may be the establishment of interracial coalitions, an idea suggested by sociologist William Julius Wilson (1999b). To work, such coalitions would obviously need to be built on an equal role for all members.

Contact between individuals occurs on the micro level. Box 10-1 (page 244) examines the interactionist research on friendships that cross ethnic and racial lines.

Table 10-2 summarizes the three major sociological perspectives on race. No matter what the explanation for racial and ethnic distinctions—functionalist, conflict, or interactionist—these socially constructed inequalities can have powerful consequences in the form of prejudice and discrimination. In the next section, we will see how inequality based on the ascribed characteristics of race and ethnicity can poison people's interpersonal relations, depriving whole groups of opportunities others take for granted.

Patterns of Intergroup Relations

Racial and ethnic groups can relate to one another in a wide variety of ways, ranging from friendships and intermarriages to hostility, from behaviors that require mutual approval to behaviors imposed by the dominant group.

One devastating pattern of intergroup relations is *genocide*—the deliberate, systematic killing of an entire people or nation. This term describes the killing of 1 million Armenians by Turkey beginning in 1915. It is most commonly applied to Nazi Ger-

many's extermination of 6 million European Jews, as well as gays, lesbians, and the Romani people ("Gypsies"), during World War II. The term *genocide* is also appropriate in describing the United States' policies toward Native Americans in the 19th century. In 1800, the Native American (or American Indian) population of the United States was about 600,000; by 1850, it had been reduced to 250,000 through warfare with the U.S. cavalry, disease, and forced relocation to inhospitable environments.

The *expulsion* of a people is another extreme means of acting out racial or ethnic prejudice. In 1979, Vietnam expelled nearly 1 million ethnic Chinese, partly as a result of centuries of hostility between Vietnam and neighboring China. In a more recent example of expulsion (which had aspects of genocide), Serbian forces began a program of "ethnic cleansing" in 1991, in the newly independent states of Bosnia and Herzegovina. Throughout the former nation of Yugoslavia, the Serbs drove more than 1 million Croats and Muslims from their homes. Some they tortured and killed; others they abused and terrorized, in an attempt to "purify" the land for the Serbian majority. In 1999, Serbs again became the focus of worldwide condemnation as they sought to "cleanse" the province of Kosovo of ethnic Albanians.

Genocide and expulsion are extreme behaviors. More typical intergroup relations follow four identifiable patterns: (1) amalgamation, (2) assimilation, (3) segregation, and (4) pluralism. Each pattern defines the dominant group's actions and the minority group's responses. Intergroup relations are rarely restricted to only one of the four patterns, although invariably one does tend to dominate. Think of these patterns primarily as ideal types.

Amalgamation

Amalgamation happens when a majority group and a minority group combine to form a new group. Through intermarriage over several generations, various groups in society combine to form a new group. This pattern can be expressed as $A + B + C \rightarrow D$, where A, B, and C represent different groups in a society, and D signifies the end result, a unique cultural-racial group unlike any of the initial groups (Newman 1973).

The belief in the United States as a "melting pot" became compelling in the first part of the 20th century, particularly since that image suggested that the nation had an almost divine mission to amalgamate various groups into one people. However, in actuality, many residents were not willing to include Native Americans, Jews, African Americans, Asian Americans, and Irish Roman Catholics in the melting pot. Therefore, this pattern does not adequately describe dominant–subordinate relations in the United States.

Assimilation

In India, many Hindus complain about Indian citizens who copy the traditions and customs of the British. In France, people of Arab and African origin, many of them Muslim, complain they are treated as

Table 10-2 Sociological Perspectives on Race

Perspective	Emphasis
Functionalist	The dominant majority benefits from the subordination of racial minorities.
Conflict	Vested interests perpetuate racial inequality through economic exploitation.
Interactionist	Cooperative interracial contacts can reduce hostility.

summingUP

Global View Genocide committed by Turkey and Nazi Germany

Global View Expulsion in Asia and Eastern Europe
Classroom Tip Another term used by sociologists to describe amalgamation is *fusion.*
Global View Assimilation in India, France, and Australia

researchIN*action*

10-1 Interracial and Interethnic Friendships

Do people really have close friends of different racial and ethnic backgrounds? Some sociologists have attempted to gauge the degree of White–Black interaction in the United States. But if these studies are not done carefully, they may overestimate the degree of "racial togetherness" in our society.

Sociologist Tom Smith, who directs the respected General Social Survey, has noticed that a high proportion of both White and African American respondents claim to have close friends of another race. But is that really true? When Smith and fellow researchers analyzed the survey data, they found that response rates varied with the way the question was phrased. When asked whether any of the friends they felt close to was Black, 42.1 percent of Whites said yes. Yet when asked to give the names of friends they felt close to, only 6 percent of Whites listed a close friend of a different race or ethnicity.

When asked the race of their best same-sex friend, most Americans choose someone of the same race as themselves. In a national study of adolescents, over 91 percent of non-Hispanic Whites claimed a non-Hispanic White as their best same-sex friend. (The General Social Survey yielded almost the same result for all adults.) Given the fact that over a third of the teens in the United States are either non-White or Hispanic, we might have expected to find more cross-race friendships. Members of minority groups seem more willing than Whites to cross racial and ethnic boundaries, however. A slightly lower 85 percent of Black adolescents selected a Black for a best friend, and a markedly lower 62 percent of Mexican Americans named another Mexican American.

Interactionists have noted significant differences in interracial and interethnic friendships. Regardless of one's racial or ethnic group, friendships that cross racial and ethnic boundaries are less likely than others to involve visits to each other's homes. They are also less likely than others to feature a sharing of personal problems.

In sum, careful research shows that to a great degree, our society's growing diversity is not reflected in our choice of friends.

> *A high proportion of both White and African American respondents claim to have close friends of another race.*

Let's Discuss

1. How common are interracial and interethnic friendships where you live or go to school? Do the results of the two surveys described here strike you as familiar?
2. What might explain the gap between the percentage of Whites claiming to have a close friend who was Black and the percentage of Whites who listed a close friend of another race or ethnicity?

Sources: Hamm et al. 2005; Kao and Joyner 2004; T. Smith 1999.

---

second-class citizens—a charge that provoked riots in 2005. In Australia, Aborigines who have become part of the dominant society refuse to acknowledge their darker-skinned grandparents on the street. And in the United States, some Italian Americans, Polish Americans, Hispanics, and Jews have changed their ethnic-sounding family names to names that are typically found among White Protestant families.

Assimilation is the process through which a person forsakes his or her own cultural tradition to become part of a different culture. Generally, it is practiced by a minority group member who wants to conform to the standards of the dominant group. Assimilation can be described as a pattern in which A + B + C → A. The majority, A, dominates in such a way that members of minorities B and C imitate it and attempt to become indistinguishable from it (Newman 1973).

Assimilation can strike at the very roots of a person's identity. Alphonso D'Abruzzo, for example, changed his name to Alan Alda. The British actress Joyce Frankenberg changed her name to Jane Seymour. Name changes, switches in religious affiliation, and dropping of native languages can obscure one's roots and heritage. However, assimilation does not necessarily bring acceptance to minority group individuals. A Chinese American such as Helen Zia (see the chapter-opening excerpt) may speak English fluently, achieve high educational standards, and become a well-respected professional or businessperson and *still* be seen as different. Other Americans may reject her as a business associate, neighbor, or marriage partner.

Use Your Sociological Imagination   www.mhhe.com /schaefer7

You have immigrated to another country with a very different culture. What steps might you take to assimilate?

Segregation

Separate schools, separate seating on buses and in restaurants, separate washrooms, even separate drinking fountains—these were all part of the lives of African Americans in the South when segregation ruled early in the 20th century. *Segregation* refers to the physical separation of two groups of people in terms of residence, workplace, and social events. Generally, a dominant group imposes this pattern on a minority group. Segregation is rarely complete, however. Intergroup contact inevitably occurs, even in the most segregated societies.

Key Person Tom Smith
Theory Interactionist analysis of interracial friendships
Let's Discuss Would students expect these patterns of interracial friendships to change in the future? Why or why not?
Classroom Tip See "Partial-Assimilation—Jews During Christmastime" (Additional Lecture Ideas).

From 1948 (when it received its independence) to 1990, the Republic of South Africa severely restricted the movement of Blacks and other non-Whites by means of a wide-ranging system of segregation known as *apartheid.* Apartheid even included the creation of separate homelands where Blacks were expected to live. However, decades of local resistance to apartheid, combined with international pressure, led to marked political changes in the 1990s. In 1994, a prominent Black activist, Nelson Mandela, was elected South Africa's president in the first election in which Blacks (the majority of the nation's population) were allowed to vote. Mandela had spent almost 28 years in South African prisons for his anti-apartheid activities. His election was widely viewed as the final blow to South Africa's oppressive policy of segregation.

Long-entrenched social patterns are difficult to change, however. In the United States today, despite federal laws that forbid housing discrimination, residential segregation is still the norm, as a recent analysis of living patterns in metropolitan areas shows. Across the nation, neighborhoods remain divided along both racial and ethnic lines. The average White person lives in an area that is at least 83 percent White, while the average African American lives in a neighborhood that is mostly Black. The typical Latino lives in an area that is 42 percent Hispanic. Overall, segregation flourishes at the community and neighborhood level, despite the increasing diversity of the nation as a whole (Lewis Mumford Center 2001).

Whatever the country, residential segregation directly limits people's economic opportunity. Sociologists Douglas Massey and Nancy Denton (1993), in a book aptly titled *American Apartheid*, noted that segregation separates poor people of color from job opportunities and isolates them from successful role models. This pattern repeats itself the world over, from South Central Los Angeles to Oldham, England, and Soweto, South Africa.

Pluralism

In a pluralistic society, a subordinate group does not have to forsake its lifestyle and traditions. *Pluralism* is based on mutual respect for one another's cultures among the various groups in a society. This pattern allows a minority group to express its own culture and still participate without prejudice in the larger society. Earlier, we described amalgamation as A + B + C → D, and assimilation as A + B + C → A. Using this same approach, we can conceive of pluralism as A + B + C → A + B + C. All the groups coexist in the same society (Newman 1973).

In the United States, pluralism is more of an ideal than a reality. There are distinct instances of pluralism—the ethnic neighborhoods in major cities, such as Koreatown, Little Tokyo, Andersonville (Swedish Americans), and Spanish Harlem—yet there are also limits to cultural freedom. To survive, a society must promote a certain consensus among its members regarding basic ideals, values, and beliefs. Thus, if a Romanian immigrant to the United States wants to move up the occupational ladder, he or she cannot avoid learning the English language.

This public housing development in suburban Paris is home to African and Asian immigrants, most of them Muslim. Such racial and ethnic enclaves are characterized by limited job opportunities and underfinanced schools. In many other parts of the world as well, the segregation of racial and ethnic minorities accentuates the gap between the haves and have-nots.

Switzerland exemplifies the modern pluralistic state. There the absence of both a national language and a dominant religious faith leads to a tolerance for cultural diversity. In addition, various political devices safeguard the interests of ethnic groups in a way that has no parallel in the United States. By contrast, Great Britain has had difficulty achieving cultural pluralism in a multiracial society. East Indians, Pakistanis, and Blacks from the Caribbean and Africa experience prejudice and discrimination within the dominant White society there. Some British advocate cutting off all Asian and Black immigration, and a few even call for expulsion of those non-Whites currently living in Britain.

Impact of Global Immigration

Worldwide, immigration is at an all-time high. Each year, about 2.3 percent of the world's population, or 146 million people, moves from one country to another. A million of them enter the United States legally, to join the 12 percent of the U.S. population who are foreign born (Schmidley and Robinson 2003; Stalker 2000).

In the 1960s, following decades of restrictive immigration policy, Congress overhauled the immigration law. U.S. policy now encourages the immigration of relatives of U.S. residents, as well as of people who have desirable skills. This change has significantly altered the pattern of sending nations. Previously, Europeans had dominated, but for the last 40 years immigrants have come primarily from Latin America, India, and Asia. Thus, in the future, an ever-growing proportion of the U.S. population will be Asian or Hispanic (see Figure 10-5, page 246). Fear and resentment of this growing racial and ethnic diversity is a key

Foreign-Born Population of the United States, from 10 Leading Countries

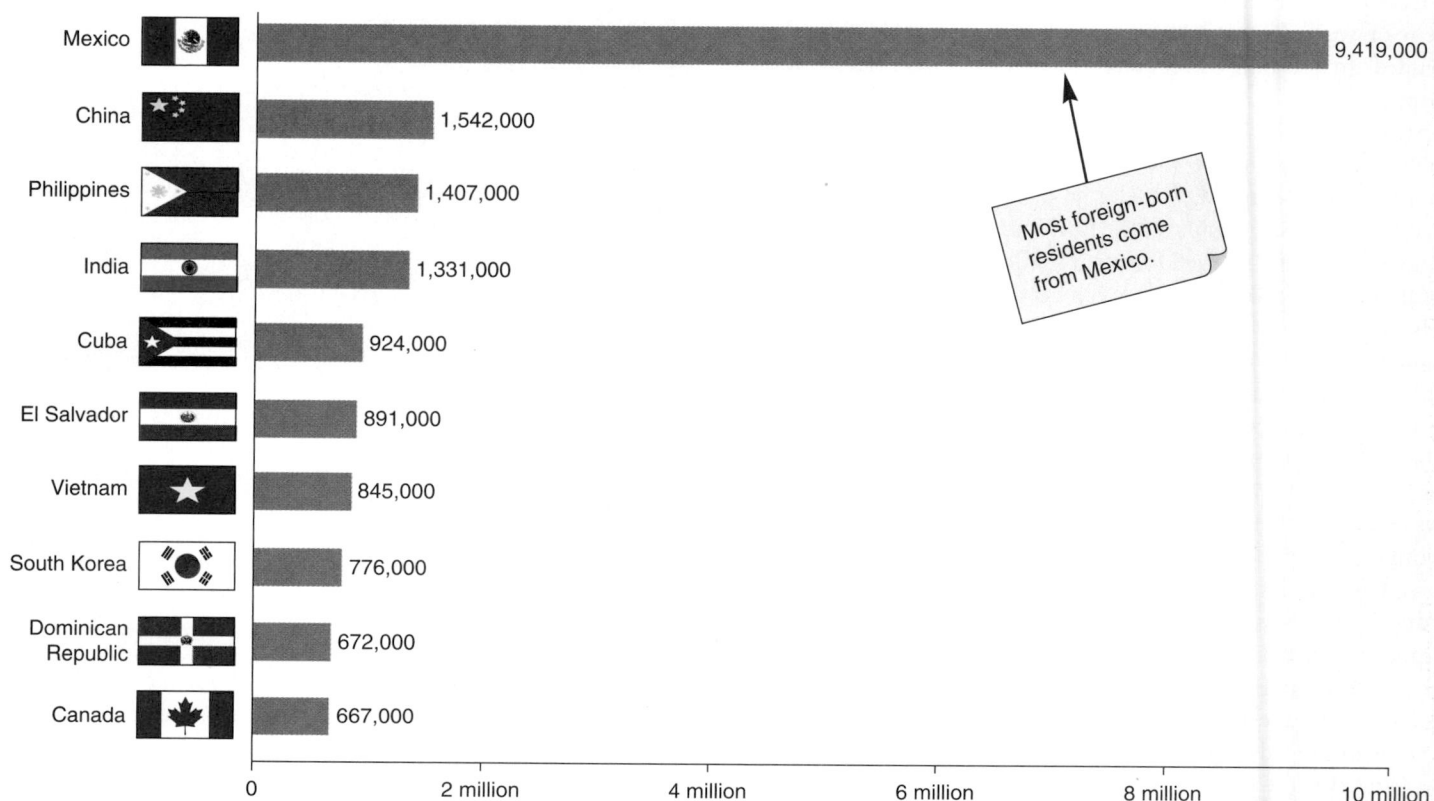

Note: Based on annualized averages of Current Population Survey. Chinese total includes Hong Kong and Taiwan.
Sources: Data for 2002 reported in Schmidley and Robinson 2003:Table A-3.

factor in popular opposition to immigration. As in many other nations, citizens in the United States are concerned that the new arrivals do not reflect the nation's cultural and racial heritage.

The long border with Mexico provides ample opportunity for illegal immigration into the United States. Throughout the 1980s, the public perception that the United States had lost control of its southern border grew. Responding to pressure for immigration control, Congress ended a decade of debate by approving the Immigration Reform and Control Act of 1986. For the first time, the hiring of illegal aliens was outlawed, and employers caught violating the law became subject to fines and even prison sentences. Just as significant a change was the extension of amnesty and legal status to many illegal immigrants already living in the United States. Twenty years later, however, the act appears to have had mixed results. Substantial numbers of illegal immigrants continue to enter the country each year, with an estimated 11 million present in March 2005 (Passel 2006).

Throughout the world, globalization has had an overwhelming impact on immigration patterns. In Europe, the European Union (EU) agreement of 1997 gave the EU's governing commission authority to propose a continentwide policy on immigration. EU policy allows residents of one EU country to live and work in another EU country—an arrangement that is expected to complicate efforts by sending nations, such as Turkey, to become members of the EU. In many EU countries, immigrants from Turkey's predominantly Muslim population are not welcome—no matter how pressing the economy's need for labor (Denny 2004).

One consequence of global immigration is the emergence of *transnationals*—people or families who move across borders multiple times in search of better jobs and education. The industrial tycoons of the early 20th century, whose power outmatched that of many nation-states, were among the world's first transnationals. But today millions of people, many of very modest means, move back and forth between countries much as commuters do between city and suburbs. More and more of these people have dual citizenship. Rather than being shaped by allegiance to one country, their identity is rooted in their struggle to survive—and in some instances prosper—by transcending international borders (Croucher 2004; Sassen 2005).

Race and Ethnicity in the United States

Few societies have a more diverse population than the United States; the nation is truly a multiracial, multiethnic society. Of

Policy Pointer Immigration Reform and Control Act of 1986.

Student Alert Sociological factors that may have led to the emergence of transnationals
Classroom Tip See "The New Immigrants" (Additional Lecture Ideas).

course, that has not always been the case. The population of what is now the United States has changed dramatically since the arrival of European settlers in the 1600s, as Figure 10-1 (see page 236) showed. Immigration, colonialism, and in the case of Blacks, slavery determined the racial and ethnic makeup of our present-day society. Figure 10-6 (below) shows where various racial and ethnic minorities are concentrated in the United States.

Racial Groups

The largest racial minorities in the United States are African Americans, Native Americans, and Asian Americans.

African Americans "I am an invisible man," wrote Black author Ralph Ellison in his novel *Invisible Man* (1952:3). "I am a man of substance, of flesh and bone, fiber and liquids—and I might even be said to possess a mind. I am invisible, understand, simply because people refuse to see me."

Over five decades later, many African Americans still feel invisible. Despite their large numbers, they have long been treated as second-class citizens. Currently, by the standards of the federal government, more than 1 out of every 4 Blacks—as opposed to 1 out of every 12 Whites—is poor.

Contemporary institutional discrimination and individual prejudice against African Americans are rooted in the history of

FIGURE 10–6

Census 2000: The Image of Diversity

MAPPING LIFE

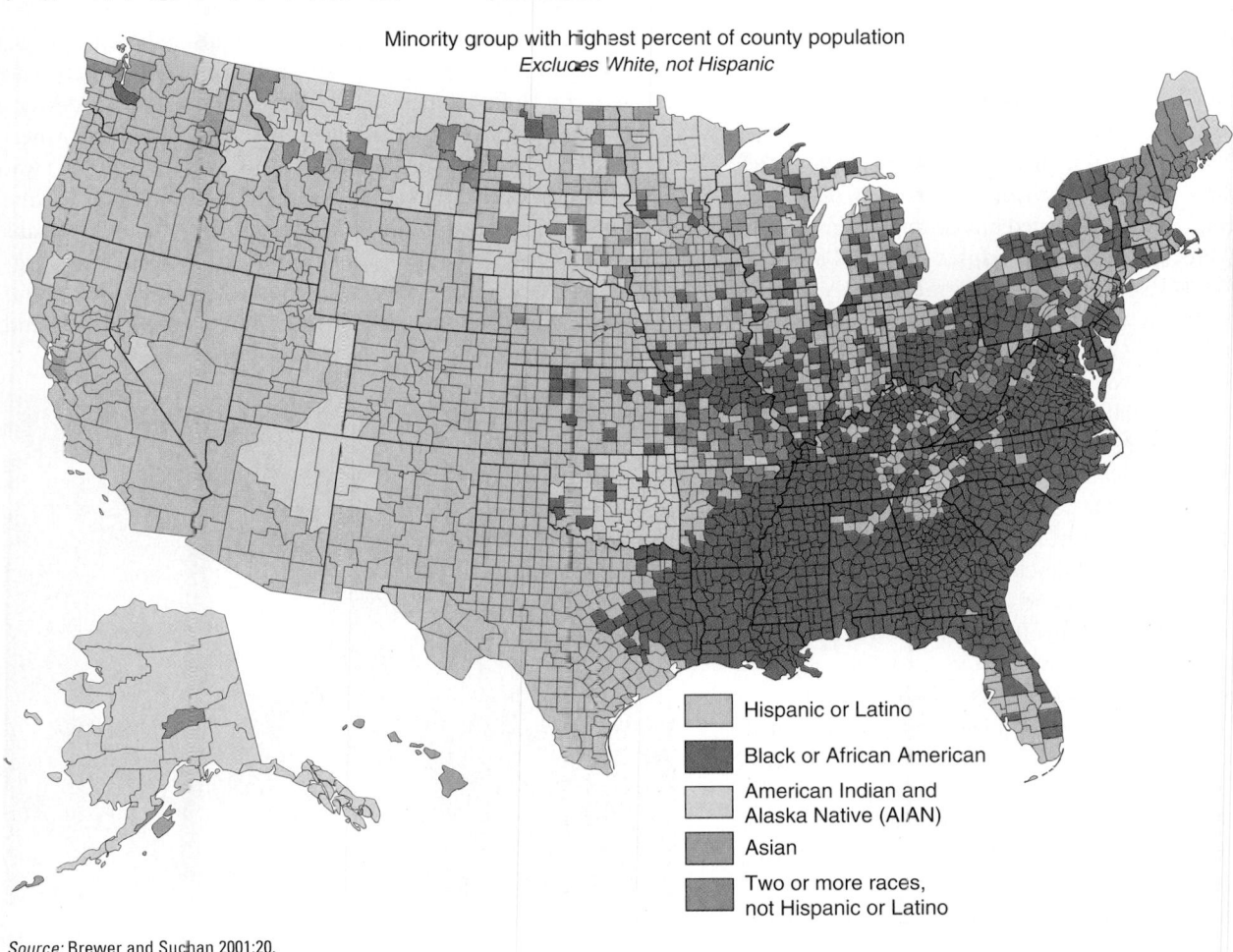

NATIONWIDE www.mhhe.com/schaefer7

Minority group with highest percent of county population
Excludes White, not Hispanic

Hispanic or Latino

Black or African American

American Indian and Alaska Native (AIAN)

Asian

Two or more races, not Hispanic or Latino

Source: Brewer and Suchan 2001:20.

Think About It
The United States is a diverse nation. Why, in many parts of the country, can't people see that diversity in their own towns?

slavery in the United States. Many other subordinate groups had little wealth and income, but as sociologist W. E. B. Du Bois (1909) and others have noted, enslaved Blacks were in an even more oppressive situation, because by law, they could not own property and could not pass on the benefits of their labor to their children. Today, increasing numbers of African Americans and sympathetic Whites are calling for *slave reparations* to compensate for the injustices of forced servitude. Reparations could include official expressions of apology from governments such as the United States, ambitious programs to improve African Americans' economic status, or even direct payments to descendants of slaves (D. Williams and Collins 2004).

The end of the Civil War did not bring genuine freedom and equality for Blacks. The Southern states passed "Jim Crow" laws to enforce official segregation, and the Supreme Court upheld them as constitutional in 1896. In addition, Blacks faced the danger of lynching campaigns, often led by the Ku Klux Klan, during the late 1800s and early 1900s. From a conflict perspective, Whites maintained their dominance formally through legalized segregation and informally by means of vigilante terror and violence (Franklin and Moss 2000).

A turning point in the struggle for Black equality came in 1954 with the unanimous Supreme Court decision in the case of *Brown v. Board of Education of Topeka, Kansas.* The Court outlawed segregation of public school students, ruling that "separate educational facilities are inherently unequal." In the wake of the *Brown* decision, there was a surge of activism on behalf of Black civil rights, including boycotts of segregated bus companies and sit-ins at restaurants and lunch counters that refused to serve Blacks.

During the 1960s, a vast civil rights movement emerged, with many competing factions and strategies for change. The Southern Christian Leadership Conference (SCLC), founded by Dr. Martin Luther King Jr., used nonviolent civil disobedience to oppose segregation. The National Association for the Advancement of Colored People (NAACP) favored use of the courts to press for equality for African Americans. But many younger Black leaders, most notably Malcolm X, turned toward an ideology of Black power. Proponents of **Black power** rejected the goal of assimilation into White middle-class society. They defended the beauty and dignity of Black and African cultures and supported the creation of Black-controlled political and economic institutions (Ture and Hamilton 1992).

Despite numerous courageous actions to achieve Black civil rights, Black and White citizens are still separate, still unequal. From birth to death, Blacks suffer in terms of their life chances. { pp.200–201 Life remains difficult for millions of poor Blacks, who must attempt to survive in ghetto areas shattered by high unemployment and abandoned housing. The median household income of Blacks is still only 60 percent that of Whites, and the unemployment rate among Blacks is more than twice that of Whites.

Some African Americans—especially middle-class men and women—have made economic gains over the last 50 years. For example, data compiled by the Department of Labor show that the number of African Americans in management increased na-

tionally from 2.4 percent of the total in 1958 to 5.9 percent in 2004. Yet Blacks still represent only 6 percent or less of all physicians, engineers, scientists, lawyers, judges, and marketing managers. In another occupation important to developing role models, African Americans and Hispanics together account for less than 11 percent of all editors and reporters in the United States (Bureau of the Census 2005a:402–403).

In many respects, the civil rights movement of the 1960s left institutionalized discrimination against African Americans untouched. Consequently, in the 1970s and 1980s, Black leaders worked to mobilize African American political power as a force for social change. Between 1970 and 2003, the number of African American elected officials increased sixfold. Even so, Blacks remain significantly *underrepresented.* That underrepresentation is especially distressing in view of the fact that sociologist W. E. B. Du Bois observed over 90 years ago that Blacks could not expect to achieve equal social and economic opportunities without first gaining political rights (Bureau of the Census 2004a:250; Green and Driver 1978).

Native Americans Today, 2.5 million Native Americans represent a diverse array of cultures distinguishable by language, family organization, religion, and livelihood. The outsiders who came to the United States—European settlers and their descendants—came to know these native peoples' forefathers as "American Indians." By the time the Bureau of Indian Affairs (BIA) was organized as part of the War Department in 1824, Indian–White relations had already included three centuries of hostile actions that had led to the virtual elimination of native peoples (see Figure 10-1). During the 19th century, many bloody wars wiped out a significant part of the nation's Indian population. By the end

{ Whose history? Native Americans took to the streets in 2005 to protest Denver, Colorado's Columbus Day parade. The demonstrators, 200 strong, sought to remember those who lost their land and lives after White Europeans "discovered" the continent.

Let's Discuss Ask for student feedback on slave reparations.
Key Persons Dr. Martin Luther King Jr., Malcolm X
Contemporary Culture Differential life chances of Blacks

Theory Conflict view of historic mistreatment of Native Americans and their subordinate position today

of the century, schools for Indians—operated by the BIA or by church missions—prohibited the practice of Native American cultures. Yet at the same time, such schools did little to make the children effective competitors in White society.

Today, life remains difficult for members of the 554 tribal groups in the United States, whether they live in cities or on reservations. For example, one Native American teenager in six has attempted suicide—a rate four times higher than the rate for other teenagers. Traditionally, some Native Americans have chosen to assimilate and abandon all vestiges of their tribal cultures to escape certain forms of prejudice. However, by the 1990s, an increasing number of people in the United States were openly claiming a Native American identity. Since 1960, the federal government's count of Native Americans has tripled, to an estimated 2.5 million. According to the 2000 census, the Native American population increased 26 percent during the 1990s. Demographers believe that more and more Native Americans who previously concealed their identity are no longer pretending to be White (Grieco and Cassidy 2001).

The introduction of gambling on Indian reservations threatens to become another battleground between Native Americans and the dominant White society. Box 10-2 (page 250) examines the controversy over the Native American gaming industry.

Use Your Sociological Imagination
www.mhhe.com/schaefer7

You are a Native American whose tribe is about to open a reservation-based casino. Will the casino further the assimilation of your people into mainstream society or encourage pluralism?

Asian Americans Asian Americans are a diverse group, one of the fastest-growing segments of the U.S. population (up 69 percent between 1990 and 2000). Among the many groups of Americans of Asian descent are Vietnamese Americans, Chinese Americans, Japanese Americans, and Korean Americans (see Figure 10-7).

Asian Americans are held up as a ***model*** or ***ideal minority*** group, supposedly because despite past suffering from prejudice and discrimination, they have succeeded economically, socially, and educationally without resorting to confrontations with Whites. The existence of a model minority seems to reaffirm the notion that anyone can get ahead in the United States with talent and hard work, and implies that those minorities that don't succeed are somehow responsible for their failure. Viewed from a conflict perspective, this attitude is yet another instance of "blaming the victims" (Hurh and Kim 1998).

The concept of a model minority ignores the diversity among Asian Americans: There are rich and poor Japanese Americans, rich and poor Filipino Americans, and so forth. In fact, Southeast Asians living in the United States have the highest rate of welfare dependency of any racial or ethnic group. Asian Americans have substantially more schooling than other ethnic

Contemporary Culture Introduction of gambling on Indian reservations
Theory Labeling Asian Americans as a "model minority" ignores their diversity, and from a conflict perspective, contributes to blaming other minorities who may have been less successful.

groups, but their median income is only slightly higher than Whites' income, and their poverty rate is higher. In 2004, for every Asian American family with an annual income of $100,000 or more, there was another earning less than $25,000 a year. Moreover, even when Asian Americans are clustered at the higher-paying end of the stratification system, the glass ceiling may limit how far they can rise (DeNavas-Walt et al. 2005).

Vietnamese Americans Each Asian American group has its own history and culture. Vietnamese Americans, for instance, came to the United States primarily during and after the Vietnam War—especially after the U.S. withdrawal from the conflict in 1975. Assisted by local agencies, refugees from the communist government in Vietnam settled throughout the United States, tens of thousands of them in small towns. But over time, Vietnamese Americans have gravitated toward the larger urban areas, establishing Vietnamese restaurants and grocery stores in their ethnic enclaves there.

In 1995, the United States resumed normal diplomatic relations with Vietnam. Gradually, the *Viet Kieu,* or Vietnamese living abroad, began to return to their old country to visit, but usually not to take up permanent residence. Today, 30 years after the end of the Vietnam War, sharp differences of opinion remain among Vietnamese Americans, especially the older ones, concerning the war and the present government of Vietnam (Lamb 1997).

Chinese Americans Unlike African slaves and Native Americans, the Chinese were initially encouraged to immigrate to the United States. From 1850 to 1880, thousands of Chinese immigrated to this country, lured by job opportunities created by the discovery of gold. However, as employment possibilities

FIGURE 10–7

Major Asian American Groups in the United States, 2000

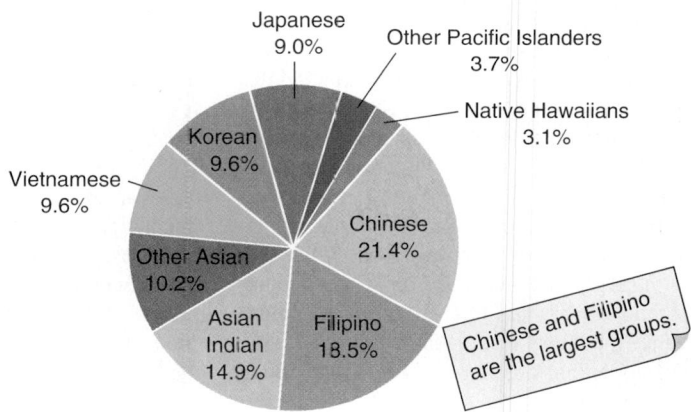

Japanese 9.0%
Other Pacific Islanders 3.7%
Native Hawaiians 3.1%
Korean 9.6%
Vietnamese 9.6%
Chinese 21.4%
Other Asian 10.2%
Asian Indian 14.9%
Filipino 18.5%

Chinese and Filipino are the largest groups.

Source: Logan 2001.

Think About It
Do Asian Americans really have a common identity?

Let's Discuss Could the "model minority" stereotype be part of our society's dominant ideology?
Theory From a functionalist perspective, even positive stereotypes of Asian Americans as "academic stars" can be dysfunctional for those Asian Americans who are not successful.

10-2 Native Americans Gamble on Gaming

On Native American reservations, economic opportunity is virtually nonexistent. For many tribes, the only viable source of employment and income is commercial gambling. When gaming began on reservations, it was an industry of last resort, a way for Native Americans to earn a living in an isolated area blessed with few natural resources. But in recent years, gaming has proved to be more than a way of getting by; for some tribes, it has become a bonanza.

Native Americans got into the gaming industry in 1988, when Congress passed the Indian Gambling Regulatory Act. The law stipulates that states must negotiate agreements with tribes interested in commercial gaming; they cannot prevent tribes from engaging in gambling operations, even if state law prohibits such ventures. By 2004, 224 tribal governments had opened a variety of gaming operations in 28 states, including off-track betting, sports betting, and telephone betting; casino games such as blackjack and roulette; high-stakes bingo; slot machines; lotteries; and video games of chance. The gamblers who patronize these operations, almost all of whom are not Native American, sometimes travel long distances for the opportunity to wager money.

Though reservation casinos are tribally owned enterprises, most are not operated by Native Americans. Nationally, 75 percent of tribal gaming operations are run by outsiders, and almost all the reservation casinos are operated by White-owned businesses. In 2004, receipts from these casinos amounted to $18.5 billion nationwide—about one-fourth the revenues from other legal gambling operations.

The income from these lucrative operations is not evenly distributed, however. About two-thirds of recognized Indian tribes are not involved in gambling ventures. Those tribes that earn substantial revenues from gambling constitute only a small fraction of Native Americans. On these reservations, about 25 very successful casinos have produced staggering windfalls. The profits from the Foxwoods Re-

sort Casino, whose annual gaming receipts total well over $1.5 billion, are shared by 820 members of the Connecticut Mashantucket Pequot Indians. The tribe provides generous benefits to anyone who can establish that he or she is at least one-sixteenth Pequot. Revenues from successful casinos have also been used to buy back tribal lands and to support the Smithsonian Museum of the American Indian, which opened in 2004.

For most Native Americans, however, income from gaming has not brought dramatic changes in lifestyle. Typically, they see a drop in unemployment and increases in household income from their moderately successful operations—benefits that are not seen on nongaming reservations. But the impact of the additional revenue is limited, given these tribes' overwhelming social and economic needs.

From some people's point of view, Native Americans have learned to play the White man's game of politics only too well.

Even on those reservations that benefit from gambling enterprises, unemployment levels are substantially higher than for the nation as a whole, and family income is significantly lower.

Criticism of Native American gambling operations exists even among Native Americans. Some feel that the tribal-themed casinos trivialize and cheapen their heritage. Native Americans gambled during tribal ceremonies and celebrations long before Europeans arrived in the Western Hemisphere, but their games were an integral part of their culture, not a commercial amusement. Other Native Americans oppose gambling on moral grounds. They are concerned about the development of compulsive gambling among members of their tribe, although the majority of gamblers are not Native American. Finally, in some tribes, the issue of who should share in the gambling prof-

its has led to heated debates over who is or is not a member of the tribe.

Not surprisingly, gaming on reservations has been a magnet for criticism from outsiders. Even though nationwide, Native Americans generate only 23 percent of the total revenue from legal gambling, including profits from lotteries and racing, White gaming interests have lobbied Congress to restrict tribal operations. They question the special status afforded to Native Americans, complaining of an uneven playing field. Tribal members counter that over the last 200 years, government policy created a playing field on which Native Americans were at a distinct disadvantage.

Though Native Americans' voting clout is weak compared to that of African Americans and Latinos, their lobbying power is significant. Casino money fueled the 2006 scandal involving lobbyist Jack Abramoff, who cheated several tribes by pretending to lobby on their behalf. But while many of the political donations Native Americans make are aimed at protecting reservation casinos, federal grants for education, roads, housing, and other projects also occupy tribes' political agendas. From some people's point of view, Native Americans have learned to play the White man's game of politics only too well.

Let's Discuss

1. What do you think of the commercial gaming operations that Native Americans run from their reservations? Would your opinion differ depending on whether you yourself were a Native American?
2. Analyze the Native American gaming industry from the functionalist, conflict, and interactionist viewpoints. Which perspective do you find most helpful?

Sources: Bartlett and Steele 2002; Drinkard 2006; Glionna 2004; National Indian Gaming Association 2005; Sahagun 2004; J. Taylor and Kalt 2005.

Policy Pointer Explain why laws governing reservations often differ from other laws.
Let's Discuss Have students ever lived on or visited a reservation? How would they describe the socioeconomic conditions?

Theory Conflict analysis of gambling on Indian reservations
Contemporary Culture How do students feel about tribal-themed casinos? Are their views related to their racial or ethnic status?

Despite their tourist appeal, Chinatowns offer their residents limited job opportunities in return for low wages and long hours.

decreased and competition for mining jobs grew, the Chinese became the target of a bitter campaign to limit their numbers and restrict their rights. Chinese laborers were exploited, then discarded.

In 1882, Congress enacted the Chinese Exclusion Act, which prevented Chinese immigration and even forbade Chinese in the United States to send for their families. As a result, the Chinese population declined steadily until after World War II. More recently, the descendants of the 19th-century immigrants have been joined by a new influx from Hong Kong and Taiwan. These groups may contrast sharply in their degree of assimilation, desire to live in Chinatowns, and feelings about this country's relations with the People's Republic of China.

Currently, about 2.7 million Chinese Americans live in the United States. Some Chinese Americans have entered lucrative occupations, yet many immigrants struggle to survive under living and working conditions that belie the model-minority stereotype. New York City's Chinatown district is filled with illegal sweatshops in which recent immigrants—many of them Chinese women—work for minimal wages. Even in legal factories in the garment industry, hours are long and rewards are lim-

ited. A seamstress typically works 11 hours per day, 6 days a week, and earns about $10,000 a year. Other workers, such as hemmers and cutters, earn only $5,000 per year (Finder 1995; Lum and Kwong 1989).

Japanese Americans Approximately 1.1 million Japanese Americans live in the United States. As a people, they are relatively recent arrivals. In 1880, only 148 Japanese lived in the United States, but by 1920 there were more than 110,000. Japanese immigrants—called the *Issei*, or first generation—were usually males seeking employment opportunities. Many Whites saw them (along with Chinese immigrants) as a "yellow peril" and subjected them to prejudice and discrimination.

In 1941, the attack on Hawaii's Pearl Harbor by Japan had severe repercussions for Japanese Americans. The federal government decreed that all Japanese Americans on the West Coast must leave their homes and report to "evacuation camps." Japanese Americans became, in effect, scapegoats for the anger that other people in the United States felt concerning Japan's role in World War II. By August 1943, in an unprecedented application of guilt by virtue of ancestry, 113,000 Japanese Americans had been forced into hastily built camps. In striking contrast, only a few German Americans and Italian Americans were sent to evacuation camps (Hosokawa 1969).

This mass detention was costly for Japanese Americans. The Federal Reserve Board estimates their total income and property losses at nearly half a billion dollars. Moreover, the psychological effect on these citizens—including the humiliation of being labeled "disloyal"—was immeasurable. Eventually, children born in the United States to the *Issei*, called *Nisei*, were allowed to enlist in the Army and serve in Europe in a segregated combat unit. Others resettled in the East and Midwest to work in factories.

In 1983, a federal commission recommended government payments to all surviving Japanese Americans who had been held in detention camps. The commission reported that the detention was motivated by "race prejudice, war hysteria, and a failure of political leadership." It added that "no documented acts of espionage, sabotage, or fifth-column activity were shown to have been committed" by Japanese Americans. In 1988, President Ronald Reagan signed the Civil Liberties Act, which required the federal government to issue individual apologies for all violations of Japanese Americans' constitutional rights, and established a $1.25 billion trust fund to pay reparations to the approximately 77,500 surviving Japanese Americans who had been interned (Department of Justice 2000).

Korean Americans At 1.2 million, the population of Korean Americans now exceeds that of Japanese Americans. Yet Korean Americans are often overshadowed by other groups from Asia.

Today's Korean American community is the result of three waves of immigration. The initial wave arrived between 1903 and 1910, when Korean laborers migrated to Hawaii. The second wave followed the end of the Korean War in 1953; most of these immigrants were wives of U.S. servicemen and war orphans. The

third wave, continuing to the present, has reflected the admissions priorities set up in the 1965 Immigration Act. These well-educated immigrants arrive in the United States with professional skills. Yet because of language difficulties and discrimination, many must settle at least initially for positions of lower responsibility than those they held in Korea and must suffer through a period of disenchantment. Stress, loneliness, and family strife may accompany the pain of adjustment.

Like many other Asian American women, Korean American women commonly participate in the paid labor force, though in Korea women are expected to serve as mothers and homemakers only. While these roles carry over to the United States, Korean American women are also pressed to support their families while their husbands struggle to establish themselves financially. Many Korean American men begin small service and retail businesses and gradually involve their wives in the ventures. Making the situation even more difficult is the hostility Korean American–run businesses often encounter from their prospective customers (Hurh 1994, 1998; Kim 1999).

In the early 1990s, the apparent friction between Korean Americans and another subordinate racial group, African Americans, attracted nationwide attention. In New York City, Los Angeles, and Chicago, Korean American merchants confronted Blacks who were allegedly threatening them or robbing their stores. Black neighborhoods responded with hostility to what they perceived as the disrespect and arrogance of Korean American entrepreneurs. In South Central Los Angeles, the only shops in which to buy groceries, liquor, or gasoline were owned by Korean immigrants, who had largely replaced White businesspeople. African Americans were well aware of the dominant role that Korean Americans played in their local retail markets. During the 1992 riots in South Central Los Angeles, small businesses owned by Koreans were a particular target. More than 1,800 Korean businesses were looted or burned during the riots (Kim 1999).

Conflict between the two groups was dramatized in Spike Lee's 1989 movie *Do the Right Thing.* The situation stems from Korean Americans' position as the latest immigrant group to cater to the needs of inner-city populations abandoned by those who have moved up the economic ladder. This type of friction is not new; generations of Jewish, Italian, and Arab merchants have encountered similar hostility from what to outsiders seems an unlikely source—another oppressed minority.

Arab Americans

Arab Americans are immigrants and their descendants who hail from the 22 nations of the Arab world. As defined by the League of Arab States, these are the nations of North Africa and what is popularly known as the Middle East, including Lebanon, Syria, Palestine, Morocco, Iraq, Saudi Arabia, and Somalia. Not all residents of those countries are Arab; for example, the Kurds, who live in northern Iraq, are not Arab. And some Arab Americans may have immigrated to the United States from non-Arab countries such as Great Britain or France, where their families have lived for generations.

The Arabic language is the single most unifying force among Arabs, although not all Arabs, and certainly not all Arab Ameri-

Entrepreneurs of all ethnic and racial backgrounds participate in a broad spectrum of commercial activities. In Hollywood, California, an Iranian American took over Mugsy Malone's ice cream store, renaming it Mashti Malone's and adding Farsi script to the Irish shamrock on this billboard. Clearly, Iranian Americans enjoy ice cream.

cans, can read and speak Arabic. Moreover, the language has evolved over the centuries so that people in different parts of the Arab world speak different dialects. Still, the fact that the Qur'an (or Koran) was originally written in Arabic gives the language special importance to Muslims, just as the Torah's composition in Hebrew gives that language special significance to Jews.

Estimates of the size of the Arab American community differ widely. By some estimates, up to 3 million people of Arab ancestry reside in the United States. Among those who identify themselves as Arab Americans, the most common country of origin is Lebanon, followed by Syria, Egypt, and Palestine. In 2000, these four countries of origin accounted for two-thirds of all Arab Americans. As with other racial and ethnic groups, the Arab American population is concentrated in certain areas of the United States (see Figure 10-8). Their rising numbers have led to the development of Arab retail centers in several cities, including Dearborn and Detroit, Michigan; Los Angeles; Chicago; New York City; and Washington, D.C. (Wertsman 2001).

As a group, Arab Americans are extremely diverse. Many families have lived in the United States for several generations; others are foreign born. Their points of origin range from the metropolis of Cairo, Egypt, to the rural villages of Morocco. Despite the stereotype, most Arab Americans are *not* Muslim, and not all practice religion. Some Arab Americans are Christian. Nor can Arab Americans be characterized as having a specific family type, gender role, or occupational pattern (David 2004).

Despite this great diversity, profiling of potential terrorists at airports has put Arab and Muslim Americans under special surveillance. For years, a number of airlines and law enforcement authorities have used appearance and ethnic-sounding names to identify and take aside Arab Americans and search their belongings. After the terrorist attacks of September 2001, criticism of this practice declined as concern for the public's safety mounted.

FIGURE 10–8

253

Racial and Ethnic Inequality

Distribution of the Arab American Population by State

MAPPING LIFE

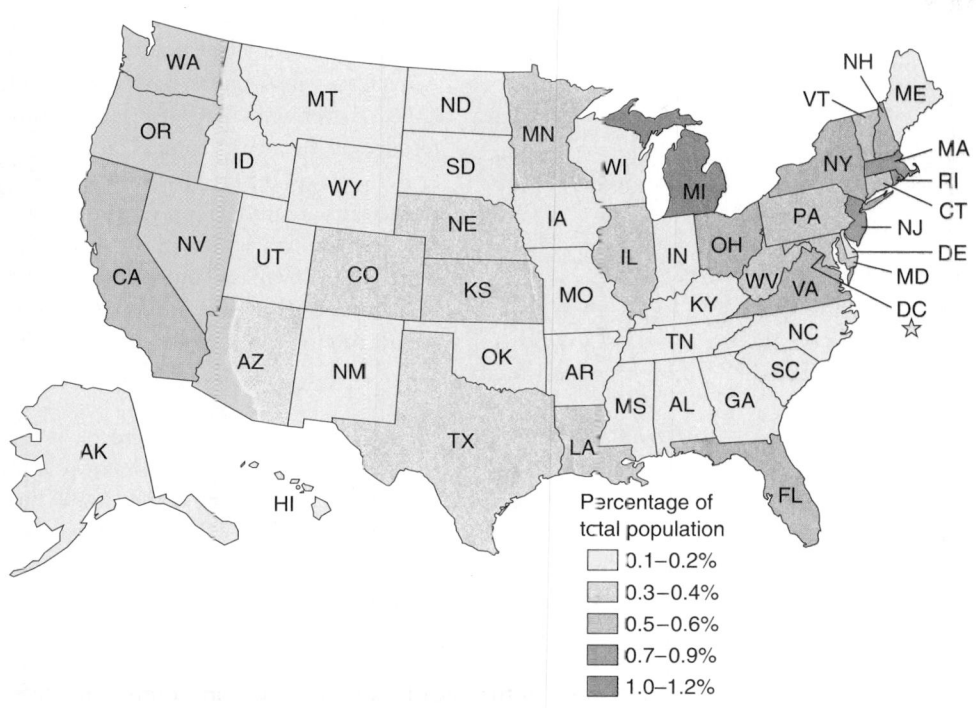

Percentage of total population

- 0.1–0.2%
- 0.3–0.4%
- 0.5–0.6%
- 0.7–0.9%
- 1.0–1.2%

Source: Data for 2000 reported in Bureau of the Census 2003c.

We will discuss racial and ethnic profiling in more detail in the Social Policy section that ends this chapter.

Ethnic Groups

Unlike racial minorities, members of subordinate ethnic groups generally are not hindered by physical differences from assimilating into the dominant culture of the United States. However, members of ethnic minority groups still face many forms of prejudice and discrimination. Take, for instance, the country's largest ethnic groups—Latinos, Jews, and White ethnics.

Latinos Together, the various groups included under the general category *Latinos* represent the largest minority in the United States. In 2002 there were more than 37 million Hispanics in this country, including 25 million Mexican Americans, more than 3 million Puerto Ricans, and smaller numbers of Cuban Americans and people of Central and South American origin (see Figure 10-9, page 254). The latter group represents the fastest-growing and most diverse segment of the Hispanic community.

According to Census Bureau data, the Latino population now outnumbers the African American population in 6 of the 10 largest cities of the United States: Los Angeles, Houston, Phoenix, San Diego, Dallas, and San Antonio. Hispanics are now the majority of residents in cities such as Miami, Florida; El

Paso, Texas; and Santa Ana, California. The rise in the Hispanic population of the United States—fueled by comparatively high birthrates and levels of immigration—has intensified debates over public policy issues such as bilingualism and immigration.

The various Latino groups share a heritage of Spanish language and culture, which can cause serious problems in their assimilation. An intelligent student whose first language is Spanish may be presumed slow or even unruly by English-speaking schoolchildren, and frequently by English-speaking teachers as well. The labeling of Latino children as underachievers, as learning disabled {p.71} or emotionally disturbed can act as a self-fulfilling prophecy for some children. Bilingual education aims at easing the educational difficulties experienced by Hispanic children and others whose first language is not English.

The educational difficulties of Latino students certainly contribute to the generally low economic status of Hispanics. In 2004 about 19 percent of all Hispanic households earned less than $15,000, compared to about 13 percent of non-Hispanic White households. As of 2003, only 12 percent of Hispanic adults had completed college, compared to 28 percent of non-Hispanic Whites. In 2004 the poverty rate for people ages 18 to 64 was 18.3 percent for Hispanics, compared to only 8.3 percent for non-Hispanic Whites. Overall, Latinos are not as affluent as White non-Hispanics, but a middle class is beginning to emerge (Bureau of the Census 2005a; DeNavas-Walt et al. 2005:33, 36, 53, 56; Tienda and Mitchell 2006).

Mexican Americans The largest Latino population is Mexican Americans, who can be further subdivided into those descended from residents of the territories annexed after the Mexican-American War of 1848 and those who have immigrated from Mexico to the United States. The opportunity for a Mexican to earn in one hour what it would take an entire day to earn in Mexico has pushed millions of legal and illegal immigrants north.

Aside from the family, the most important social organization in the Mexican American (or Chicano) community is the church, specifically the Roman Catholic church. This strong identification with the Catholic faith has reinforced the already formidable barriers between Mexican Americans and their predominantly White and Protestant neighbors in the Southwest. At the same time, the Catholic Church helps many immigrants to develop a sense of identity and assists their assimilation into the norms and values of the dominant culture of the United

Theory Labeling Latino children as underachievers or as learning disabled often acts as a self-fulfilling prophecy.
Contemporary Culture The poverty rate for Hispanics ages 18 to 64 was 18.3 percent in 2004.

Chapter 10

Major Hispanic Groups in the United States, 2002

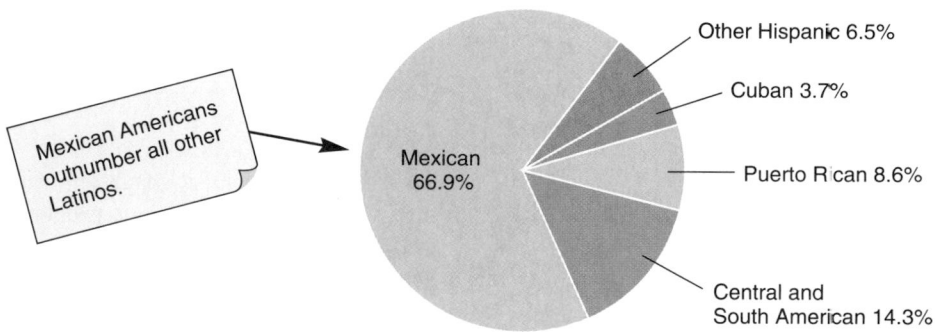

Source: R. Ramirez and de la Cruz 2003:1.

States. The complexity of the Mexican American community is underscored by the fact that Protestant churches—especially those that endorse expressive, open worship—have attracted increasing numbers of Mexican Americans.

Puerto Ricans   The second-largest segment of Latinos in the United States is Puerto Ricans. Since 1917, residents of Puerto Rico have held the status of American citizens; many have migrated to New York and other eastern cities. Unfortunately, Puerto Ricans have experienced serious poverty both in the United States and on the island. Those who live in the continental United States earn barely half the family income of Whites. As a result, a reverse migration began in the 1970s, when more Puerto Ricans were leaving for the island than were coming to the mainland (Lemann 1991).

Politically, Puerto Ricans in the United States have not been as successful as Mexican Americans in organizing for their rights. For many mainland Puerto Ricans—as for many residents of the island—the paramount political issue is the destiny of Puerto Rico itself: Should it continue in its present commonwealth status, petition for admission to the United States as the 51st state, or attempt to become an independent nation? This question has divided Puerto Rico for decades and remains a central issue in Puerto Rican elections. In a 1998 referendum, voters supported a "none of the above" option, effectively favoring continuation of the commonwealth status over statehood or independence.

Cuban Americans   Cuban immigration to the United States dates back as far as 1831, but it began in earnest following Fidel Castro's assumption of power in the Cuban revolution (1959). The first wave of 200,000 Cubans included many professionals with relatively high levels of schooling; these men and women were largely welcomed as refugees from communist tyranny. However, more recent waves of immigrants have aroused growing concern, partly because they were less likely to be skilled professionals. Throughout these waves of immigration, Cuban Americans have been encouraged to locate around the United States. Nevertheless, many continue to settle in (or return to) metropolitan Miami, Florida,

Policy Pointer Impact of the cold war on ease of immigration from Cuba.

with its warm climate and proximity to Cuba.

The Cuban experience in the United States has been mixed. Some detractors worry about the vehement anticommunism of Cuban Americans and the apparent growth of an organized crime syndicate that engages in the drug trade and ganglike violence. Recently, Cuban Americans in Miami have expressed concern over what they view as the indifference of the city's Roman Catholic hierarchy. Like other Hispanics, Cuban Americans are underrepresented in leadership positions within the church. Finally—despite many individual success stories—as a group, Cuban Americans in Miami remain behind "Anglos" (Whites) in income, rate of employment, and proportion of professionals.

Jewish Americans   Jews constitute almost 3 percent of the population of the United States. They play a prominent role in the worldwide Jewish community, because the United States has the world's largest concentration of Jews. Like the Japanese, many Jewish immigrants came to this country and became white-collar professionals in spite of prejudice and discrimination.

Anti-Semitism—that is, anti-Jewish prejudice—has often been vicious in the United States, although rarely so widespread and never so formalized as in Europe. In many cases, Jews have been used as scapegoats for other people's failures. Not surprisingly, Jews have not achieved equality in the United States. Despite high levels of education and professional training, they are still conspicuously absent from the top management of large corporations (except for the few firms founded by Jews). Until the late 1960s, many prestigious universities maintained restrictive quotas that limited Jewish enrollment. Private social clubs and fraternal groups frequently limit membership to gentiles (non-Jews), a practice upheld by the Supreme Court in the 1964 case *Bell v. Maryland.*

The Anti-Defamation League (ADL) of B'nai B'rith funds an annual tally of reported anti-Semitic incidents. Although the number has fluctuated, the 1994 tabulation reached the highest level in the 19 years the ADL has been recording them. In 2002 the total reported incidents of harassment, threats, vandalism, and assaults came to 1,559. Some incidents were inspired and carried out by neo-Nazi skinheads—groups of young people who champion racist and anti-Semitic ideologies. Such threatening behavior only intensifies the fears of many Jewish Americans, who find it difficult to forget the Holocaust—the extermination of 6 million Jews by the Nazi Third Reich during World War II (Anti-Defamation League 2003).

As is true for other minorities discussed in this chapter, Jewish Americans face the choice of maintaining ties to their long religious and cultural heritage or becoming as indistinguishable as possible from gentiles. Many Jews have tended to assimilate, as is evident from the rise in marriages between Jews and Chris-

Methods Secondary analysis (a survey of data gathered by law enforcement agencies) is used in the Anti-Defamation League's study of anti-Semitic incidents. **Theory** Conflict theorists would view anti-Semitic attacks in the United States as a reflection of continuing prejudice and discrimination.

tians. A study released in 2003 found that 47 percent of Jews who had married in the past five years chose to marry a non-Jew. Many people in the Jewish community worry that intermarriage will lead to a rapid decline in those who identify themselves as "Jewish." Yet when asked which was the greater threat to Jewish life in the United States—intermarriage or anti-Semitism—only 41 percent of respondents replied that intermarriage was the greater threat; 50 percent selected anti-Semitism (American Jewish Committee 2001; United Jewish Communities 2003).

White Ethnics   A significant segment of the population of the United States is made up of White ethnics whose ancestors arrived from Europe within the last century. The nation's White ethnic population includes about 43 million people who claim at least partial German ancestry, 31 million Irish Americans, 16 million Italian Americans, and 9 million Polish Americans, as well as immigrants from other European nations. Some of these people continue to live in close-knit ethnic neighborhoods, while others have largely assimilated and left the "old ways" behind (Brittingham and de la Cruz 2004).

Many White ethnics today identify only sporadically with their heritage. *Symbolic ethnicity* refers to an emphasis on concerns such as ethnic food or political issues rather than on deeper ties to one's ethnic heritage. It is reflected in the occasional family trip to an ethnic bakery, the celebration of a ceremonial event such as St. Joseph's Day among Italian Americans, or concern about the future of Northern Ireland among Irish Americans. Except in cases in which new immigration reinforces old traditions, symbolic ethnicity tends to decline with each passing generation (Alba 1990; Gans 1979).

White ethnics and racial minorities have often been antagonistic to one another because of economic competition—an interpretation that agrees with the conflict approach to sociology. As Blacks, Latinos, and Native Americans emerge from the lower

For practicing Jews, the Hebrew language is an important part of religious instruction. This teacher is showing flashcards of Hebrew alphabetic characters to deaf students.

class, they must compete with working-class Whites for jobs, housing, and educational opportunities. In times of high unemployment or inflation, any such competition can easily generate intense intergroup conflict.

In many respects, the plight of White ethnics raises the same basic issues as that of other subordinate people in the United States. How ethnic can people be—how much can they deviate from an essentially White, Anglo-Saxon, Protestant norm—before society punishes them for their willingness to be different? Our society does seem to reward people for assimilating. Yet as we have seen, assimilation is no guarantee of equality or freedom from discrimination. In the Social Policy section that follows, we will focus on the practice of racial profiling, in which racial minorities are placed under suspicion simply because of their race—and often in spite of their conventional appearance and lifestyle.

and Racial and Ethnic Inequality

Racial Profiling

The Issue
In the late 1980s and 1990s, Elmo Randolph, a dentist, was stopped by police dozens of times while traveling to work on the New Jersey Turnpike. Invariably, state troopers asked him whether he was carrying guns or drugs. "My parents always told me, be careful when you're driving on the turnpike," Dr. Randolph, a Black man, testified before a state commission. "White people don't have that conversation" (Purdy 2001:37).

Dr. Randolph was not the only motorist who was pulled over for what is now referred to sarcastically as a DWB offense—

Driving While Black. During the same period, African Americans constituted only 17 percent of the motorists on the New Jersey Turnpike, but 80 percent of the motorists pulled over by police (Scott Bowles 2000).

The Setting
Elmo Randolph was a victim of what is today called racial profiling. According to the Department of Justice, *racial profiling* is any police-initiated action based on race, ethnicity, or national origin rather than on a person's behavior. Generally, profiling

Methods Survey research on intermarriage involving Jewish Americans
Classroom Tip Have an officer of a White ethnic club (such as the Sons of Norway) speak to the class on the history and functions of the organization.
Theory Conflict view of the antagonism between White ethnics and racial minorities

Let's Discuss Ask whether anyone has ever heard of a White person being warned by relatives about discrimination by law enforcement officials.

occurs when law enforcement officers, including customs officials, airport security personnel, and police, assume that people who fit certain descriptions are likely to be engaged in illegal activities. Racial profiling is often based on explicit racial or ethnic stereotypes. For example, the federal antidrug initiative Operation Pipeline encouraged officers to look specifically for people wearing dreadlocks and for Latino men traveling together.

Statistics show that police rely heavily on racial profiling in their attempts to apprehend lawbreakers. A 2005 government report found that Black drivers were twice as likely as Whites, and Hispanic drivers three times more likely than Whites, to have their vehicles searched by police. Both groups were three times more likely than Whites to have force used against them (Durose et al. 2005).

Sociological Insights

Interactionists point out that when law enforcement officers or employers see people of a certain race or ethnicity as less trustworthy than others, intergroup relations suffer. Ultimately, racial profiling produces distrust on all sides. Authorities become suspicious of those who are profiled, and the victims of profiling come to disrespect those in authority.

Conflict theorists see racial profiling as one more way in which those in power seek to further social inequality. Typically, those who are profiled—African Americans, Latinos, and immigrants—are already at an economic disadvantage. Profiling, or even the threat of profiling, further stigmatizes them, decreasing their social mobility.

Policy Initiatives

In the 1990s, increased attention to racial profiling led not only to special reports and commissions, but to talk of legislation against it. But banning the practice proved difficult. In *Whren v. United States* (1996), the U.S. Supreme Court upheld the constitutionality of using a minor traffic infraction as an excuse to stop and search a vehicle and its passengers. Nonetheless, states and other government units began to devise policies and training programs to discourage racial profiling. At the same time, most law enforcement agencies rejected the idea of compiling racial data on traffic stops, arguing that it would be a waste of time and money.

The effort to stop racial profiling came to an abrupt end after the terrorist attacks of September 11, 2001. As suspicions about Muslims and Arabs in the United States mounted, police summoned foreign students from Arab countries for special questioning. Arabs or Muslims who were legal immigrants were scrutinized for any illegal activity and prosecuted for routine violations of immigration law—ones that immigration officials customarily overlooked among people of other ethnic and religious backgrounds. In 2003, President George W. Bush issued guidelines that barred federal agents from using race and ethnicity in routine investigations, but specifically exempted cases involving terrorism and national security. Though legislation dubbed the End Racial Profiling bill was introduced in Congress in 2004, it has yet to be considered.

National surveys show that those groups who are most likely to be stigmatized by racial profiling are less supportive of the practice than other groups. In a national survey done in 2004, people were asked if racial profiling of passengers at airport se-

Too often, authorities treat individuals differently based solely on their race or ethnicity. This poster dramatizes the injustice of racial profiling, a practice in which a man who looks like the Reverend Martin Luther King Jr. (left) would be treated with more suspicion than the mass murderer Charles Manson (right).

curity checkpoints was ever justified. Less than a third of all African Americans and only 40 percent of Latinos supported profiling under such circumstances, compared to 46 percent of non-Hispanic Whites. Nonetheless, racial profiling has been reaffirmed as a matter of national policy, and is becoming more common as a result. One study estimated that 32 million Americans—a number equivalent to the population of Canada—were victims of racial profiling in 2003 (Amnesty USA 2005; Carlson 2004; Coates 2004; D. Harris 1999; Lictblau 2003).

Let's Discuss

1. Have you or someone you know ever been stopped by police for a minor infraction? If so, did you suspect you were stopped because of your race or ethnicity? Do you know other people who have had a similar experience?

2. Do you support racial profiling of airplane passengers? Why or why not? Why do you think a majority of non-Hispanic Whites do not support this approach to airport security?

3. Could racial profiling ever backfire on police and intelligence agencies? Sketch a scenario in which the practice could actually undercut national security.

Theory Interactionist and conflict views of racial profiling
Contemporary Culture Far-reaching impact of September 11, 2001, terrorist attacks
Global View Scrutinization of foreign students from Arab countries
Let's Discuss Do students agree that cases involving terrorism or national security should be exempt from laws prohibiting racial profiling?

Classroom Tip See "Using Humor" (Class Discussion Topics).
Web Resource There is a true–false quiz for this chapter in the student center of the Online Learning Center (www.mhhe.com/schaefer7). Remind students that the quiz gives immediate feedback for incorrect answers.

GettingINVOLVED

To get involved in the debate over racial profiling, visit this text's Online Learning Center, which offers links to relevant Web sites. Check out the Social Policy section in the Online Learning Center as well; it provides survey data on U.S. public opinion regarding this issue.

www.mhhe.com/schaefer7

{ MASTERING THIS CHAPTER }

Summary

The social dimensions of race and ethnicity are important factors in shaping people's lives, both in the United States and in other countries. In this chapter, we examine the meaning of race and ethnicity and study the major **racial** and **ethnic groups** of the United States.

1. A **racial group** is set apart from others by physical differences; an **ethnic group** is set apart primarily by national origin or cultural patterns.

2. When sociologists define a **minority group,** they are concerned primarily with the economic and political power, or powerlessness, of the group.

3. The meaning people attach to the physical differences between races gives social significance to race, producing **stereotypes.**

4. **Prejudice** often leads to **discrimination,** but each can occur without the other.

5. **Institutional discrimination** results from the normal operations of a society.

6. Functionalists point out that discrimination is both functional and dysfunctional for a society. Conflict theorists explain racial subordination through **exploitation theory.** Interactionists pose the **contact hypothesis** as a means of reducing prejudice and discrimination.

7. Four patterns describe typical intergroup relations in North America and elsewhere: **amalgamation, assimilation, segregation,** and **pluralism.** Pluralism remains more of an ideal than a reality.

8. Worldwide, immigration is at an all-time high, fueling controversy not only in the United States but in the European Union. A new kind of immigrant, the *transnational,* moves back and forth across international borders in search of a better job or an education.

9. Contemporary prejudice and discrimination against African Americans are rooted in the history of slavery in the United States.

10. Asian Americans are commonly viewed as a **model** or **ideal minority,** a stereotype not necessarily beneficial to members of that group.

11. The various groups included under the general term *Latinos* represent the largest ethnic minority in the United States.

12. **Racial profiling** is any police-initiated action based on race, ethnicity, or national origin rather than on a person's behavior. Although the practice is based on false stereotypes of certain racial and ethnic groups, reaction to the terrorist attacks of September 11, 2001, has increased racial profiling by police and intelligence agents.

Critical Thinking Questions

1. Why is institutional discrimination even more powerful than individual discrimination? How would functionalists, conflict theorists, and interactionists study institutional discrimination?

2. Examine the relations between dominant and subordinate racial and ethnic groups in your hometown or your college. Can the community in which you grew up or the college you attend be viewed as a genuine example of pluralism?

3. What are some of the similarities and differences in the position of African Americans and Hispanics in the United States? What are some of the similarities and differences in the position of Asian Americans and Jewish Americans?

Key Terms

Affirmative action Positive efforts to recruit minority group members or women for jobs, promotions, and educational opportunities. (page 241)

Amalgamation The process through which a majority group and a minority group combine to form a new group. (243)

Anti-Semitism Anti-Jewish prejudice. (254)

Apartheid A former policy of the South African government, designed to maintain the separation of Blacks and other non-Whites from the dominant Whites. (245)

Assimilation The process through which a person forsakes his or her own cultural tradition to become part of a different culture. (244)

Black power A political philosophy, promoted by many younger Blacks in the 1960s, that supported the creation of Black-controlled political and economic institutions. (248)

Contact hypothesis An interactionist perspective which states that in cooperative circumstances, interracial contact between people of equal status will reduce prejudice. (243)

Discrimination The denial of opportunities and equal rights to individuals and groups because of prejudice or other arbitrary reasons. (238)

Ethnic group A group that is set apart from others primarily because of its national origin or distinctive cultural patterns. (234)

Ethnocentrism The tendency to assume that one's own culture and way of life represent the norm or are superior to all others. (237)

Exploitation theory A Marxist theory that views racial subordination in the United States as a manifestation of the class system inherent in capitalism. (242)

Genocide The deliberate, systematic killing of an entire people or nation. (243)

Glass ceiling An invisible barrier that blocks the promotion of a qualified individual in a work environment because of the individual's gender, race, or ethnicity. (239)

Hate crime A criminal offense committed because of the offender's bias against a race, religion, ethnic group, national origin, or sexual orientation. (237)

Institutional discrimination The denial of opportunities and equal rights to individuals and groups that results from the normal operations of a society. (240)

Minority group A subordinate group whose members have significantly less control or power over their own lives than the members of a dominant or majority group have over theirs. (234)

Model or **ideal minority** A minority group that despite past prejudice and discrimination, succeeds economically, socially, and educationally without resorting to confrontations with Whites. (249)

Pluralism Mutual respect for one another's cultures among the various groups in a society, which allows minorities to express their own cultures without experiencing prejudice. (245)

Prejudice A negative attitude toward an entire category of people, often an ethnic or racial minority. (237)

Racial group A group that is set apart from others because of physical differences that have taken on social significance. (234)

Racial profiling Any police-initiated action based on race, ethnicity, or national origin rather than on a person's behavior. (255)

Racism The belief that one race is supreme and all others are innately inferior. (237)

Segregation The physical separation of two groups of people in terms of residence, workplace, and social events; often imposed on a minority group by a dominant group. (244)

Stereotype An unreliable generalization about all members of a group that does not recognize individual differences within the group. (236)

Symbolic ethnicity An ethnic identity that emphasizes concerns such as ethnic food or political issues rather than deeper ties to one's ethnic heritage. (255)

Self-Quiz

Read each question carefully and then select the best answer.

1. Sociologists have identified five basic properties of a minority group. Which of the following is *not* one of these properties?
   a. unequal treatment
   b. physical traits
   c. ascribed status
   d. cultural bias

2. The largest racial minority group in the United States is
   a. Asian Americans.
   b. African Americans.
   c. Native Americans.
   d. Jewish Americans.

3. Racism is a form of which of the following?
   a. ethnocentrism
   b. discrimination
   c. prejudice
   d. both b and c

4. Suppose that a White employer refuses to hire a Vietnamese American and selects an inferior White applicant. This illustrates an act of
   a. prejudice.
   b. ethnocentrism.
   c. discrimination.
   d. stigmatization.

5. Suppose that a workplace requires that only English be spoken, even when it is not a business necessity to restrict the use of other languages. This would be an example of
   a. prejudice.
   b. scapegoating.
   c. a self-fulfilling prophecy.
   d. institutional discrimination.

6. Working together as computer programmers for an electronics firm, a Hispanic woman and a Jewish man overcome their initial prejudices and come to appreciate each other's strengths and talents. This is an example of
   a. the contact hypothesis.
   b. a self-fulfilling prophecy.
   c. amalgamation.
   d. reverse discrimination.

7. Intermarriage over several generations, resulting in various groups combining to form a new group, would be an example of
   a. amalgamation.
   b. assimilation.
   c. segregation.
   d. pluralism.

8. Alphonso D'Abruzzo changed his name to Alan Alda. This is an example of
   a. amalgamation.
   b. assimilation.
   c. segregation.
   d. pluralism.

9. In which of the following racial or ethnic groups has one teenager in every six attempted suicide?
   a. African Americans
   b. Asian Americans
   c. Native Americans
   d. Latinos

10. Advocates of *Marxist class theory* argue that the basis for racial subordination in the United States lies within the capitalist economic system. Another representation of this point of view is reflected in which of the following theories?
    a. Exploitation
    b. Functionalist
    c. Interactionist
    d. Contact

11. Sociologists consider race and ethnicity to be _____ statuses, since people are born into racial and ethnic groups.

12. Writing from the _____ perspective, sociologist William I. Thomas observed that people respond not only to the objective features of a situation or person but also to the *meaning* that situation or person has for them.

13. _____ are unreliable generalizations about all members of a group that do not recognize individual differences within the group.

14. Sociologists use the term _____ to refer to a negative attitude toward an entire category of people, often an ethnic or racial minority.

15. When White Americans can use credit cards without suspicion, and browse through stores without being shadowed by security guards, they are enjoying _____ _____.

16. _____ _____ refers to positive efforts to recruit minority group members or women for jobs, promotions, and educational opportunities.

17. After the Civil War, the Southern states passed "_____ _____" laws to enforce official segregation, and the Supreme Court upheld them as constitutional in 1896.

18. In the 1960s, proponents of _____ _____ rejected the goal of assimilation into White, middle-class society. They defended the beauty and dignity of Black and African cultures and supported the creation of Black-controlled political and economic institutions.

19. Asian Americans are held up as a(n) _____ or _____ minority group, supposedly because despite past suffering from prejudice and discrimination, they have succeeded economically, socially, and educationally without resorting to confrontations with Whites.

20. Together, the various groups included under the general category _____ represent the largest minority group in the United States.

Answers:
1 (d); 2 (b); 3 (c); 4 (c); 5 (d); 6 (a); 7 (a); 8 (b OR a); 9 (c); 10 (a) 11 ascribed; 12 interactionist; 13 Stereotypes; 14 prejudice; 15 White privilege; 16 Affirmative action; 17 Jim Crow; 18 Black power; 19 model; ideal; 20 Latinos OR Hispanics

{ TECHNOLOGY RESOURCES }

Online Learning Center

1. Be better prepared for your next quiz or exam by using the Flashcards at the student center in the Online Learning Center (**www.mhhe.com/schaefer7**). The Flashcards give you a fun and convenient way to brush up on the definitions of key terms and concepts from this chapter.

2. The United States has a long history of institutionalized slavery of African Americans, and of grassroots efforts to liberate them. The National Park Service maintains a Web site with an abundance of historical information about the Underground Railroad. Explore the site at **http://209.10.16.21/TEMPLATE/FrontEnd/index.cfm** to learn more.

3. The Internet has quickly become an invaluable resource for Americans who wish to research their ethnic heritage. One useful site for Jewish Americans is JewishGen (**www.jewishgen.org**). Go to the site and link to one of the Special Interest Groups toward the bottom of the page. If you were a Jew descended from this region, how might you use these resources?

*Note: While all the URLs listed were current as of the printing of this book, these sites often change. Please check our Web site (**www.mhhe.com/schaefer7**) for updates, hyperlinks, and exercises related to these sites.*

Reel Society Video Clips

Reel Society video clips, which appear on this book's Web site, can be used to spark discussion about the following topics from this chapter:
- Minority Groups
- Race
- Ethnicity
- Prejudice and Discrimination

11

Stratification by Gender and Age

inside

Social Construction of Gender

Explaining Stratification by Gender

Women: The Oppressed Majority

Aging and Society

Explaining the Aging Process

Role Transitions throughout the
    Life Course

Age Stratification in the
    United States

Social Policy and Gender
    Stratification: The Battle over
    Abortion from a Global
    Perspective

Boxes

Sociology in the Global Community:
The Head Scarf and the Veil:
Complex Symbols

Sociology in the Global Community:
Aging Worldwide: Issues and
Consequences

Research in Action: Differences in
Male and Female Physicians'
Communication with Patients

Research in Action: Naturally
Occurring Retirement Communities
(NORCs)

This billboard in Hollywood, California, produced by the feminist advocacy group Guerrilla
Girls, points out the gender inequities in the motion picture industry. In all categories,
including makeup, the overwhelming majority of Oscars have been awarded to men.

Young people sought Elvis's café [in Tehran, Iran] as refuge from the relentless ugliness that pervaded most public gathering places. Even in the rainy winter, people would crowd outside in the drizzle for an hour, smoking soggy cigarettes and waiting for a table. It was the only café in Tehran designed with innovative elegance and attracted young people starved for aesthetic beauty—the artists, writers, and musicians whose sensibilities suffered acutely in a city draped with grim billboards of war martyrs.

Elvis's coffeehouse inspired imitations all over the neighborhood and then the city. In early 2000, when Celine and I first began to haunt the tiny, modern nook, it was one of a kind. By the following summer of 2001, dozens of tastefully decorated cafés dotted the city, but Elvis's remained the original. In the Gandhi shopping complex, where it was located, at least six others sprang up, and the area became center stage in a café scene of shocking permissiveness. By that time, the dress code was so relaxed that everyone buzzed with tales of "You'll never believe what I saw this girl wearing!"; the fashion spring was likened to a silent coup.

Girls dressed in every color imaginable—veils of bright emerald, violet, buttercup—and in short coatlike tunics called *manteaus* (also known by the Farsi word *roopoosh*) that hugged their curves, Capri pants that exposed long stretches of calf, pedicured toes in delicate sandals. They sat at the tables outside, in mixed groups, alone with boyfriends, laughing and talking into the late evening, past eleven. For a few weeks, Tehran actually had something like nightlife in public, not just sequestered parties inside people's houses. . . .

Often, once we finished discussing work, men, and the new styles of head scarf we coveted, Celine and I would sit and people-watch. The throng of students and young professionals flirted brazenly, and the coquettish slipping of veils produced nothing less than social theater. The Tehran of the revolution was one of the most sexualized milieus I had ever encountered. Even the chat rooms, Celine informed me, were rife with erotic discussion. People really, really wanted to talk about sex.

. . . Made neurotic by the innate oppressiveness of restriction, Iranians were preoccupied with sex in the manner of dieters constantly thinking about food. The subject meant to be *unmentionable*—to which end women were forced to wear veils, sit in the back of the bus, and order hamburgers from the special "women's line" at fast food joints—had somehow become the most mentioned of all. The constant exposure to covered flesh—whether it was covered hideously, artfully, or plainly—brought to mind, well, flesh.

The relaxing of the dress code encouraged this tendency, by breathing sexuality back into public space. Women walked down the street with their elbows, necks, and feet exposed, their figures outlined in form-fitting tunics. After two decades in exile, skin was finally back. And so imaginations flared, everyone eagerly thought about and talked about sex a lot, as though they were afraid if they didn't exploit the new permissiveness in dress and mood, they might wake up to find it had disappeared.

(Moaveni 2005a:69–70, 71) Additional information about this excerpt can be found on the Online Learning Center at www.mhhe.com/schaefer7. ●

> " *Often, once we finished discussing work, men, and the new styles of head scarf we coveted, Celine and I would sit and people-watch. The throng of students and young professionals flirted brazenly, and the coquettish slipping of veils produced nothing less than social theater.* "

Azadeh Moaveni, the author of *Lipstick Jihad*, was born in California after her parents, both Iranian, fled the political turbulence of the Iranian revolution. In 1979, Islamic religious leaders overthrew the U.S.-backed monarchy that had ruled the country for decades. Almost overnight, the country was transformed from a relatively secular, Western-oriented society into a conservative Muslim state. Women who had been accustomed to dressing much as American women did were suddenly expected to cover themselves in dark robes. Young women, who had been required to attend school and serve in the armed forces under the old regime, were now forbidden even to appear in public without a male escort.

Though Moaveni grew up in the United States, she was conversant with her Persian cultural heritage, albeit from a distance. After graduating from college, she lived in Iran for two years, where she covered the country's affairs as a news correspondent. There she found a different society from the one her parents had fled a generation before. The lipstick jihad she refers to in the title of her book is an allusion to the recent relaxation of the strict standards for women's dress and behavior—a change that Iranian women effected by personally defying government sanctions. (*Jihad* is an Arabic term that stands for one's inner struggle against the forces of ungodliness.) Today, provocatively dressed Iranian women flirt with men in public cafés they would not have dared to visit—if the cafés had existed—25 years ago. But their place in society is still very much circumscribed by their gender (Moaveni 2005b).

How do gender roles differ from one culture to another? Are women in the United States still oppressed because of their gender? Have men's and women's positions in society changed? In this chapter we will study these and other questions by looking first at how various cultures, including our own, assign women and men to particular social roles. Then we will consider sociological explanations for gender stratification. We will see that around the world, women constitute an oppressed majority of the population.

Like gender, age is an ascribed status that dominates people's perceptions of others, obscuring individual differences. Rather than suggesting that a particular elderly person is no longer competent to drive, for instance, we may condemn the entire age group: "Those old codgers shouldn't be allowed on the

road." Such stereotypical attitudes are not likely to change unless we can begin to look at the life course as a continuum rather than a series of finite stages with inevitable consequences.

How do people's roles change as they age? What are the social implications of the growing number of elderly in the United States? How does ageism affect an older person's employment opportunities? In the second half of this chapter, we will look at aging throughout the life course. After exploring various theories of the impact of aging, we will discuss the role transitions typical of the major stages in the life course. We will pay particular attention to the effects of prejudice and discrimination on older people. Finally, in the Social Policy section we will return to the topic of gender as we close the chapter with a discussion of the controversy over a woman's right to abortion. ●

Azadeh Moaveni, author of *Lipstick Jihad,* was born in California to refugees from the Iranian revolution. In 1998 she moved to Iran and found a very different society from the one her parents had left in 1979.

Social Construction of Gender

How many airline passengers do you think are startled on hearing a female captain's voice from the cockpit? What do we make of a father who announces that he will be late for work because his son has a routine medical checkup? Consciously or unconsciously, we are likely to assume that flying a commercial plane is a *man's* job and that most parental duties are, in fact, *maternal* duties. Gender is such a routine part of our everyday activities that we typically take notice only when someone deviates from conventional behavior and expectations.

Classroom Tip/Contemporary Culture See "Stimulating Classroom Discussions about *Lipstick Jihad*" (Class Discussion Topics).
Classroom Tip See "Women's Fashions" (Class Discussion Topics).

Student Alert Gender differentiation is another example of social inequality.
Classroom Tip See "Women: The Shadow Story of the Millennium" (Class Discussion Topics).

Although a few people begin life with an unclear sexual identity, the overwhelming majority begin with a definite sex and quickly receive societal messages about how to behave. In fact, virtually all societies have established social distinctions between females and males that do not inevitably result from biological differences between the sexes (such as women's reproductive capabilities).

In studying gender, sociologists are interested in the gender-role socialization that leads females and males to behave differently. In Chapter 4, *gender roles* were defined as expectations regarding the proper behavior, attitudes, and activities of males and females. The application of dominant gender roles leads to many forms of differentiation between women and men. Both sexes are physically capable of learning to cook and sew, yet most Western societies determine that women should perform those tasks. Both men and women are capable of learning to weld and to fly airplanes, but those functions are generally assigned to men.

Most people do not display strictly "masculine" or "feminine" qualities all the time. Indeed, such standards can be ambiguous. For instance, though men are supposed to be unemotional, they are allowed to become emotional when their favorite athletic team wins or loses a critical game. Yet our society still focuses on "masculine" and "feminine" qualities as if men and women must be evaluated in those terms. Despite recent inroads by women into male-dominated occupations, our construction of gender continues to define significantly different expectations for females and males (J. Howard and Hollander 1997; West and Zimmerman 1987).

Gender roles are evident not only in our work and behavior but also in how we react to others. We are constantly "doing gender" without realizing it. If the father mentioned earlier sits in the doctor's office with his son in the middle of a workday, he will probably receive approving glances from the receptionist and from other patients. "Isn't he a wonderful father?" runs through their minds. But if the boy's mother leaves *her* job and sits with the son in the doctor's office, she will not receive such silent applause.

We construct our behavior socially so as to create or exaggerate male–female differences. For example, men and women come in a variety of heights, sizes, and ages. Yet traditional norms regarding marriage and even casual dating tell us that in heterosexual couples, the man should be older, taller, and wiser than the woman. As we will see throughout this chapter, such social norms help to reinforce and legitimize patterns of male dominance.

Gender Roles in the United States

Gender-Role Socialization Male babies get blue blankets; females get pink ones. Boys are expected to play with trucks, blocks, and toy soldiers; girls receive dolls and kitchen goods. Boys must be masculine—active, aggressive, tough, daring, and dominant—but girls must be feminine—soft, emotional, sweet, and submissive. These traditional gender-role patterns have been influential in the socialization of children in the United States.

An important element in traditional views of proper "masculine" and "feminine" behavior is **homophobia,** fear of and prejudice against homosexuality. Homophobia contributes significantly to rigid gender-role socialization, since many people stereotypically associate male homosexuality with femininity and lesbianism with masculinity. Consequently, men and women who deviate from traditional expectations about gender roles are often presumed to be gay. Despite the advances made by the gay liberation movement, the continuing stigma attached to homosexuality in our culture places pressure on all males (whether gay or not) to exhibit only narrow "masculine" behavior and on all females (whether lesbian or not) to exhibit only narrow "feminine" behavior (Seidman 1994; see also Lehne 1995).

It is *adults,* of course, who play a critical role in guiding children into those gender roles deemed appropriate in a society. {p.90} Parents are normally the first and most crucial agents of socialization. But other adults, older siblings, the mass media, and religious and educational institutions also exert an important influence on gender-role socialization, in the United States and elsewhere.

It is not hard to test how rigid gender-role socialization can be. Just try transgressing some gender norm—say, by smoking a cigar in public if you are female, or by carrying a purse if you are male. That was exactly the assignment given to sociology students at the University of Colorado and Luther College in Iowa. Professors asked students to behave in ways that they thought violated the norms of how a man or woman should act. The students had no trouble coming up with gender-norm transgressions (see Table 11-1), and they kept careful notes on others' reactions to their behavior, ranging from amusement to disgust (Nielsen et al. 2000).

Table 11-1 An Experiment in Gender Norm Violation by College Students

Norm Violations by Women	Norm Violations by Men
Send men flowers	Wear fingernail polish
Spit in public	Needlepoint in public
Use men's bathroom	Throw Tupperware party
Buy jock strap	Cry in public
Buy/chew tobacco	Have pedicure
Talk knowledgeably about cars	Apply to baby-sit
Open doors for men	Shave body hair

Source: Nielsen et al. 2000:287.

In an experiment testing gender-role stereotypes, sociology students were asked to behave in ways that might be regarded as violations of gender norms, and to keep notes on how others reacted. This is a sample of their choices of behavior over a seven-year period. Do you agree that these actions test the boundaries of conventional gender behavior?

Reel Society See Gender Roles in the Topic Index.
Web Resource The interactive activity in the student center of the Online Learning Center (www.mhhe.com/schaefer7) allows students to indicate their agreement or disagreement with the gender norm violations in Table 11-1.

Classroom Tip See "Gender Differences in Child Care" (Class Discussion Topics).
Theory Interactionist approach to the social construction of gender and gender-role socialization
Classroom Tip See "Gender Socialization" and "Homophobia" (Class Discussion Topics).

What type of body image do the media promote to young women in the United States? Over the last 80 years, one-fourth of the winners of the Miss America pageant have been so thin, they would be considered undernourished by the World Health Organization (Byrd-Bredbenner and Murray 2003).

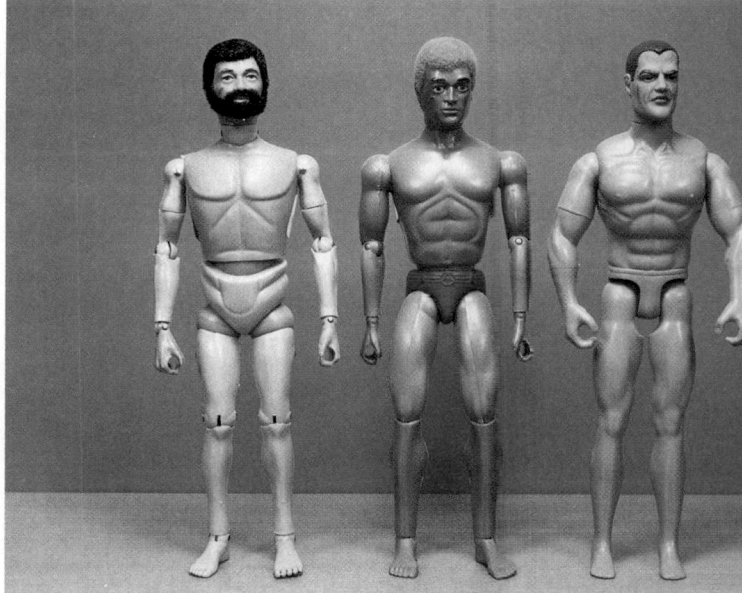

Society often exaggerates male–female differences in appearance and behavior. In 1964, the G.I. Joe doll (left) had a realistic appearance, but by 1992 (middle) it had begun to acquire the exaggerated muscularity characteristic of professional wrestlers (right). The change intensified the contrast with ultrathin female figures, like the Barbie doll (Angier 1998).

Women's Gender Roles How does a girl come to develop a feminine self-image, while a boy develops one that is masculine? In part, they do so by identifying with females and males in their families and neighborhoods and in the media. If a young girl regularly sees female television characters of all ages and body types, she is likely to grow up with a normal body image. And it will not hurt if the women she knows—her mother, sister, parents' friends, and neighbors—are comfortable with their body types, rather than constantly obsessed with their weight. In contrast, if this young girl sees only wafer-thin actresses and models on television, her self-image will be quite different. Even if she grows up to become a well-educated professional, she may secretly regret falling short of the media stereotype—a shapely, sexy young woman in a bathing suit.

Television is far from alone in stereotyping women. Studies of children's books published in the United States in the 1940s, 1950s, and 1960s found that females were significantly underrepresented in central roles and illustrations. Virtually all female characters were portrayed as helpless, passive, incompetent, and in need of a strong male caretaker. Studies of picture books published from the 1970s through the 1990s found some improvement, but males still dominated the central roles. While males were portrayed as a variety of characters, females tended to be shown mostly in traditional roles, such as mother, grandmother,

or volunteer, even if they also held nontraditional roles, such as working professional (Etaugh 2003).

Social research on gender roles reveals some persistent differences between men and women in North America and Europe. Women tend to feel pressure both to marry and to become a mother. Often, marriage is viewed as their true entry into adulthood. And women are expected not only to become mothers but to *want* to be mothers. Obviously, men play a role in marriage and parenthood, but these events do not appear to be as critical in the life course of a man. Society defines men's identities by their economic success. And even though many women today fully expect to have careers and achieve recognition in the labor force, success at work is not as important to their identity as it is for men (Doyle and Paludi 1998; Russo 1976).

Traditional gender roles have restricted females more severely than males. This chapter shows how women have been confined to subordinate roles in the political and economic institutions of the United States. Yet it is also true that gender roles have restricted males.

Men's Gender Roles Stay-at-home fathers? Until recent decades such an idea was unthinkable. Yet in a nationwide survey done in 2002, 69 percent of respondents said that if one parent stays home with the children, it makes no difference whether that parent is the mother or the father. Only 30 percent thought that the mother should be the one to stay home. But while peo-

ple's conceptions of gender roles are obviously changing, the fact is that men who stay home to care for their children are still an unusual phenomenon. For every stay-at-home dad there are 38 stay-at-home moms (Fields 2004a: 11–12; Robison 2002).

While attitudes toward parenting may be changing, studies show little change in the traditional male gender role. Men's roles are socially constructed in much the same way as women's are. Family, peers, and the media all influence how a boy or man comes to view his appropriate role in society. The male gender role, besides being antifeminine (show no "sissy stuff"), includes proving one's masculinity at work and sports—often by using force in dealing with others—as well as initiating and controlling all sexual relations.

Males who do not conform to the socially constructed gender role face constant criticism and even humiliation, both from children when they are boys and from adults as men. It can be agonizing to be treated as a "chicken" or a "sissy" as a youth—particularly if such remarks come from one's father or brothers. And grown men who pursue nontraditional occupations, such as preschool teaching or nursing, must constantly deal with others' misgivings and strange looks. In one study, interviewers found that such men frequently had to alter their behavior in order to minimize others' negative reactions. One 35-year-old nurse reported that he had to claim he was "a carpenter or something like that" when he "went clubbing," because women weren't interested in getting to know a male nurse. The subjects made similar accommodations in casual exchanges with other men (Cross and Bagilhole 2002:215).

At the same time, boys who successfully adapt to cultural standards of masculinity may grow up to be inexpressive men who cannot share their feelings with others. They remain forceful and tough, but as a result they are also closed and isolated. In fact, a small but growing body of scholarship suggests that for men as well as women, traditional gender roles may be disadvantageous. In many communities across the nation, girls seem to outdo boys in high school, grabbing a disproportionate share of the leadership positions, from valedictorian to class president to yearbook editor—everything, in short, except captain of the boys' athletic teams. Their advantage continues after high school. In the 1980s, girls in the United States became more likely than boys to go to college. By 2004, women accounted for over 56 percent of college students nationwide. And in 2002, for the first time, more women than men in the United States earned doctoral degrees.

Some of this discrepancy in achievement can be explained by noting that men can earn good hourly wages with less formal schooling than women. Yet by a number of measures, girls appear to take schooling more seriously than boys. In 2003, for example, female students taking the Advanced Placement (AP) tests outnumbered male students in 19 out of 33 subjects. Overall, they accounted for 56 percent of students who took the AP tests. Educational professionals need to look more closely at men's underperformance in school, not to mention their overrepresentation in reported crime and illegal drug use (Bureau of the Census 2005a:171; Ripley 2005).

In the last 40 years, inspired in good part by the contemporary feminist movement (examined later in the chapter), increasing numbers of men in the United States have criticized the restrictive aspects of the traditional male gender role. Some men have taken strong public positions in support of women's struggle for full equality, and have even organized voluntary associations such as the National Organization for Men Against Sexism (NOMAS), founded in 1975 to support positive changes for men. Nevertheless, the traditional male gender role remains well entrenched as an influential element of our culture (Messner 1997; National Organization for Men Against Sexism 2006).

Use Your Sociological Imagination www.mhhe.com/schaefer7

You are living in a society in which there are no gender roles. What is your life like?

Cross-Cultural Perspective

To what extent do actual biological differences between the sexes contribute to the cultural differences associated with gender? This question brings us back to the debate over "nature versus {pp.79–81 nurture." In assessing the alleged and real differences between men and women, it is useful to examine cross-cultural data.

The research of anthropologist Margaret Mead points to the importance of cultural conditioning—as opposed to biology—in defining the social roles of males and females. In *Sex and Temperament*, Mead ([1935] 2001; 1973) describes the typical behaviors of each sex in three different cultures in New Guinea. In the first culture, both men and women play the role of nurturer. In the second, both sexes behave in a stereotypically male fashion. And in the third, the gender roles are reversed: women behave as we expect men to behave, and vice versa. If biology determined all differences between the sexes, then cross-cultural differences such as those described by Mead would not exist. Her findings confirm the influential role of culture and socialization in gender-role differentiation. There appears to be no innate or biological reason to designate completely different gender roles for men and women.

In any society, gender stratification requires not only individual socialization into traditional gender roles within the family, but the promotion and support of those traditional roles by other social institutions, such as religion and education. Moreover, even with all major institutions socializing the young into conventional gender roles, every society has women and men who resist and successfully oppose the stereotypes: strong women who become leaders or professionals, gentle men who care for children, and so forth. It seems clear that differences between the sexes are not dictated by biology. Indeed, the maintenance of traditional gender roles requires constant social controls—and those controls are not always effective.

Key Person Margaret Mead
Global View Mead's cross-cultural anthropological research in New Guinea
Methods Mead conducted observation research on three New Guinea cultures.

We can see the social construction of gender roles in process in societies strained by war and social upheaval. By summer 2004, a year after the war in Iraq began, young girls in Baghdad seldom ventured out to the park or swimming pool. When they did, their parents made sure they were dressed conservatively, in loose clothing and perhaps a headscarf. The overthrow of Saddam Hussein's secular regime had emboldened Islamic fundamentalists, who had begun visiting schools, urging young women to wear long sleeves and cover their heads. Though school officials resisted, many girls dropped out, some out of fear for their safety and others because of financial hardship. In the atmosphere of violence and lawlessness that followed the 2003 invasion, young women wondered what the future would hold for them, and whether they would ever have the opportunity to become educated professionals, as their mothers had (Sengupta 2004).

Cultural conditioning is important in the development of gender role differences. Among the Bororo, a semi-nomadic people of West Africa, the *male* gender role includes ceremonial dancing (shown here), body painting, and other forms of personal adornment.

Explaining Stratification by Gender

Cross-cultural studies indicate that societies dominated by men are much more common than those in which women play the decisive role. Sociologists have turned to all the major theoretical perspectives to understand how and why these social distinctions are established. Each approach focuses on culture rather than biology as the primary determinant of gender differences. Yet in other respects, advocates of these sociological perspectives disagree widely.

The Functionalist View

Functionalists maintain that gender differentiation has contributed to overall social stability. Sociologists Talcott Parsons and Robert Bales (1955) argued that to function most effectively, the family requires adults who specialize in particular roles. They viewed the traditional gender roles as arising out of the need to establish a division of labor between marital partners.

Parsons and Bales contended that women take the expressive, emotionally supportive role and men the instrumental, practical role, with the two complementing each other. *Instrumentality* refers to an emphasis on tasks, a focus on more distant goals, and a concern for the external relationship between one's family and other social institutions. *Expressiveness* denotes concern for the maintenance of harmony and the internal emotional affairs of the family. According to this theory, women's interest in expressive goals frees men for instrumental tasks, and vice versa. Women become anchored in the family as wives, mothers, and

household managers; men become anchored in the occupational world outside the home. Of course, Parsons and Bales offered this framework in the 1950s, when many more women were full-time homemakers than is true today. These theorists did not explicitly endorse traditional gender roles, but they implied that dividing tasks between spouses was functional for the family as a unit.

Given the typical socialization of women and men in the United States, the functionalist view is initially persuasive. However, it would lead us to expect girls and women who have no interest in children to become baby-sitters and mothers. Similarly, males who love spending time with children might be programmed into careers in the business world. Such differentiation might harm the individual who does not fit into prescribed roles, as well as deprive society of the contributions of many talented people who feel confined by gender stereotyping. Moreover, the functionalist approach does not convincingly explain why men should be assigned categorically to the instrumental role, and women to the expressive role.

The Conflict Response

Viewed from a conflict perspective, the functionalist approach masks the underlying power relations between men and women. Parsons and Bales never explicitly presented the expressive and instrumental roles as being of unequal value to society, yet their inequality is quite evident. Although social institutions may pay lip service to women's expressive skills, men's instrumental skills are more highly rewarded, whether in terms of money or prestige. Consequently, according to feminists and conflict theorists,

Theory Functionalist view of gender stratification
Key Persons Talcott Parsons, Robert Bales

Theory Conflict critique of Parsons and Bales's functionalist approach
Theory Conflict view of gender stratification
Classroom Tip See "Women and Sports" (Class Discussion Topics).

any division of labor by gender into instrumental and expressive tasks is far from neutral in its impact on women.

Conflict theorists contend that the relationship between females and males has traditionally been one of unequal power, with men in a dominant position over women. Men may originally have become powerful in preindustrial times because their size, physical strength, and freedom from childbearing duties allowed them to dominate women physically. In contemporary societies, such considerations are not so important, yet cultural beliefs about the sexes are long established, as anthropologist Margaret Mead and feminist sociologist Helen Mayer Hacker (1951, 1974) both stressed. Such beliefs support a social structure that places males in controlling positions.

Conflict theorists, then, see gender differences as a reflection of the subjugation of one group (women) by another group (men). If we use an analogy to Marx's analysis of class conflict, {pp.11, 189–191 we can say that males are like the bourgeoisie, or capitalists; they control most of the society's wealth, prestige, and power. Females are like the proletariat, or workers; they can acquire valuable resources only by following the dictates of their bosses. Men's work is uniformly valued; women's work (whether unpaid labor in the home or wage labor) is devalued.

The Feminist Perspective

A significant component of the conflict approach to gender {p.16 stratification draws on feminist theory. Although use of that term is comparatively recent, the critique of women's position in society and culture goes back to some of the earliest works that have influenced sociology. Among the most important are Mary Wollstonecraft's *A Vindication of the Rights of Women* (originally published in 1792), John Stuart Mill's *The Subjection of Women* (originally published in 1869), and Friedrich Engels's *The Origin of the Family, Private Property, and the State* (originally published in 1884).

Engels, a close associate of Karl Marx, argued that women's subjugation coincided with the rise of private property during industrialization. Only when people moved beyond an agrarian economy could males enjoy the luxury of leisure and withhold rewards and privileges from women. Drawing on the work of Marx and Engels, many contemporary feminist theorists view women's subordination as part of the overall exploitation and injustice that they see as inherent in capitalist societies. Some radical feminist theorists, however, view the oppression of women as inevitable in *all* male-dominated societies, whether they are labeled capitalist, socialist, or communist (L. Feuer 1989; Tuchman 1992).

Feminist sociologists would find little to disagree with in the conflict theorists' perspective, but are more likely to embrace a political agenda. Feminists would also argue that until recently, the very discussion of women and society, however well meant, was distorted by the exclusion of women from academic thought, including sociology. We have noted the many accomplishments of Jane Addams and Ida Wells-Barnett, but {pp.12, 16 they generally worked outside the discipline, focusing on what we would now call applied sociology and social work. At the time, their efforts, while valued as humanitarian, were seen as unrelated to the research and conclusions being reached in academic circles, which of course were male academic circles (Andersen 1997; J. Howard 1999).

Feminist theorists today (including conflict theorists) emphasize that in the United States, male dominance goes far beyond the economic sphere. Throughout this textbook, we examine disturbing aspects of men's behavior toward women. The ugly realities of rape, wife battering, sexual harassment, and street harassment all illustrate and intensify women's subordinate position. Even if women reach economic parity with men, even if they win equal representation in government, genuine equality between the sexes cannot be achieved if these attacks remain as common as they are today.

Functionalist, conflict, and feminist theorists acknowledge that it is not possible to change gender roles drastically without making dramatic revisions in a culture's social structure. Functionalists perceive the potential for social disorder, or at least unknown social consequences, if all aspects of traditional gender stratification are disturbed. Yet for conflict and feminist theorists, no social structure is ultimately desirable if it is maintained by oppressing a majority of citizens. These theorists argue that gender stratification may be functional for men—who hold the power and privilege—but it is hardly in the interests of women.

The Interactionist Approach

While functionalists and conflict theorists who study gender stratification typically focus on macro-level social forces and institutions, interactionist researchers tend to examine gender

Conflict theorists emphasize that men's work is uniformly valued, while women's work (whether unpaid labor in the home or wage labor) is devalued. These women are making tents in a factory in Binghamton, New York.

Theory Feminist view of gender stratification
Key Persons Mary Wollstonecraft, John Stuart Mill, Friedrich Engels
Methods Sociological studies have traditionally focused on males to the exclusion of females.

Key Persons Jane Addams, Ida Wells-Barnett
Classroom Tip See "Gender Stratification on the Micro Level" (Class Discussion Topics).
Theory Interactionist view of gender stratification
Classroom Tip See "Gendered Spaces" (Additional Lecture Ideas).

Table 11-2 Sociological Perspectives on Gender

Theoretical Perspective	Emphasis
Functionalist	Gender differentiation contributes to social stability
Conflict	Gender inequality is rooted in the female–male power relationship
Feminist	Women's subjugation is integral to society and social structure
Interactionist	Gender distinctions are reflected in people's everyday behavior

stratification on the micro level of everyday behavior. As an example, studies show that men initiate up to 96 percent of all interruptions in cross-sex (male–female) conversations. Men are more likely than women to change the topic of conversation, to ignore topics chosen by members of the opposite sex, to minimize the contributions and ideas of members of the opposite sex, and to validate their own contributions. These patterns reflect the conversational (and in a sense, political) dominance of males. Moreover, even when women occupy a prestigious position, such as that of physician, they are more likely to be interrupted than their male counterparts (Ridgeway and Smith-Lovin 1999; Tannen 1990; West and Zimmerman 1983).

These findings regarding cross-sex conversations have been frequently replicated. They have striking implications when one considers the power dynamics underlying likely cross-sex interactions—employer and job seeker, college professor and student, husband and wife, to name just a few. From an interactionist perspective, these simple, day-to-day exchanges are one more battleground in the struggle for gender equality—as women try to get a word in edgewise in the midst of men's interruptions and verbal dominance (Hollander 2002; Okamoto and Smith-Lovin 2001; Tannen 1994a, 1994b).

Table 11-2 summarizes the major sociological perspectives on gender.

Women: The Oppressed Majority

Many people, both male and female, find it difficult to conceive of women as a subordinate and oppressed group. Yet take a look at the political structure of the United States: Women remain noticeably underrepresented. As of mid-2006, for example, only 8 of the nation's 50 states had a female governor (Arizona, Connecticut, Delaware, Hawaii, Kansas, Louisiana, Michigan, and Washington).

Women have made slow but steady progress in certain political arenas. In 1981, out of 535 members of Congress, there were only 21 women: 19 in the House of Representatives and 2 in the Senate. In contrast, the Congress that held office in mid-2006 had 81 women: 67 in the House and 14 in the Senate. Yet the membership and leadership of Congress remain overwhelmingly male (Center for American Women and Politics 2006).

In October 1981, Sandra Day O'Connor was sworn in as the nation's first female Supreme Court justice. Still, no woman has ever served as president of the United States, vice president, speaker of the House of Representatives, or chief justice of the Supreme Court.

Sexism and Sex Discrimination

Just as African Americans are victimized by racism, women in our society suffer from sexism. *Sexism* is the ideology that one sex is superior to the other. The term is generally used to refer to male prejudice and discrimination against women. In Chapter 10, we noted that Blacks can suffer from both individual acts of racism and institutional discrimination. *Institutional discrimination* was defined as the denial of opportunities and equal rights to individuals and groups that results from the normal operations of a society. In the same sense, women suffer from both individual acts of sexism (such as sexist remarks and acts of violence) and institutional sexism.

It is not simply that particular men in the United States are biased in their treatment of women. All the major institutions of our society—including the government, armed forces, large corporations, the media, universities, and the medical establishment—are controlled by men. These institutions, in their normal, day-to-day operations, often discriminate against women and perpetuate sexism. For example, if the central office of a nationwide bank sets a policy that single women are a bad risk for loans—regardless of their incomes and investments—that bank will discriminate against women in state after state. It will do so even at branches where loan officers hold no personal biases toward women, but are merely "following orders." Box 11-1 dispels the sexist myth that women cannot be good doctors, which medical schools used for years to justify their discriminatory admissions policies.

Our society is run by male-dominated institutions, yet with the power that flows to men come responsibility and stress. Men have higher reported rates of certain types of mental illness than women, and a greater likelihood of death due to heart attack or stroke. The pressure on men to succeed, and then to remain on top in the competitive world of work, can be especially intense. That is not to suggest that gender stratification is as damaging to men as it is to women. But it is clear that the power and privilege men enjoy are no guarantee of personal well-being.

Use Your Sociological Imagination www.mhhe.com/schaefer7

Think of organizations or institutions you belong to whose leadership positions are customarily held by men. What would those organizations be like if they were led by women?

Methods Experiments on dominance in cross-sex conversations
Contemporary Culture Only 8 of the nation's 50 states had a female governor in mid-2006.

Key Person Justice Sandra Day O'Connor
Student Alert Note that Justice O'Connor was appointed, not elected
Theory Conflict view of institutional discrimination against women

research IN action

11-1 Differences in Male and Female Physicians' Communication with Patients

When Perri Klass told her four-year-old son she would be taking him to the pediatrician, he replied, "Is she a nice doctor?" Klass, a professor of pediatrics, was struck by his innocent assumption that like his mother, all pediatricians were female. "Boys can be doctors too," she told him.

Not long ago, there would have been little potential for confusion on her son's part. Klass probably would not have been admitted to medical school, much less appointed a professor of medicine. But since the advent of the women's movement, the medical profession has been integrating women into its ranks. In the United States today, 42 percent of physicians under age 35 are female. Now, more than two dozen studies done over the past three and a half decades indicate that not only are women competent physicians; in some respects they are more effective than their male counterparts.

The female advantage is particularly noteworthy in physician–patient communication.

Female primary care physicians spend an extra two minutes talking with patients, or 10 percent more time than male primary care physicians They also engage in more patient-centered communication, listening more, asking questions about patients' personal well-being and counseling patients about the

> *Not only are women competent physicians; in some respects they are more effective than their male counterparts.*

concerns they bring to the doctor's office. Perhaps most important, female physicians tend to see their relationship with patients as an active partnership, one in which they discuss several treatment options with patients rather than recommending a single course of treatment. From a sociological point of view, these differ-

ences between female and male physicians correspond to the gender differences in communication style that interactionist researchers have noted.

In some respects, female and male physicians do not differ. Researchers noted no differences in the quality or amount of time the two groups spend on purely medical matters, or on the length of time they spend conversing socially with patients.

Let's Discuss

1. In your own experience, have you noted a gender difference in the way doctors communicate with their patients? Explain.
2. Why is the quality of a doctor's communication with patients important? What might be the benefit of female physicians' superior communication style?

Sources: Carroll 2003; Klass 2003:319; Kotulak 2005; Roter et al. 2002.

Sexual Harassment

The courts recognize two kinds of sexual harassment. Formally defined, **sexual harassment** is behavior that occurs when work benefits are made contingent on sexual favors (as a quid pro quo), or when touching, lewd comments, or the exhibition of pornographic material creates a "hostile environment" in the workplace. In 1998, the Supreme Court ruled that harassment applies to people of the same sex as well as the opposite. The quid pro quo type of harassment is fairly easy to identify in a court of law. But the issue of hostile environment has become the subject of considerable debate both in courts and in the general public (Greenhouse 1998; Lewin 1998).

Sexual harassment must be understood in the context of continuing prejudice and discrimination against women. Whether it occurs in the federal bureaucracy, in the corporate world, or in universities, sexual harassment generally takes place in organizations in which White males are at the top of the hierarchy of authority, and women's work is valued less than men's. One survey of the private sector found that African American women were three times more likely than White women to experience sexual

harassment. From a conflict perspective, it is not surprising that women—and especially women of color—are likely to become victims of sexual harassment. In terms of job security, these groups are typically an organization's most vulnerable employees (J. Jones 1988).

The Status of Women Worldwide

A detailed overview of the status of the world's women, issued by the United Nations in 2000, noted that women and men live in different worlds—worlds that differ in terms of access to education and work opportunities, as well as in health, personal security, and human rights. The Hindu culture of India, for example, makes life especially harsh for widows. When Hindu women marry, they join their husband's family. If the husband dies, the widow is the "property" of that family. In many cases, she ends up working as an unpaid servant; in others she is simply abandoned and left penniless. Ancient Hindu scriptures portray widows as "inauspicious" and advise that "a wise man should avoid her blessings like the poison of a snake" (Burns 1998:10).

Contemporary Culture In what other traditionally male occupations might women be more effective than men? In what ways, and why?
Classroom Tip Have an administrator visit the class to discuss the sexual harassment policy on campus.
Theory Conflict analysis of sexual harassment

Global View Analysis of the status of women worldwide
Classroom Tip See "Gender Dominance in Jobs Cross-Culturally" in Topics and Sources for Student Research.

11-2 The Head Scarf and the Veil: Complex Symbols

The wearing of a veil or head scarf by women is common to many but not all Middle Eastern societies. However, Muslim women are not alone in their observance of certain standards for dress. All Muslims, men and women alike, are expected to cover themselves and avoid revealing clothes designed to accentuate the body's contours or emphasize its physical beauty. The Qur'an (or Koran) permits Muslims to wear revealing garments in private, with their families or with members of the same sex. In keeping with this religious prescription, some Muslim countries allow beaches and public pools to be set aside exclusively for use by men or women.

The Prophet Muhammad recommended that women cover all of their bodies except for the face, hands, and feet. The Koran adds that a woman's headcovering should fall over the upper chest and neck. A variety of women's outergarments comply with these guidelines for modest attire; collectively, they are referred to as the *hijab*. Accepted Muslim head coverings include both a simple head scarf and a face veil that actually covers the face. Face veils are dictated by cultural tradition, however—not by Islam.

In effect, the veil represents a rejection of the beauty myth (see Chapter 7), which is so prevalent in Western societies. While a Muslim woman's beauty is valued, it is not to be seen or exploited by the whole world. By covering themselves almost completely, Muslim women assure themselves and their families that their physical appearance will not play a role in their contacts outside the family. Rather, these women will be known only for their faith, their intellect, and their personalities.

In the 20th century, the veil was politicized by modernization movements that pitted Western cultural values against traditional Islamic values. In Turkey, for instance, the rise to power of President Kemal Atatürk in 1923 sparked a process of sweeping social change, in which government officials attempted to subordinate traditional ethnic and religious influences to their nationalistic goals. Though women weren't forbidden to wear the veil, they were not allowed to veil themselves in public places like schools. Not surprisingly, many

> In effect, the veil represents a rejection of the beauty myth, which is so prevalent in Western societies.

Muslims resented these forced social changes. In recent decades, strict clergy in countries like Iran and Afghanistan have reinstituted the veil and other Islamic traditions.

In the United States today, Muslim women select from an array of traditional garments. They include a long, loose tailored coat and a loose black overgarment that is worn with a scarf or perhaps a face veil. However, they are just as apt to wear an overblouse and a long skirt or loose pants, which they can buy at local clothing stores.

Researchers have identified three perspectives on the *hijab* among Muslim women in the United States and other non-Islamic countries. Younger, better-educated women who support wearing the *hijab* in public draw on Western ideas of individual rights, arguing in favor of veiling as a form of personal expression. In contrast, older, less well-educated women who support the *hijab* do so without referring to Western ideology; they cannot see why veiling should be an issue. A third group of women, of all ages and educational backgrounds, opposes the *hijab*.

In some non-Muslim countries, notably France, officials have come under fire for banning the *hijab* or the head scarf in public schools (see Chapter 4). The custom generally has not been an issue in the United States, though one 11-year-old had to go to federal court to establish her right to wear a head scarf at school in Muskogee, Oklahoma. Interestingly, the U.S. Department of Justice supported her lawsuit.

Let's Discuss

1. Consider life in a society in which women wear veils. Can you see any advantages, from the woman's point of view? From the man's?

2. Do you find the Western emphasis on physical beauty oppressive? If so, in what ways?

Sources: Gole 1997; Haeri 2004; Killian 2003; *Religious Diversity News* 2004.

Though Westerners tend to view Muslim societies as being similarly harsh toward women, that perception is actually an overgeneralization. Muslim countries are exceedingly varied and complex and do not often fit the stereotypes created by the Western media. For a detailed discussion of the status of Muslim women today, see Box 11-2.

Regardless of culture, however, women everywhere suffer from second-class status. It is estimated that women grow half the world's food, but they rarely own land. They constitute one-third of the world's paid labor force, but are generally found in the lowest-paying jobs. Single-parent households headed by women, which appear to be on the increase in many nations, are typically found in the poorest sections of the population. The feminization of poverty has become a global phenomenon. As in the United States, women around the world are underrepresented politically.

Despite these challenges, women are not responding passively. They are mobilizing, individually and collectively. Given the significant underrepresentation of women in government offices and national legislatures, however, the task is difficult, as we shall see in Chapter 14.

Not surprisingly, there is a link between the wealth of industrialized nations and the poverty of women in developing countries. Viewed from a conflict perspective or through the lens of

Theory Interactionist view of veils worn by Muslim women
Global View Rejection of the beauty myth by Muslim women

Theory From a conflict view, the subordinate status of Third World women is linked to the exploitation of developing countries by Western industrialized nations.
Student Alert Refer back to the discussion of modernization in Chapter 9.
Classroom Tip See "South Asian Women" (Class Discussion Topics).

FIGURE 11–1

Gender Inequality in Industrial Nations

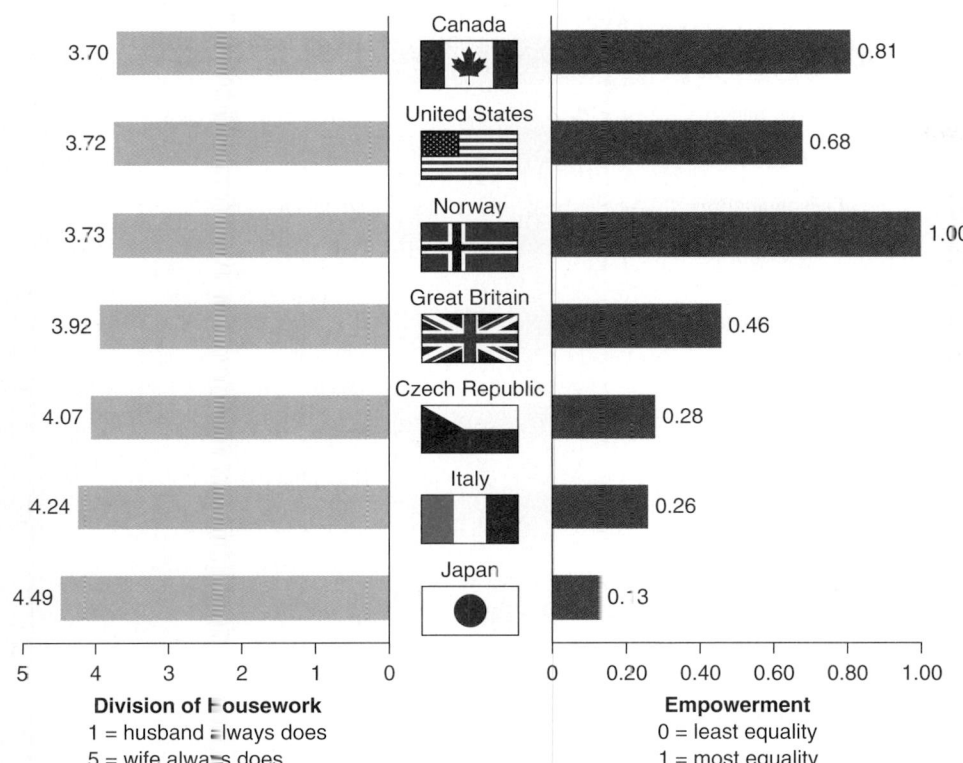

	Division of Housework	Empowerment
Canada	3.70	0.81
United States	3.72	0.68
Norway	3.73	1.00
Great Britain	3.92	0.46
Czech Republic	4.07	0.28
Italy	4.24	0.26
Japan	4.49	0.13

Division of Housework
1 = husband always does
5 = wife always does

Empowerment
0 = least equality
1 = most equality

Notes: Housework includes laundry, grocery shopping, dinner preparation, and care for sick family members. Empowerment includes the proportions of women in parliament, in management, and in professional/technical positions, as well as gender inequality in income.
Source: Adapted from Fuwa 2004:757.

{ pp.212–216 Immanuel Wallerstein's world systems analysis, the economies of developing nations are controlled and exploited by industrialized countries and multinational corporations based in those countries. Much of the exploited labor in developing na-

FIGURE 11–2

Trends in U.S. Women's Participation in the Paid Labor Force, 1890–2004

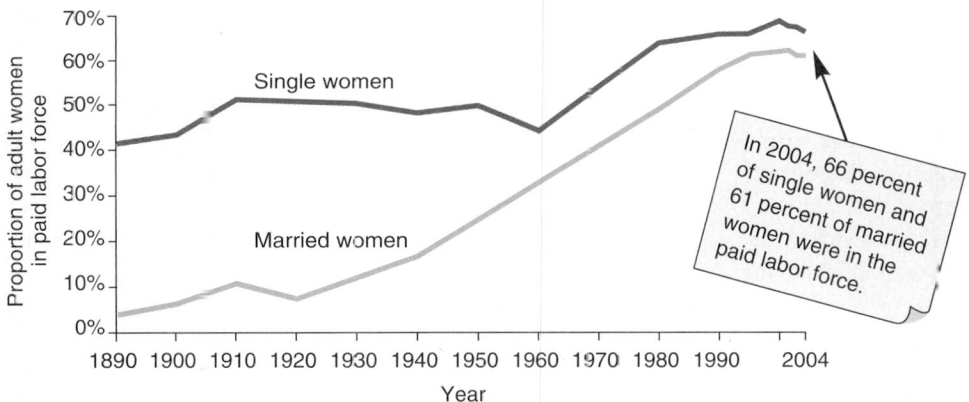

In 2004, 66 percent of single women and 61 percent of married women were in the paid labor force.

Sources: Bureau of the Census 1975; 2005a:392.

tions, especially in the nonindustrial sector, is performed by women. Women workers typically toil long hours for low pay, but contribute significantly to their families' incomes (Jacobson 1993).

In industrial countries, women's unequal status can be seen in the division of housework, as well as the jobs they hold and the pay they earn. Sociologist Makiko Fuwa (2004) analyzed gender inequality in 22 industrial countries using data from the International Social Survey Programme. Fuwa looked first at how couples divided up their housework. Then she compared that data to societywide measures of women's presence in high-status occupations, as well as their wages relative to men's. Figure 11-1 shows that while gender differences in empowerment vary widely from one country to the next, equality between the sexes is rare.

Women in the Workforce of the United States

Almost 30 years ago, the U.S. Commission on Civil Rights (1976:1) concluded that the passage in the Declaration of Independence proclaiming that "all men are created equal" has been taken too literally for too long—especially with respect to women's opportunities for employment. In this section we will see how gender bias has limited women's opportunities for employment outside the home, at the same time that it forces them to carry a disproportionate burden inside the home.

Labor Force Participation Women's participation in the paid labor force of the United States increased steadily throughout the 20th century (see Figure 11-2). No longer is the adult woman associated solely with the role of homemaker. Instead, millions of women—married and single, with and without children—are working in the paid labor force. In 2004, 59 percent of adult women in the United States held jobs outside the home, compared with 38 percent in 1960. A majority of women are now members of the paid labor force. Among new mothers, 56 percent return to the labor force within a year of giving birth. As recently as 1975, only 31 percent went back to work (Bureau of the Census 2005a:389, 392).

Yet women entering the job market find their options restricted in important ways. Particularly damaging is occupational segregation, or confinement to sex-typed "women's jobs." For example, in 2004, women accounted for 99 percent of all dental hygienists and 83 percent of all librarians. Entering such sex-typed occupations places women in "service" roles that parallel the traditional gender-role standard under which housewives "serve" their husbands.

Women are *underrepresented* in occupations historically defined as "men's jobs," which often carry much greater financial rewards and prestige than women's jobs. For example, in 2004, women accounted for approximately 45 percent of the paid labor force of the United States, yet they constituted only 12 percent of civil engineers, 22 percent of all dentists, and 29 percent of all computer systems analysts and physicians (see Table 11-3).

Such occupational segregation is not unique to the United States but typical of industrial countries. In Great Britain, for example, only 29 percent of computer analysts are women, while 81 percent of cashiers and 90 percent of nurses are women (Cross and Bagilhole 2002).

Women from all groups and men from minority groups sometimes encounter attitudinal or organizational bias that prevents them from reaching their full potential. As we saw in Chapter 10, the term **glass ceiling** refers to an invisible barrier that blocks the promotion of a qualified individual in a work environment because of the individual's gender, race, or ethnicity. A study of the Fortune 1,000 largest corporations in the United States showed that less than 15 percent of the seats on their boards of directors were held by women in 2002 (Strauss 2002).

Compensation

He works. She works. Both are physicians—a high-status occupation with considerable financial rewards. He makes $140,000. She makes $88,000.

These median earnings for physicians in the United States were released by the Census Bureau in 2004. They are typical of the results of the bureau's detailed study of occupations and income. Take air traffic controllers. He makes $67,000; she earns $56,000. Or housekeepers: he makes $19,000; she earns $15,000. What about teacher's assistants? He makes $20,000; she earns $15,000. Statisticians at the bureau looked at the median earnings for no fewer than 821 occupations ranging from dishwasher to chief executive. After adjusting for workers' age, education, and work experience, they came to an unmistakable conclusion: Across the board, there is a substantial gender gap in the median earnings of full-time workers.

Men do not always earn more than women for doing the same work. Researchers at the Census Bureau found 2 occupations out of 821 in which women typically earn about 1 percent more income than men: hazardous materials recovery and

Table 11-3 U.S. Women in Selected Occupations, 2004: Women as a Percentage of All Workers in the Occupation

Underrepresented		Overrepresented	
Aircraft pilots	5%	High school teachers	55%
Firefighters	5	Cashiers	76
Civil engineers	12	Social workers	78
Police officers	14	File clerks	80
Clergy	15	Elementary teachers	81
Dentists	22	Librarians	83
Architects	24	Tellers	88
Computer systems analysts	29	Registered nurses	92
Lawyers	29	Receptionists	92
Physicians	29	Child care workers	95
Mail carriers	37	Secretaries	97
College teachers	46	Dental hygienists	99

Note: Women constitute 45 percent of the entire labor force.
Source: Data for 2004 reported in Bureau of the Census 2005a:401–405.

telecommunications line installation. These two occupations employed less than 1 out of every 1,000 workers the bureau studied. Forecasting analyses show no convincing evidence that the wage gap is narrowing (Lips 2003; Weinberg 2004).

While women may well be at a disadvantage in male-dominated occupations, the same is not true for men in female-dominated occupations. Sociologist Michelle Budig (2002) examined a national database containing career information on more than 12,000 men, collected over the course of 15 years. She found that men were uniformly advantaged in female occupations. Though male nurses, grade school teachers, and librarians may experience some scorn in the larger society, they are much more likely than women to be encouraged to become administrators. Observers of the labor force have termed this advantage for men in female-dominated occupations the *glass escalator*—quite a contrast to the glass ceiling (J. Jacobs 2003; C. L. Williams 1992, 1995).

Social Consequences of Women's Employment

Today, many women face the challenge of trying to juggle work and family. Their situation has many social consequences. For one thing, it puts pressure on child care facilities, public financing of day care, and even the fast-food industry, which provides many of the meals women used to prepare themselves. For another, it raises questions about what responsibility male wage earners have in the household.

Who does the housework when women become productive wage earners? Studies indicate that there is a clear gender gap in the performance of housework, although it has been narrowing.

Women do more housework and spend more time on child care than men, whether on a workday or a nonworkday. Taken together, then, a woman's workday on and off the job is much longer than a man's (Sayer et al. 2004).

Sociologist Arlie Hochschild (1989, 1990, 2005) has used the phrase *second shift* to describe the double burden—work outside the home followed by child care and housework—that many women face and few men share equitably. On the basis of interviews with and observations of 52 couples over an eight-year period, Hochschild reports that the wives (and not their husbands) drive home from the office while planning domestic schedules and play dates for children—and then begin their second shift. Drawing on national studies, she concludes that women spend 15 fewer hours each week in leisure activities than their husbands. In a year, these women work an extra month of 24-hour days because of the second shift; over a dozen years, they work an extra year of 24-hour days. Hochschild found that the married couples she studied were fraying at the edges, and so were their careers and their marriages. With such reports in mind, many feminists have advocated greater governmental and corporate support for child care, more flexible {pp.94–96 family leave policies, and other reforms designed to ease the burden on the nation's families (Moen and Roehling 2005).

The greater amounts of time women put into caring for their children, and to a lesser degree into housework, takes a special toll on women who are pursuing careers. In a 2005 survey published in the *Harvard Business Review,* about 40 percent of women indicated that they had voluntarily left work for months or years, compared to only 24 percent of men. As Figure 11-3 shows, women were much more likely than men to take time off for family reasons.

Aging and Society

The Sherpas—a Tibetan-speaking Buddhist people in Nepal—live in a culture that idealizes old age. Almost all elderly members of the Sherpa culture own their homes, and most are in relatively good physical condition. Typically, older Sherpas value their independence and prefer not to live with their children. Among the Fulani of Africa, however, older men and women move to the edge of the family homestead. Since that is where people are buried, the elderly sleep over their own graves, for they are viewed socially as already dead. Like gender stratification, age stratification varies from culture to culture. One society may treat older people with great reverence, while another sees them as unproductive and "difficult" (M. Goldstein and Beall 1981; Stenning 1958; Tonkinson 1978).

It is understandable that all societies have some system of age stratification that associates certain social roles with distinct periods in life. Some of this age differentiation seems inevitable; it would make little sense to send young children off to war, or to expect most older citizens to handle physically demanding tasks, such as loading freight at shipyards. However, as is the case with stratification by gender, in the United States age stratification goes far beyond the physical constraints on human beings at different ages.

"Being old" is a master status that commonly overshadows all others in the United States. Thus, the insights of labeling theory {p.171 can help us in analyzing the consequences of aging. Once people have been labeled "old," the designation has a major impact on how others perceive them, and even on how they view themselves. Negative stereotypes of the elderly contribute to their position as a minority group subject to discrimination, as we will see later in the chapter.

The model of five basic properties of a minority or subordi- {p.234 nate group (introduced in Chapter 10) can be applied to older people in the United States to clarify their subordinate status:

1. The elderly experience unequal treatment in employment, and may face prejudice and discrimination.

FIGURE 11–3

Why Leave Work?

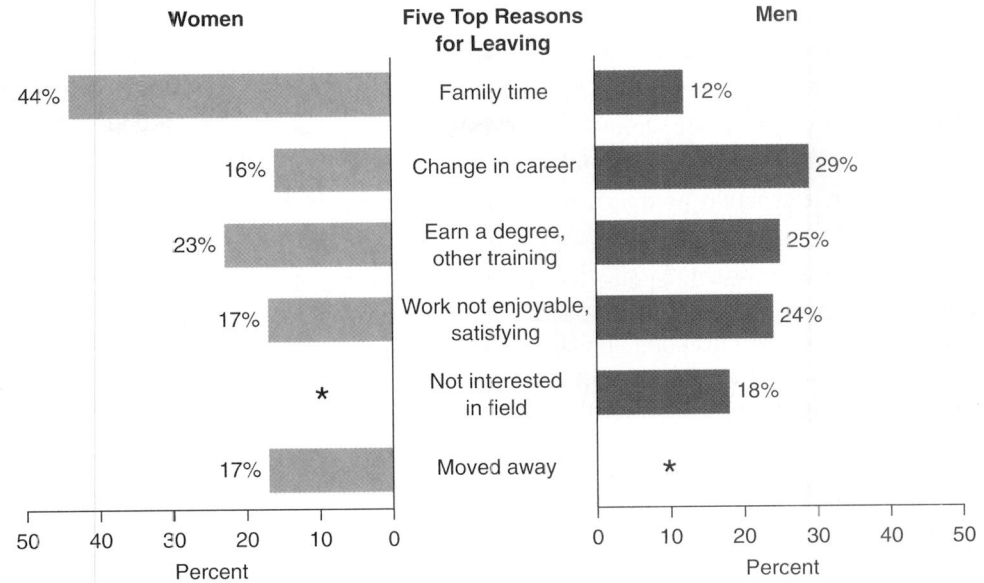

★ Not one of top 5 reasons

Note: Based on a representative Harris Interactive survey of "highly qualified" workers, defined as those with a graduate degree, a professional degree, or a high honors undergraduate degree.

Source: Figure adapted from Sylvia Ann Hewlett and Carolyn Burk Luce, 2005. "Off Ramps and On-Ramps: Keeping Talented Women on the Road to Success," *Harvard Business Review,* March 2005. Copyright © 2005 by the Harvard Business School Publishing Corporation, all rights reserved. Reprinted by permission of Harvard Business Review.

2. The elderly share physical characteristics that distinguish them from younger people. In addition, their cultural preferences and leisure-time activities often differ from those of the rest of society.

3. Membership in this disadvantaged group is involuntary.

4. Older people have a strong sense of group solidarity, as is reflected in the growth of senior citizens' centers, retirement communities, and advocacy organizations.

5. Older people generally are married to others of comparable age.

There is one crucial difference between older people and other subordinate groups, such as racial and ethnic minorities or women: *All* of us who live long enough will eventually assume the ascribed status of an older person (Barron 1953; Levin and Levin 1980; Wagley and Harris 1958).

Explaining the Aging Process

Aging is one important aspect of socialization—the lifelong process through which an individual learns the cultural norms and values of a particular society. There are no clear-cut definitions for different periods of the aging cycle in the United States. *Old age* has typically been regarded as beginning at 65, which corresponds to the retirement age for many workers, but not everyone in the United States accepts that definition. With the increase in life expectancy, writers are beginning to refer to people in their 60s as the "young old," to distinguish them from those in their 80s and beyond (the "old old"). Box 11-3 (opposite) considers some of the consequences of the growth of these age groups.

The particular problems of the elderly have become the focus of a specialized field of research and inquiry known as gerontology. *Gerontology* is the scientific study of the sociological and psychological aspects of aging and the problems of the aged. It originated in the 1930s, as an increasing number of social scientists became aware of the plight of the elderly.

Gerontologists rely heavily on sociological principles and theories to explain the impact of aging on the individual and society. They also draw on psychology, anthropology, physical education, counseling, and medicine in their study of the aging process. Two influential views of aging—disengagement theory and activity theory—can best be understood in terms of the sociological perspectives of functionalism and interactionism, respectively. The conflict perspective also contributes to our sociological understanding of aging.

Use Your Sociological Imagination
www.mhhe.com/schaefer7

Time has passed, and you are now in your 70s or 80s. How does old age in your generation compare with your parents' or grandparents' experience of old age?

In Korea, certain birthdays are celebrated as milestones, complete with formal feast. At a 60th birthday celebration, for example, all the younger family members bow before the fortunate elder one by one, in order of their ages, and offer gifts. Later they compete with one another in composing poetry and singing songs to mark the occasion. Unfortunately, not all older people are so lucky; in many other cultures, being old is considered next to being dead.

Functionalist Approach: Disengagement Theory

After studying elderly people in good health and relatively comfortable economic circumstances, Elaine Cumming and William Henry (1961) introduced their *disengagement theory,* which implicitly suggests that society and the aging individual mutually sever many of their relationships. In keeping with the functionalist perspective, disengagement theory emphasizes that passing social roles on from one generation to another ensures social stability.

According to this theory, the approach of death forces people to drop most of their social roles—including those of worker, volunteer, spouse, hobby enthusiast, and even reader. Younger members of society then take on these functions. The aging person, it is held, withdraws into an increasing state of inactivity while preparing for death. At the same time, society withdraws from the elderly by segregating them residentially (in retirement homes and communities), educationally (in programs designed solely for senior citizens), and recreationally (in senior citizens' centers). Implicit in disengagement theory is the view that society should *help* older people to withdraw from their accustomed social roles.

sociologyIN *the Global Community*

11-3 Aging Worldwide: Issues and Consequences

An electric water kettle is wired so that people in another location can determine if it has been used in the previous 24 hours. This may seem a zany use of modern technology, but it symbolizes a change taking place around the globe—the growing needs of an aging population. The Japanese Welfare Network Ikebukuro Honcho has installed these wired hot pots so that volunteers can monitor whether the elderly have used the devices to prepare their morning tea. An unused pot initiates contacts to see if the older person needs help. This technological monitoring system is an indication of the tremendous growth of Japan's elderly population, and particularly significant, the increasing numbers who live *alone*.

> An unused pot initiates contacts to see if the older person needs help.

Around the world, there are more than 453 million people age 65 and over, representing about 7 percent of the world's population. By 2050, one in three people will be over 65. In an important sense, the aging of the world's population represents a major success story that unfolded during the latter years of the 20th century. Through the efforts of both national governments and international agencies, many societies have drastically reduced the incidence of disease and the rate of death. Consequently, these nations—especially the industrialized countries of Europe and North America—now have increasingly higher proportions of older members.

The overall population of Europe is older than that of any other continent. As the propor-

tion of older people in Europe continues to rise, many governments that have long prided themselves on their pension programs have reduced benefits and raised the age at which retired workers can receive benefits.

In most developing countries, people over 60 are likely to be in poorer health than their counterparts in industrialized nations. Yet few of those countries are in a position to offer extensive financial support to the elderly. Ironically, modernization of the developing world, while bringing with it many social and economic advances, has undercut the traditionally high status of the elderly. In many cultures, the

earning power of younger adults now exceeds that of older family members.

Let's Discuss

1. For an older person, how might life in Pakistan differ from life in France?
2. Do you know an aged person who lives alone? What arrangements have been made (or should be made) for the person's care in case of emergency?

Sources: Hani 1998; Haub 2005; He et al. 2005; Kinsella and Phillips 2005; Vidal 2004.

World's "Oldest" Countries versus the United States, 2006

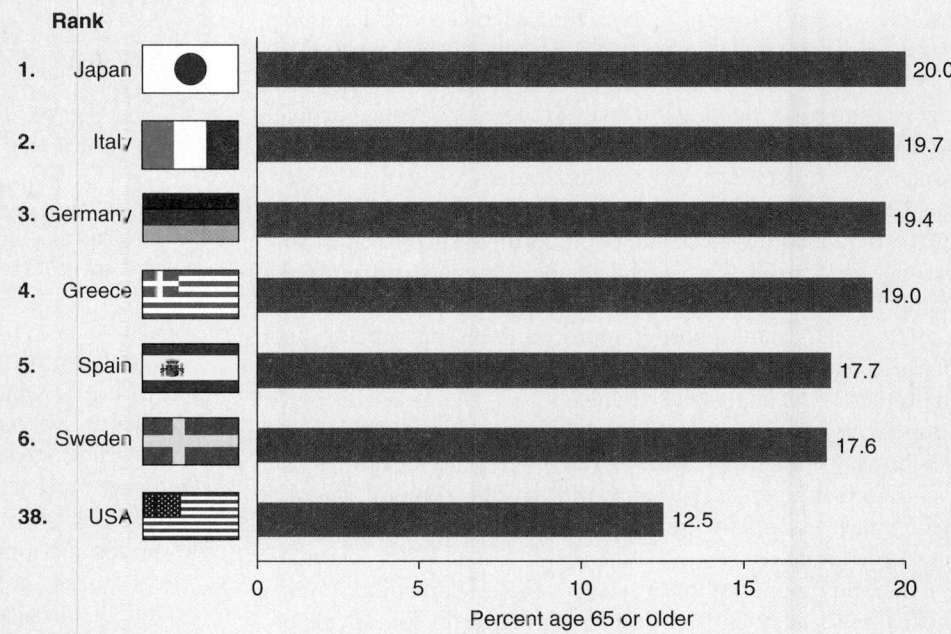

Rank		Percent age 65 or older
1.	Japan	20.0
2.	Italy	19.7
3.	Germany	19.4
4.	Greece	19.0
5.	Spain	17.7
6.	Sweden	17.6
38.	USA	12.5

Source: Bureau of the Census 2005d (projected).

Since it was first outlined more than four decades ago, disengagement theory has generated considerable controversy. Some gerontologists have objected to the implication that older people want to be ignored and put away—and even more to the idea that they should be encouraged to withdraw from meaningful social roles. Critics of disengagement theory insist that society *forces* the elderly into an involuntary and painful withdrawal from the paid labor force and from meaningful social relation-

ships. Rather than voluntarily seeking to disengage, older employees find themselves pushed out of their jobs—in many instances, even before they are entitled to maximum retirement benefits (Boaz 1987).

Although functionalist in its approach, disengagement theory ignores the fact that postretirement employment has been *increasing* in recent decades. In the United States, fewer than half of all employees actually retire from their career jobs. Instead,

most move into a "bridge job"—employment that bridges the period between the end of a person's career and his or her retirement. Unfortunately, the elderly can easily be victimized in such "bridge jobs." Psychologist Kathleen Christensen (1990), warning of "bridges over troubled water," emphasizes that older employees do not want to end their working days as minimum-wage jobholders engaged in activities unrelated to their careers (Doeringer 1990; Hayward et al. 1987).

Interactionist Approach: Activity Theory

Ask Ruth Vitow if she would like to trade her custom lampshade business in New York City for a condo in Florida, and you will get a quick response: "Deadly! I'd hate it." Vitow, in her 90s, vows to give up her business "when it gives me up." James Russell Wiggins has been working at a weekly newspaper in Maine since 1922. At age 95 he is now the editor. Vitow and Wiggins are among the 9 percent of the men and 3 percent of the women aged 75 years or older who are still participating in the nation's labor force (Himes 2001).

How important is it for older people to stay actively involved, whether at a job or in other pursuits? A tragic disaster in Chicago in 1995 showed that it can be a matter of life and death. An intense heat wave lasting more than a week—with a heat index exceeding 115 degrees on two consecutive days—resulted in 733 heat-related deaths. About three-fourths of the deceased were 65 and older. Subsequent analysis showed that older people who lived alone had the highest risk of dying, suggesting that support networks for the elderly literally help to save lives. Older Hispanics and Asian Americans had lower death rates from the heat wave than other racial and ethnic groups. Their stronger social networks probably resulted in more regular contact with family members and friends (Klinenberg 2002; Schaefer 1998a).

Often seen as an opposing approach to disengagement theory, *activity theory* suggests that those elderly people who remain active and socially involved will be best adjusted. Proponents of this perspective acknowledge that a 70-year-old person may not have the ability or desire to perform various social roles that he or she had at age 40. Yet they contend that old people have essentially the same need for social interaction as any other group.

The improved health of older people—sometimes overlooked by social scientists—has strengthened the arguments of activity theorists. Illness and chronic disease are no longer quite the scourge of the elderly that they once were. The recent emphasis on fitness, the availability of better medical care, greater control of infectious diseases, and the reduction of fatal strokes and heart attacks have combined to mitigate the traumas of growing old. Accumulating medical research also points to the importance of remaining socially involved. Among those who decline in their mental capacities later in life, deterioration is most rapid in those who withdraw from social relationships and activities. Fortunately, the aged are finding new ways to remain socially engaged, as evidenced by their increasing use of the Internet, especially to keep in touch with family and friends (Korczyk 2002).

These "silver surfers" still enjoy life to the fullest, just as they did when they were young. Staying active and involved has been shown to be healthy for the older population.

Admittedly, many activities open to the elderly involve unpaid labor, for which younger adults may receive salaries. Unpaid elderly workers include hospital volunteers (versus aides and orderlies), drivers for charities such as the Red Cross (versus chauffeurs), tutors (as opposed to teachers), and craftspeople for charity bazaars (as opposed to carpenters and dressmakers). However, some companies have recently begun programs to hire retirees for full-time or part-time work.

Though disengagement theory suggests that older people find satisfaction in withdrawal from society, conveniently receding into the background and allowing the next generation to take over, proponents of activity theory view such withdrawal as harmful to both the elderly and society. Activity theorists focus on the potential contributions of older people to the maintenance of society. In their opinion, aging citizens will feel satisfied only when they can be useful and productive in society's terms—primarily by working for wages (Civic Ventures 1999; Crosnoe and Elder Jr. 2002; Dowd 1980; Quadagno 2005).

The Conflict Approach

Conflict theorists have criticized both disengagement theorists and activity theorists for failing to consider the impact of social

structure on aging patterns. Neither approach, they say, questions why social interaction must change or decrease in old age. In addition, they often ignore the impact of social class on the lives of the elderly.

The privileged upper class generally enjoys better health and vigor and less likelihood of dependency in old age. Affluence cannot forestall aging indefinitely, but it can soften the economic hardships people face in later years. Although pension plans, retirement packages, and insurance benefits may be developed to assist older people, those whose wealth allows them access to investment funds can generate the greatest income for their later years.

In contrast, the working class often faces greater health hazards and a greater risk of disability; aging is particularly difficult for those who suffer job-related injuries or illnesses. Working-class people also depend more heavily on Social Security benefits and private pension programs. During inflationary times, their relatively fixed incomes from these sources barely keep pace with the escalating costs of food, housing, utilities, and other necessities (Atchley and Barusch 2004).

According to the conflict approach, the treatment of older people in the United States reflects the many divisions in our society. The low status of older people is seen in prejudice and discrimination against them, in age segregation, and in unfair job practices—none of which are directly addressed by either disengagement or activity theory.

Conflict theorists have noted, too, that in the developing world, the transition from agricultural economies to industrialization and capitalism has not always been beneficial to the elderly. As a society's production methods change, the traditionally valued role of older people tends to erode. Their wisdom is no longer relevant in the new economy.

In sum, the three perspectives considered here take different views of the elderly. Functionalists portray older people as socially isolated, with reduced social roles; interactionists see them as involved in new networks and changing social roles; conflict theorists see them as victimized by social structure, with their social roles relatively unchanged but devalued. Table 11-4 summarizes these perspectives.

summingUP

Table 11-4 Sociological Perspectives on Aging

Sociological Perspective	View of Aging	Social Roles	Portrayal of Elderly
Functionalist	Disengagement	Reduced	Socially isolated
Interactionist	Activity	Changed	Involved in new networks
Conflict	Competition	Relatively unchanged	Victimized, organized to confront their victimization

Classroom Tip See "Exchange Theory" (Additional Lecture Ideas).

Role Transitions throughout the Life Course

As noted in Chapter 4 and throughout this textbook, socialization is a lifelong process. We simply do not experience things the {p.86} same way at different points in the life course. For example, one study found that even falling in love differs according to where we are in the life course. Young unmarried adults tend to treat love as a noncommittal game or an obsession characterized by possessiveness and dependency. People over the age of 50 are much more likely to see love as involving commitment, and they tend to take a practical approach to finding a partner who meets a set of rational criteria. The life course, then, affects the manner in which we relate to one another (Montgomery and Sorell 1997).

How we move through the life course varies dramatically, depending on our personal preferences and circumstances. Some of us marry early, others late; some have children and some don't. These individual patterns are influenced by social factors such as class, race, and gender. Only in the most general terms, then, can we speak of stages or periods in the life course (Shanahan 2000).

One transitional stage, identified by psychologist Daniel Levinson, begins at the time at which an individual gradually enters the adult world, perhaps by moving out of the parental home, beginning a career, or entering a marriage. The second transitional period, the midlife transition, typically begins at about age 40. Men and women often experience a stressful period of self-evaluation, commonly known as the *midlife crisis,* in which they realize that they have not achieved basic goals and ambitions and have little time left to do so. Thus, Levinson (1978, 1996) found that most adults surveyed experienced tumultuous midlife conflicts within the self and with the external world.

Not all the challenges at this time of life come from career or one's partner. In the next section we will examine a special challenge faced by a growing number of middle-aged adults: caring for two generations at once.

The Sandwich Generation

During the late 1990s social scientists focused on the *sandwich generation*—adults who simultaneously try to meet the competing needs of their parents and their children. That is, caregiving goes in two directions: (1) to children, who even as young adults may still require significant direction, and (2) to aging parents, whose health and economic problems may demand intervention by their adult children.

Like the role of caring for children, the role of caring for aging parents falls disproportionately on women. Overall, women provide 60 percent of the care their parents receive, and even more as the demands of the role grow more intense and time consuming. Increasingly, middle-aged women and younger are finding themselves on the "daughter

Classroom Tip Refer to "Rethinking the Life Course" (Additional Lecture Ideas) for a discussion of Levinson's, Sheehy's, and Erikson's views on the subject.

A sandwich-generation mom cares for her bedridden parent as her older child feeds the younger one. Increasingly, members of the baby boom generation find themselves caring for two generations at once.

party, and special moments on the last day on the job. The preretirement period itself can be emotionally charged, especially if the retiree is expected to train his or her successor (Atchley 1976).

From 1950 to the mid-1990s, the average age at retirement in the United States declined, but over the last few years it has reversed direction. In 2003, 6 percent of women and 12 percent of men over 70 were still working. A variety of factors explains this reversal: changes in Social Security benefits, an economic shift away from hard manual labor, and workers' concern with maintaining their health insurance and pension benefits. At the same time, longevity has increased, and the quality of people's health has improved (He et al. 2005:89).

Gerontologist Robert Atchley (1976) has identified several phases of the retirement experience:

- *Preretirement,* a period of anticipatory socialization as the person prepares for retirement

- *The near phase,* when the person establishes a specific departure date from his or her job

- *The honeymoon phase,* an often euphoric period in which the person pursues activities that he or she never had time for before

track," as their time and attention are diverted by the needs of their aging mothers and fathers (Gross 2005).

The last major transition identified by Levinson occurs after age 60—sometimes well after that age, given advances in health care, greater longevity, and gradual acceptance by society of older people. In fact, yesterday's 60 may be today's 70 or even 75. Nonetheless, there is a point at which people transition to a different lifestyle. As we will see, this is a time of dramatic changes in people's everyday lives.

Adjusting to Retirement

Retirement is a rite of passage that marks a critical transition from one phase of a person's life to another. Typically, symbolic events are associated with this rite of passage, such as retirement gifts, a retirement

"Good news, honey—seventy is the new fifty."

research IN action

11-4 Naturally Occurring Retirement Communities (NORCs)

With recent improvements in health care, older Americans have gained new choices in where to live. Many do not reside in nursing homes or planned retirement communities. Instead, they congregate in areas that gradually become informal centers for senior citizens. Social scientists have dubbed such areas *naturally occurring retirement communities (NORCs)*. Using observation research, census data, and interviews, sociologists and urban planners have developed some interesting conclusions about NORCs.

NORCs can be as small as a single apartment building or as large as a neighborhood in a big city. Often, these settlements emerge as singles and young couples move out and older people move in. Sometimes couples simply remain where they are; as they grow older, the community becomes noticeably grayer. In time, business establishments that cater to the elderly, such as pharmacies, medical supply outlets, and small restaurants, relocate to the communities, making them even more attractive to older citizens.

The largest known NORC in the United States is Co-op City, a high-rise apartment complex in the Bronx, north of Manhattan. Built in the 1960s, the huge community was meant to house low-income workers and their families, in apartments that were relatively spacious by New York City's standards. More than three decades later, many of the buildings' first residents are still there, "aging in place," as the social workers say. Today, roughly 8,000 of Co-op City's 50,000 residents are age 65 or older.

Building managers readily admit that they could not cope with the needs of such a huge elderly population without the help they receive from the Senior Services Program. Begun by the United Hospital Fund and supported by the City Council and the New York State legislature, the program boasts a budget of $1.2 million and a staff of 40, including two nurses and four social workers. Through Senior Services, elderly residents can receive everything from Meals on Wheels and home health aides to field trips and exercise classes. With such comprehensive support, even many seriously ill seniors manage to stay out of nursing homes.

Unfortunately, residents of some high-rise communities are threatened by gentrification—the takeover of low-income neighborhoods by higher-income residents. In Chicago, a high-rise building known as Ontario Place is converting to a condominium, at prices that current residents cannot afford. About half the building's occupants are Russian immigrants; most of the others are elderly or disabled people living on fixed incomes. They are distressed not just because they will need to move, but because their community is being destroyed.

> *NORCs can be as small as a single apartment building or as large as a neighborhood in a big city.*

Let's Discuss

1. Can you think of a naturally occurring retirement community near your home or school? If so, describe the area. What kinds of services are available to elderly residents?
2. What can government or community activists do to help elderly people who are threatened by gentrification?

Sources: A. Feuer 2002; Lansprey 1995; Perry 2001; Sheehan 2005.

- *The disenchantment phase,* in which retirees feel a sense of letdown or even depression as they cope with their new lives, which may include illness or poverty
- *The reorientation phase,* which involves the development of a more realistic view of retirement alternatives
- *The stability phase,* a period in which the person has learned to deal with life after retirement in a reasonable and comfortable fashion
- *The termination phase,* which begins when the person can no longer engage in basic, day-to-day activities such as self-care and housework

Retirement is not a single transition, then, but rather a series of adjustments that varies from one person to another. The length and timing of each phase will differ for each individual, depending on such factors as financial and health status. In fact, a person will not necessarily go through all the phases identified by Atchley. For example, people who are forced to retire or who face financial difficulties may never experience a honeymoon phase.

And many retirees continue to be part of the paid labor force of the United States, often taking part-time jobs to supplement their pension income. That is certainly the expectation of baby boomers, as Figure 11-4 (page 280) shows.

During the reorientation and stability phases, an increasing number of elderly find they are living in neighborhoods where the majority of people are their own age. Box 11-4 explores this social phenomenon, called naturally occurring retirement communities (NORCs).

Like other aspects of life in the United States, the experience of retirement varies according to gender, race, and ethnicity. White males are most likely to benefit from retirement wages, as well as to have participated in a formal retirement preparation program. As a result, anticipatory socialization for retirement is most systematic for White men. In contrast, members of racial and ethnic minority groups—especially African Americans—are more likely to exit the paid labor force through disability than through retirement. Because of their comparatively lower incomes and smaller savings, men and women from racial and

Let's Discuss Are there any NORCs in your area?
Policy Pointer Role of government in assisting the elderly
Student Alert Explain some of the social processes that might lead to the emergence of NORCs.

Let's Discuss Ask students what proportion of the older people they know falls into each of Atchley's stages
Classroom Tip Compare Atchley's stages to those presented in "Typology of the Elderly" (Additional Lecture Ideas).
Gender/Race/Ethnicity Impact of gender, race, and ethnicity on retirement

Retirement Expectations

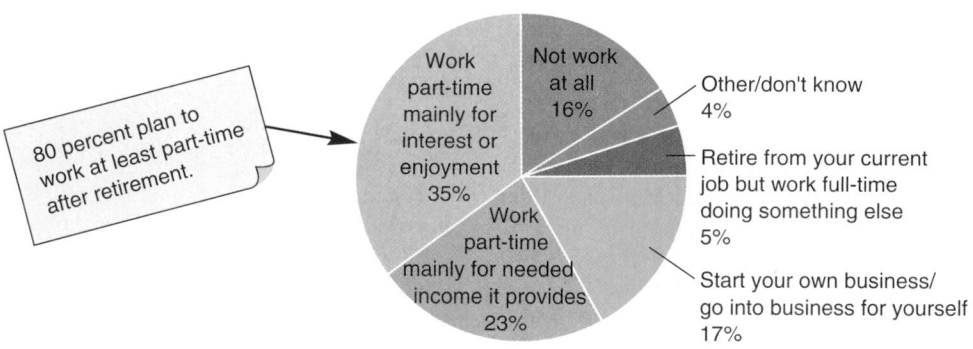

80 percent plan to work at least part-time after retirement.

Work part-time mainly for interest or enjoyment 35%

Not work at all 16%

Other/don't know 4%

Retire from your current job but work full-time doing something else 5%

Start your own business/ go into business for yourself 17%

Work part-time mainly for needed income it provides 23%

Note: Survey of the baby boom generation (people born from 1946 to 1964) conducted in 1998.
Source: AARP 1999.

ethnic minority groups work intermittently after retirement more often than older Whites (National Institute on Aging 1999; Quadagno 2005).

Death and Dying

Among the role transitions that typically (but not always) come later in life is death. Until recently, death was viewed as a taboo topic in the United States. However, psychologist Elisabeth Kübler-Ross (1969), through her pioneering book *On Death and Dying,* greatly encouraged open discussion of the process of dying. Drawing on her work with 200 cancer patients, Kübler-Ross identified five stages of the experience: denial, anger, bargaining, depression, and finally acceptance.

Despite its popular appeal, the five-stage theory of dying has been challenged. Observers often cannot substantiate these stages. Moreover, research suggests that each person declines in his or her own way. Thus, one should not expect—much less counsel—a person to approach death in any particular way (R. Epstein 2005; Fitchett 1980).

Functionalists would see those who are dying as fulfilling distinct social functions. Gerontologist Richard Kalish (1985) lists among the tasks of the dying: completing unfinished business, such as settling insurance and legacy matters; restoring harmony to social relationships and saying farewell to friends and family; dealing with medical needs; and making funeral plans and other arrangements for survivors. In accomplishing these tasks, the dying person actively contributes to meeting society's need for smooth intergenerational transitions, role continuity, compliance with medical procedures, and minimal disruption

of the social system, despite the loss of one of its members.

This functionalist analysis brings to mind the cherished yet controversial concept of a "good death." One researcher described a good death among the Kaliai, a people of the South Pacific. In that culture, the dying person calls together all his relatives, settles his debts, disposes of his possessions, and then announces that it is time for him to die (Counts 1977). The Kaliai concept of a good death has a parallel in Western societies, where people may speak of a "natural death," an "appropriate death," or "death with dignity." The practice of ***hospice care,*** introduced in London, England, in the 1960s, is founded on this concept. Hospice workers seek to improve the quality of a dying person's last days by offering comfort and by helping the person to remain at home, or in a homelike setting at a hospital or other special facility, until the end. Currently there are more than 3,200 hospice programs serving over 880,000 people a year.

Although the Western ideal of the good death makes the experience of dying as positive as possible, some critics fear that acceptance of the concept of a good death may direct both individual efforts and social resources away from attempts to extend life. Still others argue that fatally ill older people should not just passively accept death, but should forgo further treatment in

Coffins in Ghana sometimes reflect the way the dead lived their lives. This Methodist burial service honors a woman who died at age 85, leaving behind 11 children, 82 grandchildren, and 60 great-grandchildren. Her coffin, designed to resemble a mother hen, features 11 chicks nestling beneath the wings (Secretan 1995).

Key Person Elisabeth Kübler-Ross
Theory Functionalist view of the tasks of the dying
Student Alert Note the distinction between the stages of dying and the tasks of the dying.

Global View "Good death" among the Kaliai of the South Pacific
Methods The material on the Kaliai is based on observation research.
Global View Concept of hospice care introduced in London, England

order to reduce public health care expenditures. Such issues are at the heart of current debates over the right to die and physician-assisted suicide (Counts 1977; Hospice Foundation of America 2005; Mahoney 1999).

Recent studies in the United States suggest that in many varied ways, people have broken through the historic taboos about death and are attempting to arrange certain aspects of the idealized good death. For example, bereavement practices—once highly structured—are becoming increasingly varied and therapeutic. More and more people are actively addressing the inevitability of death by making wills, leaving "living wills" (health care proxies that explain their feelings about the use of life-support equipment), donating organs, and providing instructions for family members about funerals, cremations, and burials. Given medical and technological advances and a breakthrough in open discussion and negotiation regarding death and dying, it is possible that good deaths may become a social norm in the United States (La Ganga 1999; J. Riley 1992).

Age Stratification in the United States

The "Graying of America"

When Lenore Schaefer, a ballroom dancer, tried to get on the *Tonight Show*, she was told she was "too young": she was in her early 90s. When she turned 101, she made it. But even at that age, Lenore is no longer unusual in our society. Today, people over 100 constitute, proportionately, the country's fastest-growing age group. They are part of the increasing proportion of the population of the United States that is composed of older people (Himes 2001; Riner 1998).

As Figure 11-5 shows, in the year 1900, men and women age 65 and older constituted only 4.1 percent of the nation's population, but by 2010 that age group is expected to grow to 13.0 percent. According to current projections, the over-65 segment will continue to increase throughout this century. As the decades pass, the population of "old old" (people who are 85 and older) will increase at an ever-faster rate.

In 2010, 15.9 percent of non-Hispanic Whites are projected to be older than 65, compared to 8.7 percent of African Americans, 9.6 percent of Asian Americans, and 5.9 percent of Hispanics. In part, these differences reflect the shorter life spans of the latter groups. They also stem from immigration patterns among Asians and Hispanics, who tend to be young when they enter the country (Bureau of the Census 2005a:17).

The highest proportions of older people are found in Florida, Pennsylvania, Rhode Island, Iowa, West Virginia, and Arkansas. However, that will soon change. In 2000, Florida was the state most populated by the elderly, with 17.6 percent of the population over age 65. Yet as Figure 11-6 (page 282) shows, in about another 25 years, more than half the states will have an even greater proportion of elderly than Florida does now.

The graying of the United States is a phenomenon that can no longer be ignored, either by social scientists or by govern-

FIGURE 11-5   **281**

Stratification by Gender and Age

Actual and Projected Growth of the Elderly Population of the United States

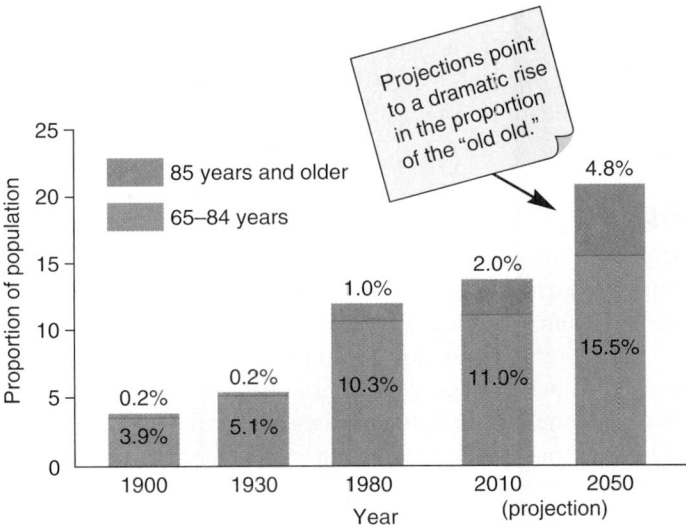

Sources: Bureau of the Census 2004a:113; He et al. 2005:9.

ment policymakers. Advocates for the elderly have spoken out on a wide range of issues. Politicians court the votes of older people, since they are the age group most likely to register and vote. In fact, in the 2000 presidential race, people 55 or older made up 35 percent of the total vote (Holder 2006).

Wealth and Income

There is significant variation in wealth and poverty among the nation's older people. Some individuals and couples find themselves poor in part because of fixed pensions and skyrocketing health care costs (see Chapter 15). Nevertheless, as a group, older people in the United States are neither homogeneous nor poor. The typical elderly person enjoys a standard of living that is much higher now than at any point in the nation's past. Class differences among the elderly remain evident, but tend to narrow somewhat: Those older people who enjoyed middle-class incomes while younger tend to remain better off after retirement, but less so than before (Denise Smith and Tillipman 2000).

To some extent, older people owe their overall improved standard of living to a greater accumulation of wealth—in the form of home ownership, private pensions, and other financial assets. But much of the improvement is due to more generous Social Security benefits. While modest when compared with other countries' pension programs, Social Security nevertheless provides 39 percent of all income received by older people in the United States. Still, about 10 percent of the nation's elderly population lives below the poverty line. At the extremes of poverty are those groups who were more likely to be poor at earlier points in the life cycle: female-headed households and racial and ethnic minorities (He et al. 2005).

Classroom Tip See "Age and Economic Hardship" (Class Discussion Topics).
Contemporary Culture How will your obligations to your parents change as they age?

Viewed from a conflict perspective, it is not surprising that older women experience a double burden; the same is true of elderly members of racial and ethnic minorities. For example, in 2004 the proportion of older Latinos with incomes below the poverty level (18.7 percent) was more than twice as large as the proportion of older non-Hispanic Whites (7.5 percent). Moreover, 23.9 percent of older African Americans fell below the federal government's poverty line (DeNavas-Walt et al. 2005:Table POV01).

Ageism

Physician Robert Butler (1990) became concerned 30 years ago when he learned that a housing development near his home in metropolitan Washington, D.C., barred the elderly. Butler coined the term *ageism* to refer to prejudice and discrimination based on a person's age. For example, we may choose to assume that someone cannot handle a rigorous job because he is "too old," or we may refuse to give someone a job with authority because she is "too young."

Ageism is especially difficult for the old, because at least youthful recipients of prejudice know that in time they will be "old enough." For many, old age symbolizes disease. With ageism all too common in the United States, it is hardly surprising that older people are barely visible on television. In 2002, the Senate Special Committee on Aging convened a panel on the media's portrayal of older people and sharply criticized media and mar-

keting executives for bombarding audiences with negative images of the aged. The social consequences of such images are significant. Research shows that older people who have positive perceptions of aging live an average of 7.5 years longer than those who have negative perceptions (M. Gardner 2003; Levy et al. 2002; E. Ramirez 2002).

Use Your Sociological Imagination

www.mhhe.com/schaefer7

It is September and you are channel-surfing through the new fall TV series. How likely are you to watch a television show that is based on older characters who spend a lot of time together?

Competition in the Labor Force

Participation in paid work is not typical after the age of 65. In 2001, 31 percent of men ages 65 to 69 and 20 percent of women participated in the paid labor force. While some people view these workers as experienced contributors to the labor force, others see them as "job stealers," a biased judgment similar to that directed against illegal immigrants. This mistaken belief not only intensifies age conflict but leads to age discrimination (Himes 2001).

While firing people simply because they are old violates federal law, courts have upheld the right to lay off older workers for economic reasons. Critics contend that later, the same firms hire young, cheaper workers to replace experienced older workers. When economic growth began to slow in 2001 and companies cut back on their workforces, complaints of age bias grew sharply as older workers began to suspect they were bearing a disproportionate share of the layoffs. According to the Equal Employment Opportunity Commission, between 1999 and 2004, complaints of age discrimination rose more than 41 percent. However, evidence of a countertrend has emerged. Some firms have been giving larger raises to older workers, to encourage their retirement at the higher salary—a tactic that prompts younger workers to complain of age discrimination (Novelli 2004; Uchitelle 2003).

A controlled experiment conducted by the AARP confirmed that older people often face discrimination when applying for jobs. Comparable résumés for two applicants—one 57 years old and the other 32 years old—were sent to 775 large firms and employment agencies around the United States. In situations

FIGURE 11–6

Twenty-Eight Floridas by 2030

MAPPING LIFE

NATIONWIDE www.mhhe.com/schaefer7

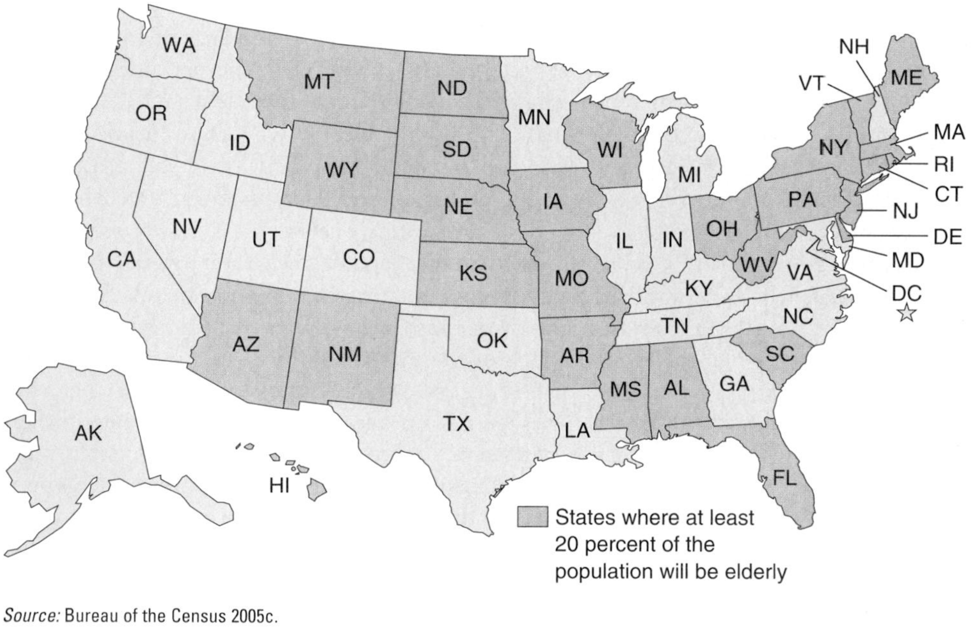

States where at least 20 percent of the population will be elderly

Source: Bureau of the Census 2005c.

Race/Ethnicity/Age Proportion of older Latinos and percentage of older African Americans who fell below the poverty level in 2004
Theory Conflict view of ageism
Theory Labeling theorists would be especially interested in stereotyping based on how old someone looks.
Methods Content analysis of television characters

Classroom Tip See "Ageism in Movies" (Class Discussion Topics).
Classroom Tip See "Ageism and Age Inequality" (Class Discussion Topics).
Methods Controlled experiment used to examine age discrimination in the economic sector

for which positions were actually available, the younger applicant received a favorable response 43 percent of the time. By contrast, the older applicant received favorable responses less than half as often (only 17 percent of the time). One Fortune 500 corporation asked the younger applicant for more information, while informing the older applicant that no appropriate positions were open (Bendick et al. 1993).

In contrast to the negative stereotypes, researchers have found that older workers can be an *asset* to employers. According to a study issued in 1991, older workers can be retrained in new technologies, have lower rates of absenteeism than younger employees, and are often more effective salespeople. The study focused on two corporations based in the United States (the hotel chain Days Inns of America and the holding company Travelers Corporation of Hartford) and a British retail chain—all of which have long-term experience in hiring workers age 50 and over. Indeed, more and more U.S. corporations, from Borders to Home Depot, are actively trying to recruit retired people, recognizing their comparatively lower turnover rates and often superior work performance (Freudenheim 2005; Telsch 1991).

About 30 percent of older workers choose to remain on the job past the usual retirement age. Research shows they can be retrained in new technologies and are more dependable than younger workers.

and Gender Stratification

The Battle over Abortion from a Global Perspective

The Issue

Few issues seem to stir as much intense conflict as abortion. A critical victory in the struggle for legalized abortion in the United States came in 1973, when the Supreme Court granted women the right to terminate pregnancies. This ruling, known as *Roe v. Wade*, was based on a woman's right to privacy. The Court's decision was generally applauded by pro-choice groups, which believe women should have the right to make their own decisions about their bodies and should have access to safe and legal abortions. It was bitterly condemned by those opposed to abortion. For these pro-life groups, abortion is a moral and often a religious issue. In their view, human life begins at the moment of conception, so that its termination through abortion is essentially an act of murder.

The Setting

The debate that has followed *Roe v. Wade* revolves around prohibiting abortion altogether, or at the very least, limiting it. In 1979, for example, Missouri required parental consent for minors wishing to obtain an abortion, and the Supreme Court upheld the law. Parental notification and consent have become especially sensitive issues in the debate. Pro-life activists argue

that the parents of teenagers should have the right to be notified about—and to permit or prohibit—abortions. In their view, parental authority deserves full support at a time when the traditional nuclear family is embattled. However, pro-choice activists counter that many pregnant teenagers come from troubled families where they have been abused. These young women may have good reason to avoid discussing such explosive issues with their parents.

Changing technology has had its impact on the debate. "Day-after" pills, which have been available in some nations since 1998, are now prescribed in the United States. These emergency contraception pills can prevent pregnancy after unprotected sex. In 2000, the U.S. government approved RU-486, an abortion-inducing pill that can be used in the first seven weeks of pregnancy. The regime requires doctor visits but no surgical procedures. In addition, doctors, guided by ultrasound, can now end a pregnancy as early as eight days after conception. Pro-life activists are concerned that the use of ultrasound technology will allow people to abort unwanted females in nations where a premium is placed on male offspring.

In the United States, people appear to support a woman's right to a legal abortion, but with reservations. According to a

Policy Pointer Legal abortion was a priority of the feminist movement in the late 1960s and early 1970s.

Let's Discuss Parental notification and parental consent—central issues in the abortion controversy—should be of special interest to college students.

2006 national survey, only 16 percent oppose a woman's right to a legal abortion under all circumstances. However, only 19 percent feel that abortion should be legal under *any* circumstances. These findings have held for the last 30 years (Benac 2006).

Sociological Insights

Sociologists see gender and social class as the defining issues surrounding abortion. The intense conflict over abortion reflects broader differences over women's position in society. Sociologist Kristin Luker (1984) has studied activists in both the pro-choice and pro-life movements. Luker interviewed 212 activists in California, overwhelmingly women, who spent at least five hours a week working for one of the two movements. According to Luker, each group has a consistent, coherent view of the world. Feminists involved in defending abortion rights typically believe that men and women are essentially similar; they support women's full participation in work outside the home and oppose all forms of sex discrimination. In contrast, most antiabortion activists believe that men and women are fundamentally different. In their view, men are best suited to the public world of work, while women are best suited to the demanding and crucial task of rearing children. These activists are troubled by women's growing participation in work outside the home, which they view as destructive to the family and ultimately to society.

In regard to social class, the first major restriction on the legal right to terminate a pregnancy affected poor people. In 1976, Congress passed the Hyde Amendment, which banned the use of Medicaid and other federal funds for abortions. The Supreme Court upheld this legislation in 1980. State laws also restrict the use of public funds for abortions (see Figure 11-7).

Another obstacle facing the poor is access to abortion providers. In the face of vocal pro-life sentiment, fewer and fewer hospitals throughout the world are allowing physicians to perform abortions, except in extreme cases. As of 2001, only about 6 percent of specialists in obstetrics and gynecology in the United States were trained and willing to perform abortions under any circumstances, and a majority of those physicians were in their 50s and 60s. To avoid controversy, many medical schools have ceased to offer training in the procedure. Moreover, some doctors who work in clinics, intimidated by death threats and actual murders, have stopped performing abortions. For poor people in rural areas, this reduction in service makes it more difficult to locate and travel to a facility that will accommodate

FIGURE 11–7

Restrictions on Public Funding for Abortion

MAPPING LIFE

NATIONWIDE www.mhhe.com/schaefer7

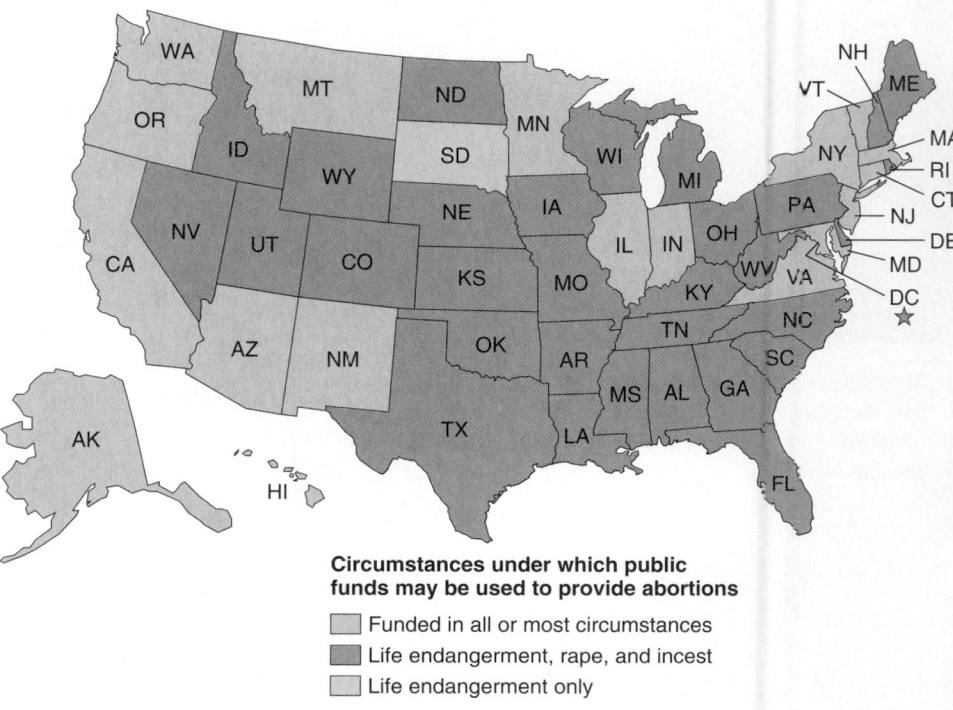

Circumstances under which public funds may be used to provide abortions

- Funded in all or most circumstances
- Life endangerment, rape, and incest
- Life endangerment only

Source: As of March 11, 2006. NARAL Pro-Choice America 2006.

their wishes. Viewed from a conflict perspective, this is one more financial burden that falls especially heavily on low-income women (T. Edwards 2001; Villarosa 2002).

Policy Initiatives

In 1973 the Supreme Court supported the general right to terminate a pregnancy by a narrow 5–4 majority. Although pro-life activists continue to hope for an overruling of *Roe v. Wade,* they have focused in the interim on weakening the decision through tactics such as limiting the use of fetal tissue in medical experiments and prohibiting certain late-term abortions, which they term "partial-birth" abortions. The Supreme Court continues to hear cases involving such restrictions. In 2005, speculation arose over a potential narrowing of the applicability of *Roe v. Wade* following the appointment of new justices, who may hold more conservative positions than those they replaced.

What is the policy in other countries? As in the United States, many European nations responded to public opinion and liberalized abortion laws beginning in the 1970s. However, many of those nations limit the procedure to the first 12 weeks of a pregnancy. (The United States, by contrast, allows abortions up to about the 24th week and beyond.) Inspired by the strong antiabortion movement in the United States, antiabortion activists

Methods Survey of U.S. citizens' attitudes about abortion rights
Methods Luker interviewed pro-choice and pro-life activists (survey research).
Theory Conflict theory used to examine the abortion issue
Theory Conflict view of how the right to legal abortions has special significance for poor women

Policy Pointer The makeup of the Supreme Court is a crucial aspect of the conflict over abortion, as has been evident in the battles over recent Court nominees.
Policy Pointer Review the most recent court rulings on abortion.
Global View Abortion policies in other countries
Global View Abortion as a controversial issue in western Europe

FIGURE 11–8

285

The Global Divide on Abortion

MAPPING LIFE

WORLDWIDE www.mhhe.com /schaefer7

Nations where abortion is permitted upon request

Note: Data current as of December 2004. Countries that prohibit abortion under any circumstances are Chile, El Salvador, Malta, and the Holy See (Vatican City).
Sources: Developed by the author based on Gonnut 2001; United Nations Population Division 1998, 2004.

in Europe have become more outspoken, especially in Great Britain, France, Spain, Italy, and Germany (*The Economist* 2003c).

The policies of the United States and developing nations are intertwined. Throughout the 1980s and 1990s, antiabortion members of Congress have often successfully blocked foreign aid to countries that might use the funds to encourage abortion. And yet those developing nations generally have the most restrictive abortion laws. As shown in Figure 11-8, it is primarily in Africa, Latin America, and parts of Asia that women are not allowed to terminate a pregnancy on request. As might be expected, illegal abortions are most common in those nations. An estimated quarter of the world's women live in countries where abortion is illegal or is permitted only if a woman's life is in jeop-

ardy. Hence, 40 percent of abortions worldwide—about 20 million procedures each year—are performed illegally (Joynt and Ganeshananthan 2003).

Let's Discuss

1. Do you know anyone who has undergone an illegal abortion? If so, what were the circumstances? Was the woman's health endangered by the procedure?

2. Do you think teenage girls should have to get their parents' consent before having an abortion? Why?

3. Under what circumstances should abortions be allowed? Explain your reasoning.

GettingINVOLVED

To get involved in the debate over abortion, visit this text's Online Learning Center, which offers links to relevant Web sites. Check out the Social Policy section in the Online Learning Center as well; it provides survey data on U.S. public opinion regarding this issue.

www.mhhe.com/schaefer7

Let's Discuss Do students believe that abortion policies will become more or less restrictive in the United States over the next decade?
Classroom Tip See "Using Humor" (Class Discussion Topics).

Summary

Gender and age are ascribed statuses that provide a basis for social differentiation. This chapter examines the social construction of gender, theories of stratification by gender, women as an oppressed majority group, theories of aging, role transitions throughout the life course, and age stratification in the United States.

1. In the United States, the social construction of gender continues to define significantly different expectations for females and males.

2. **Gender roles** show up in our work and behavior and in how we react to others.

3. Though females have been more severely restricted than men by traditional gender roles, those roles have also restricted males.

4. The research of anthropologist Margaret Mead points to the importance of cultural conditioning in defining the social roles of males and females.

5. Functionalists maintain that sex differentiation contributes to overall social stability, but conflict theorists charge that the relationship between females and males is one of unequal power, with men dominating women. This dominance shows up in people's everyday interactions.

6. As one example of their micro-level approach to the study of gender stratification, interactionists point to men's verbal dominance over women through conversational interruptions.

7. Women around the world suffer from **sexism, institutional discrimination,** and **sexual harassment.**

8. As women have taken on more and more hours of paid employment outside the home, they have been only partially successful in getting their husbands to take on more homemaking duties, including child care.

9. Like other forms of stratification, age stratification varies from culture to culture.

10. In the United States, being old is a master status that seems to overshadow all others.

11. The particular problems of the aged have become the focus for a specialized area of research and inquiry known as **gerontology.**

12. **Disengagement theory** implicitly suggests that society should help older people to withdraw from their accustomed social roles. In contrast, **activity theory** suggests that the elderly person who remains active and socially involved will be better adjusted.

13. From a conflict perspective, the low status of older people is reflected in prejudice and discrimination against them and in unfair job practices.

14. About 40 percent of those who look after their elderly relatives still have children to care for; these people have been dubbed the **sandwich generation.**

15. As we age, we go through role transitions, including adjustment to retirement and preparation for death.

16. An increasing proportion of the population of the United States is composed of older people.

17. **Ageism** reflects a deep uneasiness about growing old on the part of younger people.

18. The issue of abortion has bitterly divided the United States (as well as other nations), pitting pro-choice activists against pro-life activists.

Critical Thinking Questions

1. Imagine that you are assigned the opposite gender at birth, but that your race, ethnicity, religion, and social class remain the same. Drawing on the information contained in this chapter, describe how your life as a member of the opposite sex might differ from your life today.

2. Imagine that you have been asked to study political activism among women. How might you employ surveys, observations, experiments, and existing sources to better understand such activism?

3. Is age segregation functional or dysfunctional for older people in the United States? Is it functional or dysfunctional for society as a whole? What are the manifest functions, the latent functions, and the dysfunctions of age segregation?

Key Terms

Activity theory An interactionist theory of aging that suggests that those elderly people who remain active and socially involved will be best adjusted. (page 276)

Ageism Prejudice and discrimination based on a person's age. (282)

Disengagement theory A functionalist theory of aging that suggests that society and the aging individual mutually sever many of their relationships. (274)

Expressiveness Concern for the maintenance of harmony and the internal emotional affairs of the family. (266)

Gender role Expectations regarding the proper behavior, attitudes, and activities of males or females. (263)

Gerontology The scientific study of the sociological and psychological aspects of aging and the problems of the aged. (274)

Glass ceiling An invisible barrier that blocks the promotion of a qualified individual in a work environment because of the individual's gender, race, or ethnicity. (272)

Homophobia Fear of and prejudice against homosexuality. (263)

Hospice care Treatment of the terminally ill in their own homes, or in special hospital units or other facilities, with the goal of helping them to die easily, without pain. (280)

Institutional discrimination The denial of opportunities and equal rights to individuals and groups that results from the normal operations of a society. (268)

Instrumentality An emphasis on tasks, a focus on more distant goals, and a concern for the external relationship between one's family and other social institutions. (266)

Midlife crisis A stressful period of self-evaluation that begins at about age 40. (277)

Sandwich generation The generation of adults who simultaneously try to meet the competing needs of their parents and their children. (277)

Second shift The double burden—work outside the home followed by child care and housework—that many women face and few men share equitably. (273)

Sexism The ideology that one sex is superior to the other. (268)

Sexual harassment Behavior that occurs when work benefits are made contingent on sexual favors (as a quid pro quo), or when touching, lewd comments, or the exhibition of pornographic material creates a "hostile environment" in the workplace. (269)

Self-Quiz

Read each question carefully and then select the best answer.

1. Both males and females are physically capable of learning to cook and sew, yet most Western societies determine that women should perform these tasks. This illustrates the operation of
   a. gender roles.
   b. sociobiology.
   c. homophobia.
   d. comparable worth.

2. An important element in traditional views of proper "masculine" and "feminine" behavior is fear of homosexuality. This fear, along with accompanying prejudice, is referred to as
   a. lesbianism.
   b. femme fatalism.
   c. homophobia.
   d. claustrophobia.

3. The most crucial agents of socialization in teaching gender roles in the United States are
   a. peers.
   b. teachers.
   c. media personalities.
   d. parents.

4. In examining cross-cultural data, anthropologist Margaret Mead found that
   a. biology is the most important factor in determining the social roles of males and females.
   b. cultural conditioning is the most important factor in defining the social roles of males and females.
   c. biology and cultural conditioning have an equal impact in determining the social roles of males and females.
   d. biology and cultural conditioning have a negligible impact in determining the social roles of males and females.

5. Which sociological perspective acknowledges that it is not possible to change gender roles drastically without dramatic revisions in a culture's social structure?
   a. the functionalist perspective
   b. the conflict perspective
   c. the interactionist perspective
   d. both a and b

6. The term *sexism* is generally used to refer to
   a. female prejudice and discrimination against men.
   b. male prejudice and discrimination against women.
   c. female discrimination against men and male discrimination against women equally.
   d. discrimination between members of the same sex.

7. Which of the following statements about the elderly is correct?
   a. Being old is a master status.
   b. Once people are labeled as "old," the designation has a major impact on how others perceive them, and even on how they view themselves.
   c. Negative stereotypes of the elderly contribute to their position as a minority group subject to discrimination.
   d. all of the above

8. The text points out that the model of five basic properties of a minority or subordinate group can be applied to older people in the United States. Which of the following is *not* one of those basic properties?
   a. The elderly experience unequal treatment in employment and may face prejudice and discrimination.
   b. Statistically, the elderly represent a majority.
   c. Membership in this group is involuntary.
   d. Older people have a strong sense of group solidarity.

9. Which of the following theories argues that elderly people have essentially the same need for social interaction as any other group and that those who remain active and socially involved will be best adjusted?
   a. conflict theory
   b. functionalist theory
   c. activity theory
   d. disengagement theory

10. According to your text, which of the following statements is true?
    a. Functionalists portray the elderly as being socially isolated, with reduced social roles.
    b. Interactionists see older people as being involved in new networks of people and in changing social roles.
    c. Conflict theorists regard older people as being victimized by social structure, with their social roles relatively unchanged but devalued.
    d. all of the above

11. Talcott Parsons and Robert Bales contend that women take the _____, emotionally supportive role in the family and that men take the _____, practical role, with the two complementing each other.

12. A significant component of the _____ approach to gender stratification draws on feminist theory.

13. It is not simply that particular men in the United States are biased in their treatment of women. All the major institutions of our society—including the government, the armed forces, large corporations, the media, the universities, and the medical establishment—are controlled by men. This situation is symptomatic of institutional _____.

14. Women from all groups and men from minority groups sometimes encounter attitudinal or organizational bias that prevents them from reaching their full potential. This is known as the _____ _____.

288

15. Sociologist Arlie Hochschild has used the phrase _____ _____ to describe the double burden that many women face and few men share equitably: working outside the home followed by child care and housework.

16. _____ is the scientific study of the sociological and psychological aspects of aging and the problems of the aged. It originated in the 1930s as an increasing number of social scientists became aware of the plight of the elderly.

17. Based on a study of elderly people in good health and relatively comfortable economic circumstances, _____ theory suggests that society and the aging individual mutually sever many of their relationships.

18. During the late 1990s, social scientists focused on the _____ _____—adults who simultaneously try to meet the competing needs of their parents and their children.

19. In 2000, _____ was the state most populated by the elderly, with 17.6 percent of the population over age 65.

20. Physician Robert Butler coined the term _____ to refer to prejudice and discrimination based on a person's age.

Answers:
1 (a); 2 (c); 3 (d); 4 (b); 5 (d); 6 (b); 7 (d); 8 (b); 9 (c); 10 (d)
11 expressive; instrumental; 12 conflict; 13 discrimination; 14 glass ceiling; 15 second shift; 16 Gerontology; 17 disengagement; 18 sandwich generation; 19 Florida; 20 ageism

{ TECHNOLOGY RESOURCES }

Online Learning Center

1. Few issues stir as much intense conflict as abortion. To find out how Americans feel about abortion, visit the student center of the Online Learning Center at **www.mhhe.com/schaefer7,** and click on the Social Policy link for this chapter. Read an overview of the abortion issue and then look at the colorful pie charts and graphs.

2. About Face (**www.about-face.org**) is an organization that brings public awareness to negative stereotypes of women in the media.

Visit their site and explore the lists of "winners" and "offenders" in the media.

3. Many social and political issues are coming to the forefront as the world's aged population increases. Global Action on Aging (**www.globalaging.org**) is an advocacy organization with numerous resources to help you understand the needs of aging people around the world.

*Note: While all the URLs listed were current as of the printing of this book, these sites often change. Please check our Web site (**www.mhhe.com/schaefer7**) for updates, hyperlinks, and exercises related to these sites.*

Reel Society Video Clips

Reel Society video clips, which appear on this book's Web site, can be used to spark discussion about the following topics from this chapter:
- Gender Roles in the United States
- Cross-Cultural Perspective
- Sexism and Sex Discrimination
- The Status of Women Worldwide

The Family and Intimate Relationships

inside

Global View of the Family
Studying the Family
Marriage and Family
Divorce
Diverse Lifestyles
Social Policy and the Family:
Gay Marriage

Boxes

Sociology in the Global Community: Domestic Violence

Research in Action: Arranged Marriage, American-Style

Research in Action: The Lingering Impact of Divorce

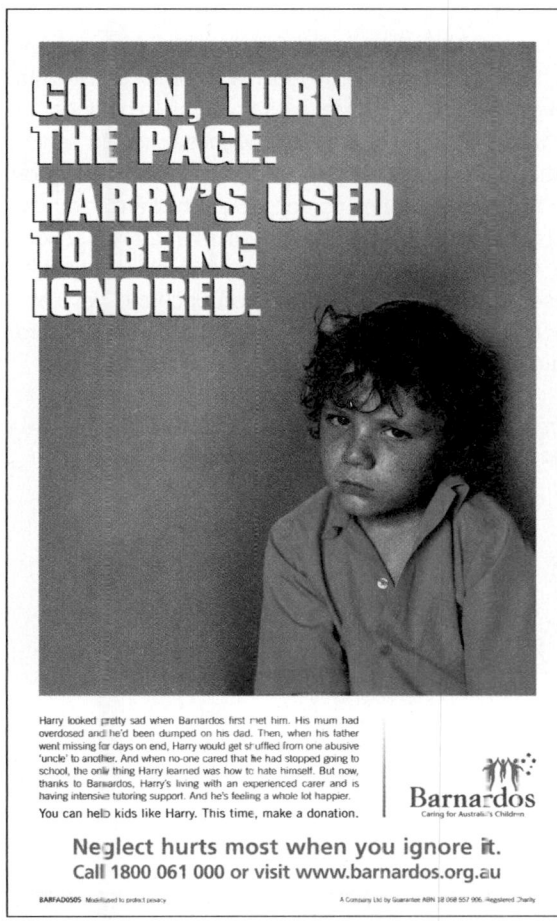

Not all children are lucky enough to grow up in a safe, loving family. These posters, sponsored by Barnardos, an Australian social service agency founded in 1921, call attention to the needs of abused and neglected children in Australia. But troubled families can be found everywhere in the world.

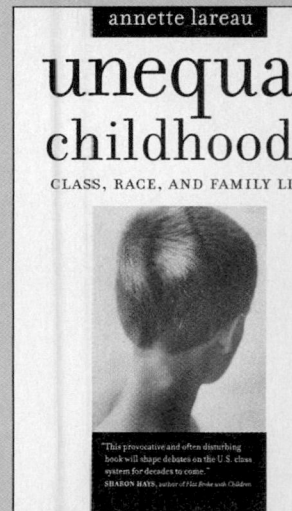

annette lareau

unequal childhoods

CLASS, RACE, AND FAMILY LIFE

"This provocative and often disturbing book will shape debates on the U.S. class system for decades to come."
SHARON HAYS, author of *Flat Broke with Children*

A Black fourth-grader, Alexander Williams, is riding home from a school open house. His mother is driving their beige, leather-upholstered Lexus. It is 9:00 P.M. on a Wednesday evening. Ms. Williams is tired from work and has a long Thursday ahead of her. She will get up at 4:45 A.M. to go out of town on business and will not return before 9:00 P.M. On Saturday morning, she will chauffeur Alexander to a private piano lesson at 8:15 A.M., which will be followed by a choir rehearsal and then a soccer game. As they ride in the dark, Alexander's mother, in a quiet voice, talks with her son, asking him questions and eliciting his opinions.

Discussions between parents and children are a hallmark of middle-class child rearing. Like many middle-class parents, Ms. Williams and her husband see themselves as "developing" Alexander to cultivate his talents in a concerted fashion. Organized activities, established and controlled by mothers and fathers, dominate the lives of middle-class children. . . . By making certain their children have these and other experiences, middle-class parents engage in a process of *concerted cultivation.* From this, a robust sense of entitlement takes root in the children. . . .

Only twenty minutes away, in blue-collar neighborhoods, and slightly farther away, in public housing projects, childhood looks different. Mr. Yanelli, a white working-class father, picks up his son Little Billy, a fourth-grader, from an after-school program. They come home and Mr. Yanelli drinks a beer while Little Billy first watches television, then rides his bike and plays in the street. Other nights, he and his Dad sit on the sidewalk outside their house and play cards. . . . Many nights Little Billy's uncle stops by, sometimes bringing Little Billy's youngest cousin. In the spring, Little Billy plays baseball on a local team. For Little Billy, baseball is his only organized activity outside of school during the entire year. . . .

Farther away, a Black fourth-grade boy, Harold McAllister, plays outside on a summer evening in the public housing project in which he lives. His two male cousins are there that night, as they often are. After an afternoon spent unsuccessfully searching for a ball so they could play basketball, the boys had resorted to watching sports on television. Now they head outdoors for a twilight water balloon fight. Harold tries to get his neighbor, Miss Lafifa, wet. People sit in white plastic lawn chairs outside the row of apartments. Music and television sounds waft through the open windows and doors.

The adults in the lives of Billy . . . and Harold want the best for them. Formidable economic constraints make it a major life task for these parents to put food on the table, arrange for housing, negotiate unsafe neighborhoods, take children to the doctor (often waiting for city buses that do not come), clean children's clothes, and get children to bed and have them ready for school the next morning. But unlike middle-class parents, these adults do not consider the concerted development of children, particularly through organized leisure activities, an essential aspect of good parenting.

(Lareau 2003:1–3) Additional information about this excerpt can be found on the Online Learning Center at www.mhhe.com/schaefer7. ●

> " *Like many middle-class parents, Ms. Williams and her husband see themselves as "developing" Alexander to cultivate his talents in a concerted fashion. Organized activities, established and controlled by mothers and fathers, dominate the lives of middle-class children. . . .* "

In this excerpt from *Unequal Childhoods: Class, Race, and Family Life,* Annette Lareau vividly illustrates how different types of stratification—class, race, gender, and age—define family life, molding the social relationships that develop among household members. Lareau, a sociologist who teaches at Temple University, based her book on the observation research she did in schools and homes. She also interviewed families from different social class backgrounds, both White and African American. Among these varied families, she found markedly different approaches to parenting—approaches, Lareau believes, that have much to do with their children's futures.

Just as stratification affects family life, so does the period in which a family lives. The family of today is not what it was a century ago, or even a generation ago. New roles, new gender distinctions, new child-rearing patterns have all combined to create new forms of family life. Today, for example, more and more women are taking the breadwinner's role, whether married or as a single parent. Blended families—the result of divorce and remarriage—are almost the norm. And many people are seeking intimate relationships outside marriage, whether it be in gay partnerships or in cohabiting arrangements.

This chapter addresses family and intimate relationships in the United States as well as other parts of the world. As we will see, family patterns differ from one culture to another, and even within the same culture. Despite the differences, however, the family is universal—found in every culture. A *family* can be defined as a set of people related by blood, marriage or some other agreed-upon relationship, or adoption, who share the primary responsibility for reproduction and caring for members of society.

What are families in different parts of the world like? How do people select their mates? When a marriage fails, how does the divorce affect the children? What are the alternatives to the nuclear family, and how prevalent are they? In this chapter we will look at the family and intimate relationships from the functionalist, conflict, and interactionist points of view. We'll examine variations in marital patterns and family life, including child rearing, paying particular attention to the increasing numbers of people in dual-income and single-parent families. We'll examine divorce in the United States, and consider diverse lifestyles such as cohabitation, lesbian and gay relationships, and marriage without children. In the Social Policy section we will confront the controversial issue of gay marriage. ●

Global View of the Family

Among Tibetans, a woman may be married simultaneously to more than one man, usually brothers. This system allows sons to share the limited amount of good land. Among the Betsileo of Madagascar, a man has multiple wives, each one living in a different village where he cultivates rice. Wherever he has the best rice field, that wife is considered his first or senior wife. Among the Yanomami of Brazil and Venezuela, it is considered proper to have sexual relations with your opposite-sex cousins if they are the children of your mother's brother or your father's sister. But if your opposite-sex cousins are the children of your mother's sister or your father's brother, the same practice is considered to be incest (Haviland et al. 2005; Kottak 2004).

As these examples illustrate, there are many variations in the family from culture to culture. Yet the family as a social institution exists in all cultures. Moreover, certain general principles concerning its composition, kinship patterns, and authority patterns are universal.

Composition: What Is the Family?

If we were to take our information on what a family is from what we see on television, we might come up with some very strange scenarios. The media don't always present a realistic view of the family. Moreover, many people still think of the family in very narrow terms—as a married couple and their unmarried children living together, like the family in the old *Cosby Show.* However, this is but one type of family, what sociologists refer to as a *nuclear family.* The term *nuclear family* is well chosen, since this type of family serves as the nucleus, or core, on which larger family groups are built.

Most people in the United States see the nuclear family as the preferred family arrangement. Yet by 2000, only about a third of the nation's family households fit this model. The proportion of households in the United States that is composed of married couples with children at home has decreased steadily over the last 40 years, and is expected to continue shrinking. At the same time, the number of single-parent households has increased (see Figure 12-1, page 294).

A family in which relatives—such as grandparents, aunts, or uncles—live in the same home as parents and their children is known as an *extended family.* Although not common, such living arrangements do exist in the United States. The structure of the extended family offers certain advantages over that of the nuclear family. Crises such as death, divorce, and illness put less strain on family members, since more people can provide assistance and emotional support. In addition, the extended family constitutes a larger economic unit than the nuclear family. If the

What Is a Family?

What makes a family? Not race, because families can be transracial. Not two generations, because families can be extended. Not the number or age of the members, because families can be big or small, young or old. Around the world, families may eat, dress, and worship differently, but all are united by a special intergenerational bond and an acknowledged responsibility to care for their kin.

German photographer Uwe Ommer (2000) took the photographs on this page and the next. For four years he traveled the world, visiting 130 countries on five continents in search of families who are typical of their societies. These three photographs, taken from Ommer's book *1000 Families,* only hint at the tremendous diversity of families around the world. The interracial family from Botswana (below) represents a departure from the norm in their society; in a country where politics is based on race, they feel they are outsiders. Still, their love for one another holds the family together. The thoroughly modern Syrian family (top right) has three children in college; of the three girls, one aspires to become a journalist, another an engineer, and the third a professional basketball player. The extended family from Armenia (bottom right) combines shoemaking, teaching, and farming to support three generations. Working with their hands and their heads, they are optimistic about the future and plan to have more children.

{Botswana}

{Syria}

{Armenia}

293

U.S. Households by Family Type, 1940–2010

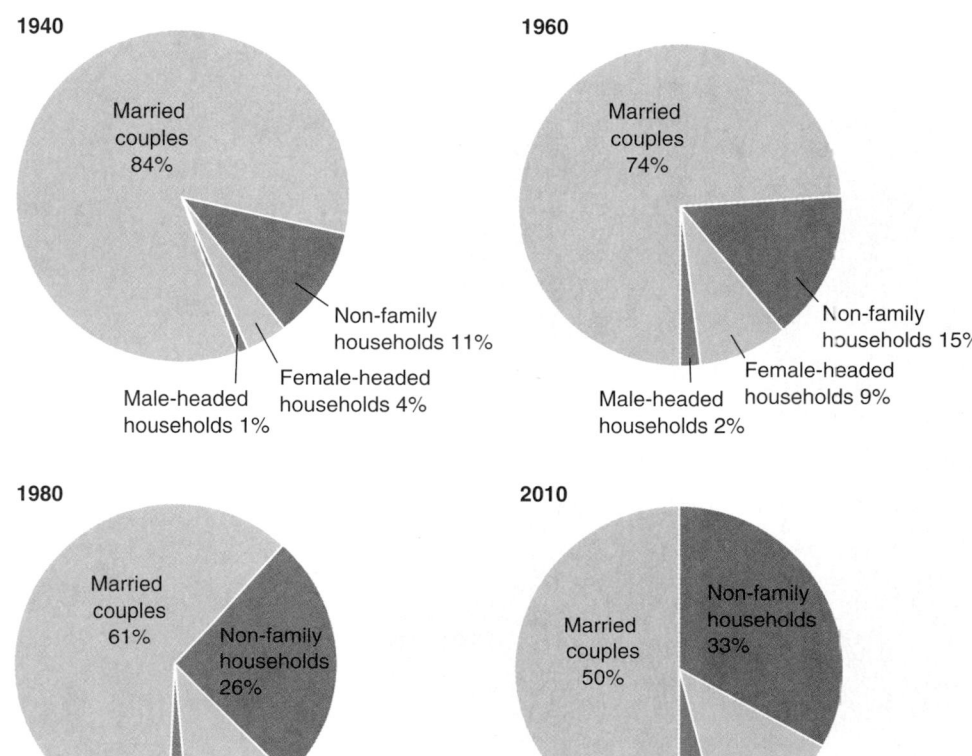

1940

Married couples 84%

Non-family households 11%

Female-headed households 4%

Male-headed households 1%

1960

Married couples 74%

Non-family households 15%

Female-headed households 9%

Male-headed households 2%

1980

Married couples 61%

Non-family households 26%

Female-headed households 11%

Male-headed households 2%

2010

Non-family households 33%

Married couples 50%

Female-headed households 13%

Male-headed households 4%

Note: Nonfamily households includes women and men living alone.

Source: Author's estimate based on Bureau of the Census 1996; Fields 2004; see also McFalls 2003:23.

family is engaged in a common enterprise—a farm or a small business—the additional family members may represent the difference between prosperity and failure.

In considering these different family types, we have limited ourselves to the form of marriage that is characteristic of the United States—monogamy. The term *monogamy* describes a form of marriage in which one woman and one man are married only to each other. Some observers, noting the high rate of divorce in the United States, have suggested that "serial monogamy" is a more accurate description of the form that marriage takes in this country. In *serial monogamy,* a person may have several spouses in his or her lifetime, but only one spouse at a time.

Some cultures allow an individual to have several husbands or wives simultaneously. This form of marriage is known as *polygamy.* In fact, most societies throughout the world, past and present, have preferred polygamy to monogamy. Anthropologist George Murdock (1949, 1957) sampled 565 societies and found that in more than 80 percent, some type of polygamy was the preferred form. While polygamy declined steadily through most

of the 20th century, in at least five countries in Africa 20 percent of men still have polygamous marriages (Population Reference Bureau 1996).

There are two basic types of polygamy. According to Murdock, the most common—endorsed by the majority of cultures he sampled—is *polygyny.* Polygyny refers to the marriage of a man to more than one woman at the same time. The wives are often sisters, who are expected to hold similar values and have already had experience sharing a household. In polygynous societies, relatively few men actually have multiple spouses. Most individuals live in monogamous families; having multiple wives is viewed as a mark of status.

The other principal variation of polygamy is *polyandry,* in which a woman may have more than one husband at the same time. Such is the case in the culture of the Todas of southern India. Polyandry, however, is exceedingly rare today. It has been accepted by some extremely poor societies that practice female infanticide (the killing of baby girls), and thus have a relatively small number of women. Like many other societies, polyandrous cultures devalue the social worth of women.

Kinship Patterns: To Whom Are We Related?

Many of us can trace our roots by looking at a family tree or by listening to elderly family members talk about their lives—and about the lives of ancestors who died long before we were born. Yet a person's lineage is more than simply a personal history; it also reflects societal patterns that govern descent. In every culture, children encounter relatives to whom they are expected to show an emotional attachment. The state of being related to others is called *kinship.* Kinship is culturally learned, however, and is not totally determined by biological or marital ties. For example, adoption creates a kinship tie that is legally acknowledged and socially accepted.

The family and the kin group are not necessarily one and the same. Whereas the family is a household unit, kin do not always live together or function as a collective body on a daily basis. Kin groups include aunts, uncles, cousins, in-laws, and so forth. In a society such as the United States, the kinship group may come together only rarely, for a wedding or funeral. However, kinship ties frequently create obligations and responsibilities. We may feel compelled to assist our kin, and we feel free to call upon them for many types of aid, including loans and babysitting.

How do we identify kinship groups? The principle of descent assigns people to kinship groups according to their relationship to a mother or father. There are three primary ways of determining descent. The United States follows the system of **bilateral descent,** which means that both sides of a person's family are regarded as equally important. For example, no higher value is given to the brothers of one's father than to the brothers of one's mother.

Most societies—according to George Murdock, 64 percent—give preference to one side of the family or the other in tracing descent. In **patrilineal** (from the Latin *pater,* "father") **descent,** only the father's relatives are significant in terms of property, inheritance, and emotional ties. Conversely, in societies that favor **matrilineal** (from the Latin *mater,* "mother") **descent,** only the mother's relatives are significant.

New forms of reproductive technology will necessitate a new way of looking at kinship. Today, a combination of biological and social processes can "create" a family member, requiring that more distinctions be made about who is related to whom.

Though spouses in an egalitarian family may not share all their decisions, they regard themselves as equals. This pattern of authority is becoming more common in the United States.

Authority Patterns: Who Rules?

Imagine that you have recently married and must begin to make decisions about the future of your new family. You and your spouse face many questions. Where will you live? How will you furnish your home? Who will do the cooking, the shopping, the cleaning? Whose friends will be invited to dinner? Each time a decision must be made, an issue is raised: Who has the power to make the decision? In simple terms, who rules the family? Conflict theorists examine these questions in the context of traditional gender stratification, under which men have held a dominant position over women. {p.266}

Societies vary in the way that power is distributed within the family. A society that expects males to dominate in all family decision making is termed a **patriarchy.** In patriarchal societies, such as Iran, the eldest male often wields the greatest power, although wives are expected to be treated with respect and kindness. A woman's status in Iran is typically defined by her relationship to a male relative, usually as a wife or daughter. In many patriarchal societies, women find it more difficult to obtain a divorce than a man does. In contrast, in a **matriarchy,** women have greater authority than men. Matriarchies, which are very uncommon, emerged among Native American tribal societies and in nations in which men were absent for long periods because of warfare or food-gathering expeditions (Farr 1999).

In a third type of authority pattern, the **egalitarian family,** spouses are regarded as equals. That does not mean, however, that all decisions are shared in such families. Wives may hold authority in some spheres, husbands in others. Many sociologists believe the egalitarian family has begun to replace the patriarchal family as the social norm in the United States.

Studying the Family

Do we really need the family? A century ago, Friedrich Engels ([1884] 1959), a colleague of Karl Marx, described the family as the ultimate source of social inequality because of its role in the transfer of power, property, and privilege. More recently, conflict theorists have argued that the family contributes to societal injustice, denies women opportunities that are extended to men, and limits freedom in sexual expression and mate selection. In contrast, the functionalist perspective focuses on the ways in which the family gratifies the needs of its members and contributes to social stability. The interactionist view considers the intimate, face-to-face relationships that occur in the family.

Functionalist View

The family performs six paramount functions, first outlined more than 65 years ago by sociologist William F. Ogburn (Ogburn and Tibbits 1934):

1. **Reproduction.** For a society to maintain itself, it must replace dying members. In this sense, the family contributes to human survival through its function of reproduction.

2. **Protection.** Unlike the young of other animal species, human infants need constant care and economic security. In all cultures, the family assumes the ultimate responsibility for the protection and upbringing of children.

3. **Socialization.** Parents and other kin monitor a child's behavior and transmit the norms, values, and language of their culture to the child.

4. **Regulation of sexual behavior.** Sexual norms are subject to change both over time (for instance, in the customs for dating) and across cultures (compare strict Saudi Arabia to the more permissive Denmark). However, whatever the time period or cultural values of a society, standards of sexual behavior are most clearly defined within the family circle.

5. **Affection and companionship.** Ideally, the family provides members with warm and intimate relationships, helping them to feel satisfied and secure. Of course, a family member may find such rewards outside the family—from peers, in school, at work—and may even perceive the home as an unpleasant or abusive setting. Nevertheless, we expect our relatives to understand us, to care for us, and to be there for us when we need them.

6. **Provision of social status.** We inherit a social position because of the family background and reputation of our parents and siblings. The family presents the newborn child with an ascribed status based on race and ethnicity that helps to determine his or her place within society's stratification system. Moreover, family resources affect children's ability to pursue certain opportunities, such as higher education and special lessons.

Traditionally, the family has fulfilled a number of other functions, such as providing religious training, education, and recreational outlets. But Ogburn argued that other social institutions have gradually assumed many of those functions. Education once took place at the family fireside; now it is the responsibility of professionals working in schools and colleges. Even the family's traditional recreational function has been transferred to outside groups such as Little Leagues, athletic clubs, and Internet chat rooms.

Conflict View

Conflict theorists view the family not as a contributor to social stability, but as a reflection of the inequality in wealth and power that is found within the larger society. Feminist and conflict theorists note that the family has traditionally legitimized and perpetuated male dominance. Throughout most of human history—and in a wide range of societies—husbands have exercised overwhelming power and authority within the family. Not until the first wave of contemporary feminism in the United States, in the mid-1800s, was there a substantial challenge to the { p.16 historic status of wives and children as the legal property of husbands.

While the egalitarian family has become a more common pattern in the United States in recent decades—owing in good

part to the activism of feminists beginning in the late 1960s and early 1970s—male dominance over the family has hardly disappeared. Sociologists have found that while married men are increasing their involvement in child care, their wives still perform a disproportionate amount of it. Furthermore, for every stay-at-home dad there are 38 stay-at-home moms (Fields 2004:11–12; Sayer et al. 2004). And unfortunately, many husbands reinforce their power and control over wives and children through acts of domestic violence. Box 12-1 (opposite) considers cross-cultural findings about violence within the home.

Conflict theorists also view the family as an economic unit that contributes to societal injustice. The family is the basis for transferring power, property, and privilege from one generation { pp.201–203 to the next. Although the United States is widely viewed as a land of opportunity, social mobility is restricted in important ways. Children inherit the privileged or less-than-privileged social and economic status of their parents (and in some cases, of earlier generations as well). As the chapter-opening excerpt showed, the social class of parents significantly influences children's socialization experiences and the degree of protection they receive. Thus, the socioeconomic status of a child's family will have a marked influence on his or her nutrition, health care, housing, educational opportunities, and in many respects, life chances as an adult. For this reason, conflict theorists argue that the family helps to maintain inequality.

Interactionist View

Interactionists focus on the micro level of family and other intimate relationships. They are interested in how individuals interact with one another, whether they are cohabiting partners or longtime married couples. For example, in a study of both Black and White two-parent households, researchers found that when fathers are more involved with their children (reading to them, helping them with homework, or restricting their television viewing), the children have fewer behavior problems, get along better with others, and are more responsible (Mosley and Thomson 1995).

Another interactionist study might examine the role of the stepparent. The increased number of single parents who remarry has sparked an interest in those who are helping to raise other people's children. Studies have found that stepmothers are more likely than stepfathers to accept the blame for bad relations with their stepchildren. Interactionists theorize that stepfathers (like most fathers) may simply be unaccustomed to interacting directly with children when the mother isn't there (Bray and Kelly 1999; Furstenberg and Cherlin 1991).

Feminist View

Because "women's work" has traditionally focused on family life, feminist sociologists have taken a strong interest in the family as a social institution. As we saw in Chapter 11, research on gender { p.272–273 roles in child care and household chores has been extensive. Sociologists have looked particularly closely at how women's work outside the home impacts their child care and

12-1 Domestic Violence

The phone rings two or three dozen times a day at the Friend of the Family Hotline in San Salvador, the capital city of El Salvador. Each time the staff receives a report of family violence, a crisis team is immediately dispatched to the caller's home. Caseworkers provide comfort to victims, as well as accumulate evidence for use in the attacker's prosecution. In the first three years of its existence, Friend of the Family handled over 28,000 cases of domestic violence.

Wife battering and other forms of domestic violence are not confined to El Salvador. Drawing on studies conducted throughout the world, we can make the following generalizations:

- Women are most at risk of violence from the men they know.
- Violence against women occurs in all socioeconomic groups.
- Family violence is at least as dangerous as assaults committed by strangers.
- Though women sometimes exhibit violent behavior toward men, the majority of violent acts that cause injury are perpetrated by men against women.
- Violence within intimate relationships tends to escalate over time.
- Emotional and psychological abuse can be at least as debilitating as physical abuse.
- Use of alcohol exacerbates family violence but does not cause it.

> *The family can be a dangerous place not only for women but also for children and the elderly.*

Using the conflict and feminist models, researchers have found that in relationships in which the inequality between men and women is great, the likelihood of assault on wives or domestic partners increases dramatically. This discovery suggests that much of the violence between intimates, even when sexual in nature, is about power rather than sex.

The family can be a dangerous place not only for women but also for children and the elderly. In 2000, public agencies in the United States received more than 3 million reports of child abuse and/or neglect. That means reports were filed on about 1 out of every 25 children. Another national study found that 1 million violent crimes a year are committed by current or former spouses, boyfriends, or girlfriends.

Let's Discuss

1. Why do you think victims of domestic violence find it difficult to seek assistance? How might they benefit from it?
2. Why might the degree of equality in a relationship correlate to the likelihood of domestic violence? How might conflict theorists explain this finding?

Sources: American Bar Association 1999; Cherlin et al. 2004; Garcia-Moreno et al. 2005; Spindel et al. 2000; Valde 1999.

Global View Domestic violence in San Salvador
Classroom Tip See "Steps to Prevent Domestic Violence" (Additional Lecture Ideas).
Theory Conflict and feminist views of family violence

housework—duties Arlie Hochschild (1989, 1990, 2005) has referred to as the "second shift." Today, researchers recognize that for many women, the second shift includes the care of aging parents as well.

Feminist theorists have urged social scientists and social agencies to rethink the notion that families in which no adult male is present are automatically a cause for concern, or even dysfunctional. They have also contributed to research on single women, single-parent households, and lesbian couples. In the case of single mothers, researchers have focused on the resiliency of many such households, despite economic stress. According to Velma McBride Murray and her colleagues (2001) at the University of Georgia, such studies show that among African Americans, single mothers draw heavily on kinfolk for material resources, parenting advice, and social support. Considering feminist research on the family as a whole, one researcher

> Interactionists are particularly interested in the ways in which mothers and fathers relate to each other and to their children. This mother and her two children are expressing a close and loving relationship, one of the foundations of a strong family.

concluded that the family is the "source of women's strength" (L. Richardson et al. 2004).

Finally, feminists who take the interactionist perspective stress the need to investigate neglected topics in family studies. For instance, in a small but significant number of dual-income households, the wife earns a higher income than the husband. Sociologist Suzanne Bianchi estimates that in 11 percent of marriages, the wife earns at least 60 percent of the family's income. Yet beyond individual case studies, little research has been done on how these families may differ from those in which the husband is the major breadwinner (Tyre and McGinn 2003:47).

Table 12-1 summarizes the four major theoretical perspectives on the family.

Marriage and Family

Currently, over 95 percent of all men and women in the United States marry at least once during their lifetimes. Historically, the most consistent aspect of family life in this country has been the high rate of marriage. In fact, despite the high rate of divorce, there are some indications of a miniboom in marriages of late.

In this part of the chapter, we will examine various aspects of love, marriage, and parenthood in the United States and contrast them with cross-cultural examples. Though we're used to thinking of romance and mate selection as strictly a matter of individual preference, sociological analysis tells us that social institutions and distinctive cultural norms and values also play an important role.

Courtship and Mate Selection

"My rugby mates would roll over in their graves," says Tom Buckley of his online courtship and subsequent marriage to Terri Muir. But Tom and Terri are hardly alone these days in turning to the Internet for matchmaking services. A generation or two ago, most couples met in high school or college, but now that people are marrying later in life, the Internet has become the new meeting place for the romantically inclined. Today, thousands of Web sites offer to help people find mates. A 2005 survey found that 12 percent of couples who visited an online

wedding site had met online. Success stories like these notwithstanding, online dating services are only as good as the people who use them. Subscribers' personal profiles—the basis for potential matches—often contain false or misleading information (Kapos 2005; B. Morris 1999:D1).

Internet romance is only the latest courtship practice. In the central Asian nation of Uzbekistan and many other traditional cultures, courtship is defined largely through the interaction of two sets of parents, who arrange marriages for their children. Typically, a young Uzbekistani woman will be socialized to eagerly anticipate her marriage to a man whom she has met only once, when he is presented to her family at the time of the final inspection of her dowry. In the United States, by contrast, courtship is conducted primarily by individuals who have a romantic interest in each other. In our culture, courtship often requires these individuals to rely heavily on intricate games, gestures, and signals. Despite such differences, courtship—whether in the United States, Uzbekistan, or elsewhere—is influenced by the norms and values of the larger society (C. J. Williams 1995).

One unmistakable trend in mate selection is that the process appears to be taking longer today than in the past. A variety of factors, including concerns about financial security and personal independence, has contributed to this delay in marriage. Most people are now well into their 20s before they marry, both in the United States and in other countries (see Figure 12-2).

Aspects of Mate Selection   Many societies have explicit or unstated rules that define potential mates as acceptable or unacceptable. These norms can be distinguished in terms of endogamy and exogamy. **Endogamy** (from the Greek *endon*, "within") specifies the groups within which a spouse must be found, and prohibits marriage with others. For example, in the United States, many people are expected to marry within their own racial, ethnic, or religious group, and are strongly discouraged or even prohibited from marrying outside the group. Endogamy is intended to reinforce the cohesiveness of the group by suggesting to the young that they should marry someone "of their own kind."

In contrast, **exogamy** (from the Greek *exo*, "outside") requires mate selection outside certain groups, usually one's own family or certain kinfolk. The **incest taboo,** a social norm common to virtually all societies, prohibits sexual relationships between certain culturally specified relatives. For those of us in the United States, this taboo means that we must marry outside the nuclear family. We cannot marry our siblings, and in most states we cannot marry our first cousins.

Endogamous restrictions may be seen as preferences for one group over another. In the United States, such preferences are most obvious in racial barriers. Until the 1960s, some states outlawed interracial marriage. Nevertheless, the number of marriages between African Americans and Whites in the

Table 12-1   Sociological Perspectives on the Family

Theoretical Perspective	Emphasis
Functionalist	The family as a contributor to social stability Roles of family members
Conflict	The family as a perpetuator of inequality Transmission of poverty or wealth across generations
Interactionist	Relationships among family members
Feminist	The family as a perpetuator of gender roles Female-headed households

FIGURE 12–2

Percentage of People Ages 20 to 24 Ever Married, Selected Countries

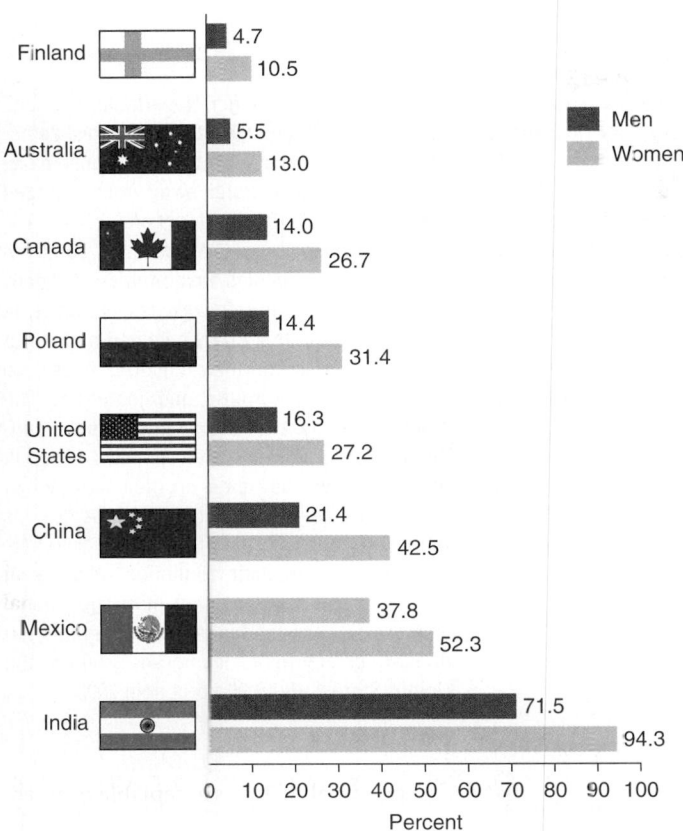

Country	Men	Women
Finland	4.7	10.5
Australia	5.5	13.0
Canada	14.0	26.7
Poland	14.4	31.4
United States	16.3	27.2
China	21.4	42.5
Mexico	37.8	52.3
India	71.5	94.3

Percent

Source: United Nations Population Division 2005.

Think About It
Why is the percentage of young women who are married particularly high in India, Mexico, and China? Particularly low in Finland and Australia?

Interracial unions, which are becoming increasingly common and accepted, are blurring definitions of race. Would the children of this interracial couple be considered Black or White?

United States has increased more than seven times in recent decades, jumping from 51,000 in 1960 to 413,000 in 2004. Moreover, 25 percent of married Asian American women and 12 percent of married Asian American men are married to a person who is not of Asian descent. Marriage across ethnic lines is even greater among Hispanics; 27 percent of all married Hispanics have a non-Hispanic spouse. But while all these examples of racial exogamy are noteworthy, endogamy is still the social norm in the United States (Bureau of the Census 1998, 2004a:48).

Another factor that influences the selection of a marriage partner is *homogamy,* the conscious or unconscious tendency to select a mate with personal characteristics similar to one's own. The "like marries like" rule can be seen in couples with similar personalities and cultural interests. However, mate selection is unpredictable. Though some people may follow the homogamous pattern, others observe the rule that opposites attract: One person is dependent and submissive—almost childishly so—while the other is dominant and controlling.

Recently, the concept of homogamy has been incorporated into the process of seeking a date or marital partner online. The Internet dating site eHarmony, which claims to be the first to use a "scientific approach" to matching people based on a variety of abilities and interests, says that it "facilitates" 46 marriages a day. Sociologist Pepper Schwartz, who works as a consultant for the competing site PerfectMatch.com, has developed a 48-question survey that covers everything from prospective mates' decision-making style to their degree of impulsivity (Gottlieb 2006).

The Love Relationship   Today's generation of college students seems more likely to "hook up" or cruise in large packs than to engage in the romantic dating relationships of their parents and grandparents. Still, at some point in their adult lives, the great majority of today's students will meet someone they love and enter into a long-term relationship that focuses on creating a family.

Parents in the United States tend to value love highly as a rationale for marriage, so they encourage their children to develop intimate relationships based on love and affection. Songs, films, books, magazines, television shows, and even cartoons and comic books reinforce the theme of love. At the same time, our society expects parents and peers to help a person confine his or

Global View Percentage of people ages 20 to 24 ever married in selected countries
Race/Ethnicity Interracial marriage in the United States
Let's Discuss What significance does the rise in interracial marriages have for the social construction of race (discussed in Chapter 10)?
Classroom Tip See "Homogamy" (Class Discussion Topics).

Contemporary Culture Love relationships on college campuses today
Reel Society See Intimate Relationships in the Topic Index.

research IN action

12-2 Arranged Marriage, American-Style

Leona Singh, a 25-year-old Californian, met her future mate, from Iowa, through her father. The two were introduced at a relative's home and later went out alone. Several months later, when they felt "90 percent certain" that their relationship would be a good one, the two Indian Americans married. Years later Leona looked back. "From the beginning, I felt there was a physical chemistry, but it took years to develop a mature bond, and I guess you could call that love" (Bellafante 2005:A15).

For many young people like Leona, the question is not "Does he or she love me?" but "Whom do my parents want me to marry?" In an *arranged marriage,* parents or matchmakers choose a marital partner for a young person based on considerations other than mutual attraction. Typically, couples whose marriages have been arranged don't even know each other. They are assumed to be compatible, however, since they have been carefully chosen to share the same social, economic, and cultural background.

The idea of an arranged marriage seems strange to Western youths, who are brought up expecting to find Mr. or Ms. Right on their own—often through "love at first sight." But this romanticized approach to courtship has its drawbacks. In a romantic or sentimental marriage, a couple starts off on high ground, in love and dreaming about their hopes (or illusions) for the future. When some of their dreams fail to materialize after marriage, there is little likelihood that their relationship will improve, and a great danger of failure. In an arranged marriage, by contrast, a couple starts off on neutral ground, without unrealistic ex-

pectations. They then work to achieve the marital happiness they have been led to expect from their union. Mutual understanding develops as their relationship matures.

Historically, arranged marriages have not been unusual; even today they are common in many parts of Asia and Africa. In cultures in which arranged marriage is the norm, young people are socialized to expect and desire such unions. But what happens in cultures that send a very different message to youths? In the United States and Canada, for example, immigrants from countries such as India, Pakistan, and Bangladesh may want to arrange their children's marriages. Their sons and daugh-

> *In cultures in which arranged marriage is the norm, young people are socialized to expect and desire such unions.*

ters, however, are growing up in a culture in which their schoolmates are obsessed with dating as a prelude to marriage. They listen as their friends engage in endless discussions of the latest episode of *Bachelor* or *Bachelorette.*

Studies of these young people, whose parents still cling to the tradition of arranging their children's marriages, document the challenges they face. Many of them do still embrace their parents' traditions. As one Princeton student of Indian ancestry put it, "In a lot of ways it's easier. I don't have pressure to look for a boyfriend" (Herschthal 2004). These youths will look to their parents and other relatives to find a mate, and may even accept a partner selected from their

parents' country of origin. Nevertheless, though systematic, nationwide studies of this demographic group are lacking, the available research points to a trend away from arranged marriage, despite family objections.

In response to cultural pressure, some Indian immigrant families have replaced formally arranged marriage with *assisted marriage,* in which the parents identify a limited number of potential mates for their children based on caste, family background, and geography. The children can then choose a mate from the candidates approved by their parents. Though these children may date on their own, when the time comes to marry they limit themselves to the very narrow field approved by their parents. Because of their continued reliance on arranged and now assisted marriage, Indian immigrants have the highest rate of ethnic endogamy of any major immigrant group in the United States: about 90 percent in 2003.

Let's Discuss

1. Can you, under any circumstances, imagine yourself accepting an arranged marriage? Take a poll of your classmates to see how many agree with you. Can you see an ethnic difference in the responses?
2. For Indian Americans as a group rather than as individuals, what might be some long-term benefits of arranged marriage? Might those benefits give them an advantage over other ethnic groups?

Sources: Bellafante 2005; Herschtha 2004; Talbani and Hasanau 2000; Zaidi and Shuraydi 2002.

---

her search for a mate to "socially acceptable" members of the opposite sex.

Though most people in the United States take the importance of falling in love for granted, the coupling of love and marriage is by no means a cultural universal. Many of the world's cultures give priority in mate selection to factors other than romantic feelings. In societies with *arranged marriages* engineered by parents or religious authorities, economic considerations play a significant role. The newly married couple is expected to develop a feeling of love *after* the legal union is formalized, if at all. Box

12-2 describes the marriages that some immigrants to the United States arrange for their children.

In some societies, neither the parents nor the bride has a say in whom she marries. Since at least the 12th century, men in the central Asian nation of Kyrgyzstan have literally kidnapped their future wives from the street in a custom known as *ala kachuu,* which translates roughly as "grab and run." In its most benign form, this custom is a kind of elopement in which the man wisks off his girlfriend. Men do it to avoid the "bride price" that parents often demand in return for their consent. But as of 2005,

Let's Discuss How does "starting off on high ground" lead to marital problems later? **Theory** Explore possible conflict, functionalist, and feminist views of arranged marriage.
Global View Arranged marriage in Asia and Africa

Contemporary Culture How would American youths respond to arranged marriages?
Web Resource The Use Your Sociological Imagination component in the student center of the Online Learning Center (**www.mhhe.com/schaefer7**) asks students how they would respond if their parents selected mates for them.

one-third of the brides in Kyrgyzstan had been abducted against their will. Many of them—perhaps 80 percent—eventually assent to the kidnapping, often at their parents' urging. For these women, romantic love does not precede marriage, though love may well develop over time (Craig Smith 2005).

Use Your Sociological Imagination

Your parents and/or a matchmaker are going to arrange a marriage for you. What kind of mate will they select? Will your chances of having a successful marriage be better or worse than if you selected your own mate?

Variations in Family Life and Intimate Relationships

Within the United States, social class, race, and ethnicity create variations in family life. Studying these variations will give us a more sophisticated understanding of contemporary family styles in our country.

Social Class Differences Various studies have documented the differences in family organization among social classes in the United States. In the upper class, the emphasis is on lineage and maintenance of family position. If you are in the upper class, you are not simply a member of a nuclear family, but rather a member of a larger family tradition (think of the Rockefellers or the Kennedys). As a result, upper-class families are quite concerned about what they see as proper training for children.

Lower-class families do not often have the luxury of worrying about the "family name"; they must first struggle to pay their bills and survive the crises often associated with a life of poverty. Such families are more likely to have only one parent at home, which creates special challenges in child care and financial management. Children from lower-class families typically assume adult responsibilities—including marriage and parenthood—at an earlier age than children from affluent homes. In part, that is because they may lack the money needed to remain in school.

Social class differences in family life are less striking today than they once were. In the past, family specialists agreed that the contrasts in child-rearing practices were pronounced. Lower-class families were found to be more authoritarian in rearing children and more inclined to use physical punishment. Middle-class families were more permissive and more restrained in punishing their children. However, these differences may have narrowed as more and more families from all social classes turned to the same books, magazines, and even television talk shows for advice on rearing children (Kohn 1970; Luster et al. 1989).

Among the poor, women often play a significant role in the economic support of the family. Men may earn low wages, may be unemployed, or may be entirely absent from the family. In 2003, 28 percent of all families headed by women with no hus-

band present were below the government poverty line. The rate for married couples was only 5.5 percent (DeNavas-Walt et al. 2005:10).

Many racial and ethnic groups appear to have distinctive family characteristics. However, racial and class factors are often closely related. In examining family life among racial and ethnic minorities, keep in mind that certain patterns may result from class as well as cultural factors.

Racial and Ethnic Differences The subordinate status of racial and ethnic minorities in the United States profoundly affects their family lives. For example, the lower incomes of African Americans, Native Americans, most Hispanic groups, and selected Asian American groups make creating and maintaining successful marital unions a difficult task. The economic restructuring of the last 50 years, described by sociologist {p.199} William Julius Wilson (1996) and others, has especially affected people living in inner cities and desolate rural areas, such as reservations. Furthermore, the immigration policy of the United States has complicated the successful relocation of intact families from Asia and Latin America.

The African American family suffers from many negative and inaccurate stereotypes. It is true that in a significantly higher proportion of Black than White families, no husband is present in the home (see Figure 12-3, page 302). Yet Black single mothers often belong to stable, functioning kin networks, which mitigate the pressures of sexism and racism. Members of these networks—predominantly female kin such as mothers, grandmothers, and aunts—ease financial strains by sharing goods and services. In addition to these strong kinship bonds, Black family life has emphasized deep religious commitment and high aspirations for achievement (Sarkisian and Gerstel 2004).

Like African Americans, Native Americans draw on family ties to cushion many of the hardships they face. On the Navajo reservation, for example, teenage parenthood is not regarded as the crisis that it is elsewhere in the United States. The Navajo trace their descent matrilineally. Traditionally, couples reside with the wife's family after marriage, allowing the grandparents to help with the child rearing. While the Navajo do not approve of teenage parenthood, the deep emotional commitment of their extended families provides a warm home environment for fatherless children (Dalla and Gamble 2001).

Sociologists also have taken note of differences in family patterns among other racial and ethnic groups. For example, Mexican American men have been described as exhibiting a sense of virility, personal worth, and pride in their maleness that is called **machismo.** Mexican Americans are also described as being more familistic than many other subcultures. **Familism** refers to pride in the extended family, expressed through the maintenance of close ties and strong obligations to kinfolk outside the immediate family. Traditionally, Mexican Americans have placed proximity to their extended families above other needs and desires.

These family patterns are changing, however, in response to changes in Latinos' social class standing, educational achievements, and occupations. Like other Americans, career-oriented

Classroom Tip See "Families in Poverty" (Class Discussion Topics).

Theory Conflict view of how African American, Native American, and immigrant families have been disrupted due to their subordinate status
Theory Interactionist view of social networks in Black and Navajo families
Gender Machismo among Mexican American men

The Family and Intimate Relationships

Latinos in search of a mate but short on spare time are turning to Internet sites. As Latinos and other groups assimilate into the dominant culture of the United States, their family lives take on both the positive and negative characteristics associated with White households (Becerra 1999; Vega 1995).

Child-Rearing Patterns in Family Life

The Nayars of southern India acknowledge the biological role of fathers, but the mother's eldest brother is responsible for her children. In contrast, uncles play only a peripheral role in child care in the United States. Caring for children is a universal function of the family, yet the ways in which different societies assign this function to family members can vary significantly. Even within the United States, child-rearing patterns are varied. We'll take a look here at parenthood and grandparenthood, adoption, dual-income families, single-parent families, and stepfamilies.

Parenthood and Grandparenthood The socialization of children is essential to the maintenance of any culture. Consequently, parenthood is one of the most important (and most demanding) social roles in the United States. Sociologist Alice Rossi (1968, 1984) has identified four factors that complicate the {p.88} transition to parenthood and the role of socialization. First, there is little anticipatory socialization for the social role of caregiver. The normal school curriculum gives scant attention to the subjects most relevant to successful family life, such as child care and home maintenance. Second, only limited learning occurs during the period of pregnancy itself. Third, the transition to parenthood is quite abrupt. Unlike adolescence, it is not prolonged; unlike the transition to work, the duties of caregiving cannot be taken on gradually. Finally, in Rossi's view, our society lacks clear and helpful guidelines for successful parenthood. There is little consensus on how parents can produce happy and well-adjusted offspring—or even on what it means to be well-adjusted. For these reasons, socialization for parenthood involves difficult challenges for most men and women in the United States.

One recent development in family life in the United States has been the extension of parenthood, as adult children continue to live at home or return home after college. In 2003, 55 percent of men and 46 percent of women ages 18 to 24 lived with their parents. Some of these adult children were still pursuing an education, but in many instances, financial difficulties lay at the heart of these living arrangements. While rents and real estate prices have skyrocketed, salaries for younger workers have not kept pace, and many find themselves unable to afford their own homes. Moreover, with many marriages now ending in divorce—most commonly in the first seven years of marriage—divorced sons and daughters often return to live with their parents, sometimes with their own children (Fields 2004:16).

Is this living arrangement a positive development for family members? Social scientists have just begun to examine the phenomenon, sometimes called the "boomerang generation" or the "full-nest syndrome" in the popular press. One survey in Vir-

FIGURE 12–3

Rise of Single-Parent Families in the United States, 1970–2000

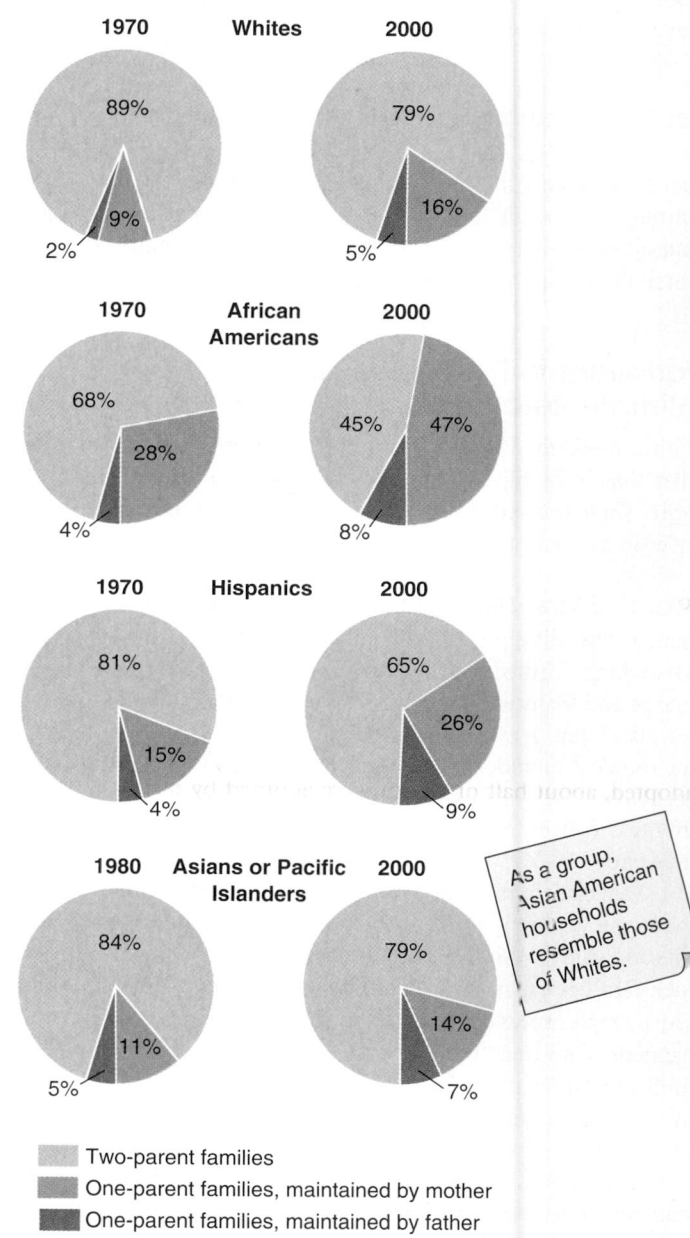

Two-parent families

One-parent families, maintained by mother

One-parent families, maintained by father

Note: "Children" refers to children under 18. Not included are unrelated people living together with no children present. Early data for Asian Americans are for 1980.
Source: Bureau of the Census 1994:63; Fields 2001:7.

ginia seemed to show that neither the parents nor their adult children were happy about continuing to live together. The children often felt resentful and isolated, but the parents suffered too: Learning to live without children in the home is an essential stage of adult life, and may even be a significant turning point for a marriage (*Berkeley Wellness Letter* 1990; Mogelonsky 1996).

In some homes, the full nest holds grandchildren. In 2002, 5.6 million children, or 8 percent of all children in the United States,

Race/Ethnicity Use of Internet sites by career-oriented Latinos in search of mates
Global View Family life among the Nayars of southern India
Student Alert Review the concept of anticipatory socialization

Contemporary Culture 2002 survey data showed that 5.6 million children lived with a grandparent.

lived in a household with a grandparent. In about a third of these homes, no parent was present to assume responsibility for the youngsters. Special difficulties are inherent in such relationships, including legal custodial concerns, financial issues, and emotional problems for adults and youths alike. Little surprise that support groups such as Grandparents as Parents have emerged to provide assistance (Fields 2003; H. Park 2005).

Adoption   In a legal sense, *adoption* is a "process that allows for the transfer of the legal rights, responsibilities, and privileges of parenthood" to a new legal parent or parents (E. Cole 1985:638). In many cases, these rights are transferred from a biological parent or parents (often called birth parents) to an adoptive parent or parents.

Viewed from a functionalist perspective, government has a strong interest in encouraging adoption. Policymakers, in fact, have both a humanitarian and a financial stake in the process. In theory, adoption offers a stable family environment for children who otherwise might not receive satisfactory care. Moreover, government data show that unwed mothers who keep their babies tend to be of lower socioeconomic status, and often require public assistance to support their children. The government can lower its social welfare expenses, then, if children are transferred to economically self-sufficient families. From an interactionist perspective, however, adoption may require a child to adjust to a very different family environment and parental approach to child rearing.

About 4 percent of all people in the United States are adopted, about half of whom were adopted by persons not related to them at birth. There are two legal methods of adopting an unrelated person: the adoption may be arranged through a licensed agency, or in some states it may be arranged through a private agreement sanctioned by the courts. Adopted children may come from the United States or from abroad. In 2005 more than 22,000 children entered the United States as the adopted children of U.S. citizens (Department of State 2006).

In some cases the adopters are not married. In 1995, an important court decision in New York held that a couple does not need to be married to adopt a child. Under this ruling, unmarried heterosexual couples, lesbian couples, and gay male couples can all legally adopt children in New York. Writing for the majority, Chief Justice Judith Kaye argued that by expanding the boundaries of who can be legally recognized as parents, the state may be able to assist more children in securing "the best possible home." With this ruling, New York became the third state (after Vermont and Massachusetts) to recognize the right of unmarried couples to adopt children (Dao 1995).

For every child who is adopted, many more remain the wards of state-sponsored child protective services. At any given time, over half a million children in the United States are living in foster care. About 113,000 of these children are eligible for adoption (Koch 2006).

Dual-Income Families   The idea of a family consisting of a wage-earning husband and a wife who stays at home has largely given way to the dual-income household. Among married people between the ages of 25 and 34, 96 percent of the men and 68 percent of the women were in the labor force in 2004.

Why has there been such a rise in the number of dual-income couples? A major factor is economic need. In 2004 the median income for households with both partners employed was 91 percent more than in households in which only one person was working outside the home ($68,892 compared to $36,149). Of course, because of such work-related costs as child care, not all of a family's second wage is genuine additional income. Other factors that have contributed to the rise of the dual-income model include the nation's declining birthrate, the increase in the proportion of women with a college education, the shift in the economy of the United States from manufacturing to service industries, and the impact of the feminist movement in changing women's consciousness (Bureau of the Census 2005a:393; DeNavas-Walt et al. 2005:HINC-01 table).

Single-Parent Families   *American Idol* winner Fantasia Barrino's song "Baby Mama" offers a tribute to young single

When nine-year-old Blake Brunson shows up for a basketball game, so do his *eight* grandparents—the result of his parents' remarriage. Blended families can be very supportive to children, but what message do they send to them on the permanency of marriage?

Let's Discuss In what ways are the concepts of resocialization, social roles, role exit, and rites of passage relevant in discussing grandparenthood?
Theory Functionalist approach to government's interest in encouraging adoption
Contemporary Culture In New York in 1995, a court decision held that a couple does not need to be married to adopt a child.

mothers—a subject she knows about. Barrino was 17 when she became pregnant with her now three-year-old daughter. Though critics charged that the song sends the wrong message to teenage girls, Barrino says it is not about encouraging teens to have sex. Rather, she sees the song as an anthem for young mothers courageously trying to raise their children alone (Blair 2005).

In recent decades, the stigma attached to unwed mothers and other single parents has significantly diminished. *Single-parent families,* in which only one parent is present to care for the children, can hardly be viewed as a rarity in the United States. In 2000, a single parent headed about 21 percent of White families with children under 18, 35 percent of Hispanic families with children, and 55 percent of African American families with children (see Figure 12-3 on page 302).

The lives of single parents and their children are not inevitably more difficult than life in a traditional nuclear family. It is as inaccurate to assume that a single-parent family is necessarily deprived as it is to assume that a two-parent family is always secure and happy. Nevertheless, life in a single-parent family can be extremely stressful, in both economic and emotional terms. A family headed by a single mother faces especially difficult problems when the mother is a teenager.

Why might low-income teenage women wish to have children and face the obvious financial difficulties of motherhood? Viewed from an interactionist perspective, these women tend to have low self-esteem and limited options; a child may provide a sense of motivation and purpose for a teenager whose economic worth in our society is limited at best. Given the barriers that many young women face because of their gender, race, ethnicity, and class, many teenagers may believe they have little to lose and much to gain by having a child.

According to a widely held stereotype, "unwed mothers" and "babies having babies" in the United States are predominantly African American. However, this view is not entirely accurate. African Americans account for a disproportionate share of births to unmarried women and teenagers, but the majority of all babies born to unmarried teenage mothers are born to White adolescents. Moreover, since 1980, birthrates among Black teenagers have declined steadily (B. Hamilton et al. 2005; J. Martin et al. 2005).

Although 82 percent of single parents in the United States are mothers, the number of households headed by single fathers more than quadrupled over the period 1980 to 2000. Though single mothers often develop social networks, single fathers are typically more isolated. In addition, they must deal with schools and social service agencies that are more accustomed to women as custodial parents (Fields 2004).

Stepfamilies Approximately 45 percent of all people in the United States will marry, divorce, and then remarry. The rising rates of divorce and remarriage have led to a noticeable increase in stepfamily relationships.

The exact nature of blended families has social significance for adults and children alike. Certainly resocialization is required when an adult becomes a stepparent or a child becomes a stepchild and stepsibling. Moreover, an important distinction

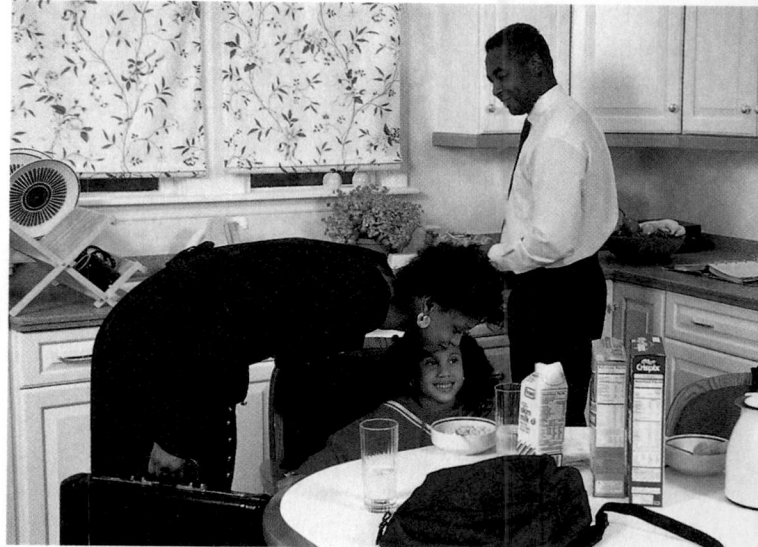

Dad takes breakfast duty while Mom rushes off to work in this dual-income family. An increasing proportion of couples in the United States rejects the traditional nuclear family model of husband as breadwinner and wife as homemaker.

must be made between first-time stepfamilies and households where there have been repeated divorces, breakups, or changes in custodial arrangements.

In evaluating the rise of stepfamilies, some observers have assumed that children would benefit from remarriage because they would be gaining a second custodial parent, and would potentially enjoy greater economic security. However, after reviewing many studies of stepfamilies, sociologist Andrew J. Cherlin (2005:455) concluded that "the well-being of children in stepfamilies is no better, on average, than the well-being of children in divorced, single-parent households."

Stepparents can play valuable and unique roles in their stepchildren's lives, but their involvement does not guarantee an

Most households in the United States do not consist of two parents living with their unmarried children.

FIGURE 12–4

305

The Family and Intimate Relationships

Trends in Marriage and Divorce in the United States, 1920–2004

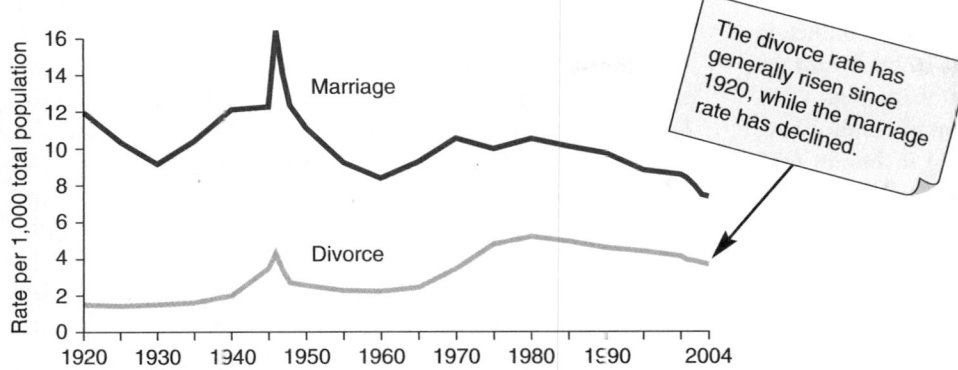

The divorce rate has generally risen since 1920, while the marriage rate has declined.

Sources: Bureau of the Census 1975:64; *National Vital Statistics Reports* 2005.

improvement in family life. In fact, standards may decline. Studies suggest that children raised in families with stepmothers are likely to have less health care, education, and money spent on their food than children raised by biological mothers. The measures are also negative for children raised by stepfathers, but only half as negative as in the case of stepmothers. These results don't mean that stepmothers are "evil"—it may be that the stepmother holds back out of concern for seeming too intrusive, or relies mistakenly on the biological father to carry out parental duties (Lewin 2000).

Divorce

"Do you promise to love, honor, and cherish . . . until death do you part?" Every year, people of all social classes and racial and ethnic groups make this legally binding agreement. Yet increasing numbers of these promises shatter in divorce.

Statistical Trends in Divorce

Just how common is divorce? Surprisingly, this is not a simple question; divorce statistics are difficult to interpret. The media frequently report that one out of every two marriages ends in divorce. But that figure is misleading, since many marriages last for decades. It is based on a comparison of all divorces that occur in a single year (regardless of when the couples were married) with the number of new marriages in the same year.

In the United States and many other countries, divorce began to increase in the late 1960s but then leveled off; since the late 1980s, it has declined by 25 percent (see Figure 12-4). This trend is due partly to the aging of the baby boomer population and the corresponding decline in the proportion of people of marriageable age. But it also indicates an increase in marital stability in recent years (Coontz 2006).

Getting divorced obviously does not sour people on marriage. About 63 percent of all divorcees in the United States have remar-

ried. Women are less likely than men to remarry because many retain custody of their children after a divorce, which complicates a new adult relationship (Bianchi and Spain 1996; Saad 2004).

Some people regard the nation's high rate of remarriage as an endorsement of the institution of marriage, but it does lead to the new challenges of a kin network composed of both current and prior marital relationships. Such networks can be particularly complex if children are involved or if an ex-spouse remarries.

Factors Associated with Divorce

Perhaps the most important factor in the increase in divorce over the last hundred years has been the greater social *acceptance* of divorce. It's no longer considered necessary to endure an unhappy marriage. More important, various religious denominations have relaxed their negative attitudes toward divorce, so that most religious leaders no longer treat it as a sin.

The growing acceptance of divorce is a worldwide phenomenon. Only a decade ago, Sunoo, South Korea's foremost matchmaking service, had no divorced clients. Few Koreans divorced; those who did felt social pressure to resign themselves to the single life. But over the last seven years, South Korea's divorce rate has doubled. Today, 15 percent of Sunoo's membership is divorced (Onishi 2003).

In the United States, several factors have contributed to the growing social acceptance of divorce:

- Most states have adopted more liberal divorce laws in the last three decades. No-fault divorce laws, which allow a couple to end their marriage without fault on either side (by specifying adultery, for instance), accounted for an initial surge in the divorce rate after they were introduced in the 1970s, but appear to have had little effect beyond that.

- Divorce has become a more practical option in newly formed families, since families tend to have fewer children now than in the past.

- A general increase in family incomes, coupled with the availability of free legal aid to some poor people, has meant that more couples can afford costly divorce proceedings.

- As society provides greater opportunities for women, more and more wives are becoming less dependent on their husbands, both economically and emotionally. They may feel more able to leave a marriage if it seems hopeless.

Impact of Divorce on Children

Divorce is traumatic for all involved, but it has special meaning for the more than 1 million children whose parents divorce each year (see Box 12-3, page 307). Of course, for some of these

Student Alert Be sure students understand why it is misleading to say that one out of every two marriages ends in divorce.

Theory Interactionist analysis of kin networks after a divorce
Classroom Tip See "Inheriting Divorce" (Additional Lecture Ideas).
Classroom Tip See "Speakers" (Class Discussion Topics).
Global View Attitude toward divorce in South Korea

children, divorce signals the welcome end to a very dysfunctional relationship. A national sample conducted by sociologists Paul R. Amato and Alan Booth (1997) showed that in about a third of divorces, the children benefit from parental separation because it lessens their exposure to conflict. But in about 70 percent of divorces, the parents engaged in a low level of conflict; in those cases, the realities of divorce appeared to be harder for the children to bear than living with the marital unhappiness.

Other researchers, using differing definitions of conflict, have found greater unhappiness for children living in homes with marital differences. Still, it would be simplistic to assume that children are automatically better off following the breakup of their parents' marriage. The interests of the parents do not necessarily serve children well.

Use Your Sociological Imagination
www.mhhe.com/schaefer7

In a society that maximizes the welfare of all family members, how easy should it be for couples to divorce? How easy should it be to get married?

Diverse Lifestyles

Marriage is no longer the presumed route from adolescence to adulthood. In fact, it has lost much of its social significance as a rite of passage. The nation's marriage rate has declined since 1960 because people are postponing marriage until later in life, and because more couples, including same-sex couples, are deciding to form partnerships without marriage.

Cohabitation

In the United States, testing the marital waters by living together before making a commitment is a common practice among marriage-wary 20- and 30-somethings. The tremendous increase in the number of male–female couples who choose to live together without marrying, a practice called *cohabitation,* is one of the most dramatic trends of recent years.

About half of all *currently* married couples in the United States say that they lived together before marriage. This percentage is likely to increase. The number of unmarried-couple households in the United States rose sixfold in the 1960s and increased another 72 percent between 1990 and 2000. Presently over 8

percent of opposite-sex couples are unmarried. Cohabitation is more common among African Americans and American Indians than among other racial and ethnic groups; it is least common among Asian Americans. Figure 12-5 (below) shows regional variations in cohabitation (Peterson 2003; T. Simmons and O'Connell 2003).

In much of Europe, cohabitation is so common that the general sentiment seems to be "Love, yes; marriage, maybe." In Iceland, 62 percent of all children are born to single mothers; in France, Great Britain, and Norway, the proportion is about 40 percent. Government policies in these countries make few legal distinctions between married and unmarried couples or households (Lyall 2002).

People commonly associate cohabitation only with college campuses or sexual experimentation. But according to a study done in Los Angeles, working couples are almost twice as likely to cohabit as college students. And census data show that in 2003, 45 percent of unmarried couples had one or more children present in the household. These cohabitants are more like spouses than dating partners. Moreover, in contrast to the common perception that people who cohabit have never been married, researchers report that about half of all people involved in cohabitation in the United States have been previously married. Cohabitation serves

FIGURE 12–5

Unmarried-Couple Households by State

MAPPING LIFE

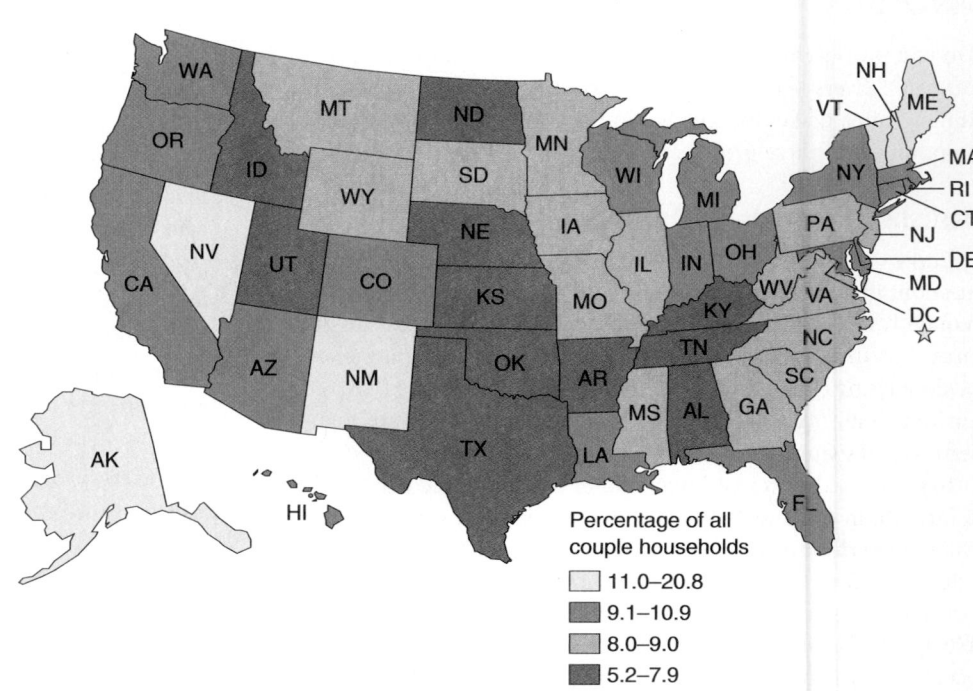

NATIONWIDE   www.mhhe.com/schaefer7

Percentage of all couple households

☐ 11.0–20.8
▨ 9.1–10.9
▨ 8.0–9.0
■ 5.2–7.9

Note: Data are for 2000 and include both opposite-sex and same-sex partners. U.S. average is 9.1 percent.
Source: T. Simmons and O'Connell 2003:4.

research IN action

12-3 The Lingering Impact of Divorce

What happens to the children of divorce? Early research suggested that the negative effects of divorce on children were confined to the first few years following a breakup. According to these studies, most children eventually adjusted to the change in family structure and went on to live normal lives. But recent studies suggest that the effects of divorce may linger much longer than scholars at first suspected, peaking in the adult years, when grown children are attempting to establish their own marriages and families.

A foremost proponent of this view is psychologist Judith A. Wallerstein, who has been conducting qualitative research on the effects of divorce on children since 1971. Wallerstein has been following the original 131 children in her study for 30 years; her subjects are now ages 28 to 43. She is convinced that these adult children of divorce have had greater difficulty than other adults in forming and maintaining intimate relationships because they have never witnessed the daily give-and-take of a successful marital partnership.

Another researcher, sociologist Paul R. Amato, agrees that divorce can affect children into adulthood, but for a different reason. Amato thinks that the parents' decision to end their marriage lies at the root of the higher-than-normal divorce rate among their children. In this study, based on telephone interviews, children whose parents had divorced had a 30 percent divorce rate themselves, which is 12 to 13 percent higher than the divorce rate among children whose parents had *not* divorced. Significantly, children of parents who did not divorce had roughly the same divorce rate regardless of whether the level of conflict in their parents' marriage was low or high. The parental example that a marriage contract can be broken—not the demonstration of poor relationship skills—is what makes an adult child more vulnerable than others to divorce, Amato thinks.

Sociologist Andrew J. Cherlin concedes that divorce can have lingering effects, but thinks the potential for harm has been exaggerated. Cherlin, who has conducted quantitative analyses of the effects of divorce on thousands of children, finds that parental divorce does elevate children's risk of emotional problems, school withdrawal, and teen pregnancy. But most children, he emphasizes, do not develop those problems. Even Wallerstein admits that the ill effects of divorce do not apply across the board. Some children seem to be strengthened by the crisis, she observes, and go on to lead highly successful lives, both personally and professionally.

> *Recent studies suggest that the effects of divorce may linger much longer than scholars at first suspected.*

Let's Discuss

1. Do you know any adult children of divorce who have had difficulty establishing successful marriages? If so, what seems to be the problem, an inability to handle conflict or a lack of commitment to the marriage?
2. What practical conclusions should we draw from the research on children of divorce? Should couples stay together for the sake of their children?

Sources: Amato 2001; Amato and Sobolewski 2001; Bumiller 2000; Cherlin 2005; Marquardt 2005; J. Wallerstein et al. 2000. For a different view, see Hetherington and Kelly 2002.

---

as a temporary or permanent alternative to matrimony for many men and women who have experienced their own or their parents' divorces (Fields 2004; Popenoe and Whitehead 1999).

Periodically, legislators attempt to bolster the desirability of a lifelong commitment to marriage. In 2002, President George W. Bush backed funding for an initiative to promote marriage among those who receive public assistance. Under the "Healthy Marriage Initiative," married couples would receive special monthly bonuses not available to others. The proposal garnered widespread support, though it drew some opposition from defenders of single-parent families. The debate became more heated when activists succeeded in legalizing gay marriage in Massachusetts: see the Social Policy section at the end of this chapter (S. Brown 2005; Cherlin 2003).

Remaining Single

Looking at TV programs today, you would be justified in thinking that most households are composed of singles. Although that is not the case, it is true that more and more people in the United States are *postponing* entry into a first marriage. Over one out of three households with children in the United States is a single-parent household. Even so, fewer than 4 percent of women and men in the United States are likely to remain single throughout their lives (Bureau of the Census 2004a:49–50; Edin and Kefalas 2005).

The trend toward maintaining a single lifestyle for a longer period is related to the growing economic independence of young people. This trend is especially significant for women. Freed from financial needs, women don't necessarily need to { p.271 } marry to enjoy a satisfying life. Divorce, late marriage, and longevity also figure into this trend.

There are many reasons why a person may choose not to marry. Some singles do not want to limit their sexual intimacy to one lifetime partner. Some men and women do not want to become highly dependent on any one person—and do not want anyone depending heavily on them. In a society that values individuality and self-fulfillment, the single lifestyle can offer certain freedoms that married couples may not enjoy.

Key Persons Judith A. Wallerstein, Paul Amato, Andrew Cherlin
Methods Wallerstein's research was qualitative.
Methods Amato's study was based on telephone interviews.
Methods Cherlin's study was quantitative.
Methods Survey data on cohabitation in the United States and other countries
Let's Discuss Why is data on cohabitation harder to obtain than data on marriage?

Gender Greater options for women in the labor force remove financial pressures to marry.

Remaining single represents a clear departure from societal expectations; indeed, it has been likened to "being single on Noah's Ark." A single adult must confront the inaccurate view that he or she is always lonely, is a workaholic, or is immature. These stereotypes help to support the traditional assumption in the United States and most other societies that to be truly happy and fulfilled, a person must get married and raise a family. To counter these societal expectations, singles have formed numerous support groups, such as Alternative to Marriage Project (www.unmarried.org).

Marriage without Children

There has been a modest increase in childlessness in the United States. According to census data, about 16 to 17 percent of women will now complete their childbearing years without having borne any children, compared to 10 percent in 1980. As many as 20 percent of women in their 30s expect to remain childless (Clausen 2002).

Childlessness within marriage has generally been viewed as a problem that can be solved through such means as adoption and artificial insemination. More and more couples today, however, choose not to have children, and regard themselves as child-free rather than childless. They do not believe that having children automatically follows from marriage, nor do they feel that reproduction is the duty of all married couples. Childless couples have formed support groups (with names like No Kidding) and set up Web sites (K. Park 2005; Terry 2000).

Economic considerations have contributed to this shift in attitudes; having children has become quite expensive. According to a government estimate made for 2004, the average middle-class family will spend $184,320 to feed, clothe, and shelter a child from birth to age 18. If the child attends college, that amount could double, depending on the college chosen. Aware of the financial pressures, some couples are having fewer children than they otherwise might, and others are weighing the advantages of a child-free marriage (Lino 2005).

Childless couples are beginning to question current practices in the workplace. While applauding employers' efforts to provide {p.94 child care and flexible work schedules, some nevertheless express concern about tolerance of employees who leave early to take children to doctors, ballgames, or after-school classes. As more dual-career couples enter the paid labor force and struggle to balance career and familial responsibilities, conflicts with employees who have no children may increase (Burkett 2000).

Use Your Sociological Imagination www.mhhe.com /schaefer7

What would happen to our society if many more married couples suddenly decided not to have children? How would society change if cohabitation and/or singlehood became the norm?

Lesbian and Gay Relationships

Twenty-one-year-old Parke, a junior in college, grew up in a stable, loving family. A self-described fiscal conservative, he credits his parents with instilling in him a strong work ethic. Sound like an average child of an average family? The only break with traditional expectations in this case is that Parke is the son of a lesbian couple (P. L. Brown 2004).

The lifestyles of lesbians and gay men are varied. Some live in long-term, monogamous relationships; others live alone or with roommates. Some remain in "empty-shell" heterosexual marriages and do not publicly acknowledge their homosexuality. Others live with children from a former marriage or with adopted children. Based on election exit polls, researchers for the National Health and Social Life Survey and the Voter News Service estimate that 2 to 5 percent of the adult population identify themselves as either gay or lesbian. An analysis of the 2000 census shows a minimum of at least 600,000 gay households, and a gay and lesbian adult population approaching 10 million (Laumann et al. 1994b:293; David M. Smith and Gates 2001).

Gay and lesbian couples face discrimination on both a personal and a legal level. Their inability to marry denies them many rights that married couples take for granted, from the ability to make decisions for an incapacitated partner to the right to receive government benefits to dependents, such as Social Security payments. Though gay couples consider themselves families, just like the ones who live down the street, they are often treated as if they are not.

Precisely because of such inequities, many gay and lesbian couples are now demanding the right to marry. In the Social Policy section that follows, we will examine the highly controversial issue of gay marriage.

Theory/Classroom Tip Indicate how interactionists and functionalists would comment on the formation of support groups among singles.
Contemporary Culture Having children has become quite expensive.

Methods The NHSLS study was an example of survey research; the census findings on gay households also relied on survey research.
Methods Use of census data to determine occurrence of gay and lesbian couples in the United States
Classroom Tip See "Joint Marriage Rights" (Additional Lecture Ideas).
Classroom Tip See "Families in the Future" (Class Discussion Topics).

Gay Marriage

The Issue

In the United States, attitudes toward marriage are complex. As always, society and popular culture suggest that a young man or woman should find the perfect mate, settle down and marry, and live "happily ever after." But young people are also bombarded by messages implying the frequency of adultery and the acceptability of divorce. In this atmosphere, the idea of same-sex marriage strikes some people as only the latest of many attacks on traditional marriage. To others, it seems an overdue acknowledgment of the formal relationships that faithful, monogamous gay couples have long maintained.

The Setting

In 2004, in his State of the Union message, President George W. Bush warned "activist judges" against attempts to broaden the definition of marriage to include same-sex couples. The only recourse to such measures, he said, would be a constitutional amendment banning same-sex unions.

What made gay marriage the focus of national attention? Events in two states brought the issue to the forefront. In 1999, Vermont gave gay couples the legal benefits of marriage through civil union, but stopped short of calling the arrangement a marriage. Then, in 2003, the Massachusetts Supreme Court ruled 4–3 that under the state's constitution, gay couples have the right to marry—a ruling the U.S. Supreme Court has refused to review.

Sociological Insights

Functionalists have traditionally seen marriage as a social institution that is closely tied to human reproduction. Same-sex marriage would at first appear not to fit that arrangement. But many same-sex couples are entrusted with the socialization of young children, whether or not their relationship is recognized by the state. Functionalists also wonder whether religious views toward marriage can be ignored. The courts have focused on civil marriage, but religious views are hardly irrelevant, even in a country like the United States, which observes a separation between religion and the state. Indeed, religious teachings have led even some staunch supporters of gay rights to oppose same-sex marriage on spiritual grounds.

Conflict theorists have charged that denial of the right to marry reinforces the second-class status of gays and lesbians. Some have compared the ban against gay marriage to past policies that until 1967 banned interracial marriage in 32 states (Liptak 2004a).

Interactionists generally avoid the policy question and focus instead on the nature of same-sex households. They ask many of the same questions about gay partner relations and child rearing that they raise about conventional couples. Of course, much less research has been done on same-sex households than on other families, but the studies published to date raise the same issues as those that apply to conventional married couples, plus a few more. For gay couples, the support or opposition of family, co-workers, and friends looms large (Dundas and Kaufman 2000; Dunne 2000).

Recently, national surveys of attitudes toward gay marriage have been showing volatile shifts in public opinion. Typically, people are more opposed to gay marriage than to civil union: about one-fourth of respondents favor legal recognition of gay marriage, while as many as half favor civil union. Still, as of 2005, the majority of the population endorsed a constitutional amendment to ban gay marriage (Saad 2005).

Policy Initiatives

The United States is not the first nation to consider this issue. Recognition of same-sex partnerships is not uncommon in Europe, including Belgium, Denmark, France, Germany, Great Britain, Italy, the Netherlands, Portugal, and Spain. Today, as many as 8 percent of all marriages in the Netherlands are same-sex. The trend is toward recognition in North America as well, since gay couples can marry legally in Canada.

Many nations strongly oppose such measures, however. For example, when Kofi Annan, secretary general of the United Nations (UN), proposed extending the benefits that married UN employees receive to employees' same-sex partners in 2004, so many countries rose in protest that he reneged. Annan decided that such benefits would extend only to those UN employees whose member nations extend the same benefits to their citizens (Cowell 2005; Farley 2004; Wines 2005).

In the United States, many local jurisdictions have passed legislation allowing for the registration of domestic partnerships, and have extended employee benefits to those relationships. Under such policies, a *domestic partnership* may be defined as two unrelated adults who share a mutually caring relationship, reside together, and agree to be jointly responsible for their dependents, basic living expenses, and other common necessities. Domestic partnership benefits can apply to couples' inheritance, parenting, pensions, taxation, housing, immigration, workplace fringe benefits, and health care. Even though the most passionate support for domestic partnership legislation has come from lesbian and gay male activists, the majority of those eligible for such benefits would be cohabiting heterosexual couples.

In the United States, marriage has traditionally been under the jurisdiction of state lawmakers. But recently, pressure has been

---

Theory Interactionist view of same-sex households
Gender How might gay marriage impact men and women differently?
Contemporary Culture What are the costs and benefits to gay couples of being married?

Let's Discuss Do you favor or oppose a ban on same-sex marriages?
Classroom Tip See "Housework within Lesbian and Gay Households" (Additional Lecture Ideas).
Methods Survey of public opinion on same-sex marriage
Global View Policies on same-sex partnerships in Europe
Let's Discuss How does a domestic partnership differ from a marriage?

310 mounting for national legislation. The Defense of Marriage Act, passed in 1996, provided that no state is obliged to recognize same-sex marriages performed in another state. However, some legal scholars doubt that the law could withstand a constitutional challenge, since it violates a provision in the Constitution that requires states to recognize one another's laws. In 2003, therefore, opponents of gay marriage proposed a constitutional amendment that would limit marriage to heterosexual couples. The measure was introduced in the Senate in 2004, but failed to receive sufficient support to come to a vote.

In the meantime, as Figure 12-6 shows, some states have moved to ban same-sex marriage, though they still prohibit discrimination against gays and lesbians. And though local jurisdictions such as the mayor's office in San Francisco may perform marriage ceremonies amid great publicity, the marriage certificates they confer on gay couples are of dubious legality.

Let's Discuss

1. If marriage is good for heterosexual couples and their families, why isn't it good for homosexual couples and their families?

2. How can interactionist studies of gay couples and their families inform policymakers who are dealing with the issue of gay marriage? Give a specific example.

FIGURE 12–6

Discriminatory Marriage and Anti–Gay Discrimination Laws

MAPPING LIFE

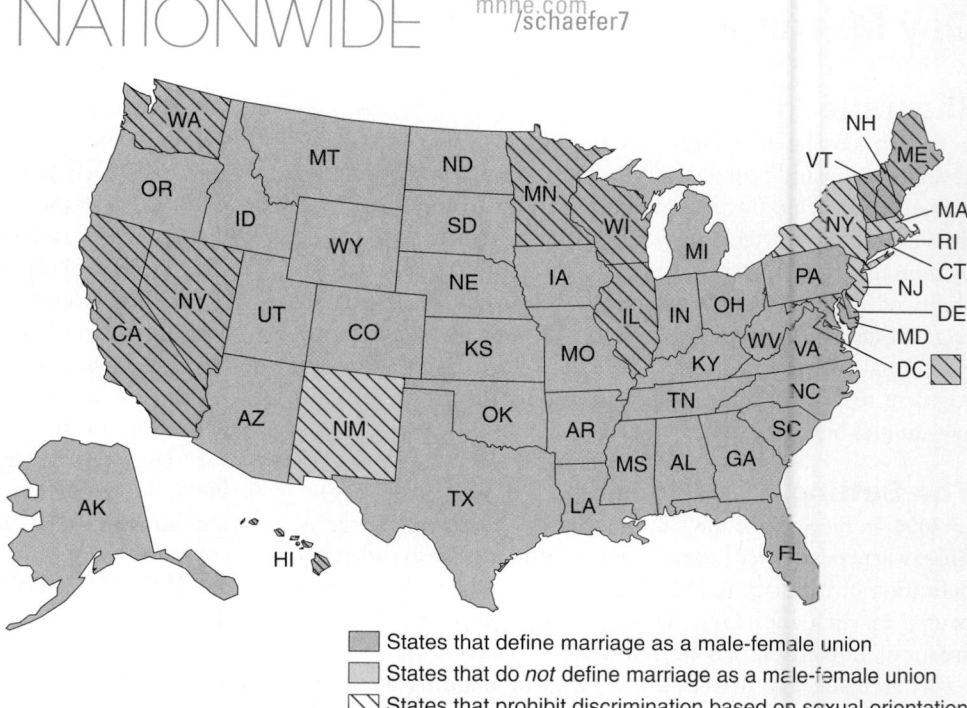

NATIONWIDE www.mhhe.com/schaefer7

■ States that define marriage as a male-female union
■ States that do *not* define marriage as a male-female union
▨ States that prohibit discrimination based on sexual orientation

Note: Current as of March 2006. Vermont prohibits same-sex marriage but provides for same-sex civil union.
Source: Human Rights Campaign 2006.

3. Who are the stakeholders in the debate over gay marriage, and what do they stand to gain or lose? Whose interest do you think is most important?

GettingINVOLVED

To get involved in the debate over gay marriage, visit this text's Online Learning Center, which offers links to relevant Web sites. Check out the Social Policy section in the Online Learning Center as well; it provides survey data on U.S. public opinion regarding this issue.

www.mhhe.com/schaefer7

{ MASTERING THIS CHAPTER }

Summary

The *family,* in its many varying forms, is present in all human cultures. This chapter examines the state of marriage, the family, and other intimate relationships in the United States and considers alternatives to the traditional *nuclear family.*

Let's Discuss How is the concept of dominant ideology relevant in examining the controversy over domestic partnerships?
Classroom Tip See "Using Humor" (Class Discussion Topics).
Classroom Tip In reviewing this chapter, ask students to take another look at the photo essay in Chapter 6.

1. *Families* vary from culture to culture and even within the same culture.
2. The structure of the *extended family* can offer certain advantages over that of the *nuclear family.*

3. Societies determine **kinship** by descent from both parents **(bilateral descent),** from the father only **(patrilineal descent),** or from the mother only **(matrilineal descent).**

4. Sociologists do not agree on whether the **egalitarian family** has replaced the patriarchal family as the social norm in the United States.

5. William F. Ogburn outlined six basic functions of the family: reproduction, protection, socialization, regulation of sexual behavior, companionship, and the provision of social status.

6. Conflict theorists argue that male dominance of the family contributes to societal injustice and denies women opportunities that are extended to men.

7. Interactionists focus on how individuals interact in the family and in other intimate relationships.

8. Feminists stress the need to broaden research on the family. Like conflict theorists, they see the family's role in socializing children as the primary source of sexism.

9. People select mates in a variety of ways. Some marriages are arranged; in other societies people choose their own mates. Some societies require mates to be chosen within a certain group **(endogamy)** or outside certain groups **(exogamy).** And consciously or unconsciously, many people look for a mate with similar personal characteristics **(homogamy).**

10. In the United States, family life varies with social class, race, and ethnicity.

11. Currently, in the majority of all married couples in the United States, both husband and wife work outside the home.

12. **Single-parent families** account for an increasing proportion of U.S. families.

13. Among the factors that contribute to the rising divorce rate in the United States are greater social acceptance of divorce and the liberalization of divorce laws in many states.

14. More and more people are living together without marrying, a practice known as **cohabitation.** People are also staying single longer, and some married couples are deciding not to have children.

15. The gay marriage movement, which would confer equal rights on gay and lesbian couples and their dependents, is strongly opposed by conservative religious and political groups.

Critical Thinking Questions

1. In an increasing proportion of couples in the United States, both partners work outside the home. What are the advantages and disadvantages of the dual-income model for women, for men, for children, and for society as a whole?

2. Consider the foster care system in the United States. Given the fact that so many children in the United States need caring homes, why do so many couples seek to adopt foreign children? Why do state agencies often deny same-sex couples the right to adopt? What can be done to improve the foster care system?

3. Given the high rate of divorce in the United States, would it be more appropriate to view divorce as dysfunctional or as a normal part of our marriage system? What would be the implications of viewing divorce as normal rather than dysfunctional?

Key Terms

Adoption In a legal sense, a process that allows for the transfer of the legal rights, responsibilities, and privileges of parenthood to a new legal parent or parents. (page 303)

Bilateral descent A kinship system in which both sides of a person's family are regarded as equally important. (295)

Cohabitation The practice of living together as a male–female couple without marrying. (306)

Domestic partnership Two unrelated adults who share a mutually caring relationship, reside together, and agree to be jointly responsible for their dependents, basic living expenses, and other common necessities. (309)

Egalitarian family An authority pattern in which spouses are regarded as equals. (295)

Endogamy The restriction of mate selection to people within the same group. (298)

Exogamy The requirement that people select a mate outside certain groups. (298)

Extended family A family in which relatives—such as grandparents, aunts, or uncles—live in the same home as parents and their children. (291)

Familism Pride in the extended family, expressed through the maintenance of close ties and strong obligations to kinfolk outside the immediate family. (301)

Family A set of people related by blood, marriage or some other agreed-upon relationship, or adoption, who share the primary responsibility for reproduction and caring for members of society. (291)

Homogamy The conscious or unconscious tendency to select a mate with personal characteristics similar to one's own. (299)

Incest taboo The prohibition of sexual relationships between certain culturally specified relatives. (298)

Kinship The state of being related to others. (294)

Machismo A sense of virility, personal worth, and pride in one's maleness. (301)

Matriarchy A society in which women dominate in family decision making. (295)

Matrilineal descent A kinship system in which only the mother's relatives are significant. (295)

Monogamy A form of marriage in which one woman and one man are married only to each other. (294)

Nuclear family A married couple and their unmarried children living together. (291)

Patriarchy A society in which men dominate in family decision making. (295)

Patrilineal descent A kinship system in which only the father's relatives are significant. (295)

Polyandry A form of polygamy in which a woman may have more than one husband at the same time. (294)

Polygamy A form of marriage in which an individual may have several husbands or wives simultaneously. (294)

Polygyny A form of polygamy in which a man may have more than one wife at the same time. (294)

Serial monogamy A form of marriage in which a person may have several spouses in his or her lifetime, but only one spouse at a time. (294)

Single-parent family A family in which only one parent is present to care for the children. (304)

Self-Quiz

Read each question carefully and then select the best answer.

1. Alice, age seven, lives in a private home with her parents, her grandmother, and her aunt. Alice's family is an example of a(n)
   a. nuclear family.
   b. dysfunctional family.
   c. extended family.
   d. polygynous family.

2. In which form of marriage may a person have several spouses in his or her lifetime, but only one spouse at a time?
   a. serial monogamy
   b. monogamy
   c. polygamy
   d. polyandry

3. The marriage of a woman to more than one man at the same time is referred to as
   a. polygyny.
   b. monogamy.
   c. serial monogamy.
   d. polyandry.

4. Which system of descent is followed in the United States?
   a. matrilineal
   b. patrilineal
   c. bilateral
   d. unilateral

5. According to the functionalist perspective, which of the following is *not* one of the paramount functions performed by the family?
   a. mediation
   b. reproduction
   c. regulation of sexual behavior
   d. affection and companionship

6. Which norm requires mate selection outside certain groups, usually one's own family or certain kinfolk?
   a. exogamy
   b. endogamy
   c. matriarchy
   d. patriarchy

7. According to the text's discussion of social class differences in family life and intimate relationships, which of the following statements is true?
   a. Social class differences in family life are more striking than they once were.
   b. The upper class emphasizes lineage and maintenance of family position.
   c. Among the poor, women usually play an insignificant role in the economic support of the family.
   d. In examining family life among racial and ethnic minorities, most patterns result from cultural, but *not* class, factors.

8. One recent development in family life in the United States has been the extension of parenthood as adult children continue to live at home or return home after college. The reason for this is
   a. the rising divorce rate.
   b. skyrocketing rent and real estate prices.
   c. financial difficulties.
   d. all of the above.

9. In the United States, the *majority* of all babies born to unmarried teenage mothers are born to whom?
   a. African American adolescents
   b. White adolescents
   c. Latina adolescents
   d. Asian American adolescents

10. Which of the following factors is associated with the high divorce rate in the United States?
    a. the liberalization of divorce laws
    b. the fact that contemporary families have fewer children than earlier families did
    c. the general increase in family incomes
    d. all of the above

11. The principle of _____ assigns people to kinship groups according to their relationship to an individual's mother or father.

12. _____ emerged among Native American tribal societies, and in nations in which men were absent for long periods because of warfare or food-gathering expeditions.

13. In the view of many sociologists, the _____ family has begun to replace the patriarchal family as the social norm in the United States.

14. As _____ theorists point out, the social class of couples and their children significantly influences the socialization experiences to which the children are exposed, and the protection they receive.

15. _____ focus on the micro level of family and other intimate relationships; for example, they are interested in whether people are cohabiting partners or are longtime married couples.

16. The rule of _____ specifies the groups within which a spouse must be found, and prohibits marriage with others.

17. Social class differences in family life are less striking today than they once were; however, in the past, _____-class families were found to be more authoritarian in rearing children and more inclined to use physical punishment.

18. Caring for children is a(n) _____ function of the family, yet the ways in which different societies assign this function to family members can vary significantly.

19. Viewed from the _____ perspective, the government has a strong interest in encouraging adoption.

20. The rising rates of divorce and remarriage have led to a noticeable increase in _____ relationships.

Answers:
1 (c); 2 (a); 3 (d); 4 (c); 5 (a); 6 (a); 7 (b); 8 (d); 9 (b); 10 (d)
11 descent; 12 Matriarchies; 13 egalitarian; 14 conflict; 15 interactions; 16 endogamy; 17 lower; 18 universal; 19 functionalist; 20 stepfamily

{ TECHNOLOGY RESOURCES }

Online Learning Center

1. Visit the student center of the Online Learning Center at **www.mhhe.com/schaefer7,** and link to "Audio Clips." Listen to Richard Schaefer, the author of this text, discuss how chat rooms are playing the role that singles' bars did in the 1980s. Professor Schaefer notes that sociologists are trying to determine whether the Internet is restructuring dating behavior or merely facilitating it.

2. More and more U.S. families include two income earners. In such households, spouses must find a way to balance their work and family obligations and accommodate each other's career needs. The Employment and Family Careers Institute at Cornell University is devoted to the study of dual-career families. Explore the institute's site (**www.lifecourse.cornell.edu/cci/default.html**) to learn more about this social trend.

3. U.S. families have undergone rapid change over the past few decades. To read about the latest trends, go to the Census Bureau's Web site (**www.census.gov**). Under Subjects A to Z, click on "Families/Households and Families Data."

Note: While all the URLs listed were current as of the printing of this book, these sites often change. Please check our Web site (**www.mhhe.com/schaefer7**) for updates, hyperlinks, and exercises related to these sites.

Reel Society Video Clips

Reel Society video clips, which appear on this book's Web site, can be used to spark discussion about the following topics from this chapter:
- Authority Patterns
- Studying the Family
- Marriage and Family
- Diverse Lifestyles

13

Religion and Education

inside

Durkheim and the Sociological Approach to Religion

World Religions

Sociological Explanations of Religion

Components of Religion

Religious Organization

Case Study: Religion in India

Sociological Perspectives on Education

Schools as Formal Organizations

Social Policy and Religion: Religion in the Schools

Boxes

Research in Action: Income and Education, Religiously Speaking

Research in Action: Islam in the United States

Sociology on Campus: The Debate over Title IX

In this billboard, Volkswagen of France compares a secular event, the introduction of a new model ("Rejoice, my friends, for a new Golf is born"), to a sacred event. While such tongue-in-cheek references to religion may offend believers, they indicate the continuing relevance of religion, even in modern, industrialized societies.

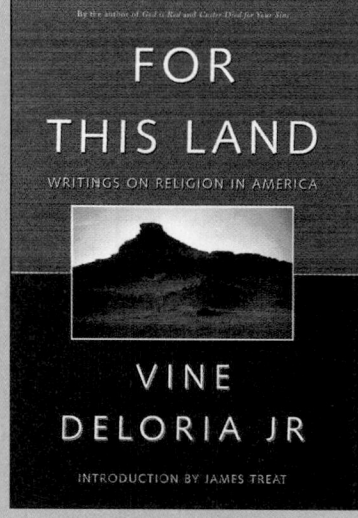

Growing up in a small mixed-blood community of seven hundred on the eastern edge of the Pine Ridge Reservation in South Dakota, I uncritically accepted the idea that the old Dakota religion and Christianity were both "true" and in some mysterious way compatible with each other. There were, to be sure, Christian fundamentalists with their intolerance and the old traditional Indians who kept their practices hidden, but the vast majority of the people in the vicinity more or less assumed that a satisfactory blend had been achieved that guaranteed our happiness.

Although my father was an Episcopal priest with a large number of chapels in a loosely organized Episcopal missionary district known (to Episcopalians) as "Corn Creek," he was far from an orthodox follower of the white man's religion. I always had the feeling that within the large context of "religion," which in a border town meant the Christian milieu, there was a special area in his spiritual life in which the old Dakota beliefs and practices reigned supreme. He knew thirty-three songs; some of them social, some ancient, and several spiritual songs used in a variety of ceremonial contexts. Driving to his chapels to hold Christian services he would open the window of the car and beat the side of the door with his hand for the drum beat and sing song after song. . . .

When I went to college I was exposed to a much larger canvas of human experience upon which various societies had left their religious mark. My first reaction was the belief that most of the religious traditions were simply wrong, that a few of them had come close to describing religious reality, but that it would take some intensive study to determine which religious traditions would best assist human beings in succeeding in the world. It was my good fortune to have as a religion and philosophy professor a Christian mystic who was trying to prove the deepest mysteries of the faith. He also had some intense personal problems which emerged again and again in his beliefs, indicating to me that religion and the specific individual path of life were always intertwined.

Over several years and many profound conversations he was able to demonstrate to me that each religious tradition had developed a unique way to confront some problems and that they had something in common if only the search for truth and the elimination of many false paths. But his solution, after many years, became untenable for me. I saw instead religion simply as a means of organizing a society, articulating some reasonably apparent emotional truths, but ultimately becoming a staid part of social establishments that primarily sought to control human behavior and not fulfill human individual potential. It seemed as if those religions that placed strong emphasis on certain concepts failed precisely in the areas in which they claimed expertise. Thus religions of "love" could point to few examples of their efficacy; religions of "salvation" actually saved very few. The more I learned about world religions, the more respect I had for the old Dakota ways.

(Deloria 1999:273–275) Additional information about this excerpt can be found on the Online Learning Center at www.mhhe.com/schaefer7. ●

> " *Although my father was an Episcopal priest with a large number of chapels in a loosely organized Episcopal missionary district known (to Episcopalians) as "Corn Creek," he was far from an orthodox follower of the white man's religion.* "

In this excerpt from *For This Land,* the late Vine Deloria—a Standing Rock Sioux—revealed his deep personal ties to the religion of his ancestors, undiluted by the overlays of missionary Christian theology. Even though his father was an Episcopal priest, Deloria was keenly aware of how tribal beliefs intruded to color his father's religious sensibility. He was also aware of the fact that Native American rites and customs had been appropriated by a generation of non-Indians seeking a kind of New Age "magic." For Deloria, Indian spiritual beliefs were an integral part of the Native American culture and helped to define that culture. Mixing those beliefs with the beliefs of other religions or systems of thought threatened to undermine the culture's strength.

Religion plays a major role in people's lives, and religious practices of some sort are evident in every society. That makes {p.58 religion a *cultural universal,* along with other common practices or beliefs found in every culture, such as dancing, food preparation, the family, and personal names. At present, an estimated 4 billion people belong to the world's many religious faiths (see Figure 13-1, page 317).

When religion's influence on other social institutions in a society diminishes, the process of *secularization* is said to be under way. During this process, religion will survive in the private sphere of individual and family life (as in the case of many Native American families); it may even thrive on a personal level. But at the same time, other social institutions—such as the economy, politics, and education—maintain their own sets of norms, independent of religious guidance (Stark and Iannaccone 1992).

Like religion, education is a cultural universal. As such, it is an important aspect of socialization—the lifelong process of learning the attitudes, values, and behavior considered appropriate to members of a particular culture. As we saw in Chapter 4, socialization can occur in the classroom or at home, through interactions with parents, teachers, friends, and even strangers. Exposure to books, films, television, and other forms of communication also promotes socialization. When learning is explicit and formalized—when some people consciously teach, while others adopt the role of learner—the process of socialization is called *education.* But students learn far more about their society at school than what is included in the curriculum.

What social purposes do education and religion serve? Does religion help to hold society together or foster social change? What is the "hidden curriculum" in U.S. schools? Do public schools offer everyone a way up the socioeconomic ladder, or do they reinforce divisions among social classes? This chapter concentrates on the formal systems of education and religion that characterize modern industrial societies. We will begin with a brief description of the sociological approach to religion, followed by an overview of the world's major religions. Next, we will explore religion's role in societal integration, social support, social change, and social control. We'll examine three important components of religious behavior—belief, ritual, and experience—as well as the basic forms of religious organization, including new religious movements. Then we'll discuss three sociological perspectives on education. We'll examine schools as formal organizations—as bureaucracies and as subcultures of teachers and students. The chapter will close with a Social Policy section on the controversy over religion in the public schools. ●

Durkheim and the Sociological Approach to Religion

If a group believes that it is being directed by a "vision from God," sociologists do not attempt to prove or disprove the revelation. Instead, they assess the effects of the religious experience on the group. What sociologists are interested in is the social impact of religion on individuals and institutions.

Émile Durkheim was perhaps the first sociologist to recognize the critical importance of religion in human societies. He saw its appeal for the individual, but more important, he {p.10 stressed the *social* impact of religion. In Durkheim's view, religion is a collective act that includes many forms of behavior in which people interact with others. As in his work on suicide, Durkheim was not so interested in the personalities of religious believers as he was in understanding religious behavior within a social context.

Durkheim defined *religion* as a "unified system of beliefs and practices relative to sacred things." In his view, religion involves a set of beliefs and practices that are uniquely the property of religion, as opposed to other social institutions and ways of thinking. Durkheim ([1912] 2001) argued that religious faiths distinguish between certain transcending events and the everyday world. He referred to those realms as the *sacred* and the *profane.*

The *sacred* encompasses elements beyond everyday life that inspire awe, respect, and even fear. People become part of the sacred realm only by completing some ritual, such as prayer or sacrifice. Because believers have faith in the sacred, they accept what they cannot understand. In contrast, the *profane* includes

FIGURE 13–1

Religions of the World

MAPPING LIFE

WORLDWIDE www.mhhe.com/schaefer7

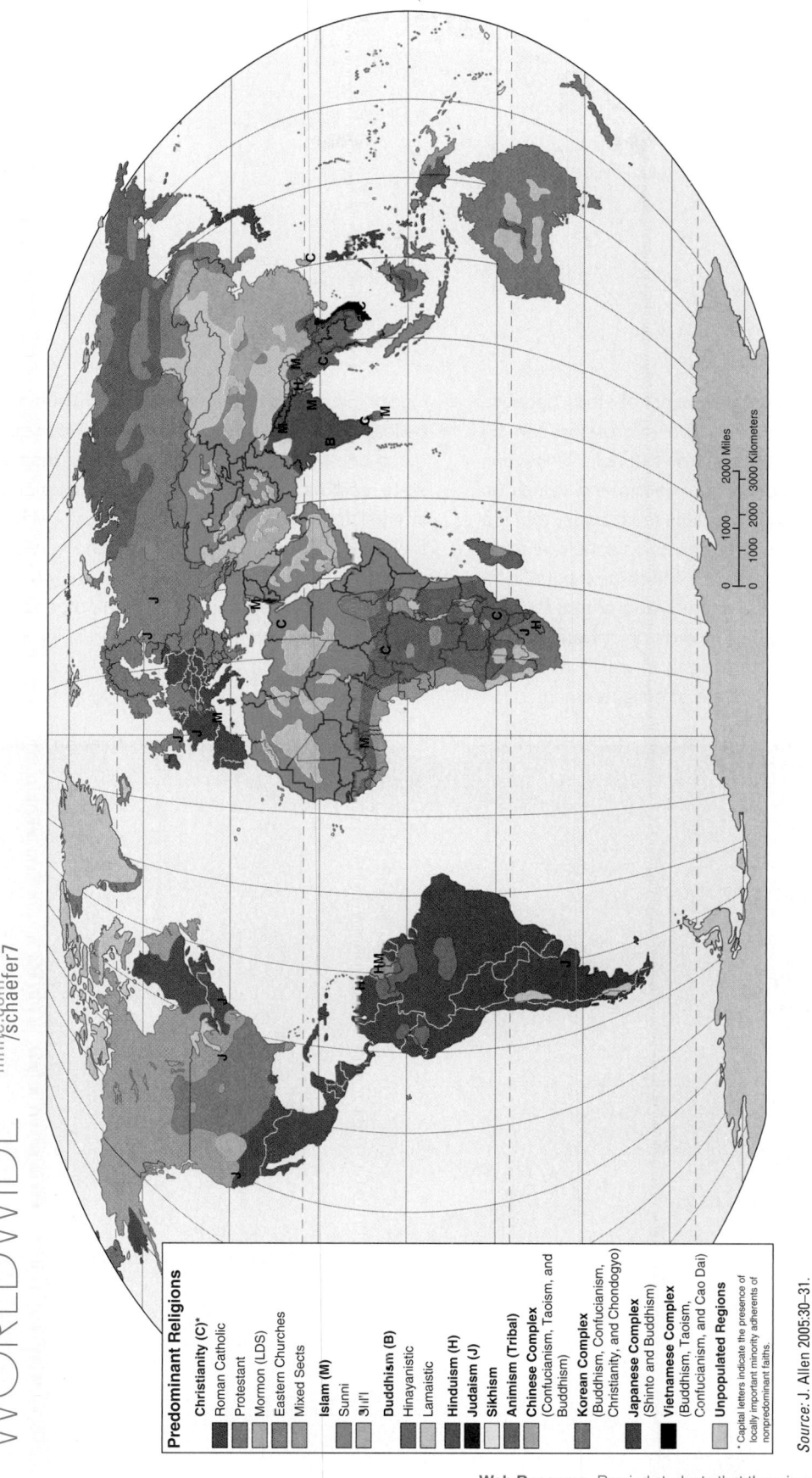

Predominant Religions

Christianity (C)*
Roman Catholic
Protestant
Mormon (LDS)
Eastern Churches
Mixed Sects

Islam (M)
Sunni
Shi'i

Buddhism (B)
Hinayanistic
Lamaistic

Hinduism (H)
Judaism (J)
Sikhism
Animism (Tribal)

Chinese Complex
(Confucianism, Taoism, and
Buddhism)

Korean Complex
(Buddhism, Confucianism,
Christianity, and Chondogyo)

Japanese Complex
(Shinto and Buddhism)

Vietnamese Complex
(Buddhism, Taoism,
Confucianism, and Cao Dai)

Unpopulated Regions

* Capital letters indicate the presence of
locally important minority adherents of
nonpredominant faiths.

0   1000   2000 Miles
0   1000   2000   3000 Kilometers

Source: J. Allen 2005:30–31.

Web Resource Remind students that there is an interactive map in the student center of the Online Learning Center (**www.mhhe.com/schaefer7**).

Why Do Sociologists Study Religion?

Sociologists find religion a fascinating subject of study because it is a cultural universal whose collective expression can be manifested in so many different ways. For example, Christians (below) worship one God and base their beliefs and values on the life and works of Jesus Christ. Muslims (next page, top) are also monotheistic, but they base their beliefs on scriptural revelations about God in the Qur'an (Koran). Hindus (next page, bottom left) hold many aspects of life sacred, and emphasize the importance of being good in this life in order to advance in the next. Buddhists (next page, bottom right) strive to overcome worldly desires in order to reach a state of enlightenment.

Sociologists are interested in how widely and strongly such beliefs are held, and what influences individuals to adopt religious beliefs. They study the impact of the family, schools, the state, and the predominant culture, among other factors. Also of interest to sociologists are the ways in which people express their faith. Do they do so by attending services? By meditating privately? By performing rituals? At the societal level, sociologists consider what impact religious organizations have on society, and conversely, how a particular culture affects the practice of religion.

{Roman Catholics at mass in Chacalte, Guatemala}

318

{Muslim men at prayer in Kurdistan, Iraq}

{Hindu holy man at the sacred Ganges River in India}

{Buddhist monks receiving food, Laos}

the ordinary and commonplace. This concept can be confusing, however, because the same object can be either sacred or profane, depending on how it is viewed. A normal dining room table is profane, but becomes sacred to some Christians if it bears the elements of a communion. A candelabra becomes sacred to Jews if it is a menorah. For Confucians and Taoists, incense sticks are not mere decorative items, but highly valued offerings to the gods in religious ceremonies that mark the new and full moons.

Following the direction established by Durkheim almost a century ago, contemporary sociologists view religion in two different ways. They study the norms and values of religious faiths by examining their substantive beliefs. For example, it is possible to compare the degree to which Christian faiths interpret the Bible literally, or Muslim groups follow the Qur'an (or Koran), the sacred book of Islam. At the same time, sociologists examine religion in terms of the social functions it fulfills, such as providing social support or reinforcing social norms. By exploring both the beliefs and the functions of religion, we can better understand its impact on the individual, on groups, and on society as a whole.

World Religions

Worldwide, tremendous diversity exists in religious beliefs and practices. Overall, about 85 percent of the world's population adheres to some religion; only about 15 percent is nonreligious. This level of adherence changes over time, and also varies by country and age group. In the United States today, those who are nonreligious account for less than 10 percent of the population;

in 1900, however, they constituted a mere 1.3 percent of all Americans. And in 2004, 25 percent of incoming U.S. college students said they either were not interested in spiritual or religious matters or had significant doubts (Barrett et al. 2005; Higher Education Research Institute 2005; Sax et al. 2005).

Christianity is the largest single faith in the world; the second largest is Islam (see Table 13-1). Although global news events often suggest an inherent conflict between Christians and Muslims, the two faiths are similar in many ways. Both are monotheistic (that is, based on a single deity); both include a belief in prophets, an afterlife, and a judgment day. In fact, Islam recognizes Jesus as a prophet, though not the son of God. Both faiths impose a moral code on believers, which varies from fairly rigid proscriptions for fundamentalists to relatively relaxed guidelines for liberals.

The followers of Islam, called *Muslims,* believe that Islam's holy scriptures were received from Allah (God) by the prophet Mohammad nearly 1,400 years ago. They see Mohammad as the last in a long line of prophets, preceded by Adam, Abraham, Moses, and Jesus. Islam is more communal in its expression than Christianity, particularly the more individualistic Protestant denominations. Consequently, in countries that are predominantly Muslim, the separation of religion and the state is not considered necessary or even desirable. In fact, Muslim governments often reinforce Islamic practices through their laws. Muslims do vary sharply in their interpretation of several traditions, some of which—such as the wearing of veils by women—are more cultural than religious in origin.

Like Christianity and Islam, Judaism is monotheistic. Jews believe that God's true nature is revealed in the Torah, which

Table 13-1 Major World Religions

summingUP

Faith	Current Following, in Millions (and Percent of World Population)	Primary Location of Followers Today	Founder (and Approximate Birth Date)	Important Texts (and Holy Sites)
Buddhism	379 (5.9%)	Southeast Asia, Mongolia, Tibet	Gautama Siddhartha (563 B.C.)	Triptaka (areas in Nepal)
Christianity	2,133 (33.1%)	Europe, North America, South America	Jesus (6 B.C.)	Bible (Jerusalem, Rome)
Hinduism	860 (13.3%)	India, Indian communities overseas	No specific founder (1500 B.C.)	Sruti and Smrti texts (seven sacred cities, including Vavansi)
Islam	1,309 (20.3%)	Middle East, Central Asia, North Africa, Indonesia	Mohammad (A.D. 570)	Qur'an, or Koran (Mecca, Medina, Jerusalem)
Judaism	15 (0.2%)	Israel, United States, France, Russia	Abraham (2000 B.C.)	Torah, Talmud (Jerusalem)

Sources: Author based on Barrett et al. 2006; Swatos 1998.

Classroom Tip See "Unitarian Universalism" (Additional Lecture Ideas).
Global View Comparison of Christianity and Islam

Contemporary Culture How have Americans' views of Islam changed since September 11, 2001?

Christians know as the first five books of the Old Testament. According to these scriptures, God formed a covenant, or pact, with Abraham and Sarah, the ancestors of the tribes of Israel. Even today, Jews believe, this covenant holds them accountable to God's will. If they follow both the letter and spirit of the Torah, a long-awaited Messiah will one day bring paradise to earth. Although Judaism has a relatively small following compared to other major faiths, it forms the historical foundation for both Christianity and Islam. That is why Jews revere many of the same sacred Middle Eastern sites as Christians and Muslims.

Two other major faiths developed in a different part of the world, India. The earliest, Hinduism, originated around 1500 B.C. Hinduism differs from Judaism, Christianity, and Islam in that it embraces a number of gods and minor gods, although most worshipers are devoted primarily to a single deity, such as Shiva or Vishnu. Hinduism is also distinguished by a belief in reincarnation, or the perpetual rebirth of the soul after death. Unlike Judaism, Christianity, and Islam, which are based largely on sacred texts, Hindu beliefs have been preserved mostly through oral tradition.

A second religion, Buddhism, developed in the sixth century B.C. as a reaction against Hinduism. This faith is founded on the teachings of Siddhartha (later called Buddha, or "the enlightened one"). Through meditation, followers of Buddhism strive to overcome selfish cravings for physical or material pleasures, with the goal of reaching a state of enlightenment, or nirvana. Buddhists created the first monastic orders, which are thought to be the models for monastic orders in other religions, including Christianity. Though Buddhism emerged in India, its followers were eventually driven out of that country by the Hindus. It is now found primarily in other parts of Asia. (Contemporary adherents of Buddhism in India are relatively recent converts.)

Although the differences among religions are striking, they are exceeded by variations within faiths. Consider the differences within Christianity, from relatively liberal denominations such as Presbyterians or the United Church of Christ to the more conservative Mormons and Greek Orthodox Catholics. Similar divisions exist within Hinduism, Islam, and other world religions (Barrett et al. 2006; Swatos 1998).

Sociological Explanations of Religion

Since religion is a cultural universal, it is not surprising that it plays a basic role in human societies. In sociological terms, it [p.14] performs both manifest and latent functions. Among its *manifest* (open and stated) functions, religion defines the spiritual world and gives meaning to the divine. It provides an explanation for events that seem difficult to understand, such as what lies beyond the grave. The *latent* functions of religion are unintended, covert, or hidden. Even though the manifest function of a church service is to offer a forum for religious worship, it might at the same time fulfill a latent social function as a meeting ground for unmarried members.

Functionalists and conflict theorists both evaluate religion's impact on human societies. We'll consider a functionalist view of religion's role in integrating society, providing social support, and promoting social change, and then look at religion from the conflict perspective, as a means of social control. Note that for the most part, religion's impact is best understood from a macro-level viewpoint that is oriented toward the larger society. Its social support function is an exception: it is best viewed on the micro, or individual, level.

The Integrative Function of Religion

Émile Durkheim viewed religion as an integrative force in human society—a perspective that is reflected in functionalist thought today. Durkheim sought to answer a perplexing question: "How can human societies be held together when they are generally composed of individuals and social groups with diverse interests and aspirations?" In his view, religious bonds often transcend these personal and divisive forces. Durkheim acknowledged that religion is not the only integrative force; nationalism or patriotism may serve the same end.

How does religion provide this "societal glue"? Religion, whether it be Buddhism, Islam, Christianity, or Judaism, gives meaning and purpose to people's lives. It offers certain ultimate values and ends to hold in common. Although they are subjective and not always fully accepted, these values and ends help society to function as an integrated social system. For example, funerals, weddings, bar and bat mitzvahs, and confirmations serve to integrate people into larger communities by providing shared beliefs and values about the ultimate questions of life.

Religion also serves to bind people together in times of crisis and confusion. Immediately after the terrorist attacks of September 11, 2001, on New York City and Washington, D.C., attendance at worship services in the United States increased dramatically. Muslim, Jewish, and Christian clerics made joint appearances to honor the dead and urge citizens not to retaliate against those who looked, dressed, or sounded different from others. A year later, however, attendance levels had returned to normal (D. Moore 2002).

The integrative power of religion can be seen, too, in the role that churches, synagogues, and mosques have traditionally played and continue to play for immigrant groups in the United States. For example, Roman Catholic immigrants may settle near a parish church that offers services in their native language, such as Polish or Spanish. Similarly, Korean immigrants may join a Presbyterian church that has many Korean American members and follows religious practices like those of churches in Korea. Like other religious organizations, these Roman Catholic and Presbyterian churches help to integrate immigrants into their new homeland.

Religion also strengthens social integration within specific faiths and denominations. In many faiths, members share certain characteristics that help to bind them together, including their race, ethnicity, and social class. Box 13-1 (page 322) examines the income and educational levels characteristic of specific denominations in the United States.

Global View Discussion of Judaism and Hinduism
Classroom Tips See 'Anti-Defamation League of B'nai Brith' (Class Discussion Topics); "Courts and Holiday Displays" (Additional Lecture Ideas).
Theory Functionalist analysis of manifest and latent functions of religion
Classroom Tip Review what is meant by both latent and manifest functions.

Theory Functionalist view of the integrative function of religion
Contemporary Culture Worship attendance in the United States increased dramatically following the terrorist attacks of September 11, 2001, but returned to normal after a year.
Race/Ethnicity Churches, synagogues, and mosques help to integrate immigrants to the United States.

research IN *action*

13-1 Income and Education, Religiously Speaking

Sociologists have found that religions are distinguished not just by doctrinal issues, but by secular criteria as well. Research has consistently shown that denominations and faiths can be arranged in a hierarchy based on their members' social class. The associated differences in financial means have a noticeable impact on the religious bodies, affecting everything from the appearance of their houses of worship to their congregations' ability to undertake social outreach activities.

Analysis of the General Social Survey shows that Jews, Presbyterians, and Episcopalians claim a higher proportion of affluent members than other faiths and denominations (see the accompanying figure, top). Their relative affluence can often be seen in the architecture and furnishings of their houses of worship. Members of less affluent groups, such as Muslims and Baptists, may compensate for their lesser means by donating their

> *Research has consistently shown that denominations and faiths can be arranged in a hierarchy based on their members' social class.*

time and talent to outreach programs. Or they may pledge a higher proportion of their income to the church.

Of course, all religious groups draw some members from each social stratum. Group differences among the faiths reflect a variety of social factors. For example, some denominations have more followers in urban areas or in the Northeast, where salaries are generally higher. Nonetheless, the existence of these income differences means that religion can become a mechanism for signaling social mobility. A family that is moving up in wealth and power may seek out a faith that is associated with a higher social ranking, moving from, say, the Roman Catholic to the Episcopal church.

Educational differences among faiths and denominations are even more striking. In the United States, Jews are three times more likely than Baptists to have a college education (see the accompanying figure, bottom). But a closer

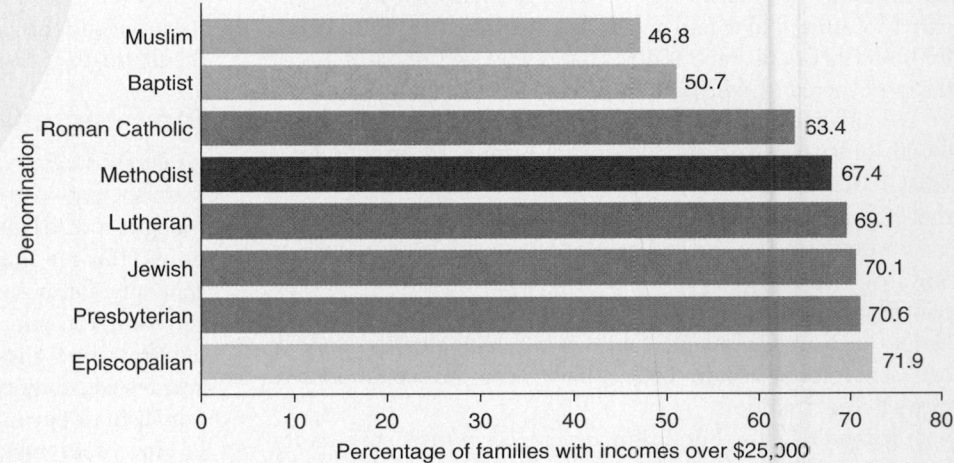

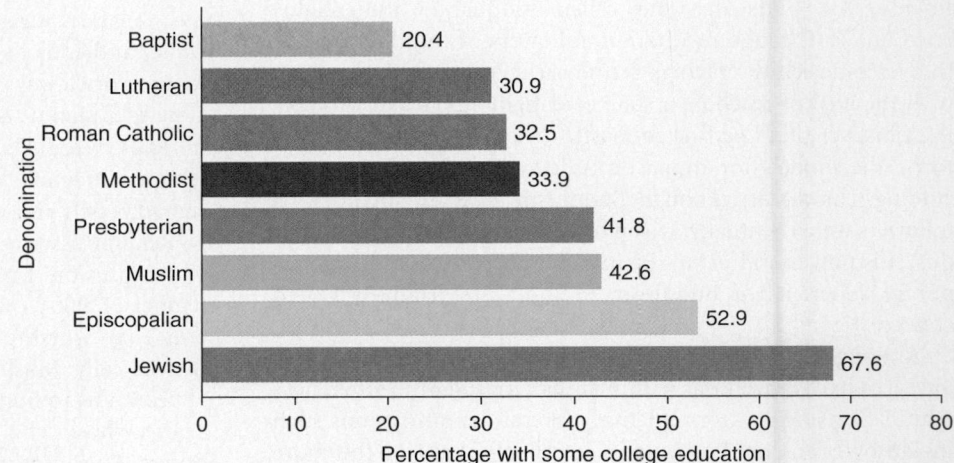

look at the data reveals a more complex picture. Those whose faiths are associated with a lower level of formal schooling—Baptists, Lutherans, and Roman Catholics—also benefit from the strongest church-sponsored educational programs. So while members of these groups may have fewer years of schooling than others, they are much more likely to have been educated in an atmosphere that encourages allegiance to their faith.

Let's Discuss

1. Which faiths and denominations maintain houses of worship in your hometown? Do

their facilities differ in terms of their size and construction? If so, do the differences mirror the size of the congregations, or do they represent social class differences as well?
2. Beside religions, what other group affiliations might suggest a person's income or educational level?

Source: Based on author's analysis of the cumulative General Social Survey 1994–2004; see J. Davis et al. 2005.

Classroom Tip Show photographs of various churches and have students guess their denominations.

Let's Discuss How homogeneous in social class and education is your religious congregation?

Classroom Tip Rank some religious faiths by class and education and discuss any patterns in religious beliefs.

322

In some instances, religious loyalties are *dysfunctional*; that is, they contribute to tension and even conflict between groups or nations. During the Second World War, the German Nazis attempted to exterminate the Jewish people; approximately 6 million European Jews were killed. In modern times, nations such as Lebanon (Muslims versus Christians), Israel (Jews versus Muslims, as well as Orthodox versus secular Jews), Northern Ireland (Roman Catholics versus Protestants), and India (Hindus versus Muslims, and more recently, Sikhs) have been torn by clashes that are in large part based on religion. (See the case study on page 332 for a more detailed discussion of religious conflict in India.)

Religious conflict (though on a less violent level) has been increasingly evident in the United States as well. Sociologist James Davison Hunter (1991) has referred to the "cultural war" taking place in the United States. In many communities, Christian fundamentalists, conservative Catholics, and Orthodox Jews have joined forces in a battle against liberal denominations for control of the secular culture. The battlefield is an array of familiar social issues, among them multiculturalism, child care (Chapter 4), abortion (Chapter 11), gay marriage (Chapter 12), school { pp.94, 283, 309 } prayer, media censorship, and government funding for the arts.

Religion and Social Support

Most of us find it difficult to accept the stressful events of life—the death of a loved one, serious injury, bankruptcy, divorce, and so forth—especially when something "senseless" happens. How can family and friends come to terms with the death of a talented college student, not even 20 years old?

Through its emphasis on the divine and the supernatural, religion allows us to "do something" about the calamities we face. In some faiths, adherents can offer sacrifices or pray to a deity in the belief that such acts will change their earthly condition. On a more basic level, religion encourages us to view our personal misfortunes as relatively unimportant in the broader perspective of human history—or even as part of an undisclosed divine purpose. Friends and relatives of the deceased college student may see his death as being "God's will," or as having some ultimate benefit that we cannot understand now. This perspective may be much more comforting than the terrifying feeling that any of us can die senselessly at any moment—and that there is no divine answer to why one person lives a long and full life, while another dies tragically at a relatively early age.

Faith-based community organizations have taken on more and more responsibilities in the area of social assistance. In fact, President George W. Bush created the Office of Faith-Based and Community Initiatives to give socially active religious groups access to government funding. From 2003 to 2005, the federal government's Compassion Capital Fund spent $100 million to support the community-oriented services of various religious groups. There is some evidence of such groups' effectiveness in helping others. Sociologist William Julius Wilson (1999b) has singled out faith-based organizations in 40 communities from California to Massachusetts as models of social reform. These organizations identify experienced leaders and assemble them into nonsectarian coalitions that are devoted to community development (DeParle 2005).

Religion and Social Change

The Weberian Thesis

When someone seems driven to work and succeed, we often attribute the Protestant work ethic to that person. The term comes from the writings of Max Weber, who carefully examined the connection between religious allegiance and capitalist development. Weber's findings appeared in his pioneering work *The Protestant Ethic and the Spirit of Capitalism* ([1904] 1958a).

Weber noted that in European nations with both Protestant and Catholic citizens, an overwhelming number of business leaders, owners of capital, and skilled workers were Protestant. In his view, this fact was no mere coincidence. Weber pointed out that the followers of John Calvin (1509–1564), a leader of the Protestant Reformation, emphasized a disciplined work ethic, this-worldly concerns, and a rational orientation to life that have become known as the **Protestant ethic.** One byproduct of the Protestant ethic was a drive to accumulate savings that could be used for future investment. This "spirit of capitalism," to use Weber's phrase, contrasted with the moderate work hours, leisurely work habits, and lack of ambition that Weber saw as typical of the times.

Few books on the sociology of religion have aroused as much commentary and criticism as Weber's work. It has been hailed as one of the most important theoretical works in the field and an excellent example of macro-level analysis. Like Durkheim, Weber demonstrated that religion is not solely a matter of intimate personal beliefs. He stressed that the collective nature of religion has consequences for society as a whole.

Weber provided a convincing description of the origins of European capitalism. But this economic system has now been adopted by non-Calvinists in many parts of the world. Studies done in the United States today show little or no difference in achievement orientation between Roman Catholics and Protestants. Apparently, the "spirit of capitalism" has emerged as a generalized cultural trait rather than a specific religious tenet (Greeley 1989).

Conflict theorists caution that Weber's theory—even if it is accepted—should not be regarded as an analysis of mature capitalism, as reflected in the rise of multinational corporations. { p.215 } Marxists would disagree with Weber not on the origins of capitalism, but on its future. Unlike Marx, Weber believed that capitalism could endure indefinitely as an economic system. He added, however, that the decline of religion as an overriding force in society opened the way for workers to express their discontent more vocally (Collins 1980).

Liberation Theology

Sometimes the clergy can be found in the forefront of social change. Many religious activists, especially in the Roman Catholic Church in Latin America, support *liberation theology*—the use of a church in a political effort to

---

Theory Functionalist view of dysfunctions of religious loyalties
Let's Discuss How is the concept of dominant ideology relevant to the "cultural war" taking place in the United States?
Classroom Tip See "Goal Multiplication and Religious Organizations" (Additional Lecture Ideas).
Theory Functionalist view of religion as a source of social assistance

Key Person Max Weber
Theory Weber's view of religion as reinforcing capitalism
Key Person John Calvin
Theory Conflict theorists' critique of Weber's analysis of religion
Global View Religious activism in Latin America

eliminate poverty, discrimination, and other forms of injustice from a secular society. Advocates of this religious movement sometimes sympathize with Marxism. Many believe that radical change, rather than economic development in itself, is the only acceptable solution to the desperation of the masses in impoverished developing countries. Activists associated with liberation theology believe that organized religion has a moral responsibility to take a strong public stand against the oppression of the poor, racial and ethnic minorities, and women (C. Smith 1991).

The term *liberation theology* dates back to the publication in 1973 of the English translation of *A Theology of Liberation*. The book was written by a Peruvian priest, Gustavo Gutiérrez, who lived in a slum area of Lima during the early 1960s. After years of exposure to the vast poverty around him, Gutiérrez concluded that "in order to serve the poor, one had to move into political action" (R. M. Brown 1980:23; G. Gutiérrez 1990). Eventually, politically committed Latin American theologians came under the influence of social scientists who viewed the domination of capitalism and multinational corporations as central to the hemisphere's problems. One result was a new approach to theology that built on the cultural and religious traditions of Latin America rather than on models developed in Europe and the United States.

Liberation theology may be dysfunctional, however. Some Roman Catholic worshipers have come to believe that by focusing on political and governmental injustice, the clergy are no longer addressing their personal and spiritual needs. Partly as a result of such disenchantment, some Catholics in Latin America are converting to mainstream Protestant faiths or to Mormonism.

Use Your Sociological Imagination
www.mhhe.com/schaefer7

The social support that religious groups provide is suddenly withdrawn from your community. How will your life or the lives of others change? What will happen if religious groups stop pushing for social change?

Religion and Social Control: A Conflict View

Liberation theology is a relatively recent phenomenon that marks a break with the traditional role of churches. It was this traditional role that Karl Marx opposed. In his view, religion *impeded* social change by encouraging oppressed people to focus on otherworldly concerns rather than on their immediate poverty or exploitation. Marx described religion as an "opiate" that was particularly harmful to oppressed peoples. He felt that religion often drugged the masses into submission by offering a consolation for their harsh lives on earth: the hope of salvation in an ideal afterlife. For example, during the period of slavery in the United States, White masters forbade Blacks to practice native African religions, while encouraging them to adopt Christianity, which taught them that obedience would lead to salvation and eternal happiness in the hereafter. Viewed from a

conflict perspective, Christianity may have pacified certain slaves and blunted the rage that often fuels rebellion.

Marx acknowledged that religion plays an important role in propping up the existing social structure. The values of religion, as already noted, tend to reinforce other social institutions and the social order as a whole. From Marx's perspective, however, religion's promotion of social stability only helps to perpetuate patterns of social inequality. According to Marx, the dominant religion reinforces the interests of those in power.

For example, contemporary Christianity reinforces traditional patterns of behavior that call for the subordination of the less powerful. The role of women in the church is an example of this uneven distribution of power. Assumptions about gender roles leave women in a subservient position both within Christian churches and at home. In fact, women find it as difficult to achieve leadership positions in many churches as they do in large corporations. A "stained glass ceiling" tends to stunt clergywomen's career development, even in the most liberal denominations.

Like Marx, conflict theorists argue that to whatever extent religion actually does influence social behavior, it reinforces existing patterns of dominance and inequality. From a Marxist perspective, religion keeps people from seeing their lives and societal conditions in political terms—for example, by obscuring the overriding significance of conflicting economic interests. {p.190} Marxists suggest that by inducing a "false consciousness" among the disadvantaged, religion lessens the possibility of collective political action that could end capitalist oppression and transform society.

Table 13-2 summarizes the three major sociological perspectives on religion.

Components of Religion

All religions have certain elements in common, yet those elements are expressed in the distinctive manner of each faith. These patterns of religious behavior, like other patterns of social behavior, are of great interest to sociologists—especially interactionists—since they underscore the relationship between religion and society.

Religious beliefs, religious rituals, and religious experience all help to define what is sacred and to differentiate the sacred from the profane. Let's examine these three components of religion, as seen through the eyes of interactionists.

Belief

Some people believe in life after death, in supreme beings with unlimited powers, or in supernatural forces. ***Religious beliefs*** are statements to which members of a particular religion adhere. These views can vary dramatically from religion to religion.

In the late 1960s, something rather remarkable took place in the expression of religious beliefs in the United States. Denominations that held to relatively liberal interpretations of religious scripture (such as the Presbyterians, Methodists, and Lutherans) declined in membership, while those that held to more conser-

---

Global View Church activists in Latin America aim to eliminate poverty, discrimination, and social injustice.
Theory Dysfunction of liberation theology
Key Person Karl Marx
Theory Conflict view of religion as a means of social control

Gender Women's subordinate role within organized religion
Classroom Tip See "Women in Clergy" (Additional Lecture Ideas).
Theory Conflict view of religion as reinforcing patterns of dominance and inequality
Reel Society See Stratification—Religion in the Topic Index.

riety of newer interpretations. The term *fundamentalism* refers to a rigid adherence to fundamental religious doctrines. Often, fundamentalism is accompanied by a literal application of scripture or historical beliefs to today's world. The phrase "religious fundamentalism" was first applied to Protestant believers in the United States who took a literal interpretation of the Bible, but fundamentalism is found worldwide among most major religious groups, including Roman Catholicism, Islam, and Judaism. Fundamentalists vary immensely in their behavior. Some stress the need to be strict in their own personal faith but take little interest in broad social issues. Others are watchful of societal actions, such as government policies, that they see as conflicting with fundamentalist doctrine.

The Adam and Eve account of creation found in Genesis, the first book of the Old Testament, is an example of a religious belief. Many people in the United States strongly adhere to this biblical explanation of creation, and even insist that it be taught in public schools. These people, known as *creationists*, are worried by the secularization of society, and oppose teaching that directly or indirectly questions biblical scripture. The Social Policy section at the end of this chapter examines the issue of religion in the schools in depth.

In general, spirituality is not as strong in industrialized nations as in developing nations. The United States is an exception to the trend toward secularization, in part because the government encourages religious expression (without explicitly supporting it) by allowing religious groups to claim charitable status, and even to receive federal aid for activities such as educational services. And although belief in God is relatively weak in formerly communist states such as Russia, surveys show a growth in spirituality in communist countries over the last 10 years (Norris and Inglehart 2004).

Ritual

Religious rituals are practices required or expected of members of a faith. Rituals usually honor the divine power (or powers) worshiped by believers; they also remind adherents of their religious duties and responsibilities. Rituals and beliefs can be interdependent; rituals generally affirm beliefs, as in a public or private statement confessing a sin. Like any social institution, religion develops distinctive norms to structure people's behavior. Moreover, sanctions are attached to religious rituals, whether rewards (bar mitzvah gifts) or penalties (expulsion from a religious institution for violation of norms).

In the United States, rituals may be very simple, such as saying grace at a meal or observing a moment of silence to commemorate someone's death. Yet certain rituals, such as the process of canonizing a saint, are quite elaborate. Most religious rituals in our culture focus on services conducted at houses of worship. Attendance at a service, silent and spoken prayers, communion, and singing of spiritual hymns and chants are common forms of ritual behavior that generally take place in group settings. From an

Women do not achieve leadership positions in religious organizations any more frequently than they do in the business world. Fewer than one in eight clergy members in the United States is female.

vative interpretations grew in numbers. Furthermore, in most faiths, those members who held strict views of scripture became more outspoken, questioning those who remained open to a va-

Table 13-2 Sociological Perspectives on Religion

Theoretical Perspective	Emphasis
Functionalist	Religion as a source of social integration and unification
	Religion as a source of social support for individuals
Conflict	Religion as a potential obstacle to structural social change
	Religion as a potential source of structural social change (through liberation theology)
Interactionist	Individual religious expression through belief, ritual, and experience

Classroom Tip See "Ritual" (Class Discussion Topics).

interactionist perspective, these rituals serve as important face-to-face encounters in which people reinforce their religious beliefs and their commitment to their faith.

For Muslims, a very important ritual is the *hajj,* a pilgrimage to the Grand Mosque in Mecca, Saudi Arabia. Every Muslim who is physically and financially able is expected to make this trip at least once. Each year 2 million pilgrims go to Mecca during the one-week period indicated by the Islamic lunar calendar. Muslims from all over the world make the *hajj,* including those in the United States, where many tours are arranged to facilitate the trip.

In recent decades, participation in religious rituals has tended to hold steady or decline in most countries. Figure 13-2 shows the change in religious participation in selected countries from 1981 to 2001.

Experience

In the sociological study of religion, the term ***religious experience*** refers to the feeling or perception of being in direct contact with the ultimate reality, such as a divine being, or of being over-come with religious emotion. A religious experience may be rather slight, such as the feeling of exaltation a person receives from hearing a choir sing Handel's "Hallelujah Chorus." But many religious experiences are more profound, such as a Muslim's experience on a *hajj.* In his autobiography, the late African American activist Malcolm X (1964:338) wrote of his *hajj* and how deeply moved he was by the way that Muslims in Mecca came together across race and color lines. For Malcolm X, the color blindness of the Muslim world "proved to me the power of the One God."

Another profound religious experience, for many Christians, is being "born again"—that is, at a turning point in one's life, making a personal commitment to Jesus. According to a 2003 national survey, 42 percent of people in the United States claim they have had a born-again Christian experience at some time in their lives. An earlier survey found that Southern Baptists (75 percent) were the most likely to report such experiences; in contrast, only 21 percent of Catholics and 24 percent of Episcopalians stated that they had been born again. The collective nature of religion, as emphasized by Durkheim, is evident in

Pilgrims on *hajj* to the Grand Mosque in Mecca, Saudi Arabia. Islam requires all Muslims who are able to undertake a pilgrimage to the Holy Land.

Classroom Tip A Muslim ritual unfamiliar to most people in the United States is Ramadan. See "Ramadan" (Class Discussion Topics).

Methods Survey of "born-again" experiences among Christians
Let's Discuss How might religious experience differ across Black and White congregations, and why?

FIGURE 13-2

Religious Participation in Selected Countries, 1981 and 2001

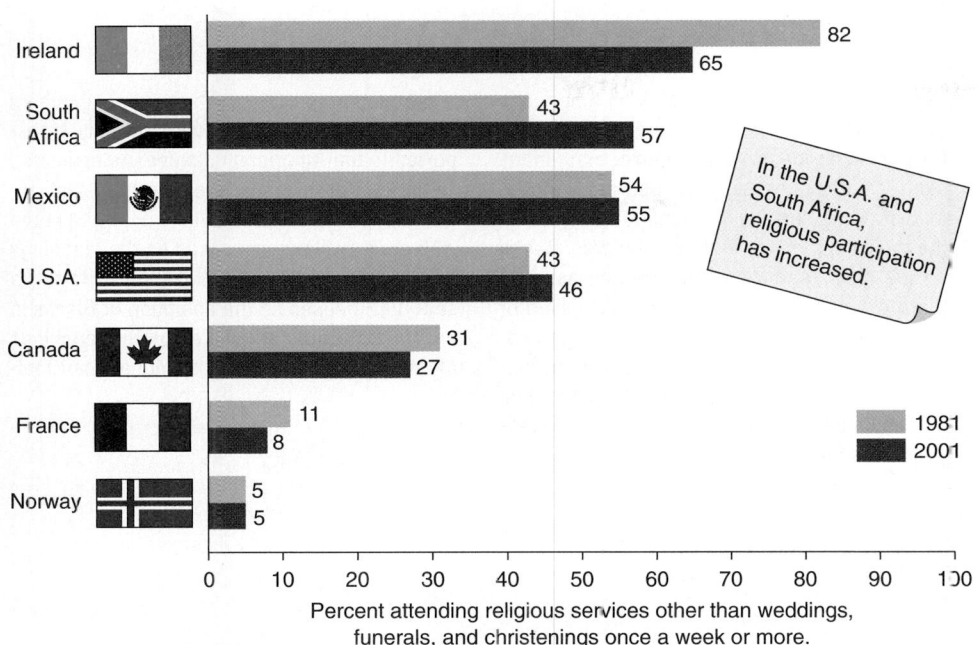

In the U.S.A. and South Africa, religious participation has increased.

Country	1981	2001
Ireland	82	65
South Africa	43	57
Mexico	54	55
U.S.A.	43	46
Canada	31	27
France	11	8
Norway	5	5

Percent attending religious services other than weddings, funerals, and christenings once a week or more.

Note: World Values survey data for 2001.
Source: Norris and Inglehart 2004:74.

Think About It
Why did religious participation decrease in Ireland but increase in South Africa?

these statistics. The beliefs and rituals of a particular faith can create an atmosphere either friendly or indifferent to this type of religious experience. Thus, a Baptist would be encouraged to come forward and share such experiences with others, whereas an Episcopalian who claims to have been born again would receive much less interest (Newport 2004).

Use Your Sociological Imagination www.mhhe.com /schaefer7

Choose a religious tradition other than your own. How would your religious beliefs, rituals, and experience differ if you had been raised in that tradition?

Religious Organization

The collective nature of religion has led to many forms of religious association. In modern societies, religion has become increasingly formalized. Specific structures such as churches and synagogues have been constructed for religious worship; individuals have been trained for occupational roles within various fields. These developments make it possible to distinguish clearly between the sacred and secular parts of one's life—a

distinction that could not be made easily in earlier times, when religion was largely a family activity carried out in the home.

Sociologists find it useful to distinguish between four basic forms of organization: the ecclesia, the denomination, the sect, and the new religious movement, or cult. We can see differences among these four forms of organization in their size, power, degree of commitment expected from members, and historical ties to other faiths.

Ecclesiae

An *ecclesia* (plural, *ecclesiae*) is a religious organization that claims to include most or all members of a society and is recognized as the national or official religion. Since virtually everyone belongs to the faith, membership is by birth rather than conscious decision. Examples of ecclesiae include Islam in Saudi Arabia and Buddhism in Thailand. However, significant differences exist within this category. In Saudi Arabia's Islamic regime, leaders of the ecclesia hold vast power over actions of the state. In contrast, the Lutheran church in contemporary Sweden holds no such power over the Riksdag (parliament) or the prime minister.

Generally, ecclesiae are conservative, in that they do not challenge the leaders of a secular government. In a society with an ecclesia, the political and religious institutions often act in harmony and reinforce each other's power in their relative spheres of influence. In the modern world, ecclesiae are declining in power.

Denominations

A *denomination* is a large, organized religion that is not officially linked to the state or government. Like an ecclesia, it tends to have an explicit set of beliefs, a defined system of authority, and a generally respected position in society. Denominations claim as members large segments of a population. Generally, children accept the denomination of their parents and give little thought to membership in other faiths. Denominations also resemble ecclesiae in that they make few demands on members. However, there is a critical difference between these two forms of religious organization. Although the denomination is considered respectable and is not viewed as a challenge to the secular government, it lacks the official recognition and power held by an ecclesia (Doress and Porter 1977).

The United States is home to a large number of denominations (see Figure 13-3, page 330). In good measure, this diversity

research IN action

13-2 Islam in the United States

The growing presence of Islam in the United States is promoting better understanding of the significant diversity *within* Islam. Throughout the world, including the United States, Muslims are divided into a variety of sects, such as Sunni and Shia (or Shiite). These divisions sometimes result in antagonism, just as rivalries between Christian denominations can cause friction. Yet the Islamic faith is expressed in many different ways, even among Sunnis or Shia. To speak of Muslims as either Sunni or Shia would be like speaking of Christians as either Roman Catholic or Baptist.

The great majority of Muslims in the United States are Sunni Muslims—literally, those who follow the *Sunnah,* or way of the Prophet. Compared to other Muslims, Sunnis tend to be more moderate in their religious orthodoxy. The Shia, who come primarily from Iraq and Iran, are the second largest group. Shia Muslims are more attentive to guidance from accepted Islamic scholars than are Sunnis. In sufficient numbers, these two Muslim groups will choose to worship separately, even if they must cross ethnic or linguistic lines to do so. That certainly is the case in U.S. cities with large and varied Muslim communities.

Estimating the number of Muslim Americans in the United States is even more difficult than estimating the number of Arab Americans (see Chapter 10). There are no census data on Muslim Americans, and Islamic institutions such as mosques tend to operate autonomously. Even the most scientific analyses of the topic vary widely in their estimates. Based on the most recent studies, we can say that there are between 3 million and 5.7 million or more Muslims in the United States. About two-thirds of those residents are native-born citizens. In terms of ethnic and racial background, the estimated breakdown of Muslim Americans is as follows:

- 20–42 percent African American
- 24–33 percent South Asian (Afghan, Bangladeshi, Indian, and Pakistani)
- 12–32 percent Arab
- 10–22 percent "other" (Bosnian, Iranian, and Turk)

All scholars agree that the Muslim population in the United States is growing rapidly, through both immigration and religious conversion.

From these data, we can determine that African Americans who embrace Islam form a significant segment of the Muslim American community. The history of Black American Islam began in the 17th century, when members of some Muslim tribes were forcibly transported to the American colonies. An estimated 10 percent of African slaves were Muslim. Today's Black Islamic community emerged in the 20th century, however, based on the teachings of Elijah Muhammad. The Nation of Islam, a sect that focuses on the condition of Blacks in the United States as well as on the teachings of the Qur'an, was formed by Muhammad's fol-

> *To many Muslim Americans, the popular culture of the United States resembles a pagan cult that celebrates money and sex.*

lowers. Today, African American adherents of Islam reflect a variety of orientations, some unique to the United States and others tied to the larger Muslim community.

Though mosques are becoming more common in the United States, these houses of worship attract a different kind of attention than a traditional church with a steeple. To many people in the United States, the mosque repre-

is a result of our nation's immigrant heritage. Many settlers brought with them the religious commitments native to their homelands. Some Christian denominations in the United States, such as the Roman Catholics, Episcopalians, and Lutherans, are the outgrowth of ecclesiae established in Europe. New Christian denominations also emerged, including the Mormons and Christian Scientists. Within the last generation, immigrants have increased the number of Muslims, Hindus, and Buddhists living in the United States.

Although by far the largest denomination in the United States is Roman Catholicism, at least 24 other Christian faiths have 1 million or more members. Protestants collectively accounted for about 49 percent of the nation's adult population in mid-2005, compared to 22 percent for Roman Catholics and 2 percent for Jews. There are also 5 million Muslims in the United States, and large numbers of people adhere to Eastern faiths such as Buddhism (3 million) and Hinduism (1 million) (Barrett et al. 2006;

Tom Smith and Kim 2004; Lindner 2006). Box 13-2 takes a closer look at Islam in the United States.

Sects

A *sect* can be defined as a relatively small religious group that has broken away from some other religious organization to renew what it considers the original vision of the faith. Many sects, such as that led by Martin Luther during the Reformation, claim to be the "true church," because they seek to cleanse the established faith of what they regard as extraneous beliefs and rituals (Stark and Bainbridge 1985). Max Weber ([1916] 1958b:114) termed the sect a "believer's church," because affiliation is based on conscious acceptance of a specific religious dogma.

Sects are fundamentally at odds with society and do not seek to become established national religions. Unlike ecclesiae and denominations, they require intensive commitments and demonstrations of belief by members. Partly owing to their out-

sents not religious freedom and diversity, but a "foreign threat." Some communities have attempted to block the construction of Muslim religious centers. In return for a permit, local authorities may require that the buildings be stripped of the usual cultural symbols, perhaps even the traditional dome. On college campuses, administrators have responded more constructively to growing numbers of Muslim students, by hiring part-time imams (prayer leaders) to minister to their needs, dedicating space for daily prayer, and providing for Muslim dietary restrictions.

How does being Muslim in the United States differ from being Muslim in an Islamic country? In the United States, Muslim Americans reflect the diversity of the worldwide Islamic faith, but they practice their faith in a nation where Christianity is the dominant cultural influence. Some Islamic scholars argue that the democracy, religious diversity, and freedom of expression that Muslims experience in the United States have encouraged a stronger, more correct Islamic practice, uninhibited by the government interference that is characteristic of many Islamic states.

Other scholars contend that what makes the Muslim American experience unique is that followers must focus even more strongly on their religion in order to survive in a culture that is so permissive. Indeed, U.S. culture encourages many behaviors that are prohibited by Islamic law or cultural tradition. To many Muslim Americans, the popular culture of the United States resembles a pagan cult that celebrates money and sex. Muslim Americans,

In the United States, Muslim Americans must focus strongly on their faith to survive within the permissive mainstream culture. This Islamic school allows Muslim girls to play basketball without compromising their modesty.

then, feel both the freedom to practice their faith as they choose and the pressure to remain Muslim.

Let's Discuss

1. Is there a mosque in your community or a Muslim congregation on your campus? If so, are the members primarily Sunni or Shia? Immigrants or African Americans?

2. Should communities be allowed to block the construction of mosques or dictate their appearance? Would your answer be the same if your community tried to block the construction of a church or temple?

Sources: Ba-Yunus and Kone 2004; Belt 2002; Institute for Social Policy and Understanding 2004; P. King 2004; Leonard 2003; McCloud 1995; N. Paik 2001; T. Smith 2001.

---

sider status, sects frequently exhibit a higher degree of religious fervor and loyalty than more established religious groups. Recruitment focuses mainly on adults, and acceptance comes through conversion.

Sects are often short-lived. Those that are able to survive may become less antagonistic to society over time and begin to resemble denominations. In a few instances, sects have been able to endure over several generations while remaining fairly separate from society. Sociologist J. Milton Yinger (1970:226–273) uses the term *established sect* to describe a religious group that is the outgrowth of a sect, yet remains isolated from society. The Hutterites, Jehovah's Witnesses, Seventh-Day Adventists, and Amish are contemporary examples of established sects in the United States.

New Religious Movements or Cults

In 1997, 38 members of the Heaven's Gate cult were found dead in Southern California after a mass suicide timed to occur with

the appearance of the Hale-Bopp comet. They believed the comet hid a spaceship on which they could catch a ride once they had broken free of their "bodily containers."

Partly as a result of the notoriety generated by such groups, the popular media have stigmatized the word *cult,* associating it with the occult and the use of intense and forceful conversion techniques. The stereotyping of cults as uniformly bizarre and unethical has led sociologists to abandon the term and refer instead to a *new religious movement (NRM).* While some NRMs exhibit strange behavior, many do not. They attract new members just like any other religion, and often follow teachings similar to those of established Christian denominations, though with less ritual.

Sects are difficult to distinguish from cults. A ***new religious movement (NRM)*** or ***cult*** is generally a small, secretive religious group that represents either a new religion or a major innovation of an existing faith. NRMs are similar to sects in that they

Let's Discuss What are the connotations of the word *cult*?
Student Alert Present case studies of new religious movements that mainstream Americans would not consider bizarre.

FIGURE 13–3

Largest Religious Groups in the United States by County, 2000

MAPPING LIFE

NATIONWIDE www.mnhe.com/schaefer7

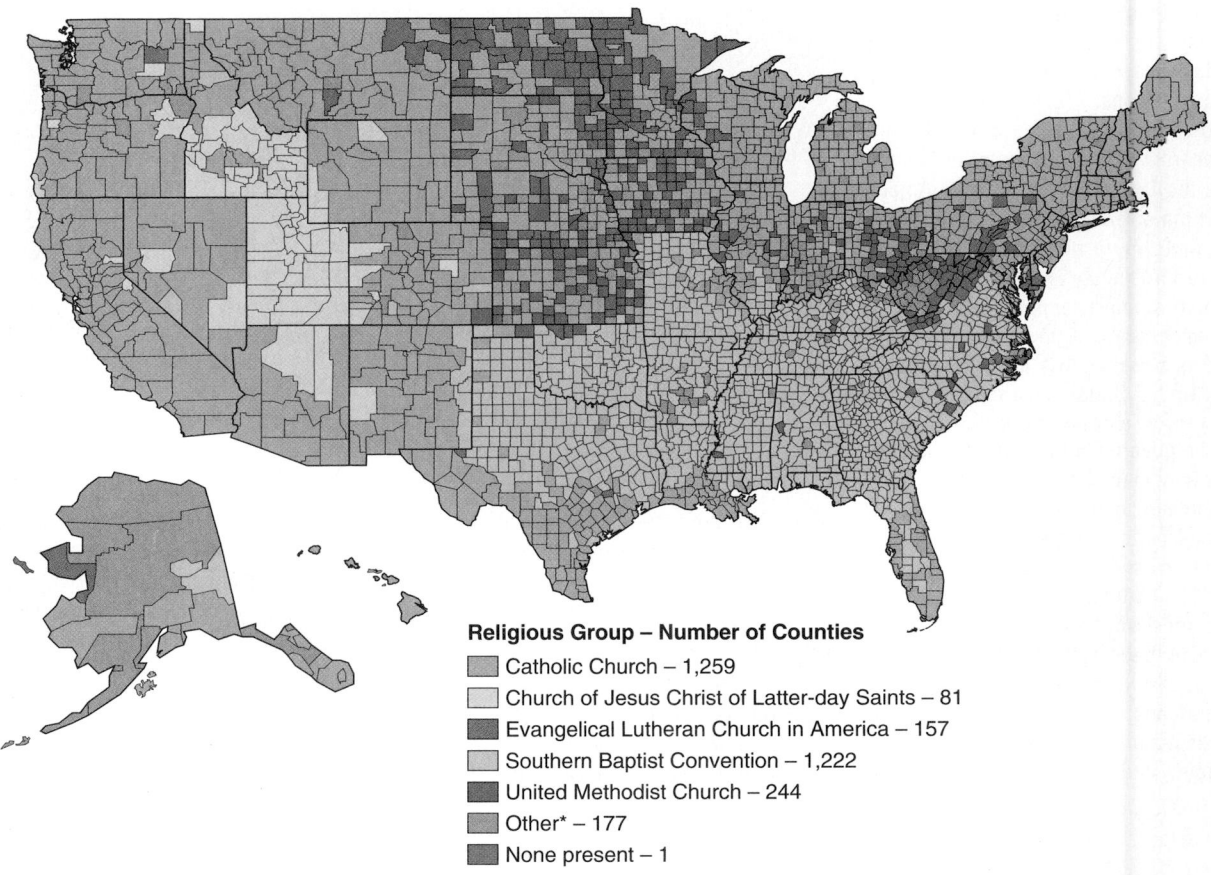

Religious Group – Number of Counties

- Catholic Church – 1,259
- Church of Jesus Christ of Latter-day Saints – 81
- Evangelical Lutheran Church in America – 157
- Southern Baptist Convention – 1,222
- United Methodist Church – 244
- Other* – 177
- None present – 1

Source: D. Jones et al. 2002:562.

This map, which shows only the largest participating religious group in each county, nevertheless suggests the large variety of faiths practiced in the United States. A total of 149 religious denominations reported the numbers of their adherents for the study on which this map is based.

tend to be small and are often viewed as less respectable than more established faiths. Unlike sects, however, NRMs normally do not result from schisms or breaks with established ecclesiae or denominations. Some cults, such as those focused on UFO sightings, may be totally unrelated to existing faiths. Even when a cult does accept certain fundamental tenets of a dominant faith—such as a belief in Jesus as divine or in Mohammad as a messenger of God—it will offer new revelations or insights to justify its claim to being a more advanced religion (Stark and Bainbridge 1979, 1985).

Like sects, NRMs may be transformed over time into other types of religious organizations. An example is the Christian Science Church, which began as a new religious movement un-

der the leadership of Mary Baker Eddy. Today, this church exhibits the characteristics of a denomination. In fact, most major religions, including Christianity, began as cults. NRMs may be in the early stages of developing into a denomination or new religion, or they may just as easily fade away through the loss of members or weak leadership (J. Richardson and van Driel 1997).

Comparing Forms of Religious Organization

How can we determine whether a particular religious group falls into the sociological category of ecclesia, denomination, sect, or NRM? As we have seen, these types of religious organization have somewhat different relationships to society. Ecclesiae are

Student Alert The role of Mary Baker Eddy in the Christian Science Church was unusual; in patriarchal societies, religious movements rarely emerge through the leadership of women.

summingUP

Table 13-3 Characteristics of Ecclesiae, Denominations, Sects, and New Religious Movements

Characteristic	Ecclesia	Denomination	Sect	New Religious Movement (or Cult)
Size	Very large	Large	Small	Small
Wealth	Extensive	Extensive	Limited	Variable
Religious services	Formal, little participation	Formal, little participation	Informal, emotional	Variable
Doctrines	Specific, but interpretation may be tolerated	Specific, but interpretation may be tolerated	Specific, purity of doctrine emphasized	Innovative, pathbreaking
Clergy	Well-trained, full-time	Well-trained, full-time	Trained to some degree	Unspecialized
Membership	By virtue of being a member of society	By acceptance of doctrine	By acceptance of doctrine	By an emotional commitment
Relationship to the state	Recognized, closely aligned	Tolerated	Not encouraged	Ignored or challenged

Source: Adapted from Vernon 1962; see also Chalfant et al. 1994.

recognized as national churches; denominations, although not officially approved by the state, are generally widely respected. In contrast, sects and NRMs are much more likely to be at odds with the larger culture.

Still, ecclesiae, denominations, and sects are best viewed as types along a continuum rather than as mutually exclusive categories. Table 13-3 summarizes some of the primary characteristics of these ideal types. Since the United States has no ecclesia, sociologists studying this country's religions have focused on the denomination and the sect. These religious forms have been pictured on either end of a continuum, with denominations accommodating to the secular world and sects protesting against established religions. While NRMs are included in Table 13-3, they lie outside the continuum, because they generally define themselves in terms of a new view of life rather than in terms of existing religious faiths.

Advances in electronic communications have led to still another form of religious organization: the electronic church. Facilitated by cable television and satellite transmission, *televangelists* (as they are called) direct their messages to more people—especially in the United States—than are served by all but the largest denominations. While some televangelists are af-

filiated with religious denominations, most give viewers the impression that they are dissociated from established faiths.

At the close of the 1990s, the electronic church had taken on yet another dimension: the Internet. According to one 2005 survey, about 1 million weblogs, or blogs (that is, online opinion columns or diaries) have been established in the United States primarily to address people's views about religion or their personal spiritual experiences. People also use cyberspace to learn more about their faith, or even just to monitor the activities of their own places of worship (D. Cohen 2005).

Use Your Sociological Imagination
www.mhhe.com/schaefer7

Suppose the political landscape in the United States has changed. The two mainstream parties, which once appealed to a broad cross-section of U.S. voters, have begun to champion specific religious beliefs. As you prepare to cast your vote, what are your concerns, both personal and societal? Assuming that one of the parties supports your religious views, would you vote for its candidates on that basis? What would you do if neither party was sympathetic to your beliefs?

Web Resource In the audio clip, Richard Schaefer, author of this text discusses how worship in cyberspace makes us reflect on Durkheim's notion of religion as a collective system of beliefs and practices relative to the sacred. Students can listen to the audio clip in the student center of the Online Learning Center (**www.mhhe.com/schaefer7**).

[RELIGION IN INDIA]

From a sociological point of view, the nation of India is large and complex enough that it might be considered a world of its own. Four hundred languages are spoken in India, 18 of which are officially recognized by the government. Besides the two major religions that originated there—Hinduism and Buddhism—several other faiths animate this society. Demographically the nation is huge, with over a billion residents. This teeming country is expected to overtake China as the most populous nation in the world in about three decades (Third World Institute 2003; United Nations Population Information Network 2003).

The Religious Tapestry in India

Hinduism and Islam, the two most important religions in India, were described on pages 320–321. Islam arrived in India in A.D. 1000, with the first of many Muslim invasions. It flowered there during the Mogul empire (1526–1857), the period when the Taj Mahal was built. Today, Muslims account for 12 percent of India's population; Hindus make up 74 percent.

The presence of one dominant faith influences how a society views a variety of issues, even secular ones. For example, India has emerged as a leader in biotechnology, due at least partly to the Hindu faith's tolerance of stem cell research and cloning—techniques that have been questioned in nations where Christianity dominates. Hinduism is open to the latest biomedical techniques, as long as no evil is intended. The only legal prohibition is that fetuses cannot be terminated for the purpose of providing stem cells. Because of its respect for life in all its forms, Hinduism has no major conflict with engineered life forms of any kind, such as clones (Religion Watch 2006).

Another religion, the Sikh faith, originated in the 15th century with a Hindu named Nanak, the first of a series of gurus (prophets). Sikhism shows the influence of Islam in India, in that it is monotheistic (based on a belief in one god rather than many). It resembles Buddhism in its emphasis on meditation and spiritual transcendence of the everyday world. *Sikhs* (learners) pursue their goal of spiritual enlightenment through meditation with the help of a guru.

Sikh men have a characteristic mode of dress that makes them easy to identify. They do not cut their beards or hair, and they wrap their heads in turbans. (Because of their distinctive dress, the 400,000 Sikhs who live in the United States are often mistaken—and discriminated against—as Muslims.) Sikhs are highly patriotic. Though their 20 million members make up just 2 percent of India's population, they account for 25 percent of India's army. Their presence in the military gives them a much larger voice in the governance of the country than might be expected, given their numbers (Fausset 2003; Watson 2005).

Another faith that has been influential beyond its numbers in India is Jainism (pronounced *Jinism*). This religion was founded six centuries before the birth of Christ—about the same time as Buddhism—by a young Hindu named Mahavira. Offended by the Hindu caste system—the rigid social hierarchy that reduces some people to the status of outcastes based solely on their birth—and by the numerous Hindu deities, Mahavira left his family and his wealth behind to become a beggar monk. His teachings attracted many followers, and the faith grew and flourished until the Muslim invasions of the 12th century.

According to the Jain faith, there is no god; each person is responsible for his or her own spiritual well-being. By following a strict code of conduct, Jains believe they can ultimately free their souls from the endless cycle of death and rebirth and attain *nirvana* (spiritual enlightenment). Jains are required to meditate; forswear lying and stealing; limit their personal wealth; and practice self-denial, chastity, and nonviolence. Because they will not knowingly harm other living beings, including plants and animals, Jains shun meat, fish, or even vegetables whose harvest kills the entire plant, such as carrots and potatoes. They will not work in the military, in farming or fishing, or in the manufacture or sale of alcohol and drugs.

Though the Jains are a relatively small group (about 4 million), they exercise considerable influence in India through their business dealings and charitable contributions. Together with

{ This Hindu temple in Khajuraho was built in the 11th century. The Hindu faith is enormously influential in India, the country where most Hindus live. }

Global View Religion in India
Student Alert Relate this discussion to the terms *religious belief, ritual,* and *experience.*

332

Christians and Buddhists, Jains make up 4 percent of India's population (Embree 2003).

Religion and the State in India

Religion was influential in India's drive to overturn British colonialism. The great Mohandas K. Gandhi (1869–1948) led the long struggle to regain India's sovereignty, which culminated in its independence in 1947. A proponent of nonviolent resistance, Gandhi persuaded Hindus and Muslims, ancient enemies, to join together in defying British domination. But his influence as a peacemaker could not override the Muslims' demand for a separate state of their own. Immediately after independence was granted, India was partitioned into two states, Pakistan for the Muslims and India for the Hindus. The new arrangement caused large-scale migrations of Indians, especially Muslims, from one nation to the other, and sparked boundary disputes that continue to this day. In many areas Muslims were forced to abandon places they considered sacred. In the chaotic months that followed, centuries of animosity between the two groups boiled over into riots, ending in Gandhi's assassination in January 1948.

Today, India is a secular state that is dominated by Hindus (see Figure 13-1 on page 317). Though the government is officially tolerant of the Muslim minority, tensions between Hindus and Muslims remain high in some states. Conflict also exists among various Hindu groups, from fundamentalists to more secular and ecumenical adherents (Embree 2003).

Many observers see religion as the moving force in Indian society. That certainly can be said of politics. When Indian political parties align themselves along religious lines, their actions polarize the nation's population. One party in particular, the Bharatiya Janata Party (BJP), is dominated by Hindu nationalists. The BJP, a major national party, led the coalition that controlled the Indian government from 1998 to 2004. Members of this party who manage to get elected to local office often tend to tolerate anti-Muslim violence. Today, however, India's prime minister is a Sikh, and its president is a Muslim woman—a combination that reflects the nation's political volatility. ●

Sociological Perspectives on Education

Besides being a major industry in the United States, education is the social institution that formally socializes members of our society. In the last few decades, increasing proportions of people have obtained high school diplomas, college degrees, and advanced professional degrees. For example, the proportion of people age 25 or over with a high school diploma increased from 41 percent in 1960 to more than 85 percent in 2004. Those with a college degree rose from 8 percent in 1960 to about 28 percent in 2004 (Bureau of the Census 2005h). Figure 13-4 shows the proportion of the college-educated population in other countries.

Throughout the world, education has become a vast and complex social institution that prepares citizens for the roles demanded by other social institutions, such as the family, government, and the economy. The functionalist, conflict, and interactionist perspectives offer distinctive views of education as a social institution.

Functionalist View

Like other social institutions, education has both manifest (open, stated) and latent (hidden) functions. The most basic *manifest* function of education is the transmission of knowledge. Schools teach students how to read, speak foreign languages, and repair automobiles. Another important manifest function is the bestowal of status. Because many believe this

FIGURE 13–4

Percentage of Adults Ages 25 to 64 Who Have Completed Higher Education

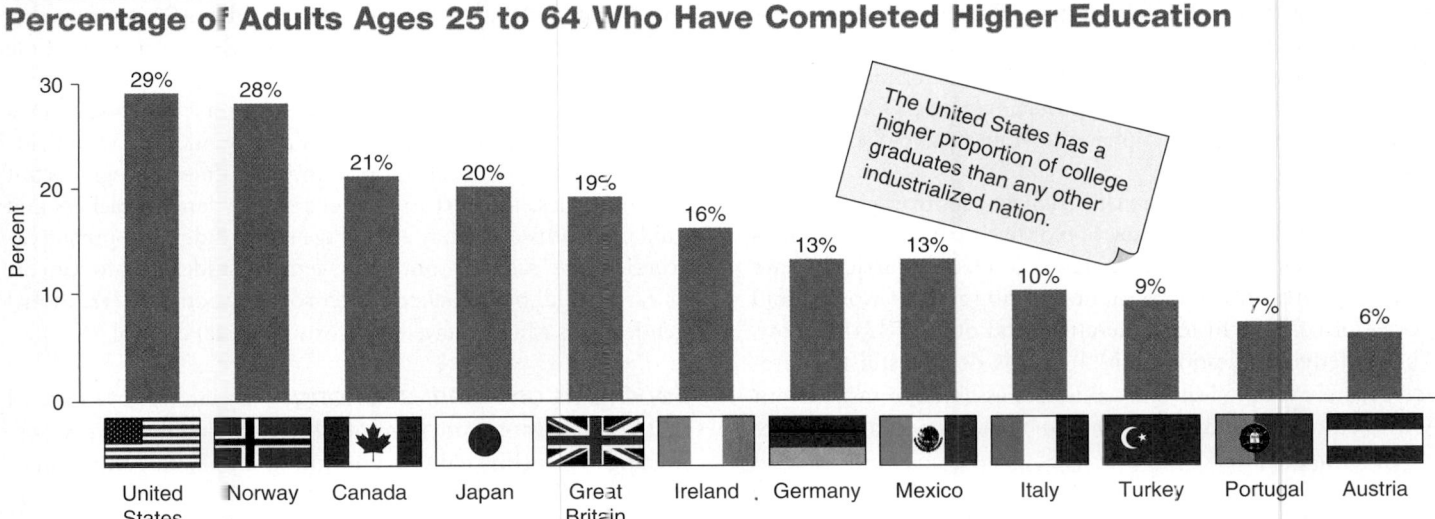

Source: Data for 2002 released in Bureau of the Census 2005a:872.

Policy Pointer Religion and political tensions between India and Pakistan

Classroom Tip See "Schools Are Not the Answer" (Class Discussion Topics).
Theory Functionalist view of the manifest and latent functions of education

function is performed inequitably, we will consider it later, in the section on the conflict view of education.

In addition to these manifest functions, schools perform a number of *latent* functions: transmitting culture, promoting social and political integration, maintaining social control, and serving as an agent of change.

Transmitting Culture

As a social institution, education performs a rather conservative function—transmitting the dominant culture. Schooling exposes each generation of young people to the existing beliefs, norms, and values of their culture. In our society, we learn respect for social control and reverence for established institutions, such as religion, the family, and the presidency. Of course, this statement is true of many other cultures as well. While schoolchildren in the United States are hearing about the accomplishments of George Washington and Abraham Lincoln, British children are hearing about the distinctive contributions of Queen Elizabeth I and Winston Churchill.

In Great Britain, the transmission of the dominant culture through schools goes far beyond learning about monarchs and prime ministers. In 1996, the government's chief curriculum adviser—noting the need to fill a void left by the diminishing authority of the Church of England—proposed that British schools should socialize students into a set of core values. The list included honesty, respect for others, politeness, a sense of fair play, forgiveness, punctuality, nonviolent behavior, patience, faithfulness, and self-discipline (Charter and Sherman 1996).

Sometimes nations may reassess the ways in which they transmit culture. Recently South Koreans began to question the content of their school curriculum. South Korean schools teach traditional Confucian values, with a focus on rote memorization. The emphasis is on accumulating facts rather than on reasoning logically. Entrance to college turns on a highly competitive exam that tests students' knowledge of facts. Once in college, students have virtually no opportunity to change their educational programs, and their instruction continues to emphasize memorization. The combination of an economic crisis and growing complaints about the educational process has caused government officials to reevaluate the nation's educational structure. Moreover, growth in juvenile crime, although low by our standards, has led the government to introduce a new civic education program emphasizing honesty and discipline (C. Woodard 1998).

On the college level in the United States, controversy has been growing over the general education or basic curriculum requirements. Critics charge that standard academic curricula have failed to represent the important contributions of women and people of color to history, literature, and other fields of study. The underlying questions raised by this debate, still to be resolved, are: Which ideas and values are essential to instruction? Which culture should be transmitted by the schools and colleges of the United States?

Promoting Social and Political Integration

Many institutions require students in their first year or two of college to live on campus to foster a sense of community among diverse groups. Education serves the latent function of promoting social and political integration by transforming a population composed of diverse racial, ethnic, and religious groups into a society whose members share—to some extent—a common identity. Historically, schools in the United States have played an important role in socializing the children of immigrants into the norms, values, and beliefs of the dominant culture. From a functionalist perspective, the common identity and social integration fostered by education contribute to societal stability and consensus (Touraine 1974).

In the past, the integrative function of education was most obvious in its emphasis on promoting a common language. Immigrant children were expected to learn English. In some instances, they were even forbidden to speak their native language {p.71} on school grounds. More recently, bilingualism has been defended both for its educational value and as a means of encouraging cultural diversity. However, critics argue that bilingualism undermines the social and political integration that education has traditionally promoted.

Maintaining Social Control

In performing the manifest function of transmitting knowledge, schools go far beyond teaching skills like reading, writing, and mathematics. Like other social institutions, such as the family and religion, education prepares young people to lead productive and orderly lives as adults by introducing them to the norms, values, and sanctions of the larger society.

Through the exercise of social control, schools teach students various skills and values essential to their future positions in the labor force. They learn punctuality, discipline, scheduling, and responsible work habits, as well as how to negotiate the complexities of a bureaucratic organization. As a social institution, education reflects the interests of both the family and another social institution, the economy. Students are trained for what is ahead, whether it be the assembly line or a physician's office. In effect, then, schools serve as a transitional agent of social control, bridging the gap between parents and employers in the life cycle of most individuals (Bowles and Gintis 1976; M. Cole 1988).

Schools direct and even restrict students' aspirations in a manner that reflects societal values and prejudices. School administrators may allocate ample funds for athletic programs but give much less support to music, art, and dance. Teachers and guidance counselors may encourage male students to pursue careers in the sciences but steer female students into careers as early childhood teachers. Such socialization into traditional gender roles can be viewed as a form of social control.

Serving as an Agent of Change

So far, we have focused on the conservative functions of education—on its role in transmitting the existing culture, promoting social and political integration, and maintaining social control. Yet education can also stimulate or bring about desired social change. Sex education classes were introduced to public schools in response to the

Classroom Tip Relate the concept of dominant ideology (Chapter 3) to the function of education in transmitting culture.
Global View Transmission of the dominant culture in Great Britain and South Korea
Reel Society See Education in the Topic Index.
Let's Discuss Do students think their college classes give enough attention to the contributions of women and people of color?

Theory Functionalist view that education promotes social and political integration
Policy Pointer The debate over bilingualism in the United States
Web Resource Refer students to the "Social Policy" link for Chapter 3 in the student center of the Online Learning Center (www.mhhe.com/schaefer7). They can see how people feel about speaking and teaching English in school.
Gender Socialization into traditional gender roles

verse opinions, and to possess the ability to make subtle distinctions in analysis. Formal education stresses both the importance of qualifying statements (in place of broad generalizations) and the need at least to question (rather than {p.30 simply accept) established truths and practices. The scientific method, which relies on *testing* hypotheses, reflects the questioning spirit that characterizes modern education (R. Williams et al. 1964).

Conflict View

The functionalist perspective portrays contemporary education as a basically benign institution. For example, it argues that schools rationally sort and select students for future high-status positions, thereby meeting society's need for talented and expert personnel. In contrast, the conflict perspective views education as an instrument of elite domination. Conflict theorists point out the sharp inequalities that exist in the educational opportunities available to different racial and ethnic groups. In 2004, the nation marked the 50th anniversary of the Supreme Court's landmark decision *Brown v. Board of Education,* which declared unconstitutional the segregation of public schools. Yet today, African Americans are still 6 percent less likely than Whites, and Latinos 32 percent less likely than Whites, to have completed high school. Furthermore, Black and Latino schoolchildren continue to underperform White schoolchildren on nationally standardized tests (Bureau of the Census 2005a:147).

Conflict theorists also argue that the educational system socializes students into values dictated by the powerful, that schools stifle individualism and creativity in the name of maintaining order, and that the level of change they promote is relatively insignificant. From a conflict perspective, the inhibiting effects of education are particularly apparent in the "hidden curriculum" and the differential way in which status is bestowed.

The Hidden Curriculum Schools are highly bureaucratic organizations, as we will see later. Many teachers rely on rules and regulations to maintain order. Unfortunately, the need for control and discipline can take precedence over the learning process. Teachers may focus on obedience to the rules as an end in itself, in which case students and teachers alike become victims of what Philip Jackson (1968) has called the *hidden curriculum.*

The term **hidden curriculum** refers to standards of behavior that are deemed proper by society and are taught subtly in schools. According to this curriculum, children must not speak until the teacher calls on them, and must regulate their activities according to the clock or bells. In addition, they are expected to concentrate on their own work rather than to assist other

In response to a high pregnancy rate among adolescent girls, many schools now offer sex education courses that promote abstinence. When schools attempt to remedy negative social trends, they are serving as an agent of social change.

{p.241 soaring pregnancy rate among teenagers. Affirmative action in admissions—giving priority to females or minorities—has been endorsed as a means of countering racial and sexual discrimination. Project Head Start, an early childhood program that serves more than 906,000 children annually, has sought to compensate for the disadvantages in school readiness experienced by children from low-income families (Bureau of the Census 2005a:376).

Education also promotes social change by serving as a meeting ground where people can share distinctive beliefs and traditions. In 2005, U.S. campuses hosted just over 565,000 international students. While that is a large number, it represented the second successive decline over the preceding academic year. This reversal in the long-term trend may be temporary, but the tightening of visa requirements that followed the terrorist attacks of September 11, 2001, has made the United States appear to be less welcoming to foreign students than in the past. Educators worry that a sustained drop in the number of international students may adversely affect engineering and science programs, which find it difficult to attract qualified U.S. students. From a larger perspective, U.S. relations around the world are nurtured on our college campuses. Thus, a long-term decline in the number of international students could eventually weaken U.S. economic and diplomatic relationships (Institute of International Education 2005).

Numerous sociological studies have revealed that additional years of formal schooling are associated with openness to new ideas and more liberal social and political viewpoints. Sociologist Robin Williams points out that better-educated people tend to have greater access to factual information, to hold more di-

students who learn more slowly. A hidden curriculum is evident in schools around the world. For example, Japanese schools offer guidance sessions that seek to improve the classroom experience and develop healthy living skills. In effect, these sessions instill values and encourage behavior useful in the Japanese business world, such as self-discipline and openness to group problem solving and decision making (Okano and Tsuchiya 1999).

In a classroom that is overly focused on obedience, value is placed on pleasing the teacher and remaining quiet rather than on creative thought and academic learning. Habitual obedience to authority may result in the type of distressing behavior documented by Stanley Milgram in his classic obedience studies. {p.159–160}

Credentialism Fifty years ago, a high school diploma was the minimum requirement for entry into the paid labor force of the United States. Today, a college diploma is virtually the bare minimum. This change reflects the process of *credentialism*—a term used to describe an increase in the lowest level of education needed to enter a field.

In recent decades, the number of occupations that are viewed as professions has risen. Credentialism is one symptom of this trend. Employers and occupational associations typically contend that such changes are a logical response to the increasing complexity of many jobs. However, in many cases, employers raise the degree requirements for a position simply because all applicants have achieved the existing minimum credential (D. Brown 2001; Hurn 1985).

Conflict theorists observe that credentialism may reinforce social inequality. Applicants from poor and minority backgrounds are especially likely to suffer from the escalation of qualifications, since they lack the financial resources needed to obtain degree after degree. In addition, upgrading of credentials serves the self-interest of the two groups most responsible for this trend. Educational institutions profit from prolonging the investment of time and money that people make by staying in school. Moreover, as C. J. Hurn (1985) has suggested, current jobholders have a stake in raising occupational requirements, since credentialism can increase the status of an occupation and lead to demands for higher pay. Max Weber anticipated this possibility as early as 1916, concluding that the "universal clamor for the creation of educational certificates in all fields makes for the formation of a privileged stratum in businesses and in offices" (Gerth and Mills 1958:240–241).

Use Your Sociological Imagination

www.mhhe.com /schaefer7

How would you react if the job you have or plan to pursue suddenly required a higher-level degree? If suddenly the requirements were lowered?

Bestowal of Status Both functionalist and conflict theorists agree that education performs the important function of be-

stowing status. As noted earlier, an increasing proportion of people in the United States are obtaining high school diplomas, college degrees, and advanced professional degrees. From a functionalist perspective, this widening bestowal of status is beneficial not only to particular recipients but to society as a whole. According to Kingsley Davis and Wilbert E. Moore (1945), society must distribute its members among a variety of social positions. Education can contribute to this process by sorting people into appropriate levels and courses of study that will prepare them for positions in the labor force. {pp.192–193}

Conflict theorists are far more critical of the *differential* way in which education bestows status. They stress that schools sort pupils according to their social class backgrounds. Although the educational system helps certain poor children to move into middle-class professional positions, it denies most disadvantaged children the same educational opportunities afforded to children of the affluent. In this way, schools tend to preserve social class inequalities in each new generation (Giroux 1988; Pinkerton 2003).

Even a single school can reinforce class differences by putting students in tracks. The term *tracking* refers to the practice of placing students in specific curriculum groups on the basis of their test scores and other criteria. Tracking begins very early, often in reading groups during first grade. Most recent research on such ability groupings raises questions about its effectiveness, especially for low-ability students. Tracks can reinforce the disadvantages that children from less affluent families may face if they haven't been exposed to reading materials, computers, and other forms of educational stimulation during their early childhood years. It is estimated that about 60 percent of elementary schools in the United States and about 80 percent of secondary schools use some form of tracking (Hallinan 2003; Sadker and Sadker 2003).

Tracking and differential access to higher education are evident in many nations around the world. Japan's educational

Studies conducted since 1987 suggest that the funding inequities between richer and poorer school districts have actually widened in recent years.

Global View The hidden curriculum in Japanese schools
Classroom Tip See "Hidden Curriculum" (Class Discussion Topics).
Key Person Stanley Milgram (See Chapter 7)
Theory Conflict view that credentialism may reinforce social inequality

Theory Functionalist view of how widening bestowal of status is beneficial to society as a whole; conflict view that schools bestow status according to students' social class background
Let's Discuss What proportion of your students were tracked during high school?

system mandates equality in school funding and insists that all schools use the same textbooks. Nevertheless, only the more affluent Japanese families can afford to send their children to *juku,* or cram schools. These afternoon schools prepare high school students for examinations that determine admission into prestigious colleges (Efron 1997).

Conflict theorists hold that the educational inequalities produced by tracking are designed to meet the needs of modern capitalist societies. Samuel Bowles and Herbert Gintis (1976) have argued that capitalism requires a skilled, disciplined labor force, and that the educational system of the United States is structured with that objective in mind. Citing numerous studies, they offer support for what they call the ***correspondence principle.*** According to this approach, schools promote the values expected of individuals in each social class and perpetuate social class divisions from one generation to the next. Thus, working-class children, assumed to be destined for subordinate positions, are likely to be placed in high school vocational and general tracks, which emphasize close supervision and compliance with authority. In contrast, young people from more affluent families are likely to be directed to college preparatory tracks, which stress leadership and decision making—the skills they are expected to need as adults.

Although the Chinese government is attempting to address educational inequalities, girls continue to receive less education than boys—especially in rural areas.

Treatment of Women in Education

The educational system of the United States, like many other social institutions, has long been characterized by discriminatory treatment of women. In 1833, Oberlin College became the first institution of higher learning to admit female students—some 200 years after the first men's college was established. But Oberlin believed that women should aspire to become wives and mothers, not lawyers and intellectuals. In addition to attending classes, female students washed men's clothing, cared for their rooms, and served them at meals. In the 1840s, Lucy Stone, then an Oberlin undergraduate and later one of the nation's most outspoken feminist leaders, refused to write a commencement address because it would have been read to the audience by a male student.

In the 20th century, sexism in education showed up in many ways—in textbooks with negative stereotypes of women, counselors' pressure on female students to prepare for "women's work," and unequal funding for women's and men's athletic programs. But perhaps nowhere was educational discrimination more evident than in the employment of teachers. The positions of university professor and college administrator, which hold relatively high status in the United States, were generally filled by men. Public school teachers, who earn much lower salaries, were largely female.

Women have made great strides in one area: the proportion of women who continue their schooling. Women's access to graduate education and to medical, dental, and law schools has increased dramatically in the last few decades as a result of the Education Act of 1972. Box 13-3 (page 338) examines the far-reaching effects of Title IX, the part of the act that concerns discrimination against women in education.

In cultures in which traditional gender roles remain the social norm, women's education suffers appreciably. Since September 11, 2001, the growing awareness of the Taliban's repression of Afghan women has dramatized the gender disparities in education in developing nations. Research has demonstrated that women are critical to economic development and good governance, and that education is instrumental in preparing them for those roles. Educating women, especially young girls, yields high social returns by lowering birthrates and improving agricultural productivity through better management (I. Coleman 2004).

Interactionist View

In George Bernard Shaw's play *Pygmalion,* later adapted as the hit Broadway musical *My Fair Lady,* flower girl Eliza Doolittle is transformed into a "lady" by Professor Henry Higgins, who changes her manner of speech and teaches her the etiquette of "high society." When Eliza is introduced to society as an aristocrat, she is readily accepted. People treat her as a "lady" and she responds as one.

The labeling approach suggests that if we treat people in par- { p.171 } ticular ways, they may fulfill our expectations. Children who are labeled as "troublemakers" may come to view themselves as delinquents. Similarly, a dominant group's stereotyping of racial minorities may limit their opportunities to break away from expected roles.

Global View Cram schools in Japan
Classroom Tip See "Both Boys and Girls Have Reason to Feel Disadvantaged in School" (Additional Lecture Ideas); and "Inequality in Education" (Additional Lecture Ideas).
Gender Treatment of women in education
Theory Conflict view of sexism in education

Global View Treatment of girls in Afghanistan
Theory Interactionist view of education introduced

13-3 The Debate over Title IX

Few federal policies have had such a visible effect on education over the last 30 years as Title IX, which mandates gender equity in education in federally funded schools. Congressional amendments to the Education Act of 1972, together with guidelines for their implementation developed by the Department of Health, Education, and Welfare in 1974–1975, have brought significant changes for both men and women at all levels of schooling. Title IX eliminated sex-segregated classes, prohibited sex discrimination in admissions and financial aid, and mandated that girls receive more opportunities to play sports, in proportion to their enrollment and interest.

Today, Title IX is still one of the more controversial attempts ever made by the federal government to promote equality for all citizens. Its consequences for the funding of college athletics programs are hotly debated, while its real and lasting effects on college admissions and employment are often forgotten. Critics charge that men's teams have suffered from proportional funding of women's teams and athletic scholarships, since schools with tight athletic budgets can expand women's sports only at the expense of men's sports. To a certain extent, non-revenue-producing men's sports such as wrestling and golf do appear to have suffered as women's teams have been added. But the high expense of some men's sports, particularly football, would be beyond many schools' means even without Title IX expenditures. And the gains for women have

more than made up for the losses to men. In 1971, when there were few opportunities for women athletes on college campuses, only 300,000 girls participated in high school sports. In 2003, three decades after Title IX opened up college athletics to women, the figure was 2.7 million.

For minority women, however, the results have been less satisfactory. Most of the women's sports that have benefited from increases in scholarships over the last 20 years, like rowing and volleyball, traditionally have not been attractive to minority women. Twenty-

> *Critics charge that men's teams have suffered from proportional funding of women's teams and athletic scholarships.*

five years ago, just 2 percent of female college athletes were African American. Today, the percentage is a disappointing 2.7 percent.

Sociologists note, too, that the social effects of sports on college campuses are not all positive. Michael A. Messner, professor of sociology at the University of Southern California, points to some troubling results of a survey by the Women's Sports Foundation. The study shows that teenage girls who play sports simply for fun have more positive body images than girls who don't play sports. But those who are "highly involved" in sports are more likely

than other girls to take steroids and to become binge drinkers and risk takers. "Everyone has tacitly agreed, it seems, to view men's sports as the standard to which women should strive to have equal access," Messner writes. "Missing from the debate is any recognition that men's sports have become sources of major problems on campuses: academic cheating, sexual violence, alcohol abuse, steroid use, serious injuries and other health issues, to name just a few" (Messner 2002:B9). Messner is skeptical of a system that propels a lucky few college athletes to stardom each year while leaving the majority, many of them African American, without a career or an education. Certainly that was not the kind of equal opportunity legislators envisioned when they wrote Title IX.

Let's Discuss

1. Has Title IX had an effect on you personally? If so, explain. On balance, do you think the increase in women's participation in sports has been good for society as a whole?

2. Are the negative social effects of men's sports evident on your campus? If so, what changes would you recommend to address the problem?

Sources: Federal Register, June 4, 1975; V. Gutierrez 2002; H. Mason 2003; Messner 2002.

Can the labeling process operate in the classroom? Because of their focus on micro-level classroom dynamics, interactionist researchers have been particularly interested in this question. Howard S. Becker (1952) studied public schools in low-income and more affluent areas of Chicago. He noticed that administrators expected less of students from poor neighborhoods, and wondered if teachers accepted their view. A decade later, in *Pygmalion in the Classroom*, psychologist Robert Rosenthal and school principal Lenore Jacobson (1968) documented what they referred to as a *teacher-expectancy effect*—the impact that a teacher's expectations about a student's performance may have on the student's actual achievements. This effect is especially evident in the lower grades (through grade three).

In this experiment, children in a San Francisco elementary school were administered a verbal and reasoning pretest. Rosenthal and Jacobson then *randomly* selected 20 percent of the sample and designated them as "spurters"—children of whom teachers could expect superior performance. On a later verbal and reasoning test, the spurters were found to score significantly higher than before. Moreover, teachers evaluated them as more interesting, more curious, and better-adjusted than their classmates. These results were striking. Apparently, teachers' perceptions that the students were exceptional led to noticeable improvements in their performance.

Studies in the United States have revealed that teachers wait longer for an answer from a student they believe to be a high achiever and are more likely to give such children a second chance.

Methods Becker did observation research in Chicago schools.
Theory Discussion of the teacher-expectancy effect draws on interactionism and labeling theory.

Methods Experiments on teacher-expectancy effect in the United States

In one experiment teachers' expectations were even shown to have an impact on students' athletic achievements. Teachers obtained better athletic performance—as measured in the number of sit-ups or push-ups performed—from those students of whom they *expected* higher numbers (Babad and Taylor 1992).

Despite these findings, some researchers continue to question the accuracy of the teacher-expectancy effect. They claim it is too difficult to define and measure. Further studies are needed to clarify the relationship between teacher expectations and actual student performance. Nevertheless, interactionists emphasize that ability alone may be less predictive of academic success than one might think (Brint 1998).

Table 13-4 summarizes the three major theoretical perspectives on education

Schools as Formal Organizations

Nineteenth-century educators would be amazed at the scale of schools in the United States in the 21st century. For example, California's public school system, the largest in the nation, currently enrolls as many children as there were in secondary schools in the entire country in 1950 (Bureau of the Census 1975:368; 2004a).

In many respects, today's schools, when viewed as an example of a formal organization, are similar to factories, hospitals, and business firms. Like those organizations, schools do not operate autonomously; they are influenced by the market of potential students. This statement is especially true of private schools, but could have broader impact if acceptance of voucher plans and other school choice programs increases. The parallels between schools and other types of formal organizations will become more apparent as we examine the bureaucratic nature of schools, teaching as an occupation, and the student subculture (K. Dougherty and Hammack 1992).

Bureaucratization of Schools

It simply is not possible for a single teacher to transmit culture and skills to children of varying ages who will enter many diverse occupations. The growing number of students being served by school systems and the greater degree of specialization required within a technologically complex society have combined to bureaucratize schools.

Max Weber noted five basic characteristics of bureaucracy, all { pp.119–121 of which are evident in the vast majority of schools, whether at the elementary, secondary, or even college level:

1. **Division of labor.** Specialized experts teach particular age levels and specific subjects. Public elementary and secondary schools now employ instructors whose sole responsibility is to work with children with learning disabilities or physical impairments.

2. **Hierarchy of authority.** Each employee of a school system is responsible to a higher authority. Teachers must report to principals and assistant principals, and may also be supervised by department heads. Principals are answerable to a superintendent of schools, and the superintendent is hired and fired by a board of education.

3. **Written rules and regulations.** Teachers and administrators must conform to numerous rules and regulations in the performance of their duties. This bureaucratic trait can become dysfunctional; the time invested in completing required forms could instead be spent in preparing lessons or conferring with students.

4. **Impersonality.** As class sizes have swelled at schools and universities, it has become more difficult for teachers to give personal attention to each student. In fact, bureaucratic norms may actually encourage teachers to treat all students in the same way, despite the fact that students have distinctive personalities and learning needs.

5. **Employment based on technical qualifications.** At least in theory, the hiring of instructors is based on professional competence and expertise. Promotions are normally dictated by written personnel policies; people who excel may be granted lifelong job security through tenure.

Functionalists take a generally positive view of the bureaucratization of education. Teachers can master the skills needed to work with a specialized clientele, since they no longer are expected to cover a broad range of instruction. The chain of command within schools is clear. Students are presumably treated in an unbiased fashion because of uniformly applied rules. Finally, security of position protects teachers from unjustified dismissal. In general, then, functionalists stress that the bureaucratization of education increases the likelihood that students, teachers, and administrators will be dealt with fairly—that is, on the basis of rational and equitable criteria.

In contrast, conflict theorists argue that the trend toward more centralized education has harmful consequences for disadvantaged people. The standardization of educational curricula, including textbooks, will generally reflect the values, interests, and

Table 13-4 Sociological Perspectives on Education

Theoretical Perspective	Emphasis
Functionalist	Transmission of the dominant culture Integration of society Promotion of social norms, values, and sanctions Promotion of desirable social change
Conflict	Domination by the elite through unequal access to schooling Hidden curriculum Credentialism Bestowal of status
Interactionist	Teacher-expectancy effect

Theory Functionalist view of the bureaucratization of education
Key Person Max Weber

summingUP

lifestyles of the most powerful groups in our society, and may ignore those of racial and ethnic minorities. In addition, the disadvantaged, more so than the affluent, will find it difficult to sort through complex educational bureaucracies and to organize effective lobbying groups. Therefore, in the view of conflict theorists, low-income and minority parents will have even less influence over citywide and statewide educational administrators than they have over local school officials (Bowles and Gintis 1976; Katz 1971).

Sometimes schools can seem overwhelmingly bureaucratic, with the effect of stifling rather than nourishing intellectual curiosity in students. This concern has led many parents and policymakers to push for school choice programs—allowing parents to choose the school that suits their children's needs, and forcing schools to compete for their "customers."

In the United States, another significant countertrend to the bureaucratization of schools is the availability of education over the Internet. Increasingly, colleges and universities are reaching out via the Web, offering entire courses and even majors to students in the comfort of their homes. Online curricula provide flexibility for working students and others who may have difficulty attending conventional classes because of distance or disability. Research on this type of learning is just beginning, so the question of whether teacher–student contact can thrive online remains to be settled. Computer-mediated instruction may also have an impact on instructors' status as employees, which we will discuss next, as well as on alternative forms of education like adult education and homeschooling.

Use Your Sociological Imagination
www.mhhe.com/schaefer7

How would you make your school less bureaucratic? What would it be like?

Teachers: Employees and Instructors

Whether they serve as instructors of preschoolers or graduate students, teachers are employees of formal organizations with bureaucratic structures. There is an inherent conflict in serving as a professional in a bureaucracy. The organization follows the principles of hierarchy and expects adherence to its rules, but professionalism demands the individual responsibility of the practitioner. This conflict is very real for teachers, who experience all the positive and negative consequences of working in bureaucracies (see Table 5-4 on page 121).

A teacher undergoes many perplexing stresses every day. While teachers' academic assignments have become more specialized, the demands on their time remain diverse and contradictory. Conflicts arise from serving as an instructor, a disciplinarian, and an employee of a school district at the same time. Burnout is one result of these stresses: 40 to 50 percent of new teachers quit the profession within five years (Gordon 2004).

Given these difficulties, does teaching remain an attractive profession in the United States? In 2005, 5.1 percent of first-year

college students indicated that they were interested in becoming elementary school teachers, and 4.8 percent, high school teachers. These figures are dramatically lower than the 13 percent of first-year male students and 38 percent of first-year female students who held those occupational aspirations in 1968 (Astin et al. 1994; Pryor et al. 2005).

Undoubtedly, economic considerations enter into students' feelings about the attractiveness of teaching. In 2004, the average salary for all public elementary and secondary school teachers in the United States was $46,597, placing teachers somewhere near the average of all wage earners in the nation. In most other industrial countries, teachers' salaries are higher in relation to the general standard of living (American Federation of Teachers 2005).

The status of any job reflects several factors, including the level of education required, financial compensation, and the respect given the occupation by society. The teaching profession (see Table 8-2, page 195) is feeling pressure in all three of these areas. First, the level of formal schooling required for teaching remains high, and the public has begun to call for new competency examinations. Second, the statistics just cited demonstrate that teachers' salaries are significantly lower than those of many professionals and skilled workers. Finally, the overall prestige of the teaching profession has declined in the last decade. Many teachers have become disappointed and frustrated and have left the educational world for careers in other professions.

Student Subcultures

An important latent function of education relates directly to student life: Schools provide for students' social and recreational needs. Education helps toddlers and young children develop interpersonal skills that are essential during adolescence and adulthood. In their high school and college years, students may meet future husbands and wives and establish lifelong friendships.

When people observe high schools, community colleges, or universities from the outside, students appear to constitute a cohesive, uniform group. However, the student subculture is actually complex and diverse. High school cliques and social groups may crop up according to race, social class, physical attractiveness, placement in courses, athletic ability, and leadership roles in the school and community. In his classic community study of "Elmtown," August B. Hollingshead (1975) found some 259 distinct cliques in a single high school. The cliques, whose average size was five, were centered on the school itself, on recreational activities, and on religious and community groups.

Amid these close-knit and often rigidly segregated cliques, gay and lesbian students are particularly vulnerable. Peer group pressure to conform is intense at this age. Although coming to terms with one's sexuality is difficult for all adolescents, it can be downright dangerous for those whose sexual orientation does not conform to societal expectations.

Teachers and administrators are becoming more sensitized to these issues. Perhaps more important, some schools are creating gay–straight alliances (GSAs), school-sponsored support groups that bring gay teens together with sympathetic straight peers. Begun in Los Angeles in 1984, these programs numbered nearly

Theory Conflict view of the bureaucratization of education as harmful to disadvantaged people
Theory Interactionist view of role conflict among teachers
Contemporary Culture Forty to 50 percent of new teachers quit the profession within five years.

Classroom Tip Review the findings on the prestige of teachers in Table 8-2.
Student Alert Review the concept of subculture (Chapter 3).
Theory Latent functions of education in meeting students' social and recreational needs
Methods Hollingshead's observation research on cliques in a high school
Contemporary Culture/Gender Some schools are creating gay–straight alliances.

3,000 nationwide in 2005; most were founded after the murder of Matthew Shepard, a gay college student, in 1998. In some districts parents have objected to these organizations, but the same court rulings that protect the right of conservative Bible groups to meet on school grounds also protect GSAs. In 2003, the gay–straight movement reached a milestone when the New York City public schools moved an in-school program for gays, bisexuals, and transgender students to a separate school of their own. The Harvey Milk High School was named in memory of San Francisco's first openly gay city supervisor, who was assassinated in 1978 (Gay, Lesbian and Straight Education Network 2005).

We can find a similar diversity of student groups at the college level. Burton Clark and Martin Trow (1966) and more recently, Helen Lefkowitz Horowitz (1987) have identified four distinctive subcultures among college students:

1. The *collegiate* subculture focuses on having fun and socializing. These students define what constitutes a "reasonable" amount of academic work (and what amount of work is "excessive" and leads to being labeled as a "grind"). Members of the collegiate subculture have little commitment to academic pursuits. Athletes often fit into this subculture.

2. The *academic* subculture identifies with the intellectual concerns of the faculty and values knowledge for its own sake.

3. The *vocational* subculture is interested primarily in career prospects, and views college as a means of obtaining degrees that are essential for advancement.

4. Finally, the *nonconformist* subculture is hostile to the college environment, and seeks out ideas that may or may not relate to academic studies. This group may find outlets through campus publications or issue-oriented groups.

Each college student is eventually exposed to these competing subcultures and must determine which (if any) seems most in line with his or her feelings and interests.

The typology used by the researchers reminds us that school is a complex social organization—almost like a community with different neighborhoods. Of course, these four subcultures are not the only ones evident on college campuses in the United States. For example, one might find subcultures of Vietnam veterans or former full-time homemakers at community colleges and four-year commuter institutions.

Sociologist Joe R. Feagin has studied a distinctive collegiate subculture: Black students at predominantly White universities. These students must function academically and socially within universities where there are few Black faculty members or Black administrators, where harassment of Blacks by campus police is common, and where the curricula place little emphasis on Black contributions. Feagin (1989:11) suggests that "for minority students life at a predominantly White college or university means long-term encounters with pervasive whiteness." In Feagin's view, African American students at such institutions experience both blatant and subtle racial discrimination, which has a cumulative impact that can seriously damage the students' confidence (see also Feagin et al. 1996).

Classroom Tip See "Subcultures on Campus" (Class Discussion Topics).
Methods Observation research by Clark and Trow, and by Horowitz, on college student subcultures
Key Person Joe Feagin
Race/Ethnicity Black student subcultures at predominantly White universities
Theory Conflict view of Black students at predominantly White universities

Student subcultures are more diverse today than they were in the past. Many adults are returning to college to obtain further education, advance their careers, or change their line of work.

Homeschooling

When most people think of school, they think of bricks and mortar and the teachers, administrators, and other employees who staff school buildings. But for an increasing number of students in the United States, home is the classroom and the teacher is a parent. More than 1.6 million students are now being educated at home. That is about 4 percent of the K–12 school population. For these students, the issues of bureaucratization and social structure are less significant than they are for public school students (R. Cox 2003:27).

In the 1800s, after the establishment of public schools, families that taught their children at home lived in isolated environments or held strict religious views that were at odds with the secular environment of public schools. But today, homeschooling is attracting a broader range of families not necessarily tied to organized religion. Poor academic quality, peer pressure, and school violence are motivating many parents to teach their children at home. The recent publicity given to school shooting sprees seems to have accelerated the move toward homeschooling.

Classroom Tip See "Online Education" (Additional Lecture Ideas).

While supporters of homeschooling believe children can do just as well or better in homeschools as in public schools, critics counter that because homeschooled children are isolated from the larger community, they lose an important chance to improve their socialization skills. But proponents of homeschooling claim their children benefit from contact with others besides their own age group. They also see homeschools as a good alternative for children who suffer from attention-deficit/hyperactivity disorder (ADHD) and learning disorders (LDs). Such children often do better in smaller classes, which present fewer distractions to disturb their concentration.

Quality control is an issue in homeschooling. While homeschooling is legal in all 50 states, 10 states require no notification that a child will be homeschooled, and another 14 require notification only. Other states may require parents to submit their children's curricula or test scores for professional evaluation. Despite the lack of uniform standards, a research review by the Home School Legal Defense Association (2005) reports that homeschooled students score higher than others on standardized tests, in every subject and every grade.

Who are the people who are running homeschools? In general, they tend to have higher-than-average incomes and educational levels. Most are two-parent families, and their children watch less television than average—both factors that are likely to support superior educational performance. The same students, with the same support from their parents, would probably do just as well in the public schools. As research has repeatedly shown, small classes are better than big classes, and strong parental and community involvement is key (R. Cox 2003:28).

and Religion

Religion in the Schools

The Issue

Should public schools be allowed to sponsor organized prayer in the classroom? How about Bible reading, or just a collective moment of silence? Can athletes at public schools offer up a group prayer in a team huddle? Should students be able to initiate voluntary prayers at school events? Each of these situations has been an object of great dissension among those who see a role for prayer in the schools and those who want to maintain strict separation of church and state.

Another controversy concerns the teaching of theories about the origin of humans and the universe. Mainstream scientific thinking holds that humans evolved over billions of years from one-celled organisms, and that the universe came into being 15 billion years ago as a result of a "big bang." These theories are challenged by people who hold to the biblical account of the creation of humans and the universe some 10,000 years ago—a viewpoint known as **creationism.** Creationists, many of whom are Christian fundamentalists, want their belief taught in the schools as the only one—or at the very least, as an alternative to the theory of evolution.

Who has the right to decide these issues, and what is the "right" decision? Religion in the schools is one of the thorniest issues in U.S. public policy today.

The Setting

The issues just described go to the heart of the First Amendment's provisions regarding religious freedom. On the one hand, the government must protect the right to practice one's religion; on the other, it cannot take any measures that would seem to "establish" one religion over another (separation of church and state).

In the key case of *Engle v. Vitale*, the Supreme Court ruled in 1962 that the use of nondenominational prayer in New York schools was "wholly inconsistent" with the First Amendment's prohibition against government establishment of religion. In finding that organized school prayer violated the Constitution—even when no student was required to participate—the Court argued, in effect, that promoting religious observance was not a legitimate function of government or education. Subsequent Court decisions have allowed *voluntary* school prayer by students, but forbid school officials to *sponsor* any prayer or religious observance at school events. Despite these rulings, many public schools still regularly lead their students in prayer recitations or Bible reading (D. Firestone 1999).

The controversy over whether the biblical account of creation should be presented in school curricula recalls the famous "monkey trial" of 1925. In that trial, high school biology teacher John T. Scopes was convicted of violating a Tennessee law making it a crime to teach the scientific theory of evolution in public schools. Today, creationists have gone beyond espousing fundamentalist religious doctrine; they are attempting to reinforce their position regarding the origins of humanity and the universe with quasi-scientific data.

In 1987, the Supreme Court ruled that states could not compel the teaching of creationism in public schools if the primary purpose was to promote a religious viewpoint. In response, those who believe in the divine origin of life have recently advanced a concept called **intelligent design (ID),** the idea that life

IT'S OK, NOW... I EVOLVED INTO A SHEEP.

KNOCK KNOCK

PS 101

INTELLIGENT DESIGN

CREATIONISM

Mike Keefe THE DENVER POST 2005

Recently, advocates of the fundamentalist doctrine of creationism have clothed their argument in a concept called intelligent design.

is so complex that it could only have been created by intelligent design. While this concept is not based explicitly on the biblical account of creation, fundamentalists feel comfortable with it. Supporters of intelligent design consider it a more accurate account of the origin of life than Darwinism, and hold that at the very least, ID should be taught as an alternative to the theory of evolution. But in 2005, *Kitzmiller v. Dove Area School District*, a federal judge ended a Pennsylvania school district's plans to require teachers to present the concept in class. In essence, the judge found ID to be "a religious belief," a subtler but similar approach to creationism in that both find God's fingerprints in nature. The issue continues to be hotly debated and is expected to be the subject of future court cases (Clemmitt 2005; Goodstein 2005; Wallis 2005b).

Sociological Insights

Supporters of school prayer and of creationism feel that strict Court rulings have forced too great a separation between what Émile Durkheim called the *sacred* and the *profane*. They insist that the use of nondenominational prayer can in no way lead to the establishment of an ecclesia in the United States. Moreover, they believe that school prayer—and the teaching of creationism—can provide the spiritual guidance and socialization that many children today do not receive from parents or regular church attendance. Many communities also believe that schools should transmit the dominant culture of the United States by encouraging prayer.

Opponents of school prayer and creationism argue that a religious majority in a community might impose viewpoints specific to its faith at the expense of religious minorities. These critics question whether school prayer can remain truly voluntary. Drawing on the interactionist perspective and small-group research, they suggest that children will face enormous social pressure to conform to the beliefs and practices of the majority.

Policy Initiatives

School education is fundamentally a local issue, so most initiatives and lobbying have taken place at the local or state level. A significant departure from the local nature of this issue came in 2003, when President George W. Bush declared that schools whose policies prevent constitutionally protected school prayer risk losing their federal education funds. At the same time, federal courts were taking a hard line on religion in the schools. In a decision that the Supreme Court reversed in 2004, a federal appeals court ruled that reciting the phrase "under God" during the Pledge of Allegiance that opens each school day violates the U.S. Constitution (Religion News Service 2003).

Religion–school debates show no sign of ending. The activism of religious fundamentalists in the public school system raises the question: whose ideas and values deserve a hearing in classrooms? Critics see this campaign as one step toward sectarian religious control of public education. They worry that at some point in the future, teachers may not be able to use books or make statements that conflict with fundamentalist interpretations of the Bible. For advocates of a liberal education and of intellectual (and religious) diversity, this is a genuinely frightening prospect (Wilgoren 2005).

Let's Discuss

1. Was there organized prayer in any school you attended? Was creationism part of the curriculum?

2. Do you think that promoting religious observance is a legitimate function of education?

3. How might a conflict theorist view the issue of organized school prayer?

GettingINVOLVED

To get involved in the debate over religion in the schools, visit this text's Online Learning Center, which offers links to relevant Web sites. Check out the Social Policy section in the Online Learning Center as well; it provides survey data on U.S. public opinion regarding this issue.

www.mhhe.com/schaefer7

Key Person Émile Durkheim
Classroom Tip See "Using Humor" (Class Discussion Topics).

Theory Interactionist view of school prayer
Web Resource Remind students that there is a multiple-choice quiz in the student center of the Online Learning Center (**www.mhhe.com/schaefer7**). This quiz gives immediate feedback for incorrect answers.

{ MASTERING THIS CHAPTER }

Summary

Religion and **education** are **cultural universals** found throughout the world in various forms. This chapter examines sociological explanations of religion, the major world religions, the three components of religion, and the four basic types of religious organization. It considers several sociological perspectives on education and analyzes schools as examples of formal organizations.

1. Émile Durkheim stressed the social impact of **religion** in attempting to understand individual religious behavior within the context of the larger society.

2. Eighty-five percent of the world's population adheres to some form of religion. Tremendous diversity exists in religious beliefs and practices, which may be heavily influenced by culture.

3. Religion helps to integrate a diverse society and provides social support in time of need.

4. Max Weber saw a connection between religious allegiance and capitalistic behavior in a religious orientation he termed the **Protestant ethic.**

5. In **liberation theology,** the teachings of Christianity become the basis for political efforts to alleviate poverty and social injustice.

6. From a Marxist point of view, religion serves to reinforce the social control of those in power. It discourages collective political action, which could end capitalist oppression and transform society.

7. Religion is expressed through **religious beliefs** (including fundamentalism), **rituals,** and **experience.**

8. Sociologists have identified four basic types of religious organization: the **ecclesia,** the **denomination,** the **sect,** and the **new religious movement (NRM),** or **cult.**

9. Advances in communications have led to a new type of church organization, the electronic church. Televangelists now preach to more people than belong to many denominations, and millions of people use the Internet for religious purposes.

10. India is a secular state that is dominated by a religious majority, the Hindus. The creation of a separate nation, Pakistan, for the Muslim minority following India's independence in 1947 did not end the centuries-old strife between the two groups, which has worsened with their political polarization.

11. The transmission of knowledge and bestowal of status are manifest functions of **education.** Among the latent functions are transmitting culture, promoting social and political integration, maintaining social control, and serving as an agent of social change.

12. In the view of conflict theorists, education serves as an instrument of elite domination by creating standards for entry into occupations, bestowing status unequally, and subordinating the role of women.

13. Teacher expectations about a student's performance can sometimes have an impact on the student's actual achievements.

14. Today, most schools in the United States are organized in a bureaucratic fashion. Weber's five basic characteristics of bureaucracy are all evident in schools.

15. Homeschooling has become a viable alternative to traditional public and private schools. An estimated 1.6 million or more American children are now educated at home.

16. Today, the question of how much religion, if any, should be permitted in the U.S. public schools is a matter of intense debate.

Critical Thinking Questions

1. From a conflict point of view, explain how religion could be used to bring about social change. Can you think of an example?

2. Are the student subcultures identified in this text evident on your campus? What other student subcultures are present? Which subcultures have the highest (and the lowest) social status? How might functionalists, conflict theorists, and interactionists view the existence of student subcultures on a college campus?

3. Do politics and religion mix? Explain your reasoning.

Key Terms

Correspondence principle The tendency of schools to promote the values expected of individuals in each social class and to prepare students for the types of jobs typically held by members of their class. (page 337)

Creationism A literal interpretation of the Bible regarding the creation of humanity and the universe, used to argue that evolution should not be presented as established scientific fact. (342)

Credentialism An increase in the lowest level of education required to enter a field. (336)

Cultural universal A common practice or belief found in every culture. (316)

Denomination A large, organized religion that is not officially linked to the state or government. (327)

Ecclesia A religious organization that claims to include most or all members of a society and is recognized as the national or official religion. (327)

Education A formal process of learning in which some people consciously teach while others adopt the social role of learner. (316)

Established sect A religious group that is the outgrowth of a sect, yet remains isolated from society. (329)

Fundamentalism Rigid adherence to fundamental religious doctrines, often accompanied by a literal application of scripture or historical beliefs to today's world. (325)

Hidden curriculum Standards of behavior that are deemed proper by society and are taught subtly in schools. (335)

Intelligent design (ID) The idea that life is so complex that it could only have been created by intelligent design. (342)

Liberation theology Use of a church, primarily Roman Catholicism, in a political effort to eliminate poverty, discrimination, and other forms of injustice from a secular society. (323)

New religious movement (NRM) or **cult** A small, secretive religious group that represents either a new religion or a major innovation of an existing faith. (329)

Profane The ordinary and commonplace elements of life, as distinguished from the sacred. (316)

Protestant ethic Max Weber's term for the disciplined work ethic, this-worldly concerns, and rational orientation to life emphasized by John Calvin and his followers. (323)

Religion A unified system of beliefs and practices relative to sacred things. (316)

Religious belief A statement to which members of a particular religion adhere. (324)

Religious experience The feeling or perception of being in direct contact with the ultimate reality, such as a divine being, or of being overcome with religious emotion. (326)

Religious ritual A practice required or expected of members of a faith. (325)

Sacred Elements beyond everyday life that inspire awe, respect, and even fear. (316)

Sect A relatively small religious group that has broken away from some other religious organization to renew what it considers the original vision of the faith. (328)

Secularization The process through which religion's influence on other social institutions diminishes. (316)

Teacher-expectancy effect The impact that a teacher's expectations about a student's performance may have on the student's actual achievements. (338)

Tracking The practice of placing students in specific curriculum groups on the basis of their test scores and other criteria. (336)

Self-Quiz

Read each question carefully and then select the best answer.

1. Which of the following sociologists stressed the social impact of religion and was perhaps the first to recognize the critical importance of religion in human societies?
   a. Max Weber
   b. Karl Marx
   c. Émile Durkheim
   d. Talcott Parsons

2. A Roman Catholic parish church offers services in the native language of an immigrant community. This is an example of
   a. the integrative function of religion.
   b. the social support function of religion.
   c. the social control function of religion.
   d. none of the above.

3. Sociologist Max Weber pointed out that the followers of John Calvin emphasized a disciplined work ethic, this-worldly concerns, and a rational orientation to life. Collectively, this point of view has been referred to as
   a. capitalism.
   b. the Protestant ethic.
   c. the sacred.
   d. the profane.

4. The use of a church, primarily Roman Catholic, in a political effort to eliminate poverty, discrimination, and other forms of injustice evident in a secular society is referred to as
   a. creationism.
   b. ritualism.
   c. religious experience.
   d. liberation theology.

5. Many people in the United States strongly adhere to the biblical explanation of the beginning of the universe. Adherents of this point of view are known as
   a. liberationists.
   b. creationists.
   c. ritualists.
   d. experimentalists.

6. The most basic *manifest* function of education is
   a. transmitting knowledge.
   b. transmitting culture.
   c. maintaining social control.
   d. serving as an agent of change.

7. Fifty years ago, a high school diploma was the minimum requirement for entry into the paid labor force of the United States. Today, a college diploma is virtually the bare minimum. This change reflects the process of
   a. tracking.
   b. credentialism.
   c. the hidden curriculum.
   d. the correspondence principle.

8. Samuel Bowles and Herbert Gintis have argued that capitalism requires a skilled, disciplined labor force and that the educational system of the United States is structured with that objective in mind. Citing numerous studies, they offer support for what they call
   a. tracking.
   b. credentialism.
   c. the correspondence principle.
   d. the teacher-expectancy effect.

9. The teacher-expectancy effect is most closely associated with
   a. the functionalist perspective.
   b. the conflict perspective.
   c. the interactionist perspective.
   d. anomie theory.

10. Sociologist Max Weber noted five basic characteristics of bureaucracy, all of which are evident in the vast majority of schools, whether at the elementary, secondary, or even college level. Which of the following is *not* one of these?
    a. division of labor
    b. written rules and regulations
    c. impersonality
    d. shared decision making

11. The _____ encompasses elements beyond everyday life that inspire awe, respect, and even fear, as compared to the _____, which includes the ordinary and the commonplace.

12. Religion defines the spiritual world and gives meaning to the divine. These are _____ functions of religion.

13. _____ is the largest single faith in the world; the second largest is _____.

14. _____ _____ are statements to which members of a particular religion adhere.

15. A(n) _____ is a religious organization that claims to include most or all members of a society and is recognized as the national or official religion.

16. Schools provide a variety of _____ functions, such as transmitting culture, promoting social and political integration, and maintaining social control.

17. Sociologist _____ _____ points out that better-educated people tend to have greater access to information, to hold more diverse opinions, and to possess the ability to make subtle distinctions in analysis.

18. The term _____ _____ refers to standards of behavior that are deemed proper by society and are taught subtly in schools. According to this curriculum, children must not speak until the teacher calls on them and must regulate their activities according to the clock or the bell.

19. _____ is the practice of placing students in specific curriculum groups on the basis of their test scores and other criteria.

20. Of the four distinctive types of subcultures among college students discussed in the text, the _____ subculture is interested primarily in career prospects, and views college as a means of obtaining degrees that are essential for advancement.

{ TECHNOLOGY RESOURCES }

Online Learning Center

1. How do you know what issues are most important as you prepare to read this chapter? The student center at the Online Learning Center at **www.mhhe.com/schaefer7** can help by providing a list of key learning objectives. Click on Learning Objectives as you get ready to read each chapter and review the major ideas and concepts that you should absorb from your reading.

2. How much do you know about current government initiatives to provide social services through religious organizations? A page on the White House Web site provides more information, from the perspective of officials who favor these programs. Visit this site at **www.whitehouse.gov/government/fbci.**

3. Humanitarian organizations are concerned about access to education in developing countries. To find out about charitable efforts to improve basic education in the world's poorest countries, go to the Oxfam Web site (**www.oxfam.org.uk/what_we_do/issues/education/index.htm**) and explore the section on education.

*Note: While all the URLs listed were current as of the printing of this book, these sites often change. Please check our Web site (**www.mhhe.com/schaefer7**) for updates, hyperlinks, and exercises related to these sites.*

Reel Society Video Clips

Reel Society video clips, which appear on this book's Web site, can be used to spark discussion about the following topics from this chapter:

- Durkheim and the Sociological Approach to Religion
- Sociological Explanations of Religion
- World Religions
- Components of Religion
- Research in Action: Islam in the United States
- Sociological Perspectives on Education
- Schools as Formal Organizations

14

Government and the Economy

inside

Economic Systems
Case Study: Capitalism in China
Power and Authority
Types of Government
Political Behavior in the United States
Models of Power Structure in the United States
War and Peace
The Changing Economy
Social Policy and the Economy: Global Offshoring

Boxes

Sociology in the Global Community: Gender Quotas at the Ballot Box

Research in Action: Why Don't More Young People Vote?

Social Inequality: Affirmative Action

Taking Sociology to Work: Richard J. Hawk, Vice President and Financial Consultant, Smith Barney

We all say

NO TO TERRORISM

جريدة الرياض

Politically oriented messages are often meant for international as well as local consumption. In 2005 the Saudi Arabian government launched a public relations campaign featuring slogans like "Islam Is Moderation" and "Say No to Terrorism." On this poster, the English translation appears in much larger type than the Arabic message.

The power elite and Congress are more diverse than they were before the civil rights movement and the social movements that followed in its train brought pressure to bear on corporations, politicians, and government. Although the power elite is still composed primarily of Christian, white men, there are now Jews, women, blacks, Latinos, and Asian Americans on the boards of the country's largest corporations; presidential cabinets are far more diverse than was the case fifty years ago; and the highest ranks of the military are no longer filled solely by white men. In the case of elected officials in Congress, the trend toward diversity is even greater for women and . . . other previously excluded groups. . . .

Perhaps it is not surprising that when we look at the business practices of the members of previously excluded groups who have risen to the top of the corporate world, we find that their perspectives and values do not differ markedly from those of their white male counterparts. When Linda Wachner, one of the first women to become CEO of a *Fortune*-level company, the Warnaco Group, concluded that one of Warnaco's many holdings, the Hathaway Shirt Company, was unprofitable, she decided to stop making Hathaway shirts and to sell or close down the factory. It did not matter to Wachner that Hathaway, which started making shirts in 1837, was one of the oldest companies in Maine, that almost all of the five hundred employees at the factory were working-class women, or even that the workers had given up a pay raise to hire consultants to teach them to work more effectively and, as a result, had doubled their productivity. The bottom-line issue was that the company was considered unprofitable, and the average wage of the Hathaway workers, $7.50 an hour, was thought to be too high. (In 1995, Wachner was paid $10 million in salary and stock, and Warnaco had a net income of $46.5 million.) "We did need to do the right thing for the company and the stockholders," explained Wachner.

Nor did ethnic background matter to Thomas Fuentes, a senior vice president at a consulting firm in Orange County, California, a director of Fleetwood Enterprises, and chairman of the Orange County Republican Party. Fuentes targeted fellow Latinos who happened to be Democrats when he sent uniformed security guards to twenty polling places in 1988 "carrying signs in Spanish and English warning people not to vote if they were not U.S. citizens." The security firm ended up paying $60,000 in damages when it lost a lawsuit stemming from this intimidation. . . . The Fanjuls, the Cuban American sugar barons, have no problem ignoring labor laws in dealing with their migrant labor force, and . . . Sue Ling Gin, one of the Asian Americans on our list of corporate directors . . . hired an all-female staff . . . "because women would work for lower wages." Linda Wachner, Thomas Fuentes, the Fanjuls, and Sue Ling Gin acted as employers, not as members of disadvantaged groups. That is, members of the power elite of both genders and of all ethnicities practice class politics.

Zweigenhaft and Domhoff 2006:229, 246–47. Additional information about this excerpt can be found on the Online Learning Center at www.mhhe.com/schaefer7.

> " *Linda Wachner, Thomas Fuentes, the Fanjuls, and Sue Ling Gin acted as employers, not as members of disadvantaged groups. That is, members of the power elite of both genders and of all ethnicities practice class politics.* "

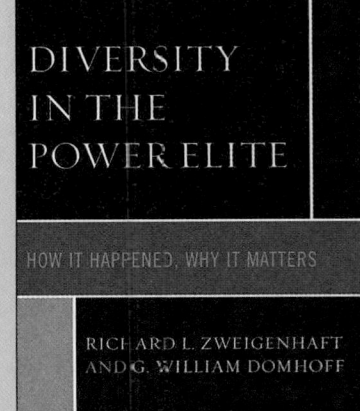

DIVERSITY IN THE POWER ELITE

HOW IT HAPPENED, WHY IT MATTERS

RICHARD L. ZWEIGENHAFT AND G. WILLIAM DOMHOFF

Half a century ago C. Wright Mills ([1956] 2000b), the originator of the phrase *the sociological imagination,* studied the political process in the United States and articulated the concept of the power elite—a White male group of decision makers who in effect ruled the country. Five decades later sociologist G. William Domhoff and psychologist Richard L. Zweigerhaft returned to the question of who rules the United States. As the opening excerpt from their book *Diversity in the Power Elite* (2006) shows, they found only modest changes in the nation's power structure. Today, a few privileged women occupy positions in the power elite, but the majority of the nation's decision makers are still men, and virtually all of them are White.

The power elite operates within the framework of the existing political system, be it local, state, national, or international. By *political system,* sociologists mean the social institution that is founded on a recognized set of procedures for implementing and achieving society's goals, such as the allocation of valued resources. Like religion and the family, the political system is a cultural universal: It is found in every society. In the United States, the political system holds the ultimate responsibility for addressing the social policy issues examined in this textbook: child care, the AIDS crisis, welfare reform, and so forth.

The term *economic system* refers to the social institution through which goods and services are produced, distributed, and consumed. As with social institutions such as the family, religion, and government, the economic system shapes other aspects of the social order and is in turn influenced by them. Throughout this textbook, you have been reminded of the economy's impact on social behavior—for example, on individual and group behavior in factories and offices. You have studied the work of Karl Marx and Friedrich Engels, who emphasized that a society's economic system can promote social inequality. And you have learned that foreign investment in developing countries can intensify inequality among residents.

It is hard to imagine two social institutions more intertwined than government and the economy. Besides serving as the largest employer in the nation, government at all levels regulates commerce and entry into many occupations. At the same time, the economy generates the revenue to support government services. This chapter will present a combined analysis of government and the economy. How does the power elite maintain its power? Is war necessary in settling international disputes? How have the trends toward deindustrialization and the outsourcing of service jobs affected our economy? The chapter begins with a macro-level analysis of two ideal types of economic system, capitalism and socialism. This theoretical discussion is followed by a case study of China's decision to allow capitalist entrepreneurial activity within its socialist economy. Next, we'll examine some general theories of power and authority, with the four major types of government in which that power and authority is exerted. We'll see how politics works, with particular attention to citizens' participation and the changing role of women. We'll look at two models of power in the United States, the elite and the pluralist models. Then we'll touch briefly on war, peace, and terrorism. In the following section we'll look at ways in which the U.S. economy is changing in response to globalization. The chapter closes with a Social Policy section on global offshoring. ●

Economic Systems

The sociocultural evolution approach developed by Gerhard {p.116 Lenski categorizes preindustrial society according to the way in which the economy is organized. The principal types of preindustrial society, as you recall, are hunting-and-gathering societies, horticultural societies, and agrarian societies.

As we noted in Chapter 5, the *industrial revolution*—which {p.117 took place largely in England during the period 1760 to 1830—brought about changes in the social organization of the workplace. People left their homesteads and began working in central locations such as factories. As the industrial revolution proceeded, a new form of social structure emerged: the *industrial society,* a society that depends on mechanization to produce its goods and services.

Two basic types of economic system distinguish contemporary industrial societies: capitalism and socialism. As described in the following sections, capitalism and socialism serve as ideal types of economic system. No nation precisely fits either model. Instead, the economy of each individual state represents a mixture of capitalism and socialism, although one type or the other is generally more useful in describing a society's economic structure.

Capitalism

In preindustrial societies, land functioned as the source of virtually all wealth. The industrial revolution changed all that. It required that certain individuals and institutions be willing to take substantial risks in order to finance new inventions, machinery, and business enterprises. Eventually, bankers, industrialists, and other holders of large sums of money replaced landowners as the most powerful economic force. These people invested their funds in the hope of realizing even greater profits, and thereby became owners of property and business firms.

The transition to private ownership of business was accompanied by the emergence of the capitalist economic system. *Capitalism* is an economic system in which the means of production are held largely in private hands and the main incentive for economic activity is the accumulation of profits. In practice, capitalist systems vary in the degree to which the government regulates private ownership and economic activity (D. Rosenberg 1991).

Immediately following the industrial revolution, the prevailing form of capitalism was what is termed *laissez-faire* ("let them do"). Under the principle of laissez-faire, as expounded and endorsed by British economist Adam Smith (1723–1790), people could compete freely, with minimal government intervention in the economy. Business retained the right to regulate itself and operated essentially without fear of government interference (Smelser 1963).

Two centuries later, capitalism has taken on a somewhat different form. Private ownership and maximization of profits still remain the most significant characteristics of capitalist economic systems. However, in contrast to the era of laissez-faire, capitalism today features government regulation of economic relations. Without restrictions, business firms can mislead consumers, endanger workers' safety, and even defraud the companies' investors—all in the pursuit of greater profits. That is why the government of a capitalist nation often monitors prices, sets safety and environmental standards for industries, protects the rights of consumers, and regulates collective bargaining between labor unions and management. Yet under capitalism as an ideal type, government rarely takes over ownership of an entire industry.

Contemporary capitalism also differs from laissez-faire in another important respect: capitalism tolerates monopolistic practices. A *monopoly* exists when a single business firm controls the market. Domination of an industry allows the firm to effectively control a commodity by dictating pricing, quality standards, and availability. Buyers have little choice but to yield to the firm's decisions; there is no other place to purchase the product or service. Monopolistic practices violate the ideal of free competition cherished by Adam Smith and other supporters of laissez-faire capitalism.

Some capitalistic nations, such as the United States, outlaw monopolies through antitrust legislation. Such laws prevent any business from taking over so much of the competition in an industry that it controls the market. The U.S. federal government allows monopolies to exist only in certain exceptional cases, such as the utility and transportation industries. Even then, regulatory agencies scrutinize these officially approved monopolies to protect the public. The protracted legal battle between the Justice Department and Microsoft, owner of the dominant operating system for personal computers, illustrates the uneasy relationship between government and private monopolies in capitalistic countries.

Conflict theorists point out that although *pure* monopolies are not a basic element of the economy of the United States, competition is much more restricted than one might expect in what is called a *free enterprise system*. In numerous industries, a few companies largely dominate the field and keep new enterprises from entering the marketplace.

As we have seen in earlier chapters, globalization and the rise of multinational corporations have spread the capitalistic pursuit of profits around the world. Especially in developing countries, governments are not always prepared to deal with the sudden influx of foreign capital and its effects on their economies. One particularly striking example of how unfettered capitalism can harm developing nations is found in the Democratic Republic of Congo (formerly Zaire). The Congo has significant deposits of the metal columbite-tantalite—coltan, for short—which is used in the production of electronic circuit boards. Until the market for cell phones, pagers, and laptop computers heated up recently, U.S. manufacturers got most of their coltan from Australia. But at the height of consumer demand, they turned to miners in the Congo to increase their supply.

Predictably, the escalating price of the metal—as much as $400 a kilogram at one point, or more than three times the average Congolese worker's yearly wages—attracted undesirable attention. Soon the neighboring countries of Rwanda, Uganda,

In the movie *Jerry Maguire,* Tom Cruise plays a successful sports agent who is fired for placing the well-being of the athletes he represents ahead of his agency's bottom line. Filmmakers often portray capitalists as selfish people who profit unfairly from the labor of others—an image that recent corporate scandals have reinforced.

Richard J. Hawk
**Vice President and Financial
Consultant, Smith Barney**

Richard Hawk had no idea what he wanted to do with his life when he entered DePauw University, and no idea what sociology was about when he registered for his first course. But he soon realized that he liked the faculty in the sociology department, and he liked the perspective the subject gave him on other subjects he was studying—economics, history, and communications. In his junior year, Hawk took a course on marriage and the family that helped him to see the "trickle-down effect" of major economic decisions on individuals and communities.

Today, Hawk credits sociology with giving him "a better overall understanding of things," one he uses daily. Asked to elaborate, he replies, "You have to realize that everyone is affected one way or another" by economic and political decisions. He points to the war in Iraq: "Half of the forces are reservists. Look at the social and financial effect on the family, the economic effect on the companies these people work for domestically, not to mention the obvious effects on the Iraqi people." Hawk sees these effects play themselves out in his clients' lives, whether they are physicians or blue-collar workers facing an early retirement. In developing their financial plans, he keeps the big picture in mind.

As a financial consultant, Hawk meets with clients, confers with money managers and financial analysts, and prepares proposals for prospective clients. He applies the same analytical perspective that he uses with clients to the economy and current business issues. "The past few years have not been particularly kind to the equity markets," he observes. "We were in a technology bubble, and as a result, we have been experiencing dramatic changes in accounting methods, compensation issues, and ethics in general."

Hawk advises first-time sociology students to approach the subject with an open mind, to "be willing to look at issues from a different perspective." Doing so, he thinks, will pay off in some valuable insights.

Let's Discuss

1. Pick an economic issue or decision that has been in the news recently and show how it could affect your family.
2. Take the same issue or decision and imagine how it might affect the people you will deal with in your future career.

A worker mines for coltan with sweat and a stick. The sudden increase in demand for the metal by U.S. computer manufacturers caused incursions into the Congo by neighboring countries hungry for capital to finance a war. Too often, globalization can have unintended consequences for a nation's economy and social welfare.

and Burundi, at war with one another and desperate for resources to finance the conflict, were raiding the Congo's national parks, slashing and burning to expose the coltan underneath the forest floor. Indirectly, the sudden increase in the demand for coltan was financing war and the rape of the environment. U.S. manufacturers have since cut off their sources in the Congo in an effort to avoid abetting the destruction. But their action has only penalized legitimate miners in the impoverished country (Austin 2002; Delawala 2002).

Socialism

{ p.11 } Socialist theory was refined in the writings of Karl Marx and Friedrich Engels. These European radicals were disturbed by the exploitation of the working class that emerged during the industrial revolution. In their view, capitalism forced large numbers of people to exchange their labor for low wages. The owners of an industry profit from the labor of workers primarily because they pay workers less than the value of the goods produced.

{ p.189 }

As an ideal type, a socialist economic system attempts to eliminate such economic exploitation. Under *socialism,* the means of production and distribution in a society are collectively rather than privately owned. The basic objective of the economic system is to meet people's needs rather than to maximize profits.

Key Persons Karl Marx, Friedrich Engels
Theory Conflict view of socialism as an alternative to capitalism

Socialists reject the laissez-faire philosophy that free competition benefits the general public. Instead, they believe that the central government, acting as the representative of the people, should make basic economic decisions. Therefore, government ownership of all major industries—including steel production, automobile manufacturing, and agriculture—is a primary feature of socialism as an ideal type.

In practice, socialist economic systems vary in the extent to which they tolerate private ownership. For example, in Great Britain, a nation with some aspects of both a socialist and a capitalist economy, passenger airline service is concentrated in the government-owned corporation British Airways. Yet private airlines are allowed to compete with it.

Socialist societies differ from capitalist nations in their commitment to social service programs. For example, the U.S. government provides health care and health insurance to the elderly and poor through the Medicare and Medicaid programs. But socialist countries typically offer government-financed medical care to *all* citizens. In theory, the wealth of the people as a collectivity is used to provide health care, housing, education, and other key services to each individual and family.

Marx believed that socialist states would eventually "wither away" and evolve into *communist* societies. As an ideal type, **communism** refers to an economic system under which all property is communally owned and no social distinctions are made on the basis of people's ability to produce. In recent decades, the Soviet Union, the People's Republic of China, Vietnam, Cuba, and nations in Eastern Europe were popularly thought of as examples of communist economic systems. However, this usage represents an incorrect application of a term with sensitive political connotations. All nations known as communist in the 20th century actually fell far short of the ideal type.

By the early 1990s, Communist parties were no longer ruling the nations of Eastern Europe. The first major challenge to Communist rule came in 1980, when Poland's Solidarity movement— led by Lech Walesa and backed by many workers—questioned the injustices of that society. Though martial law forced Solidarity underground, the movement eventually negotiated the end of Communist Party rule, in 1989. Over the next two years, Communist parties were overthrown by popular uprisings in the Soviet Union and throughout Eastern Europe. The former Soviet Union, Czechoslovakia, and Yugoslavia were then subdivided to accommodate ethnic, linguistic, and religious differences.

As of 2006, China, Cuba, and Vietnam remained socialist societies ruled by Communist parties. Even in those countries, however, capitalism had begun to make inroads. In China, fully 25 percent of the country's production originated in the private business sector. (See the case study Capitalism in China, pages 353–355, for a fuller discussion.)

As we have seen, capitalism and socialism serve as ideal types of economic system. In reality, the economy of each industrial society—including the United States, the European Union, and Japan—includes certain elements of both capitalism and socialism (see Table 14-1). Whatever the differences—whether a society more closely fits the ideal type of capitalism or socialism—all industrial societies rely chiefly on mechanization in the production of goods and services.

The Informal Economy

In many countries, one aspect of the economy defies description as either capitalist or socialist. In the **informal economy,** transfers of money, goods, or services take place but are not reported to the government. Examples of the informal economy include trading services with someone—say, a haircut for a computer lesson; selling goods on the street; and engaging in illegal transactions, such as gambling or drug deals. Participants in this type of economy avoid taxes and government regulations.

Functionalists contend that bureaucratic regulations sometimes contribute to the rise of an informal economy. In the developing world, governments often set up burdensome business regulations that overworked bureaucrats must administer. When requests for licenses and permits pile up, delaying business projects, legitimate entrepreneurs find they need to "go underground" to get anything done. Despite its apparent efficiency, this type of informal economy is dysfunctional for a country's overall political and economic well-being. Since informal firms typically operate in remote locations to avoid detection, they cannot easily expand when they become profitable. And given the limited protection for their property and contractual rights, participants in the informal economy are less likely than others to save and invest their income.

Whatever functions an informal economy may serve, it is in some respects dysfunctional for workers. Working conditions in these illegal businesses are often unsafe or dangerous, and the jobs rarely

Table 14-1 Characteristics of the Three Major Economic Systems

Economic System	Characteristics	Contemporary Examples
Capitalism	Private ownership of the means of production Accumulation of profits the main incentive	Canada Mexico United States
Socialism	Collective ownership of the means of production Meeting people's needs the basic objective	Germany Russia Sweden
Communism	Communal ownership of all property No social distinctions made on basis of people's ability to produce	Cuba North Korea Vietnam

Note: Countries listed in column 3 are typical of one of the three economic systems, but not perfectly so. In practice, the economies of most countries include a mix of elements from the three major systems.

Global View Socialist aspects of Great Britain's economy
Global View See "In Defense of Socialist Planning" (Additional Lecture Ideas).

Global View The overthrow of Communist Party rule in the former Soviet Union and Eastern Europe
Global View Capitalism was making inroads in China, Cuba, and Vietnam as of 2006.

provide any benefits to those who become ill or cannot continue to work. Perhaps more significant, the longer a worker remains in the informal economy, the less likely that person is to make the transition to the regular economy. No matter how efficient or productive a worker, employers expect to see experience in the formal economy on a job application. Experience as a successful street vendor or self-employed cleaning person does not carry much weight with interviewers (D. Light 2004a).

Use Your Sociological Imagination www.mhhe.com/schaefer7

Some of your relatives are working full-time in the informal economy—for example, babysitting, lawn cutting, house cleaning—and are earning all their income that way. What will be the consequences for them in terms of job security and health care? Will you try to persuade them to seek formal employment, regardless of how much money they are making?

CASE study

CAPITALISM IN CHINA

Today's China is not the China of past generations; it stands on the brink of becoming the world's largest economy (see Figure 14-1). In this country where the Communist Party once dominated people's lives, few now bother to follow party proceedings. Instead, after a decade of rapid economic growth, most Chinese are more interested in acquiring the latest consumer goods. Ironically, it was party officials' decision to transform China's economy by opening it up to capitalism that reduced the once omnipotent institution's influence.

The Road to Capitalism

When the communists assumed leadership of China in 1949, they cast themselves as the champions of workers and peasants and the enemies of those who exploited workers, namely landlords and capitalists. Profit making was outlawed, and those who engaged in it were arrested. By the 1960s, China's economy was dominated by huge state-controlled enterprises, such as factories. Even private farms were transformed into community-owned organizations. Peasants essentially worked for the government, receiving payment in goods based on their contribution to the collective good. In addition, they could receive a small plot of land on which to produce food for their families or for exchange with others. But while the centralization of production for the benefit of all seemed to make sense ideologically, it did not work well economically.

In the 1980s, the government eased restrictions on private enterprise somewhat, permitting small businesses with no more than seven employees. But business owners could not hold policymaking positions in the party, at any level. Late in the decade, party leaders began to make market-oriented reforms, revising the nation's legal structure to promote private business. For the first time, private entrepreneurs were allowed to compete with

FIGURE 14–1

World's Largest Economies, 2020 (Forecast)

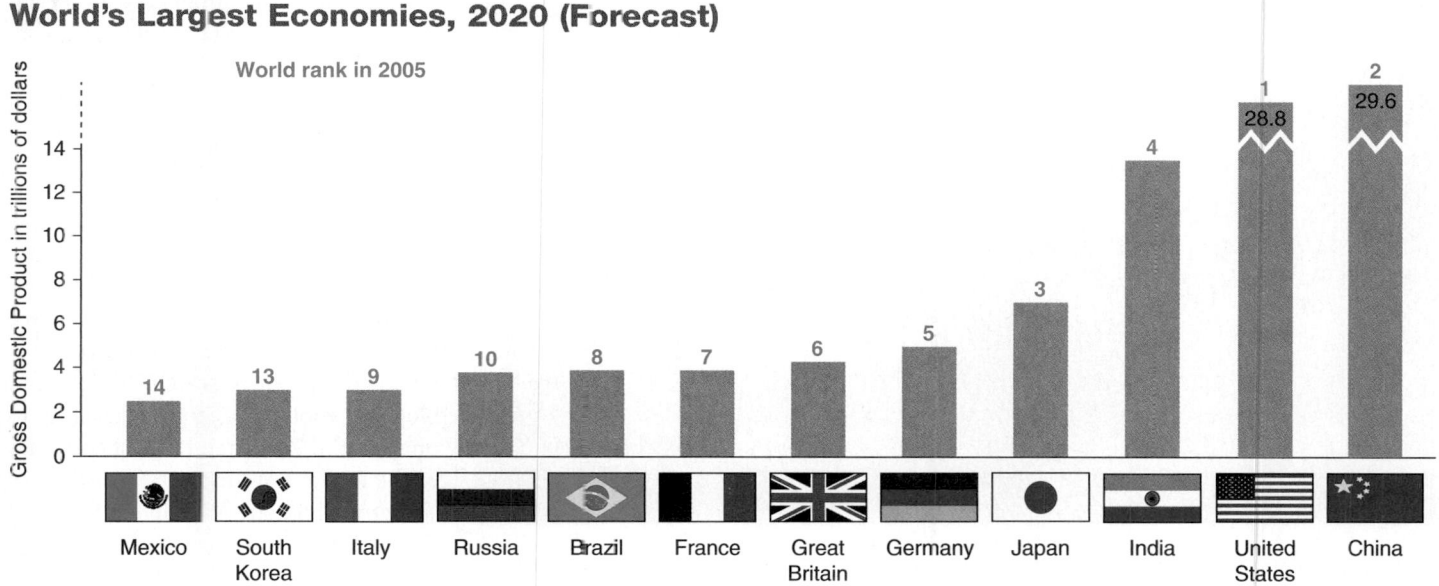

Source: The Economist 2006.
Note: Data standardized in terms of estimated purchasing power parity to eliminate differences in buying power. Countries ranked in 2005, when Spain was ranked 11, Canada 12.

Global View China's economy
Let's Discuss Is it possible to balance ideological needs with economic needs?

some state-controlled businesses. By the mid-1990s, impressed with the results of the experiment, party officials had begun to hand some ailing state-controlled businesses over to private entrepreneurs, in hopes they could be turned around.

The Chinese Economy Today

Today, the entrepreneurs who weathered government harassment during the Communist Party's early years are among the nation's wealthiest capitalists. Some even hold positions on government advisory boards. The growing free-market economy they spawned has brought significant inequality to Chinese workers, however, especially between urban and rural workers. Though the move toward market-driven development has been slowing, questions are still being raised about the accumulation of wealth by a few (Kahn 2006).

Chinese capitalists have had to compete with multinational corporations, which can operate more easily in China now, thanks to government economic reforms. General Motors (GM) first became interested in China in 1992, hoping to use the nation's low-cost labor to manufacture cars for overseas markets. But more and more, foreign-owned enterprises like GM are selling to the Chinese market. By 2003, GM's Chinese operation was producing 110,000 automobiles a year for Chinese consumers, at a profit twice as high as that in the United States (Kahn 2003a).

Chinese Workers in the New Economy

For Chinese workers, the loosening of state control over the economy has meant a rise in occupational mobility, which was severely limited in the early days of Communist Party rule. The new markets created by private entrepreneurs are allowing ambitious workers to advance their careers by changing jobs or even cities. On the other hand, many middle-aged urban workers have lost their jobs to rural migrants seeking higher wages. Moreover, the privately owned factories that churn out lawn chairs and power tools for multinational corporations offer limited opportunities and very long hours. Wages average only $75 a month—⅛ what factory workers earn in Mexico, and ⅟₄₀ of U.S. workers' wages.

In many of these small businesses, worker safety is not a priority. Just south of Shanghai, in the over 7,000 small, privately owned hardware factories that operate in the region, the unofficial injury rate is 2,500 serious injuries a year. Nationally, China recorded 140,000 workplace deaths in 2002—up 30 percent from the year before (Bradsher 2004; Iritani and Dickerson 2002; Kahn 2003b).

For the average worker, party membership is less important now than in the past. Instead, managerial skill and experience are much in demand. Hong Kong sociologist Xiaowei Zang (2002) surveyed 900 workers in a key industrial city and found that party members still had an advantage in government and state-owned companies, where they earned higher salaries than other workers. But in private businesses, seniority and either managerial or entrepreneurial experience were what counted. As might be expected, being male and well educated also helped.

Women have been slower to advance in the workplace than men. Traditionally, Chinese women have been relegated to subservient roles in the patriarchal family structure. Communist Party rule has allowed them to make significant gains in employment, income, and education, although not as quickly as promised. For rural women in China, the growth of a market economy has meant a choice between working in a factory or on a farm. Given recent economic changes, which have been massive, scholars are waiting to see whether Chinese women will maintain the progress they began under Communism (Bian 2002; Lu et al. 2002; Shu and Bian 2003).

With the growth of a middle class and increased education, many Chinese are seeking the same opportunities as their Western counterparts. The struggle has been particularly visible in the Chinese people's desire for open, unrestricted access to the World Wide Web. China requires even U.S.-based companies like Google, Yahoo, Microsoft, and Cisco Systems to alter their search engines and blogging tools so as to block access to unapproved Web sites. In most countries of the world, a Web search for images of Tiananmen Square will call up photos of the 1989 crackdown on student protesters, in which soldiers in tanks attacked unarmed students. But on the other side of what has been dubbed the Great

This burgeoning metropolis isn't located in the United States or Europe, but in China. Spurred by an influx of investment by multinational corporations, Shanghai has experienced rapid economic growth. In 1985 the city had 1 skyscraper; now it has over 300.

Student Alert Marketization has led to increased inequality in China.
Student Alert Compile a list of major U.S. companies doing business in China.
Let's Discuss In times of economic change, which groups benefit? Are they the same groups in the United States and China?
Theory Is China's path consistent or inconsistent with Marx's predictions? How?

Firewall of China, the same search yields only photos of visiting diplomats—including those from the United States—posing in the square (Grossman and Beech 2006). ●

Power and Authority

In any society, someone or some group—whether it be a tribal chief, a dictator, or a parliament—makes important decisions about how to use resources and how to allocate goods. A cultural universal, then, is the exercise of power and authority. Inevitably, the struggle for power and authority involves *politics,* which political scientist Harold Lasswell (1936) tersely defined as "who gets what, when, and how." In their study of politics and government, sociologists are concerned with social interactions among individuals and groups and their impact on the larger political and economic order.

Power

{ p.191 } Power lies at the heart of a political system. According to Max Weber, *power* is the ability to exercise one's will over others. To put it another way, whoever can control the behavior of others is exercising power. Power relations can involve large organizations, small groups, or even people in an intimate association.

"Which country is the least mad at us?"

This cartoon, published in 1957, is still relevant today. The extent of the tension between the United States and foreign countries should not be exaggerated, however. Though other countries may resent the United States' preeminent power and influence, they do not necessarily dislike the people of the United States.

Because Weber developed his conceptualization of power in the early 1900s, he focused primarily on the nation-state and its sphere of influence. Today scholars recognize that the trend toward globalization has brought new opportunities, and with them new concentrations of power. Power is now exercised on a global as well as a national stage, as countries and multinational corporations vie to control access to resources and manage the distribution of capital (Sernau 2001).

There are three basic sources of power within any political system: force, influence, and authority. *Force* is the actual or threatened use of coercion to impose one's will on others. When leaders imprison or even execute political dissidents, they are applying force; so, too, are terrorists when they seize or bomb an embassy or assassinate a political leader. *Influence,* on the other hand, refers to the exercise of power through a process of persuasion. A citizen may change his or her view of a Supreme Court nominee because of a newspaper editorial, the expert testimony of a law school dean before the Senate Judiciary Committee, or a stirring speech by a political activist at a rally. In each case, sociologists would view such efforts to persuade people as examples of influence. Now let's take a look at the third source of power, *authority.*

Types of Authority

The term *authority* refers to institutionalized power that is recognized by the people over whom it is exercised. Sociologists commonly use the term in connection with those who hold legitimate power through elected or publicly acknowledged positions. A person's authority is often limited. Thus, a referee has the authority to decide whether a penalty should be called during a football game, but has no authority over the price of tickets to the game.

Max Weber ([1913] 1947) developed a classification system for authority that has become one of the most useful and frequently cited contributions of early sociology. He identified three ideal types of authority: traditional, rational-legal, and charismatic. Weber did not insist that only one type applies to a given society or organization. All can be present, but their relative importance will vary. Sociologists have found Weber's typology valuable in understanding different manifestations of legitimate power within a society.

Traditional Authority Until the middle of the last century, Japan was ruled by a revered emperor whose absolute power was passed down from generation to generation. In a political system based on *traditional authority,* legitimate power is conferred by custom and accepted practice. A king or queen is accepted as ruler of a nation simply by virtue of inheriting the crown; a tribal chief rules because that is the accepted practice. The ruler may be loved or hated, competent or destructive; in terms of legitimacy, that does not matter. For the traditional leader, authority rests in custom, not in personal characteristics, technical competence, or even written law. People accept the ruler's authority because that is how things have always been done. Traditional authority is absolute when the ruler has the ability to determine laws and policies.

Rational-Legal Authority The U.S. Constitution gives Congress and our president the authority to make and enforce laws and policies. Power made legitimate by law is known as ***rational-legal authority.*** Leaders derive their rational-legal authority from the written rules and regulations of political systems, such as a constitution. Generally, in societies based on rational-legal authority, leaders are thought to have specific areas of competence and authority but are not thought to be endowed with divine inspiration, as in certain societies with traditional forms of authority.

Charismatic Authority Joan of Arc was a simple peasant girl in medieval France, yet she was able to rally the French people and lead them into major battles against English invaders. How was this possible? As Weber observed, power can be legitimized by the *charisma* of an individual. The term ***charismatic authority*** refers to power made legitimate by a leader's exceptional personal or emotional appeal to his or her followers.

Charisma lets a person lead or inspire without relying on set rules or traditions. In fact, charismatic authority is derived more from the beliefs of followers than from the actual qualities of leaders. So long as people *perceive* a leader as having qualities that set him or her apart from ordinary citizens, that leader's authority will remain secure and often unquestioned.

Unlike traditional rulers, charismatic leaders often become well known by breaking with established institutions and advocating dramatic changes in the social structure and the economic system. Their strong hold over their followers makes it easier to build protest movements that challenge the dominant norms and values of a society. Thus, charismatic leaders such as Jesus, Joan of Arc, Gandhi, Malcolm X, and Martin Luther King, Jr., all used their power to press for changes in accepted social behavior. But so did Adolf Hitler, whose charismatic appeal turned people toward violent and destructive ends in Nazi Germany.

Observing from an interactionist perspective, sociologist Carl Couch (1996) points out that the growth of the electronic media has facilitated the development of charismatic authority. During the 1930s and 1940s, the heads of state of the United States, Great Britain, and Germany all used radio to issue direct appeals to citizens. Now, television and the Internet allow leaders to "visit" people's homes and communicate with them. In both Taiwan and South Korea in 1996, troubled political leaders facing reelection campaigns spoke frequently to national audiences and exaggerated military threats from neighboring China and North Korea, respectively.

As we noted earlier, Weber used traditional, rational-legal, and charismatic authority as ideal types. In reality, particular leaders and political systems combine elements of two or more of these forms. Presidents Franklin D. Roosevelt, John F. Kennedy, and Ronald Reagan wielded power largely through the rational-legal basis of their authority. At the same time, they were unusually charismatic leaders who commanded the personal loyalty of large numbers of citizens.

Use Your Sociological Imagination www.mhhe.com/schaefer7

What would our government be like if it were founded on traditional rather than rational-legal authority? What difference would it make to the average citizen?

Types of Government

Each society establishes a political system through which it is governed. In modern industrial nations, these formal systems of government make a significant number of critical political decisions. We will survey five basic types of government here: monarchy, oligarchy, dictatorship, totalitarianism, and democracy.

Monarchy

A ***monarchy*** is a form of government headed by a single member of a royal family, usually a king, queen, or some other hereditary ruler. In earlier times, many monarchs claimed that God had granted them a divine right to rule. Typically, they governed on the basis of traditional forms of authority, sometimes accompanied by the use of force. By the beginning of the 21st century, however, monarchs held genuine governmental power in only a few nations, such as Monaco. Most monarchs now have little practical power; they serve primarily ceremonial purposes.

Oligarchy

An ***oligarchy*** is a form of government in which a few individuals rule. A rather old method of governing that flourished in ancient Greece and Egypt, oligarchy now often takes the form of military rule. In developing nations in Africa, Asia, and Latin America, small factions of military officers will forcibly seize power, either from legally elected regimes or from other military cliques.

Strictly speaking, the term *oligarchy* is reserved for governments that are run by a few selected individuals. However, the People's Republic of China can be classified as an oligarchy if we stretch the meaning of the term. In China, power rests in the hands of a large but exclusive ruling *group*, the Communist Party. In a similar vein, drawing on conflict theory, one might argue that many industrialized nations of the West should be considered oligarchies (rather than democracies), since only a powerful few—leaders of big business, government, and the military—actually rule. Later in this chapter, we will examine the "elite model" of the U.S. political system in greater detail.

Dictatorship and Totalitarianism

A ***dictatorship*** is a government in which one person has nearly total power to make and enforce laws. Dictators rule primarily through the use of coercion, which often includes torture and executions. Typically, they *seize* power rather than being freely elected (as in a democracy) or inheriting power (as in a monarchy). Some dictators are quite charismatic and manage to achieve a certain popularity, though their supporters'

enthusiasm is almost certainly tinged with fear. Other dictators are bitterly hated by the people over whom they rule.

Frequently, dictators develop such overwhelming control over people's lives that their governments are called *totalitarian.* (Monarchies and oligarchies may also achieve this type of dominance.) **Totalitarianism** involves virtually complete government control and surveillance over all aspects of a society's social and political life. Germany during Hitler's reign, the Soviet Union in the 1930s, and North Korea today are classified as totalitarian states.

Political scientists Carl Friedrich and Zbigniew Brzezinski (1965:22) have identified the traits that are typical of totalitarian states. They include the widespread use of ideological propaganda and state control of the media and the economy.

{ North Korea has a totalitarian government whose leadership attempts to control all aspects of people's lives. This billboard, a blatant example of government propaganda, portrays the country's ruthless leader as a benevolent father figure. }

Democracy

In a literal sense, **democracy** means government by the people. The word *democracy* originated in two Greek roots—*demos,* meaning "the populace" or "the common people," and *kratia,* meaning "rule." Of course, in large, populous nations such as the United States, government by the people is impractical at the national level. Americans cannot vote on every important issue that comes before Congress. Consequently, popular rule is generally maintained through *representative democracy,* a form of government in which certain individuals are selected to speak for the people.

The United States is commonly classified as a **representative democracy,** since the elected members of Congress and state legislatures make our laws. However, critics have questioned how *representative* our democracy really is. Do Congress and the state legislatures genuinely represent the masses? Are the people of the United States legitimately self-governing, or has our government become a forum for powerful elites? We will explore these issues in the remainder of the chapter.

Political Behavior in the United States

Citizens of the United States take for granted many aspects of their political system. They are accustomed to living in a nation with a Bill of Rights, two major political parties, voting by secret ballot, an elected president, state and local governments distinct from the national government, and so forth. Yet each society has its own ways of governing itself and making decisions. Just as U.S. residents expect Democratic and Republican candidates to compete for public office, residents of Cuba and the People's Republic of China are accustomed to one-party rule by the Communist Party. In this section, we will examine several aspects of political behavior within the United States.

Participation and Apathy

In theory, a representative democracy will function most effectively and fairly if an informed and active electorate communicates its views to government leaders. Unfortunately, that is hardly the case in the United States. Virtually all citizens are familiar with the basics of the political process, and most tend to identify to some extent with a political party. (In 2006, about 34 percent of registered voters in the United States saw themselves as Democrats, 36 percent as independents, and 30 percent as Republicans.) However, only a small minority of citizens, often members of the higher social classes, actually participate in political organizations on a local or national level. Studies reveal that only 8 percent of Americans belong to a political club or organization. Not more than one in five has ever contacted an official of national, state, or local government about a political issue or problem (Gallup 2006; Orum 2001).

By the 1980s, it had become clear that many people in the United States were beginning to be turned off by political parties, politicians, and big government. The most dramatic indication

of this growing alienation came from voting statistics. Today, voters of all ages and races appear to be less enthusiastic than ever about elections, even presidential contests. For example, in the presidential election of 1896, almost 80 percent of eligible voters in the United States went to the polls. Yet by the 2000 election, turnout had fallen to less than 47 percent of all eligible voters. Obviously, even modestly higher voter turnout could dramatically change election outcomes, as we saw in the razor-thin margin in the 2000 presidential election (Holder 2006).

While a few nations still command high voter turnout, it is increasingly common to hear national leaders of other countries complain of voter apathy. Still, among the 172 countries that have held parliamentary elections since 1945, the United States ranks only 139th in voter turnout. No other industrial nation has recorded a lower average turnout (see Figure 14-2).

In the end, political participation makes government accountable to the voters. If participation declines, government operates with less of a sense of accountability to society. This issue is most serious for the least powerful individuals and groups in the United States. Voter turnout has been particularly low among members of racial and ethnic minorities. In postelection surveys, fewer African Americans and Hispanics than Whites report that they actually voted. Many more potential voters fail to register to vote. The poor—whose focus understandably is on survival—are traditionally underrepresented among voters as well. The low turnout found among these groups is explained at least in part by their common feeling of powerlessness. Yet these low statistics encourage political power brokers to continue to

ignore the interests of the less affluent and the nation's minorities. The segment of the voting population that has shown the most voter apathy is the young: see Box 14-1 (Holder 2006).

Race and Gender in Politics

Because politics is synonymous with power and authority, we should not be surprised that political strength is lacking in marginalized groups, such as women and racial and ethnic minorities. Nationally, women did not get the vote until 1920. Most Chinese Americans were turned away from the polls until 1926. Throughout the United States, American Indians were prevented from voting until 1954. And African Americans were disenfranchised until 1965, when national voting rights legislation was passed. Predictably, it has taken these groups some time to develop their political power and begin to exercise it effectively. { p.268 } Progress has been slow. As of mid-2006, only 14 out of 100 U.S. senators were women. One was an African American, 2 were Latinos, and 2 were Asian Americans, leaving 81 White non-Hispanic men. Among the 435 members of the U.S. House of Representatives, 340 were White non-Hispanic men. Forty-six were women, 41 were African Americans (including 12 women), 23 were Latinos (including 7 Latinas), 3 were Asian Americans, and 1 was an American Indian. These numbers, though low, represent a high-water mark for these groups.

Today, with record-high numbers of Blacks and Latinos holding elective office, many critics still decry what has been termed "fiesta politics." White power brokers tend to visit racial and ethnic minority communities only when they need electoral

---

FIGURE 14-2

Voter Turnout Worldwide

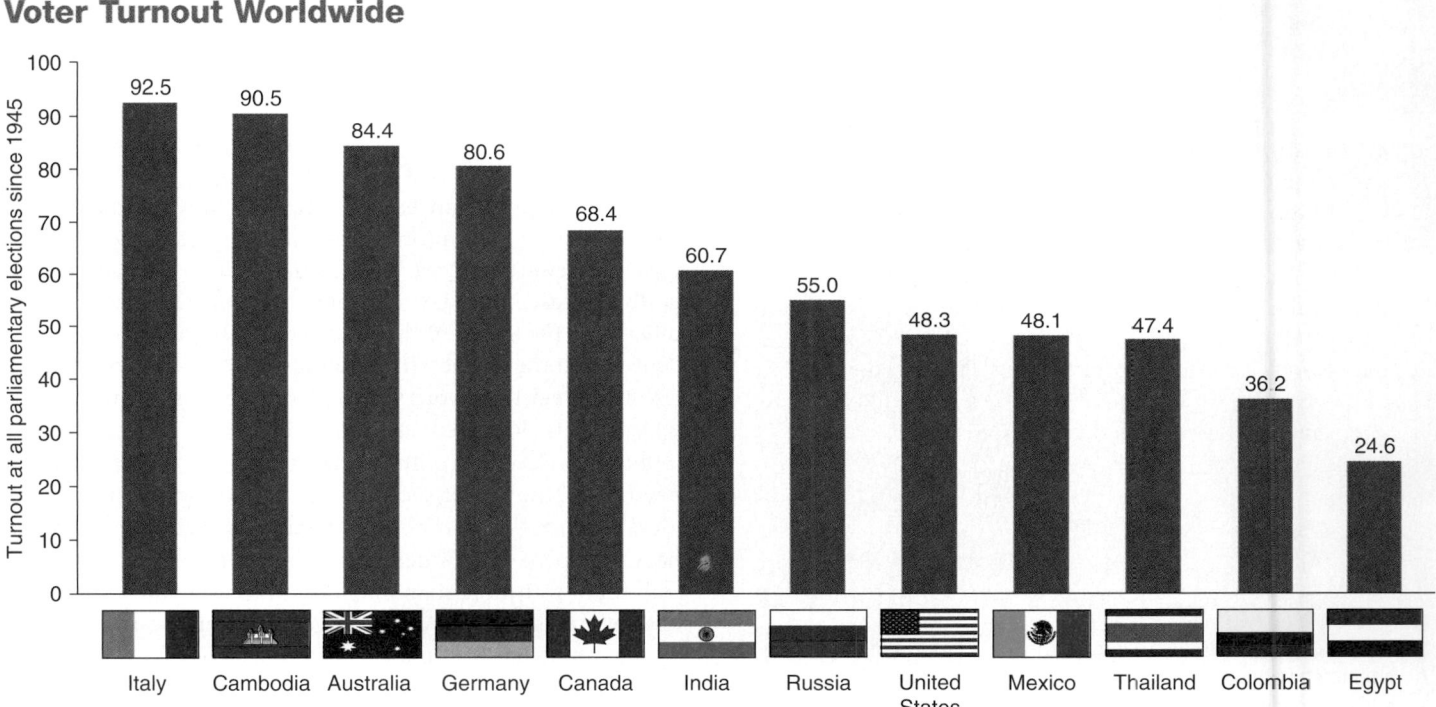

Source: International Institute for Democracy and Electoral Assistance 2005.

Methods Surveys of voter turnout in the United States and other countries
Global View Voter turnout in the United States compared with other countries
Methods/Race/Ethnicity Postelection surveys indicate fewer African Americans and Hispanics than Whites report they actually voted.

Classroom Tip See "Gender and Politics" (Class Discussion Topics).
Global View/Gender Women are underrepresented in government.
Theory Conflict view of impact of sexism in the U.S. political system

research IN action

14-1 Why Don't More Young People Vote?

All through the 1960s, young people in the United States participated actively in a range of political issues, from pushing civil rights to protesting the Vietnam War. They were especially disturbed by the fact that young men were barred from voting but were being drafted to serve in the military and were dying for their country. In response to these concerns, the 26th Amendment to the Constitution was ratified in 1971, lowering the voting age from 21 to 18.

Now, more than 30 years later, we can consider the available research and see what happened. Frankly, what is remarkable is what did *not* happen. First, young voters (those between ages 18 and 21) have not united in any particular political sentiment. We can see in the way the young vote the same divisions of race, ethnicity, and gender that are apparent among older age groups.

Second, while the momentum for lowering the voting age came from college campuses, the majority of young voters are not students at all. Many are already part of the workforce and either live with their parents or have established their own households.

Third, and particularly troubling, is their relatively low turnout. The 2004 presidential election, held against a background of war in Iraq

and an economic slump at home, did pique the interest of young voters. In that election, 51 percent of voters under age 30 turned out, compared to 42 percent in 2000. But turnout among that group was 55 percent in 1972.

What lies behind this voter apathy among the young? The popular explanation is that people—especially young people—are alienated from the political system, turned off by the shallowness and negativity of candidates and

> *While the momentum for lowering the voting age came from college campuses, the majority of young voters are not students at all.*

campaigns. True, studies have documented that young voters are susceptible to cynicism and distrust, but those qualities are not necessarily associated with voter apathy. Numerous studies show that the relationship between how people perceive the candidates and issues and their likelihood of voting is a very complex one. Young people do vote as they age. Any disaffection with the voting booth is certainly not permanent.

Other explanations for the lower turnout among the young seem more plausible. First, the United States is virtually alone in requiring citizens to vote twice, in effect. They must first *register* to vote, often at a time when issues are not on the front burner and candidates haven't even declared. Second, while citizens in the United States tend to be more active than those in other countries in politics at the community level, young people often feel unmoved by local issues such as public school financing.

Let's Discuss

1. How often do you vote? If you do not vote, what accounts for your apathy? Are you too busy to register? Are community issues uninteresting to you?

2. Do you think voter apathy is a serious social problem? What might be done to increase voter participation in your age group and community?

Sources: Alwin 2002; Clymer 2000; A. Goldstein and Morin 2002; Higher Education Research Institute 2004; Jamieson et al. 2002; Patterson 2005; Y. Rosenberg 2004.

---

support, making a quick appearance on a national or ethnic holiday to get their pictures taken and then vanishing. When the election is over, they too often forget to consult the residents who supported them about community needs and concerns.

Female politicians may be enjoying more electoral success now than in the past, but there is evidence that the media cover them differently from male politicians. A content analysis of newspaper coverage of recent gubernatorial races showed that reporters wrote more often about a female candidate's personal life, appearance, or personality than a male candidate's, and less often about her political positions and voting record. Furthermore, when political issues were raised in newspaper articles, reporters were more likely to illustrate them with statements made by male candidates than by female candidates (Devitt 1999).

Figure 14-3 (page 360) shows the representation of women in selected national legislatures. While the proportion of women in national legislatures has increased in the United States and many other nations, women still do not account for half the members of the national legislature in any country. The African Republic of Rwanda ranks the highest, with 48.8 percent of its legisla-

tive seats held by women. Overall, the United States ranked 83rd among 188 nations in the proportion of women serving as national legislators in 2006. To remedy this situation, many countries—including the world's largest democracy, India—have reserved a minimum number of legislative seats for women: see Box 14-2, page 360.

Use Your Sociological Imagination
www.mhhe.com/schaefer7

Imagine a world in which women, not men, held the majority of elective offices. What kind of world would it be?

Models of Power Structure in the United States

Who really holds power in the United States? Do "we the people" genuinely run the country through our elected representatives? Or is it true that behind the scenes, a small elite controls both the

---

Methods Content analysis of media coverage of candidates
Classroom Tip See "Class Voting Behavior" (Class Discussion Topics).
Methods Data from the Bureau of the Census
Race/Ethnicity/Gender Young voters mimic the voting behavior of adults.
Classroom Tip See "Gender Assumptions in Politics" (Class Discussion Topics).

Let's Discuss Do students believe that women are likely to hold even 25 percent of elective offices during their lifetime?

sociologyIN *the Global Community*

14-2 Gender Quotas at the Ballot Box

Worldwide, women are underrepresented in government. In national legislatures, they make up only 16 percent of the total membership—far below their share of the world's population in 2005.

To remedy this situation, many countries have adopted quotas for female representatives. In some, the government sets aside a certain percentage of seats for women, usually from 10 to 30 percent. In others, political parties have decided that 20 to 40 percent of their candidates should be women. Thirty-two countries now have some kind of female quota system.

In sheer numbers, India has seen the biggest gains in female representation. After a third of all village council seats were set aside for women, almost a million Indian women won election to local office. In South Africa, another country with quotas, women now hold 33 percent or more of the seats in both houses of Parliament. Compared with South Africa, the United States, which does not have quotas, has not done nearly as well: Women hold only 15 percent of seats in the House of Representatives and 14 percent of seats in the Senate.

In Africa, quotas have been particularly popular in countries where women contributed to independence movements. South African women fought hard against apartheid and received constitutional guarantees against discrimination in return. Ugandan women fought in the National Resistance Army in the 1980s,

> *Thirty-two countries now have some kind of female quota system.*

earning new respect—and new political power—from men. Women now comprise almost 24 percent of Uganda's parliament and form a minimum required percentage of all elected bodies in that country.

With support from President Yoweri Museveni, who appointed a woman, Wandira Kazibwe, as vice president in 1994, Ugandan women have used their newfound power to enact new privileges for themselves. Married women can now share property ownership with their husbands, and widows can retain property after their husbands' death. Women legislators have also increased educational opportunities for girls in an effort to reduce the harsh poverty in their country. In President Museveni's opinion, the presence of women in government has helped to stabilize politics in Uganda. And in a country where women produce much of the wealth, he notes, they deserve to be empowered.

Let's Discuss

1. Why do you think the United States has so few women in government compared to many other nations?
2. Should the United States adopt a quota system? Why or why not?

Sources: Center for American Women and Politics 2006; Hanes 2005; Inter-Parliamentary Union 2006; A. Simmons and Wright 2000; Vasagar 2005; Wax 2005.

FIGURE 14–3

Women in National Legislatures, Selected Countries, 2006

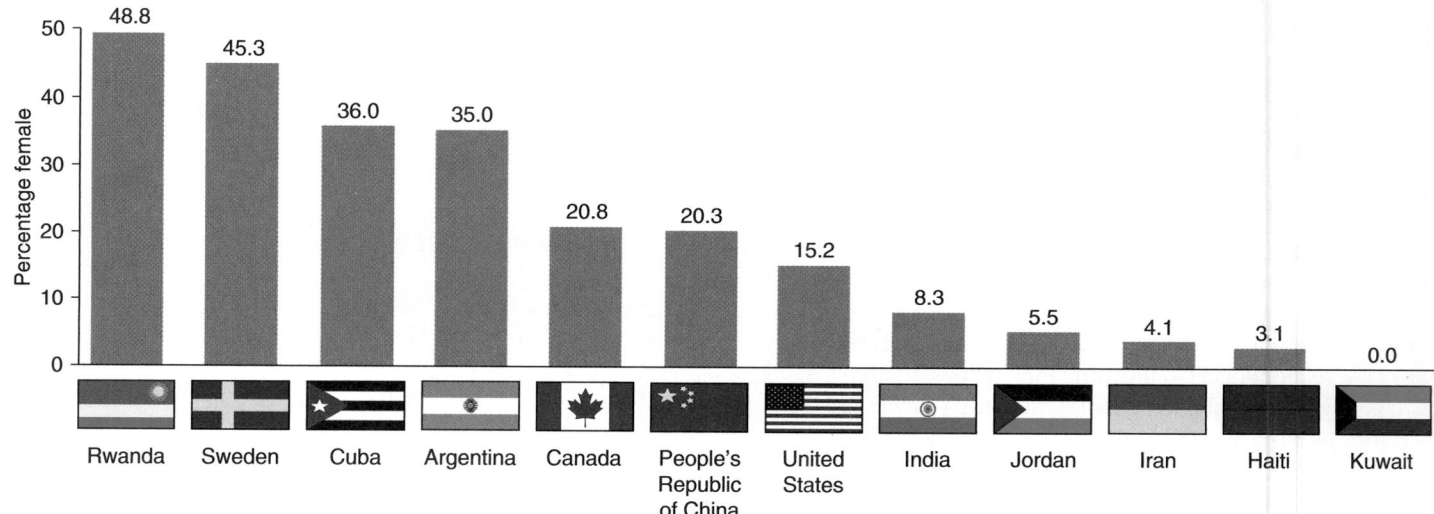

Notes: Data are for lower legislative houses only, as of March 31, 2006; data on upper houses, such as the U.S. Senate or the U.K. House of Lords, are not included. In 2005, the all-male Kuwaiti Parliament granted women the right to vote and serve in elected offices, which could allow women to run for office as soon as 2007.
Source: Inter-Parliamentary Union 2006.

Global View India, the world's largest democracy, has reserved a minimum number of legislative seats for women.

Global View/Gender The president of Uganda believes the presence of women in government has helped to stabilize politics.

government and the economic system? It is difficult to determine the location of power in a society as complex as the United States. In exploring this critical question, social scientists have developed two basic views of our nation's power structure: the power elite and the pluralist models.

Power Elite Models

Karl Marx believed that 19th-century representative democracy was essentially a sham. He argued that industrial societies were dominated by relatively small numbers of people who owned factories and controlled natural resources. In Marx's view, government officials and military leaders were essentially servants of this capitalist class and followed their wishes. Therefore, any key decisions made by politicians inevitably reflected the interests of the dominant bourgeoisie. Like others who hold an *elite model* of power relations, Marx believed that society is ruled by a small group of individuals who share a common set of political and economic interests.

Mills's Model   Sociologist C. Wright Mills, referred to earlier in this chapter, took this model a step further in his pioneering work *The Power Elite* ([1956] 2000b). Mills described a small group of military, industrial, and government leaders who controlled the fate of the United States—the *power elite.* Power rested in the hands of a few, both inside and outside government.

A pyramid illustrates the power structure of the United States in Mills's model (see Figure 14-4a). At the top are the corporate rich, leaders of the executive branch of government, and heads of the military (whom Mills called the "warlords"). Directly below are local opinion leaders, members of the legislative branch

of government, and leaders of special-interest groups. Mills contended that these individuals and groups would basically follow the wishes of the dominant power elite. At the bottom of the pyramid are the unorganized, exploited masses.

The power elite model is, in many respects, similar to the work of Karl Marx. The most striking difference is that Mills believed that the economically powerful coordinate their maneuvers with the military and political establishments to serve their common interests. Yet, reminiscent of Marx, Mills argued that the corporate rich were perhaps the most powerful element of the power elite (first among "equals"). And the powerless masses at the bottom of Mills's power elite model certainly bring to mind Marx's portrait of the oppressed workers of the world, who have "nothing to lose but their chains."

A fundamental element in Mills's thesis is that the power elite not only includes relatively few members but also operates as a self-conscious, cohesive unit. Although not necessarily diabolical or ruthless, the elite comprises similar types of people who interact regularly with one another and have essentially the same political and economic interests. Mills's power elite is not a conspiracy, but rather a community of interest and sentiment among a small number of influential people (A. Hacker 1964).

Admittedly, Mills failed to clarify when the elite opposes protests and when it tolerates them; he also failed to provide detailed case studies that would substantiate the interrelationships among members of the power elite. Nevertheless, his challenging theories forced scholars to look more critically at the democratic political system of the United States.

In commenting on the scandals that have rocked major corporations such as Enron and Arthur Andersen over the last

FIGURE 14–4

Power Elite Models

a. C. Wright Mills's model, 1956

b. G. William Domhoff's model, 2006

Source: Left, author based on C. W. Mills [1956] 2000b; right, Domhoff 2006:105

Classroom Tip See "Marx and Marxism Analyzed" (Additional Lecture Ideas).
Key Persons Karl Marx, C. Wright Mills
Theory Mills's power elite model reflects a conflict perspective.
Classroom Tip See "Corporate Power" (Class Discussion Topics).
Classroom Tip See "Military Industrial Complex" (Additional Lecture Ideas).

Student Alert Mills's power elite model may seem Marxist, but it does not conform to Marx's view that power is class-based.

decade, observers have noted that members of the business elite *are* closely interrelated. In a study of the members of the boards of directors of Fortune 1,000 corporations, researchers found that each director can reach *every* other board of directors in just 3.7 steps. That is, by consulting acquaintances of acquaintances, each director can quickly reach someone who sits on each of the other 999 boards. Furthermore, the face-to-face contact directors regularly have in their board meetings makes them a highly cohesive elite. Finally, the corporate elite is not only wealthy, powerful, and cohesive; it is also overwhelmingly White and male (G. Davis 2003, 2004; Kentor and Jang 2004; Mizruchi 1996; Strauss 2002).

Domhoff's Model Over the last three decades, sociologist G. William Domhoff (2006), coauthor of the chapter-opening excerpt from *Diversity in the Power Elite,* has agreed with Mills that a powerful elite runs the United States. He finds that it is still largely White, male, and upper class, as he wrote in his book with Richard L. Zweigenhaft (2006). But Domhoff stresses the role played both by elites of the corporate community and by the leaders of policy-formation organizations, such as chambers of commerce and labor unions. Many of the people in both groups are also members of the social upper class.

While these groups overlap, as Figure 14-4b shows, they do not necessarily agree on specific policies. Domhoff notes that in the electoral arena, two different coalitions have exercised influence. A *corporate-conservative coalition* has played a large role in both political parties, generating support for particular candidates through direct-mail appeals. A *liberal-labor coalition* is based in unions, local environmental organizations, a segment of the minority group community, liberal churches, and the university and arts communities (Zweigenhaft and Domhoff 2006).

Pluralist Model

Several social scientists insist that power in the United States is shared more widely than the elite models indicate. In their view, a pluralist model more accurately describes the nation's political system. According to the **pluralist model,** many competing groups within the community have access to government, so that no single group is dominant.

The pluralist model suggests that a variety of groups play a significant role in decision making. Typically, pluralists make use of intensive case studies or community studies based on observation research. One of the most famous—an investigation of decision making in New Haven, Connecticut—was reported by Robert Dahl (1961). Dahl found that although the number of people involved in any important decision was rather small, community power was nonetheless diffuse. Few political actors exercised decision-making power on all issues. One individual or group might be influential in a battle over urban renewal, but have little impact on educational policy.

The pluralist model, however, has not escaped serious questioning. Domhoff (1978, 2006) reexamined Dahl's study of decision making in New Haven and argued that Dahl and other pluralists had failed to trace how local elites who were promi-

nent in decision making belonged to a larger national ruling class. In addition, studies of community power, such as Dahl's work in New Haven, can examine decision making only on issues that become part of the political agenda. They fail to address the potential power of elites to keep certain matters entirely out of the realm of government debate.

Dianne Pinderhughes (1987) has criticized the pluralist model for failing to account for the exclusion of African Americans from the political process. Drawing on her studies of Chicago politics, Pinderhughes points out that the residential and occupational segregation of Blacks and their long political disenfranchisement violates the logic of pluralism—which would hold that such a substantial minority should always have been influential in community decision making. This critique applies to many cities across the United States, where other large racial and ethnic minorities, among them Asian Americans, Puerto Ricans, and Mexican Americans, are relatively powerless.

Historically, pluralists have stressed ways in which large numbers of people can participate in or influence governmental decision making. New communications technologies like the Internet are increasing the opportunity to be heard, not just in countries such as the United States but in developing countries the world over. One common point of the elite and pluralist perspectives stands out, however: in the political system of the United States, power is unequally distributed. All citizens may be equal in theory, yet those who are high in the nation's power structure are "more equal." New communications technology may or may not change that distribution of power.

Perhaps the ultimate test of power, no matter what a nation's power structure, is the decision to go to war. Because the rank and file of any army is generally drawn from the lower classes—the least powerful groups in society—such a decision has life-and-death consequences for people far removed from the center of power. In the long run, if the general population is not convinced that war is necessary, military action is unlikely to succeed. Thus, war is a risky way in which to address conflict between nations. In the following section we will contrast war and peace as ways of addressing societal conflict, and more recently, the threat of terrorism.

War and Peace

Conflict is a central aspect of social relations. Too often it becomes ongoing and violent, engulfing innocent bystanders as well as intentional participants. Sociologists Theodore Caplow and Louis Hicks (2002:3) have defined **war** as conflict between organizations that possess trained combat forces equipped with deadly weapons. This meaning is broader than the legal definition, which typically requires a formal declaration of hostilities.

War

Sociologists approach war in three different ways. Those who take a global view study how and why two or more nations become engaged in military conflict. Those who take a nation-state view stress the interaction of internal political, socioeconomic, and cultural forces. And those who take a micro view focus on

Key Person G. William Domhoff
Theory Domhoff's ruling class model reflects a conflict perspective.
Classroom Tip See "Japanese Power Elite" in Topics and Sources for Student Research.
Key Person Robert Dahl

Student Alert Pluralists see decision making as more widely shared than Mills and Domhoff do, but would agree that the disadvantaged are often excluded.
Race/Ethnicity Pinderhughes's critique of the pluralist model for failing to account for the exclusion of African Americans from the political process
Classroom Tip See "Who Rules?" (Additional Lecture Ideas).
Global View Conflict between nations

On Earth Day 2004, ecologically aware students at the University of Wisconsin, Madison, hopped on their bicycles and joined local residents at the Hummer dealership. Protesters were hoping to disrupt sales of the huge gas-guzzling vehicles by blocking traffic. When public interest groups seek to exert their power through such mass protests, they are demonstrating a belief in the pluralist model of the United States' power structure.

the public was split roughly equally on the question of whether war was an appropriate way to settle differences between nations (see Figure 14-5). This division in public opinion continued until the United States became involved in the Gulf War following Iraq's invasion of Kuwait in 1990. Since then, U.S. sentiment has been more supportive of war as a means of resolving disputes.

A major change in the composition of the U.S. military is the growing presence of women. Over 212,000 women, or about 15 percent of U.S. military forces, are now in uniform, serving not just as support personnel but as an integral part of combat units. The first casualty of the war in Iraq, in fact, was Private First Class Lori Piestewa, a member of the Hopi tribe and a descendant of Mexican settlers in the Southwest (Department of Defense 2003).

From a micro point of view, war can bring out the worst as well as the best in people. In 2004, graphic images of the abuse of Iraqi prisoners by U.S. soldiers at Iraq's Abu Ghraib prison shocked the world. For social scientists, the deterioration of the guards' behavior brought to mind Philip Zimbardo's mock prison experiment, done in 1971. Though the results of the experiment, highlighted in Chapter 5, have been applied primarily to civilian correctional facilities, Zimbardo's study was actually funded by the Office of Naval Research. In July 2004, the U.S. military began using a documentary film about the experiment to train military interrogators to avoid mistreatment of prisoners (Zarembo 2004; Zimbardo 2004).

Peace

Sociologists have considered **peace** both as the absence of war and as a proactive effort to develop cooperative relations among

the social impact of war on individuals and the groups they belong to (Kiser 1992).

The internal decision-making process that leads to war has been much studied. During the Vietnam War, Presidents Johnson and Nixon both misled Congress, painting a falsely optimistic picture of the likely outcome. Based on their intentional distortions, Congress appropriated the military funds the two administrations requested. But in 1971 the *New York Times* published a set of classified documents now known as "The Pentagon Papers," which revealed the real prospects for the war. Two years later—over Nixon's veto—Congress passed the War Powers Act, which requires the president to notify Congress of the reasons for committing combat troops to a hostile situation (Patterson 2003).

Though the decision to go to war is made by government leaders, public opinion plays a significant role in its execution. By 1971, the number of U.S. soldiers killed in Vietnam had surpassed 50,000, and antiwar sentiment was strong. Surveys done at that time showed

FIGURE 14-5

U.S. Public Opinion on the Necessity of War, 1971–2004

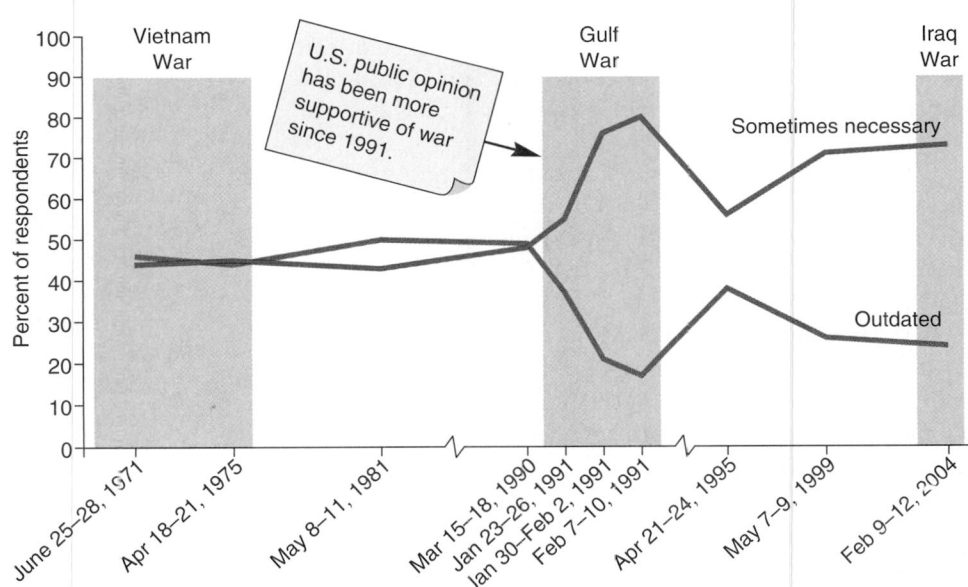

U.S. public opinion has been more supportive of war since 1991.

Note: Respondents replied to the following question: "Some people feel that war is an outmoded way of settling differences between nations. Others feel that wars are sometimes necessary to settle differences. With which point of view do you agree?"
Source: Arora 2004.

Contemporary Culture How does public sentiment about the war in Iraq compare to public sentiment about the Vietnam War?
Race/Ethnicity/Gender The role of women in the military
Let's Discuss What are some of the micro-level social impacts of the war in Iraq?

nations. While we will focus here on international relations, we should note that in the 1990s, 90 percent of the world's armed conflicts occurred *within* rather than between states. Often, outside powers became involved in these internal conflicts, either as supporters of particular factions or in an attempt to broker a peace accord. In at least 28 countries where such conflicts occurred—none of which would be considered core nations in world systems analysis—at least 10,000 people died (Kriesberg 1992; Dan Smith 1999).

Sociologists and other social scientists who draw on sociological theory and research have tried to identify conditions that deter war. One of their findings is that international trade may act as a deterrent to armed conflict. As countries exchange goods, people, and then cultures, they become more integrated and less likely to threaten each other's security. Viewed from this perspective, not just trade but immigration and foreign exchange programs have a beneficial effect on international relations.

A representative of the International Red Crescent Society delivers an aid parcel in the southern Iraqi town of Safwan. The Red Crescent provides emergency aid to victims of war and disaster in Muslim communities. Such nongovernmental organizations (NGOs) help to bind countries together, promoting peaceful relations.

Another means of fostering peace is the activity of international charities and activist groups called nongovernmental organizations (NGOs). The Red Cross and Red Crescent, Doctors Without Borders, and Amnesty International donate their services wherever they are needed, without regard to nationality. In the last decade or more, these global organizations have been expanding in number, size, and scope. By sharing news of local conditions and clarifying local issues, they often prevent conflicts from escalating into violence and war. Some NGOs have initiated cease-fires, reached settlements, and even ended warfare between former adversaries.

Finally, many analysts stress that nations cannot maintain their security by threatening violence. Peace, they contend, can best be maintained by developing strong mutual security agreements between potential adversaries (Etzioni 1965; Shostak 2002).

In recent years, the United States has begun to recognize that its security can be threatened not just by nation states, but by political groups that operate outside the bounds of legitimate authority. Indeed, terrorism is now considered the foremost threat to U.S. security—one the U.S. military is unaccustomed to fighting.

Terrorism

Acts of terror, whether perpetrated by a few or by many people, can be a powerful political force. Formally defined, **terrorism** is the use or threat of violence against random or symbolic targets in pursuit of political aims. For terrorists, the end justifies the means. They believe the status quo is oppressive, and desperate measures are essential to end the suffering of the deprived. Convinced that working through the formal political process will not effect the desired political change, terrorists insist that illegal actions—often directed against innocent people—are needed. Ultimately, they hope to intimidate society and thereby bring about a new political order.

An essential aspect of contemporary terrorism involves use of the media. Terrorists may wish to keep secret their individual identities, but they want their political messages and goals to receive as much publicity as possible. Drawing on Erving Goffman's dramaturgical approach, sociologist Alfred McClung Lee has likened terrorism to the theater, where certain scenes are played out in predictable fashion. Whether through calls to the media, anonymous manifestos, or other means, terrorists typically admit responsibility for and defend their violent acts.

Figure 14-6 shows the global reach of terrorism. Since September 11, 2001, governments around the world have renewed their efforts to fight terrorism. Though the public has generally regarded increased surveillance and social control as a necessary evil, these measures have nonetheless raised governance issues. For example, some citizens in the United States and elsewhere have questioned whether measures such as the USA Patriot Act of 2001 threaten civil liberties. Citizens also complain about the heightened anxiety created by the vague alerts issued by the federal government from time to time. Worldwide, immigration and the processing of refugees have slowed to a crawl, separating families

Let's Discuss To what extent should outside nations become involved in domestic conflicts?

Contemporary Culture What factors may make terrorism more of a threat today than in the past?

Key Person Alfred McClung Lee

Theory Compare Lee's ideas to Goffman's dramaturgical approach.

and preventing employers from filling job openings. As these efforts to combat political violence illustrate, the term *terrorism* is an apt one (R. Howard and Sawyer 2003; Lee 1983; R. Miller 1988).

The Changing Economy

As advocates of the power elite model point out, the trend in capitalist societies has been toward concentration of ownership by giant corporations, especially multinational ones. In the following sections, we will examine two related developments that have interested sociologists: the changing face of the workforce and deindustrialization. As these trends show, any change in the economy has social and political implications that soon become a concern of policymakers.

{ p.215 }

The Changing Face of the Workforce

The workforce in the United States is constantly changing. During World War II, when men were mobilized to fight abroad, women entered the workforce in large numbers. And with the rise of the civil rights movement in the 1960s, minorities found numerous job opportunities opening to them. Box 14-3 (page 366) takes a closer look at the active recruitment of women and minorities into the workplace, known as *affirmative action*.

While predictions are not always reliable, sociologists and labor specialists foresee a workforce increasingly composed of women and racial and ethnic minorities. In 1960 there were twice as many men in the labor force as women. From 1984 to 2014, however, 54 percent of new workers are expected to be women. The dynamics for minority-group workers are even

FIGURE 14–6

The Global Reach of Terrorism

MAPPING LIFE

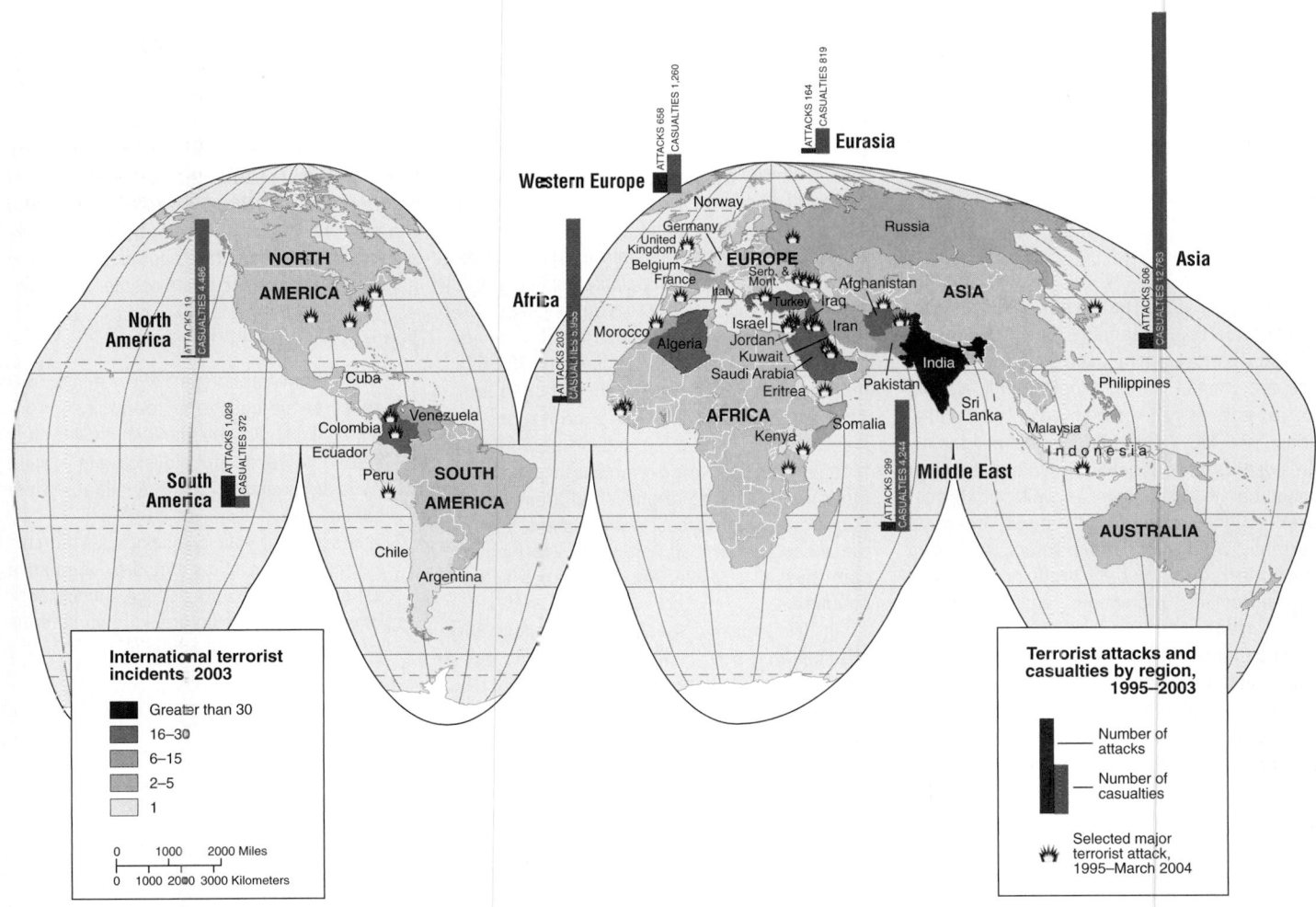

WORLDWIDE www.mhhe.com/schaefe-7

International terrorist incidents, 2003

- Greater than 30
- 16–30
- 6–15
- 2–5
- 1

0   1000   2000 Miles
0   1000 2000 3000 Kilometers

Terrorist attacks and casualties by region, 1995–2003

- Number of attacks
- Number of casualties
- Selected major terrorist attack, 1995–March 2004

Source: National Geographic 2005:17.

14-3 Affirmative Action

Jessie Sherrod began picking cotton in the fields of Mississippi when she was eight years old, earning $1.67 for a 12-hour day. Today she is a Harvard-educated pediatrician who specializes in infectious diseases. But the road from the cotton fields to the medical profession was hardly an easy one. "You can't make up for 400 years of slavery and mistreatment and unequal opportunity in 20 years," she says angrily. "We had to ride the school bus for five miles . . . and pass by a white school to get to our black elementary school. Our books were used books. Our instructors were not as good. We didn't have the proper equipment. How do you make up for that?" (Stolberg 1995:A14). Some people think it should be done through affirmative action programs.

The term *affirmative action* first appeared in an executive order issued by President John

> *Critics warn against hiring and admissions quotas, complaining that they constitute a kind of "reverse discrimination" against White males.*

F. Kennedy in 1961. That order called for contractors to "take affirmative action to ensure that applicants are employed, and that employees are treated during employment, without regard to their race, creed, color, or national origin." In 1967, the order was amended by President Lyndon Johnson to prohibit discrimination on the basis of sex as well, but affirmative action remained a vague concept. Currently, **affirmative action** refers to positive efforts to recruit minority group members or women for jobs, promotions, and educational opportunities.

Sociologists—especially conflict theorists—view affirmative action as a legislative attempt to reduce the inequality embedded in the social structure by increasing opportunities for groups who were deprived in the past,

such as women and African Americans. Despite the clear disparity in earnings between White males and other groups, however, many people doubt that everything done in the name of affirmative action is desirable. Critics warn against hiring and admissions quotas, complaining that they constitute a kind of "reverse discrimination" against White males. Thus, though a majority of 60 percent of respondents to a 2004 national survey favored affirmative action in college admissions, an analysis of the responses revealed clear racial and gender differences. Among Blacks, 87 percent favored affirmative action; among Hispanics, the rate was 77 percent. But fewer White women—60 percent—approved of the programs, and only 49 percent of White men did.

Affirmative action became a prominent issue in state and national political campaigns in 1996, when California's voters approved by a 54 to 46 percent margin the California Civil Rights Initiative. Better known as Proposition 209, this measure amends the state constitution to *prohibit* any program that gives preference to women and minorities in college admissions, hiring, promotion, or government contracts. In other words, it aims to abolish affirmative action programs. The courts have since upheld the measure. In 1998, voters in Washington state passed a similar anti–affirmative action measure.

In 2003, focusing specifically on college admissions in a pair of decisions involving policies at the University of Michigan, the Supreme Court ruled that colleges may consider race and ethnicity as one factor in their admissions decisions. However, they cannot

assign a specific value to being a minority candidate in such a way that race becomes the overriding factor in a decision. The ruling allowed many colleges and universities to continue their existing affirmative action policies. But critics complained that it permits blatant favoritism toward the children of alumni, who are more likely than others to be White, while subjecting programs that favor disadvantaged minority candidates to much greater scrutiny.

Let's Discuss

1. Is affirmative action part of the admissions policy at the college or university you attend? If so, do you think the policy has helped to level the playing field? Might it have excluded some qualified White applicants?
2. Take a poll of your classmates. What percentage of the class supports affirmative action in hiring and college admissions? How does that group break down in terms of gender, race, and ethnicity?

Sources: Pew Research Center 2004; Stolberg 1995; University of Michigan 2003.

Gender/Race/Ethnicity The issue of affirmative action has particular relevance for women and for racial and ethnic minorities.
Classroom Tip Reintroduce the concept of the glass ceiling, discussed in Chapters 10 and 11.
Policy Pointer The term *affirmative action* implies positive steps to ensure equality; civil rights legislation implies it is enough to stop discriminating.

Theory From a conflict perspective, affirmative action emerged as a result of social inequality based on gender, race, and ethnicity.
Classroom Tip See "The Efficacy of Affirmative Action" (Additional Lecture Ideas).
Classroom Tip See "Debating Affirmative Action" (Class Discussion Topics).

more dramatic, as the number of Black, Latino, and Asian American workers continues to increase at a faster rate than the number of White workers (Toossi 2005:26).

More and more, then, the workforce reflects the diversity of the population, as ethnic minorities enter the labor force and immigrants and their children move from marginal jobs or employment in the informal economy to positions of greater visibility and responsibility. The impact of this changing { pp.202–203 } labor force is not merely statistical. A more diverse workforce means that relationships between workers are more likely to cross gender, racial, and ethnic lines. Interactionists note that people will soon find themselves supervising and being supervised by people very different from themselves. In response to these changes, 75 percent of businesses had instituted some type of cultural diversity training program as of 2000 (Melia 2000).

Deindustrialization

What happens when a company decides it is more profitable to move its operations out of a long-established community to another part of the country, or out of the country altogether? People lose jobs; stores lose customers; the local government's tax base declines and it cuts services. This devastating process has occurred again and again in the last decade or so.

The term *deindustrialization* refers to the systematic, widespread withdrawal of investment in basic aspects of productivity, such as factories and plants. Giant corporations that deindustrialize are not necessarily refusing to invest in new economic opportunities. Rather, the targets and locations of investment change, and the need for labor decreases as advances in technology continue to automate production. First, companies may move their plants from the nation's central cities to the suburbs. The next step may be relocation from suburban areas of the Northeast and Midwest to the South, where labor laws place more restrictions on unions. Finally, a corporation may simply relocate *outside* the United States to a country with a lower rate of prevailing wages. General Motors, for example, decided to build a multibillion-dollar plant in China rather than in Kansas City or even in Mexico (Lynn 2003).

Although deindustrialization often involves relocation, in some instances it takes the form of corporate restructuring, as companies seek to reduce costs in the face of growing worldwide competition. When such restructuring occurs, the impact on the bureaucratic hierarchy of formal organizations can be significant. A large corporation may choose to sell off or entirely abandon less productive divisions and to eliminate layers of management viewed as unnecessary. Wages and salaries may be frozen and fringe benefits cut—all in the name of restructuring. Increasing reliance on automation also spells the end of work as we have known it.

The term *downsizing* was introduced in 1987 to refer to reductions taken in a company's workforce as part of deindustrialization. Viewed from a conflict perspective, the unprecedented attention given to downsizing in the mid-1990s reflected the continuing importance of social class in the United States. Conflict theorists note that job loss has long been a feature of de-

In Seoul in 2001, protesting employees of the dot-com industry took to the streets to demand job security and better working conditions. The year before, South Korean workers had logged longer hours than those in 199 other countries (Webb 2001).

industrialization among blue-collar workers. But when large numbers of middle-class managers and other white-collar employees with substantial incomes began to be laid off, suddenly the media began expressing great concern over downsizing. The Social Policy section that follows highlights the latest version of this issue, the outsourcing of service jobs at U.S. companies to workers in foreign countries (Richtel 2000; Safire 1996; R. Samuelson 1996a, 1996b).

The social costs of deindustrialization and downsizing cannot be overemphasized. Plant closings lead to substantial unemployment in a community, which can have a devastating impact on both the micro and macro levels. On the micro level, the unemployed person and his or her family must adjust to a loss of spending power. Painting or re-siding the house, buying health insurance or saving for retirement, even thinking about having another child must be put aside. Both marital happiness and family cohesion may suffer as a result. Although many dismissed workers eventually reenter the paid labor force, they must often accept less desirable positions with lower salaries and fewer benefits (DePalma 2002). Unemployment and underemployment are tied to many of the social problems discussed throughout

this textbook, among them the need for child care and the con-
{ pp.94, 203 } troversy over welfare. In the minds of many displaced
workers in the United States, the source of all these ills is the off-

shoring of U.S. jobs to overseas workers—the subject of the following Social Policy section.

Global Offshoring

The Issue

Anney Unnikrishnan's situation is not unusual. In fact, she is
one of 245,000 Indians who work in global call centers, answering phone calls from all over the world or dialing out to solicit
business. Anney received her MBA in India before taking the entrance exams to Purdue University. But after concluding
that she couldn't afford Purdue, she realized that because U.S.
corporations were setting up shop in India, she didn't need to
emigrate to the United States. Anney sums up what she considers her enviable position in this way: "So I still get my rice and
sambar (a traditional Indian dish). . . . I don't need to . . . learn
to eat coleslaw and cold beef . . . and I still work for a multinational. Why should I go to America?" (Friedman 2005:28).

Offshoring is global: it occurs not just between North America and India, but between North America and Europe (see Box
9-2 on page 220) and between other industrial and developing
countries. Online services in the United States enlist Romanians
to represent well-to-do video game players. Japan enlists Chinese speakers of Japanese—a legacy of Japan's bitter occupation
of China—to create databases or develop floor plans for Japanese construction firms. In Africa, over 54,000 people work in
call centers, some specializing in French and others serving the
English-speaking market. People all over the world are affected
by this issue (Friedman 2005; Lacey 2005).

The Setting

U.S. firms have been *outsourcing* certain types of work for generations. For example, moderate-sized businesses such as furniture stores and commercial laundries have long relied on outside
trucking firms to make deliveries to their customers. The new
trend toward **offshoring** carries this practice one step further, by
transferring other types of work to foreign contractors. Now,
even large companies are turning to overseas firms, many of
them located in developing countries. Offshoring has become
the latest tactic in the time-worn business strategy of raising
profits by reducing costs.

Offshoring began when U.S. companies started transferring
manufacturing jobs to foreign factories, where wage rates were
much lower. But the transfer of work from one country to another is no longer limited to manufacturing. Office and professional jobs are being exported, too, thanks to advanced
telecommunications and the growth of skilled, English-speaking
labor forces in developing nations with relatively low wage
scales. The trend includes even those jobs that require considerable training, such as accounting and financial analysis, computer programming, claims adjustment, telemarketing, and
hotel and airline reservations. Today, when you call a toll-free
number to reach a customer service representative, chances are
that the person who answers the phone will not be speaking
from the United States.

In 2003, an estimated 1.5 million service jobs were done in
lower-wage countries for customers in higher-wage economies.
By 2008, that number is expected to reach 4.1 million. Even
without further technological breakthroughs, the total could
eventually climb to over 160 million jobs worldwide. These substantial increases in overseas outsourcing would be accompanied, of course, by further job reductions in the industrialized
countries (McKinsey Global Institute 2005).

Sociological Insights

Because offshoring, like outsourcing in general, tends to improve the efficiency of business operations, it can be viewed as
functional to society. Offshoring also increases economic interdependence in the production of goods and services, both
among enterprises located just across town from one another
and among those across the globe.

Conflict theorists question whether this aspect of globalization furthers social inequality. While moving high-tech work to
India does help to lower a company's costs, the impact on those
technical and service workers who are displaced is clearly devastating. Certainly middle-class workers in industrial countries are
alarmed by the trend. Though economists favor some assistance
for workers who have been displaced by offshoring, they oppose
broad-based efforts to block the practice.

There is a downside to offshoring for foreigners, as well. Although outsourcing is a significant source of employment for
India's upper middle class, hundreds of millions of other Indians have seen little to no positive impact from the trend. Most
households in India do not possess any form of high technology:
only about 1 out of 10 have a telephone, and just 3 out of 1,000
a computer. Instead of improving these people's lives, the new
business centers have siphoned water and electricity away from

Let's Discuss Have you ever dialed a customer service number and realized that
you were connected to a foreign country?
Contemporary Culture Expansion in jobs outsourced to non-U.S. countries
Let's Discuss Are there limits to the types of jobs that can be outsourced?
Let's Discuss Do you know anyone who has lost a service-sector job because of
offshoring?

Student Alert What factors make offshoring financially feasible for U.S. companies?
Theory Functionalist and conflict views of offshoring
Let's Discuss From the Indian perspective, do the potential long-term benefits of
offshoring outweigh the short-term drawbacks?

those who are most in need. Even the high-tech workers are experiencing negative consequences. Many suffer from stress disorders such as stomach problems and difficulty sleeping; more than half quit their jobs before the end of a year. On the other hand, the new call centers have brought significant improvements in India's infrastructure, particularly in telecommunications and power generation. The long-term impact of offshoring on India and other developing nations is difficult to predict (Waldman 2004a, 2004b, 2004c).

Policy Initiatives

Offshoring became a political flashpoint in the 2004 presidential election, when Democratic candidate John Kerry branded CEOs who send jobs overseas "Benedict Arnolds." Kerry proposed repealing the tax deduction U.S. companies receive for the wages and benefits they pay to offshore workers. Despite such political rhetoric, however, little legislative action has been taken. Most policymakers, while they bemoan the loss of jobs, see offshoring as part of the "natural" process of globalization, one more manifestation of the gains that come from international trade. In their view, the resulting dislocation of workers at home is just another job change—one that more and more workers will have to adjust to at some point during their lifetimes (Friedman 2005; *Migration News* 2005b).

Let's Discuss

1. Do you know anyone whose job has been transferred to a foreign country? If so, was the person able to find a comparable job in the same town, or did he or she have to relocate? How long was the person unemployed?

2. What do you think should be done, if anything, about the growing trend toward offshoring? Do you see it as a serious political issue?

3. How might the number of foreign students who are educated in the United States contribute to the trend toward offshoring? On balance, do you think the gain from training foreign students outweighs the loss from exported jobs?

The number of jobs that can be offshored is growing. Some U.S.-based online tutoring services have begun to employ foreigners such as Somit Basak. Based in New Delhi, India, Basak earns about $200 a month, or $1.40 an hour—very little compared to the $20 or $30 an hour that online tutors in the United States earn.

GettingINVOLVED

To get involved in the debate over global offshoring, visit this text's Online Learning Center, which offers links to relevant Web sites. Check out the Social Policy section on the Online Learning Center as well; it provides survey data on U.S. public opinion regarding this issue.

www.mhhe.com/schaefer7

MASTERING THIS CHAPTER

Summary

Every society must have both an *economic system* and a *political system* through which to allocate valued resources. These two closely intertwined systems have an important influence on social behavior and social institutions, as well as on our general well-being. This chapter examines the major economic systems, the rise of *capitalism* in China, the sources of *power* and *authority,* the five major types of government, political participation and representation, two basic models of the power structure in the United States, *war* and *peace,* the changing economy, and the trend toward global *offshoring.*

1. With the industrial revolution, a new form of social structure emerged: the *industrial society.*

2. Systems of *capitalism* vary in the degree to which the government regulates private ownership and economic activity, but all emphasize the profit motive.

3. The basic objective of *socialism* is to eliminate economic exploitation and meet people's needs.

4. Marx believed that *communism* would evolve naturally out of socialism.

5. In the 1980s, the Chinese Communist Party began allowing Chinese entrepreneurs to experiment with capitalist ventures. Today, multinational corporations are capitalizing on China's huge workforce to produce goods and services for sale not just to those in industrial nations, but to the people of China.

6. There are three basic sources of *power* within any political system: *force, influence,* and *authority.*

7. Max Weber identified three ideal types of *authority: traditional, rational-legal,* and *charismatic.*

8. There are five basic types of government: *monarchy, oligarchy, dictatorship, totalitarianism,* and *democracy.*

9. Political participation makes government accountable to its citizens, but voters display a great deal of apathy both in the United States and in other countries.

10. Women are still underrepresented in politics, but are becoming more successful at winning election to public office.

11. Advocates of the *elite model* of the U.S. power structure see the nation as being ruled by a small group of individuals who share common political and economic interests (a *power elite*), whereas advocates of a *pluralist model* believe that power is shared more widely among conflicting groups.

12. *War* may be defined as conflict between organizations that possess trained combat forces equipped with deadly weapons—a definition that includes conflict with terrorist organizations.

13. The nature of the U.S. economy is changing. Sociologists are especially interested in the changing face of the workforce and the effects of *deindustrialization.*

14. *Offshoring,* or the transfer of work to foreign contractors, has become a global phenomenon involving both developed and developing nations. Today, even professional services can be outsourced to nations like India, which possess a large, well-educated English-speaking population that will work for comparatively low wages.

Critical Thinking Questions

1. The United States has long been put forward as the model of a capitalist society. Drawing on material in earlier chapters of this textbook, discuss the values and beliefs that have led people in the United States to cherish a laissez-faire, capitalist economy. To what degree have those values and beliefs changed over the past hundred years? What aspects of socialism are now evident in the nation's economy? Have our values and beliefs changed to support certain principles traditionally associated with socialist societies?

2. Who really holds power in the college or university you attend? Describe the distribution of power at your school, drawing on the elite and pluralist models where relevant.

3. Imagine that you have joined your state representative's legislative staff as a summer intern. She has assigned you to a committee that is working on solutions to the problem of school violence. How could you use what you have learned about sociology to conceptualize the problem? What type of research would you suggest the committee undertake? What legislative solutions might you recommend?

Key Terms

Affirmative action Positive efforts to recruit minority group members or women for jobs, promotions, and educational opportunities. (page 366)

Authority Institutionalized power that is recognized by the people over whom it is exercised. (355)

Capitalism An economic system in which the means of production are held largely in private hands and the main incentive for economic activity is the accumulation of profits. (350)

Charismatic authority Power made legitimate by a leader's exceptional personal or emotional appeal to his or her followers. (356)

Communism As an ideal type, an economic system under which all property is communally owned and no social distinctions are made on the basis of people's ability to produce. (352)

Deindustrialization The systematic, widespread withdrawal of investment in basic aspects of productivity, such as factories and plants. (367)

Democracy In a literal sense, government by the people. (357)

Dictatorship A government in which one person has nearly total power to make and enforce laws. (356)

Downsizing Reductions taken in a company's workforce as part of deindustrialization. (367)

Economic system The social institution through which goods and services are produced, distributed, and consumed. (349)

Elite model A view of society as being ruled by a small group of individuals who share a common set of political and economic interests. (361)

Force The actual or threatened use of coercion to impose one's will on others. (355)

Industrial society A society that depends on mechanization to produce its goods and services. (349)

Influence The exercise of power through a process of persuasion. (355)

Informal economy Transfers of money, goods, or services that are not reported to the government. (352)

Laissez-faire A form of capitalism under which people compete freely, with minimal government intervention in the economy. (350)

Monarchy A form of government headed by a single member of a royal family, usually a king, queen, or some other hereditary ruler. (356)

Monopoly Control of a market by a single business firm. (350)

Offshoring The transfer of work to foreign contractors. (368)

Oligarchy A form of government in which a few individuals rule. (356)

Peace The absence of war, or more broadly, a proactive effort to develop cooperative relations among nations. (363)

Pluralist model A view of society in which many competing groups within the community have access to government, so that no single group is dominant. (362)

Political system The social institution that is founded on a recognized set of procedures for implementing and achieving society's goals. (349)

Politics In Harold Lasswell's words, "who gets what, when, and how." (355)

Power The ability to exercise one's will over others. (355)

Power elite A small group of military, industrial, and government leaders who control the fate of the United States. (361)

Rational-legal authority Power made legitimate by law. (356)

Representative democracy A form of government in which certain individuals are selected to speak for the people. (357)

Socialism An economic system under which the means of production and distribution are collectively owned. (351)

Terrorism The use or threat of violence against random or symbolic targets in pursuit of political aims. (364)

Totalitarianism Virtually complete government control and surveillance over all aspects of a society's social and political life. (357)

Traditional authority Legitimate power conferred by custom and accepted practice. (355)

War Conflict between organizations that possess trained combat forces equipped with deadly weapons. (362)

Self-Quiz

Read each question carefully and then select the best answer.

1. Which two basic types of economic system distinguish contemporary industrial societies?

    a. capitalism and communism
    b. capitalism and socialism
    c. socialism and communism
    d. capitalism and dictatorship

2. According to the discussion of capitalism in the text, which of the following statements is true?

    a. The means of production are held largely in private hands.
    b. The main incentive for economic activity is the accumulation of profits
    c. The degree to which the government regulates private ownership and economic activity will vary.
    d. all of the above

3. Which sociological perspective points out that while *pure* monopolies are not a basic element of the economy of the United States, competition is much more restricted than one might expect in what is called a *free enterprise system*?

    a. the functionalist perspective
    b. the conflict perspective
    c. the interactionist perspective
    d. labeling theory

4. Which of the following is *not* an example of the informal economy?

    a. trading a haircut for a computer lesson
    b. selling illegal drugs on the street
    c. working as a computer programmer for a major corporation
    d. providing child care out of a private home, without reporting the income to the IRS

5. The systematic, widespread withdrawal of investment in basic aspects of productivity such as factories and plants is called

    a. deindustrialization.
    b. downsizing.
    c. postindustrialization.
    d. gentrification.

6. Political scientist Harold Lasswell defined *politics* as

    a. the struggle for power and authority.
    b. the allocation of valued resources.
    c. who gets what, when, and how.
    d. a cultural universal.

7. What are the three basic sources of power within any political system?

    a. force, influence, and authority
    b. force, influence, and democracy
    c. force, legitimacy, and charisma
    d. influence, charisma, and bureaucracy

8. Which of the following is *not* part of the classification system of authority developed by Max Weber?

    a. traditional authority
    b. pluralist authority
    c. legal-rational authority
    d. charismatic authority

9. According to C. Wright Mills, power rests in the hands of the

    a. people.
    b. representative democracy.
    c. aristocracy.
    d. power elite.

10. The use or threat of violence against random or symbolic targets in pursuit of political aims is referred to as

   a. politics.
   b. power.
   c. authority.
   d. terrorism.

11. The term _____ _____ refers to the social institution through which goods and services are produced, distributed, and consumed.

12. The principle of _____-_____, as expounded and endorsed by the British economist Adam Smith, was the prevailing form of capitalism immediately following the industrial revolution.

13. Under _____, the means of production and distribution in a society are collectively rather than privately owned, and the basic objective of the economic system is to meet people's needs rather than to maximize profits.

14. _____ is an economic system under which all property is communally owned and no social distinctions are made based on people's ability to produce.

15. The term _____ was introduced in 1987 to refer to reductions taken in a company's workforce as part of deindustrialization.

16. _____ is the exercise of power through a process of persuasion.

17. Joan of Arc, Gandhi, Malcolm X, Adolf Hitler, and Martin Luther King, Jr., all possessed _____ authority.

18. _____ involves virtually complete government control and surveillance over all aspects of a society's social and political life.

19. The United States is commonly classified as a _____ _____, because the elected members of Congress and state legislatures make our laws.

20. Advocates of the _____ model suggest that competing groups within the community have access to government, so that no single group is dominant.

Answers:
1 (b); 2 (d); 3 (b); 4 (c); 5 (a); 6 (c); 7 (a); 8 (b); 9 (d); 10 (d)
11 economic system; 12 laissez-faire; 13 socialism; 14 Communism; 15 downsizing; 16 influence; 17 charismatic; 18 Totalitarianism; 19 representative democracy; 20 pluralist

{ TECHNOLOGY RESOURCES }

Online Learning Center

1. Test your knowledge of the information in this chapter by visiting the student center in the Online Learning Center at **www.mhhe.com/schaefer7** and taking the multiple-choice quiz. This quiz will not only test your knowledge; it will give you immediate feedback on the questions you answered incorrectly.

2. The Youth Vote Coalition is a group of organizations whose goal is to reduce political apathy among young people. Visit their site at **www.youthvote.org** to read about their efforts.

3. The Bureau of Labor Statistics (**www.bls.gov**) compiles many informative statistics on the U.S. labor force. Explore the site to learn about the current unemployment rate, both in the United States and in your home state.

*Note: While all the URLs listed were current as of the printing of this book, these sites often change. Please check our Web site (**www.mhhe.com/schaefer7**) for updates, hyperlinks, and exercises related to these sites.*

Reel Society Video Clips

Reel Society video clips, which appear on this book's Web site, can be used to spark discussion about the following topics from this chapter:
   • Power and Authority
   • Economic Systems
   • The Changing Economy

Population, Communities, and Health

15

inside

Demography: The Study of Population
World Population Patterns
Fertility Patterns in the United States
How Have Communities Changed?
Urbanization
Types of Communities
Sociological Perspectives on Health and Illness
Social Epidemiology and Health
Social Policy and Health: The AIDS Crisis

Boxes

Sociology in the Global Community: Population Policy in China

Research in Action: Store Wars

Social Inequality: To Inform or Not to Inform? How Race and Ethnicity Affect Views of Patient Autonomy

Taking Sociology to Work: Jess Purmort, Research Assistant, New York Academy of Medicine

少生优生幸福一生

This billboard, photographed in China, promotes the government's policy of allowing only one child per family. For several decades, the People's Republic of China has been struggling with a population explosion that threatens to outstrip the nation's ability to provide for all its citizens.

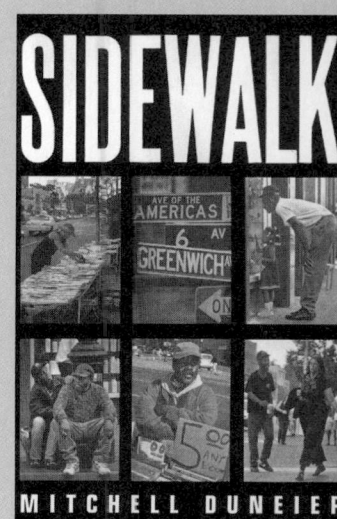

SIDEWALK

MITCHELL DUNEIER

*I*t is not hard to understand why Hakim Hasan came to see himself as a public character. Early one July morning, a deliveryman pulled his truck up to the curb behind Hakim's vending table on Greenwich Avenue off the corner of Sixth Avenue [in lower Manhattan] and carried a large box of flowers over to him.

"Can you hold these until the flower shop opens up?" the deliveryman asked.

"No problem," responded Hakim as he continued to set up the books on his table. "Put them right under there."

When the store opened for business, he brought them inside and gave them to the owner.

"Why did that man trust you with the flowers?" I later asked.

"People like me are the eyes and ears of this street," he explained, echoing [sociologist] Jane Jacobs again. "Yes, I could take those flowers and sell them for a few hundred dollars. But that deliveryman sees me here every day. I'm as dependable as any store-owner." . . .

Another day, I was present at the table when a traffic officer walked by to give out parking tickets.

"Are any of these your cars?" she asked Hakim.

"Yes, that one, and that one," said Hakim, pointing.

"What is that all about?" I asked.

"The day I met her, we got into an argument," he explained. "She was getting ready to give the guy across the street a ticket. I say, 'You can't do this!' She said, 'Why not?' I say, ''Cause I'm getting ready to put a quarter in.' She said, 'You can't do that.' I guess that, because of the way I made my argument, she didn't give out the ticket, and from that point onward we became friends. And when she comes on the block, she asks me, for every car on the block that has a violation sign, 'Is that your car?' Meaning, 'Is it someone you know?' And depending on whether I say yes or no, that's it—they get a ticket." . . .

"Are these things part of your job description as a vendor?" I asked him once.

"Let me put it to you this way, Mitch," he replied. "I kind of see what I loosely call my work on the sidewalk as going far, far beyond just trying to make a living selling books. That sometimes even seems secondary. Over time, when people see you on the sidewalk, there is a kind of trust that starts. They've seen you so long that they walk up to you. There have been occasions when I've had to have directions translated out of Spanish into French to get somebody to go someplace!"

It is not only directions and assistance that I have seen Hakim give out. He also tells people a great deal about books—so much so that he once told me he was thinking of charging tuition to the people who stand in his space on the sidewalk.

(Duneier 1999:17–18) Additional information about this excerpt can be found on the Online Learning Center at www.mhhe.com/schaefer7. ●

> " *Early one July morning, a deliveryman pulled his truck up to the curb behind Hakim's vending table on Greenwich Avenue off the corner of Sixth Avenue [in lower Manhattan] and carried a large box of flowers over to him.* "

This excerpt from *Sidewalk,* by the sociologist Mitchell Duneier, describes the social position of Hakim Hasan, a sidewalk book vendor in New York City's Greenwich Village. The author, who for two years lived just around the corner from Hasan's table, was so fascinated by street life in the Village that he decided to do observation research on it. As Duneier explains in his book, street vendors like Hasan are just as much a part of the neighborhood as the shopkeepers who occupy the storefronts behind them—even if they don't have a mailing address. In fact, their presence on the street, day in and day out, contributes to the neighborhood's safety and stability (Duneier 1999).

This chapter explores communities of all sorts, from rural towns to inner-city neighborhoods and the suburbs that surround them. In sociological terms, a **community** may be defined as a spatial or political unit of social organization that gives people a sense of belonging. That sense of belonging can be based either on shared residence in a particular city or neighborhood, such as Greenwich Village, or on a common identity, such as that of street vendors, homeless people, or gays and lesbians. Whatever the members have in common, communities give people the feeling that they are part of something larger than themselves (Dotson 1991; see also Hillery 1955).

Communities are deeply affected by two other topics of this chapter: health and population patterns. Population patterns determine which communities will grow and prosper and which will wither and die. They can also promote or undermine the health of those who live in communities. How is the world's population changing, and what effects will those changes have on our communities? Throughout the world, why have large communities grown at the expense of small villages? How do a population's health and well-being vary from one community to another, and from one part of the world to another?

In this chapter we will try to answer these questions by taking a sociological overview of the world's population and its effects on our communities and health. We will begin with Thomas Robert Malthus's analysis of population trends and Karl Marx's critical response. Brief overviews of population and fertility patterns follow, with particular emphasis on the current problem of overpopulation. Next, we will trace the development of communities from preindustrial cities to the birth of the modern megalopolis. We'll consider two different views of urbanization, one stressing its functions and the other its dysfunctions. And we'll compare three very different types of community: the city, the suburbs, and rural areas. Finally, we'll see how functionalists, conflict theorists, interactionists, and labeling theorists study health issues. We'll discover that the distribution of disease in a population varies with social class, race and ethnicity, gender, and age. In the Social Policy section that closes the chapter, we'll explore the most pressing health problem in the world today, the AIDS crisis. ●

Sociologist Mitchell Duneier *(right)* did participant observation as he worked the tables of sidewalk vendors in Greenwich Village.

Demography: The Study of Population

The study of population issues engages the attention of both natural and social scientists. The biologist explores the nature of reproduction and casts light on factors that affect **fertility,** the level of reproduction in a society. The medical pathologist examines and analyzes trends in the causes of death. Geographers, historians, and psychologists also have distinctive contributions to make to our understanding of population. Sociologists, more than these other researchers, focus on the *social* factors that influence population rates and trends.

In their study of population issues, sociologists are aware that the norms, values, and social patterns of a society profoundly affect various elements of population, such as fertility, *mortality* (the death rate), and migration. Fertility is influenced by people's age of entry into sexual unions and by their use of contraception—both of which, in turn, reflect the social and religious values that guide a particular culture. Mortality is shaped by a nation's level of nutrition, acceptance of immunization, and

provisions for sanitation, as well as its general commitment to health care and health education. Migration from one country to another can depend on marital and kinship ties, the relative degree of racial and religious tolerance in various societies, and people's evaluation of their employment opportunities.

Demography is the scientific study of population. It draws on several components of population, including size, composition, and territorial distribution, to understand the social consequences of population change. Demographers study geographical variations and historical trends in their effort to develop population forecasts. They also analyze the structure of a population—the age, gender, race, and ethnicity of its members. A key figure in this analysis was Thomas Malthus.

Malthus's Thesis and Marx's Response

The Reverend Thomas Robert Malthus (1766–1834), who was educated at Cambridge University, spent his life teaching history and political economy. He strongly criticized two major institutions of his time—the church and slavery—yet his most significant legacy to contemporary scholars is his still-controversial *Essays on the Principle of Population,* published in 1798.

Essentially, Malthus held that the world's population was growing more rapidly than the available food supply. He argued that food supply increases in arithmetic progression (1, 2, 3, 4, and so on), whereas population expands by geometric progression (1, 2, 4, 8, and so on). According to his analysis, the gap between food supply and population will continue to grow over time. Even though the food supply will increase, it will not increase nearly enough to meet the needs of an expanding world population.

Malthus advocated population control to close the gap between rising population and the food supply, yet he explicitly denounced artificial means of birth control because they were not sanctioned by religion. For Malthus, one appropriate way to control population was to postpone marriage. He argued that couples must take responsibility for the number of children they choose to bear; without such restraint, the world would face widespread hunger, poverty, and misery (Malthus et al. [1824] 1960; Petersen 1979).

Karl Marx strongly criticized Malthus's views on population. Marx pointed to the nature of economic relations in Europe's industrial societies as the central problem. He could not accept the Malthusian notion that rising world population, rather than capitalism, was the cause of social ills. In Marx's opinion, there was no special relationship between world population and the supply of resources (including food). If society were well ordered, increases in population would lead to greater wealth, not to hunger and misery.

Of course, Marx did not believe that capitalism operated under these ideal conditions. He maintained that capitalism devoted resources to the financing of buildings and tools rather than to the equitable distribution of food, housing, and other necessities of life. Marx's work is important to the study of population because he linked overpopulation to the unequal distribution of resources—a topic that will be taken up later in this chapter. His

concern with the writings of Malthus also testifies to the importance of population in political and economic affairs.

The insights of Malthus and Marx regarding population issues have come together in what is termed the *neo-Malthusian view,* best exemplified by the work of Paul Ehrlich (1968; Ehrlich and Ehrlich 1990), author of *The Population Bomb.* Neo-Malthusians agree with Malthus that population growth is outstretching the world's natural resources. However, in contrast to the British theorist, they insist that birth control measures are needed to regulate population increases. Showing a Marxist bent, neo-Malthusians condemn the developed nations, which despite their low birthrates consume a disproportionately large share of world resources. While rather pessimistic about the future, these theorists stress that birth control and sensible use of resources are essential responses to rising world population (J. Tierney 1990; Weeks 2002).

Studying Population Today

The relative balance of births and deaths is no less important today than it was during the lifetime of Malthus and Marx. The suffering that Malthus spoke of is certainly a reality for many people of the world. Malnutrition remains the largest contributing factor to illness and death among children in developing countries. Almost 18 percent of these children will die before age five—a rate over 11 times higher than in developed nations. Warfare and large-scale migration intensify problems of population and food supply. For example, recent strife in Afghanistan, the Congo, and Iraq has caused maldistribution of food supplies, leading to regional health concerns. Combating world hunger may require reducing human births, dramatically increasing the world's food supply, or perhaps both. The study of population-related issues, then, seems to be essential.

In the United States and most other countries, the census is the primary mechanism for collecting population information. A *census* is an enumeration, or counting, of a population. The Constitution of the United States requires that a census be held every 10 years to determine congressional representation. This periodic investigation is supplemented by *vital statistics,* or records of births, deaths, marriages, and divorces that are gathered through a registration system maintained by governmental units. In addition, other government surveys provide up-to-date information on commercial developments, educational trends, industrial expansion, agricultural practices, and the status of groups such as children, the elderly, racial minorities, and single parents.

In administering a nationwide census and conducting other types of research, demographers employ many of the skills and techniques described in Chapter 2, including questionnaires, interviews, and sampling. The precision of population projections depends on the accuracy of a series of estimates demographers must make. First, they must determine past population trends and establish a current base population. Next, birthrates and death rates must be determined, along with estimates of future fluctuations. In projecting a nation's population trends for the future, demographers must consider migration as well, since a significant number of individuals may enter and leave a country.

Elements of Demography

Demographers communicate population facts with a language derived from the basic elements of human life—birth and death. The **birthrate** (or more specifically, the *crude birthrate*) is the number of live births per 1,000 population in a given year. In 2002, for example, there were 14 live births per 1,000 people in the United States. The birthrate provides information on the reproductive patterns of a society.

One way demographers can project future growth in a society is to make use of the **total fertility rate (TFR)**. The TFR is the average number of children born alive to any woman, assuming that she conforms to current fertility rates. The TFR reported for the United States in 2005 was 2.0 live births per woman, compared to nearly 6 births per woman in a developing country such as Niger.

Mortality, like fertility, is measured in several different ways. The **death rate** (also known as the *crude death rate*) is the number of deaths per 1,000 population in a given year. In 2005, the United States had a death rate of 8.0 per 1,000 population. The **infant mortality rate** is the number of deaths of infants under one year old per 1,000 live births in a given year. This particular measure serves as an important indicator of a society's level of health care; it reflects prenatal nutrition, delivery procedures, and infant screening measures. The infant mortality rate also functions as a useful indicator of future population growth, since those infants who survive to adulthood will contribute to further population increases.

A general measure of health used by demographers is **life expectancy,** the median number of years a person can be expected to live under current mortality conditions. Usually the figure is reported as life expectancy *at birth*. At present, Japan reports a life expectancy at birth of 82 years—slightly higher than the United States' figure of 78 years. In contrast, life expectancy at birth is less than 45 in several developing nations, including Zambia (see Figure 15-1, page 378).

The **growth rate** of a society is the difference between births and deaths, plus the difference between *immigrants* (those who enter a country to establish permanent residence) and *emigrants* (those who leave a country permanently) per 1,000 population. For the world as a whole, the growth rate is simply the difference between births and deaths per 1,000 population, since worldwide immigration and emigration must of necessity be equal. In 2005, the United States had a growth rate of 0.6 percent, compared to an estimated 1.2 percent for the entire world (Haub 2005).

World Population Patterns

One important aspect of demographic work involves a study of the history of population. But how is that possible? After all, official national censuses were relatively rare before 1850. Researchers interested in early population must turn to archeological remains, burial sites, baptismal and tax records, and oral history sources. In the next section we will see what such detective work has told us about changes in population over time.

Demographic Transition

On October 13, 1999, in a maternity clinic in Sarajevo, Bosnia-Herzegovina, Helac Fatina gave birth to a son who has been designated the 6 billionth person on this planet. Until modern times, relatively few humans lived in the world. One estimate places the global population of a million years ago at only 125,000 people. As Table 15-1 (page 378) indicates, in the last 200 years the world's population has exploded (World Health Organization 2000:3).

The phenomenal growth of population in recent times can be accounted for by changing patterns in births and deaths. Beginning in the late 1700s—and continuing until the mid-1900s—

Throughout the world, population patterns vary widely. As this scene in Warsaw, the capital of Poland, suggests, Eastern Europe has been losing population as the birthrate falls and young people emigrate to other countries. In Africa, by contrast, the population is growing. Over the next four decades, the country of Somalia is expected to double in population.

Life Expectancy in Selected Countries, 2005

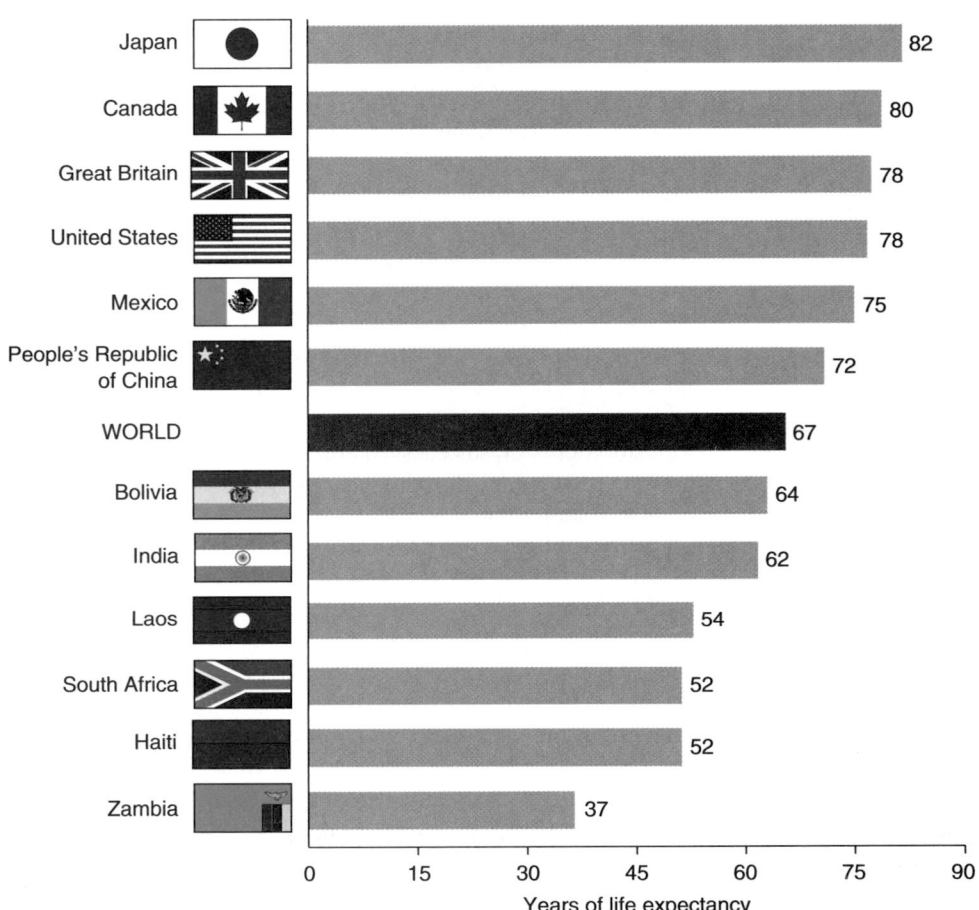

Source: Haub 2005.

1. Pretransition stage: high birthrates and death rates with little population growth.

2. Transition stage: declining death rates—primarily the result of reductions in infant deaths—along with high to medium fertility, resulting in significant population growth.

3. Posttransition stage: low birthrates and death rates with little population growth.

The demographic transition should be regarded not as a "law of population growth," but rather as a generalization of the population history of industrial nations. This concept helps us understand world population problems better. About two-thirds of the world's nations have yet to pass fully through the second stage of the demographic transition. Even if such nations make dramatic advances in fertility control, their populations will nevertheless increase greatly because of the large base of people already at prime childbearing age.

The pattern of demographic transition varies from nation to nation. One particularly useful distinction is the contrast between the rapid transition now occurring in developing nations—which include about two-thirds of the world's

death rates in northern and western Europe gradually decreased. People were beginning to live longer because of advances in food production, sanitation, nutrition, and public health care. But while death rates fell, birthrates remained high; as a result, this period of European history brought unprecedented population growth. By the late 1800s, however, the birthrates of many European countries had begun to decline, and the rate of population growth had also decreased.

The changes in birthrates and death rates that occurred in 19th century Europe serve as an example of *demographic transition*. Demographers use the term **demographic transition** to describe changes in birthrates and death rates that occur during a nation's development, resulting in new patterns of vital statistics. In many nations today, we are seeing a demographic transition from high birthrates and death rates to low birthrates and death rates. As Figure 15-2 (opposite) shows, this process typically takes place in three stages:

Table 15-1 Estimated Time for Each Successive Increase of 1 Billion People in World Population

Population Level	Time Taken to Reach New Population Level	Year of Attainment
First billion	Human history before 1800	1804
Second billion	123 years	1927
Third billion	32 years	1959
Fourth billion	15 years	1974
Fifth billion	13 years	1987
Sixth billion	12 years	1999
Seventh billion	13 years	2012
Eighth billion	15 years	2027
Ninth billion	18 years	2045

Source: Bureau of the Census 2005f.

population—and that which occurred over the course of almost a century in more industrialized countries. In developing nations, the demographic transition has involved a rapid decline in death rates without adjustments in birthrates.

Specifically, in the post–World War II period, the death rates of developing nations began a sharp decline. This revolution in "death control" was triggered by antibiotics, immunization, insecticides (such as DDT, used to strike at malaria-bearing mosquitoes), and largely successful campaigns against such fatal diseases as smallpox. Substantial medical and public health technology was imported almost overnight from more developed nations. As a result, the drop in death rates that had taken a century in Europe was telescoped into two decades in many developing countries.

Birthrates had little time to adjust. Cultural beliefs about the proper size of families could not possibly change as quickly as the falling death rates. For centuries, couples had given birth to as many as eight or more children, knowing that perhaps only two or three would survive to adulthood. Families were more willing to accept technological advances that prolonged life than to abandon fertility patterns that reflected time-honored tradition and religious training. The result was an astronomical "population explosion" that was well under way by the middle 1900s. By the middle 1970s, however, demographers had observed a slight decline in the growth rate of many developing nations, as family planning efforts began to take hold (Kent and Haub 2005).

The Population Explosion

Apart from war, rapid population growth has been perhaps the dominant international social problem of the past 40 years. Often this issue is referred to in emotional terms as the "population bomb" or the "population explosion." Such striking language is not surprising, given the staggering increases in world population recorded during the 20th century (refer to Table 15-1). The population of our planet rose from 1 billion around the year 1800 to 6.4 billion by 2005.

Beginning in the 1960s, governments in certain developing nations sponsored or supported campaigns to encourage family planning. In good part as the result of government-sponsored birth control campaigns, Thailand's total fertility rate fell from 6.1 births per woman in 1970 to only 1.7 in 2005. In China, the government's strict one-child policy actually produced a negative growth rate in some urban areas (see Box 15-1, page 380). Yet even if family planning efforts are successful in reducing fertility rates, the momentum toward growing world population is well established. Developing nations face the prospect of continued population growth, since a substantial proportion of their population is approaching the childbearing years (see the top half of Figure 15-3, page 381).

A *population pyramid* is a special type of bar chart that shows the distribution of a population by gender and age; it is generally used to illustrate the population structure of a society. As Figure 15-3 shows, a substantial portion of the population of Afghanistan consists of children under age 15, whose childbearing years are still to come. Thus, the built-in momentum for population growth is much greater in Afghanistan (and in many other developing countries in other parts of the world) than in Western Europe or the United States.

Consider the population data for India, which in 2000 surpassed 1 billion residents. Sometime between the years 2040 and 2050, India's population will exceed China's. The substantial momentum for growth that is built into India's age structure means that the nation will face a staggering increase in population in the coming decades, even if its birthrate declines sharply (Population Reference Bureau 2004).

Population growth is not a problem in all nations. Today, a handful of countries are even adopting policies that encourage growth. One such country is Japan, where the total fertility rate has fallen sharply. Nevertheless, a global perspective underscores the serious consequences that could result from continued population growth overall.

Sadly, in the last 15 years, the spread of the once unknown disease of AIDS has begun to restrict population growth. The Social Policy section at the end of this chapter considers the AIDS health crisis and its devastating effects on African communities.

FIGURE 15–2

Demographic Transition

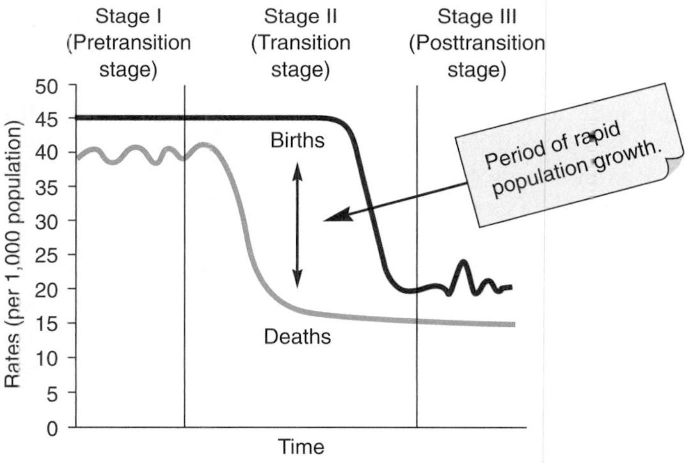

Demographers use the concept of *demographic transition* to describe changes in birthrates and death rates that occur during a nation's development. This graph shows the pattern that took place in presently developed nations. In the first stage, both birthrates and death rates were high, so that there was little population growth. In the second stage, the birthrate remained high while the death rate declined sharply, which led to rapid population growth. By the last stage, which many developing countries have yet to enter, the birthrate had declined as well, reducing population growth.

Use Your Sociological Imagination

www.mhhe.com/schaefer7

You are living in a country that is so heavily populated, basic resources such as food, water, and living space are running short. What will you do? How will you respond to the crisis if you are a government social planner? A politician?

Student Alert Population pyramids are not necessarily pyramidal in shape.
Classroom Tip See "Population Pyramid" (Class Discussion Topics).
Classroom Tip Note the relationship between demographic changes and economic problems.

sociologyIN *the Global Community*

15-1 Population Policy in China

In a residential district in Shanghai, a member of the local family planning committee knocks on the door of a childless couple. Why, she inquires, have they not started a family?

Such a question would have been unthinkable in 1979, when family planning officials, in an attempt to avoid a looming population explosion, began resorting to sterilization to enforce the government rule of one child per family. Since then, the government has quietly begun to grant exceptions to the one-child policy to adults who are only children themselves. In 2002 it extended the privilege to all families, but at a price. A new family planning law imposes "social compensation fees" to cover the cost to society of an additional child. The fee, which is substantial, is equivalent to 20 years' worth of a rural farm family's income.

Chinese families are beset, too, by the unforeseen results of their attempts to circumvent the one-child policy. In the past, in an effort to ensure that their one child would be a male capable of perpetuating the family line, many couples chose to abort female fetuses, or quietly allowed female infants to die of neglect. As a result, among children one to four years old, China's sex ratio (the ratio of males to females) is now about 119 to 100—well above the normal rate at birth of 105 to 100. This difference in birthrates translates into 1.7 million fewer female births per year than normal—and down the line, to many fewer childbearers than normal.

As a result of the rising sex ratio, Chinese officials have begun to worry about a future with too few women. The government now

> *A new family planning law imposes "social compensation fees" equivalent to 20 years' income.*

pays the parents of daughters to speak with other parents in an attempt to persuade them to raise girls. Officials have also increased the criminal penalties doctors face for performing prenatal scans and aborting pregnancies for purposes of sex selection.

Another legacy of the one-child policy is a shortage of caretakers for the elderly. Coupled with improvements in longevity, the generation-long decline in births has greatly increased the ratio of dependent elders to able-bodied children. The migration of young adults to other parts of China has further compromised the care of the elderly. To compound the crisis, barely one in four of China's elders receives any pension at all. No other country in the world faces the prospect of caring for such a large population of seniors with so little social support.

Let's Discuss

1. Does any government, no matter how overpopulated a country is, have a right to sterilize people who do not voluntarily limit the size of their families? Why or why not?

2. What do you think has been the most dramatic consequence of the one-child policy?

Sources: Glenn 2004; N. Riley 2004; Yardley 2005.

Fertility Patterns in the United States

Over the last four decades, the United States and other industrial nations have passed through two different patterns of population growth—the first marked by high fertility and rapid growth (stage II in the theory of demographic transition), the second marked by declining fertility and little growth (stage III). Sociologists are keenly aware of the social impact of these fertility patterns.

The Baby Boom

The most recent period of high fertility in the United States has often been referred to as the *baby boom*. During World War II, large numbers of military personnel were separated from their spouses. When they returned, the annual number of births began to rise dramatically. Still, the baby boom was not a return to the large families common in the 1800s. In fact, there was only a slight increase in the proportion of couples having three or more children. Instead, the boom resulted from a striking decrease in the number of childless marriages and one-child families. Although a peak was reached in 1957, the nation maintained a relatively high birthrate of over 20 live births per 1,000 population until 1964. By 2004 the birthrate had fallen to 14 live births per 1,000 population (Bureau of the Census 1975; Haub 2004).

It would be a mistake to attribute the baby boom solely to the return home of large numbers of soldiers. High wages and general prosperity during the postwar period encouraged many married couples to have children and purchase homes. In addition, several sociologists—as well as feminist author Betty Friedan (1963)—have noted the strong societal pressure on women during the 1950s to marry and become mothers and homemakers (Bouvier 1980).

Stable Population Growth

Although the total fertility rate of the United States has remained low over the last two decades, the nation continues to grow in size because of two factors: the momentum built into our age structure by the postwar population boom and continued high rates of immigration. Because of the upsurge of births

FIGURE 15–3

Population Structure of Afghanistan and the United States, 2008

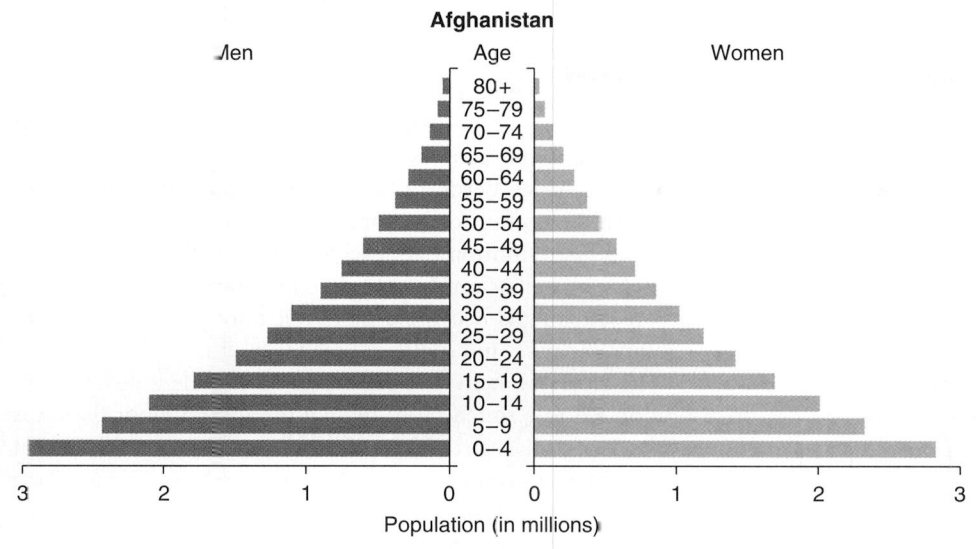

Afghanistan

Men   Age   Women

80+
75–79
70–74
65–69
60–64
55–59
50–54
45–49
40–44
35–39
30–34
25–29
20–24
15–19
10–14
5–9
0–4

Population (in millions)

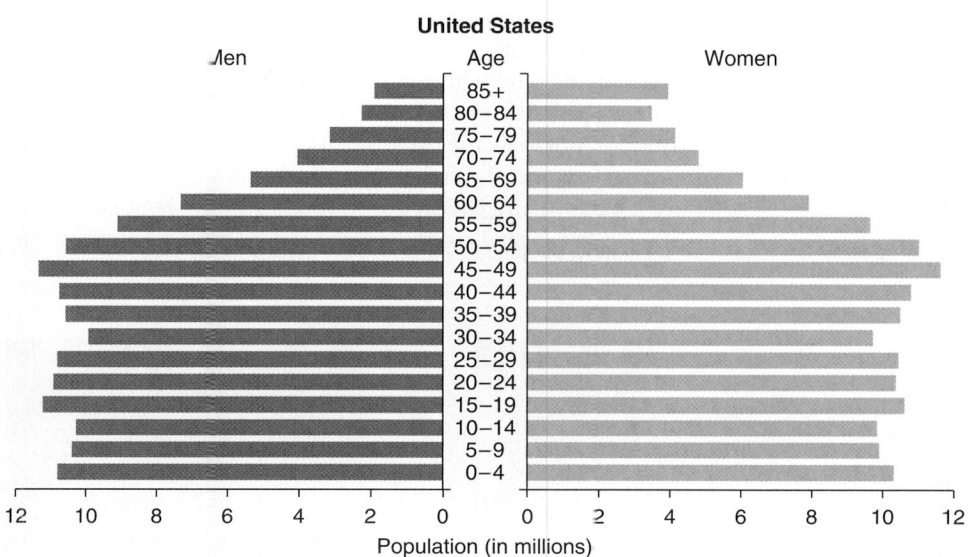

United States

Men   Age   Women

85+
80–84
75–79
70–74
65–69
60–64
55–59
50–54
45–49
40–44
35–39
30–34
25–29
20–24
15–19
10–14
5–9
0–4

Population (in millions)

Source: Projections developed by the Census in Bureau of the Census 2005i.

beginning in the 1950s, there are now many more people in their childbearing years than in older age groups (in which most deaths occur). This growth of the child-bearing population represents a "demographic echo" of the baby boom generation. Consequently, the number of people born each year in the United States continues to exceed the number who die. In addition, the nation allows a large number of immigrants to enter each year; immigrants currently account for between one-fourth and one-third of annual growth.

Despite these trends, some analysts in the 1980s and early 1990s projected relatively low fertility levels and moderate net migration over the coming decades. As a result, it seemed possible that the United States might reach **zero population growth**

(ZPG). ZPG is the state of a population in which the number of births plus immigrants equals the number of deaths plus emigrants. In the recent past, although some nations have achieved ZPG, it has been relatively short-lived. Yet today 78 countries, including all 42 in Europe, are showing a *decline* in population (Haub 2004; Longman 2004).

What would a society with stable population growth be like? In demographic terms, it would be quite different from the United States of the 1990s. There would be relatively equal numbers of people in each age group, and the median age of the population might perhaps be as high as 38 (compared to 35 in 2000). As a result, the population pyramid of the United States (as shown in Figure 15-3) would look more like a rectangle (Bureau of the Census 2004a:12–13).

There would also be a much larger proportion of older people, especially age 75 and over. These citizens would place a greater demand on the nation's social service programs and health care institutions. On a more positive note, the economy would be less volatile under ZPG, since the number of entrants into the paid labor force would remain stable. ZPG would also lead to changes in family life. With fertility rates declining, women would devote fewer years to child rearing and to the social roles of motherhood; the proportion of married women entering the labor force would continue to rise (Spengler 1978; Weeks 2002).

How Have Communities Changed?

As we noted in the chapter opening, a *community* is a spatial or political unit of social organization that gives people a sense of belonging. The nature of community has changed greatly over the course of history—from early hunting-and-gathering societies to highly modernized postindustrial cities.

For most of human history, people used basic tools and knowledge to survive. They satisfied their need for an adequate food supply through hunting, foraging for fruits or vegetables, fishing, and herding. In comparison with later industrial societies, then, early civilizations were much more dependent on the {p.116} physical environment and much less able to alter that environment to their advantage. Even when they discovered how to cultivate food rather than forage for it, their use of tools and

thus the amount of food they could produce were limited. Gradually, however, farming communities began to accumulate a surplus of food, which allowed some people to turn to the production of other goods and services. This economic breakthrough laid the foundation for social stratification and the eventual rise of preindustrial cities.

Preindustrial Cities

It is estimated that beginning about 10,000 B.C., permanent settlements free from dependence on crop cultivation emerged. By today's standards, these early communities would barely qualify as cities. The ***preindustrial city,*** as it is termed, generally had only a few thousand people living within its borders, and was characterized by a relatively closed class system and limited mobility. In these early cities, status was usually based on ascribed characteristics such as family background, and education was limited to members of the elite. All the residents relied on perhaps 100,000 farmers and their own part-time farming to provide the needed agricultural surplus. The Mesopotamian city of Ur had a population of about 10,000 and was limited to roughly 220 acres of land, including the canals, the temple, and the harbor.

Why were these early cities so small and relatively few in number? Several key factors restricted urbanization:

- **Reliance on animal power (both humans and beasts of burden) as a source of energy for economic production.** This factor limited the ability of humans to make use of and alter the physical environment.

- **Modest levels of surplus produced by the agricultural sector.** Between 50 and 90 farmers may have been required to support one city resident (K. Davis [1949] 1995).

- **Problems in transportation and the storage of food and other goods.** Even an excellent crop could easily be lost as a result of such difficulties.

- **Hardships of migration to the city.** For many peasants, migration was both physically and economically impossible. A few weeks of travel was out of the question without more sophisticated food storage techniques.

- **Dangers of city life.** Concentrating a society's population in a small area left it open to attack from outsiders, as well as more susceptible to extreme damage from plagues and fires.

A sophisticated social organization was also an essential precondition for urban existence. Specialized social roles brought people together in new ways through the exchange of goods and services. A well-developed social organization ensured that those relationships were clearly defined and generally acceptable to all parties.

Industrial and Postindustrial Cities

Imagine how harnessing the energy of air, water, and other natural resources could change a society. Advances in agricultural technology led to dramatic changes in community life, but {p.117} so did the process of industrialization. The *industrial revolution,* which began in the middle of the 18th century, focused on the application of nonanimal sources of power to labor tasks. Industrialization had a wide range of effects on people's lifestyles, as well as on the structure of communities. Emerging urban settlements became centers not only of industry but of banking, finance, and industrial management.

The factory system that developed during the industrial revolution led to a much more refined division of labor than was evident in preindustrial cities. The many new occupations that were created produced a complex set of relationships among workers. Thus, the ***industrial city*** was not merely more populous than its predecessors; it was based on very different principles of social organization. Table 15-2 contrasts preindustrial and industrial cities.

In comparison with preindustrial cities, industrial cities had a more open class system and more social mobility. After initiatives in industrial cities by women's rights groups, labor unions, and other political activists, formal education gradually became available to many children from poor and working-class families. While ascribed characteristics such as gender, race, and eth-

Over the centuries, communities of all sizes have undergone significant social change. Like the Canadian city of Toronto, many have become increasingly diverse in race and ethnicity.

nicity remained important, a talented or skilled individual had greater opportunity to better his or her social position. In these and other respects, the industrial city was genuinely a different world from the preindustrial urban community.

In the latter part of the 20th century, a new type of urban community emerged. The *postindustrial city* is a city in which {p.118} global finance and the electronic flow of information dominate the economy. Production is decentralized and often takes place outside of urban centers, but control is centralized in multinational corporations whose influence transcends urban and even national boundaries. Social change is a constant feature of the postindustrial city. Economic restructuring and spatial change seem to occur each decade, if not more frequently. In the postindustrial world, cities are forced into increasing competition for economic opportunities, which deepens the plight of the urban poor (E. Phillips 1996; D. A. Smith and Timberlake 1993).

Sociologist Louis Wirth (1928, 1938) argued that a relatively large and permanent settlement leads to distinctive patterns of behavior, which he called *urbanism.* He identified three critical factors that contribute to urbanism: the size of the population, population density, and the heterogeneity (variety) of the population. A frequent result of urbanism, according to Wirth, is that we become insensitive to events around us and restrict our attention to the primary groups to which we are emotionally attached.

Table 15-2 summarizes the differences among preindustrial, industrial, and postindustrial cities.

Use Your Sociological Imagination www.mhhe.com /schaefer7

What would the ideal city of the future look like? Describe its architecture, public transportation, neighborhoods, schools, and workplaces. What kinds of people would live and work there?

Urbanization

Urbanization has become a central aspect of life in the United States, north, south, east, and west. Only four states (Maine, Mississippi, Vermont, and West Virginia) are truly rural—that is, more than half their population lives in towns of fewer than 2,500 residents (Bureau of the Census 2004a:3–4, 28).

Urbanization can be seen throughout the rest of the world, too. In 1900, only 10 percent of the world's people lived in urban areas, but by 2000, around 50 percent of them did. By the year 2025, the number of city dwellers could reach 5 billion. During the 19th and early 20th centuries, rapid urbanization occurred primarily in Europe and North America. But since World War II, the population of cities in developing countries has exploded: see Figure 15-4 on page 384 (Koolhaas et al. 2001:3).

Some metropolitan areas have spread so far that they have connected with other urban centers. Such a densely populated area, containing two or more cities and their suburbs, has become known as a *megalopolis.* An example is the 500-mile corridor stretching from Boston south to Washington, D.C., which includes New York City, Philadelphia, and Baltimore and

summingUP

Table 15-2 Comparing Types of Cities

Preindustrial Cities (through 18th century)	Industrial Cities (18th through mid-20th century)	Postindustrial Cities (beginning late 20th century)
Closed class system—pervasive influence of social class at birth	Open class system—mobility based on achieved characteristics	Wealth based on ability to obtain and use information
Economic realm controlled by guilds and a few families	Relatively open competition	Corporate power dominates
Beginnings of division of labor in the creation of goods	Elaborate specialization in manufacturing of goods	Sense of place fades, transnational networks emerge
Pervasive influence of religion on social norms	Influence of religion limited as society becomes more secularized	Religion becomes more fragmented; greater openness to new religious faiths
Little standardization of prices, weights, and measures	Standardization enforced by custom and law	Conflicting views of prevailing standards
Population largely illiterate, communication by word of mouth	Emergence of communication through posters, bulletins, and newspapers	Emergence of extended electronic networks
Schools limited to elites and designed to perpetuate their privileged status	Formal schooling open to the masses and viewed as a means of advancing the social order	Professional, scientific, and technical personnel become increasingly important

Sources: Based on E. Phillips 1996:132–135; Sjoberg 1960:323–328.

Student Alert May need to review the concept of postindustrial society introduced in Chapter 5
Key Person Louis Wirth
Classroom Tip See "Systemic Model" (Additional Lecture Ideas).
Classroom Tip See "Community Theory and Simulation" (Class Discussion Topics) and "Land-Use Map" (Class Discussion Topics).

Global View By the year 2025, the number of city dwellers worldwide could reach 5 billion.

Global Urbanization 2015 (projected)

MAPPING LIFE

WORLDWIDE www.mhhe.com/schaefer7

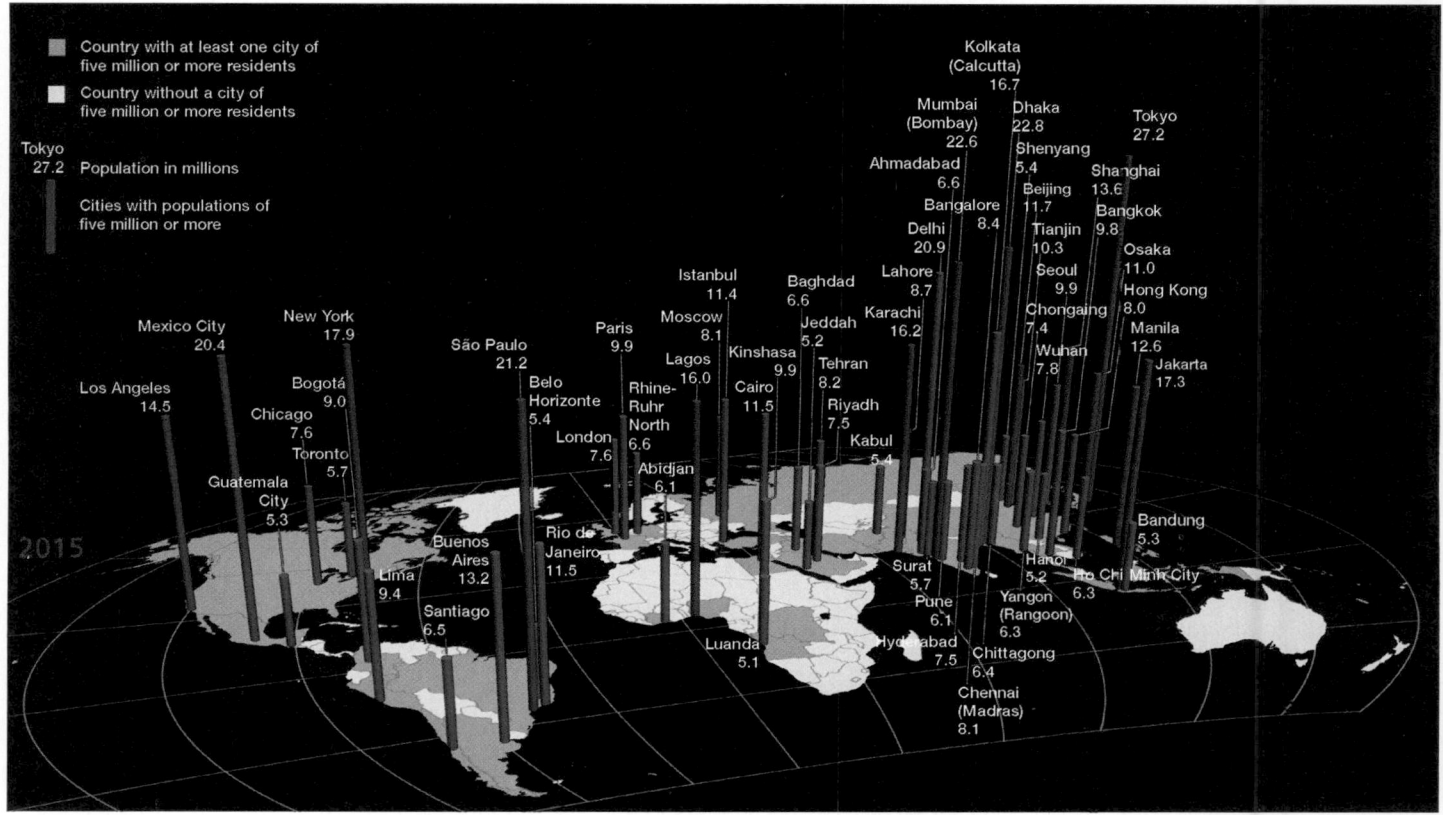

Source: National Geographic 2005:104–105.

accounts for one-sixth of the total population of the United States. Even when the megalopolis is divided into autonomous political jurisdictions, it can be viewed as a single economic entity. The megalopolis is also evident in Great Britain, Germany, Italy, Egypt, India, Japan, and China.

Functionalist View: Urban Ecology

Human ecology is an area of study that is concerned with the interrelationships between people and their environment. Human ecologists have long been interested in how the physical environment shapes people's lives (for example, how rivers can serve as a barrier to residential expansion) and in how people influence the surrounding environment (for example, how air-conditioning has accelerated the growth of major metropolitan areas in the Southwest). *Urban ecology* focuses on such relationships as they emerge in urban areas. Although the urban ecological approach focuses on social change in cities, it is nevertheless functionalist in orientation because it emphasizes how different elements in urban areas contribute to social stability.

Classroom Tip See "Human Ecology: Housing in Japan" (Additional Lecture Ideas).
Theory Urban ecology is functionalist in orientation.

Early urban ecologists such as Robert Park (1916, 1936) and Ernest Burgess (1925) concentrated on city life but drew on the approaches used by ecologists who study plant and animal communities. With few exceptions, urban ecologists trace their work back to the *concentric-zone theory* devised in the 1920s by Burgess (see Figure 15-5a). Using Chicago as an example, Burgess proposed a theory for describing land use in industrial cities. At the center, or nucleus, of such a city is the central business district. Large department stores, hotels, theaters, and financial institutions occupy this highly valued land. Surrounding this urban center are zones devoted to other types of land use, which illustrate the growth of the urban area over time.

Note that the creation of zones is a *social* process, not the result of nature alone. Families and business firms compete for the most valuable land; those who possess the most wealth and power are generally the winners. The concentric-zone theory proposed by Burgess represented a dynamic model of urban growth. As urban growth proceeded, each zone would move even farther from the central business district.

Key Persons Robert Park, Ernest Burgess

Because of its functionalist orientation and its emphasis on stability, the concentric-zone theory tended to understate or ignore certain tensions that were apparent in metropolitan areas. For example, the growing use by the affluent of land in a city's peripheral areas was uncritically approved, while the arrival of African Americans in White neighborhoods in the 1930s was described by some sociologists in terms such as *invasion* and *succession*. Moreover, the urban ecological perspective gave little thought to gender inequities, such as the establishment of men's softball and golf leagues in city parks, without any programs for women's sports. Consequently, the urban ecological approach has been criticized for its failure to address issues of gender, race, and class.

By the middle of the 20th century, urban populations had spilled beyond traditional city limits. No longer could urban ecologists focus exclusively on *growth* in the central city for large numbers of urban residents were abandoning the cities to live in suburban areas. As a response to the emergence of more than one focal point in some metropolitan areas, Chauncy D. Harris and Edward Ullman (1945) presented the **multiple-nuclei theory** (see Figure 15-5b). In their view, all urban growth does not radiate outward from a central business district. Instead, a metropolitan area may have many centers of development, each of which reflects a particular urban need or activity. Thus, a city may have a financial district, a manufacturing zone, a waterfront area, an entertainment center, and so forth. Certain types of business firms and certain types of housing will naturally cluster around each distinctive nucleus (Squires 2002).

The rise of suburban shopping malls is a vivid example of the phenomenon of multiple nuclei within metropolitan areas. Initially, all major retailing in urban areas was located in the central business district. Each residential neighborhood had its own grocers, bakers, and butchers, but people traveled to the center of the city to make major purchases at department stores. However, as metropolitan areas expanded and the suburbs became more populous, increasing numbers of people began to shop nearer their homes. Today, the suburban mall is a significant retailing and social center in communities across the United States.

In a refinement of the multiple-nuclei theory, contemporary urban ecologists have begun to study what journalist Joel Garreau (1991) has called "edge cities." These communities, which have grown up on the outskirts of major metropolitan areas, are economic and social centers with identities of their own. By any standard of measurement—height of buildings, amount of office space, presence of medical facilities, presence of leisure-time facilities, or of course, population—edge cities qualify as independent cities rather than as large suburbs.

Whether metropolitan areas include edge cities or multiple nuclei, more and more of them are characterized by spread-out development and unchecked growth. In recent years, Las Vegas has been the most dramatic example. With a new house built every 20 minutes, by 2004 the city had mushroomed from 38 to 235 square miles. The social consequences of such rapid growth are equally dramatic, from a shortage of affordable housing and

---

FIGURE 15–5

Comparison of Ecological Theories of Urban Growth

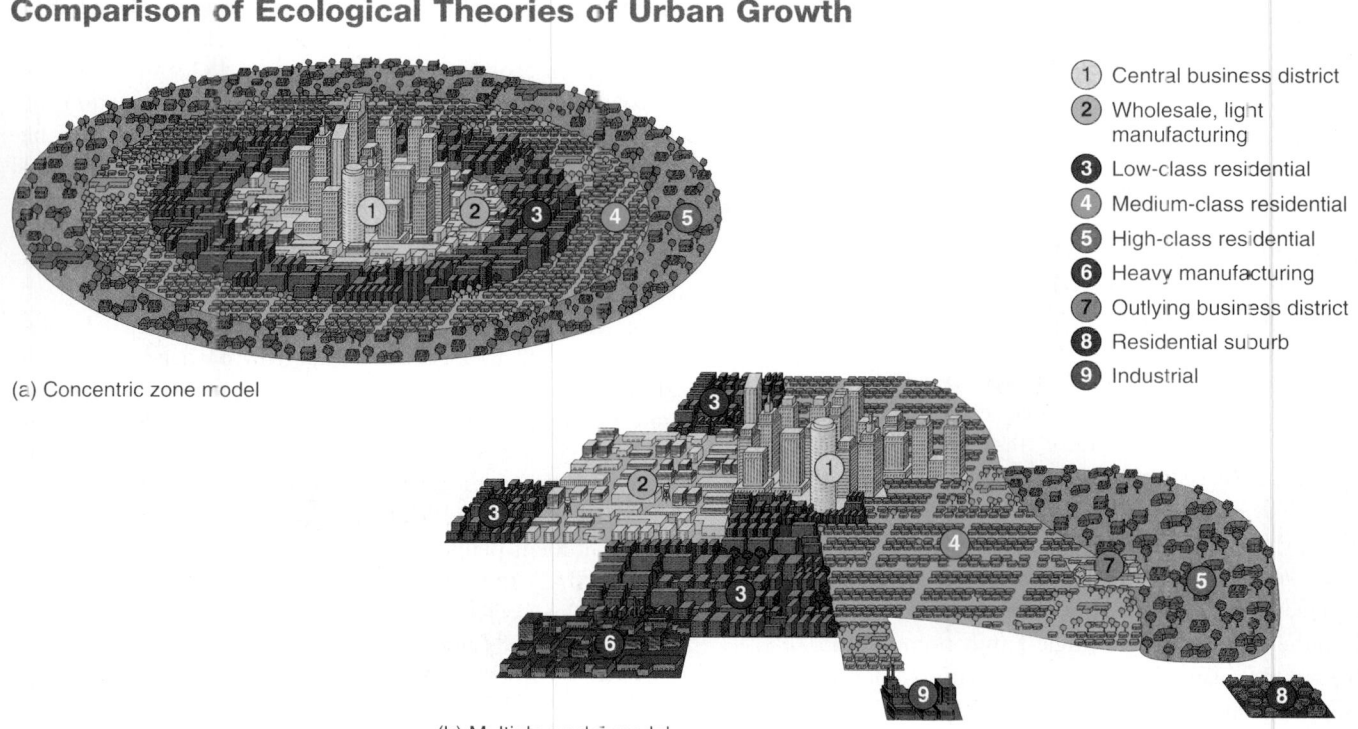

(a) Concentric zone model

(b) Multiple-nuclei model

1. Central business district
2. Wholesale, light manufacturing
3. Low-class residential
4. Medium-class residential
5. High-class residential
6. Heavy manufacturing
7. Outlying business district
8. Residential suburb
9. Industrial

Source: C. Harris and Ullmann 1945:13.

Theory Concentric zone theory has a functionalist orientation and an emphasis on stability.
Race/Ethnicity The use of terms such as *invasion* and *succession* by sociologists to describe the arrival of African Americans in White neighborhoods in the 1930s
Theory Viewed from a conflict perspective, the urban ecological approach has failed to address the issues of gender, race, and class.

Let's Discuss Are there urban centers or edge cities near your school?
Contemporary Culture Overall, 8 out of every 10 U.S. cities extended over a much greater geographical area in 2000 than they did in 1990.

Between 1990 and 2003, the population of metropolitan Las Vegas more than doubled. Cities that are undergoing such rapid growth give rise to both multiple nuclei and edge cities.

an inadequate number of food pantries to an overstretched water supply, poor health care delivery, and impossible traffic. Today's cities are very different from the preindustrial cities of a thousand years ago (D. Murphy 2004).

Conflict View: New Urban Sociology

Contemporary sociologists point out that metropolitan growth is not governed by waterways and rail lines, as a purely ecological interpretation might suggest. From a conflict perspective, communities are human creations that reflect people's needs, choices, and decisions—though some people have more influence over those decisions than others. Drawing on conflict theory, an approach that has come to be called the **new urban sociology** considers the interplay of local, national, and worldwide forces and their effect on local space, with special emphasis on the impact of global economic activity (Gottdiener and Hutchison 2006).

New urban sociologists note that proponents of the ecological approaches have typically avoided examining the social forces, largely economic in nature, that have guided urban growth. For example, central business districts may be upgraded or abandoned, depending on whether urban policymakers grant substantial tax exemptions to developers. The suburban boom in the post–World War II era was fueled by highway construction and federal housing policies that channeled investment capital into the construction of single-family homes rather than affordable rental housing in the cities. Similarly, while some observers suggest that the growth of sun-belt cities is due to a "good business climate," new urban sociologists counter that the term is actually a euphemism for hefty state and local govern-

ment subsidies and antilabor policies intended to draw manufacturers (Gottdiener and Feagin 1988; M. Smith 1988).

The new urban sociology draws generally on the conflict perspective, and more specifically on sociologist Immanuel Wallerstein's **world systems** {p.214 **analysis.** Wallerstein argues that certain industrialized nations (among them the United States, Japan, and Germany) hold a dominant position at the *core* of the global economic system. At the same time, the poor developing countries of Asia, Africa, and Latin America lie on the *periphery* of the global economy, controlled and exploited by core industrialized nations. Using world systems analysis, new urban sociologists consider urbanization from a global perspective. They view cities not as independent and autonomous entities, but as the outcome of decision-making processes directed or influenced by a society's dominant classes and by core industrialized nations. New urban sociologists note that the rapidly growing cities of the world's developing countries were shaped first by colonialism and then by a global economy controlled by core nations and multinational corporations. The outcome has not been beneficial to the poorest citizens. An unmistakable feature of many cities in developing countries is the existence of large squatter settlements just outside city limits (Gottdiener and Feagin 1988; D. A. Smith 1995).

The urban ecologists of the 1920s and 1930s were aware of the role that the larger economy played in urbanization, but their theories emphasized the impact of local rather than national or global forces. In contrast, through their broad, global emphasis on social inequality and conflict, new urban sociolo- {pp.199, 215, 367 gists concentrate on such topics as the existence of an underclass, the power of multinational corporations, deindustrialization, homelessness, and residential segregation.

For example, developers, builders, and investment bankers are not especially interested in urban growth when it means providing housing for middle- or low-income people. Their lack of interest contributes to the problem of homelessness. These urban elites counter that the nation's housing shortage and the plight of the homeless are not their fault, and insist that they do not have the capital needed to construct and support such housing. But affluent people *are* interested in growth, and they *can* somehow find capital to build new shopping centers, office towers, and ballparks. Why, then, can't they provide the capital for affordable housing, ask new urban sociologists?

Part of the answer is that developers, bankers, and other powerful real estate interests view housing in quite a different manner from tenants and most homeowners. For a tenant, an apartment is shelter, housing, a home. But for developers and in-

Theory The new urban sociology draws on the conflict perspective.

Key Person Immanuel Wallerstein
Global View Wallerstein's world systems analysis

vestors—many of them large (and sometimes multinational) corporations—an apartment is simply a housing investment. These financiers and owners are concerned primarily with maximizing profit, not with solving social problems (Feagin 1983; Gottdiener and Hutchison 2006).

As we have seen throughout this textbook in studying such varied issues as deviance, race and ethnicity, and aging, no single theoretical approach necessarily offers the only valuable perspective. As Table 15-3 shows, urban ecology and the new urban sociology offer significantly different ways of viewing urbanization, both of which enrich our understanding of this complex phenomenon.

Types of Communities

Communities vary substantially in the degree to which their members feel connected and share a common identity. Ferdinand Tönnies ([1887]1988) used the term *Gemeinschaft* to de- {p.115} scribe a close-knit community where social interaction among people is intimate and familiar. This is the kind of place where people in a coffee shop will stop talking whenever anyone enters, because they are sure to know whoever walks through the door. A shopper at the small grocery store in this town would expect to know every employee, and probably every other customer as well. In contrast, the ideal type of the *Gesellschaft* describes modern urban life, in which people have little in common with others. Social relationships often result from interactions focused on immediate tasks, such as purchasing a product. In the United States, contemporary city life generally resembles a *Gesellschaft*.

The following sections will examine different types of communities found in the United States, focusing on the distinctive characteristics and problems of central cities, suburbs, and rural communities.

Central Cities

In terms of both land and population, the United States is the fourth-largest nation in the world. Yet three-quarters of the population is concentrated in a mere 1.5 percent of the nation's land area. In 2000 some 226 million people—or 79 percent of the nation's population—lived in metropolitan areas. Even those who live outside central cities, such as residents of suburban and rural communities, find that urban centers heavily influence their lifestyles (Bureau of the Census 2003a:34).

Urban Dwellers Many urban residents are the descendants of European immigrants—Irish, Italians, Jews, Poles, and others—who came to the United States in the 19th and early 20th centuries. The cities socialized these newcomers to the norms, values, and language of their new homeland and gave them an opportunity to work their way up the economic ladder. In addition, a substantial number of low-income African Americans and Whites came to the cities from rural areas in the period following World War II.

Even today, cities in the United States are the destinations of immigrants from around the world—including Mexico, Ireland, Cuba, Vietnam, and Haiti—as well as of migrants from the U.S. commonwealth of Puerto Rico. Yet unlike those who came to this country 100 years ago, current immigrants are arriving at a time of growing urban decay. Thus they have more difficulty finding employment and decent housing.

Urban life is noteworthy for its diversity, so it would be a serious mistake to see all city residents as being alike. Sociologist Herbert J. Gans (1991) has distinguished five types of people found in cities:

1. **Cosmopolites.** These residents remain in cities to take advantage of unique cultural and intellectual benefits. Writers, artists, and scholars fall into this category.

2. **Unmarried and childless people.** Such people choose to live in cities because of the active nightlife and varied recreational opportunities.

3. **Ethnic villagers.** These urban residents prefer to live in their own tight-knit communities. Typically, immigrant groups isolate themselves in such neighborhoods to avoid resentment from well-established urban dwellers.

4. **The deprived.** Very poor people and families have little choice but to live in low-rent, often run-down urban neighborhoods.

Table 15-3 Sociological Perspectives on Urbanization

summingUP

	Urban Ecology	New Urban Sociology
Theoretical perspective	Functionalist	Conflict
Primary focus	Relationship of urban areas to their spatial setting and physical environment	Relationship of urban areas to global, national, and local forces
Key source of change	Technological innovations such as new methods of transportation	Economic competition and monopolization of power
Initiator of actions	Individuals, neighborhoods, communities	Real estate developers, banks and other financial institutions, multinational corporations
Allied disciplines	Geography, architecture	Political science, economics

Key Person Ferdinand Tönnies
Classroom Tip See "Apathy in the City?" (Additional Lecture Ideas).

Race/Ethnicity Immigration to the urban centers of the United States
Key Person Herbert J. Gans
Race/Ethnicity Racial and ethnic enclaves include Koreatown, Little Tokyo, Andersonville, Little Italy, and Little Warsaw.

5. **The trapped.** Some city residents wish to leave urban centers but cannot because of their limited economic resources and prospects. Gans includes the "downward mobiles" in this category—people who once held higher social positions, but who are forced to live in less prestigious neighborhoods owing to loss of a job, death of a wage earner, or old age.

To this list we can add a sixth type, people who live in naturally occurring retirement communities (see Box 11-4, page 279). These varied categories remind us that the city represents a choice (even a dream) for certain people and a nightmare for others.

Issues Facing Cities Within any city in the United States, people and neighborhoods vary greatly. Yet all residents of a central city—regardless of social class, racial, and ethnic differences—face certain common problems. Crime, air pollution, noise, unemployment, overcrowded schools, inadequate public transportation—these unpleasant realities and many more are an increasingly common feature of contemporary urban life.

Perhaps the single most dramatic reflection of the nation's urban ills has been the apparent death of entire neighborhoods. In some urban districts, business activity seems virtually nonexistent. Visitors can walk for blocks and find little more than deteriorated, boarded-up, abandoned, and burned-out buildings. Vacant factories mark the sites of businesses that relocated a generation ago. Such urban devastation has contributed greatly to the growing problem of homelessness.

Residential segregation has also been a persistent problem in cities across the United States. Segregation has resulted from the policies of financial institutions, the business practices of real estate agents, the actions of home sellers, and even urban planning initiatives (for example, decisions about where to locate public housing). Sociologists Douglas Massey and Nancy Denton (1993) have used the term *American apartheid* to refer to such residential patterns. In their view, we no longer perceive segregation as a problem, but rather accept it as a feature of the urban landscape. For subordinate minority groups, segregation means not only limited housing opportunities but reduced access to employment, retail outlets, and medical services.

Another critical problem for the cities has been mass transportation. Since 1950, the number of cars in the United States has multiplied twice as fast as the number of people. Growing traffic congestion in metropolitan areas has led many cities to recognize the need for safe, efficient, and inexpensive mass transit systems. However, the federal government has traditionally given much more assistance to highway programs than to public transportation. Conflict theorists note that such a bias favors the relatively affluent (automobile owners) as well as corporations such as auto manufacturers, tire makers, and oil companies. Meanwhile, low-income residents of metropolitan areas, who are much less likely to own cars than members of the middle and upper classes, face higher fares on public transit along with deteriorating service (J. W. Mason 1998; Reschovsky 2004).

C stands for "congestion." In 2003, to alleviate gridlock, officials of the city of London began to charge vehicles about $15 a day to enter designated congestion zones. At least initially, significant traffic reductions resulted, leading city planners around the world to consider adopting the idea.

Suburbs

The term *suburb* derives from the Latin *sub urbe,* meaning "under the city." Until recent times, most suburbs were just that—tiny communities totally dependent on urban centers for jobs, recreation, and even water.

Today, the term **suburb** defies simple definition. The term generally refers to any community near a large city—or as the Census Bureau would say, any territory within a metropolitan area that is not included in the central city. By that definition, more than 138 million people, or about 51 percent of the population of the United States, live in the suburbs (Kleniewski 2002).

Three social factors differentiate suburbs from cities. First, suburbs are generally less dense than cities; in some suburbs, no more than two dwellings may occupy an acre of land. Second, the suburbs consist almost exclusively of private space. For the most part, private ornamental lawns replace common park areas. Third, suburbs have more exacting building design codes than cities, and those codes have become increasingly precise in the last decade. While the suburbs may be diverse in population, their design standards give the impression of uniformity.

Distinguishing between suburbs and rural areas can also be difficult. Certain criteria generally define suburbs: Most people

work at urban (as opposed to rural) jobs, and local governments provide services such as water supply, sewage disposal, and fire protection. In rural areas, those services are less common, and a greater proportion of residents is employed in farming and related activities.

Suburban Expansion

Whatever the precise definition of a suburb, it is clear that suburbs have expanded. In fact, suburbanization was the most dramatic population trend in the United States throughout the 20th century. Suburban areas grew at first along railroad lines, then at the termini of streetcar tracks, and by the 1950s along the nation's growing system of freeways and expressways. The suburban boom has been especially evident since World War II.

Proponents of the new urban sociology contend that initially, industries moved their factories from central cities to suburbs to reduce the power of labor unions. Subsequently, many suburban communities induced businesses to relocate there by offering them subsidies and tax incentives. As sociologist William Julius Wilson (1996) has observed, federal housing policies contributed to the suburban boom by withholding mortgage capital from inner-city neighborhoods, by offering favorable mortgages to military veterans, and by assisting the rapid development of massive amounts of affordable tract housing in the suburbs. Moreover, federal highway and transportation policies provided substantial funding for expressway systems (which made commuting to the cities much easier), while undermining urban communities by building freeway networks through their heart.

All these factors contributed to the movement of the (predominantly White) middle class out of the central cities, and as we shall see, out of the suburbs as well. From the perspective of new urban sociology, suburban expansion is far from a natural ecological process; rather, it reflects the distinct priorities of powerful economic and political interests.

Suburban Diversity

In the United States, race and ethnicity remain the most important factors that distinguish cities from suburbs. Nevertheless, the common assumption that suburbia includes only prosperous Whites is far from correct. The last 20 years have witnessed the diversification of suburbs in terms of race and ethnicity. For example, by 2000, 34 percent of Blacks in the United States, 46 percent of Latinos, and 53 percent of Asians lived in the suburbs. Like the rest of the nation, members of racial and ethnic minorities are becoming suburban dwellers (El Nasser 2001; Frey 2001).

But are the suburban areas re-creating the racial segregation of the central cities? A definite pattern of clustering, if not outright segregation, is emerging. A study of suburban residential patterns in 11 metropolitan areas found that Asian Americans and Hispanics tend to reside in the same socioeconomic areas as Whites—that is, affluent Hispanics live alongside affluent Whites, poor Asians near poor Whites, and so on. However, the case for African Americans is quite distinct. Suburban Blacks live in poorer suburbs than Whites, even after taking into account differences in their income, education, and homeownership.

Again, in contrast to prevailing stereotypes, the suburbs include a significant number of low-income people from all backgrounds—White, Black, and Hispanic. Poverty is not conventionally associated with the suburbs, partly because the suburban poor tend to be scattered among more affluent people. In some instances, suburban communities intentionally hide social problems such as homelessness so they can maintain a "respectable image." Soaring housing costs have contributed to suburban poverty, which is rising at a faster rate than urban poverty (Jargowsky 2003).

Rural Communities

As we have seen, the people of the United States live mainly in urban areas. Yet according to the 2000 census, 59 million Americans, or 21 percent of the population, live in rural areas. There is quite a range in the number of rural residents from state to state: In California, fewer than 6 percent of residents live in rural areas; in Vermont, more than 60 percent. As is true of the suburbs, it would be a mistake to view these rural communities as fitting one set image. Turkey farms, coal-mining towns, cattle ranches, and gas stations along interstate highways are all part of

Rural communities like this one in Arthur, Nebraska, have been losing population as young people move away in search of employment. The decline of the family farm has contributed significantly to the depopulation.

the rural landscape in the United States (Bureau of the Census 2004a:28).

Today, many rural areas are facing problems that were first associated with the central cities, and are now evident in the suburbs. Overdevelopment, gang warfare, and drug trafficking can be found on the policymaking agenda far outside major metropolitan areas. While the magnitude of the problems may not be as great as in the central cities, rural resources cannot begin to match those that city mayors can marshall in an attempt to address social ills (Graham 2004; Osgood and Chambers 2003).

The postindustrial revolution has been far from kind to the rural communities of the United States. Of the fewer than 3 million farm and ranch operators nationwide, little more than a third consider agriculture their principal occupation. Farm residents now represent less than 1 percent of the nation's population, compared to 95 percent in 1790. The depopulation of farming areas has been especially hard on the youngest residents. It is not uncommon for rural children to travel 90 minutes each way to school, compared to a nationwide one-way commute of less than 26 minutes for urban workers (Department of Agriculture 2004; Dillon 2004).

The economic stagnation and resulting depopulation have been particularly stark in the northern Rockies and western Great Plains. These areas do not benefit much from tourism, and though agriculture thrives there, the income from farming flows disproportionately to large agribusinesses. Even food processing, an obvious potential source of employment, is lacking; area produce is shipped elsewhere to be processed (*The Economist* 2005h; Florio 2006).

In desperation, residents of depressed rural areas have begun to encourage prison construction, which they once discouraged, to bring in badly needed economic development. Ironically, in regions where the prison population has declined, communities have been hurt yet again by their dependence on a single industry (Kilborn 2001).

The construction of large businesses can create its own problems, as small communities that have experienced the arrival of large discount stores, such as Wal-Mart, Target, Home Depot, or Costco, have discovered. Although many residents welcome the new employment opportunities and the convenience of one-stop shopping, local merchants see their longtime family businesses endangered by formidable 200,000-square-foot competitors with a national reputation. Even when such discount stores provide a boost to a town's economy (and they do not always do so), they can undermine the town's sense of community and identity. Box 15-2 (opposite) chronicles the "store wars" that often ensue.

On a more positive note, advances in electronic communications have allowed some people in the United States to work wherever they wish. For those who are concerned about quality-of-life issues, working at home in a rural area that has access to the latest high-tech services is the perfect arrangement. No matter where people make their homes—whether in the city, the suburbs, or a country village—economic and technological change will have an impact on their quality of life.

Use Your Sociological Imagination www.mhhe.com/schaefer7

You have fast-forwarded to a future in which there are no central cities—just sprawling suburbs and isolated rural communities. What are the economic and social effects of the disappearance of the downtown area?

Sociological Perspectives on Health and Illness

How can we define health? Imagine a continuum with health on one end and death on the other. In the preamble to its 1946 constitution, the World Health Organization defined *health* as a "state of complete physical, mental, and social well-being, and not merely the absence of disease and infirmity" (Leavell and Clark 1965:14).

In this definition, the "healthy" end of the continuum represents an ideal rather than a precise condition. Along the continuum, people define themselves as healthy or sick on the basis of criteria established by themselves and relatives, friends, coworkers, and medical practitioners. Because health is relative, then, we can view it in a social context and consider how it varies in different situations or cultures.

Why is it that you may consider yourself sick or well when others do not agree? Who controls definitions of health and illness in our society, and for what ends? What are the consequences of viewing yourself (or of being viewed) as ill or disabled? By drawing on four sociological perspectives—functionalism, conflict theory, interactionism, and labeling

Although Western medicine has long been dominated by the scientific discoveries made in industrialized countries, more and more people are embracing alternative medicine, including herbal therapies and the Asian practice of acupuncture.

research IN action

15-2 Store Wars

No organization exists in a vacuum, especially not a corporate giant. Executives of Wal-Mart know that. The epitome of the superstore, Wal-Mart has become the center of controversy in towns and cities across the United States, despite the familiar smiley-face logo and its red, white, and blue corporate image. The reason: A new Wal-Mart can have powerfully negative effects on the surrounding community.

Wal-Mart was founded in 1962 by Sam Walton, whose strategy was to locate new stores in rural communities, where competition from other retailers was weak and unions were not organized. Over the years, as the enormously successful discount chain expanded to become the world's largest corporation, Wal-Mart began to move into the fringes of metropolitan areas as well. But the residents of the communities Wal-Mart moved into did not always welcome their new neighbor.

In Ashland, Virginia, a community of 7,200 people, residents worried that Wal-Mart would destroy the small-town atmosphere they treasured. Would their cozy grocery store, known for its personal service, survive the discount giant's competition? Would their quaint and charming Main Street fall into decline? Would full-time jobs with full benefits give way to part-time employment? (Studies have shown that superstores ultimately *reduce* employment.) Ashland's grassroots opposition to Wal-Mart, chronicled in the PBS documentary *Store Wars,* ultimately lost its battle because of Wal-Mart's promised low prices and increased tax revenues. But citizens in many other communities have won, at least temporarily.

On the urban fringes, too, residents have mobilized to stop new superstores. In Bangor, Maine, environmentalists raised an alarm over a proposed Wal-Mart superstore, to be located next to a marsh that sheltered endangered wildlife. Activists in Riverside, California, also challenged Wal-Mart, again on environmental grounds.

But the issue is more complicated in these areas, because communities on the urban fringe are hardly untouched by economic development. Wal-Mart's proposed site in Bangor, for instance, is not far from the Bangor mall. And the huge new houses that dot the suburbs surrounding new stores, built on lots carved out of farmland or forest, have had an environmental impact themselves. In fact, the trend toward the superstore seems to parallel the emergence of the megalopolis, whose boundaries push further and further outward,

> In Ashland, Virginia, residents worried that Wal-Mart would destroy the small-town atmosphere they treasured.

eating up open space in the process. Recognizing the drawbacks of urban sprawl, some planners are beginning to advocate "smart growth"—restoring the central city and its older suburbs rather than abandoning them for the outer rings.

Recently, the debate over Wal-Mart's economic impact has expanded to include health care. Given their wage level, a large proportion of Wal-Mart's employees cannot afford health insurance. In the state of Maryland, frustrated legislators passed a law requiring the state's largest private employers to spend a minimum of 8 percent of their payroll on employee health care. The law, which was later overturned in court, was aimed squarely at Wal-Mart, the only large employer in the state that was not spending the required amount on health insurance. Whatever the outcome of this controversy, there is no denying the social impact of the nation's largest employer.

Not all communities reject superstores. In countries like Mexico, where the economic outlook has been poor recently, people have welcomed Wal-Mart. From Tijuana to Cancún, in fact, public reaction to the U.S. chain's arrival has been almost universally positive. Mexican shoppers appreciate Wal-Mart's wide selection and low prices.

Wal-Mart executives are unapologetic about the chain's rapid expansion. They argue that their aggressive competition has lowered prices and raised working people's standard of living. And they say they have given back to the communities where their stores are located by donating money to educational institutions and local agencies.

Let's Discuss

1. Is there a Wal-Mart, Home Depot, or some other superstore near you? If so, was its opening a matter of controversy in your community?
2. What do you think of the "smart growth" movement? Should communities attempt to redirect business and residential development, or should developers be free to build wherever and whatever they choose?

Sources: Abelson and Barbaro 2006; Halebsky 2004; Hansen 2004; *Maine Times* 2001; PBS 2005; Saporito 2003; Smart Growth 2005; Wal-Mart 2006; Wal-Mart Watch 2006.

---

theory—we can gain greater insight into the social context that shapes definitions of health and the treatment of illness.

Functionalist Approach

Illness entails breaks in our social interactions, both at work and at home. From a functionalist perspective, being sick must therefore be controlled, so that not too many people are released from their societal responsibilities at any one time. Functionalists contend that an overly broad definition of illness would disrupt the workings of a society.

Sickness requires that one take on a social role, if only temporarily. The **sick role** refers to societal expectations about the attitudes and behavior of a person viewed as being ill. Sociologist Talcott Parsons (1951, 1975), well known for his contributions to functionalist theory, outlined the behavior required of people who are considered sick. They are exempted

{ p.13 }

Contemporary Culture Wal-Mart, the epitome of the superstore, has become the center of controversy in towns and cities across the United States.
Theory Conflict analysis of the effects of a new Wal-Mart on the surrounding community
Global View In Mexico, economically depressed communities are welcoming Wal-Mart.

Key Person Talcott Parsons
Theory Functionalist approach to health and illness introduced

from their normal, day-to-day responsibilities and generally do not suffer blame for their condition. Yet they are obligated to try to get well, which includes seeking competent professional care. Attempting to get well is particularly important in the world's developing countries. Modern automated industrial societies can absorb a greater degree of illness or disability than horticultural or agrarian societies, in which the availability of workers is far more critical (Conrad 2000).

According to Parsons's theory, physicians function as "gate-keepers" for the sick role. They either verify a patient's condition as "illness" or designate the patient as "recovered." The ill person becomes dependent on the physician, because the latter can control valued rewards (not only treatment of illness, but also excused absences from work and school). Parsons suggests that the physician–patient relationship is somewhat like that between parent and child. Like a parent, the physician helps the patient to enter society as a full and functioning adult (Segall 1976).

The concept of the sick role is not without criticism. First, patients' judgments regarding their own state of health may be related to their gender, age, social class, and ethnic group. For example, younger people may fail to detect warning signs of a dangerous illness, while the elderly may focus too much on the slightest physical malady. Second, the sick role may be more applicable to people who are experiencing short-term illnesses than to those with recurring, long-term illnesses. Finally, even simple factors, such as whether a person is employed, seem to affect one's willingness to assume the sick role—as does the impact of socialization into a particular occupation or activity. For example, beginning in childhood, athletes learn to define certain ailments as "sports injuries" and therefore do not regard themselves as "sick." Nonetheless, sociologists continue to rely on Parsons's model for functionalist analysis of the relationship between illness and societal expectations of the sick (Curry 1993).

Conflict Approach

Conflict theorists observe that the medical profession has assumed a preeminence that extends well beyond whether to excuse a student from school or an employee from work. Sociologist Eliot Freidson (1970:5) has likened the position of medicine today to that of state religions yesterday—it has an officially approved monopoly of the right to define health and illness and to treat illness. Conflict theorists use the term *medicalization of society* to refer to the growing role of medicine as a major institution of social control (Conrad and Schneider 1992; McKinlay and McKinlay 1977; Zola 1972, 1983).

The Medicalization of Society   Social control involves techniques and strategies for regulating behavior in order to enforce the distinctive norms and values of a culture. Typically, we {**p.158** think of informal social control as occurring within families and peer groups, and formal social control as being carried out by authorized agents such as police officers, judges, school administrators, and employers. Viewed from a conflict perspec-

tive, however, medicine is not simply a "healing profession"; it is a regulating mechanism.

How does medicine manifest its social control? First, medicine has greatly expanded its domain of expertise in recent decades. Physicians now examine a wide range of issues, among them sexuality, old age, anxiety, obesity, child development, alcoholism, and drug addiction. We tolerate this expansion of the boundaries of medicine because we hope that these experts can bring new "miracle cures" to complex human problems, as they have to the control of certain infectious diseases.

The social significance of this expanding medicalization is that once a problem is viewed using a *medical model*—once medical experts become influential in proposing and assessing relevant public policies—it becomes more difficult for common people to join the discussion and exert influence on decision making. It also becomes more difficult to view these issues as being shaped by social, cultural, or psychological factors, rather than simply by physical or medical factors (Caplan 1989; Conrad and Schneider 1992; Starr 1982).

Second, medicine serves as an agent of social control by retaining absolute jurisdiction over many health care procedures. It has even attempted to guard its jurisdiction by placing health care professionals such as chiropractors and nurse-midwives outside the realm of acceptable medicine. Despite the fact that midwives first brought professionalism to child delivery, they have been portrayed as having invaded the "legitimate" field of obstetrics, both in the United States and Mexico. Nurse-midwives have sought licensing as a way to achieve professional respectability, but physicians continue to exert power to ensure that midwifery remains a subordinate occupation (Friedland 2000).

Inequities in Health Care   The medicalization of society is but one concern of conflict theorists as they assess the workings of health care institutions. As we have seen throughout this textbook, in analyzing any issue, conflict theorists seek to determine who benefits, who suffers, and who dominates at the expense of others. Viewed from a conflict perspective, glaring inequities exist in health care delivery in the United States. For example, poor areas tend to be underserved because medical services concentrate where people are wealthy.

Similarly, from a global perspective, obvious inequities exist in health care delivery. Today, the United States has about 256 physicians per 10,000 people, while African nations have fewer than 1 per 10,000. This situation is only worsened by the **brain drain**—the immigration to the United States and other industrialized nations of skilled workers, professionals, and technicians who are desperately needed in their home countries. As part of this brain drain, physicians, nurses, and other health care professionals have come to the United States from developing countries such as India, Pakistan, and various African states. Conflict theorists view their emigration out of the Third World as yet another way in which the world's core industrialized nations enhance their quality of life at the expense of developing countries. One way the developing countries suffer is in lower

---

Theory Parsons's functionalist view of the "sick role"
Classroom Tip See "Disability—An Exercise" (Class Discussion Topics).
Theory Conflict view of health and medicine introduced
Theory Conflict view of medicine as a mechanism of social control

Let's Discuss How does the medical model shed light on the concept of disability as a master status?
Theory Conflict view of medical profession's opposition to chiropractors, midwives
Classroom Tip See "Professional Marginality: Chiropractors" (Additional Lecture Ideas).
Global View The "brain drain" out of Third World countries

The growing concern about obesity among the young has focused attention on their eating habits and their need for exercise.

life expectancy. In Africa and much of Latin America and Asia, life expectancy is far lower than in industrialized nations (Bureau of the Census 2004a:107; World Bank 2005a:88–90).

Conflict theorists emphasize that inequities in health care have clear life-and-death consequences. From a conflict perspective, the dramatic differences in infant mortality rates around the world (see Figure 15-6) reflect, at least in part, unequal distribution of health care resources based on the wealth or poverty of various communities and nations. Still, despite the wealth of the United States, at least 31 nations have *lower* infant mortality rates, among them Canada, Sweden, and Japan. Conflict theorists point out that unlike the United States, these countries offer some form of government-supported health care for all citizens, which typically leads to greater availability and use of prenatal care.

Interactionist Approach

From an interactionist point of view, patients are not passive; often, they actively seek the services of a health care practitioner. In examining health, illness, and medicine as a social institution, then, interactionists engage in micro-level study of the roles

played by health care professionals and patients. Interactionists are particularly interested in how physicians learn to play their occupational role. According to Brenda L. Beagan (2001), the technical language students learn in medical school becomes the basis for the script they follow as novice physicians. The familiar white coat is their costume—one that helps them to appear confident and professional at the same time that it identifies them as doctors to patients and other staff members. Beagan found that many medical students struggle to project the appearance of competence they think their role demands.

Sometimes patients play an active role in health care by *failing* to follow a physician's advice. For example, some patients stop taking medications long before they should. Some take an incorrect dosage on purpose, and others never even fill their prescriptions. Such noncompliance results in part from the prevalence of self-medication in our society; many people are accustomed to self-diagnosis and self-treatment. On the other hand, patients' active involvement in their health care can sometimes have very *positive* consequences. Some patients read books about preventive health care techniques, attempt to maintain a healthful and nutritious diet, carefully monitor any side effects of medication, and adjust the dosage based on perceived side effects. Finally, as Box 15-3 (page 394) shows, physicians may *change* their approach to a patient based on the patient's wishes.

FIGURE 15–6

Infant Mortality Rates in Selected Countries

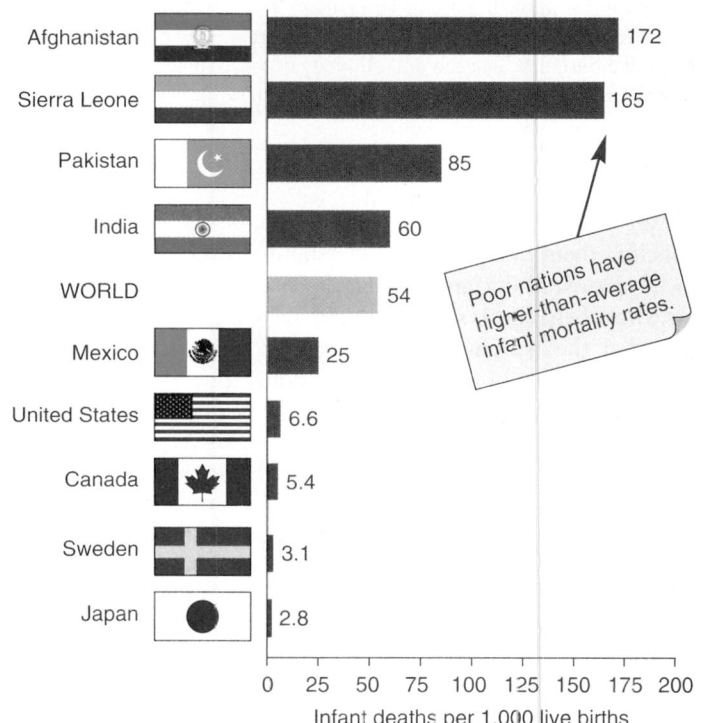

Source: Data reported in Haub 2005.

Classroom Tip Note how U.S. immigration policy has affected health care not only in the United States but especially in the Third World.
Global View Infant mortality rates around the world
Theory Conflict view of the impact of government-supported health care on infant mortality rates

Theory Interactionist view of health and illness introduced

15-3 To Inform or Not to Inform? How Race and Ethnicity Affect Views of Patient Autonomy

Should patients be told the seriousness of their illness? Should they be included in the decisions about what medical care they receive? In the last 25 years, the principle of patient autonomy has become a fundamental ideal of medical care in the United States. According to this principle, "people have the right to make informed decisions about their medical care; consequently, they need the truth about their diagnosis, their prognosis, and the risks and benefits of possible treatments." While the ideal of patient autonomy has won wide acceptance from physicians, policymakers, and the general public, some critics argue that the current focus on patient autonomy reflects an ethnocentric cultural bias that ignores other values, such as family integrity and physician responsibility.

The question of how race and ethnicity influence attitudes toward patient autonomy was studied by a team of researchers, including an internal medicine specialist and ethicist, anthropologists, translators, a statistician, and a law professor. At 31 senior centers in Los Angeles County, the researchers administered questionnaires to 800 people of diverse ethnic backgrounds, all of them age 65 or over. The major finding of the study was that there are marked differences by race and ethnicity in attitudes toward patient autonomy. While 88 percent of African Americans and 87 percent of White Americans believe that a patient should be informed of a diagnosis of cancer, the same is true of only 65 percent of Mexican Americans and 47 percent of Korean Americans. Moreover, 69 percent of Whites and 63 percent of African Americans believe that a patient should be informed of a terminal prognosis, compared with 48 percent of Mexican Americans and 35 percent of Korean Americans.

> *Navajos believe that physicians and other healers should never offer a terminal diagnosis or use any negative language that could trouble or hurt a patient.*

One reason why Korean Americans are especially opposed to hearing a terminal prognosis is their belief in the unity of mind and body. Truth-telling is like a death sentence to traditional Koreans, because of their view that the body will react to ominous news received by the mind. Many Korean Americans believe that physicians should always be optimistic and positive in their communications with patients.

Similarly, a separate study of residents of a Navajo Indian reservation in Arizona revealed that Navajo culture places a high value on thinking and speaking in a positive way. For Navajos, language can shape reality. Consequently, Navajos believe that physicians and other healers should never offer a terminal diagnosis or use any negative language that could trouble or hurt a patient. One highly regarded medicine man notes that the mention of death to a patient "is sharper than any needle" (Carrese and Rhodes 1995:828).

Let's Discuss

1. How has terminal illness been handled in your family? Have relatives who were dying been told the truth about their condition, or has it been withheld from them? Do you think your family's cultural background influenced the decision?
2. Which is more important, the patient's right to know or the patient's faith in the chance of recovery?

Sources: Blackhall et al. 1995; Carrese and Rhodes 1995; Commonwealth Fund 2002; Monmaney 1995.

Labeling Approach

Labeling theory helps us to understand why certain people are {p.171 *viewed* as deviants, "bad kids," or criminals, whereas others whose behavior is similar are not. Labeling theorists also suggest that the designation "healthy" or "ill" generally involves social definition by others. Just as police officers, judges, and other regulators of social control have the power to define certain people as criminals, health care professionals (especially physicians) have the power to define certain people as sick. Moreover, like labels that suggest nonconformity or criminality, labels that are associated with illness commonly reshape how others treat us and how we see ourselves. Our society attaches serious consequences to labels that suggest less-than-perfect physical or mental health (Becker 1963; C. Clark 1983; H. Schwartz 1987).

A historical example illustrates perhaps the ultimate extreme in labeling social behavior as a sickness. As enslavement of Africans in the United States came under increasing attack in the 19th century, medical authorities provided new rationalizations for the oppressive practice. Noted physicians published articles stating that the skin color of Africans deviated from "healthy" white skin coloring because Africans suffered from congenital leprosy. Moreover, the continuing efforts of enslaved Africans to escape from their White masters were classified as an example of the "disease" of drapetomania (or "crazy runaways"). The prestigious *New Orleans Medical and Surgical Journal* suggested that the remedy for this "disease" was to treat slaves kindly, as one might treat children. Apparently, these medical authorities would not entertain the view that it was healthy and sane to flee slavery or join in a slave revolt (Szasz 1971).

By the late 1980s, the power of one particular label—"person {p.103 with AIDS"—had become quite evident. As we saw in our discussion of the late Arthur Ashe, this label often functions as a master status that overshadows all other aspects of a person's life. Once someone is told that he or she has tested positive for

---

Race/Ethnicity Impact of race and ethnicity on attitudes toward patient autonomy
Methods The study of patient autonomy relied on survey research in Los Angeles County.
Methods Observation research among Navajos on a reservation in Arizona

Theory Labeling view of health and illness introduced
Race/Ethnicity Prejudiced views of the health and well-being of enslaved African Americans

HIV, the virus associated with AIDS, that person is forced to confront immediate and difficult questions: Should I tell my family members, my sexual partner(s), my friends, my co-workers, my employer? How will these people respond? People's intense fear of the disease has led to prejudice and discrimination—even social ostracism—against those who have (or are suspected of having) AIDS. A person who has AIDS must deal not only with the serious medical consequences of the disease, but with the distressing social consequences associated with the label.

According to labeling theorists, we can view a variety of life experiences as illnesses or not. Recently, premenstrual syndrome, posttraumatic disorders, and hyperactivity have been labeled medically recognized disorders. In addition, the medical community continues to disagree over whether chronic fatigue syndrome constitutes a medical illness.

Probably the most noteworthy medical example of labeling is the case of homosexuality. For years, psychiatrists classified being gay or lesbian not as a lifestyle but as a mental disorder subject to treatment. This official sanction by the psychiatry profession became an early target of the growing gay and lesbian rights movement in the United States. In 1974, members of the American Psychiatric Association voted to drop homosexuality from the standard manual on mental disorders (B. Adam 1995; Monteiro 1998).

Table 15-4 summarizes the four major sociological perspectives on health and illness. Though they may seem quite different, two common themes unite them. First, any person's health or illness is more than an organic condition, since it is subject to the interpretation of others. The impact of culture, family and friends, and the medical profession mean that health and illness are not purely biological occurrences, but sociological occurrences as well. Second, since members of a society (especially industrial societies) share the same health care delivery system, health is a group and societal concern. Although health may be defined as the complete well-being of an individual, it is also the result of his or her social environment, as the next section will show (Cockerham 1998).

Social Epidemiology and Health

Social epidemiology is the study of the distribution of disease, impairment, and general health status across a population. Initially, epidemiology concentrated on the scientific study of epidemics, focusing on how they started and spread. Contemporary social epidemiology is much broader in scope, concerned not only with epidemics but also with nonepidemic diseases, injuries, drug addiction and alcoholism, suicide, and mental illness. Recently, epidemiologists took on the new role of tracking bioterrorism. In 2001 they mobilized to trace the anthrax outbreak and prepare for any terrorist use of smallpox or other lethal microbes. Epidemiologists draw on the work of a wide variety of scientists and researchers, among them physicians, sociologists, public health officials, biologists, veterinarians, demographers, anthropologists, psychologists, and meteorologists.

Researchers in social epidemiology commonly use two concepts: *incidence* and *prevalence*. **Incidence** refers to the number of new cases of a specific disorder that occur within a given population during a stated period, usually a year. For example, the incidence of AIDS in the United States in 2002 was 42,745 cases. In contrast, **prevalence** refers to the total number of cases of a specific disorder that exist at a given time. The prevalence of AIDS in the United States through December 2002 was about 385,000 cases (Bureau of the Census 2004a:120–121).

When disease incidence figures are presented as rates, or as the number of reports per 100,000 people, they are called **morbidity rates.** (The term **mortality rate** refers to the incidence of *death* in a given population.) Sociologists find morbidity rates useful because they reveal that a specific disease occurs more frequently among one segment of a population than another. As we shall see, social class, race, ethnicity, gender, and age can all affect a population's morbidity rates. In 1999, the U.S. Department of Health and Human Services, recognizing the inequality inherent in U.S. morbidity and mortality rates, launched the Campaign for 100% Access and Zero Health Disparities, an ambitious undertaking (Bureau of Primary Health Care 1999).

Table 15-4 Sociological Perspectives on Health and Illness

summing**UP**

	Functionalist	Conflict	Interactionist	Labeling
Major emphasis	Control of the number of people who are considered sick	Overmedicalization Gross inequities in health care	Doctor–patient relationship Interaction of medical staff	Definition of illness and health
Controlling factors	Physician as gatekeeper	Medical profession Social inequities	Medical profession	Medical profession
Proponents	Talcott Parsons	Paul Starr Thomas Szasz Irving Zola	Doug Maynard	Thomas Szasz

Theory Impact of the label "person with AIDS"
Theory Labeling life experiences as illness

Reel Society See Health and Epidemiology in the Topic Index.
Gender/Race/Ethnicity Impact of gender, class, and race on morbidity and mortality rates

{taking SOCIOLOGY TO WORK}

Jess Purmort
Research Assistant, New York Academy of Medicine

As a public health researcher, Jess Purmort is putting the skills she learned in her sociology classes to work. At the New York Academy of Medicine, Purmort is assigned to a five-year intervention study of preschool children with asthma. She spends about half her time at participating preschools, collecting data, advising the parents of asthmatic children, and helping staff members to identify children who may be asthmatic. The rest of her time is spent at the office. "The most exciting part of my job is being involved in the research process," Purmort says. "I love learning about all of the various aspects of conducting research."

A 2004 graduate of Brown University, Purmort majored in sociology and Latin American studies. All her favorite courses were sociology courses. "I loved the diversity of the field and the fact that I could learn tangible skills, such as statistical analysis," she says. At Brown, Purmort was able to conduct her own research; her primary interest was immigrant communities. Courses on social networks and identity, in particular, helped her to better understand the diverse populations she now works with.

Purmort was interested in social issues before she went to college, "but it wasn't until I was in college that I understood that there was a field devoted to studying these issues," she admits. Her sociology courses raised her awareness, enabling her to think critically about such issues.

A year after her graduation, Purmort is glad she decided to major in sociology. "I use the practical skills and experience I have with sociological research on my job every day," she says. "Furthermore, my knowledge about various sociological and policy issues, such as poverty and welfare, has provided me with a deeper understanding about the forces that affect the lives of the individuals I encounter while working."

Let's Discuss

1. How might the research skills you develop in your sociology courses be helpful in your future career?
2. Do some research on asthma. In what kinds of community are children at high risk of developing asthma? What are the conditions that epidemiologists suspect may contribute to the prevalence of the disease?

Social Class

Social class is clearly associated with differences in morbidity and mortality rates. Studies in the United States and other countries have consistently shown that people in the lower classes have higher rates of mortality and disability than others. One study concluded that Americans whose family incomes were less than $10,000 could expect to die seven years sooner than those with incomes of at least $25,000 (Pamuk et al. 1998).

Why is class linked to health? Crowded living conditions, substandard housing, poor diet, and stress all contribute to the ill health of many low-income people in the United States. In certain instances, poor education may lead to a lack of awareness of measures necessary to maintain good health. Financial strains are certainly a major factor in the health problems of less affluent people.

Another reason for the link between class and health is that the poor—many of whom belong to racial and ethnic minorities—are less able than others to afford quality medical care. As Figure 15-7 shows, the affluent are more likely to have health insurance, either because they can afford it or because they have jobs that provide it.

{ When people who do not have health insurance seek medical care, their condition is often more critical than it would be if they had been receiving regular preventive care from a primary care provider. And the care they receive, especially if it is delivered in an emergency room, is much more expensive than the care delivered in a doctor's office. }

FIGURE 15–7

397

Population, Communities, and Health

Percentage of People without Health Insurance

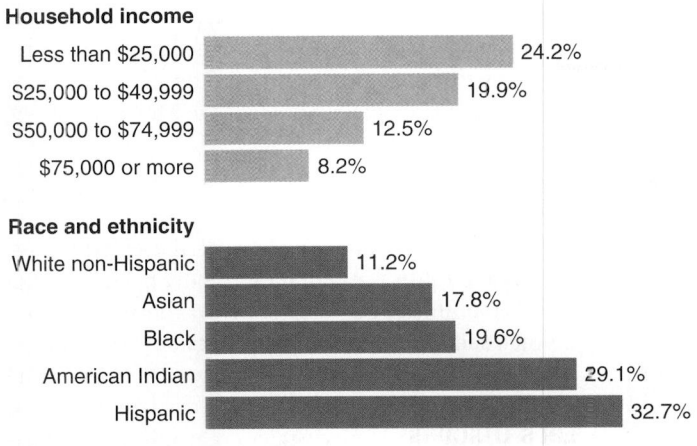

Household income

Less than $25,000 — 24.2%
$25,000 to $49,999 — 19.9%
$50,000 to $74,999 — 12.5%
$75,000 or more — 8.2%

Race and ethnicity

White non-Hispanic — 11.2%
Asian — 17.8%
Black — 19.6%
American Indian — 29.1%
Hispanic — 32.7%

Note: Based on 2-year average 2003–2004.
Source: DeNavas-Walt et al. 2005:18, 20.

Another factor in the link between class and health is evident at the workplace: The occupations of people in the working and lower classes of the United States tend to be more dangerous than those of more affluent citizens. Miners, for example, risk injury or death from explosions and cave-ins; they are also vulnerable to respiratory diseases such as black lung. Workers in textile mills who are exposed to toxic substances may contract a variety of illnesses, including one commonly known as *brown lung disease.* In recent years, the nation has learned of the perils of asbestos poisoning, a particular worry for construction workers (Berkman 2004; R. Hall 1982; J. Scott 2005).

In the view of Karl Marx and contemporary conflict theorists, capitalist societies such as the United States care more about maximizing profits than they do about the health and safety of industrial workers. As a result, government agencies do not take forceful action to regulate conditions in the workplace, and workers suffer many preventable job-related injuries and illnesses. Research also shows that the lower classes are more vulnerable to environmental pollution than the affluent, not only where they work but where they live (see Chapter 16).

Race and Ethnicity

The health profiles of many racial and ethnic minorities reflect the social inequality evident in the United States. The poor economic and environmental conditions of groups such as African Americans, Hispanics, and Native Americans are manifested in high morbidity and mortality rates for these groups. It is true that some afflictions, such as sickle-cell anemia among Blacks, have a clear genetic basis. But in most instances, environmental factors contribute to the differential rates of disease and death.

In many respects, the mortality rates for African Americans are distressing. Compared with Whites, Blacks have higher death rates from heart disease, pneumonia, diabetes, and cancer. The death rate from stroke is twice as high among African Americans. Such epidemiological findings reflect in part the fact that a high proportion of Blacks are found among the nation's lower classes. According to the National Center for Health Statistics, Whites can expect to live 77.7 years. In contrast, life expectancy for Blacks is 72.3 years (Arias 2004).

As noted earlier, infant mortality is regarded as a primary indicator of health care. There is a significant gap in the United States between the infant mortality rates of African Americans and Whites. Generally, the rate of infant death is more than twice as high among Blacks. African Americans account for 15 percent of all live births in the nation but 29 percent of infant deaths. Puerto Ricans and Native Americans have infant mortality rates that are lower than African Americans' but higher than Whites' (MacDorman et al. 2005).

The medical establishment is not exempt from racism. Unfortunately, the media often focus on obvious forms of racism, such as hate crimes, while overlooking more insidious forms in social institutions like the medical establishment. One review of more than 100 studies conducted over the last decade concluded that minorities receive inferior care even when they are insured. Despite having access to care, Blacks, Latinos, and American Indians are treated unequally as a result of racial prejudice and differences in the quality of various health care plans. Furthermore, national clinical studies have shown that even allowing for differences in income and insurance coverage, racial and ethnic minorities are less likely than other groups to receive both standard health care and life-saving treatment for conditions such as HIV infection (Caesar and Williams 2002; Smedley et al. 2002; Steyerberg et al. 2005).

Drawing on the conflict perspective, sociologist Howard Waitzkin (1986) suggests that racial tensions also contribute to the medical problems of Blacks. In his view, the stress that results from racial prejudice and discrimination helps to explain the higher rates of hypertension found among African Americans (and Hispanics) compared to Whites. Hypertension—twice as common in Blacks as in Whites—is believed to be a critical factor in Blacks' high mortality rates from heart disease, kidney disease, and stroke (Morehouse Medical Treatment and Effectiveness Center 1999).

Some Mexican Americans and many other Latinos adhere to cultural beliefs that make them less likely to use the established medical system. They may interpret their illnesses according to traditional Latino folk medicine, or **curanderismo**—a form of holistic health care and healing. *Curanderismo* influences how one approaches health care and even how one defines illness. Most Hispanics probably use folk healers, or *curanderos,* infrequently, but perhaps 20 percent rely on home remedies. Some define such illnesses as *susto* (fright sickness) and *atague* (or fighting attack) according to folk beliefs. Because these complaints often have biological bases, sensitive medical practitioners need to deal with them carefully in order to diagnose and treat illnesses accurately (Council on Scientific Affairs 1999; Trotter and Chavira 1997).

A Mexican folk healer, or *curandero,* massages a patient's feet. About 20 percent of Hispanics rely on the home remedies folk healers offer.

Gender

A large body of research indicates that compared with men, women experience a higher prevalence of many illnesses, although they tend to live longer. There are some variations—for example, men are more likely to have parasitic diseases, whereas women are more likely to become diabetic—but as a group, women appear to be in poorer health than men.

The apparent inconsistency between the ill health of women and their greater longevity deserves an explanation, and researchers have advanced a theory. Women's lower rate of cigarette smoking (reducing their risk of heart disease, lung cancer, and emphysema), lower consumption of alcohol (reducing the risk of auto accidents and cirrhosis of the liver), and lower rate of employment in dangerous occupations explain about one-third of their greater longevity than men. Moreover, some clinical studies suggest that the differences in morbidity may actually be less pronounced than the data show. Researchers argue that women are much more likely than men to seek treatment, to be diagnosed as having a disease, and thus to have their illnesses reflected in the data examined by epidemiologists.

From a conflict perspective, women have been particularly vulnerable to the medicalization of society, with everything from birth to beauty being treated in an increasingly medical context. Such medicalization may contribute to women's higher morbidity rates compared to those of men. Ironically, even though women have been especially affected by medicalization, medical researchers have often excluded them from clinical studies. Female physicians and researchers charge that sexism lies at the heart of such research practices, and insist there is a desperate need for studies of female subjects (Bates 1999; McDonald 1999; Vidaver et al. 2000).

Age

Health is the overriding concern of the elderly. Most older people in the United States report having at least one chronic illness, but only some of those conditions are potentially life threatening or require medical care. At the same time, health problems can affect the quality of life of older people in important ways. Almost half of older people in the United States are troubled by arthritis, and many have visual or hearing impairments that can interfere with the performance of everyday tasks.

Older people are also especially vulnerable to certain mental health problems. Alzheimer's disease, the leading cause of dementia in the United States, afflicts an estimated 4.5 million

FIGURE 15–8

Availability of Physicians by State

MAPPING LIFE

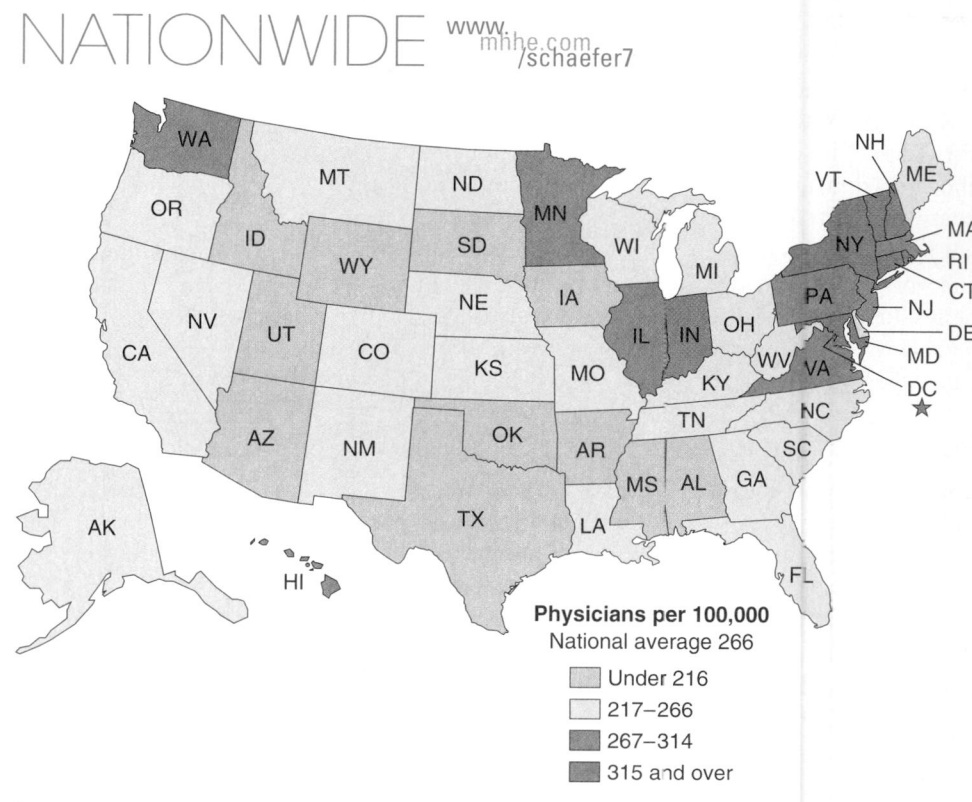

Physicians per 100,000
National average 266

- Under 216
- 217–266
- 267–314
- 315 and over

Source: Bureau of the Census 2005a:113.

Theory Conflict view of women's vulnerability to the medicalization of society

Gender Exclusion of women from clinical studies because of sexism

398

older people. While some individuals with Alzheimer's exhibit only mild symptoms, the risk of severe problems resulting from this disease rises substantially with age (Alzheimer's Association 2004).

Not surprisingly, older people in the United States (ages 75 and older) are five times more likely to use health services and to be hospitalized than younger people (ages 15–24). The disproportionate use of the U.S. health care system by older people is a critical factor in all discussions about the cost of health care and possible reforms of the health care system (Bureau of the Census 2004a:113).

In sum, to achieve the goal of 100 percent access and zero health disparities, federal health officials must overcome inequities that are rooted not just in age, but in social class, race and ethnicity, and gender. If that were not enough, they must also deal with a geographical disparity in health care resources. Figure 15-8 (opposite) shows the differences in the presence of physicians from one state to another. Dramatic differences in the availability of physicians, hospitals, and nursing homes also exist between urban and rural areas in the same state.

The AIDS Crisis

The Issue

In his novel *The Plague,* Albert Camus (1948:34) wrote, "There have been as many plagues as wars in history, yet always plagues and wars take people equally by surprise." Regarded by many as the distinctive plague of the modern era, AIDS certainly caught major social institutions—particularly the government, the health care system, and the economy—by surprise when it was first noticed by medical practitioners in the 1970s. It has since spread around the world. While encouraging new therapies have been developed to treat AIDS, there is currently no way to eradicate the disease by medical means. Therefore, it is essential to protect people by reducing the transmission of the fatal virus. But how is that to be done, and whose responsibility is it? What is the role of social institutions in preventing the spread of AIDS?

The Setting

AIDS is the acronym for *acquired immune deficiency syndrome.* Rather than being a distinct disease, AIDS is actually a predisposition to disease that is caused by a virus, the human immunodeficiency virus (HIV). The virus gradually destroys the body's immune system, leaving the carrier vulnerable to infections such as pneumonia that those with healthy immune systems can generally resist. Transmission of the virus from one person to another appears to require either intimate sexual contact or exchange of blood or bodily fluids (whether from contaminated hypodermic needles or syringes, transfusions of infected blood, or transmission from an infected mother to her child before or during birth).

The first cases of AIDS in the United States were reported in 1981. While the numbers of new cases and deaths have recently shown some evidence of decline, an estimated 1.2 million people were living with AIDS or HIV by the end of 2005. Women account for a growing proportion of new cases; racial and ethnic minorities, for 74 percent. Worldwide, AIDS is stabilizing, with an estimated 38.6 million people infected (see Figure 15-9, page 400). The disease is not evenly distributed; those areas least equipped to deal with it—the developing nations of sub-Saharan Africa—face the greatest challenge (Maugh 2004; UNAIDS 2006; World Health Organization 2005).

Sociological Insights

Dramatic crises like the AIDS epidemic are likely to bring about certain transformations in a society's social structure. From a functionalist perspective, if established social institutions cannot meet a crucial need, new social networks are likely to emerge to perform that function. In the case of AIDS, self-help groups—especially in the gay communities of major cities—have organized to care for the sick, educate the healthy, and lobby for more responsive public policies.

The label "person with AIDS" or "HIV-positive" often functions as a master status. People who have AIDS or are infected with the virus face a powerful dual stigma. Not only are they associated with a lethal and contagious disease, but they have a disease that disproportionately afflicts already stigmatized groups, such as gay males and intravenous drug users. This link to stigmatized groups delayed recognition of the severity of the AIDS epidemic. The media took little interest in the disease until it seemed to be spreading beyond the gay community.

Viewed from a conflict perspective, policymakers were slow to respond to the AIDS crisis because those in high-risk groups—gay men and IV drug users—were comparatively powerless. Furthermore, a study done in 2002 documented the fact that females and minority groups are less likely than others to receive experimental treatments for the HIV infection (Gifford et al. 2002).

On the micro level of social interaction, observers once forecasted that AIDS would lead to a more conservative sexual

Age Use of health services by older people in the United States
Gender/Race/Ethnicity/Age Inequities in provision of health care based on gender, race, ethnicity, and age
Global View The international AIDS crisis
Let's Discuss To open up class discussion, ask if any student has helped to care for a person with AIDS.

Gender/Race/Ethnicity Rates of HIV and AIDS based on gender, race, and ethnicity
Theory Functionalist analysis of the AIDS epidemic, which explains how new groups emerge to fill important needs not being met by established institutions
Theory Labeling theory used to examine the "master status" of a person with AIDS
Classroom Tip Introduce Goffman's concept of stigma in discussing HIV and AIDS as master statuses.

climate—among both homosexuals and heterosexuals—in which people would be much more cautious about becoming involved with new partners. Yet it appears that many sexually active people in the United States have not heeded precautions about "safe sex." Data from studies conducted in the early 1990s indicated a growing complacency about AIDS, even among those who were most vulnerable (Bernstein 2004).

Policy Initiatives

AIDS has struck all societies, but not all nations can respond in the same manner. Studies done in the United States show that today, people with HIV or AIDS who receive appropriate medical treatment are living longer than they did in the past. This advance may put additional pressure on policymakers to address the issues raised by the spread of AIDS.

In some nations, cultural practices may prevent people from dealing realistically with the AIDS epidemic. They may not be likely to take the necessary preventive measures, including open discussion of sexuality, homosexuality, and drug use. Pre-

vention has shown signs of working among target groups, such as drug users, pregnant women, and gay men and lesbians, but preventive initiatives are few and far between in developing nations. The prescribed treatment to reduce mother-to-baby transmission of AIDS costs about $300. That amount is roughly equivalent to the average annual income in much of the world where the risk of AIDS is greatest, such as Africa, which accounts for 71 percent of the world's deaths from AIDS in 2005. The medication for adult patients with HIV is even more costly (McNeil 2003; UNAIDS 2006:508; World Health Organization 2005:3).

The high cost of drug treatment programs has generated intensive worldwide pressure on the major pharmaceutical companies to lower the prices to patients in developing nations, especially in sub-Saharan Africa. In 2001, bowing to this pressure, several of the companies agreed to make the combination therapies available at cost. Even at these much lower prices, however, in the poorest nations, relatively few of those who were sick enough to need treatment were receiving it. In many nations,

FIGURE 15–9

Adults and Children Living with HIV/AIDS

MAPPING LIFE

WORLDWIDE www.mhhe.com/schaefer7

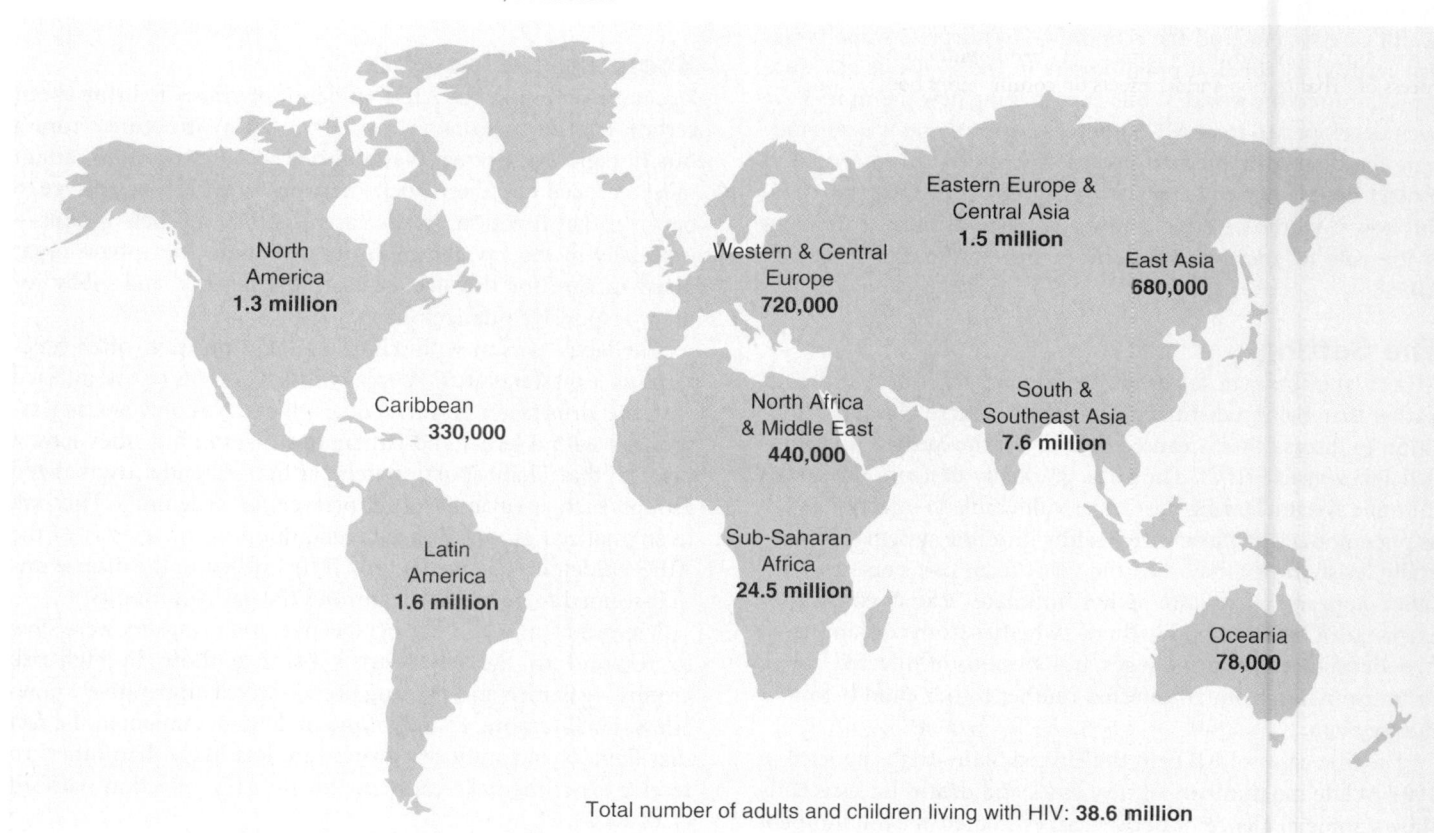

Total number of adults and children living with HIV: **38.6 million**

Note: Midpoint estimates for 2005 released in May 2006; world range is 33.4 to 46.0 million.
Source: UNAIDS 2006:505–540.

Classroom Tip See "A First-Person Commentary on AIDS" in Topics and Sources for Student Research.

Web Resource Remind students that there is an interactive map for this chapter. They can view it in the student center of the Online Learning Center **(www.mhhe.com/schaefer7).**
Classroom Tip See "Using Humor" (Class Discussion Topics).

social institutions simply are not equipped to distribute medicine to those who need it (McNeil 2004).

Let's Discuss

1. Do the people you know take few risks sexually because of the danger of becoming infected with the AIDS virus? If not, why not?

2. Look at the map in Figure 15-9. Why do you think North Africa and the Middle East had only 510,000 people living with AIDS in 2005, while sub-Saharan Africa had 25.8 million? List as many factors as you can that might account for the disparity.

3. Aside from the obvious humanitarian reasons, why should the United States help developing countries in the fight against AIDS?

GettingINVOLVED

To get involved in the debate over the AIDS crisis, visit this text's Online Learning Center, which offers links to relevant Web sites. Check out the Social Policy section in the Online Learning Center as well; it provides survey data on U.S. public opinion regarding this issue.

www.mhhe.com/schaefer7

{ **MASTERING THIS CHAPTER** }

Summary

The size, composition, and distribution of the population have an important influence on the **communities** people live in, as well as on people's **health** and well-being. This chapter examines the current problem of overpopulation and the possibility of **zero population growth,** the process of urbanization and its effects on communities both urban and rural, and several sociological perspectives on health. It closes with a discussion of the AIDS crisis.

1. Thomas Robert Malthus suggested that the world's population was growing more rapidly than the available food supply, and that the gap would increase over time. However, Karl Marx saw capitalism, rather than rising world population, as the real cause of social ills.

2. The primary mechanism for obtaining population information in the United States and most other countries is the **census.**

3. Roughly two-thirds of the world's nations have yet to pass fully through the second stage of **demographic transition.** Thus they continue to experience significant population growth.

4. Developing nations face the prospect of continued population growth because a substantial portion of their population is approaching childbearing age. Some developed nations have begun to stabilize their population growth, however.

5. Over time, cities changed and developed with their economies. In the industrial revolution, the **preindustrial city** of agricultural societies gave way to the **industrial city;** the advent of the Information Age brought with it the **postindustrial city.**

6. Urbanization is evident not only in the United States but throughout the world; by 2000, 50 percent of the world's population lived in urban areas.

7. The **urban ecological** approach is functionalist because it emphasizes how different elements in urban areas contribute to social stability.

8. Drawing on conflict theory, **new urban sociology** emphasizes the interplay of a community's political and economic interests, as well as the impact of the global economy on communities in the United States and other countries.

9. Many urban residents are immigrants from other nations who tend to live together in ethnic neighborhoods.

10. In the last three decades, cities have confronted an overwhelming array of economic and social problems, including crime, unemployment, and the deterioration of schools and public transit systems.

11. Suburbanization was the most dramatic population trend in the United States throughout the 20th century. In recent decades, **suburbs** have become more racially and ethnically diverse.

12. With the rise of agribusiness, family farms have declined, and with them the rural communities of the United States.

13. According to Talcott Parsons's functionalist perspective, physicians function as "gatekeepers" for the **sick role,** either verifying a person's condition as "ill" or designating the person as "recovered."

14. Conflict theorists use the term *medicalization of society* to refer to medicine's growing role as a major institution of social control.

15. Labeling theorists suggest that the designation of a person as "healthy" or "ill" generally involves social definition by others. These definitions affect how others see us and how we view ourselves.

16. Contemporary **social epidemiology** is concerned not only with epidemics but with nonepidemic diseases, injuries, drug addiction and alcoholism, suicide, and mental illness.

17. Studies have consistently shown that people in the lower classes have higher rates of mortality and disability than others.

18. Racial and ethnic minorities have higher rates of morbidity and mortality than Whites. Women tend to be in poorer health than men

Web Resource Remind students that the student center of the Online Learning Center (www.mhhe.com/schaefer7) offers many valuable learning tools.

but live longer. Older people are especially vulnerable to mental health problems, such as Alzheimer's disease.

19. Around the world, the AIDS epidemic has increased mortality rates, strained health care systems, and devastated those communities hardest hit by the disease.

Critical Thinking Questions

1. Some European nations are experiencing population declines. Their death rates are low and their birthrates are even lower than in stage III of the demographic transition model. Does this pattern suggest that there is a fourth stage in the demographic transition? What are the implications of negative population growth for an industrialized nation in the 21st century?

2. How has your home community (your city, town, or neighborhood) changed over the years you have lived there? Have there been significant changes in the community's economic base or its racial and ethnic profile? Have the community's social problems intensified or lessened? Is unemployment currently a major problem? What are the community's future prospects?

3. Relate what you have learned about social epidemiology to the question of universal health care coverage. If the United States were to adopt a system of universal coverage, what might be the effect on the incidence and prevalence of disease among Americans of all classes, races and ethnicities, genders, and ages? What might be the ultimate effect of such changes on health care costs?

Key Terms

Birthrate The number of live births per 1,000 population in a given year. Also known as the *crude birthrate.* (page 377)

Brain drain The immigration to the United States and other industrialized nations of skilled workers, professionals, and technicians who are desperately needed in their home countries. (392)

Census An enumeration, or counting, of a population. (376)

Community A spatial or political unit of social organization that gives people a sense of belonging, based either on shared residence in a particular place or on a common identity. (375)

Concentric-zone theory A theory of urban growth devised by Ernest Burgess that sees growth in terms of a series of rings radiating from the central business district. (384)

Curanderismo Latino folk medicine, a form of holistic health care and healing. (397)

Death rate The number of deaths per 1,000 population in a given year. Also known as the *crude death rate.* (377)

Demographic transition A term used to describe the change from high birthrates and death rates to low birthrates and death rates. (378)

Demography The scientific study of population. (376)

Fertility The level of reproduction in a society. (375)

Growth rate The difference between births and deaths, plus the difference between immigrants and emigrants, per 1,000 population. (377)

Health As defined by the World Health Organization, a state of complete physical, mental, and social well-being, and not merely the absence of disease and infirmity. (390)

Human ecology An area of study that is concerned with the interrelationships between people and their environment. (384)

Incidence The number of new cases of a specific disorder that occur within a given population during a stated period. (395)

Industrial city A relatively large city characterized by open competition, an open class system, and elaborate specialization in the manufacturing of goods. (382)

Infant mortality rate The number of deaths of infants under one year old per 1,000 live births in a given year. (377)

Life expectancy The median number of years a person can be expected to live under current mortality conditions. (377)

Megalopolis A densely populated area containing two or more cities and their suburbs. (383)

Morbidity rate The incidence of disease in a given population. (395)

Mortality rate The incidence of death in a given population. (395)

Multiple-nuclei theory A theory of urban growth developed by Harris and Ullman that views growth as emerging from many centers of development, each of which reflects a particular urban need or activity. (385)

New urban sociology An approach to urbanization that considers the interplay of local, national, and worldwide forces and their effect on local space, with special emphasis on the impact of global economic activity. (386)

Population pyramid A special type of bar chart that shows the distribution of a population by gender and age. (379)

Postindustrial city A city in which global finance and the electronic flow of information dominate the economy. (383)

Preindustrial city A city of only a few thousand people that is characterized by a relatively closed class system and limited mobility. (382)

Prevalence The total number of cases of a specific disorder that exist at a given time. (395)

Sick role Societal expectations about the attitudes and behavior of a person viewed as being ill. (391)

Social epidemiology The study of the distribution of disease, impairment, and general health status across a population. (395)

Suburb According to the Census Bureau, any territory within a metropolitan area that is not included in the central city. (388)

Total fertility rate (TFR) The average number of children born alive to any woman, assuming that she conforms to current fertility rates. (377)

Urban ecology An area of study that focuses on the interrelationships between people and their environment in urban areas. (384)

Urbanism A term used by Louis Wirth to describe distinctive patterns of social behavior evident among city residents. (383)

Vital statistics Records of births, deaths, marriages, and divorces gathered through a registration system maintained by governmental units. (376)

World systems analysis Immanuel Wallerstein's view of the global economic system as one divided between certain industrialized nations that control wealth and developing countries that are controlled and exploited. (386)

Zero population growth (ZPG) The state of a population in which the number of births plus immigrants equals the number of deaths plus emigrants. (381)

Read each question carefully and then select the best answer.

1. Which of the following argued that food supply increases in an arithmetic progression, whereas population expands by a geometric progression?
   a. Thomas Robert Malthus
   b. Karl Marx
   c. Émile Durkheim
   d. Max Weber

2. The final stage in demographic transition is marked by
   a. high birthrates and high death rates.
   b. high birthrates and low death rates.
   c. low birthrates and high death rates.
   d. low birthrates and low death rates.

3. The most recent period of high fertility in the United States, which began after the end of World War II, has often been referred to as the
   a. baby bust.
   b. baby boom.
   c. population bomb.
   d. age of Aquarius.

4. Urbanization in preindustrial cities was restricted by
   a. the ease of migration to the city.
   b. high levels of surplus produced by the agricultural sector.
   c. reliance on animal power as a source of energy for economic production.
   d. all of the above

5. The new urban sociology draws generally on the conflict perspective and more specifically on sociologist Immanuel Wallerstein's
   a. concentric-zone theory.
   b. multiple-nuclei theory.
   c. concept of edge cities.
   d. world systems analysis.

6. According to Herbert Gans, residents who remain in the city to take advantage of unique cultural and intellectual benefits of the city are called
   a. cosmopolites.
   b. ethnic villagers.
   c. urban villagers.
   d. the trapped.

7. Which of the following is a criticism of the sick role?
   a. Patients' judgments regarding their own state of health may be related to their gender, age, social class, and ethnic group.
   b. The sick role may be more applicable to people experiencing short-term illnesses than to those with recurring long-term illnesses.
   c. Even such simple factors as whether a person is employed or not seem to affect the person's willingness to assume the sick role.
   d. all of the above

8. Which of the following terms do conflict theorists use in referring to the growing role of medicine as a major institution of social control?
   a. the sick role
   b. the medicalization of society
   c. medical labeling
   d. epidemiology

9. Which sociological perspective emphasizes that a patient should not always be viewed as passive, but instead as someone who often plays an active role in his or her health care?
   a. the functionalist perspective
   b. the conflict perspective
   c. the interactionist perspective
   d. the labeling approach

10. Which of the following statements is *not* true?
    a. Compared with men, women experience a higher prevalence of many illnesses.
    b. Men are more likely than women to have parasitic diseases.
    c. As a group, women appear to be in better health than men.
    d. Women are more likely than men to become diabetic.

11. Drawing on several components, including size, composition, and territorial distribution, _____ is the scientific study of population.

12. _____ _____ are records of births, deaths, marriages, and divorces that are gathered through a registration system maintained by governmental units.

13. The _____ _____ is the number of live births per 1,000 population in a given year.

14. Louis Wirth distinguished three critical factors contributing to _____: the size of the population, the population density, and the heterogeneity of the population.

15. _____ _____ is concerned with the interrelationships between people and their environment.

16. According to the concentric-zone theory, at the core of the city is the _____ business district.

17. Ferdinand Tönnies used the term _____ to describe a close-knit community where social interaction among people is intimate and familiar.

18. As defined by the World Health Organization, _____ is a "state of complete physical, mental, and social well-being, and not merely the absence of disease and infirmity."

19. Social _____ is the study of the distribution of disease, impairment, and general health status across a population.

20. _____ refers to the number of new cases of a specific disorder occurring within a given population during a stated period, usually a year.

{ TECHNOLOGY RESOURCES }

Online Learning Center

1. A good way to help prepare for an exam or review for a class discussion is to study the outline and summary for this chapter. Outlines and summaries for all chapters in this book are available on the student center of the Online Learning Center. Go to **www.mhhe.com/schaefer7** and link to Chapter Outline or Chapter Summary.

2. The University of Michigan is the home of a research institute whose focus is on health inequalities. To view some enlightening fig-

ures that illustrate the connections among race, class, and health, visit the Michigan Center for the Study of Health Inequalities (**www.sph.umich.edu/miih/index2.html**).

3. Although you have probably heard of Habitat for Humanity—the organization that builds homes for poor families—you may not be aware of the breadth of its activities. Find out more at its Web site, **www.habitat.org.**

*Note: While all the URLs listed were current as of the printing of this book, these sites often change. Please check our Web Site (**www.mhhe.com/schaefer7**) for updates, hyperlinks, and exercises related to these sites.*

Reel Society Video Clips

Real Society video clips, which appear on this book's Web site, can be used to spark discussion about the following topics from this chapter:
- Demography: The Study of Population
- Social Epidemiology and Health

16

Globalization, the Environment, and Social Change

inside

Social Movements

Theories of Social Change

Resistance to Social Change

Global Social Change

Social Change and the Environment

Social Policy and Globalization: Transnationals

Boxes

Sociology in the Global Community: A New Social Movement in Rural India

Research in Action: The Human Genome Project

In 2002, amid charges that wealthy nations were "dumping" large quantities of surplus wheat and other commodities on the world market, jeopardizing the value of crops produced in poor countries, the global charity Oxfam launched a campaign to ensure fair trade with nations that depend on a single crop, such as wheat, coffee, or rice. These photos of well-known personalities were taken to advertise the effort, beginning in 2005. From left to right: singer/actress Alanis Morissette, actor Colin Firth, and Chris Martin (Coldplay).

RULING THE WAVES

Cycles of Discovery, Chaos, and Wealth from the Compass to the Internet

DEBORA L. SPAR

Chuck D is an unlikely hero of the digital age. With hit albums such as *Yo! Bum Rush the Show* and *Fear of a Black Planet,* the founder of the rap group Public Enemy would seem to inhabit a world far removed from the more conspicuous pioneers of cyberspace, from the Netscapes and Yahoos! and AOLs. In 1998, however, Chuck D stormed into cyberspace. Rather than giving his latest songs to Def Jam, the label that had produced his music for over a decade, the rap artist instead released his music directly onto the Internet, at www.public-enemy.com. It shouldn't have been such a big deal, really: one artist, a handful of songs, and a funky distribution method that probably reached several thousand fans. But in the music business this was very big news. For Chuck D had taken one of the industry's most sacred practices and thrown it, quite literally, into space. With just a couple of songs, he challenged how music was sold and, even more fundamentally, how it was owned. "This is the beginning," proclaimed the rapper, "of the end of domination."

As far as Chuck D was concerned, putting music online was a matter of power, of using new technologies to right old wrongs and give recording artists the influence and money that was rightfully theirs. To the recording industry, however, it was heresy. . . .

Had Chuck D been an isolated case, the studios most likely could have looked the other way. They could have dismissed Chuck D as a simple renegade, a rapper gone bad, and forgotten him and his web site. But the problem was that Chuck D, potentially, was everywhere. In cyberspace, any recording artist could distribute his or her music online; any musician could become a mini-studio, circumventing the record labels and their complex, clunky rules. . . .

Matters reached a head in 1999, when a nineteen-year-old college dropout named Shawn Fanning joined Chuck D in storming the frontier. Backed by his uncle in Boston, Fanning created Napster, a revolutionary system that allowed thousands—even millions—of users to trade their music online. Within months of its release, Napster had become a social phenomenon and a massive commercial threat. Universities complained that Napster was suddenly consuming huge chunks of their Internet bandwidth, and the music industry condemned it as piracy of the most blatant sort: "STEALING," as one music lawyer described it, "in big letters." Ironic foes such as Prince and the rock band Metallica joined the labels in pursuit of these new pirates, while prophets predicted the death of the recorded music industry. "A revolution has occurred in the way music is distributed," wrote one observer, "and the big record companies are in a state of panic."

(Spar 2001:327–329) Additional information about this excerpt can be found on the Online Learning Center at www.mhhe.com/schaefer7. ●

> *It shouldn't have been such a big deal, really: one artist, a handful of songs, and a funky distribution method that probably reached several thousand fans. But in the music business this was very big news.*

In this selection from *Ruling the Waves: Cycles of Discovery, Chaos, and Wealth from the Compass to the Internet,* political scientist Debora L. Spar (2001) describes the economic repercussions of a recent change in the way popular music is distributed. To students, the advent of Napster meant that suddenly free music was available to them over the Internet. But to recording artists and record companies, Napster was a revolutionary new technology with the potential to shift the balance of power from the corporate giants that produced popular music to the artists who created and performed it. The global distribution of digitized music via the Internet, then, changed both the way people behaved—how they selected, obtained, and listened to music—and the cultural institution that is the music business.

The invention of the personal computer and its worldwide integration into people's day-to-day lives is another example of the social change that often follows the introduction of a new technology. **Social change** has been defined as significant alteration over time in behavior patterns and culture (W. Moore 1967). But what constitutes a "significant" alteration? Certainly the dramatic rise in formal education documented in Chapter 13 represents a change that has had profound social consequences. Other social changes that have had long-term and important consequences include the emergence of slavery as a system of stratification (see Chapter 8), the industrial revolution (Chapters 5 and 15), the increased participation of women in the paid labor forces of the United States and Europe (Chapter 11), and the worldwide population explosion (Chapter 15). In many instances, the social movements covered in this chapter have played an important role in promoting social change.

How does social change happen? Is the process unpredictable, or can we make certain generalizations about it? Has globalization contributed to social change? And how has our environment been affected by social change? In this chapter we will examine the process of social change, with special emphasis on the impact of globalization and the effects on our environment. We will begin with social movements—collective efforts to bring about deliberate social change. Then we will turn to the unanticipated social change that occurs when innovations such as new technologies sweep through society. Efforts to explain long-term social change have led to the development of theories of change; we will consider the evolutionary, functionalist, and conflict approaches to change. We will see how vested interests attempt to block changes that they see as threatening. We'll see, too, that the process of globalization means that these social changes often happen on a global scale. And we'll look at what social change has done to our environment. Finally, in the Social Policy section we'll discuss a controversial effect of global social change, the creation of *transnationals*—immigrants with an allegiance to more than one nation. ●

Social Movements

Although such factors as physical environment, population, technology, and social inequality serve as sources of change, it is the *collective* effort of individuals organized in social movements that ultimately leads to change. Sociologists use the term **social movements** to refer to organized collective activities to bring about or resist fundamental change in an existing group or society (Benford 1992). Herbert Blumer (1955:19) recognized the special importance of social movements when he defined them as "collective enterprises to establish a new order of life."

In many nations, including the United States, social movements have had a dramatic impact on the course of history and the evolution of the social structure. Consider the actions of abolitionists, suffragists, civil rights workers, and activists opposed to the war in Vietnam. Members of each social movement stepped outside traditional channels for bringing about social change, yet had a noticeable influence on public policy. In Eastern Europe, equally dramatic collective efforts helped to topple Communist regimes in a largely peaceful manner, in nations that many observers had thought were "immune" to such social change (Ramet 1991).

Though social movements imply the existence of conflict, we can also analyze their activities from a functionalist perspective. Even when they are unsuccessful, social movements contribute to the formation of public opinion. Initially, people thought the ideas of Margaret Sanger and other early advocates of birth control were radical, yet contraceptives are now widely available in the United States. Moreover, functionalists view social movements as training grounds for leaders of the political establishment. Such heads of state as Cuba's Fidel Castro and South Africa's Nelson Mandela came to power after serving as leaders of revolutionary movements. Poland's Lech Walesa, Russia's Boris Yeltsin, and the Czech playwright Vaclav Havel all led protest movements against Communist rule and later became leaders of their countries' governments.

Because social movements know no borders, even nationalistic movements like those led by Castro and Walesa are deeply influenced by global events. Increasingly, social movements are taking on an international dimension from the start. Global enterprises, in particular, lend themselves to targeting through international mobilization, whether they are corporations like McDonald's or governmental bodies like the World Trade Organization. Global activism is not new, however; it began with

Social movements are not limited to local issues; globalization and the rise of the Internet have facilitated international protests. In December 2005, these South Koreans traveled to Hong Kong to protest against free trade at a meeting of the World Trade Organization.

the writing of Karl Marx, who sought to mobilize oppressed peoples in other industrialized countries. Today, activist networking is facilitated by the Internet and by relatively cheap travel costs. Participation in transnational activism is much wider now than in the past, and passions are quicker to ignite (Della Porta and Tarrow 2005; Tarrow 2005).

How and why do social movements emerge? Obviously, people are often discontented with the way things are. But what causes them to organize at a particular moment in a collective effort to effect change? Sociologists rely on two explanations for why people mobilize: the relative deprivation and resource mobilization approaches.

Relative Deprivation Approach

Those members of a society who feel most frustrated and disgruntled by social and economic conditions are not necessarily the worst off in an objective sense. Social scientists have long recognized that what is most significant is the way in which people *perceive* their situation. As Karl Marx pointed out, although the misery of the workers was important to their perception of their oppressed state, so was their position *in relation to* the capitalist ruling class (Marx and Engels [1847] 1955).

The term ***relative deprivation*** is defined as the conscious feeling of a negative discrepancy between legitimate expectations and present actualities (J. Wilson 1973). In other words, things aren't as good as you hoped they would be. Such a state may be characterized by scarcity rather than a complete lack of necessities (as we saw in the distinction between absolute and relative poverty in Chapter 8). A relatively deprived person is dissatisfied because he or she feels downtrodden relative to some

appropriate reference group. Thus, blue-collar workers who live in two-family houses on small plots of land—though hardly at the bottom of the economic ladder—may nevertheless feel deprived in comparison to corporate managers and professionals who live in lavish homes in exclusive suburbs.

In addition to the feeling of relative deprivation, two other elements must be present before discontent will be channeled into a social movement. People must feel that they have a *right* to their {p.214 goals, that they deserve better than what they have. For example, the struggle against European colonialism in Africa intensified when growing numbers of Africans decided that it was legitimate for them to have political and economic independence. At the same time, the disadvantaged group must perceive that its goals cannot be attained through conventional means. This belief may or may not be correct. Whichever is the case, the group will not mobilize into a social movement unless there is a shared perception that members can end their relative deprivation only through collective action (Morrison 1971).

Critics of this approach have noted that people don't need to feel deprived to be moved to act. In addition, this approach fails to explain why certain feelings of deprivation are transformed into social movements, whereas in other similar situations, no collective effort is made to reshape society. Consequently, in recent years, sociologists have paid increasing attention to the forces needed to bring about the emergence of social movements (Alain 1985; Finkel and Rule 1987; Orum 1989).

Resource Mobilization Approach

It takes more than desire to start a social movement. It helps to have money, political influence, access to the media, and personnel. The term ***resource mobilization*** refers to the ways in which a social movement utilizes such resources. The success of a movement for change will depend in good part on what resources it has and how effectively it mobilizes them (see also Gamson 1989; Staggenborg 1989a, 1989b).

Sociologist Anthony Oberschall (1973:199) has argued that to sustain social protest or resistance, there must be an "organizational base and continuity of leadership." As people become part of a social movement, norms develop to guide their behavior. Members of the movement may be expected to attend regular meetings of organizations, pay dues, recruit new adherents, and boycott "enemy" products or speakers. An emerging social movement may give rise to special language or new words for familiar terms. In recent years, social movements have been responsible for such new terms of self-reference as *Blacks* and

Classroom Tip See "Why Do People Join Social Movements?" (Additional Lecture Ideas).
Reel Society See Social Change in the Topic Index.
Theory The relative deprivation approach draws on the conflict perspective.
Key Person Karl Marx

Contemporary Culture About which issues do today's citizens feel strongly enough to form a social movement?
Theory Labeling theorists would be especially interested in how social movements choose new terms of self-reference.

Activists march in Washington, D.C., to protest the Supreme Court's historic *Roe v. Wade* ruling. Like most of the demonstrations held in the nation's capital, the annual pro-life event is the culmination of year-round planning and preparation. Social movements don't just happen; they require careful mobilization of resources.

African Americans (used to replace *Negroes*), *senior citizens* (used to replace *old folks*), *gays* (used to replace *homosexuals*), and *people with disabilities* (used to replace *the handicapped*).

Leadership is a central factor in the mobilization of the discontented into social movements. Often, a movement will be led by a charismatic figure, such as Dr. Martin Luther King Jr. As {p.356 Max Weber described it in 1904, *charisma* is that quality of an individual that sets him or her apart from ordinary people. Of course, charisma can fade abruptly, which helps to account for the fragility of certain social movements (A. Morris 2000).

Yet many social movements do persist over long periods because their leadership is well organized and ongoing. Ironically, as Robert Michels (1915) noted, political movements that are fighting for social change eventually take on some of the aspects of bureaucracy that they were organized to protest. Leaders tend to dominate the decision-making process without directly consulting followers. The bureaucratization of social movements is not inevitable, however. More radical movements that advocate major structural change in society and embrace mass actions tend not to be hierarchical or bureaucratic (Fitzgerald and Rodgers 2000).

Why do certain individuals join a social movement while others who are in similar situations do not? Some of them are recruited to join. Karl Marx recognized the importance of {p.190 recruitment when he called on workers to become *aware* of their oppressed status and to develop a class consciousness. Like theorists of the resource-mobilization approach, Marx held that a social movement (specifically, the revolt of the proletariat) would require leaders to sharpen the awareness of the oppressed. They would need to help workers to overcome feelings of *false*

consciousness, or attitudes that do not reflect workers' objective position, in order to organize a revolutionary movement. Similarly, one of the challenges faced by women's liberation activists of the late 1960s and early 1970s was to convince women that they were being deprived of their rights and of socially valued resources.

Gender and Social Movements

Sociologists point out that gender is an important element in understanding social movements. In our male-dominated society, women find it more difficult than men to assume leadership positions in social movement organizations. While women often serve disproportionately as volunteers in these movements, their work is not always recognized, nor are their voices as easily heard as men's. Moreover, gender bias causes the real extent of women's influence to be overlooked. Traditional examination of the sociopolitical system tends to focus on such male-dominated corridors of power as legislatures and corporate boardrooms, to the neglect of more female-dominated domains such as households, community-based groups, and faith-based networks. But efforts to influence family values, child rearing, relationships between parents and schools, and spiritual values are clearly significant to a culture and society (Ferree and Merrill 2000; Noonan 1995).

Scholars of social movements now realize that gender can affect even the way we view organized efforts to bring about or resist change. For example, an emphasis on using rationality and cold logic to achieve goals helps to obscure the importance of passion and emotion in successful social movements. It would be difficult to find any movement—from labor battles to voting

Key Person Martin Luther King Jr.
Key Person Robert Michels
Theory Marx's conflict view of false consciousness

Classroom Tip See "The Social Movement for Prostitutes' Rights" (Additional Lecture Ideas).
Classroom Tip See "Student Social Movements in Beijing" (Class Discussion Topics).

16-1 A New Social Movement in Rural India

In the mid-1980s, 5,000 striking textile workers came home from Bombay to mobilize support in their rural villages and gather food for strikers in the city. As the strike wore on, some remained in their villages and sought employment on government drought-relief projects. However, there weren't enough jobs for rural residents, much less for these new migrants from Bombay.

This experience was the origin of a new social movement in rural India. With unemployment threatening an expanded population in rural areas, activists formed what came to be called the *Shoshit, Shetkari, Kashtakari, Kamgar, Mukti Sangharsh (SSKKMS)*, which means "exploited peasants, toilers, workers liberation struggle." The initial goal of the movement was to provide drought relief for villagers, but the deeper goal was to bring more power to rural areas.

The SSKKMS was unusual compared to other social movements in India: about half its participants and many of its leaders were women. This was no accident, for the movement also sought to address gender inequities. At a meeting in 1986, Indutai Patankar—a pioneer in the rural women's movement—declared:

> We have gathered here to discuss our problems as women and a rural poor. . . . Not only do we work twice as hard as men but we also do not get equal wages, no child

care. . . . We have to organize as women with the other oppressed toilers in urban and rural areas (Desai 1996:214).

Women and men from the movement were equally involved in many forms of political activism, including such direct-action tactics as roadblocks.

In addition to addressing issues of gender stratification, the SSKKMS openly confronted the pervasive inequities associated with the *dalit*, or oppressed people from lower castes

> *The initial goal of the movement was to provide drought relief for villagers, but the deeper goal was to bring more power to rural areas.*

(previously called untouchables). Movement activists insisted that both women and landless peasants (most of whom were *dalits*) should have equal access to water once dams were completed. This is a critical issue in the lives of rural Indian women, who typically spend many hours a day in search of good drinking water.

In her analysis of the SSKKMS, sociologist Manisha Desai (1996) emphasizes that the movement does not have a single focus, but is

committed to multiple struggles for social and economic justice. Desai views the SSKKMS as an example of a new social movement because it incorporates concrete, material targets as well as broad ideological goals.

As with any social movement, there are contradictions in the SSKKMS. A middle-class leadership core generally articulates goals for the many exploited villagers in this mass movement. While in one rural area all local assemblies must be at least 30 percent female—a goal rarely achieved in the United States—rural women sometimes serve simply as fronts for the hidden agendas of their male relatives. Nevertheless, Desai's study of the SSKKMS underscores the fact that social movements in general—and new social movements in particular—are found *throughout* the world, not solely in industrialized nations.

Let's Discuss

1. Why do you think so many women participated in the SSKKMS? Describe their goals.
2. What would happen if "powerless" people in the United States formed a similar movement? Would it succeed? Why or why not?

---

rights to animal rights—in which passion was not part of the consensus-building force. Yet calls for a more serious study of the role of emotion are frequently seen as applying only to the women's movement, because emotion is traditionally thought of as being feminine (Ferree and Merrill 2000; V. Taylor 1995).

New Social Movements

Beginning in the late 1960s, European social scientists observed a change in both the composition and the targets of emerging social movements. Previously, traditional social movements had focused on economic issues, often led by labor unions or by people who shared the same occupation. However, many social movements that have become active in recent decades—including the contemporary women's movement, the peace movement, and the environmental movement—do not have the

social class roots typical of the labor protests in the United States and Europe over the past century (Tilly 1993, 2004).

The term *new social movements* refers to organized collective activities that address values and social identities, as well as improvements in the quality of life. These movements may be involved in developing collective identities. Many have complex agendas that go beyond a single issue, and even cross national boundaries. Educated, middle-class people are significantly represented in some of these new social movements, such as the women's movement and the movement for lesbian and gay rights. Box 16-1 describes a new social movement among exploited textile workers in India.

New social movements generally do not view government as their ally in the struggle for a better society. While they typically do not seek to overthrow the government, they may criticize,

Global View New social movement in rural India
Methods Observation research and existing sources were used to study the SSKKMS.
Gender About half of participants and many leaders of the SSKKMS were women.

Classroom Tip See "Social Movement Organizations" (Class Discussion Topics).

protest, or harass public officials. Researchers have found that members of new social movements show little inclination to accept established authority, even scientific or technical authority. This characteristic is especially evident in the environmental and anti–nuclear power movements, whose activists present their own experts to counter those of government or big business (Garner 1996; Polletta and Jasper 2001; A. Scott 1990).

The environmental movement is one of many new movements with a worldwide focus. In their efforts to reduce air and water pollution, curtail global warming, and protect endangered animal species, environmental activists have realized that strong regulatory measures within a single country are not sufficient. Similarly, labor union leaders and human rights advocates cannot adequately address exploitative sweatshop conditions in a developing country if a multinational corporation can simply move the factory to another country, where workers earn even less. Whereas traditional views of social movements tended to emphasize resource mobilization on a local level, new social movement theory offers a broader, global perspective on social and political activism. Table 16-1 summarizes the sociological approaches that have contributed to social movement theory. Each has added to our understanding of the development of social movements.

Use Your Sociological Imagination

www.mhhe.com/schaefer7

Try to imagine a society without any social movements. Under what conditions could such a society exist? Would you want to live in it?

Theories of Social Change

A new millennium provides an opportunity to consider *social change,* which we have defined as significant alteration over time in behavior patterns and culture. Social change can occur so slowly as to be almost undetectable to those it affects, but it can also happen with breathtaking rapidity. As Table 16-2 (page 412) shows, some changes that have occurred in U.S. society over the past century and a half have been relatively slow or slight; others have been rapid or striking in magnitude.

Explanations of social change are clearly a challenge in the diverse and complex world we inhabit today. Nevertheless, theorists from several disciplines have sought to analyze social change. In some instances, they have examined historical events to arrive at a better understanding of contemporary changes. We will review three theoretical approaches to change—evolutionary, functionalist, and conflict theory—and then take a look at resistance to change.

Evolutionary Theory

The pioneering work of Charles Darwin (1809–1882) in biological evolution contributed to 19th-century theories of social change. Darwin's approach stresses a continuing progression of successive life forms. For example, human beings came at a later stage of evolution than reptiles and represent a more complex form of life. Social theorists seeking an analogy to this biological model originated *evolutionary theory,* in which society is viewed as moving in a definite direction. Early evolutionary theorists generally agreed that society was progressing inevitably to a higher state. As might be expected, they concluded in ethnocentric fashion that their own behavior and culture were more advanced than those of earlier civilizations.

{p.9   August Comte (1798–1857), a founder of sociology, was an evolutionary theorist of change. He saw human societies as moving forward in their thinking, from mythology to the scientific method. Similarly, Émile Durkheim ([1893]1933) maintained that society progressed from simple to more complex forms of social organization.

Today, evolutionary theory influences sociologists in a variety of ways. For example, it has encouraged sociobiologists to investigate the behavioral links between humans and other animals (Maryanski 2004).

Functionalist Theory

Because functionalist sociologists focus on what *maintains* a system, not on what changes it, they might seem to offer little to the study of social change. Yet as the work of sociologist Talcott Parsons demonstrates, functionalists have made a distinctive contribution to this area of sociological investigation.

Parsons (1902–1979), a leading proponent of functionalist theory, viewed society as being in a natural state of equilibrium. {p.13 By "equilibrium," he meant that society tends toward a state of stability or balance. Parsons would view even prolonged labor strikes or civilian riots as temporary disruptions in the status quo rather than as significant alterations in social structure. Therefore, according to his *equilibrium model,* as changes occur in one part of society, adjustments must be made in other parts. If not, society's equilibrium will be threatened and strains will occur.

Reflecting the evolutionary approach, Parsons (1966) maintained that four processes of social change are inevitable. The

Table 16-1   Contributions to Social Movement Theory

Approach	Emphasis
Relative deprivation approach	Social movements are especially likely to arise when rising expectations are frustrated.
Resource mobilization approach	The success of social movements depends on which resources are available and how effectively they are used.
New social movement theory	Social movements arise when people are motivated by value issues and social identity questions.

Classroom Tip See "Steel Axes for Stone-Age Australians" (Additional Lecture Ideas).
Key Persons Charles Darwin, August Comte, Émile Durkheim
Theory Functionalist view of social change introduced
Key Person Talcott Parsons

Chapter 16

Table 16-2 The United States: A Changing Nation

Population	1850	1940	1960	2007
Total in millions	23.2	132.1	180.7	300.9
Percentage under age 15	41%	25%	31%	26%

Education	1850	1940	1960	2003
Percentage not completing high school	88%	18%	13%	15%
Percentage ages 19–24 enrolled in higher education	Under 1%	8%	40%	46%

Labor Force Participation	1850	1940	1960	2004
Men working in their 20s	94%	88%	86%	86%
Women working in their 20s	22%	39%	74%	72%

Health	1850	1940	1960	2003
Physicians per 100,000 population	176	133	150	266
Life expectancy at birth, in years	38	63	70	78

Technology	1870	1940	1960	2004
Copyrights issued	5,600	176,997	243,926	642,000
Patents issued	12,127	42,238	47,170	181,300

Family	1890	1940	1960	2003
Median age at first marriage				
Men	26	24	23	24
Women	22	22	20	22
Number of children born per family	3.25	2.7	3.65	2.0

Note: Data are comparable, although definitions vary. Definition of the United States changes between 1850 and 1940 and between 1940 and 1960. Earliest date for children born per family is 1905.
Source: Author, based on federal data collected in Bureau of the Census 2005a:9, 14, 67, 113, 144, 147, 387, 521; Kreider 2005:8; Sutch and Carter 2006:1–28/29, 391, 401–402, 440, 541, 685, 697, 709, 2–441/442, and 3–424/425, 427/428.

Think About It
Which of the social changes shown in this table surprises you the most? Which category do you think will change the most in the next 20 years?

first, *differentiation,* refers to the increasing complexity of social organization. The transition from "medicine man" to physician, nurse, and pharmacist is an illustration of differentiation in the field of health. This process is accompanied by *adaptive upgrading,* in which social institutions become more specialized in their purposes. The division of physicians into obstetricians, internists, surgeons, and so forth is an example of adaptive upgrading.

The third process Parsons identified is the *inclusion* of groups that were previously excluded because of their gender, race, ethnicity, and social class. Medical schools have practiced inclusion by admitting increasing numbers of women and African Americans. Finally, Parsons contends that societies experience *value generalization,* the development of new values that tolerate and legitimate a greater range of activities. The acceptance of preventive and alternative medicine is an example of value generalization: society has broadened its view of health care. All four processes identified by Parsons stress consensus—societal agree-

ment on the nature of social organization and values (B. Johnson 1975; Wallace and Wolf 1980).

Though Parsons's approach explicitly incorporates the evolutionary notion of continuing progress, the dominant theme in his model is stability. Society may change, but it remains stable through new forms of integration. For example, in place of the kinship ties that provided social cohesion in the past, people develop laws, judicial processes, and new values and belief systems.

Functionalists assume that social institutions would not persist unless they continued to contribute to society. This assumption leads them to conclude that drastically altering institutions will threaten societal equilibrium. Critics note that the functionalist approach virtually disregards the use of coercion by the powerful to maintain the illusion of a stable, well-integrated society (Gouldner 1960).

Conflict Theory

The functionalist perspective minimizes the importance of change. It emphasizes the persistence of social life, and sees change as a means of maintaining society's equilibrium (or balance). In contrast, conflict theorists contend that social institutions and practices persist because powerful groups have the ability to maintain the status quo. Change has crucial significance, since it is needed to correct social injustices and inequalities.

Karl Marx accepted the evolutionary argument that societies develop along a particular path. However, unlike Comte and Spencer, he did not view each successive stage as an inevitable improvement over the previous one. History, according to Marx, proceeds through a series of stages, each of which exploits a class of people. Ancient society exploited slaves; the estate system of feudalism exploited serfs; modern capitalist society exploits the working class. Ultimately, through a socialist revolution led by the proletariat, human society will move toward the final stage of development: a classless communist society, or "community of free individuals," as Marx described it in 1867 in *Das Kapital* (see Bottomore and Rubel 1956:250).

As we have seen, Marx had an important influence on the development of sociology. His thinking offered insights into such institutions as the economy, the family, religion, and government. The Marxist view of social change is appealing because it does not restrict people to a passive role in responding to inevitable cycles or changes in material culture. Rather, Marxist

{p.11

On the outskirts of Buenos Aires, Argentina, a shanty town forms a stark contrast to the gleaming skyscrapers in the wealthy downtown area. Marxists and conflict theorists see social change as a way of overcoming the kind of social inequality evident in this photograph.

points of disagreement. Indeed, Parsons spoke of new functions that result from social change, and Marx recognized the need for change so that societies could function more equitably.

Table 16-3 summarizes the differences between the three major theories of social change.

Resistance to Social Change

Efforts to promote social change are likely to meet with resistance. In the midst of rapid scientific and technological innovations, many people are frightened by the demands of an ever-changing society. Moreover, certain individuals and groups have a stake in maintaining the existing state of affairs.

Social economist Thorstein Veblen (1857–1929) coined the term *vested interests* to refer to those people or groups who will suffer in the event of social change. For example, the American Medical Association (AMA) has taken strong stands against national health insurance and the professionalization of midwifery. National health insurance could lead to limits on physicians' income, and a rise in the status of midwives could threaten the preeminent position of doctors as deliverers of babies. In general, those with a disproportionate share of society's wealth, status, and power, such as members of the American Medical Association, have a vested interest in preserving the status quo (Starr 1982; Veblen 1919).

{ p.392

theory offers a tool for those who wish to seize control of the historical process and gain their freedom from injustice. In contrast to functionalists' emphasis on stability, Marx argues that conflict is a normal and desirable aspect of social change. In fact, change must be encouraged as a means of eliminating social inequality (Lauer 1982).

One conflict theorist, Ralf Dahrendorf (1958), has noted that the contrast between the functionalist perspective's emphasis on stability and the conflict perspective's focus on change reflects the contradictory nature of society. Human societies are stable and long-lasting, yet they also experience serious conflict. Dahrendorf found that the functionalist approach and the conflict approach were ultimately compatible, despite their many

Economic and Cultural Factors

Economic factors play an important role in resistance to social change. For example, it can be expensive for manufacturers to meet high standards for the safety of products and workers, and for the protection of the environment. Conflict theorists argue that in a capitalist economic system, many firms are not willing to pay the price of meeting strict safety and environmental standards. They may resist social change by cutting corners or by pressuring the government to ease regulations.

Communities, too, protect their vested interests, often in the name of "protecting property values." The abbreviation *NIMBY* stands for "not in my backyard," a cry often heard when people protest landfills, prisons, nuclear power facilities, and even bike trails and group homes for people with developmental disabilities. The targeted community may not challenge the need for the facility, but may simply insist that it be located elsewhere. The "not in my backyard" attitude has become so common that it is almost impossible for policymakers to find acceptable locations for facilities such as hazardous waste dumps (Jasper 1997).

summingUP

Table 16-3 Sociological Perspectives on Social Change

Evolutionary	Social change moves society in a definite direction, frequently from simple to more complex.
Functionalist	Social change must contribute to society's stability. Modest adjustments must be made to accommodate social change.
Conflict	Social change can correct social injustices and inequalities.

Key Person Ralf Dahrendorf

Classroom Tip See "Resisting Social Change" (Additional Lecture Ideas).
Key Person Thorstein Veblen
Theory Conflict view of vested interests and resistance to social change
Classroom Tip See "Amish and Social Change" (Additional Lecture Ideas).
Classroom Tip See "Public Opinion and Nuclear Power" (Additional Lecture Ideas).

Like economic factors, cultural factors frequently shape resistance to change. William F. Ogburn (1922) distinguished between material and nonmaterial aspects of culture. *Material culture* includes inventions, artifacts, and technology; *nonmaterial culture* encompasses ideas, norms, communications, and so-{p.61} cial organization. Ogburn pointed out that one cannot devise methods for controlling and using new technology before the introduction of a technique. Thus, nonmaterial culture typically must respond to changes in material culture. Ogburn introduced the term **culture lag** to refer to the period of maladjustment when the nonmaterial culture is still struggling to adapt to new material conditions. One example is the Internet. Its rapid uncontrolled growth raises questions about whether to regulate it, and if so, how much.

In certain cases, changes in material culture can strain the relationships between social institutions. For example, new means of birth control have been developed in recent decades. Large families are no longer economically necessary, nor are they commonly endorsed by social norms. But certain religious faiths, among them Roman Catholicism, continue to extol large families and to disapprove methods of limiting family size, such as contraception and abortion. This issue represents a lag between aspects of material culture (technology) and nonmaterial culture (religious beliefs). Conflicts may also emerge between religion and other social institutions, such as government and the educational system, over the dissemination of birth control and family-planning information (M. Riley et al. 1994a, 1994b).

Resistance to Technology

Technological innovations are examples of changes in material {p.117} culture that often provoke resistance. The *industrial revolution,* which took place largely in England during the period 1760 to 1830, was a scientific revolution focused on the application of nonanimal sources of power to labor tasks. As this revolution proceeded, societies came to rely on new inventions that facilitated agricultural and industrial production, and on new sources of energy such as steam. In some industries, the introduction of power-driven machinery reduced the need for factory workers and made it easier for factory owners to cut wages.

Strong resistance to the industrial revolution emerged in some countries. In England, beginning in 1811, masked craft workers took extreme measures: They mounted nighttime raids on factories and destroyed some of the new machinery. The government hunted these rebels, known as **Luddites,** and ultimately banished or hung them. In a similar effort in France, angry workers threw their wooden shoes *(sabots)* into factory machinery to destroy it, giving rise to the term *sabotage.* While the resistance of the Luddites and the French workers was short-lived and unsuccessful, they have come to symbolize resistance to technology.

Are we now in the midst of a second industrial revolution, with a contemporary group of Luddites engaged in resisting? Many sociologists believe that we are living in a *postindustrial so-*{p.118} *ciety.* It is difficult to pinpoint exactly when this era began. Generally, it is viewed as having begun in the 1950s, when

for the first time the majority of workers in industrial societies became involved in services rather than in the actual manufacture of goods (D. Bell 1999; Fiala 1992).

Just as the Luddites resisted the industrial revolution, people in many countries have resisted postindustrial technological changes. The term *neo-Luddites* refers to those who are wary of technological innovations, and who question the incessant expansion of industrialization, the increasing destruction of the natural and agrarian world, and the "throw-it-away" mentality of contemporary capitalism, with its resulting pollution of the environment. Neo-Luddites insist that whatever the presumed benefits of industrial and postindustrial technology, such technology has distinctive social costs, and may represent a danger to both the future of the human species and our planet (Bauerlein 1996; Rifkin 1995; Sale 1996; Snyder 1996).

Global Social Change

We are at a truly dramatic time in history to consider global social change. Maureen Hallinan (1997), in her presidential address to the American Sociological Association, asked those present to consider just a few of the recent political events: the collapse of communism; terrorism in various parts of the world, including the United States; major regime changes and severe economic disruptions in Africa, the Middle East, and Eastern Europe; the spread of AIDS; and the computer revolution. Just a few months after her remarks came the first verification of the cloning of a complex animal, Dolly the sheep.

In this era of massive social, political, and economic change on a global scale, is it possible to predict change? Some technological changes seem obvious, but the collapse of communist governments in the former Soviet Union and Eastern Europe in the early 1990s took people by surprise. Yet prior to the Soviet collapse, sociologist Randall Collins (1986, 1995), a conflict theorist, had observed a crucial sequence of events that most observers had missed.

In seminars as far back as 1980, and in a book published in 1986, Collins had argued that Soviet expansionism had resulted in an overextension of resources, including disproportionate spending on military forces. Such an overextension will strain a regime's stability. Moreover, geopolitical theory suggests that nations in the middle of a geographic region, such as the Soviet Union, tend to fragment into smaller units over time. Collins predicted that the coincidence of social crises on several frontiers would precipitate the collapse of the Soviet Union.

And that is just what happened. In 1979, the success of the Iranian revolution had led to an upsurge of Islamic fundamentalism in nearby Afghanistan, as well as in Soviet republics with substantial Muslim populations. At the same time, resistance to Communist rule was growing both throughout Eastern Europe and within the Soviet Union itself. Collins had predicted that the rise of a dissident form of communism within the Soviet Union might facilitate the breakdown of the regime. Beginning in the late 1980s, Soviet leader Mikhail Gorbachev chose not to use military power and other types of repression to crush dissidents

Key Person William F. Ogburn
Classroom Tip Ogburn's view of the lag between change in material and nonmaterial culture was introduced in Chapter 3.
Global View Luddite movement in Europe
Contemporary Culture What might a contemporary Luddite be like? What technology would he or she resist?

Student Alert May need to review the concept of postindustrial society
Let's Discuss What are some examples of the "throw-it-away" mentality on campus or on the job?
Key Person Maureen Hallinan
Key Person Randall Collins
Global View Success of the Iranian revolution

in Eastern Europe. Instead, he offered plans for democratization and social reform of Soviet society, and seemed willing to reshape the Soviet Union into a loose federation of somewhat autonomous states. But in 1991, six republics on the western periphery declared their independence, and within months the entire Soviet Union had formally disintegrated into Russia and a number of other independent nations.

In her address, Hallinan (1997) cautioned that we need to move beyond the restrictive models of social change—the linear view of evolutionary theory and the assumptions about equilibrium in functionalist theory. She and other sociologists have looked to the "chaos theory" advanced by mathematicians to understand erratic events as a part of change. Hallinan noted that upheavals and major chaotic shifts do occur, and that sociologists must learn to predict their occurrence, as Collins did with the Soviet Union. For example, imagine the dramatic nonlinear social change that will result from major innovations in communications and biotechnology—topics we will discuss next.

In 2003 the people of Georgia, a former republic of the Soviet Union, took to the streets in protest against a rigged election. The next year they forced the peaceful overthrow of their government in a political upheaval dubbed the Velvet Revolution. The crisis further distanced the country from domination by neighboring Russia—a trend that began a decade earlier with Georgia's break from the Soviet Union.

Privacy and Censorship in a Global Village

As we saw in the chapter-opening excerpt, new technologies like the personal computer and the Internet have brought about sweeping social change. While much of that change has been beneficial, there have been some negative effects. Recent advances in computer technology have made it increasingly easy for business firms, government agencies, and even criminals to retrieve and store information about everything from our buying habits to our Web-surfing patterns. In public places, at work, and on the Internet, surveillance devices now track our every move, be it a keystroke or an ATM withdrawal. At the same time that these innovations have increased others' power to monitor our behavior, they have raised fears that they might be misused for criminal or undemocratic purposes. In short, new technologies threaten not just our privacy, but our freedom from crime and censorship (Rheingold 2003).

In recent years, concern about the criminal misuse of personal information has been underscored by the accidental loss of some huge databases. In 2006, for example, the theft of a laptop computer from the home of an employee of the Veterans' Administrator compromised the names, social security numbers, and dates of birth of up to 26.5 million veterans. Unfortunately, technologies that facilitate the sharing of information have also created new types of crime.

From a sociological point of view, the complex issues of privacy and censorship can be considered illustrations of culture lag. As usual, the material culture (technology) is changing faster than the nonmaterial culture (norms for controlling the use of technology). Too often, the result is an anything-goes approach to the use of new technologies.

Legislation regarding the surveillance of electronic communications has not always upheld citizens' right to privacy. In 1986, the federal government passed the Electronic Communications Privacy Act, which outlawed the surveillance of telephone calls except with the permission of both the U.S. attorney general and a federal judge. Telegrams, faxes, and e-mail did not receive the same degree of protection, however. In 2001, one month after the terrorist attacks of September 11, Congress passed the USA PATRIOT Act, which relaxed existing legal checks on surveillance by law enforcement officers. Federal agencies are now freer to gather data electronically, including credit card receipts and banking records (Eckenwiler 1995).

Sociologists' views on the use and abuse of new technologies differ depending on their theoretical perspective. Functionalists take a generally positive view of the Internet, pointing to its manifest function of facilitating communication. From their perspective, the Internet performs the latent function of empowering those with few resources—from hate groups to special interest organizations—to communicate with the masses. Conflict theorists, in contrast, stress the danger that the most powerful groups in a society will use technology to violate the privacy of the less powerful. Indeed, officials in the People's Republic of China have attempted to censor online discussion groups and

Web postings that are critical of the government (see Chapter 14). The same abuses can occur in the United States, civil liberties advocates remind us, if citizens are not vigilant in protecting their right to privacy (Magnier 2004).

If anything, however, people seem to be less vigilant today about maintaining their privacy than they were before the information age. Young people who have grown up browsing the Internet seem to accept the existence of the "cookies" and "spyware" they may pick up while surfing. They have become accustomed to adult surveillance of their conversation in electronic chat rooms. Many see no risk in providing personal information about themselves to the strangers they meet online. Little wonder that college professors find their students do not appreciate the political significance of their right to privacy (Turkle 2004).

Biotechnology and the Gene Pool

Another field in which technological advances have spurred global social change is biotechnology. Sex selection of fetuses, genetically engineered organisms, cloning of sheep and cows— these have been among the significant yet controversial scientific advances in the field of biotechnology in recent years. George {p.122 Ritzer's concept of McDonaldization applies to the entire area of biotechnology. Just as the fast-food concept has permeated society, no phase of life now seems exempt from therapeutic or medical intervention. In fact, sociologists view many aspects of biotechnology as an extension of the recent trend toward the medicalization of society, discussed in Chapter 15. Through genetic manipulation, the medical profession is expanding its turf still further (Clarke et al. 2003).

Today's biotechnology holds itself out as totally beneficial to human beings, but it is in constant need of monitoring. As we will see, biotechnological advances have raised many difficult ethical and political questions, among them the desirability of tinkering with the gene pool, which could alter our environment in unexpected and unwanted ways (D. Weinstein and Weinstein 1999).

One startling biotechnological advance is the possibility of altering human behavior through genetic engineering. Fish and plant genes have already been mixed to create frost-resistant potato and tomato crops. More recently, human genes have been implanted in pigs to provide humanlike kidneys for organ transplants.

One of the latest developments in genetic engineering is gene therapy. Geneticists working with mouse fetuses have managed to disable genes that carry an undesirable trait and replace them with genes carrying a desirable trait. Such advances raise staggering possibilities for altering animal and human life forms. Still, gene therapy remains highly experimental, and must be considered a long, long shot (Kolata 1999).

The debate on genetic engineering escalated in 1997 when scientists in Scotland announced that they had cloned a sheep. After many unsuccessful attempts, they had finally been able to replace the genetic material of a sheep's egg with DNA from an adult sheep, creating a lamb that was a clone of the adult. The very next year, Japanese researchers successfully cloned cows. These developments raised the possibility that in the near future, scientists may be able to clone human beings.

William F. Ogburn probably could not have anticipated such scientific developments when he wrote of culture lag 70 years earlier. However, the successful cloning of sheep illustrates again how quickly material culture can change, and how nonmaterial culture moves more slowly in absorbing such changes.

While cloning grabs the headlines, controversy has been growing concerning genetically modified (GM) food. This issue arose in Europe but has since spread to other parts of the world, including the United States. The idea behind the technology is to increase food production and make agriculture more economical. But critics use the term *Frankenfood* (as in "Frankenstein") to refer to everything from breakfast cereals made from genetically engineered grains to "fresh" GM tomatoes. Members of the antibiotech movement object to tampering with nature, and are

In Spain, Greenpeace members protest the European Union's proposed approval of a strain of genetically modified corn. The insect-resistant sweet corn produces a substance that is toxic to corn borers and earworms but not to humans. Nevertheless, transnational activists have raised questions about its potential health effects. Their vocal opposition has disrupted international trade and caused friction between the United States and Europe.

Student Alert Review the seemingly simple but genuinely complex issue of "nature versus nurture."
Classroom Tip See "Scientific Change" in Topics and Sources for Student Research.

Global View Genetically modified food in Europe

16-2 The Human Genome Project

Together with geneticists, pathologists, and microbiologists, sociologist Troy Duster of New York University has been grappling with the ethical, legal, and social issues raised by the Human Genome Project since 1989. An original member of the oversight committee appointed to deal with such matters, he does not expect that his work will be done anytime in the near future.

Duster, who is also past president of the American Sociological Association, has been asked to explain why his committee is taking so long to conclude its work. In reply, he lists the many issues raised by the massive project. First, he is concerned that the medical breakthroughs made possible by the project will not benefit all people equally. He notes that biotechnology firms have used the project's data to develop a test for cystic fibrosis in White Americans, but not for the same syndrome in Zuni Indians. Biotechnology companies are profit-making ventures, not humanitarian organizations. So while the scientists involved in the Human Genome Project hope to map the genes of all the world's peoples, not everyone may benefit from the project in practical ways.

Duster's committee has also struggled with the question of informed consent—making sure that everyone who donates genes to the project will do so voluntarily, after being informed of the risks and benefits. In Western societies, scientists commonly obtain such consent from the individuals who participate in their research. But according to Duster, many non-Western societies do not acknowledge the individual's right to make such decisions. Instead, a leader makes the decision for the group as a whole. "When Western-trained researchers descend upon a village," Duster asks, "who should they turn to for consent?" (Duster 2002:69). And what if the answer is no?

Race, too, is a knotty problem for Duster's committee. DNA analysis shows conclusively that there is no genetic difference between the races. Given that analysis, many geneticists do not want to invest more time and effort in research on racial differences. As a sociologist, Duster knows that race is socially constructed. Yet he also knows that for millions of people around the world, race has a significant effect on their health and well-being. More to the point, he knows that a group's economic and political power helps to determine which diseases scientists study.

On the other hand, Duster worries that some researchers may be putting too much emphasis on biological differences between the races. He notes that those racial groups who are socially disadvantaged suffer much higher

> *A group's economic and political power helps to determine which diseases scientists study.*

rates of disease than advantaged groups. In the United States, for example, African American men suffer from prostate cancer at twice the rate of White men. Yet in the Caribbean and sub-Saharan Africa, Black men have a much lower rate of prostate cancer than American men, White or Black. How can genes explain this disparity? Duster suspects that the explanation for African Americans' higher disease rates lies not in their genes, but in their stressful environment, where they are routinely subjected to racial profiling and other forms of institutional discrimination. "We may be 99.9 percent alike at the level of DNA," Duster writes, "but if that were the end of the story,

Troy Duster, a sociologist at NYU, also teaches and directs the American Cultures Center at the University of California, Berkeley.

we could all pack up and go home" (Duster 2002:70).

Let's Discuss

1. What other criteria besides the power of a racial or ethnic group could be used to determine how much research is done on diseases that affect the group?
2. What should a researcher do if a tribal leader refuses to allow members of the tribe to participate in a research project?

Sources: Dreifus 2005; Duster 2002

---

concerned about the possible health effects of GM food. Supporters of genetically modified food include not just biotech companies, but those who see the technology as a way to help feed the burgeoning populations of Africa and Asia (Golden 1999; Schurman 2004).

Another form of biotechnology with a potentially wide-ranging impact is the Human Genome Project. This effort involves teams of scientists around the world in sequencing and mapping all 30,000 to 40,000 human genes in existence, collectively known as the *human genome*. Supporters say that the resulting knowledge could revolutionize doctors' ability to treat and even prevent disease. But sociologists worry about the ethical implications of such research. Box 16-2 provides an overview of the many issues the project has raised.

Social Change and the Environment

Sociologists and others may debate the potential impact of biotechnology, but technological change has already had serious environmental consequences. We can see signs of despoliation almost everywhere: Our air, our water, and our land are being polluted, whether we live in St. Louis, Mexico City, or Lagos, Nigeria. In North America, each summer brings power failures or brownouts to sweltering cities as the voracious consumption of electricity exceeds the supply.

In recent years, public attention has turned to global warming, manifested in the shrinking of the polar ice caps and the increasing ferociousness of tropical storms as they cross warmer-than-normal ocean waters. Human activities have contributed to the documented warming of the planet over the last half century, through the altered chemical composition of the atmosphere and the buildup of greenhouse gases such as carbon dioxide, methane, and nitrous oxide. While environmental problems may be easy to identify scientifically, however, devising socially and politically acceptable solutions is much more difficult. In the following sections we will survey some identifiable environmental problems and see what sociologists have to say about them (Easterbrook 2006; Gore 2006).

THE FOUR TRUCK DRIVERS OF THE APOCALYPSE

Pollution, overdevelopment, warfare, and consumerism all pose a challenge to our environment.

Environmental Problems: An Overview

In recent decades, the world has witnessed serious environmental disasters. In 1986, for example, a series of explosions set off a catastrophic nuclear reactor accident at Chernobyl, a part of Ukraine (in what was then the Soviet Union). Thousands of people died, and some 400,000 residents had to be evacuated. For 19 miles in any direction, the area became uninhabitable. High levels of radiation were found as far as 30 miles from the reactor site, and radioactivity levels climbed well above normal as far away as Sweden and Japan. According to one estimate, the Chernobyl accident and the resulting nuclear fallout may ultimately result in 100,000 excess cases of cancer worldwide (Chernobyl Forum 2005).

Much more common than nuclear power plant disasters are oil spills in the ocean or coastal waters, typically from supertankers. The heavier types of crude or fuel oil, such as that carried by the *Exxon Valdez* in 1989, can contaminate the shoreline for years following a spill, even after a massive cleanup. Globally, oil spills occur regularly. In 2002 the oil tanker *Prestige* spilled twice as much fuel as the *Valdez,* greatly damaging coastal areas in Spain and France. We will discuss the impact of such disasters on water quality shortly (ITOPF 2006).

While reactor accidents, oil spills, and other environmental disasters understandably grab the headlines, it is the silent, day-to-day deterioration of the environment that ultimately poses a devastating threat to humanity. Examining all our environmental problems in detail would be impossible, but three broad areas of concern stand out: air pollution, water pollution, and the impact of globalization.

Air Pollution   Worldwide, more than 1 billion people are exposed to potentially health-damaging levels of air pollution. Unfortunately, in cities around the world, residents have come to accept smog and polluted air as normal. Urban air pollution is caused primarily by emissions from automobiles and secondarily by emissions from electric power plants and heavy industries. Smog not only limits visibility; it can lead to health problems as uncomfortable as eye irritation and as deadly as lung cancer. Such problems are especially severe in developing countries. The World Health Organization estimates that up to 700,000 premature deaths *per year* could be prevented if pollutants were brought down to safer levels (Carty 1999; World Resources Institute 1998).

People are capable of changing their behavior, but they are also unwilling to make such changes permanent. During the 1984 Olympics in Los Angeles, residents were asked to carpool and stagger their work hours to relieve traffic congestion and improve the quality of the air athletes would breathe. These changes resulted in a remarkable 12 percent drop in ozone levels. But when the Olympians left, people reverted to their normal behavior and the ozone levels climbed back up. Similarly, in the 2008 Olympics, China is prepared to take drastic action to ensure that Beijing's high levels of air pollution do not mar the games. For a two-month period, all construction work in the city will cease, polluting factories and power plants will close down, and roads will be swept and sprayed with water several times a day. But this temporary solution will hardly solve China's ongoing problem (McCright and Dunlap 2003; Nussbaum 1998; ABC Radio Australia 2006).

Global View Environmental issues are a worldwide concern.
Web Resource Students can link to the Web site of the Earthwatch Institute through the Internet Connection in the student center of the Online Learning Center (www.mhhe.com/schaefer7).
Classroom Tip See "Class Project" (Class Discussion Topics).

Reel Society See Environmental Problems in the Topic Index.

Water Pollution Throughout the United States, dumping of waste materials by industries and local governments has polluted streams, rivers, and lakes. Consequently, many bodies of water have become unsafe for drinking, fishing, and swimming. Around the world, pollution of the oceans is an issue of growing concern. Such pollution results regularly from waste dumping, and is made worse by fuel leaks from shipping and occasional oil spills. When the oil tanker *Exxon Valdez* ran aground in Prince William Sound, Alaska, in 1989, its cargo of 11 million gallons of crude oil spilled into the sound and washed onto the shore, contaminating 1,285 miles of shoreline. All together, about 11,000 { p.42 } people joined in a massive cleanup effort that cost over $2 billion. As we saw in Chapter 2, ExxonMobil continues to fight court-ordered settlements that would partially cover the cost of the cleanup.

Less dramatic than large-scale accidents or disasters, but more common in many parts of the world, are problems with the basic water supply. Worldwide, over 1 billion people lack safe and adequate drinking water, and 2.4 billion have no acceptable means of sanitation—a problem that further threatens the quality of water supplies. The health costs of unsafe water are enormous (United Nations 2003).

The Impact of Globalization Globalization can be both good and bad for the environment. On the negative side, it can create a race to the bottom, as polluting companies relocate to countries with less stringent environmental standards. Similarly, globalization allows multinationals to reap the resources of developing countries for short-term profit. From Mexico to China, the industrialization that often accompanies globalization has increased pollution of all types.

Yet globalization can have a positive impact, as well. As barriers to the international movement of goods, services, and people fall, multinational corporations have an incentive to carefully consider the cost of natural resources. Overusing or wasting resources makes little sense, especially when they are in danger of depletion (Kwong 2005).

Globalization has also encouraged efforts at multilateral environmental agreements. The Kyoto Protocol is intended to reduce global emissions of heat-trapped gases, which can contribute to global warming and climate change. To date, 141 countries have signed the accord. But the United States, which produces 24 percent of the world's carbon dioxide, has refused to sign, arguing that doing so would place the nation at a disadvantage in the global marketplace. Thirty-five other developed nations have agreed to a 5 percent reduction in the greenhouse

In a makeshift recycling center, a Chinese woman uses a hammer to open an old cathode ray tube. She wants the copper that is inside, but in the process she will release several pounds of lead into the soil and groundwater. Scientists have found alarmingly high levels of toxic heavy metals in the rivers that flow by such rural recycling operations.

Vacation in an unspoiled paradise! Increasingly, people from developed countries are turning to ecotourism as an environmentally friendly way to see the world. The new trend bridges the interests of environmentalists and businesspeople, especially in developing countries. These birdwatchers are vacationing in Belize.

gases they produce—a goal they must reach by 2012 (Landler 2005).

What are the basic causes of our growing environmental problems? Some observers, such as Paul Ehrlich and Anne Ehrlich, see the pressure of world population growth as the central factor in environmental deterioration. They argue that population control is essential in preventing widespread starvation and environmental decay. Barry Commoner, a biologist, counters that the primary cause of environmental ills is the increasing use of technological innovations that are destructive to the world's environment—among them plastics, detergents, synthetic fibers, pesticides, herbicides, and chemical fertilizers. Conflict theorists see the despoliation of the environment through the lens of world systems analysis (Commoner 1971, 1990; Ehrlich 1968; Ehrlich and Ehrlich 1990; Ehrlich and Ellison 2002).

Conflict View of Environmental Issues

In Chapter 9 we drew on world systems analysis to show how a growing share of the human and natural resources of developing countries is being redistributed to the core industrialized nations. This process only intensifies the destruction of natural resources in poorer regions of the world. From a conflict perspective, less affluent nations are being forced to exploit their mineral deposits, forests, and fisheries in order to meet their debt obligations. The poor turn to the only means of survival available to them: They plow mountain slopes, burn plots in tropical forests, and overgraze grasslands (Livernash and Rodenburg 1998).

Brazil exemplifies this interplay between economic troubles and environmental destruction. Each year more than 5.7 million acres of forest are cleared for crops and livestock. The elimination of the rain forest affects worldwide weather patterns, heightening the gradual warming of the earth. These socioeconomic patterns, with their harmful environmental consequences, are evident not only in Latin America but in many regions of Africa and Asia (*National Geographic* 2002).

Conflict theorists are well aware of the environmental implications of land use policies in the Third World, but they contend that focusing on the developing countries is ethnocentric. Who, they ask, is more to blame for environmental deterioration: the poverty-stricken and "food-hungry" populations of the world or the "energy-hungry" industrialized nations? These theorists point out that the industrialized nations of North America and Europe account for only 12 percent of the world's population but are responsible for 60 percent of worldwide consumption. The money their residents spend on ocean cruises each year could provide clean drinking water for everyone on the planet. Ice cream expenditures in Europe alone could be used to immunize every child in the world. Thus, conflict theorists charge, the most serious threat to the environment comes from the global consumer class (G. Gardner et al. 2004).

Allan Schnaiberg (1994) further refines this analysis by criticizing the focus on affluent consumers as the cause of environ-

mental troubles. In his view, a capitalist system creates a "treadmill of production" because of its inherent need to build ever-expanding profits. This treadmill necessitates creating an increasing demand for products, obtaining natural resources at minimal cost, and manufacturing products as quickly and cheaply as possible—no matter what the long-term environmental consequences.

Environmental Justice

In a stretch of land along the lower Mississippi River in Louisiana, one factory after another pours its industrial waste into the water, raising pollution counts to dangerous levels. It is no accident that the people who live nearby are African American. Poor and lacking in political clout, the communities that border these industrial sites are no match for the powerful business interests that built them (Bullard 1993).

Observations like this one have given rise to *environmental justice,* a legal strategy based on claims that racial minorities are subjected disproportionately to environmental hazards. The approach has had some success. In 1998 a chemical company called Shintech dropped plans to build a plastics plant in a poor black community in Mississippi after opponents filed a civil rights complaint with the Environmental Protection Agency (EPA). EPA administrator Carol Browner praised the company's decision: "The principles applied to achieve this solution should be incorporated into any blueprint for dealing with environmental justice issues in communities across the nation" (Associated Press 1998:18).

Following reports from the EPA and other organizations documenting the discriminatory location of hazardous waste sites, President Bill Clinton issued an executive order in 1994 that requires all federal agencies to ensure that low-income and minority communities have access to better information about their environment, and an opportunity to participate in shaping government policies that affect their health. Initial efforts to implement the policy have aroused widespread opposition because of the delays it imposes in establishing new industrial sites. Some observers question the wisdom of an order that slows economic development in areas that are in dire need of employment opportunities. Others point out that such businesses employ few unskilled or less skilled workers, and only make the environment less livable (Pellow 2002).

Meanwhile, the poor and oppressed continue to bear the brunt of environmental pollution. In the 1990s, the federal government, unable to find a disposal site for spent nuclear fuel, turned to tribal reservations. Agents eventually persuaded a tiny band of Goshute Indians in Skull Valley, Utah, to accept more than 44,000 barrels of the hot, highly radioactive substance, which will remain dangerous for an estimated 10,000 years. The government is presently attempting to implement the plan despite opposition from surrounding towns and cities, whose residents object to the movement of the material through their communities. This is not the first time the nation has prevailed on the impoverished tribe to accept environmentally

---

Key Persons Paul Ehrlich, Anne Ehrlich, Barry Commoner
Student Alert Present pollution statistics for industrializing countries.
Theory Conflict view of environmental issues introduced
Key Person Allan Schnaiberg
Theory Schnaiberg's conflict perspective on environmental issues

Race/Ethnicity Challenges to "environmental justice"
Classroom Tip See "Environmental Racism in Albany" (Additional Lecture Ideas).

objectionable installations. The military's nerve gas storage facility resides on or near the reservation, along with the Intermountain Power Project, which generates coal-fired electrical power for consumers in California (Eureka County 2006; Skull Valley Band Goshute 2005).

Use Your Sociological Imagination
www.mhhe.com/schaefer7

Your community has been designated as a site for burial of toxic waste. How will you react? Will you organize a protest? Or will you make sure the authorities carry the project out safely? How can such sites be chosen fairly?

[social|Policy]
and Globalization

TRANSNATIONALS

The Issue

Imagine that as you leave your college commencement ceremony, diploma in hand, a stranger approaches and offers you a job. If you are willing to relocate to a foreign, non-English-speaking country, he says, you can earn $300,000 a year for the kind of work you have always thought of as menial labor. You can do the job for one year or several years. The only catch is that you must enter the country illegally, and remain there until you are ready to give up your job. The opportunity he is describing isn't new to you. In fact, you have many friends and relatives who have done exactly that.

The lure of fast, easy money that is described in this story may seem incredible to you, but it is real for many people in developing nations. Incomes in developing nations are so low that the wages an immigrant can earn in the United States, even at the most menial job, seem like a fortune. Back in the home country, their purchasing power is the equivalent of a $300,000 income in the United States—a huge economic incentive to immigrate. But while the opportunity to become rich may encourage even highly skilled foreigners to immigrate, these migrant workers—even those with legal status—enjoy far fewer rights than native-born workers.

The Setting

Figure 16-1 (page 422) shows the worldwide movement of workers with and without legal authorization to immigrate. Several areas, such as the European Union, have instituted international agreements that provide for the free movement of laborers. But in most other parts of the world, immigration restrictions give foreign workers only temporary status. Despite such legal restrictions, the labor market has become an increasingly global one. Just as globalization has integrated government policies, cultures, social movements, and financial markets, it has unified what once were discrete national labor markets.

Globalization has changed the immigrant experience as well as the labor market. In generations past, immigrants read foreign-language newspapers to keep in touch with events in their home countries. Today, the Internet gives them immediate access to their countries and kinfolk. In this global framework, immigrants are less likely than they were in the past to think of themselves as residents of just one country. *Transnationals* are immigrants who sustain multiple social relationships that link their societies of origin with their societies of settlement.

Immigrants from the Dominican Republic, for example, identify with the United States, but at the same time they maintain close ties to their Caribbean homeland, returning periodically for extended stays with relatives and friends. While there, they deliver *remittances (migradollars)* to needy family members. Dominican villages reflect these close ties, both in billboards that promote special long-distance service to the United States and in the presence of expensive household appliances bought with migradollars. In poor countries, the volume of transnational remittances—perhaps $80 billion worldwide—is easily the most reliable source of foreign income, far outstripping the value of foreign aid programs (Fox 2005; Kapur and McHale 2003).

Sociological Insights

Sociologists did not begin to investigate transnationalism until the early 1990s. They are finding that new technologies which facilitate international travel and communications are accelerating the transnational movement of workers. Two other forces tend to promote transnationalism: Nationalism encourages émigrés to express continued allegiance to their homelands, and multiculturalism has legitimized the expression of those loyalties in receiving nations. Finally, international human rights organizations have joined faith-based groups in stressing universal human rights, regardless of a person's citizenship status. Whether these diverse influences will further the emergence of a global workforce composed of global citizens or simply fuel nationalistic fervor remains to be seen (Waldinger and Fitzgerald 2004).

As with other issues, sociologists differ in their opinion of transnationals, depending on their theoretical perspective.

Global View World immigration
Let's Discuss What legal rights do migrant workers lack?

Contemporary Culture Computers replacing newspapers as way for immigrants to keep in touch

Labor Migration

MAPPING LIFE

WORLDWIDE www.mhhe.com/schaefer7

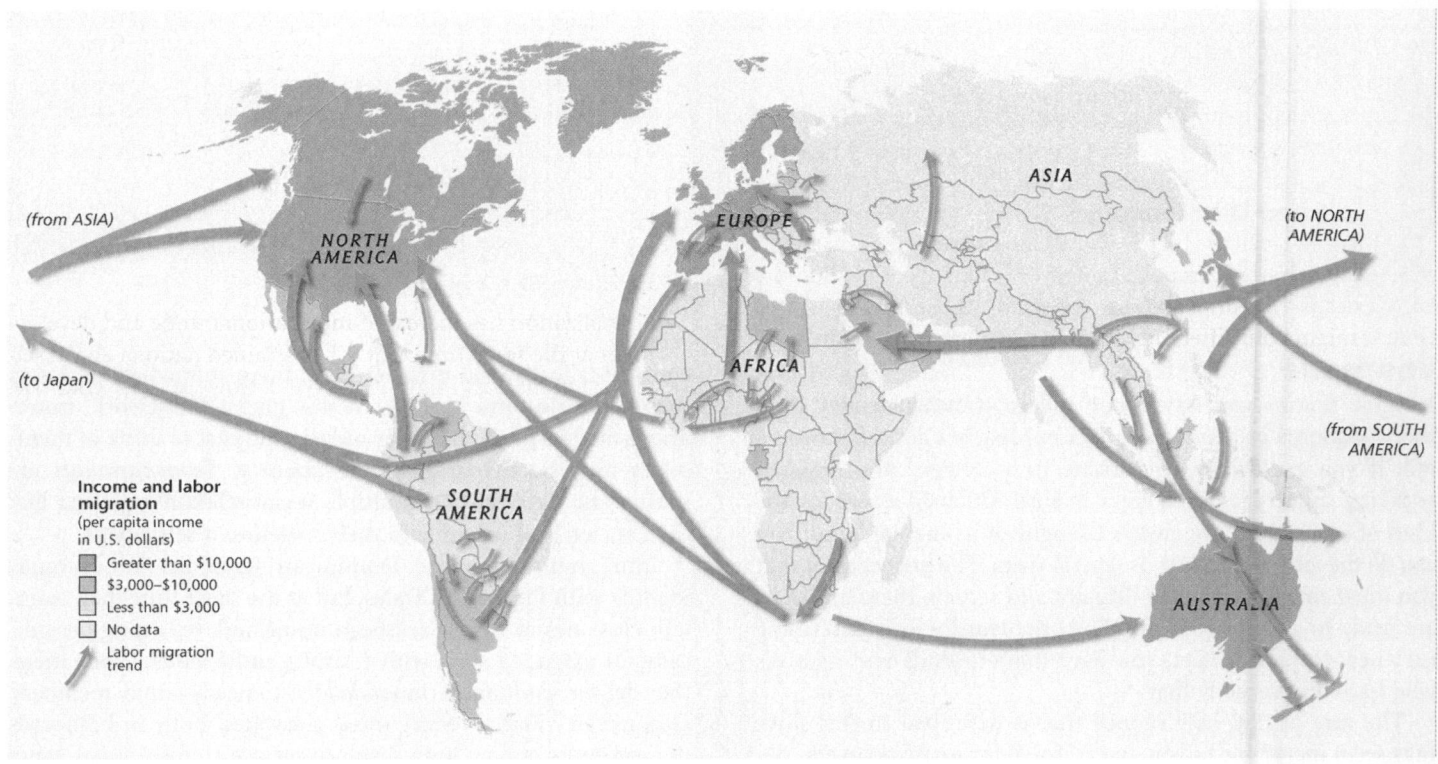

Income and labor migration
(per capita income in U.S. dollars)

- Greater than $10,000
- $3,000–$10,000
- Less than $3,000
- No data
- Labor migration trend

Source: National Geographic 2005:16.

Functionalists see the free flow of immigrants, even when it is legally restricted, as one way for economies to maximize their use of human labor. Given the law of supply and demand, they note, countries with too few workers will inevitably attract laborers, while those with too many will become unattractive to residents.

Conflict theorists charge that globalization and international migration have increased the economic gulf between developed and developing nations. Today, residents of North America, Europe, and Japan consume 32 times more resources than the billions of people who live in developing countries. Through tourism and the global reach of the mass media, people in the poorer countries have become aware of the affluent lifestyle common in developed nations—and of course, many of them now aspire to it (Diamond 2003).

Sociologists who follow world systems analysis (see Chapter 9) suggest that the global flow of people, not just goods and resources, should be factored into the relationship between core and periphery societies. The global economic system, with its sharp contrast between have and have-not nations, is responsible for the creation of the informal social networks that link those seeking a better life with those who already enjoy prosperity.

Interactionists are interested in the day-to-day relationships transnationals have with the people around them, from those of their country of origin to those of the host country and fellow workers from other countries. They are particularly concerned with how transnationals see their own identities and those of their children. In effect, transnationals negotiate their identities, depending on which social network they belong to at the moment. Some sociologists note that while being a transnational can be exhilarating, it can also isolate a person, even in a city of millions. Others worry that transnationals may become so cosmopolitan that they will lose touch with their national identities (Calhoun 2003; Plüss 2005; Rajan and Sharma 2006).

Policy Initiatives

The International Labor Organization has complained that the intense economic competition created by globalization is unraveling the social welfare systems of many countries. The United States is now only 25th on the Economic Security Index (Sweden is the most secure country). In general, Western European na-

Theory Functionalist and conflict views of transnationals
Student Alert Impact of globalization on emergence of transnationals

Theory Interactionist view introduced
Policy Pointer Policy efforts by the International Labor Organization

tions are among the most secure; Eastern European countries that once belonged to the Soviet Union are among the least secure. To alleviate the pressure created by a failing social service system, workers will often move to countries that offer both good jobs and good social services—a trend that strains receiving nations' safety nets. In 2005, voters in both France and the Netherlands rejected the proposed European Union constitution, in part because of concerns about a potential influx of workers from developing countries like Turkey (Standing 2004).

Another unresolved transnational issue is voter eligibility. Not all nations allow dual citizenship; even those countries that do may not allow absent nationals to vote. The United States and Great Britain are rather liberal in this regard, permitting dual citizenship and allowing émigrés to continue to vote. Mexico, in contrast, has been reluctant to allow citizens who have emigrated to vote. Mexican politicians worry that the large number of Mexicans who live abroad (especially those in the United States) might vote differently from local voters, causing different outcomes (Sellers 2004).

Finally, the controversial issue of illegal immigration has yet to be settled, perhaps because of culture lag. That is, both public attitudes and government policies (nonmaterial culture) have not kept pace, much less adjusted to, the increasing ease of migration around the globe (material culture). Though globalization has created a global labor market—one that many countries depend on, legal or illegal—the general public's attitude toward illegal immigrants remains hostile, especially in the United States.

Let's Discuss

1. Suppose you live in an impoverished developing country and have the opportunity to earn a much higher income by immigrating to the United States. Will you do it, even if it means entering the country illegally and working long hours doing menial labor? If so, how would you justify your decision to those who condemn illegal immigration?

2. The U.S. economy depends on the cheap labor immigrants provide. Should immigrants receive the same social services that U.S. citizens receive? What about their children who are born in the United States (and therefore are U.S. citizens)? Explain your reasoning.

3. Globalization has increased international trade and development at the same time that it has strained nations' social service systems, as migrant workers flow toward countries offering the most extensive social protection. On balance, do you think its overall effect has been beneficial or harmful? What might be done to alleviate the harmful effects of globalization?

GettingINVOLVED

To get involved in the debate over transnationals, visit this text's Online Learning Center, which offers links to relevant Web sites. Check out the Social Policy section in the Online Learning Center as well; it provides survey data on U.S. public opinion regarding this issue.

www.mhhe.com/schaefer7

{ MASTERING THIS CHAPTER }

Summary

Social change is significant alteration over time in behavior patterns and culture, including norms and values. Sometimes social change is promoted by **social movements,** but more often it is the unintended effect of technological progress. Recent changes in our environment illustrate both the effects of technology and the impact of social movements. This chapter examines social movements, sociological theories of social change and resistance to change, global social change, and the environment.

1. **Social movements** are more structured than other forms of collective behavior and persist over longer periods.

2. A group will not mobilize into a social movement without a shared perception that its **relative deprivation** can be ended only through collective action.

3. The success of a social movement depends in good part on effective **resource mobilization.**

4. **New social movements** tend to focus on more than just economic issues, and often cross national boundaries.

5. Early advocates of the **evolutionary theory** of social change believed that society was progressing inevitably toward a higher state.

6. Talcott Parsons, a leading advocate of functionalist theory, viewed society as being in a natural state of equilibrium or balance.

7. Conflict theorists see change as having crucial significance, since it is needed to correct social injustices and inequalities.

8. In general, those with a disproportionate share of society's wealth, status, and power have a **vested interest** in preserving the status quo, and will resist change.

Let's Discuss Should dual citizens be allowed to vote?

9. The period of maladjustment when a nonmaterial culture is still struggling to adapt to new material conditions is known as *culture lag.*

10. We are living in a time of sweeping social, political, and economic change—change that occurs not just on a local or national basis, but on a global scale.

11. Computer technology has made it increasingly easy for any individual, business firm, or government agency to retrieve more and more information about any of us, thereby infringing on our privacy.

12. Advances in biotechnology have raised difficult ethical questions about genetic engineering and the sex selection of fetuses.

13. Air pollution, water pollution, and the impact of globalization are three major areas of environmental concern. Though globalization can contribute to environmental woes, it can also have beneficial effects.

14. Conflict theorists charge that the most serious threat to the environment comes from Western industrialized nations.

15. *Environmental justice* addresses the disproportionate subjection of minorities to environmental hazards.

16. Globalization has increased the international migration of laborers, producing a new kind of immigrant. *Transnationals* are immigrants who sustain multiple social relationships that link their societies of origin with their societies of settlement.

Critical Thinking Questions

1. Select one social movement that is currently working for change in the United States. Analyze that movement, drawing on the concepts of relative deprivation, resource mobilization, and false consciousness.

2. In the last few years we have witnessed phenomenal growth in the use of cellular phones around the world. Analyze this form of material culture in terms of culture lag. Consider usage, government regulation, and privacy issues.

3. Imagine that you have been asked to study the issue of air pollution in the largest city in your state. How might you draw on surveys, observation research, experiments, and existing sources to study the issue?

Key Terms

Culture lag A period of maladjustment when the nonmaterial culture is still struggling to adapt to new material conditions. (page 414)

Environmental justice A legal strategy based on claims that racial minorities are subjected disproportionately to environmental hazards. (420)

Equilibrium model The functionalist view that society tends toward a state of stability or balance. (410)

Evolutionary theory A theory of social change that holds that society is moving in a definite direction. (411)

False consciousness A term used by Karl Marx to describe an attitude held by members of a class that does not accurately reflect their objective position. (409)

Luddites Rebellious craft workers in 19th-century England who destroyed new factory machinery as part of their resistance to the industrial revolution. (414)

New social movement An organized collective activity that addresses values and social identities, as well as improvements in the quality of life. (410)

Relative deprivation The conscious feeling of a negative discrepancy between legitimate expectations and present actualities. (408)

Resource mobilization The ways in which a social movement utilizes such resources as money, political influence, access to the media, and personnel. (408)

Social change Significant alteration over time in behavior patterns and culture, including norms and values. (407)

Social movement An organized collective activity to bring about or resist fundamental change in an existing group or society. (407)

Transnational An immigrant who sustains multiple social relationships that link his or her society of origin with the society of settlement. (421)

Vested interests Those people or groups who will suffer in the event of social change, and who have a stake in maintaining the status quo. (413)

Self-Quiz

Read each question carefully and then select the best answer.

1. You are a student and do not own a car. All your close friends who are attending your college or university have vehicles of their own. You feel downtrodden and dissatisfied. You are experiencing

   a. relative deprivation.
   b. resource mobilization.
   c. false consciousness.
   d. depression.

2. The text observes that it takes more than desire to start a social movement: It helps to have money, political influence, access to the media, and workers. The ways in which a social movement utilizes such things are referred to collectively as

   a. relative deprivation.
   b. false consciousness.
   c. resource mobilization.
   d. economic independence.

3. Karl Marx held that leaders of social movements must help workers overcome feelings of

    a. class consciousness.
    b. false consciousness.
    c. socialist consciousness.
    d. surplus value.

4. Organized collective activities that promote autonomy and self-determination, as well as improvements in the quality of life, are referred to as

    a. new social movements.
    b. social revolutions.
    c. resource mobilizations.
    d. crazes.

5. The text cites which of the following as a recognized definition of social change?

    a. tumultuous, revolutionary alterations that lead to changes in leadership
    b. a significant alteration over time in behavior patterns and culture
    c. regular alterations in a consistent social frame of reference
    d. subtle alterations in any social system

6. Nineteenth-century theories of social change reflect the pioneering work in biological evolution done by

    a. Albert Einstein.
    b. Harriet Martineau.
    c. James Audubon.
    d. Charles Darwin.

7. According to Talcott Parsons's equilibrium model, during which process do social institutions become more specialized in their purposes?

    a. differentiation
    b. adaptive upgrading
    c. inclusion
    d. value generalization

8. Which of the following statements regarding Karl Marx is *not* true?

    a. Marx accepted the evolutionary argument that societies develop along a particular path.
    b. Marx believed that history proceeds through a series of stages, each of which exploits a class of people.
    c. Marx accepted Parsons's equilibrium model, which states that as changes occur in one part of society, there must be adjustments in other parts if stability is to be maintained.
    d. Marx argued that conflict is a normal and desirable aspect of social change.

9. Which of the following terms did William F. Ogburn use to refer to the period of maladjustment during which the nonmaterial culture is still struggling to adapt to new material conditions?

    a. economic shift
    b. political turmoil
    c. social change
    d. culture lag

10. Conflict theorists are well aware of the environmental implications of land use policies in the Third World, but they contend that blaming developing countries for the world's environmental deterioration is an example of

    a. ethnocentrism.
    b. xenocentrism.
    c. separatism.
    d. goal displacement.

11. _____ _____ are organized collective activities to bring about or resist fundamental change in an existing group or society.

12. A person suffering from relative deprivation is dissatisfied because he or she feels downtrodden relative to some appropriate _____ group.

13. Robert Michels noted that political movements that are fighting for social change eventually take on some of the aspects of _____ that they were organized to protest.

14. Talcott Parsons used the term _____ to refer to the increasing complexity of social organization.

15. Social economist Thorstein Veblen coined the term _____ _____ to refer to those people or groups who will suffer in the event of social change.

16. The term _____ refers to those who are wary of technological innovations, and who question the incessant expansion of industrialization, the increasing destruction of the natural and agrarian world, and the "throw-it-away" mentality of contemporary capitalism.

17. In 2001, one month after the terrorist attacks of September 11, congress passed the _____ _____ Act, which relaxed existing legal checks on surveillance by law enforcement officers. Federal agencies are now freer to gather data electronically, including credit card receipts and banking records.

18. The _____ _____ Project is an effort involving teams of scientists around the world who are sequencing and mapping all 30,000 to 40,000 human genes in existence.

19. A serious environmental disaster occurred in 1986 when a series of explosions set off a catastrophic nuclear reactor accident at _____, a part of Ukraine (in what was then the Soviet Union).

20. _____ _____ is a legal strategy based on claims that racial minorities are subjected disproportionately to environmental hazards.

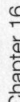

{ TECHNOLOGY RESOURCES }

 ## Online Learning Center

1. Try the crossword puzzle in the student center of the Online Learning Center (**www.mhhe.com/schaefer7**). Working the puzzle is a great way to test your familiarity with the terms and concepts related to globalization, the environment, and social change. It's also an enjoyable way to review for exams.

2. The Earthwatch Institute strives to protect the environment by organizing volunteers to participate in environmental research. To learn about the issues that concern this group, go to its Web site (**www.earthwatch.org**).

3. One way that the Internet has helped to bring about enormous social change is through Web sites like Changemakers.net (**www.changemakers.net**), an organization that seeks to promote positive social change, using the Internet as a communications tool.

*Note: While all the URLs listed were current as of the printing of this book, these sites often change. Please check our Web site (**www.mhhe.com/schaefer7**) for updates, hyperlinks, and exercises related to these sites.*

 ## *Reel Society* Video Clips

Real Society video clips, which appear on this book's Web site, can be used to spark discussion about the following topics from this chapter:
- Social Movements
- The Environment

glossary

Numbers following the definitions indicate pages where the terms were identified. Consult the index for further page references.

A

Absolute poverty A minimum level of subsistence that no family should be expected to live below. (197)

Achieved status A social position that a person attains largely through his or her own efforts. (103, 186)

Activity theory An interactionist theory of aging that suggests that those elderly people who remain active and socially involved will be best adjusted. (276)

Adoption In a legal sense, a process that allows for the transfer of the legal rights, responsibilities, and privileges of parenthood to a new legal parent or parents. (303)

Affirmative action Positive efforts to recruit minority group members or women for jobs, promotions, and educational opportunities. (241, 366)

Ageism A term coined by Robert N. Butler to refer to prejudice and discrimination based on a person's age. (282)

Agrarian society The most technologically advanced form of preindustrial society. Members are engaged primarily in the production of food, but increase their crop yields through technological innovations such as the plow. (117)

Alienation A condition of estrangement or dissociation from the surrounding society. (119)

Amalgamation The process through which a majority group and a minority group combine to form a new group. (243)

Anomie Durkheim's term for the loss of direction felt in a society when social control of individual behavior has become ineffective. (10, 168)

Anomie theory of deviance Robert Merton's theory of deviance as an adaptation of socially prescribed goals or of the means governing their attainment, or both. (168)

Anticipatory socialization Processes of socialization in which a person "rehearses" for future positions, occupations, and social relationships. (88)

Anti-Semitism Anti-Jewish prejudice. (254)

Apartheid A former policy of the South African government, designed to maintain the separation of Blacks and other non-Whites from the dominant Whites. (245)

Applied sociology The use of the discipline of sociology with the specific intent of yielding practical applications for human behavior and organizations. (18)

Argot Specialized language used by members of a group or subculture. (69)

Ascribed status A social position assigned to a person by society without regard for the person's unique talents or characteristics. (102, 186)

Assimilation The process through which a person forsakes his or her own cultural tradition to become part of a different culture. (244)

Authority Institutionalized power that is recognized by the people over whom it is exercised. (355)

B

Basic sociology Sociological inquiry conducted with the objective of gaining a more profound knowledge of the fundamental aspects of social phenomena. Also known as *pure sociology.* (20)

Bilateral descent A kinship system in which both sides of a person's family are regarded as equally important. (295)

Bilingualism The use of two or more languages in a particular setting, such as the workplace or schoolroom, treating each language as equally legitimate. (71)

Birthrate The number of live births per 1,000 population in a given year. Also known as the *crude birthrate.* (377)

Black power A political philosophy, promoted by many younger Blacks in the 1960s, that supported the creation of Black-controlled political and economic institutions. (248)

Borderlands The area of common culture along the border between Mexico and the United States. (225)

Bourgeoisie Karl Marx's term for the capitalist class, comprising the owners of the means of production. (189)

Brain drain The immigration to the United States and other industrialized nations of skilled workers, professionals, and technicians who are desperately needed in their home countries. (392)

Bureaucracy A component of formal organization that uses rules and hierarchical ranking to achieve efficiency. (119)

Bureaucratization The process by which a group, organization, or social movement becomes increasingly bureaucratic. (121)

C

Capitalism An economic system in which the means of production are held largely in private hands and the main incentive for economic activity is the accumulation of profits. (189, 350)

Caste A hereditary rank, usually religiously dictated, that tends to be fixed and immobile. (187)

Causal logic The relationship between a condition or variable and a particular consequence, with one event leading to the other. (32)

Census An enumeration, or counting, of a population. (376)

Charismatic authority Max Weber's term for power made legitimate by a leader's exceptional personal or emotional appeal to his or her followers. (356)

Class A group of people who have a similar level of wealth and income. (191)

Class consciousness In Karl Marx's view, a subjective awareness held by members of a class regarding their common vested interests and need for collective political action to bring about social change. (190)

Classical theory An approach to the study of formal organizations that views workers as being motivated almost entirely by economic rewards. (123)

Class system A social ranking based primarily on economic position in which achieved characteristics can influence social mobility. (188)

Clinical sociology The use of the discipline of sociology with the specific intent of altering social relationships or restructuring social institutions. (20)

Closed system   A social system in which there is little or no possibility of individual social mobility. (201)

Coalition   A temporary or permanent alliance geared toward a common goal. (110)

Code of ethics   The standards of acceptable behavior developed by and for members of a profession. (40)

Cognitive theory of development   Jean Piaget's theory that children's thought progresses through four stages of development. (85)

Cohabitation   The practice of living together as a male–female couple without marrying. (306)

Colonialism   The maintenance of political, social, economic, and cultural dominance over a people by a foreign power for an extended period. (214)

Communism   As an ideal type, an economic system under which all property is communally owned and no social distinctions are made on the basis of people's ability to produce. (352)

Community   A spatial or political unit of social organization that gives people a sense of belonging, based either on shared residence in a particular place or on a common identity. (375)

Concentric-zone theory   A theory of urban growth devised by Ernest Burgess that sees growth in terms of a series of rings radiating from the central business district. (384)

Conflict perspective   A sociological approach that assumes that social behavior is best understood in terms of conflict or tension between competing groups. (15)

Conformity   Going along with peers—individuals of our own status who have no special right to direct our behavior. (159)

Contact hypothesis   An interactionist perspective which states that in cooperative circumstances, interracial contact between people of equal status will reduce prejudice. (243)

Content analysis   The systematic coding and objective recording of data, guided by some rationale. (39)

Control group   The subjects in an experiment who are not introduced to the independent variable by the researcher. (38)

Control theory   A view of conformity and deviance that suggests that our connection to members of society leads us to systematically conform to society's norms. (163)

Control variable   A factor that is held constant to test the relative impact of an independent variable. (34)

Corporate welfare   Tax breaks, direct payments, and grants that the government makes to corporations. (204)

Correlation   A relationship between two variables in which a change in one coincides with a change in the other. (32)

Correspondence principle   A term used by Bowles and Gintis to refer to the tendency of schools to promote the values expected of individuals in each social class and to prepare students for the types of jobs typically held by members of their class. (337)

Counterculture   A subculture that deliberately opposes certain aspects of the larger culture. (70)

Creationism   A literal interpretation of the Bible regarding the creation of humanity and the universe, used to argue that evolution should not be presented as established scientific fact. (342)

Credentialism   An increase in the lowest level of education required to enter a field. (336)

Crime   A violation of criminal law for which some governmental authority applies formal penalties. (173)

Cross-tabulation   A table that shows the relationship between two or more variables. (48)

Cultural relativism   The viewing of people's behavior from the perspective of their own culture. (71)

Cultural transmission   A school of criminology that argues that criminal behavior is learned through social interactions. (169)

Cultural universal   A common practice or belief found in every culture. (58, 316)

Culture   The totality of learned, socially transmitted customs, knowledge, material objects, and behavior. (55)

Culture lag   A period of maladjustment when the nonmaterial culture is still struggling to adapt to new material conditions. (60, 414)

Culture shock   The feeling of surprise and disorientation that people experience when they encounter cultural practices that are different from their own. (70)

Curanderismo   Latino folk medicine, a form of holistic health care and healing. (397)

Death rate   The number of deaths per 1,000 population in a given year. Also known as the *crude death rate.* (377)

Degradation ceremony   An aspect of the socialization process within some total institutions, in which people are subjected to humiliating rituals. (89)

Deindustrialization   The systematic, widespread withdrawal of investment in basic aspects of productivity, such as factories and plants. (367)

Democracy   In a literal sense, government by the people. (357)

Demographic transition   A term used to describe the change from high birthrates and death rates to low birthrates and death rates. (378)

Demography   The scientific study of population. (376)

Denomination   A large, organized religion that is not officially linked to the state or government. (327)

Dependency theory   An approach that contends that industrialized nations continue to exploit developing countries for their own gain. (214)

Dependent variable   The variable in a causal relationship that is subject to the influence of another variable. (32)

Deviance   Behavior that violates the standards of conduct or expectations of a group or society. (163)

Dictatorship   A government in which one person has nearly total power to make and enforce laws. (356)

Differential association   A theory of deviance proposed by Edwin Sutherland that holds that violation of rules results from exposure to attitudes favorable to criminal acts. (170)

Differential justice   Differences in the way social control is exercised over different groups. (172)

Diffusion   The process by which a cultural item spreads from group to group or society to society. (59)

Discovery   The process of making known or sharing the existence of an aspect of reality. (58)

Discrimination   The denial of opportunities and equal rights to individuals and groups because of prejudice or other arbitrary reasons. (238)

Disengagement theory   A functionalist theory of aging introduced by Cumming and Henry that suggests that society and the aging individual mutually sever many of their relationships. (274)

Domestic partnership   Two unrelated adults who share a mutually caring relationship, reside together, and agree to be jointly responsible for their dependents, basic living expenses, and other common necessities. (309)

Dominant ideology   A set of cultural beliefs and practices that helps to maintain powerful social, economic, and political interests. (67, 140, 193)

Downsizing Reductions taken in a company's workforce as part of deindustrialization. (367)

Dramaturgical approach A view of social interaction, popularized by Erving Goffman in which people are seen as theatrical performers. (17, 84)

Dysfunction An element or process of a society that may disrupt the social system or reduce its stability. (14)

Ecclesia A religious organization that claims to include most or all members of a society and is recognized as the national or official religion. (327)

Economic system The social institution through which goods and services are produced, distributed, and consumed. (349)

Education A formal process of learning in which some people consciously teach while others adopt the social role of learner. (316)

Egalitarian family An authority pattern in which spouses are regarded as equals. (295)

Elite model A view of society as being ruled by a small group of individuals who share a common set of political and economic interests. (361)

Endogamy The restriction of mate selection to people within the same group. (298)

Environmental justice A legal strategy based on claims that racial minorities are subjected disproportionately to environmental hazards. (420)

Equilibrium model Talcott Parsons's functionalist view that society tends toward a state of stability or balance. (411)

Established sect J. Milton Yinger's term for a religious group that is the outgrowth of a sect, yet remains isolated from society. (329)

Estate system A system of stratification under which peasants were required to work land leased to them by nobles in exchange for military protection and other services. Also known as *feudalism*. (188)

Esteem The reputation that a specific person has earned within an occupation. (194)

Ethnic group A group that is set apart from others primarily because of its national origin or distinctive cultural patterns. (234)

Ethnocentrism The tendency to assume that one's own culture and way of life represent the norm or are superior to all others. (70, 237)

Ethnography The study of an entire social setting through extended systematic observation. (37)

Evolutionary theory A theory of social change that holds that society is moving in a definite direction. (411)

Exogamy The requirement that people select a mate outside certain groups. (298)

Experiment An artificially created situation that allows a researcher to manipulate variables. (37)

Experimental group The subjects in an experiment who are exposed to an independent variable introduced by a researcher. (38)

Exploitation theory A Marxist theory that views racial subordination in the United States as a manifestation of the class system inherent in capitalism. (242)

Expressiveness Concern for the maintenance of harmony and the internal emotional affairs of the family. (266)

Extended family A family in which relatives—such as grandparents, aunts, or uncles—live in the same home as parents and their children. (291)

Face-work A term used by Erving Goffman to refer to the efforts people make to maintain the proper image and avoid public embarrassment. (84)

False consciousness A term used by Karl Marx to describe an attitude held by members of a class that does not accurately reflect their objective position. (190, 409)

Familism Pride in the extended family, expressed through the maintenance of close ties and strong obligations to kinfolk outside the immediate family. (301)

Family A set of people related by blood, marriage or some other agreed-upon relationship, or adoption, who share the primary responsibility for reproduction and caring for members of society. (291)

Feminist view A sociological approach that views inequity in gender as central to all behavior and organization. (16)

Fertility The level of reproduction in a society. (375)

Folkway A norm governing everyday behavior whose violation raises comparatively little concern. (65)

Force The actual or threatened use of coercion to impose one's will on others. (355)

Formal norm A norm that has been written down and that specifies strict punishments for violators. (64)

Formal organization A group designed for a special purpose and structured for maximum efficiency. (119)

Formal social control Social control that is carried out by authorized agents, such as police officers, judges, school administrators, and employers. (161)

Functionalist perspective A sociological approach that emphasizes the way in which the parts of a society are structured to maintain its stability. (13)

Fundamentalism Rigid adherence to fundamental religious doctrines, often accompanied by a literal application of scripture or historical beliefs to today's world. (325)

Gatekeeping The process by which a relatively small number of people in the media industry control what material eventually reaches the audience. (139)

Gemeinschaft A term used by Ferdinand Tönnies to describe a close-knit community, often found in rural areas, in which strong personal bonds unite members. (115)

Gender role Expectations regarding the proper behavior, attitudes, and activities of males or females. (90, 263)

Generalized other A term used by George Herbert Mead to refer to the attitudes, viewpoints, and expectations of society as a whole that a child takes into account in his or her behavior. (83)

Genocide The deliberate, systematic killing of an entire people or nation. (243)

Gerontology The scientific study of the sociological and psychological aspects of aging and the problems of the aged. (274)

Gesellschaft A term used by Ferdinand Tönnies to describe a community, often urban, that is large and impersonal, with little commitment to the group or consensus on values. (115)

Glass ceiling An invisible barrier that blocks the promotion of a qualified individual in a work environment because of the individual's gender, race, or ethnicity. (239, 272)

Globalization The worldwide integration of government policies, cultures, social movements, and financial markets through trade and the exchange of ideas. (20, 214)

Goal displacement   Overzealous conformity to official regulations of a bureaucracy. (121)

Gross national product (GNP)   The value of a nation's goods and services. (216)

Group   Any number of people with similar norms, values, and expectations who interact with one another on a regular basis. (108)

Growth rate   The difference between births and deaths, plus the difference between immigrants and emigrants, per 1,000 population. (377)

Hate crime   A criminal offense committed because of the offender's bias against a race, religion, ethnic group, national origin, or sexual orientation. (237)

Hawthorne effect   The unintended influence that observers of experiments can have on their subjects. (38)

Health   As defined by the World Health Organization, a state of complete physical, mental, and social well-being, and not merely the absence of disease and infirmity. (390)

Hidden curriculum   Standards of behavior that are deemed proper by society and are taught subtly in schools. (335)

Homogamy   The conscious or unconscious tendency to select a mate with personal characteristics similar to one's own. (299)

Homophobia   Fear of and prejudice against homosexuality. (263)

Horizontal mobility   The movement of an individual from one social position to another of the same rank. (201)

Horticultural society   A preindustrial society in which people plant seeds and crops rather than merely subsist on available foods. (116)

Hospice care   Treatment of the terminally ill in their own homes, or in special hospital units or other facilities, with the goal of helping them to die easily, without pain. (280)

Human ecology   An area of study that is concerned with the interrelationships between people and their environment. (384)

Human relations approach   An approach to the study of formal organizations that emphasizes the role of people, communication, and participation in a bureaucracy and tends to focus on the informal structure of the organization. (123)

Human rights   Universal moral rights possessed by all people because they are human. (227)

Hunting-and-gathering society   A preindustrial society in which people rely on whatever foods and fibers are readily available in order to survive. (116)

Hypothesis   A speculative statement about the relationship between two or more variables. (32)

Ideal type   A construct or model for evaluating specific cases. (11, 119)

Impression management   A term used by Erving Goffman to refer to the altering of the presentation of the self in order to create distinctive appearances and satisfy particular audiences. (84)

Incest taboo   The prohibition of sexual relationships between certain culturally specified relatives. (298)

Incidence   The number of new cases of a specific disorder that occur within a given population during a stated period. (395)

Income   Salaries and wages. (186)

Independent variable   The variable in a causal relationship that causes or influences a change in a second variable. (32)

Index crimes   The eight types of crime reported annually by the FBI in the *Uniform Crime Reports*: murder, rape, robbery, assault, burglary, theft, motor vehicle theft, and arson. (174)

Industrial city   A relatively large city characterized by open competition, an open class system, and elaborate specialization in the manufacturing of goods. (382)

Industrial society   A society that depends on mechanization to produce its goods and services. (117, 349)

Infant mortality rate   The number of deaths of infants under one year old per 1,000 live births in a given year. (377)

Influence   The exercise of power through a process of persuasion. (355)

Informal economy   Transfers of money, goods, or services that are not reported to the government. (352)

Informal norm   A norm that is generally understood but not precisely recorded. (65)

Informal social control   Social control that is carried out casually by ordinary people through such means as laughter, smiles, and ridicule. (160)

In-group   Any group or category to which people feel they belong. (109)

Innovation   The process of introducing a new idea or object to a culture through discovery or invention. (58)

Institutional discrimination   The denial of opportunities and equal rights to individuals and groups that results from the normal operations of a society. (240, 268)

Instrumentality   An emphasis on tasks, a focus on more distant goals, and a concern for the external relationship between one's family and other social institutions. (266)

Intelligent design (ID)   The idea that life is so complex that it could only have been created by intelligent design. (342)

Interactionist perspective   A sociological approach that generalizes about everyday forms of social interaction in order to explain society as a whole. (16)

Intergenerational mobility   Changes in the social position of children relative to their parents. (201)

Interview   A face-to-face or telephone questioning of a respondent to obtain desired information. (35)

Intragenerational mobility   Changes in social position within a person's adult life. (201)

Invention   The combination of existing cultural items into a form that did not exist before. (58)

Iron law of oligarchy   A principle of organizational life developed by Robert Michels, under which even a democratic organization will eventually develop into a bureaucracy ruled by a few individuals. (123)

Kinship   The state of being related to others. (294)

Labeling theory   An approach to deviance that attempts to explain why certain people are viewed as deviants while others engaged in the same behavior are not. (171)

Labor union   Organized workers who share either the same skill or the same employer. (126)

Laissez-faire   A form of capitalism under which people compete freely, with minimal government intervention in the economy. (350)

Language   An abstract system of word meanings and symbols for all aspects of culture; includes gestures and other nonverbal communication. (63)

Latent function   An unconscious or unintended function that may reflect hidden purposes. (14)

, d

Law   Governmental social control. (64, 161)

Liberation theology   Use of a church, primarily Roman Catholicism, in a political effort to eliminate poverty, discrimination, and other forms of injustice from a secular society. (323)

Life chances   Max Weber's term for the opportunities people have to provide themselves with material goods, positive living conditions, and favorable life experiences. (200)

Life course approach   A research orientation in which sociologists and other social scientists look closely at the social factors that influence people throughout their lives, from birth to death. (87)

Life expectancy   The median number of years a person can be expected to live under current mortality conditions. (377)

Looking-glass self   A concept used by Charles Horton Cooley that emphasizes the self as the product of our social interactions. (82)

Luddites   Rebellious craft workers in nineteenth-century England who destroyed new factory machinery as part of their resistance to the industrial revolution. (414)

M

Machismo   A sense of virility, personal worth, and pride in one's maleness. (301)

Macrosociology   Sociological investigation that concentrates on large-scale phenomena or entire civilizations. (13)

Manifest function   An open, stated, and conscious function. (14)

Mass media   Print and electronic means of communication that carry messages to widespread audiences. (134)

Master status   A status that dominates others and thereby determines a person's general position in society. (103)

Material culture   The physical or technological aspects of our daily lives. (60)

Matriarchy   A society in which women dominate in family decision making. (295)

Matrilineal descent   A kinship system in which only the mother's relatives are significant. (295)

McDonaldization   The process by which the principles of the fast-food restaurant are coming to dominate more and more sectors of American society as well as of the rest of the world. (122)

Mean   A number calculated by adding a series of values and then dividing by the number of values. (47)

Mechanical solidarity   A collective consciousness that emphasizes group solidarity, characteristic of societies with minimal division of labor. (115)

Median   The midpoint or number that divides a series of values into two groups of equal numbers of values. (47)

Megalopolis   A densely populated area containing two or more cities and their suburbs. (383)

Microsociology   Sociological investigation that stresses the study of small groups, often through experimental means. (13)

Midlife crisis   A stressful period of self-evaluation that begins at about age 40. (277)

Minority group   A subordinate group whose members have significantly less control or power over their own lives than the members of a dominant or majority group have over theirs. (234)

Mode   The single most common value in a series of scores. (47)

Model or **ideal minority**   A minority group that despite past prejudice and discrimination, succeeds economically, socially, and educationally without resorting to confrontations with Whites. (249)

Modernization   The far-reaching process by which periphery nations move from traditional or less developed institutions to those characteristic of more developed societies. (217)

Modernization theory   A functionalist approach that proposes that modernization and development will gradually improve the lives of people in developing nations. (218)

Monarchy   A form of government headed by a single member of a royal family, usually a king, queen, or some other hereditary ruler. (356)

Monogamy   A form of marriage in which one woman and one man are married only to each other. (294)

Monopoly   Control of a market by a single business firm. (350)

Morbidity rate   The incidence of disease in a given population. (395)

Mores   Norms deemed highly necessary to the welfare of a society. (65)

Mortality rate   The incidence of death in a given population. (395)

Multinational corporation   A commercial organization that is headquartered in one country but does business throughout the world. (215)

Multiple-nuclei theory   A theory of urban growth developed by Harris and Ullman that views growth as emerging from many centers of development, each of which reflects a particular urban need or activity. (385)

N

Narcotizing dysfunction   The phenomenon in which the media provide such massive amounts of coverage that the audience becomes numb and fails to act on the information, regardless of how compelling the issue. (138)

Natural science   The study of the physical features of nature and the ways in which they interact and change. (6)

Neocolonialism   Continuing dependence of former colonies on foreign countries. (214)

New religious movement (NRM) or **cult**   A small, secretive religious group that represents either a new religion or a major innovation of an existing faith. (329)

New social movement   An organized collective activity that addresses values and social identities, as well as improvements in the quality of life. (410)

New urban sociology   An approach to urbanization that considers the interplay of local, national, and worldwide forces and their effect on local space, with special emphasis on the impact of global economic activity. (386)

Nonmaterial culture   Ways of using material objects, as well as customs, beliefs, philosophies, governments, and patterns of communication. (60)

Nonverbal communication   The sending of messages through the use of gestures, facial expressions, and postures. (16)

Norm   An established standard of behavior maintained by a society. (64)

Nuclear family   A married couple and their unmarried children living together. (291)

O

Obedience   Compliance with higher authorities in a hierarchical structure. (159)

Objective method   A technique for measuring social class that assigns individuals to classes on the basis of criteria such as occupation, education, income, and place of residence. (194)

Observation   A research technique in which an investigator collects information through direct participation and/or by closely watching a group or community. (37)

Offshoring   The transfer of work to foreign contractors. (368)

Glossary

Oligarchy   A form of government in which a few individuals rule. (356)

Open system   A social system in which the position of each individual is influenced by his or her achieved status. (201)

Operational definition   An explanation of an abstract concept that is specific enough to allow a researcher to assess the concept. (31)

Opinion leader   Someone who influences the opinions and decisions of others through day-to-day personal contact and communication. (146)

Organic solidarity   A collective consciousness that rests on mutual interdependence, characteristic of societies with a complex division of labor. (115)

Organized crime   The work of a group that regulates relations between criminal enterprises involved in illegal activities, including prostitution, gambling, and the smuggling and sale of illegal drugs. (175)

Out-group   A group or category to which people feel they do not belong. (109)

Patriarchy   A society in which men dominate in family decision making. (295)

Patrilineal descent   A kinship system in which only the father's relatives are significant. (295)

Peace   The absence of war, or more broadly, a proactive effort to develop cooperative relations among nations. (363)

Percentage   A portion of 100. (47)

Personality   A person's typical patterns of attitudes, needs, characteristics, and behavior. (79)

Peter principle   A principle of organizational life, originated by Laurence J. Peter, according to which every employee within a hierarchy tends to rise to his or her level of incompetence. (121)

Pluralism   Mutual respect for one another's cultures among the various groups in a society, which allows minorities to express their own cultures without experiencing prejudice. (245)

Pluralist model   A view of society in which many competing groups within the community have access to government, so that no single group is dominant. (362)

Political system   The social institution that is founded on a recognized set of procedures for implementing and achieving society's goals. (349)

Politics   In Harold Lasswell's words, "who gets what, when, and how." (355)

Polyandry   A form of polygamy in which a woman may have more than one husband at the same time. (294)

Polygamy   A form of marriage in which an individual may have several husbands or wives simultaneously. (294)

Polygyny   A form of polygamy in which a man may have more than one wife at the same time. (294)

Population pyramid   A special type of bar chart that shows the distribution of a population by gender and age. (379)

Postindustrial city   A city in which global finance and the electronic flow of information dominate the economy. (383)

Postindustrial society   A society whose economic system is engaged primarily in the processing and control of information. (118)

Postmodern society   A technologically sophisticated society that is preoccupied with consumer goods and media images. (118)

Power   The ability to exercise one's will over others. (191, 355)

Power elite   A term used by C. Wright Mills to refer to a small group of military, industrial, and government leaders who control the fate of the United States. (361)

Preindustrial city   A city of only a few thousand people that is characterized by a relatively closed class system and limited mobility. (382)

Prejudice   A negative attitude toward an entire category of people, often an ethnic or racial minority. (237)

Prestige   The respect and admiration that an occupation holds in a society. (194)

Prevalence   The total number of cases of a specific disorder that exist at a given time. (395)

Primary group   A small group characterized by intimate, face-to-face association and cooperation. (108)

Profane   The ordinary and commonplace elements of life, as distinguished from the sacred. (316)

Professional criminal   A person who pursues crime as a day-to-day occupation, developing skilled techniques and enjoying a certain degree of status among other criminals. (174)

Proletariat   Karl Marx's term for the working class in a capitalist society. (190)

Protestant ethic   Max Weber's term for the disciplined work ethic, this-worldly concerns, and rational orientation to life emphasized by John Calvin and his followers. (323)

Qualitative research   Research that relies on what is seen in field or naturalistic settings more than on statistical data. (35)

Quantitative research   Research that collects and reports data primarily in numerical form. (35)

Questionnaire   A printed or written form used to obtain information from a respondent. (35)

Racial group   A group that is set apart from others because of physical differences that have taken on social significance. (234)

Racial profiling   Any police-initiated action based on race, ethnicity, or national origin rather than on a person's behavior. (255)

Racism   The belief that one race is supreme and all others are innately inferior. (237)

Random sample   A sample for which every member of an entire population has the same chance of being selected. (33)

Rational-legal authority   Power made legitimate by law. (357)

Reference group   Any group that individuals use as a standard for evaluating themselves and their own behavior. (109)

Relative deprivation   The conscious feeling of a negative discrepancy between legitimate expectations and present actualities. (408)

Relative poverty   A floating standard of deprivation by which people at the bottom of a society, whatever their lifestyles, are judged to be disadvantaged *in comparison with the nation as a whole*. (198)

Reliability   The extent to which a measure produces consistent results. (33)

Religion   According to Émile Durkheim, a unified system of beliefs and practices relative to sacred things. (316)

Religious belief   A statement to which members of a particular religion adhere. (324)

Religious experience   The feeling or perception of being in direct contact with the ultimate reality, such as a divine being, or of being overcome with religious emotion. (326)

Religious ritual   A practice required or expected of members of a faith. (325)

Remittances   The monies that immigrants return to their families of origin. Also called *migradollars*. (226)

Representative democracy   A form of government in which certain individuals are selected to speak for the people. (351)

Research design   A detailed plan or method for obtaining data scientifically. (35)

Resocialization   The process of discarding former behavior patterns and accepting new ones as part of a transition in one's life. (88)

Resource mobilization   The ways in which a social movement utilizes such resources as money, political influence, access to the media, and personnel. (408)

Rite of passage   A ritual marking the symbolic transition from one social position to another. (87)

Role conflict   The situation that occurs when incompatible expectations arise from two or more social positions held by the same person. (105)

Role exit   The process of disengagement from a role that is central to one's self-identity in order to establish a new role and identity. (105)

Role strain   The difficulty that arises when the same social position imposes conflicting demands and expectations. (105)

Role taking   The process of mentally assuming the perspective of another and responding from that imagined viewpoint. (83)

Routine activities theory   The notion that criminal victimization increases when motivated offenders and suitable targets converge. (170)

Sacred   Elements beyond everyday life that inspire awe, respect, and even fear. (316)

Sample   A selection from a larger population that is statistically representative of that population. (33)

Sanction   A penalty or reward for conduct concerning a social norm. (65, 158)

Sandwich generation   The generation of adults who simultaneously try to meet the competing needs of their parents and their children. (277)

Sapir-Whorf hypothesis   A hypothesis concerning the role of language in shaping our interpretation of reality. It holds that language is culturally determined. (63)

Science   The body of knowledge obtained by methods based on systematic observation. (6)

Scientific management approach   Another name for the classical theory of formal organizations. (123)

Scientific method   A systematic, organized series of steps that ensures maximum objectivity and consistency in researching a problem. (30)

Secondary analysis   A variety of research techniques that make use of previously collected and publicly accessible information and data. (38)

Secondary group   A formal, impersonal group in which there is little social intimacy or mutual understanding. (108)

Second shift   The double burden—work outside the home followed by child care and housework—that many women face and few men share equitably. (273)

Sect   A relatively small religious group that has broken away from some other religious organization to renew what it considers the original vision of the faith. (328)

Secularization   The process through which religion's influence on other social institutions diminishes. (316)

Segregation   The physical separation of two groups of people in terms of residence, workplace, and social events; often imposed on a minority group by a dominant group. (244)

Self   According to George Herbert Mead, a distinct identity that sets us apart from others. (82)

Serial monogamy   A form of marriage in which a person may have several spouses in his or her lifetime, but only one spouse at a time. (294)

Sexism   The ideology that one sex is superior to the other. (268)

Sexual harassment   Behavior that occurs when work benefits are made contingent on sexual favors (as a quid pro quo), or when touching, lewd comments, or the exhibition of pornographic material creates a "hostile environment" in the workplace. (269)

Sick role   Societal expectations about the attitudes and behavior of a person viewed as being ill. (391)

Significant other   A term used by George Herbert Mead to refer to an individual who is most important in the development of the self, such as a parent, friend, or teacher. (83)

Single-parent family   A family in which only one parent is present to care for the children. (304)

Slavery   A system of enforced servitude in which some people are owned by other people. (187)

Social change   Significant alteration over time in behavior patterns and culture, including norms and values. (407)

Social constructionist perspective   An approach to deviance that emphasizes the role of culture in the creation of the deviant identity. (171)

Social control   The techniques and strategies for preventing deviant human behavior in any society. (158)

Social epidemiology   The study of the distribution of disease, impairment, and general health status across a population. (395)

Social inequality   A condition in which members of society have different amounts of wealth, prestige, or power. (22, 186)

Social institution   An organized pattern of beliefs and behavior centered on basic social needs. (112)

Social interaction   The ways in which people respond to one another. (101)

Socialism   An economic system under which the means of production and distribution are collectively owned. (351)

Socialization   The lifelong process in which people learn the attitudes, values, and behaviors appropriate for members of a particular culture. (79)

Social mobility   Movement of individuals or groups from one position in a society's stratification system to another. (201)

Social movement   An organized collective activity to bring about or resist fundamental change in an existing group or society. (407)

Social network   A series of social relationships that links a person directly to others, and through them indirectly to still more people. (110)

Social role   A set of expectations for people who occupy a given social position or status. (104)

Social science   The study of the social features of humans and the ways in which they interact and change. (6)

Social structure   The way in which a society is organized into predictable relationships. (101)

Societal-reaction approach   Another name for *labeling theory*. (171)

Society   A fairly large number of people who live in the same territory, are relatively independent of people outside it, and participate in a common culture. (55)

Sociobiology   The systematic study of how biology affects human social behavior. (60)

Sociocultural evolution   Long-term trends in societies resulting from the interplay of continuity, innovation, and selection. (116)

Sociological imagination   An awareness of the relationship between an individual and the wider society, both today and in the past. (3)

Sociology The scientific study of social behavior and human groups. (3)

Status A term used by sociologists to refer to any of the full range of socially defined positions within a large group or society. (102)

Status group A term used by Max Weber to refer to people who have the same prestige or lifestyle, independent of their class positions. (191)

Stereotype An unreliable generalization about all members of a group that does not recognize individual differences within the group. (140, 236)

Stigma A label used to devalue members of certain social groups. (164)

Stratification A structured ranking of entire groups of people that perpetuates unequal economic rewards and power in a society. (186)

Subculture A segment of society that shares a distinctive pattern of mores, folkways, and values that differs from the pattern of the larger society. (68)

Suburb According to the Census Bureau, any territory within a metropolitan area that is not included in the central city. (388)

Survey A study, generally in the form of an interview or questionnaire, that provides researchers with information about how people think and act. (35)

Symbol A gesture, object, or word that forms the basis of human communication. (82)

Symbolic ethnicity An ethnic identity that emphasizes concerns such as ethnic food or political issues rather than deeper ties to one's ethnic heritage. (255)

Teacher-expectancy effect The impact that a teacher's expectations about a student's performance may have on the student's actual achievements. (338)

Technology Cultural information about the ways in which the material resources of the environment may be used to satisfy human needs and desires. (60, 116)

Telecommuter An employee who works full-time or part-time at home rather than in an outside office, and who is linked to supervisor and colleagues through computer terminals, phone lines, and fax machines. (124)

Terrorism The use or threat of violence against random or symbolic targets in pursuit of political aims. (364)

Theory In sociology, a set of statements that seeks to explain problems, actions, or behavior. (8)

Total fertility rate (TFR) The average number of children born alive to any woman, assuming that she conforms to current fertility rates. (377)

Total institution A term coined by Erving Goffman to refer to an institution that regulates all aspects of a person's life under a single authority, such as a prison, the military, a mental hospital, or a convent. (88)

Totalitarianism Virtually complete government control and surveillance over all aspects of a society's social and political life. (357)

Tracking The practice of placing students in specific curriculum groups on the basis of their test scores and other criteria. (336)

Traditional authority Legitimate power conferred by custom and accepted practice. (355)

Trained incapacity The tendency of workers in a bureaucracy to become so specialized that they develop blind spots and fail to notice obvious problems. (120)

Transnational An immigrant who sustains multiple social relationships that link his or her society of origin with the society of settlement. (421)

Transnational crime Crime that occurs across multiple national borders. (176)

Underclass The long-term poor who lack training and skills. (199)

Urban ecology An area of study that focuses on the interrelationships between people and their environment in urban areas. (384)

Urbanism A term used by Louis Wirth to describe distinctive patterns of social behavior evident among city residents. (333)

Validity The degree to which a measure or scale truly reflects the phenomenon under study. (33)

Value A collective conception of what is considered good, desirable, and proper—or bad, undesirable, and improper—in a culture. (66)

Value neutrality Max Weber's term for objectivity of sociologists in the interpretation of data. (43)

Variable A measurable trait or characteristic that is subject to change under different conditions. (32)

Verstehen The German word for "understanding" or "insight"; used by Max Weber to stress the need for sociologists to take into account the subjective meanings people attach to their actions. (11)

Vertical mobility The movement of an individual from one social position to another of a different rank. (201)

Vested interests Veblen's term for those people or groups who will suffer in the event of social change, and who have a stake in maintaining the status quo. (413)

Victimization survey A questionnaire or interview given to a sample of the population to determine whether people have been victims of crime. (178)

Victimless crime A term used by sociologists to describe the willing exchange among adults of widely desired, but illegal, goods and services. (174)

Vital statistics Records of births, deaths, marriages, and divorces gathered through a registration system maintained by governmental units. (376)

War Conflict between organizations that possess trained combat forces equipped with deadly weapons. (362)

Wealth An inclusive term encompassing all a person's material assets, including land, stocks, and other types of property. (186)

White-collar crime Illegal acts committed by affluent, "respectable" individuals in the course of business activities. (175)

World systems analysis Immanuel Wallerstein's view of the global economic system as one divided between certain industrialized nations that control wealth and developing countries that are controlled and exploited. (214, 386)

Zero population growth (ZPG) The state of a population in which the number of births plus immigrants equals the number of deaths plus emigrants. (381)

references

AARP. 1999. "New AARP Study Finds Boomers Vary in Their Views of the Future and Their Retirement Years." AARP news release, June 1. Washington, DC.

ABC Radio Australia. 2006. "China: Crackdown in Air Pollution ahead of 2008 Beijing Olympics." Accessed May 2. (www.abc.net.au).

Abelson, Reed, and Michael Barbaro. 2006. "Law Aimed at Wal-Mart May Be Hard to Replicate." *New York Times,* January 16: pp. C1, C2.

Abercrombie, Nicholas, Bryan S. Turner, and Stephen Hill, eds. 1990. *Dominant Ideologies.* Cambridge, MA: Unwin Hyman.

———, Stephen Hill, and Bryan S. Turner. 1980. *The Dominant Ideology Thesis.* London: George Allen and Unwin.

Aberle, David E., A. K. Cohen, A. K. Davis, M. J. Leng, Jr., and F. N. Sutton. 1950. "The Functional Prerequisites of a Society." *Ethics* 60 (January): 100–111.

Abrahamson, Mark. 1978. *Functionalism.* Englewood Cliffs, NJ: Prentice Hall.

Acosta, R. Vivian, and Linda Jean Carpenter. 2001. "Women in Intercollegiate Sport: A Longitudinal Study: 1977–1998." Pp. 302–308 in *Sport in Contemporary Society: An Anthology.* 6th ed., edited by D. Stanley Eitzen. New York: Worth.

Adam, Barry D. 1995. *The Rise of a Gay and Lesbian Movement.* Rev. ed. New York: Twayne.

Addams, Jane. 1910. *Twenty Years at Hull-House.* New York: Macmillan.

———. 1930. *The Second Twenty Years at Hull-House.* New York: Macmillan.

Adler, Freda. 1975. *Sisters in Crime: The Rise of the New Female Criminal.* New York: McGraw-Hill.

———, Gerhard O. W. Mueller, and William S. Laufer. 2004. *Criminology and the Criminal Justice System.* 5th ed. New York: McGraw-Hill.

Adler, Patricia A. 1993. *Wheeling and Dealing: an Ethnography of an Upper-Level Drug Dealing and Smuggling Community.* 2d ed. New York: Columbia University Press.

———, and Peter Adler. 1991. *Backboards and Blackboards.* New York: Columbia University Press.

———, and ———. 1998. *Peer Power: Preadolescent Culture and Identity.* New Brunswick, NJ: Rutgers University Press

———, and ———. 2003. "The Promise and Pitfalls of Going into the Field." *Contexts* (Spring):41–47.

———, and ———. 2004. *Paradise Laborers: Hotel Work in the Global Economy.* Ithaca, NY: Cornell University Press.

———, and ———. 2005. 'Self-injurers as Loners: The Social Organization of Solitary Deviance." *Deviant Behavior.*

———, ———, and John M. Johnson. 1992. "Street Corner Society Revisited." *Journal of Contemporary Ethnography* 21 (April):3–10.

AFL-CIO. 2001. *More Workers Are Choosing a Voice at Work.* Accessed April 18 (www.aflcio.org/voiceatwork/morejoin/htm).

Alain, Michel. 1985. "An Empirical Validation of Relative Deprivation." *Human Relations* 38 (8):739–749.

Alba, Richard D. 1990. *Ethnic Identity: The Transformation of White America.* New Haven, CT: Yale University Press.

Albas, Daniel, and Cheryl Albas. 1988. "Aces and Bombers: The Post-Exam Impression Management Strategies of Students." *Symbolic Interaction* 11 (Fall):289–302.

Albiniak, P. 2000. "TV's Drug Deal." *Broadcasting and Cable,* January 17, pp. 3, 148.

Albrecht, Gary L., Katerine D. Steelman, and Michael Bury. 2001. *Handbook of Disabilities Study.* Thousand Oaks, CA: Sage.

Alfino, Mark, John S. Caputo, and Robin Wynyard. 1998. *McDonaldization Revisited: Critical Essays on Consumer Culture.* Westport, CT: Praeger.

Al Jazeera. 2006. Home page. Accessed January 30 (http://english.alijeera.net/HomePage).

Allen, Bern P. 1978. *Social Behavior: Fact and Falsehood.* Chicago: Nelson-Hall.

Allen, John L. 2005. *Student Atlas of World Geography.* 4th ed. New York: McGraw-Hill.

Allport, Gordon W. 1979. *The Nature of Prejudice.* 25th anniversary ed. Reading, MA: Addison-Wesley.

Alwin, Duane F. 2002. "Generations X, Y, and Z: Are They Changing America?" *Contexts* (Fall/Winter):42–51.

Alzheimer's Association. 2004. *Fact Sheet.* Chicago: Alzheimer's Association.

Amato, Paul R. 2001. "What Children Learn from Divorce." *Population Today,* January, pp. 1, 4.

———, and Alan Booth. 1997. *A Generation at Risk.* Cambridge, MA: Harvard University Press.

———, and Juliana M. Sobolewski. 2001. "The Effects of Divorce and Marital Discord on Adult Children's Psychological Well-Being." *American Sociological Review* 66 (December):900–921.

American Academy of Cosmetic Surgery. 2004. "2003 Estimates Total Number of Patients Treated by All U.S.-Based AACS Members." Accessed February 21 (www.cosmeticsurgery.org/media_center/stats/statistics.html).

American Association of University Women. 1998. *Gender Gaps: Where Schools Still Fail Our Children.* Washington, DC: AAUW.

American Bar Association. 1998. *Section of Individual Rights and Responsibilities. Section of Litigation (Capital Punishment).* Chicago: Division for Policy Administration, ABA.

———. 1999. "Commission on Domestic Violence." Accessed July 20 (www.abanet.org/domviol/stats.html).

American Federation of Teachers. 2005. "Teacher Salaries Lag Behind Inflation." Press release, October 6. Accessed April 11, 2006 (www.aft.org).

American Jewish Committee. 2001. "2000 Annual Survey of American Jewish Opinion." Accessed October 25 (www.ajc.org/pre/survey2000.htm).

American Lung Association. 2003. "Scenesmoking." Accessed December 19 (www.scenesmoking.org).

American Sociological Association. 1997. *Code of Ethics.* Washington, DC: American Sociological Association. Available (www.asanet. org/members/ecoderev.html).

———. 2001. *Data Brief: Profile of ASA Membership.* Washington, DC: American Sociological Association.

———. 2005a. "Need Today's Data Yesterday." Accessed December 17 (www.asanet.org).

———. 2005b. "Careers and Jobs Home." Accessed December 17 (www.asanet.org/page.ww?section=careers+and+Jobs&name=Careers+and+Jobs+Home).

———. 2006. "Current Sections." Accessed May 18 (www.asanet.org/page.ww?section=Sections&name=Overview).

———. 2007. *2006 Guide to Graduate Departments of Sociology.* Washington, DC: ASA.

Amnesty International. 1994. *Breaking the Silence: Human Rights Violations Based on Sexual Orientation.* New York: Amnesty International.

———. 2006. "Amnesty International: Facts and Figures on the Death Penalty." Accessed February 19 (www.amnesty.org).

Amnesty USA. 2005. "Racial Profiling." Accessed April 18 (www.amnestyusa.org/racial_profiling/report).

Andersen, Margaret. 1997. *Thinking about Women: Sociological Perspectives on Sex and Gender.* 4th ed. Boston: Allyn and Bacon.

Anderson, Craig A., and Brad J. Bushman. 2001. "Effects of Violent Video Games on Aggressive Behavior, Aggressive Cognition, Aggressive Affect, Physiological Arousal, and Prosocial Behavior: A Meta-Analytic Review of Scientific Literature." *Psychological Science* 12 (5):353–359.

Anderson, Elijah. 1990. *Streetwise: Race, Class, and Change in an Urban Community.* Chicago: University of Chicago Press.

Anderson, John Ward, and Molly Moore. 1993. "The Burden of Womanhood." *Washington Post National Weekly Edition* 10 (March 22–28):6–7.

Angier, Natalie. 1998. "Drugs, Sports, Body Image and G.I. Joe." *New York Times,* December 22, section D, pp. 1, 3.

436

Anti-Defamation League. 2003. *ADL Audit of Anti-Semitic Incidents, 1982–2002 (National).* (www.adl.org).

AOL Time Warner. 2003. *Factbook.* New York: AOL Time Warner.

Appelbaum, Richard, and Peter Dreier. 1999. "The Campus Anti-Sweatshops Movement." *The American Prospect* (September/October):71–78.

Argetsinger, Amy, and Jonathan Krim. 2002. "Stopping the Music." *Washington Post National Weekly Edition* 20 (December 2), p. 20.

Arias, Elizabeth. 2004. "United States Life Tables, 2002." *National Vital Statistics Report,* November 10.

Armer, J. Michael, and John Katsillis. 1992. "Modernization Theory." Pp. 1299–1304 in *Encyclopedia of Sociology,* Vol. 4, edited by Edgar F. Borgatta and Marie L. Borgatta. New York: Macmillan.

Aronson, Elliot. 1999. *The Social Animal.* 8th ed. New York: Worth.

Arora, Raksha. 2004. "Is War Still Necessary in the 21st Century?" Gallup Poll Tuesday Briefing May 11 (www.gallup.com).

Associated Press. 1998."Environmental Test Case Averted." *Christian Science Monitor,* September 21, p. 18.

Astin, Alexander, Sarah A. Parrott, William S. Korn, and Linda J. Sax. 1994. *The American Freshman: Thirty Year Trends.* Los Angeles: Higher Education Research Institute.

Atchley, Robert C. 1976. *The Sociology of Retirement.* New York: Wiley.

———, and Amanda S. Barusch. 2004. *Social Forces and Agency: An Introduction to Social Gerontology.* 10th ed. Belmont, CA: Thompson.

Austin, April. 2002. "Cellphones and Strife in Congo." *Christian Science Monitor,* December 5, pp. 11.

Axtell, Roger E. 1990. *Do's and Taboos around the World.* 2d ed. New York: John Wiley and Sons.

Azumi, Koya, and Jerald Hage. 1972. *Organizational Systems.* Lexington, MA: Heath.

Babad, Elisha Y., and P. J. Taylor. 1992. "Transparency of Teacher Expectancies Across Language, Cultural Boundaries." *Journal of Educational Research* 86:120–125.

Baby Name Wizard. 2006. "Name Voyager." Accessed January 16 (www.babynamewizard.com).

Bainbridge, William Sims. 1999. "Cyberspace: Sociology's Natural Domain." *Contemporary Sociology* 28 (November):664–667.

Baker, Therese L. 1999. *Doing Social Research.* 3d ed. New York: McGraw-Hill.

Banboza, David. 2006. "Citing Public Sentiment, China Cancels Release of 'Geisha.'" *New York Times,* February 1, p. B6.

Barr, Cameron W. 2002. "Top Arab TV Network to Hit US Market." *Christian Science Monitor,* December 26, pp. 1, 7.

Barrett, David B., Todd M. Johnson, and Peter F. Crossing. 2005. "Worldwide Adherents of All Religions, Mid-2004" and "Religions Adherents in the United States of America 1900–2005." P. 282 in *Encyclopedia Britannica, Yearbook 2005.* Chicago: Encyclopedia Britannica.

———. 2006. "The 2005 Annual Megacensus of Religions." Pp. 282–283 in 2006 *Book of the Year.* Chicago: Encyclopedia Britannica.

Barron, Milton L. 1953. "Minority Group Characteristics of the Aged in American Society." *Journal of Gerontology* 8:477–482.

Bartlett, Donald L., and James B. Steele. 2002. "Casinos: Wheel of Misfortune." *Time* 160 (December 16):44–53, 56–58.

Basso, Keith H. 1972. "Ice and Travel among the Fort Norman Slave: Folk Taxonomies and Cultural Rules." *Language in Society* 1 (March): 31–49.

Bates, Colleen Dunn. 1999. "Medicine's Gender Gap." *Shape,* October.

Bauerlein, Monika. 1996. "The Luddites Are Back." *Utne Reader* (March/April):24, 26.

Bauman, Kurt J. 1999. "Extended Measures of Well-Being: Meeting Basic Needs." *Current Population Reports,* Ser. p. 70, No. 67. Washington, DC: U.S. Government Printing Office.

Ba-Yunus, Ilyas, and Kassim Kone. 2004. "Muslim Americans: A Demographic Report." Pp. 299–322 in *Muslims in the American Public Square,* edited by Zahid H. Bukhari et al. Walnut Creek, CA: Alta Mira Press.

BBC News. 2005. "Indonesian Village Report: January 12, 2005." Accessed January 19 (www.the world.org).

Beagan, Brenda L. 2001. " 'Even If I Don't Know What I'm Doing I Can Make It Look Like I Know What I'm Doing': Becoming a Doctor in the 1990s." *Canadian Review of Sociology and Anthropology* 38:275–292.

Bearman, Peter S., James Moody, and Katherine Stovel. 2004. "Chains of Affection: The Structure of Adolescent Romantic and Sexual Networks." *American Journal of Sociology* 110 (July):44–91.

Becerra, Rosina M. 1999. "The Mexican-American Family." Pp. 153–171 in *Ethnic Families in America: Patterns and Variations,* 4th ed., edited by Charles H. Mindel, Robert W. Habenstein, and Roosevelt Wright, Jr. Upper Saddle River, NJ: Prentice Hall.

Becker, Howard S. 1952. "Social Class Variations in the Teacher-Pupil Relationship." *Journal of Educational Sociology* 25 (April):451–465.

———. 1963. *The Outsiders: Studies in the Sociology of Deviance.* New York: Free Press.

———, ed. 1964. *The Other Side: Perspectives on Deviance.* New York: Free Press.

———. 1973. *The Outsiders: Studies in the Sociology of Deviance.* Rev. ed. New York: Free Press.

Beech, Hannah. 2005. "Sex, Please—We're Young and Chinese." *Time,* December 11, p. 61.

Beeghley, Leonard. 1978. *Social Stratification in America: A Critical Analysis of Theory and Research.* Santa Monica, CA: Goodyear Publishing.

Bell, Daniel. 1953. "Crime as an American Way of Life." *Antioch Review* 13 (Summer):131–154.

———. 1999. *The Coming of Post-Industrial Society: A Venture in Social Forecasting.* With new foreword. New York: Basic Books.

Bell, Wendell. 1981. "Modernization." Pp. 186–187 in *Encyclopedia of Sociology.* Guilford, CT: DPG Publishing.

Bellafante, Ginia. 2005. "Young South Asians in America Embrace 'Assisted' Marriages." *New York Times,* August 23, pp. A1, A15.

Belt, Don. 2002. "The World of Islam." *National Geographic* (January):26–85.

Benac, Nancy. 2006. "Abortion Opinions Stay the Same as Laws Change." *Chicago Sun-Times,* March 13, p. 42.

Bendick, Marc, Jr., Charles W. Jackson, and J. Horacio Romero. 1993. *Employment Discrimination against Older Workers: An Experimental Study of Hiring Practices.* Washington, DC: Fair Employment Council of Greater Washington.

Bendix, B. Reinhard. 1968. "Max Weber." Pp. 493–502 in *International Encyclopedia of the Social Sciences,* edited by David L. Sills. New York: Macmillan.

Benford, Robert D. 1992. "Social Movements." Pp. 1880–1887 in *Encyclopedia of Sociology,* vol. 4, edited by Edgar F. Borgatta and Marie Borgatta. New York: Macmillan.

Bennett, Vivienne. 1995. "Gender, Class, and Water: Women and the Politics of Water Service in Monterrey, Mexico." *Latin American Perspectives* 22 (September), pp. 76–99.

Berger, Peter, and Thomas Luckmann. 1966. *The Social Construction of Reality.* New York: Doubleday.

Berkeley Wellness Letter. 1990. "The Nest Refilled." 6 (February):1–2.

Berkman, Lisa F. 2004. "The Health Divide." *Contexts* (Fall):38–43.

Berlin, Brent, and Paul Kay. 1991. *Basic Color Terms: Their Universality and Evolution.* Berkeley, CA: University of California Press.

Bernasek, Anna. 2006. "A Poverty Line That's Out of Date and Out of Favor." *New York Times,* August 14, p. 8.

Bernstein, Sharon. 2004. "Under the Radar, HIV Worsens." *Los Angeles Times,* October 16, pp. A1, A12.

Berry, Mary Frances. 2001. "Status Report on Probe of Election Practices in Florida During the 2000 Presidential Election." *Black Scholar* 31 (no. 2): 2–5.

Bian, Yanjie. 2002. "Chinese Social Stratification and Social Mobility." Pp. 91–116 in *Annual Review of Sociology,* edited by Karen S. Cook and John Hagan. Palo Alto, CA: Annual Reviews.

Bianchi, Suzanne M., and Daphne Spain. 1996. "Women, Work, and Family in America." *Population Bulletin* 51 (December).

Bielby, Denise D., and William T. Bielby. 2002. "Hollywood Dreams, Harsh Realities: Writing for Film and Television." *Contexts* 1 (Fall/Winter):21–25.

Black, Donald. 1995. "The Epistemology of Pure Sociology." *Law and Social Inquiry* 20 (Summer): 829–870.

Blackhall, Leslie J. et al. 1995. "Ethnicity and Attitudes toward Patient Autonomy." *Journal of the American Medical Association* 274 (September 13): 820–825.

Blair, Elizabeth. 2005. "'Baby Mama' Spurs Debate over Teen Motherhood." National Public Radio, March 24, 2005. Accessed March 1, 2006 (www.npr.org).

Blau, Peter M., and Otis Dudley Duncan. 1967. *The American Occupational Structure.* New York: Wiley.

———, and Marshall W. Meyer. 1987. *Bureaucracy in Modern Society.* 3d ed. New York: Random House.

Blauner, Robert. 1972. *Racial Oppression in America.* New York: Harper and Row.

Blumer, Herbert. 1955. "Collective Behavior." Pp. 165–198 in *Principles of Sociology,* 2d ed., edited by Alfred McClung Lee. New York: Barnes and Noble.

———. 1969. *Symbolic Interactionism: Perspective and Method.* Englewood Cliffs, NJ: Prentice Hall.

Boase, Jeffery, John B. Horrigan, Barry Wellman, and Lee Rainie. 2006. *The Strength of Internet Ties.* Washington, DC: Pew Internet and American Life Project.

Boaz, Rachel Floersheim. 1987. "Early Withdrawal from the Labor Force." *Research on Aging* 9 (December):530–547.

Bok, Sissela. 1998. *Mayhem: Violence as Public Entertainment.* Reading, MA: Addison-Wesley.

Bonczar, Thomas P., and Tracy L. Snell. 2004. "Capital Punishment, 2003." *Bureau of Justice Statistics Bulletin* (November).

Bordt, Rebecca. 2003. "Using a Research Article to Facilitate a Deep Structure Understanding or Discrimination." *Teaching Sociology* 33 (October):403–410.

Bornschier, Volker, Christopher Chase-Dunn, and Richard Rubinson. 1978. "Cross-National Evidence of the Effects of Foreign Investment and Aid on Economic Growth and Inequality: A Survey of Findings and a Reanalysis." *American Journal of Sociology* 84 (November):651–683.

Borosage, Robert L. 2003. "Class Welfare: Bush Style." *American Prospect* 14 (March):15–18.

Bottomore, Tom, and Maximilien Rubel, eds. 1956. *Karl Marx: Selected Writings in Sociology and Social Philosophy.* New York: McGraw-Hill.

Boudreaux, Richard. 2002. "Indian Rights Law Is Upheld in Mexico." *Los Angeles Times,* September 7, p. A3.

Bourdieu, Pierre. 1962. *The Algerians.* Preface by Raymond Aron. Boston: Beacon Press.

Boushey, Heather. 2005. *Student Debt: Bigger and Bigger.* Washington, DC: Center for Economic and Policy Research.

Bouvier, Leon F. 1980. "America's Baby Boom Generation: The Fateful Bulge." *Population Bulletin* 35 (April).

Bowles, Samuel, and Herbert Gintis. 1976. *Schooling in Capitalistic America: Educational Reforms and the Contradictions of Economic Life.* New York: Basic Books.

Bowles, Scott. 2000. "Bans in Racial Profiling Gain Steam." *USA Today,* June 2, p. 3A.

Bradsher, Keith. 2004. "Like Japan in the 1980's, China Poses Big Economic Challenge." *New York Times,* March 2, pp. A1, C2.

Brady, David. 2003. "Rethinking the Sociological Measurement of Poverty." *Social Forces* 81 (March):715–752.

Brannigan, Augustine. 1992. "Postmodernism." Pp. 1522–1525 in *Encyclopedia of Sociology,* vol. 3, edited by Edgar F. Borgatta and Marie L. Borgatta. New York: Macmillan.

Braverman, Amy. 2002. "Open Door Sexuality." *University of Chicago Magazine* 95 (October):20–21.

Bray, James H., and John Kelly. 1999. *Stepfamilies: Love, Marriage, and Parenting in the First Decade.* New York: Broadway Books.

Brewer, Cynthia A., and Trudy A. Suchan. 2001. *Mapping Census 2000: The Geography of U.S. Diversity.* Washington, DC: U.S. Government Printing Office.

Brint, Steven. 1998. *Schools and Societies.* Thousand Oaks, CA: Pine Forge Press.

Brittingham, Angela, and G. Patricia de la Cruz. 2004. *Ancestry: 2000. Census Brief* C2KBR-35. Washington, DC: U.S. Government Printing Office.

Brown, David K. 2001. "The Social Sources of Educational Credentialism: Status Cultures, Labor Markets, and Organizations." *Sociology of Education* 74 (Extra Issue):19–34.

Brown, Patricia Leigh. 2004. "For Children of Gays, Marriage Brings Joy." *New York Times,* March 19, p. A13.

Brown, Robert McAfee. 1980. *Gustavo Gutierrez.* Atlanta: John Knox.

Brown, Susan I. 2005. "How Cohabitation Is Reshaping American Families." *Contexts* (Summer): 33–37.

Bryant, Adam. 1999. "American Pay Rattles Foreign Partners." *New York Times,* January 17, sec. 6, pp. 1, 4.

Budig, Michelle J. 2002. "Male Advantage and the Gender Composition of Jobs: Who Rides the Glass Escalator?" *Social Problems* 49 (2):258–277.

Bullard, Robert, D. 1993. *Dumping in Dixie: Race, Class, and Environmentalist Quality.* 2d ed. Boulder, CO: Westin Press.

Bulle, Wolfgang F. 1987. *Crossing Cultures? Southeast Asian Mainland.* Atlanta: Centers for Disease Control.

Bumiller, Elisabeth. 2000. "Resolute Adversary of Divorce." *New York Times,* December 16, pp. A17, A19.

Bunzel, John H. 1992. *Race Relations on Campus: Stanford Students Speak.* Stanford, CA: Portable Stanford.

Bureau of Justice Statistics. 2004. *First Release from State Prisons 2001.* Washington, DC: Bureau of Justice Statistics.

Bureau of Labor Statistics. 2002. "Number of Jobs Held, Labor Market Activity, and Earnings Growth Among Young Baby Boomers." News release of August 27 (www.bls.gov/nls).

———. 2004. "Current Labor Statistics." Accessed January 28 (www.bls.gov/opub/mlr/mlrhome.htm).

———. 2005. *Union Members in 2004.* Accessed February 28 (www.bls.gov).

Bureau of Primary Health Care. 1999. Home page. Accessed January 18, 2000 (www.bphc.hrsa.gov/bphcfactsheehtm).

Bureau of the Census. 1975. *Historical Statistics of the United States, Colonial Times to 1970.* Washington, DC: U.S. Government Printing Office.

———. 1994. *Statistical Abstract of the United States, 1994.* Washington, DC: U.S. Government Printing Office.

———. 1996. "Percent Distribution of Projected Households by Type: 1995 to 2010." Released May 1996. Accessed March 1, 2006 (www.census.gov).

———. 1998. "Race of Wife by Race of Husband." Internet release of June 10.

———. 2003a. *Statistical Abstract of the United States, 2003.* Washington, DC: U.S. Government Printing Office.

———. 2003b. *Characteristics of American Indians and Alaska Natives. By Tribe and Language: 2000.* Washington, DC: U.S. Government Printing Office.

———. 2003c. TM-PCT023 *Percent of Persons of Arab Ancestry 2000.* Accessed March 4, 2004 (http://factfinder.census.gov).

———. 2003d. *Summary Tables on Language Use and English Ability, 2000* (PHC-T-20). Accessed January 14, 2004 (www.census.gov/population/www/cen2000/phc-t20.html).

———. 2004a. *Statistical Abstract of the United States, 2004–2005.* Washington, DC: U.S. Government Printing Office.

———. 2005a. *Statistical Abstract of the United States 2006.* Washington, DC: U.S. Government Printing Office.

———. 2005b. "Total Midyear Population for the World: 1950–2050." Updated April 26. Accessed June 1 (www.census.gov/ipc/www/worldpop.html.)

———. 2005c. *Florida, California and Texas Future Population Growth,* Census Bureau Reports, CB05-52. Washington, DC: U.S. Government Printing Office.

———. 2005d. "International Data Base." Accessed April 26 (www.census.gov/ipc/www/idbnew.html).

———. 2005e. World Population: 1950–2050. April 2005 version. Accessed May 3, 2006 (www.census.gov/ipc/www/img/worldpop.gif).

———. 2005f. "American Fact Finder: Places with United States." Accessed December 12 (http://factfinder.census.gov).

———. 2005g. "Hurricane Katrina Disaster Area." Accessed December 15 (www.census.gov).

———. 2005h. *Educational Attainment CPS 2004.* Washington, DC: US Government Printing Office.

———. 2005i. "International Database Pyramids." Updated April 26. Accessed June 1 (www.census.gov/ipc/www.idbpyr.htm).

Burgess, Ernest W. 1925. "The Growth of the City." Pp. 47–62 in *The City,* edited by Robert E. Park, Ernest W. Burgess, and Roderick D. McKenzie. Chicago: University of Chicago Press.

Burkett, Elinor. 2000. *The Baby Boom: How Family Friendly America Cheats the Childless.* New York: Free Press.

Burns, John R. 1998. "Once Widowed in India, Twice Scorned." *New York Times,* March 29, p. A1.

Bushway, Shawn D., and Anne Mourison Piehl. 2001. "Judging Judicial Discretion Legal Factors and Racial Discrimination Legal Factors and Racial Discrimination in Sentencing." *Law and Society Review* 35 (4):733–764.

Butler, Daniel Allen. 1998. *"Unsinkable": The Full Story.* Mechanicsburg, PA: Stackpole Books.

Butler, Robert N. 1990. "A Disease Called Ageism." *Journal of American Geriatrics Society* 38 (February):178–180.

Byrd-Bredbenner, Carol, and Jessica Murray. 2003. "Comparison of the Anthropometric Measurements of Idealized Female Body Images in Media Directed to Men, Women, and Mixed Gender Audiences." *Topics in Clinical Nutrition* 18 (2):117–129.

Caesar, Lena G., and David R. Williams. 2002. *The ASHA Leader Online: Socioculture and the Delivery of Health Care: Who Gets What and Why.* Accessed December 1 (www.asha.org).

Calhoun, Craig. 2003. "Belonging in the Cosmopolitan Imaginary." *Ethnicities* 3 (December): 531–553.

Campbell, Mary, Robert Haveman, Gary Sandefur, and Barbara Wolte. 2005. "Economic Inequality and Educational Attainment Across a Generation." *Focus* 23 (Spring):11–15.

Camus, Albert. 1948. *The Plague.* New York: Random House.

Caplan, Ronald L. 1989. "The Commodification of American Health Care." *Social Science and Medicine* 28 (11):1139–1148.

Caplow, Theodore, and Louis Hicks. 2002. *Systems of War and Peace.* 2d ed. Lanham, MD: University Press of America.

Carey, Anne R., and Elys A. McLean. 1997. "Heard It Through the Grapevine?" *USA Today,* September 15, p. B1.

Carlson, Darren K. 2004. "Racial Profiling Seen as Pervasive, Unjust." Accessed July 20 (www.gallup.com).

Carrese, Joseph A., and Lorna A. Rhodes. 1995. "Western Bioethics on the Navaho Reservation: Benefit or Harm?" *Journal of the American Medical Association* 274 (September 13):826–829.

Carroll, John. 2003. "The Good Doctor." *American Way* (July 15):26–31.

Carroll, Joseph. 2006. "Public: National Anthem Should Be Sung in English." Gallup Poll, May 3, 2006.

Carter, Bill, and Jim Rutenberg. 2003. "Shows' Creators Say Television Will Suffer in New Climate." *New York Times,* June 3, pp. C1, C8.

Carty, Win. 1999. "Greater Dependence on Cars Leads to More Pollution in World's Cities." *Population Today* 27 (December):1–2.

Castañeda, Jorge G. 1995. "Ferocious Differences." *Atlantic Monthly* 276 (July):68–69, 71–76.

Castells, Manuel. 1983. *The City and the Grass Roots.* Berkeley: University of California Press.

———. 1997. *The Power of Identity.* Vol. 1 of *The Information Age: Economy, Society and Culture.* London: Blackwell.

———. 1998. *End of Millennium.* Vol. 3 of *The Information Age: Economy, Society and Culture.* London: Blackwell.

———. 2000. *The Information Age: Economy, Society and Culture* (3 vols.). 2d ed. Oxford and Malden, MA: Blackwell.

———. 2001. *The Internet Galaxy: Reflections on the Internet, Business, and Society.* New York: Oxford University Press.

Catalano, Shannon M. 2005. *Criminal Victimization, 2004.* Washington, DC: U.S. Government Printing Office.

CBS News. 1979. Transcript of *Sixty Minutes* segment, "I Was Only Following Orders." March 31, pp. 2–8.

Center for Academic Integrity. 2006. *CAI Research.* Accessed January 10 (www.academicintegrity.org).

Center for American Women and Politics. 2006. *Fact Sheet: Women in the U.S. Congress 2006 and Statewide Elective Women 2006.* Rutgers, NJ: CAWP.

Cerulo, Karen A., Janet M. Ruane, and Mary Chagko. 1992. "Technological Ties that Bind: Media Generated Primary Groups." *Communication Research* 19:109–129.

Chalfant, H. Paul, Robert E. Beckley, and C. Eddie Palmer. 1994. *Religion in Contemporary Society.* 3d ed. Itasca, IL: F. E. Peacock.

Chambliss, William. 1973. "The Saints and the Roughnecks." *Society* 11 (November/December): 24–31.

Charter, David, and Jill Sherman. 1996. "Schools Must Teach New Code of Values." *London Times,* January 15, p. 1.

Chase-Dunn, Christopher, and Peter Grimes. 1995. "World-Systems Analysis." Pp. 387–417 in *Annual Review of Sociology,* 1995, edited by John Hagan. Palo Alto, CA: Annual Reviews.

———, Yukio Kawano, and Benjamin D. Brewer. 2000. "Trade Globalization Since 1795: Waves of Integration in the World System." *American Sociological Review* 65 (February):77–95.

Cherlin, Andrew J. 2003. "Should the Government Promote Marriage?" *Contexts* 2 (Fall): 22–29.

———. 2005. *Public and Private Families: An Introduction.* 4th ed. New York: McGraw-Hill.

———, Linda M. Burton, Tera R. Hurt, and Diane M. Purvin. 2004. "The Influence of Physical and Sexual Abuse on Marriage and Cohabitation." *American Sociological Review* 69 (December): 768–789.

Chernobyl Forum. 2005. *Chernobyl's Legacy: Health, Environmental and Socio-economic Impacts and Recommendations to the Governments of Belarus, the Russian Federation and Ukraine.* Geneva, Switzerland:International Atomic Energy Agency.

Chesney-Lind, Meda. 1989. "Girls' Crime and Woman's Place: Toward a Feminist Model of Female Delinquency." *Crime and Delinquency* 35:5–29.

Children Now. 2004. *Fall Colors: 2003–04 Prime Time Diversity Report.* Oakland, CA: Children Now.

Chin, Ko-lin. 1996. *Chinatown Gangs: Extortion, Enterprise, and Ethnicity.* New York: Oxford University Press.

China Daily. 2004. "Starbucks Takes Aim at China Chain." Accessed July 21 (www2.chinadaily.com.cn).

Christensen, Kathleen. 1990. "Bridges over Troubled Water: How Older Workers View the Labor Market." Pp. 175–207 in *Bridges to Retirement,* edited by Peter B. Doeringer. Ithaca, NY: IRL Press.

Chronic Poverty Research Center. 2005. "Chronic Poverty." Accessed March 3, 2006 (www.chronicpoverty.org).

Chu, Henry. 2005. "Tractors Crush Heart of a Nation." *Los Angeles Times,* July 10, p. A9.

Civic Ventures. 1999. *The New Face of Retirement: Older Americans, Civic Engagement, and the Longevity Revolution.* Washington, DC: Peter D. Hart Research Associates.

Clark, Burton, and Martin Trow. 1966. "The Organizational Context." Pp. 17–70 in *The Study of College Peer Groups,* edited by Theodore M. Newcomb and Everett K. Wilson. Chicago: Aldine.

Clark, Candace. 1983. "Sickness and Social Control." Pp. 346–365 in *Social Interaction: Readings in Sociology,* 2d ed., edited by Howard Robboy and Candace Clark. New York: St. Martin's.

Clarke, Adele E., Janet K. Shim, Laura Maro, Jennifer Ruth Fusket, and Jennifer R. Fishman. 2003. "Bio Medicalization: Technoscientific Transformations of Health, Illness, and U.S. Biomedicine." *American Sociological Review* 68 (April): 161–194.

Clausen, Christopher. 2002. "To Have . . . or Not to Have." *Utne Reader* (July–August): 66–70.

Clawson, Dan and Naomi Gerstel. 2002. "Caring for Our Young: Child Care in Europe and the United States." *Contexts* 1 (Fall/Winter):23–35.

Clemmitt, Marcia. 2005. "Intelligent Design." *CQ Researcher* 15 (July 29):637–660.

Clinard, Marshall B., and Robert F. Miller. 1998. *Sociology of Deviant Behavior.* 10th ed. Fort Worth: Harcourt Brace.

Clymer, Adam. 2000. "College Students Not Drawn to Voting or Politics, Poll Shows." *New York Times,* January 2, p. A14.

Coates, Rodney D. 2004. "Critical Racial and Ethnic Studies—Profiling and Reparations." *American Behavioral Scientists* 47 (March):873–878.

Cockburn, Andrew. 2003. "21st Century Slaves." *National Geographic* 203 (September):2–29.

Cockerham, William C. 1998. *Medical Sociology.* 7th ed. Upper Saddle River, NJ: Prentice Hall.

Cohen, Debra Nussbaum. 2005. "Questions, Answers and Minutiae of the Faithful Can Be Found in the Blogosphere." *New York Times,* March 5, p. A13.

Cohen, Lawrence E., and Marcus Felson. 1979. "Social Change and Crime Rate Trends: A Routine Activities Approach." *American Sociological Review* 44:588–608.

Cole, Elizabeth S. 1985. "Adoption, History, Policy, and Program." Pp. 638–666 in *A Handbook of Child Welfare*, edited by John Laird and Ann Hartman. New York: Free Press.

Cole, Mike. 1988. *Bowles and Gintis Revisited: Correspondence and Contradiction in Educational Theory.* Philadelphia: Falmer.

Coleman, Isobel. 2004. "The Payoff from Women's Rights." *Foreign Affairs* 83 (May/June):80–95.

Coleman, James William. 2006. *The Criminal Elite: Understanding White-Collar Crime.* 6th ed. New York: Worth.

Collins, Randall. 1975. *Conflict Sociology: Toward an Explanatory Sociology.* New York: Academic.

———. 1980. "Weber's Last Theory of Capitalism: A Systematization." *American Sociological Review* 45 (December):925–942.

———. 1986. *Weberian Sociological Theory.* New York: Cambridge University Press.

———. 1995. "Prediction in Macrosociology: The Case of the Soviet Collapse." *American Journal of Sociology* 100 (May):1552–1593.

Commission on Civil Rights. 1976. *A Guide to Federal Laws and Regulations Prohibiting Sex Discrimination.* Washington, DC: U.S. Government Printing Office.

———. 1981. *Affirmative Action in the 1980s: Dismantling the Process of Discrimination.* Washington DC: U.S. Government Printing Office.

Commoner, Barry. 1971. *The Closing Circle.* New York: Knopf.

———. 1990. *Making Peace with the Planet.* New York: Pantheon.

Commonwealth Fund. 2002. *Unequal Treatment: Confronting Racial and Ethnic Disparities in Health Care.* Washington, DC: National Academy of Sciences.

Comstock, P., and M. B. Fox. 1994. "Employer Tactics and Labor Law Reform." Pp. 90–109 in *Restoring the Promise of American Labor Law*, edited by S. Friedman, R. W. Hurd, R. A. Oswald, and R. L. Seeber. Ithaca, NY: ILR Press.

Conrad, Peter, ed. 2000. *The Sociology of Health and Illness: Cultural Perspectives.* 6th ed. New York: Worth.

———, and Joseph W. Schneider. 1992. *Deviance and Medicalization: From Badness to Sickness.* Expanded ed. Philadelphia: Temple University Press.

Cooley, Charles. H. 1902. *Human Nature and the Social Order.* New York: Scribner.

Coontz, Stephanie. 2006. "A Pop Quiz on Marriage." *New York Times*, February 19, p. 12.

Cortese, Anthony J. 1999. *Provocateur: Images of Women and Minorities in Advertising.* Lanham, MD: Rowman and Littlefield.

Coser, Lewis A. 1977. *Masters of Sociological Thought: Ideas in Historical and Social Context.* 2d ed. New York: Harcourt, Brace and Jovanovich.

Côté, James E. 2000. *Arrested Adulthood: The Changing Nature of Identity and Maturity in the Late World.* New York: New York University.

Couch, Carl J. 1996. *Information Technologies and Social Orders.* Edited with an introduction by David R. Maines and Shing-Ling Chien. New York: Aldine de Gruyter.

Council on Scientific Affairs. 1999. "Hispanic Health in the United States." *Journal of the American Medical Association* 265 (January 9): 248–252.

Counts, D. A. 1977. "The Good Death in Kaliai: Preparation for Death in Western New Britain." *Omega* 7:367–372.

Cowell, Alan. 2005. "Gay Britons Signing Up as Unions Become Legal." *New York Times*, December 5.

Cox, Oliver C. 1948. *Caste, Class, and Race: A Study in Social Dynamics.* Detroit: Wayne State University Press.

Cox, Rachel S. 2003. "Home Schooling Debate." *CQ Researcher* 13 (January 17):25–48.

Cressey, Donald R. 1960. "Epidemiology and Individual Contact: A Case from Criminology." *Pacific Sociological Review* 3 (Fall):47–58.

Cromwell, Paul F., James N. Olson, and D'Aunn Wester Avarey. 1995. *Breaking and Entering: An Ethnographic Analysis of Burglary.* Newbury Park, CA: Sage.

Crosnoe, Robert, and Glen H. Elder Jr. 2002. "Successful Adaptation in the Later Years: A Life Course Approach to Aging." *Social Psychology Quarterly* (No. 4), pp. 309–328.

Cross, Simon, and Barbara Bagilhole. 2002. "Girls' Jobs for the Boys? Men, Masculinity and Non-Traditional Occupations." *Gender, Work, and Organization* 9 (April):204–226.

Croteau, David, and William Hoynes. 2001. *The Business of the Media: Corporate Media and the Public Interest.* Thousand Oaks, CA: Pine Forge.

———. 2003. *Media/Society: Industries, Images, and Audiences.* 3d ed. Thousand Oaks, CA: Pine Forge.

Croucher, Sheila L. 2004. *Globalization and Belonging: The Politics of Identity in a Changing World.* Lanham, MD: Rowman and Littlefield.

Crouse, Kelly. 1999. "Sociology of the Titanic." *Teaching Sociology Listserv.* May 24.

Crowe, Jerry, and Valli Herman. 2005. "NBA Lists Fashion Do's and Don'ts." *Los Angeles Times*, October 19, pp. A1, A23.

Cuff, E. C., W. W. Sharrock, and D. W. Francis, eds. 1990. *Perspectives in Sociology.* 3d ed. Boston: Unwin Hyman.

Cullen, Francis T., Jr., and John B. Cullen. 1978. *Toward a Paradigm of Labeling Theory*, ser. 58. Lincoln: University of Nebraska Studies.

Cumming, Elaine, and William E. Henry. 1961. *Growing Old: The Process of Disengagement.* New York: Basic Books.

Currie, Elliot. 1985. *Confronting Crime: An American Challenge.* New York: Pantheon.

———. 1998. *Crime and Punishment in America.* New York: Metropolitan Books.

Curry, Timothy Jon. 1993. "A Little Pain Never Hurt Anyone: Athletic Career Socialization and the Normalization of Sports Injury." *Symbolic Interaction* 26 (Fall):273–290.

Curtiss, Susan. 1977. *Genie: A Psycholinguistic Study of a Modern Day "Wild Child."* New York: Academic Press.

———. 1985. "The Development of Human Cerebral Lateralization." Pp. 97–116 in *The Dual Brain*, edited by D. Frank Benson and Eran Zaidel. New York: Guilford.

Dahl, Robert A. 1961. *Who Governs?* New Haven, CT: Yale University Press.

Dahrendorf, Ralf. 1958. "Toward a Theory of Social Conflict." *Journal of Conflict Resolution* 2 (June):170–183.

———. 1959. *Class and Class Conflict in Industrial Sociology.* Stanford, CA: Stanford University Press.

Daley, Suzanne. 1999. "Doctors' Group of Volunteers Awarded Nobel." *New York Times*, October 16, pp. A1, A6.

Dalla, Rochelle L., and Wendy C. Gamble. 2001. "Teenage Mothering and the Navajo Reservation: An Examination of Intergovernmental Perceptions and Beliefs." *American Indian Culture and Research Journal* 25 (1):1–19.

Daniszewski, John. 2003. "Al-Jazeera TV Draws Flak Outside—and Inside—the Arab World." *Los Angeles Times*, January 5, pp. A1, A5.

Dao, James. 1995. "New York's Highest Court Rules Unmarried Couples Can Adopt." *New York Times*, November 3, pp. A1, B2.

Darwin, Charles. 1859. *On the Origin of Species.* London: John Murray.

Dash, Erich. 2006. "Executive Pay: A Special Project." *New York Times*, April 9, sect. 3, pp. 1, 5.

David, Gary. 2004. "Scholarship on Arab Americans Distorted Past 9/11." *Al Jadid* (Winter/Spring): 26–27.

Davies, Christie. 1989. "Goffman's Concept of the Total Institution: Criticisms and Revisions." *Human Studies* 12 (June):77–95.

Davis, Darren W. 1997. "The Direction of Race of Interviewer Effects Among African-Americans: Donning the Black Mask." *American Journal of Political Science* 41 (January): 309–322.

Davis, Donald B., and Karen A. Polonko. 2001. *Telework America 2001 Summary.* Accessed March 3, 2003 (www.workingfromanywhere.org/telework/twa2001.htm).

Davis, Gerald. 2003. *America's Corporate Banks Are Separated by Just Four Handshakes.* Accessed March 7 (www.bus.umich.edu/research/davis.html).

———. 2004. "American Cronyism: How Executive Networks Inflated the Corporate Bubble." *Contexts* (Summer):34–40.

Davis, James A. 1982. "Up and Down Opportunity's Ladder." *Public Opinion* 5 (June/July):11–15, 48–51.

———, Tom W. Smith, and Peter V. Marsden. 2005. *General Social Surveys, 1972–2004: Cumulative Codebook.* Chicago: National Opinion Research Center.

440

Davis, Kingsley. 1940. "Extreme Social Isolation of a Child." *American Journal of Sociology* 45 (January):554–565.

———. 1947. "A Final Note on a Case of Extreme Isolation." *American Journal of Sociology* 52 (March):432–437.

———. [1949] 1995. *Human Society.* Reprint, New York: Macmillan.

———, and Wilbert E. Moore. 1945. "Some Principles of Stratification." *American Sociological Review* 10 (April):242–249.

Davis, Mike. 2005. *Planet of Slums.* London: Verso.

Davis, Nanette J. 1975. *Sociological Constructions of Deviance: Perspectives and Issues in the Field.* Dubuque, IA: Wm. C. Brown.

Davis, Robert, and Anthony DeBarros. 2006. "In College, First Year Is by Far the Riskiest." *USA Today,* January 25.

Death Penalty Information Center. 2006. "Number of Executions by State and Region Since 1976." Accessed February 19 (www.deathpenalty info.org).

Deegan, Mary Jo, ed. 1991. *Women in Sociology: A Bio-Biographical Sourcebook.* Westport, CT: Greenwood.

———. 2003. "Textbooks the History of Sociology, and the Sociological Stock of Knowledge." *Sociological Theory* 21 (November):298–305.

Deflem, Mathieu. 2005. "'Wild Beasts Without Nationality': The Uncertain Origins of Interpol, 1898–1910." Pp. 275–285 in *Handbook of Transnational Crime and Justice,* edited by Philip Rechel. Thousand Oaks, CA: Sage.

Delany, Kevin J. 2005. "Big Mother Is Watching." *Wall Street Journal,* November 26, pp. A1, A6.

Delawala, Imtyaz. 2002. "What Is Coltran?" January 21, 2002 (www.abcnews.com).

Della Porta, Donatella, and Sidney Tarrow, eds. 2005. *Transnational Protest and Global Activism.* Lanham, MD: Rowman and Littlefield.

Dellios, Hugh. 2002. "Desperate Migrants Accept Risks." *New York Times,* October 20, pp. 1, 7.

Deloria, Vine, Jr. 1999. *For This Land: Writings on Religion in America.* New York: Routledge.

DeNavas-Walt, Carmen, Bernadette D. Proctor, and Cheryl Miller. 2005. "Income, Poverty and Health Insurance Coverage in the United States: 2004." *Current Population Reports.* ser. P-60, no. 229. Washington, DC: U.S. Government Printing Office.

Denny, Charlotte. 2004. "Migration Myths Hold No Fears." *Guardian Weekly* (February 26):12.

Denzin, Norman K. 2004. "Postmodernism." Pp. 581–583 in *Encyclopedia of Social Theory,* edited by George Ritzer. Thousand Oaks, CA: Sage.

DePalma, Anthony. 1995. "Racism? Mexico's in Denial." *New York Times,* June 11, p. E4.

———. 1996. "For Mexico Indians, New Voice but Few Gains." *New York Times,* January 13, pp. B1, B2.

———. 2002. "White-Collar Layoffs, Downsized Dreams." *New York Times,* December 5, pp. A1, A38.

DeParle, Jason. 2005. "Hispanic Group Thrives on Federal Aid." *New York Times,* May 3, pp. A1, A16.

Department of Agriculture. 2004. *2002 Census of Agriculture: Preliminary Report AC-02-A-PR.* Washington, DC: U.S. Government Printing Office.

Department of Defense. 2003. "Selected Manpower Statistics Fiscal Year 2002." Washington, DC: Department of Defense.

Department of Health and Human Services. 2004. "Percent Change in AFDC/TANF Families and Receipts." Accessed February 22 (www.acfhhs.gov).

Department of Homeland Security. 2006. *The Federal Response to Hurricane Katrina: Lessons Learned.* Washington, DC: U.S. Government Printing Office.

Department of Justice. 2000. *The Civil Liberties Act of 1988: Redress for Japanese Americans.* Accessed June 29 (http://www.usdoj.gov/crt/ora/main. html).

———. 2005. *Crime in the United States, 2004.* Washington, DC: U.S. Government Printing Office.

Department of Labor. 1995a. *Good for Business: Making Full Use of the Nation's Capital.* Washington, DC: U.S. Government Printing Office.

———. 1995b. *A Solid Investment: Making Full Use of the Nation's Human Capital.* Washington, DC: U.S. Government Printing Office.

———. 2005. *Union Members in 2004.* Washington, DC: Bureau of Labor Statistics.

Department of State. 2006. "Immigrant Visas Issued to Orphans Coming to the US." Accessed March 21 (http://travel.state.gov/family/adoption/stats/ stats_451.html).

Derné, Steve. 2003. "Arnold Swarzenegger, Ally McBeal, and Arranged Marriages: Globalization on the Ground Media." *Contexts* 2 (Summer): 12–18.

Deutsch, Claudia H. 2005. "My Big Fat CEO Paycheck." *New York Times,* April 3, sect. 5. pp. 1, 11–12.

Desai, Manisha. 1996. "If Peasants Build Their Own Dams, What Would the State Have Left to Do?" Pp. 209–224 in *Research in Social Movements, Conflicts and Change,* vol. 19, edited by Michael Dobkowski and Isidor Wallimann. Greenwich, CT: JAI Press.

Devitt, James. 1999. *Framing Gender on the Campaign Trail: Women's Executive Leadership and the Press.* New York: Women's Leadership Conference.

Diamond, Jared. 2003. "Globalization, Then." *Los Angeles Times,* September 14, pp. M1, M3.

Dighton, Daniel. 2003. "Minority Overrepresentation in the Criminal and Juvenile Justice Systems." *The Compiler* (Summer):1, 3–6.

Dillon, Sam. 1998. "Sex Bias at Border Plants in Mexico Reported by U.S." *New York Times,* January 13, p. A6.

———. 2004. "Education Can Be Long, Hard Haul for Nation's Rural Kids." *Chicago Tribune,* May 28, p. 13.

DiMaggio, Paul, Eszter Hargittai, W. Russell Neuman, and John P. Robinson. 2001. "Social Implications of the Internet." Pp. 307–336 in *Annual Review of Sociology, 2001,* edited by Karen S. Cook and John Hogan. Palo Alto, CA: Annual Reviews.

Directors Guild of America. 2002. *Diversity Hiring Special Report.* Los Angeles: DGA.

Dodds, Klaus. 2000. *Geopolitics in a Changing World.* Harlow, England: Pearson Education.

Doeringer, Peter B., ed. 1990. *Bridges to Retirement: Older Workers in a Changing Labor Market.* Ithaca, NY: ILR Press.

Domhoff, G. William. 1978. *Who Really Rules? New Haven and Community Power Reexamined.* New Brunswick, NJ: Transaction.

———. 2006. *Who Rules America?* 5th ed. New York: McGraw-Hill.

Dominick, Joseph R. 2005. *The Dynamics of Mass Communication: Media in the Digital Age.* 8th ed. New York: McGraw-Hill.

Doress, Irwin, and Jack Nusan Porter. 1977. *Kids in Cults: Why They Join. Why They Stay, Why They Leave.* Brookline, MA: Reconciliation Associates.

Dotson, Floyd. 1991. "Community" P. 55 in *Encyclopedic Dictionary of Sociology.* 4th ed. Guilford, CT: Dushkin.

Dougherty, John, and David Holthouse. 1999. "Bordering on Exploitation." Accessed March 5 (www.phoenixnewtime.com/issies/1998-07-09/ feature.html).

Dougherty, Kevin, and Floyd M. Hammack. 1992. "Education Organization." Pp. 535–541 in *Encyclopedia of Sociology,* vol. 2, edited by Edgar F. Borgatta and Marie L. Borgatta. New York: Macmillan.

Dowd, James J. 1980. *Stratification among the Aged.* Monterey, CA: Brooks/Cole.

Doyle, James A., and Michele A. Paludi. 1998. *Sex and Gender: The Human Experience.* 4th ed. New York: McGraw-Hill.

Dreifus, Claudia. 2006. "A Sociologist Confronts 'the Messy Stuff' of Race, Genes and Disease." *New York Times,* October 18.

Drinkard, Jim. 2006. "Tribes' Political Giving Targeted." *USA Today,* January 31, p. A1.

Du Bois, W. E. B. 1909. *The Negro American Family.* Atlanta University. Reprinted 1970. Cambridge, MA: M.I.T. Press.

———. [1940] 1968. *Dusk of Dawn.* New York: Harcourt, Brace. Reprinted New York: Schocken Books.

Dukes, Richard L., Tara M. Bisel, Karoline N. Burega, Eligio A. Lobato, and Matthew D. Owens. 2003. "Expression of Love, Sex, and Hurt in Popular Songs: A Content Analysis of All-Time Greatest Hits." *Social Science Journal:*643–650.

Dundas, Susan, and Miriam Kaufman. 2000. "The Toronto Lesbian Family Study." *Journal of Homosexuality* 40 (20):65–79.

Duneier, Mitchell. 1994a. "On the Job, but Behind the Scenes." *Chicago Tribune,* December 26, pp. 1, 24.

———. 1994b. "Battling for Control." *Chicago Tribune,* December 28. pp. 1, 8.

———. 1999. *Sidewalk.* New York: Farrar, Straus and Giroux.

Dunne, Gillian A. 2000. "Opting into Motherhood: Lesbians Blurring the Boundaries and Transforming the Meaning of Parenthood and Kinship." *Gender and Society* 14 (February):11–35.

Durkheim, Émile. [1912] 2001. *The Elementary Forms of Religious Life.* A new translation by Carol Cosman. New York: Oxford University Press.

———. [1893] 1933. *Division of Labor in Society.* Translated by George Simpson. Reprint, New York: Free Press.

———. [1897] 1951. *Suicide.* Translated by John A. Spaulding and George Simpson. Reprint, New York: Free Press.

———. [1895] 1964. *The Rules of Sociological Method.* Translated by Sarah A. Solovay and John H. Mueller. Reprint, New York: Free Press.

Durose, Matthew R., Erica L. Schmitt, and Patrick A. Langan. 2005. *Contacts between Police and the Public: Findings from the 2002 National Survey.* Washington, DC: Office of Justice Programs, Bureau of Justice Statistics.

Duster, Troy. 2002. "Sociological Stranger in the Land of the Human Genome Project." *Contexts* 1 (Fall):69–70.

———. 2003. *Backdoor to Eugenics.* 2d ed. New York: Routledge.

Dworsky, Amy, Mark Courtney, Irving Pitauin. 2003. *What Happens to Families Under W-2 in Milwaukee County, Wisconsin?* Chicago: Chapin Hall Center for Children, University of Chicago.

Easterbrook, Gregg. 2006. "Case Closed: The Debate about Global Warning Is Over." Working paper. Washington, DC: Brookings Institution.

Ebaugh, Helen Rose Fuchs. 1988. *Becoming an Ex: The Process of Role Exit.* Chicago: University of Chicago Press.

Eckenwiler, Mark. 1995. "In the Eyes of the Law." *Internet World* (August):74, 76–77.

The Economist. 2003a. "Race in Brazil: Out of Eden." (July 5):31–32.

———. 2003b. "The One Where Pooh Goes to Sweden." (April 5):59.

———. 2003c. "The War That Never Ends." 360 (January 18):24–26.

———. 2003d. "No Rush to Death." 368 (August 16):47.

———. 2004a. "Veil of Tears." (January 15).

———. 2004b. "Battle on the Home Front." (February 21):8–10.

———. 2005a. "Back to the Beach?" (January 8):54–55.

———. 2005b. "We Are Tous Québécois." (January 8):39.

———. 2005c. "Behind the Digital Divide." (March 2):22–25.

———. 2005d. "Chasing the Dream." (August 6): 53–55.

———. 2005e. "The Mountain Man and the Surgeon." (December 24):24–26.

———. 2005f. "The Hidden Wealth of the Poor." (November 5):1–14.

———. 2005g. "Not Here, Surely?" 377 (December 10):31–32.

———. 2006. "The World's Largest Economies." (April 1):84.

Edin, Kathryn, and Maria Kefalas. 2005. "Unmarried with Children." *Contexts* (Spring):16–22.

Edwards, Harry. 1973. *Sociology of Sport.* Homewood, IL: Dorsey Press.

Edwards, Tamala M. 2001. "How Med Students Put Abortion Back in the Classroom." *Time* 157 (May 7):59–60.

Efron, Sonni. 1997. "In Japan, Even Tots Must Make the Grade." *Los Angeles Times,* February 16, pp. A1, A17.

Ehrenreich, Barbara. 2001. *Nickel and Dimed: On (Not) Getting By in America.* New York: Metropolitan.

Ehrlich, Paul R. 1968. *The Population Bomb.* New York: Ballantine.

———, and Anne H. Ehrlich. 1990. *The Population Explosion.* New York: Simon and Schuster.

———, and Katherine Ellison. 2002. "A Looming Threat We Won't Face." *Los Angeles Times.* January 20, p. M6.

Eitzen, D. Stanley. 2003. *Fair and Foul: Beyond the Myths and Paradoxes of Sport.* 2d ed. Lanham, MD: Rowman and Littlefield.

Ellingwood, Ken. 2001. "Results of Crackdown and Border Called Mixed." *Los Angeles Times,* August 4, p. B9.

Elliott, Barry J. 1999. "Road Rage: Media Hype or Serious Road Safety Issue?" Accessed December 14, 2005 (www.drivers.com).

Ellison, Ralph. 1952. *Invisible Man.* New York: Random House.

El Nasser, Haya. 2001. "Minorities Reshape Suburbs." *USA Today,* July 9, p. 1A.

Ely, Robin J. 1995. "The Power of Demography: Women's Social Construction of Gender Identity at Work." *Academy of Management Journal* 38 (3):589–634.

Embree, Ainslie. 2003. "Religion." Pp. 101–220 in *Understanding Contemporary India,* edited by Sumit Ganguly and Neil DeVotta. Boulder, CO: Lynne Rienner.

Engels, Friedrich [1884] 1959. "The Origin of the Family, Private Property, and the State." Pp. 392–394, excerpted in *Marx and Engels: Basic Writings on Politics and Philosophy,* edited by Lewis Feuer. Garden City, NY: Anchor.

Entine, Jon, and Martha Nichols. 1996. "Blowing the Whistle on Meaningless 'Good Intentions.'" *Chicago Tribune,* June 20, sec. 1, p. 21.

Epstein, Robert. 2005. "Pychology's Top 10 Misguided Ideas." *Psychology Today* 38 (January/February):55–58, 60.

Erard, Michael. 2005. "How Linguistics and Missionaries Share a Bible of 6,912 Languages." *New York Times,* July 10, p. D3.

Ericson, Nels. 2001. "Substance Abuse: The Nation's Number One Health Problem." *OJJDP Fact Sheet* 17 (May):1–2.

Erikson, Kai. 1966. *Wayward Puritans: A Study in the Sociology of Deviance.* New York: Wiley.

Etaugh, Claire. 2003. "Witches, Mothers and Others: Females in Children's Books." *Hilltopics* (Winter): 10–13.

Etzioni, Amitai. 1964. *Modern Organization.* Englewood Cliffs, NJ: Prentice Hall.

———. 1965. *Political Unification.* New York: Holt, Rinehart, and Winston.

Eureka County. 2006. "EPA Hears Testimony on Proposed Radiation Rule." *Nuclear Waste Office Newsletter* (Eureka County Yucca Mountain Information Office) 11 (Winter).

FAIR. 2001. "Fear and Favor 2000." Accessed December 29, 2001 (www.FAIR.org).

Faith, Nazila. 2005. "Iranian Cleric Turns Blogger in Campaign for Reform." *New York Times,* January 16, p. 4.

Fallows, Deborah. 2006. *Pew Internet Project Data.* Washington, DC: Pew Internet and American Life Project.

Farley, Maggie. 2004. "U.N. Gay Policy is Assailed." *Los Angeles Times,* April 9, p. A3.

Farr, Grant M. 1999. *Modern Iran.* New York: McGraw-Hill.

Farrar, Melissa. 2005. "Road Rage and Aggressive Driving." Unpublished paper, Depaul University, Chicago.

Fausset, Richard. 2003. "Sikhs Mark New Year, Fight Post-September 11 Bias." *Los Angeles Times,* April 14, pp. B1, B7.

Feagin, Joe R. 1983. *The Urban Real Estate Game: Playing Monopoly with Real Money.* Englewood Cliffs, NJ: Prentice Hall.

———. 1989. *Minority Group Issues in Higher Education: Learning from Qualitative Research.* Norman, OK: Center for Research on Minority Education, University of Oklahoma.

———. 2001. "Social Justice and Sociology: Agenda for the Twenty-First Century." *American Sociological Review* 66 (February):1–20.

———, Harnán Vera, and Nikitah Imani. 1996. *The Agony of Education: Black Students at White Colleges and Universities.* New York: Routledge.

Featherman, David L., and Robert M. Hauser. 1978. *Opportunity and Change.* New York: Aeodus.

Federal Register, June 4, 1975.

Feinglass, Joe. 1987. "Next, the McDRG." *The Progressive* 51 (January):28.

Feketekuty, Geza. 2001. "Globalization—Why All the Fuss?" P. 191 in *2001 Britannica Book of the Year.* Chicago: Encyclopedia Britannica.

Felson, David, and Akis Kalaitzidis. 2005. "A Historical Overview of Transnational Crime." Pp. 3–19 in *Handbook of Transnational Crime and Justice,* edited by Philip Reichel. Thousand Oaks, CA: Sage.

Felson, Marcus. 2002. *Crime and Everyday Life.* 3d ed. Thousand Oaks, CA: Pine Forge Press.

Ferree, Myra Marx. 2005. "It's Time to Mainstream Research on Gender." *Chronicle of Higher Education* 51 (August 21):B10.

———, and David A. Merrill. 2000. "Hot Movements, Cold Cognition: Thinking about Social Movements in Gendered Frames." *Contemporary Society* 29 (May):454–462.

Feuer, Alan. 2002. "High-Rise Colony of Workers Evolves for Their Retirement." *New York Times,* August 5, pp. A1, A15.

References

Feuer, Lewis S. 1989. *Marx and Engels: Basic Writings on Politics and Philosophy.* New York: Anchor Books.

Fiala, Robert. 1992. "Postindustrial Society." Pp. 1512–1522 in *Encyclopedia of Sociology,* vol. 3, edited by Edgar F. Borgatta and Marie L. Borgatta. New York: Macmillan.

Fields, Jason. 2001. "America's Families and Living Arrangements." *Current Population Reports,* ser. P-20, no. 537. Washington, DC: U.S. Government Printing Office.

————. 2003. "Children's Living Arrangements and Characteristics: March 2002." *Current Population Reports,* ser. P-20, no. 547. Washington, DC: U.S. Government Printing Office.

————. 2004. "America's Families and Living Arrangements: 2003." *Current Population Reports,* ser. P-20, no. 553. Washington, DC: U.S. Government Printing Office.

Fields, Jessica. 2005. "'Children Having Children': Race, Innocence, and Sexuality Education." *Social Problems* 52 (4):549–571.

Finder, Alan. 1995. "Despite Tough Laws, Sweatshops Flourish." *New York Times,* January 6, pp. A1, B4.

Fine, Gary Alan. 1987. *With the Boys: Little League Baseball and Preadolescent Culture.* Chicago: University of Chicago Press.

————. 2004. "Forgotten Classic: The Robbers Care Experiment." *Sociological Forum* 19 (December): 663–666.

Finkel, Steven E., and James B. Rule. 1987. "Relative Deprivation and Related Psychological Theories of Civil Violence: A Critical Review." *Research in Social Movements* 9:47–69.

Firestone, David. 1999. "School Prayer Is Revived as an Issue in Alabama." *New York Times,* July 15, p. A14.

Fiss, Peer C., and Paul M. Hirsch. 2005. "The Discourse of Globalization: Framing of an Emerging Concept." *American Sociological Review* (February):29–52.

Fitchett, George. 1980. "It's Time to Bury the Stage Theory of Death and Dying." *Oncology Nurse Exchange II* (Fall).

Fitzgerald, Kathleen J., and Diane M. Rodgers. 2000. "Radical Social Movement Organization: A Theoretical Model." *The Sociological Quarterly* 41 (4):573–592.

Flacks, Richard. 1971. *Youth and Social Change.* Chicago: Markham.

Flavin, Jeanne. 1998. "Razing the Wall: A Feminist Critique of Sentencing Theory, Research, and Policy." Pp. 145–164 in *Cutting the Edge,* edited by Jeffrey Ross. Westport, CT: Praeger.

Fletcher, Connie. 1995. "On the Line: Women Cops Speak Out." *Chicago Tribune Magazine,* February 19, pp. 14–19.

Florio, Gwen. 2006. "Vacant Seat Tough to Fill If 'Districts' Empty, Too." *USA Today,* January 24, p. 3A.

Forsythe, David P. 1990. "Human Rights in U.S. Foreign Policy: Retrospect and Prospect." *Political Science Quarterly* 105(3):435–454.

Fortune. 2005. "Fortune Global 500." 152 (July 25), 97–142.

Fox, Jonathan. 2005. "Unpacking 'Transnational' Citizenship." Pp. 171–201 in *Annual Review of Political Science 2005.* Palo Alto, CA: Annual Reviews.

Fox, Susannah, and Lee Rainie. 2001. *Time Online: Why Some People Use the Internet More Than Before and Why Some Use It Less.* Washington, DC: Pew Internet and American Life Project.

Franklin, John Hope, and Alfred A. Moss. 2000. *From Slavery to Freedom: A History of African Americans.* 8th ed. Upper Saddle River, NJ: Prentice Hall.

Freidson, Eliot. 1970. *Profession of Medicine.* New York: Dodd, Mead.

French, Howard W. 2000. "The Pretenders." *New York Times Magazine,* December 3, pp. 86–88.

————. 2002. "Teaching Japan's Salarymen to Be Their Own Men." *New York Times,* November 27, p. A4.

————. 2003a. "Insular Japan Needs, but Resists, Immigration." *New York Times,* July 24, pp. A1, A3.

————. 2003b. "Japan's Neglected Resource: Female Workers." *New York Times,* July 25.

————. 2004. "Despite an Act of Clemency, China Has Its Eye on the Web." *New York Times,* June 27, p. 6.

Freudenburg, William R. 2005. "Seeing Science, Courting Conclusions: Reexamining the Intersection of Science, Corporate Cash, and the Law." *Sociological Forum* 20 (March):3–33.

Freudenheim, Milt. 2005. "Help Wanted: Oldest Workers Please Apply." *New York Times,* March 23, pp. A1, C3.

Frey, William H. 2001. *Melting Pot Suburbs: A Census 2000 Study of Suburban Diversity.* Washington, DC: The Brookings Institution.

Fridlund, Alan. J., Paul Erkman, and Harriet Oster. 1987. "Facial Expressions of Emotion; Review of Literature 1970–1983." Pp. 143–224 in *Nonverbal Behavior and Communication,* 2d ed., edited by Aron W. Seigman and Stanley Feldstein. Hillsdale, NJ: Lawrence Erlbaum Associates.

Friedan, Betty. 1963. *The Feminine Mystique.* New York: Dell.

Friedland, Jonathon. 2000. "An American in Mexico Champions Midwifery as a Worthy Profession." *Wall Street Monitor,* February 15, pp. A1, A12.

Friedman, Thomas L. 2005. *The World Is Flat: A Brief History of the Twenty-first Century.* New York: Farrar, Straus and Giroux.

Friedrich, Carl J., and Zbigniew Brzezinski. 1965. *Totalitarian Dictatorship and Autocracy.* 2d ed. Cambridge, MA: Harvard University Press.

Fronczek, Peter. 2005. *Income, Earnings, and Poverty from the 2004 American Community Survey.* Washington, DC: U.S. Government Printing Office.

Frost, Greg. 2003. "U.S. Anti-War Movement Breaks Ranks with the 60's." *Washington Post,* March 31.

Fujimoto, Kayo. 2004. "Feminine Capital: The Forms of Capital in the Female Labor Market in Japan." *Sociological Quarterly* 45 (1):91–111.

Furstenberg, Frank, and Andrew Cherlin. 1991. *Divided Families: What Happens to Children When Parents Part.* Cambridge, MA: Harvard University Press.

Furstenberg, Sheela Kennedy, Jr., Vonnie C. McCloyd, Rubén G. Rumbaut, and Richard A. Setterstein, Jr. 2004. "Growing Up Is Harder to Do." *Contexts* 3:33–41.

Fuwa, Makiko. 2004. "Macro-Level Gender Inequality and the Division of Household Labor in 22 Countries." *American Sociological Review* 69 (December):751–767.

Gallup. 2004. *The Gallup Poll of Baghdad.* Omaha, NE: Gallup.

————. 2006. "Party Affiliation May 12–13, 2006." Accessed June 2 (www.gallup.com).

Gamson, Joshua. 1989. "Silence, Death, and the Invisible Enemy: AIDS Activism and Social Movement 'Newness.'" *Social Problems* 36 (October): 351–367.

————, and Pearl Latteier. 2004. "Do Media Monsters Devour Diversity?" *Contexts* (Summer): 26–32.

Gans, Herbert J. 1979. "Symbolic Ethnicity: The Future of Ethnic Groups and Cultures in America." *Ethnic and Racial Studies* 2 (January): 1–20.

————. 1991. *People, Plans, and Policies: Essays on Poverty, Racism, and Other National Urban Problems.* New York: Columbia University Press and Russell Sage Foundation.

————. 1995. *The War against the Poor: The Underclass and Antipoverty Policy.* New York: Basic Books.

Ganzeboom, Harry B. G., Donald J. Treiman, and Woult C. Ultee. 1991. "Comparative Intergenerational Stratification Research." Pp. 277–302 in *Annual Review of Sociology, 1991,* edited by W. Richard Scott. Palo Alto, CA: Annual Reviews.

Garcia-Moreno, Claudia, Henrica A. F. M. Jansen, Mary Ellsberg, Lori Heise, and Charlotte Watts. 2005. *WHO Multi-country Study on Women's Health and Domestic Violence Against Women.* Geneva, Switzerland: WHO.

Gardner, Gary, Erik Assadourian, and Radhika Sarin. 2004. "The State of Consumption Today." Pp. 3–21 in *State of the World 2004,* edited by Brian Halweil and Lisa Mastny. New York: W. W. Norton.

Gardner, Marilyn. 2003. "This View of Seniors Just Doesn't 'Ad' Up." *Christian Science Monitor,* January 15, p. 15.

Garfinkel, Harold. 1956. "Conditions of Successful Degradation Ceremonies." *American Journal of Sociology* 61 (March):420–424.

Garner, Roberta. 1996. *Contemporary Movements and Ideologies.* New York: McGraw-Hill.

————. 1999. "Virtual Social Movements." Presented at Zaldfest: A conference in honor of Mayer Zald. September 17, Ann Arbor, MI.

Garreau, Joel. 1991. *Edge City: Life on the New Frontier.* New York: Doubleday.

Gay, Lesbian and Straight Education Network. 2005. "About GLSEN." Accessed May 12 (www.glsen.org).

Gecas, Viktor. 1992. "Socialization." Pp. 1863–1872 in *Encyclopedia of Sociology*, Vol. 4, edited by Edgar F. Borgatta and Marie L. Borgatta. New York: Macmillan.

Geist, Eric L., Vasily V. Titov, and Costas E. Synolakis. 2006. "Tsunami: Wave of Change." *Scientific American* 294 (January):56–63.

Gerth, H. H., and C. Wright Mills. 1958. *From Max Weber: Essays in Sociology*. New York: Galaxy.

Gertner, Jon. 2005. "Our Ratings, Ourselves." *New York Times Magazine*, April 10, pp. 34–41, 56, 58, 64–65.

Giddens, Anthony. 1991. *Modernity and Self-Identity: Self and Society in the Late Modern Age*. Cambridge, UK: Polity.

Gifford, Allen L., et al. 2002. "Participation in Research and Access to Experimental Treatments by HIV-Infected Patients." *New England Journal of Medicine* 346 (May):1400–1402.

Giordano, Peggy C. 2003. "Relationships in Adolescence." Pp. 257–281 in *Annual Review of Sociology, 2003*, edited by Karen S. Cook and John Hagan. Palo Alto, CA: Annual Reviews.

———, Stephen A. Cernkovich, and Alfred DeMaris. 1993. "The Family and Peer Relations of Black Adolescents." *Journal of Marriage and Family* 55 (May): 277–287.

Giroux, Henry A. 1988. *Schooling and the Struggle for Public Life: Critical Pedagogy in the Modern Age*. Minneapolis: University of Minnesota Press.

Gitlin, Todd. 2002. *Media Unlimited: How the Torrent of Images and Sounds Overwhelms Our Lives*. New York: Henry Holt and Company.

Glauber, Bill. 1998. "Youth Binge Drinking Varies Around World." *St. Louis Post-Dispatch*, February 9, p. E4.

Glaze, Lauren E, and Seri Palla. 2005. "Probation and Parole in the United States, 2004." *Bureau of Justice Statistics Bulletin* (November).

Glenn, David. 2004. "A Dangerous Surplus of Sons?" *Chronicle of Higher Education* 50 (April 30):A14–A16, A18.

Glionna, John M. 2004. "Finding a Voice in Politics." *Los Angeles Times*, May 22, pp. A1, A22.

Global Alliance for Workers and Communities. 2003. *About Us*. Accessed April 28 (www.the globalalliance.org).

Goffman, Erving. 1959. *The Presentation of Self in Everyday Life*. New York: Doubleday.

———. 1961. *Asylums: Essays on the Social Situation of Mental Patients and Other Inmates*. Garden City, NY: Doubleday.

———. 1963a. *Stigma: Notes on Management of Spoiled Identity*. Englewood Cliffs, NJ: Prentice Hall.

———. 1979. *Gender Advertisements*. Cambridge, MA: Harvard University Press.

Golden, Frederic. 1999. "Who's Afraid of Frankenfood?" *Time*, November 29, pp. 49–50.

Goldstein, Amy, and Richard Morin. 2002. "The Squeaky Wheel Gets the Grease." *Washington Post National Weekly Edition* 20, October 28, p. 34.

Goldstein, Melvyn C., and Cynthia M. Beall. 1981. "Modernization and Aging in the Third and

Fourth World: Views from the Rural Hinterland in Nepal." *Human Organization* 40 (Spring): 48–55.

Gole, Nilofer. 1997. "Lifting the Veil—Reform vs. Tradition in Turkey—An Interview." *Manushi*, May 1.

Gonnut, Jean Pierre. 2001. Interview. June 18, 2001.

Gonzalez, David. 2003. "Latin Sweatshops Pressed by U.S. Campus Power." *New York Times*, April 4, p. A3.

Goodman, Peter S., and Akiko Kashiwagi. 2002. "In Japan, Housewives No More." *Washington Post National Weekly Edition*, November 4, pp. 18–19.

Goodstein, Laurie. 2005. "Issuing Rebuke, Judge Rejects Teaching of Intelligent Design." *New York Times*, December 21, pp. A1, A21.

Gordon, Gary. 2004. "Teacher Retention Statistics with Great Principals." *Gallup Poll Tuesday Briefing*, February 17. Accessed March 18 (www.gallup.com).

Gordon, Raymond G., Jr., ed. 2005. *Ethnologue: Languages of the World*. 15th ed. Dallas, TX: SIL International.

Gore, Al. 2006. *An Inconvenient Truth: The Planetary Emergency of Global Warming and What We Can Do About It*. New York: Rodale Books.

Gornick, Janet C. 2001. "Cancel the Funeral." *Dissent* (Summer):13–18.

Gornick, Vivian. 1979. "Introduction" to *Gender Advertisements*. Cambridge, MA: Harvard University Press.

Gottdiener, Mark, and Joe R. Feagin. 1988. "The Paradigm Shift in Urban Sociology." *Urban Affairs Quarterly* 24 (December):163–187.

———, and Ray Hutchinson. 2006. *The New Urban Sociology*. 3d ed. Boulder, CO: Westview.

Gottfredson, Michael, and Travis Hirschi. 1990. *A General Theory of Crime*. Palo Alto, CA: Stanford University Press.

Gottlieb, Lori. 2006. "How Do I Love Thee?" *Atlantic Monthly* (March): 58, 60, 62–68, 70.

Gould, Larry A. 2002. "Indigenous People Policing Indigenous People: The Potential Psychological and Cultural Costs." *Social Science Journal* 39:171–188.

Gouldner, Alvin. 1960. "The Norm of Reciprocity." *American Sociological Review* 25 (April):161–177.

———. 1970. *The Coming Crisis of Western Sociology*. New York: Basic Books.

Graham, Judith. 2004. "Kids of Addicts Bear Scars as Meth Sweeps Rural Areas." *Chicago Tribune*, March 7, pp. 1, 14.

Gramsci, Antonio. 1929. *Selections from the Prison Notebooks*. Antonio Gramsci. Edited and translated by Quintin Hoare and Geoffrey Nowell Smith. London: Lawrence and Wishort.

Greeley, Andrew M. 1989. "Protestant and Catholic: Is the Analogical Imagination Extinct?" *American Sociological Review* 54 (August):485–502.

Green, Dan S., and Edwin D. Driver. 1978. "Introduction." Pp. 1–60 in *W. E. B. DuBois on Sociology and the Black Community*, edited by Dan S. Green and Edwin D. Driver. Chicago: University of Chicago Press.

Greenblatt, Alan. 2005. "Upward Mobility." *CQ Researcher* 15 (April 29).

Greenhouse, Linda. 1998. "High Court Ruling Says Harassment Includes Same Sex." *New York Times*, March 5, pp. A1, A17.

———. 2005. "Justices Say U.S. May Prohibit the Use of Medical Marijuana." *New York Times*, June 7, pp. A1, A15.

Grieco, Elizabeth M., and Rachel C. Cassidy. 2001. "Overview of Race and Hispanic Origin." *Current Population Reports Series* CENBR/01–1. Washington, DC: U.S. Government Printing Office.

Grier, Peter. 2005. "Rich-Poor Gap Gaining Attention." *Christian Science Monitor*, June 14.

Gross, Jane. 2005. "Forget the Career. My Parents Need Me at Home." *New York Times*, November 24: A1, A20.

Grossman, Ler, and Hannah Beech. 2006. "Google Under the Gun." *Time*, February 13, p. 53.

Groza, Victor, Daniela F. Ileana, and Ivor Irwin. 1999. *A Peacock or a Crow: Stories, Interviews, and Commentaries on Romanian Adoptions*. Euclid, OH: Williams Custom Publishing.

Gundersen, Edna. 2006. "Ring-Tone Sales Ring Up Music Profits." *USA Today*, January 20, p. D1.

Guterman, Lila. 2000. "Why the 25-Year-Old Battle over Sociology Is More than Just 'An Academic Sideshow.'" *Chronicle of Higher Education*, July 7, pp. A17–A18.

Gutiérrez, Gustavo. 1990. "Theology and the Social Sciences," in Paul E. Sigmund, *Liberation Theology at the Crossroads: Democracy or Revolution?* New York: Oxford University Press, pp. 214–225.

Gutierrez, Valerie. 2002. "Minority Women Get Left Behind by Title IX." *Los Angeles Times*, June 23, pp. D1, D12.

Gwynne, S. C., and John E. Dickerson. 1997. "Lost in the E-Mail." *Time* 149 (April 21):88–90.

Hacker, Andrew. 1964. "Power to Do What?" Pp. 134–146 in *The New Sociology*, edited by Irving Louis Horowitz. New York: Oxford University Press.

Hacker, Helen Mayer. 1951. "Women as a Minority Group." *Social Forces* 30 (October):60–69.

———. 1974. "Women as a Minority Group, Twenty Years Later." Pp. 124–134 in *Who Discriminates against Women?* edited by Florence Denmark. Beverly Hills, CA: Sage.

Haeri, Shaykh Fadhilalla. 2004. *The Thoughtful Guide to Islam*. Alresford, UK: O Books.

Hafner-Burton, Emilie M., and Kiyoteru Tsutsui. 2005. "Human Rights in a Globalizing World: The Paradox of Empty Promises." *American Journal of Sociology* 110 (March):1373–1411.

Halebsky, Stephen. 2004. "Superstores and the Politics of Retail Development." *City and Community* 5 (June):115–134.

Hall, Mimi. 2005. "Senators 'to Demand Answers' on Slow Action." *USA Today* September 6, p. 4A.

Hall, Robert H. 1982. "The Truth about Brown Lung." *Business and Society Review* 40 (Winter 1981–82):15–20.

Haller, Max, Wolfgang Konig, Peter Krause, and Karin Kurz. 1990. "Patterns of Career Mobility and Structural Positions in Advanced Capitalist

444

Societies: A Comparison of Men in Austria, France, and the United States." *American Sociological Review* 50 (October): 579–603.

Hallinan, Maureen T. 1997. "The Sociological Study of Social Change." *American Sociological Review* 62 (February):1–11.

———. 2003. "Ability Grouping and Student Learning." Pp. 95–140 in *Brookings Papers on Education Policy,* edited by Diane Ravitch. Washington, DC: Brookings Institute Press.

Hamilton, Brady E., Joyce A. Martin, Stephanie J. Ventura, Paul D. Sutton, and Fay Menacker. 2005. "Births: Preliminary Data for 2004." *National Vital Statistics Reports* 54 (December 29).

Hamm, Jill V., B. Bradford Brown, and Daniel J. Heck. 2005. "Bridging the Ethnic Divide: Students and School Characteristics in African American, Asian-Descent, Latino, and White Adolescents' Cross-Ethnic Friend Nominations." *Journal of Research on Adolescence* 15 (1):21–46.

Hanes, Stephanie. 2005. "Woman Quota Changes Dynamics of Lesotho Vote," *USA Today,* June 10, p. 12A.

Hani, Yoko. 1998. "Hot Pots Wired to Help the Elderly." *Japan Times Weekly International Edition,* April 13, p. 16.

Hank, Karsten. 2001. "Changes in Child Care Could Reduce Job Options for Eastern German Mothers." *Population Today* 29 (April):3, 6.

Hansen, Brian. 2004. "Big-Box Stores." *CQ Researcher* 14 (September 10).

Hanson, Ralph E. 2005. *Mass Communication: Living in a Media World.* New York: McGraw Hill.

Harlow, Harry F. 1971. *Learning to Love.* New York: Ballantine.

Harrington, Michael. 1962. *The Other America: Poverty in the United States.* Baltimore: Penguin.

———. 1980. "The New Class and the Left." Pp. 123–138 in *The New Class,* edited by B. Bruce Briggs. Brunswick, NJ: Transaction.

Harris, Chauncy D., and Edward Ullman. 1945. "The Nature of Cities." *Annals of the American Academy of Political and Social Science* 242 (November):7–17.

Harris, David A. 1999. *Driving While Black: Racial Profiling on Our Nation's Highways.* New York: American Civil Liberties Union.

Harris, Judith Rich. 1998. *The Nurture Assumption: Why Children Turn Out the Way They Do.* New York: Free Press.

Hartman, Chris, and Jake Miller. 2001. *Bail Outs That Work for Everyone.* Boston: United for a Fair Economy.

Haub, Carl. 2004. *World Population Data Sheet, 2004.* Washington, DC: Population Reference Bureau.

———. 2005. *2005 World Population Data Sheet.* Washington, DC: Population Reference Bureau.

Hauser, Robert M., and David B. Grusky. 1988. "Cross-National Variation in Occupational Distributions, Relative Mobility Chances, and Intergenerational Shifts in Occupational Distributions." *American Sociological Review* 53 (October):723–741.

Haviland, William A. 2002. *Cultural Anthropology.* 10th ed. Belmont, CA: Wadsworth.

———, Harald E. L. Prins, Dana Walrath, and Bunny McBride. 2005. *Cultural Anthropology—The Human Challenge.* New York: McGraw-Hill.

Hawkins, Darnell F., et al. 2000. "Race, Ethnicity, and Serious and Violent Juvenile Offending." *Juvenile Justice Bulletin* (June):107.

Hayden, H. Thomas. 2004. "What Happened at Abu Ghraib." Accessed August 7 (www.military.com).

Hayward, Mark D., William R. Grady, and Steven D. McLaughlin. 1987. "Changes in the Retirement Process." *Demography* 25 (August):371–386.

He, Wan, Manisha Sengupta, Victoria A. Velkoff, and Kimberly A. DeBarros. 2005. "65+ in the United States: 2005." *Current Population Reports,* ser. P-23, no. 209. Washington, DC: U.S. Government Printing Office.

Health Canada. 1993. *Gender and Violence in the Mass Media.* Ottawa, Canada: Health Canada.

Heckert, Druann, and Amy Best. 1997. "Ugly Duckling to Swan: Labeling Theory and the Stigmatization of Red Hair." *Symbolic Interaction* 20 (4):365–384.

Hedley, R. Alan. 1992. "Industrialization in Less Developed Countries." Pp. 914–920 in *Encyclopedia of Sociology,* vol. 2, edited by Edgar F. Borgatta and Marie L. Borgatta. New York: Macmillan.

Heilman, Madeline E. 2001. "Description and Prescription: How Gender Stereotypes Prevent Women's Ascent up the Organizational Ladder." *Journal of Social Issues* 57 (4):657–674.

Hellmich, Nanci. 2001. "TV's Reality: No Vast American Waistlines." *USA Today,* October 8, p. 7D.

Henly, Julia R. 1999. "Challenges to Finding and Keeping Jobs in the Low-Skilled Labor Market." *Poverty Research News* 3 (1):3–5.

Herschthal, Eric. 2004. "Indian Students Discuss Pros, Cons of Arranged Marriages." *Daily Princetonian* (October 20).

Hetherington, E. Mavis, and John Kelly. 2002. *For Better or For Worse.* New York: Norton.

Hewlett, Sylvia Ann, and Carolyn Buck Luce. 2005. "Off-Ramps and On-Ramps: Keeping Talented Women on the Road to Success." *Harvard Business Review* (March):43–53.

Hickman, Jonathan. 2002. "America's 50 Best Corporations for Minorities." *Fortune* 146 (July 8):110–120.

Higher Education Research Institute. 2004. *Trends in Political Attitudes and Voting Behavior Among College Freshmen and Early Career College Graduates: What Issues Could Drive This Election?* Los Angeles: HERI, University of California, Los Angeles.

———. 2005. *The Spiritual Life of College Students.* Los Angeles: HERI.

Hill, Michael R., and Susan Hoecker-Drysdale, eds. 2001. *Harriet Martineau: Theoretical and Methodological Perspectives.* New York: Routledge.

Hillery, George A. 1955. "Definitions of Community: Areas of Agreement." *Rural Sociology* (2):111–123.

Himes, Vristine L. 2001. "Elderly Americans." *Population Bulletin* 56 (December).

Hipp, John R., Daniel J. Bauer, Patrick J. Curran, and Kenneth A. Bollen. 2004. "Crimes of Opportunity or Crimes of Emotion? Testing Two Explanations of Seasoned Change in Crime." *Social Forces* 82 (4):1333–1372.

Hirsch, Barry, and David Macpherson. 2006. "Union Membership and Coverage Database." Accessed April 12 (www.unionstats.com).

Hirschi, Travis. 1969. *Causes of Delinquency.* Berkeley: University of California Press.

Hirst, Paul, and Grahame Thompson. 1996. *Globalization in Question: The International Economy and the Possibilities of Governance.* Cambridge, UK: Polity Press.

Hitlin, Steven, and Jane Allyn Piliavin. 2004. "Values: Reviving a Dormant Concept." Pp. 359–393 in *Annual Review of Sociology, 2004,* edited by Karen S. Cook and John Hagan. Palo Alto, CA: Annual Review of Sociology.

Hochschild, Arlie Russell. 1990. "The Second Shift: Employed Women Are Putting in Another Day of Work at Home." *Utne Reader* 38 (March/April):66–73.

———. 2005. *The Commercialization of Intimate Life: Notes from Home and Work.* Berkeley: University of California Press.

———, with Anne Machung. 1989. *The Second Shift: Working Parents and the Revolution at Home.* New York: Viking Penguin.

Hodge, Robert W., and Peter H. Rossi. 1964. "Occupational Prestige in the United States, 1925–1963." *American Journal of Sociology* 70 (November):286–302.

Hoffman, Adonis. 1997. "Through an Accurate Prism." *Los Angeles Times,* August 8, p. M1.

Hoffman, Lois Wladis. 1985. "The Changing Genetics/Socialization Balance." *Journal of Social Issues* 41 (Spring):127–148.

Holden, Constance. 1980. "Identical Twins Reared Apart." *Science* 207 (March 21): 1323–1328.

———. 1987. "The Genetics of Personality." *Science* 257 (August 7):598–601.

Holder, Kelly. 2006. "Voting and Registration in the Election of November 2004." *Current Population Reports,* ser. P-20, no. 556. Washington, DC: U.S. Government Printing Office.

Hollander, Jocelyn A. 2002. "Resisting Vulnerability: The Social Reconstruction of Gender in Interaction." *Social Problems* 49 (4):474–496.

Hollingshead, August B. 1975. *Elmtown's Youth and Elmtown Revisited.* New York: Wiley.

Homans, George C. 1979. "Nature versus Nurture: A False Dichotomy." *Contemporary Sociology* 8 (May):345–348.

Home School Legal Defense Association. 2005. "State Laws" and "Academic Statistics on Home-schooling." Accessed May 12 (www.hslda.org).

Hoover, Eric. 2002. "Binge Thinking." *Chronicle of Higher Education* 49 (November 8):A34–A37.

Horgan, John. 1993. "Eugenics Revisited." *Scientific American* 268 (June):122–128, 130–133.

Horovitz, Bruce. 2003. "Smile! You're the Stars of the Super Ad Bowl." *USA Today,* January 24, pp. B1, B2.

Horowitz, Helen Lefkowitz. 1987. *Campus Life.* Chicago: University of Chicago Press.

Hosokawa, William K. 1969. *Nisei: The Quiet Americans.* New York: Morrow.

Hospice Foundation of America. 2005. *What Is Hospice?* Accessed April 28 (www.hospice foundation.org/what_is).

Houghton County. 2005. "MTV Student Electrifies NBC's 'Fear Factor.'" Accessed March 1 (www.wluctv6.com).

Hout, Michael. 1988. "More Universalism, Less Structural Mobility: The American Occupational Structure in the 1980s." *American Journal of Sociology* 91 (May):1358–1400.

Howard, Judith A. 1999. "Border Crossings between Women's Studies and Sociology." *Contemporary Sociology* 28 (September):525–528.

———, and Jocelyn Hollander. 1997. *Gendered Situations, Gendered Selves.* Thousand Oaks, CA: Sage.

Howard, Michael C. 1989. *Contemporary Cultural Anthropology.* 3d ed. Glenview, IL: Scott, Foresman.

Howard, Russell D., and Reid L. Sawyer. 2003. *Terrorism and Counterterrorism: Understanding the New Security Environment.* Guilford, CT: McGraw-Hill/Dushkin.

Huang, Gary. 1988. "Daily Addressing Ritual: A Cross-Cultural Study." Presented at the annual meeting of the American Sociological Association, Atlanta.

Huber, Bettina J. 1985. *Employment Patterns in Sociology: Recent Trends and Future Prospects.* Washington, DC: American Sociological Association.

Huddy, Leonie, Joshua Billig, John Bracciodieta, Lois Hoeffler, Patrick J. Moynihan, and Patricia Pugliani. 1997. "The Effect of Interviewer Gender on the Survey Response." *Political Behavior* 19 (September):197–220.

Huffstutter, P. J. 2003. "See No Evil." *Los Angeles Times,* January 12, pp. 12–15, 43–45.

Hughes, Everett. 1945. "Dilemmas and Contradictions of Status." *American Journal of Sociology* 50 (March):353–359.

Human Rights Campaign. 2006. *Equality in the States: Gay, Lesbian, Bisexual and Transgender. Americans and State Laws and Legislation in 2006.* Washington, DC: HRC.

Hunt, Darnell. 1997. *Screening the Los Angeles "Riots": Race, Seeing, and Resistance.* New York: Cambridge University Press.

Hunter, Herbert M., ed. 2000. *The Sociology of Oliver C. Cox: New Perspectives: Research in Race and Ethnic Relations,* vol. 2. Stamford, CT: JAI Press.

Hunter, James Davison. 1991. *Culture Wars: The Struggle to Define America.* New York: Basic Books.

Hurh, Won Moo. 1994. *Korean Immigrants in America: A Structural Analysis of Ethnic Confinement and Adhesive Adaptation.* Rutherford, NJ: Fairleigh Dickinson University Press.

———. 1998. *The Korean Americans.* Westport, CT: Greenwood Press.

———, and Kwang Chung Kim. 1998. "The 'Success' Image of Asian Americans: Its Validity, and Its Practical and Theoretical Implications." *Ethnic and Racial Studies* 12 (October):512–538.

Hurn, Christopher J. 1985. *The Limits and Possibilities of Schooling,* 2d ed. Boston: Allyn and Bacon.

Inglehart, Ronald, and Wayne E. Baker. 2000. "Modernization, Cultural Change, and the Persistence of Traditional Values." *American Sociological Review* 65 (February):19–51.

Institute for Social Policy and Understanding. 2004. *The USA PATRIOT Act: Impact on the Arabs and Muslim American Community.* Clinton Township, MI: ISPU.

Institute of International Education. 2005. "Open Doors 2005 Fast Facts." Accessed April 11, 2006 (www.iie.org).

Instituto del Tercer Mundo. 2005. *The World Guide 2005/2006.* Oxford: New Internationalist Publications.

Internal Revenue Service. 2004. "Selected Income and Tax Items from Inflation. Indexed Individual Tax Returns, 1990–2001." *Statistics of Income* (Spring):200–212.

International Crime Victim Survey. 2004. *Nationwide Surveys in the Industrialized Countries.* Accessed February 20 (www.ruljis.leidenuniv.nl/group/jfcr/www/icvs).

International Institute for Democracy and Electoral Assistance. 2005. "Turnout in the World—Country by Country Performance." Modified March 7, 2005. Accessed April 18, 2006 (www.idea.int).

International Monetary Fund. 2000. *World Economic Outlook: Asset Prices and the Business Cycle.* Washington, DC: International Monetary Fund.

Inter-Parliamentary Union. 2006. *Women in National Parliaments.* February 27. Accessed March 2 (www.ipu.org).

Iritani, Evelyn, and Marla Dickerson. 2002. "People's Republic of Products." *Los Angeles Times,* October 20, pp. A1, A10.

ITOPF. 2006. "Statistics: International Tanker Owners Pollution Federation Limited." Accessed May 2 (www.itopf.com/stats.html).

Jackson, Elton F., Charles R. Tittle, and Mary Jean Burke. 1986. "Offense-Specific Models of the Differential Association Process." *Social Problems* 33 (April):335–356.

Jackson, Philip W. 1968. *Life in Classrooms.* New York: Holt.

Jacobs, Jerry. 2003. "Detours on the Road to Equality: Women, Work and Higher Education." *Contexts* (Winter):32-41.

Jacobson, Jodi. 1993. "Closing the Gender Gap in Development." Pp. 61–79 in *State of the World,* edited by Lester R. Brown. New York: Norton.

Jamieson, Arnie, Hyon B. Shin, and Jennifer Day. 2002. "Voting and Registration in the Election of November 2000." *Current Population Reports,* ser. P-20, no. 542. Washington, DC: U.S. Government Printing Office.

Jargowsky, Paul A. 2003. *Stunning Progress, Hidden Problems: the Dramatic Decline of Concentrated Poverty in the 1990s.* Washington, DC: Brookings Institute.

Jasper, James M. 1997. *The Art of Moral Protest: Culture, Biography, and Creativity in Social Movements.* Chicago: University of Chicago Press.

Jencks, Christopher, Joe Swingle, and Scott Winship. 2006. "Welfare Redux." *American Prospect* (March):36–40.

Jenkins, Richard. 1991. "Disability and Social Stratification." *British Journal of Sociology* 42 (December):557–580.

Johnson, Anne M., Jane Wadsworth, Kaye Wellings, and Julie Field. 1994. *Sexual Attitudes and Lifestyles.* Oxford: Blackwell Scientific.

Johnson, Benton. 1975. *Functionalism in Modern Sociology: Understanding Talcott Parsons.* Morristown, NJ: General Learning.

Johnson, Jeffrey, et al. 2002. "Television Viewing and Aggressive Behavior During Adolescence and Adulthood." *Science* 295 (March 29):2468–2471.

Johnson, Julia Overturf. 2005. "Who's Minding the Kids? Child Care Arrangements: Winter 2002." *Current Population Reports,* ser. P-70, no. 101. Washington, DC: U.S. Government Printing Office.

Johnston, David Cay. 1994. "Ruling Backs Homosexuals on Asylum." *New York Times,* June 12, pp. D1, D6.

Jolin, Annette. 1994. "On the Backs of Working Prostitutes: Feminist Theory and Prostitution Policy." *Crime and Delinquency* 40 (2):69–83.

Jones, Dale E., Dherri Doty, James E. Horsch, Richard Houseal, Mac Lynn, John P. Marcum, Kenneth M. Sanchagrin, and Richard H. Taylor. 2002. *Religious Congregations and Membership in the United States 2000: An Enumeration by Religion, State and Country Based on Data Reported by 149 Religious Bodies.* Nashville, TN: Glenmary Research Center.

Jones, James T., IV. 1988. "Harassment Is Too Often Part of the Job." *USA Today,* August 8, p. 5D.

Jones, Jeffrey M. 2005. "Americans' Views of Death Penalty More Positive This Year." May 19. Accessed May 24 (www.gallup.com).

Jones, Nicholas A. 2005. *We the People of More Than One Race in the United States.* Census 2000 Special Reports, CENSR-22. Washington, DC: U.S. Government Printing Office.

Jones, Stephen R. G. 1992. "Was There a Hawthorne Effect?" *American Journal of Sociology* 98 (November):451–568.

Jost, Kenneth. 2005. "Death Penalty Controversies." *CQ Researcher* 15 (September 23):785–808.

Joynt, Jen, and Vasugi Ganeshananthan. 2003. "Abortion Decisions." *Atlantic Monthly* 291 (April):38–39.

Juhasz, Anne McCreary. 1989. "Black Adolescents' Significant Others." *Social Behavior and Personality* 17 (2):211–214.

Kahn, Joseph. 2003a. "Made in China, Bought in China." *New York Times,* January 5, sec. 3, pp. 1, 10.

———. 2003b. "China's Workers Risk Limbs in Export Drive." *New York Times,* April 7, p. A3.

————. 2006. "A Sharp Debate Erupts in China over Ideologies." *New York Times,* March 12, pp. 1, 8.

Kaiser Family Foundation. 2001. *Few Parents Use V-Chip to Block TV Sex and Violence.* Menlo Park: Kaiser Family Foundation.

————. 2005. *Sex on TV: 2005.* Santa Barbara, CA: Kaiser Family Foundation.

Kaiser Family Foundation. 2005. *Sex on TV.* Menlo Park, CA: Kaiser Family Foundation.

Kalish, Richard A. 1985. *Death, Grief, and Caring Relationships.* 2d ed. Monterey, CA: Brooks/Cole.

Kalita, S. Mitra. 2006. "On the Other End of the Line." *Washington Post National Week Edition,* January 9, pp. 20–21.

Kamenetz, Anya. 2006. *Generation Debt.* New York: Riverhead.

Kao, Grace, and Kara Joyner. 2004. "Do Race and Ethnicity Matter among Friends? Activities among Interracial, Interethnic, and Interethnic Adolescent Friends." *Sociology Quarterly* 45 (3):557–573.

Kapos, Shia. 2005. "Bloom Falls Off the Rose for Internet Matchups." *Chicago Tribune,* February 14, sect. 4, pp. 1, 7).

Kapur, Deutsch, and John McHale. 2003. "Migration's New Payroll." *Foreign Policy* (November/December):48–57.

Katel, Peter. 2005. "Ending Poverty." *CQ Researcher* 15 (September 9):733–760.

Katovich, Michael A. 1987. Correspondence. June 1.

Katz, Michael. 1971. *Class, Bureaucracy, and the Schools: The Illusion of Educational Change in America.* New York: Praeger.

Kent, Mary M., and Carl Haub. 2005. "Global Demographic Divide." *Population Bulletin* 60 (December).

Kentor, Jeffrey, and Yong Suk Jang. 2004. "Yes, There Is a (Growing) Transnational Business Community:" *International Sociology* 19 (September), 355–368.

Kerbo, Harold R. 2003. *Social Stratification and Inequality: Class Conflict in Historical, Comparative, and Global Perspective.* 5th ed. New York: McGraw-Hill.

Kilborn, Peter T. 2001. "Rural Towns Turn to Prisons to Reignite Their Economies." *New York Times,* August 1, pp. A1, A11.

Kilbourne, Jean. 2000a. *Can't Buy My Love: How Advertising Changes the Way We Think and Feel.* New York: Touchstone Book, Simon and Schuster.

————. 2000b. *Killing Us Softly* 3. Videorecording. Northampton, MA: Media Education Foundation (Cambridge Documentary Films).

Killian, Caitlin. 2003. "The Other Side of the Veil: North Africa Women in France Respond to the Headscarf Affair." *Gender and Society* (August 17):576–590.

Kim, Kwang Chung. 1999. *Koreans in the Hood: Conflict with African Americans.* Baltimore: Johns Hopkins University Press.

King, Leslie. 1998. "France Needs Children: Pronatalism, Nationalism, and Women's Equity." *Sociological Quarterly* 39 (Winter):33–52.

King, Peter H. 2004. "Their Spiritual Thirst Found a Desert Spring." *Los Angeles Times,* August 4, pp. A1, A10, A11.

Kinkade, Patrick T., and Michael A. Katovich. 1997. "The Driver Adaptations and Identities in the Urban Worlds of Pizza Delivery Employees." *Journal of Contemporary Ethnography* 25 (January):421–448.

Kinsella, Kevin, and David R. Phillips. 2005. "Global Aging: The Challenge of Success." *Population Bulletin* 60 (March).

Kinsey, Alfred C., Wardell B. Pomeroy, and Clyde E. Martin. 1948. *Sexual Behavior in the Human Male.* Philadelphia: Saunders.

————, Wardell B. Pomeroy, and Paul H. Gebhard. 1953. *Sexual Behavior in the Human Female.* Philadelphia: Saunders.

Kirp, David L. 2004. "Life Way After Head Start." *New York Times,* November 21, pp. 31–33, 38.

Kiser, Edgar. 1992. "War." Pp. 2243–2247 in *Encyclopedia of Sociology,* edited by Edgar F. Borgatta and Marie L. Borgatta. New York: Macmillan.

Kitchener, Richard F. 1991. "Jean Piaget: The Unknown Sociologist." *British Journal of Sociology* 42 (September):421–442.

Klass, Perri. 2003. "This Side of Medicine." P. 319 in *This Side of Doctoring: Reflection for Women in Medicine,* edited by Eliza Lo Chin. New York: Oxford University Press.

Klein, Naomi. 1999. *No Logo: Money, Marketing, and the Growing Anti-Corporate Movement.* New York: Picador (St. Martin's Press).

Kleiner, Art. 2003. "Are You In with the In Crowd?" *Harvard Business Review* 81 (July):86–92.

Kleinknecht, William. 1996. *The New Ethnic Mobs: The Changing Face of Organized Crime in America.* New York: Free Press.

Kleniewski, Nancy. 2002. *Cities, Change, and Conflict: A Political Economy of Urban Life.* 2d ed. Belmont, CA: Wadsworth.

Klinenberg, Eric. 2002. *Heat Wave: A Social Autopsy of Disaster in Chicago.* Chicago: University of Chicago Press.

Klug, Heinz. 2005. "Transnational Human Rights: Exploring the Persistence and Globalization of Human Rights." Pp. 85–103 in *Annual Review of Law and Social Sciences.* Palo Alto, CA: Annual Reviews.

Koch, Wendy. 2006. "Relatives Open Hearts and Homes." *USA Today,* March 20, p. 3A.

Kochhar, Rakesh. 2004. *The Wealth of Hispanic Households: 1996 to 2002.* Washington, DC: Pew Hispanic Center.

Kohn, Melvin L. 1970. "The Effects of Social Class on Parental Values and Practices." Pp. 45–68 in *The American Family: Dying or Developing,* edited by David Reiss and H. A. Hoffman. New York: Plenum.

Kolata, Gina. 1999. *Clone: The Road to Dolly and the Path Beyond.* New York: William Morrow.

Koolhaas, Rem, et al. 2001. *Mutations.* Barcelona, Spain: Actar.

Kopinak, Kathryn. 1995. "Gender as a Vehicle for the Subordination of Women Maquiladora Workers in Mexico." *Latin American Perspectives* 22 (Winter):30–48.

Korczyk, Sophie M. 2002. *Back to Which Future: The U.S. Aging Crisis Revisited.* Washington, DC: AARP.

Kottak, Conrad. 2004. *Anthropology: The Explanation of Human Diversity.* New York: McGraw-Hill.

Kotulak, Ronald. 2005. "Increase in Women Doctors Changing the Face of Medicine," *Chicago Tribune,* January 12, pp. 1, 4.

Kraul, Chris. 2003. "After Initial Boom, Mexico's Economy Goes Bust." *Los Angeles Times,* January 2, pp. A71, A36, A37.

Kreider, Rose M. 2005 "Number, Timing, and Duration of Marriages and Divorces: 2001." *Current Population Reports,* pp. 70–97. Washington, DC: U.S. Government Printing Office.

Kriesberg, Louis. 1992. "Peace." Pp. 1432–1436 in *Encyclopedia of Sociology,* edited by Edgar F. Borgatta and Marie L. Borgatta. New York: Macmillan.

Kristof, Nicholas D. 1998. "As Asian Economies Shrink, Women Are Squeezed Out." *New York Times,* June 11, pp. A1, A12.

Kroeger, Brooke. 2004. "When a Dissertation Makes a Difference." Accessed January 15, 2005 (www.racematters.org/devahpager.htm).

Kroll, Luisa, and Lea Goldman. 2005. "The World's Billionaires." Accessed March 15 (www.forbes.com).

Kübler-Ross, Elisabeth. 1969. *On Death and Dying.* New York: Macmillan.

Kwong, Jo. 2005. "Globalization's Effects on the Environment." *Society* 42 (January/February): 21–28.

Labaton, Stephan. 2003. "10 Wall St. Firms Settle with U.S. in Analyst Inquiry." *New York Times,* April 29, pp. A1, C4.

Lacey, Marc. 2005. "Accents of Africa: A New Outsoaring Frontier." *New York Times,* February 2, pp. C1, C6.

Ladner, Joyce. 1973. *The Death of White Sociology.* New York: Random Books.

La Ganga, Maria L. 1999. "Trying to Figure the Beginning of the End." *Los Angeles Times,* October 15, pp. A1, A28, A29.

Lamb, David. 1997. "Viet Kieu: A Bridge Between Two Worlds." *Los Angeles Times,* November 4, pp. A1, A8.

Landler, Mark. 2005. "Mixed Feelings as Kyoto Pact Takes Effect." *New York Times,* February 16, pp. C1, C3.

Landtman, Gunnar. [1938] 1968. *The Origin of Inequality of the Social Class.* New York: Greenwood (original edition 1938, Chicago: University of Chicago Press).

Lang, Eric. 1992. "Hawthorne Effect." Pp. 793–794 in *Encyclopedia of Sociology.* vol. 2, edited by Edgar F. Borgatta and Marie L. Borgatta. New York: Macmillan.

Lansprey, Susan. 1995. "AAAs and 'Naturally Occurring Retirement Communities' (NORCs)." Accessed August 4, 2003 (www.aoa.gov/housing/norcs.html).

Lareau, Annette. 2003. *Unequal Childhoods: Class, Race, and Family Life.* Berkeley: University of California Press.

Laska, Shirley. 2005. "The Role of Social Science Research in Disaster Preparedness and Response." Testimony before U.S. House of Representatives, Science Committee Subcommittee on Research.

Lasn, Kalle. 2003. "Ad Spending Predicted for Steady Decline." *Adbusters* (January/February).

Lasswell, Harold D. 1936. *Politics: Who Gets What, When, How.* New York: McGraw-Hill.

Lauer, Robert H. 1982. *Perspectives on Social Change.* 3d ed. Boston: Allyn and Bacon.

Laumann, Edward O., John H. Gagnon, and Robert T. Michael. 1994a. "A Political History of the National Sex Survey of Adults." *Family Planning Perspectives* 26 (February):34–38.

———, John H. Gagnon, Robert T. Michael, and Stuart Michaels. 1994b. *The Social Organization of Sexuality: Sexual Practices in the United States.* Chicago: University of Chicago Press.

Lazarsfeld, Paul, Bernard Beretson, and H. Gaudet. 1948. *The People's Choice.* New York: Columbia University Press.

———, and Robert K. Merton. 1948. "Mass Communication, Popular Taste, and Organized Social Action." Pp. 95–118 in *The Communication of Ideas,* edited by Lymon Bryson. New York: Harper and Brothers.

Leavell, Hugh R., and E. Gurney Clark. 1965. *Preventive Medicine for the Doctor in His Community: An Epidemiologic Approach.* 3d ed. New York: McGraw-Hill.

Lee, Alfred McClung. 1983. *Terrorism in Northern Ireland.* Bayside, NY: General Hall.

Lehne, Gregory K. 1995. "Homophobia among Men: Supporting and Defining the Male Role." Pp. 325–336 in *Men's Lives,* edited by Michael S. Kimmel and Michael S. Messner. Boston: Allyn and Bacon.

Leinwand, Donna. 2000. "20% Say They Used Drugs with Their Mom and Dad." *USA Today,* August 24, pp. 1A, 2A.

Lemann, Nicholas. 1991. "The Other Underclass." *Atlantic Monthly* 268 (December):96–102, 104, 107–108, 110.

Lengermann, Patricia Madoo, and Jill Niebrugge-Brantley. 1998. *The Women Founders: Sociology and Social Theory, 1830–1930.* Boston: McGraw-Hill.

Lenski, Gerhard. 1966. *Power and Privilege: A Theory of Social Stratification.* New York: McGraw-Hill.

Leonard, Koren Isakser. 2003. *Muslims in the United States: The State of Research.* New York: Russell Sage Foundation.

Leonhardt, David. 2004. "As Wealthy Fill Top Colleges Concerns Grow Over Fairness." *New York Times,* April 22, pp. A1, A12.

Levin, Jack, and William C. Levin. 1980. *Ageism.* Belmont, CA: Wadsworth.

Levinson, Daniel J. 1978. *The Seasons of a Man's Life.* With Charlotte N. Darrow et al. New York: Knopf.

———. 1996. *The Season of a Woman's Life.* With Judy D. Levinson. New York: Knopf.

Levitt, Steven D., and Stephen J. Dubner. 2005. *Freakonomics: A Rogue Economist Explores the Hidden Side of Everything.* New York: William Morrow.

Levy, Becca R., Martin D. Slade, Suzanne R. Kunkel, and Stanislav V. Kasl. 2002. "Longevity Increased by Positive Self-Perceptions of Aging." *Journal of Personality and Social Psychology* 83 (2):261–270.

Lewin, Tamar. 1998. "Debate Centers on Definition of Harassment." *New York Times,* March 22, pp. A1, A20.

———. 2000. "Differences Found in Care with Stepmothers." *New York Times,* August 17, p. A16.

Lewis Mumford Center. 2001. *Ethnic Diversity Grows, Neighborhood Integration Is at a Standstill.* Albany, NY: Lewis Mumford Center.

Lichter, Robert S., Linda S. Lichter, Daniel R. Amundson, and Trevor Buterworth. 2002. *Hollywood Cleans Up Its Act: Changing Rates of Sex and Violence in Entertainment Media.* Washington DC: Center for Media and Public Affairs.

Lichtblau, Eric. 2003. "Bush Issues Racial Profiling Ban but Exempts Security Awareness." *New York Times,* June 18, pp. A1, A14.

Lieberson, Stanley. 2000. *A Matter of Taste: How Names, Fashions, and Culture Change.* New Haven, CT: Yale University Press.

Light, Donald W. 2004. "From Migrant Enclaves to Mainstream: Reconceptualizing Informal Economic Behavior." *Theory and Society* 33:705–737.

Lin, Nan, and Wen Xie. 1988. "Occupational Prestige in Urban China." *American Journal of Sociology* 93 (January):793–832.

Lindner, Eileen, ed. 2006. *Yearbook of American and Canadian Churches, 2006.* Nashville: Abingdon Press.

Linn, Susan, and Alvin F. Poussaint. 1999. "Watching Television: What Are Children Learning About Race and Ethnicity?" *Child Care Information Exchange* 128 (July):50–52.

Lino, Mark. 2005. *Expenditures on Children by Families, 2004.* Washington, DC: U.S. Department of Agriculture, Center for Nutrition Policy and Promotion.

Lips, Hilary M. 2003. "The Gender Pay Gap: Concrete Indicator of Woman's Progress Toward Equality." *Analysis of Social Issues and Public Policy* 3 (1):87–109.

Lipset, Seymour Martin. 1996. *American Exceptionalism: A Double-Edged Sword.* New York: Norton.

Lipson, Karen. 1994. "'Nell' Not Alone in the Wilds." *Los Angeles Times,* December 19, pp. F1, F6.

Liptak, Adam. 2004a. "Bans on Interracial Unions Offer Perspective on Gay Ones." *New York Times,* March 17, p. A16.

———. 2004b. "Study Revises Texas's Standing as a Death Penalty Leader." *New York Times,* February 14, p. A8.

———. 2006. "The Ads Discriminate, but Does the Web?" *New York Times,* March 5, p. 16.

Liska, Allen E., and Steven F. Messner. 1999. *Perspectives on Crime and Deviance.* 3d ed. Upper Saddle River, NJ: Prentice Hall.

Livernash, Robert, and Eric Rodenburg. 1998. "Population Change, Resources, and the Environment." *Population Bulletin* 53 (March).

Liveplasma.com. 2006. "Music Maps." Accessed January 30 (www.liveplasma.com).

Livingstone, Sonia. 2004. "The Challenge of Changing Audiences." *European Journal of Communication* 19 (March):75–86.

Loeb, Susanna, Bruce Fuller, Sharon Lynn Kagan, and Bidemi Carrol. 2004. "Child Care in Poor Communities: Early Learning Effects of Type, Quality, and Stability." *Child Development* 75 (January/February):47–65.

Lofland, Lyn H. 1975. "The 'Thereness' of Women: A Selective Review of Urban Sociology." Pp. 144–170 in *Another Voice,* edited by M. Millman and R. M. Kanter. New York: Anchor/Doubleday.

Logan, John R. 2001. "From Many Shores: Asians in Census 2000." Accessed November 29 (http://mumford1.dyndns:org/cen2000/Asianpop).

Longman, Phillip. 2004. "The Global Baby Bust." *Foreign Affairs* 83 (May/June):64–79.

Lu, Ming, Jianyong Fan, Shejan Liu, and Yan Yan. 2002. "Employment Restructuring During China's Economic Transition." *Monthly Labor Review* (August):25–31.

Lukacs, Georg. 1923. *History and Class Consciousness.* London: Merlin.

Luker, Kristin. 1984. *Abortion and the Politics of Motherhood.* Berkeley: University of California Press.

Lum, Joann, and Peter Kwong. 1989. "Surviving in America: The Trials of a Chinese Immigrant Woman." *Village Voice* 34 (October 31):39–41.

Lumpe, Lora. 2003. "Taking Aim at the Global Gun Trade." *Amnesty Now* (Winter):10–13.

Lupton, Deborah. 1999. "Monster in Metal Cocoons: 'Road Rage' and Cyborg Bodies." *Body and Soul* 3 (N.1):57–92.

———. 2001. "Constructing 'Road Rage' as News: An Analysis of Two Australian Newspapers." *Australian Journal of Communication* 28 (N.3):25–36.

Luster, Tom, Kelly Rhoades, and Bruce Haas. 1989. "The Relation between Parental Values and Parenting Behavior: A Test of the Kohn Hypothesis." *Journal of Marriage and the Family* 51 (February):139–147.

Lyall, Sarah. 2002. "For Europeans, Love, Yes; Marriage, Maybe." *New York Times,* March 24, pp. 1–8.

Lynn, Barry C. 2003. "Trading with a Low-Wage Tiger." *The American Prospect* 14 (February): 10–12.

MacDorman, Marian, et al. 2005. "Explaining the 2001–2002 Infant Mortality Increase: Data from the Linked Death/Infant Death Data Set." *National Vital Statistics Reports* 53 (January 24).

Mack, Raymond W., and Calvin P. Bradford. 1979. *Transforming America: Patterns of Social Change.* 2d ed. New York: Random House.

448

MacLeod, Scott, and Vivienne Walt. 2005. "Live from Qatar." *Time,* Bonus Section, June, pp. A6–A8.

Magnier, Mark. 2004. "China Clamps Down on Web News Discussion." *Los Angeles Times,* February 26, p. A4.

Mahoney, Robert J. 1999. "Lessens from a Rose: Sociological Reflections on Eight Years of Long Term Care." *Illness, Crisis and Loss* 7 (1):77–90.

Maine Times. 2001. Article on Wal-Mart's Plan to Build Near the Penja. January 4.

Malcolm X, with Alex Haley. 1964. *The Autobiography of Malcolm X.* New York: Grove.

Malthus, Thomas Robert, Julian Huxley, and Frederick Osborn. [1824] 1960. *Three Essays on Population.* Reprint. New York: New American Library.

Mangum, Garth L., Stephen L. Magnum, and Andrew M. Sum. 2003. *The Persistence of Poverty in the United States.* Baltimore: Johns Hopkins University Press.

Marijuana Policy Project. 2004. *State-by-State Medical Marijuana Laws: How to Remove the Threat of Arrest.* Washington, DC: MPP.

———. 2006. *Marijuana Policy Project.* Accessed February 20 (www.mpp.org).

Mark, Gloria, Victor M. Gonzalez, and Justin Harris. 2005. "No Task Left Behind? Examining the Nature of Fragmented Work." Paper presented at CHI 2005, Portland, Oregon.

Marquardt, Elizabeth. 2005. *Between Two Worlds: The Inner Lives of Children of Divorce.* New York: Institute for American Values.

Marr, Phebe. 2003. "Civics 101, Taught by Saddam Hussein: First, Join the Paramilitary." *New York Times,* April 20.

Marriott, Michel. 2004. "The Color of Mayhem, in a Wave of Urban Games." *New York Times,* August 12.

Martelo, Emma Zapata. 1996. "Modernization, Adjustment, and Peasant Production." *Latin American Perspectives* 23 (Winter):118–130.

Martin, Joyce A., Brady E. Hamilton, Paul D. Sutton, Stephanie J. Ventura, Fay Menacker, and Martha L. Munson. 2005. "Births: Final Data for 2003." *National Vital Statistics Reports* 54 (September 8).

Martin, Marvin. 1996. "Sociology Adapting to Changes." *Chicago Tribune,* July 21, sec. 18, p. 20.

Martin, Susan E. 1994. "Outsider Within the Station House: The Impact of Race and Gender on Black Women Politics." *Social Problems* 41 (August):383–400.

Martineau, Harriet. [1837] 1962. *Society in America.* Edited, abridged, with an introductory essay by Seymour Martin Lipset. Reprint. Garden City, NY: Doubleday.

———. [1838] 1989. *How to Observe Morals and Manners.* Philadelphia: Leal and Blanchard. Sesquentennial edition, edited by M. R. Hill, Transaction Books.

Marx, Karl, and Friedrich Engels. [1847] 1955. *Selected Work in Two Volumes.* Reprint, Moscow: Foreign Languages Publishing House.

Maryanski, Alexandra R. 2004. "Evaluation Theory." Pp. 257–263 in *Encyclopedia of Social Theory,* edited by George Ritzer. Thousand Oaks, CA: Sage.

Mason, Heather. 2003. "What Do Americans See in Title IX's Future?" *Gallup Poll Tuesday Briefing.* Accessed January 28, 2003 (www.gallup.com).

Mason, J. W. 1998. "The Buses Don't Stop Here Anymore." *American Prospect* 37 (March):56–62.

Massey, Douglas S. 1998. "March of Folly: U.S. Immigration Policy After NAFTA." The *American Prospect* (March/April):22–23.

———, and Nancy A. Denton. 1993. *American Apartheid: Segregation and the Making of the Underclass.* Cambridge, MA: Harvard University Press.

Maugh, Thomas H., II. 2004. "AIDS Epidemic Continues to Grow, U.N. Reports." *Los Angeles Times,* July 7, p. A3.

McCall, Tommy. 2006. "Pay for Performance? Sometimes, but Not Always." *New York Times,* April 9, sect. 3, p. 6.

McCarthy, Ellen. 2004. "A Voice for the Mideast." *Washington Post National Weekly Edition* 22 (October 25):30–31.

McCloud, Aminah Beverly. 1995. *African American Islam.* New York: Routledge.

McCormick, John, and Claudia Kalb. 1998. "Dying for a Drink." *Newsweek,* June 15, pp. 30–34.

McCright, Aaron M., and Riley E. Dunlap. 2003. "Defeating Kyoto: The Conservative Movement's Impact on U.S. Climate Change Policy." *Social Problems* 50 (3):348–373.

McDonald, Kim A. 1999. "Studies of Women's Health Produce a Wealth of Knowledge on the Biology of Gender Differences." *Chronicle of Higher Education* 45 (June 25):A19, A22.

McFalls, Joseph A., Jr. 2003. "Population: A Lively Introduction." 4e, *Population Bulletin* 58. (December).

McGue, Matt, and Thomas J. Bouchard, Jr. 1998. "Genetic and Environmental Influence on Human Behavioral Differences." Pp. 1–24 in *Annual Review of Neurosciences.* Palo Alto, CA: Annual Reviews.

McIntosh, Peggy. 1988. "White Privilege and Male Privilege: A Personal Account of Coming to See Correspondence Through Work and Women's Studies." Working Paper No. 189, Wellesley College Center for Research on Women, Wellesley, MA.

McKinlay, John B., and Sonja M. McKinlay. 1977. "The Questionable Contribution of Medical Measures to the Decline of Mortality in the United States in the Twentieth Century." *Milbank Memorial Fund Quarterly* 55 (Summer):405–428.

McKinsey Global Institute. 2005. "The Emerging Global Labor Market." Accessed April 18, 2006 (www.mckinsey.com).

McLuhan, Marshall. 1964. *Understanding Media: The Extensions of Man.* New York: New American Library.

———, and Quentin Fiore. 1967. *The Medium Is the Message: An Inventory of Effects.* New York: Bantam Books.

McNeil, Donald G., Jr. 2003. "Africans Outdo U.S. Patients in Following AIDS Therapy." *New York Times,* September 3, pp. A1, A5.

McNeil, Donald G., Jr. 2004. "Plan to Battle AIDS Worldwide Is Falling Short." *New York Times,* March 28, pp. 1, 14.

Mead, George H. 1934. In *Mind, Self and Society,* edited by Charles W. Morris. Chicago: University of Chicago Press.

———. 1964a. In *On Social Psychology,* edited by Anselm Strauss. Chicago: University of Chicago Press.

———. 1964b. "The Genesis of the Self and Social Control." Pp. 267–293 in *Selected Writings: George Herbert Mead,* edited by Andrew J. Reck. Indianapolis: Bobbs-Merrill.

Mead, Margaret. 1973. "Does the World Belong to Men—Or to Women?" *Redbook* 141(October):46–52.

———. [1935] 2001. *Sex and Temperament in Three Primitive Societies.* New York: Perennial, Harper-Collins.

MediaGuardian. 2001. "Censorship of News in Wartime Is Still Censorship." October 15. Accessed January 25, 2003 (http://media.guardian.co.uk/attack/story/0,1301,57445,00.html).

Medina, Jennifer. 2004. "Housewives, Try This for Desperation." *New York Times,* December 22, pp. A1, A28.

Melia, Marilyn Kennedy. 2000. "Changing Times." *Chicago Tribune,* January 2, sec. 17, pp. 12–15.

Mencimer, Stephanie. 2002. "Children Left Behind." *The American Prospect,* December 30, pp. 29–31.

Mendez, Jennifer Bickman. 1998. "Of Mops and Maids: Contradictions and Continuities in Bureaucratized Domestic Work." *Social Problems* 45 (February):114–135.

Menzel, Peter. 1994. *Material World.* Berkeley: University of California Press.

Merton, Robert. 1948. "The Bearing of Empirical Research upon the Development of Social Theory." *American Sociological Review* 13 (October):505–515.

———. 1968. *Social Theory and Social Structure.* New York Free Press.

———, and Alice S. Kitt. 1950. "Contributions to the Theory of Reference Group Behavior." Pp. 40–105 in *Continuities in Social Research: Studies in the Scope and Methods of the American Soldier,* edited by Robert K. Merton and Paul L. Lazarsfeld. New York: Free Press.

Messner, Michael A. 1997. *Politics of Masculinities: Men in Movements.* Thousand Oaks, CA: Sage.

———. 2002. "Gender Equity in College Sports: 6 Views." *Chronicle of Higher Education.* 49 (December 6):B9–B10.

Meyers, Thomas J. 1992. "Factors Affecting the Decision to Leave the Old Order Amish." Presented at the annual meeting of the American Sociological Association, Pittsburgh.

Michals, Jennifer M. 2003. "The Price We Pay to Get Richer: A Look at Student Indebtedness." Unpublished M.A. paper, DePaul University, Chicago, IL.

Michels, Robert. 1915. *Political Parties.* Glencoe, IL: Free Press (reprinted 1949).

Migration News. 2002c. "Mexico: Bush, IDs, Remittances." (December). Accessible online at (http://migration.ucdavis.edu).

———. 2004. "NAFTA at 10." *Migration News* 11 (January). Accessible online at (http://migration.ucdavis.edu).

———. 2005a. "Mexico: Migrants, Mexicans in U.S. Economy." (April). Accessed (http://migration.ucdavis.edu).

———. 2005b. "Offshoring" (January). Accessed (http://migration.ucdavis.edu).

———. 2005c. "Maquiladoras" (July). Accessed (http://migration.ucdavis.edu).

Milgram, Stanley. 1963. "Behavioral Study of Obedience." *Journal of Abnormal and Social Psychology* 67 (October):371–378.

———. 1975. *Obedience to Authority: An Experimental View.* New York: Harper and Row.

Miller, David L. 2000. *Introduction to Collective Behavior and Collective Action.* 2d ed. Prospect Heights, IL: Waveland Press.

———, and JoAnne DeRoven Darlington. 2002. *Fearing for the Safety of Others: Disasters and the Small World Problem.* Paper presented at Midwest Sociological Society, Milwaukee, WI.

Miller, Reuben. 1988. "The Literature of Terrorism." *Terrorism* 11 (1):63–87.

Mills, C. Wright. [1959] 2000a. *The Sociological Imagination. 40th Anniversary Edition: New Afterword by Todd Gitlin.* New York: Oxford University Press.

———. [1956] 2000b. *The Power Elite.* A New Edition. Afterword by Alan Wolfe. New York: Oxford University Press.

Minnesota Center for Twin and Family Research. 2006. "Minnesota Center for Twins and Family Research." Accessed January 11 (www.psych.umn.edu).

Mirapaul, Matthew. 2001. "How the Net Is Documenting a Watershed Moment." *New York Times,* October 15, p. E2.

Mizruchi, Mark S. 1996. "What Do Interlocks Do? An Analysis, Critique, and Assessment of Research on Interlocking Directorates." Pp. 271–298 in *Annual Review of Sociology,* 1996, edited by John Hagan and Karen Cook. Palo Alto, CA: Annual Reviews.

Moaveni, Azadeh. 2005a. *Lipstick Jihad. A Memoir of Growing Up Iranian in America and American in Iran.* New York: Public Affairs.

———. 2005b. "Fast Times in Tehran," *Time* (June 12): 38–42.

Moeller, Susan D. 1999. *Compassion Fatigue.* London: Routledge.

Moen, Phyllis, and Patricia Roehling. 2005. *The Career Mystique: Cracks in the American Dream.* Lanham, MD: Rowman and Littlefield.

Mogelonsky, Marcia. 1996. "The Rocky Road to Adulthood." *American Demographics* 18 (May): 26–29, 32–35, 56.

Monaghan, Peter. 1993. "Sociologist Jailed Because He 'Wouldn't Snitch' Ponders the Way Research Ought to Be Done." *Chronicle of Higher Education* 40 (September 1):A8, A9.

Monmaney, Terence. 1995. "Ethnicities' Medical Views Vary, Study Says." *Los Angeles Times,* September 13, pp. B1, B3.

Monteiro, Lois A. 1998. "Ill-Defined Illnesses and Medically Unexplained Symptoms Syndrome." *Footnotes* 26 (February):3, 6.

Montgomery, Marilyn J., and Gwendolyn T. Sorrell. 1997. "Differences in Love Attitudes Across Family Life Stages." *Family Relations* 46:55–61.

Moore, David W. 2002. "Americans' View of Influence of Religion Settling Back to Pre-September 11 Levels." *Gallup Poll Tuesday Briefing.* December 31

Moore, Wilbert E. 1967. *Order and Change: Essays in Comparative Sociology.* New York: Wiley.

———. 1968. "Occupational Socialization." Pp. 861–883 in *Handbook of Socialization Theory and Research,* edited by David A. Goslin. Chicago: Rand McNally.

Morehouse Medical Treatment and Effectiveness Center. 1999. *A Synthesis of the Literature: Racial and Ethnic Differences in Acccess to Medical Care.* Menlo Park, CA: Henry J. Kaiser Family Foundation.

Morin, Richard. 2000. "Will Traditional Polls Go the Way of the Dinosaur?" *Washington Post National Weekly Edition* 17 (May 15):34.

Morris, Aldon. 2000. "Reflections on Social Movement Theory: Criticisms and Proposals." *Contemporary Sociology* 29 (May):445–454.

Morris, Bonnie Rothman. 1999. "You've Got Romance! Seeking Love on Line." *New York Times,* August 26, p. D1.

Morrison, Denton E. 1971. "Some Notes toward Theory on Relative Deprivation, Social Movements, and Social Change." *American Behavioral Scientist* 14 (May/June):675–690.

Mosley, J., and E. Thomson. 1995. Pp. 148–165 in *Fatherhood: Contemporary Theory, Research and Social Policy,* edited by W. Marsiglo. Thousand Oaks, CA: Sage.

Moss, Michael, and Ford Fessenden. 2002. "New Tools for Domestic Spying, and Qualms." *New York Times,* December 10, pp. A1, A18.

MRI+. 2005. "MRI Cyberstats," Accessed March 29 (www.mriplus.com).

Mueller, G O. 2001. "Transnational Crime: Definitions and Concepts." Pp. 13–21 in *Combating Transnational Crime: Concepts, Activities, and Responses,* edited by P. Williams and D. Vlassis. London Franklin Cass.

Mumola, Christopher J. 2000. *Incarcerated Parents and Their Children.* Washington, DC: U.S. Government Printing Office.

Murdock, George P. 1945. "The Common Denominator of Cultures." Pp. 123–142 in *The Science of Man in the World Crisis,* edited by Ralph Linton. New York: Columbia University Press.

———. 1949. *Social Structure.* New York: Macmillan.

———. 1957. "World Ethnographic Sample." *American Antaropologist* 59 (August): 664–687.

Murphy, Caryle. 1993. "Putting Aside the Veil." *Washington Post National Weekly Edition* 10 (April 12–18):10–11.

Murphy, Dean E. 1997. "A Victim of Sweden's Pursuit of Perfection." *Los Angeles Times,* September 2, pp. A1, A8.

———. 2004. "Desert's Promised Land: Long Odds for Las Vegas Newcomers." *New York Times,* May 30, pp. A1, A16.

Murray, Velma McBride, Amanda Willert, and Diane P. Stephens. 2001. "The Half-Full Glass: Resilient African American Single Mothers and Their Children." *Family Focus,* June, pp. F4–F5.

NARAL Pro-Choice America. 2006. *Who Decided? A State-by-State Report on the Status of Women's Reproductive Rights.* Accessed March 11 (www.naral.org).

Nash, Manning. 1962. "Race and the Ideology of Race." *Current Anthropology* 3 (June):285–288.

National Advisory Commission on Criminal Justice. 1976. *Organized Crime.* Washington, DC: U.S. Government Printing Office.

National Center on Women and Family Law. 1996. *Status of Marital Rape Exemption Statutes in the United States.* New York: National Center on Women and Family Law.

National Geographic. 2002. "A World Transformed." *National Geographic* (September): map.

———. 2005. *Atlas of the World.* 8th ed. Washington, DC: *National Geographic.*

National Indian Gaming Association. 2005. *An Analysis of the Economic Import of Indian Gaming in 2004.* Washington, DC: NIGA.

National Institute on Aging. 1999. *Early Retirement in the United States.* Washington, DC: U.S. Government Printing Office.

National Organization for Men Against Sexism. 2006. Home page. Accessed March 11, 2006 (www.nomas.org).

National Right to Work Legal Defense Foundation. 2006. *Right to Work States.* Accessed January 18 (www.nrtw.org/rtws.htm).

National Vital Statistics Reports. 2005. "Births, Marriages, Divorces, and Deaths: Provisional Data for October 2004." *National Vital Statistics Reports* 53 (April 19).

Navarro, Mireya. 2002. "Trying to Get Beyond the Role of the Maid." *New York Times,* May 16, pp. E1, E4.

Neary, Ian. 2003. "Burakumin at the End of History." *Social Research* 70 (Spring):269–294.

Nelson, Emily. 2004. "Goodbye, 'Friends'; Hello, New Reality." *Wall Street Journal,* February 9, pp. B6, B10.

Neuman, W. Lawrence. 2000. *Social Research Methods: Qualitative and Quantitative Approaches.* Boston: Allyn and Bacon.

Newman, William M. 1973. *American Pluralism: A Study of Minority Groups and Social Theory.* New York: Harper and Row.

Newport, Frank. 2004. "A Look at Americans and Religion." Accessed April 14 (www.gallup.com).

Newsday. 1997. "Japan Sterilized 16,000 Women." September 18, p. A19.

New York Times. 1991. "For 2, an Answer to Years of Doubt on Use of Peyote in Religious Rite." July 9, p. A14.

NICHD. 1998. *Early Childhood Care.* Accessed October 19, 2000 (www.nichd.nih.gov/publications/pubs/ early_child_care.htm).

450

Nielsen, Joyce McCarl, Glenda Walden, and Charlotte A. Kunkel. 2000. "Gendered Heteronormativity: Empirical Illustrations in Everyday Life." *Sociological Quarterly* 41(2): 283–296.

Nolan, Patrick, and Gerhard Lenski. 2006. *Human Societies: An Introduction to Macrosociology.* 10th ed. Boulder, CO: Paradigm.

Noonan, Rita K. 1995. "Women Against the State: Political Opportunities and Collective Action Frames in Chile's Transition to Democracy." *Sociological Forum* 10:81–111.

Norris, Poppa, and Ronald Inglehart. 2004. *Sacred and Secular: Religion and Politics Worldwide.* Cambridge: Cambridge University Press.

Novelli, William D. 2004. "Common Sense: The Case for Age Discrimination Law." *Global Report on Aging,* pp. 4, 7. Washington, DC: AARP.

Nussbaum, Daniel. 1998. "Bad Air Days." *Los Angeles Times Magazine,* July 19, pp. 20–21.

Oberschall, Anthony. 1973. *Social Conflict and Social Movements.* Englewood Cliffs, NJ: Prentice Hall.

O'Brien, Steve. 2005. "The Gallup Poll of China." Accessed January 6 (www.gallup.com).

O'Connor, Anne-Marie. 2004. "Time of Blogs and Bombs." *Los Angeles Times,* December 27, pp. E1, E14–E15.

O'Donnell, Jayne, and Richard Willing. 2003. "Prison Time Gets Harder for White-Collar Crooks." *USA Today,* May 12, pp. A1, A2.

O'Donnell, Mike. 1992. *A New Introduction to Sociology.* Walton-on-Thames, United Kingdom: Thomas Nelson and Sons.

Office of Justice Programs. 1999. "Transnational Organized Crime." *NCJRS Catalog* 49 (November/December):21.

Ogburn, William F. 1922. *Social Change with Respect to Culture and Original Nature.* New York: Huebsch (reprinted 1966, New York: Dell).

———, and Clark Tibbits. 1934. "The Family and Its Functions." Pp. 661–708 in *Recent Social Trends in the United States,* edited by Research Committee on Social Trends. New York: McGraw-Hill.

O'Hare, William P., and Brenda Curry White. 1992. "Is There a Rural Underclass?" *Population Today* 20 (March):6–8.

Okamoto, Dina G., and Lynn Smith-Lovin. 2001. "Changing the Subject: Gender, Status, and the Dynamics of Topic Change." *American Sociological Review* 66 (December):852–873.

Okano, Kaori, and Motonori Tsuchiya. 1999. *Education in Contemporary Japan: Inequality and Diversity.* Cambridge: Cambridge University Press.

Oliver, Melvin L., and Thomas M. Shapiro. 1995. *Black Wealth/White Wealth: New Perspectives on Racial Inequality.* New York: Routledge.

Ommer, Uwe. 2000. *1000 Families: The Family album of Planet Earth.* Cologne, Germany: Taschen for Unicef.

Onishi, Norimitsu. 2003. "Divorce in South Korea: Striking a New Attitude." *New York Times,* September 21, p. 19.

Ormond, James. 2005. "The McDonaldization of Football." Accessed January 23, 2006 (http://courses.essex.ac.uk/sc/sc111).

Orum, Anthony M. 1989. *Introduction to Political Sociology: The Social Anatomy of the Body Politic.* 3d ed. Englewood Cliffs, NJ: Prentice Hall.

———. 2001. *Introduction to Political Sociology.* 4th ed. Upper Saddle River, NJ: Prentice Hall.

Osgood, D. Wayne, and Jeff M. Chambers. 2003. "Community Correlates of Rural Youth Violence." *Juvenile Justice Bulletin* (May):1–9.

Ouchi, William, 1981. *Theory Z: How American Businesses Can Meet the Japanese Challenge.* Reading, MA: Addison-Wesley.

Page, Charles H. 1946. "Bureaucracy's Other Face." *Social Forces* 25 (October):89–94.

Pager, Devah. 2003. "The Mark of a Criminal Record." *American Journal of Sociology* 108 (March):937–975.

———, and Lincoln Quillian. 2005. "Walking the Talk? What Employers Say Versus What They Do." *American Sociological Review* 70 (June): 355–380.

Paik, Haejung, and George Comstock. 1994. "The Effects of Television Violence on Anti-social Behavior: A Meta-analysis." *Communication Research* 21:516–546.

Paik, Nancy. 2001. *One Nation: Islam in America.* Accessed March 15 (www.channelonenews.com/special/islam/media.html).

Pamuk, E., D. Makui, K. Heck, C. Reuban, and K. Lochren. 1998. *Health, United States 1998 with Socioeconomic Status and Health Chartbook.* Hyattsville, MD: National Center for Health Statistics.

Parents Television Council. 2003. *TV Bloodbath: Violence on Prime Time Broadcast TV.* Los Angeles: PTC.

———. 2005. "Top Ten Best and Worst Shows for Family Viewing on Prime Time Broadcast Television." News release, October 19 (www.parentstv.org). Accessed January 30, 2006.

Park, Hwa-Ok. 2005. "Grandmothers Raising Grandchildren: Family Well-Being and Economic Assistance." *Focus* 24 (Fall):19–27.

Park, Kristin. 2005. "Choosing Childlessness Weher's Typology of Action and Motives of the Voluntarily Childless." *Sociological Inquiry* (August):372–402.

Park, Robert E. 1916. "The City: Suggestions for the Investigation of Human Behavior in the Urban Environment." *American Journal of Sociology* 20 (March):577–612.

———. 1922. *The Immigrant Press and Its Control.* New York: Harper.

———. 1936. "Succession, an Ecological Concept." *American Sociological Review* 1 (April):171–179.

Parker, Alison. 2004. "Inalienable Rights: Can Human-Rights Law Help to End U.S. Mistreatment of Noncitizens?" *American Prospect* (October):A11–A13.

Parsons, Talcott. 1951. *The Social System.* New York: Free Press.

———. 1966. *Societies: Evolutionary and Comparative Perspectives.* Englewood Cliffs, NJ: Prentice Hall.

———. 1975. "The Sick Role and the Role of the Physician Reconsidered." *Milbank Medical Fund Quarterly Health and Society* 53 (Summer): 257–278.

———, and Robert Bales. 1955. *Family: Socialization, and Interaction Process.* Glencoe, IL: Free Press.

Passel, Jeffrey S. 2006. *The Size and Characteristics of the Unauthorized Migrant Population in the U.S. Estimates Based on the March 2005 Current Population Survey.* Washington: Pew Hispanic Center.

Passero, Kathy. 2002. "Global Travel Expert Roger Axtell Explains Why." *Biography,* July, pp. 70–73, 97–98.

Patterson, Thomas E. 2003. *We the People.* 5th ed. New York: McGraw-Hill.

———. 2005. "Young Voters and the 2004 Election." Cambridge, MA: Vanishing Voter Project, Harvard University.

Pattillo-McCoy, Mary. 1999. *Black Picket Fences: Privilege and Peril among the Black Middle Class.* Chicago: University of Chicago Press.

PBS. 2005. "Store Wars: When Wal-Mart Comes to Town." Accessed August 31 (www.pbs.org).

Pear, Robert. 1997. "Now, the Archenemies Need Each Other." *New York Times,* June 22, sec. 4, pp. 1, 4.

Pearlstein, Steven. 2001. "Coming Soon (Maybe): Worldwide Recession." *Washington Post National Weekly Edition* 19 (November 12):18.

Pellow, David Naguib. 2002. *Garbage Wars: The Struggle for Environmental Justice in Chicago.* Cambridge, MA: MIT Press.

Pelton, Tom. 1994. "Hawthorne Works' Glory Now Just So Much Rubble." *Chicago Tribune,* April 18, pp. 1, 6.

Perrow, Charles. 1986. *Complex Organizations.* 3d ed. New York: Random House.

Perry, Joellen. 2001. "For Most, There's No Place Like Home." *U.S. News and World Report* 130 (June 4):66.

Peter, Laurence J., and Raymond Hull. 1969. *The Peter Principle.* New York: Morrow.

Petersen, William. 1979. *Malthus.* Cambridge, MA: Harvard University Press.

Peterson, Karen. S. 2003. "Unmarried with Children: For Better or Worse?" *USA Today,* August 18, pp. 1A, 8A.

Pew Internet Project. 2005. "Demographics of Internet Users." Updated December 5, 2005. Accessed January 26, 2006 (www.pewinternet.org).

Pew Research Center. 2004. "Conflicted Views of Affirmative Action." News release, May 14, 2004. Washington, DC: Pew Research Center.

Phillips, E. Barbara. 1996. *City Lights: Urban—Suburban Life in the Global Society.* New York: Oxford University Press.

Phillips, Susan A. 1999. *Wallbangin': Graffiti and Gangs in L.A.* Chicago: University of Chicago Press.

Piaget, Jean. 1954. *The Construction of Reality in the Child.* Translated by Margaret Cook. New York: Basic Books.

Pierre, Robert E. 2002. "When Welfare Reform Stops Working." *Washington Post National Weekly Edition,* January 13, pp. 29–30.

Pinderhughes, Dianne. 1987. *Race and Ethnicity in Chicago Politics: A Reexamination of Pluralist Theory.* Urbana: University of Illinois Press.

Pinkerton, James P. 2003. "Education: A Grand Compromise." *Atlantic Monthly* 291 (January/February):115–116.

Plomin, Robert. 1989. "Determinants of Behavior." *American Psychologist* 44 (February):105–111.

Plüss, Caroline. 2005. "Constructing Globalized Ethnicity." *International Sociology* 20 (June): 201–224.

Polletta, Francesca, and James M. Jasper. 2001. "Collective Identity and Social Movements." Pp. 283–305 in *Annual Review of Sociology, 2001,* edited by Karen S. Cook and Leslie Hogan. Palo Alto, CA: Annual Review of Sociology.

Poniewozik, James. 2001. "What's Wrong with This Picture?" *Time* 157 (May 28):80–81.

———. 2005. "The Decency Police." *Time,* March 28.

Popenoe, David, and Barbara Dafoe Whitehead. 1999. *Should We Live Together? What Young Adults Need to Know About Cohabitation Before Marriage.* Rutgers, NJ: The National Marriage Project.

Population Reference Bureau. 1996. "Speaking Graphically." *Population Today* 24 (June/July):b.

———. 2004. "Transitions in World Population." *Population Bulletin* 59 (March).

Power, Samantha. 2002. *A Problem from Hell: America and the Age of Genocide.* New York: Perennial.

Prah, Pamela M. 2005. "Labor Unions' Future." *CQ Researcher* 15 (September 2):709–731.

Pryor, John H., Sylvia Hurtado, Victor B. Saenz, Jennifer A. Lindholm, William S. Kom, and Kathryn M. Mahoney. 2005. *The American Freshman: National Norms for Fall 2005.* Los Angeles: Higher Education Research Institute, UCLA.

Purdy, Matthew. 2001. "Ignoring and Then Embracing the Truth about Racial Profiling." *New York Times,* March 11, p. 37.

Quadagno, Jill. 2005. *Aging and the Life Course: An Introduction to Social Gerontology.* 3d ed. New York: McGraw-Hill.

Quart, Alissa. 2003. *Branded: The Buying and Selling of Teenagers.* New York: Perseus.

Quinney, Richard. 1970. *The Social Reality of Crime.* Boston: Little, Brown.

———. 1974. *Criminal Justice in America.* Boston: Little, Brown.

———. 1979. *Criminology.* 2d ed. Boston: Little, Brown.

———. 1980. *Class, State and Crime.* 2d ed. New York: Longman.

Rainey, Richard. 2004. "Groups Assail 'Most Violent' Video Games, Industry Rating System." *Los Angeles Times,* November 24, p. A34.

Rainie, Lee. 2001. *The Commons of the Tragedy.* Washington, DC: Pew Internet and American Life Project.

———. 2006. *Sports Fantasy Leagues Online.* Washington, DC: Pew Internet and American Life Project.

———, and Andrew Kohut. 2000. *Tracking Online Life: How Women Use the Internet to Cultivate Relationships with Family and Friends.* Washington, DC: Pew Internet and American Life League.

Rajan, Gita, and Shailja Sharma. 2006. *New Cosmopolitanisms: South Asians in the US.* Stanford, CA: Stanford University Press.

Ramet, Sabrina. 1991. *Social Currents in Eastern Europe: The Source and Meaning of the Great Transformation.* Durham, NC: Duke University Press.

Ramirez, Eddy. 2002. "Ageism in the Media Is Seen as Harmful to Health of the Elderly." *Los Angeles Times,* September 5, p. A20.

Ramirez, Roberta R., and G. Patricia de la Cruz. 2003. "The Hispanic Population in the Current United States: March 2002." *Current Population Reports,* ser. P-20, no. 545. Washington, DC: U.S. Government Printing Office.

Rantala, Ramona R. 2004. "Cybercrime against Businesses." *Bureau of Justice Statistics Technical Report* (March).

Reeves, Terrence, and Claudette Bennett. 2003. "The Asian and Pacific Islander Population in the United States: March 2002." *Current Population Reports* ser. P-20, no. 540. Washington, DC: U.S. Government Printing Office.

Reinharz, Shulamit. 1992. *Feminist Methods in Social Research.* New York: Oxford University Press.

Religion News Service. 2003. "New U.S. Guidelines on Prayer in Schools Get Mixed Reaction." *Los Angeles Times,* February 15, p. B24.

Religion Watch. 2006. "Hinduism Shaping India's Pragmatic Use of Biotechnology." April.

Religious Diversity News. 2004. "The Oklahoma Headscarf Case." Accessed October 16 (www.pluralism.org).

Religious Tolerance. 2005. "Female Genital Mutilation (FGM): Informational Materials." Accessed March 15 (www.religioustolerance.org).

Remnick, David. 1998. "Bad Seeds." *New Yorker* 74 (July 20):28–33.

Reschovsky, Clara. 2004. *Journey to Work: 2000.* Census 2000 Brief C2KBR-23. Washington, DC: U.S. Government Printing Office.

Rheingold, Howard. 2003. *Smart Mobs: The Next Social Revolution.* Cambridge, MA: Perseus.

Richardson, James T., and Barend van Driel. 1997. "Journalists' Attitudes toward New Religious Movements." *Review of Religious Research* 39 (December):116–136.

Richardson, Laurel, Verta Taylor, and Nancy Whittier, eds. 2004. *Feminist Frontiers.* 6th ed. New York: McGraw-Hill.

Richtel, Matt. 2000. "www.layoffs.com." *New York Times,* June 22, pp. C1, C12.

Rideout, Victoria, Donald F. Roberts, and Ulla G. Foehr. 2005. *Generation M: Media in the Lives of 8–18-Year-Olds.* Menlo Park, CA: Kaiser Family Foundation.

Ridgeway, Cecilia L., and Lynn Smith-Lovin. 1999. "The Gender System and Interaction." Pp. 191–216 in *The Annual Review of Sociology 1999,* edited by Karen Cook and John Hagan. Palo Alto, CA: Annual Review.

Riding, Alan. 1998. "Why 'Titanic' Conquered the World." *New York Times,* April 26, sec. 2, pp. 1, 28, 29.

———. 2005. "Unesco Adopts New Plan Against Cultural Invasion." *New York Times,* October 21, p. B3.

Rifkin, Jeremy. 1995. "Afterwork." *Utne Reader* (May/June):52–62.

Riley, John W., Jr. 1992. "Death and Dying." Pp. 413–418 in *Encyclopedia of Sociology,* vol. 1, edited by Edgar F. Borgatta and Marie L. Borgatta. New York: Macmillan.

Riley, Matilda White, Robert L. Kahn, and Anne Foner. 1994a. *Age and Structural Lag.* New York: Wiley InterScience.

———, Robert L. Kahn, and Anne Foner, in association with Karin A. Mock. 1994b. "Introduction: The Mismatch between People and Structures." Pp. 1–36 in *Age and Structural Lag,* edited by Matilda White Riley, Robert L. Kahn, and Anne Foner. New York: Wiley InterScience.

Riley, Nancy E. 2004. "China's Population: New Trends and Challenges." *Population Bulletin* 59 (June).

Rimer, Sara. 1998. "As Centenarians Thrive, 'Old' Is Redefined." *New York Times,* June 22, pp. A1, A14.

Ripley, Amanda. 2005. "Who Says a Woman Can't Be Einstein?" *Time* (March 7):51–60.

Ritzer, George. 2002. *McDonaldization: The Reader.* Thousand Oaks, CA: Pine Forge Press.

———. 2004a. *The McDonaldization of Society.* Revised New Century Edition. Thousand Oaks, CA: Pine Forge Press.

———. 2004b. *The Globalization of Nothing.* Thousand Oaks, CA: Pine Forge Press.

Rivoli, Pietra. 2005. *The Travels of a T-Shirt in the Global Economy: An Economist Examines the Markets, Power, and Politics of World Trade.* Hoboken, NJ: John Wiley.

Roberson, Debi, Ian Davies, and Jules Davidoff. 2000. "Color Categories Are Not Universal: Replications and New Evidence From Stone Age Culture." *Journal of Experimental Psychology* 129 (3):369–398.

Roberts, D. F., Lisa Henriksen, Peter G. Christiansson, and Marcy Kelly. 1999. "Substance Abuse in Popular Movies and Music." Accessible online (www.whitehousedrugpolicy.gov/news/press/042 899.html). Washington, DC: Office of Juvenile Justice.

Robertson, Roland. 1988. "The Sociological Significance of Culture: Some General Considerations." *Theory, Culture, and Society* 5 (February):3–23.

Robinson, Thomas N., Marta L. Wilde, Lisa C. Navracruz, K. Farish Haydel, and Ann Varady. 2001. "Effects of Reducing Children's Television and Video Game Use on Aggressive Behavior." *Archives of Pediatric Adolescent Medicine* 155 (January):17–23.

452

Roethlisberger, Fritz J., and W. J. Dickson. 1939. *Management and the Worker.* Cambridge, MA: Harvard University Press.

Rose, Arnold. 1951. *The Roots of Prejudice.* Paris: UNESCO.

Rose, Peter I., Myron Glazer, and Penina Migdal Glazer. 1979. "In Controlled Environments: Four Cases of Intense Resocialization." Pp. 320–338 in *Socialization and the Life Cycle,* edited by Peter I. Rose. New York: St. Martin's.

Rosenberg, Douglas H. 1991. "Capitalism." Pp. 33–34 in *Encyclopedic Dictionary of Sociology,* 4th ed., edited by Dushkin Publishing Group. Guilford, CT: Dushkin.

Rosenberg, Howard. 2003. "Snippets of the 'Unique' Al Jazeera." *Los Angeles Times,* April 4, pp. E1, E37.

Rosenberg, Yuval. 2004. "Lost Youth." *American Demographics* (March):18–19.

Rosenthal, Elizabeth. 2001. "College Entrance in China: 'No' to the Handicapped." *New York Times,* May 23, p. A3.

Rosenthal, Robert, and Lenore Jacobson. 1968. *Pygmalion in the Classroom.* New York: Holt.

Rossi, Alice S. 1968. "Transition to Parenthood." *Journal of Marriage and the Family* 30(February): 26–39.

———. 1984. "Gender and Parenthood." *American Sociological Review* 49 (February):1–19.

Rossi, Peter H. 1987. "No Good Applied Social Research Goes Unpunished." *Society* 25 (November/December):73–79.

Rossides, Daniel W. 1997. *Social Stratification: The Interplay of Class, Race, and Gender.* 2d ed. Upper Saddle River, NJ: Prentice Hall.

Roszak, Theodore. 1969. *The Making of a Counterculture.* Garden City, NY: Doubleday.

Roter, Debra L., Judith A. Hall, and Yutaka Aoki. 2002. "Physician Gender Effects in Medical Communication: A Meta-analytic Review." *Journal of the American Medical Association* 288 (August 14):756–764.

Ruane, Janet M., and Karen A. Cerulo. 2004. *Second Thoughts: Seeing Conventional Wisdom Through the Sociological Eye.* Thousand Oaks, CA: Pine Forge.

Rubin, Alissa J. 2003. "Pat-Down on the Way to Prayer." *Los Angeles Times,* November 25, pp. A1, A5.

Russo, Nancy Felipe. 1976. "The Motherhood Mandate." *Journal of Social Issues* 32:143–153.

Rutenberg, Jim. 2002. "Fewer Media Owners, More Media Choices." *New York Times,* December 2, pp. C1, C11.

Ryan, William. 1976. *Blaming the Victim.* Rev. ed. New York: Random House.

Rymer, Russ. 1993. *Genie: An Abused Child's Flight from Science.* New York: HarperCollins.

Saad, Lydia. 2003. "What Form of Government for Iraq?" Accessed September 26 (www.gallup.com).

———. 2004. "Divorce Doesn't Last." *Gallup Poll Tuesday Briefing,* March 30 (www.gallup.com).

———. 2005. "Gay Rights Attitudes a Mixed Bag." Accessed May 20 (www.gallup.com).

Sabbathday Lake. 2004. Interview by author with Sabbathday Lake Shaker Village. July 28.

Sachs, Jeffrey D. 2005a. *The End of Poverty: Economic Possibilities for Our Time.* New York: Penguin.

———. 2005b. "Can Extreme Poverty Be Eliminated?" *Scientific American* 293 (September): 56–65.

Sadker, Myra Pollack, and David Miller Sadker. 2003. *Teachers, Schools and Society,* 6th ed. New York: McGraw-Hill.

Safire, William. 1996. "Downsized." *New York Times Magazine,* May 26, pp. 12, 14.

Sagarin, Edward, and Jose Sanchez. 1988. "Ideology and Deviance: The Case of the Debate over the Biological Factor." *Deviant Behavior* 9 (1):87–99.

Sahagun, Louis. 2004. "Tribes Fear Backlash to Prosperity." *Los Angeles Times,* May 3, pp. B1, B6.

Sale, Kirkpatrick. 1996. *Rebels against the Future: The Luddites and Their War on the Industrial Revolution* (with a new preface by the author). Reading, MA: Addison-Wesley.

Salem, Richard, and Stanislaus Grabarek. 1986. "Sociology B.A.s in a Corporate Setting: How Can They Get There and of What Value Are They?" *Teaching Sociology* 14 (October):273–275.

Samuelson, Paul A., and William D. Nordhaus. 2005. *Economics.* 18th ed. New York: McGraw-Hill.

Samuelson, Robert J. 1996a. "Are Workers Disposable?" *Newsweek* 127, February 12, p. 47.

———. 1996b. "Fashionable Statements." *Washington Post National Weekly Edition* 13 (March 18):5.

Sanders, Edmund. 2004. "Coming of Age in Iraq." *Los Angeles Times,* August 14, pp. A1, A5.

Saporito, Bill. 2003. "Can Wal-Mart Get Any Bigger?" *Time,* January 13, pp. 38–43.

Sarkisian, Natalia, and Naomi Gerstel. 2004. "Kin Support among Blacks and Whites Race and Family Organizations." *American Sociological Review* 69 (December):812–837.

Sassen, Saskia. 2005. "New Global Classes: Implications for Politics." Pp. 143–170 in *The New Egalitarianism,* edited by Anthony Giddens and Patrick Diamond. Cambridge: Policy.

Sax, Linda J., Jennifer A. Lindholm, Alexandra W. Astin, William S. Korn, and Kathryn M. Mahoney. 2005. *The American Freshman National Norms for Fall 2004.* Los Angeles: Higher Education Research Institute, UCLA.

Sayer, Liana C., Suzanne M. Bianchi, and John P. Robinson. 2004. "Are Parents Investing Less in Children? Trends in Mothers' and Fathers' Time with Children." *American Journal of Sociology* 110 (July):1–43.

Scarce, Rik. 1994. "(No) Trial (But) Tribulations: When Courts and Ethnography Conflict." *Journal of Contemporary Ethnography* 23 (July):123–149.

———. 1995. "Scholarly Ethics and Courtroom Antics: Where Researchers Stand in the Eyes of the Law." *American Sociologist* 26 (Spring):87–112.

———. 2005. "A Law to Protect Scholars." *Chronicle of Higher Education* (August 12):324.

Schaefer, Richard T. 1998a. "Differential Racial Mortality and the 1995 Chicago Heat Wave." Presentation at the annual meeting of the American Sociological Association, August, San Francisco.

———. 1998b. *Alumni Survey.* Chicago, IL: Department of Sociology, DePaul University.

———. 2006. *Racial and Ethnic Relations.* 10th ed. Upper Saddle River, NJ: Prentice Hall.

Scharnberg, Kirsten. 2002. "Tattoo Unites WTC's Laborers." *Chicago Tribune,* July 22, pp. 1, 18.

Schmidley, A. Dianne, and J. Gregory Robinson. 2003. *Measuring the Foreign-Born Population in the United States with the Current Population Survey: 1994–2002.* Washington, DC: Population Division, Bureau of the Census.

Schnaiberg, Allan. 1994. *Environment and Society: The Enduring Conflict.* New York: St. Martin's.

Schor, Juliet B. 2004. *Born to Buy: The Commercialized Child and the New Consumer Culture.* New York: Scribner.

Schur, Edwin M. 1965. *Crimes without Victims: Deviant Behavior and Public Policy.* Englewood Cliffs, NJ: Prentice Hall.

———. 1968. *Law and Society: A Sociological View.* New York: Random House.

———. 1985. "'Crimes without Victims': A 20 Year Reassessment." Paper presented at the annual meeting of the Society for the Study of Social Problems.

Schurman, Rachel. 2004. "Fighting 'Frankenfoods': Industry Opportunity Structures and the Efficacy of the Anti-Biotech Movement in Western Europe." *Social Problems* 51 (2):243–268.

Schwartz, Howard D., ed. 1987. *Dominant Issues in Medical Sociology.* 2d ed. New York: Random House.

Schwartz, John. 2004. "Leisure Pursuits of Today's Young Man." *New York Times,* March 29.

Schwartz, Shalom H., and Anat Bardi. 2001. "Value Hierarchies Across Cultures: Taking a Similarities Perspective." *Journal of Cross-Cultural Perspective* 32 (May):268–290.

Scott, Alan. 1990. *Ideology and the New Social Movements.* London: Unwin Hyman.

Scott, Greg. 2005. "Public Symposium: HIV/AIDS, Injection Drug Use and Men Who Have Sex with Men." Pp. 38–39 in *Scholarship with a Mission,* edited by Susanna Pagliaro. Chicago: DePaul University.

Scott, Gregory. 2001. "Broken Windows behind Bars: Eradicating Prison Gangs through Ecological Hardening and Symbolic Cleansing." *Corrections Management Quarterly* 5 (Winter):23–36.

Scott, Jenny. 2005. "Life at the Top in America Isn't Better, It's Longer." *New York Times,* May 16, pp. A1, A19–A20.

Scott, W. Richard 2003. *Organizations: Rational, Natural, and Open Systems.* 5th ed. Upper Saddle River, NJ: Prentice Hall.

———. 2004. "Reflections on a Half-Century of Organizational Sociology." Pp. 1–21 in *Annual Review of Sociology 2004,* edited by Karen S. Cook and John Hagan. Palo Alto, CA: Annual Reviews.

Seabrook, Jeremy. 2005. "In Death, Imperialism Lives On." *Guardian Weekly Edition,* July 7, p. 5.

Secretan, Thierry. 1995. *Going into Darkness: Fantastic Coffins from Africa.* London: Thames and Hudson.

Seefeldt, Kristin S. 2004. "After PRWOA: Barriers to Employment, Work, and Well-Being among Current and Former Welfare Recipients." *Poverty Research Insights* (Fall):1–6.

Segall, Alexander. 1976. "The Sick Role Concept: Understanding Illness Behavior." *Journal of Health and Social Behavior* 17 (June): 163–170.

Segerstråle, Ullica. 2000. *Defense of the Truth: The Battle for Science in the Sociobiology Debate and Beyond.* New York: Oxford University Press.

Seidman, Steven. 1994. "Heterosexism in America: Prejudice against Gay Men and Lesbians." Pp. 578–593 in *Introduction to Social Problems,* edited by Craig Calhoun and George Ritzer. New York: McGraw-Hill.

Sellers, Frances Stead. 2004. "Voter Globalization." *Washington Post National Weekly Edition,* November 29, p. 22.

Sengupta, Somini. 2004. "For Iraqi Girls, Changing Land Narrows Lines." *New York Times,* June 27, pp. A1, A11.

Senior Action in a Gay Environment (SAGE). 2005. Home page. Accessed April 26 (www.sageusa.org).

Sernau, Scott. 2001. *Worlds Apart: Social Inequalities in a New Century.* Thousand Oaks, CA: Pine Forge Press.

Shanahan, Michael J. 2000. "Pathways to Adulthood in Changing Socities: Variability and Mechanisms in Life Cause Perspective." Pp. 667–692 in *Annual Review of Sociology 2000,* edited by Karen S. Cook. Palo Alto, CA: Annual Reviews.

Shapiro, Joseph P. 1993. *No Pity: People with Disabilities Forging a New Civil Rights Movement.* New York: Times Books.

Sheehan, Charles. 2005. "Poor Seniors Take On Plans of Condo Giant." *Chicago Tribune,* March 22, pp. 1, 9.

Shenon, Philip. 1995. "New Zealand Seeks Causes of Suicides by Young." *New York Times,* July 15, p. 3.

Shin, Hyon B., and Rosalind Bruno. 2003. "Language Use and English-Speaking Ability: 2000." *Census 2000 Brief,* C2KBR-29. Washington, DC: U.S. Government Printing Office.

Shinkai, Hiroguki, and Ugljea Zvekic. 1999. "Punishment." Pp. 89–120 in *Global Report on Crime and Justice,* edited by Graeme Newman. New York: Oxford University Press.

Shipler, David K. 2005. *The Working Poor: Invisible in America.* New York: Alfred A. Knopf.

Short, Kathleen, Thesia Garner, David Johnson, and Patricia Doyle. 1999. "Experimental Poverty Measures: 1990 to 1997." *Current Population Reports,* ser. P-60, no. 205. Washington, DC: U.S. Government Printing Office.

Shostak, Arthur B. 2002. "Clinical Sociology and the Art of Peace Promotion: Earning a World Without War." Pp. 325–345 in *Using Sociology: An Introduction from the Applied and Clinical Perspectives,* edited by Roger A. Straus. Lanham, MD: Rowman and Littlefield.

Shu, Xialing, and Yanjie Bian. 2003. "Marketing Transition and Gender Gap in Earnings in Urban China." *Social Forces* 81 (4):1107–1145.

Shupe, Anson D., and David G. Bromley. 1980. "Walking a Tightrope." *Qualitative Sociology* 2:8–21.

Silicon Valley Cultures Project. 2004. The Silicon Valley Cultures Project Web site. Accessed February 3, 2005 (www2.sjsu.edu/depts/anthropology/svcp).

Silver, Ira. 1996. "Role Transitions, Objects, and Identity." *Symbolic Interaction* 10 (1):1–20.

Simmons, Ann M. 1998. "Where Fat Is a Mark of Beauty." *Los Angeles Times,* September 30, pp. A1, A12.

———, and Robin Wright. 2000. "Gender Quota Puts Uganda in Role of Rights Pioneer." *Los Angeles Times,* February 23, p. A1.

Simmons, Tavia, and Martin O'Connell. 2003. "Married-Couple and Unmarried-Partner Households: 2000." *Census 2000 Special Reports* CENBR-5. Washington, DC: U.S. Government Printing Office.

Simons, Marlise. 1997. "Child Care Sacred as France Cuts Back the Welfare State." *New York Times,* December 31, pp. A1, A6.

Sjoberg, Gideon. 1960. *The Preindustrial City: Past and Present.* Glencoe, IL: Free Press.

Skull Valley Band Goshute. 2006. Home page. Accessed May 2 (www.skullvalleygoshutes.org).

Slavin, Robert E., and A. Cheung. 2003. *Effective Reading Programs for English Language Learners: A Best-Evidence Synthesis.* Baltimore, MD: Johns Hopkins University, Center for Research on the Education of Students Placed at Risk.

Smart, Barry. 1990. "Modernity, Postmodernity, and the Present." Pp. 14–30 in *Theories of Modernity and Postmodernity,* edited by Bryan S. Turner. Newbury Park, CA: Sage.

Smart Growth. 2005. "About Smart Growth." Accessed May 31 (www.smartgrowth.org.).

Smedley, Brian D., Adrienne Y. Stith, and Alan R. Nelson, eds. 2002. *Unequal Treatment: Confronting Racial and Ethnic Disparities in Health Care.* Washington, DC: Institutional Medicine.

Smeeding, Timothy, Lee Rainwater, and Gary Burtless. 2001. "United States Poverty in a Cross-National Context." *Focus* 21 (Spring):50–54.

Smelser, Neil. 1963. *The Sociology of Economic Life.* Englewood Cliffs, NJ: Prentice Hall.

———. 1981. *Sociology.* Englewood Cliffs, NJ: Prentice Hall.

Smith, Christian. 1991. *The Emergence of Liberation Theology: Radical Religion and Social Movement Theory.* Chicago: University of Chicago Press.

Smith, Craig S. 2005. "Abduction, Often Violent, a Kyrgyz Wedding Rite." *New York Times,* April 30, pp. A1, A7.

Smith, Dan. 1999. *The State of the World Atlas.* 6th ed. London: Penguin.

Smith, David A. 1995. "The New Urban Sociology Meets the Old: Rereading Some Classical Human Ecology." *Urban Affairs Review* 20 (January): 432–457.

———, and Michael Timberlake. 1993. "World Cities: A Political Economy/Global Network Approach." Pp. 181–207 in *Urban Sociology in Transition,* edited by Ray Hutchison. Greenwich, CT: JAI Press.

Smith, David M., and Gary J. Gates. 2001. *Gay and Lesbian Families in the United States: Same-Sex Unmarried Partner Households.* Washington, D.C.: Human Rights Campaign.

Smith, Denise, and Hava Til(lipman. 2000. "The Older Population in the United States." *Current Population Reports,* ser. P-20, no. 532. Washington, DC: U.S. Government Printing Office.

Smith, James F. 2001. "Mexico's Forgotten Find Cause for New Hope." *Los Angeles Times,* February 23, pp. A1, A12, A13.

Smith, Michael Peter. 1988. *City, State, and Market.* New York: Basil Blackwell.

Smith, Tom. 1999. *GSS News: Trendlets: An Inter-Racial Friendship.* Accessed December 17, 2001 (www.icpsr.uonich.edu/GSS/about/news/trends.htm).

Smith, Tom W. 2001. *Estimating the Muslim Population in the United States.* New York: American Jewish Committee.

———. 2003. *Coming of Age in 21st Century America: Public Attitudes Toward the Importance and Timing of Transition to Adulthood.* Chicago: National Opinion Research Center.

———, and Seokho Kim. 2004. "The Vanishing Protestant Majority." *GSS Social Change Report No. 49.* Chicago: NORC.

Snyder, Thomas D. 1996. *Digest of Education Statistics 1996.* Washington, DC: U.S. Government Printing Office.

Sorokin, Pitirim A. [1927] 1959. *Social and Cultural Mobility.* New York: Free Press.

Southern Poverty Law Center. 2005. "Active Hate Groups in the United States 2004." Accessed April 28 (www.splcenter.org/images/dynamic/intel/hatemaps,3/ir117_hate_mao2004.pdf).

Spar, Debora. 2001. *Ruling the Waves: Cycles of Discovery, Chaos, and Wealth from the Compass to the Internet.* Harcourt.

Spengler, Joseph J. 1978. *Facing Zero Population Growth: Reactions and Interpretations, Past and Present.* Durham, NC: Duke University Press.

Spielmann, Peter James. 1992. "11 Population Groups on 'Endangered' List." *Chicago Sun-Times,* November 23, p. 12.

Spindel, Cheywa, Elisa Levy, and Melissa Connor. 2000. *With an End in Sight.* New York: United Nations Development Fund for Women.

Spitzer, Steven. 1975. "Toward a Marxian Theory of Deviance." *Social Problems* 22 (June):641–651.

Squires, Gregory D., ed. 2002. *Urban Sprawl: Causes, Consequences and Policy Responses.* Washington: Urban Institute.

Staggenborg, Suzanne. 1989a. "Stability and Innovation in the Women's Movement: A Comparison of Two Movement Organizations." *Social Problems* 36 (February):75–92.

———. 1989b. "Organizational and Environmental Influences on the Development of the Pro-Choice Movement," *Social Forces* 36 (September): 204–240.

Stalker, Peter. 2000. *Workers Without Frontiers.* Boulder, CO: Lynne Reinner.

Standing, Guy. 2004. *Economic Security for a Better World.* Geneva: International Labour Organization.

Stark, Rodney, and William Sims Bainbridge. 1979. "Of Churches, Sects, and Cults: Preliminary Concepts for a Theory of Religious Movements." *Journal for the Scientific Study of Religion* 18 (June):117–131.

———, and William Sims Bainbridge. 1985. *The Future of Religion.* Berkeley: University of California Press.

———, and Laurence R. Iannaccone. 1992. "Sociology of Religion." Pp. 2029–2037 in *Encyclopedia of Sociology,* vol. 4, edited by Edgar F. Borgatta and Marie L. Borgatta. New York: Macmillan.

Starr, Paul. 1982. *The Social Transformation of American Medicine.* New York: Basic Books.

Stavenhagen, Rodolfo. 1994. "The Indian Resurgence in Mexico." *Cultural Survival Quarterly,* Summer/Fall, pp. 77–80.

Steele, Jonathan. 2005. "Annan Attacks Britain and U.S. over Erosion of Human Rights." *Guardian Weekly,* March 16, p. 1.

Steffensmeier, Darrell, and Stephen Demuth. 2000. "Ethnicity and Sentencing Outcomes in U.S. Federal Courts: Who Is Punished More Harshly?" *American Sociological Review* 65 (October): 705–729.

Stenning, Derrick J. 1958. "Household Viability among the Pastoral Fulani." Pp. 92–119 in *The Developmental Cycle in Domestic Groups,* edited by John R. Goody. Cambridge, England: Cambridge University Press.

Stevenson, David, and Barbara L. Schneider. 1999. *The Ambitious Generation: America's Teenagers, Motivated but Directionless.* New Haven: Yale University Press.

Steyerberg, Ewout, Craig Earle, Bridget Neville, and Jane Weeks. 2005. "Racial Differences in Surgical Evaluation, Treatment, and Outcome of Locoregional Esophageal Cancer: A Population-Based Analysis of Elderly Patients." *Journal of Clinical Oncology* 23:510–517.

Stolberg, Sheryl. 1995. "Affirmative Action Gains Often Come at a High Cost." *Los Angeles Times,* March 29, pp. A1, A13–A16.

Strauss, Gary. 2002. "'Good Old Boys' Network Still Rules Corporate Boards." *USA Today,* November 1, pp. B1, B2.

Suitor, J. Jill, Staci A. Minyard, and Rebecca S. Carter. 2001. "'Did You See What I Saw?' Gender Differences in Perceptions of Avenues to Prestige Among Adolescents." *Sociological Inquiry* 71 (Fall):437–454.

Sullivan, Harry Stack. [1953] 1968. *The Interpersonal Theory of Psychiatry.* Edited by Helen Swick Perry and Mary Ladd Gawel. New York: W.W. Norton.

Sumner, William G. 1906. *Folkways.* New York: Ginn.

Sunstein, Cass. 2002. *Republic.com.* Rutgers, NJ: Princeton University Press.

———, Reid Hastie, John W. Payne, David A. Schkade, W. Kip Viscusi, and George L. Priest, eds. 2003. *Punitive Damages: How Juries Decide.* Chicago: University of Chicago Press.

Sutch, Richard, and Susan B. Carter. 2006. *Historical Statutes of US: Earliest Time to the Present.* Cambridge University Press.

Sutcliffe, Bob. 2002. *100 Ways of Seeing an Unequal World.* London: Zed Books.

Sutherland, Edwin H. 1937. *The Professional Thief.* Chicago: University of Chicago Press.

———. 1940. "White-Collar Criminality." *American Sociological Review* 5 (February):1–11.

———. 1949. *White Collar Crime.* New York: Dryden.

———. 1983. *White Collar Crime: The Uncut Version.* New Haven, CT: Yale University Press.

———, Donald R. Cressey, and David F. Luckenbill. 1992. *Principles of Criminology.* 11th ed. New York: Rowman and Littlefield.

Swatos, William H., Jr., ed. 1998. *Encyclopedia of Religion and Society.* Lanham, MD: Alta Mira.

Sweet, Kimberly. 2001. "Sex Sells a Second Time." *Chicago Journal* 93 (April):12–13.

Swiss Re. 2005. "Catastrophes." *The Economist* (March 26):98.

Szasz, Thomas S. 1971. "The Same Slave: An Historical Note on the Use of Medical Diagnosis as Justificatory Rhetoric." *American Journal of Psychotherapy* 25 (April):228–239.

———. 1974. *The Myth of Mental Illness* (rev. ed.). New York: Harper and Row.

Talbani, Aziz, and Parveen Hasanav. 2000. "Adolescent Females between Tradition and Modernity: Gender Role Socialization in South Asian Immigrant Culture." *Journal of Adolescence* 23:615–627.

Talbot, Margaret. 1998. "Attachment Theory: The Ultimate Experiment." *New York Times Magazine,* May 24, pp. 4–30, 38, 46, 50, 54.

Tannen, Deborah. 1990. *You Just Don't Understand: Women and Men in Conversation.* New York: Ballantine.

———. 1994a. *Talking from 9 to 5.* New York: William Morris.

———. 1994b. *Gender and Discourse.* New York: Oxford University Press.

Tarrow, Sidney. 2005. *The New Transnational Activism.* Boulder, CO: Rowman and Littlefield.

Taylor, Jonathan B., and Joseph P. Kalt. 2005. *American Indians on Reservations: A Data Book of Socioeconomic Change between the 1990 and 2000 Censuses.* Cambridge, MA: The Harvard Project on American Indian Development.

Taylor, Verta. 1995. "Watching for Vibes: Bringing Emotions into the Study of Feminist Organizations." Pp. 223–233 in *Feminist Organizations: Harvest of the New Women's Movement,* edited by Myra Marx Ferree and Patricia Yancy Martin. Philadelphia: Temple University Press.

Tedeschi, Bob. 2004. "Social Networks: Will Users Pay to Get Friends?" *New York Times,* February 9, pp. C1, C3.

———. 2006. "Those Born to Shop Can Now Use Cellphones." *New York Times,* January 2.

Telsch, Kathleen. 1991. "New Study of Older Workers Finds They Can Become Good Investments." *New York Times,* May 21, p. A16.

Terry, Sara. 2000. "Whose Family? The Revolt of the Child-Free." *Christian Science Monitor,* August 29, pp. 1, 4.

Therrien, Melissa, and Roberto R. Ramirez. 2001. "The Hispanic Population in the United States, March 2000." *Current Population Report,* ser. P-20, no. 535. Washington, DC: U.S. Government Printing Office.

Third World Institute. 2003. *The World Guide 2003–2004.* Oxford, England. New Internationalist Publishers.

Thomas, R. Murray. 2003. "New Frontiers in Cheating." In *Encyclopedia Britannica 2003 Book of the Year.* Chicago: Encyclopedia Britannica.

Thomas, William I. 1923. *The Unadjusted Girl.* Boston: Little, Brown.

Thompson, Clive. 2005. "Meet the Life Hackers." *New York Times Magazine,* October 16, pp. 40–45.

Thompson, Ginger. 2001a. "Chasing Mexico's Dream into Squalor." *New York Times,* February 11, pp. 1, 6.

———. 2001b. "Why Peace Eludes Mexico's Indians." *New York Times,* March 11, sec. WK, p. 16.

Thompson, Tony. 2005. "Romanians Are Being Paid to Play Computer Games for Westerners." *Guardian Weekly,* March 25, p. 17.

Thornton, Russell. 1987. *American Indians Holocaust and Survival: A Population History Since 1492.* Norman: University of Oklahoma Press.

Tienda, Marta, and Faith Mitchell, eds. 2006 *Hispanics and the Future of America.* Washington, DC: National Academics Press.

Tierney, John. 1990. "Betting the Planet." *New York Times Magazine,* December 2, pp. 52–53, 71, 74, 76, 78, 80–81.

———. 2003. "Iraqi Family Ties Complicate American Efforts for Change." *New York Times,* September 28, pp. A1, A22.

Tilly, Charles. 1993. *Popular Contention in Great Britain 1758–1834.* Cambridge, MA: Harvard University Press.

———. 2004. *Social Movements, 1768–2004.* Boulder, CO: Paradigm.

Time Warner. 2004. "America Online and AOL International: Who We Are." Accessed February 6 (www.timewarner.com).

Tolbert, Kathryn. 2000. "In Japan, Traveling Alone Begins at Age 6." *Washington Post National Weekly Edition* 17 (May 15):17.

Tonkinson, Robert. 1978. *The Mardudjara Aborigines.* New York: Holt.

Tönnies, Ferdinand. [1887] 1988. *Community and Society.* Rutgers, NJ: Transaction.

Toosi, Mitra. 2005. "Labor Force Projections to 2014: Returning Boomers." *Monthly Labor Review* (November):25–44.

Touraine, Alain. 1974. *The Academic System in American Society.* New York: McGraw-Hill.

Treiman, Donald J. 1977. *Occupational Prestige in Comparative Perspective.* New York: Academic Press.

Trotter III, Robert T., and Juan Antonio Chavira. 1997. *Curanderismo: Mexican American Folk Healing.* Athens, GA: University of Georgia Press.

Trumbull, Mark. 2006. "America's Younger Workers Losing Ground on Income." *Christian Science Monitor,* February 27.

Tuchman, Gaye. 1992. "Feminist Theory." Pp. 695–704 in *Encyclopedia of Sociology,* vol. 2, edited by Edgar F. Borgatta and Marie L. Borgatta. New York: Macmillan.

Tumin, Melvin M. 1953. "Some Principles of Stratification: A Critical Analysis." *American Sociological Review* 18 (August):387–394.

———. 1985. *Social Stratification.* 2d ed. Englewood Cliffs, NJ: Prentice Hall.

Ture, Kwame, and Charles Hamilton. 1992. *Black Power: The Politics of Liberation.* Rev. ed. New York: Vintage Books.

Turkle, Sherry. 2004. "How Computers Change the Way We Think." *Chronicle of Higher Education* 50 (January 30):B26–B28.

Turner, Bryan S., ed. 1990. *Theories of Modernity and Postmodernity.* Newbury Park, CA: Sage.

Turner, C. F., et al. 1998. "Adolescent Sexual Behavior, Drug Use, and Violence Increased Reporting with Computer Survey Technology." *Science* 280:867–873.

Tyre, Peg, and Daniel McGinn. 2003. "She Works, He Doesn't." *Newsweek,* 141, May 12, pp. 45–52.

Uchitelle, Louis. 2003. "Older Workers Are Thriving Despite Recent Hard Times." *New York Times,* September 8, pp. A1, A13.

UNAIDS. 2004. *AIDS Epidemic Update: December 2004.* Geneva, Switzerland: UNAIDS.

———. 2006. *Report on the Global AIDS Epidemic.* Geneva, Switzerland: UNAIDS.

United Jewish Communities. 2003. *The National Jewish Population Survey 2000–2001.* New York: UJC.

United Nations. 2003. *Water For People, Water for Life: Executive Summary.* New York: United Nations World Water Assessment Programme.

———. 2005a. *The Millennium Development Goals Report.* Washington, DC: United Nations.

———. 2005b. *In Larger Freedom: Towards Development, Security and Human Rights for All.* New York: United Nations.

United Nations Development Programme. 1995. *Human Development Report 1995.* New York: Oxford University Press.

———. 2000. *Poverty Report 2000: Overcoming Human Poverty.* Washington, DC: UNDP.

United Nations Office on Drugs and Crime. 2005. "The United Nations Convention Against Transnational Organized Crime and Its Protocols." Accessed March 13, 2005 (www.unodc.org).

United Nations Population Division. 1998. *World Abortion Policies.* New York: Department of Economic and Social Affairs, UNPD.

———. 2004. *World Population Monitoring 2002: Reproductive Rights and Reproductive Health.* New York: United Nations.

———. 2005. *World Fertility Report 2003.* New York: UNPD.

United Nations Population Information Network. 2003. *World Population Prospects: The 2003 Revision.* Accessed May 20 (www.un.org/popin.data.html).

University of Michigan. 2003. *Information on Admissions Lawsuits.* Accessed August 8 (www.umich.edu/~urel/admissions).

Urbina, Ian. 2002. "Al Jazeera: Hits, Misses and Ricochets." *Asia Times,* December 25.

———. 2004. "Disco Rice, and Other Trash Talk." *New York Times,* July 31, p. A11.

U.S. English. 2006. *Official English: States with Official English Laws.* Accessed January 10, 2006 (www.us-english.org/inc/official/states.asp).

U.S. Surgeon General. 2001. *Youth Violence: A Report of the Surgeon General.* Washington, DC: U.S. Government Printing Office.

U.S. Trade Representative. 2003. *2002 Annual Report.* Washington, DC: U.S. Government Printing Office.

Utne, Leif. 2003. "We Are All Zapatistas." *Utne Reader* (November–December):36–37.

Valdez, Enrique. 1999. "Using Hotlines to Deal with Domestic Violence: El Salvador." Pp. 139–142 in *Too Close to Home,* edited by Andrew R. Morrison and Maria Loreto Biehl. Washington, DC: Inter-American Development Bank.

van den Berghe, Pierre. 1978. *Race and Racism: A Comparative Perspective.* 2d ed. New York: Wiley.

van Vucht Tijssen, Lieteke. 1990. "Women between Modernity and Postmodernity." Pp. 147–163 in *Theories of Modernity and Postmodernity,* edited by Bryan S. Turner. London: Sage.

Vasagar, Jeeran. 2005. "'At Last Rwanda Is Known for Something Positive.'" *Guardian Weekly,* July 22, p. 18.

Veblen, Thorstein. [1899] 1964. *Theory of the Leisure Class.* New York: Macmillan. New York: Penguin.

———. 1919. *The Vested Interests and the State of the Industrial Arts.* New York: Huebsch.

Vega, William A. 1995. "The Study of Latino Families: A Point of Departure." Pp. 3–17 in *Understanding Latino Families: Scholarship, Policy, and Practice,* edited by Ruth E. Zambrana. Thousand Oaks, CA: Sage.

Vernon, Glenn. 1962. *Sociology and Religion.* New York: McGraw-Hill.

Vidal, John. 2004. "One in Three People Will Be Elderly by 2050." *Guardian Weekly,* April 1, p. 5.

Vidaver, R. M., et al. 2000. "Women Subjects in NIH-Funded Clinical Research Literature: Lack of Progress in Both Representation and Analysis by Sex." *Journal of Women's Health Gender-Based Medicine* 9 (June):495–504.

Villarosa, Linda. 2002. "New Skill for Future Ob-Gyns: Abortion Training." *New York Times,* June 11, p. D6.

Villarreal, Andrés. 2004. "The Social Ecology of Rural Violence: Land Scarcity, the Organization of Agricultural Production, and the Presence of the State." *American Journal of Sociology* 110 (September):313–348.

Wages for Housework Campaign. 1999. *Wages for Housework Campaign.* Circular. Los Angeles.

Wagley, Charles, and Marvin Harris. 1958. *Minorities in the New World: Six Case Studies.* New York: Columbia University Press.

Waite, Linda. 2000. "The Family as a Social Organization: Key Ideas for the Twentieth Century." *Contemporary Sociology* 29 (May):463–469.

Waitzkin, Howard. 1986. *The Second Sickness: Contradictions of Capitalist Health Care.* Chicago: University of Chicago Press.

Waldinger, Roger, and David Fitzgerald. 2004. "Transnationalism in Question." *American Journal of Sociology* 109 (March):1177–1195.

Waldman, Amy. 2004a. "India Takes Economic Spotlight, and Critics Are Unkind." *New York Times,* March 7, p. 3.

———. 2004b. "Low-Tech or High, Jobs Are Scarce in India's Boon." *New York Times,* May 6, p. A3.

———. 2004c. "What India's Upset Vote Reveals: The High Tech Is Skin Deep." *New York Times,* May 15, p. A5.

Waldrop, Judith, and Sharon M. Stern. 2003. *Disability Status: 2000.* Census 2000 Brief C2KBR-17. Washington, DC: U.S. Government Printing Office.

Wallace, Ruth A., and Alison Wolf. 1980. *Contemporary Sociological Theory.* Englewood Cliffs, NJ: Prentice Hall.

Wallerstein, Immanuel. 1974. *The Modern World System.* New York: Academic Press.

———. 1979a. *Capitalist World Economy.* Cambridge, England: Cambridge University Press.

———. 1979b. *The End of the World as We Know It: Social Science for the Twenty-First Century.* Minneapolis: University of Minnesota Press.

———. 2000. *The Essential Wallerstein.* New York: The New Press.

Wallerstein, Judith S., Judith M. Lewis, and Sandra Blakeslee. 2000. *The Unexpected Legacy of Deviance.* New York: Hyperion.

Wallerstein, Michael, and Bruce Western. 2000. "Unions in Decline? What Has Changed and Why." Pp. 355–377 in *Annual Review of Political Science,* edited by Nelson Polsby. Palo Alto, CA: Annual Reviews.

Wallis, Claudia. 2005a. "A Snapshot of Teen Sex." *Time,* February 7, p. 58.

———. 2005b. "The Evolution Wars." *Time,* August 15, pp. 26–35.

Wal-Mart. 2006. "Wal-Mart News: Our Commitment to Communities." Accessed April 24 (www.walmartstores.com).

Wal-Mart Watch. 2006. *Wal-Mart Watch: Breaking News.* Accessed April 24 (www.walmartwatch.com).

Watson, Paul. 2005. "Defying Tradition." *Los Angeles Times,* April 24, p. 56.

Watts, Duncan J. 2004. "The 'New' Science of Networks." Pp. 243–270 in *Annual Review of Sociology 2004,* edited by Karen S. Cook and John Hagan. Palo Alto, CA: Annual Reviews.

Wax, Emily. 2005. "Where Woman Rule." *Washington Post National Weekly Edition* July 18, p. 18.

Webb, Cynthia L. 2001. "The Workweek Gets Longer." *Washington Post National Weekly Edition,* September 10, p. 21.

Weber, Max. [1913–1922] 1947. *The Theory of Social and Economic Organization.* Translated by A. Henderson and T. Parsons. New York: Free Press.

———. [1904] 1949. *Methodology of the Social Sciences.* Translated by Edward A. Shils and Henry A. Finch. Glencoe, IL: Free Press.

———. [1904] 1958a. *The Protestant Ethic and the Spirit of Capitalism.* Translated by Talcott Parsons. New York: Scribner.

———. [1916] 1958b. *The Religion of India: The Sociology of Hinduism and Buddhism.* New York: Free Press.

Wechsler, Henry, J. E. Lee, M. Kuo, M. Seibring, T. F. Nelson, and H. Lee. 2002. "Trends in College Binge Drinking During a Period of Increased Prevention Efforts: Findings from Four Harvard School of Public Health College Alcohol Surveys: 1993–2001." *Journal of American College Health* 50 (5):203–217.

———, Mark Seibring, I-Chao Liu, and Marilyn Ahl. 2004. "Colleges Respond to Student Binge Drinking: Reducing Student Demand or Limiting Access." *Journal of American College Health* 52 (4):159–168.

Weeks, John R. 2002. *Population: An Introduction to Concepts and Issues.* 8th ed. Belmont, CA: Wadsworth.

———. 2005. *Population: An Introduction to Concepts and Issues.* 9th ed. Belmont, CA: Wadsworth.

Weinberg, Daniel H. 2004. *Evidence from Census 2000 About Earnings by Detailed Occupation for Men and Women.* CENSR-15. Washington, DC: U.S. Government Printing Office.

Weinstein, Deena, and Michael A. Weinstein. 1999. "McDonaldization Enframed." Pp. 57–69 in *Resisting McDonaldization,* edited by Barry Smart. London: Sage.

Weinstein, Henry. 2002. "Airport Screener Curb Is Regretful." *Los Angeles Times,* November 16, pp. B1, B14.

Weinstein, Michael A., and Deena Weinstein. 2002. "Hail to the Shrub." *American Behavioral Scientist* 46 (December):566–580.

Weisbrot, Mark, Dean Baker, and David Rusnick. 2005. *The Scorecard on Development: 25 Years of Diminished Progress.* Washington, DC: Center for Economic and Policy Research.

Wells-Barnett, Ida B. 1970. *Crusade for Justice: The Autobiography of Ida B. Wells.* Edited by Alfreda M. Duster. Chicago: University of Chicago Press.

Wentz, Laurel, and Claire Atkinson. 2005. "'Apprentice' Translators Hope for Hits All Over Globe." *Advertising Age,* February 14, pp. 3, 73.

Wertsman, Vladimir. 2001. "Arab Americans: A Comparative and Critical Analysis of Leading Reference Sources." *Multicultural Review* (June):42–57.

West, Candace, and Don H. Zimmerman. 1983. "Small Insults: A Study of Interruptions in Cross Sex Conversations between Unacquainted Per-

sons." Pp. 86–111 in *Language, Gender, and Society,* edited by Barrie Thorne, Cheris Kramarae, and Nancy Henley. Rowley, MA: Newbury House.

———. 1987. "Doing Gender." *Gender and Society* 1 (June):125–151.

White, Jonathan R. 2002. *Terrorism: An Introduction.* Belmont, CA: Wadsworth.

Whyte, William Foote. 1981. *Street Corner Society: Social Structure of an Italian Slum.* 3d ed. Chicago: University of Chicago Press.

Wickman, Peter M. 1991. "Deviance." Pp. 85–87 in *Encyclopedic Dictionary of Sociology,* 4th ed., edited by Dushkin Publishing Group. Guilford, CT: Dushkin.

Wilford, John Noble. 1997. "New Clues Show Where People Made the Great Leap to Agriculture." *New York Times,* November 18, pp. B9, B12.

Wilgoren, Jodi. 2005. "In Kansas, Darwinism Goes on Trial Once More." *New York Times,* May 6, p. A14.

Williams, Carol J. 1995. "Taking an Eager Step Back." *Los Angeles Times,* June 3, pp. A1, A14.

Williams, Christine L. 1992. "The Glass Escalator: Hidden Advantages for Men in the 'Female' Professions." *Social Problems* 39 (3):253–267.

———. 1995. *Still a Man's World: Men Who Do Women's Work.* Berkeley: University of California Press.

Williams, David R., and Chiquita Collins. 2004. "Reparations." *American Behavioral Scientist* 47 (March):977–1000.

Williams, Robin M., Jr. 1970. *American Society.* 3d ed. New York: Knopf.

———, with John P. Dean and Edward A. Suchman. 1964. *Strangers Next Door: Ethnic Relations in American Communities.* Englewood Cliffs, NJ: Prentice Hall.

Williams, Wendy M. 1998. "Do Parents Matter? Scholars Need to Explain What Research Really Shows." *Chronicle of Higher Education* 45 (December 11):B6–B7.

Wilson, Edward O. 1975. *Sociobiology: The New Synthesis.* Cambridge, MA: Harvard University Press.

———. 1978. *On Human Nature.* Cambridge, MA: Harvard University Press.

———. 2000. *Sociobiology: The New Synthesis.* Cambridge, MA: Belknap Press, Harvard University Press.

Wilson, John. 1973. *Introduction to Social Movements.* New York: Basic Books.

Wilson, William Julius. 1980. *The Declining Significance of Race: Blacks and Changing American Institutions.* 2d ed. Chicago: University of Chicago Press.

———. 1987. *The Truly Disadvantaged: The Inner City, the Underclass and Public Policy.* Chicago: University of Chicago Press.

———, ed. 1989. *The Ghetto Underclass: Social Science Perspectives.* Newbury Park, CA: Sage.

———. 1996. *When Work Disappears: The World of the New Urban Poor.* New York: Knopf.

———. 1999a. "Towards a Just and Livable City: The Issues of Race and Class." Address at the Social Science Centennial Conference, April 23. Chicago, IL: DePaul University.

———. 1999b. *The Bridge over the Racial Divide: Rising Inequality and Coalition Politics.* Berkeley: University of California Press.

Wines, Michael. 2005. "Same-Sex Unions to Become Legal in South Africa." *USA Today,* December 2, p. A6.

Wirth, Louis. 1928. *The Ghetto.* Chicago: University of Chicago Press.

———. 1931. "Clinical Sociology." *American Journal of Sociology* 37 (July):49–60.

———. 1938. "Urbanism as a Way of Life." *American Journal of Sociology* 44 (July):1–24.

Witte, Griff. 2005. "The Vanishing Middle Class." *Washington Post National Weekly Edition,* September 27:6–9.

Wolf, Naomi. 1992. *The Beauty Myth: How Images of Beauty Are Used Against Women.* New York: Anchor.

Wolff, Edward N. 2002. *Top Heavy.* Updated ed. New York: New Press.

Wolraich, M., et al. 1998. "Guidance for Effective Discipline." *Pediatrics* 101 (April):723–728.

Wood, Julia T. 1994. *Gendered Lives: Communication, Gender and Culture.* Belmont, CA: Wadsworth.

Woodard, Colin. 1998. "When Rote Learning Fails against the Test of Global Economy." *Christian Science Monitor,* April 15, p. 7.

World Bank. 2000. *World Development Report 2000/2001.* Washington, DC: World Bank.

———. 2001. *World Development Report 2002. Building Instructions for Markets.* New York: Oxford University Press.

———. 2003a. *World Development Report 2003: Sustainable Development in a Dynamic World.* Washington, DC: World Bank.

———. 2003b. *Development Indicators 2003.* Washington, DC: World Bank.

———. 2004. *World Development Report 2005. A Better Investment Climate for Everyone.* Washington, DC: World Bank.

———. 2005. *World Development Indicators 2005.* Washington, DC: World Bank.

———. 2006. *Repositioning Nutrition as Central to Development: A Strategy for Large-Scale Action.* Washington, DC: World Bank.

World Development Forum. 1990. "The Danger of Television." 8 (July 15):4.

World Economic Forum. 2005. *The Global Information Technology Report 2004–2005.* Davos, Switzerland: World Economic Forum.

World Health Organization. 2000. *The World Health Report 2000. Health Systems: Improving Performance.* Geneva, Switzerland: WHO.

———. 2002. *Global Report on Health and Violence.* Geneva: WHO.

———. 2005. *AIDS Epidemic Update, December 2005.* Geneva, Switzerland: WHO.

World Resources Institute. 1998. *1998–1999 World Resources: A Guide to the Global Environment.* New York: Oxford University Press.

Wortham, Robert A. 2005. "The Early Sociological Legacy of W. E. B. DuBois." Pp. 74–95 in *Diverse Histories of American Sociology,* edited by Anthony J. Blasi. Boston: Brill.

Wright, Charles R. 1986. *Mass Communication: A Sociological Perspective.* 3d ed. New York: Random House.

Wright, Eric R., William P. Gronfein, and Timothy J. Owens. 2000. "Deinstitutionalization, Social Rejection, and the Self-Esteem of Former Mental Patients." *Journal of Health and Social Behavior* (March).

Wright, Erik Olin, David Hachen, Cynthia Costello, and Joy Sprague. 1982. "The American Class Structure." *American Sociological Review* 47 (December):709–26.

Yamagata, Hisashi, Kuang S. Yeh, Shelby Stewman, and Hiroko Dodge. 1997. "Sex Segregation and Glass Ceilings: A Comparative Statistics Model of Women's Career Opportunities in the Federal Government over a Quarter Century." *American Journal of Sociology* 103 (November):566–632.

Yardley, Jim. 2005. "Fearing Future, China Starts to Give Girls Their Due." *New York Times,* January 31, p. A3.

Yinger, J. Milton. 1970. *The Scientific Study of Religion.* New York: Macmillan.

Young, Alford A., Jr., and Donald R. Deskins, Jr. 2001. "Early Traditions of African-American Sociological Thought." Pp. 445–477 in *Annual Review of Sociology, 2001,* edited by Karen S. Cook and John Hagan. Palo Alto, CA: Annual Reviews.

Young, Gay. 1993. "Gender Inequality and Industrial Development: The Household Connection." *Journal of Comparative Family Studies* 124 (Spring):3–20.

Zaidi, Arshia U. 2002. "Perceptions of Arranged Marriages by Young Pakistani Muslim Women Living in a Western Society." *Journal of Comparative Family Studies* 33 (Autumn), pp. 495–515.

Zang, Xiaowei. 2002. "Labor Market Segmentation and Income Inequality in Urban China." *Sociological Quarterly* 43 (1):27–44.

Zarembo, Alan. 2003. "Funding Studies to Suit Need." *Los Angeles Times,* December 7, pp. A1, A20.

———. 2004. "A Theater of Inquiry and Evil." *Los Angeles Times,* July 15, pp. A1, A24, A25.

Zellner, William M. 1995. *Counter Cultures: A Sociologica Analysis.* New York: St. Martin's Press.

———, and Richard T. Schaefer. 2006. *Extraordinary Groups.* 8th ed. New York: Worth.

Zernike, Kate. 2002. "With Student Cheating on the Rise, More Colleges Are Turning to Honor Codes." *New York Times,* November 2, p. A10.

Zia, Helen. 2000. *Asian American Dreams: The Emergence of an American People.* New York: Farrar, Straus, and Giroux.

Zimbardo, Philip G. 1972. "Pathology of Imprisonment." *Society* 9 (April):4, 6, 8.

———. 2004. "Power Turns Good Soldiers into 'Bad Apples.'" *Boston Globe,* May 9. Also available at www.prisonexp.org.

———. 2005. "What Do You Believe Is True Even Though You Cannot Prove It?" *New York Times,* January 4, p. D3.

———, Craig Haney, W. Curtis Banks, and David Jaffe. 1974. "The Psychology of Imprisonments: Privation, Power, and Pathology." In *Doing Unto Others: Joining, Molding, Conforming, Helping, and Loving,* edited by Zick Rubin. Englewood Cliffs, NJ: Prentice Hall.

———, Ann L. Weber, and Robert Johnson. 2003. *Psychology: Core Concepts.* 4e. Boston: Allyn and Bacon.

Zola, Irving K. 1972. "Medicine as an Institution of Social Control." *Sociological Review* 20 (November):487–504.

———. 1983. *Socio-Medical Inquiries.* Philadelphia: Temple University Press.

Zweigenhaft, Richard L., and G. William Domhoff. 2006. *Diversity in the Power Elite: How It Happened, Why It Matters.* 2d ed. New York: Rowman and Littlefield.

acknowledgements

Chapter 1

P. 2: Quotation from Barbara Ehrenreich. 2001. *Nickel and Dimed: On (Not) Getting By in America.* © 2001 by Barbara Ehrenreich. Reprinted by permission of Henry Holt and Company, LLC, and by permission of International Creative Management, Inc.

P. 17: Figure 1–3 Out of Code by Perry Perez in Jerry Crowe and Valli Herman. 2005. "NBA Lists Fashion Do's & Don'ts," Los Angeles Times (October 19):A23. Copyright 2005 *Los Angeles Times.* Reprinted by permission.

P. 23: Figure 1–4 From the American Sociological Association, 2005. Used by permission.

Chapter 2

P. 29: Quotation from Patricia A. Adler and Peter Adler. 2004. *Paradise Laborers: Hotel Work in the Global Economy.* © 2004 by Cornell University. Used by permission of Cornell University Press.

P. 34: Figure 2–4 Author's analysis of General Social Survey 2004 in J. A. Davis et al. 2005. Used by permission of National Opinion Research Center.

P. 34: Cartoon, DOONESBURY " 1989 G. B. Trudeau. Reprinted with permission of UNIVERSAL PRESS SYNDICATE. All rights reserved.

P. 39: From Devah Pager, "The Mark of a Criminal Record," *American Journal of Sociology.* Copyright © 2003 by the University of Chicago Press. All rights reserved.

P. 41: Figure from Laura Wattenberg. 2006. *The Baby Name Wizard.* Used by permission.

P. 46: Figure 2–6 From Henry J. Kaiser Family Foundation. February 2005. Executive Summary of Sex on TV 4:4; a Biennial Report of the Kaiser Family Foundation (#3324). This information was reprinted with permission from the Henry J. Kaiser Family Foundation. The Kaiser Family Foundation, based in Menlo Park, CA, is a nonprofit, private operating foundation focusing on the major health care issues facing the nation and is not associated with Kaiser Permanente or Kaiser Industries.

P. 47–48: Figure in Appendix I—General Social Survey in J. A. Davis et al. 2005. Used by permission of National Opinion Research Center.

Chapter 3

P. 54: Quotation from Juliet B. Schor. 2004. *Born to Buy.* Copyright © 2004 by Juliet Schor. Reprinted with permission of Scribner, an imprint of Simon & Schuster Adult Publishing Group. All rights reserved.

P. 62: Figure 3–1 From Michael Erard. 2005. "How Linguists and Missionaries Share a Bible of 6,912 Languages," *New York Times* (July 19): D4. New York Times Copyright © 2005 The New York Times. Reprinted by permission.

P. 67: Figure 3–2 as reported in Astin et al. 1994; Pryor et al. 2005. From UCLA Higher Education Research Institute. 2005. The American Freshman: National Norms for Fall '05. Reprinted by permission of UCLA.

P. 70: Cartoon by Sidney Harris. © ScienceCartoonsPlus.com.

Chapter 4

P. 78: Quotation from Mary Pattillo-McCoy. 1999. *Black Picket Fences: Privilege and Peril among the Black Middle Class:*100–02. Copyright 1999. Reprinted by permission of University of Chicago Press.

P. 85: Quotation from Daniel Albas and Cheryl Albas. 1988. "Aces and Bombers: The Post-Exam Impression Management Strategies of Students." *Symbolic Interaction* Copyright 1988 by University of California Press—Journals. Reproduced by permission of University of California Press—Journals via Copyright Clearance Center.

P. 87: Table 4–2 From Tom Smith. 2003. "Coming of Age in 21st Century America: Public Attitudes Toward the Importance and Timing of Transition to Adulthood." Based on the 2002 General Social Survey of 1,398 people. Used by permission of National Opinion Research Center.

P. 92: Table 4–3 Adapted from Jill Suitor, Staci A. Minyard, and Rebecca S. Carter, "Did You See What I Saw? Gender Difference in Perceptions of Avenues to Prestige Among Adolescents," *Sociological Inquiry* 71 (Fall 2001):445, Table 2. University of Texas Press. Reprinted by permission of Blackwell Publishing Ltd. via Copyright Clearance Center.

Chapter 5

P. 100: Quotation from Philip G. Zimbardo. 1972. "Pathology of Imprisonment," *Society,* 9 (April):4. Copyright © 1972 by Transaction Publishers. Reprinted by permission of the publisher. And quotation from P. G. Zimbardo, C. Haney, W. C. Banks, & D. Jaffe. 1974. "The Psychology of Imprisonment: Privation, Power, and Pathology." In Z. Rubin (Ed.), *Doing Unto Others: Explorations in Social Behavior:*61–63. Used by permission of Philip G. Zimbardo, Inc.

P. 111: Figure adapted from Peter S. Bearman, James Moody, and Katherine Stovel. 2004. "Chains of Affection: The Structure of Adolescent Romantic and Sexual Networks," Figure 2, p. 58. *American Journal of Sociology* Copyright 2004. Used by permission of University of Chicago Press.

P. 112: Cartoon by TOLES © 2000 The Washington Post. Reprinted with permission of UNIVERSAL PRESS SYNDICATE. All rights reserved.

P. 120: Cartoon by Chris Wildt. www.CartoonStock.com

P. 125: Figure 5–2 Barry T. Hirsch and David A. MacPherson, "Union Membership and Coverage Database from the Current Population Survey," *Industrial and Labor Relations Review* 56 (2), Jan. 2003, pp. 349–54, and accompanying database at www.unionstats.com. Used by permission.

Chapter 6

P. 133: Quotation from Don Tapscott. 1999. *Growing Up Digital: The Rise of the Net Generation.* © 1999. Reprinted by permission of the McGraw-Hill Companies.

P. 144: Figure 6–1 Adapted from *National Geographic Atlas of the World* 8e. National Geographic Society, 2005. The Fuller Projection Map design is a trademark of the Buckminster Fuller Institute™ © 1938, 1967 & 1992. All rights reserved. www.bfi.org. NG Maps/National Geographic Image Collection. Used by permission of National Geographic Image Sales and the Buckminster Fuller Institute.

P. 145: Figure 6–2 From the Pew Internet & American Life Project.

P. 146: Figure 6–3. Figure from liveplasma.com. Used by permission.

P. 147: Cartoon by Daryl Cagle. Copyright Daryl Cagle 2004 and Cagle Cartoons. All rights reserved.

P. 151: Cartoon by Kirk Anderson. Used by permission of Kirk Anderson, www.kirktoons.com.

P. 151: Table 6–3 From Parents Television Council news release October 15, 2005. Used by permission.

Chapter 7

P. 157: Quotation from Susan A. Phillips. 1999. *Wallbangin': Graffiti and Gangs in L.A:*21, 23, 134–35. Copyright 1999. Used by permission of University of Chicago Press.

P. 162: Figure from Henry Wechsler et al. 2002. "Trends in College Binge Drinking During a Period of Increased Prevention Efforts," *Journal of American College Health,* 2002:208. Copyright © 2002 Heldref Publications. Reprinted with permission of the Helen Dwight Reid Educational Foundation. Published by Heldref Publications, 1319 18th St. NW, Washington, DC 20036-1802.

P. 165: © The New Yorker Collection 2002 Alex Gregory from cartoonbank. com. All rights reserved.

P. 168: Table 7–1 From Robert K. Merton. 1968. *Social Theory and Social Structure.* Adapted by permission of The Free Press, a Division of Simon & Schuster Adult Publishing Group. Copyright © 1967, 1968 by Robert K. Merton. All rights reserved.

P. 175: Cartoon by Sidney Harris. © ScienceCartoonsPlus.com.

P. 180: Death Penalty Information Center 2006. Used with permission.

Chapter 8

P. 185: Quotation from David K. Shipler. 2005. *The Working Poor: Invisible in America.* Copyright © 2004, 2005 by David K. Shipler. Used by permission of Alfred A. Knopf, a division of Random House, Inc.

P. 195: Table 8–2 from James. A. Davis, Tom W. Smith, Peter B. Marsden. 2005. *General Social Surveys, 1972–2004: Cumulative Codebook.* Chicago: National Opinion Research Center. Used by permission.

P. 196: Data on wealth from Edward N. Wolff. 2002. "Recent Trends in the Distribution of Household Wealth Ownership." In *Back to Shared Prosperity: The Growing Inequality of Wealth and Income in America,* ed. Ray Marshall. New York: M.E. Sharpe. Reprinted by permission of the author.

P. 197: Figure 8–6 From Timothy Smeeding, Lee Rainwater, and Gary Burtless. 2001. "United States Poverty in a Cross-National Context." *Focus,* newsletter of the Institute for Research on Poverty, 21 (Spring):51. Used by permission of Institute for Research on Poverty.

P. 204: Cartoon by Mike Konopacki. Used with permission, Mike Konopacki, Huck / Konopacki Labor Cartoons.

Chapter 9

P. 210: Quotation from Steve Derné. 2003. "Schwarzenegger, McBeal and Arranged Marriages: Globalization on the Ground in India" in *Contexts,* a publication of the American Sociological Association. Copyright 2003 of University of California Press—Journals. Used by permission of University of California Press—Journals via the Copyright Clearance Center.

P. 212: Figure 9–1 Adapted from Bob Sutcliffe. 2002. *100 Ways of Seeing an Unequal World,* Fig 1, p. 18. London: Zed Books. Reprinted by permission.

P. 213: Figure 9–2 Adapted in part from John R. Weeks. 2002, 2005. *Population: An Introduction to Concepts and Issues,* with InfoTrac 8th ed. and 9th ed. Belmont, CA: Wadsworth. © 2002 and © 2005. Reprinted with permission of Wadsworth, a division of Thomson Learning, www.thomsonrights.com. Fax (800) 730-2215. And adapted in part from Carl Haub. 2005. *World Population Data Sheet 2005.* Used by permission of Population Reference Bureau.

P. 217: Table 9–1 Adapted in part from *Fortune.* 2005. FORTUNE Global 500, *Fortune,* July 25. © 2005 Time Inc. All rights reserved. And adapted in part from World Bank. 2005. *World Development Indicators 2005* © World Bank, used by permission of the World Bank via the Copyright Clearance Center.

P. 218: Figure 9–4 From Chronic Poverty Research Center. 2005. Administered by Institute for Development Policy and Management, School of Environment and Development, University of Manchester, UK. Used by permission.

P. 220: Table from Dutta, *The Global Information Technology Report* 2004–2005. Reproduced with permission of Palgrave Macmillan.

P. 221: Figure 9–5 Data from World Bank. 2005. *World Development Indicators 2005.* © World Bank. Used by permission of the World Bank via Copyright Clearance Center.

Chapter 10

P. 233: Quotation from Helen Zia. 2000. *Asian American Dreams: The Emergence of an American People.* Copyright © 2000 by Helen Zia. Reprinted by permission of Farrar, Straus & Giroux, LLC.

P. 238: Figure 10–3 From Southern Poverty Law Center Intelligence Project. 2005. Used by permission of Southern Poverty Law Center.

P. 240: Figure 10–7 From John R. Logan. 2001. *From Many Shores: Asians in Census 2000.* Accessed at http://mumford1.dyndns.org/cen2000/AsianPop/AsianReport/page1.html. Used by permission.

Chapter 11

P. 261: Quotation from Azadeh Moaveni. 2005. *Lipstick Jihad: A Memoir of Growing up Iranian in America and American in Iran.* Copyright © 2005 by Azadeh Moaveni. Reprinted by permission of PublicAffairs, a member of the Perseus Books Group LLC.

P. 263: Table 11–1 From Joyce McCarl Nielsen, et al. 2000. "Gendered Heteronormativity: Empirical Illustrations in Everyday Life," *Sociological Quarterly* 41 (No. 2):287. © 2000 by Blackwell Publishing. Reprinted by permission of Blackwell Publishing via Copyright Clearance Center.

P. 271: Figure 11–1 From Makiko Fuwa. 2004. "Macro-level Gender Inequality and the Division of Household Labor in 22 Countries." *American Sociological Review* 69: December 2004, Table 2, page 757. Used by permission of the American Sociological Association and the author.

P. 278: © The New Yorker Collection 2000 Victoria Roberts from cartoonbank. com. All rights reserved.

P. 280: Figure 11–4 © AARP. Reprinted by permission of the American Association of Retired Persons.

P. 284: Figure 11–7 From NARAL Pro-Choice America Foundation 2006. Used by permission of NARAL, Washington, DC.

Chapter 12

P. 290: Quotation from Annette Lareau. 2003. *Unequal Childhoods: Class, Race, and Family Life.* Copyright 2003 The Regents of the University of California. Used by permission.

P. 294: Figure 12–1 In part from Joseph A. McFalls, Jr. 2003. "Population: A Lively Introduction." 4e, *Population Bulletin* 58 (December):23. Used by permission of the Population Reference Bureau.

P. 299: Figure 12–2 From *World Fertility Report 2003.* © 2004 United Nations Population Division. Used by permission.

P. 304: Cartoon by Signe Wilkinson, Cartoon Arts International. Used by permission of Signe Wilkinson, Cartoonists & Writers Syndicate/cartoon-web.com.

P. 310: Figure 12–6 From Human Rights Campaign accessed at www.hrc.org, "Statewide Anti-Discrimination Laws and Policies" and "Statewide Discriminatory Marriage Laws". Used with permission.

Chapter 13

P. 315: Quotation from Vine Deloria, Jr. 1999. *For This Land: Writings on Religion in America:*273–275. Copyright © 1999 by Routledge Publishing Inc. Reproduced by permission of Routledge Publishing Inc. via Copyright Clearance Center.

P. 317: Figure 13–1 From John L. Allen. 2005. *Student Atlas of World Geography* 4e. Copyright © 2005 by The McGraw-Hill Companies, Inc. All rights reserved. Reprinted by permission of McGraw-Hill / Contemporary Learning Series.

P. 327: Figure 13–2 Adapted from Pippa Norris and Ronald Inglehart. 2004. *Sacred and Secular: Religion and Politics Worldwide:* Table 3.6, p.74. Cambridge University Press © 2004. Reprinted with permission of Cambridge University Press.

P. 330: Figure 13–3 From Dale E. Jones et al. 2002. "Largest Participating Religious Group," from *Religious Congregations and Membership in the United States: 2000.* Nashville: Glenmary Research Center. ©2002 Association of Statisticians of American Religious Bodies. Reprinted with permission. All rights reserved.

P. 336: Cartoon by Kirk Anderson. Used by permission of Kirk Anderson, www.kirktoons.com.

P. 343: Cartoon by Mike Keefe, The Denver Post. Used by permission.

Chapter 14

P. 348: Quotation from Richard L. Zweigenhaft and G. William Domhoff. 2006. *Diversity in the Power Elite: How It Happened, Why It Matters.* Copyright 2006 Rowman & Littlefield. Used by permission of the publisher.

P. 353: © 2006 The Economist Newspaper Ltd. All rights reserved. Reprinted with permission. Further reproduction prohibited. www.economist.com.

P. 355: Cartoon © The New Yorker Collection 1957 Chon Day from cartoonbank.com. All rights reserved.

460

P. 358: Figure 14–2 © International Institute for Democracy and Electoral Assistance, www.idea.int. Used by permission.

P. 360: Figure 14–3 From Inter-Parliamentary Union (IPU), 2006, Women in National Parliaments, www.ipu.org/wmn-e/classif.htm. Used by permission.

P. 361: Figure 14–4 (right) From G. William Domhoff. 2001. *Who Rules America,* 4th ed.:96. © 2001 by The McGraw-Hill Companies, Inc. Reproduced by permission of the publisher.

P. 363: Figure 14–5 From 1971—2004 The Gallup Poll. All rights reserved. Reprinted with permission from The Gallup Organization.

P. 365: Figure 14–6 Adapted from *National Geographic Atlas of the World* 8e. National Geographic Society, 2005. NG Maps/National Geographic Image Collection. Used by permission.

P. 366: Cartoon by Mike Peters. © King Features Syndicate. Reprinted by permission

P. 366: Quotation from Sheryl Stolberg. 1995. "Affirmative Action Gains Often Come at a High Cost," Los Angeles Times (March 29):A14. Copyright 1995 *Los Angeles Times.* Reprinted by permission.

Chapter 15

P. 374: Quotation from Mitchell Duneier. 1999. *Sidewalk.* Copyright © 1999 by Mitchell Duneier. Reprinted by permission of Farrar, Straus & Giroux, LLC.

P. 378: Figure 15–1 From Carl Haub. 2005. *World Population Data Sheet 2005.* Used by permission of Population Reference Bureau.

P. 383: Table 15–2 Based on Gideon Sjoberg. 1960. *The Preindustrial City: Past and Present:*323–328. Adapted with permission of The Free Press, a Division of Simon & Schuster Adult Publishing Group. Copyright © 1960 by The Free Press. Copyright © renewed 1968 by Gideon Sjoberg. All rights reserved. And based on E. Barbara Phillips. 1996. *City Lights: Urban-Suburban Life in the Global Society,* 2/e. Copyright © 1981 by E. Barbara Phillips and

Richard T. LeGates, 1996 by E. Barbara Phillips. Oxford University Press. Used by permission.

P. 384: Figure 15–4 Adapted from *National Geographic Atlas of the World* 8e. National Geographic Society, 2005. NG Maps/National Geographic Image Collection. Used by permission.

P. 385: Figure 15–5 From Chauncy Harris and Edward Ullmann. 1945. "The Nature of Cities," *Annals of the American Academy of Political and Social Science,* 242 (November):13. Reprinted by permission of American Academy of Political and Social Science, Philadelphia.

P. 393: Figure 15–6 From Carl Haub. 2005. *World Population Data Sheet 2005.* Used by permission of Population Reference Bureau.

P. 400: Figure 15–9 From UNAIDS. 2006. Adapted with permission from UNAIDS, Geneva, Switzerland. For further information, please view the *2006 Report on the global AIDS epidemic* at www.unaids.org.

Chapter 16

P. 406: Quotation from Debora L. Spar. 2001. *Ruling the Waves: Cycles of Discovery, Chaos and Wealth from the Compass to the Internet.* Copyright © 2001 by Debora L. Spar. Reprinted by permission of Harcourt, Inc. and the William Morris Agency.

P. 410: Quotation from Manisha Desai. 1996. "If Peasants Build Their Own Dams, What Would the State Have Left to Do?" *Research in Social Movements, Conflicts and Change,* 19:214, ed. Michael Dobkowski and Isidor Wallimann. Greenwich, CT: JAI Press. Used with permission from Elsevier.

P. 418: Cartoon by Chris Madden. Used by permission.

P. 422: Figure 16–1 Adapted from *National Geographic Atlas of the World* 8e. National Geographic Society, 2005. NG Maps/National Geographic Image Collection. Used by permission.

Acknowledgements

credits

Chapter 1

p. 1: © United Air Lines, Inc. All rights Reserved. By permission of Fallon Minneapolis. Photography: © 2005 Kevin Peterson (left) and Matthew Phillips/Jupiter (right); p. 4, p. 5 (T), p. 5 (b): ©1994 Peter Menzel www.menzelphoto.com. From the book Material World, Sierra Club Books.; p. 7: © Kyle Niemi/U.S. Coast Guard via Getty Images; p. 8 (L): © AJ Mast/AP Photo; p. 9 (R): ©James Marshall/The Image Works; p. 10: "Harriet Martineau" By Richard Evans. National Portrait Gallery, London.; p. 12 (L): Bibliothèque Nationale de France; p. 12 (M): The Granger Collection, New York; p. 12 (R): Archivo Iconografico, S.A./Corbis; p. 12: Jane Addams Memorial Collection (JAMC neg. 613), Special Collections, The University Library, The University of Illinois at Chicago; p. 14: © Earl & Nazima Kowall/CORBIS; p. 15: U.S. Postal Service; p. 16: Department of Special Collections, The University of Chicago Library; p. 19: © Gavin Lawrence/Getty Images; p. 20: © Topham/The Image Works

Chapter 2

p. 28: © 1990 Erika Rothenberg; p. 31: © Van Bucher/Photo Researchers, Inc.; p. 36: © 2003 The Gallup Poll; p. 37: © Robert Fried/Alamy; p. 38: Courtesy of AT&T Archives and History Center, Warren, NJ.; p. 42: © Stephen Shugerman/Getty Images; p. 43: © John Gaps III/AP Photo; p. 44 (T): Collection of Richard Schaefer; p. 44 (B): © Bob Daemmrich/The Image Works; p. 46: © Jose Luis Pelaez, Inc./CORBIS

Chapter 3

p. 53: © Mike Clark /AFP/Getty Images; p. 56: © Eddie Gerald/Lonely Planet Images; p. 57 (T): AP/Wide World Photos; p. 57(B): © Patrick Zachmann/ Magnum Photos, Inc.; p. 58: © UPPA/ZUMA Press; p. 63: Courtesy of the Oneida Nation; p. 64 (T): © Jim Watson/AFP/Getty Images; p. 64 (B): AP/Wide World Photos; p. 65: © Topham/The Image Works; p. 69: © Mark Henley/Panos Pictures; p. 72: © Andre Jenny/Alamy

Chapter 4

p. 77: © David H. Wells/The Image Works; p. 80: Reprinted from Genie: A Psycholinguist Study of a Modern Day "Wild Child" by Susan Curtis, 1977, p. 274, with permission from Elsevier.; p. 81: © Bob DeBris/Corbis; p. 82: © Tony Freeman/PhotoEdit, Inc; p. 83: © AP/Wide World Photos; p. 84: © Ryan McVay/Getty Images; p. 86: © Thomas S. England/Photo Researchers, Inc.; p. 87: © AP/Wide World Photos; p. 88: © A. Ramey/Photo Edit ; p. 89: © Carlos Osorio/AP Photo; p. 90: © Dennis Macdonald/Index Stock; p. 91: Courtesy of Rakefet Avramovitz; p. 93: © Jim West/The Image Works; p. 95: © Svenn Nordlöv/Trifoto/Nordic Photos

Chapter 5

p. 99: Courtesy of America's Promise; p. 102: © Don Murray-Pool/Getty Images; p. 103: © Vincent DeWitt/Stock Boston, LLC; p. 105: © Anna Clopet/Corbis; p. 106: © Scott Fisher/Woodfin Camp & Associates; p. 107 (T): © Randy Faris/Corbis; p. 107 (B): © STAN HONDA/AFP/Getty Images; p. 108: © Viviane Moos/CORBIS; p. 109: Courtesy of the New York Unicycle Club; p. 110: Landov; p. 113: © AP/Wide World Photos; p. 114: © Charles & Josette Lenars/Corbis; p. 115: © Pablo Corral V/CORBIS; p. 117: © David Frazier/PhotoEdit; p. 118: © Vladimir Sichov/SIPA Press; p. 120: © AP/Wide World Photos; p. 122: © Koichi Kamoshida/Getty Images; p. 124: © Peter R. Hvizdak/The Image Works

Chapter 6

p. 132: Courtesy of Michael Horse; p. 135: © Khalil Hamra; p. 136 (L): © CBS/Photofest; p. 136 (R): © ABC/Photofest; p. 137 (T L): © NBC/ Photofest; p. 137 (T R): © Fox Broadcasting/Photofest; p. 137 (B L):

© HBO/Photofest; p. 137 (B R): © CBS/Warner Bros./Photofest; p. 138 (L): Photo by Stan Wayman/Time Magazine, Copyright Time Inc./Time Life Pictures/Getty Images; p. 138 (M L): PEOPLE Weekly © Time Inc. All Rights Reserved; p. 138 (M R): © Vince Bucci/Getty Images; p. 138 (R): Courtesy of Rolling Stone; p. 139: Courtesy of Everett Collection; p. 140: © Ellen Emendorp/The New York Times; p. 141: Courtesy of Everett Collection; p. 142: Photofest; p. 147 (L): © Danny Moloshok/AP; p. 147 (R): © Royalty Free/Corbis; p. 149: © Jeffery Aaronson/Network Aspen; p. 150: © Frederic Stevens/SIPA Press

Chapter 7

p. 156: Courtesy of Bozell New York; p. 159 (T): © Alliance Atlantis/Dod Eat Dog/United Broadcasting/The Kobal Collection; p. 159 (B): © Lehtikuva/Jussi Nukari; p. 160: © 1965 by Stanley Milgram. From the film OBEDIENCE, distributed by Penn State, Media Sales; p. 161: © George Steinmetz; p. 164: Los Angeles Times Photo by Luis Sinco; p. 165: © Duane Burleson/AP Photo; p. 166: © Jerry Alexander/Getty Images; p. 167 (T): © Bob Krist/Corbis; p. 167 (B): Kevin Moloney for The New York Times; p. 169: © AP/Wide World Photos; p. 172: © Michael Newman/PhotoEdit; p. 173: © Stock Montage; p. 176: Courtesy of Tiffany Zapata-Mancilla

Chapter 8

p. 184: ConAgra Foods Feeding Children Better Foundation. Courtesy of The Ad Council; p. 189: © Roger Ball/Corbis; p. 191: © Bettmann/Corbis; p. 192: © Steven S. Miric/SuperStock ; p. 193: © Paul A. Souders/Corbis; p. 199: © Rubber Ball Productions/Index Stock; p. 200: © AP Photos; p. 203: © Suzanne Opton; p. 209: Agency: Springer & Jacoby Werbung GmbH, Hamburg; creative directors: Betina Olf, Timm Weber; copywriter: Sven Keitel; art director: Claudia Todt; photographer: Jan Burwick; p. 210: © Margo Silver/Stone/Getty; p. 211: © Alan Dejecacion/Getty; p. 212 (L): © Seth Wenig/Reuters/Corbis; p. 212 (R): © Photofusion Picture Library/ Alamy; p. 215: © K. Hamilton/Corbis; p. 216: © Catherine Karnow/Woodfin Camp & Associates; p. 217: © James Leynse/Corbis; p. 223: © Stuart Franklin/Magnum Photos; p. 224: © Gregory Bull/AP Photo; p. 225: © Eduardo Verdugo/ AP Photo; p. 228: © Simon C. Roberts/NB Pictures/Contact Press Images

Chaper 10

p. 232: © Courtesy of the American Indian College Fund; p. 237: © Mark Richards/Photoedit; p. 240: © Tom McCarthy/Photoedit; p. 241: Courtesy of Prudence Hannis; p. 242: © Elliot Erwitt/Magnum Photos; p. 245: © Mandatory Credit: Alexandra Boulat/VII/AP Photo; p. 248: AP Photo/David Zalubowski; p. 251: © Roy Ooms/Masterfile; p. 252: © Photo by Brian Vander Burg. Copyright 2002, Los Angeles Times. Reprinted with permission.; p. 255: © Photo by David Bohrer. Copyright 2002, Los Angeles Times. Reprinted with permission.; p. 256: Courtesy of Devito/Verdi, New York, NY

Chapter 11

p. 260: © 2006 by Guerrilla Girls, Inc.; p. 262: Courtesy of Azadeh Moaveni; p. 264 (L): © Laura Farr/Zuma Press; p. 264 (R): Picture provided by Harrison G. Pope, Jr. adapted from THE ADONIS COMPLEX by Harrison G. Pope, Jr., Katherine Phillips, Roberto Olivardia. The Free Press, © 2000; p. 266: © Steve McCurry/Magnum; p. 267: © Bob Mahoney/The Image Works; p. 274: © Robert Brenner/Photoedit; p. 276: © Catherine Karnow/ Woodfin Camp & Associates; p. 278: © Spencer Grant/Photoedit; p. 280: © Thierry Secretan/Woodfin Camp & Associates; p. 283: © Gabe Palmer/Corbis

p. 289 (L & R): Courtesy of Barnardos; p. 292, p. 293 (T), p. 293 (B): Uwe Ommer from 1000 families; p. 295: © Ariel Skelley/CORBIS; p. 297: © Richard Hutchings; p. 299: © Colin Young-Wolff/PhotoEdit; ;p. 303: © Lori Waselchuck/New York Times Pictures; p. 304: © Blair Seitz/Photo Researchers, Inc.

Chaper 13

p. 314: © Thomas Coex/AFP/Getty Images; p. 318: © Sean Sprague/Peter Arnold, Inc.; p. 319 (T): © Sebastian Bolesch/Peter Arnold, Inc; p. 319 (B L): © Lindsay Hebberd/Corbis; p. 319 (B R): © Jorgen Schytte/Peter Arnold, Inc.; p. 325: © Syracuse Newspapers/The Image Works; p. 326: AP Photo; p. 329: © Robert Davis; p. 332: © Lindsay Hebberd/Corbis; p. 335: © Mary Kate Denny/PhotoEdit, inc.; p. 337: © Marc Ribound/Magnum Photos; p. 341: © Bob Daemmrich/Stock Boston, LLC

Chapter 14

p. 347: © Mike Nelson/epa/Corbis; p. 350: © Andrew Cooper/Columbia Tri Star/The Kobal Collection; p. 351 (T): Courtesy of Richard J. Hawk; p. 351 (B): © Ramadhan Khamis/Panapress; p. 354: © Jose Fuste Raga/Corbis; p. 357: © Joren Gerhard/Corbis Sygma; p. 363: © Jaron Berman Photography; p. 364: © Yannis Behrakis/Reuters/Landov; p. 367: © Reuters/Corbis; p. 369: © MANAN VATSYAYANA/AFP/Getty Images

Chapter 15

p. 373: © GOH CHAI HIN/AFP/Getty Images; p. 375: © Ovie Carter; p. 377: © Josef Polleross/The Image Works; p. 382: © Mark Henley/Panos Pictures; p. 386: © Sarah Leen/National Geographic/Getty Images; p. 388: AP/Wide World Photos, Max Nash; p. 389: © Philip Gould/CORBIS; p. 390: © Robert Harding Picture Library Ltd/Alamy; p. 393: © Bob Daemmrich/The Image Works; p. 396 (T): Courtesy of Jess Purmort; p. 396 (B): © Ryan McVay/Photodisc Green/Getty; p. 398: © Reuters/Corbis

Chapter 16

p. 405 (all): Courtesy of the Make Trade Fair Campaign, Oxfam and Greg Williams, Photographer; p. 408: © Ryan Pyle/Corbis; p. 409: AP/Wide World Photos; p. 413: © 2002 Joseph Rodriguez/Stockphoto.com; p. 415: © Viktor Drachev/AFP/Getty Images; p. 416: © Pedro Armestre/Reuters; p. 417: Courtesy of Troy Duster; p. 419 (T): Basel Action Network; p. 419 (B): © Macduff Everton/Corbis

name index

A

Abelson, Reed, 391
Abercrombie, Nicholas, 193
Aberle, David F., 112
Abrahamson, Mark, 168
Abramoff, Jack, 250
Acosta, Vivian R., 19
Adam, B., 395
Addams, Jane, 12, 13, 17, 22, 43, 267
Adler, Fred, 173, 174
Adler, Patricia, 29, 36, 37
Adler, Peter, 29, 36, 37
Alain, Michel, 408
Alba, Richard D., 255
Albiniak, P., 135
Alfino, Mark, 60
Ali, Muhammad, 102, 138
Allen, B., 160
Allport, Gordon, 242, 243
Alwin, Duane F., 359
Amato, Paul R., 306, 307
Andersen, Margaret, 267
Anderson, C., 152
Anderson, Elijah, 17
Anderson, J., 221
Angier, Natalie, 264
Anniston, Jennifer, 138
Appelbaum, Richard, 211
Argetsinger, Amy, 68
Arias, Elizabeth, 397
Aristotle, 7, 8
Armer, J. Michael, 220
Arnaz, Desi, 136
Aronson, Elliot, 158
Ashe, Arthur, 103
Astin, Alexander, 67, 340
Astin, Alexandra W., 7
Ataturk, Kemal, 270
Atchley, Robert C., 277, 278
Atkinson, Claire, 142
Austin, April, 351
Avramovitz, Rakefet, 91
Axtell, Roger E., 82
Azumi, Koya, 119

B

Babad, Elisha Y., 339
Bagilhole, Barbara, 265, 272
Bainbridge, William Sims, 45, 316, 328, 330
Baker, Dean, 219
Baker, Therese L., 37
Baker, Wayne E., 220
Bales, Robert, 266
Ball, Lucille, 136
Barbaro, Michael, 391
Barboza, David, 142

Bardi, Anat, 66
Barr, Cameron W., 150
Barrett, David B., 320, 321, 328
Barron, Milton L., 274
Bartlett, Donald L., 250
Barusch, 277
Basso, Keith H., 61
Bates, Colleen Dunn, 398
Bauerlein, Monika, 414
Bauman, Kurt J., 196
Beagan, Brenda L., 393
Beall, 274
Bearman, Peter, 111
Becerra, Rosina M., 302
Becker, Howard, 171, 174, 338, 394
Beech, Hannah, 355
Beeghley, Leonard, 189
Bell, Daniel, 118, 175, 414
Bell, Wendel, 217
Bellafante, Ginia, 300
Benac, Nancy, 284
Bendick, Marc Jr., 283
Bendix, B. Reinhard, 43
Benford, Robert D., 407
Bennett, Vivienne, 225
Berger, Peter, 114
Berkman, Lisa F., 397
Berlin, Brent, 63
Bernasek, Anna, 198
Bernstein, Sharon, 400
Berry, Halle, 138
Best, Amy, 164
Bian, Yanjie, 354
Bianchi, Suzanne M., 273, 296, 305
Bielby, D., 141
Bielby, William T., 320
Black, Donald, 64, 161
Blackhall, Leslie J., 394
Blair, Elizabeth, 304
Blau, Peter M., 121, 201
Blauner, Robert, 242
Blumer, Herbert, 101, 407
Boase, Jeffery, 143
Boaz, Rachel Floersheim, 275
Bogart, Humphrey, 138
Bok, Sissela, 152
Bonczar, Thomas P., 180
Booth, Alan, 306
Bordt, Rebecca, 39
Bornschier, Volker, 221
Borosage, Robert L., 126
Bottomore, Tom, 412
Bouchard, Thomas, 81
Boudreaux, Richard, 224
Boushey, Heather, 202
Bouvier, Leon F., 380
Bowles, Samuel, 91
Bowles, Scott, 255, 334, 337, 340
Bradford, Calvin, 112
Bradsher, Keith, 354
Brannigan, Augustine, 118

Brauman, Rony, 228
Bray, James H., 296
Brint, Steven, 339
Brittingham, Angela, 255
Bromley, David, 37
Brown, D., 336
Brown, P. L., 308
Brown, R. M., 324
Brown, S., 307
Bruno, Rosalind, 71
Brzezinski, Zbigniew, 357
Buckley, Tom, 298
Budig, Michelle, 272
Bullard, Robert D., 420
Bulle, Wolfgang F., 65
Bunzel, John H., 237
Burgess, Ernest, 384
Burkett, Elinor, 308
Burns, John R., 269
Burtless, Gary, 197
Bush, George H. W., 138
Bush, George W., 39, 64, 138, 309
Bushman, 152
Butler, D., 200
Butler, Robert, 282
Byrd-Bredbenner, Carol, 264

C

Caeser, Lena G., 397
Calhoun, Craig, 422
Calvin, John, 323
Campbell, Mary, 202
Camus, Albert, 399
Caplan, Ronald L., 392
Caplow, Theodore, 362
Caputo, John S., 60
Carey, Anne R., 110
Carlson, Darren K., 256
Carpenter, Linda Jean, 19
Carrese, Joseph A., 394
Carroll, Diahann, 138
Carroll, John, 269
Carter, Bill, 148
Carter, Jimmy, 138
Carter, Rebecca S., 92
Carty, Win, 418
Cassidy, Rachel C., 236, 249
Castaneda, Jorge, 224
Castells, Manuel, 112, 125, 149, 220
Castro, Fidel, 254, 407
Catalano, Shannon M., 178
Cerulo, Karen A., 7, 143
Chalfant, H. Paul, 331
Chambers, Jeff M., 390
Chambliss, William, 171
Charter, David, 334
Chase-Dunn, Christopher, 214, 215, 216
Chavira, 397

Cherlin, Andrew, 24, 296, 304, 307
Chesney-Lind, Meda, 173, 174
Cheung, A., 72
Chin, Ko-lin, 175
Christensen, Kathleen, 276
Churchill, Winston, 334
Clark, Burton, 341, 390
Clark, C., 394
Clarke, Adele E., 416
Clausen, Christopher, 308
Clawson, Dan, 95
Clemmitt, Marcia, 343
Clinard, Marshall B., 169
Clinton, Bill, 138
Clymer, Adam, 359
Coates, Rodney D., 256
Cockburn, Andrew, 187
Cockerham, William C., 395
Cohen, D., 331
Cohen, L., 170
Cole, E., 303
Cole, M., 334
Coleman, I., 337
Coleman, J., 175
Collins, Chiquita, 248
Collins, Randall, 193, 323, 414
Commoner, Barry, 420
Comstock, P., 126, 152
Comte, Auguste, 9, 10, 13, 411
Conrad. Peter, 392
Cooley, Charles Horton, 11, 13, 18, 82, 84, 85, 86, 89, 108
Coontz, Stephanie, 305
Cortese, Anthony J., 143
Cosby, Bill, 138
Coser, L., 11, 193
Costner, Kevin, 63
Coté, James E., 87
Couch, Carl, 356
Counts, D. A., 280, 281
Cowell, Alan, 309
Cox, Oliver, 242
Cox, R., 341, 342
Cressey, Donald R., 170
Cromwell, Paul F., 171
Crosnoe, Robert, 276
Cross, Simon, 265, 272
Crossing, Peter F., 320, 321, 328
Croteau, David, 146, 149
Croucher, Sheila, 246
Crouse, Kelly, 200
Cruise, Tom, 350
Cuff, E. C., 193
Cullen, Francis T., 171
Cullen, John B., 171
Cumming, Elaine, 274
Currie, Elliot, 178, 179
Curry, Timothy Jon, 392
Curry-White, Brenda, 199
Curtiss, Susan, 80

Name Index

D

Dahl, Robert, 362
Dahrendorf, Ralf, 15, 193, 413
Daley, Suzanne, 228
Dalla, Rochelle L., 301
Daniszewski, John, 150
Dao, James, 303
Darwin, Charles, 10, 60, 411
Dash, Erich, 191
Davidoff, Jules, 63
Davies, Christie, 88
Davies, Ian, 63
Davis, D. B., 124
Davis, D. W., 35
Davis, G., 362
Davis, J. A., 34, 48, 195, 202
Davis, K., 80
Davis, Kingsley, 192, 336, 382
Davis, N., 168, 171
Davis, Robert, 162
Davis, Sammy Jr., 138
De la Cruz, G. Patricia, 255
DeBarros, Anthony, 162
Deegan, Mary Jo, 12
Deflem, Mathieu, 177
Delaney, Kevin J., 140
Delawala, Imtyaz, 351
Della Porta, Donatella, 408
Dellios, Hugh, 226
Deloria, Vine, Jr., 315, 316
DeNavas-Walt, Carmen, 32, 48, 188, 190, 195,
    196, 198, 199, 239, 249, 253, 282, 301, 303
Denny, Charlotte, 246
Denton, Nancy, 245, 388
Denzin, Norman, 118
DePalma, Anthony, 224
DeParle, Jason, 323
Derné, Steve, 210, 211
Desai, Manisha, 410
Desegrais, Helene, 203
Deskins, Donald R., Jr., 15
Devitt, James, 359
Diamond, Jared, 422
Diaz, Cameron, 135
Dickerson, Marla, 354
Dickson, W. J., 123
Dillon, Sam, 225, 390
DiMaggio, Paul, 125
Dodge, Hiroko, 239
Doeringer, Peter B., 276
Domhoff, G. William, 348, 349, 362
Dominick, Joseph R., 142
Doress, Irwin, 327
Dotson, Floyd, 375
Dougherty, John, 225
Dougherty, Kevin, 339
Dowd, James J., 276
Doyle, James A., 264
Dreier, Peter, 211
Drinkard, Jim, 250
Driver, Edwin D., 248
Du Bois, W. E. B., 15, 17, 18, 22, 43, 248
Dubner, Stephen J., 41
Dukes, Richard L., 39
Duncan, Otis Dudley, 201
Dundas, Susan, 309
Duneier, Mitchell, 114, 374, 375
Dunlap, Riley E., 418
Dunne, Gillan A., 309
Durkheim, Emile, 9, 10, 11, 12, 13, 18, 38, 43,
    101, 114, 115, 118, 119, 158, 168, 174,
    316, 320, 326, 411
Durose, Matthew R., 256
Duster, Troy, 417
Dylan, Bob, 138

E

Earle, Craig, 397
Easterbrook, Gregg, 418
Ebaugh, Helen Rose Fuchs, 105
Eberbach, Dave, 44
Eckenwiler, Mark, 415
Eddy, Mary Baker, 330
Edin, Kathryn, 307
Edwards, H., 19
Edwards, T., 284
Efron, Sonni, 337
Ehrenreich, Barbara, 2–3, 37, 196, 198
Ehrlich, Paul, 376, 420
Eisenhower, Dwight, 138
Eitzen, D. Stanley, 19
Ellison, Ralph, 247, 420
Ely, Robin J., 119
Embree, Ainslie, 333
Engels, Friedrich, 11, 21, 408
Entine, Jon, 216
Epstein, R., 280
Erard, Michael, 62
Ericson, Nels, 135
Erikson, Kai, 168
Estevez, Ramon, 141
Etaugh, Claire, 264
Etzioni, Amitai, 119, 364

F

Faith, Nazila, 112
Fallows, Deborah, 143
Falwell, Jerry, 150
Fanning, Shawn, 406
Farley, Maggie, 309
Fausset, Richard, 332
Feagin, Joe R., 341, 386, 387
Featherman, David L., 201
Feketekuty, Geza, 215
Fellini, Federico, 152
Felson, D., 177
Felson, Marcus, 170, 174
Ferree, Myra Marx, 16, 409, 410
Fessenden, Ford, 161
Feuer, L., 215, 267
Fiala, Robert, 414
Fields, Jason, 265, 296, 302, 303, 304, 307
Fields, Jessica, 16
Finder, Alan, 251
Fine, Gary Alan, 19, 243
Finkel, Steven E., 408
Fiore, Quentin, 149
Firestone, D., 342
Firth, Colin, 405
Fiss, Peter C., 21
Fitchett, George, 280
Fitzgerald, David, 421
Fitzgerald, Kathleen J., 409
Flacks, Richard, 69
Flavin, Jeanne, 174
Fletcher, Connie, 105
Florio, Gwen, 390
Foehr, Ulla G., 93
Ford, Gerald, 138
Forsythe, David P., 227
Foster, Jodie, 79, 152
Fox, Jonathan, 421
Fox, M. B., 126
Franklin, John Hope, 248
Freidson, Eliot, 392
French, Howard W., 84, 139, 222
Freud, Sigmund, 84, 86
Freudenburg, William B., 43
Freudenheim, Milt, 283
Frey, William H., 389
Fridlund, Alan J., 64
Friedan, Betty, 380
Friedland, Jonathan, 392
Friedrich, Carl, 357
Fuentes, Thomas, 348
Fujimoto, Kayo, 222
Furstenberg, S., 87, 296
Fuwa, Makiko, 271

G

Gagnon, John H., 46, 308
Gamble, Wendy, 301
Gamson, Joshua, 149, 408
Gandhi, Mohandas K., 333
Ganeshananthan, Vaugi, 285
Gans, Herbert, 200, 255, 387
Ganzeboom, Harry B. G., 221, 222
Gardner, G., 420
Gardner, M., 282
Garner, Roberta, 411
Garreau, Joel, 385
Gates, Gary J., 308
Geist, Eric L., 21
Gerstel, Naomi, 95, 301
Gerth, H. H., 11, 191, 200, 336
Gertner, Jon, 140
Ghirda, Bogdan, 220
Gifford, Allen L., 399
Gin, Sue Ling, 348
Gintis, Herbert, 91, 334, 337, 340
Giordano, Peggy C., 84, 92
Giroux, Henry A., 336
Gitlin, Todd, 149
Glauber, Bill, 162
Glaze, Lauren E., 161
Glionna, John M., 250
Goffman, Erving, 17, 18, 39, 84, 86, 88, 143,
    164, 364
Golden, Frederic, 417
Goldstein, A., 359
Goldstein, M., 274
Gonzalez, David, 216
Goodman, Peter S., 222, 224
Goodstein, Laurie, 343
Gorbachev, Mikhail, 414
Gordon, R., 61, 62, 340
Gore, Al, 418
Gornick, J., 205
Gornick, Vivian, 143
Gottdiener, Mark, 386, 387
Gottfredson, Michael, 163
Gottlieb, Lori, 299
Gould, Larry, 105
Gouldner, Alvin, 43, 412
Grabarek, Stanislaus, 23
Graham, Judith, 390
Gramsci, Antonio, 67
Greeley, Andrew M., 323
Green, Dan S., 248
Greenblatt, Alan, 190, 196
Greenhouse, Linda, 269
Greenspan, Alan, 196
Grieco, Elizabeth M., 236, 249
Grier, Peter, 196
Grimes, Peter, 214, 216
Gross, Jane, 278
Grossman, Ler, 355
Groza, Victor, 80
Grusky, David, 221
Gundersen, Edna, 147
Guterman, Lila, 61
Gutierrez, Gustavo, 324

H

Hacker, A., 361
Hacker, Helen Mayer, 267
Hafner-Burton, Emilie M., 228
Hage, Jerald, 119
Halebsky, Stephen, 391
Hall, R., 397
Haller, Max, 221
Hallinan, Maureen T., 336, 415
Hamilton, Brady E., 248, 304
Hamilton, Charles, 248
Hamm, Jill V. B., 244
Hammack, Floyd M., 339
Hank, Karsten, 96
Hannis, Prudence, 241
Hansen, Brian, 391
Hanson, Ralph E., 139
Harlow, Harry, 80
Harrington, Michael, 118, 158
Harris, 234
Harris, Chauncy D., 385
Harris, D., 256
Harris, J., 89
Harris, Marvin, 274
Harrison, George, 138
Hartman, Chris, 204
Hasan, Hakim, 374, 375
Haub, Carl, 198, 213, 219, 224, 377, 379, 380,
    381
Hauser, Robert M., 201, 221
Havel, Vaclav, 407
Haviland, William A., 61, 63, 291
Hawk, Richard, 351
Hayden, H. Thomas, 160
Hayward, Mark D., 276

He, Wan, 278, 281
Heck, Makui K., 396
Heckert, Druann, 164
Hedley, R. Alan, 220
Heilman, Madeline E., 203
Hendrix, Jimi, 138
Henly, Julia R., 110
Henry, William, 274
Hepburn, Katherine, 138
Herschthal, Eric, 300
Hickman, Jonathan, 239
Hicks, Louis, 362
Hill, Michael R., 10
Hillery, George A., 375
Himes, Vristine L., 276, 231, 282
Hipp, John R., 171
Hirsch, Paul M., 21
Hirschi, Travis, 163
Hirshfeld, Marc, 141
Hitlin, Steven, 66
Hochschild, Arlie, 273, 297
Hodge, Robert W., 194
Hoecker-Drysdale, Susan, 10
Hoffman, A., 141
Hoffman, Lois, 60
Holden, Constance, 81
Holder, Kelly, 281, 358
Hollander, Jocelyn A., 263, 268
Hollingshead, August B., 340
Holthouse, David, 225
Homans, George C., 79
Hoover, Eric, 162
Horgan, John, 82
Horne, Lena, 138
Horovitz, Bruce, 138
Horowitz, Helen Lefkowitz, 341
Hosokawa, William K., 251
Houston, Whitney, 138
Hout, Michael, 202
Howard, J., 263, 267
Howard, M., 82
Howard, Russell D., 365
Hoynes, William, 146, 149
Huber, Bettina J., 24
Huddy, Leonie, 35
Huffstutter, P. J., 143
Hughes, Everett, 103
Hull, Raymond, 121
Hunt, Darnell, 147
Hunter, Herbert M., 242
Hunter, James Davison, 323
Hurh, Won Moo, 249, 252
Hurn, Christopher J., 336
Hussein, Saddam, 35
Hutchison, Ray, 386, 387

Inglehart, Ronald, 220, 325
Iritani, Evelyn, 354

Jackson, E., 170
Jackson, Janet, 138
Jackson, Michael, 138
Jackson, Philip, 335
Jacobs, J., 272
Jacobson, Jodi, 271
Jacobson, Lenore, 338
Jagger, Mick, 138
Jamieson, Arnie, 359
Jang, Yong Suk, 362
Jargowsky, Paul A., 199
Jasper, James M., 411, 413
Jencks, Christopher, 204
Johnson, A., 46
Johnson, B., 412
Johnson, J., 94, 152
Johnson, Lyndon, 138
Johnson, Todd M., 320, 321, 328
Johnston, David Cay, 228
Jolin, Annette, 174
Jones, Jeffrey, 180, 269
Jones, N., 235
Jones, S., 38
Joplin, Scott, 58
Jost, Kenneth, 179
Joyner, Kara, 244
Joynt, Jen, 285
Juhasz, Anne McCreary, 84

Kahn, 354
Kahn, Joseph, 354
Kalaitzidis, 177
Kalish, Richard, 280
Kalt, Joseph P., 250
Kamenetz, Anya, 202
Kao, Grace, 244
Kapos, Shia, 298
Kapur, Deutsch, 421
Karzai, Hamid, 139
Kashiwagi, Akiko, 222
Katel, Peter, 219
Katovich, Michael A., 160
Katsillis, John, 220
Katz, Michael, 340
Kaufman, Miriam, 309
Kay, Paul, 63
Kaye, Judith, 303
Kefalas, Maria, 307
Keith, Kenton, 150
Kelly, John, 296
Kennedy, John F. Jr., 133, 191, 356
Kent, Mary M., 379
Kentor, Jeffrey, 362
Kerbo, Harold R., 193, 216, 221
Kidman, Nicole, 138
Kilborn, Peter T., 390
Kilbourne, Jean, 143
Kim, Kwang Chung, 249, 252, 328
King, L., 96
King, Martin Luther, 256, 409
King, Stephen, 172
Kirp, David L., 95
Kiser, Edgar, 363
Kitchener, Richard F., 86
Kitt, Alice S., 109
Klass, Perri, 269

Klein, N., 149
Kleiner, Art, 124
Kleinknecht, William, 175
Kleniewski, Nancy, 388
Klinenberg, Eric, 276
Klug, Heinz, 228
Knowles, Beyonce, 42
Koch, Wendy, 303
Kochhar, Rakesh, 203
Kohn, Melvin L., 301
Kolata, Gina, 416
Koolhaas, Rem, 383
Kopinak, Kathryn, 224
Korczyk, Sophie M., 276
Korn, William S., 7, 340
Kottak, Conrad, 291
Kotulak, Ronald, 269
Kriesberg, Louis, 364
Krim, Jonathan, 68
Kristof, Nicholas D., 221
Kroeger, Brooke, 39
Kroll, Luisa, 224
Kubler-Ross, Elisabeth, 280
Kuo, M., 162
Kurosawa, Akira, 58
Kwong, Jo, 419
Kwong, Peter, 251

La Ganga, Maria L., 281
Labaton, Stephan, 176
Ladner, Joyce, 43
Lamb, David, 249
Landler, Mark, 420
Landtman, Gunnar, 192
Lang, Eric, 38
Langan, Patrick A., 256
Lareau, Annette, 290, 291
Laska, Shirley, 6
Lasn, Kalle, 138
Lasswell, Harold, 355
Latteier, Pearl, 149
Lauer, Robert H., 413
Laumann, Edward O., 46, 308
Lazarsfeld, Paul, 134, 146
Leavell, Hugh R., 390
Lee, Alfred McClung, 364, 365
Lee, Bruce, 53
Lee, J. E., 162
Lee, Spike, 252
Lehne, Gregory K., 263
Lemann, Nicholas, 254
Lengermann, Patricia, 12
Lennon, John, 138
Lenski, Gerhard, 60, 101, 116, 117, 118, 194, 349
Leonhardt, David, 202
Levin, Jack, 274
Levin, William C., 274
Levinson, Daniel, 277
Levitt, Steven D., 41
Levy, Becca R., 282
Lewin, Tamar, 269, 305
Lichter, Linda S., 151
Lichter, Robert S., 151

Lictblau, Eric, 256
Lieberson, Stanley, 41
Light, D., 353
Lin, Nan, 194
Lincoln, Abraham, 334
Lindner, Eileen, 328
Linn, Susan, 90
Lino, Mark, 308
Lips, Hilary M., 272
Lipset, Seymour Martin, 196
Lipson, Karen, 79
Liptak, Adam, 239, 309
Liska, Allen E., 171
Livernash, Robert, 420
Livingstone, Sonia, 145
Lochen, K., 396
Loeb, Susanna, 95
Lofland, L., 37
Longman, Philip, 381
Lu, Ming, 354
Luckmann, Thomas, 114
Luijkx, Ruud, 222
Lukacs, Georg, 67
Luker, Kristin, 284
Lum, Joann, 251
Lumpe, Lora, 175
Luster, Tom, 301
Luther, Martin, 328, 356
Lyall, Sarah, 306

McAllister, Harold, 290
McCabe, Donald, 68
McCall, Tommy, 191
McCarthy, Ellen, 150
McCartney, Paul, 138
McCright, Aaron M., 418
McDonald, Kim A., 398
MacDorman, Marian, 397
McGinn, Daniel, 298
McGue, Matt, 81
McHale, John, 421
McIntosh, Peggy, 239, 240
Mack, Raymond, 112
McKinlay, John B., 392
McKinlay, Sonja M., 392
McLean, Elys A., 110
MacLeod, Scott, 150
McLuhan, Marshall, 149
McNeil, Donald G., 212, 400, 401
McVeigh, Timothy, 179, 180
Magnier, Mark, 416
Mahoney, Kathryn M., 7
Mahoney, Robert J., 281
Malcolm X, 103, 104, 326
Malthus, Thomas Robert, 375, 376
Mandela, Nelson, 245, 407
Mangum, Garth L., 199
Mangum, Stephen L., 199
Manson, Charles, 256
Mark, Gloria, 125
Marr, Phebe, 92
Marriott, Michel, 237
Martelo, Emma Zapata, 224
Martin, Chris, 405

Name Index

Martin, Joyce A., 304
Martin, M., 18
Martin, S., 105
Martineau, Harriet, 9, 10
Marx, Karl, 11, 12, 13, 15, 18, 21, 22, 67, 118, 186, 189, 191, 192, 193, 214, 242, 267, 324, 349, 352, 361, 375, 376, 397, 408, 412
Maryanski, Alexandra R., 411
Mason, J. W., 388
Massey, Douglas S., 226, 245, 388
Maugh, Thomas H., II, 399
Mead, George Herbert, 17, 18, 82, 83, 84, 85, 86, 89
Mead, Margaret, 265, 267
Mencimer, Stephanie, 95
Mendez, Jennifer Bickman, 121
Menzel, Peter, 4
Merrill, David A., 409, 410
Merton, Robert, 13, 14, 35, 49, 109, 134, 138, 158, 168, 169, 174
Messner, Michael A., 171, 265, 338
Meyer, Marshall W., 121
Michael, Robert T., 46, 308
Michaels, Stuart, 46
Michals, Jennifer M., 202
Michels, Robert, 123, 126, 409
Milgram, Stanley, 159, 160, 336
Mill, John Stuart, 267
Miller, D. L., 135
Miller, Jake, 204
Miller, Reuben, 365
Miller, Robert F., 169
Mills, C. Wright, 3, 6, 11, 139, 191, 200, 336, 349, 361
Minyard, Staci, 92
Mirapaul, Matthew, 135
Mitchell, Faith, 253
Mizruchi, Mark S., 362
Moaveni, Azadeh, 261, 262
Moeller, Susan D., 139
Moen, Phyllis, 273
Mogelonsky, Marcia, 302
Monaghan, Peter, 41
Monmaney, Terence, 394
Monteiro, Lois A., 395
Montgomery, Marilyn J., 277
Moody, James, 111
Moore, D., 321
Moore, Molly, 221
Moore, Wilbert E., 93, 192, 336, 407
Morin, Richard, 45, 359
Morissette, Alanis, 405
Morris, A., 409
Morris, B., 298
Morrison, Denton E., 408
Mosley, J., 296
Moss, Michael, 161, 248
Muir, Terri, 298
Murdock, George, 58, 294
Murphy, C., 221
Murphy, D., 386
Murray, Jessica, 264
Murray, Velma McBride, 297

N

Naipaul, V. S., 58
Nash, Manning, 241, 242
Navarro, M., 141
Navracruz, Lisa C., 152
Neary, Ian, 222
Nelson, E., 134
Neuman, W. Lawrence, 33
Neville, Bridget, 397
Newman, William M., 243, 244
Newport, Frank, 327
Nichols, Martha, 216
Niebrugge-Brantley, Jill, 12
Nielsen, Joyce McCarl, 263
Nixon, Richard, 138
Nolan, Patrick, 116, 194
Noonan, Rita K., 409
Nordhaus, William D., 195
Norris, Poppa, 325
Novelli, William D., 282
Nussbaum, Daniel, 418

O

Oberschall, Anthony, 408
O'Brien, Steve, 36
O'Connell, Martin, 306
O'Connor, Anne-Marie, 112
O'Connor, Sandra Day, 268
O'Donnell, Jayne, 176
O'Donnell, M., 195
Ogburn, William F., 60, 295, 414
O'Hare, William P., 199
Okamoto, Dina G., 268
Okano, Kaori, 336
Oliver, Melvin L., 196, 203
Ommer, Uwe, 292
Onassis, Jackie, 138
Onishi, Norimitso, 305
Ormond, James, 122
Orum, Anthony M., 357, 408
Orwell, George, 158
Osgood, D. Wayne, 390
Ouchi, William, 124

P

Page, Charles, 123
Pager, Devah, 38, 39, 239, 240
Paik, H., 152
Palla, Seri, 161
Paludi, Michele A., 264
Pamuk, E. D., 396
Park, H., 303
Park, K., 308
Park, Robert, 134, 384
Parker, Alison, 227
Parrott, Sarah A., 340
Parsons, Talcott, 13, 266, 391, 392, 411, 413
Passel, Jeffrey S., 246
Passero, Kathy, 64
Patrick, Danica, 19
Patterson, Thomas E., 359, 363

Pattillo-McCoy, Mary, 90
Pear, Robert, 110
Pearlstein, Steven, 215
Pellow, David Naguib, 420
Pelton, Tom, 38
Perrow, Charles, 123
Peter, Laurence J., 121
Petersen, William, 376
Peterson, Karen S., 306
Phillips, E., 383
Phillips, Susan, 157–158, 169
Piaget, Jean, 85, 86
Pierre, Robert E., 203
Piestewa, Lori, 363
Piliavin, Jane Allyn, 66
Pinderhughes, Dianne, 362
Pinkerton, James P., 336
Pitt, Brad, 138
Plomin, Robert, 82
Plüss, Caroline, 422
Poe, Edgar Allan, 158
Poitier, Sidney, 138
Polletta, Francesca, 411
Polonko, James, 124
Poniewozik, James, 141, 151
Popenoe, David, 307
Porter, Jack Nusan, 327
Poussaint, Alvin F., 90
Power, Samantha, 227
Prah, Pamela M., 126
Presley, Elvis, 261
Pryor, John H., 67, 340
Purdy, Matthew, 255
Purmort, Jess, 396
Pythagoras, 7, 8

Q

Quadagno, Jill, 276, 280
Quart, Alissa, 138
Quillian, Lincoln, 39
Quinney, Richard, 171, 172, 174

R

Rainey, Richard, 151
Rainie, Lee, 135, 143
Rainwater, Lee, 197
Rajan, Gita, 422
Ramet, Sabrina, 407
Ramirez, Eddy, 282
Ramirez, Roberto R., 235
Randolph, Elmo, 255
Rantala, Ramona R., 175
Reagan, Ronald, 138, 356
Reardon, Danny, 162
Reinharz, Shulamit, 37
Reschovsky, Clara, 388
Reuban, C., 396
Rheingold, Howard, 415
Rhodes, Lorna A., 394
Richards, Keith, 138
Richardson, James T., 330
Richardson, L., 298
Rideout, Victoria, 93
Ridgeway, Cecilia, 268

Riding, Alan, 142, 200
Rifkin, Jeremy, 414
Riley, J., 281
Riley, M., 414
Rimer, Sara, 281
Ripley, Amanda, 265
Ritzer, George, 59, 60, 122
Rivoli, Pietra, 211
Roberson, Debi, 63
Roberts, D. F., 135
Roberts, Donald F., 93
Roberts, Julia, 138, 139
Robertson, Roland, 193
Robinson, J. Gregory, 245, 246
Robinson, John P., 273
Robinson, Thomas N., 152
Robison, 265
Rodenburg, Eric, 420
Rodgers, Diane M., 409
Roehling, Patricia, 273
Roethlisberger, Fritz J., 123
Roosevelet, Franklin D., 356
Rose, Arnold, 242
Rose, P., 88
Rosenberg, D., 189, 350
Rosenberg, Howard, 150
Rosenberg, Y., 359
Rosenthal, Robert, 338
Rossi, Alice, 302
Rossi, Peter, 43, 194
Rossides, Daniel, 188
Roszak, Theodore, 69
Ruane, Janet M., 7
Rubel, Maximilien, 412
Rubin, Alissa J., 65
Rule, James B., 408
Rusnick, David, 219
Russo, Nancy Felipe, 264
Rutenberg, Jim, 148
Ryan, William, 200
Rymer, Russ, 80

S

Saad, Lydia, 305, 309
Sachs, Jeffrey D., 212, 217, 219
Sadker, David Miller, 336
Sadker, Myra Pollack, 336
Sagarin, Edward, 168
Sale, Kirkpatrick, 414
Salem, Richard, 23
Samuelson, Paul, 195
Sanchez, Jose, 168
Sanders, Edmund, 92
Saporito, Bill, 391
Sarkisian, Natalia, 301
Sassen, Saskia, 246
Sawyer, Reid L., 365
Sax, Linda J., 7, 67, 320
Sayer, Liana C., 273, 296
Scarce, Rik, 40, 41, 42
Schaefer, Richard T., 72, 237, 239, 276
Scharnberg, Kirsten, 17
Schmidley, A. Dianne, 245, 246
Schmitt, Erica L., 256
Schnaiberg, Allan, 420

Schneider, Barbara, 109, 392
Schor, Juliet B., 54
Schur, Edwin M., 161, 174
Schurman, Rachel, 417
Schwartz, H., 394
Schwartz, J., 149
Schwartz, Pepper, 299
Schwartz, Shalom H., 66
Schwarzenegger, Arnold, 210
Scopes, John T., 342
Scott, A., 411
Scott, G., 15, 18
Scott, J., 397
Scott, W., 124
Seabrook, Jeremy, 21
Secretan, Theirry, 280
Seefeldt, Kristin S., 205
Segall, Alexander, 392
Segerstrale, Ullica, 61
Seibring, T. F., 162
Seidman, Steven, 263
Sellers, Frances Stead, 423
Sengupta, Somini, 266
Sernau, Scott, 203, 355
Shanahan, Michael J., 277
Shapiro, Joseph P., 203
Shapiro, Thomas M., 196
Sharma, Shailja, 422
Shaw, George Bernard, 337
Sheen, Martin, 141
Shepard, Matthew, 341
Sherman, Jill, 334
Shin, Hyon B., 71
Shinkai, Hiroguki, 179
Shipler, David K., 185, 186, 190, 196
Shostak, Arthur B., 364
Shu, Xialing, 354
Shue, Elisabeth, 152
Shupe, Anson, 37
Simmons, A., 164, 360
Simmons, Tavia, 306
Simons, Marlise, 203
Singh, Leona, 300
Slavin, Robert E., 72
Smart, Barry, 118
Smedley, Brian D., 397
Smeeding, Timothy, 197
Smelser, Neil, 350
Smith, Adam, 350
Smith, Craig, 135, 301, 324
Smith, D. A., 383
Smith, Dan, 364
Smith, David M., 308
Smith, Denise, 281
Smith-Lovin, Lynn, 268
Smith, M., 386
Smith, Tom, 244, 328
Smits, Jimmy, 141
Snell, Tracy L., 180
Snyder, Thomas D., 414
Sorell, Gwendolyn T., 277
Spain, Daphne, 305
Spar, Debora L., 406, 407
Spears, Britney, 59
Spencer, Herbert, 13, 15
Spengler, Joseph J., 381
Spielmann, Peter James, 228

Spitzer, Steven, 172
Springsteen, Bruce, 138
Squires, Gregory D., 385
Staggenborg, Suzanne, 408
Stalker, Peter, 245
Standing, Guy, 423
Stark, Rodney, 316, 328, 330
Starr, Paul, 392, 413
Stavenhagen, Rodolfo, 224
Steele, James B., 227, 250
Stenning, Derrick J., 274
Stevenson, David, 109
Stewman, Shelby, 239
Steyerberg, Ewout, 397
Stohr, Oskar, 81
Stone, Lucy, 337
Stovel, Katherine, 111
Strauss, 272, 362
Suitor, Jill, 92
Sullivan, Harry Stack, 84
Sumner, William Graham 109, 234
Sunstein, Cass, 43, 143
Sutcliffe, Bob, 212
Sutherland, Edwin, 169, 170, 174, 175
Swatos, William H., Jr., 321
Sweet, Kimberly, 46
Szasz, Thomas, 394

Talbot, Margaret, 80
Tannen, Deborah, 268
Tapscott, 133
Tarrow, Sidney, 408
Taylor, Elizabeth, 138
Taylor, Jonathan, 250
Taylor, P. J., 339
Taylor, Verta, 410
Tedeschi, Bob, 112
Telsch, Kathleen, 283
Terry, Sara, 308
Therrien, Melissa, 235
Thomas, R., 68
Thomas, William I., 102, 236
Thompson, C., 125
Thompson, G., 224, 226
Thompson, T., 220
Thomson, E., 296
Thornton, Russell, 236
Tienda, Marta, 253
Tierney, J., 70, 376
Tillipman, Hava, 281
Tilly, Charles, 410
Timberlake, Justin, 145
Timberlake, Michael, 383
Tolbert, Katherine, 89
Tonkinson, Robert, 274
Tönnies, Ferdinand, 101, 115, 116, 118, 119, 387
Touraine, Alain, 334
Treiman, Donald, 194, 222
Trotter, Robert T., III, 397
Trow, Martin, 341
Trumbull, Mark, 202
Tsuchiya, Motonori, 336
Tsutsui, Kiyoteru, 223

Tuchman, Gaye, 267
Tumin, Melvin M., 193
Ture, Kwame, 248
Turkle, Sherry, 416
Turner, B., 118
Twai, Mark, 158
Twain, Shania, 145, 146f
Tyre, Peg, 298

U

Uchitelle, Louis, 282
Ullman, Edward, 385
Urbina, Ian, 150
Usher, 146f
Utne, Leif, 224

V

van Driel, Barend, 330
van Vucht Tijssen, Lieteke, 118
Vasagar, Jeeren, 360
Veblen, Thorstein, 192, 413
Vega, William A., 302
Ventura, Stephanie J., 304
Vermeer, Jan, 58
Vernon, Glenn, 331
Vidaver, R. M., 398
Villarosa, Linda, 284
Villarreal, Andres, 173
Vitow, Ruth, 276

W

Wachner, Linda, 348
Wagley, Charles, 234, 274
Waite, Linda, 143
Waitzkin, Howard, 397
Waldinger, Roger, 421
Walesa, Lech, 407
Wallace, Ruth A., 412
Wallerstein, Immanuel, 214, 215, 216, 225, 271
Wallerstein, Judith A., 307
Wallerstein, M., 126
Wallis, Claudia, 343
Walt, Vivienne, 150
Washington, George, 334
Watson, Paul, 332
Watts, Duncan J., 110
Wax, Emily, 360
Weber, Max, 12, 13, 43, 46, 71, 101, 119, 121, 122, 123, 186, 191, 192, 200, 323, 328, 339, 355
Wechsler, Henry, 162
Weeks, Jane, 397
Weeks, John R., 376, 381
Weinberg, Daniel H., 272
Weinstein, Deena, 143, 416
Weinstein, H., 240
Weinstein, Michael A., 143, 416
Weisbrot, Mark, 219
Wells-Barnett, Ida, 12, 16, 22, 267
Wentz, Laurel, 142

Wertsman, Vladimir, 252
West, Candace, 263, 268
Whitehead, Barbara Dafoe, 307
Whyte, William F., 37
Wickman, Peter M., 163
Wilde, Marta L., 152
Wilford, John Noble, 116
Wilgoren, Jodi, 343
Williams, Alexander, 290
Williams, C. J., 298
Williams, C. L., 272
Williams, David R., 248, 397
Williams, R., 335
Williams, W., 89
Willing, Richard, 176
Wilson, E., 60, 61
Wilson, J., 408
Wilson, William Julius, 110, 199, 203, 243, 301, 323, 389
Wines, Michael, 309
Wirth, Louis, 383
Witte, Griff, 190
Wolf, Alison, 412
Wolf, Naomi, 163
Wolff, Edward N., 196
Wollstonecraft, Mary, 267
Wolraich, M., 161
Wood, Julia T., 142
Woodard, C., 334
Wortham, Robert A., 15
Wright, C., 134, 146, 360
Wright, E. O., 193
Wright, E. R., 171
Wynyard, Robin, 60

X

Xie, Wen, 194

Y

Yamagata, Hisashi, 239
Yeh, Kuang S., 239
Yinger, J. Milton, 329
Young, Alford A., Jr., 15
Young, G., 224
Yufe, Jack, 81

Z

Zang, Xiaowei, 354
Zapata-Mancilla, Tiffany, 176
Zarembo, Alan, 43, 101, 363
Zellner, William M., 70
Zernike, Kate, 68
Zhang, Ziyi, 142
Zia, Helen, 233, 234, 244
Zimbardo, Philip, 100, 101, 102, 104, 363
Zimmerman, Don H., 263, 268
Zola, Irving K., 392
Zvekic, Uglijea, 179
Zweigenhaft, Richard L., 348, 349, 362

subject index

Page numbers followed by *f* refer to figures.
Page numbers followed by *t* refer to tables.

A

AARP (American Association for Retired Persons), 282
Abortion, 283–285
  public funding, by state, 284f
  for sex selection, 380
  worldwide, 285–286
Absolute poverty, 197, 206
Abu Graib prison, 101, 160
Achieved status, 103, 128, 186, 206
Activists, social. *See* Social activists
Activity theory, 276, 286
Adolescents
  gay and lesbian, 340–341
  and popularity, 92t
  and religion, 7, 8
  sexual networks, 111
  subcultures, 340–341
Adoption, 303, 311
Adulthood, transitional milestones to, 87t
Advertising, 138, 314
  and market research, 145–146
Affirmative action, 241, 338, 365, 366
  definition, 370
Afghanistan
  infant mortality rate, 393t
  languages used in, 62f
  population structure, 381f
  poverty level, 218f
  religious fundamentalism, 414
  terrorist incidents, 365f
AFL-CIO (American Federation of Labor-Congress of Industrial Organizations), 125
Africa, 212f. *See also* individual countries
  labor migration, 422f
  terrorist incidents, 365f
African Americans
  and criminal justice system, 171, 172
  health and illness, 394, 397
  infant mortality rate, 397
  marriage and family, 301
  media portrayal, 140, 141
  median income, 239f
  middle class, 203, 248
  and politics, 358
  population distribution, United States, 247f
  in poverty, 247–248, 282
  single-parent families, 302f
  in slavery, 248, 394
  as social activists, 103
  social mobility of, 204
  as sociologists, 12, 16, 17
  in U.S. population, 235
    projected, 236f
African entrepreneurs, 60
African Queen (film), 138
Age
  and health and illness, 398–399

Internet use by, 145f
Ageism, 282–283, 286
Aging, 273–283. *See also* Elderly
  activity theory, 276, 277t
  conflict perspective, 276–277
  disengagement theory, 274, 275, 277t
  functionalist perspective, 274–275
  interactionist perspective, 277t
  of population, 281
    by state, 282f
  and retirement, 278–279
  worldwide, 275
Agrarian societies, 117, 117t, 128
AIDS/HIV, 18, 399–400
  and drug abuse, 18, 20
  effect on population, 379
  as master status, 394–395
  people living with, worldwide, 400f
  sufferer, as master status, 103
Air pollution, 418
Al Hurra, 150
Al Jazeera, 150
Al-Qaeda, 120, 150
Alabama
  abortion funding, 284f
  anti-gay laws, 310f
  Arab American population, 253f
  cohabitation, 306f
  educational level, 32f
  elderly population, projected, 282f
  executions, since 1972, 170f
  household income, 32f
  median household income, 187f
  medical marijuana, 163f
  physicians, availability of, 398f
  union membership, 127f
Alaska
  abortion funding, 284f
  anti-gay laws, 310f
  Arab American population, 253f
  cohabitation, 306f
  educational level, 32f
  elderly population, projected, 282f
  executions, since 1972, 170f
  household income, 32f
  median household income, 187f
  physicians, availability of, 398f
  union membership, 127f
Albania, languages used in, 62f
Algeria
  languages used in, 62f
  terrorist incidents, 365f
Alienation, 119, 128
Amalgamation, 243
Amazon.com, 59
American Academy of Cosmetic Surgery, 164
American Academy of Pediatrics, 138, 161
American Dad (TV show), 151t
American Federation of Teachers, 340
American Idol (TV show), 151t, 303
American Indians. *See* Native Americans
American Jewish Committee (AJC), 255
American Lung Association, 39
American Medical Association (AMA), 413

American Sociological Association (ASA), 14t, 22, 23, 23f, 24, 40, 41, 414
  Code of Ethics, 42, 46
American Sociological Society, 12
Americans with Disabilities Act, 124
Amish, 90
Amnesty International, 228, 364
Amnesty USA, 256
Andorra, languages used in, 62f
Angola
  computer network readiness, 220
  income per capita, 213f
Animism, 317f
Anomie, 10, 168, 181
Anomie theory of deviance, 168–169, 174f
Anti-Defamation League (ADL), 254
Anti-Semitism, 254
Anticipatory socialization, 88, 97
AOL (America Online), 148
Apartheid, 245
  American, 388
Appalachian Mountains, 198
Applied sociology, 18
Apprentice, The (TV show), 139
Arab Americans, 252, 253
  after September 11, 161, 171, 237, 253, 256
  population, by state, 253f
Arab cultures, 64, 65
Argentina
  Gross Domestic Product (GDP), 217t
  income per capita, 213f
  languages used in, 62f
  terrorist incidents, 365f
  women in, 360
Argot, 69, 74
Arizona
  anti-gay laws, 310f
  Arab American population, 253f
  cohabitation, 306f
  educational level, 32f
  elderly population, projected, 282f
  executions, since 1972, 170f
  household income, 32f
  median household income, 187f
  medical marijuana, 163f
  physicians, availability of, 398f
  union membership, 127f
Arkansas
  abortion funding, 284f
  anti-gay laws, 310f
  Arab American population, 253f
  cohabitation, 306f
  educational level, 32f
  elderly population, projected, 282f
  household income, 32f
  median household income, 187f
  medical marijuana, 163f
  physicians, availability of, 398f
  union membership, 127f
Armenia, languages used in, 62f
Arthur Andersen, 361
Artifacts, cultural, 4–5, 60
Ascribed status, 102, 102–103, 119, 128, 186
Asia, 212f. *See also* individual countries
Asia, terrorist incidents, 365f
Asian American Dreams (Zia), 233–234

Asian Americans, 233–234, 249, 251–252
  major groups, United States, 249f
  as model minorities, 249
  and politics, 358
  population distribution, United States, 247f
  single-parent families, 302f
  in U.S. population, 235
    projected, 236f
Assimilation, 244
Audience, media, 145–146
Audience networks, 146f
Australia
  absolute poverty, 197f
  labor migration, 422f
  languages used in, 62f
  people ever married, percentage, 299f
  terrorist incidents, 365f
  voter turnout, 358f
Austria
  culture, 60
  educational level, 333f
  income per capita, 213f
Authority
  definition, 370
  types of, 355–356
Aviation and Transportation Security Act, 240
Avon Corporation, 203

B

Baby boom, 380
Baby Name Wizard, 41
Baghdad, Iraq, 36
  urbanization, projected, 384f
Bahrain, 150
Bangalore, urbanization, projected, 384f
Bangkok, urbanization, projected, 384f
Bangladesh
  computer network readiness, 220
  Gross Domestic Product (GDP), 217t
  income distribution, 221f
  income per capita, 213f
  poverty level, 218f
Baptists, 330f
Basic sociology, 20
Beauty myth, 163
Beijing, urbanization, projected, 384f
Belarus, languages used in, 62f
Belgium
  income per capita, 212, 213f
  languages used in, 62f
  terrorist incidents, 365f
Benin
  languages used in, 62f
  poverty level, 218f
Berkeley Wellness Letter, 302
Bernie Mac (TV show), 151t
BET (Black Entertainment Television), 141, 148
Beverly Hills 90210 (TV show), 145
Bhutan, 149
  languages used in, 62f
Bilateral descent, 295, 311

Bilingualism, 71, 71–74, 7–
Billboard magazine, 39
Binge drinking, 162
Biology, and social behavior, 60, 61
Biotechnology, 416
Birthrate, 377, 402
Black Americans. *See African Americans*
Black Picket Fences (Pattillo), 78–79
Black power, 248, 258
Black separatists, 238f
Bogata, urbanization, projected, 384f
Bolivia
    computer network readiness, 220
    languages used in, 62
    poverty level, 218f
Borderlands, 225, 226f, 2 0
Born to Buy (Schor), 54–55
Bosnia, war crimes, 227
Boston Pops, 119
Botswana, 104
Bourgeoisie, 189, 206
Bosnia & Herzogovena, languages used in, 62f
Brady Bunch (TV show) 136
Brain drain, 392, 402
Brand marketing, 54
Brazil
    economic forecast, 3–3f
    income distribution, 221f
    income per capita, 2 3f
    languages used in, 62f
    poverty level, 218f
British Petroleum (BP) revenues, 217t
Brown University, 396
*Brown v. Board of Education of Topeka,
        Kansas,* 248, 435
Buddhism, 317f, 318, 3 9, 320t, 321
Buenos Aires, urbanization, projected, 384f
Bulgaria, languages used in, 62f
Bureau of Indian Affairs (BIA), 248
Bureau of Labor Statistics, 93, 125, 127f
Bureaucracy, 119, 128
    characteristics of, 119–121, 121t
        at McDonald's, 122
    and organizational culture, 123–124
    in school systems, 339–341
Bureaucratization, 121, 123, 129
    and labor unions, 126
Burkina Faso, poverty level, 218f
Burundi, languages used in, 62f

Cairo, urbanization, projected, 384f
California
    abortion funding, 284f
    anti-gay laws, 310
    Arab American population, 253f
    cohabitation, 306f
    educational level, 32f
    elderly population, projected, 282f
    executions, since 1972, 170f
    medical marijuana, 163f
    physicians, availability of, 398f
California Civil Rights Initiative, 366
Calvinism, 323
Cambodia
    poverty level, 218f
    voter turnout, 358f
Cambridge University, 376
Cameroon, languages used in, 62f
Canada
    absolute poverty, 197f

bilingualism, 72
computer network readiness, 220
educational level, 333f
gender stratification, 271f
income distribution, 221f
infant mortality rate, 392t
life expectancy, 378f
media penetration, 148f
religious participation, 327f
voter turnout, 358f
women in, 360
Canadian immigrants, in U.S. population,
        246f
Capital punishment, 179–180
    executions, by state, 170f
Capitalism, 189, 206, 349–350, 352t
    in China, 353, 354–355
    definition, 350, 370
Careers in sociology, 22–24, 44
    community activist, 24
    research assistant, 396
    research coordinator, 44
    victim witness specialist, 176
Caribbean Islands, 212f
    people living with AIDS, 400f
Casinos, Native American, 250
Castes, 187, 188, 206
Catholic Church, 330f
Catholicism, 322, 323–324
Caucus for Producers, Writers & Directors,
        141
Causal logic, 32, 33f, 50
CBS News, 160
Censorship, 139, 354
    in global community, 415–416
Census, 376, 402
Census Bureau, 7, 71, 190 197, 201, 224, 235t,
        239, 248, 271f, 303, 307, 333, 334,
        335, 339t, 380, 399
Center for Academic Integrity, 68
Center for American Women and Politics, 360
Centers for Disease Control and Prevention
        (CDC), 111
Central African Republic, languages used in,
        62f
Central Europe, people living with AIDS, 400f
Central Intelligence Agency (CIA), 120
Chad
    computer network readiness, 220
    languages used in, 62f
Charismatic authority, 356, 370
Cheating, academic, 68
Chernobyl Forum, 418
Chicago Coalition for the Homeless, 43
Child abuse, 289
Child care, 94–96
Children, and marketing, 54, 55
Children Now, 2004, 141
Chile
    income per capita, 213f
    languages used in, 62f
    terrorist incidents, 365f
China
    bilingualism, 72
    capitalism in, 353, 354–355
    censorship, 139, 354–355, 415–416
    culture, 56, 58, 70
    death penalty, 179
    economic forecast, 353f
    education in, 337
    environmental problems, 418
    female infanticide, 221, 380
    income per capita, 213f

Internet access, 139, 415–416
Internet access in, 354–355
life expectancy, 378f
people ever married, percentage, 299f
population control, 373, 380
poverty level, 218f
sexuality in, 46–47
social mobility in, 222
women in, 354, 360
China Daily, 58
Chinese Americans, 233–234, 249, 251
Chinese Exclusion Act, 251
Chinese immigrants, in U.S. population, 246f
Christianity, 317f, 318, 320t. *See also*
        Catholicism; Protestant
        denominations
    fundamentalist, 342–343
CIA (Central Intelligence Agency), 120
Circumcision, female, 227–228
Cities, 382–383
City of Angels, 141
Civil Liberties Act, 251
Civil Rights Act, 1964, 241, 242
Civil rights, after September 11, 11, 161, 237,
        253, 256, 364, 415
Civil rights model of disability, 104
Civil rights movement, 248
Class consciousness, 190, 206
Class, social, 206
    and childraising, 290–291
    definition, 171, 191
    and education, 337
    and educational access, 202
    and health and illness, 396–397
    and marriage, 301
    measuring, 194–195
Class system, 188, 188–189, 194–201, 206
    shrinking middle class, 190
Classical theory, 123, 129
Clinical sociology, 20
Closed system, 201, 206
CNN network, 142
Coalition, 110, 129
Cockfighting, 6
Code of ethics, 40, 50
Code of Ethics (American Sociological
        Association), 40, 42, 46
Cognitive theory of development, 85, 86t, 97
Cohabitation, 306, 311
    by state, 306f
Cold War era, 63
Collective decision making, 124
College students
    binge drinking, 162
    cheating, 68
    impression management, 85
    life goals, 66, 67, 67f
    and religion, 7, 8
    subcultures, 341
Colombia
    income distribution, 221
    languages used in, 62f
    poverty level, 218f
    terrorist incidents, 365f
    voter turnout, 358f
Colonialism, 214, 230
Colorado
    abortion funding, 284f
    anti-gay laws, 310f
    Arab American population, 253f
    cohabitation, 306f
    educational level, 32f
    elderly population, projected, 282f

executions, since 1972, 170f
    household income, 32f
    median household income, 187f
    medical marijuana, 163f
    physicians, availability of, 398f
    union membership, 127f
Columbia University, 31
Columbine High School, 109, 152
Commission on Civil Rights, 240, 271
Common sense, and research, 7, 8
Communication
    nonverbal, 64
    verbal. *See* Language
Communism, 352, 352t, 370
Communist League, 11
Communist Manifesto, The (Marx), 11, 12, 119
Communities, types of, 387–389
Community, 375, 402
    changes in, 381–382
Comoros, poverty level, 218f
Compassion Capital Fund, 323
Computer Security Institute, 176
Concentric-zone theory, 384, 385f, 402
Confidentiality, 40, 41, 42
Conflict perspective, 15, 15–16, 18t
    on aging, 276–277, 277t
    on bureaucracies, 119–120
    on crime, 171, 172–173
    on culture, 67, 69, 71t
    on deviance, 171, 173
    on education, 334–335, 336, 337, 339–340,
        339t
    on environmental problems, 420–421
    on the family, 296, 298t
    on global immigration, 422
    on health and illness, 392–393, 395t, 397
    on the Internet, 415–416
    on labor unions, 123
    on the media, 139–140, 142, 146t
    on multinational corporations, 215–216,
        221t
    on poverty, 199
    on race, 242, 243t
    on religion, 324, 325t
    on social change, 413, 413t
    on social institutions, 113–114
    on sports, 19
    on status, 102
    on stratification, 193, 194f
    on stratification by gender, 266–267, 268t,
        270
    on urbanization, 386–387, 387t
Conformity, 159, 169, 181
Confucianism, 317f, 320
Congo, Democratic Republic of, 198, 350, 351
    income per capita, 213f
    poverty level, 218f
Congo, languages used in, 62f
Connecticut
    abortion funding, 284f
    anti-gay laws, 310f
    Arab American population, 253f
    cohabitation, 306f
    educational level, 32f
    elderly population, projected, 282f
    executions, since 1972, 170f
    household income, 32f
    median household income, 187f
    medical marijuana, 163f
    physicians, availability of, 398f
Conspicuous consumption 192
Conspicuous leisure, 192
Consumerism, 54–55

Contact hypothesis, 242–243, 258
Content analysis, 39, 50
Contexts (journal), 210–211
Control group, 38, 50
Control theory, 163, 181
Control variable, 34, 50
Core nations, and periphery nations. *See*
  World systems analysis
Cornell University, 68
Corporal punishment, 161
Corporate crime, 175, 176
Corporate Policy Institute, 141
Corporate welfare, 204, 206
Corporations
  media, 147–149
  multinational. *See* Multinational
    corporations
  scandals, 361–362
Correlation, 32, 50
Correspondence principle, 337, 344
Cosby Show, The, 136
Costa Rica
  income per capita, 213*f*
  languages used in, 62*f*
Council on Scientific Affairs, 397
Countercultures, 69–70, 70, 74
  theoretical perspectives on, 71*t*
Courtship, 298, 300
Craigslist.com, 239
Creationism, 342, 343, 344
Credentialism, 336, 344
Crime, 173, 173–174, 175, 176–179
  conflict perspective, 171, 172–173
  corporate, 175, 176
  definition, 173
  organized, 175, 182
  professional, 174, 175
  technology-based, 175, 176
  transnational, 176–177, 182
  victimless, 174, 182
  victims, 176
  white-collar, 175, 176, 182
Crime rates, 178–179
Crime statistics, 177–179
Criminal justice system
  conflict perspective, 171, 172–173
  Navajo Nation Police Department, 105
Croatia, languages used in, 62*f*
Cross-tabulation, 48, 50
C.S.I. (Crime Scene Investigation) (TV show),
  151*t*
Cuba
  languages used in, 62*f*
  terrorist incidents, 365*f*
  women in, 360
Cuban Americans, 254
Cuban immigrants, in U.S. population, 246*f*
Cults, religious, 329–330, 331*t,* 345
Cultural diffusion, 58–60
Cultural relativism, 71, 74
Cultural transmission, of deviance, 169, 174*f,*
  181
Cultural universals, 58, 74, 316, 344
Culture, 55, 74
  biological bases of, 60, 61
  elements of
    language, 55, 58, 61–64
    nonverbal communication, 64
    norms, 67
    sanctions, 65–66
    values, 66
  exporting, of United States', 141–142
  and food, 56–57

globalization of, 58–60
  organizational, 123–124
  subcultures, 68–69
  theoretical perspectives on, 71*t*
Culture lag, 60, 74, 414, 424
Culture shock, 70, 74
Culture, 59, 74
Culture wars, 323
Curanderismo, 397, 402
Curandero, 398
Current Population Survey, 246*f*
Czech Republic
  gender stratification, 271*f*
  languages used in, 62*f*

Daimler Chrysler Corporation, revenues, 217*t*
Dalit, 188
Dances With Wolves (film), 63
Dancing with the Stars (TV show), 151*t*
Darwinism, 343
Das Kapital (Marx), 12
Data analysis, 47–48
Data collection, 33, 35, 36–37, 38, 39, 40*t*
D.C., The (TV show), 151*t*
Death and dying, 280–281
Death of White Sociology, The (Joyce Ladner),
  43
Death of White Sociology, The (Ladner), 43
Death penalty, 179–180
  executions, by state, 170*f*
Death Penalty Information Center, 179, 181
Death rate, 377, 402
Defense Intelligence Agency, 120
Degradation ceremony, 89, 97
Deindustrialization, 370
Delaware
  abortion funding, 284*f*
  Arab American population, 253*f*
  cohabitation, 306*f*
  educational level, 32*f*
  elderly population, projected, 282*f*
  executions, since 1972, 170*f*
  household income, 32*f*
  median household income, 187*f*
  medical marijuana, 163*f*
  physicians, availability of, 398*f*
  union membership, 127*f*
Dell Corporation, 140
Democracy, 357, 371
Demographic transition, 378, 402
Demography, 375–377, 376, 402
  definition, 376
  elements of, 377
  world population patterns, 377–380
Denmark
  aid to developing nations, 216
  computer network readiness, 220
  languages used in, 62*f*
  suicide rate, 9
Denominations, religious, 327, 328, 331*t,* 344
Department of Agriculture, 390
Department of Health, Education and
  Welfare, 338
DePauw University, 351
Dependency theory, 214, 219, 221*t,* 230
Dependent variable, 32, 50
Desperate Housewives (TV show), 151*t*
Developing countries. *See also* Social
  inequality, global
    aid to, 216
    cultural domination of, 59, 142, 149

exploitation, in global economy, 214–226,
  350–351
  hunger in, 211
  and Internet access, 144*f,* 220
  women in, 221, 222
Deviance, 163, 163–164
  conflict perspective, 171, 173
  definition, 181
  feminist perspective, 173, 174*f*
  functionalist perspective, 168–169, 173
  interactionist perspective, 169–171, 174*f*
  labeling theory of, 171
  routine activities theory, 170, 174*f*
  as social construct, 166–167
  social constructionist perspective, 171,
    174*f*
  and technology, 165
Dharma and Greg (TV show), 141
Dictatorship, 371
Differential association, 169, 174*f,* 181
Differential justice, 172, 181
Diffusion, 59, 74
Digital divide, 144*f,* 145*f,* 200–201
Digital Solidarity Fund, 220
Directors Guild of America, 141
Disability, as master status, 103, 104
Disabled people
  and Hurricane Katrina, 7
  status of, 189
Disasters, community reaction to, 7
Discovery, 58, 74
Discrimination, 238–243, 258
  and affirmative action, 241, 338
  age, 282–283
  benefits, for dominant group, 239–240,
    241
  gender, 268, 269–273
  institutional, 240, 286
  vs. prejudice, 238–239
  racial, 39, 238–240
  reverse, 366
  sexual preference, 310*f*
  wage, 272
Disengagement theory, 274, 275, 277*t,* 286
Disney Corporation, 142, 148
Disneyworld, Paris, 118
Diversity: *See specific* ethnic, gender,
  racial, and religious groups
Diversity in the Power Elite (Zweigenhaft and
  Domhoff), 348–349, 362
Division of labor
  in bureaucracies, 119
  and social structure, 114–115
Division of Labor in Society (Durkheim),
  12, 114
Divorce
  impact on children, 305–306, 307
  trends in, 305*f*
Do the Right Thing (film), 252
Doctors Without Borders, 228, 364
Domestic partnership, 309
Domestic violence, 297, 311. *See also* Child
  abuse
Dominant ideology, 67, 67–68, 75, 140, 193
  definition, 206
Dominican immigrants, in U.S. population,
  246*f*
Dominican Republic
  income per capita, 213*f*
  languages used in, 62*f*
Doonesbury (cartoon), 34
Downsizing, 367, 371
Dramaturgical approach, 17, 84, 97

Driving while Black (DWB), 171, 255
Drug abusers, and AIDS/HIV, 18, 20
Drunk driving, 174
Djibouti, languages used in, 62*f*
Dugum Dani language, 63
Duke University, 68
Dysfunction, 14, 14–15

E-mail, in the workplace, 125
E. T. (film), 138
East Asia, people living with AIDS, 400*f*
Eastern Europe, 212*f. See also* individual
  countries
    economic security, 423
    people living with AIDS, 400*f*
    social change, 414–415
EBay, 59
Ebony magazine, 138
Ecclesiae, 327, 331*t,* 344
Economic Security Index, 422–423
Economic system, definition, 349
Economic systems, 350–352, 352, 352*t,* 371
  pluralist model, 362
  power elite models, 361–362
Economies, world's largest, 353*f*
Economist, The, 21, 83, 142, 151, 198, 220,
  285, 390
Ecuador
  computer network readiness, 220
  income per capita, 213*f*
  poverty level, 218*f*
  terrorist incidents, 365*f*
Edge cities, 385
Education, 316. *See also* Schools
  conflict perspective, 334–335, 336, 337,
    339–340, 339*t*
  definition, 344
  financial aid, 202
  functionalist perspective, 336, 339, 339*t*
  homeschooling, 341–342
  and household income by state, 32*f*
  and income, 31, 34*f*
  interactionist perspective, 337, 338, 339*t*
  and Internet usage, 145*f*
  in Japan, 336–337
  level, by country, 333*f*
  by religion and income, 322
  and social class, 337
  and status, 336
  for women, 221, 337
Egalitarian families, 295, 311
Egocasting, 143
Egypt
  languages used in, 62*f*
  voter turnout, 358*f*
El Salvador
  domestic violence, 297
  income per capita, 213*f*
  languages used in, 62*f*
El Salvadoran immigrants, in U.S. population,
  246*f*
Elderly, 102–103. *See also* Aging
  caring for, 277–278
  growth, of population, 281*f*
  in labor force, 282–283
  in poverty, 281–282
Electric shock experiments, of Milgram,
  159–160
Electronic Communications Privacy Act, 415

Elementary Forms of Religious Life (Durkheim), 12
Elite model, 361, 371
Employment
    and discrimination, 35, 271–272
    for elderly, 282–283
    loss of, 367–368
    reasons for leaving, by gender, 273f
    retirement from, 278–279
    women's, 271–273
Employment based on technical qualifications, 121
Endogamy, 298, 311
Engle v. Vitale, 342
English language, 63, 71–74
Enron, 361
Environmental justice, 420, 424
Environmental problems, 418–421
    conflict perspective, 420–421
Environmental Protection Agency (EPA), 420
Environmental sociology, 18
Equatorial Guinea, languages used in, 62f
Equilibrium model, 411, 424
Eritrea, 211
    terrorist incidents, 365f
Essays on the Principle of Population (Malthus), 375
Established sect, 329, 344
Estate system, 188, 206
Esteem, 194, 206
Estonia
    income per capita, 213f
    languages used in, 62f
Ethics, research, 40, 41
    and funding, 42, 43
    and value neutrality, 43
Ethiopia
    computer network readiness, 220
    languages used in, 62f
Ethnic cleansing, 227, 243
Ethnic group, definition, 234, 258
Ethnic groups, United States, 236, 237
    percentage of population, 235t
        projected, 236f
    white, 255
Ethnocentrism, 70, 75, 237, 258
Ethnograph software, 44
Ethnography, 37, 50
Eurasia, terrorist incidents, 365f
Europe
    labor migration, 422f
    poverty level, 218f
    terrorist incidents, 365f
European Union (EU), 246
Euthanasia, 280–281
Evangelical Lutheran Church, 330f
Everybody Hates Chris (TV show), 151t
Evolutionary perspective, on social change, 413t, 424
Evolutionary theory, 411
Exogamy, 298, 311
Experience, religious, 326–327
Experiment, 37
Experimental group, 38, 50
Exploitation theory, 242, 258
Expressiveness, 266, 286
Extended family, 291, 311
Extreme Makeover (TV show), 151t
Exxon Mobil Corporation, 42, 43, 46, 418, 419
    revenues, 217t
Exxon Valdez oil spill, 43, 418

Face-work, 84, 86t, 97
False consciousness, 190, 206, 324, 409
Families
    dual-income, 303
    egalitarian, 311
    grandparents' role, 302
    single-parent, 301, 302f, 303–304
    step, 304–305
Familism, 301, 311
Family, 291
    conflict perspective, 298t
    defining, 291, 292
    definition, 311
    extended, 291, 311
    feminist perspective, 296–298
    functionalist perspective, 295–296, 298t
    gender stratification in, 295
    and kinship, 294–295
    media portrayal, 136
    nuclear, 291, 311
Family Guy, The (TV show), 136, 151t
Fattening room, Nigeria, 164
FBI (Federal Bureau of Investigation), 67, 120, 175
    Uniform Crime Reports, 178
FCC (Federal Communications Commission), 148
Federal Bureau of Investigation (FBI), 67, 120, 174
Federal Register, 338
Federal Reserve Board, 251
Female genital mutilation (FGM), 227–228
Female infanticide, 221, 380
Feminist activists, 195
Feminist perspective, 16
    on deviance, 173, 174f
    on the family, 296–298
    on language, 63
    on the media, 142–143, 146t
    on social institutions, 113, 114
    on stratification by gender, 267
Feminization of poverty, 199, 203–204
Fertility, 375, 402
    patterns, United States, 380–383
Filipino immigrants, in U.S. population, 246f
Finland
    absolute poverty, 197f
    computer network readiness, 220
    languages used in, 62f
    people ever married, percentage, 299f
    prisons, 159
First Nations communities, 241. *See also* Native Americans
Florida
    abortion funding, 284f
    anti-gay laws, 310f
    Arab American population, 253f
    cohabitation, 306f
    educational level, 32f
    elderly population, projected, 282f
    executions, since 1972, 170f
    household income, 32f
    median household income, 187f
    medical marijuana, 163f
    physicians, availability of, 398f
    union membership, 127f
Folkways, 65, 75
Food, and culture, 56–57
For This Land (Deloria), 315–316

Forbes magazine, 224
Force, 355, 371
Ford Motor Corporation, revenues, 217t
Formal norms, 64, 66t, 75
Formal organization, 119, 129
Formal social control, 161, 181
Fortune magazine, 217t, 239
Fox Entertainment, 141
France
    absolute poverty, 197f
    culture, 56, 83
    economic forecast, 353f
    income per capita, 213f
    religious participation, 327f
    suicide rate, 9
    terrorist incidents, 365f
    welfare programs, 203
Frankenfood, 416
French Guiana, languages used in, 62f
Friend of the Family Hotline, 297
Friends (TV show), 140
Functionalist perspective, 13, 13–15, 18t
    to aging, 274–275
    on aging, 277t
    on culture, 67, 69, 71t
    on deviance, 168–169, 173
    on education, 333–335, 336, 339, 339t
    on the family, 295–296, 298t
    on health and illness, 391–392, 395t
    on the Internet, 415
    on labor unions, 126
    on the media, 134–135, 138–139, 146t
    on multinational corporations, 215, 221t
    on poverty, 200
    on race, 241–242, 243t
    on religion, 316, 320, 321, 323, 325t
    on social change, 413t
    on social institutions, 112–113
    on sports, 19
    on stratification, 191, 192–193, 194f
    on stratification by gender, 266, 268t
    on urbanization, 384–386, 386, 387t
Fundamentalism, religious, 325, 342–343, 345
Furman v. Georgia, 179

Gabon, languages used in, 62f
Gallup Organization, 36
Gambia, languages used in, 62f
Gambling industry, Native American, 250
Gaming industry, Native American, 250
Gap clothing, 216
Gatekeeping, 139
Gay, Lesbian, and Straight Education Network, 341
Gay marriage, 308–310
Gay-straight alliances, 340–341
Gays and lesbians, adolescents, 340–341
Gemeinschaft, 115, 116t, 119, 124, 129, 387
Gender
    and communication, 269
    and health and illness, 398
    and Internet use, 143
    and language, 63
    and occupational prestige, 194–195
    social construction of, 262–266
    and social mobility, 203, 222–223
    stratification by, 265–273
        in developing countries, 270, 271
        in the family, 295
        industrial nations, 271f

Gender norms, 263–264
Gender-role socialization, 263
Gender roles, 90, 97, 262, 264–265
    across cultures, 265–266
    definition, 263, 286
    in religion, 324, 325
General Electric, 124
    revenues, 217t
General Motors, 354, 367
    revenues, 217t
General Social Survey (GSS), 33, 34f, 45, 244, 322
Generalized other, 83, 86t
Genetic engineering, 416
Genetics
    Human Genome Project, 417
    and socialization, 81–82
Genocide, 243, 258
Georgia
    abortion funding, 284f
    anti-gay laws, 310f
    Arab American population, 253f
    cohabitation, 306f
    educational level, 32f
    elderly population, projected, 282f
    executions, since 1972, 170f
    household income, 32f
    median household income, 187f
    medical marijuana, 163f
    physicians, availability of, 398f
    union membership, 127f
Gerontology, 274
Gesellschaft, 115, 116t, 119, 124, 129, 387
Ghana
    culture, 280
    poverty level, 218f
Ghost Whisperer (TV show), 151t
G.I. Joe, 264
Glass ceiling, 239, 258, 272, 286
Glass Ceiling Commission, 239
Global Alliance for Workers and Communities, 216
Global community, sociology in
    aging, worldwide, 275
    Amish children, 90
    Brazilian culture, 61
    Internet readiness, 220
    al Jazeera, 150
    McDonaldization, 122
    population policy, China, 380
    poverty, relative, 198
    poverty, cutting 219
    tsunami, 2004, 21
    veil, meaning in Islamic cultures, 270
    women in public office, 369
Global economy
    and exploitation, 59, 60, 214–226, 350–351
    and job outsourcing, 216, 225, 367, 368–369
    marketing in the, 53, 59–60
    workers in the, 29–30, 69
    and world debt crisis, 224–225
Global view of the family, 291–295

Globalization, 20, 69. *See also World Systems Analysis*
  and 2004 tsunami, 21
  and culture, 58–60, 77, 141–142
  and cultural domination, 59, 214
  definition, 230, 237
  effect on manufacturing in Mexico, 223–227
  of entertainment media, 150
  and environmental problems, 419–421
  and exploitation, 59, 60, 214–226, 361, 386
  and global debt crisis, 212–215, 224–225
  in the global village, 122
  and international relations, 364
  and the Internet, 215
  and job outsourcing, 216, 235, 367, 368–369
  and labor unions, 126
  and McDonaldization of society, 59–60, 122
  and multinational corporations, 215
  in postmodern societies, 118
  and technology, 59
  and tourism, 21, 29–30
  and war, 364
GM foods (genetically modified foods), 416, 417
Goal displacement, 121, 129
Google, 140
Government, types of, 356–357
Graffiti, 157–158
Grand Theft Auto (video game), 151
Grandparenting, 302
Gray Panthers, 102–103
Great Britain. *See* United Kingdom
Greece
  aging population, 275
  Gross Domestic Product (GDP), 217*t*
  income per capita, 213*f*
  languages used in, 62*f*
Greenpeace, 416
Gregg v. Georgia, 179
Grinnell College, 44
Gross national product, 216
Gross national product (GNP), definition, 230
Groups, 108, 108–110, 129
Growing Up Digital (Tapscott), 133–134
Growth rate, 377, 402
Guatemala, urbanization, projected, 384*f*
Guinea, languages used in, 62*f*
Guyana, languages used in, 62*f*

Haiti
  income per capita, 213*f*
  languages used in, 62*f*
  life expectancy, 378*f*
  poverty level, 218*f*
  women in, 360
Hamas, 135
Harvard Business Review, 273
Harvard University, 16, 42, 162
Harvey Milk High School, 341
Hate crimes, 237, 258, 341
  categorization of reported, 237*f*
Hate groups, 238*f*
Hawaii
  abortion funding, 284*f*
  anti-gay laws, 310*f*
  Arab American population, 253*f*
  cohabitation, 306*f*
  educational level, 32*f*

executions, since 1972, 170*f*
household income, 32*f*
median household income, 187*f*
physicians, availability of, 398*f*
union membership, 127*f*
Hawthorne effect, 38, 51
Hawthorne studies, 123
Health and illness, 391, 392–401. *See also* Physicians
  and age, 398–399
  AIDS/HIV. *See* AIDS/HIV
  conflict perspective, 397
  functionalist perspective, 391–392, 395*t*
  and gender, 398
  interactionist perspective, 393, 395*t*
  Marxist perspective, 397
  and patient autonomy, 394
  and social epidemiology, 395, 396, 397–399
Health beliefs, and race, 394, 397
Health Canada, 152
Health care, nationalized, 204
Health, definition, 390, 402
Health insurance, people without, by race and income, 397*f*
Heredity, and socialization, 81–82
Hidden curriculum, 335, 345
Hierarchy of authority, 120
Higher Education Research Institute, 320, 359
Hijab, 270
Hinduism, 269, 317*f*, 319, 320*t*, 321, 332
Hispanics, 41, 253–254
  and criminal justice system, 172
  health and illness, 394
  marriage and family, 301–302
  media portrayal, 140, 141
  median income, 239*f*
  and politics, 358
  population distribution, United States, 247*f*
  in poverty, 282
  single-parent families, 302*f*
  in U.S. population, 235*t*
  projected, 236*f*
HIV (human immunodeficiency virus). *See* AIDS/HIV
Home Depot, 390, 391
Homeland Security, Department of, 200
Homeschooling, 341–342
Homogamy, 299, 311
Homophobia, 263, 286, 341
Homosexuality, as illness, 395
Homosexuals. *See also* Gays
  anti-gay laws, by state, 310*f*
  persecution, by governments, 228
Honduras
  computer network readiness, 220
  income per capita, 213*f*
  languages used in, 62*f*
Hong Kong
  computer network readiness, 220
  income per capita, 213*f*
  urbanization, projected, 384*f*
Horizontal mobility, 201, 206
Horticultural societies, 116, 117*t*
Hospice care, 280, 286
Hospice Foundation of America, 281
Housework, and gender, 272–273
Hull House, 12
Human ecology, 402
Human Genome Project, 417
Human relations approach, 123, 129
Human rights, definition, 227, 230
Hungarian language, 63

Hunger, 211
Hunting-and-gathering society, 116, 117*t*, 129
Hurra, al, 150
Hurricane Katrina, 6, 7, 22, 200
Hypothesis, 32, 51
  formulating, 31, 31*f*, 32
  supporting, 34

I Love Lucy (TV show), 136
Idaho
  abortion funding, 284*f*
  anti-gay laws, 310*f*
  Arab American population, 253*f*
  cohabitation, 306*f*
  educational level, 32*f*
  elderly population, projected, 282*f*
  executions, since 1972, 170*f*
  household income, 32*f*
  median household income, 187*f*
  physicians, availability of, 398*f*
  union membership, 127*f*
Ideal minority, 249, 258
Ideal type, 11, 119, 129
Identity theft, 415
Illinois
  abortion funding, 284*f*
  Arab American population, 253*f*
  cohabitation, 306*f*
  educational level, 32*f*
  elderly population, projected, 282*f*
  executions, since 1972, 170*f*
  household income, 32*f*
  medical marijuana, 163*f*
  physicians, availability of, 398*f*
  union membership, 127*f*
Illness. *See* Health care system
Immigrants, 187
  illegal, 223, 225–226, 251, 421–423
  in U.S. population, by origin, 246*f*
Immigration, 245–246
  and international relations, 364
  worldwide, 422*f*
Immigration Act, 1965, 252
Immigration Reform and Control Act, 246
Impersonality, 121
Impression management, 84, 85, 86*t*, 97
In-group, 109, 129
Incest taboo, 298
Incidence, 395, 402
Income, 186, 206
  distribution, within nations, 221*f*, 224
  and education, 34*f*
  and education, by state, 32*f*
  for the elderly, 281
  and health and illness, 396, 397*f*
  and Internet usage, 145*f*
  median, by race, ethnicity, and gender, 239*f*
  median household, by state, 187*f*
  by religion and education, 322
  and wealth, 195–196
Independent variable, 32, 51
Index crimes, 174, 181
India
  economic forecast, 353*f*
  in global economy, 368, 369
  income per capita, 213*f*
  infant mortality rate, 393*t*
  languages used in, 62*f*
  life expectancy, 378*f*
  middle class, 210–211

religions of, 332–333. *See* Buddhism; Hinduism
  social mobility in, 222
  stratification in, 187, 188
  subcultures, 69
  terrorist incidents, 365*f*
  voter turnout, 358*f*
  women in, 221, 269, 359, 360
Indian Americans, 300
Indian Gambling Regulatory Act, 250
Indian immigrants, in U.S. population, 246*f*
Indiana
  abortion funding, 284*f*
  anti-gay laws, 310*f*
  Arab American population, 253*f*
  cohabitation, 306*f*
  educational level, 32*f*
  executions, since 1972, 170*f*
  household income, 32*f*
  median household income, 187*f*
  medical marijuana, 163*f*
  people ever married, percentage, 299*f*
  physicians, availability of, 398*f*
  union membership, 127*f*
Indonesia
  cockfighting, 6
  languages used in, 62*f*
  poverty level, 218*f*
  tsunami in, 21
Industrial city, 382, 383*t*, 402
Industrial society, 117, 117*t*, 118, 129, 349, 371
Infant mortality rate, 377, 402
  by country, 393*t*
  Mexico vs. United States, 224
  and race, 394
  worldwide, 393*t*
Infanticide, female, 221, 380
Influence, 355, 371
Informal economy, 352, 371
Informal norms, 65, 66*t*, 75
Informal social control, 160, 182
Innovation, 58, 75
Institute for Social Policy and Understanding, 329
Institute of International Education, 335
Institutional discrimination, 240, 258, 268, 286
Instrumentality, 266, 287
Intelligent design (ID), 342–343, 345
Inter-Parliamentary Union, 224
Interactionist perspective, 15, 16–17, 18*t*
  on aging, 276, 277*t*
  on culture, 71*t*
  on deviance, 169–171, 174*f*
  on education, 337, 338, 339*t*
  on health and illness, 393, 395*t*
  on the media, 143, 144
  on race, 242–243, 243*t*
  on religion, 324–327, 325*t*
  on social institutions, 114
  on social structure, 102
  on sports, 19
  on stratification, 192, 194*t*
  on stratification by gender, 267–268, 268*t*
Internal Revenue Service, 196*f*
International Labor Organization, 422
International Monetary Fund, 214–215
International Social Survey Programme, 271
International Women Count Network, 195
Internet
  access, and censorship, 139, 354–355
  access, and inequality, 145, 200–201, 220

conflict perspective, 415–416
crime, 175, 176
and cultural diffusion, 60
dating, 298, 302
functionalist perspective, 415
government surveillance, 139–140, 415
and media distribution, 148–149, 149, 406–407
online networking, 110, 112
piracy, 165
regulation of, 139
sexual content, 143
and social research, 44–45
telecommuting, 124–125
use, by demographic, 143, 145f
video games, 151
in the workplace, 124–125
Internment camps, for Japanese Americans, 251
Interview, 35, 51
Intragenerational mobility, 201, 206
Invention, 58
Invisible Man (Ellison), 247
Iowa
abortion funding, 284f
anti-gay laws, 310f
Arab American population, 253f
cohabitation, 306f
educational level, 32f
executions, since 1972, 170f
household income, 32f
physicians, availability of, 398f
union membership, 127f
Iran
death penalty, 179
income per capita, 213f
languages used in, 62f
life in, 261–262
terrorist incidents, 365f
women in, 360
Iraq
Abu Graib prison, 101, 160
culture, 65
income per capita, 213f
languages used in, 62f
opinion polls in, 36
poverty level, 218f
terrorist incidents, 365f
Ireland
computer network readiness, 220
educational level, 333f
Gross Domestic Product (GDP), 217t
income per capita, 213f
languages used in, 62f
religious participation, 327f
Iron Chef, 142
Iron law of oligarchy, 123, 126, 129
Islam, 317f, 318, 319, 320, 320t. *See also* Middle Eastern cultures; Muslim culture
rituals, 326
sects of, 328
in the United States, 328, 329
Islamic culture, 70, 83, 89. *See also* Middle Eastern cultures
religious fundamentalism, 414–415
Isolation, impact on socialization, 79–81
Israel
income per capita, 213f
languages used in, 62f
terrorist incidents, 365f
Istanbul, urbanization, projected, 384f

Italy
aging population, 275
economic forecast, 353f
educational level, 333f
gender stratification, 271f
income per capita, 213f
languages used in, 62f
voter turnout, 358f
Ivory Coast, languages used in, 62f

J

Jainism, 332–333
Jamaica
income distribution, 221f
income per capita, 213f
languages used in, 62f
Japan
aging population, 275
computer network readiness, 220
culture, 56, 60
economic forecast, 353f
education in, 336–337
educational level, 333f
family possessions in, 4
gender stratification, 271f
income distribution, 221f
income per capita, 212, 213f
infant mortality rate, 393t
languages used in, 62f
life expectancy, 378f
media penetration, 148f
religions of, 317f, 320
stratification in, 222
Japanese Americans, 251
Jazeera, al, 150
Jerry Maguire (film), 350
Jewish Americans, 254–255
Jim Crow laws, 242, 248
Jordan, 150
languages used in, 62f
terrorist incidents, 365f
women in, 360
Judaism, 320–321, 320t, 322
Justice Department, 237f

K

Kaiser Family Foundation, 45, 46f, 152
Kansas
abortion funding, 284f
anti-gay laws, 310f
Arab American population, 253f
cohabitation, 306f
educational level, 32f
elderly population, projected, 282f
executions, since 1972, 170f
household income, 32f
median household income, 187f
medical marijuana, 163f
physicians, availability of, 398f
union membership, 127f
Kansas State University, 68
Katrina (hurricane). *See* Hurricane Katrina
Kayan tribe, of Thailand, 166
Kentucky
abortion funding, 284f
anti-gay laws, 310f
Arab American population, 253f
cohabitation, 306f
educational level, 32f

elderly population, projected, 282f
executions, since 1972, 170f
household income, 32f
median household income, 187f
medical marijuana, 163f
physicians, availability of, 398f
Kenya
languages used in, 62f
terrorist incidents, 365f
King of the Hill (TV show), 141
Kinsey Report, 45
Kinship, 294–295, 311
KISS (band), 156
Kitzmiller v. Dove Area School District, 343
Koran (Qur'an), 253, 270, 320
Korea, religions of, 317f
Korean Americans, 251–252
health beliefs, 394
Ku Klux Klan, 238f
Kuwait
income per capita, 213f
languages used in, 62f
terrorist incidents, 365f
women in, 360
Kyoto Protocol, 419
Kyrgyzstan
languages used in, 62f
marriage, 300–301

L

Labeling theory, 171, 173, 182, 337, 338
and health and illness, 394–395
Labor Department, 248
Labor unions, 123, 126, 129, 191
and social policy, 125–127
Lagos, urbanization, projected, 384f
Laissez-faire, 350, 371
Lakota Indians, 63
Language, 63, 75
bilingualism, 71–74
and culture, 55, 58, 61–64
feminist perspective, 63
and subcultures, 69
Languages of the World, 62f
Laos
income per capita, 213f
life expectancy, 378f
Las Vegas, 384
Latent functions, 14
Latin America, 212f, 323, 324
people living with AIDS, 400f
Latinos. *See* Hispanics
Latvia, languages used in, 62f
Law, 64, 75, 161, 163
definition, 182
Law and Order (TV show), 135
Leaving Las Vegas (film), 152
Lebanon
income per capita, 213f
languages used in, 62f
Lesbians. *See* Gay marriage
Lesotho, languages used in, 62f
Lewis Mumford Center, 245
Liberation theology, 323–324, 345
Liberia
languages used in, 62f
poverty level, 218f
Library of Congress, 135
Libya
income per capita, 213f

languages used in, 62f
Life chances, 200, 206
Life course approach, 87, 97
Life expectancy, 377, 402
by country, 378f
worldwide, 378f
Lipstick Jihad (Moaveni), 261–262
Literature review, 31
Liveplasma.com, 146f
London, urbanization, projected, 384f
Looking-glass self, 82, 86t, 97
Los Angeles, urbanization, projected, 384f
Louisiana
abortion funding, 284f
anti-gay laws, 310f
Arab American population, 253f
cohabitation, 306f
educational level, 32f
elderly population, projected, 282f
environmental problems, 420
executions, since 1972, 170f
household income, 32f
median household income, 187f
medical marijuana, 163f
physicians, availability of, 398f
union membership, 127f
Love, and marriage, 299, 300
Love, and social expectations, 7, 8
Luddites, 414
Luxembourg
aid to developing nations, 216
languages used in, 62f

M

Macedonia, languages used in, 62f
Machismo, 301, 311
Macrosociology, 13, 31, 119, 145
Madagascar
income per capita, 213f
poverty level, 218f
Maid in Manhattan (film), 201
Maine
abortion funding, 284f
anti-gay laws, 310f
Arab American population, 253f
cohabitation, 306f
educational level, 32f
elderly population, projected, 282f
executions, since 1972, 170f
household income, 32f
median household income, 187f
medical marijuana, 163f
physicians, availability of, 398f
rural character, 383
union membership, 127f
Maine Times, 391
Malawai
languages used in, 62f
poverty level, 218f
Mali
languages used in, 62f
poverty level, 218f
Malthusian thesis, of population growth, 376
Manifest functions, 14
Maquiladoras, 225
Marijuana, medical use, by state, 163f
Market research, 145–146
Marketing
and children, 54, 55
in the global economy, 53

Marriage
  arranged, 298, 300
  child-free, 308
  and divorce, 305–306
    trends in, 305f
  forms of, 294
  gay, 308–310
  interracial, 299
  and love, 299, 300
  mate selection, 298–299
  people ever married, by country, 299f
  and race and ethnicity, 301–302
  and social class, 301
  and social expectations, 7, 8
Marxist class theory, 242
Marxist perspective, 16, 67. *See also* Conflict Perspective
  on bureaucracies, 119–120
  on economic systems, 361
  on health and illness, 397
  on labor unions, 126
  on overpopulation, 376
  on religion, 324
  on stratification, 189, 190–191
Maryland
  abortion funding, 284f
  anti-gay laws, 310f
  Arab American population, 253f
  cohabitation, 306f
  educational level, 32f
  elderly population, projected, 282f
  household income, 32f
  median household income, 187f
  medical marijuana, 163f
  physicians, availability of, 398f
  union membership, 127f
Mass media, 134
Massachusetts
  abortion funding, 284f
  anti-gay laws, 310f
  Arab American population, 253f
  cohabitation, 306f
  educational level, 32f
  elderly population, projected, 282f
  executions, since 1972, 170f
  household income, 32f
  median household income, 187f
  medical marijuana, 163f
  physicians, availability of, 398f
  union membership, 127f
Massachusetts Institute of Technology (MIT), 190
Master status, 103–104
  AIDS sufferer as, 103
  disabled person as, 103
  old age as, 274
Material culture, 4–5, 60, 75, 414
Material World: A Global Family Portrait, 4–5
Matriarchy, 295
Matrilineal descent, 295, 311
Matrix Reloaded, 148
Mauritania
  income per capita, 213f
  poverty level, 218f
McDonaldization, 122, 129
McDonaldization of society, 59–60
McDonaldization of Society, The (Ritzer), 122
McDonalds corporaton, 406
McKinsey Global Institute, 368
Mean, 47, 51
Mechanical solidarity, 115
Médecins San Frontières (Doctors Without Borders), 228, 364

Media, 149
  advertising, 138, 145–146
  as agent of socialization, 135
  audience, 145–146
  conflict perspective, 139–140, 142, 146t
  feminist perspective, 142–143, 146t
  functionalist perspective, 134–135, 138–139, 146t
  interactionist perspective, 143, 144
  ownership, 147–149
  piracy, 165
  sexuality in, 45, 46
  violence, 151–152
Media monitoring, 139–140
Media penetration in selected countries, 148f
Median, 47, 51
Medical model, 392
  of disability, 104
Medical sociology, 18
Medicalization of society, 392
Megalopolis, 383, 402
Memoirs of a Geisha (film), 142
Men. *See* Gender, Gender Roles
Mesopotamia, 382
Mexican Americans, 253–254, 301
  health beliefs, 394, 397
Mexican immigrants, in U.S. population, 246f
Mexico
  borderlands, 225–226
  crime, 173
  economic forecast, 353f
  educational level, 333f
  family posessions in, 5
  income distribution, 221, 221f, 224
  income per capita, 223
  infant mortality, 224
  infant mortality rate, 393t
  languages used in, 62f
  life expectancy, 378f
  media penetration, 148f
  people ever married, percentage, 299f
  religious participation, 327f
  stratification in, 223–227
  voter turnout, 358f
  women in, 224
Michigan
  abortion funding, 284f
  anti-gay laws, 310f
  Arab American population, 253f
  cohabitation, 306f
  educational level, 32f
  elderly population, projected, 282f
  executions, since 1972, 170f
  household income, 32f
  median household income, 187f
  medical marijuana, 163f
  physicians, availability of, 398f
  union membership, 253f
Microsociology, 13, 31, 119, 145
Microsoft Corporation, 140, 350
Middle East, terrorist incidents, 365f
Middle Eastern cultures, 64, 70, 135
  Islamic fundamentalist revolution, 414–415
  media in, 150
  women in, 221
Middle Eastern people, media portrayal, 141
Midlife crisis, 277, 287
Migradollars, 226, 421
Migration News, 225, 226
Millennium Project, 216, 219
Minimal heirarchy, 124
Minimum wage, 197f

Minnesota
  abortion funding, 284f
  anti-gay laws, 310f
  Arab American population, 253f
  cohabitation, 306f
  educational level, 32f
  elderly population, projected, 282f
  executions, since 1972, 170f
  household income, 32f
  median household income, 187f
  medical marijuana, 163f
  physicians, availability of, 398f
  union membership, 127f
Minnesota Center for Twin and Family Research, 81
Minnesota Twin Family Study, 81
Minority group, definition, 234, 258
Miss America pageant, 264
Mississippi
  abortion funding, 284f
  anti-gay laws, 310f
  Arab American population, 253f
  cohabitation, 306f
  educational level, 32f
  elderly population, projected, 282f
  executions, since 1972, 170f
  household income, 32f
  median household income, 187f
  union membership, 127f
Missouri
  abortion funding, 284f
  anti-gay laws, 310f
  Arab American population, 253f
  cohabitation, 306f
  educational level, 32f
  elderly population, projected, 282f
  executions, since 1972, 170f
  household income, 32f
  median household income, 187f
  physicians, availability of, 398f
  rural character, 383
  union membership, 127f
Mobility, social. *See* Social mobility
Mode, 47, 51
Model minority, 249, 258
Modernization, 217, 218, 230
Modernization theory, 218, 221t, 230
Moldova, languages used in, 62f
Monarchy, 356, 371
Mongolia, income per capita, 213f
Monkeys, impact of social isolation, 80–81
Monogamy, 294, 311
Monopoly, 350, 371
Montana
  abortion funding, 284f
  anti-gay laws, 310f
  Arab American population, 253f
  cohabitation, 306f
  educational level, 32f
  executions, since 1972, 170f
  household income, 32f
  median household income, 187f
  medical marijuana, 163f
  physicians, availability of, 398f
  union membership, 127f
Morbidity rates, 395, 402
Mores, 65, 75
Mormons (Church of Jesus Christ of Latter-day Saints), 330f
Morocco, terrorist incidents, 365f
Mortality, 375–376
Mortality rate, 395, 402
Mothers Against Drunk Driving (MADD), 174

Mozambique, 211
  income per capita, 213f
  languages used in, 62f
  poverty level, 218f
MTV network, 142
Multinational corporations, 59, 215–217, 221t, 350–351
  compared to nations, 217t
  definition, 215, 230
  offshoring, 216, 225, 367, 368–369
Multiple-nuclei theory, 385, 385f, 402
Multiracial people, 235–236, 237
Muslim culture, 65, 89, 253, 264
  women in, 261–262, 270
Muslims, 317f, 318, 319, 320, 320t
  in India, 332
  rituals, 326
  Sunni vs. Shiite, 328
  in the United States, 328, 329
My Fair Lady (play), 337
Myanmar
  income per capita, 213f
  languages used in, 62f
  poverty level, 218f

NAACP (National Association for the Advancement of Colored People), 15, 248
Namibia
  income distribution, 221
  income per capita, 213f
Napster, 406
Narcotizing dysfunction, 138, 138–139
NASCAR, 19
Nation of Islam, 328
National Advisory Committee on Criminal Justice, 174
National Basketball Association (NBA), 17
National Center for Health Statistics, 397
National Crime Victimization Survey, 178–179
National Geographic magazine, 144f
National Geographic Society, 45
National Health and Social Life Survey (NHSLS), 46
National Indian Gaming Association, 250
National Institute of Child Health and Human Development, 46
National Institute on Aging, 280f
National Opinion Research Center (NORC), 33
National Reconnaissance Office, 120
National Right to Work Legal Defense Fund, 127f
National Science Foundation, 42
National Security Agency (NSA), 120
Native Americans, 63, 232, 248–249, 315–316
  decimation, of population, 243, 248
  gaming industry, 250
  health and illness, 394
  health beliefs, 394
  media portrayal, 140
  median income, 239f
  and politics, 358
  population distribution, United States, 247f
  religion, 315–316
  in U.S. population, 235t
    projected, 236f
Natural science, 6
Natural selection, 60

Naturally occurring retirement communities (NORCs), 279
Nature vs. nurture, 81–82
Navajo Nation Police Department, 105
NBA (National Basketball Association), 144
NBC (National Broadcasting Company), 141
Nebraska
    abortion funding, 284f
    anti-gay laws, 310f
    Arab American population, 253f
    cohabitation, 306f
    educational level, 32f
    elderly population, projected, 282f
    executions, since 1972, 170f
    household income, 32f
    median household income, 187f
    physicians, availability of, 398f
    union membership, 127f
Neighborhoods, segregated, 388
Neo-Confederates, 238f
Neo-Nazi hate groups, 238f
Neocolonialism, 214, 230
Nepal
    culture, 273–274
    income per capita, 213f
    languages used in, 62f
    poverty level, 218f
Netherlands
    aid to developing nations, 216
    income per capita, 213f
    languages used in, 62f
Network Readiness Index (NRI), 220
Networking, 110–112
Nevada
    abortion funding, 384f
    anti-gay laws, 310f
    Arab American population, 253f
    cohabitation, 306f
    educational level, 32f
    elderly population, projected, 282f
    executions, since 1972, 170f
    household income, 32f
    median household income, 187f
    physicians, availability of, 398f
    union membership, 127f
New Guinea, 265
New Hampshire
    abortion funding, 284f
    anti-gay laws, 310f
    cohabitation, 306f
    educational level, 32f
    elderly population, projected, 282f
    executions, since 1972, 170f
    handicap access in, 104
    household income, 32f
    median household income, 187f
    medical marijuana, 163f
    physicians, availability of, 398f
    union membership, 127f
New Jersey
    abortion funding, 284f
    anti-gay laws, 310f
    Arab American population, 253f
    cohabitation, 306f
    educational level, 32f
    elderly population, projected, 282f
    executions, since 1972, 170f
    household income, 32f
    median household income, 187f
    medical marijuana, 163f
    physicians, availability of, 398f
    union membership, 127f
New Line Cinema, 148

New Mexico
    abortion funding, 284f
    anti-gay laws, 310f
    Arab American population, 253f
    cohabitation, 306f
    educational level, 32f
    executions, since 1972, 170f
    household income, 32f
    median household income, 187f
    medical marijuana, 163f
    physicians, availability of, 398f
    union membership, 127f
New Orleans, 6, 7, 200
New Orleans Medical and Surgical Journal, 394
New religious movement (NRM), 329
New religious movements (NRMs), 330, 331, 331t, 345
New social movements, 410, 424
New urban sociology, 386, 402
New York Academy of Medicine, 396
New York City, urbanization, projected, 384f
New York State
    abortion funding, 384f
    anti-gay laws, 310f
    Arab American population, 253f
    cohabitation, 306f
    educational level, 32f
    elderly population, projected, 282f
    executions, since 1972, 170f
    household income, 32f
    median household income, 187f
    medical marijuana, 163f
    union membership, 127f
New Zealand, suicide rate, 9
Newsday, 104
NGOs (nongovernmental organizations), 228, 364
Nicaragua, computer network readiness, 220
Nickel And Dimed (Ehrenreich), 2–3, 198
Niger
    languages used in, 62f
    poverty level, 218f
Nigeria
    income distribution, 221
    income per capita, 213f
    languages used in, 62f
    poverty level, 218f
Nights of Cabiria (film), 152
Nike corporation, 53, 216
NIMBY (not in my back yard), 413
Nonmaterial culture, 60, 75, 414
Nonverbal communication, 16, 64
Norms, 64, 64–65, 66t, 75
    enforcing, 135, 158–163
    gender, 263–264
    theoretical perspectives on, 71t
    violating, 263. *See also* Deviance
North Africa, people living with AIDS, 400f
North America
    labor migration, 422f
    people living with AIDS, 400f
    terrorist incidents, 365f
North Carolina
    abortion funding, 284f
    anti-gay laws, 310f
    Arab American population, 253f
    cohabitation, 306f
    educational level, 32f
    elderly population, projected, 282f
    executions, since 1972, 170f
    household income, 32f
    median household income, 187f

medical marijuana, 163f
    physicians, availability of, 398f
    union membership, 127f
North Dakota
    abortion funding, 284f
    anti-gay laws, 310f
    Arab American population, 253f
    cohabitation, 306f
    educational level, 32f
    elderly population, projected, 282f
    executions, since 1972, 170f
    household income, 32f
    median household income, 187f
    medical marijuana, 163f
    physicians, availability of, 398f
    union membership, 127f
North Korea
    income per capita, 213f
    languages used in, 62f
Norway
    absolute poverty, 197f
    aid to developing nations, 216
    educational level, 333f
    gender stratification, 271f
    Gross Domestic Product (GDP), 217t
    languages used in, 62f
    religious participation, 327f
    terrorist incidents, 365f
Nuclear family, 291
Nuclear reactor accident, 418
NU*DIST software, 44
Nurses, 127
NYPD Blue, 141

Obedience, 159, 182
Obesity, 393
Objective method, 194, 206
Observation, 37, 51
Observation, for data collection, 36–37
Occupation, and social class, 194–195
Occupational mobility, 201–202
Occupations, prestige rankings, 195t
Occupations, women as percentage in selected, 272t
Oceania, people living with AIDS, 400f
Offshoring, in global economy, 216, 225, 367, 368–369, 371
Ohio
    abortion funding, 284f
    anti-gay laws, 310f
    Arab American population, 253f
    cohabitation, 306f
    educational level, 32f
    elderly population, projected, 282f
    executions, since 1972, 170f
    household income, 32f
    median household income, 187f
    medical marijuana, 163f
    physicians, availability of, 398f
    union membership, 127f
Oklahoma
    abortion funding, 284f
    anti-gay laws, 310f
    Arab American population, 253f
    educational level, 32f
    elderly population, projected, 282f
    executions, since 1972, 170f
    household income, 32f
    median household income, 187f
    medical marijuana, 163f

physicians, availability of, 398f
    union membership, 127f
Oligarchy, 371
Olin Center for Law, Harvard University, 42
Oman, income per capita, 213f
1000 Families (Ommer), 292–294
On the Origin of Species (Darwin), 10
Online networking, 110, 112
Open system, 201, 206
Operational definition, 31
Opinion leader, 146
Oprah Winfrey Show, 149
Oregon
    abortion funding, 384f
    anti-gay laws, 310f
    Arab American population, 253f
    educational level, 32f
    elderly population, projected, 282f
    executions, since 1972, 170f
    median household income, 187f
    medical marijuana, 163f
    physicians, availability of, 398f
    union membership, 127f
Organic solidarity, 115, 129
Organizational culture, 123–124
Organized crime, 175, 182
Out-group, 109, 129
Overpopulation
    and environmental problems, 420
    Malthus vs. Marx, 376

Pacific Islanders, single-parent families, 302f
Pacific Islands, 212f
Pakistan
    Gross Domestic Product (GDP), 217t
    income per capita, 213f
    infant mortality rate, 393t
    languages used in, 62f
    poverty level, 218f
    terrorist incidents, 365f
    women in, 221
Palestine, 135, 150
Pan Arab Research Center, 56
Pan-Cordillera Women's Network for Peace, 223
Panama
    income per capita, 213f
    languages used in, 62f
Papua New Guinea
    culture, 56
    languages used in, 62f
Paradise Laborers (Adler and Adler), 29–30
Paraguay
    computer network readiness, 220
    income per capita, 213f
Parents Television Council, 151t
Patriarchy, 295, 311
Patrilineal descent, 295, 312
Patriot Act, 67, 161, 364, 415
PBS (Public Broadcasting Service), 391
Peace, 363–364
    definition, 371
Peer groups, 92
Pennsylvania
    abortion funding, 384f
    anti-gay laws, 310f
    Arab American population, 253f
    cohabitation, 306f
    educational level, 32f
    elderly population, projected, 282f

executions, since 1972, 170f
household income, 32f
    median household income, 187f
    medical marijuana, 163f
    physicians, availability of, 398f
    union membership, 127f
People magazine, 135, 138
Percentage, 47, 51
Personal Responsibility and Work
        Opportunity Reconciliation Act,
        204
Personality, 79, 97
Peru
    Gross Domestic Product (GDP), 217t
    income per capita, 213f
    languages used in, 62f
    poverty level, 218f
    terrorist incidents, 365f
Peter principle, 121, 129
Pew Internet Project, 145f
Pew Research Center, 366
Philippines
    languages used in, 62f
    poverty level, 218f
    terrorist incidents, 365f
    women in, 223
Photo opportunities, 143
Physicians
    availability, by state, 398f
    gender differences in, 269
    racism of, 394, 397
    status quo, vested interest in, 413
Pica, 211
Piracy, media, 165
Pluralism, 245, 258
Pluralist model, 362, 371
Poland
    Gross Domestic Product (GDP), 217t
    languages used in, 62f
    people ever married, percentage, 299f
Political behavior, 357–359
    and race, 358–359
Political system, 349, 371
Politics, 355, 371
    women in, 358, 359, 360, 360f
Pollution, environmental, 418–421
Polyandry, 294, 312
Polygamy, 294, 312
Polygyny, 294, 312
Poor, 199
Poor people, demographic characteristics of,
        199t
Pop Idol, 142
Popularity, high school, 92t
Population Bomb, The (Ehrlich), 376
Population pyramid, 379, 402
Population Reference Bureau, 379
Population structure, of U. S. and
        Afghanistan, 381f
Population studies. *See* Demography
Population, world, 377–380
    time for each one billion increase, 378t
Pornography, 143
Portugal
    educational level, 333f
    Gross Domestic Product (GDP), 217t
    income per capita, 213f
    languages used in, 62f
Postal Service, United States, 119
Postindustrial city, 383, 383t, 402
Postindustrial society, 117t, 118, 129
Postmodern society, 117t, 118, 129
Poverty, 196–201

absolute, 197
    conflict perspective, 199
    and the elderly, 281–282
    and exposure to pollutants, 420–421
    feminization of, 199, 203–204
    functionalist perspective, 200
    global, 210
    and Hurricane Katrina, 6, 7, 22, 200
    and life chances, 200–201
    and race, 199
    relative, 198
    welfare programs, 203–205
    women in, 301
    working poor, 2–3, 198, 199
    worldwide, 216–217
        by country, 218f
Power, 191, 206, 355, 355–356
    and authority, 355–356
    definition, 371
Power elite, 349, 361
Power elite models, 361–362
Power Elite, The (Mills), 361
Prayer, in schools, 343
Preindustrial city, 382, 383t, 402
Prejudice, 237, 258
    vs. discrimination, 238–239
Prestige, 194, 206
Pretty Woman (film), 152
Prevalence, 395, 402
Primary groups, 108, 108t, 129
Primate studies, on social isolaton, 80–81
Prison experiments, of Zimbardo, 100–101,
        102, 104
Prisoner abuse, at Abu Graib prison, 101
Proctor & Gamble, 124
Product placement, 138
Profane, 316, 345
Professional criminal, 174
Program, The (film), 152
Proletariat, 190, 206
Protestant denominatons, 322
Protestant ethic, 323, 345
Protestant Ethic and the Spirit of Capitalism
        (Weber), 12, 323
Psychoanalysis, 86t
Psychology, 6
Public Enemy (rap group), 406
Puerto Ricans, 254
Purdue University, 368
Pygmalion in the Classroom (Rosenthal), 338

Qaeda, -al, 120, 150
Qatar, 150
Qualitative research, 35, 51
Quantitative research, 35, 51
Questionnaires, 33, 35, 51
Qur'an (Koran), 253, 270, 320

Race
    conflict perspective, 242, 243t
    definition, 235
    functionalist perspective, 241–242
    and health and illness, 394, 397f
    and health beliefs, 394, 397
    and infant mortality, 394
    interactionist perspective, 242–243, 243t
    and Internet usage, 145f

and language, 63
    in the media, 140, 141
    multiracial people, 235–236, 237
    and political behavior, 358–359
    and poverty, 199
    as social construct, 235, 417
    and social mobility, 202–203, 204
    and wealth and income, 196
Race riots, 146–147
Racial and ethnic groups
    intergroup relations, 243–245
    interracial friendships, 244
Racial and ethnic groups, United States, 235t
    projected populations, 236f
Racial and ethnic inequality, 232–259
Racial group, definition, 234, 258
Racial profiling, 171, 253, 255–256, 258
Racism, 237. *See also* Discrimination; Racial
        profiling
    and criminal justice system, 171, 172
    and employment, 39
    in Japan, 222
    in the medical community, 397
    in Mexico, 224
    and segregation, 242, 244, 258, 388
    and war crimes, 227
Random sample, 33, 51
Rational-legal authority, 356, 371
Reality, constructing, 140
Reba (TV show), 151t
Red Crescent Society, 364
Red Cross, 364
Reebok, 216
Reference group, 109
Relative deprivation, 408, 424
Relative poverty, 198, 206
Reliability, 33, 51
Religion, 316
    components of, 324–327
    conflict perspective, 324, 325t
    Durkheim defines, 316
    functionalist perspective, 316, 320, 321,
        323, 325t
    fundamentalism, 325
    by income and education, 322
    interactionist perspective, 324–327, 325t
    Max Weber's thesis, 323
    Native American, 315–316
    purpose, of study, 318
    in the schools, 342–343
    and social activism, 323–324
    and social change, 414
    social issues and, 323
    and suicide, 9
    and wars, 323
    women's role, 324, 325
    and youth, 7, 8
Religion Watch, 332
Religions, world, 317f, 320t
Religious beliefs, 324
Religious cults, 329–330, 331t
Religious Diversity News, 270
Religious experience, 326, 345
Religious organizations, 327, 328, 329–331,
        331t
    comparing, 330–331
Religious participation, by country, 327f
Religious Tolerance, 228
Remittances, 226, 230, 421
Representative democracy, 357, 371
Research
    and common sense, 7, 8
    funding, 42–43

interpreting, 47–48
    software for, 44
    writing reports, 48–49
Research in action
    adolescent sexual networks, 111
    arranged marriage, 300
    communication, physicians and, 269
    divorce, 307
    Human Genome Project, 417
    interracial friendships, 244
    Islam, in the United States, 328–329
    middle class, shrinking, 190
    religion, and income and education, 322
    retirement communities, 279
    sports, 19
    superstores, opposition to, 391
    voting, and young adults, 359
Research designs, 35, 51
    comparison of, 42t
Research methods. *See also* Scientific method
    data collection, 33, 35, 36–37, 38, 39
    defining research problem, 31
    experiments, 37–38
    hypothesis, formulating, 31, 32
    importance of understanding, 30
    major research designs, 35, 36, 37–38, 39,
        40, 42
    reliability and validity, 33
    sampling, 33
    and technology, 43, 44–45
Resocialization, 88, 97
Resource mobilization, 408, 424
Retirement, 278–280
    expectations in, 280f
Rhode Island
    abortion funding, 284f
    anti-gay laws, 310f
    Arab American population, 253f
    cohabitation, 306f
    educational level, 32f
    elderly population, projected, 282f
    executions, since 1972, 170f
    household income, 32f
    median household income, 187f
    medical marijuana, 163f
    physicians, availability of, 398f
    union membership, 127f
Rite of passage, 97
Rites of passage, 87
Rituals, religious, 325–326, 345
Road rage, 172
Roe v. Wade, 284
Role conflict, 104–105, 105, 129
Role exit, 105, 105, 108, 129
Role strain, 105, 129
Role taking, 83, 97
Roles, 104–105, 108
Rolling Stone magazine, 138
Romania
    Gross Domestic Product (GDP), 217t
    languages used in, 62f
Roomate.com, 239
Routine activities theory, 170, 174f, 182
Royal Dutch/Shell, revenues, 217t
Ruling the Waves (Spar), 406–407
Rural communities, 389–390
Russia
    economic forecast, 353f
    income per capita, 213f
    languages used in, 62f
    media penetration, 148f
    poverty level, 218f
    voter turnout, 358f

Russian language, 63
Rutgers University, 68
Rwanda
    languages used in, 62f
    women in, 359, 360f

Sacred, 316, 345
Sample, 33, 51
Sampling methods, 33
Sanctions, 65–66, 66t, 75, 158, 182
Sandwich generation, 277, 287
Sao Paulo, urbanization, projected, 384f
Sapir-Whorf hypothesis, 63
Saudi Arabia, 150
    culture, 64
    Gross Domestic Product (GDP), 217t
    income per capita, 213f
    terrorist incidents, 365f
    women in, 221
Schools, 338–343
    as agent of socialization, 91–92
    bureaucratization of, 339–341
    homeschooling, 341–342
    religion in the, 342–343
Scientific management approach, 123, 129
Scientific method, 30, 31f, 51
Scopes monkey trial, 342
Second shift, 273, 287
Secondary analysis, 38, 51
Secondary groups, 108, 108–109, 108, 129
Sects, religious, 328, 329, 330, 331t, 345
Secularization, 316, 345
Securities and Exchange Commission (SEC), 119
Segregation, 242, 244, 258
    residential, 388
Self, 82, 97
    development of, 86t
September 11, 2001, 6, 16, 21, 134–135, 139
    and global awareness, 70
    and immigration, 335
    memorial service, 113
    national security, breach in, 120
    security, after, 161, 226, 227, 240
        and civil rights violations, 67, 237, 253,
        256, 364, 415
Serbia
    ethnic cleansing, 227, 243
    languages used in, 62f
    terrorist incidents, 365f
Serial monogamy, 294, 312
Sex and Temperament (Margaret Mead),
    264–265
Sex selection, 59, 380
Sexism, 268. *See also* Feminist perspective;
    Women
    definition, 237
    in Japan, 222
    in the media, 143, 152
    in professional sports, 19
Sexual harassment, 269, 287
Sexual networks, adolescent, 111
Sexual orientation. *See* gay marriage, gays,
    homosexuality, and sexuality
Sexuality
    in China, 46–47
    in the media, 45, 46f
    and social policy, 45–47
Sherpas, 273–274
Shiite Muslims, 328

Shintoism, 317f
Sick role, 391, 402
Sidewalk (Duneier), 374–375
Sierra Leone
    income per capita, 213f
    infant mortality rate, 393t
    languages used in, 62f
    poverty level, 218f
Significant others, 83, 97
Sikhism, 317f, 332
Silicon Valley Cultures Project, 93f
Singapore
    computer network readiness, 220
    Gross Domestic Product (GDP), 217t
Single lifestyle, 307–308
Single-parent families, 301, 303–304, 304, 312
    rise of, 302f
Skinheads, 238f
Slavery, 187, 206, 394
Slovakia, languages used in, 62f
Slovenia, languages used in, 62f
Social activism, and defining reality, 102
Social activists, 12–13, 17–18, 195
    global, 406–407, 416
    and religion, 323–324
Social change, 407
    conflict perspective, 413, 413t
    definition, 424
    functionalist perspective, 413t
    global, 414
    resistance to, 413–414
Social constructionist perspective, 171, 182
Social control, 158, 158–163, 182
    formal vs. informal, 160–161
Social epidemiology, 397–399, 402
    definition, 395
Social inequality, 2–3, 22, 186, 206. *See also*
    Poverty
    and employment, 39
    global, 210–231
        and hunger, 211–212
        measures of, 212f
    significance of, 22
Social institutions, 112, 129
Social interaction, 101, 129
Social mobility, 201–203, 206
    in developing nations, 222
    and education, 202
    and gender, 203
    and race, 202–203, 204
    worldwide, 221–222
Social movements, Wo
Social network, 110, 129
Social policy
    abortion, 283–285
    AIDS crisis, 399–400
    bilingualism, 71–73
    child care, 94–96
    the death penalty, 179–180
    gay marriage, 309–311
    global offshoring, 368–369
    labor unions, 125–127
    media violence, 151–152
    racial profiling, 255–256
    religion in the schools, 342–343
    sexuality, 45–47
    transnationals, 421–423
    universal human rights, 227–228
    welfare, 203–205
Social reality, defining, 101–102
Social research, and common sense, 7, 8
Social role, 104
Social science, 5

Social Security Administration, 41
Social Security benefits, 281
Social structure, 101, 129
    elements of
        groups, 108
        roles, 104–105, 108
        statuses, 102–104
    global perspective, 114–119
Socialism, 351, 351–352, 352t
Socialization, 79, 97
    agents of, 89, 90, 91–94
        family, 89, 90, 91
        media, 134–134
        school, 91–92
        workplace, 92
    and the self, 82
Societal-reaction approach, 171, 182
Society, 55, 75
Society in America (Martineau), 9
Sociobiology, 60, 75
Sociocultural evolution, 116, 129
Sociological imagination, 2–3
    developing, 20, 21, 22
    using, 4–6
Sociological Practice Association, 20
Sociological Practice (journal), 20
Sociologists, early, 9–13
    as social activists, 12–13, 17–18
Sociology, 3
    careers in. *See* Careers, in Sociology
Somalia
    income per capita, 213f
    languages used in, 62f
    terrorist incidents, 365f
Sony Corporation, 148
Sopranos, The (TV show), 136
South Africa
    family possessions in, 2–3
    income distribution, 221
    income per capita, 213f
    languages used in, 62f
    life expectancy, 378f
    media penetration, 148f
    religious participation, 327f
    women in, 360
South America
    labor migration, 422f
    terrorist incidents, 365f
South Asia, people living with AIDS, 400f
South Carolina
    abortion funding, 284f
    anti-gay laws, 310f
    Arab American population, 253f
    cohabitation, 306f
    educational level, 32f
    elderly population, projected, 282f
    executions, since 1972, 170f
    household income, 32f
    median household income, 187f
    medical marijuana, 163f
    physicians, availability of, 398f
    union membership, 127f
South Dakota
    abortion funding, 284f
    anti-gay laws, 310f
    Arab American population, 253f
    cohabitation, 306f
    educational level, 32f
    elderly population, projected, 282f
    executions, since 1972, 170f
    household income, 32f
    median household income, 187f
    medical marijuana, 163f

physicians, availability of, 398f
union membership, 127f
South Korea
    economic forecast, 353f
    income per capita, 213f
    languages used in, 62f
South Korean immigrants, in U.S. population,
    246f
South Pacific Islander, 1
Southeast Asia, people living with AIDS, 400f
Southern Baptist Convention, 330f
Southern Christian Leadership Conference
    (SCLC), 248
Soviet Union (Russia), 63
    fall of, 414–415
Spain
    aging population, 275
    gm foods in, 416
    income per capita, 213f
    nationalized healthcare, 204
Spider-Man II (film), 152
Sports, 19, 165
    school, 338
Sri Lanka
    income per capita, 213f
    languages used in, 62f
    terrorist incidents, 365f
Stanford University, 100
Starbucks, 58, 216
Starvation, 211
Statistics, crime, 177–179
Statistics, using, 47–48
Status, 102, 102–104, 129
    achieved, 103, 103f, 206
    ascribed, 102–103, 103f, 119, 206
    and education, 336
Status group, 191, 206
Stepfamilies, 304–305
Stereotypes, 140, 236, 258
    age, 274
    gender, 63, 143, 152, 272
    racial, 63, 141, 161, 236
Sterilization, involuntary, 104
Stigma, 164–165
    definition, 164, 182
Store Wars (documentary), 391
Stratification, 206
    by age, 274
    castes, 187, 188
    class system, 188–189, 194–201
    conflict perspective, 193, 194f
    definition, 186
    estate system, 188
    functionalist perspective, 192–193, 194f
    gender, 194–195, 265–273
        conflict perspective, 266–267, 268t,
        270
        feminist perspective, 267
        functionalist perspective, 266, 268t
        industrial nations, 271f
        interactionist perspective, 267–268,
        268t
    global, 212–220
    interactionist perspective, 192, 194f
    in Japan, 222
    Lenski's viewpoint, 194
    Marxist perspective, 189, 190–191
    in Mexico, 223–227
    within nations, 220, 221–227
    open vs. closed systems, 201
    slavery, 187
    Weber's view, 191
Students Against Drunk Driving (SADD), 174

Sub-Saharan Africa, people living with AIDS, 400f
Subculture, definition, 75
Subcultures, 68, 68–69
    student, 340–341
    theoretical perspectives on, 71t
Suburb, 388, 402
Sudan, languages used in, 62f
Suicide, 9
    Native Americans, 248
    physician-assisted, 280–281
Superstores, opposition to, 391
Suicide (Durkheim), 12
Sunni Muslims, 328
Super Bowl, 138
Supreme Court, United States, 42, 163, 179,
    241, 248, 284, 309, 335, 342, 366
Surgeon General's Report, 2001, 152
Surveillance, government, 67, 139–140, 161,
    415
Survey, 35, 51
Surveys, 33
Survivor (TV show), 110, 142
Swaziland, languages used in, 62f
Sweatshops, 251
Sweden
    aid to developing nations, 216
    computer network readiness, 220
    culture, 56
    Gross Domestic Product (GDP), 217t
    income distribution, 221f
    infant mortality rate, 393t
    women in, 360
Switzerland
    computer network readiness, 220
    income per capita, 212, 213f
    languages used in, 62f
Symbolic ethnicity, 255
Symbolic interactionism, see Interactionist
    perspective
Symbols, 16–17, 82, 97, 101
Syria, income per capita, 213f

Tables, reading, 48
Tajikstan, languages used in, 62f
Tanzania, poverty level, 218f
Taoism, 317f, 320
Tattoos, 16, 101
Taxi Driver (film), 152
Teacher-expectancy effect, 338, 339, 345
Teachers, as employees, 340
Technology, 60, 75, 116, 129. *See also* Internet
    and cultural diffusion, 59, 60
    and networking, 110, 112
    resistance to, 414
    and social research, 43, 44–45
Telecommuters, 124, 129
Telemundo network, 141
Television, 136
    best and worst shows, 2005–2006, 151t
Tennessee
    abortion funding, 384f
    anti-gay laws, 310f
    Arab American population, 253f
    cohabitation, 306f
    educational level, 32f
    elderly population, projected, 282f
    executions, since 1972, 170f
    household income, 32f
    median household income, 187f

physicians, availability of, 398f
union membership, 127f
Terrorism, 364–365. *See also* September 11,
    2001
    definition, 364, 371
Terrorist groups, 70, 109, 120
    and the Internet, 143
Terrorist incidents, by region, 365f
Texas
    abortion funding, 284f
    anti-gay laws, 310f
    Arab American population, 253f
    cohabitation, 306f
    educational level, 32f
    elderly population, projected, 282f
    executions, since 1972, 170f
    household income, 32f
    median household income, 187f
    medical marijuana, 163f
    physicians, availability of, 398f
    union membership, 127f
Texting, 111
Thailand
    income per capita, 213f
    Kayan tribe, 166
    tsunami in, 21
    voter turnout, 358f
That '70s Show, 151t
Theology of Liberation, A (Gutiérrez), 324
Theoretical perspectives, major, 13–20, 18t
Theory, 8–9
Third World countries. *See* Developing
    countries
Third World Institute, 332
Three Wishes (TV show), 151t
Time magazine, 138, 139, 148
Time Warner Corporation, 148
Titanic (film), 142, 200
Title IX, 338
Togo
    languages used in, 62f
    poverty level, 218f
Torah, 320–321
Total corporation, revenues, 217t
Total fertility rate (TFR), 377, 402
Total institution, 88, 97
Totalitarianism, 357, 371
Toyota, revenues, 217t
Tracking, in education, 336, 337, 345
Traditional authority, 355, 371
Trained incapacity, 120, 129
Transnational crime, 176, 182
Transnationals, 421–423
    conflict perspective, 422
    definition, 421, 424
Tsunami, of 2004, 21
Tunisia, languages used in, 62f
Turkey
    educational level, 333f
    income per capita, 213f
    languages used in, 62f
TV, percentage of shows with sexual content,
    45, 46f
Twins studies, 81–82
Two and a Half Men (TV show), 136, 151t

Uganda
    languages used in, 62f
    women in, 360
Ukraine, languages used in, 62f

UNAIDS, 400, 400f
Unatics (unicycle club), 109
Underclass, 199, 207
Unemployment, 367–368
Unequal Childhoods (Lareau), 290–291
UNESCO (United Nations Educational,
    Scientific, and Cultural
    Organization), 142
Uniform Crime Reports (FBI), 178
Union membership, by state, 127f
Unions, labor, 191
United Arab Emirates
    Gross Domestic Product (GDP), 217t
    income per capita, 213f
United Kingdom
    absolute poverty, 197f
    economic forecast, 353f
    educational level, 333f
    income distribution, 221f
    income per capita, 213f
    labor unions, 127
    language, 58
    languages used in, 62f
    life expectancy, 378f
    nationalized healthcare, 204
    suicide rate, 9
    terrorist incidents, 365f
United Methodist Church, 330f
United Nations, 269, 419
    Development Programme, 195, 223
    Digital Solidarity Fund, 220
    domestic partnership policy, 309
    Human Rights Commission, 227
    Millennium Project, 216, 219
    Population Division, 285f
    Population Information Network, 332
United States
    absolute poverty, 197f
    aging population, 275
    class system, 188–189
    computer network readiness, 220
    economic forecast, 353f
    educational level, 333f
    elderly population, growth of, 281f
    gender stratification, 271f
    household income, 188f
    income distribution, 221f
    income per capita, 212, 213f
    infant mortality rate, 393t
    languages used in, 62f
    life expectancy, 378f
    minimum wage, 197f
    norms and values, 66, 67
    people ever married, percentage, 299f
    population patterns, 380–383
    poverty level, 218f
    religious participation, 327f
    voter turnout, 358f
    wealth and income distribution, 195–196
    welfare programs, 203, 204
United States Naval Academy, 68
United States Trade Representative, 215
United Students Against Sweatshops, 211
Universal Declaration of Human Rights, 187,
    227–228
University of Chicago, 17
University of Maryland, 162
University of Michigan, 366
University of Montreal, 241
University of Québec, 241
University of Wisconsin, 80–81, 363
Univision network, 141
Urban dwellers, 387–388
Urban ecology, 384, 402

Urbanism, 383, 402
Urbanization, 383–384
    conflict perspective 386–387, 387t
    functionalist perspective, 384–386, 387t
    global, projected, by region, 384f
USA, media penetration, 148f
Utah
    abortion funding, 284f
    anti-gay laws, 310f
    Arab American population, 253f
    educational level, 32f
    elderly population, projected, 282f
    executions, since 1972, 170f
    household income, 32f
    median household income, 187f
    medical marijuana, 163f
    physicians, availability of, 398f
    union membership, 127f
Uzbekistan, courtship, 298

Validity, 33, 51
Value, 75
Value neutrality, 30, 43, 51
Values, 56
    theoretical perspectives on, 71t
Variable, 51
Variables, 32
    control, 34–35
    operationalizing, 31
Vatican Television Center, 60
Veil, in Middle Eastern cultures, 270
Venezuela
    languages used in, 62f
    terrorist incidents, 365f
Vermont
    abortion funding, 384f
    anti-gay laws, 310f
    Arab American population, 253f
    cohabitation, 306f
    educational level, 32f
    elderly population, projected, 282f
    executions, since 1972, 170f
    household income, 32f
    median household income, 187f
    medical marijuana, 163f
    physicians, availability of, 398f
    rural character, 383
    union membership, 127f
Verstehen, 11
Vertical mobility, 201, 207
Vested interests, 413, 424
Viacom, 148
Victimization surveys, 178, 182
Victimless crime, 174, 182
Vietnam
    death penalty, 179
    income per capita, 213f
    poverty level, 218f
    religions of, 317f
Vietnamese Americans, 249
Vietnamese immigrants, in U.S. population,
    246f
Violence
    domestic, 297, 311. *See also* Child abuse
    in the media, 151–152
Virginia
    abortion funding, 284f
    anti-gay laws, 310f
    Arab American population, 253f
    cohabitation, 306f

educational level, 32f
elderly population, projected, 282f
executions, since 1972, 170f
household income, 32f
median household income, 187f
physicians, availability of, 398f
union membership, 127f
Vital statistics, 376, 402
Voting behavior, 357–359
    voter turnout, by country, 358f
    of youth, 359

W

Wage discrimination, 272
Wal-Mart, 216, 390, 391
    revenues, 217t
Wallbangin' (Phillips), 157–158
War, 362, 362–363
    definition, 371
    deterrents, 364
    public opinion of, 1971–2004, 363f
War at Home, The (TV show), 151t
War crimes, 227
Warner Brothers, 148
Washington, D.C.
    abortion funding, 284f
    anti-gay laws, 310f
    Arab American population, 253f
    cohabitation, 306f
    elderly population, projected, 282f
    executions, since 1972, 170f
    median household income, 187f
    medical marijuana, 163f
    physicians, availability of, 398f
Washington State
    abortion funding, 284f
    anti-gay laws, 310ff
    Arab American population, 253f
    cohabitation, 306f
    educational level, 32f
    elderly population, projected, 282f
    executions, since 1972, 170f
    median household income, 137f
    medical marijuana, 163f

physicians, availability of, 398f
    union membership, 127f
Water pollution, 418
Wealth, 186, 207
    of the elderly, 281
    and income, 195–196
Welfare, corporate, 204
Welfare programs, 203–205
West Virginia
    abortion funding, 284f
    anti-gay laws, 310f
    Arab American population, 253f
    cohabitation, 306f
    educational level, 32f
    elderly population, projected, 282f
    executions, since 1972, 170f
    household income, 32f
    median household income, 187f
    medical marijuana, 163f
    physicians, availability of, 398f
    rural character, 383
    union membership, 127f
Western Europe
    people living with AIDS, 400f
    terrorist incidents, 365f
White-collar crime, 175, 176, 182
White ethnic groups, 255
Whites, privileges of, 239–240, 241
Who Wants to Be a Millionaire (TV show),
    142
Will and Grace (TV show), 141
Wiretapping, 140
Wirtschaft und Gesellschaft (Weber), 12
Wisconsin
    abortion funding, 384f
    anti-gay laws, 310f
    Arab American population, 253f
    cohabitation, 306f
    educational level, 32f
    elderly population, projected, 282f
    executions, since 1972, 170f
    household income, 32f
    median household income, 187f
    medical marijuana, 163f
    physicians, availability of, 398f
    union membership, 127f

Women
    African American, 239f
    Asian, 239f
    Asian American, 252
    body image, 163–164
    and college sports, 338
    criminal behavior, 178
    education for, 221, 337
    genital mutilation, 227–228
    and health and illness, 398
    Hispanic, 239f
    in India, 269
    in Japan, 222
    Korean American, 252
    in labor force, 271–273
        consequences of, 272–273
    labor force participation, 271f
    median income, by race, 239f
    in Mexico, 224
    in Middle Eastern cultures, 221, 261–262,
        270
    in national legislatures, by country, 360f
    as percentage, in selected occupations,
        272t
    in the Philippines, 222
    and politics, 358, 359, 360
    portrayal, in the media, 143, 152
    in poverty, 281–282, 301. *See*
        Feminization of poverty
    and religion, 324, 325
    as sociologists, 9–10, 12, 17
    unpaid labor of, 195
    in the workplace, 365, 366, 367
Working poor, 2–3, 198, 199
Working Poor, The (Shipler), 185–186, 190
Workplace
    as agent of socialization, 93–94
    management styles, 124–126
    school as, 340
    women in, 365, 366, 367
World Bank, 204, 214, 217t, 222, 224, 393
World Economic Forum's Networked
    Readiness Index (NRI), 220
World Health Organization, 9, 377, 390, 399,
    400, 418

World systems analysis, 214, 221t, 230, 386,
    402
    and gender stratification, 271
    and urbanization, 386
World Trade Center attacks, 6, 7, 16, 21,
    134–135, 139
    and civil rights, 67
    memorial service, for victims, 113
    national security, breach in, 120
    security, after, 161
World Trade Organization, 407
Writing research reports, 48–49
Written rules and regulations, 120
Wyoming
    abortion funding, 284f
    anti-gay laws, 310f
    Arab American population, 253f
    cohabitation, 306f
    educational level, 32f
    elderly population, projected, 282f
    executions, since 1972, 170f
    household income, 32f
    median household income, 187f
    physicians, availability of, 398f
    union membership, 127f

Y

Yahoo search engine, 140
Yale University, 159
Young people
    and politics, 359
    and religion, 7, 8

Z

Zambia
    languages used in, 62f
    life expectancy, 378f
Zapatista National Liberation Army, 225
Zero population growth (ZPG), 381, 402
Zimbabwe, income per capita, 213f

Applications of *sociology's* Major Theoretical Approaches

Sociology provides comprehensive coverage of the major sociological perspectives. This summary table includes a sample of the topics in the text that have been explored using the major approaches. The numbers in parentheses indicate the pertinent chapters.

FUNCTIONALIST PERSPECTIVE

Defined and explained (1)
Adoption (12)
AIDS and social networks (15)
Anomie theory of deviance (7)
Bilingualism (3)
Bureaucratization of schools (13)
Cow worship in India (1)
Culture (3, 13)
Davis and Moore's view of stratification (8)
Disengagement theory of aging (11)
Dominant ideology (3)
Durkheim's view of deviance (7)
Dysfunctions of racism (10)
Ethnocentrism (3)
Family (12)
Formal organizations (6)
Functions of dying (11)
Functions of racism (10)
Gans's functions of poverty (8)
Gay marriage (12)
Gender stratification (11)
Health and illness (15)
Human ecology (15)
Human rights (9)
In-groups and out-groups (5)
Integrative function of religion (13)
Media and social norms (6)
Media and socialization (6)
Media and status conferral (6)
Media promotion of consumption (6)

Modernization theory (9)
Multinational corporations (9)
Narcotizing effect of the media (6)
Offshoring (14)
Population policy (15)
Social change (13, 16)
Social control (7, 13)
Social institutions (5)
Socialization in schools (4, 13)
Sports (1)
Subcultures (3)
Transnationals (16)
Urban ecology (15)

CONFLICT PERSPECTIVE

Defined and explained (1)
Abortion (11)
Access to health care (15)
Affirmative action (14)
Age stratification (11)
AIDS crisis (15)
Bilingualism (3)
Bureaucratization of schools (13)
Capitalism (13, 14)
Corporate welfare (8)
Correspondence principle (13)
Credentialism (13)
Culture (3)
Day care funding (4)
Deviance (7)
Disability as a master status (5)
Domestic violence (12)
Dominant ideology (3, 6, 8)
Downsizing (14)
Elite model of the U.S. power structure (14)
Environmental issues (16)
Exploitation theory of discrimination (10)
Family (12)
Gay marriage (12)
Gender stratification (11)
Gender equity in education (13)
Hidden curriculum (13)

Iron Law of Oligarchy (5)
Labor unions (5)
Marx's view of stratification (8)
Media gatekeeping (6)
Media stereotypes (6)
Media violence (6)
Medicalization of society (15)
Model minority (10)
Multinational corporations (9)
New urban sociology (15)
Offshoring (14)
Population policy (15)
Poverty (8)
Privacy and technology (16)
Racial profiling (10)
Racism and health (15)
Religion and social control (13)
Social change (16)
Social control (7)
Social institutions (5)
Socialization in Schools (4)
Sports (1)
Subcultures (3)
Tracking (13)
Transnationals (16)
Victimless crimes (7)
White-collar crime (7)
World systems analysis (9, 15)

INTERACTIONIST PERSPECTIVE

Defined and explained (1)
Activity theory of aging (11)
Adolescent sexual networks (5)
Adoption (12)
Affirmative action (14)
AIDS and its impact (15)
Charismatic authority (14)
Conspicuous consumption (8)
Contact hypothesis (10)
Culture (3)
Differential association (7)
Dramaturgical approach (4, 14)
Electronic communication (6)
Family (12)
Gay marriage (12)

Gender stratification (11)
Health and illness (15)
Human relations approach (5)
Interracial and interethnic friendships (10)
Labor unions (5)
Media violence (6)
Obedience (7)
Presentation of the self (4)
Racial profiling (10)
Routine activities theory (7)
School prayer (13)
Social institutions (5)
Sports (1)
Tattoo symbols of 9/11 (1)
Teacher-expectancy effect (13)
Teenage pregnancy (12)
Transnationals (16)

FEMINIST PERSPECTIVE

Defined and explained (1)
Day care funding (4)
Deviance (7)
Domestic violence (12)
Dominant ideology (3)
Ethnographic research (2)
Family (12)
Gender stratification (11)
Language (3)
Media stereotypes (6)
Media violence (6)
Population policy (15)
Pornography (6)
Rape (7)
Sports (1)
Victimless crimes (7)

LABELING THEORY

Defined and explained (7)
AIDS and labeling (15)
Disabilities and labeling (5)
Health and illness (19)
Societal reaction approach (7)
Teacher-expectancy effect (13)
Victimless crimes (7)